NOTABLE AMERICAN WOMEN
The Modern Period
A Biographical Dictionary

Prepared under the auspices of
Radcliffe College

NOTABLE AMERICAN WOMEN
The Modern Period

A Biographical Dictionary

Edited by

Barbara Sicherman   Carol Hurd Green

with

Ilene Kantrov   Harriette Walker

The Belknap Press of Harvard University Press
Cambridge, Massachusetts, and London, England
1980

PRINTED IN THE UNITED STATES OF AMERICA

LIBRARY OF CONGRESS CATALOGING IN PUBLICATION DATA

Main entry under title:

Notable American women: the modern period.

　　1. Women—United States—Biography.　I. Sicher-
man, Barbara.　2. Green, Carol Hurd.
CT3260.N573　　920.72′0973　　80–18402
ISBN 0–674–62732–6

ADVISORY BOARD

Funding for research and editing was provided in part
by grants to Radcliffe College from the Research Materials
Program of the National Endowment for the Humanities.

CONTENTS

PREFACE

The publication of *Notable American Women* in 1971 marked a new era in the writing of women's history. The three-volume biographical dictionary, the first full-scale scholarly work of its kind, appeared at a time when the women's movement, and its academic offshoot, women's studies, had created an unparalleled interest in understanding women's past. Recounting the biographies of hundreds of women who had made a distinctive contribution to American life, the volumes provided an essential research base for the study of American women over the centuries.

As a work of collective biography, *Notable American Women* demonstrated women's achievements not only in such enterprises as primary education, nursing, and home economics, often designated as women's work, but also in fields where women's role had been little appreciated, in medicine and religion, for example, and in such mainstream historical movements as abolitionism and progressivism. The stimulus that the work provided to scholarship is already apparent in the burgeoning monographic literature on women's history. Beyond that, *Notable American Women* has attracted a wide general readership, as the search for roots, role models, and strategies for the future has increasingly led to a study of women's past.

In response to public and scholarly demand, Radcliffe College and the Harvard University Press decided to undertake a supplementary volume that would bring the story of American women's achievements further into the twentieth century. The original work, edited by Edward T. James, Janet Wilson James, and Paul S. Boyer, spanned the years from 1607 to 1950. The volumes included only women who died before January 1, 1951, and only five of the subjects were born after 1900. For this reason, they could say little about women's activities or about what had happened to the women's movement after ratification of the nineteenth amendment in 1920. To help bring the story of American women up to date, the National Endowment for the Humanities provided funding for research and editing of a new volume, to include subjects who died between January 1, 1951, and December 31, 1975.

Work on *Notable American Women: The Modern Period* began in July 1976 following the appointment of the editors and an advisory board of eight leading scholars representing several disciplines. The first task was the identification of potential subjects for the new volume. The editors conducted as wide a search as time and resources allowed, beginning with the reading of all the obituaries of women that appeared in the *New York Times* between 1951 and 1975. The research staff also examined professional journals, yearbooks, directories of manuscript collections, and state compilations of notable women; the project benefited greatly from the work done by many state bicentennial commissions. Because women's achievements are often inadequately recorded in published sources, the editors solicited suggestions for subjects from hundreds of professional, labor, political, cultural, social, scientific, and religious organizations, and from individuals—historians, practitioners in the many fields covered in this volume, and persons interested in specialized branches of women's studies. Requests for suggestions also went to all state libraries and historical societies, as well as to those of many cities.

Recognizing that racial and ethnic prejudice have worked against the career aspirations of minority women, the editors and the advisory board made a particular effort to consult representatives of Afro-American, Native American, Asian American, and Hispanic American organizations, as well as individuals knowledgeable about the history of these groups. The achievements of black women, particularly in education, religion, politics, and the arts, are well documented in this volume. Asian, Hispanic, and Native American women are less well represented, a consequence of the history of these minorities in American society and of women within these groups. Nevertheless, a glimpse of the story of Puerto Rican feminism appears in the lives of Julia de Burgos and María Cadilla de Martínez, the emergence of Chinese women into scholarly careers is reflected in the biography of Rose Hum Lee, and the significant accomplishments of Indian women are suggested in the accounts of Ella Deloria and Alice Lee Jemison.

Some 4,000 names emerged from the original search. Many major figures were obvious choices from the outset, among them Eleanor Roosevelt, Margaret Sanger, Helen Keller, and Mary McLeod Bethune. Beyond these, however, the editors were conscious of the risks and problems involved in choosing among women whose lives had only recently ended, and who represented fields as diverse as film, anthropology, and engineering. In consultation with the advisory board, they devised four basic criteria for selecting subjects: the individual's influence on her time or field; the importance and significance of her achievement; the pioneering or innovative quality of her work; and the relevance of her career for the history of women. The durability of a career was also taken into account in making final selections.

Concepts such as innovation and influence are susceptible of many interpretations. The editors and the board determined that, within the limitations imposed by the scope of a single volume, it was important not only to suggest the wide variety of fields in which women worked but also to take account of the diverse ways in which women have defined themselves and made an impact on their culture—to include both those who moved beyond traditional roles and those who worked within them. In practice the criteria favored individuals who had founded new fields or institutions, those who had made important discoveries, and those who had worked to advance opportunities for their sex. Individuals who had succeeded in breaking barriers or in overcoming difficult odds in fields hitherto difficult of access for women received particular consideration, although the editors exercised caution in accepting claims of notable firsts.

In defining an American career, all agreed that a foreign-born woman might be included if she had done important work in the United States and had significant influence here. Though this decision excluded women who came to the United States late in life, it permitted the inclusion of the remarkable group of émigrés from Nazi Germany and Austria who made especially important contributions in the sciences and social sciences, among them Hannah Arendt, Else Frenkel-Brunswik, and Tilly Edinger. American-born women who spent most of their lives abroad were also included if their work met the other criteria.

In making the final selections, the editors relied on consultants in many fields. Fifty-three lists of prospective subjects (narrowed down on the basis of preliminary research to approximately 2,400 names) went for evaluation to more than seven hundred experts in all parts of the country, among them historians, specialists in many branches of women's studies, and distinguished practitioners who had often known some of the women suggested for inclusion. Though many choices became obvious at this stage, further extensive research was often needed before final decisions could be made. In the sciences as well as in other specialized branches of knowledge, individual evaluations had to be secured before a particular geneticist or pathologist could be chosen for inclusion. Knowing that family responsibilities more often restricted the opportunities of women than of men, the editors decided to include some individuals who had exerted an important influence on their city or region but were not well known nationally. Some promising subjects had to be eliminated because insufficient material existed on which to base a scholarly article. Eventually 442 women were selected for inclusion.

A wide range of individuals—historians in several fields, novelists and literary critics, journalists, and scientists—contributed to this volume. Each was asked to do the impossible: to present within a very limited space the life and personality of a woman of achievement, while also evaluating her career and placing it in historical context. Contributors were expected to base their articles on primary sources, but in some cases a subject's papers had not yet been collected or were unavailable for research. Several collections of manuscript materials discovered during the course of the project have since been deposited in archives.

Each article presents the basic information about the woman's life: the crucial dates, her ancestry, parents, birth order, education, marital status, children, and cause of death. Because many of the essays are the first, or among the first, scholarly biographical appraisals of their subject, such information was often difficult to establish. Birth dates proved particularly elusive and some have remained in question. Information from death certificates could be used only with caution; furthermore, because laws in some states and municipalities, including New York City, forbid the publication of cause of death and, in some cases, even the distribution of death certificates, that information is missing from a number of articles.

In making selections, and in giving directions to contributors, the editors sought to produce a volume that would reflect new directions in women's scholarship and would be accessible to general readers as well. Beyond recording the essentials of the life and death of the subject, contributors and editors worked to shape the entries to indicate the reasons why a woman chose a particular way of life, the major stages in the evolution of her career, and the relationship between her public and personal life. (In order to avoid anachronistic usage in the accounts of public careers, titles such as chairman have been retained.) As family, friends, teachers and other mentors are of considerable importance in understanding how and why women have sought and attained a measure of achievement, the articles note such influences whenever possible. They consider, too, the responsibilities individual women assumed for parents, siblings, husbands, and children, and the effects of such commitments on their careers. In articles as brief as these must be, such concerns can receive only limited consideration, and difficult decisions had to be made. The choice of emphasis—like the choice of subjects for the volume—reflects both the requirements of a reference work and the ideas about women's history current in the late 1970s.

This book represents the contributions of many people. Our particular thanks go to Edward T. James and Janet Wilson James, who have given generously of their time and experience throughout the project. We also wish to acknowledge the support of Radcliffe College and its president, Matina Horner, and of the Harvard University Press, its director, Arthur J. Rosenthal, executive editor Aida D. Donald, and managing editor Catherine Bayliss. Elizabeth Suttell, senior editor at the Harvard University Press, worked closely with the project and was consistently helpful and encouraging.

Members of the advisory board provided thoughtful and important guidance throughout, contributing their time and their rich store of knowledge about American history in general and about women in particular. Special mention should be made of the late Ellen Moers, whose understanding of literary women was of inestimable value, and whose interest in the project is reflected in several outstanding articles.

We are also grateful for the advice offered by the several hundred consultants who evaluated lists of potential subjects or made individual recom-

Preface

mendations, and by the committee of consultants: the late Elizabeth Bishop, Mary I. Bunting, Eleanor Flexner, Elizabeth Hardwick, Susan M. Hartmann, Lillian Hellman, Edward T. James, Janet Wilson James, Alice Kessler-Harris, Katharine Kuh, Mary McGrory, Dorothy Porter, Alden Whitman, and Joan Hoff Wilson. Dr. Thomas Zant guided us through the difficulties of understanding and translating the information on death certificates into accurate and comprehensible language. Jeannette Bailey Cheek, Ann J. Lane, and Elizabeth Pleck made helpful comments on the introduction.

The project would not have been possible without the dedicated assistance of librarians and archivists in hundreds of institutions across the country. Their generous responses to our numerous requests for biographical information not only saved us from many errors but also enabled us to track down new facts about some subjects. Elizabeth Mason and the late Louis M. Starr of the Oral History Research Office of Columbia University searched their files for references to all subjects in this volume. We were also fortunate in having the resources of Harvard's Widener Library and of other libraries within the University to draw on for research and checking; the Harvard Theatre Collection and its assistant curator Martha Mahard deserve special mention. The publishers kindly granted permission to quote from *The Poems of John Dewey*, edited by Jo Ann Boydston. Copyright © 1977 by Southern Illinois University Press.

Central to the success of this project were the holdings of the Arthur and Elizabeth Schlesinger Library on the History of Women in America at Radcliffe College, whose staff, including director Patricia King, Barbara Haber, and Eva Moseley, were of unfailing assistance. The Schlesinger Library is the repository for research materials on subjects who appear in the volume as well as on those who were considered but not included.

Students at the library schools of the University of North Carolina at Chapel Hill, Columbia University, Emory University, San José State University, Western Michigan University, the University of Texas at Austin, the University of Michigan at Ann Arbor, Simmons College, Drexel University, Louisiana State University at Baton Rouge, the University of Illinois at Urbana-Champaign, and the University of Wisconsin at Madison provided biobibliographies which were of great value to contributors. The individual students are acknowledged in the relevant articles; we wish here also to thank their teachers, who made the assignments for *Notable American Women* and worked to ensure their usefulness. The biobibliographies are on file in the Schlesinger Library.

We have benefited as well from a staff who gave more than time to the project, becoming engaged with the idea behind it and working harder than anyone imagines to complete the book. Harriette Walker was both project coordinator, responsible for the smooth functioning of the business end of the project, and editor for theater, entertainment, and film. In the latter capacity, she conducted research, suggested subjects and contributors, and contributed to the successful completion of many articles. As senior staff

Preface

editor, Ilene Kantrov was responsible for the editing of a disproportionately large number of the articles; in addition, she shared in the direction of the work of research assistants and staff editors. Joan Feinberg and Stephen Hyslop served the project over a long period, first as research assistants and then as staff editors. Christopher Corkery and Maria Kawecki also worked in an editorial capacity. During the early stages Catherine Lord and Marilyn B. Weissman served as primary researchers. Many individuals assisted in tracking down information on subjects and verifying the details of each article. Those who worked for more than a few weeks include Florence Bartoschesky, Christopher Cornog, Leslie Gould, Karen Reed Hadalski, Sheryl Kujawa, Carol Lasser, Blanche Linden, Cynthia McLoughlin, Dee Ann Montgomery, Linda ole-MoiYoi, Patricia Palmieri, Judith Schwarz, Joëlle Stein, Susan Wendell, Kate Wittenstein, and Shoshana Zax. A number of undergraduates also helped with our varied research and office needs: Mary Lou Brewster, Paula Grant, Kim Jones, Megan Lesser, Emily Schneider, and Elise Wang. In the final stages of the project Susan Jane Pizzolato served as an admirable proofreader. Clare McGorrian worked with élan as researcher, office worker, and proofreader. We were fortunate also in having Valerie Abrahamsen and Linda Lord on our office staff, and everyone on the project benefited from the wit, wisdom, and skills of Grace Clark, who not only typed the vast majority of articles and masses of correspondence, but also called our attention to inaccuracies, infelicities, and boners. Without the assistance of all these people, often working under great pressure, *Notable American Women: The Modern Period* could not have been completed.

B.S.
C.H.G.

INTRODUCTION

Notable American Women: The Modern Period offers the biographies of 442 women, spanning the years from the late nineteenth through the mid-twentieth centuries. No work of collective biography can define an era or a group. What such a work can do, and what this volume sets out to do, is to present lives that are important in themselves and suggestive as well of the larger social and cultural issues of their time.

The women who appear in these pages exemplify a wide variety of career patterns, philosophical outlooks, and personal styles. As notable women, they are by definition atypical. They are a small and highly select group, and their inclusion in one volume is in part the result of the historical accident of having died within a twenty-five-year period. Large generalizations about American women's lives drawn solely from this volume would therefore be misleading. Some comments about the subjects and their achievements may nevertheless be helpful to readers.

The birth years of the subjects range from 1857 (Marian Nevins Mac-Dowell) to 1943 (Janis Joplin). More than three quarters were born in the nineteenth century. As a group they were exceptionally long-lived: fewer than 12 percent died before the age of sixty, while almost half lived to be eighty or more. Most of the subjects were of white Protestant origin, many with American roots reaching back to the colonial period. They came from all parts of the country: the largest number were born in the mid-Atlantic states, followed in order by the midwest, New England, the southeast, the Great Plains, the west, and the mountain states. More than one-tenth of the subjects were born abroad, principally in Russia, Poland, and the Austro-Hungarian Empire; many of these were Jewish.

By and large the subjects came from comfortable backgrounds or from families that encouraged the education of daughters. At a time when few women attended college or had careers, the vast majority of subjects received some education beyond high school. Close to half attained bachelor's degrees; twelve institutions provided almost half of these degrees, with nearly one-third coming from the Seven Sister colleges, led by Bryn Mawr and Smith. More than a third of the subjects received graduate or professional degrees: Columbia University granted the most master's degrees; the University of

Introduction

Chicago (followed by Columbia) the most doctorates, and Johns Hopkins Medical School the most medical degrees. Though most of the subjects began life with either material or cultural advantages, many financed their own educations in whole or in part; the pages of the volume are crowded with women who began their careers as teachers in primary and secondary schools. Among those from less advantaged backgrounds, the principal avenues of mobility were in theater, film, labor, and business.

Demographically, the subjects of this volume stand apart from their contemporaries: they married less often, had fewer children, and divorced more frequently. As in the earlier volumes, a large proportion—almost 40 percent—remained single. Thirty percent of the ever-married women had no children who survived infancy; over 45 percent raised one or two children, including adopted, step, and foster children, while fewer than 6 percent raised more than four. Of the married subjects, over 40 percent were divorced, some more than once. More than 10 percent of the married subjects were widowed either within the first ten years of their married lives or while their children were young.

These demographic findings suggest that there was more than a little truth to the conventional wisdom that it was difficult for women to have both careers and children, or at least full-time careers and several children. Lillian Gilbreth, who had twelve children—the largest number—and a distinguished career as an engineer and psychologist, was unique. But combining a profession with three children was also uncommon. Those who managed to do so usually had the assistance of servants or relatives. Although a large proportion of the married subjects maintained their involvement in the world outside the home while their children were young, many began their sustained public efforts only after their children were grown. Whether single, married, widowed, or divorced, many subjects formed close and long-lasting bonds with other women, continuing the tradition of mutual support that had characterized women's lives in an earlier era.

The subjects of *Notable American Women: The Modern Period* came to public attention for their achievements in many fields. Some continuities with those in the earlier volumes are apparent in the careers of such long-lived settlement leaders and reformers as Vida Scudder and Mary Kingsbury Simkhovitch, in the alliance of working- and middle-class women in the Women's Trade Union League (Rose Schneiderman, Mary Dreier), in the continued efforts of black women to provide educational opportunities for members of their race (Mary McLeod Bethune, Charlotte Hawkins Brown, Anna Julia Cooper), and in the leadership of women in the progressive education movement (Flora Cooke, Lucy Sprague Mitchell). The businesswomen in this volume, as in the earlier ones, often catered to a women's market, specializing in the cosmetics and beauty industries (Helena Rubinstein, Elizabeth Arden, Annie Turnbo-Malone), women's apparel (Hattie Carnegie), and products for children (Gertrude Muller). As in the cases of Ida Rosenthal and Margaret Rudkin, publicity for their products often emphasized

Introduction

the personalities of the founders and the home origins of their enterprises.

The concern with public issues that motivated earlier reformers is reflected here in the lives of the many women who were active in the peace, labor, and settlement movements, and in those who sought to improve the well-being of women and children, through voluntary organizations or through such federal agencies as the Women's and Children's Bureaus. Women's resourcefulness in shaping organizations for the public good is particularly apparent in the biographies of several women who worked first with the YWCA, among them Edith Terry Bremer and Louise Leonard McLaren. It is seen as well in the many courageous black and white civil rights reformers whose work provides a history of the ongoing struggle for civil rights through such organizations as the National Association for the Advancement of Colored People (Mary White Ovington, Daisy Lampkin), the Association of Southern Women for the Prevention of Lynching (Jessie Daniel Ames), the Commission on Interracial Cooperation and the Fellowship of the Concerned (Dorothy Rogers Tilly), and the Student Non-Violent Coordinating Committee (Rubye Doris Smith Robinson). In addition to their efforts on behalf of civil rights, many women, among them Dorothy Thompson and Fannie Hurst, were active in efforts to bring European refugees from Nazi Germany to the United States.

Women's efforts to change society took a variety of forms. A few, notably Elizabeth Gurley Flynn, Ella Reeve Bloor, and Anna Louise Strong, made careers as radicals, protesting against many forms of injustice. The ideal of a world without war motivated social reformers like Emily Greene Balch who saw the forms of injustice as interconnected. Others concentrated on a particular issue. The story of women's leadership in the birth control movement appears here in the lives of reformers such as Margaret Sanger and Katharine Dexter McCormick as well as physicians Lena Levine and Sophia Kleegman. Women such as Mildred Edie Brady and Persia Campbell played an important part in the consumer movement, while the prophetic writings of Rachel Carson influenced the conservation movement.

Like its predecessors, this volume records the lives of several well-known musicians, entertainers, and actresses. Included here are singers in a variety of modes, from opera through gospel and jazz to rock. The passing of vaudeville is reflected in the careers of performers such as Gracie Allen and Fanny Brice, who successfully adapted their talents to the new medium of radio, while the transition from silent to talking motion pictures is marked by the stories of actresses who survived the transition as well as those who did not. The Hollywood star system is vividly recalled in the careers of Judy Garland and Marilyn Monroe, while the problems of minorities in American culture are echoed in the film careers of Hattie McDaniel and Anna May Wong. The difficulties women had in establishing themselves as composers and instrumentalists are reflected here in the lives of Ethel Leginska and of Hazel Harrison, whose career also illustrates the barriers encountered by minority artists.

Introduction

In the theater, women successfully struck out in new directions in the twentieth century, making their mark not only as actresses but increasingly in other capacities as well: in the development of regional theater (Margo Jones), in the evolution of lighting and stage design (Jean Rosenthal, Aline Bernstein), and in the creation of children's theater (Winifred Ward). Katharine Cornell led her own company; Theresa Helburn was a moving force behind the Theatre Guild; and Margaret Webster became known as a foremost interpreter of Shakespeare for American audiences. Hallie Flanagan's achievements as head of the Federal Theatre Project provide a vivid reminder of the importance of women in the unparalleled national experiment of the Works Progress Administration's federal arts projects.

There is continuity with the earlier careers of women in the lives of the several artists and writers included here. The work of composer Ruth Crawford-Seeger, fiction writer Flannery O'Connor, poet Marianne Moore, choreographer Doris Humphrey, sculptor Eva Hesse, and others reflects as well the experimental nature of the arts in the twentieth century. Women in this period also continued to create opportunities for artists as they had in the past. Marian Nevins MacDowell gave her life to creating and sustaining the MacDowell Colony; Mary Curtis Bok Zimbalist founded and fostered the Curtis Institute of Music; Elizabeth Sprague Coolidge worked to create an audience for chamber music in the United States and provided places for its performance. Katherine Dreier and Marion Bauer were ardent advocates of contemporary painting and music, while Natalie Barney and Mabel Dodge Luhan brought artists together and encouraged and inspired their work.

Newer careers for women in the twentieth century reflect not only women's changing historical situation—more direct access to political power, for example—but also the growing specialization of modern life. In comparison to the earlier volumes, the proportion of women who made their mark in voluntary endeavors—as missionaries and women's club leaders, for example—is smaller. Nor are there as many generalists, the gifted amateurs who before the establishment of fixed professional boundaries moved easily and successfully among a variety of endeavors.

Specialization is especially apparent in the careers of the physicians and scientists, many of whom became renowned for achievements of a highly technical nature. Most of the physicians in the earlier volumes, clustered in the women's medical colleges or hospitals and often concentrating on the care of women and children, worked in an essentially separate women's medical sphere. Some physicians in this volume, including Bertha Van Hoosen, founder of the American Medical Women's Association, and Esther Pohl Lovejoy, head of the American Women's Hospitals Service, remained staunch advocates of separate medical organizations for women. But the newer trend, necessitated in any event by the closing of all but one of the women's medical colleges, was to try to break down barriers and to enter the mainstream of medicine. While they were often promoted at slower rates than their male colleagues, several physicians in this volume held appointments in highly

Introduction

specialized fields in major academic and research institutions: Florence Sabin at Johns Hopkins and the Rockefeller Institute, Alice Hamilton at Harvard, and an impressive number at the College of Physicians and Surgeons of Columbia University (Hattie Alexander, Dorothy Andersen, Virginia Apgar, and Virginia Kneeland Frantz). Several also became the first woman to serve as president of a specialized professional society. Given the limited opportunities for women in medicine during the early twentieth century, the successes of such women must be viewed as truly extraordinary.

Scientists, working in a milieu that was inhospitable to women, sometimes proved remarkably resourceful in creating niches, usually on the margins of their profession, that permitted them to lead productive professional lives. The internationally recognized work of biologists Ethel Browne Harvey and Libbie Hyman was in marked contrast to their professional status, as measured by such indicators as academic appointments and research grants. Margaret Morse Nice, who was self-trained and held no academic appointment, was a world-renowned ornithologist. And two women won Nobel prizes, Maria Goeppert Mayer—who because of nepotism laws was long unable to obtain suitable employment—in physics, and Gerty Cori in medicine and physiology.

The trend toward professionalization is apparent in fields more traditional for women, including home economics, nursing, and social work. Leaders of the home economics profession such as Agnes Fay Morgan, Katharine Blunt, and Hazel Kyrk placed increasing emphasis on training in the sciences and in economics. The efforts of nurses to upgrade their profession, recorded in the earlier volumes in such figures as Isabel Hampton Robb and Adelaide Nutting, were extended by their contemporary Lavinia Dock, and by Annie Goodrich and Isabel Stewart. Women's leadership in the professionalization of social work is especially striking, as social workers with advanced education gradually replaced the self-trained women and men who had opened and run settlements and other social agencies in the late nineteenth century. Some, like Edith Abbott, tried to incorporate the reform values of the settlement movement into the curriculum. Others were active in developing new specialties, including casework, group work, medical social work, and psychiatric social work.

Women often found their opportunities in developing fields or in new specializations within established ones. The volume records the lives of several women who made their mark in the radio and television industries (station manager Judith Waller, writers Gertrude Berg and Irna Phillips, and television commentator and journalist Aline Saarinen). Also included are several major photographers whose work sketches a history of changing styles and attitudes toward photography as an art form and whose success illustrates the opportunities for women in that emerging field. Among scientists, too, several pioneered in new specialties: Anna Wessels Williams and Alice Evans in bacteriology, Maud Slye and Madge Macklin in genetics, Alice Hamilton in industrial medicine, and Elda Anderson in health physics. Women also

Introduction

attained prominence as leaders and innovators in the new specialty of psychoanalysis; Karen Horney and Clara Thompson were early critics of Freud's theories of female psychosexual development. In the social sciences there were two pioneer demographers, Irene Taeuber and Margaret Jarman Hagood. Mary Beard articulated a theoretical base for the study of women's history. Constance McLaughlin Green was an early practitioner of urban history, while Mary Clabaugh Wright was among the first serious scholars of modern Chinese history.

In addition to their primary vocations, many subjects took a deep interest in national and international affairs. World War I drew philanthropists, nurses, and volunteer Red Cross workers to the European front, while others participated in war-related activities at home. An important minority of women, however, opposed the war, and subsequently established a separate peace movement, the Women's International League for Peace and Freedom. That story is told in part in the life of Jane Addams in an earlier volume, and of Emily Greene Balch in this one; both women won the Nobel Peace Prize. Their interest in international affairs took many American women to conferences in Europe and Latin America in search of ways in which they could promote peace. This international outlook is strikingly illustrated by the large numbers who attended the founding conference of the United Nations in San Francisco in 1945. Virginia Gildersleeve was the only woman member of the official United States delegation to the conference, but many others attended as representatives of organizations or special interest groups. A number of subjects subsequently took part in the work of the United Nations, as members of commissions and in other capacities that reflected women's international perspective. Of these, Eleanor Roosevelt's achievement in shaping the Universal Declaration of Human Rights was the most notable. A few women were able to make careers in international affairs, among them Vera Micheles Dean, Esther Caukin Brunauer, and Muna Lee.

The story of women who worked for passage of the nineteenth amendment, including not only the older generation of suffragists, but also younger women like Sara Bard Field and Lucy Burns, Alice Paul's important associate, is extended here. (Paul herself died in 1977, too late for inclusion in this volume.) The suffrage movement, particularly its more dramatic manifestations during World War I, has captured the imagination of many, and has led some to conclude that the women's movement died after 1920. These pages provide material, however, for a study of women's continued involvement in politics after passage of the federal suffrage amendment. Their activism took several, sometimes conflicting, directions. Leaders of the League of Women Voters, the successor organization of the National American Woman Suffrage Association (Maud Wood Park, Belle Sherwin, and Marguerite Wells), worked not only to educate the new voters, but also to attain social welfare legislation on behalf of women and children. In this latter goal they were joined by officers of the National Federation of Business and Professional Women (Lena Madesin Phillips), as well as by women from

Introduction

labor and reform backgrounds (Mary Anderson and Mary van Kleeck). Other women, often younger, put feminist issues first, and worked through the National Woman's party for passage of the Equal Rights Amendment (Anita Pollitzer, Mabel Vernon). Still others emphasized women's direct participation in the political process, whether through a major party (Emma Guffey Miller, Emily Newell Blair), or in a separate women's campaign (Anne Martin).

Women sought and attained a wide variety of political offices. Southerners Nellie Nugent Somerville and Minnie Fisher Cunningham initially gained political power through their leadership of the temperance and woman suffrage movements in their states. Lawyers Florence Allen, Genevieve Cline, and Mary Bartelme, who cultivated ties to the woman suffrage and women's club movements as well as to their political parties, rose to the judiciary, while Annette Abbott Adams and Mabel Willebrandt each served as assistant attorney general of the United States; in a later period Frieda Hennock was appointed to the Federal Communications Commission. Women also served in Congress, beginning with Jeannette Rankin, who was elected even before passage of the nineteenth amendment. Like Rankin, most held office briefly, but representatives Edith Nourse Rogers and Mary Norton, Republican and Democrat respectively, became powerful figures during their long congressional careers.

Probably the most interesting political story that emerges from these pages is the importance of women in the New Deal. The unique position of Eleanor Roosevelt, a social reformer and political figure in her own right by the time her husband became president of the United States, was central to this development. Roosevelt's close working relationship with Mary Dewson, head of the Women's Division of the Democratic National Committee, paved the way for high-level appointments of women in the federal government. The most important of these was Frances Perkins, who had already worked closely with Franklin Delano Roosevelt in New York state. Her appointment as the first woman cabinet officer not only symbolized women's new standing in the Democratic party, but also recognized women's long-standing efforts to reform industrial society through social legislation. There were other appointments as well, including Ellen Sullivan Woodward as director of the Women's and Professional Division of the Works Progress Administration; the first two female diplomats (Ruth Bryan Owen Rohde and Florence Jaffray Harriman); Mary McLeod Bethune in the National Youth Administration; and numerous participants on National Recovery Administration boards. Eleanor Roosevelt's leadership was felt too in the formation of a Washington women's press corps that included May Craig and Bess Furman. During these years women also attained significant positions in the federal bureaucracy, notably Jane Hoey in the Bureau of Public Assistance of the Social Security Administration, and Mary Switzer, later head of the Office of Vocational Rehabilitation. It is possible to view women's participation in the New Deal as the culmination of the tradition of progressive social reform,

Introduction

inspired especially by Jane Addams and Florence Kelley. Perkins and Dewson, among others, were the direct heirs of the earlier reformers.

The history revealed by this volume thins out after World War II. The consequences of the McCarthy era appear in the stories of Esther Caukin Brunauer and Ethel Rosenberg, while fleeting suggestions of the histories of the new civil rights and feminist movements of the 1960s are seen in the truncated lives of Rubye Doris Smith Robinson and Ann London Scott. The full story of women's participation in these events, and others, must await the future, as must an understanding of the collective impact of the lives of the women recorded in this volume.

BARBARA SICHERMAN
CAROL HURD GREEN

NOTABLE AMERICAN WOMEN

Subjects who appear either in *Notable American Women, 1607–1950,* or elsewhere in *Notable American Women: The Modern Period* are designated by small capitals.

A

ABBOTT, Edith, Sept. 26, 1876–July 28, 1957. Social work educator, social reformer.

Edith Abbott was born in Grand Island, a small town on the Nebraska prairie, the second of four children and the older of two daughters of Othman Ali and Elizabeth (Griffin) Abbott. Her mother's parents, with other members of their substantial and close-knit Quaker-abolitionist family, emigrated in the late 1830s from New York to Illinois. Elizabeth Abbott, a graduate of Rockford Seminary in Illinois, had been a highly regarded high school principal. Othman Abbott, whose English ancestors were among the earliest settlers of New England, grew up in Illinois, served in the Civil War, and then settled in Nebraska. Active throughout his life in the practice of law and politics, he became Nebraska's first lieutenant governor.

Both Edith and her sister GRACE ABBOTT identified with their mother's concern for the oppressed, her interest in progressive ideas and social reform, her pacifist beliefs, and her commitment to equal rights for women. Othman Abbott demonstrated a vigor and love of new experiences, and from the sharing of his legal experiences his daughters learned reasoned and orderly thinking. To benefit from better educational opportunities than the small town schools offered, Edith Abbott was sent at age twelve to Brownell Hall, a girls' boarding school in Omaha. She graduated in 1893, but was unable to go to college when a severe Nebraska drought and the national financial panic brought heavy losses to the Abbott family. Instead, she began teaching high school in Grand Island.

Feeling a heavy responsibility to succeed and to become independent, Abbott combined correspondence courses, summer sessions, and then full-time work at the University of Nebraska to obtain an A.B. degree in 1901. She taught in the Lincoln, Neb., public schools for two years and attended the 1902 summer session at the University of Chicago, where she attracted the attention of economists James L. Laughlin and Thorstein Veblen. Aided by a small fellowship in political economy, Edith Abbott left Nebraska for full-time study at the University of Chicago in 1903.

Upon receiving a Ph.D. degree with honors in economics in 1905, Abbott accepted a Women's Trade Union League secretaryship in Boston and a research assignment for the Carnegie Institution. The award of a Carnegie fellowship took her in 1906 to England, where she studied at the University of London's University College and London School of Economics and Political Science. This experience shaped the direction and focus of Abbott's career. Exposed at the London School of Economics to the influence of Beatrice and Sidney Webb, she adopted their convictions about the need to abolish demeaning poor laws and establish programs to eradicate poverty. In addition, off and on during her stay in London, Abbott lived and worked in an East End settlement, where she began to learn about the poor person behind the statistics.

Upon her return to the United States in the fall of 1907, Edith Abbott served for one year as instructor of economics at Wellesley College. But she felt a strong commitment to coeducation as well as to what she and her sister termed "our western heritage." She preferred "the vigorous activity of Chicago's Halstead Street," where Hull House was located, to "the cool aloofness of a New England college for women." Aware of these preferences, SOPHONISBA BRECKINRIDGE, then director of social research at the Chicago School of Civics and Philanthropy, and JULIA LATHROP of Hull House offered her the opportunity to serve as Breckinridge's assistant. Abbott accepted and by the fall of 1908 she had joined her sister at Hull House, where they both lived most of the time until 1920, becoming associated with the remarkable women and men whom JANE ADDAMS attracted to her cause.

A far-ranging and effective partnership between the Abbott sisters began when Edith Abbott returned to Chicago. Strongly committed to common values and goals, the two put their different personality traits and competencies to work in complementary ways. Edith Abbott was the scholar; Grace Abbott, especially during her tenure as chief of the United States Children's Bureau (1921–34), took the initiative in translating knowledge into action. While they lived at Hull House, they worked for woman suffrage, a ten-hour law to protect working women, the admission of women to trade unions, the rights of immigrants, the improvement of tenement housing, and child labor legislation. Attempting to provide an exact base of knowledge for such efforts, Edith Abbott produced studies of *Women in Industry* (1910) and *The Real Jail Problem* (1915), and, together with Breckinridge, *The Delinquent Child and the Home* (1912) and *Truancy and Non-Attendance in the Chicago Schools* (1917).

These were among the more than one hundred books and articles Abbott wrote on a wide range of topics. Always in her research and writing she sought to establish the facts to the end that rational solutions could be found to the problems of society. Adding her own insightful introductions and interpretations to documentary evidence, she built a sound historical, legal, and philosophical basis for the resolution of policy issues. Her work earned her the title "passionate statistician" in the pages of *The Nation*.

Edith Abbott's most significant contributions to social work education came after 1920, when, with the School of Civics and Philanthropy in serious financial straits, she and Breckinridge helped to arrange its transfer to the University of Chicago. Renamed the School of Social Service Administration, it became the first graduate school of social work within a university. Rejecting as too narrow the prevailing apprenticeship model of training social workers in philanthropic agencies, Abbott was convinced that social work education belonged under university auspices where students could be offered a broad intellectual grasp of social issues. She was committed to making human services more scientific and insisted that social work education should include access to advanced social science courses and research facilities and that faculty teaching and research should be subject to rigorous standards of university scholarship.

In 1924 Edith Abbott became dean of the School of Social Service Administration. Together with Breckinridge, she formulated a curriculum that included knowledge from political science, economics, law, medicine, and studies of immigration, labor problems, and governmental processes. Sent to work in the community, students were expected to apply scientifically disciplined methods of social investigation to document needed changes in public policy. Always the focus was on social reform and public social service administration.

The long friendship and professional collaboration of Edith Abbott and Sophonisba Breckinridge, remarkable for its absence of personal competition, was so close that it is often difficult to differentiate their individual contributions. They jointly established the *Social Service Review* in 1927, which became a highly esteemed and influential professional journal. As part of their attempt to establish a curriculum broad in scope and scholarly in method, the two women also launched the distinguished University of Chicago Social Service Series of books and monographs, making use of case records and public documents in a novel and striking way.

Among these books, which became classics in social welfare, were two of Abbott's own studies, *Immigration: Select Documents and Case Records* (1924) and *Historical Aspects of the Immigration Problem: Select Documents* (1926). As a leading scholar of immigration, she spoke out for legislation that would restrict the exploitation of the foreign born. Her expertise was recognized by her appointment as chairman of the Committee on Crime and the Foreign Born of the Wickersham National Commission on Law Observance and Enforcement (1929–31).

Abbott also contributed to the formulation of public policy on the issue of public assistance to the poor. A longtime advocate of a network of professional public social services, she attacked the evils of patronage in existing public welfare programs, and spoke out in the 1920s against tax subsidies to private agencies, which she believed would delay the development of basic public services. Persuasively outspoken about the outworn concept of local responsibility for public assistance, Abbott called on the federal government to assume leadership in providing relief to individual citizens affected by the deepening economic crisis of the 1930s. At the same time she staunchly held that make-work programs would not solve the relief problems of the period and that comprehensive social insurance measures were required. Her views on these issues appeared from 1911 on in professional journals, government bulletins, and such publications as *The New Republic* and *The Nation*, as well as in her book *Public Assistance* (1941).

Edith Abbott was a beautiful woman, tall and slender, with blonde hair, brown eyes, and fine features. As she grew older, always working at a tremendous pace, her face showed lines of fatigue and stress; more and more she dressed plainly and rather severely. She had a keen sense of humor, but her wit sometimes had a biting edge, and, particularly after the death of her sister in 1939, her manner became more brusque. Abbott made heavy and uncompromising demands upon students for academic achievement and commitment to her goals. Some feared her; few if any forgot her. To all she offered a model of integrity, intellectualism, and commitment to social justice.

After giving up her post as dean in 1942, Edith Abbott continued to teach and to edit the *Social Service Review* until her retirement in 1953. She spent the rest of her life with her brother Arthur in the family home in Grand Island, becoming increasingly infirm until her death there of pneumonia at the age of eighty.

[The major source is the large collection of personal and professional papers of Edith and Grace Abbott in the Joseph Regenstein Library, Univ. of Chicago, which includes a draft of a proposed book about Grace Abbott by Edith Abbott. Family correspondence is held by a niece, Charlotte Abbott, in Grand Island. There are manuscript materials in *The Survey* Papers at the Archives of Social Welfare Hist., Univ. of Minn., and the Neb. State Hist. Soc. An annotated bibliography of Edith Abbott's publications appears in Rachel Marks, "The Published Writings of Edith Abbott: A Bibliography," *Social Service Rev.*, March 1958, pp. 51–56. Abbott's significant publications include Nat. Commission on Law Observance and Enforcement, *Report on Crime and the Foreign Born* (1931); *Social Welfare and Professional Education* (1931; 2d ed. 1942); *Some American Pioneers in Social Welfare: Select Documents with Editorial Notes by Edith Abbott* (1937); and in the *Social Service Rev.*: "Grace Abbott: A Sister's Memories," Sept. 1939, pp. 351–407; "Sophonisba Preston Breckinridge Over the Years," Dec. 1948, pp. 417–47; "Grace Abbott and Hull House, 1908–21," Sept. 1950, pp. 374–94, and Dec. 1950, pp. 493–518. *Women in Industry* was reprinted in 1918, 1969, and 1970. The *Social Service Rev.* published three accounts and evaluations of her career: Helen Wright, "Three Against Time: Edith and Grace Abbott and Sophonisba P. Breckinridge," March 1954, pp. 41–53; Elizabeth Wisner, "Edith Abbott's Contributions to Social Work Education," March 1958, pp. 1–10; and Stephen J. Diner, "Scholarship in the Quest for Social Welfare: A Fifty-Year History of the *Social Service Review*," March 1977, pp. 1–66. Other sources of biographical information include *Nat. Cyc. Am. Biog.*, C, 371, and *Current Biog.*, 1941. Additional information was provided by Martha Eliot, Katharine Lenroot, Robert Hutchins, Frank Bane, Dorothy Bradbury, Elisabeth Shirley Enochs, Arlien Johnson, Phyllis Osborn, Mary Macdonald, and Lillian Ripple. Death certificate supplied by Neb. Dept. of Health.]

LELA B. COSTIN

ADAMS, Annette Abbott, March 12, 1877–Oct. 26, 1956. Lawyer, judge.

Annette Abbott Adams began her law career as the first woman to handle federal prosecutions; she completed her career as the first woman appellate judge in California. She was born in Prattville (Plumas County), Calif., and her legal and political career was rooted in and grew with that state. Her father, Hiram Brown Abbott of Ohio, was a forty-niner who with her mother, Annette Frances (Stubbs), a Maine schoolteacher, ran a country store; he also served as justice of the peace. Hiram Abbott's rigid ideas about sex roles, as applied to Annette and her younger brother, and the local community's rejection of her mother—the best educated person in the county—as a school board member led to her early determination to be independent and successful despite her sex. She was drawn toward a legal career after her father's death when, then in her teens, she read the California code to give her mother business and legal advice.

After attending local schools and graduating from the State Normal School at Chico in 1897, Adams's first job was teaching in a country school. In 1901 she entered the University of California at Berkeley. She received a bachelor of letters degree in 1904, and returned again to teaching, taking a high school post in Alturas, Modoc County, in 1905.

She broke tradition on marrying Martin H. Adams on Aug. 13, 1906, by continuing to teach; she also served as principal from 1907 to 1910. In that year, with the encouragement of John E. Raker, the county trial judge, Annette Adams entered Boalt Hall, the school of jurisprudence at Berkeley, and worked her way to the J.D. in 1912, the only woman in the graduating class. Although the school's dean recommended to Western Pacific Railway that it hire her as house counsel, the railway was not ready to employ a woman and she opened an office in Plumas County, where Judge Raker, by then a Democratic congressman, persuaded her to organize women for Woodrow Wilson's presidential campaign in the summer of 1912. Adams moved to San Francisco, leaving her husband behind, and by 1914 apparently allowed it to be assumed that she was a widow. Martin Adams lived in Susanville, Calif., until his death in 1947; the couple evidently did not divorce.

Becoming president of the Women's State Democratic Club Adams worked throughout the Wilson campaign, promoting him as a supporter of women's rights. In 1913 she traveled to Washington to celebrate his victory and apply for a patronage appointment. On her return to San Francisco she started a practice with Marguerite Ogden, the daughter of an Alameda judge. The firm took pro bono and criminal cases but its specialty was probate.

Annette Adams's reward for her political work was the post of assistant United States attorney for the northern district of California. She received it not as a symbol of the Wilson administration's support for women's rights, however, but as the fruit of her heavy pressure through federal officials, Democratic party leaders, women's clubs, and her friends, Congressman Raker and the new United States attorney for northern California, John Preston. Especially resistant to her appointment was Attorney General James C. McReynolds, and it was not until after President Wilson named him to the Supreme Court that she was sworn in, on Oct. 13, 1914, as the first woman federal prosecutor. As assistant attorney she won important cases against the German consul in San Francisco and against a group of Hindu revolutionaries, both on grounds of conspiring to violate the neutrality law. In 1918 Wilson named her special United States attorney in San Francisco. She vigorously prosecuted radicals for sedition and after the war went after food hoarders and prohibition violators.

Knowing of Adams's prestige in California, Attorney General A. Mitchell Palmer, candidate for the Democratic presidential nomination in 1920, invited her to become an assistant attorney general in Washington, D.C. She was sworn in late in June 1920, the first woman to hold the rank; her first duties were at the Democratic National Convention in San Francisco garnering women's backing for Palmer. There she began her own bid for the vice presidential spot and received one token vote for president on the thirty-seventh ballot.

In Washington beginning in August 1920 her major assignment was to supervise the prosecution of violators of the Volstead Act, although she was not herself a prohibitionist. Also responsible for federal prisons, she had to ensure the efficient utilization of prison labor and supervise policy on the treatment of prisoners. She had a narrow view of prisoners' rights to health care and to privacy of mail, and followed the Palmer policy of valuing law enforcement more than freedom of speech or press.

In August 1921 President Warren G. Harding replaced Adams with Republican MABEL WILLE-BRANDT. Adams returned to private practice in San Francisco with her friend John Preston. Out of office, she criticized the country for being "hysterical about booze" and the government for the laxity of enforcement of prohibition laws. She also urged women to "bore from within" to gain their rightful place in government. When Preston went on the California Supreme Court,

Adams practiced alone but handled San Francisco affairs for Jesse W. Carter, then a Redding attorney. He arranged a regular income for her from the California dental board and between 1927 and 1935 paid her to prepare and argue cases for his firm, exploiting the considerable legal talents which she could not market directly. During this time she won some significant water and public utility cases in the state courts as well as the notorious "Painless Parker" case (1932). She received $250 for taking the side of the professional board against Parker's inexpensive, business-sponsored dental services for the public.

Annette Adams continued to participate in state and national Democratic politics after the 1920 Democratic defeat. Her aggressive campaign for a seat on the San Francisco Board of Supervisors in 1923 was unsuccessful; she lost labor support because of her prohibition prosecutions and she blamed the passivity of women voters for her defeat. Working to involve women in the Democratic party organization, she won a commitment for half of the California delegate-at-large seats for the 1924 national convention to go to women. In 1932 she campaigned for Franklin D. Roosevelt, and the Women's Division of the Democratic National Committee relied on her organizational skills for the development of clubs in northern California. As a political reward in 1933 Adams was invited to replace the Republican woman incumbent, Annabel Matthews, on the Federal Board of Tax Appeals. But she preferred to remain in California, and the appointment went to another California lawyer, Marion Harron.

Early in 1935 Adams decided to campaign for the vacancy on the federal bench in the Northern District of California. She sought and gained the support of local Democratic leaders, legal colleagues, and women's groups, but the judgeship went to a male candidate. In 1935 President Roosevelt offered Adams a consolation prize, the post of assistant special counsel under John Preston to prosecute two important cases, one to secure restoration to the federal government of two sections in Elk Hills Naval Oil Reserve No. 1 and the other to recover compensation for oil and gas extracted by Standard Oil and other companies between 1918 and 1932. She moved to Los Angeles, a city she did not like, and through brilliant and painstaking work at trial and appeal won both the land and a judgment of more than seven million dollars against Standard Oil. After another brief assignment for the Justice Department she returned home in 1939 to San Francisco.

In 1942, Democratic Gov. Culbert Olson appointed Adams presiding justice of the three-judge intermediate appellate court in Sacramento; in November 1942 she won election for a twelve-year term. In 1950 she was assigned for a single case to the California Supreme Court, the first woman to sit on the Court. Adams suffered from arteriosclerosis after 1947 and retired on Nov. 20, 1952, when her ten years of service entitled her to a pension. She died in Sacramento of myocarditis in October 1956.

During her long political and professional career Annette Adams joined and led professional societies—including the prestigious American Law Institute—and many women's groups. Tall, slender, and attractive, she dressed in conservative but expensive style for work, but also enjoyed the informality of golf, horse-raising, and trips to her beloved California mountains. Early in her legal career she went to a voice instructor to lower her voice from soprano to baritone, to suit her advocate's role. From the 1920s into the 1950s, she shared her home with her brother.

Annette Adams gained her power and public positions through a series of male sponsors, each of whom recognized her ability and her contribution to their careers. Although she once claimed that in common with other women lawyers she had a tendency to an inferiority complex, Annette Adams accurately gauged her own abilities and achievements. She paid her professional and political dues in full, and knew that only sex discrimination prevented her from reaching the highest legal positions in government and private firms.

[There are letters and other material relevant to Adams's career in the Jesse W. Carter, William Denman, and James Phelan collections, all in the Bancroft Library, Univ. of Calif., Berkeley. Information on Adams's federal work is in the records of the Dept. of Justice, Criminal Div., Nat. Archives, Washington, D.C., and Suitland, Md. Important opinions written by Justice Adams include *San Diego Electric Railway Company v. State Board of Equalization*, 200 P 2d 573 (1948) and *People v. Gallow*, 235 P 2d 660 (1951). The "Painless Parker" case appears as *Parker v. Calif. Board of Dental Examiners*, 14 P 2d 67 (1932). Biographical material appears in Arthur Dunn, "A Portia in the Federal Court," *Sunset Mag.*, Feb. 1915; "New Post for Brilliant Annette Adams," *Democratic Digest*, March 1936; June Hogan, "Annette Abbott Adams, Presiding Justice," *The Trident*, Oct. 1950; and Joan M. Jensen, "Annette Abbott Adams, Politician," *Pacific Hist. Rev.*, May 1966. An obituary appeared in the *N.Y. Times*, Oct. 27, 1956. The death certificate for Martin H. Adams gives his occupations as bookkeeper, clerk, and cook and lists him as the husband of Aneta A. Adams; her death certificate shows her as widowed. Both certificates were provided by the Calif. Dept. of Health. Additional information supplied by Gladys Morgan, her court reporter.]

BEVERLY BLAIR COOK

ADAMS, Maude, Nov. 11, 1872–July 17, 1953. Actress.

Maude Adams, one of the most popular actresses of her generation, was born Maude Ewing Adams Kiskadden in Salt Lake City, Utah. She was the youngest and only surviving child of James Henry Kiskadden, a businessman of Scottish descent, and Asenath Ann (Adams) Kiskadden, an actress; their twin sons had died shortly after birth. Annie Adams, as her mother was known professionally, was a Mormon whose parents had joined Brigham Young on his way to Utah in 1847. She became a member of Young's theatrical stock company and later, until her retirement in 1897, appeared on stage with her daughter. The Kiskaddens moved to Virginia City in 1874, and a year later moved to San Francisco. There, billed as "La Petite Maude," Maude Adams became a salaried juvenile on Oct. 17, 1877, in a production of *Fritz*, a popular melodrama. She continued to play similar roles —frequently listed as "Little Maude"—in stock companies, until, at ten, she grew too tall for children's parts. While her parents remained in San Francisco, Maude was sent to school at the Collegiate Institute in Salt Lake City, where she lived with her grandmother.

After her father's sudden death on Sept. 22, 1883, having already resolved to become a great actress, she left school to join the traveling stock company to which her mother then belonged. Maude Adams experienced a long and difficult theatrical apprenticeship before reaching New York in August 1888, where she first appeared as the maid in *The Paymaster*. The same year she played in E. H. Sothern's company and two years later in Charles Frohman's stock company, most notably as Nell in an 1891 production of *Lost Paradise*. In October 1892 Frohman, correctly appraising her talent, made Maude Adams leading lady to John Drew. Then, as later, she took infinite pains in studying her parts. After her initial success in *The Masked Ball* as Suzanne Blondet, she appeared with Drew for four seasons in a succession of light comedies. They last appeared together in *Rosemary*.

Frohman had been urging Scottish playwright James Barrie to dramatize his novel *The Little Minister*, but the author was stymied. Attending a performance of *Rosemary* in 1896, Barrie saw Adams and hurried to the producer, exclaiming, "Behold my Babbie!" A year later, Adams, now head of her own company, made a dazzling success as Babbie; thus began a relationship between actress and playwright that continued until Barrie's death in 1937. Other glorious roles, all written by Barrie, followed: *Quality Street* (1901), *Peter Pan* (1905), *What Every Woman Knows* (1908), *The Legend of Leonora* (1914), and *A Kiss for Cinderella* (1916). Adams once said that whenever she acted, she was aware of one unseen spectator—Barrie.

Maude Adams's affinity for James Barrie's art was based on a mutual gift of humor and pathos —and on a perception of fantasy as a vehicle of spiritual truth. "So much of Barrie's life is second nature to me that I have to remind myself that other people do not know it so well," she wrote her biographer. The affinity was never so obvious as in *Peter Pan*. In the summer of 1905, Adams spent a month in the Catskills preparing for the monumental role. She designed a costume different from the one used in the London production; it quickly became vogue and the round collar and peaked hat were copied by young and old. As the child who would not grow up, Maude Adams captivated audiences with her demure charm and grace, and with her voice, with its blend of laughter and tears. *Peter Pan* was the pinnacle of her career; she performed the role more than 1,500 times.

Adams also appeared in the works of other playwrights, most notably in Rostand's *L'Aiglon* (1900) and *Chantecler* (1911)—at which, during the opening performance, she received twenty-two curtain calls. Not immune to failure, she was miscast in *The Squire of Dames* (1896), and was not up to the breadth of range needed for tragedy. Adams herself admitted that she "was very bad as Juliet" in an 1899 production of *Romeo and Juliet*, but greatly valued her one appearance in Schiller's *Joan of Arc*, performed in the Harvard University stadium in June 1909. Peter Pan and Chantecler remained, however, her most unforgettable achievements. In November 1918, while on tour in *A Kiss for Cinderella*, she fell dangerously ill with influenza. Only after thirteen years did she act again, playing Portia to Otis Skinner's Shylock in a national tour of *The Merchant of Venice*. Early in 1934, Adams participated in a radio series of six plays. Then, playing Maria in *Twelfth Night*, she toured summer theaters, making her final stage appearance on September 8 at the Dennis Playhouse on Cape Cod. After this her only contact with the public was a cross-country lecture tour in January 1939.

At forty-nine, Maude Adams began another life in the theater, first as a lighting designer. "As all my life had been in the theater, it was natural to turn to something akin, not too remote from my former profession," she explained (Robbins, *Maude Adams*, pp. 203–4). In 1921, after receiving an honorary A.M. from Union College, Adams moved to Schenectady, N.Y., and went to work with General Electric. There she conducted lighting experiments, displaying a competence which astonished the experts with whom she collaborated. After two years she developed an incandescent bulb widely used in color film, but failed to secure the patent. Advised to sue, Adams refused, not wishing such notoriety.

In the mid-1920s, at the request of the editors of *Ladies' Home Journal*, Maude Adams wrote an account of her life. Written in the third person, "The One I Knew Least of All" appeared in seven installments between March 1926 and May 1927. She turned next to teaching, accepting in 1937 an invitation to become a professor of drama at Stephens College in Columbia, Mo. There Maude Adams gave the same devotion to her teaching that she had given to her acting. She directed plays as diverse as *Everyman* and *Chantecler*, and compiled an unpublished textbook, "The First Steps in Speaking Verse," which she used to teach choral reading. Her teaching became intermittent after 1946, and four years later she retired.

In the face of immense popularity Maude Adams sought seclusion, and having experienced it during the summer of 1901 in a convent in France, she found a like refuge at the Cenacle Convent in New York City, where she often withdrew in strict secrecy from 1915 onward. In 1922 she gave to the Cenacle her large estate at Ronkonkoma, Long Island; she donated a second estate, at Onteora in the Catskills, in 1949. She had purchased both estates in 1900 and continued to divide her time between them until her death from a heart attack in 1953 in Tannersville, N.Y. As she had requested, she was buried in the private cemetery of the Cenacle at Ronkonkoma.

[The Maude Adams Coll. in the Library of Congress includes annotated typescripts and copies of her writings, among which are unpublished textbooks, "The First Steps in Speaking Verse"; "The Spoken Word"; and "A Pamphlet on English Speech and English Verse." Both the Billy Rose Theatre Coll., N.Y. Public Library, and the Harvard Theatre Coll. have extensive clipping files. A biography by Acton Davies, *Maude Adams* (1901), depends in part on accounts by Annie Adams and David Belasco. Other biographies are Ada Patterson, *Maude Adams: A Biography* (1907), and Phyllis Robbins, *Maude Adams: An Intimate Portrait* (1956), and *The Young Maude Adams* (1959). See also Isaac F. Marcosson, *Charles Frohman, Manager and Man* (1916); John Drew, *My Years on the Stage* (1922), a valuable study by her associate; Cyril Clemens, "Theatreana: Some Recollections of

Maude Adams," *Hobbies,* Nov. 1953; H. I. Brock, "Her Light Still Glows in the Theatre," *N.Y. Times Mag.,* Nov. 8, 1942; and Louise Dudley, "Notes on the Dramatic Theory of Maude Adams," *Theatre Arts,* Aug. 1954, an article read and approved by Adams. George D. Pyper, *The Romance of an Old Playhouse* (1928) provides background on theater in Salt Lake City. A portrait of Adams by Sigismond de Ivanowski (discussed in *Century Mag.,* Dec. 1906) is in the Pioneer Memorial Theatre, Univ. of Utah. Obituaries appeared in the Salt Lake City *Deseret News and Telegram* and the *N.Y. Times,* both July 18, 1953; death record from the Register of Deaths, Tannersville, N.Y. Further information was provided by Adams's colleague at Stephens College, Zay Rusk Sullens, and by college officials; by Judith Kalin; and by the Religious of the Cenacle.]

COLUMBA HART, O.S.B.

ADLER, Polly, April 16, 1900?–June 9, 1962. Madam.

Polly Adler, manager of a prominent New York bordello, was born Pearl Adler in Yanow, Russia, the eldest of the two daughters and seven sons of Morris and Gertrude (Koval) Adler. The family was well off by Yanow standards, but her father, a tailor, left the family on occasion to travel to Berlin, Warsaw, and New York in search of more favorable business opportunities. While aiding the family at home, Polly began her education under the tutelage of the village rabbi.

When Polly was twelve her parents sent her to the United States. For two years she lived in Holyoke, Mass., with family friends, the Grodeskys, doing housework for them and attending public school. Shortly after her fourteenth birthday she began work in the local paper mills. The next year she moved to Brooklyn, N.Y., and lived with her cousins Lena and Yossell Rosen, working successively in a corset factory, as a seamstress at home, and as a machine operator in a shirt factory.

An attractive teenager eager to escape the grinding poverty of immigrant life, Adler refused the penniless suitor her relatives had chosen for her and instead sought glamour in the local dance halls. At the age of seventeen she was raped by her supervisor from the shirt factory. After a family quarrel and an abortion she moved to Manhattan, where she found part-time work, once more in a corset factory. Through a family friend Adler became acquainted with a young actress living on Manhattan's fashionable Upper West Side who introduced her to a world of show business celebrities and the flashy, flourishing world of the prohibition bootleggers. Disturbed by the actress's addiction to drugs, Adler wanted to move out in the spring of 1920. As she had little money, she accepted the assistance of an acquaintance, a gangster and bootlegger, who offered to pay her rent if he and his girlfriend could use her apartment as a meeting place. Adler began procuring for him and his friends, and her informal activities rapidly developed into a thriving business.

When she had saved enough to finance a legitimate business Adler established a lingerie shop, but the shop failed after a year. Discouraged and penniless, in 1924 she went back to running a house. "In the world of the Twenties," she wrote in her autobiography, "the only unforgivable sin was to be poor"; adopting the credo that whatever is economically right is morally right, she determined "to be the best goddam madam in America."

Adler began a well-organized publicity campaign to make " 'going to Polly's' a euphemism for the world's most popular indoor sport." Short (four feet eleven), plump, dark-haired, and flamboyantly dressed, she became a familiar figure at New York's best-known nightclubs, spending freely, attracting attention to her beautiful girls, and providing material for newspaper columnists. Her shrewd business sense resulted in a skyrocket rise to popularity, and her liberal bribes to law enforcement officials kept her establishment open.

Adler moved farther downtown to a lavish apartment near the center of Manhattan, and at the age of twenty-four found herself with a business so successful that she had no time to devote to her private life. The patronage of her New York establishment ranged from the wits of the Algonquin Round Table to motion picture stars, business tycoons, and notable members of the social register set. In an effort to attract a more elite clientele, Adler also established a summer business in fashionable Saratoga Springs. She became increasingly estranged from her parents, who had come to the United States in 1923; although she visited them, she did her best to keep them from learning the nature of her work.

In 1930–31 the house received publicity, ironically, from a widespread crackdown on corruption in New York City government. Polly Adler became a frequent and sensational courtroom sight during investigations, led by Judge Samuel Seabury, which sought to determine the connections between prostitution, police payoffs, and organized crime. Adler was questioned about her many arrests, which had consistently failed to bring convictions, but she yielded no information on the witness stand. She admitted entertaining such notable underworld figures as George McManus, Jack "Legs" Diamond, Al Capone, Charles "Lucky" Luciano, and Arthur

"Dutch Schultz" Flegenheimer, but asserted her independence from racket control over her operations.

In 1935 Adler's house was raided as part of an investigation led by the young prosecutor Thomas Dewey into an alleged prostitution syndicate. Although this charge remained unproved, she served her only jail term (twenty-four days, under the alias Joan Martin) in May 1935 for possession of pornographic films.

Although Adler considered retiring several times during the late 1930s and early 1940s she remained in business throughout World War II. In January 1943, while seriously ill with pleurisy, she was arrested for the last time. After charges were dismissed, she retired to the Los Angeles area, where she enrolled in a community college to continue her long-suspended formal education. She died of cancer in 1962 at the Cedars of Lebanon Hospital in Hollywood. Her autobiography, *A House Is Not a Home* (1952), brought her international fame; a best seller, it was translated into eleven languages and later appeared as a movie. The book offers an intimate history of the 1920s and 1930s, as well as an inside view of life in a house. But Adler considered it significant above all as "an American success story."

[The best single source on Adler is her autobiography, *A House Is Not a Home*; all quotations are from that source. The *N.Y. Times* covered her career and arrests; accounts in the *N.Y. Journal*, the *N.Y. Graphic*, and the *N.Y. Daily Mirror* are more colorful. Herbert Mitgang, *The Man Who Rode the Tiger* (1979), describes her role in the Seabury investigations. Martin Gosch and Richard Hammer, *The Last Testament of Lucky Luciano* (1974), details the case against Adler in the Dewey investigations. Reviews of her book appeared in *Newsweek*, June 8, 1953; *Am. Mercury*, Oct. 1953; and the *N.Y. Times*, June 14, 1953. Other biographical information is available in *Celebrity Register* (1959), and obituaries in *Time*, June 22, 1962, and the *N.Y. Times*, June 11, 1962. Her literary agent, Armitage Watkins, has some correspondence. In her autobiography Adler gives her parents' names as Isadore and Sarah; the names Morris and Gertrude Koval, and a birth date for Adler of April 16, 1899, appear on her death certificate, obtained from the Calif. Dept. of Health. Information for the death certificate was supplied by her brother.

CAROL S. LASSER

AKELEY, Mary Lee Jobe, Jan. 29, 1878–July 19, 1966. Explorer, photographer.

Mary Jobe Akeley, who "brought the jungle to Central Park West," was born Mary Leonore in Tappan, Ohio, the younger daughter of Rich-

ard Watson and Sarah Jane (Pittis) Jobe. Her father's family came to the United States from the west of England during colonial times. Richard Jobe, who was born in Missouri, fought in the Civil War, enlisting before he was sixteen. Her mother, born in Ohio, was also of English descent.

Mary Jobe attended Scio College (later Mt. Union College) in Alliance, Ohio, and received her Ph.B. in 1897. She apparently taught school in Ohio before enrolling at Bryn Mawr in 1901 for two years of graduate study in English and history. While at Bryn Mawr, she taught at Temple College in Philadelphia (1902–03). Enrolling at Columbia University for an A.M. in history and English (1909), she simultaneously taught history at the Normal College of the City of New York, which became Hunter College; she remained on the Hunter faculty until 1916.

During her years in New York, Mary Jobe's career as an explorer began. In 1909 she requested a month's leave to join an exploration party in British Columbia, but her travels as an explorer in the Canadian northwest seem to have begun in earnest in 1913. Studying the habitat of Indian groups in the region, she also explored the Canadian Rockies, and made several journeys into the Canadian wilderness for botanical research, mountain climbing, and photography during the summers of 1914 and 1915 and the winters of 1917 and 1918. Her goal was "to go whither we knew not . . . to do the individual thing which we ourselves had chosen, and to do it because, in obtaining a bit of real knowledge hitherto unobtained, it gave unmeasurable satisfaction" ("My Quest," p. 814). The Canadian government gave her a commission to explore and map the headwaters of the Fraser River and she also made the first two attempts to climb Mt. Sir Alexander, one of the highest peaks in the Canadian Rockies (then unmapped and unnamed). In recognition of her accomplishments, the Canadian government later named another of the highest peaks Mt. Jobe. Her work in Canada led to her nomination as a fellow of the Royal Geographic Society of London.

Mary Jobe's interest in the energetic outdoor life led in 1914 to her purchase of land in Mystic, Conn., as a camp for girls. From the first full camp season in 1916 until the camp closed in 1930, she presided over Camp Mystic, where the daughters of the well-to-do learned the techniques of outdoor living and heard famous explorers such as Martin and Osa Johnson and Vilhjalmur Stefannson talk of their adventures.

It may have been Stefannson who introduced her to the noted explorer Carl Akeley, whom she married in 1924. Two years later she went with him to Africa on an expedition designed to collect animal and plant specimens of the region for the Great African Hall he had planned for the American Museum of Natural History in New York City. Mary Jobe Akeley served as field assistant, safari manager, secretary, and photographer for the expedition; she made especially valuable photographs of lions and antelope as well as portraits of animals in their natural habitats. With Carl Akeley she went to Mount Mikeno in the Kivu District of the Belgian Congo to study gorillas, long a central interest of his. He planned a gorilla habitat for the Museum of Natural History and had also been asked by King Albert of Belgium to survey the recently established Parc National Albert and study the best means to provide sanctuary for the large primates.

Carl Akeley died suddenly of a fever in November 1926 and Mary Jobe Akeley took over as leader of the expedition. For several weeks she remained in the Parc National Albert, continuing her husband's study of the great gorillas. In addition she mapped much of Kenya, Tanganyika, and the Congo, and collected plants which, with her photographs, would be used to complete the exhibition at the Great African Hall. Before leaving Africa, she traveled to Uganda to do a photographic study of the pink flamingos indigenous to that region. On her return to New York in 1927, she became a special adviser and assistant at the Hall; dedicated in 1936, it was renamed in memory of Carl Akeley.

In 1928, Mary Jobe Akeley was invited to Belgium to work on reports of the African expedition with J. M. Derscheid, the Belgian zoologist and conservationist who had worked with the Akeleys in the Congo. While there she received from King Albert the Cross of the Knight, Order of the Crown, in recognition of her work in Africa. She was also invited to participate in an effort to enlarge the national park and to initiate a broader program to preserve the large primates, an enterprise she welcomed. Her time in Africa had made her aware of both the destruction of African wildlife by game hunters and the debilitation of African tribal life by the influx of European settlers. She had become a crusader for the establishment of game preserves and a serious student of tribal customs and ceremonies, and worked to protect the African pygmies in the area of the Parc National Albert.

Akeley returned to Africa in 1935, heading her own expedition to the Transvaal, Southern Rhodesia, and Portuguese East Africa to collect further materials for the Museum of Natural History. She surveyed the wildlife in Kruger National Park, and made a study of the Zulu and Swazi people, returning to the Museum with films of the customs and ceremonies of the tribes and with a renewed conviction of the need for a policy for wildlife conservation in the parks. Knowing that "a vanished species can never be recalled, that wild life is easily changed by upsetting the balance of nature, and that primitive men have many customs which should be preserved free from the influence of so called civilization," she saw her work as having both scientific and humanitarian goals.

While her interests centered almost exclusively on Africa from the time of her marriage, Akeley did return to British Columbia in 1938 for a "journey of rediscovery" on the Canoe River. She also made a survey of the Canadian women's war effort and a study of Alaskan defenses, including Kodiak Island, in 1941.

After World War II, Akeley returned to Africa to see the newly enlarged Parc National Albert and to visit her husband's gravesite. The next year, 1947, she was commissioned by the Belgian government to make another survey of wildlife sanctuaries and national parks in the Congo. She also filmed the great African mammals, several of them rare and almost extinct species, and collected plant accessories for the African habitats at the Museum of Natural History.

Mary Jobe Akeley's work in Africa brought her international recognition, but more important it helped to inform the world that Africa's greatest treasures were being plundered almost to extinction. Her several books recognized the beauty and unique promise of Africa and her expeditions realized her desire "to continue to learn of the primitive, to arouse an interest in its preservation."

Mary Akeley spent part of each year at the home she had built on Great Hill in Mystic, Conn., and she retired there. Until her death of a stroke in Stonington, Conn., in 1966, she remained on her hill, holding herself aloof from the town, a "fiercely independent" and legendary figure in the eyes of Mystic residents (Kimball, p. 11).

[The Am. Museum of Natural History has Akeley's personal papers, photographs, diaries, and newspaper clippings. The collection includes her 1941 application for a Guggenheim fellowship, from which unidentified quotes are taken. She published her report to the Museum on the 1926–27 Akeley-Eastman-Pomeroy African Hall Expedition and Carl Akeley's journal of the expedition as *Carl Akeley's Africa* (1929). *Adventures in the African Jungle* (1930) and *Lions, Gorillas and Their*

Neighbors (1932) are based on studies made by Carl Akeley. Her other books are *The Restless Jungle* (1936), *The Wilderness Lives Again: Carl Akeley and the Great Adventure* (1940), *Rumble of a Distant Drum* (1946), and *Congo Eden* (1950). She also wrote numerous magazine articles, book reviews, and travel pieces on Canada and Africa. Those on her early explorations include "My Quest in the Canadian Rockies," *Harper's Mag.*, May 1915; "Mt. Kitchi: A New Peak in the Canadian Rockies," *Bull. Am. Geographical Soc.*, July 15, 1915; and three articles in *Canadian Alpine Jour.*: 6 (1915), 188–200; 7 (1916), 82–99; and 9 (1918), 79–89. Among her writings on her husband and on the 1926–27 expedition are "Carl Akeley's Last Journey," *World's Work*, July 1928, and "In the Land of His Dreams," *Natural Hist.*, Nov.-Dec. 1927. Several articles on her activities in the late 1920s and the 1930s appear in the *N.Y. Times*, for which she also wrote reviews and articles. Carol W. Kimball, "Camp Mystic in the Good Old Summertime," *Historical Footnotes: Bull. Stonington* (Conn.) *Hist. Soc.*, Feb. 1978, includes some biographical information on Akeley, as do the obituaries in the *Geographical Jour.*, Dec. 1966, and the *N.Y. Times*, July 22, 1966. A biobibliography by Janet Marie Harbour assisted in research. A death certificate was provided by Conn. Dept. of Health. Printed sources and the death certificate give Jan 29, 1888, as Akeley's date of birth. The 1878 date is confirmed by the 1880 U.S. Census and by records in the Bryn Mawr College Archives.]

MARY MCCAY

ALEXANDER, Hattie Elizabeth, April 5, 1901–June 24, 1968. Pediatrician, microbiologist.

Hattie Alexander was born in Baltimore, Md., the second daughter and second of eight children of Elsie M. (Townsend) and William Bain Alexander. The ancestors of both her mother and her father, a merchant, were Scottish. The family lived in the heart of Baltimore, and Hattie attended the city's Western High School for girls. A partial scholarship enabled her to enroll at Goucher College where she was an enthusiastic athlete and a not very ambitious C student. Yet Alexander showed even then the qualities of character and intellectual tastes that later contributed to her success as a physician and a scientist. The college yearbook recognized her fundamental attributes: "Ambition fires her; hygiene claims her; kindness portrays her." Her interest in "hygiene" led her to prefer courses in bacteriology and physiology.

After graduating from Goucher with an A.B. in 1923, Alexander worked for three years as a bacteriologist, first for the United States Public Health Service and then for the Maryland Public Health Service. She saved enough money to enroll in the Johns Hopkins School of Medicine where she made a brilliant record. After receiving her M.D. in 1930, Alexander served a one-year internship in pediatrics at the Harriet Lane Home in Baltimore. There she developed an interest, which was to be lifelong, in influenzal meningitis, a disease caused by *Hemophilus influenzae* (unrelated to the influenza virus). In 1931 Alexander interned at Babies Hospital of the Columbia-Presbyterian Medical Center in New York City, accepting at the completion of her service an appointment as instructor in the medical school's department of pediatrics. Thereafter she rose steadily in the ranks of the teaching and attending staff of this medical center, becoming full professor in 1958. From 1966 until her death, Alexander was professor emeritus and special lecturer in pediatrics, as well as consultant to the Presbyterian Hospital.

At Babies Hospital, in the pediatric service of Rustin McIntosh, Alexander was in full charge of the microbiological laboratory, which exercised both a service and a research function. She established such rigid standards that the laboratory soon became a model of excellence, the envy of the other pediatric services. She also undertook a heavy load of clinical teaching. A diffident and almost reluctant lecturer, Alexander excelled in the give-and-take of bedside teaching. Always she insisted on objective evidence to back up clinical judgment, training her students to develop a healthy skepticism.

Her first research studies were in the diagnosis and treatment of bacterial meningitis, especially that caused by *Hemophilus influenzae*. Treatment of this disease by anti-influenzal serum prepared in horses had uniformly failed. But, learning that Rockefeller Institute scientists had prepared in rabbits a serum highly successful for the treatment of pneumonia, Alexander applied this knowledge to her own problem. She immunized rabbits with large doses of influenza bacilli and worked in collaboration with immunochemist Michael Heidelberger to determine in the test tube the potency of the serum thus obtained. In 1939 she reported that treatment with the rabbit serum had brought about complete cure in infants critically ill with influenzal meningitis—the first successful treatment of this previously fatal disease. In the early 1940s Alexander began experimenting with drug treatment, first with the sulfas and then with other antibiotics, and eventually succeeded in substantially reducing the mortality of influenzal meningitis. Noting the resistance to antibiotics often developed by cultures of influenza bacilli, she was one of the first to realize that this phenomenon was a consequence of genetic mutation. Thus she was led into the study of microbiological genetics, then just beginning to emerge as one of the most exciting biological sciences.

Alexander immediately recognized the importance of the 1944 report by Rockefeller Institute scientists that they had been able to change the hereditary characteristics of pneumococci by means of the genetic constituent now known as DNA, a discovery that many others received with initial skepticism. In collaboration with Grace Leidy she developed techniques which made it possible in 1950 to produce hereditary changes in *Hemophilus influenzae* with DNA obtained from this organism, thus confirming and extending the work done at Rockefeller Institute. To the end of her life Alexander continued her research in genetics with other bacterial species and with various types of viruses. At the same time, she remained active on the wards and even extended her clinical studies to tuberculosis.

The successful integration of achievements in theoretical biology with the practice of clinical medicine required skillful management of her time and much intellectual discipline. These qualities are reflected in the precision and organization of Alexander's writings, which won her in 1954 the Stevens Triennial Prize for the best essay on a medical subject. The recipient of many other honors, including the E. Mead Johnson Award for Research in Pediatrics (1942), she was the first woman to receive the Oscar B. Hunter Memorial Award of the American Therapeutic Society (1961), and the first woman president of the American Pediatric Society (1964).

Alexander was a fun-loving person, fond of music, of travel, and of her speedboat; she also cultivated exotic flowers. With Dr. Elizabeth Ufford, her companion for many years, she lived in Port Washington, N.Y., until her death of cancer in New York City in 1968.

[Columbia-Presbyterian Medical Center has compiled a list of some 150 articles published by Hattie Alexander. A list of publications and a curriculum vitae are also available from Goucher College. Sources of biographical information include Mary Jane Hogue, "The Contribution of Goucher Women to the Biological Sciences," *Goucher Alumnae Quart.*, Summer 1951, pp. 21–22; Lenore Turner, "From C Student to Winning Scientist," *Goucher Alumnae Quart.*, Winter 1962, pp. 18–20; *Nat. Cyc. Am. Biog.*, J, 106 (with photograph). An evaluation of Alexander's work and appreciation of her personality are contained in Rustin McIntosh's letter to the editor of *Pediatrics*, Sept. 1968, p. 544. Edward C. Curnen's memorial to Hattie Alexander, delivered July 29, 1968, is available from Columbia-Presbyterian Med. Center. Obituaries appeared in *N.Y. Times*, June 25, 1968, and *Goucher Alumnae Quart.*, Fall 1968. A biobibliography prepared by Susan Finer assisted in the research for this article. Additional information was supplied by Alexander's brother, William B. Alexander.]

RENÉ DUBOS

ALLEN, Florence Ellinwood, March 23, 1884–Sept. 12, 1966. Judge, lawyer, suffragist.

Florence Allen was born in Salt Lake City, Utah, the third daughter of seven children of Clarence Emir and Corinne Marie (Tuckerman) Allen. Her seventeenth-century English ancestors had pioneered in New England; their descendants had settled in the Ohio and Pennsylvania wilderness and her parents were pioneers in the Utah territory. Florence Allen would pioneer in her own way, becoming the first woman on the Ohio Supreme Court and the United States Court of Appeals, as well as an active supporter of women's advances into all areas of public life.

She was a favorite of her paternal grandfather, Edwin R. Allen, justice of the peace in Girard, Pa. Her maternal grandfather, Jacob Tuckerman, a graduate of Oberlin College, was an early advocate of higher education for women. Florence attended his school, New Lyme Institute, in Ashtabula County, Ohio, from 1895 to 1897, while her father served in Congress as the first representative from the state of Utah. Clarence Allen had passed the Utah bar, served in the state legislature, managed mines, and taught his children Greek and Latin; Florence Allen considered him a brilliant scholar and her best friend. She also admired the industry of her mother, the first student admitted to Smith College, who in addition to raising a large family was a leader of the Mothers' Congress and the Utah Federation of Women's Clubs.

Florence Allen attended Salt Lake College from 1897 to 1899, and in 1900 matriculated at Western Reserve University in Cleveland, Ohio, where her father had once taught classics. Elected president of her freshman class and editor of the college magazine, she graduated Phi Beta Kappa in 1904. The next two years were spent with her family in Berlin, Germany, where she studied piano and wrote on music for several English-language periodicals. Returning to Western Reserve, she received an A.M. in political science in 1908, and the following year entered the University of Chicago Law School. In 1910, however, she left Chicago at the request of FRANCES KELLOR to work for the New York League for the Protection of Immigrants. In New York she lived at the Henry Street Settlement, assisted MAUD WOOD PARK at the College Equal Suffrage League, and became acquainted with other leaders of the social welfare and suffrage movements. She also enrolled at New York University Law School, which had a reputation for encouraging women students, and graduated second in her class in 1913. The school later established the Florence E. Allen scholarship fund.

Admitted to the Ohio bar in 1914, Allen opened her own office in Cleveland, volunteered for legal aid work, and participated in local Democratic party politics. She also took on the legal chores of the Woman Suffrage party in Cleveland, arguing in favor of municipal suffrage for women before the Ohio Supreme Court and aiding in legal battles for presidential suffrage. Inspired by Maud Wood Park, and encouraged by HARRIET TAYLOR UPTON, she spoke on women's rights in every Ohio county and across the United States.

A decade of work for woman suffrage developed large state and national female constituencies for Florence Allen. She considered running for the state legislature and later ran unsuccessfully in the 1926 Democratic primary for United States Senate and in the 1932 congressional election. She was more successful in achieving nonpartisan judicial office. Her first appointment was as assistant county prosecutor of Cuyahoga County, Ohio, in 1919. After ratification of the nineteenth amendment, she announced her candidacy for common pleas court judge, and members of the Woman Suffrage party carried her petitions. She won support from unions, church and professional groups, newspapers, and both political parties, and ran first against nine male candidates. As the first woman on any general jurisdiction court, she set about improving judicial administration.

In 1922, sixty-six Florence Allen Clubs canvassed the state to elect her to the Ohio Supreme Court by a large majority. Driving a Model T Ford, she campaigned to become the first woman on an appellate court of last resort, and was reelected in 1928 by a larger majority.

In 1934 friends and supporters from labor, academic, business, and reform groups backed her nomination to the Sixth Circuit Court of Appeals. They persuaded Ohio Senator Robert J. Bulkley and President Franklin D. Roosevelt of the political wisdom of ending the male monopoly in the federal court system and Allen was appointed. Attorney General Homer Cummings commented: "Florence Allen was not appointed because she was a woman. All we did was to see that she was not rejected because she was a woman" (*To Do Justly*, p. 95).

Allen's most notable decision as a federal judge concerned the constitutionality of the powers granted the Tennessee Valley Authority (TVA). Private utility companies from nine southern and border states had sued the TVA, challenging the scope of its authority. Allen's legal and administrative abilities were tested by the trial, which ran for several weeks in 1937 and required consideration of masses of technical data. Her opinion upheld the right of the TVA to buy transmission lines from private companies, sell electricity generated by its dams, and build new dams. The ruling, which had widespread implications for New Deal public works programs, was upheld by the United States Supreme Court. The public attention she received at the time encouraged speculation that she would be elevated to the Supreme Court. But Allen had been correct in predicting in a 1934 letter, "That will never happen to a woman while I am living."

Praised at her death as "a great patriot," throughout her career Allen had delivered speeches on the Constitution, which were later collected in *This Constitution of Ours* (1940). But her patriotism did not conflict with her strong desire for world peace, intensified by the loss of two younger brothers in World War I. She advocated a flexible use of international law to settle disputes and at a 1925 conference of women chaired by CARRIE CHAPMAN CATT, she spoke forcefully for the outlawry of war. In the 1930s she worked for good relations with Mexico at a series of church-sponsored seminars, and by 1948 she was calling for international cooperation in regulating space exploration. In addition to these efforts, Allen was active in the American Bar Association, chaired committees of the International Bar Association and the International Federation of Women Lawyers, and visited women law leaders in Europe and Asia.

Florence Allen combined great ambition with common sense, pride with sensitivity, and humor with rectitude. She viewed life as a series of small personal and large social struggles. Although strong and stocky in appearance, she suffered illnesses which sometimes interfered with her reading, piano playing, and daily walks for pleasure and exercise. She also experienced continual financial distress, paying off a note she cosigned for friends before the depression, helping to support her parents, one sister, and a niece, and often finding her judge's salary insufficient to meet the costs of her national and international responsibilities.

As a judge, Allen's aim was to perform so that the public and her peers would find female authority appropriate. The appreciation of her fellow judges was particularly important to her, and she was satisfied at the end of her career that "judges who were at first opposed to women officials accepted us when we handled our work steadily and conscientiously" (*To Do Justly*, p. 96). Judge Allen retired in 1959; she was widely honored both before and after her retirement for her achievements on and off the bench. She died in 1966 of a stroke in Cleveland, Ohio.

[The Florence E. Allen Papers at the Western Reserve Hist. Soc., Cleveland, Ohio, include personal and work diaries for 1901–66, notes on cases, opinion drafts, speeches, scrapbooks and clippings, and correspondence. A "Register of Papers" was prepared by Ellen B. Heinbach in 1971. Duplicates of some of these materials are in the Schlesinger Library, Radcliffe College. Other books by Allen are *To Do Justly* (1965), a short autobiography, and *The Treaty as an Instrument of Legislation* (1952). Her support for women in public life rings through her article, "Participation of Women in Government," Am. Acad. of Political and Social Sci., *Annals*, May 1947, pp. 94–103. Allen's numerous appellate opinions can be found in the *Ohio Reports*, 1923–28, and the *Federal Reporter*, 1935–65. Sources of biographical information include "From Covered Wagon to the Judge's Bench," Youngstown, Ohio, *Sunday Vindicator*, Oct. 28, 1928; Grace Izant, "The Life Story of Ohio's First Lady," *Cleveland Plain Dealer*, Oct. 6, 1935; Marion J. Harron, "In Memoriam: Honorable Florence Ellinwood Allen," *Women Lawyers Jour.*, Fall 1966; Eleanor Roosevelt and Lorena Hickok, *Ladies of Courage* (1954), pp. 195–98; and *Nat. Cyc. Am. Biog.*, LII, 111–12. The speeches given at the portrait presentation ceremonies and dinner for Allen's retirement show her relationship to the federal bar and bench: West's Reporter series 278 F 2d 4–35 (1960). Her portrait hangs in the federal building, Sixth Circuit Court of Appeals, Cincinnati, Ohio; other photographs can be found in the pictures collection of the Allen papers. An obituary appeared in the *N.Y. Times*, Sept. 14, 1966; death record provided by Ohio Dept. of Health.]

                                        BEVERLY BLAIR COOK

ALLEN, Gracie, July 26, 1895–Aug. 27, 1964. Comedian, actress.

Gracie Allen was born Grace Ethel Cecile Rosalie Allen in San Francisco, the daughter of Margaret (Darragh) and George W. Allen. Reputed to be the best clog- and buck-dancer in San Francisco, her father later taught dancing and physical education. The youngest of five (three older sisters and a brother), Allen first came on stage before the age of six at a benefit, in a dress suit and top hat, although she refused to wear the red whiskers that went with the costume. (Badly scalded as a baby, she was left with a scar on her right arm and always wore long-sleeved costumes.) When she was fourteen her education at the Star of the Sea Convent School was interrupted when she joined her sister Bessie in a vaudeville act in Chicago, dancing the Highland reel. At sixteen, she was booked for "singles" in the San Francisco area, her mother serving as her dresser. Her first three-days' salary was fifteen dollars.

Gracie Allen and her sisters joined an act called the Larry Reilly Company, playing colleen parts in a brogue that she had difficulty losing later on. As her sisters dropped out one by one, Gracie stayed on to become the star attraction, but quit after a quarrel over billing. She then worked a six-a-day act that featured Boylan Brazil as a smooth-talking jewelry salesman and herself as a simple country girl. Disgusted with poor bookings, however, she left the act in Wilkes-Barre, Pa., went to New York, and entered a secretarial school where she remained for three months.

In 1922, Allen met George Burns (born Nathan Birnbaum), then a minor song-and-dance man; in his words "she made me a success after years and years of failure." Initially, Allen played straight to Burns's comedy but Burns soon recognized that her set-ups got more laughs than his punch lines. The rewritten act, called "Sixty-Forty," was first booked in Newark, N.J., for $10 and initiated the soon-to-be-famous combination of Gracie, the scatterbrained ingenue, and George, the long-suffering boyfriend. Gracie's persona of endearing dizziness differed from that of other "dumb Doras" then in variety by eschewing grotesque outfits and slapstick, by dressing with chic, and by dealing in what Burns called "illogical logic": "Gracie gets her laughs—we hope—because we often *think* the way Gracie *talks*, but we pride ourselves that *we* never talk the way Gracie thinks." Burns slowly developed her stage character from a wisecracker to a garrulous, flirtatious, addlepated flapper, rattling on about her relations: "My uncle eats concrete. Mother asked him to stay to dinner, but he said he was going to eat up the street." Despite what she reported as intense stage fright, Allen powerfully impressed reviewers, who found the act original, clean, and "devilish clever." It toured the Orpheum circuit at $400 a week.

As "Dizzy," the act was booked for nineteen weeks on Loew's circuit, and a new version, "Lamb Chops," was signed to a six-year contract by the Keith theaters to tour the United States and Europe beginning in 1926. The success enabled Burns and Allen to marry in Cleveland, Ohio, on Jan. 7, 1926. (Burns had been married once before.) In London, they made so popular a debut on the BBC that their radio show was extended for twenty weeks. In 1930, after they appeared with Eddie Cantor at the Palace Theatre in New York, Cantor asked Allen to do a guest stint on his radio program. Their first joint appearance on American radio was on the Rudy Vallee show. That job was followed by two years on the Guy Lombardo show, which led to an offer from the Columbia Broadcasting System (CBS) of a contract for their own show, "The Adventures of Gracie," which premiered on Feb. 15, 1932. By 1940 Burns and Allen had more than forty-five million listeners and made over $9,000 a week. Gracie's recurring, "Oh, George, I'll bet you tell that to all the girls" and "I don't get it" became national catchphrases, and "Gracie Allen" a fond nickname for any female nitwit.

Allen herself had only a minimal part in the development of her stage character. The radio scripts were written by three men and edited by Burns, to whom she entrusted all of her career decisions. The scripts were submitted to her only on the day of the broadcast, when she omitted all "smartalecky" or double entendre lines, coined characteristic remarks, and then went on the air giving a perfect illusion of spontaneity. Her freshness, staccato delivery, high-pitched voice, and total unconsciousness of the studio audience contributed to her authenticity as a living zany in American mythology.

Some of the most celebrated publicity stunts in radio history were connected with Gracie Allen's persona. In 1933 she began a radio search for an imaginary lost brother, popping up unexpectedly on soap operas, mysteries, and daytime serials in lunatic pursuit. In 1938, to make money for the China Aid Council, she exhibited a set of "surrealistic" pastels at the Julien Levy Gallery in New York; the works bore such titles as "Eyes Adrift as Sardines Wrench at Your Heart Strings." In 1940 Allen ran for president on the Surprise party ticket and received a few hundred write-in votes.

Allen's first film was an improvised short subject made for Warner Brothers; she signed her first movie contract with RKO in 1930, transferring to Paramount a year later. Her cinematic career was trivial, consisting primarily of excerpts from the vaudeville routines or segments sandwiched into anthology films, although she managed to steal focus from W. C. Fields in *International House* (1933) and *Six of a Kind* (1934). She was also the first movie actress to have a film named after her: *The Gracie Allen Murder Case* (1939), from the novel by S. S. Van Dine. Allen abandoned film work in the late 1930s to spend more time with her adopted children, Sandra Jean (b. 1934) and Ronald John (b. 1935).

A decline in ratings made Burns and Allen

realize that audiences no longer accepted a bantering boy-girl relationship from a middle-aged married couple. In 1945, moving to the National Broadcasting Company, they changed the format of their show to a domestic situation comedy; in October 1950, they transferred to CBS television in a highly successful biweekly series. Allen moved to television reluctantly, but filmed before a live audience, a process which required intensive rehearsals. In 1955, Burns and Allen added a brief excerpt from their old variety routines as the standard closing and their son Ronald joined them as a featured player, enhancing the sense of reality in the comedy. In the late 1950s Allen began to grow tense and withdrawn, and to suffer migraine headaches brought on, according to George Burns, by the "chronic strain of making like someone she isn't." She retired in 1958 on her doctor's orders, devoting her time to her grandchildren and to card-playing. On Aug. 26, 1964, the five-foot tall, auburn-haired comedian, who always protested that she had never enjoyed show business, suffered a heart attack and entered Cedars of Lebanon Hospital in Hollywood where she died the next day.

[Gracie Allen's papers have been deposited at the Univ. of Southern Calif. There are clipping files in the Billy Rose Theatre Coll., N.Y. Public Library, and at the Harvard Theatre Coll.; also see back issues of *Radio Guide* and *Radio Mirror*. Allen's memoirs are reported in Katharine Best, "Nitwits of the Networks," *Stage*, May 1 and May 15, 1939, and "Gracie Allen's Own Story: 'Inside Me' as Told to Jane Kesner Morris," *Woman's Home Companion*, March 1953. Her one book, *How to Become President* ("The Gracie Allen Self-Delusion Institute," 1940), was actually written by Charles Palmer, and her column, which appeared in 125 newspapers, was similarly ghosted. A filmography appears in *Who Was Who on Screen* (1974). Columbia Records has issued two sets of recordings of Burns and Allen broadcasts from 1930 and 1933; recordings of their radio shows have also been released by Mark and by Radiola. George Burns gives much information in his two reminiscences, *I Love Her That's Why* (1955) and *Living It Up* (1977), and in an interview in *Educational Theatre Jour.*, Oct. 1975. See also the joint entry "George Burns and Gracie Allen" in *Current Biog.*, 1951. Obituaries appeared in the *N.Y. Times*, Aug. 29, 1964, and *Variety*, Sept. 2, 1964. Allen's birth date is most often given as 1902; the 1895 date is confirmed by the 1900 U.S. Census. A marriage certificate was provided by the Cuyahoga Cty. Probate Court, Cleveland; death record from Calif. Dept. of Public Health. Shirley Staples, who is preparing a doctoral dissertation at Tufts University relating Burns and Allen to the tradition of male-female comedy acts in American vaudeville, was of major assistance in preparing this article.]

LAURENCE SENELICK

AMES, Blanche Ames, Feb. 18, 1878–March 1, 1969. Suffragist, artist, feminist.

Blanche Ames, best known as a botanical illustrator and an advocate of birth control, was born in Lowell, Mass., the fourth of six children and third of four daughters of Adelbert and Blanche (Butler) Ames. Both parents descended from early settlers of New England. Her father, a native of Rockland, Maine, and a general in the Civil War, served as United States senator and governor of Mississippi during Reconstruction. Her mother was the daughter of Benjamin F. Butler, a Civil War general and later a congressman from Massachusetts, and Sarah (Hildreth) Butler, a popular Shakespearean actress.

For most of Blanche's youth, the family lived in Lowell, where the Butlers owned woolen mills. Her father's investments in family flour mills in Northfield, Minn., meant long separations. Nevertheless, they were an unusually close and happy family, the parents taking an active role in the education of their children. Blanche learned golf, tennis, football, and yachting—her grandfather owned the yacht *America*. Privilege also meant learning self-discipline and the highest standards of conduct. "I have no doubt you will keep up the reputation of the family while we are away," General Ames wrote to his children in 1893.

Blanche Ames graduated from Rogers Hall School in Lowell in 1895 and entered Smith College. There she excelled in art, played basketball, and was president of her class. She received an A.B. in 1899. In May of that year she displayed her early interest in women's rights: "I am out of temper because of the Debate in History: 'Resolved, that women should be given the right of suffrage,' and they put me on the negative side, *me* of all people!"

On May 15, 1900, Blanche Ames married Oakes Ames (unrelated), an instructor in botany at Harvard University. "You and I are forming a contract . . . we have an equal voice," he wrote to her before their wedding. They settled in his home in North Easton, Mass., the site of the prosperous Ames Shovel and Tool Company. There the couple planned and built Borderland, an elaborate estate where they farmed and raised cattle. They had four children: Pauline (b. 1901), Oliver (b. 1903), Amyas (b. 1906), and Evelyn (b. 1910).

The marriage of Blanche and Oakes Ames began a remarkable, lifelong collaboration in the discovery, study, and illustration of the world's orchids. Working from their extensive collection of living orchids as well as with dried specimens, Blanche Ames executed drawings and analytical sketches of hundreds of new species which were published in a seven-volume series, *Orchidaceae: Illustrations and Studies of the Family Orchidaceae* (1905–22). Oakes Ames became the leading orchidologist of his day, serving as Arnold Professor of Botany at Harvard, and also becoming director of the Botanical Museum and supervisor of the Arnold Arboretum. Together they made numerous collecting trips around the world. They developed the Ames Charts, using water colors executed by Blanche Ames to show the phylogenetic relationships of the more important useful plants.

Close collaboration was evident in their political activity as well. Both Republicans, they lobbied the Republican National Convention delegates in 1914 to support a suffrage plank. Blanche Ames was an officer of the Massachusetts Woman Suffrage League, and her husband headed a men's suffrage league. She also produced a widely used series of prosuffrage cartoons with incisive captions. In 1918 she chaired a committee of Massachusetts women who organized a campaign against Sen. John W. Weeks, an opponent of the suffrage amendment. Her husband noted in his diary: "Walsh defeated Weeks. Blanche danced around the library table!"

No issue was as central to Ames's belief in self-determination for women as birth control. In 1916 she cofounded the Birth Control League of Massachusetts (BCLM), an affiliate of the national group led by MARGARET SANGER. Through debates, mass meetings, and private persuasion, the BCLM sought to make birth control a public issue. Ames used her social and political connections to enlist the support of prominent people. She also did research on maternal health statistics, planned a parents' petition to the Massachusetts Medical Society, and engaged in a public debate with leaders of the Roman Catholic church. In 1935 she resigned from the BCLM in protest over a fundraising advertisement that appealed to taxpayers by citing the 250,000 babies born to families on relief.

When all attempts to modify the law prohibiting the dissemination of birth control information were defeated, Ames wrote: "Women must resort to their old expedient of self-help. They must tell each other how to regulate conception. Mothers must teach their daughters, since their doctors may not supply the means." She illustrated methods for making a diaphragm starting with a baby's teething ring, or a jam jar ring, and wrote down formulas for spermicidal jellies.

Ames's strong belief in freedom of choice led

her in 1941 to become a member of the corporation of the New England Hospital for Women and Children (NEH), founded in 1862 to afford women medical care by members of their sex and to train women physicians and nurses. By 1950 the hospital was in financial difficulties, and its board of directors accepted recommendations to include men on the active staff. Ames objected, citing the original charter of the NEH, and when she became president of the board in 1952 she led a broad fund-raising effort to maintain the unique character of the hospital. A number of wealthy donors, including KATHARINE DEXTER MCCORMICK, came to the aid of the NEH at Ames's request. The hospital survived, and in 1955 its directors established the Blanche Ames Fund for Medical Education of Women.

At the age of eighty, prompted by references to Adelbert Ames as a carpetbagger in John F. Kennedy's *Profiles in Courage*, Ames began to compile data on her father's career. Her book, *Adelbert Ames, Broken Oaths and Reconstruction in Mississippi, 1835–1933*, a spirited defense of the career of General Ames, was published in 1964. She also painted many oil portraits of her father, one of which hangs at the state capitol in Jackson, Miss. Other oil paintings by Blanche Ames are displayed at Dartmouth College, Columbia University, and Phillips Exeter Academy.

An avid inventor, Ames applied for patents on a hexagonal lumber cutter, propeller snares for catching low-flying enemy aircraft during World War II, and an antipollution toilet. During her last year of life she was involved in refurbishing the Oakes Ames Hall in North Easton, a prime example of the architecture of H. H. Richardson. She survived her husband by nineteen years, dying at Borderland of a stroke in 1969.

In everything she did, Blanche Ames Ames was remarkable for her energy and commitment. Her daughter Pauline has written: "For her to have an idea was to act, no matter how difficult or how impossible. We were never allowed to say 'I can't,' even if we might think it."

[Blanche Ames Ames's collected papers, diaries, and letters are part of the Ames Family Papers, Sophia Smith Coll., Smith College, as are notebooks of drawings, art albums, charts showing her theory of color, suffrage cartoons, and photographs of her oil paintings. The collection also contains Pauline Ames Plimpton, "Ancestry of Blanche Butler Ames and Adelbert Ames," a genealogy compiled in 1977. Pauline Plimpton also edited *Oakes Ames: Jottings of a Harvard Botanist* (1980). The Blanche Ames Ames Papers at the Schlesinger Library, Radcliffe College, contain material on the New England Hospital, some of Ames's suffrage correspondence (1892–1919), birth control correspondence (1931–

43), and some birth control literature. Her drawings and etchings of orchids are at the Ames Orchid Herbarium, Harvard Univ. Her book *Drawings of Florida Orchids* was published in 1959. Biographical information is also found in Richard Evans Schultes, "Blanche Ames Ames, 1878–1969: An Appreciation," Botanical Museum Leaflet, Harvard Univ., vol. 22, no. 7, 1969, and *Nat. Cyc. Am. Biog.*, LIII, 573. Family background is contained in entries for Benjamin Butler, Adelbert Ames, and Oakes Ames, *Dict. Am. Biog.*, vol. three, Supp. One, and Supp. Four, respectively, and in Blanche Butler Ames, comp., *Chronicles from the Nineteenth Century: Family Letters of Blanche Butler and Adelbert Ames*, 2 vols. (1957). At Borderland, a state park, her art studio is intact; several of her portraits and suffrage cartoons are also there. Obituaries appeared in the March 3, 1969, *Boston Globe* and *N.Y. Times*. Further information was provided by Pauline Ames Plimpton, Susan Boone, William Nelson, Richard Schultes, and Lesley Garay. Death certificate was supplied by Mass. Dept. of Public Health.]

JANET NELSON FRIEDELL

AMES, Jessie Daniel, Nov. 2, 1883–Feb. 21, 1972. Antilynching reformer, suffragist.

Jessie Daniel Ames was born in Palestine, Texas, the third of four children and the younger daughter of James Malcom and Laura Maria (Leonard) Daniel. Her mother had grown up on an Indiana farm, attended Battle Ground Methodist Institute, and taught briefly before marrying James Daniel, a Scots-Irish orphan from Buffalo, N.Y., who worked as a train dispatcher and telegraph operator. The family moved from Palestine to the small railroad crossing of Overton and then in 1893 to Georgetown, Texas.

Loneliness clouded Jessie Daniel's early life. She admired her self-educated father, but he reserved his affection for his first-born daughter. As a student at the primary school and, later, at the college of Southwestern University, a Methodist school in Georgetown, her painful feeling of unworthiness hampered her friendships. Graduating in 1902, she faced what she regarded as the purgatory of spinsterhood. Her mother was a strong-willed Methodist church worker who nursed the sick and played an active role in community affairs, but the only female relative who might have provided a model for a dignified alternative to marriage was her father's half-sister ANNIE STURGIS DANIEL, an early suffragist and physician. James Daniel disapproved of his sister, however, and Jessie met her only after she had launched her own career.

In 1905, Jessie Daniel married a friend of her father's, Roger Post Ames, an Army physician thirteen years her senior who had worked on Walter Reed's yellow fever experiments in Cuba. She saw her wedding as belated proof of her desirability as a woman. But the marriage was an unhappy one, marred by sexual incompatibility and financial problems. In 1907, Ames gave birth to a son, Frederick, and six years later to a daughter, Mary. During most of her nine-and-a-half-year marriage, she and her husband lived separately; he practiced medicine in Central America, while she stayed with her parents or older sister and visited him periodically. In 1914, when Jessie Ames was pregnant with her third child, Lulu, her husband died of black water fever in Guatemala.

A widow at thirty-one, with three young children to support, Ames began her emergence into public life. She and her mother, who had been widowed three years earlier, managed a local telephone company and shared in the care of Ames's children, the youngest of whom was crippled by polio in 1920. The self-confidence and economic independence Ames acquired in this period encouraged her incipient feminism. In 1916, with her mother's enthusiastic support, she organized a county suffrage association. As a protégée of Texas Equal Suffrage Association president MINNIE FISHER CUNNINGHAM, Ames was soon writing and speaking in behalf of women's rights. She was elected treasurer of the state association in 1918 and, in this position, helped to secure suffrage for women in primary elections and to make Texas the first southern state to ratify the nineteenth amendment.

Ames moved in many directions to mobilize newly enfranchised women. In 1919, she became the founding president of the Texas League of Women Voters (LWV) and was a representative of the National LWV to the Pan-American Congress of 1923. She also served as a delegate-at-large to the national Democratic party conventions of 1920 and 1924 and as an alternate delegate to the convention of 1928. As an organizer and president of the Texas branch of the American Association of University Women and an officer of the Joint Legislative Council, the Committee on Prisons and Prison Labor, and the Federation of Women's Clubs, she sought to enlist women behind the social welfare goals of southern progressivism.

Unlike most of her allies, however, Jessie Daniel Ames soon perceived the limitations of the movement in which she found her start. The female voting bloc that she expected did not materialize. More important, her political work in an era dominated by the Ku Klux Klan forced her to confront the contradiction of a women's humanitarian reform movement that excluded black women from its ranks and racial oppres-

sion from its concerns. In 1924, she became director of the Texas council of the Atlanta-based Commission on Interracial Cooperation (CIC), as well as field representative for the southwest. Five years later, she moved to Georgia to accept the directorship of the Woman's Committee of the CIC.

Jessie Daniel Ames made her major contribution to the interracial movement through the Association of Southern Women for the Prevention of Lynching (ASWPL), which she founded in 1930 and directed until its disbandment. The ASWPL proposed to use the moral and social leverage of enfranchised white women for preventing mob violence in the rural south. It hoped to affect public opinion by challenging the justification commonly given for lynching: that it was necessary for the defense of white womanhood. Ames collected statistics that showed that only 29 percent of lynch victims were accused of rape or other crimes against white women. She also encouraged women to dispute the stereotype of the vulnerable white female in need of protection.

The ASWPL, which was sponsored and largely financed by the CIC, worked through existing women's groups, primarily Protestant women's missionary societies. It formed state councils in each southern state; council members garnered endorsements from other women's groups, solicited antilynching pledges from local women, and issued press statements denouncing the claim that lynchers acted "solely in the defense of womanhood." The organization's central strategies were, first, to convince police officials to protect their prisoners and bring mob members to trial and, second, to urge the wives and daughters of the men who lynched to act as a restraining influence on masculine violence.

Like FRANCES WILLARD, who used temperance to channel women into the political arena, Jessie Daniel Ames sought to link mob violence to the special concerns of women and to lead them toward an increasingly sophisticated understanding of the roots and implications of lynching. She made ingenious use of southern institutions and of the modes of influence available to middle-class women. Her personal control over ASWPL policy, however, limited the group's ability to evolve in response to new issues and opportunities. Largely at her insistence, the ASWPL refused to lobby for federal antilynching legislation. Such a shift to federal initiatives, she feared, would undermine her own regional leadership position, divert attention from underlying social dynamics to legislative panaceas, and obviate the campaign's function as a means of liberation for white women as well as for blacks. Ames's obduracy on this issue helped alienate her from the thrust of southern liberalism in the New Deal era.

With a decrease in the number of lynchings, the ASWPL dissolved in 1942. During World War II, Ames set in motion a series of conferences designed to reinvigorate the CIC. When, instead, the result of the conferences was the dissolution of the organization and its replacement by the Southern Regional Council, she was forced into reluctant retirement. From 1944 until 1968, she lived in Tryon, N.C., active in local Democratic party politics and vitally interested in world affairs, but no longer the dedicated, energetic reformer she had been for a quarter of a century.

Friends remember Jessie Daniel Ames in her latter years as "animated, positive, and full of determination." But no amount of determination could compensate for her loss of the work in which she had achieved her greatest sense of authenticity and self-fulfillment. In a period of antifeminist reaction, she found herself prey to doubts about her own contravention of sex-role prescriptions. Forced out of the public arena, she proved vulnerable once more to the emotional isolation that had blighted her youth and young womanhood. In the late 1960s, suffering from crippling arthritis, Ames gave up her struggle to live alone and returned to Texas to be cared for by her younger daughter, Lulu. She died of pneumonia in 1972 at the age of eighty-eight in a nursing home in Austin, Texas.

[The Jessie Daniel Ames Papers in the Southern Hist. Coll., Univ. of N.C. at Chapel Hill, contain correspondence, clippings, and other materials concerning her work with the CIC and the ASWPL. The other principal MS. collection is the ASWPL papers, Trevor Arnett Library, Atlanta Univ., which contain correspondence and records of the association, records of state councils, and lynching data. The CIC Coll., also at Atlanta Univ., has correspondence and records by and related to Ames and her CIC work. Smaller holdings in the Dallas Hist. Soc. include biographical material, clippings, and other papers on the Texas woman suffrage campaign, the LWV, and Ames's Democratic party work. The Texas State Library in Austin has biographical data, professional correspondence, and papers on the LWV and the Texas Equal Suffrage Association. Private family papers and photographs are in the author's possession. Among Ames's own writings are *Southern Women Look at Lynching* (1937) and *The Changing Character of Lynching* (1942). For a fuller description and bibliography see Jacquelyn Dowd Hall, *Revolt Against Chivalry: Jessie Daniel Ames and the Women's Campaign Against Lynching* (1979). Also useful are Henry E. Barber, "The Association of Southern Women for the Prevention of Lynching, 1930–1942" (M.A. thesis, Univ. of Ga., 1967) and "The Association of Southern Women for the Prevention of Lynching,

1930–1942," *Phylon*, Dec. 1973, pp. 378–89; Wilma Dykeman and James Stokely, *Seeds of Southern Change: The Life of Will Alexander* (1962); John Shelton Reed, "An Evaluation of an Anti-Lynching Organization," *Social Problems*, Fall 1968, pp. 172–82; Kathleen Atkinson Miller, "The Ladies and the Lynchers: A Look at the Association of Southern Women for the Prevention of Lynching," *Southern Studies*, Fall 1978; and Anne Firor Scott, *The Southern Lady: From Pedestal to Politics, 1830–1930* (1970). Additional information was provided by Lulu Daniel Ames. Death record from Texas Dept. of Health.]

JACQUELYN DOWD HALL

ANDERSEN, Dorothy Hansine, May 15, 1901–March 3, 1963. Pathologist, pediatrician.

Dorothy Hansine Andersen was born in Asheville, N.C., the only child of Hans Peter and (Mary) Louise (Mason) Andersen. Her father, a native of the Danish island of Bornholm, grew up on a farm in Danville, Vt. He was a YMCA secretary and a member of the national advisory board of the YMCA. Her mother was a descendant of Sir John Wentworth, colonial governor of New Hampshire, and of Benning Wentworth, for whom the town of Bennington, Vt., was named. Following the death of her father in 1914, Dorothy Andersen moved her invalid mother to Saint Johnsbury, Vt.; Louise Andersen died there in 1920, leaving her daughter with not a single close relative.

Dorothy Andersen graduated from Saint Johnsbury Academy (1918), Mount Holyoke College (1922), and Johns Hopkins Medical School (1926). Her first two papers, on the blood vessels and lymphatics of the ovary and fallopian tube of the sow, were accepted by *Contributions to Embryology* while she was still a medical student; research for these papers was done in the laboratory of FLORENCE SABIN. She taught anatomy for a year at Rochester School of Medicine before interning in surgery at Strong Memorial Hospital in Rochester, N.Y.

Unable to obtain a residency in surgery and denied an appointment in pathology because she was a woman, Andersen left Rochester to become an assistant in the department of pathology at the College of Physicians and Surgeons, Columbia University. At the same time she began postdoctoral research on the relationship of the endocrine glands to the female reproductive cycle. In 1930 Andersen was appointed to the teaching staff at the medical school, with the title of instructor in pathology. She received the degree of D.Med.Sc. from Columbia in 1935 and that year moved to Babies Hospital at the Columbia-Presbyterian Medical Center as assistant pathologist. There she began a collection of infants' hearts with congenital defects to which she continued to add over the years.

In December 1935 a child who had presented the clinical picture of celiac disease was found at postmortem examination to have a lesion in the pancreas. Her researcher's sixth sense alerted, Dr. Andersen searched for similar cases in the autopsy files and in the literature. Analysis of the collected material provided a clear picture of a previously unrecognized disease entity, which she called cystic fibrosis. Andersen presented the paper summarizing her research at a joint meeting of the American Pediatric Society and the Society for Pediatric Research in Cincinnati, May 5, 1938, and received the E. Mead Johnson Award for her discovery.

The pathologist's task was now accomplished, but Andersen was unwilling to stop there. She began to search for a way of diagnosing cystic fibrosis in the living patient and for methods of saving patients from what was, at that time, certain death. Acquiring on her own the necessary skills of a chemist and clinical pediatrician, Andersen contrived techniques for obtaining duodenal fluid and analyzing its enzyme content, which ultimately enabled her to diagnose the disease. Some colleagues openly disapproved of her assumption of these new roles, but she ignored them.

Appointed assistant attending pediatrician in 1945, Andersen continued her research on cystic fibrosis. Her major publications in the 1940s included papers on chemotherapy for respiratory tract infections in cystic fibrosis and on the genetics of this hereditary disease. The discovery by her research group of an increase of salinity in the sweat of cystics led to the development of a simple, definitive diagnostic test to replace the complicated one she had pioneered. From time to time Andersen digressed from the main thrust of her research to study and report on other problems that intrigued her, particularly glycogen storage disease.

Dorothy Andersen was appointed chief of pathology at Babies Hospital following the retirement of Beryl Paige in 1952. She was a controversial figure at the hospital, where some staff members admired her with almost fanatical devotion while others criticized everything she did. Supporters cited the hours she spent helping others with their research projects, her outstanding talents as a teacher, and her consideration for her subordinates. Detractors complained of her disregard of convention and the untidiness of her person and of her laboratory. A tidy mind was important to her; superficial neatness was not. Ashes from the cigarette that

usually dangled from the corner of her mouth were virtually a part of her costume, and her hair was always in disarray. Opponents condemned her hobbies, branding as unfeminine her penchant for canoeing, swimming, skiing, hiking, and carpentry. But Andersen's friends, including interns and residents, were delighted to spend weekends at her farm in the Kittatinny range of northwest New Jersey. At this farm she built with her own hands a fireplace and chimney, a new roof, and some of the furniture. Dr. Andersen belonged to no formal feminist organization, but she fought valiantly for professional equality, spoke out against sex discrimination when colleagues remained silent, and refused to pattern her life according to others' ideas of what was suitable for a lady.

During World War II surgeons pioneering in open-heart surgery, whose knowledge of cardiac embryology and anatomy was limited, sought Andersen's assistance. Asked to develop a training program, she did so, using her collection of congenital cardiac defects as illustrations. The sessions proved so valuable that no surgeon who had failed to complete her course was permitted to open a child's chest in a Babies Hospital operating room. At the request of cardiologists from other hospitals, she agreed to conduct seminars for them as well.

In 1958 Andersen became full professor at the College of Physicians and Surgeons. Her last major paper on cystic fibrosis (1959) dealt with the disease in young adults—a new category of patients; formerly all cystic fibrosis patients had died in childhood. During her last years she published several papers on cardiac malformations. Among her many honors were the Borden Award for research in nutrition (1948); a citation for outstanding performance from Mount Holyoke College (1952); and the distinguished service medal of the Columbia-Presbyterian Medical Center (conferred posthumously). Operated on for lung cancer in 1962, Andersen died of the disease the following year in New York City.

[Dorothy Andersen's personal papers are held by one of her heirs, Bessie Coombs Haskell. A curriculum vitae and list of her publications are available from the Columbia Univ. College of Physicians and Surgeons. The research summarized in her D. Med. Sc. thesis was published as a series of nineteen papers, most of which appeared in the *Jour. Physiology* and *Am. Jour. Physiology*, 1932–38. Sources of personal information include an autobiographical sketch available from Mount Holyoke College; progress reports in the form of letters to the Commonwealth Fund, available at the Fund's New York City office; and Louise Andersen's application for membership in the Daughters of the Am. Revolution. The eulogy given by Douglas S. Damrosch at the memorial service for Dr. Andersen was published in the *Jour. Pediatrics,* Oct. 1964, pp. 477–79. Obituaries appeared in *The Stethoscope* (published by the Columbia-Presbyterian Medical Center), April 1963, and the *Jour. Am. Medical Assoc.,* May 25, 1963, p. 670. Additional information was supplied by Andersen's colleagues and friends, including Rustin McIntosh, Paul A. di Sant'Agnese, Carolyn Denning, Hilde Bruch, Bessie Coombs Haskell, Ruth Terborgh Murray, and Marian Beman Chute.]

LIBBY MACHOL

ANDERSON, Elda Emma, Oct. 5, 1899–April 17, 1961. Health physicist.

A member of the team of scientists who developed the atomic bomb during World War II, Elda Anderson went on to become a leader in health physics, the study of radiation protection. She was born in the small Wisconsin town of Green Lake, the second of three children and younger daughter of Edwin A. and Lena (Heller) Anderson. Her father, a local automobile dealer and mortician, had been a foundling left on a doorstep in Green Lake; her mother had been brought to Wisconsin from Germany by her parents at about age six. As a child Elda was fascinated by numbers, and aspired to be a kindergarten teacher. In subsequent years, she set her ambitions on a scientific career, influenced by her sister, who served for a time as an assistant instructor of chemistry. Her entire family supported her academic plans, rather expecting her to achieve success because of her early display of intellectual ability. After graduating from high school in Green Lake, she attended nearby Ripon College, earning her A.B. in 1922. She then obtained a graduate assistantship in physics at the University of Wisconsin, which awarded her an A.M. in 1924. Later, in 1941, she received the Ph.D. in physics from Wisconsin.

Elda Anderson began her career as a teacher. At Estherville Junior College in Iowa from 1924 to 1927, she served as dean of physics and mathematics, teaching those subjects as well as chemistry. She then returned to her native Wisconsin, where she taught science at Menasha High School before leaving in 1929 to help organize the physics department at Milwaukee-Downer College. There she served as professor of physics, becoming chairman of the department in 1934.

Anderson's career took a dramatic turn in late 1941. On a sabbatical leave from teaching, she became a staff member in the Office of Scientific Research and Development at Princeton University. The office was a forerunner of the Manhattan Engineering District, and Anderson's work led her in 1943 to the Los Alamos Scientific Laboratory in New Mexico, where she joined other scientists working at feverish pace to develop an atomic bomb. Part of the cyclotron group at Los Alamos, Anderson's research efforts dealt primarily with spectroscopy and experimental measurements of neutron cross-sections, vital to the successful construction of the bomb and also of use in nuclear reactor design. In the summer of 1945, she witnessed the "Trinity event," the explosion in the New Mexico desert of the first atomic bomb.

Elda Anderson left Los Alamos in 1947 to resume the chairmanship of the physics department at Milwaukee-Downer College, teaching physics concurrently at Wisconsin State Teachers College. Classroom and administrative chores seemed tame by comparison to the hectic eighteen-hour days at Los Alamos, and in 1949 she returned to the field, becoming the first chief of education and training for the Health Physics Division at Oak Ridge National Laboratory in Tennessee. Health physics, the science of protecting people and their environment from the effects of ionizing radiation, was barely five years old when Anderson came to Oak Ridge; she spent the rest of her life there bringing it to maturity. In conjunction with several scientists who had pioneered in health physics, including Karl Z. Morgan and James C. Hart, she established a training program for the new discipline at Oak Ridge; she was also teacher and adviser to graduate fellows in health physics from 1949 on. She later cooperated with Vanderbilt University to inaugurate a master's degree program in the field.

Anderson worked on several fronts to promote health physics as a profession. Abroad, she organized the first international course in her field at Stockholm in 1955, followed by courses in Belgium in 1957, and Bombay, India, in 1958. At home, she encouraged her students at Oak Ridge to seek independent status for their new discipline, contributing to the formation of the Health Physics Society in 1955. Anderson served as secretary pro tem, charter secretary, then from 1959 to 1960, as president of the society. In 1960 she also helped institute the American Board of Health Physics, a professional certifying agency, for which she acted as secretary, then chairman until her death. A member of various scientific groups, she was elected to the honorary societies Sigma Xi and Sigma Delta Epsilon and named a fellow of the American Association for the Advancement of Science. Anderson continued to perform research at Oak Ridge, publishing a *Manual of Radiological Pro-*

tection for Civil Defense (1950), and developing a set of spectrometer standards in cooperation with L. J. Beaufait, Jr., one of her students.

Elda Anderson was a slight woman, of medium height, with a warm smile and soft speech. Her solitary hobbies of gardening, music, and camping contrasted with her gregariousness among students, whom she lent both knowledge and counsel. To many new arrivals at the seemingly remote and primitive Oak Ridge site, she became a confidante and friend, dispensing small loans and an occasional nip from a bootleg bottle in times of distress. Anderson was stricken by leukemia in 1956, yet remained extremely active. Then in 1961 she developed breast cancer as well and died in April of that year at Oak Ridge Hospital. In her memory, the Health Physics Society established the Elda E. Anderson Award, providing a certificate and honorarium annually to an outstanding health physicist under the age of forty. The students she helped became Anderson's broader legacy, realizing her vision of a body of professionals devoted to the study of radiation's effects on human health.

[Documents concerning Anderson's efforts in the Health Physics Soc. and the Am. Board of Health Physics are on deposit in the Center for Hist. of Physics, Am. Inst. of Physics, N.Y. City. Anderson's important publications include "Education and Training of Health Physicists," *Radiology*, Jan. 1954, pp. 83–87; and "Isotope Milker Supplies Ba-137 from Parent Cs-137," *Nucleonics*, May 1957, pp. 122–25. She also coauthored "Development and Preparation of a Set of Gamma Spectrometer Standards," *Analytical Chemistry*, 30 (1958), 1762–64, with L. J. Beaufait, Jr., and Paul Peterson; and three articles on neutron cross-sections for gold, boron, and hydrogen, published in *Physical Review*, 71 (1947), 272; 72 (1947), 729 and 1147–56. Anderson's role in the growth of her field is discussed in Ronald Kathren and Natalie Tarr, "The Origins of the Health Physics Society," *Health Physics*, Nov. 1974, pp. 419–28. See also *Nat. Cyc. Am. Biog.*, L, 281–82; and tributes by S. Marshall Sanders, Jr., *Health Physics*, Sept. 1968, pp. 217–18; and William Mills, *Health Physics*, Sept. 1969, pp. 403–4. Obituaries appeared in *Oak Ridger*, Oak Ridge, Tenn., April 18, 1961; *Health Physics*, 5 (1960), 244; and *Physics Today*, July 1961, p. 68. Family and personal information provided by Anderson's niece Roanne McConnell Klaver, and career information by numerous colleagues, including Karl Z. Morgan, J. C. Hart, John A. Auxier, Francis L. Bradley, Allen Brodsky, Natalie Tarr Millemann, Walter S. Snyder, and Mary Jane Cook Hilyer.]

RONALD L. KATHREN

ANDERSON, Margaret Carolyn, Nov. 24, 1886–Oct. 19, 1973. Editor, writer.

Margaret Anderson, founder of the *Little Review*, was born in Indianapolis, the eldest of three daughters of Jessie (Shortridge) and Arthur Aubrey Anderson. Her father, of Scottish Presbyterian descent, was an electric railway executive who later became president of the Interurban Electric Lines which operated in five midwestern states. His father had brought his family west from Virginia and then deserted them when he joined the army during the Civil War. Jessie Anderson came from a distinguished Indiana political family.

After leaving high school in Anderson, Ind., in 1903, Margaret Anderson entered the two-year junior preparatory class at Western College in Miami, Ohio. Her passion, however, was the piano, and by 1906, at the end of her freshman year, she left Western intending to have a beautiful life founded upon a love of ideas and music. In a major break with her prosperous family Anderson argued her case for freedom, particularly from the restraints of a socially ambitious mother. She taught herself typing and, with the encouragement of her gentle father, left home for Chicago in the fall of 1908, accompanied by her sister Lois.

A young woman of luminous beauty and refreshing exuberance, Margaret Anderson arrived in Chicago during a renaissance of the arts. At first guided by editor Clara E. Laughlin, she wrote book reviews for a religious weekly, *The Continent*. She then worked for Francis F. Browne as a bookstore clerk and also gained experience on the staff of his magazine, *The Dial*. She frequented the bohemian literary gatherings of Margery Currey and her husband Floyd Dell, attended performances at Maurice Browne's Little Theatre, and especially enjoyed recitals by pianists and singers.

As a book critic for the *Chicago Evening Post*, under the tutelage of Floyd Dell, by 1913 Anderson was reviewing over one hundred books a week. Overwhelmed by drudgery, she hit upon a way to overcome her boredom. As she recalled it in the opening volume of her autobiography, *My Thirty Years War* (1930), the idea came after a day of depression: "In the night I wakened. First precise thought: I know why I'm depressed—nothing inspired is going on. Second: I demand that life be inspired every moment. Third: the only way to guarantee this is to have inspired conversation every moment. Fourth: most people never get so far as conversation; they haven't the stamina, and there is no time. Fifth: if I had a magazine I could spend my time filling it up with the best conversation the world has to offer. Sixth: marvelous idea—salvation. Seventh: decision to do it. Deep sleep."

With very little money and an indomitable will, Margaret Anderson launched the *Little Review* as a monthly in March 1914. Its central aim was the publication of creative criticism that "shall be fresh and constructive, and intelligent from the artist's point of view." The first number featured praise of feminism, Nietzsche, and psychoanalysis; it also included works by Chicago poets EUNICE TIETJENS, Arthur Davidson Ficke, and Vachel Lindsay. Through her compelling presence and her enthusiastic promotion of the magazine, Anderson attracted contributors and, initially, patrons. By fall the magazine included the poetry of AMY LOWELL; for the next two years Anderson both published and encouraged the Imagist poets. By late 1914 she was also featuring the anarchist writings of EMMA GOLDMAN, a choice which resulted in the loss of her principal backer.

In early 1916 Jane Heap (1887–1964), a painter of English and Lapp descent who was born in Topeka, Kans., joined the *Little Review*. Heap had graduated from the Art Institute of Chicago in 1905, and had studied painting in Germany and costume jewelry design at Chicago's Lewis Institute. After her arrival the magazine took on a new appearance with modern typographical design and reproduction of contemporary artists' works. Heap preferred to remain in the background, however, appearing on the masthead only as "jh," and her influence on the magazine has never been fully assessed. Anderson's association with Heap remained close until 1922. Initially charmed by her skills as a conversationalist, Anderson came to value Heap's "mind, her imagination, her formulations, her vision, her 'creativeness,'" and frequently cited Heap's influence on her.

In March 1917 the editors moved the *Little Review* to New York. In the next years it became increasingly committed to literary experiment, publishing Dorothy Richardson, T. S. Eliot, and, most notably, James Joyce. From May 1917 to April 1919 Ezra Pound acted as foreign editor, contributing criticism, and attracting British and European writers, including Joyce. In 1918 the magazine began a serialization of *Ulysses*. During the three years in which the magazine ran installments of the novel, four issues were confiscated and burned by the Post Office Department. In December 1920 the editors were put on trial for obscenity; they were convicted and fined on Feb. 21, 1921. By fall of that year the magazine had become a quarterly for lack of funds and henceforth appeared only irregularly, suspending publication between 1926 and the final issue—published in Paris—in 1929.

During the years of its American publication the magazine made significant contributions to the history of modern literature. In addition to introducing readers to Joyce, it also printed early works by Sherwood Anderson, GERTRUDE STEIN, Hart Crane, William Carlos Williams, Ernest Hemingway, HILDA DOOLITTLE, and others who were giving new directions to literature. As Frederic J. Hoffman later noted, without "the sacrifices and limitless enthusiasms of Margaret Anderson, it is quite likely that postwar American fiction and poetry would have been slower in its experimental course." HARRIET MONROE, editor of *Poetry*, described the editors as having a kind of courage she could never attain, the "courage to run into debt and print issue after issue without knowing, or indeed caring, where the money would come from to pay for it. And frequently it didn't come, and printers and editors alike were perilously near starvation" (*Poetry*, Nov. 1930, p. 98).

In 1922 Margaret Anderson moved to Paris and in 1923 she turned over the editorship of the *Little Review* to Jane Heap. During that year she also adopted her sister Lois's two children for the duration of their mother's prolonged illness, although Jane Heap, as legal partner in the adoption, actually assumed the responsibility for their care and education. (The children later returned to their mother.) Anderson left the *Little Review* to share her life with the French singer Georgette Leblanc; she planned to study the piano, write, and serve as Leblanc's accompanist. Until Georgette Leblanc's death at their home in Le Cannet, France, in 1941, the two women lived together in a relationship of rare mutual understanding.

Under Jane Heap's editorship, the focus of the *Little Review* shifted from literature to an emphasis on international experimental art movements such as dada and surrealism. Although Heap too moved to Paris in 1927, during the twenties she operated an art gallery on lower Fifth Avenue in New York City, where she exhibited the artists whose work appeared in the *Little Review*. In New York she organized both an International Theatre Exposition (1926) and the highly original Machine Age Exposition (1927).

In 1924, at Jane Heap's urging, Anderson had begun to attend lectures at Fontainebleau-Avon given by George I. Gurdjieff. The philosopher and spiritual master, who taught that human beings merely "sleepwalk" unless awakened to full consciousness through stages of shocks and self-observation, became an important influence on her life. Although she never committed herself totally to his work, Anderson later recorded the depth of her experience in *The Unknowable Gurdjieff* (1962). The book was dedicated to

Jane Heap, who no longer corresponded with her, but "without whose illuminations," she wrote, "I would have understood less of Gurdjieff's doctrine of the 'Fourth Way.' "

On her return to the United States from France in 1942, Margaret Anderson met Dorothy Caruso (widow of the singer Enrico Caruso), with whom she lived for the next thirteen years. The second volume of her autobiography, *The Fiery Fountains*, appeared in 1951. After Dorothy Caruso's death in 1955, Anderson returned to Le Cannet, where she wrote "This Thing Called Love," based in part upon an unrequited love affair, and her final autobiographical volume, *The Strange Necessity* (1969). She dedicated this volume to the poet and novelist Solita Solano, who was Anderson's most challenging critic and also a devoted student of Gurdjieff. Although gifted in the arts of communication, Margaret Anderson seemed at last to fulfill herself most when alone, living at the Hotel Reine des Prés, writing, and listening to music. "I think life has been too kind to me," she concluded in an article for *Prose* (1971). "Even my losses, through death, have been transmutations."

After much suffering from emphysema, she died of heart failure in 1973 at the Clinique Beausoleil in Cannes; she was buried in Notre Dame des Anges Cemetery besides Georgette Leblanc.

[Much of the material on which this article and a forthcoming biography of Margaret Anderson are based may be found in the Janet Flanner–Solita Solano Coll. at the Library of Congress, in the extensive collection pertaining to the *Little Review* at the Univ. of Wisconsin-Milwaukee, and in smaller collections at the Univ. of Chicago, the Houghton Library of Harvard Univ., the Newberry Library, and in private hands. Anderson's three-volume autobiography remains the best source of information about her life; the first two volumes were reprinted in 1969. Her other writings include "The Art of Prose," "Conversation," and "Chambre d'Hotel" in *Prose* 1970, 1971, and 1973, and *The Little Review Anthology* (1953, 1970). For further biographical information see Georgette Leblanc, *La Machine à Courage* (1947). Frederic J. Hoffman in *The Little Magazine* (1946) and Jackson Robert Bryer in his remarkably thorough dissertation, "A Trial-Track for Racers: Margaret Anderson and the *Little Review*" (Univ. of Wis., 1965) have compiled the history of the magazine. See also Abby Ann Arthur Johnson, "The Personal Magazine: Margaret C. Anderson and the *Little Review*," *So. Atlantic Quart.*, Summer 1976, pp. 351–63. For an account of Gurdjieff groups in Paris in the 1930s see Kathryn Hulme, *Undiscovered Country* (1966). Anderson's date of birth is often given as 1891; the 1886 date is confirmed by her sister Lois Anderson Karinsky, born in 1888. Obituaries appeared in the *N.Y.*

Times, Oct. 20, 1973, and the *Wash. Post,* Oct. 22, 1973.]

MATHILDA M. HILLS

ANDERSON, Mary, Aug. 27, 1872–Jan. 29, 1964. Labor leader, federal official.

Mary Anderson, head of the federal Women's Bureau from 1920 to 1944, was born on her parents' farm near the small town of Lidköping in southwestern Sweden. Magnus and Matilda (Johnson) Anderson had seven children, of whom Mary was the youngest and the fourth daughter. Sturdy in physique, she loved the outdoor work of the farm but shunned housework. Her only formal education came at a local Lutheran school, where she graduated at the head of her class. When a severe agricultural depression hit Sweden in the late 1880s, Mary and a sister, with their mother's encouragement, decided to migrate to America and join their oldest sister in the Michigan lumbering area.

Crossing the ocean as a steerage passenger in 1889, the sixteen-year-old Mary, who knew no English, secured her first job as dishwasher in a lumberjacks' boardinghouse in Ludington, Mich. A succession of housework positions followed, until Mary and her sister Anna moved in 1892 to Chicago. After working briefly in a garment factory, Mary Anderson found employment as a stitcher at a shoe factory in West Pullman. The company failed in the depression of 1893, but by the fall of 1894 she had secured a steady job at Schwab's, a larger Chicago factory.

Anderson's first contact with trade unionism came in 1899, when she and other women at her shop joined the International Boot and Shoe Workers Union. A year later she was elected president of the women stitchers' Local 94 and soon afterward became its representative on the union's citywide joint council and its delegate to the Chicago Federation of Labor. Through a fellow Chicagoan, Emma Steghagen, whom she later succeeded as a member of the union's national executive board (1906–19), Anderson first learned of the Women's Trade Union League (WTUL); she joined its Chicago branch in 1905. Thus began her long friendship with the League's president, MARGARET DREIER ROBINS, whom she found a constant source of inspiration and support and "the finest person I ever knew" (*Woman at Work*, pp. 37–38).

A hard-fought strike of Chicago clothing workers (1910–11) brought Anderson new responsibilities. The strike, in which the WTUL played an integral role, secured a trade agreement with the firm of Hart, Schaffner & Marx that provided arbitration machinery for worker grievances. But the employees, new to unionism and mostly young women, needed guidance to put the system into effect. For this job Robins picked Mary Anderson, who gave up working at her craft in July 1911 to become a salaried League organizer. For two years she made a daily round of visits to various of the company's forty shops, explaining trade unionism, hearing and responding to workers' complaints, and forestalling or ending a succession of wildcat strikes; during these two years she attended 570 meetings. Her part in this pioneering venture in industrial arbitration she later regarded as her most important achievement.

Four years of general organizing work for the League followed, until World War I brought Anderson a new role. In April 1917 Samuel Gompers, labor representative on the Advisory Commission of the United States Council of National Defense, appointed her to a subcommittee on women in industry. Through the committee she met MARY VAN KLEECK, director of industrial studies of the Russell Sage Foundation. When in January 1918 van Kleeck was chosen to head a women's branch in the Army's Ordnance Department, she called Anderson to her staff. Six months later, the Department of Labor set up a wartime bureau, the Women in Industry Service, with Mary van Kleeck as director and Mary Anderson as assistant director.

To her new post Anderson brought a first-hand knowledge of working women, a calm common sense, and the capacity to learn from experience. She absorbed much from van Kleeck, a seasoned administrator and social investigator. Her experience was further broadened by a mission for the National WTUL early in 1919. Margaret Dreier Robins, concerned that the labor representatives meeting in conjunction with the Paris Peace Conference included no women, sent Anderson and ROSE SCHNEIDERMAN to Paris to represent women workers. During the trip Anderson met women labor leaders in England and France; she made further such friendships that fall as a delegate to the WTUL-sponsored International Congress of Working Women in Washington. She remained an active member of the WTUL throughout her government career.

In August 1919, following Mary van Kleeck's resignation, Anderson became director of the Women in Industry Service. Then pressure from the National WTUL and other women's groups secured an act of Congress in June 1920 converting the Service into a permanent Women's Bureau within the Department of Labor, and President Woodrow Wilson appointed Anderson as director. The Republican

triumph that fall placed her tenure in doubt. Renewed support, however, from organized women and the strategic efforts of two prominent Republicans, HARRIET TAYLOR UPTON and Corinne Roosevelt Robinson, moved President Warren G. Harding to reappoint Anderson, and her post was thereafter secure.

From the start the basic mission of the Women's Bureau was to perform a fact-finding, coordinating, and advocacy role on behalf of women workers. Anderson hired able associates, worked closely and supportively with them, and inspired their loyalty and hard work. The Bureau's field investigations won a reputation for reliability. As early as 1925 Anderson was hailed as the best known and most popular woman in the federal service.

Anderson got along well with the two Republican secretaries of labor of the 1920s, both old trade unionists like herself. Yet she welcomed the appointment in 1933 of FRANCES PERKINS as a person "who really understood our problems" and "a friend to whom I could go freely and confidently" (*Woman at Work*, p. 183). The expected entree never materialized. Perkins, sensitive to prejudice against her as a woman, may have sought to distance herself from women's causes; but it seems clear that she and Anderson simply did not hit it off. While the failure puzzled and troubled Anderson, her disappointment was partly offset by the friendship of Franklin and ELEANOR ROOSEVELT; she had known Franklin during World War I and Eleanor through the WTUL. President Roosevelt in 1933 insisted on appointing Anderson as chief of the United States delegation to the International Labor Organization, to the annoyance of Perkins (Margaret Dreier Robins to Raymond Robins, Aug. 21, 1939).

Of medium height and stocky build, Anderson had fair coloring, penetrating blue eyes, and what MARY DEWSON once called "a poker face." By all accounts she was an effective public speaker; her sincerity, expert knowledge, and warm concern for working women far outweighed her Swedish accent and sometimes shaky English syntax. A supporter of woman suffrage, Anderson had become a naturalized citizen in 1915 when it looked as though Illinois women might get the vote. She kept her political preferences to herself while in government service but later confided that she had voted regularly for Democratic presidential candidates. Within the Women's Bureau and outside, she consistently and vigorously opposed the National Woman's party's proposed Equal Rights Amendment on the grounds that it would destroy hard-won protective legislation for wage-earning women.

Anderson's task at the Women's Bureau expanded in the early 1940s, as the Lend-Lease Act and the American war effort brought a new influx of women workers into defense plants. Applying the experience of World War I, Mary Anderson established procedures to assure women's access to jobs and training and to uphold high working standards. Then, disheartened by the failure of Frances Perkins to support an increase in the Bureau's budget to match its new duties, she retired in June 1944. Her successor was FRIEDA MILLER.

To a large degree, Mary Anderson's work was her life. A fellow trade unionist, Pauline Newman, found her surprisingly lacking in intellectual curiosity. Remaining unmarried, Anderson lived in a succession of Washington apartments, at first with her sister Anna and, after Anna's death, with occasional government colleagues. She received an honorary degree from Smith College in 1941, and on her ninetieth birthday, in 1962, Secretary of Labor Arthur Goldberg presented her the department's Award of Merit. She died at her Washington home a year and a half later, of a stroke.

By developing and backing Mary Anderson, the Women's Trade Union League made what was perhaps its most enduring contribution to American life. Anderson firmly established concern for the special needs of working women as part of federal policy, at a time when such protection seemed more urgent than equality of rights.

[The basic manuscript sources are the Mary Anderson Papers, Schlesinger Library, Radcliffe College; the Margaret Dreier Robins Papers, Univ. of Fla. Libraries; and the Mary Winslow Papers, Schlesinger Library. The first two collections have been microfilmed as part of the Papers of the Women's Trade Union League and Its Principal Leaders, to be issued with a detailed printed guide. The Schlesinger Library also has a taped interview of Mary Anderson by Esther Peterson (1963?) and a tape of the memorial services held at the Dept. of Labor, with remarks by Pauline Newman, Frances Perkins, and others. Anderson's official correspondence is in the records of the Women's Bureau in the Nat. Archives. The basic biographical source is her autobiography, *Woman at Work* (1951), written with Mary Winslow. The only extended study of her career is Sister John Marie Daly, "Mary Anderson, Pioneer Labor Leader" (Ph.D. diss., Georgetown Univ., 1968). Gustavus A. Weber, *The Women's Bureau* (1923), is a brief administrative analysis. Other secondary sources include *Union Labor Advocate* (Chicago), Dec. 1905, pp. 19, 22; *Current Biog.*, 1940; and George Martin, *Madam Secretary: Frances Perkins* (1976). Death certificate supplied by D.C. Dept. of Human Resources.]

EDWARD T. JAMES

ANDRUS, Ethel Percy, Sept. 21, 1884–July 13, 1967. Educator, organization founder and executive.

Ethel Andrus, founder of the National Retired Teachers Association and of the American Association of Retired Persons, was born in San Francisco, the second of two daughters of Lucretia Frances (Duke) and George Wallace Andrus, a lawyer. Her father had moved to California from New York state. While in law school, he married Lucretia Duke, the daughter of a British sea captain who had remained in California after docking there on the day that gold was discovered. The family moved to Chicago after the birth of their daughters so that George Andrus could continue his law studies at the University of Chicago. His daughter later described him as a man who believed everyone should do some good somewhere; her career followed his belief.

Ethel Andrus grew up in Chicago, graduating from Austin High School in 1900 and attending the University of Chicago, where she received her bachelor's degree in 1903. From 1903 until 1910 Andrus taught English and German at Lewis Institute (later the Illinois Institute of Technology), and worked at Hull House and at the Chicago Commons, two settlement houses. While teaching at Lewis, Andrus also took courses there, later (1918) receiving a B.S. from the Institute.

In 1910, Andrus moved back to California and remained there for the rest of her life. She taught for a year at Santa Paula High School and from 1911 to 1916 at the Manual Arts High School, where she was acting principal for one year. In 1916 she became vice principal and then principal of Abraham Lincoln High School in Los Angeles. The first woman high school principal in the state of California, she remained at the Lincoln School until her retirement. Committed to higher education for women, Andrus also became a student again, earning an M.A. (1928) and a Ph.D. (1930) from the University of Southern California. Her dissertation, on the development of a high school curriculum for girls "based on a critical study of [their] nature and [their] needs," stressed the need for an education that would develop all of women's capacities.

The Lincoln School was a large urban institution which served over 2,500 students of varied ethnic, racial, and cultural backgrounds. The school was plagued by a high delinquency rate, and the district was said to take a perverse pride in its lawlessness. Parents of the pupils were often suspicious of the school, the teachers, and the principal. In this milieu, Ethel Andrus began her campaign to give her students a sense of self and of community. Her goal was "to bring to each a sense of his own worth by treating him with dignity and respect, by honoring his racial background, not as a picturesque oddity, but as a valued contribution to the rich tapestry of American life." She intended that the school would help each student "to find fulfillment according to his own unique nature, then to find worthy of his respect his neighbor of a different race or color."

Ethel Andrus strove for twenty-eight years to make this goal a reality. While she was principal the delinquency rate in the neighborhood dropped sharply, and in 1940 the school and Andrus were awarded special citations by the judge of the juvenile court for East Los Angeles for this achievement. Also in 1940, the school was chosen by the National Education Association as its case study in *Learning Ways of Democracy,* a textbook used in schools all over the world. Not content just with teaching high school students, Andrus formed an Opportunity School for the parents of her pupils. The Lincoln Heights Adult Evening School offered courses of all types to members of the community and was a measure of the progress that Andrus had made in overcoming community hostility. Abraham Lincoln High became the center of the East Los Angeles community.

When Andrus retired in 1944 to care for her ailing mother, her state pension was a little over sixty dollars a month. Although she herself had additional income, she realized that many teachers who had devoted their lives to the profession ended their days struggling to live on meager pensions. Her concern led her in 1947 to found the National Retired Teachers Association (NRTA).

Under Andrus's leadership, the NRTA moved in a variety of directions to ensure a better life for its members. Since almost no health or accident insurance was then available for those over retirement age, she fought for low-cost insurance for retired teachers, reaching her goal with the establishment in 1956 of the nation's first health insurance plan for people over sixty-five. She also established a low-cost mail-order pharmaceutical program to provide prescription medicines at reasonable rates. In addition, the NRTA created a retirement home (Grey Gables), a geriatric nursing home, a travel service, and a quarterly journal which Andrus edited.

In 1958, under pressure from retired persons in other professions, Ethel Andrus founded and became president of the American Association of Retired Persons (AARP). Open to all retired people over the age of fifty-five, the AARP extended the insurance and other benefits Andrus had won for teachers to a broad segment of the population. By 1958, she had already set up retirement readiness programs all over the United States, and had begun to make her organization a powerful lobbying force in Congress. In 1961, her work received recognition with her appointment to the advisory committee of the White House Conference on Aging. She had given the elderly in America a voice.

The second career of Ethel Andrus, serving the elderly in America, and later all over the world, was as rich and rewarding as the first had been. Andrus regarded the scarcity of jobs for older Americans as a national tragedy and consistently urged retired persons to try to begin second careers. For this purpose she established the Institute of Life Long Learning to provide classes and seminars geared to their needs. The first Institute opened in Washington, D.C., in 1963 and other centers followed in California and in Florida; the Institute's educational broadcasts were carried on more than 500 radio stations. She also established and edited *Modern Maturity,* the monthly AARP magazine.

Andrus's philosophy on aging was similar to the philosophy that had guided her throughout her teaching career. She helped the elderly, as she had helped her students, by urging them to find and use their strengths and to accept their limitations without being victims of them. When Andrus died in Long Beach, Calif., in 1967, of a massive pulmonary embolism, she left two strong retirement organizations, a legacy of service to the community, and a commitment to the growing retired population of America. In 1973, the Ethel Percy Andrus Gerontology Center at the University of Southern California was dedicated in memory of her work for the elderly.

[Ethel Andrus's published articles include "An Experiment in Social Living," Jan. 1935; "Core Curriculum at the Lincoln High School," Jan. 1937; and "Social Living Classes for the Underprivileged," Nov. 1939, all in *Calif. Jour. of Secondary Education.* She also wrote "What the Girl of Today Asks of the School," *Jour. of Am. Assoc. of Univ. Women,* April 1932, and "Retirement Readiness," *NEA Jour.,* April 1952. An unpublished autobiographical sketch, written in 1962, is available from the central office of the AARP in Long Beach, Calif. Andrus also edited the *Jour. of the Assoc. of Retired Persons International* and *Dynamic Maturity.* The Jan. 1968 issue of *Modern Maturity,* dedicated to Andrus, is the most extensive source of information on her life and work; unidentified quotations are taken from this source. Her obituary appeared in the *N.Y. Times,*

July 15, 1967; death record provided by Calif. Dept. of Health. Dorothy Crippen, Andrus's niece and Associate Director of Publications and Membership Processing for the AARP, provided family information.]

MARY MCCAY

APGAR, Virginia, June 7, 1909–Aug. 7, 1974. Physician, anesthesiologist.

Virginia Apgar was born in Westfield, N.J., the younger of two surviving children and only daughter of Helen May (Clarke) and Charles Emory Apgar, an insurance executive interested in astronomy and wireless telegraphy. Apgar was fond of describing her family as one that "never sat down." From her father, an amateur musician, she acquired an interest in music, and the family often held impromptu living-room concerts. While attending public schools in Westfield, N.J., Apgar developed a fascination with medicine. An excellent student in the sciences, she nearly failed her cooking classes.

Apgar entered Mount Holyoke College in 1925. She majored in zoology and minored in chemistry, while supporting herself by working in the college library, waiting on tables, and catching stray cats for comparative anatomy classes. In college, as in high school, she demonstrated the seemingly limitless energy which became her trademark. She played on seven varsity teams, reported for the college newspaper, acted in dramatic productions, and played violin in the orchestra. After receiving her A.B. from Mount Holyoke in 1929, she entered the College of Physicians and Surgeons, Columbia University, as one of its few women students. She received her M.D. degree in 1933 and immediately began a prestigious internship at the Columbia-Presbyterian Medical Center in surgery, a field which women rarely entered.

After two years and two hundred operations, Apgar decided not to complete her training in surgery, turning instead to the young field of anesthesiology. Having been convinced that as a woman she would be unable to support herself as a surgeon, Apgar also saw in anesthesiology an opportunity to do pioneering work. Previously, nurses had administered anesthetics, but as surgery grew more sophisticated, medical specialists started to take over the work. In search of the best training then available, Apgar began her instruction under the nurse-anesthetists at Columbia, and then studied with Ralph M. Waters at the University of Wisconsin and Emery A. Rovenstine at Bellevue Hospital in New York City. In 1938 she was appointed director of the division of anesthesiology at the Columbia-Presbyterian Medical Center, thus becoming the first woman to head a department there.

In her eleven years in this position, Apgar created an entire academic department that included a staff of physician-anesthesiologists, a program to train residents, and courses for medical students. In 1949 Columbia appointed her as its first full professor of anesthesiology, thereby recognizing anesthesiology as a distinct and increasingly important specialty; she also became the first woman to hold a full professorship there.

That same year she chose to give up her administrative responsibilities as department head to devote herself to the study of anesthesia in childbirth, and it is for this work that she is best remembered. After years of clinical observation of newborns, she devised a scoring system—which measured the infant's heart rate, respiration, muscle tone, reflexes, and color—to predict which babies would need special medical attention in the crucial first minutes and hours of life. Presented in 1952, her system, known as the Apgar Score, became the standard means of evaluating infants immediately after birth.

Apgar's research, which yielded more than sixty scientific papers, reflected the great depth and variety of her interests. Her other contributions to medicine were essentially practical and directly affected the care of her patients.

At the base of her work lay a fundamental pleasure in taking care of people and an eagerness to be helpful. Nothing was too much trouble. She carried a child up nine flights of stairs when she learned that he was afraid of elevators. She kept in her handbag equipment to resuscitate or perform emergency tracheotomies on accident victims, claiming: "Nobody, but nobody is going to stop breathing on me."

Apgar's deepening commitment to maternal and child health led her to Johns Hopkins University, from which she received a master's degree in public health in 1959, at the age of forty-nine. Intended as a sabbatical, this year proved to be a turning point in her career. Instead of returning to Columbia she accepted an executive position with the National Foundation–March of Dimes in 1959 and devoted the rest of her life to fostering public support for research on birth defects. With missionary zeal, she traveled throughout the world, educating the public to the need for research into the prevention and treatment of birth defects and raising funds toward this end. Largely as a result of these efforts, the annual income of the National Foundation increased from $19 million when she arrived to $46 million at the time of her death.

In addition to her work at the National Foundation, Apgar held the first faculty positions in the United States which named birth defects as a subspecialty, serving as lecturer (1965–71) and then as clinical professor of pediatrics (teratology) at Cornell University Medical College. In 1973 she was appointed lecturer in the department of medical genetics at the Johns Hopkins School of Public Health. A gifted and much-loved teacher—she taught on airplanes and in churches as well as in class—she was fond of using unorthodox methods. She taught medical students the anatomy of the spinal cord by having them feel her own unusually prominent coccyx; and in explaining the origin of various congenital defects to concerned parents, she often passed around a tiny preserved fetus which she carried in a bottle in her purse.

After her rise to national prominence, Apgar received numerous awards including several honorary degrees. In 1973 she became the first woman to receive the Gold Medal for Distinguished Achievement in Medicine from the Alumni Association of the Columbia College of Physicians and Surgeons; the same year she received the Ralph M. Waters Award given by the American Society of Anesthesiology and was named Woman of the Year in Science and Research by the *Ladies' Home Journal.* Throughout her life she remained devoted to Mount Holyoke, serving as an alumna trustee from 1966 to 1971.

Apgar never married, insisting: "It's just that I haven't found a man who can cook." She made her home in Tenafly, N.J., and cared for her mother who lived in the same apartment building. Maintaining her lifelong interest in music, she built her own stringed instruments and delighted in the tale of how she and a friend crept into the Presbyterian Medical Center late at night to steal a wooden shelf from a telephone booth because it was "just right" for the back of a viola which Apgar was making. Fishing, golfing, and stamp collecting were great loves and, long past the age of fifty, she began taking flying lessons, hoping one day to fly under the George Washington Bridge.

Her fundamental optimism and mischievous wit pervaded everything in her life and shaped her attitudes toward her own career and the careers of other women. She insisted that "women are liberated from the time they leave the womb." Despite her acknowledged disappointment at not having become a surgeon, she believed that her sex had placed no obstacles in the path of her career; indeed, she transcended traditional boundaries, achieving prominence both as a scientist and as a humanitarian.

In the last years of her life, Apgar suffered from progressive cirrhosis of the liver. She died in New York City at the age of sixty-five. A tall and physically imposing woman who appeared in later years as "a kindly grandmother," Virginia Apgar was fiercely independent and active until the day she died. She bequeathed to medicine a legacy of knowledge which continues to affect the lives of women and of children who are yet to be born.

[Apgar's personal papers, including office files, speeches, and biographical materials, are in the Williston Memorial Library, Mount Holyoke College. She wrote one book, *Is My Baby All Right?* (1972), coauthored with Joan Beck, and published numerous articles in scientific and popular journals. See especially "Proposal for a New Method of Evaluation of the Newborn Infant," *Anesthesia and Analgesia,* July–Aug. 1953, pp. 260–67. Two informative memorial tributes are Christianna Smith, "In Memoriam: Dr. Virginia Apgar '29," *Mount Holyoke Alumnae Quart.,* Fall 1974, pp. 178–79; and L. Stanley James, "Fond Memories of Virginia Apgar," *Pediatrics,* Jan. 1975, pp. 1–4. See also *Current Biog.,* 1968, pp. 25–27. Obituaries appeared in the *N.Y. Times* and the *Holyoke* (Mass.) *Transcript-Telegram,* Aug. 8, 1974. L. Stanley James, Carleen M. Hutchins, and Lawrence Apgar provided useful information.]

ROBERT J. WALDINGER

ARBUS, Diane Nemerov, March 14, 1923–July 27(?), 1971. Photographer.

Diane Arbus was born in New York City, the second of three children and the older daughter of David and Gertrude (Russek) Nemerov. The son of Jewish immigrants from Kiev who settled in Brooklyn, Nemerov would eventually own Russeks Fifth Avenue, the fashionable fur and women's clothing store founded in the 1890s by his father-in-law, who had come to New York from Poland. Nemerov kept his family in affluence, preserving highly visible symbols of success: large apartments, first on Park Avenue, and after the depression on Central Park West, and a staff of servants. Arbus later viewed what she called her "nouveau" surroundings with a tentative humor. To her, it was a facade supported by a "humiliatingly gross kingdom" of fur salesmen. She felt painfully "exempt from circumstances," reduced to fabricating theories about the rest of the world from clues as rudimentary as the remarks of elevator men (Terkel interview). She told of such disparate but modest acts of rebellion as daring herself to stand on the window ledge of the apartment and asking her parents for a sewing machine to make her own clothes.

All three children were educated at the progressive Fieldston School and encouraged by their father (who took up painting when he retired) to study the arts. Arbus painted with the Russeks fashion artist, but soon stopped: "I had a sense that if I was so terrific at it, it wasn't worth doing, and I had no real sense of wanting to do it" (Terkel interview). She did not go on to college after graduating from Fieldston in 1940, but briefly studied fashion drawing.

Although Diane Arbus later blamed her parents for leading her to expect that she would live "under the wing of a man" (Terkel interview), she married at eighteen, on April 10, 1941. She had met Allan Arbus, five years her senior, at thirteen, when he was a paste-up boy in the Russeks advertising department, and they had since seen each other as much as possible, often surreptitiously. Arbus was a choice the Nemerovs had to regard as inevitable, and they finally gave the couple their support.

Shortly after their marriage, Allan Arbus bought a camera for his wife. She rapidly learned the fundamentals in the darkroom at her parents' apartment building and in a short course with the photographer Berenice Abbott. Both Diane and Allan Arbus immersed themselves in the work of major photographers, and, with David Nemerov's unfailing encouragement embarked upon a career in the then relatively open field of fashion photography. They began by doing six or eight pictures a week for Russeks, and soon became prominent as a team. Diane Arbus did the creative work before the actual shooting, conceiving the approach to be taken; during the sessions, Allan, who handled the technical side, took over.

Diane Arbus grew to hate the work. In a competitive field, and with two daughters (Doon, born in 1945, and Amy, born in 1954), the Arbuses lived by monetary brinksmanship. It was also a strenuous job, and she found little time for work of her own. She quit in 1957, after bursting into tears while describing her day to a dinner guest.

Arbus's initial efforts to take pictures on the streets of New York were hampered by her diffidence in approaching people. A course with Alexey Brodovitch led her nowhere. The turning point came in 1958, when she began two years of study with Lisette Model, the Austrian-born documentary photographer who became a close friend. Model pushed her student, who had always felt vaguely that she had something significant to say, to identify her subject. Arbus started, in her daughter Doon's phrase, with "the forbidden."

Although she moved with the children into her own apartment in 1960, she remained friends with Allan Arbus and relied on him to teach her the technical craft of photography, at which she came to excel. Freed by the move from orthodox household routine, she could now explore in earnest the world to which she had never been exposed, build the courage she felt her mother had failed to teach her. "I seek danger and excitement now," she told Studs Terkel. "It may be frivolous of me, but . . . I've come to feel that you can only learn by being touched by something."

Arbus called her work "collecting things" and chalked lists of subjects on a blackboard above her bed. They formed "a sort of contemporary anthropology": beauty contestants, families, giants, midgets, drag queens, fat ladies, junkie hippies, nudists, twins married to twins. She was drawn to and awed by those unprotected by the invisibility of normality, and attracted by eccentricity, whether physically determined or deliberately cultivated. She was fascinated, too, by the flaw in any public persona, the gap between "what you want people to know about you and what you can't help people knowing about you" (Aperture monograph). Her portraits pose mythic riddles of identity: what is it to inhabit a body virtually indistinguishable from one's twin, to tower three feet above one's parents, to choose to appear either man or woman? Gradually overcoming her initial shyness, Arbus learned to approach strangers, make friends, follow leads, wait, and come back until she had her portrait and the tale of an adventure. Energetic, witty, charming, and capable of a genuine and disarming curiosity, she persuaded her subjects to reveal themselves in an act of conscious collaboration. In her last year, photographing the mentally retarded whom she found "enveloped in innocence" (Israel interview), she moved to pictures no longer catalyzed mainly by her presence.

Although a joint account with Allan provided partial security until their divorce in 1969, Arbus had to earn money independently. She taught (Parsons School of Design, 1965–66; Cooper Union, 1968–69; privately, 1970–71; Hampshire College, June 1971), photographed for publications such as *Esquire* and *Harper's Bazaar*, and researched press photography for the Museum of Modern Art (1971). She won two Guggenheim fellowships, in 1963 and 1966, and her reputation grew steadily within the photographic community. A 1967 exhibition at the Museum of Modern Art aroused popular curiosity in her work and gained her imitators among photographers. She kept on, as her friend Marvin Israel said, "endlessly pursuing and pursued."

Diane Arbus's body was found in her West-beth apartment on July 28, 1971; she had committed suicide one or two days before. After her death, she became a cult figure, both damned for voyeurism and lauded for compassion. A posthumous exhibition at the Museum of Modern Art in 1972—which later traveled throughout the United States and in Europe—drew vast crowds. In slightly over ten years, Arbus claimed as part of her material a world previously recorded by only a few photographers, brought new dimensions to documentary portraiture, and achieved an international reputation.

[Important publications by Diane Arbus are "The Full Circle," *Infinity*, Feb. 1962, and "The Vertical Journey: Six Movements of a Moment within the Heart of the City," *Esquire*, July 1960. Most Arbus negatives and prints other than those in museum collections are part of the estate of Diane Arbus, of which Doon Arbus is executor. There is a clipping file, as well as a collection of her photographs, at the Museum of Modern Art. Papers held privately include letters, 1968–71, by Peter Crookston of the London *Observer;* papers for an honors literature class at Fieldston, by Elbert Lenrow; a transcript of a 1971 Arbus class, by the Visual Studies Workshop, Rochester, N.Y. A tape of Studs Terkel's interview with Arbus was provided by WFMT, Chicago. The Aperture monograph *Diane Arbus* (1972) is the best source of reproductions of photographs and also contains partial transcriptions of some interviews and classes. A comprehensive, annotated bibliography was compiled by Robert B. Stevens for *Exposure*, Sept. 1977. Major biographical sources are: Doon Arbus, "Diane Arbus: Photographer," *Ms.*, Oct. 1972, pp. 44–53; Marvin Israel, "Diane Arbus," *Infinity*, Nov. 1972; and Anne Tucker, "Diane Arbus, 1923–1971," *The Woman's Eye* (1973), pp. 109–23. See also Peter Bunnell, "Diane Arbus," *Print Collector's Newsletter*, Jan.-Feb. 1973, pp. 128–30, and Susan Sontag, "Freak Show," *N.Y. Rev. of Books*, Nov. 15, 1973, pp. 13–19. Information about Arbus's death furnished by Campbell's Funeral Chapel, Manhattan. Assistance was also provided by interviews and/or correspondence with Allan Arbus, Doon Arbus, Gertrude Nemerov, Howard Nemerov, Renée Nemerov Sparkia, Spencer Brown, Allan Gussow, Marvin Israel, Elbert Lenrow, Joan Morgan, Neil Selkirk, Eugene Tulchin, and Adam Yarmolinsky.]

CATHERINE LORD

ARBUTHNOT, May Hill, Aug. 27, 1884–Oct. 2, 1969. Educator, children's literature specialist.

When May Hill Arbuthnot died at the age of eighty-five, the fourth edition of her major work, *Children and Books,* was in preparation. In the preface to that volume, her collaborator said: "Her knowledge, her enthusiasm, her practical commonsense, and her boundless imagination have guided countless parents, teachers, librar-

ians, and students . . . May Hill Arbuthnot is still with us in her books, a wise and blithe spirit."

Born in Mason City, Iowa, where her parents Frank and Mary Elizabeth (Seville) Hill, were visiting friends, May Hill spent some part of her early childhood years in Newburyport, Mass., where she and her brother attended school. She had a happy childhood in which books were enjoyed and shared; she later recalled that her "absorption in books" was the result of a "reading mother, a reading-aloud father, and the *Book of Common Prayer*," which gave her "a sensitivity to the beauty and power of words." The family moved frequently, and she also went to school in Minneapolis and Chicago, where she graduated from Hyde Park High School. Family finances prevented her from going immediately to college. In 1913 she received a kindergarten-primary supervisor's certificate from the University of Chicago; nine years later, she completed her Ph.B. degree at that university. At Chicago, she met the eminent educator William S. Gray, who later became her colleague in writing textbooks for children.

May Hill received a master's degree from Columbia University in 1924. While working on her degree programs, she taught kindergarten, worked as a kindergarten director at the Superior (Wis.) State Normal School (1912–17), and participated in the teacher training program at the Ethical Culture School in New York City (1918–21). Between 1913 and 1922 she taught courses in children's literature at the summer school of the University of Chicago.

In the fall of 1922 May Hill moved to Cleveland to become principal of the Cleveland Kindergarten-Primary Training School. Five years later the school was made a department of elementary education of Western Reserve University (later Case Western Reserve University). She became an associate professor of education, remaining at that rank until her retirement in 1950.

A strong believer in the value of preschool education, May Hill established the first nursery schools in both Cleveland and the state of Ohio. The University Nursery School (located on the campus of Western Reserve) which she founded in 1929 became a nationally known laboratory school and, with the other day nurseries established under her direction, made Cleveland an important center for the study of early childhood education. They also brought her national recognition. From 1927 to 1929 she was national vice president of the International Kindergarten Union (later renamed Association for Childhood Education). In 1930 she was a member of the original committee for the White House Conference on Children and three years later participated in a national committee concerned with the establishment of emergency nursery schools for the depression years.

In 1932, at forty-eight, May Hill married Charles Crisswell Arbuthnot, a professor of economics at Western Reserve. He was always supportive of his wife's work and theirs was a notably happy marriage. Long active as a writer, lecturer, reviewer, and teacher of children's literature, May Arbuthnot's major contributions to the field did not appear until the 1940s. Between 1933 and 1943 she was review editor for children's books for *Childhood Education;* she later served in the same capacity for *Elementary English* (1948–50). In 1939, the friendship that had begun at the University of Chicago led William Gray to impress on Scott, Foresman, the publishing firm which he served as both editor and author, the advisability of inviting Arbuthnot to join the staff. With Gray she co-authored *Basic Readers: Curriculum Foundation Series* (1940, 1946), better known as the "Dick and Jane" books. For many years these were the major readers for more than half the children in the United States. As literary products, however, the books were not universally acclaimed.

Perhaps for that reason the first edition of Arbuthnot's college textbook, *Children and Books* (1947), was not warmly welcomed. It is also possible that critics felt that Arbuthnot, as an educator, valued function over literary merit. As the years passed, however, the integrity of her work, her high standards of evaluation, and her insistence on the prime importance of literary quality made it inevitable that her eminence be recognized. While she was concerned with function, with how books were introduced to children and how they served in the teaching of language arts, she was even more concerned with the goals of reading enjoyment and of giving children the best in world literature— well-written books that stirred the imagination and awoke sympathy for others and an understanding of self. In the late 1970s, *Children and Books,* in its revised editions, remained the best-selling textbook on children's literature published in the United States.

During the early 1950s, Arbuthnot edited a series of anthologies designed to provide reading-aloud material to accompany reading instruction in the elementary grades. *Time for Poetry* (1951), *Time for Fairy Tales, Old and New* (1952), and *Time for True Tales* (1953) were published together in 1953 as *The Arbuthnot Anthology.* It, too, went into several later editions.

Arbuthnot's later years were marked by honors, and by her continued contribution to her field. She received the Constance Lindsay Skinner Medal in 1959 from the Women's National Book Association for a distinguished contribution to the field of books, and the Regina Medal of the Catholic Library Association for distinguished contributions to the field of children's literature (1964). After their retirement from teaching, the Arbuthnots kept homes in both Cleveland and Pasadena, Calif.; Charles Arbuthnot died in 1963. Although beset by arthritis and failing eyesight, May Arbuthnot continued to write articles and revise her books into her eighties. In June 1969, Scott, Foresman announced the establishment of the May Hill Arbuthnot lectureship. She died the following October in a Cleveland nursing home of cancer.

A woman who throughout her adult life had known material comfort, a lifelong Episcopalian, a Republican, a scholarly research worker, May Hill Arbuthnot might have become narrow in the intensity of her concentration on her work. She was, instead, a person of warmth and humor, broad-minded and compassionate. In all of her writing and lecturing she made readers and listeners conscious of the needs and rights of the poor, the members of minority groups, and the young; she valued intellectual curiosity and deplored narrow judgments. Her work was characterized by a dedication to bringing children and books together, and by a zeal tempered by her understanding of practical problems. Above all, she had that rare quality: a truly open mind. She made a permanent and significant contribution to children's literature.

[The archives at Case Western Reserve Univ. has a public relations file on Arbuthnot, containing articles, some biographical data, a list of publications, a useful "Biographical Essay on May Hill Arbuthnot" by Gladys F. Blue, and a biographical sketch by Dora Lawthorn. There is no published bibliography, although *Contemporary Authors* (1974) lists all of her books and the revisions through 1972. The fifth edition of *Children and Books* appeared in 1977, with Zena Sutherland as primary author. *New Basic Readers: Curriculum Foundation Series* appeared in 1951, coauthored by Arbuthnot, Gray, and A. Sterl Artley; a revision of this series was published in 1956, with Marion Monroe as a fourth coauthor. Articles about her include Marie C. Corrigan and Adeline Corrigan, "May Hill Arbuthnot," *Catholic Library World,* Feb. 1964, pp. 337–39; Mary C. Austin, "May Hill Arbuthnot: Teacher, Author, Friend," *The Alumnae Folio,* Western Reserve Univ., March 1951; "May Hill Arbuthnot," *Education,* March 1958, pp. 446–47. Obituaries appeared in *Library Jour.,* Nov. 15, 1969; *Cleveland Plain Dealer,* Oct. 3, 1969. A biobibliography by Carol Crider provided useful information. Death certificate supplied by the Ohio Dept. of Health.]

ZENA SUTHERLAND

ARDEN, Elizabeth, Dec. 31, 1878?–Oct. 18, 1966. Entrepreneur.

Between 1920 and 1940, swift and significant changes occurred in ideas of feminine grooming. Influenced by motion pictures and by the growth of the toiletries industry, these changes were also importantly the work of two women, Elizabeth Arden and her greatest rival, HELENA RUBINSTEIN.

Elizabeth Arden was born Florence Nightingale Graham in the village of Woodbridge, near Toronto, Ont., Canada, the fourth of five children and third of four daughters of William and Susan (Tadd) Graham. Her father, a Scotsman, and her mother, from Cornwall, England, had emigrated to Canada after their marriage, and leased a tenant farm in Woodbridge. Susan Graham died when Florence was still a child, and the children were reared in near poverty. Even a small allowance which her mother had obtained for the children from an aunt ended before Florence could finish high school. She moved aimlessly from one job to another—dental assistant, cashier, stenographer—until she decided to follow her brother, William, to New York. By then she was thirty years old.

Florence Graham knew that few women were blessed with the smooth, fair complexion that at thirty made her look ten years younger. But she soon realized that a fine complexion need not depend upon chance. In 1908, as the modern cosmetic industry was about to be born, she took a clerical job with Eleanor Adair, whose beauty salon, in which "facials" were given, was one of the first of its kind. Graham insisted that Adair teach her the art of giving facials, and soon was pronounced to have "healing hands." At this critical stage she recognized, like the true entrepreneur, that she would never get anywhere working for somebody else. In 1909 she and Elizabeth Hubbard, who made and sold beauty products, opened a salon, under Hubbard's name, at 509 Fifth Avenue.

The two strong-minded women failed to get along, and Hubbard left to open her own salon. Florence Graham, with a small loan from her brother, lavished upon the little shop the talent for elegant decor for which she was to become famous. The entrance featured a red door with brass name-plate. Wondering what to call herself, she hit upon the name Arden while, she said, reading Tennyson's poem *Enoch Arden.* If she merely had the sign painter scrape Hubbard off the front window of the salon, she realized, she could save a large bill for the gold leaf work. So Elizabeth stayed, and Elizabeth Arden—the woman and the business—was

born. While she never legally changed her name, she used Graham seldom except in horse racing circles.

Recognizing that the real profits lay in cosmetics, Elizabeth Arden got in on the ground floor of the new industry. She gradually introduced face makeup, which had not been used by "respectable" women, under the guise of facial treatments. Ignoring the war that had just broken out in Europe, in 1914 Arden went to Paris, where she had a facial in nearly every beauty establishment in that fashion-conscious city. The only exception, she later insisted, was the salon of "that woman," as she always referred to Rubinstein. She was impressed by the striking effects produced by the skillful use of mascara and eye shadow, then quite new.

In 1914 Arden also opened a small shop in Washington, the first of many branches. By the 1920s, her main business was in creating makeups for her customers, and in the sale of creams and other cosmetics. Among other products, she introduced a fluffy cream, Amoretta, which proved a great improvement over old-fashioned greasy preparations. As the range of cosmetics that respectable women considered proper increased, Arden was ready with such innovations as lipsticks to match not only one's skin coloring but one's clothing as well. She ultimately added hairdressing, advice on diet and exercise, and both ready-made and custom clothing to her services; at one time or another she operated salons in over 100 different locations throughout North and South America and Europe.

Cosmetics sales soon outpaced the salons in dollar volume, and ultimately made up for losses in the salons. The person who ran this branch of the business for nearly twenty years was her first husband, Thomas Jenkins Lewis, whom she had met in 1914 while applying for a loan in the bank where he worked; they were married on Nov. 29, 1915. The union succeeded better as a business partnership than as a personal relationship. She divorced Lewis in 1934 and in 1942 married Prince Michael Evlanoff, a Russian émigré from whom she was divorced in 1944. Meanwhile, her business continued to grow, in spite of or perhaps because of the depression. By 1930 she had achieved a place just within the magic circle of New York society, largely by cultivating ELISABETH MARBURY, member of a prominent old New York family, influential literary agent, and house mate of the popular interior designer ELSIE DE WOLFE.

Arden had a short-lived radio program in the 1930s; she also opened a health resort at Maine Chance Farm, her former country home in Mount Vernon, Maine. In 1947 she opened another in Phoenix, Ariz. She loved travel, and did her duty in sponsoring charity balls which were probably the best advertising investment she made. But for the most part she worked industriously at the business, of which she owned every share of stock, and saw annual sales grow to $60,000,000. Her other real passion was horses. Her Maine Chance Stables in Lexington, Ky., won purses totaling $589,000 in 1945, more than any other stable. In 1946 her racing success won her a place on the cover of *Time* magazine, and in 1947 her horse, Jet Pilot, won the Kentucky Derby.

Elizabeth Arden fits the classic model of the entrepreneur as closely as any other man or woman in the history of American business. She was innovative and even inventive, but her forte was in recognizing good ideas, putting them into effect, and making them succeed. Although she mastered the pose of the demure little girl who wanted everything to be pink, she drove home her message with the force of a steel executive. "Hold fast to life and youth," her advertisements warned, and she never stopped working. When she died in New York in her eighty-eighth year, she was still the sole owner of the business. Her legacies included $4,000,-000 to be divided among longtime employees of the company. Another $4,000,000 went to her sister Gladys (Vicomtesse de Maublanc), who had worked for Arden, helping to develop the wholesale business, initiating the first sales trips, and expanding the business into France, where she ran the Paris and Nice salons. Most of the remainder went to her brother William's surviving daughter, Patricia Young, who had been Arden's constant companion. The business was sold to Eli Lilly and Company to satisfy government inheritance taxes. Apparently she could not conceive of a life for Elizabeth Arden after Florence Graham was gone.

[Material published during Elizabeth Arden's lifetime is highly undependable, especially as to her date of birth. The Office of the Registrar General, Toronto, Ont., has no record of her birth for the period 1876–80. The 1878 date is used by Alfred Allan Lewis and Constance Woodworth, *Miss Elizabeth Arden* (1972). This book, prepared with the cooperation of relatives and former employees, marshals the important facts, but is not a definitive biography. Earlier articles, which better capture the spirit of the times in which she lived, include a profile in the *New Yorker*, April 6, 1935; "I Am a Famous Woman in This Industry," *Fortune*, Oct. 1938; the *Time* cover story, May 6, 1946; Hambla Bauer, "High Priestess of Beauty," *Sat. Eve. Post*, April 24, 1948. There is also an entry in *Current Biog.*, 1957; obituaries appeared in the *N.Y. Times*, Oct. 19, 1966, and the Oct. 28, 1966, issues of *Time*, *Life*, and *Newsweek*.]

ALBRO MARTIN

ARENDT, Hannah, Oct. 14, 1906–Dec. 4, 1975. Philosopher, political theorist.

Hannah Arendt was born in Hanover, Germany, the only child of Paul Arendt, an engineer, and Martha (Cohn) Arendt. Both parents had been born in Königsberg, East Prussia, to middle-class Jewish families of Russian descent. Several years after their daughter's birth, the Arendts moved back to Königsberg, where Paul Arendt was institutionalized in 1911 with tertiary syphilis. He died in 1913, as did his father, Max Arendt, a leader in the Jewish community, who had also been very close to Hannah.

Arendt was precocious as a child, learning to read before she entered kindergarten. Her mother was a broadminded, progressive woman, and a Social Democrat; she was very supportive of her daughter, even when Hannah was expelled from the gymnasium for a breach of discipline. In 1920 Martha Arendt married Martin Beerwald, a merchant with two teenage daughters, and the Beerwald home became a center for Arendt's talented young friends. For two years (1922–24) Arendt prepared for the abitur, the final examination for university entrance, by auditing courses at the University of Berlin and working with a private tutor. An attractive but shy young woman, she enjoyed company but was also given to long periods of solitary reading and poetry writing.

Arendt's university career began in 1924 at Marburg, where she studied Greek, New Testament theology with Rudolf Bultmann, and philosophy with Martin Heidegger, who became a close friend. She spent one semester at Freiburg studying with Edmund Husserl, and then went to Heidelberg where she received a doctorate in philosophy in 1929. Her dissertation, *Der Liebesbegriff bei Augustin*, was supervised by Karl Jaspers, who became like a second father for her. Both Heidegger's and Jaspers's philosophies shaped Arendt's later work, supplying her with insights and categories to which she gave a specifically political turn.

In 1929 Arendt married Gunther Stern, a writer whose pen name was Gunther Anders. While he worked on his habilitation in philosophy, Arendt, supported by a stipend from the Notgemeinschaft der Deutschen Wissenschaft, began writing *Rahel Varnhagen: The Life of a Jewess*. This biography of the late eighteenth-century Berlin salon hostess (not published until 1957) stresses the personal struggle Varnhagen waged to accept her Jewish identity. Arendt's work was interrupted by her flight from Germany in 1933. She left Berlin after a week of imprisonment by the Gestapo, having been arrested not for harboring communists, as she might have been, but for collecting materials on German anti-Semitism at the behest of Zionist friends. Arendt was not a Zionist, but she was sympathetic to Zionism, particularly as advocated by her friend Kurt Blumenfeld, the leader of the German Zionist Organization.

Arendt took refuge in Paris, where she worked for various Jewish organizations, including Youth Aliyah, and joined refugee discussion circles, including one that met at the home of the literary critic, Walter Benjamin. Her marriage to Stern, which had begun to dissolve by the time he left Berlin for Paris early in 1933, ended in 1936 when she met Heinrich Blücher, a non-Jewish Berliner of working-class origins who was, until 1939, a communist. Shortly after their marriage in 1940, Arendt and Blücher were interned for six weeks in separate camps in the south of France. During the German occupation of Paris, they were able to escape and, with Arendt's mother, they secured visas and sailed to New York in the spring of 1941.

During the war, living with Blücher and her mother in a New York rooming house, Arendt wrote a political column for the German-Jewish weekly *Aufbau* in which she called for the formation of a Jewish army and discussed Jewish history. Helped by other Europeans, including Paul Tillich, Salo Baron, and Waldemar Gurian, she placed essays in *Jewish Social Studies, Jewish Frontier,* and the *Review of Politics.* Blücher worked in factories until he found a position at the National Broadcasting Company preparing German-language broadcasts; Martha Arendt kept their house and did factory piecework. Slowly, the Blüchers were able to make enough to live without help from friends. They learned English, relishing every new idiomatic expression, but their circle was German-speaking until after the war, when they began to meet "the American friends"—Alfred Kazin, Randall Jarrell, Mary McCarthy, Phillip Rahv, and others.

Arendt was employed as a director of research by the Conference on Jewish Relations (1944–46), and as a part-time teacher of history at Brooklyn College. From 1946 to 1948 she was a senior editor at Schocken Books. During these years she also wrote for *Partisan Review,* the *Review of Politics,* and *The Nation,* and published articles in support of a binational Arab-Jewish state in Palestine. These articles came to the attention of Judah Magnes, the president of Hebrew University, who invited her to work

with him in advocating a binational state. When that campaign failed, Arendt turned her attention away from exclusively Jewish concerns.

Drawing on her published essays, she began to write *The Origins of Totalitarianism,* a three-part work tracing the history of anti-Semitism, imperialism, and totalitarianism, and stressing the unprecedented nature of the totalitarian form of government. Arendt's was the first major study of totalitarianism published after the war and, particularly in the 1950s, it was enormously influential. The book is intricate, with many themes developed simultaneously; the main theme is the decline and fall of the eighteenth-century nation-states of Europe with their stable class structures. Arendt charted the nineteenth-century emergence of the bourgeoisie as a political force bent on imperialistic expansion and showed how this emergent group's actions and ideologies—particularly racism—undermined the nation-state, rendering "superfluous" or stateless those to whom the nation-state had given place, meaning, and political rights. Eventually, even the bourgeoisie was drawn into the collapse of the nations, and from that came "the masses," those without collective interests, the atomistic members of mass movements like Nazism. Mass society is the precondition for totalitarian regimes, with their ideologies of world conquest and their essential means—total terror.

Particularly in the first edition (subsequent editions were heavily revised) Arendt issued a call for European federation, an ideal she shared with Heinrich Blücher, who advocated a "League for the Rights of Peoples" to supplant the lost "Rights of Man" theories. Blücher's collaboration on *The Origins of Totalitarianism* was crucial; although he had almost no formal schooling, he was Arendt's political mentor, and until his death in 1970 he continued to influence her thought. Blücher was never a writer, but he was an enthusiastic talker and a successful teacher of philosophy at the New School for Social Research in New York City and at nearby Bard College.

When *The Origins of Totalitarianism* appeared in 1951—the year she acquired United States citizenship—it was immediately acclaimed and Arendt emerged as a historian and political thinker of importance. The book's success allowed Arendt and Blücher to leave the rooming house for an apartment, and it led to opportunities for her to pursue her work under easier financial circumstances. Despite her pleasure in its success, Arendt was uncomfortable with the publicity she received. She was, and remained, reticent, uneasy in public, and very protective of her privacy. She had a wide and appreciative circle of acquaintances—many would have agreed that she was the most incisive, intelligent person they had ever met—but few ever came to know her well.

In 1952 Arendt received a Guggenheim Foundation fellowship to begin a study of the Marxist elements of Soviet totalitarianism, a dimension of her subject which she had left for a separate treatment. (Many critics had noted that *The Origins of Totalitarianism* did not fully substantiate its claim that Bolshevism was, in form, like Nazism.) The study outgrew her original conception and she shifted its focus, evolving a series of categories for considering the *vita activa,* the active life. In articles and in lectures at leading universities throughout the 1950s Arendt developed the ideas of her next book, *The Human Condition* (1958), in which she emphasized man's properly political capacities, action and speech, and distinguished these from work and labor. Arendt considered these activities in light of the fundamental conditions of human existence—plurality, natality, mortality, life itself, worldliness, and earthboundness—and in light of a vast historical shift, from the classical period, when each activity had its place in the private or the public realm, to the modern period when both private and public realms atrophied and a hybrid realm, called the social, emerged.

In six essays published in 1961 as *Between Past and Future,* Arendt further developed her idea that the social realm had, in the modern world, usurped the public realm, the realm for action and speech. In "What Is Authority?" for example, she considered "the Roman trinity"— religion, authority, tradition—and asked how authority might exist without the images of future reward and punishment supplied by religion and the images of past origins or foundations supplied by tradition. Between past and future, in the modern situation, Arendt looked for a concept of authority—not rulership, not *raisons d'état,* not power, not violence—in which foundations and new initiatives, precedents and actions, could combine. This led her to the most important modern political phenomenon, revolution, in which liberation and constitution-making or -founding can combine.

In 1959 Arendt was invited to Princeton as a visiting professor, the first woman full professor at that institution. There she delivered the lectures that later became *On Revolution* (1963), which focused on the American version of the revolutionary council system, local township government. In comparison to her writings of the 1940s, which were calls to resist loss of personal identity, chauvinistic nationalism, and the general deterioration of political life, her work

in the 1950s was constructive, informed by a qualified hope for the possibility of political renewal.

In the spring of 1961, as a reporter for *The New Yorker,* Arendt attended the trial of the Nazi Adolf Eichmann in Jerusalem. Her report on the trial appeared in the magazine in February and March 1963. Amid a growing controversy, she prepared it for book publication as *Eichmann in Jerusalem: A Report on the Banality of Evil* (1964). Disputes arose over three aspects of Arendt's account: the issues she raised about the legality of Eichmann's trial and the inadequacy of existing legal categories to deal with a "crime against humanity"; her portrait of Eichmann as a banal, thoughtless man, no demon and no psychopath; and her presentation of the role of the European Jewish Councils (*Judenräte*) in the implementation of the Nazis's deportation and extermination policy. The debates on matters of historical fact and interpretation overshadowed the philosophical issues implicit in the book's subtitle; they also alienated Arendt from many she had considered to be friends. Although she faced the controversy courageously, she was shocked and hurt by its vehemence.

Preoccupied with the arguments over her book and with her duties as a professor with the University of Chicago's Committee on Social Thought (1963–67), Arendt wrote only essays in the mid-1960s. "Truth and Politics," her response to the Eichmann debate, was included in the revised edition of *Between Past and Future* (1968). Much of her work during these years, however, reappeared in *Men in Dark Times* (1968), a diverse collection of portraits of modern men and women who offered, in their lives and works, "some illumination," which she believed "even in the darkest times we have a right to expect" (p. ix). These portraits of courage reveal Arendt's abiding concern with personal integrity and dignity. In 1962 and 1966, the two volumes in English of Karl Jaspers's *The Great Philosophers,* which Arendt edited, appeared. She lectured widely in America during the 1960s and traveled to Europe almost yearly to lecture and to visit with friends, including Heidegger and Jaspers.

Arendt accepted a professorship at the New School for Social Research in 1967 and gave courses which contributed to "Thinking and Moral Considerations" (*Social Research,* Autumn 1971), and to her final work, the philosophical study that became *The Life of the Mind.* Her plan to return to her "first amour," philosophy, was interrupted several times as she stopped to analyze the tumultuous events of 1968, the Pentagon Papers, and the Watergate scandal. Arendt's political essays of the late 1960s and early 1970s are collected in *Crises of the Republic* (1972), which is dedicated to her closest American friend, the writer Mary McCarthy.

The Life of the Mind, published posthumously in two volumes in 1979, was to have consisted of three parts: "Thinking," "Willing," and "Judging." It was conceived as a complement to *The Human Condition*; the earlier book had considered the *vita activa*, the later one would deal with the *vita contemplativa*. Arendt had nearly completed the first two parts, but hardly begun the third, when she died in her New York apartment in December 1975 of heart failure. In the last months of her life, there were two public acknowledgments of the worldwide influence of Arendt's work: the Danish government's Sonning Prize for "contributions to European civilization," and the American Political Science Association's Lippincott Award for a work of enduring and exceptional quality, which went to her 1958 book, *The Human Condition*.

The traditional relation of the active and contemplative lives was the focus of Arendt's study and criticism over the course of her thirty-five years in America. Most western philosophers, she thought, had looked upon the political realm from without, from above. Arendt, who refused the title philosopher and called herself, until the last years of her life, a political theorist, wanted to avoid that traditional perspective. In the major books which precede *The Life of the Mind* she considered, first, what politics means, setting out to define what is properly political, namely action and speech. From this fundamental orientation toward public action, a host of conceptual distinctions followed. She set apart "the political space," the space in which men act purposively through words and deeds, from what she called "the social," by which she meant the relations men develop for the maintenance of life. Acting together in the political space, human beings can attain power, Arendt believed. She distinguished power from violence, which she saw as an instrument or means which did not stem from cooperative action and which could not, therefore, secure power for any but a short period. Acting and speaking are always limited, but there are compensations, Arendt pointed out: the outcomes of human action are unpredictable, but promises protect human beings from this unpredictability; actions are irreversible but the act of forgiveness can redeem the doers; human actions disappear from memory, but poetry and history preserve them for future generations.

Revolutions, she believed, are successful only insofar as their end is the establishment of free institutions within which citizens can act together. She emphasized the council system—which she saw as the spontaneous outgrowth of revolution—as the political form which most effectively offered space to those who wished to act, and warned that representative government neglected such grassroots institutions at its peril. A place for the "public happiness" of speaking and acting is the condition of freedom. Forms of government can therefore be assessed according to the space they offer for such action; revolutions can be judged by whether or not they lead to constitution-making. In looking at revolutions in history, Arendt saw only the American revolution as having been successful in these terms, as the Constitution had emerged from it as a commonly agreed on principle of authority.

The distinctions that made up Hannah Arendt's political philosophy were complemented by the series of distinctions she began to elaborate in *The Life of the Mind*: between knowing and thinking, science and philosophy, the pursuit of truth and the search for meaning. Arendt "located" thinking, which she called "a silent dialogue between me and myself," far from the political realm. She tied it, however, to the human ability to project into the future—willing—and to judge the past, and suggested that thinking has a political role in times when most are swept up unthinkingly in political movements. She asked and replied affirmatively: "Could the activity of thinking as such, the habit of examining whatever comes to pass or to attract attention, regardless of results and specific content, could this activity be among the conditions that make men abstain from evil-doing or even actually 'condition' them against it?"

Even when she applied her conceptual schemes to studies of particular events Arendt often baffled her readers, as neither her schemes nor her specific analyses could be conventionally classified as conservative or liberal, reactionary or progressive. She was never a political activist or what she called an intellectual streetfighter, but neither was she a contemplative in the traditional sense. Although she was profoundly disturbed by the events of her age and the tendencies she saw in them, particularly by the transformation of politics into social administration, it is inadequate to call her a pessimist. Such categorizations are tied to philosophies of history, which Arendt felt deflected truly political understanding: "Each time the modern age had reason to expect a new political philosophy it received a philosophy of history instead."

Hannah Arendt's work was as highly regarded in the United States as that of any postwar political philosopher; internationally, she was perhaps the best known American theorist of her generation. In the twentieth century, theorists of many persuasions, including philosophers of history, have seen the need to bridge the gap between philosophy and politics. Arendt's great contribution was that she understood that this bridge could not be built unless the entire range of political concepts, formulated while the gap was open, was reexamined and rethought. To this end, she cleaned and polished the tarnished words of political discourse, uncovering their original meanings and linking them together again to articulate a new science of politics. Participants in public and private discussions felt this articulation process going on as Hannah Arendt practiced distinction-making and sorted concepts, using a story to illustrate, a poem to illuminate, a joke to startle. Her mother had been amused when her five-year-old played school at home—*immer ist Sie die Lehrerin*, she wrote in a journal—and so Arendt remained, always the teacher.

[A collection of Arendt's papers, manuscripts, and correspondence, numbering over 30,000 items, is in the Library of Congress. Correspondence with Jaspers and Heidegger is in the Deutsches Literaturarchiv, Marbach, Fed. Rep. of Germany. An archive of articles on *Eichmann in Jerusalem* and on the controversy surrounding it is in the Leo Baeck Inst., N. Y. City, and a bibliography is available in R. Braham, *The Eichmann Case: A Source Book* (1969). Arendt's response to a book-length critique, Jacob Robinson, *And The Crooked Shall Be Made Straight* (1965), appeared in the *N.Y. Rev. of Books,* Jan. 20, 1966, and was collected, with other articles, in R. Feldman, ed. *Hannah Arendt: The Jew as Pariah* (1978). Also see Friedrich A. Krummacher, ed., *Die Kontroverse: Hannah Arendt, Eichmann und die Juden* (1964). Many of Arendt's essays remain uncollected; six early essays appear in *Die Verborgene Tradition* (1976). Excerpts from *The Life of the Mind* appeared in the *New Yorker*, Nov. 21, 28, and Dec. 5, 1977; the book was published in two volumes, *Thinking* and *Willing*, edited by Mary McCarthy (1978). Melvyn Hill, ed., *Hannah Arendt: The Recovery of the Public World* (1979), a collection of essays on her ideas with commentary by Arendt, contains a bibliography. A biography by Elisabeth Young-Bruehl is forthcoming. For analysis of Arendt's thought see Margaret Canovan, *The Political Thought of Hannah Arendt* (1974). The Spring 1977 issue of *Social Research* was devoted to Arendt; Peter Stern and Jean Yarbrough discuss her as a teacher in "Hannah Arendt," *Am. Scholar*, Summer 1978. Obituaries appeared in the *N.Y. Times*, Dec. 6, 1975; in *PS* (newsletter of the Am. Political Sci. Assoc.), Summer 1976; and (by Judith Shklar) in the *New Republic*, Dec. 27, 1975.

Reminiscences appeared in "Talk of the Town," the *New Yorker*, Dec. 22, 1975, and the *N.Y. Rev. of Books*, Jan. 22, 1976 (by Mary McCarthy) and May 13, 1976 (by Robert Lowell).]

ELISABETH YOUNG-BRUEHL

ARNSTEIN, Margaret Gene, Oct. 27, 1904– Oct. 8, 1972. Public health nurse, nursing educator.

Known for her work in promoting systematic research on health care among nurses, Margaret Arnstein was born in New York City, the second of four children and younger daughter of Leo and Elsie (Nathan) Arnstein. Her parents were second-generation Americans of German-Jewish descent, who engaged in the social and cultural activities of the Jewish tradition but did not follow its religious practices. Leo Arnstein, a graduate of Yale, was a successful businessman who became New York City welfare commissioner and president of Mt. Sinai Hospital. Both parents were closely associated with the Henry Street settlement, Elsie Arnstein taking part in its vocational advisory service. The children all later served in health-related fields. Margaret's interest in nursing and public health developed early, encouraged by LILLIAN WALD, the founder of Henry Street and a close family friend.

Graduating in 1921 from the Ethical Culture School in New York, Margaret Arnstein attended Smith College, where she received the A.B. in 1925. She went on to earn a diploma from the New York Presbyterian Hospital School of Nursing in 1928 and an A.M. in public health nursing from Teachers College, Columbia University, in 1929. She then served five years as staff nurse and later supervisor at the Westchester County Hospital in White Plains, N.Y. After receiving her master's degree in public health from Johns Hopkins University (1934), she applied her training first as consultant nurse in the Communicable Disease Division of the New York State Department of Health (1934–37), then as a teacher of public health and nursing in the University of Minnesota's Department of Preventive Medicine (1938–40). Eager to resume field work, Arnstein returned as consultant nurse to the New York Department of Health in 1940.

There she stimulated field studies in public health nursing, an activity which became the focus of her career. Seeking to bring the nursing profession abreast of the dramatic changes in health care, she later observed that this goal had been delayed because nurses, preoccupied with patient care, rarely had the chance to contribute to the analysis of health issues; yet many nurses had "an intuitive grasp of the ways in which their patient might fare better." Arnstein designed field studies to analyze and systematize the observations and insights of nurses and to explore ways of modernizing their profession. Also interested in using applied research in the public health field, she collaborated with physicians in 1941 on a study of the contributing factors in the incidence of respiratory infections and coauthored with Gaylord Anderson the widely used text *Communicable Disease Control* (1941). She went on leave from the New York Department of Health to work with the United Nations Relief and Rehabilitation Administration (1943–45), advising nurse training programs in the Balkan countries.

In 1946 Margaret Arnstein began a twenty-year career in the United States Public Health Service, rising to chief of the Division of Nursing in 1960. During these years, she directed national field studies on nursing and helped individual hospitals conduct their own research to improve patient care. Even as an administrator and consultant with an international reputation, she often outpaced her colleagues in visiting the programs under her jurisdiction, whether in urban ghettos or Appalachia, finding new ideas in the field and putting them to use. She also studied health issues abroad, preparing for the World Health Organization *A Guide for National Studies of Nursing Resources* (1953), and directing in 1956 the first International Conference on Nursing Studies in Sèvres, France. She took leave from the government for a semester in the spring of 1958 to become the first holder of the ANNIE W. GOODRICH Chair of Nursing at Yale.

In 1964, while still affiliated with the Public Health Service, Arnstein moved from the Division of Nursing to the Office of International Health. There, supported by the Rockefeller Foundation and the Agency for International Development, she joined American and British physicians to study health service needs in developing countries. As part of the project, Arnstein visited India, concluding that much could be learned from nurses and midwives in the field and that planned parenthood programs must be accompanied by improvements in child welfare: "Before Indian families can accept the principle of birth control, they must be shown that their present children have a good chance of living" (*Smith Alumnae Quart.*). Leaving government service in 1966, Arnstein spent a year as professor of public health nursing at the University of Michigan, then became dean of the Yale School of Nursing until her retirement in 1972. She died of cancer at her apartment in New Haven, Conn., in October 1972.

Margaret Arnstein's contributions to public health nursing were widely recognized. She received several honorary degrees and became the first woman to be awarded the $10,000 Rockefeller Public Service Award (1965); she also received the Sedgwick Memorial Medal, the highest honor of the American Public Health Association, in 1971. Free from serious illness until that year, she led an active life of travel, hiking, and tennis, while also enjoying the arts. Cancer slowed her down but did not immobilize her. Into her last week, Arnstein maintained her own calendar and received calls from around the country. She faced death securely, as she had the other challenges of living.

[The Margaret Arnstein Papers, including notes of speeches and articles, course outlines, consultant reports, correspondence between 1956 and 1972, and a curriculum vitae, are in the Nat. Nursing Archives, Mugar Library, Boston Univ. Published writings include: "Secondary Attack Rates in Pneumonia," *Am. Jour. Public Health*, Feb. 1941, with Edward S. Rogers and Morton Robins; "Nursing in UNRRA Middle East Refugee Camps," *Am. Jour. Nursing*, May 1945; "Public Health Work in England: How It Is Like and Unlike Ours," *Am. Jour. Public Health*, Jan. 1947; "Research in the Nursing Field," *Am. Jour. Public Health*, Aug. 1950; "A Training Program for Nurses' Aides and Auxiliaries," *Hospital Management*, July 1956; *International Conference on the Planning of Nursing Studies* (1957), with Ellen Broe; and "Training Nurses for Research Work," *Internat. Nursing Rev.*, Oct. 1959. Useful articles on Arnstein include "Yale Nursing School Alumnae Meet New Visiting Professor," New Haven *Sunday Register*, Feb. 23, 1958; and "We See by the Papers," *Smith Alumnae Quart.*, Winter 1966. An obituary (with photograph) appeared in the *N.Y. Times*, Oct. 9, 1972, and a tribute by Myron Wegman in *Am. Jour. Public Health*, Feb. 1973. Information was also derived from personal acquaintance and from her brother Robert Arnstein. Death certificate supplied by Conn. Dept. of Health.]

NANCY MILIO

AUERBACH, Beatrice Fox, July 7, 1887–Nov. 29, 1968. Business executive, philanthropist.

Beatrice Fox Auerbach, the elder of two daughters of Moses and Theresa (Stern) Fox, was born in Hartford, Conn., into a mercantile dynasty. (Her father had one daughter by a previous marriage who died in early adolescence.) Both her grandfathers were part of the antebellum German-Jewish migration, and both had established locally important dry goods stores—Gerson Fox in Hartford about 1845 and Ferdinand Stern in Newburgh, N.Y., about 1857. Moses Fox took over the ever-enlarging Hartford store after the death of his father. Eventually his elder daughter inherited a major share of the stock in the store as well as the family's style of personalized business management.

Beatrice Fox attended local public and private schools and spent some time at the Benjamin-Deane School, a private boarding school in New York City. She later joked that she had never received a diploma, "not even from Sunday School." Throughout her youth she often traveled in Europe with her family; on one such trip she met her future husband.

On April 15, 1911, Beatrice Fox married George Auerbach, whose father had been among the first Jewish settlers in Salt Lake City, Utah, and a founder of its largest non-Mormon department store. George Auerbach worked in the family business. Beatrice Auerbach, a small, slight woman of great verve and charm, fulfilled family expectations by devoting herself to household and community affairs. The couple had two daughters, Georgette Fox (b. 1916) and Dorothy Brooks (b. 1919).

G. Fox & Company was destroyed by fire in 1917, and, when Moses Fox decided to rebuild, George and Beatrice Auerbach were persuaded to move to Hartford. There George Auerbach took a major role in managing the new and enlarged store, and became secretary-treasurer of the company. In the 1920s, the Auerbachs bought Auerfarm, where they raised prize Guernsey cows, and, as her children grew, Beatrice Auerbach extended her community activities and commitments. The death of her husband in 1927 marked a turning point in her life. She went to work for her father, at first part-time, but gradually increasing her managerial responsibilities. Her aging, ailing parents moved into her home, and a household staff helped care for the extended family. When Moses Fox died in 1938, Beatrice Fox Auerbach became president of G. Fox & Company.

Beatrice Auerbach ran G. Fox & Company from 1938 until 1965. During that time the business reportedly increased tenfold, making Fox's the largest privately owned department store in the country, and the largest in business volume between Boston and New York. More important, Auerbach was among the pioneers in such labor programs as the five-day-week, retirement plans, medical and nonprofit lunch facilities for employees, and a revolving fund (the Theresa Stern Fox Fund) to lend employees interest-free money in times of personal crisis. Fox's was also the first large department store to hire black employees for positions which offered advancement. Many of Auerbach's merchandising practices were also bold or innovative: a statewide toll-free telephone order department, free delivery service, and fully automated billing. By 1959 an eight-million-dollar addition was required for floor space; it included Centinel Hill Hall, famous throughout the state for its free meeting facilities for non-profit organizations. Although her daughters' husbands eventually became key figures in the company's operation, Auerbach remained president until 1965, when she supervised the exchange of the privately held stock of Fox's (owned by herself, her sister, and the Beatrice Fox Auerbach Foundation) for about forty million dollars worth of the publicly held stock of the May Department Stores Company.

Auerbach's activities as a philanthropist and civic leader were consonant with her ideas about the role of a wealthy and cultivated woman in business. She supported and served on the boards of several schools, hospitals, and cultural organizations. One of her earliest and most continuous philanthropies, an example of her concern about professional education for women, was the Auerbach program in retailing and allied arts at Connecticut College for Women. From 1938 to 1959 the program provided an undergraduate major that combined academic preparation and apprenticeship. In 1941 she established the Beatrice Fox Auerbach Foundation which helped finance educational and civic activities. Her carefully planned educational philanthropies were recognized by honorary degrees and citations from several colleges and universities.

An important beneficiary of the Auerbach Foundation was the Service Bureau for Women's Organizations, founded in 1945. The bureau trained women's groups in techniques of community organization and engaged in topical studies that made it an informational resource for organizations throughout the state. The Service Bureau also became a center of local concern about international affairs and served as the host organization for the State Department's foreign visitor program. These activities also reflected Auerbach's growing interest in international affairs as she sought to reestablish contact with her European suppliers after World War II. Accompanied on a series of trips through Europe, Africa, and the Far East by Chase Going Woodhouse, a former congresswoman and professor at Connecticut College and then director of the Auerbach Service Bureau, she had an opportunity to look at the problems as well as the products of the countries they visited. By the time she died in Hartford in 1968, Beatrice Fox Auerbach had earned national recognition as an innovative merchandiser and a civic-minded philanthropist.

[The Utah Biographic Sketches Coll. at the Bancroft

Library, Berkeley, Calif., contains information on the Auerbach family. Beatrice Fox Auerbach's uncatalogued personal papers are in her former home, donated to the Univ. of Hartford by her daughters. A collection of photographs of the Fox family, including Beatrice Fox Auerbach, is at the Jewish Hist. Soc. of Greater Hartford. The annual reports and other records of the Auerbach Service Bureau for Conn. Organizations (formerly the Service Bureau for Women's Organizations) have been deposited in the Schlesinger Library, Radcliffe College. The best published source of information about her travels, public appearances, statements, honors, and awards is the file of clippings at the *Hartford Courant*. In particular see a series of eight articles by Roger Dove, "Inside a Great Store," April 10–April 17, 1955. Auerbach's career is also outlined in Irene D. Neu, "The Jewish Businesswoman in America," *Am. Jewish Hist. Quart.*, Sept. 1976, pp. 137–54. Entries on Auerbach, her husband, her father, and her grandfather can be found in Rabbi Morris Silverman, *Hartford Jews, 1659–1970* (1970). Biographical information about her maternal grandparents is in Wallkill Valley Publishing Association, *The Historic Wallkill and Hudson River Valleys A.D. 1913*, pp. 84–85. The history of her husband's family is outlined in Leon L. Watters, *The Pioneer Jews of Utah* (1952), Studies in American Jewish History, no. 2, published by the Am. Jewish Hist. Soc. A biobibliography prepared by Glenda Hughes assisted in the research for this article. Additional information was provided by Auerbach's daughter Georgette Koopman and by Chase Going Woodhouse. Birth record supplied by Conn. State Dept. of Health.]

DOROTHY ANN LIPSON

B

BAKER, Josephine, June 3, 1906–April 12, 1975. Entertainer.

Josephine Baker was born Freda Josephine McDonald in St. Louis, Mo., the daughter of Carrie Martin McDonald, who was of African ancestry; her father, Edward Cason, was said to be of Spanish descent. Her mother later married Arthur Baker and had three other children, a son and two daughters. The family was desperately poor. They lived in East St. Louis, Ill., when the riots occurred there in 1917; the memory of white thugs burning and killing in her neighborhood affected Josephine Baker deeply.

A born entertainer who starred in basement theatricals as a child, Baker ran away from home at the age of thirteen to join a traveling vaudeville company. Her natural dancing and comic ability attracted attention and within three years she was appearing on Broadway, both in shows by Noble Sissle and Eubie Blake (*Shuffle Along*, 1921) and at the famed Plantation Club.

Baker traveled to Paris with a show called *La Revue Nègre* in 1925. Since black entertainers and their hot jazz had caught on in the United States, the show's promoters hoped Parisians would respond similarly. But there was too much tap dancing, a dance form unknown to the French and horrible to their sensitive ears. The show soon closed and Baker was stranded in Paris.

Fortunately, the director of the Folies Bergère, famous for its lavish sets and scantily clad performers, decided to introduce a black act into the revue currently at the Folies and auditioned the members of *La Revue Nègre* who had remained. Baker's comic style attracted him, and she became the first black to star in a solo revue on the Paris stage. Clad in a G-string made of bananas and little else, she was supposed to do a dance number only, but the excited audience reaction stimulated the natural performer in her. She put on a one-woman show. She danced, she scat-sang, she clowned, and in a burst of abandon she leaped into the air and landed in a prop banana tree. It was pure vaudeville, but to the French it was the epitome of the new hot jazz, and the audience went wild.

For the next four decades, Baker would evoke the same kind of excitement, for she never did the same thing twice. Billed only as "Josephine," she became a symbol of everything spontaneous, madcap, and full of the driving energy that was associated with jazz, not only in Paris but in the rest of Europe and in Latin America as well. She lived accordingly. Her lavish wardrobe, crowds of suitors, menagerie of exotic pets, and impulsive behavior became legendary.

But Baker was unsuccessful in achieving two things she wanted: motherhood and stardom in the United States. In 1937 she married Jean Lion, a wealthy industrialist, and converted to Judaism. She also became a French citizen. The marriage effectively ended after Baker had a miscarriage in 1938, although she and Lion were not divorced until 1941.

When World War II began, Baker went to

work for the Red Cross. Soon she was approached by the French Resistance because her entrée into the upper levels of European society and the ease with which she traveled about Europe made her valuable as a gatherer of intelligence. She eagerly accepted the assignment, and her work for the Resistance and her tireless entertaining of troops in Africa and the Middle East earned her the highest French military honors.

After the war, Baker plunged into another cause. With her second husband, Jo Bouillon, a successful band leader whom she married in 1947, she took steps to create a "showplace for brotherhood" at Les Milandes, her property in the Dordogne. There, they planned to raise adopted children of all races and religions. Baker eventually adopted twelve children. But her vision of Les Milandes as a World Village with accommodations for hundreds of tourists became ever more complicated and costly to realize. To finance her dream, she had to go back to work.

Returning to the stage in the early 1950s, Baker was as successful as ever, and her success, coupled with her annoyance at an incident at the Stork Club in New York City, led to her involvement in yet another cause. In October 1951, while on tour in the United States, Baker was refused service at the Stork Club. Columnist Walter Winchell was in the club at the time. After Baker berated him for not coming to her aid, Winchell launched a vicious attack on her, branding her a communist and charging that she had consorted with Nazis and fascists during the war. The charges were completely unfounded, but the blot on Baker's name remained. In the United States, she began a crusade for racial equality. She refused to appear anywhere in her native country where blacks were not admitted and succeeded in integrating theaters and night clubs from Miami to Las Vegas. In 1963, at the climax of the famous March on Washington, she stood in front of the Lincoln Memorial with Martin Luther King, Jr., and delivered an impassioned speech to the huge crowd.

Baker failed to achieve her World Village. By the late 1950s, she and Bouillon were separated. Bills for construction and staff at Les Milandes were astronomical, and she could not earn enough to pay them. In 1969, wrapped in an old blanket and clutching a kitten, Josephine Baker was dragged from her chateau, and Les Milandes was sold at auction for debts, for a fraction of its value. Nor did she realize her dream of an ideal *arc-en-ciel tribu* (rainbow family). By returning to work she had deprived her children of what they needed most—her presence. Starved for her attention, they could not be managed by the succession of nurses and nannies and tutors who cared for them after Bouillon left.

Princess Grace of Monaco provided a villa for Baker and the children who were not away at school, and in 1973 the irrepressible Baker made a comeback. She triumphed at Carnegie Hall and in April 1975 she repeated her success on the Paris stage. Two days after her last performance she died of a stroke.

In the 1970s Josephine Baker considered the possibility of a film biography, but the project never materialized. As she told reporters in Los Angeles in 1973: "I would like to meet the woman who has the courage even to play my life story in a film . . . I do not believe the woman exists who would have the courage to have *lived* it as I have done."

[The principal sources are Josephine Baker, *Les Memoires* (1949); Josephine Baker and Jo Bouillon, *Josephine*, translated from the French by Mariana Fitzpatrick (1977); and Stephen Papich, *Remembering Josephine* (1976). Articles about her include "Josephine," *Ebony*, Dec. 1973; Charles L. Sanders, "A Farewell to Josephine," *Ebony*, July 1975; and Gossie Harold Hudson, "Not for Entertainment Only," *Negro Hist. Bull.*, March-April 1977, pp. 682–83. Also see the entries in *Current Biog.*, 1964, and Wilhelmena S. Robinson, *Hist. Negro Biographies*, vol. II (1968). *The Biog. Encyc. and Who's Who of the Am. Theatre* (1966) lists Baker as a Chevalier of the Legion of Honor, recipient of the Croix de Guerre (1939–45) and the Rosette de la Résistance, and NAACP Woman of the Year (1951). An obituary appeared in the *N.Y. Times*, April 13, 1975. Confirmation of her date of birth and her father's name was provided by the U.S. Passport Office. Several sources report that Baker's first marriage was to her manager, Pepito Abbatino, but this cannot be confirmed.]

JIM HASKINS
KATHLEEN BENSON

BALCH, Emily Greene, Jan. 8, 1867–Jan. 9, 1961. Peace advocate, social reformer, economist.

Emily Greene Balch's steadfast labor for freedom and cooperation among individuals and peoples brought her the Nobel Peace Prize in 1946. Of old New England origin, she was born in Jamaica Plain, Mass., near Boston, the second daughter and second of the six surviving children (five girls and one boy) of Francis Vergnies and Ellen Maria (Noyes) Balch. Her father, a Harvard graduate and enlisted man by choice in the Civil War, served as secretary to Senator Charles Sumner before starting his career as a Boston lawyer. Her mother, who had been an advanced student at the Ipswich Female Academy in Byfield, Mass., taught school in Mattoon, Ill., before her marriage. The Balches, liberal Unitarians, examined religious and ethical precepts critically and Emily made their demanding standard her own. The family was close, with grandparents and unmarried aunts living in the home or nearby. Irish domestics helped with the children. Emily Balch remembered her mother as "quick-tempered and loving . . . the center of my life and its chief influence as long as she lived." Seventeen when her mother died, she then found in her selfless, learned father her most important guide and model.

Though reserved and self-effacing, Emily Balch became a leader at Miss Catherine Ireland's School in Boston, where teachers nurtured independence of thought. At Bryn Mawr College, which she entered in 1886, she studied widely in the classics, philosophy, and modern languages before she found in economics a field which had a direct relation to "the social question." Earning her A.B. in 1889, she became the first recipient of the Bryn Mawr European Fellowship. The faculty perceived her as a woman of "unusual ability" and "extraordinary beauty of moral character." She herself hoped she would "not get lost in study or pursue it for pleasure beyond its best measure for my purpose, unknown to me as yet." Balch was dissatisfied with her pursuit of political economy at the Sorbonne (1890–91), for she studied the poor but met not one. The American Economic Association published the results of her research as *Public Assistance of the Poor in France* (1893).

Eager for practical experience, Balch apprenticed herself to Charles W. Birtwell of the Boston Children's Aid Society. She found stimulus in working with such reform-minded Boston Brahmins as MARY MORTON KEHEW, and with trade union leaders John F. and MARY KENNEY O'SULLIVAN. More important, at Felix Adler's Summer School of Applied Ethics in 1892, she made friends of three contemporaries, JANE ADDAMS, KATHARINE COMAN, and VIDA SCUDDER. A founder of Denison House, Balch agreed to head the new Boston settlement until her college classmate HELENA STUART DUDLEY arrived. By then she had rejected a career in social work, deciding that she could have greater impact as a college teacher by awakening "the desire of women students to work for social betterment." Encouragement and financial assistance from her father led to brief study at the Harvard Annex (1893) and the University of Chicago (1895). She also spent a year at the University of Berlin (1895–96) that included travel with fellow student MARY KINGSBURY (SIMKHOVITCH).

Balch began her academic career at Wellesley College in 1896 as assistant to Katharine Coman in an economics course. Her own innovative courses treating socialism and Karl Marx, immigration, the theory of consumption, and the economic roles of women, drew on her experiences as a reformer. During the Wellesley years Balch served on numerous state commissions, including the first commission on minimum wages for women in the United States; she became cofounder and president of the Boston Women's Trade Union League (1902), supported striking workers, and spoke out against racial discrimination and class exploitation. In 1906 she declared herself a socialist and three years later she and Vida Scudder organized a socialist conference in Boston.

Because of her radical extracurricular activities, Balch advanced slowly on the academic ladder. But in 1913 she received a five-year appointment as professor and chairman of the department of economics and sociology. By this time she had also established herself as a scholar of distinction. Her major work, *Our Slavic Fellow Citizens* (1910), was a comprehensive study of immigrants from eastern and southern Europe, for which Balch did two years of research in the United States and abroad. The book was unique not only in presenting the first-hand viewpoints of immigrants but also in countering the nativist racial assumptions of her society.

Not bound by conventional attitudes toward women, Balch believed that as an unmarried professional she could take personal risks for the public good. World War I was her proving ground. A pacifist since the Spanish-American War, she took an active role in working for an early peace and joined the American delegation to the International Congress of Women at The Hague (1915). There she saw women from belligerent and neutral countries struggle with their differences and reach agreement on a plan to bring about peace by instituting continuous mediation before armistice. As one of the envoys chosen to gain support for the plan, Balch visited the neutral Scandinavian countries and Russia, and later conferred with British leaders and with President Woodrow Wilson. Although nothing came of these efforts, she remained hopeful about the prospects for peace, and in 1916 took part in the International Committee on Mediation in Stockholm, supported by Henry Ford.

Based in New York City during a sabbatical (1916–17) and an unpaid leave (1917–18), during which she wrote for *The Nation*, Balch became a political activist. She opposed the war, conscription, and espionage legislation, and defended the civil liberties of conscientious objectors and the foreign born. She served as liaison among peace groups including the American Union Against Militarism (the predecessor of the American Civil Liberties Union), the national Woman's Peace party with Jane Addams as president, the more outspoken Woman's Peace party of New York led by CRYSTAL EASTMAN, and the Collegiate Anti-Militarism League. In 1917 Balch helped found the Emergency Peace Federation and supported its even more radical successor, the People's Council of America, an organization that called for a new social order. Unlike most reformers of her generation, Balch acceded to the flamboyant tactics of her young associates. She was conspicuous in newspaper accounts of mass meetings and demonstrations that linked her name with the socialist-Bolshevist fringe of pacifists.

In 1919 the trustees of Wellesley College voted not to renew Balch's appointment, which had expired the previous year. At fifty-two, she was without a job or the security it had provided. Yet she ignored suggestions that she make her "firing" into an academic freedom case; she had knowingly risked her position in order to live her faith. As she wrote Wellesley's president, she could not "reconcile war with the truths of Jesus' teaching." During this period of crisis, Balch's religious convictions sustained her. Joining the London Society of Friends in 1921, for the rest of her life she found in Quakerism support for her vision of openness and cooperation. Significantly, this choice coincided with her rejection of socialism, which she believed had become too narrowly identified with Marxism.

Balch was an important participant in the International Congress of Women held in Zurich, in May 1919, which issued the first public criticisms of the Versailles Treaty and established itself as a permanent organization, the Women's International League for Peace and Freedom (WILPF). Balch, serving as paid international secretary-treasurer until 1922, set up the office in Geneva, established guidelines for the new organization, and made its primary focus the study and elimination of the causes of war. Setting out to influence the development of the new League of Nations, Balch lobbied for enlarging its membership, democratizing its structure, and recognizing the rights of minorities. She took special satisfaction in the admission of Albania in 1921 and in the League's protection of women and children deported from Asia Minor. She did not expect the League of Nations to resolve national and political rivalries, but perceived that the organization could bring peoples together through joint economic, scientific, and cultural efforts.

In 1922 Balch resigned from her demanding executive post. Thereafter her far-ranging influence in the WILPF was as a voluntary leader. She held many offices in the organization, serving as one of three cochairmen of the executive committee (1929–31), taking a brief second term as international secretary, this time without pay (1934–35), and succeeding Jane Addams as president of the American section (1931) and as honorary international president (1937). But Balch's leadership was much more than a matter of formal titles. A tireless writer, traveler, and organizer, she had a talent for enlisting the cooperation of diverse individuals and groups in the cause of peace. She had organized the third international congress in Vienna in 1921, traveling extensively in central Europe and the Balkans to encourage women to attend. She promoted peace education at several of the WILPF's summer schools, and in time she also helped develop sections of the organization in fifty countries. Holding together the WILPF's mixed international constituency—which included, among others, supporters of international revolution and absolute pacifists—was no easy feat. While some colleagues found Balch too patient, most recognized her genius for steering a group to consensus.

Balch also undertook special missions for the WILPF. In 1926, with five other Americans, including two black women, she investigated conditions in Haiti, which had been occupied by United States marines since 1915. The resulting study, *Occupied Haiti* (1927), edited and written primarily by Balch, recommended removal of the troops and restoration of self-government to the native black population. In 1930 President Herbert Hoover established an official commission; its conclusions, similar to those of the WILPF group, brought the occupation to an end in 1934.

A gradualist in her work for peace, Balch remained flexible and pragmatic, judging each situation on its merits. Thus, despite her strong advocacy of disarmament and endorsement of the 1928 Kellogg-Briand Pact to outlaw war, she believed that Germany should be allowed to rearm because other nations possessed that right and because clandestine rearmament seemed to her more dangerous. She also advocated the use of collective economic and political force to prevent war, urging President Hoover in 1932 to institute sanctions against Japan for invading Manchuria. During later crises in Ethiopia and Spain, she circulated proposals for mediation. In *Refugees as Assets* (1939) she appealed to the United States to welcome refugees from Nazi Germany on economic and cultural as well as humanitarian grounds. Deeply concerned about the threat of Hitler's domination of Europe and his treatment of the Jews, after Pearl Harbor Balch chose what she considered the lesser evil and supported the United States war effort. Unlike some interventionists, she did not resign from the WILPF. Rather she encouraged its members to aid the Japanese-Americans detained in camps in the United States.

The idea of nominating Emily Balch for a Nobel Peace Prize originated with Mercedes Randall, who had met Balch as a young protester during World War I and had worked with her during the 1930s. Randall, with the help of her husband, Professor John H. Randall, Jr., found support for Balch's candidacy among distinguished leaders in many fields who attested to her courage, judgment, and dedication on behalf of people irrespective of race, religion, class, sex, or nationality. With this award the Nobel Peace Prize Committee recognized not only Balch herself but also the work of the WILPF, affirming women's separate leadership in effecting social change. Balch, who shared the prize with John R. Mott of the Student Christian Movement, thus became the second American woman honored with the prize, the first being Jane Addams, with whom she felt the deepest personal kinship.

After 1924, when the Jamaica Plain home she had shared with relatives became too expensive to maintain, Balch moved to Wellesley, Mass., where she created her "Domichek," the separate wing of a house owned by college friends. She lived frugally on a modest income that was augmented by occasional subsidies from affluent friends. Diminishing funds and old age forced Balch to spend her last four years in the Mt. Vernon Nursing Home in Cambridge, Mass. She died there of pneumonia in January 1961.

Emily Balch, the plainest of gaunt New Englanders, had the gift of Yankee humor expressive of her common sense. The enduring impression she gave to all who met her was of an inner radiance and serenity. To the end she was outspoken on any issue of concern to her. During the cold war she did not condemn communism for those who chose it, but neither did she condone passivity in the face of Soviet expansion. At the height of China's isolation from the world, Balch wrote a poem, "A Letter to the Chinese People" (1955), declaring that ideological differences need not be a "barrier to love." To her delight, it was translated for its Chinese audience.

Balch comprehended the layers of history that shape individuals, families, and nations. Valuing her own New England past, out of her respect for different cultural traditions she ultimately identified herself as a citizen of the world. On a deeper level, Balch remained essentially private, trying to "live not only in the ordinary dimensions but also . . . in that other dimension which we call God." A fragment of her writing catches the limitless, enigmatic aspiration Emily Greene Balch held for human beings: "Speak of the great things/ Above Peace, above Freedom./ These are means, not ends."

[Emily Balch's papers are in the Swarthmore College Peace Coll. Also at Swarthmore are the Mercedes M. Randall Papers and those of WILPF and other peace organizations. There is Balch material in the Wellesley College Archives; the Erin-Go-Bragh Papers, Schlesinger Library, Radcliffe College; and the O. G. Villard Papers, Houghton Library, Harvard Univ. Trustees minutes are in the Office of the President, Wellesley College. For a complete list of Balch's prolific writings see Mercedes M. Randall, ed., *Beyond Nationalism: The Social Thought of Emily Greene Balch* (1972), pp. 243–49. Of particular interest are "Who's Who Among Pacifists: The Position of the Emergency Peace Federation," March 20, 1917, in the Balch papers on microfilm, Swarthmore College Peace Coll.; "The Effects of War and Militarism on the Status of Women," *Publications of the American Sociological Society*, 1915, pp. 39–55; Balch's letter to Jane Addams, in Addams, *The Second Twenty Years at Hull House* (1930), p. 197; *Women at The Hague: The International Congress of Women and Its Results*, with Jane Addams and Alice Hamilton (1915, 1972); Balch's tribute to Jane Addams in *Beyond Nationalism*, pp. 205–11; "The Earth Is My Home," in *Beyond Nationalism*, pp. 238–39; and *The Miracle of Living* (1941), a collection of poems. Mercedes M. Randall, *Improper Bostonian: Emily Greene Balch* (1964), is a full-length biography. See also John Herman Randall, Jr., *Emily Greene Balch of New England, Citizen of the World* (1946); Elizabeth Stix Fainsod, "Emily Greene Balch," *Bryn Mawr Alumnae Bull.*, May 1947; and Barbara Miller Solomon, *Ancestors and Immigrants* (1956), chap. 9. For studies of American peace movements see Gertrude Bussey and Margaret Tims, *Women's International League for Peace and Freedom, 1915–1965* (1965); Charles Chatfield, *For Peace and Justice: Pacifism in America, 1914–1941* (1971); and Lawrence S. Wittner, *Rebels Against War: The American Peace Movement, 1941–1960* (1969). For perspectives on the young radicals with whom Balch worked in World War I see *The Reminiscences of Frances Witherspoon and Tracy Mygatt* (1966), New York Times Oral History Program, in the Oral History Coll., Columbia Univ.; *Four Lights* (1917), the antiwar periodical for which Balch wrote occasionally (available at the Swarthmore College Peace Coll.); and Blanche Wiesen Cook, ed., *Crystal Eastman on Women and Revolution* (1978). Two doctoral dissertations were useful: Blanche Wiesen Cook, "Woodrow Wilson and the Antimilitarists, 1914–1917" (Johns Hopkins Univ., 1970), and Barbara Steinson, "Female Activism in

World War I: The American Women's Peace, Suffrage, Preparedness, and Relief Movements, 1914–1919" (Univ. of Michigan, 1977). Helpful information was provided by Brand Blanshard, Blanche Wiesen Cook, Dorothy Detzer Denny, Patricia A. Palmieri, Anne-Margaret Osterkamp Lewenz, Bernice Nichols, Barbara Sicherman, and Wilma Slaight. An obituary appeared in the *N.Y. Times*, Jan. 11, 1961.]

BARBARA MILLER SOLOMON

BAMBACE, Angela, Feb. 14, 1898–April 3, 1975. Labor organizer and leader.

Angela Bambace was born in Santos, Brazil, to Italian parents, Antonio and Giuseppina (Calabrese) Bambace. Her father, the owner and operator of a small shipping company, had migrated to Brazil from Calabria, her mother from Sicily. Angela was the oldest of their three surviving children (two girls and a boy); a younger sister died in childhood. After moving back to Calabria in about 1900 when Antonio Bambace became ill, the family emigrated to New York in 1901, settling in East Harlem. There Giuseppina Bambace found work trimming plumes for ladies' hats in order to support her children and ailing husband.

At age eighteen, after attending high school, Angela Bambace started to work as a bookkeeper and clerk in a laundry. In 1918 she and her sister, Maria, went to work as operators in a shirtwaist factory, and the following year participated in the International Ladies' Garment Workers' Union (ILGWU) organizing strike. Both Bambace daughters developed reputations as effective organizers among Italian women; visiting workers' homes, they appealed to fathers to let their daughters participate in union activities. Giuseppina Bambace sometimes marched with her daughters on the picket line, rolling pin in hand, to protect them from thugs hired to beat up strikers.

In June 1919 Angela Bambace married Romolo Camponeschi, a man chosen by her father who had emigrated from Rome and worked as a waiter in a Manhattan hotel. After the marriage, she left work to stay at home. The couple had two sons: Oscar, born in 1920, and Philip, born in 1923. During this period, she supported Italian-American antifascist and anarchist causes, including the defense of Nicola Sacco and Bartolomeo Vanzetti. These activities conflicted with her husband's conventional views on politics and the role of women. In 1925 she decided to return to work, not only to supplement her husband's income but also to resume her organizing career.

Taking a job as a dressmaker in a Manhattan shop, Angela Camponeschi became embroiled in a power struggle within the ILGWU. She grew close to communists in the union, including Charles and Rose Zimmerman; joining the party herself, she backed communist-supported elements in several locals in their efforts to gain control of the ILGWU's governing board. The attempt failed, however, and her commitment to the union outlived that to the Communist party, which she left in 1929 following the party's expulsion of the Zimmermans for factional deviation.

This period of intense political involvement also brought changes in Camponeschi's personal life. In 1927 she and her husband were divorced; soon after he won custody of their children, using her radical activities as evidence against her. Resuming her maiden name, Angela Bambace sought friendship among those who shared her convictions: Clara Larson, an anarchist who had emigrated from the Ukraine, became one of her closest comrades, and Luigi Quintilliano, an Italian anarchist writer and organizer, her companion. Working for the ILGWU and the Amalgamated Clothing Workers of America from 1927 to 1933, Bambace expanded her predominantly Italian network of colleagues to include a number of Jewish union officials, welcoming them to the Flushing, N.Y., home she purchased and shared with her mother. While no longer their legal guardian, she remained close to her two sons for the rest of her life.

In 1934 David Dubinsky, president of the ILGWU, acting on the recommendation of union leaders, including Charles Zimmerman, offered Bambace an important temporary assignment in Baltimore. Union efforts in that city had been slowed by the refusal of male cloakmakers to extend membership to less well-paid women in the industry; Bambace responded by organizing a local composed entirely of women. She fought against manufacturers' efforts to manipulate National Recovery Administration codes and expanded the work of the ILGWU by following "runaway" shops into small communities where they hoped to avoid union influence. Remaining in Baltimore, she assumed responsibility for dress and cotton shops with a high percentage of women workers and soon began to conduct organizing drives in outlying districts, serving as assistant manager of the ILGWU's Maryland Department. She also became involved in New Deal politics, modifying her earlier radical views and encouraging union members to support prolabor politicians.

Bambace reunited her family in her new environment: Luigi Quintilliano joined her in the late 1930s, and both her sons attended Maryland colleges and later settled nearby. She also retained close ties with friends and family in New York, including her mother, whose Flushing home remained a center for weekend gatherings.

During World War II, her duties increased as war production stimulated the cotton garment branches of the industry in Virginia, West Virginia, and southern Pennsylvania. Bambace was appointed manager in 1942 of the newly created Maryland-Virginia District, which included all but the cloakmakers in Baltimore. Keeping in constant touch with union organizers in the field from her Baltimore office, she made a special effort to fight the prejudices she encountered in the upper south—the anti-Semitism directed against the union's largely Jewish leadership and the racism encountered by the black workers it recruited.

Bambace became an important figure in the trade union movement despite the limited leadership opportunities it afforded to women. In New York, as a member of the Italian Dressmakers' Local 89, she could not advance beyond business agent; in Baltimore, however, operating in a looser power structure, she progressed from district manager to chief official of the Upper South Department (formerly the Maryland-Virginia District) in 1947. She achieved success as an administrator as well as an organizer, helping to establish an outpatient clinical service for union members in 1956 and a pension fund the following year. She was elected a vice president of the ILGWU's General Executive Board. The first non-Jewish woman to hold the post, her appointment reflected the increasing role of Italians in the union.

Angela Bambace's career of service extended from her union to the broader problems of its communities. She was active in war relief programs, Histadrut (the Zionist labor movement), the Italian American Labor Council, the Americans for Democratic Action, and the American Civil Liberties Union. In 1962 President John F. Kennedy named her to his Commission on the Status of Women. Retiring as a vice president of the ILGWU in 1972, into her last year she remained alert to the issues of labor and social justice to which she had responded with determination for nearly six decades. She died in Baltimore of cancer in April 1975.

[Sources for a study of Angela Bambace are scarce. The Immigration Hist. Research Center, Univ. of Minn., St. Paul, holds some personal correspondence, photographs, and clippings on Bambace's career; it also houses the papers of her brother-in-law Antonio Capraro. Records beginning about 1939 for the Upper South Dept. of the ILGWU are deposited at the union's archives in N.Y. City. Bambace's role in the 1919 East Harlem strike is mentioned in Salvatore Amico, *Gli Italiani e L'Internationale Dei Sarti Da Donna Di Storie E Memorie Contemporanee* (1944), p. 42. See also Marianne Alexander, "Angela Bambace, 1898–1975: Labor Organizer," in Winifred Helms, ed., *Notable Maryland Women* (1977), pp. 14–16; A. D. Glushakow, *A Pictorial History of Maryland Jewry* (1955), pp. 131–32; and *Who's Who in Labor* (1946), p. 15. An obituary appeared in the Baltimore *Sun*, April 4, 1975. Information provided by the Enoch Pratt Free Library, and the Museum and Library of Maryland Hist., both in Baltimore, and by her sister, Maria Bambace Capraro, her sons, Philip Camponeschi and Oscar Camp, and by Charles and Rose Zimmerman, Clara Larson, Abraham and Edith Rosenfield, Margaret Frank, Edward Milano, May Lewis, Sarah Barron, Dora Feleman, and Henoch Mendelsund. Death certificate provided by Md. Dept. of Health.]

JEAN A. SCARPACI

BANCROFT, Jessie Hubbell, Dec. 20, 1867– Nov. 13, 1952. Physical education specialist.

Jessie Bancroft, the first woman to direct a physical training program in a large public school system, was born in Winona, Minn., the daughter of Susan Maria (Hubbell) and Edward Hall Bancroft. Both parents came from New York, and both were of English ancestry. Edward Bancroft, like his father a pioneer in the development of rail transportation, had been superintendent of the Syracuse Northern Railway before moving westward with the railroads and settling in Winona, where he met his wife. After Jessie was born, the family moved to New York for a period of time, but returned to Minnesota during her teenage years.

Bancroft's earliest interests in systematic exercise developed out of concern for her own health. Not a robust teenager, in the early 1880s she attended a lecture on exercise, diet, and hygiene. Becoming interested in the subject, she took private lessons to learn more about the exercises. In 1888 Bancroft attended the Minneapolis School of Physical Education to study anatomy, physiology, Swedish and German gymnastics, and the techniques of directing exercises for groups. Still undecided about whether she wanted to teach physical education, she enrolled at the Winona State Normal School (1888–89), completing the two-year kindergarten training course in one year. She decided, however, to choose physical education because it offered "larger possibilities for the future and greater assurance of my own health."

Since it was difficult to find regular employment in an emerging field dominated by men, and not yet firmly established as a field for women, Bancroft began teaching "parlor classes" in various types of exercise. She also gave exercise demonstrations at "churches, welfare societies or schools, using for the purpose a public hall, church, or assembly room, with admission charged and receipts divided between the society and the lecturer." After two years of this nomadic lecture circuit through Illinois and Iowa, she left the midwest to go to the Harvard Summer School of Physical Education (1891), one of the first schools of its kind. There she studied applied anatomy, mechanics of exercise, and dance gymnastics, and gained a "broad, eclectic view of 'systems' of exercise."

Encouraged by friends to seek a teaching position in New York City, she soon learned that physical education there was not the advanced profession she had expected. Only after visiting all the teaching agencies and many of the private schools for girls in the city, and seeking the help of her friends, did she secure a series of part-time positions. For the next two years she lectured and taught at several schools and colleges. These part-time positions led to Bancroft's appointment in 1893 as director of physical training in the Brooklyn Public Schools, a post she held until 1903 when Brooklyn became one of the boroughs of New York City. In the reorganization of the city's physical training department in 1904, Bancroft was appointed assistant director for the New York City Schools, a post she held until her retirement in 1928.

Bancroft attained both positions with neither a college degree nor the medical degree which was the chief credential of physical educators at the time. Her work was characterized by numerous and diverse accomplishments. She organized a graded course of gymnastic exercises for use by classroom teachers; classified games according to age groups and introduced them into the school curriculum; and added light apparatus to the exercise program, resulting in the establishment of the first public school gymnasium. She also used anthropometric measures of thousands of children in adjusting school furniture to their sizes and established methods for sight and hearing tests, reorganizing classroom seating from the results.

Bancroft was a prolific lecturer and writer, publishing seven books and numerous periodical articles aimed at arousing interest in physical education. Her book *Games for the Playground, Home, School and Gymnasium* (1909; rev. ed. 1937) was considered "the most comprehensive and scholarly book on games then published in English" (Gerber, p. 361). A modest and reserved individual who felt keenly her lack of formal education, Bancroft nevertheless played a significant role in the development of public school physical education. She also founded and was president of the American Posture League. Her research was used to apply new principles to foot measuring and shoemaking; to the manufacture of school, factory, and office furniture; and to seating in subway trains. Honored for her accomplishments, Bancroft was the first woman to receive the Gulick Award for distinguished service in physical education (1924); the first woman member of the American Academy of Physical Education; and the first woman to receive an honorary degree from Springfield College (1926). She was the first woman to serve as executive secretary of the American Association for the Advancement of Physical Education (later the American Alliance for Health, Physical Education, and Recreation).

Following her retirement Bancroft lived and traveled in England, France, and Italy. She died in Pittsfield, Mass., in 1952 of a heart attack.

[For insight into Bancroft's professional ideas see her own works: *School Gymnastics, Free-Hand* (1896), *Recess Games* (1895), *School Gymnastics with Light Apparatus* (1897), *The Posture of School Children* (1913), *Handbook of Athletic Games for Players, Instructors, and Spectators* (1916), and numerous articles in the *Am. Physical Education Rev.* beginning as early as 1898. The best source of information on her career is her autobiography, "Pioneering in Physical Training," in the supplement to the *Research Quart.*, Oct. 1941, pp. 666–78 (unidentified quotations are from this source). Additional biographical information may be found in Janice Carkin, "Recipients of the Gulick Award" (Ed.D. diss., Stanford Univ., 1952); Ellen Gerber, *Innovators and Institutions in Physical Education* (1971), pp. 357–62; and a short sketch in Emmett Rice, John Hutchinson, and Mabel Lee, *A Brief History of Physical Education* (5th ed., 1969), pp. 329–30. Her professional contributions are detailed in George J. Fisher, "Jessie H. Bancroft, Educator-Author-Pioneer-Philanthropist," *Am. Physical Education Rev.*, Oct. 1924, pp. 476–80; Albert K. Aldinger, "Reports of Local Societies," *Am. Physical Education Rev.*, Nov. 1924, pp. 540–43; and Ruth Evans, "Jessie H. Bancroft," *Jour. Health, Physical Education and Recreation*, May–June 1960, p. 50. An obituary appeared in the *N.Y. Times*, Nov. 14, 1952, with a photograph. Death certificate supplied by Mass. Dept. of Public Health.]

MARY L. REMLEY

BANKHEAD, Tallulah Brockman, Jan. 31(?), 1902–Dec. 12, 1968. Actress.

Tallulah Bankhead, with sheer perseverance and with little help from studios or agents, successfully made herself famous. Her eccentricities were staggering, her performances varied enormously, and most of her career was devoted to mediocre exhibitions of her legendary style. But no stage actress in this century has been so successful at molding her own life into a stunning theatrical role.

Although her father at one time aspired to a theatrical career, it was into a prominent political family that Tallulah Brockman Bankhead was born in Huntsville, Ala. Both her father and her grandfather had long careers in the United States Congress, her father, William Brockman Bankhead, serving as House speaker from 1936 to 1940. Tallulah's mother, Adelaide Eugenia (Sledge) Bankhead, died only weeks after the birth of Tallulah, her younger daughter, and the two girls were raised in turn by aunts, by grandparents, and, at times, by their father. It was from her paternal grandmother that Tallulah got her universally recognized first name. She revered her father, spoke glowingly of her family and her southern heritage, and predictably became an active Democrat, campaigning vigorously for Roosevelt, Truman, and Stevenson well before it was customary for entertainers to involve themselves in politics.

Although the Bankheads were Episcopalian, Tallulah was educated in a number of Catholic girls' schools. In 1917, after her photograph won a contest in *Picture Play Magazine,* she abandoned school and won her family's consent to attempt an acting career in New York. A few low-budget films and her first stage appearance as an extra in *The Squab Farm* (1918) followed. But more important, by chance she and an aunt took a room at the Algonquin Hotel, the focal point of New York's theatrical and literary set. There she made numerous acquaintances (one of them, the actress Estelle Winwood, remained throughout Bankhead's life her most devoted friend), attracting them not only with her stunning looks but with the deliberately outrageous manners she was already cultivating. Although no important engagements resulted, she won a recommendation from British producer Charles Cochran, and, in what must surely have been the major decision of her career, sailed for England early in 1923.

In very little time, Bankhead became a sensation in London, both as an actress with an enormous following (especially among the "gallery girls," young women in cheap seats who idolized her) and as a model for the "bright young things," the new generation that had emerged from the war determined to abandon the proprieties of the Edwardian age. In the eight years she spent in London, which she later called the happiest of her life, she appeared for the most part in dreadful plays; exceptions were Noël Coward's *Fallen Angels* (1925) and Sidney Howard's *They Knew What They Wanted* (1926). But her roles were what her public craved: daring creatures, dressed in Mayfair chic, dedicated to insouciant wit.

In 1931 Bankhead succumbed to the lure of money and returned to America to make pictures for Paramount, which tried, with no success at all, to make her a "femme fatale" in the mold of Marlene Dietrich. Bankhead's various attempts at film acting were failures, with the exception of Alfred Hitchcock's *Lifeboat* (1944), which won her the New York Film Critics' Award as Best Actress. The films themselves were no doubt to blame, although Bankhead's rather mannered acting and her impulses to crowd-pleasing were certainly better suited to the stage than to films. She came very close, however, to landing Scarlett O'Hara, the most sought-after film role in history.

Bankhead's stage presence, which her contemporaries praised more than any other aspect of her acting, was in part a product of her stunning appearance. Although she was only five feet three, she dominated audience attention with her large, rather sorrowful eyes, luxurious blonde hair, and, particularly, her famous baritone voice. Most of her New York plays were memorable only because she was in them, but in 1939 Bankhead appeared in what she always considered her greatest role: the predatory Regina Giddens in Lillian Hellman's vicious portrayal of the postbellum south, *The Little Foxes.* With both play and actress receiving vast acclaim, Bankhead, for the first time, found herself regarded as a serious actress. She delighted in this new image and in 1942 showed herself worthy of it in a far more daring part, the "eternal temptress," Sabina, in Thornton Wilder's *The Skin of Our Teeth.*

Bankhead also appeared in plays by Clifford Odets, Jean Cocteau, Philip Barry, and George Kelly. Never afraid of the unusual play or the daring role, at the same time she preferred acclaim and a long run to real artistry. Consequently, she spent much of her time with badly written, shoddily produced plays on the road, or with lengthy runs of revivals such as Noël Coward's *Private Lives* and Tennessee Williams's *A Streetcar Named Desire.* She yearned for great parts, but not enough to keep her away from easier successes, and Regina and Sabina remain the roles for which she is remembered. Bankhead was hindered too by her lack of training, either realistic or classical. Although she always insisted that acting should be entirely instinctive, her talents were definitely limited, as her one disastrous attempt at Shakespeare clearly revealed: she appeared as Cleopatra in 1937. Actor John Emery, who played Octavian in that production, was her only husband; they were married Aug. 31, 1937, and divorced June 13, 1941.

In the 1940s, Bankhead began working more and more in radio—and later, television—which, along with her lecture tours and nightclub and stock appearances, brought her to millions who had previously known her only by her vast reputation. Whether in guest appearances or as the hostess of "The Big Show" (1950–52), the National Broadcasting Company's star-studded radio attempt to forestall the inevitability of television, Bankhead always played the same role: the woman of wealth and sophistication at sea in the real world. She handled these assignments effectively, and it is unfortunate that the rise of television corresponded with her physical decline, since her stylized comedy may have been ideally suited to the new medium.

In the theater, however, Bankhead was slipping, and her last stage appearance, in Williams's revision of *The Milk Train Doesn't Stop Here Anymore* (1964)—said to have been written for her—was a disaster. For some time she had been succumbing to a dependency on alcohol and pills and rapidly was reduced to appearing only in unfortunate parodies of her once-esteemed image: her last role was the Dragon Lady in the American Broadcasting Company's "Batman." Bankhead died in New York of emphysema complicated by pneumonia.

How good Bankhead was can no longer be answered since her few films are no measure of her abilities. She certainly lacked the versatility of such a contemporary as KATHARINE CORNELL, while the numerous shallow parts she played kept her from displaying the depth of a Vivien Leigh. Least of all could she ever subordinate herself to a script as any number of character players can effectively do. Her stature must depend on the strength of the Tallulah legend, a monumental achievement, to be sure, but one which must inevitably fade with time.

[The Tallulah Brockman Bankhead Coll. in the Ala. Dept. of Archives and History, Maps and MSS. Div., consists of personal and family correspondence (1916–51) and press clippings (1917–69). An uncataloged collection of photographs, letters, scripts, and scrapbook items is in the Walter Hampden–Edwin Booth Theatre Coll. and Library, N.Y. City. Bankhead's autobiography, *Tallulah,* appeared in 1952. Largely ghostwritten by Richard Maney, it cannot be entirely trusted. The most complete biography, Lee Israel, *Miss Tallulah Bankhead* (1972), is overly derogatory. Brendan Gill, *Tallulah* (1972), first published as a profile in the *New Yorker,* Oct. 7 and 14, 1972, includes a brief life, numerous photographs, and a full record of films, plays, and radio and television appearances. Kieran Tunney,

Tallulah—Darling of the Gods: An Intimate Portrait (1973), is a rather sentimental memoir. *Biog. Encyc. and Who's Who of the Am. Theatre* (1966) contains an almost complete list of her film and theater credits. See also *Current Biog.,* 1941 and 1953, and obituary in the *N.Y. Times,* Dec. 13, 1968. No birth record is available, and Lee Israel presents some evidence that she was born around Feb. 12, 1902, not Jan. 31.]

JOHN DAVID SHOUT

BARA, Theda, July 20, 1885–April 7, 1955. Film actress.

Theda Bara was born Theodosia Goodman in Cincinnati, Ohio, the oldest of three children and elder daughter of Bernard and Pauline Louise (de Coppet) Goodman. She always kept her year of birth a secret, feeling that a woman who would tell her real age would tell anything. Her father was a prosperous Jewish tailor from Poland; her mother, born in Switzerland of French parents, was in the hair products business before her marriage.

Goodman graduated from Cincinnati's Walnut Hills High School in 1903 and attended the University of Cincinnati from 1903 to 1905. Although her early theatrical career is obscure, she was apparently encouraged by her family, who moved to New York around 1905. In 1908, as Theodosia de Coppet, she appeared on Broadway in Molnar's *The Devil.* But she had no stirring success on the stage, and when in 1914 she was offered the leading female role in the film *A Fool There Was,* she readily accepted. She would later say proudly that she was one of the few who came into the movies directly as a star. The film was based on a Broadway play inspired by Rudyard Kipling's poem "The Vampire" and portrayed the machinations of a woman who ensnares and ruins a prosperous married man.

Goodman was given a new name, Theda Bara (derived from the middle name of her maternal grandfather). She and her family approved sufficiently to change their names legally to Bara in 1917. A whole personality was fabricated for her as well, and Theda (pronounced Thayda) Bara became one of the most successful examples of press agentry. Readers of fan magazines were told that Bara was Arab spelled backwards; that her whole name was an anagram for Arab death; that she was born on an oasis in the shadow of the sphinx; that she was a child of exotic parents; that she had been a star of the Parisian theater. In order to preserve her mystery, Bara was kept distant from the public and from interviewers, and her rare personal appearances were carefully staged. Although the facts about her life were apparently available by 1915, journalists, as well as the public, preferred to foster the legend. *Photoplay* in September 1915 said that it chose "to disbelieve those stupid people who insist that Theda Bara's right name is Theodosia Goodman and that she is by, of, and from Cincinnati."

A Fool There Was, released in 1915, was a significant box office success, helping to establish William Fox as a major producer. It also became the prototype of countless other films (many starring Bara herself) depicting a woman destroying a man. Bara's victims were wrecked morally, financially, and even physically, and seemed to die from sexual excess. Previously, films had most often depicted women as good and vulnerable creatures—hard-working seamstresses or faithful wives. American movie audiences in a puritanical age had seen nothing like this "bad" woman, and they flocked to see how she exercised her seductive talents. Men enjoyed her scanty clothes, her earrings, and her spangles. A number of women grew irate at this "husband stealer," wrote her vicious letters, and even defaced lobby posters. However, many women were avid fans, and adopted her sultry costumes, heavy makeup, and so-called exotic ways.

A Fool There Was, with its famous line, "Kiss me, my fool!" made Theda Bara an institution. A new word entered the English language: to vamp, meaning to seduce, and the term vampire signified a Bara-like person until Béla Lugosi restored its former meaning. Between 1914 and 1919 Bara appeared in thirty-nine movies for Fox; only the first one survives. Her famous parts included Carmen and the notorious title role in *Cleopatra* (1917), in which she was scantily clad and rather busily seductive. The film was censored heavily in some states. Bara did not like being typecast and appeared as a poor girl in *The Two Orphans* (1915) and as Juliet in *Romeo and Juliet* (1916). But audiences did not want their stars to break their molds. Like Mary Pickford (d. 1979) who was compelled to play the adolescent, Theda Bara was doomed to be the vamp.

Although Bara at times relished her parts and enjoyed her eventual $4,000 a week salary, her portrayal of woman was not kind to her sex. In defense, she explained her role as the vengeance of women on men. The woman vampire is loved but does not love in return; she exploits men for their money and their sex, and, when they are exhausted of both, abandons them.

The absurdity of Bara's vamp personifications seemed to go unnoticed by the public at first, but after much repetition and much imitation,

by other stars and other studios, as well as some healthy satire, the exotic woman soon became ridiculous. After her contract with Fox ended in 1919, Bara announced that she wanted to be a "symbol of purity" and that her purpose was "to spread happiness." No one seemed to be interested in the new Bara and she reverted to type in a poor play, *The Blue Flame*, which was received with derision when it appeared on Broadway in March 1920. Although audiences laughed at it, they liked her, and the play did well at the box office on tour. In 1921 Bara married one of her film directors, Charles J. Brabin, and the couple had one of Hollywood's few successful marriages. She tried to make a comeback in *The Unchastened Woman* (1925), appeared in a Hal Roach comedy, *Madame Mystery*, in 1926, and then retired from the movies.

Bara showed no bitterness. She and her husband lived in Beverly Hills and entertained frequently. Short, bosomy, and a trifle plump, Bara became a hostess famous for her gourmet meals. Her mother lived nearby, and she retained a strong sense of family. In February 1955 Bara entered a hospital in Los Angeles where she died two months later of cancer.

[The Theda Bara Coll. in the Billy Rose Theatre Coll., N.Y. Public Library, contains photographs, portfolios, scrapbooks, press books, reviews, and manuscript notes about Bara and her early years in Cincinnati. Additional material is in the Robinson Locke Scrapbooks in the same library. The Harvard Theatre Coll. has a clipping file. *Cumulated Dramatic Index, 1909–1949*, and Mel Schuster, *Motion Picture Performers* (1971) contain bibliographies of articles about Bara. Sources of information about her life and career include DeWitt Bodeen, "Theda Bara," *Films in Review*, May 1968, pp. 266–87 (which contains a list of her films); Alexander Walker, *The Celluloid Sacrifice: Aspects of Sex in the Movies* (1966); and an entry in *Dict. Am. Biog.*, Supp. Five. The 1885 birth date is confirmed by the U.S. Census (1900), which also shows her to be the oldest of three children. An obituary appeared in the *N.Y. Times*, April 8, 1955; a death record was provided by Calif. Dept. of Public Health. Additional information was provided by Bara's goddaughter, June Millarde.]

ARTHUR LENNIG

BARKER, Mary Cornelia, Jan. 20, 1879–Sept. 15, 1963. Educator, labor leader.

Mary Cornelia Barker was born in Atlanta, the eldest of three daughters of Dora Elizabeth (Lovejoy) and Thomas Nathaniel Barker. Both parents were of English descent, her father the son of a sea captain in the Bahama Islands, her mother the daughter of a plantation owner and local preacher in Greenville, Ga. Both were trained as teachers. They lived briefly in Atlanta before settling in Rockmart, Ga., where Thomas Barker was employed at the Methodist-affiliated Piedmont Institute and Dora Lovejoy Barker taught in the local public schools.

Mary Barker entered Agnes Scott Institute in Decatur, Ga., in 1894. After her father's sudden death in 1896 the rest of the family moved to Decatur to live with Dora Barker's retired father. Living with her mother and sisters, Barker completed the diploma normal course and graduated from Agnes Scott College in 1900. She began her teaching career with one-year appointments in the small Georgia communities of Stockbridge and McDonough, followed by two years at the Decatur Orphans Home. In 1904 Mary Barker commenced her forty-year career with the Atlanta public schools, teaching until 1921 and then serving as principal of the Ivy Street School (1922–23) and the John B. Gordon School (1923–44). Barker and her two sisters, both educators, maintained a home in Atlanta throughout their adult lives; their mother lived with them until her death in 1931.

Mary Barker's life combined dedication to public education and the teaching profession with an allegiance to the American labor movement. A proponent of John Dewey's philosophy of education, she was a creative force in the classroom, offering students an innovative curriculum and the newest teaching methods. A stern disciplinarian and a meticulously organized administrator, as a principal Barker combined the best of traditional school regime with the most stimulating of progressive techniques. She believed that administrators should operate schools democratically and protect both the rights of students and the freedom of teachers. Likewise, she encouraged teachers to work for better teaching conditions.

Central to Barker's notion of teachers' rights, autonomy, and participation in the educational process was the development of a professional organization. In 1905 she was a founding member of the Atlanta Public School Teachers' Association (APSTA); by 1907 two-thirds of the teachers in the system had joined. Barker served on the board of the association and supported the group's efforts to increase salaries, to fight favoritism in the renewal of teacher contracts, and to assist the city's board of education in obtaining additional financial support for the schools. In early 1919 the city council finally met the association's demands for a significant salary increase. In May of that year an APSTA committee of which Barker was a member recommended affiliation with the American Federation of Teachers (AFT). The membership

approved, and the group became Local 89 of the three-year-old national union. In January 1920 Barker was one of five delegates of the teachers' union who took their places in the Atlanta Central Labor body, proud to be consummating the alliance between teachers and organized labor.

For Atlanta's organized teachers, affiliation with the AFT and the Atlanta Federation of Trades meant increased clout with the board of education on the issue of salary increases, and a new sense of community responsibility. During Barker's tenure as president of the local, from 1921 to 1923, issues ranged from the perennial salary question to the matter of continuing education for teachers and the passage of a tenure law. In 1924 she vigorously supported the AFT's campaign for adoption of the constitutional amendment to end child labor. Barker gave Local 89 the firm leadership it needed in its early years and her demand that public officials, the school administration, and especially teachers themselves value and support the local had wide impact.

For Barker personally, alignment with the AFT offered new opportunities for leadership. She attended her first national AFT convention in 1923 and in 1925 that body, in need of strong direction in an era of declining support, chose her as its third president. The AFT was then under both internal and external attack and membership had dropped precipitously. Under Barker's direction a special organizing fund was established, and by 1930 there had been a 50 percent increase in membership. During her six-year presidency, the AFT adopted a specific legislative program advocating the improvement of school facilities, reduction in class size, the abolition of "factory standards" of production for schools, just compensation for teachers, and the provision of opportunities for all children to receive an adequate education. The program also dealt with the issues of academic freedom and tenure. Barker worked to protect the rights of members to speak freely and participate openly in union affairs.

From early in her career Mary Barker was especially concerned about the welfare of southern women workers, particularly those who labored long hours in factory jobs for inadequate wages. In 1926 she was invited to join the organizing committee of the Southern Summer School for Women Workers in Industry. The school, directed by LOUISE MCLAREN, brought together workers from textile mills, garment factories, and the tobacco industry to teach them economics, principles of organizing, and labor history and train them as labor leaders. From 1927 until 1944 Barker chaired the school's central committee, finding there a community of women whose commitment to democracy in education and to the organization of women workers paralleled her own. A leader in the biracial movement in Atlanta, Mary Barker belonged to the Atlanta Urban League, the Committee on Interracial Cooperation, and the American Civil Liberties Union. She served on the board of the Phyllis Wheatley Branch of the local YWCA and encouraged black teachers to organize a union and negotiate for an equal salary schedule. In the thirties, Barker supported numerous appeals for political justice, including the campaign to free Angelo Herndon, a black communist convicted in Atlanta under an 1866 law of inciting insurrection.

Despite her poor health in the years following her retirement in 1944, Barker remained active in organizations committed to social change, and retained both her sense of public responsibility and the security of her convictions. She died at her home in Atlanta of heart failure in 1963.

[The principal manuscript sources are the Mary C. Barker Papers in the Emory Univ. Special Collections, which include correspondence, organizational records, clippings, and other printed material; and the Atlanta Public School Teachers' Assoc. Papers in the Southern Labor Archives at Ga. State Univ., which include correspondence, records of conventions and meetings, financial and other reports, office files, clippings, newsletters, and pamphlets. The papers of Mary Barker's sister Meta Barker are in the Atlanta Hist. Soc. Coll. Articles by or about Mary Barker were published in the AFT's *Am. Teacher* magazine, March 1928, Oct. 1930, and Feb. 1964, and in the *Jour. of Labor,* published by the Atlanta Federation of Trades, 1925–40. Her article, "The Public-School Teacher Awakes" appeared in *The Labor World* Supp., May 1, 1931. Information about her career is available in the *American Labor Year Book* for 1926 and 1932. Other sources that include references to her work are the Commission on Educational Reconstruction, *Organizing the Teaching Profession: The Story of the American Federation of Teachers* (1955); William Edward Eaton, *The American Federation of Teachers, 1916–1961: A History of the Movement* (1975); Joseph W. Newman, "A History of the Atlanta Public School Teachers' Association, Local 89 of the American Federation of Teachers, 1919–1956" (Ph.D. diss., Georgia State Univ., 1978), and "The Social Origins of Atlanta's Teachers: 1881, 1896, 1922," *Urban Education,* April 1976, pp. 115–22; Aileen W. Robinson, *A Critical Evaluation of the American Federation of Teachers* (1934); Wayne J. Urban, "Organized Teachers and Educational Reform During the Progressive Era: 1890–1920," *Hist. of Education Quart.,* Spring 1976, pp. 35–52. An obituary appeared in *Am. Teacher,* Feb. 1964, p. 19. Information about the Barker and Lovejoy families was supplied by Mary Barker's sister Tommie Dora Barker, and recollections of Barker as teacher and principal were provided by Frances Waggoner Strother. A biobibliography by Stephen H. Dew assisted in the research for this article. Death certificate supplied by Ga. Dept of Public Health.]

MARY E. FREDERICKSON

BARNEY, Natalie Clifford, Oct. 31, 1876–Feb. 2, 1972. Salon hostess, writer.

Natalie Barney, hostess of a literary salon in Paris, was born in Dayton, Ohio, the elder of two daughters of Alice (Pike) and Albert Clifford Barney. Both of her grandfathers had made large fortunes, which left her parents and eventually Natalie and her sister, Laura, independently wealthy and free to follow their inclinations. Her mother was a remarkable woman who studied painting under Whistler and other masters and became an accomplished artist as well as a generous patron of the arts. Natalie's father, heir to a fortune made in building railroad cars, seems never to have done much of anything. He was chiefly interested in the social life of Washington, D.C., where the family moved when the girls were growing up, and Bar Harbor, Maine, where they spent summers.

The two girls received their earliest education from a French governess and their first regular schooling at a boarding school, Les Ruches in Fontainebleau, while their mother studied painting in Paris. Before she entered her teens, Natalie Barney was completely bilingual, able to express herself with equal ease in French and English. She completed her formal education at Miss Ely's School for Girls in New York City (1894), spent the following summer on a European tour, and stayed on for another seven months in Germany, taking lessons in the violin, which she played quite well.

Natalie Barney was born with every advantage—not only wealth but beauty, talent, intelligence, and an extraordinary magnetism. Launched in society in Washington at the age of eighteen, she enjoyed dancing and flirting with the rich and titled young men who courted her assiduously—French and English as well as American—and even went so far as to become engaged to several of them. But she had discovered at an early age that she was only attracted to her own sex, and she was destined to become the most daring and candid lesbian of her time. Returning to Paris in 1898 with her mother and sister, she became notorious when one of the great courtesans of the *belle époque,* Liane de Pougy, published the story of her seduction by a young American woman in a thinly disguised novel, *Idylle saphique* (1901).

It was but the first of a number of novels about Natalie Barney's many love affairs.

By this time Natalie Barney was launched on a writing career of her own, having published in French a volume of love poems, *Quelques portraits-sonnets des femmes* (1900), illustrated by her mother. She continued to write until her old age, not only poetry but drama, fiction, memoirs, and epigrams, but never to take her writing very seriously. Instead, she believed in making her life a work of art, of which her writings were merely the by-product: her poems were addressed to the women she loved, her dialogues expressed her Sapphic ideals, her plays were designed as entertainments to be performed by friends.

Barney's early work is occasionally interesting for her emancipated views, although even as a feminist she seems never to have dedicated herself wholeheartedly. She did attempt to encourage women writers, giving receptions in her salon in celebration of new books by friends and establishing in the late 1920s an Académie des Femmes to give women writers an opportunity to read from their work. For some years she gave an annual prize to a woman writer, named in honor of Renée Vivien, a fragile English poet who died young, with whom Barney had had a celebrated love affair.

Most of Barney's writing is in French, as she found its spirit more akin to her own than English. Like her mother, she also preferred Paris and the company of creative people to the fashionable society of Washington. After 1902, when the death of her father left her financially independent, she settled permanently in Paris. There she exercised all her charms, not only in her love affairs but also in cultivating the friendship of writers, scholars, and statesmen, older men for the most part, who appreciated her personal radiance, intelligence, and wit. Her most famous conquest was of the writer Remy de Gourmont who, old and disfigured by illness, had become a complete recluse. He made Barney famous by addressing her in his *Lettres à l'Amazone*, essays inspired by their conversations and published in the influential fortnightly *Mercure de France* during 1912–13.

In 1909 she had moved to a house at 20 rue Jacob that was to become a literary landmark, the setting for her international salon. Here Natalie Barney found her true calling, presiding over her weekly receptions for some sixty years. The salon—at its height in the 1920s and 1930s—provided a focus for her best writing, which appeared in the form of epigrams and memoirs. The epigrams give some idea of the conversation of the salon, distilling its essence in wise and witty observations, most of them

her own, as suggested by the title of one collection, *Pensées d'une Amazone* (1920). Her three volumes of memoirs, of which the best known was *Aventures de l'esprit* (1929) and the best *Souvenirs indiscrets* (1960), chronicle her literary friendships and provide a roster of those who came to the salon at one time or another. She included such names as Rilke, D'Annunzio, Valéry, Cocteau, Gide, Colette, Bernard Berenson, Max Jacob, and GERTRUDE STEIN, but omitted others who came but were less known in France–T. S. Eliot, Ezra Pound, Ford Madox Ford, Edith Sitwell, Janet Flanner, and Djuna Barnes. Barney's last book was another volume of memoirs, *Traits et portraits* (1963), completed in her eighty-seventh year.

She continued to conduct her salon almost to the end. But long before this the salon had become an anachronism and dwindled to a small band of frail survivors. Natalie Barney herself had long outlived her own era and all her contemporaries. The last to go was her beloved friend the painter ROMAINE BROOKS, who died in December 1970. After a relationship that survived more than fifty years, they became estranged in 1969, Brooks refusing to share Barney's love and home with a third woman, Janine Lahovary. Devastated by Brooks's death, Natalie Barney lived on for a little more than a year as an invalid in the Hôtel Meurice in Paris. She died there quietly at the age of ninety-five.

[Natalie Barney's papers are at the Fonds Littéraire Jacques Doucet in Paris, which has published a catalog, *Autour de Natalie Clifford Barney* (1976), comp. François Chapon, Nicole Prévot, and Richard Sieburth. Some of her letters and other MSS. are in the Beinecke Rare Book and Manuscript Library, Yale Univ. Two biographies have been published, both with illustrations: George Wickes, *The Amazon of Letters* (1976), and Jean Chalon, *Portrait d'une Séductrice* (1976), translated as *Portrait of a Seductress: The World of Natalie Barney* (1979).]

GEORGE WICKES

BARNEY, Nora Stanton Blatch, Sept. 30, 1883–Jan. 18, 1971. Civil engineer, architect, suffragist.

Nora Blatch was born in Basingstoke, England, where her English father, William Henry Blatch, owned a brewery. Her mother, HARRIOT STANTON BLATCH, and her maternal grandmother, ELIZABETH CADY STANTON, descendants of pre-revolutionary English settlers in America, led successive generations of the American women's rights movement. Nora's younger sister and only sibling died in childhood, and Nora was raised with the help of a governess. The Blatches lived in a large house in Basingstoke where British suffrage leaders and members of the Fabian Society were frequent visitors. During the 1890s, the family traveled often between England and the United States, before moving to New York City when William Blatch retired.

In 1901, after graduating from the Horace Mann School in New York, Nora Blatch entered Cornell University. Her high math aptitude and the scarcity of women in the field led Blatch to study civil engineering: she was elected to Sigma Xi, an honorary scientific society, and worked on a survey of New York state water resources. Blatch also organized a woman suffrage club at Cornell before graduating cum laude in 1905, the first woman at Cornell to receive a degree in civil engineering. After college, Nora Blatch worked from 1905 to 1906 as a draftsman for the American Bridge Company and for the New York City Board of Water Supply the following year.

In 1906 Blatch met Lee de Forest, an American inventor who developed the radio vacuum tube. Blatch studied electricity and mathematics with Michael Pupin at Columbia University in order to become de Forest's laboratory assistant. Married in February 1908, Lee and Nora de Forest spent their honeymoon in Europe demonstrating radio equipment to win contracts for de Forest's newly organized company. Despite her husband's wish that she stop working, Nora de Forest became involved in the company's manufacturing and criticized its financial practices; her judgment proved accurate for the company soon failed. These professional strains were accompanied by personal ones. When she became pregnant, Nora de Forest moved alone to a rented cottage near the company factory in New Jersey; after the birth of their daughter, Harriet, in June 1909, the de Forests filed separately for divorce.

Nora de Forest then returned to New York City, where she worked first as assistant engineer and chief draftsman for the Radley Steel Construction Company for three years, and then as an assistant engineer for the New York Public Service Commission. In May 1912, she was granted a divorce; she received custody of her daughter and the legal right to use her maiden name. (She does not seem to have used it, however.) She drew public attention in 1916 in another court case, this one involving the American Society of Civil Engineers. The first woman member of the ASCE, Nora de Forest was dropped from the society when she passed the age limit for junior status; her suit for reinstatement was unsuccessful.

Throughout this period, from 1909 to 1917, Nora de Forest devoted much time and energy to winning the vote for women in New York state. She was a key member of the Women's Political Union, editing its publication, *Women's Political World,* and serving first as executive secretary and later as president of the organization upon her mother's resignation from that post in 1915. She marched, made street-corner speeches, and rode on horseback in a parade across the state in 1913 as part of the organization's dramatic efforts to publicize women's demands for the vote, finally granted in 1917. Like her mother, she later worked through the National Woman's party for a federal Equal Rights Amendment and opposed protective legislation for working women.

In 1919 she married Morgan Barney, a successful naval architect who designed yachts and commercial boats. The Barneys had two children, Rhoda (b. 1920) and John (b. 1922). In 1923, with money from her father's estate, Nora Barney established herself as a real estate developer in Greenwich, Conn. Earlier she had done some work as an architect and developer on Long Island, beginning around 1914. But in Greenwich, building homes became a full-time venture. While completing a house, she moved in with her family, including her childhood nurse and governess, who now cared for Barney's three children. Once the house was sold, the family moved to another semifinished dwelling. Finally, in 1935, Nora Barney designed a waterfront home in Greenwich for her family and they settled there permanently. She continued to build large, gracious, traditional, and expensive residences for the wealthy suburban community. Until her death at home of a stroke in January 1971, she made her living primarily from real estate development, although in 1934 she accepted an appointment as an engineering inspector for the Public Works Administration in Connecticut and Rhode Island. Morgan Barney died in 1943.

In her later years, Nora Barney remained politically active. World War II aroused her concern for achieving peace and in her pamphlet *World Peace Through a Peoples Parliament* (1944) she argued for the creation of a democratic house of world government consisting of one woman and one man representing sixty different economic and professional groups. She hoped such a body would cut through ideology and nationalism and give women a large role in winning peace. Barney supported Henry A. Wallace for president in 1948 and urged an immediate cease-fire in Korea four years later. In 1950, she was investigated by the House Committee on Un-American Activities for her membership in the Congress of American Women. Though she never testified, Barney

Barron

Memorial Library
Mars Hill College **Barron**
Mars Hill, N. C.

denounced the committee's investigations in a letter to Representative John Wood, describing the movements for racial justice and sexual equality as profoundly American.

A forceful, energetic woman, Nora Barney combined political activism with professional success. In her writings and her life, she revealed a strong sense of continuity with the democratic and feminist tradition of which her grandmother and mother had been an important part. She carried that tradition forward by her insistence that women seek full legal and professional, as well as political, equality.

[Nora Stanton Barney's publications include an engineering article, "Discussion on 'Works for the Purification of the Water Supply of Washington, D.C.,'" *Transactions of the Am. Soc. of Civil Engineers*, Dec. 1906, pp. 400–8. Barney also wrote two other pamphlets, *Women as Human Beings* (1946) and *Life Sketch of Elizabeth Cady Stanton* (1948). Barney's life and thought is best traced in letters and articles which appeared in the *N.Y. Times* between 1909 and 1945. Other sources include Lee de Forest, *Father of Radio: The Autobiography of Lee De Forest* (1950); Georgette Carneal, *A Conqueror of Space: an Authorized Biography of the Life and Work of Lee De Forest* (1930); and Harriot Stanton Blatch and Alma Lutz, *Challenging Years* (1940), which contains two photographs of Barney. For the House Committee on Un-American Activities profile of Nora Stanton Barney see 81st Cong., 2d sess., House Report 1953 (1950), pp. 102, 103. Obituaries appeared in the *N.Y. Times*, Jan. 20, 1971, and *Civil Engineering*, April 1971, p. 87. Barney's high school graduation date is confirmed by the Horace Mann School; death certificate provided by Conn. Dept. of Health. Additional information was provided by Barney's children, Rhoda Barney Jenkins and John Barney. They have a collection of their mother's correspondence as well as photographs of her and of many of the houses she designed.]

TERRY KAY ROCKEFELLER

BARRON, Jennie Loitman, Oct. 12, 1891– March 28, 1969. Judge, lawyer, suffragist, community leader.

Jennie Loitman was born in Boston's West End, the third of four daughters of Morris and Fannie (Castleman) Loitman, Jewish immigrants who had left eastern Russia to escape the tsar's conscription. Their Boston home became a center for new immigrants, for whom Jennie's mother, who knew five languages, acted as interpreter. The Loitmans worked in the needle trades until Morris Loitman became an agent for New York Life Insurance Company. A founder of the Hebrew Progressive Lodge, he often took Jennie to meetings where he would stand her on a table to recite poetry.

Jennie Loitman's parents brought up their daughters as they would have raised sons; three of them later became professionals. After graduating from Girls' High School in 1907, together with her two older sisters, Jennie entered Boston University, earning her A.B. (1911), LL.B. (1913), and LL.M. (1914). To meet her college expenses, she taught Americanization classes and worked in the Women's Educational and Industrial Union's department of law. Becoming active in the woman suffrage movement, she organized Boston University's league for equal suffrage. She was invited by MAUD WOOD PARK to speak at open-air meetings of the Boston Equal Suffrage Association for Good Government and later took part as a street-corner speaker in the successful New York suffrage campaign in 1917.

Loitman married her childhood sweetheart, Samuel Barron, Jr., a distant cousin, on June 23, 1918. Barron, who had come to Chelsea, Mass., from the Ukraine as a child, had recently graduated from Harvard Law School. He was always supportive of his wife's career goals. Together they set up a Boston law firm, Barron and Barron; Jennie Barron remained in practice with her husband until 1937.

She also continued her work for women's rights. As president of the Massachusetts Association of Women Lawyers, Barron organized the successful campaign to allow women to become notaries (1918). Working with the League of Women Voters (LWV) in its efforts to organize the newly won women's vote, she served as chairman of the state League's committee on uniform laws and as delegate to a federal commission on uniform marriage and divorce laws. She also wrote the national LWV statement arguing for women's service on juries.

After the birth of her daughters Erma (1919) and Deborah (1923; died 1956), Barron increasingly emphasized the values of motherhood and family in her work. She later had a third daughter, Joy (b. 1931). Soon after Erma entered public school, Barron ran for a seat on the five-member Boston School Committee. Although she was active in the Woman's Republican Club, she gained support from a nonpartisan group of women. Running on the slogan "Put a Mother on the Boston School Committee," she received the second highest vote. The only woman member from 1926 through 1929, Barron exposed substandard school conditions and advocated an adequate building program. She also urged the appointment of a Yiddish-speaking attendance officer.

Barron decided not to seek reelection in 1929 because she could not accomplish her goals. In that year's mayoralty race, she campaigned for the candidate opposing James Michael Curley, focusing on school issues. Curley attacked her on the false charge of having secured an old brewery for storing school supplies instead of supporting new school construction. Barron retaliated in a dramatic midnight radio appeal, accusing him of smearing "the fair name of all womanhood in Boston," but Curley won the election. Despite this defeat, Barron was well connected politically. She became a director of the Home Owners Federal Savings and Loan Association, which her husband acquired and reorganized in 1933, with the support of her brother-in-law Joseph Grossman, a prominent Republican and member of the Governor's Executive Council (1933–37).

Barron reentered public life in 1934, beginning her thirty-year career as a judge. She was appointed by the governor as a special justice (part time) of the Western Norfolk District Court, serving until 1937. Concurrently she served as an assistant attorney general for Massachusetts (1934–35). Her greatest opportunity came in 1937 when the governor named her an associate justice of the Boston Municipal Court, a position she held from 1938 to 1959. The first woman in the Commonwealth to become a full-time judge and the only woman until 1977 to serve on the nine-member court, she was known for her empathy with defendants. Her decisions were pragmatic ones, emphasizing the reconciliation of families and rehabilitation rather than upholding the letter of the law. She often placed youthful offenders on probation, rather than in prison, sometimes assigning them to do volunteer community work. In 1959 Barron was elevated to associate justice of the Massachusetts Superior Court, and became known for encouraging litigators to settle their own differences. The first woman to hold the associate justice position, she served until her death.

Over the years, Barron served on the boards of many organizations, particularly in the Jewish community. As first president of the Women's Auxiliary of Beth Israel Hospital from 1926 to 1929, she pulled together separate auxiliaries to form essential support for a new building. She also served on the first board of the Brandeis University National Women's Committee (1949–55), as first president of the New England Women's Division of the American Jewish Congress, and on the national boards of Hadassah and the National Conference of Christians and Jews. In 1955 she was the only woman delegate to the first United Nations Congress on crime prevention.

Throughout her career, Barron remained close to her family, who assembled at her table every Friday night for the beginning of the Sabbath.

In 1959, the year in which she also received an honorary LL.D. from Boston University, Barron won the honor she considered her greatest achievement: American Mother of the Year. To celebrate the Barrons toured Europe, Israel, and the Soviet Union. In 1963 they visited the Far East and Africa under the People to People program. The Barrons observed their fiftieth anniversary in June 1968; Sam Barron died a week later. Less than a year later, Jennie Loitman Barron died in Beth Israel Hospital in Boston a few days after suffering a heart attack.

[A small collection of Barron's papers in the Schlesinger Library, Radcliffe College, includes biographical material, articles by and about her, and speeches. Her LWV pamphlet, *Jury Service for Women* (Dec. 1924), is in the library's Woman's Rights Coll. The library also has Dick Horne, "Women Who Won," typescript, WEEI–CBS radio broadcast, Aug. 25, 1960, in which Barron and several other women speak about the suffrage movement. Clipping files are available at the School of Public Communication, Boston Univ., the *Boston Herald-American*, and the *Boston Globe*. Barron's career can be traced in *Manual for the General Court of the Commonwealth of Massachusetts*, 1929–30 through 1977–78, and *Proc. of the School Committee of the City of Boston*, 1926–29. See also Durward Howes, ed., *American Women, 1935–1936*, and Dorothy Thomas, ed., *Women Lawyers in the United States* (1957). An obituary appeared in the *Boston Globe*, March 29, 1969. Additional information was provided by Barron's sisters Rose Loitman and Dr. Clara Loitman Smith, her daughter Erma Barron Wernick, and Judge Jacob Lewiton. Death certificate from the Mass. Dept. of Public Health.]

POLLY WELTS KAUFMAN

BARRY, Iris, March (?) 1895–Dec. 22, 1969. Film historian and critic, writer.

Iris Barry knew earlier and perhaps better than anyone the importance of motion pictures. From 1913 on she went to the movies steadily, and by the time she died, she had seen more than 15,000 films and "made a profession of her vice." She organized an exceptional film archives at the Museum of Modern Art in New York City, and it was her work that led to the serious consideration in the United States of film as art.

Iris Barry was born Iris Sylvia Crump in Washwood Heath, near Birmingham, England, probably in March 1895–the year the movies were invented. She was the daughter of Alfred Charles Crump, a brass founder, who left the family while she was a baby, and Annie Crump, a gypsy-like woman with a fondness for fortune-telling and crystal-gazing. Iris's mother and grandparents, who were dairy farmers, raised her and sent her to convent school, first in England and then to the Ursuline Convent in Verniers, Belgium. Although she passed the qualifying examinations for Oxford in 1911, her entry was deferred, and she went to France. World War I intervened, and she returned to Birmingham where she worked at routine jobs, went to the movies as often as possible, and wrote verse.

Some of her poems were published in *Poetry* magazine and caught the attention of Ezra Pound, with whom she began to correspond. Eager for the literary life, in 1916 or 1917 she went to London. She was, in her words, "serious as all get out and fairly fresh out of a convent, an only child and a solitary one, very romantic." Pound introduced her into the liveliest circle of artists and writers of the time, including the author and painter Wyndham Lewis, just returned to London from the front. He and Barry became lovers, and Lewis was the father of her two children, a son born in 1919, and a daughter born in 1920. The children were raised by Iris Barry's mother and only came to know their mother later in life.

During these early years in London Barry proved herself a clever and resolute young woman. She knew everyone there was to know, tried various jobs, and not only went to the movies every day but also began writing about them, having been given the chance to review films for theaters controlled by business executive and film enthusiast Sidney Bernstein. Her first book, *Splashing Into Society,* an amusing story about art and success, was published in 1923, and in the same year she was invited to review films for the *Spectator.* The first woman film critic in England, for four years she wrote bright and penetrating criticism for the magazine. Soon after joining the *Spectator,* she married its literary editor, Oxford poet Alan Porter.

Barry soon established herself as a devoted *cinéaste* of rare talent with an omniscient knowledge of films. In 1925, with Sidney Bernstein, filmmaker and writer Ivor Montagu, and others, she took on the censors and the film trade to found the London Film Society, the first organization to promote and support the showing of films. Her second book, *Let's Go to the Pictures* (1926), about "why we slink into the cinema and what happens to us there," was a trenchant and illuminating analysis of the cinema as both entertainment and art. In 1925 Barry became film critic for *The Daily Mail,* but that job ended in 1930, when she was fired for writing an unfavorable review. Her marriage to Alan Porter, which seems not to have had much importance for either of them, ended as well, though both left England for the United States,

he to teach English at Vassar College, and she to make her own way in Hollywood and New York. (Porter died in the early 1940s.)

Iris Barry arrived in New York, as she had in London, with little money but with much ingenuity and intelligence. She confidently established herself in the circles of such wealthy patrons of art as Philip Johnson and Kirk and Constance Askew and thus gained entry into the Museum of Modern Art. In 1932 she was hired to begin its library; three years later the Film Library was established and Iris Barry was there to become its first curator.

Her knowledge and her undeviating devotion to the cause of the cinema made her outstandingly qualified to accumulate, catalog, preserve, exhibit, distribute, and circulate films, and to begin the process of defining the motion picture as an art form. The task was enormous: she had to win the attention and understanding of the motion picture industry, collaborate with the trade, and convince Hollywood and others that films were art and should be respected and saved in order to be seen again and again. To these ends Iris Barry wrote innumerable catalogs, screen programs, and film notes for the museum bulletins and for Film Library publications.

She also began immediately to acquire films, going first to Hollywood to win over that community to her cause, and in 1936 making the first of many trips to Europe to visit film archives, and to search for and collect films. She also lectured and taught, developed film programs for distribution to colleges and museums, and published two more books, a translation of *The History of Motion Pictures* by Maurice Bardèche and Robert Brasillach (1938), and *D. W. Griffith, American Film Master* (1940). In 1939 Barry became the founder-president of the International Federation of Film Archives, a significant achievement for the cause of film study, preservation, and cooperation among supporters of the cinema.

Iris Barry became a naturalized citizen of the United States in 1941. She married again in the early 1940s; her second husband was John E. "Dick" Abbott, a Wall Street financier who shared her interest in film. He became the first director of the Film Library at the Museum of Modern Art. Barry was generally regarded as the more intelligent and talented of the two and the marriage seems to have been one of convenience. Abbott eventually moved on to other administrative positions within the museum and Barry became director as well as curator of the Film Library. By 1950 they were divorced.

Barry left the museum for Europe at the

end of 1949 and did not return; the reasons for her departure remain unclear. In that year, she had been made a Chevalier of the Legion of Honor for her work on behalf of French film. She continued as the museum's representative abroad, attending film festivals, acquiring movies for its collection, and encouraging film scholarship, but she seldom returned to New York. With a young Frenchman named Pierre Kerroux she settled in Fayence, Var, in the south of France, where they gardened, renovated houses, and opened an antique shop. In 1955, suspected of communist sympathies, she had difficulty renewing her United States passport, but after friends at the museum confirmed her affiliation the problem was resolved.

By 1969 Iris Barry was ill, alone, and, as had often been the case throughout her life, in need of money; loyal and affectionate colleagues and friends from the museum came to her aid with funds for hospital bills and expenses. She died that year of cancer in Marseilles after a dramatic, pioneering life, full of loves and adventures, as well as difficulties and regrets, and marked always by her determination to get what she wanted for herself and for films.

[There is no collection of Iris Barry's papers. Some of her correspondence with Ezra Pound is published in the *Letters of Ezra Pound, 1907–1941* (1950) and there are unpublished letters between them in the Poetry Coll. at the State Univ. of N.Y. at Buffalo. There is also interesting correspondence with Wyndham Lewis in the Cornell Univ. Library and with Virgil Thomson in the Yale Univ. Music Library. The Humanities Research Center of the Univ. of Texas has some letters, and unpublished letters exist between Barry and Nelson A. Rockefeller, with whom she maintained a very warm correspondence, and with museum director A. Everett Austin, in whose house she lived in Fayence. In addition to the books mentioned above, Barry wrote a novel, *The Last Enemy* (1929–published in England as *Here Is Thy Victory*); *Portrait of Lady Mary Montagu* (1928); and countless film reviews and articles about motion pictures. *The Film Index* (1941), for which she wrote the foreword, is the beginning of a good bibliography for many of these pieces. *Let's Go to the Pictures* was published in the United States as *Let's Go to the Movies*. Important articles include "The Museum of Modern Art Film Library," *Sight and Sound*, Summer 1936; "Challenge of the Documentary Film," *N.Y. Times Mag.*, Jan. 6, 1946; "Why Wait for Posterity?" *Hollywood Quart.*, Jan. 1946; "Retrospect with Lament and Motto," *Sat. Rev. of Lit.*, Aug. 6, 1949; and "The Film Library and How It Grew," *Film Quart.*, Summer 1969. She also wrote the preface to Lewis Jacobs, *The Rise of the American Film* (1939), and to Parker Tyler, *The Hollywood Hallucination* (1944). For information about her earlier years see her article, "The Ezra Pound Period," *The Bookman*, Oct. 1931. The best published sources on her life are Ivor Montagu, "Students of Film Throughout the World Have Lost Their Most Respected Pioneer," *Sight and Sound*, Spring 1970; Alistair Cooke, "To Iris Barry (1895–1969)," *N.Y. Times*, Jan. 18, 1970; and Arthur Knight, "I Remember MOMA," *The Hollywood Reporter*, April 21, 1978. See also Russell Lynes's informative book, *Good Old Modern* (1973). An obituary appeared in the *N.Y. Times*, Dec. 23, 1969; the London *Times* published an obituary, Jan. 1, 1970, and a tribute, Jan. 3, 1970. A baptismal record, confirming her parents' names and giving the date of baptism as June 2, 1895, was provided by the parish of Saltley, Birmingham. Correspondence and conversations with friends of Iris Barry including Margareta Akermark of the Museum of Modern Art, Arthur Knight, Elsa Lanchester, Jay Leyda, Dorothy Miller, Ivor Montagu, Elodie Osborne, Alan Porter, Paul Rotha, and Virgil Thomson, were invaluable.]

MISSY DANIEL

BARRYMORE, Ethel, Aug. 16, 1879–June 18, 1959. Actress.

Ethel Barrymore was born in Philadelphia, Pa., into a family of actors and grew up amid the emblems and traditions of a theatrical dynasty. She was the only daughter and second of three children of Anglo-American matinee idol Maurice Barrymore and comedienne GEORGIANA EMMA DREW BARRYMORE. Her maternal grandparents were Irish-American comedian John Drew and actress-manager LOUISA LANE DREW, whose English parents and grandparents were also performers. Both of Ethel's brothers, Lionel and John, became prominent actors.

Ethel Barrymore was raised largely by her grandmother, manager of the Arch Street Theatre in Philadelphia, and saw her parents infrequently. Her mother, who had converted to Catholicism, had Ethel baptized a Catholic, and she was sent at age six to the Academy of Notre Dame, a convent boarding school in Philadelphia. In May 1893, she was taken from school to accompany her ailing mother to California, and she handled funeral arrangements when Georgiana Barrymore died in Santa Barbara in July. Ethel Barrymore remembered her mother as "the gayest and most gallant person I have ever known." She later praised the "naturalness" of her mother's acting, "twenty-five years ahead of its time," and credited Georgiana Barrymore with her technique of throwing away a comedy point.

In the fall Ethel returned to the convent school, but after her father's remarriage in 1894 she was sent to Montreal. There she joined her grandmother and her uncle, Sidney Drew, at the Academy of Music, where she made her stage debut as Julia in Sheridan's *The Rivals.* "I had thought I was going to be a great pianist," she wrote in *Memories: An Autobiography* (1955). "I had never known I was to go on the stage . . . But suddenly there was no money, no Arch Street Theatre, no house, and I must earn my living." Louisa Drew soon left for New York and Barrymore went on tour with her uncle and the company.

Then in 1895 she was sent to New York to join her grandmother and her other uncle, light comedian John Drew, Jr. He arranged for a three years' apprenticeship ("some understudying chores and a little tray carrying") with him and his costar, MAUDE ADAMS, under the management of Charles Frohman. The young actress played the rustic servant Priscilla in Drew's production of *Rosemary* in New York and on the road; she went to London in the summer of 1897 to support William Gillette in *Secret Service,* and afterwards appeared with Sir Henry Irving and Ellen Terry.

Barrymore remained under Charles Frohman's aegis until his death in 1915, and continued as a member of the Frohman organization until 1921. She joined the stock company at his Empire Theatre in 1898, toured as comedy adventuress Stella de Gex, her first leading role, in Frohman's road production of *His Excellency the Governor* in 1900, and in 1901 advanced to stardom as Madame Trentoni in *Captain Jinks of the Horse Marines.* In all, Barrymore's association with Frohman embraced twenty-five separate plays, in many of which she played ingenue roles.

On March 14, 1909, Barrymore married Russell Griswold Colt, son of United States Rubber Company board chairman Samuel Pomeroy Colt. During intervals between productions, she bore three children. Samuel Pomeroy, born in 1909, Ethel Barrymore, born in 1912, and John Drew, born in 1913, often accompanied their mother on cross-country tours.

Barrymore had bolted Frohman in 1911, in the absence of an acceptable script, to play Kate, the liberated typist in *The Twelve-Pound Look.* The play initially achieved only thirty-two performances, but—intermittently in vaudeville—"was to serve as a life-saver for the next twenty years." She returned to the Frohman management for such long-running successes as *Tante* (1913), *Our Mrs. McChesney* (1915), and *The Lady of the Camellias* (1917). But in 1919 she defied Frohman's successor, Al Hayman, by spearheading the Actors' Equity contract strike, starring in outlaw Equity benefits,

and, as the union's appointee, initialing the resulting five-year pact with the New York producers. In *Déclassée* (1919), Barrymore broke the Empire Theatre house record with 200 sold-out performances, made a sensation on tour, then played another season in New York.

During the early twenties, both her career and her personal life foundered for a time. She was legally separated from her husband in 1921, and divorced him in 1923 on grounds of desertion and nonsupport. Although Barrymore obtained the divorce, as a Catholic she considered it "merely legal," and she never remarried. On the stage, she failed as Juliet in Arthur Hopkins's 1922 revival of *Romeo and Juliet,* and *The Laughing Lady* (1923) was panned by the New York critics. A 1923 production of *The School for Scandal,* with Barrymore as Lady Teazle, ran for only one week. She won praise in *The Second Mrs. Tanqueray* in 1924 and in Shakespearean roles (Portia, Ophelia) with Walter Hampden, but her next real triumph in the theater did not come until 1926, when she starred as Constance Middleton in *The Constant Wife.* She played this part on Broadway for 295 performances and toured in the play for over two years. In 1928, as Sister García (aging through the play from nineteen to seventy) in *The Kingdom of God,* she opened the Shuberts' Ethel Barrymore Theatre in New York.

Barrymore successfully met a new challenge with the title role in *Scarlet Sister Mary* (1930), in which she portrayed a black woman and spoke her lines in the Gullah dialect of South Carolina. In 1931 she collapsed on stage in Denver during a performance of *The School for Scandal.* The tour folded and, with other unsuccessful tours, placed her in severe financial straits. She had almost no work until 1934, with the exception of a film in 1932 and a month (July 1933) of five-a-day appearances in *The Twelve-Pound Look.* Subsequent unemployment, relieved only by occasional performances on radio and a short tour in *The Constant Wife* during the winter of 1935–36, eventually led to her despairing announcement in August 1936 that she would "never appear in another play." But the National Broadcasting Company forestalled Barrymore's retirement with a radio series in which she acted half-hour abridgements of her most popular plays.

Acquiescing to a series of character parts in the late thirties, Barrymore created for American audiences the memorable role of Miss Moffat, the Welsh schoolmistress, in Herman Shumlin's 1940 production of *The Corn Is Green.* It ran for fourteen months in New York and for two years on the road. Barrymore's final

Broadway venture was *Embezzled Heaven* (1944), which also prospered but was suspended by her near-fatal bout with pneumonia. Her last performance before a theater audience was in *The Twelve-Pound Look* for an American National Theatre Academy benefit, Jan. 29, 1950.

In her last years, Barrymore continued to act in the movies and for television. Her movie career had begun in 1914, with a five-year foray into silent films. She starred in *The Nightingale*, for which she reputedly earned $15,000, *The Awakening of Helena Richie*, and ten others. As the czarina, at a reported fee of $57,000 for eight weeks' work, she later costarred with brothers Lionel and John in the 1932 sound feature *Rasputin and the Empress*.

In the forties her national tour of *The Corn Is Green* had been curtailed in California so she might costar with Cary Grant in *None But the Lonely Heart*. Her portrayal of the frumpy charwoman Ma Mott in this film earned her an Academy Award as best actress in 1944. Settling in Palos Verdes, Calif., Barrymore appeared in twenty films from 1946 through 1957. She made her network television debut in 1953, and performed in various drama and comedy-variety series through the mid-1950s.

Ethel Barrymore, for good or ill, epitomized the star system. The focus of a real Barrymore cult from her earliest starring days, the beautiful actress inspired imitators of her hairstyle, her regal walk, her cool, fierce, Barrymore eyes, and her low, breathless, haunting voice (which detractors found monotonous). Like her illustrious forebears and her famous brothers, she readily managed transitions from comedy to drama and, in her later years, to eccentric parts. She believed that "the thought running through the person's mind is what the actor has to capture . . . Years of experience at acting give a player the ability to call on his thought and be sure of it. It's like a good serve at tennis." Barrymore made her last public appearance during a testimonial for her seventy-eighth birthday; she died in 1959 of a pulmonary infarction at her Beverly Hills apartment.

[The Robinson Locke Scrapbooks in the Billy Rose Theatre Coll., N.Y. Public Library, are the best source of information on Barrymore's career. *Cumulated Dramatic Index, 1909–1949*, lists articles and books by and about the Barrymores. In addition to her autobiography, Barrymore wrote "My Reminiscences," *Delineator*, Sept. 1923–Feb. 1924, and "How Can I Be an Actress?" *Ladies' Home Journal*, March 15, 1911. Other major sources of information are Hollis Alpert, *The Barrymores* (1964); Robert Downing, "Ethel Barrymore, 1879–1959," *Films in Review*, Aug.–Sept. 1959; Barbara Birch Jamison, "Ethel Barrymore—In Mid-Career at 75," *N.Y. Times Mag.*, Aug. 15, 1954; S. J. Woolf, "Miss Barrymore Refuses to Mourn the 'Good Old Days,'" *N.Y. Times Mag.*, Aug. 13, 1939; a book by Barrymore's press agent, Richard Maney, *Fanfare* (1957); and *Current Biog,,* 1941. Additional background about the Barrymore family can be found in Lionel Barrymore with Cameron Shipp, *We Barrymores* (1951), and James Kotsilibas-Davis, *Great Times, Good Times; The Odyssey of Maurice Barrymore* (1977). Most sources give Barrymore's birth date as Aug. 15, 1879, but her birth record from the City of Philadelphia gives Aug. 16. A death record was provided by the Calif. Dept. of Public Health. An obituary appeared in the *N.Y. Times*, June 19, 1959. Photographs are in the autobiography as well as in Alpert and Jamison.]

PAT M. RYAN

BARTELME, Mary Margaret, July 24, 1866– July 25, 1954. Lawyer, judge.

Mary Bartelme was born in Chicago to Jeannette (Hoff) and Balthazar Bartelme. Both parents had emigrated from Alsace, and her father worked in the building trades. During much of her life, Mary Bartelme continued to live with her older brother, Alfred, and her younger sister, Adeline.

After graduating from Chicago's Western Division High School in 1882, Mary Bartelme attended the Cook County Normal School and then taught in Chicago schools for eight years. In 1892 she entered Northwestern University Law School, graduating in 1894, the only woman in her class. MYRA BRADWELL, a prominent Illinois lawyer, encouraged Bartelme's career and published the young woman's thesis, "Spendthrift Trusts," in the *Chicago Legal News*. Bartelme won first prize in a case annotation competition sponsored by the *American Law Register and Review* in 1895. She had been admitted to the Illinois bar in 1894 and, after her admission to the United States bar in 1896, she began private legal practice in Chicago. With her appointment in 1897 by the governor of Illinois as public guardian for Cook County, Bartelme began a lifetime of public service. Until 1913 she served in this office, assuming responsibility for the placement of orphans.

Mary Bartelme's major contribution to juvenile reform occurred within the Chicago juvenile court, which she helped to establish in 1899, along with other members of the Chicago Woman's Club. In 1911, during the "white slave" scare which heightened concerns about female delinquency, and after an investigation of the probation department raised criticisms of the court, juvenile court judge Merritt W. Pinckney recommended the appointment of a woman probation officer to hear the cases of delinquent girls. He chose Mary Bartelme to fill the new office of assistant to the judge.

Bartelme began hearing cases on March 3, 1913, in private judge's chambers. The press and public were excluded in order to protect the reputations of the ten- to seventeen-year-old offenders, most of whom were charged with immoral behavior or incorrigibility. Bartelme interviewed each girl and her parents, attempted to gain the child's confidence, and took her side when necessary. She then made her recommendation to the judge, who almost automatically acted upon it. A grand jury that investigated this arrangement in 1915 commended Bartelme's work. Journalists wrote about her "court of another chance" for girls and praised her "professional mothering."

One of Bartelme's methods earned her the nickname "Suitcase Mary." With financial support from local women's clubs, Bartelme established residential halfway houses for dependent girls (1914) and "semidelinquent" girls (1916). The first such residence was in her own home. Whenever a resident left one of the homes, she received a suitcase full of clothes, which, Bartelme believed, would enhance the girl's self-esteem. Women's groups continued to support three Chicago area residences bearing her name long after Bartelme had retired.

For ten years Bartelme served as assistant to the judge of the juvenile court. Then in 1923, possibly motivated by the recent enfranchisement of women, the county Republican party nominated Bartelme as a candidate to complete the unexpired term of a Cook County Circuit Court judge. She won the election. As associate justice of the juvenile court she continued to hear girls' cases, but now had complete judicial authority. In 1927 she won election to a full six-year term and became the presiding judge of the juvenile court, a position she held until her retirement in 1933.

In social outlook, Bartelme typified Progressive era social feminists and juvenile reformers. She had advocated woman suffrage as early as 1895, held office in the Chicago Suffrage Club, and belonged to the League of Women Voters. She supported the work of the Juvenile Protective Association and helped raise funds for the Institute for Juvenile Research. Along with her Chicago colleagues JULIA LATHROP and JANE ADDAMS, Bartelme believed that female delinquency resulted in part from the lack of respectable amusements for urban youth. She called for chaperoned dances to replace dance halls, sex education to warn girls of temptations, and the extension of the minimum age for women's em-

ployment to sixteen in order to keep girls in school. Women parole and police officers, she felt, should process the cases of female offenders. Although like other Progressives she criticized institutional commitments for delinquents, court records show that she herself sentenced girls to reformatories more frequently than she placed them on probation.

In 1933 Mary Bartelme retired to Carmel, Calif., with her sister, her brother, and her niece. There she enjoyed over twenty years of tending her gardens and household. She died in Carmel of a stroke at the age of eighty-eight.

[A newspaper clippings file at the Northwestern Univ. Archives is useful for tracing Bartelme's career. Some Bartelme letters appear in the Ethel Sturges Dummer Papers at the Schlesinger Library, Radcliffe College. Bartelme discussed her views in "Woman's Place at the Bar," *Chicago Legal News*, 43 (1911), 370; "The Opportunity for Women in Court Administration," Am. Acad. of Political and Social Sci., *Annals*, March 1914, pp. 188–90; and "Prevention Not Punishment," *Dept. of Elementary School Principals Bull.*, 11th Yearbook, April 1932, pp. 521–24. The reports of the Chicago juvenile court, in the *Charity Service Reports*, Cook Cty., Ill., contain aggregate data on court cases and describe the origins and operation of Bartelme's court, as does Helen Rankin Jeter, *The Chicago Juvenile Court* (1922). On Bartelme's legal education and early career see the *Chicago Legal News* for 1894, 1895, and 1900. Her court is described in the *N.Y. Times Mag.*, May 25, 1913, p. 4 (with photograph), and in Betsy Greenbaum, "The Court of 'Another Chance' Where Judge Mary Bartelme Presides," *Woman Citizen*, Aug. 1927, pp. 12–14. See also the *Nat. Cyc. Am. Biog.*, XLVII, 626. Obituaries appeared in the July 26, 1954, issues of the *N.Y. Times* and *Chicago Tribune*. A biobibliography prepared by Sally Nichols assisted in the research for this article. Death certificate supplied by Calif. Dept. of Health Services.]

ESTELLE B. FREEDMAN

BASS, Charlotta Spears, Oct. 1880?–April 12, 1969. Editor, civil rights reformer.

For more than forty years Charlotta Bass edited *The California Eagle*, the oldest black newspaper on the west coast. She was born in Sumter, S.C., the sixth of eleven children and third of four daughters of Hiram and Kate Spears. Leaving South Carolina sometime before 1900, she went to live with her oldest brother, Ellis, in Providence, R.I. There she worked as office help and advertising solicitor for a local newspaper. In September 1910 she went to Los Angeles, planning what she called a two-year health recuperation stay; she remained a California resident for the rest of her life.

In Los Angeles she took a job collecting and

soliciting subscriptions for *The Eagle* newspaper, then edited by John Neimore. Plagued by ill health, he came increasingly to depend on Spears to run the paper. In May 1912, after Neimore's death, *The Eagle*'s new owner, a Captain Hawkins, handed the paper over to Spears on the promise of future payment. Recognizing that she would have to print social items to keep her readership, Spears determined also that the paper (renamed *The California Eagle*) would discuss the important issues of the day for the "patriotically inclined."

Also in 1912 Joseph Bass, a founder of the *Topeka* (Kans.) *Plaindealer*, came to California. He became editor of *The California Eagle* and he and Charlotta Spears were married. She subsequently became managing editor. Under their combined direction the paper began to wage its "fearless war against segregation and discrimination." Charlotta Bass campaigned against D. W. Griffith's *Birth of a Nation*, calling it "the big lie," and she vociferously opposed the injustice to black soldiers in the 1917 Houston, Texas, race riot. The same year, she supported the establishment in southern California of the Progressive Educational Association, which marked the beginnings there of interracial organization in defense of Negro and other minorities' rights.

After World War I Charlotta and Joseph Bass battled the Ku Klux Klan; in 1925 the Klan brought the paper to court on libel charges. The *Eagle* won the case and continued its fight against racism. In the 1930s the Basses supported the nine black defendants in the Scottsboro (Ala.) trials, backed organizing efforts among waterfront workers, and opposed labor racketeering. They also joined A. Philip Randolph in his struggle to end discriminatory hiring practices on the railroads. Charlotta Bass was one of the organizers in 1930 of the Industrial Business Council, designed to encourage blacks to go into business and to work against discriminatory employment practices. She also organized a militant integrated group, the Home Protective Association, which defended the right of blacks to live in formerly all-white neighborhoods and fought to abolish restrictive covenants.

Running *The California Eagle* on her own after her husband's death in 1934, Charlotta Bass also became increasingly prominent in civic and political affairs. A longtime Republican, in 1940 she served as western regional director for Wendell Willkie's presidential campaign. In 1943 she became the first Negro grand jury member for the Los Angeles County Court. Two years later she ran unsuccessfully as a "people's candidate" for City Council from the Seventh District. Her platform emphasized job security, a building plan to construct houses for those in need of shelter, and other progressive measures.

During the years immediately after World War II, Bass intensified her campaigning for civil rights and civil liberties. She again fought the Klan and the barbarous lynching which plagued the south, particularly in the summer of 1946, and joined other national black leaders in calling for the establishment of a permanent fair employment practices committee. She also supported the Hollywood Ten. With the growing repression of the left during the late 1940s her outspoken crusading led to suspicion of her as "un-American" and in 1946 she was called before the Tenney Committee, the California version of the House Committee on Un-American Activities.

With her mounting awareness of the failure of the traditional parties to address civil rights issues, Bass abandoned the Republican party to become a founding member of the Progressive party, led by Henry A. Wallace. In 1948 she supported Wallace's presidential candidacy, serving as national cochairman of Women for Wallace, presiding over the candidate's Los Angeles appearances, and traveling to Philadelphia as a candidate to the party's national convention.

During the next two years she traveled extensively, going in 1950 to Paris and to Prague for the Peace Committee of the World Congress. There Bass supported the "Stockholm Appeal," calling for a ban on the atomic bomb. Later that year she was a delegate at the World Student Congress in Prague and made a brief visit to the Soviet Union. Describing her visit in a November 1950 article in *Soviet Russia Today*, she praised the lack of racial discrimination there.

Returning to California, Bass ran unsuccessfully for Congress in the Fourteenth Congressional District on the Independent Progressive party ticket. Two years later the Progressive party, fragmented by the question of support of United States action in Korea, chose her as vice presidential candidate, the first black woman to run for the nation's second-highest office. For president, the party nominated California attorney Vincent Hallinan, a strong supporter of civil liberties who was then serving a jail sentence for contempt of court.

During the campaign Bass stressed with pride, "Win or lose, we win by raising the issues." Denouncing both Democrats and Republicans as in favor of war and as antilabor and anti-Negro, Bass and Hallinan linked domestic and foreign policy issues, calling for an end to the cold war, an immediate cease-fire in Korea, an end to poverty in the United States, and equal rights for minorities and for the oppressed of the nation and the world. Praised by W. E. B. Du Bois as representing "black America and American womanhood," Bass made an analogy between the plight of women and of blacks, noted the small number of women serving in Congress, and urged women to run for political office. Hallinan and Bass received a very small percentage of the vote (0.2 percent according to Gerald Gill), but their campaign focused attention on significant issues.

Bass had retired from *The California Eagle* in the early 1950s. In 1960, after a lifetime of crusading, she published *Forty Years: Memoirs from the Pages of a Newspaper,* her autobiography and the biography of the paper. Over the years Charlotta Bass had encouraged many young blacks to enter the professions, and had provided jobs and training on the *Eagle.* In retirement she established a library for neighborhood youth in the garage of her home in the Elsinore section of Los Angeles. She died in Los Angeles in April 1969, as the nation again confronted the issues of racism and violence to which she had called attention and which she had worked to eradicate.

[Charlotta Bass's library and some of her papers are at the California Library for Social Studies in Los Angeles. The Schomburg Coll. of the N.Y. Public Library and the Moorland-Spingarn Coll. at Howard Univ., Washington, D.C., both have clipping files on Bass. There are some letters from her in the Calvin Benham Baldwin Papers, Univ. of Iowa. Her acceptance speech for the vice presidential nomination appeared in the *Nat. Guardian,* April 2, 1952, p. 3. Biographical information is scanty; *Forty Years* is the best source. An entry appears in Harry Ploski, ed., *The Afro-American: The Negro Almanac* (1976). On her candidacy see Gerald R. Gill, " 'Win or Lose—We Win'; The 1952 Vice Presidential Campaign of Charlotta A. Bass," in Sharon Harley and Rosalyn Terborg-Penn, eds., *The Afro-American Woman: Struggles and Images* (1978). Bass's year of birth frequently appears as 1890 and her place of birth as Little Compton, R.I. The birth date, place, and family names from U.S. Census 1880 and 1900. Death record from Calif. Dept. of Public Health gives 1874 birth date. Assistance provided by Arthur Freed, Sheryl Kujawa, and Joseph Spears.]

ANDREW BUNI
CAROL HURD GREEN

BASS, Mary Elizabeth, April 5, 1876–Jan. 26, 1956. Physician.

Elizabeth Bass, founder of an outstanding biographical collection on medical women and lifelong advocate of women physicians in the south, was the first of four daughters and second of eight children born to Isaac Esau and Mary Eliza (Wilkes) Bass. The family home was located in Carley, Marion County, Miss., where Isaac Bass ran a gristmill and a dry goods store. After losing his property during the depression of the mid-1890s, he moved his family to Lumberton, Miss. (1899), and established a large pecan nursery. Elizabeth's mother, whom she deeply loved and admired, was well known for her sense of humor and took an active interest in the welfare of her community. Both of Elizabeth's parents were devout Baptists. Wishing to remain free to dance, however, they did not join the church until 1882, eight years after their marriage. A sense of loyalty, duty, and honesty pervaded the Bass household; "none can work as hard as a Bass" was a commonly spoken tribute.

Elizabeth Bass attended Bunker Hill and other nearby elementary schools and assisted teachers in these schools while attending Columbia (Miss.) High School. She graduated in 1893, and received teaching certificates from normal schools in 1892 and 1896. Bass taught in public schools in Mississippi and Texas for several years, until her older brother, Charles, who had graduated from the Tulane School of Medicine in 1899, encouraged her and her sister Cora to study medicine.

Because women were not allowed in the medical schools of the south, the sisters matriculated at the Woman's Medical College of Pennsylvania in the fall of 1900. After graduating in 1904 they, like Charles, began private practice in New Orleans. In reaction to the policy that barred women doctors from the city's existing clinical and hospital facilities, Elizabeth Bass and five other women established in 1905 a free dispensary, in a house loaned by a friend. Hospital beds were added two years later and the institution—one of five American hospitals founded and managed by women practitioners—was dedicated in 1908 as the New Orleans Hospital and Dispensary for Women and Children (later the Sara Mayo Hospital). Women physicians in New Orleans now had adequate medical facilities, which they used to provide medical care to women and children of limited means.

In December 1911 Elizabeth Bass and Edith Ballard became the first women faculty members of the School of Medicine at Tulane University. After two years Bass advanced from assistant demonstrator of surgical pathology (nonsalaried) to instructor in the laboratory of clinical medicine, receiving a salary of $500 for the academic year 1914–15. In the same year the administration permitted women to matriculate as medical students, a decision undoubtedly influenced by the Equal Rights Association of New Orleans. Bass was a member of this women's group, which lobbied aggressively for woman suffrage and improved child labor laws. She taught pathology, clinical laboratory diagnosis, bateriology, and clinical medicine during her thirty years at Tulane, becoming a full professor in 1920. An excellent teacher, she took a personal interest in her students, providing friendship, counsel, and money to those in need, especially women students.

Through her work with professional and social organizations, Elizabeth Bass did much to advance the cause of women physicians. She became the first woman elected to active membership in the Orleans Parish Medical Society (1913), serving as secretary (1921 and 1922), vice president (1923), and editor of the Society's bulletin (1939). In 1915 she joined the recently founded Women Physicians of the Southern Medical Association, becoming first vice president in 1919, and president from 1925 to 1927. As a member of the Medical Women's National Association (later the American Medical Women's Association), she served as fifth president (1921–22) and contributed essays and a column to the Association's journal. In 1924 she became secretary of the Section of Pathology for the Southern Medical Association, and subsequently vice chairman (1938) and chairman (1939) of that section.

Bass enjoyed traveling and attended conferences in Canada, France, Sweden, Austria, Italy, and Greece. Chosen to represent the United States at international forums, she was a delegate in 1928 to the first Pan Pacific Women's Conference, held in Honolulu, Hawaii, and was a representative at the conferences of the Medical Women's International Association held in Stockholm (1934) and Edinburgh (1937). A trim, slender, well-dressed woman, she also participated in the cultural and social endeavors of many women's groups in New Orleans and was a devoted member of the famous Le Petit Théâtre du Vieux Carré.

When Elizabeth Bass resigned from the Tulane faculty in 1941, she was professor of clinical laboratory diagnosis in the Graduate School of Medicine and associate professor of medicine in the School of Medicine. Because of the shortage of doctors during World War II, she returned to private practice and became house physician at the Jung Hotel, where she had lived for many years.

During the 1940s Bass devoted time to expanding her extraordinary collection of manuscripts, correspondence, pictures, press clippings, pamphlets, and books by and about women in medicine. The collection served as a basis for her numerous historical and biograph-ical essays, and for a regular column on outstanding women physicians, "These Were the First," published in the *Journal of the American Medical Women's Association* (1946–56). During the latter half of 1949, Bass decided to cease medical practice. She spent much time caring for her aged mother at the family home in Lumberton, returning to New Orleans periodically for meetings and social functions.

In 1952 Elizabeth Bass received the Alumni Achievement Award from the Woman's Medical College of Pennsylvania, and in 1953 the American Medical Women's Association presented her the Elizabeth Blackwell Centennial Medal Award. She died of cancer in 1956 at the Foundation Hospital in New Orleans and was buried in Lumberton. After her death, her friends at Tulane established the Elizabeth Bass Memorial Medical Student Loan Fund as a tribute to her lifelong dream of improving opportunities for women in the profession of medicine.

[The Elizabeth Bass Coll. on Women in Medicine, located in the Matas Medical Library of Tulane Univ., consists of some 290 monographs and 1,400 clippings and pictures on women in medicine. It also contains the MS. of Bass's unpublished book, "History of Medicine in Louisiana." Correspondence between Elizabeth Bass and Florence Sabin is located in the Sophia Smith Coll., Smith College. The alumnae file of the Medical College of Pa. contains some useful information. Bass's own writings, all in the *Jour. Am. Medical Women's Assoc.* (JAMWA), include "Dispensaries Founded by Women Physicians in the Southland," Dec. 1947, pp. 560–61; her acceptance speech for the Elizabeth Blackwell Centennial Medal Award, Sept. 1953, p. 307; several articles on aspects of clinical medicine; and a number of tributes, obituaries, and histories of women physicians. Articles about Bass include: "In Memoriam Elizabeth Bass, 1876–1956," *Bull. Orleans Parish Medical Soc.*, April 9, 1956; "In Memoriam," *JAMWA*, Sept. 9, 1956; Durward Howes, ed., *American Women*, 1939–40, p. 57; *Nat. Cyc. Am. Biog.*, XLV, 350; James P. Morris, "Elizabeth Bass, M.D. (1876–1956), Tulane's Woman Pioneer in Medicine," *Tulane Medicine*, Spring 1973. Details of family history can be found in Ivan E. Bass, *Wilkes Family History and Genealogy* (1965); Ivan E. Bass, *Bass Family History* (1955); Rudolph Matas, "Dr. Charles C. Bass: An Appreciation," *Mississippi Doctor*, Aug. 1943. Other published sources include Vera Morel, "Dr. Elizabeth Bass Assembles Notable Collection," *Mississippi Doctor*, Aug. 1943, and an unsigned note, "Women Physicians of the Southern Medical Association," *JAMWA*, Dec. 1947. For information regarding various organizations to which Bass belonged see A. E. Fossier, *History of the Orleans Parish Medical Society 1878–1928* (1930), which contains a photo, and C. P. Loranz, *A History of the Southern Medical Association* (1960). Obituaries appeared in *New Orleans States*, Jan. 28, 1956; *New Orleans Times-Picayune*, Jan. 28, 1956; *N.Y.*

Times, Jan. 28, 1956; and Jour. Am. Medical Assoc., March 31, 1956.]

CHESTER BURNS
MELINDA NELSON

BAUCHENS, Anne, Feb. 2, 1881?–May 7, 1967. Film editor.

Anne Bauchens was one of the earliest and most distinguished of American film cutters. In a craft that has had many women practitioners, she was the first woman to receive an Academy Award for film editing, and the first recipient of the ACE, the Achievement Award of the American Cinema Editors. Born in St. Louis, she was the only daughter and older child of Luella (McKee) and Otto Bauchens, a porter who was of German-American descent.

Anne Bauchens aspired to become an actress. In St. Louis she studied drama under actor-director Hugh Ford, while working as a telephone operator at the St. Louis Post-Dispatch. She also studied gymnastics and dancing and eventually left for New York to try her luck on Broadway. Unsuccessful, she became a secretary in a real estate firm. When that company went bankrupt, Anne Bauchens found employment as secretary to William C. DeMille, well-known playwright and incipient film director. Shortly after, he was called to Hollywood by his brother Cecil B. DeMille to set up the first studio scenario department. Anne Bauchens soon followed. Fascinated by the movies, Bauchens took to the studio job immediately, assisting C. B. DeMille on the set as well as serving as his brother's secretary. She created the position of script clerk, the indispensable production secretary who records every detail of individual film shots so that they can be properly matched for later assemblage or editing.

In 1917 a studio crisis arose, requiring someone to edit a film left unassembled by a director. William DeMille recommended Bauchens for the task, personally guaranteeing to reimburse the studio if her work proved unsatisfactory. It did not—and she entered upon a new career. With C. B. DeMille she coedited his film We Can't Have Everything (1918). Dissatisfied with the editing on the first two films of his career, DeMille had been serving as his own editor; after working with Bauchens he entrusted to her the sole editing responsibility for all of his films. Between 1918 and DeMille's death in 1959, Bauchens's professional life was entirely meshed with his. She became one of the seven "loyal female followers" who made up the center of his staff, and edited the remaining thirty-nine films of his prestigious career.

Sometimes called "Trojan Annie . . . because she can take so much," in the early days Bauchens worked sixteen- to eighteen-hour days when a movie was in the editing phase; even in her seventies she was known to work ten to fourteen hours a day. A small, soft-spoken woman, she had confidence in her own skills and was willing to argue with DeMille over points of editing and interpretation. "Annie is stubborn," an acquaintance once commented, "and Mr. DeMille is three times as stubborn. If they disagree, one of them has to bring the other around because neither of them will give in" (Sammis, "Film Editor Indefatigable"). Although Bauchens once commented that she had never been thanked by the actors whose work she had improved through her editing, DeMille appreciated her value to him. He would not sign a contract for a film unless it was specified that Bauchens be the editor, explaining: "That is not sentiment, or at least not only sentiment. She is still the best film editor I know" (DeMille, p. 120).

Film editing is essentially a collaborative art, seldom recognized by the public and requiring the kind of self-effacing devotion which Anne Bauchens brought to it. Her skills brought her the Academy Award in 1940 for the editing of North West Mounted Police and three nominations for the Oscar: in 1934 for Cleopatra, in 1952 for The Greatest Show on Earth (for which she also received the ACE), and in 1956 for the last of DeMille's epic films, The Ten Commandments.

More than any other film of Bauchens's career, The Ten Commandments, made when she was seventy-five, demanded all of the skills she had learned and taught to others over the years. For the movie, DeMille used sixteen cameras and shot more than 100,000 feet of film. She had to reduce the footage to 12,000 feet while retaining and heightening the drama of the story. It was, DeMille noted, "the most difficult operation of film editing in motion picture history." Earlier DeMille epic films had prepared her for the task: for Union Pacific (1938) she had had to blend the work of two directors and reduce the film from 14,000 to 10,000 feet; The Greatest Show on Earth required massive editing to bring it down to two hours and thirty-one minutes.

Interviewed when she was working on The Ten Commandments, Bauchens compared film editing to magazine editing: "You must make the story flow evenly . . . splice in the close-ups and the distance shots so the audience is not conscious of any break in the story." Earlier, in her contribution to We Make the Movies (1937), one of the first serious volumes to explain the techniques of filmmaking to the public,

Bauchens had discussed her concept of film editing. The editor's main concern, she believed, was to tell the story well: "Unusual angles should not be employed merely for their own interest, unless they are effective in telling the story. The moment the audience is aware of the various cuts and devices used, the story will suffer."

Anne Bauchens gave most of her life to her work, although she also enjoyed gardening and was active in church and civic organizations. A movie fan, she had her favorite actors—Wally Reid was her "all-time favorite"—and she felt that the love of the dramatic which had sent her in search of an acting career had been satisfied through her work. With DeMille's death in January 1959, Bauchens retired from film editing. Her final work for DeMille was a tribute to him, published in France the year after her death. After suffering a stroke, Anne Bauchens died of pneumonitis in 1967 at the Motion Picture Country House and Hospital in Woodland Hills, Calif. Over more than forty years in Hollywood, her work had helped to establish the standards of her craft.

[There are clipping files on Bauchens in the Herrick Library, Acad. of Motion Picture Arts and Sciences, and in the Am. Film Inst., both in Beverly Hills, Calif. Bauchens wrote two articles: "Cutting the Film," in Nancy Naumburg, ed., *We Make the Movies* (1937); and a "témoignage" in Michel Mourlet, *Cecil B. DeMille* (1968). Biographical information is scanty and repetitive. See Phil A. Koury, "A Very Handy Lady with the Shears," *N.Y. Times*, April 6, 1947, sect. II, p. 4; William Waller, "She 'Cuts' Those Super Movies," *St. Louis Globe-Democrat*, May 3, 1947; Constance Sharp Sammis, "Film Editor Indefatigable," *Christian Science Monitor*, Feb. 11, 1957, p. 4; Art Arthur, "A Tribute to Anne Bauchens," *Am. Cinema Editors Mag.*, Feb. 1961; and Evelyn Scott, *Hollywood When Silents Were Golden* (1972). Many works dealing with C. B. DeMille have material on Bauchens; see Donald Hayne, ed., *The Autobiography of Cecil B. DeMille* (1959); William C. DeMille, *Hollywood Saga* (1939); Gene Ringgold and DeWitt Bodeen, *The Films of Cecil B. DeMille* (1969); Gabe Essoe and Raymond Lee, *DeMille: The Man and His Pictures* (1970); Phil A. Koury, *Yes, Mr. DeMille* (1959); and Charles Higham, *Cecil B. DeMille* (1973). Obituaries appeared in the *N.Y. Times* and the *L.A. Times*, both May 9, 1967. A death record, provided by the Calif. Dept. of Public Health, gives her birth date as Feb. 2, 1882, but the 1900 U.S. Census gives a date of February 1881 and lists her as Rosanna.

HAROLD J. SALEMSON

BAUER, Catherine Krouse, May 11, 1905–Nov. 22, 1964. Housing expert, planner.

Catherine Bauer, whose work helped lead to the passage of the first federal housing act in the United States, was born in Elizabeth, N.J., the oldest of three children (two girls and a boy) of Jacob Louis and Alberta Louise (Krouse) Bauer. Her father, as chief highway engineer for the state of New Jersey, achieved some fame for his pioneering designs, such as cloverleafs and banked curves. Through her mother, who frequently took the children on nature walks, Catherine Bauer acquired a love of the outdoors; she became an avid swimmer and hiker, and an ardent supporter of conservation efforts. From early childhood Bauer exhibited a rebellious nature. She clashed with her mother, a strong-minded, domineering woman, and openly ridiculed her old-fashioned, middle-class ways. Known to her friends as "Casey," she possessed a quick intelligence, a lively sense of humor, and a frank and forthright manner.

Bauer attended the Vail-Deane School for Girls in Elizabeth, and went on to Vassar College. She transferred to Cornell University for her third year to study architecture, but returned to graduate from Vassar in 1926. After graduation she spent a year in Paris, living alone in a rented apartment on the Ile Saint Louis, and associating with an arty and intellectual bohemian group. She wrote several articles on the new functionalist domestic architecture of Europe, one of which later appeared in the *New York Times Magazine* (April 15, 1928).

Returning to New York with no particular career objective, she held various routine jobs until 1928, when she became advertising manager at the Harcourt Brace publishing house. A bright and engaging conversationalist and a rebel against established taste and standards, Bauer made the acquaintance of writers and social critics, and was accepted into their circles. Her most important friendship was with Lewis Mumford, who was to become her intellectual mentor and close friend. He helped to cure her of a sterile aestheticism by calling her attention to the social dimensions of architecture, an awareness that shaped her future career.

The depression having cost Bauer her job, she returned to Europe in 1930 to examine architectural developments in Sweden, the Netherlands, and Germany, as well as in France. Her study of new European housing communities and her introduction there to the new social, technical, and economic research on housing, transformed her from a "dilettante" into a housing reformer and convinced her that an entirely new kind of human environment was not only possible but inevitable. Upon her return to New York in 1931 she became the executive secretary of the Regional Planning Association of America (established in 1923 by Lewis Mumford and other architects, economists, and social critics). The association challenged the remedial and restrictive approach that characterized most housing legislation and sought instead to set housing activity within the broader framework of regional planning.

Encouraged by Mumford, Bauer submitted an article on the architectural aspects of modern housing in Germany to a contest sponsored by *Fortune* magazine. It won first prize and was published in the May 1931 issue ("Prize Essay: Art in Industry," pp. 94–110). Overnight Bauer became known as an expert on housing. From May 1931 to the spring of 1932 she published nine articles on art and architecture in *The New Republic, Creative Art,* and *Arts Weekly,* where she was a member of the staff. In the summer of 1932 she returned to Europe as Mumford's research assistant, gathering information on European housing communities for a series of articles he was to write for *Fortune.* After three articles had appeared, the series was canceled as too radical and Mumford persuaded Bauer to use the mass of unused material she had helped collect as the basis for a book.

In *Modern Housing* (1934) Bauer described the northern European housing movement not merely as a demonstration of advanced architectural design but as proof that an organized demand for quality housing at a price accessible to all could bring results. A comparable housing movement could develop in the United States, she believed, if those having a direct stake in new, low-cost housing—the workers and consumers—similarly took an active role in its development.

In the spring of 1934 Bauer helped to organize the American Federation of Labor Housing Conference (LHC) to promote the involvement of labor in the move to create a federal housing program. As executive secretary of the LHC, Bauer succeeded in establishing some seventy-five local labor housing committees; their efforts were the principal political force behind the 1937 Wagner-Steagall Housing Act, the country's first public housing legislation.

In 1936 Bauer received a Guggenheim Foundation fellowship to study housing in Scandinavia and the Soviet Union, the first Guggenheim award in that field. When the United States Housing Authority was established in 1937 to administer the public housing program, she became director of research and information. The federal bureaucracy was not to her taste, however, and in 1940 she began her teaching career, going to the University of California at Berkeley as Rosenberg Professor of Public Social Services. There she met William Wilson

Wurster, a prominent Bay area architect ten years her senior, whom she married on August 13, 1940.

While Bauer and her husband developed separate careers, their professional interests overlapped. In 1943 they moved to Cambridge, Mass., where a year later Wurster became dean of the School of Architecture and Planning at the Massachusetts Institute of Technology. Catherine Bauer taught a seminar on housing at Harvard University and participated in the ongoing arguments about urban development. In August 1945, at the age of forty and after several miscarriages, she gave birth to a daughter, Sarah Louise, known as Sadie. The Wursters returned to Berkeley in 1950; from that time until her death in 1964 Bauer taught at the Berkeley campus of the University of California, becoming professor of city and regional planning and associate dean of the College of Environmental Design.

With seemingly boundless energy, Catherine Bauer not only taught but served as consultant to local, national, and international agencies; she was an active contributor to the urban development programs of the United Nations. She also wrote articles, gave speeches, and traveled throughout the country and abroad on behalf of a campaign for better housing communities. She called for active citizen involvement in planning and managing housing communities, and came to see the public housing movement as giving off a "fatal charity smell." Bauer had hoped that American architects would be challenged by the sociological implications of the housing program. But a failure of architectural imagination coupled with the parsimonious federal legislation (which set strict limitations on dwelling unit and design costs) had resulted instead in a housing program that seemed to her in 1957 to be in a "dreary deadlock." Public housing advocates, she acknowledged, had too uncritically embraced functionalist architectural theories and had thus given inadequate attention to subtler aesthetic values and basic social needs.

Throughout her career, Bauer urged the balance of social and aesthetic concerns in housing and urban planning. She was among the earliest to warn that urban renewal would result in removing people from their neighborhoods. She argued for diversity in housing scale and for public and private support of community facilities. Actively interested in the form and structure of metropolitan areas, she pleaded for the unification of housing and transportation policies and regional land controls. Her critical study of such issues, "Framework for an Urban Society," served as a basis for the 1960 report of the President's Commission on National Goals.

Catherine Bauer was a founding member of the National Association of Housing Officials, a member of the board and vice president of the National Public Housing Conference, and an honorary member of the American Institute of Planners. In November 1964 her important contribution to the housing movement in the United States was cut short by her death from a brain concussion and exposure, the result of a fall during a hike on Mount Tamalpais in California.

[Catherine Bauer's papers, dating from her arrival in California in 1940 to her death in 1964, are in the Bancroft Library at the Univ. of Calif. at Berkeley. LHC files are in the State Hist. Soc. of Wis. "Framework for an Urban Society" was published in President's Commission on Nat. Goals, *Goals for Americans* (1960). She also wrote *Labor and the Housing Program* (1938); *A Citizen's Guide to Public Housing* (1940); and *Social Questions in Housing and Town Planning* (1952). Important articles include "Housing: Paper Plans or a Workers' Movement," in Carol Aronovici, ed., *America Can't Have Housing* (1940); and *Social Questions in Housing* Cahill and Alfred H. Barr, Jr., eds., *Art in America in Modern Times* (1934); "Elements of English Housing Practice," in *Modern Architecture in England* (1937); "Redevelopment: A Misfit in the Fifties," in Coleman Woodbury, ed., *The Future of Cities and Urban Redevelopment* (1953); and "The Form and Structure of the Future Urban Complex," in Lowdon Wingo, ed., *Cities and Space: The Future Use of Urban Land* (1963). An early autobiographical statement, "We Present Catherine Bauer in Her Own Words," is in *Jour. of Housing*, Nov. 1944, pp. 27 and 31. For biographical information see Mary Mix Foley, "Housing's White Knight Is a Handsome Blonde with Brunette Economic Ideas," *Architectural Forum*, March 1946, pp. 116–19; Suzanne Stephens, "Voices of Consequence: Four Architectural Critics," in Susana Torre, ed., *Women in Architecture: A Historic and Contemporary Perspective* (1977); and *Nat. Cyc. Am. Biog.*, LI, 268–69. Susan Cole, "Catherine Bauer and the Public Housing Movement: 1926–1937," (Ph.D. diss., George Washington Univ., 1975), provides background and details on Bauer's activities and bibliography. Her relationship with Lewis Mumford is reflected in his *My Works and Days: A Personal Chronicle* (1979). Bauer's body was found on Nov. 23, 1964; a death record was provided by Calif. Dept. of Public Health. Further information was provided by Bauer's sister, Elizabeth Bauer Kassler, by her daughter, Sadie Wurster Super, and by Frederick Gutheim, Lewis Mumford, Coleman Woodbury, and Ernest J. Bohn.]

SUSAN COLE

BAUER, Marion Eugénie, Aug. 15, 1887–Aug. 9, 1955. Music educator, composer.

Marion Bauer, an influential advocate of modern music and musicians, was born in Walla Walla, Wash., the youngest of seven children, five of whom survived. Her father, Jacques Bauer, a grocer and amateur musician, and her mother, Julie (Heyman) Bauer, an accomplished linguist and language teacher, were both French-born Jews. After her father died in 1890 the family moved to Portland, Ore. Marion Bauer attended the public schools there, and then St. Helen's Hall, where her mother taught and from which she graduated in 1903. Soon afterward she moved to New York City to live with her eldest sister, Emilie Frances, a pianist and writer who had become established as a music critic there. From her sister, who had helped to care for her as a child, Marion Bauer received her first serious music lessons as well as consistent encouragement and financial assistance. In New York she began to study piano and harmony with the composer Henry Holden Huss; she also began to compose, at first chiefly songs.

In 1906 Bauer went to France, where she studied piano with Raoul Pugno, the noted violinist. He encouraged her to compose and arranged for her to study harmony with Nadia Boulanger. Thus Bauer became one of the first Americans to study with this great French teacher. In 1907 Bauer returned to New York, where for the next four years she taught piano and theory and herself studied with Eugene Heffley. During this period her first published song, "Light," was introduced by the famous contralto ERNESTINE SCHUMANN-HEINK. In 1910 and 1911 Bauer studied counterpoint and form with Paul Ertel in Berlin. When she returned to America, the publishing firm of Arthur P. Schmidt offered her a seven-year contract for her songs, and she also began to work with the conductor Walter Henry Rothwell.

As she gained confidence, Bauer started to compose piano works, choral pieces, and chamber music. She wrote a tone poem for violin and piano, *Up the Ocklawaha* (1913), for her friend, violinist MAUD POWELL. Other works of this period include *Fair Daffodils* (1913), a trio for women's voices; *The Lay of the Four Winds* (1915), for men's voices; and *Allegretto giocoso* (1920), for eleven instruments, her most ambitious work up to that time.

In 1923 Bauer returned to Europe for a third time, again to France. She later described this period as one of the richest of her life, for she studied fugue with the celebrated teacher André Gédalge and met many prominent musicians and composers. But her sister fell ill, and in January 1926 Bauer returned to New York to be with her, remaining there until Emilie Bauer's death later that year.

Throughout her career, Marion Bauer was a prolific writer and a popular teacher. She had begun quite early to write for music journals, and in 1925 she published the first of several popular books on music history, *How Music Grew*, written with Ethel Peyser. After her return from Europe she replaced her sister as New York correspondent for *Musical Leader*, a post she retained for the rest of her life. She also joined the faculty of New York University, where she remained for twenty-five years. In 1928 Bauer became a lecturer on contemporary music at the Chautauqua Institute, and she returned nearly every summer for over twenty years. She also taught summer sessions elsewhere, and in the early 1940s she joined the faculty of the Juilliard School as well.

In addition to these activities, Bauer continued to compose, especially chamber, choral, and orchestral works. Notable among her chamber works are *Fantasia quasi una sonata*, for violin and piano (1928); a string quartet first performed in 1928; *Sonata* for viola and piano (1935); *Concertino* for oboe, clarinet, and string quartet (1939–43); and a trio sonata for flute, cello, and piano (1951). Of her large works, *Symphonic Suite for Strings*, opus 34, was given its premiere at Chautauqua in 1941; *American Youth Concerto* for piano and orchestra was performed in New York in 1943; *China*, for chorus and orchestra, was performed at the Worcester Festival in 1945; and the tone poem *Sun Splendor* was performed by the New York Philharmonic under Leopold Stokowski in 1947.

In her own compositions Bauer retained a largely impressionist style, in the vein of Claude Debussy and Charles Griffes, whose music had made a deep impression on her in her youth. But her later works show increasing use of dissonance, and in her teaching and writing Bauer was a tireless champion of more innovative styles. Urging music teachers to use modern pieces to accustom young pupils to dissonance and other "unusual" sounds, she gave lecture recitals to explain modern music to the general public. She also served on the executive board of the League of Composers, an organization influential in promoting contemporary American music.

In addition to two more books written with Peyser, *Music Through the Ages* (1932) and *How Opera Grew* (1955), Bauer wrote *Twentieth Century Music* (1933) and *Musical Questions and Quizzes* (1941) and contributed articles to music encyclopedias and journals. Highly regarded by other musicians and musicologists, she was honored upon her retirement from New York University by a program devoted entirely to her works, which was given at New York's Town Hall in May 1951. Bauer spent her last summer completing the book *How Opera Grew* at the South Hadley, Mass., home of her longtime friend and colleague, Harrison Potter. She died there of a heart attack in 1955, a few days before her sixty-eighth birthday.

[*How Music Grew* was revised in 1939; *Music Through the Ages*, in 1946; *Twentieth Century Music*, in 1947. Representative of Bauer's writings on modern music is her article "Why Not Teach Music of Today?" *Associated Music Teachers League Bull.*, Nov. 1951. A brief autobiographical sketch by Marion Bauer is included in David Ewen, ed., *American Composers Today* (1949) and *Composers Since 1900* (1969). Claire R. Reis, *Composers in America* (1947), and Madeleine Goss, *Modern Music Makers* (1952), contain biographical information as well as lists of Bauer's compositions. See also Gdal Saleski, *Famous Musicians of Jewish Origin* (1949); Irwin A. Bazelon, "Woman with a Symphony," *The Baton*, March 1951; Olin Downes, *N.Y. Times*, May 9, 1951; and *Nat. Cyc. Am. Biog.*, XLIII, 121. Obituaries appeared in the *N.Y. Times*, Aug. 11, 1955, and *Musical Leader*, Sept. 1955. Additional information for this article was supplied by Harrison Potter; a biobibliography prepared by Annette Le Clair assisted in the research. A death record was provided by Mass. Dept. of Public Health. A fuller treatment appears in Christine Ammer, *Unsung: A History of Women in American Music* (1980).]

CHRISTINE AMMER

BEACH, Sylvia Woodbridge, March 14, 1887–June 16, 1962. Bookshop proprietor, publisher.

In 1922, when no English or American publisher would risk it, Sylvia Beach, a minister's daughter, brought out a legally obscene book, James Joyce's *Ulysses*. The book was published under the imprint of Shakespeare and Company, an American bookshop and lending library that Beach established in Paris in 1919. In the 1920s Shakespeare and Company became a focus of expatriate literary activity, Beach herself an important, if unheralded champion of modern literature.

To her bookshop and the writers who frequented it, to Joyce above all, Sylvia Beach brought a sense of service often found in the women of American clerical families. Her mother, Eleanor Thomazine Orbison, was born in India, the daughter of a medical missionary whose colonial ancestors founded the Allegheny town of Bellefonte, Pa. In 1880, as a student at Bellefonte Academy, she became engaged to the Rev. Sylvester Woodbridge Beach, a ninth generation Presbyterian minister, then a Latin teacher recently graduated from Princeton College. Upon their marriage in 1882, the couple went to Baltimore. There the second of their three daughters was born and christened Nancy, a name soon changed at the mother's insistence to the patronymic, Sylvia.

From Baltimore the family moved to Bridgeton, N.J., and in 1901, to Paris, where Sylvester Beach had been appointed assistant pastor of the American Church and director of an American student center. During these early years in France, Sylvia Beach, whose chronic migraine headaches prevented regular school attendance, received the only formal education she ever acknowledged—two or three months in a restrictive Lausanne school. In 1906 her father began his final ministry, as pastor of the prestigious First Presbyterian Church of Princeton, N.J. Among his parishioners were Woodrow Wilson and his family. The Beaches' "veritable passion for France" took them back frequently, however, and inspired in Sylvia Beach an interest in contemporary French literature.

In 1917, with her younger sister Cyprian, then a popular screen actress, she came to wartime Paris to pursue her studies "at the source." They took her to La Maison des Amis des Livres, the Left Bank bookshop of Adrienne Monnier. With Monnier, an approachable and dedicated bookseller, Beach developed a personal and professional friendship that would last almost forty years and make the rue de l'Odéon the center, in T. S. Eliot's phrase, of "the Franco-Anglo-American literary world of Paris."

Monnier's shop, established in 1915 as "the first lending library in France," was a gathering place for many of the writers Beach admired and wished to make better known at home—André Gide, Paul Valéry, Valéry Larbaud, and Léon-Paul Fargue. It was initially Beach's intention to open a branch of La Maison in New York, an idea that "had become an obsession" by the time she returned to Paris after nine months as a Red Cross volunteer in Serbia. Her regret was brief, however, when the project appeared prohibitively expensive. Through Monnier, she soon saw the possibilities of an English-language bookshop in Paris, where the cost of living was low and she could count on the Frenchwoman's help and experience. On Nov. 19, 1919, financed by her mother's life savings, Sylvia Beach opened Shakespeare and Company in the rue Dupuytren. Later, with the help of her older sister, Holly, the shop was moved to 12 rue de l'Odéon, across from La Maison.

The opening anticipated a wave of American tourists and expatriates anxious to exchange the social and literary suppressions of their country for the openness and excitement of Montparnasse. Among Beach's earliest customers were such expatriate writers as Ezra Pound, Robert McAlmon, and GERTRUDE STEIN, to whose studio Beach later escorted, among others, Sherwood Anderson and Ernest Hemingway. She was to be disappointed by Anderson's defection to Stein, but Hemingway, who called himself her "best customer," remained a favorite. Beach was also uniquely supportive of women writers not ordinarily welcomed by Stein, including McAlmon's wife, Bryher (Winifred Ellerman), and Bryher's intimate friend, the poet HILDA DOOLITTLE, Janet Flanner (1892–1978), and Katherine Anne Porter.

For these "pilgrims of the twenties," a term Beach preferred to Stein's "lost generation," Shakespeare and Company quickly became an indispensable stopping-off place. It was at once a post office, bank, and informal club, a conduit to the editors of little reviews and Paris-based American publishers, and, most important, a place where apprentice writers could count on the reassurance and resourcefulness of the proprietor.

James Joyce and Sylvia Beach met on July 11, 1920; the next day he began his regular visits to Shakespeare and Company. In 1921 official censorship prevented Harriet Weaver in England and MARGARET ANDERSON and Jane Heap in the United States from publishing *Ulysses* in its uncut entirety. Joyce was close to despair. "My book," he told Beach, "will never come out now." With characteristic impetuosity, she asked for the "honor" of seeing that it did.

The task of publishing *Ulysses* was enormous. Beach engaged a Dijon printer and solicited subscriptions to the first edition. As the author struggled against deteriorating eyesight, Beach all but single-handedly prepared the barely decipherable manuscript for the printer, nearly ruining her own sight in the process. She allowed Joyce the unheard-of privilege of composing a third of *Ulysses* on corrected proofsheets, yet managed to have the first two copies of the novel delivered to Paris in time for the author's fortieth birthday on Feb. 2, 1922.

Subsequently Beach was called upon by Joyce to act as unpaid agent, private secretary, business manager, occasional nursemaid, and constant maid-of-all-work, receiving a daily "grocery list" of tasks to perform. In spite of a contract that promised her payments from future publishers, she was pressured by a friend of Joyce into resigning her rights to *Ulysses* after its eleventh printing in 1933, the year the Supreme Court permitted its publication in the United States. Beach received no royalties from the Random House editions of *Ulysses* and suffered financially during the depression, when many of her American customers left Paris. In 1936, the year she received the Legion of Honor, Shakespeare and Company had to be rescued by a committee of her French friends, joined by Hemingway and T. S. Eliot, who sponsored a benefit series of readings from their works.

What the depression could not accomplish, the Nazi occupation did. In December 1941, Beach refused to sell a copy of *Finnegans Wake* to a German officer who threatened to confiscate the contents of the shop. Within two hours, she had them removed to a vacant apartment above her own and all traces of Shakespeare and Company eradicated. Beach herself was later interned for some seven months in Vittel but returned to the rue de l'Odéon in time for its liberation and the dramatic return of Hemingway, at the head of a squad of French and American soldiers, on Aug. 26, 1944.

Beach never reopened her shop. The climax of what she ironically called her "official period" occurred in 1959, when she organized and prepared the catalog for a Paris exhibition devoted to writers she had known there in the twenties. The same year saw the publication of her autobiography and an honorary degree from the University of Buffalo. On "Bloomsday," June 16, 1962, Beach spoke at the dedication of Dublin's Martello Tower, the site of the opening chapter of *Ulysses,* as a center for Joyce studies. It was her last service for the author, who died the year Shakespeare and Company closed. On Dec. 6, 1962, she was discovered in her apartment above where her bookshop had been, the victim apparently of a heart attack. Her ashes were brought to the family plot in Princeton, her papers to the Princeton University Library.

[The Beach papers at Princeton consist primarily of material relating to her bookshop. See Howard Rice, Jr., "The Sylvia Beach Collection," *Princeton Univ. Library Chronicle,* Autumn 1964, pp. 7–13. Photographs of Beach and her friends may be found in her autobiography, *Shakespeare and Company* (1959). Her other writings include introductions to her translation of Henri Michaux's *A Barbarian in Asia* (1949) and to a collection of essays, *Our Exagmination Round His Factification for Incamination of Work In Progress* (1962). A memorial edition of *Mercure de France,* Aug.–Sept. 1963, contains her account of wartime imprisonment, "Interned," and remembrances by T. S. Eliot, Archibald MacLeish, Allen Tate, Janet Flanner, and others. Her relations with Joyce are documented in Jane Lidderdale and Mary Nicholson, *Dear Miss Weaver* (1970); with Monnier in *The Very Rich Hours of Adrienne Monnier,* translated with an introduction and commentaries by Richard McDougall (1976).

Reflective reviews of her autobiography are by Justin O'Brien, "What Is She?" *Reporter,* Oct. 1, 1959; Alice B. Toklas, *New Republic,* Oct. 19, 1959; Janet Flanner, *New Yorker,* Oct. 24, 1959. See also Richard Ellman, *James Joyce* (1959); W. G. Rogers, *Ladies Bountiful* (1968); Noel Riley Fitch, "An American Bookshop in Paris: The Influence of Sylvia Beach's Shakespeare and Company on American Literature" (Ph.D. diss., Wash. State Univ., 1961). A biobibliography by Karen Knight assisted the discovery of these and other sources.]

HERBERT R. HABER

BEARD, Mary Ritter, Aug. 5, 1876–Aug. 14, 1958. Historian, feminist.

Mary Ritter Beard, who provided an intellectual foundation for women's history, was born in Indianapolis, the third of six children and the elder of two daughters of Narcissa (Lockwood) and Eli Foster Ritter. Both her father, a lawyer devoted to temperance and Methodism, and her mother, an academy-educated woman who had taught school, came from westward-migrating southern Protestant families. During Mary's girlhood the Ritters lived comfortably in a suburban part of Indianapolis.

Mary Ritter extended the horizons of this secure world when she left, at sixteen, to study political science, languages, and literature at DePauw University in Asbury, Ind., a Methodist institution attended by her father and all her siblings. There she met Charles Austin Beard (1874–1948), a young Indianan of similar background. Ritter graduated in 1897 and taught high school German in Indiana before she married Beard in March 1900.

Marriage provided one element of continuity in Mary Ritter Beard's life. Her interest in the history, needs, status, and social views of her sex provided another. That interest was first manifest in her involvement in the woman suffrage and women's trade union movements. Influenced, as was Charles Beard, by the reform currents of the 1890s, she immersed herself in social action in England immediately after her marriage. At Oxford, where her husband was studying history and helping to found the workingman's college Ruskin Hall, Mary Beard plunged into the woman suffrage movement. Her involvement familiarized her both with militant tactics and with the needs and priorities of working-class women.

Returning to New York in 1902, a year after the birth of their daughter Miriam, the Beards enrolled at Columbia University. Mary Beard's iconoclastic combination of graduate study in sociology with young motherhood lasted only until 1904. Whether family considerations or intellectual predisposition dictated her termination of graduate study is not clear. For the duration of her scholarly life she criticized academic narrowness and remained bent on self-education instead. In 1907 she bore a son, William. Shortly afterward she joined the National Women's Trade Union League in organizing the New York shirtwaistmakers' strike of 1909 and in protesting the Triangle factory fire. She also entered the mainstream of the woman suffrage movement, as a fundraiser and organizer, in 1910, and within a year was editing *The Woman Voter,* published by the Woman Suffrage party of New York. Her special interest in working women led her in 1912 to resign the editorship to concentrate instead on the Wage Earners' League, the Woman Suffrage party's adjunct for working women. When a militant faction within the national suffrage movement coalesced around the leadership of Alice Paul (1885–1977), Beard was won over. She spoke, wrote, organized, and raised money in cooperation with Paul's Congressional Union (later the National Woman's party) between 1913 and 1917. When her support lapsed in the 1920s it was because she gave priority to protective legislation for working women, and consequently opposed Paul's Equal Rights Amendment.

Gradually Beard found her authentic vocation in writing and lecturing, rather than in activism. Her first book, *Woman's Work in Municipalities* (1915), published when she was thirty-nine, and her second, *A Short History of the American Labor Movement* (1920), focused on social reform and the working class. Subsequently Beard gave rein to her interest in universal questions about women in a succession of books, speeches, and articles. From her apprenticeship in Progressive social reform, political agitation, and labor organization, she brought to her scholarship pragmatism, political savvy, and a profound awareness of the significance of class and gender. To these she added intellectual flexibility and vision. She did most of her writing at the bustling home in Milford, Conn., where the family had moved after Charles Beard resigned his Columbia University professorship in 1917 in protest against the firing of three colleagues who had opposed American entry into World War I.

Mary Beard brought a unique point of view to her writing. Insisting that women's contributions were central to human society, she drew a direct connection between women's primary responsibility for the care of life and their potential for enacting progressive social change. She refused to see women merely as subject to or victimized by male domination. Without

denying that women had legitimate grievances, she maintained that feminist protest from the eighteenth century to the twentieth had devalued women's history by expounding women's subordination. Beard's work consisted therefore in bringing to light women's neglected past: through her historical studies, such as *On Understanding Women* (1931) and *Woman as Force in History* (1946); through her collections of documents, *America Through Women's Eyes* (1933) and *Laughing Their Way: Women's Humor in America* (1934); in her unique study guide, "A Changing Political Economy as It Affects Women"; and in her brilliant 1942 critique of the omissions and distortions about women in the *Encyclopedia Britannica.* Moreover, in the 1930s Beard attempted to establish a World Center for Women's Archives to preserve the records of women's lives. Although she led a group of women in incorporating and setting up an office for the archives in New York, the project failed for lack of funds and support.

The years in which Mary Beard pursued her "calling" as woman's historian (Lane, p. 8) were also those in which she collaborated with Charles Beard to produce a justly famous series of volumes of American history. Their first, the highly praised *The Rise of American Civilization* (1927), has been called "probably the most successful synthesis in American historical writing" (Beale, p. 263). Besides that series, which had an extensive general audience, the Beards coauthored three textbooks for classroom use. If in her own work Mary Beard sought to combat what she saw as a false and pernicious impression that "all history is but the story of the 'man's world,'" the historical syntheses written with her husband were attempts to implement her vision of integrated human knowledge. That vision colored, but did not wholly inform, the structure and content of the coauthored volumes. Comprising social, economic, cultural, intellectual, and political history, and characterized by grand interpretive sweep, the series took more cognizance of women's roles and contributions than any comparable survey. Although it is impossible to separate their individual contributions to the volumes, Charles Beard has received most of the credit for them. Such was the reward of a prolific woman scholar married to an even more prolific and more famous man.

In the 1940s, frequently facing hostility from male academics and indifference or hostility from professional women, Beard intensified her lecturing and writing efforts to transform the curricula of higher education to encompass women's points of view. At seventy, she published her best book, *Woman as Force in His-*

tory. In it she developed her critique of nineteenth-century feminists' emphasis on women's subjection, locating their mistake in a misreading of women's status in English common law. Harshly reviewed by male historians when first published, the book served as a beacon for feminist scholars rediscovering women's history two decades later.

Mary Beard continued her compelling interest and diverse projects in women's history into old age. She outlived Charles Beard by a decade, and spent her last years in Phoenix, Ariz., where she died of kidney failure in 1958 after a long illness.

A feminist at heart who decried the counterproductiveness of feminist ideology, a polemicist for woman's point of view whose real goal was to integrate human culture, a woman whose ideas about her sex shared more with her grandmother's and granddaughter's generations than with her own, Mary Beard embodied paradox. Yet she lived a highly unified life, symbolized by her working relationship with her husband. She refused to accept a definition of sexual equality that expected women to conform to male-defined standards, and maintained instead that genuine autonomy and self-confidence for women would emerge from a more complete knowledge of their own past.

[Mary Beard destroyed the bulk of her personal papers. What remains can be found in small collections at the Schlesinger Library, Radcliffe College; the Sophia Smith Collection, Smith College; and the DePauw Univ. Archives. The papers of the Nat. Woman's party at the Library of Congress contain some information on her early activist days. In addition to the works mentioned above, Beard wrote *The Force of Women in Japanese History* (1953) and *The Making of Charles A. Beard* (1955); she collaborated with her husband on *America in Midpassage* (1939) and *The American Spirit: A Study of the Idea of Civilization in the United States* (1942). Ann J. Lane's excellent compilation, *Mary Ritter Beard: A Sourcebook* (1978), contains the only extensive appraisal of Beard's life and work, judicious selections from her writings, and a thorough bibliography. Other useful evaluations are Berenice A. Carroll, "Mary Beard's *Woman as Force in History*: A Critique," *Mass. Rev.*, Winter–Spring 1972, and Carl N. Degler, "*Woman as Force in History* by Mary Beard," *Daedalus*, Winter 1974. See also Howard K. Beale, ed., *Charles A. Beard: An Appraisal* (1954). An obituary appeared in the *N.Y. Times*, Aug. 15, 1958; death record provided by Ariz. Dept. of Health.]

NANCY F. COTT

BERG, Gertrude Edelstein, Oct. 3, 1899–Sept. 14, 1966. Radio, television, and screen writer, actress.

Gertrude Berg, who became famous on radio and television as Molly Goldberg, was born in New York City, the only child of Jacob and Dinah Netta (Goldstein) Edelstein. An important source for her humor and knowledge of Jewish life was her paternal grandfather, Mordecai Edelstein, an immigrant from Russian Poland. In the decade before World War I, her father, who had worked in the restaurant business, undertook the operation of a Catskill mountain boardinghouse at Fleischmanns, N.Y., where the young Gertrude Edelstein began writing entertainments to amuse the vacationers. Her mother assumed responsibility for the management of the hotel kitchen and did the bookkeeping.

As a teenager, Gertrude Edelstein attended Wadleigh High School in New York City but did not graduate. In 1918 she married Lewis Berg, a student from Brooklyn Polytechnic Institute and a guest at the hotel. After a brief stint on a Louisiana sugar plantation where Lewis Berg worked as an engineer, the couple returned to New York City where their children Cherney (1922) and Harriet (1926) were born. Lewis Berg continued to work as a mechanical engineer and manager of Arbuckle Brothers Sugar Refinery until the 1940s.

With the advent of commercial radio, both Bergs saw the potential for capitalizing on Gertrude's playwriting skills. Going to radio station WMCA in the hope of selling a script, she instead found herself hired to read recipes in Yiddish for Consolidated Edison commercials. As she spoke no Yiddish, she read from phonetic translations. A year later, she developed her first radio series, "Effie and Laura," which was canceled after a single performance. Fortunately, she tried again, this time drawing upon the immigrant experience of her grandparents' generation and her own knowledge of Jewish family life. On Nov. 20, 1929, Gertrude Berg began broadcasting "The Rise of the Goldbergs," the radio program which catapulted her to celebrity status and made her one of the most successful women writers in the history of the entertainment industry.

The program quickly gained an audience and in 1931 picked up a sponsor, Pepsodent; the series then ran without interruption, six times a week, for three years. In 1934, the troupe began a personal appearance tour of vaudeville houses in key cities. When "The Rise of the Goldbergs" was discontinued in 1934 because Pepsodent was having business difficulties, the sponsor received 30,000 letters of complaint within the first month. Berg then came up with the idea for "The House of Glass," a half-hour serial about a Catskill mountain resort that was broadcast for a few months in 1935 but never reached the popularity of the Goldberg series. During the winter of 1936, Berg temporarily relocated herself in Hollywood and wrote screenplays for producer Sol Lesser and child star Bobby Breen. In the summer of 1937 her family joined her in California; that August, before returning to New York, Berg signed a one million dollar contract, committing her to five more years of writing and starring in the Goldberg series. From 1938 until 1945, the program was carried by both NBC and CBS, allegedly making it second only to "Amos 'N' Andy" in the annals of radio popularity.

Berg wrote all her own scripts and acted the part of the central character, the mother, Molly Goldberg. Her radio family remained basically the same for the next two decades. Her husband, Jake Goldberg (played by James R. Waters), was a cloak and suiter in the garment trades; Rosalie (played by Rosalyn Silbur) and Sammy (played by Alfred Ryder and others) were their children. Over the years the family moved, the children grew up and began to date, and Sammy went off to war. In each fifteen-minute segment, Molly, a good-natured meddler, involved herself, her Jewish relatives, and her polyglot New York neighbors in a variety of problems which inevitably gave her the opportunity to moralize about human behavior. While the character Berg created displayed elements of her own personality and values, her private domestic arrangements were a far cry from the struggling Goldbergs. In the midst of the depression, Berg had the resources to employ three persons to help her manage her domestic life and maternal responsibilities.

Millions of Americans were involved in the problems and delights of the Goldberg family. Both the volume and character of Berg's fan mail indicate that a significant portion of the audience found the program inspirational as well as amusing. Listeners from diverse religious and geographical backgrounds commented on the manner in which Molly "symbolized the importance of Motherhood," while the program "stressed home and family as the nucleus of society." Considered by many as good as any sermon, "The Rise of the Goldbergs" was an important secular source of moral inspiration.

This wide national acceptance and benevolent interest in the aspirations of the Goldberg family were important to those in the Jewish community who feared radio's potential as an additional source of Jewish stereotyping. The Jewish *Daily Forward* complimented Gertrude Berg for the authenticity of both her dialect and her portrayal of Jewish life. In fact, American Jews wrote Berg consistently, both to comment on those programs which portrayed their religious observances and to request her support in fund raising on behalf of American and European Jewry. She responded with increasing regularity, as the specter of fascism grew, intermingling her work for Jewish groups with participation in the larger war effort.

Fan mail from non-Jews indicated that "The Goldbergs" was widely perceived as a catalyst in the development of interfaith and interracial understanding. "You are doing a masterly job of fighting anti-Semitism," wrote a typical Christian listener who considered Molly, Jake, and the kids to be close friends. Non-Jews identified with the family's quest for improved economic and social status and liked Molly Goldberg's homiletics, often more American than ethnic.

The successful transition of "The Goldbergs" to television in 1949 was seen by CBS as a model, "pointing to a reservoir of program talent and ideas," drawn from radio. With an estimated thirteen million viewers, Berg's opening line for each show, "Yoo hoo, Mrs. Bloom," became a national cliché. In 1950, the National Academy of Television Arts and Science awarded Gertrude Berg an Emmy for her role as Molly Goldberg.

Berg's career on the stage and in films was, to a large extent, based on her identity as Molly Goldberg. She appeared on Broadway in *Me and Molly* (1948) and in a 1951 film entitled *Molly*. Her other theater credits include *A Majority of One*, for which she received an Antoinette Perry Award in 1959, and *Dear Me, the Sky Is Falling* (1963). Gertrude Berg died in New York City of a heart condition, while she was in production for the starring role in *The Play Girls*, a script based on her idea.

[The best source of information on Gertrude Berg's professional life is the Gertrude Berg Coll., George Arents Research Library, Syracuse Univ. It includes correspondence, scrapbooks, radio and television scripts, and published materials. Her autobiographical work *Molly and Me* (1961) documents her career. See also *The Rise of the Goldbergs* (1931) and the *Molly Goldberg Cook Book* (1955), with Myra Waldo. Biographical information is contained in *Current Biog.* 1941, 1960; *Who Was Who in America*, vol. IV (1968); *Biog. Encyc. and Who's Who of the Am. Theatre* (1966); and a *N.Y. Times* obituary, Sept. 15, 1966. Personal information was supplied by Lewis Berg, her husband, and Harriet Berg Schwartz, her daughter.]

JOAN JACOBS BRUMBERG

BERNSTEIN, Aline Frankau, Dec. 22, 1880– Sept. 7, 1955. Stage and costume designer.

Aline Bernstein was America's first woman theatrical designer to achieve professional importance. In a working career that stretched from the mid-1920s to the early 1950s, Bernstein became one of a half dozen designers whose work represented the best of the American theater.

She was born Hazel Frankau in New York City, the elder of two daughters of Rebecca (Goldsmith) and Joseph Frankau, an actor of German-Jewish ancestry. Her father chose the name Hazel, but her mother had it changed to Aline. She was raised in the actor's milieu of theatrical boarding houses and drafty backstages. Following the early deaths of both parents (her mother in 1895 and her father in 1897), Aline became the ward of her Aunt Rachel Goldsmith, who was addicted to drugs. Fortunately, Tom Watson, who had been a close friend of the family, perceived in her drawings a definite talent. A member of the board of directors of the New York School of Applied Design, Watson arranged for Aline to receive a scholarship to study drawing there. She later studied with Robert Henri, one of the most important American painters of the early twentieth century.

Aline Frankau married Wall Street broker Theodore Bernstein on Nov. 19, 1902. They had two children, Theodore (b. 1904) and Edla (b. 1906). In the years following her marriage, Aline Bernstein focused mostly on portrait painting, but she also started working at the Henry Street Settlement as a backstage volunteer on productions and pageants presented by her friends the Lewisohn sisters. Alice (1884–1972) and IRENE LEWISOHN were wealthy young women who started the Neighborhood Playhouse in an attempt to bring the European "art theatre" movement to America. Between 1915 and 1924, Bernstein served her apprenticeship at the playhouse, designing and executing costumes for at least fifteen plays. By 1924 she had also begun working part-time for the Theatre Guild.

That year she turned out her first significant designs—for *The Little Clay Cart* at the Neighborhood Playhouse. This production of the ancient Indian classic marked Bernstein's emergence as a major designer of sets and costumes. She captured a simplicity and beauty in her unified visual treatment that was based on the Rajput style of miniature painting.

In the summer of 1925 Bernstein met the writer Thomas Wolfe (1900–1938), twenty years her junior, and began an affair which lasted more than five years. She urged Wolfe to abandon his awkward attempts at playwriting, and, while they were touring Europe together, he began work on his first novel, *Look Home-*

ward, Angel (1929). Bernstein also became his financial benefactor and his unofficial agent, eventually finding a publisher for his work. Esther Jack, a major character in Wolfe's *The Web and the Rock* (1939) and *You Can't Go Home Again* (1940), is based essentially on Bernstein. She in turn wrote and published novels and short stories, some of which—the final story in the volume *Three Blue Suits* (1933) and the novel *The Journey Down* (1938)—were based on Wolfe's early days in New York City. Bernstein was very disturbed when the relationship with Wolfe ended; her marriage, however, survived.

Meanwhile Bernstein's career as a theatrical designer progressed rapidly. At the Neighborhood Playhouse in the fall of 1925 she designed the settings and costumes for the first American production of *The Dybbuk*. Her famous expressionistic designs for this classic Jewish folktale were more and more grotesquely distorted as the play reached its climax with a leap into mysticism. Some of her satiric designs for the Grand Street Follies, an annual parody of the Broadway season performed from 1924 through 1929 at the Neighborhood Playhouse, were strikingly apt in their burlesque of the visual styles of various designers.

In early 1928 Bernstein began working with Eva Le Gallienne at her Civic Repertory Theatre. During the next four years she was the resident designer for the Civic Repertory company, turning out an average of five shows each year. Her major contribution at the Civic was the unit setting she created for the later seasons. She designed a basic neutral skeleton frame which, with the addition of dozens of different inserts, doors, and windows, could accommodate almost any dramatic need. This concept of design allowed the Civic to save large sums of money during the early years of the depression and to continue to run in repertory fashion.

Both the Neighborhood Playhouse and the Civic Repertory Theatre had closed by 1934, but Bernstein continued working with the Theatre Guild and other independent producers. One such production matched her with playwright Lillian Hellman and director Herman Shumlin, for Hellman's first play, *The Children's Hour* (1934). The three worked together again on four other Hellman scripts between 1934 and 1949.

After a brief stint in Hollywood, designing two RKO spectaculars for the 1935 season (*She* and *The Last Days of Pompeii*), Bernstein gladly returned to New York to design such well-known plays as Hellman's *The Little Foxes* (1939, sets only), *The Male Animal*, by James

Thurber and Elliott Nugent (1940, sets only), and Samuel Taylor's *The Happy Time* (1950). From 1943 to 1949 she was an instructor in costume design and consultant to the Experimental Theatre at Vassar College. At the age of seventy, Bernstein won an Antoinette Perry Award for her costume designs for the opera *Regina* (1949); she also designed three other shows that season. Her last project as a designer for the stage was the creation of the costumes for the off-Broadway production of *The World of Sholom Aleichem* in 1953.

In addition to her long and stunning career as a theatrical designer, Aline Bernstein helped Irene Lewisohn to establish the Museum of Costume Art, which became the Costume Institute of the Metropolitan Museum of Art, a collection of authentic clothing from different periods and countries. She succeeded Lewisohn as president of the institute in 1944 and held that position until her death in New York in 1955. Bernstein's technical expertise and experience were of great importance in making the collection a valuable source for costume designers and scholars alike.

[A collection of Aline Bernstein's unpublished notebooks, drawings, and photographs is in the Billy Rose Theatre Coll., N.Y. Public Library. The William B. Wisdom Coll., Houghton Library, Harvard Univ., contains substantial correspondence between Bernstein and Wolfe, and some between Bernstein and numerous Wolfe scholars. In addition to the books mentioned, her publications include her autobiography, *An Actor's Daughter* (1941); *The Martha Washington Dollbook* (1945); the novel *Miss Condon* (1947); *Masterpieces of Women's Costume of the 18th and 19th Centuries* (1959); "Scissors and Sense," *Theatre Arts Monthly*, Aug. 1925; "Off-Stage: A Harp String Breaks," *Vogue*, Dec. 1939; "In Production," *Atlantic Monthly*, Sept. 1940. A biography, *Aline*, by Carole Klein was published in 1979. Mike Barton, "Aline Bernstein: A History and Evaluation" (Ph.D. diss., Indiana Univ., 1971), has an extensive bibliography. Other sources of information about her life and career include Alice Lewisohn Crowley, *The Neighborhood Playhouse* (1959); Norris Houghton, "The Designer Sets the Stage: Aline Bernstein," *Theatre Arts*, Feb. 1937; Eva Le Gallienne, *At 33* (1934); Florence Von Wien, "Women Who Are Stage Designers," *Independent Woman*, May 1946; *Nat. Cyc. Am. Biog.*, XLVII, 598; and entries in the *Dict. Am. Biog.* on Wolfe (Supp. Two) and Bernstein (Supp. Five). John Skally Terry, ed., *Thomas Wolfe's Letters to His Mother Julia Elizabeth Wolfe* (1943), provides some evidence that Bernstein attempted suicide in March 1931. An obituary appeared in the *N.Y. Times*, Sept. 8, 1955. An excellent photograph is in *Theatre Arts*, Feb. 1951. Marriage certificate supplied by Office of the City Clerk, City of N.Y.]

MIKE A. BARTON

BETHUNE, Mary McLeod, July 10, 1875–May 18, 1955. Educator, civil rights reformer, federal government official.

Mary McLeod Bethune was the most influential black woman in the United States through more than three decades. Her remarkable skills as a leader and her ability as an orator enabled her to translate the problems of Afro-Americans into terms that brought national attention. Although she favored conciliation over confrontation, she persisted throughout her career in seeking for all blacks, but especially for black women, the opportunity for education and for the chance to emerge from the social and political invisibility that kept them oppressed. Battling for the creation of united Afro-American political and organizational efforts, she pushed blacks to a keener recognition of the federal government's potential to advance the race, and to an awareness that they should work to influence government policies.

Born near Mayesville, S.C., Mary McLeod was the fifteenth of seventeen children of Sam and Patsy (McIntosh) McLeod. Her parents were slaves freed as a result of the Civil War. After the war, they farmed and did domestic work. Even with freedom, the McLeods had few material or cultural advantages, a situation aggravated during the post-Reconstruction era as whites gained political control of the overwhelmingly black Sumter County. Yet, in 1871 they had begun purchasing land where they built a cabin and grew mostly corn and cotton. Her family recognized and nurtured Mary's abilities as a leader and inspired her to work hard and believe in Christian teachings.

Mary McLeod's schooling began at a small black mission school near Mayesville. She quickly mastered its offerings and with the help of a scholarship went in 1888 to Scotia Seminary (later Barber-Scotia College) in Concord, N.C., a Presbyterian school for black girls that emphasized religion and industrial education. The school was conducted by a faculty of both blacks and whites, enabling Mary McLeod to develop greater confidence in both racial groups. She took the normal and scientific course which qualified her to teach, and graduated in 1894. In July of that year, again through a scholarship, she entered the Bible Institute for Home and Foreign Missions (later the Moody Bible Institute) in Chicago to prepare for a career as a missionary to Africa. After a year's stay, she applied to the Presbyterian Mission Board for an assignment only to learn that it had no openings in Africa for black missionaries.

Mary McLeod went instead to teach at the Haines Normal and Industrial Institute in

Augusta, Ga. There she met LUCY LANEY, the dynamic black founder and principal of the school, who became McLeod's model for serving others. After a year, she returned to South Carolina to teach at Kindell Institute in Sumter, where she met Albertus Bethune, five years her senior, formerly a teacher but then a menswear salesman. They were married in May 1898 and moved to Savannah to further his business career. Their only child, Albert McLeod Bethune, was born in 1899. Later that year the family moved again, as Mary McLeod Bethune went to Palatka, Fla., to open a Presbyterian mission school. Albertus Bethune did not share his wife's missionary ardor, however. Their marriage foundered and they separated; Albertus Bethune died in 1918.

After five years in Palatka, Mary Bethune resettled in Daytona Beach, Fla., to establish a school for girls patterned after Scotia Seminary. Daytona had a rapidly increasing black population for whom public education was not available; it also had a large number of wealthy northern whites who might be called on to support a school. Beginning with only $1.50, Bethune collected dry goods boxes for benches, begged for other essentials, and in October 1904 opened her school in a rented house with six students, five little girls and her own son. With Bethune's business skills and the assistance of much of the black community and of some influential whites, the school's growth was phenomenal.

Mary Bethune's powerful personality and indomitable energy pervaded all aspects of her well-administered school. A deeply religious person, she did all she could for the school and trusted in God to promote its development. Like most other black schools of the period, the Daytona Normal and Industrial Institute stressed religion and industrial education; emphasis was placed on the production and handling of food to meet the school's needs and to provide income. But Bethune also championed the need for broader educational, social, and political opportunities for blacks. After World War I, she devoted increased attention to the high school program and to encouraging ambitious students to attend college. In 1920, underlining her belief in the importance of black participation in all aspects of American life, she led a successful black voter registration drive for recently enfranchised women, despite threats from the terrorist Ku Klux Klan. Well aware of her own worth, she wanted her students and other black women to transcend society's barriers and to develop "Self-Control, Self-Respect, Self-Reliance and Race Pride."

The Daytona Institute was also deeply involved in the life of the local black community through a variety of programs, including celebrated Sunday afternoon community meetings which brought black and white visitors to the campus. In 1911 Bethune established under the school's sponsorship a much-needed hospital for blacks in Daytona; the school maintained it until 1927 when it was taken over by the city. Her skills as an administrator were reflected in the school's expansion. In less than twenty years the Daytona Normal and Industrial Institute for girls acquired twenty acres and had an attractive campus with eight buildings and a farm. In 1923, the school employed a faculty and staff of 25 for a student body of 300 girls. Although most were in the elementary grades, the secondary and teacher-training programs were growing.

Bethune's next step was to transform Daytona Institute into a college. In 1923 she won the crucial sponsorship of the Board of Education for Negroes of the Methodist Episcopal church in her drive to make this change. The board merged the school with Cookman Institute of Jacksonville, thus making it coeducational. Although Bethune's deepest interest was the education and development of women, she was flexible enough to accept the new arrangement and reoriented the curriculum. In 1929 the institution was officially renamed Bethune-Cookman College. Three years later it was recognized by the regional accreditation agency as a standard junior college and in 1936 the high school department was discontinued. In 1943, the college conferred degrees in teacher education upon its first four-year graduates.

Mary McLeod Bethune maintained firm personal control over the college until June 1936 when she began a second career with the federal government in Washington, D.C. She continued as president of Bethune-Cookman until December 1942, however, reflecting a tendency to dominate that also marked other areas of her life. As a college president, she took on the enormous task of raising funds. The college had almost no endowment, so Bethune had to solicit financial support from whites. Traveling through both the south and the north to woo potential donors, she used her talent as a singer to present Negro songs and her even greater talent as an orator to tell her life's story.

Bethune sometimes suppressed her outrage at racist practices to appear positive and understanding and on occasion even minimized the overwhelming segregation and discrimination of the era, saying in a 1915 interview, for example, that Daytona offered "a fair measure of justice to the negro." Her basic approach, however, was to stress the identity of interest between the races and to a large extent she obtained funds from sympathetic individuals through carefully cultivated personal relationships. In the early years of the depression the college was in severe financial need, but in April 1934, through Bethune's efforts, the General Education Board awarded the school a $55,000 grant.

While directing the school, Mary McLeod Bethune rose to national prominence through her work with the National Association of Colored Women (NACW). From 1917 to 1924 she served as president of the Florida Federation of Colored Women, which opened a home for "wayward" and delinquent girls in Ocala during these years. In 1920, she founded and became president of a regional association which developed into the Southeastern Federation of Colored Women. Four years later her work culminated in the presidency of NACW, an office regarded by many as the highest to which a black woman could then aspire. During her four years as head of the Association, she continued its commitment to a scholarship fund and to the preservation of the Frederick Douglass home in Washington, D.C., as a national memorial.

She also worked aggressively to project a positive image of black women to whites through her travels in the United States and abroad and through NACW affiliation with the National Council of Women. By her oratory and her example Mary McLeod Bethune inspired black women to greater levels of service. Most important, however, she strengthened the structure of the 10,000-member organization by revising the constitution, improving the Association's periodical, *National Notes,* and in other ways promoting greater communication between members. Through a strenuous financial campaign, she succeeded in establishing in Washington, D.C., the organization's first fixed headquarters, and employing its first paid executive secretary.

In December 1935, in New York City, Bethune created the National Council of Negro Women (NCNW), formed by uniting the major national black women's associations. Although she remained active in the NACW, she had come to believe that its member federations and clubs were too deeply involved in local matters and too much oriented toward self-help for the association to speak as the authoritative national voice that black women needed. Serving as president of the NCNW from its founding until December 1949, she focused the Council's activities on segregation and discrimination especially as they affected black women, on the cultivation of better international relationships through visitation programs and attendance at

international conferences, and on national liberal causes. She also represented the NCNW at the 1945 founding conference of the United Nations. To strengthen the organization, Bethune expanded the membership by creating chapters in major cities. She again established an impressive permanent headquarters in Washington, D.C., employed a full-time staff, and launched the *Aframerican Woman's Journal.*

Forceful and articulate, Bethune was a natural leader. She served as president of the National Association of Teachers in Colored Schools, vice president of the Commission on Interracial Cooperation, and president of the Association for the Study of Negro Life and History. Her support was important to the Southern Conference for Human Welfare, as well as to the National Urban League and the NAACP. Her greatest influence as a black leader came, however, through her role in the administration of President Franklin D. Roosevelt. It was she who primarily educated ELEANOR ROOSEVELT (whom Bethune had met through her NCNW work) on the problems of blacks in the United States. And, with the exception of NAACP executive secretary Walter White, she was the only black who then had access to the White House.

In August 1935, through Eleanor Roosevelt's influence, Bethune was appointed to the thirty-five-member National Advisory Committee to the National Youth Administration (NYA). The agency's primary purpose was to help young people both in and out of school to find work during the depression and later during the World War II defense effort. Bethune used her relatively minor advisory position as a springboard; in June 1936 she was put in charge of Negro affairs within the NYA and in January 1939 became director of the division of Negro affairs. Like a number of other blacks who entered the federal government as specialists on Negro problems during the New Deal, she was responsible for ensuring that an equitable share of her agency's program went to blacks. Although this ideal was generally unrealized, especially in terms of proportionate expenditures for black youth as compared to white, Bethune influenced the agency to adopt nondiscriminatory policies and to recognize special black needs. She persuaded the NYA to expand the office of Negro affairs at the national level, to employ black administrative assistants at the state level, and, when the agency adopted a regional structure in 1942, to employ regional Negro affairs representatives. Bethune also guided the NYA toward broadening Negro participation in the school aid program, where she succeeded in creating a special fund, administered through her office, for Negro graduate students and Negro colleges. In the training program for youth out of school, she pressed for opportunities for blacks to learn skilled trades and argued for programs to assist black youth in finding jobs. Though her demands generally went unheeded during the depression, her persistent efforts later resulted in the employment of some NYA-trained Negro youth in defense industries that had not previously hired blacks.

The aggressive and indefatigable Bethune did not limit her concern to the NYA, but effectively and self-confidently assumed the role of advocate to the government for all black interests. It was, she believed, her "sacred trust" to interpret to the administration "the dreams and the hopes and the problems of my long-suffering people."

Since blacks across the country hailed her as a charismatic leader and believed that she understood their problems, Bethune could speak with authority as an individual. But she knew, as a political leader, that she needed in addition a unified power base. Believing in the efficacy of widespread cooperative efforts among blacks—an important factor in the founding of the NCNW—in August 1936 she organized the Federal Council on Negro Affairs. Popularly called the black cabinet, the Council was an informal group of blacks in government who worked together to strengthen Negro support of the New Deal and to promote nondiscrimination in government facilities, greater opportunities for government jobs, and prevention of government actions potentially harmful to Negroes. The black cabinet met weekly at Bethune's home and she was its influential "mother superior" (Sitkoff, p. 81), urging that its energies be directed to the support of the emerging drive for civil rights. Bringing to the group her prestige and her power as dispenser of NYA funds to black communities, she strengthened its will and voice, and succeeded in creating a channel of communication between civil rights organizations and the national administration. In turn, the Federal Council increased attention in the black press and among blacks across the nation to the political process and to government opportunities for blacks. Bethune also drew on her national power and influence to gain government support for two important National Negro Conferences, in January 1937 and January 1939. Sponsored by the NYA and widely covered in the press, these conferences spotlighted the plight of blacks in the United States and provided a forum through which blacks could make policy recommendations to the government.

Backed by the NCNW, the Federal Council, and the National Conferences, all of which she dominated, Bethune personally urged President Roosevelt to advance civil rights and continually appealed to Eleanor Roosevelt to promote Negro interests. She apparently concentrated, although with indifferent success, on trying to have blacks appointed to top level jobs, believing that this was an essential step toward elevating the Negro people. Outside the NYA, she was generally able to secure only particular exceptions to common discriminatory policies and procedures.

Bethune also worked for civil rights reform outside government channels. She marched and picketed businesses in Washington that refused to hire blacks, spoke and demonstrated in support of the drives to free the nine defendants in the Scottsboro case and to gain rights for black sharecroppers in the south, and was a regular and effective speaker at conferences of the NAACP and other civil rights organizations. Speaking to white organizations, she often cultivated a down-home style that attracted listeners: "You white folks have long been eating the white meat of the chicken. We Negroes are now ready for some of the white meat instead of the dark meat" (quoted in Ross, p. 5).

In addition, Bethune had to represent the administration to her race. Traveling throughout the country, she cast the New Deal and black participation in it in the most favorable light possible. With the coming of World War II, she exhorted blacks to forget "traditional customs of social standing, caste, and privilege" in order to unite with their fellow Americans to win the war. She hailed the president's executive order 8802 (1941) banning racial discrimination in government and defense industries. Personally loyal to the Roosevelts, she separated Franklin Roosevelt in her mind from the Democratic party, especially its flagrantly racist southern wing, and clung fervently to his idealism. She was even more devoted to the president's wife, who supported Bethune's national activities and her college, and led others in the administration to solicit her counsel on race-related issues.

Mary McLeod Bethune left government when the NYA ceased operation in 1944; she resigned as president of the NCNW in 1949 to go into retirement at her home in Daytona Beach, which she transformed into an educational foundation. She remained a popular public figure, receiving many honors as a black leader and in January 1952 traveling to Liberia as a United States representative to the second inaugural of President William Tubman. In April of that year, the Board of Education of Englewood, N.J., canceled her engagement to speak in a public school because some whites had branded her a communist. Undaunted, she continued to champion democratic values and faith in the American creed until she died in 1955 from a heart attack at her home. She was buried on the campus of Bethune-Cookman College.

Using a style of leadership characterized by negotiation and cooperation with white leaders, Mary McLeod Bethune struggled for Negro equality in an era when there was no national commitment to improve the inferior status and material condition of blacks in American life. Her career has been compared to that of Booker T. Washington; like his, her public views were sensitively attuned to the racial climate of the times and her ever-increasing advocacy of Negro equality reflected the gradual improvement of race relations.

Though she tended to overpower those about her and on occasion to gloss over unpleasant truths in the interest of political harmony, Bethune was a dazzling and magnetic personality. She had a keen understanding of human behavior, the ability to inspire others by her words, and the facility to adapt to changing times. As one of the most influential black leaders of her day, and as the most prominent black woman, she received many honors and awards. Blacks and whites, both the famous and the obscure, respected and honored her as the personification of achievement and dignity.

[The Mary McLeod Bethune Papers at the Bethune Fdn., Bethune-Cookman College, Daytona Beach, Fla., include papers dating from about 1915 to 1955 dealing with the varied aspects of Bethune's life, and photographs. A smaller and more narrowly focused group of Bethune's papers are located at the Amistad Research Center, Dillard University, New Orleans. Bethune's activities in black women's organizations are recorded in the Mary Church Terrell Papers at the Library of Congress, and in the Nat. Archives for Black Women's History, NCNW, Washington, D.C. Papers relating to Bethune's federal government work are in the NYA records, Record Group 119, Nat. Archives, and in the Eleanor Roosevelt Papers at the Franklin D. Roosevelt Library, Hyde Park, N.Y.; there are also limited references to her work in the Franklin D. Roosevelt Papers and in the Aubrey Williams Papers, both at the Roosevelt Library. An extensive annotated bibliography can be found in Dolores C. Leffall and Janet L. Sims, "Mary McLeod Bethune—The Educator," *Jour. Negro Education*, Summer 1976, pp. 342–59. Representative of Bethune's writings are: "I'll Never Turn Back No More," *Opportunity*, Nov. 1938, pp. 324–26; "Certain Unalienable Rights," in Rayford Logan, ed., *What the Negro Wants* (1944), pp. 248–58; "My Secret Talks with FDR," *Ebony*, April 1949, pp. 42–51; "The Negro in Retrospect and Prospect," *Jour. Negro Hist.*, Jan. 1950, pp. 9–19; and most notably, "My Last Will and Testament," *Ebony*, Aug. 1955, pp. 105–10. She also wrote a weekly column for the *Pittsburgh Courier* in the late 1930s and for the

Chicago Defender in the late 1940s and early 1950s. Bethune has been the subject of three idealized biographies: Catherine Owens Peare, *Mary McLeod Bethune* (1951); Emma Gelders Sterne, *Mary McLeod Bethune* (1957); and Rackham Holt, *Mary McLeod Bethune: A Biography* (1964). Important accounts of Bethune's school include: Helen W. Ludlow, "The Bethune School," *Southern Workman*, March 1912, pp. 144–54; Clara Stillman, "A Tourist in Florida," *The Crisis*, Feb. 1924, pp. 171–74; Sadie Iola Daniel, *Women Builders* (1931), pp. 79–106; James P. Brawley, *Two Centuries of Methodist Concern: Bondage, Freedom and Education of Black People* (1974); and Florence L. Roane, "A Cultural History of Professional Teacher Education at Bethune-Cookman College" (Ed.D. diss., Boston Univ., 1965). For Bethune's leadership in the NACW see: Elizabeth Lindsay Davis, *Lifting as They Climb* (1937) and *National Notes*, 1913–35, scattered issues of which are located at the Tuskegee (Ala.) Inst. Library. The founding of the NCNW is reviewed in the Council's *Women United: Souvenir Year Book* (1951). The major studies of Bethune's government career are: B. Joyce Ross, "Mary McLeod Bethune and the National Youth Administration: A Case Study of Power Relationships in the Black Cabinet of Franklin D. Roosevelt," *Jour. Negro Hist.*, Jan. 1975, pp. 1–28; and Elaine M. Smith, "Mary McLeod Bethune and the National Youth Administration," in Mabel E. Deutrich and Virginia C. Purdy, eds., *Clio Was a Woman: Studies in the History of American Women* (1979). See also Harvard Sitkoff, *A New Deal for Blacks* (1978) and the entry on Bethune in *Dict. Am. Biog.*, Supp. Five. De Witt Dykes provided information on the death certificates of Patsy McLeod and Albertus Bethune, the birth certificate of Albert McLeod Bethune, and other documentation. A death certificate was provided by the Fla. Dept. of Health and Rehabilitative Services.]

ELAINE M. SMITH

BLAINE, Anita Eugénie McCormick, July 4, 1866–Feb. 12, 1954. Philanthropist.

Through wide-ranging and often adventurous philanthropy in education, social welfare, and the cause of world peace, Anita Blaine carried forward through her long life the tradition of Progressive reform. She was born in Manchester, Vt., the fourth of seven children (five of whom survived) and the second of three daughters of Cyrus Hall and NETTIE FOWLER MCCORMICK. Cyrus McCormick, of Scots-Irish descent, achieved national prominence as the inventor and manufacturer of the reaper and was known as well for his philanthropies. Nancy Marie Fowler (later called Nettie), the daughter of a storekeeper and small manufacturer of English descent, attended several seminaries before her 1858 marriage to Cyrus McCormick;

she became a well-known philanthropist and businesswoman.

Anita McCormick was schooled by tutors and governesses in France, New York City, and Chicago because of her father's business-related travels. She graduated from the Kirkland School in Chicago in 1884. She was somewhat introspective and given to critical self-examination, a trait reinforced by her strict Presbyterian upbringing. From her mother she absorbed a strong sense of Christian stewardship and duty, tempered by a love of nature, and an interest in education and social welfare.

On Sept. 26, 1889, she married Emmons Blaine, a lawyer and businessman and the son of James G. Blaine, who was defeated by Grover Cleveland in the presidential election of 1884. A son, Emmons Jr., was born in 1890. After the death of her husband two years later, she devoted her attention to the education of her son and to philanthropic activities.

Like her parents, Anita Blaine believed that personal wealth was a trust to be used for the good of others. The McCormicks gave extensively to religious organizations and were preoccupied with rural life and activities. In contrast Anita Blaine, who developed some antipathy toward religious organizations, oriented her philanthropy toward secular concerns, especially toward the solution of urban problems. Her concerns and methods reflected those of her era. Whereas her mother favored an individualistic approach to giving, she supported the trend toward scientific investigation and more organized philanthropy and served as a member of many charity societies, committees, and boards. Nettie McCormick's beliefs in stewardship and humanitarianism were transmuted in Anita Blaine into the Progressive ideals of organization and group cooperation. Convinced that the world's wealth was unjustly distributed and repelled by the idea of competition, she suggested in a 1910 speech that a portion of the national wealth be allocated to a public organization for more equitable administration.

Anita Blaine's concern for her son's educational future broadened her own interests. In 1897 she enrolled him in the laboratory school of the Cook County (subsequently the Chicago) Normal School, headed by the noted Progressive educator Francis W. Parker. She shared Parker's beliefs in the child-centered approach, in learning by doing, in the school as a preparation for future life, and in the value of nature study. In 1899 she founded the Chicago Institute, with Parker as head, to train teachers and educate children according to Progressive methods; the Institute was merged into the University of Chicago School of Education in 1901. In the same year Anita Blaine founded the Francis W. Parker School, to be directed by FLORA COOKE, one of Parker's most trusted followers. She contributed more than three million dollars to the school during her lifetime. Blaine was also a member of the Chicago Board of Education from 1905 to 1907, and served on its Juvenile Court and Truancy committees.

Increasingly concerned for the city's poor, Anita Blaine contributed to and participated in a number of social welfare organizations. In 1900, she and JANE ADDAMS formed the City Homes Association, which sought to investigate tenement conditions in Chicago; Blaine was appointed chairman of its tenement committee. She also served on the board of the Bureau of Charities and on the National Child Labor Committee. After 1912, she devoted her philanthropic activity less to social welfare groups and more to cases of individual need. Urban reform, she felt, had largely been accomplished.

After her son's death from influenza in 1918, Anita Blaine's philanthropic and organizational activities became the focus of her life. The entry of the United States into World War I had turned her attention to international concerns, and after the war she became an ardent advocate of world cooperation. She campaigned for American entry into the League of Nations and was a financial backer of the League of Nations Association until the late 1930s. She also promoted international cooperation through her involvement in the World Foundation and the World Citizens Association, of which she became vice chairman.

During the 1940s her activities became more political in nature. Despite the fact that her family had been Republican, she became a supporter of President Franklin D. Roosevelt, favored aid to Britain and France, and urged a declaration of war against Germany in May 1941. In 1943 she gave $100,000 to Madame Chiang Kai-shek for the aid of Chinese war orphans. A supporter of the 1945 San Francisco Conference and of the United Nations, in 1948 she contributed over one million dollars to establish the Foundation for World Government, which advocated the limitation of national sovereignty, the enforcement of world law, and the complete control of atomic development. During the 1948 election campaign Blaine backed the Progressive party and the candidacy of Henry Wallace. In the following years she made substantial contributions to two fledgling New York papers, *The Daily Compass*, which she hoped would popularize the idea of world government, and the more radical *National Guardian*. Blaine underwent an operation in December 1949 from which she never fully recovered; she remained in ill health until her death in Chicago from bronchial pneumonia in 1954.

In her later years, Anita Blaine seemed odd to some; she was also accused of being a radical and a socialist. A determined and vivacious woman, in some ways she was personally eccentric; she reportedly felt, for example, that big hats caused mental strain, and she refused to buy any hat that weighed more than four ounces. She was also very effective. During her lifetime, Anita Blaine's philanthropies totaled over ten million dollars; she willed another twenty million dollars (out of an estate of thirty-eight million dollars) to charitable causes, notably to the New World Foundation, for the improvement of education and social welfare. Her activities both reflected and stimulated the growth of the American reform tradition in the early twentieth century.

[Blaine's papers are in the McCormick Coll., State Hist. Soc. of Wis. They total 1,117 boxes and include letters, business papers, copies of her writings, diaries, and information relating to her estate and those of her husband and son. Papers of the latter two are also in the McCormick Coll. For a more extended description of the Blaine papers see Margaret R. Hafstad, ed., *Guide to the McCormick Collection of the State Historical Society of Wisconsin* (1973), pp. 28–38. The Chicago Hist. Soc. has some Blaine items, including several speeches made in her memory in 1955: "My Grandmother," by Nancy Blaine Harrison; "Mrs. Blaine and the Francis W. Parker School," by Charlotte Kuh; and "Mrs. Blaine —Citizen of the World," by Katharine Taylor. The Newberry Library, Chicago, has several unpublished articles on Blaine. See Gilbert A. Harrison, *A Timeless Affair: The Life of Anita McCormick Blaine* (1979) and *Dict. Am. Biog.*, Supp. Five. Brief references can be found in Charles O. Burgess, *Nettie Fowler McCormick: Profile of an American Philanthropist* (1962); Stella Virginia Roderick, *Nettie Fowler McCormick* (1956); and Jack K. Campbell, *Colonel Francis W. Parker: The Children's Crusader* (1967). See Cedric Belfrage and James Aronson, *Something to Guard: The Stormy Life of the National Guardian, 1948–1967* (1978), for an account of Blaine's involvement with that paper. Obituaries appeared in the *Chicago American* and *Chicago Daily Tribune*, Feb. 13, 14, 1954; *Chicago Daily News*, Feb. 13, 1954; *N.Y. Herald Tribune*, Feb. 14, 1954; *N.Y. Times*, Feb. 13, 1954; *Newsweek* and *Time*, both Feb. 22, 1954.]

                                                        BRUCE WHITE

BLAIR, Emily Jane Newell, Jan. 9, 1877–Aug. 3, 1951. Suffragist, feminist, Democratic party official, writer.

In 1910 Emily Newell Blair was a "contented" Missouri wife and mother; by 1924 she was vice president of the Democratic National Committee, its only woman national officer. Born in Joplin, Mo., she was the oldest daughter of James Patton and Anna Cynthia (Gray) Newell. After graduating from high school in Carthage, Mo., in 1894 she enrolled at the Woman's College of Baltimore (later Goucher College). Her father, a Civil War veteran, was a successful mortgage broker, but when he died there was not enough money for her to continue her education. Needed at home to help bring up and educate her younger brother and three sisters, she returned after one year in college. She attended classes at the University of Missouri but did not graduate, and she taught school.

On Dec. 24, 1900, Emily Newell married Harry Wallace Blair, a law student. He established a law practice in Carthage and they became the parents of a daughter, Harriet, and a son, Newell. She kept house, did some civic work and, because her husband was interested in politics, worked for candidates for county office. Although she enjoyed her husband and children she wanted to do something in addition, to move out "of the narrow confines into a larger sphere."

In 1909 Emily Newell Blair sold her first short story to a national magazine. Over the next few years her writing was published in *Cosmopolitan, Harper's Magazine, Woman's Home Companion,* and other magazines. With the money she earned she hired help for the house and children to free herself to write.

Around 1910, when the woman suffrage campaign was revived, Blair began her active career in politics. She saw the law that prevented women from voting as denying civil rights as well. A woman had "no property rights, no parental rights, practically no economic freedom, since professions, trades and business were closed to her," she later recalled (*Missouri Hist. Rev.*, April 1920). Determined to gain political power for women, she joined the Missouri Equal Suffrage Association, and in 1914 became press and publicity chairman and the first editor of the *Missouri Woman*, a monthly suffrage publication. A diminutive woman, Blair's gentle manner concealed a cool analytical mind and a strong will. She used her charm to win over the Missouri press, which to a large extent backed her cause. She also persuaded both the state Parent-Teachers Association and the Federation of Women's Clubs to endorse the *Missouri Woman* as their official organ, thus securing broad support.

Blair rose to national prominence during World War I. When the war broke out she became vice chairman of the Missouri Woman's Committee of the Council of National Defense, a preparedness agency. Her work was so effective that she was appointed to the executive committee of the council's national Woman's Committee. Based in Washington, and chaired by suffrage leader ANNA HOWARD SHAW, the committee was charged with providing "a direct and organized channel through which the government could convey to women its requests and directions for war work" (*Interpretative Report*, p. 18). Blair, who was in charge of news and publicity, learned about women's problems throughout the country and about the workings of national politics.

With her husband, who had served overseas during the war, Emily Newell Blair returned to Joplin in 1919. Her official history of the Woman's Committee, which appeared in 1920, emphasized the potential for political power among organized women and the role women could play in government when they had the vote. After the passage of the nineteenth amendment, Blair helped found the League of Women Voters in 1920 but then rejected it, feeling that nonpartisanship was not an effective use of the vote. Neither did she join the more militantly feminist National Woman's party. Blair believed there were only two ways for women to get political power: by holding office and by becoming effective in political organizations. She joined the Democrats and began to work for the party. In 1920 the Democratic party added one committeewoman from each state, doubling its National Committee. These women were appointed, not elected, however, and they had no voting power. Blair worked with others to put pressure on the party, and in 1921 women were elected to the National Committee and had the same votes as the men. Elected that year to represent Missouri, Emily Blair was soon chosen by the committee as national vice chairman with particular responsibility for organizing women voters and for women's activities. She worked hard: in the next two years she made 200 speeches in twenty-two states, organized more than 2,000 Democratic Women's Clubs, and built up regional training programs for women party workers. She was reelected to the Democratic National Committee in 1924 and chosen first vice president. Serving until 1928, she prepared a history of the Democratic party, an organization primer, and many leaflets. Blair also helped to found the Woman's National Democratic Club, serving as its secretary from 1922 to 1926 and as its president in 1928.

Reviewing the results of ten years of suffrage in a 1930 interview Blair concluded that women had accomplished little with the vote; they had neither solidarity nor power and, in fact, had slipped backwards. She wondered if it had been a mistake to join men in the existing parties, and noted that her acceptance of the argument that

women must work along party lines had led to nothing more than individual recognition for herself. She had not been able to create a position of power for other women. A "new feminism" was needed, Blair believed, to urge women to run for public office and to support them when they did.

Blair continued her writing career, focusing on books and the home as well as on feminist topics. She was associate editor of *Good Housekeeping* magazine from 1925 to 1933, and published a book on decorating, *The Creation of a Home*, in 1930. A novel, *A Woman of Courage*, appeared the following year. In 1933, when the Democrats regained the presidency, Blair returned with her husband to Washington where she was appointed to the Consumers' Advisory Board under the National Industrial Recovery Act, serving as its chairman in 1935. She then turned again to free-lance writing, but published little. Her last public office was a 1942 War Department appointment as chief of the women's interests section in the department's bureau of public relations. In 1944 Emily Blair suffered a stroke which incapacitated her; she died in Alexandria, Va., seven years later.

[There are a few letters in the Sue Shelton White Papers and some clippings in the Woman's *Rights* Coll., both at the Schlesinger Library, Radcliffe College. Blair's writings also include *The Woman's Committee, U.S. Council of Nat. Defense: An Interpretative Report* (1920); *Letters of a Contented Wife* (1931); "Are Women a Failure in Politics?" *Harper's Mag.*, Oct. 1925, pp. 513–22, and two articles in *The Woman's Journal*, "Why I Am Discouraged about Women in Politics," Jan. 1931, pp. 20–22, and "Putting Women into Politics," March 1931, pp. 14–15, 29. She wrote an introduction to the history of suffrage activity in Missouri in the *Missouri Hist. Rev.*, April–July 1920, which also contains an article by Mary Semple Scott, "The Missouri Woman," on Blair's suffrage work. An interview with Blair by Mary Carroll, "Wanted—A New Feminism," appeared in *Independent Woman*, Dec. 1930, pp. 499 and 544. For information on her life and activities see Ernestine Evans, "Women in the Washington Scene," *Century Mag.*, Aug. 1923, pp. 507–17; Anne Hard, "Emily Blair 'Politician,'" *Woman Citizen*, April 1926, pp. 15–16; and a profile in *Missouri Hist. Rev.*, Fall 1968. The entry in *Dict. Am. Biog.*, Supp. Five, is particularly useful. Obituaries appeared in the *N.Y. Times* and *Wash. Post*, Aug. 4, 1951; death record provided by Va. Dept. of Health.]

MARGOT JERRARD

BLANCHFIELD, Florence Aby, April 1, 1882–May 12, 1971. Nurse, military officer.

Florence Blanchfield, superintendent of the Army Nurse Corps and the first woman commissioned in the regular army, was born in Front Royal, Va., the second of three daughters and fourth of eight children of Mary Louvenia (Anderson) and Joseph Plunkett Blanchfield, a stonemason and cutter. Her father was of English and Irish ancestry; her mother's ancestors were German and French. Shortly after her birth the family moved to Oranda, Va. Florence attended public school in Walnut Springs, Va. (1889–98), and the Oranda Institute, a private school (1898–99).

Florence Blanchfield's mother practiced nursing, and her maternal grandfather and an uncle were physicians. All three Blanchfield daughters became trained nurses; the youngest, Ruth, later studied under Florence. In addition to the family orientation toward medicine, the illness and eventual death of a favorite brother influenced Florence Blanchfield's choice of career.

She graduated from South Side Hospital Training School for Nurses in Pittsburgh in 1906, and, while engaged as a private duty nurse, undertook postgraduate study in Baltimore at Dr. Howard Kelly's Sanatorium and at Johns Hopkins Hospital. She then held supervisory positions at Pittsburgh's South Side and Montefiore Hospitals, and served as superintendent at Suburban General Hospital in Bellevue, Pa. (1909–13). Determined to broaden her experience and knowledge of nursing, in 1913 Blanchfield joined the staff at Ancon Hospital, Panama Canal Zone. She returned aboard one of the first ships to sail through the newly opened locks. Turning to industrial nursing she became emergency surgical nurse at the United States Steel Corporation plant in Bessemer, Pa. (1914–15). Blanchfield briefly resumed her former position in Bellevue but resigned to join the Army Nurse Corps (ANC) in 1917, serving during World War I in Angers and at Camp Coetquidan, France. Although she returned once again to Bellevue in 1919, Blanchfield's wartime experiences drew her to a career in the military, which promised more opportunities for nurses. Having chafed under the orders of officers who knew little of nursing, she vowed to work toward gaining full military status for nurses.

Blanchfield reentered the ANC in 1920 and completed tours of duty in San Francisco, Washington, D.C., Michigan, Indiana, Georgia, the Philippines, and China. She joined the Surgeon General's staff in Washington in 1935, became lieutenant colonel in 1942, and was promoted to superintendent of the ANC in 1943, receiving the rank of colonel.

As superintendent, Colonel Blanchfield was an effective administrator who oversaw the dramatic increase in the number of nurses during World War II—from a few hundred to over 50,000. Among her innovations were the establishment of training schools to teach nurses military regulations, and the assignment of nurses to hospitals near the front lines to provide surgical nursing care. The Army Nurse Branch of Technical Information in the Surgeon General's Office, which she helped to create, informed the public about the work of army nurses and aided recruiting efforts. To gain a better understanding of nursing care and to oversee the welfare of the army nurses, Blanchfield toured extensively in war areas.

Florence Blanchfield's major interest and accomplishment was obtaining full military rank for nurses, for which she worked tirelessly with Congresswoman Frances Payne Bolton (1885–1977) and others. In 1944 temporary full military rank was granted. The Army–Navy Nurse Act of 1947 secured permanent status, and Blanchfield received the first regular army commission held by a woman in the United States.

In 1945 the army awarded Blanchfield the Distinguished Service Medal for "devotion to duty" and "administrative and executive ability of the highest order." She also received the Florence Nightingale Medal from the International Red Cross (1951) and West Virginia's Distinguished Service Medal (1963). In 1978 the army named the United States Army hospital under construction in Fort Campbell, Ky., in her honor.

In addition to writing articles on military nursing and participating in nursing associations, Blanchfield took courses in business, public speaking, English composition, and dressmaking. Her car provided a major interest and pleasure which prompted her to study automobile mechanics. An avid sports fan, she was also pleased when the army named a tennis trophy after her.

After Col. Blanchfield's retirement from the ANC in 1947, she traveled and worked with Mary W. Standlee on a manuscript history of the ANC. Asked in 1964 about her current interests, she replied: "They are the same as ever, an intense interest in the nursing service, its professional progress; the broadening educational field . . . together with the art of nursing." Blanchfield shared a home with a sister and brother-in-law in Washington, D.C., where she died in 1971 at Walter Reed General Hospital of atherosclerotic heart disease.

[The official records of the ANC are with those of the Surgeon General's Office, Record Group 112, Nat. Archives. Additional materials, including correspondence, speeches, memorabilia, and photographs, are in the Col. Florence A. Blanchfield Coll.,

Nursing Archives, Mugar Library, Boston Univ., and the U.S. Army Center of Military Hist., Washington, D.C. Her writings include "The Needs of the Army Nurse Corps," *Am. Jour. Nursing*, Nov. 1943, pp. 991–92, and "New Status in Military Nursing," *Am. Jour. Nursing*, Sept. 1947, pp. 603–05. The main biographical sources are Doris W. Egge, "A Concise Biography of Colonel Florence Aby Blanchfield, ANC," prepared in 1974 for the U.S. Army Center of Military Hist.; Edith A. Aynes, "Colonel Florence A. Blanchfield," *Nursing Outlook*, Feb. 1959, pp. 78–81; and *Current Biog.*, 1943. Blanchfield was interviewed by Evelyn Dent for the Wash. *Star*, Feb. 23, 1964. Also helpful are Mary M. Roberts, *The Army Nurse Corps Yesterday and Today* (1957), and Edith A. Aynes, *From Nightingale to Eagle: An Army Nurse's History* (1973). An obituary appeared in the *Wash. Post*, May 14, 1971. Family information was provided by Florence Blanchfield's sister, Ruth Orndorff. Although almost all sources give her year of birth as 1884, a birth record provided by the Va. Dept. of Health confirms the 1882 date. A death certificate was supplied by D.C. Dept of Public Health.]

LINDA J. HENRY

BLOOR, Ella Reeve, July 8, 1862–Aug. 10, 1951. Radical, labor organizer, journalist, suffragist.

Ella Reeve Bloor was born on Staten Island, N.Y., to Harriet Amanda (Disbrow) and Charles Reeve; she was the oldest of ten children (three girls and seven boys). Her father's Dutch and English ancestors had settled on Staten Island in the eighteenth century; her mother's family, French and English in origin, had arrived in Connecticut in the seventeenth century. Ella grew up on Staten Island, and later in Bridgeton, N.J., where her parents enjoyed a certain social standing. Her father was a relatively prosperous owner of a drugstore there, and her mother was active in the community. After attending local public school, and then, briefly, the Ivy Hall Seminary, Ella was taught at home by her mother. When Harriet Reeve died in childbirth in 1879, Ella, as the oldest daughter, became responsible for tending her younger siblings.

Although her mother had intensely disliked intolerance and social pretense, Ella's parents—and especially her father—had tended toward conservative political and religious beliefs. Therefore, when Ella Reeve became interested in social and political reform in her teens she sought out her great-uncle, Dan Ware, an abolitionist, greenbacker, Unitarian, and freethinker, who introduced her to the works of the agnostic Robert Ingersoll. Ella Bloor later acknowledged her uncle's strong influence on her intellectual development.

At the age of nineteen, following her father's remarriage, Ella Reeve married Lucien Ware, Dan Ware's son. An aspiring lawyer, Ware had been a court stenographer at the trial of the Molly Maguires, radical miners accused of conspiracy. Over the next eleven years Ella Ware gave birth to six children: Pauline (b. 1882), Charles (b. 1883), Grace (b. 1885), Helen (b. 1887), Harold (b. 1889), and Hamilton Disbrow (b. 1892); Pauline and Charles died, on the same day, in 1886.

During these years, her associations with Quakers and Unitarians introduced her to the issues of women's equality and woman suffrage. She also became active in the Ethical Culture Society in Philadelphia, and in the Woman's Christian Temperance Union, serving as president of its branch in Woodbury, N.J., where the Wares had moved. Becoming interested in the labor movement, she organized Philadelphia streetcar workers in the early 1890s. Increasing tension between Lucien and Ella Ware over her political activities caused the marriage to deteriorate; a separation was followed by divorce in 1896.

For several years after the separation, Ella Ware enjoyed her independence and explored possible occupations. She took courses at the University of Pennsylvania, wrote two children's books, and contributed occasionally to newspapers. With her children, she lived in the utopian community of Arden, Del., which had been established by single-taxers and socialists. In 1897 she married Louis Cohen, a socialist associated with Daniel DeLeon, who later worked for the Socialist party. He was also a persistent but quite unsuccessful entrepreneur. After the birth of two children, Richard in 1898 and Carl in 1900, the couple separated in 1902 and later divorced.

Ella Cohen then embarked on her long and contentious career as a political activist. Her interest in improving the status of women continued throughout her life. She advocated communal sharing of basic housekeeping duties in a 1903 article for *Wilshire's Magazine,* and participated in both the 1913 Ohio referendum campaign for the woman suffrage amendment and the mass demonstration of suffragists in Washington, D.C., at the time of Woodrow Wilson's inauguration. Initially a supporter of the National Woman's party, she later opposed the organization and its Equal Rights Amendment as antilabor. She also fought for women's interests in the Socialist and Communist parties.

But it was to labor organizing and left-wing politics that she most fully devoted her energies and talents. Eugene Debs, whom she met in

1895, had convinced her of the necessity for socialism. After working for a time with Daniel DeLeon's Socialist Labor party, Ella Cohen joined the Socialist party soon after its founding in 1901. In 1905 she moved to Connecticut, where she became a state organizer for the party and also wrote for the Waterbury (Conn.) *American*. A particularly blunt article on child labor practices in the state cost her this job.

In 1906 her friend Upton Sinclair, who had lived at Arden, persuaded Ella Cohen to investigate the Chicago meat-packing industry. She was to gather evidence for a government investigating commission to document the charges Sinclair had made against the industry in *The Jungle*. Richard Bloor, a young pottery worker and fellow socialist, went along to protect her. Sinclair, who feared that the public would be scandalized by an unmarried team of investigators, convinced her to publish her reports under the name Ella Bloor. She later denied any romantic attachment, but the reports became well known, and so did the reporter. Although the pair soon split up, she continued to use the name Bloor for the rest of her life.

After her Chicago trip, Ella Bloor spent the next dozen years organizing for the Socialist party and for various labor unions, including the United Cloth Hat and Cap Makers. A state organizer for the party in Connecticut, she also traveled frequently, visiting party locals in Ohio, West Virginia, and southern Illinois on one swing, rallying support for the strikers at Ludlow, Colo., and at Calumet, Mich., on others. Her efforts in the coal fields earned her honorary membership in the United Mine Workers of America. During this period she also ran for political office on the Socialist party ticket, first in Connecticut and later in New York.

Bloor joined those socialists who opposed World War I as imperialist, and came to the aid of individuals arrested for antiwar activities. She served as field organizer for the Workers' Defense Union, which, with ELIZABETH GURLEY FLYNN and others, she had formed to raise money and support for the legal defense of political prisoners and conscientious objectors. Denied the right to speak at a number of meetings, Bloor was slated for arrest during the postwar Red Scare; she managed to escape, at one point fleeing Worcester, Mass., leaving all her possessions behind.

In 1919 Ella Bloor—who had been disillusioned by the support of many Socialist party leaders for the war—participated in the formation of the Communist party. For the rest of her life she worked assiduously on its behalf.

As a trade union delegate to the Red International of Labor Unions conference in Moscow in 1921, she made her first visit to the Soviet Union. Four years later, at the age of sixty-three, Bloor set off on an exhausting cross-country tour for the *Daily Worker*. Hitchhiking from New York to San Francisco, she held recruiting and subscription meetings in several dozen cities along the way. Through the International Labor Defense, Bloor was also active in the unsuccessful campaign to free Nicola Sacco and Bartolomeo Vanzetti. Continuing her work in labor organizing as well, she appeared frequently in the coal fields, traveled to Gastonia, N.C., to raise support for arrested strikers, and participated in demonstrations of the unemployed as they began their hunger marches on Washington in the early 1930s.

By the 1930s Mother Bloor, as she had come to be called, was in considerable demand as a speaker; in her seventies, she still traveled extensively for the Communist party. She went to the Dakotas in 1930 to take charge of the party's election campaign and to win support for the United Farmers' League. There she met Andrew Omholt, a farmer and Communist candidate for Congress in North Dakota, who soon became her third husband. On another cross-country tour in 1936, she campaigned for the party's national candidates, and in the late 1930s worked in its organizing drives in eastern Pennsylvania. In 1937 she returned to the Soviet Union as an honored guest at the celebration of the twentieth anniversary of the October Revolution. Bloor undertook her last major campaign during World War II: on several multicity tours, she spoke at public rallies and private meetings, granted interviews, and made radio talks on the theme of "Win the War Against Fascism." In addition to serving the party as a speaker, Bloor was also a member of its Central Committee from 1932 to 1948.

Throughout her career, Bloor had to make a variety of arrangements for the care of her children. In the early years she sometimes took one or two with her on speaking tours, while the older children were on occasion placed in boarding schools. When the children were older, she kept in touch through a blizzard of letters, and saw them when her travels permitted; Bloor also occasionally took one or another granddaughter with her. While the children resented her absences, they supported her work and remained emotionally close to her; two sons also worked for the Communist party.

Always an activist, Ella Bloor had little interest in ideological debates. She served the Communist party as a perpetual and indefatigable organizer; her role was to build support, recruit members, and rally morale for the party's programs. Her singular objective seemed to be, as *Life* magazine described it, "to make life happier for the world's unfortunates." To this end she suffered over thirty arrests—one at the age of seventy-two for assault and inciting to riot—innumerable threats of physical violence, and frequent harassment by police and vigilantes.

In 1937 Ella Bloor retired to eastern Pennsylvania; soon after, she and Andrew Omholt acquired a working apple farm near Coopersburg. She frequently noted how much she liked "her first real home." At the age of eighty-nine, she died of a stroke in a convalescent home in Richlandtown, Pa.

[Ella Bloor's personal papers, temporarily stored at Hollins College, contain approximately 2,000 personal letters, transcripts of speeches, programs, clippings, photographs, and personal souvenirs. Her children's books are *Three Little Lovers of Nature* (1895) and *Talks about Authors and Their Works* (1899). Much information is contained in Bloor's autobiography, *We Are Many* (1940), although it is occasionally unreliable. Ann Barton's *Mother Bloor: The Spirit of '76,* a pamphlet published in 1937, provides a brief biographical account. Elizabeth Gurley Flynn writes of Bloor's work and character in her autobiography, *The Rebel Girl* (1973), and in *Daughters of America: Ella Reeve Bloor and Anita Whitney* (1942). There are references to Bloor in *The Reminiscences of Charles E. Taylor* in the Oral History Collection, Columbia Univ. See also *Dict. Am. Biog.,* Supp. Five. Bloor's Socialist party activities are mentioned in James Weinstein, *The Decline of Socialism in America, 1912–1925* (1967). Her Communist party experiences are referred to in Theodore Draper, *The Roots of American Communism* (1957), and *American Communism and Soviet Russia* (1960), and in Joseph Starobin, *American Communism in Crisis, 1943–1957* (1972). William Z. Foster, *History of the Communist Party of the U.S.* (1952), notes Bloor's assertion of women's rights within the party. Upton Sinclair's *Autobiography* (1962) speaks of her role in investigating conditions in meat-packing plants. Radical newspapers such as the *N.Y. Call,* the *Daily Worker,* and *Farmers Nat. Weekly* chronicle her travels and labors. *Life,* July 26, 1937, contains a good photograph and brief assessment of her activities. Additional information for this article was obtained from FBI documents released under provisions of the Freedom of Information Act and from interviews with Bloor's contemporaries. Information on the number of children in the Reeve family comes from *Genealogy of the Descendants of Joseph Ware* (1891; rev. 1922). An obituary appeared in the *N.Y. Times,* Aug. 11, 1951; death record provided by Pa. Dept. of Health.]

THOMAS L. EDWARDS
RICHARD C. EDWARDS

BLUNT, Katharine, May 28, 1876–July 29, 1954. College administrator, home economics educator, nutritionist.

Katharine Blunt was born in Philadelphia, the first of three daughters of Stanhope English and Fanny (Smyth) Blunt. Her father, a distinguished professional soldier then stationed at the Frankford Arsenal, was an expert in gunnery and small arms who retired as a full colonel after serving as commander of the Rock Island (Ill.) Arsenal and the Springfield (Mass.) Armory. He spent part of his early career as an instructor at West Point.

Until Katharine Blunt became determined to attend college, none of the women of her comfortable, upper-middle-class family had aspired beyond finishing school. Blunt attended the Porter School in Springfield, Mass., and in 1894 entered Vassar College, from which she received her A.B. in 1898. After graduation, Blunt spent four years at home at the urging of her family, doing church and civic work, before resuming her education at the Massachusetts Institute of Technology in 1902. The following year she took the first of two appointments at Vassar, serving as an assistant in chemistry. She left Vassar in 1905 for further scientific training at the University of Chicago, where she received her Ph.D. in organic chemistry in 1907. That same year Blunt accepted the post of instructor in chemistry in the domestic science department at Pratt Institute in Brooklyn, N.Y. Returning to Vassar in 1908, she remained there as instructor in chemistry until 1913, when she entered the department of home economics at the University of Chicago as assistant professor. She was named associate professor in 1918, when she began serving informally as the department chairman; she became full professor and official chairman of the department in 1925.

During Blunt's tenure, the department grew to seventeen staff members and produced many outstanding researchers, administrators, and nutritionists. Concerned with the importance of establishing home economics as a profession, she worked to gain acceptance of home economics as an appropriate subject of instruction and to plan a scientific curriculum for training professionals. In a 1928 tribute the American Home Economics Association observed that her administration had enhanced the quality of graduate work in the field, and that Blunt's own devotion to research had provided an invaluable example to students. Her major research field was nutrition, and she did valuable work on calcium and phosphorus metabolism and on the basal metabolism of women and children.

In 1917 Blunt was drafted from her duties at

the university to work for the United States Department of Agriculture and the Food Administration as an expert on nutrition. For the war effort, she wrote pamphlets on food conservation and collaborated with Florence Powdermaker (1894–1966) to prepare food conservation lessons which were disseminated to colleges and later published as a textbook, *Food and the War* (1918).

Throughout this period of heavy administrative and public service commitments, Blunt continued to publish articles on food chemistry and nutrition in scholarly journals. Her work culminated in 1930 with the publication of *Ultra-Violet Light and Vitamin D in Nutrition,* a summary of research in the field, written with Ruth Cowan. The book was praised for its usefulness to both professional and lay readers concerned with public health and welfare. During these years Blunt also served as editor of the University of Chicago's Home Economics Series.

In September 1929, Katharine Blunt was named the third president of Connecticut College for Women, a four-year liberal arts college founded in 1911. The first woman to hold the post, she applied her administrative skills to enlarging the college's physical plant, increasing its financial resources, and upgrading its faculty. These improvements resulted in the institution's accreditation in 1932. A wealthy woman, Blunt was not only a skilled fund raiser, but personally generous to the college. When she retired in 1943, Connecticut College was on a sound financial basis and boasted twenty-one buildings, about 750 students, and a faculty of over 100. Recalled to the presidency in 1945, she retired again the following year.

A vigorous and gregarious person, Blunt was determined that education should prepare the college woman for a life of active public service and stimulate an interest in civic concerns. The college, she believed, should train women so that their desires for public service do not "evaporate into vague benevolence, but develop into well-considered action." She invited many outstanding women whose lives exemplified this ideal—among them JANE ADDAMS, ALICE HAMILTON, FRANCES PERKINS, and ELEANOR ROOSEVELT—to speak on the campus.

Blunt was active in many professional and civic organizations and served from 1924 to 1926 as president of the American Home Economics Association. She was on the Connecticut State Board of Education (1931–40), and devoted much time and interest to local groups in New London.

As a young woman, Katharine Blunt enjoyed the outdoors, went mountain climbing, and traveled widely. The love of travel persisted into old age, and she made trips to Turkey and Israel in her retirement. In her last years, Blunt suffered from progressive blindness, but was otherwise healthy until incapacitated in July 1954 by a broken hip. While in a New London hospital recovering from this injury, she died of a pulmonary embolism.

[Some letters and documents concerning Katharine Blunt's tenure at Conn. College are in the college archives in New London, Conn., along with some of her journal articles and several pictures. During her time at the Univ. of Chicago, Blunt's scholarly work was published regularly in professional journals, including the *Jour. Biological Chemistry* and the *Jour. Home Economics.* After she became president of Conn. College, her speeches appeared in a number of educational journals; for example, see the *Jour. Assoc. of Am. Univ. Women,* Oct. 1938. A brief biography of Blunt by Gertrude Noyes appeared in *Conn. Teacher,* Jan. 1950. There are substantial entries in *Current Biog.,* 1946, and *Nat. Cyc. Am. Biog.,* B, 385. References to her personality occur in Irene Nye, comp., *Chapters in the History of Connecticut College* (1943). On her Chicago career see Marie Dye, *Home Economics at the University of Chicago 1892–1956* (1972), and *Home Economists: Portraits and Brief Biographies of Women Prominent in the Home Economics Movement in the United States* (1929). Obituaries appeared in the *N.Y. Times,* July 30, 1954, and *Jour. Home Economics,* Sept. 1954. Personal information for this article was obtained from Gertrude Noyes and Louise Potter. Death certificate was provided by Conn. Dept. of Health.]

JANICE LAW TRECKER

BOGAN, Louise, Aug. 11, 1897–Feb. 4, 1970. Poet, critic.

Louise Bogan was born in Livermore Falls, Maine, the second child and only daughter of Mary Helen (Shields) and Daniel Joseph Bogan. Both parents were of Irish descent. Her paternal grandfather left Londonderry as a boy to become a captain of sailing vessels out of Portland Harbor, Maine, and her mother's people, to whom the poet felt she owed her Celtic gift for language and her remarkable energy, came from Dublin.

Louise Bogan spent her childhood in New Hampshire and Massachusetts milltowns, where her father held various white-collar jobs in paper companies. She learned to read at the relatively late age of eight, finding refuge from her family's insular and troubled existence in *Grimm's Fairy Tales* and the adventure stories belonging to her older brother Charles, who was killed in World War I. As described in Bogan's journals, her mother was a beautiful, tempestuous, unhappy woman, who quarreled with her husband and on occasion disrupted the family with unexplained absences which were particularly hard on her daughter. During one such absence, in 1907, Bogan was sent as a boarding student to Mount St. Mary's Academy in Manchester, N.H., where she conceived the ambition of becoming an opera singer. In March 1909, the Bogan family, now reunited, moved from Ballardvale, Mass., to Boston. The city's cultural advantages and the rigorous classical education she received at the Girls' Latin School (1910–15) soon awakened Bogan to the difference between provincial life and high civilization. But she had entered an alien world as well, where "it was borne in upon me, all during my adolescence, that I was a 'Mick,' no matter what my other faults or virtues might be." From this realization came her lifelong antipathy to snobbery and pretension.

At the age of fourteen, Louise Bogan began to write verse; by seventeen, she had mastered the essentials of English versification and developed an elegant prose style. Like the young T. S. Eliot, Bogan was especially influenced by Arthur Symons's *The Symbolist Movement.*

Upon graduation from high school, Bogan enrolled for a year (1915–16) at Boston University. Although she published a number of apprentice poems in the *Boston University Beacon,* she was finding her home life oppressive, and, to break away, married a young army officer, Curt Alexander, in September 1916. She accompanied him to the Panama Canal Zone, where, in October 1917, she gave birth to her only child, a daughter, Mathilde. She also published her first mature poems in 1917, in *Others,* a magazine devoted to experimental verse. By the time Curt Alexander died in 1920, Bogan had been living alone in New York for at least a year; by 1921, her poems had begun to appear in *The New Republic* and other magazines.

After a year in Vienna (1922), she published her first book, *Body of This Death* (1923). The volume received considerable critical acclaim, and established Louise Bogan as one of the foremost lyric poets of her generation. Bogan relied on her mother for help in caring for her child, while she struggled to make a living, working in a bookstore, and later, through her friend Margaret Mead (1901–1978), finding a cataloging job at Columbia University.

In July 1925, Louise Bogan married Raymond Holden, poet and former Princeton classmate of Bogan's good friend, the critic Edmund Wilson. The couple spent nearly a year in Santa Fe, N.M., for reasons of Holden's health, and then bought a fruit farm in Hillsdale, N.Y., where

the subsequently peaceful months found issue in Bogan's second book, *Dark Summer* (1929). Containing her two longest poems, "The Flume" and "Summer Wish," as well as such lyrics as "Simple Autumnal" and "Come, Break with Time," the collection was marked by a formal perfection which demanded comparison "with the best songs of the sixteenth and seventeenth centuries" (Winters, 247).

On Dec. 26, 1929, a fire destroyed the Hillsdale house, and with it the books, letters, and manuscripts gathered over the previous decade. Determined to start anew, Bogan and Holden went back to New York early in 1930, but Bogan soon began to show signs of discouragement and exhaustion. In March 1931 she wrote her first poetry review for *The New Yorker,* beginning her thirty-eight-year association with the magazine, but she soon suffered an emotional collapse. With the benefit of psychiatric attention, she began to regain strength, exorcising despair and unsealing the past in a series of superb prose memoirs, "Journey Around My Room," "Dove and Serpent," and "Letdown," published in *The New Yorker* in 1933 and 1934.

Awarded a Guggenheim fellowship, Louise Bogan traveled through Italy, France, and Austria in the spring and summer of 1933, hoping to find new bearings as a poet. She came back to New York to be confronted with the failure of her marriage, as Raymond Holden had become involved with another woman. His betrayal opened the psychic wounds inflicted during her childhood, and once again she suffered an emotional collapse. Bogan emerged from this ordeal a changed woman, however, and the poems published in *The Sleeping Fury* (1937) bear witness to her hard-won liberation from rage and despair. Discovering the poetry of Rainer Maria Rilke in 1935, Bogan embraced his belief in the necessity of openness to emotion and acceptance of oneself and one's past; from his principles of spiritual and artistic freedom she drew the vision of existence she henceforth brought to her work as both poet and critic.

Laboring so hard for autonomy and insight, Louise Bogan passionately opposed the 1930s tendency to bend art to political dogma and insisted that art's true source lay in private experience. Writing at the time of her mother's death in 1936, she asserted: "What we suffer, what we endure, what we muff, what we kill, what we miss, what we are guilty of, is done by us, as individuals." It was "a sin and a shame," she added, "to try to organize or dictate" emotions.

Evicted from her apartment in 1935, divorced

in 1937, responsible for the support of her father and the education of her daughter, Bogan faced difficulties with courage, humor, and an extreme devotion to responsibility. Writing to Edmund Wilson about the delay of a promised poem, she reminded him that she was "a housewife, as well as a writer; I have no one to sweep floors or get meals . . . All these tasks are very good for me, but they are tasks I never can allow to slip."

By 1940, Bogan's daughter was living on her own, though remaining good friends with her mother. Having faced her furies, Bogan was able to give free play to her spirit in the occasional and epigrammatic verse of *Poems and New Poems* (1941). She continued to write verse departments for *The New Yorker*, although for five years (1943–48) she did not write a poem. In 1945–46, she occupied the Chair in Poetry at the Library of Congress, and in 1948 began a new career as a teacher with visiting lectureships at the University of Washington and the University of Chicago. In the same year, she collaborated with her friend Elizabeth Mayer on translations of Goethe and Ernst Jünger; in later years she translated Valéry with May Sarton and Jules Renard with Elizabeth Roget.

In 1951, Bogan published a critical history, *Achievement in American Poetry, 1900–1950*, and in 1954, *Collected Poems, 1923–1953*, followed a year later by *Selected Criticism*. As a critic, Bogan was just, witty, and generous, both with poets of her own generation and with such younger talents as Richard Eberhart and Richard Wilbur. At her best as a correspondent, her letters to Theodore Roethke and May Sarton are models of insight into the problems of artistic growth. Those addressed to such friends as Rolfe Humphries, Edmund Wilson, and the scholar-critic Morton Dauwen Zabel show as well her gift for burlesque and parody.

From time to time in the 1950s and 1960s, Bogan worked on her memoirs, left unfinished at the time of her death, and published posthumously in *The New Yorker* (1978). Although poems were "given" to her rarely, she wrote the magnificent "Song for the Last Act," "March Twilight," and "Night" in these years. A visit to Boston in 1965 revived painful memories and precipitated her last severe depression, out of which came the three superb lyrics with which she closed her final collected edition, *The Blue Estuaries: Poems, 1923–1968* (1968). Living in increasing seclusion, Bogan never stopped working; she had only recently approved the text of her collected criticism, *A Poet's Alphabet* (1970), when she died in February 1970, alone

in her Washington Heights apartment, from a heart attack.

Although most often identified with the severe tradition of the seventeenth-century lyric, Louise Bogan's poetry was nourished by the technical discoveries and spiritual concerns of such modern masters as Hopkins, Yeats, Eliot, and Auden. With major gifts, she forged a perfect minor mode out of her unparalleled ear for rhythm, purity of diction, and variety of cadence and filled her meditative and dramatic lyrics with the seasons and terrain of her New England childhood, transformed into symbol by "memory and desire." She wrote about the divided heart and the deceiving mind which must face truth, and be chastised into peace, love, and a part in the unconscious life of the universe. In W. H. Auden's words, what is most impressive about Bogan's poems "is that unflinching courage with which she faced her problems, her determination never to surrender to self-pity, but to wrest beauty and joy out of dark places." Surviving her quarrel with the world, and such quarrels as she may have had with herself, she could look back, late in life, and say: "Ignorant, I took up my burden in the wilderness/ Wise with great wisdom, I shall lay it down upon flowers."

[The Louise Bogan Papers in the Amherst College Library contain correspondence, drafts of poems, short fiction, critical notes, journals, and notebooks. There is no biography; the author is preparing a critical volume with biographical foundations. For the most complete view to date see Ruth Limmer, ed., *What the Woman Lived: Selected Letters of Louise Bogan, 1920–1970* (1973), and "Louise Bogan: From the Journals of a Poet," *New Yorker*, Jan. 30, 1978. See also Bogan's reply to a questionnaire, "The Situation in American Writing: Seven Questions," *Partisan Rev.*, Fall 1936. There are two bibliographies, both incomplete: William Jay Smith, *Louise Bogan: A Woman's Words* (1970), and Jane Couchman, "Louise Bogan: A Bibliography of Primary and Secondary Materials, 1915–1975," in two parts, *Bull. of Bibliography* (1976). For critical assessments see Yvor Winters, "The Poetry of Louise Bogan," *New Republic*, Oct. 16, 1929, and W. H. Auden, "Louise Bogan," *Proc., Am. Acad. of Arts and Letters, Nat. Inst. of Arts and Letters* (1970). Obituaries appeared in the *New Yorker*, Feb. 14, 1970, and the *N.Y. Times*, Feb. 5, 1970. There are photographs of Bogan in Nancy Milford's review of *What the Woman Lived*, in *N.Y. Times Book Rev.*, Dec. 16, 1973. Information was also provided by Ruth Limmer, executor of the Bogan estate.]

ELIZABETH PERLMUTTER

BOK, Mary Louise Curtis. *See* ZIMBALIST, Mary Louise Curtis Bok.

BOOLE, Ella Alexander, July 26, 1858–March 13, 1952. Temperance leader.

Ella Boole, fifth president of the National Woman's Christian Temperance Union (WCTU), was born in Van Wert, Ohio, the oldest of three children and elder of two daughters of Rebecca (Alban) and Isaac Newton Alexander, a prominent lawyer. Both parents were natives of Ohio. A paternal great-grandfather migrated from Scotland to Virginia in the mid-eighteenth century; her mother's ancestors were English. Ella Alexander grew up in a scholarly, pious environment. From her father, who had edited a free-soil newspaper and during Reconstruction became an ardent advocate of the rights of freedmen, she acquired a lifelong belief in the power of law to effect reform. Her mother also provided a strong model of social responsibility.

A bright, serious student, Ella Alexander was educated in the public schools of Van Wert, then studied classics at the College of Wooster, where she excelled in natural science and developed a flair for public speaking. She earned an A.B. in 1878 and, also from Wooster, an A.M. in 1881. From 1878 until 1883 Alexander taught high school in Van Wert, conducted a Sunday school class at the First Presbyterian Church, and lectured at teachers' institutes. At one of these conferences she met William Hilliker Boole, a twice-widowed Methodist minister thirty-one years her senior. They were married July 3, 1883, and moved to William Boole's pastorate in Brooklyn, N.Y. They had one child, Florence Alexander (b. 1887); three daughters from William Boole's former marriages were also part of the family.

Influenced by her husband, an active prohibitionist and temperance orator, Ella Boole joined a local union of the WCTU in 1883. Displaying a talent for organizing new unions and for increasing membership, by 1891 she had become vice president of the New York state union. After her husband's death in 1896, income from her temperance work and speaking engagements, supplemented by an inheritance from her father, supported the family. In 1898 Boole was elected president of the New York WCTU, a position she held until 1925, except for six years during which she felt called to serve as corresponding secretary of the Woman's Board of Home Missions of the Presbyterian Church (1903–09).

During her tenure as state president, the New York union shifted from the tactic of collecting petitions to the practice of exerting pressure by writing legislators directly. Boole became an extremely skilled lobbyist and spoke frequently at hearings in Albany. In addition to temperance, she applied her energies to other issues she believed were of special concern to women, including protective legislation for women and children in industry, the establishment of special courts and separate deputies for juvenile offenders, and woman suffrage. At the national level, Boole participated in successful efforts to remove liquor from military locations, Indian reservations, and government buildings. In 1913 she attended a Washington demonstration in support of a national prohibition amendment and delivered an eloquent speech in its favor from the Capitol steps. After the eighteenth amendment was passed, she worked for its ratification in the New York legislature.

The enfranchisement of women encouraged Boole to take an even more active role in politics. At the request of the League of Women Voters, she ran for the Senate in 1920 against the incumbent James W. Wadsworth, who had voted against prohibition, woman suffrage, and child labor laws. After losing to him in the Republican primary, she ran in the general election on the Prohibition party ticket, adopting the slogan "Send a mother to the Senate," and conducting a vigorous campaign. Although she lost, she received over 150,000 votes, mostly from upstate. Two later bids for the Senate in 1922 and 1926 were also unsuccessful.

Elected in 1925 to succeed ANNA ADAMS GORDON as president of the National WCTU, Boole set as her main goal the retention of prohibition and directed a campaign of education to increase public support. In 1927 she organized a conference in Washington, D.C., where WCTU members lobbied their representatives for better law enforcement. In the presidential campaign in 1928, Boole urged her membership to support the candidacy of Herbert Hoover and later claimed that the votes of southern women accounted for Hoover's strong showing in that region.

As public sentiment for prohibition declined in the late 1920s and early 1930s, Boole increased her efforts to retain the eighteenth amendment. She wrote a history of women in the temperance movement, spoke throughout the country on social and economic benefits of prohibition, and exhorted her followers to place principle above party by voting for dry candidates. At the National WCTU convention of 1933, Boole attempted to rally the opponents of repeal by delivering her annual address on radio. Perhaps sensing defeat, at that meeting she resigned as head of the national organization; she continued, however, as president of the World's WCTU, a post she had held since 1931.

As head of the international organization,

Boole focused her energies on peace and disarmament, abolition of the international drug traffic, and the condition of women around the world. She had displayed an interest in peace earlier, joining in 1925 with CARRIE CHAPMAN CATT and other leaders of women's organizations in calling for a Conference on the Cause and Cure of War. During World War II, Boole's correspondence with all member nations sustained the World's WCTU. After the war she was instrumental in securing recognition for the international organization by the United Nations.

Ella Boole retired as president of the World's WCTU in 1947, at age eighty-eight. During the last twenty years of her life, she also held executive positions in several national organizations as well as in the International Temperance Union. She died of a stroke in 1952 at the Brooklyn home she shared with her daughter and stepdaughter.

A large woman of dignified bearing, Ella Boole, an ordained deaconess in the Presbyterian church, was always strongly motivated by her religious beliefs. She was described by contemporaries as a person of "unassailable integrity" and as "a born organizer." In devoting her life to moral reform, Boole exemplified what she herself referred to as "the organized civic conscience of women."

[The minutes of the National WCTU, which contain records of Boole's terms of office and her annual addresses, are found in the annual report of each convention; these, together with the *Union Signal*, are located in the WCTU headquarters, Evanston, Ill. The minutes, records, and publications of the N.Y. state WCTU are in its headquarters in Syracuse, N.Y. Boole's correspondence while secretary of the Woman's Board of Home Missions is held by the Presbyterian Hist. Soc. in Philadelphia. Her writings consisted chiefly of temperance articles for WCTU publications, as well as *Give Prohibition Its Chance* (1929). Other principal sources are *The Reminiscences of Ella A. Boole* (1950), in the Oral History Coll., Columbia Univ., and Frances W. Graham, *Sixty Years of Action: A History of Sixty Years' Work of the W.C.T.U. of the State of New York* (1934). See also *Dict. Am. Biog.*, Supp. Five; *Nat. Cyc. Am. Biog.*, B, 492, and XXXVIII, 531–32; Helen E. Tyler, *Where Prayer and Purpose Meet* (1949); Stanley Walker, "With Ella in the Desert," *Outlook and Independent*, April 9, 1930; Owen P. White, "The Same Old Fight," *Collier's*, Nov. 5, 1932. Information about Boole's father is in R. Sutton, *History of Van Wert and Mercer Counties, Ohio* (1882). The *N.Y. Times* carried an obituary on William Boole, Feb. 25, 1896, and one on Ella Boole, March 14, 1952. A biobibliography compiled by Sally Lohr assisted in the research for this article.]

SUSAN DYE LEE

BORCHARDT, Selma Munter, Dec. 1, 1895–Jan. 30, 1968. Educator, lawyer, labor leader and lobbyist.

Selma Munter Borchardt was the only daughter and second of three surviving children of Newman and Sara (Munter) Borchardt, both born in Germany. Newman Borchardt served as an officer during the Civil War, then went west to work as a civilian quartermaster for the United States Army, fought in the Indian wars, and held government appointments in Custer County, Mont. The Borchardts had four children who died in the west before they returned to the east where Selma and her brothers were born in Washington, D.C.

Selma Borchardt graduated in 1914 from Washington's Central High School, completed an A.B. degree at Syracuse University in 1922, and a B.S. in education, also at Syracuse, the following year. In 1933 she graduated from the Washington College of Law (later American University College of Law). Four years later she received an A.M. in sociology from Catholic University where she continued graduate work, completing all of the requirements for a Ph.D. in sociology except for the dissertation. Despite the breadth and quality of her formal education, "the trade union movement," she insisted, "has been my greatest teacher."

Borchardt eventually combined careers as a teacher, lawyer, and labor lobbyist, but began her professional career as a playground instructor. In 1919 and 1920 she directed teacher training for Montgomery County, Md., and then served as supervisor of the county's rural schools (1920–21). She joined the faculty of the Washington, D.C., public schools in 1922. Although she developed a sizable legal practice and was admitted to the select group of lawyers permitted to appear before the Supreme Court of the United States, she chose to remain a teacher. Until her retirement in December 1960, except for an educational leave to serve on the Wartime Education Commission (1941–45), Borchardt worked in public education. She was chairman of the English department at Washington's Eastern High School when she retired.

The Washington school district where Borchardt taught formed a charter local of the American Federation of Teachers (AFT) and she quickly became active in the teachers' union. In 1924 she became a vice president of the AFT, and the following year organized its Research Department. From 1929 until 1955 she also served as secretary of the Education Committee of the American Federation of Labor (AFL). Both the AFT and the AFL made extensive use of Borchardt's legal talent, which she volunteered in the cause of education and labor. For more than thirty years she acted as congressional representative for the AFT, representing the union in the capital and publishing annually an extensive report of her activities.

As a labor lobbyist Borchardt first worked with AFL legislative representative Edward McGrady, who later became assistant secretary of labor, and with MAUD WOOD PARK, president of the League of Women Voters. Among the legislation she promoted on behalf of the teachers' union were bills calling for federal aid to raise teachers' salaries, to provide health services for children, to eradicate adult illiteracy, to aid public school construction, and to provide loans and scholarships to needy students (*Am. Teacher*, Oct. 1950, pp. 25–26).

Early in the 1930s Borchardt joined with such noted educators as John Dewey, Henry Linville, and George Counts to rid the AFT of radical influence. She cautioned the teachers to be on their guard equally against communists and against the police state methods being used to control them. The job of keeping communist propaganda out of the classroom was the teachers' alone: "If you don't do it," she told them, "you ought to be fired." She also believed that only professionally trained educators were competent to make educational judgments and opposed attempts by noneducators to control curricula or textbook content.

In addition to her congressional liaison work for organized labor, Borchardt drafted legislation and monitored its passage through Congress for the national board of the YWCA and the Women's Bar Association. She chaired the Subcommittees on Federal Aid to Education and Child Labor Standards for the Women's Joint Congressional Committee, a national clearinghouse for the legislative work of women's groups which had a common interest in education and in welfare programs. Although a champion of women's rights, like many other women in the labor movement she opposed the Equal Rights Amendment on the grounds that it denied women the benefit of protective legislation.

Borchardt was active in a number of other organizations of educators, both national and international. In 1927 she became a director of the World Federation of Education Associations (WFEA), an organization that promoted cooperation among educators of all nations. She served until the federation disbanded in 1946. From 1931 until her retirement she was the consultant on education for the American Association of University Women. She was also a director and a member of the Educational Planning Committee of the Institute of World Studies (1946–48), which operated resident study centers throughout the world. In addition, Borchardt wrote extensively and traveled widely in the cause of education, accepting as many as 200 speaking invitations a year.

Borchardt's knowledge and talents were recognized by appointments to government commissions. In 1935 President Franklin D. Roosevelt named her to the National Advisory Board of the National Youth Administration (NYA). As the only classroom teacher on the NYA national board, she chaired the Subcommittee on Coordination of Training Programs with Schools and Colleges and directed her efforts toward drafting and implementing work-study programs. During World War II she served as the teacher member of the United States Office of Education Wartime Commission, and as director of its High School Victory Corps (1941–43). In 1946 Secretary of State James F. Byrnes appointed her to the United States Commission on UNESCO, where she served on the committee which drafted the UNESCO charter. She remained a delegate until 1951.

Throughout her long career as an educator within the labor movement Selma Borchardt addressed the problems of child welfare, juvenile delinquency, and child labor. In 1930, 1940, and 1950 she was a delegate to the White House Conferences on Children and Youth and in 1955 to the White House Conference on Education. Deploring the disintegration of the American family, which she blamed largely on the development of fast foods, she told a 1954 teachers' union convention that the passing of the American dining room and the tradition of families eating together were the root cause of juvenile delinquency.

Borchardt retired from her teaching job in 1960 and in 1962 from her positions as vice president and legislative representative of the AFT (1924–35 and 1942–62). She died of arteriosclerosis in a Washington, D.C., nursing home in 1968.

[The Selma Borchardt Coll., Archives of Labor History and Urban Affairs, Walter P. Reuther Library, Wayne State Univ., consists of 89 linear feet of documents from 1911 through 1967; it includes correspondence, minutes, reports, speeches, press releases, and notes. The bulk of Borchardt's writings were published by the AFT's *Am. Teacher* and other educational and trade union journals. A list of studies she conducted for the AFT and WFEA is in the entry in *Who Was Who in Am.*, V. As president of the Washington Women's Trade Union League, 1925–27, she wrote a regular column for the Washington *Herald* on the problems of working women. Philip Taft, *United They Teach: The Story of the American Federation of Teachers* (1974), describes Borchardt's role in the AFT's anticommunist campaign. Death certificate supplied by D.C. Dept. of Public Health.]

DONALD L. HAYNES

BOURKE-WHITE, Margaret, June 14, 1904– Aug. 27, 1971. Photographer.

Margaret Bourke-White, commercial and industrial photographer and photojournalist, was born in New York City, the second child of Joseph and Minnie (Bourke) White. Her father was a successful engineer-designer in the printing industry; her self-taught mother worked on publications for the blind.

When she began college at age seventeen, at Rutgers University summer school, Margaret White's interests were in engineering and biology. While at Columbia University in 1922 and 1923, she studied photography with Clarence H. White; as a student of herpetology at the University of Michigan (1923–25), she also took pictures for the yearbook. In 1925 she married Everett Chapman, a graduate student in engineering at the university. The marriage lasted only a year. After her divorce in 1926 she began using the hyphenated compound of her middle and last names.

Bourke-White also attended Western Reserve University before matriculating as a senior at Cornell University, where she received an A.B. in 1927. At Cornell, she made an impressive and painterly photographic record of the campus, an idyllic region defined by gorges, hills, and valleys. The romance of nature, however, soon gave way to the romance of technology. Along with many other artists working in the 1920s and 1930s, Bourke-White became a partisan of the machine esthetic, discovering and celebrating the beauty of the products of modern technology. In 1927 she moved to Cleveland to begin a photographic career as a specialist in architectural and industrial subjects. Within two years she had not only mastered her medium but also managed to articulate the basis of her work to a wide audience. In the September 1929 issue of *World's Work*, she stated with assurance that "whatever art will come out of this industrial age will come from the subjects of industry themselves, which are sincere and unadorned in their beauty, and close to the heart of the people."

A turning point in Bourke-White's adventurous career occurred in 1929 when she began working as one of the first photographers for the new *Fortune* magazine. She established a studio in the Chrysler Building in New York City and worked half the year for the magazine and the other half as a commercial freelancer, developing a successful advertising business. In 1930

she made the first of a number of photographic surveys through the Soviet Union. This trip yielded about 800 photographs, of which 40 were printed, along with a text, in *Eyes on Russia* (1931).

The context and direction of her life changed again during the mid-1930s when she shifted her interest from industrial to human subjects. A *Fortune* assignment to cover the drought-stricken Dust Bowl area of the midwest resulted in "The Drought" (*Fortune*, Oct. 1934). This early social documentary is a poignant account of the havoc wrought by a combination of economic depression and mismanagement of land. The drought experience, Bourke-White said later, "was the beginning of my awareness of people in a human, sympathetic sense as subjects for the camera and photographed against a wider canvas than I had perceived before" (*Portrait of Myself*, p. 110).

In 1935 Bourke-White, along with Alfred Eisenstaedt and other renowned photographers, joined the as yet unborn *Life* magazine, designed by publisher Henry Luce as a vehicle for photojournalism. Sent on her first assignment to a dam under construction at New Deal, Mont., she photographed a variety of engineering forms and, on her own initiative, also produced a human interest picture story of nearby frontier towns. The editors, struck by the combination of industrial objects and people, used her material for the cover and lead article of the first issue (Nov. 23, 1936).

Also in 1935 Bourke-White met the writer Erskine Caldwell, who was planning a documentary account of sharecropper life in the south. They agreed to collaborate; writer and photographer traveled together for several months during 1936, documenting the appalling living conditions of southern sharecroppers. The resulting book, *You Have Seen Their Faces* (1937), is probably the most historically significant single work of Bourke-White's career. Its pictures are grouped to illustrate environmental, social, and personal decay. A number of the people photographed, suffering from malnutrition, are grotesquely malformed; rusted hulks lie beside rotting shacks; desperate faces express a lifetime of futility.

Bourke-White and Caldwell, who were married in 1939 and divorced in 1942, also collaborated during the late thirties and early forties on two timely books: *North of the Danube* (1939), a sketch of life in Czechoslovakia before the Nazi takeover, and *Say, Is This the U.S.A.* (1941), a panoramic survey of the United States shortly before its entrance into World War II. They were in Moscow during the spring and summer of 1941 when the Germans attacked the city, and they covered the events in words and photographs. Bourke-White was the only foreign photographer in the USSR at the time.

After the United States entered the war, Bourke-White received accreditation as an official Army Air Force photographer, her work to be used jointly by the military and *Life*. She went to England as American B-17 squadrons were assembling for attacks on the Continent, and when Air Force action shifted to North Africa, she moved with it. Denied permission to fly with the men, she traveled instead on a ship which was torpedoed near North Africa. Later she was allowed to accompany a mission, participating in a January 1943 raid on a German airfield at El Aouina, north of Tunis. In Italy, she photographed the extraordinary violence in Cassino Valley, and during the closing days of the war she moved along the Rhine with General George Patton's Third Army, recording the last days of the Third Reich. Entering death camps, she produced, among many pictures, "The Living Dead of Buchenwald" (1945), a classic in the history of photography.

Life continued to send Bourke-White abroad after the war ended. Her first postwar assignment was to India, where she worked intermittently through 1948. While there she produced the famous "Gandhi at His Spinning Wheel" (1946). In 1949 and 1950 she did a number of studies of life in South Africa, and during the Korean War she concentrated on the human aspects of guerrilla warfare, on families split by opposing political allegiances.

Margaret Bourke-White's career was cut short by Parkinson's disease; by the mid-fifties its effects had curbed her professional activities, and she fought the illness until her death in 1971 at Stamford, Conn. As a photojournalist the substance of her work was news, not art. Yet among the hundreds of thousands of works that she produced are some of the most successful artistic statements of the twentieth century.

[Margaret Bourke-White's publications not cited above include *U.S.S.R. Photographs* (1934); *Shooting the Russian War* (1942); *They Called It "Purple Heart Valley"* (1944); *"Dear Fatherland, Rest Quietly"* (1946); *Halfway to Freedom: A Study of the New India* (1949); *A Report on the American Jesuits* (1956), with John La Farge, S.J.; and *Portrait of Myself* (1963). For an extensive sampling of her photographs see Sean Callahan, ed., *The Photographs of Margaret Bourke-White* (1972). Theodore M. Brown, *Margaret Bourke-White,*

Photojournalist (1972), contains a complete bibliography of her publications as well as a full account of her career. See also Anne Tucker, ed., *The Woman's Eye* (1973). William Stott, *Documentary Expression and Thirties America* (1973), provides a contrasting opinion of *You Have Seen Their Faces.* An obituary appeared in the *N.Y. Times*, Aug. 28, 1971.]

THEODORE M. BROWN

BOW, Clara Gordon, July 29, 1905–Sept. 27, 1965. Film actress.

Clara Bow, renowned for her film personification of sexuality in the 1920s, was born into poverty in Brooklyn, N.Y. She was the third and only surviving child of Sarah (Gordon) and Robert Bow, who were of French, Scottish, and English ancestry. Her childhood was fraught with tragedy. A good friend burned to death despite Bow's efforts to save him. She was close to her father, a waiter and handyman, but he was often unemployed and deserted the family for varying periods of time, leaving Bow to care for her mother, who was chronically depressed. Bow believed that her mother attempted to kill her when she was sixteen. Permanently hospitalized two years later, Sarah Bow died soon after. In response to early privations, Clara Bow became both a devoted movie fan and a tomboy. She left school during the eighth grade to work as a receptionist.

In 1921 Bow won a "Fame and Fortune" beauty contest sponsored by three movie magazines, but it did little to promote the promised film career. She landed a part in *Beyond the Rainbow* (1922), only to have her footage cut. (It was restored after she attained stardom.) Soon, however, director Elmer Clifton, who liked her magazine photographs, cast her in the low-budget *Down to the Sea in Ships*. The film became a popular success, and Bow received excellent reviews. Now determined that his daughter succeed, Robert Bow brought her to the attention of agent Maxine Alton, who negotiated Bow's first contract with Preferred Pictures in Hollywood in 1923. The contract paid her fifty dollars a week for three months, plus her fare to Hollywood.

Her success in films was testimony to Bow's real talent as well as to her willingness to accept long working hours and difficult schedules. By the end of 1924 she had made thirteen films and was regularly referred to as a rising star. From the first she was cast as a flapper, a popular figure borrowed from novels and from real life, whose free and easy ways presumably mirrored the emancipated young woman of the 1920s. Other actresses had already established the type in films. But Clara Bow became overwhelmingly identified as the flapper after Elinor Glyn, a popular and flamboyant English author and scriptwriter, singled out Bow as possessing "It," Glyn's idiosyncratic euphemism for sex appeal; the word had recently captured the public fancy. Paramount, the studio to which Bow had moved in 1925, now trumpeted her to the public and cast her in a film dramatization of Glyn's novelette, *It* (1927). The role established Bow's epic stature: soon the volume of her fan mail was greater than that of any other Hollywood actress.

In her films, Bow exuded both an earthy sensuality and a childish innocence, accompanied by frenetic and flirtatious movement. Her figure was boyish; her face pixyish; her hair red. Before Bow's time, most female "sex symbols" had derived from European models of exotic, sophisticated sensuality. Bow combined the innocence of Mary Pickford (died 1979) with the guile of THEDA BARA and added her own distinctly American brashness and vitality. She became a symbol for an age which combined a freer sensuality with lingering Victorian propriety. The plots of her flapper movies, including the best-known—*The Plastic Age* (1925), *Dancing Mothers* (1926), and *It*—were all similar. Bow played a lower-class working woman who gained a certain emancipation through dancing, smoking, drinking, and wearing short skirts. But beneath her rebellious behavior her morality was strict: the flapper was a "nice" girl and invariably left her job for marriage.

Off the screen Bow led a sensational life. Her love affairs with such men as director Victor Fleming and actors Gilbert Roland and Gary Cooper were Hollywood legends. Independent, brash, and unsophisticated, she made no attempt to become part of the group of film actors who lived like aristocrats and dominated Hollywood's film society. She seemed happiest with extras, crew members, and her own servants. Bow's closest intimate was probably her father, whom she supported in various business enterprises while he lived in her home. By the late 1920s a number of scandals threatened both her career and her emotional stability. The wife of a Texas doctor who had been Bow's lover sued her for alienation of affection. In 1931 she prosecuted her then secretary and companion, Daisy DeVoe, for embezzling funds. The experience was traumatic, particularly when DeVoe, in retaliation, released to the press letters containing alleged details of Bow's love affairs.

For some time Bow had suffered from overwork, depression, and insomnia and had had periodic nervous breakdowns. Fear that she had inherited her mother's mental instability haunted her. Shortly after the DeVoe affair, she retired from the screen and moved to Nevada to live quietly with Rex Bell (George F. Beldam), a rancher and minor movie actor who later served as Nevada's lieutenant governor. A secure man of strong character, he provided stability in her life. In December 1931 she and Bell were married. Bow returned to Hollywood in 1932 to make the successful *Call Her Savage*, followed in 1933 by *Hoopla*, a financial and critical failure. As a result of bad reviews, her inability to summon her old energy for work, and her desire for a family, Bow retired permanently from the screen.

Bow's first son, Rex Anthony, was born in 1934; her second, George Robert in 1938. Though settled in Nevada, she periodically returned to Hollywood with her husband. For a time in the mid-1930s she owned a Hollywood coffeehouse, and for some weeks in 1947 she was the mystery voice, Mrs. Hush, on radio's most popular program, "Truth or Consequences." By the early 1950s marital discord and increasing emotional difficulties prompted Bow to move permanently to Los Angeles to be near her psychiatrists and the sanitarium where she was occasionally hospitalized. For the most part, she lived quietly at home and spent her time swimming and watching television. Clara Bow died at her home of a heart attack in 1965.

Many critics judged Bow to be a talented actress and regretted her identification with the flapper role. Still, she was an artistic success in several nonflapper parts, including roles as a World War I ambulance driver in *Wings* (1927) and an illegitimate halfbreed and prostitute in *Call Her Savage*. The common belief that she failed in sound movies is debatable, although given her restless acting style, she found the stationary microphone supremely frustrating. Bow herself recognized that her own personality meshed with that of the screen flapper, but she grew to hate the role. In the 1930s a more mature symbol of beauty replaced the flapper. Ironically, just when more varied parts might have been available, Bow's emotional instability made it impossible for her to continue her career.

[Clipping files of articles about Bow's life and career, photographs, and reviews of her films are located in the Margaret Herrick Library, Acad. of Motion Picture Arts and Sciences, Beverly Hills; the Film Library of the Museum of Modern Art; and the Billy Rose Theatre Coll., N.Y. Public Library. A bibliography of articles and obituaries on Bow appears in Mel Schuster, *Motion Picture Performers: A Bibliography of Magazine and Periodical Articles, 1900–1969* (1971). The major biography is Joe Morella and Edward Z. Epstein, *The "It" Girl: The*

Incredible Story of Clara Bow (1976). James Robert Parish, *The Paramount Pretties* (1972), contains a lengthy biographical and critical essay, as well as annotated credits for all her films. Brief interpretations of Bow's career are contained in Alexander Walker, *The Celluloid Sacrifice: Aspects of Sex in the Movies* (1966); Norman Zierold, *Sex Goddesses of the Silent Screen* (1973); and David Thomson, ed., *Biog. Dict. of the Cinema* (1975). Background information is in Lary May, "Reforming Leisure: The Birth of Mass Culture and the Motion Picture Industry, 1896–1920" (Ph.D. diss., Univ. of Calif., Los Angeles, 1977). For earlier biographical accounts, based on interviews with Bow, see Rudy Behlmer, "Clara Bow," *Films in Review*, Oct. 1963, and Adela Rogers St. Johns, "Clara Bow: My Life Story," *Photoplay*, April 1928. An obituary appeared in the *N.Y. Times*, Sept. 28, 1965. The death certificate supplied by the Calif. Dept. of Health lists acute drug intoxication as a significant condition contributing to death but not related to the terminal disease.]

LOIS W. BANNER

BOWEN, Catherine Shober Drinker, Jan. 1, 1897–Nov. 1, 1973. Biographer, essayist.

Catherine Drinker Bowen was born on the Haverford (Pa.) College campus, the youngest of six children (four sons and two daughters) of Aimée Ernesta (Beaux) and Henry Sturgis Drinker. She grew up in a talented, loving, competitive family for whom, according to her son, Ezra, "excellence was the starting point." In an active household presided over by a gentle but demanding father and a supportive, domestic mother, Catherine Drinker developed the three great passions of her life—family, music, and writing.

She could trace her ancestry to the first American-born English child in Pennsylvania, and the "vigor and sinew" of her family's history was always a source of strength (*Family Portrait*). Drinker was influenced, too, by her mother's sister, the portrait painter CECILIA BEAUX, and by her brothers who, she recalled, "had spurred themselves—and me—to competition." Her oldest brother, Harry, a lawyer, shared with her a love for music. Another brother, Philip, invented the iron lung, and a third, Cecil, served as dean of the Harvard School of Public Health.

At the time of Catherine Drinker's birth, her father was general solicitor of the Lehigh Valley Railroad. In 1905 he became president of Lehigh University and the Drinker family moved to Bethlehem, Pa. At first tutored by local school mistresses and young Lehigh faculty, Catherine was sent in 1905 to Miss Kellogg's dame school where she was pleased to find herself for the first time surrounded by her equals,

instead of by her older brothers and beautiful sister. After a brief period in 1907–08 at a school attended by the daughters of wealthy steel magnates, she enrolled at the Moravian Academy in Bethlehem, Pa. Between the ages of eleven and eighteen Catherine Drinker was only occasionally in school as she traveled widely with her mother and sister, Ernesta, and later her father; Henry Drinker's interest in engineering projects took them to the Panama Canal before the Culebra Cut was completed and to the Suez Canal. From 1914 to 1916 she attended St. Timothy's School in Catonsville, Md.

Drinker's early love of music led her to consider a career as a violinist and she enrolled at the Peabody Conservatory in Baltimore after graduation from St. Timothy's. She continued to study at Peabody and subsequently at the Institute of Musical Art (later the Juilliard School) in New York, because, as she explained later, she loved it. Throughout her life she was a talented and enthusiastic violinist.

Catherine Drinker married Ezra Bowen, an associate professor of economics at Lehigh University, in 1919. The couple moved the next year to Easton, Pa., when he became head of the economics department at Lafayette College. Catherine Bowen began her writing career by winning a ten-dollar prize in a contest sponsored by the *Easton Express*. During the next few years she sold her first stories and began writing a daily column for the paper, stopping just before the birth of her first child, a daughter, Catherine Drinker (1924). Her son, Ezra, was also born in Easton (1927). Bowen credited her husband with starting her writing: "And once I saw my product in print, nothing mattered but to get on with the work" ("We've Never Asked a Woman Before," p. 85).

Bowen's first two books appeared in 1924: *The Story of the Oak Tree*, a children's book, and *A History of Lehigh University*. In the latter, a commissioned study, she was identified as the daughter of Dr. H. S. Drinker '71 and wife of Professor Ezra Bowen '13. Asked in later years why she had never written the biography of a woman she replied that "a woman's biography—with about eight famous historical exceptions—so often turns out to be the story of a man and the woman who helped his career."

Rufus Starbuck's Wife, her only novel, appeared in 1932. Praised for its sympathetic characters and psychological accuracy, this semiautobiographical account of the stresses in a marriage between two talented people offers valuable insights into her developing independence and self-definition. Catherine and Ezra Bowen separated in the 1930s (they were divorced in 1936) and she and her children returned to Lehigh to live with her parents. In 1939 she married Thomas McKean Downs, a surgeon. The marriage lasted until his death in 1960.

During the 1930s Bowen tried various literary forms. In 1935 she published a charming and widely read book of essays on music and amateur musicians, *Friends and Fiddlers.* Her sensitivity to music was evident in her next project as well: *"Beloved Friend": The Story of Tchaikowsky and Nadejda von Meck* (1937), was the first of the series of distinguished biographies on which Catherine Drinker Bowen's reputation rests. That venture led to *Free Artist: The Story of Anton and Nicholas Rubinstein* (1939), a study of the pianists who had helped to popularize Tchaikovsky's music. A diligent researcher in printed sources, for this book she traveled to the Soviet Union in 1937 for first-hand experience of scenes and atmosphere.

Disappointed by her discovery of some less than desirable characteristics in the private lives of various musicians, Bowen determined to write about a good man. *Yankee from Olympus: Justice Holmes and His Family* (1944) began her series of biographies of men involved in forming and interpreting the constitutional government of the United States. Although Holmes's literary executors refused her access to all unpublished material, Bowen's extensive research resulted in a superb portrayal of urban life in Boston and Washington as well as a remarkable range of character portraits.

For the second book in this series, *John Adams and the American Revolution* (1950; reissued 1976), Bowen was again refused permission to read unpublished material and she embarked on five years of research. The book continued in the pattern of what critics called "fictionalized biography," a term to which Bowen objected. "The facts on which my narrative is based are available to everyone," she pointed out. "I aim not to startle with new material but to persuade with old" (*John Adams,* p. 62). Bowen went on to seek "the foundations of our constitutional government" in the study of seventeenth- and eighteenth-century England, specifically in the life of Edward Coke. With the enthusiastic support of her husband, she undertook what became a six-year research effort. At Cambridge, Coke's university, she encountered many obstacles: "Even Bluebeard did not consider women more expendable than does a Cambridge don," she later remarked. The work caused a temporary breakdown in health but resulted in her greatest book, *The Lion and the Throne: The Life and Times of Sir Edward Coke, 1552–1634* (1957). Here Bowen "turned once and for all to writing

biography that contained no fictional devices and documented every quotation." In 1957 she received the Phillips Prize, given by the American Philosophical Society for "the best essay . . . on the science and philosophy of jurisprudence"; she was also invited to membership in the society. The following year *The Lion and the Throne* won a National Book Award.

Francis Bacon, discovered during her research on Coke, fascinated Bowen because of his genius and his literary style, as well as his courage in adversity. (She rejected opportunities to write about men who had not themselves written well.) In *Francis Bacon: The Temper of a Man* (1963), a series of essays on Bacon in crucial periods, she offered a more relaxed, though equally meticulous approach to biography. The book was probably Bowen's favorite among her own works.

In the last of her books on the development of constitutional government she moved away from individual biography. *Miracle at Philadelphia: The Story of the Constitutional Convention* (1966), the fifth of her books to be a Book-of-the-Month Club selection, succeeded, a reviewer noted, "much better than any previous book" on the subject, in "present[ing] a vivid recreation of the 'tenseness of the moment'" (Greene, pp. 218–19).

Bowen described her work methods in three collections of essays: *The Writing of Biography* (1951), *Adventures of a Biographer* (1959), and *Biography: The Craft and the Calling* (1969). "Writing biography is exciting business," she said, and the biographer must examine and record with excitement and precision "the nature or motivation of man." Her view of history as shaped by individuals led Bowen to focus on character and personality. To create the proper atmosphere she surrounded her work area with portraits of her subject and his contemporaries and pored over the material until she could hear the person speaking in his own authentic voice. Challenging professional historians for draining the life from history, Bowen also resented the condescension of some historians toward popular books, observing that "books that are well written seemed doomed to popularity; the public is avid for history." Biography was not a lesser art; rather, she argued, it was a craft requiring "so total an effort that one's life actually must be planned around it."

Family Portrait (1970), the biography of Bowen's family, reveals little about herself and nothing of her marriages. Nonetheless the abiding values in her life emerge clearly: love of family, a deep appreciation of the past and of old age; deep respect for hard work; and an unflagging zeal for achievement, for doing something worthwhile. She felt she had an advantage as a woman in perceiving character because women "are trained from childhood to notice the relationships between people." A strong supporter of the rights of women to exercise their talents independent of home and family, in a speech near the end of her life Bowen observed that "no woman of spirit can focus her entire life on the raising of two children"; she must also use her "vital energies in national causes, world causes."

At the time of her death Catherine Drinker Bowen was working with "zest and the sense that work was sacred" on a study of Benjamin Franklin. The book was published posthumously in 1974 as *The Most Dangerous Man in America: Scenes from the Life of Benjamin Franklin.* Following a year's illness Catherine Drinker Bowen died at seventy-six of cancer, in Haverford, a mile from the place of her birth.

[Bowen's papers, which include correspondence, notes, and drafts, are at the Library of Congress. Other articles by Bowen of interest to the biographer are: "An Alumna Looks Back—and Ahead," St. Timothy's School *Alumnae Bull.*, Spring 1951; "Discipline and Reward: A Writer's Life," *Atlantic Monthly*, Dec. 1957, pp. 87–92; "The Nature of the Artist," *Scripps College Bull.*, 1961; "We've Never Asked a Woman Before," *Atlantic*, March 1970, pp. 82–86; "For American Women Again It Is the Time to Move Mountains," *Smithsonian*, July 1970, pp. 24–31. A comprehensive biographical memoir by Whitfield J. Bell, Jr., is in the *Am. Phil. Soc. Yearbook, 1974* (1975). Ezra Bowen, *Henry and Other Heroes: An Informal Memoir of High Dreams and Vanished Seasons* (1974) gives a son's warm and appreciative recollection of his mother in the course of his own autobiographical memories. For an insight into Bowen's personality see Harvey Breit, "Talk with C. D. Bowen," *N.Y. Times Book Rev.*, July 2, 1950, and Robert Clurman, "Talk with Mrs. Bowen," *N.Y. Times Book Rev.*, March 16, 1957. A short film in which Bowen discusses her work, *Catherine Drinker Bowen: Other People's Lives*, is in the Free Library of Philadelphia. Important reviews of Bowen's books include Henry S. Commager on *Yankee from Olympus*, in *Weekly Book Rev.*, April 23, 1944; C. H. McIlwain on *The Lion and the Throne*, in *Am. Hist. Rev.*, Oct. 1957; and Jack P. Greene on *Miracle at Philadelphia*, in *Am. Hist. Rev.*, Oct. 1967. See also the entry in *Contemporary Authors* (1969) and in *Current Biog.*, 1944. Obituaries in the *Phila. Inquirer*, Nov. 2, 1973, and the *N.Y. Times*, Nov. 3, 1973, include useful summaries of her life and work. Further information was given by Ezra Bowen and by Barbara Rex, her editor and longtime friend. A biobibliography by Frank Friedman, Diane Lovelace, and Donna Zientek assisted with research. A death record was provided by Pa. Dept. of Health.]

MARGARET STEINHAGEN

BOWEN, Louise deKoven, Feb. 26, 1859–Nov. 9, 1953. Philanthropist, community leader, suffragist.

Louise deKoven Bowen was born in Chicago, where she devoted most of her adult life to the support of social welfare efforts. The only child of Helen (Hadduck) and John deKoven, a successful banker, she was the granddaughter of Edward Hiram Hadduck, who built a large fortune through investments in land that eventually became the center of Chicago's Loop. Louise deKoven grew up conscious of this wealth; her grandfather informed her one day that he had just sold the corner of Washington Street and Wabash Avenue "for a good sum," one he promptly divided between Louise and her mother. At the same time, she was taught to be responsible for her inheritance, learning that "God would hold me accountable for the manner in which I used my talents."

Louise deKoven's interest in social work developed gradually. As a youth she enjoyed the privileges accorded Chicago's elite and attended the prestigious Dearborn Seminary, graduating at sixteen near the top of her class. About that time she appealed to her pastor at St. James Episcopal Cathedral for appropriate social service work. He reluctantly offered her a Sunday school class of "bad boys," a responsibility other more experienced church members had refused. Louise deKoven took on the task and quickly established order and discipline—her trademarks throughout her social service life. She led the class for eleven years, attracting many new members and establishing for their benefit one of the first boys' clubhouses in Chicago, the Huron Street Club. This experience helped shape her commitment to child welfare and the prevention of juvenile crime.

DeKoven's Sunday school work ended with her marriage to Chicago businessman Joseph Tilton Bowen on June 1, 1886. The Bowens had four children: John deKoven (b. 1887), Joseph Tilton, Jr. (b. 1889), Helen Hadduck (b. 1891), and Louise deKoven (b. 1893). While maintaining social service activities, Louise deKoven Bowen spent much of her early married life raising her children and managing complex households in Chicago and at their summer estate in Bar Harbor, Maine.

Bowen's career took a critical turn about 1893, when JANE ADDAMS, founder of Hull House, asked her to help with the settlement's fledgling Woman's Club. Bowen accepted, guiding the neighborhood women in parliamentary procedure and debate; during her seventeen years as an officer of the organization, it grew to a membership of over 2,000. She became a Hull House trustee in 1903 and beginning in 1907 served as treasurer. A financial mainstay of the settlement, what funds she did not provide herself, she raised from others.

Some of Bowen's key welfare efforts grew out of her association with Hull House. In the late 1890s she joined Jane Addams and her Hull House colleague JULIA LATHROP on the Juvenile Court Committee of Chicago; Bowen later became its president. Seeking separate treatment and counsel for young offenders, the committee succeeded in establishing the Juvenile Court and Detention Home across the street from Hull House. After the city of Chicago and Cook County assumed responsibility for that institution in 1907, the Court Committee reorganized itself as the Juvenile Protective Association, with Bowen as first president. There she supervised research, carried out in large part by Jessie Binford (1876–1966), examining the moral and physical effects on young people of poor working conditions, racial prejudice, prostitution, and popular entertainment. Among such studies, Bowen herself wrote *The Colored People of Chicago* (1913). The following year she published a book, *Safeguards for City Youth at Work and at Play*.

Louise deKoven Bowen was a vital link in the social welfare network of her city and nation. She possessed not only access to power and money, but also the leadership ability and commitment to see that ideas for welfare programs became realities. Acting on the advice of ALICE HAMILTON, in 1911 she pressured the managers of the Pullman Company, of which she was a stockholder, into acknowledging health hazards to Pullman workers and improving medical facilities. Through her friend Cyrus McCormick, she then obtained a minimum wage for women employed at the International Harvester Company. In 1912 Bowen raised more than $12,000 to provide food for the children of striking garment workers, took part in a suffragist march on the Republican National Convention in Chicago (she lectured nationally for woman suffrage), and supported the efforts of the Progressive party that fall. She later returned to the Republican fold as a national committeewoman from Illinois. A figure to be reckoned with in Chicago, she monitored charges of municipal corruption as president of the Woman's City Club, and investigated requests for financial assistance as vice president of the United Charities (1911–15).

For all her diverse activities, Bowen's attention rarely wandered far from Hull House. During her years as its treasurer, she personally funded the construction of two settlement buildings, the Woman's Club and the Boys' Club, and

donated to Hull House a seventy-two-acre summer campsite in memory of her husband, who had died in 1911. Bowen's loyalty to Hull House survived World War I, which she supported, while Jane Addams became one of the nation's leading pacifists. After Addams's death in 1935, Bowen was the moving force in the settlement, serving as president of the board for nine years. Small in stature, with a straightbacked carriage and determined tread, she handled all situations with brisk authority, brooking no opposition. She saw herself as the guardian of the image and ideals of Addams as she understood them, a stance which brought her into conflict with succeeding head residents of the settlement. Although Bowen's need to be involved in all managerial decisions sometimes caused consternation, Hull House as an institution might not have survived the death of Jane Addams without Bowen's financial support and organizational abilities.

Bowen was honored on numerous occasions by Hull House, and by other civic and educational groups. Her long service as an adviser and financial contributor to hospitals and health organizations was recognized in 1939, when she was made a citizen-fellow of the Chicago Institute of Medicine. She ceased most of her official activities in 1944, at the age of eighty-five, yet remained honorary president of both Hull House and the Juvenile Protective Association. Bowen underwent an operation for cancer in October 1953, and died the following month of a stroke at her Chicago home.

[The Louise deKoven Bowen Papers in the Chicago Hist. Soc. consist primarily of three scrapbooks containing some correspondence as well as newspaper clippings, photographs, and other memorabilia relating to her public life. In addition there is a collection of Bowen correspondence, clippings, articles, and photographs in the Jane Addams Memorial Coll., Univ. of Ill. at Chicago. The papers of Hull-House Associates and of the Juvenile Protective Assoc., also at the Univ. of Ill., provide information on Bowen's activities. Bowen offered accounts of her own life and career in three books: *Growing Up with a City* (1926), a useful, though uneven, autobiography; *Baymeath* (1944), written for and about her family; and *Open Windows: Stories of People and Places* (1946), which includes a tribute to Jane Addams. See also Mary E. Humphrey, ed., *Speeches, Addresses and Letters of Louise deKoven Bowen, Reflecting Social Movement in Chicago* (1937). Helpful secondary sources include Allen Davis and Mary Lynn McCree, eds., *80 Years at Hull-House* (1969), and Anthony Platt, *The Child Savers: The Invention of Delinquency* (1969), which includes a critical portrait of Bowen and her efforts at moral reform. Bowen is included in *Who Was Who in America*, III; and *Dict. Am. Biog.*, Supp. Five. An obituary appeared in *N.Y. Times,* Nov. 10, 1953; death certificate furnished by Ill. Dept. of Public Health.]

MARY LYNN MC CREE

BRADY, Mildred Edie, June 3, 1906–July 27, 1965. Consumer advocate, editor, journalist.

Mildred Edie Brady, a central figure in the history of the Consumers Union, was born in Little Rock, Ark., the only daughter and eldest of three children of Maude (White) and Stewart Carson Edie. Both parents were natives of Missouri and of Scots-Irish ancestry. Stewart Edie, a pharmacist, worked in and then refurbished a series of drugstores and restaurants in several states before settling down to employment by a chain of drugstores in Kansas City, Mo. Absorbed in his work, he provided his children with a strong sense of professional dedication and pride. Maude Edie, the thirteenth child of a poor family, was a self-educated woman who had become an expert railroad telegraph operator at age twelve. A perfectionist who felt she must continually prove herself, she instilled in her children the same need to excel.

Because both parents worked and because of the frequent moves and changes of schools, Mildred Edie and her brothers early became self-reliant. After the family settled in Kansas City, around 1920, she attended Northeast High School. An honor student, she graduated in 1923 and entered a junior college in Kansas City. Her college career was stormy; after being expelled from the first school for her work on an irreverent student newspaper, she studied for some time at two other midwestern colleges, but never graduated. During these years her main interests were literature and theater. She lived briefly in Chicago, working at various jobs, including modeling. Also during this period her parents were divorced; they later remarried.

In 1929, rebelling against her family and her midwestern origins, and seeking wider experience, Mildred Edie moved to New York City. Not long after her arrival she married an old boyfriend, Gerald Fling, editor of a hotel trade journal. (They divorced in 1931.) For a time she worked under EDITH ISAACS as associate editor of *Theatre Arts Monthly.* Then in 1930 she met Dexter Masters, editor of *Tide* (an offshoot of *Time*), a publication concerned with the world of marketing and advertising, who hired her to work for him. For *Tide* she reported on the boom period in American advertising, focusing particularly on the impact of New Deal programs on the business. Within a few years she was recognized as a knowledgeable reporter and analyst of Madison Avenue as well as of

Washington. Along with Masters, she met and became friendly with people in the worlds of theater, journalism, and politics, and with the leaders of the new consumer movement. Among these leaders were Frederick J. Schlink, head of a new publication, *Consumers Research,* and his colleague Arthur Kallet. When in 1935 a series of internal conflicts resulted in a strike at *Consumers Research,* Edie did a major story on the situation for *Tide.*

Also in 1935, Edie met Robert Brady, an economist and author of *The Spirit and Structure of Fascism.* They began living together the following year, and she later took the name Brady, but they could not marry because his first wife would not grant a divorce. (They were married in Berkeley, Calif., in 1956.) The couple had two daughters.

In 1936 Arthur Kallet and others split from *Consumers Research* to found Consumers Union (CU), a competing organization. Dexter Masters became editor of CU publications and Mildred Edie and Robert Brady joined the new group, which conducted and publicized laboratory tests of consumer products and services. Robert Brady, who was then a professor of economics at the University of California, Berkeley, where the couple had moved, became vice president of the organization; Mildred Edie became manager of the short-lived western branch of CU, which was established at her suggestion. Her early work for CU consisted mainly of writing, editing, and promotion.

Mildred Edie Brady remained active in the consumer movement through the 1940s, while also building a considerable reputation as a writer for national magazines. In 1940 she went to New York as managing editor of the reform publication *Friday* and then helped to launch a new weekly publication for CU. Called *Bread & Butter,* it dealt with the inflationary tendencies of a defense economy. She worked briefly during World War II in Washington, D.C., for the Consumer Division of the Office of Price Administration, and she edited a Washington consumer newsletter for *McCall's.* In April 1947 she wrote a famous article for *Harper's Magazine* based on an investigation of therapist Wilhelm Reich and some of his associates. Her work also appeared in *Collier's* and *The New Republic.*

In 1950 Mildred Brady rejoined CU as a feature writer for *Consumer Reports.* From her base in California, which provided a rich field for consumer reform, she produced a series of investigative reports on marketing practices. Business in California enthusiastically endorsed so-called "fair trade laws," designed to restrain product competition by means of resale price maintenance restrictions, and banks and financial institutions there welcomed the new era of easy credit and small down payments. Uniquely in that state, she could discern the impact of new marketing practices and the decline of price competition.

In 1958 Dexter Masters, who had become executive director of CU four years earlier, brought Brady to Mount Vernon, N.Y., as editorial director and senior editor of *Consumer Reports*. Her work focused on such themes as truth in lending, truth in packaging, product safety, restraint of trade, and price fixing, and she urged the passage of strong legislation to protect the consumer in these areas. In 1961 Brady's story "The Great Ham Robbery" focused public concern on the practice of injecting hams with water to increase their weight.

Though she was burdened by Robert Brady's illness (he suffered a stroke in 1952 and was an invalid until his death in 1963), Mildred Brady was through the 1950s and early 1960s an influential and creative force in the consumer movement, as well as a mainstay of *Consumer Reports*. She participated in the International Organization of Consumers Unions, founded in 1960, and lectured on the role of consumer testing before technical groups in the United States, Europe, and Asia. A careful journalist who, in her words, "did her homework," she articulated the consumer position on a wide range of national and international issues, and her investigations laid the groundwork for the rise of world consumerism. When she died of heart failure in 1965, while in the midst of a conference with CU leaders about product standardization, *Consumer Reports* paid tribute to her "intelligence and drive" in guiding the publication and noted the widespread impact of her work.

[Copies of articles and speeches by Mildred Brady are in the CU archives in Mount Vernon, N.Y. Biographical material is nearly nonexistent. Brief obituaries appeared in the *N.Y. Times*, July 29, 1965, and *Consumer Reports*, Sept. 1965. A tribute to Brady in *Consumer Reports*, Oct. 1965, includes comments from a number of public officials at her death. Further information for this article was provided by her brother Leslie Edie, by Judy Syfers, and by Dexter Masters.]

COLSTON WARNE

BRAUN, Emma Lucy, April 19, 1889–March 5, 1971. Botanist, conservationist.

Emma Lucy Braun, one of the truly dedicated pioneer ecologists of the first half of the twentieth century, was an original thinker in the fields of plant ecology, vascular plant taxonomy, plant geography, and conservation. Throughout her life, E. Lucy Braun, as she preferred to be known, gathered facts from the field, garden, and laboratory. She synthesized them into over 180 publications, including four books. Her work, coinciding with the recognition of plant ecology as a scientific discipline in the United States, was instrumental in the development of that discipline.

Born in Cincinnati, Braun was the younger of two daughters of Emma Moriah (Wright) and George Frederick Braun, a school principal. Her paternal ancestors were of German-French descent, her maternal ancestors of English origin. Braun's early interest in the natural world, like that of her older sister, Annette (1884–1978), was fostered by their parents, who took the girls to the woods and identified wildflowers. Their mother was especially interested in botany and had prepared a small collection of dried pressed plants for study.

Braun received her primary and secondary education in the Cincinnati public schools. At the University of Cincinnati she earned an A.B. in 1910, an A.M. in geology in 1912, and a Ph.D. in botany in 1914. (Her sister had obtained a Ph.D. from the university in 1911.) At the same institution Braun was an assistant in geology (1910–13), assistant in botany (1914–17), instructor in botany (1917–23), assistant professor of botany (1923–27), associate professor of botany (1927–46), and professor of plant ecology (1946–48). Early retirement from teaching allowed her to conduct research in areas of special interest that resulted in field work and significant publications nearly to the end of her life.

Braun's early scientific publications in plant ecology dealt with the physiographic ecology and vegetation of the Cincinnati region, the unique vegetation of the unglaciated limestone in Adams County, Ohio, and the forests of the Illinoian Till Plain of southwestern Ohio and of the Cumberland Plateau and Mountains in Kentucky. From this research she developed a classic book, *Deciduous Forests of Eastern North America* (1950). Based on twenty-five years of field study and over 65,000 miles of travel, the book gives a comprehensive and coordinated account of the entire hardwood forest. It lays the foundation for the measurement and evaluation of all future ecological changes in the hardwood forest and remains her most remembered and lasting scholarly achievement.

Braun also contributed extensively to the field of floristics and taxonomy of vascular plants. In the 1920s and 1930s she catalogued the flora of the Cincinnati area and compared it with the flora of the same region a hundred years earlier. This study, one of the first of its type in the United States, provided a model for comparing the changes in a given flora over a span of time. Her other writings included a key to the deciduous trees of Ohio, articles on selected plants of southwestern Ohio and eastern Kentucky, descriptions of plants new to science, and *An Annotated Catalog of the Spermatophytes of Kentucky* (1943). With these contributions as a foundation and the desire to continue advancing knowledge of the flora, in 1951 she organized an Ohio Flora Committee within the Ohio Academy of Science. Its objective was to prepare a comprehensive study of the vascular flora of Ohio. Braun chaired the committee and moved the project forward by writing two authoritative books, *The Woody Plants of Ohio: Trees, Shrubs, and Weedy Climbers, Native, Naturalized, and Escaped; A Contribution Toward the Vascular Flora of Ohio* (1961), and *The Monocotyledoneae: Cat-tails to Orchids* (1967).

The field studies Braun conducted led naturally into the study of plant distribution. She expanded on the theory that the southern Appalachians were the center of the survival of plants during glaciation and that from there the forest communities spread. This phytogeographic knowledge culminated in an extensive analytical summary, "The Phytogeography of Unglaciated Eastern United States and Its Interpretation," published in 1955 in *Botanical Review*. Braun's ideas on the origin of the prairie elements within the forest constitute an often overlooked but innovative viewpoint. Although she drew freely from the work of others, her botanical and ecological studies diverged from those of her contemporaries, exhibiting originality in methodology and philosophy.

Braun's varied contributions to conservation were also significant. She wrote articles stressing the importance of saving natural habitats, founded the Cincinnati chapter of the Wild Flower Preservation Society, and edited the society's national magazine, *Wild Flower*. Particularly concerned about the prairie remnants in Adams County, Ohio, she fought to save natural areas and to establish preserves.

Annette Braun, an entomologist who became internationally known as an authority on Microlepidoptera (moths), accompanied and assisted her sister in her field studies. Retaining the strict way of life of their parents, the sisters lived together in Mount Washington, in suburban Cincinnati. Their home and garden, surrounded by mostly natural, undisturbed woods, contained an area they called the science wing, which served as their laboratory. Their garden was an experimental one, where many rare and unusual plants were transplanted for close observation and study.

E. Lucy Braun's stature in the scientific community is well demonstrated by her election as the first woman president of both the Ohio Academy of Science (1933–34) and the Ecological Society of America (1950). For her achievements, she received many honors and awards, among them the Mary Soper Pope Medal for achievement in the field of botany (1952) and a Certificate of Merit from the Botanical Society of America (1956). She died of congestive heart failure in her home at the age of eighty-one and is buried in Spring Grove Cemetery, Cincinnati.

[Braun's *Deciduous Forests of Eastern North America* was reprinted in 1964, 1967, and 1972; *The Woody Plants of Ohio* was reprinted in 1969. The major biographical source is Ronald L. Stuckey, "E. Lucy Braun (1889–1971), Outstanding Botanist and Conservationist: A Biographical Sketch, with Bibliography," *Mich. Botanist*, vol. 12, March 1973, pp. 83–106, which contains a complete list of Braun's popular and scientific writings. Two popular articles are Perry K. Peskin, "A Walk Through Lucy Braun's Prairie," *The Explorer*, vol. 20, no. 4 (1978), pp. 15–21 (with photographs), and Lucile Durrell, "Memories of E. Lucy Braun" Sixth North American Prairie Conference, *Proceedings* (1980). For more technical background on the history of plant ecology in North America see Paul B. Sears, "Plant Ecology," in Joseph Ewan, ed., *A Short History of Botany in the United States* (1969), and Robert P. McIntosh, "Ecology Since 1900," in Benjamin J. Taylor and Thurman J. White, eds., *Issues and Ideas in America* (1976). An obituary appeared in *Ohio Jour. Science,* July 1971, pp. 247–48. Annette Braun provided family information. A death certificate was supplied by Ohio Dept. of Health.]

RONALD L. STUCKEY

BRECKINRIDGE, Mary, Feb. 17, 1881–May 16, 1965. Nurse-midwife, organization founder.

Mary Breckinridge, founder and director of the Frontier Nursing Service and pioneer in American midwifery, was born in Memphis, Tenn. First daughter and second of four children of Clifton Rodes and Katherine (Carson) Breckinridge, she was descended from old southern families through both her parents. Her mother had been born on a Louisiana plantation, and her father, a cotton planter and commission merchant, was the son of John C. Breckinridge, United States vice president and Confederate general.

Because her father served as a United States representative from Arkansas, Breckinridge spent most of her childhood in Washington, D.C., where she was educated by governesses.

When he was appointed American minister to Russia during the 1890s, the family moved to Saint Petersburg. Breckinridge attended the Rosemont-Dézaley School in Lausanne, Switzerland, from 1896 to 1898, when she returned to the United States and enrolled in the Low and Heywood School in Stamford, Conn. In 1899 she returned to live with her parents in Arkansas. She found life at home frustrating and "chafed at the complete lack of purpose in the things I was allowed to do."

In 1904 Mary Breckinridge married Henry Ruffner Morrison, who died of appendicitis in 1906. Deeply grieved, she sought some way to make her life useful. Deciding she would like to care for children, in February 1907 she entered Saint Luke's Hospital School of Nursing in New York City, graduating as a registered nurse in 1910. At her ailing mother's request, Breckinridge returned again to her family in Fort Smith, Ark. On Oct. 8, 1912, she married Richard Ryan Thompson, president of Crescent College and Conservatory for Young Women in Eureka Springs, Ark., where she taught French and hygiene. A son, Breckinridge, was born in 1914, followed in 1916 by a daughter, Mary, who died within six hours of her birth. Just after his fourth birthday, the adored Breckie was taken suddenly ill; he died on Jan. 23, 1918.

Once again Mary Breckinridge turned to nursing as an outlet for her sorrow, with an intensified commitment to "raise the status of childhood everywhere" in memory of her own children. In June 1918 she left her husband and with their divorce in 1920 legally resumed use of her maiden name.

To meet wartime need, Breckinridge volunteered to serve with the American Red Cross in France. While awaiting an assignment, she spent several months as a public health nurse in Boston and Washington, D.C. Finally embarking for Europe after the armistice, under the auspices of the American Committee for Devastated France, headed by ANNE MORGAN, Breckinridge organized disaster relief in Vic-sur-Aisne and inaugurated a special program to provide food and medical care for children and pregnant and nursing women. She later regarded this work as the most important preparation she had for founding the Frontier Nursing Service.

Her work in France and several visits to England convinced her that the nurse-midwife was the "logical response to the needs of the young child in rural America," and she determined to introduce the position to an area of the United States neglected by other social and medical agencies. After her return from France in 1921, she prepared for this work at Teachers College, Columbia University, through studies in public health nursing with ADELAIDE NUTTING and others. In the fall of 1923, she departed for London to enroll at the school of the British Hospital for Mothers and Babies, where four months later she was certified as an English midwife. After an additional postgraduate course at the York Road General Lying-In Hospital in London, Breckinridge joined the Midwives Institute in 1924. She completed her program of self-preparation with a trip to Scotland to observe the Highlands and Islands Medical and Nursing Service, which in its effective delivery of medical care to a widely scattered population was to serve as the direct model for the Frontier Nursing Service.

Breckinridge had earlier explored the Kentucky mountain area she aspired to serve, surveying its existing medical personnel, which consisted of elderly, untrained midwives and no licensed physician. Although she had never lived in Kentucky, her family was well known there; moreover, the challenge of bringing services to such an isolated area appealed to her, and the state's health commissioner was supportive. Early in 1925 Breckinridge began her nursing experiment in Leslie County. By May she had enlisted support from prominent citizens in founding the Kentucky Committee for Mothers and Babies, which in 1928 became the Frontier Nursing Service (FNS). For the first three years Breckinridge underwrote the entire operation with capital inherited from her mother. She hoped that the undertaking would demonstrate the effectiveness of nurse-midwifery as a solution to America's alarmingly high maternal and infant death rate, and therefore determined to keep complete statistics.

Since most of the residents of Leslie County lived in areas inaccessible by roads, the Service was designed around outpost nursing centers, each approximately ten miles apart. The nurse-midwives, who traveled on horseback, were no more than five or six miles from any patient. Breckinridge viewed the hospital, which opened at Hyden in 1928, and the physician who was its medical director, as "the palm of a hand from which fingers radiate in several directions." The FNS provided preventive as well as crisis nursing and within five years claimed responsibility for serving the medical needs of more than 1,000 rural families. Staff members of the FNS also formed the nucleus of what became in 1929 the American Association of Nurse-Midwives.

Breckinridge directed the project, edited its quarterly bulletin, and raised funds, traveling to speak on behalf of the Service in major American cities. A tiny woman, the "blessed old gray-haired critter" beloved by the Kentucky mountaineers was at the same time an effective speaker and fund raiser among the wealthy, some of whom were old family friends. Although they sometimes despaired of her unfashionable clothes, and self-administered haircuts, they nevertheless supported Breckinridge's cause. Her administrative and practical skills were complemented by a deep spirituality, and, as a member of the London Spiritualist Alliance, she maintained an active interest in psychical research. Always close to her family, Breckinridge brought her widowed father to live with her.

The success of the FNS in lowering the rate of death in childbirth in the area it served to substantially below the national average has served as a frequently cited proof of the potential of nurse-midwifery as a method of delivering quality health care services at a manageable cost. The recipient of many honors, Mary Breckinridge remained the director of the FNS and editor of its bulletin until she died, of leukemia and a stroke, in Hyden, Ky., at the age of eighty-four. The FNS, the Hyden Hospital, and the Frontier Graduate School of Midwifery, a training program for nurse-midwives which she had established in 1939, continued to flourish after her death.

[Mary Breckinridge destroyed her personal papers after completing her autobiography, *Wide Neighborhoods: The Story of the Frontier Nursing Service* (1952). Quotations are from the autobiography. A few Breckinridge letters survive in the Louis I. Dublin Papers, Nat. Library of Medicine, Bethesda, Md. Her articles, both signed and unsigned, appear in the *Frontier Nursing Service Quart. Bull.*, which she edited from 1925 to 1965. Other writings by Breckinridge of particular interest include "The Nurse-Midwife—A Pioneer," *Am. Jour. of Public Health*, Nov. 1927, and "Is Birth Control the Answer?" *Harper's*, July 1931. Useful secondary sources include Caroline Gardner, *Clever Country: Kentucky Mountain Trails* (1931); Judy Barrett Litoff, *American Midwives, 1860 to the Present* (1978); Ernest Poole, *Nurses on Horseback* (1932); Barbara Schutt, "Frontier's Family Nurses," *Am. Jour. of Nursing*, May 1972; Katherine Elliott Wilkie and Elizabeth R. Mosely, *Frontier Nurse: Mary Breckinridge* (1969); Carol Crowe-Carraco, "Mary Breckinridge and the Frontier Nursing Service," *Register, Ky. Hist. Soc.*, July 1978. Information about Breckinridge's private life was gathered in part from correspondence and interviews with her sister-in-law, Dorothy Throckmorton Thomson Breckinridge, and with Peggy Elmore of the FNS, and Amelia Martin of the Fort Smith (Ark.) Hist. Soc. Assistance in the research for this article was provided by a biobibliography prepared by Lauren K. Lee. Photographs of Breckinridge appeared periodically in the *Frontier Nursing Service Quart.*

Bull. during her editorship. An obituary appeared in the *N.Y. Times*, May 17, 1965; death record from Ky. Registrar of Vital Statistics.]

DREW GILPIN FAUST

BREMER, Edith Terry, Oct. 9, 1885–Sept. 12, 1964. Organization founder, social worker.

Edith Terry Bremer, pioneer leader in immigrant social service work and founder of the International Institute movement, was born in Hamilton, N.Y., the second of three children and elder daughter of Benjamin Stites and Mary (Baldwin) Terry. Her father, a descendant of Northwest Territory pioneers, had graduated from Colgate University in 1878 and served as a Baptist minister. At the time of Edith's birth he was teaching history at Colgate, and in 1892 he became professor of English history at the University of Chicago. Her mother, of English ancestry, was the daughter of a Baptist minister.

Edith Terry grew up in Chicago and received an A.B. from the University of Chicago in 1907. While attending the Chicago School of Civics and Philanthropy (1907–08), she did field research on women in industry for the Chicago Women's Trade Union League. This experience turned her interest to the problems of immigrants, as did her work as a field investigator for the Chicago Juvenile Court (1908) under the direction of JULIA LATHROP. She then served as a special agent for the United States Immigration Commission, and as a resident at University of Chicago Settlement and at the Union Settlement in New York City. In 1910, she began work with immigrant girls as a national field secretary for the National Board of the YWCA in New York. On Sept. 4, 1912, Edith Terry married Harry M. Bremer, a resident at the Greenwich House settlement in New York City and later a special agent with the National Child Labor Committee.

Edith Terry Bremer made her most important contribution to immigrant social welfare as founder and leader of the International Institute movement. Concerned that the existing public and private agencies serving immigrants largely ignored women, she established the first International Institute in New York City as a YWCA experiment in December 1910. Its purpose was to assist newly arrived and second-generation immigrant girls and women by providing English classes, recreational and club activities, and assistance with employment, housing, naturalization, and other problems. Most of the Institute's teaching, visiting, counseling, and casework was conducted by nationality workers —trained social workers who were immigrants themselves.

The advent of World War I temporarily diverted Bremer's attention from establishing new International Institutes. She assumed direction of work for foreign-born women under the YWCA's War Work Council and was also chiefly responsible for the recruitment and training of the Polish Gray Samaritans, young Polish-American women who went to Poland to do postwar relief and social service work. After the war, the International Institute movement proliferated, and by the mid-1920s, fifty-five Institutes had been established, primarily in industrial cities with large ethnic populations.

During the 1920s and early 1930s, as head of the YWCA's Department of Immigration and Foreign Communities (renamed in March 1932 the Bureau of Immigration and Foreign-Born), Edith Bremer provided inspiration and central direction for the International Institutes. She helped local YWCAs organize new Institutes, made field visits to advise on programs, sponsored annual meetings of Institute workers, and publicized the immigrant cause in articles and speeches. Through a stream of newsletters and memos from the national office, she alerted Institute workers to new developments in immigration law and urged sensitivity in dealing with ethnic communities. During these years, Bremer also testified as an expert witness at congressional hearings on immigration policies and lobbied in Washington for more flexible and humane immigration laws. In 1927, she was awarded the Order of the White Lion by President Thomas G. Masaryk of Czechoslovakia for her immigrant welfare work.

Bremer formulated a philosophy for the International Institute movement which opposed the ruthless Americanization and forced assimilation common in the postwar years. In a 1911 report, she had rejected the "prevailing notion that work for immigrants must be either shaking hands on Ellis Island or making them learn English." As the movement developed, she gradually elaborated a policy of cultural pluralism. Institute nationality workers not only engaged in traditional settlement work, but also, following Bremer's ideas, tried to foster a sense of cultural identity among newcomers. They encouraged pride in the immigrant heritage, advocated cooperation and understanding among ethnic groups, and urged immigrants to retain their languages and folkways while simultaneously learning American ways. At the same time, they encouraged Americans to understand immigrant customs and recognize ethnic contributions to American life.

In December 1933, after several years of discussion and planning, and with YWCA approval, Edith Bremer founded the National Institute of Immigrant Welfare (which became the American Federation of International Institutes in 1944). This new national agency took over the functions of the YWCA's Bureau of Immigration and Foreign-Born and became the umbrella organization for the International Institutes, most of which separated from their local YWCAs. Bremer became executive director of the new agency, which continued to oversee the efforts of the individual International Institutes, and worked to reform and humanize the immigration laws and to promote cultural pluralism.

During World War II the agency sought to secure fair treatment for immigrant aliens and eliminate conflicts among different ethnic groups. It subsequently aided in the resettlement of European refugees, displaced persons, and Japanese-Americans who had been incarcerated during the war. In the postwar years, Bremer remained active in a number of organizations dedicated to the assistance of immigrants and refugees. She retired as executive director of the American Federation of International Institutes in 1954, but from 1955 to 1958 served as acting director of the International Institute of New York, the agency she had founded in 1910. Edith Terry Bremer died in 1964 of cancer at her home in Port Washington, N.Y., and was survived by her husband. In a letter to the editor of the *New York Times* following her death, Edward Corsi, a former United States commissioner of immigration, paid tribute to Bremer's "passionate concern for people of all nationalities and the tireless effort she devoted to the welfare of immigrant and refugee, to helping them adjust to American life and to encouraging their contribution toward . . . a richer and more varied America."

[There is no collection of Edith Terry Bremer papers, but four manuscript collections have information about her work in the International Institute movement: the archives of the Nat. Board, YWCA, N.Y. City; the YWCA papers in the Sophia Smith Coll., Smith College; the Edward Corsi papers, the George Arents Research Library, Syracuse Univ.; and the Am. Council for Nationalities Service papers, at the Immigration History Research Center, Univ. of Minn., which contain the papers of the Am. Fed. of International Institutes. Bremer's writings include "Education for 'Immigrant Women': What Is It?" *Educational Foundations*, 1916; "Foreign Community and Immigration Work of the National Young Women's Christian Association," *Immigrants in America Rev.*, Jan. 1916; "Our International Institutes and the War," Nat. Conference of Social Work, *Proc.*, 1918; "The Foreign Language Worker in the Fusion Process," Nat. Conference of Social Work, *Proc.*, 1919; *The International Institutes in Foreign Community Work: Their Program and Phi-*

losophy (1923); "Immigrants and Foreign Communities," *Social Work Yearbook, 1929* (1930); "Development of Private Social Work with the Foreign Born," Am. Acad. of Political and Social Sci., *Annals*, March 1949; three articles in *The Survey*, May 15, 1924, Jan. 15, 1925, Dec. 15, 1930; and two dozen articles in the YWCA magazine, *Association Monthly* (renamed *Womans Press* in 1922), 1913–34. A photograph appears in *Womans Press*, Nov. 1927. Useful secondary sources are: Mary S. Sims, *The Natural History of a Social Institution— the Young Women's Christian Association* (1936); Julia Talbot Bird, "Immigrant Women and the International Institutes of the Young Women's Christian Association" (M.A. thesis, Yale Univ., 1932); Raymond A. Mohl, "The American Federation of International Institutes," in Peter Romanofsky, ed., *Greenwood Encyc. of Am. Institutions: Social Service Organizations* (1978), vol. I. The latter also contains a useful bibliography. Edith Terry Bremer's birth date and information about the Terry family were provided by the Colgate Univ. Archives. See also *Who Was Who in America*, I (1942), and an obituary in the *Port Washington News*, Sept. 17, 1964; death record provided by N.Y. State Dept. of Health.]

RAYMOND A. MOHL

BRICE, Fanny, Oct. 29, 1891–May 29, 1951. Comedian.

Fanny Brice made America laugh for forty years. Like many other great comedians, she was born on Manhattan's Lower East Side. She was the second daughter and third of four children of Rose (Stern) Borach, who emigrated from Hungary at age ten, and Charles Borach, known as "Pinochle Charlie," who was a heavy-gambling, happy-go-lucky Alsatian. Fanny grew up in Newark, N.J., where her parents eventually owned seven saloons. While Rose ran the businesses, Pinochle Charlie spent the profits and encouraged young Fanny to sing on tables and bartops. Finally, Rose sold the saloons, left Charlie, and moved with her children to Brooklyn, where she went into the real estate business. Like her mother, Fanny later became a strong, independent, professional woman with marital problems.

Even as a girl, Fanny knew performing was to be her life, and theater audiences were to be her best teachers. By the age of fourteen, she had quit school, won her first amateur contest, and taken the name of family friend John Brice. At fifteen, she discovered that she was too tall and skinny to become a chorus girl in the age of the short, chunky chorine, so she learned to rely on her talent and humor, not her figure. In 1910, while she was touring on the Columbia burlesque circuit, Irving Berlin gave her a song

to perform called "Sadie Salome," a Yiddish dialect parody of the Salomé dance. For her first performance of it, Brice wore a heavily starched sailor suit that made her squirm and make faces as she sang. The audience loved it, and from then on she built her act on parody, dialect, and physical humor.

Brice quickly moved to stardom in the *Ziegfeld Follies* and the other major forms of contemporary show business—vaudeville, musicals, drama, movies, and radio. Her big break came in the *Follies of 1910*, in which her first number earned her twelve encores. Blending serious material like the pathos of "Second Hand Rose" (who "never had a t'ing that ain't been used") and the heartbreak of "My Man" with comedy numbers that included lampooning Camille, vamping THEDA BARA, and tripping through "The Dying Swan," Brice became Florenz Ziegfeld's greatest female star. She was in nine *Follies* from 1910 to 1936; she toured big-time vaudeville, headlining at the Palace Theatre in New York in 1923; and she was in a number of musicals, from *The Honeymoon Express* (1913) and *Music Box Revue* (1924) to *Fioretta* (1929), *Sweet and Low* (1930), and *Crazy Quilt* (1931). Her only stage failure was *Fanny* (1926), a serious drama. She also made six movies, including *My Man* (1928), *The Great Ziegfeld* (1936), and *Ziegfeld Follies* (1946).

Brice, who was forceful and blunt, always insisted on controlling her own material. Even in her first big break, the 1910 *Follies*, she refused to change her song lyrics at the orders of producer Abe Erlanger, who fired her before Ziegfeld smoothed things over. "Fanny had a consideration for artistic integrity that I've never encountered elsewhere," Katharine Hepburn noted.

Brice became a household word to a new generation because of radio and her most distinctive character, "Baby Snooks," a devilish infant whose impish wisecracks made audiences think about the human condition as they roared with laughter. Brice had created Snooks in 1912 for vaudeville, but she did not develop her onstage until *Sweet and Low* and the *Ziegfeld Follies* of 1934 and 1936. Snooks appeared on radio in 1936 on "The Ziegfeld Follies of the Air" and was a regular on "Good News," starting in 1937, and "Maxwell House Coffee Time." In 1944 Brice began her own very popular "Baby Snooks" radio show, which ran until her death.

But Brice's personal life lacked the happiness and fulfillment that she found professionally. On Feb. 14, 1910, while touring with the revue *College Girls*, she impulsively married Frank

White, a barber from Springfield, Mass.; they probably never lived together and she divorced him in 1913, the year after she began living with dashing gambler Jules W. "Nick" Arnstein, whom she married on Oct. 18, 1918. She could accept Arnstein's squandering of her money and his two jail terms for fraud and theft (1915–17, 1924–25), but she could not accept his infidelity. She divorced him in September 1927 but never stopped loving him, despite her marriage to producer Billy Rose, which lasted from 1929 to 1938.

With Arnstein, she had two children, Frances (b. 1919) and William (b. 1921), who were raised by servants while Brice worked. She spent as much time with her children as possible, but she missed the full family life that she felt her career precluded. "I didn't want my daughter to have a career," she reflected. "Because if a woman has a career, she misses an awful lot. And I knew it then, that if you have a career, then the career is your life."

Brice's career proved that women could excel as comedians without exploiting their sexuality or making fools of themselves or other women. She did not joke about her home life or about domestic topics. She based her career on what the *Literary Digest* in 1934 called her "talent for sly dissection of all that is fake and preposterous." Whether parodying opera singers, fan dancers, evangelists, cockneys, Indians, boxers, or royalty, she always did it with humanity and sensitivity. "Because when I did a character," she explained, "I was that character." Based on human nature as it was, Brice's humor had a timeless appeal. As film director George Cukor observed, "Fanny was one of the great, great clowns of all time." In 1951, a few months before her sixtieth birthday, Brice died in Los Angeles of a stroke.

[The Billy Rose Theatre Coll., N.Y. Public Library, has a clipping file on Brice. The only full-length biography of Brice, from which the quotations here are taken, is Norman Katkov's *The Fabulous Fanny* (1953). Weak on facts and details of her career, it is still very valuable for insights into Brice as a person, combining interviews with her friends and family and her unpublished autobiography. For details of Brice's career see *Dict. Am. Biog.*, Supp. Five, and *Current Biog.*, 1946. Information and reminiscences on her early career are in Eddie Cantor, *As I Remember Them* (1963), and Niven Busch, Jr., *Twenty-One Americans* (1930). A sketch of her life and career is in Marjorie Farnsworth, *The Ziegfeld Follies* (1956). A birth certificate provided by the N.Y. City Municipal Archives reflects changes made in 1950; marriage certificate for Fannie Borach and Frank White from Mass. Dept. of Public Health; death record from Calif. Dept. of Public Health. Her obituary appeared in the *N.Y. Times*, May 30, 1951.]

ROBERT C. TOLL

BRONNER, Augusta Fox, July 22, 1881–Dec. 11, 1966. Psychologist.

Augusta Fox Bronner, clinical psychologist and expert on juvenile delinquency, was born in Louisville, Ky., to Hanna (Fox) and Gustave Bronner, a wholesale milliner. Both sets of grandparents had migrated from Germany, and her maternal grandfather had been a leader of the Jewish community of Louisville and a founder of the Reform Temple. The Bronners were comfortable financially, and Augusta grew up in a close-knit, richly cultured family. Her relationships with her brother, one year older, and two older male cousins were close and competitive; she took a maternal and protective attitude toward her younger sister. Bronner's mother and her independent maternal grandmother both urged her to pursue a career; she was not required to learn to do housework.

After attending schools in Cincinnati, where the family lived for several years, and in Louisville, Bronner graduated from public high school in Louisville in 1898. From the age of six she had wanted to be a teacher, and she entered Louisville Normal School. Eye problems caused Bronner to drop out after one year, and she spent a *Wanderjahr* in Europe with an aunt. Returning, she finished normal school in 1901; later that year she took over an unruly class of fourth graders, whom she quickly brought under control. In 1903 she went to Teachers College, Columbia University (B.S., 1906; A.M., 1909), where she held a position grading papers for Edward L. Thorndike, the creative educational psychologist.

From 1906 to 1911, Bronner taught English in Louisville at the girls high school from which she had graduated. Her experiences with students were extremely rewarding; in later years, in the clinics, she took special responsibility for adolescent girls. After her father died in 1911, Bronner returned to Teachers College, acting again as Thorndike's assistant. She studied with both the theoretically oriented Columbia psychologists and the practical-minded psychologists at Teachers College, but inclined toward the latter. For her dissertation she conducted a study of groups of girls to determine the relationship between mental defect and delinquency. Mental testing was just beginning, and retardation was often regarded as a cause of delinquency. Bronner's dissertation, completed and published in 1914, became a standard work showing that character rather than intelligence distinguished the offenders from the others.

In 1913 Bronner attended the Harvard summer school course given by William Healy (1869–1963), a Chicago neurologist, on the motivations of juvenile offenders. Healy had begun research on juvenile delinquency in 1909, at the instance of ETHEL STURGES DUMMER and other associates of Hull House. Seeking to draw conclusions only after thorough physical, psychological, and social investigation, he pioneered in the individual study of delinquents. Healy recognized Bronner's interest and ability and offered her a position as psychologist at the Chicago Juvenile Psychopathic Institute that he headed.

Because their work in Chicago was limited to research, both Bronner and Healy came to feel frustrated by their inability to follow up diagnosis with understanding treatment. Learning from Bronner that some Boston philanthropists were interested in his type of work, Healy agreed to move, knowing that there would be effective social agencies available to give treatment there. The Judge Baker Foundation (later Guidance Center), the model for hundreds of child guidance clinics in the United States and abroad, opened in 1917 with Healy as director and Bronner as assistant director.

In her early work with Healy, Bronner did most of the psychological testing; she also interviewed adolescent girls and sometimes younger children. As the guidance center expanded, Bronner increasingly did the administrative work and most of the supervision of psychologists and social workers, while Healy supervised the medical work. By 1930 Bronner felt the need for more administrative authority and was named codirector. After Healy's wife died, Bronner married him, in September 1932. The only change that marriage made in their professional collaboration was to facilitate their working together evenings and weekends, while complicating administration of the clinic when they took vacations together.

For some years Bronner had continued to publish on her own. *The Psychology of Special Abilities and Disabilities* (1917), which was reprinted several times, was important not only in emphasizing the limitations of mental testing but also in helping to inspire the vocational testing movement. Her widely cited article, "Attitude as It Affects Performances of Tests" (1916), similarly emphasized the affective factors that help determine test results. But increasingly Bronner published jointly with Healy. They worked closely together, and sometimes

one, sometimes the other, made a first draft from a jointly composed outline.

Together they had a powerful influence on both clinical psychology and criminology. *A Manual of Individual Mental Tests and Testing* (1927), a fundamentally important guide, appeared just as the mental testing movement was getting under way. After about 1930, when they began to combine treatment with diagnosis, they were able to do remarkable pioneer work in following up their cases. Particularly significant was their development of the widely adopted "team" concept in psychiatric practice —which brought the psychologist, the social worker, and others into a case conference with the physician. The prototypical nonphysician who came on an equal basis, Bronner scheduled the case conferences and oversaw the many students who served in residence at the clinic. Over the years she also did much outside lecturing, to the public, at Boston University and Simmons College, and in special courses, such as one offered jointly with Healy to FBI agents in training.

Bronner, who served as president of the American Orthopsychiatric Association in 1932, limited her influence by failing to publish results of a number of interesting psychological research projects and by deliberately staying in Healy's shadow. Another limiting factor was Healy and Bronner's joint decision to keep the Judge Baker Guidance Center small enough to be personal. Nevertheless her work enriched the fields of mental testing, mental health, and criminology. She also aided, both directly and indirectly, countless children who had deviated from the norms of society.

Bronner and Healy planned to retire during World War II, but lack of staff kept them on the job until late 1946. After 1950 they lived in Clearwater, Fla. Bronner died at home in December 1966.

[The Judge Baker Guidance Center is establishing an archives in the Francis A. Countway Library of Medicine, Boston, that will contain some Bronner papers, but most of her papers were destroyed upon her retirement. Some of the Center's informal publications contain photographs of Bronner at work. There are occasional Bronner letters in the Ethel Sturges Dummer Papers in the Schlesinger Library, Radcliffe College. A full but still incomplete list of Bronner's publications may be found in *Author Index to Psychological Index, 1894 to 1935* (1960), and *Psychological Abstracts, 1927 to 1958* (1960), vols. 1 and 2. "Attitude as It Affects Performances of Tests" appeared in *Psychological Rev.*, July 1916. In addition to such standard biographical directories as *The Psychological Register*, the main source of information is a typescript of oral history interviews with Healy and Bronner conducted in 1960 and 1961 by John C. Burnham, copies of which are available at the Judge Baker Guidance Center and at the Houghton Library, Harvard Univ. The chief published autobiographical account is William Healy and Augusta F. Bronner, "The Child Guidance Clinic, Birth and Growth of an Idea," in Lawson G. Lowrey and Victoria Sloane, eds., *Orthopsychiatry, 1923–1948, Retrospect and Prospect* (1948), which also contains a useful bibliography. An obituary appeared in the *Boston Globe*, Dec. 12, 1966. A biobibliography prepared by Kathy Blythe was useful in preparing this article.]

JOHN C. BURNHAM

BROOKS, Romaine, May 1, 1874–Dec. 7, 1970. Artist.

Romaine Brooks was born Beatrice Romaine Goddard in Rome, Italy, where her American mother, Ella (Waterman) Goddard, was staying after being deserted by her husband, Major Harry Goddard. Both parents were of English ancestry and had been born in Pennsylvania. Harry Goddard's father was a well-known preacher, and the Waterman family were wealthy owners of coal mines. Romaine was the youngest of four children, three girls and a boy. (The eldest daughter died in infancy.) The object of Ella Goddard's European travels was to seek help for her much-loved son, Henry St. Mar, who already, at age seven, showed signs of being mentally disturbed. Because he was more manageable when Romaine was with him, much of her childhood was spent as his companion and keeper. St. Mar's madness, however, seemed mild to Romaine compared to the more exacting and autocratic madness of their mother, who was both vindictive and entirely unpredictable.

When Romaine Goddard was only six or seven her mother left her with their laundress in a crowded New York tenement while she took St. Mar to Europe to consult another physician. An arrangement for money to be forwarded each week for her care was soon forgotten, but after almost six months she was rescued by her grandfather's secretary and sent to the Chestnut Hill, Pa., home of an aunt and uncle. They chose St. Mary's Hall, an Episcopal school in Burlington, N.J., where Romaine Goddard stayed for four years (1882–86) before joining her mother and brother in London. Two years later she was placed in a convent school in northern Italy, returning for holidays to Menton, in southeastern France, where her mother had three villas. From 1891 until 1893 she attended a private finishing school in Geneva and then boarded with a family in Paris, where she studied music and art (1893–95). Forbidden by her mother to draw, she could only indulge her talent and love for drawing while she was away at school. Finally, when she was twenty-one, after briefly attempting a singing career, Goddard set off for Rome to study painting. With the help of the Waterman family lawyer, her mother was prevailed upon to give her a monthly allowance of 300 francs, just enough for a meager living.

In Rome Goddard attended the free Scuola Nazionale during the day and the Circolo Artistico in the evenings. In the summer of 1899 she discovered the island of Capri, where she felt very much at home, enjoying its beauty, making friends, and starting to paint portraits, some of which she sold. Her peaceful life in Capri was disturbed in December 1901 when she received word that St. Mar had died. Summoned to Nice, she was caught again in the maelstrom of her mother's irascible nature. But her mother was seriously ill with diabetes, of which she died within a year. Goddard inherited the family fortune, becoming financially independent. She returned to Capri, resuming her friendships there including that with Charles Lang Freer, donor of the Freer Gallery of Art in Washington, D.C. Freer urged her to go to London to see the paintings of his friend James McNeill Whistler and to settle in Cornwall where Whistler had worked. This she did, after an "ephemeral marriage" to John Ellingham Brooks, an English dilettante who accompanied her to London, but whom she shortly discarded, giving him an annuity.

Finding that the vivid colors she had used at Capri were not appropriate for the landscape of England, Romaine Brooks spent long hours at St. Ives in Cornwall training her eyes to detect and her brushes to note down an endless variety of grays. She found the resulting subtle palette most congenial and continued to use it during her entire career.

By 1908 Brooks felt that she was ready to seek an artistic career in Paris. Furnishing her apartment there in her customary color scheme of black, white, gray, and beige, she produced a dramatic effect comparable to that of Whistler's white rooms in London some years before. She became well known as an interior decorator among her friends in Parisian society, who also clamored to have her paint their portraits. In 1910 she was invited to exhibit her paintings at the prestigious Galeries Durand-Ruel in Paris. Claude Roger-Marx, in his introduction to the catalog of the exhibition, described the paintings as "faithful effigies, innocent of fraud," in which "the soul is identified with the flesh," and the aesthete Robert de Montesquiou called her a "thief of souls."

The most striking painting in the exhibition, a reclining nude entitled "White Azaleas," was one of a series for which the model was Ida Rubinstein, who had been introduced to Paris in 1909 by Sergei Diaghilev as Cleopatra in the first of his Ballet Russe presentations. Brooks was fascinated by Rubinstein, finding in her thin, lithe figure the living incarnation of her own artistic ideal. In "Le Trajet" (The Crossing), a symbolic painting in the art nouveau manner, a lovely nude closely resembling Rubinstein rests on a long, unadorned white wing floating over an extensive black background. In Brooks's only formal portrait of Rubinstein she appears as a rare beauty, wrapped in a flowing black cloak with sharply highlighted white revers.

In 1912 Brooks painted an incisive portrait of the poet and playwright Gabriele D'Annunzio called "The Poet in Exile." D'Annunzio, who had settled in Paris after bad debts barred him from his native Italy, became her close friend; she said that knowing him lifted her out of a state of despondency. A group of sonnets he wrote to accompany her 1914 painting of Rubinstein, "La France Croisée," inspired by the outbreak of World War I, was exhibited with the canvas to benefit the Red Cross. For most of World War I she lived in Italy, settling in Venice to be near D'Annunzio, who was taking a heroic role in Italy's aerial combat.

Around 1915 Romaine Brooks first met NATALIE CLIFFORD BARNEY, an American writer whose Paris salon was frequented by Marcel Proust, André Gide, D'Annunzio, Paul Valéry, and Remy de Gourmont, as well as by members of a circle of lesbian artists and writers. Brooks and Barney formed a passionate friendship and lived together during most of the next forty years.

Brooks's work had three important showings, giving a comprehensive view of her achievement, in 1925. Thirty-five paintings were exhibited first at the Galerie Jean Charpentier in Paris, then at the Alpine Club Gallery in London, and finally at Wildenstein's in New York. As fine as any of her paintings was her self-portrait: it depicts an isolated figure whose face expresses a temperate calm and a strength that defies the twilight of color and the ruined landscape behind her. A triumph of introspection and perception, the painting reflects her postwar belief that she was an outcast.

After the 1925 exhibitions Brooks withdrew further into herself and began to concentrate entirely on her drawings. At the same time she decided to write about her life with her mother

and her brother, calling the document "No Pleasant Memories." As she reconstructed this nightmare existence she produced more than a hundred drawings which represent the most exciting, original aspect of her art. Linear fantasies, resembling the visions of Poe, Wilde, and Valéry, they are strange, mysterious, and poetic, and display a passionate intelligence that commanded the respect and admiration of some of the foremost critics of her time.

Brooks returned to the United States in 1935 for a show of her drawings at the Arts Club of Chicago; she then lived for a time at Carnegie Hall in New York City. Returning to Europe just before the outbreak of World War II in 1939 Brooks, with Natalie Barney, left France for Florence. They later moved to nearby Fiesole, where they lived until 1967.

Despite a cataract in one eye, which she diagnosed and treated herself, Romaine Brooks still painted even in her eighties. In her final years she lived increasingly as a recluse, with a housekeeper as her only companion. Barney had returned to Paris and was living with another woman. Romaine Brooks died at her home in Nice at the age of ninety-six.

[There is no collection of Brooks's papers. Reproductions of her work appear in the privately printed *Romaine Brooks: Portraits—Tableaux—Dessins* (1952) and *Romaine 70 Dessins* (n.d.). There is a biography by Meryle Secrest, *Between Me and Life: A Biography of Romaine Brooks* (1974); it includes a bibliography. Another major biographical account is the introduction by Adelyn Breeskin to *Romaine Brooks: "Thief of Souls"* (1971), the catalog of an exhibition at the Nat. Coll. of Fine Arts, Smithsonian Institution. A brief biographical sketch and evaluation of her work is in Linda Nochlin and Ann S. Harris, *Women Artists* (1977). See also George Wickes, *The Amazon of Letters: The Life and Loves of Natalie Barney* (1977), and Jean Chalon, *Portrait of a Seductress: The World of Natalie Barney* (1979).]

ADELYN D. BREESKIN

BROWN, Charlotte Eugenia Hawkins, June 11, 1883?–Jan. 11, 1961. Educator, school founder.

Charlotte Hawkins Brown was born Lottie Hawkins in Henderson, N.C., the daughter of Caroline Frances Hawkins (sometimes called Carrie) and Edmund H. Hight. Caroline Hawkins was a direct descendant of the English navigator John D. Hawkins through her mother, a former house slave named Rebecca. Educated in the elementary department of Shaw University, Caroline Hawkins early imbued her daughter with high cultural and educational aspirations.

The prospects of increased opportunities

caused the large Hawkins clan to move in the late 1880s to Cambridge, Mass. By this time Caroline Hawkins had married a man named Willis who helped support the family by doing odd jobs, including brick masonry. Lottie Hawkins helped out by caring for infants and working for the hand laundry operated by the Willises. Such industry did not prevent her from attending grammar school and the Cambridge English High School, where she excelled academically.

With the approach of high school graduation in 1900, Hawkins decided to upgrade her name, becoming Charlotte Eugenia. It was during the same period that she by chance encountered ALICE FREEMAN PALMER, president of Wellesley College. Hawkins so impressed Palmer with her intelligence that she provided the financial aid and sponsorship which enabled Hawkins to attend the two-year State Normal School at Salem beginning in 1900. Much to the amazement of her mother, who was a strong influence throughout her life, Hawkins left Salem at the beginning of her second year. (A later reevaluation of her record resulted in her being granted a diploma.) Through another chance encounter, on a train, Hawkins had been recruited by a representative of the American Missionary Association to teach in one of its schools near McLeansville (later Sedalia), N.C. Influenced by her exposure to liberal New England thinking and to the cause of racial uplift preached at the family's Union Baptist Church, Hawkins had decided to use her talents and skills for the education of blacks in the rural south. She started teaching in October 1901 at Bethany Institute, in little more than a run-down country church. When the American Missionary Association phased out the school the following year, it was taken over by the Sedalia community with Hawkins determinedly at its head. She returned for a time to New England, giving concerts at resorts to raise funds for the school that in 1902 she renamed the Palmer Memorial Institute in memory of her mentor.

Though it began as a rural grammar school with emphasis on agriculture and manual training, Palmer was to exercise an influence in education and social circles understandable only in light of the dedicated and dynamic personality of its leader. Hawkins's single-minded determination perhaps accounts for her less than five years of marriage to Edward S. Brown. Brown taught school in New Orleans before completing his education at Harvard University, where he met Charlotte Hawkins, who was in Cambridge often and attended summer school at Harvard in 1901 and 1909. They were married in 1911. He served as both a teacher and dormitory head at Palmer until they separated and he relocated in another school farther south. Although she had no children of her own, Charlotte Hawkins Brown raised the three daughters of her widowed half brother, Mingo, and the two daughters and two sons of her mother's sister, Ella Brice. She also cared for her ailing mother, who spent her final days at Palmer, dying in 1938.

Despite these family responsibilities, Brown built Palmer into a thriving school which graduated its first accredited high school class in 1922. Through her lifelong fund-raising efforts, she won contributions both from wealthy northerners and from southerners and was able to expand the physical facilities of Palmer and increase its staff and enrollment. Dedicated to interracial cooperation, Brown introduced exchange programs and encouraged interracial contact in cultural activities. She integrated the school into the Sedalia community, working on local health problems and urging blacks to vote and seek home ownership. Until 1937, when the town opened a public school, Palmer was subsidized by the county to educate local children. Thereafter, it was forced to rely exclusively on private funding, and focused on its secondary and junior college levels (the latter introduced in the mid-1920s).

Palmer's reputation and that of its founder increasingly attracted black middle-class students from other parts of the country. The school was recognized for its strong academic program, which emphasized the arts, self-discipline, and cultural attainments. By 1941, with the publication of her book *The Correct Thing to Do, to Say, and to Wear,* Brown had become known as the "First Lady of Social Graces." She was invited to lecture at many schools and colleges about her interests in education and interracial cooperation, as well as her views on manners and morality.

Her growing reputation as an educator brought Brown honorary master's degrees and honorary doctorates from Lincoln University in Pennsylvania, Wilberforce University in Ohio, Howard University, and Tuskegee Institute. Her avid pursuit of excellence in the academic achievements and character development of Palmer students did not preclude her serving other institutions in which she believed. Brown was a founding member of the National Council of Negro Women. From 1915 to 1936 she served as president of the North Carolina State Federation of Negro Women's Clubs, and she was also president of the North Carolina Teachers Association (1935–37). In 1945 she was a Council of Congregational Churches delegate to England and spoke at the Congrès International des

Femmes in Paris. Brown was the first black woman selected for membership in the Twentieth Century Club of Boston (1928), an organization honoring distinction in the fields of religion, education, art, and science. She also served on the national board of the YWCA, and was the first black woman on the North Carolina Council of Defense (1940). Despite her accomplishments, she never missed the opportunity for self-improvement, taking advanced courses at several universities.

Charlotte Hawkins Brown retired as president of Palmer Memorial Institute in 1952, but remained active as vice president of the board and director of finances until 1955. After a lingering illness, she died of heart failure in Greensboro, N.C., in 1961, a decade before Palmer was forced to close because of financial difficulties. For nearly a half century, Charlotte Hawkins Brown had set her mark upon American education, graduating young black men and women into leading colleges and universities from which they went forth to leadership positions in their professions and communities throughout the country.

[The Charlotte Hawkins Brown Papers at the Schlesinger Library, Radcliffe College, contain speeches, correspondence, biographical material, memorabilia, and materials concerning the Palmer Memorial Institute. The vertical file and aids index at the Schomburg Center for Research in Black Culture, N.Y. Public Library, also has material on Brown and the Palmer Institute; papers concerning her work with the Nat. Council of Negro Women are in the NCNW's Nat. Archives for Black Women's Hist., Washington, D.C. Her other publications are *Mammy: An Appeal to the Heart of the South* (1919) and a series of articles, "The Correct Thing," in *Norfolk Jour. and Guide*, 1940. The best published sources of information are a biography by Constance Marteena, *The Lengthening Shadow of a Woman* (1977); Sadie I. Daniel, *Women Builders* (1931); *Who's Who in Colored America*, 1927 and 1930–32; and "A Bit of New England in North Carolina," *Brown American*, Summer 1958. An obituary appeared in the *N.Y. Times*, Jan. 12, 1961. Additional information for this article was provided by Wilhelmina Crosson, and Salem State College. Most sources list Brown's year of birth as 1883, although it is sometimes given as 1882 or 1884. No birth record is available. Death certificate supplied by N.C. Board of Health.]

RUTH ANN STEWART

BROWN, Margaret Wise, May 23, 1910–Nov. 13, 1952. Children's author.

Margaret Wise Brown, innovator in the field of picture books, was born in New York City, the second of three children and elder daughter of Robert Bruce and Maude Margaret (John-son) Brown. Her mother was born in Kansas, her father in Missouri. Robert Brown, an executive with the American Manufacturing Company, was the son of Benjamin Gratz Brown, governor of Missouri (1871–73). When Margaret was three the Browns moved from Brooklyn to Whitestone Landing, Queens, a suburban community near Long Island Sound. There the children had a profusion of pets—rabbits, squirrels, guinea pigs, goldfish, a cat, and a dog.

After attending Long Island schools, Margaret Brown went to the Château Brillantmont School in Switzerland and to Dana Hall School in Wellesley, Mass. She received her A.B. in 1932 from Hollins College in Virginia (which her mother had also attended), majoring in English. Her ambition to become a writer was temporarily dampened by a writing course she took at Columbia University; she felt that she would never master the technique of plotting a short story. In 1935 she enrolled in the Bureau of Educational Experiments (later the Bank Street College of Education) in New York City. LUCY SPRAGUE MITCHELL, who ran the school, encouraged Brown to try writing for preschool children and to follow the precepts of the Here-and-Now ideas that Mitchell herself had originated: to tell stories about the child's own world from the child's point of view, free from fantasy, fairy tales, and talking animals. While Brown soon moved beyond didactic explanations, Here-and-Now concepts influenced much of her work. She enjoyed testing stories by reading preliminary drafts aloud to children; upon becoming a member of the Bureau's publications staff she read manuscripts in progress to the children in the model school's nursery and kindergarten classes.

Even after leaving Bank Street, Brown continued to "borrow" classes of three- to five-year-olds to use as "guinea pigs." The children reacted to the presence of any element that was complicated, false, or adult, suggested new subjects and ideas, and indicated words and phrases they liked. They were interested in sights, smells, tastes, and textures, and were excited by contrasts, similarities, and surprises.

Within two years (1937–38) Brown wrote five books, translated and adapted stories for *The Children's Year* (1937), contributed to the second *Here and Now Story Book*, and edited *The Log of Christopher Columbus*. Her first book, a fairy tale reminiscent of a Chekhov story, was *When the Wind Blew* (1937), about an old, old lady with a toothache, seventeen cats, and a kitten who comforted her. In 1938 Harper published *The Streamlined Pig* and E. P. Dutton *The Fish with the Deep Sea Smile*, a collection of Brown's stories. The same year she became an editor at William R. Scott's publishing house, and within twelve months three of her books appeared under the Scott imprint: *Bumblebugs and Elephants* (1938), *The Little Fireman* (1938), and *Noisy Book* (1939). In the last, a blindfolded dog named Muffin listens to the city's noises and identifies their sources, with assistance from any five-year-old who is hearing the story being read. *Noisy Book*'s success led to *Country Noisy Book* and *The Seashore Noisy Book* (1941), *Indoor Noisy Book* (1942), *The Noisy Bird Book* (1943), *The Winter Noisy Book* (1947), *The Quiet Noisy Book* (1950), and *The Summer Noisy Book* (1951). Of this series Brown wrote that "their design and creation came right from the children themselves—from listening to them, watching them and letting them into the story . . . I was merely an ear and a pen" (*Hollins Alumnae Mag.*).

Margaret Brown left editing in 1941. By the mid-forties she was completing six or seven books a year, more than Scott or any one publishing house could handle. Harper became her main publisher, and Ursula Nordstrom her chief editor; in all, Harper issued thirty-four of her books, including *Goodnight Moon* (1947) and *Wait till the Moon Is Full* (1948), and acquired five of the Noisy Books from Scott. She was also published by ten other firms, among them Doubleday, Random House, Simon and Schuster, and T. Y. Crowell, and she used several noms de plume, such as Golden Macdonald, Timothy Hay, and Juniper Sage—the last for the six books on which she collaborated with Edith Thacher Hurd. She was concerned about the quality of her texts and made sure that the same high standards were met by the illustrations and the physical design of her books, including the way the pages turned—the "only action," she said, of a picture book. She worked with forty different artists, including Garth Williams, Leonard Weisgard, Clement Hurd, Esphyr Slobodkina, Jean Charlot, Remy Charlip, and Charles Shaw, striving for a perfect match between the text and its depiction—a goal that ordinarily involved numerous revisions in both. Brown once remarked that she finished the rough draft of a book in twenty minutes and then spent a year polishing. In fifteen years (1937–52) she produced more than a hundred books and wrote the lyrics for twenty-one children's records—drawn, in most cases, from her written works.

Margaret Brown lived and worked in New York City. She had an apartment and a studio —a small, ancient (ca. 1810) wooden farmhouse in the back yard of a Manhattan apartment building—and summered in Vinal Haven, Maine, in an isolated house that once belonged to a granite cutter. She was seldom without her Kerry Blue terrier, Smoke, or his successor, Crispian. She was unmarried, but was contemplating marriage when she died unexpectedly in 1952 at Nice, France, after an operation. Her books increased in popularity after her death, and many were republished. In the late 1970s, after more than a quarter of a century, almost half of all the work she completed was in print —proof of its classic quality.

[A collection of Margaret Brown's books and MSS. and some biographical material is at the Westerly Public Library, Westerly, R.I. An essay, "Writing for Children," appeared in *Hollins Alumnae Mag.*, Winter 1949. For additional information on her work see: Barbara Bader, *American Picturebooks* (1976); Louise Seaman Bechtel, "Margaret Wise Brown, 'Laureate of the Nursery,'" *Horn Book Mag.*, June 1958; Bruce Bliven, Jr., "Child's Best Seller," in *The Finishing Touch* (1978), reprinted from *Life*, Dec. 2, 1946; Lucy Sprague Mitchell, "Margaret Wise Brown, 1910–1952," *Children Here and Now: Notes from 69 Bank Street*, vol. I, no. 1, 1953; and an entry in *Dict. Am. Biog.*, Supp. Five. The essays by Bliven and Bechtel are accompanied by photographs. Obituaries appeared in the *N.Y. Times*, Nov. 15, 1952; *Publishers Weekly*, Nov. 22, 1952; *Time*, Nov. 24, 1952; and *Newsweek*, Nov. 24, 1952.]

BRUCE BLIVEN, JR.

BRUNAUER, Esther Delia Caukin, July 7, 1901–June 26, 1959. International affairs specialist, federal official.

Esther Brunauer was born near Jackson, Calif., the older of two daughters—an earlier girl had been stillborn—of Ray Oakheart and Grace Elizabeth (Blackwell) Caukin, both native Californians of English stock. Her father, an electrician, moved frequently in construction jobs, and served for a time as postmaster of Sierra Madre. A strong liberal whose beliefs verged on socialism, he later wrote a book about his economic theories. Her mother began work as a clerk in 1903; an active suffragist and one of the earliest supporters of Woodrow Wilson, she was rewarded in 1914 for her tireless campaign work with the position of receiver of the United States Land Office, apparently one of the earliest federal appointments for a woman.

During the first eight years of public school in the Berkeley-San Francisco area, Esther Caukin moved thirteen times. She graduated from Girls' High School in San Francisco in 1920 by living with friends and relatives during her parents' absence. Entering Mills College, she became the protégée of President AURELIA HENRY REINHARDT, receiving her B.A. in 1924. By 1927 she had completed a Ph.D. in history at Stanford University, aided by a fellowship from the

American Association of University Women (AAUW). She then joined the AAUW headquarters staff in Washington, D.C., in charge of its international education program, a position she filled until 1944. Notable among her contributions there was the International Problem of the Month Series. She made numerous visits to Europe, attending councils of the International Federation of University Women.

Esther Caukin was married on July 8, 1931, to Stephen Brunauer, a Hungarian who had arrived in the United States in 1921 and later became a commander in the United States Navy. A chemist, his research and writings led to international recognition. The Brunauers had three children: Louis (July-December 1934), Kathryn (b. 1938), and Elizabeth (b. 1942). Once the children arrived, Brunauer led an exceedingly busy life, balancing both family and professional responsibilities. In 1936, her mother-in-law came from Hungary to assume the major responsibility for running the home.

In 1933, with a fellowship from the Carl Schurz Foundation, Esther Brunauer spent a year in Germany, becoming an eyewitness to the rise of Adolf Hitler. At the University of Berlin, she concentrated her studies on the effects of the Nazi revolution and ideology on all aspects of German life, and even secured an interview with Hitler. She returned to speak with authority at congressional hearings and elsewhere on the Nazi threat to the United States. In the ensuing years Brunauer's brilliant and tireless work helped to make the AAUW the best informed women's organization in the country on foreign affairs; she also played a vital role in the association's decision in May 1941 to advocate all-out aid to the Allies ("Women on the Ramparts," p. 20). Her official report on national defense in relation to foreign policy, *National Defense, Institutions, Concepts, and Policies* (1937), was later credited by Admiral W. H. Standley, then Chief of Naval Operations, as being "largely responsible for converting various pacifistic organizations in this country and thus making possible an immediate program of rearmament" (*Dept. of State Bulletin*, April 10, 1950, p. 576). She became a founder of the Committee to Defend America by Aiding the Allies and chaired the committee that established the Women's Action Committee for Victory and Lasting Peace (1943–44).

In March 1944, Brunauer joined the United States Department of State as a specialist in international organizational affairs. She became heavily involved in drafting plans for the United Nations and particularly for the United Nations Educational, Scientific, and Cultural Organization (UNESCO). In February 1946 she became the third woman in the United States to hold the diplomatic rank of minister when she was appointed the United States representative on the Preparatory Commission to UNESCO. Thereafter she served as senior adviser at general conferences in Paris, Mexico City, Beirut, and Florence. Her outstanding service with UNESCO won wide recognition and national awards as well as the high praise of important public officials.

In early 1950, at the height of her professional career, Brunauer's world came crashing down. On February 11 of that year Senator Joseph R. McCarthy mentioned her name as one of four cases justifying his claim that there were communists in the Department of State. In the following weeks her case was highly, even sensationally, publicized and such prominent individuals as Milton S. Eisenhower defended her. Brunauer was fully cleared by the State Department's Loyalty Board and by a Senate subcommittee, chaired by Senator Millard B. Tydings, which denounced as "a fraud and a hoax" McCarthy's charges that Brunauer was a "security risk" because of such alleged communist-front activities as associating with Alger Hiss at the United Nations San Francisco Conference. In the meantime, Stephen Brunauer, having been cleared by the Navy Department four times, refused to subject himself to a fifth clearance; he resigned. The State Department then suspended Brunauer in April 1951 and terminated her employment in June 1952. Of the many great men and women who knew Esther Brunauer, none believed that the Department had acted fairly or that there was a shred of evidence to support McCarthy's accusation. It was a tragedy of the time that McCarthy, later shown to be a compulsive liar, was able to destroy the public career of such a capable and dedicated woman.

After her dismissal Esther Brunauer worked briefly for the Library of Congress. The Brunauers moved to Evanston, Ill., in September 1952, and she worked in the Chicago area as associate director of the Film Council of America and as an editor for Rand McNally and Company. Her final position was as textbook editor for the Follett Publishing Company. She died quietly in Evanston in June 1959 of a heart condition.

[Sources are scanty and widely scattered. This article is based chiefly on selected correspondence and papers in the custody of Stephen Brunauer and D. H. Brunauer, Potsdam, N.Y., and Kathryn Brunauer Horvat, Deerfield, Ill.; selected papers provided by the national headquarters of the AAUW and the Alumnae Office of Mills College; and government documents. Among Brunauer's many works published by the AAUW were: *European Diplomacy* (1930); *Germany, the National Socialist State* (1934); *Russia, A Study Course* (1931). She also contributed many articles to the *Jour. of the Am. Assoc. of Univ. Women*. Other significant articles or pamphlets by Brunauer include: "A Course for American Women at Oxford University," *School and Society*, Feb. 6, 1932; "Facing the Nazi Menace," *Vital Issues*, June 1941; "Women on the Ramparts," *Vital Issues*, July 1941; *Has America Forgotten? Myths and Facts About World Wars I and II* (1941), published by the Am. Council on Public Affairs; *International Council of Scientific Unions, Brussels and Cambridge* (1945), published by the Dept. of State; "The Peace Proposals of December, 1916–January, 1917," *Jour. of Modern Hist.*, Dec. 1932, a condensation of her dissertation; "Power, Politics and Democracy," Am. Acad. of Political and Social Science, *Annals*, July 1941; "The United States in the Transition to a New World Order," *International Conciliation*, April 1942. For her positions on critical foreign policy issues see government reports of hearings in which she participated, including two documents from the Committee on Foreign Affairs, U.S. House of Representatives: *Hearings, Am. Neutrality Policy*, 75th Cong., 1st sess., April 11–28, 1939 and May 2, 1939, and *Hearings, Membership and Participation by the United States in the United Nations Educational, Scientific, and Cultural Organization*, 79th Cong., 2nd sess., H. J. Res. 305, April 3–5, 1946. See also U.S. Senate, Subcommittee of the Committee on Foreign Relations, *State Dept. Employee Loyalty Investigation*, 81st Cong., 2nd sess., Pursuant to S. Res. 251, 1950. Articles about Brunauer and McCarthy's allegations appear in the *U.S. Dept. of State Bulletin* on March 27, 1950, April 10, 1950, and April 23, 1951. Helpful secondary articles include: "A Sketch and Portrait," *Independent Woman*, Nov. 1936; "Two Women Appointed to Important Policymaking Posts," *Independent Woman*, April 1946; "Brunauer Enigma," *Newsweek*, April 23, 1951; and *Current Biog.*, 1947. See also Ray O. Caukin, *Economics and American Democracy* (1955).]

BETTY MILLER UNTERBERGER

BUCK, Pearl, June 26, 1892–March 6, 1973. Writer.

Pearl Comfort Sydenstricker Buck, extraordinarily productive author and humanitarian, was born in Hillsboro, W. Va., in the home of her maternal grandparents, where her parents, Absolom and Caroline (Stulting) Sydenstricker, were on furlough from Presbyterian missionary work in China. She was the third of four daughters and the fifth of seven children, only three of whom reached maturity; Pearl grew up as the elder daughter. Her forebears had migrated to America to find religious freedom—her father's from Bavaria in the 1760s, her mother's from Utrecht in 1847.

Taken to China as an infant, the American missionary child grew up in the worlds of East and West, becoming "mentally bifocal," a process detailed in her autobiography, *My Several Worlds* (1954). Her early education consisted of her nurse's Chinese legends, her father's biblical readings, basic instruction and American history from her mother, and her own reading of Victorian novelists, especially Dickens. She often won the prize offered by the *Shanghai Mercury*, an English newspaper, for the best children's writing. After her family's escape during the 1900 Boxer Rebellion and their furlough in America, Pearl received private tutoring in Chinese subjects until 1905. She then attended missionary and boarding schools until 1910, when she went to Randolph-Macon Woman's College in Virginia, where she excelled. After earning her B.A. in 1914 she held a teaching assistantship in psychology until recalled to China later that year to nurse her ill mother.

Returning to politically restive China, Pearl ran her parents' household, taught in a boys' school, and studied Chinese literature. Readily attracted to John Lossing Buck, a young, handsome American agricultural expert, she married him in May 1917 after a brief courtship. They moved to North China, where she gained the knowledge of peasant life she portrayed so memorably in later books. After the birth of a daughter in March 1920, and Buck's subsequent hysterectomy in New York, they moved south to the University of Nanking, where he taught agriculture, she English literature.

In 1922, Buck began writing articles and short stories about China which appeared in various American magazines. During a leave in America in 1924–25, learning that her daughter was mentally retarded, she responded characteristically: while caring for the child at home, she took a master's degree in English at Cornell University, wrote an essay on "China and the West" to win the $200 Messenger Prize in History, and adopted another daughter.

Back in China, she helped support her enlarged family by teaching at Southeastern (1925–27) and Chung Yang Universities (1928–30), as well as at Nanking (1921–31). Compelled by creative and financial need, she began to write longer works. Her first novel perished in the 1927 revolutionary uprising in Nanking, in which the Bucks narrowly escaped death. In 1929, after placing her retarded daughter in the Vineland (N.J.) Training School, she returned to China and devoted herself to writing. Finding an agent's name in a handbook, she submitted an expanded short story, set in China, about the clash of old and new values—Buck's favorite theme. After many rejections, it was published in 1930 as *East Wind: West Wind* by the fledgling John Day Company, headed by Richard J. Walsh. Their publication of her next, most famous, novel, *The Good Earth* (1931), transformed her life.

Buck's realistic, sympathetic portrayal of a Chinese peasant family, the first in Western literature, proved an unprecedented success. Heading the best-seller lists for months, it sold nearly two million copies, was translated into over thirty languages, inspired a Broadway play (1932) and an award-winning Hollywood film (1937), received the Pulitzer Prize (1932), and figured in the innumerable later awards and honorary degrees given its author. The novel's exotic subject, its focus on universal processes in man and nature, and its lucid, flowing style (mentally translated from Chinese, according to Buck) attracted a worldwide audience.

Buck's subsequent books, including two successors to *The Good Earth* published as *The House of Earth* trilogy (1935), were successful. Few have remained highly esteemed, however. Most memorable are a novel, *The Mother* (1934), with its pioneering scenes of childbirth and abortion; her two-volume translation of the famous Chinese saga, *Shui Hu Chuan* (1933); and the companion biographies *The Exile* and *The Fighting Angel* (both 1936), the stories of her parents, whom she deftly made symbols as well as vivid individuals.

During a sabbatical at Cornell in 1932, Buck grew closer to her publisher-editor, Richard Walsh. They were married on June 11, 1935, after her divorce from Lossing Buck from whom she had separated in China in 1934. After her remarriage, Buck followed a disciplined writing schedule, compelled still by both her innate creativity and her obligations as the main family support. She published from one to five books annually, while managing the expanding farm she had bought in Perkasie, Pa., a New York City apartment, and, later, properties in Vermont. She also supervised all the help for her offices and residences, and for her six adopted and two foster children, who came from a variety of racial backgrounds.

Buck now began to treat American subjects and themes in a more conventional, journalistic style in novels like *This Proud Heart* (1938). A dramatization of her own conflict between work and marriage, the work met with less favor than her earlier novels. In 1938, however, she became the first American woman to win the Nobel Prize for literature, awarded for her earlier portrayals of China and for her parents' biographies. Although some objected because

she was a woman, too young, and not really American, the award revived her reputation and self-confidence, and convinced her to write for the masses, as Chinese novelists did. Her subsequent works, often serialized first in popular magazines, were always readable and informative. They sold very well in America and even better abroad, where even into the 1970s she remained widely translated. Because of their frequency, facility of plot and characterization, and, perhaps, their special appeal to women, her books were increasingly ignored by serious critics and academics.

When the United States entered the Second World War, one which Buck had anticipated, she devoted her talents to the Allied effort. Long active in United China Relief, she provided data for servicemen's Asian guidebooks and wrote radio plays for broadcast to China. As China's most famous Western interpreter, she publicized the war there in three novels—of which *Dragon Seed* (1942) is the best known and most timeless—as well as in propagandistic fiction which generated both sympathy and funds. In such essay collections as *Of Men and Women* (1941) and *American Unity and Asia* (1942), she strove to clarify the war's underlying issues, prophesying that ignorant white imperialist, racist, and sexist attitudes would undermine the Allied struggle as well as any future peace. Her advanced ideas on women's rights and responsibilities were lost on a war-absorbed public. She also tried to disseminate knowledge of Asia through the East and West Association, which she founded in 1941 to bring cultural figures from Asia to America; through *Asia Magazine*, which she and Walsh owned and directed from 1941 to 1946; and even through juvenile fiction such as *The Chinese Children Next Door* (1942), involving young Asians and Americans, and later *The Big Wave* (1948).

As the war ended, Buck continued to foster international understanding with her five "Talk Books." Based on extended interviews with knowledgeable participants, the books publicized important historic developments. These included the effect of the 1917 Russian Revolution (*Talk About Russia*, 1945), events in Germany between 1914 and 1933 (*How It Happens*, 1947), and interracial problems (*American Argument*, 1949).

Changing Asia continued to provide material for Buck's postwar fiction which, however, seemed less compelling as the subjects became more remote from her own experience. Her novels about prewar China, such as *Pavilion of Women* (1946), featuring a distinguished, mature heroine, and *Imperial Woman* (1956), a history of the last Empress, are more convincing than the four novels she published between 1949 and 1973 that dramatize the excesses in Communist China—and anticommunist America—both of which she abhorred. Her study of an interracial marriage, *The Hidden Flower* (1952), partly set in occupied Japan, her two portrayals of India (1953, 1970), and even her ambitious history of Korea, *The Living Reed* (1963) are also lacking in immediacy. Despite their varied literary quality, the books all sold widely and helped to inform readers about Asian countries.

Buck also wrote novels set wholly in America, often drawing on her family's experiences to explore subjects from the post-Civil War to the present. She issued the first five (1945–53) under the pseudonym, "John Sedges," lest she be dismissed, especially by male critics, as too prolific, or only competent to write about China. The first "Sedges" novel, *The Townsman* (1945), won particular praise for its accurate depiction of early Kansas. Reverting to her own name, she published *Command the Morning* (1959), a carefully researched account of the development of the atomic bomb. Her concern with the negative implications of nuclear science was also reflected in her Broadway play, "Desert Incident" (1959). Though the play failed, she characteristically utilized the experience in a credible novel about the theater, *The Rainbow* (1974). In 1956, with producer Tad Danielewski, she had cofounded Stratton Productions, Inc., which generated various theater, television, and film projects, none commercially successful. However, these varied literary activities helped to make her an effective president of the Authors' Guild, Inc. (1958–65).

Though she continued to advocate freedom and peace for all peoples, Buck disbanded the East and West Association (1951) during the cold war when any interest in Asia, especially in Communist China, was suspect. She then focused her humanitarian impulses on disadvantaged children. In 1949 she founded Welcome House, an adoption agency for Asian-Americans, which prompted two nonfictional books, *Children for Adoption* and *Welcome Child* (both 1964). Long privately engaged in mental retardation work, she courageously publicized her experiences with her retarded daughter in *The Child Who Never Grew* (1950), described advances in the field in three other nonfictional works, and began to help state and national organizations. These activities, together with the care of her adult and adolescent children, travel, French and dance lessons, and a deepening relationship with Harvard philos-

opher William Ernest Hocking, kept her going through the difficult years of her husband's illness and death (1953–60). She recounted this period in *A Bridge For Passing* (1962), and fictionalized her early widowhood in *The Goddess Abides* (1972).

In 1964 Buck founded the Pearl S. Buck Foundation to assist fatherless, and often stateless, half-American children throughout Asia. As its head, she appointed Theodore F. Harris, a young dance instructor from whom she had taken lessons. His experience in organizing charity balls proved valuable in raising funds. Their developing companionship and early work for the Foundation, largely endowed by Buck's properties and royalties, was related by both of them in *For Spacious Skies* (1966). The Foundation's concerns also inspired the novel *The New Year* (1968) and a moving children's story, *Matthew, Mark, Luke, and John* (1967), while its needs prompted the publication of an earlier autobiographical fiction, *The Time is Noon* (1967 [written 1937]), and two essay collections.

In 1969, a *Philadelphia Magazine* article accused Harris of misusing Foundation funds for private purposes, causing his resignation despite Buck's loyal support. Both later moved to Danby, Vt., where Harris had established Creativity, Inc., a multipurpose firm which also managed most of Buck's later projects. She continued to publish both adult and juvenile fiction, most written earlier, and general works such as *Pearl Buck's America* (1971) and *Pearl Buck's Oriental Cookbook* (1972). In 1973, in her eighty-first year, weakened by heart attacks and by gall bladder and lung surgery, she died of lung cancer in Danby. She left a contested estate and many manuscripts. Some have been issued posthumously, including a volume of poetry, *Words of Love* (1974), and several short story collections. Buck's controversial last years and her overwhelming productivity as author of over one hundred books, as well as countless speeches, articles, and scripts, have obscured her enduring literary and humanitarian achievements. It is those achievements which make her an eminent world figure.

[Many of Buck's MSS. are at the Pearl S. Buck Birthplace Fdn., Hillsboro, W. Va., and most have been cataloged by Mary Lee Welliver in a master's thesis, "Pearl S. Buck's Manuscripts: The Harvest of Half a Century" (W. Va. Univ., 1977). The other sizable collection of Buck materials is in the Lipscomb Library, Randolph-Macon Woman's College, Lynchburg, Va. Lucille Zinn, the Birthplace Fdn. bibliographer, has prepared a bibliography, "The Works of Pearl S. Buck," for the 1979 *Bull. of Bib-*

liography. A biobibliography by Lucy B. Flynn lists several reference book entries. Theodore Harris, *Pearl S. Buck, A Biography,* 2 vols. (1969 and 1971), written with Buck's cooperation, contains a bibliography of her books through 1967. Paul A. Doyle, *Pearl S. Buck* (1965), a short, useful critical study, includes a selected list of secondary sources. Other helpful secondary sources include Cornelia Spencer, pseud. [Grace S. Yaukey, Buck's sister], *Exile's Daughter: A Biography of Pearl S. Buck* (1944); Irvin Block, *The Lives of Pearl Buck* (1973); Michael H. Hunt, "Pearl Buck—Popular Expert on China, 1913–49," *Modern China,* Jan. 1977, pp. 33–63; Greg Walter, "The Dancing Master," *Philadelphia Mag.,* July 1969, pp. 55–59, 112–26; Frederic H. Birmingham, "Pearl Buck and The Good Earth of Vermont," *Sat. Eve. Post,* Spring 1972, pp. 70–73ff.; Thomas Lask, "A Missionary Heritage," *N.Y. Times,* March 7, 1973, p. 40; and Helen F. Snow, "Pearl S. Buck, 1892–1973: An Island in Time," *New Republic,* March 24, 1973, pp. 28–29. See also reviews by Elizabeth Janeway, "The Optimistic World of Miss Buck," *N.Y. Times Book Rev.,* May 25, 1952, and V. S. Pritchett, "Command the Morning," *Scientific American,* July 1959, pp. 159–60. An obituary appeared in the *N.Y. Times,* March 7, 1973. Other information is based on records from Cornell Univ.; Washoe Cty. Court, Reno, Nev.; and Rutland Cty., Vt., Dept. of Health (death record) and Superior Court (Trial re Estate, July 22–26, 1974); and on interviews and correspondence with Buck's relatives, friends, associates, and lawyers. Portraits of Buck are in the National Portrait Gallery, Washington, D.C., and the Buck Birthplace Fdn., W. Va., and the Buck Fdn., Bethlehem, Pa., both National Historic Sites.]

JANE R. COHEN

BÜHLER, Charlotte Bertha, Dec. 20, 1893–Feb. 3, 1974. Psychologist.

Charlotte Bühler was born in Berlin, the older child and only daughter of Rose (Kristeller) and Hermann Malachowski. Her father was an innovative and talented architect who helped to build the first department store in Germany. Of Slavic Jewish background, he rose to a position of prominence and affluence. Rose Malachowski, a beautiful and ambitious woman, poured into her daughter her own aspirations and frustrations. Bored with her upper-class life, she resented the constraints on women of her class that had prevented her from pursuing a career as a singer. Charlotte found her parents somewhat remote, but was very close to her brother, five years younger, with whom she enjoyed music and hiking.

From both parents she acquired a deep interest in culture (she later wrote about aesthetics and literature even while establishing herself as a psychologist). Encouraged by her father's nurturance, but also driven by her mother's ele-

gance and unrequited brilliance, the schisms that would later torment Charlotte Bühler developed early. A visionary with gaping blind spots, she had a love of humanity and a sense of superiority to the commoner, a tremendous warmth and an imperious coldness.

At seventeen, Charlotte Malachowski became interested in psychology following a period of severe religious doubt. She had been baptized a Protestant, a common practice among upper-class Jewish families trying to escape the anti-Semitism rampant in Germany. But her doubt was a matter of questioning the existence of God rather than of denominational choice. Rejecting her pastor's advice that she accept the catechism on faith, she read widely in the works of the great metaphysicians and philosophers of religion. She concluded that metaphysical problems could not be solved by studying religion, and decided to inform herself about the nature of thought processes. She disagreed with the view of the psychologist Hermann Ebbinghaus, whom she read at this time, that thought is merely a matter of associations, and began to conduct experiments on her own.

After attending private schools, Malachowski entered the University of Freiburg in 1913, where she studied medicine, philosophy, and psychology. The following spring she went to the University of Kiel. There she fell in love with a handsome geographer who became a shell-shock casualty during the early days of World War I, leaving her a "war victim by proxy." She completed her undergraduate studies at the University of Berlin (1914–15) under Carl Stumpf, a pioneer experimental psychologist. With characteristic independence, Malachowski refused Stumpf's offer of a graduate assistantship—an unprecedented honor for a woman—because she wished to study thought processes rather than feelings. Stumpf referred her to Oswald Külpe, a leading investigator of thought processes, whose psychological laboratory at the University of Munich was one of the foremost in Europe.

After Külpe's death in December 1915, a few months after she had arrived in Munich, his chief assistant, Karl Bühler (1879–1963), returned from the battlefield to take over his mentor's work. Even before meeting Bühler, a physician and a psychologist, Malachowski had learned that he was conducting experiments for studying thought process similar to those she had improvised earlier. Teacher and pupil were drawn to each other and married on April 4, 1916. They had two children, Ingeborg (b. 1917), and Rolf (b. 1919), who were cared for by a governess. Charlotte Bühler completed her Ph.D. at Munich in 1918 with a dissertation on thought processes. The same year she published a highly original study of fairy tales and children's fantasies.

For the next twenty years, Karl and Charlotte Bühler produced and inspired innovative work in psychology. While most European psychologists were oriented toward physics, the Bühlers took a biological approach, becoming central figures in the development of new research methods. They worked at the Dresden Institute of Technology, where Charlotte Bühler became the first woman privatdozent (1920–22). In 1923 she received one of the first Rockefeller Exchange fellowships and went to the United States to study with psychologist Edward Thorndike at Columbia University. The behaviorist methods she encountered there reinforced her own devotion to direct observation. On her return, she joined her husband at the University of Vienna, where he had become head of the psychology department. At Vienna she helped her husband found and run a psychological institute and herself became head of an innovative child psychology department.

Charlotte Bühler concentrated initially on the periods of childhood and adolescence. For a study of the psychic life of adolescents, she collected diaries (which she knew from her personal experience to be significant) and made major use of the life biography approach that became one of her major contributions to research. Published in 1922 as *Das Seelenleben des Jugendlichen*, the book on adolescents established her as an important psychologist. At the institute, she and her students pioneered in conducting experimental studies on the child during the first year of life. By 1925 she was editing her own monograph series in child psychology. A major European authority on child-rearing, she believed that her work on the sequences of child development had also influenced such American psychologists as Arnold Gesell. But although she made her reputation in child psychology, she always viewed that field as part of the general subject of developmental psychology. This remained her greatest interest, and she explored it in *Der Menschliche Lebenslauf als Psychologisches Problem* (1932), one of her best-known books.

The Vienna years were happy and productive. Bühler wrote each morning at her desk and published regularly, amassing a long bibliography of significant contributions. She and her husband were surrounded by a lively group of graduate students, including ELSE FRENKEL (-BRUNSWIK) and Paul Lazarsfeld. Then in 1938, Charlotte Bühler learned while abroad that her husband had been detained by the Nazis because of her Jewish background. Their possessions were confiscated and they were stripped of their positions. The sought-after and touted Bühlers became just another refugee family.

After living for two years in Oslo, the Bühlers came to the United States in 1940. For the next five years they took a succession of posts and moved from place to place. Charlotte Bühler taught at the College of St. Catherine in St. Paul, Minn., at Clark University in Worcester, Mass., and at the City College of New York. She took up the practice of clinical psychology (which initially consisted chiefly of administering psychological tests) and became chief clinical psychologist at the Minneapolis General Hospital.

In 1945, the year Charlotte Bühler became a citizen, she and her husband moved to Los Angeles to be near their son. There she worked as chief clinical psychologist at the Los Angeles County General Hospital (1945–53) and as assistant clinical professor of psychiatry at the University of Southern California School of Medicine (1945–59). But never again were significant research funds or facilities available to her. Undaunted, she began a successful private practice in individual and group psychotherapy, adapting her ideas to the by-then predominantly Freudian outlook of the Americans. Still a prolific writer, in 1962 she published one of her most important books, *Psychologie im Leben unserer Zeit*.

Charlotte Bühler, along with Abraham Maslow, Carl Rogers, and Viktor Frankl, arranged what became known as the Old Saybrook Conference which in 1964 gave birth to the humanistic psychology movement. The movement became an important force in American psychology, emphasizing (in contrast to both the Freudian and behaviorist approaches) the importance of growth and self-fulfillment as motives of human behavior. The excitement of this evolving approach helped somewhat in Bühler's efforts to overcome the mourning that followed her husband's death in October 1963. She became president of the new Association for Humanistic Psychology (1965–66), and wrote two books: *The Course of Human Life*, with Fred Massarik (1968), and *An Introduction to Humanistic Psychology*, with Melanie Allen (1972). As a member of this group, which shared her religious and holistic interests, Charlotte Bühler finally found a secure professional niche in her adopted country.

Remaining vitally involved in her work during her last years, Bühler tried to validate her theory of human behavior which encompassed both tension-reduction and growth motivations. By 1972, however, she was physically incapacitated and returned to her children in Stuttgart, Germany. She started a practice there, but yearned for "her country, America," and for the intellectual companionship she had lost. Charlotte Bühler died in her sleep in Stuttgart in February 1974 following a series of strokes.

[James Birren conducted oral history interviews in 1967–68; tapes and transcripts are located in the archives of the Am. Psychiatric Assoc., Washington, D.C. A collection of Bühler's papers, including letters to and from colleagues, drafts of published and unpublished MSS., and personal correspondence, are in the possession of Melanie Allen. A bibliography of Bühler's work through 1969 appears in *Revue de Psychologie Appliquée*, vol. 19 (1969), 141–47. The major published source on Bühler's life is her autobiographical statement in *Psychologie in Selbsdarstellungen*, ed. Ludwig J. Pongratz and others (Berne, 1972), pp. 9–42, also available in pamphlet form. There is information in Akademie der Wissenschaften Wien, vol. 265, *Karl Bühler, Die Uhren der Lebewesen und Fragmente aus dem Nachlass* (Vienna, 1969). See also *Contemporary Authors* (1965); *Psychological Register*, vol. 2 (1929); *Int. Encyc. Psychiatry, Psychology, Psychoanalysis and Neurology*, II (1977); Robert J. Havighurst, "Charlotte Bühler, December 20, 1893–February 3, 1974," *Human Development*, vol. 17 (1974); Fred Massarik, "Charlotte Bühler: A Reflection," *Jour. Humanistic Psychology*, Summer 1974. June Clee's excellent biobibliography was of assistance in writing this article. Information was also derived from personal acquaintance; Susan Wendell provided research assistance. Background material may be found in Bernard Bailyn and Donald Fleming, eds., *The Intellectual Migration: Europe and America, 1930–1960* (1969).]

                                          MELANIE ALLEN

BURCHENAL, Elizabeth, 1876?–Nov. 21, 1959. Folk dance educator.

Elizabeth Burchenal, who generated a widespread and enduring interest in folk dance and the folk arts, influenced not only the American physical education movement, but also the social, cultural, and recreational life of the United States, Canada, and Europe. Through her work, she enriched the lives of both the sophisticated and the unworldly, and she helped to break down barriers between them.

Born in Richmond, Ind., Elizabeth Burchenal was introduced early to music, dance, and internationalism by her musician mother, Mary Elizabeth (Day) Burchenal, and her father, Judge Charles Henry Burchenal. Mary Burchenal, a native of Ohio, bore six children: Elizabeth Burchenal was her second child and the second eldest of four daughters. Judge Burchenal, who traced his paternal ancestors to the earliest English settlers of Maryland, was an attorney who refused a political career; he was a lover of literature and art, family and friends. Burchenal once said that her career began in childhood when European visitors, warming up in her "musically gifted family circle, passed many an hour dancing and singing songs of the old country." She accompanied her mother on horseback to remote mountain cabins to chat and "surreptitiously to pick up what they could of musical interest."

Maintaining her interest in music, literature, and dance, Burchenal graduated in 1896 with an A.B. in English from her hometown college, Earlham, and went to Boston to study at Dr. Sargent's School of Physical Training (later affiliated with Boston University). Initially interested in Sargent's medical approach to physical education, she directed the Medical Gymnasium in the department of orthopedics (later Boston Children's Hospital Medical Center) after receiving her Sargent diploma in 1898. From 1898 until 1902 Burchenal also taught in and ran physical education programs in Chicago and Boston. Her interest in the role of dance in education had been aroused by the dance educator Melvin Gilbert. In 1903 Burchenal joined the faculty of Teachers College, Columbia University, with the intention of implementing Gilbert's belief that dance should be incorporated in physical education. Contact with the New York immigrant population convinced her of the value of folk dance in particular; with that realization, her career was launched.

Yielding to the persuasive encouragement of Luther Gulick, then director of physical training in the New York City public schools, Burchenal went to work for the city, accepting positions of increasingly greater authority and scope. As executive secretary of the Girls' Branch of the New York Public Schools Athletic League (1906–16), she taught athletics and folk dancing to teachers. In this position and as inspector of athletics for the New York Department of Education (1909–16), she provided models for the entire country by introducing folk dancing into the public school curriculum and by organizing folk festivals such as the gigantic May Day celebrations in Central Park.

Burchenal's influence extended to other countries as well. In 1913, impressed by the sight of 2,000 girls folk dancing in a Manhattan public school, the Irish Lady Aberdeen persuaded Burchenal to train a group of teachers in Ireland. By the end of the year, national folk dances were introduced into the Irish schools as part of the standard physical education program.

Burchenal traveled throughout the United States, Canada, and Europe both to train teachers of folk dance and, as there were very few known dances, to gather source material. Frequently joined by her younger sister Emma Howells, who was her piano accompanist, she lived in isolated communities and participated in every type of folk occasion and celebration, notating dance steps while her sister took down the accompanying music. Burchenal's research resulted in the publication of some fifteen volumes of collected folk dances, which for decades were the authoritative reference sources in the field.

In 1916, resigning from the Public Schools Athletic League, Burchenal became assistant state inspector of the Military Training Commission of the New York State Department of Education (1916–18). By promulgating her philosophy of vigorous, wholesome, character-building, but noncompetitive athletics for all girls, she was influential in framing early policies on female athletics in schools. Also in 1916, Gulick convinced her of the need for a national folk dance organization and persuaded her to head it. Thus the American Folk Dance Society was formed; and Burchenal, joined by her older sister, Ruth, began to provide direction to a nationwide movement. She gave demonstrations and lectures and spoke at conferences, teaching the value of folk dancing as "a spontaneous emotional expression of every-day life." It was also, as she wrote in *The Playground* (Oct. 1920), one of the few opportunities for people of different nationalities to join together "unembarrassed by differences in language, viewpoint, education, social status, culture, religion, occupation, dress and manners." Appointed jointly by the United States Department of Labor and the National Recreation Association as special national representative of the War Workers Community Service (1918–22), Burchenal helped ease racial and ethnic conflicts through her social, recreational, and cultural programs.

In 1929 the American Folk Dance Society became a division of a new, larger organization, the National Committee of Folk Arts, which Burchenal, again with the help of her sister Ruth, directed from its inception until a few years before her death. She headed the Folk Arts Center in New York, which housed a museum, a library, and a national information bureau, and she established an Archive of American Folk Dance. As America's leading authority on folk dance and the folk arts, Burchenal represented the United States at various international congresses and festivals. With a research fellowship from the Oberlaender Trust she studied folk dances in rural Germany for two years (1933–34); she also chaired several national and international committees and organizations and received many honors, including physical education's highest, the Gulick Award (1950).

Elizabeth Burchenal died in Brooklyn, N.Y., in 1959. Memorial services for her ended with a uniquely appropriate tribute: the floor was cleared, the music began, and the mourners joined hands to dance her favorite folk dances.

[The Elizabeth Burchenal Papers, Mugar Library, Boston Univ., contain Burchenal's personal library of about 500 volumes, scrapbooks of clippings, correspondence, materials related to the Folk Arts Center, and other Burchenal memorabilia, including photographs. Her books include *Folk-Dances and Singing Games* (1909), *American Country Dances* (1918), and *Rinnce Na Eirann: National Dances of Ireland* (1924). *Who's Who in America*, 1954–55, has a bibliography of her volumes of collected folk dances. The best sources of information about Burchenal's career and philosophy are Janice W. Carkin, "Recipients of the Gulick Award" (Ed.D. diss., Stanford Univ., 1952), and Ellen W. Gerber, *Innovators and Institutions in Physical Education* (1971), also an excellent source of information about the early physical education movement; it contains a useful, though incomplete, bibliography of Burchenal's short articles. Josephine Dorgan, *Luther Halsey Gulick* (1934), and Norma Schwendener, *A History of Physical Education in the United States* (1942), also contain information about Burchenal and the early physical education movement. Frances Drewry McMullen, "Folk Dances for Fox Trots," *Woman Citizen*, June 1927, and a piece by Emma Bugbee in the *N.Y. Herald Tribune*, May 31, 1943, are informative popular articles. The latter has a photograph, as do Schwendener and an obituary in the *Jour. Health, Physical Education and Recreation*, May 1, 1960. Census information for 1880 indicates that Burchenal was born between June 12, 1875, and June 11, 1876, and that her name at birth was Flora Elizabeth. Family and friends confirm that, in keeping with family tradition, she pronounced her name "Burchenélle." Valuable information for this article was provided by George Makechnie, Mabel Lee, and Selden Day Burchenal. Death record supplied by N.Y. City Dept. of Health.]

MARILYN B. WEISSMAN

BURGOS, Julia de, Feb. 17, 1914?–July 6, 1953. Poet, journalist.

Julia de Burgos is significant not only for the exquisite poetry she wrote but also because of the example of freedom that her unorthodox pattern of life and behavior provided to the Puerto Rican women of her times. She was born Julia Constancia Burgos García in Carolina, Puerto Rico, the oldest of thirteen children of Paula García de Burgos and Francisco Burgos Hans. Only seven of the children survived to maturity.

Her father farmed and worked for the National Guard, but the family remained very poor. Contributions from townspeople allowed Julia to attend the local school. She grew up in the humble rural barrio of Santa Cruz, near a tributary of the powerful Río Grande de Loíza. The river would later be a recurrent and haunting subject in her poems, transformed into the image of a lover: "Muy señor río mío. Río hombre. Unico hombre/ Que ha besado en mi alma al besar en mi cuerpo" ("Río Grande de Loíza"). Her childhood, in the poet's words, was a "poem to the river."

Classmates at the University of Puerto Rico High School in San Juan, where Julia de Burgos enrolled in 1928, remember her as a shy, sensitive, and brilliant girl. From early on, she was committed both to learning and to social change. When she completed her secondary education with honors (1931), she entered the University of Puerto Rico. After receiving a teaching certificate, she began work in the rural town of Naranjito in 1933. The following year she married Ruben Rodríguez Beauchamp; they were divorced in 1937. After her marriage, she worked for a day care center run by the Puerto Rico Emergency Reconstruction Administration (PRERA). In 1936–37 she wrote librettos for the Escuela del Aire (School of the Air), a division of the Department of Education of Puerto Rico which broadcast educational programs.

Her first published poems appeared in 1937 in a private edition: *Poemas Exactos A Mí Misma* (Exact Poems to Myself). The following year she published *Poema en Veinte Surcos* (Poem in Twenty Furrows) and in 1939 *Canción de la Verdad Sencilla* (Song of the Simple Truth), a celebration of love, which merited an award from the Institute of Puerto Rican Literature.

Julia de Burgos left Puerto Rico early in 1940. She went first to New York, where she wrote for newspapers and pursued further studies. Later that year, with her lover, she moved to Cuba, where she also worked as a journalist; in Cuba as in New York she suffered social isolation. In 1941 she enrolled at the University of Havana to study philosophy and literature but returned to New York in 1942. She worked at a variety of jobs and, the following year, married for the second time; her husband was Armando Marín, a poet and writer who was devoted to her. With the friendship and support of members of the Circle of Ibero-American Writers and Poets (CEPI), she continued to write. Between 1943 and 1945 she worked for *Pueblos Hispanicos*, a publication founded in New York by the Puerto Rican poet, Juan Antonio Corretjer. She wrote editorials, news stories, and interviews, and won a second Institute of Puerto Rican Literature prize for one of her editorials (1945).

A woman of great sensibility, rebellious spirit, and exceptional intelligence, Julia de Burgos no doubt felt imprisoned by circumstances. Her discomfort with social ills, her love for Puerto Rico, and her preoccupation with justice and death, all come out in the torrents of her poetry with its richly emotional metaphors. She firmly believed in the need for social reform and for the radical improvement of living conditions for the working class in Puerto Rico; she was also a staunch supporter of political independence for the island.

As a poet, Julia de Burgos deserves to be ranked with such major contemporary poets as the Uruguayan Juana de Ibarburu. Her poems reveal her gift for lyricism, while their erotic content and their cosmic symbolism provide autobiographical glimpses into a troubled and pagan soul which often felt itself lost and abandoned. In "Donde Comienzas Tú," she described herself metaphorically: "Soy ola de abandono, derribada, tendida,/ sobre un inmenso azul de sueños y de alas."

Her work shows the influence of Luis Llorens Torres, perhaps the most famous of Puerto Rican poets, who saw in her a "propensity for Kantian abstraction." The influence of modernism and of the work of the great Chilean poet Pablo Neruda can also be felt in such poems as "Río Grande de Loíza," "Nada," and her most frequently anthologized poem, "A Julia de Burgos." In that poem, and in "Yo Misma Fuí Mi Ruta," de Burgos calls attention sharply to the restrictions imposed on women by a society that forces them to live by laws and by social and ethical patterns not of their making.

Because she was dedicated to the cause of social change, de Burgos may often have felt that what she had to say was more important than how she said it; literary craftsmanship thus gave way at times to her impulse to speak out and to her irredentist theories. She believed poetry should be both a means to self-discovery and a herald of new truths; as such it could become a weapon against the dead forms of the past, a weapon of the revolution. In "A Julia de Burgos" she looked forward to the coming of revolution: "Cuando las multitudes corran alborotadas/dejando atrás cenizas de injusticias quemadas,/ . . . yo iré en medio de ellas con la tea en la mano."

In her last years, Julia de Burgos was often ill. She suffered from alcoholism and was frequently hospitalized for treatment of cirrhosis of the liver. In 1952 she was operated on for papaloma of the vocal cords. The following July she died tragically in New York of pulmonary disease. Her body was found in the street, taken to Harlem Hospital, and later buried in the potter's field. Some days later Armando Marín and friends from the CEPI were able to find out what had occurred and had her body returned for burial to Puerto Rico, near the Río Grande de Loíza.

A posthumous volume, *El Mar y Tú y Otros Poemas*, appeared in 1954. Seven years later the Institute of Puerto Rican Culture, following a resolution by the Puerto Rican legislature, published her collected works, the *Obra Poetica* of Julia de Burgos, "Criatura del Agua."

[A volume of selections from her work, *Cuadernos de Poesía, Julia de Burgos*, was published in 1964. The most complete biographical discussion is contained in Yvette Jiménez de Baez, *Julia de Burgos: Vida y Poesía* (1966), which also includes commentary on the poems and a bibliography. See also Josefina Rivera de Alvarez, *Diccionario de Literatura Puertorriqueña*, vol. I (1974); Adolfo de Hostos, *Diccionario Historico Bibliografico Comentado de Puerto Rico* (1976); Carmen Delgado Votaw, *Puerto Rican Women: Some Biographical Profiles* (1978); and *Enciclopedia: Grandes Mujeres de Puerto Rico*, vol. I (1978). For criticism of her poetry see José Emilio González, *La Poesía Contemporánea de Puerto Rico, 1930–1960* (1972), and Cesáreo Rosa-Nieves, *Historia Panorámica de la Literatura Puertorriqueña, 1589–1959* (1963).]

CARMEN DELGADO VOTAW

BURNS, Lucy, July 28, 1879–Dec. 22, 1966. Suffragist.

Lucy Burns, who with Alice Paul invigorated the American campaign for a federal woman suffrage amendment, was a leader of the militant wing of the suffrage movement between 1912 and 1919. She was born in Brooklyn, N.Y., the fourth child and fourth of five daughters in a family of eight children. Her parents, Ann (Early) and Edward Burns, were Catholic, and both of Irish descent. Her father, who became a bank president, supported his daughters' educational aspirations, and Lucy followed her sisters to the Packer (Collegiate) Institute in Brooklyn, from which she graduated in 1899.

Hailed as a brilliant scholar at Vassar College, from which she received an A.B. in 1902, she appeared to be headed for an academic career. She studied etymology at the Yale University Graduate School (1902–03), taught English at Erasmus Hall High School in Brooklyn from 1904 to 1906 (where, despite her dismay at the public school system, she made a vivid impression on students), and then resumed her study of languages at the Universities of Berlin (1906–08) and Bonn (1908–09). Burns described

herself as "languishing" in Germany, but occasional trips to England exposed her to the militant leaders of the woman suffrage movement there. By the time she began work toward her doctorate at Oxford in 1909, "Votes for Women" had already become "the one subject in the world."

The English experience proved exhilarating, and Lucy Burns soon gave up scholarship for action. Working closely with the Women's Social and Political Union (WSPU) led by the Pankhursts, Burns joined British women in deputations to Parliament, pressuring Cabinet members to declare for woman suffrage. She also spoke on street corners, helped to stage pageants, and, with Emmeline Pankhurst, campaigned for suffrage in Scotland. The WSPU bestowed a special medal of valor on Burns, who was arrested several times and joined in prison hunger strikes in July and September 1909. At the request of Christabel Pankhurst, she served as a salaried organizer in Edinburgh and east Scotland from 1910 to 1912.

In England, Burns crossed paths with Alice Paul (1885–1977), a young American student who was also close to the Pankhursts. When Burns returned to the United States in 1912, she and Paul cemented a friendship that created a suffrage team as staunch as that of ELIZABETH CADY STANTON and SUSAN B. ANTHONY. Although they believed that suffrage could be attained more quickly through a constitutional amendment than through the state-by-state campaigns favored by the National American Woman Suffrage Association (NAWSA), Paul and Burns began their suffrage work as chairman and vice chairman respectively of NAWSA's Congressional Committee. Setting up shop in Washington early in 1913, they organized the spectacular suffrage parade the day before Woodrow Wilson's inaugural. In April they formed a national organization, the Congressional Union for Woman Suffrage (CU), to work solely for a federal amendment. Friction between the CU and NAWSA, then led by ANNA HOWARD SHAW, increased steadily. In late 1913, following the failure of an attempted compromise that would have made Lucy Burns head of NAWSA's Congressional Committee if she accepted new regulations governing its activities and those of the CU, Alice Paul was removed from the Committee and Lucy Burns resigned. The CU and NAWSA subsequently went their separate ways.

With Alice Paul, Lucy Burns shaped the major policies of the CU and of its successor after 1916, the National Woman's party (NWP). If Paul was the chief strategist, Burns was the major organizer. There was virtually no task she did not perform for the cause. She took charge of the early lobbying activity of the CU, of which she was vice chairman, and held suffrage schools to educate followers in campaign methods and suffrage history. To implement the CU's policy of holding the party in power responsible for congressional failure to enact a suffrage amendment, she led the campaigns in 1914 and 1916 to defeat Democratic candidates in states where women were already enfranchised. The best known of these ventures was the "Suffrage Special," a railroad car that in 1916 took more than twenty women through the far west. Burns also edited the CU newspaper, *The Suffragist*, from the spring of 1915 to the end of 1916; her editorials were considered models of clarity, conciseness, and "accumulative force of expression."

Lucy Burns brought a fierceness and resoluteness to the American woman suffrage movement that was rarely equaled. Praised by Alice Paul as "a thousand times more valiant than I," Burns in her poise and strength of character was a rallying symbol for the more faint-hearted. First arrested in the United States for chalking suffrage ads on the pavements of Washington, D.C., in 1913, by 1919, when the militant phase of the NWP ended, she had spent more time in jail than any other American suffragist. She headed the well-publicized demonstrations against President Wilson during World War I; following her arrest in November 1917, she went on a nineteen-day hunger strike, during which she was forcibly fed. Burns also managed the publicity tour of NWP prison veterans in 1919 aboard the railroad car dubbed the "Prison Special."

Burns was an eloquent and forceful speaker. With a mass of red hair piled high on her head, she was an arresting figure at hundreds of open air meetings across the country. Warm-hearted and quick-witted, Burns had an Irish wit that injected levity in difficult situations. For all her militance, Burns impressed her coworkers with her gentleness and tact. The flood of telegrams at the NWP headquarters in June 1919, following congressional passage of the suffrage amendment, touted the joint Paul-Burns leadership that had made victory possible.

Exhausted from the long campaign, Lucy Burns refused to take on new battles, such as those designed to help married women fight for greater professional equality. Always close to her family, she abruptly retired to the quiet of home life with two unmarried sisters in Brooklyn. Following the death of her youngest sister in childbirth in 1923, Burns took responsibility for raising an infant niece. Forty-four at the

time, she spent the next quarter century principally in domestic pursuits. Though at times she felt like an "impassioned baby-minder . . . in need of someone to come along and emancipate me," Burns became a model for her niece whom she impressed with her "love, understanding, [and] encouragement," as well as with her absolute fearlessness. A devout Catholic, she remained close to the church. Incapacitated by the late 1950s, Lucy Burns died in Brooklyn in December 1966.

[Lucy Burns's letters are scattered throughout the NWP Papers at the Library of Congress, but a series containing editorial correspondence of *The Suffragist*, located in boxes 259–65, has hundreds of exchanges. Burns's entries in the Vassar College alumnae bulletins between 1902 and 1951 provide a rare personal glimpse, while interviews with Alice Paul, Mabel Vernon, and Hazel Hunkins completed by the Regional Oral History Office, the Bancroft Library, Univ. of Calif., Berkeley, contain valuable recollections. Other accounts by fellow suffragists include: Sylvia Pankhurst, *The Suffragette* (1911); Inez Haynes Irwin, *The Story of the Woman's Party* (1921); Doris Stevens, *Jailed for Freedom* (1920); and Caroline Katzenstein, *Lifting the Curtain* (1955). *The Suffragist*, which contains photographs, is a valuable source on Burns and the CU; the *Brooklyn Daily Eagle* reported Burns's more sensational exploits. On the early history of the NWP see Sidney R. Bland, "Techniques of Persuasion: The National Woman's Party and Woman Suffrage, 1913–1919" (Ph.D. diss., George Washington Univ., 1972), and Loretta Ellen Zimmerman, "Alice Paul and the National Woman's Party, 1912–1920" (Ph.D. diss., Tulane Univ., 1964). See also *Woman's Who's Who of America, 1914–15*. Janet Burns Appleton Campbell, the niece raised by Burns, provided useful information.]

SIDNEY R. BLAND

BURROUGHS, Nannie Helen, May 2, 1878?– May 20, 1961. Educator, school founder.

Nannie Burroughs, who dedicated her life to the education of young black women, was born in Orange, Va., the older of two daughters of John and Jennie (Poindexter) Burroughs. Her maternal grandfather, called Lija, the slave carpenter, purchased land at the end of the Civil War and earned a comfortable living for his wife and children as a skilled craftsman. Her paternal grandparents, freed during the early 1860s, owned a sizable farm by the end of the war.

Burroughs's sister died in infancy. Her father, a farmer and preacher, died a few years later. When she was five years old, her mother, seeking better educational opportunities for her, took her to Washington, D.C. There she attended school while her mother worked as a cook. At the M Street High School, Nannie Burroughs studied business and domestic science and organized the Harriet Beecher Stowe Literary Society; she graduated in 1896 with honors. Failing to acquire a job as a domestic science teacher in the District of Columbia public schools, which had a reputation for favoring the fairer skinned among black students, she determined that she would "have a school . . . in Washington, that school politics had nothing to do with" and that "would give all sorts of girls a fair chance without political pull" (Harrison, p. 10).

After a year in Philadelphia as associate editor of a Baptist paper, *The Christian Banner,* Burroughs returned to Washington, expecting to be appointed as a clerk after having obtained a high rating on a civil service examination. She was told, however, that there were no openings for "a colored clerk." She then worked as janitor in office buildings, and for a short time as bookkeeper for a manufacturer, before moving to Louisville, Ky., in 1900 to accept a position as secretary for the Foreign Mission Board of the National Baptist Convention. In her spare time Burroughs organized the Woman's Industrial Club, which served lunches at moderate cost to office workers in the Louisville business district. In addition, she held evening classes in typing, shorthand, bookkeeping, millinery, sewing, handicrafts, and cooking for members of the club, who paid ten cents a week to attend. Finally, acting on the advice and with the financial help of an influential white woman, she increased the tuition, hired teachers, and freed herself to supervise and develop the evening school.

A tall, handsome woman with a strong, vigorous voice and a direct manner, Nannie Burroughs was an impressive speaker. In 1900 she attracted the notice of delegates to the annual meeting of the National Baptist Convention in Richmond, Va., with a stirring speech entitled "Hindered from Helping." At the meeting she was elected corresponding secretary of the National Baptist Woman's Convention, a newly formed auxiliary to the men's convention. The Woman's Convention, like most women's missionary societies, aimed to reinforce Christianity in the United States and ultimately to Christianize the world by training missionaries and supporting missions.

The work of the auxiliary became the center of Burroughs's life. She was its leading spirit and its major strategist, drawing widespread attention to its needs and attracting funds for its good works even during the depression. Her eloquence, which first occasioned widespread comment when she addressed the First Baptist World Alliance meeting in London in 1905 on "Women's Work," made her especially valuable as a speaker. Traveling thousands of miles in the interests of the auxiliary, Burroughs served as secretary until 1948, when she became president. She established a retreat home for missionaries returning from their work, and, in the 1950s, a camp in Michigan for the youth department of the Woman's Convention. In the preamble to her will, Nannie Burroughs summarized her work with the auxiliary: "Without stint I have given my entire life to the Woman's Convention and have proudly built it and watched it grow from the humblest beginnings to world service and security."

Burroughs first mentioned her deferred dream of founding a training school for girls in Washington, D.C., to the fledgling Woman's Convention in 1900. Arguing that some missionary work must be done at home, she recommended that the Baptist women establish and manage a national school to prepare black girls for homemaking and respectable careers. It was not until 1906 that the Woman's Convention agreed to underwrite the purchase of a six-acre site on a hill in northeast Washington, previously selected by Burroughs as the location for the National Training School for Women and Girls (later the National Trade and Professional School for Women and Girls).

The school opened free of debt on Oct. 19, 1909, with seven students and a staff of eight women. By the end of the first year thirty-one students had enrolled. The Convention remained the continuing sponsor of the school, but during the early years most of the money for maintenance and expansion came from Burroughs's nationwide fund-raising campaigns. She also supported her mother as well as Alice Smith, a young student who came to the school in 1928 and became Burroughs's assistant and confidante. Over the years Burroughs purchased more land and sustained an ambitious building program. By the 1960s thousands of black women, living in almost every state and in South Africa, Haiti, and Puerto Rico, had attended the school.

Under the motto "We specialize in the wholly impossible," Burroughs sought "the highest development of Christian womanhood" through a curriculum designed to train Negro women to be self-sufficient wage earners as well as "expert homemakers." Various departments offered courses in sewing, home economics, practical and home nursing, bookkeeping, shorthand, typing, gardening, laundering, and interior decorating, among others. Disregarding stereotypical occupational roles for women, Burroughs also initiated such courses as printing, shoe repairing, gardening, and barbering. Similarly, she rejected the contemporary assumption that black Americans had made no significant contributions to the history of the nation, installing a department of Negro history, and requiring that each student take at least one course in the discipline.

Burroughs believed in the ideology of self-help which urged black Americans to establish and support the growth of their own institutions, despite the severe limitations imposed upon them by segregation and discrimination. But, although she and Booker T. Washington had a similar approach to vocational education, at no time during the history of the training school did the curriculum emphasize vocational education to the exclusion of academic subjects. As she said in her second annual report to the Woman's Convention: "We believe that an industrial and classical education can be simultaneously attained, and it is our duty to get both" (Harrison, p. 26). A purist who found grammatical errors almost physically painful, Burroughs took special care to require courses on a high school and junior college level that developed language skills. She herself was a prolific writer with a witty, candid style, and her columns appeared regularly in such periodicals as the *Afro-American* and the *Pittsburgh Courier*. In 1934 she began publication of *The Worker*, a devotional quarterly.

The National Trade and Professional School also maintained a close connection between education and religion. The school's creed, enunciated by Nannie Burroughs, consisted of the "three B's—the Bible, the bath, the broom: clean life, clean body, clean home."

Establishing a self-sufficient school for black women was not the only way in which Burroughs pioneered. During the depression, she organized a self-help cooperative in the northeast Washington community which provided facilities, without charge, for a medical clinic, a variety store, farming, canning, and hairdressing. The project, later called Cooperative Industries, Inc., became a permanent establishment managed by Burroughs.

During her later years Nannie Burroughs suffered from arthritis, diabetes, and heart disease. In 1961 she died of a stroke at Georgetown University Hospital in Washington. Among many honors accorded her, in 1964 the school she founded was renamed the Nannie Burroughs School, and in 1975, in recognition of her courage and wisdom in espousing education for black women against the consensus of society, Mayor Walter E. Washington proclaimed May 10 Nannie Helen Burroughs Day in the District of Columbia.

[The Nannie Helen Burroughs Papers in the Library of Congress include correspondence, reports, school records, scrapbooks, clippings, printed matter, photographs, and memorabilia. "Nannie Helen Burroughs Papers," *Quart. Jour. Library of Congress*, Oct. 1977, pp. 356–60, describes the collection and includes a biographical sketch and photograph of Burroughs. A number of her pamphlets and monographs, as well as *The Worker*, are distributed by the school. Also available from the school is Earl L. Harrison, *The Dream and the Dreamer* (1956, 1972), an account of her life and a history of the school. Other sources are: Elizabeth L. Davis, ed., *Lifting As They Climb* (1933); William Pickens, *Nannie Burroughs and the School of the Three B's* (n.d.); Sadie I. Daniels, *Women Builders* (1931), pp. 107–32; and Gerda Lerner, ed., *Black Women in White America: A Documentary History* (1972), pp. 132–33. An obituary appeared in the *Wash. Post*, May 21, 1961. Certificate of death from the D.C. Dept. of Public Health. There is no birth record; date of birth is from an insurance form she signed, used by the school to verify her official birth date.]

JUANITA FLETCHER

BUTLER, Selena Sloan, Jan. 4, 1872?–Oct. 7, 1964. Community leader, organization founder.

Publicly, life for Selena Sloan Butler began in 1888 when she was about sixteen years old and a graduate of Spelman Seminary (later Spelman College), the Baptist home mission school for black women in Atlanta. Achieving prominence later as founder of the National Congress of Colored Parents and Teachers, Butler never freely issued information about her earliest years. She was born in Thomasville, Ga., to Winnie Williams, a woman of African and Indian descent, and William Sloan, a white man. Sloan is said to have taken care of the family, but he did not live with them: the early household consisted of Selena, her somewhat older sister, and their mother. Winnie Williams apparently died young, Selena lost touch with her married sister sometime during her years at Spelman, and she could not publicly acknowledge her father, leaving her with few ties to her birthplace.

After receiving an elementary school training from missionaries in Thomas County, Selena Sloan was sponsored for admission to Spelman by her mother's minister. One of 100 boarders among nearly 500 students, Sloan took every advantage of her six years there, studying the higher normal and scientific course, and working on the school magazine. She received her high school diploma with Spelman's second graduating class in 1888.

For the next five years, Sloan eked out a living as a teacher of English and elocution, first in the Atlanta public school system, and then, around 1891, in the State Normal School at Tallahassee, Fla. In 1893 she married Henry Rutherford Butler, a graduate of Meharry Medical School about ten years her senior. Both gracious and gifted leaders, the Butlers shared for nearly four decades professional interests and common values, European travel, and a commitment to serve their community and race. In 1894 they traveled to Cambridge, Mass., where Selena Butler attended Emerson School of Oratory while her husband took special courses at Harvard in childhood diseases and surgery. Returning to Atlanta the following year, he practiced medicine and she taught school and tutored in public speaking. On Nov. 1, 1899, their only child, Henry Rutherford, Jr., was born.

Selena Butler's involvement in parent-teacher associations grew out of her efforts to educate her son. The Butlers lived comfortably in the better section of black Atlanta, where in addition to his practice, Dr. Butler became a partner in the first black-owned drugstore in Georgia. Still, the family was hampered by the city's bias against blacks, particularly in education. When Selena Butler and neighboring mothers could not find a preschool teacher for their children, Butler set up a kindergarten in her own home, enrolling her son along with the others. In time she followed the children to the neighborhood public grammar school on Yonge Street, where she established the first black parent-teacher association in the country. From this base Butler developed in 1920 the Georgia Colored Parent-Teacher Association (PTA) and served as its president for several years.

Selena Butler expanded her efforts decisively beyond the state level in May 1926, when the National Congress of Colored Parents and Teachers was formed at a meeting in Atlanta, held under the aegis of the Sixth Annual Convention of the Georgia Colored PTA and the Thirtieth Annual Convention of the National Congress of Parents and Teachers. As founding president of the new organization, Butler created a successful working relationship with the white National Congress, adopting that body's policies and programs and receiving in return assistance and encouragement through an integrated advisory committee. Although the black National Congress served principally those states then maintaining segregated schools, the arrangement with its sister organization fostered greater cooperation between black and white groups in school systems, especially at the local level, where such communication was unprecedented. Butler obtained the support of several white Georgian leaders and the organization became, in her words, a channel for "effective interracial education work."

While principally occupied with the black National Congress, Butler played an important part in several other bodies. She was a delegate at the founding convention of the National Association of Colored Women, first president of the Georgia Federation of Colored Women's Clubs, and a member of the Georgia Commission on Interracial Cooperation. She also belonged to an elite social club, The Chautauqua Circle, and was both an organizer of the Ruth Chapter of the Order of the Eastern Star in Atlanta and for many years Grand Lecturer of the lodge in Georgia.

In 1931 Butler's husband died, and a few years later she traveled to Europe with her son, a graduate of Harvard Medical School. Residing in London, she kept up her child welfare activities by working in the Nursery School Association, the British equivalent of the PTA. World War II brought her back to the United States, where she followed Henry Butler, Jr., to Arizona and organized a Gray Lady Corps at the hospital in Fort Huachuca where he served. In 1947 she returned to her home in Atlanta, staying until 1953, when she moved for the last time to live with her son and daughter-in-law in Los Angeles. Butler remained active there in the Congregational church and in several welfare organizations, including the board of the Sojourner Truth Home and Las Madrinas. She died of congestive heart failure in Los Angeles in October 1964; her body was returned to Atlanta for burial next to her husband in Oakland Cemetery.

Selena Butler's devotion to interracial cooperation and child welfare earned her many tributes in her lifetime—from the Lord Mayor of London, the American Red Cross, her alma mater, and President Herbert Hoover, who appointed her to the White House Conference on Child Health and Protection. After her death, she continued to be honored. The black and white PTAs, after their integration in 1970, elevated her to national founder status alongside ALICE MCLELLAN BIRNEY and PHOEBE HEARST. Atlanta renamed the Yonge Street School after her husband and the park adjacent to it after her; and the state of Georgia had her portrait painted for the Capitol, recognizing Butler as one of the state's outstanding educator citizens.

[Selena Butler's personal papers remain with her family. Manuscript sources include the Selena Sloan Butler file, Alumni Office, Spelman College, which contains a copy of a major speech, "The Rise and Growth of the Nat. Congress of Parents and Teachers," delivered at Spelman in 1929; and three collections housed at the Trevor Arnett Library, Atlanta Univ.: Chautauqua Circle Papers, Assoc. of Southern Women for the Prevention of Lynching Papers, and Neighborhood Union Papers. See also at Atlanta Univ. the typescript, "Phyllis Wheatley YWCA, A Historical Sketch." Butler's other major speech, the "Chain-Gang System," was delivered before the Nat. Assoc. of Colored Women in 1897. A useful secondary source is Florence Read, *The Story of Spelman College* (1961); see also Elizabeth Davis, *Lifting as They Climb* (1933). Butler's PTA work is described in "The Convention of Colored Parents and Teachers," *Child Welfare*, Oct. 1931, p. 88; Cecie P. Henry, "A Founder's Day Quiz," *Our National Family*, Nov. 1966, pp. 5, 6; Ga. Congress PTA, "Pioneering Presidential Personalities, Mrs. H. R. Butler" (n.d.); and in several publica-

tions of the Ga. Congress CPTA, including *Founder, The Georgia Congress* (1971), *Through the Years, the 51st Annual Convention* (1971), and *Golden Anniversary History* (1971). The latter three are in the Williams Coll., Atlanta Public Library. Obituaries and related stories appeared in *Atlanta Daily World*, Oct. 8, 10, 1964; and in *Atlanta Journal* and *Atlanta Constitution*, Oct. 7, 8, 9, 1964. Butler was circumspect about her age; it is not reported in obituaries and is incorrect on her death certificate. The date used here is that furnished by her son, who also supplied other information. Biobibliography provided by Robyn Rosenblatt, and death record by Registrar of Los Angeles Cty., Calif.]

DARLENE R. ROTH

C

CADILLA DE MARTÍNEZ, María ("Liana"), Dec. 21, 1886–Aug. 23, 1951. Educator, folklorist, writer, feminist.

The contribution made by María Cadilla de Martínez to the Puerto Rican and Hispanic heritage was both outstanding and unique for its time. Through her research, her teaching, and her writings, she worked to recreate and preserve the culture of her people. Born in Arecibo, Puerto Rico, she was the daughter of Armindo Cadilla y Fernández and Catalina Colón y Nieves. Her father, born in Spain, was an official in the Spanish navy; her mother was a native of Puerto Rico. María Tomasa Cadilla y Colón grew up in a town and during an era that cherished popular expression.

The early years of the twentieth century in Puerto Rico were marked, however, by strong pressures toward conformity and acculturation. In addition, poor agricultural development and the ravages of hurricanes created conditions unfavorable to cultural expression. María Cadilla determined early in her life to work to preserve the rich indigenous culture of Puerto Rico.

After graduating from a private Catholic secondary school in Arecibo, her intellectual curiosity led María Cadilla both to study painting and in 1902 to go to the United States to attend a normal school. She had begun to write when she was fifteen, and for the rest of her life combined teaching and writing careers. Licensed as a primary and secondary education teacher by the University of Puerto Rico, she became a "humble rural teacher" while still in her teens.

In 1903 Cadilla married Julio Tomas Martínez Mirabal, an architect who has also been called the first surrealist painter in Puerto Rico. With him Cadilla shared both her intellectual concerns and her interest in drawing, teaching the subject at a preparatory school he founded in Arecibo. She bore several children, but only two daughters, María and Tomasita, reached maturity.

A lifelong love of learning led Cadilla to continue her education after marriage. She received a certificate as a teacher of English from the University in 1910, studied agriculture and home economics at the College of Agricultural and Mechanical Arts in Mayaguez in 1913, and completed both an A.B. in education (1928) and an A.M. (1930) at the University of Puerto Rico. With a thesis on *La Poesía Popular en Puerto Rico* she earned a doctorate in philosophy and literature from the Universidad Central of Madrid in 1933; her thesis became a popular textbook in many Latin American universities. Cadilla was also a gifted student of the Puerto Rican master painter, Francisco Oller, and studied the piano under such noted pianists as Doña Trina Padilla de Sanz.

Throughout these years she also continued to teach at all levels from primary to university, receiving an appointment in 1916 as professor of Hispanic history and literature in the University of Puerto Rico. One of those rare educators whose work shapes the consciousness of generations of students, Cadilla helped to stimulate teachers, researchers, and writers to study and preserve Hispanic and Puerto Rican literature and culture.

María Cadilla de Martínez brought to her

teaching the vision that also enabled her to prepare a framework for the study and preservation of Puerto Rican folklore. Her research into the mode of dress of Puerto Rican women and men during the nineteenth century provided valuable insights into such customs as those of mourning and celebration of the feasts of patron saints. Her zeal in collecting the rich lore of children's songs and games and her descriptions of other folkloric traditions rescued from extinction important aspects of Puerto Rican culture.

A prolific writer, sometimes using the pseudonym "Liana," Cadilla both produced original work and brought together traditional stories. *Cuentos a Lillian* (1925) is a collection of twenty-six stories and legends, retold in a contemporary idiom and conveying her feeling for the customs and mores of the island. In 1941, in *Raices de la Tierra*, she combined twenty-two short folktales, collected through the oral method, with essays on traditional customs. *Hitos de la Raza* (1945) reproduces other stories from memory. She was also a poet; her best work includes "La Rosa," "Vespertina," and "Torre de Marfil."

While working to preserve the cultural heritage of Puerto Rico, Cadilla also looked to the future. A dedicated feminist, she served as vice president of both the Suffrage Association of Puerto Rico and, after women won the right to vote, the Insular Association of Women Voters. One of the first Puerto Rican feminists, she spoke out for women's causes both in her writings in the press and through speeches at the Atheneum of Puerto Rico. Her belief that women's aspirations to equality could best be realized through education was echoed in a poem she included in *La Poesía Popular in Puerto Rico*: "Sigue en tu afán de aprender/ conquistando tu renombre/ que el derecho y el saber/ elevan a la mujer/ hasta el respeto de un hombre." In an article, "Doña Ana Roqué as a Feminist," published in the *Review of Women Graduates of the University of Puerto Rico* in 1945, Cadilla bemoaned the fact that "women are condemned to automatically consent to the orders or caprices of the opposite sex," and praised the "closely knit and militant group which campaigned for the right to vote and claim the equal right of women to join men in the conduct of public affairs."

Also active in civic and national organizations, Cadilla served as president of the Women's Club of Arecibo, and as vice president of both the Civic League of Puerto Rico and the Union of American Women (UMA). She was also honorary president of the Association of Women Graduates of the University of Puerto Rico.

The many honors she received in her lifetime reflect the range of Cadilla's accomplishments

and the extent of her recognition. Among them were a prize from the Society of Writers and Artists of Puerto Rico (1913) for her story *El Tesoro de Don Alonso;* the Medal of the Atheneum of Puerto Rico for her painting "El Río de mi Pueblo" (1917); election in 1934 as the only female member of the Puerto Rican Historical Academy; and a citation from the UMA as "Woman of Puerto Rico" (1936). Among her several foreign honors were a gold medal from the Société Académique d'Histoire Internationale at the Sorbonne in Paris (1921) for her essay "Ethnography of Puerto Rico," and the Medal of St. Louis of France. Awards and honors also came from the Soviet Union, India, Mexico, Brazil, Peru, Argentina, the Dominican Republic, and the United States.

María Cadilla de Martínez died of cancer in 1951 in her native Arecibo, where she and her husband had continued to make their home. She is a figure to be revered for her contributions to Puerto Rican traditions, folklore, and feminist ideals.

[Cadilla's books include *El Hogar Puertorriqueño* (1926); *Cazadora en el Alba y Otros Poemas* (1933); *La Mística de Unamuno y Otros Ensayos* (1934); *Costumbres y Tradicionalismos de mi Tierra* (1938); *Juegos y Canciones Infantiles de Puerto Rico* (1940); *Alturas Paralelas: Ensayos sobre Rafael del Valle Rodríguez y Manuel Corchado Juarbe* (1941); and *Rememorando el Pasado Heroico* (1946). For biographical information and commentary on her writing see Marcelino Canino, *La Gran Enciclopedia de Puerto Rico*, vol. 12 (1976); Carlos Carreras, ed., *Hombres y Mujeres de Puerto Rico* (1974), pp. 174–76; Osiris Delgado, ed., *La Gran Enciclopedia de Puerto Rico*, vol. 8 (1976); Isabel Cuchí Coll, *Oro Nativo* (1936); Adolfo de Hostos, *Diccionario Histórico Bibliográfico Comentado de Puerto Rico* (1976); an entry in *Grandes Mujeres de Puerto Rico*, vol. I, pp. 117–19; and Carmen Delgado Votaw, *Puerto Rican Women: Some Biographical Profiles* (1978). Articles include Josefina Guevara Castañeira, "Obra y Personalidad de la Sra. Cadilla de Martínez," *Del Yunque a los Andes* (1959); and Angela Negrón Muñoz, "María Cadilla de Martínez," in *Puerto Rico Illustrado*, Jan. 1934. A death certificate was provided by the Puerto Rico Dept. of Health.]

CARMEN DELGADO VOTAW

CAMERON, Donaldina Mackenzie, July 26, 1869–Jan. 4, 1968. Missionary, social reformer.

Donaldina Mackenzie Cameron was born on a sheep station at the Clutha (then Molyneux) River, in the upper Clydevale area, Otago Land District, on the South Island of New Zealand, the youngest of the six girls and seven children of Allan and Isabella (Mackenzie) Cameron.

Her Scottish parents, descendants of Highland sheep ranchers and devout Presbyterians, had come to New Zealand a few years earlier. In 1871 sheep raising attracted Allan Cameron to California, where the family began ranching in the San Joaquin Valley.

Drought, rustlers, and Isabella Mackenzie Cameron's death in 1874 did not shake the tight-knit family. Allan Cameron took his children to The Willows, near San Jose, and worked for other ranchers while his oldest daughters kept house and helped to raise Donaldina. She attended Castleman School for Girls before the Camerons moved to Oakland, where she went to high school. When she was fifteen, her father became manager of a sheep ranch in the San Gabriel Valley, and the family moved to La Puente, near Los Angeles. Donaldina began a teacher-training course at Los Angeles Normal School, but her father's death in 1887 ended her college plans. At nineteen she became engaged to a friend of her brother, but they did not marry and she remained at La Puente.

When Mary Ann Frank Browne, mother of an Oakland schoolmate, suggested mission work in San Francisco, Donaldina Cameron, who shared her family's forthright Christianity, was ready to try this new venture. Mary Browne was president of the Woman's Occidental Board of Foreign Missions, established in 1873 in San Francisco to maintain a refuge for Chinese women. It was to this Mission Home that she brought Donaldina Cameron in 1895 to teach sewing and assist its director, Margaret Culbertson. Cameron shared responsibilities immediately; after Culbertson's death in 1897, she served briefly under Mary H. Field. Following Field's resignation in 1900, Cameron became superintendent of the home to which she would devote her life. Some time later she again became engaged, but both she and her fiancé, a student at Princeton Seminary, decided to place religious work above marriage. In 1911 she agreed to marry Nathaniel Tooker, a well-to-do widower and supporter of missionary work. With his sudden death in July of that year, she reaffirmed her commitment to her work and guided the mission like a second family until her retirement in 1934.

The home at 920 Sacramento Street gave Cameron a base on the fringe of San Francisco's Chinatown from which she could pursue her prime objective, the destruction of the Chinese slave trade. Assisted by Chinese and American friends, she became a living legend as a crusader, and was credited with helping more than two thousand women and girls who had been smuggled into the United States from China. Cameron broke into brothels and gambling clubs in response to calls for help, brought the women and girls she rescued to "920," fought in court for their custody, and exposed the importers of slave girls. She also developed educational programs at the home, and found staff positions, schools, homes, and husbands for the women assigned by the courts to her as foster daughters. In 1925 she established in Oakland a second home, designed by JULIA MORGAN, as a refuge for young children.

Donaldina Cameron's actions and her persistence corrected American and Chinese neglect of the slave trade and contributed to its demise. Although the last slave girl was admitted to the home as late as 1938, the trade had begun to weaken after the destruction of the old Chinatown in the San Francisco fire of 1906 and as a result of the reforms that followed the Chinese Revolution of 1911. The home continued to serve as a refuge, but by the 1920s its original function had been increasingly replaced by educational and community activities. In the early 1920s all the work of the Presbyterian church related to the Chinese on the west coast was transferred to the Board of National Missions, and the Mission Home became a social service center of the church in the 1930s. Donaldina Cameron, following the national board's mandatory retirement rule, left the home in 1934 at the age of sixty-five.

Cameron remained in San Francisco to assist her successor, Lorna Logan, until the needs of three older unmarried sisters brought her to their Oakland home in 1939. She and her two remaining sisters moved to Palo Alto in 1942, the year she finally consented to have "920" renamed Donaldina Cameron House. World War II, elevating Great Britain to the bastion of freedom in Europe, reinforced her Scottish heritage and her British citizenship. Cameron's sister Annie, her second mother, died in 1950 leaving her the only survivor. For eighteen more years she enriched the lives of relatives and friends, until her death from a pulmonary embolism in January 1968 at the age of ninety-eight, several months after breaking her hip.

A memorial tribute by the California legislature, introduced by Assemblywoman March Fong, praised Donaldina Cameron as a "distinguished Californian," who "will be remembered for the . . . integral part which she played in the history of San Francisco and the Chinese community." Although by her work against the slave trade she had interfered with ways of life sanctioned by another culture, the Christianity she lived enabled her to effect change in others' lives without malice and in defense of a common humanity. Cameron's work mirrored her diverse personality. She was at once a strict taskmaster and an affectionate "Lo Mo" (Mama); an imperious superintendent and a humble Presbyterian; a British citizen and an American heroine; a dignified public figure and a reticent private person; the youngest sister of a large and close family and a solitary mind seeking her own way. Her life belied the potential for conflict inherent in the complication of her character.

[Cameron's personal papers, correspondence, and diary for 1909 are in the possession of her niece Caroline Bailey, Palo Alto; files of letters, records, papers, and mementos of the Woman's Occidental Board of Foreign Missions are at the Donaldina Cameron House. *Annual Reports* of the Woman's Occidental Board, 1874–1921, are in the Archives, San Francisco Theological Seminary, San Anselmo, Calif.; other correspondence is in the Presbyterian Church Archives, Phila. Studies of Cameron's life and work are Carol Green Wilson, *Chinatown Quest: The Life Adventures of Donaldina Cameron* (1931, 1950; reissued 1974); Lorna E. Logan, *Ventures in Mission: The Cameron House Story* (1976); and Mildred Crowl Martin, *Chinatown's Angry Angel: The Story of Donaldina Cameron* (1977), which has a selected bibliography. An obituary appeared in the Oakland *Tribune*, Jan. 6, 1968. An interview with Mildred Crowl Martin provided further information. Death certificate provided by Calif. Dept. of Health Services.]

GUNTHER BARTH

CAMPBELL, Persia Crawford, March 15, 1898–March 2, 1974. Economist, consumer advocate.

Persia Campbell was born near Sydney, Australia, the daughter of Rodolphe and Beatrice (Hunt) Campbell. Her father was a primary school teacher. She attended local public schools and Sydney University, receiving her A.B. in 1918. After taking an A.M. at Sydney, Campbell received a two-year fellowship to the London School of Economics where in 1923 she completed an M.Sc. and published her first book, *Chinese Coolie Emigration*. She spent the following year on fellowship at Bryn Mawr College, studying American immigration problems.

Returning to Australia in 1924, Campbell became an assistant editor of the *Australian Encyclopedia*, an experience that taught her a great deal about national economic problems in their historical setting. From 1926 to 1930 she served as a research economist with the Industrial Commission of New South Wales, a wage-fixing tribunal; she collected material relating to the setting of minimum wages, specifically to factors determining the standard of living at different income levels. While employed full-time, Campbell began teaching university extension courses in economics to working men and women, in cooperation with the Workers' Educational Association.

In 1930 a two-year Rockefeller International fellowship in economics brought Campbell to Harvard University, where she studied American agricultural policy and its effect on rural living conditions; her research and her travels throughout the United States formed the basis of her next book, *American Agricultural Policy* (1933). In 1931 she married an American electrical engineer, Edward Rice, Jr.; five years later she became an American citizen.

During the 1930s Campbell became increasingly interested in consumer advocacy. She took graduate courses in public law at Columbia, and studied the work of the Consumers' Advisory Board of the National Recovery Administration and the Consumers' Council of the Agricultural Adjustment Administration. In her doctoral dissertation, published as *Consumer Representation in the New Deal* (1940), she examined the first attempts to represent the consumer point of view in government.

In 1939 her husband died, leaving Campbell with a six-year-old son, Edward Boyden, and a five-year-old daughter, Sydney. Campbell became an instructor in the economics department at Queens College; she remained at Queens until 1965, advancing to full professor and head of the department of social science (1960), and becoming emeritus professor of economics in 1965. She was named Bryan Professor of Economics at the University of North Carolina (1965–66).

Campbell came to correlate lack of "consumer-mindedness" with political apathy and economic illiteracy; educating and organizing consumers became her goal. She combined her academic interests in consumer economics with her work as an adviser to government organizations at all levels, devoting special attention to the plight of low-income groups. During World War II she directed the Consumer Services Civil Defense Voluntary Organization, which administered a broad educational program. She worked to create an independent consumer movement and helped establish participatory grassroots organizations such as the Consumers' National Federation (1930s), the National Association of Consumers (1947), and the Consumer Federation of America (1960). To alert consumers to their rights, Campbell wrote pamphlets, articles, and books on such subjects as trading stamps and installment buying. Later she conducted weekly radio broadcasts called "Report to Consumers" and the first series for public television, "You, the Consumer" (1962–63).

In 1954 Gov. Averell Harriman appointed

Campbell the first consumer counsel of New York state. This was a pioneering move, bringing the voice of the consumer directly into government. Granted a leave of absence by Queens College, Campbell spent four years in Albany, where she worked to promote legislation to curb bait-and-switch selling and to eliminate fraud in radio and television repair services. The passage of New York's first law on general installment buying was owing largely to her efforts.

Persia Campbell continued to act as an adviser to various government bodies and to give expert testimony when needed. In 1959 she served as a consultant to the United States Senate's Antitrust and Monopoly Subcommittee. She also helped state officials in California and Massachusetts develop consumer representation plans based on the New York model. In 1962 she was appointed by President John F. Kennedy to the President's Council of Economic Advisers. She was reappointed in 1964 by President Lyndon Johnson, and the same year received an appointment to the national advisory committee to the President's Representative on International Trade Negotiation.

Campbell was involved in many international programs, and was especially interested in those affecting the Pacific and Southeast Asia. In accord with her faith in international cooperation and her interests in women, in education, and in the consumer, she attended and arranged numerous international conferences on these subjects. She carried out three missions for UNESCO between 1948 and 1951 and led the United States delegation to the Eighth Triennial Conference of the Pan-Pacific and Southeast Asia Women's Association in Tokyo (1958 and 1961). She also chaired this organization (which had consultative status to the United Nations) for several years.

In 1959 Campbell was elected to the board of directors of Consumers Union (CU), publisher of *Consumer Reports;* she held this post until her death. Her focus was on CU's place in the larger consumer movement, on consumer representation in government, and on educational aid to low-income consumers. Much of her time and energy was devoted to representing the International Organization of Consumers Unions (IOCU) at the United Nations.

Always wearing one of her collection of hats, Campbell almost lived at the UN. She pressed for accent on the needs of developing countries and her contagious enthusiasm brought regional conferences of IOCU to the Caribbean, to Israel, and to Southeast Asia. She encouraged consumer organizations in all countries and placed the consumer movement on the agenda of a wide range of UN agencies. Working through the specialized agencies of the UN, Campbell accented consumer education, consumer standards, and consumer organizations in her lifelong effort to foster higher living standards throughout the world. Shortly before her death in Queens, N.Y., in 1974, against doctor's orders she carried the crusade to an IOCU conference on consumer problems in Southeast Asia. In a last letter she wrote: "When it came to the final moment . . . I confess that I could not bear not to be present at the birth of the Asian consumer movement, so long gestating. It was that which really overcame me."

With extraordinary energy, high expectations of herself and others, personal integrity, great warmth, impeccable scholarship, a faculty for enlisting the cooperation of others, and a deep interest in the welfare of the economically or socially disadvantaged, Persia Campbell carried forth her crowded agenda of items that had to be accomplished. She dedicated herself to helping people get their money's worth and improve their lives.

[The Persia Campbell Coll. at the Center for the Study of the Consumer Movement, Mount Vernon, N.Y., contains correspondence, writings, résumés, legislative testimony, conference documents, financial records, newspaper clippings, photographs, and Campbell's personal library. The Averell Harriman papers at Syracuse Univ. contain further information relating to Campbell's work as N.Y. state consumer counsel. In addition to numerous articles and speeches, Campbell wrote *The Consumer Interest* (1949) and *Mary Williamson Harriman* (1960) and was joint editor of *Studies in Australian Affairs* (1928). Details relating to her career can be found in "Consumer Representation in Government," *Consumer Reports,* Nov. 1958; and in Colston E. Warne, "Remarks at the Memorial Service Held for Persia Campbell at Queens College, Flushing, New York," March 23, 1974. Obituaries appeared in the *N.Y. Times,* March 3, 1974; *Wash. Post,* March 4, 1974; *Long Island Press,* March 3, 1974; and *Consumer Reports,* May 1974.]

SYBIL SHAINWALD

CANFIELD, Dorothy. *See* FISHER, Dorothy Canfield.

CANNON, Ida Maud, June 29, 1877–July 7, 1960. Social worker.

Ida Cannon, a pioneer in medical social work, was born in Milwaukee, the third of four children and second of three daughters of Colbert Hanchett and Sarah Wilma (Denio) Cannon. A former high school teacher, Wilma Cannon was descended from French-Canadian emigrants to New England in the eighteenth century. Colbert Cannon, who worked for the Great

Northern Railroad, was the descendant of Scots-Irish emigrants to eighteenth-century New England who eventually settled in the midwest. Ida's mother died when she was four, and her father subsequently married a woman who was devoted to his young children.

Growing up in St. Paul, Ida Cannon graduated from high school in 1896. Her interest in medicine was probably aroused by the examples of her brother, Walter Bradford Cannon, who was attending Harvard Medical School and later became a world-renowned physiologist, and of her father who had once aspired to a medical career. She later acknowledged the influence of an article by ISABEL HAMPTON ROBB in *Harper's Bazaar*. After graduating from the City and County Hospital Training School for Nursing in 1898, Cannon took charge of the hospital at the State School for the Feeble-Minded at Faribault, Minn., and then studied psychology and sociology at the University of Minnesota for a year. Her next position, visiting nurse for the St. Paul Associated Charities (1903–06), was the turning point in her career; it led to a lifelong commitment to the integration of medical treatment and social service. Working with a social casework agency in the river-front slums of St. Paul, she was exposed to the environmental conditions which generated disease and to the poverty which often made sound medical treatment impossible. A talk she attended by JANE ADDAMS reinforced her emerging dissatisfaction with current medical education and with treatment which ignored the patient's living and working conditions.

In order to overcome the limitations of her nursing training, she left for Boston in 1906 to attend the Boston School for Social Workers (later the Simmons College School of Social Work). There she met Dr. Richard Clarke Cabot who had launched an experiment in medical social work in the outpatient department of Massachusetts General Hospital (MGH) a year earlier. The project intrigued Cannon and, at Cabot's invitation, she joined the staff, at first as a volunteer. After graduation in 1907, and a summer visiting hospitals in London and Paris, she became a full-time member of the medical social work staff, and head worker in 1908. In 1915 she was named chief of social service, a title she retained until her retirement in 1945.

In collaboration with Cabot, her lifelong friend and mentor, Ida Cannon's singular achievement was to translate the tentative, limited experiment in medical social work at MGH into a nationwide institution. This required considerable tact; social work in the rigid, authoritarian hospital setting was a diffi-cult, sometimes threatening, innovation for administrators, physicians, and nurses. Cannon always emphasized the necessity of winning the support of physicians by force of example and explanation and the importance of avoiding any conflict over the physician's authority in patient care.

Although not an original thinker or theorist, as Richard Cabot was, Ida Cannon was a talented administrator and advocate. More diplomatic and down-to-earth than Cabot, but tenacious as well, Cannon had first to overcome the resistance of administrators of her own hospital. Members of her department worked closely with sympathetic physicians to ensure that clinic patients, often poor and foreign born, understood the prescribed therapies for tuberculosis, psychoneuroses, venereal diseases, and cardiac complaints, among others, and had the necessary assistance to follow them through. They also investigated the environmental conditions that caused illness, engaging in what may have been the first systematic study of industrial diseases in any American hospital. Restricted for some years to work with outpatients, the social service department proved its usefulness, and in 1919 was officially incorporated into the hospital organization. Over the years, the department participated in training medical students and also attracted numerous American and foreign observers who wanted to establish or upgrade similar programs.

Cannon recognized that the acceptance and growth of medical social work would require the development of an educational curriculum to produce trained practitioners. In this context she played a significant role in the professionalization of social work. Like other social workers in the early twentieth century who were seeking to substitute professional competence for the paternalistic and volunteer tradition of the past, she emphasized that effective social work required more than dedication and good intentions —the physician or nurse might possess these qualities. Kindness and sympathy had to be reinforced, if the social worker was to make a distinctive contribution in the hospital setting, by an understanding of the psychological and social conditions which influenced mental or physical health and treatment plans. Conscious of the need to create an image of professional competence for medical social work in order to ensure its acceptance, Cannon pioneered in the development of a specialized educational curriculum at the Boston School for Social Workers in 1912; she directed this program until 1925. She later taught at the Boston College School of Social Work (1937–45).

Ida Cannon became the leading advocate and

publicist for medical social work during its formative years. Apart from extensive conference participation and consultation, her outstanding achievement during the first decade was publication of *Social Work in Hospitals: A Contribution to Progressive Medicine* (1913; rev. 1923). She visited most of the existing medical social service departments while preparing the book, which became the first comprehensive analysis of the development and principles of the field. Cannon also played a major role in the organization of the American Association of Hospital Social Workers in 1918, and served as its second president in 1920. She received honorary degrees from the University of New Hampshire and Boston University, and the Lemuel Shattuck Award for distinguished service in public health from the Massachusetts Public Health Association.

Ida Cannon was an amateur student of astronomy and found a congenial hobby in bookbinding. For many years she and her sister Bernice lived in Cambridge, Mass., with their brother and his wife, Cornelia James Cannon (1876–1968), a novelist. A warm and generous woman, Ida Cannon took great pleasure in her nieces and nephews. She died of a stroke in Watertown, Mass., shortly after her eighty-third birthday.

[The Ida Cannon Papers, in the Archives of the Social Service Dept., MGH, are a rich source of material on Cannon's career and the development of medical social work. They contain autobiographical material, fragmentary diary entries, correspondence, and reprints. The annual reports of the Social Service Dept. at MGH, beginning with the first (Oct. 1, 1905 to Oct. 1, 1906) are also valuable. There is some correspondence between Cannon and Cabot in the Richard Clarke Cabot Papers, Harvard Univ. Archives. Other important publications by Cannon include *On the Social Frontier of Medicine: Pioneering in Medical Social Service* (1952); "The Function of the Social Service Department in Relation to the Administration of Hospitals and Dispensaries," *Hospital Social Service*, Feb. 1921, pp. 117–26; and "Medicine as a Social Instrument: Medical Social Service," *New England Jour. Med.*, May 10, 1951, pp. 717–24. Cannon's career is examined in Harriett M. Bartlett, "Ida M. Cannon: Pioneer in Medical Social Work," *Social Service Rev.*, June 1975, pp. 208–29. The early development of medical social work is discussed in Roy Lubove, *The Professional Altruist: The Emergence of Social Work as a Career 1880–1930* (1965). Material on family background is included in the article on Walter Bradford Cannon in *Dict. Am. Biog.*, Supp. Three; see also Marian Cannon Schlesinger, *Snatched from Oblivion* (1979). Ida Cannon's nieces, Marian Schlesinger and Linda Burgess, provided information on the family; the Mass. Dept. of Public Health supplied a copy of the death certificate.]

ROY LUBOVE

CARNEGIE, Hattie, March 15, 1886?–Feb. 22, 1956. Fashion designer, entrepreneur.

Hattie Carnegie, founder of a million dollar fashion industry, began life in poverty. Born Henrietta Königeiser in Vienna, the second of seven children (five girls and two boys) of Hannah (Kraenzer) and Isaac Königeiser, at the age of six she migrated with her family to New York City, where her father worked in the garment industry. She attended public school on the Lower East Side but left school when she was thirteen, after her father died, and went to work at Macy's. A beauty, she caught the attention of a neighbor, Rose Roth, a seamstress who encouraged her to open her first business, Carnegie–Ladies Hatter, in 1909. The name Carnegie was borrowed from the steel tycoon, whose wealth she envied.

By 1913 Carnegie and Roth were partners, with a shop near fashionable Riverside Drive. Carnegie modeled and sold the clothes that Roth designed and manufactured, and she designed the hats. The business became Hattie Carnegie, Inc., after World War I when Roth left the partnership. Carnegie was president, owned most of the stock, and had a working capital of $100,000. By 1929 the business had sales of three and a half million dollars a year, and Carnegie was able to employ many members of her family. She remained an active force in all aspects of the business, and manufactured all her own designs.

Although strongly influenced by the world of French fashion, Hattie Carnegie designs were originals. She traveled abroad frequently and brought back models, but redesigned them to satisfy an American taste and temperament. A collection might include 100 to 150 models of great range and variety—all reflecting Carnegie's preferences. The "Carnegie look" evolved from a belief that clothes should never be extreme, and that women should dress to please men. Her line included spangled cocktail suits, velvet dresses trimmed with mink, tweeds, and sleek evening gowns. Retail stores fought to steal her designs, and once her entire collection was stolen before a show by her own head designer, who hoped to set himself up in business. In three weeks she had designed and manufactured a whole new collection in time for the show. The "little Carnegie suit" became a basic garment and was later translated by Hattie Carnegie into the WAC uniform; she also created a modernized habit for an order of Carmelite nuns.

Her retail dresses were always expensive, even at the beginning, and by the onset of the depression even the rich could no longer afford her clothes. In 1932 Carnegie was involved in two famous lawsuits which she filed over unpaid bills—one against New York mayor James Walker and his wife, and the other against the writer Clarence Budington Kelland. She began to market a less expensive ready-to-wear line in her New York retail shop, and eventually established Spectator Sports, a low-priced wholesale line of her own, sold nationwide. The business also began to include other items besides clothes, and in the early 1940s, Carnegie introduced a line of cosmetics hoping to rival ELIZABETH ARDEN and HELENA RUBINSTEIN.

Carnegie was briefly married in 1918 to an Englishman, then married again in 1922, a marriage that counted even less, "since Hattie, on their wedding night, sailed for Paris in lonely grandeur" (Maloney, p. 68). Her third marriage, to Major John Zanft in 1927, lasted until her death. Zanft spent most of his time on the west coast involved in the film business, while Carnegie remained in New York or Paris involved in her work. She reportedly told people: "I've had three husbands, but my romance is my work" (Bauer, p. 27).

Hattie Carnegie was slender and attractive, with blonde hair and blue eyes; she wore thick, black horn-rimmed glasses. She could be girlish and charming but had a ferocious temper, and her manner was once described as "that of a shrewd, tough, highly suspicious business woman" (Bauer, p. 27). Her own wardrobe featured Schiaparelli and Vionnet, and she never wore hats. She made no attempt to educate women to fashion, resented ugly customers, and hated fashion lunches, newspaperwomen, and fashion experts. Preferring her employees to be stylish, good looking, and blonde, she was fiercely loyal to those she liked.

Among her clientele were many famous women, including actresses who wore her clothes in their films. Her film work spanned decades, and ranged from the clothes she designed for Constance Bennett in *Two Against the World* (1932) and *Our Betters* (1933) to those designed for Claudette Colbert in *The Secret Fury* (1950) and Joan Fontaine in *Born To Be Bad* (1950). It was considered a status symbol for a customer to have her own personalized dummy kept in the workrooms, a favor accorded to only a few.

Carnegie loved her work and devoted long hours to it, but disliked shop talk and avoided associating with business people. Her amusements were dining out, attending lively parties, and gambling. At her death in 1956 at her home in New York, she headed an eight-million-dollar fashion, jewelry, perfume, and cosmetics business and paid wages to more than a thousand employees.

[The most informative and entertaining account of Carnegie's career is Hambla Bauer, "Hot Fashions by Hattie," *Collier's*, April 16, 1949. "Profiles: Luxury, Inc.," *New Yorker*, March 31, 1934, also presents a vivid portrait. Russell Maloney, "Hattie Carnegie," *Life*, Nov. 12, 1945, is lively and informative, and analyzes her position in the world of fashion, her approach as a designer, and her manufacturing and marketing techniques. See also *Current Biog.*, 1942, and "Portrait," *House and Garden*, Oct. 1948. Obituaries appeared in the *N.Y. Times*, Feb. 23, 1956, and the March 5, 1956, issues of *Time* and *Newsweek*. Additional information for this article was provided by Sally Kirkland and Howard Mandelbaum. Carnegie's family name appears as Kanengeiser in some sources. The death certificate, provided by N.Y. City Dept. of Health, gives her date of birth as March 15, 1886; most printed sources say 1889.]

ALMA L. KENNEY

CARR, Emma Perry, July 23, 1880–Jan. 7, 1972. Chemist.

Emma Perry Carr was born in Holmesville, Ohio, the third of five children and the second of three daughters of Edmund Cone and Anna Mary (Jack) Carr. Before Emma was a year old, her family moved to Coshocton, Ohio, where her mother was active in the Methodist church and community affairs. Her father, a descendant of seventeenth-century English settlers, was a general practitioner and pediatrician.

After high school in Coshocton, Carr attended Ohio State University for one year (1898–99). She then transferred to Mount Holyoke College for two years of study and three years as a chemistry assistant. In 1905 Carr finished her B.S. degree in chemistry at the University of Chicago under the tutelage of Alexander Smith and Julius Stieglitz, both leading educators and researchers. After several years as an instructor at Mount Holyoke (1905–08), she returned to Chicago and received her Ph.D. in physical chemistry in 1910. Between 1910 and 1913 Carr was associate professor of chemistry at Mount Holyoke; thereafter until her retirement in 1946 she was professor of chemistry and head of the department.

Carr was successful as a teacher, administrator, and researcher. In general chemistry courses, as well as advanced classes in physical chemistry, she was an inspiring and popular teacher whose lectures were characterized by clear logic, numerous demonstrations, and abundant enthusiasm. As an administrator, she was a demanding, but not petty, leader. She expected, and got, quality work from the department's staff and students.

Most often, however, Carr could be found in the laboratory. She regarded research as a vital element in both teaching and learning science. In 1913 that conviction led her to introduce a departmental research program designed to train honors students and master's candidates through cooperative work with faculty members who had various specialties. She saw group research as a means of heightening the appeal and quality of the department's graduate assistantships. What began as a modest effort to train postgraduates evolved into the department's trademark: a variety of ongoing collaborative research projects that combined the concepts and techniques of organic and physical chemistry.

Although there were other projects and other teams over the years, none had the success or renown of the research under Carr's leadership in the challenging but promising field of spectroscopy. For approximately the first ten years, Carr, her colleague Dorothy Hahn (an organic chemist), and various students synthesized complex organic molecules and analyzed their structures, using absorption spectroscopy and other techniques. Although similar work in the application of ultraviolet absorption spectroscopy to organic compounds was under way in Europe, the investigations at Mount Holyoke were among the first American entries into this difficult field of research. To improve her own knowledge of spectroscopy, Carr studied at Queen's University in Belfast (1919) and under Victor Henri at the University of Zurich (1925 and 1929–30).

By the late 1920s, Carr and the other members of the group realized the theoretical limitations of their work. The analysis of a complex compound, as she noted later, does not answer "*why* certain wave-lengths of light are absorbed by certain atomic groups in the molecule and what happens inside the molecule when this light energy is absorbed." Concluding that "for any theoretical analysis we must use simple molecules with fewer variable factors," around 1928 Carr and her group undertook a systematic study of the ultraviolet absorption spectra of a series of simple unsaturated hydrocarbons. By changing the position of the carbon-carbon double bond, the team hoped to understand the electronic structure of that important chemical unit. During the 1930s and 1940s, the project grew to include the difficult but accurate method of far ultraviolet vacuum spectroscopy and the analysis of more complicated substances. For her work she received highly prized grants from the National Research Council and the Rockefeller Foundation in the 1930s.

By the time Carr retired in 1946, the research program was a marked success, producing dozens of honors and master's theses and thirty-five

published papers on spectroscopy. Carr and the team made significant empirical and theoretical contributions to the problem of the relationship of absorption spectra, electronic energy transitions, and molecular structure, especially the nature of the carbon-carbon double bond.

In the process, Emma Perry Carr achieved national and international prominence. She served as a consulting expert on spectra for the International Critical Tables, a catalog of scientific data and standards, and was a delegate to the International Union of Pure and Applied Chemistry three times between 1925 and 1936. Awarded four honorary degrees, Carr in 1937 became the first recipient of the Garvan Medal, established to honor an American woman annually for distinguished service in chemistry.

Although her life revolved around the classroom and the laboratory, Carr was anything but a narrow chemist. A campus leader and strong member of many college committees, she was distinguished by her good judgment and outspokenness. In 1937, for example, she questioned both the procedure and choice when the college hired a man to succeed president MARY WOOLLEY. An enthusiastic New Deal Democrat, she was informed and vocal about current events and was also fond of music, sports, gardening, and travel. Her home, which she shared with her colleague and friend Mary Lura Sherrill (1888–1968), was a lively social center in South Hadley. Intense, forceful, and demanding, Carr was also gracious, friendly, and considerate. Tall, slim, and always well dressed, she was a striking figure noted for her "infectious enthusiasm," her interest in "everything and everybody," and her delightful way of telling stories.

Carr's life reflected her commitment to education and careers for women. The model she provided to her students of the possibility and joy of a life in science and her program of group research proved effective. During her tenure, scores of departmental majors and A.M. recipients from Mount Holyoke earned further degrees and obtained jobs in science, a record that was unparalleled among women graduates of other institutions.

Carr lived in South Hadley for eighteen years after retirement and remained active in college and civic affairs. In 1964 she moved to the Presbyterian Home in Evanston, Ill., where she died of heart failure in 1972.

[The archives of the chemistry department and Williston Memorial Library at Mount Holyoke College contain valuable records, reports, and unpublished material, including a speech by Carr entitled "Hydrocarbon Research at Mount Holyoke College." Her more than two dozen professional papers may be traced in *Chemical Abstracts*. She also wrote several pieces about science education at Mount Holyoke, including "Chemical Education in American Institutions: Mount Holyoke College," *Jour. Chemical Education*, Jan. 1948, pp. 11–15; "Scientific Research in a Liberal Arts College," *Nucleus*, June 1957, pp. 216–20; and three articles which appeared in the *Mount Holyoke Alumnae Quart.*: "The Department of Chemistry: Historical Sketch," Oct. 1918, pp. 159–62; "New Horizons for the Chemist," April 1926, pp. 13–18; and "One Hundred Years of Science at Mount Holyoke College," Nov. 1936, pp. 135–38. Biographical articles are in *Industrial and Engineering Chemistry*, May 10, 1938, pp. 263–64; *Nat. Cyc. Am. Biog.*, F, 364; *Current Biog.*, 1959; and *Am. Men of Science* (1965). Several colleagues and former students have published recollections: "Emma Perry Carr," *Mount Holyoke Alumnae Quart.*, Aug. 1946, pp. 53–55; C. Pauline Burt, "Emma Perry Carr," *Nucleus*, June 1957, pp. 214–16; and "In Memoriam: Emma Perry Carr," *Mount Holyoke Alumnae Quart.*, Spring 1972, pp. 23–25. Obituaries appeared Jan. 8, 1972, in the *N.Y. Times* and the *Holyoke* (Mass.) *Transcript-Telegram*. General background is found in Margaret W. Rossiter, "Women Scientists in America Before 1920," *Am. Scientist*, May–June 1974, pp. 312–23. Additional information was obtained from Marian Craven, George E. Hall, Anna J. Harrison, Vera Kistiakowsky, Jyette Muus, Lucy W. Pickett, and her nephew Edmund A. Carr. Death certificate supplied by Ill. Dept. of Public Health.]

MARTHA H. VERBRUGGE

CARSON, Rachel Louise, May 27, 1907–April 14, 1964. Writer, biologist, conservationist.

Rachel Carson refused to believe that damage to nature was the inevitable cost of progress. Through her writing she created a worldwide awareness of environmental dangers from which the modern environmental movement grew. Born in Springdale, Pa., in the lower Allegheny Valley, Rachel was the youngest of three children (a son and two daughters) of Robert Warden and Maria (McLean) Carson. Her father, of Scottish ancestry, came from Pittsburgh. He sold insurance and dealt in real estate; the family was not well off. Her mother was the dominant influence in Rachel Carson's early life. Daughter of a Presbyterian minister, a graduate of the Female Seminary in Washington, Pa., and for a short time a schoolteacher, Maria Carson was both musical and bookish. She also had a deep love of nature, and encouraged Rachel, while still an infant, to become aware of the beauty and mystery of the natural world.

"I can remember no time when I wasn't interested in the out-of-doors and the whole world of nature," Rachel Carson said later. "I was rather a solitary child and spent a great deal of time in woods and beside streams, learning the birds and the insects and flowers." She also loved books, and always assumed that she was going to be a writer; at the age of ten she had a story published in *St. Nicholas* magazine.

Not given to easy friendships, imbued by her mother with intellectual ambition, she was noticed at school more by her teachers than by her schoolmates. After attending public grammar and high schools in Springdale and Parnassus, Pa., she entered Pennsylvania College for Women (later Chatham College) with the aid of a scholarship. She assumed that the way to become a writer was to major in English, and she had the good fortune to study under a dedicated teacher, Grace Croff, "a wonderful woman who . . . exerted quite an influence on my life." A classmate remembered Rachel Carson as "quiet and self-effacing," an earnest scholar, self-contained, not socially popular. In her junior year she made a decision which, in retrospect, was a turning point in her life. A required course in biology, given by a brilliant teacher, Mary Scott Skinker, so fascinated her that she switched to that field, believing that she had abandoned her dream of a literary career. The contrary proved to be true. "I have always wanted to write," she said to a college friend, "but I know I don't have much imagination. Biology has given me something to write about. I will try in my writing to make animals in the woods and waters where they live as alive and as meaningful to others as they are to me."

In the 1920s, there was still a strong prejudice against women in science. "They [the college administration] would be just as happy if there were no science majors," Rachel Carson wrote. With Skinker's help, however, she was able to get a scholarship at Johns Hopkins University, after graduating from college magna cum laude in 1929. At Johns Hopkins she studied genetics under two distinguished teachers, H. S. Jennings, professor of experimental zoology, and the biologist and statistician, Raymond Pearl. Even before she received her A.M. in zoology in 1932, she began teaching summer school at Johns Hopkins and also joined the zoology department at the University of Maryland. Most important for her career, however, were her summers at the Marine Biological Laboratory in Woods Hole, Mass. Since childhood she had had a passion for the sea, which she knew only from books. Now it became a part of her life.

Rachel Carson's father died suddenly in 1935. Her married sister died a year later, leaving two young daughters to be brought up by Rachel Carson and her mother. Fortunately she was able to find a job with the United States Bureau of Fisheries in Washington as a junior aquatic biologist—one of the first two women to be hired by the Bureau in other than a clerical capacity. In her spare time, she wrote feature articles on fisheries and other subjects for the Baltimore *Sunday Sun.* A writing assignment from the Bureau itself led indirectly to her first article for a national magazine. Entitled "Undersea," it was published by *The Atlantic Monthly* in September 1937. From that essay, she later recalled, "everything else followed." Quincy Howe, editor for Simon and Schuster, and Hendrik Willem Van Loon, author of *The Story of Mankind,* both urged her to develop it into a book. The result was *Under the Sea-Wind—* published, unluckily, in November 1941, just before Pearl Harbor. Though it contains some of her best writing and received appreciative reviews, especially from the scientific community, sales were small. Ten years later, when the author had become famous, it was reissued and became a best seller.

During World War II, Rachel Carson wrote conservation bulletins for the government, and took over the management of the publications program of what had become the United States Fish and Wildlife Service; by 1949 she had risen to the position of biologist and chief editor. Her colleague and close friend Shirley Briggs recalled that "her qualities of zest and humor made even the dull stretches of bureaucratic procedure a matter for quiet fun, and she could instill a sense of adventure into the editorial routine of a government department." Every spare moment she spent outdoors, birding or pursuing other nature studies. After the war, she had an opportunity to engage in the sort of field work she most enjoyed, writing (or editing) a series of twelve illustrated booklets on the national wildlife refuges. Published under the title *Conservation in Action,* they set a new standard for government publications.

During these years, Rachel Carson was in the classic position of the would-be writer who cannot afford the time for creative work. Her job at the Fish and Wildlife Service allowed her little literary outlet. Her salary was modest, and she had a household to support. "If I could choose what seems to me the ideal existence," she wrote to a friend, "it would be just to live by writing. But I have done far too little to dare risk it." She did manage to supplement her income by doing a number of magazine articles on natural history subjects. Meanwhile she had for years been quietly working on the book that would make her famous.

The Sea Around Us, written under great pressure at night and during brief leaves of absence from the Service, was published in the summer of 1951. Aided by advance serialization in *The New Yorker,* and by universally enthusiastic reviews, it became an immediate best seller and remained so for more than a year and a half. The author, a notably private person, suddenly found herself in the role of a public figure and the subject of much speculation, some of it amusing. One reader (disregarding the name Rachel) wrote: "I assume from the author's knowledge that he must be a man." *The Sea Around Us* won the John Burroughs Medal and the National Book Award and was chosen by the *New York Times* poll as the outstanding book of the year. Other honors and awards poured in from all over the world; eventually the book was published in thirty-two languages.

After years of struggle to support her mother and her nieces, Rachel Carson at last had some financial independence. A 1951 Guggenheim Foundation fellowship allowed her to take a year's leave from her job, and in 1952 she was able to resign from the Fish and Wildlife Service to devote full time to her writing. The following year she realized her deep desire to own a summer home by the sea. She bought land in West Southport, Maine, and built a cottage on the rocks overlooking Sheepscot Bay, within a few steps of the tide pools. There she completed her next book, *The Edge of the Sea* (1955), which she saw as a biological counterpart to *The Sea Around Us,* balancing and complementing its predecessor. Always more interested in future projects than in past accomplishments, she had begun to plan this book while she was still a relatively unknown government employee. Her aim was "to take the seashore out of the category of scenery and make it come alive . . . An ecological concept will dominate the book." Though it never reached record-breaking sales, it won several more awards and confirmed Rachel Carson's reputation as an eloquent interpreter of natural science for the public.

In 1957 one of her nieces died, leaving a five-year-old boy, Roger Christie, whom she adopted. Added to the care of her aging mother, this new responsibility curtailed her time for writing. However, it was Roger, to whom Rachel Carson had been very close since his birth, who served as the inspiration for an outstanding magazine article, "Help Your Child to Wonder," published by the *Woman's Home Companion* in 1956 and posthumously as an illustrated book, *The Sense of Wonder* (1965).

Rachel Carson's most influential book, *Silent Spring* (1962), was a far cry from anything she had previously written, or had ever expected to write. Ever since the end of World War II, when the insecticide known as DDT first came into agricultural and other civilian use, she had been aware of the dangers inherent in such synthetic, nonselective, and persistent poisons, and she had tried unsuccessfully to interest some magazine in an article on the subject. Finally in 1958 she felt she had to speak out: "There would be no peace for me if I kept silent."

The immediate occasion for *Silent Spring* was a request from her friend Olga Owens Huckins, whose private bird sanctuary in Duxbury, Mass., had been sprayed with DDT under the state's mosquito control program. Distressed by the wholesale killing of birds and harmless insects, Huckins begged Rachel Carson to find someone in Washington to help prevent such destruction. As she searched for such help, Rachel Carson realized she had to write the book. Other projects were abandoned, and the pleasurable research that had gone into her books on the sea was replaced by an almost religious dedication as she gathered her evidence from scientists throughout America and Europe.

What was to have been an article grew into a book that dealt not only with the dangers of DDT but also with other and still more toxic chemicals with which modern man was poisoning earth, air, and water on a worldwide scale. It was violently attacked—as the author knew it would be—by the agricultural chemical industry and others who felt their interests threatened. Treating the matter as a public relations problem, the industry spent enormous sums to ridicule both the book and its author. However, these attempts to discredit her facts were not successful. A direct result of the revelations in *Silent Spring* was the formation, at the direction of President John F. Kennedy, of a special panel of the President's Science Advisory Committee to study the effects of pesticides on the environment. Its report amounted to an official endorsement of Rachel Carson's position.

In retrospect, *Silent Spring* has been given a major share of credit for initiating the environmental movement. As one editorial put it, "A few thousand words from her, and the world took a new direction." Rachel Carson was questioning not only the indiscriminate use of poisons but also the basic irresponsibility of an industrialized, technical society toward the natural world.

The writing of *Silent Spring* represented a remarkable act of moral courage. Before she had finished the last chapters, Rachel Carson was already suffering from (in her own words) "a whole catalogue of illnesses," and she was barely able to accept the many new honors that were bestowed upon her after it appeared. Crippled by arthritis and suffering from bone

cancer, she continued to do as much as her strength allowed. She testified before Congress, and played an important role in the initial steps toward legislative action. Meanwhile, she never lost interest in the creatures in the tide pools near her summer cottage. And though confined to a wheelchair, she fulfilled a lifelong ambition to see the California redwoods. But her health was steadily declining and in 1964, at the age of fifty-six, she died at her home in Silver Spring, Md.

Though *Silent Spring* had an impact far beyond her expectations, Rachel Carson never saw herself as a crusader. She was, first and last, a scientist and writer, and she had a rare ability to fuse these two professions into one. A *New York Times* reviewer, on publication of *The Sea Around Us*, wrote that rarely "does the world get a physical scientist with literary genius." She herself challenged the notion that science belongs in "a separate compartment of its own, apart from everyday life." The aim of science, like the aim of literature, is "to discover and illuminate truth . . . If there is poetry in my book about the sea, it is not because I deliberately put it there, but because no one could write truthfully about the sea and leave out the poetry."

Rachel Carson's personal life was, on the whole, inseparable from her work. Her choice of reading, as an adult, was closely related to her professional interests: Henry Thoreau, Richard Jefferies, Joseph Conrad, H. M. Tomlinson, Henry Williamson, Henry Beston. She had close friends and a growing number of correspondents as her fame grew. But the writer's occupation, she felt, "is one of the loneliest in the world, even if the loneliness is only an inner solitude and isolation."

In her work she was a perfectionist. She did not write easily, but she never worried that the scientific discipline in which she was trained would dull her pen. Nor was she ashamed of her emotional response to the forces of nature. Though she had the broad view of the ecologist, she nonetheless felt a spiritual closeness to the individual creatures about whom she wrote. As she was finishing *Silent Spring*, Rachel Carson expressed the hope that the "ugly facts" would not dominate the book. "The beauty of the living world I was trying to save has always been uppermost in my mind."

[The Rachel Carson Papers in the Yale Univ. Library include texts of speeches, articles on the public debate over *Silent Spring*, and fan mail. There is also correspondence with her publishers, with her literary agent and close friend Marie Rodell, and other friends, including Edwin Way Teale, Clarence Cottam, Lois Crisler, Judge Curtis Bok, and Dorothy

Freeman. A complete bibliography of Rachel Carson's publications, including magazine articles and foreign editions of her books, is in Paul Brooks, *The House of Life: Rachel Carson at Work* (1972). This book, based on the papers, is the principal biographical source and the source of all quotations not otherwise cited. The controversy that followed the publication of *Silent Spring* is described in detail by Frank Graham, Jr., in *Since Silent Spring* (1970). In addition to the many articles and editorials written about Rachel Carson after she became famous, there is a biography for children by Philip Sterling, *Sea and Earth: The Life of Rachel Carson* (1970). An obituary appeared in the *N.Y. Times*, April 15, 1964; death record provided by Md. Dept. of Health.]

PAUL BROOKS

CARTER, Eunice Hunton, July 16, 1899–Jan. 25, 1970. Lawyer, community leader.

Eunice Hunton Carter was the third of four children of William Alphaeus and ADDIE WAITES HUNTON. Only she and a younger brother, William, survived infancy. Born in Atlanta, where her father was a well-known national executive with the YMCA, she later moved with her family to Brooklyn, N.Y., because of the reign of terror following the 1906 race riots in Atlanta. William Hunton, who had migrated from Canada, had pioneered in establishing YMCA services for blacks in Virginia and other states. Addie Hunton, daughter of a middle-class family from Norfolk, Va., was a teacher and an active participant in the work of the YWCA. During World War I she did field service work with the YMCA in France. Eunice Hunton learned from her parents a commitment to public service that marked her career.

Hunton attended public schools in Brooklyn and spent two years (1909–10) in Strassburg, where her mother studied at Kaiser Wilhelm University. She enrolled at Smith College in 1917, where she was an outstanding student and graduated with both an A.B. and an A.M. in 1921. Her master's thesis was on reform in state government, with special attention to the state of Massachusetts. After graduation she took courses at Columbia and, for the next eleven years, worked with various family service agencies.

In 1924, Eunice Hunton married Lisle Carter, a Barbados-born dentist who practiced in New York. Their only child, Lisle Jr., was born the following year. Although her unusual talents had swiftly brought her recognition in the social work field, Eunice Carter's religious beliefs—she was a devout Episcopalian—and her commitment to the improvement of society led her to want a more active and public life. In 1927 she enrolled in night classes in law at Fordham

University; she received her LL.B. in October 1932, and was admitted to the New York bar in 1934. Active in Republican politics and civic organizations, she also opened a private practice.

A year later, following the Harlem riots in the spring of 1935, Eunice Carter was appointed by Mayor Fiorello La Guardia as secretary of the Committee on Conditions in Harlem. In August of that year Special Prosecutor Thomas E. Dewey named her as the only woman, and the only black, on his ten-member staff for an extraordinary grand jury investigation into rackets and organized crime. Newspaper accounts noted that Dewey was focusing especially on the Harlem policy rackets dominated by "Dutch" Schultz (Arthur Flegenheimer); Carter's knowledge of conditions in Harlem made her a valuable choice for the staff. She is credited with having developed the crucial evidence in the case against "Lucky" Luciano. Later in 1935, in recognition of her work with the investigation, Dewey (then District Attorney) named her Deputy Assistant District Attorney for New York County. She served in that post until 1945 (when she returned to private practice) and amassed a distinguished record as a trial prosecutor.

Eunice Carter was a staunch Republican and was prominent in New York Republican politics for many years. Her only attempt at political office, however, was an unsuccessful campaign in 1934 for the New York state assembly. She remained a close associate of Dewey, and of Nelson Rockefeller.

Throughout her career, Eunice Carter was actively involved with women's organizations, at both the national and international level, and was a strong supporter of equal rights for women. A close friend of MARY MCLEOD BETHUNE, she was a charter member of the National Council of Negro Women (NCNW) and served the organization as legal adviser and as both a member and chairman of the board of trustees. In 1945 she and Bethune went to San Francisco as representatives of the NCNW at the founding conference of the United Nations; Carter was the accredited NCNW observer at the UN until 1952. She was made a consultant to the Economic and Social Council of the UN for the International Council of Women in 1947, and served as chairman of its Committee of Laws. At the 1955 conference of the UN in Geneva, she was elected to chair the International Conference of Non-Governmental Organizations. A regular traveler to Europe, Carter was a guest of the German government in 1954 as an adviser to women in public life.

Following in the tradition of her family, Carter also served in key positions for the

YWCA: as a member of its National Board, and of the administrative committee for the foreign division, and as cochairman of its committee on development of leadership in other countries. She was also actively associated with the Upper Manhattan YWCA (earlier the Harlem branch).

Carter retired from active law practice in 1952, and was widowed in 1963. Throughout the last years of her life, she remained active with the NCNW and in the many other organizations to which she volunteered her assistance. A charming and strong-willed woman, Eunice Carter was a stimulating conversationalist who was at ease with people from all walks of life. After an illness of a few months she died in Knickerbocker Hospital in New York City in January 1970.

[The Trevor Arnett Library at Atlanta Univ. has material relating to Eunice Hunton Carter in three vertical files: a biography file, the file on women, and the NCNW file. Papers concerning her work with the NCNW are in the Nat. Archives for Black Women's Hist., NCNW, Washington, D.C. There is also a clipping file on Carter at the Schomburg Center of the N.Y. Public Library. An article by Carter, "Following the U.N.," appears in *Women United, Souvenir Year Book* for the sixteenth anniversary of NCNW (1951). A biographical sketch appeared in *N.Y. Age*, Nov. 5, 1955, pp. 1–2; and an article on her appointment to the rackets investigation was in the *N.Y. Herald-Tribune*, Aug. 6, 1935. Carter's birth date sometimes appears as 1900; 1899 is confirmed by the Registrar, Smith College. There were obituaries in the *N.Y. Amsterdam News*, Jan. 31, 1970, and in the *N.Y. Times*, Jan. 26, 1970. A biobibliography by Jessie Satyanesan was very useful in the research for this article; further information was supplied by Lisle Carter, Jr.]

JEAN BLACKWELL HUTSON

CASTLE, Irene, April 7, 1893–Jan. 25, 1969. Dancer.

Irene Castle, fashion-setting dancer, film star, and a leader in animal rescue work, was born Irene Foote in New Rochelle, N.Y., the second daughter of Hubert Townsend and Annie Elroy (Thomas) Foote. Her father, a physician, loved animals and was a breeder of Manchester and wire-haired terriers. Her mother was educated in Germany and France and spoke four languages. The daughter of David Thomas, a press agent for the P. T. Barnum circus, as a girl Annie Foote once ascended in a balloon from the roof of New York's Madison Square Garden.

Irene was sent at age seven to St. Mary's Episcopal Convent, Peekskill, N.Y., where her older sister, Elroy, was a student. As a child she also studied dancing with Rosetta O'Neill, who taught her skirt and gypsy dances. Later she

attended National Park Seminary near Washington, D.C., but did not graduate. By 1909 Irene Foote was participating in amateur theatricals, imitating Broadway star Bessie McCoy singing "The Yama, Yama Man." Irene Castle later attributed features of her own dancing to McCoy, including such Castle mannerisms as the high shoulder and the way she held her hands. Her mother took her on rounds of the Broadway producers, with no success.

In 1910 Irene Foote met English-born actor Vernon Castle (1887–1918) at the Rowing Club in New Rochelle. A graduate of Birmingham University with a degree in engineering, he had come to the United States in 1906 and made his debut as a stage comedian in 1907, changing his name from Blythe to Castle. Through Vernon Castle's influence, Irene Foote obtained an audition with Lew Fields and was hired as a dancer for *The Summer Widowers*. Despite her father's reservations, Irene Foote married Vernon Castle on May 28, 1911. After a brief honeymoon in England, they returned for the reopening of *The Hen-Pecks*, in which Vernon Castle was playing. His wife was hired for the show as a singer at twenty-five dollars per week.

In 1912, when Vernon Castle was engaged for a French revue, the Castles went to Paris, where they were discovered as a dance team in an informal act at the Café de Paris. During a six-month engagement they became popular favorites and created a demand for American dancers. Returning to New York City, they danced at the Café de l'Opéra for three hundred dollars a week, a salary which was soon doubled. Irene Castle attributed their success to the fact that they were "young, clean, married and well-mannered." Credit must also be given to Irene Castle's appearance: extraordinarily graceful, slim and boyish, dressed in expensive but simple fashions, she was a refreshing change from the jewel-bedecked, elaborately dressed ladies of fashion. The Castles loved dancing together and were able to infect others with their enthusiasm.

Among the dances they made popular were the Maxixe, Castle Polka, Tango, Hesitation Waltz, Texas Tommy, and Castle Walk. The Castles gave to the "dance craze" an aura of elegance and respectability. They succeeded in integrating ragtime and Latin elements into popular social dancing and performed to the music of a black orchestra directed by James Reese Europe and Ford Dabney. Yet they deemphasized the sensuality of the dances, playing up instead their grace and their value as exercise. Irene Castle also had a tremendous influence on fashion. In emulation of her, women across the country bobbed their hair and adopted the headache band, the little Dutch cap, and the light, floating "Castle frocks."

The last years of the Castles' career were marked by new ventures. In 1913 they appeared in Charles Frohman's production of *The Sunshine Girl*. They also opened their dancing school, Castle House, across from the Ritz Hotel in New York, and Sans Souci, a supper club. Castle House catered to the sons and daughters of the wealthy. The Castles lived in Manhattan and at their estate in Manhasset, Long Island, with Vernon's German shepherd dogs, polo ponies, and monkeys.

In 1914, after a whirlwind tour of the United States, they opened at the New Amsterdam Theatre in New York in *Watch Your Step*, written for them by Irving Berlin. In the same year they published an instructional book, *Modern Dancing*, and in 1915 made *The Whirl of Life*, a film based on their lives. When her husband left for England in 1916 to join the Royal Flying Corps, Irene Castle remained in *Watch Your Step*. She also continued her film career, appearing in the fifteen-episode serial *Patria* (1917) as an American heiress to a munitions fortune who combats the activities of foreign agents. Her final Broadway appearance was in *Miss 1917*, which ran only forty-eight performances.

Vernon Castle died in a plane crash on Feb. 15, 1918, at Fort Worth, Texas, where he was training Canadian flyers. On May 4, 1919, Irene Castle married Robert E. Treman, an Ithaca, N.Y., businessman. Continuing to perform, in 1921 she hired William Reardon to play vaudeville theaters with her in an act designed for them by Fred and Adele Astaire. By 1922 she had also made seventeen more films.

The marriage to Treman ended in divorce in 1923, and Irene Castle's performing career ended the same year. After she married Frederic McLaughlin, a wealthy Chicago coffee heir and sportsman, on Nov. 26, 1923, she lived the life of a socialite. She had three children: Barbara Irene, born in 1925; Michael, who died at birth in 1926; and William Foote, born in 1929. During this period, Irene McLaughlin plunged herself into animal rescue work. In 1928 she founded Orphans of the Storm, a shelter for homeless animals in Deerfield, Ill., gave annual "Pooch Balls" to raise money for the shelter, and brought area residents into court on charges of cruelty to animals.

After years of conflict in her marriage, in 1937 Irene McLaughlin sued her husband for divorce. The suit was dropped after two years of litigation, but the McLaughlins were rarely seen together and maintained separate residences.

Frederic McLaughlin died in 1944. On Nov. 26, 1946, Irene Castle McLaughlin married George Enzinger, a Chicago advertising executive who had been involved in the 1937 divorce suit. In addition to her continued activities on behalf of animals, Irene Enzinger ran a wholesale millinery company with her husband, taught children's dancing classes, wrote a fashion column for the Chicago *Herald and Examiner*, and was costume designer and technical adviser for the 1939 Fred Astaire–Ginger Rogers film *The Story of Vernon and Irene Castle*. In 1939–40 and again in 1959 she appeared in plays in New Jersey and Florida.

Irene Castle survived her fourth husband by ten years. In her later years she suffered from emphysema. She also had an embolism and three strokes before dying in 1969 in Eureka Springs, Ark., of acute congestive heart failure. She was buried next to Vernon Castle at Woodlawn Cemetery, New York City.

[The Irene and Vernon Castle Scrapbooks are located in the Billy Rose Theatre Coll., N.Y. Public Library. Irene Castle's dance costumes are at the Metropolitan Museum of Art and the Museum of the City of N.Y. The archives of the Chicago *Tribune* are rich in clippings about Irene Castle, her career, and her life in Chicago. The Harvard Theatre Coll. also has a file of clippings. *The Whirl of Life* and segments of *Patria* are in the film archives of the Museum of Modern Art, N.Y. Irene Castle published *My Husband* (1919), about Vernon Castle, as well as her autobiography, as told to Bob and Wanda Duncan, *Castles in the Air* (1958). *Dance Magazine* printed two articles about Castle by Donald Duncan: "Irene Castle in 1956," Oct. 1956, and "Irene Castle 'Comeback,'" March 1958. Lewis A. Erenberg interprets the Castle phenomenon in "Everybody's Doin' It: The Pre-World War I Dance Craze, the Castles, and the Modern American Girl," *Feminist Studies*, Fall 1975. Obituaries appeared in the *N.Y. Times*, Jan. 26, 1969, and in the March 1969 issue of *Dance Magazine;* death record provided by Ark. Dept. of Health. Irene Castle's daughter, Barbara McLaughlin Kreutz, supplied information for this article.]

IRIS M. FANGER

CHACE, Marian, Oct. 31, 1896–July 20, 1970. Dance therapist, dancer.

Marian Chace, who created dance therapy as a profession, was born in Providence, R.I., the oldest of four children, three girls and a boy. Her father, Daniel Champlain Chace, descendant of an old New England family, was an editor and journalism teacher. Her mother, Harriet Edgaretta (Northrup) Chace, a publicist and poet, was especially sensitive to Marian's spiritual and physical well-being. In a journal she described her young daughter as "energetic . . . sensitive, happy, sympathetic, stubborn . . . honest and courageous." In later life Marian Chace's ability to blend honesty, energy, and courage with sensitivity led to her success in the use of dance as therapy for the mentally ill.

Chace attended Pembroke College in Providence for one year, then moved with her family to Washington, D.C., where she studied at the Corcoran School of Art in 1915. She began to dance in an attempt to release tension in her back muscles caused by an accident, and soon found that dance was her natural means of expression. In Washington she met and fell in love with Lester Shafer, a young dancer who urged her to study with him in New York at the Denishawn School, directed by RUTH ST. DENIS and her husband, Ted Shawn.

Marian Chace and Lester Shafer were married in New York, July 29, 1924, before beginning a tour in vaudeville with a dance act they had created. They settled in Los Angeles, where their daughter, Marian Lester, was born in 1925. Rejoining the Denishawn dancers four years later, Chace appeared in the Denishawn concerts in Lewisohn Stadium in New York City in August 1929 and again a year later. For two years she also taught children at the Denishawn School. Ted Shawn and Ruth St. Denis taught Chace their concepts of movement and their theory of the relation between the cultural histories of individuals and their ways of moving. Also at Denishawn she learned to work as a member of a group, which influenced her later belief in the power of dance as a means of group communication.

Moving to Washington in 1930, where their daughter had been living with Chace's parents, Marian Chace and her husband opened a branch of the Denishawn School. Her career from then on centered in the capital. After her marriage ended in divorce in 1938, she continued to direct the school.

Increasingly Chace's students included both adults and children for whom dance was a means of therapy. For some years she also continued to train creative dancers and to direct and choreograph for her own group. As more doctors referred patients to her, however, she soon became better known for her use of movement and rhythmic action as tools for reaching those in need of psychiatric care; by 1940, her school was almost equally divided between the two groups. Looking back, Chace recalled the 1930s as a period of "intense absorption in learning about non-verbal communication." In addition to her classes, she gave a series of seminars for elementary school teachers on the use of movement for communication. These were followed by work with troubled adolescents at the National Training School for Girls and classes in a Washington orphanage. Her reputation led to an invitation in 1942 from Dr. Winfred Overholser, superintendent of Saint Elizabeths, the federal psychiatric hospital in Washington, to start a dance program at the hospital. Working as a part-time Red Cross volunteer, Marian Chace led a "dance for communication" group, developing techniques and tools never before attempted with the mentally ill in a hospital setting. The staff at Saint Elizabeths gave enthusiastic support and Chace began to feel torn between her school and her therapeutic work: "When I was at the hospital, I felt needed at the studio, and when I was at the studio, I felt needed at the hospital."

In 1944 she somewhat reluctantly gave up her school for full-time work at Saint Elizabeths. At the hospital Chace had the opportunity to observe changing techniques in psychotherapy. In addition, she attended daily clinical conferences at the hospital and took courses at the Washington School of Psychiatry, where she studied with the psychoanalyst FRIEDA FROMM-REICHMANN. Combining her knowledge of music and music therapy with dance, Chace helped patients produce plays and pageants they wrote themselves, including "Cry for Humanity," which was later televised, and "Hotel Saint Elizabeth," a satire on institutional life. She also trained other therapists in her techniques, serving for them, as one trainee recalled, as both therapist and teacher. Demanding from her students the perfection she would never ask of patients, Chace tried to make trainees confront their own problems as they learned to solve those of others.

In 1946 Chace was invited to join the staff of Chestnut Lodge, a private psychiatric hospital in Rockville, Md., where Frieda Fromm-Reichmann was a staff member. There she became both dance therapist and leader of the program in psychodrama. Between 1946 and her retirement from Saint Elizabeths in 1966, she also lectured at other hospitals and at universities and clinics throughout the country. In addition, in 1955 Chace joined the faculty of the Turtle Bay Music School in New York City and in 1957 instituted a dance therapy training workshop there, which she offered every summer until her death.

In July 1964, at the age of sixty-seven, Marian Chace took her only trip abroad, going to Israel to discuss and demonstrate her techniques and philosophy with mental health workers there. Her visit was welcomed as the start of an important new direction in therapy. In 1965, mainly on Chace's initiative, a small group of dance therapists joined in founding the American Dance Therapy Association, of which she was first president. Her work had earlier been recognized by the Oveta Culp Hobby Award in 1955 and an award for outstanding service from the United States Department of Health, Education, and Welfare (1956). Chace continued to work as a member of the Chestnut Lodge staff until her death in 1970 of a heart attack at the Washington home she shared with her daughter.

Marian Chace described dance therapy as the combination of "verbal and non-verbal communication to enable a patient or group member to express feeling, to participate in human relationships, to increase personal self-esteem, to develop a more realistic concept of his body image and through all of these, to achieve some feelings of relaxation and enjoyment." Her belief that the human body was the "most easily available . . . freest means of healthful self-expression and emotional release" led to the development of techniques that have helped to free many from the bondage of mental illness.

[The major source is Harris Chaiklin, ed., *Marian Chace: Her Papers*, published by the Am. Dance Therapy Assoc. (1975). It contains her mother's journal, various autobiographical statements, her published and unpublished articles, transcripts of panel discussions in which she participated, her journal and newspaper accounts of her trip to Israel, two articles and a poem about her, and a bibliography. All quotations are taken from this source. See also Catherine Pasternak, "Marian Chace," Am. Dance Therapy Assoc., *Proc. of Fifth Annual Conference*, 1970. Obituaries appeared in *Am. Dance Therapy Assoc. Newsletter*, Sept. and Dec. 1970; *Dance Mag.*, Sept. 1970 (with photograph); *Jour. of Music Therapy*, Winter 1970; *Wash. Post*, July 22, 1970; death record provided by D.C. Dept. of Public Health. Information for this article was also provided by Chace's daughter, Marian L. Barb.]

NORMA CANNER

CHASE, Edna Woolman, March 14, 1877– March 20, 1957. Fashion editor.

Edna Chase, editor-in-chief of *Vogue* magazine and moving force of American fashion, was born in Asbury Park, N.J., the only child of Franklyn and Laura (Woolman) Alloway. Her parents separated shortly after her birth and her mother later remarried, moving with her new husband to New York City. Edna was left in the care of her maternal grandfather and stepgrandmother, who raised her in a modest Quaker environment (one of her ancestors was the fa-

mous Quaker John Woolman). She adopted the Woolman name as her own.

Never very revealing about herself, in her autobiography *Always in Vogue* (1954) Chase offered few details about her youth. She claimed to have had a simple "country school education," although this disarming label probably cloaked tutoring and perhaps private schooling as well. In later years, she attributed many of her qualities to her sober Quaker upbringing, but she was not strongly bound to that faith: she sent her own child to Catholic schools and dabbled intermittently in Christian Science. Her elusive account of her own past emphasized her lack of college education or professional training and even suggested a kind of self-creation. In 1895, at the age of eighteen, she became a temporary worker in the circulation department at *Vogue*, at that time a small weekly written "by society for society." The magazine, then only three years old, became her life.

Chase used her early years at *Vogue* as an apprenticeship. She gradually absorbed all the details of the magazine's activities and assumed more and more de facto responsibility. Attracting the attention of *Vogue*'s first publisher, Arthur Turnure, she participated increasingly in layouts and other business. By the time Condé Nast bought the magazine in 1909, she had become thoroughly familiar with its workings and spirit and had established herself as a reporter of fashion.

Against her passionate involvement with her work, her private life paled. About 1902 she married the scion of an old Boston family, Francis Dane Chase, whose personal charm failed to offset his lack of business acumen; he left the merchant marine for the hotel business, but did not make a success of it. On April 8, 1905, Edna Chase gave birth to her only child, Ilka (d. 1978), who later became a noted actress and writer. Although delighted with her daughter, Chase did not let motherhood interfere with her work. A close friend, Claire Avery, and a loyal secretary looked out for Ilka in her mother's absence, and the child was sent to a convent school at the age of five. Chase and her husband gradually drifted apart and in 1914 she began seeing one of her early suitors, Richard Newton, an English engineer whose own first marriage was disintegrating. Sometime after 1914 she divorced Chase (although at Condé Nast's request she retained the name by which *Vogue* readers knew her) and in November 1921 she married Newton, to whom she remained devoted until his death in 1950.

Condé Nast, however, proved the most important partner in Chase's life. With his keen understanding of the relationship between advertising and the luxury trades, Nast appreciated Chase's genius for editing an unabashedly elite publication. In 1911 he promoted her to managing editor and in 1914 to editor-in-chief. By 1920 both the French and the British editions of *Vogue* were in her charge.

Chase's knowledge of the European fashion industry helped to transform the American scene in the years after World War I. When Paris fashion houses were forced to close because of the war, she called upon New York designers to present their own creations and staged the first American fashion show. In 1924 she initiated the policy of crediting the New York shops that sold the European fashions depicted in *Vogue*, assuming that readers would buy only in New York. But the magazine was soon carrying the names of such western-based stores as Nieman-Marcus and I. Magnin. The French government awarded her the Legion of Honor in 1935 in testimony to her services to French fashion. As she herself approvingly noted, the French well understood the importance of fashion to a nation's economy and culture.

Chase's career bridged the two industries of fashion and publishing, and she came to know each of them intimately. She worked closely with designers, merchants, and advertisers. Her day-to-day schedule was far from routine: she might spend her time trying to persuade Henri Bendel or Mrs. Stuyvesant Fish to support her projects, or lugging clothes back and forth from Seventh Avenue in cabs, or chaperoning a group of American models to a Paris fashion show. She never questioned the structure or importance of fashionable society; she merely tried to lead it down the path of refinement. Under her guidance, *Vogue* published DOROTHY PARKER, Robert Benchley, and Robert Sherwood; reported on the world of contemporary art; and reflected the most modern trends in decoration, design, illustration, and photography. She maintained the strictest editorial standards, claiming that her wastebasket—into which she threw anything that was bad or merely "good enough"—was her strongest ally. Condé Nast gave her complete control, and under her direction the magazine gained a reputation for high editorial and graphic quality and assumed an important role in the world of international fashion.

In the *Vogue* offices Chase trained a whole generation of fashion and society reporters and editors, including Carmel Snow (1890–1961), who became editor of *Harper's Bazaar*, and Jessica Daves, who succeeded Chase at *Vogue*. She held her profession in high esteem and retained fierce standards of what she deemed good taste. Rooted in a pre-World War I notion of polite society, these standards tended toward an almost Proustian snobbishness. Next to entertainment, Chase believed, fashion provided the most enticing career for a woman, and of the two, fashion was preferable because it was more lucrative. Indeed, at her retirement in 1952, at which time she became chairman of the board, Chase was earning between $50,000 and $75,000 a year. When she died in 1957 in Sarasota, Fla., of heart disease, she left an impressive record: as a fashion promoter, editor, and businesswoman, she had demonstrated an initiative, determination, and commitment to elite style that would be hard to equal. The promotional structure and international standing of American fashion owe much to her efforts.

[At her retirement, Chase destroyed her entire correspondence. Her autobiography, *Always in Vogue*, which she wrote with her daughter, Ilka Chase, is entertaining but gracefully eludes hard questions and precise information. Some details relating to her life and work can be found in Ilka Chase, *Past Imperfect* (1942); Helen Lawrenson, *Stranger at the Party* (1972); and an entry in *Current Biog.*, 1940. Articles dealing with her opinions and achievements have appeared in *Newsweek*, Aug. 24, 1935; *Time*, May 22, 1939; and the *N.Y. Times*, Sept. 27, 1940, and March 13, 1957. For information on the world of *Vogue* and Chase's role see Allene Talmey, comp., *People are Talking About . . . People and Things in Vogue* (1969), and Margaret Story, *Individuality and Clothes* (1930). Obituaries appeared in the *N.Y. Times* and the *N.Y. Herald-Tribune* on March 21, 1957. Further information was provided by Chase's son-in-law, Norton Brown; Mary Salerno, her personal secretary; and *Vogue* editors Virginia Massenesi and Allene Talmey. Death certificate provided by Fla. Board of Health.]

ELIZABETH FOX-GENOVESE

CHASE, Mary Agnes, April 20, 1869–Sept. 24, 1963. Botanist, suffragist.

Agnes Chase, a botanist who contributed significantly to the knowledge of grasses, was born Mary Agnes Meara (alternately spelled Mera) in Iroquois County, Ill. She was the third daughter and second youngest of six children of Martin J. Meara, a railroad blacksmith who came from Tipperary, Ireland, and Mary (Cassidy) Brannick Meara, who was from Louisville, Ky. (The youngest child died in infancy.) Following her father's death in 1871, her mother moved the family to Chicago and changed the family name to Merrill. After attending public grammar school, Mary Agnes worked at various jobs to help her mother with expenses.

One of her jobs was reading proof and setting type for a periodical, the *School Herald*. She married its editor, William Ingraham Chase, on Jan. 21, 1888. He was thirty-four; she was eighteen. This happy marriage was terminated on Jan. 3, 1889, by William Chase's untimely death. Determined to pay off the many debts he had incurred, Agnes Chase raised money by reading proof for the *Inter-Ocean* newspaper of Chicago while subsisting on a diet of oatmeal and beans. Chase then worked briefly in her brother-in-law's general store in Wady Petra, Ill. She became a good friend of her nephew, Virginius Chase, who later proudly claimed that he had introduced his aunt to botany by enlisting her help in using a manual of wildflowers to identify some Stark County plants.

Chase returned to Chicago and the *Inter-Ocean* newspaper in 1890. After a visit with her nephew to the exhibit on plant collecting at the Columbian Exposition in 1893, she began to develop a keen interest in the flora of northern Illinois and Indiana, and, in 1897, started to record her collections. In 1898, while collecting in the swampy areas around the Des Plaines River, she met Rev. Ellsworth Jerome Hill, a bryologist, and they became friends. Hill taught Chase as much as he could about local flora and from 1898 to 1903 employed her to draw many of the new species which he described. Charles Frederick Millspaugh, curator of botany of the Field Museum of Natural History, recognized and employed Chase's talent in two Museum publications: *Plantae Utowanae* (1900) and *Plantae Yucatanae* (1904). Hill also taught Chase the use of the compound microscope and encouraged her to apply for a job as a meat inspector for the United States Department of Agriculture (USDA) at the Chicago stockyards, where she worked from 1901 to 1903. Again at Hill's urging, she applied for a position as botanical artist at the USDA Bureau of Plant Industry in Washington, D.C. She moved to the capital and began working on Nov. 1, 1903, at a salary of $720 per year.

Chase illustrated publications in the Division of Forage Plants until 1905. Then she began her close collaboration with Albert Spear Hitchcock, first as illustrator, then as scientific assistant in systematic agrostology, assistant botanist, and associate botanist; in 1936 she succeeded Hitchcock as principal scientist in charge of systematic agrostology, and also became senior botanist. The names of Hitchcock and Chase became synonymous with North American agrostology.

In a career that spanned nearly sixty years, Chase made outstanding contributions to the knowledge of grasses, especially those of the western hemisphere. Particularly important was her work of updating and augmenting the collections of the grass herbarium, originally part of the United States National Herbarium at the USDA and in 1912 returned to the

Smithsonian Institution. By the time of her last collecting trip in 1940, Chase had gathered over 12,200 sets of plants, most of which were grasses. From 1905 to 1912 she collected grasses along the eastern and southern coast of the United States, in the southwestern states, in northern Mexico, and in parts of California. Much of the information Chase obtained on the distribution of the various species she had collected was incorporated into the range maps of Hitchcock's *Manual of Grasses of the United States* (1935) and into specialized monographs on the genera *Panicum* and *Paspalum*. She almost entirely financed her own expeditions to Puerto Rico in 1913 and, in 1924–25 and 1929–30, to Brazil, where she established good relations with many scientists and government officials. During a total of twelve months in Brazil, Chase collected over 4,500 grasses. Many of the plants she collected over the years were new to science, and her contributions helped to make the herbarium a unique resource for taxonomic research on grasses in the Americas. Like Hitchcock, Chase donated her own agrostological library to the Smithsonian, further enhancing the usefulness of its collections.

Chase's work was intended in part to furnish agricultural scientists with a precise knowledge of the plants with which they experimented to provide nutritionally better and more disease-resistant food crops. To this end she visited many European herbaria in 1922 and again in 1925. While helping to identify grasses in these foreign research institutions, she also obtained valuable duplicates of type specimens (those from which the original descriptions of new species had been made). She deposited many of these in the National Herbarium.

Chase, the author of some seventy publications, made important contributions to systematic botany. Besides her monographs on various genera of grasses, she wrote the popular *First Book of Grasses* (1922) and, with Cornelia D. Niles, the *Index to Grass Species* (1962), a bibliographic register of types. She was also responsible for the 1950 revised edition of the *Manual of the Grasses of the United States*. People interested in grasses came from all over the world to study with her; many lived at her house at her expense for the duration of their stay.

Active in various reform movements throughout her life, during World War I Chase marched with Alice Paul (1885–1977) and other suffragists, and was jailed and forcibly fed. At one time she vowed to burn any publication by President Woodrow Wilson in which the words liberty and freedom were mentioned until women were granted the right to vote. Chase was also a prohibitionist, and thought it unhealthy and unseemly for anyone to drink or smoke. Although raised a Roman Catholic, she abandoned church attendance. Friends said that her version of Christianity was socialism; and she favored the perennial socialist presidential candidate Norman Thomas. She contributed to the Fellowship of Reconciliation, the NAACP, the National Woman's party, and the Women's International League for Peace and Freedom.

Chase remained active and vigorous to the end, balancing professional and personal concerns. Slightly under five feet tall, she never weighed more than ninety-three pounds; yet her energy rivaled that of any gymnast. No one else has matched the volume of specimen identifications done in the grass herbarium in Agnes Chase's day. Officially retiring in 1939, she continued her work at the herbarium for the rest of her life. At the age of seventy-one she was asked to visit Venezuela to assist its department of agriculture in developing a range management program. Chase cared for her sister Rose from 1936 until her death in 1954. After 1953 she shared her Washington home with Florence Van Eseltine, a longtime friend. Agnes Chase died of congestive heart failure in a Bethesda, Md., nursing home in 1963.

Agnes Chase had neither diplomas nor degrees, only the knowledge that a curious mind could acquire from nature, people, and literature of all kinds. Yet the honors she received in her later years illustrate the esteem of her colleagues. The Botanical Society of America awarded her a certificate of merit in 1956 "for distinguished achievement in the contributions to the advancement of botanical science." In 1958 she received an honorary D.Sc. from the University of Illinois and a medal for her service to the botany of Brazil. The same year the Smithsonian Institution made Agnes Chase its eighth honorary fellow. Three years later she was unanimously elected a fellow of the Linnean Society of London.

[The major manuscript source is the Albert S. Hitchcock and Mary Agnes Chase Papers at the Hunt Inst. for Botanical Documentation, Carnegie-Mellon Univ., which contain microfilm copies of the records of the Div. of Grasses, 1884, 1888, 1899–1963, from the Smithsonian Institution Archives, and additional personal papers and letters. Her bound field books (seven vols., 1897–1959) are in the botany branch of the Smithsonian Institution Libraries. Reprints of Chase's articles as well as various unpublished talks and manuscripts are located at the Hitchcock-Chase Library, also at the Smithsonian. Correspondence between Chase and Charles Millspaugh is in the botany dept. of the Field Museum of Natural Hist., Chicago. The publications on which they collaborated were part of the *Field Columbian Museum Botanical Series*, no. 50, Aug. 1900, pp. 113–24; no. 69, Feb. 1903, pp. 15–84; no. 92, April 1904, pp. 85–151. Transcripts of Sept. 1977 interviews about Chase with her colleagues and friends, Gerie Davis, Ruth Drury McClure, and Mildred Gilman Wohlforth, and of March 1979 with Florence, Marian, and William Van Eseltine, are in the Oral History Coll., Hunt Inst. Chase's *First Book of Grasses* was revised in 1937 and 1968 and reissued in 1977. Her article, "Eastern Brazil through an Agrostologist's Spectacles," appeared in *Annual Report Smithsonian Institution, 1926* (1927), pp. 383–403. Agnes Chase, "Rev. E. J. Hill," *Rhodora*, April 1917, pp. 61–69, offers some information on her early association with Hill. See her illustrations in E. J. Hill, "A New Biennial-Fruited Oak," *Botanical Gazette*, March 1899, pp. 204–8, and her memorial to Hitchcock, *Science*, March 6, 1936, pp. 1–6. F. R. Fosberg and J. R. Swallen, "Agnes Chase," *Taxon*, June 1959, pp. 145–51, contains a bibliography and brief biography. See also Michael T. Stieber, "Manuscripts Written and/or Annotated by Agnes Chase Pertinent to the Grass Collections at the Smithsonian Institution," *Huntia*, vol. 3, no. 2, 1979. A biographical sketch is included in Leonard Carmichael's foreword to the third edition of *First Book of Grasses*. Also see Liz Hillenbrand, "87-Year-Old Grass Expert Still Happy with Subject," *Wash. Post and Times Herald*, April 30, 1956; Bess Furman, "Grass Is Her Lifroot," *N.Y. Times*, June 11, 1958; Gladys Baker, "Women in the U.S. Department of Agriculture," *Agricultural Hist.*, Jan. 1976, pp. 190–201. An obituary appeared in the *N.Y. Times*, Sept. 26, 1963. Data on birth and birth order were supplied by Iroquois Co., Ill., census records for 1870; death record provided by Md. Dept. of Health.]

MICHAEL T. STIEBER

CHRISTMAN, Elisabeth, Sept. 2, 1881–April 26, 1975. Labor organizer and reformer.

Elisabeth Christman was born in Germany to Henry and Barbara (Guth) Christman. Her father was a native of Bavaria, and her mother was from Baden. The family emigrated to the United States within a few years of Elisabeth's birth. They settled in Chicago, where Henry Christman worked as a laborer and supplemented his income by playing clarinet in a union band. Barbara Christman, a lively, energetic woman, was a housewife who encouraged the independence of her children. The eldest of four daughters and two sons (one of whom was a cousin raised by the family), Elisabeth attended a German Lutheran school until the age of thirteen, when she began work in a Chicago glove factory.

Her public career began in 1902, when she emerged as a leader, along with AGNES NESTOR, during a strike of workers at the Eisendrath

Glove Factory. The operatives were victorious, and a union was formed which later that year joined with twenty-seven other glove workers' locals to form the International Glove Workers Union of America (IGWUA). Christman was president of her local from 1912 to 1917; when in 1913 she was elected secretary-treasurer of the IGWUA, she became one of the very few women in the country to be an officer of an international union. She remained secretary-treasurer until 1931 and served as vice president from 1931 to 1937.

Christman's commitment to trade unionism and the cause of women workers found its main expression through the National Women's Trade Union League (WTUL). A coalition of women workers and middle- and upper-class women reformers, the WTUL was established in 1903 to organize working women and educate the public about labor conditions. Christman joined the Chicago branch in 1904 and served on its executive board from 1910 to 1929. She was also centrally involved from 1914 to 1926 in the administration of the WTUL's Training School for Women Organizers, a pioneering venture in workers' education.

Christman's abilities as a leader and organizer of women workers were particularly evident during a 1915 strike at the Herzog Manufacturing Company. Representing both her union and the Chicago WTUL, she chaired one of the most dramatic meetings of the strike when over 800 workers met to discuss a proposed contract. Most of the strikers were young women, new to the ideas and practices of trade unionism, and many of them spoke no English. Years later Christman's conduct of this meeting was still remembered as a triumph of patience and skill which played a crucial role in the successful resolution of the strike.

During World War I Christman served the government as chief of the women field representatives under the National War Labor Board. This was the first of a series of government appointments which enhanced her reputation as a national leader and advocate of the cause of women workers. At the end of the war, in 1919, Christman was elected to the national executive board of the WTUL. Her dedication and competence made her the unanimous choice in 1921 for WTUL secretary-treasurer, a full-time position she held until 1950. The mainstay of the WTUL, she worked heroically to raise funds and to keep alive the organization and the causes with which it was concerned as the social climate became less sympathetic to labor and feminism. She edited the League's monthly newsletter, *Life and Labor Bulletin,* and was a central figure in efforts to secure and retain protective legislation for women workers. She was also active in the League's southern campaign of the late 1920s, one of the first attempts to bring trade unionism to the growing number of women industrial workers in the south.

In addition to her union and WTUL responsibilities, Christman devoted considerable energy to the presidential committees on unemployment, child welfare, and vocational education to which she was appointed during the 1920s and particularly after 1930 when the WTUL moved its national headquarters from Chicago to Washington, D.C. In 1934 Elisabeth Christman became the first woman appointed to a National Recovery Administration code authority. During World War II, MARY ANDERSON, head of the United States Women's Bureau and a close friend and colleague from the WTUL, named Christman head of the Bureau's efforts to secure trade union support for equal pay for women workers in war-related industries. Her tact, tenacity, and skill as a negotiator with male employers and unionists resulted in gains for women workers at many plants throughout the country.

After the WTUL disbanded in 1950, Christman worked briefly as the legislative representative for the Amalgamated Clothing Workers of America, the union with which part of the IGWUA had merged in 1937. Even after her retirement in 1952, she continued a variety of labor-related activities. In ill health during her later years, Christman nonetheless retained her interest in helping women workers; from her hospital bed she counseled a group of female employees negotiating with the hospital management. She died at the age of ninety-three of cerebral arteriosclerosis in Delphi, Ind., at the home of a niece.

Modest and unassuming, but steadfast in the pursuit of her goals, Elisabeth Christman was an indefatigable administrator as well as an effective organizer, negotiator, and public speaker. However, she could never bring herself to accept positions of primary leadership. Despite her intense dedication and loyalty to the WTUL, Christman refused all suggestions that she be a candidate for the WTUL presidency, preferring to remain second in command. She also insisted on returning to the moribund WTUL rather than remain at the Women's Bureau. Engaged as a young woman, to her regret she never married. She was well-liked and respected by family, friends, and colleagues, who recall the integrity, loyalty, and effectiveness she brought to her trade union and social reform activities.

[The WTUL papers at the Library of Congress and the Schlesinger Library of Radcliffe College, the

Mary Anderson Papers, also at the Schlesinger Library, and the Margaret Dreier Robins Papers at the Univ. of Florida are the most important MS. sources for information about Christman's personality and career. They contain little about her private life. Among the published sources, the most valuable books are Mary Anderson, *Woman at Work* (1951); Gladys Boone, *The Women's Trade Union Leagues in Great Britain and the United States of America* (1942); Mary E. Dreier, *Margaret Dreier Robins: Her Life, Letters, and Work* (1950); and Agnes Nestor, *Woman's Labor Leader* (1954). Useful journal articles include Alice Henry, "Service Is Their Watchword," *Life and Labor*, July 1921, pp. 205–7; Eleanor Ellis Perkins, "Elisabeth Christman: 'Co-Worker,'" *Christian Sci. Monitor Mag.*, Jan. 19, 1946, p. 6; "The National Women's Trade Union League," *Life and Labor*, Oct. 1913, p. 320; "Trade Union Women Serving Uncle Sam," *Life and Labor*, Oct. 1918, pp. 213–15; "Who's Who— National League Officers," *Life and Labor Bull.*, Oct. 1926, pp. 2–4. Further information, including detailed listings of her government appointments, may be found in *Biog. Dict. Am. Labor Leaders* (1974); *Current Biog.*, 1947; and *Who's Who in Labor* (1946). An obituary appeared in the *Wash. Post*, April 29, 1975. Additional information for this article was provided by a 1971 interview with Christman and by her niece, Betty Hansen. The year and place of her birth were obtained from the 1900 U.S. Census, which spells her family name Christmann. Other, later sources list Chicago as her place of birth and 1882 as the year. Contemporary sources give the date of her assumption of the WTUL secretary-treasurer post as 1913, rather than 1916 as usually cited. Death certificate was supplied by Indiana Board of Health.]

ROBIN MILLER JACOBY

CLAPP, Margaret Antoinette, April 10, 1910– May 3, 1974. College administrator, historian, federal official.

Margaret Clapp was the youngest of four children and second daughter of Alfred Chapin Clapp, an insurance broker whose ancestors emigrated from England and Scotland in the seventeenth century, and Anna (Roth) Clapp, of German Lutheran descent. She was born and grew up in East Orange, N.J., in a modest home rich in words. Heady dinner discussions led by Alfred Clapp made consulting the dictionary a family ritual. At these round tables Margaret Clapp cultivated the clarity and eloquence which later stamped her Pulitzer Prize-winning biography of John Bigelow, and distinguished too her terms as president of Wellesley College and as United States cultural attaché to India.

Graduating from East Orange High School in 1926, Clapp attended Wellesley on scholarship. There, under the influence of Elizabeth Donnan and Henry Mussey, her interest in languages,

sparked by her father, was replaced by history and then by economics. Her academic achievements made her a Wellesley College Scholar, but, receiving her A.B. in 1930, during the depression, she was forced to defer graduate work.

Hired by Todhunter, a private school for girls in Manhattan, to teach English literature, a subject she had avoided in college, Clapp quickly learned on the job—as she was to do in each of her several careers. During her tenure at Todhunter she earned an A.M. in history from Columbia University (1937). An outstanding teacher, Clapp remained at Todhunter for twelve years, through its merger with the Dalton School. She left in 1942 to take short-term instructorships in the history departments of City College of New York (1942–44), Douglass College (1945–46), and Columbia University's general sessions (1946–47).

Concurrently, Clapp pursued a doctorate in American history at Columbia, under the direction of Allan Nevins. Intrigued by recurrent references to John Bigelow, a little-known nineteenth-century editor, reformer, and diplomat, she meticulously reconstructed his life in a dissertation which earned her the Ph.D. (1946). In 1947 she worked as a government researcher in Washington, D.C. That year *Forgotten First Citizen: John Bigelow*, her first publication, appeared. Brooklyn College then offered Clapp an assistant professorship. Happy to leave the minor leagues of academe, she quipped, "I've been sold to the Dodgers."

No championship season ensued. Living with her mother, Clapp commuted daily to teach American history to the veterans crowding the campus, and after classes did research at the Columbia library. Pleasantly shocked in May 1948 that her biography of Bigelow had won the Pulitzer Prize, she still recognized that advancement within the history profession was problematic for a woman. Thus, despite her lack of administrative experience, Clapp "took a gamble" and accepted the offer of the presidency of Wellesley College, becoming one of only five women presidents of major liberal arts colleges.

As Wellesley's eighth president, Margaret Clapp gave forceful leadership to an institution which had languished during the long wartime absence of her predecessor, Mildred McAfee Horton, commander of the WAVES. At thirty-nine, Clapp brought to her office a youthful, almost student vigor. An effective administrator who "always did her homework," she labored each day late into evening, rarely took vacations, and managed to be remarkably well informed about what occurred on campus. Her high standards were contagious. Never authoritarian, she earned the faculty's respect for her ability to penetrate to the heart of an issue, rendering decisions possible. Of her duties as hostess, Clapp, who remained single, noted, "I am not only the president, but the president's wife as well."

A canny fund raiser and financial manager who tripled Wellesley's endowment, Clapp remodeled all of the college's existing dormitories and built three new ones, as well as an arts center, a faculty club, and a new wing for the library. To attract and hold distinguished scholars, she increased faculty salaries by 150 percent and instituted the most liberal leave policy in the country for junior faculty.

Presiding over a prestigious women's college during the era of the feminine mystique, Margaret Clapp often opposed publicly the notion that women be educated solely for motherhood. Scorning facile magazine analyses that attributed women's frustration to overeducation, Clapp blamed instead cultural attitudes and a socioeconomic system that made it impossible for a woman to combine career and marriage. The modest proposals she offered—that women enter college at sixteen and that older women organize voluntary day care and domestic services to free younger ones for careers—were bold enough at the time to draw national media attention. Hardly an activist, Margaret Clapp nevertheless kept the beacon of feminism aloft in a period she astutely assessed as one in which the "old feminism is dead and the new feminism, inchoate."

Dashing hopes that she would serve until Wellesley's 1975 centennial, Clapp retired in 1966, citing Wellesley's need for a fresh vision and her own need for a fresh horizon. This she sought as interim head of Lady Doak, a women's college in Mandurai, South India, then undergoing what she termed a yeasty period. Not given the free hand she had expected, Clapp resigned in November 1967.

Traveling about India while consulting for the Danforth Foundation, Clapp broke her semiretirement in 1968 to serve as cultural attaché to India for the United States Information Agency (USIA). In 1970 the agency made her the first woman ever to hold its highest ranking post, minister councilor of public affairs. Despite strained India–United States relations, Clapp successfully directed the USIA's largest educational and cultural program. Her effectiveness hampered by staff cutbacks, she resigned in 1971 and returned to Tyringham, Mass., where she lived with her sister until her death from cancer in 1974. As a scholar, administrator, and cultural envoy, Margaret Clapp upheld the tradition of excellence in education. Her legacy is most visible at Wellesley; there the library bears her name and the modern college she created endures.

[Margaret Clapp's papers, in the Wellesley College Archives, consist of her presidential correspondence, speeches, chapel talks, and newspaper clippings, as well as some pertinent materials relating to her tenure at Lady Doak and her work for the Danforth Foundation. Especially relevant is a 1972 oral interview done in preparation for the Wellesley centennial. Various USIA news releases concerning Clapp and an officer evaluation report are available from the USIA. In addition to the biography of Bigelow, Clapp wrote a chapter entitled "The Social and Cultural Scene" for Allan Nevins and John Krout, eds., *The Greater City: New York, 1898–1948* (1948), and edited *The Modern University* (1950), which also contains her essay "Contemporary Universities: Some Problems and Trends." Her educational philosophy can best be traced in the short articles and speeches that span her career as president, including "Realistic Education for Women," *Jour. Am. Assoc. Univ. Women,* Summer 1950; "Journey into the Future," *Wellesley Alumnae Mag.,* March 1958; and "Retrospect and Prospect, Wellesley, 1951–1971," *Wellesley Alumnae Mag.,* Nov. 1961. Jean Glasscock, ed., *Wellesley College, 1875–1975: A Century of Women* (1975), briefly chronicles the Clapp presidency and places it in historical context. The *Wellesley Alumnae Mag.,* July 1966, contains an extensive retrospective of Clapp and her presidency, along with photographs of her. For a journalistic account of post-World War II college life see "Wellesley's Margaret Clapp," *Time,* Oct. 10, 1949. Obituaries appeared in the *Wash. Post* and *N.Y. Times,* May 4, 1974. Useful information for this article was also provided by Sylvia Berkman, Virginia Onderdonk, and Miriam Berlin. Death record was obtained from the Mass. Dept. of Public Health.]

PATRICIA A. PALMIERI

CLARKE, Edith, Feb. 10, 1883–Oct. 29, 1959. Electrical engineer.

Edith Clarke was born in Howard County, Md., where her father, John Ridgely Clarke, was a well-to-do lawyer and farmer. Her family's ancestors had settled in Maryland before 1800, her father's family coming from northern Ireland and her mother's from England. Edith was the fifth of seven daughters and the sixth of nine children, three of whom died in childhood. She attended a country grade school and later went to Briarley Hall, a girls' boarding school in neighboring Montgomery County. Although she did not read well as a child, she loved arithmetic and games.

When Edith was seven her father died. Her mother, Susan Dorsey (Owings) Clarke, ran the farm until her death five years later. A maternal uncle became guardian, but Edith's oldest sister,

Mary, cared for the Clarke children. Despite relatives' disapproval, Edith Clarke used her inheritance to go to college; she claimed to remember her mother's praising a man who spent his estate to gain an education. After private tutoring, she went to Vassar College, where she earned an A.B. in mathematics and astronomy in 1908 and was elected to Phi Beta Kappa. Following graduation she taught mathematics and physics for one year at Miss West's School in San Francisco and for two years at Marshall College, Huntington, W. Va. It was the wrong career, she decided: "Teaching is not at all like a game of Duplicate Whist! I therefore turned to something else."

While searching for a new career, she suffered a serious illness in 1911. "Thinking that I was going to die," Clarke later told an Austin, Texas, reporter, "I just decided to do what I wanted to do—study engineering." Healthy again, she took civil engineering courses at the University of Wisconsin (1911–12). A summer job at American Telephone and Telegraph (AT&T) as a computer, solving mathematical equations, proved so interesting that she stayed with AT&T in New York City for six years (1912–18).

With the United States' entry into World War I, she enrolled as a graduate student at the Massachusetts Institute of Technology, feeling she needed more education to do her share for the war effort. In 1919, Clarke received the first M.S. in electrical engineering granted to a woman by that institution. However, the war was over and no one would hire a woman engineer. She took a job at General Electric (GE) in Schenectady, N.Y., training and directing a force of women computers. Dissatisfied with this job and desiring to travel, Clarke left in 1921 to spend a year in Turkey teaching physics at Constantinople Woman's College. She returned to GE in 1922, as an engineer in the Central Station Engineering Department, and stayed for twenty-three years.

Edith Clarke's work at GE focused on large electrical power systems which were being newly constructed or created through the interconnection of smaller systems. Engineers needed to know how currents were distributed within these systems and how the systems would perform under fault conditions, lightning strikes, or short circuiting. Building upon fundamental theories of alternating current developed by Charles P. Steinmetz, Clarke prepared charts and calculating devices from which engineers could predict the behavior of a system without the repetitive solving of complicated equations. The calculating device that she developed to perform these operations was patented in 1925. In 1930, Clarke took charge of a group of engineers studying power system stability, and then in 1933 she moved to GE's Analytical Division to do apparatus and system analysis. During this period Clarke authored or coauthored numerous articles, two of which received prizes from the American Institute of Electrical Engineers (AIEE): "Three-Phase Multiple-Conductor Circuits," published in 1932, and "Stability Limitations of Long-Distance A-C Power Transmission Systems," published in 1941. Her two-volume work, *Circuit Analysis of A-C Power Systems* (1943, 1950), became a standard graduate text.

Planning to retire in 1945, Clarke bought a farm in Howard County, Md. She changed her mind and accepted a professorship in electrical engineering at the University of Texas, Austin. Remaining there from 1947 to 1956, she supervised a number of graduate theses and encouraged both graduate students and assistant professors to publish. Among many professional honors, she was the first woman elected a fellow of the AIEE (1948), and she received the Society of Women Engineers' Achievement Award (1954).

Edith Clarke was a square-faced, broad-shouldered woman of great vitality. Her childhood love of the out-of-doors continued throughout her life. She took up tennis, skiing, and camping, and spent many weekends at one of two cabins she owned on Lake George, a retreat favored by GE employees. Clarke lived on her farm during her last years and died in 1959 in Olney, Md., of a heart attack. In a 1948 interview Clarke observed that she had not been handicapped by being a woman. Though she felt that women engineers often had to be better than men at mathematics, she claimed that in engineering "there is a demand for ability regardless of sex." Because of her ability, Clarke overcame initial barriers to become the leading woman electrical engineer of her day.

[Clarke's engineering articles appeared in the *General Electric Rev.* between 1923 and 1941, the *Transactions* of the Am. Inst. of Electrical Engineers (1926–45), and *Electrical Engineering* (1933–39). The employee files at GE, Schenectady, N.Y., and the files of the Dept. of Electrical Engineering, Univ. of Texas at Austin, contain bibliographies of Clarke's writings as well as biographical information. The best published source on Clarke's life is Alice C. Goff, *Women Can Be Engineers* (1946). See also Dudley Early, "Miss Edith Clarke," *Sunday–American Statesman*, Austin, Texas, Oct. 10, 1948, and articles about Clarke in the *Bridgeport* (Conn.) *Post*, March 24, 1941, the *Dallas Morning News*, Dec. 12, 1948, and the *N.Y. Times*, Feb. 19, 1956.

Obituaries appeared in *The Times,* Ellicott City, Md., Nov. 4, 1959, and *The Schenectady Gazette,* Nov. 19, 1959. All newspaper stories are accompanied by a photograph; the Historical Collections at MIT also has two photographs of Clarke. Additional information came from an interview with Clarke's nephew, James Macgill; death record from the Md. State Dept. of Health.]

TERRY KAY ROCKEFELLER

CLINE, Genevieve Rose, July 27, 1878?–Oct. 25, 1959. Lawyer, judge.

The first woman appointed a United States federal judge, Genevieve Cline was born in Warren, Ohio, the youngest of Edward and Mary (Fee) Cline's two girls and two boys. Her father, a lunch room proprietor, had emigrated from Hungary, her mother from Canada. Graduating from Warren High School in 1896, Cline enrolled in Cleveland Spencerian College, a business school, where she learned stenographic skills. She then worked for two years for a manufacturing firm in Cleveland, before returning to her parents' home in Warren. In 1904 she enrolled at Oberlin College, where she studied for a year.

Cline moved to Cleveland in 1905, taking a position as a clerk to her brother John A. Cline, a lawyer and subsequently prosecutor of Cuyahoga County, Ohio. The job served as part of her apprenticeship in politics and law; equally important was her role in women's club work on the city and state level. For several years, she spoke widely on legislative issues of interest to women. In 1916 she chaired the Committee on Legislation and State Institutions for the Ohio Federation of Women's Clubs, organizing support for child labor bills, civil service reform, proper care for the mentally retarded, and pure food laws. Lobbying in Columbus and Washington, D.C., Cline learned how to deal with legislators and sharpened her speaking skills.

In 1917 Cline entered the law school of Baldwin-Wallace College in Cleveland; she graduated and passed the Ohio bar exam in 1921. During these years, she broadened her political experience, moving from the presidency of the Cleveland Federation of Women's Clubs to a position of influence in the state's Republican party. As president of the Women's Republican League of Cuyahoga County, and vice president for Ohio of the Women's National Republican Association, Cline came to the attention of party leaders in Washington. President Warren G. Harding appointed her in 1922 to the post of appraiser of merchandise in Cleveland. The first woman named to such a position in the United States, she was responsible for the inspection and appraisal of all foreign merchandise shipped through customs to Ohio and northwestern Pennsylvania. Cline combined a knowledge of tariff law with sound business instincts in her work to determine the precise value of imported goods. Aspiring unsuccessfully to the Board of General Appraisers in 1923, she remained at her post in Cleveland until 1928.

During the 1920s, Genevieve Cline continued to expand her activities within the Republican party and among women's groups. In 1927 she became vice president for Ohio of the National Association of Women Lawyers. The executive committee of that association, along with such prominent Ohio Republicans as Senator Simeon Fess, then urged her appointment by President Calvin Coolidge to a vacancy on the United States Customs Court. Coolidge nominated her for the post in the spring of 1928. Judges in the Customs Court had jurisdiction over cases involving the classification and value of imported merchandise taken before the court on protest or appeal of actions taken by custom collectors and appraisers. Although Cline had six years of experience in the field, her nomination received some initial opposition, notably from Senator William King of Utah and members of the New York Customs Bar Association. King withdrew his objections as the Senate judiciary committee reported favorably on her qualifications, however, and on May 25, 1928, the Senate confirmed the nomination in executive session, marking Cline as the first woman to sit as a judge on the federal bench. With her appointment, she joined a pair of Cleveland woman jurists elected to office, FLORENCE ALLEN, associate justice of the Ohio Supreme Court, and Mary B. Grossman of the Cuyahoga County Court of Common Pleas.

Cline remained at the United States Customs Court in New York City for twenty-five years. An indefatigable worker who always kept up with her case load, she brought to her rulings a thorough study of tariff law and trade policy. Appreciating the support the National Association of Women Lawyers had shown her, Judge Cline remained close to that organization, serving on its executive committee from 1930 to 1932, and speaking frequently at its annual conventions. In 1932 she offered a prize for the best thesis by an Association member on the subject of "Adherence by the United States to the Permanent Court of International Justice." She retired from the bench on March 1, 1953, and returned to Cleveland, where she died of bronchopneumonia six years later.

[The Frank Willis Papers at the Ohio Hist. Soc. contain numerous letters relating to Cline's court appointment and her Republican party activities.

The Cleveland Public Library holds a newspaper clipping file on her career. There is no biography, but her professional activities are covered in issues of the *Women Lawyer's Jour.* (1927–59) and in the annual proceedings of the Ohio Federation of Women's Clubs. Obituaries appeared in the *Cleveland Press,* Oct. 27, 1959, and *Warren Tribune Chronicle,* Oct. 27, 1959. A birth date of July 27, 1877, appears on Cline's death certificate, and the obituaries conform to this; the Ohio census of 1900, however, lists the date as July 1878. Transcript and alumnae questionnaire furnished by Oberlin College, and death certificate by the Ohio Dept. of Health.]

FRANK R. LEVSTIK

COHN, Fannia Mary, April 5, 1885?–Dec. 24, 1962. Labor educator and leader.

Fannia Cohn was born in Kletzk, Minsk, Russia, the fourth of five children (four girls and one boy) of Hyman Cohn, the manager of a family-owned flour mill, and Anna (Rosofsky) Cohn. The Cohn children were privately educated and encouraged to undertake professional careers. Although prosperous, their parents espoused radical political views, perhaps influencing Fannia to join the outlawed Socialist Revolutionary party in 1901. Three years later she emigrated to New York City, and worked briefly as representative of the American Jewish Women's Committee on Ellis Island.

Determined to pursue a career, Cohn prepared for pharmacy school, intending to join a drug supply company owned by her American relatives. But in 1905, having decided on a career in the trade union movement, she abandoned her studies and took a job in a garment factory as a sleevemaker. Of her decision to forsake her middle-class privileges, she wrote in 1951: "I realized then that if I wanted to really understand the mind, the aspirations of the workers, I should experience the life of a worker in a shop."

Cohn was elected to the executive board of the newly organized Wrapper, Kimono, and House Dress Makers', Local 41 of the International Ladies' Garment Workers' Union (ILGWU), in 1909, and chaired the board from 1913 to 1914. In 1914 she attended the National Women's Trade Union League's Training School for Women Organizers in Chicago, but withdrew after a few months because she was dissatisfied with the courses. She remained in Chicago as general organizer for the ILGWU, reaching the high point of her organizing career in August 1915, when she led the first successful strike of Chicago's dress and white goods workers.

When Cohn returned to New York in early 1916, her name was known throughout the union; that year she became the first woman elected to a vice presidency of the ILGWU. Aware of the problems facing women in the male-dominated labor movement, she demanded that more women be organized and hoped that her example would encourage other women to seek union office. She was appointed to the ILGWU's General Education Committee in 1917, and succeeded Juliet Stuart Poyntz as executive secretary of the Educational Department in 1918. Under Cohn's leadership, programs initiated by Poyntz—Unity Centers, Unity Houses, the Workers' University, cultural and recreational activities—were expanded, giving the ILGWU the largest union education department in the country.

In 1921, by helping to establish the Workers' Education Bureau, a clearinghouse for workers' education programs, and Brookwood Labor College, the first residential college for workers in the United States, Cohn emerged as a leader of the workers' education movement. In 1924 she helped to organize the Manumit School for Workers' Children and the Pioneer Youth of America, a recreational program for working-class children. For Cohn, workers' education had several aims: to develop well-informed labor leaders, to create union loyalty, and to instill in workers "a social conscience" which would lead to "a world where economic and social justice will prevail." She believed that the programs should provide workers with a liberal education, thus affording them opportunities for self-expression and personal development, but insisted that their primary effect would be to strengthen the union. To Cohn, workers' education offered the best hope of bridging the gap between workers and those middle-class intellectuals who believed that workers would remake society. Her single-minded devotion to the cause may have originated in the contradiction that she perceived between her own middle-class background and her dedication to the labor movement.

During the 1920s, when communists battled the leadership for control of the ILGWU, Cohn refused to take sides, not wanting to associate workers' education with factional ideology. In 1925 she was defeated in her bid for a fifth term as vice president. Cohn blamed the loss on her political neutrality, but her lack of a power base in the locals and the view of many unionists that workers' education was an irrelevant luxury were equally important. Cohn continued as head of the Educational Department, but the ILGWU could provide funds neither for its educational programs nor for her salary. Forced to rely on her family for financial support, Cohn kept the ideal of workers' education alive through her speeches and numerous articles in the labor press.

By the late 1920s the workers' education movement was in disarray. Cohn staunchly defended Brookwood Labor College when in 1929 the Workers' Education Bureau, now dominated by the conservative American Federation of Labor, expelled the college for alleged radical activities. In 1933 political controversy divided the school and led to the resignation of its director, A. J. Muste. Cohn, who had become disillusioned with Muste's left-wing views, fought to preserve Brookwood as a nonpolitical school for union organizers, but uninspired leadership and the labor movement's indifference led to its closing in 1937.

In 1933, following the defeat of the communists and the passage of the National Industrial Recovery Act, the ILGWU launched a massive and successful organizing drive. David Dubinsky, the president, viewed workers' education as a means to bind new recruits to the union and to present a favorable image of the ILGWU to the public. Because Cohn represented the older, foreign-born members, Dubinsky would not entrust her with the supervision of a department whose aim was to appeal to younger, American-born workers, who were more interested in bowling leagues, folk dancing, and courses in union management than in classes in literature and socialism. After Dubinsky hired Mark Starr as educational director in 1935, Cohn retained the title of executive secretary but was increasingly relegated to such marginal activities as planning panel discussions, museum trips, and hikes. During the next two decades her duties were whittled away until, by the 1950s, her sole responsibility was the book division. Frustrated, increasingly irritable and idiosyncratic, she refused to consider retirement until the union forced the issue by staging a retirement luncheon for her in August 1962. Four months later she died of a stroke in New York City.

Cohn's difficulties stemmed not only from the bias of male unionists against women leaders and from changing trends in workers' education, but also from her personality. Both male and female colleagues found her demanding, domineering, and self-centered. But the same zeal which contributed to many of her career reversals enabled her to keep the ideal of workers' education alive. Her legacy to the labor movement was her vision of a union as more than an economic entity. "While organization gives the workers power," she wrote in the Feb. 1934 issue of *American Federationist*, "purposeful, dynamic education gives them the ability to use that power intelligently and effectively."

[Fannia Cohn's papers are at the N.Y. Public Library. Her articles appeared in *Labor Age, Am. Federationist, Justice,* and *Workers' Education Bureau of Am. Quart.* Biographical details are sparse. The major source is Ricki Carole Myers Cohen, "Fannia Cohn and the International Ladies' Garment Workers' Union" (Ph.D. diss., Univ. of Southern Calif., 1976). Cohn's work in Chicago is discussed by Wilfred Carsel, *A History of the Chicago Ladies' Garment Workers' Union* (1940), pp. 87–101. On her work in the ILGWU Educational Department see Robert Schaefer, "Educational Activities of the Garment Unions" (Ph.D. diss., Columbia Univ. Teachers College, 1951); Benjamin Stolberg, *Tailor's Progress* (1944), pp. 281–304; Louis Levine, *The Women's Garment Workers* (1924), pp. 482–505. Also see Alice Kessler-Harris, "Organizing the Unorganizable: Three Jewish Women and Their Union," *Labor Hist.,* Winter 1976, pp. 5–23. The most probable year of Cohn's birth is 1885, as indicated in *Am. Labor Who's Who* (1925), but later publications, *Who's Who in Am. Jewry* (1938) and *Who's Who in Labor* (1946), list the date as 1888. Additional information for this article was provided by Cohn's niece Clarice Selub and by Mark and Helen Norton Starr, Leon Stein, and Theodore Bernstein of the ILGWU.]

SUSAN STONE WONG

COLCORD, Joanna Carver, March 18, 1882–April 8, 1960. Social worker.

Joanna Carver Colcord was born aboard her father's sailing ship near New Caledonia in the southwest Pacific. Her parents, Jane French (Sweetser) and Lincoln Alden Colcord, were descended from families who had made their living from the sea for several generations. Joanna spent her first seventeen years with her parents and younger brother, Lincoln, either at sea or in Searsport on Penobscot Bay, Maine. Tutored by her mother, she also learned geography and mathematics from first-hand experience. There were other lessons, Colcord recalled in mid-career: the equality of all races; self-control and orderliness; "contempt for sham and double-dealing, because you cannot fool the sea"; and "the inexorability of duty." Although she was never sheltered from danger and harsh conditions, she recalled that her brother enjoyed the run of the ship, while she was expected to "behave quietly, like a little lady."

Colcord made her own way, nevertheless, first as a rural schoolteacher, then as a student at the University of Maine. She majored in chemistry, earning a B.S. in 1906 and an M.S. in biological chemistry in 1909, while also working in the Maine Agricultural Experiment Station. Encouraged by a former teacher to explore a career in social service, she studied at the New York School of Philanthropy (1910–11), where she came under the influence of MARY E. RICHMOND. Employed in 1911 by the New York Charity Organization Society (COS), Colcord became, in three years, supervisor of its twelve district offices. Except for a brief leave of absence in 1920 as field representative for the Red Cross in the Virgin Islands, she held that position until 1925, when she became general secretary of the Minneapolis Family Welfare Association.

Named in 1929 to succeed Mary Richmond as director of the Charity Organization Department of the Russell Sage Foundation, Joanna Colcord quickly became a powerful national figure in the field of public assistance and social policy. An efficient administrator, she directed a research staff and wrote reports, articles, and a number of pamphlets and books on a variety of depression-related issues—unemployment, relief, public works, social insurance, self-help cooperatives, subsistence gardens, and public health. Her comprehensive guide for welfare workers— *Your Community: Its Provisions for Health, Safety, and Welfare* (1939)—provided sound information on all aspects of community planning, health, education, employment, housing, crime, and recreation, together with practical advice to community leaders. Because of the prestige of the Russell Sage Foundation and her own personal authority as scholar and administrator, her work enlarged the scope of family services to include social policy and community action as well as guidance in the traditional field of individual and family counseling.

Although management, research, and writing occupied much of her time, Colcord contributed in diverse ways to the profession; she frequently conducted surveys in the field, consulted with local welfare officials, and lectured at regional and national professional conferences. She was a regular contributor to *The Survey*, the leading journal in social work and social welfare, and a member of its editorial board throughout the depression, editing a monthly department, "Unemployment and Community Action," from November 1932 until December 1935. Active in professional affairs through the American Association of Social Workers and the National Conference of Social Work, she also served as secretary and then as chairman of Hospites, a voluntary association which assisted fellow professionals imprisoned in German concentration camps and provided aid and counsel to refugee social workers. During the early months of World War II, Colcord served as consultant to the Office of Defense Health and Welfare Services and redirected the focus of her department from hard times to war. But failing health made it difficult to maintain her pace; by the summer of 1944 she had become incapable of sustained effort, and she soon resigned her position.

On Thanksgiving day 1950, in Bangor, Maine, Colcord, sixty-eight, married Frank J. Bruno, then seventy-four, whose first wife had died six months earlier. Bruno, professor of applied sociology at Washington University in St. Louis, was a distinguished social worker and educator. Close friends for many years, Colcord and Bruno had first met when both worked for the New York COS, and their professional careers and lives had touched at many points. She wrote of him soon after his death in 1955: "Frank was my guiding light—the summer of my heart—ever since I first met him years ago."

Colcord's last years were marred by sickness and pain. Circulatory troubles, probably related to diabetes, which had become acute as early as 1944, continued to plague her. In the fall of 1955 her right leg was amputated above the knee. She died of a stroke in 1960 in Lebanon, Ind., where she had been living with her stepson.

Of Colcord's contributions during the depression, the historians of the Russell Sage Foundation wrote: "Experience with gales and hurricanes, and the need to change course in heavy weather, was a useful background for piloting her department through a tumultuous fifteen years" (Glenn, Brandt, and Andrews, p. 514). A friendly critic of New Deal welfare policies, she fought for federal assumption of the responsibility for public assistance, for the coordination and regularization of work relief, for the maintenance of sound professional standards even in times of crisis, and for the establishment of comprehensive systems of social security (including health insurance). In all her work she insisted that citizens in need be treated with respect and continued to express her faith in the power of regeneration inherent in all persons. She also labored to upgrade the training of social workers. Although disappointed in what she judged to be the inadequacies of many New Deal measures, Colcord worked for the reelection of Franklin D. Roosevelt in 1940 and was an enthusiastic supporter of Adlai Stevenson in 1952. Best known for her contributions to social work and public policy, her spirited personality is evidenced in her compilation of American sea chanties, *Roll and Go* (1924), which was reissued in expanded form as *Songs of American Sailormen* (1938), and in her salty analysis of the enrichment of American idiom by the common speech of sailors, *Sea Language Comes Ashore* (1945).

[Materials by and about Joanna Colcord can be

found in the papers of the Survey Associates, the Am. Assoc. of Social Workers, Louis Towley, and Benjamin Youngdahl, all in the Social Welfare Hist. Archives, Univ. of Minn. In addition to the books cited, her other major works include *Broken Homes: A Study of Family Desertion and Its Social Treatment* (1919); *The Long View: Papers and Addresses by Mary E. Richmond* (1930), which she compiled and edited; *Community Planning in Unemployment Emergencies* (1930); *Emergency Work Relief* (1932), with William C. Koplovitz and Russell H. Kurtz; *Community Programs for Subsistence Gardens* (1933), with Mary Johnston; and *Cash Relief* (1936). Many of her articles appeared in *The Survey*, 1930–42. Quotations on her childhood are from an autobiographical article published in the *Portland Sunday Telegram*, July 12, 1936. A summary of her career appears in the *Encyc. of Social Work*, vol. 17 (1977), pp. 186–87. John W. Glenn, Lilian Brandt, and F. Emerson Andrews, *Russell Sage Foundation, 1907–1946* vol. II (1947), pp. 514–30, discusses her role in that organization, 1929–45. The obituary of Jane Sweetser Colcord in the *N.Y. Times*, Dec. 12, 1939, includes family information, as does Lincoln Colcord's entry in *Dict. Am. Biog.*, Supp. Four. A popular account of Colcord's childhood is J. M. Stenbuck, "The World Was Their Back Yard," *Coronet*, Feb. 1946, pp. 38–41. There are brief obituaries in *Social Service Rev.*, June 1960, p. 233, and the *N.Y. Times*, April 9, 1960. Death certificate supplied by Boone Cty. Dept. of Health, Lebanon, Ind.]

CLARKE A. CHAMBERS

COMSTOCK, Ada Louise, Dec. 11, 1876–Dec. 12, 1973. College administrator.

Ada Comstock, the first full-time president of Radcliffe College, was the oldest of the two daughters and a son born in Moorhead, Minn., to Solomon Gilman and Sarah Ann (Balls) Comstock. Her father was an ambitious Yankee lawyer from Maine who acquired considerable land in Minnesota through association with the railroad financier James J. Hill. Her mother, born in Ontario to English immigrant parents, was a schoolteacher in Minnesota until her marriage. Over the years the prospering Comstocks took the lead in bringing education to their frontier community: Sarah Comstock as a founder of the women's club and supporter of the public library, and S. G. Comstock as state legislator, advocate of the Moorhead Normal School, and regent of the University of Minnesota.

Ada Comstock grew up confident of her father's love and approval; their close relationship lasted until his death in 1933. Her mother, teaching her at home in the early years, was the only one who thought the forceful daughter needed checking. An exuberant tomboy, Ada climbed trees, walked on fences, and played baseball, but also liked to make corncob dolls.

Indoors she could not be pried from books and soon took over from her father reading to the family. She quickly outgrew a small private school and graduated from the local high school at fifteen.

After attending the University of Minnesota from 1892 to 1894, Ada Comstock received her B.L. from Smith College in 1897. Although she made friends at the university and remembered her professors enthusiastically, she liked still more "the great richness in female companionship" offered by the woman's college. Enjoying languages and literature and avoiding the sciences, she had time for theatricals and pranks but was also elected to Phi Beta Kappa. With her father's encouragement to prepare to earn a living, she acquired a diploma at Moorhead Normal School. But teacher training did not satisfy her and in 1899 she gained an A.M. in English, history, and education at Columbia University.

Comstock eagerly accepted an assistantship in 1900 in the department of rhetoric and oratory at the University of Minnesota, where she taught under the supervision of MARIA SANFORD. Becoming the first dean of women at Minnesota in 1907, Comstock held a joint appointment as dean and full professor of rhetoric and oratory (1909–12). She was conspicuous as the only woman administrator in the predominantly male faculty and student body. Young scholars, including the historian Wallace Notestein, whom she married many years later, were drawn to the "tall, stately woman of great presence, absolute sincerity and wonderful charm." Proposals of marriage were abundant, but, absorbed in her own career and with the concerns of the new academic women, Comstock declined them.

Joining the Association of Collegiate Alumnae (ACA), Comstock felt the direct stimulus of older leaders like M. CAREY THOMAS and MARION TALBOT, and made friends among younger members. She also participated in the first meetings of deans of women and later helped to found the Association of Women Deans. At Minnesota Comstock made it the dean's responsibility to improve housing, find jobs for students, and bring women from the periphery into the center of the university. By the time she left to become the first dean of Smith College in 1912, Comstock had acquired a national reputation and had been awarded the first of fourteen honorary degrees (which would include Harvard's and Oxford's).

At Smith Ada Comstock had broad academic and social responsibilities. In addition to her earlier interests, she made it her concern to study the costs of private collegiate education and to expand scholarships for women. After the departure of Smith's president Marion Le Roy Burton, Comstock ran the college (1917–18), even though the trustees refused her the title of acting president because of her sex. She never forgot "the insult," but nonetheless she formed an unusually close partnership with William A. Neilson, Smith's next president.

Outside the college the quality of Comstock's leadership was recognized. She was one of the American delegates to the organizing conference for the International Federation of University Women in London in 1920. When the ACA merged with the Southern Association of College Women in 1921, she became first president of the American Association of University Women (AAUW), serving until 1923.

A new era began for Ada Comstock and for Radcliffe College when she assumed the presidency in 1923. She saw her challenge as that of transforming a provincial school into a national institution. Her vision encompassed the needs of undergraduates, graduate students, trained scholars, and self-supporting women at all levels. Since the college had no faculty of its own, each year Radcliffe's president was forced to negotiate with the Harvard faculty to ensure full academic programs. With ingenuity Comstock tapped the academic riches of Harvard. For undergraduates, she also established the tutorial system and regional scholarships. Through the tutorial system, and through Harvard-Radcliffe professorial appointments and joint projects like those of the Bureau of International Research, Comstock opened new opportunities for women scholars. In addition, by establishing doctoral and research fellowships, she made Radcliffe a leading graduate center for foreign as well as American women. Her concern for the vocational needs of Radcliffe women resulted in the Summer Secretarial School (1931) and the Management Training Program (1937).

Throughout her presidency Comstock's genius for administration was most severely tested by efforts to redefine Radcliffe's ambiguous relationship with Harvard. For years President A. Lawrence Lowell's desire to sever or reduce Harvard's connection threatened to destroy Radcliffe's ability to fulfill the terms of its charter. Comstock triumphed when the Harvard Corporation agreed in 1931 to continue to certify Radcliffe degrees. But she knew that Radcliffe instruction required a more secure and logical basis. Under Harvard's next president, James Bryant Conant, a reevaluation of faculty hiring and tenure policy took place which, combined with the emergencies of World War II, finally led to an agreement, engineered by Comstock and provost Paul Buck in 1943, by which Harvard took responsibility for educating women in the liberal arts. Coeducation was not integral to the plan, but Comstock hoped that the contractual agreement would make the "complete inclusion" of Radcliffe College within Harvard University "inevitable."

From the time women got the vote, Comstock relished "the new circumstances of full and active citizenship" and expected students to take stands on public issues. She herself set an example of participation in public affairs. As the only woman on the National Commission of Law Observance and Enforcement (the Wickersham Commission) in 1929, she was one of five who recommended revision, though not repeal, of the eighteenth amendment. In Massachusetts she supported jury duty for women and opposed discrimination in the employment of married women. She also served on the National Committee for Planned Parenthood (1941). Between the two world wars Comstock became increasingly concerned about international affairs. Visiting China in 1931 for the Institute of Pacific Relations (of which she was vice chairman), she reported on the Manchurian crisis. She protested actively against Hitler, favored freer admission of immigrant children, and helped place Russian and German refugee students and scholars. William A. Neilson summed up the public's respect for her: "In a different world, Miss Comstock would have sat on the Supreme Bench of the United States" (Thorp, p. 231).

A week after retiring from Radcliffe in 1943, Comstock astounded friends, staff, and alumnae by marrying her old suitor, Wallace Notestein, Yale professor emeritus. The couple made their home in New Haven, where she remained after his death in 1969. During these years Ada Comstock Notestein continued to generate support for Smith and Radcliffe Colleges. She found marriage at sixty-six an adventure prompting new thoughts on women's lives. Even before marrying, she had come to believe that institutions should encourage gifted women who desired to combine marriage and career. As wife, she wrote to a friend in 1946 that professional women should learn from men not to be "distracted" by petty "details of living," and by contrast "a woman with a home and a husband" needed to sustain "an interesting piece of work and . . . keep a thread of continuity in her life." She survived her husband by several years, dying in New Haven of congestive heart failure in 1973.

In private and public life Ada Comstock Notestein sustained deep and lasting friendships with women and men. Strong, wise, and humorous, she knew how to put people at ease with a toss of her head and a great laugh. For students her large presence was both awesome and charismatic. She was a speaker of magnificent voice and elegant phrasing; her letters, essays, and reviews show that she was a stylist of the written word as well. To generations of college women Ada Comstock, with her record of academic firsts and her pioneer efforts to widen choices for educated women, provided an extraordinary model.

[The archives of the Univ. of Minn., Smith College, Harvard Univ., and the S. G. Comstock House in Moorhead, Minn., contain published and unpublished materials by and relating to Ada Comstock Notestein, but the largest collection is in the Radcliffe College Archives. Many private papers are held by Susan Comstock Clemedtson. The Schlesinger Library at Radcliffe College and the Sophia Smith Coll. at Smith College have some personal letters. Especially useful are a transcript of reminiscences, Roberta Yerkes Blanshard, "Ada Louise Comstock, the Years 1876–1973 of Ada Notestein's Life, as She Recalled Them," and a memorial talk given at Harvard by John H. Finley, Jr., Feb. 8, 1974, both in the Schlesinger Library. Among Ada Comstock's numerous articles, the most pertinent are "The Fourth R for Women," *Century Mag.,* Feb. 1929; "Inaugural Address," Oct. 20, 1923, *School and Society,* vol. XVIII, no. 463; "Office of the Dean of Women," in E. Bird Johnson, ed., *Forty Years at the University of Minnesota* (1910); and "Aims and Policies of the AAUW," *Jour. AAUW,* 43 (1949). A valuable source is Jacqueline Van Voris, "Interview with Ada Comstock Notestein," *Smith Centennial Study* (1971). Informative secondary sources include Susan M. Smith's essay in Barbara Stuhler and Gretchen Kreuter, eds., *Women in Minnesota* (1977), although it is not entirely accurate; Margaret Farrand Thorp, *Neilson of Smith* (1956); and the *N.Y. Times* obituary, Dec. 13, 1973. Additional information was provided by a niece, Susan C. Clemedtson, and by Bernice Brown Cronkhite, Frances R. Jordan, Edith Stedman, Roberta Y. Blanshard, Marjorie Sprague Friis, Helen Smith, Sidney Lovett, Marjory Archer Haggart, Mina Curtiss, and Robert Loeffler. Death certificate supplied by Conn. Dept. of Health.]

BARBARA MILLER SOLOMON

COOKE, Flora Juliette, Dec. 25, 1864–Feb. 21, 1953. Educator.

Flora Juliette Cooke, who as principal of the Francis W. Parker School in Chicago became a leader in progressive education, was born in Bainbridge, Ohio. She was the second daughter and fourth of six children of Sumner and Rosetta (Ellis) Hannum. When Flora was barely five her mother died, and her father sought adoption for his children. Her brothers and sisters were easily placed; but Flora, considered a headstrong child, was in and out of six different homes within one year. Finally, she was sent to

live with her mother's close friends Charles and Luella (Miller) Cooke of Youngstown, Ohio. The Cookes, of English ancestry like the Hannums, had strong religious ideals, much patience, and a firm belief in the value of education. Flora responded to them almost immediately and in 1881 they legally adopted her.

Flora Cooke attended public elementary schools in Youngstown and graduated from the local high school in 1884. At nineteen she began her teaching career in a succession of rural schools. By 1885 she was teaching at the Hellman Street School in Youngstown, where she remained until 1889—the last two years as principal. There she began a lifelong association with geographer and teacher Zonia Baber, who inspired her to further study and to an eventual career in Chicago. Baber, a graduate of Chicago's Cook County Normal School, was an ardent disciple of the school's principal, Col. Francis W. Parker. A well-known educational reformer, Parker believed in child-centered education and had introduced a number of innovations in curriculum, materials, and pedagogical style.

In 1889 Colonel Parker invited Cooke to become a student at the Cook County Normal School, where Baber was then teaching. Cooke graduated in 1890 and Parker asked her to join his faculty as critic-teacher of the practice school's first grade. In one year she had developed, according to Parker, into "the best primary teacher I ever saw." Like him, she refused to accept the notion of a "bad child." And, perhaps mindful of her own difficult early years, she refused to "lose faith in any child" (*Progressive Education,* Dec. 1937).

As interest in Francis W. Parker's educational ideas increased, he sent his teachers throughout the country to promote them. Flora Cooke was especially valuable because, better than most, she was able to explain Parker's often nebulously worded theories. During her ten years at the Cook County Normal School, she lectured on his work in twenty-eight states and, in 1899, went as far as the newly annexed territory of Hawaii. She also served as Parker's representative at conferences in Switzerland and Denmark.

In 1899 Flora Cooke followed Parker to the new Chicago Institute, a private school financed by Chicago philanthropist ANITA MCCORMICK BLAINE to serve as a laboratory for Parker's ideas. In 1901, with the merger of the Chicago Institute with the University of Chicago, Parker became the first director of the new School of Education at the university. Cooke was named principal of the Francis W. Parker School, built on the north side of the city—again with Anita Blaine's assistance—to replace the Institute. After Parker's death in 1902, the school, which included both the elementary grades and high school, severed its relations with the University of Chicago; Flora Cooke remained its principal until her retirement in 1934.

Under her leadership the Francis W. Parker School became a model of progressive education in the United States. Her professional reputation grew as she not only furthered Parker's ideas but also developed programs and materials reflecting her own educational views. She insisted upon enrolling students of varied economic, racial, and cultural backgrounds, believing that the school, though private, should serve as a model for public education. Under her guidance, the Parker School was run democratically, with the cooperation of principal, teachers, and students. Cooke also adamantly upheld the rights of individual students, in one instance (during World War I) defending a student who had written a pacifist essay against a group of parents who sought his expulsion. A twelve-volume series, *The Francis W. Parker Studies in Education* (1912–34), written by teachers at the Parker School under Cooke's direction and edited by her, deals with teaching the various subjects in the curriculum and reflects her ideas on curricular and methodological issues. She incorporated her views on reading instruction and on the significance of reading in the total social and creative development of the child in *Reading in the Primary Grades*, which served as a manual of instruction for her primary teachers.

Like Parker and John Dewey (whose children she had taught in the Cook County Normal practice school), Cooke regarded the school as a learning laboratory. In 1932 she readily agreed to participate in the important Eight-Year Study initiated by the Commission on the Relation of School and College of the Progressive Education Association. Among its benefits she saw in the study's provision for more flexible college entrance an opportunity for the high school she directed to carry on the kinds of progressive experiments her elementary school had begun thirty years earlier. As a result of participation in the study, the Francis W. Parker School enhanced its reputation as a showplace for visitors from all over the world.

After her retirement, Cooke became a trustee of the Parker School (1934–48); she was also one of the founders of the North Shore Country Day School in Winnetka, Ill., and was a founder and trustee of the Graduate Teachers College of Winnetka and of Roosevelt University in Chicago. In her last years, Cooke remained active in a number of social, civic, and educational organizations. At the age of eighty she engaged in a celebrated controversy with Sen. Theodore Bilbo of Mississippi over his attempts to prevent passage of fair employment practices legislation. Flora Cooke died of a heart attack in Chicago in 1953. As one memorial to her records: "She gave of herself lavishly everywhere."

[The Flora Juliette Cooke Papers at the Chicago Hist. Soc. contain correspondence, speeches, reports, and printed materials, mostly concerning the educational policies and administration of the Parker School. References to Cooke's activities are also found in the Anita McCormick Blaine Papers in the McCormick Coll. at the State Hist. Soc. of Wis., and in the Chicago Teachers College historical files at Chicago State Univ. Her book *Nature Myths and Stories for Little Children* (1895) outlines ideas about the use of myths to capture the curiosity of children which were later incorporated into the Parker School science curriculum. Some of Cooke's speeches and articles can be found in *Elementary School Teacher* (1912), NSSE [Nat. Soc. for the Study of Education] *Yearbook* (1926), *Chicago Schools Jour.* (1930–38), *Progressive Education* (1937), and *Ill. School Teacher* (1936). She also edited the 1937 edition of Francis W. Parker's *Talks on Pedagogics* (1894). *Coronet*, Oct. 1947, pp. 77–83, contains a biographical sketch. An article on her exchange of letters with Sen. Bilbo appeared in the *Chicago Sun*, Aug. 24, 1945. See also Lawrence Cremin, *The Transformation of the School* (1961), and Marie Kirchner Stone, ed., *Between Home and Community: Chronicle of the Francis W. Parker School* (1976). Obituaries appeared in the *N.Y. Times* and *Chicago Tribune*, Feb. 22, 1953. Adoption record supplied by Probate Court, Mahoning Cty., Ohio; death certificate provided by Cook Cty., Ill.]

ROSEMARY V. DONATELLI

COOLIDGE, Elizabeth Penn Sprague, Oct. 30, 1864–Nov. 4, 1953. Music patron.

Elizabeth Sprague Coolidge was born in Chicago, the oldest child of Albert Arnold and Nancy (Atwood) Sprague, and the only one to reach maturity. Originally English, the Spragues and the Atwoods had settled by the middle of the eighteenth century in Vermont, and both families lived a rugged farm existence.

In 1861 Albert Sprague, a Yale graduate, moved to Chicago, where, with his younger brother Otho, he established what became one of the largest wholesale grocery businesses in the world. At home Albert Sprague was easy going and gentle. By comparison his wife Nancy, with whom Elizabeth enjoyed a close relationship, had an abundance of executive energy and an uninhibited tongue, two characteristics that her daughter also exhibited. According to her cousin, LUCY SPRAGUE MITCHELL, Elizabeth Sprague "was always a determined individualist, with 'social' leanings that were rather confusing to her conservative father, who greatly admired her, though a bit uncomprehendingly" (Mitchell, p. 41).

Privately educated, Elizabeth Sprague began at the age of eleven to play the piano. This activity, to which she devoted hours of daily rehearsal, became not only a lifelong interest but a safeguard against emotional turmoil as well. An accomplished pianist, she later believed that her piano teacher's "exaction from me, throughout my girlhood, of reverence for duty, of coordinated self-control, and uncompromising fidelity to standards" was the foundation of her mental and moral strength. "Without the mechanical stabilizer of hard piano practice and its concomitant sense of power and balance, my emotional equilibrium must have been wrecked." Coolidge also began to compose music in the 1890s. Though she continued to write music for many years, composition later became for her primarily a spiritual refuge from the deafness which began to afflict her in her thirties.

On Nov. 12, 1891, Elizabeth Sprague married Frederic Shurtleff Coolidge, an orthopedic surgeon at the Rush Medical College in Chicago. Their only child, Albert Sprague Coolidge, was born on Jan. 23, 1894. In 1902 Dr. Coolidge acquired an infection while performing surgery. After two years in a sanatorium, he established a medical practice in Pittsfield, Mass., but contracted tuberculosis in 1911 and died in 1915. Elizabeth Coolidge's father died the same year, her mother some months later.

It was after these events that Coolidge began in earnest her well-calculated service to chamber music. Her purpose, she said, was to foster "the triumph of Spirit over Brute Force . . . the immortality of Human Inspiration in the face of threatened mechanical destruction" and to emphasize "our hopeful privilege and duty to keep Art alive." Her style was that of a Victorian autocrat and her imposing height (five feet eleven) and ample figure made an impression that contributed to her success in accomplishing her goals.

After her father's death, Coolidge and her mother had given over $200,000 for the construction of Sprague Memorial Hall, Yale University's first music building. In 1916, in memory of both her parents, Coolidge endowed the first pension fund for the Chicago Symphony Orchestra. In the same year, she agreed to contribute up to $50,000 a year for ten years to support Lucy Sprague Mitchell's Bureau of Educational Experiments, gave $100,000 to the Anti-Tuberculosis Association in Pittsfield, and underwrote the first performance of what was to become, through her efforts, the Berkshire String Quartet.

From 1918 to 1924, Coolidge sponsored annual South Mountain (later Berkshire) Chamber Music Festivals, held in the South Mountain Temple of Chamber Music which she had built near her Pittsfield estate. The festivals brought chamber music to a new peak in the United States. Each featured new compositions, commissions, and prizes and Coolidge herself was occasionally performer as well as manager and patron.

In 1923 she sponsored a festival in Rome, the first of many foreign festivals produced under her sponsorship. Wishing to establish the South Mountain festivals on a more lasting basis, and wanting to commit the federal government to the support of the musical arts, in 1925 she established the Elizabeth Sprague Coolidge Foundation at the Library of Congress. She endowed the foundation—which was to be administered by the Library's Music Division—with the income from two substantial trust funds, ensuring a yearly income of approximately $25,000; the principal of the funds went to the foundation after her death. An additional $60,000 (later substantially increased) made possible the construction at the Library of the Coolidge Auditorium, a hall for chamber music.

The sources of Coolidge's wealth were several trust funds containing Chicago municipal bonds. The defaulting of these securities between 1931 and 1933 and changes in her tax assessment forced her to cut back on her contributions. But she continued her lifelong support of the English composer Frank Bridge, and through the early thirties also supported the work of the Italian composer Gian Francesco Malipiero and several others. Increasingly troubled by poor health, she began to winter in California instead of near her son and his family in inclement Cambridge, Mass. Her loneliness was relieved by two favorite recreations, automobile rides and the movies. Despite illness, she never lost her humor. Asked why she did not support modern art, she replied: "I may be deaf but I am not blind."

Increasingly her musical efforts were channeled through the Coolidge Foundation which, with her encouragement, supported modern music. In 1944, a foundation commission, Aaron Copland's *Appalachian Spring*, was choreographed by Martha Graham and had its premiere in the Coolidge Auditorium. The foundation also commissioned new works from such composers as Béla Bartók, Walter Piston, Sergei

Prokofiev, and Igor Stravinsky and introduced these and other works, as well as major performing artists, to audiences all over the country through radio broadcasts and concerts. Consistent with Elizabeth Coolidge's purposes, it acted as a national bureau of musical standards while also demonstrating the vast resources of the Library of Congress Music Division through its support of performances by the best available artists. Coolidge participated actively in the foundation's work and also gave much unrecorded assistance to individual performers and composers. In recognition of her work, France awarded her the medal of the Legion of Honor, and Belgium presented her with the Order of Leopold and the Order of the Crown.

Elizabeth Sprague Coolidge died in Cambridge, Mass., in November 1953 of a stroke. Her efforts and her generosity made an incalculable contribution to the development of an audience for chamber music in the United States.

[The Elizabeth Sprague Coolidge Papers at the Library of Congress contain business and personal correspondence as well as books from her library; all unidentified quotations are from these papers. The Library of Congress also holds the papers of the Elizabeth Sprague Coolidge Fdn., which contain correspondence and autograph scores by many major twentieth-century composers, as well as programs, photographs, and other materials relating to contemporary music and musicians. Coolidge's musical compositions are listed in the Library of Congress Catalogs, vol. 27 (1953–57): Music and Phonorecords. She also wrote "The Order of the Garden," *Atlantic Monthly*, June 1911, and "Da Capo; A Paper Read Before the Mother's Club, Cambridge, Mass., March 13, 1951" (1952). The Library of Congress has published *The Elizabeth Sprague Coolidge Foundation Autograph Music Scores* (1950). See also William C. Bedford, "Elizabeth Sprague Coolidge, the Education of a Patron of Chamber Music: The Early Years" (Ph.D. diss., Univ. of Mo., 1964); Jay Rosenfeld, *Elizabeth Sprague Coolidge: A Tribute on the One Hundredth Anniversary of Her Birth* (1964); Lucy Sprague Mitchell, *Two Lives* (1953), and *Dict. Am. Biog.*, Supp. Five. Death record provided by Mass. Dept. of Public Health.]

GILLIAN ANDERSON

COOLIDGE, Grace Anna Goodhue, Jan. 3, 1879–July 8, 1957.

Grace Goodhue Coolidge, who became the wife of a president and a champion of the deaf, was born in Burlington, Vt., the only child of Lemira (Barrett) and Andrew Issachar Goodhue. She attended local schools and, although spinal problems forced her to take off a year,

graduated from Burlington High School in 1897. Her upbringing was thoroughly middle class, consonant with her father's status as an engineer and steamboat inspector. Her parents, both of whom came from old New England families, were practicing Methodists until their daughter, then in college, persuaded them to attend the Congregational church. Grace Goodhue attended the University of Vermont, where she sang in the glee club, acted in plays, served as vice president of the sophomore class, and was a founder of the school's chapter of Pi Beta Phi, the first national "women's fraternity." She had a highly expressive face, made even more attractive by her gray-green eyes, and was noted then, and throughout her life, for her irrepressible gaiety.

After receiving a Ph.B. in 1902, Grace Goodhue went to Northampton, Mass., for training and employment as a teacher of the deaf at the Clarke Institute. Her interest in teaching the deaf had been stimulated by CAROLINE A. YALE, head of the Clarke Institute, whose brother was the Goodhues' Burlington neighbor. In Northampton, she met Calvin Coolidge, an attorney and fellow Vermonter. Her extroversion and his introversion were complementary, and each found the other's broad, though often different, interests attractive. Her mother disliked Coolidge and never completely changed her mind about him. Nonetheless, Grace Goodhue and Calvin Coolidge were married on Oct. 4, 1905.

The couple resided in Northampton until 1921. Their life there was happy, though simple; until 1916 they had no servants and entertained little. Calvin Coolidge's only extravagance was in seeing that his wife was handsomely clothed. Grace Coolidge gave birth to two sons, John in 1906 and Calvin, Jr., in 1908. While her husband advanced up the political ladder, she cared for their children and home, engaged in Congregationalist and community work, and remained active in the affairs of Pi Beta Phi, of which she became eastern regional president in 1915. Except for occasional social duties, she kept out of politics. When Calvin Coolidge moved to Boston as lieutenant governor (1916–19) and governor (1919–21) of Massachusetts, she traveled there frequently. Because of his frugality, however, she and the children continued to live in Northampton. Nevertheless, his increasing political prominence involved her more in social and charitable affairs.

When Calvin Coolidge became vice president in 1921, the family took rooms in Washington's New Willard Hotel. Grace Coolidge, befitting her new status, presided over the Senate Ladies'

Club and plunged into the capital's social and cultural activities. She became the nation's first lady in 1923, when her husband succeeded to the presidency upon the death of Warren G. Harding. After three weeks in her new role, Grace Coolidge wrote: "Being wife to a government worker is a very confining position." Although she found abundant scope for entertaining and repartee, at both of which she excelled, many things were forbidden her. By presidential edict, she could not express her political views, ride horses, fly in airplanes, bob her hair, or be free from escort. Her husband grew even more protective of her after their younger son died in 1924. She found her compensations in charitable work, especially for the deaf; visits to disabled veterans; cultural functions; needlework; and the restoration of the White House. Her warm, outgoing personality and her multifarious interests made her greatly admired and beloved, and she gained a popularity matched by few first ladies. A baseball enthusiast, for years she was known as the number one fan of the Boston Red Sox.

After she and her husband left the White House in 1929, Grace Coolidge emerged more fully as an individual. Some of her articles and poems were published, and in 1932 she lent her name to Republican campaign efforts. After Calvin Coolidge's death in 1933, she became a trustee of Mercersburg Academy in Pennsylvania, which their sons had attended, and in 1935 she became president of the board of the Clarke School for the Deaf. During the rest of her life, she continued her charitable and church works and she occasionally spoke out politically, most notably for world peace and then for American intervention early during World War II. Her forte was rallying public support to deal with the problems of the deaf and other handicapped people.

For much of her life Grace Goodhue Coolidge subordinated herself to others, first to her strong-willed, though loving, mother, then to her husband. Yet she never lost her charm, good humor, curiosity, and compassion. If she contributed to society only in traditional ways, she did so vivaciously and effectively. An active person almost to the end, she died in Northampton in 1957 of heart disease.

[The Forbes Library, Northampton, Mass., contains a large amount of unpublished and other pertinent material, including Grace Coolidge's letters to her friend Therese C. (Mrs. Reuben B.) Hills. Her articles include "How I Spent My Days at the White House," Oct. 1929; "Making Ourselves at Home in the White House," Nov. 1929; "Home Again!" Jan. 1930, all in *American Mag. Good Housekeeping*

published her poems "The Open Door" (Oct. 1929) and "The Quest" (Oct. 1930). The best printed source of biographical information is Ishbel Ross, *Grace Coolidge and Her Era: The Story of a President's Wife* (1962). Material on Grace Coolidge can also be found in biographies of her husband, including Donald R. McCoy, *Calvin Coolidge, The Quiet President* (1967). She was often the subject of newspaper and magazine pieces, especially during the 1920s and 1930s. The *New Yorker*, May 15, 1926, contains a profile of the first lady by Paul A. Burns. An obituary appeared in the *N.Y. Times*, July 9, 1957.]

DONALD R. MCCOY

COOPER, Anna Julia Haywood, Aug. 10, 1859?–Feb. 27, 1964. Educator, scholar.

Anna Julia Cooper, self-styled "Black Woman of the South," who dedicated her life to the advancement of her fellow blacks, was born in Raleigh, N.C. She was the daughter of Hannah Stanley, a slave, by a white father, George Washington Haywood, presumably her mother's master. A child at the time of the Emancipation Proclamation, she had scant personal recollection of slavery and her writings tell little of her childhood save her devotion to her slave mother. Her remarkable career offers unusual insights into the postwar experience of former slaves; her faith in education as essential to true liberation was unshakable.

At seven "Annie" Haywood entered St. Augustine's Normal School and Collegiate Institute, a freedmen's school in Raleigh, founded by an Episcopal clergyman to train teachers for southern black schools. Here she spent twelve years, beginning as pupil, presently "pupil-teacher," then teacher, and finally as matron. St. Augustine's brought her into contact with ex-slaves of all ages and degrees of literacy, a revealing experience of slavery at second hand. It also led to her lifelong membership in the Episcopal church. A precocious child—she was a pupil-teacher at eight—Annie Haywood was admitted to more advanced classes and ultimately to special studies under the principal's direction. In June 1877 she married a colleague, the Rev. George C. Cooper, a former slave who had become an Episcopal minister. The marriage was cut short by his death two years later and she never remarried. In 1881 she took the next step in her education, applying to Oberlin College. Her impressive list of subjects offered for entrance resulted in her admission there as a sophomore.

Oberlin, a white community hospitable to blacks, offered unlimited resources of learning and music. It also offered Anna Julia Cooper a home with the family of a distinguished professor of mathematics and physics—Charles Henry Churchill. Oberlin became for her "that scene of happy memories." She received her A.B. in 1884, and an A.M. in 1888. After teaching for a year at Wilberforce University (1884–85), she returned to teach at St. Augustine's for two years. In 1887, through a recommendation from Oberlin, she secured a post as teacher of Latin at the Washington High School (later the M Street High School and then Dunbar High School). A preparatory school for blacks, it offered a classical curriculum supplemented by business courses. For nearly forty years—with one brief interval—it furnished the stage for Anna Cooper's career.

Her first years at M Street High School coincided with a mounting emphasis in Washington and elsewhere on vocational—rather than classical—training for blacks, a point of view exemplified by Booker T. Washington at Tuskegee. Anna Cooper spoke out in public appearances and especially in her first book, *A Voice from the South by a Black Woman of the South* (1892), for higher education for blacks. While paying high tribute to Tuskegee Institute, she argued that race should not be a criterion, that aptitude alone should determine who is admitted to further education. She argued as well against the use of sex as a criterion, taking to task those black educators and clergymen who failed to support education for black women as well as for black men.

When she became principal at M Street in 1901, Anna Cooper stressed high academic standards, developed a college preparatory program for qualified students, and led a concerted effort to secure consideration for her students at prestigious colleges. She succeeded with Harvard, Yale, and Brown, meanwhile enlisting her staff in the quest for scholarship aid where needed. It was an outstanding victory in the face of strong opposition from supporters of the Tuskegee approach and from the school authorities in Washington, D.C. Ironically her success incurred sharp criticism from local school officials, who ordered her to discontinue the practice. She refused to comply. In 1906 she was summarily dropped from the staff of the M Street School.

Anna Cooper may have been the victim of male resentment against a woman holding an important government position. It seems clear, however, that there was also pressure from Tuskegee to drop her. Booker T. Washington was a friend of Robert Terrell, her predecessor as principal, and of W. T. S. Jackson, her successor; he was also friendly with the superintendent of the District of Columbia public schools. She was not called back to M Street until 1910, and then as a teacher of Latin, not as principal. By then a new superintendent had taken office, and Jackson had stepped down to become head of the high school's business department.

Anna Cooper's ouster was a humiliating experience. As principal she had brought new distinction to her school in the educational world. Her recall to the rank and file involved a loss of status for which she had to seek compensation. During her four "years of exile" teaching languages at the Lincoln Institute in Jefferson, Mo., she spent summers at her beloved Oberlin, where her ambition to attain the doctorate revived. Herein lay compensation.

With her program at M Street confined to teaching, Anna Cooper devoted her spare time and vacations to graduate studies in French history and literature, a new interest. The summers of 1911, 1912, and 1913 were spent studying at the Guilde Internationale in Paris. She matriculated for the doctorate at Columbia University, and spent four summers (1914–17) completing the necessary course work. There remained a year's residency requirement and a thesis to prepare. Her subject was a college edition of an eleventh-century epic, *Le Pèlerinage de Charlemagne*. (The edition was published in Paris in 1925.) The difficulties involved in taking time away from her teaching to do this work were further complicated by her responsibilities for five children whom she had "taken under her wing with the hope and determination of nurturing their growth into useful and creditable American citizens" ("The Third Step," p. 4).

As the war years receded, the lure of France led her to transfer her credits and thesis to the Sorbonne in Paris, a venture made possible with the aid of Abbé Felix Klein, who had visited her school on a tour of the United States in 1905. This "third step," as she called it in an autobiographical sketch, was her greatest triumph, although it too was marred by the obstructionist tactics of the school authorities. With much difficulty she had secured what she understood to be a year's leave from teaching, and sailed for Paris in 1924. The authorities had assumed—but did not say—that she was being given only sixty days. On the fiftieth day, they wired her to return in ten days or lose her job. Working with amazing rapidity, she gained approval for a subject for the new thesis required by the Sorbonne, began preliminary research, and, with the aid of Abbé Klein, secured the research assistance she needed to complete her work away from Paris.

The thesis, written in French, was entitled *L'Attitude de la France à l'Égard de l'Esclavage pendant la Révolution* (published in Paris in 1925). It deals with the attitude of revolutionary

France toward its slave colony of St. Domingue (Haiti) in the Caribbean, the impact of the ideals of "Liberty, Equality, and Fraternity" on the colony, and the failure of the revolutionaries in France to extend these ideals to the slaves. It is a carefully documented study—a pioneer in its field—by a writer uniquely qualified both as a scholar and by personal experience. Of slave background herself, Anna Cooper brought to her subject both understanding and scholarly objectivity.

In 1925, at the age of sixty-five, Anna Cooper was awarded the coveted degree from the Sorbonne. Her return from Paris was without fanfare at the Dunbar High School although students regarded her new title of "Dr. Cooper" with awe. She retired from the school in 1930.

Retirement meant only a shift in the scene of her activities. In the same year Anna Cooper accepted the presidency of an evening school for employed blacks, the Frelinghuysen Group of Schools for Employed Colored Persons (later Frelinghuysen University). A unique institution, privately supported, it had been established as a result of the shrinking of educational facilities open to blacks in Washington, D.C. She served as its president until 1942; the school remained open until 1961.

Even after her retirement, she continued to write. Her last major work, *The Grimké Family* (1951) details the career of her closest friend, CHARLOTTE FORTEN GRIMKÉ, and her family. The book affords unusual insight into various aspects of slavery in the United States and into the aftermath of emancipation.

In February 1964, Anna Cooper died of a heart attack at her Washington home. She was buried in Hargett Street Cemetery, Raleigh, N.C., beside the grave of her husband.

[The Anna Julia Cooper Papers at the Moorland-Spingarn Research Center, Howard Univ., contain correspondence, speeches, articles by and about Cooper, and the privately printed "The Third Step" (1925). She also edited the diaries of Charlotte Forten Grimké, whose papers were left in Cooper's care. A full-scale biography by Leona Gabel is in preparation. Sources with information on Cooper's career are Abbé Felix Klein, *Au Pays de "La Vie Intense"* (1907); Bert Loewenberg and Ruth Bogin, eds., *Black Women in Nineteenth Century American Life* (1976); indirectly, Mary Church Terrell, *A Colored Woman in a White World* (1940). A discussion of her Sorbonne thesis is Frances Richardson Keller, "The Perspective of a Black American on Slavery and the French Revolution: Anna Julia Cooper," *Proc. of the Third Annual Meeting of the Western Society for French History* (1976), pp. 165–76. See also *Who's Who in Colored America* (1927; 1930–32). For background information see E. B. Chamberlin, *The Churchills of Oberlin*

(1965); Constance M. Green, *Washington, Capital City, 1879–1950* (1963); Cecil D. Halliburton, *A History of St. Augustine's College, 1867–1937* (1937); L. R. Harlan, *Booker T. Washington: The Making of a Black Leader, 1856–1901* (1972). The exact date of Cooper's birth is uncertain; the Aug. 10, 1859 date is taken from Oberlin alumni records and from the death record provided by D.C. Dept. of Public Health. Obituaries appeared in the *Wash. Post* and the Wash. *Eve. Star*, Feb. 29, 1964.]

LEONA GABEL

CORI, Gerty Theresa Radnitz, Aug. 15, 1896–Oct. 26, 1957. Biochemist, physician.

Gerty Cori, the first American woman to win the Nobel Prize for medicine and physiology, was born in Prague, then part of the Austro-Hungarian Empire, the eldest of three daughters of Otto and Martha (Neustadt) Radnitz. Her father was a businessman and manager of a sugar refinery. She was educated by private tutors until the age of ten, then attended a private girls' school. At sixteen, probably influenced by a maternal uncle who was a professor of pediatrics at the University of Prague, Gerty decided to study medicine. She lacked the necessary training in Latin and mathematics, but she managed to remedy these deficiencies in a remarkably short time at the Realgymnasium at Tetschen, from which she graduated in 1914. In that same year, at the age of eighteen, she entered the Medical School of the German University of Prague, from which she received her M.D. in 1920.

While in medical school, she met Carl Ferdinand Cori, a fellow student who shared her love of the outdoors and of mountain climbing and skiing, as well as her interest in laboratory research. Gerty Radnitz and Carl Cori collaborated on a research project on the immune bodies of blood which led to a publication in 1920. On Aug. 5, 1920, they were married in Vienna, where she had accepted a position as assistant in the Karolinen Children's Hospital and where he served as assistant in the medical clinic and the pharmacological institute of the University of Vienna. Both were interested in pursuing careers in medical research rather than in medical practice.

In 1922 Carl Cori emigrated to the United States to join the staff of the New York State Institute for the Study of Malignant Diseases (later Roswell Park Memorial Institute) in Buffalo. Gerty Cori joined him a few months later, becoming an assistant pathologist at the institute, a position that she held until 1925, when she was made an assistant biochemist. The Coris became naturalized citizens of the United States in 1928.

At the state institute both Carl and Gerty Cori had routine laboratory duties to perform, but they also had time to pursue research of their own choosing. At one point, however, the director of the institute threatened to dismiss Gerty Cori if she did not end her collaborative work with her husband. Carl Cori later recalled that after "sitting out this storm," they were free to work together whenever they chose. The question of collaboration arose only once more, when Carl Cori was offered a position at another university where one of the conditions was that he end his collaborative research with his wife. On a visit to that university, Gerty Cori was told that she was standing in the way of her husband's career and that it was un-American for a man to work with his wife.

Though some of their work in Buffalo was related to cancer research (for example, their studies on the metabolism of tumors), the Coris' main interest was normal carbohydrate metabolism and its regulation. Although the direction of their research was not questioned, they eventually began to feel uneasy about pursuing investigations that were not directly relevant to the purpose of the institute, and they decided to move elsewhere.

In 1931 Carl Cori accepted the position of chairman of the department of pharmacology of the Washington University School of Medicine in St. Louis. University rules at the time prohibited faculty appointment of two members of the same family, but Gerty Cori was given a research position at a token salary in the same department. The Coris later moved to the department of biochemistry, where Gerty Cori was finally made professor of biochemistry in 1947, the same year in which she shared the Nobel Prize in medicine and physiology with her husband and with Bernardo Houssay of Argentina. She was the third woman ever to receive this honor and the first from the United States. It was one of many awards and recognitions bestowed upon her during her career, among them her appointment by President Harry S Truman to the board of the newly organized National Science Foundation.

The Coris' early work in Buffalo was concerned with the overall processes of carbohydrate metabolism in the body, including the effect of hormones such as epinephrine and insulin on the rate of conversion of glycogen to glucose. Glycogen, a starchlike substance consisting of large numbers of glucose molecules bound together, is the form in which sugar is stored in the animal body; it is broken down as

needed to provide glucose for the body's energy needs. The Coris later focused their attention on the intermediary metabolism of carbohydrates, that is, the specific chemical reactions that carbohydrates undergo within the organism. This was a new and exciting area of biochemical research which required the use of tissue preparations rather than whole animals. Though the Coris began their investigations in this field before coming to St. Louis, their major discoveries were made there, and their laboratory became a focal point for all workers interested in carbohydrate metabolism.

It was widely believed at the time that glycogen was metabolized to glucose by hydrolysis. The Coris demonstrated in the 1930s, however, that the breakdown of glycogen involved the formation of a substance known as glucose-1-phosphate, which came to be referred to as the "Cori ester." This reaction was catalyzed by an enzyme—isolated by the Coris and named phosphorylase—which was involved in both the synthesis and cleavage of glycogen. The Coris later identified and isolated other enzymes that were involved in the formation and breakdown of the glycogen molecule and in 1939 they carried out the first synthesis of glycogen in a test tube.

In her later work, Gerty Cori and her collaborators used the enzymes involved in the breakdown of glycogen to determine its molecular structure. They also elucidated the nature of glycogen storage diseases in children, demonstrating for the first time that a human heritable disease can stem from a defect in an enzyme.

Gerty Cori had one son, Carl Thomas Cori, born in August 1936. She worked in her research laboratory up until the last moment before going to the maternity hospital, and the responsibilities of motherhood did not interrupt her career. Cori retained her interest in art, music, and literature, as well as her love of the outdoors, throughout her life. It was while climbing Snow Mass peak in Colorado in the summer of 1947 that the symptoms of myelofibrosis, a rare disease of the bone marrow, first began noticeably to affect her. She suffered bravely with this fatal disease for ten years, refusing to give up her work, but finally succumbed to its effects, dying of kidney failure in St. Louis in 1957. Her philosophy of life was summed up in a statement for the Edward R. Murrow radio series, "This I Believe": "I believe that in art and science are the glories of the human mind. I see no conflict between them . . . Contemplation of the great human achievements through the ages is helpful to me in moments of despair and doubt. Human meanness and folly then seem less important . . .

Honesty, which stands mostly for intellectual integrity, courage and kindness are still the virtues I admire, though with advancing years the emphasis has been slightly shifted and kindness now seems more important to me than in my youth. The love for and dedication to one's work seem to me to be the basis of happiness."

[Useful biographical articles include those by Joseph Fruton, *Dict. Sci. Biog.*, vol. 3 (1971), pp. 415–16; Edna Yost, *Women of Modern Science* (1964), pp. 1–16; Carl Cori, *Am. Chemists and Chemical Engineers* (1976), pp. 94–95. Valuable biographical information can also be found in Carl Cori's autobiographical article, "The Call of Science," in *Annual Rev. of Biochemistry*, vol. 38 (1969), pp. 1–20. See also the biographical sketches of the Coris in *Current Biog.*, 1947, and one by Bernardo Houssay in *Biochemica et Biophysica Acta*, vol. 20 (1956), pp. 11–16. There is no comprehensive published bibliography of Gerty Cori's publications, but Fruton refers to several of her most important papers and a partial bibliography, through 1954, is on file at the Nat. Acad. of Sciences. Among the more substantial obituary notices are those by E. A. Doisy, *Am. Phil. Soc. Yearbook* (1958), pp. 108–11, and by Severo Ochoa and H. M. Kalckar, *Science*, vol. 128 (1957), pp. 16–17. Her obituary also appeared in the *N.Y. Times*, Oct. 27, 1957. Death record was supplied by Mo. Division of Health. Carl Cori provided a typescript of Gerty Cori's statement from "This I Believe" (Columbia Records).]

JOHN PARASCANDOLA

CORNELL, Katharine, Feb. 16, 1893–June 9, 1974. Actress, producer.

Katharine Cornell was the only child of Peter and Alice Gardner (Plimpton) Cornell. Her parents, both from socially prominent Buffalo, N.Y., families, were on a year's honeymoon in Berlin when their daughter was born. After Peter Cornell completed his postgraduate work in medicine at the University of Berlin in July 1893, the family returned to Buffalo. Dr. Cornell held only a passing interest in medicine, but he was devoted to the theater, and in 1901 he abandoned medicine to become part owner and manager of the Star Theatre in Buffalo. It was here, six years later, that Katharine, seeing MAUDE ADAMS fly across the stage in *Peter Pan*, began her passionate affair with the theater.

Alice Cornell suffered from severe timidity; although she could not share her family's passion for the theater, she did support it. In later years, Cornell recalled her mother as having "a childlike quality about her—simple and direct" (*I Wanted to Be an Actress*, p. 57), and her father as "a disciplinarian, in fact . . . a martinet" (Funke & Booth, p. 203). The tension between her parents' contradictory natures was the

basis for Katharine's unhappy and lonely childhood.

Katharine Cornell attended St. Margaret's, an Episcopal day school for the children of Buffalo's elite, graduating from eighth grade in June 1908. That fall her father sent her to Oaksmere, a finishing school in Mamaroneck, N.Y. After graduation in 1911 and a summer's trip abroad with her aunt, Lucy Plimpton, Cornell returned to Oaksmere to teach dramatics and coach athletics, remaining there until 1916.

Three people figured in Katharine Cornell's decision to give up teaching and attempt an acting career. Alice Cornell died in June 1915, leaving a considerable fortune to her only child, and rendering Cornell financially independent of her domineering father. THERESA HELBURN directed Oaksmere's production of *Twelfth Night*, and played Sir Toby Belch to Cornell's Malvolio, giving Cornell her first chance at serious acting. Edward Goodman, a founder of the Washington Square Players, also directed Oaksmere productions. After one such performance, of *Play*, written by Cornell, Goodman said what she had longed to hear: "If you're thinking of going into the theatre, let me know when you get to New York" (Mosel, p. 57).

Cornell took Goodman at his word. She moved to New York with her aunt, and began attending Washington Square Players' rehearsals. In November 1916, when the actress whom she was understudying in the role of Samurai Mother became ill, Cornell made her New York debut in the Nō play *Bushido*. The entire role consisted of four words, "My son . . . my son." She was twenty-three. For two years Cornell remained with the troupe, playing minor roles. Here she received her first notices and her first salary, forty dollars for the 1917–18 season.

In 1918, when Katharine Cornell was asked by JESSIE BONSTELLE to join her highly accomplished stock company, she accepted at once. Beginning the first of three seasons, Cornell performed minor roles in a new play each Monday, ten performances a week, fourteen weeks at the Star Theatre in Buffalo and eighteen weeks at the Garrick in Detroit. Bonstelle, a good friend of the theater's manager and owner, Peter Cornell, became his daughter's mentor. After the 1918 season, Cornell (again with Bonstelle's assistance), graduated to second leads, playing Marcelle, a fallen woman and drug addict, in the third road company of *The Man Who Came Back*. This was her first tour and by its end she was eager to return to stock for the 1919 season.

Bonstelle had years before commanded Cornell: "Hurry and grow up so you can play Jo for me." On Nov. 20, 1919, Cornell made her

London debut in *Little Women,* staged by Bonstelle. Although at twenty-six Cornell was too old to play Jo, the audiences and critics acclaimed her originality and manner of expression and overlooked her age. When the run ended in February 1920, Cornell returned to Detroit for her final stock season to play alternating leads at the Garrick, where Guthrie McClintic (1893–1961) had been named director. McClintic replaced Bonstelle as the primary influence on Cornell's artistic development. It was not until she met him that her desire to be a great actress crystallized: "She had become serious about acting to please Guthrie," her biographer later noted (Mosel, p. 370). They were married Sept. 8, 1921; it was his second marriage.

Cornell returned to New York in 1921 to play Eileen Baxter Jones in RACHEL CROTHERS's *Nice People.* She withdrew from the cast in September to take the role of Sydney Fairchild, the daughter of a man suffering from hereditary madness, in *A Bill of Divorcement.* Initial reviews were mixed but later notices were raves, one critic calling hers a performance of "memorable understanding and beauty." The play ran for 173 performances.

Similar parts followed: Mary Fitton in *Will Shakespeare* (1923), Laura Pennington in *The Enchanted Cottage* (1923), Henriette in *Casanova* (1923), Talage Sturdee in *The Outsider* (1924), and Suzanne Chaumont in *Tiger Cats* (1924). Cornell felt it better to take any part than to wait for a good one. The one fine role which did come her way, Candida in the 1924 Actors' Theatre production of Shaw's play, was accepted in passing, but became a monumental role for Cornell. At last she was comfortable with her acting; her noble and compassionate Candida was in such demand that a commercial run of five months followed.

During the 1920s Cornell drew increasingly better notices in meretricious plays. After *Candida,* Cornell played Iris March in *The Green Hat,* her first starring vehicle. Although Cornell did not embody the flapper type, physically or artistically, she elevated the character, playing against type. McClintic hated the play but agreed to direct; *The Green Hat* was successful, running twenty-nine weeks, then touring through the summer of 1927. The rest of the 1920s were marked by similar femme fatale parts for Cornell as she appeared as Leslie Crosbie in *The Letter* (1927), Ellen Olenska in *The Age of Innocence* (1928), and Madeline Carey in *Dishonored Lady* (1930). In retrospect Cornell remarked: "Every part I've played I've twisted and turned in my mind until I've made it something of my own."

Cornell and McClintic Productions, Inc., was formed in December 1930. The company was financed by longtime friends and admirers of Cornell—Stanton Griffis and A. Conger Goodyear, and Cornell's indispensable assistant, Gertrude Macy—who wanted to free Cornell from financial worries. All profits were to be used for future productions; all plays were to feature Cornell as star and McClintic as director. The company's first production was *The Barretts of Wimpole Street* (1930), the last *Dear Liar* (1959–60). In the intervening years, $12,000,000 was grossed from the initial investment of $30,000.

Twenty-seven producers had turned down *The Barretts of Wimpole Street* before Cornell bought it as a gift for her husband. Originally she had not wanted to play Elizabeth Barrett: she thought the character too passive and the role too taxing. The play opened on Feb. 9, 1931, at the Empire Theatre, ran for a year, and toured for twenty weeks. Cornell was triumphant. "Her acting is quite as remarkable for the carefulness of its design as for the fire of her presence," a *New York Times* critic wrote. Elizabeth Barrett would become her most famous role, and this production the first of many.

During the next six years Cornell aimed much higher. After one poor play, *Lucrece* (1932), and one middling success, *Alien Corn* (1933), Cornell was urged to play Juliet. Insecure with the technique required for Shakespeare, she combined *Romeo and Juliet* in repertory with established vehicles, *The Barretts* and *Candida,* as her company toured thirty-four states, playing to an estimated total audience of a half million. This commitment to touring was a hallmark of her career; she believed that actors who did not tour missed "a lot of the covered-wagon feeling about the theatre."

After seven months on tour, Cornell felt prepared to brave the New York audiences and critics; *Romeo and Juliet* began its run there in December 1934. Cornell's lyrical and haunting Juliet received unqualified praise, and she received the New York Drama League Award for her performance. In 1936 Cornell reached the pinnacle of her career, playing Shaw's *Saint Joan.* In meeting the dramatic range demanded by the role, Cornell established firmly the high standard of acting upon which her reputation rests. Her Joan combined the radiance of simple presence with eloquent speech and unequaled grace.

Following two slight plays and a revival of *Candida* (1937), Cornell appeared as Linda Easterbrook in *No Time for Comedy.* The role was a difficult one. She had little experience with comedy and little success with modern plays; moreover, when the play opened in April 1939, Cornell was forty-six, fourteen years older than the character and her costar, Laurence Olivier. Cornell gave an admirable performance; her beauty and discipline were sufficient.

Although Cornell's career began to decline in the 1940s, she set a record in 1941 for a New York run of a Shaw play, appearing for fifteen weeks in *The Doctor's Dilemma*. The following year, however, *Rose Burke* closed in San Francisco. Critics acclaimed her performance in the 1942 all-star revival of *Candida* as the definitive portrayal. Wit, nobility, and great whistling were the finest points of Cornell's performance of Masha in *Three Sisters* (1942), and they contributed much to the success of this run.

Asked once what her greatest experience was in the theater, Katharine Cornell told of touring with her company in *The Barretts of Wimpole Street* during World War II. From August 1944 to February 1945 the troupe, financed by the American Theatre Wing and sponsored by the United States Army, barnstormed Europe, playing to G.I.s in camps and hospitals.

Cornell made two forays into movies. In *Stage Door Canteen* (1943), she delivered a sampling of Juliet's lines while handing out oranges to servicemen. Eleven years later, she was the narrator for *Helen Keller in Her Story*, a documentary produced by Cornell's housemate, Nancy Hamilton, for their good friend. It won an Academy Award in 1955.

In her fifties, Cornell was criticized for facets of her character and ability that had before been heralded. "Formal, good-mannered, a little fastidious," one critic wrote of her Cleopatra, her final Shakespearean role. Then, too, she was perceived as inflexible, unable to acclimate herself to contemporary drama. By the 1950s, changing tastes, combined with the rigors of age, kept Cornell more and more from the stage. There was the commercially successful run of *The Constant Wife* (1951)—the last success—but little more. She last appeared as Mrs. Campbell in *Dear Liar*. Guthrie McClintic—who had once said, "I believe in Will Shakespeare, Bernard Shaw, and Katharine Cornell"—died Oct. 29, 1961. Katharine Cornell never again acted. She died of pneumonia at her summer retreat in Tisbury, Mass., thirteen years later.

Exacting in her standards, Cornell surrounded herself with people of the first rank. She was a bad study and suffered from preperformance fright; but she proved herself an actress of the highest distinction through discipline and hard work. Her intriguing beauty—Shaw once described her as "a gorgeous dark lady from the cradle of the human race"—statuesque carriage, and mellifluous voice were equally captivating.

Cornell's portrayal of emotions in their fullest dimensions, combined with her dedication to audiences across the country, elevated the standards of American culture. This was Katharine Cornell's finest and most enduring achievement.

[The Katharine Cornell/Guthrie McClintic Archives are located in the Billy Rose Theatre Coll., N.Y. Public Library; additional manuscript collections are housed in the Sophia Smith Coll., Smith College, and the Poetry Coll., Lockwood Memorial Library, State Univ. of N.Y., Buffalo. Nancy Hamilton, to whom Cornell left her estate, has some papers. *The Reminiscences of Katharine Cornell* (1960), in the Popular Arts Project, Oral History Coll., Columbia Univ., appear in similar form in Lewis Funke and John Booth, *Actors Talk About Acting* (1961). Cornell wrote an autobiography, as told to Ruth Sedgwick, *I Wanted to Be an Actress* (1938), which was published in serial form in *Stage* magazine; the book is most useful for its appended cast listings and abbreviated reviews. Gladys Malvern, *Curtain Going Up* (1943), recounts most of the autobiography. The most complete and accurate account of Cornell's life is contained in Tad Mosel with Gertrude Macy, *Leading Lady* (1978), which gives much personal detail before unpublished. Differing accounts of events appear in Guthrie McClintic, *Me and Kit* (1955); a more scholarly appraisal of Cornell is contained in Lynda Moss, "A Historical Study of Katharine Cornell as an Actress and Manager, 1931–60" (Ph.D. diss., Univ. of Southern Calif., 1974), which has a complete bibliography to date. See also *Current Biog.*, 1952; *N.Y. Times Mag.*, Feb. 15, 1948; *Newsweek*, Jan. 19, 1948; and *New Yorker*, Feb. 14, 1931. A complete list of Cornell's credits appears in *Biog. Encyc. and Who's Who of the Am. Theatre* (1966). An obituary appeared in the *N.Y. Times*, June 10, 1974. Cornell's birth date is confirmed by U.S. Census, 1900; death record from Mass. Dept. of Public Health. Assistance in research was provided by a biobibliography by Alison Landus. Almost all major works on Cornell contain photographs; Cornell may be heard on a Caedmon record, *Sonnets from the Portuguese and Barretts of Wimpole Street*.]

PAUL MYERS

COYLE, Grace Longwell, March 22, 1892– March 9, 1962. Social work educator.

Grace Coyle was born in North Adams, Mass., the only daughter and younger of two children of Mary (Cushman) and John Patterson Coyle. Her ancestors were farmers, teachers, and preachers—Pennsylvania Scots-Irish on the Coyle side, New England Puritans on the Cushman side. Although John Coyle, a successor of Washington Gladden as minister of the North Adams Congregational Church and an emerging leader of the social gospel movement, died in 1895, his vigorous personality and liberal theology left a strong imprint on his family and community. His brothers and sisters helped Mary Coyle raise Grace and her brother, David. According to an older cousin, Grace made up a language of her own, understood only by her mother, which she used until she went to school.

In 1910, after attending public schools, Coyle entered Wellesley College where she majored in English and was elected to Phi Beta Kappa. On an alumnae form she cited "friends made" as her most valuable college experience. "I would like to rank democratic community living first," she commented, "but I do not think we were very democratic." On graduation in 1914 she won a College Settlements fellowship for study at the New York School of Philanthropy, and received a certificate in 1915.

Coyle's professional career began in 1915 at the West Side Settlement in Kingston, Pa. In 1917 she joined the YWCA as a field worker in Pittsburgh and from 1918 to 1926 was industrial secretary of the YWCA National Board in New York City. In this office she opposed the view that the YWCA "should be seen and not heard" and strove to ensure that opinionmaking in matters of public policy was as important in the organization's program as recreation, education, and service.

While taking graduate work at Columbia University (A.M., economics, 1928; Ph.D., sociology, 1931) Coyle did research for the Inquiry, an agency interested in discussion and conference methods, and lectured on labor problems at Barnard College. Robert M. MacIver, professor of political philosophy and sociology, directed her dissertation, which was influenced by the writings of MARY FOLLETT. She dedicated the published version, *Social Process in Organized Groups* (1930), to the memory of FLORENCE SIMMS, first director of the YWCA industrial department. In 1930 she returned to the YWCA National Board as executive of the Laboratory (research and program) Division.

Coyle accepted an appointment as assistant professor of group work in the School of Applied Social Sciences (SASS) at Western Reserve University in Cleveland in 1934. She remained on the faculty for the rest of her life, advancing to associate professor in 1936 and professor in 1939. Throughout her teaching career she remained active in the profession, serving as president of the three major social work organizations: National Conference of Social Work (1940), American Association of Social Workers (1942–44), and Council on Social Work Education (1958–60).

Coyle is best known for her contributions to group work, the branch of social work which stemmed from the efforts of settlement houses

and other agencies to provide recreation and informal education during leisure time. She helped extend group work to new settings such as hospitals, clinics, and children's institutions; at a time when group work might have sought professional identification with recreation or education, she was instrumental in establishing it as a field of social work. Her writings and teachings equipped a generation of group workers with methods and techniques derived from progressive education and sociological and psychological study of group behavior. Inherent in all her professional activities was the conviction that group work could and should become "part of that schooling in real democracy and in the newer forms of collective effort upon which so much of our future may depend" ("Group Work and Social Change," p. 397).

Coyle described herself as "a group worker with great concern for social action especially in the field of industrial problems" (*The Survey*, April 1937, p. 102). Critical of American society as "wasteful of its material and human resources, torn by class and social conflicts," she called on social workers to take a more active part in social change. "In a society such as ours," she wrote in 1937, it is folly "to continue to pick up the pieces without even attempting to stop the breakage" (*The Survey*, May 1937, p. 138).

Coyle stressed the value of social science research for social work and emphasized its inclusion in the social work curriculum. In 1960 CHARLOTTE TOWLE of the University of Chicago hailed her achievement "in making social work whole again through reviving its roots in the social sciences." One of Coyle's favorite courses was the history of social work. In personal and professional life she had a sense of continuity and change, particularly in the way her generation faced experiences and problems related to but distinct from those of the past.

"The most basic need of human nature," she wrote, "is the need to be loved and to love" (*Group Experience and Democratic Values*, p. 117). She never married but, on the death of her sister-in-law, became the beloved surrogate mother of her brother's three young children and later "grandmother" of their children. She was devoted to her housemate and longtime friend, Abbie Graham, biographer of YWCA leader GRACE DODGE. They shared a love of Vermont, built a summer home there, and for several summers in the 1930s drove a horse-drawn milkman's cart about the state, camping at night in farmers' fields.

Professional in appearance and manner, Coyle had a cryptic sense of humor and delighted in people, nature, and literature. Possessed of a powerful, disciplined mind she had the ability to recognize and the grace to acknowledge the contributions of others. She died in Cleveland of a heart attack in 1962, several months before her scheduled retirement.

[The Grace Coyle Papers at Case Western Reserve Univ. Archives contain correspondence, class materials, lecture notes, material on committees and workshops, publications and speeches, and testimonials. Other important publications include *Studies in Group Behavior* (1937); *Group Experience and Democratic Values* (1948); *Group Work with American Youth* (1948); *Social Science in the Professional Education of Social Workers* (1938); "Changing Emphasis in the Y.W.C.A.," *The Womans Press*, Jan. 1926; "Group Work and Social Change," Nat. Conference of Social Work (NCSW), *Proceedings*, 1935; "Group Dynamics and the Practice of Social Group Work," NCSW, *Proceedings*, 1950. *Encyc. Social Work* (1977) contains a biographical sketch as well as references in articles on Social Group Work. Obituaries and memorial notices appeared in *Cleveland Plain Dealer*, March 9, 1962; *N.Y. Times*, March 10, 1962; *Social Service Rev.*, June 1962; *Social Casework*, July 1962; *Am. Sociological Rev.*, Feb. 1963. Information provided by Marion C. Plack, Coyle's cousin, Anne Coyle Howard, her niece, Esther I. Test, and Marjorie White Main was helpful in the preparation of this article. Death certificate was obtained from Ohio Dept. of Health.]

ROBERT H. BREMNER

CRAIG, Elisabeth May Adams, Dec. 19, 1888– July 15, 1975. Journalist.

May Craig was born Elisabeth May Adams into a Presbyterian family in Coosaw Mines, Beaufort County, S.C., the sixth of nine children and fourth of seven girls. Her father, Alexander Adams, of Scottish descent, was born in Chippenham, Wiltshire, England. A blacksmith before migrating to Beaufort County in the 1870s, he was employed there in the local phosphate mines. Her mother, Elizabeth Ann (Essery) Adams, a native of Barnstaple, Devonshire, England, died when Elisabeth May was only four, a week after giving birth to twin daughters, who also died soon after.

At the age of six, Elisabeth May Adams found a foster home with Frances and William Weymouth, owners of the phosphate mines in which Alexander Adams worked. Theirs was not an affectionate household, and the child, left much on her own, eagerly read the books in the family library. She attended the Beaufort Elementary School and, after the Weymouths moved to Washington, D.C., when she was twelve, she published articles and poems in her Washington Central High School newspaper.

After Alexander Adams moved to Charleston, S.C., with two of his children and remarried (about the same time that the Weymouths left for Washington), Elisabeth May saw him only twice. As part of a lifelong pattern of independence, after high school she pursued a dual career in writing and nursing, enrolling in George Washington University Nursing School rather than attending finishing school as the Weymouths wished. This ambitious rebellion and her marriage in 1909 to Donald A. Craig, a journalist and columnist with the Washington bureau of the *New York Herald*, led to a complete rupture with the Weymouths.

The Craigs had a son, Donald A. (b. 1910), and a daughter, Betty Adams (b. 1915). They hired Louise Jacobs as a housekeeper and nursemaid, enabling Elisabeth May Craig to continue her writing career and to participate in various reform activities in the fields of women's rights and children's education. She marched in the homemakers' section of the suffragist parade at Woodrow Wilson's inauguration, and organized and served as the first president of the Parent-Teachers Association for Washington's Bryant Elementary School. Although she collected rejection slips for short stories and screenplays, Craig occasionally sold feature articles to newspapers such as Joseph Pulitzer's New York *World*; and she tried to convince editors of the worth of a column which presented a "woman's view of Washington news." With journalist Florence Yoder of the *Washington Times-Herald*, she attempted to launch a newspaper for children.

After her husband, then chief of the Washington bureau of the *Herald*, was severely injured in 1923 in an automobile accident (from which he never fully recovered), Craig began to help him with his work, especially the column "On the Inside in Washington" which he wrote for the Gannett Publishing Company's chain of newspapers in Maine. In 1931 she organized a news bureau with Buck Bryant, a colleague from the *World* whom she credited with teaching her the trade. Her columns on congressional activities appeared in newspapers in New York, Montana, and North Carolina. Also in 1931 she obtained a by-line for the Gannett papers column. The political columnist's role was new to journalism when May Craig chose to focus her career on it, and its future was uncertain. By the late 1930s the columnist achieved prestige and influence, and Craig's early start put her in an enviable position.

Craig was active in professional organizations and in efforts of women journalists to achieve recognition. She joined the American Newspaper Guild shortly after it was organized in 1933 and also became an active member of the Washington Newspaper Guild, serving on its executive committee for ten years, several times as president or vice president. Excluded from the National Press Club because of her sex, Craig, along with her friends Isabel Griffin, DORIS FLEESON, Ruby Black, and Christine Sadler, joined the Women's National Press Club; she served as its president in 1943. Like other women who covered the Washington political scene during the New Deal era, Craig became a friend of ELEANOR ROOSEVELT, and she helped to organize women correspondents into the Eleanor Roosevelt Press Conference Association. Annually she attempted to attend the all-male dinner of the White House Correspondents' Association, and in 1945 she won a battle to obtain washroom facilities for women outside the congressional press galleries.

By 1936, the year her husband died, Craig was recognized as an established Washington journalist. She renegotiated the Maine column as "Inside in Washington," and it appeared in four Maine papers. Though a southerner, she became identified as a Maine Yankee. A small woman with striking blue eyes and brown hair wrapped in a bun, she dressed in blue and wore flowered hats so that she would be remembered at White House, Capitol Hill, and government department press conferences. With a mind "as tough as a very old down-East lobster," she was known for her short, generally issue-oriented questions designed to prevent evasive answers. Her queries sometimes produced responses such as President Franklin D. Roosevelt's description of his position on the political spectrum as "left of center."

Craig maintained many friendships in Washington, with Margaret Chase Smith, the Roosevelts, and Lyndon Baines Johnson in particular. She refused to join a political party or express political preferences, believing that journalists should remain nonpartisan. She identified herself as a liberal, however, one who recognized the New Deal as a "long overdue" social movement. In the 1940s she opposed a movement by left-wing members of the Newspaper Guild to control the organization.

During the early 1940s Craig began a regular radio broadcast, "Inside Washington," for two Maine stations, shortening her professional name to May Craig. She also completed a series of articles for *Independent Woman*. Both her radio broadcasts and her columns frequently focused on legislation pertaining to women. Although women journalists had enormous difficulty gaining accreditation as war correspondents, Craig was able to obtain hers in 1944. She toured American bases in England during the buzz bomb raids, visited the front lines in France and Germany as the war drew to a close, and reported on the Mediterranean theater after Germany's surrender.

After the war Craig became a popular panelist on the "Meet the Press" radio and television programs. The methodical newswoman prepared for her first television appearance by observing other women on the medium and decided: "I'd rather be grim than giggly."

Between 1944 and 1956 May Craig traveled to every continent except Australia, and was reportedly the first woman correspondent to live on a combat ship at sea, to participate in the Berlin airlift, to attend the Kaesong truce talks in Korea, to fly over the North Pole, and to be accredited as a war correspondent by the United States Navy. Craig visited defense facilities around the world, made an editors' tour of the Soviet Union and Eastern Europe, and took several trips to Latin America. Throughout the 1950s and early 1960s her columns emphasized a "duel between democracy and communism" and the need for American foreign aid to newly independent nations, a strong national defense budget, and unity at home.

May Craig retired in 1965 as a radio commentator and panelist with "Meet the Press" and completed her last newspaper column in December. She lived in retirement with her daughter's family in Maryland until 1970, then moved to the Althea Woodland Nursing Home in Silver Spring, Md., where she died in 1975 as a consequence of arteriosclerotic cardiovascular disease. Throughout her career, May Craig had remained a critical, often acerbic, questioner of government and its representatives.

[The papers of Elisabeth May Craig at the Library of Congress include correspondence, scrapbooks, clippings, and outlines and early drafts of her uncompleted autobiography. The Franklin D. Roosevelt, Harry S Truman, Dwight D. Eisenhower, John F. Kennedy, and Lyndon B. Johnson presidential libraries have small collections of correspondence between Craig and the presidents and their staffs. The Roosevelt library also contains correspondence between Craig and Eleanor Roosevelt. The Guy Gannett Publishing Co. and the archives of "Meet the Press," NBC News, Washington, D.C., have small holdings of clippings and biographical materials. There are brief sketches in Ishbel Ross, *Ladies of the Press* (1936), pp. 335–36, and Marion Marzolf, *Up from the Footnote: A History of Women Journalists* (1977). Lengthier biographical articles include Ruth Montgomery, "'Little Woman in Blue' Who Outquips President," *Wash. Times-Herald*, Jan. 7, 1945; Patricia Schroth, "Meet May Craig," *Down East*, Aug. 1959, pp. 32–35, 59; and Eleanor Harris, "May Craig: TV's Most Unusual Star," *Look*, April 26, 1962. Photographs of her accompany the entry in *Current Biog.*, 1949, and

"Lady with a Hatpin," *Newsweek*, Aug. 12, 1957. See also obituaries in the *N.Y. Times* and Portland *Press Herald*, July 16, 1975. Death certificate was obtained from Md. Dept. of Health and Mental Hygiene. Information was also supplied by her grandson, Craig A. Clagett, and a niece, Jennie K. Padgett.]

JENNIFER L. TEBBE

CRAWFORD-SEEGER, Ruth Porter, July 3, 1901–Nov. 18, 1953. Composer, folk music scholar, teacher.

Ruth Crawford-Seeger was born in East Liverpool, Ohio, the younger child and only daughter of Clark and Clara Alletta (Graves) Crawford. Ruth's mother taught school for several years prior to her marriage to Clark Crawford, a Methodist minister who held pastorates in several midwestern towns before settling his family in Jacksonville, Fla., in 1911. After his death in 1914, Clara Crawford supported her two children by operating a rooming house.

Introduced to the piano by her mother, Ruth took lessons in Jacksonville at the School of Musical Art, where she continued to study and teach piano after graduating from high school in 1918. In the fall of 1920, with money enough for one year, Crawford entered the American Conservatory in Chicago, studying piano with Heniot Levy and theory and composition with Adolf Weidig. She received her teacher's certificate in 1921, but decided to remain at the Conservatory in Chicago, supporting herself by ushering at local theaters and teaching piano. Although she went on to study that instrument for several years, by 1923 her main interest had shifted to composition. Under Weidig's guidance she completed her master's degree in 1929. Crawford's most important works during these years were *Five Preludes for Piano* (composed 1924–25), *Suite for Small Orchestra* (1926), and *Four Preludes for Piano* (1927–28). On the recommendation of composer Henry Cowell, the *Four Preludes* were published in *New Music*. Cowell also arranged for her later study in New York with Charles Seeger.

Crawford's financial situation eased considerably during her last years in Chicago. She taught piano and theory at the American Conservatory from 1924 to 1929, and from 1926 to 1929 taught piano as well at the Elmhurst College of Music, outside Chicago. Among her students in Elmhurst were the children of Carl Sandburg. Crawford wrote some of the accompaniments for songs in Sandburg's *American Songbag* (1927), beginning an involvement in the collection and publication of folk music which later became a principal occupation.

Leaving Chicago, Ruth Crawford spent the summer of 1929 at the MacDowell Colony in New Hampshire, where she met and received encouragement from her fellow composer MARION BAUER. Then in September Crawford began a year's study in New York with Charles Seeger (1886–1979), the prominent musicologist who encouraged the experimental thrust of her music. Living in the apartment of Blanche Walton, a patron of modern music, Crawford worked steadily, completing her *Piano Study in Mixed Accents* (1930), four *"Diaphonic" Suites* for various wind and string instrument combinations, and one song, "Rat Riddles," with text by Sandburg, which later became the first of *Three Songs* for contralto, oboe, piano, and percussion.

On the strength of her work, Crawford was awarded a Guggenheim Foundation fellowship in late 1930 for European study in composition. She chose not to spend the year with any one teacher; instead through letters of introduction from the Foundation, she met and discussed her work with many of Europe's leading composers, including Bartók, Berg, and Ravel. Freed from financial worry and building on the new ideas she had developed in New York, Crawford composed some of her best works during this fellowship year, including *Chants* for women's chorus (1930), *String Quartet* (1930–31), and the second of her *Three Songs*, "In Tall Grass" (1931).

Crawford returned to the United States in November 1931 and spent the following year in New York, where she and Charles Seeger were married on Oct. 3, 1932. Earlier that year Crawford and Seeger, along with Henry Cowell and the folklorists John and Alan Lomax, joined the Composers Collective, a group seeking to explore connections between their musical and political values. As part of the collective, Crawford wrote the song, "Sacco, Vanzetti." The same year she also composed "Chinaman, Laundryman," and "Prayers of Steel," the latter completing her *Three Songs*, chosen in 1933 for performance at the festival of the International Society for Contemporary Music at Amsterdam.

In subsequent years, family responsibilities and the depression combined to change the direction of Ruth Crawford-Seeger's career. She and her husband now increasingly turned their interests to the place of music in society. In 1935 they moved to Silver Spring, Md., near Washington, D.C., where Charles Seeger worked as a musicologist for various government agencies until 1953. During this period, Crawford-Seeger collaborated with John and Alan Lomax as musical editor for the anthology *Our Singing Country* (1941) and transcribed more than a

173

thousand songs from the Library of Congress Archive of Folk Song. A specialist in folk music for young people, she taught at several schools in the Washington area and published *American Folk Songs for Children in Home, School and Nursery School* (1948), *Animal Folk Songs for Children* (1950), and *Christmas Folk Songs for Children* (1953). Crawford-Seeger shared her enthusiasm and interest in this direction with her large family, including stepson Pete, Michael (Mike, b. 1933), Margaret (Peggy, b. 1935), Barbara Mona (b. 1937), and Penelope (b. 1943). The children of Charles and Ruth Crawford Seeger continued the family's key role in the American folk music revival, bringing its resources to a wide audience through performances and recordings.

Although she devoted herself freely to her family and to the study of folk music, Crawford-Seeger often expressed the desire to return to composing. After 1932, however, she completed only two works: "Rissolty Rossolty" (1940) and *Suite for Wind Quintet* (1952). At the age of fifty-two, she was stricken by cancer, and died at her home in Chevy Chase, Md., in November 1953.

Ruth Crawford-Seeger's career as a composer was brief yet significant. As Charles Seeger wrote of her in 1933, few American composers were as "uncompromisingly and successfully radical." Although her total output was slender, it is possible to trace the stylistic changes in her work. The compositions from Chicago show strong traces of Debussy and Scriabin, such as shifting, nondirectional harmonies and the use of parallel progressions, particularly in her second set of piano preludes. The application of Charles Seeger's theories of dissonant counterpoint and dissonant rhythm is seen in her New York compositions, especially in the *Piano Study in Mixed Accents*. This work also reflects Crawford-Seeger's growing interest in the unusual treatment of dynamics, a trait which blossomed fully in her *String Quartet,* written during her European sojourn. Formal unity, although present from Crawford-Seeger's earliest works, became more and more highly organized, culminating in the *Three Songs.* Charles Seeger believed that had she lived, she would have pursued further the use of folk material seen in "Rissolty Rossolty." The majority of Crawford-Seeger's instrumental works were cast in an intimate chamber music style; most of her vocal music used a declamatory and word-oriented approach. Crawford-Seeger's compositions, which show wide understanding of the past and present and an intuitive grasp of avant-garde ideas, have left a deep impression on twentieth-century American music.

[Crawford-Seeger's papers are held by family members: diaries by her daughters Barbara and Penelope; letters to her mother by her brother, Carl Crawford; and letters to her husband by the Charles Seeger estate. A short biography, and a detailed analysis of Crawford-Seeger's compositions, can be found in Matilda Gaume, "Ruth Crawford Seeger: Her Life and Works" (Ph.D. diss., Indiana Univ., 1973). Useful discussions of the music include Charles Seeger, "Ruth Crawford," in Henry Cowell, ed., *American Composers on American Music* (1933), pp. 110–18; George Perle, "Atonality and the Twelve-Note System in the United States," *The Score,* July 1960, pp. 51–60; and B. Jepson, "Ruth Crawford-Seeger: A Study in Mixed Accents," *Feminist Art Jour.,* Spring 1977. An obituary appeared in *Wash. Post,* Nov. 20, 1953; death record provided by Md. Dept. of Health.]

MATILDA GAUME

CROTHERS, Rachel, Dec. 12, 1870–July 5, 1958. Playwright.

Rachel Crothers was born in Bloomington, Ill., the youngest of three children and the second daughter of Marie Louise (De Pew) and Eli Kirk Crothers, a physician. Her mother, at the age of forty, decided to study medicine and became the first woman physician in central Illinois. Although theater was foreign to her deeply religious and conservative midwestern upbringing, Rachel Crothers asserted her interest at the age of thirteen when she and a friend, May Fitzwilliam, wrote and acted all the roles of a romantic four-act melodrama entitled *Every Cloud Has a Silver Lining.*

Crothers graduated from high school in Bloomington in 1891; a severe attack of typhoid at the age of eighteen had delayed her education and almost cost her her life. After more playwriting in conjunction with the Bloomington Dramatic Society, which she founded, Rachel Crothers traveled to Boston and then to New York to study drama. At the Stanhope-Wheatcroft School of Acting, where she spent four years as pupil and instructor, she began to direct some of her one-act plays. During these years she had three professional engagements as an actress, but playwriting was her forte. Her first professionally produced play, a one-act comedy titled *The Rector,* opened at New York's Madison Square Theatre on April 3, 1902.

Crothers's early plays set the tone for her life's work. The heroine of *The Three of Us* (1906) is a strong and independent woman who defends her right to freedom and demands the respect of others. *A Man's World* (1909), which expresses defiance of accepted social attitudes, both interested and provoked critics and audiences: having discovered that her fiancé has fathered a child for whom he feels no responsibility, the heroine castigates the "man's world" in which she must live and breaks her engagement. In *He and She* (first version titled *The Herfords,* 1911) the heroine is a sculptor who wins a national competition but surrenders the commission she has won to her husband (who has placed second) in favor of caring for her teenage daughter. Although this play depicts the usual male and female stereotypes and rejects an ending in which family sex roles would be reversed, social standards are consciously challenged in a structure where She is superior to He in both artistic and economic worlds.

Rachel Crothers wrote mainly for a middle-class audience, but she offered a wide-ranging commentary on the condition of twentieth-century women. Her plays deal with the double standard (*A Man's World*); woman's moral responsibility (*Ourselves,* 1913); trial marriages (*Young Wisdom,* 1914); the generation gap (*Nice People,* 1921); honesty in marriage (*Mary the Third,* 1923); freedom to express oneself (*Expressing Willie,* 1924); divorce (*Let Us Be Gay,* 1929); relations between men and women (*When Ladies Meet,* 1932); and domestic upheaval (*Susan and God,* 1937). Basically, she wrote social comedy and melodrama and stoutly disclaimed any conscious effort to chronicle women's causes or changing attitudes toward women or to evaluate sex roles (*N.Y. Times Mag.,* May 4, 1941, pp. 10, 27). Rather, she wrote about life as she understood it, conceding only that most great modern plays are studies of women and that because women prevail in theater audiences they largely determine the kind of plays that will be produced. "Drama is drama," she explained in a speech in Boston in February 1912 before the Drama League, "and what difference does it make whether women or men are working in it?"

During her long career Rachel Crothers wrote at least thirty-eight plays. After a hiatus following the success of *Susan and God,* she completed a final comedy titled *We Happy Few* (1955), which was not produced. For nearly a third of a century she provided Broadway audiences with a new play almost every year. If she did not chronicle the life of modern woman, she emphasized her problems. If she was not a profound commentator on life, she certainly had thoughtful opinions. And if she shocked some of her contemporaries (Ludwig Lewisohn considered *Mary the Third* an attack on marriage), she is a disappointment to women of later generations. Although she raised the right questions, she never provided radical solutions, and her plays inevitably climaxed with an emphasis upon traditional means for reaching traditional values—

happiness, mutual faith, and love, which she regarded as the one great emotion of which woman was capable. Yet her plays—"well-bred, witty, and wise," according to Barrett Clark (*Drama Mag.,* April 1931)—exhibited a craftsmanship and a vitality in dialogue which made her the most commercially successful American woman playwright prior to World War II.

With as passionate a concern for the staging of her plays as for the plays themselves, Rachel Crothers firmly believed in her own ability to guide her work through production. A strong and independent woman who drifted away from her family and never married, she readily expressed her views on modern drama, theater audiences, the importance of directors, and women playwrights. An active member of the Society of American Dramatists, the Authors League of America, and P.E.N., she won the Megrue Prize in 1933 for *When Ladies Meet* and the Theatre Club's gold cup in 1937 for *Susan and God.* Her patriotic and humanitarian impulses led her to establish the Stage Women's War Relief Fund during World War I, and, with producer John Golden, the Stage Relief Fund in 1932, of which she remained a board member until it disbanded in 1951. In 1940 she helped create the American Theatre Wing, which after 1941 operated such war services as the Stage Door Canteen; she served as the organization's executive head until 1950. Rachel Crothers died in her sleep at her home in Danbury, Conn., at the age of eighty-seven.

[The Billy Rose Theatre Coll., N.Y. Public Library, has clippings, reviews, and typescripts, some containing significant revisions to the plays. There is a small collection of Crothers's correspondence at the Library of the Am. Acad. of Arts and Letters, N.Y. City. In an interview with Catherine Hughes, "Women Playmakers," *N.Y. Times Mag.,* May 4, 1941, Rachel Crothers revealed her attitude toward women's causes. An unsigned interview, "Future of American Stage Depends on Directors," *N.Y. Times Mag.,* Dec. 3, 1916, pp. 136–37, shows her appreciation of the role of stage director. See also two other essays by Crothers: "Troubles of a Playwright," *Harper's Bazaar,* Jan. 1911, pp. 14, 46, and "Our Own Daisy Ashford Urges Dramatists as Directors," *N.Y. Herald,* April 1, 1923. A biography by Lois Gottlieb, *Rachel Crothers* (1979), contains a bibliography. See also her "Obstacles to Feminism in the Early Plays of Rachel Crothers," *Univ. of Mich. Papers in Women's Studies,* June 1975, pp. 71–84. Arthur H. Quinn provides one of the best and most extensive analyses of Crothers's work in *A History of the American Drama from the Civil War to the Present Day,* II (1927), 50–61. He also includes a fine photograph. The anonymous "Rachel Crothers, Pacemaker for American Social Comedy," *Theatre Arts Monthly,* Dec. 1932, pp. 971–72, gives a good production list. Cynthia Sutherland, "American

Women Playwrights as Mediators of the 'Woman Problem,' " *Modern Drama*, Sept. 1978, pp. 319–36, provides, as does Gottlieb's work, evidence of newer feminist interest in Crothers. Ludwig Lewisohn's comments on *Mary the Third* appeared in the *Nation*, March 7, 1923. An obituary appeared in the *N.Y. Times*, July 6, 1958; a letter to the editor of the *N.Y. Times*, July 12, 1958, supplied early family history. Crothers's date of birth is most often listed as 1878. The 1870 date is confirmed by the 1900 U.S. Census and is also given on her death certificate, provided by the Conn. Dept. of Health.]

WALTER J. MESERVE

CUNNINGHAM, Minnie Fisher, March 19, 1882–Dec. 9, 1964. Suffragist, politician, community leader.

Minnie Fisher was born in New Waverly, Texas, the sixth of seven children and youngest of five daughters of Horatio White Fisher, a plantation owner, Confederate cavalry officer, and local politician, and Sallie Comer (Abercrombie) Fisher, daughter of a neighboring plantation owner. She inherited her Methodist faith from both the Fisher and Abercrombie families and learned her Democratic politics from her father, who served a term as a member of the Texas legislature. Minnie Fisher decided at an early age to emulate her father's political success.

Educated by her mother until the age of sixteen, Fisher then obtained a teaching certificate by passing a state examination. She taught for a year at Gourd Creek Community School, near New Waverly, before entering the University of Texas Medical Branch located in Galveston. Graduating in 1901 with a degree in pharmacy, she practiced her profession for a year preceding her marriage to Beverly Jean Cunningham, an insurance executive and lawyer, Nov. 27, 1902. The marriage foundered because of her husband's drinking and Minnie Fisher Cunningham's increasing political activities.

Because of her disappointment in her marriage and her childhood interest in her father's political career, Minnie Fish, as her friends called her, channeled her energies into the causes of civic reform. Earlier she had been an active supporter of modern health and sanitary facilities for the city of Galveston in the aftermath of the 1900 hurricane there. Soon after her marriage Cunningham became involved in the suffrage campaign in Galveston. Her work came to the attention of Annette Finnigan, president of the state suffrage association formed in 1903. At Finnigan's request, Cunningham toured the state to promote the cause of suffrage. Small in stature, she was formidable in debate. "She

looked like a wren [but] she behaved like a hawk," one admirer recalled.

Becoming president of the state suffrage organization in 1915, Cunningham proved a skillful political leader. She led the suffrage campaign in Texas, concentrating on lobbying for a primary suffrage bill and encouraging the impeachment of Gov. James Ferguson, an outspoken foe of woman suffrage. The capstone of her presidency came in 1918, when Gov. William P. Hobby, Ferguson's successor, signed into law an amendment to the Texas constitution which ensured Texas women a vote in primary elections. Because of the one-party politics of the state, women in Texas effectively received the vote two years before the nineteenth amendment enfranchised all women in the nation.

Cunningham's leadership extended beyond her suffrage work. During World War I she served as the state chairman of the Women's Liberty Loan Committee for the third and fourth loan drives and chaired the Texas Women's Anti-Vice Committee. Conducting what was popularly known as a "white zone" campaign, the antivice group demanded an end to both prostitution and liquor traffic in the vicinity of military training camps in the state.

In 1919 CARRIE CHAPMAN CATT, president of the National American Woman Suffrage Association, invited Cunningham to Washington, D.C., to serve as the secretary of the association's Congressional Committee. During the final stage of the national suffrage campaign, she successfully utilized the lobbying techniques that had been effective in Texas in the halls of Congress. After the passage of the nineteenth amendment, Cunningham remained in Washington, becoming in 1920 executive secretary of the National League of Women Voters. She coordinated the activities of the League's national office and helped organize new branches throughout the country. Turning to party politics, in 1923 she became executive secretary of the Woman's National Democratic Club and editor of its *Democratic Bulletin*. Under the Club's auspices Cunningham conducted training schools in political organization for the newly enfranchised women voters.

In 1927, following the death of her husband, Minnie Fisher Cunningham returned to Texas to settle his estate. His legacy enabled her to announce her candidacy for the United States Senate, seeking to upset incumbent Sen. Earle B. Mayfield. The first woman from Texas to run for that office, Cunningham used the novelty of her campaign to focus the attention of voters on issues she deemed important to all Texans. She advocated prohibition, tariff and tax reduction, farm relief and an adequate flood control program, and opposed the Ku Klux Klan. She placed fifth out of six candidates in the Democratic primary.

Her financial resources depleted by the campaign, Cunningham joined the Texas Agricultural Extension Service at Texas A & M College in 1930 as associate editor, later becoming editor. In 1939 she returned to Washington as an information specialist in the Women's Division of the Agricultural Adjustment Administration (AAA). She served until 1943, when she resigned in protest of a gag rule imposed on AAA employees. Her resignation reflected her commitment to freedom of expression and her concern that information flow freely to farmers who were aiding the war effort.

Returning to Texas, Cunningham announced her candidacy for the office of governor. Her campaign was based upon her promise to give full support to the war effort. She criticized incumbent Gov. Coke Stevenson's obstruction of the federal gasoline rationing program and his use of cuts in old age pensions to decrease the state deficit. Her campaign created considerable interest, and, although she lost to Stevenson by a large margin in the primary, she placed second in the field of nine candidates.

Following her 1944 defeat, Cunningham and Jane Y. McCallum, a friend and former secretary of state of Texas, formed the Women's Committee for Educational Freedom, which publicly criticized the conservative policies of Governor Stevenson. The committee supported the 1946 gubernatorial candidacy of Homer P. Rainey, former president of the University of Texas, who had been fired in 1944 for defending academic freedom. In the 1950s Cunningham organized the Texas Democratic Women's State Committee, and was also a founder of the liberal state Democratic organization, the Democrats of Texas. She was a force in liberal journalism as well as politics. In 1944 she began writing a column for the liberal *State Observer* entitled "By Countryside and Town," and in 1954 she offered to mortgage part of her 1,200-acre estate, Fisher Farms, to save the newspaper from a conservative buyer. In that year she organized a coalition of liberals to buy the paper, which then became *The Texas Observer*.

Financially straitened in her later years, Cunningham retired to her farm where she opened a roadside garden stand to supplement the earnings from her pecan orchards and tended a small herd of cattle without assistance. She remained actively interested in Texas Democratic politics and became a symbol and rallying point for embattled Texas liberals throughout the 1950s. Cunningham died in 1964 in a Conroe, Texas, nursing home of heart failure and complications arising from a broken arm.

[The principal sources are manuscript collections. The Minnie Fisher Cunningham Papers at the Houston Public Library contain correspondence, reports, clippings, and other material, particularly concerning the Texas Equal Suffrage Assoc. Other correspondence is in the Carrie Chapman Catt Papers and the Nat. Am. Woman Suffrage Assoc. Records in the Manuscript Div., Library of Congress; the Maud Wood Park Papers and the Dorothy LaRue Brown Papers at the Schlesinger Library, Radcliffe College; and the Mrs. Percy Pennybacker Papers, Barker Texas Hist. Center, Univ. of Texas at Austin. Private manuscript collections are the Elizabeth Hill McCoy Coll., New Waverly, Texas, which contains Cunningham's "Life of Sallie Abercrombie Fisher"; Franklin P. Jones Coll., Marshall, Texas; Creekmore Fath Coll., Austin; and Margaret Reading-Jimmy Demaret Coll., in the possession of John Eudy, Houston. The League of Women Voters, Washington, D.C., has a file of newspaper clippings on Cunningham. A brief biographical sketch may be found in Eldon Stephen Branda, ed., *Handbook of Texas: A Supplement* (1976). An account of her role in the Texas suffrage campaign is in John Carroll Eudy, "The Vote and Lone Star Women: Minnie Fisher Cunningham and the Texas Equal Suffrage Association," *East Texas Hist. Jour.*, 14 (1976), 52–59. Death certificate supplied by Texas Dept. of Health.]

JOHN CARROLL EUDY

CURTIS, Mary Louise. See ZIMBALIST, Mary Louise Curtis Bok.

D

DANIELS, Mabel Wheeler, Nov. 27, 1878– March 10, 1971. Composer.

The only child of Sarah (Wheeler) and George Frank Daniels, Mabel Daniels was born in Swampscott, Mass., of old New England stock on both sides. Her father's family had prospered as painter-decorators, jewelers, stock brokers, and circus producers. Both grandfathers were church organists. George Daniels, active in shoe manufacturing, became president of the Boston Boot and Shoe Club and vice president of the

Boston Board of Trade. Both of Mabel Daniels's parents played a role in Boston musical life through lifelong involvement in the Handel and Haydn Society (her father was president), which boasted ten members of the Daniels family. Listening to her father sing the Verdi *Requiem* gave young Mabel her first intense musical experience. Her mother had leisure to devote to encouraging her daughter to develop both her literary gifts and the musical talent she revealed during early piano lessons.

After graduating from Girls' Latin School in Boston in 1896, Daniels went to Radcliffe College where singing in the Glee Club and composing and conducting operettas clarified the direction her career would take. At Radcliffe she began to take herself seriously as a composer and she remained grateful to the college (which later commissioned two of her most important choral pieces), gladly serving as trustee and later sharing her wealth with the school through generous bequests. Graduating magna cum laude in 1900, Daniels continued to study orchestration with George Chadwick at the New England Conservatory of Music. In 1902 she went to Germany, accompanied by her mother, to become the first woman enrolled in Ludwig Thuille's score-reading class at the Royal Conservatory of Munich. Returning to America, she published *An American Girl in Munich* (1905) which recorded her appreciation of artistic discipline: "No matter how deeply an artist's feelings may be stirred . . . he must always be the master of his emotions."

Attached to Boston for the abundance and quality of its music, Daniels directed the Radcliffe Glee Club and became music director at Simmons College (1913–18). She also sang with the Cecilia Society, which strengthened her composer's understanding of choral textures (she always preferred writing for voices), and she played a social role as musical adviser to the Boston school system. Boston also provided her with many friends and with an audience for her music.

Daniels never married; she focused her creative energy on her music and, with the domestic help of her "faithful retainer," Norah, the constant encouragement of her teachers, and the facilities of the MacDowell Colony in Peterborough, N.H., she was able to produce a body of varied musical compositions that defined her as an outstanding woman composer of her generation. Yet she was never able to support herself as a composer; family wealth remained her main source of income.

The only woman to have had three different works played by the Boston Symphony (*Exultate Deo*, 1929; *Deep Forest*, 1931; and *A Psalm of Praise*, 1954); the only American woman composer represented at the Carnegie Hall Festival in 1939; and the only woman among thirty-one composers recorded by the Boston Symphony under Charles Munch, Mabel Daniels would nonetheless have preferred not to be known as a woman composer, but rather, as Randall Thompson insisted, as "one of our finest composers." She believed strongly that all art should be judged solely on merits which have nothing to do with sex. There were only two kinds of music—good or bad, she wrote: "What difference whether written by a man or a woman or a Hottentot or a Unitarian."

Perhaps because she had strong support from her family and, like the circus performers in her background, relished challenge, Daniels was able to laugh at the prejudice she encountered: the conductor who expressed surprise that her piece would have to be rehearsed, the near-sighted concertgoer who asked her why a woman was on the stage after a Worcester performance of her cantata, *Jael*. On a 1901 program she listed herself as M. W. Daniels because she felt that as a woman she would be patronized.

Although her temperament was conservative—she had little sympathy for atonal music and was a lifelong Republican—Daniels became active in the woman suffrage movement. She later compared the suffragists to the demonstrators for civil rights: like them, she wrote, "we would die for our cause." She did not call herself a feminist, but commented in her memoirs: "When I hear of a man putting on his hat after breakfast and striding off to a secluded study, free from all cares (due no doubt to the maneuvering of an understanding female) I have a pang of envy." Daniels expressed satisfaction that changing conditions had made it easier for women to be professional musicians, but continued to feel that social demands militated against women, and that the endurance necessary to a successful career in composition was hard for her sex to come by.

"A composer must have a strong constitution, perseverance, ingenuity, [and] above all, courage," Daniels believed. Her own perseverance and musical achievement were acknowledged by several awards and honorary degrees. She also received two prizes from the National Federation of Music Clubs (1911 and 1913), and the MacDowell Colony supported the first performance of *The Desolate City* (1913), one of her most popular cantatas. Aware that young artists needed encouragement, she provided money to establish several prizes and tried to foster a competition at Tanglewood, the summer home of the Boston Symphony Orchestra, which serves as a training and performance center for young musicians. She also established a scholarship for a student at the New England Conservatory. Her friendship with MARIAN MACDOWELL led to her enthusiastic participation in the development of the MacDowell Colony.

Mabel Daniels's last principal composition was *Piper, Play On*, written in 1960; she died of pneumonia in Cambridge, Mass., in 1971 at ninety-three. Her music was cautiously experimental; she tried to be modern without being avant-garde. Critics often greeted performances of her work with enthusiasm, appreciative of her knowledge of the voice and her skill in handling instrumentation; her music gave the listener memorable pleasure. The gift of song and the pursuit of perfection that Randall Thompson found characteristic of Mabel Daniels's work should guarantee its place in the canon of American music.

[The extensive collection of Daniels's papers at the Schlesinger Library, Radcliffe College, includes her unpublished memoirs, correspondence, a complete file of reviews and press interviews, photographs and family mementos, some scores, and complete publication lists of her more than thirty compositions. There is also considerable information in the alumnae files, Radcliffe Archives. The Fleisher Music Library in Philadelphia has copies of her out-of-print scores. For biographical information and comment on her work, see Madeleine Goss, *Modern Music Makers: Contemporary American Composers* (1952); Claire Reis, *Composers in America* (1938, 1947); three books by John Tasker Howard, *Annals of Music in America* (1922), *Our American Music* (1939), and *Our Contemporary Composers* (1941); and a longer account in Christine Ammer, *Unsung: A History of Women in American Music* (1980). Two articles appeared in the *Christian Science Monitor*: Pearl Strachan Hurd, "Composer Joins Grace and Vigor: Modern But Not Ultra," Dec. 28, 1955, and "Murals of Wool—Mabel Daniels Reads Through Her Score of Memories," April 2, 1961. For her work with the MacDowell Colony, see Rollo Walter Brown, "Mrs. MacDowell and Her Colony," *Atlantic Monthly*, July 1949, and Rudolph Elie, "The MacDowell Colony Enters Its 45th Year," *Boston Herald*, Jan. 6, 1951. See also Dwight Shepler, "More Glory Than Profits in Music," *Boston Herald*, May 24, 1936; Robert Taylor, "Women Composers of Merit Rare, So Hail Mabel Daniels," *Boston Globe*, Nov. 1, 1964; the speech by Randall Thompson at the dedication of Daniels Hall at Radcliffe, Nov. 17, 1966 (in the Radcliffe Archives); and three reviews in the *N.Y. Times*, April 12, 1931, p. 8; April 12, 1935, p. 5; June 18, 1939, p. 6. David McCord, "Radcliffe and Education for Women," *N.Y. Times Mag.*, Dec. 5, 1954, relates Daniels's achievement to her education. An obituary article by Robert Taylor appeared in the *Boston Globe*, March 11, 1971. A death record was provided by the Mass. Dept. of Public Health.]

EUGENIA KALEDIN

DAVIS, Adelle, Feb. 25, 1904–May 31, 1974. Food writer.

Adelle Davis, popular writer and lecturer on food and health, was born Daisie Adelle Davis in Lizton, Ind., the youngest of the five daughters of Charles Eugene Davis, a farmer, and Harriet (McBroom) Davis. She later dropped the name Daisie because she associated it with cows and pigs. Ten days after the baby's birth, Harriet Davis became paralyzed; she died seventeen months later. This blow and the strict upbringing by her father, Davis later asserted, created a sense of loneliness and lack of self-esteem which only seven years of psychoanalysis, beginning in 1953, eventually dispelled. As a girl, Davis worked on the farm, learned to cook before learning to read, and won 4-H Club ribbons for baking and canning.

After graduating from Lizton High School, Davis studied home economics at Purdue University (1923–25), then transferred to the University of California at Berkeley, receiving a B.A. in household science in 1927. She obtained further training in dietetics at New York's Bellevue and Fordham Hospitals, then supervised nutrition in the Yonkers, N.Y., public schools and served as consulting nutritionist for New York obstetricians. Davis returned to California in 1931, launching a private consulting practice in nutrition which continued until 1958, for two years in Oakland, thereafter in the Los Angeles area. In 1939 she received an M.S. degree in biochemistry from the University of Southern California. From 1948 on she made her home in Palos Verdes Estates, near Los Angeles.

Davis married George Edward Leisey, a surveyor ten years her junior, in 1946. An adopted son and daughter, George Davis (b. 1946) and Barbara Adelle (b. 1950), were given the Leisey name. This marriage ended in divorce in 1953, and in 1960 Davis married Frank V. Sieglinger, a retired accountant and lawyer.

Davis's first publication was a 1932 promotional pamphlet for a milk company. There followed two privately printed tracts, *Optimum Health* (1935) and *You Can Stay Well* (1939), and a nutrition handbook, *Vitality through Planned Nutrition* (1942). Davis's public acclaim, however, rested on four books: *Let's Cook It Right* (1947), *Let's Have Healthy Children* (1951), *Let's Eat Right to Keep Fit* (1954), and *Let's Get Well* (1965). The four *Let's* books and their revisions sold ten million copies, mostly in paperback, during Davis's lifetime, and made her, as *Time* put it in 1972, "the high priestess of a new nutrition religion." Davis began to travel widely on the lecture circuit, especially to college campuses, speaking also in Latin America and Europe. She became a sought-after guest on television talk shows.

In her heyday as a food guru, the matronly Davis conveyed a feisty, down-to-earth forthrightness. Bright blue eyes dominated her lined face and she wound her gray hair into a chignon. The pitch of her voice was unusually low—she sang tenor in her church choir—and her use of it commanding. Writing and speaking with an ex cathedra air, she offered simple, easy-to-follow advice about diet. She radiated assurance that abiding by her precepts—as she herself did—would ward off or cure most personal illnesses. Moreover, in proper diet lay societal well-being. To Davis, "Alcoholism, crime, insanity, suicide, divorce, drug addiction and even impotency are often merely the results of bad eating" (Deutsch, p. 4).

Davis benefited from and contributed to the phenomenal growth, from the 1950s onward, of the health food movement, which thrived on publicity about pesticide residues and food additives. Scientific nutritionists particularly regretted that Davis, with her proper academic credentials and powerful public appeal, gave support to the movement's exaggerated claims by recommending oversimplified and at times unsound solutions to problems of nutritional deficiency. Although she gave some useful advice, advocating physical exercise and warning Americans of the risks of nutritional imbalance, her books were marred by the unreliability of her numerous citations of scientific literature and the lack of evidence to support her bold and sometimes dangerous advice. An analysis of *Let's Eat Right* found mistakes averaging one per page ("Americans Love Hogwash," pp. 3, 4). Checks of references in *Let's Get Well*, conducted by Edward Rynearson of the Mayo Clinic and by Roslyn Alfin-Slater of the University of California at Los Angeles, found numerous inaccuracies and misquotations.

Some errors might merely amuse, like Davis's insistence on the nutritional superiority of fertile over infertile eggs. But examples of hazardous counsel included the recommendation of massive daily doses of Vitamins A, D, and E; the assertion that magnesium alone offered useful treatment for epilepsy; the suggestion that nephrosis patients should take potassium chloride; the criticism of the pasteurization of milk. The panel on deception and misinformation of the 1969 White House Conference on Food,

Nutrition and Health deemed Davis probably the nation's most harmful single source of false nutrition information. When challenged, Davis would sometimes retract her position; usually she shrugged off the charges or responded by attacking her accusers. Criticism by scientific nutritionists, in any case, offered but slight counterweight to the widespread favorable publicity given her by the popular media and to adulation from the faithful.

In 1973, at the height of her popularity, Davis was shocked to learn that she had contracted multiple myeloma, a cancer of the bone marrow. She attributed the cancer to "too many X-rays." In less than a year Adelle Davis died at her home of this disease.

[Davis also wrote *Exploring Inner Space*, an account of her experience in taking LSD, published in 1961 under the pseudonym Jane Dunlap. *Vitality through Planned Nutrition* was revised in 1949, *Let's Cook It Right* in 1970, *Let's Have Healthy Children* in 1972, and *Let's Eat Right to Keep Fit* in 1970. Her publishing career is summed up in *Publishers Weekly*, June 21, 1971. For biographical facts see Jane Howard, "Earth Mother to the Food Faddists," *Life*, Oct. 22, 1971; Daniel Yergin, *N.Y. Times Mag.*, May 20, 1973; Jean Wixen, *Chi. Sun-Times*, Dec. 23 and 24, 1973; *Current Biog.*, 1973. John Poppy interviewed Davis for *Look*, "Adelle Davis and the New Nutrition Religion," Dec. 15, 1970. Her confrontations with nutritionists are documented in *Glamour*, July 1971; *Wash. Eve. Star*, May 3, 1972; *Wash. Post*, May 4, 1972; *Time*, Dec. 18, 1972. Critiques of her ideas are found in Ruth Baker, "Encounter with Adelle Davis," *Jour. Nutrition Education*, Summer 1972; Edward H. Rynearson, *Medical Insight*, July-Aug. 1973, and "Americans Love Hogwash," *Nutrition Rev.*, July 1974; Chicago Nutrition Assoc., *Nutrition References and Book Reviews* (1975); Ronald M. Deutsch, *The New Nuts among the Berries* (1977). Obituaries appeared in the *N.Y. Times*, June 1, 1974, and *Wash. Post*, June 2, 1974. The marriage certificate of Adelle Davis and George Leisey indicates a prior marriage for Davis; details on this marriage were unavailable. A death record was provided by the Calif. Dept. of Health Services. Helpful information for this article was supplied by Roslyn B. Alfin-Slater, William E. Braunig, William J. Darby, Thomas H. Jukes, Gilda Knight, Bonnie McMullen, E. Neige Todhunter, and Philip L. White.]

JAMES HARVEY YOUNG

DAVIS, Frances Elliott, April 28, 1882?–May 2, 1965. Nurse, community leader.

On July 2, 1918, through her dedication to nursing and a quiet persistence that was to mark her career, Frances Elliott became the first black nurse to be officially enrolled by the American National Red Cross. Later, as a nursing supervisor and administrator and as a community visiting nurse, she helped and encouraged other blacks to pursue an education and to better their living conditions.

Elliott was born in North Carolina, probably in the town of Shelby, to Emma Elliott, the white daughter of a plantation owner and Methodist minister, and Darryl Elliott, a part black and part Cherokee Indian sharecropper. Darryl Elliott's mother had assumed the Elliott name while a slave on their plantation in Asheville, N.C. Frances Elliott's childhood was lonely, as her mother died when she was five and her father had long since fled for his life. Shifted from one place and one guardian to another, she nonetheless managed through her own efforts to be educated intermittently in the public schools of Pittsburgh, Pa. There, against the wishes of her guardian, who wanted her to leave school and work for him, Elliott worked as household help for the Joseph Reed family. She developed a lifelong attachment to the Reeds, later assuming their name; they helped her run away to Knoxville (Tenn.) College in 1899, encouraged her to complete the teacher training program there, and provided for her expenses until she graduated in 1907.

But Elliott knew that nursing was her vocation, and despite the Reeds' fears that it would tax her frail health, she entered the small School Hospital, newly organized by Knoxville College. Remaining for over a year, she had to leave because of illness. After her recovery she taught school in Henderson, N.C., and, in the spring of 1910, enrolled at the Freedmen's Hospital Training School for Nurses in Washington, D.C. She graduated on June 2, 1913.

Elliott did private duty nursing in Washington for three years after her graduation. Feeling the need for broader nursing challenges, she applied to the American Red Cross (ARC) for work, despite her fears of rejection because of her race. She was accepted and became the first black nurse to take the Town and Country Nursing Service course (sponsored by the ARC) at Teachers College, Columbia University. The course included conferences each week with ADELAIDE NUTTING, head of the department of nursing and health, and practice work at the Henry Street Settlement and the New York Board of Charities; it did not carry with it, however, official acceptance by the Red Cross. Elliott was assigned temporarily to Henry Street in 1917, until a suitable assignment could be found. In July of that year she was sent by the ARC Town and Country Nursing Service to Jackson, Tenn. There she provided nursing care, including midwifery, and attempted to teach the basics of sanitation and prenatal care.

Although Elliott was deeply involved in her work in Jackson, she was also concerned about the need for nurses to serve in World War I. The United States had entered the war in April 1917, and at that time the ARC began serving as the procurement agency for the Army Nurse Corps. All Town and Country nurses were automatically enrolled as ARC nurses, given official Red Cross pins, and thereby made eligible for the Army Nurse Corps; Frances Elliott was the exception. ADAH THOMS, president of the National Association of Colored Graduate Nurses, had been urging the acceptance of black nurses in the ARC since the beginning of the war. In the spring of 1918, Elliott notified MARY S. GARDNER, director of the Bureau of Public Health Nursing, that her Red Cross pin had never arrived. At first told that the Red Cross had not begun to enroll black nurses, Elliott soon heard from Gardner that she was the first black nurse to be enrolled. On July 2, 1918, she was awarded badge number 1-A. (The letter "A" identified all black nurses until 1949, when the "A" system was abolished.) She was still not accepted by the Army Nurse Corps, which enrolled no black nurses until after the war.

Elliott's only direct work for the war effort was a month (May 1918) spent at Chickamauga, Tenn., with the ARC Public Health Service (the new name for the Town and Country Service), working with the thousands of soldiers in training there. Returning to Jackson in June, she remained with the ARC until December 1918, nursing victims of the influenza epidemic. Elliott contracted a severe case of influenza, which left her heart permanently damaged. In 1919 she moved to Tuskegee, Ala., to become director of nurses' training at John A. Andrew Memorial Hospital.

Later that year Elliott was invited to organize the first Michigan training school for black nurses, at Dunbar Hospital in Detroit. After the first class graduated, passed their state board examinations, and were admitted to practice in Michigan, in August 1920 she began a dedicated, though interrupted, service on the staff of the Detroit Visiting Nurses' Association (VNA).

In the midst of her busy career, Frances Elliott married William A. Davis on Dec. 24, 1921. A graduate of the Detroit Conservatory, he was a band musician and gave private piano lessons. Their only child was stillborn in 1922. Frances Davis returned to Dunbar in 1923 to take over her former job as superintendent of nurses and director of nurses' training. Determined to upgrade the nursing program, she managed to secure funds from a wealthy Michigan philanthropist, Senator James Couzens, but the hospital's staff physicians refused to accept the money for nursing purposes, and tried to change the terms of Couzens's offer. Davis resigned and in March 1927 she began to work with the Child Welfare Division of the Detroit Health Department, conducting prenatal, maternal, and child health clinics.

With her husband's support and encouragement, Davis returned to Teachers College in the fall of 1929 to work on her B.S. degree, having received a Rosenwald Fellowship, but she was unable to complete the program because of ill health. Shortly after her return the Davises moved to Inkster, Mich., a black community outside Detroit. During the depression Frances Davis worked at the Ford Motor plant commissary distributing food to Inkster residents, as well as continuing to work for the Detroit Health Department. She helped to convince Henry Ford to aid Inkster by paying utility bills, providing clothing, and repairing homes. In return Inkster men worked for pay to improve the physical appearance of the community.

In 1932 Davis again left the Health Department to devote more time to the commissary. She returned to work for the VNA in 1935, by which time she was also serving on the Inkster school board. She left the VNA in 1940 to begin a day nursery for Inkster. Through her efforts, the nursery attracted the attention of ELEANOR ROOSEVELT, who helped to provide funds. From 1945 until the onset of another illness in 1951 Davis worked at Eloise Hospital in Wayne County; after that time she remained at home to care for her husband who died in 1959.

Davis was admired for the manner in which she met challenges among blacks and broke down racial barriers among whites with unflagging persistence and quiet dignity. She was to be honored at the ARC national convention in Detroit on May 11, 1965, but died in Mount Clemens, Mich., of a heart attack shortly before the event. Her Red Cross pin was presented to officials at the convention to be displayed in the ARC historical collection.

[The most extensive source is a biography by Jean Maddern Pitrone, *Trailblazer: Negro Nurse in the American Red Cross* (1969). For further information and background see Adah B. Thoms, *Pathfinders: A History of the Progress of Colored Graduate Nurses* (1929), pp. 46–51. Davis is mentioned in Anna B. Coles, "The Howard University School of Nursing in Historical Perspective," *Jour. Nat. Medical Assoc.*, March 1969, pp. 105–18. No birth record is available. The 1882 birth date comes from the death certificate, provided by the Mich. Dept. of Health; facts in the Pitrone biography also point to this date, although Frances Elliott gave 1883 on her application to Freedmen's.]

JOYCE ANN ELMORE

DAVIS, Hallie Flanagan. *See* FLANAGAN, Hallie Mae Ferguson.

DAVIS, Pauline Morton. *See* SABIN, Pauline Morton.

DEAN, Vera Micheles, March 29, 1903–Oct. 10, 1972. International affairs specialist, editor.

Vera Dean, best known for her work for the Foreign Policy Association (FPA), helped to shape American opinion on international relations for three decades. Especially during periods of national hysteria in the late 1940s and the 1950s, hers was the cool voice of a moderate who advocated above all understanding and cooperation abroad combined with defense of basic freedoms at home.

She was born in St. Petersburg, Russia, the eldest of three children of Nadine (Kadisch) and Alexander Micheles. Her father, of German-Jewish ancestry, emigrated from Russia to the United States in 1888 and spent eight years in New York City reporting for Jewish newspapers. His command of English enabled him, on his return to Russia in 1896, to gain employment as a sales representative for American firms. Vera's mother, born in Russia to Polish and German Jews who had been baptized in the Russian Orthodox Church, was educated in England and Germany. After her marriage in 1899, she translated English novels into Russian and helped her husband with his business ventures.

Vera Micheles's parents had a profound influence on their children, instilling in them a sense of duty to serve country and community, and exposing them to liberal political, economic, and religious ideas. Vera and her sister and brother were provided with an education that prepared them to earn a living. They were tutored in languages, and she became fluent in seven, including—besides Russian—English, German, and French. This knowledge aided her later as a world affairs analyst, when she visited the countries she wrote about and talked with cab drivers and street venders as well as presidents and prime ministers.

During the 1917 revolution in Russia the Micheles family remained at their summer home in Finland; they were prevented from returning to St. Petersburg because Alexander Micheles was threatened by arrest. In 1919 they left for London, and Vera Micheles was sent to the United States to live in Boston under the care of William Nickerson, an executive of the Gillette Company for whom her father had worked.

Haunted by a tutor's comment that it was fortunate she had a good mind because she lacked her sister's beauty, Micheles attended business school in order to be able to support herself. After working briefly as a stenographer, she enrolled at Radcliffe College in 1921, graduating with distinction in 1925 after earning Phi Beta Kappa honors as a junior. She then received a Carnegie Endowment fellowship in international law, which enabled her to earn an A.M. from Yale University in 1926. That year she returned to Radcliffe and in 1928 obtained a doctorate in the then new fields of international law and international relations.

Vera Micheles became an American citizen in 1928 and the same year began her long career with the FPA. In August 1929 she married William Johnson Dean, a New York City attorney. When William Dean died in 1936, she was left with a three-year-old daughter, Elinor, and a son, William, who was born five weeks after her husband's death. With little money, Vera Dean worked unremittingly "to keep our little family together." Yet she did not consider her extensive lecturing, writing, and teaching a burden endured for the sake of the children. In an outline for an autobiography, she described her activities as "sheer, unadulterated joy."

Dean's greatest impact as an authority on world affairs resulted from her work for the FPA. Beginning in 1922, the FPA pioneered in the field of popular education in international relations. In its publications the Association presented information and opinion on world affairs to help the public reach decisions about the course of American foreign policy. As director of research and editor of publications, including the influential bimonthly *Foreign Policy Bulletin,* Dean had to determine which subjects would be of current interest and to anticipate future developments.

An advocate of collective security as the best means to preserve world peace, Dean decried American isolationist tendencies and during and after World War II she encouraged Americans to support membership in world organizations. In recognition of her efforts, the State Department invited her to advise the American delegation at the founding conference of the United Nations in 1945. For many years she served as UN correspondent for India News and Feature Alliance, an Indian news syndicate.

Following the war, the subject of Soviet-American relations dominated Dean's work. Believing that permanent world peace depended on détente with the Russians, she stressed the importance of improving American understanding of the Soviet Union. In her book *The United States and Russia* (1947), Dean argued that the "inevitable" war should be "the war against hunger, disease, illiteracy, poverty, and fear. In this war there are no frontiers, and there should

be no ideological differences. In this war the United States and Russia can fight side by side as peace-time allies." Her opinions proved controversial during the McCarthy era, and she warned, in *Foreign Policy without Fear* (1953): "As long as any American who does not agree one hundred per cent with a given set of doctrines can be called 'subversive' . . . the United States will find it increasingly difficult to inspire confidence in its common sense, its integrity, and its reliability in time of crisis."

Vera Dean was a "stately, dark blonde," with a "brusque and direct" manner. She taught at Barnard College (1946), Harvard University (1947–48), Smith College (1952–54), the University of Rochester (1954–62), and New York University's Graduate School of Public Administration (1962–71). To reach a wider audience, she wrote books, countless pamphlets, and articles on world affairs for such diverse magazines as *The New Republic, Christian Century,* and *Parents' Magazine.* She also appeared frequently on radio and television public affairs broadcasts, and lectured widely at colleges and before civic groups. For her articulate and open-minded opinions and for her dedicated commitment to making world affairs understandable to the public, Dean received the French Legion of Honor (1947), the Jane Addams Medal (1954), and more than a dozen honorary doctorates.

Resigning as research director of the FPA in 1961, Vera Dean continued to teach until 1971, the year before her death in New York City from a heart attack following a series of strokes. Appropriately, memorial services were held at the United Nations chapel.

[The Vera Micheles Dean Papers in the Schlesinger Library, Radcliffe College, contain an outline for an autobiography with an introduction by her son, sparse correspondence, and her mother's autobiography, which provides insight into the early years in Russia. The library also has a clippings file on Dean. Among Dean's most noted books are *The Four Cornerstones of Peace* (1946), *Russia: Menace or Promise* (1947), and *The Nature of the Non-Western World* (1957). The publications of the FPA, particularly the *Foreign Policy Bulletin, Foreign Policy Reports,* and the Headline Series of books, contain the bulk of her writings. Biographical sketches can be found in *Current Biog.,* 1943, and an obituary in the *N.Y. Times,* Oct. 12, 1972. William Dean provided additional information. Death certificate supplied by N.Y. City Dept. of Health.]

ROBERTA J. MILLIGAN

DE BURGOS, Julia. *See* BURGOS, Julia de.

DELORIA, Ella Cara, Jan. 30, 1888–Feb. 12, 1971. Linguist, anthropologist.

Ella Deloria, a Dakota (Sioux) Indian who devoted her life to the study of her people's language and culture, was born on the Yankton Indian Reservation, near the present town of Lake Andes, S. Dak. The first of four children and elder daughter of Philip Joseph and Mary (Sully) Deloria, she also received the name Anpetu Waśte Win, "Beautiful Day Woman," in commemoration of the blizzard that raged the day of her birth. Her father was a Yankton Dakota whose Indian name was Tipi Sapa, "Black Lodge." His grandfather was a Frenchman named Des Lauriers who had married a Yankton woman. Ella's mother was of mixed Yankton and Irish ancestry, the granddaughter of the artist Thomas Sully. Both parents had children by previous marriages. Philip Deloria, a convert to Christianity who had been ordained an Episcopal minister, was in charge of St. Elizabeth's Mission, which he had founded in 1885 at Wakpala, S. Dak., on the Standing Rock Reservation.

Ella Deloria was raised on the reservation and attended the mission school until age fourteen. She continued her education at All Saints, an Episcopal school in Sioux Falls, S. Dak. Winning a college scholarship, she studied from 1911 until 1913 at Oberlin College in Ohio, then transferred to Teachers College, Columbia University, where she received her B.S. in 1915. That year she began teaching at All Saints. In 1923 she went to Haskell Indian School in Lawrence, Kans., as a teacher of physical education and dancing.

Deloria had a deep intellectual interest in her native Dakota language and in the traditional Indian culture. While at Columbia she had attracted the attention of Franz Boas, the dean of American anthropologists and leader in the study of Native American languages. In 1927 he proposed that she work seriously on Dakota linguistics and offered her minimal financial support. She resigned her teaching position to devote herself to scholarly study of the Dakota, working with Boas until his death in 1942, and with RUTH BENEDICT until her death in 1948. Deloria did field research whenever possible, returning periodically to New York to assist Boas in preparing translations and publications, including *Dakota Grammar* (1941), which they coauthored. During this period, she traveled to the various Dakota reservations to interview elders on traditional culture and all other aspects of Dakota life. She sent this information, with translations, to Boas and Benedict. In 1932, Deloria published *Dakota Texts*, a compilation of the myths and tales she collected on her journeys.

Her correspondence with Boas, who repeatedly urged her to return to Columbia, reflects a continuing conflict between Deloria's commitment to her work and her deeply felt sense of obligation to her family. She cared for her father during a long illness, and helped to support her sister, Mary Susan, with whom she lived for much of her life. Mary Susan, an artist known professionally as Mary Sully, did the artwork for Deloria's 1944 book, *Speaking of Indians,* a popular account of the traditional Dakota way of life. Deloria was supported by small research grants, the proceeds from speaking engagements, writing and consulting work, and the generosity of friends.

Through her sixties and seventies, Ella Deloria continued her Dakota research, always hampered by monetary difficulties and other demands on her time. From 1955 to 1958 she returned to St. Elizabeth's to take charge of the mission school. Later she worked briefly for the Sioux Indian Museum in Rapid City and served as assistant director of the W. H. Over Museum at the University of South Dakota. Between 1962 and 1966 she was supported by a National Science Foundation grant to that university's Institute of Indian Studies.

During these later years she worked under many disadvantages. Her constant traveling had taken its toll in lost notes and manuscripts. Without Deloria's knowledge, her earlier manuscripts were transferred by Columbia to the American Philosophical Society Library in Philadelphia. She learned of their location near the end of her life but never had the opportunity to work with them again. Without stable economic support, she was never able to organize her scattered materials and prepare them for publication. She suffered a stroke in 1970 and died the next year in Tripp, S. Dak., of a pulmonary embolus.

Ella Deloria's studies provide some of the best material ever recorded on Dakota culture and are the fullest accounts in the native language. Her work is also unique in emphasizing an understanding of the culture from the woman's perspective, a perspective lacking in most studies of Native American peoples. Her research had three main goals: first, to edit and translate a series of linguistic texts that had been written or dictated by various Indians in the Dakota language; second, to provide a thorough description of traditional Dakota social and religious life; third, to produce a definitive dictionary and grammar. Deloria was a perfectionist who worked slowly and cautiously, rewriting many times and attempting to be as completely objective as possible. As a result she published relatively little, but her work is invaluable.

Ella Deloria was a scholar through and through, yet she never let her dedication to scholarship overcome her sense of responsibility as a Dakota woman, with family concerns taking precedence over her work. Nor did she ever lose her deep faith in Christianity. She was a warm and gracious human being whose kindness and personality were inspirational. Her constant goal was to be an interpreter of an Indian reality to other peoples. Her studies of the Dakota remain as a monument to her talent and industry.

[Thousands of pages of texts, translations, and notes are preserved among Ella Deloria's papers in the Amer. Phil. Soc. Library, which also holds the Deloria-Boas correspondence, and in the Inst. of Indian Studies, Univ. of S. Dak. A bibliography and the fullest account of Deloria's life and career are in Janette K. Murray, "Ella Deloria: A Biographical Sketch and Literary Analysis" (Ph.D. diss., Univ. of N. Dak., 1974). For information on the Deloria family see Sarah Emelia Olden, *The People of Tipi Sapa* (1918). A brief biographical sketch with a portrait appears in Marion E. Gridley, ed., *Indians of Today* (1947; 2d ed. 1971). This article is based in part on interviews with Ella Deloria in 1970 and on correspondence with her brother Vine V. Deloria. A death record was provided by S. Dak. Dept. of Health.]

RAYMOND J. DEMALLIE

DENSMORE, Frances Theresa, May 21, 1867– June 5, 1957. Ethnomusicologist.

Frances Densmore's singular accomplishment was recording on nearly 2,500 wax cylinders the songs of Native Americans at a time when their culture was in rapid decline. Thus she preserved a vital though still relatively neglected segment of North American cultural history. No other collector of American Indian music has been so prolific, no student more productive of scholarly publications based upon such recordings.

Densmore was born in Red Wing, Minn., the elder of two daughters of Benjamin and Sarah (Greenland) Densmore. The family was prominent: her paternal grandfather was a judge and amateur scientist; her father, a civil engineer. Her formal education in music began in childhood with keyboard and harmonic studies at home. This training was both thorough and comprehensive—"Spartan in its severity," as she later observed. At seventeen Densmore entered Oberlin Conservatory of Music, where she studied for three years. (Forty years later, Oberlin awarded her an honorary A.M. degree.) In 1889–90 she sought out the best music

teachers in Boston for private instruction. By the age of thirty-five she had taught piano, served as church organist, trained a boys' choir, lectured on Richard Wagner's operas, and published an account of Felix Mendelssohn's boyhood.

Densmore's first encounter with American Indian music had been as a child in Red Wing, when at night she heard the distant singing of the Sioux. Her initial reaction was curiosity; the music held appeal only as a novelty. Upon closer exposure to Indian song and dance at the Chicago World's Fair in 1893, she remarked that she "heard them yell, and was scared almost to death." But she became genuinely interested after reading *A Study of Omaha Music* (1893) by ALICE CUNNINGHAM FLETCHER, a pioneer in the study of American Indian music and in the use of sound recordings in the field. Fletcher came to be a model for Densmore, offering encouragement and permitting the use of her Omaha songs in one of Densmore's piano lectures.

Densmore's success in lecturing on Indian music eventually led her into field work and publication in the new discipline of ethnomusicology, at the time as yet unnamed. Since she had little to guide her, Densmore developed her own methods. Seeking original material for her studies and for lectures, she began to explore the music of the Minnesota tribes. Her first field trip was to a Chippewa (Ojibwa) village near the Canadian border in 1905. Accompanied by her sister, Margaret, who became her lifelong traveling companion, Densmore visited Little Spruce, who enacted for her a private religious ceremony. Drawing on notes entered in her diary, Densmore subsequently published her observations of the event in the *American Anthropologist* (April-June 1907). The following year, she found her first real informants in two Sioux women, who dictated songs for her while she transcribed them in musical notation.

Soon realizing the inadequacy of transcriptions alone ("nothing is lost so irrevocably as the sound of a song"), Densmore began in 1907 to record the music. With a borrowed phonograph in a music store near the White Earth Reservation in northern Minnesota, she persuaded Big Bear to fill twelve cylinders with his songs, thus launching her career. Because she feared that traditional Indian music would soon be lost, she appealed to the Smithsonian Institution's Bureau of American Ethnology for assistance. Densmore was particularly concerned that the oldest singers be recorded before they died. With the Bureau's initial allotment in 1907 of $150 for the study of American Indian music, she purchased an Edison Home phonograph to continue her work among the Chippewa. Thus began her fifty-year association with the Bureau, which granted her a yearly stipend and gave her the title of collaborator.

Densmore's monographs, based on the recordings, were incorporated into the Bureau's bulletin series. As the scope of her field work expanded, the study of one tribe would overlap with that of another. By the time *Chippewa Music–II* (Bulletin 53) was published in 1913, Densmore had completed three studies of Teton Sioux music and had begun collecting Mandan and Hidatsa songs in North Dakota. By 1954—at age eighty-seven still collecting Seminole music and lecturing in Florida—Densmore had recorded songs from more than thirty tribes.

Although her work required extensive travel, Densmore maintained a lifelong residence in Red Wing. She died in a hospital there of bronchopneumonia shortly after her ninetieth birthday.

Densmore's energy and perseverance were remarkable. For a middle-aged, single woman to venture into the wilderness was surely viewed as unorthodox in her day. Furthermore, field recording at the time was not easy. The equipment was heavy, cumbersome, and often unreliable, and her "recording studios" were improvised in whatever space was available—a Red Cross supply shack, a vacant jail cell, or a mice-ridden coal shed. When the places where she wanted to do field work were inaccessible by car, she would travel by boat or even by birchbark canoe.

Taking advantage of scientific techniques of studying music, Densmore constantly strove for accuracy in her data. She devised new experiments, such as recording the same Omaha singers Fletcher had recorded fifty years earlier to determine what changes their songs had undergone. She also submitted her melodies to recent inventions in phonophotography. As an amateur photographer, Densmore documented many of the events she attended and the singers who performed at them, as well as musical instruments and other artifacts.

Frances Densmore's work reflected her traditional western musical training and beliefs. Yet she explored some of the ways in which Indian music differed from western music. She was also aware that her data would be subject to new interpretation, and, writing in the 1941 *Smithsonian Annual Report*, she modestly assessed her purpose: "Other students, scanning the material, may reach other conclusions. My work has been to preserve the past, record observations in the present, and open the way for the work of others in the future."

[Densmore's papers are held by the Nat. Anthro-pological Archives (Smithsonian Institution) and the Music Div. of the Library of Congress. Her largest and most valuable studies were *Chippewa Music* (1910) and its companion volume, *Chippewa Music–II* (1913), and *Teton Sioux Music* (1918), Bulletins 45, 53, and 61 of the Bureau of Am. Ethnology. *Chippewa Customs*, originally published in 1929, was reprinted in 1979 by the Minn. Hist. Soc. Her own summary of her career is in "The Study of Indian Music," *Smithsonian Annual Report for 1941*, pp. 527–50. Several of her recordings are available from the Laboratory Services, Library of Congress, the repository for most of her original cylinders. The most comprehensive treatment of Densmore is Charles Hofmann, ed., *Frances Densmore and American Indian Music*, Contributions from the Museum of the Am. Indian, Heye Foundation, vol. XXIII (1968), which contains a complete bibliography, chronology of Densmore's life, excerpts from her correspondence and diaries, several of her most important articles, unpublished poems, photographs, and annotated Bureau of Am. Ethnology Reports outlining the progress of her work. See also Nina M. Archabal, "Frances Densmore, Pioneer in the Study of American Indian Music," in *Women of Minnesota* (1977), pp. 94–115. For a critique of her early procedures and findings see the introduction by Thomas Vennum, Jr., to Frances Densmore, *Chippewa Music* (1973 reprint of Bulletins 45 and 53). An obituary appeared in the *N.Y. Times*, June 7, 1957; a "Memorial to Frances Densmore" by Gertrude P. Kurath appeared in *Ethnomusicology*, May 1958. Death record supplied by Minn. Dept. of Health.]

THOMAS VENNUM, JR.

DEREN, Maya, April 29, 1917–Oct. 13, 1961. Filmmaker.

Maya Deren, a major figure in the history of avant-garde film in the United States, was born Eleanora Derenkowsky in Kiev, Russia. Before emigrating to the United States in 1922, her father, Solomon Derenkowsky, had served as a captain in the Russian medical corps, and her mother, Marie (Fiedler) Derenkowsky, had received a rigorous education at an arts conservatory in Kiev. The family settled in Syracuse, N.Y., and soon shortened their name. After completing a second medical training in the United States, Solomon Deren became first assistant physician at the Syracuse State School for Mentally Defective Children and a lecturer in mental hygiene at Syracuse University, while Marie Deren taught. She encouraged her only child to pursue a broad education; to that end, Eleanora Deren attended L'École Internationale in Geneva, Switzerland. Subsequently, she attended Syracuse University (1933–35), New York University (A.B. 1936), and the New School for Social Research (1937–38). In 1939 she received an A.M. in literature from Smith College.

During the 1930s Deren, like many of her contemporaries, became interested in socialism. She was a member of the Young People's Socialist League, serving in 1936 as national student secretary, and she wrote for various left-wing periodicals. In 1935 she married fellow student Gregory Bardacke, who was also a labor organizer; they were divorced three years later.

In 1940 Deren, drawing on her literary training and her extensive interest in dance, proposed to Katherine Dunham that they collaborate on a young people's book about the origins of dance movement. The book never materialized but Deren became Dunham's personal secretary and accompanied her on a national tour of *Cabin in the Sky* (1940–41), ending in California. Deren's research on dance resulted in her first article, "Religious Possession in Dancing"; focusing on Haitian culture, which was to be a lifelong interest, it was published in *Educational Dance* in 1942. That year she married Czech cinematographer Alexander Hammid whom she had met in California. Although the marriage ended in divorce five years later, Deren acknowledged her debt to Hammid for teaching her "the mechanics of film expression and . . . the principle of infinite pains."

In 1943, Deren and Hammid produced *Meshes of the Afternoon,* probably the most widely known of her films. (It was during this time that Deren began to use Maya as a first name.) After completing the film, Deren returned to New York City and began her first independent attempt to produce a film. Made at the surrealist Art of This Century Gallery, *Witch's Cradle* (1943), featuring Marcel Duchamp and Pajarito Matta, was left incomplete. According to Deren's program notes, it was intended to compare the surrealists' defiance of time and space with that of medieval magicians and witches.

Deren's next film, *At Land* (1944), was her most experimental up to that time. In contrast to *Meshes,* it is an outdoor film, a series of disquieting encounters with objects in landscape, intended to reveal "the hidden dynamic of the external world" (Deren, *Film Culture*). In 1945 she made *Study in Choreography for Camera.* Focusing on a dancer, played by Talley Beatty, it was considered a pioneering work in cinedance. *Ritual in Transfigured Time* (1946) shows the passage of a woman from widow to bride; like *Meshes* and *At Land,* it uses Deren herself as a protagonist. *Ritual* has been seen as both an attempt to construct a myth for contemporary times and a film about the nature of artistic creativity.

The year 1946 was Deren's most fruitful. Early in the year she arranged the first presentation of independent art film ever held in the United States, showing *Meshes, At Land,* and *Choreography* under the title of "Three Abandoned Films" at the Provincetown Playhouse in Greenwich Village. Later that year she received a Guggenheim fellowship for "creative work in the field of motion pictures." And, in the autumn, she published her major theoretical treatise, *An Anagram of Ideas on Art, Form and Film.*

The following summer Deren became the first woman—and the first American—to receive the Cannes Grand Prix Internationale for Avant-Garde Film, awarded in the sixteen millimeter category for her first four films. That fall she made her first, long-awaited trip to Haiti (World War II had prevented her going earlier) to view firsthand the island's voudoun culture. The film she began there was never completed, although she shot extensive footage of dances and rituals and taped hours of music. Her book, *Divine Horsemen: The Living Gods of Haiti,* was published in 1953 and soon received international acclaim.

During her several years of travel between Haiti and New York Deren also produced *Meditation on Violence* (1948), a film based on three types of Chinese martial arts, and began work on what would be her last completed film, *The Very Eye of Night.* With choreography by Antony Tudor danced by members of the Metropolitan Opera Ballet School, the film concerns the process of ritual metamorphosis. Deren had begun the film in 1951 under the title "Ensemble for Somnambulists"; it was completed in 1954 but not released in the United States until 1959. Soon after the film's 1955 premiere in Haiti, Deren confided that *Very Eye* had "taken me out in space about as far as I can go . . . there truly seems no place to go from here" (*Film Culture,* p. 31).

Throughout her career Deren wrote, taught, lectured, and traveled in her unceasing advocacy of film as art. In 1955 she founded the Creative Film Foundation to "help other independent filmmakers obtain recognition and funding for their works." Maya Deren died in 1961 from a stroke at the St. Albans Naval Hospital in Queens, N.Y.; she was survived by her third husband, composer Teiji Ito, whom she had married in 1960 and with whom she had collaborated since the mid-1950s. At her death, she left several projects unfinished; most noteworthy was a film adaptation of the poetic form, the haiku, on which she had worked since 1959.

As American experimental film gained national and international stature, Deren's reputation also grew. Her energy and sense of commitment were extraordinary, and she was remembered by fellow filmmakers as, in James Broughton's words, "the mother of us all."

[Maya Deren's papers, including photographs, sound tapes, and miscellaneous material, are located in Special Collections, Mugar Library, Boston Univ. Her completed films and related film material are housed at the Anthology Film Archives, N.Y. City. Material on Deren's early family history supplied by Syracuse Univ. Archives. The film community she worked hard to organize honored her with a memorial issue of *Filmwise*, no. 2 (1962), ed. P. Adams Sitney; a selection of her own writings, including a complete reprint of *Anagram*, and a bibliography of articles and reviews by and about her, was published in *Film Culture*, no. 39 (1965). A bibliography of Deren's writings is also included in Rosemary Kowalski, comp., *Women in Film* (1976). Deren is mentioned in almost all texts on American experimental or avant-garde cinema; however, extended discussions of her work are rare and no published monograph yet exists. The most useful sources are Jeanne Betancourt, *Women in Focus* (1974); P. A. Sitney, *Visionary Film*, 2d ed. (1979); S. Grossmann and M. Bronstein, "Zu Maya Derens Filmarbeit; analyse von Ritual in Transfigured Time," *Frauen und Film*, Winter 1976–77; Raffaele Milani, "Maya Deren, il tempo trasfigurato," *Filmcritica*, Sept. 1975; Am. Federation of Arts, *A History of American Avant-Garde Cinema* (1976); Sheldon Renan, *An Introduction to the American Underground Film* (1967); and Liz-Anne Bawden, ed., *Oxford Companion to Film* (1976). A discussion of Deren's work with dance is included in *Dance Perspectives*, Summer 1967. Obituaries appeared in the *N.Y. Times*, Oct. 14, 1961, and *Village Voice*, Oct. 19, 1961. Assistance in research was provided by a biobibliography by Ashley Kerst, and by VeVe A. Clark, Millicent Hodson, Catrina Neiman, and Francine Bailey, eds., the Legend of Maya Deren Project, who are preparing a three-volume documentary biography to be published in three special issues of *Film Culture* beginning in 1980.]

WANDA BERSHEN

DEWSON, Mary Williams, Feb. 18, 1874–Oct. 21, 1962. Social worker, reformer, suffragist, Democratic party official.

Mary Dewson, generally known as Molly, was born in Quincy, Mass., the youngest of the four sons and two daughters of Edward Henry and Elizabeth Weld (Williams) Dewson. Her grandfather Francis Dewson was an English sea captain who married into an old New England family. Her father became a leather merchant in partnership with his future father-in-law but never prospered because of chronic stomach trouble which made him an invalid. His family had to practice strict economy but lived comfortably. Elizabeth Dewson, who came from an old and well-to-do New England family and had no formal education, was the backbone of the

family because of her husband's poor health. Her one interest outside the home was the Unitarian church. Molly Dewson always remembered the happiness her mother found in being wife and mother. From her father, who read widely, Dewson acquired a strong interest in history and government.

Other influences on Dewson as she grew up included a number of female relatives and neighbors—especially her aunt Elizabeth Cabot Putnam, a leader in prison reform—whose idealism found more public expression than her mother's. Among her childhood playmates, mainly her four brothers and numerous boy cousins, she was a natural leader. In school she was pitcher on the boys' baseball team; she also became an excellent tennis player, winning local tournaments.

Dewson began her education at Miss French's School in Quincy from 1880 until 1889. She then attended Miss Ireland's School in Boston for two years and Dana Hall School in Wellesley for two more. There she developed a close friendship with the school's founder and principal, Julia Eastman, who did much to strengthen her desire to go to college. Entering Wellesley College in 1893, Dewson pursued her studies with her usual intensity. She was inspired by professors such as KATHARINE COMAN and EMILY GREENE BALCH who related economics, history, and sociology to the emerging problems of industrial America. As senior class president, she showed great ability to plan and organize; the class prophecy predicted she would be elected president of the United States.

Graduating with an A.B. in 1897, Dewson accepted a job as full-time secretary of the Domestic Reform Committee of the Women's Educational and Industrial Union, the largest and most influential of the women's social and reform clubs in Boston. The invitation came from ELIZABETH GLENDOWER EVANS, chairman of the committee, which was charged with finding ways to professionalize housework. The objectives were to provide working women a more attractive and better paying alternative to factory work and to free middle-class women to pursue careers and activities outside the home. To these ends, Dewson conducted statistical studies of the home (on the basis of which she published three articles), reorganized the Union's employment office for domestics, formed social clubs for them, and taught at a school of housekeeping organized by ELLEN RICHARDS. In connection with the course she published her *Twentieth Century Expense Book* (1899) as an aid to women in purchasing household goods and budgeting expenses. The Union's optimism never left Dewson, who always saw reformed households and a science of consumption as keys to a better society.

In 1900 Elizabeth Glendower Evans and Elizabeth Putnam persuaded Dewson to set up and become superintendent of the parole department of the Massachusetts State Industrial School for Girls. Under Dewson the department began to keep careful records of all offenders in order to develop a better understanding of the problems of female delinquency and crime and to aid in rehabilitation. Dewson also applied to penal reform many of the evolving techniques of modern social work, such as individualized care outside state institutions, in-depth investigation of the social and psychological aspects of each ward's problems, and close and continual contact between the social worker and the ward and her family. She wrote several articles on her work and presented a paper, "The Delinquent Girl on Parole," at the National Conference of Charities and Correction in 1911.

Although Dewson did not leave her probation work until May 1912, Evans had already brought her into the minimum wage movement in 1911. Under the leadership of FLORENCE KELLEY and the National Consumers' League, Massachusetts reform organizations had successfully lobbied the state legislature to set up a minimum wage investigating commission. Evans supported Dewson's appointment as the commission's executive secretary, in charge of planning and carrying out a statistical study of wages of women and children in the state. The commission's report became the basis for the minimum wage act passed in 1912, the first in modern industrial America.

The report brought Dewson national recognition among reformers as the preeminent authority on minimum wage legislation; it also resulted in several job offers. Dewson declined these, feeling the need for a rest and suffering from depression as a result of the death of her mother, with whom she had lived in the family's Quincy home since graduating from college. In 1913 she and her old friend Mary G. Porter settled down to run a small dairy farm near Worcester, Mass. Dewson shared a home with Porter for the rest of her life.

After two years of country living, however, Dewson, who had come to believe that woman suffrage would promote social justice legislation, was drawn into the Massachusetts suffrage movement. Becoming active in suffrage work in Worcester County during the state suffrage referendum campaign of 1915, she soon was chairman of the county suffrage organization and a member of the state association's executive board. After the failure of the 1915 campaign, Dewson also became leader of the state associa-

tion. During World War I, like many other American social workers, Dewson went to Europe to aid in the war effort. From 1917 to 1919 she was in France with the American Red Cross's Bureau of Refugees, becoming chief of its Mediterranean Zone.

After the war Florence Kelley made Dewson her chief assistant in the National Consumers' League drive for state minimum wage laws for women and children. Dewson's most notable work in the campaign was compiling and writing up the factual parts of the briefs which Felix Frankfurter, the League's lawyer, used to defend the California and District of Columbia minimum wage laws before the courts. Adverse court decisions and public apathy, however, led her to conclude that a national minimum wage crusade was hopeless. In 1924 she resigned her position, over Kelley's strong objections, to concentrate her reform energies in New York state. As president of the New York Consumers' League between 1925 and 1931, Molly Dewson quickly became the leader of the lobbying effort of the Women's Joint Legislative Conference, a coalition of organizations including the Consumers' League and the Women's Trade Union League. She played a central part in the passage of a 1930 New York law limiting the working hours of women to forty-eight a week.

Impressed by the willingness of New York Democratic party leaders to respond to the reform efforts initiated by women, Molly Dewson came to believe that she could most effectively further the passage of social justice legislation by helping to strengthen women's activities within the Democratic party. At ELEANOR ROOSEVELT's request, Dewson agreed to organize Democratic women in Alfred E. Smith's presidential campaign of 1928. She performed the same office for Franklin D. Roosevelt in his 1930 gubernatorial campaign and in his successful bid for the presidency two years later.

Eleanor Roosevelt and Molly Dewson extended their close political collaboration to the national scene during Franklin Roosevelt's presidency. In 1933 Eleanor Roosevelt used her influence to secure Dewson a position in the Women's Division of the Democratic National Committee. Dewson agreed to reorganize the Division to try to create within the Democratic party a nationwide group of party workers similar to the one which had sustained the reform efforts in New York.

As a first step, Dewson concentrated on finding government jobs for women party workers. Although she hated patronage as a symbol of the kind of politics she wished to supplant, she thought it necessary to find jobs for women in order to motivate party members and to demonstrate to would-be recruits that the Division was taken seriously by the party hierarchy and by the administration. Dewson managed to win important jobs for key women party workers in most states, more than any other administration had given to women. Her quietly organized campaign is generally credited with securing the appointment of FRANCES PERKINS as secretary of labor. With Eleanor Roosevelt's behind-the-scenes support, she also secured high-level appointments for many women in New Deal agencies, especially the Social Security Administration and the National Recovery Administration. With the motivation more of a reformer than a feminist—she opposed the equal rights amendment because she feared it would undo protective legislation for women—Dewson promoted women in politics because she believed they had a special sensitivity to human welfare that was badly needed in public life.

In early 1934 Dewson began to push for the passage of state laws or state party rulings to provide for fifty-fifty representation of women in membership and in leadership positions on all party committees from the precinct level on up. The same year she launched the Reporter Plan, a national program to train women campaign workers to understand and explain New Deal programs. The Plan was an attempt to make the party more attractive to issue-oriented citizens of both sexes, thereby transforming politics into a debate on issues and ensuring victory at the polls for a reform-minded Democratic party. To establish the Reporter Plan Dewson persuaded President Roosevelt in 1934 to allocate Democratic National Committee funds for a between-elections headquarters for the Women's Division with a paid director, occasional field organizers, and its own publication, the monthly *Democratic Digest*. In 1935 the Women's Division began to hold regional conferences to show Democratic women how to carry on the Reporter Plan as well as more traditional campaign work. On the eve of the 1936 presidential election, Democratic women trained by the Women's Division were better prepared for the campaign than any other group organized by the party. The campaign literature prepared by Dewson and her division, the so-called Rainbow Fliers, made up a large proportion of all campaign literature issued in 1936 by the Democratic National Committee.

After the 1936 election Dewson gave up everyday leadership of the Women's Division because of heart trouble, but until about 1941 she was responsible for the appointment of its directors and was available with eagerly sought advice. She occasionally used her considerable influence within the party and administration to ensure financial and patronage support for the Women's Division.

During the 1930s Dewson was the decisive force in bringing many women into Democratic party politics, especially in the middle levels of party leadership, and in increasing their political leverage within the party. Under her leadership, the number of women campaign workers increased to 73,000 by 1936 and to 109,000 by 1940. Her success in mobilizing women derived not only from her high seriousness as a reformer but also from complete self-confidence in her ability to lead. While communicating a sense of deep dedication, she was decidedly not stuffy. Her talk was unusually direct and often irreverent, and her vivid and forceful expression came across as well in her writing as in her speech. She worked easily and effectively with men as well as women and was respected by many seasoned politicians. One of her major victories came in 1936 when she persuaded Democratic party leaders to draw up a new party rule providing for an alternate as well as a regular member from each state on the Platform Committee and specifying that one of each pair be male and one female.

Dewson's influence extended beyond the realm of the Women's Division. Combining the weight of her national political position with her reformer's zeal, she was instrumental in gaining passage of a New York unemployment insurance act in 1935 and in securing minimum wage laws in Ohio and Illinois. She was a member of the President's Commission on Economic Security, which did much to shape the Social Security Act of 1935, and served Frances Perkins as an official industrial consultant. Dewson's greatest contribution to New Deal labor and welfare legislation came when, in August 1937, President Roosevelt nominated and the Senate confirmed her as a member of the Social Security Board. The Board was bogged down in its dealings with Congress and in its attempts to establish workable relationships with the states; Dewson did much to encourage the establishment of effective systems of federal-state cooperation in the administration of unemployment and old age assistance programs and to achieve better relations with Congress. These accomplishments, as well as her keen intelligence and irrepressible sense of humor, helped to raise the morale of the Board.

Dewson resigned from the Social Security Board in 1938 because of continued ill health, which kept her in semiretirement for the rest of her life. The women's activities she developed in the 1930s failed to maintain their momentum after 1940 due to Franklin Roosevelt's deemphasis of partisan politics during World War II and the shifting of Eleanor Roosevelt's interests away from the Women's Division, as well as Dewson's diminished involvement. In her retirement Dewson shared a home in Castine, Maine, with Mary Porter. She acted as elder stateswoman to the Women's Division of the Democratic National Committee and to the Democratic party of Maine, becoming vice president of the state's Democratic Advisory Committee in 1954. She died in Castine of bronchopneumonia following a stroke in 1962.

[The principal source is the Mary W. Dewson Papers at the Schlesinger Library, Radcliffe College, which contain two volumes of autobiography covering the years 1928–40. The Elizabeth Glendower Evans and Sue Shelton White Papers, also at the Schlesinger Library, have additional information. The basic sources for her Democratic party activities are in the Franklin D. Roosevelt Library, Hyde Park, N.Y., especially the Mary W. Dewson Papers, including the indispensable Dewson letterbooks; the massive collection of papers of the Women's Division of the Democratic Nat. Committee, which contain many valuable Dewson letters, especially in the state correspondence; the Eleanor Roosevelt Papers; the Louis M. Howe Papers; and President Roosevelt's official and personal files. Published articles by Dewson are in her papers at the Schlesinger and Roosevelt Libraries. Revealing books by people who knew her well are Eleanor Roosevelt and Lorena Hickok, *Ladies of Courage* (1954), and Bess Furman, *Washington By-line* (1949). The N.Y. State Democratic party's women's division publication, *Women's Democratic News*, May 1925–Dec. 1930, reports on the work of Dewson and other women party members in N.Y. The *Democratic Digest*, Nov. 1933–Dec. 1940, documents the development of the Dewson program for the Women's Division of the Democratic Nat. Committee. Secondary sources containing information about her work for industrial legislation are James T. Patterson, "Mary Dewson and the American Minimum Wage Movement," *Labor Hist.*, Spring 1964, pp. 134–52, and Clarke A. Chambers, *Seedtime of Reform* (1963). Susan Ware, "Political Sisterhood in the New Deal: Women in Politics and Government, 1933–1940" (Ph.D. diss., Harvard Univ., 1978), covers Dewson's career in the 1930s. Secondary works which mainly concern her political achievements are Arthur M. Schlesinger, Jr., *The Politics of Upheaval* (1960); Joseph P. Lash, *Eleanor and Franklin* (1971); William Henry Chafe, *The American Woman* (1972); and George Martin, *Madam Secretary: Frances Perkins* (1976). For background on earlier efforts of women in American politics see Paul C. Taylor, "The Entrance of Women into Party Politics: the 1920's" (Ph.D. diss., Harvard Univ., 1966). An obituary appeared in the *N.Y. Times*, Oct. 25, 1962. Additional information for this article was provided by interviews with Dewson, Oct. 16 and 17, 1961, and with May Thompson Evans and Dorothy S. McAllister. Death certificate supplied by Maine Dept. of Health and Welfare.]

PAUL C. TAYLOR

DICK, Gladys Rowena Henry, Dec. 18, 1881– Aug. 21, 1963. Microbiologist, physician.

Gladys Henry Dick was born in Pawnee City, Neb., the second daughter and youngest of three children of William Chester and Azelia Henrietta (Edson) Henry. Her father, who had been a cavalry officer during the Civil War, raised carriage horses and was also a grain dealer and banker. Shortly after Gladys's birth the family moved to Lincoln, presumably for the children's education. She attended the public schools there, and obtained her B.S. from the University of Nebraska in 1900. She hoped to attend medical school, but her mother initially opposed the idea. For a year Gladys Henry taught high school biology in Carney, Neb.; she also took graduate courses, mainly in zoology, at the University of Nebraska (1900–02). In 1903, having won out, she left for Baltimore to attend the Johns Hopkins University School of Medicine.

Though Hopkins admitted female students it provided no residences. Gladys Henry early demonstrated her independence and business acumen by organizing the women to buy their own house. She received her M.D. in 1907 and remained at Hopkins as an intern and house staff member. She also took a requisite year of foreign postgraduate training in Berlin. These years marked her introduction to biomedical research, and she engaged in studies on experimental cardiac surgery and blood chemistry with such then and future luminaries of American medicine as Harvey Cushing, W. G. MacCallum, and Milton Winternitz.

In 1911 Gladys Henry moved to Chicago, where her mother had settled. At the University of Chicago she worked on kidney pathochemistry with H. Gideon Wells and on the etiology of scarlet fever with George Frederick Dick (1881–1967). She and Dick were married on Jan. 28, 1914. After an extended honeymoon in Egypt and the Balkans they settled in Evanston, Ill., where she practiced medicine and served as a pathologist to the Evanston Hospital. Later in 1914 she joined her husband as a member of Chicago's John R. McCormick Memorial Institute for Infectious Diseases, which had been founded by EDITH ROCKEFELLER MCCORMICK and her husband after their son's death from scarlet fever in 1901. Gladys Dick remained at the Institute until her retirement in 1953. During World War I she also served as a United States Public Health Service bacteriologist and replaced her husband on the staff of St. Luke's Hospital in Chicago.

Gladys and George Dick, working closely together, made enduring contributions to the prevention and treatment of scarlet fever. The disease, then endemic to North America and Europe, principally struck children, causing crippling complications and up to 25 percent mortality. For more than a decade the Dicks attempted to surmount a series of technical difficulties involved in implicating the hemolytic streptococcus as the causative agent of scarlet fever. Finally, on Oct. 6, 1923, they reported producing the experimental disease in two human volunteers who were injected with streptococcal cultures isolated from typical scarlet fever cases. Hemolytic streptococci, previously thought by many investigators to be important secondary invaders, were established as the true cause. Within the year they demonstrated that these bacteria release a toxin which causes the disease's characteristic red rash. The Dicks's isolation of the toxin afforded a foundation for developing a skin test for susceptibility to scarlet fever similar to the Schick test for diphtheria, a method of active immunization by larger doses of toxin, and antitoxin for treatment, prevention, and diagnosis. The skin test, known as the "Dick test," proved most valuable and was rapidly employed across the globe.

The hallmark of the Dicks's research was a systematic, rather than original, approach. Others, notably Gladys Dick's Hopkins classmate A. Raymond Dochez, were working along similar lines. In 1924 and 1926, when the Dicks took the unusual steps of securing United States and United Kingdom patents for their methods of toxin and antitoxin production, criticism developed over the issues of originality and whether or not there was a bona fide invention. Charges of commercialism were forthcoming from the medical presses of both countries and in 1935 the League of Nations health organization claimed that the patent terms restricted research and hampered biological standardization. In their own defense the Dicks asserted, with some justification, that they received no personal gain and only sought to ensure the quality of preparations. In fact, Gladys Dick waged a time-consuming but successful lawsuit during the late 1920s against the Lederle Laboratories for patent infringement and improper toxin manufacture. The advantages of the Dicks's methods of serum manufacture over others were not altogether clear, but the substitution of antibiotics for immunization as the preferred means of treating streptococcal throat infections closed the issue in the 1940s.

The scarlet fever research brought the Dicks wide celebrity. In 1925 they were contenders for the Nobel Prize in medicine, but no prize was awarded that year. They received the Mickle Prize of the University of Toronto (1926), the Cameron Prize of the University of Edinburgh for their work in practical therapeutics (1933), and several honorary degrees.

Gladys Dick had a lifelong interest in child welfare. She was a founder of the Cradle Society in Evanston, reputed to be the first American professional organization for the adoption of children, and served it from 1918 to 1953. When she was forty-nine years old she and her husband themselves adopted two infants, Roger Henry Dick and Rowena Henry Dick. Devoted to her children, she also continued her research, mainly on polio. In addition to her scientific accomplishments, Gladys Dick was an adept businesswoman and avid traveler. The vitality of her early and middle years contrasted with the last decade of her life, when she suffered from a debilitating cerebral arteriosclerosis. The Dicks retired to Palo Alto, Calif., in 1953; ten years later Gladys Dick died of a stroke in nearby Menlo Park.

[The most significant scarlet fever studies coauthored by the Dicks appear in the *Jour. Am. Med. Assoc.*: vol. 81, 1923, pp. 1166–67; vol. 82, 1924, pp. 265–66, 301–02, 544–45, 1246–47; vol. 84, 1925, pp. 802–03; vol. 115, 1940, pp. 2155–56. See also "Scarlet fever" (Cameron Prize lecture), *Edinburgh Med. Jour.*, vol. 41, 1934, pp. 1–13, and *Scarlet Fever* (1938). For details over the patent row see *Jour. Am. Med. Assoc.*, vol. 85, 1925, p. 996 and vol. 88, 1927, pp. 1324, 1341–42; *Am. Jour. Public Health*, vol. 16, 1926, pp. 919–20; *Brit. Med. Jour.* 1, 1927, pp. 479–80, 526, 881–82. Biographical information is scanty, but see *Science News-Letter*, Oct. 22, 1927 (with portrait); *Who Was Who in America*, IV, 248; *Nat. Cyc. Am. Biog.*, LI, 107; obituaries in *Chicago Tribune*, Aug. 23, 1963, and *Jour. Am. Med. Assoc.*, Dec. 28, 1963. On George F. Dick see *Nat. Cyc. Am. Biog.*, LIV, 240, and an obituary in the *N.Y. Times*, Oct. 14, 1967. Excellent surveys of early scarlet fever discoveries are found in: Arthur L. Bloomfield, *A Bibliography of Internal Medicine: Communicable Diseases* (1958), *Stanford Med. Bull.*, vol. 10, 1952, pp. 114–29, and Harry F. Dowling, *Fighting Infection* (1977). For the court opinion which summarizes the issues involved in scarlet fever bacteriology see *Dick et al. v. Lederle Antitoxin Laboratories* (1930). Information was provided by Rowena Dick Kelley. Gladys Dick's transcript is available from the Univ. of Nebraska-Lincoln. Death record provided by Calif. Dept. of Public Health.]

LEWIS P. RUBIN

DICKASON, Gladys Marie, Jan. 28, 1903–Aug. 31, 1971. Labor economist, organizer, and leader.

Gladys Dickason was born in Galena, Oklahoma Territory, the second of four children and younger daughter of Simon Milton and Linnie

(Kellerman) Dickason. Both sides of the family had migrated to America in the eighteenth century, the Dickasons from England to Massachusetts, the Kellermans from Germany to Pennsylvania. In 1904 Gladys's parents moved to Okemah, Indian Territory (which became part of the state of Oklahoma); there Simon Dickason engaged in farming, in stock raising, and later in real estate.

A precocious child, Dickason graduated at the head of her high school class in 1918. After receiving her A.B. from the University of Oklahoma in 1922, she earned an A.M. in economics and political science at Columbia University (1924), taught at the Hamilton Grange School in New York City, briefly attended the London School of Economics, and then joined the economics department at Sweet Briar College in Virginia in 1926. Two years later, Dickason entered, but did not complete, the doctoral program at Columbia, returning to Sweet Briar in 1929, and then becoming an instructor in political science at Hunter College in 1930. Although she always maintained warm ties with her family, Dickason left behind her conservative, evangelical Christian past in these years. Increasingly restless with academic life, she became a friend of Jacob Potofsky, secretary-treasurer of the Amalgamated Clothing Workers of America (ACWA); she took a job with the union in 1933.

After a stint on the industrial committee of the National Recovery Administration's Cotton Garment Code Authority (1933–34), Gladys Dickason was named research director of the ACWA in 1935. She excelled as the union's representative before public bodies, skillfully advocating minimum wage standards for the Fair Labor Standards Act of 1938. Government controls during World War II further increased the importance of her work; industrial statistics gathered by Dickason and her staff provided support for union cases before the War Labor Board, and helped forestall the proliferation of new shops at a time when excess capacity existed in union shops. At the ACWA's 1944 convention, president Sidney Hillman singled out Dickason's work for praise. In 1946 she took part in national negotiations in the cotton-garment industry; she later spearheaded the union's 1948–49 campaign to raise the minimum wage.

From the outset, her union career had taken Dickason into the field. During the 1930s, she participated regularly in organizing drives among cotton-garment workers, mainly the wives and daughters of industrial workers in northern mining and manufacturing areas. Dickason was at her best representing these workers in formal proceedings. Always well-prepared, cool, and resourceful, she was regarded as a formidable opponent by employers and an articulate champion by the female operatives. Appointed a special cotton-garment representative, Dickason in 1937 took charge of the campaign against Cluett, Peabody & Co., the nation's largest shirt manufacturer. Victory in February 1941 established her as a top organizer for the union.

While remaining nominally head of the research department until 1954, after World War II Dickason's interests shifted decisively away from research to organizing. When the CIO launched Operation Dixie in the south in 1946, she became an assistant director of the organizing drive. She also headed the ACWA's southern department. In a decade of unremitting effort, Dickason established a strong union bridgehead among southern clothing workers: roughly 30 percent became covered by collective bargaining during her years of leadership.

Elected a vice president of the ACWA in 1946, Dickason took her place as one of the highest ranking women trade unionists in the country. In addition to serving on a variety of government commissions in Washington and New York in the postwar years, she spent several months in Japan in 1951, sponsored by the United States Army, addressing workers and studying the role of women in the Japanese labor movement. Her report stressed the need to change the repressive attitudes of male trade unionists, and to expand opportunities for Japanese working women to assert themselves. This liberating function was, in fact, as important to Dickason's concept of trade unionism as was the task of ending the economic exploitation of women. Her feminism stopped short of the equal rights amendment, however, which she regarded as a threat to protective legislation. She saw common ground for the women's and labor movements in the struggle against the arbitrary division of people "by race or sex or class, into superiors and inferiors." Both strove for "equal opportunity for all men and women to participate actively in shaping the conditions of their lives" (Annals, pp. 70, 74). In 1951 the National Council of Negro Women honored her for work on behalf of women in the labor movement in Japan and the United States.

A tall, slender, auburn-haired woman, who looked and talked "like a college professor" (Fortune, p. 149), Dickason always seemed something of an anomaly among the Jewish and Italian men who led the Clothing Workers. Yet the union became her life; her energies were absorbed by its campaigns and most of her emotions by the working women of the cotton-garment factories, north and south. In the early 1930s Dickason formed a close attachment to Arthur S. Harrison, a New York building contractor, that lasted throughout her life; they may have been briefly married. Increasingly troubled by ill health during the 1950s, she retired from the ACWA in December 1963. Among the many tributes she received following her death of lung cancer in New York City in August 1971, the ACWA lawyers memorialized her as "a gracious lady" (*N.Y. Times*, Sept. 2, 1971). They could also have said that she was a tough and dedicated fighter for the rights of her working-class sisters.

[The most important source on Dickason's career is the biennial ACWA convention proceedings, which contain useful historical accounts of the union's affairs and Dickason's official reports. Additional materials may be found in the union's archives in N.Y. City. See her "Women in Labor Unions," Am. Acad. of Political and Social Sci., *Annals*, May 1947. There is an excellent likeness and brief assessment of her career in "Ten Who Deliver," *Fortune*, Nov. 1946, p. 149. Obituaries appeared in the *N.Y. Times*, Sept. 1, 1971, and in the ACWA journal, *Advance*, Sept. 17, 1971. Genealogical material, letters, and clippings were provided by her brother Don L. Dickason, and career information by Charles English, for many years Dickason's assistant and then successor in charge of the ACWA Southern Department. Death certificate furnished by N.Y. City Dept. of Health.]

DAVID BRODY

DIDRIKSON, Mildred (Babe). *See* ZAHARIAS, Mildred Ella Didrikson.

DILLER, Angela, Aug. 1, 1877–May 1, 1968. Music educator.

Angela Diller introduced a new approach to music education in America when she systematically sought to blend the study of theory with the study of instrumental technique. She was born Mary Angelina Diller in Brooklyn, N.Y., where she attended the public schools. She was the youngest of four children, two boys and two girls, of Mary Abigail (Welles) and William A. M. Diller. In the environment of the Diller home—her father was a church organist and choir master—she was free to exercise her musical inclinations long before she had any formal training in music. She played by ear, improvising and exploring sounds at the piano by the hour. Her older sister taught her to read music and they played piano duets together. At eight Diller earned German lessons at school by accompanying the children's folk singing in the German classes. By the time she began to study piano with a teacher at twelve, she was already

experimenting in teaching piano to younger children. From fourteen to seventeen, she studied with an "inspiring" piano teacher, Alice Fowler, who introduced her to the great literature for piano.

Diller's first teaching position, shortly after leaving Fowler in 1894, was at the Saint John the Baptist School for Girls, a boarding school in New York. There she was allowed to develop a music curriculum that included a class in musicianship for piano students. For seven years, from 1896 until 1903, she studied harmony, counterpoint, orchestration, composition, and piano with Edward MacDowell at Columbia University, and concurrently was enrolled at Barnard College as a special student in music (1896–1901). In 1899 Angela Diller was the first recipient of the Mosenthal fellowship for musical composition at the university. During this time she continued teaching at the boarding school. She also studied briefly with Johannes Schreyer in Dresden, Germany.

In 1899 Diller joined the staff of the Music School Settlement in New York City, and later became head of the theory department; she remained there until 1916. Founded by Emilie Wagner in 1894 and later directed by David Mannes, this school was intended to provide music education for underprivileged children. Diller became a devoted and inspiring teacher to the hundreds of students, young and old, whom she met at the settlement. There she learned much about "what to teach and how to do it."

At the Music School Settlement Diller and Elizabeth Quaile (1874–1951) became colleagues and lifelong friends. Quaile was largely self-taught, but had studied briefly with Franklin Robinson and Harold Bauer. Diller and Quaile held many musical ideas in common and together began to formulate theories of music education, emphasizing emotional and musical values and yet not minimizing the development of technique. In 1916 both joined the David Mannes School of Music where they taught together for five years—Diller as head of the theory department and Quaile as head of the piano department.

In 1921 they founded the Diller-Quaile School of Music, a school for teaching children and adults and for training teachers. Putting into practice their ideas on pedagogy, they developed a new graded curriculum which emphasized the development of musicianship in a program closely coordinated with the individual instrumental lessons. What the pupils studied in theory class they immediately put to practical use at the lesson: "The door was wide open between the room where a student wrote in counterpoint, and the room where he played a Fugue" (*Music Jour.*, p. 37). Their approach was later widely integrated into the music curriculum of many schools. After administering the Diller-Quaile School for twenty years, until 1941, Diller became a director and taught part-time until the last years of her life, when she became director emeritus.

The school's philosophy of teaching music reached a larger audience through the materials Diller and Quaile published illustrating their approach. During the summer of 1917 Thomas Whitney Surette, whose Concord, Mass., summer school for teachers they attended, urged them to collaborate in the publication of a beginner's piano book based on folk tunes. Thus began a long association resulting in the well-known Diller-Quaile series of teaching materials. Diller also collaborated in publications with Kate Stearns Page, who shared a home with her for many years, and with Harold Bauer. Over forty volumes of music, useful and in good taste, circulated extensively in America and Europe, and were extraordinarily influential in improving music instruction.

In a 1958 interview in *The New Yorker* Angela Diller commented, "I'd rather teach teachers than anyone else." Her lively and sensible approach to teaching was imparted with warmth and love to music educators. During the years 1930 to 1950 she was visiting instructor at various universities and conservatories, and lectured widely in America and Europe. In 1953 Diller received a Guggenheim Foundation award to write *The Splendor of Music*, a volume that reflects a lifetime of teaching experience. It is written wisely and sympathetically for the student, the teacher, and the parent. In addition to her other activities, Diller, together with Margarethe Dessoff, founded the Adesdi Chorus of women's voices in 1924, and in 1929 the A Cappella Chorus of mixed voices; the two later merged into the Dessoff Choirs.

An Episcopalian for most of her life, in her later years Diller became interested in New Thought. During the last twenty years, she fought courageously against hearing difficulties and limited peripheral vision. Yet she remained active as a music educator until shortly before she died of heart failure in Stamford, Conn., in 1968.

[Diller's important published writings include *First Theory Book* (1921); *Keyboard Harmony Course*, Books 1–4 (1936, 1937, 1943, 1949); *Keyboard Music Study*, Books 1 and 2 (1936–37); and *The Splendor of Music* (1957). Biographical material and critical studies are limited to short articles, notices, and reviews in periodicals and newspapers. Diller's "Personal Recollections of a Music Teacher,"

Music Jour., April-May 1958, pp. 36–37, 64, contains a good likeness of her as well as material on Quaile. An interview, "Teachers' Teacher," in the *New Yorker*, Sept. 20, 1958, pp. 33–34, also includes information on the Quaile association. Significant reviews of *The Splendor of Music* are found in *Notes*, Sept. 1958, p. 573, and *Juilliard Rev.*, Winter 1958–59, p. 23. See also Oscar Thompson, ed., *Internat. Cyc. of Music and Musicians* (1975). An obituary appeared in the *N.Y. Times*, May 2, 1968. Death record provided by Conn. Dept. of Public Health. Information was provided by Barbara Diller, her niece, and Dorothy Weeks, a colleague at the Diller-Quaile School.]

ELFRIEDA HIEBERT

DIX, Dorothy. *See* GILMER, Elizabeth Meriwether.

DOCK, Lavinia Lloyd, Feb. 26, 1858–April 17, 1956. Nurse, settlement house worker, suffragist.

Lavinia Dock was born in Harrisburg, Pa., the second daughter and second of the six children of Gilliard and Lavinia Lloyd (Bombaugh) Dock. Both families traced their descent from eighteenth-century Pennsylvania Germans. The parents inherited property in land, from which their five daughters in turn derived comfortable incomes until the great depression. Lavinia Dock, who remembered a happy-go-lucky childhood, had a conventional education at a girls' academy in Harrisburg. Both parents were liberal in their views: "Father had some whimsical masculine prejudices but Mother was broad on all subjects and very tolerant and charitable toward persons."

After her mother's death when Dock was eighteen, she helped her older sister in the care of the younger ones. She was, she later recalled, living "a very free and happy life" when she read in *Century* magazine an article describing the school for nurses at Bellevue Hospital in New York. In 1884 "Vin" went into training at Bellevue, the first American school to follow Florence Nightingale's principles. Dock survived the twelve-hour workday among the sick poor on the wards, learned all she could from the skimpy evening instruction, and graduated in 1886.

With no need to earn a living, she was free to explore. She worked as a visiting nurse among the poor, with the Woman's Mission of the New York City Mission and Tract Society, and then for a ladies' charitable society in Norwich, Conn. During the yellow fever epidemic in Jacksonville, Fla., in 1888, she ran a ward in a temporary hospital under the direction of JANE DELANO, a Bellevue classmate. She rushed to the scene of the Johnstown, Pa., flood the next spring, and met CLARA BARTON. The real beginning of her career came later that year. While serving as night superintendent at Bellevue for six months, she compiled from medical texts the first nurses' manual of drugs. Her brother, George Dock, a medical school professor, gave helpful advice, and her father financed publication in 1890. *Materia Medica for Nurses* remained the standard nursing school text for a generation.

In November 1890 she became assistant superintendent of nurses at the new Johns Hopkins Hospital in Baltimore under ISABEL HAMPTON (ROBB). The serenely forceful Hampton commanded Dock's loyalty at once. Dock took over the first-year classes and much of the ward teaching, making a reputation for her vigorous though fair distribution of praise and rebuke. Among the students was ADELAIDE NUTTING, like Hampton and Dock in her early thirties. The three women were to become preeminent in the coming professionalization of nursing. Hampton was already advocating improvements in education and practice, and the establishment of professional organizations to control standards. At an international conference on hospitals, organized by the Johns Hopkins doctors in Chicago in conjunction with the Chicago World's Fair of 1893, Hampton and Dock were featured speakers. Dock's address called for the separation of medical and nursing spheres of authority. As the meeting ended, Hampton organized the nurse administrators present into an American Society of Superintendents of Training Schools.

Dock stayed in Chicago to become superintendent of the Illinois Training School at the Cook County Hospital, the leading school in the midwest. In her brief two years there, she recognized her deficiencies as an administrator; she candidly recalled in old age that her "principles, aims, and endeavors were right and sound, but I showed no diplomatic skill in personal relations." From Chicago she returned home to Harrisburg, where, after her father's death, she spent a year in charge of the household so that her older sister, Mira Lloyd Dock, could take university training in horticulture. Late in 1896, Lavinia Dock took up residence at the Nurses' Settlement on the Lower East Side in New York City.

The community of women that LILLIAN WALD had created at 265 Henry Street was to be a congenial home for twenty years. "Dockie" became a member of Wald's inner circle. The affectionate mutual support of the Henry Street "family," and Wald's radiant confidence in their power to relieve not only human suffering but also the burdens of poverty, released creative energies. Dock's intellect came into focus with her ingrained humanitarian and libertarian sympathies. Caring for the sick among the immigrant poor was not a new experience, but the settlement nurses were virtually independent practitioners. With sick care went preventive care, health education, and pilot projects like school nursing that could point the way to public assumption of responsibility for society's welfare.

At Henry Street Dock rejected Social Darwinism for the philosophical anarchist Kropotkin's theories of social evolution through mutual aid and cooperation. She was introduced to the Social Reform Club of trade unionists and middle-class sympathizers, and met the eloquent LEONORA O'REILLY. The two women were soon organizing a women's local of the United Garment Workers of America. Each new experience fortified the feminism Dock had absorbed by the time she was twelve from reading "some of the earliest challenges thrown out by defiant women."

The professional organization of nurses remained her central concern. A faithful attender and speaker at meetings, she was Isabel Hampton Robb's chief aide in nurturing the Society of Superintendents in the early years, and its secretary from 1896 to 1901. Her research into the structure of other women's organizations and of the American Medical Association laid the base in 1896 for a general membership group, the Nurses Associated Alumnae, later the American Nurses Association. When Robb and Adelaide Nutting, now superintendent of the Johns Hopkins School, managed to establish a postgraduate course for nurses at Teachers College, Columbia University, Dock was one of the volunteer faculty.

Nurses knew her best, however, as a contributing editor of the *American Journal of Nursing*, established by SOPHIA PALMER in 1900. A tireless writer, she urged nurses to join together and stand on their own feet, while stressing their obligation to be socially useful. Most important, Lavinia Dock brought to the *Journal* an international outlook. A trip to London with Mira Dock in 1899 to attend meetings of the International Council of Women opened a transoceanic world of female amity and cooperation in the cause of public health. Dock joined Ethel Gordon Fenwick, the dynamic organizer of British nursing, in founding the International Council of Nurses (ICN), and was made its secretary.

She now became the communications center of the professional nursing world. In Europe she found the lines more sharply drawn between the professional movement in nursing and the medical and hospital establishments. Through the ICN she urged on the sisters in Europe in their challenge to medical authority, while in the

American Journal of Nursing she conducted a monthly "Foreign Department," reporting the progress of nursing, public health, and social legislation overseas.

Of the elements of professionalism, nursing now lacked only its history. At Johns Hopkins, Dock and Nutting had taken note of the doctors' cultivation of the past. They planned *A History of Nursing* together, and the two volumes published in 1907 bore both names. The research, and the writing of all but two chapters, however, were Dock's. Pointing to historians' neglect of the "usual and homely," she traced the care of the sick from primitive humanity up through the ages. Women's autonomy, she found, had been lost when men took control of health care systems in the seventeenth century, bringing "general contempt" to the nurse and "misery" to the patient until Florence Nightingale came to the rescue. Thoroughly documented, the book conveyed the excitement of Dock's discoveries of women's past in libraries in France and Germany and the United States surgeon general's library in Washington. In 1912 she brought the *History of Nursing* up to date in two additional volumes by recording the experience of her own generation on four continents.

As she approached fifty, Lavinia Dock gave up nursing practice. Professional affairs still claimed some of her time; she helped ADAH THOMS and other black nurses organize a national association. But nursing problems had come to seem only a part of the larger question of women's economic, sexual, and political bondage. An early member of the New York Women's Trade Union League, she walked the picket line in the shirtwaist strike of 1909. In 1913, in a major convention speech, she appealed to the American Nurses Association for understanding of the labor movement and a sense of sisterhood with other working women.

Nurses had taken many local initiatives in the Progressive era's campaign against tuberculosis, but Lavinia Dock was the profession's lone crusader against venereal disease. She allied herself with the physicians who in 1905 launched a voluntary organization to bring the forbidden subject into the open; she was one of the earliest members, only a handful of them women, of the American Society of Sanitary and Moral Prophylaxis. That year she began printing news of action against venereal disease in Europe in the *Journal*'s Foreign Department. Dock rejected "any treatment which would make it hygienically safe for men to continue a brutal misuse of women." Her real target was prostitution, and in 1910 she took a leading part in demonstrations against a state law which leaned toward regulation rather than suppression. In *Hygiene and Morality* (1911), "a manual for nurses and others," she called for abolition of the double standard of morality, for self-control by men, and for suffrage for women.

Lavinia Dock had been arrested for attempting to vote in 1896, but New York's police commissioner, Theodore Roosevelt, refused to put her in jail. The suffrage remedy was laid aside in the glow of hopes for economic reform, but in 1907 she enlisted in the Equality League of Self-Supporting Women, just founded by HARRIOT STANTON BLATCH with a program adapted from the British movement.

Confident hope and the joy of battle carried Dock through the turmoil of the next decade. She ran a suffrage newsstand in front of the Equality League's office and was "shoved about by police" as a pioneer poll watcher. In December 1912 she was one of the five women who made the thirteen-day "suffrage hike" from New York to Albany, speaking to crowds along the way. On trips to London for ICN business she hawked suffrage papers in Piccadilly. For the suffrage parade of 1913 she organized the Lower East Side into a contingent carrying banners in ten languages, and two years later was interviewed while campaigning in a Bowery flophouse. Dock's activities shifted to Washington when Alice Paul (1885–1977) began her militant campaign for a federal suffrage amendment. She became a member of Paul's advisory council, one of the few elders in this group of predominantly young women. In January 1917 she led the first group of suffrage pickets from the National Woman's party headquarters to the White House; she was jailed three times that year and the next for taking part in militant demonstrations.

Few nurses or social reformers approved the tactics of the National Woman's party. Relations grew strained; Dock moved out of Henry Street in 1915 and resigned from its board. When the suffrage victory came, the great expectations were already clouded by World War I. To Dock, war was the monster twin of poverty, spawned by men's greed and competitiveness; she determined that the conflict should have no advertising from the secretary of the ICN and refused to mention it in the *Journal* except to condemn it. In the early 1920s her *Journal* columns predicted worse slaughter, "perhaps [by] disease germs," if war were not outlawed. She shocked *Journal* readers for the last time in 1921, calling for the conservation of life through birth control, and praising MARGARET SANGER "for teaching to poor working women what all well-to-do women may learn from reliable authority, if they wish it."

By 1922 Lavinia Dock had rejoined her sisters

at home; the five women, none of whom had married, lived together in the country outside Fayetteville, Pa. She resigned as foreign editor of the *Journal* that year, and as secretary of the ICN the next. Dock's years in retirement were to outnumber those of her active career. Handicapped by increasing deafness, she seldom left home. Her arguments for the Equal Rights Amendment, introduced by the National Woman's party in 1923, only widened the breach with former associates. The bonds of affection with Lillian Wald held, and she resumed correspondence with Adelaide Nutting, mending an old rift. Successive revisions, with ISABEL STEWART, of an abridged *History of Nursing* grew burdensome, but the income from royalties saw her through the depression. She followed the course of the New Deal eagerly, especially in labor reform, hoping that what she saw was "socialism in the egg." The Second World War revived the anger of the First; in the onset of the cold war she saw "conspiracy against Russia and socialism, *everywhere.*"

At eighty-nine, Lavinia Dock was guest of honor, with ANNIE GOODRICH, at the ICN convention held in 1947 at Atlantic City. Her tiny figure and her enthusiasm, humor, and resistance to eulogy captivated the delegates. In 1956, she broke a hip in a fall and died in Chambersburg (Pa.) Hospital of bronchopneumonia. Through helping to frame the institutions of professional nursing, and by writing its history, she had done much to establish its identity. Her legacy was a feminist ideal of the nurse as independent practitioner and social reformer in a world free of barriers between nations.

[A very small group of Dock's papers is at the Library of Congress, which also has papers of Mira Lloyd Dock. A collection of family papers is also in the Pa. State Archives at Harrisburg. Dock's "Self-Portrait" of 1932, published in *Nursing Outlook*, Jan. 1977, is the source of the autobiographical quotations. Her other writings include *Short Papers on Nursing Subjects* (1900) and, with others, *History of American Red Cross Nursing* (1922). Biographical details have been assembled from widely scattered sources, including Lillian Wald Papers, Columbia Univ. and N.Y. Public Library; Adelaide Nutting Papers, Teachers College, Columbia Univ.; *Am. Jour. Nursing* Coll., Nursing History Archives, Boston Univ. (including clippings by and about Dock from the *British Jour. Nursing*); Leonora O'Reilly Papers, Schlesinger Library, Radcliffe College; oral history interviews with Isabel M. Stewart, in the Oral History Coll., Columbia Univ., and with Alice Paul, in the Bancroft Library, Univ. of Calif. at Berkeley; Sidney Howard Bland, "Techniques of Persuasion: The National Woman's Party and Woman Suffrage, 1913–1919" (Ph.D. diss., George Washington Univ., 1972); James Frank Gardner, Jr., "Microbes and Morality: The Social

Hygiene Crusade in New York City, 1892–1917" (Ph.D. diss., Indiana Univ., 1974); Lillian D. Wald, *The House on Henry Street* (1915); R. L. Duffus, *Lillian Wald* (1938); Blanche W. Cook, "Female Support Networks and Political Activism: Lillian Wald, Crystal Eastman, Emma Goldman," *Chrysalis*, 1977; Mary M. Roberts, *American Nursing: History and Interpretation* (1954), and "Lavinia Lloyd Dock—Nurse, Feminist, Internationalist," *Am. Jour. Nursing*, Feb. 1956; Victor Robinson, *White Caps* (1946); Margaret Breay and Ethel Gordon Fenwick, *The History of the International Council of Nurses, 1899–1925* (1931); Mabel K. Staupers, *No Time for Prejudice: A Story of the Integration of Negroes in Nursing in the U.S.* (1961); Janet Wilson James, "Isabel Hampton and the Professionalization of Nursing in the 1890s," in Morris J. Vogel and Charles E. Rosenberg, eds., *The Therapeutic Revolution* (1979); Am. Soc. of Superintendents of Training Schools, *Proceedings*, 1894–1900; files of *Am. Jour. Nursing*; Doris Daniels, "Building a Winning Coalition: The Suffrage Fight in New York State," *N.Y. History*, Jan. 1979; Ida H. Harper, ed., *History of Woman Suffrage*, vol. VI (1922); Harriot Stanton Blatch and Alma Lutz, *Challenging Years* (1940); Inez Haynes Irwin, *The Story of the Woman's Party* (1921); Doris Stevens, *Jailed for Freedom* (1920); obituaries in *Am. Jour. Nursing*, May 1956, and *N.Y. Times*, April 18, 1956; death certificate from Pa. Dept. of Health.]

JANET WILSON JAMES

DODGE, Mabel. *See* LUHAN, Mabel Dodge.

DOOLITTLE, Hilda (H.D.), Sept. 10, 1886– Sept. 27, 1961. Poet, writer.

Hilda Doolittle, who published her writings as H.D., was born in Bethlehem, Pa., the only surviving daughter of Helen Eugenie (Wolle) and Charles Leander Doolittle. At the time of their marriage in 1882, Charles Doolittle was a widower with two sons and a daughter (who died in childhood). In addition to her half-brothers, Hilda Doolittle also had a younger and an older brother. She later described herself as a "girl between two boys" and felt that everyone else in the family belonged to a duo: parents, half-brothers, brothers. Only she was without a partner, an idea later reflected in her idea of a universe made up of opposites and dualities, finding and complementing each other.

Charles Doolittle was born in Indiana of parents who had moved to the midwest from New England. Hilda Doolittle's was the eighth generation of the family in America. She remembered her father as a Puritan—cold, strict, and preoccupied; yet she attributed her scholarly side to his influence. A scientist by temperament and training, in 1874 he became professor of mathematics and astronomy at Lehigh University. From there he moved his family to Philadelphia, where he was director of the Flower Astronomical Observatory at the University of Pennsylvania. H.D. later claimed she was her father's favorite; imagery borrowed from astronomy, and certain characters in H.D.'s fiction, reflect his influence. Tall, blond, blue-eyed, she was said to resemble him.

Helen Wolle was born and raised in Bethlehem, Pa. Her family belonged to the Moravian brotherhood, one of the earliest mystical groups of Palatinate Protestants in America, and her father, a biologist, headed the Moravian seminary where she had taught music and painting. H.D. attributed her imaginative faculties to her mother's influence, referring to Helen as "creator" and "muse." Yet she recalled her mother, for all her warmth, as inaccessible and as "morbidly self-effacing" (*Tribute to Freud*, pp. 121 and 164). H.D. never stopped seeking a "fusion or transfusion" of her mother's art and the choice of her mother's name for *Helen in Egypt* was deliberate (*End to Torment*, p. 41). H.D.'s Moravian background is the subject of her unpublished novel, "The Mystery" (written in 1951) and characterizes the ambience of her later work.

Despite the disconnection she felt between her mother's music and her father's stars, H.D. remembered childhood as happy. Her maternal grandparents, her older half-brothers, and a wide circle of friends provided support. "Peaceful Bethlehem" would later be contrasted to wartime London and summer trips to Maine and Rhode Island would suggest the redemptive landscape imagery of her mature work. She attended the Gordon School and graduated in 1905 from the Friends Central School in Philadelphia. At the house of mutual friends she met Ezra Pound. She was fifteen; he sixteen. At first her tutor and literary guide, later, despite her family's objections, he became her fiancé. William Carlos Williams, when introduced to Pound's protégé, remarked her "bizarre" beauty and her "provocative indifference to rule and order" (Williams, p. 68).

In 1905 Hilda Doolittle entered Bryn Mawr College. She stayed less than two years, having had a "slight breakdown" and "flunked" English. She left, too, because she was involved with Pound—her "first serious love-conflict" (*Tribute*, p. 181). For some years, she wrote and studied at home. (Her first poems were translations of Heine and of Latin lyrics.) But the need to "get away" sent her to New York briefly in 1910, where her first published writing appeared in a syndicated paper. In 1911 she sailed to Europe with a girlhood friend, to be with Pound and to begin her career. Thereafter she lived in Europe, mainly in England and Switzerland. Her parents frequently joined her, but she seldom returned to the United States.

In Europe Hilda Doolittle met, among others, D. H. Lawrence, William Butler Yeats, and the poet and translator Richard Aldington. She became associated with Imagism, a poetic movement that HARRIET MONROE said "shook the Victorian tradition and discarded its excesses." Imagism helped Hilda Doolittle to learn her craft. In 1913, her first poems appeared in *Poetry*, signed, at Pound's suggestion, "H.D. Imagiste"; from then on she preferred to be known as H.D. With Aldington she translated Greek poetry. Her first volume, *Sea Garden* (1916), and her early translations of Euripides show her dependence on the classical world for models on which to base modern poetic innovation. H.D. married Aldington in 1913, with her parents and Pound attending.

World War I brought a set of major life crises. In 1915 she suffered a miscarriage. The following year, anticipating Aldington's conscription, H.D. took over his editorial duties on the literary magazine *The Egoist*, the only position other than writer and mother she ever held. By 1917, Aldington was in action in France and the breakup of their marriage, retold many years later in the novel *Bid Me To Live*, had begun. These pressures exhausted her mentally and physically. Her older brother was killed in action in 1918. At the news, her father suffered a stroke from which he did not recover; he died in 1919. That year, despite double pneumonia and emotional depression, H.D. bore her only child, a daughter, Perdita. By then she and Aldington were separated. Divorce proceedings, not begun until 1937, were concluded in 1938.

H.D. was "saved" (her word) by a wealthy English friend, the novelist Winifred Ellerman, who had met H.D. in 1918. Bryher, as she was called, arranged for H.D.'s rehabilitation and shared in Perdita's care. An important support for H.D. throughout her life, Bryher's became the most significant of several major friendships. (Other close friends, besides Pound, included a girlhood friend, Viola Jordan, with whom she corresponded for many years, and the critic Norman Holmes Pearson, who became H.D.'s literary executor.) Bryher and H.D. usually shared a home, and frequently traveled together. At the time of the Aldingtons' divorce, Perdita was legally adopted by Bryher, then married to Kenneth MacPherson, and took the MacPherson name (letter to Viola Jordan, Sept. 15, 1946).

In the 1920s H.D. expanded her artistic media

and materials, although the death of her mother in March 1927 left her feeling "overburdened and lost." Her half-brother Eric had died in 1920. Trips with Bryher to Greece (1920), Egypt (1923), and twice to America (1921 and 1926) proved stimulating. In the two years following her *Collected Poems* (1925), H.D. wrote a verse drama (*Hippolytus Temporizes*, 1927) and three novels (*Palimpsest*, 1926; *Hedylus*, 1928; and the short, privately printed, *The Usual Star*, 1934). She gave serious attention to the medium of film, writing reviews for the film magazine *Close-Up*, and trying her hand at film writing and directing with Bryher and Kenneth MacPherson. They produced *Foothills* (1928) and *Borderline* (1930), featuring Paul and ESLANDA ROBESON, in which H.D. also appears.

Although poetically dry, the next decade brought reflection and consolidation. H.D. continued her study of the occult in both western and eastern religions; this research, she wrote to Viola Jordan, "feeds some imaginative center." So too did her brief psychoanalysis with Freud (in 1933 and 1934), described in *Tribute to Freud* (1956). "Without the analysis and the illuminating doctrine or philosophy of Sigmund Freud," H.D. later said, "I would hardly have found the clue or the bridge between the child-life, the memories of peaceful Bethlehem, and the orgy of destruction, later to be witnessed and lived through in London" (quoted by Pearson, foreword, *Hermetic Definition*).

Between *Red Roses for Bronze* (1931) and the wartime poetry of the mid-1940s, she published no verse. Instead, she wrote stories for children, including *The Hedgehog* (1936), and, in 1937, a translation, with commentary, of Euripides's *Ion*. In her commentary, modern life is seen as at a turning point, and an Athene-like new world woman is predicted. The relationship of mothers to children and the leadership of women are persistent themes in this period; H.D. felt that the Aquarian age, "coming in with such agony, is a woman's age and we must stick together" (undated letter to Jordan, 1941). She linked the "hieroglyphs" of her personal unconscious to a complex typology from the Bible, astrology, the Tarot, the Kaballah, and certain Moravian and Rosicrucian rituals familiar from her youth. This synthesis of history, art, and religion was made in order to "act out the legend" of herself on which to base the major late poems ("The Mystery," p. 77).

H.D. was both "energized" and brought to emotional exhaustion by World War II. Her *Trilogy* ("The Walls Do Not Fall"; "Tribute to the Angels"; "The Flowering of the Rod," 1944–46) affirms the resurrection of new life from the devastation of London. In 1944 H.D. completed the novel *Bid Me To Live*, which draws on her relationship with D. H. Lawrence as well as with Aldington; it was not published until 1960. Both are works "infused with the action and memory of an ancient past that exist within the mutations of the present tense" (Horace Gregory, introduction, *Helen in Egypt*, p. x). History for H.D. does not progress; it is a "changeless repetition of the true" (Watts, p. 297). In *By Avon River* (1949) she celebrated the peace by celebrating Shakespeare and the Renaissance poets.

Following a mental breakdown after World War II, H.D. moved to Küsnacht, Switzerland, where she lived and wrote until her death in a Zurich hospital in 1961. In 1956 she made her first visit to the United States since 1926. After her return to Switzerland, she fell and broke her hip, an accident from which she never fully recovered. In semi-invalidism she intensified her studies and writing, completing a reminiscence of Pound, *End to Torment*, in 1958. Her final visit to the United States came in 1960, when she accepted the Award of Merit Medal for Poetry from the American Academy of Arts and Letters. H.D.'s last, and some feel strongest, works were *Helen in Egypt* (1961), a reimagining of the Helen-Achilles myth, and the posthumously published *Hermetic Definition* (1972). There the poet's quest for wholeness is made as a passionately personal statement, although cast, again, as myth.

Critical judgments of H.D.'s poetry have been divided between those who consider her the poet of a "few gems" (Engel, p. 507), those who designate her best poems as Imagist (Quinn, p. 146), and those who admire the "energy and sweep" of the later volumes (Bogan, p. 94). In the critical reassessment of H.D.'s work begun in the 1970s, wide-ranging significances have been attributed to the development of her poetic method, particularly in the later poetry. For its syncretistic method, her mature work is frequently compared to *The Wasteland, Cantos, Paterson*, and *Ulysses*.

Some critics see her as a major American artist. H.D. claimed that she was, despite her removal, always American, and that her expatriation had enabled her to come closer to self and to origins. Not confessional, hers is recognized nevertheless as a poetry of quest for identity. Pearson placed it therefore in the mainstream of twentieth-century poetry. H.D.'s research into and uses of mythological, astrological, and psychological sources of identity for women has made her an important poet for women, as Denise Levertov has testified. That the reappraisal of her work is not complete is suggested in Pearson's remark that "we may not yet know how to read her."

[The H. D. Coll. at the Beinecke Library, Yale Univ., contains many MSS. of published and unpublished work, both poetry and prose, extensive correspondence, and autobiographical notes from 1910 to 1939. Her letters to Viola Jordan are open to research with permission from Perdita Schaffner, H.D.'s daughter; the correspondence with Pound, Bryher, and Norman Holmes Pearson is closed. Unpublished MSS. at Yale include "The Mystery." There are also some poems and correspondence in the *Poetry* magazine papers at the Regenstein Library, Univ. of Chicago. H.D.'s memoir of Ezra Pound, *End to Torment*, was published in 1979. The most complete listing of H.D.'s works is Jackson R. Bryer and Pamela Roblyer, "H.D.: A Preliminary Checklist," *Contemporary Lit.*, Autumn 1969. There is no biography, and there are only three book-length studies: Thomas Swann, *The Classical World of H.D.* (1962); Vincent Quinn, *Hilda Doolittle* (1967), which is limited and occasionally inaccurate; and an excellent dissertation, Susan S. Friedman, "Mythology, Psychoanalysis, and the Occult in the Late Poetry of H.D." (Univ. of Wis., 1973). Especially helpful for both biographical detail and critical commentary are the introductions by Norman Holmes Pearson to *Hermetic Definition* (1972), *Trilogy* (1973), and *Tribute to Freud* (reissued in 1974 and including "Advent," H.D.'s notes on her sessions with Freud). The Autumn 1969 issue of *Contemporary Lit.* is devoted to H.D.; among the several articles included are "Norman Holmes Pearson on H.D.: An Interview," and Bernard F. Engel, "H.D.: Poems that Matter and Dilutations." Other useful articles are R. P. Blackmur, "The Lesser Satisfactions," *Poetry*, Nov. 1932; an essay by Louise Bogan in the *New Yorker*, Oct. 21, 1944; Denise Levertov, "H.D.: An Appreciation," *Poetry*, June 1962; F. D. Reeves, "H.D. Reviva," *Poetry*, June 1974; Harold H. Watts, "H.D. and the Art of Myth," *Sewanee Rev.*, Spring 1948. See also *Twentieth Century Authors* (1942), p. 391, and William Carlos Williams, *Autobiography* (1951). An obituary appeared in the *N.Y. Times*, Sept. 29, 1961. Assistance with research was provided by a biobibliography prepared by Charlene Bird.]

ROSAMOND ROSENMEIER

DRAPER, Ruth, Dec. 2, 1884–Dec. 30, 1956. Actress, monologuist.

In a career that spanned four decades, Ruth Draper made of the dramatic monologue a lively, personal art form that won her international acclaim. Draper created and brought to the stage a remarkable array of characters, ranging from the preoccupied society matron who would interrupt her tutor in "The Italian Lesson" ("Signorina, my little manicurist has ar-

rived . . . You don't mind if I have my nails done?") to the resilient Irish charwoman who could console her coworker in a New York business office ("We're lucky to have a place like this to clean . . . A cousin o' mine, Mary Flynn, works down to the Tombs Prison . . . *That's* a cheerful hole!").

Ruth Draper's performances were not merely recitals or satirical sketches; they were short, coherent dramas. Alone on the stage, Draper managed through words and gesture to give her audience a vivid impression of the invisible figures to whom her characters spoke, as in her piece, "Three Women and Mr. Clifford," where Draper played the parts of Clifford's wife, his secretary, and the woman he loved. Clifford himself never appeared in the act, but as Draper's friend and critic Iris Origo recalled: "Most of us would agree with the member of the audience who, on his way out of the theatre, said to his companion: 'Wasn't Clifford the most long-suffering jackass . . . ?'—and only a moment later added, 'My God, he wasn't there!' "

Ruth Draper was born in New York City, the fifth of six children and third of four daughters of Dr. William Henry Draper, a well-known physician, and his second wife, Ruth (Dana) Draper, daughter of Charles A. Dana, editor of the New York *Sun*. William Draper had two other children by his first marriage. Ruth's education was largely with a governess, although she attended Miss Spence's School in New York City in 1894 and again briefly in 1896. As a child, she often entertained family and friends with her impersonations. After making her debut in 1903, she devoted herself in the next decade to developing her character sketches, and frequently entertained at the homes of friends and at benefits.

During these years, while Ruth Draper was in her twenties, several influences helped shape her art and move her toward a professional stage career. Draper found a model for her work in the performances of Beatrice Herford, the English-born actress who helped to make the monologue a popular theater form. She was also impressed by the 1912 production of *The Yellow Jacket*, a play based on a Chinese tale, employing words and gestures rather than elaborate scenery to evoke its setting, a technique Draper used to great effect. Finally, several prominent artists encouraged her: the pianist Paderewski saw her perform and urged her to try a career, and during Draper's frequent visits to England, both Henry Adams and Henry James came to admire her work. James wrote a monologue for Draper in 1913, and though she found herself unable to perform it, the author remained devoted to her. "You have woven your own very beautiful little Persian carpet," James told her. "Stand on it!"

Heartened by such support, Draper began to perform publicly. The *New York Times* of April 15, 1916, favorably reviewed her "first public appearance in monologues," but it was another four years before Draper was ready to make a full professional commitment in this direction. Briefly in May 1916 Draper played a small part in a Broadway play with Marie Tempest's company, and she staged a one-act play by Strindberg the following year. Neither effort bore fruit and Draper never appeared again in a play with other actors or used any but her own material. Toward the close of World War I, she entertained servicemen at home and overseas. Traveling widely in Europe and the British Isles, Draper used her exceptional ear for foreign languages and dialects to expand her repertoire of character sketches.

Finally, on Jan. 29, 1920, Ruth Draper made her formal professional debut in monologues at London's Aeolian Hall. The engagement was a success and the following year Aurelien-François Lugné-Poe, director of the Théâtre de l'Oeuvre, sponsored her on a percentage basis in Paris. Draper made a similar arrangement with Max Reinhardt in Germany, and over the next three decades, European tours became a regular part of her schedule. Draper's following was truly international, as she performed eventually in Latin America, Africa, and Asia. She quickly won wide recognition in the United States, appearing before President Warren G. Harding at the White House in December 1921; by 1928 her popularity in New York was great enough to sustain a run of nineteen weeks at the Comedy Theater. During her long career, Draper's repertoire grew to fifty-four characters in some thirty-five sketches, all of them her own compositions. Audiences around the world were enthralled by this woman who, alone on the stage, with only a shawl for costume, and a table or chair for setting, could create the illusion of a full drama being enacted.

Although Ruth Draper spent much of her adult life traveling and performing, she maintained a home in Dark Harbor, Maine, where she returned to rest between tours. (This home provided the setting for one of her most famous monologues, "On a Porch in a Maine Coast Village.") Draper made a number of close friends among actors and artists in the United States and Europe, including the Italian poet Lauro de Bosis, some of whose work she translated. Draper met de Bosis on one of her periodic trips to Italy and sympathized with his liberal opposition to Mussolini; she gave refuge at Dark Harbor to several Italian friends who fled the

regime. After the poet's death in 1931, Draper established the Lauro de Bosis Lectureship in the History of Italian Civilization at Harvard University.

Ruth Draper received many awards over the years, including several honorary degrees from British and American institutions; in 1951 she was made a Commander, Order of the British Empire. Her greatest pride, however, was that in her entire career she missed only one performance, an engagement she fulfilled the following month. In December 1956, following two performances in New York, Ruth Draper died in her sleep. As she had requested, her coffin was draped with the shawls she had used to create her remarkable cast of characters.

Draper attributed her success to her own curiosity and energy, and to the receptive imaginations of her audience. Her unique gifts were an eye for the finest details of gesture and movement, and an ear for the faintest nuances of speech. As John Ciardi wrote in tribute to her: "She *heard* her lives; heard them in every intonation and shift and flutter of their voices." Those who heard Ruth Draper, and watched her evoke her characters, came to delight in these gifts.

[Primary sources include Neilla Warren, ed., *The Letters of Ruth Draper, 1920–1956* (1979), and an album of several records, *The Art of Ruth Draper* (Spoken Arts, 1960–61). A book, *The Art of Ruth Draper* (1960), contains transcriptions of Draper's sketches, along with a list of costumes, props, and characters portrayed and evoked in each sketch. The transcriptions are preceded by Morton Zabel's biographical memoir, the most extensive published account of Draper's life and career. A valuable article is Iris Origo, "Ruth Draper and Her Company of Characters," *Cornhill*, Winter 1957/58, pp. 382–93; a shorter version of this article appears in *Atlantic Monthly*, Oct. 1958. Reviews of Draper's work include John Ciardi, "The Genius of Ruth Draper," *Sat. Rev.*, Oct. 14, 1961, p. 90; Francis Hackett, "Miss Ruth Draper," *New Republic*, March 23, 1921, p. 111; and Alexander Woollcott, *Going to Pieces* (1928), pp. 99–109. An interview with Draper appeared in the *New Yorker*, March 6, 1954, and an obituary in the *N.Y. Times*, Dec. 31, 1956. A biobibliography prepared by Eugenia Loyster assisted in research.]

MURIEL R. MC KENNA

DREIER, Katherine Sophie, Sept. 10, 1877– March 29, 1952. Art patron, artist.

Katherine Dreier, the fifth surviving child and youngest daughter of Theodor and Dorothea Adelheid (Dreier) Dreier, was born in the family home in Brooklyn, N.Y. Throughout her life she sought to combine a steadfast commitment to social reform, the hallmark of the Dreier family, particularly of her sisters, MARGARET DREIER ROBINS and MARY DREIER, with her own intense attraction to the arts. An artist herself, she became the patron, publicist, and friend of other artists. Her lifelong endeavor to enlarge public support and understanding for modern art centered upon the exhibitions and activities of the Société Anonyme, of which she was the guiding spirit.

Theodor Dreier came to New York from Bremen, Germany, in 1849. By the time he married his cousin Dorothea in 1864, he was the manager of the New York branch of Naylor, Benson and Company, international distributors of iron and steel products. The socially prominent Dreiers were a close-knit and affectionate family. Katherine was closest to her sister Mary, whom she regarded as goodness personified, especially in contrast to her own determined inclination, demonstrated from an early age, to get her own way.

Dreier's parents encouraged personal achievement, independent judgment, social service, and democratic ideals. Privately educated at George Brackett's school in Brooklyn, Katherine Dreier shared her mother's love for music and her older sister Dorothea's interest in painting. She began a weekly art class when she was twelve and studied at the Brooklyn Art Students League from 1895 to 1897. Her parents died within two years of one another, in the late 1890s, leaving a legacy guaranteeing her financial independence.

Continuing the family tradition of community service, from 1900 until 1909 Dreier worked as volunteer treasurer for the German Home for Recreation for Women and Children, which had been founded by her mother. In 1905 she cofounded and served as president of the Little Italy Neighborhood Association in Brooklyn. Also sharing her sisters' commitment to the campaign for woman suffrage, Dreier was a delegate to the Sixth Convention of the International Woman Suffrage Alliance, which met in Stockholm in June 1911. She later (1915) headed the German-American Committee of the Woman Suffrage party in New York City.

Mainly, however, she was intent on becoming a painter. In 1900 she enrolled for a year of art study at the Pratt Institute, where her sister Dorothea was a student, and in 1902 and 1903 traveled in Europe with Dorothea and MARY QUINN (SULLIVAN) to study the old masters. Returning to New York impatient with the academicism of her earlier training, Dreier began art lessons with Walter Shirlaw, who encouraged individuality in his pupils. In 1905 her first commission, an altar painting for the chapel of Saint

Paul's School in Garden City, N.Y., was installed. She studied in Paris with Raphaël Collin for three months in 1907, then in 1909 moved to London. Living in a Chelsea neighborhood redolent of associations with Whistler and Wilde, she devoted herself to painting, despite periods of self-doubt and intermittent illness. The American actress and feminist Elizabeth Robins (1862–1952), sister of Dreier's brother-in-law Raymond Robins, introduced her into a circle of artists and literati. Dreier became engaged to Edward Trumbull (who was also known as Trumbull-Smith), an American painter working in London, and returned to her family home in Brooklyn for their wedding in August 1911. The marriage was annulled soon after when it was learned that Trumbull had a wife and children.

She returned to Europe, where her first exhibition opened at the Doré Galleries in London in September 1911 and toured Germany in 1912. Critics noted the Whistlerian character of her landscapes, commenting on her soft tones, rich color harmonies, and poetic rendering of atmospheric effects. Settling in Munich for the winter of 1911–12, she studied with Gustav Britsch, whom she regarded as her most gifted teacher.

Dreier's return to New York late in 1912 inaugurated a new era in her life and work. Invited to exhibit in the 1913 Armory Show, she was inspired by the vitality and originality of the avant-garde painters who were represented there and who had earlier attracted her attention in Europe. Dismayed by the lack of understanding of modern art apparent in the generally derisive response to the Armory Show, she determined to work for the cause of free artistic expression and promote public appreciation for art.

In 1914 she launched the Cooperative Mural Workshop, a combination art school and workshop in the Ruskin-Morris tradition, which operated until 1917. In the fall of 1916 she was invited to help found the Society of Independent Artists, which brought her into the circles of the European and American avant-garde who gathered in the New York home of collector and patron Walter Arensberg. The iconoclastic art and antics of this group, in which Marcel Duchamp was prominent, earned its members a reputation as the creators of New York Dada. While Dreier's own expressions of rebellion against established artistic convention tended to be earnest rather than irreverent, she enjoyed the gaiety of their gatherings, and shared the general admiration for Duchamp, becoming his patron, partner, and friend.

In 1920, deciding that the modernist cause was still in need of a sustaining champion, Dreier enlisted Duchamp and Man Ray to assist her in founding a new organization—the Société Anonyme, "a center for the study and promotion of modern art." The Société Anonyme opened its first season on April 30, 1920, in rented gallery space decorated by Duchamp. Dreier's funds and efforts supported its ambitious program, which included publications, lectures, and occasional performances as well as exhibitions. Throughout the twenties the Société, New York's first "museum of modern art," presented an international array of cubists, constructivists, expressionists, futurists, Bauhaus artists, and dadaists. The Société introduced to the American public the work of contemporary German, East European, and Russian artists, as well as of American modernists. One-man shows, their first in America, were held for Kandinsky, Klee, Campendonk, and Léger. The major event of a remarkable decade of activity was the huge exhibition of international modern art in Brooklyn in 1926.

The opening of the New York Museum of Modern Art in 1929 diminished Dreier's hope of establishing the Société Anonyme as a permanent museum. But she continued to invoke its name in connection with her activities, including an extensive exhibition and lecture series at the Rand School (1930–31) and the New School for Social Research (1931). An exhibition of thirteen women artists (1934–35) demonstrated her enduring feminist concerns. She also supported dance performances by Ted Shawn, who became a friend, and about whom she wrote a book, *Shawn the Dancer* (1933). Undaunted by a crippling illness in the last decade of her life, Dreier remained active, writing, lecturing, and managing an extensive correspondence. Concerned with the permanent safeguarding of the Société Anonyme collection, in 1941 Dreier and Duchamp presented it to Yale University, and later worked together on the catalog published in 1950. Dreier died in 1952 of nonalcoholic cirrhosis of the liver at her Milford, Conn., home.

Dreier continued to paint throughout her life. The first American show of her work opened at New York's Macbeth Gallery in 1913. A 1918 "psychological" portrait of Duchamp indicated the predominantly abstract style that characterized her later work. In 1933 a Dreier retrospective was shown in New York at the Academy of Allied Arts, followed in 1935 by a showing at the Annot Art School of "40 Variations," abstractions conceived as a parallel to musical variations on a theme.

Like the painter Wassily Kandinsky, whom she knew and admired, Katherine Dreier looked upon form as the outward expression of inner spiritual meaning. Kandinsky's conception of an underlying mystical source for creative expression confirmed her own views, elaborated in her lectures and in *Western Art and the New Era* (1923). Insofar as her interpretive vocabulary derived from a continuing interest in theosophy and numerology, her explanations of the meaning of art sometimes lacked clarity and sophistication. Dreier's major achievement lay neither in her writings nor in her painting, however, but in her early recognition and championship of such artists as Duchamp and Kandinsky, as well as Klee, Gabo, Villon, Léger, and Mondrian, and in her determined attempts to create both an institution and a climate of acceptance for their work.

[The Katherine S. Dreier Papers, containing correspondence and manuscripts relating primarily to her activities on behalf of the Société Anonyme, are in the Beinecke Library, Yale Univ. Additional material may be found in the Margaret Dreier Robins Papers, Univ. of Florida; the Raymond Robins Papers, State Hist. Soc. of Wis.; the Mary E. Dreier Papers, Schlesinger Library, Radcliffe College; and the Dorothea Dreier Papers, Archives of American Art. Katherine Dreier also translated and wrote the introduction to Elizabeth du Quesne Van Gogh's *Personal Recollections* of her brother, Vincent Van Gogh (1913). A chapter on Dreier as a collector appears in Aline B. Saarinen, *The Proud Possessors* (1958). See also Ruth L. Bohan, "Katherine Sophie Dreier and New York Dada," *Arts Mag.*, May 1977, and an entry in *Nat. Cyc. Am. Biog.*, XLII, 78–79. Société Anonyme exhibitions, lectures, and publications are listed in the *Collection of the Société Anonyme* (1950), which includes a biographical entry for Dreier listing her publications and exhibitions of her paintings. Reprints of most of the Société publications are in *Selected Publications: Société Anonyme* (1972). Selections from Dreier's personal art collection are described in "In Memory of Katherine S. Dreier," *Bull. of the Associates in Fine Arts at Yale Univ.*, Dec. 1952; see also Donald G. Wing, "The Katherine S. Dreier Collection of Oscar Wilde," *Yale Univ. Lib. Gazette*, Oct. 1953. Her marriage and the subsequent annulment are documented in several articles in the *N.Y. Times* between Aug. 9 and Sept. 15, 1911 (indexed under Edward Trumbull-Smith). Obituaries appeared in the *N.Y. Times* and *N.Y. Herald Tribune*, March 30, 1952. A death record was supplied by Conn. Dept. of Health.]

ELEANOR S. APTER

DREIER, Mary Elisabeth, Sept. 26, 1875–Aug. 15, 1963. Labor reformer, suffragist.

Mary Dreier was born in Brooklyn, N.Y., the

fourth of five surviving children and the third of four daughters of Theodor and Dorothea Adelheid (Dreier) Dreier. Her parents were cousins who descended from a long line of merchants and civic leaders in Bremen, Germany, a Hanseatic city whose history, according to the Dreiers, embodied "the golden thread of democracy." In 1849, at the age of twenty-one, Theodor Dreier emigrated to the United States and within fifteen years rose from clerk to partner in the New York branch of Naylor, Benson and Company, an English iron firm. In 1864 he revisited Bremen and married Dorothea Dreier, daughter of a country parson. They returned to America and settled in a comfortable Brooklyn Heights brownstone home. Civic-minded and devout members of the German Evangelical Church, the Dreiers surrounded their children with warmth and gaiety but emphasized disciplined self-development.

Few families could claim four such distinguished daughters. Mary Dreier and her eldest sister, MARGARET DREIER ROBINS, after whose social reform career Mary closely modeled her own, pioneered in labor reform for working women. Dorothea Dreier (1870–1923) became known for her postimpressionist paintings, KATHERINE DREIER for her work as an early proponent and benefactor of modern art. Privately educated and tutored, the daughters attended George Brackett's school in Brooklyn. Although Mary Dreier later took courses at the New York School of Philanthropy (ca. 1904), none of the Dreier children attended college: their parents felt American colleges neglected the arts and humanities.

Shy by nature, Mary Dreier took little interest in Brooklyn Heights social life and in 1895 began searching for useful work. Around 1899 at Asacog House, a Brooklyn settlement, she met LEONORA O'REILLY. A garment worker who at that time was head of the settlement, O'Reilly introduced her to the problems of working women. More important, she later recruited Dreier and her sisters for the Women's Trade Union League (WTUL), a coalition of women workers and middle- and upper-class women reformers founded in 1903 both to organize working women and to educate the public about labor conditions.

While presiding over the New York WTUL from 1906 until 1914, Dreier found her life's work. Arrested in 1909 during a strike of shirtwaistmakers leading to the great "Uprising of the Twenty Thousand" in New York City, she confirmed reports of police brutality and stimulated widespread interest in the strike among both workers and the general public. Previously terrified of public speaking, she emerged from the strike a forceful and deliberate advocate of women workers. Rare among middle-class reformers, Dreier won the complete trust of working women. "She didn't carry a trade union card," militant labor organizer Pauline Newman recalled, "but there was no more devoted trade unionist than Mary Dreier."

While the WTUL under Dreier's leadership worked primarily to organize unskilled women into unions, it also looked to legislation as a means of curbing industry's abuses. On March 25, 1911, with the Triangle Shirtwaist Company fire, the League's worst fears were realized: 146 workers, mostly women and children, jumped to their deaths or died behind the factory's locked doors. Out of the shock following this tragedy emerged the New York State Factory Investigating Commission, a landmark in labor history. From 1911 to 1915, Mary Dreier, along with chairman Robert F. Wagner and vice chairman Alfred E. Smith, undertook the most comprehensive study of American industrial conditions up to that time. Investigating fire prevention, safety standards, hours and wages, and industrial disease, the nine commissioners drafted legislation that revolutionized New York's labor laws. Dreier, the only female member, combined compassion with toughness as she doggedly upheld the sanctity of individual human life. "Bob Wagner was the brain behind the commission," Al Smith reportedly said, "but Mary Dreier was its soul."

After completing her work with the commission, Dreier turned to the suffrage campaign. Explaining that the attitude of male trade unionists toward her working sisters had changed her from "an ardent supporter of labor to a somewhat rabid supporter of women," she chaired New York City's Woman Suffrage party and headed the industrial section of that party's state organization. She also displayed an active and lasting concern with national politics, serving as a delegate-at-large to the Progressive party convention of 1912 (though she supported Charles Evans Hughes in 1916) and voting for Robert M. La Follette in 1924. A friend of the Roosevelts from the 1920s when ELEANOR ROOSEVELT was active in the New York WTUL, Dreier became an enthusiastic supporter of Franklin D. Roosevelt and the New Deal. In 1948 she backed Henry Wallace's presidential candidacy on the Progressive ticket, to the dismay of some of her oldest and closest union friends.

Dreier's other interests never completely displaced her original commitment to labor, however. Active in the National WTUL until its demise in 1950, she frequently served on government boards and private organizations concerned with labor and women. During World War I, for example, she presided over the New York State Committee on Women in Industry of the Advisory Commission, Council of National Defense.

After the war, peace and international concerns seemed a natural extension of Dreier's domestic reform activities and claimed an increasing share of her time and financial resources. She became a strong advocate of United States–Soviet friendship and of the outlawry of war movement, and during the 1930s she helped mobilize public opinion against Nazism. The growing split after World War II between the United States and the Soviet Union deeply concerned her, and she aided a variety of organizations promoting international cooperation and the curtailment of atomic weapons. During the McCarthy era the FBI investigated her as a possible subversive.

Throughout her life, Dreier enjoyed writing, especially poems and pageants for WTUL activities. Around 1914 she began a novel entitled *Barbara Richards*. Never published, this somewhat autobiographical novel explores the relationship between working- and middle-class women. In 1950 she published *Margaret Dreier Robins: Her Life, Letters, and Work*, an adulatory biography of her sister.

Dreier had several serious suitors (including Gifford Pinchot) but never seemed interested in marriage. An affectionate person, she remained close to her family and became a doting aunt to her brother's children. She admired Raymond Robins, her brother-in-law, and looked to him for guidance, constantly seeking his advice about her work. In 1905 FRANCES KELLOR, a fellow reformer, began living in the Dreier household at Mary Dreier's invitation; they continued to share a home until Kellor's death in 1952. Dreier, who had inherited around $600,000 in 1899, viewed her wealth as a trust and often aided other reformers financially. She helped support Kellor and her work during their forty-seven-year friendship and in 1908 gave Leonora O'Reilly a lifetime annuity.

Of medium height with blonde hair and blue eyes, Dreier radiated a gentleness and sincerity that carried considerable appeal. Her passionate commitment to reform was religiously motivated and her mystical interior life nourished her activism and sharpened her loyalties. Democracy, she thought, required a basic reshaping of human relationships; any injustice seemed an insult to her belief that "we all are God's children, economically as well as spiritually." Often

critical of organized religion, she nevertheless retained institutional ties. Originally German Evangelical, she became a Presbyterian in 1943 and closely allied herself with the policies of the National Council of Churches. As a member of the Industrial Department and later of the National Board of the YWCA, she enlisted that organization's support in the cause of working women. Mary Dreier's influence grew primarily out of personal relationships; for her, fellowship was the key to leadership.

Still active in her eighties, Dreier could be seen handing out antinuclear proliferation flyers or gathering signatures to petition for a favorite cause. She died in 1963 of a pulmonary embolism in Bar Harbor, Maine, near Southwest Harbor, her summer home for thirty-five years.

[No biography of Mary Dreier exists. Important manuscript collections include the Mary E. Dreier Papers, Schlesinger Library, Radcliffe College; Margaret Dreier Robins Papers, Univ. of Fla.; Raymond Robins Papers, State Hist. Soc. of Wis.; N.Y. WTUL Papers, N.Y. State Labor Library, N.Y. City; and Nat. WTUL Papers, Library of Congress. Other sources of biographical information are an entry in the *Nat. Cyc. Am. Biog.*, I, 266, and an obituary in the *N.Y. Times*, Aug. 19, 1963. Dreier's biography of her sister and a privately printed family history, *In Memory of the One Hundredth Anniversary of the Birth of Dorothea Adelheid Dreier* (1940), provide family background. Also see George Martin, *Madam Secretary: Frances Perkins* (1976); Leon Stein, *The Triangle Fire* (1962); J. Joseph Huthmacher, *Senator Robert F. Wagner and the Rise of Urban Liberalism* (1968); and Nancy Schrom Dye, "The Women's Trade Union League of New York, 1903–1920" (Ph.D. diss., Univ. of Wis., 1974). Additional information for this article was supplied by Lisa von Borowsky, Pauline Newman, and Dreier's nephews, Theodore and John Dreier. A death certificate was provided by the Maine Dept. of Health and Welfare.]

ELIZABETH PAYNE MOORE

DREXEL, Mother Mary Katharine, Nov. 26, 1858–March 3, 1955. Founder, religious order.

Katharine Drexel, founder of the Sisters of the Blessed Sacrament for Indians and Colored People, was born in Philadelphia to Francis Anthony Drexel, a prosperous banker whose father had emigrated from Austria, and Hannah Jane (Langstroth) Drexel, a Quaker of German descent. Her mother died five weeks after Katharine's birth; with her three-year-old sister, Elizabeth, she was cared for by relatives until her father married Emma Bouvier in 1860. The family, completed by the birth of Louise in 1863, was doubly outstanding among Philadelphia's social elite, for its piety and for its philanthropy. Emma Drexel, who wished her daughters to understand the obligations of Christian womanhood, opened her home three times a week to distribute aid to the poor. The family regularly made substantial contributions to mission work among blacks and Indians.

Private tutors and extensive travel provided the sisters' early education. At twelve Katharine met her most important teacher, Rev. James O'Connor, whose parish included the Drexels' summer home. O'Connor, later bishop of Omaha, served as Katharine Drexel's spiritual guide for twenty years.

The 1880s were a time of change for Katharine Drexel. Her mother, whom she nursed during a three-year illness, died in 1883; Francis Drexel died two years later. The daughters, beneficiaries of a $14,000,000 estate, resolved to continue their parents' charitable activities. Katharine Drexel was particularly drawn to the needs of the Indians in the west, where she traveled and gave money to mission schools. Sharing her sisters' concern with advancing Christian education, she went with them to Europe to survey the newest educational techniques. At an audience with Pope Leo XIII in January 1887, she pleaded for missionary priests and nuns for the Indians. The Pope replied, "Why not, my child, yourself become a missionary?"

Katharine Drexel had long considered a religious vocation, but Bishop O'Connor had counseled her, "Think, pray, and wait." After the visit to the Pope and long hours of prayer, she wrote to O'Connor of her final decision to enter a convent and consecrate herself to Jesus Christ. Convinced of her vocation, and familiar with her interests, the Bishop immediately suggested the founding of a new order to aid Indians and blacks. He recommended the Sisters of Mercy as the most appropriate order in which to receive her training and on May 6, 1889, she entered their novitiate in Pittsburgh. Despite the deaths of both Bishop O'Connor and her sister Elizabeth in 1890, she managed to complete plans for the new order during her two-year novitiate; in July of that year Pope Leo XIII gave his apostolic blessing to her and the other women who would join her. Sustained by the guidance of Archbishop Patrick J. Ryan of Philadelphia and the support of Louise, she made her vows as the first of the Sisters of the Blessed Sacrament for Indians and Colored People, on Feb. 12, 1891. She added a special vow: "To be the mother and servant of the Indian and Negro races."

By December 1892, Drexel had directed the establishment of a novitiate and motherhouse,

St. Elizabeth's at Cornwells Heights, Pa. From there in June 1894, the first four missionary sisters departed for St. Catherine's School, a boarding school for Pueblo Indians in Santa Fe, N.M. The Rules and Constitution for the new order were established the same year; they incorporated a strict interpretation of the vow of poverty. A Decree of Definitive Approbation was granted by the College of Cardinals in 1907, and the first Chapter General of the order elected Drexel superior general, a position she held until 1937. The formal papal Decree of Approbation was granted by Pope Pius X in May 1913.

For forty years, Mother Katharine directed every aspect of the order's work as her sisters founded and staffed missions and schools throughout the south, the urban north, and the Indian territories. Her keen understanding of race problems led to the founding of a high school for black girls in Virginia, a manual arts school for Navahos in Arizona, and a mission in Harlem. The sisters combined religious instruction with training in vocational skills, liberal arts, and native culture; they also served as missionaries in the surrounding communities. In 1915, with the aid of Archbishop Francis Janssens of New Orleans, Mother Katharine initiated plans for a teachers college in that city. In 1925, the college received a charter as Xavier University, the only Catholic college for blacks in the United States.

Throughout these years, Drexel made annual trips to plan missions, investigate race relations, promote lay participation, and survey the work of the order; she also directed its administration. In the mid-1930s, following two heart attacks, she began to withdraw from her administrative work and travels into a more contemplative life, although she continued to give spiritual guidance to her order. As this transition began, she summarized her view of their life in a 1936 address to the sisters: "People out in the world think we are doing something great in giving ourselves to God . . . It is God who is great in giving us the chance to be His spouses." Despite the attempts of many journalists to unveil the life of "the richest nun in the world," Drexel shunned publicity. Insisting that her accomplishments were the work of the order and of God, she explained: "It is more pleasing to God to do things quietly." She remained very close to her sister Louise, who died in 1943.

By 1955, the year of Katharine Drexel's death, her order numbered 501 sisters in fifty-one convents. In addition to Xavier University, the order conducted sixty-one schools, a study house in Washington, D.C., and three social service houses. Katharine Drexel died of pneumonia and heart failure at St. Elizabeth's in Cornwells Heights. The cause of her beatification was opened in 1964 and her writings were approved in 1973, a further step toward canonization.

[Mother Mary Katharine Drexel's letters, diaries, and papers, including her long letters recounting her missionary travels, are at St. Elizabeth's, the motherhouse of the Sisters of the Blessed Sacrament, Cornwells Heights, Pa. A full account of her life is Consuela Marie Duffy, *Katharine Drexel: A Biography* (1966, 1972) which contains a good likeness. See also Sister M. Delores (Marie Elisabeth Letterhouse), *The Francis A. Drexel Family* (1939); Katherine Burton, *The Golden Door: The Life of Katharine Drexel* (1957); Helen Grace Smith, "Apostles of the Negro," *Sign*, July 1934, and "Sketch of the Life of Mother Katharine," *Am. Catholic Hist. Soc. Records*, March 1956; "Fifty Years of Service," *Interracial Rev.*, March 1941; and *Dict. Am. Biog.*, Supp. Five. Obituaries appeared in the Phila. *Eve. Bull.*, the *Catholic Standard and Times*, and the *N.Y. Times*, all March 4, 1955. On her beatification see *Ave Maria*, May 1964; the *Catholic Star Herald*, May 1967; and *Peacemaker*, the Mother Katharine Guild newsletter. A bio-bibliography compiled by John R. Daggett, Margaret Gardner, Deborah Ricketts, and Sister Alma Marie Walls, I.H.M., provided assistance with research. Sisters of the Blessed Sacrament at St. Elizabeth's, particularly archivist Sister Roberta Smith, supplied valuable assistance, including personal reminiscences. A death record was provided by the Pa. Dept. of Health.]

NANCY A. HEWITT

DUMMER, Ethel Sturges, Oct. 23, 1866–Feb. 25, 1954. Philanthropist.

Ethel Sturges Dummer, whose wide-ranging interests included education, mental hygiene, and the problem of prostitution, practiced an active and personal style of philanthropy. Through correspondence, conferences, and direct financial aid, she sought to encourage the creation of new knowledge and to establish connections between people whose work she thought would be mutually stimulating.

Born in Chicago, Ethel Sturges was the third of nine children and first of six girls of George and Mary (Delafield) Sturges. Her ancestry on both sides was English. Family life, though saddened by the early death of Ethel's two older brothers, was characterized by spirited discussions of public events. George Sturges, president of the Northwestern National Bank, took an active role in community affairs. In 1885 Ethel Sturges finished her formal education at the private Kirkland School. Her teachers, including ELLEN GATES STARR, cofounder of Hull House,

emphasized the social service obligations of wealthy women. Through the Kirkland Alumnae Association, which established a lunch room for Chicago shop girls in 1894, Ethel Sturges developed some sense of the problems of working women.

In 1888 Ethel Sturges married William Francis Dummer (1851–1928), a banker and descendant of the distinguished Massachusetts Dummer family. Frank Dummer, born and educated in downstate Illinois, was vice president of the Northwestern National Bank and, like George Sturges, civic-minded. The Dummers had four daughters, Marion (b. 1890), Katharine (b. 1892), Ethel Sturges (b. 1895), and Frances (b. 1899). A last-born boy, William Francis, died in infancy, in 1902. Ethel and Frank Dummer firmly believed in the value of education through planned activity and raised their daughters accordingly. By using phonetic exercises that he had observed at a school for the deaf, Frank Dummer taught his daughters to speak by their first birthday. Ethel Dummer assisted the family tutors to educate the girls through handicrafts, home dramatics, and anagrammatic play with foreign languages. At their Michigan Avenue townhouse in Chicago and at vacation homes in Lake Geneva, Wis., and Coronado, Calif., the family became the hub of the Sturges and Dummer clans.

Ethel Dummer wrote in 1914 that this leisured and family-centered life had given her "no conception of the other 98 percent of humanity." Her public role began in 1905, when articles about child labor in *The Outlook* aroused her to join the National Child Labor Committee and the Chicago Juvenile Protective Association. "From a trim and orderly garden," she recalled, "I slipped into a jungle." Dummer's philanthropy was initially guided by her concern with the conditions of urban life, particularly as these affected children. In 1908 she became a founding trustee of the Chicago School of Civics and Philanthropy and, soon thereafter, underwrote two University of Chicago lecture series on social problems. She also supported a survey of sanitation policies in European cities conducted by MARY MCDOWELL of the University of Chicago Settlement.

In 1909, Dummer made her first and probably most important contribution to the field of mental hygiene by providing the funds to establish the Juvenile Psychopathic Institute. There the neurologist William Healy began *The Individual Delinquent* (1915), a pioneering psychological study of youthful recidivists in the Chicago juvenile court. By relating persistent misbehavior to incorrect nurture, Healy's case studies challenged the then dominant hereditarian viewpoint. Led by Healy and his assistant, psychologist AUGUSTA BRONNER, the Institute utilized the teamwork of psychiatrists, psychologists, and social workers, thereby providing a model for the child guidance clinics that proliferated in the 1920s.

During and after World War I, Ethel Dummer's interests expanded to include study of prostitution and unwed motherhood. Rejecting the conventional belief that prostitutes were inferior and unchangeable types, she opposed forced marriages and legal penalties for prostitution. She also believed that prostitutes, like trench warfare combatants, had suffered shell shock, and she envisioned their return to "constructive living in the community" through sympathetic institutional treatment. Later, she aided the development of therapeutic detention homes such as MIRIAM VAN WATERS's El Retiro in Los Angeles. Dummer also examined European laws and programs affecting unwed mothers and, impressed by Norway's Castberg Law and the feminist writings of Katharine Anthony (1877–1965), she urged the repeal of state laws discriminating against these women and their children.

Throughout her public life, Ethel Dummer drew intellectual support from the ideas of English writer Mary Everest Boole, wife of the logician George Boole. Mary Boole sought to integrate progressive educational values into a philosophy synthesizing Darwinian biology and religion. Thus, she maintained that organized play encouraged the development of conscious mind, which was both the means through which the unconscious found expression and the basis for social activity. Conversely, criminal or antisocial behavior indicated the continued dominance in adult life of the child's animal or instinctual mind and reflected a person's neglected or prematurely abstract education.

Boolean ideas not only confirmed the Dummer family's traditional education practices but also guided Ethel Dummer's philanthropic aid to sympathetic men and women in the new social science professions. In an era before the widespread availability of fellowships and research grants, she personally supported the work of several notable scholars. She assisted Miriam Van Waters's 1922 Survey Graphic study of schools for delinquent girls and also aided her during the writing of Youth in Conflict (1925). When University of Chicago sociologist William I. Thomas lost his job, she provided him with research funds and living expenses and later assisted Thomas and his second wife, Dorothy Swaine Thomas (1899–1977), in the prepara-

tion of their survey of child study programs, The Child in America (1928). Through the 1930s and 1940s, Dummer's enduring philanthropic interest remained the encouragement of educational programs seeking to coordinate the development of children's minds and bodies. In Chicago, she financed Florence Beaman's class for retarded, truant, and delinquent boys at the Montefiore School. In 1932 Neva Boyd (1876–1963) of Hull House used the Dummers' living room to instruct elementary school teachers on the development of exercise programs. "If I could live to see every seat in the first grade rooms removed," Ethel Dummer said, "I should feel that I had not lived in vain." Later, she helped her daughter Ethel D. Mintzer, principal of San Diego's Francis W. Parker School, promote Boole blocks, which were designed to teach algebraic formulas and fractional parts. In the 1940s, she sponsored child development courses at Northwestern University that introduced the work of Jean Piaget.

Although she avoided publicity, Dummer received numerous awards, most notably an honorary doctorate from Northwestern (1940). Unpretentious in dress and manner, she was always eager to discuss new ideas. To the end, she retained an almost mystical faith that humanity would continue to improve. Confronted by Hitler and the holocaust, she paraphrased William Blake: "God has given a body to evil that he may cast it out."

Crippled by arthritis, Ethel Dummer spent the last seven years of her life at the home of her daughter Katharine D. Fisher in Winnetka, Ill. She died there in 1954 of a stroke. Her ashes were scattered among the trees at her Lake Geneva summer home.

[The Ethel Sturges Dummer Papers at the Schlesinger Library, Radcliffe College, are especially informative as a portrait of genteel family life and as the repository of her remarkable professional correspondence. All quotations come from the papers. In addition to those mentioned, her correspondents included Scott Buchanan, Ernest W. Burgess, Marion E. Kenworthy, Julia Lathrop, Adolf Meyer, John B. Watson, and William Alanson White. Some of Dummer's essays appear as prefaces or introductions in the following studies: William I. Thomas, The Unadjusted Girl (1923); The Unconscious: A Symposium (1928); The Collected Works of Mary Everest Boole (1931). Her other writings include The Evolution of a Biological Faith (1943); What Is Thought? (1945); Mary E. Boole: A Pioneer Student of the Unconscious (1945). The principal biographical sources are the papers and Dummer's autobiography, Why I Think So–The Autobiography of an Hypothesis (1937). For family information see Ebenezer Buckingham, comp., *Solomon Sturges and His Descendants* (1907). Obituaries appeared in the *N.Y. Times,* Feb. 27, 1954; *Proceedings,* Inst. of Medicine in Chicago (1954), 201–2; *Am. Jour. Orthopsychiatry,* July 1954; death record provided by Ill. Dept. of Public Health. Additional information was provided by Ethel Dummer's daughter Frances D. Merriam and her grandson Roger D. Fisher.]

ROBERT M. MENNEL

DUNBAR, Helen Flanders, May 14, 1902–Aug. 21, 1959. Psychiatrist, psychoanalyst.

Helen Flanders Dunbar, pioneer in psychosomatic medicine and in clinical training for ministers, and a Dante scholar, dropped her first name at the beginning of her career. Known for a time as H. Flanders Dunbar and finally as Flanders Dunbar, she did not take the names of her husbands, but maintained her own name by law.

Both of her parents were descended from old New England families. Dunbar's mother, Edith Vaughan (Flanders) Dunbar, daughter of a Protestant Episcopal clergyman, was a genealogist who published an account of the Flanders family. She also translated *La Neuvaine de Colette,* and served in the National League for Women's Service. Dunbar's father, Francis William Dunbar, a mathematician and patent attorney, received an electrical engineering degree from the Massachusetts Institute of Technology; one of his first projects was to wire Madison Square Garden. After his marriage, Frank Dunbar worked in Chicago, where Helen Flanders Dunbar was born.

In her first year Dunbar suffered from malnutrition caused by feeding problems. The resulting "pseudo infantile paralysis"—which she later called polio—undoubtedly had an impact on her life, but any physical effects were unnoticeable. She grew up in robust health, delighting in dancing, horseback riding, and challenging her younger brother, Francis. Dunbar was profoundly influenced by the religious faith of her grandmother, Sarah Flanders, who lived with the family; until she opposed Dunbar's decision to attend college, Dunbar revered her.

Dunbar's early schooling was erratic. A tense, sensitive girl, she stayed only a few weeks in public school. At eight she entered the University of Chicago Laboratory School. She was eleven when her father, following an arduous lawsuit in which he successfully represented his company, moved the family to Manchester, Vt., and withdrew increasingly into isolation. For the next three years, Dunbar and her brother studied with tutors until, at her insistence, the

family traveled to the Caribbean, Central and South America, and California. Dunbar studied briefly at the Bishop's School in La Jolla, Calif. (1917), and then entered the Brearley School in New York City (class of 1919). Her mother and brother followed, taking up residence in New York and then in Philadelphia when Dunbar entered Bryn Mawr (A.B. 1923).

The years at Brearley and Bryn Mawr were difficult. Lonely and overprotected, Dunbar wanted friends, but was shunned. She blamed her mother for not giving her proper opportunities and turned to a socially prominent aunt to learn the amenities. Intensely unhappy about her short, fat appearance—she was four feet eleven—"Little Dunbar" withdrew into her studies. She felt empathy for those who suffered and became determined to make her mark by helping alleviate pain.

Flanders Dunbar's brilliance is demonstrated by her stunning graduate career: she earned four advanced degrees within seven years. Interested in Dante Alighieri and the function of symbolism in integrating religion and science, she enrolled in Columbia University in 1923 to study with the Dante scholar Jefferson B. Fletcher and earned an A.M. in 1924 and a Ph.D. in 1929. Her doctoral dissertation, *Symbolism in Mediaeval Thought and Its Consummation in the Divine Comedy* (1929, reprinted 1961) won her an enduring reputation as a Dante scholar. While working for her doctorate, Dunbar entered Union Theological Seminary, where in 1927 she received a B.D. magna cum laude. She enrolled at the Yale University School of Medicine in 1926 while still a student in philosophy at Columbia and in theology at Union, and kept up with classes and research by employing two secretaries.

Dunbar spent her final year of medical school abroad. In Vienna she was hospitant at the General and Psychiatric-Neurological Hospital and Clinic of the University of Vienna and she began psychotherapy with Helene Deutsch. Then in Zurich she became an assistant at the Burghölzli Psychiatric Clinic, meeting periodically with Carl Jung, whose views on religion she found more acceptable than Freud's. To observe the relation of faith to healing, she visited the shrine at Lourdes before returning home to receive her M.D. in 1930.

The months abroad transformed Flanders Dunbar. She returned slender, strikingly pretty, and adept at using her feminine charm. Choosing among several suitors, in 1932 she married Dr. Theodor P. Wolfensberger (later Theodore P. Wolfe), a Swiss psychiatrist whom she had met in Zurich. Wolfe later brought orgone therapist Wilhelm Reich to America and became his English translator.

By temperament and training Dunbar had a special capacity for synthesizing. Seeking to integrate religion and science, medicine and psychiatry, she anticipated later interdisciplinary work in these fields. In 1925 she had worked at the Worcester (Mass.) State Hospital, where the Rev. Anton Boisen was introducing divinity students into a clinical setting so that they might learn from "living human documents." She became director in 1930 of the newly formed Council for the Clinical Training of Theological Students, an organization that grew phenomenally under her leadership and became influential in theological seminaries. Through her efforts and those of the organization countless divinity graduates have begun their ministries better prepared to deal with human problems.

Flanders Dunbar is remembered chiefly for her psychosomatic approach to medicine. In the 1930s she conducted with others a study of 1,600 consecutive patients admitted to Columbia Presbyterian Hospital with such illnesses as coronary heart disease, high blood pressure, diabetes, and asthma. Examining patients' backgrounds and environments, as well as their emotional makeup, she found distinctive personality profiles characteristic of each disease. Unexpectedly, she also identified an accident-prone personality, whose emotional disturbances found outlet in unconscious self-injury. The results of this research were published in *Psychosomatic Diagnosis* (1943). Although her concept of a specific personality profile for certain diseases was later largely abandoned, her work had a far-reaching influence, particularly in calling the attention of the American medical profession to the importance of emotional factors in disease. Dunbar founded *Psychosomatic Medicine*, a journal which she served as editor-in-chief from 1938 to 1947, and its derivative, the American Psychosomatic Society (1942). She also compiled a massive bibliography, *Emotions and Bodily Changes* (1935), a standard reference work that she revised several times. The same year she received another graduate degree (Med. Sc.D., Columbia University) on the basis of this study. Believing that her work had value for preventive medicine and mental health, Dunbar presented her findings to the public in *Mind and Body* (1947), a book that exemplifies her lucid prose style.

Predictably, Dunbar's professional career was complex: she held many positions concurrently and drove herself and others to the limits of endurance. She never traveled without a load of journals, books, notes, manuscripts, and a secretary for dictation. From 1931 to 1949 Dunbar held appointments in medicine and psychiatry at Presbyterian Hospital and Vanderbilt Clinic in New York City. During this period she taught at Columbia University's College of Physicians and Surgeons and, from 1942 to 1947, at the New York Psychoanalytic Institute. She was also engaged in private practice, and was especially successful in inspiring patients, notably women, to creative effort.

In December 1939 Ted Wolfe and Flanders Dunbar were divorced. Eighteen days later her father died. Within six months she married the liberal economist George Henry Soule, Jr., an editor of *The New Republic*, who was fifteen years her senior. In 1941, when she was almost forty, she gave birth to Marcia Dunbar-Soule. Mother and daughter were very close, and Dunbar's scientific articles tended to parallel child's development. Her popular book, *Your Child's Mind and Body,* appeared in 1949; *Your Pre-Teenager's Mind and Body* and *Your Teenager's Mind and Body* were published posthumously.

In her later years, Dunbar devoted herself increasingly to private practice. The quality of her work deteriorated as she relied increasingly on alcohol to deal with emotional pain. Unhappy with Soule, she lived with Dr. Raymond Squier, a gynecologist who was her patient and colleague. When he committed suicide in 1951, press accounts erroneously identified him as Dunbar's second husband. She spent her final years with Soule.

In 1954 Dunbar barely escaped death as a passenger in an automobile accident that damaged her beauty and her health. She was also troubled by a lawsuit, brought by a former patient, that was finally settled out of court. In August 1959, on the day of publication of *Psychiatry in the Medical Specialties,* her daughter found her drowned in the swimming pool of their home in South Kent, Conn. She was fifty-seven. Although her death was an accident, newspapers implied that it might have been a suicide.

Flanders Dunbar was a pathfinder who contributed significantly to psychiatry and medicine. She was, in her daughter's words, "a magnetic, charismatic woman, with a disturbed and beautiful soul and an almost magical gift of insight and intuition."

[There is no Dunbar manuscript collection, but the Union Theological Seminary Library has a box of materials about her association with the Council for Clinical Training. Other papers are still in family hands. Robert C. Powell's dissertation, "Healing and Wholeness: Helen Flanders Dunbar (1902–59) and an Extra-Medical Origin of the American Psychosomatic Movement" (Duke University, 1974), covers in detail Dunbar's life and thought with a complete bibliography to 1939. Powell has published "Helen Flanders Dunbar (1902–1959) and a Holistic Approach to Psychosomatic Problems," in *Psychiatric Quart.*, 1977 and 1978. See also "Bibliography: Flanders Dunbar," *Psychiatry*, 1939, p. 318. Two "In Memoriam" articles assess Dunbar's contribution and character: Franz Alexander, *Am. Jour. of Psychiatry*, Aug. 1960, pp. 189–90, and [George Soule, Jr.], *Psychosomatic Med.*, Oct. 1959, pp. 349–52. The same photograph accompanies both tributes. See also obituaries in the *N.Y. Times* and *N.Y. Herald Tribune*, both on Aug. 23, 1959, and *Dict. Am. Biog.*, Supp. Six. A biobibliography compiled by C. Ross Burns assisted research for this article. Information was also obtained from interviews with Marcia Dunbar-Soule Dobson and Rosamond Grant Fisher; from letters in private hands; and from research shared by Robert C. Powell. A death record was provided by the Conn. Dept. of Health.]

G. ALLISON STOKES

DUNHAM, Ethel Collins, March 12, 1883–Dec. 13, 1969. Pediatrician.

Ethel Dunham, specialist in the care of premature infants, was born in Hartford, Conn., the eldest of five daughters and one son of Alice (Collins) and Samuel G. Dunham. Her father, a highly successful businessman, succeeded his brother as president of the Hartford Electric Light Company in 1912. Her mother, whom she described as "shy, retiring, and gentle," enjoyed art and painted landscapes and miniatures. The ancestors of both parents had migrated from England to Massachusetts in the seventeenth century and had settled in Hartford after 1835.

Ethel Dunham enjoyed the security of a wealthy family and the companionship of fourteen cousins who lived in seven neighboring houses. After graduating from Hartford High School in 1901, she spent two years at Miss Porter's School in Farmington, Conn. The next six years, filled with social activities, golf, two European tours, and some volunteer social work, left her dissatisfied. With unusual determination, she reenrolled at Hartford High School at the age of twenty-six to complete entrance requirements for Bryn Mawr College. Graduating from Bryn Mawr in 1914, Dunham was admitted to Johns Hopkins Medical School, one of eleven women in a class of ninety-five. Entering with her was Martha May Eliot (1891–1978), a Radcliffe graduate who had spent one year at Bryn Mawr, where their enduring friendship began. During their Hopkins years, they attended suffrage meetings together as well

as lectures on philanthropy and midwifery. Thereafter they shared a home, except for a few years when they held appointments in different cities.

In 1918 Dunham interned in pediatrics under John Howland at the Harriet Lane Home of the Johns Hopkins Hospital, while Eliot began an internship in medicine at the Peter Bent Brigham Hospital in Boston. A year later, Dunham went to the New Haven Hospital as one of its first women house officers. Eliot joined her there in 1920 in the newly established department of pediatrics, under Edwards A. Park and Grover Powers. The same year Dunham became director of the outpatient clinic of the New Haven Dispensary and was also put in charge of the nursery for newborn infants. In addition, she served as instructor in the School of Medicine at Yale University, advancing to assistant professor in 1924 and associate clinical professor in 1927. From 1935 until 1950 she returned periodically to speak at Yale, retaining the title of lecturer in clinical pediatrics. Quick to identify problems and to devise solutions, Dunham soon displayed the abilities that marked her later career. Dismayed at the crowded, disorganized dispensary, within a year she had instituted an appointment system that improved patient care and eased the burden on physicians. Despite the resistance of the obstetrician-in-chief who considered the nursery his province rather than that of the pediatrician, Dunham was able to work productively there. Gentle in manner, with a quick sense of humor, she initiated an era of cooperation between the two specialties.

Dunham early discovered what became the central interest of her career: the newborn infant, especially the prematurely born. She published a series of clinical papers on diseases and abnormalities of very young infants, but soon recognized the need for a more systematic study of the factors associated with infant death or survival. In 1927 GRACE ABBOTT, chief of the United States Children's Bureau, appointed Dr. Dunham medical officer in charge of neonatal studies. Under an unusual arrangement, she was permitted to remain at the New Haven Hospital and to conduct her studies there. By 1933 she was able to present to the American Pediatric Society a report on morbidity and mortality among 1,000 newborns. She found prematurity the most important cause of death. The society responded to the report by establishing a committee on neonatal studies chaired by Ethel Dunham.

In 1935 Dunham and Eliot moved to Washington, D.C., where Dunham became director of the division of research in child development of the Children's Bureau, and Eliot the assistant chief of the Bureau. Dunham was convinced that the high mortality rates of newborn and especially premature infants could be reduced if sound standards were established, existing knowledge more widely disseminated, and research encouraged. In her new post, her major goal was the development of standards for the care of newborn infants. In an informal survey of 105 hospitals in 1935, she found that the majority made no special provision for the care of premature babies. The standards that Dunham and her colleagues at the Children's Bureau prepared were published in 1943 as *Standards and Recommendations for the Hospital Care of Newborn Infants, Full Term and Premature.* Recognized as a pioneering work, an expanded version published in 1948 by the American Academy of Pediatrics became one of the Academy's most widely distributed publications.

Dunham's interest in broadening access to existing information culminated in the publication of her book *Premature Infants, a Manual for Physicians* (1948). In this book she brought together the knowledge gained from research in specialized centers in the United States and in other countries. Drawing also on her own clinical and statistical studies, she considered the public health as well as clinical aspects of prematurity. Her book was both a symbol of and a stimulus for marked advances in clinical investigation and public health organization for the care of premature infants.

Among Dunham's other accomplishments at the Children's Bureau was a model effort in the late 1930s aimed at extending infant care from the hospital into the home and community. Dunham assigned a public health nurse and a social worker to collaborate with a pediatrician in follow-up care. This experiment led to greater coordination of activities of members of different professions, and of public and private agencies, for the benefit of premature infants.

Between 1949 and 1951 Dunham and Eliot worked for the World Health Organization in Geneva, Switzerland. As consultant to the maternal and child health section, Dunham organized an expert group on prematurity, which promoted interest in the care of premature infants, in the training of personnel for specialized services, and in the need for research on social and economic as well as biological problems. Returning to Washington when Eliot became chief of the Children's Bureau in 1951, Dr. Dunham began her studies of childbearing and childrearing patterns among primates in their natural habitat. In 1957 the two women moved to Cambridge, Mass.

The same year, Dunham was the first woman to be honored with the Howland Medal, the American Pediatric Society's highest award. In accepting the medal, she showed her continued interest in new research, proposing the use of a marsupial, the Virginia opossum, as a possible subject for studies of the immaturely born young. Ethel Dunham died at home of bronchopneumonia in 1969.

[In addition to the works already mentioned, Dunham published some forty papers, almost all related to problems of premature infants and requirements for their care. A bound volume of reprints is in the Yale Univ. Medical Library. The 1940 edition of *Infant Care*, the Children's Bureau's most widely distributed publication, was the work of Dunham and Marian M. Crane. *Premature Infants, a Manual for Physicians*, was revised by Dunham in 1955 and by William Silverman in 1961. Dunham also published privately a book about her family, *Samuel G. Dunham, Alice Collins Dunham, Their Descendants and Antecedents* (1955). The Children's Bureau records in the Nat. Archives contain approximately 700 of Dunham's letters written between 1921 and 1940. See also "Expert Group on Prematurity—Final Report," Technical Report Series, no. 27, World Health Organization, Geneva, Switz., Oct. 1957. Sources of biographical information include the letters of Martha Eliot to her parents, 1914–18, in the Martha May Eliot Collection, and Eliot's oral history (1976), both at the Schlesinger Library, Radcliffe College. An excellent appreciation of Dunham's life and work is Harry H. Gordon, "Presentation of the John Howland Medal and Award of the American Pediatric Society to Dr. Ethel C. Dunham," *Am. Jour. of Diseases of Children*, Oct. 1957. Dunham's acceptance speech is printed in the same issue. Her professional contributions are ably discussed in Harry H. Gordon, "Perspectives on Neonatology—1975," in Gordon B. Avery, ed., *Neonatology: Pathophysiology and Management of the Newborn* (1975). Helpful information was obtained from Harry H. Gordon, Katherine Bain, and Katharine Lenroot, and from the biobibliography prepared by Sarah M. Fain. Obituaries appeared in the *N.Y. Times*, Dec. 14, 1969, and *Wash. Post*, Dec. 15, 1969; death record from Mass. Dept. of Public Health.]

WILLIAM M. SCHMIDT

E

EAMES, Emma Hayden, Aug. 13, 1865–June 13, 1952. Opera and concert singer.

Emma Eames was the younger of two children of Ithama Bellows and Emma (Hayden) Eames. She was born in Shanghai, China, where her father was a lawyer in the international courts. Her parents were of Scottish and English ancestry. Due to her mother's ill health the family moved to Bath, Maine, in 1870, and from there to Portland. For several years the young girl lived chiefly with her maternal grandparents in Bath. From the age of fifteen she studied singing with her mother in Portland. Encouraged to seek further training, in 1882 she went to Boston, where her light soprano was noticed and she obtained remunerative church work. Three years later she moved to the studio of Clara Munger, a concert soprano who had had Parisian vocal training. At the insistence of composer John Knowles Paine and other influential Bostonians that she go to Paris for completion of her studies, Eames and her mother borrowed money and sailed in June 1886.

The teacher chosen was Mathilde Marchesi, whose school was then the most renowned in Europe for the training of young female voices. Eames's voice, which was already perfectly placed, needed attention only in a few minor aspects, but she undertook the regular Marchesi curriculum: sight-reading, languages, mime, and stage deportment. After two years with Marchesi, whom the singer later referred to as a "Prussian drill-master," Eames was offered a debut at the important Théâtre de la Monnaie of Brussels. Meanwhile, at the school she had made the acquaintance of Australian Nellie Melba, who was already singing in Brussels. Pretending friendship with Eames, Melba successfully blocked the debut. A second theater backed out of another contract. But Marchesi then introduced Eames to Charles Gounod, who was seeking a youthful soprano for his *Roméo et Juliette* at the Paris Opéra. He was impressed and coached her in the part. Eames made her stage debut as Juliette at the tenth performance of the opera, in March 1889, opposite the matinee idol Jean de Reszke. She was an immediate success, as much for her beauty, her svelte figure, and her graceful acting as for the clarity and perfection of her voice. She was taken up at once by the most influential Parisian social, musical, and literary salons and met such figures as Henry James and the future King Edward VII, who remained a lifelong friend.

In 1890 the Opéra management engaged Melba, who made life so nightmarish for Eames

that she refused to renew her contract. Instead, she signed with London's Covent Garden and with the New York Metropolitan Opera for the winter of 1891–92. Her roles in London were Marguerite in *Faust*, Elsa in *Lohengrin*, Mireille in Gounod's *Mireille*, and Desdemona in *Otello*. She repeated her Parisian success and was readily admitted into London social circles. In subsequent years she often sang privately for Queen Victoria. In London in August 1891 Eames married Julian Story, expatriate painter and scion of a distinguished New England family, whom she had met two years earlier. The marriage was a happy one at first but ended in divorce in 1907. Eames earned a fortune early in her career and was able to maintain two European homes, a townhouse in Paris and a castle in Tuscany.

The singer's American debut took place during the Metropolitan Opera's preseason tour in Chicago in the fall of 1891. The vehicle was *Lohengrin*. In December she was introduced to New York as Juliette. Audiences and critics were enthusiastic about her extraordinarily pure voice, her aristocratic art, and the radiance of her person. As in Paris and London, an exclusive social world welcomed her.

The Eames voice, after only three years of professional work, was darkening and growing in power so that, though it retained its early flexibility, it was big enough to enable her to venture into a wide repertory. In her thirteen seasons at the Metropolitan, between 1891 and 1909, she sang many of the major roles in both Italian and German operas. A particular success as *Tosca*, she also appeared in *Aida, Cavalleria Rusticana, Falstaff, Il Trovatore*, and *Don Giovanni*, as well as in *The Magic Flute, The Marriage of Figaro*, and Wagner's *Die Meistersinger, Tannhäuser*, and *Die Walküre*. Eames continued to sing during most seasons in London through 1901, and also performed in Madrid (1893) and Monte Carlo (1896). In New York and London she created a number of roles in new operas that failed. An interesting failure was the world premiere of César Franck's *Giselle* at Monte Carlo.

As a result of what Eames termed her grandmother's puritanical standards, she developed an icy and disdainful air which prompted one reviewer to comment on her Aïda, "There was skating on the Nile last night." She was noted also for her stubbornness, which met its match in the intractability of Giulio Gatti-Casazza and Arturo Toscanini, the new directors of the Metropolitan Opera in 1908–09. The result was her withdrawal from opera at the end of that season. She then devoted herself to concerts, often singing with the Brooklyn-born Emilio de Gogorza. The two were married in 1911, after a scandal-ridden suit for alienation of affection brought by de Gogorza's first wife, but separated a few years later. In spite of her aloofness, Eames was generally much beloved by a large public. She returned to opera briefly in 1911 to sing in *Tosca* and *Otello* with the Boston Opera, and retired finally in 1916. She divided her time between the United States and France until 1936, when she settled in New York City where she taught singing and where she died in 1952.

[Files on Eames at the N.Y. Public Library, Music Div., contain newspaper clippings, portraits, and pictures. Eames wrote an autobiography, *Some Memories and Reflections* (1927), which is generally candid, although guarded concerning her marriages. Her friend Henry T. Finck, in *Success in Music and How It Is Won* (1909), pp. 169–74, and *My Adventures in the Golden Age of Music* (1926), pp. 208–12, gives the best summation of her career. Hermann Klein writes about her London career in *Thirty Years of Musical Life in London* (1903). See also Oscar Thompson, *The American Singer* (1937), pp. 174–83 (which contains several mistakes); Desmond Shawe-Taylor, "A Gallery of Great Singers: Emma Eames (1865–1952)," *Opera*, Jan. 1957, pp. 8–13, 64–65. Irving Kolodin, *The Metropolitan Opera* (1966), deals rather summarily with her New York appearances. An obituary appeared in the *N.Y. Times*, June 14, 1952. A biobibliography prepared by Gale Scharf assisted in the research for this article.]

CHARLES JAHANT

EASTMAN, Linda Anne, July 17, 1867–April 5, 1963. Librarian.

Linda Anne Eastman, the first woman to head a metropolitan library system in the United States, was born in Oberlin, Ohio, to William Harvey and Sarah (Redrup) Eastman. In 1874 the family moved to Cleveland, where Linda, along with her three sisters and two brothers, attended public schools. Her father, of English ancestry, was in the produce business; her mother was a graduate of Oberlin College.

As a schoolgirl, Linda Eastman was impressed by the sympathetic attention of William H. Brett, head of the Cleveland Public Library, who helped her obtain a book she needed. After graduation from West High School in 1885 she attended Cleveland Normal School for a year. Until 1892 she taught fourth graders and was among the first to use classroom collections lent by the Cleveland Public Library. Impressed by the children's eagerness to read, she turned to library work—a field in which she felt she could better aid and educate those with a desire to learn. During 1892 she began working at the Cleveland Public Library and soon became an assistant at the West Side Branch. After she completed an extension course from the New York State Library School in Albany, William Brett appointed her librarian of the new Miles Park Branch in 1894.

In 1895 Eastman, Brett, and Electra C. Doren of the Dayton (Ohio) Public Library founded the Ohio Library Association; eight years later, Eastman became its first woman president. During 1895 she gained additional experience in Dayton as Doren's vice librarian, and the following year Brett invited his protégée to return to the Cleveland Public Library in the same capacity.

Together Eastman and Brett arranged several short library training courses. On the basis of this experience they organized a full-time School of Library Science at Western Reserve University, with the aid of a $100,000 endowment from Andrew Carnegie. The school opened in 1904; Doren became director, and Eastman an instructor in library administration.

In 1894 Eastman heard a speech on "Reading for the Young," given by LUTIE STEARNS, an early advocate of library access for children. Eastman subsequently reshelved Cleveland's children's books in one alcove available to every child. During 1897 she recruited over 14,000 children to a Library League designed to awaken interest in books, and the following year opened a separate children's room.

Linda Eastman also brought the library's services to people in the community, especially to immigrants and the handicapped. Foreign language books and English language study groups provided a bridge toward Americanization. Eastman established libraries in hospitals and sanitariums, and added a Braille collection (1903) and reading group (1906) for the blind; by the time she retired, the library was serving 30,000 blind readers.

Following Brett's death in 1918 Eastman was unanimously elected his successor. In 1925 a five million dollar six-floor building, planned since 1896, was opened under Eastman's supervision. This was the first large public library that successfully used, beginning in 1913, a divisional plan—an arrangement that grouped together books on similar subjects, rather than separating all the books into reference and circulating departments, as had been the practice. Staff with specialized backgrounds were assigned to each reading room and limited-access shelves were eliminated, making books directly available to readers. In the 1920s Eastman began a county extension service; she also established a municipal reference service, a travel service, and a business information bureau that was considered one of the best in the nation.

When the library's tax base was severely reduced during the depression, Eastman was forced to cut services at a time when circulation increased by 20 percent and the library was serving as many as 12,000 persons daily. Nonetheless, she provided current vocational materials, a directory of adult-education opportunities, and advisers to counsel the influx of jobless borrowers. In 1936, with Works Progress Administration funds and assistance from Girl Scouts, she organized a book delivery service to shut-ins. By the time Eastman retired in 1938, the Cleveland Public Library had grown from a collection of 57,000 volumes with a staff of 18 to one of over 2,000,000 volumes with a staff of over 1,100.

Eastman belonged to many civic and professional organizations. She served on the American Library Association's council and executive board, was made a vice president in 1917, and became its president in 1928. She received honorary degrees from three universities, a Carnegie Corporation award for educational leadership (1927), and the Cleveland Medal for Public Service (1929). The Cleveland Public Library's Eastman Branch (1947) and the Eastman Reading Garden (1960) were named in her honor. She died in Cleveland of bronchopneumonia in 1963.

Linda Eastman's best-known work, her biography of William Brett, provides insight into her own philosophy of service. Drawn to librarianship by her love of literature and her desire to aid those eager to learn, she devoted her life to the enrichment of Cleveland's people. She supplied books and information adapted to their age, education, and interest level, and extended library services into the community. Throughout her long life she was honored and admired for her practical vision, her organizational power, and her personal integrity.

[Primary source materials are at the Schlesinger Library, Radcliffe College, which contains Eastman's papers, 1925–58; the School of Library Science, Case Western Reserve Univ.; and the Cleveland Public Library. Numerous professional articles by Eastman are listed in a bibliography dated Nov. 1937 at the Archives of Case Western Reserve Univ. Her most important published work is *Portrait of a Librarian: William Howard Brett* (1940). Two master's theses that include interview information are Cecil Olen Phillips, "Linda Anne Eastman: Librarian" (School of Library Science, Case Western Reserve Univ., 1953), and Alice Edwards Wright, "Linda Anne Eastman: Pioneer in Librarianship" (Kent State Univ., 1952). Basic published sources are C. H. Cramer, *Open Shelves and Open Minds: A*

History of the Cleveland Public Library (1972), and *Annual Report* of the Cleveland Public Library, 1892–1938. Short biographies can be found in *Dict. Am. Library Biog.* (1978); *Nat. Cyc. Am. Biog.*, C, 465; and *Who's Who in Library Service*, 1933. Obituaries appeared in the *ALA Bull.*, Sept. 1963, pp. 783–85; the *Library Jour.*, May 1963, p. 1974; and the *Cleveland Press*, April 8, 1963. Death certificate was obtained from the Ohio Dept. of Health.]

VALMAI FENSTER

EASTWOOD, Alice, Jan. 19, 1859–Oct. 30, 1953. Botanist.

Alice Eastwood was born in Toronto, Canada, eldest of the two daughters and one son of Colin Skinner and Eliza Jane (Gowdey) Eastwood, who came from northern Ireland. Her paternal grandfather, a native of Yorkshire, England, founded the Unitarian church in Toronto; her father was steward of the Toronto Asylum for the Insane. At six, after her mother's death, Alice was placed in the care of her uncle William Eastwood, a physician, who taught her Latin plant names. A French priest who gardened at Oshawa Convent, where she lived for six years, taught her gardening practices. When she was fourteen the family was reunited in Denver, Colo., where her father was a storekeeper and invested in real estate. While keeping house, acting as nursemaid, and working in a millinery factory, she attended public schools, graduating from East Denver High School in 1879 as valedictorian.

For the next ten years Alice Eastwood taught a medley of subjects at East Denver High. Studying plants was her joy, and by foot, horseback, buckboard, stage, and train she botanized in the Colorado mountains. David Moffat, railroad builder, issued her a pass, and so characteristically she later commemorated him in *Penstemon moffatii*. The English naturalist Alfred Russel Wallace accompanied her on a walk up 14,000-foot Grays Peak in 1887 and recalled: "We luxuriated here in plants which were altogether new to me." In 1890, with a modest income from real estate sales and rentals, Eastwood resigned her teaching job and toured California, meeting botanists who encouraged her to join them. Returning to Colorado, she visited remote places for botanical explorations, from Thompson Springs, Utah, to Mancos, Colo. Later, at her own expense, she published *A Popular Flora of Denver, Colorado* (1893).

In 1892 Alice Eastwood returned to California, accepting a modest assistantship offered by KATHARINE BRANDEGEE at the California Academy of Sciences in San Francisco. She was assigned the task of founding the California

Botanical Club and directed its activities thereafter. When Katharine and Townshend Stith Brandegee moved to San Diego in 1894, Eastwood succeeded Katharine Brandegee as curator of the herbarium at the academy and briefly took over T. S. Brandegee's post as editor of the journal *Zoe*. In addition to her responsibilities at the academy, she was able to do extensive field work in California, beginning in the little-known inner south Coast Ranges, where she found a xerophytic shrubby daisy named *Eastwoodia* by T. S. Brandegee. An avid outdoorswoman, she climbed Mt. Whitney with the Sierra Club in 1903. One product of her botanical forays was *A Handbook of the Trees of California* (1905), of which she noted in her preface: "The aim has always been brevity and clearness—the desire to help rather than to shine." The line drawings in this book and her other papers were her own.

For some years preceding the San Francisco earthquake and fire of 1906, Alice Eastwood had been enlarging the academy's botanical collection and prophetically segregating critical type specimens from the herbarium's 100,000 sheets. When the earthquake and fire left the academy in shambles, through her fortitude and prompt action the segregated specimens were rescued. She described the disaster in a letter printed in the May 25, 1906, issue of *Science* and in an article in *Torreya* in June 1906. Alone and with devotees of the academy she set out to rebuild the crippled botany department with field trips to the Coast Ranges and Sierra Nevada. To verify the accurate application of plant names against the original specimens from which the descriptions were published, she made study visits to the historic herbaria of Harvard University, the New York Botanical Garden, and the National Herbarium in Washington, D.C. Her travel included extended stays at the British Museum of Natural History, the Royal Botanic Gardens, Kew, and the Natural History Museum at Paris.

In 1912 Alice Eastwood returned to the United States and resumed her post at the academy. From then until her retirement in 1949, over 340,000 specimens were added to the herbarium. One of her aims was to verify the classification of tropical and subtropical exotics grown in California. Her own large personal contributions also made possible the reassembly of an outstanding botanical library. In 1932, together with her assistant John Thomas Howell, she founded and edited the much needed journal *Leaflets of Western Botany*. For a time she had also assisted in editing Willis Jepson's journal *Erythea*. Her own bibliography exceeds 300 titles, including semipopular articles on California gardens.

Forceful, energetic, and outgoing, Alice Eastwood not only provided professional botanists with critical specimens but also stimulated fuchsia fanciers to grow novelties, instructed travelers in the best methods of plant collecting, and helped to arouse the public to save native species, from the endemic lowly salt marsh sanicle to the giant redwoods. To popularize botany she maintained changing exhibits of freshly gathered flowers in the academy's foyer. She was the "gardener's botanist" to west coast horticulturists—to Golden Gate Park superintendent John McLaren and his associate Eric Walther, and to KATE SESSIONS of San Diego. Recognition and awards came from garden clubs as well as from the Seventh International Botanical Congress in Stockholm in 1950, which elected her honorary president. Her name was starred in every edition of *American Men of Science*.

Alice Eastwood lived alone in a small cottage on San Francisco's Russian Hill and was in good health up to her final illness. She died of cancer in San Francisco in her ninety-fifth year.

[Eastwood's correspondence and memorabilia from 1906 on are at the Calif. Acad. of Sciences. Depositories of her plant collections are listed in J. Lanjouw and F. A. Stafleu, "Index Herbariorum, Part II (2)," *Regnum Vegetabile* 9 (1957), 175. A bibliography of her publications in Calif. Acad. of Sciences *Proceedings*, 1949, pp. xv–xxiv, is supplemented by the list in the ten-year index, 1932–66, of *Leaflets of Western Botany* (1968), pp. 114–16. Carol Green Wilson, *Alice Eastwood's Wonderland: The Adventures of a Botanist* (1955) is the official biography. A short illustrated biography by Susanna Bryant Dakin, *Perennial Adventure: A Tribute to Alice Eastwood, 1859–1953* (1954), includes a reprint of her "Early Botanical Explorers on the Pacific Coast and the Trees They Found There," with additional notes by John Thomas Howell. Relevant articles in the Aug. 28, 1953, issue of *Leaflets of Western Botany*, commemorating the centennial of the Calif. Acad. of Sciences, include Carol Green Wilson, "The Eastwood Era at the California Academy of Sciences," and "A Partial Gazetteer and Chronology of Alice Eastwood's Botanical Explorations," and Victor Reiter, Jr., "Horticulture and the California Academy of Sciences." See also John Thomas Howell, "I Remember . . . ," *Leaflets of Western Botany*, Aug. 26, 1954, pp. 153–76. A distinctive photograph of the youthful Alice Eastwood appears in Olga Reifschneider, *Biographies of Nevada Botanists* (1964). A. R. Wallace, *My Life: A Record of Events and Opinions* (1905), vol. 2, pp. 180–84, tells of his 1887 visit with her. Two obituaries by Howell complement each other: *Taxon*, May 1954, pp. 98–100, and *Sierra Club Bull.* 39 (6), 78–80. An obituary also appeared in the *N.Y. Times*, Oct. 31, 1953. Death certificate supplied by Calif. Dept. of Health Services.]

JOSEPH EWAN

EDINGER, Tilly, Nov. 13, 1897–May 27, 1967. Vertebrate paleontologist, paleoneurologist.

Tilly Edinger was born Johanna Gabrielle Ottelie in Frankfurt am Main, Germany, the last of three children and younger daughter of Ludwig and Anna (Goldschmidt) Edinger. Her parents, both independently wealthy, were among the most prominent citizens of Frankfurt. Tilly's mother came from a family of bankers and was a widely respected leader of social welfare movements, while Ludwig Edinger was a famous medical researcher who helped found the science of comparative neurology.

Tilly Edinger studied at the universities of Heidelberg and Munich from 1916 to 1918 and received her doctorate in natural philosophy at Frankfurt in 1921, submitting a dissertation on the skull and cranial cavity of a fossil reptile, Nothosaurus. She remained at Frankfurt for the next six years as a research assistant in paleontology. In 1927 she became curator of the vertebrate collection at the Senckenberg Museum in Frankfurt, working without pay. Two years later she published Die Fossilen Gehirne (Fossil Brains), one of her two major works. Edinger did not take up the study of brains as a passive follower in her father's footsteps. In fact, her father had not thought highly of professional careers for women, and she had initially hoped to be a geologist, giving up her studies in that field when she learned that opportunities for women scarcely existed.

Edinger, with a good job and a wealthy family rooted for centuries in Frankfurt, would never have joined the ranks of American scientists but for one fact: she was Jewish. After the Nazis came to power, the director of the Senckenberg Museum managed to keep her there for five years by removing her name from the door and having her use a side entrance whenever visitors were present. In 1938, however, she was discovered and forced to leave her position. Edingerstrasse, a street dedicated to her father, had its name changed and a bust of her mother was removed from the town park. Later her brother Fritz died in a concentration camp. In May 1939 Tilly Edinger fled Germany for London, where she found work as a translator.

She came to the United States in 1940 to work at Harvard University, which had designated funds for the temporary employment of displaced European scholars. Thanks to the intercession of A. S. Romer, director of the Museum of Comparative Zoology, Edinger became a research associate under this program. Except for a year when she taught zoology at Wellesley College (1944–45), she remained at the Museum for the rest of her life; she became a United States citizen in 1945. She continued her study of fossil brains, publishing her second great work, The Evolution of the Horse Brain, in 1948. She also pursued a variety of anatomical investigations with fossil vertebrates (advancing the controversial argument that the pineal opening of lower vertebrates was originally a light-sensitive organ, or "third eye"), and later collaborated with three other authors on a two-volume bibliography of vertebrate paleontology from the sixteenth to twentieth centuries. Her comprehensive bibliography on fossil brains was published posthumously.

Assisted in her work by fellowships from the Guggenheim Foundation (1943–44) and the American Association of University Women (1950–51), Edinger earned the respect of her colleagues, who named her president of the Society of Vertebrate Paleontology for 1963–64. She also received honorary degrees from Wellesley (1950) and from the German Universities of Giessen (1957) and Frankfurt (1964)—the last she particularly treasured as she remained strongly loyal to her native city, despite her ill treatment there. She was feisty, strong-willed, opinionated, and warm-hearted—a most engaging, if sometimes trying, combination. Edinger, who was very hard of hearing, was struck by an automobile near her home in Cambridge on May 26, 1967, and died the next day.

Tilly Edinger surely ranks among the dozen or so major figures of twentieth-century vertebrate paleontology. She virtually established the field of paleoneurology (the study of fossil brains) with her groundbreaking work on the casts of the cranial cavity, often preserved as fossils. In mammals, as opposed to nonmammalian vertebrates, the brain tends to fill the cranial cavity tightly, and a cranial cast can be a virtually exact replica of the brain's external structure. Fossil brain casts had been described before Edinger's time, but usually as curiosities only: hers was the first systematic work. She used this evidence to shed new light on the brain's evolution, which had been conventionally (but quite invalidly) discussed in terms of a supposedly "progressive" and unilinear sequence of modern vertebrates—the rat, the cat, the monkey, and the human, for example—a scheme reviving the discredited scala naturae (or chain of being) in vogue among eighteenth-century philosophers.

Edinger proved that the brain's evolution could and should be studied directly from fossils, not from a misleading hierarchy of separate modern species, each adapted to its own mode of life. She railed against the chain-of-being approach in several articles. And in her work on the horse brain, she showed that an enlarged forebrain evolved several times, independently among advanced groups of mammals; no single evolutionary scale embraced them all. Moreover, she showed how rates and styles of change varied in different lineages, and how relationships among parts of the brain differed with varying ecologies and adaptations among groups of mammals. Thus Edinger contributed to the understanding of evolution as a complex branching bush, rather than a ladder to perfection. Thanks to her pioneering work, paleoneurology became one of the most active and exciting subdisciplines of vertebrate paleontology.

[Tilly Edinger's papers, including professional correspondence, drafts of articles, and photographs, are held in the archives of the Museum of Comparative Zoology at Harvard. The Edinger family papers are at the Leo Baeck Institute, N.Y. City. The AAUW Foundation in Washington, D.C., holds a file on her, which includes her fellowship application and reports. Among Edinger's major works are *Bibliography of Fossil Vertebrates, Exclusive of North America, 1509–1927*, Geological Soc. of Am., Memoir 87, 2 vols. (1962), with A. S. Romer, N. E. Wright, and R. v. Frank; and "Paleoneurology, 1804–1966: An Annotated Bibliography," *Advances in Anatomy, Embryology and Cell Biology*, 49, parts 1–6 (1975), which includes a foreword by Bryan Patterson reviewing Edinger's career. A complete bibliography of Edinger's works, along with an assessment of her career, may be found in H[elmut] Hofer, "In Memoriam Tilly Edinger," *Gegenbaurs Morphologisches Jahrbuch*, 113, no. 2 (1969), 303–13. See also *Am. Men and Women of Science*, 11th ed. (1965); A. S. R[omer], "Tilly Edinger, 1897–1967," *News Bull., Soc. of Vertebrate Paleontology*, Oct. 1967, pp. 51–53; H. Tobien, "Tilly Edinger," *Paläontologische Zeitschrift*, vol. 42 (1968). Obituaries appeared in the *N.Y. Times, Boston Herald*, and *Boston Globe*, all on May 29, 1967. Death certificate furnished by Mass. Dept. of Public Health.]

STEPHEN JAY GOULD

EVANS, Alice Catherine, Jan. 29, 1881–Sept. 5, 1975. Microbiologist.

Alice Evans's discovery and confirmation of the etiology of the disease brucellosis has been cited as one of the outstanding achievements in medical science in the first quarter of the twentieth century. Yet it took extraordinary perseverance for this woman scientist without a medical or Ph.D. degree to convince the scientific establishment of the validity of her work.

Alice Catherine Evans was born in Neath, Pa., the only daughter and younger of two children of William Howell and Anne (Evans) Evans. Both parents were of Welsh descent; her paternal grandfather had settled in Pennsylvania in 1831 and her mother had emigrated from Wales at age fourteen. William Evans was a surveyor, teacher, and farmer who fought in the Civil War. Alice Evans attended a rural elementary school and obtained her secondary education at Susquehanna Collegiate Institute in Towanda, Pa. (1898–1901). She taught school for four years, then took her meager savings and went to Ithaca, N.Y., to enroll in a two-year nature study course for rural teachers offered by Cornell University.

At Cornell Evans became interested in science and, aided by a scholarship, continued for a B.S. degree (1909), with a major in bacteriology. Receiving a scholarship at the University of Wisconsin at Madison, she obtained an M.S. degree in bacteriology in 1910, under the direction of E. G. Hastings of the university's College of Agriculture. Professor E. V. McCollum, the discoverer of vitamin A, encouraged her to continue for a Ph.D. and offered her a fellowship in chemistry. She accepted instead Hastings's offer of a research position working for the Dairy Division, Bureau of Animal Industry of the United States Department of Agriculture. Assigned to study the bacteriology of milk and cheese, Evans began work in July 1910 at the state agricultural experiment station in Madison.

In 1913, when the new research laboratories of the Dairy Division were ready for occupancy, she was transferred to Washington, D.C. There she became involved in one of the Division's major research programs: the identification of sources of bacterial contamination of milk products. (This work was in accord with the then prevailing opinion that fresh, unpasteurized whole milk was quite healthful if uncontaminated.) On her own Evans also studied the bacterial flora of milk freshly drawn from healthy cows' udders.

This latter work led to her pioneering studies on brucellosis and to her discovery of a common origin for what had previously been considered two separate diseases, one affecting humans, the other cattle. In 1887 David Bruce, a British army surgeon, had isolated the *Micrococcus melitensis* in the bodies of British soldiers who had died from the mysterious Mediterranean or Malta fever. Goats on Malta were found to be the means by which the disease was transmitted; it was subsequently prevented by stopping the consumption of raw goats' milk. The second organism, *Bacillus abortus*, was identified in 1897 by the Danish veterinarian Bernhard Bang as the cause of contagious abortion in cattle. The true relationship between these very similar organisms was clouded by the difference in classification and by the lack of contact between physicians and veterinarians.

Evans's investigations of milk flora showed that varieties of *B. abortus* were common in the milk of normal cows. She then compared *B. abortus* from cattle, *M. melitensis* from goats, and a third organism recently discovered in diseased pigs and found that they all appeared and behaved in culture nearly identically. She reported her results at the 1917 meeting of the Society of American Bacteriologists and published them in 1918 in the *Journal of Infectious Diseases*. At this time Evans warned that raw cows' milk might present a danger to human health and that ordinary pasteurization readily destroyed *B. abortus*. The announcement was greeted with skepticism on the part of many scientists and physicians and with outright hostility on the part of dairymen. No human cases of undulant fever, as Malta fever had come to be designated, had yet been discovered with a bovine source. The disease was in fact exceedingly difficult to diagnose; its acute symptoms simulated those of typhoid fever, malaria, tuberculosis, influenza, and rheumatism.

Transferring in 1918 to the Hygienic Laboratory of the United States Public Health Service (later the National Institutes of Health), Evans worked on epidemic meningitis and influenza. At the conclusion of World War I, she resumed her investigations of *B. abortus* and *M. melitensis*. Her work now received confirmation by other scientists, and by 1920 Karl F. Meyer of the University of California proposed a new genus, *Brucella*, to include both organisms. Evans continued to extend knowledge of the *Brucellae*, examining samples from all over the world and demonstrating that they could be grouped into several strains by serological tests. In 1922, while working with *Br. melitensis*, Evans herself became infected, and suffered recurrent episodes of chronic brucellosis over the next twenty-three years.

Despite the mounting evidence, some scientists still resisted Evans's conclusions. Her most formidable opponent was Theobald Smith, perhaps the foremost authority in the United States on animal and human infections. Smith, who had earlier challenged the view that the transmission of bovine tuberculosis to humans through milk and meat was a major source of that disease, apparently also believed that *Br. abortus* from cattle was not dangerous except perhaps under unusual circumstances. Attempting to explain Smith's determined opposition, Evans later observed: "The nineteenth amendment was not a part of the constitution of the United States when the controversy began and he was not accustomed to considering a scientific idea proposed by a woman." In 1925, through the mediation of William Henry Welch of the Johns Hopkins University, the disagreement was resolved to the extent that Smith agreed to chair the Committee on Infectious Abortion of the National Research Council to which Evans had been appointed.

Evans's work had widespread repercussions. By the late 1920s, as numerous cases of human brucellosis were being reported from all over the world and from diverse animal sources, the disease came to be recognized as an important hazard for occupational groups which come in close contact with domestic animals, and as a worldwide threat to human and animal health and to food supply industries. Further studies in the 1930s eventually forced the dairy industry to accept the pasteurization of all milk, a measure that greatly diminished the incidence of brucellosis in the United States.

In 1928 Alice Evans's accomplishments were recognized by the Society of American Bacteriologists, which elected her its first woman president. Other honors followed. She was a United States delegate to the First International Congress of Microbiology in Paris in 1930, and again at the Second Congress in London in 1936. She also received several honorary degrees. Around 1939 she began investigating immunity to streptococcal infection, and continued to study streptococci until her retirement in 1945. After she retired Evans became honorary president of the Inter-American Committee on Brucellosis, serving until 1957, and in 1975 she was elected honorary member of the American Society for Microbiology (ASM). She moved in 1969 to a retirement home in Arlington, Va., where in 1975 she died following a stroke.

Alice Evans was an imaginative researcher, intrepid in the face of opposition, and courageous during the long period of recurring illness. Outspoken in her beliefs, at age eighty-five she protested the disclaimer of communist affiliation on the Medicare application as a denial of constitutional rights.

[Alice Evans's unpublished autobiography, "Memoirs," personal papers, and photographs are at the Nat. Library of Medicine, Bethesda, Md., and the ASM Archives, Univ. of Md. There are also Evans papers, mainly correspondence relating to brucellosis, at the Cornell Univ. Libraries. Another copy of "Memoirs," which includes a bibliography, is in the Schlesinger Library, Radcliffe College. The correspondence of Evans, Smith, and Welch is in the dept. of bacteriology, Univ. of Wis. Evans's earliest publications on her discovery include "The large numbers of *Bact. abortus* var. *lipolyticus* which may be found in milk," *Jour. Bacteriology*, March 1917, and a series of three articles under the general title of "Further Studies on *Bacterium Abortus* and Related Bacteria," in vols. 22 and 23 (1918) of the *Jour. Infectious Diseases*. Several earlier publications are brought together in "Studies on Brucella (Alkaligenes) melitensis," Hygienic Lab. Bull., Aug. 1925. In 1950 the AAAS Symposium, Brucellosis, printed her "Comments on the Early History of Human Brucellosis." A bibliography listing most of her publications, compiled by W. J. B. Morgan and M. J. Corbel, appears in an issue of Annali Sclavo dedicated to Evans, Feb. 1977. Two major articles about Evans are Elizabeth M. O'Hern, "Alice Evans, Pioneer Microbiologist," ASM News, Sept. 1973,

and "Alice Evans and the Brucellosis Story," Annali Sclavo, Feb. 1977. See also Current Biog., 1943. In 1947 the DuPont Co.'s "Cavalcade of America" on NBC presented a radio program dramatizing Evans's life and work. Obituaries appeared in the N.Y. Times and Wash. Post, Sept. 8, 1975; NIH Record, Sept. 23, 1975; and ASM News, vol. 42 (1976). Death certificate provided by Va. Dept. of Health.]

ELIZABETH M. O'HERN

F

FARRAND, Beatrix Jones, June 19, 1872–Feb. 27, 1959. Landscape architect.

Beatrix Jones Farrand, the finest woman landscape architect of her generation, was born in New York City, the only child of Mary Cadwalader (Rawle) and Frederick Rhinelander Jones. Her father came from a wealthy family of Dutch and English ancestry; her mother's ancestors were English. Beatrix Jones was, as she put it, "the product of five generations of garden lovers." Her grandmother owned one of the first espaliered fruit gardens in Newport, R.I. At eight Beatrix observed the laying out of the grounds of Reef Point, her parents' summer home at Bar Harbor, Maine. Reef Point was later the site of one of the most ambitious projects of her career.

Beatrix Jones grew up in the tightly knit world of New York society. Tutored at home, she frequently traveled abroad with her mother and with her father's sister, EDITH WHARTON. The novelist aided her niece and sister-in-law financially after the Joneses were divorced (sometime before Beatrix was twelve). Mary Cadwalader Jones managed the New York assembly balls for a number of years. She was a close friend of Henry James and often entertained other such distinguished writers and artists as Henry and Brooks Adams and John La Farge.

Before she was twenty, Beatrix Jones lived for several months at Holm Lea, the estate of Charles Sprague Sargent, near Brookline, Mass. With Sargent, the founder and first director of the Arnold Arboretum, she studied horticulture and was introduced to the principles of landscape design. Although she developed her own philosophy of design, she always followed Sargent's early advice "to make the plan fit the ground and not twist the ground

to fit a plan." Encouraged by Sargent to become a professional, she began taking private landscape commissions in 1897. Within a short time she was able to establish a distinguished list of clients and could count among her patrons on Long Island and in Maine Edward Whitney, Willard Straight, and J. P. Morgan. She was also consulting landscape architect for ABBY ALDRICH ROCKEFELLER's garden at Seal Harbor, Maine, for nearly fifty years. In 1899 Beatrix Jones joined Frederick Law Olmsted, Charles Eliot, and others in founding the American Society of Landscape Architects. Interviewed shortly afterward, she remarked, "Society, yes, it is very agreeable," but "this grand art of mine is a noble art."

Beatrix Jones's earliest designs were formal in character but reflected the influence of William Robinson, the English landscape architect and author of The Wild Garden. She also admired the work of the celebrated English landscape gardener Gertrude Jekyll who, like Robinson, advocated the use of wild and native materials. Jones shared with Jekyll too a subtle and harmonious approach to color. Her lifelong associate, the landscape architect Robert Patterson, later wrote that Beatrix Jones Farrand's work had a "freedom of scale," "a subtle softness of line and an unobtrusive asymmetry." Her designs combined the best elements of Baroque and English landscape gardening.

Beatrix Jones gained among her private clients a reputation for thoroughness and certainty of approach. At Dartington Hall, an English estate of more than 2,000 acres, she is said to have understood the complexities of the whole site at a glance and laid out terraces, the great lawn, and encircling system of paths. This reputation also extended to her public work. At Princeton University, beginning in 1916, she designed the Graduate College gardens, achieving quiet, simple effects through broad stretches of lawn, espaliered ivy, and wisteria.

Jones married Max Farrand, a distinguished constitutional historian and chairman of the Yale University history department, on Dec. 17, 1913. Both were dedicated to their work, and the marriage seems to have been a happy and constructive one. At Yale, beginning in 1923, Beatrix Farrand designed the Memorial Quadrangle gardens and, in cooperation with the departments of botany and forestry, established a maintenance program which long remained in effect. She also served as landscape consultant to Vassar College, the University of Chicago, and Oberlin College. Her college work was marked by good sense and careful attention to detail; she noted in her Yale instructions that "spaces must be kept free . . . and nothing should be attempted in the way of ornamentation that is flimsy in character or inappropriate to the use of thousands of young men."

It was at Dumbarton Oaks in Washington, D.C., that Farrand achieved her finest work. Working closely with her friend Mildred Bliss (1880–1969), who was herself an imaginative gardener, she transformed what had once been a farm into one of the finest gardens in this country. Mildred Bliss had cherished the idea of a garden throughout her years as the wife of diplomat Robert Woods Bliss. The Blisses purchased the property in 1920, and the gardens evolved under Farrand's direction over the next twenty years. Terraced formal gardens near the Georgian manor house reflected its architectural character. Gardens removed from the house were increasingly informal and designed to express the wooded character of the land below. The entire composition reflects a clear understanding of the topographic subtleties of the site. "Never . . . did Beatrix Farrand impose on the land an arbitrary concept," wrote Mildred Bliss. "She 'listened' to the light and wind and grade of each area." The gardens are marked by a richness of architectural detail and imaginative choice of materials, as well as a sense of delicacy and restraint, qualities associated with all of her best work. Writing of the copse at Dumbarton Oaks, Farrand said that the "idea of the planting was to keep it as poetic and delicate as possible" and to make it "the sort of place in which thrushes sing and dreams are dreamt." Of all her designs, only the gardens at Dumbarton Oaks survived essentially unchanged.

Farrand brought to her art a discriminating and critical intelligence which earned her the respect of her contemporaries. She received many awards, including the Garden Club of America Medal of Achievement (1947) and the New York Botanical Garden Distinguished Service Award (1952). Formal and reserved in both appearance and manner, she was admired for her integrity and dedication.

Keeping a small office in New York, Farrand traveled constantly among assignments in Maine, New York, and Washington, supervising the planting and construction of her garden designs. In 1927 Max Farrand became director of research at the Huntington Library in San Marino, Calif., but the Farrands made their home principally at Bar Harbor. Beatrix Farrand devoted the last years of her life to Reef Point Gardens, a project she and her husband had begun some twenty years before his death in 1945. Designed for both scholarly and experimental purposes, Reef Point ultimately included a test garden of native flora, a library (which included the original garden plans of Gertrude Jekyll), and a herbarium. In 1955, concerned about the survival of Reef Point Gardens, Farrand decided to transfer the contents of the library, the herbarium, and her own correspondence to the department of landscape architecture at the University of California, Berkeley. Beatrix Farrand died at Bar Harbor in 1959.

[The Beatrix Farrand Coll. on Landscape Design, in the College of Environmental Design Documents Coll., Univ. of Calif., Berkeley, contains her landscape plans, drawings, correspondence, and unpublished manuscripts. The collection is described in H. L. Vaughan, "Library Gift to California," *Landscape Architecture*, Oct. 1956, pp. 298–300. The Dumbarton Oaks Center for Studies in Landscape Architecture holds some correspondence between Farrand and Mildred Bliss as well as plans for the gardens at Dumbarton Oaks. There are several letters from Henry James to Mary Cadwalader Jones and a few to Beatrix Jones in the Roger Sherman Green Papers, Houghton Library, Harvard Univ. The Max Farrand Memorial Fund published the *Reef Point Gardens Bulletins*, Aug. 1946–June 1956. Farrand contributed two articles on landscape gardening at Princeton to the *Princeton Alumni Weekly*, June 9, 1926, and May 29, 1931. Sources of information about her life and work include Robert W. Patterson, "Beatrix Farrand—1872–1959: An Appreciation of a Great Landscape Gardener," *Landscape Architecture Quart.*, Summer 1959; and a volume of the same title published by Mildred Bliss (1960), which contains Bliss's article, "An Attempted Evocation of a Personality," and articles by Lanning Roper and Robert Patterson. See also *Dict. Am. Biog.*, Supp. Six; Walter Muir Whitehill, *Dumbarton Oaks: The History of a Georgetown House and Garden* (1967); Marlene Salon, "Beatrix Jones Farrand: Pioneer in Gilt-Edged Gardens," *Landscape Architecture*, Jan. 1977, pp. 69–77; and Georgina Masson, *Dumbarton Oaks: A Guide to the Gardens* (1968). Family background is provided in Louis

Auchincloss, *Edith Wharton: A Woman in Her Time* (1971). Death record supplied by Maine Dept. of Health and Welfare.]

ELEANOR M. MCPECK

FARRAR, Geraldine, Feb. 28, 1882–March 11, 1967. Opera singer.

Geraldine Farrar was born in Melrose, Mass., the only child of Henrietta (Barnes) and Sidney D. Farrar. Her father kept a small store in Melrose and, in the summer, played baseball for the Philadelphia team of the old National League. Both parents were amateur singers.

The possibilities inherent in Geraldine's voice became apparent when she was twelve, and she was recommended to Mrs. John H. Long, a prominent Boston teacher. Henrietta Farrar was ambitious for her daughter and, as Geraldine's voice developed, decided to send her to New York for intensive study with the country's leading concert soprano, EMMA THURSBY. In Thursby's studio she was heard by Nellie Melba and LILLIAN NORDICA, both of whom insisted on European training for the young singer. A substantial loan was arranged and in 1899 the Farrar family set out for Paris, where Geraldine was enrolled in the class of Antonio Trabadelo for one winter. Again on Nordica's advice, she moved on to Berlin for work with Giorgio Graziani. Soon she auditioned at the Berlin Court Opera and was accepted on a trial basis. She made her first professional appearance there in October 1901 as Marguerite in Gounod's *Faust.*

Because of her youth, her innate acting ability, and her great beauty, Farrar became an immediate sensation. She was permitted the luxury of singing her first three roles in Italian until she could master German. As soon as possible, she placed herself under the tutelage of the noted Wagnerian soprano, Lilli Lehmann. She became an intimate of the German royal family and especially of Crown Prince Frederick Wilhelm, and rumors of a liaison persisted.

Word of Farrar's talents spread quickly, and contract offers flowed in. The Berlin Opera lent her to Monte Carlo in 1904 for appearances in *La Bohème* with Enrico Caruso. An invitation by the tsarist theaters for 1904–05 was accepted, but the singer got only as far as Warsaw when the 1905 revolution broke out, and she returned to Berlin. During these years she was also heard in Stockholm and Munich.

Noting her European successes, the Metropolitan Opera approached Farrar with a contract for 1906–07. En route to New York she stopped off for a Paris debut and her first creation of a role: as the leading soprano in Camondo's *Le Clown* at the Théâtre Nouveau. Her initial American appearance occurred on Nov. 26, 1906, opening night of the Metropolitan season, when she sang Juliette in Gounod's *Roméo et Juliette.* She delighted audiences from the outset. Critics, too, welcomed her, although they found a certain hardness in her top register. Soon after the debut, she became the original Metropolitan Madame Butterfly opposite Caruso. From then on they made many appearances as a team.

During this period, Farrar's voice was a strong lyric soprano with dramatic accents, and she was able to encompass a wide range of roles in the French and Italian repertoire, as well as in works by Mozart and Wagner. She had the advantage of working under such divergent conductors as Gustav Mahler and Arturo Toscanini, whose mistress she was for seven years. But her studies under so many teachers with differing theories, and the strain she imposed on her voice by singing too frequently, ultimately told. In 1913 her voice broke during a performance. Following a period of rest it gradually returned. It was no longer the silvery instrument it had been, although it remained serviceable for a dozen or more years thereafter. In New York alone, Farrar sang 493 performances of twenty-nine roles, ninety-five of them as the hapless Butterfly.

Geraldine Farrar was the first opera star to be summoned to Hollywood. Between 1915 and 1920 she made fourteen films, including *Carmen* (1915) and *Joan the Woman* (1917). Her 1916 marriage to Lou Tellegen, an actor whom she met in Hollywood, was possibly the greatest mistake of her life. A scandalous and painful divorce case ensued, during which Tellegen threatened to reveal the truth about her Berlin escapades. Farrar's lawyers countered with the information that Tellegen had a criminal record in France, and she won her divorce in 1923.

The much acclaimed performance of Maria Jeritza at the Metropolitan in 1921 in the favorite Farrar opera of *Tosca* confirmed Farrar's decision to withdraw at the end of the season. Her farewell appearance was the occasion for stormy demonstrations of loyalty by hundreds of young woman fans who called themselves "Gerry-flappers." Farrar retired to an estate in Ridgefield, Conn., but returned to the concert stage between 1924 and 1931. In 1925 she organized a tour of her own revised version of *Carmen,* a somewhat avant-garde production featuring Art Deco costumes for herself and dances by a Broadway choreographer. Audiences were "horrified and charmed," to quote one critic. The following year she attempted an operetta,

Romany Love by Franz Lehar, but it closed after one performance.

In retirement Farrar engaged in civic affairs, wrote poetry, and composed songs. For one season she was intermission commentator on the Saturday Metropolitan Opera broadcasts, sometimes singing and playing the piano as well. During World War II she was a Red Cross volunteer, a member of the American Women's Volunteer Service Transport Corps, and a frequent correspondent with servicemen stationed overseas. She died of bronchopneumonia at her home in Ridgefield at the age of eighty-five.

Geraldine Farrar made an important place for herself in musical history. She sang in the first performances anywhere of Mascagni's *Amica*, Saint-Saëns's *L'Ancêtre*, and, at the Metropolitan Opera, Giordano's *Madame Sans-Gêne*, Humperdinck's *Königskinder*, and Puccini's *Suor Angelica*. She was admired and loved for her verve, her beauty, her unfailing flair for the pictorial in both her wardrobe and her sense of staging, and her singleness of purpose toward her art. Although evaluations of Farrar's career often stress her acting rather than her technical proficiency, WILLA CATHER described her voice as "feeling which manifests itself in sound." That voice lives on, in the more than 100 phonograph records Farrar made, from 1904 throughout her career.

[Geraldine Farrar's autobiography, *Such Sweet Compulsion*, was published in 1938. The most complete account of her career is Edward Wagenknecht, *Geraldine Farrar: An Authorized Record of Her Career* (1929), which includes a list of her operatic roles, a chronology of her appearances in New York, and lists of her movies and recordings. Biographical sketches appear in Henry T. Finck, *Success in Music and How It Is Won* (1909), which also prints excerpts from her letters; Oscar Thompson, *The American Singer* (1937); and David Ewen, *Living Musicians* (1940). Evaluations of her operatic career include Willa Cather, "Three American Singers," *McClure's Magazine*, Dec. 1913; Irving Kolodin, *The Metropolitan Opera* (1966); and Henry Pleasants, *The Great Singers: From the Dawn of Opera to Our Own Time* (1966). Henry T. Finck, *My Adventures in the Golden Age of Music* (1926), is a more personal account. Obituaries appeared in the *N.Y. Times*, March 12, 1967; *Opera News*, April 15, 1967; and *Opera*, May 1967.]

CHARLES JAHANT

FAUSET, Crystal Dreda Bird, June 27, 1893– March 28, 1965. Race relations specialist, state legislator.

Crystal Bird Fauset, the first black woman elected to any American state legislature, was born in Princess Anne, Md. She was one of the youngest of nine children and the second youngest daughter of Portia E. (Lovett) and Benjamin Oliver Bird. A light complexion evidenced her mixed racial background. Her father was born in Gettysburg, Pa., in 1853, and her mother in Virginia to a family newly freed. Benjamin Bird, a graduate of Centenary Biblical Institute, was the first principal of Princess Anne Academy for black youth (later part of the University of Maryland), a post Portia Bird held for three years following her husband's death in 1897. Portia Bird died in 1900 and Crystal was raised by her mother's sister in Boston. She attended integrated public schools there and, in 1914, graduated from Boston Normal School. After three years as a teacher in Boston she resigned in 1918 to become a field secretary for the National Board of the Young Women's Christian Association (YWCA). In this position she traveled throughout the country with responsibility for Girl Reserves programs aimed at Negro students and working girls.

In 1927 the Interracial Section of the American Friends Service Committee (AFSC) engaged Crystal Bird for an innovative program designed to communicate the human aspirations and longings of blacks. Endowed with extraordinary charm and intensity, she spoke "with great vividness and with the utmost frankness, but without rancor or bitterness" (Jones, p. 169), and fulfilled her mission, an AFSC observer noted, with exceptional "fire and magnetism." In a 1928 report to the AFSC, prior to her departure for Europe to rest and study, Crystal Bird said that her 210 speeches had reached almost 50,000 people in a single year. She also completed her formal education during these years, receiving a B.S. from Teachers College, Columbia University, in 1931. That year she married Arthur Huff Fauset, a Philadelphia school principal. They soon separated, although it was not until 1944 that Arthur Fauset initiated divorce proceedings.

Continuing her efforts at interracial understanding, Crystal Bird Fauset helped to create the Swarthmore College Institute of Race Relations in 1933 and for two years was joint executive secretary of the Institute's summer seminars. In 1935 she became assistant to the director of the Philadelphia Works Progress Administration (WPA). She also began to work in party politics, organizing the Philadelphia Democratic Women's League and in 1936 serving as Director of Colored Women's Activities for the Democratic National Committee.

Philadelphia Democratic party leaders, recognizing her ability as a public speaker and her deep involvement in local civic and political life, urged Fauset to run for the state legislature in

1938. After a bitter primary contest, she won election in a district where two-thirds of the voters were white, gaining strong support from women through an innovative telephone appeal. "My interest is no way limited to my race," she said after her victory, "but is universal." Slum clearance and low-cost housing projects were her top priorities; she also campaigned for fair employment legislation to ban discrimination against blacks and other minorities.

Election to the legislature gained Fauset national renown. She received Pennsylvania's Meritorious Service Medal in 1939 but resigned from the Assembly late that year to become assistant state director of the Education and Recreation Program of the WPA and race relations adviser in all sectors of the WPA in Pennsylvania.

Through her work for the Institute of Race Relations Fauset had met ELEANOR ROOSEVELT; she later drew on her campaign role to renew this relationship. Eleanor Roosevelt provided a link between Negro leadership and President Franklin D. Roosevelt, giving Fauset the chance to press black concerns at the centers of governmental power. On Oct. 20, 1941, Fauset became a special assistant in the Office of Civilian Defense, a post permitting her to monitor black participation on the American "home front." She resigned on Jan. 3, 1944, to work for the Democratic National Committee on the forthcoming election. By mid-August, however, she had come to feel the new party leadership rejected Negro women's campaign efforts. Political pressures kept Eleanor Roosevelt from intervening in the dispute, and, although it meant the sacrifice of her connection to the White House, in September Fauset publicly declared for the Republican presidential candidate.

From 1945 on world affairs claimed Fauset's energies. A founder that year of the United Nations Council of Philadelphia (afterward the World Affairs Council), she went to San Francisco as an observer at the inaugural session of the United Nations. Later she developed educational programs to foster understanding between white and nonwhite peoples. In 1950 she journeyed with an associate in these projects, Sophia Yarnall Jacobs, to attend India's independence ceremonies as guests of Madame Vijaya Lakshmi Pandit. Extensive travel in India, the Middle East, and Nigeria led Fauset to seek a high-level diplomatic post in Africa. In 1957 she protested in a telegram to the White House that the United States delegation to mark Ghana's independence should have included "a woman like myself . . . to represent the millions of slave mothers" in America's past.

Crystal Bird Fauset's determination to engage her strengths in public undertakings, and her bitterness at the bruises she and other blacks endured in a white-dominated world, sometimes overwhelmed her earlier optimistic expectations. In her last years she made her home in New York City; while visiting Philadelphia in 1965 she died in her sleep.

[The principal manuscript sources are in the Archives of the Nat. Board of the YWCA in N.Y. City. The General Files, Interracial Section, AFSC Archives, Philadelphia, has material relating to her employment by AFSC. There is some correspondence in the Franz Boas Papers, Am. Phil. Soc. Library; in the Eleanor Roosevelt Papers, Franklin D. Roosevelt Library, Hyde Park, N.Y.; and in the Dwight D. Eisenhower Presidential Library, Abilene, Kans. The Moorland-Spingarn Research Center, Howard Univ., has clippings on Fauset's career. Scattered newspaper coverage includes an article on Fauset's election in the *N.Y. Amsterdam News*, Dec. 3, 1938. Mary Hoxie Jones, *Swords into Ploughshares* (1937), pp. 169–70, discusses Fauset's work; her portrait appeared in *The Crisis*, Dec. 1938, cover, and July 1943, p. 207. Obituaries appeared in the *N.Y. Times*, Philadelphia *Inquirer*, and Wash. *Star*, all March 30, 1965, and the *N.Y. Amsterdam News*, April 3, 1965; death record provided by Pa. Dept. of Health. Further information was provided by Anna Arnold Hedgeman and Sophia Yarnall Jacobs.]

RUTH BOGIN

FAUSET, Jessie Redmon, April 26, 1882–April 30, 1961. Writer, editor, teacher.

Jessie Fauset, novelist, poet, and editor, was the seventh child and fifth daughter of Anna (Seamon) and Redmon Fauset. She was born in Fredericksville, N.J., one of several small towns in which her father, a minister in the African Methodist Episcopal church, held pastorates. Redmon Fauset's forebears had lived in Philadelphia since the eighteenth century. Like them, he had been born free and because of his relatively privileged social status, he was able to provide his children with a measure of economic security and to encourage their ambitions for education. Anna Fauset died when Jessie was a child and her father married Belle Huff, a widow with three children. Two sons and a daughter were born of this marriage.

Her mother's early death strengthened the bond between Jessie Fauset and her father. When she was denied admission to a local teachers' college after her graduation from the Philadelphia High School for Girls, he was able to intervene. His influence, coupled with her superior academic abilities, won her admission to Cornell University, from which she was graduated in 1905. At Cornell, she was elected to Phi Beta Kappa, probably the first black woman to receive that honor. She later pursued her studies in French at the University of Pennsylvania (A.M., 1919) and at the Sorbonne. Her student experiences, exceptional as they were, helped convince Fauset that prejudice was an obstacle that could be overcome.

Jessie Fauset began her professional life in 1906 as a teacher of French and Latin at the M Street High School (later Dunbar High School) in Washington. Her strong commitment to racial uplift soon found expression outside the classroom. In 1912 she began to publish occasional articles and book reviews in *The Crisis*, the influential journal (edited by W. E. B. Du Bois) of the National Association for the Advancement of Colored People (NAACP). From 1919 to 1926 Fauset was its literary editor. She also wrote biographical sketches of diverse figures and reported on contemporary events. One of the few women to participate in the 1921 Pan-African Congress, Fauset shared her vivid impressions of that meeting with *Crisis* readers; later she described her travel in Europe and the Middle East during 1925 and 1926. As Du Bois proselytized for a more international political perspective among blacks, Fauset offered reviews and translations of works by French-speaking black writers from Africa and the Caribbean.

By far the most significant achievement of Fauset's tenure at *The Crisis* was her provision of a showcase for the young writers of the Harlem Renaissance. It was she who chose the poetry and fiction that appeared in the magazine and, according to Langston Hughes, Jessie Fauset was one of those "who midwifed the so-called New Negro literature into being." In her role as mentor, she also wrote encouraging and critical letters to authors, published numerous reviews, and opened her home as a literary salon. Fauset played an analogous part on the progressive children's magazine, *The Brownies' Book*, edited by Du Bois in 1920 and 1921. Many of the female authors of the Harlem Renaissance were first published there, among them novelist Nella Larsen (d. 1964). As an editor, Fauset demonstrated sound critical judgment, admirable receptivity to new intellectual and political thought, and an appreciation for innovative literary ideas.

Fauset's own fiction and poetry often lacked the adventurous quality she admired and nurtured in others. Her writing is important, however, for its revelations of the lives and aspirations of those middle-class blacks who, for Fauset, exemplified the "New Negro." Her poetry, of which "La Vie C'est La Vie" is the best known, is most aptly described as *vers de société*. Marked by French phrases and a so-

phisticated tone, it seems intended primarily for a refined middle-class audience.

In Fauset's fiction young men and women struggle against prejudice without succumbing to bitterness. For Joanna Marshall, the heroine of *There Is Confusion* (1924), racism is merely a complication in the larger ordeal of attaining womanhood and achieving fulfillment. She aspires to a career as a concert singer and discounts race as a barrier to realizing her goals. By contrast, her lover Peter Bye is disillusioned by the discrimination he meets in his efforts to become a doctor. Absorbed in her own pursuits throughout much of the novel, in the end Joanna sacrifices her ambition to ensure his success and he disavows bitterness to achieve their now common goal.

To emerge victorious, Fauset's characters must learn to sacrifice, as Joanna and Peter do. The protagonist of *Plum Bun* (1929), Fauset's best-written novel, attempts to escape this responsibility by "passing" as white. Although subtitled "a novel without a moral," *Plum Bun* clearly argues that one must accept not only one's self but also one's obligation to the race. *The Chinaberry Tree* (1931) suggests a reason for the disproportionate share of sacrifice required of Fauset's female characters. During slavery, the mother of the novel's heroine had been the mistress of a wealthy white man; although their love was genuine they could not legitimize it through marriage. After slavery, however, the black woman was free to be virtuous, and for Fauset this was a precious freedom indeed. Her last novel, the ironically titled *Comedy: American Style* (1934), tells the tragic story of a woman's self-hatred and its devastating effect on her family. An ambitiously conceived novel, it impresses more for its choice of subject than for its execution.

In 1927 Fauset had joined the faculty of De Witt Clinton High School in New York City as a teacher of French. Two years later she married Herbert E. Harris, an insurance agent and businessman. They moved to Montclair, N.J., in 1939 but she continued to teach in New York until 1944. Although she maintained contact with some black writers and intellectuals through the thirties, Fauset did not continue to take an active part in black cultural affairs. In 1949 she spent a semester at Hampton (Va.) Institute as a visiting professor of English. Following a lengthy illness, Jessie Fauset died at the home of her stepbrother, Earl Huff, in Philadelphia in 1961.

[Letters of Jessie Fauset may be found in Herbert Aptheker, ed., *The Correspondence of W. E. B. Du Bois*, vol. 1 (1973); the Moorland-Spingarn Research Center, Howard Univ.; and the Jean

Toomer Coll., Fisk Univ. Archives. The Schomburg Center for Research in Black Culture, N.Y. Public Library, has a useful clipping file. Important critical assessments of Fauset's writings appear in Robert Bone, *The Negro Novel in America* (1965); William Stanley Braithwaite, "The Novels of Jessie Fauset," *Opportunity,* Jan. 1934, pp. 24–28; Sterling Brown, *Negro Poetry and Drama* and *The Negro in American Fiction* (1937, 1969); Addison Gayle, *The Way of the New World* (1975); Nathan Huggins, *Harlem Renaissance* (1971); and Marion L. Starkey, "Jessie Fauset," *The Southern Workman,* May 1932, pp. 217–20. Hiroko Sato, "Under the Harlem Shadow: A Study of Jessie Fauset and Nella Larsen," in Arna Bontemps, ed., *The Harlem Renaissance Remembered* (1972), also includes an extended bibliography of Fauset's writings which is the best guide to her publications in *The Crisis.* There are two dissertations: Cheryl A. Wall, "Three Novelists: Jessie Fauset, Nella Larsen, and Zora Neale Hurston" (Harvard Univ., 1976), and Carolyn Wedin Sylvander, "Jessie Redmon Fauset, Black Writer" (Univ. of Wis., 1976). Langston Hughes, *The Big Sea* (1940), and Claude McKay, *A Long Way from Home* (1937), provide personal reminiscences. An obituary appeared in the *N.Y. Times,* May 3, 1961. Fauset's birth order is confirmed by the U.S. Census, 1880 and 1900. Family information was provided by Arthur Huff Fauset.]

CHERYL A. WALL

FERBER, Edna, Aug. 15, 1885–April 16, 1968. Writer, playwright.

Edna Ferber recorded in her novels the growth and particular vitality of many regions of the United States, among them Oklahoma, Texas, Alaska, New Orleans, and Appleton, Wis., where she spent most of her childhood. She was born in Kalamazoo, Mich., the second of two daughters of Julia (Neumann) and Jacob Charles Ferber. She was early aware that her mother had badly wanted her to be a boy, to be called Edward. From the beginning Edna Ferber was one of those striving, precocious, active girls known as tomboys who find insipid the usual girlish pursuits.

Ferber's parents were Jewish, but did not practice their religion. She early in life rejected conventional belief in God but always thought of herself as privileged because a Jew. "Being a Jew makes it tough to get on, and I like that," she later wrote; perhaps this attitude was confirmed by an early childhood spent in what she described as an anti-Semitic middle western town. The effects of anti-Semitism remained a consuming interest throughout her life.

Julia Ferber came of an established family of merchants and bankers that had reached America in the 1840s; she grew up on Chicago's North Side. Her mother had ruled the family as a matriarch, and she became the dominant personality in her own marriage. Jacob Ferber was born in Hungary and came to the United States at seventeen. His eyesight began to fail when his daughter was a child; once blindness had overtaken him, the entire support of the family, financial and emotional, fell upon his wife, who ran the family store.

The Ferbers moved from Kalamazoo to Chicago to Ottumwa, Iowa, back to Chicago, then to Appleton, where they remained until Jacob Ferber's death. During her childhood, Edna Ferber read a book a day, and the whole family attended the theater, a practice they did not abandon even as their misfortunes mounted. Ferber from early childhood hoped to be an actress, an ambition not wholly abandoned until she appeared, at the age of fifty-five, in a production of her own play *The Royal Family.*

At seventeen, Ferber graduated from Appleton's Ryan High School; her high school days were particularly happy because of a gifted principal who ran the school along advanced lines. Ferber describes herself at this time as a plump, stocky, and ugly girl in eyeglasses, with thick black hair in a wiry bush. She did not lack boyfriends, but seems early to have decided that her life would not be lived along conventional lines. Taking her mother as a role model, Ferber determined upon a life of competence and self-reliance. Her admiration for her mother, and her sense of emulating her, is told in *Fanny Herself* (1917), Ferber's only autobiographical novel.

Just before graduation Ferber had won the Wisconsin State Declamatory Contest, and she wanted to attend the Northwestern University School of Elocution, but there was no money. She could not leave home, and so went to work for the *Appleton Daily Crescent* as a reporter at the salary of three dollars a week. She still wished to be an actress, not a writer, but her lifelong profession was determined.

The first woman reporter in Appleton was a phenomenon; she covered a regular beat, often frightened and offended, but learning to write concisely, to observe, to remember without taking notes—rare lessons for a novelist. Her salary eventually rose to eight dollars a week. At nineteen she went to work for the *Milwaukee Journal,* earning fifteen dollars a week, and for the first time leaving her tightly knit family. For two more years Ferber underwent what she was to call good training, but brutal, and at the end of this time collapsed from fatigue; her reporting days were over. Convalescing, she turned to the writing of fiction. When Jacob Ferber died in 1909, the family sold the store in Appleton and moved to Chicago, where Julia Ferber invested her money in real estate.

Ferber's first published story, "The Homely Heroine," appeared in *Everybody's Magazine* in 1910; her first novel, *Dawn O'Hara*, was published in 1911. There followed many short stories set in Chicago, all with the sound sociological basis Ferber always claimed for her writing. Beginning in 1912, her stories were collected into volumes, the first called *Buttered Side Down*, because the stories were mainly about working-class people and eschewed the usual, almost obligatory happy ending. Some reviewers saw the stories as clearly the work of a man using a female pseudonym, a fact of which Ferber was proud. She believed that a writer's sex should not be evident in the work. Soon after this, she began writing the Emma McChesney stories, about a woman drummer (saleswoman), which appeared in *The American Magazine* and *Cosmopolitan*. These stories, still readable, were very new then, particularly in their understanding that assertiveness in women was necessary to success. They were collected in three volumes, from 1913 to 1915. Ferber received extraordinary offers for more Emma McChesney stories, but realized that she no longer enjoyed writing them.

When her sister Fannie married Jacob Fox, Ferber began a lifetime of traveling. She first moved to New York City in 1912, but returned to Chicago that year to cover the national political conventions for the George Matthew Adams Newspaper Syndicate. There she met William Allen White, of the *Emporia Gazette*, who was to remain a close friend and adviser.

In 1914 she took her first trip to Europe, and remained grateful that she had seen that civilization before World War I destroyed it. She returned to New York for a dramatization of the McChesney stories, *Our Mrs. McChesney* (1915), starring ETHEL BARRYMORE, Ferber's first experience in the production of a Broadway play. Her next work, however, was the novel *Fanny Herself*, the story of a Jewish family in Wisconsin. With this novel she established the pattern of writing 1,000 words a day, whenever possible.

Ferber's career as a playwright began in 1919, when she collaborated on a play produced by George M. Cohan which failed. From this experience, she learned much that would serve her in later collaborations with George S. Kaufman. Their association began in 1924 with *Minick*, and included such famous productions as *The Royal Family* (1927), *Dinner at Eight* (1932), and *Stage Door* (1936). *Show Boat*, based on the Ferber novel of 1926, has been in almost constant production since it was first adapted for the stage in 1927.

Ferber's first best seller was *So Big*, the story of a woman dirt farmer with a no-good son, published in 1924 and awarded the Pulitzer Prize for the best novel of that year. It sold 300,000 copies, in a time before the invention of book clubs. Thereafter, her novels, which continued to achieve enormous sales, created many places and conditions she had experienced only briefly or not at all. As she wrote, "I can project myself into any age, environment, condition, situation, character or emotion that interests me deeply." She claimed that no reviewer ever criticized the veracity of her novels. In all, Ferber published more than twenty-five volumes, including two of autobiography, thirteen novels, eight plays, and many collections of stories. Her late novels, especially *Saratoga Trunk* (1941) and *Giant* (1952) were made into highly profitable movies.

A major event in Ferber's life was the building of Treasure Hill, a vast and luxurious estate in Connecticut, the fulfillment of a childhood dream. This home gave her years of happiness, but she determined to sell it when she realized it was taking her attention and energies away from her writing. Ferber proudly believed herself to be one of only 250 people in the United States who earned a living entirely from writing, without salary. Edna Ferber died in New York City of cancer at the age of eighty-two; her wealth, reputed to be over a million dollars, was left to her sister and two nieces.

Edna Ferber is an example of that uniquely modern phenomenon, the best-selling novelist ignored by the critics and condemned to the category of middlebrow by those culture-watchers who notice, or fail to notice, their work. Probably she was ignored because, as a best seller, she not only reinforced the fantasies of American readers in the 1920s and after, but ignored those themes which obsessed many of the critics of her time: the oppressiveness of American society; the politics of depression; the validity of Marxism; the rough sexuality of male, as opposed to female, fantasy. Her friends were mostly men, including those in the famous circle that gathered at New York's Algonquin Hotel, but her major portraits were all of women, unusual in the relentlessly masculine world of American fiction. Her gallery of compelling women characters testifies to her belief in female determination and autonomy.

Ferber's female characters are the essence of her originality. Strong, ambitious women, often exploited by the men they love, they nonetheless order their lives to the ends they have chosen. Emma McChesney, however victimized by her son, will not have an inferior hotel room palmed off on her. Molly Brandeis and Fanny after her, in *Fanny Herself*, make their own lives in the way of modern women, with only token regret for lost male lovers. Selina, in *So Big*, typifies the strength of America's frontier women. Clio Dulaine, in *Saratoga Trunk* (1941), plans her own triumph and lands the strong man in the bargain. Ferber's novels offered an American success fantasy, but offered it in the person of accomplished and ambitious women.

[The Edna Ferber Papers at the State Hist. Soc. of Wis. contain correspondence; research materials, notes, manuscripts, and galleys for her stories, novels, plays, and autobiographies; as well as reviews, speeches, clippings, and photographs. Some Ferber correspondence, as well as a clipping file, are in the Billy Rose Theatre Coll., N.Y. Public Library; additional correspondence is held by the Manuscripts and Archives Div., N.Y. Public Library, and by the Beinecke Library, Yale Univ. Works about Ferber, except for her two autobiographies, *A Peculiar Treasure* (1939) and *A Kind of Magic* (1963), of which the former is by far the more important, are slight. Vito J. Brenni and Betty Lee Spencer, "Edna Ferber: A Selected Bibliography," *Bull. of Bibliography*, Sept.-Dec. 1958, pp. 152–56; the entry in *Contemporary Authors*, vol. 5–8, which also contains a bibliography; DeWitt Bodeen, "Edna Ferber into Film," *Films*, June-July 1978, pp. 321–30, which includes a filmography; and Miles Kreuger, *Show Boat: The Story of a Classic American Musical* (1978), are useful. The 1978 biography, *Ferber*, by her great-niece Julie Goldsmith Gilbert, is far from satisfactory: it airs many family antagonisms which seem unfair to its subject. Based on a conventional view of women, it depicts Ferber as suffering from spinsterhood; and it is written backwards, from Ferber's death to her birth, conveying little sense of her development and extraordinary career. For brief accounts of her life and career see Annabel Douglas McArthur, "Edna Ferber," State Hist. Soc. of Wis. Women's Auxiliary, *Famous Wisconsin Women*, IV (1974), pp. 4–8, and *Nat. Cyc. Am. Biog.*, C, 298. In Lewis Nichols, "Talk with Edna Ferber," *N.Y. Times Book Rev.*, Oct. 5, 1952, she discusses her writing. Articles about her work include Grant Overton, "The Social Critic in Edna Ferber," *The Bookman*, Oct. 1926, pp. 138–43, and William Allen White, "A Friend's Story of Edna Ferber," *English Jour.*, Feb. 1930, pp. 101–06. Malcolm Goldstein, *George S. Kaufman: His Life, His Theater* (1979), discusses Ferber's collaboration with Kaufman. An obituary appeared in the *N.Y. Times*, April 17, 1968. A biobibliography prepared by Anita Wilburn Gauthier assisted in research. Ferber's date of birth is recorded in her mother's diary and confirmed by the Mich. Dept. of Public Health; however, she habitually cut two years from her age, so the date is widely reported as 1887.]

CAROLYN G. HEILBRUN

FERGUSON, Margaret Clay, Aug. 20, 1863–Aug. 28, 1951. Botanist.

Margaret Clay Ferguson was born in Orleans,

N.Y., the third of four daughters and fourth of six children of Robert Bell and Hannah Mariah (Warner) Ferguson. Her mother was of English descent. Her father, of Scottish ancestry, farmed in the township of Phelps, N.Y. At fourteen, Margaret Ferguson began teaching in the public schools in the Phelps area, becoming an assistant principal in 1887. During these years, she also studied at Genesee Wesleyan Seminary in Lima, N.Y., graduating in 1885. She later maintained that her experience there was second only to her mother in influencing the course of her life.

Ferguson became a special student at Wellesley College (1888–91), combining course work in botany with chemistry, a science few botanists then pursued. After spending two years as head of the science department of Harcourt Place Seminary in Gambier, Ohio (1891–93), she was asked to return to Wellesley by Susan Maria Hallowell, professor and head of the botany department, whom she had impressed as a student. Ferguson served there as an instructor in botany until 1896, traveled briefly to Europe, and then returned to the United States in 1897 to complete her formal education at Cornell University under the direction of George F. Atkinson. Cornell awarded her a B.S. in 1899 and a Ph.D. in 1901.

At Cornell, Ferguson initiated important research on the reproductive process and life history of a species of native pine *(Pinus strobus)*. In 1903 she submitted a greatly extended version of her doctoral thesis to a contest held to publicize the American Women's Table at the Naples Zoological Station. Although FLORENCE SABIN won the prize that year, Ferguson earned honorable mention; her work was published by the Washington Academy of Sciences in its 1904 *Proceedings* and subsequently became widely known. Exemplifying her gifts as a painstaking observer and illustrator, the study was one of the first to give a detailed analysis of the functional morphology and cytology of a pine native to North America, setting a standard for further investigations of plant life histories.

For many years Margaret Ferguson combined research with teaching and administrative responsibilities at Wellesley College. Returning there as an instructor in botany in 1901, five years later she become full professor; she served as head of the department from 1902 until 1930. An excellent teacher and efficient administrator, Ferguson built a modern and innovative department, emphasizing laboratory work and the importance of chemistry and physics, in addition to zoology, to botanical studies. She planned, designed, and raised funds for new college greenhouses and for a botany building, which was completed in 1927. Besides insisting that this building be attached to the greenhouses—a radical departure from the norm in the early twentieth century—she furnished space in these glass laboratories for the students to grow plants and conduct experiments in genetics, horticulture, and physiology, another innovation. During these years, she also saw to the increase in number and diversity of specimens in the college herbarium and to the acquisition of current research periodicals as well as rare botanical works by the college library. Ferguson helped make her department one of the nation's leading undergraduate centers for the study of plant science, and many of her students pursued careers in botany or related fields.

During the 1920s, the focus of Margaret Ferguson's research and advanced level courses shifted to genetics. Beginning with her "Preliminary Announcement of Cytological and Genetical Study of *Petunia*" (*Anatomical Record*, Dec. 1924), she proceeded to demonstrate the potential of *Petunia* as a tool for studying higher plant genetics. Ferguson wrote a number of papers describing pollen color and chromosome numbers and revising the taxonomy of the then confused state of the horticultural varieties. She found no cases of Mendelian inheritance for flower color or pattern, suggesting that these alleles are unstable; experiments in the 1970s confirmed her findings. She continued work with *Petunia* as a research professor at Wellesley from 1930 until her formal retirement in 1932; that same year she received a grant-in-aid from the National Research Council and exhibited her work on *Petunia* at the Sixth International Congress of Genetics.

Concluding research in 1938 at the age of seventy-five, Ferguson left Wellesley to live near family members in Seneca Castle, N.Y. She later moved to Florida and in 1946, to San Diego, Calif., where she died five years later of a heart attack.

Margaret Ferguson received several major honors during her lifetime, including election as the first woman president of the Botanical Society of America (1929). She received an honorary D.Sc. at Mount Holyoke College's centennial (1937) and became a fellow of the New York Academy of Science (1943). Wellesley honored her in 1946 by naming after her the greenhouses she had designed and directed.

[Ferguson's papers, including lecture notes, MSS., correspondence, and a list of publications, are in the Wellesley College Archives. See also the Minutes of the Trustees, Office of the President, Wellesley College. For information on her family and early years see *The Ferguson Family in Scotland and America* (1905), pp. 114–28. Other published biographical sources include Sophie C. Hart, "Margaret Clay Ferguson," *Wellesley Mag.*, June 1932, pp. 408–10; Harriet B. Creighton, "The Margaret C. Ferguson Greenhouses," *Wellesley Alumnae Mag.*, Feb. 1947, pp. 172–73; and *Am. Men of Science*, 9th ed. (1955). An obituary by Harriet B. Creighton appeared in *Wellesley Alumnae Mag.*, Jan. 1952, p. 106. Documents were furnished by Cornell Univ. and Mount Holyoke College, and personal information by F. Leah Andrews, Town Clerk, Phelps, N.Y., Ada Ferguson Caves, and Harriet Creighton. Death certificate supplied by Calif. Dept. of Health Services.]

ANN M. HIRSCH
LISA J. MARRONI

FERGUSON, Miriam Amanda Wallace (Ma), June 13, 1875–June 25, 1961. Governor.

Miriam Amanda Ferguson, who served two terms as governor of Texas, was born in Bell County, Texas. She was the eldest of three daughters and third of six children of Eliza (Garrison) Wallace, a native of Texas, and Joseph Lapsley Wallace, who came to Texas from Kentucky at the age of twelve. Both parents were of British ancestry. Her father dealt in land and cattle and became wealthy by the standards of the community. Raised on the family farm, Miriam Wallace received her early education from a tutor at home. Later she attended Salado College, a preparatory school, and Baylor Female College (later Mary Hardin-Baylor College).

On Dec. 31, 1899, she married James Edward Ferguson, her cousin by marriage. The couple lived in Belton, Texas, where Jim Ferguson was a rising young lawyer with interests in real estate and banking. They had two daughters, Ouida Wallace (b. 1900) and Ruby Dorrace (b. 1903). In 1907 Jim Ferguson moved his family from Belton to nearby Temple, where he founded and became president of the Temple State Bank. As the family prospered, he was active in civic as well as business affairs, while Miriam Ferguson devoted herself almost exclusively to her home and family. In 1914 her husband ran for governor and in January 1915 she became first lady of Texas. Besides entertaining, her main contribution was the greenhouse she had built in 1915 to foster her hobby of gardening. There was little criticism of her as first lady, but much criticism of her husband's handling of finances. Though reelected in 1916, the following year, amid bitter controversy, he was impeached, convicted, and removed from office.

With her husband's conviction Miriam Ferguson's political career began. Having been banned from holding office in Texas by the terms of his conviction, Jim Ferguson spent seven years battling this restriction. When the exclusion from office provision was upheld by the Texas Supreme Court in June 1924, Jim Ferguson (who had been an active opponent of woman suffrage) announced that his wife would be a candidate for governor. There was never any doubt that Miriam Ferguson was a stand-in for her husband. They campaigned together, and her slogan was "Two Governors for the Price of One." She quietly appealed to "the mothers, sisters, and wives of Texas to help clear her family's name" (Nalle, p. 169).

It was during this campaign that, in the interest of brevity, a newspaperman substituted the initials "MA" for Miriam Amanda. Thereafter she was known as Ma, a nickname she disliked but which proved fortuitous politically. "Me for Ma" became a popular slogan, and "Put on Your Old Gray Bonnet" became the campaign song. These folksy tactics had a great appeal in the rural and small town areas of the state, where the Fergusons drew their strongest support.

Ma Ferguson came in second out of nine candidates in the 1924 Democratic primary and won the runoff by 100,000 votes. In the primaries, and again in the general election, the major issue, in addition to her husband's record and the prospect of government by proxy, was the Ku Klux Klan. Both Fergusons were passionate opponents of the Klan and publicly supported tolerance for Catholics and Jews. Ma Ferguson's platform also promised economy in government, better administration of state penitentiaries, and easing of the prohibition laws. This last was one subject on which the Fergusons publicly disagreed: while Jim Ferguson was a notorious "wet," Ma Ferguson supported prohibition and, once in office, called for strengthening the laws preventing the sale of liquor.

Elected easily in November, she became the nation's second woman governor, inaugurated fifteen days after Wyoming's Nellie Tayloe Ross (1880–1977). The record of her first term is undistinguished. Little significant legislation was passed, and her efforts to lower state expenditures and raise taxes to build highways and aid education failed. She was successful, however, in gaining passage of an antimask law, directed against the Ku Klux Klan, and of an amnesty act, later declared unconstitutional by the Texas Supreme Court, restoring her husband's political rights. Much controversy arose over her liberal use of the power to pardon and parole. Defended by the Fergusons as humanitarian, and as a means of decreasing the expenses of the state prison system, the large numbers of pardons were seen by many as a further sign of the corruption of "Fergusonism." Critics of the ad-

ministration charged that pardons were for sale; they also claimed that highway construction contracts were being awarded to friends of highway commissioner Jim Ferguson, who had been appointed by his wife. The *Ferguson Forum*, a newspaper founded by Jim Ferguson in 1917, defended the governor's policies. During her term in office Ma Ferguson wrote a syndicated column which was published in the *Forum* and other papers.

Defeated in the primary in her bid for reelection in 1926, and again in 1930, Ma Ferguson won a second term as governor in 1932. Incumbent governor Ross Sterling, her opponent in the 1932 primary, challenged her victory, claiming that the number of votes cast in many "Ferguson" counties exceeded the number of eligible voters. The Texas Supreme Court upheld Ferguson and she went on to win the November election.

Governor Ferguson's second administration was dominated by the depression. Finding the state on the brink of bankruptcy, she called for drastic reductions in expenditures. Anticipating a wave of bank failures, she proclaimed a Texas bank holiday on March 3, 1933, two days before President Franklin D. Roosevelt ordered a national bank holiday. A strong Roosevelt supporter, she took advantage of the aid offered the state by New Deal programs. Legislation enacted during her tenure included a congressional redistricting law and legalization both of gambling on horse races and prizefighting. Attempting to deal with the threat of overproduction by the unregulated oil industry, she secured passage of a tax of two cents a barrel on oil. But the legislature failed to respond to her requests for a sales tax to meet state expenses and aid the schools or to a later proposal for an income tax on the earnings of corporations. She also resumed her liberal pardoning policy, and met with renewed criticism.

Ferguson did not seek reelection in 1934, but ran again in 1940 at the age of sixty-five. By that time the Fergusons' influence in Texas politics was declining, and their campaign was less spirited. Ma Ferguson finished fourth in the Democratic primary. Four years later, on Sept. 21, 1944, her husband died. As an elderly widow, she lived in Austin as the "grand old lady" of Texas politics. In 1961 she died of congestive heart failure at her home.

Described by her daughter as dignified and "brutally frank and honest," Ma Ferguson in later years prided herself on the family's modest style of living and on its liberal political record. Motivated to run for political office by her strong sense of family loyalty, the key to Ma Ferguson's political success, as to that of her husband, was the ability to identify with the common people and to capitalize on timely issues.

[Ferguson's official governor's papers are on file in the Texas State Archives in Austin. For information about her political campaigns see Seth Shepard McKay, *Texas Politics, 1906–1944* (1952). Ouida Ferguson Nalle, *The Fergusons of Texas or "Two Governors for the Price of One"* (1946), is a partisan account of her public and private life by her daughter. See also a long article by Billy M. Jones, "Miriam Amanda Ferguson," in *Women of Texas* (1972); the entry in Eldon Stephen Branda, ed., *Handbook of Texas: A Supplement*, vol. 3 (1976); and Jack Lynn Calbert, "James Edward and Miriam Amanda Ferguson: The 'Ma' and 'Pa' of Texas Politics," (Ph.D. diss., Indiana Univ., 1968). The entry on James Ferguson in *Dict. Am. Biog.*, Supp. Three, provides useful background information. Death certificate was supplied by Texas Dept. of Health.]

A. ELIZABETH TAYLOR

FIELD, Jessie. *See* SHAMBAUGH, Jessie Field.

FIELD, Sara Bard, Sept. 1, 1882–June 15, 1974. Suffragist, poet.

Sara Bard Field was born in Cincinnati, the fourth of five daughters and of six children of Annie Jenkins (Stevens) and George Bard Field. (The third daughter died in infancy.) Her father traced his ancestors to English and French colonists, and her mother, who passed on to Sara a love of literature and history, descended from English Quakers with roots in Rhode Island. George Field, a purchasing agent for a wholesale food company, moved his family to Detroit in 1885, where Sara Field grew up "the child of ultra-orthodoxy and respectability."

George Field's strict Baptist beliefs ordered his family's life. He banished from his house his two eldest daughters—Mary for analyzing Christianity in a college philosophy course and Alice for disobedience. Mary Field (Parton [1878–1969]), who later became a teacher, social worker, and writer, protected Sara, and took her along to classes at the University of Michigan. Sara Field planned to enroll there after graduating from Detroit Central High School in 1900, but her father refused support because he feared the university would weaken her faith, as it had her sister's. A dedicated and excellent student, Field was disappointed and ready for a break with her family. On Sept. 12, 1900, she married Albert Ehrgott, who was twice her age. A minister and friend of her parents, Ehrgott was about to leave for the Eurasian Baptist Church in Rangoon, Burma.

The couple's trip through India and their stay in Burma constituted an important turning point in Sara Field Ehrgott's life. The sight of Indians starving in the streets before indifferent wealthy natives and British colonials shocked her. She acquired a "sense of inequality in a world where the privileged had too much and the underprivileged far too little." In addition, her contact with Asian religions deepened her doubts about Baptist orthodoxy.

Injuries resulting from the birth of her son, Albert Field, in 1901 forced Sara Ehrgott to return to the United States in 1902. The family lived in New Haven, Conn., where Albert Ehrgott attended Yale Theological School. Sara Ehrgott audited a course in English poetry given by Robert Lounsbury, who encouraged her to write poetry.

In 1903 her husband was assigned to a poor parish in Cleveland, Ohio, where she established a soup kitchen and kindergarten which attracted the attention of reform Mayor Tom L. Johnson. Increasingly concerned with a "practical application of Christianity," Sara Ehrgott was drawn to the fringe of municipal reform activities. Mary Field, at the time head of a settlement house in Chicago, also promoted her sister's turn to socialism, urged her to write, and introduced her to Clarence Darrow. While Albert Ehrgott objected to his wife's political activities, his own advocacy of Christian Socialism led to his dismissal from his post in Cleveland. The family, which now included a daughter, Katherine Louise (b. 1906), moved to a pastorate in Portland, Oreg., in 1910.

In Oregon Sara Ehrgott first became involved in the campaign for woman suffrage. She joined the Oregon College Equal Suffrage League, a group of young women who took up ABIGAIL SCOTT DUNIWAY's work; she became the paid state organizer for the campaign that won suffrage in Oregon in 1912. Leaving her children with a maid, she canvassed the state in the summers of 1911 and 1912, gaining a reputation as an eloquent orator whose youth and beauty enhanced her appeal. She obtained her credentials as a reporter in the fall of 1911, when she covered the trial of the McNamara brothers, union members who were accused of bombing a Los Angeles newspaper office, for the *Oregon Daily Journal*.

By this time Ehrgott had come to differ with her husband "on every important question" and resented her duties as a minister's wife. In 1913 and 1914 she assisted in the Nevada suffrage campaign and meanwhile sought a divorce. The Nevada divorce was granted in November 1914 over the bitter protest of her husband, who had moved to Berkeley, Calif., and was given custody of the children. Resuming her maiden name, Field went to San Francisco to be near her children.

Thereafter she worked for national suffrage with the Congressional Union, the militant off-shoot of the National American Woman Suffrage Association, and its successor, the National Woman's party. In 1915 Alice Paul (1885–1977) chose Field to carry across the continent by automobile a petition signed by 500,000 people in support of the woman suffrage amendment. Preceded by MABEL VERNON, who organized greeting parades along the way, Field and two drivers left San Francisco Sept. 16, 1915. Often stopping to offer the support of enfranchised western women to the voteless women of the east, they found the transcontinental highway in many places only a poorly marked wagon road, and endured Wyoming blizzards, midwestern mud, and continual mechanical breakdowns. The envoys presented their petition to President Woodrow Wilson on Dec. 6, 1915. Field also participated in the formation of the National Woman's party, speaking at its Chicago convention in 1916 and throughout the west. She was a member of another deputation to President Wilson in January 1917, and in 1918 stumped Nevada in ANNE MARTIN's senatorial campaign. Field, a pacifist, also supported the San Francisco People's Council after the United States entered World War I.

Personal tragedy halted her suffrage and anti-war work in October 1918, when a car she was driving crashed, killing her son. Field suffered a breakdown lasting almost a year, and she was plagued by nervous illnesses for the rest of her life.

When Field resumed public life it was as a poet and, with Charles Erskine Scott Wood, a champion of liberal causes. Field had met Wood, a West Point graduate and corporate lawyer in Portland, through Clarence Darrow in 1910. She was introduced to Wood, a philosophical anarchist, as a fellow radical. A handsome, wealthy man of fifty-eight at the time, he solicited Field's advice about his poetry, and edited some of her work, thereby initiating a thirty-four-year literary collaboration. They soon acknowledged mutual love, and lived together after 1918, although Wood's wife refused him a divorce. He retired from legal practice in 1918, and wrote poetry and political satire fulltime, while Field turned intensively to poetry. Many of her poems, which were published in literary and political magazines, were meditations on the death of her son. Her first collection, The Pale Woman, appeared in 1927.

In addition to their own creative efforts, Field and Wood encouraged other artists by their friendship, support, and example. In the early twenties their San Francisco home became a focus for writers and artists in the Bay area. Ralph Stackpole, George Sterling, GENEVIEVE TAGGARD, Benjamin Bufano, and John and Llewelyn Powys visited frequently. In 1923–24 Field and Wood sponsored the School of the Arts of the Theatre in San Francisco. Remaining interested in social causes, they also supported a birth control clinic and sought the pardon of radical labor organizer Tom Mooney.

Field and Wood found little leisure to write in San Francisco, so they built a house, "The Cats," in the Los Gatos hills south of the city. There Field wrote a long narrative poem, Barabbas (1932), which won the Book Club of California gold medal, and also composed her second volume of poems, Darkling Plain (1936). Portraying Barabbas as a rebel rather than a thief, she attempted to combine her knowledge of scripture with her political creed. The couple's reputation as poets and critics of social injustice, and their warmth, attracted artists and political radicals to The Cats, among them Lincoln Steffens, Robinson Jeffers, and William Rose Benét.

Field married Wood on Jan. 20, 1938, after his wife's death. When he died in 1944, much of her creative impulse vanished. During the remaining decades of her life she edited Wood's Collected Poems (1949), arranged his papers for the Huntington Library, and lent her name to the activities of the American Civil Liberties Union. In 1955 Sara Field Wood moved to Berkeley, near her daughter. There she died of arteriosclerotic heart disease in 1974.

[The Huntington Library, San Marino, Calif., holds an extensive collection of manuscripts, correspondence, and memorabilia of Sara Bard Field and C. E. S. Wood, including Field's brief manuscript autobiography. Additional correspondence and an oral history, taken from interviews with Field between Oct. 1959 and Oct. 1963, are in the Bancroft Library, Univ. of Calif., Berkeley. An example of her arguments for suffrage can be found in her article, "Nevada's Fight for Woman Suffrage," Out West, Aug. 1914. For an account of Field's 1915 transcontinental journey see Amelia Fry, "Along the Suffrage Trail: From West to East for Freedom Now," American West, Jan. 1969 (with photographs). Edwin R. Bingham discusses Field's relationship with Wood in "Oregon's Romantic Rebels: John Reed and Charles Erskine Scott Wood," Pacific Northwest Quart., July 1959, and William Rose Benét describes their Los Gatos home in The Dust Which Is God (1941). Field's role in the Nat. Woman's party is reported in Inez Haynes Irwin, The Story of the Woman's Party (1921). On Field see also entries in Biog. Cyc. of Am. Women, I (1924), and Twentieth Century Authors

(1942); on Wood see *Dict. Am. Biog.*, Supp. Three. Obituaries appeared in the *Berkeley Gazette, San Francisco Chronicle,* and *Oakland Tribune,* June 18, 1974; death certificate supplied by Calif. Dept. of Health Services. Additional information was provided by Field's daughter, Katherine Field Caldwell, and by her niece, Margaret Parton Hussey.]

CATHERINE M. SCHOLTEN

FIELDS, Dorothy, July 15, 1904–March 28, 1974. Lyricist.

Dorothy Fields, who turned out lyrics for others' melodies for nearly fifty years, was never well known to the public. By her colleagues, however, she was long regarded as one of the finest and most versatile lyricists in the business —a peer of Hart, Hammerstein, and Ira Gershwin. In 1971 she won election to the Songwriters' Hall of Fame—the first woman ever thus honored.

Unquestionably, Fields's career was in great part a product of her upbringing. Her father, Lew Fields (Lewis Maurice Schanfield), was already something of a legend as the vaudeville and music hall partner of Joseph Weber by the time his daughter was born (in Allenhurst, N.J.). Both he and his wife, Rose (Harris) Fields, were second generation Polish immigrants with little education who had grown up on New York's Lower East Side. They strongly disapproved of stage careers for their children. Despite this, only Dorothy's elder sister Frances "remained a civilian"; both of her brothers, Joseph and Herbert, were dabbling in stage writing by the 1920s, when Dorothy, the youngest, began to try her own hand at poetry and song lyrics.

The mid-1920s was a period of considerable change in the form of the stage musical, as the loosely integrated, mildly risqué escapist entertainments with which Lew Fields was associated gave way to the plot-centered, sedate shows for which Jerome Kern was composing. As songs became more important for conveying plot and character, audiences began paying closer attention to their lyrics. For Fields the time was right and her ear for contemporary speech idioms as well as her ability to compress complex sentiments into a few words served her well from the start. Although she began by writing lyrics for revue songs, it was in the integrated musical comedy, a form generally acknowledged to have begun in 1927 with *Show Boat,* that she achieved her success.

There were some disasters (such as "They Needed a Songbird in Heaven So They Took Caruso Away"), but by 1927 Fields and Jimmy McHugh were writing songs for black entertainers at Harlem's Cotton Club. Their first Broadway show, *Blackbirds of 1928,* became one of the most successful all-black revues in Broadway history. Here and elsewhere the collaborators established a style in keeping with white notions of black entertainment. From *Blackbirds* came "I Can't Give You Anything But Love," while "Exactly Like You" and "On the Sunny Side of the Street" appeared in the 1930 *International Revue,* by which time the team was writing for white performers. Fields's later career is better typified, though, by the blues quality of "Porgy" (from *Blackbirds*) or the absolute simplicity of "I'm in the Mood for Love" (from *Every Night at Eight,* 1935).

These successes led to Fields's contact with Jerome Kern, who became something of an idol for her. "Lovely to Look At," which Fields wrote to an already existing Kern melody for the film *Roberta,* so pleased the composer that Fields spent the greater part of the 1930s in Hollywood collaborating principally with him. They wrote many fine songs together but surprisingly only one superb score: *Swing Time,* arguably Fields's finest work. In no other of her plays or films are the songs so well integrated into the action and so suited to the moment; words and phrases are even repeated from song to song to add cohesiveness. "The Way You Look Tonight" became a standard and won Fields a 1936 Academy Award. The song, a comic device in the film, is unique in its evocation of wistful longing in some future time. At once silly and tender, it also illustrates Fields's ability to eliminate all but the essential emotional statements so that the few touches of detail ("the laugh that wrinkles your nose") take on a special significance.

Returning to New York at the end of the 1930s, Fields married Eli Lahm, a dress manufacturer, in 1938; the marriage lasted until Lahm's death in 1958. (A first marriage, in 1925, to Dr. J. J. Weiner, a surgeon, had lasted seven years.) The Lahms had one son, David, born in 1941, and a daughter, Eliza, born in 1944.

In the late 1930s Fields also embarked on a partnership with her brother Herbert, turning out competent but on the whole undistinguished musical comedy librettos, chiefly for Cole Porter (*Let's Face It, Something for the Boys, Mexican Hayride*). She added her own lyrics to Sigmund Romberg's music in *Up in Central Park,* a pleasant if anachronistic operetta-musical evoking a Currier-and-Ives New York. A soldier who had won prizes at Coney Island for his sharpshooting gave Fields the inspiration for an Ethel Merman vehicle based on the legendary Annie Oakley. Fields was to do the lyrics and Jerome Kern the music, but after Kern's unexpected death in 1945, Irving Berlin was recruited for both words and music, with the Fields duo writing the book. The result was one of the greatest of all successes in the musical theater, *Annie Get Your Gun.*

After this, Fields wrote lyrics principally for the actresses' vehicles which dominated the musical stage in the 1950s and early 1960s. With Arthur Schwartz she wrote two scores for Shirley Booth, *A Tree Grows in Brooklyn* and *By the Beautiful Sea.* These were only limited successes but the first one, her only attempt at a rather serious piece of musical theater, is frequently extraordinary, especially in its rather daring evocations of poverty and dreariness that open the acts: "Mine Till Monday" and "That's How It Goes."

In 1959 Fields collaborated with Albert Hague on *Redhead,* a vehicle for Gwen Verdon, which won her both a Tony Award for best lyrics and a Grammy. Vehicles are generally the most temporal of shows, but in 1965 Fields's second musical for Verdon (and her first collaboration with composer Cy Coleman) achieved real distinction. *Sweet Charity's* lyrics unerringly evoked New York of the mid-1960s, a remarkable achievement for a lyricist whose best-known songs date from the 1920s. More important, these lyrics reveal what Fields could do best: reflect precisely a particular emotional situation. In each of Verdon's six solos, song projects character, rather than remaining incidental to it, a far greater accomplishment than the simple creation of some pleasant sentiments. Fields's last show, *Seesaw* (1973), was also written with Coleman, reflecting her continued desire to work with young composers in order to avoid anything passé.

Dorothy Fields died in 1974 of a heart attack in her New York apartment, leaving many intriguing projects unfinished. Asked once if she would retire, Fields responded: "Are you crazy? Listen, honey, I've got songs coming out of me I haven't even thought about yet. I plan to write until I can no longer hold a pencil."

[The most important sources are Fields's lyrics and their music. As of 1980, recordings of her major shows (*Blackbirds, Arms and the Girl, A Tree Grows in Brooklyn, By the Beautiful Sea, Sweet Charity, Seesaw, Roberta, Swing Time,* and selections from *Up in Central Park*) were still in print; *Redhead* was also recorded. Most of Fields's librettos are available in manuscript from the Billy Rose Theatre Coll., N.Y. Public Library, which also has a detailed clipping file on her career. Fields's recollections are included in two oral history compilations: the Popular Arts Project in the Oral History Coll., Columbia

Univ., and Max Wilk, *They're Playing Our Song* (1973). Her obituary appeared in the *N.Y. Times* on March 29, 1974. Additional information came from correspondence with Stephen Sondheim and James Maher, who confirmed that Fields wrote the lyrics to "I Can't Give You Anything But Love" and "Sunny Side of the Street."]

JOHN DAVID SHOUT

FISHER, Dorothy Canfield, Feb. 17, 1879– Nov. 9, 1958. Writer.

Dorothy Canfield Fisher, prolific writer and longtime member of the selection board of the Book-of-the-Month Club, was born Dorothea Frances in Lawrence, Kans., the second child and only daughter of James Hulme and Flavia (Camp) Canfield. Her father and mother, both born in the midwest, descended from old Vermont families. At the time of Dorothea's birth, James Canfield was a professor at the University of Kansas. Flavia Canfield was an artist; she also organized and became the first president of the Columbus (Ohio) Federation of Women's Clubs. Both parents were ardent feminists.

Dorothy Canfield attended public schools in Kansas and spent summers with her father's relatives in Arlington, Vt. When she was eleven, her mother took her to Paris for a year, where she was placed in a Catholic girls' school while her mother studied art; there she acquired a fluent command of French. The return from Paris coincided with her family's move to Nebraska, where James Canfield became chancellor of the state university. In Nebraska Dorothy Canfield began her lifelong friendship with the author WILLA CATHER, a university classmate of her brother, James. In 1895 her father became president of Ohio State University and she entered that university, graduating in 1899 with a degree in French. Immediately following her graduation, she again accompanied her artistic mother to Paris and studied at the Sorbonne and the École des Hautes Études. She continued her work in French literature at Columbia University, where in 1899 her father had become university librarian, and completed the Ph.D. in 1904.

That year she was offered a teaching position at Western Reserve University in Cleveland, but because her parents could not bear to have her move so far from home she accepted an administrative post at the experimental Horace Mann School in New York instead. During her spare time she began to write short stories, and a journey alone to Norway in the summer of 1905 provided material for her first novel, *Gunhild*

(1907). Responsibility for her ailing mother forced her to give up her work at the Horace Mann School, and she turned gradually to full-time writing. Her stories were published in several popular magazines; a few appeared in *Munsey's Magazine* under the pen name Stanley Crenshawe.

In 1907 Dorothy Canfield married John Redwood Fisher, a 1904 graduate of Columbia. The young couple moved to one of the Canfield properties in Arlington, Vt., with the plan that both would write for a living. Her work was commercially more successful, however, and he gradually abandoned his own writing, although he provided general editorial assistance and collaborated with her on some essays. They had two children: Sarah, born in 1909, and James Canfield, born in 1913.

She continued to write, and a steady stream of short stories, articles, novels, and nonfiction books poured from her pen. Her fiction carried the name Dorothy Canfield; she wrote nonfiction as Dorothy Canfield Fisher. In addition, the Fishers were both active in local and state civic and educational affairs: Dorothy Canfield Fisher was the first woman appointed to the Vermont state board of education, and John Fisher served in the Vermont legislature and was appointed chairman of the state board of education. In 1911, during one of their many trips to Europe, Dorothy Canfield Fisher visited the innovative school of Maria Montessori. She introduced and popularized the Montessori method of early childhood education in the United States in *A Montessori Mother* (1912, reprinted 1965 as *Montessori for Parents*), *A Montessori Manual* (1913), *Mothers and Children* (1914), and *Self-Reliance* (1916). She also treated the Montessori method fictionally in two novels, *The Bent Twig* (1915) and the popular children's story *Understood Betsy* (1916).

During the First World War, the entire Fisher family went to France. John Fisher served in the ambulance corps; Dorothy Canfield Fisher founded a press to print books in Braille for the war blind and established a refugee center in the Basque country for children from Paris, supporting these activities by writing articles and short stories. The war stories were gathered into two volumes: *Home Fires in France* (1918) and *The Day of Glory* (1919). Experiences of this period are also reflected in *The Deepening Stream* (1930) and *Basque People* (1931). Her novels all employ settings with which she was intimately familiar. *The Brimming Cup* (1921), which William Allen White called "the other side of Main Street," and its sequel *Rough-Hewn* (1922) contrast American and French values.

Three novels set in midwest America discuss the problems of women of three different ages: *The Squirrel-Cage* (1912) describes the tragedy of a young woman's "suitable marriage"; *The Home-Maker* (1924) releases an energetic woman trapped in domesticity by an exchange of roles with her gentler husband; *Her Son's Wife* (1926), called her best novel by William Lyon Phelps, sensitively portrays the effects on a mother's personality of her deliberate sacrifice of her daughter-in-law.

In 1926 Dorothy Canfield Fisher became a member of the first board of selection of the Book-of-the-Month Club. Serving as the only woman on the board for twenty-five years, she played an important role in the success of PEARL BUCK, Isak Dinesen, Richard Wright, and others. She also served on the American Youth Commission and on the boards of trustees of Goddard College and Howard University. During World War II she organized and led the Children's Crusade to encourage American children to help young victims of war in other lands.

Her last two novels, both set in Vermont, were *Bonfire*, published in 1933, and *Seasoned Timber*, which appeared in 1939. After that, burdened by the advent of war, and nearly crushed by the death of her son, a doctor, in combat in the Philippines in 1945, she turned almost completely to nonfiction. Her last major work was *Vermont Tradition: The Biography of an Outlook on Life* (1953). She died at home in Arlington, Vt., of a stroke. Her husband survived her by less than six months.

Dorothy Canfield Fisher is best remembered for her fiction. Her novels and short stories are rich in descriptive detail and carefully crafted, blending humanistic idealism with realistic portrayal.

[The Wilbur Collection of the Univ. of Vt. contains the largest collection of Dorothy Canfield Fisher's works, letters, and manuscripts, as well as photocopies of the most important documents in other collections. The correspondence with her first publisher, Henry Holt, is in the Princeton Univ. Library, while her letters to her later publisher, Alfred Harcourt, are in the files of Harcourt Brace Jovanovich. Columbia Univ. holds the letters to her literary agent Paul Reynolds, many letters to Harry Sherman of the Book-of-the-Month Club, and (in the Oral History Collection) an interview in which she discusses her work on the Book-of-the-Month Club board. Medals, diplomas, and hoods from honorary degrees, as well as some pictures, are at the Univ. of Vt.; other memorabilia are in the Martha H. Canfield Library in Arlington, Vt. Her works were widely translated into other languages. In addition to those mentioned, her published works include several volumes of short stories: *Hillsboro People* (1915), *The Real*

Motive (1916), *Raw Material* (1923), *Made-to-Order Stories* (1925), *Fables for Parents* (1937), *Four-Square* (1949), *A Harvest of Stories* (1956). Among her works of nonfiction are two historical narratives for young people: *Paul Revere and the Minute Men* (1950) and *Our Independence and the Constitution* (1950). Her doctoral dissertation was reprinted in 1966 as *Corneille and Racine in English*. No scholarly biography exists. There is one biography for young people by Elizabeth Yates: *Pebble in a Pool* (1958, reprinted as *The Lady from Vermont*, 1971). Further biographical material may be found in *Threescore* (1936), the autobiography of Sarah N. Cleghorn; *The Autobiography of William Lyon Phelps* (1939); Zephine Humphrey, "Dorothy Canfield," *Woman Citizen*, Jan. 1926; David Baumgardt, "Dorothy Canfield on Her Seventieth Birthday," *Educational Forum* (1950); and an essay by Robert Frost in *Dorothy Canfield Fisher, In Memoriam* (Book-of-the-Month Club, 1958). Significant autobiographical material is contained in the introduction to *A Harvest of Stories*, in *Memories of Arlington, Vermont* (1957), and in *American Portraits* (1946). An unusually articulate description of the author's experience in writing a short story is found in Dorothy Canfield, "How 'Flint and Fire' Started and Grew," in *Americans All*, ed. B. A. Heydrick (1920, reprinted in Jay B. Hubbell, *American Life in Literature*, 1936). Among the more important critical evaluations of her work are Edward Wagenknecht, *Cavalcade of the Novel* (1952); Edward A. Post, "The Neo-Puritanism of Dorothy Canfield," *The Christian Register*, Aug. 17, 1933; Elizabeth Wyckoff, "Dorothy Canfield: A Neglected Best Seller," *The Bookman* (Sept. 1931); William Allen White, "The Other Side of Main Street," *Collier's*, July 30, 1921; and Friderike Maria Zweig, *Güte, Wissen, Verstehen, Drei Lebensbilder grosser amerikanischer Erzieher* (1949). An obituary appeared in the *N.Y. Times*, Nov. 10, 1958; death record from Office of the Secy. of State, Vt.]

IDA H. WASHINGTON

FLANAGAN, Hallie Mae Ferguson, Aug. 27, 1890–July 23, 1969. Theater educator and administrator, director.

Few careers have had the continuity of activity and unity of purpose that marked that of Hallie Flanagan. From her college days she learned to regard "art, music, and theatre as necessary and normal expressions of life." As educator, playwright, director, and administrator, she devoted herself to innovative ways of keeping theater "part of, and not apart from, everyday existence." This vision led her to nurture new plays, to experiment with new modes of staging, to link drama and education, and to direct during the depression the only federally funded national theater in American history.

She was born Hallie Mae Ferguson in Redfield, S.D., the eldest of three children of Frederic Miller and Louisa (Fischer) Ferguson; she had a younger brother and a sister. Her mother, who came from a large German family from Illinois, was a devoted homemaker, reserved but artistic and literary. Her father, son of Scottish pioneers, worked at various business enterprises; he was a dynamic, volatile, charming man whose example taught his daughter to regard every new experience as an adventure. She looked back on a "serene" childhood of travel, visits to relatives, games, and celebrations.

Because of economic reverses, the family moved frequently, living in several midwestern states before settling in Grinnell, Iowa, where Hallie Ferguson attended the public schools and was graduated from Grinnell College in 1911. "The main thing that happened to me at College," she was to recall, "was Murray Flanagan." Hallie Ferguson married (John) Murray Flanagan on Christmas Day, 1912, after she had spent one year teaching at Sigourney High School. The couple went to live in St. Louis, where he was employed by an insurance firm. It was, she said, a "rapturous" marriage. A son, John Murray, was born in 1915, and soon they moved to Omaha. Shortly after the birth of a second son, Frederic, in 1917, Murray Flanagan was sent to Colorado Springs to be treated for tuberculosis.

In between visits to her dying husband, Hallie Flanagan lived with her two infant sons in the Grinnell home of her parents. Secretly she set about earning some money, and, renting a studio in downtown Colorado Springs, advertised for students in drama. After her husband's death at the end of 1919, Flanagan taught high school and assisted a professor at Grinnell College who gave her lessons in voice, fencing, and dance. He suggested that she go on the stage, but she preferred writing plays in order to be with her children. While teaching English courses at the college, she also organized performances. Her play, *The Curtain*, won a $100 prize in the Des Moines Little Theatre Contest and helped gain her entry to Harvard professor George Pierce Baker's esteemed 47 Workshop for playwrights.

The second tragic event of Flanagan's young life occurred in 1922 when her elder son, Jack, died of spinal meningitis. She gathered her courage, however, and with funds from her husband's insurance policy, she went off to Cambridge with her younger son. There Flanagan served as production assistant to Baker, who encouraged her writing. With her child and her increasingly dependent parents to support, however, she could not follow her creative desire. In 1924, with her A.M. degree from Radcliffe and her greatly increased knowledge of theater, she returned to Grinnell College. Some performances of her plays attracted the attention of Vassar College president Henry Noble Mac-Cracken, and she was invited to teach there, beginning in the fall of 1925. The following spring, sponsored by Frederick Keppell of the Carnegie Foundation, she was awarded a Guggenheim Foundation fellowship to visit the theaters of Europe.

In her book *Shifting Scenes* (1928), Hallie Flanagan recorded her experiences during her extraordinary year of European travel. Increasing her understanding of the relationship of the arts and public life, she learned about the various types of government sponsorship of the theater. She was especially influenced by her conversations with English theater visionary Gordon Craig, who spoke of theater as a communion in which performers and spectators are linked by their shared beliefs. In the Soviet Union, she was impressed by the use of powerful theatrical events to make theater an instrument of social change.

Newly inspired, Flanagan returned to teach at Vassar. In her work there she discovered her talent for directing, and it was as director as well as teacher and playwright that she shaped productions, plays, and students at her famous Vassar Experimental Theatre, founded in 1925. Among her many productions were a fresh staging of *Antony and Cleopatra* (1934) and the innovative and influential *Can You Hear Their Voices?* (1931). Written by Flanagan and a former student, this play about the plight of starving Arkansas dirt farmers and the inaction of Congress anticipated the documentary techniques later used by the Federal Theatre Project's Living Newspapers.

These were challenging years for her. In 1930 Flanagan returned to the Soviet Union with a group of students to attend a theater festival, and in 1934, during a sabbatical from Vassar, she directed the theater at the progressive school, Dartington Hall, in England. The same year she married Vassar professor of Greek Philip H. Davis, a widower ten years her junior who had three young children. (She kept the name Flanagan professionally.) It was a marriage of shared interests, shared responsibilities, and shared expenses.

In 1935 her Grinnell contemporary, Harry Hopkins, director of the Works Progress Administration, asked Hallie Flanagan to undertake the formation of what was to become the Federal Theatre Project. From her initial conversations with Hopkins about how unemployed actors could be put to work until the untimely demise of the Project in 1939, she turned all her efforts to structuring a unique institution. She

took what was intended as a relief measure for destitute theater people and turned it into a daring, innovative national network of regional theaters dedicated to education, social comment, and entertainment. In the first year of its existence the Federal Theatre Project put over 12,000 people to work in theaters all across the country. During the next four years, in 1,200 or more productions, these theaters provided entertainment for more than twenty-five million people, many of whom had never seen live theater before.

This "free, adult, uncensored" entertainment included almost every kind of theater—circuses and vaudeville, musical theater, Shakespeare, ethnic plays, and contemporary drama. The roster of artists who contributed to the Project or got their start with it forms a who's who of American theater. It includes playwrights from the established Elmer Rice to the very young Arthur Miller, directors Orson Welles and Joseph Losey, set and lighting designers Howard Bay and Ben Edwards, and innumerable actors from Arlene Francis to Canada Lee and E. G. Marshall. Such noted playwrights as Eugene O'Neill and George Bernard Shaw released their plays to the Federal Theatre for reduced royalties; the Project also promoted black theater at a time when opportunities for black artists were limited. Determined to make theater "conscious of the implications of the changing social order," Flanagan negotiated the presentation of Sinclair Lewis and John C. Moffitt's warning of the dangers of fascism, *It Can't Happen Here*, simultaneously in twenty-two theaters in eighteen cities. The Living Newspapers, which documented such central social issues as the lack of housing, the loss of farms, and labor's struggle to organize, also reflected her conviction of the theater's social responsibility.

As administrator of this vast, unruly complex, Hallie Flanagan, gentle but possessed of an incredible will, was called admiringly "the soft-spoken slave driver." She had to balance many conflicting forces to get her shows on. The theatrical unions that did not want their members working under union scale had to be placated at the same time that artists and administrators who did not need relief had to be attracted to provide leadership for the Project. She wanted to draw on the creative verve of amateurs in regional and educational theaters yet could only hire professional performers who were located mainly in New York and a few other urban centers. In a decade of economic and political upheaval she tried to encourage an artistic drama of social significance in the face of government censorship and radical activism among her ranks. The witch-hunting activities of the House

Committee on Un-American Activities found an easy target in the volatile and varied Theatre Project which Flanagan had hoped would be "part of a tremendous re-thinking, re-building, and re-dreaming of America." Despite the many successes of the Project and Flanagan's spirited defense of it before the Committee, all was lost to congressmen like Joseph Starnes, who challenged her comments about Orson Welles's production of *Doctor Faustus* with the question: "You are quoting from this Marlowe. Is he a Communist?" The Federal Theatre Project came abruptly to an end on June 30, 1939, when Congress refused to appropriate funds for its continued life.

Flanagan returned to Vassar College where, with funding from the Rockefeller Foundation, she and a staff wrote *Arena* (1940), the story of the Federal Theatre. In 1940, during her first year back with her family, her husband died suddenly, a blow which made "everything seem unreal." She remained at Vassar until 1942, mounting a widely acclaimed production of T. S. Eliot's *Murder in the Cathedral* in 1941. The following year, lured by the possibility of needed financial security, and by the chance to develop some of her ideas about general education as well as theater education, she accepted an offer to become the dean of Smith College and professor in a new theater department there.

Flanagan served as dean from 1942 to 1946, and then devoted herself to the growing Smith theater department until her retirement in 1955. She continued her pioneer efforts, integrating the teaching of theater into the liberal arts curriculum. With her students, she wrote new plays, among them a documentary about atomic power, $E = MC^2$. She sought ways to enlarge the role of women during World War II and the postwar period, planned ways to adjust the curriculum to war needs, and offered Smith's resources to the government. During her last years at the college Flanagan was stricken by Parkinson's disease, which was to afflict her until her death in Old Tappan, N.J., at the age of seventy-eight.

In 1957 Hallie Flanagan was given one of the first of the Creative Arts Awards presented by Brandeis University. The year before her death she received the first annual citation of the National Theatre Conference, an organization of theater leaders which she had helped to found. Both Smith and Vassar named theaters in her honor. This "small, red-haired lady with the firm mouth and the ferocity of a roused lion," as John Houseman described her, left a deep mark on all those who knew her. She changed their lives by her strong interest in them and their work, and especially by her vision of theater as

the central art of a humane, democratic people.

[Hallie Flanagan's personal papers, including scrapbooks, correspondence, photographs, articles, and reviews, are in the Billy Rose Theatre Coll., N.Y. Public Library. The Smith College Archives faculty section has clippings, typescripts, correspondence, articles about Flanagan, and a chronology of her life. Additional information may be found in the project records at the Research Center for the Federal Theatre Project, George Mason Univ., Fairfax, Va., and in the Vassar College Archives. Autobiographical notes made in 1948 are in the possession of her stepdaughter, Joanne Davis Bentley. The best published sources are her own books, which also include *Dynamo: The Story of a College Theatre* (1943), an account of her work at Vassar. Jane De Hart Mathews, *The Federal Theatre, 1935–1939: Plays, Relief, and Politics* (1967), has a great deal of biographical information, although it is primarily a history of the Federal Theatre, as is Willson Whitman, *Bread and Circuses* (1937). John O'Connor and Lorraine Brown, *Free, Adult, Uncensored: The Living History of the Federal Theatre Project* (1978), has some material on Hallie Flanagan but is mainly a review of the rich store of material on Federal Theatre productions at George Mason Univ. Barbara Mendoza, "Hallie Flanagan: Her Role in American Theatre, 1924–1936" (Ph.D. diss., N.Y. Univ., 1976), covers her work as an educator. An obituary appeared in the *N.Y. Times*, July 24, 1969. Additional information for this article was provided by Joanne Davis Bentley.]

HELEN KRICH CHINOY

FLEESON, Doris, May 20, 1901–Aug. 1, 1970. Journalist.

Doris Fleeson was not just the first syndicated woman political columnist; she was the only one of either sex to approach national affairs like a police reporter.

"Avoid mere opinion as you would the pestilence," her friend H. L. Mencken once counseled her in a letter. It was needless advice. While there was never any doubt about where she stood, or who or what she thought was wrong, Doris Fleeson's opinions were based on hard facts of her own collection. "I like to see the whites of their eyes," she told an interviewer. "I like to watch the demeanor of a witness."

Doris Fleeson became a columnist in 1945. Her copy was carried, five times a week, under the banner of the United Features Syndicate, in more than 100 papers around the country. Until sickness sidelined her in the mid-sixties, she roamed the Capitol, a tiger in white gloves and a Sally Victor hat, stalking explanations for the stupidity, cruelty, fraud, or cant that was her chosen prey. Every day, she went to the White House, frequently to put the disemboweling question to the press secretary of the moment;

then she headed for Capitol Hill, where she called senators and congressmen off the floor—whether to be asked for information or to be given a piece of her mind they were never sure.

It was the crispness of her prose, just barely containing her passionate convictions, which gave her columns their special bite and edge—and caused John Kennedy to say that he "would rather be Krocked than Fleesonized." (Arthur Krock of the *New York Times*, confidant of the mighty, often startled, but seldom wounded.) Another contemporary, Walter Lippmann, wrote from heights which Doris Fleeson scorned to scale. She was always in the thick of the scrap. When she struck, she drew blood.

During her long career, she scolded four presidents: Truman, Eisenhower, Kennedy, and Johnson. Franklin D. Roosevelt, the one chief executive whom she almost unreservedly admired—for his character, political skills, and liberal views—died the year before she began her column. His wife, Eleanor, was a long-time friend and one of Doris Fleeson's few idols.

To be a woman reporter in the man's world of Washington in the 1940s and 1950s was to be patronized or excluded, or both. Doris Fleeson submitted to these indignities with tearful rage. She knew that few of the men were her peers and none her superior, and she was, well in advance of the women's liberation movement, a militant feminist. She fought for the underdog as she breathed—she was a founder of the American Newspaper Guild, and a pioneer in helping blacks to break race barriers in the trade. But her most burning concern was for her sisters. In those days, the struggle was over such matters as the installation of women's restrooms in congressional galleries. She was in the front line of the charge. She warned her colleague Frank Kent: "If you laugh, I will never speak to you again." She was notoriously kind to younger women reporters, indulgent and encouraging to a degree that caused wonderment and envy among the male politicians whom she had skewered.

If Doris Fleeson was feared and respected, she was also widely liked. She was an attractive person, always immaculately turned out. She had bright, large hazel eyes and a sudden, wide smile. Five minutes in her company was sufficient to convince most people that she was an honest woman, who adored her friends, hated her enemies, and remembered every slight or kindness that had ever been dealt her.

Her professionalism was nothing short of breathtaking. Her early training in deadlines had focused her mind. She would go from a press conference, a debate, or a convention floor directly to the typewriter, and in the time it took other people to sort out what had happened, turn out 700 words of cogent prose that proceeded straight to the heart of the matter.

Doris Fleeson was born May 20, 1901, in Sterling, Kans., where her father, William Fleeson, ran a clothing store, and, she often said, "the town—from the backroom." Her mother, Helen (Tebbe) Fleeson, was the daughter of immigrants from Schleswig-Holstein who had settled in St. Louis. Doris was the second daughter and the youngest of six children: she particularly admired and confided in her sister Elizabeth, one of the first women to receive a doctorate from Yale, who consistently supported and encouraged her. She attended local schools and graduated from the University of Kansas, where she studied journalism, in 1923. Her first newspaper jobs were at the Pittsburg (Kans.) *Sun* and the Evanston (Ill.) *News Index*.

In 1926, she established a base at the *Great Neck News* in Long Island, N.Y., from which she laid siege to the *New York Daily News*. Finally, in November 1927, she was given a staff job and began covering police, courts, investigations, and eventually, New York politics. In 1930, she married a fellow *Daily News* reporter, John O'Donnell. They had a daughter, Doris (b. 1932). In 1933, they arrived in Washington to write a political column, "Capitol Stuff," under a double by-line.

The marriage began to collapse under the strain of irreconcilable personal and political differences. Doris Fleeson was an ardent New Dealer; John O'Donnell was not. They were divorced in 1942. In the fashion of the times, he was kept on as a Washington correspondent, and she was recalled to New York to write radio news. Doris Fleeson landed a job as a war correspondent for the *Woman's Home Companion* (1943–44). With her usual verve and nerve, she covered battlefronts from Salerno to Omaha Beach.

When she came home, she struck out on her own as a political columnist. Only the editors of the Washington *Evening Star* and the *Boston Globe* promised to print her copy. Her clientele swiftly grew with her reputation for beats and tough analysis, and, in 1952, she was awarded the abominable accolade, "Capitol's top newshen" by *Newsweek* magazine. She traveled often with her friend, MAY CRAIG, and cast a clear eye on world figures. But her abiding passion was domestic politics. Once in Rome, she happened upon Richard Cardinal Cushing of Boston. Her antipathy to the hierarchy of the Roman Catholic church, an institution she found insufficiently democratic, was renowned. But the pair fell instantly fathoms deep into an esoteric discussion of Kennedy's reelection chances in the mid-Atlantic states.

In 1958, she married Dan Kimball, a big, bluff industrialist and former Secretary of the Navy (1951–53), who matched her in generosity and kindness and enjoyed her rages. He called her "my little bride," and they were aggressively happy in their house on S Street. She was fiercely domestic, and a perfectionist about her appointments. Sunday afternoon often found the scourge of statesmen sewing fresh white collar and cuffs on her dark-blue dress, looking for all the world like Kitty Foyle.

The Johnson campaign of 1964 was her last. She collapsed on the trail, suffering from circulatory disorders. She had had grave doubts about Lyndon Johnson's character. She saw them epitomized in the Vietnam war, of which she felt herself a casualty. On July 30, 1970, Dan Kimball died. On being told, Doris Fleeson responded with her astonishing presence of mind, quoting lines from Macaulay that begin, "The house that was the happiest within the Roman walls . . ."

Thirty-six hours later, she was dead of a stroke. No one has taken her place, either personally or professionally, on the Washington scene.

[Doris Fleeson's papers are at the Spencer Research Library, Univ. of Kans. in Lawrence. They include correspondence, typescripts of speeches, scrapbooks, photograph albums, and memorabilia. Among the correspondents are her sister, Elizabeth Fleeson Jordan, Eleanor Roosevelt, Bess and Harry Truman, and H. L. Mencken. Articles containing biographical information are "Lady About Town," *Time*, April 21, 1952; "Mad Over Politics," *Newsweek*, Oct. 7, 1957; "Newswomen Who Cover the New Frontier," *Editor and Publisher*, Aug. 19, 1961; and an entry in *Current Biog.*, 1959. Obituaries appeared in the *N.Y. Times*, the *N.Y. Daily News*, the Wash. *Star*, and the *Wash. Post*, all Aug. 2, 1970, and the *Kansas City Star*, Aug. 1, 1970. A death record was supplied by D.C. Dept. of Public Health. Assistance with research was provided by a biobibliography prepared by Rick Harlowe. Doris Fleeson's daughter, Doris O'Donnell, gave family information.]

MARY MC GRORY

FLÜGGE-LOTZ, Irmgard, July 16, 1903–May 22, 1974. Engineer, mathematician.

Irmgard Flügge-Lotz was born in Hameln, Germany, the daughter of Oscar and Dora (Grupe) Lotz. Her interest in technical subjects was motivated by her mother, whose family had been involved in construction for several generations, and by her father, a mathematician.

As a child, she visited construction sites with her uncle and attended half-price Sunday matinee showings of technical films at local theaters. She later said of her choice of engineering as a profession: "I wanted a life which would never be boring. That meant a life in which always new things would occur . . . I wanted a career in which I would always be happy even if I were to remain unmarried" (*Stanford Engineering News*, May 1969).

In 1923 Irmgard Lotz entered the Technische Hochschule of Hanover, where she studied applied mathematics and fluid dynamics, financing her education by tutoring students in technical subjects. Often, she was the only female student in her classes. In 1927 she received her *diplom ingenieur*, and stayed on at Hanover to study for her doctorate in engineering, which was granted in 1929 for a dissertation examining problems in thermodynamics.

Influenced in part by childhood memories of watching the flight testing of zeppelin rigid airships, she determined to enter the field of aeronautics. Her first position was as a junior research engineer at the Aerodynamische Versuchsanstalt (AVA) at Göttingen, one of the most prominent aeronautical research establishments in Europe. There she worked closely with Ludwig Prandtl, one of the founders of the modern science of aerodynamics, and his pupil and senior assistant Albert Betz. In 1931 she developed what became known as the Lotz method for calculating the spanwise (wingtip to wingtip) distribution of a wing's lifting force, even for wings of diverse shapes. Lotz built up the theoretical department of the AVA, establishing her own research program and assisting other researchers.

While at Göttingen, Lotz met Wilhelm Flügge, an authority on thin shell construction and a member of the Göttingen faculty. They were married on June 4, 1938, shortly before leaving Göttingen to join the staff of the government's central aeronautics research institute, Deutsche Versuchsanstalt für Luftfahrt (DVL). Following her marriage, Irmgard Lotz decided to retain the name under which her work was known; she became Irmgard Flügge-Lotz.

While at Göttingen, Wilhelm Flügge had been denied promotion because of his anti-Nazi views. He later recalled that while he was refused academic advancement because of his political opinions, his wife was additionally "blocked from any possibility of ever getting into a university career, just because of being a woman." His acceptance of an offer as department head in the DVL "was absolutely determined by the political situation." The apparent anomaly of two anti-Nazi academics being invited to work in a government research facility is attributable to the policy of Hermann Göring, who had absolute authority over all aeronautical research, and valued technical expertise even when unaccompanied by ideological purity. "The balance of power was . . . always precarious," Flügge remembered, "but it lasted to the end."

At the DVL Wilhelm Flügge worked as chief of structures research; Flügge-Lotz served as a scientific adviser in the fields of aerodynamics, flight dynamics, and navigation. During this time she also began her major research in the field of flight controls, the work for which she is best known. As a result of discussions with her husband, who was interested in flight dynamics as a hobby, she became interested in electronic automatic control theory. She developed the theory of discontinuous (that is, on and off) control systems, a pioneering effort which had many implications for the development of simple, automatic flight control equipment for aircraft. The press of wartime research demands, however, limited the time she could give to this work.

As a result of the frequent bombing of Berlin, Flügge-Lotz and her husband had to evacuate their research staffs to the town of Saulgau. At the end of the war, Saulgau came under French occupation, and in 1947 the couple were invited to join the Office National d'Études et de Recherches Aéronautiques (ONERA) at Paris. After a year at ONERA doing fundamental aeronautical research, they came to Stanford University in California, where Wilhelm Flügge was appointed a professor of engineering and Irmgard Flügge-Lotz became a lecturer in engineering mechanics and research supervisor. She quickly established graduate-level programs in mathematical aerodynamics and hydrodynamics at Stanford, initiated a weekly fluid mechanics seminar, and resumed her controls research. In 1954 she became a naturalized American citizen.

Irmgard Flügge-Lotz had published her first book, *Discontinuous Automatic Control*, in 1953; she continued to write technical papers, eventually publishing more than fifty. In 1960, as a result of her outstanding work in controls theory, and because of her invitation as the only woman delegate from the United States to the First Congress of the International Federation of Automatic Control in Moscow, she was finally appointed a full professor of engineering mechanics, aeronautics, and astronautics, becoming Stanford's first woman professor of engineering. Her second book, *Discontinuous and Optimal Control*, was published in 1968, the

year of her retirement. Despite increasingly severe attacks of arthritis, Flügge-Lotz continued a busy schedule of individual research on such problems as satellite control and the heat transfer and drag characteristics of high-speed flight vehicles. She also enjoyed her hobbies of music and gardening.

During her lifetime, Flügge-Lotz received many honors. Named professor emerita of applied mechanics and of aeronautics and astronautics by Stanford in 1968, she was in 1970 appointed a fellow of the American Institute of Aeronautics and Astronautics (AIAA), the second woman ever so honored. That same year, the Society of Women Engineers presented her with its Achievement Award in recognition of "her significant contributions to the field of fluid mechanics, in particular, wing theory and boundary layer theory." In 1971 Flügge-Lotz was appointed von Kármán lecturer of the AIAA, and she spoke on "Trends in the Field of Automatic Control in the Last Two Decades." Following a lengthy illness, she died of an intra-abdominal hemorrhage at Stanford University Medical Center in 1974.

[The Stanford Univ. Archives has a listing of Irmgard Flügge-Lotz's publications from 1961 to 1968. " 'A Life Full of Work'–The Flügges," *Stanford Engineering News*, May 1969, is a particularly useful source of biographical information. Another excellent reference is a "Memorial Resolution: Irmgard Flügge-Lotz, 1903–1974," by John R. Spreiter, Milton D. Van Dyke, and Walter G. Vincenti of Stanford. Other sources include the Engineers Joint Council, *Engineers of Distinction: A Who's Who in Engineering* (1973); the Society of Women Engineers, *SWE Achievement Award, 1952–1976;* and *Stanford Engineering News*, Nov. 1973. Flügge-Lotz's awards are listed in the Nat. Air and Space Museum Library, *Internat. Handbook of Aerospace Awards and Trophies* (1978). Obituaries appeared in the *N.Y. Times*, May 23, 1974; *Stanford Engineering News*, May 1974; and *SWE Newsletter*, Sept. 1974. Additional information was provided by Wilhelm Flügge. A death record was supplied by the Calif. Dept. of Health Services.]

RICHARD P. HALLION

FLYNN, Elizabeth Gurley, Aug. 7, 1890–Sept. 5, 1964. Labor organizer, radical.

Elizabeth Gurley Flynn, who for more than fifty years functioned as a professional revolutionary in American society, was born in Concord, N.H., the eldest of three daughters and one son of Thomas and Annie (Gurley) Flynn, and a descendant of a long line of Irish rebels. Her father spent his early years as a stonecutter with his father and brothers in the Maine granite quarries, then studied engineering at Dartmouth

College. He worked erratically for the rest of his life as an itinerant civil engineer and map-maker. Annie Gurley migrated to the United States from Ireland in 1876. When her father died three years later, she went to work in a tailor shop to help support her large family. An Irish nationalist and a feminist, she approved of her daughter's political activities and lent her lifelong material and moral support.

Both Thomas and Annie Flynn were socialists, and Elizabeth Gurley Flynn later thought that her father had relied heavily on his radicalism as an excuse for being unemployed much of the time. The family moved often during her early years as her father sought employment, but in 1900 her mother insisted that they establish a permanent home in a working-class district of the south Bronx. The poverty Flynn saw as a child in New England mill towns and in New York City left a lasting impression. In the Bronx she attended P.S. 9 and Morris High School. An introduction to EMMA GOLDMAN and Alexander Berkman by a high school friend led to a brief flirtation with anarchism, alarming her parents and their friends at the Socialist Forum that the Flynn family had been attending for some years. The Marxist pamphlets her parents gave her to read contributed to a socialist ideology that had already fed on the utopian writings of Edward Bellamy and William Morris.

Flynn's career as a radical agitator began in January 1906, when she was sixteen, with a speech to the Harlem Socialist Club on the subject of women under socialism. By late summer she was so successful as a soapbox speaker that she was arrested for blocking traffic in the heart of the New York theater district. Her black hair and blue eyes made her a striking figure, and her powerful voice, eloquence, and youthful good looks attracted and held crowds easily. A Philadelphia reporter noted that a working-class crowd gathered around her were soon "frowning when she frowned, laughing when she laughed, growing terribly earnest when she merely grew moderately so." By the time she stepped down, he claimed: "The perpetual inebriate forgot about the swinging doors. The corner loungers stood straight."

By 1907 Gurley Flynn, as she came to be called, was speaking often under the auspices of the Socialist party, the Socialist Labor party, and the Industrial Workers of the World (IWW). She had joined the IWW in 1906, and for a decade it provided a focus for her activity. When in the summer of 1907 members of the Metal and Machinery Workers Union turned to the IWW for help in their walkout against the American Tube and Stamping Company, she traveled to Bridgeport, Conn., to participate in her first strike. At the IWW national convention held that fall in Chicago she met John Archibald Jones, a Mesabi Iron Range organizer. Invited by Jones to join a Minnesota speaking tour, she dropped out of high school, with her parents' consent, and began her national career. As she recalled later: "I felt that socialism was just around the corner and I had to get into the struggle as fast as I could."

In January 1908 Flynn and Jones were married. She later realized that she had fallen in love with the mining frontier and had married the first miner she met. The marriage had little chance. Her love of her work and the couple's financial needs kept her on the road, and they lived together for only brief periods. A premature baby, born in 1909, did not live out the day; a son, Fred, was born in 1910. After Fred's birth, Jones wanted her to give up her work, but she refused and the two did not live together again; he divorced her in 1920. As she continued to travel, her mother and her sister Kathie often cared for the child, who was always called Fred Flynn.

Elizabeth Gurley Flynn quickly acquired a national reputation as an effective speaker and organizer. In 1909 she led successful free speech fights in Missoula, Mont., and Spokane, Wash., after local authorities had prohibited the IWW workers from speaking in the streets. Arrested and imprisoned in Spokane, she protested conditions in the jail, attracting widespread press coverage. She continued to organize and was arrested again and charged with conspiracy. At the trial her moving speech to the jury resulted in her acquittal, though her codefendant was convicted. In 1910 Flynn returned to New York City; as long as the IWW remained an active force, she worked as a national organizer in the northeast, participating in all of its major efforts in that area.

The most spectacular of these were the textile strikes at Lawrence, Mass., in 1912 and at Paterson, N.J., in 1913. The Lawrence strike, won after a three-month walkout by over 10,000 workers, owed much of its success to the publicity generated by Flynn and MARGARET SANGER, who arranged to have the children of striking workers taken to New York City and placed temporarily in foster homes. When police tried to stop a group of children from boarding a train in Lawrence, their action attracted national attention and the threat of a congressional investigation. The IWW was unable to follow up its Lawrence success, however, and the 1913 Paterson strike failed.

In Lawrence, Elizabeth Gurley Flynn met Carlo Tresca, a strikingly handsome man who had fled Italy in 1904 to escape a prison sentence for his radical political activities and had become a leader of the Italian anarchists in the United States. In 1913 he moved his Italian language newspaper to New York City, and he and Flynn lived together for more than twelve years while each was still legally married. Their relationship was sensual and stormy. Although they worked together for the IWW, he resented her devotion to the cause when it interfered with their private lives. She was no more willing to subordinate her career to him than she had been to Jack Jones. Flynn and Tresca separated in 1925, shortly after her sister Bina had borne Tresca's son. An unknown assassin murdered Tresca in 1943; her poetry indicates that she mourned him for years, keeping his memory in her heart "like a battered ikon."

Although she continued to appear occasionally under IWW auspices, Flynn had less to do with the organization after a feud developed between her and William D. (Big Bill) Haywood, its secretary and chief officer, in the fall of 1916. At issue was her handling of the defense of Tresca and two other IWW organizers arrested during a strike in the Mesabi Iron Range. In September 1917 both she and Tresca were among 169 members of the IWW indicted by a federal grand jury for violation of the Espionage Act. Charges against them were dropped because they had not been active in the IWW during the period in question.

In the wake of the postwar "red scare" which contributed to the demise of the IWW, Flynn turned from organizing workers to defending them and upholding their rights. In December 1918 she was instrumental in establishing the Workers' Defense Union (WDU), which provided relief funds and obtained legal aid for the large numbers of immigrants arrested and threatened with deportation. It also brought the Sacco-Vanzetti case to the attention of the English-speaking community. The organization was affiliated with the National Civil Liberties Bureau, forerunner of the American Civil Liberties Union (ACLU), of which Flynn was a founding member in 1920. By 1925 the WDU had completed its work, and it merged with the International Labor Defense (ILD), an organization of lawyers and civil libertarians, many affiliated with the Communist party. In 1926 Flynn became chairman of the ILD, a post she retained until 1930.

Also in 1926 Flynn applied for membership in the American branch of the Communist party (CPUSA). She had never surrendered her youthful attachment to Marxism and it required no significant ideological shift for her to move, as many others on the left were doing, into the Communist party. Her political journey was also affected by the personal crisis brought on by the end of her relationship with Tresca and her strong desire to return to labor activism. Before her application could be processed, however, she became critically ill while on a west coast speaking tour. Doctors diagnosed the problem as heart disease, and warned Flynn that continuing her public career would endanger her life. She was cared for by an old friend, Dr. Marie Equi, who had also been active in the radical labor movement, and for the next ten years she lived with Equi in Portland, Oreg.

Conflicts developed between the two women after Equi herself became ill in 1928. As Flynn improved, she became increasingly restive, particularly as the labor movement grew more militant in the mid-1930s and began successfully organizing large numbers of workers. Deciding that she must resume her career no matter what the cost, in the summer of 1936 Elizabeth Gurley Flynn returned to New York City and finally joined the Communist party, which welcomed her eagerly. She became a national organizer and a member of the party's women's commission, and began writing a column for the *Daily Worker*, covering economic, political, and social issues from her own feminist vantage. Like most women labor leaders, she advocated equality of employment opportunity and equal pay for equal work, yet believed in special legislative protection for women workers. She approved of Lilly Daché designer coveralls for women aviation workers, and also thought women capable of going into combat in case of enemy invasion. In 1938 Flynn was elected to the party's national committee. Under the party's united front policy, she maintained her old liberal and union associations in the late 1930s, speaking often before groups ranging from the Ethical Culture Society to CIO locals.

In 1940, as the Nazi-Soviet pact of the previous year deepened fears of the Soviet Union, the ACLU expelled Flynn from its executive board because of her Communist party membership. She had refused to resign, and, despite her grief over the recent death of her son from lung cancer, had conducted a strong defense before the board of directors. (The ACLU rescinded her expulsion in 1976.)

With the wartime alliance between the United States and the Soviet Union, and the end of the CPUSA's uncomfortable acquiescence in the Nazi-Soviet pact, the party became nearly respectable. In 1941 Flynn was elected to the party's political bureau (later known as the national board), elevating her to the inner circles of leadership. The following year, as two party members were elected to the city council in

New York City, Elizabeth Gurley Flynn ran for congressman-at-large in New York state. Basing her campaign largely on women's issues, she received 50,000 votes. For the duration of the war she publicized women's contributions to the war effort. She also urged the unionization of the thousands who poured into war production plants, the establishment of public day care centers, and the drafting of women for industrial service and for the Women's Army Corps.

After the war, in November 1945, Flynn was part of the American delegation to the socialist-dominated Women's Congress in Paris, out of which came the Women's International Democratic Federation and its United States affiliate, the Congress of American Women. With others in the American delegation, she supported a proposed alternative to the National Woman's party-sponsored equal rights amendment (ERA), trying to overcome objections that the ERA would undercut protective labor legislation for women.

Flynn survived the Communist party's factional disputes of the early 1940s, although she relinquished her support of party chairman Earl Browder grudgingly and deeply resented the interference of the international communist movement in the internal affairs of the CPUSA. In the increasingly menacing atmosphere of the late 1940s she remained a vigorous supporter of the party, and headed the defense committee formed to aid the top party leaders arrested in July 1948 under the Smith Act (for conspiring to teach and advocate the overthrow of the United States government by force and violence). Flynn was indicted on the same charge in 1951. After a nine-month trial she was convicted and sentenced to three years in the federal penitentiary for women at Alderson, W. Va.; she served from January 1955 until May 1957.

When Flynn returned to New York City after completing her prison term, she found the Communist party in a serious crisis provoked by further factional dissent. By supporting the moderate leadership of Eugene Dennis, she was able to remain within the party's inner circle, and in March 1961, after Dennis's death, she became the first woman selected as national chairman. The following year the State Department revoked her passport after the Supreme Court upheld the validity of the 1950 McCarran Act, which prohibited entry into the United States of anyone who had been a member of a totalitarian organization. Flynn and the historian Herbert Aptheker took a test case to the Supreme Court on this issue and won.

Flynn finally had her first look at a communist society in April 1960 when she visited the Soviet Union. After attending the midsummer Bucharest Conference, she made an eight-month tour of the communist bloc nations. In the fall of 1961 Flynn returned to Moscow to attend the funeral of William Z. Foster, chairman emeritus of the CPUSA, and stayed on for the twenty-second party congress. The events of that congress convinced her that Stalin was a "madman," but did not lead her to abandon her commitment to the American Communist party. On a third visit to Moscow in the late summer of 1964 Flynn became ill. She died there of acute gastroenterocolitis and was given a state funeral in Red Square.

Elizabeth Gurley Flynn drew her strength and her dedication from the struggles of the working class—struggles that she saw firsthand from the picket lines, from the backs of flatbed trucks, and from prison cells. She propagandized generations of working men and women to join and support the labor movement; she defended the civil liberties of radicals; and she proudly persevered in her own beliefs when doing so meant going to prison. She never publicly criticized the American Communist party, although she believed privately that it had made a number of serious mistakes, particularly in its "idolatry" of the Soviet Union and its lack of "self-criticism." She felt, too, that the struggles of the American comrades were often underrated by their own party. However, the sins of the international communist movement could not reconcile her to capitalism. Her vision of a socialist America was a humane one, a dream of a utopian society in which genuine equality and brotherhood could be realized.

[The Elizabeth Gurley Flynn Papers are housed at the Am. Inst. for Marxist Studies, N.Y. City. The WDU Papers are at the State Hist. Soc. of Wis. The IWW collection, Archives of Labor History and Urban Affairs, Wayne State Univ., Detroit, has some references to Flynn's activities as well as a tape recording of a speech, "Personal Recollections of the Industrial Workers of the World," given at Northern Ill. Univ., Nov. 8, 1962. There are letters from Flynn in the Mary Heaton Vorse Papers, also at Wayne State Univ. The Labadie Coll., Univ. of Mich., Ann Arbor, has a file on Flynn containing pamphlets, clippings, and some correspondence. She wrote two books about her experiences: *I Speak My Own Piece* (1955), an autobiography tracing her life up to 1925, which was later reissued as *The Rebel Girl* (1973); and a memoir of her prison experiences, *Alderson Story* (1955, 1963). Her articles and columns appeared regularly in the *Daily Worker* and *Sunday Worker*, and in *Political Affairs*, the Communist party's theoretical journal. Margaret Gerteis examines Flynn's IWW career in "Coming of Age with the Industrial Workers of the World: The Early Career of Elizabeth Gurley Flynn" (M.A. thesis, Tufts Univ., 1975). Audrey P. Olmsted traces her entire career in "Agitator on the Left: The Speech-making of Elizabeth Gurley Flynn" (Ph.D. diss., Ind. Univ., 1971). The entry in *Current Biog.*, 1961, is also useful. Some information about Flynn may also be found in Melvyn Dubofsky, *We Shall Be All: A History of the Industrial Workers of the World* (1969). An obituary appeared in the *N.Y. Times,* Sept. 6, 1964.]

HELEN C. CAMP

FORBES, Esther, June 28, 1891–Aug. 12, 1967. Writer.

Esther Forbes, novelist and biographer, was born in Westborough, Mass., the youngest of three daughters and of five children who survived infancy. Both parents came from established families long identified with Westborough and nearby Worcester. Her father, William Trowbridge Forbes, a lawyer, was appointed judge of probate in Worcester in 1888. Her mother, Harriette (Merrifield) Forbes (1856–1951), was a gifted writer of local history whose achievements included the rediscovery of early New England gravestone art. In the mid-1890s the family moved to a spacious new house in Worcester that replaced a mansion belonging to Harriette Forbes's father.

The older children all went on to college and graduate school. Esther Forbes, less academically motivated, managed to graduate from Bradford Academy in Haverhill, Mass., in 1912. As a child she loved to make up stories, and by her early teens had written several novels set in ancient Troy and Renaissance Europe. In 1916 she accompanied an older sister to Wisconsin and took courses in writing at the state university in Madison, remaining there until 1918. In December of the following year she joined the editorial department of the Houghton Mifflin Company in Boston as an assistant to Ferris Greenslet. She left in 1926 after marrying Albert Hoskins, a lawyer. The Hoskinses lived in New York and later in Boston, but the marriage was not a success and ended in divorce at her initiative in 1933. Esther Forbes returned to the family house in Worcester, rejoining her mother, a bachelor brother who was notably shy, and a retiring sister.

Professional recognition came first for a short story, "Break-neck Hill," which won an O. Henry Award in 1920. She was immediately successful as a novelist with *O Genteel Lady!* (1926), which sold well. Her strongest novels all focus on the struggle to accommodate fantasy and reality, sexual passion and prudent gentility. *O Genteel Lady!* tells of a would-be woman writer in nineteenth-century Boston who is entranced by the sexuality of a man of "demon" appearance. The remarkably inventive *A Mirror for Witches* (1928) is the story of a young woman

in seventeenth-century Salem who imagines she has taken the devil for her lover. The spinster heroine of *Miss Marvel* (1935), inspired by Forbes's glimpses of a local character, writes impassioned letters to imaginary lovers. *The General's Lady* (1938), based loosely on the real life story of Bathsheba Spooner, tells of a woman who dies to save her lover from execution. Less successful are the panoramic novels of New England life: *Paradise* (1937), about a seventeenth-century town, and *The Running of the Tide* (1948), winner of the 1948 Metro-Goldwyn-Mayer Novel Award, which traces the decline of Salem in the early nineteenth century. *Rainbow on the Road* (1954) uses the travels of an itinerant limner to describe the making of Yankee folklore.

Widely recognized by the end of the 1930s as a leading historical novelist, Forbes used her skills at recreating everyday life in a biography of *Paul Revere and the World He Lived In* (1942), for which she won the Pulitzer Prize in history, the second woman to do so. A novel for children, *Johnny Tremain* (1943), drawn from the same materials, won the Newbery Medal (1944) and was made into a motion picture. Conceived as her contribution to the war the United States was then fighting, it tells of ordinary people who must suddenly grow up and become soldiers. At her death, she left unfinished a study of witchcraft in early New England.

Esther Forbes believed strongly in the validity of her art. She did not hesitate to change publishers rather than revise a manuscript. Nor was she comfortable in a marriage that threatened her life as a writer. In preferring Worcester to Boston or New York as her home after 1933, she acted out her self-confessed identity as a provincial writer. Indeed her strengths came from close identification with a region, and most especially with her mother. The two collaborated on the research that went into the biography of Revere, and Esther Forbes inherited not only a passion for New England history but also the fascination with witchcraft that became a persistent motif of her fiction. The family matrix made hers a distinctive voice among the many historical novelists of the interwar period.

Scrupulous about the facts, she was nonetheless more concerned with personal character, and wrote novels set in the past because she thereby gained essential distance on human nature. Her portraits of women are for the most part portraits of desperate persons seeking to live intensely. At her best, as in *A Mirror for Witches*, the fusion of historical setting and this search for fulfillment links her with Hawthorne and EDITH WHARTON. Like those writers, she was drawn to the darker colors of New England life.

Other honors that came to Esther Forbes included election in 1960 as the first woman member of the American Antiquarian Society. She died in Worcester in 1967 of heart failure.

[The MSS. of Forbes's early stories and novels and letters relating to the editorial revision of *Paradise* are in the Jefferson Library, Clark Univ., Worcester. The Am. Antiquarian Soc., also in Worcester, owns the manuscript of the unfinished history of witchcraft. Letters between Forbes and her editors are in the Houghton Mifflin Co. Papers, Houghton Library, Harvard Univ. Her writings include *America's Paul Revere* (1946), with Lynd Ward; *The Boston Book* (1947), with photographer Arthur Griffin; "Why the Past?" in Dale Warren, ed., *What Is a Book?* (1935); "The Newbery Medal Acceptance," *Horn Book Mag.*, July-Aug. 1944; "Memoirs of an Author," *Bradford Alumnae Assoc. Bull.*, April 1944; and "The Historical Novel," in Herschel Brickell, ed., *Writers on Writing* (1949). An authoritative biography is Margaret Erskine, *Esther Forbes* (1976), published by the Worcester Bicentennial Commission. Written by a member of the family, it is based on papers still in the keeping of the Forbeses and on long friendship with Esther Forbes. There are entries in *Twentieth Century Authors* (1942) and *First Supplement* (1955); *Nat. Cyc. Am. Biog.*, LIII, 296; and *Contemporary Authors* (1975). Obituaries appeared in *Proc. Am. Antiquarian Soc. at the Annual Meeting Held in Worcester*, Oct. 18, 1967 (1968), and in the *N.Y. Times*, Aug. 13, 1967.]

DAVID D. HALL

FRANTZ, Virginia Kneeland, Nov. 13, 1896–Aug. 23, 1967. Surgical pathologist, medical educator.

Virginia Kneeland Frantz was born in New York City, the first of two children and only daughter of Yale and Anna Ilsley (Ball) Kneeland. Both parents came from prominent, upper-class New York families, with ancestors emigrating from England as early as the seventeenth century. Her father ran a successful grain business, while her mother served on the Board of Trustees of the Presbyterian Hospital. The family also owned and operated a dairy farm in Vermont.

In 1906, Virginia Kneeland entered the prestigious Brearley School in New York City, where she received her secondary education. Graduating in 1914, she matriculated at Bryn Mawr College. She excelled as a chemistry major, and Bryn Mawr's president, M. CAREY THOMAS, encouraged her to seek a career in medicine. The student body elected Kneeland president of the Undergraduate Association, a group that coordinated war-related activities at the college during the First World War. In 1918, she graduated first in her class and entered the College of Physicians and Surgeons of Columbia University, which, because of a drop in male applicants during the war, broke its all-male admissions policy for the first time in 1917. Kneeland joined five other women in the class of 1922, which included seventy-four graduates.

Compiling an outstanding record as a medical student, Kneeland ranked second in her class. Upon completion of her M.D. in 1922, she became the first woman ever appointed to a surgical internship at the Presbyterian Hospital, the major affiliate of the College of Physicians and Surgeons. From 1924 to 1927, she served as assistant surgeon to the out-patient department, as well as at the College of Physicians and Surgeons. In 1920, as a third year medical student, she married Angus Macdonald Frantz, a classmate. She had three children: Virginia Hathaway (b. 1924), Angus Macdonald, Jr. (b. 1927), and Andrew Gibson (b. 1930). Nurses and housekeepers assisted at home, enabling Virginia Frantz to meet her commitments at the hospital.

In a profession where women were the exception, Frantz had chosen a specialty in which they were virtually forbidden. Many male surgeons believed that women could not sustain the physical and emotional strain of conducting operative procedures. Probably because of these prejudices, but also because she wanted to free more time for her family and avoid competing in the clinical arena with her husband, a neurologist, she switched to surgical pathology. In 1935, nevertheless, the marriage ended in divorce.

In the late 1920s, she joined noted pathologists William C. Clarke and Arthur Purdy Stout in the Surgical Pathology Laboratory at Presbyterian Hospital. The skills which Frantz derived from her surgical training—a keen sense of the technical requirements of surgical procedure—served her well in this new role.

During the ensuing years, Frantz contributed a series of important pathological studies, particularly relating to tumors of the pancreas, thyroid, and breast. In 1935, she received national attention when she collaborated with the renowned surgeon Allen O. Whipple in describing insulin-secreting tumors of the pancreas for the first time. Her monograph on tumors of the pancreas for the *Armed Forces Atlas of Tumor Pathology* (1959) remains a standard reference work. In the 1940s, Frantz was among the first researchers to demonstrate the effectiveness of radioactive iodine for identifying and treating metastatic thyroid carcinoma. In another pioneering study, she attempted to determine the incidence of chronic cystic disease in the so-called normal female breast through a series of postmortem examinations.

The office of Scientific Research and Development, established during the Second World War, provided Frantz with a grant to investigate the control of bleeding in surgery. This work, done in collaboration with Raffaele Lattes, led to the discovery of the effectiveness of oxidized cellulose for hemostasis. Placed directly into the wound, this gauzelike substance was absorbed into the body. Its use was widely adopted, and in 1948 Frantz received the Army-Navy Certificate of Appreciation for Civilian Service.

Frantz's professional peers recognized her contributions to medical science as well as her engaging personality. The New York Pathological Society elected her president in 1949 and 1950; in 1961, the American Thyroid Association selected her as its first woman president. The New York Infirmary presented her with an Elizabeth Blackwell Award in 1957, given to a woman for distinguished service to medicine. Frantz considered rejecting this honor because it emphasized her gender rather than her profession. "I can accept recognition as a doctor," she explained, "but not as a female doctor. I'm not a medical oddity." In the late 1930s she was offered the presidency of Bryn Mawr, a position she declined because she did not want to leave medicine.

Although she achieved prominence through her research, Frantz's first commitment was to medical education. From 1924 to 1962, the year of her retirement, she taught surgery to second year medical students at the College of Physicians and Surgeons, where she rose from the position of instructor, eventually becoming a full professor in 1951. Using the Socratic method, she deemphasized rote memorization in favor of an inquisitive, experimental approach. With a sharp but easy humor, she attempted to instill a modicum of levity into a rigorous medical curriculum. Sensitive to the pressures of medical education, Frantz became an accessible and valued counselor for students.

After her retirement, she maintained an office at the Columbia-Presbyterian Medical Center and continued as a consultant in surgery. Frantz died of cancer at her home in New York City in 1967.

[Among Frantz's most important publications (most of them coauthored) are: "Adenoma of Islet Cells with Hyperinsulinism," *Annals of Surgery*, June 1935, pp. 1299–1335; "Storage of Radioactive Iodine in a Metastasis from Thyroid Carcinoma," *Science*, April 3, 1942, pp. 362–63; *Introduction to Surgery* (1943); "Hemostasis with Absorbable Gauze," *Annals of Surgery*, Aug. 1944, pp. 181–98; "Radioactive Iodine Studies of Functional Thyroid Carcinoma," *Radiology*, Oct. 1948, pp. 531–52; "An Evaluation of Radioactive Iodine Therapy in Metastatic Thyroid Cancer," *Jour. Clinical Endocrinology*, Sept. 1950, pp. 1084–91; "Incidence of Chronic Cystic Disease in So-Called 'Normal Breasts,'" *Cancer*, July 1951, pp. 762–83; "Pathology of the Thyroid," in Sidney C. Werner, ed., *The Thyroid* (1955). For her view of the problems of women in the medical profession see *Brearley Bull.*, Spring 1957, pp. 9–11. For biographical material see *Nat. Cyc. Am. Biog.* LIII, 346; *P & S Quart.*, Jan. 1968, p. 30; *Who Was Who in Am.*, IV. An obituary appeared in the *N.Y. Times*, Aug. 24, 1967. Information was supplied by Dr. Andrew Gibson Frantz.]

ALLAN M. BRANDT

FRAZIER, Maude, April 4, 1881–June 20, 1963. Educator, state legislator.

Maude Frazier was born in rural Sauk County near Baraboo, Wis., the oldest of the six daughters and three sons of William Henry and Mary Emma (Presnall) Frazier. The Fraziers were Quakers who had migrated from a Friends community in Indiana. William Frazier worked successively as a plasterer, mason, and farmer. Mary Frazier, a well-read, vivacious woman, cared for her large family and found time for weaving, quilting, and gardening.

Maude Frazier attended the Baraboo high school, graduated from the state teachers' college at Stevens Point, and taught briefly in rural Wisconsin schools. Early in the twentieth century, when Nevada's mines received worldwide attention, Maude Frazier followed other adventurers west. From 1906 to 1921 she taught in Nevada's small towns: Genoa, Lovelock, Seven Troughs, Beatty, Goldfield, and Sparks. School facilities and living conditions were very primitive, but Frazier grew to love the rough desert country and its thriving new communities.

In 1921 a post as deputy state superintendent of public instruction opened in the southern part of the state, and Frazier won the appointment over several male applicants. Although she apparently had never driven an automobile, she bought a car, took driving lessons, and learned about auto mechanics; she needed to cover a district that embraced more than 40,000 square miles, a population of only 14,000, a school enrollment of about 2,800, sixty-three elementary schools, ten high schools, and two kindergartens. During her six years on the job, Frazier became well known and was affectionately greeted by those who recognized her on her travels through the rough back roads of her southern Nevada district. Her successors claimed that her records for driving on unpaved roads remained unbroken.

In 1927 Maude Frazier abandoned the back

roads to become superintendent of the Las Vegas Union School District, a position she retained for nearly twenty years. As her district was then feeling the effects of a boom stemming from the construction of Hoover Dam, she initiated a building program that extended through the next several years. In 1929 she spurred construction of the town's second permanent public building, the Las Vegas High School; six more school buildings soon followed. These formed the basis of what was to become the largest school district in Nevada. After her retirement in 1946, Frazier continued for a year as consultant to the district she had supervised.

In 1948, still energetic, Frazier filed as a candidate for the Nevada state legislature. She lost, but tried again in 1950 and won, thus beginning a new career that spanned the next twelve years.

A member of the majority (Democratic) party in the assembly, Frazier became chairman of the education committee and made this post into one of the most powerful gifts in the hands of the party caucus; she retained the chair through six terms in the legislature. She also served on the important ways and means committee through part of her tenure.

As head of the education committee, Maude Frazier wrote or steered to passage dozens of important measures. Probably her most outstanding contribution involved the reorganization in 1955 of the Nevada state school system: a conglomeration of over 230 large and small districts, mostly underfinanced or poorly led, was reduced to 17, and a patchwork tax system was reworked to provide support for quality education.

Maude Frazier's other legislative accomplishments included the establishment of Nevada Southern University (later the University of Nevada, Las Vegas), whose first building was named for her; revised election laws that have been widely copied; and the state's first attempt to hold annual legislative sessions. In recognition of her governmental acumen, Maude Frazier was appointed lieutenant governor to fill a vacancy in 1962. Although she served only part of one year, she was the first woman to attain that high state office in Nevada.

Maude Frazier died of a heart attack at her home in Las Vegas in 1963. She seemed never to have thought of her attainments as feminist achievements, remarking only that she had held a number of positions usually held by men, and had "got by all right"; she was confident that she would do well in any government post, even that of state governor. Her tall, spare, sturdy frame indicated that she could take care of herself. To all who knew and admired her, she exemplified self-sufficiency and independence.

[An unpublished autobiography is in the Manuscript Coll. at the Univ. of Nev., Las Vegas. An informal biography is Elbert B. Edwards, *Maude Frazier, Nevadan* (Southern Nev. Retired Teachers Assoc., 1970). Information on her political career is given in Mary Ellen Glass, "Nevada's Lady Lawmakers: Women in the Nevada Legislature," *Nev. Public Affairs Report,* Oct. 1975. Other sources include reports of the Nev. Deputy State Supt. of Public Instruction, 1921–27; Nev. State Legislature, *Journals of the Assembly,* 1951–61; and newspaper articles. An obituary appeared in the *Las Vegas Sun,* June 21, 1963. Photograph is available at the Univ. of Nev., Reno Library Special Coll. Dept. Assistance was given by Frazier's niece Marie M. Dawn. Death certificate obtained from the Nev. Dept. of Human Resources.]

MARY ELLEN GLASS

FREDERICK, Christine McGaffey, Feb. 6, 1883–April 6, 1970. Household efficiency specialist, businesswoman.

Christine Frederick was born in Boston, the only child of Mimi (Scott) and William R. Campbell, a clergyman. Her parents separated shortly after her birth. Her mother took Christine to Russia, where she lived with an aunt in Moscow while her mother worked as a governess. After about seven years, Christine returned with her mother to the United States to live with her maternal grandparents, Scottish immigrants, in St. Louis. In 1894 her mother married Wyatt MacGaffey, a Chicago lawyer who legally adopted Christine; there were two sons from this marriage. Christine McGaffey (the spelling she later adopted) graduated from Chicago's Northwest Division High School in 1901, and a year later entered Northwestern University, where she was elected to Phi Beta Kappa and earned her B.S. in 1906.

The following year Christine McGaffey married Justus George Frederick (1882–1964), a business executive, writer, and editor active in advertising and marketing research. They had four children: David (b. 1908), Jean (b. 1910), Phyllis (b. 1915), and Carol (b. 1917). As a well-educated housewife with a growing family, Christine Frederick soon became interested in improving household efficiency. When the Fredericks moved to Greenlawn, Long Island, around 1910, she transformed several rooms of their house into the Applecroft Home Experiment Station, a model efficiency kitchen and laundry in which she tested household equipment, utensils, and products. Her work there contributed to the standardization of the height of sinks and working surfaces at a comfortable level. She also compiled food charts, recipes, and booklets on household products; produced a film on housekeeping; and lectured, with dramatic flair, on efficient home management.

Frederick's ideas began to reach a wide audience in 1912, when she was appointed household editor for *Ladies' Home Journal.* Four articles she wrote for the magazine that year on the domestic applications of scientific management were subsequently expanded into a book, *The New Housekeeping* (1913). This was followed by *Household Engineering: Scientific Management in the Home* (1915), a work that marked Frederick as a pioneer in applying to domestic chores the principles of scientific management devised by Frederick Winslow Taylor to standardize work in factories and offices. Christine Frederick hoped to liberate women from household tasks by introducing efficient management of the home, but later critics charged that some of her "efficiency" measures were in fact quite time consuming, and therefore restricted women's aspirations. Nevertheless her ideas gained wide currency: *The New Housekeeping* was translated into several foreign languages; *Household Engineering* served students as a home economics textbook; and the author became a sought-after lecturer, touring the country on the Chautauqua circuit in 1917 as one of its chief orators.

Known principally for her books and speeches on household efficiency, Christine Frederick also developed a related career in advertising. Shortly after the Applecroft Home Experiment Station was established, manufacturers began to send her their products for comparison with advertised claims; if they passed her inspection, she prepared promotional literature. Finding no advertising association in New York that would admit women, in 1912, with her husband's support, she founded the League of Advertising Women (later Advertising Women of New York). She testified two years later before a House committee on trust legislation, advocating a "general law against unfair competition," and proceeded in subsequent years to advance her own brand of consumerism, one that urged women to become trained "purchasing agents" as well as efficient household "managers." For many years, she served as household editor for *American Weekly,* a periodical on advertising read by manufacturers and dealers across the country. Her third book, *Selling Mrs. Consumer* (1929), was based on one of the first surveys of the buying habits of women, conducted by Christine Frederick at the suggestion of her husband. It counseled manufacturers and advertisers on ways of interpreting the habits of women in the marketplace and on the need to maintain the reliability of brand names.

Throughout the 1920s and 1930s, Frederick continued to write for magazines and newspapers, lectured widely in the United States, and reached thousands of people with her radio talks. She also spoke in Europe, where her books and theories had preceded her and where the idea of the functional planning of space was winning acceptance. Abroad, she toured a number of low-cost housing projects that provided convenience in compact quarters and exemplified her own ideas on interior design, Frederick's main occupation in later years.

Her children grown, Frederick moved to New York City in 1939; she and her husband separated somewhat later. She traveled frequently during the 1940s, settling in Laguna Beach, Calif., in 1950. There she taught extension courses in interior design at Orange Coast College and worked in her own interior design and decorating consulting business until her retirement in 1957. Christine Frederick died of a heart attack in Newport Beach, Calif., in April 1970, at the age of eighty-seven.

[Christine Frederick's papers—including the typescript of an unpublished and unfinished autobiography written in 1969, speeches, correspondence, and other business records—are in the Schlesinger Library, Radcliffe College. Her work is discussed in Sigfried Giedion, *Mechanization Takes Command* (1955), and in Susana Torre, ed., *Women in American Architecture* (1977). See also *Who's Who in America,* 1920–21. Critiques of Frederick's writings are offered by Stuart Ewen, *Captains of Consciousness: The Social Roots of American Advertising* (1976), and by Barbara Ehrenreich and Deirdre English, *For Her Own Good: 150 Years of the Experts' Advice to Women* (1978). Obituaries appeared in the *N.Y. Times* and *L.A. Times,* April 8, 1970. Personal information provided by Frederick's daughter Jean Joyce. Transcript and alumni information furnished by Northwestern Univ. Archives; birth certificate by Mass. Dept. of Public Health; death certificate by Calif. Dept. of Public Health.]

CAROLINE SHILLABER

FRENKEL-BRUNSWIK, Else, Aug. 18, 1908– March 31, 1958. Psychologist.

Else Frenkel was the second of three daughters born to Abraham and Helene (Gelernter) Frenkel in Lemberg, a Polish town then part of the Austro-Hungarian empire. The family moved to Vienna in 1914 to escape the pogrom of that year. There Abraham Frenkel became a bank director, then owner of a private bank. There Else was educated, graduating from the gymnasium in 1926 and taking her doctorate in psychology at the University of Vienna in 1930, where she remained as the equivalent of assistant professor at the Psychological Institute until the *Anschluss* of 1938 that incorporated Austria into Nazi Germany.

The plainest of the sisters, Else Frenkel-Brunswik later attributed her intellectual achievements to her older sister's extraordinary beauty; she also referred cryptically to her "Cordelia complex" as it emerged in her psychoanalysis (*Selected Papers*, pp. 36–57). Their mother was especially proud of the beautiful oldest sister, and tended to baby the youngest. Else was closest to their father, who regretted the lack of a son and appreciated Else's intellectual accomplishments. When Else shocked her observantly Jewish parents by her attachment and subsequent marriage to her psychologist teacher and colleague Egon Brunswik (1903–1955), from a gentile family of minor Hungarian nobility, it was her father who forgave her and maintained contact.

The Psychological Institute during the decade of Else Frenkel's participation was a benign but absolute monarchy presided over by Karl and CHARLOTTE BÜHLER. Her dissertation with Karl Bühler sought a rapprochement between the older theories of psychological association and the newer Gestalt doctrines; she also assisted Charlotte Bühler in her biographical studies which foreshadowed later research on personality in life course perspective. If her status as plainest daughter thrust her into intellectual life, her Vienna colleagues remembered her as lively and assertive but also slim, elegant, flirtatious, and an excellent dancer. The sequels to a severe attack of rheumatic fever in 1932 interfered with her dancing but not with her assiduous work. Her illness interrupted her first venture in personal psychoanalysis after eight months, and left her with a lifelong concern about her heart.

Two of the currents that made interwar Vienna a center of European intellectual culture contributed to Frenkel-Brunswik's career as a psychologist. One was psychoanalysis. She resumed analysis in 1937 with the renowned psychoanalytic ego psychologist Ernst Kris, terminating only when she emigrated. The other was logical positivism and the Unity of Science movement as expounded by Moritz Schlick, Rudolf Carnap, and other members of the "Vienna Circle," in which her husband-to-be also participated. More than the ideas of the Bühlers, these intellectual sources, together with the experience of being a Jew during the Hitler years, underlay the problems that she addressed during her two very productive decades in the United States.

Egon Brunswik had gone to the University of California at Berkeley in 1937. A philosophically and historically oriented scholar alien to the predominantly behaviorist American style, he had a distinguished though truncated career as a theorist and methodologist of experimental psychology. After the *Anschluss*, Else Frenkel joined him; they married on June 9, 1938. Nepotism rules prevented her from being considered for a tenured appointment in psychology. Instead, in 1939 she became a research psychologist in the Institute of Child Welfare (later the Institute of Human Development) at Berkeley, which remained her principal employment thereafter. As a lecturer, she often taught seminars in the psychology department, where she had many devoted students, including some who apprenticed themselves to her in research.

Soon after arriving in the United States, she published "Mechanisms of Self Deception," work that she had done in Vienna when first influenced by psychoanalysis. In 1940 there followed her first major discussion of the bearing of psychoanalysis on the psychology of personality, a contribution to an influential symposium in which prominent psychologists commented on their psychoanalyses (*Selected Papers*, pp. 36–57).

The time was ripe. Frenkel-Brunswik had arrived in the United States just as a new and self-conscious psychology of personality was emerging, led by Gordon Allport, Henry A. Murray, and Gardner Murphy, and a new profession of clinical psychology was beginning to take form. Frenkel-Brunswik participated centrally in these developments, both much influenced by psychoanalysis, which was difficult for American psychologists to assimilate. Her sophistication in both psychoanalysis and Vienna-Circle logical positivism enabled her to champion the scientific respectability of psychoanalytic constructions. American positivism in psychology (behaviorism) had come forth with a crasser "operationism" that insisted upon tying concepts tightly to operations of measurement, thus rejecting the "speculative" and "mentalistic" formulations of psychoanalysis and other nonbehaviorist psychology. Frenkel-Brunswik was in a firm position to counter this attack (*Selected Papers*, pp. 161–231).

After publishing an important monograph, *Motivation and Behavior* (1942), showing how clinical ratings of adolescents' underlying drives could bring discrepant data from self-reports and ratings of social behavior into congruence, she joined forces with Nevitt Sanford and Daniel Levinson (then their student) in designing and launching major psychological studies of anti-Semitism. In 1945 the American Jewish Committee supported an expansion of these studies provided that Theodor Adorno, the well-known émigré scholar of the Frankfurt School, joined the group. Publication in 1950 of the resulting book, *The Authoritarian Personality*, was a major event. In addition to her central role in the conception of the studies, Frenkel-Brunswik contributed the systematic analysis of clinical interviews which distinguished between highly prejudiced and unprejudiced persons. The research was widely acclaimed for bringing the clinical insights of psychoanalysis and the empirical methods of American social psychology jointly to bear on the study of prejudice and proto-fascist attitudes, and for presenting a well-developed model of the relations between childrearing, character structure, and ideology. It was sharply criticized for overplaying the characterological roots of prejudice as compared with class- or situation-based sources, for focusing on the authoritarianism of the right to the neglect of left authoritarianism (the cold war was beginning), and for a variety of technical flaws. Identifying and correcting the latter so preoccupied psychologists in the ensuing decade that intellectual fashions changed before the substantive issues raised by the research had been adequately clarified. Nevertheless the book has enduring importance as a classic of American social science.

In addition to her major part in *The Authoritarian Personality*, Frenkel-Brunswik conducted related research on prejudice in children, wrote on "intolerance of ambiguity" as a cognitive style of personality that had emerged saliently in her studies of prejudice (*Selected Papers*, pp. 58–91), and began a major study of aging in the postwar years before her life crumbled.

Else and Egon Brunswik were devoted to each other in a childless marriage. On July 7, 1955, near the end of her year as a fellow of the Center for Advanced Study in the Behavioral Sciences at Stanford, Egon Brunswik ended a long and painful struggle with severe hypertension by suicide. He had had a sympathectomy and was being treated with the depressive drug reserpine. The loss to Else Frenkel-Brunswik was heartbreaking and permanently disruptive. A year as Fulbright fellow at the University of Oslo did not put her world back together. Her husband's death coincided with profound midlife doubts about both psychoanalysis and logical positivism as pillars of her intellectual life. She had continued for several years to mine the rich ore of *The Authoritarian Personality;* now an inner intellectual crisis became an integral aspect of her personal crisis.

Meanwhile, with the nepotism barrier removed, her colleagues in psychology at Berkeley sought to obtain a full professorship for her in recognition of her eminence in child and developmental psychology, psychoanalytic theory, and personality and cognition; the appointment was endorsed unanimously by the full professors on Dec. 4, 1957. The recognition (which would have taken effect the following July) came too late, and in no way compensated for her sense of loss—nor, indeed, did it assuage her bitterness about aspects of her career that were attendant upon her female role. Else Frenkel-Brunswik died of an overdose of barbital on March 31, 1958, in her fiftieth year.

[Nanette Heiman and Joan Grant, eds., *Else Frenkel-Brunswik: Selected Papers*, in *Psychological Issues*, VIII, Monograph 31 (1974) contains a substantial biographical essay and an annotated bibliography of her publications in German and English. Other major writings are "Mechanisms of Self-Deception," *Jour. Soc. Psychol.*, Aug. 1939, pp. 409–20, and *Motivation and Behavior, Genetic Psychology Monographs*, XXVI, Nov. 1942, pp. 121–265. See also Daniel J. Levinson, "Else Frenkel-Brunswik," *Int. Encyc. Social Sciences* (1968). Robert I. Watson, ed., *Eminent Contributors to Psychology*, 2 vols. (1974, 1976) includes primary and secondary bibliographical references. On Egon Brunswik see Kenneth R. Hammond, ed., *Psychology of Egon Brunswik* (1966). Donald Fleming and Bernard Bailyn, eds., *The Intellectual Migration: Europe and America, 1930–1960* (1969) contains background information on the contributions of European émigrés to American thought. Helpful information came from Frenkel-Brunswik's sisters, Johanna Urabin and Marta Fischler; from Hedda Bolgar, Donald T. Campbell, Norma Haan, Marie Jahoda-Albu, Daniel J. Levinson, Read Tuddenham, Ann Vollmar, and Edith Weisskopf-Joelson; from Nanette Heiman, Murray Jarvik, and Vivien March; and from personal acquaintance. The Univ. of Calif., Berkeley, provided her biographical employment form, and the Calif. Dept. of Public Health her death certificate.]

M. BREWSTER SMITH

FROMM-REICHMANN, Frieda, Oct. 23, 1889–April 28, 1957. Psychoanalyst, psychiatrist.

Frieda Fromm-Reichmann, who pioneered in psychotherapy with schizophrenic patients, was born in Karlsruhe, Germany, the eldest of three daughters of Klara (Simon) and Adolf Reichmann, an orthodox Jew and a merchant. By the time she entered school in 1894 the Reichmann family had moved to Königsberg, East Prussia, where her father became a bank director.

Frieda Reichmann's emancipated mother, who had been trained as a schoolteacher, impressed upon her daughters the need to become financially independent so that they might have an alternative to marriage. Well endowed with talent and energy, Frieda Reichmann readily absorbed these precepts, and excelled at her studies in the arts and sciences. As girls were not yet permitted to attend the gymnasium, Klara Reichmann founded a club which organized a private course of instruction for her oldest daughter and a select group of other young women.

After Frieda Reichmann passed her examination for university entrance (abitur) in 1907, she and her family decided that the study of medicine would provide the greatest opportunities. She entered the medical school of Königsberg's Albertus University the following year and graduated in 1913. There were only a handful of women medical students at the time, and Reichmann, who was little more than four feet ten and still wore her braids pinned around her ears, experienced considerable discriminatory treatment by members of the faculty.

Because of her small stature and lack of physical strength she had to abandon an early interest in obstetrics. Becoming aware of her natural empathy toward severely disturbed mental patients, she decided to pursue a career in psychiatry instead. From 1913 to 1920 Reichmann engaged in various postgraduate studies under Kurt Goldstein, a holistic neurologist whose notions she later adapted for use in psychiatry. She served as an intern (1913), then as an assistant and instructor (1914–16) at the University of Königsberg's psychiatric hospital, later becoming, under Goldstein's guidance, physician-in-charge (1916–18) of Königsberg's new 100-bed hospital and dispensary for brain-injured soldiers. At the outbreak of World War I she had also worked briefly in Berlin at the Municipal Hospital Moabit and its attached neurological dispensary. Her work with brain-injured soldiers was especially important for her later psychotherapeutic efforts with schizophrenic patients: the soldiers' deep anxieties ("catastrophic reactions") prepared her to understand psychotic panic states; their functional losses also disposed her to emphasize nonverbal understanding rather than verbal interpretation.

After the war Reichmann's professional interests diversified. She continued research under Goldstein at the University of Frankfurt am Main Neurological Institute (1918–20) and then worked at J. H. Schultz's Weisser Hirsch, a sanitarium near Dresden that practiced relaxation therapy. She also began her personal psychoanalysis, first under Wilhelm Wittenberg in Munich, then under the training analyst Hanns Sachs in Berlin. During this period she was greatly influenced by Georg Groddeck, a

psychoanalytic theorist interested in symbolic communication who was using psychoanalytic principles in the treatment of somatic disorders. In 1923 she served as visiting physician at Emil Kraepelin's psychiatric clinic at the University of Munich.

Her encounter with the psychoanalytic movement was a turning point in her life. In the early years, she believed that this revolutionary new method would not only alleviate human suffering but also lead to social change. To this end she analyzed many members of the Zionist movement, in which she was then vitally interested. Still under the sway of these ideas, she headed a private psychoanalytic sanitarium in Heidelberg from 1924 to 1928. Social philosopher Erich Fromm, eleven years her junior, joined her in this endeavor; she and Fromm were married on March 26, 1926. In October, with five others, they founded the Frankfurt subsection of the German Psychoanalytic Society; three years later she and her colleagues organized the Psychoanalytic Institute of South-Western Germany at Frankfurt. By this time she had become disillusioned with psychoanalysis as a political approach and had abandoned the practice of orthodox Judaism. She had also become interested in socialism.

In 1933, with the rise of National Socialism and its attendant anti-Semitism, Fromm-Reichmann moved across the border to Strasbourg, France, where she continued the analyses of her German patients. Two years later she briefly visited Palestine, and then immigrated to the United States, arriving in April 1935; she became a naturalized citizen in April 1941. The following year she and Fromm, who had been separated since the early 1930s, were divorced.

Fromm-Reichmann spent her entire American career as a staff member at Chestnut Lodge, a private psychoanalytic sanitarium in Rockville, Md. There she became a close colleague of Harry Stack Sullivan, leader of the interpersonal school of psychoanalysis. She was active in all three of the Sullivanian psychoanalytic training organizations, serving in the Washington-Baltimore (later the Washington) Psychoanalytic Society as a training and supervising analyst after 1935, and as president (1939–41); in the Washington School of Psychiatry after 1936; and in the William Alanson White Institute of Psychiatry, Psychoanalysis, and Psychology in New York City after 1943.

Sullivan's emphasis on interpersonal rather than intrapsychic theories of behavior influenced Fromm-Reichmann's already developing interest in using intensive psychotherapy with schizophrenic and manic-depressive patients, who were usually considered beyond the reach of such treatment. An extraordinarily gifted therapist, Fromm-Reichmann had the capacity to listen closely, to wait out a patient's silences or rages, and ultimately to make even extremely disturbed patients aware that she understood and accepted them as they were. Measuring improvement by the direction of change rather than by any absolute norm, she viewed the patient as one who needed practical help in overcoming illness rather than as one defined by it. She also considered the psychiatrist as an active healer rather than as a detached observer. While known mainly as a clinician, Fromm-Reichmann also disseminated her ideas, publishing two classic works: *Principles of Intensive Psychotherapy* (1950) and "An Intensive Study of Twelve Cases of Manic-Depressive Psychosis" (1954), the latter coauthored with four colleagues from Chestnut Lodge. But it is probably Joanne Greenberg's *I Never Promised You a Rose Garden* (1964; published under the pseudonym Hannah Green) that, in the character of Dr. Fried, best captures the special quality of Fromm-Reichmann's work.

For many colleagues, students, and patients, Fromm-Reichmann's chief contribution was her sensitivity to the "assets of the mentally handicapped," the title of her best known lecture series given in the Washington School of Psychiatry and in the White Institute in New York. She gave special emphasis to the relationship between art and mental illness and to the creative potential of patients, an interest probably stimulated by her close friendship with Gertrud Jacob (1893–1940), a German-born psychiatrist and artist who worked at Chestnut Lodge after 1937. In an unforgettably dramatic fashion, Fromm-Reichmann used the pictures of Van Gogh, the writings of Schopenhauer, and the music of Robert Schumann to illustrate the ways in which the experiences of the mentally handicapped contributed to the development of artistic and intellectual expression. Younger colleagues in training with her developed a sensitivity to the intellectual and artistic gifts of their patients; and she helped many of her own patients toward creative expression that was recognized in the larger world.

Toward the end of her life Fromm-Reichmann gained wide recognition from her professional colleagues: she received the Adolf Meyer Award from the Association for the Improvement of Mental Hospitals (1952), primarily because of her insistence that psychotherapy was possible with psychotic patients, and delivered the prestigious Academic Lecture (on the "Psychotherapy of Schizophrenia") before the American Psychiatric Association (1954). At the age of sixty-six she held a fellowship at the Center for Advanced Study in the Behavioral Sciences in Palo Alto, Calif., which she used to study more formally the nature of nonverbal communication in psychotherapy. The only woman in the group, she made a deep impression on her colleagues.

Indeed, to all her friends and associates she was a vital presence, one who lifted their spirits; aware of the needs and expectations of others, she kept any private unhappiness to herself. Always generous, during most of her adult life, and especially during the years of the Holocaust, she contributed to the financial support of family and friends.

Frieda Fromm-Reichmann's last years were plagued by a hereditary form of deafness. She died of a heart attack at her home in Chestnut Lodge in April 1957.

[Some of Frieda Fromm-Reichmann's papers were destroyed, as stipulated by her will. The rest are in the possession of her executor, Virginia Gunst. Many of her English writings, including "An Intensive Study of Twelve Cases of Manic-Depressive Psychosis," are collected in Dexter M. Bullard, ed., *Psychoanalysis and Psychotherapy: Selected Papers of Frieda Fromm-Reichmann* (1959); it also contains a bibliography of her papers written in German. Other published writings include two edited works: *The Philosophy of Insanity—by a Late Inmate of the Royal Asylum for Lunatics at Gartnavel* ([1860] 1947) and *Progress in Psychotherapy—1956* (1956), with J. L. Moreno. One chapter, "Psychiatric Aspects of Anxiety," of a work in progress at the time of her death appeared in Clara Thompson and others, eds., *An Outline of Psychoanalysis* (1955). Some translated extracts of her German writings appear in Jarl Dyrud, "The Early Frieda and Traces of Her in Her Later Writings," unpublished MS. delivered at Chestnut Lodge, 1969. A complete bibliography appears in Alexander Grinstein, ed., *The Index of Psychoanalytic Writings* (1956, 1967). The most useful secondary sources are Edith Weigert, "In Memoriam: Frieda Fromm-Reichmann, 1889–1957," *Psychiatry*, Feb. 1958; Marianne Marschak, "One Year Among the Behavioral Scientists: In Memory of Frieda Fromm-Reichmann," *Psychiatry*, Aug. 1960; and Gregory Bateson, "Language and Psychotherapy—Frieda Fromm-Reichmann's Last Project," *Psychiatry*, Feb. 1958. See also the entry in *Who's Who in World Jewry* (1955) and Hannah Green, "In Praise of My Doctor," *Contemporary Psychoanalysis*, Fall 1967. Other secondary sources are listed in Robert I. Watson, ed., *Eminent Contributors to Psychology*, II (1976). A helpful source on the Washington psychoanalytic milieu is Douglas Noble and Donald L. Burnham, "History of the Washington Psychoanalytic Society and the Washington Psychoanalytic Institute" (1969). On Gertrud Jacob see Dexter Means Bullard, "Gertrud Jacob, M.D., 1893–1940," *Psychiatry*, May 1940, and William V. Silverberg, "The Art of Dr. Gertrud Jacob, 1893–1940: Portraits of Psychotics," *Psychiatry*, May

1941. Naturalization information provided by U.S. Dept. of Justice; death certificate provided by Md. State Dept. of Health.]

ROBERT C. POWELL
SYLVIA G. HOFF

FULLER, Meta Vaux Warrick, June 6, 1877– March 13, 1968. Sculptor.

Meta Warrick Fuller was born in Philadelphia, Pa., the youngest of three children of Emma (Jones) and William H. Warrick. Henry Jones, her maternal grandfather, was a well-known caterer in Philadelphia. Her father owned barber shops and her mother a hairdressing parlor. Meta was named after one of her mother's clients, Meta Vaux, the daughter of Senator Richard Vaux.

Meta Warrick's early knowledge and appreciation of art began with her father's self-instructed interest in paintings and sculpture in the Philadelphia Academy of Fine Arts. When she completed high school in Philadelphia in 1894, she won a three-year scholarship to the Pennsylvania Museum and School of Industrial Art (later the Philadelphia College of Industrial Art). Her prizewinning bas-relief frieze of thirty-seven medieval figures, "The Procession of Arts and Crafts," earned her a postgraduate scholarship for an additional year of study in sculpture. At her graduation in 1898, she won an honorable mention for modeling and a prize for a metalwork piece, "Crucifixion of Christ in Agony."

With the encouragement of her teachers and friends, Meta Warrick went to Paris in October 1899 for further study. She was not permitted because of her race to stay at the American Girls Club, so a family friend, Henry O. Tanner, the American-born Negro painter who had won acclaim in Paris, found her a room in a small hotel. Despite limited financial resources, she attended the École des Beaux Arts (1899), and the Colarossi Academy (1900–02) where she studied modeling under such notable French artists as Injalbert, Gauqui, and Rollard. Introduced to the sculptor Auguste Rodin, she showed him a plaster model of her "Secret Sorrow" (also known as "Man Eating His Heart"). He praised her work and with his encouragement she exhibited several sculptures, including "The Thief on the Cross," "The Impenitent Thief," "The Wretched," and "Man Carrying a Dead Comrade"—all examples of the powerful combination of the romantic and the macabre that marks her early work—in L'Art Nouveau, an important Paris gallery.

Despite her successful years in Paris, race prejudice denied Meta Warrick similar recognition after her return to Philadelphia in 1902. Art dealers asserted that there was no interest in the "domestic" works she produced in her Philadelphia studio, but they also belittled the sculptures she had done in Paris. It was not until 1907, when she won a gold medal for her tableaux of 150 figures illustrating the progress of the Negro in America (a commission for the Jamestown Tercentennial Exhibition), that she began to receive recognition.

On Feb. 3, 1909, Meta Warrick married Dr. Solomon Carter Fuller of Boston and Framingham, Mass. A Liberian by birth, he was a graduate of the Boston University School of Medicine. Then working in the fields of pathology and neurology, he later became a noted psychiatrist. They moved to a house he had had built in Framingham, which was their home for the remainder of their lives. In 1910 a fire in a Philadelphia warehouse where Meta Fuller's sculptures were stored destroyed practically all her work of the past sixteen years.

Her opportunities for professional work were somewhat limited by the birth of three sons: Solomon Carter, Jr., born in 1910; William Thomas, born in 1911; and Perry J., born in 1916. But in 1913, at the request of W. E. B. Du Bois, famous author and editor of *The Crisis* magazine, she molded a statue depicting a black boy and girl for the fiftieth anniversary celebration in New York of the Emancipation Proclamation. This sculpture marked the beginning of her use of Afro-Americans as her models and the start of fifty prolific years, working at first in a studio on the top floor of her house and after 1929 in a separate studio building on the shore of nearby Learned Pond. In 1922 Meta Fuller showed a life-size sculpture, "Awakening Ethiopia" (now in the Schomburg Collection of the New York Public Library) at New York's Making of America Exposition. During the 1930s she exhibited at local libraries, the Boston Art Club, and at churches, where she gained increased popularity. Her later work, usually small pieces, is more reserved than that done before 1910. It shows "greater self-consciousness . . . check-reined technic," and an "ingratiating charm" (Porter, p. 78) that distinguish it from the more emotionally demanding work of the earlier period.

In 1950 Meta Warrick Fuller left her studio to a former pupil in order to care for her ailing and blind husband. He died on Jan. 16, 1953, and shortly thereafter she contracted tuberculosis which required confinement for two years in a sanatorium. She returned to Framingham and began to work again, completing a bust of CHARLOTTE HAWKINS BROWN in 1956 and the following year producing for the National Council of Negro Women doll models of ten famous American Negro women. In the early 1960s she sculpted a bronze plaque of a doctor and two nurses for the Framingham Union Hospital where her husband had practiced. This period is also marked by one of her most notable works, "The Crucifixion," with the head of Christ raised, done in memory of the four Negro girls killed in the church bombing in Birmingham, Ala., in 1963. A bronze piece, "Storytime" (depicting a mother reading to her three children) was unveiled in the Framingham Center Library in 1964.

Although much of her early work was destroyed, several of her important pieces were placed in museums: "The Talking Skull" in the Museum of Afro-American History in Boston; "The Wretched" in the Palace of the Legion of Honor in San Francisco, a museum built by Alma Spreckels (1881–1968) which features the work of Rodin, his students, and those whom he inspired; her statuette of Richard B. Harrison as "De Lawd" in *Green Pastures* in the art gallery of Howard University; a bas-relief of a black youth rising from a kneeling position to meet the rising sun in the YMCA building in Atlanta, Ga.; a bronze bust of her husband in the Boston University School of Medicine; and "The Dancing Girl" in the Cleveland Museum of Art. In addition to her many prizes, she was a fellow of the Academy of Fine Arts and was one of three sculptors receiving special honor in March 1961 at the "New Vistas in American Art" exhibit at Howard University. Meta Warrick Fuller died in Framingham at the age of ninety.

[A bibliography on Meta Fuller, as well as lists of her work, exhibitions, and awards, and the collections in which her sculpture may be found are included in Theresa Dickason Cederholm, ed., *Afro-American Artists: A Bio-bibliographical Directory* (1973). Sylvia G. L. Dannett, "Meta Warrick Fuller," *Profiles of Negro Womanhood*, vol. II (1966), pp. 31–46, is the most complete biographical sketch. See also Elwin Greene, "Profile: Sculptress Meta Warrick Fuller," Worcester (Mass.) *Sunday Telegram*, May 18, 1958; Mary White Ovington, *Portraits in Color* (1927), pp. 216–26; *The Crisis*, Jan. 1918, p. 133, Jan. 1919, p. 135, Nov. 1919, p. 350, April 1920, p. 337; and Velma G. Hoover, "Meta Vaux Warrick Fuller: Her Life and Her Art," *Negro Hist. Bull.*, March-April 1977, pp. 678–81. The best brief critical evaluation is in James A. Porter, *Modern Negro Art* (1943, 1969) pp. 62, 77, 86–87, 92, 94. An obituary appeared in *Jet*, March 28, 1968. A birth certificate was provided by the Dept. of Records, City of Phila. Personal information was supplied by Solomon C. Fuller, Jr.]

RAYFORD W. LOGAN

FURMAN, Bess, Dec. 2, 1894–May 12, 1969. Journalist.

Bess Furman was born in Danbury, Neb., the second of five children and oldest of three daughters of Mattie Ann (Van Pelt) and Archie Charles Furman. Her father's family migrated to Nebraska from the Susquehanna valley of Pennsylvania in the 1870s; her mother was a native of State Center, Iowa. The family home doubled as the storefront office of *The Danbury News*, which Bess's father edited and published. "I learned to set type as I learned to read," Furman remembered. Her lifelong interest in journalism had begun.

After her graduation from high school in Kirksville, Mo., in 1910, Bess Furman spent seven years teaching in rural Missouri and Nebraska schools while attending college in the summer. She graduated from Kearney (Neb.) State Teachers College in 1918, where she was the first woman editor of the school newspaper, *The Antelope*. But Furman gladly gave up her teaching career when she landed a job at the *Kearney Daily Hub*. From 1920 until 1929, she worked for the *Omaha Daily News*. Occasionally writing under the pseudonym Bobbie O'Dare, Bess Furman enjoyed her "catch-as-catch-can, girl-in-the-street sort of reporting," but her ambition was to establish her reputation outside Nebraska. Furman's chance came in 1928 when her prizewinning story on an Omaha campaign appearance by presidential candidate Alfred E. Smith ("We Want Al! Crowd Shouts") brought her to the attention of the Associated Press (AP), where by-lines by women were just beginning to appear. From 1929 to 1936 Furman worked for the Washington bureau of AP. The first woman reporter regularly assigned to the House of Representatives by a press association, she also covered the White House and national political events from the woman's angle. Her principal AP assignment after 1932 was ELEANOR ROOSEVELT, whose press conferences, activities, and travels Furman extensively chronicled. "No newspaperwoman could have asked for better luck," Furman recalled. During these years, Furman and other newspaperwomen such as LORENA HICKOK, Emma Bugbee, and Ruby Black (1896–1957) developed lasting friendships with Eleanor Roosevelt.

During her early years in the House Press Gallery Furman met her future husband, Robert J. Armstrong, Jr. (1903–1955), then a reporter with the *Los Angeles Times* and later with the *St. Louis Globe-Democrat*. After some hesitation because of the difference in their ages, Furman finally consented to one of Armstrong's frequent marriage proposals. Her close friend RUTH BRYAN OWEN (ROHDE) arranged their wedding on March 18, 1932, in Washington. Furman continued to use her given name professionally.

The marriage was successful, despite early financial problems (most reporters faced salary cuts in the depression) and Armstrong's occasional bouts with alcoholism. The couple was surprised yet delighted when Furman realized she was pregnant at the age of forty-one. Even while pregnant, she kept up a hectic reporting pace through the last months of the 1936 campaign. In December she resigned from the AP and soon after returned home to McCook, Neb., where on April 4, 1937, twins were born: Ruth Eleanor (named for her godmothers Ruth Owen Rohde and Eleanor Roosevelt) and Robert Furman. Fellow journalist Geno Herrick wired, "The AP always did make carbon copies," and Eleanor Roosevelt volunteered to knit a second baby blanket. Furman combined motherhood and career with the help of a sympathetic husband and flexible working arrangements while the twins were young. Of crucial help, both in childrearing and journalism, was her sister Lucile (1895–1961) who had come from Nebraska in 1936 to live with the Armstrongs. From 1937 to 1941, the sisters ran Furman Features, a free-lance outfit which did publicity and writing for national women's organizations, including the American Association of University Women, the League of Women Voters, and the Women's Division of the Democratic party. From 1938 to 1940 they wrote the "Know Your Government" feature for the *Democratic Digest* and prepared the "Rainbow Fliers," summarizing the Roosevelt position on a wide range of issues, for the 1940 presidential campaign.

During World War II, Bess Furman worked in the Office of War Information, but by the mid-1940s she was anxious to return to newspaper journalism. In 1943 she joined the Washington bureau of the *New York Times*, where she remained until 1961. While on the *Times* staff, Furman continued her coverage of women's activities and the White House, but her by-line was much more likely to appear on stories concerning health and education. Unlike her days as a flamboyant girl reporter in Nebraska, Furman was now more concerned with

informing the public about new trends in science, medicine, and education than with ferreting out scoops or exclusive interviews. Her thorough and balanced reportage won her the respect of the other Washington newspaperwomen, who honored Furman by electing her president of the National Women's Press Club in 1946. In addition to her successful career in journalism, Furman also aspired to be a serious writer, and took a short story writing seminar at Columbia University in 1926. She later published two books, her autobiography, *Washington By-Line* (1949), and *White House Profile* (1951), a social history of the White House from the Adamses to the Trumans.

In the 1960s, Furman returned to government service. Her *Times* coverage had made her a familiar figure around the Department of Health, Education, and Welfare, and in 1961 she joined the department as assistant in public affairs, becoming head of its Press Information Section in 1962. Later that year, she accepted a three-year special assignment to write a history of the United States Public Health Service. Bess Furman died of arteriosclerosis in May 1969 at her home in Woodacres, Md.

In her autobiography, Bess Furman summed up her own career: "Well, I got what I wanted, and I wanted what I got." She began as a cocky, redheaded "girl reporter" in Nebraska, who succeeded as a nationally recognized newspaperwoman despite ingrained prejudice against women in the journalism field. But Furman never lost her identification with the prairie. Her decision to return to McCook to have her children showed her determination to pass on to them the strength and inspiration she had drawn from her Nebraska roots throughout her long and active life.

[Bess Furman's extensive papers are at the Library of Congress, and include diaries, correspondence, and newspaper clippings spanning her entire career. Also of great help on her journalism career is her autobiography, from which all quotes are taken. See also Ishbel Ross, *Ladies of the Press* (1936), pp. 345–47. A death record was provided by the Md. Dept. of Health. Obituaries appeared in the *N.Y. Times* and the Omaha *World-Herald*, May 13, 1969.]

SUSAN WARE

G

GAINES, Irene McCoy, Oct. 25, 1892?–April 7, 1964. Civil rights reformer, community leader, clubwoman.

Irene McCoy Gaines was born in Ocala, Fla., the younger daughter of Mamie (Ellis) and Charles Vivien McCoy; her older sister died in childhood. Her father was a barber and postal carrier; he also loved literature and wrote poetry. Taken to Chicago as an infant, Irene stayed with her mother when her parents were divorced in 1903. She attended Chicago public schools and graduated from Wendell Phillips High School. After attending Fisk Normal School in Nashville, Tenn. (1905–10), she returned to Chicago and became a typist in the complaint department of the Juvenile Court. This formal and informal education helped rouse Irene McCoy's consciousness of the problems of her race, and of women and youth in particular. She devoted her life to their betterment.

Well organized, with plenty of driving force, she also had a talent for written and oral expression and won three oratorical essay contests in the years between 1910 and 1914. Just before she married Harris Barrett Gaines, a law student, in 1914, she won a popularity contest at a carnival given by the NAACP. Such qualities helped bring success to her many projects.

From the beginning of her career as a community worker, Irene McCoy Gaines strove to end the segregation which limited opportunities for black youth. During World War I, at the urging of MARY CHURCH TERRELL, she joined the War Camp Community Service. In 1920 she became industrial secretary for the YWCA in Chicago at their first branch for Negroes. During these years she also recruited for the Urban League and took classes in social work at the University of Chicago. (Later, in the 1930s, she also studied at Loyola University of Chicago.)

After her sons, Harris Barrett, Jr. (b. 1922) and Charles Ellis (b. 1924), were in school, in the early 1930s she became a social worker in the Cook County welfare department. She remained associated with the department until 1945, while also becoming increasingly active in civic and community affairs. Critical of the Chicago schools, she used her positions as a member of the Citizens Advisory Committee and as president from 1939 to 1953 of the Chicago Council of Negro Organizations (CCNO) to protest against inferior conditions in the schools and against the inequality of segregation. Her successes included the improvement of facilities for the education of pregnant teenagers, and the establishment of one of the first integrated nursery schools in Chicago.

Gaines also joined the struggle to provide better employment for blacks. She investigated the working conditions of domestics, most of whom were Negro women, and tried to organize them and improve their training. Through the CCNO Gaines organized in March 1941 what has been called the first march on Washington. She led a group of fifty Chicagoans to Washington where with other protesters from around the country they formed committees to visit heads of government agencies and protest discrimination against blacks in employment. This action helped to lay the groundwork for the celebrated march scheduled by A. Philip Randolph for July. In June, however, President Franklin D. Roosevelt issued Executive Order 8802 banning discrimination in federal and defense employment and the march was canceled. Gaines continued to protest and testified before congressional committees for fair employment practices legislation. A lifelong Republican, she worked for political candidates, regardless of party, who supported these reforms.

Gaines's many activities increasingly involved her in politics. As president (1924–35) of the Illinois Federation of Republican Colored Women's Clubs, she helped to organize the first network of Republican women's clubs in the state. In 1928 she served as Republican state central committeewoman for the First Congressional District. Active in the 1928 and 1930 congressional campaigns of RUTH HANNA MCCORMICK (SIMMS), Gaines herself ran for office without success. In 1940 she was the first Negro woman to run for the state legislature (her husband served for eight years, 1928–36), and she was the first to appear on a party slate for county office when she led the Republican ticket in 1950 as candidate for county commissioner.

Gaines's political experience and her organizational skills bore fruit in her other club work. During her years with the welfare department, she had started clubs for young people and joined Negro organizations. Rapidly assuming leadership roles, she stressed the need to end segregation and helped organize such cooperative efforts as a Negro in Art Week cosponsored by the Northern District Association of Club Women, of which she was fine arts and literature chairman, and the Chicago Woman's Club. She also founded and served as president of the Chicago and Northern District Association of Club Women and Girls.

Most significant was Gaines's work with the National Association of Colored Women's Clubs

(NACWC). After serving as historian and then as recording secretary, in 1952 she was nominated from the floor at the biennial convention and elected president. Her first two terms (1952–56) saw great progress, with the establishment of a new clubhouse in Washington and maintenance and further restoration of the Frederick Douglass Home at Anacostia, Md.

In 1956 Gaines obtained a $50,000 grant from the Sears Foundation for a contest in neighborhood improvement to be conducted by the NACWC. Her interest in housing problems dated from her service on President Herbert Hoover's Housing Commission in 1930, and she was eager to supervise this contest and to see the momentum it generated carry on in further neighborhood improvement. She broke all precedents and ran for a third term as president, winning by two votes in a contested election that required legal aid to settle.

Gaines was in great demand as a speaker, and as president of the NACWC she traveled widely in the United States for speaking engagements and to help with local projects. A very religious woman (she belonged to three Protestant churches and was also active in the Theosophical Society and Moral Rearmament), she drew on biblical stories and quotations in her speeches.

Gaines was also internationally minded, and thought in terms of worldwide sisterhood. In 1947, as vice president of the Congress of American Women (Chicago Area), recording secretary of the NACWC, and president of the CCNO, she presented a statement to United Nations Secretary General Trygve Lie, protesting the "inferior status" accorded the "colored women of America . . . [and] of the world."

The family spent summers at Idlewild, Mich., a Negro resort where Gaines was president of the Lot Owners Association for fourteen years and received an award for building the resort into a major recreational center. From 1951 on she was the recipient of many awards, among them the George Washington Honor Medal, given by the Freedoms Foundation at Valley Forge in 1958 for the NACWC neighborhood improvement contest, the Fisk University Distinguished Alumni Service Award (1959), and an honorary degree from Wilberforce University (1962). Irene McCoy Gaines died in Chicago of cancer in April 1964.

[The Irene McCoy Gaines Papers at the Chicago Hist. Soc. include memorabilia, clippings, and records of some of her speeches. An interview by B. S. Decker appeared in the *Christian Science Monitor*, Dec. 2, 1957, and there are countless stories about her in the *Chicago Defender*, the *Pittsburgh Courier*, and the *Washington* (D.C.) *Courier*. *Negro Hist. Bull.*, Summer 1953, has a biographical article and cover photo. Entries on Gaines appear in *Who's Who in Colored America*, 1928–29, p. 140, and 1950, pp. 200–1; and in *Who's Who of Am. Women*, 1950, p. 359, and 1958, p. 456. Elizabeth Lindsay Davis, *Story of Ill. Federation of Colored Women's Clubs* (1922), p. 52, includes a photograph; in *Lifting as We Climb* (1933) Davis gives Gaines only one line, however. Date of birth taken from Fisk Univ. records; death certificate provided by Chicago Board of Health.]

ADADE MITCHELL WHEELER

GARDEN, Mary, Feb. 20, 1874–Jan. 3, 1967. Opera singer.

In her values, her way of life, and her approach to her profession, Mary Garden was a woman ahead of her time. Pursuing her career with determination and style, she could look back and state: "I began . . . at the top, I stayed at the top, and I left at the top."

Born in Aberdeen, Scotland, the second of four daughters of Robert and Mary (Joss) Garden, she came to the United States at the age of six with her family. They settled first in Brooklyn, N.Y., then moved to Chicopee, Mass., where Mary first sang in public at a church social at the age of ten. She briefly studied the violin but abandoned the instrument when her teacher told her she would "probably be a good amateur in twenty years." On a short visit to Aberdeen, she started piano lessons, but she did not care much for the instrument. Her nonmusical education was equally slight. Around 1888 the family moved to Chicago, where Robert Garden, an engineer, was employed by the Pope Company, which manufactured bicycles. At the age of sixteen Mary Garden began singing lessons with Sarah Robinson-Duff, who encouraged her to study in Paris and found a patron from Chicago, Mrs. David Mayer, to underwrite the trip.

Settled in Paris by 1897, Garden tried and rejected several teachers before becoming the student of two excellent vocal coaches, Antonio Trabadelo and Lucien Fugère. Through Sybil Sanderson, an American singer, she met Albert Carré, director of the Opéra-Comique. He invited her to attend his rehearsals of Charpentier's new opera *Louise* and urged her to study the score. On Friday, April 13, 1900, holding ticket number 113, Garden was suddenly called upon to replace Rioton, who became ill after having sung the first two acts. The conductor, André Messager, at first furious at Carré's use of an unknown, changed his mind after Garden's overnight success in the role. Soon after he became her lover. Only a few years later, Carré left his wife and asked Garden to marry him.

Following her success in *Louise* (a role she sang more than 100 times), Garden performed in Paris in *La Traviata*, Offenbach's *La Fille du Tambour-Major,* and *L'Ouragon* by Alfred Bruneau. On April 30, 1902, she first sang the role for which she became best known, Mélisande in Claude Debussy's *Pelléas et Mélisande.* She displayed such empathy for the character that Debussy later said, "I have nothing to tell her. In some mysterious way, she knows or senses everything" (Garden, p. 63). Another role with which she became identified was Thaïs in Massenet's opera of that name. Garden made her American debut in the New York premiere of *Thaïs* on Nov. 25, 1907, at Oscar Hammerstein's Manhattan Opera House. This was followed by performances of *Louise, Pelléas et Mélisande,* and Massenet's *Le Jongleur de Notre Dame,* in which she played the role of the juggler, originally written for a tenor. (Only a woman of her build could have portrayed the juggler—a boy of fifteen. Garden ate only one meal a day and remained at 112 pounds all her adult life.) A spectacular success in all these roles, she occasionally ran into conflict with the censors over her erotic Dance of the Seven Veils in Strauss's *Salomé,* which she first performed in New York in 1909.

Garden negotiated her own contracts both in Europe and America. She favored French opera and often sang her part in French while others sang in Italian. (She also sang Salomé in French, rather than the original German.) In 1910 she joined the Chicago Opera Company, and in the twenty years she remained there created a bastion of French opera in America; the French government awarded her the medal of the Legion of Honor in recognition of her services to French music and the Ministère des Beaux Arts gave her a decoration for her creations of roles in French opera. During the 1921–22 season Garden also served as director of the Chicago company. Encountering considerable personal hostility, she also incurred many debts by hiring additional performers and accepting a number of new operas for production.

Garden never married, although she had several liaisons and countless suitors, many of whom showered her with jewels, of which she was very fond. She insisted that she was not the marrying kind; her independence and her career came first, in that order. "I never lost my heart . . . I never knew what it was to have that mad passion, where you say mad things and sometimes do them," she said. Garden gave herself completely to the stage, becoming each character she portrayed. Except on her first visit to London, when her voice gave out as it suc-cumbed to British weather, she never experienced stage fright. Even those who were less than flattering in their judgment of her vocal abilities praised her style and her acting. She convinced her audiences, and she cared far more for their approval than for the plaudits of the critics.

Garden's last great personal success came in 1925, with the American premiere of Alfano's *Resurrection.* She retired from the Chicago Opera after the 1930–31 season, although she continued to make occasional concert and opera appearances and taught master classes at the Chicago Musical College. Later, she returned to Aberdeen, making periodic trips to the United States to lecture and to participate on juries convened to select promising young singers. Mary Garden died shortly before her ninety-third birthday at the House of Daviot, the nursing home in Aberdeen where she had spent her final years.

[Garden's autobiography, *Mary Garden's Story* (1951), written with Louis Biancolli, is the major source of biographical information. Accounts and assessments of her career appear in Oscar Thompson, *The American Singer* (1937), and Henry Pleasants, *The Great Singers: From the Dawn of Opera to Our Own Time* (1966). Also see John K. Winkler, "Salomé Redivivus," a profile in the *New Yorker,* Dec. 11, 1926; Edward C. Moore, *Forty Years of Opera in Chicago* (1930); Quaintance Eaton, *The Boston Opera Company* (1965); and entries in *Nat. Cyc. Am. Biog.,* XV, 209, and *Baker's Biog. Dict. of Musicians* (1971). Numerous books on Debussy, particularly Edward Lockspeiser, *Debussy, His Life and Mind,* 2 vols. (1962 and 1965), contain bits of information about Garden. An obituary appeared in the *N.Y. Times,* Jan. 5, 1967. Birth record provided by Registrar, Dist. of Aberdeen, Scotland.]

ELAINE BRODY

GARDNER, Julia Anna, Jan. 26, 1882–Nov. 15, 1960. Geologist, stratigraphic paleontologist.

Julia Gardner was born in Chamberlain, S. Dak., the only child of Charles Henry Gardner, a physician, and his second wife Julia M. Brackett, a schoolteacher from Dixon, Ill. Gardner, many years his wife's senior, had seven grown children from an earlier marriage. Julia Gardner was only four months old when her father died. She and her mother remained in South Dakota through the 1880s; by 1895 they had returned to Dixon. Three years later they moved to North Adams, Mass., where Julia attended Drury Academy for two years. After her graduation, the Gardners moved to Vermont.

Julia Gardner enrolled at Bryn Mawr College in September 1901. Supported by an inheritance from her grandmother, in 1903 she began course work in geology and paleontology with FLORENCE BASCOM and Benjamin L. Miller. Bascom, an important influence on Gardner's career, became a lifelong friend, as did fellow students ELEANORA F. BLISS (KNOPF) and Anna I. Jonas (Stose, 1881–1974), who later served with her in the United States Geological Survey (USGS). After receiving her A.B. in 1905, Gardner taught grammar school for a year in Chamberlain, then returned to Bryn Mawr where she received an A.M. in 1907.

Bascom and Miller encouraged her to begin doctoral studies at Johns Hopkins University, where she enrolled in 1907. The following year, after a summer course in invertebrate zoology at the Marine Biological Laboratory in Woods Hole, Mass., Gardner received a year's salaried fellowship and the USGS supported one summer of her field work. At Johns Hopkins, stratigrapher William B. Clark, who with paleobotanist E. W. Berry guided her work in paleontology, drew Gardner into his investigations of the Mesozoic-Cenozoic sedimentary rocks and biotas of the Atlantic coastal plain. She earned her Ph.D. in 1911 with a dissertation "On Certain Families of Gasteropoda from the Miocene and Pliocene of Virginia and North Carolina." Her research on mollusks continued throughout her career. She later joined Clark and Berry in investigations for the Maryland Geological Survey, and also worked on Miocene mollusks from South Carolina. Between 1911 and 1917, Gardner was a sometime salaried research assistant in paleontology at Hopkins, and occasionally taught laboratory and other classes for Berry.

In 1915, Julia Gardner and her mother moved to Washington, D.C. Under the direction of T. Wayland Vaughan, head of the Coastal Plain section of the USGS, she continued work on a contract investigation, begun in 1914 for the USGS, on the taxonomy of Oligocene mollusks from the Alum Bluff Group of northern and western Florida. Her contract completed, she accepted a renewed assistantship at Hopkins for 1917–18, but the overwhelming reports of the destruction of World War I prompted her, at great personal sacrifice, to join the war effort. Her mother died in October 1917 and by the end of that year Gardner was in France, serving, often near the front, with the Red Cross and later, after the armistice, with the American Friends Service Committee. In the summer of 1919, she was hospitalized after a service-related accident near Rheims.

Returning to the United States in March 1920, Gardner was hired by the USGS at Vaughan's recommendation and assigned to the Coastal Plain section. She worked first on A. C. Trowbridge's geologic mapping project in the lower Rio Grande (Texas) area, evaluating Eocene invertebrates. Gardner advanced rapidly in the USGS, becoming associate geologist in 1924 and geologist four years later. In 1936, when the Coastal Plain unit was abolished, she transferred to the Paleontology and Stratigraphy section.

Through her own field work and information exchanges with other geologists, Julia Gardner extended her knowledge of Cenozoic stratigraphic paleontology of the Coastal Plain westward through Texas to the Rio Grande Embayment in northeastern Mexico. She gave special attention to the taxonomy and paleoecology of molluscan faunas from the Midway (Paleocene) and Wilcox (Eocene) Groups. Gardner's work was valuable to petroleum geologists in establishing standard stratigraphic sections for Tertiary rocks around the Caribbean's southern rim.

Active in professional organizations, in 1926, 1929, and 1937 Gardner traveled widely in Europe, attending two International Geological Congresses, promoting exchanges of data and museum specimens, and visiting type-localities of the stratigraphic units she employed in the United States. Her research during the 1920s and 1930s culminated in *Correlation of the Cenozoic Formations of the Atlantic and Gulf Coastal Plain and the Caribbean Region* (1943), coauthored with her colleagues C. Wythe Cooke and Wendell Woodring. By the 1940s, Gardner's work in stratigraphic paleontology was of national and international importance, contributing especially to studies of economic geology in the western hemisphere.

During World War II, Julia Gardner joined the USGS Military Geology Unit (MGU). Sponsored and funded by the Army Corps of Engineers, the unit provided strategic and tactical information through analyses of maps, aerial photographs, and other sources. Among her many contributions, Gardner helped to pinpoint some of the beaches in Japan from which balloon-borne incendiary bombs were being launched against the Pacific northwest forests of the United States by identifying the origin of shells in the sand ballast of the balloons. Her geological skills, fluency in languages, resourcefulness, energy, and gentle humor made her invaluable to the MGU and she was revered by her colleagues.

After the war, in 1947–48, Gardner visited Japan and the Palau Islands under the auspices of the Office of the Chief of Engineers. Assigned to the National Resources Section, Headquarters of the Supreme Commander, she participated in the geological mapping of the

West Pacific islands, and studied the area's living faunas to enhance her interpretations of its fossils.

Julia Gardner retired from the USGS in January 1952. She received the Interior Department's Distinguished Service Award in September and also served that year as president of the Paleontological Society. The Geological Society of America elected her one of its vice presidents for 1953.

Immediately after retirement, she was rehired on a yearly contract basis and joined the USGS project studying the Cenozoic mollusks of the West Pacific islands. Gardner had planned to continue in retirement an earlier collaboration with L. R. Cox on the gastropod volume for the *Treatise on Invertebrate Paleontology.* But a cerebral hemiplegia, and subsequent progressive arteriosclerosis, terminated her investigations in 1954. In November 1960, at seventy-eight, she suffered a fatal stroke at her home in Bethesda, Md.

As mentor or by example, Julia Gardner encouraged and generously aided the careers of many colleagues, including Esther E. Richards Applin (1895–1972), Alva Ellisor (1892–1964), WINIFRED GOLDRING, and other women paleontologists. She maintained an active social life and was equally at ease with scientists, business people, writers, and artists. In a poem composed for Gardner's retirement, a woman colleague captured her spirit: "Julia is skilled in that high art: To read with love the human heart."

[The Nat. Personnel Records Center, General Services Admin., St. Louis, maintains Gardner's official personnel folder of her service with the USGS. The Branch of Paleontology and Stratigraphy, USGS, Washington, D.C., has her professional correspondence, 1911–62, but principally for the period 1924 to 1950; 36 field notebooks (1913–49); and 168 letters to her on her retirement. The Field Records Coll., USGS Library, Denver, holds two manuscript maps used in preparing the 1932 edition of the geologic map of Texas, and manuscript and field notes on the foraminiferids of southwest Ark. Gardner's literary executor destroyed most of her personal papers. The Bryn Mawr College Archives has a transcript of her course work; lists of courses taken at Johns Hopkins and at Woods Hole and some correspondence are in the Ferdinand Hamburger, Jr., Archives, Johns Hopkins Univ. There are a few letters in the Florence Bascom Papers, Sophia Smith Coll., Smith College, and in the Tasker Howard Bliss (Addition) Papers, Library of Congress. Gardner recalled events in her field work for the USGS in "Notes on Travel and Life," *Johns Hopkins Alumni Mag.,* April 1940. Biographies include those by H. S. Ladd in *Geological Soc. Am. Proc. 1960,* with a bibliography; by A. N. Sayre in *Am. Assoc. Petroleum Geologists Bull.,* Aug. 1961; and by Druid Wilson in *Nautilus,* Jan. 1962. See also E. B.

Knopf, "Julia Gardner, A.B., M.A., '07" in *Bryn Mawr Bull.,* Winter 1961, and *Am. Men of Science,* 3d through 10th eds. For an evaluation of women's contributions to the USGS see Jane House Wallace, "Women in the Survey," *Geotimes,* March 1979. A death record was provided by the Md. Dept. of Health. Family information was verified by records of the town clerk, Braintree, Vt., and the Brule Cty. Register of Deeds, Chamberlain, S.Dak.]

CLIFFORD M. NELSON
MARY ELLEN WILLIAMS

GARDNER, Mary Sewall, Feb. 5, 1871–Feb. 20, 1961. Public health nurse.

Mary Sewall Gardner entered the profession of public health nursing in its early years and, over the course of a long career, helped to shape its goals, character, and functions. She was born in Newton, Mass., the only child of Mary (Thornton) and William Sewall Gardner. Her mother, a descendant of Matthew Thornton of New Hampshire, a signer of the Declaration of Independence, had a son, Charles Thornton Davis, by a previous marriage. William Gardner, who was born in Maine, was a judge of the superior court of Massachusetts. Both her father and her half brother, who also became a judge, were important influences on Mary Gardner; to them she owed her logical and orderly habits of mind and her keen sense of civic responsibility.

Her mother died when she was four and her father soon remarried; her stepmother, Sarah Gardner, was a physician. The family was well off, and Mary was educated in private schools and, for a time, by a French governess. At sixteen she became severely ill with tuberculosis, but by 1888, the year her father died, she was well enough to enroll at Miss Porter's School in Farmington, Conn., where she remained until 1890. The next years she spent at home, helping to care for her invalid stepmother and becoming active in volunteer and community work. By 1892 the family had moved to Providence, R.I., and in 1901, at the age of thirty, Mary Gardner finally fulfilled an early ambition by enrolling at the Newport (R.I.) Hospital Training School for Nurses.

Immediately upon her graduation in 1905, Gardner became superintendent of nurses (later director) of the five-year-old Providence District Nursing Association (PDNA). When she assumed her responsibilities at the PDNA, she saw immediately that it "lacked . . . professional leadership." In order to fill this gap, she visited similar services elsewhere, including LILLIAN WALD's Henry Street Visiting Nurse Service in New York, and began a dialogue with other public health nurses. The encounter with

Wald led to a lifelong friendship. Among Gardner's first steps at the PDNA were the establishment of its first record system, the institution of regular meetings, and the introduction of uniforms. She was committed to improving education for public health nurses and encouraged in-service training programs. Concerned as well with the interrelationship of health and social problems, she urged the involvement of nurses and other medical personnel in community planning. Under Gardner the PDNA greatly expanded and became a model for other Rhode Island district nursing associations, to whom she freely offered advice and assistance.

Although she remained as director of the PDNA until 1931 (when she was made honorary director), Mary Gardner took several leaves of absence to engage in other nursing activities. Gardner and Lillian Wald urged the formation of the National Organization of Public Health Nursing (NOPHN), which came into being in 1912. Mary Gardner served as first secretary of the new organization (1912–13), and in 1913 she succeeded Wald as president. Reflecting in 1937 on the conditions which prevailed at the time the NOPHN was created, Gardner wrote: "There were no generally accepted standards for anything. Eligibility and preparation of the nurse, working conditions, objectives, salary rates, content of visit—all these things, like my own spelling, 'lay wholly within the field of conjecture.' "

As with the PDNA, Gardner's work as president of the NOPHN was aimed at expanding the membership, setting standards for training and service, and collecting and distributing information. In both cases, her work reflected a trend toward specialization and professionalization characteristic of all branches of nursing during this period. Gardner was particularly interested in the organization's publication, *Public Health Nurse* (later *Public Health Nursing*). She headed the committee in charge of the magazine, supported its growth, and wrote numerous articles and editorials. After she left the presidency of the NOPHN in 1916, Gardner continued to be actively involved with both the organization and its periodical. Appreciated by her colleagues for her ability to think in broad and logical terms about organizations and to assess their efficiency, she was twice called on, in 1925 and 1936, to study and evaluate the structure and workings of the NOPHN. In 1922 Mary Gardner was made honorary president of the organization, an honor she shared only with Lillian Wald.

Gardner's nursing activities and interests were not confined to the United States. On leave from the PDNA, in April 1918 she became di-

rector of the American Red Cross's Town and Country Nursing Service (soon renamed the Bureau of Public Health Nursing). Several months later she left this position for a wartime mission as chief nurse of the American Red Cross Tuberculosis Commission for Italy. Leading a group responsible for setting up training programs for Italian women interested in nursing, she defined the aim of her mission as the stimulation of local initiative to assess and meet local needs. Gardner returned to the United States in 1919 but again went abroad for the Red Cross in 1921 to study public health nursing and child welfare in eastern Europe and France. In other international activity, she chaired the standing committee on public health nursing of the International Council of Nurses from 1925 to 1933.

Mary Gardner's greatest contribution to her profession was probably her book *Public Health Nursing* (1916), long and widely hailed as a classic. Revised twice, in 1924 and 1936, and translated into a number of languages, the book was praised as "everywhere concrete, specific, and practical," yet informed by "the current of a high idealism." It reflected the dominant characteristics of its author, who combined a gentle manner and "unusual understanding of, and respect for, human relationships" with a clear, sharp mind and great determination.

In 1931 Mary Gardner was awarded the Walter Burns Saunders Medal for distinguished service to nursing. In retirement she continued to write articles on a variety of public health matters and also produced two works of fiction about nursing, *So Build We* (1942) and the autobiographical *Katherine Kent* (1946). Throughout her last years Gardner remained an informal adviser to her successors in the organizations she had served and to many other nurses who admired her work. She died in Providence at age ninety.

[The Mary Sewall Gardner Papers at the Schlesinger Library, Radcliffe College, contain correspondence, the unpublished MS. of a collection of short stories entitled "I Wonder," and material on public health nursing around the world. The Nat. League for Nursing in N.Y. City has on microfilm records of the NOPHN, 1912–28. Gardner's publications include "Problems Met by the District Nurse," *Providence Medical Jour.*, March 1913; "A Report of Six Months' Study of the NOPHN," *Public Health Nurse*, July 1926; "Twenty-Five Years Ago," *Public Health Nursing*, March 1937; and "Functions of the NOPHN," *Public Health Nursing*, April 1938. The best published source of biographical information is Sophie Nelson, "Mary Sewall Gardner," *Nursing Outlook*, Dec. 1953 and Jan. 1954. A briefer account of her career is in Meta Rutter Pennock, *Makers of Nursing History* (1940), p. 70. Mary M. Roberts, *American Nursing: History and Interpretation*

(1954), provides background on the development of the nursing profession, with mention of Gardner's role. Her work for the Red Cross is described in Lavinia Dock and others, *History of American Red Cross Nursing* (1922), and Portia B. Kernodle, *The Red Cross Nurse in Action, 1882–1948* (1949). Material on the origins and history of the NOPHN is in M. Louise Fitzpatrick, *The National Organization of Public Health Nursing, 1912–1952: Development of a Practice Field* (1975). Obituaries appeared in the Providence *Evening Bull.*, Feb. 21, 1961, and *Am. Jour. Nursing*, April 1961. Additional information was obtained from the 1880 U.S. Census and the birth certificate, supplied by Mass. Dept. of Public Health.]

ILENE KANTROV
KATE WITTENSTEIN

GARLAND, Judy, June 10, 1922–June 22, 1969. Singer, actress, entertainer.

Judy Garland was born Frances Ethel Gumm in Grand Rapids, Minn., the third and last child of Ethel (Milne) and Frank Avent Gumm. While appearing as a song illustrator at a movie house in Superior, Wis., Frank Gumm had met Milne who, equally musical, was employed there as a pianist. Shortly after their 1914 marriage, the Gumms moved to Grand Rapids, Minn., where he became manager and co-owner of the local movie house. In 1924, Frances and her two older sisters, Mary Jane and Dorothy Virginia, began performing there between features. The Gumm Sisters, accompanied on the piano by their mother, soon became a popular local attraction.

In 1927 the family moved to Lancaster, Calif., where Frank Gumm again managed a movie house. While attending public schools, Frances and her sisters were enrolled in weekly classes at the Ethel Meglin Dance School, a training school for professional children in Los Angeles, about sixty miles from their home. At eleven, Frances left public school to enroll in the Lawlor School for Professional Children. This training led to vaudeville bookings and, beginning in 1927, The Gumm Sisters toured theaters mainly in California and appeared in film shorts. Although she was the youngest, Frances was featured in the act. In the summer of 1934, while performing in Chicago during a brief visit to the World's Fair, the sisters, at the suggestion of George Jessel, changed their name to the more euphonious Garland Sisters. Shortly after, Frances took the stage name of Judy, after a Hoagy Carmichael–Sammy Lerner song of that name.

As her appearances multiplied, Judy Garland's reputation as a prodigious child talent grew. The impact of her performances was doubled by the contrast between her appearance and the maturity and power of her voice. One of her earliest professional reviews described her at twelve: "Possessing a voice that, without a P.A. system, is audible throughout a house as large as the Chinese [Grauman's Chinese Theatre], she handles ballads like a veteran, and gets every note and word over with a personality that hits audiences . . . she has never failed to stop the show" (*Variety*, Nov. 4, 1934). This widening reputation brought Garland to the attention of Louis B. Mayer and, in the fall of 1935, at thirteen, she entered into a contract with Metro-Goldwyn-Mayer (MGM). Her high school education was completed at MGM, where she joined the ranks of child performers being groomed for stardom.

Garland's first movie under contract, *Every Sunday* (1936), was a film short in which she played opposite Deanna Durbin, another child performer. It established her image as a wholesome and high-spirited American girl-next-door. In contrast to Durbin's more formal and operatic vocal style, Garland sang in the swing idiom with verve and brilliance. A natural screen performer, she brought a special quality of innocence and conviction to both her acting and her singing. Garland at this time came under the influence of Roger Edens, a vocal coach, composer, lyricist, and later a producer, who became a major force in helping her shape her vocal style and in selecting and arranging her musical material. Edens's special arrangement of the song "You Made Me Love You," which she sang as a tribute to Clark Gable in *Broadway Melody of 1938* (1937), brought Garland her first widespread public recognition. This was followed by several other films, including *Everybody Sing* (1938) and *Listen Darling* (1938).

The most celebrated role of Garland's early career was that of Dorothy, the Kansas schoolgirl blown by a tornado into the magical world of *The Wizard of Oz* (1939). This film established her as a star, and her performance won her a special Academy Award. In the film she introduced "Over the Rainbow," a song by Harold Arlen and E. Y. Harburg, in which Dorothy first wistfully imagines Oz. It became Garland's signature song, and in later years she made it the traditional and highly emotional ending to her concerts.

Garland's appearances with Mickey Rooney in *Thoroughbreds Don't Cry* (1937), and then as Betsy Booth in three of the "Andy Hardy" series (1938–41), established a screen relationship that culminated in four "backyard" musicals: *Babes in Arms* (1939), *Strike Up the Band* (1940), *Babes on Broadway* (1941), directed by Busby Berkeley, and *Girl Crazy* (1943), directed by Norman Taurog with some dance direction by Berkeley. These films were all variations on the theme of young theatrical hopefuls who "put on a show," a format that allowed Garland to demonstrate the scope of her talent as she sang a wide variety of American songs. As the female counterpart of the Mickey Rooney character, the sturdy, optimistic teenager became the embodiment of MGM's— and the nation's—ideal of American middle-class adolescence. The popularity Garland gained from these musicals was enhanced by personal appearances, radio performances, and recordings. Enduring a grueling schedule, she made nineteen films in her first eight years at MGM, aided by her ability to learn her parts at first reading.

The 1940s saw Garland's emergence into adult roles. Becoming one of the most important performers in film musicals, she made twenty films during this decade, including *For Me and My Gal* (1942), *Meet Me in St. Louis* (1944), *The Harvey Girls* (1946), *The Pirate* (1948), *Easter Parade* (1948), and *In the Good Old Summertime* (1949), all popular successes. Her image remained that of the girl-next-door, now grown up but retaining some of the tomboyish ebullience and childlike wistfulness of her adolescent persona. Quick witted and sensitive, with expressive brown eyes, long slim legs, and tremulous hands, Garland was a distinctive and compelling screen presence who conveyed a warmth and vulnerability that evoked a powerful audience response.

For many of her important films at MGM, Garland was associated with the Arthur Freed production unit, a group that made many of the finest musicals in Hollywood. The best of these films were characterized by an exceptionally high level of musical material and a format that stressed integration of music, dance, and plot. This format was well suited to Garland, a singing actress without peer, who excelled at giving both musically and dramatically sensitive readings of a song. Moving fluently and easily from song to dialogue to dance, Garland had full command of the diverse and complex skills necessary for performing in a film genre that demanded the widest range of talents from its performers. Garland could also make a mediocre musical (like *Presenting Lily Mars,* 1943) memorable by the quality of her performance alone.

Meet Me in St. Louis (1944) marked the beginning of a close personal and professional relationship with director Vincente Minnelli, whom she married in 1945. (Garland had married musician David Rose in 1941 and had divorced him two years later.) Minnelli's talent as a director matched hers as a performer, and

Meet Me in St. Louis gave her, for the first time since *The Wizard of Oz,* a superior setting for her talents. Her characterization of Esther Smith, one of the sisters in Sally Benson's story of family life in turn-of-the-century St. Louis, and her interpretation of the score (written by Hugh Martin and Ralph Blane, it included "The Boy Next Door" and "The Trolley Song") helped to make this film a classic.

Minnelli continued to direct Garland, first in a segment of *Ziegfeld Follies* (1944, released in 1946), then in her first dramatic film, *The Clock* (1945), the story of a wartime romance. Following *The Harvey Girls* (1946), directed by George Sidney, Garland was again directed by Minnelli in a cameo appearance in *Till the Clouds Roll By* (1946), a film under the overall direction of Richard Whorf. Soon after completing this film she gave birth to her first child, Liza May. She returned to the screen in another distinguished Minnelli musical with a Cole Porter score, *The Pirate* (1948). Costarring with Gene Kelly, she demonstrated her gifts for both subtle comedy and slapstick.

Garland's next film, *Easter Parade* (1948), directed by Charles Walters and with an Irving Berlin score, paired her happily with Fred Astaire. The success of the partnership led to an attempt to reunite them in *The Barkleys of Broadway,* from which Garland, suffering from nervous exhaustion, was forced to withdraw. She recovered for a cameo appearance in *Words and Music* (1948), a biography of Rodgers and Hart in which she sang two of their songs. This was followed by *In the Good Old Summertime,* a musical set in turn-of-the-century Chicago. In May 1949, MGM suspended Garland from her next project, *Annie Get Your Gun,* and sent her to Peter Bent Brigham Hospital in Boston for treatment. In late summer 1949, she returned to make her last MGM film, *Summer Stock* (1950), which reunited her with Gene Kelly. Under psychological stress, Garland found it increasingly difficult to maintain her working schedule and was suspended from one more film (*Royal Wedding*). In June 1950, after a much-publicized suicide attempt, she terminated her contract with MGM.

Garland then continued her career as a singer-entertainer, appearing mainly in concert, but also in cabaret and on radio and television. She made the transition from film to stage easily, drawing on her ability, developed in childhood, to make an immediate and powerful impact on a live audience. Her concert repertoire consisted in part of songs associated with her films and she developed a large and loyal following in the United States and England. Her charismatic stage presence—and the fervent emotional response she generated in her audience—became well known. A *New York Times* critic described one concert as "something not too remote from a revival meeting." From the beginning she attracted sellout audiences. In a series of performances at New York's Palace Theater beginning in October 1951, she set attendance and box-office records during a nineteen-week engagement for which she received an Antoinette Perry Award.

By 1950 Garland had met Michael Sidney Luft, who became her manager. After her divorce from Minnelli in 1951, she and Luft were married the following year. They had two children, Lorna (b. 1952) and Joseph (b. 1955). Spurred by successful concert tours in the United States and abroad, she and Luft produced a musical remake of the 1937 film *A Star Is Born* (1954). This film marked another association with composer Harold Arlen, and Garland's performance of his songs, including "The Man That Got Away," added to the list of songs associated with her. For her performance as Esther Blodgett, an actress whose rising career eclipses that of her alcoholic actor-husband, she was nominated for an Academy Award for best actress. Garland did not appear in films again until 1961, when her portrayal of a German housewife, a nonsinging role, in *Judgment at Nuremberg* also resulted in an Academy Award nomination for best supporting actress.

That same year a recording of one of her most notable concerts (held April 23, 1961), *Judy at Carnegie Hall,* became the first two-record album to sell over one million copies and won her two Grammy Awards. Garland made three more films in the 1960s. She was one of the voices in *Gay Purr-ee* (1962), a cartoon feature, and took leading roles in *A Child Is Waiting* (1962) and *I Could Go On Singing* (1963), in which the central character was modeled on Garland. During this time she made guest appearances on television and, from September 1963 through March 1964, starred in her own weekly television program.

Garland's popularity led to the publicizing of all aspects of her life and she was plagued, especially during her later years, by the widespread attention given to her personal problems, including her dependence on stimulants and sedatives. Garland attributed her problems in part to the physical and emotional pressures she had endured during the early years of her career. Whatever the cause, her later concert performances varied greatly in quality. She had increasing difficulty in controlling her voice, and the distinctive vibrato that had been a hallmark of her style became "more tremulous than vibrant." Her powerful stage presence and her

near-legendary status continued to draw audiences and she became a cult figure for a sizable audience of vocal followers who made it a tradition to shout out encouragement during her performances and to rush the stage at a concert's end to touch hands with their idol. *New York Times* critic Vincent Canby aptly described her at this time as "a raffish, sequin-sprinkled female Lazarus," her voice "now a memory." He noted that although "those sad and forlorn tales of her personal life . . . inevitably color our reaction to her actual performance," she was still "one of the most remarkable personalities of the contemporary entertainment scene."

In May 1965, Garland divorced Luft and six months later married Mark Herron, whom she divorced in February 1969. She married Michael de Vinko (Mickey Deans) in March 1969, three months before her accidental death in London, at forty-seven, from "an incautious self-overdosage" of barbiturates. Her funeral in New York City was attended by an estimated 20,000 people.

Within the history of popular entertainment, Garland ranks not merely as a public phenomenon but as one of the major figures of the century. She gave definitive performances of songs by the best of American songwriters, often in works commissioned especially for her films. Equally important, her consistently brilliant performances helped to shape and define the film musical during a period that saw this uniquely American art form at its height.

[For information on Judy Garland's films, including production details, consult the Arthur Freed and Roger Edens Collections. These papers, along with Edens's collection of vocal arrangements written for her, are in the Special Collections, Doheny Library, Univ. of Southern Calif. Clipping files on Garland may be consulted in the Billy Rose Theatre Coll., N.Y. Public Library, and the Margaret Herrick Lib., Acad. of Motion Picture Arts and Sciences, Beverly Hills, Calif. Garland herself discusses her early years in "There'll Always Be an Encore," *McCall's,* Jan. 1964. Research is made difficult because most secondary sources focus more on her troubled personal life than on analysis of her vocal and acting styles and because biographies often distort the facts or include outright fabrications. Garland herself often embellished stories of her early and later years. The most detailed and generally reliable biography is Gerold Frank, *Judy* (1975), authorized by her family. David Dahl and Barry Kehoe, *Young Judy* (1975), deals with her career through 1935, includes a list of her earliest performances, and contains a fairly accurate look at her earliest history. Other biographies include Christopher Finch, *Rainbow* (1975); Anne Edwards, *Judy Garland* (1974), which includes publication of her adolescent poetry; and James Juneau, *Judy Garland* (1974). Joe Morella and Edward Epstein, *Judy* (1969), a catalog of her films, reprints excerpts of some reviews for each film. Mickey Deans, *Weep No More My Lady* (1972), with Anne Pinchot, is an account of their life together. An account of Vincente Minnelli's life with Garland is included in his autobiography, *I Remember It Well* (1974), with Hector Arce. Mel Tormé, *The Other Side of the Rainbow* (1974), gives a detailed account of working with Garland in television. Henry Pleasants devotes a chapter to an analysis of her vocal style in *The Great American Popular Singers* (1974). See also *Current Biog.*, 1941 and 1952; Robert Rosterman, "Judy Garland," *Films in Review*, April 1962, pp. 209–16; and David Thomson, *Biog. Dict. of the Cinema* (1975). A bibliography of magazine articles about Garland appears in Mel Schuster, comp., *Motion Picture Performers* (1971). An obituary appeared in *N.Y. Times*, June 23, 1969. Birth certificate obtained from Itasca Cty., Minn.; death certificate from General Registry Office, London, England. Assistance was provided by James T. Maher.]

BETH GENNÉ

GAYLE, Newton. *See* LEE, Muna.

GEIRINGER, Hilda, Sept. 28, 1893–March 22, 1973. Applied mathematician, statistician.

Hilda Geiringer was born to a Jewish family in Vienna, the only daughter of Martha (Wertheimer) and Ludwig Geiringer, who was a textile manufacturer. Her younger brother Karl later became a noted musicologist. Hilda Geiringer possessed a prodigious memory, especially for mathematical relations, and by the time she was in the gymnasium it was clear that mathematics was her major interest. With her parents' financial support, she went to the University of Vienna where she studied pure mathematics under Wilhelm Wirtinger. In July 1917, she received her Ph.D. on the strength of a thesis on double trigonometric series (*trigonometrische Doppelreihen*), which was published in the following year.

From 1919 to 1920 Geiringer worked under Leon Lichtenstein editing the *Fortschritte der Mathematik*. In 1921 she went to the University of Berlin where she worked as first assistant under Richard Martin Edler von Mises at the Institute of Applied Mathematics. The same year she married a mathematician, Felix Pollaczek; their daughter, Magda, was born July 6, 1922. They were divorced by 1925, and Geiringer brought up the child herself while she pursued her professional interests.

The move to Berlin marked a major change: for the rest of her life, Geiringer's interests were in applied rather than pure mathematics. She held the position with von Mises until 1927, when she became Privatdozent (lecturer) at the University of Berlin. There she made significant contributions to probability theory and also worked on the mathematical development of plasticity theory, which led in 1930 to the fundamental Geiringer equations for plane plastic deformations.

The faculty at Berlin had just proposed Geiringer's nomination as an extraordinary professor when Hitler came to power in 1933. Like other Jewish academics, she lost her job. She left Germany with her child, going first to Belgium, where Geiringer became a research associate at the Institute of Mechanics, and then (1934) to Istanbul University in Turkey where she was professor of mathematics. She remained there until 1939, eventually learning Turkish so she could lecture.

With the outbreak of war, Geiringer was among the Europeans who left Turkey, fearing their refuge was no longer safe. She and her daughter came to the United States. From 1939 to 1944 Geiringer was a lecturer at Bryn Mawr College. (She became a naturalized citizen in 1945.) During the summer of 1942, she was one of a number of distinguished Europeans who taught at Brown University in a program for advanced instruction and research in mechanics.

On Nov. 5, 1943, Hilda Geiringer married Richard von Mises, who had also emigrated to Turkey from Germany and then come to the United States, where he was lecturer on aerodynamics and applied mathematics at Harvard University. She left Bryn Mawr in 1944 to become professor and chairman of the mathematics department at Wheaton College in Norton, Mass., a position she held until her retirement in 1959. During her tenure at Wheaton the department expanded considerably, and a number of her students went on to pursue careers in mathematics. Geiringer lived and worked at Wheaton during the week, coming to Cambridge on weekends to be with her husband who was named Gordon McKay Professor of Aerodynamics and Applied Mathematics at Harvard in 1945.

Despite the difficulties imposed by the war and the demands of her jobs, Geiringer worked steadily on her own research. In 1953 she wrote: "I have to work, scientifically, besides my college work. This is a necessity for me; I never stopped it since my student days, it is the deepest need in my life." Of central importance to her were issues in statistics, especially the mathematical basis of Mendelian genetics. She also continued research in plasticity.

Von Mises died in 1953 and Geiringer felt a strong responsibility to complete his work. From 1954, when she was awarded a grant by the Office of Naval Research and began to work as research fellow in mathematics at Harvard, Geiringer devoted most of her time to finishing von Mises's work and developing her own interests. With Geoffrey S. S. Ludford she finished an incomplete von Mises manuscript that was published in 1958 as *Mathematical Theory of Compressible Fluid Flow*. She also collaborated with A. M. Freudenthal, and contributed the mathematical part of the article "The Mathematical Theories of the Inelastic Continuum" for the *Encyclopedia of Physics* (1958).

During the same period, Geiringer turned her attention to the foundations of probability theory. Before leaving Germany, von Mises had developed the view that probability theory was a science based on observable phenomena rather than an extension of mathematical set theory. Geiringer reintroduced this idea in a new edition of von Mises's work, *Probability Statistics and Truth* (1957). In 1964 she published a revised edition of his *Mathematical Theory of Probability and Statistics* in which she reworked a number of concepts and, by developing a new mathematical interpretation, removed an inconsistency which had flawed the original presentation. During the 1960s Geiringer lectured frequently and published several articles supporting this controversial view of probability theory.

Hilda Geiringer's work received considerable recognition. In 1960 Wheaton awarded her an honorary degree. The University of Berlin elected her professor emeritus with full salary in 1956, and in 1967, the fiftieth jubilee of her graduation, she was given a special presentation by the University of Vienna. She was also a member of Sigma Xi and a fellow of the American Academy of Arts and Sciences.

Geiringer's range of interests, noticeable in the breadth of her professional work, also extended beyond the field of mathematics. She was an avid mountain climber, and had an impressive knowledge of literature, poetry, and classical music. She died in 1973 of influenzal pneumonia in Santa Barbara, Calif., while visiting her brother.

[Hilda Geiringer's papers in the Harvard Univ. Archives include a bibliography of her published work, correspondence 1944–73, manuscripts, speeches, notebooks, and lecture notes. The Schlesinger Library, Radcliffe College, has the German text of a speech delivered when she was honored in Vienna in 1967; it contains an invaluable description of her mathematical contributions. There are partial lists of Geiringer's publications in J. C. Poggendorff, *Biographisch-literarisches Handworterbuch der exakten Naturwissenschaften*, 1923–1931, ser. 6, vol. 2, p. 865, and 1932–1953, ser. 7a, vol. 2,

pp. 179–80. A brief article about her is in the *Wheaton Newsletter*, Sept. 1959. The program in which she participated at Brown is described in Dean R. G. D. Richardson, "Advanced Instruction and Research in Mechanics," *Am. Jour. of Physics*, 1943, pp. 67–73, and in a pamphlet "Applied Mathematics at Brown: A Description and History of the Division of Applied Mathematics at Brown University on the Occasion of its 25th Anniversary Celebration. September 7–10, 1971." Background about the scientific immigration to the United States is given in Laura Fermi, *Illustrious Immigrants* (1968) and in Donald Fleming and Bernard Bailyn, eds., *The Intellectual Migration: Europe and America, 1930–1960* (1969). Obituaries appeared in *Boston Sunday Globe*, March 25, 1973, and the *N.Y. Times*, March 24, 1973. Additional information was provided by Geiringer's daughter, Magda Tisza, her brother, Karl Geiringer, and her colleague Geoffrey S. S. Ludford. A birth certificate was provided by the Israelitische Kultusgemeinde Wien, Vienna, Austria; death record from Calif. Dept. of Public Health.]

JOAN L. RICHARDS

GELLHORN, Edna Fischel, Dec. 18, 1878– Sept. 24, 1970. Community leader, suffragist.

Edna Fischel Gellhorn, best known for her work with the League of Women Voters, was born in St. Louis, the only daughter and eldest of four children of Washington Emil and Martha (Ellis) Fischel. Her inspired career in public service benefited from the encouragement and example provided by her parents, both leaders in the Ethical Culture Society. Her father, a native St. Louisan whose ancestors came from Prague, was a prominent physician and professor of clinical medicine at Washington University. A founder and president of the medical staff of the Barnard Free Skin and Cancer Hospital, Washington Fischel was respected for his dedication to his patients, both rich and poor. Martha Fischel, a descendant of early English settlers, moved to St. Louis as a child from her native Mississippi. An educator and civic worker before her marriage, she led the movement to provide homemaking and manual training for St. Louis youngsters, and in 1908 was named director of the St. Louis School of Philanthropy (later the George Warren Brown School of Social Work at Washington University).

Edna Fischel attended Mary Institute, graduating as class president in 1896, and briefly attended the Baldwin School in Bryn Mawr, Pa. She received an A.B. in 1900 from Bryn Mawr College. A popular student, she was chosen lifetime president of her class; she later served as an elected trustee of the college.

On Oct. 21, 1903, Edna Fischel married

George Gellhorn (1870–1936), a gynecologist who came to the United States from Germany in 1899. Beginning his St. Louis practice in 1900, he later became professor of obstetrics and gynecology at St. Louis University and Washington University, and president of the American Gynecological Society. The Gellhorns had four children: George Jr. (b. 1904), Walter (b. 1906), Martha (b. 1908), and Alfred (b. 1913). They had a housekeeper and other servants, but both parents spent as much time as possible with their children. A warm and affectionate mother, Edna Gellhorn once observed: "We always expected them to do their best." The children became, in order of birth, a naval officer and international businessman, a law professor, a writer, and a medical educator.

Although she never ran for public office or received a salary, Edna Gellhorn became a powerful force for reform in her native city and state. Asking nothing for herself, and turning down responsibilities that would take her too far from her family, she exemplified the influence a woman could exert by virtue of high ideals, hard work, and the ability to mobilize others into action. A woman of great beauty and charm, she brought out the best in everyone. Beginning as a successful organizer of charity drives, as a young mother she worked in campaigns to purify the city water supply and, together with her husband, to secure inspection of milk. She went on to lend her talents to a variety of causes, most notably those devoted to environmental improvement, good government, and, above all, suffrage and the League of Women Voters (LWV). During World War I, she worked full-time as regional administrator of the food program directed by Herbert Hoover. George Gellhorn encouraged his wife in all her undertakings, and she credited him with sparking her own enthusiasm for suffrage.

Convinced that without the vote women were not even second-class citizens, Edna Gellhorn joined the suffrage movement in 1910. She held office in both the Missouri and St. Louis Equal Suffrage Leagues, and was an organizer of the "Walkless-Talkless Parade" at the Democratic National Convention in St. Louis (1916). For this event 7,000 women in yellow sashes lined the streets, and a tableau depicted women representing suffrage and nonsuffrage states, the latter dressed in deep mourning.

Gellhorn served as arrangements chairman for the national suffrage convention in St. Louis at which the League of Women Voters was organized (1919). She agreed to become first vice president of the new organization. Also elected first president of the state branch, Gellhorn began her many years of service to the League—which she considered her "profession"—by leading its campaign for citizenship schools to educate the new voters for intelligent participation in government. Often riding in milk train cabooses, in the 1920s she visited many Missouri towns to teach voter education classes; in an effort to appear ladylike, she pretended to knit.

Edna Gellhorn's reform interests kept pace with the emergence of new political and social problems. She led the successful efforts of the LWV to institute the merit system in government hiring in Missouri in the 1930s and to secure passage of a new state constitution (1945). In addition to her work for good government, she participated in programs for slum clearance and smoke abatement. After World War II, she organized local chapters of the American Association for the United Nations and was a founder of the Citizens Committee on Nuclear Information. She reduced her commitments in the 1960s, but kept charge of League finances, still impressing her colleagues with her willingness to do even the most menial job as if it were a real privilege. A proponent of racial integration, she regretted that she had not joined the 1963 March on Washington. While she always maintained that the best person should receive any job, over the years she advanced the careers of many women whom she recommended for local office. In 1964, she was appointed to the Missouri Commission on the Status of Women. Despite her wide-ranging interests, Edna Gellhorn never lost the personal touch. She even served as a local representative for ELEANOR ROOSEVELT, who referred to her personal requests for aid originating in St. Louis.

Edna Gellhorn's long years of public service were honored by, among others, Lindenwood College (LL.D., 1956) and Washington University, which awarded her an honorary LL.D. (1964) and established the Edna Fischel Gellhorn Professorship of Public Affairs (1968). In 1973, three years after her death in St. Louis of cardiac arrhythmia, the Women's Political Caucus and the National Organization of Women sponsored the first Edna Gellhorn Award Dinner.

[The principal source of primary material, the Edna Fischel Gellhorn Coll. at the Washington Univ. Archives, St. Louis, contains both personal and professional papers. Photographs and materials pertaining to her LWV activities are also among the papers of the LWV of Mo. at the Western Hist. Manuscripts Coll., Univ. of Mo.-St. Louis. The Mo. Hist. Soc. has a small collection of papers on the LWV. Some of Gellhorn's papers are located at the Schlesinger Library, Radcliffe College. Letters between Gellhorn and Eleanor Roosevelt are among the holdings of the Franklin D. Roosevelt Library, Hyde Park, N.Y. Edna Gellhorn outlined the aims of the LWV in "Ratification, Schools, and League of Women Voters," *Missouri Hist. Rev.*, vol. XIV, April-July 1920. Feature articles on Gellhorn appeared in the *St. Louis Post-Dispatch* on Dec. 15, 1963, Dec. 18, 1967, and Oct. 8, 1973. On Edna Gellhorn, her parents, and her husband see *Missouri Biography* (1943), vol. III. Portions of family information were supplied by Walter Gellhorn. Obituaries appeared in the *St. Louis Post-Dispatch* and the *St. Louis Globe-Democrat* on Sept. 25, 1970; death record provided by St. Louis Division of Health.]

SUSAN M. SABRIN

GERSTEN, Berta, Aug. 20, 1896?–Sept. 10, 1972. Actress.

Berta Gersten, a leading performer in Yiddish theater, was born in Cracow, Poland, the older child and only daughter of Avrom and Meshe (Kopps) Gerstenman. Her father, an impoverished scholar who had been born in Byelorussia, moved to Cracow where he became a religious teacher in a Jewish school; both of her parents were orthodox Jews. In 1899 the Gerstenmans migrated to the United States and settled in New York City. While Berta's father eked out a meager income there as a courthouse translator, a position he obtained because of his fluency in seven languages, Meshe Gerstenman became the main support of the family. An excellent dressmaker, she won a following among the actresses in the then burgeoning Yiddish theater, whose lively entertainments, running the gamut from tragedy to musical comedy, had become a staple of Jewish cultural life on the Lower East Side. An actress who patronized Meshe Gerstenman needed a child in her act and borrowed Berta for the part, thus inaugurating a notable career.

On finishing elementary school, Berta took a job in a paper box factory to supplement the family income. Her ambitions remained set on an acting career, though, and she haunted the theater. After her first formal role in 1908, as a little boy in Jacob Gordin's *Mirele Efros*, she appeared in vaudeville sketches, in movie nickelodeons, and in minor roles in operettas. By 1915 she was appearing in the company of the famous character actor David Kessler, who cast her as an ingenue. She then played various roles in Boris Thomashefsky's company, before being recruited in 1918 by the young impresario Maurice Schwartz, who was seeking distinguished artists for his new company at the Irving Place Theatre, a venture that was to become the historic Yiddish Art Theatre two years later.

Berta, who had changed her name for professional purposes from Gerstenman to Gersten, became an original member of the Theatre together with Celia Adler, Jacob Ben-Ami, and Ludwig Satz. She continued as ingenue and then leading lady in Schwartz's company until 1950, when the Yiddish Art Theatre officially disbanded.

From 1918 until her death in 1972, Gersten appeared each and every season on stage. One of the mainstays of the Yiddish theater, she starred with acting companies in New York City and with traveling troupes in the major cities of North and South America and Europe, including Warsaw, where for several years in the late 1930s she was the leading actress in the resident Yiddish theater. She appeared in stellar roles in such Yiddish standards as Sholom Asch's *Salvation* (1939), Simon Wolf's *Believe Your Mother* (1941), and Sholom Aleichem's *Yosele, the Nightingale* (1949). Gersten became most closely identified with the title role in *Mirele Efros*, starring in the screen version (1939) of Gordin's drama as well as in stage productions. Like several other characters she portrayed, Gersten's Mirele Efros was a sturdy matriarch whose trials served only to confirm her strength and integrity. Gersten would not be confined to a single ethnic type, however: "I love the Jewish mother," she told the *New York Times* in 1955, "but I'm an actress." In Yiddish versions of the classics from Shakespeare to Shaw, she took on such parts as Hedda Gabler, St. Joan, and Gertrude in *Hamlet*. In all, she played more than 150 roles.

With the decline of Yiddish theater after 1950, Gersten turned her talents to the English-speaking stage, making her debut there in a Chicago production of *The World of Sholom Aleichem* (1954). The year after, she received critical acclaim as Noah's wife Esther, opposite Menasha Skulnik in a Broadway production of Clifford Odets's *The Flowering Peach*. Other important appearances included a tour with Sir Cedric Hardwicke in *A Majority of One* (1959), a role she took over from her friend GERTRUDE BERG, and her performance as SOPHIE TUCKER's mother in the Broadway musical *Sophie*. A versatile artist, Gersten adapted herself successfully to melodrama, musicals, and sophisticated comedy. She complemented her theater work with television appearances during the 1950s and 1960s and with roles in two films: the screen version of Gordin's *God, Man, and the Devil* (1950) and *The Benny Goodman Story* (1955).

Berta Gersten was married for forty-eight years to Issak Hershel Finkel, the son of a manager and an actress, both active in the Yiddish theater. Finkel met Gersten in his mother's dressing room; still in their teens, the two fell in love and were married on July 10, 1911. Exactly one year later, their son, Albert, was born. Issak Finkel had to Anglicize his name to Irwin Henry Fenn in order to secure a position as a faculty member at Brooklyn Polytechnic Institute, where he taught physics and mathematics for over forty years. He died in 1960 and eight years later Gersten began to live with Jacob Ben-Ami, her longtime friend and a distinguished actor who appeared with her frequently on the Yiddish stage. Her last appearance was opposite Ben-Ami in the dramatization of Isaac Bashevis Singer's *In My Father's Court* at the Folksbiene Theater in New York City in the 1971–72 season. The two remained together until Berta Gersten's death in New York City of cancer in September 1972.

The years of Berta Gersten's triumphant career in the Yiddish theater did not yield her awards. Lacking an Oscar, an Emmy, or a Tony, she found her reward instead in unfailingly good reviews in the press, and in the applause not only of theatergoers but also of audiences at hospitals, old age homes, and charitable functions, where she generously performed the great dramas of the Yiddish and world repertoires. Her career was in the grand tradition of a dependable, resourceful, talented, dignified, and devoted trouper.

[Documents pertaining to Berta Gersten's career can be found in the Billy Rose Theatre Coll., N.Y. Public Library (clippings, reviews, and press interviews); in the Yiddish Theatre Coll., Museum of the City of N.Y. (clippings, playbills, programs, critiques in English and Yiddish, and photographs); and in the archives and Theatre Coll., YIVO Inst. for Jewish Research, N.Y. City (miscellaneous memorabilia, mostly in Yiddish). Her work can be followed over many years in issues of the *Jewish Daily Forward*, available on microfilm in the Judaica Div., N.Y. Public Library. A major secondary source for Gersten and her tradition is David S. Lifson, *Yiddish Theatre in America* (1965). A useful article, quoting her extensively, is Bernard Kalb, "A Cinderella in Her Middle Age," *N.Y. Times*, March 20, 1955. See also Nahma Sandrow, *Vagabond Stars* (1976), and Irving Howe, "The Yiddish Theater: A Blaze of Glory and Claptrap," *New York Mag.*, Jan. 1976, pp. 31–38. Sketches of Gersten are included in Zalmen Zylbercwaig, *Leksikon fun Yidishn Teatr*, vol. 1 (1931), and in *Encyc. Judaica*, vol. 15 (1972). An obituary appeared in *N.Y. Times*, Sept. 11, 1972. Sources vary as to her year of birth: the *Leksikon fun Yidishn Teatr* and *N.Y. Times* indicate 1894, while Gersten herself offered 1897 during a meeting with D. S. Lifson. The year 1896 is suggested by the *Jewish Daily Forward* and by her son, Albert Fenn, who, along with Jacob Ben-Ami, supplied further personal information.]

DAVID S. LIFSON

GILBRETH, Lillian Evelyn Moller, May 24, 1878–Jan. 2, 1972. Engineer, household efficiency expert, industrial psychologist.

Lillian Moller Gilbreth was born in Oakland, Calif., the first of eight surviving children, three boys and five girls, of William and Annie (Delger) Moller. Her father was the son of a prosperous New York sugar refiner; her mother was the daughter of a wealthy Oakland real estate developer. All four of her grandparents had been born in Germany. William and Annie Moller moved from New York to California soon after the death, in infancy, of their first child. There William Moller was a partner in a large retail hardware business, and the Mollers became one of Oakland's leading families.

Lillian Moller was tutored at home by her mother until the age of nine and then attended public elementary and high schools in Oakland. Her mother's frequent illness, and frequent pregnancies, placed special burdens on Lillian; at the age of thirteen she was given almost complete responsibility for the care of a baby sister. Nonetheless, as the oldest child of a prosperous and particularly doting father, she also enjoyed special opportunities, and before she had graduated from high school she had traveled across the country three times. By her own account she was a shy and introverted child who enjoyed studying and was especially interested in poetry and music. Although her parents had at first opposed her plan to attend the University of California in nearby Berkeley, they eventually relented and she enrolled after graduating from high school. When Moller received her B.Litt. degree in 1900 she was the first woman to be chosen as a commencement day speaker. For a brief period after graduation she lived in New York City, studying for a master's degree in English literature at Columbia University. Unhappy there, she returned to California and lived at home while she continued her studies. She received her master's degree in English from the University of California, following completion of a thesis on Ben Jonson's *Bartholomew Fair*.

Moller began studying for a doctorate but took a leave in the spring of 1903 in order to tour Europe. While in Boston prior to her departure, she met Frank Bunker Gilbreth, a cousin of her chaperon. Frank Gilbreth, a native of Maine, was then thirty-five years old. A self-made man, he was in 1903 one of Boston's leading building contractors and was acquiring a nationwide reputation for what was then termed speed building. Later called motion study, it involved the development of various techniques, both managerial and technological, for building quickly. Lillian Moller and Frank Gilbreth were married in the Moller home in Oakland on Oct. 19, 1904. They lived in New York, and Lillian Gilbreth quickly became a partner in her husband's growing motion study business.

The Gilbreths had twelve children in the space of seventeen years. In the early years of their marriage, when there were small children at home and Frank Gilbreth was traveling for a good part of the year, Lillian Gilbreth assisted him principally by editing his many publications. Later, when he had closed the construction business and had become a management consultant in Providence, R.I., she earned a Ph.D. in psychology at Brown University (1915). She became a member of the firm, Gilbreth Inc., which they subsequently established in Montclair, N.J., as well as an author in her own right: her book *Psychology of Management* was published in 1914. Martha Bunker Gilbreth, Frank Gilbreth's mother, lived with the family, freeing Lillian Gilbreth to pursue her education and career; they also employed several servants over the years.

The Gilbreths pioneered in the application of motion study in industry; by studying each part of the work process in minute detail (using motion pictures as the principal form of analysis), they aimed to discover the "one best way" to do any given task. By defining the best way as that which required the least exertion, they assumed that less strain would mean better health and consequently increased production, which would, of course, be economically advantageous for the employer.

In the decade following 1910 the Gilbreths attempted to promote motion study principally as a tool for industry. They established a private laboratory in their home, where they also periodically offered instruction for managers of businesses. They lectured widely, principally at schools of engineering and business, and they published in both professional and popular magazines. During this decade they also co-authored several books: *A Primer of Scientific Management* (1912), *Motion Models* (1915), *Fatigue Study* (1916), *Applied Motion Study* (1917), and *Motion Study for the Handicapped* (1920).

When Frank Gilbreth died in 1924, Lillian Gilbreth discovered that factory owners, for whom her husband had worked as a consultant, were not confident that she could carry on in his stead. Most of his contracts were canceled, and the family experienced financial difficulty. But she continued lecturing as well as offering courses in their laboratory. She kept her family together, put all of her eleven surviving children through college, and went on with her own work—and she did it, according to her children

and friends, with humor, with energy, with relish, and without long-term financial help from her family in California.

To some extent the Gilbreths had always used their household routines to experiment with motion study. Following her husband's death Gilbreth discovered that home economists and the various businesses that catered to the needs of housewives were interested in the methods that she and her husband had pioneered. After 1924 she began intensive studies of the application of modern business methods in the home. Her research on this subject continued, with occasional interruptions, for the next two decades and was reported in two major publications, *The Home-Maker and Her Job* (1927) and *Management in the Home* (1954), as well as in numerous articles in popular periodicals such as *Good Housekeeping* and *Better Homes and Gardens*. As a consultant to university departments of home economics beginning in 1926, Gilbreth had considerable influence on the development of home management courses throughout the country.

Ironically, after she had gained worldwide recognition for her studies of housework, Gilbreth remained a virtual stranger in her own kitchen. She never installed modern kitchen equipment in her home—partly because she could not afford to and partly because her servants did not wish to have it.

Gilbreth also served at various times on the faculties of several colleges and universities. Asked in 1924 to take her husband's place as visiting lecturer at Purdue University, she lectured there every year and in 1935 became professor of management. She held that position until 1948 and helped to establish a time and motion study laboratory at Purdue. From 1939 on she also served Purdue as a consultant on careers for women; she has been credited with bringing "a more realistic attitude among faculty and students toward the human factor in management and . . . the place of women in industry" (Potter, p. 4).

Equally influential as Gilbreth's research in home economics was her innovative use of the techniques of motion analysis to design special equipment and routines to make housework possible for handicapped persons. Her most significant results were reported in *Normal Lives for the Disabled* (1944), coauthored with Edna Yost. Gilbreth later became a consultant to the Institute of Rehabilitation Medicine at the New York University Medical Center, where she developed a model kitchen adapted to the needs of the handicapped. The kitchen became an internationally known training center.

As both lecturer and author, Lillian Gilbreth

was a superb publicist for the methodology that she and her husband had created. She became an accomplished and stimulating speaker and worked unceasingly to gain acceptance for the techniques of motion study both in professional circles and among the public at large. Although home economists readily adopted her techniques, proponents of scientific management were at first less receptive to her message because it emphasized motion rather than time, seeking to maximize the worker's comfort rather than the employer's profit. By 1931, however, when the Society of Industrial Engineers created the Gilbreth Medal (named for Frank Gilbreth), motion study had become part of the accepted methodology for industrial engineers, industrial psychologists, and personnel specialists. The first recipient of the medal was Lillian Gilbreth.

Extraordinarily energetic as well as public-spirited, Gilbreth found time to be active in volunteer work for the Girl Scouts of America, for various organizations helping the handicapped, and for churches and libraries in her community. She also responded to calls to serve the government: as a member of the President's Emergency Committee for Unemployment Relief in 1930; as an educational adviser to the Office of War Information during World War II; and as a member of the Civil Defense Advisory Commission in 1951.

Lillian Gilbreth continued her research past the age of seventy and was still writing and lecturing in her eighties. Over the years she received many honors, beginning in 1921 when she was named an honorary member of the Society of Industrial Engineers (which did not then admit women to membership). In 1966 she was the first woman to receive the Hoover Medal for distinguished public service by an engineer. In all she accumulated more than twenty honorary degrees and special commendations from professional societies. Throughout her life Gilbreth actively encouraged other women to become and remain engineers; she was honored for her commitment to women in her profession by a fellowship in her memory established by the Society of Women Engineers.

The Gilbreth family and the application of their management theories to homemaking and childraising became widely known through the humorous reminiscences of their childhood by Frank Gilbreth, Jr., and Ernestine Gilbreth Carey, *Cheaper by the Dozen* (1948) and *Belles on Their Toes* (1950). Lillian Gilbreth died in Scottsdale, Ariz., of a stroke at the age of ninety-three.

[The Lillian Gilbreth Coll. in the Dept. of Special Collections and Archives, Purdue Univ. Library, contains a considerable amount of professional and personal correspondence, reprints of articles, newspaper clippings, conference records, films, slides, photographs, and other material. The Frank Gilbreth Coll., containing his business files, his correspondence, and his books, is also at Purdue; MSS. are in Special Collections, books in the library of the School of Industrial Engineering. Lillian Gilbreth's writings can be sampled in William R. Spriegel and Clark E. Meyers, eds., *The Writings of the Gilbreths* (1949). She also contributed a chapter on "Women in Industry" to Beverly Benner Cassara, ed., *American Women: The Changing Image* (1962). Some autobiographical material can be found in her biography of her husband, *The Quest for the One Best Way: A Sketch of the Life of Frank Bunker Gilbreth* (1926). The best available biography was written during her lifetime by her friend Edna Yost: *Frank and Lillian Gilbreth: Partners for Life* (1949). A more anecdotal but also more personal account is in Frank Gilbreth, Jr., *Time Out for Happiness* (1970). Information about her work for the handicapped can be found in Elizabeth Eckhardt May, "Lillian Moeller Gilbreth, 1878–1972," *Jour. Home Economics*, April 1972, pp. 13–16. See also the entry in *Current Biog.*, 1951; Andrey A. Potter, "Reminiscences of the Gilbreths," *Purdue Alumnus*, Feb. 1972, pp. 4–6; and Soc. of Women Engineers *Newsletter*, Jan. 1972. An obituary appeared in the *N.Y. Times*, Jan. 3, 1972. A biobibliography prepared by Gail M. Upton assisted in the research for this article. Death certificate supplied by Ariz. Dept. of Health.]

RUTH SCHWARTZ COWAN

GILDERSLEEVE, Virginia Crocheron, Oct. 3, 1877–July 7, 1965. College administrator.

Virginia Gildersleeve, dean of Barnard College, and a leader in international affairs, was born in New York City, the youngest of five children born to Henry Alger and Virginia (Crocheron) Gildersleeve. The first two children were sons, and of the three daughters who followed, the first died in infancy and the second was stillborn. The Crocherons were of French Huguenot ancestry from Alabama, mingled with south German stock from Philadelphia, while the English Gildersleeves had settled on Long Island and later in Dutchess County, N.Y. Henry Gildersleeve was a judge who became a justice of the state supreme court. Raised in a townhouse in Manhattan, Virginia enjoyed a secure and comfortable childhood. Her beloved brother Harry's sudden death when she was fourteen was the saddest event of her childhood and probably gave her a seriousness beyond her years.

Educated at the Brearley School in New York City (1892–95) and encouraged by a mother who sensed her intellectual potential, Gildersleeve entered Barnard College in 1895. There she studied Greek under the brilliant dean, EMILY JAMES SMITH PUTNAM, and was taught by a succession of renowned Barnard and Columbia University faculty, including George Odell in English, Nicholas Murray Butler in philosophy, and James Harvey Robinson in history. After taking her A.B. (1899) and winning the Fiske Graduate Scholarship in Political Science, she received an A.M. in medieval history from Columbia in 1900. Shortly thereafter she began teaching English composition and argumentation at Barnard and in 1908 acquired a Ph.D. in English and comparative literature at Columbia.

Turning down the offer of an associate professorship from the University of Wisconsin because she did not want to leave her parents, Gildersleeve accepted an appointment as lecturer at Barnard. She soon became the obvious candidate to succeed Laura Gill as dean in 1911. During the thirty-six years that she held the college's highest office, Virginia Gildersleeve was synonymous with Barnard College. A woman of wide-ranging curiosity and judicious outlook like that of her father, she combined the life of a devoted college administrator with that of a busy public figure. She remained single, enjoying the companionship of Caroline Spurgeon (1869–1942), the British literary scholar, and later of Elizabeth Reynard (1897–1962), professor of English at Barnard, who was active in the organization of the WAVES, the women's naval unit in World War II.

Gildersleeve quickly asserted her authority in the Barnard deanship. While retaining a sound working relationship with Nicholas Murray Butler, who had become president of Columbia, she took the initiative in a number of ways, strengthening Barnard departments, championing a paid maternity leave policy for women faculty, and systematically encouraging Columbia to make its professional schools more accessible to women. Despite her conservative temperament, she presided over shifts in entrance requirements and curriculum that retained Barnard's high academic standards while accommodating changes in the educational climate. During her administration the classics lost their dominant role and greater flexibility in course selection was introduced. But distribution requirements for the A.B. degree, instituted in 1926, ensured that students became acquainted with each of the broad areas of human knowledge through courses in specific academic disciplines. This approach differed from the Columbia system of broadly designed general education courses, and continued to distinguish the curricula of the two affiliated institutions.

While maintaining a not unfriendly reserve with students, Gildersleeve faithfully looked after their interests. Ever a champion of young women with scholarly talents, regardless of their means, she also contended that more affluent students were often disadvantaged by the opposition to female intellectual activity common in their social circles. Her practical efforts for students were numerous. She early initiated the system of academic advising that reduced the impersonality of the urban college, established a vocational advisory office, enlarged campus facilities for students, encouraged the evolution of Greek Games into a major campus tradition that combined athletic prowess with literary and artistic skills, and adroitly assisted students in dissolving sororities.

Early in her career Gildersleeve became a recognized advocate for women's education, fostering the expansion of educational opportunities for women. She criticized the existence of separate curricular tracks that might prematurely segregate girls headed for college from those who were not. Such a "double curriculum," she felt, could discriminate unjustly against the young woman whose potential for higher education had not been recognized early enough. Gildersleeve also deplored the assumption that wives and mothers were less in need of college training than working women. Indeed, she believed that "we may be partially different from men in our tastes and our talents, without thereby being necessarily of less dignity and value to the community and to ourselves" ("Some Guides for Feminine Energy," pp. 372–73). While acknowledging that college women typically entered professions identified as female, she refused to deny them the fullest equality of aspiration. Under Gildersleeve's leadership Barnard in the 1920s pioneered among women's colleges in granting the professional option, which substituted the first year of professional school for the final undergraduate year. During World War II, with her plea for "trained brains," Gildersleeve urged young women to eschew high-paying jobs in favor of the college education that would provide them with the foundation for later training in all fields of intellectual work.

Undaunted by the disruptions of two world wars and an intervening depression, Gildersleeve secured Barnard's academic reputation and widened its appeal to students outside New York and from foreign countries. She also spread her influence locally to secondary schools, serving as trustee of the Spence School in New

York City and the Masters School in Dobbs Ferry, N.Y. Her other activities extended well beyond her college and her city. With Caroline Spurgeon, Gildersleeve in 1919 founded the International Federation of University Women, which she twice served as president. She also chaired the American Council on Education and was instrumental in the founding of the Seven College Conference of Women's Colleges. Her francophile sympathies inspired her long support of Reid Hall as a center for visiting scholars in Paris, and her interest in the Near East resulted in leadership roles with both the American College for Girls in Istanbul and the Near East College Association.

Gildersleeve's involvement in international affairs increased significantly during the 1940s. She chaired the advisory council of the WAVES (1942–45), and in February 1945 was the only woman member of the United States delegation to the founding conference of the United Nations in San Francisco. It was the high point of her career. She assisted in drafting the United Nations charter and worked on behalf of human rights. Shortly thereafter she became a member of the United States Educational Mission to Japan and helped design a restructuring of the Japanese educational system. Gildersleeve later actively opposed the creation of a Jewish state in Palestine, which she believed would produce more problems than it would solve.

In 1947 Gildersleeve retired and moved to Navarre, Elizabeth Reynard's federal home in Bedford Village, N.Y. She died of a heart attack in a nursing home in Centerville, Mass., in July 1965. During her lifetime, Gildersleeve received numerous honorary degrees as well as the Legion of Honor of France. The Virginia Gildersleeve International Fund for University Women was established in 1969 to promote educational projects and international understanding among women. Gildersleeve's formidable presence, together with her aversion to parochialism and her commitment to women's intellect, left a permanent impress upon the college which she headed for so long. Barnard's academic intensity, its cosmopolitan personality, and its sober feminism were largely the product of her leadership.

[Virginia Gildersleeve's papers are in the Rare Book and Manuscript Library, Columbia Univ. The materials relating to her Barnard career, consisting of dean's office correspondence, occasional papers, clippings, pamphlets, photographs, and memorabilia, can be found in the Barnard College Archives. Her major writings are her 1908 Columbia Univ. dissertation, published in 1975 as *Government Regulation of the Elizabethan Drama;* her informa-

tive autobiography, *Many A Good Crusade* (1954); and *A Hoard for Winter* (1962), a collection of meditative essays on diverse subjects. Her educational philosophy can be traced in published articles that span her career, including "Some Guides for Feminine Energy," *Columbia Univ. Quart.,* Sept. 1915; "The Question of the Women's Colleges," *Atlantic Monthly,* Nov. 1927; and "Educating Girls for the War and the Post-War World," a brochure published by Barnard College, Jan. 1943. Marian Churchill White, *A History of Barnard College* (1954), provides a detailed account of the Gildersleeve era. Also useful is Alice Duer Miller and Susan Myers, *Barnard College: The First Fifty Years* (1939). For Gildersleeve's role in the Am. Assoc. of Univ. Women and the Internat. Federation of Univ. Women see Marion Talbot and Lois Kimball Mathews Rosenberry, *The History of the American Association of University Women, 1881–1931* (1931), and Edith C. Batho, *A Lamp of Friendship: A Short History of the International Federation of University Women* (1969). More personal accounts include Ruth McAneney Loud and Mary C. St. John, "Virginia Crocheron Gildersleeve," *Brearley Bull.,* Dec. 1938, and "Barnard: Gildersleeve & Mrs. Mac," in Joseph Gerard Brennan, *The Education of a Prejudiced Man* (1977), pp. 113–29. An obituary appeared in the *N.Y. Times,* July 9, 1965; death record from Mass. Dept. of Public Health. Memorials and selections from obituaries are gathered in "In Memoriam: Virginia Crocheron Gildersleeve, 1877–1965," *Barnard Alumnae,* Fall 1965. A biobibliography prepared by Randall Erickson assisted in the research for this article. Additional information was provided by Jean Palmer.]

ANNETTE K. BAXTER

GILLMORE, Inez. *See* IRWIN, Inez Haynes Gillmore.

GILMER, Elizabeth Meriwether (Dorothy Dix), Nov. 18, 1861–Dec. 16, 1951. Journalist.

Elizabeth Meriwether Gilmer, who as Dorothy Dix became an enormously popular and successful advice columnist, was born in Montgomery County, Tenn. Her father, Will Douglas Meriwether, was a member of a well-connected southern family who had come to Tennessee from Virginia and before that from Wales. Her mother, Maria (Winston) Meriwether, bore another daughter and a son after Elizabeth, at Woodstock, the family farm on the Kentucky-Tennessee border. By the time of Elizabeth's birth, the Meriwether family was experiencing economic difficulties. Her childhood was also marred by the Civil War and by the illness of her mother, who, Gilmer later said, had had no real part in her life. Upon the death of his first wife, Will Meriwether married a cousin, Martha Gilmer Chase, and the Meriwether children spent their teenage years under her guidance, a good deal stricter than what their own mother had been able to provide.

Elizabeth Meriwether was largely self-educated. Taught to read by an elderly family retainer, she devoured the books in her great-grandfather's impressive library, and always felt that her most substantial education took place there. She did attend the Female Academy in Clarksville, Tenn., and completed one semester at Hollins Institute in Virginia, where she was very unhappy.

On Nov. 21, 1882, Elizabeth Meriwether married George O. Gilmer, her stepmother's brother. The marriage was problematic at the outset and, subsequently, tragic. George Gilmer, ten years her senior, was in poor physical and mental health at the time of their marriage, and his problems steadily worsened. He achieved some success as an inventor in developing new methods for distilling turpentine, but the Gilmers' personal life was disrupted by his serious illnesses and by long periods of separation. They had no children, and George Gilmer died in a mental institution in 1929 after being hospitalized by his family. Though Elizabeth Gilmer rarely alluded specifically to her marital difficulties, and never saw fit to break the marriage contract of forty-seven years, she often wrote or spoke of her "suffering" as the basis of her extraordinary empathy for the problems of others.

In the early 1890s Elizabeth Gilmer suffered a nervous collapse and was taken by her father to Bay Saint Louis, a Mississippi Gulf coast town, to recover. There she met ELIZA NICHOLSON, owner and editor of the New Orleans *Daily Picayune*. For about a decade Gilmer had been writing short stories and sketches for newspaper publication. Nicholson encouraged her writing, purchased a story from her, and in 1894 brought her to New Orleans to work for the *Daily Picayune*. Beginning by writing obituaries and recipes, the talented Gilmer soon had her own weekly column, which first appeared May 5, 1895, under the pen name Dorothy Dix.

Her early columns were witty, literate pieces of social satire. A significant number were on topics of interest to women; some, like "Some New Women Problems" and "Give the Girls a Chance," had a distinctly angry feminist edge. Her work was an immediate success, and readers began to write to Dorothy Dix at the paper, a phenomenon that was to shape her later career. By 1897 she was able to repay her father for his sacrifices during her illness, and they took a three-month trip to Europe for the Diamond Jubilee of Queen Victoria.

By the turn of the century, Dorothy Dix—a name she now used as her own—had begun to draw national attention. In 1901 she accepted an assignment from William Randolph Hearst to cover the activities of CARRY NATION in Kansas. Her vivid and unusually sympathetic accounts of the hatchet crusade won her coast-to-coast fame, and in April 1901 she went to work for Hearst's *New York Journal*. There Dix became a celebrated crime reporter known for her coverage of all the sensational murder trials of the period, including the Nan Patterson, Ruth Wheeler, and Thaw-White-Nesbit cases. Her sympathy for the sufferings of the accused as well as for the victims led many of the principals in these cases to talk freely with her. And her sense of the drama of an individual life contributed to powerful, and often advocacy, journalism. Dix also continued to write her feature columns, which now ran five times a week and drew an increasing volume of mail which she felt obliged to answer personally. Probably as the result of this heavy workload, she suffered a protracted period of ill health in 1905.

Her commitment to women's interests helped to make Dix, by the mid-1910s, an active suffragist. In 1903 she had shared a platform with SUSAN B. ANTHONY at the National American Woman Suffrage Association convention in New Orleans, and she later made many public appearances for the cause of woman suffrage. The financial vulnerability of women, which she had experienced in traumatic fashion during the early years of her marriage, was a persistent theme of her columns, and she was always the particular champion of the woman who had to work for a living. Though the polemic cast of her columns diminished late in her career, Dix never abandoned the conviction that "being a woman has always been the most arduous profession any human being could follow."

At the end of 1917, tired of crime reporting, Dix left the *Journal*, joined the nationwide Wheeler Newspaper Syndicate, and returned to New Orleans to devote full time to her advice column, which she now began to write in letter and answer format. She was based in New Orleans for the rest of her life, although she covered the Hall-Mills murder case in New York in 1926. Her popularity continued to grow. In June 1928 the city of New Orleans declared Dorothy Dix Day and thousands thronged to a public park to greet her. A factory worker paid a significant tribute: over 500 women in her factory read Dorothy Dix every day. "Nobody knows how much she means to us . . . More than anything else she keeps us going" (*Times-Picayune*, June 11, 1928). By the 1930s Dix was receiving 400 to 500 letters a day; by the end of her career she had an estimated 60 million readers and earned around $100,000 a year.

During the last decades of her career, years of increasing work and prosperity, Dix, assisted by her secretary and close friend Ella Bentley Arthur, followed a rigorous and disciplined schedule. In addition to a daily column and volumes of direct correspondence, she had published seven books by 1939. She wrote her own column until April 1949, and one year later suffered a stroke which required her hospitalization. Dorothy Dix, an American legend, died of kidney failure in New Orleans in 1951.

[Dix's work appeared Sundays in the New Orleans *Daily Picayune*, 1895–1901, and in the New York *Journal*, 1901–17; after 1917 her column was widely syndicated. She also contributed regular features to *Good Housekeeping* and other women's magazines. Biographical information about Dix in print is often inaccurate, particularly about her age. The one full-length biography, Harnett T. Kane, *Dear Dorothy Dix: The Story of a Compassionate Woman* (1952), written in collaboration with Ella Bentley Arthur, is highly anecdotal and not precise about sources of information. See also "My Philosophy of Life," in *Dorothy Dix—Her Book* (1926); John Elfreth Watkins, introduction to Dorothy Dix, *How to Win and Hold a Husband* (1939); Herman Deutsch, "Dorothy Dix Talks," in *Post Biographies of Famous Journalists* (1942); *Dict. Am. Biog.*, Supp. Five, and *Current Biog.*, 1940. Archival material on Dix exists at a number of Louisiana libraries, including some letters at Tulane Univ. and the Meriwether family papers, which include some of Dorothy Dix's letters, at Western Kentucky Univ. For a discussion of Dix's early work see Margaret Culley, "Sob-Sisterhood: Dorothy Dix and the Feminist Origins of the Advice Column," *Southern Studies*, Summer 1977. Birth and marriage dates supplied by Tenn. State Archives; death record by La. Office of Vital Records.]

MARGARET CULLEY

GISH, Dorothy, March 11, 1898–June 4, 1968. Actress.

The second child of Mary (McConnell) and James Lee Gish was born Dorothy Elizabeth in Dayton, Ohio. Her father, a grocer, suffered a number of business failures: the first in Springfield, Ohio, where her older sister Lillian was born, and the second in Dayton. James Gish abandoned his family in New York City in 1900. Mary Gish took in boarders to supplement income earned by occasional stage work and clerking. At the suggestion of one boarder, the Gish sisters began stage careers in stock productions of popular melodramas.

Dorothy's appearance in an early role, "Little Willie" in *East Lynne*, required her to wear boy's apparel, a requirement she resented. However, she was not bothered by a later role in *Her First False Steps* for which the six-year-old Dorothy had to enter a cage with two real lions. The pert juvenile told an interviewer at the time that she "had been on the stage for three years, that she just loves the stage, and that she is going to be an actress all her life" (quoted in L. Gish, *Dorothy & Lillian*, p. 13). A pattern was set early: the family toured during the season and rested at a family home in Massillon, Ohio. In 1907 Dorothy made her New York stage debut as an Irish girl in *Dion O'Dare*. At that time she had a four-year contract with the Fiske O'Hare Company which utilized her in conventional juvenile roles.

The Gishes hoped to give up their vagabond existence when Mary Gish went into the confectionery business in 1910. For a year Dorothy attended boarding school in Virginia, but her mother's store burned down and the family was once again forced to seek work in the theater. For Dorothy, the impoverishment strengthened their relationship: "The intimacy with mother was promoted by our sharing in the work, we know all that she went through. We were part of it all" ("And So I Am a Comedienne," p. 7).

In 1911, watching *Lena and the Geese*, the Gishes saw an actress they recognized as their friend Gladys Smith. The Gish and Smith families had met earlier when both were touring, and had a friendship while living for a summer in New York City. When the Gishes appeared at the Biograph Studios, asking for Gladys, they were surprised to find she was now Mary Pickford. She persuaded D. W. Griffith to hire the Gish sisters: they soon began work as extras earning five dollars a day and were first given recognizable parts in *An Unseen Enemy*, released in September 1912.

Griffith found Dorothy's pert manner far less appealing than Lillian's soulfulness, and he used her in major parts only at the behest of Lillian. Dorothy Gish's apprenticeship under Griffith was long and labored: she appeared in sixty-one films before gaining a star-status contract in 1915. The contract, awarded for her role in *Old Heidelberg*, called for eleven feature films, which were made during the next two years.

In 1918, Gish's career surged when her sister urged Griffith to use her instead of Constance Talmadge for the role of The Little Disturber in *Hearts of the World*. The part was her favorite and her portrayal of a vagabond minstrel in war-ravaged France was one of her best. Gish stole the show with her delightfully humorous performance, the film became immensely popular, and, as a direct result, Paramount-Artcraft Studios offered her a million-dollar, two-year contract. Believing that "at my age all that money would ruin my character" (*Dorothy and Lillian*, p. 81), Gish turned down the offer. Ironically, her subsequent films—all variations of The Little Disturber—were sold by Griffith to Paramount for release.

In 1920 Lillian Gish directed her sister in the feature film *Remodeling Her Husband*, a romantic comedy in which the new bride overhauls her husband to suit her notions of propriety. The husband was played by James Rennie; on Dec. 20, 1920, he and Dorothy Gish were married. Although separated in the early 1930s and divorced in 1935, they remained friends.

After appearing in three other films, Gish was united with her sister for their final Griffith picture, *Orphans of the Storm* (1922). She played Louise, a blind girl who becomes separated from her sister on their arrival in Paris and is forced to beg and sing in the streets. The piteous role prevented her from displaying her comic talents, although she had a few light moments. It was the last great success of her career. After middling successes as a Cuban dancer in *The Bright Shawl* (1923) and as Tessa, a peasant girl seduced into a sham marriage, in *Romola* (1924), Gish appeared in three mediocre films before British producer Herbert Wilcox brought her to England. There Wilcox used her in four pictures, of which the first, *Nell Gwyn* (1926), was the best. Of her performance in the title role *Variety* said: "She is Gish, Pickford, Negri and Swanson in one." Her last Wilcox film, *Wolves* (1930) was also her first talkie and a distinct failure.

Dorothy Gish returned to the stage in a 1928 production of *Young Love* (in which she appeared with her husband) and during the remainder of her life worked periodically in the theater. She appeared on Broadway in, among others, *The Inspector General* (1930), *The Pillars of Society* (1931), *Brittle Heaven* (1934), in which she played Emily Dickinson, *The Magnificent Yankee* (1946), *The Man* (1950), and *The Chalk Garden* (1956), her last stage appearance. She again found work in Hollywood: in 1944 she gave a delightful portrayal of Mrs. Skinner in *Our Hearts Were Young and Gay*. The occasional film appearances then consisted of character roles, all mothers: *Centennial Summer* (1946), *The Whistle at Eaton Falls* (1951), a quasi-documentary about labor strife, and *The Cardinal* (1964).

In her last years, Gish suffered from memory loss and subsequent depression, and in the early 1960s her sister moved her to a sanatorium in Rapallo, Italy. There, in 1968, Dorothy Gish died of bronchial pneumonia.

Gish's achievement was adversely affected by comparison to her sister's. She felt that audiences "did not want to see a woman play outright comedy" ("And So I Am a Comedienne," p. 7), but her comedic talent was sometimes compared to that of Chaplin and Keaton. Her versatility as a performer gives Dorothy Gish an enduring—yet, because of the loss of most of her comic films, diminished—place in cinema history.

[There are extensive clipping files on Dorothy Gish in the Billy Rose Theatre Coll., N.Y. Public Library; in the Harvard Theatre Coll.; in the Am. Film Institute; and in the Margaret Herrick Library, Acad. of Motion Picture Arts and Sciences, Beverly Hills, Calif. "And So I Am a Comedienne," *Ladies' Home Journal*, July 1925, is Gish's only account of her career. Lillian Gish's two autobiographies, *The Movies, Mr. Griffith and Me* (1967) and *Dorothy and Lillian* (1973), include a wealth of material concerning her sister. De Witt Bodeen, "Dorothy Gish," *Films in Review*, Aug.-Sept. 1968, and Anthony Slide, "Dorothy Gish" in *The Griffith Actresses* (1973), offer insightful biographical accounts, particularly of the early Biograph days. A full bibliography of magazine articles appears in Mel Schuster, comp., *Motion Picture Performers* (1971), p. 279. See also *Current Biog.*, 1944. *Biog. Encyc. and Who's Who of the Am. Theatre* (1966) gives complete stage credits; Evelyn Mack Truitt, ed., *Who Was Who on Screen* (1977), gives screen credits; and James Parrish, ed., *Actors' Television Credits, 1950–1972* (1972), gives Gish's few television credits. Obituaries appeared in *N.Y. Times*, June 6, 1968, *Newsweek*, June 17, 1968, and *Time*, June 17, 1968. A biobibliography, prepared by Nancy Snowden, was of assistance in research. A copy of record of birth, provided by Montgomery Cty. Probate Court, gives her name as Dorthy and her mother's name as May McConnell.]

ARTHUR LENNIG

GLUECK, Eleanor Touroff, April 12, 1898–Sept. 25, 1972. Criminologist, social worker.

Eleanor Glueck was born Leonia Touroff in Brooklyn, N.Y., the older of two children and only daughter of Bernard Leo and Anna (Wodzislawska) Touroff, immigrants respectively from Russia and Poland. Her father, who had legal training, worked in the real estate business; her mother was extraordinarily well read. After graduating from Hunter College High School in 1916, Touroff went to Barnard College, where she majored in English; she received her A.B. in 1920.

Determined to have a career, and considering journalism, she entered the New York School of Social Work in the hope of acquiring more knowledge of the world than her sheltered life had afforded her. Before receiving her diploma in 1921, however, she had become enthusiastic about the possibilities in social work, in part because of her studies with Bernard Glueck, a psychiatrist interested in criminology and social work. Glueck not only helped her to obtain her first job as head social worker at the Dorchester Community Center in Boston (1921–22) but also introduced her to his brother, Sheldon, a young lawyer interested in relating law to psychiatry. Eleanor Touroff and Sheldon Glueck were married on April 16, 1922.

The same year, Eleanor Glueck entered the Harvard Graduate School of Education, receiving her M.Ed. in 1923 and her Ed.D. in 1925; her doctoral thesis, *The Community Use of Schools,* was published in 1927. But it was a seminar with Richard C. Cabot in Harvard's department of social ethics, in which Sheldon Glueck was then a student, that most fully engaged her. Cabot, a distinguished physician, had pioneered in the development of medical social work and in the use of long-term follow-up studies as the ultimate test of medical therapies. His interdisciplinary seminar underscored for the Gluecks the fact that adequate follow-up of criminals sentenced to reformatories had never been carried out.

Eleanor and Sheldon Glueck were to spend the rest of their lives studying criminal careers, not after the fact, but as they unfolded. In 1925, under the auspices of the Department of Social Ethics, they began work on their first joint book, *Five Hundred Criminal Careers* (1930), a study of offenders incarcerated in the Massachusetts Reformatory whom they followed for five years after completion of their parole. Using the discipline of social case work, and working closely with her husband, Eleanor Glueck demonstrated a special knack for extracting the relevant facts from a web of hearsay, and for imposing order on the mass of data. Tracing virtually all of their first 500 criminals in a follow-up study fifteen years later, their thoroughness made one fact disturbingly clear: reformatories did not reform.

The Gluecks collaborated on more than a dozen books. Their early work included a study of former inmates of the Massachusetts Reformatory for Women, initiated by superintendent JESSIE D. HODDER, which appeared in 1934 as *Five Hundred Delinquent Women. One Thousand Juvenile Delinquents,* published the same year, was a study of delinquents referred by the Boston juvenile court to the Judge Baker Foundation, a treatment center directed by William Healy and AUGUSTA BRONNER. In these works the Gluecks attempted to predict—statistically at least—the likelihood of criminality, and, once delinquents were in prison, the likelihood of their rehabilitation.

The Gluecks worked together closely on each book: Sheldon had a penchant for the legal, psychiatric, and literary aspects of the work, while Eleanor's province was the practical, statistical, and field work. Sheldon Glueck always referred to his wife as the "scientist." Her training in social case work and her abiding character traits of determination and perseverance made possible the planning and completion of the immense field investigations that characterized their in-depth studies of over 3,000 criminals.

From small beginnings, the Gluecks' researches developed into a large-scale enterprise, devoted principally to determining the effectiveness of various methods of correction and to studying the causes, prevention, prediction, and treatment of juvenile delinquency. In 1940, the Gluecks began the ambitious study that culminated in 1950 in *Unraveling Juvenile Delinquency.* They compared 500 boys in reform schools with 500 nondelinquents, matched for intelligence, ethnicity, and residence. Remarkably eclectic, the study examined the significance of peer-group associations, genetic background, early childhood, neighborhood influences, projective tests, and body type in predicting future delinquency. The careers of the delinquents and matched controls were reevaluated at ages seventeen, twenty-five, and thirty-one. The accuracy of inferences made at one period could be checked later, and paths out of, as well as into, delinquency could be charted.

This research resulted in the Gluecks' Social Prediction Tables, which attempted to identify potential delinquents at the age of six, on the basis of information collected about older offenders. The Gluecks maintained that the absence of family cohesion, maternal supervision, and maternal affection were the most important etiological factors in delinquency. Though criticized by sociologists for methodological defects, and by social reformers concerned about their possible misuse, the Gluecks' tables have been validated in prospective studies in several countries.

The Gluecks enjoyed a closely knit family as well as professional life. During their fifty years of marriage, they took thirty-seven trips abroad, often combining work with vacation. Eleanor Glueck's Sunday teas for law students became legendary. The Gluecks also took great pride in their only child, Anitra Joyce (b. 1924), who became a poet; her premature death in 1956 was a major tragedy in their lives.

From 1928 to the end of her life, Eleanor

Glueck worked at the Harvard Law School, where her husband had become a professor. She was a research assistant (1929–53), and later a research associate (1953–72) of the Harvard Law School Research Project into the Causes, Treatment, and Prevention of Juvenile Delinquency. From 1966 to 1972, with Sheldon Glueck, she was also codirector of the program. In their later years, the Gluecks shared numerous honors, at home and abroad, for their work in criminology. Harvard awarded each of them an Honorary Sc.D. in 1958, and Eleanor Glueck received the Distinguished Alumna Award from Barnard College in 1969. Following their retirement in the 1960s, the Gluecks continued to harvest their data until Eleanor Glueck's death, of an accidental drowning, in Cambridge in 1972.

Eleanor Glueck always maintained a strong professional identity as a social worker. Despite a life committed to her family and research, she found time to do case work with delinquent girls, and for four decades served as a trustee of the Judge Baker Guidance Center in Boston. Her commitment to improving methods of research was revealed in *Evaluative Research in Social Work* (1936), a book published on her own. In their joint efforts, Eleanor and Sheldon Glueck always sought to bring the principles of experimental medicine—especially that of meticulous follow-up—to the administration of criminal justice. As Felix Frankfurter aptly noted of the Gluecks' trailblazing work: "It means much to have speculation supplanted by facts, to prove quantitatively that which was previously merely surmised." Eleanor Glueck was one of those who did most to elevate the artisan craft of social work into one of the social sciences.

[The joint papers of Sheldon and Eleanor T. Glueck at the Harvard Law School contain 30,000 items spanning the years 1911–72. The collection relates mainly to their research on delinquency, but it also contains some personal material on Eleanor Glueck's precollege, college, and graduate school years (including a diary for 1916–22), and photographs. Other books by Eleanor Glueck include *Adventure in Japan* (1962), and, with Sheldon Glueck, *Physique and Delinquency* (1956), *Predicting Delinquency and Crime* (1959), *Family Environment and Delinquency* (1962), *Ventures in Criminology* (1964), *Later Criminal Careers* (1966), *Juvenile Delinquents Grown Up* (1966), *Delinquents and Nondelinquents in Perspective* (1968), and *Toward a Typology of Juvenile Offenders* (1970). A bibliography of her work is available in the Glueck Papers and in Sheldon Glueck, *Lives of Labor, Lives of Love* (1977), which also contains biographical information. See also the entry on Eleanor and Sheldon Glueck in *Current Biog.*, 1957; an interview with Eleanor Touroff Glueck by Elizabeth Waterman Gilboy in *Barnard College Alumnae Monthly,* Oct. 1936, pp. 11–12, and Eleanor Glueck's *N.Y. Times* obituary, Sept. 26, 1972. Birth record provided by N.Y. City Dept of Health; death record by the Mass. Dept. of Public Health.]

GEORGE E. VAILLANT

GOEPPERT-MAYER, Maria. *See* MAYER, Maria Gertrude Goeppert.

GOLDMAN, Hetty, Dec. 19, 1881–May 4, 1972. Archaeologist.

Hetty Goldman was born in New York City, the third of four children and middle daughter of Julius and Sarah (Adler) Goldman. Both parents were of German Jewish descent. Her father was a lawyer; her grandfather, Marcus Goldman, was cofounder of Goldman, Sachs and Co., an investment banking firm in New York City. The intellectual and social concerns of the family had a lasting influence on Hetty Goldman. Her mother was actively interested in social work, and Hetty attended Dr. J. Sachs School for Girls in New York, founded by her uncle Julius Sachs, an educator and classicist with an interest in archaeology.

In 1899 Hetty Goldman entered Bryn Mawr College, where she majored in Greek and English, receiving her A.B. in 1903. During the next several years, she took graduate courses in Greek at Columbia University and worked briefly as a manuscript reader with the Macmillan Company. Despite a strong interest in literature, she decided that her special gifts were in scholarly rather than creative writing. In 1909 Goldman went to Radcliffe College to continue her studies in classical languages and archaeology, earning an A.M. in 1910. That year she also published her first article, "The *Oresteia* of Aeschylus as Illustrated by Greek Vase-Painting," on the strength of which she became the first woman awarded the Charles Eliot Norton fellowship to attend the American School of Classical Studies at Athens. She studied there from 1910 to 1912.

In Greece Hetty Goldman became interested in archaeological field work, following in the path of a small group of women, among them HARRIET BOYD HAWES and EDITH HALL (DOHAN), who had begun to work independently as excavators on Crete. Under the auspices of the school in Athens, she undertook her first excavation jointly with Alice Walker, a Vassar graduate, at the small coastal town of Halae in central Greece. Beginning in 1911, they excavated classical remains but also revealed some of the earliest traces of Neolithic village occupation in

Greece, a discovery that stimulated Goldman's interest in prehistoric archaeology. Terracottas from the necropolis of Halae became the subject of her doctoral dissertation, for which she received her Ph.D. from Radcliffe in 1916.

Goldman's excavations at Halae were interrupted first by the Balkan wars from 1912 to 1913, when she served as a volunteer nurse in a Greek hospital, and then by World War I. She left Greece in 1914 to work for the Red Cross in New York City, returning four years later to report on Jewish communities in Greece and the Balkans for the American Jewish Joint Distribution Committee. Goldman revisited Halae in 1921, and the following spring undertook the first of her excavations in Asia Minor, at the site of Colophon in ancient Ionia. There she directed the project for the Fogg Museum of Harvard University, supervising a team of young archaeologists who were to become famous in their own right (among them the prehistorian Carl Blegen, the architect Leicester B. Holland, and the epigraphist Benjamin D. Meritt). The Graeco-Turkish war in 1922 put an end to work at Colophon; villagers in the 1950s still remembered with awe the energetic woman who ran the project.

With two important excavations to her credit, Hetty Goldman's direction in the field of prehistoric archaeology was set. One of the pioneers in the investigation of the pre-Greek and earliest Greek peoples, she expanded her geographical horizons to explore the near eastern contacts of the earliest inhabitants of the Greek mainland. The archaeological relationships between Greece and the lands of the eastern Mediterranean remained one of her major interests.

Goldman returned to Greece in 1924, where for the next three years, as director of excavations for the Fogg Museum, she worked in central Greece. *Excavations at Eutresis in Boeotia* (1931), which documents her findings there, has remained a classic for its lucid exposition and its interpretation of the stages of prehistoric life in Greece. After some interim advisory work in Yugoslavia in 1932, Goldman selected the site for her fourth major excavation, at Tarsus near the southeast coast of Turkey. Sponsored jointly by Bryn Mawr College, Harvard University, and the Archaeological Institute of America (AIA), the excavation was motivated by the search for prehistoric links between Greece and Anatolia. Goldman's approach to the problem was characteristically sober and systematic; she avoided the speculative flights of Emil Forrer, who had accompanied her on the first exploration at Tarsus in 1934, and tried to find literary references in Hittite cuneiform texts to the heroes of Homer and the Trojan War. She searched for hard his-torical facts and was duly rewarded as her team of young apprentices unearthed inscribed tablets, seals, and seal impressions proving the importance of the site at Tarsus and documenting its relations with the Hittite kings of central Anatolia. By 1939 excavations had reached down to levels of about 3000 B.C. when, once again, war interrupted Goldman's efforts.

During World War II, Goldman resided in Princeton, N.J., where in 1936 she had become the first woman appointed professor at the Institute for Advanced Study. She devoted her time at the Institute to research and writing, preparing the findings at Tarsus for publication. Keenly aware of political developments, she also sponsored many German refugees who fled the Nazi regime. Finally in 1947, Goldman was able to return to Tarsus, where two years later excavations reached the deepest levels. Retiring in 1948, she devoted much of the next fifteen years to publishing the results of the Tarsus excavation in collaboration with her associates. The three volumes of *Excavations at Gözlü Kule, Tarsus* (1950, 1956, and 1963) are major documents of the prehistoric and historical growth of a prosperous near eastern town from the sixth millennium B.C. to the Roman period.

In 1966 Hetty Goldman received the gold medal for Distinguished Archaeological Achievement from the AIA. A visiting lecturer at Johns Hopkins in 1928, Goldman did little other formal teaching, but shared her knowledge and insights with her excavating and research staff, whom she taught accuracy in field work and reporting, and clarity in interpretation. It was this careful, exacting approach to the craft of archaeology, as much as the discoveries of her major excavations, which distinguished Goldman's achievement.

Hetty Goldman had a wide range of cultural interests, read widely, and played the piano and violin. She remained close to her family, including nieces and nephews, until the end of her life. After a period of failing health, she died in Princeton of pulmonary edema in May 1972.

[Notes and manuscripts relating to the excavations at Halae, Colophon, and Tarsus and a small number of letters are in the Bryn Mawr College Archives; the Radcliffe College Archives contain Goldman's transcripts and alumnae questionnaires. Published sources on Goldman include Saul Weinberg, ed., *The Aegean and the Near East* (1956), a collection of essays written by Goldman's friends and colleagues on the occasion of her seventy-fifth birthday. It contains a selected bibliography, as does *The Institute for Advanced Study. Publications of Members: 1930–1954* (1955). Biographical sketches appear in *A Symposium in Memory of Hetty Goldman: 1881–1972* (1974), a report of the meeting held at the Institute for Advanced Study in May 1973. The text of the AIA Award and Goldman's response were published in *Archaeology*, April 1967, p. 83. See also *Nat. Cyc. Am. Biog.*, LVI, 507–10, and an obituary in the *N.Y. Times*, May 6, 1972. Goldman's sister Agnes G. Sanborn, her niece Elizabeth Lehmann, and Dr. Frances F. Jones provided information. Death certificate supplied by N.J. State Health Dept.]

MACHTELD J. MELLINK

GOLDRING, Winifred, Feb. 1, 1888–Jan. 30, 1971. Paleontologist.

Winifred Goldring was the fourth of Frederick and Mary (Grey) Goldring's eight daughters; their ninth and last child was a boy. She was born in Kenwood, near Albany, N.Y., where her father maintained an orchid collection on the Erastus Corning estate. He had trained at Kew Gardens in London before emigrating in 1879 to the United States and marrying Winifred's mother, a teacher and the daughter of Corning's head gardener. Shortly after Winifred's birth the family moved to Slingerlands, an Albany suburb, where Frederick Goldring started his own business as a florist. Growing up there, Winifred explored the surrounding countryside whose rocks and fossils became the focus of her later work.

Goldring graduated as class valedictorian of the high school of the New York State Normal School in 1905, and then entered Wellesley College, where she was elected Phi Beta Kappa and appointed a Durant Scholar for her junior and senior years. She received her A.B. in 1909 and remained at Wellesley, as assistant to geology professor Elizabeth F. Fisher. Goldring also earned an A.M. there in 1912 with a thesis on "The Geographer and His Subject," completed under the supervision of Harvard's William M. Davis. From 1912 to 1914 she was an instructor in petrology and geology at Wellesley while assisting in geography and field geology. During those two years, she also taught geography at the Teachers' School of Science, a special evening and Saturday program begun by LUCRETIA CROCKER and affiliated with the Boston Society of Natural History, which had elected Goldring a member in 1911. She supplemented her graduate training in the summer of 1913, studying at Columbia University, and again in 1921, working with paleobotanist Edward W. Berry at Johns Hopkins University.

Goldring was anxious to return to Albany and introduced herself to John M. Clarke, director of the New York State Museum there. In 1914 he offered her a temporary summer appointment as "scientific expert" to develop exhibits at the museum's recently opened Hall of Invertebrate Paleontology. She stayed on and by 1916 began her own research on Devonian crinoids ("sea lilies" from the middle of the Paleozoic era), which provided the subject for her major monograph, published in 1923. Her permanent affiliation with the State Museum was guaranteed by her appointment as associate paleontologist in 1920. Paleobotany was then an area of particular excitement as researchers sought the connecting link between algae and vascular plants, and Goldring became internationally known in this discipline; her field work helped make the Devonian plant collection at Albany one of the best in the world. When state funds became constricted in the late 1920s, the museum staff turned to more applied geological projects. Goldring geologically mapped the Coxsackie and Berne quadrangles of New York, a project occupying several of her summers between 1928 and 1937. She also maintained and developed the State Museum's public programs in paleontology during these years.

Although she disliked public lecturing, Goldring's exhibitions and handbooks were unusually effective. Her initial museum assignment had been simply to "fill the cases," but she took the opportunity to explore educational techniques as well. Two of her displays, "What Is a Fossil" and "What Is a Geological Formation," were considered model teaching exhibits. Goldring's most notable presentation, though, was the large Gilboa (Upper Devonian) Fossil Forest of Seed Ferns, completed after nearly two years' effort in 1924, which juxtaposed an impressionistic background painting of an ancient forest with life-size restorations of the fern trees and fossil stumps. Her success with exhibits led Goldring to produce several popular handbooks. The first, an introduction to fossils published in 1929, was accessible to general readers but also served as a college textbook for many years. Similarly her *Guide to the Geology of John Boyd Thacher Park* (1933) was a case study well suited to college courses. While Goldring never pursued an academic appointment, she worked actively with graduate students who studied New York formations and often arranged for their summer support.

On April 1, 1939, Winifred Goldring was officially appointed state paleontologist, attracting attention as the first woman to hold that post. The appointment reflected her impressive credentials and the support of Rudolf Ruedemann, her predecessor in the position and her mentor at the State Museum who had recommended her for the honorary doctorate she received from Russell Sage College two years earlier. Goldring remained state paleontologist until her retirement in 1954.

Winifred Goldring's life centered on her work and family in Albany. She lived, from 1914 until her death, in the family home in Slingerlands, with her parents and various sisters. She never married, explaining in her Wellesley class report in 1919 that she had "as yet discovered no one more attractive than my work." As few women then studied paleontology, most of her professional friends and correspondents were men. Nor could Goldring encourage women to enter the field; when asked in 1929 to discuss their prospects, she noted pessimistically that there were almost no women paleontologists in higher education and that those employed were in museums or doing micropaleontology for oil companies. Her unsuccessful efforts to gain a position with the United States Geological Survey the previous year—she was told that the Survey was looking for a "he-man" paleontologist—along with her perception that she was not as well paid as her male colleagues, undoubtedly fueled her cynicism.

New York state offered unusually rich resources for geological study and nearly all of Goldring's research was performed there. Colleagues in paleontology rarely invited her on expeditions outside the state, commenting to her in letters about the limitations of taking women into the field. Nonetheless, she made her presence felt at professional meetings and, in some cases after debate, participated in associated field trips. Generally quiet, Winifred Goldring could be adamant when she felt her legitimate ambitions were thwarted. Her determination led her to design a bloomer outfit for field work and to learn to shoot a revolver so that she could work alone when necessary.

Friends and advisers could not always dissuade her from overwork and in 1925, and on several subsequent occasions, she suffered a nervous collapse which required a leave of absence. Later, she enjoyed the recognition accompanying her election as the first woman president of the Paleontological Society (1949) and as vice president of the Geological Society of America (1950). In 1957 she was awarded a second honorary degree, from Smith College. By choice, Goldring stopped scientific work after her retirement; for the next sixteen years she read, took long walks in the nearby Helderberg Mountains she had studied since her youth, and visited with friends. She died in Albany, N.Y., in 1971, two days before her eighty-third birthday, after a brief gastrointestinal illness.

[For a list of publications and official correspondence see the Winifred Goldring Papers, along with a few Goldring letters in the John M. Clarke Papers, both at the N.Y. State Archives, Albany. Several letters are in the Charles Schuchert Papers, Yale Univ. Archives. Personal letters are held by Katherine Van Winkle Palmer, Am. Paleontological Inst., Ithaca, N.Y.; Wellesley College has a copy of Goldring's M.A. thesis, letter of evaluation from Elizabeth Fisher, and useful alumnae class records. Goldring's major works include *The Devonian Crinoids of the State of New York* (1923); and the two volumes of her *Handbook of Paleontology for Beginners and Amateurs: Pt. 1, The Fossils* (1929) and *Pt. 2, The Formations* (1931). See also Donald W. Fisher, *Memorial to Winifred Goldring, 1888–1971* (Geological Soc. of America, Nov. 1971), which includes a bibliography and photograph. She is listed in *Am. Men of Science*, 9th ed. (1955). Personal information supplied by her sister Joyce Goldring. Death certificate furnished by N.Y. State Dept. of Health.]

SALLY GREGORY KOHLSTEDT

GOLDSMITH, Grace Arabell, April 8, 1904–April 28, 1975. Physician, nutritionist, public health educator.

Grace Goldsmith was born in St. Paul, Minn., the only child of Arthur William and Arabell (Coleman) Goldsmith. Her father, an accountant, emigrated from Canada in 1883 and settled in St. Paul. Her mother, of British ancestry, was a native of New England. Grace Goldsmith attended public school and studied at the University of Minnesota for two years before transferring to the University of Wisconsin, where she received the B.S. degree in 1925.

Physically active, skilled in many sports, and a superb dancer, Goldsmith became physical education director of the New Orleans YWCA. There a friend persuaded her to enter the Tulane University School of Medicine, where she was one of six women in a class of 108 students. She taught dancing at the YWCA to pay her school bills. Goldsmith graduated at the top of her class in 1932, edging out Michael E. DeBakey, who became a famous cardiovascular surgeon.

From the first she was interested in internal medicine and nutrition. After a year's internship at Touro Infirmary in New Orleans (1932–33), she worked as a fellow in internal medicine at the Mayo Clinic in Rochester, Minn., from 1933 to 1936. With her cousin, Dr. George Brown, she published in 1934 an article on pain associated with heart disease; this was the first of over 150 publications. At Mayo Dr. Russell Wilder further encouraged Goldsmith's interest in the diseases of nutrition and metabolism, to which she would devote the rest of her life. In 1936 she earned the M.S. degree in medicine at the University of Minnesota and returned to Tulane University School of Medicine as an instructor. Thirteen years later she was a full professor.

Vitamin deficiency diseases were a serious

problem in New Orleans; at Charity Hospital there were dozens of pellagra patients and much malnutrition. Goldsmith's first research was on vitamin C deficiency, for which she developed measurement tests. In 1940 she was coauthor of a report, "Vitamin C Nutrition in Pellagra," the first of a remarkable series of studies which unraveled many of the mysteries of nutritional deficiency diseases, proved the effectiveness of nutritional enrichment of cereals, and applied the new knowledge of nutrition to the advancement of public health.

Her work with pellagra led to extensive studies on the B-complex vitamins. She collaborated on research which proved that the amino acid tryptophan was a precursor of the pellagra-preventive vitamin, niacin; she also helped establish recommended dietary allowances for niacin. Stimulated by this success, she turned her attention to other B-complex vitamins, riboflavin, folic acid, and B_{12}. She was the first to report on the treatment of macrocytic anemia with folic acid (1946). As deficiency diseases were conquered, Goldsmith turned her attention to the relationship between nutrition and other diseases in both prevention and treatment and did important work on the effect of diet in atherosclerosis.

The magnitude of nutritional problems in Louisiana attracted Goldsmith's attention to the problems of community nutrition. She did a nutritional survey of Louisiana school children in 1943 and twice went to Newfoundland (1944, 1948), to study diet and the effects of vitamin enrichment of foods. Although she was a strong advocate of enrichment, Goldsmith recognized that the problem of world hunger was not easily solved. A rapidly expanding world population and the failure of the food supply to increase at the same rate presented the world with a race against starvation. She was optimistic, however, that family planning, proper diet, and a better distribution of food would reverse the trend.

In the early 1940s Goldsmith instituted at Tulane the first nutrition training for medical students anywhere in the world. Appointed director of the nutrition and metabolism section of the department of medicine in 1946, she served in that capacity for twenty-one years. In 1967 she was instrumental in founding the Tulane School of Public Health and Tropical Medicine and became its dean, the first woman ever to head a school of public health in the United States. She also served as president of three major organizations devoted to nutrition: the American Institute of Nutrition (1965), the American Board of Nutrition (1966–67), and

the American Society for Clinical Nutrition (1972–73). The American Medical Association presented its Goldberger Award in Clinical Nutrition to her in 1964.

Goldsmith maintained a deep interest in her patients and in internal medicine and kept abreast of medical advances in other areas. Administrative duties reduced her time for laboratory work after 1967, but not her extensive publication. Although she retired as dean, she remained on the Tulane faculty until her death, of cancer, in New Orleans in 1975.

Energetic and superbly organized, Grace Goldsmith excelled in everything she did. An avid gardener and a gourmet cook, she enjoyed giving parties and was always the last to leave the dance floor. She never felt handicapped because she was a woman, but admitted that "on the whole women have to work harder and do more, and seldom are equally paid." She moved up faster than other women in academic medicine, she said, but added modestly, "There were not too many women in medicine."

[In addition to her many articles for professional journals, Goldsmith wrote chapters for twenty-five books and was the author of one book, *Nutritional Diagnosis* (1959). A bibliography of her published work is available from the Howard-Tilton Memorial Library, Tulane Univ. "Tulane Nutritionist Wins Many Distinctions: Sees Hope for Solution to World's Food Problems," *Tulane Report,* Winter 1972, surveys Goldsmith's career and writings. Other sources include an article in the *Jour. La. State Med. Soc.,* June 1967, and an entry in *Nat. Cyc. Am. Biog.,* J, 204. Obituaries appeared in the *N.Y. Times,* April 29, 1975; *Nutrition Reviews,* Oct. 1975; *Tulane Medicine,* Summer 1975. An hour-long videotaped interview with Goldsmith, conducted in 1974 for the *Leaders in Am. Medicine* series of Alpha Omega Alpha, is available through the Nat. Library of Medicine. A portrait hangs in the School of Public Health and Tropical Medicine at Tulane Univ. Assistance in the preparation of this article was received from her colleagues Paul Beaver, Claudia Odom, Ann Metzinger, and Gladys Emerson.]

ELIZABETH W. ETHERIDGE

GOODENOUGH, Florence Laura, Aug. 6, 1886–April 4, 1959. Developmental psychologist.

Florence Goodenough was born in Honesdale, Pa., the cherished youngest of eight children, two boys and six girls, of Alice (Day) and Linus North Goodenough, a farmer. She attended a rural school in Rileyville, Pa., and in 1908 received a B.Pd. from Millersville (Pa.) Normal School. After some years as a teacher in rural schools in Pennsylvania she moved on, from 1919 to 1921, to teaching and research in the public schools of Rutherford and Perth Amboy, N.J., and at the Vineland (N.J.) Training School for retarded children. During these years she earned her B.S. (1920) and A.M. (1921) at Columbia University.

Goodenough completed her graduate training at Stanford University. Her adviser, Lewis M. Terman, a scholar distinguished for his work in mental measurements, was beginning his notable investigations of gifted children. Goodenough became a chief research assistant in these studies. They convinced her of the essential importance to psychology of the individual differences she had observed earlier in her varied teaching and research experiences. After completing work on her Ph.D. in 1924 she moved to Minnesota (1925) to become chief psychologist at the Minneapolis Child Guidance Clinic. The following year she joined the faculty of the newly organized Institute of Child Welfare at the University of Minnesota, where in a few years she became research professor, working primarily with graduate students while pursuing her own research and writing. Illness forced her retirement in 1947.

Goodenough's doctoral thesis, published in 1926 as *Measurement of Intelligence by Drawings,* was an impressive standardization, with hundreds of subjects, of the "Draw-a-Man" test she was devising in her work with retardates and with children in the public schools. To draw a man was the task set for children ages three through thirteen; the test was predicated on the thesis that a child's drawing of a very familiar object is an index of the complexity of his general concepts that, with age and ability, improve in organization and relationships. The results showed striking individual differences both within and between age groups through ages eleven or twelve. Cognitive rather than aesthetic, this unique test had very wide use.

Goodenough recognized that there were multiple problems in research methodology in the growing field of child psychology. In "Measuring Behavior Traits by Means of Repeated Short Samples" (*Jour. Juvenile Research,* 1928) she provided a striking method of episode-sampling in researching children's social behavior, while her book with John E. Anderson, *Experimental Child Study* (1931), presented the pros and cons of many research methodologies. In *Anger in Young Children* (1931), she used careful and continuous recordkeeping by the mothers of preschool children to furnish an important body of new data on age changes in the forms of behavior and the objects of anger. These early studies remain a basic source in developmental social behavior. Described by W.

W. Hartup as an "innovator of the first magnitude in the observational study of child behavior," she was instrumental in guiding studies of leadership, quarrels, social participation, and play.

Many of her professional contemporaries focused on the study of single units of behavior and did not explore beyond adolescence. Goodenough, however, contended—in *Developmental Psychology* (1934) and in "The Development of Human Behavior" (*Acta Psychologica,* 1935)—that the most penetrating approach to a scientific human psychology was through the study of individual differences in reactions both to the environment and to developmental sequences or growth stages. Her position at Minnesota kept her own research largely in childhood, but she continued to urge the study of the total life span.

In the often heated debates during the 1930s and 1940s over mental measurements and their correlations with demographic and situational variables, and over the comparative influence of heredity and environment, Goodenough was both an incisive critic and an originator. Between 1929 and 1946 she prepared evaluative conference reports for the National Research Council, the White House Conferences on Children and Youth, and the prestigious *Handbook of Child Psychology* (1931, 1933, 1946). Speaking to anthropologists at a 1935 meeting of the American Association for the Advancement of Science, she argued against naive research claims of the superiorities and inferiorities of primitive peoples, pointing out that researchers ignored the pervasive cultural patterns that affected not only intelligence tests, but even measures of sensory acuity (*Am. Anthropology,* Jan.–March 1936).

Goodenough also devised the Minnesota Preschool Scale (1932, 1940, 1942), which provided estimates of mental status. With Katherine Maurer, she wrote *The Mental Growth of Children from Two to Fourteen Years* (1942); their assessments of the predictive value of preschool scores for later ones proved important in challenging the assumption that the intelligence quotient (IQ) was a constant. The idea persisted, however, and practitioners and parents tended to put children's IQs in cubbyholes, like so many marbles—an unparalleled example, according to Goodenough, of the "misinterpretations of experimental evidence."

Goodenough's most highly charged controversy was with the University of Iowa Research Group, headed by Beth Wellman (1895–1952) and supported by George Stoddard. They began in 1932 to claim that nursery school attendance and advantageous foster homes "could raise the (true) IQ to an outstanding degree" and could even move a child "from average intelligence to . . . genius levels," a view publicized on radio and in the *New York Times* (July 17, 1938). In a 1939 address to a large audience at Columbia University ("Look to the Evidence!", *Educational Method*, Nov. 1939), and in the 1940 National Society for the Study of Education *Yearbook,* Goodenough exposed serious errors in both the research methods of the Iowa group and the conclusions they drew from their research, maintaining that "the Iowa statistical laboratory had a greater effect on the 'intelligence' of children than the Iowa nursery school." She did not dispute the social and "basic learning" advantages of nursery school, but argued that evidence for raised mental capacity was not demonstrable, and that definitive causative factors should not be assigned "when so many variables . . . must inevitably remain uncontrolled." The Iowa controversy abated after 1941–42, although the nature-nurture issue remained unsettled.

In the early 1940s Goodenough developed for the Women's Army Corps's officer-selection process a projective test using free associations with words having several meanings. Although the test was later used with such other groups as teacher trainees, illness prevented Goodenough from standardizing the instrument. Through the work, however, she came to appreciate Alfred Binet's neglected contribution to projective methods.

Florence Goodenough received many honors: in 1936 she was a starred scientist in *American Men of Science,* a rare honor for a woman. In 1942 she became president of the National Council of Women Psychologists (a section of the American Psychological Association formed "for the war effort"). Believing, however, that psychologists should not be differentiated by sex, she hoped for the "early demise" of the Council. In 1946–47 she was president of the Society for Research in Child Development, and president of Division 7 of the American Psychological Association in 1947. Colleagues at the University of Minnesota established there a psychology reference library bearing her name.

Goodenough was affectionately regarded by students and colleagues as "a character," with "a pixielike, almost epigrammatic humor." Widely influential because of her integrity and her scrupulous creative scholarship, she was also a delightful companion who shared her fondness for music, nature study, and photography, and her bibliophilism. In religion she called herself "a comfortable agnostic."

Despite diabetes, deafness, and almost total blindness, in her last years (with the assistance

of a niece, Lois M. Rynkiewicz) Goodenough completed *Exceptional Children* (1956) and collaborated with Leona Tyler on the third revision of her acclaimed *Developmental Psychology* (1959). She died of a stroke in Lakeland, Fla., while visiting a sister.

[Some of Goodenough's papers are in the Archives of the Univ. of Minn.; others are in the files of the Institute of Child Welfare. They include letters to and from her between 1935 and 1947 and statements from many who knew her. Goodenough's mature experience with problems of mental growth was brought together in "The Measurement of Mental Growth in Childhood," in the *Manual of Child Psychology* (1946), and in her book *Mental Testing, Its History, Principles and Applications* (1949). Other notable writings include: with J. E. Anderson, *Your Child Year by Year* (1930); annual annotated "Selected References on Preschool and Parental Education," *Elementary School Jour.,* 1934–45; "Trends in Modern Psychology," *Psychological Bull.,* 1934; and her critiques of personality evaluations, "Semantic Choice and Personality Structure," *Science,* Nov. 15, 1946, and "The Appraisal of Child Personality," *Psychological Rev.,* May 1949. Robert I. Watson, ed., *Eminent Contributors to Psychology* (1974), contains a partial bibliography of her writings (vol. I, pp. 157–58) and a list of secondary sources (vol. II, pp. 365–68). Annotated bibliographies of her work from 1925 to 1947 appear in publications of the faculty of the Institute of Child Welfare, Univ. of Minn.; there is no separate brochure of Goodenough's publications. Two articles in Paul Mussen, ed., *Manual of Child Psychology* (1970), show particular appreciation of her contributions to research in social behavior: S. Fesbach, "Aggression," and W. W. Hartup, "Peer Interaction and Social Organization." See also W. W. Hartup, "Aggression in Childhood, Developmental Perspectives," *Am. Psychologist,* May 1974. An obituary, with a photograph, by Dale B. Harris appeared in *Child Development,* 30 (1959), 305–6. Death record provided by the Fla. Dept. of Health and Rehabilitative Services. Correspondence from Mildred Templin, Dale Harris, Willard W. Hartup, and E. Adamson Hoebel, and from several relatives, including Lyman Moore, Howard Goodenough, Howard Goodenough, Jr., Merle Patten, and Olive Robinson, was very helpful for this article, as was the assistance of the staff of the Institute of Child Welfare.]

THETA HOLMES WOLF

GOODRICH, Annie Warburton, Feb. 6, 1866– Dec. 31, 1954. Nursing educator, nurse.

Annie Goodrich was born in New Brunswick, N.J., the second of seven children of Samuel Griswold and Annie (Butler) Goodrich. Both parents came from distinguished New England families; her maternal grandfather, Dr. John Butler, was a pioneer psychiatrist who headed the famous Hartford Retreat (later the Institute of Living) for thirty years. Samuel Goodrich, a representative of the Equitable Life Assurance Company, maintained his family in very comfortable circumstances. Annie, the second of four daughters, was educated by governesses until the age of twelve; she then attended private schools in Connecticut, and later in London and Paris, when her father's work took the family to Europe. After finishing her education, Goodrich entered into the social life of Hartford, Conn., where her family had settled in her late teens.

When her father suffered financial reverses and became ill, Goodrich had to think of supporting herself. Practical experience gained in nursing her maternal grandparents, as well as her grandfather Butler's influence, contributed to her decision to become a nurse. With her parents' consent, she enrolled in the New York Hospital Training School for Nurses in 1890.

When Annie Goodrich came to the New York Hospital, formal nursing education had existed in the United States for less than two decades. In the early training schools administered by individual hospitals, student nurses provided patient care in exchange for room, board, and a small cash allowance, with a diploma and the title of "trained nurse" conferred at the end of two years. Spending twelve hours a day on the wards, primarily doing routine unskilled chores, Goodrich was often too tired to absorb even the limited curriculum offered by her overworked nursing supervisors. This fundamental conflict between educational goals and the demand for patient care disturbed her, as did the restrictions placed on her independence and judgment by the rigid discipline and absolute obedience demanded of nurses. She began then to think that nursing education had to change.

Annie Goodrich's intelligence, administrative skill, and social background led to her recruitment, soon after her 1892 graduation, into the elite of the nursing profession, the hospital training school administrators. Hospital administration then provided the chief means of career mobility for nurses, and Goodrich took on a series of challenging posts. Beginning as a head nurse at the New York Hospital (1892), she became superintendent of nurses, first at the New York Post-Graduate Hospital (1893–1900), and later at St. Luke's Hospital (1900–02), the New York Hospital (1902–07), and the Bellevue and Allied Hospitals (1907–10). In all these institutions, Goodrich pursued the same objectives: to raise educational requirements for entering students; to expand and systematize the nursing curriculum; to develop more varied clinical experience, particularly in obstetrical

and public health nursing; and to instill high professional standards in her students. In 1910, she was appointed State Inspector of Training Schools under New York's nurse registration law.

Goodrich carefully maintained the boundaries between nursing and medicine in her efforts to improve the status of her profession. She did not challenge the supremacy of the medical profession in diagnosis or treatment; nursing, as she defined it, involved an entirely different set of skills, those of organizing and administering patient care. Yet Goodrich often found doctors to be at best uncertain allies in her attempts to improve nursing education. In 1907 she resigned as superintendent of nurses at the New York Hospital because she felt the doctors and administrators there did not support her goals.

In 1914, Annie Goodrich realized a long-cherished ambition and began to teach fulltime in the department of nursing at Teachers College, Columbia University, where she had lectured since 1904. During these years, Goodrich also became a leader in state and professional nursing organizations. As president of the International Council of Nurses (1912–15) and the American Nurses Association (1915–18), she was a national advocate of state registration and licensing, the most pressing professional issues for nurses in the prewar period. She also campaigned for woman suffrage, and joined Alice Paul's National Woman's party.

In 1917, Annie Goodrich became director of the Henry Street Visiting Nurses Service, founded by LILLIAN WALD to provide health care for the poor of New York. The work appealed to Goodrich's interest in public health nursing, and to her strong sense of social responsibility. With the coming of World War I, she left Henry Street to lead another significant professional battle. In a major victory for the profession, Annie Goodrich convinced the military to use trained nurses overseas, rather than volunteers, as had been planned, and to set up training schools to provide nursing care in the military hospitals at home. In 1918, the Army School of Nursing was established, with Annie Goodrich as its dean. For her work in the war, she received a Distinguished Service Medal in 1923.

In 1919, Goodrich returned to Henry Street and to Teachers College. Four years later, she received the most important appointment of her career, as dean of the School of Nursing at Yale University, an experimental school funded by the Rockefeller Foundation after the publication in 1923 of JOSEPHINE GOLDMARK's *Nursing and Nursing Education in the United States.* As Goodrich had long advocated, the school required high school and soon college diplomas for

287

admission and specified two years of course work uninterrupted by routine ward duties. Students had an eight-hour workday and received varied clinical experience in obstetrical, public health, and psychiatric nursing. In contrast to earlier practice, instructors were paid. Most important, under Goodrich's direction Yale became the first independent university school of nursing in the United States to grant the bachelor's degree. Though the first years were not without difficulties, the Rockefeller Foundation recognized the school's success by giving it a million dollar endowment in 1929.

Despite the success of the Yale program, Goodrich felt a sense of failure that her democratic vision of nursing education was not more fully realized in her lifetime. The principles she espoused were still too innovative and expensive to be widely adopted by other institutions. Not until the 1950s did collegiate schools of nursing begin to multiply.

Goodrich retired from Yale in 1934 and moved to Colchester, Conn., to be near her older sister. She continued to act as a consultant and lecturer at several institutions and received many awards and testimonials, including the Mary Adelaide Nutting Award in 1948 and the Yale Medal in 1953. She died in Cobalt, Conn., in 1954, of a stroke.

Annie Goodrich was a woman of great brilliance, wit, and vitality. The same qualities that made her a great leader—her convictions, her ambition, her energy—sometimes made her a difficult person to work with, and she often inspired hero worship rather than intimacy. Yet her comradeship with her students and other nursing colleagues provided great emotional support throughout her career. In all, Goodrich's accomplishments make her possibly the most influential figure in twentieth-century nursing.

[The major collection of Annie Goodrich's papers is at the Yale School of Nursing. See also papers in the Dept. of Archives and TCana, Teachers College Library; Nursing Archives, Mugar Library, Boston Univ. Goodrich's published works consist of *The Social and Ethical Significance of Nursing* (1932), a collection of essays, and extensive contributions to professional journals, especially the *Am. Jour. of Nursing* and *Modern Hospital*. There are two biographies: Esther A. Werminghaus, *Annie W. Goodrich: Her Journey to Yale* (1950), and Harriet B. Koch, *Militant Angel* (1951). See also Virginia Henderson, "Annie Warburton Goodrich," *Am. Jour. of Nursing*, Dec. 1955, pp. 1488–92. Biographical sketches appear in *Nat. Cyc. Am. Biog.*, XLII, 326–27, and *Dict. Am. Biog.*, Supp. Five. Marcia Curtis, "Autonomy: An Institutional Study: Yale University School of Nursing," *Nursing Research Conference*

(1972), pp. 229–47, and Mary Roberts, *American Nursing* (1954), also discuss Goodrich's role in the history of nursing education. There is a portrait at the Yale School of Nursing. A death record was provided by Conn. Dept. of Health.]

NANCY TOMES

GORDON, Dorothy Lerner, April 4, 1889–May 11, 1970. Radio and television producer and performer, singer.

The youngest of four girls, Dorothy Lerner was born in Odessa, Russia, to American parents, Leo and Rosa (Schwartz) Lerner. Her father, a lawyer associated with the foreign service, moved from post to post during her childhood; the family left Russia when she was still very young and she spent her early years largely in the Balkans and Italy. There she began to develop her versatility in European folk music and languages (she eventually claimed to speak seven fluently). In addition to tutoring and other intermittent schooling, she received formal training in voice and piano in Italy before moving to the United States. Dorothy Lerner married Bernard Gordon, a New York lawyer, on June 28, 1910. Deferring plans for a musical career, she devoted the next several years largely to raising her two sons, Frank Harmon (b. 1911), who became a lawyer, and Lincoln (b. 1913), who became a State Department official and later president of Johns Hopkins University.

Dorothy Gordon returned to singing in 1923 with a classical recital at Town Hall in New York City; the *New York Times* reviewer credited her with "personal charm and [a] pleasing voice, light and birdlike." She achieved her greatest success, though, with a different repertoire—folk songs for children. In November 1926 she offered a program of American traditional songs in costume before an audience of children at New York's Princess Theatre. Within three years, such concerts had become popular enough to be institutionalized as the "Young People's Concert Hour," which furnished the material for the first of Gordon's ten books, *Sing It Yourself* (1929). The concerts continued, with varying frequency, until 1941.

Singing for children led Dorothy Gordon into broadcasting, where she made her major contribution. She presented one of the first American radio programs for children, an appearance on New York station WEAF in April 1924. Subsequently in the 1920s, she sang on another New York station, WJZ, and on an entertainment program, the "Evening Journal Variety Hour."

After a stay in England to work with the British Broadcasting Corporation on children's programs (1929–30), Dorothy Gordon returned to assume a major role in American network radio. In 1931 the Columbia Broadcasting System (CBS) named her director of musical programs for that era's leading experiment in classroom radio, the five-day-a-week "American School of the Air." As the program's "Song and Story Lady," she persuaded James M. Barrie to authorize the first radio adaptation of his *Peter Pan* and won A. A. Milne's permission to broadcast songs from *Winnie the Pooh*. In 1936, she originated at CBS a program of dramatic adaptations, "Children's Corner," for which she wrote scripts and performed; she also set strict standards for commercials by the program's sponsor, Wheatena cereal. Late in 1938, she moved "Children's Corner" for a season to the Mutual Broadcasting System, before joining the National Broadcasting Company (NBC) as a consultant. There she was host of a new program, "Yesterday's Children" (1940), featuring adaptations of the favorite childhood books of public figures, who often appeared with Gordon on the air. Among the participants were Franklin and ELEANOR ROOSEVELT.

With United States entry into World War II, Gordon shifted her efforts decisively to public affairs programming for young people. Early in the war, she offered news commentaries for children on station WQXR in New York. She also did part-time work for the government developing children's programs for the Office of Civilian Defense and writing scripts for broadcast overseas. In 1943, asked to preside over a panel about the impact of war on children, Gordon responded that she would rather hear from the children themselves. The result was a session on April 3, 1943, sponsored by the *New York Times*, in which an audience of adults listened to a panel of nine-to-thirteen-year-olds. The meeting was the germ of the Youth Forums with which Gordon was identified for the rest of her career.

As they developed, the Youth Forums brought together youngsters chosen by classmates and teachers from local public, parochial, and private schools to discuss with an adult guest such issues as world peace, juvenile delinquency, or political ideologies. The success of the first sessions brought Gordon an offer from Iphigene Ochs Sulzberger, wife of the publisher of the *Times*, to conduct the forums as a member of the newspaper's staff. Gordon accepted, and the "*New York Times* Youth Forum" was broadcast regularly on WQXR from 1945, when the newspaper purchased the station, until 1960, when the NBC radio network took over the program under a new title, the "Dorothy Gordon Youth Forum." During this period, the broadcast changed from a children's forum to one featuring

high school and, once a month, college students.

The success of Gordon's program owed much to her skill at seeking out new issues and guests of international stature, while serving as an informed and impartial moderator for the weekly broadcasts. She brought the Forum to television in 1952, and though *Times* critic Jack Gould took her to task at one point for an "excess of classroom formality," the program continued to be seen on the Dumont network until 1958 and then on WNBC-TV in New York (1958–70). In a quarter century on the air, the Youth Forum collected more than a hundred citations and awards, including the George Foster Peabody Award for radio broadcasting (1959, 1964, 1966), and an Emmy from the National Academy of Television Arts and Sciences.

Dorothy Gordon never retired. In 1965, then in her mid-seventies, she called the Youth Forum "*the* important work of my life"; she believed that "when we encourage a flow of ideas between young people of varying backgrounds, and encourage them to think about the world and humanity, we are planting the seeds of democracy." She continued the broadcasts until her death in May 1970, at her home on West 57th Street in New York City. On May 17 NBC broadcast a memorial to Gordon in the time originally scheduled for the Forum, bringing together students, journalists, and public figures who had appeared on her program, to pay tribute to the "flow of ideas" she had set in motion.

[*The Reminiscences of Dorothy Gordon* (1951), in the Oral History Coll., Columbia Univ., should be used cautiously with regard to chronology and dates. Gordon's views on broadcasting for children are set forth most fully in *All Children Listen* (1942). Her other books include *Around the World in Song* (1930), *Come to France* (1939), *Dorothy Gordon's Treasure Bag of Game Songs* (1939), *You and Democracy* (1951), and *Who Knows the Answer?* (1965). A biographical summary appeared in *Current Biog.*, 1955, and an obituary by Alden Whitman in *N.Y. Times*, May 12, 1970; both are accompanied by a 1953 photograph. Although Gordon sometimes gave her year of birth as 1893, her obituary lists 1889, the year confirmed by her son Frank Gordon. Sources spell her mother's maiden name alternately as Schwartz or Schwarz. Press releases were furnished by NBC, and a biobibliography by Anne Jones.]

JAMES BOYLAN

GRABLE, Betty, Dec. 18, 1916–July 2, 1973. Actress.

Betty Grable, Hollywood film star, was the highest-salaried American woman in the mid-1940s, earning $300,000 a year. She had achieved little success in films until the early forties, when historical events produced a cultural need: the harsh realities of war engendered a national desire, shared by men and women alike, to fantasize and to dream, and her films met this need.

Betty Grable was a sex symbol to millions of servicemen; a series of films, all emphasizing her figure and her famous legs, drew over 3,000,000 requests for pin-up photos; 60,000 copies were once mailed in a single week. Her film characterizations denoted innocence, however, and to the lonely homesick men who watched them they supported the fantasy of the sweet, wholesome, innocent girl who was also a sexual bombshell. But women liked Betty Grable too. Her acting, singing, and dancing were adequate but not exceptional, a fact partly responsible for her success; girls with average talent could identify with her. As one writer observed, to "the ambitious stenographer, the Hollywood-hungry mother dragging her little daughter off to dancing school, Betty represents . . . a daydream that might come true" (*Time*, 1948, p. 40).

Betty Grable was born Ruth Elizabeth in St. Louis, Mo., one of two daughters of Leon and Lillian (Hoffman) Grable. Her father was an accountant and stockbroker. Lillian Grable was an archetypal stage mother who insisted that Betty take acting, singing, dancing, and music lessons from the age of four, denying her privileges if she missed even one lesson. "I dreaded every lesson and I especially hated acrobatics," Grable recalled (*Time*, 1948, p. 40). Her mother even tried to make her perform in hotel lobbies, but "I wouldn't. I died inside at the thought of it" (*Sat. Eve. Post*, p. 110). Eventually she took her daughter to Hollywood, leaving her husband behind. Betty Grable recognized that her mother was the "driving force" of her life, but accepted her constant surveillance.

Claiming to be fifteen in order to get the part, Betty Grable first appeared as a chorine in *Let's Go Places* (1930). Using the name Frances Dean, she moved from studio to studio playing small parts and appearing in film shorts. Her brightest moment at RKO was her performance in Fred Astaire's *The Gay Divorcee* (1934), which won her a contract from the studio. She did a zany number with Edward Everett Horton and projected a winsome charm. In 1936, she moved to Paramount Pictures where she made several of the then popular college films as the studio tried to establish her as "Betty Coed."

The following year, after a long engagement, Betty Grable married Jackie Coogan (her contract forbade her to marry before she was twenty-one), and helped him finance his famous

lawsuit over his misappropriated salary. They were divorced in 1940, the same year her parents divorced. She married bandleader Harry James in 1943 and they had two daughters, Victoria (b. 1944) and Jessica (b. 1946). Their marriage ended in divorce in 1965.

Betty Grable's career had failed to take hold until 1939 when she appeared in the Broadway show *Du Barry Was a Lady* with Ethel Merman. Its success led to a contract with Twentieth Century-Fox, and she replaced an ailing Alice Faye in *Down Argentine Way* (1940). Fox promoted her legs as a publicity angle, she caught on, costarred with Faye in *Tin Pan Alley* (1940), and eventually starred throughout the decade in an assortment of lush technicolor musicals, among them *Song of the Islands* (1942), *Footlight Serenade* (1942), *Springtime in the Rockies* (1942), and *Four Jills in a Jeep* (1944). Her films were extraordinarily successful at the box office. Grable frequently worked with Dan Dailey (*Mother Wore Tights*, 1947; *My Blue Heaven*, 1950; and others) and was reunited with him for a condensed Las Vegas stage version of *Guys and Dolls* (1962). She shared star billing with MARILYN MONROE and Lauren Bacall in *How to Marry a Millionaire* (1953), her best-known film of the 1950s.

Grable had no pretensions about her abilities, but her movies were fun. She worked hard, was thoroughly professional, down-to-earth, and likable. Blue-eyed, five feet three and a half inches tall, she had a chronic weight problem that necessitated severe dieting before every film. Her appeal diminished with time, and although she was only thirty-four when she made *Wabash Avenue* (1950) her career was already beginning to slip.

After her last film, *How to Be Very, Very Popular* (1955), she made many comeback attempts on the nightclub circuit and the stage; a 1959 review described her as "trembling with fatigue" after a show (*Time*, 1959, p. 68). Many of her old fans remained loyally vociferous but she never regained her former popularity. She made some television appearances in the late 1950s and in the 1960s, bought a home in Las Vegas (she liked gambling), and enjoyed seeing her many friends. Betty Grable died of lung cancer in 1973 in Santa Monica, Calif.

[A short but detailed biography appears in James Parish, *The Fox Girls* (1970); it captures some of the period during which Grable starred and also includes a complete filmography. "Living the Daydream," *Time*, Aug. 23, 1948, is a detailed and sympathetic article, stressing the hardships of Grable's upbringing. Equally sympathetic and vivid is Pete Martin, "The World's Most Popular Blonde," *Sat. Eve. Post*, April 1950, which profiles her personality at work and at home. Also useful are G. Ringgold, "Betty Grable," *Screen Facts*, vol. 4, no. 1 (n.d.); Kyle Crichton, "Out on Two Limbs," *Collier's*, May 17, 1941; "Ham and Legs," *Time*, April 13, 1959; Jeffrey Gorney, "Betty Grable, 1916–1973," *Films in Review*, Aug.-Sept. 1973; "Betty Grable," in David Thomson, *Biog. Dict. of Film* (1975); and an obituary in the *N.Y. Times*, July 4, 1973. A birth certificate was provided by the St. Louis City Registrar; death certificate from Calif. Dept. of Public Health.]

ALMA L. KENNEY

GREEN, Constance McLaughlin, Aug. 21, 1897–Dec. 5, 1975. Historian.

Constance Winsor McLaughlin was born in Ann Arbor, Mich., the fourth of six children and first of three daughters of Lois Thompson (Angell) and Andrew Cunningham McLaughlin. Her mother was the daughter of the University of Michigan's distinguished president James B. Angell, and her father taught history at the university. Andrew McLaughlin moved his family in 1903 to Washington, D.C., where he organized the Bureau of Historical Research for the Carnegie Institute while writing *The Confederation and the Constitution* (1905). The much-acclaimed book led to his appointment as chairman of the history department of the University of Chicago.

Connie, as she was known from early youth, started school in Washington and later attended the Laboratory School begun by John Dewey and ALICE CHIPMAN DEWEY at the University of Chicago. Her mother, disappointed that she had been denied a college education, encouraged her daughters to prepare for careers. McLaughlin entered the University of Chicago in 1914, but transferred two years later to Smith College "to see whether I had anything to offer on my own." A history major, she received her A.B. in 1919 and then taught English briefly at the University of Chicago. In February 1921 she married Donald Ross Green, an executive of the Farr Alpaca Co. in Holyoke, Mass. Avid for more intellectual stimulation than the town of Holyoke provided, she taught English part-time at nearby Smith College (1921–22), received an A.M. in history from Mount Holyoke College (1925), and served as a part-time instructor there from 1925 to 1932. Her three children were born during this period: Lois in 1922, Donald Ross, Jr., in 1925, and Elizabeth in 1928 (d. 1970).

When the depression forced curtailments at Mount Holyoke, with the encouragement of her husband and support from her mother-in-law she resumed her graduate studies, this time at Yale University. She was granted credits for teaching experience and encouraged by Professor Ralph Gabriel to take the history of Holyoke as a thesis topic. With a scholarly scent for documentary sources acquired from her father and with assistance from her husband's business connections, Constance Green located and examined mill records, newspaper files, and family papers. She produced an illuminating history of a small industrial city that won her a Ph.D. from Yale in 1937. *Holyoke, Massachusetts: A Case History of the Industrial Revolution in America,* published in 1939, was one of the early scholarly works in the new field of urban history. A source of some controversy in Holyoke, the book received Yale's Eggleston prize in history.

Working largely outside the traditional confines of academic life, Constance Green held a series of research appointments and published an impressive number of books. From 1939 to 1946 she was director of research for the Smith College Council of Industrial Relations and supervised dissertations that explored the industrial development of the Connecticut Valley. She also taught occasionally part-time in the economics department. During the war, she served as official historian to the United States Army Ordnance Department in Springfield, Mass. She moved to Washington, D.C., following her husband's death in 1946, working first as historian for the American National Red Cross and then, with more satisfaction, as the chief historian for the Army Ordnance Corps (1948–51) and as historian in the Department of Defense (1951–54). Possessed of a gracious manner, a sparkling wit, and a firm grasp of historical techniques, she was able, despite her modest stature and gentle voice, to win the respect of army officials. She coauthored one volume of the series on *The United States Army in World War II*. While finding the army associations agreeable, she was not deflected from the nascent field of urban history. An assignment to write the history of Naugatuck and an invitation to give a series of lectures on American cities at the University of London, published in book form as *American Cities in the Growth of the Nation* (1957), made her the most versatile pioneer in the field.

By the 1950s urban history was coming of age. Green became an active participant in the American Historical Association's Urban History Group formed in 1953. Her report to that group on her projected history of Washington precipitated a debate over the nature and objectives of urban history in which Green, while not unappreciative of the techniques of the new urban history, including use of the computer, advanced a view of the field that left room for narrative sweep and colorful detail. She had been invited by the Rockefeller Foundation to write a pilot study of American urban history that analyzed the process of urbanization, but proposed instead, and secured backing for, the writing of a rounded history of the nation's capital. Working at American University, with able assistants, she tackled Washington's voluminous documentary and other records, tracing the city's development from a model plan through its crude early stages into a beautiful though still hectic national capital.

The first volume, *Washington: Village and Capital, 1800–1878*, published in 1962, won the Pulitzer Prize in history in 1963, twenty-seven years after her father had received a similar award. A second volume, published a year later, carried Washington's history forward to 1950. The books, hailed as the most distinguished of the new urban biographies, gave considerable attention to the large and active contingent of blacks in the city's population. In the mounting concern for civil rights during the sixties, Green, an ardent member of Americans for Democratic Action, added a third volume, *The Secret City: A History of Race Relations in the Nation's Capital* (1967).

These and other writings, including her study of *The Role of Women as Production Workers in War Plants of the Connecticut Valley* (1946), were models of objective scholarship. They reflected as well Constance Green's confidence, inherited from her father, that an understanding of the origins and course of racial and other minority problems and of urban developments in all their complexity would enable citizens to perform their functions more satisfactorily. Her readiness, despite a pressing scholarly schedule, to serve on civic and institutional boards (the Landmark Committee of the National Capital Planning Commission, the Committee on the History of Social Welfare, among others) further demonstrated her democratic commitment. Poor health in her last years forced a curtailment of her researches. She died in December 1975 of generalized arteriosclerosis in Annapolis, Md., where she had moved to live with her daughter, also a historian.

[The Smith College Archives contain a folder of Constance McLaughlin Green's letters, photographs, and clippings, including an early tribute by Mina Curtiss, and an oral history tape. Green's published works not named above include: "The Value of Local History," in Caroline F. Ware, ed., *The Cultural Approach to History* (1940), pp. 275–86; *History of Naugatuck, Connecticut* (1948); *The Ordnance Department: Planning Munitions for War* (1955), with Henry C. Thomson and Peter C. Roots; *Eli Whitney and the Birth of American Technology* (1956); *Washington: Capital City, 1879–1950*

(1963); *The Rise of Urban America* (1965); *The Church on Lafayette Square: A History of St. John's Church, Washington, D.C. 1810–1970* (1970); and *Vanguard: A History* (1971), with Milton Lomask. She also wrote numerous book reviews for historical journals and contributed articles to the *Encyc. Britannica* and the *Encyc. Americana*. The most complete account of Green's career is "A Conversation with Constance McLaughlin Green," in Bruce M. Stave, *The Making of Urban History* (1977), pp. 103–42, which includes a selected bibliography. See also *Contemporary Authors*, vol. 9–12, pp. 343–44 and *Dict. Am. Biog.*, Supp. Four, on Andrew Cunningham McLaughlin. Obituaries appeared in *Holyoke Transcript & Telegraph*, Dec. 8, 1975; *N.Y. Times*, Dec. 8, 1975; and *Wash. Post*, Dec. 7, 1975. A death certificate was provided by Md. Dept. of Health.]

BLAKE MC KELVEY

GRIFFIN, Marion Lucy Mahony, Feb. 14, 1871–Aug. 10, 1961? Architect, delineator.

Marion Lucy Mahony was born in Chicago, the older of two daughters and second of five children of Clara (Perkins) and Jeremiah Mahony. Her mother was a descendant of early settlers of New England; her father, who became a poet, journalist, schoolteacher, and principal in Chicago, came as a child to Illinois from his native Cork, Ireland. After her father's death in 1882, her mother, a teacher who became principal of the Kamensky School, supported the family. Marion Mahony attended public schools in Winnetka, Ill., and Chicago. In 1890, with financial help from Chicago civic leader Mary Wilmarth, she entered the architecture course at the Massachusetts Institute of Technology (MIT), then strongly influenced by the École des Beaux Arts. She may have been directed toward this career by her cousin, Dwight Perkins, a Chicago architect who had also graduated from MIT and with whom she worked briefly following her 1894 graduation. She was the second woman to complete the MIT course. Mahony became the first woman registered to practice architecture in Illinois. In 1895 she began an association with the architect Frank Lloyd Wright, and worked at his Oak Park, Ill., studio. The studio was the source of the Prairie School, the most important indigenous movement in American architecture, and as both designer and delineator Mahony made fundamental contributions to the work done there.

Mahony's decisive moment at the studio came in 1909 when Wright departed suddenly for Europe, leaving behind a number of uncompleted commissions. Prior to leaving, Wright had asked Mahony to take over direction of the studio, but she refused. The architect H. V. Von Holst agreed to take charge on condition that Mahony would work as his designer. Architect Walter Burley Griffin (1876–1937), who had been office manager of the studio from 1901 to 1906, worked with Von Holst and Mahony as landscape consultant.

It has been established that during Wright's absence Marion Mahony designed the David Amberg house, Grand Rapids, Mich. (1909–11); the Adolph Mueller house, Decatur, Ill. (1910); and a fully designed but unexecuted house for Henry Ford. Earlier, she had completed an independent commission for the Church of All Souls in Evanston, Ill. (1902–03). After 1909, Mahony's relations with Wright came to an end. Wright accused her of stealing clients and architectural projects; bitter at the false accusations, and disapproving of Wright's private life, Mahony never forgave him.

Marion Mahony's marriage to Walter Burley Griffin on June 29, 1911, in Michigan City, Ind., brought an important change in her life. While she continued to be professionally active, she claimed no credit for her work on projects designed by her husband. She assisted him in winning the 1912 competition for the design of Canberra, the new capital city of Australia, and she accompanied him there in 1914. For over twenty years they worked together in Australia, living in both Sydney and Melbourne, where they were also successful amateur horticulturists. Walter Griffin moved his practice to Lucknow, India, in October 1935, and Marion Mahony Griffin joined him there in June 1936. When he died the following year, Marion Griffin wound up the work of the Lucknow office, spent several months in Australia, and, at the age of sixty-seven, returned to Chicago and resumed independent practice. Remaining active for over two decades, she produced some subdivision plans reminiscent of her husband's work, and some house designs. She also wrote a rambling autobiographical and philosophical manuscript, "The Magic of America," which incorporated the biography of her husband and reflected her belief in anthroposophy.

The designs attributed to Marion Griffin demonstrate the high order of her professional skills as an architect. Less clear, but perhaps more important in the total view of her career, are her contributions to the designs of Wright and Walter Burley Griffin. In these associations she was an incomparable delineator, as her drawings of their designs and plans demonstrate. The art of the delineator was fully recognized in the early years of the century, and such drawings were often signed, Griffin's by her distinctive

monogram. Her drawings frequently assumed a vertical composition, with the elevation of the building at the top of the plate, and plans and details below. Carefully drawn trees, with well-defined columnar trunks and highly detailed foliage, were characteristic but also echoed the contemporary art nouveau. Ink wash was her favorite medium, and while she frequently drew on tracing paper, a typical medium of the period, she also worked on linen drafting cloth (even window shades). Many of her large and spectacular renderings, such as that of Griffin's Rock Crest–Rock Glen group of houses at Mason City, Iowa, used colored inks and gold on sateen or silk. Her renderings constituted the bulk of the richly presented *Ausgeführte Bauten und Entwürfe von Frank Lloyd Wright* (1910), known as the Wasmuth Portfolio, which represented the first international recognition of Wright's significance.

Marion Mahony Griffin was remembered by an associate at the Oak Park studio as "so homely that she looked almost distinguished. She had a fragile frame and walked as though she were falling forward. She was a good actress, talkative, and when around Wright there was a real sparkle" (*The Prairie School*, p. 79). She may have been "more an artist than an architect," as H. Allen Brooks has observed; but an architect she was indisputably, by education, qualification, and demonstrated ability. If her contribution was more to the presentation of the work of Wright and others of the Prairie School, and was subsequently merged with the career of her husband, it was not less significant.

[Marion Mahony Griffin's drawings are at the Northwestern Univ. art department; the N.Y. Hist. Soc.; Avery Library, Columbia Univ.; and the Burnham Library, Art Inst. of Chicago. Both the Burnham Library and the N.Y. Hist. Soc. have copies of "The Magic of America." Her professional life has been detailed by H. Allen Brooks, *The Prairie School: Frank Lloyd Wright and His Midwest Contemporaries* (1972), which reproduces and discusses many of her drawings and considers her relationships with Wright and other contemporaries. An important study is David Van Zanten, "The Early Work of Marion Mahony Griffin," *Prairie School Rev.*, vol. 3, no. 2, 1966. Her work with Griffin is described in David Van Zanten, ed., *Walter Burley Griffin: Selected Designs* (1970). Further details, including color plates, are in Donald L. Johnson, *Architecture of Walter Burley Griffin* (1977). The first adequate appreciation of Mahony's significance was in Grant Carpenter Manson, *Frank Lloyd Wright to 1910, the First Golden Age* (1958). See also the critical appraisal by Susan Fondiler Berkon and Jane Holtz Kay, "Marion Mahony Griffin, Architect," *Feminist Art Jour.*, Spring 1975; Mark L. Peisch, *The Chicago School* of Architecture: Early Followers of Sullivan and Wright (1964); and H. Allen Brooks, "Frank Lloyd Wright and the Wasmuth Drawings," Art Bull., June 1966, pp. 193–202. Some sources give 1962 as the date of Griffin's death. The Aug. 10, 1961, date was provided by the MIT Alumni Office. James Weirick, who is preparing a biography of Walter Burley Griffin, provided information on family history and other details. Additional assistance was supplied by Cecilia Chin of the Art Inst. of Chicago.]

FREDERICK GUTHEIM

GROSSINGER, Jennie, June 16, 1892–Nov. 20, 1972. Hotel executive, philanthropist.

Jennie Grossinger was born in Baligrod, a small village in Galicia, Austria, the elder daughter and oldest of three children of Asher Selig and Malka (Grumet) Grossinger. Her father was an estate overseer, a common occupation for village Jews in eastern Europe; her mother was the daughter of a Galician country innkeeper.

Leaving his family behind, Selig Grossinger migrated to New York City in 1897 in search of better economic opportunities. His wife and two daughters joined him in 1900, settling on the Lower East Side. There Grossinger earned a modest livelihood as a coat presser in a garment factory. On their arrival Jennie was enrolled in a traditional Jewish elementary school, as well as at P.S. 174, but her formal education ended four years later, when she quit school to take a job as a buttonholemaker. Working an eleven-hour day while attending night school, she helped to support her father and sent money to her mother, who had returned to Europe seeking a cure for Jennie's brother, a deaf-mute.

She married her cousin Harry Grossinger on May 25, 1912, and they moved into an apartment next door to her parents. While her husband worked as a production man in a garment factory, Jennie Grossinger joined her parents as a waitress in their new enterprise, a dairy restaurant. Her first child, born prematurely in 1913, died within two days.

In 1914 the ailing Selig Grossinger decided to move to the country for his health. With borrowed money he bought a small farm in Ferndale, N.Y., in the Catskill Mountains. To meet expenses the Grossingers followed Jewish immigrant custom and took in summer boarders. Their guests were fellow immigrants from New York City, who, as they moved into the middle classes, sought low-cost vacations in the country in hotels with kosher food and warm hospitality. While Malka Grossinger presided over the kitchen and won renown as a cook, her elder daughter assumed responsibilities as chamber-

maid, bookkeeper, and hostess. Harry Grossinger assisted his in-laws and wife by doing the marketing in New York City and actively recruiting guests. Despite its modest facilities—no heat, electricity, or indoor plumbing—the boarding house succeeded, boosted by word-of-mouth advertising from guests who appreciated large portions of good food and inexpensive rates. In 1919, partly at Jennie Grossinger's initiative, the family sold the original farmhouse and purchased nearby property with more extensive grounds and a suitably equipped hotel building.

Jennie Grossinger had given birth to a son, Paul, in September 1915, but she continued to work long hours at the hotel. With some feelings of guilt, she shared his care with members of her extended family and the hotel staff. When her daughter, Elaine Joy, was born in December 1927 she hired a nurse-governess to look after the child.

Jennie Grossinger's role as hostess and business manager was an increasingly important asset to the hotel. Her charm, friendly smile, and personal concern for her guests' satisfaction inspired clients to return yearly, allowing Grossinger's to compete successfully with other Catskill Mountain resorts. She provided the ambience of a family-run enterprise even as the hotel expanded in the economic boom which followed World War I. Drawing on the advice of guests and a visit to a rival resort, by the mid-1920s Grossinger had introduced tennis courts, a bridle path, a children's camp, a social director, and resident professional entertainers, many of whom went on to fame as singers and comedians. Attuned to innovative business techniques, she made effective use of advertising and hired a public relations man as early as 1927. "Grossinger's has everything" became the hotel's slogan.

Even though the hotel barely broke even during the depression, Jennie and Harry Grossinger continued to improve their property and to develop a year-round luxury resort. To attract publicity, in 1934 they brought the boxer Barney Ross to the hotel, the first of many fighters to train at Grossinger's.

Jennie Grossinger's career was shadowed by ill health. She suffered from severe headaches, chronic high blood pressure, and bouts of depression and back ailments for which she was hospitalized. After the death of her father in December 1931, she was hospitalized again. In both 1941 and 1946 she underwent major surgery.

Because of her ill health, Grossinger began to delegate many of her former responsibilities at the hotel. Beginning in the mid-1930s, she devoted much of her energy to numerous philanthropic causes, both nonsectarian and Jewish. She received many awards for philanthropy, as well as two honorary degrees, and in 1954 was the subject of the television program *This Is Your Life.*

Jennie Grossinger's fame helped the resort to diversify its clientele and in the 1940s and 1950s she presided over its further transformation. Increasingly, in the years after World War II, the resort catered to guests who were not Orthodox Jews; in recognition of this fact Grossinger's began in 1948 to offer entertainment on the Jewish Sabbath.

After her husband's death in July 1964, Grossinger turned over responsibility for administering the resort to her children, who had long been involved in its management. By then Grossinger's included 1,200 acres and thirty-five buildings, and served 150,000 guests a year. Jennie Grossinger died in her cottage at Grossinger's in November 1972 of a stroke. She had become the best-known hotelkeeper in America.

[Grossinger published a book of recipes used at the hotel, *The Art of Jewish Cooking* (1958). The best biography is Joel Pomerantz, *Jennie and the Story of Grossinger's* (1970), which includes information on her philanthropic activities. More anecdotal is Harold Jaediker Taub, *Waldorf-in-the-Catskills: The Grossinger Legend* (1952). A more critical view is presented in Tania Grossinger, *Growing Up at Grossinger's* (1975). Also useful are articles by Morris Freedman, "The Green Pastures of Grossinger's," *Commentary,* July 1954, pp. 56–63 and Aug. 1954, pp. 147–54; David Boroff, "The Saga of the 'G'," *Coronet,* July 1959, pp. 163–69; Quentin Reynolds, "Jennie," *Look,* July 13, 1965, pp. 86–88ff. An obituary appeared in the *N.Y. Times,* Nov. 21, 1972; death record from N.Y. State Dept. of Health.]

PAULA E. HYMAN

GRUENBERG, Sidonie Matsner, June 10, 1881–March 11, 1974. Parent education leader.

Sidonie Gruenberg, writer and director of the Child Study Association of America, was born near Vienna, Austria, the oldest of the four daughters and two sons of Idore and Augusta Olivia (Basséchés) Matzner. Her mother was the daughter of a wealthy German grain exporter. Her father, the son of an Austrian town mayor, was educated at the University of Cracow and inherited a share in the family distillery business. In 1895, after several visits to the United States, Idore Matzner took his family to live in New York, but two years later he suffered a paralyzing stroke. Having had a sixth child, Augusta Matzner was determined to stay in New York, and with assistance from her

brothers in Europe she began an unusual career as an importer of scrap rubber.

Sidonie Matsner (the spelling of the family name was changed) was tutored at the family home near Vienna and briefly attended the Höhere Töchterschule in Hamburg. Shortly after arriving in the United States she was enrolled in Felix Adler's Ethical Culture School in New York City, then called the Workingman's School. She came to share Adler's belief in science and reform, and his philosophy of "deed before creed." Matsner graduated in 1897. As a result of her father's death in 1902, she became her mother's partner in managing the household and business. She also augmented the family income as a bilingual secretary.

In 1903 Sidonie Matsner married Benjamin Charles Gruenberg (1875–1965), in an Ethical Culture ceremony. He, too, came from an educated Jewish background and was attracted by Adler's reformist and egalitarian ideas. Gruenberg was a biologist, author, and educator. He headed the biology and science department of the New York public school system from 1902 to 1920, and later was a consultant and writer on issues relating to science and education. In a lifelong blend of partnership and affection, the Gruenbergs coauthored three books and frequently collaborated as consultants and lecturers. They had four children: Herbert (b. 1907); Richard (b. 1910); Hilda (b. 1913); and Ernest (b. 1915).

After one year of marriage Sidonie Gruenberg began advocating employment for married women. She continued her education at the Ethical Culture Normal School, graduating in 1906, and participated in the woman suffrage and child labor reform movements. Gruenberg eventually went to work for Ethical Culture, compiling a catalog of part-time jobs for women, and began graduate courses at Teachers College, Columbia University. After the birth of her first child, she joined a mother's study group sponsored by the Federation of Child Study.

The Federation, begun in 1888, was an association of Ethical Culture mothers interested in the study of infancy and early childhood development. Their readings on the subject ranged from Plato, Rousseau, and Locke to modern psychologists and educators such as John Dewey and A. A. Brill, Sigmund Freud's first translator and popularizer in America. The Federation was eclectic in its approach to child study and open to a variety of innovative ideas.

In 1912 Gruenberg wrote *Your Child Today and Tomorrow,* in which she first articulated the recurrent themes of her career. The book, which developed from topics discussed in Federation study groups, dealt clearly and informally with such subjects as discipline, imagination, sex education, and fear, and offered personal experiences in illustration. Parenthood, Gruenberg believed, encompassed skills and knowledge that could be learned and applied; traditional methods of childrearing should give way to more flexible methods derived from recent advances in the biological and behavioral sciences. Gruenberg skillfully collected and synthesized the newest scientific research and translated it into language parents could understand, a talent that doubtless contributed to her growing popularity as a speaker and lecturer. She integrated her private and professional lives with assistance from household help, and a large extended family. The education and development of her children were consistently her main interests.

In 1924, with a grant from the Laura Spelman Rockefeller Foundation, the Federation of Child Study expanded to become the Child Study Association of America (CSAA), with Sidonie Gruenberg as director. She also served as chairman and board member of the National Council of Parent Education, established with CSAA sponsorship in 1925 under the direction of EDNA NOBLE WHITE.

An energetic executive, Gruenberg expanded educational services to parents, recruited memberships, managed fund raising, and spoke persuasively in behalf of parent education across the country. From 1928 to 1937 she taught courses in parent education leadership at Columbia University and New York University, and published scores of articles on topics of interest to parents. In 1933 she and her husband coauthored *Your Child and Money,* in which they advocated a progressive, learn-by-doing approach to teaching the value of money.

Gruenberg brought the CSAA to national prominence by promoting parent education as an information exchange between professional researchers and families, given impetus by the needs of parents themselves: "We have long since abandoned the quaint notion that we acquire the arts and skills of parenthood by instinct" ("Parent Education," pp. 81–87). The CSAA played an important part in the burgeoning progressive education movement in New York City, and generally favored a psychoanalytic approach to childrearing.

In the 1940s, as the war in Europe gained momentum, Sidonie Gruenberg and her husband helped relatives escape from Germany; all three of their sons served in active duty. As women felt the tension between the need to do patriotic work and to maintain stability at home, parent education gradually became less child-centered and began to focus on the family as a whole. Gruenberg served as an adviser to the United States Children's Bureau on issues of children in wartime, and edited *The Family in a World at War* (1942), written to help parents contend with the devastating effects of war on family life.

After her retirement from the CSAA in 1950, Sidonie Gruenberg became a special consultant to Doubleday for education and children's literature. Her most successful books, *The Wonderful Story of How You Were Born* (1952) and *The Encyclopedia of Child Care and Guidance* (1954) were written during this period. She also coauthored *The Many Lives of Modern Women* (1952) with her daughter, Hilda Krech; the book chronicles changes in the family and in women's roles. Gruenberg died of cancer at her home in New York City at the age of ninety-two.

Sidonie Gruenberg favored flexible methods of childrearing and expanded roles for women, and emphasized the need for women to pursue meaningful work in addition to domestic responsibilities. In 1931, in a *Delineator* article on vocational guidance for girls, she had written: "The present high school girl will have to visualize her life as made up of successive phases . . . and choose not once, but many times." Throughout her career, she encouraged women who were seeking wider possibilities for their lives.

[The Benjamin and Sidonie Gruenberg Coll. at the Library of Congress contains extensive family and general correspondence from 1892 to 1970, including diaries, scrapbooks, and unpublished MSS. Information about Gruenberg's early life can be found there in an unpublished MS. by Augusta O. Matzner and an unfinished autobiography. The Social Welfare Hist. Archive at the Univ. of Minn. has the CSAA papers, containing Gruenberg's professional collection. There is no adequate biography. For general information see: *Who's Who of Am. Women,* 1974–75; *Current Biog.,* 1940; *N.Y. Times* obituary, March 13, 1974. See Howard B. Radest, *Toward Common Ground: The Story of the Ethical Societies in the United States* (1969), for her association with the Ethical Culture Society. Interviews with Herbert Gruenberg, Ernest Gruenberg, and especially Hilda Krech provided valuable information about the family. Steven Schlossman provided background on the CSAA.]

ROBERTA WOLLONS

H

HAGOOD, Margaret Loyd Jarman, Oct. 26, 1907–Aug. 13, 1963. Sociologist, statistician, demographer.

Margaret Jarman Hagood was born in Newton County, Ga., the second child and second daughter among the four daughters and two sons of Lewis Wilson and Laura Harris (Martin) Jarman. Her mother and father were strict Presbyterians, of Scots-Irish and English descent, respectively. Lewis Jarman, a mathematician by training, combined farming and school teaching and actively encouraged his daughters' education.

Margaret was a precocious youngster, who organized a Sunday school class for mill children when she was thirteen, and gave violin lessons at an early age. She studied at Emory-at-Oxford, a preparatory school in Covington, Ga., and then at Agnes Scott College in Atlanta. In 1926 she left college to marry a childhood sweetheart, Middleton Howard Hagood, and in 1927 gave birth to her only child, also named Margaret. Meantime Lewis Jarman had become president of Queen's College in Charlotte, N.C., and she matriculated there, graduating in 1929.

At Emory University in Atlanta, where her husband was studying dentistry, Margaret Hagood completed an A.M. in mathematics in 1930. With the onset of the depression, she decided she should contribute to the family exchequer; to this end she took a job at the National Park Seminary in College Park, Md., where she taught for four years.

In 1935 Howard Odum, a family friend from Newton County and at that time head of the Institute for Research in Social Science at the University of North Carolina, offered her a graduate fellowship in sociology. She joined the group of young scholars clustered around Odum—Rupert Vance, Katharine Jocher, Guy and Guion Johnson—all of whom were engaged in pioneering sociological studies in the southern region.

"Marney," as she was called, soon became a key figure in this group, noted for her intensity of purpose and her capacity to become totally immersed in her work. Her strong bent toward mathematics took her into two rapidly developing and related fields: sociological statistics and demography. She was destined to make original contributions to both.

Associates from this period of her life remember her as tolerant and thoughtful, always willing to listen to other people's problems but singularly unrevealing of herself. Among her friends were some of the Chapel Hill radicals of the 1930s (a fact that brought her a small encounter with McCarthyism twenty years later, when she was prevented by the FBI from attending an international conference in Rome because of her alleged communist sympathies). She is pictured in recollections as a person so caught up in her work that she sometimes forgot to comb her hair, or even to eat regular meals.

In 1936, after living apart for some time, Margaret Hagood and her husband were formally divorced. A year later she finished her dissertation, a pioneering statistical analysis of the fertility patterns of white women in the rural southeast—the region of highest population growth in the nation. She was then appointed to the department of sociology and made a research associate in the Institute for Research in Social Science. Soon after Hagood decided to examine the same population from a different perspective: traveling through several southern states, she interviewed at length more than 240 wives of tenant farmers and wrote a careful social study of tenant life. Published as *Mothers of the South,* this book is a sensitive document of a vanishing way of life, and one of the best records available of the daily experience of poverty-stricken white southern farmers in the midst of the depression.

Hagood then began another project, which also belongs with the documentary expression of the thirties. With a fellow sociologist, Harriet Herring, and two photographers from the staff of the Farm Security Administration, Marion Post and DOROTHEA LANGE, she compiled a detailed photographic record of the patterns of agriculture and farm life in the southeast. This striking study formed the basis for an exhibit at the University of North Carolina in 1940, and, but for the disruption of World War II, would doubtless have been made into a book.

Hagood continued to refine and expand her studies in statistics and demography. *Statistics for Sociologists,* published in 1941 and in several later editions, was a landmark work that influenced a whole generation of graduate students, and hence the direction of the discipline. The social sciences were then in the process of becoming far more quantitative, relying to an increasing extent on complex statistical methods; thanks to Hagood's work, sociology was among the first to move in this direction.

When the war drew students away from Chapel Hill, Hagood decided she could work more usefully at the United States Department of Agriculture: in the Bureau of Agricultural Economics (1942–52) and in the Farm Population and Rural Life Branch of the Agricultural

Marketing Service (which she headed after 1952), she was able to initiate demographic studies of farm populations. Among her achievements was the invention of the "level-of-living index" for each county in the United States—an index that could be modified after each successive census and that enabled policymakers in Washington to make useful comparisons among counties. Alone, and with colleagues in other parts of the government as well as in the United Nations, she published numerous reports and articles. She also represented the department in interagency discussions of agricultural manpower, farm population, and general labor-force concepts. Her work won national recognition when she was elected president of the Population Association of America in 1954, and of the Rural Sociological Society in 1956.

In the mid-1950s Hagood developed a rheumatic heart condition; the sturdy young woman who had climbed Mt. Mitchell three times gradually became a frail and sedentary person whose capacity for work and research was sadly diminished. She retired in 1962 and died of a heart attack in 1963 in San Diego, Calif., the home of one of her brothers.

Hagood's intensity of purpose and capacity for hard work may have shortened her life, but they also enabled her to accomplish a prodigious amount of work. She takes her place as a pioneer in two fields, statistics and demography, which were to become central to the study of sociology in the late twentieth century.

[There is no collection of papers; some information may be found in the Alumni Office, Univ. of N.C., and the alumnae files of Queens College. Hagood's 1940 photographic study is in the Howard Washington Odum Papers, Southern Hist. Coll., Univ. of N.C. Something of her personality emerges in *Mothers of the South*, but few personal documents seem to have survived. During her tenure at the Dept. of Agriculture, Hagood published a number of studies and reports; they are listed in the *Nat. Agricultural Library Dict. Catalog*. Some biographical information is available in obituaries in *Am. Statistician*, Oct. 1963; *Rural Sociology*, Jan. 1964; and *Population Index*, Jan. 1964, which includes a bibliography of her publications in demography. The introduction by Anne Firor Scott to the reprint edition of *Mothers of the South* (1977) contains an analysis of Hagood's career. Further assistance was provided by her sister Alice Jarman Browder and her colleague Daniel O. Price. Death certificate provided by the Calif. Dept. of Public Health.]

ANNE FIROR SCOTT

HAINES, Helen Elizabeth, Feb. 9, 1872–Aug. 26, 1961. Librarian.

Helen Haines's work in the art of book selec-

tion and her defense of intellectual freedom during the 1940s and 1950s earned her a permanent place in the history of American librarianship. Helen Haines was born in New York City, the eldest of five daughters of Benjamin Reeves and Mary (Hodges) Haines. Her mother was Irish; her father, a merchant, was from old New Jersey Quaker stock. He died when Helen was a girl. She was educated at home, where the close family unit of mother and five daughters provided an intellectually stimulating and emotionally supportive environment which continued throughout their lives. Each of the sisters followed a literary or library career.

To contribute to the family's income, Haines obtained a commission to write a brief *History of New Mexico from the Spanish Conquest to the Present Time, 1530–1890* (1891), which she completed with the help of her mother. She failed to obtain a position at the Pratt Institute Library, near the family home in Brooklyn, because she could not afford the prerequisite training program. However, in 1892 Mary W. Plummer, family friend and librarian at Pratt, suggested she apply for a secretarial position with Richard R. Bowker.

A successful businessman, Bowker was a benefactor of libraries and of the book trade, and supported pioneering ventures in recording the activities of American publishing and of the library profession. He soon recognized the talents of his new assistant and gave her major editorial responsibilities for his publications *Library Journal, Publishers Weekly, The American Catalogue* for 1890–95, and others. In addition, she wrote articles and book reviews, presented papers, and gave talks to library groups, constantly emphasizing the librarian's role in introducing books to readers. In 1896 Haines became managing editor of *Library Journal* as well as recorder of the American Library Association, responsible for compiling, editing, and indexing its annual proceedings, published in the *Journal*.

Her productivity was prodigious, but the pace of her activities contributed to a breakdown in her health in 1906. Haines spent the winter of 1907–08 in the Adirondacks in outdoor treatment for tuberculosis, and in March 1908 she resigned from the Bowker office as well as from the American Library Association, of which she had been elected second vice president in June 1906. Library benefactor Andrew Carnegie settled a pension on her, and, on doctors' recommendations that she move west, Haines, her mother, and two of her sisters moved first to Colorado and then to Pasadena, Calif. Another sister was already established in Pasadena as a librarian at the state library.

Forced by her health to limit her activities, Haines only gradually began to resume her career, publishing several articles in library periodicals in 1909 and 1910. Also in 1910 she began a book review column for the *Pasadena News;* she contributed a weekly column to its successor the *Pasadena Star-News* until 1950. By 1914 Haines was able to begin teaching in the Los Angeles Public Library training class (later training school), giving lectures on book selection, modern fiction, and library history. When the training school was supplanted by the School of Library Science at the University of Southern California, she became a member of its faculty.

Having developed into a specialist on the subject, she prepared home study courses in book selection for a Syracuse-based correspondence school (1925) and for Columbia University's Home Study Department (1928–34). In 1923, 1924, and 1926 Haines lectured on contemporary fiction to the book selection class at the University of California at Berkeley, and from 1937 until her retirement in 1950 she divided her time between summer sessions at Columbia University and the rest of the academic year at the University of Southern California.

Haines's preeminence in the area of book selection was firmly established by the publication of *Living With Books: The Art of Book Selection* in 1935. A document of her belief in self-education through books, of which she was an exemplar, it became a standard text in library schools. *What's in a Novel?* (1942), written on a grant from Columbia University Press (1938–39), was a less successful treatment of modern fiction.

Prominent in professional library activities in California, Haines was especially proud of her role in fighting censorship and in helping to establish the Intellectual Freedom Committee of the California Library Association (1940), which she chaired for ten years. Her opposition to censorship both from within libraries and from outside was reflected in the many articles she wrote for professional and other publications over the years. Another favorite theme was the defense of the literary rather than technical approach to librarianship, a position which was increasingly challenged as automation and information systems became many librarians' chief concerns.

Haines continued her literary activities and her championship of intellectual freedom in her later years. When in the early 1950s a revised and expanded edition of *Living With Books* (1950) was criticized for allegedly pro-Soviet bias, she attracted few supporters among her colleagues. Nevertheless, honors came at the end of her career, including a scholarship founded in her name by the alumni association of the University of Southern California library school and the American Library Association's Lippincott Award. In her acceptance speech for the award in 1951, Haines declared: "We must face controversial violences and prevailing hatreds, must counteract mass pressures from super-patriots, must continue to make material on all sides of any subject available to readers."

Helen Haines died in 1961 of heart disease at an Altadena nursing home. During a career which spanned a transitional period in the book trade and library world, which saw dramatic technological developments and the professionalization of library education, Haines remained constant in her concern for the content of the book as central to the librarian's role.

[Helen Haines's papers are in the possession of Robert D. Harlan, School of Library and Information Studies, Univ. of Calif., Berkeley. Personal recollections and a sense of Haines's style and philosophy are found in her article about her years in the Bowker office, " 'Tis Fifty Years Since: PW Office in an Earlier Day," *Publishers Weekly,* Jan. 18, 1947, pp. 278–83; her commencement address at Western Reserve Univ. School of Library Science, "Technics or Humanization in Librarianship?" *Library Jour.,* Sept. 1, 1938, pp. 619–24; and her acceptance speech for the Lippincott Award, "Living With Books," *Library Jour.,* Oct. 1, 1951, pp. 1494–95. Mary Robinson Sive, "Helen Haines, 1872–1961: An Annotated Bibliography," *Jour. Library Hist.,* April 1970, pp. 146–64, gives a brief account of Haines and a comprehensive listing of writings by and about her. Biographical sketches include the entry in *Dict. Am. Library Biog.* (1978); Faith Holmes Hyers, "Our Frontispiece: Helen E. Haines," *Bull. Bibliography,* Sept.-Dec. 1951, pp. 129–31; and Althea Warren, Foreword to *Living With Books* (2d ed., 1950). An obituary by Robert D. Harlan appeared in *Library Jour.,* Oct. 15, 1961, p. 3459; death record issued by Calif. Dept. of Public Health. A biobibliography prepared by Betsy Jones assisted in the research for this article.]

ANNE C. EDMONDS

HALL, Rosetta Sherwood, Sept. 19, 1865–April 5, 1951. Physician, missionary.

Rosetta Hall, founder of hospitals and a medical college in Korea, was born on a farm in Liberty, N.Y., the elder daughter and second of three children of Rosevelt Rensler and Phoebe (Gildersleeve) Sherwood, both of English ancestry. Her father, twenty-four years older than her mother, also had several children by his first wife. He was an official of the local Methodist church. Rosetta attended the Chestnut Ridge district school, the Liberty Normal Institute, and the Oswego State Normal School, graduating in 1883. After student teaching in the nearby town of Bethel, she returned to the Chestnut Ridge district school as a teacher of both elementary and high school subjects. In 1886, inspired by a visiting lecturer's plea for medical missions in India, she enrolled in the Woman's Medical College of Pennsylvania in Philadelphia, receiving her M.D. three years later.

After serving a six-month internship at the Nursery and Children's Hospital on Staten Island, N.Y., Rosetta Sherwood accepted a temporary appointment from the Methodist Deaconess's Home to work at the Madison Street Mission Dispensary in lower Manhattan. There she met and became engaged to Canadian-born William James Hall, medical superintendent at the dispensary and a candidate for the China mission of the Methodist Episcopal Church of Canada. Rosetta Sherwood soon applied to the (Methodist) Woman's Foreign Missionary Society in New York for a similar appointment, but in August 1890 she was sent instead to Seoul, Korea. She replaced Meta Howard, the first woman physician in Korea and founder of a small women's hospital. William Hall, released from his commitment to his own mission board, joined Sherwood in Seoul the following year under the auspices of the Methodist Episcopal Church (North). They were married on June 27, 1892, and the following year had a son, whom they named Sherwood. William Hall made frequent trips north to Pyong Yang, where he opened a new mission. Rosetta Hall founded the Baldwin Dispensary in Seoul, which later became the Lillian Harris Memorial Hospital.

In May 1894 the Halls moved to Pyong Yang, although the city was officially forbidden to foreign residents. As a result of anti-Christian disturbances and the impending Sino-Japanese War they were soon recalled to Seoul by the British Legation, which was responsible for them as Canadian citizens. (Rosetta Hall lost her United States citizenship on marriage.) After the Japanese victory in the battle of Pyong Yang in September, William Hall revisited the city briefly but contracted typhus fever while treating wounded soldiers; he died in Seoul in November 1894. His widow, seven months pregnant and uncertain of her own and her son's health, returned to her parents' home in Liberty, N.Y. On Jan. 18, 1895, four days after her arrival, she gave birth to a daughter, Edith Margaret. Rosetta Hall spent the next two and a half years in the United States, lecturing and fund raising for the Korea mission, editing a biography of her husband, serving as examining physician for a children's mission program at Nyack-on-Hudson, and advising medical students at the International Medical Missionary Union in New York City.

Determined to continue her missionary career, she returned to Seoul with her children in the fall of 1897. By May of the following year she had resumed her work in Pyong Yang, with her son and daughter under the care of a Korean *amah,* or nursemaid. A second family tragedy struck on May 23, 1898, when her daughter died of amoebic dysentery.

Rosetta Sherwood Hall continued her missionary labors in Korea for thirty-five years, at first in Pyong Yang and after 1917 in Seoul. Despite a pronounced curvature of the spine from which she suffered all her life, she managed to carry on a long and arduous career as a single mother and missionary physician in the difficult Korean mission field. Described as "naturally reticent and reserved," she was said to have "never pushed herself ahead, but when called to a task . . . has always done it patiently and perseveringly, going far beyond her strength when duty led her in difficult paths" (Wilton, p. 5). In 1899 she established the Edith Margaret Memorial Wing of the Women's Dispensary in Pyong Yang in memory of her daughter. After its destruction by fire in November 1906, she supervised the construction of a larger building, the Women's Hospital of Extended Grace, completed in 1908.

Rosetta Hall took an early interest in the medical training of Korean women. In the 1890s she sponsored the medical education in the United States of Esther Kim Pak, who became the first Korean physician trained abroad to practice western medicine in that country. Hall was one of the founders of the Women's Medical (Training) Institute in Seoul in 1928, and was head of the Institute for the Blind and the Deaf in Pyong Yang. A pioneer in the education of sight- and hearing-impaired persons in Korea, she devised a braillelike system of embossed printing for the Korean alphabet. In 1915 the Japanese Government-General of Korea honored her many accomplishments by presenting her with three silver cups and a certificate of merit.

During her years of service in Korea, Hall spent five furloughs traveling and studying in the United States and other parts of the world. In 1910, accompanied by her son, she went to Edinburgh, Scotland, as a delegate to the International Missionary Convention. Sherwood Hall, following in his parents' footsteps, later became a physician and joined the fight against tuberculosis in Korea and India.

In October 1933, nearing the mandatory retirement age of seventy, Rosetta Hall returned permanently to the United States, settling in

Gloversville, N.Y., to care for an ailing step-brother. She remained active for another decade, writing, lecturing, and practicing medicine in Gloversville and later in Liberty. In 1943 she retired to a rest home for Methodist missionaries in Ocean Grove, N.J., where her United States citizenship was restored by court order in 1948. She died there of influenzal pneumonia in 1951; her remains were cremated and buried along-side the graves of her husband and daughter in Seoul.

[Rosetta Hall's diaries, journals, and miscellaneous papers are in the possession of her granddaughter, Phyllis H. King. The alumnae files of the Medical College of Pennsylvania contain two folders of material on her. Hall was the editor of the *Life of Rev. William James Hall, M.D.* (1897) and the author of several articles in medical and missionary journals. The best account of her life is found in the first volume of Sherwood Hall's autobiography, *With Stethoscope in Asia: Korea* (1978), which also contains a bibliography of writings by and about her. Briefer notices are found in two undated pamphlets, Frances J. Baker, *A Woman Doctor in the Land of the Morning Calm,* and Mary Wilton (pseud.), *The Mother of Pyong Yang.* See also Rhoda Kim Pak, "Medical Women in Korea," *Jour. Am. Medical Women's Assoc.,* March 1950, pp. 116–17; Esther P. Lovejoy, *Women Doctors of the World* (1957); *Who's Who in New York* (1938); and articles in the Liberty (N.Y.) *Gazette,* June 7, 1934, and March 9, 1939, and the Middletown (N.Y.) *Times Herald,* Sept. 25, 1935. Obituaries appeared in the Ocean Grove (N.J.) *Times,* April 13, 1951, and in the Liberty *Gazette.* Extremely helpful were Phyllis H. King, Juanita Lindenberg, Betty Ihlo-Morganstern, and Sandra L. Chaff. Death certificate was provided by the N.J. Dept. of Health.]

CLIFTON J. PHILLIPS

HALPERT, Edith Gregor, April 25, 1900?–Oct. 6, 1970. Art dealer, collector.

A pioneer in the American art world, Edith Halpert introduced contemporary American art, as well as American folk art, into the realm of commercial galleries and, by her promotion and sponsorship, created a public for them. Born in Odessa, Russia, the second of two daughters of Gregor and Frances (Lucom) Fivoosiovitch, Edith and her sister were brought to the United States in May 1906 by their mother, then a widow. Edith grew up in Manhattan. At four-teen, while attending Wadleigh High School, she enrolled in the National Academy of De-sign by convincing the instructors she was six-teen. At the Academy, she met the artist Samuel Halpert, whom she married in 1918; they were divorced in 1930, after a long separation. He

died a few weeks later. In the summer of 1939 she married Raymond Davis, who, she said, knew "nothing about art." The marriage was apparently short-lived.

Between 1914 and 1918 Edith Halpert dis-covered the galleries of Alfred Stieglitz and Newman Montross. They introduced her to modern art, which the Academy instructors had discouraged her from seeing, and taught her to feel a boundless love for American art. When she married, Edith Halpert gave up painting, saying that one artist in the family was enough, and began a business career. She joined the ad-vertising department of Stern Brothers depart-ment store in 1917 but switched to management in 1918 when she was hired by the Cohen Goldman firm as an efficiency expert. In 1920, having donned shell-rim glasses to make herself appear older and thus justify a weekly salary of $50, Halpert was hired by S. W. Straus & Com-pany, an investment banking firm. Beginning as a personnel manager, she eventually became a member of the board, drawing the then remark-able salary of $6,000 a year and receiving bonuses that would later help her begin her gal-lery work.

In 1925, she was invited to reorganize the Galeries Lilloises, a department store in Lille, France. The move to France led her back to art. Seeing that French artists were both more re-spected and freer to experiment and exhibit than their American counterparts, she returned to the United States resolved to open a gallery that would give new American artists a place to ex-hibit. Her decision involved an enormous chal-lenge, since no one believed it was aesthetically or financially worthwhile to establish a gallery specializing in unorthodox contemporary art. Characteristically—and to the great benefit of American art—Edith Halpert disagreed and was determined to prove her point.

On Nov. 6, 1926, Halpert opened the Down-town Gallery of Contemporary Art at 113 West 13th Street in Greenwich Village, the first com-mercial gallery in that area. She had said that the Downtown Gallery would fulfill "a new need in the art life of New York." It did that and much more. Located in the geographic and spiritual center of the city's artistic activity, the Downtown Gallery featured artists unappre-ciated or ignored by most other dealers: Stuart Davis, Charles Demuth, Arthur Dove, Yasuo Kuniyoshi, John Marin, Ben Shahn, Charles Sheeler, Niles Spencer, Max Weber, and Wil-liam Zorach. Relying on her own unshakable conviction of the importance of contemporary art, Halpert insisted: "Our gallery has no special prejudice for any school. Its selection is directed by what is enduring—not by what is in vogue."

During the 1920s Halpert often spent summer vacations in Ogunquit, Maine. At the Perkins Cove art colony established by folk art enthusiast Hamilton Easter Field, artists introduced her to the beauty of American folk art painting. Together with Holger Cahill, writer and later director of the Federal Arts Project, she began to collect the ship figureheads, weathervanes, furniture, portraits, and other artifacts that were gathering dust in the barns and attics of New York, Pennsylvania, and New England. Always shrewd, Halpert realized that these forgotten pieces of Americana would soon be financially and aesthetically valuable and inaugurated the American Folk Art Gallery within the premises of the Downtown Gallery in September 1931. During the depression, folk art was, in Halpert's words, "the reliable sugar daddy" that brought in the working capital she needed to support her main project. Unlike many other galleries, the Downtown Gallery did not ask its artists to pay any part of exhibition costs, but only the 33⅓ percent consignment fee. Thus the Folk Art Gallery, which became tremendously popular in its own right, provided a much needed subsidy. As a result of Halpert's work in folk art, ABBY ALDRICH ROCKEFELLER asked her to assemble the collection of American artifacts that was installed at Colonial Williamsburg in 1940. Later, Electra Havemeyer Webb (1888–1960) depended on Halpert to assist her in gathering the folk art collection of the Shelburne Museum in Vermont. In addition, her advocacy of the nineteenth-century trompe l'oeil painter William Harnett led to the rediscovery of an entire movement in American art.

Halpert's work was not confined to the world of galleries, collectors, and museums. She introduced the concept of the municipal art exhibition, organizing the first one in Atlantic City, N.J., in 1929. In 1934 she convinced Mayor Fiorello La Guardia to endorse a municipal exhibition in Rockefeller Center, the first time in New York that a chief executive gave public endorsement to living American artists. In 1941 the Downtown Gallery was the first commercial gallery in the United States to show an exhibition of black artists; among the show's sponsors were Mayor La Guardia and ELEANOR ROOSEVELT. Halpert also worked with the Works Progress Administration, selecting and promoting exhibitions of work by project artists.

By the 1940s it was evident that Edith Halpert's vision of the beauty and worth of contemporary American art had prevailed. The homey Downtown Gallery had grown into a major commercial establishment representing artists beginning to be revered as the old masters of twentieth-century American art. By 1945 she owned an entire building on East 51st Street, in which both her apartment and the gallery were located; in 1965 the gallery moved to the Ritz Towers at 57th Street and Park Avenue.

In 1952 Halpert established the Edith Gregor Halpert Foundation, which lobbied for the rights of artists to control the sale and reproduction of their work, published a code of relations between museums and living artists, and quietly endowed universities with pictures they could sell to create scholarships in American art. One of Halpert's greatest triumphs was her curatorship, in 1959, of the Moscow-bound National Art Exhibition, a State Department-sponsored show of American art from Thomas Hart Benton to Marca-Relli. Overcoming objections by the House Committee on Un-American Activities that some of the artists involved might have been Communist sympathizers, Halpert then surmounted difficult working and display conditions in Moscow. The exhibit was so thronged with visitors that Halpert had to discontinue her public lectures. Resolved to get her message across, she closed the exhibit for two hours a day to all but artists, museum workers, and professors. During this time, speaking in Russian, she defended modern painting and sculpture against charges of decadence.

During the late 1960s Halpert's health began to fail, and it became more difficult for her to promote her artists. Misunderstandings began to occur and some left her for personal or financial reasons. In 1970 she died at New York Hospital of cancer. Halpert's collection of paintings and sculpture was auctioned in 1973 for over three million dollars.

Quick to anger at those who scoffed at what she had to show, but an unstinting and loyal worker on behalf of creative artists, Edith Gregor Halpert was instrumental in establishing native themes, styles, and traditions as respected subjects for art and the art-buying public. Her willingness to take the risk of supporting unpopular progressive artists was unusual and brave. The artists whom she knew, assisted, or represented, in Marvin Sadik's phrase, "constitute a litany which no exhibition of twentieth-century American art can fail to recite."

[The papers of the Downtown Gallery, a transcript of a talk given by Edith Halpert in 1959, and several photographs are held by the Archives of American Art, Washington. No biography of Edith Gregor Halpert has been written; the fullest accounts are Avis Berman's profile in *Museum News*, Nov.-Dec. 1975 (from which portions of this entry are adapted), and Marvin Sadik's introduction to *Edith*

Halpert & the Downtown Gallery (1968). *The Edith G. Halpert Collection of American Paintings* (1973) is an annotated Sotheby Parke Bernet catalog of the Halpert estate. See also *Current Biog.*, 1955; *Art Digest*, Oct. 15, 1945; *College Art Journal*, Autumn 1949; *Life*, March 17, 1952; *Art in America*, Fall 1959; *Art Voices*, Oct. 1962; *Time*, Nov. 27, 1964; and *Newsweek*, Sept 20, 1965. The entry on Halpert in *Who Was Who in America*, V, says she became a naturalized citizen in 1921. Passport office records show that Samuel Halpert became a naturalized citizen in 1906 and, under the laws then in effect, Edith Halpert automatically acquired citizenship through his naturalization. On a 1925 passport application, he gave Edith Halpert's birth date as April 25, 1899. An obituary appeared in the *N.Y. Times*, Oct. 7. 1970. Further biographical information was furnished by Halpert's niece, Nathaly Baum, and by Diane Tepfer Robbins, who is writing a dissertation on Halpert.]

AVIS BERMAN

HAMILTON, Alice, Feb. 27, 1869–Sept. 22, 1970. Physician, social reformer.

Alice Hamilton, pioneer in industrial toxicology, was the second of four girls born in six years to Montgomery and Gertrude (Pond) Hamilton; her only brother was seventeen years her junior. Born in New York City, she grew up in privilege and comfort in Fort Wayne, Ind., on the family estate presided over by her widowed Hamilton grandmother, a leader in the city's charitable and religious life. Her father, a Princeton graduate and lover of the classics, had settled for a partnership in a wholesale grocery store, a situation arranged for him by his family. Gregarious in his youth and middle age, after the failure of his business in 1885 he retreated from public life. Gertrude Hamilton, a woman of generous sympathies, encouraged her daughters' aspirations, despite opposition from her conventional and clannish in-laws and the stress attendant on her husband's business losses and his excessive drinking. Alice Hamilton was especially close to her mother, from whom she learned that "personal liberty was the most precious thing in life."

The intellectually stimulating, religious, and socially protected environment of her youth left Alice Hamilton with high aspirations and a deep attachment to her family that lasted throughout her life. Educated at home, she and her sisters learned languages, history, and literature. Their only playmates were two sets of cousins; except when they attended the First Presbyterian Church, the Hamiltons rarely associated with "outsiders." Alice's moral earnestness was tempered by a zest for outdoor sport, a delicious sense of humor and eye for the absurd, and an insatiable curiosity that even at thirteen manifested itself in her eagerness to meet new people. These she encountered mainly during summers at Mackinac Island, Mich., and at Miss Porter's School in Farmington, Conn., which, following a family tradition begun by her aunts, she attended from 1886 to 1888.

Finding it necessary to support herself, Alice Hamilton chose medicine, over her family's objections, as the only profession open to women that would satisfy her desire to be both independent and useful. She made up her deficiencies in science at the Fort Wayne College of Medicine, convinced her father of her seriousness of purpose, and entered the medical department of the University of Michigan in March 1892. Although she already knew she did not want the responsibility of caring for patients, after receiving her M.D. in 1893 she interned at the Northwestern Hospital for Women and Children in Minneapolis and the New England Hospital for Women and Children in Boston (1893–94).

In the next few years, Hamilton acquired a scientific training equaled by few contemporaries, male or female. She returned to Ann Arbor in February 1895 to assist in the bacteriology laboratory of F. G. Novy, and the following fall, with her older sister, EDITH HAMILTON, she departed for Germany where she studied bacteriology and pathology at the Universities of Leipzig and Munich. On balance the year proved disappointing: she learned little she had not already known, none of her experiments worked out, and she was repelled by German militarism, anti-Semitism, and "woman-despising." After spending a final postgraduate year at the Johns Hopkins Medical School, she left for Chicago in the fall of 1897 to begin her first job: as professor of pathology at the Woman's Medical School of Northwestern University.

In Chicago she fulfilled a longstanding ambition by becoming a resident of Hull House. The move plunged her into a world of poverty, trade unions, radical talk, and social action far removed from the protected environment of Fort Wayne. Typically apprehensive in a new situation—she felt like "a lonely stranded heathen among many elect"—Alice Hamilton soon made her way into the inner circle that included JANE ADDAMS, FLORENCE KELLEY, and JULIA LATHROP. At Hull House she found companionship, intellectual stimulation, and the excitement of being caught up in an important cause. But her own efforts there—teaching evening classes, taking Italian children on outings, even the well-baby clinic which she established and which gave her genuine pleasure—seemed hopelessly inadequate to the need. Struggling to reconcile conflicting personal imperatives, her scientific work seemed "remote and useless," while the demands of settlement life left her with "the feeling of being pulled about and tired and yet never doing anything definite." Family obligations also weighed heavily on Alice Hamilton during these years, particularly her sister Norah's breakdown and slow recovery, which she oversaw.

Still hoping to bring her two lives together, when the Woman's Medical School closed in 1902 Hamilton accepted a position as bacteriologist at the new Memorial Institute for Infectious Diseases. Encouraged by the Institute's director, Ludwig Hektoen, she published scientific papers, studied at the Pasteur Institute in Paris, and became active in Chicago medical and reform circles. She gained acclaim for an investigation of a typhoid epidemic in her neighborhood, and tried, unsuccessfully, to end the cocaine traffic there. But the work she wanted still eluded her, and in her tenth year at Hull House she concluded that she would "never be more than a fourth-rate scientist."

Then a muckraking article and a copy of Sir Thomas Oliver's *Dangerous Trades* called her attention to industrial diseases. Appalled by the callous disregard of human life that permitted workers to be poisoned for doing their jobs, she immersed herself in the subject. In contrast to Germany and England, which had reasonably effective factory inspection systems, the United States ignored diseases of the workplace: there were no occupational safety laws, few unions to press the workers' claims, and virtually no medical records. In 1908 Governor Charles S. Deneen appointed Hamilton to the Illinois Commission on Occupational Diseases and early in 1910 she became supervisor of the state's survey of industrial poisons, the first to combine modern laboratory techniques with field study. She concentrated on lead, the most widely used—and insidious—industrial poison. By following up every rumor, searching hospital records, and visiting workers at home, she and her assistants identified 77 lead-using industrial processes and 578 certain victims of poisoning. The survey and the ensuing state law requiring safety measures and medical examinations were important milestones in the mounting campaign to improve industrial conditions.

Early in 1911, Hamilton accepted an appointment as special investigator for the United States Bureau (later Department) of Labor. Starting with the lead trades, by 1916 she had become the leading American authority on lead poisoning and one of a handful of specialists on industrial diseases. Although she avoided the sensationalism of her muckraking contemporaries, her surveys dramatically documented high mortality and morbidity rates, first in the lead industries, and later in rubber and munitions plants. In view of the prevailing ignorance, mere exposure of such conditions was a major achievement. Dissatisfied with the "cold, printed report," Hamilton also had extraordinary success in persuading owners to improve safety conditions; her scrupulous accuracy and persistence helped her in this self-assigned task.

Combining the unlikely roles of scientific investigator, skilled negotiator, advocate for the helpless, and crusader for the public health, Alice Hamilton pursued her specialty with an intensity that many found incongruous in a woman of exquisite, "almost fragile," appearance. Scientific in part, but "human and practical in greater measure," the work she began in her forties permitted her to achieve a goal she had articulated in her twenties: to leave behind some "definite achievement, something really lasting . . . to make the world better." Initially cautious in her politics—she had felt safest on the fence— her latent empathy for the underprivileged had been intensified by her years at Hull House. She found her voice as champion of the mainly poor and foreign-born victims of industrial diseases, "a class that is not really free." Hating conflict of any kind, she still looked instinctively for ways to reconcile opponents. But when a choice had to be made, she stood with the rebel and the underdog: she believed in being "fair but not too fair."

Her experiences during World War I completed Hamilton's transformation from "a doubting Thomas and a pessimist" into an effective political person. Characterizing herself as a "confidante in white linen," in 1915 she accompanied Jane Addams to the International Congress of Women at The Hague, and then on a mission to the war capitals to present the women's peace proposal. Hamilton also visited German-occupied Belgium, which ever after remained for her a symbol of oppression. Unable to view the war as a contest between good and evil, she became a pacifist, happy to leave "muddled thinking behind." (She continued her government investigations, tackling the secret munitions industries that sprang up during the war.) After attending the second International Congress of Women in Zurich (1919) she visited Germany to investigate the famine there; it was the most searing experience of her life.

Soon after her return, she took up her duties as assistant professor of industrial medicine at the Harvard Medical School (after 1925 at the School of Public Health). Harvard's first woman professor, Hamilton had accepted Dean David L. Edsall's invitation only after he agreed to a half-time appointment that would leave her free for field work. She stayed on her own terms as well, refusing to halt her fund-raising appeals on behalf of the Quaker famine relief, which a financial backer of the school considered pro-German. Barred from entering the Harvard Club, from marching in commencement, and from claiming her quota of football tickets, Hamilton remained an anomaly at Harvard, and an assistant professor. Nevertheless she contributed significantly to the work of the department, chiefly through her successful fund-raising efforts and her support of the *Journal of Industrial Hygiene*.

After World War I, as the medical profession became more interested in industrial diseases and state compensation laws forced owners to make their plants safer, Hamilton's role changed from that of pioneer investigator to that of consultant, codifier, and troubleshooter. She continued to do field studies, for the Department of Labor right after the war, and later with Harvard colleagues; but, compared to her earlier investigations, these efforts seemed like attending an "infant class in Sunday School." Still the most visible person in the field, Hamilton solicited funds from foundations for research and field studies, and worked with reform, government, and labor groups interested in industrial diseases. Most important, she publicized the dangers of the new industrial poisons that multiplied as American industry expanded. Her book *Industrial Poisons in the United States* (1925) was the first American text on the subject and established her as one of the two leading authorities in the world. She also had a major part in prompting the surgeon general to call national conferences to discuss two new poisons, the first on tetraethyl lead in 1925, the second on radium in 1928.

Although never a political infighter, Hamilton became a persuasive proponent of reform. Whether testifying for the federal child labor amendment or state health insurance, speaking for peace or birth control, or debating supporters of the Equal Rights Amendment (which she feared would eliminate protective legislation for women), her measured and ironic voice conveyed the depth of her feelings. Profoundly stirred by the Sacco-Vanzetti case, she joined a small group of citizens in a futile last minute appeal for clemency to Governor Alvan Fuller. As a member of the President's Research Committee on Social Trends (1930–32), she proved an incisive critic of American welfare capitalism.

Hamilton also became an avid student of international affairs. Her two terms as a member of the Health Committee of the League of Nations (1924–30) completed her conversion to a pro-League position. (She had initially opposed it as a League of Victors.) A visit to the

Soviet Union in 1924 left her admiring the Bolshevist ideal of equality but dismayed by the concentration of power and the suppression of free speech. By contrast, her response to Nazi Germany, which she visited in April 1933, was unequivocal: in an influential series of articles published soon after her return, she deplored Nazi anti-intellectualism, stifling of dissent, and persecution of the Jews. She continued to support pacifist measures, but after Hitler's conquest of western Europe in 1940 she concluded that the antiwar movement had become narrow and nationalistic and that the United States must "throw our strength on the side we think the right one."

Her forced retirement from Harvard in 1935, coinciding with the death of Jane Addams, left her in search of new directions. Declining an invitation to become head resident of Hull House (where she had continued to spend part of each year), with her sister Margaret she took up year-round residence in the Hadlyme, Conn., home they had purchased in 1916. Still vigorous and with her funds reduced by the depression, in the fall of 1935 Hamilton eagerly accepted an invitation to become a consultant in the Division of Labor Standards which FRANCES PERKINS had recently established in the Department of Labor. In that capacity she assisted state labor departments, testified at hearings, and, most important, conducted her last field survey—an investigation of the viscose rayon industry (1937–38). The study not only demonstrated the toxic nature of the industry but also prompted passage of Pennsylvania's first compensation law for occupational diseases.

Hamilton remained active during her early retirement years, continuing to lecture and serving as president of the National Consumers' League (1944–49). She also wrote her autobiography, *Exploring the Dangerous Trades* (1943), which, while it minimized the conflict in her life, nevertheless conveyed her passionate determination. With Harriet L. Hardy, a specialist on beryllium poisoning, in 1949 Hamilton published a revised edition of her 1934 textbook, *Industrial Toxicology*.

In her "old-old age," politics remained her absorbing interest. She prided herself on keeping up to date and in 1952 withdrew her opposition to the ERA. In letters to editors, congressmen, and friends, Hamilton deplored the obsessive anticommunism of American foreign policy and the concomitant threat to civil liberties at home. She early favored recognition of the People's Republic of China and in 1963 signed an open letter calling for an end to American military efforts in Vietnam. Still able to enjoy an hour of "gentle gardening" in her eighties, in her nineties the deficits of age began to overtake her. She died at home of a stroke at the age of 101.

A living legend in her later years, Alice Hamilton received numerous honorary degrees and awards. Retaining the faith in progress she had shared with reformers of her generation, she emphasized the improvements in workers' health, which she attributed to compensation laws, increased medical concern, and voluntary cooperation between business and government. Always a pragmatist, she still preferred "half a loaf rather than no bread."

In maturity Alice Hamilton impressed others as a "perfectly harmonious woman." Few knew of her dramatic transformation from a spirited but hesitant and self-deprecating girl into the woman who rebelled against her family's social values while remaining close to its members, risked her life doing "breakneck stunts" in mines, and refused to accept work on any but her own terms. Through it all she retained the graciousness, humor, and concern for others that led Walter Lippmann to say: "She has the most satisfying taste of all personalities I've ever met —wine and silver and homespun." About her own precedent-breaking career, Alice Hamilton remained modest, summing up her achievements at eighty-eight: "For me the satisfaction is that things are better now, and I had some part in it."

[The principal manuscript sources are the Alice Hamilton Papers, which include correspondence, clippings, and reprints, and the Hamilton Family Papers, which contain personal letters, pocket diaries, and photographs; both are in the Schlesinger Library, Radcliffe College. Connecticut College, New London, has a collection of Hamilton MSS. There are important Hamilton letters on World War I in the Swarthmore College Peace Collection. Information about the Harvard years may be found in the records of the Harvard School of Public Health, Countway Library of Medicine, which also has a 1963 taped interview with Hamilton, and in the A. Lawrence Lowell Papers, Harvard Univ. Archives. Hamilton was a prolific writer. Her field investigations were published as bulletins of the U.S. Bureau of Labor Statistics; some have been reissued. An excellent bibliography appears in Wilma Ruth Slaight, "Alice Hamilton: First Lady of Industrial Medicine" (Ph.D. diss., Case Western Reserve Univ., 1974). Her nonmedical writings include: *Women at The Hague: The International Congress of Women and Its Results*, with Jane Addams and Emily Greene Balch (1915); "Protection for Women Workers," *The Forum*, Aug. 1924; "What About the Lawyers?" *Harper's*, Oct. 1931; "An Inquiry into the Nazi Mind," *N.Y. Times Mag.*, Aug. 6, 1933; "A Woman of Ninety Looks at Her World," *Atlantic*, Sept. 1961. The basic biographical source is still *Exploring the Dangerous Trades*, which can be supplemented by Hamilton's "Nineteen Years in the Poisonous Trades," *Harper's*, Oct.

1929, and "Edith and Alice Hamilton: Students in Germany," *Atlantic*, March 1965. See also Elizabeth Shepley Sergeant, "Alice Hamilton, M.D.: Crusader for Health in Industry," *Harper's*, May 1926, and Elizabeth Glendower Evans, "People I Have Known: Alice Hamilton, M.D., Pioneer in a New Kind of Human Service," *The Progressive*, Nov. 29 and Dec. 20, 1930; *Current Biog.*, 1946; *Nat. Cyc. Am. Biog.*, G, 107–8; S. J. Woolf, "Triumphs of a Pioneer Doctor," *N.Y. Times Mag.*, Nov. 9, 1947; and the special issue of *Jour. Occupational Med.*, Feb. 1972. An edition of Hamilton's letters, with an introduction by Barbara Sicherman, is in preparation. Useful information for this article was provided by Dorothy Detzer Denny, Madeleine P. Grant, Holman Hamilton, W. R. G. Hamilton, Frances Hamilton, Harriet Hardy, Jarmila and Jane Petrzelka, and the Fort Wayne Public Library. Death certificate provided by Conn. Dept. of Health.]

BARBARA SICHERMAN

HAMILTON, Edith, Aug. 12, 1867–May 31, 1963. Writer, classicist, educator.

Edith Hamilton, eldest of the five children of Gertrude (Pond) and Montgomery Hamilton, was born in Dresden, Germany, where her parents were visiting. She had three sisters, close in age, and one brother, considerably younger. Her paternal grandfather, Allen Hamilton, emigrated from the north of Ireland to the United States, settling in Fort Wayne, Ind., where he made a fortune in business. His wife, Emerine Holman Hamilton, was of English ancestry. An insatiable reader, she was active in First Presbyterian Church affairs and in the temperance and woman suffrage movements. Montgomery Hamilton, partner in a wholesale grocery business, was fond of good books and good conversation. In later life his heavy drinking alienated his daughters. Gertrude Hamilton was of mixed Dutch, Irish, and English descent on her mother's side; her father was a wealthy New York sugar merchant. A lover of literature, fluent in several languages, and plain speaking in a prudish age, she encouraged independence in her daughters.

Edith Hamilton's childhood was spent in the company of her sisters and cousins on the family estate in downtown Fort Wayne. Educated at home by parents and tutors, they learned Latin and Greek (Edith started Latin with her father at age seven) and became fluent in French and German. Associating mainly with each other, they developed intense and lasting ties. Religion was important: they attended the First Presbyterian Church, studied the Bible, and were drilled by Montgomery Hamilton in theology. At seventeen, Edith Hamilton went to Miss Porter's School in Farmington, Conn. (1884–

86), where her three Hamilton aunts had been and where her sisters followed her.

The failure of their father's business in 1885 made the sisters aware of the need to be self-supporting. Deciding on a career as a teacher, Edith Hamilton made up her deficiencies in science and mathematics by study at home, passed the Bryn Mawr College entrance examinations, and was admitted in 1891. She majored in Greek and Latin and received an A.B. and A.M. in 1894, was a fellow in Latin in 1894–95, and received the college's highest honor, the Mary E. Garrett European Fellowship. Already at Bryn Mawr certain lifelong dispositions began to appear in Edith Hamilton, as revealed in her letters. A sense of family obligation made her apply for the Latin fellowship, in spite of an already strong distaste for conventional scholarship: it was, as she wrote, "a matter of common sense, and duty to the other three girls." Combining intellectual aspiration with self-deprecation, she found it "harder to resign myself to not being clever than to anything else in the whole world." Even at this early date, she anticipated the tone and emphasis of her books, favoring a religious approach to art over the aesthetic outlook of her close friend LUCY DONNELLY.

The European fellowship made it possible for Edith and her sister ALICE HAMILTON to pursue graduate studies in Germany (1895–96). They spent part of the year in Leipzig, where she was impatient with the philological preoccupations of her professors, and part in Munich, where the lectures were more rewarding, but she was required to sit in isolation on the lecture platform, apart from the male students.

In 1896 Bryn Mawr president M. CAREY THOMAS invited Hamilton to be headmistress of the recently founded Bryn Mawr School in Baltimore, the only girls' school in the country with an exclusively college preparatory curriculum. She accepted out of practical necessity, renouncing her aspiration to be a classical scholar. Her sister Margaret, also a Bryn Mawr College graduate, came to live with her in 1901, becoming a science teacher and then head of the primary school. (She later served as acting headmistress.) After their father's death in 1909, their mother also lived with them. At the time Hamilton arrived, the school was in difficulties; barely twenty-nine and without experience, she was at first very frightened. However, with a mixture of shrewdness, force, and personal magnetism, she convinced Baltimore's conservative parents of the value of rigorous academic training for women, and she built the school into one of the foremost in the country.

Her intellectual and moral ideals, distilled from her reading of Greek literature and conveyed with characteristic fervor and intensity, informed the program and inspired the students, to whom she was a venerated presence—remote, terrifying, and incredibly demanding. She made senior Vergil, her only course, a memorable experience. A confrontation with Thomas, culminating a long period of strained relations, probably contributed to the exhaustion and ill health which were the ostensible reasons for Hamilton's resignation as headmistress in 1922. After her retirement she admitted she had never liked the work.

In 1923, after a period of rest and reorientation, Hamilton bought and moved to a house at Sea Wall, Mount Desert Island, Maine, with Doris Fielding Reid, a daughter of old Baltimore friends, who had attended the Bryn Mawr School. The two women shared a home for the rest of Hamilton's life, moving in 1924 to an apartment at 24 Gramercy Park in New York City, though keeping Sea Wall as their summer retreat. They provided a second home for the children of Reid's brother. The eldest, Dorian, who came to them when he was five, lived with them permanently, and Hamilton legally adopted him. In 1929 Doris Reid went to work for the investment firm of Loomis Sayles & Co.

In New York Hamilton kept house and began a larger life—making friends among members of the New York literary and theatrical worlds, traveling, and embarking on her extraordinarily successful second career as a writer. Authorship came almost accidentally. Rosamond Gilder, fascinated by the extempore translation and exposition of Greek dramatists offered at weekly tea parties at Gramercy Park, prevailed on a reluctant Hamilton to write some articles on ancient drama and culture for *Theatre Arts Monthly*, which she edited. Six articles and a verse translation of Aeschylus's *Prometheus* appeared between 1927 and 1929. Still reluctant to publish, Hamilton finally yielded to Elling Aannestad, an editor for W. W. Norton, and wrote *The Greek Way* (1930).

The book brought her immediate acclaim. The prose was vivid and graceful, and salted with the same quotations and moral exhortations that inspired students at the Bryn Mawr School. Hamilton's sense of literature as a source of ideas to live by gave meaning and immediacy to a past which had become inaccessible to the general reader. Her readings of ancient writers were idiosyncratic, however, and sometimes marred by distortion or mistranslation. Her certainty about what Aeschylus or Plato really meant, which fascinated the nonscholarly public and reviewers, disconcerted most scholarly reviewers, who praised her, if at all, for her lively prose and for reviving interest in antiquity. But Hamilton was established as a writer from then on, producing articles and reviews on ancient and modern literary topics for the *Saturday Review of Literature, Saturday Evening Post, New York Times Book Review,* and *Theatre Arts Monthly,* as well as a series of books on Greek, Roman, and biblical antiquity which brought her ever-increasing recognition. By 1943, when she moved to Washington, D.C., where Reid had been made head of her firm's Washington office, Hamilton had published four more books, including *Prophets of Israel* (1936), her first venture into the biblical field.

In Washington, her home for the rest of her life, Hamilton continued to produce articles, wrote two more books, and added speaking engagements and radio talks to her activities. In her nineties she edited *The Collected Dialogues* of Plato (1961) with Huntington Cairns for the Bollingen Series. She was visited by the eminent and famous, ranging from Isak Dinesen, Robert Frost, and Harvard classicist Werner Jaeger to labor leader John L. Lewis. Awards and honors poured in. In addition to several honorary degrees, she was recognized by election to the American Institute of Arts and Letters in 1955, and to the American Academy of Arts and Letters in 1957. That same year, and most prized of all, she was made an honorary citizen of Athens. The public ceremony, preceding a performance of her translation of Aeschylus's *Prometheus* in the ancient theater of Herodes Atticus at the foot of the Acropolis, received national coverage. In 1957 and again in 1958 she was interviewed for National Broadcasting Company television programs, and in 1957 *The Greek Way* (1930) and *The Roman Way* (1932) were selected as the Book-of-the-Month Club summer dividend. In 1960, at ninety-two, Hamilton made a motor trip through France, the last of her many trips to Europe. John F. Kennedy invited her to his inauguration (she declined), and sent an emissary to Maine asking advice about a new cultural center (she would not give any). At the time of her death of heart failure at her Washington home in 1963, she was planning a book on Plato.

Though she became a symbol of scholarship for a large public, Edith Hamilton was not, and did not claim to be, a scholar, or even a popularizer of the scholarly work of others. Throughout her career her commitment was not the scholar's commitment to the facts of the past that require demonstration, but to the unverifiable "truths of the spirit," which she thought she found in ancient writers. Her life was ruled by a passionately nonconformist vision that was the source of her phenomenal strength and vitality and her almost magical appeal as public figure and author.

[The Hamilton family papers in the Schlesinger Library, Radcliffe College, are a rich source of correspondence by, to, and about Hamilton from her girlhood until her death. Quotations are from this collection. The M. Carey Thomas Papers, Bryn Mawr College Archives, contain a small amount of material on Hamilton and the Bryn Mawr School. The W. W. Norton and Co. Papers in the Special Collections, Columbia Univ. Libraries, and the Huntington Cairns Papers in the Library of Congress Manuscript Div., also contain material on Hamilton. Hamilton's publications included *Three Greek Plays* (1937), verse translations with introductions and explanatory chapters; *Mythology* (1942); *The Great Age of Greek Literature* (1942), an expanded version of *The Greek Way,* subsequently reissued under that title; *Witness to the Truth* (1948); and *The Echo of Greece* (1957). The text of the 1958 NBC interview by Huntington Cairns is published in James Nelson, ed., *Wisdom for Our Time* (1961). *The Ever Present Past* (1964), with a prologue by Doris Fielding Reid, is a collection of articles, reviews, and talks by Hamilton, 1927–63. Published biographical material is meager. The fullest, but still very selective, account is Doris Fielding Reid, *Edith Hamilton: An Intimate Portrait* (1967). Alice Hamilton's "Edith and Alice Hamilton: Students in Germany," *Atlantic Monthly,* March 1965, pp. 129–32, gives a firsthand account of the year in Germany, and her autobiography, *Exploring the Dangerous Trades* (1943), is informative about the family, particularly in the early years. Rosamond Randall Beirne, *Let's Pick the Daisies* (1970), a history of the Bryn Mawr School published by the school, and the *Bryn Mawr School Bull.,* 75th anniversary issue, 1960–61, provide information about her years as headmistress. There are brief appreciations by John Mason Brown, "The Heritage of Edith Hamilton," *Sat. Rev.,* June 22, 1963, pp. 16–17, and by Brooks Atkinson, *Tuesdays and Fridays* (1963), pp. 60–63. See also the brief biographical sketches in Hope Stoddard, *Famous American Women* (1970); *Current Biog.,* 1963; and *Nat. Cyc. Am. Biog.,* LII, 289. Obituaries appeared in the *N.Y. Times,* June 1, 1963; *Time,* June 7, 1963; and *Newsweek,* June 10, 1963. A biobibliography by Anne Haimes assisted in the research for this article. Valuable information was also provided by George P. Brockway, Rosamond Gilder, Francesca Gilder Palmer, Millicent Carey McIntosh, Barbara Sicherman, Lucy Fisher West, and Hortense Zera. Death certificate supplied by D.C. Dept. of Public Health.]

HELEN H. BACON

HAMILTON, Gordon, Dec. 26, 1892–March 10, 1967. Social work educator.

Amy Gordon Hamilton was born in Tenafly, N.J., the youngest of four children, two daughters and two sons, of Bertha (Torrance) and

George Hamilton. Her father, born in Scotland into an aristocratic family, came to the United States as a young man. He became an importer of goods from the Far East. The Torrances, after emigrating from Canada in the 1870s, lived in a rambling Victorian house in Tenafly, where Bertha Hamilton brought her husband to live after their marriage. According to the family story, George Hamilton, overwhelmed by the exuberant and competitive Torrances, "turned to the demon rum." Bertha Hamilton became deeply involved in Christian Science and was a close associate of MARY BAKER EDDY, but Gordon Hamilton, as she was always known, never embraced her mother's religion. Bertha Hamilton, who lived to be 103, was a reserved and critical woman who vigorously opposed her children marrying; neither daughter married and the sons did so late.

Gordon's childhood was not an easy one. She suffered from respiratory ailments, which plagued her throughout her life. Along with her siblings, she was educated at home. Though she had a lively and curious mind and wanted to go to college, she was discouraged by her family and was poorly prepared, particularly in the sciences, of which her mother disapproved. She finally obtained permission to be tutored in geography, and in 1911 entered Bryn Mawr College. Majoring in Greek and English, she hoped to make writing and journalism her career.

After graduation in 1914, Hamilton spent a year in London. World War I brought her home and into the American Red Cross. Moving to Colorado for her health, she worked from 1917 until 1920 for the Red Cross Home Service in Colorado Springs. There she met MARY RICH-MOND who encouraged her to seek a position as a caseworker at the Charity Organization Society (COS) of New York City. With Richmond's recommendation, Hamilton obtained the position and thus began her career in social work. After two years as a caseworker (1920–21), she was forced by ill health to leave this strenuous work. She turned to research for the COS, investigating mental retardation and participating in the Pittsburgh study of social agencies.

In 1923 Gordon Hamilton left the COS to join the faculty of the New York School of Social Work (NYSSW), which remained her professional home for thirty-four years. An inspired teacher, Hamilton was both model and mentor to generations of student social workers, many of whom went on to occupy positions of leadership in the profession. Her effectiveness as a teacher was built on mastery of her subject and the ability to stimulate creative thinking in her

students. Witty and articulate, she brought to the classroom a brilliant mind, a broad classical education, and varied and constantly renewed practical experience.

From 1925 to 1932, in addition to her teaching, Hamilton served as associate director of social service and then as adviser on research at New York's Presbyterian Hospital; this work resulted in her first book, *Medical Social Terminology* (1927), which attempted to link the languages of medicine and of social work. Responding to the crisis created by the depression, Hamilton worked for the emergency relief agencies established by the federal government and helped set up the first Federal Emergency Relief Administration training program. She then took a two-year leave from teaching to be director of social service of the Temporary Emergency Relief Administration of New York state. Deeply concerned with international as well as national social problems, in the aftermath of World War II she worked to form a nonsectarian refugee organization. When that effort failed, she joined the Board of Christian Refugees and went to Germany for Church World Service. She was also a staff member and consultant for the United Nations Relief and Rehabilitation Administration.

Gordon Hamilton's most influential work, *Theory and Practice of Social Casework* (1940), was the first major book about casework to appear since Mary Richmond's *Social Diagnosis* (1917). The major text used in schools of social work for many years, it defined the primary concern of casework as the delivery of concrete services. In the late 1940s, as the influence of psychoanalysis shook the assumptions upon which casework practice was based, Hamilton, skeptical at first, began to attend sessions on psychoanalytic theory and consulted with leaders in the psychoanalytic movement. From 1947 to 1950 she served as research consultant to the Jewish Board of Guardians, where psychoanalytic theory had been translated into child guidance practice. Her 1951 revision of *Theory and Practice of Social Casework* reflected her conviction that casework could indeed treat psychological problems of considerable depth as well as deal with the social function and needs of the individual. Her definition of the profession's special way of helping stressed its "ability to operate at both ends of the psychosocial event," maintaining a balance between "manipulation of external factors" and "treatment of inner factors."

Continuing to struggle with ill health, Hamilton resigned from the New York School of Social Work in 1957. That year she returned to her original interest in writing and journalism, becoming the first editor-in-chief of *Social Work*, the professional journal of the newly formed National Association of Social Workers. As editor, Hamilton, who had fought for the unification of all the practitioners of social work into the Association, was its leading voice. Her most controversial editorial, appearing shortly before her retirement in 1962, recommended that income maintenance be separated from social services and be administered by trained civil servants, not caseworkers. Overturning the long-held assumptions that recipients of public assistance were in need of rehabilitation and that relief should be used as a tool in treatment, the editorial represented a major departure for the former charity worker. Hamilton, who had shared a home in New York with her close associate Anna Kempshall, spent her last years in British Columbia, where she lived with her friend Ruby McKay. She died there in 1967.

A complex woman of great personal charm, Gordon Hamilton was capable of being both stern and generous, aloof and warm. Above all, she was loyal and devoted to family, friends, colleagues, and her convictions. The recipient of many honors throughout her career, Hamilton in 1958 was awarded the Florina Lasker Award for superior achievement as "practitioner, educator, scholar, author, thinker and leader" in the profession of social work.

[The Columbia Univ. School of Social Work library has some informal notes about her professional life that Gordon Hamilton dictated at the time of her retirement, as well as copies of the speeches given on May 16, 1957, in honor of her retirement. Hamilton also wrote *Principles of Social Case Recording* (1946) and *Psychotherapy in Child Guidance* (1947). Her articles appeared regularly in *Jour. Social Casework* (formerly *The Family*) and in the Nat. Conference of Social Work (NCSW), *Proceedings*, throughout her career. Of particular interest are "Progress in Social Casework," NCSW, *Proceedings*, 1923; "Refocussing Social Casework," NCSW, *Proceedings*, 1931; "Basic Concepts in Social Casework," *The Family*, Feb. 1938; and "The Underlying Philosophy of Casework Today," NCSW, *Proceedings*, 1941. Two other articles, "Psychoanalytically Oriented Casework and Its Relation to Psychotherapy," *Am. Jour. Orthopsychiatry*, April 1949, and "The Role of Social Casework in Social Policy," *Social Casework*, Oct. 1952, outline the development of her thought over the course of her career. The editorials in *Social Work* published during her tenure as editor, 1957–62, express her thinking on many issues. There is little published material about her life and career. See the entry in *Encyc. Social Work* (1977) and Anna Kempshall, "Gordon Hamilton: Some Intimate Glimpses," *NYSSW Newsletter*, June 1957, pp. 11–12. Excerpts from the tributes given at a memorial service for Hamilton at the Columbia Univ. School of Social Work were reprinted in the *Alumni Newsletter*, Spring 1967. An obituary appeared in the *N.Y. Times*, March 11, 1967. Other information was provided by her nephew Richard Hamilton, by her nieces Minard Hamilton and Lisa H. Wear, and by Dorothy Sumner and Beatrice Saunders. Death certificate supplied by British Columbia Ministry of Health.]

ANN HARTMAN

HANSBERRY, Lorraine, May 19, 1930–Jan. 12, 1965. Playwright, civil rights reformer.

Lorraine Hansberry, best known for her plays, was also an early and active advocate of the civil rights movement, and gave much of her energy to that cause. Born in Chicago, Hansberry grew up on the South Side of that city. Her father, Carl Augustus Hansberry, was a very successful real estate broker and, in 1930, a United States deputy marshal. Her mother, Nannie (Perry) Hansberry, was thirty-two when Lorraine, the second daughter and youngest of four children, was born. Both parents were active in Republican politics; Nannie Hansberry, who became a major force in her daughter's life, had also been a hairdresser, cashier, and schoolteacher in the south.

Carl Hansberry, a graduate of Alcorn College in his native Mississippi, was knowledgeable about both law and history and believed in the potential for justice in the American system. Because of that belief, in 1938 he deliberately moved his family into a restricted neighborhood. Lorraine Hansberry later recalled a mob gathering on their porch and a brick crashing through a window, just missing her. She also praised her mother's courage in staying on alone with the children for eight months while Carl Hansberry fought their case in Washington. The Hansberrys' determination to stay had resulted in one of the NAACP's most celebrated housing cases: *Hansberry* v. *Lee* (311 U.S. 32). In November 1940 the Supreme Court reversed a lower court's decision that whites had a right to bar blacks from their neighborhoods, and the Hansberrys could legally occupy their property. The court decision made little real difference to the ghetto-bound blacks of Chicago, however. Becoming disillusioned, Carl Hansberry later went to Mexico to try to establish a new home for his family; he died there in 1945 at age fifty-one. Lorraine Hansberry believed that "American racism helped kill him" (*The New Yorker*, p. 34).

In spite of the privileges available to the black middle class, the Hansberrys chose not to send their children to private schools. Lorraine Hansberry had a ghetto education, which meant that she was given "half an education" in a segregated school system that opened schools for blacks for half-day sessions.

After graduating from Englewood High School in Chicago in 1948, Hansberry spent two years at the University of Wisconsin (1948–50), an experience that she found, for the most part, dull and seemingly irrelevant. As a student there she wandered one day into a rehearsal of Sean O'Casey's *Juno and the Paycock.* She later wrote that that experience "consumed all my senses." Although her formal education ended by 1950, she took classes wherever she was, and continued to educate herself through voracious reading. A particularly important book for her was Simone de Beauvoir's *The Second Sex.*

When Hansberry first moved to New York City in 1950, she lived on the Lower East Side; she worked as a typist, taking home $31.70 per week. Early in 1951 she began to work in Harlem for Paul Robeson's newspaper, *Freedom,* first as a reporter and then as associate editor. The paper shared offices with the Council on African Affairs, so she was able to meet and to talk with W. E. B. Du Bois and visiting African leaders. At that time Hansberry was, according to Robert Nemiroff, "on fire with black liberation not only here but in Africa." She met Nemiroff, then a graduate student and also a playwright, at an NAACP protest against racist practices on the New York University basketball team, an event she was covering for *Freedom.* Both were active in the civil rights and peace movements, and they married on June 20, 1953. After her marriage, Hansberry gave more time to writing, ultimately for the stage. She had a fruitful working relationship with Nemiroff, with whom she shared a home in Croton-on-Hudson, N.Y.; in later years Hansberry also had an apartment on Bleecker Street.

Hansberry's first completed play, *A Raisin in the Sun,* was written to counteract a distorted view of blacks that had been perpetuated on American stages. The play avoids both exotic and minstrel stereotypes and succeeds in creating characters who are credible black Americans intent upon surviving. Those who faulted the play for its "happy ending," with the black family moving into a white neighborhood, did not realize that their real struggle would begin with that move.

A Raisin in the Sun opened at the Ethel Barrymore Theatre on March 11, 1959, the first play by a black woman ever to appear on Broadway. It was an instant and extraordinary success with audiences and with critics. After a Broadway run of 530 performances, it had an extensive tour and became a popular film. Hansberry was

the youngest American, the fifth woman, and the only black playwright to win the New York Drama Critics' Circle Award for the Best Play of the Year. In 1961 the film version of *A Raisin in the Sun* won the Cannes Film Festival Award.

While writing plays, Hansberry continued to be an active and vocal participant in the growing movement for civil rights. Between 1959 and 1964, in interviews, letters, and speeches, the successful young playwright made clear her political philosophy and spoke out with increasing vehemence against racism. Observing in 1959 that "Negroes are in a hostile circumstance in the United States" and have "a great deal to be angry about," by 1964 she urged "the white liberal to stop being liberal and become an American radical" (*To Be Young,* p. 239). Protesting the House Committee on Un-American Activities, she saw the United States as a "laggard and oppressive nation" and also urged Americans to "oblige all governments to say no to war anymore."

These political concerns were reflected in her second Broadway play, *The Sign in Sidney Brustein's Window,* which opened on Oct. 15, 1964, at the Longacre Theatre. It came as a surprise to many that her new play was set in Greenwich Village and had an all-white cast, with the exception of one "passing" black. Dedicated "to the committed everywhere," the play has at its center the struggle of Sidney Brustein, a disillusioned liberal who learns in the course of the play to reject complacency and despair and to take a step toward involvement with other human beings.

The Sign in Sidney Brustein's Window became a cause célèbre, while Lorraine Hansberry lay in the hospital during much of the rehearsal and production period, fighting what was finally diagnosed as cancer. The play ran for 101 performances, kept alive as long as its author lived by people who sincerely believed in the "politics of caring" expressed in the play. Although she and Nemiroff had been divorced the previous spring, he worked to keep the play open, and remained close to her in her last months. Lorraine Hansberry died in New York in January 1965, at age thirty-four.

[All of Lorraine Hansberry's unpublished correspondence and papers are in the hands of Robert Nemiroff, whom she named as her sole executor. *The Movement, Documentary of a Struggle For Equality* (1964), *A Raisin in the Sun,* and a few articles constituted her published works at the time of her death. Robert Nemiroff later edited *The Sign in Sidney Brustein's Window* (1965) and *Les Blancs: The Collected Last Plays of Lorraine Hansberry* (1972), which includes two television plays, *The Drinking*

Gourd and *What Use Are Flowers? Les Blancs* was produced on Broadway in 1970. *To Be Young, Gifted and Black* (1969), also edited by Nemiroff, is the best source for information about her life and works; it includes selections, photographs of Hansberry, and some of her drawings. As a theater piece *To Be Young, Gifted and Black* was produced off-Broadway in 1968–69. A bibliography by Nemiroff is included in *Freedomways,* Fourth Quarter 1979, an issue devoted to Hansberry. Outstanding magazine articles are James Baldwin, "Sweet Lorraine," *Esquire,* Nov. 1969; Ossie Davis, "The Significance of Lorraine Hansberry," *Freedomways,* Summer 1965; Julius Lester, "Remembering Lorraine Hansberry/Young, Gifted, and Black: The Politics of Caring," the *Village Voice,* May 28, 1970. Hansberry was interviewed for a brief profile in the *New Yorker,* May 9, 1959, and an entry appears in *Current Biog.,* 1959. A bibliography of both Hansberry's work and critical pieces on her is included in Esther Spring Arata and Nicholas John Rotoli, *Black American Playwrights, 1800 to the Present: A Bibliography* (1976). An excellent recording of her speeches is Caedmon's *Lorraine Hansberry Speaks Out: Art and the Black Revolution* (1972). An obituary appeared in the *N.Y. Times,* Jan. 13, 1965. Research for this article was assisted by a biobibliography prepared by Janis Clark.]

DORIS ABRAMSON

HARKNESS, Georgia Elma, April 21, 1891–Aug. 21, 1974. Theologian, religious educator.

Georgia Harkness was the second daughter and youngest of four children of J. Warren and Lillie (Merrill) Harkness. Born in Harkness, N.Y., she grew up on a farm which had belonged to her father's family since 1801, when her Scots-Irish forebears migrated to the Lake Champlain region. The Harknesses were eminent and prosperous members of their small rural community, the village having been named in honor of Georgia's grandfather.

The one-room school Georgia attended also housed, on Sundays, the Methodist congregation to which her parents belonged. Stirred to experience conversion once a year when the traveling revivalist came to town, around the age of nine she resolved what she later claimed was the only crisis of faith of her life. She joined the church at the age of fourteen after what she considered her definitive conversion; she maintained her membership in this church, and strong ties to the people of Harkness, for the rest of her life.

Upon her graduation from high school in nearby Keeseville, Harkness won a state scholarship to Cornell University. Never before more than twenty miles from home, she found the large university lonely until she joined the Student Christian Association and the Student Volunteer Movement. Through the latter group, Harkness pledged her life to service as a foreign missionary. The Social Gospel's vision of progress toward an earthly millennium thus combined with the deep personal piety of her childhood to shape her underlying faith.

Upon receiving her A.B. from Cornell in 1912, Harkness felt that she was needed by her parents, so she taught in high schools in Schuylerville and Scotia, N.Y., until 1918. The experience proved unsatisfying, and she was delighted to learn of a new profession which opened access to theological education and church employment to women: religious education. Master's degrees (M.R.E. and A.M.) from the Methodist-affiliated Boston University School of Religious Education (1920) whetted her appetite for more study, and she overcame the doubts of her male professors to earn a Ph.D. in philosophy from Boston University in 1923.

Harkness went to Elmira College in Elmira, N.Y., as an assistant professor of religious education in 1922, and taught in the philosophy department from 1923 to 1937. During this period she spent academic leaves at Harvard and Yale, and occasionally returned to Harkness to care for her aged parents. Ever an active Methodist, Georgia Harkness was ordained in 1926 as a local deacon and in 1938 as a local elder. Local ordination, the only form available to Methodist women until 1956, permitted her to exercise most ministerial roles but denied her membership in Annual Conference. She accepted frequent invitations to preach, and was a steady advocate of women's rights within the church. In 1931 she began to write poetry, and in 1935 *Holy Flame,* the first of several books of devotional poetry, was published. While at Elmira she also published five other books on the philosophy of religion and ethics.

A year and a half at Union Theological Seminary in New York City (1935–37) marked Harkness's shift of intellectual allegiance from philosophy to theology. As one of the "younger theologians" who met regularly for discussion, she held up the side of theological liberalism then under attack from continental theologians such as Karl Barth. Her liberalism was "chastened and deepened," however, by both theological criticism and the social turmoil of the 1930s. She never abandoned her commitment to a personalist philosophy, but she added to her beliefs in progress, continuing revelation, and the teachings of modern science an increased attention to the Bible as well as a more frequent reiteration of her faith that "only in Christ is revelation ultimate and unequivocal."

Her father, from his deathbed in 1937, gave her a personal motive for abandoning the quest for "an ideal of philosophical objectivity," as he urged her to "write more about Jesus Christ." Calling herself an evangelical liberal, she wrote the rest of her thirty-eight books unabashedly from the perspective of faith. Partly for this reason, Harkness was happy to leave Elmira's philosophy department in 1937 to teach religion at Mount Holyoke College. But she was unhappy there and left after two years to teach applied theology at Garrett Biblical Institute (later Garrett-Evangelical Theological Seminary) in Evanston, Ill.

A tour of war-ravaged Europe in 1924 had made Harkness a pacifist. Unlike many other Christian pacifists, she refused to abandon that position in the 1930s as war broke out in Europe and threatened America. Lending crucial support to her pacifism was her active involvement during the late thirties in the international ecumenical movement. The unity of Christians across national boundaries, Harkness argued, enabled the church to preach reconciliation to the world. Although she never supported World War II, Harkness voiced her public opposition in typically conciliatory fashion. Later, she did support the United Nations action in Korea, and, although continuing to call herself a pacifist, resigned her long-standing membership in the Fellowship of Reconciliation in 1951 because she objected to such tactics as tax and draft resistance.

The period between 1939 and 1945 was one of pain and change for Georgia Harkness. Suffering a severe fever and later a back injury as well as insomnia and depression, she sought psychiatric help. In *The Dark Night of the Soul* (1945) she wrote on suffering and its religious meaning. In 1944 Harkness began to share a home with Verna Miller, a musician. First in Evanston, and later in Berkeley and Claremont, Calif., they created a warm home where students and colleagues were entertained and served "theological cookies and pies" baked by Harkness. There the somewhat formal reserve which strangers noted in Harkness gave way to humor and an unaffected concern for others.

In a series of lectures at the Pacific School of Religion in Berkeley, published in 1949 as *The Gospel and Our World*, Harkness argued that the task of theologians was to make Christianity meaningful to the people in the pews. The lecture series won her an invitation to teach applied theology at the Berkeley school, which she accepted in 1950, and set the tone for the many books and articles she produced from 1950 until her death. Although the simplicity of her language earned her some academic condescension as a popularizer, her style should rather be seen as integrally related to her theology, which emphasized the importance of the laity and the correlation of doctrine and experience.

Harkness's claim to ecclesiastical leadership was well established by the 1950s. She continued to work for international ecumenism through the World Council of Churches, as well as serving her own denomination on several boards and commissions. In 1961, she retired and moved to Claremont, Calif., where she continued to write almost a book a year and to speak out on ecclesiastical and social issues. Widely respected for her graceful combination of personal piety and courageous social stands, including support of civil rights and opposition to the war in Vietnam, she won numerous honors. In 1974 she suffered a heart attack at home and died at Pomona Valley Community Hospital.

The most visible woman theologian in mid-century America, Georgia Harkness disclaimed what she called "militant feminism" but was not reluctant to call the church a "bastion of male dominance" or to argue forcefully for the full participation of women, most notably in a debate with Karl Barth at a 1948 meeting of the World Council of Churches. Her success was a source of encouragement to many women, and Garrett-Evangelical Theological Seminary honored her contribution by establishing a chair for a woman theologian, the Georgia Harkness Professorship of Applied Theology.

[A large manuscript collection at Garrett-Evangelical Theological Seminary contains an autobiography written for the Pacific Coast Theological Group during the 1950s; many letters to Harkness and some from her; printed articles; clippings; and manuscripts of sermons, articles, poems, hymns, lectures, and syllabi. *Conflicts in Religious Thought* (1929) and *The Recovery of Ideals* (1937) are illustrative of her early philosophical approach, while *Prayer and the Common Life* (1948), *Toward Understanding the Bible* (1954), *Christian Ethics* (1957), and *Women in Church and Society* (1971) represent her later perspectives. Devotional writings include *Through Christ Our Lord* (1951) and *The Bible Speaks to Daily Needs* (1959). Harkness was the only woman contributor to the *Christian Century's* series "How My Mind Has Changed in This Decade," March 15, 1939. Between 1938 and 1942 she also wrote a number of articles on pacifism for *Christian Century*. Other articles on pacifism, women in the church, and ecumenism appeared in the Methodist periodicals *Zion's Herald* (1925–40) and *Christian Advocate* (1924–46). Margaret Frakes, "Theology Is Her Province," *Christian Century*, Sept. 24, 1952, and Helen Johnson, "She Made Theology Understandable," *United Methodists Today*, Oct. 1974, based on interviews with Harkness, are important sources. Also see the entry in *Current Biog.*, 1960. Obituaries appeared in the *N.Y. Times*, Aug. 22, 1974, and the *Methodist Christian Advocate*, Sept. 10, 1974. Birth certificate from the N.Y. State Dept. of Health; death certificate from the Registrar of Los Angeles Cty., Calif. Charlotte Williams Conable, *Women at Cornell* (1978), contains a photograph of Harkness. Additional information was provided by the Abingdon Press, John C. Bennett, C. Douglas Hayward, Harland E. Hogue, and Verna Miller.]

DOROTHY C. BASS

HARRIMAN, Florence Jaffray Hurst, July 21, 1870–Aug. 31, 1967. Democratic party official, diplomat.

Florence Harriman, who became the United States minister to Norway, was born in New York City to Caroline Elise (Jaffray) and Francis William Jones Hurst. Both her parents' families were English; her father's family had come to America from Bermuda before the Civil War. Two older brothers had died in infancy; Daisy (as she was called all her life) was the eldest of the three surviving children, all daughters. Caroline Hurst died at twenty-nine of puerperal fever following childbirth; Daisy was then three years old. She and her sisters were raised by their father, the head of a steamship company and president of the New York Yacht Club, in their maternal grandfather's home on Fifth Avenue. Her education was, as she put it, rather sketchy, consisting only of private classes from 1880 to 1888, which she attended at the home of ANNE MORGAN, daughter of J. Pierpont Morgan. Daisy Hurst made her debut in 1888 and in November 1889 married J. Borden Harriman, a New York banker. She had several miscarriages before her only child, Ethel Borden Harriman, was born on Dec. 11, 1897.

Harriman soon moved beyond the narrow circles prescribed for young society matrons at the turn of the century. She was a founder and the first president of the exclusive Colony Club, New York's first social club for women—a daring innovation at the time. Harriman felt that its members would discover that "union in social, as in business and working life, is strength." She formed a department in the club to investigate working conditions in stores, hotels, and factories.

Harriman entered politics in the 1912 presidential campaign of Woodrow Wilson, who remained her hero for the rest of her life. At Wilson's request, she chaired the Women's National Wilson and Marshall Association, giving campaign speeches and acting as a "curtain-raiser." In return for her campaign work, Wilson made Harriman one of three representatives of the public on the Federal Industrial Relations Commission (FIRC), which had been established to investigate the causes of industrial unrest. Harriman traveled to strike sites during this period and tried to blunt criticisms that she lacked expertise by consulting with such prominent social reformers as LILLIAN WALD, JANE ADDAMS, and FLORENCE KELLEY. Her four-year term on the FIRC, from 1913 to 1916, required a move from Mt. Kisco, N.Y., to Washington, D.C., which became her permanent home. Harriman's husband supported the move wholeheartedly, but he died after a long illness in December 1914. Although J. Borden Harriman was a first cousin of railroad magnate E. H. Harriman, the Harrimans had never been wealthy, and finances were often a problem for Daisy Harriman after her husband's death.

During World War I Daisy Harriman organized a Red Cross motor corps in France and chaired the Committee on Women in Industry for the Council of National Defense. A former suffragist, Harriman increased her political activities during the 1920s. In 1922 she headed the committee of the National Consumers' League that organized the league's opposition to the Equal Rights Amendment. In the same year Harriman cofounded the Women's National Democratic Club, of which she was president for eight years. The following year, she published a volume of memoirs entitled *From Pinafores to Politics* and in 1924 began a thirty-two-year term as Democratic National Committeewoman from Washington, D.C. The 1920s also saw the initiation of Harriman's "Sunday night suppers," which brought Washington's most interesting people to Uplands, her Foxhall Road home. These suppers, while nominally nonpartisan, helped maintain the spirits of out-of-power Democrats throughout the 1920s.

Daisy Harriman supported Newton D. Baker over Franklin D. Roosevelt for the 1932 Democratic nomination, believing that Baker's views were closer to Wilson's ideals; her defection was widely noted by Roosevelt and his advisers. During Roosevelt's first term, Harriman's role was limited, though she participated vicariously in the New Deal through her friends MARY HARRIMAN RUMSEY, who was chairman of the Consumers' Advisory Board of the National Recovery Administration, and FRANCES PERKINS, who shared Uplands with her in the summer of 1933. Harriman had so much spare time during these years that she tried to write a novel—a romance about a love triangle in England and America. It was unsuccessful, and she destroyed the only copies.

In April 1937, Harriman's banishment from official Democratic duties ended when she was named minister to Norway, the second American woman to so represent her country abroad. (RUTH BRYAN OWEN [ROHDE], minister to Denmark from 1933 to 1936, was the first.) Harriman hesitated because of her age, but her daughter's strong support convinced her to accept the challenge. Her three years in Norway were happy ones; she loved the country and enjoyed her diplomatic duties. In November 1939, Harriman negotiated the release of the American ship *City of Flint*, which had been captured by a German warship and sent into the Norwegian port of Haugesund. Franklin Roosevelt had not intended to send a woman to any country likely to become involved in European hostilities, but the situation changed dramatically when Germany invaded Norway on April 9, 1940; Harriman was the first diplomat to cable news of the invasion. Sometimes in personal danger, she continued to report to Washington as she followed the Norwegian government from Oslo to asylum in Sweden. She also arranged for the evacuation of hundreds of United States citizens, and finally in August 1940 she and her party (which included the Crown Princess of Norway and her children) were picked up by a transport ship returning to the United States.

Harriman's daughter died in 1953. Daisy Harriman lived fourteen years longer, remaining active in the Democratic party and in Washington affairs. At the age of eighty-four, she led a march through Washington in 1955 to protest the disfranchisement of the District of Columbia. In 1963, she received a special Citation of Merit and the Medal of Freedom from President John F. Kennedy in a White House ceremony. Harriman died at her Washington home in 1967 after suffering a stroke. In her ninety-seven years she had, as she said in her memoirs, "a box seat at the America of my times." In turn, she had won the country's respect.

[The Florence Jaffray Harriman Papers in the Library of Congress concentrate on her public career and are best on the years in Norway. There are some Harriman letters in the Katie Louchheim Papers, Library of Congress. The first volume of Harriman's memoirs, *From Pinafores to Politics* (1923), captures the spirit of one woman's entrance into public life at the beginning of the twentieth century. The second volume, *Mission to the North* (1941), tells the compelling story of her flight from the Nazis. Less useful are *The Reminiscences of Florence Jaffray Harriman* (1950) in the Oral History Coll., Columbia Univ. For a more personal glimpse of Harriman see the chapter "Tea with Daisy" in Katie Louchheim, *By the Political Sea*

(1970). An obituary appeared in the *N.Y. Times,* Sept. 1, 1967; death record provided by D.C. Dept. of Public Health. Assistance with research was provided by an excellent biobibliography prepared by Betty Jo Keppel.]

SUSAN WARE

HARRIS, Mary Belle, Aug. 19, 1874–Feb. 22, 1957. Prison administrator.

Mary Belle Harris was best known for her work as a prison administrator. That career did not begin until she was almost forty; she had been before that a scholar and teacher of the classics. Born in Factoryville, Pa., she was the oldest of three children and only daughter of John Howard and Mary Elizabeth (Mace) Harris. Her father was a Baptist minister and president of Bucknell University (1889–1919). Her mother died in 1880. A year later, John Harris married Lucy Adelaide Bailey, a first cousin of Mary Mace and close friend of the Harris family, who was to be a much-loved stepmother. Six children, all boys, were born of this second marriage. Mary Harris and her brothers were educated at the Keystone Academy, a Baptist secondary school founded by her father, and at Bucknell.

Harris began her college work in 1890. She received a music degree in 1893, an A.B. in 1894, and an A.M. in Latin and classics in 1895, all from Bucknell. A year later she enrolled at the University of Chicago, obtaining the Ph.D. in Sanskrit and Indo-European Comparative Philology in 1900. At Chicago, Harris became friends with KATHARINE BEMENT DAVIS, who was later to change the direction of Harris's life from classical studies to prison work.

Between 1900 and 1910, Harris taught Latin in Chicago and at the Bryn Mawr School in Baltimore, then under the direction of EDITH HAMILTON, and studied archaeology and numismatics at Johns Hopkins University. In June 1912 she sailed for Europe to become a teacher-chaperone at the American Classical School in Rome and to study Roman coins in Italy and at the Kaiser Friedrich Museum in Berlin. By May 1914, when Harris returned to the United States, Katharine Davis had become a prominent penologist and prison reformer and was then Commissioner of Corrections in New York City. She offered Harris the newly created post of superintendent of women and deputy warden of the Workhouse on Blackwell Island; Harris, who had neither job nor prospects, accepted. Without prior corrections experience, she began on July 1, 1914, the career in prison administration that would bring her renown.

The severely overcrowded Workhouse, an

institution with an average daily population of 700 women, was a "depressingly grim place" to begin. Inmates, serving sentences ranging from three days to six months for alcoholism, prostitution, and drug offenses, were crowded into 150 cells and given little to do. Harris introduced changes which, while common at women's prisons, were not available at the Workhouse: she created a library, permitted card-playing and knitting in the cells, fenced off part of the yard to allow daily outdoor exercise, and renovated the dining room and lounge for staff. Besides the direct benefits, these policies also released matrons from enforcing petty rules which had increased the boredom and tension. Early in her new career, Harris thus earned a reputation for success based on common sense tactics.

Harris remained at the Workhouse for three and a half years, until the defeat of reform mayor John Purroy Mitchel in 1917 forced her resignation. Despite suspicions that penal work was merely an "interlude" in her teaching career, Harris assumed the superintendency of the State Reformatory for Women at Clinton, N.J., in February 1918. There she continued or expanded many of the programs initiated by her predecessor. By encouraging such measures as self-government in the cottages, a dairy run mostly by inmates and their "student officer," and an Exit Club for women about to be paroled, Harris provided the inmates with some freedom and responsibility for institutional management, a policy which became her trademark.

In September 1918 Harris was granted a leave of absence from Clinton to join MARTHA P. FALCONER at the War Department's Commission on Training Camp Activities. As assistant director of the Section on Reformatories and Detention Houses, which was responsible for dealing with women and girls arrested in the camp areas, Harris set up detention homes and health facilities in Florida, South Carolina, Virginia, and Georgia. When this assignment ended, she returned briefly to Clinton, but in May 1919 she became superintendent of the State Home for Girls, a juvenile institution in Trenton, N.J., which was known as a place inhabited by dangerous girls. Despite continual problems, Harris successfully inaugurated an inmate self-government system and the local press praised her as a miracle worker who quietly instituted revolutionary changes with wonderful results. It was an image she retained throughout her life.

Harris resigned from the Trenton institution at the end of 1924 and on Jan. 1, 1925, went to Washington, intending to become executive secretary of the International Policewoman's Association. Instead, MABEL WALKER WILLEBRANDT, the assistant attorney general responsible for federal prisons, offered her the opportunity to head the newly authorized Federal Industrial Institution for Women, to be built at Alderson, W. Va. On March 12, 1925, Mary Belle Harris was sworn in as Alderson's first superintendent.

She immediately became involved with the plans for the new prison, working with the architects to see that it conformed both to its congressional mandate and to her own ideas about the best environment for rehabilitating women prisoners. Harris believed that traditional institutions prohibited change because they also imprisoned the personalities of inmates and staff. She intended Alderson to be a place where women would be educated and active, trained to be good citizens and self-supporting individuals, strong enough to resist temptations once outside. The prison began operation April 30, 1927, when the first inmates arrived; it opened officially on Nov. 24, 1928.

Alderson was admired and applauded for its modern and innovative features: the absence of a massive surrounding wall or heavily armed guards, the extensive farming and physical activities, an individualized classification system, an inmate self-governing system, and the promotion of education and vocational training—all with few escapes or serious disciplinary problems. Its image was that of a model institution, resembling a fashionable girls' boarding school.

Harris retired reluctantly from Alderson at the age of sixty-six in March 1941. Returning to Pennsylvania, she served briefly on the state Board of Parole until it was abolished by the legislature in 1943. She then settled in Lewisburg, Pa., continuing to serve as a trustee of Bucknell University and of the First Baptist Church of Lewisburg and lecturing and writing about her penal work. In 1953 Harris embarked on an extended European and North African tour, visiting her diplomat nephew in Cyprus, and inspecting two Libyan prisons. She returned to Lewisburg in July 1954 and died there three years later of a heart attack, at the age of eighty-two.

Mary Belle Harris shared with contemporary penal reformers belief in a classification system geared to individual needs and talents, education and training in employable fields, exercise and outdoor activities to develop physical and mental discipline, and an indeterminate sentence that would permit the reeducation process to occur at the inmate's own pace. These visions of change were constrained by the values of her time, so racial segregation of inmates, for example, was acceptable to her. She believed that women's criminality was largely due to economic or psychological dependency, particularly upon men. Thus she was outspoken about the need for women to "build within them a wall of self-respect" and to learn employable skills which would free them from being dependent on a man or a burden on the community. Despite the fears of some Washington bureaucrats that men would not serve on a staff dominated by women, she was uncompromising about the importance of operating Alderson with a predominantly female staff. A tough and powerful administrator, Harris understood and successfully used a variety of political weapons to create and maintain at Alderson the oft-praised "community of women working together under the guidance of other women."

[The Archives and Bertrand Library of Bucknell Univ. contain personal and professional materials on Harris and her family, including educational records, books by Harris, alumni magazine reports, and newspaper clippings. Information about her nonpenal life may also be found in her inactive personnel file at the National Personnel Records Center (NPRC), St. Louis, and in the Ferdinand Hamburger, Jr., Archives at Johns Hopkins Univ. The basic sources on her penal career are her autobiography, *I Knew Them in Prison* (1936); Eugenia Lekkerkerker, *Reformatories for Women in the United States* (1931); the NPRC file; and the Bureau of Prisons boxes of the Dept. of Justice files at the Nat. Archives. "The Alderson Saga," a scrapbook and diary of the early years, is currently stored at Alderson. Harris published several books and articles, including her doctoral thesis, *Kalidasa, Poet of Nature* (1936); *The Pathway of Mattie Howard to and from Prison: True Story of the Regeneration of an Ex-Convict and Gangster Woman* (1937); "Personality in Prison," *Proceedings* of the Am. Prison Assoc. (1929), pp. 292–300; "I Suppose I Was Stupid," *Survey*, Nov. 15, 1928, pp. 235–37; and "Women's Reformatory," *The Prison World: A Jour. of Crime and Corrections*, Oct. 15, 1924. Harris was the subject of news articles at each stage of her career: see "Woman to Rule Women," *N.Y. Times*, June 18, 1914; "Jail for Women to Be Unwalled," *N.Y. Times*, Aug. 22, 1926; and "Four Named to Parole Board," *Harrisburg Patriot*, April 15, 1942. Frequently in the press during or because of her Alderson tenure, the portraits of her were always adoring; see, for example, those in *World's Work*, March 1931; *Rotarian*, June 1942; and *Country Gentleman*, June 1938. See also Elizabeth Munger, "The Federal Institution at Alderson," *Policewoman's Internat. Bull.*, Feb. 1929, and Martha P. Falconer, "The Segregation of Delinquent Women and Girls As a War Problem," Am. Acad. of Political and Social Sci., *Annals*, Sept. 1918. An obituary (aging her by seven years) appeared in the *N.Y. Times*, Feb. 23, 1957; death certificate provided by the Pa. Dept. of Health. A biobibliography by Patti Peery assisted with research.]

CLAUDINE SCHWEBER

HARRISON, Hazel Lucile, May 12, 1883–April 28, 1969. Pianist.

Hazel Harrison, American concert pianist, was born in La Porte, Ind., the only child of Hiram and Olive Jane (Woods) Harrison. Her parents were direct descendants of pioneering black people who had fled the slave system in southern states and followed legendary escape routes to the midwestern United States and southern Ontario. Olive Harrison, who had been born in Canada, was a hairdresser and manicurist whose customers came from La Porte's most prominent families. Hiram Harrison, born in Michigan, worked as a laborer and rural postman and was, by 1884, coproprietor of Stevesand and Harrison, a barber shop close to the central business district of La Porte. He had a beautiful tenor voice, sang with the choir of the Central Presbyterian Church, and was organizer, director, and accompanist of its Sunday school choir.

Hazel Harrison's exceptional talents, manifest at an early age, were fostered by her father. She began piano lessons at four with Richard Pellow, an accomplished English organist and choirmaster of the Harrisons' church. By age eight Hazel was supplementing the family income by playing for dancing parties. At one such party, according to La Porte legend, a distinguished German musician, Victor Heinze, heard her and offered to become her teacher.

Heinze's tutelage and influence were major factors in Hazel Harrison's development as a pianist. Through her study with him, she acquired a remarkable keyboard technique, a lyrical quality of playing, and a large repertory. She remained his student for many years, commuting to Chicago when Heinze moved all his teaching activity there from La Porte. In Chicago, devoted and knowledgeable patrons of music praised her as Heinze's most accomplished student; encouragement also came from prominent members of the city's black community.

In 1902, Hazel Harrison graduated from La Porte High School. She remained at home, intensifying preparations for a career as a concert pianist and teaching music to the children of La Porte's leading families. The trips to Chicago for lessons continued, as did employment as a dance pianist in both cities.

The horizons of Harrison's career widened when in the spring of 1904 she received an invitation to appear as soloist with the Berlin Philharmonic Orchestra under August Scharrer. The concert took place on October 22 at the Berlin Singacademie; she performed two concerti, the A minor by Grieg and the E minor of Chopin. It was the first appearance with an orchestra in Europe of an American artist whose entire musical education had taken place on home soil. Berlin critics were unanimous in praise: she was described as a "musical wonder," a "sensation," and a "virtuoso."

She returned at once to La Porte, resuming the cycle of teaching, studying, and performing. A recital at Kimball Hall in Chicago in 1910 brought critical acclaim and an appeal from a veteran musical critic for financial assistance to enable her to return to Germany for further study. Response came from two Chicago music philanthropists and Harrison began lessons early in 1911 in Berlin with Hugo van Dalen. He arranged an audition for her with Ferruccio Busoni, the world-renowned Italian pianist and composer. Busoni responded to the "strength, rhythm, and poetry" of the young pianist and agreed to supervise her training, reversing his earlier decision not to accept new pupils.

Hazel Harrison was drawn immediately into the closely knit circle in Berlin of the Busoni family, pupils, and intimate associates, and a close bond was established between teacher and student. She embraced the unique Busonian precepts and dicta: recognition of similitudes among the arts, musical eclecticism, program-building on the grand scale, and recognition of the sonorities of the piano as echoing those of orchestral sound. Busoni exhorted the young artist to visit art galleries, to study German philosophy and folk literature, to engage in ensemble playing, and to "live more . . . all will show in your playing." During Busoni's absences from Berlin, Harrison worked on keyboard technique with his young protégé and assistant, the Dutch pianist Egon Petri.

This remarkable experience ended in 1914 with the outbreak of World War I. Hazel Harrison returned to the United States and moved from La Porte to Chicago. She was joined there by her mother in 1920 and shortly thereafter by Hiram Harrison who had been separated from the family for many years. On Sept. 1, 1919, she married Walter Bainter Anderson, a beauty products manufacturer and salesman; the marriage ended in divorce in the late 1920s.

Hazel Harrison's fame as a pianist grew to considerable proportions during the 1920s, as recital tours under various managements took her many times across the country. In 1927 she returned to Germany to study for a brief period with Petri. The depression years took their toll, however, forcing her into an expanded teaching career but in no way causing her to abandon her efforts as a concert artist. She worked indefatigably on enlarging a repertory recognized for its brilliance and technical difficulty. Harrison was an early proponent of contemporary composers of the Soviet Union, Poland, and Germany and of "synesthesia," the association of color and sound on a systematic and consistent basis. Her programs included compositions of polysensory intent by Alexander Scriabin and Alexander Laszlo and unpublished works by black composers of her acquaintance, as well as the more familiar but stunning variations and fantasies built on the waltzes of Johann Strauss and the transcriptions for piano of organ works of Bach written by Liszt and by Busoni.

Recitals at Aeolian and Town Halls in New York City, at Jordan Hall in Boston, at Kimball Hall in Chicago, and in major American and Canadian musical centers brought Harrison continued praise. In 1940 Glenn Dillard Gunn, music critic of the Washington (D.C.) Times-Herald, wrote: "She has today a technical equipment that is definitely that of a virtuoso, and her gift for pianistic address is vivid, urgent and eloquent." Nonetheless, access to the mainstream of the concert business in the United States—annual performances in the great concert halls, appearances with major symphony orchestras, and contracts with the important recording companies—was denied her because of her race. The 1904 Berlin engagement was Hazel Harrison's only appearance as soloist with a major symphony orchestra during its normal concert season. She played with the Minneapolis Symphony under Eugene Ormandy in 1932 in a concert at the Tuskegee (Ala.) Institute, and with the Hollywood Bowl Symphony under Izeler Solomon in August 1949 during a convention of the National Association of Negro Musicians, both appearances under special circumstances and before special audiences.

An enthusiastic review of a 1922 Chicago recital had ended in a somber prophetic vein: "She is extremely talented . . . it seems too bad that the fact that she is a Negress may limit her future plans." The pattern of segregated audiences and management systems characterizing the business of concert performance of the day yielded rarely to include this exceptional artist and her audiences remained largely those of her own race. She gained an enormous following throughout the United States, however, and was the unrivaled pianist of the day for the nation's black music lovers.

Hazel Harrison's accomplishments as a teacher of piano are also of great significance. During a long and distinguished teaching career she was instrumental in developing a number of outstanding younger musicians. In November 1931 Harrison had joined the faculty of the School of Music at Tuskegee Institute, newly organized by her friend William Dawson, noted composer and choir director. Leaving Tuskegee in 1937, she became head of the piano faculty at Howard University in Washington, D.C. She also taught for brief periods at Alabama State College in Montgomery and at Jackson College in Mississippi. In 1945 she established at Howard the Olive J. Harrison Piano Scholarship Fund in memory of her mother. Subsequent annual recitals by her students and her own appearances served as benefits for the fund. During the 1940s and 1950s she also gave benefit recitals for war relief and for partisan causes sponsored by groups sympathetic to civil uprisings in the Soviet Union, Spain, and Latin America. On leave from Howard from 1947 to 1950 she toured the United States, and in 1952 the western provinces of Canada.

For a short period during the 1950s Harrison was married to Allen Moton, an Alabama businessman and a friend of long standing. The marriage ended in divorce. She resigned from Howard in 1957 and moved to New York City. In 1965 she went south, to La Grange, Ga., and Montgomery, Ala., seeking a gentler climate. Returning to Washington, D.C., she lived in the home of a former student, the Reverend Alphonso Harrod, and then in the nursing home where she died in 1969 of congestive heart failure. During her last years she became immersed in reading philosophy. She had continued as long as possible to teach, practiced daily, and played for small groups of friends in the Harrod home.

[Correspondence between Harrison and members of the Harreld family from 1903 to 1965, clippings, photographs, and recital programs are held by Josephine Harreld Love. There is also some material in the Moorland-Springarn Coll., Howard Univ. Her career may be traced in the files of the La Porte, Ind., *Daily Record* and *Argus Bulletin,* and the *Chicago Tribune, Inter-Ocean,* and *Record-Herald.* Family information was verified through municipal and county records in La Porte. Published biographical information and commentary is scanty; see Maude Cuney Hare, *Negro Musicians and Their Music* (1936); "Men of the Month," in *The Crisis,* Dec. 1912; and a tribute to her in an article by Ralph Ellison, her student at Tuskegee, "The Little Man at Chehaw Station: The American Artist and His Audience," *Am. Scholar,* Winter 1978–79. Assistance was provided by William Dawson of Tuskegee; by Florence Andrew, Rev. John Deason, and Ruth Tallant, all of La Porte; and by Catherine Moton Patterson, Portia Trenholm Jenifer, Doris McGinty, Benjamin Ward, Rev. Alphonso Harrod, and Vivian Scott. A death certificate was obtained from the D.C. Dept. of Health.]

JOSEPHINE HARRELD LOVE

HARVEY, Ethel Browne, Dec. 14, 1885–Sept. 2, 1965. Cell biologist, embryologist.

Ethel Browne Harvey, known for her findings about cell division in sea urchin eggs, was born in Baltimore, Md., the last of two sons and three daughters of Jennie R. (Nicholson) and Bennet Bernard Browne. Both her maternal and paternal ancestors came to America from England in the seventeenth century. Her father— a successful Baltimore obstetrician-gynecologist —was professor of gynecology at the Woman's Medical College of Baltimore and an early practitioner of ovariotomy and other sexual surgery for diseases of women. Both of her sisters, Mary Nicholson and Jennie Browne, became Baltimore physicians. The Brownes supported women's education and sent their daughters to the Bryn Mawr School, the first solely preparatory girls' school in the United States, whose headmistress was the classicist EDITH HAMILTON.

Graduating from the Bryn Mawr School in 1902, Ethel Browne earned an A.B. at the Woman's College of Baltimore (later Goucher College) in 1906. After spending the first of many summers in Woods Hole, Mass., where she studied at the Marine Biological Laboratory (MBL), she enrolled at Columbia University, earning an A.M. in 1907 and Ph.D. in 1913 under the cell biologist Edmund Beecher Wilson. Her doctoral thesis, a study of male germ cells of the aquatic carnivorous insect genus *Notonecta,* marked the beginning of a lifelong interest in the role of the nucleus and cytoplasm in inheritance and development. Publishing several papers while a graduate student, Browne supported herself with a series of fellowships and jobs. She received fellowships from Goucher (1906–07) and the Society for the Promotion of University Education for Women (1911–12), and, because of World War I, used the Sarah Berliner Fellowship, intended for study in Germany, at the Hopkins Marine Station, University of California (1914–15). From 1908 until 1911 she was an instructor in science and mathematics at the Bennett School for Girls in Millbrook, N.Y., and she spent a year teaching biology at the Dana Hall School in Wellesley, Mass. (1913–14). She also served as a laboratory assistant in biology at Princeton (1912–13) and in histology at Cornell Medical College (1915–16).

On March 12, 1916, Ethel Browne married Edmund Newton Harvey, a biology professor at Princeton whose widely recognized work was on bioluminescence. They shared scientific passions, but worked independently. Their social and cultural lives centered around Princeton and the international world of marine biology. The Harveys had two children, Edmund Newton Harvey, Jr. (b. 1916), who became a chemist, and Richard Bennet Harvey (b. 1922), who became a physician.

Ethel Harvey's career illustrates some of the complexities encountered by women scientists of her generation in obtaining support for their work. After her marriage, she engaged in part-time research until 1927, aided by a mother's helper who spent summers with the family at Woods Hole, by Catherine Bates, their maid in Princeton, and by governesses during a year spent in Monaco at l'Institut Océanographique (1920–21) and another year in Naples at the Stazione Zoologica (1925–26). From 1928 until 1931 Harvey was instructor in biology at Washington Square College, New York University. But for most of her career, from 1931 until 1962, she was an independent investigator in the biology department at Princeton, where she received office space in Edwin G. Conklin's laboratory. Princeton paid her summer fees at the MBL, where she shared space with her husband. Otherwise, except for one grant in 1937 from the American Philosophical Society, her internationally recognized work was unsupported.

The MBL provided Harvey with a professional base—as it and similar laboratories did for other women who had no regular scientific appointments. Over the years Harvey also conducted research at marine stations in Japan, Bermuda, North Carolina, and California. Having benefited from education in women's institutions and fellowships for women, she also profited, in 1925–26 and 1932, from the American Women's Table in Naples, which had been established by physiologist IDA HENRIETTA HYDE and other scientific women of the previous generation. Subsequently Harvey was awarded use of the Rockefeller Institute's Jacques Loeb Memorial Table at Naples (1933, 1934, 1937).

Culminating in the publication of *The American Arbacia and Other Sea Urchins* (1956), Ethel Harvey's scientific contributions were in descriptive and experimental cytology in early development, particularly of sea urchin eggs. From the time of the origin of modern experimental embryology in the late nineteenth century, researchers have tried to determine the relative contributions of parts of the germ cell to development. Most attention focused on the chromosomes in the cell nucleus, which often appeared uniquely to "direct" development. Harvey's work, however, concentrated mainly on the egg cytoplasm, the nonnuclear substance of the cell which is the site of many other structures, such as mitochondria. She examined cell structures in the light microscope and conducted physiological experiments on such physical-chemical factors in development as oxygen, ultraviolet light, and sonic waves. She also helped design and adapt technically advanced apparatus to study early embryos.

Her most important work began in the 1930s. To investigate the optically empty "ground substance" of the sea urchin egg, Harvey developed a technique to stimulate cell divisions of sea urchin egg fragments (merogones) which had no nuclear material, and were thus, according to contemporary scientific opinion, without "directing" genes or chromosomes. Centrifuging eggs at forces of 10,000 times gravity, she placed resulting nuclei-free egg fragments in concentrated sea water. The fragments divided into as many as 500 cells and lived up to a month, but underwent no further development. Cell division without either maternal or paternal nucleus was unexpected and stimulated scientific controversy about the active role in development of cytoplasmic structures and processes. Harvey's work also was important to further investigations of mechanisms of cell division.

The popular press hailed Ethel Harvey's work as a "creation of life without parents." Although her interpretations of the merogones were very cautious, she worked in the tradition of Jacques Loeb, famous in the early twentieth century for his mechanistic conception of life and his pioneering studies of parthenogenesis. Harvey's work, like Loeb's, drew popular attention to the modern biologist's intervention in the life process. Harvey speculated that her parthenogenetic merogones might mean that fundamental characteristics of living matter (such as cell division) were cytoplasmic, while genes controlled later, more specialized characteristics (like eye color).

Among the honors earned by Ethel Harvey were an honorary D.Sc. from Goucher College (1956) and election as fellow of the American Association for the Advancement of Science, l'Institut International d'Embryologie in Utrecht, and the New York Academy of Sciences. In 1950 she was elected a trustee of the MBL, the first woman trustee since CORNELIA CLAPP. After an attack of acute appendicitis, Ethel Harvey died of peritonitis in Falmouth, Mass., in 1965.

[Ethel Harvey published about 100 papers in scientific journals, especially *Biological Bull.* and *Jour. Experimental Zoology*. Bound volumes of her collected papers are held by her son Richard B. Harvey, and reprints are held in the MBL Library, Woods Hole. See especially "A Study of the Male Germ Cells in Notonecta," *Jour. Experimental Zoology*, Jan. 1913; "A Review of the Chromosome Numbers in the Metazoa," *Jour. Morphology*, Dec. 1916, and June 1920; "Parthenogenetic Merogony or Cleavage Without Nuclei in *Arbacia punctulata*," *Biological Bull.*, Aug. 1936; "Fertilization," *Encyc. Britannica*, 1946 and 1961. Popular response to her discovery of parthenogenetic merogony may be followed in articles in *Science News Letter*, Oct. 12, 1935, p. 227; *Life*, Sept. 13, 1937, p. 70; *N.Y. Herald Tribune*, Nov. 28, 1937, pp. 1, 32; *N.Y. Times*, Nov. 28, 1937, pp. 1, 41; *Newsweek*, Dec. 6, 1937, pp. 36–37; and *Time*, Dec. 6, 1937, p. 32. Biographical material may be found in E. G. Butler, "Memorials: Ethel Browne Harvey," *Biological Bull.*, Aug. 1967. See also Mary Jane Hogue, "The Contribution of Goucher Women to the Biological Sciences," *Goucher Quart.*, Summer 1951; articles in the *Goucher Quart.*, Summer 1956, and Bryn Mawr School *Bull.*, 14 (1957); Jan Burtin Sloan, "The Founding of the Naples Table Association for Promoting Scientific Research by Women, 1897," *Signs*, Autumn 1978; and Margaret Rossiter, "Women Scientists in America Before 1920," *Am. Scientist*, May-June 1974. Biographical information about Harvey's family is in "A Sketch of the Life of Bennet Bernard Browne, M.D.," in M. Y. Ridenbaugh, *The Biography of Ephraim McDowell, M.D.* (1890); and Frank H. Johnson, "Edmund Newton Harvey, 1887–1959," *Biog. Memoirs of the Nat. Acad. of Sci.*, vol. 39 (1967). For the scientific traditions in which she worked see Jacques Loeb, *Artificial Parthenogenesis and Fertilization* (1913), and *The Mechanistic Conception of Life* (1912, 1964), and E. B. Wilson, *The Cell in Development and Inheritance* (1896; 2d ed. 1900). Additional information was provided by Richard B. Harvey and Edmund N. Harvey, Jr. An obituary appeared in the *N.Y. Times*, Sept. 3, 1965; death certificate from Mass. State Dept. of Public Health.]

DONNA J. HARAWAY

HAWES, Elizabeth, Dec. 16, 1903–Sept. 6, 1971. Fashion designer, writer, feminist.

Elizabeth Hawes was a fashion designer who announced that "fashion is spinach." She was also a journalist, a union organizer, an advocate of publicly supported child care centers, and a prolific author. Her books offer both a continuous anecdotal autobiography and explanations in defense of the oppressed in America, especially of women.

Born in Ridgewood, N.J., Elizabeth Hawes was the second oldest of four children and the second of three daughters of John and Henrietta (Houston) Hawes. A granddaughter of Theodore Houston of Oswego, N.Y., a railroad executive, she was raised in an educated middle-class family. Her father became general freight manager of the Southern Pacific steamship line. It was her mother, however, who most encouraged her daughter's ambitions. An 1891 graduate of Vassar, Henrietta Hawes was an active member of the community; from 1932 to 1936 she directed the Emergency Relief Administration for Bergen County, N.J.

From the age of ten, Elizabeth made her own clothes and also sewed for her mother's friends. She made her first commercial sale—to a store in Haverford, Pa.—when she was twelve. After graduation from Ridgewood High School, she went to Vassar, as did her sisters, and majored in economics. Graduating in 1925, she sailed for Paris, intending to become a couturiere.

Paris introduced her to the realities of the fashion business. She worked for a copy house and then for an American dressmaking firm which hired her to make clandestine sketches of designer collections. At first Hawes was excited and challenged by the secrecy and by the chance to use her sketching and observation skills. Eventually, however, she became disturbed at her employers' ethics and took jobs in the Paris offices of two New York department stores, first Macy's and, later, Lord & Taylor. In 1928 she finally got her chance to design clothes, going to work at very low wages for the couturiere Nicole Groult. She also continued to do fashion reporting, writing about Paris fashions for various newspapers and for *The New Yorker*. Deciding, however, that the lives led by French women were not in accord with the clothes she wanted to design, Hawes returned to the United States.

On her twenty-fifth birthday, Dec. 16, 1928, Elizabeth Hawes, in partnership with Rosemary Harden, opened her own fashion business in Manhattan. The following year, her friend Alexander Calder gave a performance of his wire circus at Hawes-Harden. Harden withdrew in 1930 and the business was reorganized as Hawes Inc.

On Dec. 12, 1930, Hawes married Ralph Jester, a sculptor she had known in Paris. She gave Jester credit for making her think of clothes architecturally. They both believed in "building clothes to fit the body, and not being scared at curves." The couple separated in 1933 and were divorced in 1935.

During the 1930s, when Americans looked to Europe for innovations in the arts, Elizabeth Hawes proved that Americans could develop their own fashion ideas. In contrast to the sharp, wide-shouldered silhouette of the period, she designed softly fitting bias-cut dresses. On July 4, 1931, she became the first American to display a fashion collection in Paris, and in 1932 Lord & Taylor gave her nationwide publicity as one of three American designers promoted by DOROTHY SHAVER. Success led to a need for more space and in mid-1933 Hawes Inc. moved to a townhouse on East 67th Street. In 1935, she gave a showing of her clothes in the Soviet Union, the first such exhibit by an American woman designer since 1917.

With her move, Hawes added ready-to-wear clothes to her custom-made lines and began to sell designs to garment manufacturers. Becoming quickly frustrated when manufacturers changed her fabrics and designs, she refused to adapt to their ways; by the spring of 1937, she had severed relations with the Seventh Avenue garment district. On July 24, 1937, she married Joseph Losey, film and theater director; their son Gavrik, was born in July 1938.

Hawes reflected her disagreements with manufacturers in her best-selling first book, *Fashion Is Spinach* (1938). Rich with lively anecdotes of her career in Paris, the book attacks the American fashion industry for demanding continuous change in order to improve sales. She argued instead for "style," which would meet basic needs with simplicity.

Convinced that the day of made-to-order clothes was over (*Why Is a Dress?* p. 2), she closed Hawes Inc. in January 1940. From June 1940 to February 1942, she wrote a weekly column for the New York newspaper *PM*, advocating pants for women, skirts for men, and child care centers for working mothers. Despite opposition from Mayor Fiorello La Guardia, she attempted during 1941–42 to promote child care centers as a leader of the Committee for the Care of Young Children in Wartime.

Abandoning fashion, Hawes became preoccupied with helping women adjust to the dislocations of wartime. She worked the midnight shift at the Wright Aeronautical plant in Paterson, N.J., for a short time in 1943 and supported unionizing efforts there, joining the United Auto Workers (UAW) local. *Why Women Cry,* an account of her experiences at the plant, appeared in 1943; it defends women's need to be free of domestic routine while also detailing the hardships they suffer as "workingwomen." In 1944, the year of her divorce from Losey, Hawes moved to Detroit, where she spent ten months in the education department of the UAW.

Union work led Hawes to question the Equal Rights Amendment because of her fear, shared by most labor women, that it would eliminate protective legislation for women workers. *Hurry Up Please It's Time* (1946) recounts her UAW experience, both her friendships with women in the union and her criticism of them for their submissiveness in accepting arbitrary pay cuts and dismissals.

In late 1944, when the UAW reduced its staff, Hawes returned to New York and remained there until 1947. She continued to write for newspapers; in 1945 she was also an editorial adviser for the Labor Book Club. For much of 1947 she was in St. Croix. *Anything But Love,*

which appeared in 1948, is a satiric compilation of the rules of feminine behavior as promulgated by films, radio, and newspapers.

In 1948, Hawes returned to fashion design, opening Elizabeth Hawes Inc. on Madison Avenue in February. Everything about the business was more difficult and more expensive than it had been in the 1930s and it lasted only until Aug. 1, 1949. In 1950, dismayed by the growing political conservatism in the United States, she moved to the Virgin Islands.

In California around 1952, Hawes tried again for the fame that had been hers. She was not successful: the clothes she designed for a handful of women failed to provide financial security and writing no longer provided an alternate source of income. Her final book, *It's Still Spinach* (1954), restated her plea for men as well as women to break away from the inanities of fashion. In the late 1960s, Hawes returned to New York for the last time and lived at the Hotel Chelsea. She died there of a gastrointestinal hemorrhage in 1971.

As an unconventional designer, Elizabeth Hawes proved Americans could work independently of the French legend. In 1967 the Fashion Institute of Technology recognized her contribution as a trailblazer for American fashion with a retrospective show of her designs.

[What remains of Elizabeth Hawes's papers are in private hands. In addition to those mentioned above, her books include *Men Can Take It* (1939) and *But Say It Politely* (1951). Her correspondence with Bennett Cerf and other Random House executives regarding *Fashion Is Spinach* and *Men Can Take It* is in Box 84 of the Random House Papers in the Rare Book and Manuscript Library at Columbia Univ. Many of Hawes's sketches are in the Brooklyn Museum's Art Reference Library and some of her clothes are in that museum's collection. Her clothes are also in the collection of the Fashion Inst. of Technology and in the Costume Inst. of the Metropolitan Museum of Art, both N.Y. City. See also *Current Biog.*, 1940, pp. 370–72, and Elinor Lambert, *World of Fashion* (1977), p. 324. A birth certificate was provided by the N.J. Bureau of Vital Statistics; death record from N.Y. City Dept. of Health. Her obituary appeared in the *N.Y. Times,* Sept. 8, 1971. Helpful information was furnished by Hawes's son, Gavrik Losey, and by her older sister, Charlotte Adams.]

PATRICK R. MAHONEY

HAYDEN, Sophia Gregoria, Oct. 17, 1868–Feb. 3, 1953. Architect.

Sophia Hayden was born in Santiago, Chile. Her father, George Henry Hayden, a dentist from a New England family, married a South

American woman; Sophia was one of two daughters and three sons. In 1874 Sophia Hayden came to live with her paternal grandparents in the Jamaica Plain section of Boston. There she attended the Hillside School and went on to West Roxbury High School (1883–86).

In 1886 Hayden entered the Massachusetts Institute of Technology, the first woman admitted to study architecture in the program developed by Eugène Létang according to the principles of the École des Beaux Arts in Paris. Hayden's MIT training emphasized the ability to produce first an appropriate plan for a monumental building and then magnificent watercolor renderings. She demonstrated these skills in her thesis, "Design for a Museum of Fine Arts" in the neoclassical style. She learned basic structural engineering as well. President Francis Amasa Walker of the Institute stated that he considered her "competent to build a railroad bridge, if necessary, as she has gone thoroughly into her work" (Stern, p. 69). Hayden received her bachelor of architecture degree with honors in 1890 and took a job teaching mechanical drawing to students in the Eliot School in Jamaica Plain.

In 1891 an opportunity for public recognition of her talent and professional training appeared, in the announcement of "An Unusual Opportunity for Women Architects." This was the Board of Lady Managers' competition for the design of the Woman's Building of the World's Columbian Exposition in Chicago. The rules stated that the creator of the winning design would be appointed the architect of the building and would receive an honorarium of $1,000, plus expenses. Hayden set to work in her home designing a suitable building. Awarded first prize in the competition for her design, done in Italian Renaissance style, she was summoned to Chicago by Daniel Burnham, chief of construction at the Exposition, to complete the working drawings. For complete eighth-inch scale working drawings of the building, which cost over $150,000, she received a total of less than $1,500. Male architects commissioned to design Exposition buildings received honoraria and reimbursements three to ten times higher (Bethune, p. 21).

Working under tremendous pressure, Hayden prepared her plans, and hers was the first Exposition building to commence construction, as well as the first one finished, in 1892. According to Enid Yandell, a young sculptor from Kentucky engaged in work on the building, and Laura Hayes, secretary to Board of Lady Managers president BERTHA HONORÉ PALMER: "It was generally known about the Construction Department that no one could change, by any amount of persuasion, one of her plans when she was convinced of its beauty or originality. She was always quiet but generally carried her point" (Yandell and Hayes, p. 64). Hayden's stamina and her good temper were tested again and again, and she later regretted "the rather vague conditions under which I had undertaken the work" (Hayden, report to the Board). Not only was she underpaid, but Palmer and other members of the Board were demanding clients, constantly pressing the architect to incorporate various materials designed or produced by women into the interior decoration of the building, whether or not they were suitable. Despite such difficulties, Hayden received an award "for delicacy of style, artistic taste, and geniality and elegance of the interior hall" from the Exposition; the Artist's Medal from Daniel Burnham; and a gold medal from the Board of Lady Managers.

Perhaps because she was tired of arguing with her clients, as well as exhausted from long months of work, Sophia Hayden did not appear at the Exposition after the dedication ceremony for the Woman's Building in October 1892. Rumors of her mental collapse appeared. The editors of *American Architect and Building News* suggested in November 1892 that the reports about her failing health provided "a much more telling argument against the wisdom of women entering this especial profession than anything else could." Hayden was not only told that architecture was a masculine field but also informed that her building was clearly feminine. The structure was described by one critic as "dainty but tasteful" (Millet, p. 879). The architect Henry Van Brunt claimed that its "graceful timidity or gentleness, combined however with evident technical knowledge, at once differentiate[s] it from its colossal neighbors, and reveal[s] the sex of its author" (Stern, p. 75).

The Woman's Building was the major work of Hayden's career. In 1894 she designed another structure as a memorial for women's clubs in the United States, but it was never built. She lived in Winthrop, Mass., and was active in the Floral Emblem Society and the Winthrop Business League in 1895. By 1900 she had married an artist, William Blackstone Bennett, who had one daughter, Jennie (b. 1890), by a previous marriage. A widow by 1913, she continued to list herself in the Winthrop city directory as an artist until 1939. Since the Woman's Building was only a temporary structure, Sophia Hayden left no architectural monument to mark her brief career. She died at the Winthrop Convalescent Nursing Home in 1953 of pneumonia after suffering a stroke.

[A major unpublished source is Sophia Hayden's report to the Board of Lady Managers, April 28, 1894, Chicago Hist. Soc. MIT's Hist. Collections contain records from her student years. Two published accounts of her career are Madeleine Stern, "Sophia G. Hayden," *We the Women: Career Firsts of Nineteenth-Century America* (1963), pp. 67–76, and Judith Paine, "Sophia Hayden and the Woman's Building Competition," in Susana Torre, ed., *Women in American Architecture: An Historic and Contemporary Perspective* (1977), pp. 71–73. The Torre book also contains Hayden's report to the board, an account of the Woman's Building competition, and a plan and picture of her building. The full story of the Woman's Building will be treated by Jeanne Madeline Weimann in a forthcoming book. The rumors of "brain fever" were printed in *Am. Architect and Building News*, Nov. 26, 1892, and Dec. 10, 1892. The professional situation for women in the 1890s is discussed in Louise Bethune, "Women and Architecture," *Inland Architect and News Record*, March 1891, pp. 20–21. See also Enid Yandell and Laura Hayes, *Three Girls in a Flat: The Story of the Woman's Building* (1892), an anecdotal account of the building's creation. The best likeness available is in F. D. Millet, "The Designers of the Fair," *Harper's New Monthly Mag.*, Nov. 1892. Entries in the Woman's Building competition are illustrated in *Inland Architect and News Record*, Aug. and Sept. 1891. Assistance in the research for this article was provided by Madeleine Stern, Judith Paine, Jeanne Weimann, the Winthrop (Mass.) Public Library, and the Chicago Hist. Soc. Death certificate supplied by Mass. Dept. of Public Health.]

DOLORES HAYDEN

HAYNES, Elizabeth Ross, July 30, 1883–Oct. 26, 1953. YWCA official, social researcher, community leader.

Elizabeth Haynes devoted her life to the improvement of economic and social opportunities for blacks. The scope of her efforts ranged from a pioneering statistical study on black domestic workers to public service in New York City and throughout the nation.

She was born in Mount Willing, Lowndes County, Ala., the daughter of Henry and Mary (Carnes) Ross, former slaves. Her father served in the Union army and used his bounty to buy land in Alabama, which he and his wife enlarged by decades of hard work into a 1,500-acre plantation. Elizabeth was a bright child and her parents had high aspirations for her; they provided her with educational opportunities that were exceptional for a black farm girl. As class valedictorian at the State Normal School in Montgomery (later Alabama State University), she won a scholarship to Fisk University, earning an A.B. in 1903. She taught high school in Galveston, Texas, and other southern cities for several years and spent summers between 1905 and 1907 attending graduate school at the University of Chicago.

In 1908 Ross was invited, probably on the recommendation of ADDIE WAITES HUNTON, to work for the Student Department of the National Board of the Young Women's Christian Association. She spent more than two years working among black college students, traveling extensively and providing detailed observations on student life. In a 1910 report, she wrote that through YWCA efforts the thoughts of young women "are being turned inward to their own beliefs and ideals, and outward to the part they can play in helping to better . . . social conditions."

Ross resigned to marry George Edmund Haynes on Dec. 14, 1910, and settled in Nashville, Tenn. George Haynes had also graduated from Fisk in 1903 and attended the University of Chicago in the summers of 1906 and 1907. Formerly a professional worker for the YMCA among black collegians, in 1910 he joined the Fisk faculty to develop its sociology department. Although Elizabeth Ross Haynes no longer sought paid employment after her marriage, she undertook volunteer commitments in social service and temperance work; her career paralleled that of her husband for much of her life. Her only child, George Edmund Haynes, Jr., was born in 1912.

In 1918, when her husband went to Washington as director of the Negro Economics Division in the Department of Labor, Elizabeth Haynes became his assistant director; she was also a "dollar-a-year" worker for the department's Women in Industry Service, an antecedent of the Women's Bureau. Between January 1920 and May 1922 she helped reorganize the Domestic Service Section of the United States Employment Service, and served as minimum wage consultant. She drew on these experiences in "Negroes in Domestic Service in the United States," her master's thesis at Columbia University where she studied sociology in 1922 and 1923. More than half a century later this work was recognized as "the first and still most thorough study of black domestics" (Katzman, p. 347).

Elizabeth Haynes rejoined the YWCA in 1922 when she was named to the newly created Council on Colored Work. Two years later she became the first black member of the association's National Board. Remaining on the Board until 1934, she was active in developing the Industrial Division. Haynes also served in the Department of Race Relations of the Federal Council of the Churches of Christ in America (later the National Council of Churches), working as a volunteer in close association with her husband, who was secretary of the department from 1922 to 1946. She belonged to the National Association of Colored Women and to Alpha Kappa Alpha sorority.

Turning her attention to the Harlem community, where she and her family moved in the 1920s, Elizabeth Haynes entered Democratic politics. In November 1935 she was elected coleader of New York's Twenty-first Assembly District, and in 1936 she was a member of the Colored Division of the National Democratic Speakers' Bureau. She aligned herself with the New Deal wing of the party. Haynes asserted in 1936 that women should no longer be willing to remain in subsidiary roles in the party structure but should "aspire for political plums."

In 1937 Gov. Herbert H. Lehman appointed her—the only woman—to the New York State Temporary Commission on the Condition of the Urban Colored Population. At the commission's hearings, Haynes designed her questions to expose the prejudice in the state government's employment and promotion policies. She also stressed the economic and social circumstances underlying stark racial differentials in health statistics.

Haynes worked to upgrade schools and library services in Harlem and to integrate the nursing and social work staffs in city hospitals. She served on Mayor Fiorello La Guardia's City Planning Commission, and on the National Advisory Committee on Women's Participation in the 1939 New York World's Fair. During and after the Second World War she supported the Emergency Committee to Save the Jewish People of Europe.

Haynes's belief in the value of black history led her to write inspirational material. *Unsung Heroes* (1921) recounts the lives of celebrated blacks for a juvenile audience. The year before her death in New York City she published *The Black Boy of Atlanta* (1952), a biography of Richard Robert Wright, a banker and "unsung American Negro whose life and solid achievements would be an inspiration." Through her writings and organizational work Haynes encouraged individuals to overcome impediments and better their lives, emphasizing interracial understanding and cooperation.

[The principal sources are a small group of Haynes's papers (including an unfinished novel) in the James Weldon Johnson Memorial Coll., Yale Univ., and the Archives of the Nat. Board of the YWCA in N.Y. City. Her publications include "Negroes in Domestic Service in the United States," a slightly revised version of her thesis, *Jour. Negro Hist.*, Oct. 1923; "Two Million Negro Women at Work," *Southern Workman*, Feb. 1922; and "Margaret Murray Wash-ington," *Opportunity*, July 1925. For commentary on Haynes's work see Richard Bardolph, *The Negro Vanguard* (1959); David M. Katzman, *Seven Days a Week* (1978); and N.Y. State Temporary Commission on the Condition of the Urban Colored Population, *Public Hearings*, 2 (1937), 630–34, 681, 735–36. Obituaries appeared in *N.Y. Times*, Oct. 27, 1953; and in *N.Y. Amsterdam News* and *N.Y. Age*, both on Oct. 31, 1953. *Fisk News*, Nov.-Dec. 1935, contains a likeness. Information was obtained from an interview with Olyve Jeter Haynes, Dec. 14, 1978.]

RUTH BOGIN

HAYWARD, Susan, June 30, 1917?–March 14, 1975. Film actress.

Susan Hayward, believing "it's what you achieve on your own that counts," made herself a movie star. The youngest of three children and the second daughter of Walter and Ellen (Pearson) Marrener, she was born Edythe Marrener in Brooklyn, N.Y., and spent her next nineteen years attempting to leave the harsh tenement life of Flatbush. Her father descended from Irish and French ancestors, her mother from Swedish; he was a carnival barker and a transit worker, she a homemaker. Edythe attended public schools, leaving Girls' Commercial High School in 1935.

Within two years, Edythe Marrener got as far as Manhattan, where she began work as a model for the Walter Thornton Agency. Her photogenic features, particularly the combination of red hair and green eyes, were well suited to the demands of color photography: she modeled for national advertisements of products ranging from pedicare scissors to crackers. Thornton chose Marrener to pose for photographs to accompany his article "The Merchant of Venus" (*Sat. Eve. Post*, Oct. 30, 1937). It was a fortunate choice: when director George Cukor saw the magazine, he persuaded producer David O. Selznick to give the model a screen test, thinking she might be just the actress to play the much sought-after role of Scarlett O'Hara.

Edythe Marrener, chaperoned by her sister, eagerly left for Hollywood. Selznick was unimpressed by her screen test, however, and told her to go home and take acting lessons. Undaunted, she hired an agent who took the test to Warner Brothers. That studio quickly gave her a six-month contract, renamed her Susan Hayward, used her sparingly in bit parts and publicity shots, then dropped her.

Hayward realized that she must rid herself of her Brooklyn accent and gain technical skill; she formally began acting lessons and informally, by repeatedly viewing the same movie, improved her speech through imitation. Such endeavors were soon rewarded by a $200 a week contract at Paramount. There she appeared in a minor, romantic role in *Beau Geste* (1939), and was used minimally for the next seven years. Hayward complained often and vehemently to all who would listen. At the studio's annual convention in 1942, unannounced she screamed to the audience: "Would you like to see Susan Hayward in pictures? They won't put me in pictures. Do something about it" (quoted in McClelland, *Films in Review*, p. 268). But such action secured only unflattering attention, not featured roles. Hayward's apprenticeship continued to be labored. *Adam Had Four Sons* (1941), *Reap the Wild Wind* (1942), and *The Hairy Ape* (1944) are the only noteworthy films of the sixteen she made during this period.

Soon after leaving Paramount, Hayward got the break she wanted: she signed on with Walter Wanger, an independent producer who appreciated her emotional range. In her second Wanger film, *Smash-up, the Story of a Woman* (1947), Hayward was shown to advantage portraying a screen character that later—in variously contrived plots and settings—became her trademark: a desperate woman in an even more desperate situation. Her performance of the alcoholic Angie Evans, who once had had a successful career and then became a neglected homemaker, held great appeal for postwar audiences; Hayward was nominated for an Academy Award for best actress. After *They Won't Believe Me* (1947); *The Lost Moment* (1947), loosely adapted from Henry James's *The Aspern Papers; Tap Roots* (1948), in which Hayward appears as a "latter-day Scarlett"; and *Tulsa* (1949), Wanger sold her contract to Twentieth Century-Fox.

Hayward, unsatisfied with popular and material success—and spurred on by a compelling sense of her own merits—now strove to attain artistic success. Her aim was often at odds with studio demands; from 1950 on her films were generally divided between inconsequential Technicolor spectacles and blockbuster, two-tissue dramas. *David and Bathsheba* (1951), *Demetrius and the Gladiators* (1954), and *Thunder in the Sun* (1959) best represent the studio ideal. Hayward gained increasing critical acclaim for her sensitive portrayals of women facing crises and hardship: the unmarried, pregnant Eloise Winter in *My Foolish Heart* (1950); singer Jane Froman in *With a Song in My Heart* (1952); performer Lillian Roth in *I'll Cry Tomorrow* (1956); and Barbara Graham, a woman condemned to execution, in *I Want to Live* (1958). She won the Cannes Film Festival award for her portrayal of Roth, and captured the Oscar she so coveted for her role in

I Want to Live. Hayward finally was satisfied.

Susan Hayward married Jeffrey (Jess) Thomas Barker, an actor, in 1944, and gave birth to twin sons, Timothy and Gregory, the following year. The distrustful Hayward had Barker enter into a prenuptial contract that specified her income would remain forever separate from his; she divorced Barker in 1954, retaining custody of the children and of her money. Two years later she found the "reliability, tenderness, strength, and an equal income" she sought in a husband in Floyd Eaton Chalkley, a lawyer and businessman. When they married in 1957, Hayward willingly exchanged her hectic Hollywood existence for the serenity of their Carrollton, Ga., retreat. Until Chalkley's death in 1966, she appeared in only a few minor film roles.

Hayward then returned sporadically to California, appearing in occasional films—*Valley of the Dolls* (1968) was perhaps the best—and on stage and television. There were few gratifying roles available to the once in-demand Hayward, however. She died of brain cancer in March 1975 in her Beverly Hills home.

Susan Hayward's native defiance of systems—whether star or social—and her gut determination to succeed heightened her image both on and off the camera, distinguishing her from a generation of actresses noted for their conformity to type.

[Hayward's life is replete with legend. Eduardo Moreno, *The Films of Susan Hayward* (1979), offers biography and film-by-film analysis of her career and includes complete credits, reprints of reviews, and extensive photographs. Douglas McClelland has written extensively on her career: *The Divine Bitch* (1973), revised and reprinted as *The Complete Life Story of Susan Hayward* (1975); "Susan Hayward," *Films in Review* (May 1962); and "The Brooklyn Bernhardt," *Films and Filming* (March 1965). See also *Current Biog.*, 1953; *N.Y. Times*, April 20, 1953, sec. II, p. 5; and David Thomson, *Biog. Dict. of the Cinema* (1975). Hayward's stormy life was chronicled in the popular press: Mel Schuster, comp., *Motion Picture Performers* (1971), gives the most complete list of these articles. Evelyn Mack Truitt, *Who Was Who on Screen* (2d ed., 1977), cites some of Hayward's earliest credits. An obituary appeared in the *N.Y. Times*, March 15, 1975; death certificate from Calif. Dept. of Health.]

HARRIETTE L. WALKER

HAZEN, Elizabeth Lee, Aug. 24, 1885–June 24, 1975. Microbiologist, mycologist.

Elizabeth Lee Hazen, codiscoverer of the antifungal antibiotic nystatin, was born in Rich, Miss., the second daughter and middle of three children of William Edgar and Maggie (Harper) Hazen. Her father and mother, Baptists and cotton farmers, both died before she was four years old. Elizabeth and her sister (her brother died at age four) were raised by an uncle and his wife. She attended public schools in Coahoma County, Miss., and later entered the Mississippi Industrial Institute and College (later Mississippi University for Women) in Columbus.

Early in life Elizabeth Hazen set herself the goal of a career in science. After obtaining her B.S. in 1910, she became a high school science teacher in Jackson, Miss., and devoted her summers to further study at the Universities of Tennessee and Virginia. In 1916 she went to Columbia University to study bacteriology, and received an M.S. in 1917. During and immediately following World War I she worked in United States Army diagnostic laboratories in Alabama and New York and in the laboratory of a West Virginia hospital. Hazen then returned to Columbia, where she remained, in one or another capacity, for nearly a half century. She earned her Ph.D. in microbiology there in 1927, when she was forty-two. Her journey from a poor Mississippi farm had been marked by considerable adversity and personal sacrifice.

During the next four years Hazen served as an instructor at Columbia's College of Physicians and Surgeons. In 1931 she joined the New York City Branch Laboratory of the New York State Department of Health, Division of Laboratories and Research. Throughout the 1930s and early 1940s she engaged in laboratory diagnosis, analysis of vaccines and serums, and microbiological research, concentrating on a variety of infectious diseases of viral, bacterial, and rickettsial origin.

During World War II Hazen turned increasingly to work with the poorly characterized fungal, or mycotic, infections afflicting humans. She studied in the Columbia University Mycology Laboratory, established by J. Gardner Hopkins and Rhoda W. Benham (1895–1957), and began to build a collection of fungal cultures and slides for the state's Central Laboratory in Albany. Encouraged by the recent discovery of the antibacterial antibiotic penicillin, Hazen began to look for a naturally occurring antifungal antibiotic. Gilbert Dalldorf, the newly appointed director of the Division of Laboratories, introduced her to a collaborator with the required chemical skills, Rachel Brown of the Central Laboratory. Hazen collected and assayed soil samples, cultured soil microorganisms of suspected activity, and forwarded the cultures to Brown for chemical testing. Their efforts paid off in 1948: a soil sample which

Hazen had collected on the Virginia farm of some friends named Nourse yielded a streptomycete (*Streptomyces noursei*) extract possessing the desired properties. The existence of this new antibiotic, fungicidin (later named nystatin for the New York State Department of Health), was revealed at the October 1950 meeting of the National Academy of Sciences.

The announcement elicited immediate interest from several pharmaceutical firms. Dalldorf put Hazen and Brown in contact with Research Corporation, a New York foundation which had previous experience administering a medical patent. Nystatin patent rights were signed over and commercial production commenced in 1954, initially by E. R. Squibb and Sons. Half the royalties were placed in the Brown-Hazen Fund for the support of scientific work in fields of the codiscoverers' interests; the remainder was made available for other Research Corporation grant programs. By the time the patent expired, in 1974, over thirteen million dollars had been generated. Nystatin has proved effective against yeast (*Candida albicans*) vaginal infections and a range of similar infections of the intestine, skin, and mucous membranes. It also has found application in combating molds in livestock feed and foodstuffs, and in the restoration of murals and manuscripts following the 1966 flooding of Florence, Italy.

Elizabeth Hazen's work routine and way of life were little altered by the discovery of nystatin. After the state's Branch Laboratory was disbanded in 1954, she continued her rigorous schedule of research and diagnostic screening at the Central Laboratory in Albany. In 1958 she accepted an associate professorship at Albany Medical College, and after her retirement in 1960 she became a full-time guest investigator in the Columbia University Mycology Laboratory. In 1973 Hazen visited her ailing sister in Seattle; complications from the ulcers she had suffered for many years, sometimes severely, and the debilities of age prevented her return to New York. She remained at the nursing home where her sister was living. Less than two years later she died there of acute cardiac arrhythmia.

According to her friends, the passion of Hazen's life was her work. She shunned publicity, never presenting any of the papers which she coauthored with Brown and avoiding reporters and photographers. Among acquaintances, however, she was warm, outgoing, and opinionated about matters of science and politics. She devoted a portion of her time to the Brown-Hazen Fund Advisory Committee. The fund, officially terminated in 1978, was in its time the single most important source of support for medical mycology in the United States. In her later years Hazen shared with Brown an interest in encouraging women to enter scientific careers. Consequently, the fund allocated fellowship grants to the women's colleges they had each attended.

In 1955 Elizabeth Hazen shared with Rachel Brown the Squibb Award in Chemotherapy. She also received a Distinguished Service Award from the New York State Department of Health (1968). Just a month before her death, she and Brown became the first women to receive the Chemical Pioneer Award of the American Institute of Chemists.

[The initial reports on nystatin are E. L. Hazen and R. Brown, "Two Antifungal Agents Produced by a Soil Actinomycete," *Science*, Oct. 1950, p. 423, and "Fungicidin, a New Antibiotic," N.Y. State Assoc. of Public Health Laboratories, *Proceedings*, 1950, pp. 56–57. Also of interest is their "The Discovery, Development, and Applications of Nystatin," N.Y. State Assoc. of Public Health Laboratories, *Proceedings*, 1955, pp. 58–62. In addition to her over fifty scientific articles, Hazen wrote a widely used text, *Laboratory Diagnosis of Pathogenic Fungi Simplified* (1955; 2nd ed., 1960; 3rd ed., with Morris A. Gordon, 1970). The major biographical source is W. Stevenson Bacon, "Elizabeth Lee Hazen, 1885–1975," *Mycologia*, Sept.-Oct. 1976, pp. 961–69, which contains a photograph. Richard S. Baldwin of Research Corporation is preparing a book on Hazen and Brown. For background on the period in which Hazen entered science see Margaret W. Rossiter, "Women Scientists in America Before 1920," *Am. Scientist*, May-June 1974, pp. 312–23. Brief obituaries appear in the Miss. Univ. for Women *Alumnae News*, Fall 1975, p. 43; Research Corp. *Quart. Bull.*, Summer 1975, p. 4; and *The Stethoscope* (published by Columbia-Presbyterian Medical Center), Sept. 1975, p. 6. Hazen occasionally reported her birth year incorrectly as 1886 and her birthplace as Lula, Miss.; these inaccuracies are reproduced in most of the obituaries. Information was supplied by Richard S. Baldwin and Rachel Brown. Death certificate provided by Wash. Dept. of Social and Health Services.]

LEWIS P. RUBIN

H.D. *See* DOOLITTLE, Hilda.

HEAP, Jane. *See* ANDERSON, Margaret Carolyn.

HELBURN, Theresa, Jan. 12, 1887–Aug. 18, 1959. Theatrical producer.

In more than thirty years with the Theatre Guild, Theresa Helburn became more powerful and more influential than any American woman had ever been in the production of drama. Born on West Forty-Sixth Street in New York City, which later became the center of Broadway, she

was the younger child and only daughter of Julius Helburn, an immigrant from Germany, and his wife, Hannah (Peyser). While her father commuted between Salem, Mass., where he owned a leather manufacturing company, and New York City, her mother ran an experimental primary school in their home. As a child she was taken to the theater by her mother, who stressed the importance of literary and cultural attainments. Watching ADA REHAN's stock company, Theresa Helburn found her vocation: "I entered a world that was unlike anything I have ever imagined, but that I recognized at once as my own. The theatre was not a dream, or a goal—it was home."

Theresa was educated by her mother until the family moved to Boston in 1900. That year she entered the fashionable Winsor School, graduating in 1903. The following year she enrolled at Bryn Mawr College. The college offered no drama courses, but Helburn read plays, writing a sophomore thesis on Arthur Wing Pinero with the resources of the Philadelphia library, and produced and directed college plays. In 1908, after graduating "with éclat and all the senior prizes," Helburn suffered a breakdown. "With that physical collapse, I started the pattern of my life: a wild spurt of activity followed by total exhaustion."

After recuperating on the Cape Ann farm her mother and brother had bought her, Helburn enrolled in George Pierce Baker's playwriting course at Radcliffe. The short exposure to Baker's English 47 Workshop—and its high dramatic standards—was probably her single most important educational experience. Baker treated his students with respect as present or potential partners in the professional theater. On Theresa Helburn, laboring at writing a play of her own, that made a deep impression.

During the next few years Helburn progressed slowly in her pursuit of a career in the theater. Returning to New York with her parents, she made a modest social debut in 1910. Within a year she was thoroughly involved in writing; she found friends in the Poetry Society of America, among them Edward Arlington Robinson and Vachel Lindsay, and she enjoyed moderate success publishing verse and short stories. In 1911 Theresa Helburn met Lawrence Langner, an Englishman who had come to New York as a patent attorney, and who later became her longtime associate in the theater. She was asked to join a weekly play-reading group, which included Langner, Lee Simonson, and Philip Moeller; they combined talent with the determination to elevate American theater. Within three years they had established the Washington Square Players, an amateur company that presented European plays in the belief that there was an audience for something other than what was then being offered on Broadway. Helburn was offered the role of the mother in the Players' first production, *Licensed,* but had to withdraw because her parents found that "the subject was immoral, the part was unladylike."

Helburn twice traveled abroad, spending much of 1913 in Paris. In 1916, she assisted KATHARINE CORNELL in directing a production of *Twelfth Night* at the Oaksmere School where Cornell taught at the time. The same year, *Enter the Hero,* Helburn's first play, was put in rehearsal by the Washington Square Players, with EDNA ST. VINCENT MILLAY in a principal role. But Millay proved a better poet than player, and *Enter the Hero,* a one-acter, was scratched. Similarly, Helburn's later plays were produced without much success; they were published, however, and later performed by community theater companies.

During the 1918 season Helburn served a further apprenticeship in the theater by working as a drama critic for *The Nation.* Then in December of that year, the Washington Square Players, reorganized as a subscription-based repertory company, became the Theatre Guild. Theresa Helburn's association with the Guild began as a play reader; however, within a year, when the organization was experiencing its first of many managerial crises, she was made executive secretary pro tem, a job no one wanted because it was vaguely defined and unprofitable.

The Guild began its first season in 1919, which Helburn later called the most important year of her life. She married that year; her husband was John Baker Opdycke, a former press correspondent, and a high school English teacher who later wrote a number of books on proper English usage. The marriage lasted until his death in 1956.

In the 1919 season the Guild offered two plays to its 135 patrons: the first was little more than a failure; the second, *John Ferguson,* made theater history and its financial and artistic success established the Theatre Guild as the country's premiere art theater. During that first season, Helburn quickly learned the dos and don'ts of theater management and production. The Guild's five directors (Langner, Simonson, Moeller, Helen Westley, an actress, and Maurice Wertheim, a financier), impressed with her business sense, made Helburn executive director. Now a member of the Guild's board, Helburn had equal say in all decisions, choosing, then casting, scrutinizing, and then criticizing, productions. She took an aggressive and creative part in over a hundred Theatre Guild productions; the Guild became the most important

force for development and improvement in the American theater.

During its first decade, the Guild grew to over 25,000 patrons, built its own playhouse, compiled a record unequaled in theater annals with the production of fourteen successful plays between 1926 and 1928, and fulfilled its promise to produce quality works unsuited to commercial theater. But success spurred dissension among board members, and Helburn took a leave of absence to try her hand at film. From 1934 to 1935 she worked as an adviser and producer for Columbia Pictures, but quickly realized her talents were better utilized in the theater. Returning to New York, Helburn established the Bureau of New Plays, which ultimately held national competitions for new playwrights and ran seminars for the most promising winners. Under Helburn's aegis, the seminars were later offered at the New School for Social Research and were modeled after Baker's 47 Workshop. In 1935 she also attempted directing, at Langner's summer stock theater in Westport, Conn.

All these activities were important to Helburn, but none as important as the Theatre Guild. Besieged with growing economic and managerial problems, and public and critical dissent (several productions failed during the 1930s), in 1939 the Guild reorganized and changed its fundamental design and policy. The board of six directors was replaced by Helburn and Langner as coadministrative directors, and the Guild lowered its artistic aim, producing commercial plays. Helburn's control enlarged measurably; now she was both actively and aggressively involved in every step of production.

She was largely responsible for the casting, the selection of actors, and, whether the playwrights liked it or not, for suggesting—sometimes ordering—changes. Helburn had never lost the itch to write plays and eventually was able to sublimate it through advising and counseling some of the foremost American playwrights, becoming, in effect, a "play doctor." Many Guild productions were altered and some improved by her; however, not all authors were pleased with her role, and several major writers abandoned their Guild association to form the Playwrights Company. By 1939 Helburn had lost that certain diffidence which earlier had marked her personality and had become dogmatic and didactic.

Although the Guild rebounded to its former financially secure state with a production in 1939 of *The Philadelphia Story,* within four years it again verged on bankruptcy. Then, in 1943, Theresa Helburn had the idea that Lynn Riggs's play *Green Grow the Lilacs* could be made into a musical and she brought together Richard Rodgers and Oscar Hammerstein II to write it. Initially dismissed as "Helburn's Folly," *Oklahoma!* saved the Guild from financial ruin, and, as Helburn had insisted, brought distinction to the form. When the state of Oklahoma officially adopted the show, the Kiowa Indian tribe honored Helburn as a chief with the appropriate title, "Little Lady Who Sees Far."

Still seeing far beyond most of her contemporaries, two years later she again brought Rodgers and Hammerstein together, urging them to do for Ferenc Molnar's *Liliom* what they had done for *Green Grow the Lilacs*. Utilizing the concept of a totally integrated musical with which *Oklahoma!* had revolutionized American musical theater, *Carousel* was equally successful. Helburn's characteristic persistence was largely responsible for the regeneration of the Theatre Guild.

Throughout her career with the Guild, Helburn maintained a close relationship with both George Bernard Shaw and Eugene O'Neill, the Guild's most famous dramatists, asking the former to make cuts in his plays—which he refused to do—and encouraging the latter to make more of his works available for production. She also fought personally against the censorship of *Strange Interlude* and *A Moon for the Misbegotten*. She was instrumental in producing the major plays of S. N. Behrman and Philip Barry, and was enmeshed in every one of the Theatre Guild's subsidiary interests, most notably the Group Theatre and Theatre Guild on the Air. In 1947 Bryn Mawr, recognizing her contribution to the American theater, named a chair in her honor.

A practical idealist, and an organizer who coped with tough Broadway showmen and temperamental stars, Helburn remained a strong presence in the Theatre Guild until 1953. In failing health in the late 1950s, she died of a heart attack at her Weston, Conn., home, Terrytop, in August 1959.

[The Theatre Guild Coll., in the Yale Coll. of Am. Literature, Beinecke Library, includes Helburn's professional correspondence; some personal correspondence is in the Edward Goodman Coll., Billy Rose Theatre Coll., N.Y. Public Library, which also has extensive clipping files on both Helburn and the Theatre Guild. There are also clipping files in the Harvard Theatre Coll. and the Radcliffe College Archives. Typescripts of Helburn's plays are in the Bryn Mawr College Archives. All quotations in the article are from Helburn's memoir, *A Wayward Quest* (1960), completed after her death by her assistant Elinore Denniston. Her published plays are *Allison Makes Hay* (1919) and *Enter the Hero* (1919). A colorful portrait of Helburn is Marya Mannes, "Behind the Throne," *New Yorker*, Dec. 6, 1930; a dual entry on Langner and Helburn in *Current Biog.*, 1944, is indicative of the press they received after the success of *Oklahoma!* All studies of the Theatre Guild contain information on Helburn: Walter Eaton, *The Theatre Guild: The First Ten Years* (1929), includes a chapter by Helburn; Roy Waldau, *Vintage Years of the Theatre Guild* (1972), has a complete bibliography and list of credits. An obituary appeared in the *N.Y. Times*, Aug. 19, 1959. A birth certificate, filed in 1938, was supplied by the N.Y. City Municipal Archives. Personal and family information provided by Helburn's sister-in-law Margaret Helburn and her niece Margaret Helburn Kocher.]

ELLIOT NORTON

HENIE, Sonja, April 8, 1912–Oct. 12, 1969. Figure skater, film actress.

"Family, home, circumstances, the country I lived in and the weather I was born in all conspired" to make a figure skater of Sonja Henie. Born during a blizzard in Oslo, Norway, she was the younger child and only daughter of Selma (Lochman-Nielsen) and Hans Wilhelm Henie, a well-to-do fur wholesaler, and one-time world bicycle champion. Winner of nearly 160 trophies in a variety of sports, he actively encouraged his children's athletic development.

Skiing was a part of winter life from early childhood; ballet lessons began at age five; when she was eight, Sonja received a long-coveted pair of figure skates. Tagging after her brother Leif, she spent hours at Oslo's outdoor ice rink. With Leif's help, she quickly mastered the basics and attracted the attention of a member of the local skating club, who gave her informal lessons. At age nine, Sonja Henie entered and won her first competition, for the children of Oslo. Another victory the following year convinced the Henie family to take skating seriously. They decided on the national championship of Norway as their goal and Sonja began the practice and training regime that was to dominate her life, and her family's. Private tutoring replaced school attendance and summers included ballet lessons in London.

In 1923 Sonja Henie became national champion of Norway. Three years later she placed second in the world championships; the next year, 1927, skating at her home rink in Oslo, she won her first world figure skating championship. She wore a trim white velvet dress designed by her mother, a radical change from the usual longer, black skating attire. In her autobiography, *Wings on My Feet* (1940), she attributed her 1927 victory and her first Olympic gold medal, won in 1928, to the intensive preparation supervised by her father, her experience in skating exhibitions, and the influence of Anna Pavlova whom she had seen dance the year before.

Henie's free skating programs attempted to follow the choreographic form of ballet solos; it was through her efforts to fuse dance and skating that Sonja Henie most profoundly affected the development of figure skating. She sought to achieve a graceful total effect rather than merely to perform a series of technically difficult but disconnected moves as had been the style.

With the world championship Sonja Henie began a decade of travel, exhibitions, and parties, incessant rivalry with other competitors, and a constant pressure to train. Family wealth and encouragement helped enormously: her father paid the bills and made the arrangements; her mother was a tireless chaperone and traveling companion. Yet life was not only skating; skiing, swimming, horseback riding, and ballet were also important. In the summer of 1932, she was runner-up in the Norwegian national tennis tournament and finished second in a three-day cross-country auto race in Sweden.

Sonja Henie first visited the United States in 1929. She returned for the 1932 Olympics at Lake Placid, where the seven judges unanimously awarded her first place in both the compulsory school figures and free skating. Reporters commented on her sureness and confidence, her lilting, graceful style, and her flair for the theatrical.

Discarding brief thoughts of retirement, Henie previewed her version of Pavlova's *Dying Swan* solo at a Milan exhibition in 1933; it was a further development of the blending of dance and skating that reached its fullest expression in 1940 when she staged *Les Sylphides* in her "Hollywood Ice Revue." Prior to the 1935–36 season, during which she won her third Olympic gold medal and defended her world title, Henie announced her decision to end her amateur career.

Her next objective was a movie contract, and Henie pursued it with the same cool determination that had won ten consecutive world championships and three Olympic gold medals. Within thirty days of turning professional, she signed a contract with Arthur Wirtz for a series of exhibitions in the United States. When the tour failed to produce suitable results, the Henie family stormed Hollywood, renting the Polar Palace for two performances preceded by extensive advertising. The shows were a success and offers poured in. With shrewd bargaining, Henie won the starring role she sought and a five-year contract with Twentieth Century-Fox.

Her first film, *One in a Million,* predictably the story of the development of a skater, was an immediate success on its release at Christmas 1936. Between 1937 and 1939 Henie starred in five more successful movies; in a 1939 poll she ranked behind only Clark Gable and Shirley Temple as a box office attraction. Five later films were less popular, however.

The death of Wilhelm Henie in the spring of 1937 was a profound blow. She had already proved herself astute in making business deals on her own, however, and with Arthur Wirtz, she worked out plans to star in her own professional ice show. Drawing on the new audience created by her films, Henie's "Hollywood Ice Revue" premiered to sell-out crowds in the winter of 1937–38. She also coproduced with Wirtz a permanent ice show (in which she did not appear) which ran at the Centre Theatre in New York City from 1940 to 1950.

Until World War II made travel impossible, Henie returned each summer to her villa outside Oslo. In 1937 King Haakon made her a Knight of the First Class of the Order of St. Olav, the youngest person ever to be so honored. In 1941 she became a citizen of the United States.

Rumors of impending marriages had circulated for years, but it was not until July 4, 1940, that Sonja Henie married sportsman Daniel Reid Topping. Divorced in 1946, she married Winthrop Gardiner, Jr., on Sept. 15, 1949. A divorce in 1956 was soon followed by marriage to wealthy Norwegian shipowner and art patron Niels Onstad. Henie began investing much of her fortune in the paintings of the impressionists and expressionists. In 1961 she and Onstad began planning a center for the visual and performing arts to be built outside Oslo. In August 1968 the Sonja Henie–Niels Onstad Art Center opened. Fourteen months later, at the age of fifty-seven, Sonja Henie died of leukemia on an ambulance plane flying her from Paris to Oslo.

[Scrapbooks and clippings are preserved at the Sonja Henie–Niels Onstad Foundations, Høvikodden, Norway. *Skating* magazine, especially from 1924 through the 1930s, is the best source of information on Henie's competitive career; the Dec. 1969 issue has a summary of her life by Marjorie Wilson. Evelyn Mack Truitt, *Who Was Who on Screen* (1974), lists her film credits. Also useful are *Current Biog.,* 1940 and 1952; *Time,* March 30, 1936, July 17, 1939, and Feb. 2, 1948; *Newsweek,* Jan. 29, 1940, and Oct. 25, 1948; and *Who Was Who in Am.,* V. Information on the art collection at the Sonja Henie–Niels Onstad Center can be found in *Prisma* and other publications of the center. An obituary appeared in the *N.Y. Times,* Oct. 13, 1969.]

PATRICIA KING

HENNOCK, Frieda Barkin, Sept. 27, 1904–
June 20, 1960. Lawyer, federal official.

Frieda Hennock, the first woman appointed
to the Federal Communications Commission
(FCC), was born in Kovel, Poland, the youngest
of six girls and two boys of Boris and Sarah
(Barkin) Hennock. She came to the United
States in 1910 with her parents and acquired
citizenship in 1916 upon the naturalization of
her father, who became a real estate broker and
banker in New York City. After attending
Morris High School in the Bronx, Hennock
entered Brooklyn Law School. She clerked in
several New York law offices to help pay for her
education, since her parents opposed her choice
of career. She graduated in 1924, but could not
be admitted to the bar until she was twenty-one.

Hennock became one of New York's most
successful women lawyers. She began her practice in 1926 with fifty-six dollars, in the office
of a woman friend. The following year, she
formed a partnership with Julius Silver, later
explaining that it had seemed beneficial to practice with a man because of the barriers encountered by women lawyers. The two dissolved the
firm in 1934 because of disagreements, and
Hennock eventually received $9,000 and court
costs from a suit against Silver over a partnership share in Edwin H. Land's invention, the
Polaroid camera. A successful criminal lawyer,
Hennock said she changed to corporate law
because the emotional drain was less and because as a woman she had to work doubly hard
to win criminal cases. She served as assistant
counsel to the New York Mortgage Commission
(1935–39), studying low-cost housing, and
lectured on current developments in law and
economics at the Brooklyn Law School (1936).
In 1941 Hennock had the distinction of being
the first woman and the first Democrat to be associated with Choate, Mitchell and Ely, one of
New York City's most prestigious law firms.

Hennock's appointment as the first woman
FCC commissioner in 1948 was due to her role
as an energetic campaigner and financial contributor to New York Democratic party politics
and to the strong support of India Edwards,
director of the Women's Division of the Democratic National Committee, who pressured
President Harry S Truman to appoint women
to federal jobs. The Senate confirmed the appointment on June 20, 1948, despite the strong
Democratic partisanship she had revealed to the
Republican majority on the committee. Hennock gave up a substantial income from her law
practice to take the FCC position, but said she
had "sufficient means" to accept the relatively
low government salary. In her acceptance
speech Hennock observed: "It seems fundamental that in this field [communications]—so
peculiarly affecting women—the viewpoint of
this sex should be represented." To a *Milwaukee Journal* reporter she remarked: "Women
haven't had nearly the recognition they deserve.
If they have brains and ability they should not
be penalized merely because they wear a skirt."
Hennock represented women well, generally
working from 8:30 A.M. until 10:00 or 10:30
P.M.; she also studied electronics and engineering to master communications technicalities. On
occasion, however, she tempered work with
dancing, riding, tennis, golf, and swimming.

At the FCC, Commissioner Hennock's major
effort was directed toward reserving channels in
the developing television medium for educational use. Although she argued unsuccessfully
that a minimum of 500 channels should be saved
for noncommercial purposes, the commission
did agree in 1952 to reserve 242 channels. Hennock next prodded educators to apply for channels even though funds to operate the stations
might not be immediately available. She told a
New York Daily News reporter that "educators
were asleep at the switch in standard radio"
and she feared they would also fail to utilize
educational television. Dramatizing her cause,
Hennock spent countless weekends in cities from
coast to coast promoting educational television,
and wrote a dozen articles for magazines
ranging from the *Saturday Review of Literature*
to *Broadcasting.* Many more stories were written
about her and her quest. In June 1953, Hennock
spoke at the opening ceremony of the first educational television station KUHT–TV, in Houston. She later wrote of this event: "They said I
would not get a channel, that I would not get an
application and that a station would never get
on the air. Well, it was a pretty good feeling
to be there in Houston and see educational television become a reality."

Hennock dissented from FCC majority decisions in most aspects of broadcast regulation.
She advocated FCC preferential treatment for
the weaker transmitters of UHF stations,
opposed editorializing by broadcasters, and,
convinced that television was "just too important
a medium," denounced multiple ownership of
broadcast facilities. Hennock also argued for
stricter controls on children's programming. She
told the investigating Senate subcommittee that
the continued subjection of children to a television diet of violence, brutality, crime, and horror
should be sufficient cause for loss of license.
Her persistent efforts and forceful arguments
helped to ensure that serious attention was paid

to these issues. As a gadfly, Madame Commissioner, as she was frequently called, did not rely on her energy and legal knowledge alone, but used her photogenic appeal, penchant for high fashion and spectacular hats, and even an occasional deluge of tears.

In June 1951, toward the end of her FCC career, Hennock became a focus of controversy when she was nominated by President Truman for a federal judgeship. Probably because she was female, Hennock failed to win the support of the American and New York City bar associations, although several women's bar associations, several women judges, and her FCC colleagues, including Chairman Wayne Coy, backed her. The ultimate reason for her failure to win Senate support was probably her friendship with a married federal judge. Subjected to unusually personal questioning by the Senate Judiciary Committee, Hennock denied an improper relationship, called the charge malicious and unfounded, and asserted that she had merely helped the man in various political campaigns. In her testimony, she also explained the details of her lawsuit against Silver and admitted to a small private wager that Franklin D. Roosevelt would be elected to a third term, relatively minor improprieties. Nevertheless, she withdrew her name.

After President Dwight D. Eisenhower failed to reappoint her, Hennock left the FCC in 1955 and assumed a less hectic pace. She married William H. Simons, a Washington, D.C., real estate broker, in March 1956, and they lived in the capital. Her husband recalled that she observed the Orthodox Jewish prayer ritual nightly and had strong and affectionate ties to her family. She helped her parents financially until their deaths, and also aided a sister and a niece. After leaving the FCC, she practiced corporate law, first with the firm of Davies, Richberg, Tydings, Beebe and Landa, and then on her own. Hennock remained active in Washington society and politics until her death there in 1960 of a brain tumor. Her memorial is educational television.

[The principal manuscript sources are the Frieda (Hennock) Simons Papers at the Harry S Truman Library, Independence, Mo., and at the Schlesinger Library, Radcliffe College. The latter include lists of articles by and about her; clippings; correspondence; a summary of FCC decisions, illustrating her role; and transcripts of the testimony before the Senate Judiciary Committee. Extensive files of personal papers and scrapbooks were also retained by the late William H. Simons. The best insight into Hennock's philosophy of broadcast regulation and her contributions to the FCC can be found in the various opinions, concurring opinions, and dissents

she wrote from 1948 through 1955, which appear in the *FCC Reports*, as well as in her recorded testimony before a number of Senate committees. There are at least a dozen articles written by Hennock, including "TV 'Conservation,'" *Sat. Rev. of Lit.*, Dec. 9, 1950, and more than a hundred articles about her and her FCC crusade for educational television, including Mary Scott Welch, "Donna Quixote," *Look*, July 17, 1951; an article by John Chabot Smith in the *N.Y. Herald Tribune*, June 12, 1951, which discusses her nomination as a federal judge; and "Portia on the FCC," *Milwaukee Jour.*, Sept. 2, 1948, which contains a brief biography. Also see the entries in *Current Biog.*, 1948, and *Nat. Cyc. Am. Biog.*, H, 337. Obituaries appeared in the *N.Y. Times* and *Wash. Post*, June 21, 1960. A death record was provided by D.C. Dept of Public Health. Additional information for this article was provided by many FCC staff members and Washington reporters, and by William H. Simons.]

MARYANN YODELIS SMITH

HERBST, Josephine, March 5, 1892–Jan. 28, 1969. Writer, journalist.

Josephine Herbst belongs to the histories of literature and of radicalism, to both of which she remained committed during a vigorous, independent, and idiosyncratic career as writer and journalist. Between the publication of her first short stories in the 1920s and the partial publication of her memoirs during the 1960s, she wrote seven novels, including a major trilogy, a biography, a number of first-hand journalistic reports about important political events of the 1930s, and dozens of short stories and critical essays. She also devoted much energy to letters, diaries, and other private writings, sending thousands of personal letters over the years to friends who treasured them as literary documents.

Herbst was at once uniquely representative of the political and cultural conditions of her time and unusually vulnerable to them. Her career paralleled the major political and literary currents of the twentieth century: bohemian in the 1920s, political in the 1930s, withdrawn from public life in the 1940s and 1950s, revived in the 1960s. She exercised an immense personal as well as literary influence, and in her last years presided over something of an American salon at her Bucks County (Pa.) farmhouse.

Herbst was born in Sioux City, Iowa, the third of four daughters of Mary (Frey) and William Benton Herbst, who had moved from Pennsylvania a few years before. Neither parent had any formal education, but Mary Herbst had a cultivated eastern outlook, loved reading, and encouraged her daughters to look to literature for adventure and enlightenment. Her stories about her ancestors, the Freys, who had begun emigrating from Switzerland around 1700, were told so memorably that they became the basis for her daughter's trilogy. William Herbst was a salesman of farm implements who came west to start his own business; it was unsuccessful and the family was always poor. After graduating from high school in Sioux City in 1910 Herbst wanted to go to college, but poverty made it impossible to do so easily; for the next nine years she alternated periods of work, usually clerical jobs, and periods of schooling. She completed her bachelor's degree at the University of California at Berkeley in 1918, having attended Morningside College (1910–12), the University of Iowa (1912–13), and the University of Washington (1916) along the way.

In the fall of 1919 Herbst moved to New York and quickly became part of the radical literary and political circles generally associated with *The Masses* and *The Liberator*. Her innately radical temperament had expressed itself in her revulsion against the war fervor on the Berkeley campus, but it was in New York that it first became associated with a way of life. Her friends there included GENEVIEVE TAGGARD, Max Eastman, and Albert Rhys Williams; through them she met Maxwell Anderson, then a young socialist newspaper writer and poet, who became her first serious lover. Anderson was married at the time and had two children but Herbst, accepting the ideology of "free love," plunged ahead. In her case it had a price. In the summer of 1920, somewhat reluctantly, she had an abortion. A few months later her younger sister also had an abortion, and the sister died. This combination of events brought Herbst close to an emotional breakdown. Although she had just begun her first literary job—as a reader in the magazine empire of H. L. Mencken—she decided to leave New York City and write.

In 1922 she moved to Berlin where she lived alone for more than a year working on her first novel (unpublished), an autobiographical account of her affair with Anderson. In Paris, in 1924, she met John Herrmann (1900–59), a charming and talented but unserious and ultimately alcoholic writer, and fell in love again. They returned to America in the fall of 1924, set up housekeeping in a Connecticut farmhouse the following year, and were legally married on Sept. 2, 1926. In 1928, after a few years of doing odd jobs around New York, they bought the farmhouse in Erwinna, Pa., that remained her home until she died.

The move to Erwinna coincided with a long productive period. Herbst's first novel, *Nothing Is Sacred*, was published to critical praise in 1928, and except for her second novel, *Money for Love* (1929), her work, for over a decade, was well received. Her writing was compared to both the "Hemingway school" of the 1920s and the proletarian literature of the 1930s. While she shared certain characteristics with each, the development of her style was largely autonomous and her subject matter was almost always autobiographical. After the publication of the first volume of her trilogy, *Pity Is Not Enough* (1933), she came to be regarded as a major figure in American letters, the peer of such close personal friends as Katherine Anne Porter, Ernest Hemingway, and John Dos Passos. The trilogy, also including *The Executioner Waits* (1934) and *Rope of Gold* (1939), is the retelling of the Frey family saga from the Civil War until Herbst's own adulthood; Harvey Swados accurately described it as one of the most "sweeping and ambitious" fictional reconstructions of American life ever attempted by any writer.

Although Herbst had wished to devote her major energy to fiction, as the political crisis of the 1930s progressed she gave more time to journalism, reporting on the midwestern farmers' strikes, on an uprising in Cuba, on the German resistance to Hitler, and on the civil war in Spain. Her articles appeared in a variety of publications, from the *New York Post* to *New Masses*, and enlarged her reputation, particularly on the left.

Herrmann also continued to write, but after *Pity Is Not Enough* Herbst's reputation outdistanced his. The disparities between her ambition and his, her successes and his, as well as political and sexual difficulties, led eventually to the breakup of their marriage. Herrmann joined the Communist party and became active in party activities in Washington, D.C., to which he moved in 1934. Herbst's radicalism brought her close to the Communist party in the early 1930s, but while she was something more than a fellow traveler she was never technically a party member. Her criticism of Herrmann's underground party activities further disrupted their marriage. In addition, Herbst became involved with a woman and Herrmann also became involved with another woman. The marriage was effectively over by the winter of 1935, although it was not legally dissolved until 1940.

In February 1937, Herbst went to Spain to report on the civil war and remained there until July. It was a critical moment in her life. She left the United States thinking that even if she had failed in her personal life, there was still hope in political action. She came home believing that political life was far too complicated to be sustaining. After her return she began gradually to withdraw from her political associations, and although she never became anticommunist, and remained very much on the left, politics never again had for her the centrality or the simplicity of the earlier years.

The last part of Herbst's life was divided between years of loneliness and years of renewed activity and recognition. In 1942 she was fired from a government job on political grounds. Although she was cleared of the charges, this was the onset of a period of harassment which did not end until 1954 when she successfully challenged an attempt to deny her a passport. She lived by herself at the house in Erwinna, isolated and poor, her private suffering over the outcome of her marriage very great. The novels from this period, *Satan's Sergeants* (1941) and *Somewhere the Tempest Fell* (1947), were scantily and indifferently reviewed.

By the middle of the 1950s she began to be active again, writing in a new, increasingly poetic, literary style. Her major efforts went now to her memoirs and to a projected volume of interrelated novellas about writers who were her friends. Although neither was completed, portions of both were published before her death and were the foundation of what briefly appeared to be a literary revival. She also published *New Green World* (1954), a delicate biographical appreciation of two eighteenth-century botanists, John and William Bartram, and a number of shorter critical essays. In addition to rekindling old friendships, she formed lively and powerful relationships with such younger writers as Jean Garrigue (1913–1972), Alfred Kazin, Hilton Kramer, and Saul Bellow. The house in Erwinna became something closer to what it had once been, a gathering place for people who loved literature and writing, and Herbst's last years had in them far more companionship than those that had come before. When she died of cancer in New York Hospital in January 1969, many friends were by her side.

[Herbst's papers, including extensive personal correspondence, journals, manuscripts, and photographs, are at the Beinecke Library, Yale Univ. The permission of her literary executor, Hilton Kramer, is required for access. In addition to her books, all of which are cited in the text, her important writings include the three published sections of her memoirs: "The Starched Blue Sky of Spain" in *Noble Savage*, 1 (1960); "A Year of Disgrace" in *Noble Savage*, 3 (1961); "Yesterday's Road" in *New Amer. Rev.*, 3 (1968); and a novella, *Hunter of Doves* (*Botteghe Oscure* III, Spring 1954), a fictional evocation of Nathanael West that is the only completed portion of her projected collection of novellas. A bibliography prepared in 1968 by Martha Elizabeth Pickering, "A Biography and Checklist of Josephine Herbst," is at the Beinecke Library; it is largely complete. Apart from the excellent brief analysis of the trilogy in Walter B. Rideout, *The Radical Novel in the United States, 1900–1954* (1966), there are no major published discussions of her work. There are three dissertations: Winifred Farrant Bevilacqua, "The Novels of Josephine Herbst" (Univ. of Iowa, 1977); John M. Gourlie, "The Evolution of Form in the Works of Josephine Herbst" (New York Univ., 1975); and Dion Quintin Kempthorne, "Josephine Herbst: A Critical Introduction" (Univ. of Wis., 1973). A biography by the author is forthcoming. Herbst's obituary appeared in the *N.Y. Times*, Jan. 29, 1969. A eulogy delivered by Alfred Kazin at a memorial service was published in the *N.Y. Rev. of Books*, March 27, 1969. Herbst's date of birth is sometimes given as 1894, and most frequently, in Library of Congress and other government records, as 1897. The 1892 date is correct, established on the basis of discussions with relatives and from such corroborating material evidence as her enrollment in the Edith Everett Elementary School in Sioux City on Sept. 23, 1897.]

ELINOR LANGER

HERRICK, Elinore Morehouse, June 15, 1895–Oct. 11, 1964. Labor relations specialist, journalist.

Elinore Morehouse Herrick was born in New York City, the older child and only daughter of Martha Adelaide (Bird) and Daniel Webster Morehouse, both descendants of old New England families. Because of the failing health of her father, a Unitarian minister, the family moved to Springfield, Mass., in Elinore's early childhood. Martha Morehouse, who had been registrar at Pratt Institute in Brooklyn, resumed work as secretary and registrar of the MacDuffie School for Girls after her husband's death in 1904. Elinore attended the Technical High School and the MacDuffie School in Springfield.

In 1913 Morehouse enrolled at Barnard College, majoring in economics and taking courses at Columbia University's School of Journalism while earning her tuition as a cub reporter for the *New York World*. Her most important mentors were Talcott Williams, dean of the Columbia School of Journalism, and the historian Charles A. Beard, at whose homes she met notable reformers and journalists. Neglecting those classes which interested her least, she failed history and left college in 1915. The next year she married Horace Terhune Herrick, a chemical engineer. After three miscarriages their first son, Snowden Terhune, was born in 1919, and their second, Horace Terhune, Jr., in 1920. With the dissolution of her marriage soon after, Herrick was forced to take a series of factory jobs; her mother came to live with her and care for the two small boys. At a DuPont rayon plant in Buffalo, where she was then living, Herrick quickly advanced from pieceworker to training supervisor. When the company opened a new factory in Old Hickory, Tenn., she moved there in 1923 to become production manager of the textile division. Since DuPont did not promote women beyond this level, she left a few years later for Antioch, Ohio.

At the age of thirty-two, Herrick resumed her education at Antioch College. She also ran a boarding house with her mother, lectured on industrial problems, and worked as an administrative assistant to the president. She studied economics and labor relations with William L. Leiserson and received her A.B. in 1929.

Herrick spent the next five years, interrupted by treatment for tuberculosis, as executive secretary of the New York Consumers' League. She prepared studies of labor conditions in the canning, laundry, and candy industries. With ROSE SCHNEIDERMAN, MARY DEWSON, Felix Frankfurter, and others, she helped draft and lobbied for state minimum wage and child labor laws. After passage of the bill in 1933, she served on New York's first minimum wage board. She maintained her commitment to the Consumers' League although she left the paid staff in 1934, serving later as vice president and member of its board of directors.

In 1933 Herrick was appointed to the New York City Mediation Board established to promote national recovery by assisting in the settlement of labor disputes. Later in the year when the National Labor Board was created to handle disputes arising under National Recovery Administration codes, its chairman Robert F. Wagner recommended her to be executive vice chairman of the Regional Labor Board, whose jurisdiction covered most of New York and Connecticut. Handling more than 1,000 cases during her first year on the job, Herrick was convinced of the need for more effective machinery to protect workers in their efforts to organize and so testified before the Senate Committee on Education and Labor in 1934. When in 1935 the Wagner Act was passed, creating the National Labor Relations Board (NLRB), Herrick became regional director of the district which included eastern New York, northern New Jersey, and most of Connecticut. One of twenty-one regional boards, it handled more than 20 percent of the nation's disputes and had the only woman director.

Profoundly sympathetic to labor's need to organize and equally determined to avoid strikes, Herrick developed a reputation for independence and fair-mindedness. Although at-

tacked at various times by employers and by AFL and CIO unions and at odds at times with the staff of the national board, she was generally regarded as competent and impartial. She had a forceful personality and often employed blunt and salty language, but was also adept at using tact and humor to facilitate negotiations. The NLRB worked to convince employers to bargain collectively with employee unions, and to see that elections were held to choose these unions. On occasion, it also ran the elections. By 1942 Herrick's office had dealt with more than 5,000 disputes, the vast majority of which were settled without recourse to litigation.

Previously a nominal Democrat, Herrick embarked on her first political activity in 1936 when Sidney Hillman, president of the Amalgamated Clothing Workers of America, asked her to direct the campaign of the newly formed American Labor party (ALP). During her three-months leave from the labor board, she conducted a highly successful campaign which polled almost 300,000 votes for the party. She continued her ALP participation as a member of its executive committee until 1940.

In 1942 Herrick resigned from the labor board to become director of personnel and labor relations for Todd Shipyards Corporation, an enterprise consisting of ten shipyards and 150,000 employees. Her duties included assisting with the integration of women and blacks into the work force and preventing labor problems from hindering maximum war production. In demand as a speaker, during the war she emphasized the need to provide employment for women who wanted to remain in the labor force after demobilization.

When the war ended, Herrick moved to the *New York Herald Tribune* where she was director of personnel and a member of the editorial staff, writing occasional articles and editorials on labor and economic problems. By the late 1940s she had joined the ranks of moderate Republicans and her columns and editorials reflected the rightward tendency of her political views. Amidst the wave of postwar labor disputes, Herrick cautiously supported the Taft-Hartley Act. An anticommunist since the 1930s, she favored judicious investigation of communist infiltration into government. When ill health necessitated her resignation from the newspaper in 1955, she retired to Orford, N.H. In 1963 she moved to Chapel Hill, N.C., and died there of cirrhosis of the liver the following year.

[The Elinore Herrick Papers in the Schlesinger Library, Radcliffe College, contain an autobiographical manuscript drafted in the late 1930s, professional correspondence, speeches, and articles. There are also Herrick letters in the papers of the Nat. Consumers' League, Library of Congress. Articles by her appear in *The Woman's Press,* May 1939, Sept. and Nov. 1947; *N.Y. Times Mag.,* Jan. 24 and Sept. 5, 1943; *The Forum and Century,* Dec. 1934; and Am. Acad. of Political and Social Science, *Annals,* Nov. 1946. The most extensive secondary work on Herrick is Maybelle Mann, "Elinore Morehouse Herrick: Regional Labor Board Director of New York, 1933 to 1942" (M.A. thesis, N.Y. Univ., 1967). Articles about her include: Beverly Smith, "Shipyard Trouble Shooter," *Am. Mag.,* Sept. 1944; Dorothy Dunbar Bromley, "Mrs. Herrick of the Labor Board," *Harper's Mag.,* Oct. 1941; Beulah Amidon, "Office Hours for Mrs. Herrick," *Survey Graphic,* July 1937; Rose C. Feld, "The Woman Who Unravels Labor Knots," March 25, 1934, and S. J. Woolf, "A Woman's Way with Labor and Industry," May 16, 1937, both in the *N.Y. Times Mag.*; and an article in the *N.Y. Times,* Aug. 30, 1942, p. 1. See also *Current Biog.,* 1947. An obituary appeared in the *N.Y. Times,* Oct. 12, 1964; death record from N.C. Board of Health.]

SUSAN M. HARTMANN

HESSE, Eva, Jan. 11, 1936–May 29, 1970. Sculptor.

Born in the Israelite Hospital in Hamburg, Germany, Eva Hesse was the younger of two daughters of Wilhelm and Ruth (Marcus) Hesse. In November 1938, Nazi pogroms forced the Hesses to send their children to a Catholic home in Amsterdam until they also could escape. The family was reunited in Amsterdam and went from there to New York in June 1939. Wilhelm Hesse, a criminal lawyer, began a new career as an insurance broker. He and his wife were soon divorced and he remarried; Eva chose to live with her father and his second wife, and became a United States citizen in 1945. In 1946, Ruth Hesse, who had long been severely depressed, committed suicide. Eva Hesse was to see her rejection of, and then by, her mother as a formative influence on her art.

Hesse attended public schools in New York and received her high school diploma from the School of Industrial Arts in 1952. She decided in her mid-teens to be an artist, writing at that time that she wanted "to do more than just exist, live happily and contented with a home, children, to do the same chores every day." She attended Pratt Institute and the Art Students League and worked at *Seventeen* magazine before enrolling in Cooper Union, where she studied from 1954 to 1957. A scholarship to the Yale-Norfolk summer art school led her to the Yale School of Art and Architecture, where between 1957 and 1959 she studied painting with Rico Lebrun and Bernard Chait and was a fa-

vorite student of Josef Albers. At Yale, Hesse was torn between the expressionist and the formalist factions, between feeling and intellect—a conflict she resolved only years later with the fusion of these and other polarities in her mature work.

On graduating from Yale with a B.F.A. in 1959, Hesse returned to New York and energetically set about finding her professional place in the highly competitive art world. Her ambition and her need to be loved and respected were equally intense. In 1960 she met the conceptual sculptor Sol LeWitt, then also unknown, whose friendship and intellectual support were to be crucial for the rest of her life. By the spring of 1961 her drawings (always more successful and original than her paintings) were being shown in group exhibitions. At the same time, she met Tom Doyle, a sculptor somewhat older than Hesse, whose structural expressionist work was beginning to attract attention; they were married on Nov. 21, 1961. The marriage provided Hesse with the intense emotional relationship and the social place in the art world she wanted, but did not allay her personal insecurities. She was justifiably anxious about the inevitable competition and role playing that are generated when two ambitious and dedicated artists live together. A charming and beautiful woman, Hesse was seen for the next four years as Doyle's wife rather than as a serious artist in her own right. Though she had her first one-woman show —of drawings—at the Allan Stone Gallery in March 1963, her work developed little.

In June 1964, Hesse and Doyle left for Kettwig-am-Ruhr under the sponsorship of a German industrialist who had offered Doyle an abandoned factory in which to work for a year in exchange for some of his sculpture. Ironically, it was Hesse who was to gain most from this period, an extremely unhappy one during which she had to confront her German-Jewish background, the deterioration of her marriage, and her own lack of professional accomplishment. Doyle's suggestion that she experiment with string and found objects in the factory where they worked led to her first small reliefs and sculptures and, eventually, to the breakthrough she had sought for so long.

On her return to New York in the fall of 1965, Hesse's marriage came to a painful end. Her father, to whom she had remained very close, died soon after. She began, nonetheless, to come into her own as a mature artist and from then until her death less than five years later, Hesse's art developed with extraordinary clarity and passion. From tightly wound and bound black organic forms she moved into a more strictly geometrical period, focusing on serialism, the color gray, grids, and spheres, while retaining variations on the long, flexible "umbilical cords" and tangled skeins that subverted structural purism with elements of pathos, humor, and eroticism. After 1967, with the discovery of the malleable, sensuous, and near-ugly properties of latex and the translucent surfaces of fiberglass, her work became increasingly free. By the time she had her first one-woman sculpture show at the Fischbach Gallery in the fall of 1968, she was exhibiting in major museums as a respected younger artist. In 1969 the Museum of Modern Art bought her group of dented fiberglass bucket forms titled *Repetition Nineteen*. In April of that year, at the height of her first successes, Hesse collapsed and underwent the first of three operations for a brain tumor that was later found to be cancerous.

Though Hesse has been associated with so-called Minimal Art, anti-form, and Process Art, these terms do not convey the strengths of her work. Her aesthetic significance lies in the unique synthesis she made of the pictorial and the sculptural, the organic and the geometric, soft and hard, internal and external, subjective and objective. Hesse's sculpture is entirely abstract, but it evokes ambiguous erotic, symbolic, and psychological associations, which she accepted as part of "the total absurdity of life." Eva Hesse wanted to break rules and take risks: "I am interested in solving an unknown factor of art and an unknown factor of life." The emotive power she forged from apparently dumb, neutral forms, from layers, repetitions, delicate obsessive detail, and body associations, as well as her conviction that her life and art were not separate, have made her a model for many women artists. Although she resisted the category of feminist as she had others, Hesse was well aware of the part her femaleness played in her life and her art. In 1965 she wrote: "A woman is sidetracked by all her feminine roles . . . She's at [a] disadvantage from the beginning . . . She also lacks the conviction that she has the 'right' to achievement . . . that her achievements are worthy . . . A fantastic strength is necessary and courage. I dwell on this all the time."

During the last year of her life Hesse worked with strength and courage and with increased intensity, creating some of her major works despite operations, chemotherapy, and, finally, the knowledge of imminent death. When she died in New York Hospital in May 1970, she had achieved her goal of being an important and acknowledged artist. Two years after her death the Solomon R. Guggenheim Museum presented a memorial exhibition of her work, the first retrospective ever given there to a woman artist. Eva Hesse had disproved the stereotypes in which she once felt herself trapped.

[All quotations are taken from Hesse's diaries, writings, interviews, and conversations as cited in *Eva Hesse*, by Lucy R. Lippard (1976). See also "An Interview with Eva Hesse," *Artforum*, May 1970, pp. 59–63, and "Eva Hesse: Her Life," *Feminist Art Journal*, Winter 1973, both by Cindy Nemser; *Eva Hesse: A Memorial Exhibition*, Solomon R. Guggenheim Museum, Dec. 7, 1972–Feb. 11, 1973, with texts by Linda Shearer and Robert Pincus-Witten; Kasha Linville Gula, "Eva Hesse: No Explanation," *Ms.*, April 1973, pp. 39–42; *Strata: Nancy Graves, Eva Hesse, Michelle Stuart, Jackie Winsor*, Vancouver Art Gallery, Oct. 9–Nov. 6, 1977, text by Lucy R. Lippard. Hesse's obituary appeared in the *N.Y. Times*, May 30, 1970.]

LUCY R. LIPPARD

HICKOK, Lorena A., March 7, 1893–May 1, 1968. Journalist.

Lorena Hickok was born in East Troy, Wis., the eldest of three daughters of Addison J. and Anna (Waite) Hickok. Her mother, who came of a moderately prosperous farming family, had been a dressmaker before her runaway marriage. Her father, a buttermaker, lost one job after another, whipped his children, and dashed out the brains of Lorena's pet kitten. The family's constant moving disrupted schooling and friendships, and contributed to her loneliness. Her mother's gentle cousin, "Aunt" Ella C. Ellis— "the only person I really trusted"—gave her love. Lorena was taught, and believed, that "we could get anything we wanted out of life if we wanted it hard enough and worked for it."

When Lorena was thirteen, in Bowdle, S. Dak., her mother died. The following year she took the first of a series of jobs as a "hired girl." Gaining independence, she soon realized that she was no longer in her father's power. Aunt Ella came to her aid, and at fifteen Lorena went to live in Battle Creek, Mich., where, encouraged by an English teacher, she completed high school. In succeeding years, she briefly attended Lawrence College in Appleton, Wis., and the University of Minnesota, but never sustained interest long enough to graduate.

Hickok began her journalistic career in 1913 on the *Battle Creek Evening News*, then moved on to the *Milwaukee Sentinel*. Transferred from the society pages onto the city staff, she soon earned a by-line and wrote feature stories on visiting celebrities. In 1917 she moved to Minneapolis and the *Minneapolis Tribune*, where, after a brief interlude in New York City, she became Sunday editor and then a star reporter. The managing editor, Thomas J. Dillon, gave Hickok varied opportunities: she covered murder trials, football, and politics. The "Old Man," she gratefully remembered, "taught me the newspaper business, how to drink, and how to live." While in Minneapolis she also wrote speeches for the mayor. A male interviewer described "Hick" as "good natured, overweight, erratic," and claimed she was "the cleverest interviewer in this part of the country" (newspaper clipping, box 14, Hickok Papers).

In 1926 Hickok left Minneapolis and, after a short stay in San Francisco, arrived in New York in 1927. After a stint on the *Daily Mirror,* she shifted to the Associated Press the following year. Again, she covered front-page stories: tennis at Forest Hills, the Lindbergh kidnapping, and politics—state party conventions, the Alfred E. Smith campaign of 1928, the Democratic National Committee, and Franklin D. Roosevelt.

In 1932, when at her suggestion the Associated Press assigned her to cover ELEANOR ROOSEVELT during the presidential campaign, Hickok entered upon a friendship that became the pivot of her existence. With sympathetic insight, she perceived the misgivings of the candidate's wife, and, by the inauguration in March 1933, had become a close friend of the "reluctant first lady." They took extended trips together: to the Gaspé peninsula, to Puerto Rico, and to the west coast. When separated the two women corresponded and unburdened themselves of anxieties, whether about the marital troubles of the Roosevelt children, or about the depression and feelings of worthlessness that frequently seized upon the outwardly confident newspaperwoman.

Feeling that her friendship with Eleanor Roosevelt interfered with her objectivity as a reporter, Hickok left the Associated Press in the spring of 1933 and undertook her most memorable piece of work. Traveling around the country, she reported confidentially to Harry Hopkins, head of the Federal Emergency Relief Administration, on the effectiveness of New Deal programs and on the condition and attitudes of ordinary people hit by the great depression. Circulated among a few officials, her candid observations provided vital information to those who were groping for a policy to relieve immediate human needs. She wrote vividly and often with anger. In parts of West Virginia, diphtheria, tuberculosis, and typhoid flourished, and babies routinely died of dysentery; yet there was not "a single city or county hospital with free clinics or free beds." Writing from North Dakota in November, she insisted that "these

people have GOT to have clothing—right away." In assessing local responses to the deprivation she witnessed, Hickok spoke approvingly of certain officials who rounded up suspected communists; yet she also suggested that the unemployed were too patient. In eastern Kentucky she found it hard to understand why the mountain people "don't go down and raid the Blue Grass country."

After Roosevelt's reelection in 1936, Hickok left the government and took a position in public relations for the New York World's Fair. Freed from constant travel, she worked in New York City and retreated on weekends to a beloved country cottage in Moriches, Long Island. Early in 1940 she joined the Democratic National Committee, first in the publicity section and then in the Women's Division, where she served four years as executive secretary. During that time she lived at the White House, saw Eleanor Roosevelt constantly, and had the status almost of a member of the family. She also enjoyed rewarding friendships with Howard Haycraft, Helen Gahagan Douglas, Marion Harron (1903–1972) of the United States Tax Court, MARY DEWSON, and Congresswoman MARY T. NORTON, to whom she was much attached.

Having suffered from diabetes since the mid-1920s, Hickok was forced by ill health to give up her job, and she left Washington in March 1945. Poor health kept her from regular employment thereafter, although in 1947 she joined the Women's Division of the State Democratic Committee of New York. In 1954 Hickok and Eleanor Roosevelt coauthored *Ladies of Courage.* Between 1956 and 1962 she published six more books, including biographies of Franklin D. Roosevelt, Eleanor Roosevelt, HELEN KELLER, and ANNE SULLIVAN MACY. Before she died she had begun a biography of Walter Reuther which was completed by a collaborator.

In the mid-1950s Lorena Hickok moved to Hyde Park, N.Y. Her later years were saddened by the death of Eleanor Roosevelt in 1962, by failing eyesight, and by a crippling condition caused by diabetes. She died in Rhinebeck, N.Y., in 1968 of pneumonia following amputation of a leg.

[The Lorena Hickok Papers, Franklin D. Roosevelt Library, Hyde Park, N.Y., consist of correspondence, principally from the 1930s and 1940s, with Eleanor Roosevelt, Mary Norton, and many others, her reports to Harry Hopkins, and an unfinished autobiography which offers details of her childhood and youth. Quotations in the article about her early life are from the autobiography. The papers of Eleanor Roosevelt and of Mary Dewson, in the same repository, also contain relevant material. Eleanor Roosevelt speaks affectionately of

Hickok in *This I Remember* (1949), and Hickok's *Reluctant First Lady* (1962) illuminates both their friendship and her own personality. Her other books were *The Story of Franklin D. Roosevelt* (1956); *The Story of Helen Keller* (1958), *The Story of Eleanor Roosevelt* (1959), *The Touch of Magic: The Story of Helen Keller's Great Teacher, Anne Sullivan Macy* (1961), *The Road to the White House* (1962), and, with Jean Gould, *Walter Reuther: Labor's Rugged Individualist* (1972). Some of her reports to Hopkins are quoted at length in Bernard Sternsher, "Depression and New Deal in Ohio: Lorena A. Hickok's Reports to Harry Hopkins, 1934–1936," *Ohio Hist.*, Autumn 1977, pp. 258–77. Ishbel Ross, *Ladies of the Press* (1936) contains an account of her career. A biography by Doris Faber, *The Life of Lorena Hickok* (1980), appeared when this volume was in press. An obituary appeared in the *N.Y. Times*, May 3, 1968. Rev. Gordon Kidd, retired pastor of St. James Church in Hyde Park, contributed information about her later years. A birth record supplied by Walworth Cty., Wis., Register of Deeds gives her name as Alice Loraine Hickok; death certificate supplied by N.Y. State Dept. of Health.]

JEAN CHRISTIE

HIGGINS, Marguerite, Sept. 3, 1920–Jan. 3, 1966. Journalist.

Marguerite Higgins was the first woman to win a Pulitzer Prize for foreign correspondence, awarded her in 1951 for her coverage of the Korean War. Admired and envied for her tenacity in getting a story, and for her courage and drive, she quickly ascended to the top of her profession. Born in the British crown colony of Hong Kong, China, she was the only child of Marguerite (Godard), a Frenchwoman, and Lawrence Daniel Higgins, an American Army Air Corps veteran who was freight manager of a steamship company. Marguerite received her early education in California, where the family settled after their return to the United States in 1923. She attended the Anna Head School in Berkeley and in 1941 graduated with honors from the University of California at Berkeley. She received her M.S. in journalism in 1942 from Columbia University.

Higgins's first reporting experiences were in California at the *Tahoe Tattler*, the *Daily Californian*, and the Vallejo *Times-Herald*. She was Columbia's campus correspondent to the *New York Herald Tribune* and was hired as a reporter there in 1942. Because the draft was taking away the men, the paper had several women reporters in the early forties. Her city editor, Lessing Engleking, said Higgins was "intensely competitive" and had more "fire and zeal than most." In 1944 she obtained her first overseas

assignment, having bypassed her editors and gone directly to publisher HELEN ROGERS REID with her request. Just turned twenty-four, she was assigned first to the London bureau, and then to Paris.

Named the paper's Berlin bureau chief in 1945, Higgins "covered the news with a single mindedness and determination . . . that brooked no interference," recalled Whitelaw Reid. She earned a large share of front-page headlines with her coverage of the capture of Munich and Berchtesgaden and the liberation of Buchenwald and Dachau. Her vivid and moving accounts of the German concentration camps won her the New York Newspaper Women's Club Award as best foreign correspondent of 1945. She also reported on the treason trial of Marshal Henri Pétain, the Nuremberg war trials, and the Berlin blockade, and became adept at obtaining exclusive interviews.

Higgins was sent to Tokyo in May 1950 to be the *Herald Tribune*'s Far East bureau chief; almost immediately she was in Korea covering a new war. The newspaper soon sent its star war correspondent, Homer Bigart, to Korea, and the intense competition between the two reporters resulted in excellent news coverage and Pulitzer Prizes for both. Higgins prided herself on accepting the hardships and dangers of war zone reporting along with her colleagues, and most of them learned to accept her as one more reporter. But the officers frequently told her she did not belong on the front lines. Eighth Army Commander Lt. Gen. Walton H. Walker ordered her out of Korea and had her escorted to a waiting airplane. Higgins protested this unfair decision to Gen. Douglas MacArthur, who quickly lifted the ban and wired her editors to indicate his support.

An attractive blonde, Higgins was the victim of much unfair and untrue gossip, said Chicago *Daily News* correspondent Keyes Beech, who served with her in Korea. "Maggie didn't need to use her sex to do a good job as a war correspondent. She had brains, ability, courage and stamina."

Higgins returned to the United States in late 1950 in triumph, something of a heroine as the best known woman correspondent serving in the Korean War. She was showered with some fifty awards and honors in the next few years, including the Overseas Press Club's George Polk Memorial Award, Theta Sigma Phi Award, Marine Corps Reserve Officers Award, and the 1951 Woman of the Year Award from the Associated Press. Her best-selling book, *War in Korea: The Report of a Woman Combat Correspondent* (1951), was followed by *News Is a Singular*

Thing (1955) and *Red Plush and Black Bread* (1955), all highly personalized recollections of her journalistic experiences.

Higgins's 1942 marriage to Stanley Moore, later a professor of philosophy, had ended in divorce in 1948. In 1952 she married Lt. Gen. William E. Hall, former director of United States intelligence in Berlin. In 1955 they settled in Washington, D.C., where Higgins covered the State Department and wrote a Monday editorial page column. Her first child, Sharon Lee, born in 1953, was a premature baby who lived only five days. She had two more children: Lawrence O'Higgins, born in 1958, and Linda Marguerite, born in 1959.

Through the 1950s and early 1960s Higgins continued to travel abroad, covering international meetings and presidential trips. Long a vigorous opponent of communism, she was outspoken on the subject in her column. In 1962 she warned early of Soviet military activity in Cuba. Following two trips to Vietnam in 1963 to report on the religious crisis, Higgins alleged that the Buddhist self-burnings were politically inspired to help bring down the Diem regime. She charged that President Ngo Dinh Diem's overthrow was the result of American pressures and policy. *Our Vietnam Nightmare* (1965) detailed her firsthand investigations and her criticisms of American policy on Vietnam.

Higgins left the *Herald Tribune* in the fall of 1963, moving to *Newsday* of Long Island to write a thrice weekly column which was syndicated in ninety-two other newspapers. Her death at the age of forty-five, after another long reporting tour in Vietnam, India, and Pakistan, was caused by a tropical infection, leishmaniasis, picked up during the journey. She was hospitalized in Washington, D.C., in November 1965, and died there two months later of complications of the disease.

[The Marguerite Higgins Papers in the George Arents Research Library, Syracuse Univ., contain correspondence, a diary, scrapbooks and other memorabilia, notes, manuscripts, and articles by and about Higgins. Two other books by Marguerite Higgins are *Overtime in Heaven: Adventures in the Foreign Service* (1964), written with Peter Lisagor, and *Jessie Benton Fremont* (1962), a children's book. Her "Thoughts on the Death of a Five-day-old Child" appeared in *Good Housekeeping*, Aug. 1954. Sources of information about her life and career include Carl Mydans, "Girl War Correspondent," *Life*, Oct. 2, 1950; *Current Biog.*, 1951; Keyes Beech, *Tokyo and Points East* (1954); Ansel Talbert, "Korea: Along the 38th Parallel," *Dateline*, 1966; Kathleen Kearney Lewis, "Maggie Higgins," (M.A. thesis, Univ. of Md., 1973); Margaret Parton, *Journey Through A Lighted Room* (1973); Marion

Marzolf, *Up From the Footnote: A History of Women Journalists* (1977). Obituaries appeared in the *N.Y. Herald Tribune*, Jan. 4, 1966; *N.Y. Times*, Jan. 4, 1966; *Wash. Post*, Jan. 4, 1966; *Time*, Jan. 14, 1966; *Newsweek*, Jan. 17, 1966; *Editor and Publisher*, Jan. 8, 1966; *Publishers Weekly*, Jan. 17, 1966; death record provided by D.C. Dept. of Public Health. Information was also obtained from documents from the Eighth U.S. Army in Korea (July 1950) and from correspondence with Whitelaw Reid, Lessing Engleking, Richard L. Tobin, Margaret Parton, Carl Mydans, Keyes Beech, Louise Fitzsimons, and Harry W. Baehr. Carl Mydans's photographs of Marguerite Higgins are available through the *Time-Life* Picture Agency.]

                                                    MARION MARZOLF

HILL, Lillie Rosa Minoka. *See* MINOKA-HILL, Lillie Rosa.

HILL, May. *See* ARBUTHNOT, May Hill.

HOEY, Jane Margueretta, Jan. 15, 1892–Oct. 6, 1968. Social worker, federal official.

Jane Hoey, first director of the Bureau of Public Assistance, Social Security Board, was born in Greeley County, Neb., the youngest of nine children of John and Catherine (Mullen) Hoey; of the children surviving in 1900, there were three boys and four girls. The Hoeys, who had lived in New York City for at least twenty years following their emigration from Ireland shortly after the Civil War, returned to New York from the west when Jane was about six years old. A rancher in Nebraska, John Hoey had worked as a laborer in the city. The family was modestly well off, their economic status improving as Jane's older brothers and sisters obtained work; these brothers and sisters later financed her education and European travels. Catherine Hoey introduced Jane to social work at an early age, taking her on charitable visits to New York's Welfare Island.

Jane Hoey graduated from Wadleigh High School in 1910, then attended Hunter College for two years. In 1912 she transferred to Trinity College, Washington, D.C., where her teachers included sociologist William J. Kerby and economist John A. Ryan, both prominent Catholic clergymen and reformers, who helped shape Hoey's social philosophy. Throughout her life Jane Hoey remained committed to Catholicism and did not hesitate to employ broad religious themes in her policy statements. Graduating from Trinity College in 1914, Hoey continued her education at Columbia University, earning an A.M. in political science in 1916 and a diploma from the New York School of Philanthropy, where she studied under MARY

RICHMOND, a leading exponent of professionalism in social work.

Hoey's first job (1916–17) was as assistant to Harry L. Hopkins, then head of the Board of Child Welfare of New York City and later director of the Federal Emergency Relief Administration. At the Board of Child Welfare, Hoey helped administer a mothers' aid program which helped needy mothers to keep their children at home rather than place them in institutions. In January 1918, after the United States entered World War I, Hoey joined the Home Service of the American Red Cross, where she remained until June 1921. Later that year, she began work with two members of the faculty of the New York School of Social Work on a survey of local affiliates of national social work agencies. As assistant director of the project, Hoey studied social services in twelve cities and two rural counties across the country. She then headed the Bronx division of the New York Tuberculosis and Health Association from 1923 to 1926, during which time she helped organize the influential Welfare Council of New York City, an association of social service agencies. Hoey served as assistant director and secretary of the Health Division of the Welfare Council from 1926 to 1936.

In a decade of work for the Welfare Council, Hoey made use of her professional training as well as her valuable connections in the state's Democratic party: her brother, James J. Hoey, had served in the New York State Assembly from 1907 to 1911, and through him Hoey came to know such prominent figures as Alfred E. Smith, Franklin D. Roosevelt, and Robert Wagner, Sr. As governor, Smith named Jane Hoey to the New York State Crime and Correction Commissions in 1926; she later served on the Commission of Education of Inmates of Penal Institutions from 1933 to 1936. While fully realizing the usefulness of her political connections, Hoey insisted on a civil service classification when the Roosevelt administration in Washington sought her out. In February 1936 she was named director of the Bureau of Public Assistance, Social Security Board (later Social Security Administration).

The Bureau Hoey directed for seventeen years was responsible for the welfare provisions of the Social Security Act of 1935 (Old Age Assistance, Aid to the Blind, and Aid to Dependent Children). Hoey's task was complicated by the fact that she did not have full control over these programs; they were administered by the states whose expenditures were matched by Washington at rates of from one-third to one-half. State welfare plans were subject to approval by the federal government, but the law left to state discretion the all-important standards of eligibility for assistance as well as the level of assistance payments. Accordingly Hoey defined her role at the Bureau as one of helping the states to develop adequate programs. Where state officials were reluctant to be helped, Hoey worked to persuade them, meeting with governors and key legislators, counseling and cajoling, pressing for better welfare services, standards, personnel, and management.

Hoey's career at the Bureau of Public Assistance reflected a coherent welfare philosophy, spelled out in her many public addresses and articles. She regarded money payments to the needy as a great step forward from the poor law days of hand-me-down clothing and grocery orders. Money payments reinforced recipients' capacity for self-reliance, Hoey believed, but she also realized that careful fiscal management was required. Public welfare had become big money—in 1953 the Bureau's budget exceeded one billion dollars—and Hoey saw to it that the states and the federal government established statistical reporting systems to ensure accountability and measure trends. Hoey also believed that money was wasted in the absence of services provided by trained social workers, and established a unit within the Bureau of Public Assistance to assist states in staff development. As a result, standards for employment of personnel, in-service training, and liberal educational leave policies became an integral part of many state programs.

As an administrator, Hoey was sensitive yet firm. She asked for and listened carefully to the recommendations of her staff, but assumed full responsibility for program decisions. A warm and generous person, Hoey broke the rules for professional women of her day by displaying emotion, losing her temper or shedding tears on occasion. But even her critics agreed that she was persuasive, even inspirational, at a time when the Bureau of Public Assistance required a dynamic leader.

Devoted to her job and reluctant to surrender it, when Dwight D. Eisenhower captured the presidency in 1952 and proceeded to replace Democrats in top jobs, she argued in vain that hers was not a policymaking position and that the law required administration by a qualified professional. Jane Hoey was removed as director of the Bureau of Public Assistance on Nov. 3, 1953.

Retired on full pension and by now a wealthy woman—she inherited and helped manage her brother's insurance business—Hoey chose nonetheless to take another job, serving as director of social research for the National Tuberculosis Association until 1957.

Hoey received wide recognition for her leadership in social welfare. The recipient of several honorary degrees, she served as president of the National Conference of Social Work (1940–41) and later represented the United States at several sessions of the UN Social and Economic Commission. In 1955 she became the first recipient of the Florina Lasker Social Work Award, and received the René Sand Award for her distinguished contribution to international social work in 1966. A strong advocate of the rights of minorities, she received the James J. Hoey award from the Catholic Interracial Council of New York, which her brother had founded.

Jane Hoey spent her last years in New York City. Following a stroke, she died there in October 1968. She divided the bulk of her estate between Trinity College and the Columbia University School of Social Work, bequeathing nearly a million dollars to each institution.

[Information on Hoey's public life may be found in the records of the Bureau of Public Assistance, Social Security Administration, Record Group 47, Washington Nat. Records Center, Suitland, Md. *The Reminiscences of Jane Hoey* (1965) are in the Oral History Coll., Columbia Univ.; also useful are interviews with staff members of the Social Security Administration, including Arthur J. Altmeyer, Lavinia Eagle, Kathryn Goodwin, and Maurine Mulliner. The archives of Trinity College contain clippings about Hoey and copies of articles by her. Trinity College also has a copy of her will; a portrait hangs in the college entrance hall. Revealing articles by Hoey include: "The Federal Government and Desirable Standards of State and Local Administration," Nat. Conference of Social Work, *Proceedings*, 1937; "Our Common Stake in the Development of the Social Security Program," *The Family*, Jan. 1938; "The Significance of the Money Payment in Public Assistance," *Social Security Bull.*, Sept. 1944; and "Public Welfare—Burden or Opportunity?" *Social Service Rev.*, Dec. 1953. Biographical information on Hoey appears in *Current Biog.*, 1950; *Encyc. of Social Work* (1971); and Dorothy A. Mohler, "Jane Hoey and Agnes Regan, Women in Washington," in Robert Trisco, ed., *Catholics in America, 1776–1976* (1976). The *N.Y. Times* reported her dismissal from the Bureau of Public Assistance on Nov. 4, 1953, and published an obituary on Oct. 7, 1968. The following works contain useful background information: June Axinn and Herman Levin, *Social Welfare: A History of the American Response to Need* (1975); Winifred Bell, *Aid to Dependent Children* (1965); Roy Lubove, *The Struggle for Social Security, 1900–1935* (1968); and Edwin E. Witte, *The Development of the Social Security Act* (1962). Additional information was supplied by Dorothy Lally and Ruth Pauley.]

BLANCHE D. COLL

HOFFMAN, Malvina Cornell, June 15, 1885–July 10, 1966. Sculptor.

Malvina Hoffman, internationally recognized sculptor, was born in New York City to Richard and Fidelia (Lamson) Hoffman, the fourth girl and youngest of six children. (The eldest daughter died in infancy.) Her father, English by birth, was a piano teacher and soloist with the New York Philharmonic. Her mother, born of a socially prominent New York family of English origin, was a talented amateur pianist and lover of French literature.

Electric batteries, mechanical toys, and toy horses fascinated Malvina as a child. Her father encouraged these interests and guided her intellectual development by devising games that sharpened her power of observation and developed her memory. He explained musical principles of construction, rhythm, balance, and harmony as paradigms for the practice of any art form. From her father, Malvina Hoffman gained a lifelong sense of the artist's vocation. She attended the Chapin and Brearley Schools in New York City and, during her teens, studied at the Women's School of Applied Design and at the Art Students League. Later, at the Veltin School, she studied painting with John W. Alexander and modeling with Herbert Adams and George Grey Barnard.

Hoffman's career as a sculptor developed as a result of the successful reception of two early works. Her clay portrait of her father, done about 1909, gained her important criticisms from Gutzon Borglum, who encouraged her to carve it in marble. The finished work was exhibited in 1910 at the National Academy of Design. During the same year she received honorable mention at the Paris Salon for a bust of Samuel Bonarios Grimson, an English violinist friend of her father's who later became her husband. They married on June 6, 1924, and divorced in 1936.

Determined to study with Auguste Rodin, Hoffman, accompanied by her mother, made her first trip to Europe in 1910, a year after her father's death. After persistent efforts she received an audience with Rodin and her work convinced him of her talent. She studied with him for sixteen months until her funds ran out. Once back in New York City she undertook, on Rodin's advice, the study of dissection and anatomy at the Columbia University College of Physicians and Surgeons. Hoffman resumed her studies with Rodin during the two summers before the outbreak of World War I in 1914. While studying with Rodin and the sculptor Emanuele Rosales, she also learned bronze casting, chasing, and finishing at foundries.

After returning to New York to work for the Red Cross, with which her sister Helen Draper (1871–1951) was associated, Hoffman became the American representative of Appui aux Artistes, a French war charity benefiting needy artists which she had helped to found before leaving France. For the United States government she reported on relief work in Greece and the Balkans.

In Paris Hoffman knew GERTRUDE STEIN, the artists Monet, Matisse, and Brancusi, and the dancer Nijinsky; she became a good friend of Anna Pavlova. Like many other artists of the period, she was influenced by the Ballet Russe of Sergei Diaghilev. Inspired by Pavlova and others, she attempted to capture in her sculpture "that new kind of freedom in the dance" and to convey its "sense of motion and immediacy." Hoffman's "Russian Dancers," which won first honorable mention at the Paris Salon in 1911, and "Bacchanale Russe," awarded the Shaw Memorial Prize by the National Academy of Design in 1917, are based on the figures of Pavlova and Mikhail Mordkin. Other works interpreting the dance are "Pavlowa Gavotte," "La Péri," "Les Orientales," and a series of twenty-six bas-relief panels never exhibited.

Several large pieces typify Hoffman's work of the twenties. She completed her war monument, "The Sacrifice," in 1922. Commissioned by Martha W. Bacon and given to Harvard University, the sculpture depicts a mother kneeling at the head of a recumbent crusader in armor. Between 1923 and 1925, Hoffman concentrated on the heroic group "To the Friendship of English-Speaking Peoples," designed for the entrance of Bush House in London. In 1925, she did an over-life-size portrait in bronze of the Yugoslavian sculptor Ivan Meštrović, with whom she later studied architectural and monumental sculpture.

Hoffman's first extensive exhibition came in 1929 at Grand Central Art Gallery in New York City. It included 105 pieces of sculpture in sixteen different materials and many life-size crayon portraits. For five years the exhibit traveled to museums throughout the country.

The work that brought Malvina Hoffman international recognition resulted from a commission by Chicago's Field Museum of Natural History in 1930. For this project—her most demanding and comprehensive—she traveled for two years in remote countries, accompanied by her husband. Returning with models of a series of racial types, Hoffman spent three more years completing the work. The collection, consisting of over 100 heads and figures of men and women from Africa, Asia, Europe, the Pacific Islands, and North America, was dedicated on June 6, 1933. Although impressive, the heads and figures in the museum's Hall of Man are more anthropological studies than works of art.

In the late forties and fifties Hoffman received two major commissions for bas-reliefs. To commemorate American soldiers killed in battles near Épinal, France, the United States Fine Arts Commission in 1948 engaged her as sculptor for the American War Memorial Building located in the Vosges Mountains of France; her principal contributions were two bas-relief panels on the façade. In 1956 she completed thirteen bas-relief panels depicting the evolution of medicine for the facade of the Joslin Hospital in Boston.

In appearance, Malvina Hoffman was tall and slim; in manner, alert and direct. Strong-willed and hardworking, she created an enormous oeuvre including fountains, statuettes, architectural sculpture, portrait busts, and even a series of models for medical studies in prenatal care. From Rodin she learned to give vitality and emotion to her creations, but she kept them tied to realistic images. Her work is characterized by breadth of subject matter, careful attention to detail, and psychological insight.

Hoffman's artistry is most fully displayed in her naturalistic portrait busts of friends and acquaintances. An unending interest in people led her beyond the mere recording of physical features to seek the depths of personalities. She once wrote that "probing for what lies beneath the surface has been the search of my whole life." Hoffman employed her naturalistic style for a diverse range of subjects: from the simple humanity of a Parisian mattress mender to the fashionable portrait of MARY HARRIMAN; from the dynamic image of Meštrović to the quiet strength of Fidelia Hoffman, her mother. During the fifty years before she retired in 1963, Malvina Hoffman modeled such diverse personalities as Paderewski (four busts, "The Statesman," "The Man," "The Artist," and "The Friend," done in 1922 and 1923), Pavlova (1924), Wendell L. Willkie (1944), Teilhard de Chardin (1948), and KATHARINE CORNELL (1961).

Malvina Hoffman won numerous prizes and medals, including the National Sculpture Society's Gold Medal of Honor (1964), and was awarded five honorary degrees. She wrote a textbook, *Sculpture Inside and Out* (1939), and two autobiographies, *Heads and Tales* (1936) and *Yesterday Is Tomorrow* (1965). Her last book was published the year before her death, from a heart attack, at her New York City studio.

[About seventy-five items of Hoffman's correspondence, chiefly relating to the Nat. Inst. of Arts and Letters, are located in the Am. Acad. of Arts and Letters Library, N.Y. City. The principal sources of personal information are Hoffman's autobiographies. All quotations in the article are from *Yesterday Is*

Tomorrow. See also the biographical sketch in her *Malvina Hoffman* (1948), a volume in a series sponsored by the Nat. Sculpture Soc. Other references include Pauline Carrington Bouvé, "The Two Foremost Women Sculptors in America: Anna Vaughn Hyatt and Malvina Hoffman," *Art and Archaeology*, June 1928, pp. 74–82; *Current Biog.*, 1940; Margaret French Cresson, "A Great Lady of Sculpture," *Nat. Sculpture Rev.*, Summer 1962, pp. 16–17, 24; Marianne Moore, "Malvina Hoffman: 1887–1966," *Nat. Sculpture Rev.*, Fall 1966; and Beatrice G. Proske, *Brookgreen Gardens Sculpture* (1968). An obituary appeared in the *N.Y. Times*, July 11, 1966. In *Yesterday Is Tomorrow* Hoffman wrote that although the records of her birth were lost and her mother gave her birth date as 1887, family documents proved the date was 1885. A biobibliography prepared by James V. Wroblewski assisted in the research for this article.]

MYRNA GARVEY EDEN

HOGG, Ima, July 10, 1882–Aug. 19, 1975. Philanthropist.

The platitude about being a legend in one's own time was actually true of Ima Hogg for the last fifty years of her long life. Two pervasive myths about "Miss Ima," as she was known in Texas, are that she had a sister Ura and that these harshly punning names were chosen by a wealthy, puritanical father to protect his daughters from the sin of vanity. In truth, Ima Hogg's father had no such moralistic intentions: Ima, born in Mineola, Texas, was named for the heroine of an epic poem written by her father's brother. And there was no Ura Hogg; Ima, the second of four children, had only brothers with the more prosaic names of William, Michael, and Thomas.

Ima Hogg grew up in the heat and turbulence of Texas politics. Her father, James Stephen Hogg, elected to posts of political combat— county attorney, district attorney, attorney general, and finally governor of Texas—was drawn into political and economic frays from which he emerged as a fighting reformer and a perennial booster of Texas. Ima Hogg was only nine years old when her father was inaugurated in 1891 for his one four-year term as governor. Her mother, Sarah Ann (Stinson) Hogg, was in chronically poor health. Partly because of this, partly because of her own temperament, and partly because of her father's high regard for her, Ima Hogg played a strong role in James Hogg's political and business life from a very early age. She traveled extensively with him, both while he was governor and after he had left office. In some ways she filled the role of her mother, who died of what was diagnosed as

tuberculosis in 1895. James Hogg's extraordinary relationship with his daughter and his respect for her character and influence are reflected in a letter he wrote to her in 1902 concerning her brothers: "Now, Ima, that dream of yours won't work. I shall not indulge those boys in a 'trip to England' . . . *My boys must work their way!* . . . Your influence over them will make fine men out of them. Of course I shall be glad to take you anywhere, if I have to make the boys work to defray the expenses. In other words, you shall have *carte blanche*, as you have always had and never abused" (Cotner, p. 542).

As an adult Ima Hogg took the "carte blanche" of her family's wealth and political connections and put it to use in a variety of civic and philanthropic projects. One of her lifelong causes was mental health. After their father's death in 1906, the Hogg children were left with what was to become a substantial fortune in oil-producing land in West Columbia, Texas. When Ima's older brother, William, died in 1930— like Ima, he never married—the major part of his large estate went to the University of Texas, with the stipulation that Ima Hogg and her brother Michael should determine how the funds would be used. Ima Hogg conceived of a program that would disperse a variety of university mental health services across the state; the result in 1940 was the Hogg Foundation for Mental Hygiene (later changed to "Mental Health"). She also founded the Houston Child Guidance Center, a pioneering institution in child psychiatry.

Another of Ima Hogg's lifelong interests was music. After two years at the University of Texas (1899–1901) and several years of music study in New York and abroad, she moved in 1909 to Houston, where she was to live until 1975. She played a major role in organizing the Houston Symphony and served as president of the Symphony Society for a number of years. It was once said of Ima Hogg that she had "an exceptional combination of gracious firmness, insistence on seeking perfection, and impatience with obstacles or excuses." With this combination of graciousness and imperiousness, she exerted her considerable influence to build the orchestra and bring world-famous conductors to Houston.

Although a woman of her wealth might have been politically conservative, Ima Hogg was consistently liberal. She did not inherit her father's taste for politics; the only time she ran for public office was in 1943 when she won a six-year term on the Houston School Board. She later complained: "I really don't think I'm suited for that kind of public service. It is too involved with extraneous influences" (Iscoe, p. 25). More to her taste was public service by means of direct, personal philanthropy.

Historic preservation was another of Ima Hogg's causes, and in Texas, a state governed more than most by an all-consuming ideal of economic growth, her efforts to preserve and maintain historic buildings were particularly valuable. She initiated and supervised the restorations of her parents' first home in Quitman, Texas, the Varner-Hogg Plantation in Bravoria County, and historic buildings at Winedale, Texas. Her most personal and meticulous effort can be seen at Bayou Bend in Houston, her home for thirty-nine years, which she gave to Houston's Museum of Fine Arts in 1966. She provided there a carefully researched, artful assemblage of American antiques and furnishings—the first of its kind in the American southwest and the product of almost forty years of work on her part—within the setting of a splendid building and acres of lawn and formal gardens. Bayou Bend, like Ima Hogg's other restorations, has been left with an endowment to help maintain the building and keep it open to the public.

Both Presidents Eisenhower and Kennedy appointed Ima Hogg to advisory committees on the arts, but her primary recognition came from within Texas, where, among her other accomplishments, she became in 1948 the first woman president of the state's Philosophical Society. A perfectionist and sometimes an autocrat, she also knew how to value and enjoy what she had. Before leaving Houston on a trip to London in 1975, at the age of ninety-three, she told friends that she was going there in order to "hear the greatest music in the world one last time." She died there in August of a heart attack subsequent to a fall.

[Ima Hogg's "Life in the Governor's Mansion," a typescript in the James Stephen Hogg Coll. in the archives of the Univ. of Texas Library, describes that period of her childhood. Robert C. Cotner, *James Stephen Hogg: A Biography* (1959), contains extensive information about the history of the Hogg family. Louise Kosches Iscoe, *Ima Hogg: First Lady of Texas* (1976), is an unabashedly laudatory collection of reminiscences. It contains a number of good photographs of Ima Hogg. In 1969 the Rotary Club of Houston produced a booklet in honor of Ima Hogg's receiving its Distinguished Citizen Award; it contains speeches on Hogg and her family. David Warren, *Bayou Bend* (1975), contains numerous photographs of the furnishings at Bayou Bend and includes a foreword by Ima Hogg. *The Hogg Foundation for Mental Health: The First Three Decades* (1970) is a history of the Founda-

tion and its programs. An interview with McClelland Wallace provided further information.]

VIRGINIA ROTAN YOUNGREN

HOLIDAY, Billie, April 7, 1915?–July 17, 1959. Singer.

Billie Holiday was born in Baltimore, Md., probably in the spring of 1915, to Sadie Fagan and Clarence Holiday, both in their early teens and both black. Given the name Eleanora Fagan, she chose early on to adopt the first name of her screen idol, Billie Dove. She acquired the name Holiday upon the marriage of her parents when she was about three years old; she was their only child.

Clarence Holiday, a guitarist and banjoist, abandoned his wife and Billie to travel with a band. A divorce followed and each remarried. Sadie, widowed shortly thereafter, went to New York to work as a maid, leaving her daughter to be reared by relatives in impoverished and unhappy circumstances. She began to work before she was ten, performing menial chores and errands for a madam in her neighborhood. The experience exposed her to intimate adult behavior; it also provided her opportunities to hear the recorded blues and jazz music of BESSIE SMITH and Louis Armstrong. Both the social and the musical experiences profoundly influenced the course of her life.

Her mother returned briefly to Baltimore but soon went back to New York. Billie joined her there in the summer of 1927, having finished the fifth grade of school in Baltimore. This ended her formal education. In New York she began work as a maid but soon left that job. By 1931, the depression was deeply affecting Billie Holiday and her ailing mother, to whom she remained very close. She sought employment as a dancer in Harlem nightclubs; in one, she was asked to sing. In her words: "The whole joint quieted down. If someone had dropped a pin, it would have sounded like a bomb" (*Lady Sings the Blues*, p. 34).

She sang every night from midnight into the morning for a few dollars plus tips. Moving from club to club in Harlem, she began to attract well-known admirers from the entertainment world. During this time she acquired her lasting nickname, "Lady," bestowed sarcastically by other female performers. Her dignity, like the gardenias she wore in her hair, became part of her legend.

Her public and her career began to grow, in part through the agency of jazz enthusiast John Hammond, who organized her first recording, with clarinetist Benny Goodman in 1933. This record went unnoticed but in mid-1935 Hammond arranged for her to record as vocalist with Teddy Wilson and his band. That series sold well and was favorably reviewed, especially abroad, although it was not financially rewarding for Holiday. Also in 1935, she appeared in a short film, "Symphony in Black," and made her successful stage debut at the Apollo, a theater then of singular importance to black performers. Holiday began recording under her own name in 1936 and also began to sing outside of New York, mainly with Fletcher Henderson's band. She toured extensively during 1937 and 1938 with the Count Basie and the Artie Shaw bands.

On tour, Billie Holiday was almost everywhere subjected to prevailing racial hostilities and discriminatory practices. In 1938, in St. Louis, Shaw was told that he could not have a black singer with a white band; in New York she was asked to enter and leave the hotel where she performed by the kitchen door. The tours were further marred for her by personality clashes with managers. While traveling, she indulged the habit of smoking marijuana which she had begun in her teens.

At jam sessions in Harlem, Billie Holiday met many outstanding jazz musicians; throughout her career she was known for her empathy with other jazz performers. Particularly important to her was saxophonist Lester Young with whom she developed an extraordinary and enduring friendship. He called her "Lady Day"; she called him "Prez," to show her admiration. Young's style was as distinctive as her own, and completely compatible with it: they made several memorable recordings.

From 1939 to 1941 Holiday sang at Café Society Downtown, a club in Greenwich Village. There she created her unique interpretations of the antilynching song, "Strange Fruit," written for her by poet Lewis Allen, and of "God Bless the Child," both of which remained closely identified with her. Singing directly and intimately to her audience, occasionally and meditatively snapping her fingers in time to the music, she had an impact on her hearers like no other singer of her time.

In 1941 Billie Holiday married James N. (Jimmy) Monroe, a nightclub manager. While they remained together (they divorced in 1949 after a long separation) she joined him in smoking opium and her drug use became serious.

Public recognition for Holiday increased during the 1940s, but her personal problems also mounted. Between 1941 and 1945, she performed in New York and other major cities. In 1944 she won the Esquire Jazz Critics Poll and in 1946 received the Metronome Vocalist of the Year Award. But between these professional triumphs, her mother died (1945), leaving her with no close family and emotionally stricken. She met Joe Guy, a jazz trumpeter with whom she formed a liaison; they organized a band, and toured briefly in 1945. Problems resulting from her addiction had worsened with her use of heroin. Nevertheless, she sang at the Downbeat Club before and after the tour until the fall of 1946 when she went to Hollywood to play a role in the film *New Orleans*. She was cast as a maid, not an artist. This experience with racial stereotyping frustrated and humiliated her though the film expanded her exposure to the public.

Returning from Hollywood, Holiday resumed her nightclub engagements in New York City. In the spring of 1947, she voluntarily entered a private sanitarium there to be cured of her drug addiction. But her abstention was short-lived and in May she was convicted of narcotics violations in Philadelphia and sentenced to Alderson, the federal reformatory for women in West Virginia, where she was kept for over nine months.

Ten days after her release, she received a tumultuous welcome at a come-back concert in Carnegie Hall in New York City and she later starred in a revue. Because of her felony conviction, however, she was denied legal license to perform in New York nightclubs. She never regained it, though for a while she sang without incident at a club managed by John Levy. For three years she appeared in clubs and theaters in major American cities.

In 1949 Billie Holiday was arrested again for possession of narcotics but she was acquitted. Levy, who had succeeded Joe Guy in her affections, managed, exploited, and finally abandoned her while she was touring with a band in 1950. The following year Louis McKay became her manager and common-law husband.

Continuing to make records in the 1950s, she also sang again at the Apollo, and appeared with Duke Ellington, with Stan Kenton, and on television. In 1954 Holiday made a highly successful tour through western Europe; returning to the United States she resumed a heavy schedule of concert and club appearances through 1957. She and Louis McKay had been legally married in 1956. Both had been arrested the same year, again in Philadelphia, she for narcotics possession and he on a weapons offense. Once more, Billie Holiday committed herself briefly for clinical treatment of her addiction. She and McKay separated in 1957 but there was no divorce. Until 1959 she continued to record and perform publicly at home and abroad though she was visibly and vocally debilitated by alcoholism, now acute after years of drinking.

In March 1959 Lester "Prez" Young died. A

few months later Billie Holiday was admitted to Metropolitan Hospital in New York, a victim of drug and alcohol abuse. She was arrested for the last time in her hospital bed for alleged drug possession and died in July.

Billie Holiday became "Lady Day," a legend, and she has been hailed as the most influential female jazz singer of all time. Her style was unique and her vocal quality distinctive. The many musicians who heard and played with her praised her inventiveness with melody and time, her flexible phrasing, intuitive inflections, and compelling interpretations, and the freedom and sparkle she brought to all of these when she was at her best. Forty-one of Billie Holiday's forty-four years were marked by abandonments, divorces, arrests, notoriety, misfortune, and endless humiliations in pursuit of her career. They were also illuminated by sensitivity and her oft-exploited generosity, by celebrity status, performance awards, and a long recording career, but they ended with the ravages of sustained narcotics abuse. Recollections of her personal tragedies, reappraisals of her significance in jazz history, reissues of her recordings, and a film (*Lady Sings the Blues*, 1972) based on her autobiography have combined in a final irony to give her a secure place, that which she sought but never found.

[Billie Holiday, *Lady Sings the Blues* (1956), with William Dufty, contains disputed chronology but is an invaluable source. John Chilton, *Billie's Blues: Billie Holiday's Story, 1933–1959* (1975), is the principal biographical source; in two parts, it also includes an extensive bibliography of secondary sources and a discography. Single records and albums are listed in Jorgen Grunnet Jepsen, *A Discography of Billie Holiday* (1969), published in Denmark. Mention of Holiday appears in much of the historical and critical literature on jazz since 1933. Ralph Gleason gives a forceful and gripping description of her style in the liner notes to the Columbia albums, *Billie Holiday: The Golden Years* (I), reprinted in his book, *Celebrating the Duke* (1975). Other discussions include comment on her vocal style in Whitney Balliett, *Such Sweet Thunder* (1966); and reminiscences in Stanley Dance, *The World of Swing* (1974) and in John Hammond, *On Record* (1978). She is evaluated within the context of jazz history in Robert Goffin, *Jazz, from the Congo to the Metropolitan* (1944); Marshall Stearns, *The Story of Jazz* (1962, 1970); and Samuel Charters and Leonard Kundstadt, *Jazz: A History of the New York Scene* (1962). See also Spike Hughes, *Second Movement* (1951); Nat Shapiro and Nat Hentoff, *Jazz Makers* (1957); Benny Green, *The Reluctant Art: The Growth of Jazz* (1963); Jack Schiffman, *Uptown: The Story of Harlem's Apollo Theatre* (1971); Bruce Cook, *Listen to the Blues* (1973); Hampton Hawes and Don Asher, *Raise Up Off Me* (1974); and Hettie Jones, *Big Star Fallin'*

Mama: Five Women in Black Music (1974). A biobibliography by James Carmichael provides a short biography of Holiday and includes an annotated bibliography and discography.]

GEORGIA A. RYDER

HOLLIDAY, Judy, June 21, 1921–June 7, 1965. Actress.

In an acting career spanning less than twenty years, Judy Holliday appeared in only six plays and eight films; most are of minor significance. Yet critics and directors compared her to Charlie Chaplin; Katharine Hepburn credited her with stealing *Adam's Rib* from her and Spencer Tracy; and Jack Benny studied her performances to improve his timing. She brought incredible artistic thoroughness to her handful of comic creations; few performers have ever endeared themselves to audiences so thoroughly.

She was born Judith Tuvim in Manhattan, the only child of Abraham and Helen (Gollomb) Tuvim. Both parents were of Russian-Jewish descent, her maternal grandparents having emigrated to escape a czarist pogrom. Abraham Tuvim was a professional fund raiser for socialist and Jewish organizations, while Helen Tuvim taught piano. After her parents' separation (she was only six and it left her somewhat embittered), Judith lived with her mother and grandmother. She graduated from Julia Richman High School in 1938, and then worked briefly as a switchboard operator for Orson Welles's Mercury Theatre. At seventeen, with a few friends, including Betty Comden and Adolph Green, she launched her performing career. Their group, "The Revuers," developed a topical cabaret act which began in New York nightclubs and eventually shifted to Hollywood. It brought some attention in film circles for Judith Tuvim—who at this time took the name Holliday, an English derivative of the Hebrew Tuvim. Although all three appeared in a few films, their screen time was largely cut and, with Comden and Green beginning the book and lyrics for what became *On the Town*, the group disbanded. Back in New York, Holliday made her stage debut, a small "moronic" role in a farce called *Kiss Them For Me* (1945) which earned her the Clarence Derwent and Theatre World Awards.

It was late in 1945 that Holliday's storybook leap to stardom occurred. Producer Max Gordon found himself in trouble in Philadelphia when Jean Arthur, the star of Garson Kanin's *Born Yesterday*, a new comedy, became ill and left the show. He summoned Holliday and gave her seventy-two hours to learn and rehearse the role of Billie Dawn, a megalomaniac junkman's empty-headed mistress whose latent sensitivities are awakened and temper aroused, and who scores a moral and financial victory on behalf of little people. The play struck all the right chords with postwar audiences, and Holliday and *Born Yesterday* were stunning successes. Between 1946 and 1950 she played Billie more than 1,600 times and, except for a leave of absence during which she played a similar role in *Adam's Rib* (1949) for MGM, she never missed a performance.

Despite her huge success, Harry Cohn of Columbia Pictures found her type unusual; he was further put off by her insistence on a contract which would require of her only a single picture a year. She was jealous of her private life, having married David Oppenheim, a clarinetist and later an executive with Columbia Records, on Jan. 4, 1948 (they were divorced in 1957); her only child, Jonathan, was born in 1952. Because of his reservations, Cohn launched the longest and most thorough star search since that for *Gone with the Wind* to cast Billie Dawn for the screen. After two years, when it became clear that no one could touch what Holliday brought to the role, she recreated Billie on film, winning an Academy Award in 1950. (She defeated, among others, Bette Davis in *All About Eve* and Gloria Swanson in *Sunset Boulevard*.) Subsequently, she made five more comedies for Columbia.

Holliday turned up frequently on television variety shows in the early 1950s, but this side of her career was cut short by her appearance before the Senate Internal Security Subcommittee in 1952 and the partial blacklisting which followed. Her Senate testimony was evasive; apparently, she intentionally confounded the committee by once again becoming the scatterbrained Billie Dawn, allowing her to exonerate herself—she had actively supported various causes alleged by the committee to be communist-front—and to avoid naming others. Garson Kanin later remarked: "Of all those who were harassed in the ugly days of Red Channels and blacklisting, no one was more steadfast or less craven. Her behavior under pressure was a poem of grace."

In 1956 Holliday returned to the stage in her musical debut, as Ella Peterson in *Bells Are Ringing*. Her old friends Comden and Green tailored the role to both her expressive vulnerability and her varied talents as a vaudevillian and mimic. Four years later she appeared in MGM's screen version. She toured in Elmer Rice's *Dream Girl* in the late 1950s, still searching for roles which would allow her to escape the more and more confining Billie Dawn stereo-

type. Sadly, the play which meant the most to her in developing herself as an actress, Samuel Taylor's *Laurette* (1960), based on her idol Laurette Taylor, had to be canceled in New Haven when the throat affliction which had bothered her for many years made acting impossible. She made one more acting attempt, in an ill-fated musical called *Hot Spot* (1963), before her death in New York from cancer in 1965.

George Cukor, the director of most of Judy Holliday's films, said that "she had in common with the great comedians—with Chaplin—that depth of emotion, that unexpectedly touching emotion, that thing which would unexpectedly touch your heart." Nor should any assessment of her artistry ignore the amazing rapport she could establish with her audiences. In every one of her dumb blonde caricatures, she would endow her character with a sort of primeval intelligence that could instantly transport her far beyond her surroundings. But she did it too well: audiences always wanted another Billie Dawn. In 1955 Holliday observed: "One writer said that I started as a moron in 'Kiss Them For Me' and I worked up to be an imbecile in 'Adam's Rib.' What I want to know is: where does a girl go from being an imbecile. Maybe, if I'm lucky, I can be an idiot or a cretin?"

[All of Holliday's plays are mentioned. Her other films are *The Marrying Kind* (1952), *It Should Happen to You* (1954), *Phfft* (1954), *The Solid Gold Cadillac* (1956), and *Full of Life* (1956). The original cast album of *Bells Are Ringing* is the only recording on which Judy Holliday can be heard. There are masses of articles on Holliday, not all of them to be trusted: after her rise to fame, she became a favorite subject for the less reliable screen magazines. An ample clipping file is in the Billy Rose Theatre Coll., N.Y. Public Library; another clipping file is in the Harvard Theatre Coll. Also see Mel Schuster, *Motion Picture Performers: A Bibliography of Magazine and Periodical Articles, 1900–1969* (1971). The best articles are Winthrop Sargeant, "Judy Holliday," *Life*, April 2, 1951; V. Bird, "Holliday's Blond Surprise," *Sat. Eve. Post*, Dec. 31, 1955; William Peters, "Judy Holliday," *Redbook*, June 1957; and Lee Israel, "Judy Holliday," *Ms.*, Dec. 1976. Entries appear in *Current Biog.*, 1951, and *Biog. Encyc. and Who's Who of the Am. Theatre* (1966). One must read cautiously the accounts of her Senate committee appearance: *N.Y. Times*, April 5, 1951, p. 1; *N.Y. Times*, Sept. 25, 1952, p. 12; "Off on a Holliday," *Newsweek*, Oct. 6, 1952, pp. 38–39. An obituary appeared in the *N.Y. Times*, June 8, 1965. A biobibliography prepared by June Parker assisted in the research for this article. Dates of birth and death verified by N.Y. City Dept. of Health.]

JOHN DAVID SHOUT

HOPPER, Hedda, May 2, 1885–Feb. 1, 1966. Journalist, actress.

Hedda Hopper, the Hollywood gossip columnist, was born Elda Furry in Hollidaysburg, Pa., the fifth of nine children of David and Margaret (Miller) Furry, who were of German Quaker ancestry. She was the second daughter of the three girls and four boys who survived. When Elda was three, the family moved to Altoona, Pa., where her parents operated a butcher shop. It went bankrupt and her father set out for the Klondike, relying on his eldest sons' salaries and their bill collecting to support the family. When the boys' efforts in extracting money from creditors failed, Elda pitched in to become "the fightingest 14-year-old bill collector in Altoona."

Rebellious and resentful of male privilege, Elda Furry quit school after finishing the eighth grade and ran away to join a theatrical troupe. Brought home, she then went to study piano and voice at the Carter Conservatory in Pittsburgh. Furry made her stage debut in 1907 in the chorus of the Aborn Light Opera Company and her New York debut on Dec. 3, 1908, in the musical comedy *The Pied Piper* at the Majestic Theatre. In the latter production, she met fifty-year-old (William) DeWolf Hopper, a legendary ham celebrated for his roles in Gilbert and Sullivan and his recitations of "Casey at the Bat." She became the fifth of his six brides on May 8, 1913, and spent most of the following season accompanying him on tour, then returned to Manhattan alone. To quell rumors of a rift, she scheduled a luncheon for Jan. 26, 1915, but labor pains interrupted the party. At seven that evening she gave birth to her only child, William DeWolf Hopper, Jr.

Traveling to Hollywood with her husband that summer, Hopper accepted her first film role in Fox's *The Battle of Hearts*. When DeWolf Hopper's Hollywood career foundered, the couple returned east where she worked steadily in films and theater. Sometime in 1918, upon the advice of a numerologist, she adopted the name she believed changed her luck—Hedda Hopper.

The Hoppers maintained a precarious emotional balance until 1920 when her film salary reached $1,000 a week, equaling what her husband could command after years on the stage. The relationship deteriorated rapidly as Hedda Hopper appeared simultaneously in the play *Six-Cylinder Love* and, with John Barrymore, in the silent film *Sherlock Holmes*. DeWolf Hopper's career difficulties and philandering caused their divorce in 1922. Unable to rely on him, Hopper took out insurance on their lives to protect their son, to whom she attempted to play both mother and father.

In 1923, for security, she signed a modest $250-a-week contract at Metro-Goldwyn-Mayer and by 1927 found herself labeled "Queen of the Quickies." During the next decade, Hopper appeared in up to a dozen films a year. In addition, she ran for the Los Angeles County Central Committee, worked briefly as an actor's agent, sold real estate, and modeled for mail-order clothes.

Almost fifty and a failure, under the tutelage of personal manager Dema Harshbarger, Hopper took her first step toward establishing herself as a major personality with a serial and a gossip stint in radio. In 1937, when studio executives searched for someone to build as a rival to the increasingly demanding LOUELLA PARSONS, they chose Hedda Hopper as someone who knew who was doing what to whom, but who, they assumed, could be controlled.

On Feb. 14, 1938, the Hopper column, distributed by Esquire Syndicate, made its debut in thirteen newspapers, including the important *Los Angeles Times*, which gave her Hollywood readership. Hopper began with a benign approach but failed to attract attention until she ran her first scandal-tinged item. "The minute I started to trot out the juicy stuff my phone began to ring," she said.

Both the movie moguls and columnist Parsons were startled in October 1939 when Hopper scooped Parsons on the divorce announcement of James Roosevelt, the president's eldest son. Hopper and Parsons began feuding, and Hopper began to aspire to omniscience and omnipotence as she not only tattled on movie stars but also preached isolationism, harried union racketeers, hobnobbed with socialites, and promoted opera and theater as well as films. In 1940, Cowles's larger Register-Tribune Syndicate took over her column; by 1942 she had switched to the Chicago Tribune–New York Daily News combine, which offered her even wider circulation plus a wire service.

Working 130 hours a week, Hopper, manager Harshbarger, and a staff of seven plus innumerable informants—milkmen, obstetricians, beauticians, even morticians—turned out daily columns and material for radio broadcasts. Shying away from remarriage or affairs, Hopper channeled her energies into work, building her syndication to eighty-five metropolitan and 3,000 small-town dailies plus 2,000 weeklies. With her earnings she bought an impressive Beverly Hills home, which she often wryly referred to as "The House That Fear Built."

With the outbreak of World War II, Hopper abandoned her isolationism and enthusiastically plunged into the war effort. In 1945 the Columbia Broadcasting System hired her to cover the founding of the United Nations in San Francisco, an occasion she airily dismissed as "the greatest clambake in history." Always conservative, she became increasingly so. By 1947 Hopper was urging a boycott of films by writers, actors, and directors "with communist connections," and she joined the ultra-right-wing Motion Picture Alliance for the Preservation of American Ideals. Denouncing Larry Parks, among others, for telling "too little, too late" to the House Committee on Un-American Activities, she dealt his career a blow from which it never recovered. She helped persuade Richard Nixon to run against Helen Gahagan Douglas for Congress and espoused the causes of Senators Robert A. Taft, Everett Dirksen, Barry Goldwater, and Joseph McCarthy. Hopper so often praised J. Edgar Hoover, Gen. Douglas MacArthur, and Ronald Reagan ("after he got over being foolishly liberal") and attacked ELEANOR ROOSEVELT and Adlai Stevenson that some editors refused to run her column, claiming that show business gossip, not politics, was her beat.

Hedda Hopper published two best-selling books, her autobiography, *From Under My Hat* (1952), and *The Whole Truth and Nothing But* (1963), coauthored by James Brough. The latter was dedicated "To my son, Bill, who never took any sass from his mother and never gave her any," indicating that a once-troubled relationship had finally been calmed.

Riding high as undisputed queen of Hollywood gossips after Parsons's retirement in 1964, Hopper was slightly subdued in the aftermath of a disastrous libel suit by Michael Wilding, which was settled out of court in 1965. She died the following year in Los Angeles of acute pulmonary edema.

Hedda Hopper's life suggests how far a high-spirited, witty, yet basically simple and uneducated person can climb. By cultivating a vivid personality—mixing the ingredients of aggressiveness and sympathy, courage and neurosis—she achieved fulfillment of the American dream for herself while turning it into a nightmare for many others.

[In addition to Hopper's two books, scrapbooks containing most of her columns, some of her magazine articles, and some of the magazine articles about her, as well as her files containing unpublished articles, tape transcripts of interviews, and correspondence, can be found in the Margaret Herrick Library of the Acad. of Motion Picture Arts and Sciences, Beverly Hills, Calif. A list of her film credits appears in Evelyn Mack Truitt, ed., *Who Was Who on Screen* (1974). George Eells, *Hedda and Louella* (1972), contains a full-length biographical study. A brief biographical sketch is in *Current Biog.*, 1942. Other sources include *Look*, Sept. 10, 1940; *Life*, July 14, 1941; *Time*, July 28, 1947. An obituary appeared in the *N.Y. Times*, Feb. 2, 1966. Although Hopper reported her birth date as June 2, 1890, Patsy Gaile and Susie Traynor, her long-time employees and friends, as well as her cousin, sister, and son, confirm the May 2, 1885 date. A death record was provided by the Calif. Dept. of Health Services.]

GEORGE EELLS

HORNEY, Karen Danielsen, Sept. 16, 1885–Dec. 4, 1952. Psychiatrist, psychoanalyst.

Karen Horney was born in the village of Blankenese, near Hamburg, Germany. Her father, Berndt Heinrich Wackels Danielsen, a ship captain with the Hamburg-American lines, was Norwegian by birth but became a naturalized German; he had four grown children from an earlier marriage. Her mother, Clotilde Van Ronzelen, eighteen years younger than her husband, was of Dutch background. Their differences in personality and outlook led to their eventual separation and profoundly affected their daughter's personality. Gruff, earthy, and intensely religious, Berndt Danielsen believed in the patriarchal family, expecting women to be homebound and compliant. Karen had strongly ambivalent feelings toward him, admiring but also fearing and resenting his authority, often hating him yet seeking and needing his approval.

Clotilde Danielsen, a religious freethinker, was more educated, liberal, and cultured than her husband, and advocated a greater independence for women. When her husband opposed Karen's plans to attend college and to become a doctor, she was instrumental in overcoming his disapproval. After completing elementary school, Karen attended a private parochial school, but soon rebelled against its religious teachings, which represented the oppressive restrictions of her father. At seventeen she became —and remained—a self-styled "skeptic."

Karen Danielsen was endowed with a high intelligence, a zest for learning, and a determination to succeed. Believing that her parents favored her older brother, Berndt, she felt unwanted and rejected, even ugly, although she was a strikingly beautiful girl. She decided that if she could not be beautiful she would be smart. She had decided to study medicine at twelve, a goal she retained in spite of short-lived interests in teaching and drama. After attending the

Hamburg Realgymnasium for girls for four years, she studied medicine at the universities of Freiburg-im-Breisgau, Göttingen, and Berlin. In 1909, while still a student, she married Oskar Horney, a student of political science and economics. They had three daughters, Brigitte (b. 1911), Marianne (b. 1913), and Renate (b. 1915). Horney was so permissive a mother that her daughters later complained of her being disinterested and detached. Occupied with her work, she soon relied on governesses for their care.

After receiving her M.D. from the University of Berlin in 1911, Horney interned in Berlin's Urban Hospital, and then did residencies in the Neurology Clinic of Hermann Oppenheim and the psychiatric service of Karl Bonhoeffer, both in the Berlin Charité. Her doctoral thesis in 1915 on the "Post-Traumatic Psychoses" addressed the question of whether immediate organic precipitating factors or previous underlying temperamental or psychological factors were primarily responsible for mental symptoms—a central issue in the ensuing struggle over the validity of psychoanalysis. During World War I she worked in the Lankwitz Sanitarium, a private women's hospital temporarily turned into a war hospital.

Horney was first drawn to psychoanalysis as a treatment for her own depression and fatigue that began in 1911. Contributing to these symptoms were the death of her mother, her long-standing ambivalence toward her father, the conflict between her roles as mother and homemaker and her career, and beginning marital difficulties. She entered into analysis with Karl Abraham, one of Freud's foremost Berlin disciples, but terminated after a year. Dissatisfied with the results (as she noted in her diary), she nevertheless remained committed to the principles of psychoanalysis and underwent an additional six months of treatment in 1921 with Hans Sachs. She took her first analytic patients in 1919 and was actively involved with the Berlin Psychoanalytic Clinic and Institute for the next twelve years, first as lecturer (mainly on subjects relating to women) and as treating analyst, then as training and supervising analyst.

The already strained relationship between Karen Horney and her husband deteriorated still further in the early 1920s. Oskar Horney, who had prospered as general manager of the Stinnes Corporation, an investment firm that expanded rapidly during and immediately after World War I, was forced to declare personal bankruptcy following the runaway inflation of 1923. This trauma, soon followed by a severe neurological illness, caused a radical change in his personality. The Horneys separated in 1926 and were divorced in 1937.

In a series of papers written in the 1920s and 1930s Horney addressed the subjects of female psychology and sexuality. From the start she rejected Freud's phallocentric psychology, with its emphasis on castration, female inferiority, and the primacy of "penis envy" in the psychosexual development of women. Insisting that female psychosexual development must be viewed on its own terms, rather than as derivative of male development, Horney affirmed the special functions of womanhood—childbearing, nursing, and motherhood—as positive and fulfilling in themselves; she also suggested that men secretly envied these activities, an attitude writers later termed "womb-envy." During the period of her own separation and its aftereffects, Horney also wrote a series of important papers on marital problems and the relations between the sexes.

In 1932 Horney accepted an invitation to become assistant director of the new Chicago Institute for Psychoanalysis by its director, Franz Alexander, a former Berlin colleague. Disillusioned with the strict atmosphere of the Berlin Institute, she believed that the United States offered greater opportunity for freedom of expression. Moreover, although she was neither Jewish nor political, she was concerned because the Nazis were already attacking psychoanalysis as a "Jewish science." Horney also wished to leave behind the emotional effects of her marital breakup. Her daughter Renate left with her, and Marianne followed a year later to enter the University of Chicago Medical School.

Horney remained in Chicago for only two years. Her departure was hastened by a personality clash with Alexander and by her disagreement with practices he was introducing at the institute. They had theoretical differences as well. Stimulated by the opportunity to observe women in a new environment, Horney had already begun to emphasize the importance of cultural factors in female psychology, departing still further from orthodox Freudianism; Alexander regarded her new emphasis as revolutionary.

Moving to New York in 1934, Horney quickly built an active analytic practice, while teaching at the New York Psychoanalytic Institute and the New School for Social Research. In her first book, *The Neurotic Personality of Our Time* (1937), she discussed the role of social practices in causing neuroses, while her second, *New Ways in Psychoanalysis* (1939), spelled out her differences with Freudian theory. She took issue with Freud's basic concepts of psychosexual development, the death instinct, and the Oedipus complex, and with such derivatives as regression and repetition compulsion. While she believed that these phenomena derived from social inequities and pressures, as yet she did not advance any theories of her own.

Horney's ideas generated great controversy at the institute, and she felt obliged to resign after her training privileges were curtailed. She and several like-minded analysts—including CLARA THOMPSON, Erich Fromm, and Harry Stack Sullivan—organized in 1941 their own Association for the Advancement of Psychoanalysis and its teaching arm the American Institute for Psychoanalysis. She was dean of the American Institute and editor of the Association's *American Journal of Psychoanalysis*, which she founded, until her death. Some of her early colleagues, objecting either to her influence or her ideas, later split off to form their own analytic groups.

Throughout her life Horney derived her concepts from clinical observations of patients and felt uncomfortable with abstract or metaphysical thought. Nonetheless, in her subsequent books, *Self-Analysis* (1942), *Our Inner Conflicts* (1945), and *Neurosis and Human Growth* (1950), she attempted to systematize her own theory of neurotic development, character structure, and moral philosophy. In contrast to orthodox psychoanalysts, she placed greater emphasis on the importance of sociocultural factors in producing neurosis. She also became more concerned with purely psychological factors—both within the individual and in relation to others—and stressed the concept of self-realization, the innate tendency for growth toward fulfilling one's potential. To clarify this concept, she again turned to religion during her last years. Her new direction reflected an intense spiritual struggle. During this period she was influenced by her old friend the existentialist theologian Paul Tillich, and by Daisetz Suzuki, the revered Buddhist sage, with whom she spent a month in Japan in 1951, studying and discussing Zen principles. Though she was never able to fit these principles into her theory of neurosis, some of them influenced her methods of therapy.

Until her death Horney—who needed work as an outlet—remained astonishingly active writing, teaching, practicing, and lecturing. In November 1952 she fell ill of a late diagnosed cancer of the bile ducts which spread rapidly to her lungs. She died within two weeks in New York City.

Karen Horney was a reserved person who rarely confided in others. She had many friendships, made and broken off easily, but few intimate or long-standing ones. In her work she had an uncanny ability to grasp intuitively the feelings of others, but in her personal relations she

could be quite insensitive. A complex personality, with often conflicting feelings and attitudes, she disliked organizational leadership, which she left to her followers. Yet she needed behind-the-throne power, while also wanting to be loved. She possessed great personal magnetism, and no one who knew her remained unaffected by her. As a lecturer she drew large audiences; she spoke in low, vibrant tones, yet with great intensity and sincerity. Her capacity to simplify a complex concept by going straight to the central idea was particularly impressive.

Although not allied with any political movement, Horney was an early feminist who fought for equality of the sexes. While she spoke for women's freedom to have careers without prejudice, she also praised the joy and creative possibilities in being homemakers and mothers. In addition to her contributions to understanding the psychology of women, Horney's work is also important for emphasizing sociocultural factors in producing neurosis and for developing a new noninstinctivist psychoanalytic theory and therapy. Since her death, her followers have extended her theories to new problems and to conditions other than the neuroses. Most of her ideas have quietly entered the mainstream of psychology. Some—including her emphasis on self-realization, neurotic narcissism, analysis of the total self, and the interaction between intrapsychic and social factors—have been rediscovered and appropriated by other schools.

[A collection of reprints, MSS., letters, and photographs is in the possession of Jack L. Rubins. Horney's papers on women are collected in Harold Kelman, ed., *Feminine Psychology* (1966). Frederick A. Weiss, "Karen Horney: A Bibliography," *Am. Jour. Psychoanalysis*, Jan. 1954, lists works in German and English. It is part of a special issue devoted to Horney. For a full-scale biography see Jack L. Rubins, *Karen Horney: Gentle Rebel of Psychoanalysis* (1978). Biographical sketches include Joseph M. Natterson, "Karen Horney: The Cultural Emphasis," in Franz Alexander, ed., *Psychoanalytic Pioneers* (1966); Harold Kelman, *Helping People: Karen Horney's Psychoanalytic Approach* (1971); Jack L. Rubins, "Karen Horney: A Biographical Study," in *Developments in Psychoanalysis* (1972); and *Dict. Am. Biog.*, Supp. Five. For reviews of her work see Y. Bres, *Freud et la psychanalyse Americaine Karen Horney* (1970); I. Portnoy, "The School of Karen Horney," in S. Arieti, ed., *Am. Handbook of Psychiatry*, I (2d ed., 1974); Paul L. Wachtel, "Karen Horney's Ironic Vision," *New Republic*, Jan. 6, 1979; Rona and Lawrence Cherry, "The Horney Heresy," *N.Y. Times Mag.*, Aug. 26, 1973. For her role in American psychoanalysis see Marianne Horney Eckardt, "Organizational Schisms in American Psychoanalysis," in Jacques M. Quen and Eric T. Carlson, eds.,

American Psychoanalysis: Origins and Development (1978).]

JACK L. RUBINS

HUGHAN, Jessie Wallace, Dec. 25, 1875–April 10, 1955. Pacifist, socialist, educator.

Jessie Hughan was born in Brooklyn, N.Y., the second of three daughters and third of four children, to Margaret (West) and Samuel Hughan; her brother died in infancy. Her parents were cultured but of modest circumstances. Samuel Hughan, born in England to a Scottish family, came to New York as an importer in 1863 and was at various times a writer, accountant, treasurer, and librarian. Margaret Hughan's English, Scottish, and French ancestors migrated to the United States in the seventeenth and eighteenth centuries. She became a writer and composer. Both were convinced by Henry George's single tax plan; Margaret Hughan was president of the Brooklyn Women's Single Tax Club, while Samuel Hughan wrote a book on the British land question. Their religious affiliations were successively Presbyterian, Episcopalian, Swedenborgian, and Unitarian, but Jessie Hughan—at one time a Sunday school teacher and superintendent—was a lifelong Unitarian.

From grammar school in Staten Island, Jessie Hughan went on to Northfield Seminary in Massachusetts. Enrolling at Barnard College in 1894, she joined three classmates in founding the national sorority Alpha Omicron Pi and was elected to Phi Beta Kappa. Her college parodies and a long class ode were forerunners of her later, more serious, poetry, most notably her collection *The Challenge of Mars and Other Verses* (1932). She earned her A.B. in 1898, with a thesis entitled "Recent Theories of Profits."

Continuing her study of economics at Columbia University, Hughan pursued the family interest in the single tax theory in her A.M. thesis, "The Place of Henry George in Economics" (1899). She chose socialism as the subject of her doctoral thesis, and followed the suggestion of her adviser, J. P. Clark, that she attend meetings and get acquainted with socialists. Hughan later explained that at the start she feared that "Socialists might be dangerous people" but soon found herself sympathetic to their ideas. She became a socialist in 1907, "by conviction and not merely by emotion," and served on the executive committees of both the Socialist party and the Inter-Collegiate Socialist Society (later the League for Industrial Democracy). In 1910 she was awarded a Ph.D. for her dissertation, "The Present Status of Socialism in America."

Her teaching career began at schools in Naugatuck, Conn. (1899–1900) and White Plains, N.Y. (1900–02). Hughan then taught in Brooklyn (1902–07), and between 1906 and 1911, while continuing to teach and work on her Ph.D., she assisted Roswell Johnson with his writings on eugenics. From 1907 on she taught in a series of New York public high schools, chairing the English department at Textile High School in the twenties and then heading its Cooperative Annex. She also chaired the character education and national committees of the teachers union.

Hughan made several attempts to be elected to public office, beginning in 1915 when she became a candidate for alderman in New York on the Socialist party ticket. She also ran for secretary of state (1918), for lieutenant governor (1920), and for United States senator (1924). Although never elected to any of these offices, she believed that socialist votes were not wasted because they pressured the winning party to grant some of the reforms that socialists sought.

In 1915, following the outbreak of World War I, Hughan initiated the Anti-Enlistment League, to mobilize individuals to declare themselves opposed to military service and other support of the war. In this effort she obtained the assistance of John Haynes Holmes and Tracy Mygatt who, like Hughan, saw the need for new, militant pacifist organizations to counter the American drift toward entering the war. Hughan also became a charter member of the Fellowship of Reconciliation (FOR), the Christian pacifist organization founded in 1915. In 1917 she was warned that her uncompromising antiwar stand might result in her dismissal from the school system, but she remained firm. For years she was denied the Lusk Certificate of Character and Loyalty because she added to her teachers' oath of loyalty the words: "This obedience being qualified always by dictates of conscience."

Following the war, Hughan maintained her commitment to organized pacifism, and in 1922, under the auspices of the FOR, she formed a Committee for Enrollment Against War. In 1923 she brought together representatives of the FOR, the Women's Peace Union, and the Women's Peace Society to form the War Resisters League (WRL), which also affiliated with War Resisters International. Hughan became secretary of the new organization, a position she held until 1945, when she became honorary secretary. The WRL, officially organized to enroll the names of all those who opposed war and refused to take part in it, gradually expanded to support not only all forms of conscientious objection but also nonviolent efforts to secure social justice.

Believing the profit motive to be the main source of economic and social injustice as well as the incentive for war, throughout the 1920s and 1930s Hughan continued to focus most of her considerable energies on the propagation of both socialism and pacifism. She encouraged participation in "No More War" parades sponsored by the WRL, and in 1938 helped to organize the United Pacifist Committee, a coalition of pacifist organizations which coordinated peace education and support of conscientious objectors. Two years later she founded the Pacifist Teachers League, and when conscription was enacted she was among the first to oppose the government's establishment of Civilian Public Service camps where objectors were forced to work without pay. Increasingly disturbed by rumors of Nazi extermination plans for Germany's Jews during World War II, Hughan urged an immediate armistice, predicting that millions more would otherwise be killed.

A tall woman with prominent features and bobbed hair, Hughan for many years helped care for her widowed mother and contributed to the support of her sister's four children. Following World War II and her retirement from the school system in 1945, she continued to be active in the WRL, serving on its executive committee up to the time of her death. In April 1955 she died at her Manhattan home of arteriosclerotic heart disease. The following December a memorial meeting was held for her at New York's Community Church, where the Jessie Wallace Hughan Memorial Fund was established to publish materials furthering the cause of peace.

[Some material about Jessie Hughan may be found in the Barnard College Archives and the Swarthmore College Peace Coll. Her published works include *The Present Status of Socialism in America* (1911), her doctoral thesis, also issued as *American Socialism of the Present Day* (1911); *The Facts of Socialism* (1913); *A Study of International Government* (1923); the WRL pamphlets *If We Should Be Invaded: Facing a Fantastic Hypothesis* (1940) and *Three Decades of War Resistance* (1942); and *New Leagues for Old: Blueprints or Foundations?* (1947). Sources of biographical information include an article in the Barnard College *Alumnae Monthly*, Oct. 1932, based on an interview with Hughan, and *Report and Register of the Associate Alumnae of Barnard College*, 1904 and subsequent issues. References to her life and work appear in Lawrence S. Wittner, *Rebels Against War: The American Peace Movement, 1941–1960* (1969); Charles Chatfield, *For Peace and Justice: Pacifism in America, 1914–1941* (1971); and Vera Brittain, *The Rebel Passion* (1964). Additional information for this article was provided by Hughan's niece Margaret Rockwell Finch, and by Abraham Kaufman and Bernice Nich-

ols. Death certificate from N.Y. City Dept. of Health.]

ANN MORRISSETT DAVIDON

HULL, Hannah Hallowell Clothier, July 21, 1872–July 4, 1958. Pacifist, suffragist.

Hannah Clothier Hull was born in Sharon Hill, Pa., third of five daughters and fourth child of nine, to Isaac Hallowell and Mary Clapp (Jackson) Clothier. Descendant of a Quaker family that settled in Pennsylvania in the early seventeenth century, Hannah Clothier adopted the Quaker principles of peacemaking and reconciliation and devoted her energies to establishing world peace.

Her father founded the Philadelphia department store, Strawbridge and Clothier, which became the largest store in the United States devoted solely to dry goods. His many philanthropic interests centered largely in the Society of Friends and Swarthmore College. Hannah Clothier, bright and high-spirited but serious, attended Friends Central School in downtown Philadelphia and, in 1889, enrolled at Swarthmore College, where she received a B.L. in 1891. Prevented from taking a job by her family's conservatism, she devoted her energies to volunteer settlement work in Philadelphia and later undertook graduate work in history and biblical literature at Bryn Mawr College (1896–97).

On Dec. 27, 1898, Hannah Clothier married William Isaac Hull, an associate professor of history and political science at Swarthmore College, whom she had met while they both were engaged in volunteer social work. For the next forty-one years they shared a devotion to each other and to the cause of world peace. Their two daughters, Mary Clothier (b. 1900) and Elizabeth Powell (b. 1904), were born at their home near the Swarthmore College campus.

Hannah Hull was introduced to organized peace efforts when in 1907 she joined her husband at the Second Hague Conference for International Peace. Also active in the campaign for woman suffrage, she served as vice president of the Pennsylvania Woman Suffrage Association (1913–14). During World War I, Hull remained committed to absolute pacifism, although many former peace advocates supported the American war effort after April 1917. She was chairman of the Pennsylvania branch of the Woman's Peace party from 1917 to 1920. Mindful of her Quaker heritage, she also worked with the American Friends Service Committee (AFSC) on its programs of reconstruction among civilians in France and the Soviet Union, and later on those for feeding children in Germany and Austria. She served as vice chairman of the board of the AFSC (1928–47) and was a member both of its peace section and of the executive committee of the foreign service section responsible for overseas work.

While she continued to be active in other organizations, for more than forty years Hannah Hull's major interest was the Women's International League for Peace and Freedom (WILPF), founded in 1919. She was a delegate to an emergency International Conference of Women called by the WILPF in December 1922 at The Hague to press for a reasonable settlement of reparation claims and for the withdrawal of armies of occupation from the Rhineland. When JANE ADDAMS became the international chairman of the WILPF in 1924, Hannah Hull succeeded her as national chairman of the United States section. Through the years, until Addams's death in 1935, the two women were close friends as well as coworkers. Except for a year (1928–29) during which she and her husband sailed around the world in the interest of international good will for the WILPF and the Society of Friends, Hull held national office in the WILPF until 1939, serving as chairman of the national board (1929–38) and as president of the United States section (1933–39).

During this period Hull promoted the efforts of the WILPF in a variety of ways. Joining the WILPF Peace Caravan organized by MABEL VERNON in 1931, she crossed the country from California to Washington, D.C., participating in public demonstrations and gathering signatures to petitions on disarmament for presentation to President Herbert Hoover. The following year Hull attended the World Disarmament Conference in Geneva. Later she worked with Vernon as chairman of the executive committee of the Peoples Mandate to Governments to End War, a committee of the WILPF organized in 1935 which secured 8,000,000 signatures to a peace petition from people of all nations. When her husband died suddenly in November 1939, Hannah Hull resigned the national presidency. In recognition of its development into a national power for peace under her leadership, the WILPF persuaded her to continue as honorary national president, a post she held until her death.

The year after her husband's death Hull wrote: "I feel utterly lost and in no way have I been able to adjust myself to the situation." She gradually recovered and returned to her peace work and other activities. Maintaining her commitment to the WILPF and AFSC, attending every Philadelphia-area meeting of both until her death, Hull also served for many years on the Friends Peace Committee and the Representative Meeting of Philadelphia Yearly Meeting of Friends. She was a devoted member of the board of directors of Pendle Hill, a Quaker center for social and religious study in Wallingford, Pa. (1929–55). In addition, she held executive positions in a variety of women's organizations, ranging from the Swarthmore Woman's Club to the Pennsylvania State Federation of Women's Clubs. Hull was appointed by the governor to the Pennsylvania Mothers Assistance Fund and served on Herbert Hoover's National Committee on Food for the Five Small Democracies (1940).

Hannah Hull died of a heart attack at her home in Swarthmore in 1958. At a memorial service held in the Swarthmore Friends Meeting House, neighbors and friends recalled her sympathy and vision, her sense of humor, her marked executive ability, and her effort to live, in the words of George Fox, seventeenth-century Quaker leader, "in the virtue of that life and power that took away the occasion of all wars."

[The Hannah Clothier Hull Papers in the Swarthmore College Peace Coll. contain most of her writings as well as correspondence relating to her official roles in the WILPF and other organizations, but there is little on her personal life. Other collections at Swarthmore which contain material on Hull are the papers of Jane Addams and Lucia Ames Mead and the records of the Woman's Peace party and the WILPF. The Swarthmore College alumni office has some biographical material and clippings. Howard H. Brinton, ed., *Byways of Quaker History* (1944), contains a combined biographical account of William and Hannah Hull, as does Frederick B. Tolles, "Partners for Peace," *Swarthmore College Bull.*, Dec. 1958. Charles Chatfield, *For Peace and Justice: Pacifism in America, 1914–1941* (1971), has information on her peace activities. See also *Friends Intelligencer*, Feb. 9, 1929, and May 19, 1945; *Friends Jour.*, Aug. 23, 1958, and Jan. 17, 1959. Additional information was obtained from William W. Hinshaw, *Am. Quaker Genealogy*, vol. 2 (1938), and Gertrude Bussey and Margaret Tims, *Women's International League for Peace and Freedom, 1915–1965* (1965). Both Hull and her husband were included in Elizabeth Dilling, *The Red Network* (1934), a book attacking so-called subversive organizations. Personal information was provided by Hull's daughter Elizabeth Powell Roberts and by Mildred Scott Olmsted. A biobibliography prepared by Mary Kaufman assisted in the research for this article. Death certificate from Pa. Dept. of Health.]

BERNICE BERRY NICHOLS

HUMPHREY, Doris, Oct. 17, 1895–Dec. 29, 1958. Choreographer, dancer.

Doris Batcheller Humphrey was born in Oak Park, Ill., the only child of Julia Ellen (Wells) and Horace Buckingham Humphrey. Both parents' ancestors had come from England in the seventeenth century. Her father was a sometime hotel manager, sometime photographer, her mother a trained musician.

Given dancing lessons at an early age, Doris soon showed talent that was encouraged by her teacher, Mary Wood Hinman. When she graduated from the Francis W. Parker School in Chicago in 1913, she wanted to perform. But the family was in need of money, so Julia Humphrey installed her daughter as a teacher of social dancing, with herself as accompanist, in a network of suburban schools. It was a period of great frustration.

In 1917 Doris Humphrey managed to enroll at the Denishawn school in Los Angeles and soon became a performer with the company of RUTH ST. DENIS and Ted Shawn, participating in their Oriental tour in 1925 and 1926. While with Denishawn, Humphrey began to choreograph her first dances, but her urge to experiment with new movement forms was frowned upon by the company, and she was forced to resign in June 1928.

That fall, along with her former Denishawn colleagues Pauline Lawrence and Charles Weidman, Doris Humphrey opened a New York studio where classes in dance technique paid production costs for concerts of new choreography. The Humphrey-Weidman company was not interested in the kind of elaborate, exotic spectacles they had known at Denishawn; instead, they wanted to create a dance of their own time and place. Doris Humphrey defined her principle as "moving from the inside out." Unlike the contemporary ballet, which started with a set of vocabulary, the American modern dance started with feeling and then devised such movements as were necessary to communicate it. Spectacle and virtuosity were shunned, for this was serious art, not frivolous entertainment.

Some of her early experimental work, such as *Water Study* (1928) and *Life of the Bee* (1929), was based on movements of nature. *Drama of Motion* (1930) used neither conventional plot, sound, nor theatrical costumes. In 1931, having made her point about abstraction, she choreographed *The Shakers*, its roots deep in the specific facts of American history.

For the Humphrey-Weidman company, which now began to traverse the United States on what became known as the "gymnasium circuit" of college towns, Doris Humphrey created some of her finest works. Notable was the 1935–36 trilogy (*New Dance, Theatre Piece, With My Red Fires*), which envisioned an ideal society where each person is fulfilled as an individual while contributing to the harmony of the group. In 1938 she choreographed the noble *Passacaglia* to the music of Bach, proclaiming the grandeur of the human spirit in a dance of majestic architectural design.

The Humphrey-Weidman company disbanded in 1940, and four years later Doris Humphrey, crippled by arthritis, retired as a dancer. In 1946, however, she joined her former student José Limón as artistic director of his company. Humphrey created for the Limón company some of her finest dances: experiments combining the poetry of Federico García Lorca with the movement in *Lament for Ignacio Sánchez Mejías* (1946); a poignant study of the family of man in *Day on Earth* (1947); an attack on escapism in *Ruins and Visions* (1953); an innovative venture into mixed media in *Theatre Piece No. 2* (1956).

A slender, attractive woman with red hair, Doris Humphrey was in her mid-thirties before she found time for marriage. When Charles Francis Woodford began to talk of marriage, she warned him that she was "an artist first and afterwards a woman," but he was a merchant seaman, away from home for long periods of time, and she chose him wisely. They were married on June 10, 1932, and their son, Charles Humphrey Woodford, was born in July the following year. Although the couple were separated more often than not, the marriage survived until her death.

The creative achievements of Doris Humphrey were recognized slowly, but eventually there were some honors: a Guggenheim Foundation fellowship to write on choreography in 1949, the Capezio Award in 1954, and the Dance Magazine Award four years later. Her material rewards were few, and she was well over fifty before she was somewhat free of constant financial worry. Throughout much of her career, she helped to support her parents. Though she disliked teaching, she taught constantly: in her New York studio, at a series of summer schools, and finally in 1951 at the Juilliard School of Music where she was provided not only with talented students but also with funding to produce new works. It was a luxury she had never known before. In 1955, with the assistance of Martha Hill, director of dance at the Juilliard School, Humphrey founded the Juilliard Dance Theater. There she choreographed, revived some of her major works, and invited guest choreographers to present their work. She remained at Juilliard until her death in New York City of cancer in 1958.

Along with Martha Graham, Doris Humphrey created the form of the American modern dance, using movement to communicate depths of human feeling. One of the most musical of choreographers, Humphrey devised intricate but always expressive devices for working with and against the rhythms of musical scores. Unable to afford scenery, she made miracles with a set of rectangular boxes that could be assembled in an infinite number of ways to represent a scene or set a mood. But her greatest contribution came from her idea of dance as existing in the arc between two deaths: the body lying prone or standing firmly balanced, both secure, both lacking in theatrical excitement. Kinetic interest, she asserted, is stirred when the body, venturing from its position of stability, encounters the pull of gravity, defies it, and triumphantly reclaims its equilibrium. The theory of fall and recovery was at once a pure movement idea and a dramatic concept, symbolizing the eternal conflict between the longing for security and the desire to dare the unknown. From the theory came both a movement technique and a rationale for choreographic structure. The brilliance of the insight was matched only by the beauties of its applications.

[Doris Humphrey's book on choreography, *The Art of Making Dances*, was published posthumously in 1959. Her autobiography, which covered the years up to 1928, was published as *New Dance: An Unfinished Autobiography* by *Dance Perspectives*, Spring 1966. It was completed and edited by Selma Jeanne Cohen, using letters and papers in the Dance Coll., N.Y. Public Library, in *Doris Humphrey: An Artist First* (1972). The most perceptive contemporary remarks about Doris Humphrey may be found in John Martin's reviews in the *N.Y. Times*. See also Margaret Lloyd's discussion in *The Borzoi Book of Modern Dance* (1949). A detailed discussion of the Humphrey movement theory as interpreted by an early member of her company is Ernestine Stodelle, *The Dance Technique of Doris Humphrey and Its Creative Potential* (1978). Marcia Siegel, *The Shapes of Change: Images of American Dance* (1979), contains analyses of six works by Doris Humphrey. The Dance Notation Bureau has published its notation of three Humphrey scores, with notes on the history and style of each dance, in *Doris Humphrey: The Complete Works*, vol. I (1978); other notated scores are available from the bureau. An obituary appeared in the *N.Y. Times*, Dec. 30, 1958.]

SELMA JEANNE COHEN

HUNTINGTON, Anna Vaughn Hyatt, March 10, 1876–Oct. 4, 1973. Sculptor.

Anna Hyatt Huntington, prolific and successful sculptor, was born in Cambridge, Mass., the younger of two daughters and third child of Audella (Beebe) and Alpheus Hyatt II. Her ancestors came from England to America as early as 1629; the Hyatts went to Maryland, and the Beebes settled in Virginia.

Anna enjoyed a comfortable, intellectually stimulating home life and was encouraged to develop her creative talents. From her father, a noted professor of paleontology and zoology at the Massachusetts Institute of Technology and Boston University, she gained a keen knowledge of animal behavior and physiology. Her artistically talented mother, who frequently painted the sketches and diagrams for her husband's books, also encouraged her daughter Anna to observe and to draw. The technical mastery of her great equestrian monuments was also rooted in her early years. She loved horses and even as a child could recognize the distinguishing traits of a hundred thoroughbreds; she later became an expert horsewoman.

After attending private grade and high schools in Cambridge, Hyatt studied briefly in the late 1890s in Boston with Henry Hudson Kitson, and in the early 1900s in New York with George Grey Barnard (at the Art Students League), Hermon MacNeil, and Gutzon Borglum. She was primarily self-trained, however, and preferred to study independently, modeling a variety of animals at zoos and circuses. Nature itself she always regarded as her most important teacher.

Anna Hyatt had her first exhibition in 1900 at the Boston Arts Club, and became nationally known within a few years. Although she generally worked alone, she collaborated with ABASTENIA ST. LEGER EBERLE on at least two statues: "Men and Bull," which was awarded a bronze medal at the Louisiana Purchase Exposition of 1904, and "Boy and Goat Playing," which was exhibited in 1905 at the gallery of the Society of American Artists.

Between 1906 and 1910 she traveled and worked in France and Italy. At the Paris Salon she exhibited a pair of life-sized jaguars in 1908, a Joan of Arc equestrian in 1910 (awarded Honorable Mention), and two life-sized Great Danes in 1911.

Returning to her New York studio in 1911, she began work on another large equestrian of Joan of Arc, emplaced at New York City's Riverside Drive, and a wall statue of the same subject for the city's Cathedral of St. John the Divine. Her works sold well, were exhibited widely, and received numerous awards.

In 1923, at the height of her career, Anna Hyatt married Archer Milton Huntington, Hispanic scholar, poet, philanthropist, and adopted son of Collis Potter Huntington, the railroad magnate. Archer Huntington encouraged his wife's work, and the two collaborated on philanthropic projects benefiting a considerable number of museums and other cultural institutions. They also joined in efforts for the preservation of wildlife.

Following her marriage, Anna Huntington created a remarkable variety of sculpture, including portrait busts, studies of domestic and wild animals, and other large-scale works. Among these was her standing equestrian, "El Cid Campeador," erected in Seville, Spain; a replica was placed on the terrace of the Hispanic Society of America in New York, which was founded by Archer Huntington. This prolific period was interrupted in 1927 when she contracted tuberculosis. Despite her struggle with the illness during the following decade, she continued her work. Although less productive during this period, she received widespread recognition, including the Gold Medal for Distinction in 1930 from the American Academy of Arts and Letters, which in 1936 also held a retrospective exhibition of 171 of her works.

The Huntingtons continually sought ways to support traditional American sculpture, and in 1932 they opened Brookgreen Gardens in South Carolina as an outdoor museum. Originally intended as a winter residence and showcase for Anna Huntington's sculpture, it became the home of one of the finest collections of American sculpture of the late nineteenth and early twentieth centuries.

In 1940 the Huntingtons settled at Stanerigg, an estate in Redding Ridge, Conn., where Anna Huntington, in addition to practicing organic farming, maintaining a bird sanctuary, and raising Scottish deerhounds, continued her sculpture. During the 1940s she became increasingly critical of modern art and what she considered "a tasteless machine age." Although disappointed that traditional sculpture was being superseded by a growing public interest in more innovative forms, Huntington went on working and continued to receive recognition and awards.

Despite Archer Huntington's death in 1955, she entered a period of renewed creative activity. During the late 1950s and early 1960s, she completed a full range of works from small animal studies to monumental equestrians. In her studio at Stanerigg, she modeled the last five larger-than-life equestrian statues of her career, including the monument to Gen. Israel Putnam, the American revolutionary hero, completed in 1966 when she was ninety. In the year before her death, Huntington suffered several dozen small strokes; she died at Stanerigg in 1973 at the age of ninety-seven.

A tall, handsome, dignified woman, Anna Hyatt Huntington was gracious yet unassuming, tactful yet forthright. An article in *Connecticut Life* described her at eighty-five as "a woman of vigorous wit and charm who could scamper up a ten foot ladder to work on her massive sculptures or knock down with her .22 calibre any squirrels molesting the birds on her estate." Her academic sculpture was characterized by meticulous craftsmanship. Following the French naturalistic tradition of Barye, Frémiet, and Falguière, her method was realistic. She maintained a lifelong interest in realistic detail and undertook extensive documentary research for her historical subjects. The full range of Anna Hyatt Huntington's extraordinary output over a period of seventy years, from the graceful portrayal of a playful fawn or the poised ferocity of tigers to the heroic equestrian monument, is represented in the collections of more than 200 museums and in parks and gardens of major cities throughout the world.

[Anna Hyatt Huntington left the bulk of her papers to Syracuse Univ.; they contain correspondence, MSS., photographs, scrapbooks, and diaries, in addition to critical and biographical material. Other sources include "A Giant's Horse for the Asking," *Connecticut Life*, Oct. 5, 1961; Doris E. Cook, *Woman Sculptor: Anna Hyatt Huntington* (1976); three studies by Myrna G. Eden, a dissertation, "Anna Hyatt Huntington, Sculptor, and Mrs. H. H. A. Beach, Composer: A Comparative Study of Two Women Representatives of the American Cultivated Tradition in the Arts" (Syracuse Univ., 1977), and "The Significance of the Equestrian Monument 'Joan of Arc' in the Artistic Development of Anna Hyatt Huntington," and "The Sculpture of Anna Hyatt Huntington in the Syracuse University Art Collection," both in *The Courier* of Syracuse Univ., Fall 1975; Anna C. Ladd, "Anna V. Hyatt—Animal Sculptor," *Art and Progress*, Nov. 1912; Beatrice G. Proske, *Brookgreen Gardens Sculpture* (1968); J. Walker McSpadden, *Famous Sculptors of America* (1924); Katharine L. Weems, "Anna Hyatt Huntington," *Nat. Sculpture Rev.*, Winter 1973–74; and an entry in *Current Biog.*, 1953. An obituary appeared in the *N.Y. Times*, Oct. 5, 1973. A death certificate was provided by the Conn. Dept. of Health.]

MYRNA GARVEY EDEN

HURST, Fannie, Oct. 18, 1889–Feb. 23, 1968. Writer.

Relief for the oppressed Jews in eastern Europe, the right of a woman to retain her maiden name after marriage, equal pay for equal work, the social and medical problems of the homosexual—all of these issues preoccupied Fannie Hurst, America's most highly paid "sob sister" novelist of the first half of the twentieth century. This image of Hurst may come as a surprise to a generation which, if it remembers her at all, probably associates her with such late night, three-handkerchief reruns as *Imitation of Life* and *Back Street*. Though she demonstrated her concern for these social causes as early as the 1920s, Hurst was considered neither a radical nor an intellectual. She was, in fact, frequently dismissed by critics of the time as sentimental or, as one 1929 reviewer caustically remarked, merely "a speaker in the voice of the pee-pul."

Born at a farm belonging to her mother's family in Hamilton, Ohio, and reared in St. Louis in a "middle-western world of assimilated Jews," Fannie Hurst was the only child of Rose (Koppel) and Samuel Hurst, a successful shoe factory owner. The families of both her parents had emigrated from Bavaria around 1860. Her early training was not one to prepare her for sympathy with the social misfits who fill the central role in most of her works, and her mother insisted that "Fannie does not know them from home. Mr. Hurst and I always surrounded her with the best." Hurst, however, did know such people in New York, where she moved in 1910, after receiving an A.B. from Washington University in St. Louis in 1909. Leaving home despite her parents' protests, she went ostensibly to do graduate work at Columbia University, but actually "to study people" and pursue her career as a writer. Working as a waitress in Child's and as a salesgirl, acting bit parts on Broadway, attending night court sessions, and wandering through the slums, the young author became "passionately anxious to awake in others a general sensitiveness to small people," an awareness of "causes, including the lost and the threatened."

The realization of Hurst's ambitions came arduously. Although her first story, "Ain't Life Wonderful," had been published in *Reedy's Mirror*, a St. Louis weekly, when she was still in college, it was followed by a host of rejections, some thirty-five from the *Saturday Evening Post* alone. Then, in 1912, a second story was accepted for $30, and shortly thereafter *Saturday Evening Post* not only bought "Power and Horse Power" for $300 but also wanted first chance at all her future work. By 1914 Harper's had published her first collection of stories, *Just Around the Corner*, launching a career that was to span five decades and include seventeen novels, nine volumes of short stories, three plays, innumerable articles, and a television talk show, as well as a host of speaking engagements and collaboration on several films.

By 1925 Hurst held with MARY ROBERTS RINEHART and Booth Tarkington the distinction of being the highest paid writer in America; by 1940 she reputedly held the field alone. In spite of her commitment to her craft, she also found time to speak out for numerous social causes and to assume an active role in organizations dedicated to social welfare. A long-time friend of ELEANOR ROOSEVELT, Hurst was an ardent supporter of labor and New Deal policies. She chaired a national housing commission (1936–37) and the committee on workmen's compensation (1940); in addition, she was a member of the national advisory committee to the Works Progress Administration (1940–41) and the board of directors of the New York Urban League.

Hurst also firmly allied herself with Jewish causes. In the 1920s she was the keynote speaker in the campaign for the relief of Jews in eastern Europe; in the 1940s she was active in raising funds for refugees from Nazi Germany; and in the 1950s she was a staunch promoter of the state of Israel. She gave support to members of her own craft as well, donating most of her 1925 $50,000 prize from *Liberty* and Famous Players–Lasky Corporation to the support of writers. In her will she left approximately one million dollars to both Brandeis and Washington Universities to establish professorships in creative literature. Of all the causes to which Hurst contributed, however, the one which most consistently preoccupied her was the rights of women.

Her revelation in 1920 that she had been secretly married to the pianist Jacques Danielson since 1915, although they had maintained separate residences, was met by a caustic editorial in the *New York Times*. It took the Danielsons to task particularly for occupying "two domiciles . . . under the present housing shortage." Hurst retaliated by stating that "nine out of ten marriages . . . were merely sordid endurance tests overgrown with the fungi of familiarity." She was determined that her marriage "should not lessen my capacity for creative work or pull me down into a sedentary state of fatmindedness." Declaring that she considered the notion of " 'two souls with but a single thought' a horrible and siamese state of freak mentality," she defended the right of a married woman to retain her own name, her own social life, and her own personal liberty. Only in such a way, she asserted, would "the dust stay on the butterfly wings . . . the dew on the rose." The dew evidently did remain on the rose for the Danielsons, who apparently remained happily married until Jacques's death in 1952. Even after his death, Hurst continued to write weekly letters addressed to him, and she always wore a calla lily, the first flower that he had ever sent her.

Like her marriage, much of Hurst's fiction exemplifies her belief that a woman's "place is not at the front door waiting for the steps of her John and fearful lest the roast be overdone. Her place is where she can give the most service and get the most out of life." That women are frequently the victims of preconceived attitudes or of social and economic discrimination is a major theme in many of her works. In *Lummox* (1923), for example, her own favorite and probably the best of her novels, the heroine, an inarticulate domestic servant who has great warmth and capacity for life, barely survives the systematic injustice of a callous society. That she does survive must be attributed to plot manipulation rather than natural events. In *Back Street* (1931) the heroine's capacity for life is frustrated by her lover's adherence to social prescriptions, and in *Imitation of Life* (1933) the villain is again a social code that will not allow an individual to realize her own potential. In each of these novels, however, women's own passivity, a trait Hurst deplored, conspires in their victimization.

Unfortunately Hurst's fictions are not always capable of communicating the high seriousness of her intent. Frequently her characters slip into stereotypes. The Cad, the Alcoholic, the Egotist, the Self-Absorbed Rich Lady, the Golden-Hearted Whore, the Brave Wife, the Pure-Minded Virgin, and the Honest Burgher stalk through even her best works. When Hurst is most successful, as in *Lummox*, *Back Street*, and *Imitation of Life*, as well as *A President Is Born* (1928) and isolated short stories, these characters assume a minor role and their effect is mitigated by the author's power to perceive and communicate real human anxiety and frustration. In her less successful work, when these characters assume a central role, as in *Hallelujah* (1944), or when the apparently good evoke less sympathy than the apparently evil, as in *Any Woman* (1950), more sentiment than illumination, more confusion than insight, is generated. Hurst's last novel, *Fool, Be Still*, appeared in 1964. She died in New York City in 1968 at the age of seventy-eight.

If Fannie Hurst's point was sometimes obscure when expressed through her novels, it was never obscure when she spoke in her own voice. Thus, for example, when in 1962 Justice Arthur Goldberg declared: "It is time we evaluated women on merit and fitness alone when they apply for a job," Hurst crisply retorted, "Time, Sir! You are almost half a century too late."

[The Hurst Coll. at Brandeis Univ., which contains several notebooks, letters, and MSS., is an invaluable primary source. The Berg Coll. in the N.Y. Public Library contains letters from 1913 to 1942 from Robert Hobart Davis, editor of *Munsey's Mag.*, who encouraged Hurst and later became a close friend; this correspondence provides insight into Hurst's personality. The collection is catalogued in *Dict. Catalog of the Berg Coll.*, vol. 2 (1969). For a complete bibliography of Hurst's work, except for *Fool Be Still* (1964), and for her various activities, see *Who's Who of Am. Women*, 1969. Her autobiography, *Anatomy of Me* (1958), says a great deal about Hurst's background and tastes and gives the general flavor of her life, but it fails to provide precise chronological details. In addition, there are, as she admitted herself, some large omissions. Many of the details can be filled in by a perusal of the *N.Y. Times Index*, 1920–68. Particularly useful are the articles on her marriage, *N.Y. Times*, May 4, May 5, and May 7, 1920, an interview with Rose Feld, Dec. 9, 1923, and her obituary, Feb. 24, 1968. For Hurst's views on her career see Harry Salpeter, "Fannie Hurst: Sob Sister of American Fiction," *Bookman*, Aug. 1931. Her comments on women's rights appear in the *N.Y. Times*, Feb. 20, 1921, and Fannie Hurst, "The Trouble with Women Is Women," *Reader's Digest*, Feb. 10, 1962. Assistance in the research for this article was provided by a biobibliography prepared by Jean Seaman.]

ANTOINETTE FREDERICK

HURSTON, Zora Neale, Jan. 7, 1901?–Jan. 28, 1960. Writer, folklorist.

Zora Neale Hurston was born in Eatonville, Fla., seventh of eight children and the third daughter of John and Lucy (Potts) Hurston. The Hurstons had been tenant farmers in their native Alabama, but in Eatonville, the first incorporated all-black town in the United States, John Hurston, a Baptist preacher, was thrice elected mayor and wrote the village laws. His daughter, who inherited some of his egotism and flair for showmanship, was a source of concern, as he feared that her strong spirit would be a liability. But Lucy Hurston urged her precocious daughter to "jump at de sun." The town of Eatonville also provided a supportive environment. The Hungerford School, run by disciples of Booker T. Washington, offered instruction in the basic academic skills and in self-reliance, and the townspeople educated Zora to the wit, wisdom, and beauty of the folk culture.

Her mother's death when she was nine and her father's remarriage shortly thereafter effectively ended Hurston's childhood. In her autobiography, *Dust Tracks On A Road* (1942), she characterized her life after these events as "a series of wanderings." She first left home at fourteen to join a traveling Gilbert and Sullivan troupe as wardrobe girl. After eighteen months Hurston left the company in Baltimore. There, while working at menial jobs, she managed to attend Morgan Academy. Moving on to Washington, D.C., in 1918, she studied part-time at Howard University. She also began to write and to gain the attention of some of the major figures of the Harlem Renaissance, including Alain Locke and the poet Georgia Douglas Johnson (1886–1966). In January 1925, Hurston arrived in New York City, where she broadened her contacts with the black literary community. Through the novelist FANNIE HURST, for whom Hurston worked first as secretary, then chauffeur, she made acquaintances in the white literary world as well.

For the next two years, Hurston regularly published essays and short fiction. She was convinced that the people and places she had known as a child could fascinate readers as they had fascinated her. But with the exception of a remarkable story entitled "Sweat," she was not yet able to make her experiences come alive as memorable literature. She was learning to look at her past differently, however, as the result of anthropology courses taken at Barnard College. Awarded a scholarship in September 1925, Hurston studied with the famous anthropologist Franz Boas. The school's first known black graduate, she received an A.B. in 1928.

From 1927 to 1932, Zora Neale Hurston devoted all her energies to her work as a social scientist. On trips to Florida, Alabama, Louisiana, and the Bahamas, she signed on at labor camps and apprenticed herself to hoodoo doctors. The folktales, songs, children's games, prayers and sermons, and hoodoo practices she collected were published in *Mules and Men* (1935), and her ethnographic studies became vehicles for communicating the richness and complexity of rural black life. Hurston brought unusual gifts to her work: the ability to be assimilated into the way of life she was researching, the daring to undertake the strange and rigorous initiation rites of religious cults in Louisiana (and later in Haiti and Jamaica, as recorded in *Tell My Horse*, 1938), and an ear sensitive to the rhythms of folk speech. Although her training had taught her to view the people whose culture she studied as objects of scientific inquiry, Hurston could not sustain this posture. She was more participant than observer, and her response was personal and engaged. She first presented her research dramatically in a series of folklore concerts.

Hurston's professional commitments had numerous personal consequences. As well as being physically and psychologically demanding, field work was costly. Charlotte Osgood Mason, a wealthy Park Avenue matron, agreed to sponsor Hurston's research from 1927 to 1932, but then claimed ownership of the material and forced Hurston to delay its publication. Other close relationships were similarly problematic. In the spring of 1927, Hurston married Herbert Sheen, a medical student whom she had met when both were students at Howard University. She could not reconcile the competing demands of marriage and career, however, and the couple soon separated; they were divorced in 1931. A second marriage in 1939 to Albert Price, a former Works Progress Administration (WPA) playground worker fifteen years her junior, also ended in divorce. Hurston herself was employed briefly (1935–36) by the WPA Federal Theatre Project in New York as a drama coach, and in 1938 became an editor for the Federal Writers' Project in Florida.

Hurston made intermittent efforts to establish an academic career, but only twice held full-time academic jobs: a semester at Bethune-Cookman College in Daytona Beach, Fla. (spring 1934), and a year at North Carolina College at Durham (1939). Awarded a Rosenwald Fellowship in December 1934, she enrolled at Columbia University for graduate study in anthropology but did not complete the course. In 1936 and 1937 she received Guggenheim fellowships for field work in the Caribbean. She chose, however, to be a writer rather than a scholar, becoming the most prolific black woman author of her day, and perhaps the most accomplished figure in Afro-American letters in the 1930s.

The collective folk imagination was the soil that nourished the individual expression of Hurston's novels. In *Jonah's Gourd Vine* (1934), her protagonist is John Buddy Pearson, a preacher and the symbolic bearer of the folk tradition. The novel afforded Hurston an opportunity to display her masterful command of the folk idiom, but Pearson fails to emerge as a fully realized character, and the folk material threatens to overwhelm the formal narrative. Her second novel, *Their Eyes Were Watching God* (1937), is the finest expression of Hurston's talent. A beautifully written work, it traces a woman's search for self-fulfillment. Janie Starks dreams of exploring life to the fullest, and she resists anything or anyone that threatens to encroach upon her dream. An independent, spirited woman, she sees no reason to exchange the oppression of slavery and racism for the vapidity of life on a pedestal. Janie and Tea

Cake, her third husband, represent the ideal sought by most characters in Hurston's fiction. They trust emotion over intellect, value the spiritual over the material, preserve a sense of humor, and are comfortable with their sensuality. In this novel folklore complements the narrative without overwhelming it. In her last two novels, *Moses, Man of the Mountain* (1939) and *Seraph on the Suwanee* (1948), Hurston moved away from the Eatonville milieu, with generally disappointing results.

While Eatonville fueled Hurston's creative powers, it served her less well in other ways. She revered Booker T. Washington, the town's patron saint, and clung to his ideas long after they had been discredited. Her increasingly conservative political philosophy was revealed in essays written during the 1940s and 1950s for such publications as the *American Legion Magazine* and *American Mercury*. In a widely reprinted letter to the editor of a Florida newspaper, Hurston attacked the Supreme Court's 1954 school desegregation decision, arguing that the pressure for integration denied the value of existing black institutions. According to her biographer, Hurston refused "to admit that one could both celebrate Afro-American culture and deplore many of the conditions that helped to shape it" (Hemenway, p. 333).

By the 1950s Zora Neale Hurston had largely withdrawn from public view and was struggling financially. Her name was in the news briefly in 1950 when it was reported that the Miami woman who employed her as a maid had discovered an article Hurston had written in the *Saturday Evening Post*. The most important project of this period was a biography of Herod the Great. Despite numerous revisions, the purpose of the work remained obscure, the language unrelentingly stilted. Although she did some substitute teaching and wrote for a local paper, Hurston had no steady income and lived her last years in poverty and ill health. Refusing to ask help of her relatives after suffering a stroke in January 1959, she was eventually confined to the county welfare home in Ft. Pierce, Fla., where she died a year later of hypertensive heart disease. After an appeal was made to raise funds for her burial, Zora Neale Hurston was buried in the Negro cemetery of Ft. Pierce.

[The Zora Neale Hurston Coll. at the Univ. of Florida contains MSS. and correspondence, particularly from her later years. Letters and MSS. from Hurston's early career are in the James Weldon Johnson Memorial Coll. and the Carl Van Vechten Papers at the Beinecke Library, Yale Univ. Other correspondence and documents are held by the Am. Phil. Soc. Library, the Moorland-Spingarn Re-

search Center at Howard Univ., and the Special Collections of the Fisk Univ. Library. Robert E. Hemenway's *Zora Neale Hurston: A Literary Biography* (1977) is the best single source of information on Hurston's life and work; it includes a checklist of her writings. Critical assessments appear in Addison Gayle, *The Way of the New World: The Black Novel in America* (1975); Darwin Turner, *In A Minor Chord: Three Afro-American Writers and Their Search for Identity* (1971); Cheryl A. Wall, "Three Novelists: Jessie Fauset, Nella Larsen and Zora Neale Hurston" (Ph.D. diss., Harvard Univ., 1976). Two important articles are Alice Walker, "In Search of Zora Neale Hurston," *Ms.*, March 1975, and Mary Helen Washington, "Zora Neale Hurston: The Black Woman's Search for Identity," *Black World*, Aug. 1972. Hurston claimed various birth dates, and birth records of the period do not survive. Hemenway reports that she used 1901 most often and that date is consistent with verifiable facts about her life. The U.S. Census (1900), however, lists a Zora L. Hurston, daughter of John and Lucy Hurston, born in 1891; a death record, from the Fla. Dept. of Health, gives 1903. Marjorie Silver Adler, Dr. C. C. Benton, C. E. Bolen, Matilda Clark Moseley, Louise Thompson Patterson, and Arthur Huff Fauset provided information in interviews.]

CHERYL A. WALL

HUTCHINS, Grace, Aug. 19, 1885–July 15, 1969. Labor researcher, social reformer.

Grace Hutchins was born in Boston, Mass., the third daughter and third of five children of Edward Webster and Susan Barnes (Hurd) Hutchins. Her two sisters died in childhood. Both parents were of English ancestry, descendants of early Massachusetts settlers; they were members of Boston's Trinity Church (Episcopal), as were many of the city's social elite. Edward W. Hutchins was a prominent Boston attorney, a founder of the Legal Aid Society, and an incorporator of the Boston Bar Association. Susan Hutchins devoted her energies to the Baldwinsville Hospital for Crippled Children, the Home for Aged Women, and the Society of Colonial Dames.

Grace Hutchins attended private schools, traveled around the world with her parents (1898–99), and received her A.B. from Bryn Mawr College in 1907. During her college years she developed suffragist sympathies distressing to her parents. Wanting to do missionary work Hutchins went to China, where from 1912 to 1916 she served as teacher and then principal of the Episcopal St. Hilda's School for Chinese Girls, in Wuchang. Her notebooks from this period are filled with observations of the medical, educational, and social conditions of Chinese women. Ill health and parental pressure brought her back to Boston in 1916.

After returning from China Hutchins became active in the labor movement in the United States and taught at a "social training school" in New York City. As a protest against United States participation in World War I she joined the Socialist party, and nearly lost her teaching job as a result. She studied labor problems at the New York School of Philanthropy (1920–21), and spent several months as a worker in the Seidenberg cigar factory in New York City to complete a course requirement. In 1922–23 Hutchins also took graduate courses at Teachers College, Columbia University.

During this time Hutchins met Anna Rochester (1880–1966), Marxist economist and historian, who became her close friend and co-worker. Rochester, too, had attended Bryn Mawr (1897–99) but had left school after her father's death to help care for her mother. She had received musical training in New York and Germany and had participated in Episcopal church work. After meeting VIDA SCUDDER in 1908, she became interested in Christian socialism. She worked in a Boston settlement house (1909), lobbied for the nine-hour bill for women workers as a member of the New Jersey Consumers' League (1911–12), investigated child labor conditions (1912–15), and served as an analyst under JULIA LATHROP, chief of the United States Children's Bureau (1915). Rochester and Hutchins remained devoted friends for over forty years; in 1924 they moved to an apartment in Greenwich Village in Manhattan, where they lived together for the rest of their lives.

Hutchins's pacifist principles led her to join the Fellowship of Reconciliation (FOR), a Christian pacifist organization. She served as business executive (1925–26), press secretary (1924–26), and contributing editor to the FOR's monthly paper, *The World Tomorrow* (1922–24); Anna Rochester was editor-in-chief from 1922 to 1926. Together Hutchins and Rochester wrote and traveled on behalf of the FOR. Their book, *Jesus Christ and the World Today* (1922), challenged Christians to confront modern social issues. In 1923 they attended the International Fellowship of Reconciliation conference in Denmark, and a meeting of the German Youth Movement in Hellerau, Germany; they traveled to the Far East, India, Europe, and the Soviet Union in 1926–27, meeting Toyohiko Kagawa, Gandhi, and other leading social reformers, visiting factories, and sending dispatches to various American publications. Disillusioned with *The World Tomorrow*, which seemed increasingly conservative, and

impressed with the Soviet Union's social reforms, Hutchins and Rochester left the church and joined the Communist party in 1927. Hutchins also became a correspondent for the Federated Press.

In August 1927 Hutchins was arrested during a Boston demonstration in support of Nicola Sacco and Bartolomeo Vanzetti. Her mother wrote: "Father lowered his head and said one word 'disgrace' which sums it all up." Despite differing political and social views, Hutchins remained close to her family, continued to receive a substantial allowance from her father, and inherited a considerable portion of his estate.

Hutchins spent five months in 1927–28 as an investigator for the New York Department of Labor's Bureau of Women in Industry, resigning because of ill health. In 1927 she, Rochester, and Robert W. Dunn formed the Labor Research Association (LRA), which was devoted to providing information—books, reports, statistics—to labor organizations and publications. Remaining on the staff from 1929 to 1967, Hutchins wrote pamphlets on labor, children, and women's issues, jointly edited seventeen volumes of the LRA's series of Labor Fact Books, and edited its *Railroad Notes* (1937–62). In 1929, after participating in textile strikes in Paterson, N.J. (1924), and New Bedford, Mass. (1928), she wrote *Labor and Silk*, an account of conditions in the industry. She produced three editions of her *Women Who Work* (1933, 1934, 1952), an analysis of the struggle to improve working conditions for women. Hutchins was also a major stockholder in the *Daily Worker* from 1940 to 1956.

Grace Hutchins remained an active member of the Communist party; in New York state she ran (unsuccessfully) as the party's candidate for alderman (1935), controller (1936), and lieutenant governor (1940). She was also treasurer of the Communist National Election Campaign Committee in 1936. Hutchins personally furnished $10,000 bail in 1951 for ELIZABETH GURLEY FLYNN and $5,000 for Alexander Trachtenberg, both indicted under the Smith Act. As designated trustee of the Bail Bond Fund of the Civil Rights Congress, a Communist party-backed organization formed in support of Smith Act defendants, she was involved in litigation concerning the Fund's liquidation (1951–56).

In 1948 Hutchins became involved in a public controversy when Whittaker Chambers, key witness in the trial of Alger Hiss, accused her during congressional hearings of making threats against his life after he had broken with the Communist party; he repeated these accusations in his autobiography, *Witness* (1952). Hutchins vigorously refuted his charges in journal articles and interviews, labeling them "unutterable nonsense" and claiming that she had simply wanted him to return to his job. Despite mounting pressure in the 1940s and 1950s against such organizations as the Civil Rights Congress and the American Committee for Protection of Foreign Born for their radical sympathies, Hutchins continued to support them. In 1964 she served as secretary of the Elizabeth Gurley Flynn Memorial Committee.

Hutchins's long association with Anna Rochester influenced both her career and her private life. A prominent Marxist scholar, Rochester wrote numerous articles and books, among them *Rulers of America: A Study of Finance Capital* (1936) and *Why Farmers Are Poor: The Agricultural Crisis in the United States* (1949). She died of pneumonia in 1966 in New York City; Hutchins died there three years later of arteriosclerosis.

Throughout her career Grace Hutchins was concerned with the health and welfare of the working classes, particularly women and children. Although deeply involved in politics, she kept in touch with her Bryn Mawr classmates. Letters from friends, associates, and family members evoke the image of a kind, thoughtful, and generous individual.

[Manuscript sources include the Grace Hutchins, Anna Rochester, and Robert W. Dunn Colls. at the Univ. of Oreg. Library; the Devere Allen Coll. at the Swarthmore College Peace Coll.; and documents provided by Bryn Mawr College. Photographs of Hutchins and Rochester are at the Univ. of Oreg. Library. *The World Tomorrow*, 1922–26, gives a chronology of Hutchins's association with that publication. Other sources include: Sidney Streat, "Grace Hutchins—Revolutionary," *Daily Worker*, Sept. 16, 1935; Betty Feldman, "Grace Hutchins Tells about 'Women Who Work,'" *The Worker*, March 1, 1953; Meyer A. Zeligs, *Friendship and Fratricide: An Analysis of Whittaker Chambers and Alger Hiss* (1967); U.S. Senate Committee on the Judiciary, Subcommittee to Investigate the Administration of the Internal Security Act and Other Internal Security Laws of the Committee on the Judiciary, *The Communist Party of the United States of America: What It Is, How It Works; A Handbook for Americans* (1955). Obituaries on Hutchins appeared in *N.Y. Times,* July 16, 1969, and *Daily World,* July 17, 1969. Other writings by Anna Rochester include *Lenin on the Agrarian Question* (1942); *The Nature of Capitalism* (1946); and *American Capitalism, 1607–1800* (1949). For information on her life and work see: Stephen Peabody, "Rochester Papers, Please Copy!" *Daily Worker,* April 29, 1940; Julia Martin, "Greetings to Anna Rochester," *The Worker,* March 27, 1953; James S. Allen, "Anna Rochester—Marxist Scholar,"

The Worker, May 24, 1966; *Who Was Who Among North Am. Authors, 1921–1939* (1976). Obituaries on Rochester appeared in *N.Y. Times,* May 12, 1966; *The Worker,* May 24, 1966; and *Publishers Weekly,* June 20, 1966.]

ELAINE A. KEMP

HYATT, Anna. *See* HUNTINGTON, Anna Hyatt.

HYMAN, Libbie Henrietta, Dec. 6, 1888–Aug. 3, 1969. Zoologist.

Libbie Hyman, internationally recognized authority on the taxonomy and anatomy of invertebrates, was born in Des Moines, Iowa, the daughter of Jewish immigrants. Her father, Joseph Hyman (whose original surname was Russian) was a tailor who had left Poland at age fourteen. As a child, she learned some Russian from him. Her mother, Sabina (Neumann) Hyman, had been born in Stettin, Germany.

Libbie Hyman grew up in Fort Dodge, Iowa, the only daughter and the third of four children. According to her longtime colleague Horace W. Stunkard, the family was beset by financial difficulties and home life was unhappy; the mother, who was twenty years her husband's junior, was domineering and demanding. As a child Libbie roamed the fields and woods near her home, collecting and identifying flowers, butterflies, and moths. She graduated from high school in 1905, the valedictorian and youngest member of her class. After Joseph Hyman died in 1907, his widow moved the family to Chicago. Libbie Hyman lived at home until her mother's death in 1929, pursuing her career despite the ill-tempered disapproval of her mother and her bachelor brothers.

The year following graduation, before the move to Chicago, Hyman took additional courses in science and German at the high school and worked in a Mother's Rolled Oats factory pasting labels. Mary Crawford, a Radcliffe graduate and language teacher at Fort Dodge High School, arranged for her to enter the University of Chicago on a scholarship in 1906. Reacting to what she perceived as anti-Semitism in the botany department, Hyman switched to zoology. In this department, built to excellence under Charles Otis Whitman, she received a B.S. in 1910 and a Ph.D. in 1915. She took what she called an "outstanding" undergraduate invertebrate zoology course from Charles Manning Child and did her graduate work under his direction, continuing as his research assistant until about 1930. She was also employed for a number of years as laboratory instructor in the undergraduate courses in comparative vertebrate anatomy and in elementary zoology.

Most of Hyman's articles published between 1916 and 1932 were contributions to Child's project, which consisted of demonstrating the integration of organisms through studies of regeneration or the metabolism of adjacent tissues. More important, she published her *Laboratory Manual for Elementary Zoology* in 1919 (2d ed. 1926) and her *Laboratory Manual for Comparative Vertebrate Anatomy* in 1922 (expanded as *Comparative Vertebrate Anatomy* in 1942)— texts of clarity, honesty, and vigor that became widely used. Not until 1925, ten years after her doctorate, did Hyman's first taxonomic paper appear, an anatomical study of a species of flatworm.

Child's experiments were performed mainly on lower invertebrates such as hydra and planaria. There were few knowledgeable specialists in the area of invertebrate taxonomy, and Hyman soon found herself cast in that role by colleagues who sent her specimens to identify. She found she enjoyed taxonomic research more than experimentation. The lack of a comprehensive reference work in English on the invertebrates, combined with the success of her textbooks, suggested to Hyman the major service she could render to science.

In 1931, her mother dead, her books earning her a small income, Professor Child on leave, Hyman resigned from the University of Chicago and embarked on an independent career. She spent fifteen months visiting scientific centers in Europe, including the Naples Zoological Station. In her mid-forties she settled in New York City. Living very modestly, she began to write, in her own apartment, a treatise on the invertebrates. In 1937 the American Museum of Natural History, whose library she had been using, gave her the unsalaried status of research associate, plus office and laboratory space in the museum.

Hyman did not have many close friends; her manner was rough and her appearance unprepossessing. (Most of her colleagues believed and repeated the story that she smoked cigars; in fact, she never smoked or drank.) But although she lived and worked alone, she was not a recluse and was acquainted with hundreds of colleagues in her profession. She spent several summers at the Marine Biological Laboratory, Woods Hole, Mass., and other marine stations, and she made at least one visit to South America. She carried on a lively correspondence with scientists from around the world who sent her specimens or otherwise consulted her. While president of the Society of Systematic Zoology (1959–63) she took over the editorship of its journal, *Systematic Zoology*.

Hyman's research on flatworms, her wide-ranging and detailed work in a neglected field, earned her the respect of the scientific world. Her six-volume encyclopedic survey of the biology of invertebrates, published between 1940 and 1967, was recognized as possessing a scientific value rarely found in works of such broad scope. She had a deep and abiding fondness for her subject matter. "I don't like vertebrates," she once said. "It's hard to explain but I just can't get excited about them, never could. I like invertebrates. I don't mean worms particularly, although a worm can be almost anything, including the larva of a beautiful butterfly. But I do like the soft delicate ones, the jellyfishes and corals and the beautiful microscopic organisms."

At age seventy-eight, because of her health, she had to give up hope of completing projected volumes on the higher mollusks and on arthropods; but for the myriad other animal forms, *The Invertebrates* achieved great stature. A systematic digestion of scattered information, plentifully illustrated and based on careful reading of German and other foreign sources, was bound to be of value to English-speaking zoologists. Hyman's intelligent, forceful, and independent mind shone through her task. On points of controversy or inconsistency in the literature, Hyman did not hesitate to pronounce her own judgment, and she often took it upon herself to explain the unacceptability of a term or idea widely used by experts. Nearly all zoology books accepted the Hemochordates as part of the Chordates, for example, but she carefully analyzed their differences and denied their relationship.

Although handicapped by Parkinson's disease during the last ten years of her life, Hyman continued to work at the American Museum of Natural History until her death in New York City in 1969. Her approach was in the best tradition of comparative anatomy, histology, morphology, and physiology. The contribution of her great labor was not merely in making information about invertebrates more accessible but also in demonstrating the value of the comparative descriptive method, with concern for detail and scorn of speculation.

[Information for this essay comes from Horace W. Stunkard's "In Memoriam," in Nathan W. Riser and M. Patricia Morse, eds., *Biology of the Turbellaria* (1974); Stunkard first met Hyman in 1914 and was a colleague of hers at the Am. Museum of Natural Hist. from 1955. His account agrees with that of Edna Yost, *American Women of Science* (1943), pp. 122–38. *Biology of the Turbellaria* contains a bibliography of her writings, compiled by William K. Emerson. Miscellaneous recollections of Hyman, with three photographs, may be found in the *Jour.*

Biological Psychology, 12 (1970), 1–15. A biographical sketch by Richard Blackwelder, and recollections by two colleagues appear in *Worm Runners' Digest,* Oct. 1970, pp. 3–23. Obituaries appeared in *Nature,* Jan. 24, 1970, pp. 393–94; *Transactions of the Am. Microscopical Soc.,* April 1970, p. 196; the *N.Y. Times,* Aug. 5, 1969; and the *Wash. Post,* Aug. 6, 1969.]

MARY P. WINSOR

HYSLOP, Beatrice Fry, April 10, 1899–July 23, 1973. Historian.

Beatrice Fry Hyslop was born at home in New York City, the youngest of three children (two girls and a boy) of Mary Fry (Hall) and James Hervey Hyslop. Both parents were of Scottish ancestry. Mary Hyslop, daughter of a wealthy Philadelphia merchant, was a pianist; she died when Beatrice was eighteen months old. James Hyslop, a native of Ohio, was professor of philosophy and ethics at Columbia College; he later founded the American Society for Psychical Research.

Beatrice Hyslop was educated in New York City public schools and at the Barnard School for Girls (1912–15). Entering Mount Holyoke College at sixteen, she came under the influence of NELLIE NEILSON, and majored in history and art. Hyslop played on the college basketball team, was elected to Phi Beta Kappa, and graduated with honors in 1919. After teaching for two years at Mrs. Day's School in New Haven, Conn., she began graduate work at Columbia University in 1921. Working with Carlton J. H. Hayes, she concentrated on the French revolutionary era, and won the A.M. in 1924 with a thesis on French guilds based partly on French archival research. Hyslop taught at Rosemary Hall (1924–26) and Mount Holyoke (1926–28) before resuming her studies at Columbia in 1928. At Hayes's suggestion she studied the *cahiers de doléances* of 1789, the lists of grievances drawn up in connection with the elections to the Estates-General of 1789. Hyslop, who considered the *cahiers* an important source of public opinion for the period, spent three years in France working on the project. She became so well known that in 1931 the French government commissioned her to verify and catalog the *cahiers.* The result was her *Répertoire critique des cahiers de doléances pour les États-généreaux de 1789* (1933; *Supplément,* 1952). This work, together with her doctoral thesis, *French Nationalism in 1789 According to the General Cahiers* (1934), and *A Guide to the General Cahiers* (1936) established Hyslop as the leading American authority on the *cahiers.* Through these works, Hyslop not only made the *cahiers* accessible to scholars, but also exploited them in her own analysis of French public opinion on the eve of the Revolution. They remain essential to serious students of the era.

Hyslop received the Ph.D. from Columbia in 1934, in the midst of the depression. Unable to find a university position, she taught at the Kingswood School for Girls in Bloomfield, Mich., from 1934 to 1936. Her long association with Hunter College began in 1936, when she was appointed instructor of history. She became assistant professor in 1941, associate professor in 1949, and professor in 1954. A kind and generous teacher, she exacted the highest standards from her students, whether the freshmen she sent off to analyze colonial furniture at the Metropolitan Museum of Art or students in her advanced course, "The Age of Democratic Revolution." Only toward the end of her career did she direct graduate students, serving as a member of the graduate faculty of the City University of New York from 1964 until her retirement in 1969.

A small energetic woman with bright blue eyes, Beatrice Hyslop devoted her considerable energies to her work, her friendships, and to community and professional activities. Her intense love of the history and culture of France was manifested through her writings, her efforts to promote French historical studies in the United States, her many trips to France for research and recreation, her friendships with leading French scholars and archivists, and her acts of personal generosity following World War II. Scores of younger American scholars benefited from her advice, drawn from her rich knowledge of French archives and libraries and of French historical scholars.

In addition to her work on the *cahiers,* Hyslop published four books, in the United States and France, the most notable being *L'Apanage de Philippe-Égalité, duc d'Orléans, 1785–1791* (1965), and, in collaboration with Jacques Godechot and David Dowd, *The Napoleonic Era in Europe* (1970). She also wrote numerous articles and from 1947 until 1968 edited the "France" section of "Recently Published Articles" for the *American Historical Review.* A founder of the Society for French Historical Studies (1955), Hyslop suggested the name for the association and served as its third president. Her commitment to international cooperation at all levels is perhaps best illustrated by her organizational role in three Franco-American colloquia during the 1960s and by her vigorous support of the United Nations. An active member of several professional societies, including the Berkshire Conference of Women Historians and the American Association of University Women, Hyslop vigorously protested the lack of equality for women historians in a letter to the editor of the *American Historical Review* in 1956.

Hyslop received many honors for her several contributions. The French government made her a Chevalier des Palmes académiques (1931), later elevating her to an Officier (1952); in 1961 she became a Chevalier de la Légion d'Honneur. She also received an honorary degree from Mount Holyoke in 1959. Following her retirement, she served as visiting scholar at the University of Kentucky (1969) and at Winthrop College (1970). She died of a heart attack in July 1973 while visiting her sister in Rochester, N.Y.

Beatrice Hyslop occupied a unique place among American historians of France. No one else in her time contributed as much as she to the organization of French historians in the United States and to the establishment and maintenance of ties between historians in the United States and in France.

[There are two principal manuscript collections on Beatrice Hyslop: the Thomas Cooper Library, Univ. of S.C., has correspondence and other materials from her private papers; the Williston Memorial Library, Mount Holyoke College, contains a valuable collection of Hyslop's letters to the Alumnae Assoc. of Mount Holyoke (1922–69) as well as a complete list of her memberships in learned societies and publications to 1952. Similar information for the period 1952–73, as well as a full biographical treatment, may be found in Ellen Furlough, "Beatrice Fry Hyslop: Historian of France" (M.A. thesis, Univ. of S.C., 1978). Works about Hyslop include: John Hall Stewart, "Beatrice Fry Hyslop: A Tribute," *French Hist. Studies*, Fall 1972, pp. 473–78, which appears in a special issue of the journal dedicated to Hyslop, and the obituaries by Georgia Robison Beale, *Am. Hist. Rev.*, Feb. 1975, pp. 208–09, and Marc Bouloiseau, *Annales Historiques de la Révolution Française*, Jan.-March 1974, pp. 154–55. A good likeness may be found in the *N.Y. Times*, May 28, 1951. Hyslop's educational records are available from Mount Holyoke College and Columbia Univ.; her employment record at Hunter College is held by the Personnel Services Office. For information on James H. Hyslop, see *Dict. Am. Biog.*, vol. 9. An obituary on Beatrice Hyslop appeared in the *N.Y. Times*, July 27, 1973; death record provided by N.Y. State Dept. of Health.]

ELLEN FURLOUGH

I

IRWIN, Inez Leonore Haynes Gillmore, March 2, 1873–Sept. 25, 1970. Suffragist, feminist, writer.

Inez Haynes Irwin was born in Rio de Janeiro, Brazil, where her parents, Emma Jane (Hopkins) and Gideon Haynes, had moved from New England, hoping to make a fortune in the coffee trade. The venture soon collapsed, and the family returned to manage hotels in Boston. Inez Irwin was proud of coming from the "oldest American stock": on her father's side a long line of farmers led back to 1636; on her mother's side the family could be traced to the Mayflower. Stories of heroic revolutionary ancestors and of her idealistic and adventurous parents fueled her imagination as a child. Her father had been an actor, politician, author, and celebrated prison reformer; her mother had worked before her marriage in the Lowell mills. The Haynes family was large and exuberant. Gideon Haynes, a widower twenty-two years older than his second wife, had five children, and together they had ten more. Inez was the third youngest of twelve surviving children, eight girls and four boys.

Although her parents' marriage was a happy one, Irwin felt from girlhood "a profound horror of the woman's life," with its monotony, drudgery, and endless childbearing. Through discussions with her father and his two unmarried sisters—one a spiritualist, the other an ordained minister—she was early introduced to ideas of women's independence, and to the vision of life as an adventure. Despite genteel poverty, the Haynes children were encouraged to pursue education and to take advantage of the resources of Boston culture: libraries, lectures, and the symphony. Inez, however, longed for a career of travel and exploration, and envied her father and brothers.

At the Bowdoin Grammar School in Boston, from which she graduated as valedictorian in 1887, a teacher assigned as a composition topic "Should Women Vote?" and Inez Haynes became a fervent and lifelong supporter of women's rights. She went on to study at Girls' High School (1887–90) and Boston Normal

School; after graduating in 1892 she taught briefly in the city. On Aug. 30, 1897, she married Rufus Hamilton Gillmore, a newspaper reporter. With his encouragement she entered Radcliffe College as a special student (1897–1900), concentrating in English. At a time when few undergraduates were suffragists, her closest friend was MAUD WOOD PARK, later a leader of the National American Woman Suffrage Association and the League of Women Voters. Together they invited ALICE STONE BLACKWELL to the college to speak about the woman's movement; in 1900 they were cofounders of the College Equal Suffrage League, an influential organization of undergraduates and alumnae which soon expanded to become national.

The marriage to Gillmore allowed her considerable independence. They moved to New York where she began to publish short stories, articles, and, in 1908, her first novel, *June Jeopardy*. A long trip to Europe the following year brought her into contact with American expatriates such as Leo and GERTRUDE STEIN; there are pungent details of these encounters in her unpublished memoirs. By 1911 the Gillmores had become a part of the Greenwich Village community. Inez Haynes Gillmore became the first fiction editor of Max Eastman's radical periodical *The Masses,* and was one of the original members of Heterodoxy, a lively feminist society organized in 1912. Through Heterodoxy and later through Query, another woman's club, she met many of the eminent suffragists, artists, and professional women of the period.

During these years she also met William Henry Irwin, a dynamic California journalist who had come to New York as managing editor of *McClure's Magazine.* Leaving Gillmore in 1913, she obtained a divorce in California, and on Feb. 1, 1916, she married Irwin, who was also divorced and had one son. This second marriage was profoundly satisfying; the couple shared a deep affection and many professional interests. During World War I Inez Irwin accompanied her husband to Europe and reported on many of the major battles in France and Italy for various American magazines. Illness forced her to return alone to New York in 1918, but she recovered from surgery and plunged into the activities of the militant suffrage campaign.

A member of the National Advisory Council of the National Woman's party, Irwin's chief contribution was her colorful history of the suffrage campaign, *Story of the Woman's Party* (1921), a detailed account which emphasizes the courage and personality of the party's leaders, Alice Paul (1885–1977) and LUCY BURNS. Irwin's engaging and informal style, and her careful use of documentation, made her an effective feminist historian. In a later book, the wide-ranging *Angels and Amazons: A Hundred Years of American Women* (1933), she relates the development of women's organizations of all kinds to broader changes in public policy and social status.

She also continued her career as a writer of fiction and books for children; two early novels, *Angel Island* (1914) and *The Lady of Kingdoms* (1917), reflect her feminism. In 1924 Irwin's short story "The Spring Flight" won the O. Henry Memorial Prize. This was to be the height of her literary success; none of her more than a dozen novels (described by one critic as "sympathetic studies of family relations") achieved distinction. The popular "Maida" series of children's books, based on her own childhood, is among her best work. *Maida's Little Shop* was published in 1910, followed by *Maida's Little House* (1921), and *Maida's Little School* (1926). Eight more volumes in the series appeared between 1939 and 1951.

Like her husband, whose career as a political journalist and biographer of Herbert Hoover she lovingly supported, Inez Irwin devoted herself to professional writers' associations. She served as president of the Authors Guild (1925–28) and of the Authors' League of America (1931–33), and as vice president of the New York chapter of P.E.N. (1941–44). Irwin also chaired the board of directors of the World Center for Women's Archives, which was organized in 1936 by the historian MARY BEARD to collect and preserve materials about women. She worked for the center until lack of funding and professional staff forced it to close in 1940.

Overall, Irwin's contributions were made more in the role of follower than as leader. An energetic publicist of feminist ideas, she never had enough faith in her own work to give it the attention she generously provided for others. After her husband's death in 1948, she retired to their summer home in Scituate, Mass., and published only the two final "Maida" books, in 1949 and 1951. Inez Haynes Irwin died in a nursing home in Norwell, Mass., of arteriosclerosis at the age of ninety-seven.

[The principal source is the Inez Haynes Irwin Coll. at the Schlesinger Library, Radcliffe College, which includes a 1950 MS. autobiography, "Adventures of Yesterday," diaries, photographs, and notes for novels. Irwin wrote about her family in "The Making of a Militant," *The Nation,* Dec. 1, 1926, pp. 553–55, and about womanhood in "Why I Am Glad I Am a Woman," *Harper's Bazaar,* July 1912. She talks about her writing and the suffrage campaign in "Will Irwin Interviews His Wife," an unidentified clipping in the Irwin Coll. at the Schlesinger Library. There are brief entries in *Twentieth Cen-*

tury Authors (1942) and the *First Supplement* (1955), and in the *Nat. Cyc. Am. Biog.*, F, 535. See also the entry on Will Irwin in *Dict. Am. Biog.*, Supp. Four, and his autobiography, *The Making of a Reporter* (1942). On the World Center for Women's Archives see Ann J. Lane, ed., *Mary Ritter Beard: A Source Book* (1977). An obituary appeared in the *N.Y. Times*, Oct. 1, 1970. Death certificate supplied by Mass. Dept. of Public Health.]
ELAINE SHOWALTER

ISAACS, Edith Juliet Rich, March 27, 1878–Jan. 10, 1956. Editor, critic.

Edith Isaacs, longtime editor of *Theatre Arts* magazine, was born in Milwaukee, the third daughter in a family of five girls and one boy born to Adolph Walter and Rosa (Sidenberg) Rich. The family lived in Milwaukee, where her Hungarian-born father had settled after leaving Europe as part of a small group of emigrants, led by Carl Schurz, who pooled their resources in order to come to the United States. In Milwaukee, Adolph Rich worked his way up from peddling eyeglasses to become the owner of a prosperous shoe factory. The Sidenbergs had been in the lace business in Breslau, and became successful stockbrokers and realtors in New York City.

Edith Rich was educated in the public schools of Milwaukee, graduating from East Side High School. She received an A.B. from Milwaukee-Downer College (later Lawrence University) in 1897 and began her writing career as a reporter on the *Milwaukee Sentinel*, becoming its literary editor in 1903. At about this time, she met Lewis Montefiore Isaacs, a New York lawyer and composer with whom she collaborated as librettist on a children's operetta. They were married on Nov. 28, 1904, and moved to New York to begin a long, happy, and fruitful life together. The couple had three children: Marian (b. 1906), Lewis (b. 1908), and Hermine (1915–1968).

Motherhood did not stifle Edith Isaacs's writing career. Besides being drama critic for *Ainslee's Magazine* (1913), she contributed articles to *The Delineator, Ladies' Home Journal*, and other magazines, often signing the pieces "Mrs. Pelham" after the town where the family lived. Although informal and anecdotal, the articles encouraged women to widen their interests, to understand family finances, and to take an active interest in the quality of local schools. During World War I Isaacs also became chief of the Women's Publicity Committee for the 1917–18 Liberty Loan Campaign in New York.

In 1918 Edith Isaacs joined the editorial board of *Theatre Arts,* a quarterly founded by Sheldon Cheney two years earlier. By 1922 she was in charge of the magazine, and in 1924 expanded it to a monthly. As the guiding force and chief stockholder of *Theatre Arts,* Isaacs began to make her tremendous contributions to the theater. In articles and editorials, she defined theater in the broadest sense—to include dance, music, and art. She coined the term "tributary theatre" to describe the contributions which community, college, and regional groups—the whole Little Theatre Movement—could make toward developing a truly national theater. Isaacs worked tirelessly and successfully for creation of the National Theatre Conference (1925) and the American National Theatre and Academy (1935). During the 1930s she was active in the Federal Theatre Project, providing office space for its director, HALLIE FLANAGAN, and assisting her in choosing the heads of the project's regional centers.

Isaacs also had an uncanny eye for discovering new talent and bringing it to public attention in the pages of *Theatre Arts.* Some of those she aided, and with whom she developed lasting friendships, were dramatists Eugene O'Neill and Thornton Wilder; dancer Martha Graham; designers Robert Edmond Jones, Jo Mielzner, and Donald Oenslager; critic John Mason Brown; and Rosamond Gilder, who succeeded Isaacs as editor of *Theatre Arts.* People who worked with Isaacs at the time recall her as a "unique and compelling presence"; sensitive, stimulating, and forthright; an able administrator; a "fantastic editor" who could suggest a few trenchant ideas during casual conversation to guide an author; a "mother conscience" who made one wish to do well both artistically and ethically. Lewis Isaacs, a distinguished musician, shared his wife's interests and enthusiasms, and the doors of the Isaacs home were thrown open to artists of all ages and nationalities.

Edith Isaacs combined her activity in the theater with a lifelong interest in black culture. In the 1920s she arranged with Alain Locke for the exhibition of the Blondiau-Theatre Arts Collection of Primitive African Art, the first large collection of this type to be shown in New York. After the exhibition, it was feared that the collection would be dispersed, but Isaacs bought it and the items were ultimately divided between Howard University and the Schomburg Center for Research in Black Culture (part of the New York Public Library). She also wrote the narrative for the August 1942 issue of *Theatre Arts,* entirely devoted to the Negro in the American theater.

A series of crippling attacks of arthritis, beginning in 1929, eventually forced Isaacs to rely on a wheelchair, but she still arrived at the *Theatre Arts* office at 8:30 every morning. Even when she became bedridden, she continued to write and edit books on the theater from her home. While physical infirmity could not defeat her spirit, the death of her husband in 1944 was a severe blow. In 1951 Edith Isaacs gave up her home in New York City and moved to a small private nursing home in White Plains. Among the many friends who visited her there was Martha Graham, who helped her to develop limited-motion movements and to utilize simple movement-saving devices. After suffering a stroke, she died in White Plains in January 1956.

In 1958, a Theatre Arts Project for East Harlem was established in her honor at the James Weldon Johnson Community Center. The project was dedicated to Edith J. R. Isaacs because the founders believed with her that "the theatre is both a means and an end in education, an important form of recreation, and a social force to be reckoned with."

[The Edith J. R. Isaacs Papers at the Wis. Center for Theatre Research in Madison contain correspondence, clippings, typescripts, and other materials relating to Isaacs, her family, and *Theatre Arts*. There is a clipping file on Isaacs in the Billy Rose Theatre Coll., N.Y. Public Library, which also holds her five scrapbooks on the Liberty Loan Campaign. Isaacs was the author of *The American Theatre in Social and Educational Life: A Survey of Its Needs and Opportunities* (1932) and *The Negro in the American Theatre* (1947, 1968), an expanded version of the Aug. 1942 issue of *Theatre Arts*. She edited *Theatre: Essays on the Arts of the Theatre* (1927); a series of essays, *Architecture for the New Theatre* (1935); and a collection, *Plays of American Life and Fantasy* (1929), which had appeared in various issues of *Theatre Arts*. A short biographical sketch by Rosamond Gilder is in Phyllis Hartnoll, ed., *The Oxford Companion to the Theatre* (1967). A photograph can be found in *Vanity Fair*, Dec. 1933. Invaluable assistance in the preparation of this article was provided by Isaacs's children, Marian R. I. Brody and Lewis M. Isaacs, Jr., and by Rosamond Gilder, George Beiswanger, and Martha Hill Davies. An obituary appeared in the *N.Y. Times*, Jan. 11, 1956; death certificate from N.Y. State Dept. of Health.]

DOROTHY L. SWERDLOVE

J

JACKSON, Mahalia, Oct. 26, 1911–Jan. 27, 1972. Gospel singer.

Mahalia Jackson was born and raised in New Orleans, the daughter of John Jackson and Charity Clark. She had at least one older brother. Her father, descended from slaves who had labored on a Louisiana rice plantation, supplemented the money he earned as a longshoreman by cutting hair in the evenings and preaching the gospel on Sundays. However, it was her mother's family, the Clarks, that had the most decisive influence on her upbringing. Her grandfather, Paul Clark, was born a slave on the Merrick cotton plantation along the Atchafalaya River in Louisiana's Pointe Coupee Parish. He raised his eleven children (nine of whom survived childhood) in an atmosphere of strict Christian respectability. His son Porter was the first of the Clarks to leave the plantation. Working as a cook on the Mississippi River steamboats, he gradually helped most of his family to migrate to New Orleans by the early years of the twentieth century.

Mahalia Jackson was five years old when her mother died. She lived for more than a decade with her mother's sister, Mahalia Paul, after whom she was named. Aunt Duke, as she was known, "wasn't one for showing much affection. She believed in the church and hard work and no frills . . . In our house we shut everything down from Friday night until Monday. Either you were a Christian and acted like it or you were put out of the church." The severity of her aunt's regimen was relieved by the affection shown her by her uncle Emanuel Paul and several of her other aunts, by occasional visits with her father at his barber shop, and by the music that filled her life. "I was singing almost as soon as I was walking and talking. I always had a big voice, even as a small child, and I was raised with music all around me." Although her happiest childhood memories were those associated with singing in the congregation of the Mount Moriah Baptist Church, the music that influenced her was not confined to her church. There was the music of the brass bands and of such local jazz musicians as Jelly Roll Morton and King Oliver which one could scarcely avoid hearing on the streets of New Orleans. There was the recorded blues of Ma Rainey, Mamie Smith, and especially BESSIE SMITH which Jackson heard through the open windows and thin partitions of the houses and which she played on her worldly cousin Fred's recordings when her Aunt Duke was away cooking for her white employers. Finally, there was the music of the Sanctified Church next door to her house. "Everybody in there sang and they clapped and stomped their feet and sang with their whole bodies. They had a beat, a powerful beat, a rhythm we held on to from slavery days, and their music was so strong and expressive it used to bring the tears to my eyes." It was to be Jackson's role to aid in amalgamating these musical styles into the new gospel music which she was to help spread throughout the world.

Forced to go to work as a laundress before finishing elementary school, Jackson began to nurture the dream of leaving the south for the greater opportunities of the north. In 1928 she moved to Chicago where two of her mother's sisters had already settled. During her early years in Chicago she sustained herself by doing laundry for white residents of the North Side and by working as a hotel maid. Increasingly her life centered around the Greater Salem Baptist Church where she sang first in the choir, then as a soloist. In 1930, with the three sons of her minister and another young woman, she formed the Johnson Gospel Singers with whom she traveled and sang for the next few years. By the mid-1930s, Jackson's reputation earned her invitations to sing in black churches from New York to California.

The music which Jackson brought with her as she traveled from church to church, though it included the traditional hymns and spirituals, consisted primarily of the gospel songs that were rapidly becoming the single most important form of black religious music in America. The religious consciousness expressed in their lyrics came closer to the ethos of modern religion than slave spirituals ever had and thus manifested black acculturation to the larger white world. Conversely, in the nature of their music and the style of their performance, gospel songs constituted an important force for the preservation of black musical tradition. The roots of gospel music lay in the Holiness and Spiritualist sects that developed at the turn of the century. At a time when many black churches sought respectability by reacting against the past, discouraging all forms of enthusiastic religion, and adopting more sedate hymns and concertized versions of the spirituals, the Holiness churches constituted a revitalization movement by emphasizing such traditional religious practices as spirit possession and religious dance. Musically, they reached back to the traditions of the slave past and out to the rhythms of the secular black world around them, incorporating into their services not only the sounds and spirit of slave music but the sounds and instruments of ragtime, blues, and jazz. The spirit of their music was summed up by a church patriarch who paraphrased Martin Luther: "The devil should not be allowed to keep all this good rhythm" (Levine, chap. 3).

Mahalia Jackson, who had been influenced by all of these components of black music during her youth in New Orleans, became one of the most important instruments for the spread and legitimization of the new gospel sound. She performed the songs of such pioneer gospel composers as Thomas A. Dorsey in the uninhibited manner of traditional Afro-American sacred music: shouting, employing a rocking, swaying rhythm, utilizing her entire body while singing, interpolating cries of "Lord have mercy," "Well, well, well," "Yeah, yeah, yeah," interacting intimately with her audiences—"sometimes I get right down off the stage on my knees and sing with the folks." This style prompted one of her fellow gospel singers to comment: "Mahalia took the people back to slavery times" (Heilbut, p. 94). It also prompted many ministers and church elders to criticize her for a lack of dignity. Her response never varied: "I had been reading the Bible every day most of my life and there was a Psalm that said: 'Oh, clap your hands, all ye people! Shout unto the Lord with the voice of a trumpet!' If it was undignified, it was what the Bible told me to do . . . I want my hands . . . my feet . . . my whole body to say all that is in me."

Her insistence upon uninhibited religion confined Jackson at first to small churches usually of the basement or store-front variety, but as her popularity grew so did her access to the larger and more influential churches. The recordings she cut after World War II, a series of annual Carnegie Hall concerts beginning in 1950, increasing exposure on radio and television, and triumphant tours through Asia and Europe extended her influence and popularity beyond the black world. Her emergence as one of the best known religious singers in the world increased the pressure upon Jackson to expand her repertory to include secular music—especially the blues for which her voice seemed particularly well suited. Always she refused, arguing that "Blues are the songs of despair, but gospel songs are the songs of hope. When you sing them you are delivered of your burden." Nor would she bring her gospel music into night clubs: "To me it's a mockery to religion to sing religious songs to people who are drinking and dancing."

She attributed her 1943 divorce from Isaac Hockenhull, whom she married in 1936, in part to her refusal to accept the lucrative offers to sing secular songs, which he felt were an art form superior to her gospel songs, in part to the amount of time she spent traveling: "Ike's life wasn't within the church the way mine was. He loved me, but he didn't love my songs . . . A man doesn't want his wife running all over the country, even if it's for the Lord." She also pointed to her career as a major source of her marital difficulties with Sigmund Galloway, a business-man and musician whom she married in 1964, divorced in 1967, and with whom she seems to have been reconciled before her death: "When a woman marries a man with a big ego, a man with a desire to accomplish great things—and hasn't, but the woman has—he becomes frustrated. He begins to belittle her talents and to boost his own. . . . Suddenly she is unable to speak for herself, he assumes, or to take care of the business or career she built" (*Ebony,* April 1968).

Jackson was active in the civil rights movement after 1955, when she went to Montgomery, Ala., to support the bus boycott led by Martin Luther King, Jr. During the 1963 March on Washington, she preceded King's famous speech at the Lincoln Memorial by singing the old slave spiritual:

I been 'buked and I been scorned.
I'm gonna tell my Lord
 When I get home,
Just how *long* you've been treating me wrong.

Her final years were hampered by a series of illnesses culminating in a heart condition from which she finally died in Evergreen Park, Ill., a Chicago suburb. Her body was returned to New Orleans and buried in Providence Memorial Park.

Mahalia Jackson was one of those rare individuals whose life and career epitomized the developments shaping an entire group. Through her career one can better understand the intricate relationships between the secular and the sacred in twentieth-century Afro-American culture and the complex process by which black Americans have intensified their degree of acculturation within the larger American society even while they continually reaffirmed and revitalized many of the central facets of their traditional culture.

[Until there is an authoritative scholarly study, many aspects of Jackson's upbringing and personal life will remain obscure. The only biography, Laurraine Goreau, *Just Mahalia Baby* (1975), is inadequate. More interesting, though too sketchy, is the auto-biography Jackson wrote with Evan McLeod Wylie, *Movin' On Up* (1966). All otherwise unidentified quotations come from this work. Jackson's reflections on her two marriages can be found in her article, "Marital Bliss Vs. Single Blessedness," *Ebony,* April 1968, pp. 89–100. The cultural context within which Jackson's career took place is portrayed in Lawrence W. Levine, *Black Culture and Black Consciousness* (1977), chap. 3. There are chapters on Jackson's career in Tony Heilbut, *The Gospel Sound* (1971), Henry Pleasants, *The Great American Popular Singers* (1974), and Hettie Jones, *Big Star Fallin' Mama* (1974). See also *Current Biog.,* 1957. The best introduction to Jackson's music are her recordings. Her early Apollo records were reissued on Kenwood 474, *In the Upper Room,* Kenwood 479, *Just As I Am,* and Kenwood 486, *Mahalia.* Her later career is represented on Columbia CL 644, *World's Greatest Gospel Singer,* Columbia CL 1726, *Mahalia Jackson Live in Europe,* and Columbia CL 1643, *Every Time I Feel the Spirit.* An obituary appeared in the *N.Y. Times,* Jan. 28, 1972. See also "Two Cities Pay Tribute to Mahalia Jackson," *Ebony,* April 1972, pp. 62–72. Death record provided by Ill. Dept. of Health.]

LAWRENCE W. LEVINE

JACKSON, Shirley Hardie, Dec. 14, 1916–Aug. 8, 1965. Writer.

Her comic, grotesque style blends ordinary events, folk ritual, the occult, strange architecture, and a girl facing an identity crisis into a recognizable entity—the Shirley Jackson story. Her protagonists are outsiders; some strive for acceptance, but most flee into a seductive fantasy world characterized by the magic thinking, vivid imagination, and uncivilized perversity of childhood.

Shirley Jackson was born in San Francisco and grew up in nearby Burlingame, where she and her younger brother, Barry, attended the local schools. Her father, Leslie H. Jackson, was an English immigrant who eventually became the president of Stecher-Traung Label and Lithographing Company. Her mother, Geraldine (Bugbee) Jackson, was the daughter and great-granddaughter of prominent California architects. In 1933, Jackson's father was transferred to Rochester, N.Y., where she entered Brighton High School. Her diaries and juvenilia show Jackson's feeling of being an overweight outsider there (Friedman, pp. 18–20). After graduation in 1934, she enrolled at the University of Rochester but withdrew in 1936 to write at home.

The following year, Jackson enrolled at Syracuse University. There she, Stanley Edgar Hyman (later a noted literary critic), and others created a literary magazine, *Spectre,* which was controversial for attacking racial segregation in the dormitories, for criticizing faculty writings, and for attempting to publish male nudes. Directly after graduation, Jackson and Hyman were married, on June 3, 1940. The marriage was welcomed by neither of their families, as Hyman was Jewish and Jackson's family was Protestant.

The couple moved to New York and embarked on literary careers. Hyman worked first at *The New Republic*, which launched Jackson's national career by publishing "My Life With R. H. Macy" (1941). He became a staff writer on *The New Yorker* in 1941 and remained affiliated with the magazine for the rest of his life. In 1943, *The New Yorker* published Jackson's "After You, My Dear Alphonse"; five years later, in June 1948, it printed "The Lottery," which remains her best known work. In this terrifying story a seemingly innocent folk ritual, the drawing of one townsperson's name, turns out to be the yearly selection of a scapegoat to be brutally stoned to death.

The Hymans moved to Vermont in 1945, and Stanley Hyman taught for a year at Bennington College. Bennington remained their home for the rest of Jackson's life except for the years 1949 to 1951, when they lived in Westport, Conn. In *Life Among the Savages* (1953) and *Raising Demons* (1957), her humorous accounts of raising four children (Laurence, b. 1942; Joanne, b. 1945; Sarah, b. 1948; and Barry, b. 1951), Jackson recorded life in Bennington and her experiences as a faculty wife. (Hyman rejoined the college faculty in 1953.) Highly fictionalized autobiography, the books present Jackson as a tolerant, jovial, but harassed suburban mother coping with the frustrations of raising children, cleaning house, cooking, and chauffeuring. Amidst the chaos, Hyman reads, writes, and prepares classes for adoring college girls who patronize his wife.

The books do not mention Jackson's agoraphobia, which perhaps began in the early 1950s and for which she sought therapy (Friedman, p. 37), nor the heavy drinking described by friends and acquaintances. Neither do they record her discipline in writing about three hours a day, producing stories, novels, magazine articles, and books for children.

Jackson's novels became progressively more skillful in their focus, style, depth, and characterization, and increasingly reflected her fascination with the occult. *The Road Through the Wall* (1948), which introduces the families of a California neighborhood by describing their houses, suggests the omnipresence of evil. The characters remain insufficiently individualized, however, and the book has a weak ending, as do her next two novels. In *Hangsaman* (1951), Jackson explores the seductiveness of an imaginary world. Her satire of intellectuals, academic parties, and women's colleges enhances the theme of schizoid withdrawal. *The Bird's Nest* (1954), an original study of a multiple personality, has the stylistic energy and the irony of Jackson's best work.

In Jackson's novels, houses are both symbols and characters. Houses not inhabited by married women are sick. The house in *The Sundial* (1958) embodies the distorted personalities of its residents, and the book suggests that even a new world would be blighted by human failures. In *The Haunting of Hill House* (1959), Jackson presents a house "deranged" since the death of its intended mistress. This most gothic of her novels develops important themes: rivalry between sisters, loss of identity while traveling, solidarity among outcasts, and the seductiveness of secluding oneself in a house.

In Jackson's most satisfying novel, the best-selling *We Have Always Lived in the Castle* (1962), the house becomes sick because Mary Katherine, the book's protagonist, is rejected by her cold mother. Mary Katherine then poisons most of her family, barricades herself and her mothering sister in the house, and becomes a writer, the narrator of a novel that is focused and controlled, as well as terrifying and funny.

In 1964, although she was not physically well (she was overweight and suffered from asthma and arthritis), Jackson was becoming freer of her anxieties about venturing into public. Throughout the difficult years she had remained a warm and generous hostess in her home, and had participated on occasion in writers' conferences. When she died unexpectedly in Bennington in 1965 of a heart attack, she left a novel fragment, published in *Come Along With Me* (1968). It concerned a middle-aged widow who "dabbles in the supernatural" and who has moved to a new city, experiencing for the first time the exhilarating freedom of doing as she pleases.

"The Lottery" and other Jackson stories were selected for prize collections and "Louisa, Please" won the Edgar Allan Poe Award in 1961. Stanley Edgar Hyman described Jackson's attitude toward not receiving other, more prestigious awards as "wry amusement." Since Jackson's death her work has gained increased critical attention.

[The extensive collection of Jackson papers at the Library of Congress includes high school diaries, correspondence, manuscripts, scrapbooks, college notebooks, and miscellaneous material. The George Arents Research Library, Syracuse Univ., has manuscripts of four stories; a complete file of *Spectre* is in the Syracuse Univ. archives. Jackson's works for children are *Witchcraft of Salem Village* (1956); *The Bad Children* (1959), a play; and *Nine Magic Wishes* (1963). She contributed thirteen articles to

Special Delivery (1960), an overly cute advice book for new mothers. Collections of her work include *The Lottery, or The Adventures of James Harris* (1949), and two volumes edited by Stanley Edgar Hyman, *The Magic of Shirley Jackson* (1966), which includes Hyman's memoir, "Shirley Jackson, 1919–1965," first published in *Sat. Eve. Post*, Dec. 18, 1965, and *Come Along With Me* (1968). Lenemaja Friedman, *Shirley Jackson* (1975), a biographical and critical study, includes a selected bibliography and a late photograph; "Shirley Jackson: A Chronology and a Supplementary Checklist," *Bibliographical Soc. of Am. Papers*, April 1966 was approved by Jackson. See also Raymond R. Miller, Jr., "Shirley Jackson's Fiction: An Introduction" (Ph.D. diss., Univ. of Del., 1974); John G. Parks, "The Possibility of Evil: The Fiction of Shirley Jackson" (Ph.D. diss., Univ. of N.M., 1973); and Helen E. Nebeker, "'The Lottery': Symbolic Tour de Force," *Am. Lit.*, March 1974. Brendan Gill discusses Jackson and Hyman in *Here at the New Yorker* (1975), pp. 244–50, as does Phoebe Pettingell (Hyman's widow) in her introduction to *The Critic's Credentials* (1978), a collection of Hyman's essays. Obituaries appeared in the *N.Y. Times*, Aug. 10, 1965, and *Publishers Weekly* and *Newsweek*, both Aug. 23, 1965. Jackson's birth date is usually given as 1919, but a birth certificate from the Calif. Board of Health confirms the 1916 date. Death record supplied by the state of Vt. Assistance with research was provided by a biobibliography by Martha A. Powell, and by correspondence with Ann Malamud and Lionel Nowak.]

CAROL AMES

JARRELL, Helen Ira, July 27, 1896–Aug. 27, 1973. Superintendent of schools, union leader.

Ira Jarrell was born in Meriwether County, Ga., the seventh of nine children and youngest of three daughters of William Henry and Emma (Hutchison) Jarrell. Both parents were of Scots-English ancestry. During Ira's early years her father worked as a farmer, but an agricultural depression drove him to seek opportunities in Atlanta, where the family moved in 1901. There he entered the grocery business and the family took up residence with relatives. In 1904 their difficulties multiplied when William Jarrell died of a heart ailment. However, thanks to a modest income from life insurance, assistance from relatives, the labor of the older children, and, above all, her own efforts as head of the household, Emma Jarrell was able to buy a house and send her three youngest children to the local public schools. There Ira Jarrell excelled in her studies. Those who knew her as a child recalled that she possessed a winning personality that charmed all she met, child and adult. At twelve she joined the Woodward Avenue Baptist Church and two years later began teaching the beginner's class

in Sunday school, a responsibility she discharged for the next fifty years.

It was during these early years that Ira Jarrell decided to become a teacher. In 1910 she enrolled in Girls' High School in Atlanta. After graduating in 1914 she spent two years at the Atlanta Normal School, completing her preparation for teaching. Her life's work began in 1916, when she became a teacher of the fifth and sixth grades in an elementary school in Atlanta. She quickly established herself in the hearts of her pupils, one of whom remembered her as "kind, understanding, and always willing to assist us in any of our problems" (Harper, p. 3). Determined to improve her educational qualifications, Jarrell enrolled at Oglethorpe University in Atlanta where, in 1928, she received an A.B., and, in 1931, an A.M. Atlanta school officials rewarded her effort and ability by promoting her to the position of senior teacher in 1930 and by naming her a principal in 1934. During these years she was also responsible for the care of her aging mother and aunt.

A turning point in her life came when Jarrell began to play an active role in the Atlanta Public School Teachers' Association (APSTA), serving first as recording secretary (1929) and then as member of the executive board, first vice president (three terms), and delegate to the Atlanta Federation of Trades. She helped to make the APSTA the largest American Federation of Teachers local in the nation, and gained valuable political experience in struggling with sometimes penurious and hostile city officials. In 1936 she was elected to the presidency of the local.

As head of the thousand-member union, Jarrell displayed considerable administrative and political skill. She labored hard to secure better working conditions and higher salaries, believing that "you can't pay a good teacher too much." Involving herself in municipal politics, she enlisted union energies to defeat a mayor regarded as unfriendly to the welfare of teachers and formed an alliance with William B. Hartsfield, helping to secure his election as mayor in 1936. Together, Jarrell and Hartsfield dominated Atlanta city politics for the next two decades. She next turned to the conquest of the Board of Education. With the help of the Atlanta Federation of Trades, the teachers' union in 1937 engineered the election of a board composed of business and professional men who proved friendly to the teachers. To her political skills Jarrell added a magnetic personality; she could be jovial or flinty as the occasion demanded. Five and one-half feet tall and weighing nearly two hundred pounds, she conveyed a sense of warmth, dignity, and solidity.

In 1944 Ira Jarrell became superintendent of the Atlanta schools, elected by the Board of Education only eight days after the retirement of the incumbent superintendent. Not only was she the first woman in Atlanta history to hold the post, but she was also one of the few women in the nation to direct a large school system. She proved herself an extraordinarily effective administrator, running the Atlanta public schools with the same firm hand she had displayed as head of the teachers' union, while remaining friendly to the teachers' cause. She gave high priority to the reduction of class size and to the steady increase of teachers' salaries, thus gaining the wholehearted cooperation of most members of the union. Under Jarrell the APSTA became, in effect, a "quasi-company union."

Ira Jarrell governed during a period of unprecedented growth in the Atlanta public schools, and she labored to move the Atlanta system into the mainstream of American public education. She secured the approval of a series of bond issues, presided over a doubling in the enrollment and in the number of schools, and sponsored a tripling in the number of teachers. In addition, she supervised a building program amounting to nearly forty million dollars, reorganized and decentralized the administrative structure of the schools, engineered a change making the schools financially independent of city hall, established a radio station and later a television station as part of the school operation, and promoted special programs for gifted and handicapped children.

Among her more controversial innovations was the appointment of male principals to the elementary schools. Even more controversial was her decision in 1947 to replace Atlanta's five high schools, each of which drew students from the entire city and thus laid a heavy burden on the city's transportation system, with ten coeducational high schools, each serving only the students residing in the immediate area. The plan also abolished separate junior high schools. Despite a protest from the alumni and faculty of Boys' High and Girls' High, who complained about the breach of tradition and saw a threat to the quality of secondary education in Atlanta, in this matter, as in most others, Ira Jarrell had her way.

In 1952 the annexation of suburbs led to the addition of three new members to the Board of Education, ending more than a decade of harmony between the superintendent and the board. To some, Jarrell's strengths as an administrator and politician were a vice. Charges followed that the superintendent and the teachers' union were embroiled in political activity, and that Jarrell and Mayor Hartsfield were "dictators." Other controversies ensued, but none seemed to disturb Jarrell. "You can't exist without some controversy," she once said. "People think different, and if you have the courage to do things you think are right, you are going to have disagreements" (Barnwell, p. 11).

Additional criticism came from some of Atlanta's black citizens, who found Jarrell less than firmly committed to the goal of racial equality. Historians of the Atlanta public schools disagree about whether she actually endorsed the idea of granting equal pay for black teachers. There is no doubt, however, that as early as 1944 she and the board ignored petitions from black citizens' groups to secure equal facilities for black children. After the 1954 Supreme Court decision declaring racial segregation of the public schools unconstitutional, both the superintendent and the board engaged in a variety of delaying tactics. She privately welcomed retirement in 1960 before the Atlanta public schools were plunged fully into the desegregation controversy.

Upon retirement as superintendent, Jarrell accepted an appointment as director of the division of curriculum development for the Georgia State Department of Education. Forced to withdraw from public life altogether in 1967 because of ill health, she occupied herself chiefly with civic affairs and her duties as a Sunday school teacher. She spent most of her remaining years with her brother Fitz Hugh in Little Rock, Ark., where she died of breast cancer in 1973.

[The chief sources of information about Ira Jarrell are in the archives of the Atlanta Board of Education, which hold school records, minutes of the board of education, a clipping file, a taped interview with Jarrell, photographs, and copies of all known secondary sources on her career. Principal secondary sources are Melvin W. Ecke, *From Ivy Street to Kennedy Center: Centennial History of the Atlanta Public School System* (1972), especially chap. 4; Joseph W. Newman, "A History of the Atlanta Public School Teachers' Association, Local 89 of the American Federation of Teachers, 1919–1956" (Ph.D. diss., Ga. State Univ., 1978), especially chaps. 6 and 8; and Philip Noel Racine, "Atlanta's Schools: A History of the Public School System, 1869–1955" (Ph.D. diss., Emory Univ., 1969), pp. 305–43. See also C. L. Harper, "My Fifth Grade Teacher," *Atlanta Teacher*, Jan. 1944, and Katherine Barnwell, "Ira Jarrell Looks Back," *Atlanta Journal and Constitution Mag.*, April 3, 1960. Other articles about her appeared in the *Atlanta Journal*, Jan. 29, 1948; *Atlanta Constitution*, Feb. 8, 1957; *Jour. of Labor*, Nov. 12, 1943, and April 14, 1944; *North Side News*, Sept. 5, 1956; *Atlanta Journal and Constitution Mag.*, Dec. 3, 1972. An obituary appeared in the *Atlanta Constitution*, Aug. 28, 1973. Additional information for this article was provided by Mrs. S. L. Calder, Mrs. O. W. Hornbuckle, Walter

Bell, J. Everette De Vaughn, Mark Huie, and Fitz Hugh Jarrell. Death certificate was supplied by Ark. Dept. of Health.]

CHARLES E. STRICKLAND

JARRETT, Mary Cromwell, June 21, 1877–Aug. 4, 1961. Social worker, social work educator.

Mary Jarrett, a founder of Smith College School for Social Work and pioneer in psychiatric social work and health care planning, was born in Baltimore, Md., the only child of Frank Asbury and Caroline Watkins (Cromwell) Jarrett. Her mother's ancestors were English settlers in Maryland before the Revolution. Her father was a bookkeeper, a partner in a tailoring business, and later a reporter. He died when Mary Jarrett was fifteen.

After graduating from Western High School, Jarrett entered Woman's College of Baltimore (later Goucher College) in 1895. She specialized in English and worked on the college publication *Kalends*, receiving her A.B. degree in 1900. After two years of teaching, Jarrett began volunteer work for the Baltimore Charity Organization Society. In 1903 she moved to Boston, where she was employed by the Boston Children's Aid Society. Trained by the director, Charles W. Birtwell, a persuasive advocate of individualizing services to the needy, Jarrett worked with delinquent girls and boys. She advanced from general assistant to head of the casework department and, on leave, established the York County Children's Aid Society in Saco, Maine.

In 1913 the director of Boston Psychopathic Hospital, E. E. Southard, invited Mary Jarrett to develop a social service department. Her original contribution there was the application of social casework methods to the treatment of psychiatric patients, which no one had previously done systematically. In 1916 she gave this approach the name psychiatric social work. With Southard she was an early proponent of the clinical team. As part of the team, social workers brought their knowledge of family and social conditions to bear on the diagnosis and treatment of psychiatric inpatients and outpatients. Jarrett identified the special skills needed for this work—objective observation, self-awareness, understanding of personality development, and knowledge of mental disorders. On this basis, she formulated systematic requirements for training. An efficient administrator, she was determined to develop a dedicated professional staff who would serve as models for others.

Jarrett's association with Southard, a man of strong social conscience, was pivotal to her career. In 1919 she resigned from Boston Psychopathic to work with him on a comprehensive study of psychiatric problems in industry for the Engineering Foundation of New York. She found that many workers suffering from nervous breakdowns could be rehabilitated and rehired after special counseling. Later Jarrett characterized her discoveries in this area as her one original contribution to research. Her efforts in this new field of industrial psychiatry were cut short by Southard's death in 1920. Southard and Jarrett's book *Kingdom of Evils* (1922) is a record of their joint thinking and collaborative research.

Believing that all social work would be enriched by the application of psychiatric concepts of human behavior, Jarrett also campaigned vigorously to establish special training in psychiatric social work. Her own contribution to social work education began with a combined seminar and apprenticeship program at Boston Psychopathic, initiated in 1914. There she developed a comprehensive educational plan to attract able college graduates for advanced studies in mental hygiene. In 1918, when the large number of shell-shocked soldiers returning from the battlefields of World War I had become a national concern, Jarrett became director of the first training program for psychiatric social workers, offered during the summer at Smith College in response to the war emergency. Operated under the joint auspices of Boston Psychopathic and the National Committee for Mental Hygiene, the experimental program proved so successful that the following year a permanent graduate school, originally known as the Smith College Training School for Social Work, was established. Stuart Chapin, Smith professor of sociology, was director, and Mary Jarrett was associate director. The curriculum of the Smith School reflected Jarrett's convictions, providing a broad base in social work theory along with courses in psychiatry, sociology, government, and economics taught by experts in these fields. The program's block plan, also suggested by Jarrett, represented a radical departure in social work education. Under this plan students alternated periods of intensive theoretical study with periods of supervised practice and research.

Jarrett became an acknowledged leader in efforts to develop psychiatric social work as a specialty. Her influential paper, "The Psychiatric Thread Running Through All Social Case-Work," presented at the 1919 meeting of the National Conference of Social Work, criticized MARY RICHMOND's classic formulation of casework in *Social Diagnosis* (1917) as deficient in recognition of the psychopathology of her clients. Jarrett insisted that good casework must focus on the personality of the individual and must include "the habitual recognition of mental causes of conduct." In 1920 she organized the Psychiatric Social Workers Club (later the American Association of Psychiatric Social Workers). The same year the National Committee for Mental Hygiene endorsed as the national norm the definition of functions and training requirements for psychiatric social work which Jarrett had institutionalized at Smith. Throughout the decade from 1913 to 1923, Jarrett insistently called for a new professional attitude that would abandon the still prevalent moralistic tone in favor of objective observation and impersonal friendliness. The success of her efforts was evident in the integration of instruction in psychiatric concepts into all aspects of social work training.

In 1923, when the Smith School underwent some reorganization, Jarrett was eased out of her position as associate director. Bitterly disappointed at losing her academic base, she worked subsequently for the United States Public Health Service (USPHS), studying the social adjustment of immigrants, and for the Veterans Bureau in Boston. In 1927 Jarrett and Katrine Collins, with whom she shared a home from 1919 on, moved to New York City. There she began work in a new and neglected field: health care planning for the chronically ill.

When Jarrett entered this field, care of the chronically ill was scarce, haphazard, and demeaning. Working from 1927 to 1943 for the Research Bureau of the Welfare Council of New York City (later the Community Council of Greater New York), Jarrett conducted major studies of chronic diseases. A Health Inventory of New York City (1929), coauthored with medical economist Michael M. Davis, prepared the way for Jarrett's Chronic Illness in New York City (1933). A comprehensive analysis of the problem, her book contradicted the prevalent notion that chronic illness was restricted to the aged and incurable. It also included a guide to systematic community planning.

Following the publication of Chronic Illness, the Welfare Council appointed a Committee on Chronic Illness, with cardiologist Ernst P. Boas as chairman and Jarrett as secretary. For the next decade she was in a key position to promote some of the recommendations specified in her book. An immediate result of the committee's work was the construction of a medical center for the chronically ill on Welfare Island (later Goldwater Memorial Hospital). Jarrett's main goal, however, was to develop an integrated program for the care and prevention of chronic illness in New York City that would serve as a model for the rest of the nation.

Jarrett's research for the Welfare Council was used extensively in the National Health Survey undertaken by the USPHS in 1935 and influenced the provisions for the chronically ill under the Social Security Act of 1935. In related work, from 1935 to 1940 Jarrett directed a widely influential interagency project for the Works Progress Administration in New York to demonstrate the use of home care with the chronically ill. In 1939 she initiated the formation of the Subcommittee on Arthritis (later the New York Rheumatism Association), which developed uniform criteria in diagnosis. From 1943 until her retirement in 1949, Jarrett served as consultant on the planning of long-term health care facilities in several cities.

Jarrett's retirement was marred by ill health. For the last three years of her life she was confined to a wheelchair and could no longer enjoy traveling—a major outlet during her busy career. An ample, dark-haired woman with an abrasive personality, Jarrett made a strong impression on those who knew her because of her seriousness and her forcefulness in expressing her convictions. Although embittered about the lack of appreciation in the academic community, she was gratified that many of her ideas were absorbed into the mainstream of social work thought. Mary Jarrett died in New York City in 1961.

[Original MSS. and extensive professional correspondence, as well as photographs, are in the Sophia Smith Coll. at Smith College and in the files of the Alumnae Assoc. of the Smith College School for Social Work. The Michael M. Davis Coll. of Social and Economic Aspects of Medicine at the N.Y. Acad. of Medicine sheds light on her thinking and style of collaborative work in public health. Also useful is the oral memoir of Maida Herman Solomon, in the William E. Wiener Oral Hist. Library of the Am. Jewish Committee in N.Y. City; a copy is in the Schlesinger Library, Radcliffe College. Jarrett summarized the guiding principles of health care planning in "Combatting Chronic Illness," Public Welfare, June 1945. The most useful secondary sources are L. Vernon Briggs, History of the Psychopathic Hospital (1922); Frederick P. Gay, The Open Mind: Elmer Ernest Southard, 1876–1920 (1938); Lois French, Psychiatric Social Work (1940); Howard J. Parad, "The Smith College School for Social Work in Perspective," Smith College Studies in Social Work, Feb. 1960; Ernst P. Boas, The Unseen Plague: Chronic Disease (1940); and Commission on Chronic Illness, Prevention of Chronic Illness, I (1957). An obituary appeared in the N.Y. Times, Aug. 5, 1961. A biobibliography prepared by Linda Hardin assisted in the research for this article. Additional information was derived from interviews with Jarrett's associates and students, from Goucher College, and from Baltimore census records. Jarrett's birth year is sometimes given as 1876. The 1877 date comes from her personnel form provided by Boston State Hospital, from the death certificate provided by N.Y. City Dept. of Health, and from the records of Greenmount Cemetery, Baltimore.]

VIDA SIMENAS GRAYSON

JEMISON, Alice Mae Lee, Oct. 9, 1901–March 6, 1964. Indian political leader, journalist.

Alice Jemison was born at Silver Creek, N.Y., just off the Cattaraugus Reservation of the Seneca, one of the Six Nations of the Iroquois. She was the first of three children and elder daughter of Daniel A. Lee and Elnora E. Seneca, both graduates of Hampton Institute. Although her father, a cabinetmaker, was Cherokee, Alice Lee was raised in the matrilineal society of the Seneca, in which her mother's family was prominent. From the ancient Iroquois tradition of behind-the-scenes political participation by women, she acquired a self-confidence that stood her well in her later crusades.

Lee's formal education was limited by her family's financial exigencies; she attended Silver Creek High School, working in the evenings as an usher and beautician until her graduation in 1919. Later that year, on December 6, she married LeVerne Leonard Jemison, a Seneca steelworker from her own reservation. The marriage ended in separation in December 1928, and subsequently Alice Jemison had to support her mother as well as her two children, LeVerne "Jimmy" Lee (b. 1920) and Jeanne Marie (b. 1923). She struggled to provide for her family in a variety of jobs: as factory worker, clerk, peddler, dressmaker, practical nurse, secretary, paralegal researcher, free-lance journalist, and in 1930, Bureau of the Census employee.

Disturbed by the terrible living conditions of her people, Jemison became increasingly active on behalf of the Senecas. Becoming secretary in 1929 to Ray Jimerson, then president of the Seneca Nation, she proved her political skills decisively the following year during the Marchand murder case, in which two Seneca women were accused of killing a white woman in Buffalo. Working closely with other Iroquois leaders, Jemison aided the defense through letters to public figures and articles for the Buffalo newspapers; the defendants eventually were freed. She followed this campaign with a series of syndicated columns for the North American Newspaper Alliance from 1932 to 1934 and appearances in Washington as a lobbyist for the Seneca.

Her articles and speeches during this period expressed a firm belief in the sanctity of Indian treaty rights, particularly the guarantees ex-pressed to the Six Nations of the Iroquois by the Treaty of Canandaigua of 1794. She was also influenced by the writings of Carlos Montezuma, the noted Pan-Indian leader, and adopted his conviction that the Bureau of Indian Affairs (BIA) should be abolished. For the rest of her life, Jemison clung to these two principles.

In the mid-1930s Jemison emerged as a vocal opponent of the Franklin D. Roosevelt administration. Sharing the historic distrust of western New Yorkers for Washington-directed policies, a suspicion heightened by her native American heritage of betrayal by white authorities, she attacked liberal efforts to extend a "New Deal" to Indians. Her vehicle for this fight was the American Indian Federation, whose president, Joseph Bruner, appointed her his spokesperson in 1935. For several years she edited the Federation's newspaper, *The First American*; she served as the organization's major lobbyist on Capitol Hill until her resignation in 1939.

Jemison appeared at more congressional hearings on Indian affairs than any other Indian in the late 1930s, urging representatives to repeal the Indian Reorganization Act of 1934, remove Commissioner of Indian Affairs John Collier, and abolish the bureau he headed. Collier, a reformer, had promoted the Indian Reorganization Act as a means of establishing his concept of home rule among the nation's tribes. Jemison challenged his authority, however, and insisted that no act or uniform program dictated by Washington could do justice to the needs of all Native Americans across the United States.

In her testimony and writings, Jemison consistently criticized federal intervention in tribal affairs. She accused Collier of authoritarian measures in the herd reduction program among the Navaho, opposed construction of the Blue Ridge Parkway through the Cherokees' North Carolina reservation, and supported Sioux who questioned the legality of the Indian Reorganization Act referendum. She also charged Collier's bureau with administrative incompetence and wasting taxpayers' funds.

Jemison's attacks were on occasion overblown. Sometimes branding her opponents as communists or atheists, Jemison herself was accepted by right-wing critics of the Roosevelt administration, ranging from the Daughters of the American Revolution to William Dudley Pelley, the extremist leader of the Silver Shirts of America. In her relentless war against the BIA, she was willing to appear at the same hearing with self-styled fascists, as she did in 1938 and 1940 before the House Committee on Un-American Activities. Such tactics, coupled with Jemison's strong opposition in 1940 to the Selective Service Act, allowed the Interior Depart-

379

ment to portray her as an Indian Nazi, a charge belied by the fact that she passed every loyalty check made by the FBI and was able to secure government employment in the Bureau of the Census during World War II. After the war, despite repeated government harassment for her past activities, she continued to call for the BIA's abolition in the pages of *The First American*, which she revived and published independently from 1953 to 1955.

Jemison spent the remainder of her life in the Washington, D.C., area, maintaining ties to her people through Cornelius Seneca, her uncle and president of the Seneca Nation. While her militancy anticipated much of the Red Power Movement of the 1970s, she never lived to see her ideas espoused by a new generation of Indians, dying in Washington of cancer in March 1964. Her body was returned to New York and buried at the United Mission Cemetery on the Cattaraugus Indian Reservation.

[Jemison correspondence can be found in BIA Central Classified Files, 1907–39, and in the Office File of Commissioner John Collier, Record Group 75, Nat. Archives. Some documents relating to her, including a resumé, are located in the Indian Coll., Buffalo and Erie Cty. Hist. Soc. Her career is discussed in detail in Laurence Hauptman, "Alice Jemison: Seneca Political Activist, 1901–1964," *Indian Historian*, Summer 1979, pp. 15–22, 60–62. For a different view of Jemison and the Am. Indian Federation see Kenneth Philp, *John Collier's Crusade for Indian Reform, 1920–1954* (1977). An obituary appeared in *Buffalo Evening News*, March 10, 1964. Personal information supplied by Francis and Winifred Kettle, Pauline Seneca, Robert Galloway, Rev. W. David Owl, Genevieve Plummer, Catherine Bauer, Rupert Costo, and Jeanne Marie Jemison. Jemison's FBI file was obtained through the Freedom of Information and Privacy Act; a death certificate was furnished by D.C. Dept. of Public Health.]

LAURENCE M. HAUPTMAN

JOHNSON, Adelaide, Sept. 26, 1859–Nov. 10, 1955. Sculptor, feminist.

Adelaide Johnson was the sculptor of the monument to the woman's movement that stands in the United States Capitol. Somewhat eccentric in the fashion of her time, intrigued by spiritualism and the occult, Johnson often attracted dramatic publicity. But her portrait busts of suffragists and feminists gave women a physical and artistic embodiment of their own historical significance during a time when such public recognition was scarce.

Johnson was born in Plymouth, Ill.; her father, Christopher William Johnson, was a farmer from Indiana. Her mother, Margaret Huff (Hendrickson) Johnson came from Kentucky.

It was the third marriage for each; Adelaide, originally named Sarah Adeline, was the first child of their union. She had several older siblings from the previous marriages, as well as a younger brother and sister.

Johnson was educated in country schools and in her teens studied art at the St. Louis School of Design, boarding with an older half brother. In 1877 she was awarded first and second prizes at a state exposition in competition with professional woodcarvers. A year later, manifesting a dramatic flair exhibited throughout her life, she changed her name to Adelaide. While studying in Chicago and supporting herself by decorating and woodcarving, she fell down an elevator shaft in the Central Music Hall, breaking her hip. She used the $15,000 obtained from a casualty suit to finance her study of sculpture in Europe.

In 1883, Johnson studied painting in Dresden, then, in 1884, moved on to Rome, becoming a pupil of Giulio Monteverde. She studied with him for eleven years and maintained a studio in Rome for the next twenty-five; at various times in her career Johnson had studios in Carrara, London, New York, Chicago, and Washington.

Johnson developed a feminist perspective early. Perceiving feminism as the greatest revolutionary force in history and "the mightiest thing in the evolution of humanity," she saw it as her mission to record and immortalize the history of the movement. She began this life work by exhibiting busts of suffragists LUCRETIA MOTT, ELIZABETH CADY STANTON, and SUSAN B. ANTHONY, and of the pioneer physician Caroline B. Winslow, at the Woman's Pavilion of the World's Columbian Exposition in Chicago in 1893.

On Jan. 29, 1896, Johnson married Alexander Frederick Jenkins, an English businessman. She falsified her age on the marriage certificate, listing it as twenty-four, one year younger than her husband, though she was actually thirty-six. Married in her Washington studio, with busts of Anthony and Stanton serving as "bridesmaids," the couple was united by a woman minister and became Mr. and Mrs. Johnson. The groom, like Johnson, was a vegetarian and a spiritualist; he took her name as "the tribute love pays to genius." Their marriage, however, was characterized by long separations in which Johnson felt that her husband had lost the spiritual consciousness they had shared. In 1908 she obtained a divorce, retaining much bitterness about their relationship.

Johnson had a lifelong dream of creating a gallery and museum to house the history of the woman's movement. Lacking public support and funding, she eventually regarded her home-studio in Washington, D.C., as the locus of this museum. She also hoped that the National American Woman Suffrage Association (NAWSA) would underwrite the costs of a woman's monument for the United States Capitol. In 1904 differences with Susan B. Anthony, who opposed the placement of a monument in the Capitol, preferring the Library of Congress, caused a disruption in their friendship and in Johnson's relationship with NAWSA. She turned then to New York suffragist ALVA BELMONT of the National Woman's party, and later secured a commission for the national monument. Her seven-ton sculpture of white Carrara marble, "The Woman Movement," containing portrait busts of Mott, Stanton, and Anthony, was presented to the nation on behalf of American women by the National Woman's party, which had financed and lobbied for it, on Anthony's birthday, Feb. 15, 1921. The reception for Johnson on that day was the first ever given for a woman in the Capitol building. In 1936, Johnson's sculpture of Anthony was used as the model for the three-cent postage stamp commemorating the sixteenth anniversary of woman suffrage.

Johnson was a supporter of numerous women's organizations. A founder and lifelong member of the National and International Councils of Women, she was also a charter member of the Lyceum Club, founded in London in 1904, and its American organizer. She held a "veteran's certificate" from NAWSA. Throughout her life Johnson spoke on the topic of the woman's rights movement, though her perspective was inspirational rather than political. Speaking on Anthony's birthday in 1934, she referred to "the awakening of woman" as "the central and supreme fact in the world of today."

After the 1930s, Johnson's career declined. Financial problems, which had always beset her, became worse, and she relied for support on family and friends. Unable, and often unwilling, to sell her sculpture because she considered the prices offered an affront, she faced eviction and sale of her home to pay taxes. In 1939, frustrated and convinced that her dream of a studio-museum would never be realized, she mutilated many of her sculptures and called in the press to witness the destruction. Though she denied indignantly that she intended to arouse sympathy, she benefited from public generosity and from the intervention of Congressman Sol Bloom of New York who prevented her eviction. Efforts to pass a bill through Congress granting her $25,000 were unsuccessful, however.

Financial distress and ebbing strength caused her to move in with friends on Capitol Hill about 1947. Attempting to raise money to repurchase her home, she appeared on several television quiz programs and won prize money, but to no avail. Seeing that advanced age could convey special privilege, she reversed her earlier falsification, made herself twelve years older than she was, and celebrated every birthday from "100" to "108" with friends and newspaper publicity. Johnson died in Washington in 1955, at the age of 96, of a stroke. Her Capitol sculpture remains the only national monument to the woman's movement.

[The most important source is the Adelaide Johnson Collection of correspondence, diaries, speeches, and articles in the Manuscript Div. of the Library of Congress. A collection in the Div. of Political Hist. of the Smithsonian Institution contains material collected by Johnson on her various interests, clippings, a number of her marble and plaster portrait busts, and numerous items of clothing. Her published articles include "The Import of the Woman Movement," *Equal Rights Mag.*, March 10, 1934. The best secondary source is Charles E. Fairman, *Art and Artists of the Capitol of the United States* (1927). See also Ralph C. Smith, *A Biog. Index of Am. Artists* (1932); *Am. Art Annual* (1923); *Contemp. Am. Sculpture* (1924); and Jean B. Cook Smith, "Life in Marble—Speech in Silence: Adelaide Johnson and Her Work," *The New Am. Woman*, June 1917. Newspaper clippings in the National Portrait Gallery Library and in the office of the Architect of the (U.S.) Capitol, as well as correspondence and records located there about the installation of the monument, are useful. Obituaries, all giving the incorrect age, appeared in the *Wash. Post*, the *Wash. Evening Star*, and the *Wash. Daily News* on Nov. 11, 1955, and the *N.Y. Times*, Nov. 12. Her birth date was obtained from the Div. of Political Hist. accession records provided by Mrs. Romola Johnson Cristal, the donor and a niece, and confirmed by the U.S. Census (1860). Her marriage and death records were obtained from the Vital Statistics Bureau in Washington, D.C. Interviews and correspondence with Romola Johnson Cristal and another niece, Alathena Johnson Smith, provided valuable information on her family background, early life, and personality.]

EDITH MAYO

JOHNSTON, Frances Benjamin, Jan. 15, 1864–May 16, 1952. Photographer.

Frances Benjamin Johnston's long career incorporates almost every aspect of the early history of American photography and photojournalism. In more than fifty years of making photographs, she was often a pioneer, a role well suited to her adventurous temperament.

As early as 1897, in an article for the *Ladies'*

Home Journal, Johnston was advising young women to look for careers in photography, while reminding her readers that "the woman who makes photography profitable must have . . . good common sense, unlimited patience to carry her through endless failures, equally unlimited tact, good taste, a quick eye, a talent for detail, and a genius for hard work." By this time, Johnston was supporting herself solely on her income as a photojournalist and lecturer.

Frances Benjamin Johnston was born in Grafton, W. Va., an only child. Her family moved to New York City, to Rochester, N.Y., and finally to Washington, D.C., where her father, Anderson Dolophon Johnston, became head bookkeeper at the Treasury Department. Her mother, Frances Antoinette (Benjamin) Johnston, was related to the wife of Grover Cleveland, a connection that later helped her daughter to establish herself as the unofficial "court" photographer of the White House in the 1890s.

Johnston had originally planned to become an artist. Graduating from Notre Dame Convent, Govanston, Md., in 1833, she went to Paris and studied drawing and painting at the Julien Academy from 1884 to 1885. Returning to Washington, she continued her education as a member of the Art Students League and decided to become a journalist. At first she illustrated her articles with her own drawings, but soon followed the technical developments of the day and acquired her own camera in 1887. After a brief and unsatisfactory apprenticeship with a commercial photographer, she studied photography with Thomas William Smillie, then director of the Division of Photography at the Smithsonian Institution. Her first published photographs—illustrations for her article on the United States Mint—appeared in *Demorest's Family Magazine* in December 1889. By 1890 she had her own professionally equipped portrait studio in Washington, and was also providing photographs not only to *Demorest's* but to the *Ladies' Home Journal* and other magazines as well. By the mid-1890s she was concentrating almost exclusively on photography, no longer writing the articles she was illustrating.

In the early 1890s Johnston did numerous photographs of the interior of the White House; these were published as a book, *The White House,* in 1893. As in this case, most of her early work was done on commission. She never neglected the artistic side of photography, however, and the artistic quality of her work was recognized when, together with GERTRUDE KÄSEBIER and Clarence White, she was made a member of the jury for the Philadelphia Photographic Society exhibition in 1899. In 1904

Johnston became an associate member of the Photo-Secession, the group of photographers, led by Alfred Stieglitz, organized to promote photography as one of the fine arts. She made only one contribution to their publication, *Camera Work,* a short note on Käsebier.

While in agreement with the photosecessionist point of view, Johnston was especially drawn to the documentary possibilities of photography. She rapidly developed her own documentary style, a combination of photographic didacticism, humanistic portrayal, and a journalistic concentration on elementary information. In 1899, on a summer trip to Europe, she won national recognition for her photographs of Admiral George Dewey and his fleet in Naples as they returned from victory at Manila Bay. Between 1891 and 1910, however, her work was primarily devoted to industry and education, two areas of particular concern to Progressive reformers. To study the effects of industrialization on workers and their environment she visited the Kohinoor Mines at Shenandoah City, Pa. (1891), the iron ore mines near Lake Superior (1903), a shoe factory in Lynn, Mass. (1895), and a cigar box factory (1910). Concerned with the aesthetic restoration of personal dignity, Johnston's portrayals of working women are undramatic accounts, stressing the workers' individuality rather than their deprivation as a result of poor working conditions.

Like her friend Jacob Riis and many other reformers of her time, Johnston believed in the possibility of social change as a result of both education and social engineering, a belief reflected in her remarkable photographic record of progressive education. In 1900 she gained international recognition when her photographs of the public schools of Washington, D.C., and of the Hampton (Va.) Institute, a training school for black youths, won a gold medal at the Paris Exposition. The Hampton photographs document the benefits of progressive education for blacks through a series of didactic before and after shots. They also portray in detail both the educational practices of the Institute and the life of poor blacks in Virginia. Because of this work she was invited to attend the Third International Photographic Congress, also held in Paris in 1900. The only American female photographer present, she was awarded the Palmes Académique for her contributions to the congress.

Johnston continued her work on educational institutions with a series of photographs of the Carlisle (Pa.) Indian School (1900) and of Tuskegee Institute (1902, 1906), neither of them as didactically composed as the Hampton photographs. At the same time, she was doing portrait photography, producing many sensitive character studies of national celebrities, including presidents William McKinley and Theodore Roosevelt (and his family) as well as authors Mark Twain and Joel Chandler Harris and woman's rights champion SUSAN B. ANTHONY. In her portraits, she successfully caught the personal characteristics of her subjects, rather than duplicating in studied poses their established public images.

Johnston also developed a style very distinctively her own in her pioneering work in architectural photography. In addition to her early White House pictures, Johnston photographed the "White City" of the World's Columbian Exposition (1893) and the Louisiana Purchase Exposition (1904). Between 1913 and 1917 she worked with a partner, Mattie Edward Hewitt, out of a studio in New York, specializing in photographs of architecture, estates, and gardens; during the 1920s she counted the Vanderbilts, Whitneys, and Astors among her clients and also became known as a lecturer on gardens. Most important, however, was her work on southern colonial architecture which began in 1927 with a commission to photograph a Virginia estate. Realizing that the more ordinary colonial buildings in southern towns were not being photographed for posterity, she obtained a commission in the same year to do a photographic survey of Fredericksburg, Va. The Fredericksburg photographs were later exhibited at the Library of Congress (1929), leading to commissions for surveys of buildings and homes in Virginia and other southern states. Between 1933 and 1940, she made more than 7,000 negatives in nine southern states. The work was financed by a series of Carnegie Foundation grants, beginning in 1933. In their careful attention to detail and in their recording of buildings soon to disappear, Johnston's photographs made a major contribution to the history of southern colonial architecture and of southern life.

Although not a feminist in any conventional sense, Johnston retained throughout her career the quality of bohemian individualism that characterized her Washington days and enjoyed her conspicuous role as an independent photographer and businesswoman. She based the course of her career entirely upon her own judgment, leaving its practical management to her agents, who had to remind her constantly of deadlines, assignments, and financial obligations which she was prone to ignore. In 1947 she donated her prints, negatives, and correspondence to the Library of Congress; they are an invaluable record of her times.

In the early 1940s, Johnston moved to New Orleans where she remained until her death in 1952 at the age of eighty-eight. In 1895 the Washington Times had described her as an "ambitious young woman . . . ranking with the foremost amateur photographers in this country." After her death, however, she was remembered above all for her relentless professionalism and for the standards she had set as a pioneer in photojournalism, and in portrait and architectural photography.

[In addition to the MSS., papers, and negatives at the Library of Congress, 1,200 of Johnston's negatives and cyanotype copies are in the Huntington Library, San Marino, Calif. She also published *Descriptive Sketches* (1890), *Mammoth Cave by Flash Light* (1893), and a series of six articles, "The Foremost Women Photographers in America," in *Ladies' Home Jour.* (1890). Her photographs of southern architecture are in three books, *Colonial Churches in Virginia*, with H. I. Brock (1930); *The Early Architecture of North Carolina*, with T. T. Waterman (1941); and Frederick D. Nichols, *The Early Architecture of Georgia* (1957). The *Hampton Album*, with an introductory essay by Lincoln Kirstein, was republished in 1966. Pete Daniel and Raymond Smock, *A Talent for Detail: The Photography of Miss Frances Benjamin Johnston* (1974), provides samples of her work and biographical information. See also Paul Vanderbilt, "Frances Benjamin Johnston," *Jour. of the Am. Inst. of Architects,* Nov. 1952; Robert Sidney Kahan, *The Antecedents of American Photojournalism* (1969); John C. L. Andreassen, "Frances Benjamin Johnston and Her Views of Uncle Sam," *Louisiana Hist.,* 1960, 130–36; Anne Tucker, "Frances Benjamin Johnston, 1864–1952," *The Woman's Eye* (1973); and *Dict. Am. Biog.,* Supp. Five.]

OLAF HANSEN

JONES, Margo, Dec. 12, 1912–July 24, 1955. Producer, director.

Margo Jones, regional theater pioneer, passionate advocate of theater-in-the-round, and patron saint of new playwrights, was born in Livingston, Texas, the second daughter and one of four children of Richard Harper Jones, a lawyer, and Martha Pearl (Collins) Jones, a teacher. Born Margaret Virginia Jones, she preferred to be called by the more theatrical name of Margo. In her book, *Theatre-in-the-Round* (1951), she recalls that until she was eleven she wanted to be a lawyer and often sat in the local courtroom watching her father argue cases. "Then one day it occurred to me that the reason I enjoyed the courtroom sessions was that they were so much like plays." So at eleven she knew what she wanted to do: "put on plays—and up went a sheet in the barn where my sister and my brothers joined me in my first producing-directing venture."

An avid reader of Shakespeare from childhood on, Jones first saw a professional production of a play in Fort Worth at the age of fifteen: Walter Hampden as Cyrano de Bergerac. Her high school grades were so high that she enrolled in the College of Industrial Arts, Denton, Texas (now Texas Woman's University) at fifteen, receiving a B.S. in speech in 1931. The college offered no graduate degree in theater; instead Jones took her M.A. in psychology, in 1932. The subject of her thesis was taken not from the clinic but from the stage: "The Abnormal Ways Out of Emotional Conflict as Reflected in the Dramas of Henrik Ibsen."

In college, Jones directed several plays; she occasionally acted, "but always with the understanding that I was doing it to acquaint myself with the actor's viewpoint and problems, never with any ambition to become an actress myself." She also began her practice of reading at least one play each day. When she left college, she obtained a job as a "glorified office girl" in the newly organized Southwestern School of the Theatre in Dallas. She observed and studied all phases of theater for a year, then in 1933 directed at the Pasadena Summer School of the Theatre in California. That fall Jones got her first full-time directing job, with the Ojai (Calif.) Community Players. She directed *Hedda Gabler* and wrote and produced two successful one-act plays. As with acting, she did not intend to become a professional playwright, but "wanted to walk in the shoes of a dramatist."

Soon after her year at Ojai, she traveled around the world as companion and secretary to a wealthy woman, attending the theater in Japan, China, India, France, and England. In the fall of 1935, for the first time in her life, she arrived in New York, where she was inspired by the work of the Group Theatre. She returned to Texas to become assistant director of the short-lived Houston Little Theatre, part of the Federal Theatre Project. In 1936 Jones went to Europe again for the Moscow Art Theatre Festival, which she covered for the *Houston Chronicle*.

In November 1936, the Houston recreation department hired her to teach playground directors how to stage children's plays. She convinced the city officials to let her start an adult group, the Houston Community Players. Miraculously, it became self-supporting by means of ticket sales; Jones switched to it as a full-time job, and the nine original members of the company expanded to six hundred. Among her notable productions were Elmer Rice's *Judgment Day*, actually staged in the main courtroom of the Harris County Courthouse, and two

world premieres (almost unheard of among community theaters): *Special Edition,* by *Houston Post* city editor Harold Young (1938–39), and Edwin Justus Mayer's *Sunrise in My Pocket* (1941).

In May 1939, as delegate from the south at the Confederacy of American Community Theatres in Washington, D.C., Jones was first introduced to theater-in-the-round. Impressed by an arena-style production of the Blue Room Players of Portland, Oreg., performed in a hotel ballroom, she determined to attempt something similar in Houston, and experimented with the technique in the mezzanine of the Rice Hotel in Houston. She longed, however, for a full-time professional theater.

The Houston Community Players suspended operations during World War II. In October 1942, Margo Jones accepted a teaching-directing assignment in the drama department of the University of Texas at Austin, continuing her search for new plays and working largely on experimental theater projects. She took a leave of absence to stage *You Touched Me,* a new play by Tennessee Williams and Donald Windham, first at the Cleveland Play House and then at the Pasadena Playhouse. At Pasadena in the summer of 1944 she directed another Williams work, *The Purification.*

The plan for a permanent, professional repertory theater in Dallas took shape in her mind in December 1943. In the summer of 1944, she received a grant from the Rockefeller Foundation and infinite help from John Rosenfield, drama editor and critic of the *Dallas Morning News.* The Dallas project was interrupted in 1944 while Jones directed Tennessee Williams's first Broadway production, *The Glass Menagerie,* and again in 1946, when she returned to Broadway to direct Maxine Wood's *On Whitman Avenue* and Maxwell Anderson's *Joan of Lorraine.*

Margo Jones realized her dream with the opening of Theatre '47 on June 3, 1947. (The theater changed names each New Year's Eve.) The permanent, professional theater-in-the-round opened on the grounds of the State Fair Association in Dallas with William Inge's *Farther Off from Heaven.* That same year, the theater presented Williams's *Summer and Smoke,* which moved to Broadway in 1948. At Theatre '55, in January of that year, she presented one of her most famous and successful discoveries, *Inherit the Wind* by Jerome Lawrence and Robert E. Lee, which she then coproduced on Broadway. Throughout the life of her theater, Jones was dedicated to new plays and new playwrights; of the eighty-five plays she produced in Dallas, fifty-seven were new scripts.

Jones's accidental death in 1955 was an indirect result of her newest hobby, painting. Cleaning fluid had been used to remove paint spilled on her carpet; she fell asleep, inhaled the fumes from the fluid, and died shortly after of acute kidney failure. She was mourned throughout the international theater community. Without her dedication and enthusiasm, her own theater did not long continue, but Jones's influence was epidemic. A theater evangelist, her passion for "theater everywhere" inspired many theaters and theater workers, among them Zelda Fichandler of Washington's Arena Stage and Nina Vance of Houston's Alley Theatre. *Theatre-in-the-Round* became the bible of decentralized theater. In one of her written comments about Soviet audiences, Jones perhaps described herself: "They seem to find in the theatre not only glamour, but life itself!"

[The files of the Dallas Theatre in the Margo Jones Coll., Dallas Public Library, contain production data, scripts, professional and personal correspondence, and business material. Jones's career is documented in clipping files in the Billy Rose Theatre Coll., N.Y. Public Library, and the Harvard Theatre Coll. Margo Jones traces the development of her theater and her theater philosophy in "Theatre '50: A Dream Come True," in David Harrison Stevens, ed., *Ten Talents in the American Theatre* (1957). In addition to her own book, sources of biographical information include Don B. Wilmeth, "A History of the Margo Jones Theatre" (Ph.D. diss., Univ. of Ill., 1964); J. Wesley Ziegler, "Margo Jones: Legacy and Legend," *Theatre Today*, Summer 1970; and Ronald L. Davis, "Margaret Virginia (Margo) Jones," *Handbook of Texas* (1976). See also Murray Schumach, "A Texas Tornado Hits Broadway," *N.Y. Times Mag.*, Oct. 17, 1948; William Shapard, "Margo Jones and Her Theatre in Dallas, 1945–49" (M.A. thesis, Southern Methodist Univ., 1960). Her discovery of *Inherit the Wind* is further documented in Jerome Lawrence, *Actor: The Life and Times of Paul Muni* (1974). Information on the Margo Jones award, established by Jerome Lawrence and Robert E. Lee and presented annually to a producing manager who presents new works in the tradition of Margo Jones, is available from Silverstone and Rosenthal, Attorneys, New York City. Obituaries appeared in the *N.Y. Times*, July 25, 1955, and the *Dallas Morning News*, July 26, 1955.]

JEROME LAWRENCE

JOPLIN, Janis Lyn, Jan. 19, 1943–Oct. 4, 1970. Singer.

Janis Joplin, the "first female superstar of rock music," was born in Port Arthur, Texas, an oil refinery town on the Texas-Louisiana border.

Her mother, Dorothy (East), was born in Nebraska; Seth Joplin, whom she married in 1936, was a Texas native. Janis was the first of their three children, two daughters and a son.

Seth Joplin worked for a canning company and later as an engineer for Texaco; Dorothy Joplin later became the registrar of a local business college. Although their second daughter, Laura, born when Janis was six, was a colicky baby who monopolized her mother's attention, Janis had a "very protective relationship" to her sister, Dorothy Joplin recalled (Friedman, p. 11). As a child, Janis showed an early interest in art and had private lessons when she was nine and ten. Her mother sang, although not professionally, and Janis was in the church choir and the junior high school glee club.

During her high school years Janis Joplin and her friends listened to jazz. She memorized songs from records by BESSIE SMITH, Odetta, and Leadbelly. Joplin remembered singing an Odetta number at a beach party: "They told me I had a good voice, and I thought, wow, that's far out, and when I played records, I'd sing them to myself" (Dalton, p. 39). She graduated from Thomas Jefferson High School in Port Arthur in 1960, and then drifted for two years, taking a business course at a local college, moving between Texas and California, working as a part-time keypunch operator in Los Angeles. For a time in 1961 she hung out in the North Beach area of San Francisco, drawn there by her interest in beatnik poets and by her identification with the beats: "In Texas I was a beatnik, a weirdo," she later told an interviewer. "Texas is OK if you want to settle down and do your thing quietly, but it's not for outrageous people, and I was always outrageous" (quoted in *Rolling Stone*, Oct. 29, 1970).

Joplin returned periodically to Port Arthur, where she began to sing in local coffeehouses. In the summer of 1962 she left for Austin to become an art student at the University of Texas. Her first professional engagements were in Austin, singing with a bluegrass band, the Waller Creek Boys. But in January 1963, humiliated by her nomination as "ugliest man on campus," she again left Texas for San Francisco. Her last attempt at life in Port Arthur came in the summer of 1965 when she went home to try to kick a growing drug habit and to get ready for her marriage to a man she had met in San Francisco. He was, according to Myra Friedman, a "soft-spoken charmer . . . gentle and . . . romantic." He was also a drug pusher and he had a reputation for using and then casually discarding women (pp. 56–57). For ten months she tried to live as Port Arthur wished. Then she was jilted.

In June 1966 fellow Texan Chet Helms, then a successful rock promoter in San Francisco, suggested that the rock group Big Brother and the Holding Company might use Joplin as a singer. Her first concert with them came that month. Before, singing with a bluegrass band, she had not sung so loud. But "with all that rhythm and power" and amplifiers, she "found herself moving and dancing like another rhythm instrument . . . She was a mean blues singer and she looked it, with her trailing draperies and tangled hair. San Francisco fell in love with her" (Roxon, p. 47). A year later, at the first Monterey International Pop Festival, she sang "Love Is Like a Ball and Chain" and the press and big music names from New York agreed: "Janis Joplin is it!"

She had a second big success in the summer of 1967, at the Monterey Jazz Festival. Joplin then signed a personal management contract with Bob Dylan's manager, Albert Grossman, who became a father, companion, and adviser to her. Under his management she was soon earning over $150,000 a year.

Janis Joplin made her New York City debut in February 1968 at the Anderson Theatre. There she "controlled the entire audience with her body . . . [she] made her whole performance a frantic, sweating, passionate, demanding sexual act" (Roxon, pp. 47–48). Capitalizing on the momentum of her career, she appeared later in 1968 at the Newport (R.I.) Folk Festival and in New York City at Fillmore East. Her first album, *Cheap Thrills*, was also released that year, and sold over a million copies in a few months. In 1969 she toured the United States and also made an enormously successful London debut at the Albert Hall. She capped the year with a performance in Madison Square Garden in December 1969 that brought the audience to a frenzy of excitement.

Joplin realized that her recordings made with Big Brother did not capture the sound and excitement of their live concerts. At the end of 1968 she decided to form her own band, and asked Sam Andrew, a guitarist with Big Brother, to come with her. After trying for a time in 1969 with the Kozmic Blues Band (as well as with a few other groups earlier), she finally built a new band she said she loved. The Full Tilt Boogie Band debuted in Louisville in June 1970.

At the same time, Joplin was drinking heavily and again taking drugs; a bottle of Southern Comfort became her trademark. She saw herself as "a victim of my own insides . . . It's not what isn't but what you wish *was* that makes unhappiness. The hole, the vacuum . . . I think I think too much. That's why I drink" (Dalton, pp. 39, 53). She believed, however, that performing

provided a release, that it had taught her to make feeling "work *for* me . . . If you're on stage and it's really working, and you've got the audience with you, it's a *oneness* you feel" (Dalton, p. 39).

Janis Joplin had a continuing love affair with her audiences. In her private life, by her own account, she had many "one-night stands" as well as highly publicized longer romances with Country Joe McDonald and Kris Kristofferson. In the fall of 1970 she was planning to marry Seth Morgan, a Berkeley student and son of a wealthy New York family. But in October, with a dozen concerts booked, a new record being made, and wedding plans underway, Joplin died in a Los Angeles motel of acute heroin-morphine intoxication.

The controversy and comment that followed her death revealed Joplin's power as a cultural image for the late 1960s. *The New Yorker*, calling her death "in all likelihood a miserable accident," saw her addiction to drugs as "not a personal but a cultural idiosyncrasy." Her defiance of convention made her a folk hero to her followers. So, too, did her attempts to use not only the language of rock music but also the language of clothes and of the movement of her body to free her generation from the inhibitions of their parents.

Taking raw emotion, organizing it into music, and transmitting it to her audience directly, freely, and without limits, Joplin suggested a new direction and new possibilities for women performers. Her recordings cannot approximate the impact of experiencing Joplin in concert. But they can provide intense pleasure from her sound, her phrasing, and her concentrated explosive emotion, and they suggest the liberation Joplin experienced by expressing her feelings through the blues. Some argued that a white woman had no right to sing the blues, but Joplin introduced a new generation of Americans to this music, and her effort brought forth new appreciation for great singers like Bessie Smith and Big Mama Thornton. She helped to create a new variation of this distinctly American music, a marriage of rhythm and blues with rock.

Joplin brought to her music a distinctive sound and look, passion, and an honest interpretive ability. Her hold over an audience was as great as that of Elvis Presley and her success was an extraordinary and unprecedented feat in the male-dominated rock and music world.

[Songs written solely by Janis Joplin include "Down on Me," "Mary Jane," "Daddy, Daddy, Daddy," "No Reason for Livin'," "What Good Can Drinkin' Do," "Turtle Blues," "Move Over," and "Mercedes Benz." She coauthored "I Need a Man to

Love" and "Oh, Sweet Mary." All of Joplin's albums were on the Columbia label. Early recordings from 1963 and 1965 in Austin and 1965 in San Francisco have been reproduced on *Janis* (1975). Other albums are *Big Brother and the Holding Company* (1968); *Cheap Thrills* (1968); *I Got Dem Ol' Kozmic Blues Again Mama!* (1969); *Pearl* (1970); *Joplin in Concert* (1970); and *Janis Joplin's Greatest Hits* (1972). The best biographical account is Myra Friedman, *Buried Alive: The Biography of Janis Joplin* (1973), based on Friedman's working relationship and friendship with Joplin as well as on interviews with countless people who knew and worked with her. There are twelve pages of photographs. A controversial account of Joplin during the San Francisco years is Peggy Caserta as told to Dan Knapp, *Going Down with Janis* (1973). David Dalton, *Janis* (1971), is a long, warm memoir interspersed with transcriptions of many hours of taped interviews with Joplin; it includes excellent photographs, a record of Joplin singing and talking, and reprints of important articles from *Rolling Stone* magazine. A series of articles by Jane Perlez in the *N.Y. Post*, Feb. 20–March 18, 1974, covers the lawsuit by Joplin's manager against the insurance company that issued him an accidental death policy on her life. For a description of Joplin working live with Big Brother and the Holding Company see Lillian Roxon's article on Joplin in her *Rock Encyclopedia* (1971), pp. 46–49. A series by Dolores Barclay for Associated Press, "Music Was '60s' Conscience" appeared in the *Omaha* (Neb.) *World-Herald*, May 1979. Peter Barnes, "Rebirth of the Blues," *Newsweek*, May 26, 1969, sets Joplin within the music world of the 1960s. See also *Current Biog.*, 1970, and Ellen Willis, "Rock, Etc.," *New Yorker*, Aug. 14, 1971. Films about Joplin include: *Janis*, produced by Crawley Films, distributed by Universal, and *Monterey Pop*, which shows the performance that brought her to national prominence. Death certificate obtained from Calif. Dept. of Public Health.]

MEGAN TERRY

JORDAN, Sara Claudia Murray, Oct. 20, 1884–Nov. 21, 1959. Physician.

Sara Murray Jordan, director of the department of gastroenterology at the Lahey Clinic in Boston, was born in Newton, Mass., the second of seven children and first of four daughters in the family of Patrick Andrew and Maria (Stuart) Murray. Her father, a native of County Cork, Ireland, owned and operated a carriage and auto body repair shop in Newton. Her mother was born in Maine of Scots-English descent. Sara Murray graduated from the Newton public schools and entered Radcliffe College in 1901. Though her father disapproved of her childhood ambition to practice medicine, he and her mother gave critical assistance during her years of medical training and early practice.

Another enduring family tie was her close, lifelong relationship with her sister Mary.

At Radcliffe Sara Murray completed her undergraduate degree in classics in three years, receiving an A.B. in 1904. That year she entered the doctoral program in classical philology and archaeology at the University of Munich. Her dissertation, an analysis of two sixteenth-century translations of a tenth-century Greek text, was completed in 1908 and published in Germany two years later. After teaching briefly at Adelphi Academy in Brooklyn, Murray returned to Munich and on Jan. 14, 1913, married Sebastian Jordan, a young German lawyer she had met when both were students. Their daughter, Mary Stuart, was born in 1914 while the young couple lived in Traunstein. Five months later, at her father's insistence, Sara Murray Jordan returned to her parents' home in Newton with her infant daughter. World War I separated the Jordans permanently and they were divorced in 1921.

Sometime between 1914 and 1917 Jordan determined to become a doctor. She was admitted to Tufts College Medical School in 1917 at the age of thirty-three on condition that she complete courses in chemistry and zoology. When her probationary status was continued despite fulfillment of these requirements, Jordan threatened to seek an investigation by the American Medical Association (AMA). Her regular standing was acknowledged, and in 1921 she graduated at the top of her class.

In her second year at medical school, Jordan was selected by Frank H. Lahey, then a young and enterprising surgeon, as his assistant in a study of his patients admitted to the New England Deaconess Hospital. Her responsibilities included administration of a relatively new procedure for evaluating thyroid function, a test of the basal metabolism rate. This research led in 1921 to her first scientific paper, "Basal Metabolism as an Index of Treatment in Diseases of the Thyroid," coauthored with Lahey. Impressed with Jordan's ability and perseverance, Lahey helped arrange an internship for her at the Worcester (Mass.) Memorial Hospital, followed by training in gastroenterology under Dr. Bertram Sippy in Chicago.

In July 1922 Jordan returned to Boston to join Lahey, surgeon Howard M. Clute, and anesthesiologist Lincoln F. Size in what soon emerged as an unusual group practice. While this venture was getting under way in Lahey's Beacon Street office, Jordan opened a small general practice from the Brookline home in which she lived with her school-age daughter. When the Lahey Clinic moved to its own well-equipped building in 1926, Jordan was a full-time and essential member of the team. As a resourceful specialist in diseases associated with the tensions of public life, she contributed significantly to establishing the stellar reputation of the Lahey Clinic in a community traditionally dominated by the well-established private practices of physicians linked to Boston's three medical schools. An emphasis on diagnosis and on the coordination of surgical and medical treatment established both the clinic's position and Sara Jordan's eminence as an authority on the diseases of the gastrointestinal tract.

Her management of famous patients whose peptic ulcers were part of their renown flourished on catchy aphorisms as well as sound medical practice. Jordan was widely quoted as advising that "every businessman over 50 should have a daily nap and nip—a short nap after lunch, and a relaxing highball before dinner." Her clinical skills won patients to the prescribed regimen of diet, recreation, and rest, while this conservative therapy earned the approval of fellow physicians. She consistently favored medical over surgical intervention.

Encouraged by her patient Harold W. Ross, editor of *The New Yorker*, Sara Jordan and Sheila Hibben, the magazine's culinary expert, wrote a cookbook, *Good Food for Bad Stomachs* (1951). Many of Jordan's publications, including the annual oration to the Massachusetts Medical Society in 1953, "Medicine and the Doctor in Word and Epigram," reflected her earlier scholarship in classical history and literature. From her first scientific article to the daily syndicated column "Health and Happiness," which she wrote after her retirement in 1958, Jordan was known for her erudition and flawless prose.

Her colleagues recognized Sara Jordan's contributions to medicine, electing her the first woman president of the American Gastroenterological Association (1942–44) and secretary, vice chairman, and chairman of the AMA Section on Gastroenterology (1941–48). She was one of five American women awarded the Elizabeth Blackwell Citation in 1951 for the teaching and practice of medicine; she also received the Julius Friedenwald Medal for outstanding achievement in her specialty (1952). Her standing as a community leader led to her election to the board of directors of the Boston Chamber of Commerce (1948) and to the board of trustees of Tufts University (1951). During

World War II she chaired the Women's Committee on Procurement and Assignment of the War Manpower Commission. On numerous occasions Jordan spoke to the issue of women's personal and public roles, usually stressing her conviction that femininity need not conflict with professional achievement. In a 1954 article, "The Woman Doctor of Today," she acknowledged the "sex prejudice" of male physicians in the past, but concluded optimistically that such prejudice "no longer exists in medicine today."

Always an advocate of personal and medical moderation, Dr. Jordan led a full but carefully regulated life. She enjoyed a round of golf early in the morning and gave up smoking at the age of fifty-one. With Penfield Mower, a Boston stockbroker whom she married in 1935, she maintained a home in Marblehead, Mass., and was an attentive grandmother to her daughter's five children. She diagnosed her own final illness, cancer of the colon, of which she died in 1959 at the New England Baptist Hospital, one of the three Boston hospitals where she had practiced medicine.

[Small collections of personal papers and memorabilia, consisting mainly of letters written to Sara Jordan, are in the Schlesinger Library, Radcliffe College, and the Tufts Univ. Archives. Also useful is the Frank H. Lahey folder at the Tufts Archives. The Lahey Clinic has a bibliography of her scientific articles, which include "Basal Metabolism as an Index of Treatment in Diseases of the Thyroid," *Boston Med. and Surgical Jour.*, April 7, 1921, pp. 348–58, and "Medicine and the Doctor in Word and Epigram," *New England Jour. Med.*, May 21, 1953, pp. 875–83. Also of interest are her doctoral dissertation, *A Study of the Life of Andreas: The Fool for the Sake of Christ* (1910), and "The Woman Doctor of Today," *Radcliffe Quart.*, Aug. 1954, pp. 27–29. Information about her early life can be found in the privately published *Sara Murray Jordan: A Memorial Volume* (1944), a copy of which is at the Schlesinger Library, Radcliffe College. A biographical sketch is in *Current Biog.*, 1954. Obituaries appeared in the *N.Y. Times* and *Boston Globe*, Nov. 22, 1959. Additional information was provided by Jordan's daughter, Mary Stuart Logan, and granddaughter, Deborah Ann Logan, and by Dr. David P. Boyd. Death certificate supplied by Mass. Dept. of Public Health.]

BARBARA GUTMANN ROSENKRANTZ

JOSEPH, Mother Mary. *See* ROGERS, Mother Mary Joseph (Mary Josephine).

K

KELLER, Helen, June 27, 1880–June 1, 1968. Writer, feminist, advocate for the handicapped.

Helen Keller was born in Tuscumbia, Ala., the oldest of three children, two daughters and one son, of Arthur H. and Kate (Adams) Keller. Her father, a Confederate veteran and publisher of a country weekly, was married to Memphis belle Kate Adams, some twenty years his junior, after the death of his first wife, by whom he had two sons. Her mother was related to the John Adams family of New England.

At the age of nineteen months Helen Keller was stricken by acute congestion of the stomach and brain, which left her deaf, blind, and mute. Her afflictions turned her into a wild destructive child; yet she also displayed a native brightness, contriving sixty signs to indicate what she wanted. Kate Keller, a cultivated woman as well as a prodigious housekeeper, was interested to read in Charles Dickens's *American Notes* of Samuel Gridley Howe's success at the Perkins Institution in Boston with the deaf-blind LAURA BRIDGMAN. Brought to Alexander Graham Bell at six, Helen impressed him with her liveliness, and he also suggested Perkins. Howe's successor there, Michael Anagnos, promptly recommended a recent Perkins graduate, the formerly blind ANNE SULLIVAN (MACY), then twenty, as teacher and governess.

Within two weeks after her arrival in Tuscumbia in March 1887, Sullivan, with an inspired mixture of love and discipline, established her mastery over the unruly Helen. Two weeks later in the episode of the water pump—immortalized in William Gibson's play *The Miracle Worker*—Helen learned that everything had a name and that the manual alphabet was the key to everything she wanted to know. On fire with this realization, Helen in a few months learned 300 words. By mid-July she wrote her first letter to her mother, and by the end of 1887, through Anagnos's flair for publicity, she was known internationally as "one of the most remarkable children in existence."

In May 1888 Annie Sullivan brought her charge to Boston; they stayed with Anagnos, who persuaded them to come to Perkins on a permanent basis. Helen Keller took Boston by storm, but while it lionized her it ignored her teacher. In a defiant press interview Sullivan asserted that Helen was not a "regular" pupil at Perkins and "I have the whole charge of her." An intuitive teacher, she was also temperamental and high-handed. She did not, for example, wish Helen to learn to speak, and only Helen's pleadings overcame her resistance.

Helen Keller's life mission—to help the disadvantaged, particularly the blind and the deaf—already manifested itself at Perkins. Hearing about four-year-old Tommy Stringer, triply afflicted like herself, she persuaded Anagnos to take him in, then raised a fund for him.

Her relationship to Perkins crumbled after a story she wrote that Anagnos published in *The Mentor*, the school's alumni association magazine, proved to have been taken almost word for word from a book published in the 1870s. Sullivan, who had sent the story to Anagnos, claimed she had never read the original or even heard of the book and that it had been read to Helen without her knowledge. A court of investigation, set up by Anagnos at the insistence of jealous teachers, divided four to four over their guilt. Although he cast a tie-breaking vote in their favor, Anagnos gradually became persuaded that Sullivan had duped him. When she decided her pupil should not return to Perkins, he turned against them, whispering that one or both was "a living lie." But Boston remained faithful and eminent citizens like Alexander Graham Bell and John Hitz, the superintendent of the Volta Bureau (which disseminated information regarding the deaf), stood by them. At Bell's request Hitz made an independent inquiry into the affair; his conclusions vindicating Sullivan and Keller were published by the Volta Bureau in its first *Helen Keller: Souvenir*.

In the autumn of 1894, with Bell's blessing, Helen Keller and Annie Sullivan moved to New York, so Keller could attend the Wright-Humason School, established to teach oral language to deaf children. Their expenses were underwritten by John Spaulding, a sugar millionaire. Her speech did not improve, but she and Sullivan met and conquered New York society. Through the bibliophile Lawrence Hutton they met Mark Twain and William Dean Howells, and the poets Edmund Clarence Stedman and Richard Gilder. Although Keller's father had come upon hard times and John Spaulding died, Sullivan managed to spur a group of Keller's friends into setting up a fund for her further education.

With this backing Helen Keller enrolled in 1896 in the Cambridge School for Young Ladies, headed by Arthur Gilman, to prepare for Radcliffe College. After only nine months she passed the first battery of admission tests triumphantly. Sullivan wanted her to take the remaining tests within two years, but Gilman opposed so heavy a schedule. When he insisted, Sullivan flouted his authority. He moved to separate her from Keller, but Keller's mother

389

as well as her close friends, whatever their misgivings about Sullivan's methods, recoiled from such a step. They recognized that these two, for better or for worse, were bound to each other.

They left Gilman's academy and took refuge with a friend on his farm in Wrentham, Mass. Keller worked with a private tutor for two years, took the remaining admission tests, and received a certificate of admission for Radcliffe College, along with notice that she had passed with credit in advanced Latin. Radcliffe resisted admitting her, but finally yielded, and she entered in September 1900. She carried a full schedule, accompanied to every class by Sullivan, who spelled the lectures into her hands. She took seventeen and one half courses to fulfill the requirements for an A.B., but no science, mathematics, or fine arts.

Through Charles Copeland's composition course, her writing came to the attention of the *Ladies' Home Journal*, which persuaded her to write her autobiography. When she and Teacher (as Keller now always called Sullivan) ran into difficulties, mutual friends suggested they employ a young Harvard University literature instructor, John Albert Macy, to assist them. *The Story of My Life* appeared in 1902. Public reception was little short of lyrical and the book in time became, as the publisher predicted, a classic. An old controversy revived—which was the genius, Helen Keller or her teacher? Some contended that Sullivan's methods were not original, that it was Keller who was the miracle; others, including at times Sullivan herself, argued that the teacher could have accomplished the same with any deaf-blind child. Most were content to see miracle and miracle worker as one.

With the book's proceeds and some shares of sugar stock Spaulding had given them, they bought a seven-acre farm in Wrentham. While still an undergraduate, Helen Keller wrote a 7,500-word essay on the "goodness of life" which was published as a book, *Optimism* (1903). Religion bolstered her optimistic faith, but she rebuffed a Catholic effort to convert her. She preferred the doctrines of Emanuel Swedenborg, to which she had been introduced at the age of sixteen by Hitz and to which she remained faithful until her death, somewhat to the distress of her Presbyterian family.

In June 1904 Keller graduated from Radcliffe cum laude, with the additional citation, "excellent in English letters," an unprecedented achievement for a deaf-blind woman. Her classmates wrote, "Beside her task our efforts pale," and gave her an ovation when she received her diploma, but she and Sullivan hurried away, both bitter that Sullivan had received no recognition.

They settled down in Wrentham. In 1905 Annie Sullivan married John Macy, eleven years her junior, but only after he agreed to her stipulation that Keller would continue to come first in the household. John Macy joined his wife as Keller's collaborator. Encouraged by Richard Gilder of the Century publishing house, Keller wrote several essays about her ways of knowing the world, beginning with one called "The Seeing Hand." The collection, entitled *The World I Live In* (1909), ended with a Whitmanesque poem, "The Chant of Darkness." William James praised her "for the success with which you have told so much truth about human nature which nobody had suspected." A 600-line patriotic poem, *A Song of the Stone Wall*, was published in 1910. "And whence comes this power over sound?" asked an astonished London *Times* reviewer. How much the Macys contributed to these poems remains conjectural, but after their marriage ended Keller never again wrote with such lyric power.

Busy though she was as a writer, Keller pitched in to help improve the conditions of the blind. When Massachusetts established its pioneering State Commission for the Blind, Gov. Curtis Guild, Jr., in 1906 appointed Helen Keller to it. She led the campaign against ophthalmia neonatorum, the blindness of newborn infants. Because it is caused by venereal disease in the mother, this was an unmentionable subject in polite circles until Keller broke the taboo.

The Wrentham trio flirted briefly with the thesis that Bacon was the author of Shakespeare's plays but abandoned this crusade for the more fundamental one of socialism. In 1909 Keller followed John Macy and became a member of the Socialist party. She was already a militant suffragist who preferred the aggressive tactics of Emmeline Pankhurst to the moderation of CARRIE CHAPMAN CATT. Anne Macy held back; the women's movement did not interest her and she was a pessimist about human perfectibility, male or female. All three, however, ardently supported the Lawrence, Mass., textile strike led by the Industrial Workers of the World (IWW). A red flag hung on the wall of Helen Keller's study. Socialism gave direction and excitement to her life and provided a theme for her writing. A collection of her socialist essays, *Out of the Dark*, was published in 1913.

Keller and Anne Macy had begun to make paid appearances on the lecture platform to supplement their income. But they were still unable to make ends meet and in 1913, despite her socialist convictions, Keller finally accepted a

$5,000-a-year lifetime pension offered by Andrew Carnegie.

The Wrentham idyll fell apart when John Macy moved away in 1913. In marrying Annie Sullivan, he later explained, he found that he had married an institution. She never reconciled herself to his departure and refused to give him a divorce. Without him, the two women preferred to be on the road and became standbys of the Chautauqua lecture circuit. Mary Agnes (Polly) Thomson (1885–1960), a young Scotswoman, joined them in 1914 as secretary, hairdresser, and housekeeper, and accompanied them on their cross-country tours. These took them to the 1915 San Francisco Exposition, where Maria Montessori and Annie Sullivan Macy exchanged glowing words of praise and Helen Keller proclaimed herself "a product of the Montessori method."

As President Woodrow Wilson abandoned neutrality in the European conflict, Keller turned into a passionate advocate of the general strike against war and joined the IWW. Invited to sail on Henry Ford's Peace Ship, she pulled away because she became persuaded of its futility. She embraced a whole arsenal of reforms, including the abolition of child labor and capital punishment and MARGARET SANGER's birth control movement. Her public support of the NAACP outraged her Alabama relatives and friends. As a consequence of these stands, the attacks on her multiplied, the most insidious being that she was a pawn in the hands of others —notably Annie Sullivan Macy.

In late 1916 Macy fell ill with what was diagnosed as tuberculosis. At the same time Keller fell in love with her socialist secretary, Peter Fagan. Macy and Kate Keller managed to break this up just before Macy, accompanied by Polly Thomson, left for a sanitarium in upstate New York. She wanted the love of a man, Keller later wrote, but in reality felt herself unfitted for marriage, and "I faced consciously the strong sex-urges of my nature and turned that life energy into channels of satisfying sympathy and work."

In the period just before the United States entered World War I, Macy and Thomson were in Puerto Rico, while Keller was in Montgomery, Ala., with her mother, effectively sidelined as the final struggles against entering the war and for suffrage reached their climax. When Macy recovered and returned to the United States in 1917, they sold the property in Wrentham and purchased a house in Forest Hills, N.Y. They then went to Hollywood and made a film, *Deliverance* (1918), based on Keller's life. It received good notices but was not a box office success. From 1920 until 1924 they were

in and out of vaudeville, touring the Keith circuit.

Keller's mother died in 1921; her father had died in 1896. Whatever Kate Keller may have felt about Macy's usurpation of her role she kept to herself, grateful for what Macy had done for her child. By 1924, just as their vaudeville bookings were running out, the newly established American Foundation for the Blind asked Keller to assist in its drive for funds. She accepted and her identification with the Foundation quickly established it in the awareness of the public. Almost all doors were open to her. Although in 1924 she supported the third party candidacy of Robert M. LaFollette, President Calvin Coolidge accepted the honorary chairmanship of the Foundation and received Keller at the White House. Because her work for the blind drew support from all political parties, she decided to mute her own political views and did not publicly support another presidential candidate until Franklin D. Roosevelt's fourth term race in 1944.

Major M. C. Migel, the Foundation's president, realized Keller's indispensability, as much in the legislative field as in fund raising. By the early 1930s, as Macy started to fail, Migel made the Foundation responsible for the three women, considering Keller in particular a national asset entrusted to the Foundation's guardianship.

In 1923 the publishing house Doubleday and Page had assigned a young editor, Nella Braddy Henney, to help Helen Keller bring her story up to date. Keller diverted her into first helping with *My Religion*, which she was writing at the invitation of the Swedenborg church. It was published in 1927, and two years later the autobiographical *Midstream* appeared. Cooperating with Henney on *Midstream* awakened Macy's desire to do her own autobiography and, inviting Henney to work with her, for the first time she spoke about the difficulties of her early life.

Macy was becoming blind again, and the next few years were devoted mainly to her care, with many trips abroad. Polls placed Helen Keller among the nation's greatest women and *The Pictorial Review* in 1932 gave her its annual award for a noteworthy contribution by a woman. Temple University went a step further and awarded honorary degrees to both Keller and Macy. Keller, who was always ready to allow scientists to test her capabilities, underwent tests by Frederick Tilney, an eminent neurologist, of her senses of taste, touch, and smell and was surprised to learn that they were average. But the tests also showed, said Tilney, how much the human brain is capable of when pushed hard.

In 1933, a year after the ailing Macy received the news of her husband's death, the book about her, *Anne Sullivan Macy*, appeared, with Nella Henney alone listed as the author. "The book does not present Teacher to me as I know her," Keller commented, and determined to do her own. Macy died on Oct. 20, 1936.

Keller went abroad with Polly Thomson to adjust to a world without Macy. As a form of therapy and self-vindication she began a journal. "People will see that I have a personality, not gifted, but my own," she wrote. At the invitation of the Japanese blind, she and Thomson went to Japan, visiting thirty-nine cities and giving ninety-seven lectures. *Helen Keller's Journal*, which appeared in 1938, was a revealing book and put to rest the question: "What will Helen do without Teacher?"

Keller's work with the American Foundation for the Blind took on a different character during the thirties. She lobbied effectively in Washington for legislation on behalf of the blind and had measurable influence on the passage of the Pratt bill to provide federally funded reading services for the blind. With her help this was later broadened into the production of talking-book records. Perhaps her most significant intervention was on behalf of the inclusion of Title X in the 1935 Social Security Act, which established the blind as a category to receive federal grant assistance. Keller continued to prod state legislatures and governors to mandate preventive measures against ophthalmia neonatorum. Amid all the calls upon her, the book about Macy progressed slowly. She sold the Forest Hills house and in early 1939 moved to a house in Easton, Conn., built for her by the pharmaceutical manufacturer and Foundation trustee Gustavus A. Pfeiffer.

With the outbreak of World War II, Keller abandoned her pacifism and supported President Roosevelt's policy of aid to the democracies. After Pearl Harbor she searched for a job connected with the war and found her niche in morale-building tours of military hospitals. Through her friend the sculptor Jo Davidson, she became a sponsor of an Independent Voters Committee for Roosevelt. She called her tours of the military hospitals "the crowning experience of my life." As they drew to an end she went to Europe for the American Foundation for the Overseas Blind. In Rome in November 1946 she heard the news that fire had destroyed her Connecticut house, including her unfinished manuscript about Macy. "To lose all your possessions at my age is hard," she commented, and quickly turned to the greater horrors occurring in Europe. The house was rebuilt for her, a replica of the first.

Although Keller supported Henry Wallace in his break with President Harry S Truman, she declined to back his presidential candidacy in 1948, pleading her commitments to the blind. Among those commitments was a trip to Australia and New Zealand, and, at the invitation of Gen. Douglas A. MacArthur and the Japanese blind, a return visit to Japan. She spoke in atom-devastated Hiroshima and Nagasaki, experiences that confirmed her resolve "to fight against the horrors of atomic warfare and for the constructive uses of atomic energy." A planned tour of China and India was abruptly canceled when Polly Thomson suffered a stroke.

Their close friends had become increasingly concerned over what might happen to Keller if Thomson became incapacitated, but they had been unable to prevail upon the latter to train a substitute. Instead Thomson became increasingly possessive, refusing to permit anyone to converse with Keller except through her. She accompanied Keller on tours of South Africa in 1951 and of the Middle East in 1952. Next came a swing around Latin America and, although Keller had supported Adlai E. Stevenson for the presidency, a call on President Dwight D. Eisenhower.

KATHARINE CORNELL had become one of Keller's closest friends, and in 1953–54 Nancy Hamilton, Cornell's manager, produced a documentary about Helen Keller's life, *The Unconquered* (later called *Helen Keller in Her Story*). The film won an Academy Award in 1955 but, like *Deliverance*, was not a commercial success. Keller returned from a trip to Japan and India in time to receive an honorary LL.B. from Harvard University on her seventy-fifth birthday. A few weeks later *Teacher* (1955), the book about Macy, appeared. It lacked sharpness, but a careful reader could learn a great deal from it about the realities of the relationship between the two women.

Through the good offices of Nella Henney, Keller agreed to cooperate in the production of William Gibson's *The Miracle Worker*. Unfortunately the play irritated Thomson, who no longer liked to be reminded of Macy's role in Keller's life. A dispute with Henney over *The Miracle Worker* and over the power-of-attorney Keller had once given her left Keller more isolated than ever.

After Thomson died in 1960, Keller carried on. Her nurse, Winifred Corbally, and a secretary, Evelyn Seide, served as her interpreters. Interviewed on her eightieth birthday about her plans for the future, she replied: "I will always—as long as I have breath—work for the handicapped." Like Major Migel before him, the investment banker James Adams, who lived nearby, made Helen Keller his special responsibility. In October 1961 while at his home she suffered a slight stroke, the first in a series. Although she lived nearly seven more years, she no longer was in active communication with the outside world and sent a nephew and niece to Washington in 1964 to accept the Presidential Medal of Freedom conferred upon her by President Lyndon B. Johnson.

Helen Keller died at home of arteriosclerotic heart disease in 1968. Although she had wanted a Swedenborgian minister to participate in her funeral service, the rites at the National Cathedral, where her ashes were deposited next to Macy's and Thomson's, were presided over by the cathedral's dean.

Among American heroines Helen Keller is most widely known by school children. The appeal of her story is easily understood: If Helen Keller was able to transcend her handicaps to leave her mark upon the times as a writer, feminist, lobbyist for remedial legislation, and as a sheer charismatic presence, "Who am I to complain?"

[The main archival materials on Helen Keller, including personal and professional correspondence, intermittent diaries, MSS., and large holdings of clippings, are at the Am. Fdn. for the Blind. The Perkins School, in Watertown, Mass., has some papers of Anne Sullivan Macy and all the papers of Nella Braddy Henney, including her diaries, which are quite detailed for the postwar years. The Volta Bureau has the correspondence of Helen Keller and Anne Sullivan Macy with Alexander Graham Bell and John Hitz. Keller's socialist writings and speeches were collected in Philip S. Foner, ed., *Helen Keller: Her Socialist Years* (1967). Writings about Helen Keller include Van Wyck Brooks, *Helen Keller: Sketch for a Portrait* (1956), and Richard Harrity and Ralph G. Martin, *The Three Lives of Helen Keller* (1962). See also the annual reports of the Perkins Institution, 1887 through 1892, written by Michael Anagnos. John A. Macy's perceptive essay, "Helen Keller as She Really Is," which originally appeared in the *Ladies' Home Journal*, Oct. and Nov. 1902, was used in modified form in *The Story of My Life*. The Volta Bureau published two *Souvenirs* of Helen Keller, 1891 and 1899. A profile by Robert M. Coates appeared in the *New Yorker*, Jan. 25, 1930. There is a biography by Joseph Lash, *Helen and Teacher* (1980). See also Thomas D. Cutsforth, *The Blind in School and Society* (1933); Pierre Villey, *The World of the Blind* (1930); and Frances A. Koestler, *The Unseen Minority: A Social History of Blindness in America* (1976). The Sept. 1968 issue of *The New Outlook for the Blind*, which was devoted to Keller, contains a biographical sketch, an article by M. Robert Barnett about her work for the Am. Fdn. for the Blind, an excerpt from Brooks's book, and excerpts from Keller's writings. There is an entry in *Current Biog.*, 1942; an obituary appeared in the

N.Y. Times, June 2, 1968. Death certificate supplied by Conn. Dept. of Health.]

JOSEPH P. LASH

KELLOR, Frances, Oct. 20, 1873– Jan. 4, 1952. Social investigator and reformer, arbitration specialist.

Frances Alice Kellor was born in Columbus, Ohio, the younger of two daughters of Daniel and Mary (Sprau) Kellor. In 1875 she moved with her mother and her sister, who was twenty-four years older, to live in Coldwater, Mich. Nothing is known of Daniel Kellor.

In Coldwater Mary Kellor did washing and housecleaning for wealthier families to support herself and young Alice (as she was then known), who later did the same work to put herself through high school. Leaving high school in 1890 after only two years, she became a reporter and columnist on local affairs for the *Coldwater Republican*. In 1891 she joined the First Presbyterian Church, whose liberal pastor, Henry P. Collin, interested her in social problems. Another strong influence on Kellor in Coldwater was a pair of sisters, Mary A. and Frances E. Eddy, with whom she lived in 1894–95 before leaving to enroll at Cornell Law School.

Admitted to Cornell on the basis of an examination, Kellor put herself through law school, earning an LL.B. in 1897. More concerned with contemporary social problems than with law, however, she then enrolled in 1898 at the University of Chicago, combining part-time work with the study of sociology. Her first article in a professional journal, appearing shortly after her arrival at Chicago, as well as a book she later coauthored, reflected her early interest in the benefits of physical education for women.

During the years Kellor was enrolled at the University of Chicago, she undertook studies of female criminals, southern black migrants, and unemployed women, all of which supported her growing conviction of the causal connection between environmental factors and crime. In her first book, *Experimental Sociology* (1901), she wrote that juvenile crime was related to unemployment, lack of education, and childhood experiences, and suggested that reformatories and rehabilitation programs be established in prisons. Becoming interested in the problems faced by black migrants in northern cities, in 1900 Kellor, supported by the Chicago Woman's Club, traveled through the south to study conditions among blacks there. Her findings and analysis appeared in a series of eight articles for *The Arena* in 1901 and *Charities* in 1903. As remedies for poverty and neglect, she recommended the establishment of special school programs, labor organizations, employment bureaus, and vocational training programs.

In 1902 Kellor enrolled in the New York Summer School of Philanthropy and received a New York College Settlements Association fellowship to study employment bureaus for women in New York and Chicago. She lived at the College Settlement House intermittently until 1905, occasionally returning to Chicago to live at Hull House. The result of her research was *Out of Work: A Study of Employment Agencies* (1904; rev. 1915), a comprehensive work which concluded that unemployment was a national problem requiring federal government action.

The insistence upon government responsibility and the search for legislative remedies were characteristic of Kellor's approach to social reform, as they were of other reformers during the Progressive era. In 1904 Kellor became general director of the newly founded Inter-Municipal Committee on Household Research, whose legislative committee, headed by MARY DREIER, prepared proposals for remedial legislation concerning child labor, employment agencies, and tenement houses. Kellor's growing friendship with Mary Dreier and MARGARET DREIER (ROBINS) influenced her decision to settle permanently in New York City. In 1905 Mary Dreier invited Kellor to live with the family, and she shared a home with Dreier for the rest of her life.

Kellor's continuing interest in the plight of southern black women in the urban north led her in 1906 to call a meeting of concerned men and women out of which emerged the National League for the Protection of Colored Women. Kellor, assisted by Mary Dreier and MARY WHITE OVINGTON, served as executive secretary of the organization, which was dedicated to providing protection and guidance to migrant women while they looked for jobs and homes in New York.

In 1908 Gov. Charles Evans Hughes appointed Kellor secretary of the newly created New York State Immigration Commission. Charged with investigating the living and working conditions of immigrants, the committee concluded that they were exploited and their welfare ignored by the state. It recommended the creation of a Bureau of Industries and Immigration, which was established in 1910, with Frances Kellor as director and chief investigator. The Bureau encouraged English language classes, prepared foreign language pamphlets about life in the United States, and promoted job safety to prevent industrial accidents.

Kellor's reform interests led her naturally into the Progressive party. She served as a national Progressive party committeewoman in Theodore Roosevelt's unsuccessful 1912 presidential campaign, and, at Roosevelt's suggestion, was appointed to the administrative board of the party. She also headed the party's publicity and research committee, helped prepare campaign statements, and enlisted the support of other social reformers. According to one historian, Kellor "did more than anyone else to direct Roosevelt's growing reformist zeal toward the special plight of the urban immigrant" (Higham, p. 190). With the decline of the Progressive party by 1916, Kellor campaigned for Charles Evans Hughes, the Republican candidate for president that year, and also served as a Republican party committeewoman.

Although she had resigned from the Bureau of Industries by 1913, Kellor remained actively involved in immigrant affairs. In 1909 she had organized a New York branch of the Boston-based North American Civic League for Immigrants, and in 1913 she became director of its legislative committee. In this role she investigated the possibilities of government action in matters pertaining to immigrants' employment, education, naturalization, and standard of living. As the Boston group moved away from the liberal, social welfare oriented policies supported by Kellor, the New York branch broke away in 1914, forming the Committee for Immigrants in America. Kellor served as a vice chairman of the committee, which acted as a clearinghouse for information useful to immigrants.

Kellor continued to pursue social welfare goals for immigrants, but with the onset of World War I the emphasis of her efforts shifted to the promotion of naturalization, citizenship, and English classes. In 1915 the Committee for Immigrants in America established the National Americanization Day Committee to publicize Americanization in cities around the country. The aim of this organization and its successor, the National Americanization Committee, was to encourage national unity. As the war progressed, Kellor's writing took a new tone, reflecting her growing fear that large numbers of dissatisfied aliens would be a threat to the country. Though the Americanization Committee disbanded after the war, Kellor continued Americanization work into the early 1920s through such organizations as the Inter-Racial Council, which she founded, and the Association of Foreign Language Newspapers, of which she was director.

In the last phase of her career, Kellor applied her energies to yet another new interest. A founding member, first vice president (1926–52), and chief executive of the American Arbitration Association, she sought ways to bring efficiency, order, and justice to the resolution of industrial and international problems. As a member of the editorial board of *Arbitration Journal*, she prepared a code of ethics for arbitration that remained in effect for many years. Her commitment to arbitration as a method for settling international as well as industrial disputes led her to support the League of Nations and the Court of International Justice as vehicles for achieving permanent peace and national security. As a member of the executive board of the Pan American Union, Kellor promoted arbitration and better economic relations between North and South America. She continued these efforts until her death in New York City at the age of seventy-eight.

Described as brusque and businesslike, Frances Kellor, though not unfriendly, discouraged closeness. Highly intelligent, independent, and self-directed, she approached everything she did with great determination and drive. Her success in so many and various activities is attributable to her persistence, her skill at generating publicity, and her extraordinary organizational ability.

[Some of Frances Kellor's letters, reports, and papers can be found in various collections in the Manuscript Div. of the Library of Congress. Some of her correspondence with friends and associates is in the possession of William Joseph Maxwell and some additional materials, including newspaper clippings, photographs, and letters, are in the files of Phyllis Holbrook. The results of Kellor's early studies of physical education appeared in "A Psychological Basis for Physical Culture," *Education*, Oct. 1898, and *Athletic Games in the Education of Women* (1909), coauthored by Gertrude Dudley. The subtitle of the 1915 edition of *Out of Work* was *A Study of Unemployment*. Among Kellor's other books were *A Call to National Service* (1916), *Immigration and the Future* (1920), *The United States of America in Relation to the Permanent Court of International Justice of the League of Nations and in Relation to The Hague Tribunal* (1923), *Arbitration in the New Industrial Society* (1934), *Arbitration in Action: A Code for Civil, Commercial and Industrial Arbitration* (1941), and *American Arbitration: Its History, Functions and Achievements* (1948). With Antonia Hatvany she wrote *Security Against War* (1924), *The United States Senate and the International Court* (1925), and *Protocol for the Pacific Settlement of International Disputes in Relation to the Sanction of War* (1925). She was also coauthor of *Code of Arbitration, Practice and Procedure of the American Arbitration Tribunal* (1931) and *Arbitration in International Controversy* (1944). The fullest biographical account is in William Joseph Maxwell, "Frances Kellor in the Progressive Era: A Case Study in the Professionalization of Reform" (Ph.D. diss., Teachers College, Columbia Univ., 1968). See also the entry in *Dict. Am. Biog.*, Supp. Five. Interpretations of her Americanization work can be found in Edward George Hartmann, *The Movement to Americanize the Immigrant* (1948); John Higham, *Strangers in the Land* (1955); and Gerd Korman, *Industrialization, Immigrants, and Americanizers: The View from Milwaukee, 1866–1921* (1967). See also Phyllis Maynick Palmer, "Two Friends of the Immigrant, 1908–1920" (M.A. thesis, Ohio State Univ., 1967). Kellor's early work with black women is discussed in Gilbert Osofsky, *Harlem: The Making of a Ghetto* (1966), and her work within the context of the settlement movement is mentioned in Allen F. Davis, *Spearheads for Reform* (1967). An obituary appeared in the *N.Y. Times*, Jan. 5, 1952, and an editorial comment appeared in the *Times* the following day.]

LUCILLE O'CONNELL

KENYON, Dorothy, Feb. 17, 1888–Feb. 11, 1972. Lawyer, feminist, civil libertarian, judge.

Dorothy Kenyon was born in New York City, the oldest of three children and only daughter of Maria Wellington (Stanwood) and William Houston Kenyon, a pioneer in patent law. Her mother's lineage reached back to colonial Massachusetts; her paternal ancestors emigrated from Scotland in the 1830s. Reared on Manhattan's Upper West Side and at the family summer home in Connecticut, she graduated from the Horace Mann High School in New York City in 1904. At Smith College Kenyon combined an active social life with music, athletics, and an outstanding academic record. She received her A.B. in economics and history in 1908.

A self-described social butterfly until a trip to Mexico awakened her to social injustice, Kenyon entered New York University Law School, obtaining a J.D. degree and admission to the New York Bar in 1917. Her brothers also became lawyers; unlike them, she declined an offer to join her father's firm. Her first jobs were with the government, doing research on wartime labor and preparing studies for the 1919 peace conference. Then, for a few years she worked in other law firms and, during the 1930s, in partnership with Dorothy Straus. But most of her fifty-four-year legal career was spent in a wide-ranging independent practice. Challenging the male exclusivity of the New York City bar association, she was among the first women to gain admittance in 1937.

Throughout her career, Kenyon devoted much of her considerable energy to liberal causes. Her legal expertise and commitment to social justice brought her appointments to public commissions dealing with the issues of relief, minimum wage legislation, public housing, and women's court procedures. As a founder and director of several consumer corporations and legal counsel to the Cooperative League of the United States, she pursued a lifelong interest in the cooperative movement. Kenyon also served on the national board of directors of the American Civil Liberties Union (ACLU) from 1930 to her death and was among the minority that opposed the expulsion of ELIZABETH GURLEY FLYNN in 1940 because of her membership in the Communist party. A vital woman with abundant wit and good humor, Kenyon had a wide circle of friends, many of whom belonged with her to Barnhouse, a colony of artists, intellectuals, and reformers at Martha's Vineyard.

Kenyon was an active participant in the liberal wing of New York politics. A reform Democrat most of her life, she worked with the anti-Tammany City Fusion party in the early 1930s and served on committees of the American Labor party later in the decade. Mayor Fiorello La Guardia appointed her first deputy commissioner of licenses in 1936 and chose her to fill a municipal court judgeship vacancy in 1939. Unopposed for both the Republican and American Labor party nominations, she lost her bid for reelection to the judgeship in 1940 to the regular Democratic candidate.

Having played a minor role in the suffrage movement, Kenyon gained national recognition for her feminist activism in the 1920s and 1930s. An officer in several women's organizations, she worked to advance the status of women of all socioeconomic classes through lobbying, public advocacy, and private persuasion. In 1938 her commitment to women's rights was afforded a broader scope when the council of the League of Nations named her to a seven-member committee of jurists to study the legal status of women throughout the world. From 1946 to 1950 Kenyon resumed this work as United States delegate to the United Nations Commission on the Status of Women. To her disappointment, and despite high praise for her work, when her term ended she was replaced by a woman active in regular Democratic party politics.

In 1950 Sen. Joseph R. McCarthy charged Kenyon with membership in numerous Communist-front organizations. The first person to appear before the Senate Foreign Relations Subcommittee that investigated McCarthy's charges, Kenyon acknowledged that along with many prominent figures she had lent her name to a number of liberal, antifascist organizations, but denied that she was disloyal, a Communist, or a fellow-traveler. Her defense evoked widespread support from respected lawyers, public figures, and the liberal press. Nonetheless, Kenyon received no further public appointments

and, although she had been granted four honorary degrees from 1948 to 1950, she was not similarly recognized for another sixteen years.

Kenyon continued her law practice and her involvement in New York City politics and liberal movements. A longtime resident of the Chelsea section of the city, she was active in community improvement and at eighty played a major role in the establishment of the first legal services for the poor on the Lower West Side. Believing that her experiences as a woman gave her an insight into the frustrations of black Americans, Kenyon supported the civil rights movement, prepared briefs for the NAACP Legal Defense Fund and for ACLU suits, promoted integration in the New York City schools, and marched with sanitation workers after the assassination of Martin Luther King, Jr., in Memphis in 1968. She participated in the anti-Vietnam War movement and was an organizer of a women's coalition to divert federal spending from military to social purposes.

Feminist issues occupied high priority among Kenyon's activities in the 1960s. Since early in her career, she had campaigned for jury service for women, equality in marriage, and educational and economic opportunities. She was a vocal opponent of discrimination against married women workers during the depression and a leader in the struggles to obtain military commissions for female physicians in World War II and to promote women into government policy-making positions. Along with many feminists, Kenyon had staunchly opposed the Equal Rights Amendment (ERA) as a threat to protective legislation. But by 1970 her frustration over the Supreme Court's hesitancy in striking down legal differentiations based on sex led her to join the pro-ERA ranks. A supporter of birth control from the 1920s, Kenyon began to challenge restrictive abortion laws in the 1950s. Her vehicles for feminist protest were the ACLU, where with lawyer and civil rights activist Pauli Murray she championed women's issues on the board of directors, and the emerging women's liberation movement in New York, where she testified, marched, and demonstrated with younger feminists.

Active in the cause of social justice until the end, Dorothy Kenyon died of cancer in New York City in 1972.

[A large collection of Kenyon's papers, currently in the possession of her brother and sister-in-law, W. Houston Kenyon and Mildred Adams Kenyon, will be deposited in the Sophia Smith Coll. at Smith College, whose archives contain an oral history interview with Kenyon (1971). The papers include speech and clipping files, correspondence, and records from her League of Nations, United Nations, and ACLU work. Her articles appear in *Birth Control Rev.*, Oct. 1930; *Am. Labor Legislation Rev.*, Sept. 1936; *Independent Woman*, May 1937, June 1938, March 1949; *Women Lawyers Journal*, Spring 1947, Fall 1948; *N.Y. Law Forum*, July 1960; Robert L. Carter and others, *Equality* (1965); and *Americana Annual* (1971). Isabella Taves, *Successful Women* (1943), and William F. Buckley and L. Brent Bozell, *McCarthy and His Enemies* (1954), contain chapters on Kenyon. Also see "Judge Kenyon Meets the Press," *Am. Mercury,* June 1950, and *Current Biog.*, 1947. Obituaries appeared in the *Chelsea Clinton News,* Feb. 17, 1972, and *N.Y. Times,* Feb. 14, 1972. Kenyon's death date is generally given as Feb. 12, 1972; the Feb. 11 date is confirmed by the N.Y.C. Dept. of Health and by Mildred Adams Kenyon.]

SUSAN M. HARTMANN

KING, Carol Weiss, Aug. 24, 1895–Jan. 22, 1952. Lawyer, civil libertarian.

Carol King tried to make the law serve those who were traditionally its victims. Her clients were aliens, radicals, union members; a few were famous, most were rank-and-filers. She could not win their cases by representing them individually. They were a class, and she had to force discussion and decision on the underlying issues leading to their arrests, while providing narrow, technical reasons for letting each individual go. In the process, she enlightened and influenced a generation of lawyers on the strategy and tactics of constitutional litigation.

Her major adversaries were officials of the United States immigration service. To save her clients from deportation, she contrived new arguments and procedures based on the principle that the foreign born have legal rights the government must respect. She measured victory by her ability to keep her clients in this country, relatively free of restrictions on their political activity, until they died.

In her work, Carol King exhibited the self-confidence that characterized her father, Samuel Weiss, who had organized one of the first successful corporate law firms in New York City. He, like his wife, Carrie (Stix) Weiss, had come to the United States from Germany with his family in 1848. The Stix family were well-to-do merchants; Samuel Weiss was a self-made man. The couple had four children, two daughters and two sons; their youngest child, named Caroline, was born in New York City. Her parents provided her with the best in education and culture. She gained from them a taste for art, conversation, and friendship—and an understanding of the uses of power. Her two brothers became lawyers; her sister married a lawyer.

Carol Weiss graduated in 1912 from the Horace Mann School in New York City and went on to Barnard College. There her history teacher, Juliet Stuart Poyntz, directed her attention to workers' problems and the solutions offered by trade unionism. After graduation in 1916 Weiss worked as a research fellow for the American Association for Labor Legislation. Confident that she could make a better contribution to the labor movement by becoming a lawyer, she enrolled in the New York University Law School in 1917.

In the same year, she married Gordon Congdon King, a writer. Her mother helped them buy a small apartment house in which they lived and rented apartments, and suggested a housekeeper, Mrs. Matthew Barkley, who remained with Carol King for the next thirty years.

There were few women in her class when King received her J.D. in 1920. She could not find a job with a labor law firm, so she rented an office from Hale, Nelles and Shorr, a leading liberal firm busy with the defense of foreign-born workers arrested in the massive raids conducted by Attorney General A. Mitchell Palmer. King was thrown into immigration and civil liberties cases—from Ellis Island deportation hearings to Supreme Court briefs. In 1925 she became a full partner in the successor firm of Shorr, Brodsky, and King—and the delighted mother of a son, Jonathan.

When Gordon King died suddenly of pneumonia in 1930, Carol King rejected the role of "young, widowed mother." She was a practicing lawyer, determined to fill her life with work, family, old friends like Wall Street lawyer Walter H. Pollak, and young lawyers and artists seeking encouragement. Pollak, like many other lawyers and law professors, permitted King to persuade him to work on her constitutional law cases, gratis, to make his mark in legal history.

In 1932, after an inspiring trip to the socialist Soviet Union, and a frightening glimpse of fascism in Germany, King returned home to found an important journal on human rights, the *International Juridical Association Bulletin*. The monthly *IJA Bulletin* provided a national forum for developments in constitutional theory and the practice of immigration, labor, civil rights, poverty, and landlord-tenant law. King was the moving spirit on the *Bulletin*—which was described by the dean of a leading law school as "by far the best legal publication in this country" in its field (Stern, p. 55)—until its merger with the *Lawyers Guild Review* in 1942.

Carol King learned from experience what her father had represented: the strength of corporate power, often acting through government officials. She worked constantly to build a countervailing force of lawyers and civil libertarians. Success in this effort required that she eschew competition with her colleagues for paying clients and publicity. Her partner, Joseph Brodsky, helped organize the International Labor Defense (ILD) during the great depression; she promptly joined. As a member of the ILD legal advisory committee, she worked to prevent the execution of nine young blacks arrested in Scottsboro, Ala. To this end, she prepared arguments for the Supreme Court against the exclusion of blacks from juries trying black defendants, and for the right of indigent defendants to have effective counsel provided by the state. She worked on hundreds of "little" cases, and lobbied repeatedly for legislative changes and administrative reform. In 1936 she helped found the National Lawyers Guild and long chaired its immigration committee. She also began working with the American Committee for Protection of Foreign Born, and served as its general counsel during the last decade of her life.

Her best known client was Harry Bridges, the west coast labor leader arrested for deportation in 1938 for membership in the Communist party. After a lengthy administrative hearing, the hearing officer dismissed the charge: he did not believe the government witnesses. Arrested again, tried again, Bridges lost. On appeal, the Supreme Court reversed the deportation order: the government witnesses did not hold up. In 1942, King represented Communist party leader William Schneiderman against government efforts to revoke his citizenship. When the case reached the Supreme Court, King secured as counsel Wendell Willkie, Republican presidential candidate in 1940 on a One-World platform. In 1943, during the World War II alliance of the Soviet Union and the United States, he won the case.

In 1948 King won her greatest victory when the Supreme Court accepted her theory concerning the legal rights of aliens, and stopped all deportation hearings in the nation until the Immigration Service at last provided some measure of due process to aliens. Like many of her victories, it was soon blunted by cosmetic reforms.

Carol King's frequent representation of communists arrested for deportation, or simply for making speeches, led to accusations that she was a communist sympathizer. A *Saturday Evening Post* article (Feb. 17, 1951) described this "stubby, stoutish woman with the gift of invective and a fine disdain for fashion" as "the Communist's dearest friend." She refused to answer questions about her political affiliations, particularly during the cold war period, arguing that they were not proper in a free country. Among friends, she was known to be an independent radical, proud of being retained by all kinds of political activists while following only her own convictions.

In 1948, Carol King formed a partnership with Blanch Freedman (1909–1967), a New York lawyer long active in the Women's Trade Union League. The following year, King ran unsuccessfully for municipal judge on the American Labor party ticket. The Association of the Bar of the City of New York commented grudgingly: "Notwithstanding doubts as to her judicial temperament, the Committee, by a divided vote, finds her to be 'qualified' because of her unquestioned ability and experience."

After the brief victories for the foreign born won during the war against fascism, King had to return to the defense when the Immigration Service again began arresting aliens and activists. She fought hard; she won seldom. Increasingly judges denied bail to aliens charged solely with being deportable. Late in 1951 she made her first argument to the Supreme Court, a deportation case which she lost. In January 1952 she died of cancer in New York City.

Carol King made a permanent mark on the law, on lawyers, and on the people of her country. She brought the Bill of Rights to Ellis Island and to many criminal and appellate courts where it had long been treated as an alien.

[The Carol King Coll. at the Meiklejohn Civil Liberties Institute, Berkeley, Calif., contains correspondence, briefs, transcripts, legal documents, and periodicals. In addition to her work for the *IJA Bull.*, King edited the *ACLU Law Bull.* from 1924 to 1931, was an associate editor for the *Lawyers Guild Rev.* in 1943–44, and wrote articles for that journal between 1945 and 1951. Other writings include "Contempt by Publication in the United States," *Columbia Law Rev.*, April-May 1928, pp. 401–31, 525–62, with W. Nelles; "The Willkie I Knew," *New Masses*, 1944; "The McCarran Act and the Immigration Laws," *Lawyers Guild Rev.*, Summer 1951, pp. 128–41, with Ann Fagan Ginger. There is a biography by Ann Fagan Ginger, "Call My Lawyer, Carol King," in preparation. An account of a testimonial for Carol King, held March 5, 1948, appeared in *The Lamp* (Am. Comm. for Protection of Foreign Born), April 1948. Two tributes, both containing biographical information, are Thomas I. Emerson, "In Memoriam: Carol King," *Lawyers Guild Rev.*, Winter 1952, pp. 54–56, and Carl S. Stern, "Carol King," *Memorial Book* of the Assoc. of the Bar of the City of N.Y. (1952), pp. 52–56. See also *Dict. Am. Biog.*, Supp. Five. An obituary appeared in the *N.Y. Times*, Jan. 23, 1952.]

ANN FAGAN GINGER

KLEEGMAN, Sophia Josephine, July 8, 1901– Sept. 26, 1971. Gynecologist, obstetrician.

Born in Kiev, Russia, Sophia Kleegman was the youngest of the four surviving children (all girls) of Israel and Elka (Siergutz) Kleegman; four sons died in childhood. Her eldest sisters, Mary and Rae, migrated to the Lower East Side of New York City and worked in garment industry sweatshops to earn ship passage for their parents and their two younger sisters. The family arrived in the United States around 1906, when Sophia was five years old. She was naturalized in 1923.

From the outset, Sophia and Anna Kleegman (1893–1970) were encouraged to become educated professional women. Neither was expected to do household chores. Mary and Rae provided the bulk of the family income, while their father, a Talmudic scholar, worked in a laundry and their mother, a fastidious housekeeper, cared for the family and several boarders.

Influenced by Anna Kleegman's choice of medicine as a career, Sophia Kleegman entered the University and Bellevue Hospital Medical College (later the New York University College of Medicine) in 1920 as a member of its second coeducational class. Following her graduation in 1924, and a residency at Chicago Lying-In Hospital, she began to practice obstetrics and gynecology (again, like her sister Anna). She was the first woman appointed to the NYU College of Medicine faculty of obstetrics and gynecology (1929); the same year she became a member of the attending staff of Bellevue Hospital. In 1953 she became clinical professor of obstetrics and gynecology.

On Dec. 31, 1932, Kleegman married Dr. John H. Sillman, an orthodontist and expert on the growth and development of the jaw. She retained her maiden name because she was already established professionally. Their first child, Frederick Holden, was born in 1937 and their second, Anne Marice, in 1941. (Their son later became a physician and their daughter a social worker.) Sophia Kleegman found it difficult to reconcile the claims of family and profession; to minimize night duties Kleegman gave up obstetrical practice when her first child was born and hired a full-time maid and a babysitter.

Kleegman's lifelong professional interest in the study of conception manifested itself early in her career. Believing that gynecologists had a responsibility for helping as well as preventing conception, her most important contribution was as a pioneer in the study of infertility. Her research on methods of improving the diagnosis and treatment of sterility in men and women yielded several papers beginning in the 1930s and culminated in 1966 in a book, *Infertility in Women*, coauthored with Sherwin Kaufman. By

discussing male sterility, she did much to dispel the common practice of attributing a couple's infertility to the woman. Although there was religious opposition to the practice, she early advocated artificial insemination, and also favored the establishment of semen banks "with the same scientific attitude . . . found in all other therapies for helping the infertile."

Kleegman belonged to the medical vanguard which recognized the importance of the psychological aspects of gynecological practice. She noted that sexual dysfunction often resulted from a repressive upbringing (particularly among women), from fear of conception, and from emotional or situational stress between husbands and wives. Her interest in these matters extended beyond the problem of conception to that of promoting happier marriages. Extraordinarily successful in her own practice, Kleegman lived up to her dictum that success in psychosomatic medicine required "a personality able to establish warm rapport" with patients. In addition to her private practice, she directed the Infertility Clinic at NYU-Bellevue Medical Center from 1958 until her death.

Although best known for her work in the social aspects of medicine, Kleegman was also interested in technical procedures. Most notably, she extended the diagnostic value of Dr. George Papanicolau's smear test for cervical cancer by adding the endometrial aspiration test and developing the necessary techniques for instrumentation.

Kleegman was an ardent advocate of birth control and of planned parenthood clinics, and she supported the clinic established in New York by MARGARET SANGER. In the early 1930s, when birth control was still an unpopular topic, she toured the United States lecturing on the subject. She became medical director of the New York State Planned Parenthood Association in 1936 and held that post until 1961, when she became a medical consultant to the Eastern Planned Parenthood League. Consistent with her view that women had the right to decide when and how many children to have, Kleegman publicly advocated the legalization of abortion. She also favored more liberal divorce laws.

Convinced that improved sex education and marriage counseling would save many marriages, Kleegman urged physicians, social workers, nurses, lawyers, the clergy, and, most important, parents to become better informed about sexual relations. She pinned her greatest hope on the education of physicians, believing that every medical student should learn how to conduct an adequate premarital examination and interview. After twelve years of persistent effort, she was able to convince the NYU Medical Center to include a one-hour lecture on the premarital interview in its curriculum. She finally succeeded as well in securing the addition of lectures on sex and sex education to the curriculum. Kleegman was a forthright and colorful lecturer and her course quickly became both popular and influential as a forum for new ideas.

Despite her demanding schedule, Kleegman was an active member of many organizations. She served as president of both the Women's Medical Association of New York (1942–44) and the American Association of Marriage Counselors (1960). In 1965 she became the first woman to be elected president of the NYU Medical Alumni Association.

Sophia Kleegman was active in medicine until her death from cancer in New York in September 1971. After her death friends and grateful patients made possible the establishment of the Sophia J. Kleegman professorship in human reproduction at the NYU Medical Center.

[The Institute for Sex Research, Indiana Univ., has correspondence between Kleegman and Alfred Kinsey, 1945–56. Kleegman contributed to two texts, R. J. Lowrie, ed., *Gynecology* (1952), and J. V. Meigs and S. Sturgis, eds., *Progress in Gynecology*, 2 vols. (1946, 1950); she also published articles in the popular press, especially *Parents' Magazine*. Her best-known works are: "Medical and Social Aspects of Birth Control," *Journal-Lancet*, Nov. 15, 1935; "Recent Advances in the Diagnosis and Treatment of Sterility," *Med. Woman's Jour.*, Jan. 1939; "Diagnosis and Treatment of Infertility in Women," *Med. Clinics of North America*, May 1951; "Therapeutic Donor Insemination," *Fertility and Sterility*, Jan.-Feb. 1954; "Frigidity in Women," *Quart. Rev. of Surgery, Obstetrics, and Gynecology*, Oct.-Dec. 1959; "Educate the Educators," *Fertility and Sterility*, March-April 1966. Biographical material on Kleegman may be found in Joy Daniels Singer, *My Mother, The Doctor* (a book about Anna Kleegman by her daughter); *Who Was Who in America*, V (1973); *Med. Tribune*, Dec. 5, 1966; *Newsday*, Feb. 24, 1965; *NYU Alumni News*, March 1965 and June 1968; and the *N.Y. Times* obituary for John Sillman, May 22, 1967. Kleegman's obituaries include the *N.Y. Times* and the *N.Y. Daily News*, both on Sept. 27, 1971; and *N.Y. State Jour. Med.*, Nov. 15, 1971. Information was also obtained from Walter Levy and Charles H. Debrovner; from Kleegman's children, Frederick Holden Sillman and Anne Bobrik; and from the NYU School of Medicine.]

DEBORAH DWORK

KNOPF, Blanche Wolf, July 30, 1894–June 4, 1966. Editor, publisher.

Blanche Knopf was born in New York City, the younger of two children and the only daughter of Julius W. Wolf, a jeweler, and his wife Bertha Wolf. As the daughter of a well-to-do

Jewish family of Viennese origins on the paternal side, she was reared in a cultivated and cosmopolitan milieu. Her education at New York's Gardner School was supplemented by French and German governesses. She met Alfred A. Knopf, two years her senior, around 1911, when her family was summering near the Knopf residence at Lawrence, Long Island. They were married on April 4, 1916; their only child, Alfred Jr., was born on June 17, 1918.

Alfred Knopf had entered book publishing with Doubleday, Page & Company soon after his graduation from Columbia College in 1912, and with his fiancée's encouragement he launched his own firm in 1915. From the first, the corporate name Alfred A. Knopf referred in reality to a shared enterprise in which Blanche Knopf played a central role. Soon after their son's birth the couple hired a full-time nurse to enable Blanche Knopf to devote herself to the business, of which she became a director and vice president in 1921. Initially functioning mainly as an office manager, she soon began to deal directly with authors, particularly the foreign ones for which the Knopf imprint would become famous. Her first trip to Europe was a joint one with her husband in 1920, during which they met with some of the principal publishers of England, France, Germany, and Scandinavia. In the 1930s Blanche Knopf began a series of independent European trips on which (making good use of her flawless French and her facility in other languages) she arranged to publish the United States editions of such writers as André Gide, Ilya Ehrenburg, Mikhail Sholokhov, and Thomas Mann. In 1938 she persuaded Sigmund Freud to publish his last book, *Moses and Monotheism*, with Knopf.

During World War II, when travel in Europe was restricted, she made several trips to Latin America in search of new authors. She signed Brazilian sociologist Gilberto Freyre and other notable writers of the region, beginning what was to be a continued interest of the firm throughout her lifetime. Returning to Europe after the war, she added Jean Paul Sartre, Albert Camus, and Simone de Beauvoir to the Knopf list. Not solely interested in books of such a high intellectual level, Blanche Knopf also had a keen eye for the potential best seller, and it was she who signed and principally dealt with James M. Cain, author of hard-boiled crime stories; with mystery writers Dashiell Hammett and Raymond Chandler; and with journalist William L. Shirer, whose *Berlin Diary* (1941) became one of the firm's biggest sellers.

The Knopf style was always a highly individualistic one, which Blanche Knopf helped establish and sustain. Her intellectual interests and her acuity in sensing emerging literary trends were matched by her social prowess. She always dealt with the more prestigious authors on a personal basis, supervising the English translations of their work, entertaining them extensively both abroad and in New York, and occasionally assisting them in moments of crisis. Geoffrey T. Hellman described her in 1948: "Aggressive, hunchy, dynamic, sociable, politically minded, and capable of exerting a very considerable charm, she courts writers the firm would like to publish . . . and keeps those already on the roster happy with celebrity-studded parties, and promises, which she is in a position to implement, of liberal advertising and other promotion." As the firm matured and prospered, her role remained central. In 1957, when her husband became chairman of the board, she became president.

The professional relationship between Blanche Knopf and her husband was not without its stresses. Both were gifted, ambitious, and strong-willed, and their personalities often clashed. By the 1950s the two had established their own distinct domains within the company, each with a stable of established authors, promising newcomers, and loyal staff members. The Knopfs' publicity director in these years later described their relationship as one of strained politeness punctuated by outbursts of rage on his part followed by "quick sarcasm" on hers. The firm's Manhattan headquarters he saw, perhaps somewhat unfairly, as resembling an "intimate royal court of eighteenth century Germany, with its tyrannical Emperor, devious Empress, and ebullient, if somewhat apprehensive, Crown Prince" (Lemay, pp. 231–32). Alfred Knopf, Jr., left the firm in 1959 to begin an independent career in book publishing as one of the founders of Atheneum Publishers. This decision was a blow to both parents, and a year later, with annual sales of about four million dollars and a reputation for excellence almost unmatched in the contemporary publishing world, they sold their firm to Random House, Inc. The Alfred A. Knopf imprint continued as an independent editorial entity, however, and Blanche Knopf, retaining her position as president, remained actively involved in Knopf's operations.

Blanche Knopf's personal life, too, had over the years increasingly followed an independent course from that of her husband. The Knopfs had moved from Manhattan to Purchase, N.Y., in 1928, but by the late 1940s Blanche Knopf had returned to the city where, from her apartment on West Fifty-Fifth Street, she mostly carried on her own social life. Her life and her career were integral to each other; her friends were drawn almost entirely from the ranks of Knopf authors—several of whom were devoted to her—and the world of publishing. Her few intimates found her loyal, witty, and amusing. A petite and frail-looking woman, she was fond of jewelry and high fashion. Increasingly plagued by ill health, she died in her sleep at home in June 1966.

A brilliant woman of cosmopolitan outlook and an intuitive publishing sense, Blanche Wolf Knopf carved out for herself a position near the summit of a profession historically dominated by men and even openly discriminatory against women. (She was never admitted to the Publishers' Lunch Club, the Book Table, or other social organizations to which her husband belonged.) The tinge of bitterness that characterized her later years may have been related to resentment over such slights and, more broadly, to the frustrations of a professional career spent in her husband's looming shadow. Clearly she merits a large share of credit for the success of the firm that bore her husband's name, and in particular for its receptivity to the newer literary currents—a fact which Alfred A. Knopf himself would fully acknowledge in later years. In introducing American readers to a larger world of letters and high literary culture, Blanche Knopf helped shape the intellectual and cultural contours of her own and future generations.

[Blanche Knopf's articles include "An American Publisher Tours South America," *Sat. Rev.*, April 10, 1943, pp. 7–10, and "Albert Camus in the Sun," *Atlantic Monthly*, Feb. 1961. For biographical sketches see *Current Biog.*, 1957; *Who Was Who in America*, IV (1968); and part 3 of Geoffrey T. Hellman's profile of her husband in the *New Yorker*, Dec. 4, 1948, pp. 40–53. Also interesting is Harding Lemay's *Inside, Looking Out* (1971). Blanche Knopf's obituary appeared in the *N.Y. Times*, June 5, 1966. Information supplied by Alfred A. Knopf was helpful in compiling this article.]

PAUL BOYER

KNOPF, Eleanora Frances Bliss, July 15, 1883–Jan. 21, 1974. Geologist.

Eleanora Knopf was born in Rosemont, Pa., the older child and only daughter of Tasker Howard and Eleanora Emma (Anderson) Bliss. Her father's ancestors had migrated from England in the seventeenth century, as had her maternal grandmother in the nineteenth century. Tasker Howard Bliss graduated from West Point, taught there eight years, and was a career army officer, rising to chief of staff during

World War I and later playing an important part in peace negotiations. A scholar with a special interest in languages, he at first knew little about geology but grew to share his daughter's enthusiasm for it. Eleanora's mother was privately educated; she too studied languages and also wrote poetry in the little time she could spare from the duties of an army officer's wife.

Eleanora Frances Bliss prepared for college at the Florence Baldwin School, adjacent to the campus of Bryn Mawr College, where she enrolled in 1900. Graduating in 1904 with an A.B. in chemistry and an A.M. in geology, she continued her graduate work at Bryn Mawr under the eminent geologist FLORENCE BASCOM, and became lifelong professional and personal friends with two other Bascom protégées, JULIA GARDNER and Anna Isabel Jonas (1881–1974). Between 1904 and 1909, Bliss served several years as an assistant curator in the Geological Museum of Bryn Mawr College and as a demonstrator in the college's geological laboratory. Bascom assigned Bliss and Jonas a very difficult area near Bryn Mawr for a joint dissertation; their study of the folded, faulted, and metamorphosed rocks of the region cleared up a number of the questions posed by the material. On completion of this work in 1912, Bliss received a Ph.D. in geology from Bryn Mawr. Earlier she had taken courses at the University of California at Berkeley (1910–11), and later she held a postdoctoral fellowship in geology at Johns Hopkins University (1917–18).

In 1912 Eleanora Bliss passed the federal civil service examinations and was hired as geologic aide by the United States Geological Survey (USGS) in Washington, D.C. The USGS assigned her field terrains adjacent to her former dissertation site for several years, and she reported on the chrome ores, metamorphism, and erosional history of the area, often in papers coauthored with Jonas. Independently in 1913, she announced in the *American Museum of Natural History Bulletin* her discovery of the mineral glaucophane in Pennsylvania, the first American sighting of that substance east of the Pacific coast. The USGS promoted her to assistant geologist in 1917, and for the next three years she worked jointly with the federal survey and the Maryland State Geological Survey.

In 1920 Bliss married Adolph Knopf, a fellow geologist with the USGS, and they moved to New Haven, where he became a professor at Yale University. Eleanora Knopf acquired three stepchildren by her marriage, but since they were all of school age by 1920 (George Dillon was ten years old, Theresa eight, and Agnes seven), she had many hours free to work on geology in her husband's office. When both parents were in the field, relatives or paid help took care of the children. Knopf never held a staff position at Yale, but she was a visiting lecturer there and at Harvard during the 1930s and shared her knowledge generously with students.

Eleanora Knopf continued to perform important assignments periodically for the USGS from 1920 until 1955, serving at the rank of full geologist. (During the depression, when the federal survey had to economize drastically, Knopf made up shortfalls in research funding with grants from the National Research Council and the Penrose Fund of the Geological Society of America.) In the early 1920s she coauthored with Jonas reports on the Pennsylvania and Maryland piedmont, but in 1925 Knopf began a separate USGS assignment farther north that was to engage her attention for the rest of her life. She studied the mountainous region along the New York–Connecticut border, a region about which geologists had disagreed since the 1840s, centering her work on Stissing Mountain, a site of metamorphism, overturned folds, and thrust faults even more complex than that of her dissertation assignment. Knopf gained a reputation for her Stissing Mountain publications and her laboratory work on metamorphic rocks (those transformed not by the surface processes of weathering or sedimentation, but by changes in temperature or pressure).

By the mid-1920s, having exhausted most of the laboratory techniques known among American geologists for studying metamorphic rocks, she began to look overseas for new methods of analysis. She found them in the petrofabrics (the study of the texture, grain orientation, and optical characteristics of minerals in rocks as evidence for their origin and geologic history) of Bruno Sander of Innsbruck University. Knopf translated Sander's work, and explained and applied it in the United States for the next forty years. She brought to this project a long-standing interest in European geology, a facility in German, and a thorough grounding in statistics and crystallography. The publication of her major book on the subject, *Structural Petrology* (1938), was followed by a series of significant appointments for Knopf in the Geological Society of America and the National Research Council, including chairmanship of the latter's committees on experimental deformation of rocks (1945–49) and on a glossary on structural petrology (1951–53). Bryn Mawr College formally recognized her work as a researcher and writer with a citation in 1960.

Knopf moved with her husband in 1951 from Yale to Stanford University, where she became a research associate in the geology department. Until Adolph Knopf's death in 1966, she accompanied him on studies at several Rocky Mountain locales, noting examples from them occasionally in her publications. Apart from the hazards of her profession ("I counted 43 chigger bites upon my anatomy and quit!" she once wrote from the field), Eleanora Knopf enjoyed good health into her early eighties. She died of arteriosclerosis in January 1974 in Menlo Park, Calif.

[About one thousand letters to, from, or mentioning Eleanora Bliss Knopf are located in the Family Correspondence Series of the Tasker Howard Bliss Papers, Manuscript Div., Library of Congress; the collection is especially helpful for the period 1905 to 1925. A few Knopf letters are in the Florence Bascom Papers, Sophia Smith Coll., Smith College. The Bryn Mawr College Archives has background material on the geology department useful for evaluating Knopf's education; field notebooks for her Stissing Mountain research (1925–1954) are preserved at the Denver branch of the USGS. For a survey of her life and career see John Rodgers, *Memorial to Eleanora Bliss Knopf, 1883–1974* (Geological Soc. of America, 1977), which includes a thorough bibliography and photograph. See also *Am. Men and Women of Science* (1972), and Jane H. Wallace, "Women in the Survey," *Geotimes*, 24 (1979), 34. For information on Knopf's father, husband, and Anna Jonas Stose, see the article on Tasker Howard Bliss in *Dict. Am. Biog.*, Supp. One; Frederick Palmer, *Bliss, Peacemaker* (1934); Charles Park, "Memorial to Adolph Knopf, 1882–1966," Geological Soc. of America *Proceedings for 1966* (1968), pp. 261–66; Robert Coleman, "Memorial to Adolph Knopf (December 2, 1882–November 23, 1966)," *Am. Mineralogist*, 53 (1968), 567–76; and Richard Dietrich, *Memorial to Anna I. Jonas Stose, 1881–1974* (Geological Soc. of America, 1977). An obituary on Eleanora Knopf appeared in Redwood City (Calif.) *Tribune*, Jan. 23, 1974. Death certificate furnished by Calif. Dept. of Public Health.]

MICHELE L. ALDRICH

KOHUT, Rebekah Bettelheim, Sept. 9, 1864– Aug. 11, 1951. Social welfare leader, educator.

Rebekah Kohut's career was multifaceted: she was a social worker within the American and eastern European Jewish communities, one of the developers of volunteer Jewish women's organizations, an early supporter of national unemployment insurance, and a patron of Judaic and near eastern scholarship. Born in Kaschau, Hungary, she was the youngest daughter and third child of the three daughters and two sons of Albert Siegfried and Henrietta (Wientraub) Bettelheim. The Bettelheim family tradition encouraged eldest sons to become either rabbis or physicians; Rebekah's father became both a rabbi and a doctor, pursuing lifelong interests in religious scholarship and in the natural sciences.

His daughter admired him deeply. Henrietta Bettelheim was a schoolteacher, an occupation generally reserved for males in Hungarian Jewish communities. Her unconventionality was viewed as a radical protest for equal rights and full participation of women in the society. In her autobiography, *My Portion* (1925), Rebekah Kohut stated that it was her mother who inspired her "to seek out all kinds of less sheltered activities."

In 1867 Albert Bettelheim, as a result of theological disagreements with Jewish leaders in Hungary, brought the family to the United States. He became rabbi of a synagogue in Philadelphia, then in 1869 of one in Richmond, Va., which had recently altered its religious practices from Orthodox to Reform Judaism. In 1870 Rebekah's mother died. Her father remarried and another child was born, but within a few years his new wife became an invalid and Rebekah and her sisters assumed care of the household and the younger children.

In 1875 the family moved to San Francisco, where Rebekah earned diplomas from the high school and the normal school and took courses at the University of California, Berkeley. During these years she experienced religious doubts, but succeeded in overcoming them. She also discovered her vocation: "It appeared to me that my real mission in life," she wrote in *My Portion*, "should be as a worker in the front ranks of American Jewish womanhood." Acting upon this belief, she became involved in community work. Her first experience in social welfare was as a member during her high school years of the Fruit and Flower Mission of San Francisco, an organization of young Christian women who collected funds from the rich and aided the sick and the poor. She aspired to a "career of service" rather than to a "life limited to housewifely duties."

In 1886, however, she met Alexander Kohut, an eminent Hungarian rabbinic scholar twenty-two years her senior, a widower with eight children, and a recent immigrant to the United States. They were married on Feb. 14, 1887. "I go to New York to be the wife of a great man and to become a mother to the motherless," she wrote her sister.

In the first years of their marriage Rebekah Kohut cared for her large family, maintained her husband's correspondence, and translated his sermons from German into English for publication. Despite his mild disapproval, she launched a career as a volunteer by participating in the New York Women's Health Protective Association, which campaigned for better city sanitation. As a rabbi's wife she also became a leader in organizing women's groups, or sisterhoods, within the Reform synagogues. Occasionally she taught classes at the Educational Alliance, a school founded on the Lower East Side of New York by wealthy German Jewish Americans whose goal was to Americanize their poorer eastern European immigrant brethren. Kohut became well known as a communal innovator, and in 1893 her reputation brought her an invitation to deliver an address at the first Congress of Jewish Women, held at the Chicago World's Fair. Because her ailing husband wished her to remain at home, Kohut's sister presented the address in her stead. "The disappointment was keen," she wrote in *My Portion*. "I felt it was one of the finest sacrifices I had ever made for Alexander Kohut." In May 1894 he died, leaving her with his family to raise.

After widowhood, Kohut's career in communal social work continued but was tempered by the need to contribute to the family's income. She lectured on cultural topics to groups associated with the Reform sisterhoods, and taught confirmation classes for young Jewish girls. From 1894 to 1898 she was president of the New York section of the newly founded National Council of Jewish Women, the volunteer women's organization of the Reform Jewish movement. In 1899, with the financial assistance of the financier-philanthropist Jacob Schiff, who also handled her investments, she founded the Kohut School for Girls. It lasted five years.

Kohut was also a patron of Jewish scholarship and the special endowments she made to Yale University subsidized important scholarly research and publication. In 1912 she established the Alexander Kohut Memorial Collection, giving the university several thousand volumes of near eastern literature from her husband's library. Three years later the Alexander Kohut Memorial Publication Fund was instituted, as the combined gift of the Kohut family and the university, to support the Yale Oriental Series, and in 1919 the family established the Alexander Kohut Research Fellowship for graduate students in Semitics.

Kohut also turned her energies to employment planning and counseling for women. As early as 1914 she established the Employment Bureau of the Young Women's Hebrew Association. During World War I she chaired the Employment Committee of the Women's Committee for National Defense, organized under New York Mayor John Purroy Mitchel in April 1917. The committee attempted to act as a clearinghouse for New York working women, placing workers either in positions vacated by soldiers or in war-related jobs. By August of that year Kohut was doing similar work on a national level as part of the newly formed United States Employment Service. She also served as a member of President Woodrow Wilson's Federal Employment Committee and as industrial chairman of the National League for Women's Service. Praised by the press as a "Dollar-a-Year" patriot, Kohut volunteered her administrative skills to the government.

After the war, Kohut worked to help Jews in eastern Europe who had been impoverished by the war. Under her direction the National Council of Jewish Women began its Reconstruction United organization for relief work among Jewish refugees in Europe. She made many trips to Europe in the 1920s to study conditions and to determine the kind of aid needed; in 1923 in Vienna she was elected president of the World Congress of Jewish Women. Kohut saw women's organizations as deserving the recognition that comes with major responsibilities: "We refuse as women to be used merely to raise money and to act as figureheads in the management of sewing societies and ladies' auxiliaries," she told a conference of the National Council of Jewish Women (Baum, Hyman, Michel, pp. 51–52).

In 1931 Governor Franklin D. Roosevelt appointed her to the New York State Advisory Council on Employment and to the Joint Legislative Commission on Unemployment. The following year she alone of the sixteen members of the commission offered the New York legislature a minority report recommending unemployment insurance. Remaining active in her seventies, Kohut returned to school administration in 1934, administering a boys' private school, the Columbia Grammar School, for several years. During World War II and until her death in New York City in 1951, Rebekah Kohut continued to play a leading role in philanthropic, governmental, religious, and women's organizations.

[The major source of information on Rebekah Kohut is the Am. Jewish Hist. Soc., Waltham, Mass., which contains papers, correspondence, and clippings. There are also correspondence and clippings in the Rebekah Kohut Papers, Am. Jewish Archives, Hebrew Union College, Cincinnati. Her most important writings include *As I Know Them: Some Jews and a Few Gentiles* (1929); *His Father's House: The Story of George Alexander Kohut* (1938); "Freidus: A Personal Reminiscence," in *Studies in Jewish Bibliography and Related Subjects* (1929); Harold U. Ribalow, ed., "Emergence of the Jewess," in *Autobiographies of American Jews* (1965); and her two autobiographies *My Portion* (1925) and *More Yesterdays* (1950). Information about her life and ideas can be found in Dora Askowith, *Three Outstanding Women* (1941); Charlotte Baum, Paula Hyman, and Sonya Michel, *The Jewish Woman in America* (1976); a biobibliography by Hedy L. Haas; and entries in the *Universal Jewish Encyc.*

(1942), pp. 438–39, *Encyc. Judaica* (1972), pp. 1149–52, and the *Nat. Cyc. Am. Biog.*, XLI, 53. Numerous articles about her work, reviews of her books, and an obituary (Aug. 12, 1951) appeared in the *N.Y. Times.* Obituaries also appeared in the *Wilson Library Bull.*, Oct. 1951, and the *Am. Jewish Yearbook* (1952), p. 539.]

NORMA FAIN PRATT

KYRK, Hazel, Nov. 19, 1886–Aug. 6, 1957. Consumer economist.

Hazel Kyrk, a pioneer in the field of consumer economics, was born in Ashley, Ohio, the only child of Elmer and Jane (Benedict) Kyrk. Her mother's ancestors were English, her father's Scots-Irish; they migrated to the United States in the mid-eighteenth century and her paternal grandparents settled in Ohio a century later. Her father worked as a drayman. Her mother, a homemaker, died when Hazel was in her teens, and she early found it necessary to support herself. After three years as a schoolteacher she enrolled at Ohio Wesleyan University (1904–06), then found employment as a mother's helper in the home of economics professor Leon Carroll Marshall. When he moved to the University of Chicago, Hazel Kyrk accompanied the family and continued her studies at Chicago, then a seedbed for new ideas in the social sciences. She earned a Ph.B. degree in economics and a Phi Beta Kappa key in 1910.

After a year as an instructor at Wellesley College, Hazel Kyrk pursued a Ph.D. in economics at Chicago, combining her studies after 1914 with a teaching position at Oberlin College. Granted leave to complete her thesis, she decided to join the war effort and in 1918 followed her adviser, James Alfred Field, to London where she worked as a statistician for the American Division of the Allied Maritime Transport Council. Coming back to the United States in 1919, she returned to teaching at Oberlin and resumed work on her dissertation. Her firsthand observation of regulated consumption in wartime England shaped the final draft, completed in 1920 and published as *A Theory of Consumption* in 1923. Selected by a distinguished panel of economists for the thousand-dollar Hart, Schaffner and Marx prize for research in economics, it remains a classic exposition of the social basis of consumer behavior.

A Theory of Consumption drew on the new field of social psychology to explain why consumers act as they do; it analyzed the constraints placed by the market on the consumer's "formal freedom of choice," and drew attention to the changing role of women in twentieth-century economics. Production had moved out of the home, the study noted, and the housewife had become largely a "director of consumption." A later study by Kyrk, *The Economic Problems of the Family* (1929), expanded on this theme, outlining a program for educating the woman consumer and urging the formation of more cooperatives and research bureaus to simplify her task.

After a year with the Food Research Institute at Stanford University (1923–24) and a stint as professor at Iowa State College (1924–25), Hazel Kyrk was invited to join the faculties of economics and home economics at the University of Chicago. She remained from 1925 until 1952, and became full professor in 1941. During her tenure there, she broadened the economics curriculum to include consumer topics and established Chicago as the premier university for the study of family and consumer economics. Several generations of graduate students, most of them women, trained under her; many distinguished themselves in government and academic careers.

Hazel Kyrk's interest in consumer economics was not merely academic; she also served the consumer cause as a consultant to the federal government and was principal economist in the Bureau of Home Economics of the Department of Agriculture in the summers between 1938 and 1941. There, she contributed to the Bureau's massive Consumer Purchases Study, undertaken with Works Progress Administration funding in cooperation with the Bureau of Labor Statistics. Published in more than twenty volumes, it was the most comprehensive consumer survey ever attempted, breaking down consumption patterns by five different regions and by urban, village, and farm categories. It established base year prices for the cost-of-living index (later called the consumer price index), an important economic barometer and, increasingly, a reference point in labor-management negotiations.

Hazel Kyrk's work on this study led to her appointment in 1943 as chairman of the Consumer Advisory Committee to the Office of Price Administration (OPA). In this position, and later as a member of a similar committee for the Office of Price Stabilization, she forcefully represented the consumer's point of view, arguing particularly for standards in consumer goods and for more gradual price decontrol. After World War II she joined her colleagues in urging President Harry Truman to establish a permanent consumer service bureau, as well as consumer advisory committees in each federal agency.

Hazel Kyrk was pressed into government service again in 1945–46 when, in response to congressional requests, the Bureau of Labor Statistics undertook to formulate a "standard family budget." The Technical Advisory Committee, which she chaired, helped to draw up this yardstick for measuring the economic health of American families and for setting levels of income tax exemption. She was also involved in the various attempts to revise the consumer price index to reflect postwar inflation.

Her activities during these years were not limited to the federal government. She was an early organizer and active board member of a consumer cooperative in the Hyde Park section of Chicago. Her concern for working women led her to teach at the Bryn Mawr Summer School for Women Workers from 1922 to 1925, and to serve on the board of the Chicago Women's Trade Union League. She also took responsibility for raising and educating a teenage cousin.

Upon her retirement from the University of Chicago in 1952, Hazel Kyrk settled in Washington, D.C. She subsequently had time to complete her textbook, *The Family in the American Economy* (1953; rev. 1967). In 1953 Ohio Wesleyan honored her with the degree of doctor of humane letters. She died in 1957 of a stroke while vacationing at her summer home in West Dover, Vt., and was buried in Ashley, Ohio.

[Information on Hazel Kyrk can be found in the archives of Oberlin College (report on war service) and in the files of the Am. Home Economics Assoc. in Washington, D.C. (including an autobiographical statement). Records of her service with the OPA are in the Nat. Archives, Industrial and Social Branch, Record Group 188. She coauthored *The American Baking Industry* (1925), *Food Buying and Our Markets* (1940), and several volumes of the Consumer Purchases Study, notably *Family Expenditures for Housing and Household Operation* (1940). She was a frequent contributor to the *Jour. Home Economics* and the *Am. Economic Rev.* Details of her life are contained in: Margaret Reid, "Hazel Kyrk," in Marie Dye, ed., *History of the Department of Home Economics at the University of Chicago* (1972); a biographical sketch in *Ohio Wesleyan Alumni Mag.*, June 1952; and an entry in *Who Was Who in America*, III (1960). Information about her work with the Bureau of Labor Statistics was gleaned from current staff members and from "Workers' Budgets in the United States: City Families and Single Persons, 1946 and 1947," U.S. Dept. of Labor, Bureau of Labor Statistics, Bull. 927 (1948). H. I. Hartmann's doctoral dissertation, "Capitalism and Women's Work in the Home, 1900–1930" (Yale, 1974), contains an extended analysis of Hazel Kyrk's work from a Marxist point of view. Obituaries appeared in *Wash. Post* and Wash. *Eve. Star*, Aug. 8, 1957, and in *N.Y. Times*, Aug. 7, 1957. Assistance was provided by her foster daughter, Ruth Struie Bellstrom. Birth certificate obtained from Court of Common Pleas, Del. Cty., Ohio; death certificate from town clerk, Brattleboro, Vt.]

ELIZABETH NELSON

L

LAMPKIN, Daisy Elizabeth Adams, Aug. 9, 1883?–March 10, 1965. Civil rights reformer, suffragist, community leader.

Daisy Adams Lampkin, national field secretary for the NAACP and vice president of the *Pittsburgh Courier*, was born in Washington, D.C., the only child of Rosa Anne (Proctor) and George S. Adams, a porter. After her father's death, her mother married John Temple. The family lived in Reading, Pa., where Daisy Adams attended public schools. In 1909 she moved to Pittsburgh, where on June 18, 1912, she married William Lampkin, a chauffeur who was later in the restaurant and catering business.

Daisy Lampkin began her public career in Pittsburgh, making street-corner speeches to organize black housewives into consumer protest groups. In 1915 she was elected president of the Lucy Stone Woman Suffrage League, an organization of black Pittsburgh women dedicated to promoting interest in suffrage among black women; the league cooperated with other local, state, and national suffrage organizations. After women won the right to vote, the league became the Lucy Stone Civic League and concentrated on raising money for scholarships for black students. Representing the league at the national conference of the National Association of Colored Women (NACW) in Baltimore in 1916, Lampkin learned "that I, too, was a woman with a spiritual interest in the world of women, brown women" ("Faith and Our Future," p. 16). She subsequently served the NACW as national organizer and as chairman of the executive board.

With the experience she gained from the league and the NACW, Lampkin moved first into county and then into national politics. In 1928 she served as an alternate delegate-at-large to the Republican national convention and became vice chairman of the Colored Voters' Division of the Republican National Committee. She was also active in state organizations as the chairman of the Negro Women's Republican League of Allegheny County, Pa., and as vice chairman of the Negro Voters League of Pennsylvania.

During the 1920s, Lampkin was active in the Pittsburgh branch of the NAACP, as a member of its executive committee and its women's auxiliary. In 1929 she headed a campaign that secured 2,000 new members and that was credited by national leaders with rejuvenating the dormant Pittsburgh branch. As a result of her success, Lampkin was invited to join the NAACP staff as regional field secretary. She served in that capacity from 1930 to 1935, and as national field secretary from 1935 to 1947. Through constant traveling and speaking, she helped establish NAACP chapters in cities all over the United States and pioneered in developing mass support for a civil rights organization by means of individual memberships. Lampkin stressed the importance of organizing women's groups, believing that: "Our male leadership . . . is so busy with their private interests that nothing is done unless the women do it." A remarkably effective fund raiser, she played an important role during the 1930s in NAACP efforts to raise funds for its antilynching campaign.

Lampkin's success was attributed to her seemingly endless energy, her forceful and persuasive personality, her imposing appearance, and her organizational skills. In 1944 the National Council of Negro Women (NCNW) honored her for building the largest membership enrollment in NAACP history. The same year, the NAACP *Bulletin* reported that she had "served longer than any other executive of the NAACP except Walter White and . . . raised more money." Although she retired as field secretary in 1947 in order to spend more time at home, she was elected to the NAACP national board, a signal honor for a staff member. She continued to raise funds for the organization.

In addition to her work for the NAACP, Lampkin was active on behalf of many local and national black causes. She was a member of the executive board of the Pittsburgh Urban League, served on the Committee on Negro Housing for the President's Conference on Home Building and Home Ownership, and worked closely with MARY MCLEOD BETHUNE in the formation of the National Council of Negro Women. She also had a long-standing interest in

the *Pittsburgh Courier,* an important black weekly. She had become involved with the paper in 1913 when she won a contest for raising the largest number of new subscribers and received *Courier* stock as a prize. In 1929, Lampkin became vice president of the paper. She served on the board of directors until her death.

Daisy Lampkin felt she had been called by God to her life's work and retained a strong commitment to her church. As a participating member of Grace Memorial Presbyterian Church in Pittsburgh, she raised money and served as one of its first woman elders. She also served on the board of the Council of Churches in Pittsburgh.

Her marriage was also extremely important to Daisy Lampkin. Friends described William Lampkin as a mild man who remained in the background but was proud of his wife's achievements; she believed that his support contributed to her success. She also felt that her work helped her marriage: "The woman who is pursuing a career makes a more successful wife. She is more broadminded. She has too much on her mind to have room for petty unpleasantnesses" (*Philadelphia Tribune*). The couple had no children, but they considered Daisy Lampkin's goddaughter, Romaine Jackson Childs, and her husband and son, to be their family.

Lampkin received many honors. In December 1964, she was the recipient of the first Eleanor Roosevelt–Mary McLeod Bethune World Citizenship Award, given by the National Council of Negro Women. The award was accepted for her by the actress Lena Horne as, in October of that year, Lampkin had suffered a stroke in Camden, N.J., while conducting an NAACP membership drive. She did not recover, and died in Pittsburgh in March 1965.

[Lampkin correspondence can be found in the NAACP Papers, Library of Congress. A scrapbook compiled by Daisy E. Lampkin is in the possession of Romaine Childs, as are pamphlets from the Lucy Stone Civic League. There is also material on Lampkin in the Nat. Archives for Black Women's Hist., NCNW, Washington, D.C. Daisy E. Lampkin, "Faith and Our Future," *The Message Mag.*, Oct. 1955, pp. 16–17, contains autobiographical information. See also Elizabeth L. Davis, ed., *Lifting as They Climb* (1933), a history of the Nat. Assoc. of Colored Women; Andrew Buni, *Robert L. Vann of The Pittsburgh Courier* (1974); Robert Zangrando, *The NAACP Crusade Against Lynching, 1909–1950* (1980); August Meier and Elliott Rudwick, *Along the Color Line: Explorations in the Black Experience* (1976), pp. 94–127. Articles on Lampkin appeared in the NAACP *Bulletin*, March 1944; the *Philadelphia Tribune*, April 28, 1932; and various issues of the *Pittsburgh Courier*. Obituaries appeared in the *Pittsburgh Courier*, March 20, 1965, and in the *Pittsburgh Post Gazette* and the *N.Y. Times,* March 12, 1965. Lampkin's birth date is uncertain. The Aug. 9, 1883, date comes from the marriage certificate of Daisy Adams and William Lampkin. Information from 1900 U.S. Census; death certificate from Pa. Dept. of Health. Romaine Jackson Childs, Wilhelmina Byrd Brown, Lucille Cuthbert, Gertrude Holmes, Norrine Cyrus, Fanny Howard, and Harold Tolliver provided useful information. Sheryl Kujawa and Janet Rumbarger provided research assistance.]

ELIZABETH FITZGERALD HOWARD

LANE, Rose Wilder. *See* WILDER, Laura Ingalls.

LANGE, Dorothea, May 26, 1895–Oct. 11, 1965. Photographer.

Dorothea Lange was born in Hoboken, N.J., the elder child of Joanna (Lange) and Henry Martin Nutzhorn. Her father abandoned the family when Dorothea and her brother, Martin, were in elementary school. Their maternal grandmother, Sophie Vottler Lange, a seamstress who had emigrated from Germany, took them in, and Dorothea transferred to Public School 62 on New York's Lower East Side to be near the public library where her mother worked. After her divorce in 1907, Joanna Nutzhorn resumed her maiden name, and her children also took the Lange name. Dorothea's feeling of alienation from her classmates was accentuated by a marked limp, the result of polio at age seven. She attended school erratically, preferring to wander through the city, carefully noting what she saw. By the time she graduated from Wadleigh High School in 1913, she knew she wanted to become a photographer, although she had never made a photograph.

At her family's insistence, Lange attended the New York Training School for Teachers from 1914 to 1917. Meanwhile, she apprenticed herself to photographers, including Arnold Genthe and theatrical photographer Charles H. Davis. She also enrolled in Clarence H. White's photography class at Columbia University.

In 1918 Lange left New York, convinced she knew enough to earn her way around the world making photographs. She went as far as San Francisco, where she took a job as a photo finisher and joined a camera club. A friend provided money for her to start a portrait business in 1919, and Lange's studio at 540 Sutter Street became a gathering spot for many artists. There she met the painter Maynard Dixon, twenty-one years her senior, whom she married on March 21, 1920. They had two sons, Daniel Rhodes (b. 1925) and John Eaglefeather (b. 1928).

Lange's portrait business provided the main support for the family. For over ten years she concentrated on making photographs for her clients, members of San Francisco's merchant elite. As the depression deepened, the sight of unemployed men in the streets drew Lange out of her studio. "The discrepancy," she said, "between what I was working on in the printing frames and what was going on in the street was more than I could assimilate." Her first attempt to capture that social reality produced one of her most widely used photographs, "White Angel Breadline," which shows a crowd of well-dressed, newly unemployed men in line for food. One man in the foreground, looking down into the cup he holds between his hands, dominates the photograph, symbolizing the impact of the depression on individual lives. In 1934 Lange exhibited her documentary photographs, still unsure what purpose they served, at the Oakland studio of Willard Van Dyke. Paul S. Taylor, a social economist at the University of California who had used photography in his field work, was impressed with Lange's exhibit and they began working together, documenting in words and photographs the living conditions of migrant workers in California. Their reports for the California State Emergency Relief Administration were instrumental in securing federal funds to build the first sanitary facilities for migrants. Lange married Taylor on Dec. 6, 1935, two months after she and Dixon were divorced.

Their California reports impressed Roy Stryker, head of the Historical Section of the newly formed federal Resettlement Administration, who had been looking for a way to use documentary photography to further his agency's mission. In mid-1935 he hired Lange. Her work was influential in the development of the agency, renamed the Farm Security Administration (FSA) in 1937, the year it was absorbed into the Department of Agriculture. "Migrant Mother," Lange's famous photograph of a prematurely aged woman in a tattered tent with her children, epitomized the concerns of the FSA. The range of her work was well represented in the magazine articles, illustrated books, and exhibits which used photographs to document the effects of the depression on rural Americans and the agency's efforts to remedy their problems. The impact of her migrant photographs was enormous: Pare Lorentz wrote that Lange and author John Steinbeck "have done more for these tragic nomads than all the politicians of the country."

Lange worked full-time for a year and part-time for several more years as the principal FSA photographer in California. She and Taylor devoted the summers of 1936–38 to extended field trips through the dust bowl and southern states, where mechanization and harsh weather were forcing people off the land. Lange then spent months editing the photographs and combining them with appropriate text, often quotations from her subjects. *An American Exodus: A Record of Human Erosion* (1939), coauthored by Lange and Taylor, set a standard for other FSA work in its blending of words and documentary images.

In 1940 Lange worked briefly for the Bureau of Agricultural Economics, documenting the migrants and the collectively organized cotton farms of the southwest in a style similar to that of her FSA work. In 1941 she received one of the first Guggenheim fellowships awarded to a photographer, to photograph "the American social scene." She had barely begun a project on traditional cooperative societies when fatigue and the imminence of war convinced her that the project was inappropriately timed, and she returned home. When Executive Order 9066 forced all Japanese aliens and Japanese-Americans into internment camps, Lange was hired by the War Relocation Authority to record the process. She joined families as they left their homes and businesses and followed them into the crowded camps. Her sympathies lay with the internees, causing suspicions among her supervisors, and many of her photographs were impounded until after the war. Most were not seen until thirty years later when they appeared as part of an exhibit and book by Maisie and Richard Conrat, *Executive Order 9066* (1972). Lange also worked for the Office of War Information from 1943 to 1945, and her photographs appeared uncredited in *Victory* magazine. Most of the negatives from this period have been lost.

In 1945, while photographing the United Nations Conference in San Francisco for the State Department, Lange had to be hospitalized for ulcers. Her convalescence took several years, during which she redefined her ideas about photography. By 1951, when she resumed photographing, she had decided to focus on "the familiar," the aspects of everyday life and subtleties of relationships that are widely shared and seldom noticed. Her home and, as grandchildren were added to the circle, her family's life were favorite subjects, but she also undertook assignments for *Life,* including "Three Mormon Towns" (Sept. 6, 1954), on which she collaborated with Ansel Adams, and "The Irish Country People" (March 21, 1955), for which her son Daniel Dixon wrote the text. Lange also carried out a study of a public de-

fender (with Pirkle Jones), and recorded the devastation caused by dam construction in California's Berryessa Valley—published in *Aperture* in 1960 as "Death of a Valley."

Lange made several overseas journeys with Taylor, whose work took him to Asia for six months in 1958–59, to Venezuela and Ecuador in 1960, and to Egypt in 1962–63, although their work was not linked as it had been in the 1930s. Poor health limited Lange's activities, but when she could she photographed, working close to her subjects to document expressions she considered to be universally understood.

In August 1964, Lange's recurring illness was diagnosed as cancer of the esophagus. During the last year of her life she put aside the photographic record she was making of her family to design a retrospective exhibition of her work for the Museum of Modern Art in New York (shown in 1966). She also compiled a sequence of photographs of the American country woman and worked on plans for a center for photographic studies which would emphasize the potential of documentary photography. When Lange died in San Francisco in 1965 she left behind, in addition to her photographs, a vision of photography as uniquely capable of exploring and revealing the human condition.

[The Dorothea Lange Coll. at the Oakland Museum includes the majority of her nongovernmental photographs; FSA photographs are in the Library of Congress; Bureau of Agricultural Economics and War Relocation Authority photographs are in the Nat. Archives. Other published selections of her photographs are *Dorothea Lange* (1966); *Dorothea Lange Looks at the American Country Woman* (1967); Lange and Margaretta Mitchell, *To a Cabin* (1973); and Therese Thau Heyman, *Celebrating a Collection: The Work of Dorothea Lange* (1978). The major sources of biographical information are 1960–61 interviews with Lange, *The Making of a Documentary Photographer* (1968), in the collection of the Regional Oral History Office, Univ. of Calif., Berkeley, and Milton Meltzer, *Dorothea Lange: A Photographer's Life* (1978), the most complete account; it contains a bibliography. See also Pare Lorentz, "Dorothea Lange, Camera with a Purpose," *U.S. Camera Annual*, 1941; Lange and Daniel Dixon, "Photographing the Familiar," *Aperture*, 1952; Anne Tucker, "Dorothea Lange 1895–1965," *The Woman's Eye* (1973); Milton Meltzer and Bernard Cole, "Dorothea Lange," *The Eye of Conscience: Photographers and Social Change* (1974); Karin Becker Ohrn, "What You See Is What You Get: Dorothea Lange and Ansel Adams at Manzanar," *Journalism Hist.*, 1977; and Karin Becker Ohrn, *Dorothea Lange and the Documentary Tradition* (1980). Lange appears in two films produced by KQED for National Educational Television: "Under the Trees" (1965) and "The Closer for Me" (1966). For her role in the FSA see

Lange-Stryker correspondence, Roy Stryker Coll., Univ. of Louisville Photographic Archives; Museum of Modern Art, *The Bitter Years, 1935–1941* (1962); F. Jack Hurley, *Portrait of a Decade: Roy Stryker and the Development of Photography in the Thirties* (1972); Stryker and Nancy Wood, *In This Proud Land: America 1935–43 as Seen in the Farm Security Administration Photographs* (1973); William Stott, *Documentary Expression and Thirties America* (1973); Hank O'Neal, *A Vision Shared* (1976). Obituaries appeared in the *S.F. Chronicle*, Oct. 13, 1965, and the *N.Y. Times*, Oct. 14, 1965. A death record was provided by the Calif. Dept. of Health Services.]

KARIN BECKER OHRN

LAUGHLIN, Gail, May 7, 1868–March 13, 1952. Lawyer, suffragist, feminist, state legislator.

Born Abbie Hill Laughlin in Robbinston, Maine, Gail Laughlin vowed at age twelve "to study law and dedicate my entire life to the freeing of women and establishing their proper place in this 'man's world.'" For the next seventy years she adhered to this plan unflinchingly, rewriting old laws, submitting new ones for passage, and demolishing legal barriers to woman's emancipation.

Her youthful decision may have been sparked by her widowed mother's difficult life raising a large family alone. Gail Laughlin was the eighth of nine children, the youngest of five daughters, two of whom died in infancy. When her Irish-born father, Robert C. Laughlin, an ironworker, died, her Canadian mother, Elizabeth P. (Stuart) Laughlin, returned with her children to her family in Saint Stephen, New Brunswick. In 1880 the Laughlins moved to Portland, Maine, where the oldest son was working as a clerk, and the family's circumstances gradually improved.

In 1886 Gail Laughlin graduated from Portland High School, receiving the Brown Medal for the highest grades. She worked for four years as a bookkeeper for a china importer, finally saving enough to enter Wellesley College. Enrolled as Abigail over her objections, Laughlin was called Gail by some Wellesley friends and decided to take that name legally.

In her freshman year Laughlin organized the Agora Society to promote the study of politics and civics and to sponsor political debates; she served as its president for four years. At the society's final program just prior to her graduation, her dynamic speech on tariffs attracted an offer from the Home Market Club of Boston to print 100,000 copies.

Receiving her A.B. from Wellesley in 1894,

Laughlin began writing for the *American Economist*, earning enough to enter law school at Cornell University two years later. She graduated with an LL.B. in 1898, passed the New York bar examination the following year, and opened her first office in New York City. In 1900 Col. Albert Clarke, who had been responsible for printing her speech on tariffs, obtained her appointment as an expert agent for the United States Industrial Commission, comprised of representatives from business and from the Congress. Her work for the commission included a report on domestic service containing statistics on rural, immigrant, and black women employed as servants in private homes; it documented their meager salaries and the unreasonable demands placed on them.

Her two years of research for the commission led Laughlin to give up her law practice and devote herself full-time to the cause of women. From 1902 until 1906 she campaigned on behalf of the National American Woman Suffrage Association. Traveling throughout the country, she lectured, organized, and roused women to demand consideration for their opinions.

In 1906 Laughlin decided to return to law practice and settled in Denver because Colorado women had been enfranchised. Admitted to the bar, she opened her second office in 1908. While living in Colorado, she served on the state board of pardons (1911–14), the (Denver) Mayor's Advisory Council (1912), and the state executive committee for the Progressive party (1912–14). Her work brought to her attention the injustices rendered by all-male juries, and she added the cause of jury duty for women to her list of goals.

Moving to San Francisco in 1914, Laughlin opened her third office. During the next ten years, she served on the Republican state central committee (1920–22), sat as a judge in the police courts, founded and was director of the state branch of the National League for Women's Services, and joined the National Woman's party. Drafting a law to permit women to serve on juries in California, she lobbied successfully for its passage.

In July 1919 Laughlin traveled to St. Louis for the first convention of the National Federation of Business and Professional Women (NFBPW). Making the opening speech and several more, she was unanimously elected the organization's first national president. Under her leadership, in its first year the new federation grew to a membership of 26,000, with 287 clubs in forty-seven states. Speaking in February 1920 before the New York state convention of the federation, she declared: "Our ultimate goal

... is the absolute elimination of the consideration of the sex of the person in occupation or opportunity or remuneration ... We must establish in the mind of everyone that women have an absolute right in industry, in business and in the professions ... The work belongs to the one who can do it best—be that one man or woman" (*Independent Woman*, Feb. 1920).

As an opponent of protective legislation which applied only to women, and as a leading member of the National Woman's party, Laughlin worked on behalf of the Equal Rights Amendment (ERA). In July 1927, as vice chairman of the party, she led a 200-car motorcade over dirt roads through Kansas, Colorado, Nebraska, and Wyoming to call upon President Calvin Coolidge, who was summering in the Black Hills National Forest in South Dakota. Invading his police-guarded privacy, 700 determined women begged his support in passing the ERA in the next session of Congress. The incident received national publicity.

Earlier, Gail Laughlin had become homesick for northern New England. By 1924 she had returned to Portland, where she shared an office with her younger brother, Frederick, also a lawyer. When she was approached by a delegation of club women to consider running for the state legislature, Laughlin welcomed the political challenge, believing that by holding office she could assist all the women of Maine, rather than just a small list of clients. She ran first in 1929. Winning easily, she went on to serve three terms, making her presence known as a ready speaker who stated her views pointedly, but with a sense of humor. Among the many bills submitted by Laughlin that became law, several were aimed at improving the quality of women's lives. These included a law raising the marriage age for girls from thirteen to sixteen and an act designed to prevent the commitment of women to mental institutions solely on their husbands' testimony. She was also instrumental in organizing the state department of health. In other areas, Laughlin favored a billboard control law and related measures to preserve and beautify state resources.

Remaining an advocate of the inclusion of women on juries, she was admitted to practice before the United States Supreme Court in 1931 to argue this question; she also traveled to other states to assist women convicted by all-male juries. Another favorite issue was prohibition, which she strongly supported, calling the day in 1933 that beer sales were legalized "the most shameful day in the history of Maine."

In 1935 Laughlin stepped up to the state senate, where she served until 1941. A loyal Republican, she vigorously opposed the New Deal and in 1936 chaired a legislative committee investigating the usefulness of federal relief expenditures in Maine. After her term in the senate she became the first woman recorder of court decisions, serving until 1945.

An ardent angler and golfer, Gail Laughlin was also an active member of the community, serving on numerous boards and committees. Laughlin continued her law practice until a minor stroke suffered in 1948 forced her into semiretirement. She died four years later at her home in Portland.

[There is no collection of Laughlin papers; some biographical clippings are available from the Resources Office, Wellesley College, and from the NFBPW, Washington, D.C. Laughlin's writings include the "Report on Domestic Service," *U.S. Industrial Commission Reports*, vol. 14 (1901), pp. 739–67, and "Equal Suffrage and Nevada Prosperity," *Out West*, Aug. 1914. Articles on her appeared in the *St. Louis Post-Dispatch*, July 18, 1919; *Independent Woman*, Feb. 1920, Jan. 1927, and April 1952; *N.Y. Times*, Feb. 7, 1925, May 19, July 15, July 16, Sept. 11, 1927, and July 7, 1932; *Equal Rights*, Feb. 14, 1925, and Feb. 12, July 16, and July 23, 1927. See also *Woman's Who's Who of America, 1914–15; Who Was Who in America*, III (1960); and Laura Miller Derry, ed., *Digest of Women Lawyers and Judges* (1949). Obituaries appeared in the *N.Y. Times*, March 14, 1952, and the *Portland* (Maine) *Evening Express*, March 13, 1952. A biobibliography by Anna Stewart was of assistance with research.]

RUTH SARGENT

LEE, Gypsy Rose, Jan. 9, 1914?–April 26, 1970. Entertainer, writer.

"Zip, I was reading Schopenhauer last night;/ Zip, and I think that Schopenhauer was right." These lines from the Rodgers and Hart musical *Pal Joey* (1940) paid satiric tribute to the best-known, best-read, best-self-educated, and most-quoted burlesque queen in America: Gypsy Rose Lee. Tall, gray-eyed, and willowy, with an upswept hair-do, she brought to the striptease a self-ironic presence which made "a wry and terribly funny comment on American hang-ups with sex" (*N.Y. Times*, May 10, 1970).

Gypsy Rose Lee was born Rose Louise Hovick on the west coast. Her father, John Hovick, was a newspaperman. Her mother, Rose (Thompson) Hovick, was to become one of the nation's most closely observed stage mothers. When Rose Louise was four, her parents were divorced. She, her mother, and her younger sister Ellen June (later the actress June Havoc) moved in with the Thompsons, in Seattle. It was there that Rose Louise, aged four, and

June, two and a half, made their singing and dancing debut at a Knights of Pythias lodge entertainment.

Their mother, who arranged engagements, was frugal, brutal, and "in a ladylike way, ruthless"; she could also be charming. She pushed the girls, terrified theater managers, and wrote anonymous letters of abuse to other performers. The girls never went to school. Once in a while policewomen would come around the theater where they were playing, and Rose Hovick would hire a "tutor" until the heat was off.

In 1922 the girls toured the Pantages Circuit as "Baby June and Her Pals." But their first long contract was on the Orpheum circuit in an act most often known as "Dainty June and Her Newsboy Songsters." It included Rose Louise, June, six young boys, and assorted animals; from 1924 to 1928 they toured vaudeville theaters all over the country, sometimes making as much as $1,250 a week. The future stripper dressed in boy's clothes and always sang the same song, "Hard-boiled Rose."

"Dainty June" escaped her mother by eloping at age thirteen with one of the newsboys. The act was reassembled as an all-girl act, but vaudeville bookings grew scarce. In 1929 Rose Hovick and her older daughter found themselves stranded in Kansas City, and "Rose Louise and Her Hollywood Blondes" had to turn to playing burlesque houses. In Toledo, they discovered that the burlesque star of the show with which they were traveling had been thrown into jail in another town. So, at age fifteen, Rose Louise Hovick stepped into a solo strip spot. It was a great triumph, and Gypsy Rose Lee (as she decided to call herself) went on to become a star at Minsky's at seventeen (1931) and a performer in the Ziegfeld Follies by 1936. It was at that first performance in Toledo, in 1929, that fright or modesty or showmanship induced her to wrap the curtain around herself at the end of the act and toss into the audience her garter with a rose attached. The gestures became her trademark.

Intellectuals and artists adored her. Jean Cocteau cried: "How vital!" A Vertès sketch of her nude at the typewriter appeared in Vogue in 1935. H. L. Mencken, in admiration of her art, called her an "ecdysiast," combining the Greek for "getting out" and "the act of molting." Such refinements amused her. She said of her act that it was like holding a toy in front of a baby, just out of reach, to make it laugh. Of her audiences she said affectionately: "Why, the little rascals, I adore them. Let me freshen up on my philosophy. I don't subscribe to St. Augustine's view that man is born in filth and predisposed to evil; I incline more to Clement of Alexandria who wrote that man should not be ashamed to love that which God was not ashamed to create. Meaning, of course, women."

In 1940 Gypsy Rose Lee wrote a mystery novel, The G-String Murders, which Janet Flanner of The New Yorker took to Simon and Schuster; it became a 1941 best seller. She followed it with Mother Finds a Body (1942) and a play, The Naked Genius (1943). Her articles, on a variety of subjects, appeared throughout the forties and fifties in The New Yorker, American Mercury, and Collier's. She had an instinctive and original sense of style and threw off criticism lightly: "Whom in the hell says whom?"

Her most successful work was Gypsy, A Memoir (1957), more a hilarious celebration of her mother's ruthlessness and of vaudeville and burlesque in the 1920s and 1930s than a history of her life. It was authentic Americana, with Mother Rose Hovick as the protagonist (although Gypsy said she was really the antagonist). It was later made into a successful musical comedy (1959); a film based on the musical appeared in 1965.

Gypsy Rose Lee the writer continued on the runways of burlesque: The Streets of Paris at the New York World's Fair (1940), and Star and Garter, burlesque for the carriage trade, after Mayor Fiorello H. La Guardia closed down the burlesque houses in New York (1942). She appeared in several movies, including Stage Door Canteen (in a famous satire on striptease, 1942) and Belle of the Yukon (1944). Earlier, after her first retirement from burlesque, she had gone to Hollywood and as Louise Hovick made five films, all flops, in 1937 and 1938. She also had roles in the film made from The G-String Murders (1943) and in Doll Face (1945), based on The Naked Genius.

Of the many Gypsy quotations that appeared in the press, none was press-agentry; she was quotable, and widely syndicated columnists used her witticisms eagerly and regularly. She sued theater managers who failed to pay up, defied an American Legion official who opposed her open support of the loyalists in the Spanish Civil War, and in the late 1930s caused even the Dies Committee (later the House Committee on Un-American Activities) to back off from a subpoena to appear before them; she had made too much fun of them at a press conference.

Gypsy Rose Lee was married and divorced three times: in 1937 to Arnold R. Mizzy (they were married in a water taxi off the coast of California and divorced in 1941); to Alexander Kirkland, the actor, in 1942 (divorced 1944); and to Julio De Diego, painter and designer, in 1948 (divorced 1955). In December 1944 she had a son, Erik; the director and producer Otto Preminger later acknowledged him as his son (*N.Y. Times*, Feb. 6, 1971).

By the 1960s the gypsy had become a full-fledged lady. She designed and decorated houses (most notably, a twenty-six-room townhouse with a pool and marble floors on Manhattan's East 63d Street); collected art and antiques (earlier, she had exhibited some of her own paintings in Peggy Guggenheim's "Art of This Century" show); gardened, cooked, and sewed with consummate skill; graciously received interviewers at home, among the objets d'art; appeared in television episodes and as hostess for a nationally syndicated television talk show in California; and became the dowager stripper whose times had finally caught up with her.

Gypsy Rose Lee died in 1970 of lung cancer, in Los Angeles; she had been living in Beverly Hills for ten years. Feminists may contemplate with delight the history of a sex object who made America laugh at sex—Sister Carrie without tears.

[There is a clipping file in the Billy Rose Theatre Coll., N.Y. Public Library; much of the material is undated, however. The best source is *Gypsy*; she also wrote two articles which appeared in the *New Yorker*, "Mother and the Knights of Pythias," April 10, 1943, and "Just Like Children Leading Normal Lives," July 3, 1943. For her further comment on her burlesque career see "My Burlesque Customers," *Am. Mercury*, Nov. 1942. *Biog. Encyc. and Who's Who of the Am. Theatre* (1966) gives a list of credits; Mel Schuster, comp., *Motion Picture Performers: A Bibliography of Magazine and Periodical Articles, 1900–1969* (1971), lists secondary sources. Several articles on Lee appeared in the *N.Y. Times* throughout the 1930s and 1940s. Her effects were auctioned in 1971 and 1978; see articles in the *N.Y. Times*, March 10, 1971, and April 17 and 20, 1978. A fascinating sidelight on Lee's career is given in her mother's series of articles, "A Stage Mother Tells of the Trials and Tribulations of Guiding Two Talented Daughters Along the Road to Success," which appeared in the *N.Y. Journal American* in July 1944. See also June Havoc, *Early Havoc* (1959). Portraits of her include John Richmond, "Gypsy Rose Lee, Striptease Intellectual," *Am. Mercury*, Jan. 1941, and those in *Cue Mag.*, July 17, 1943; *Variety*, Jan. 6, 1943; *N.Y. Times*, Dec. 8, 1941; and *Current Biog.*, 1943. See also "Fighting the Blacklist," *New Republic*, Oct. 2, 1950. The "senior stateswoman" appears in an article by Stanley Richards in *Theatre*, Jan. 1960. Obituaries appeared in the *L.A. Times*, April 27, 1970, and the *N.Y. Times*, April 27 and 28, 1970; there was also a memorial article by Leonard Spigelgass in the *N.Y. Times*, May 10, 1970. Gypsy Rose Lee's birth date is given variously as Jan. or Feb. 1914; no birth record is available for her. Death record provided by Calif. Dept. of Public Health.]

MARYLEA MEYERSOHN

LEE, Muna, Jan. 29, 1895–April 3, 1965. International affairs specialist, writer, feminist.

Muna Lee grew up in Mississippi and Oklahoma, but her career reflected her enduring attachment to Latin America. Her parents, Benjamin Floyd Lee, a druggist, and Mary (McWilliams) Lee, both college graduates and both descendants of early British settlers, nurtured their daughter's idealistic spirit and her devotion to learning. The family enjoyed a modest but genteel life in the quiet town of Raymond, Miss., where Muna Lee was born, the eldest of nine children (five girls and four boys), three of whom died in infancy. In 1902 her father moved the family to Hugo, Okla., then part of Indian Territory.

Lee returned to Mississippi at fourteen to attend Blue Mountain College, her mother's alma mater. With encouragement from her teacher, David Guyton, she began to write large numbers of poems. After a year at Blue Mountain and another year at the University of Oklahoma, she enrolled at the University of Mississippi, where she obtained her B.S. in 1913. The same year she published a three-line poem in *Smart Set*. From 1916, when she won *Poetry* magazine's Lyric Prize for a group of poems entitled "Footnotes," until the 1930s, Lee published well over a hundred poems in a variety of magazines. Her most representative lyrics are collected in her only book of poetry, *Sea-Change* (1923).

After teaching school in Oklahoma for several years, Lee went to New York to work as a confidential translator for the government. She had qualified for the job by teaching herself Spanish in two weeks. Dark-haired, dark-eyed, full of extraordinary vitality, she had already claimed some attention with her poetry when Luis Muñoz Marin, poet and journalist, presented himself to her, carrying with him a sheaf of her poems which he had translated. Lee and Muñoz Marin, the son of Luis Muñoz Rivera, one of Puerto Rico's most famous statesmen, married in 1919 and soon established their West Side apartment as a gathering place for literary figures. They had two children: Luis (b. 1920) and Muna (b. 1926).

In 1926 the family moved to Puerto Rico where Muñoz Marin edited his father's newspaper and pursued a career in politics. Energetic as always, Muna Lee ran their large household, helped her husband in his fight for Puerto Rican democracy, and held a job as director of international relations at the University of Puerto Rico. She loved the intensity of the rich tropic island whose landscape inspired her writing. Continuing to write poetry, she also branched out into translations and murder mysteries. Between 1934 and 1938, under the pen name of Newton Gayle, Lee coauthored five mystery novels with Maurice Guinness. She wrote in Spanish and English, and her poetry and prose were published in periodicals in both the United States and Latin America.

A woman of determination and independence, Lee was drawn to the fight for women's rights. In 1928 she joined a large group from the National Woman's party (NWP) who stormed the sixth Pan-American Conference in Havana, demanding an audience for women's rights. The speeches delivered by seven women, Lee among them, brought about the formation of the Inter-American Commission of Women. Her March 14, 1928, report of the event in *The Nation* said, "The women of no country will look upon the cause as won until it is won for all." Lee later took a leave of absence from her job to work as director of national affairs for the NWP (1931–33). In accord with the NWP position, she argued against protective legislation for women workers.

Even before Muñoz Marin was elected to the Puerto Rican Senate in 1940, his and Lee's lives had diverged. (Puerto Rico's most popular politician, in 1948 he became the island's first elected governor.) Lee returned with her children to Washington in 1941 and went to work for the State Department. By 1946 she and Luis Muñoz Marin were officially divorced.

Muna Lee spent the next twenty-five years working to promote a closer understanding between the United States and Latin America. As specialist in the State Department's Division of Cultural Relations, she arranged the international exchange of literature, art, and films. With Archibald MacLeish, then the Librarian of Congress, she collaborated on *The American Story* radio series in 1944. He credited her with the success of the program, praising her as "a poet . . . a sound scholar, a mistress of tongues, and a profound believer in a cause."

In spite of her demanding job, Lee still managed to translate several books and numerous poems from the Spanish, write a children's book, and coauthor, with Ruth McMurry, *The Cultural Approach: Another Way in International Relations* (1947). She also cared for her mother until her death in 1954. In 1950 Lee received a commendable service award from the State Department for "exceptional contributions in the field of Latin-American republics," and in 1951 she was promoted to cultural coordinator in the Office of Public Affairs. Much sought after as an adviser, in the remaining fifteen years of her life she appeared as a United States delegate at many conferences around the world. When she

retired in February 1965, she returned to San Juan, where her children lived and where she had purchased a home. Two months later Lee died there of lung cancer, surrounded by the "flame-trees and tree-ferns and frail white orchises," she had celebrated in her 1930 poem, "Rich Port."

[The papers of Archibald MacLeish in the Library of Congress contain official correspondence between MacLeish and Lee. In addition to the five mysteries and the volume of poetry, Lee wrote a book of children's stories, *Pioneers of Puerto Rico* (1945), and edited *Modern Haiti* (1936) with Richard Pattee, and *Art in Review*, the Dec. 1937 issue of the *Univ. of Puerto Rico Bull.* She translated Gen. Rafael de Nogales, *Four Years Beneath the Crescent* (1926), Rafael Altamira, *The History of Spain* (1949), and Jorge Carrera Andrade, *Secret Country* (1946). Her article, "The Inter-American Commission of Women," *Pan-American Mag.*, Oct. 1929, pp. 105–14, contains information about her work for women's rights as well as a photograph. An early bibliography can be found in Mary Frances Schumpert, "Mississippi Fiction and Verse Since 1900" (M.A. thesis, Univ. of Miss., 1931). Mary Reid, "Muna Lee: Poet and Feminist," *Hollands, The Magazine of the South*, April 1940, pp. 6, 25, contains biographical information and a small photograph. She is mentioned in Thomas Aitken, Jr., *Poet in the Fortress: The Story of Luis Muñoz Marin* (1964), and Joseph Blotner, *Faulkner* (1974). An obituary appeared in the *N.Y. Times*, April 4, 1965. Information was provided by Lee's relatives, especially her sister Virginia Reppy. Death record supplied by Puerto Rico Dept. of Health.]

ELAINE HUGHES

LEE, Rose Hum, Aug. 20, 1904–March 25, 1964. Sociologist.

An authority on Chinese-American life and the first woman of Chinese ancestry to chair a department at an American university, Rose Hum Lee was born in Butte, Mont., the second daughter and second of seven children (four girls and three boys) of Hum Wah-Lung and Hum Lin Fong. Hum Wah-Lung, born in Kwangtung province, China, migrated to California and worked his way to Montana as a ranch hand, miner, and laundry worker. He had his own business in Butte by 1900, when he married Lin Fong, a mail-order bride, also from Kwangtung province, and many years his junior. After her husband's death, Hum Lin Fong took over his business. Illiterate herself, she encouraged her children's studies despite the objections of more traditional relatives who felt that children should provide immediate income for their parents.

Rose Hum took the commercial course at Butte High School, graduating in 1921. Sometime thereafter she married Ku Young Lee, a Chinese citizen then studying in Philadelphia, whom she met while she was working as a secretary; the marriage was for love and met with her mother's disapproval. Rose Hum Lee went with her husband to China in the late 1920s and lived there for a decade, working for government bureaus and American corporations in Canton. When the Japanese invaded China in 1937, she aided the Chinese government by helping to organize emergency social services for refugees and war orphans, one of whom became her adopted daughter.

After surviving the bombing of Canton, Rose Hum Lee returned with her daughter to the United States, determined to pursue a career as a writer and teacher. Once again, Lee's mother supported her academic ambitions despite opposition from certain relatives who insinuated that she was trying to escape parental supervision and lead a promiscuous life. Lee persisted, financing her studies through lectures and free-lance writing. She received her B.S. in social work from Carnegie Institute of Technology in 1942 and then entered the graduate program in sociology at the University of Chicago, where she earned an A.M. in 1943 and a Ph.D. four years later. During this period, she also wrote two children's plays, including the popular *Little Lee Bo-Bo: Detective for Chinatown*, produced at Chicago's Goodman Theatre (1945–46).

In 1945 Rose Hum Lee joined the sociology department at newly founded Roosevelt University in Chicago. She became chairman of the department in 1956 and three years later was promoted to full professor. A woman of great personal charm, her striking success in overcoming the considerable obstacles she faced as a Chinese-American woman was due not only to her own determination and ability but also to Roosevelt's explicit commitment to equal opportunity.

Lee is best remembered for her pioneering work on the social structure and assimilation patterns of Chinese-Americans. In her dissertation she had analyzed the growth and decline of Chinese communities in the Rocky Mountain area. A grant from the Social Science Research Council in 1949 enabled her to study new Chinese immigrant families in the San Francisco area. Her major work, *The Chinese in the United States of America*, appeared in 1960. An original and comprehensive study, the book explored such problems as the conflict between "American-Chinese" who strove to enter the cultural mainstream and less-assimilated "sojourners" who opposed such efforts. Drawing on her own experience, she argued that the Chinese community's parochialism impeded its members' efforts to enter the larger society. Her own relationship to that community was severely strained. In a passage presumed to be autobiographical, Lee noted the hostility an educated woman encountered from sojourners and the efforts of a tong (secret society) to discredit her after she reported its leaders to the police for operating a "white slave" ring. Despite such tensions, Lee's position as an insider helped her define the distinctive features of Chinese-American experience, providing a strong foundation for further study. In addition to her work on Chinese-Americans, during the 1950s and 1960s Lee also produced comparative academic and policy-oriented studies on racial and urban problems, including *The City: Urbanism and Urbanization in Major World Regions* (1955).

A pacifist and a Quaker, Lee's commitment to integration extended beyond her scholarly work. She deeply believed in ecumenical cooperation and was an active participant in the National Conference of Christians and Jews and the Chicago Commission on Human Relations; in 1959 she received the Woman of Achievement Award of B'nai B'rith. She was interested as well in efforts to promote international understanding, and during the 1950s traveled in Europe and Asia, where she observed the modernizing efforts of developing nations. In 1951 she had married Glenn Ginn, a Chinese-American lawyer from Phoenix, Ariz. Lee took a leave of absence from Roosevelt University in 1961 to teach at Phoenix College (1962–63). She died in Phoenix of a stroke in March 1964.

[Sources of information on Rose Hum Lee are meager in detail. There is a file on Lee, including several photographs of her, at the Roosevelt Univ. Library. She includes incidents from her own life in *The Chinese in the United States of America* (1960), pp. 387–88. A partial bibliography of Lee's work appears in Hermann Bowersox, ed., *Faculty Publications to 1959: Roosevelt University* (1959). See also *Who Was Who in America*, IV. Obituaries appeared in *Chicago Sun Times*, March 26, 1964; and the *N.Y. Times* and *N.Y. Herald Tribune*, both on March 27, 1964. Information provided by Arthur Hillman, Mary Senoda, Robert Robertson, Roma Rosen, and Alva Maxey. Birth certificate furnished by Mont. Board of Health; transcript by Butte High School; and death certificate by Ariz. Dept. of Health.]

WILLIAM BURR

LEGINSKA, Ethel, April 13, 1886–Feb. 26, 1970. Musician.

Ethel Leginska, concert pianist and teacher, composer, conductor, and organizer of women's symphony orchestras, was born Ethel Liggins in Hull, England, to Thomas and Annie (Peck) Liggins. A child prodigy as a pianist, Leginska attracted the interest of Mary Emma Wilson, the wife of Arthur Wilson, a shipowning magnate in Hull. With the Wilsons' patronage, she studied at the Hoch Conservatory in Frankfurt, with Theodor Leschetizky in Vienna for three years, and in Berlin. She adopted the name Leginska early in her career, presumably because its Polish sound was thought to be advantageous to her as a musician. In 1907 she married Roy Emerson Whittern, an American studying abroad, who later became a composer and changed his name to Emerson Whithorne. They had one child, Cedric Whittern, born in 1908.

Leginska was a well-known pianist in England and on the continent when she made her New York debut in a solo recital in Aeolian Hall on Jan. 20, 1913. She was hailed by the *New York Herald* as a "remarkably sound, intelligent, and finished player." Soon thereafter dubbed the "Paderewski of women pianists" and compared favorably with her legendary predecessor TERESA CARREÑO, Leginska concertized in recitals and with orchestras throughout the United States each season, reaching a plateau in critical acclaim in 1916–17. She was an extremely popular artist and won praise from the press for her demanding programs, her magnetism as a performer, and her innovations—for example, playing an entire Chopin program without an intermission.

Leginska's bobbed hair and experimentation in concert dress in lieu of formal evening gowns also attracted notice, and around 1915 she decided upon an outfit that remained standard throughout her career, a black velvet jacket and a trim skirt, with a white shirt. She commented that the attire was "always the same and always comfortable, so that I can forget my appearance and concentrate on my art" (*Minneapolis Journal*, Oct. 11, 1915). In a similar vein, between 1915 and 1920 Leginska began to speak out on the various problems confronting professional women, such as arranging for child care, as well as on the need for women to strike out in new directions. The latter theme forecast her own bold move toward conducting in the 1920s. That she was sensitive on the issue of child care is not surprising, since in the winter of 1917–18 she lost a custody suit for her son in the course of obtaining a divorce. During the proceedings Leginska offered to give up her concert career and instead to teach piano exclusively, maintaining that she could earn $300 a week through teaching.

In 1909, 1925, and 1926, Leginska suffered nervous breakdowns. After several prolonged absences from the concert stage, in 1926 she announced her permanent retirement as a pianist in favor of composition and conducting. She had, in fact, been active as both a composer and a conductor for a number of years. As early as 1914 she was writing songs and piano music, and in the summer of 1918 she studied composition with Ernest Bloch in New York. Leginska's *oeuvre* is relatively small and dates chiefly from the late 1910s and early 1920s. Her style is modern in its rhythmic interest and use of tonality, and she achieved a certain distinction in that her orchestral and stage works, including symphonic poems, a fantasy for piano and orchestra, and the opera *Gale*, were performed by major organizations at a time when women's compositions rarely received such recognition.

More significant was her work as a woman pioneer in symphonic conducting and as organizer or conductor of three different women's symphony orchestras in Boston, Chicago, and New York. By performing as a conductor of leading American orchestras, beginning in 1925, Leginska dispelled the long-held assumption that women were not equal to the demands of orchestral conducting and symphonic repertory. Similarly, through her work with women's orchestras, she helped women gain credibility as orchestral players as well as the experience necessary to create the "mixed" orchestra of the future.

In establishing herself as a conductor, Leginska planned carefully. During 1923 she studied conducting with Eugene Gossens in London and Robert Heger in Munich. In 1924 she appeared as guest conductor with major orchestras in Munich, Paris, London, and Berlin, drawing on contacts developed during her years as a pianist. She seems also to have capitalized on her reputation as a pianist in securing most of her conducting engagements, by agreeing to perform in a concerto on the programs. Leginska's American debut as a conductor occurred on Jan. 9, 1925, with the New York Symphony Orchestra. It was followed by appearances with the Boston People's Orchestra in the spring and a triumphant performance at the Hollywood Bowl in the summer of 1925. Clearly she was a novelty, and, as the reviews indicate, skepticism abounded. The legitimacy of Leginska's conducting, however, won over the majority of her critics, who in turn announced that a new field had been opened to women.

Between 1925 and 1930 Leginska was based in Boston, where she founded and conducted the Boston Philharmonic Orchestra (1926–27) and headed the Boston Woman's Symphony Orchestra from 1926 until 1930, making two extensive tours with the orchestra in 1928 and 1929. During the late twenties she also established and directed the Boston English Opera Company and assumed the directorship of the Woman's Symphony Orchestra of Chicago, winning praise for the orchestra's progress during her tenure.

Always ambitious, Leginska left the United States in 1930 to conduct at a number of important opera houses in Europe where she met with great success. Upon her return in 1931 she conducted the revival of Franz von Suppe's *Boccaccio* on Broadway, and the following year organized the National Women's Symphony Orchestra, also in New York, which proved short-lived. Other notable performances at this time included Beethoven's Ninth Symphony in Havana and Dallas as well as the 1935 premiere of her one-act opera *Gale* by the Chicago City Opera. John Charles Thomas created the title role in an all-American cast, with Leginska conducting.

After 1935 conducting opportunities diminished for Leginska. Her novelty had faded, and her age also probably worked against her. In 1938 and 1939 she taught piano in London and Paris, and in 1940 she announced the permanent location of her studio in Los Angeles, where she was a respected teacher into the 1950s. In 1943, with Mary Holloway, Leginska founded a concert bureau, New Ventures in Music, mainly as a vehicle for her pupils. She also presented students at public concerts in performances of concertos with orchestra, which she conducted. In 1957 she conducted in Los Angeles the premiere performance of her first opera, *The Rose and the Ring*, which she had written in 1932. Ethel Leginska died in Los Angeles of a stroke in 1970, at the age of eighty-three, concluding a rich and varied career in music, one unparalleled for women in the United States up to that time.

[Leginska's unpublished works not mentioned above include chamber music: *String Quartet after Four Poems by Tagore* and *Triptych for Eleven Instruments;* orchestral works: *Beyond the Fields We Know, Two Short Poems,* and *Quatre Sujets Barbares.* Her published compositions include piano music: *The Gargoyles of Notre Dame, Scherzo after Tagore,* and *Three Victorian Portraits;* songs: "At Dawn," "Bird Voices of Spring," "The Frozen Heart," "The Gallows' Tree," "Six Nursery Rhymes," and "In a Garden." The Boston Public Library holds a scrapbook covering Leginska's Boston years. The N.Y. Public Library has clipping files. Other sources of information include a number of articles in *Musical Courier,* 1913–40, and *Who Is Who in Music* (1951). A photograph appears in *Musical Courier,* July 16, 1932, inside cover. Death certificate from Calif. Dept. of Public Health.]

CAROL NEULS-BATES

LEONARD, Louise. *See* MCLAREN, Louise Leonard.

L'ESPERANCE, Elise Strang, Jan. 1878?–Jan. 21, 1959. Physician, pathologist, clinic founder.

Born in Yorktown, N.Y., Elise Strang was the second of three daughters of Albert Strang, a physician, and Kate (Depew) Strang, a sister of Chauncey M. Depew, railroad president and United States senator. After attending St. Mary's School in Peekskill, N.Y., and St. Agnes Episcopal School in Albany, in 1896 Elise Strang entered the Woman's Medical College of the New York Infirmary for Women and Children established by ELIZABETH BLACKWELL. Greatly influenced by the institution's concern for women patients and by its pioneering efforts in preventive medicine, she developed a strong sense of identity as a woman in medicine. She was a member of the last class to be graduated (1899) from Woman's Medical College but, because of an attack of diphtheria, did not receive her M.D. degree until 1900. Her marriage to David A. L'Esperance, Jr., a lawyer, was short-lived.

Following graduation, L'Esperance interned for one year at New York Babies Hospital under L. Emmett Holt, a leading pediatrician. She then turned to private practice in pediatrics, working for two years in Detroit, and then in New York until 1908. Frustrated by the inability of medicine to meet many clinical needs, she turned to research, and was appointed a member of the Tuberculosis Research Commission in New York under Dr. William H. Park.

L'Esperance became increasingly interested in pathology, and took a position in 1910 as assistant to James Ewing, chairman of the department of pathology of Cornell University Medical College. His specialty was cancer—it was he who transformed Memorial Hospital, an affiliate of Cornell, into a famous cancer center—and it was with him that L'Esperance acquired the knowledge and skills necessary for her future research. From 1910 to 1932 her work centered on the pathology and treatment of malignant tumors. In 1914 she was awarded the Mary Putnam Jacobi Fellowship and spent six months in Munich studying malignant hepatoma. Her work, which was interrupted by the war and finished at Cornell, was published in the *Journal of Medical Research* in 1915. Other research yielded publications on the Wassermann reaction, gynecological tumors, and Hodgkin's disease.

L'Esperance's academic association with Cornell Medical College dates from 1912, when she was made an instructor in the pathology department. In 1920, when she was promoted to an assistant professorship, she became the first woman to attain that rank, which she held until 1932. After ten years' absence, she returned to Cornell as assistant professor of preventive medicine (1942–50), becoming full clinical professor shortly before she retired in 1950.

She also served at many hospitals in the New York area as a clinical pathologist. Among these was the New York Infirmary, where she was appointed pathologist (1910–17) and director of laboratories (1917–27, 1929–54). She was also instructor in surgical pathology on the second surgical division of Bellevue Hospital (1919–32).

L'Esperance's concern for the early treatment of cancer led to her greatest achievement: the establishment of the Strang clinics. With her sister and close companion May Strang (1880–1952), in 1933 she founded the Kate Depew Strang Tumor Clinic at the New York Infirmary with a gift of $30,000, in memory of their mother who had died of cancer. Thereafter she turned her energies to directing the clinic, which was established specifically for the diagnosis and treatment of cancer in women. Recognizing that the intensive education campaign of the New York City Cancer Committee had created concern among healthy women about the risks of cancer, L'Esperance founded the Kate Depew Strang Cancer Prevention Clinic in May 1937. The first organized attempt to prevent cancer by early diagnosis, it offered complete physical examinations to apparently healthy women to determine the presence of cancer anywhere in the body, and provided referrals for treatment. The clinic, which she directed, was staffed entirely by female physicians, a probable reason for its success in L'Esperance's view. At the invitation of Dr. Ewing, a second Strang Cancer Prevention Clinic, directed by L'Esperance from 1940 to 1950, was opened in New York at Memorial Hospital for Cancer and Allied Diseases. Originally for women only, this clinic soon included men and children. As a result of L'Esperance's successful initiative, clinics based on the same principles were opened in cities all over the United States. The clinic that originally opened at Memorial Hospital became the Preventive Medical Institute/Strang Clinic, with its own facilities.

Several major advances in cancer detection technology resulted from the work at the Strang clinics. Clinical evidence amassed by Dr. George Papanicolaou supported the value of exfoliative cytology (the "Pap" smear) in the diagnosis of cervical cancer. Early studies on the value of proctoscopy for evaluation of asymptomatic neoplasms of the colon and rectum were also conducted there. The clinics further served as a teaching forum where both physicians and patients were taught the value of a yearly physical exam.

L'Esperance was active in several women's medical associations, which she considered essential for promoting the equality of women in the profession. She was president of the Women's Medical Society of New York State (1935–36) and of the American Medical Women's Association (1948–49). She also served as editor of the *Medical Woman's Journal* from 1936 to 1941, and as the first editor of the *Journal of the American Medical Women's Association* (JAMWA) from 1946 until 1948.

Among her many honors and awards, she received the Clement Cleveland Medal "for outstanding contribution to cancer control work" presented by the New York City Cancer Committee in 1942. In 1951, L'Esperance was awarded the prestigious Albert Lasker Award of the American Public Health Association, for her "application of preventive medicine to cancer control."

In her seventies L'Esperance continued to be active as a member of numerous medical and scientific societies, and as a consultant in pathology at New York Infirmary (1954–55). She also served on several hospital boards. Her favorite pastime was raising and showing hackney horses and she had a unique collection of carriages to go with them. She died at the home she had shared for many years with her sister May Strang in Pelham Manor, N.Y., in January 1959.

[The Medical Archives of Cornell University Medical Center has some of L'Esperance's reprints bound in volumes of *Publications of Cornell University Medical College*. She published about thirty papers in medical journals, especially *Jour. Immunology, JAMWA,* and *Medical Woman's Jour.* Her best known works are: "Modification of the Teaching of the Wassermann Reaction," *Archives of Internal Medicine,* Jan. 1913; "Primary Splenic Hodgkin's Disease," *Proc. of the N.Y. Pathological Soc.,* Jan.-May 1924; "Early Carcinoma of the Cervix," *Am. Jour. Obstetrics and Gynecology,* Oct. 1924; "Embryonal Carcinoma of the Ovary," *Archives of Pathology,* March 1928; and a series of articles on cancer prevention and the Strang clinics in *Medical Woman's Jour.,* Feb. 1940, Jan. 1944, and *Bull. of the N.Y. Acad. of Medicine,* July 1947. Articles by L'Esperance on women in medicine include *N.Y. State Jour. Medicine,* July 1946; *Medical Woman's Jour.,* June 1936, and *JAMWA,* June 1949. Biographical information about L'Esperance is extremely scarce. See Miriam Zeller Gross, "Men of Medicine," *Postgraduate Medicine*, Aug. 1952, and *Current Biog.*, 1950. Several brief articles which follow her career are found in *Medical Woman's Jour.*, 1936–60; *JAMWA*, 1946–60; the *N.Y. Times*, 1942–50. Obituaries include the *N.Y. Times*, Jan. 22, 1959; *JAMWA*, May 1959; *The Necrology of the Faculty of Cornell University, 1958–59*, pp. 16–18. Information was obtained from the Strang clinics, the N.Y. Infirmary, the N.Y. Academy of Medicine, and the Medical Archives of Cornell Univ. Medical Center. L'Esperance's birth year is uncertain. The 1878 date comes from the 1900 U.S. Census, as does the information about birth order. Frances Sarli of the Field Library, Peekskill, N.Y., provided useful information.]

DEBORAH DWORK

LEVINE, Lena, May 17, 1903–Jan. 9, 1965. Gynecologist, psychiatrist.

Lena Levine, pioneer in marriage counseling and in the birth control movement, was born in Brooklyn, N.Y., the youngest of the four daughters and three sons of Sophie (Levine) and Morris H. Levine, a clothing manufacturer. Her parents were Russian Jews who had emigrated from the Vilno area of Russian Lithuania in the 1890s. The Levines were relatively prosperous among the many poor Jews living in the Brownsville section of Brooklyn. Lena Levine attended Girls High School in Brooklyn, Hunter College (A.B., 1923), and University and Bellevue Hospital Medical College (M.D., 1927). In 1929 she married a fellow student, Louis Ferber, and they did residencies together at Brooklyn Jewish Hospital.

Retaining her maiden name, Lena Levine became a gynecologist and obstetrician, while her husband remained a general practitioner; they practiced together in their large house in Brooklyn. A daughter, Ellen Louise, was born in 1939, and a son, Michael Allen, in 1942. In early infancy Michael contracted viral encephalitis and became severely retarded. Levine cared for him at home for five years with the assistance of a nurse and Pearl Harrison, a black housekeeper from New Orleans. Afterward he was institutionalized, and Lena Levine visited him regularly until her death.

In 1943 Louis Ferber died of a heart attack. This tragedy necessitated major changes in Levine's private and professional life, some of which ultimately encouraged her ambition. She increased her reliance on Pearl Harrison, who remained with the family until Levine's death. The all-female household, mother, daughter, and housekeeper, were extremely close.

Her husband's death also stimulated Levine to give up obstetrics, because she was unwilling to have to leave her children to perform sudden deliveries. She narrowed her practice to gynecology, then reoriented her medical interests toward psychiatry. Levine underwent psychoanalysis by Sandor Rado at the Columbia Psychoanalytic Institute. She became a Freudian, and later integrated Freudian theories with her concern for women's psychological and reproductive health and freedom. She opened a private practice in psychiatry at 30 Fifth Avenue, while continuing a small gynecological practice at her Brooklyn home. In 1957, when her daughter left for college, Levine moved permanently to Greenwich Village in Manhattan, maintaining her professional offices in her house.

During the 1920s Levine had become committed to the cause of birth control—that is, legalized contraception—and had met and come to admire MARGARET SANGER. In the 1930s she began to work for the Birth Control Federation of America (later the Planned Parenthood Federation of America). She also became the medical secretary of the London-based International Planned Parenthood Federation and was probably more prominent as an international advocate for birth control than she was in the United States. In the 1940s and 1950s her educational and organizational work became the major focus of her career, somewhat overshadowing but meshing with her private practice; her experiences with private patients formed the basis of her writings.

Levine's concerns encompassed a wide range of women's medical problems. With Hannah Stone (1893–1941) and Abraham Stone she conducted marriage counseling at the Community Church of New York. After Hannah Stone's death she and Abraham Stone, under the aegis of Planned Parenthood, organized a group counseling program on sex and contraception—perhaps the first such program in the United States. From the 1930s she worked at the Margaret Sanger Research Bureau, one of the main New York City Planned Parenthood birth-control clinics, and became its associate director under Abraham Stone. At the clinic she acted as supervisor of medical services and offered group therapy for sexual problems. She ran a Special Consultation Bureau for pregnant women, dispensing medical advice and helping some obtain abortions. Like almost all others in the birth control movement at this time, she declined to support abortion publicly in order to avoid jeopardizing the movement in favor of legalizing contraception.

Lena Levine worked effectively on both the individual and organizational levels. As a physician and psychiatrist she helped women with physical and emotional problems, and counseled them on the use of contraceptives. She was also an effective publicist, and wrote numerous books, pamphlets, and papers on women's medical and psychological problems for both professional and lay readers. Her topics included menopause, frigidity, virginity, contraception, and sexual relations in marriage. She lectured widely in the United States and abroad on planned parenthood, sex education, the sexuality of youth, marriage, and the family, until her death of a stroke in New York City in 1965.

A woman concerned with a broad range of social issues, Levine was a supporter of the New Deal, and she was sympathetic as well to socialist ideas. She was also committed to revitalizing and reforming the family along more egalitarian lines. Levine's writing and speaking helped erode some of the misogynist myths that surrounded women's physiology and psychology —myths about menstruation, menopause, virginity, and sexual arousal. She believed that women's sexual enjoyment, free access to birth control, and frankness about sexual technique would contribute to stronger marriages and psychologically healthier children. She supported women's economic and emotional independence, encouraged them to seek happiness in family life and in marriage, and worked to eliminate Victorian prudery and obscurantism about sex.

[Most of Levine's papers are still in private hands, but papers pertaining to her work are in the Planned Parenthood MSS. at the Sophia Smith Collection, Smith College. Her major published writings are: *The Doctor Talks with the Bride* (1936; 2d ed. 1938); *The Menopause* (1952), with Beka Doherty; *The Premarital Consultation* (1956), with Abraham Stone; *The Modern Book of Marriage: A Practical Guide to Marital Happiness* (1957); *The Frigid Wife: Her Way to Sexual Fulfillment* (1962), with David Loth; and *The Emotional Sex: Why Women Are the Way They Are Today* (1964). Levine's sex-counseling work is discussed in Linda Gordon, *Woman's Body, Woman's Right: A Social History of Birth Control in America* (1976). An obituary appeared in the *N.Y. Times*, Jan. 11, 1965. Assistance was provided by Ellen Louise Ferber.]

LINDA GORDON

LIEBES, Dorothy Katherine Wright, Oct. 14, 1897–Sept. 20, 1972. Textile designer, businesswoman.

Dorothy Wright Liebes, "the mother of modern weaving," was born in Guerneville, Calif., the eldest of four children (two girls and two boys) of Frederick L. and Elizabeth (Calderwood) Wright. Her parents met when both were teachers in one-room schoolhouses. Her father went on to become Sonoma County Clerk, founder of a telephone and light company, a land developer, and rancher. As a schoolgirl in Santa Rosa, where she graduated from high school, Dorothy Wright sold her first works—hand-painted flower pots. She attended San Jose Normal School, taught art for one year, and in 1921 received an A.B., Phi Beta Kappa, from the University of California at Berkeley. She then studied weaving and design, first at Hull House in Chicago, then at Columbia University and the California School of Fine Arts. By selling small handwoven items, she earned money for her first trips to visit European museums and weavers.

In 1928 Dorothy Wright married Leon Liebes, a wealthy San Francisco businessman. Leon Liebes, who had sponsored a number of young artists, gave his wife studio space in the building which housed his store. With his backing she began experimenting on a grand scale, and her weaves, commissioned by friends, attracted an ever-widening audience. Her first group show was in 1933 at the Decorator's Club in New York City. In 1934 she founded Dorothy Liebes Design, Inc., of San Francisco, and the following year received her first major commissions, from the Ahwahnee Hotel in the Yosemite Valley and the San Francisco Stock Exchange Club. By 1940 Liebes was well on her way to revolutionizing American textiles. Director of the influential Decorative Arts Exhibition of the 1939 San Francisco World's Fair, she had also won several awards and had shows in the United States and abroad.

When Liebes began, most weavers were making only standard cloths (twills, plain weaves, and damasks) of cotton, wool, silk, or linen. But Liebes saw weaving as an art with unlimited creative possibilities. She worked with unconventional colors—lacquer red, chartreuse, fuchsia, tangerine, turquoise. "There is no such thing as bad color," she claimed, "only bad color combinations." She used not only yarns, but also strings of beads, strips of bamboo, cellophane, metallic threads, leather, straw, and metal rods. Experimenting with the hand loom, she adapted it for open mesh (leno) and dobby weaves. She wove colorful window blinds; she bunched yarns to create sculptural weavings; she designed rugs, upholstery material, and gauzelike draperies. Her weaves, colors, and designs became the standard complement to modern architecture. Liebes's San Francisco studio employed twenty weavers from all over the world who executed one-of-a-kind, commissioned articles: materials for ocean liners, hotels, and private houses, theater curtains, and even gold and silk fabrics for the traveling throne room of King Ibn Saud of Saudi Arabia.

In 1940, when Goodall Fabrics hired her to design twelve fabrics, Liebes began a major new phase of her career, bringing her art and her craft to industry. She believed that beauty need not be sacrificed to mass production. Since machine looms, with their more uniform tensions of warp and weft, tend to create less interesting weaves than hand looms, Liebes experimented with new yarns, colors, and weaves that contained their own interest, translating hand weaving to power looms "with little or no compromise."

Her ability to create with whatever materials she had at hand and to forecast public taste led to many other industrial contracts. Dorothy Liebes was the dominating aesthetic influence in the textile industry's postwar conversion to manmade fibers and new technologies in dyes and finishes. She was design and color consultant for Lurex metallic yarns for Dobeckmun, and at DuPont for acrylics, synthetic straw, and nylon rug yarns. Through her work with Sears, Roebuck, she brought colorful fabrics and good design to a wide market.

Liebes's designs were used for everything from mattress ticking and sound-filter screens for radios to wallpaper and airplane upholstery, clothing and home furnishings. She gradually moved her work from San Francisco to New York, completing the move in 1952; by 1958 she was designing solely for industry from her New York studio. Her ideas seemed inexhaustible: she alone produced about 2,500 swatches a year. "There is no more esthetic delight in the world," she believed, "than putting beautiful colors together in a loom, watching the juxtaposition of thread as it winds its way in and out, and the resulting vibration of tonal qualities" (McCausland, p. 132). Often called "the greatest weaver in the world," Liebes was considered responsible for the excellence of American textile design.

Dorothy Liebes also sat on the boards of many organizations, including Save the Redwoods, the San Francisco Art Institute, and the Museum of Modern Art Advisory Council; she was the first woman on the board of the United States Finishing Corporation. During the war she was director of arts and skills for the American Red Cross. She and Leon Liebes were divorced in 1946, and two years later she married Relman Morin (1907–73), author and twice winner of the Pulitzer Prize for journalism. Their loom-filled New York apartment was decorated with her own weavings and works of Picasso, Matisse, and Calder. Her friends included fashion designers, artists, craftsmen,

architects, and Hollywood celebrities, attracted by her vitality, charm, and beauty. Liebes was active until her death of a heart attack in New York City in 1972. With creativity, intelligence, and business acumen she had influenced an entire industry and helped to transform the world's textiles.

[Mills College Library, Oakland, Calif., has a small collection of letters from Dorothy Liebes. Collections of her work are in the Brooklyn Museum; Detroit Institute of Arts; Oakland (Calif.) Museum; and Victoria and Albert Museum, London, England. Liebes's writings include two articles for *Craft Horizons*: "Designing Textiles for Industry," May 1952, pp. 19–21, and "All Is Grist . . . to Our Mill," Jan. 1950, pp. 16–17; and "Color as I See it," *House and Garden*, Sept. 1946, pp. 74–75. For biographical information see *Current Biog.*, 1948, and the catalog of the Dorothy Liebes Retrospective Exhibition, Museum of Contemporary Crafts, N.Y. City, 1970, which contains lists of commissions, awards, honors, and an essay by Nell Znamierowski. Discussions of Liebes's work include "Pioneers in Modern," *House and Garden*, April 1941; Yousef Karsh, "Meet Dorothy Liebes," *House Beautiful*, April 1945; Elizabeth McCausland, "Dorothy Liebes, Designer for Mass Production," *Mag. of Art*, April 1947; "Top Weaver," *Life*, Nov. 24, 1947; "Dorothy Liebes," *Handweaver and Craftsman*, Spring 1960; "Dorothy Liebes, Her Approach to Design and Weaving," *Am. Artist*, April 1971; and Jack Lenor Larsen, "Dorothy Liebes: A Tribute," *Craft Horizons*, Dec. 1972. An obituary appeared in the *N.Y. Times*, Sept. 21, 1972. Additional assistance was provided by William P. Wright, Liebes's brother, and by a biobibliography prepared by Janet Schwabe. Liebes gave 1899 as her year of birth, but 1897 is confirmed by the U.S. Census, 1900. Divorce decree came from Second Judicial District Court, Washoe Cty. Courthouse, Reno, Nev. Death record supplied by N.Y. City Dept. of Health.]

SARAH V. DUNLAP

LITTLEDALE, Clara Savage, Jan. 31, 1891– Jan. 9, 1956. Editor, writer.

Clara Savage was born in Belfast, Maine, the youngest of five children of John Arthur and Emma (Morrison) Savage who were of Scots and Irish ancestry. Only Clara and two sisters survived. Her mother was a strong, self-possessed person; her father, a brilliant man of classical training, could converse fluently in both Latin and Hebrew. Originally a Methodist minister, in the late 1870s he switched his denominational affiliation to Unitarianism. After Clara was born, he had a parish in Medfield, Mass.

Savage went to school primarily in Medfield, although she graduated in 1909 from high school in Plainfield, N.J., where her family moved to live with her older sister Grace after her father's retirement in 1907. From her brother-in-law, Charles A. Selden, then editor of the *New York Post,* Savage acquired her initial interest in journalism. As a high school student, she wrote for the school magazine. When she went on to Smith College, she became a member of the Press Board, and on occasion wrote articles for major newspapers, including the *New York Times.*

Graduating from Smith in 1913, Savage initially applied for teaching jobs, but went into journalism when a school principal pointed out that she clearly wanted to write. Her first job was with the *New York Evening Post,* where she was one of the first woman reporters in the city room. Quickly made editor of the woman's page, she was a frequent observer at suffrage meetings and in 1914 became press chairman for the National American Woman Suffrage Association (NAWSA). Later, she expressed dismay at having marched in parades carrying a banner that said: "If Idiots and Morons Can Vote Why Can't I?"

Discovering that she did not like publicity work, Savage left NAWSA in 1915 and became an associate editor of *Good Housekeeping.* She covered Washington politics from the woman's point of view and in June 1918 was sent overseas to report on the war. Her stories from the front were enthusiastically received. Told to come home at the end of six months, she cabled back: "Resigning and remaining."

In 1920, soon after her return to the United States, Savage married Harold Aylmer Littledale, a Pulitzer Prize-winning reporter, and later managing editor of the *New York Times,* whom she had met while working on the *Evening Post.* She continued to work as a free-lance writer; her stories, most of which dealt with marriage and family life, were published in *Good Housekeeping, The New Republic,* and *McCall's.* In 1923, the Littledales had a daughter, Rosemary, followed in 1927 by a son, Harold, Jr.

George J. Hecht, founder of *Children, The Magazine for Parents,* asked Clara Littledale—because she was both a mother and a writer—to become the managing editor of his new magazine. She refused at first because she planned to spend all of her time raising her daughter, but accepted in 1926. Littledale remained with the magazine (which changed its name to *Parents' Magazine* in 1929) until her death.

As editor of *Parents' Magazine,* Littledale attempted to provide "new knowledge in . . . health, mental hygiene, education and other fields" in readable form, and sought to make parents "more enlightened, more competent,

and more self-reliant" ("We Believe in Parents"). She advocated gentle discipline: punishment was necessary only when parents did not "guide" their children wisely. Encouraging parents to think of themselves as educators, *Parents' Magazine* suggested how they might use libraries, movies, and other community resources. The magazine also attempted to show them the relationship between their role as parents and the welfare of society, emphasizing national issues such as child labor legislation and federal aid for education.

Under Littledale's leadership, *Parents' Magazine* became "the Family Bible in many an American home." Its circulation, which was 400,000 in 1936, reached 1,000,000 by 1946. The magazine also provided study outlines—distributing more than 2,000,000 by 1936—which were used by mothers' clubs, Parent-Teacher Associations, and child study groups throughout the nation. In addition it brought out a number of book-length advice manuals, and gave awards for movies and books that provided outstanding family entertainment, as well as a medal for distinguished service to children. Clara Littledale's frequent speeches at meetings and over the radio extended *Parents' Magazine's* influence beyond even its large readership.

A devoted mother, Littledale worked at home three days a week and at the office four days a week while her children were young. In addition to her work and her children, she was interested in gardening and the theater; she had acted with the Provincetown Players during the 1917–18 season. In 1941, she and her husband were in an airplane crash that left him permanently paralyzed. Thereafter, their relationship, which had been strained for a long time, became untenable, and in 1945 they were divorced.

Six years later, Clara Littledale discovered that she had cancer. Despite a number of operations and severe pain, she continued to work until her death in 1956 in New York City. According to her son: "Her last years were happy ones . . . she was generally pleased with the way things turned out for her . . . it was a life that got better and made sense."

[Clara Littledale's diaries are held by her daughter, Rosemary Rieser. "Adam at Home," Aug. 1922, and "So This Is Marriage," Jan. 1925, both in *Good Housekeeping,* are typical of Littledale's early articles. Two articles in *Parents' Mag.,* "We Believe in Parents," Aug. 1936, and "Our First Ten Years," Oct. 1936, explain her philosophy as an editor. Her account of the plane crash is in the *Smith Alumnae Quart.,* May 1941. The Smith Alumnae Assoc. has clippings of her contributions to class notes in the *Smith Alumnae Quart.* from 1913 to 1955 and her obituary from the May 1956 issue; unidentified quotations are from these sources. For a summary of her life see *Current Biog.*, 1946, which includes a photograph. An obituary appeared in the *N.Y. Times*, Jan. 10, 1956. Her children, Rosemary Rieser and Harold A. Littledale, Jr., and her niece Eva S. Banks provided helpful information.]

ELLEN CONDLIFFE LAGEMANN

LLOYD, Alice Spencer Geddes, Nov. 13, 1876–Sept. 4, 1962. Educator.

Alice Lloyd came to the Kentucky hills at forty, a victim of spinal meningitis; she died there more than forty years later, leaving behind a college, a community center, and a legend. Born in Athol, Mass., the only child of William Edwin Geddes, a merchant, and Ella Mary (Ainsworth) Geddes, Alice Lloyd later rejected queries about her early life, and it remains shrouded by questions.

Her family had been well-to-do, and she graduated from Chauncy Hall, a Boston preparatory school (1894), and traveled abroad with her parents. Geddes enrolled in Radcliffe in 1895 but left in 1896, when her father died and finances became a problem; she returned as a special student in 1899–1900. In 1904, living with her grandmother (also named Alice Geddes) in Cambridge, Mass., she was publisher of *The Cambridge Press*, "a live newspaper published every Wednesday." Arthur Lloyd, whom she later married, was the paper's advertising manager. In 1905, she and her grandmother moved to Wakefield, Mass., where she was at first managing editor of the *Wakefield Citizen and Banner*, and later a freelance writer and lecturer.

Alice Geddes married Arthur Lloyd on Feb. 16, 1914; it was his second marriage (*Wakefield Town Report*, 1914). They moved to Gilmanton, N.H., in 1915, but left there in 1916. That year Alice Lloyd, apparently separated from her husband, left with her mother for the south, following her doctor's advice to seek a warmer climate. Her health, always frail, had further deteriorated in her thirties, when she was partially paralyzed by spinal meningitis.

The two women chose to settle in the mountains of eastern Kentucky, having heard from friends of an abandoned church-mission shack on Troublesome Creek in Knott County, an isolated and impoverished area. Knott County in 1916 had only one college graduate; few of its citizens could read or write and there was no public high school in an area encompassing parts of four counties. The average annual income was under twenty-five dollars. The hills had been depleted of timber; coal, which ultimately revolutionized the economy of the area, was only an insignificant source of income for mountain farmers.

Within a year Lloyd and her mother moved to Caney Creek at the request of Abisha Johnson, a landowner who offered her fifty acres of land if she would educate his children. There was a dilapidated schoolhouse on the creek but it was apparent that a better building was needed. Through letters to northern friends, Alice Lloyd and her mother raised enough money to begin construction on a six-room schoolhouse and to purchase the rest of the Johnson farm for a Caney Creek community center. Over the next forty-six years Alice Lloyd would laboriously type hundreds of such letters on her battered typewriter, soliciting the funds to support her schools.

From the beginning the school's mission was to train mountain youth to be leaders in their communities. The first few years were spent in cooperating with the county to develop an improved grammar school and to establish community organizations. In 1919 Alice Lloyd opened a high school with two pupils. Enrollment advanced rapidly, as did accreditation, and in 1924 it became the Knott County High School at Pippa Passes, the name Alice Lloyd suggested for the growing community on Caney Creek.

Within five years of her arrival, Lloyd had opened seven other high schools in surrounding areas. Each was started with gifts of money solicited from friends and staffed with eastern college graduates, often serving without salaries and paying their own expenses. Some, like June Buchanan, a Wellesley College graduate who became Alice Lloyd's friend and assistant, remained and dedicated their lives to serving mountain youth.

In 1922, acting on her belief that education was the means to leadership, Lloyd founded Caney Junior College. The college quickly became her central concern. She usually worked twelve hours, seven days a week, and ran the school almost single-handedly for more than forty years. The college relied entirely on contributions and accepted no state or federal aid during Lloyd's lifetime. Yet no tuition was charged and scholarships were given to promising graduates to further their education. Lloyd was able to attract trained professional faculty, drawn by the idea of the college, but its isolated location, coupled with economic insecurity, led to frequent faculty turnover.

Many of the traditions established by Lloyd in the early days of the college persisted through her lifetime and for some years thereafter. Students wore uniforms and all were required to work, both to provide necessary services and to help maintain the school. In addition, graduates pledged to use their training to help serve mountain people. Lloyd, a freethinker, had earned the respect and support of the mountain people by pledging never to interfere with their politics, religion, or moonshining. Within the college, however, she laid down a strict code of conduct: there was to be neither tobacco, whiskey, playing cards, or firearms, nor unauthorized meetings with the opposite sex. Boys and girls did not mix, even in classrooms. Believing that this Spartan way of life would thrive best in an isolated environment, Lloyd opposed the building of a paved road to the school.

Alice Lloyd also brought to Caney Creek her belief in traditional education. Convinced that youthful energy could compensate for lack of training, Lloyd instituted a rigorous curriculum, including Latin and Greek, literature, mathematics, philosophy, and the sciences. The school participated in no athletic program. It did, however, send students, Caney "crusaders," on tour to arouse interest in the college. During Lloyd's lifetime more than 200 graduates went on to universities, all expenses paid, while over 1,200 served as educators in mountain counties. Most graduates remained in the mountain regions, as Lloyd had intended.

Alice Lloyd's personal life was completely entwined with her work. Other than her mother, who died in 1945, her only close associate was June Buchanan. She was never well; her right arm was helpless, and she walked with pain after a leg fracture in the 1940s. William Hayes, Lloyd's handpicked successor as college president, once said: "The only picture in her bedroom was of Christ at Gethsemane—she identified with that. She pulled herself around campus, stooped and crippled by paralysis." She usually avoided publicity and refused any form of remuneration. In 1951, however, she was lured to California by the prospect of raising funds and found herself on December 7 the subject of Ralph Edwards's television program, "This Is Your Life." Edwards's appeal for funds for Caney Creek brought over $50,000 to the school by the end of the year. Alice Lloyd, feeling "rather ashamed of all the personal attention," said, "Caney is the important thing, not me. I will never leave it again."

She never did. In September 1962, with over half of her almost eighty-six years devoted to serving the isolated mountain people of eastern Kentucky, she died of a stroke. Following a simple service in line with her wishes, she was buried on a hillside overlooking the educational complex she had created. Almost immediately after her death the college was renamed Alice Lloyd College. While some of the traditions she established did not survive her, her goal of providing leaders to serve the people of Appalachia continued to dominate the institution's outlook in the 1970s.

[The Special Collections section of the King Library of the Univ. of Ky. has an excellent clipping file on Alice Lloyd and the college. Also in the King Library is a critical but fair report on the college, the result of a 1938 accreditation study directed by Maurice Seay for the Bureau of School Service of the Univ. of Ky. College of Education. The archives at Alice Lloyd College, Pippa Passes, Ky., contain the official college files, clippings, and general material pertaining to the college and its founder, and the tapes of a continuously expanding oral history program pertaining to the college and region. William S. Button, *Stay On, Stranger* (1950) is a popular uncritical study of Lloyd and the Caney Creek schools. See also "School in Caney Valley," *Time*, April 8, 1940, and Laurel Anderson, "The School at Pippa Passes," *Appalachian Heritage*, Fall-Winter 1974–75, pp. 108–10. An obituary appeared in the *Boston Globe*, Sept. 5, 1962. Information on Alice Lloyd's earlier career from the Cambridge and Wakefield, Mass., city directories and town reports; death certificate from Ky. Dept. of Health.]

RICHARD LOWITT

LOTZ, Irmgard Flügge. *See* FLÜGGE-LOTZ, Irmgard.

LOUCHHEIM, Aline Bernstein. *See* SAARINEN, Aline Milton Bernstein.

LOVEJOY, Esther Pohl, Nov. 16, 1869–Aug. 17, 1967. Physician, administrator, feminist.

Esther Lovejoy was born in a logging camp near Seabeck, Washington Territory, the third of six children of Edward and Annie (Quinton) Clayson and the first of three daughters. During a career of more than seventy years she established an international reputation as a skillful physician and administrator, a persuasive advocate of women's rights, and a scholarly author.

Her father, Edward Clayson, born to a poor English family, was a seaman in the British navy; her mother, also English, was the daughter of a tailor. In 1864 Clayson jumped ship on the west coast of the United States and made his way to Washington Territory, where his wife and son Edward joined him in 1867. Edward Clayson had a quick wit and a sharp mind, but his successive attempts to support his family—as lumber merchant, hotel manager, newspaper editor, and farmer—were all unsuccessful. In 1887 Annie Clayson moved to Portland, Ore., so the children could find work on their own, leaving her husband on the farm.

Esther Clayson was a sturdy, attractive, blue-eyed girl with an independent mind, a lively sense of humor, and an outgoing manner. Impressed with the woman doctor who attended her mother at the birth of her youngest sister, she resolved to study medicine, though she lacked both training and money. Her education consisted of a few years at a lumber-camp school and some lessons in Latin and history with an impoverished classics professor at one of her father's hotels. With only sixty dollars saved from a year's work in a department store and with help from a sympathetic dean, she entered the recently opened Medical School of the University of Oregon in 1890. By borrowing money and dropping out for a year to work, she was able to complete her M.D. in 1894, and received a medal for consistent academic achievement. She was the school's second woman graduate, the first to practice medicine.

Three weeks after graduation Esther Clayson married a fellow student of Czech birth, Emil Pohl, and they began private practice—he as a surgeon, she as an obstetrician. In 1896 she went for further training to the West Side Postgraduate School in Chicago. Upon returning to Portland, she and her husband were persuaded by her brothers to move to Skagway, Alaska, where the Clayson brothers sold supplies to gold prospectors in the Klondike. The Pohls became the first physicians in the area. They lived in a log cabin, visited patients on dogsleds, and helped establish the Union Hospital. After the mysterious murder of Frederick Clayson in 1899, Esther Pohl returned to Portland; her husband, however, stayed on in Alaska where she visited him summers.

In 1901 the couple had a son, whom they named Frederick Clayson Pohl. The boy was cared for by his maternal grandmother, leaving Esther Pohl free to pursue her career; she was even able to attend a clinic in obstetrics and gynecology in Vienna in 1904. She also started to take an active part in the woman suffrage movement and joined the fight against tuberculosis, becoming a member of the newly organized Portland Board of Health in 1905 and its director in 1907—the first woman to hold such a position in a major American city. She secured the first ordinance regulating the supply of milk, provided funds for school nurses, and helped Portland gain a national reputation for high sanitation standards. Ironically, the death of her son from septic peritonitis in September 1908 was attributed to contaminated milk.

In 1909 Esther Pohl returned to private practice, and the following year went to Berlin for more advanced training. On her return from Germany she received the news of yet another personal loss: her husband had died in the Klondike on May 11, 1911, during an encephalitis epidemic. Her bereavements drew her closer to the rest of her family, especially her nephews, to whom she remained close throughout her busy career.

In the next few years, besides maintaining her private practice, Esther Pohl became active in politics, continued to work for woman suffrage, and also supported the prohibition movement. In 1913 she married a Portland businessman, George A. Lovejoy, but divorced him seven years later because he was using her name to promote projects of which she did not approve.

During World War I Esther Pohl Lovejoy, as a member of the American Medical Women's Association (AMWA), attempted unsuccessfully to secure the right of women physicians to serve in the United States armed forces overseas. In 1917 she went to France, and although over age (she was forty-eight and her hair was snow white) she was assigned to the American Red Cross to investigate claims for assistance. Working to aid the civilian population of war-torn Paris, she served in a Red Cross center by day and did volunteer work in a charity hospital at night, often until two or three in the morning. Her experiences are recorded in her book, *The House of the Good Neighbor* (1919).

Early in 1918 Lovejoy returned to the United States. The emergency war-relief committee set up by the AMWA was expanded into the American Women's Hospitals (AWH), and $24,000 was collected for its work. Lovejoy gave frequent lectures on conditions in Europe, prompting citizens to contribute an additional $300,000 to the AWH treasury. She returned to Europe in 1919 as head of the group.

The first AWH hospital had been established in July 1918 at Neufmoutiers near Paris, moving a few months later to an old chateau in Luzancy. This AWH No. 1 set the pattern for the many similar hospitals in various parts of the world that the AWH established during Lovejoy's forty-eight years as director. The organization also founded outpatient clinics, orphanages, and public health services. Lovejoy personally visited troubled areas and returned again and again to the United States to appeal for funds, putting special emphasis on the need to prevent disease. She was one of the founders of the Medical Women's International Association in 1919, serving as its first president until 1924 and as president of the AMWA from 1932 to 1933.

In Portland in 1920 Lovejoy ran unsuccessfully for Congress on the Democratic ticket, campaigning for equal rights for women, prohibition, and the League of Nations. She subsequently gave up politics and concentrated her energies on the American Women's Hospitals Service (AWHS), as the AWH was later called. In her book, *Certain Samaritans* (1927, 1933), Lovejoy wrote of her work with this organization during the 1920s and of the efforts to relieve the suffering of the uprooted peoples of Europe, especially in Greece and Turkey. She devoted herself to aiding the impoverished, saving money by skimping on her own meals, hotels, and travel.

The AWHS aided victims of the Tokyo earthquake of 1923, the Florida hurricane of 1926, pellagra in South Carolina, and chronic poverty in Appalachia. During World War II the organization brought relief to people in Britain, France, and Greece, and in the postwar period expanded its activities to the Far East and Latin America.

Lovejoy did much to encourage women in medicine; in 1936, when she endowed the Pohl Scholarships for medical students at the University of Oregon in memory of her husband and son, she stipulated that a third of the awards be given to women. Her success in raising money for AWHS activities created more health-related jobs for women. Her last books, *Women Physicians and Surgeons* (1939) and *Women Doctors of the World* (1957), record the service and achievements of women physicians around the world.

In 1959 the AWHS separated from the AMWA to form an independent corporate body. Lovejoy left the directorship to become president of the corporation, but resigned this office in March 1967 at the age of ninety-seven. She died of pneumonia in New York City five months later. During her long life, she had received numerous honors at home and abroad, including the medal of the Legion of Honor (France), the Gold Cross of Saint Sava (Yugoslavia), the Gold Cross of the Holy Sepulcher (Jerusalem), the Gold Cross of the Order of George I (Greece), and, on two occasions, the Elizabeth Blackwell Medal of the AMWA, the only individual so honored.

[Estelle Fraade, former executive director of the AWHS, has letters and an unpublished autobiographical MS. by Esther Clayson. Biographical information, medals, diplomas, and photographs are located in the library of the Univ. of Oregon Health Sciences Center. Biographical information, photographs, and letters can be found in the archives of the Oregon Hist. Soc. The AWHS in N.Y. City has photographs, publications, and information about her career. Lovejoy's publications include: "American Women's Hospitals: 'a Cullinan,' " *Medical Rev. of Reviews*, Feb. 1934, pp. 104–8; and "My Medical School, 1890–1894," *Oregon Hist. Quart.*, March 1974, pp. 7–35, with an introduction by Bertha Hallam. See also Alma Dea Morani, "Reflections," *Jour. Am. Medical Women's Assoc.*, Aug. 1967, p. 571; "Esther Pohl Lovejoy, M.D., Founder and First President, Medical Women's International Association," Medical Women's Internat. Assoc. Golden Jubilee *Souvenir* (1970); Olive W. Burt, *Physician to the World* (1973); Libman Block, "The Doctor Was an Adventuress," *Today's Health*, 48 (1970), 20, 63; Marguerite N. Davis, "Dr. Esther Lovejoy, State Pioneer Woman in Medicine," *Oregon Jour.*, Feb. 14, 1968; and "Esther Pohl Lovejoy," *N.Y. State Jour. Medicine*, 77 (1977), 1161–65. Obituaries appeared in the *N.Y. Times*, Aug. 18, 1967, and the *Oregon Jour.*, Aug. 21, 1967. Assistance was also provided by Estelle Fraade, Bertha Hallam, and by Lovejoy's nephews John C. and Frederick H. Snook.]

ELIZABETH H. THOMSON

LOVEMAN, Amy, May 16, 1881–Dec. 11, 1955. Editor, literary critic.

Amy Loveman, one of the founding editors of the *Saturday Review of Literature*, was for over thirty years a mainstay of that magazine and a quiet but well-loved figure in the New York literary world. She derived both her interest in literature and many of the qualities of her personality and her work from her family. Her mother, Adassa (Heilprin) Loveman, descended from a long line of distinguished Jewish writers and scholars. Adassa Heilprin's father, Michael, left his native Piotrków, in Russian-dominated Poland, in 1842 to join Louis Kossuth's short-lived Hungarian revolution. Well-educated and an expert linguist, Michael Heilprin migrated with his family to the United States in 1856, eventually settling in Brooklyn. There he became a noted encyclopedist, regular contributor to *The Nation*, and outspoken foe of slavery. Adassa Heilprin exhibited briefly in public the family interest in politics and aptitude for writing, as well as its members' characteristic modesty, contributing unsigned political columns in the early 1870s to the *Week*, a New York periodical. Privately, she assisted in her father's and brother Louis's work in revising and editing encyclopedias. Amy Loveman's father, Adolph P. Loveman, had emigrated with his family from Hungary to the United States around 1850. A cotton broker, he was also a lover of books and spoke six languages.

Amy Loveman was born into this cultured family in New York City, the second of five children; the eldest child and only other daughter died in infancy. Educated at the Horace Mann School in New York, she graduated in 1897 and entered Barnard College. She received her A.B. in 1901 at age twenty, but it was some time before she found her niche as an editor and literary critic. Engaging briefly in private tutoring and volunteer settlement work, she eventually developed her skills as an editor, as well as expanded her general knowledge, by assisting her uncle Louis in encyclopedia revisions. For another uncle, Gustav Pollak, Loveman worked in the offices of the *New York Evening Post,* choosing articles for his book marking the fiftieth anniversary of *The Nation.* When the project was completed in 1915, she was asked to stay on at the *Evening Post* as a book reviewer. In 1920 she joined fellow staffers Henry Seidel Canby, Christopher Morley, and William Rose Benét in founding the *Post's Literary Review,* and in 1924 was one of the same group who put out the first issue of the independent *Saturday Review of Literature.*

As associate editor, Amy Loveman contributed unsigned editorials, assigned books to be reviewed, wrote reviews, and handled "The Clearing House," a column which answered readers' queries. She also edited copy, dummied pages, and read proof, seeing the magazine through all the stages preliminary to printing. Always devoted to her work, to the *Saturday Review,* and to her coworkers, who became her friends, she also saw that the office ran smoothly. It was she who volunteered to find lost copy, to stay late, and to mollify authors and publishers.

Norman Cousins, a later addition to the magazine's staff, has praised Amy Loveman for displaying in her work a rare "combination of incisiveness and kindness." Her prose was crisp and clear, her opinions moderate but direct. Like her favorite author, Jane Austen, Loveman exhibited great tolerance for human weakness while defending enduring ethical as well as aesthetic standards. Writing about her profession in the *Saturday Review* in 1941, she declared: "It becomes, then, the critic's primary business . . . from the welter of activity about him to isolate those manifestations which make for permanent good or ill, and in season and out to wage a lusty fight for or against them." In the novel, the subject of much of her writing, Loveman valued above all fully realized portraits of human character and conduct. Commenting in the twenties on modern fiction, she suggested that "so long as fiction concerns itself more with states of mind and emotion than with conduct we may continue to get from it admirable psychographs but hardly figures to be loved and cherished." Not that she decried experimentation; she befriended and praised the efforts of a number of the American novelists who were breaking new literary ground during the period that she served as an editor of the *Saturday Review.* However, she distinguished between "the new and the tentative" on the one

hand and "the bizarre and the sensational" on the other.

Loveman also had the chance to shape the reading habits of the public through her long association with the Book-of-the-Month Club, as head of the reading department from soon after the club's inception in 1926 and later as a member of the editorial board, succeeding DOROTHY CANFIELD FISHER in 1951. Undertaking what nearly amounted to another full-time job, she sifted through hundreds of manuscripts and reported on twenty or more every month. Like her role on the *Saturday Review,* her work for the Club earned Loveman little public recognition but a great deal of respect from colleagues, authors, and publishers. In June 1942 many of these people paid her tribute at a surprise dinner in her honor. She also received the Columbia University Medal for Excellence (1945) and the Constance Lindsay Skinner Award from the Women's National Book Association (1946).

Loveman continued her work at the Book-of-the-Month Club and the *Saturday Review,* where she had also become poetry editor in 1950, for a year and a half after an operation for cancer in 1954. She lived alone in a Manhattan apartment but remained close to her three brothers. Characteristically, she brought along her reports for the Book-of-the-Month Club when she entered the New York hospital where she died of cancer in 1955. Described as an optimist and a rationalist, and as unfailingly modest, Amy Loveman is best remembered by her colleagues for her ability to bring out the best in others.

[The Amy Loveman Coll. at Butler Library, Columbia Univ., consists entirely of correspondence. The Book-of-the-Month Club Records, Manuscript Div., Library of Congress, contain editorial correspondence and readers' reports. *The Reminiscences of Amy Loveman* (1955), in the Oral History Coll., Columbia Univ., is largely an account of the way books were selected for the Club. Also at Columbia are the Women's Nat. Book Assoc. Papers, which document the Amy Loveman Award, established in 1962 and awarded annually for the best personal library collected by a college student. Loveman collaborated with Canby and Benét on *Saturday Papers: Essays on Literature from the Literary Review* (1921) and with Canby, Benét, Morley, and May Lamberton Becker on *Designed for Reading: An Anthology Drawn from The Saturday Review of Literature, 1924–1934* (1934). Her *I'm Looking for a Book* (1942) grew out of the "Clearing House" column. She also edited *Varied Harvest: A Miscellany of Writing by Barnard College Women* (1953), with Frederica Barach and Marjorie M. Mayer. The *Saturday Review of Literature Index, 1924–1944* lists her contributions to the magazine during that period. Entries in the *Report and Register of the Associate Alumnae of Barnard College,* 1900–47, outline her activities. Loveman was interviewed for the *Barnard College Alumnae Monthly*, April 1934, by Clare Howard. The major sources of information about her career are the memorial by Norman Cousins in *Sat. Rev.*, Dec. 24, 1955, pp. 20–32, and "The World of Amy Loveman," consisting of tributes by Harrison Smith, Henry Seidel Canby, George Stevens, and Harry Scherman, *Sat. Rev.*, Dec. 31, 1955, pp. 19–21. Biographical sketches appear in *Nat. Cyc. Am. Biog.*, XLIV, 307; *Current Biog.*, 1943; and *Dict. Am. Biog.*, Supp. Five. See also Bennett Cerf, "Trade Winds," *Sat. Rev. Lit.*, June 27, 1942, p. 20; *Publishers Weekly*, April 6, 1946, p. 1961, and March 3, 1951, p. 1136; and Marjorie Shuler, Ruth Adams Knight, and Muriel Fuller, *Lady Editor: Careers for Women in Publishing* (1941), pp. 157–59. Information about the Heilprin family can be found in Gustav Pollak, *Michael Heilprin and His Sons* (1912); entries for Angelo and Michael Heilprin, *Dict. Am. Biog.*, VIII; entries for Michael and Phineas Mendel Heilprin, *Jewish Encyc.* (1904); the entry on Michael Heilprin, *Nat. Cyc. Am. Biog.*, VIII, 168–69; and Henry Samuel Morais, *The Jews of Philadelphia* (1894). Additional information for this article was provided by Hilda Loveman Wilson, Marion Pollak, and Ann Loveman Zimmerman. Birth certificate supplied by N.Y. City Dept. of Records and Information Services; death certificate by N.Y. City Dept. of Health.]

ILENE KANTROV

LOWE-PORTER, Helen Tracy, June 15, 1876–April 26, 1963. Translator, writer.

Helen Tracy Lowe-Porter made her most important contribution to twentieth-century letters as the English translator of Thomas Mann. From 1922 to 1951 she labored painstakingly to render the monumental, intellectually and stylistically complex works of this major German writer accessible to British and American readers. Her translations of almost all of Mann's novels (except *The Black Swan* and *Confessions of Felix Krull*) and of a great number of his short stories and essays played a significant role in winning a large non-German audience and international recognition for the author who lost both his home and his native audience when Hitler came to power in 1933.

While assessments of the quality of Helen Lowe-Porter's translations vary, there can be no doubt that her achievement is impressive. Thomas Mann's style and vocabulary posed endless difficulty: he exploited fully the German language's potential for constructing long involved sentences, and he often employed a highly specialized vocabulary from diverse fields of knowledge and time periods. His translator —who signed her work as H. T. Lowe-Porter— was an intellectual, keenly interested in the large historical, cultural, and social questions that he dealt with, and a writer sensitive to his art. She met Mann first in 1923 and over the years became a warmly supportive friend who sympathized strongly with the author's growing political commitment.

Publicly quite modest about her work, Helen Lowe-Porter was nonetheless convinced of its worth and meticulously perfectionist about it. She cooperated closely with Mann, read the books that he had studied as background material, and often sought the advice of experts. In general she felt committed to the tone of the whole rather than to individual phrasing and above all she decided, "English is what I want it to be." Mann often acknowledged her devoted services and her "linguistic talent." Skeptical about the possibility of translating "superior prose" at all, he still believed strongly that she had accomplished all that "is humanly possible."

Besides Thomas Mann, Helen Lowe-Porter translated the work of other German authors, such as Arthur Schnitzler, Hermann Sudermann, Bruno Frank, Franz Werfel, Frank Thiess, and Hermann Broch. Thiess, like Mann, was published in the United States by Alfred and BLANCHE KNOPF, who had originally urged Lowe-Porter to continue her work with Mann. She also translated papers and letters for her friend Albert Einstein and did some renderings from French, Italian, Dutch, and Latin as well.

Important as these translations were to her, Helen Lowe-Porter's great ambition was to be recognized for her own original work. All her life she wrote—poems, plays, prose fiction, and essays—but very little was ever published. On Sept. 28, 1948, her blank-verse drama *Abdication* was performed at the Gate Theatre in Dublin to good reviews, and in 1950 it appeared as a book. The play deals with contemporary history, the abdication of Edward VIII of England, in the manner of a Shakespearean chronicle. In 1957 Oxford University Press brought out a small volume of her poetry, *Casual Verse*. "Sea Change," a novel, remained in manuscript; of her many essays on political, social, and literary subjects only those concerning Thomas Mann ever saw print. Helen Lowe-Porter was disappointed by the lack of success in her creative endeavors and after 1951 retired from the consuming task of translating Mann in order to make one last concerted effort at establishing herself as a writer in her own right. By that time, however, advanced age and ill-health only exacerbated her failure.

Intellectual ambition was not unusual for women in the old New England family into which Helen Tracy Porter was born. She was the younger daughter and second of three children of Clara (Holcombe) and Henry Clinton Porter. Her father, a pharmacist, had moved from Connecticut to Towanda, Pa., the small town where Helen was born and grew up. A distinguished aunt, CHARLOTTE ENDYMION PORTER, editor of Shakespeare, Robert Browning, and the Boston literary magazine *Poet Lore*, was both a role model and a strong influence in her formative years. Helen Porter attended her aunt's alma mater, Wells College in Aurora, N.Y., and became an editor for the *Wells College Chronicle*, which her aunt had helped to found. After her graduation in 1898, she contributed translations and book reviews to *Poet Lore* and worked on the Shakespeare edition.

In 1906–07, while visiting her sister who was in Germany training to become a singer, Helen Porter met Elias Avery Lowe, an American three years her junior who was studying at the University of Munich. They were married in Berne in 1911. The couple had three daughters: Prudence Holcombe (b. 1912), Frances Beatrice (b. 1913), and Patricia Tracy (b. 1917).

Helen Lowe-Porter encouraged and aided her husband's early career, learning Latin to be able to do so. He became a very distinguished paleographer, receiving an appointment at Oxford University in 1913. From 1912 to 1915, and again from 1919 to 1936, their principal home—international and hospitable—was in Oxford. During World War I they lived in the United States. In 1936 Elias Lowe was invited to join the faculty at the Institute for Advanced Study in Princeton, N.J., and after 1937 they had a home in Princeton.

Helen Lowe-Porter held strong, somewhat radical social and political convictions. Under her aunt's tutelage she had become a firm believer in women's rights, and the experience of the Reading, Pa., coal strike in 1902 turned her toward a Fabian kind of socialism. Although a pacifist, she never questioned the need to fight fascism. After World War II, however, she again spoke for international understanding and deplored both the nationalism and the anti-communist campaigns of the McCarthy era, always regretting how little influence she had as a private citizen. Full of spirit and energy she remained active till late in life. She was increasingly plagued by ill health, however, and spent her last six years in Merwick, a nursing home of Princeton Hospital, where she died of heart failure. Among translators, a profession at once indispensable and thankless, she well deserves a place of honor.

[Helen Lowe-Porter's papers, including correspondence, MSS., and typescripts, mostly connected with Mann, are at the Beinecke Library, Yale Univ. *In Another Language* (1966), by John C. Thirlwall, on her association with Mann, has some biographical information but for the most part excerpts letters between them. It also contains two of her essays: "On Translating Thomas Mann" and "Doctor Faustus." Hans Bürgin, *Das Werk Thomas Manns: eine Bibliographie* (1959) has a list of all her Mann translations. Assessments of these translations were often included in reviews of Mann's books as they appeared in English; see *Book Review Digest* for the years 1924–51. A general discussion is E. Koch Emmery, "Thomas Mann in English Translation," *German Life and Letters*, July 1953. See also Klaus W. Jonas, "In Memoriam: Helen T. Porter Lowe," *Monatshefte*, Nov. 1963, and a *N.Y. Times* obituary, with portrait, April 27, 1963; death record provided by N.J. Dept. of Health. Assistance with research was provided by a biobibliography by Norbert Black McLean. Patricia Lowe gave further helpful information.]

CHRISTIANE ZEHL ROMERO

LOWRY, Edith Elizabeth, March 23, 1897– March 11, 1970. Religious leader, organization executive.

For more than three decades Edith Lowry was the national director of interdenominational Protestant work among agricultural migrants. Though for much of this time she also held important executive posts in national home mission agencies, she became the most conspicuous and best-informed leader in the ministry to migrants. She was a persistent advocate of these workers, whom she described in many speeches and writings as the loneliest, the most inarticulate, and the most forgotten group in America.

Edith Lowry was born in Plainfield, N.J., the only daughter of Elizabeth (Darling) and Robert Hanson Lowry, Jr. A brother died before her birth. Her paternal great-grandfather, a Scots-Irishman, had migrated to the United States from northern Ireland in the early nineteenth century. Robert Lowry worked in the loan department of the Chemical Corn Exchange Bank of New York. The family lived comfortably in Plainfield, where Elizabeth Lowry, of a family said to be of English and French descent which traced its American history back into the colonial period, had been born.

Edith Lowry was educated in the town's public schools and graduated from Plainfield High School in 1915. At Wellesley College she majored in languages and received an A.B. in 1920. After some volunteer YWCA service and substitute teaching and tutoring, in 1922 she commenced her lifelong career in home mission work by joining the staff of the Department of Education and Publicity of the Board of National Missions of the Presbyterian Church in the USA. Throughout her life, however, she remained a member of the First-Park Baptist Church of Plainfield.

In 1926 Lowry accepted a position as assistant to the executive secretary and assistant to the director of work with agricultural migrants of the Council of Women for Home Missions, an agency sponsored by the women's home missionary societies of a number of denominations. Long before most people were aware of the plight of migrants, she became deeply involved in the needs of these roving, poorly paid, ill-housed seasonal workers. In 1929 she was promoted to the directorship of the program. Her executive abilities were quickly displayed as, through the difficult depression years and after, she undertook frequent travel, working with migrants and visiting their camps to observe living conditions. She also directed a growing permanent and volunteer staff of nurses, social workers, teachers, and ministers, made speeches, and wrote articles about the work. Under her forceful leadership, the program mushroomed; over three decades the permanent staff increased from three to twenty-five, the work spread from five states to thirty-one, and there was growing public recognition of the migrants' problems.

In 1936 Edith Lowry's talents were further recognized when she became executive secretary of the Council of Women. When that agency merged in 1940 with the Home Missions Council of North America, the cooperative agency of the denominational boards, she became coexecutive secretary of the unified agency. In 1950 the Home Missions Council in turn united with other interdenominational agencies to form the National Council of Churches, and Lowry was named an executive secretary of the division of home missions. Throughout these changes, she retained the directorship of the migrant program and continued to develop new services. In the 1940s she established day care centers for the children of migrants; in the next decade she took steps to reach workers in remote camps, packing station wagons with films and records, health supplies, and on occasion a portable altar. She also directed a drive to inform migrants about their eligibility for Social Security benefits.

Edith Lowry retired from the National Council in January 1962. Long active on many related committees and boards, she had also devoted much attention to the interdenominational work of church women. In 1939 she was the first woman to occupy the National Radio Pulpit, broadcasting on the theme "Women in a Changing World." In addition to preparing many articles for church periodicals and contributing a monthly article to *The Church Woman,* she compiled a widely read booklet, *They Starve That We May Eat* (1938), and with two associates compiled *Tales of Americans on Trek* (1940).

Edith Lowry was an even-tempered, alert person of middle height with a ready smile; she was a firm but gentle leader of the many women and men who conducted the migrant ministry. From 1962 to 1964 she was a part-time consultant in Washington with the National Council on Agricultural Life and Labor, a clearinghouse for thirty-five private national organizations concerned with farm labor problems. She retired in 1965, settling on a farm in Perkinsville, Vt., which she refurbished. She died of arteriosclerotic heart disease in Claremont (N.H.) General Hospital shortly before her seventy-third birthday and was buried in her native Plainfield.

[Edith Lowry's papers, in the archives of the Nat. Council of Churches at the Presbyterian Hist. Soc. in Philadelphia contain correspondence, personal papers, and drafts of speeches, articles, and reports. There is also a clipping file on Edith Lowry at the Wellesley College Alumnae Assoc. There are several references to her work in Robert Handy, *We Witness Together: A History of Cooperative Home Missions* (1956); she was interviewed several times during its writing. Paul Marcus, "The Ladies Have the Answer," *Sat. Eve. Post,* Oct. 4, 1952, discusses the work of the Home Missions Div. of the Nat. Council of Churches. See also entries in *Who's Who in America* between 1952 and 1967. Obituaries appeared in the (Plainfield, N.J.) *Courier-News,* March 13, 1970, and the *N.Y. Times,* March 14, 1970. An informative biobibliography by Virginia L. Munford lists articles by and about Lowry; assistance was also provided by Elizabeth Gustafson, a second cousin. Death record provided by State of N.H.]

ROBERT T. HANDY

LUHAN, Mabel Dodge, Feb. 26, 1879–Aug. 13, 1962. Writer, patron, salon hostess.

In 1924, Mabel Dodge Luhan began her memoirs, four volumes of which were published in the 1930s. In these books, which are a significant contribution to American social and intellectual history, Mabel Luhan offered herself as a metaphor for the decline and the potential regeneration of American civilization. D. H. Lawrence, in a letter to Luhan, called the opening volume, *Intimate Memories* (1933), "perhaps the most heart destroying revelation of the American life-process that ever has or ever will be produced." The writing of her memoirs epitomized her life's calling: the search for and the creation of her identity. They trace as well her attempts to create a series of model communities, most notably the artist colony at Taos, N.M., to replace the disintegrating Victorian culture which had failed her.

Mabel Luhan's search for an identity and a community in which she could root herself took on symbolic dimensions not only in her own works but also in those of numerous writers who borrowed her to define their own views of American character and culture. Her extraordinary vitality and magnetism and her lust for experience, as well as the cruelty of which she was capable, took dramatic hold in the works of such writers as Carl Van Vechten, John Reed, Max Eastman, and, particularly, D. H. Lawrence. Believing herself to be a woman without a center, seeking to unify her fragmented sensibility through art, politics, love affairs, psychoanalysis (with A. A. Brill), even mind cures and astrology, Mabel Dodge Luhan paradoxically succeeded best in creating a subject for the art of others, a fact which has obscured the value of the work she herself did.

Born in Buffalo, N.Y., Mabel was the only child of Sarah (Cook) and Charles Ganson, members of Buffalo's upper class who lived on inherited wealth. A moody and highly neurotic man, Charles Ganson was trained in law, but, according to his daughter, "did nothing and finally died of having nothing to do." Sarah Ganson was a beautiful woman who expended her restless energies in a social life that often left her irritable. Looking back, Luhan remembered herself as a psychic orphan who craved the sensory and emotional stimulation denied by her parents and by her conventional upper-class education. She attended St. Margaret's School in Buffalo until she was sixteen, then Miss Graham's in New York City, with a final year at a finishing school in Chevy Chase, Md.

In 1900, at twenty-one, Mabel Ganson married Karl Evans, a young man from her set who she later claimed abducted her into marriage. The birth of her only son, John, in 1901, was soon followed by the accidental hunting death of her husband and, within a few months, the death of her father. She suffered a nervous breakdown and was sent to recuperate in Europe with a nurse and the child in whom she had lost interest at the moment of his birth. On the boat to Europe, she met Edwin Dodge, an architect from Boston, whom she married in Paris in 1905. Her second marriage was succeeded by the first of the severe neurasthenic depressions that occurred whenever she felt "unlucky in love." When the Dodges moved to Florence and purchased a magnificent Medician

villa, however, Mabel Dodge found her "life flow" in alignment with a "spirit of place"; her depression lifted, as it always did when she found herself in the presence of a person or a place to which her creative instincts could respond.

In Florence from 1905 to 1912 Mabel Dodge adopted Renaissance modes of dress and behavior, attempting to give form to her anomic American spirit by appropriating a ready-made European past. She lavishly entertained emigré royalty and American expatriate artists and involved herself in flirtations that twice led her to attempt suicide. A friendship with Leo and GERTRUDE STEIN, whom she met in 1911, emancipated her from this self-willed past into a future which seemed to offer the possibility of constant self-regeneration through art.

In the fall of 1912, Mabel Dodge moved to New York City, separated from her husband, and instituted at 23 Fifth Avenue the most famous salon in American history. Seeing herself as the vanguard of a revolutionary age, she cultivated EMMA GOLDMAN, MARGARET SANGER, Lincoln Steffens, Alfred Steiglitz, and scores of other modernists whose debates over anarchism, Freudian psychology, abstract art, and sexuality made her gatherings internationally famous. Besides collecting people who she hoped would transform her life into a work of art, she was drawn to numerous political and social causes, to which she gave time and money (the almost constant supply of which came from her mother). She promoted the Armory Show, worked to further Gertrude Stein's reputation, and supported struggling artists and imprisoned radicals. She also wrote for avant-garde journals, and for a time popularized Freudian psychology in a weekly column for the Hearst papers (1917–18). In the mode of the times, she experimented with free love; in a rare maternal moment, she adopted an orphaned girl, whom she later disregarded. Making herself a leading advocate of modernism, Mabel Dodge also became, according to a contemporary news account, a "national institution."

One major impulse for her activism between 1913 and 1915 was her affair with John Reed, the radical journalist. With him she planned and raised money for the spectacular but unsuccessful Madison Square Garden pageant designed to give support to striking textile workers in Paterson, N.J. Reed's failure to give her his undivided loyalty drove her to another attempted suicide, and, finally, to a retreat from radical politics into the pastoral world of Croton-on-Hudson, N.Y. There, in 1916, she met Maurice Sterne, a postimpressionist painter with whom she lived for a year, before marrying him in 1917 with the hope of turning him into a sculptor.

Her relationship with Sterne epitomized her dilemma. Claiming to believe that women were capable only of "secondary" creativity, she turned her remarkable energies to serving as a muse to male genius. The results for her male friends and lovers were sometimes fruitful, but sometimes disastrous. For her the role was never satisfying, but she also found herself unable to accept the other options society seemed to offer: motherhood or a professional career. She continued throughout her life to search for a way to direct her energies and impulses that would satisfy her sense of mission.

In 1918, the Sternes moved to Taos, N.M., her final "cosmos" and the place where she came closest to realizing her hopes. In the spring of that year she met Tony Lujan, a full-blooded Pueblo Indian who became her lover; divorcing Sterne, she married Lujan in April 1923. Through her contact with him and with the Pueblo Indians, Mabel Dodge Luhan underwent a conversion experience so compelling that she spent much of the rest of her life trying to convert others to the Indian way of life. Believing that she and her husband were fated to be messiahs, she envisioned Taos, "the beating heart of the universe," as the center of spiritual and cultural redemption for a bankrupt white civilization.

The Pueblos had what Mabel Luhan (her phonetic spelling of the name) had been seeking: a society in which each individual achieved integrity through commitment to personal, artistic, and religious values that were also integral expressions of an organic, communal way of life. For twenty years she called others to Taos to help celebrate and preserve the Eden she had discovered: Georgia O'Keeffe and Andrew Dasburg to immortalize its beauty; Leopold Stokowski to capture the rhythms of native American music; John Collier to protect the Indians' territorial rights and way of life; and Robinson Jeffers and D. H. Lawrence to write its gospel. Her personality and her vision were at once attractive and repellent to Lawrence and her presence can be felt in most of his American works.

Throughout the 1920s and 1930s, Mabel Luhan used her money and influence to fight for land reform, self-determination, and medical benefits for the Indians. In the many articles she wrote, she was an articulate advocate for the culture which she tried, but failed, to adopt for her own. In 1935 she published *Winter in Taos*, a powerfully lyrical testament to the land

and people she believed had redeemed her.

Mabel Dodge Luhan died in Taos in 1962 of a heart attack. She never fulfilled her messianic dream, but she had, in the words of Claire Morrill, "acknowledged the wonder" of Taos's spirit of place and had drawn there men and women of achievement and vision who did the same. This act of creation, with her books and the force of her presence, give her a unique place in American cultural history.

[The Mabel Dodge Luhan Papers in the Beinecke Library, Yale Univ., contain twenty-three volumes of autobiographical materials, most of Luhan's published and unpublished poetry, essays, short stories, and the MSS. of two unpublished novels. The autobiographical MSS. are not open to scholars, but the several volumes of letters to and by Mabel Luhan are, as are her scrapbooks and other MSS. The Bancroft Library, Univ. of Calif., Berkeley, contains Mabel Luhan's extensive correspondence with Robinson and Una Jeffers. Her other published books are *Lorenzo in Taos* (1932); *European Experiences* (1935); *Movers and Shakers* (1936); *Edge of the Taos Desert: An Escape to Reality* (1937); *Taos and Its Artists* (1947). There are two biographies: Emily Hahn's anecdotal account of her life, *Mabel* (1977), and Lois Rudnick's dissertation, "The Unexpurgated Self: A Critical Biography of Mabel Dodge Luhan" (Brown Univ., 1977), which includes a bibliographical checklist of most of Luhan's published essays, stories, and poetry. For accounts of her character and significance see: Christopher Lasch, *The New Radicalism in America* (1965); Hutchins Hapgood, *A Victorian in the Modern World* (1939); *The Autobiography of Lincoln Steffens*, vol. II (1931); Robert Crunden, *From Self to Society, 1919–1941* (1972); Joseph Foster, *D. H. Lawrence in Taos* (1972); Maurice Sterne, *Shadow and Light* (1952); Claire Morrill, *A Taos Mosaic* (1973); Martin Green, *The Von Richtofen Sisters* (1974). A death record was provided by the N.M. Dept. of Health.]

LOIS RUDNICK

LUNDBERG, Emma Octavia, Oct. 26, 1881–Nov. 17, 1954. Social worker.

Emma Lundberg, a specialist in child welfare, was born at Tranegärdet, Humle Socken, Västergötland, Sweden, the third of four children and middle daughter of Frans Vilhelm and Anna Kajsa (Johanson) Lundberg; her younger sister died in infancy. In 1884 the family migrated to the United States, where they settled eventually in Rockford, Ill., site of a large Swedish community. There her father, a machine hand, worked for several furniture manufacturers. After first studying in Swedish at home, Emma Lundberg attended public school, and graduated from Rockford High School in 1901.

For the next few years, in order to save money for college, she worked as a bookkeeper and stenographer for a local firm.

In the fall of 1903, Lundberg entered the University of Wisconsin at Madison. While supporting herself by doing secretarial work, she earned an A.B. in English in 1907 and an A.M. in 1908. Her courses in sociology and political economy with social progressives Lester F. Ward and John R. Commons influenced her ultimate choice of career. In 1910, she enrolled in a doctoral program in philology at the university. Although she never completed it, she maintained a deep interest in language, as well as a love of poetry, which she both read and wrote throughout her life.

Lundberg began her long career in social service in 1908 by conducting a cost-of-living study in Buffalo, under Frederic Almy, a leader of the charity organization movement. In the next two years, she conducted studies of immigrants in several cities for the United States Immigration Commission, served on the staff of the United Charities of Chicago, and attended lectures on relief at the Chicago School of Civics and Philanthropy; she later completed two summer sessions at the New York School of Philanthropy. During these years, Lundberg also lived in settlement houses in several cities. After working with the Associated Charities in both Madison and Milwaukee (1910–12), she became a deputy for the recently established Wisconsin Industrial Commission. In that capacity Lundberg continued to advance her skills as an investigator and author, studying the problems of women and children in industry, producing such reports as *Cost of Living of Wage Earning Women in Wisconsin* (1916), and helping to implement the state's labor laws for women and children. In 1913 a young graduate of the University of Wisconsin, Katharine Fredrica Lenroot, began to serve as her assistant, initiating a close friendship which lasted until Lundberg's death.

Lundberg's long affiliation with the United States Children's Bureau began in November 1914, when the Bureau's chief, JULIA LATHROP, named her head of the new social service division. Her work at the Children's Bureau set high standards for research in an emerging profession and promoted acceptance of public welfare services for children. For eleven years Lundberg, who traveled extensively, directed investigations on such problems as the care of mentally defective children, child dependency and neglect, juvenile delinquency, state laws for children, and, especially, illegitimacy. In the 1920s and early 1930s, she also became known

as a specialist on mothers' pensions, government payments to destitute women with children. Lundberg, who maintained that mothers' pensions kept families together and gave children the benefits of their mothers' care, helped to reshape professional opinion into accepting this type of assistance as a form of child welfare. She sounded the same theme in her approach to illegitimacy. On the basis of evidence that she and the Bureau staff had compiled, she contended that unmarried mothers should keep, nurse, and raise their babies rather than surrender them for adoption. One of the Children's Bureau's leading specialists on illegitimacy, she wrote studies and planned conferences on the subject, and influenced the acceptance of this principle into social casework in the 1920s and early 1930s. Her Bureau publications encouraging states to provide public welfare services for children developed her reputation as an expert on the subject, and, during World War I and in the early 1920s, Lundberg advised several state child welfare commissions that were revising and adopting new state child welfare laws.

Her service at the Bureau was interrupted at the end of 1925 when she accepted an offer from the Child Welfare League of America (CWLA), with headquarters in New York City. She worked for the organization for nearly five years, first as director of institutional care and later as director of studies and surveys. On leave from the CWLA, in late 1929 and 1930 she served as research secretary to Section IV of the 1930 White House Conference on Child Health and Protection, which dealt with handicapped, dependent, neglected, and delinquent children. In Lundberg's report on the child welfare services of federal agencies, she again emphasized the need to develop and strengthen public welfare provisions for children. Her experimental statistical study, conducted for the CWLA and published as *Child Dependency in the United States* (1933), collected data on dependent and neglected children not, as had been done previously, from the Bureau of the Census but from various state welfare departments. The study prompted public departments to improve their collection of statistics and reports on such children.

Emma Lundberg accepted a position with the New York State Temporary Emergency Relief Administration in New York City in 1931, and soon became its director of research and statistics. The experience broadened her interests and expertise to include such problems as public relief and food costs. Her reputation as a researcher also led various public agencies to engage her as a consultant. Studies she conducted in this capacity included *Unmarried Mothers in the Municipal Court of Philadelphia* (1933) and *Social Welfare in Florida* (1934).

When Katharine Lenroot became chief of the Children's Bureau in 1934, she called quickly for Lundberg's return. In 1935 Lundberg became the assistant director of the Bureau's child welfare division. There she helped to establish and strengthen state child welfare services under the Social Security Act of 1935, which provided federal funds to states to create and improve public welfare services for dependent, neglected, and potentially delinquent children, primarily in rural areas. Lundberg, who had participated in each but the first of the White House conferences on children, served as assistant secretary of the White House Conference on Children in a Democracy in 1940 and was responsible for the conference's administrative work. In the last of several Bureau positions, in 1942 she became consultant in social services for children.

Declining health forced Lundberg to resign from the Bureau at the end of 1944. Lenroot, who still served as Bureau chief, cared for Lundberg, now an invalid, at their Washington, D.C., home. Years of work culminated for Lundberg with the publication in 1947 of *Unto the Least of These*, a lively history of child welfare and a personal statement of children's needs and rights. After Lenroot retired from the Bureau in 1951, the two women moved to a country home in Hartsdale, N.Y., where Emma Lundberg died three years later of a stroke.

[The Emma Lundberg Papers in Butler Library, Columbia Univ., which consist of unpublished and published speeches, articles, and pamphlets, contain virtually no personal information or correspondence. Several Lundberg letters in the files of the Children's Bureau at the Nat. Archives also refer exclusively to her work. The most helpful source of biographical information is *The Reminiscences of Katharine Lenroot* in the Oral History Coll., Columbia Univ. The Rockford (Ill.) Public Library has a small file on Lundberg, including local newspaper articles and obituaries. *Illegitimacy as a Child-Welfare Problem*, part I (1920) and part II (1922), Children's Bureau publications no. 66 and no. 75, coauthored by Lenroot, are Lundberg's most important publications on illegitimacy. Lundberg's "A Man of Good Will," *The Family*, March 1946, contains information about her early career. An accessible tribute to Lundberg by Lenroot is in *Child Welfare*, Jan. 1955; another brief evaluation of her work appeared in Lenroot, "Origins of the Social Welfare Provisions," *Children*, July-Aug. 1960, reprinted in Robert Bremner, ed., *Children and Youth in America: A Documentary History*, vol. III (1974). An obituary appeared in the *N.Y. Times*,

Nov. 18, 1954. A photograph of Lundberg appeared in *Survey Midmonthly*, Feb. 1945. Clarence McDermaid, Lundberg's nephew, supplied information helpful in preparing this article. Birth and immigration information were provided by First Lutheran Church, Rockford, Ill., and Nat. Central Bureau of Statistics, Stockholm, Sweden; death record supplied by N.Y. State Dept. of Health.]

PETER ROMANOFSKY

LUSK, Georgia Lee Witt, May 12, 1893–Jan. 5, 1971. Educator, state government official, congresswoman.

Georgia Lusk, often referred to as "the first lady of New Mexico politics," was born on Blue Spring Ranch in Eddy County, near Carlsbad, N.Mex., eldest of the three daughters and one son of George and Mary Isabel (Gilreath) Witt. Her parents were Methodists of English and Welsh ancestry, and her father was a surveyor as well as a rancher. She grew up on the ranch and, after graduating from Carlsbad High School in 1912, enrolled at New Mexico State Teachers College (later Western New Mexico University) in Silver City. She began her teaching career in Eddy County in 1914. The following year she married Dolph Lusk, a rancher and banker, quitting teaching temporarily as she and her husband settled on a ranch near Lovington. Dolph Lusk died suddenly in 1919, leaving his wife with two sons, Virgil Witt (b. 1916) and Morgan Dolph (b. 1918), and pregnant with a third, Thomas Eugene, who was born in 1920.

The next few years were difficult ones for Lusk. She resumed her teaching career while continuing to manage the family ranch and raise her three sons. Her parents gave her some help with the children, and she often took the younger boys to school with her. During this period Lusk developed the independence which later helped to make her a successful politician.

Lusk's political career spanned thirty-five years, from 1924 when she successfully ran for superintendent of Lea County schools until 1959 when she retired after twelve years as superintendent of public instruction for the state of New Mexico. Defeated in her first race for the post in 1928, she was elected superintendent of public instruction six times between 1930 and 1956 and elected to Congress once, in 1946. From 1935 until 1942, Lusk devoted her energies to her 16,000-acre ranch and to her family, although she did serve as rural school supervisor in Guadalupe County in 1941 and 1942. From 1949 until 1953 she held appointive office as a member of the War Claims Commission.

As superintendent of public instruction, Georgia Lusk dramatically upgraded the quality of education in New Mexico. She was instrumental in putting free textbooks in all of the state's public schools, and in convincing a reluctant state legislature to finance school building programs, dramatic increases in teachers' salaries, and a teacher retirement program. She improved the quality of education in the state's remote rural areas, hired the state's first director of physical education, and expanded the instructional programs offered in the state's schools. Pleased that she may have helped to open the way for other women to enter school administration, Lusk nevertheless believed that women "still have to work . . . indirectly, not on terms of full equality. Men will listen to women, but they are unwilling to give them recognition" (*Ladies of Courage*, p. 135).

In 1946, Lusk was barred by state law from running for a third consecutive term as superintendent of public instruction. Free of family and business obligations (her eldest son had been killed in the war, the others were grown, and she had sold the ranch in 1943), Lusk, a Democrat, announced her candidacy for Congress. Her election made her the first New Mexico woman to be sent to Congress. The well-liked, mild-mannered congresswoman served only one term, losing her bid for renomination in 1948.

As congresswoman, Lusk supported federal aid to education, including vocational and rehabilitation programs, and improved school lunch programs; she also favored the creation of a cabinet-level department of education. Assigned at her request to the Veterans Affairs Committee, she worked for increased benefits for veterans. She supported the foreign policy of President Harry S Truman, voting in favor of foreign aid appropriations, including Truman's request for military assistance to Greece and Turkey.

Although Lusk was involuntarily retired from Congress on Jan. 3, 1949, she remained out of public life only a short time. In July 1949 Truman appointed her to the newly created War Claims Commission, charged with distributing $179 million of enemy assets to servicemen and civilians who had been interned in enemy prison camps during World War II. Lusk served on the commission until December 1953, when President Dwight D. Eisenhower replaced her with a Republican.

After once again serving for four years as superintendent of public instruction in New Mexico, Lusk retired in 1959. Her political activity in her later years was directed mainly at advising her son Eugene, the majority leader of

the New Mexico state senate for four years and the Democratic nominee for governor in 1966. (He was defeated in the general election.) In 1971, two years after Eugene Lusk committed suicide, Georgia Lusk died in Albuquerque of thyroid cancer.

[The Georgia L. Lusk Coll. at the N.Mex. State Records Center and Archives in Santa Fe contains her congressional correspondence, records of her years on the War Claims Commission, and ten scrapbooks of newspaper clippings covering some of her years as superintendent of public instruction. Her congressional activities are recorded in the *Congressional Record*, 80th Cong., vols. 93 and 94. The results of Lusk's elections can be found in *New Mexico Election Returns, 1911–1969* (1970). The only comprehensive treatment of her life is Roger D. Hardaway, "Georgia Lusk of New Mexico: A Political Biography" (M.A. thesis, N.Mex. State Univ., 1979). Lusk's election to Congress in 1946 is the subject of Roger D. Hardaway, "New Mexico Elects a Congresswoman," *Red River Valley Hist. Rev.*, Fall 1979. Her accomplishments as superintendent of public instruction are highlighted in Alice Fraser, "Two New But Not Too New," *Independent Woman*, Jan. 1947, pp. 2–3, 27, and (with some inaccuracies) in Eleanor Roosevelt and Lorena A. Hickok, *Ladies of Courage* (1954), pp. 130–36. For an accurate account of her life up to 1947 see *Current Biog.*, 1947, and for a good brief biographical sketch see *Biog. Directory of the Am. Cong., 1774–1971* (1971), p. 1316. Obituaries appeared in the *Albuquerque Journal*, Jan. 6, 1971, and the *N.Y. Times*, Jan. 6, 1971. Additional information for this article was provided by Lusk's relatives Patti Witt Wright, Alene Q. Witt, Pat Watson, and Frances M. Wilcox. Death certificate supplied by N.Mex. Health and Environment Dept.]

ROGER D. HARDAWAY

LYMAN, Mary Ely, Nov. 24, 1887–Jan. 9, 1975. Theologian.

Mary Redington Ely was born in St. Johnsbury, Vt., the youngest of four daughters of Henry Guy and Adelaide (Newell) Ely. She praised her parents for sparing her the "disappointment" she believed they suffered at having a fourth daughter. Both parents were from New England families. Henry Ely, "a scholar turned factory manager," left Dartmouth College to join the Union army; after the war he went to work for the Ely Hoe and Fork Company in St. Johnsbury, eventually becoming manager and remaining with the firm until his death. Because Adelaide Ely was frequently ill, the younger girls became the responsibility of their older sisters, who were seventeen and twenty when Mary was born. The second oldest, Caroline, who did not marry, was especially important to Mary throughout her childhood and youth.

The Ely family was respected, but not prosperous. As a child, Mary felt like a "poor relation" to the town's prominent families. She described her home as "conservatively Puritan . . . We never had a Christmas tree for instance." Henry Ely was a deacon in the Congregational church, and the children were expected to attend church and Sunday school, and later to go to Christian Endeavor classes on Sunday evenings, and to Wednesday evening prayer meetings as well. Mary went to local schools, graduating in 1906 from St. Johnsbury Academy.

At seven, during a visit with her mother to her oldest sister in Brooklyn, N.Y., Mary Ely became very ill with something she later believed to have been "incipient TB." Soon after, her mother suffered the first of her many "breakdowns" and Mary Ely always believed that her own illness was partly responsible for her mother's condition. A long series of illnesses darkened her childhood; she was never really well until she went away to Mount Holyoke College, which she later described as "the open door on life for me."

Mary Ely graduated from college in 1911, taught high school in Connecticut for two years, then returned to Mount Holyoke as general secretary of the YWCA (1913–16). In that capacity she conducted evening Bible classes—a job she loved, and one which eventually led her to enroll at Union Theological Seminary. From this point on, her major professional goal was to teach the Bible. Throughout her life, hers was a teaching ministry.

In 1919, Mary Ely received her B.D. from Union Seminary. She was the only woman in her class, and was not allowed to attend the commencement luncheon; she had to sit in the balcony with the faculty wives during the graduation ceremony. As the ranking scholar of her class, Mary Ely received the Philadelphia Traveling Fellowship and went to England to spend two years (1919–20) at Cambridge. The university would neither grant a theological degree nor issue a transcript to a woman. When she applied to the Ph.D. program at the University of Chicago, she carried individual letters from her Cambridge professors. She earned her doctorate (magna cum laude) from Chicago in 1924 with a dissertation on "The Knowledge of God in the Fourth Gospel" (published in 1925 as *Knowledge of God in Johannine Thought*). While working on her doctorate she taught at Vassar College (1920–26), where in 1923 she became Weyerhauser Professor of Religion.

On Feb. 13, 1926, Mary Ely married Eugene W. Lyman, fifteen years her senior; he was Marcellus Hartley Professor of the Philosophy of Religion at Union Seminary. The marriage was outstandingly happy and successful, and Mary Ely Lyman adopted the two children of her husband's first marriage, Charles Eugene (b. 1915) and Laura (b. 1916). Mary Lyman always believed that she was especially fortunate, that "marriage and profession were united in a very remarkable way in my life."

Mary Lyman taught religion at Barnard College from 1929 to 1940, while both Lymans taught at Union Seminary. They lived in a large faculty apartment and the household was famous for its elegant hospitality. They spent summers in Cummington, Mass., where Eugene Lyman had grown up. Both used the mornings to work on their books, scandalizing neighbors who believed Mary Lyman was sitting on the porch "do[ing] nothing." When she became a Congregational minister in 1949, she chose to be ordained in the church at Cummington.

Eugene Lyman retired from Union in 1940, and the seminary "took it for granted" that his wife would retire also. They moved to Virginia, where Mary Lyman became dean and professor of religion at Sweet Briar College. Eugene Lyman died in 1948, and two years later Mary Lyman returned to Union as Morris K. Jessup Professor of English Bible and dean of women students. She was the first woman to hold a faculty chair at Union, and one of the first to be a full professor at any American seminary.

Women were enrolling in Union in significant numbers in 1950, and, although she neither sought nor welcomed the job as dean, Lyman realized that "someone ought to be thinking of and for them." Recognizing that religion tended to be a conservative force, she had decided very early not to attack the woman question directly, but to do her work to the best of her ability, and to trust that that would help to open doors for other women. But her experiences in seminary, her service on the World Council of Churches Commission on the Life and Work of Women in the Churches (1948–54), and her awareness of the difficulties faced by women in parish ministry gradually overcame her dislike of "crusading." Recognizing the compelling needs of the women, the theological schools, and the churches, she took more and more of an advocacy role.

After her official retirement from Union in 1955, Mary Lyman lectured at Union, Vassar, and Sweet Briar, served one semester as visiting professor at Randolph-Macon Woman's College, and kept up her long and fruitful connection with various boards and commissions of the World Council of Churches. In 1956 she published *Into All the World*, an account of an eight-month trip to visit former students throughout Asia and the Near East.

Mary Lyman moved in 1961 to Pilgrim Place, a community of retired church workers and seminary faculty in Claremont, Calif. In 1964–65 she taught at Scripps College; for the last ten years of her life she was active as a teacher and speaker to church and Bible study groups. She kept up her many friendships with students and colleagues around the world, her love of music, and her close ties to her family. On one joyous occasion, she presided at the ordination of her grandson, Eugene Lyman Boutilier, and the christening of his daughter. Mary Lyman died in Claremont of a stroke, after a very brief period of illness, at the age of eighty-seven.

The recipient of many honors, Mary Lyman never defined her work in narrow academic terms. Such major works as *The Fourth Gospel and the Life of To-day* (1931) and *The Christian Epic* (1936) reflect her intention to make the Bible, and the higher criticism of the Bible, available to all faithful Christians. She wrote articles for church papers as well as academic journals, always with the intention of teaching the Bible, helping others to do so, and encouraging scholars and ministers to share their faith and knowledge widely.

In her inaugural address to her colleagues at Union Seminary, Mary Lyman described her own life work: "Here is the culminating phase of our work as interpreters—to bring the writings of the Bible into direct relation to the life being lived today."

[Union Theological Seminary has several folders containing clippings, articles, biographical sketches, and photographs of Mary Lyman; the Seminary Library has books, reprints of articles, the manuscripts of four lectures, and the memorial minute of the Union faculty written by Paul W. Hoon. Besides the books mentioned above, Lyman wrote *Paul the Conqueror* (1919). Pamphlets for churches and study groups include *Jesus* (1937), *Death and the Christian Answer* (1960), and *In Him Was Life: A Study Guide on the Gospel of John* (1960). "The Liberal Spirit in the New Testament" was written for David E. Roberts and Henry P. Van Dusen, eds., *Liberal Theology: An Appraisal* (1942), a festschrift in honor of Eugene Lyman. Her inaugural address as Morris K. Jessup Professor appears in the *Union Seminary Quart. Rev.*, Jan. 1951, pp. 21–31. She was also a frequent contributor to *Advance*, the newspaper of the Congregational church. A biobibliography by Lillian K. Lehto assisted in research. A death certificate was provided by Calif. Dept. of Health. Laura Lyman Hackett provided memories of her mother and the transcript of a tape made by Mary Lyman for her family. Additional information came from John C. Bennett, Blanche Britton, Robert T. Handy, and Thomas P. Slavens.]

CLARISSA W. ATKINSON

M

McCARDELL, Claire, May 24, 1905–March 22, 1958. Fashion designer.

Claire McCardell was born in Frederick, Md., the eldest of four children and only daughter of Adrian Leroy and Frances (Clingan) McCardell. Her father, of Scots, English, and Irish ancestry, was president of the Frederick County National Bank, as well as a state senator, a member of the state tax commission, and an elder in the Evangelical and Reformed Church. Her mother was a southern belle from Jackson, Miss., who kept a portrait of General Robert E. Lee on the parlor wall.

Claire had a comfortable but unpretentious small-town girlhood. She attended public schools in Frederick, graduating from Girls High School in 1922. Although her three brothers kept her active in sports, she showed her interest in fashion at an early age, cutting paper dolls from her mother's sophisticated fashion magazines.

She learned about clothes construction from observing the family dressmaker; by the time she was in high school she was making all of her own clothes.

McCardell attended Hood College in Frederick (1923–25), but her interest was low as were her marks. Her father eventually gave in to her desire for a fashion education, and in 1925 she enrolled at the New York School of Fine and Applied Arts (later the Parsons School of Design). She spent her second year at the school's Paris branch where she attended couture showings. As was the custom at the season's end, McCardell bought and dissected shopworn dress models, particularly those of her idol Madeleine Vionnet, the inventor of the bias cut. From them she mastered the technique of cutting on the diagonal of the fabric, to give clothes greater flexibility and fit. McCardell later applied this technique, used in Paris mainly for formal wear, to casual clothes.

After graduation from Parsons in 1928, McCardell took the only job she could find—painting rosebuds on lampshades for twenty dollars a week. Modeling stints, an occasional sketching assignment, and some unsuccessful months as assistant to a knitwear manufacturer followed. Finally in 1930 she became assistant designer at the sportswear firm of Townley Frocks. After the designer's sudden death a year later, in the middle of the season, McCardell took his place. With the exception of a period (spent at the firm of HATTIE CARNEGIE) when Townley closed because of the owner's illness, she stayed with the firm until her death, becoming a partner in 1952.

American fashion houses, still under the influence of French couture in the 1930s, sent their designers to the Paris collections twice a year to buy models for copying or adapting. Despite McCardell's admiration for the tradition of haute couture dressmaking, she came to feel that such clothes were too formal, and too costly for busy young women like herself to buy and maintain. Experimenting with designs that used the casual comfort and easy fit of sportswear for all-occasion clothes, she created the first "separates": a bare and a covered top, a long and a short skirt, plus a culotte, all in black wool jersey and untrimmed to be "dressed up or down" with accessories. Although it became an American classic, the "separates" wardrobe was not at first understood by the buyers. Another McCardell innovation, inspired not by Paris but by a Moroccan robe she had worn to a Beaux Arts ball, was an immediate and widely copied success when it appeared in 1938. Called the Monastic dress, it was cut completely on the bias with no difference in the back or front and no fixed waistline; it fit almost any figure.

World War II confronted American designers with the dilemma of making clothes without the elegant designs of the French and within the limits of fabric restrictions and a labor shortage. McCardell was in the vanguard with innovative solutions, such as the Popover, a denim wraparound designed for women whose maids had gone to the war plants. A stylish substitute for a housedress, it also launched denim on a fashionable career. The leotard or "body suit" was another McCardell wartime design. Originally designed in wool jersey to be worn under jumpers or separate skirts in college dormitories that were unheated because of wartime fuel shortages, it was soon taken up by women everywhere.

Beyond these well-known innovations, McCardell also contributed to the overall design of American fashion, particularly for moderately priced, ready-to-wear clothes. Her designs were easy to fit: most had no waistline or one which could be adjusted by string ties, and sleeves were either cut in one with the bodice or came from a dropped shoulder line. To make reasonably priced clothes that did not look cheap or dull, she avoided imitations of expensive satins and brocades, instead introducing wool jersey for evening clothes. McCardell made American cotton, previously confined to housedresses or golfing garb, a fabric for coats, suits, and evening as well as day dresses. Unlike other moderate price designers, McCardell did not confine herself to one category of clothing. From sports dresses, she moved on to street and evening clothes, bathing suits, and all of the accessories shown with the clothes.

In 1943 Claire McCardell married Irving Harris, a New York consulting architect. Harris was a widower with two teenaged children, with whom McCardell established a good and enduring relationship. She continued to design four collections a year for Townley, and made frequent public appearances all over the country. She also served as an officer of the Fashion Group (an organization of women in the business), an adviser to the Costume Institute of the Metropolitan Museum, and a teacher-critic at the Parsons School. In addition, she ran an eleven-room apartment in New York, a summer house at Fishers Island, N.Y., and a year-round weekend cottage in Frenchtown, N.J. A tall lithe blonde, she was described as her own best model at the age of fifty.

During the 1940s McCardell earned all of the fashion industry's awards, including the two most prestigious: the American Fashion Critics Award and the Neiman-Marcus Award for the best in international design in all fields. In 1950 she was the first fashion designer to be voted one of America's Women of Achievement by the National Women's Press Club. The 1953 retrospective show of her designs from 1933 to 1953 in the Perls Gallery, a major art dealer in Los Angeles, was hailed as "the first one-man show of dress designs exhibited just like any other works of art." In 1956 McCardell published *What Shall I Wear?* In it she explained the spirit behind her designs: "For me, it's America—it looks and feels like America. It's freedom, it's democracy, it's casualness, it's good health. Clothes can say all that."

McCardell died of cancer in New York City in 1958. Fourteen years later the Fashion Institute of Technology in New York had a retrospective show of her designs that *Newsweek* reported as "the smash fashion collection of the season." The show proved, as McCardell had earlier written, that "good fashion somehow earns the right to survive."

[The Costume Institute of the Metropolitan Museum and the Design Laboratory of the Fashion Institute of Technology, both in N.Y. City, have comprehensive collections of McCardell's designs. There is a smaller collection at the Los Angeles Cty. Museum. The Parsons School has every McCardell sketch for the twenty-five years she was an established designer. An extended study of McCardell by Sally Kirkland appears in Sarah Tomerlin Lee, ed., *American Fashion* (1975). Discussions of her life and career are in Beryl Williams, *Fashion Is Our Business* (1945); *Current Biog.*, 1954; and "The American Look," *Time*, May 2, 1955, pp. 85–90. *Newsweek*, June 5, 1972, has a review of the 1972 retrospective. An obituary appeared in the *N.Y. Times*, March 23, 1958. Additional information was provided by Robert Riley and Stella Blum.]

SALLY KIRKLAND

McCORMICK, Anne Elizabeth O'Hare, May 16, 1880–May 29, 1954. Journalist.

Anne O'Hare McCormick, the first woman to serve on the *New York Times* editorial board, was born in Wakefield, Yorkshire, England, the eldest of three daughters of Thomas J. and Teresa Beatrice (Berry) O'Hare. The O'Hare family immigrated to the United States shortly after her birth, settling briefly in Massachusetts and finally moving to Columbus, Ohio, where Anne was raised and educated in the Catholic faith of her Irish ancestors. In 1898 she graduated from Saint Mary of the Springs Academy in Columbus. A year or so earlier, her father, the central Ohio regional manager for Home Life Insurance Company of New York, had encountered business problems and permanently deserted his family. Teresa O'Hare struggled to support her daughters by operating a dry goods store and selling door-to-door a book of her poetry, *Songs at Twilight* (1898). Following Anne's graduation from Saint Mary's, the O'Hares moved to Cleveland, where both mother and daughter worked for the weekly *Catholic Universe Bulletin*. Anne O'Hare became the associate editor, thus embarking upon her journalistic career; her mother wrote a column and edited the women's section.

O'Hare worked for the *Bulletin* until her marriage to Francis J. McCormick, a Dayton importer and engineer eight years her senior, on Sept. 14, 1910. After moving to Dayton, she began writing on a free-lance basis. Eventually her articles were accepted by such publications as *Catholic World, Reader Magazine,* and the *New York Times Magazine*. She also wrote poetry, which appeared in *Smart Set, Bookman,* and other magazines, and published a short architectural and ecclesiastical history of her former parish church. A lifelong Catholic, her

strong religious convictions greatly influenced her views throughout her career.

After her marriage, Anne O'Hare McCormick traveled extensively with her husband, whose business required frequent purchasing trips to Europe. She was not content to be a mere tourist, and was particularly eager to study and record the changes occurring in Europe in the wake of World War I. In 1921 McCormick wrote to Carr V. Van Anda, managing editor of the *New York Times*, for permission to send the paper regular dispatches from overseas. The *Times* agreed and printed many of her articles on conditions abroad, including her analyses of the rise of Italian fascism and the growing power of Benito Mussolini. So pleased were the paper's editors with her work that they made her a regular correspondent in 1922. After 1925 she wrote exclusively for the *Times*, with the exception of a series on contemporary Europe published in the *Ladies' Home Journal* (1933–34).

Throughout the 1920s and early 1930s, Anne O'Hare McCormick unfailingly displayed the broad knowledge and penetrating insight which would ultimately propel her to the top of her profession. Her articles from Europe accurately analyzed the social, political, and economic events of the postwar world. She became known for the personal interviews she obtained with world leaders, including Roosevelt, Churchill, Hitler, Mussolini, and Stalin. Spiritual leaders, too, came under her scrutiny, as she reported from Rome on the history, organization, and contemporary influence of the Catholic church. Her thrice-weekly column "In Europe" (from 1936 titled "Abroad") won a wide readership not only in the United States but also among journalists and government officials in Europe and Asia. McCormick also traveled extensively throughout the United States, covering national political conventions, describing life in the modern south, and reporting on the hardships inflicted by the depression.

Arthur Hays Sulzberger, president and publisher of the *Times*, recognized McCormick's achievements by inviting her to join the newspaper's editorial board as "freedom editor," enjoining her "to stand up and shout whenever freedom is interfered with in any part of the world." Remaining on the board from June 1936 until her death, she regularly wrote editorials. She also continued to produce her column and contributed special features to the paper's magazine section. The McCormicks were based in New York after 1936, although they continued to live in hotels.

Further recognition of her work soon followed. In 1937 McCormick became the first woman to win the Pulitzer Prize for foreign correspondence. Over the years she received numerous honorary degrees, including an A.B. from the College of Saint Mary of the Springs (1928), and many awards, including the Medal of the National Institute of Social Science (1942) and the Laetare Medal of the University of Notre Dame (1944).

McCormick's greatest influence came during the 1940s through her articles delineating America's position in the postwar world. Her writings reflected her belief in the existence of an unchanging moral order; drawing strength from her convictions, she refused to despair even in the bleakest days of World War II and the cold war. As a recognized expert on current events, McCormick was besieged by publishers to write books, but she refused to take time away from her newspaper work. During her long career she wrote only one full-length book, *The Hammer and the Scythe: Communist Russia Enters the Second Decade* (1928), a study of the Soviet Union ten years after the Bolshevik Revolution. During World War II, she was named to the Advisory Committee on Post-War Foreign Policy, a select government body that was secret at the time. She served as a delegate to UNESCO conferences in 1946 and 1948 and was mentioned as a candidate for influential diplomatic positions.

A petite, energetic, and vivacious woman, McCormick was exceptionally modest. She took little credit for her ability to unearth major news stories, once remarking that "crises were popping all over Europe at the time, so it isn't strange that I bumped into a few." Believing that journalists should not become celebrities, McCormick consistently refused to reveal details of her private life, or to permit articles to be written about her. She feared that personal fame would interfere with "the kind of impersonal and uncolored reporting . . . on which the maintenance of a free press and therefore a free society depend."

Although not an activist on behalf of feminist causes, McCormick did encourage women to enter all professions and urged government and business leaders to employ women's talents. Her correspondence with DOROTHY THOMPSON, Clare Boothe Luce, and others reveals an avid interest in women's issues. Discussing her success and that of other prominent newspaperwomen of her time, she said: "We had tried hard not to act like ladies or to talk as ladies are supposed to talk—meaning too much—but just to sneak toward the city desk and the cable desk, and the editorial sanctum and even the publisher's office with masculine sang-froid."

Anne O'Hare McCormick died in 1954 in New York City. Upon her death, the *Times*

blackened the borders of her "Abroad" column and paid tribute to her in a special editorial, describing her as "a reporter in a rare sense. She understood politics and diplomacy but for her they were not the whole truth and no abstraction was ever the whole truth. The whole truth lay in people."

[The principal sources of information are the Anne O'Hare McCormick Papers (1936–54), including correspondence, lectures, editorials, columns, clippings, and pamphlets, at the N.Y. Public Library; a collection of her *N.Y. Times* articles on microfilm in the State Hist. Soc. of Wis.; and the pages of the *N.Y. Times* (1920–54). McCormick's *St. Agnes Church, Cleveland, Ohio: An Interpretation* was published in 1920. Two volumes of her writings culled from the files of the *N.Y. Times*, both edited by Marion Turner Sheehan, were published posthumously: *The World at Home* (1956) and *Vatican Journal, 1921–1954* (1957). Accounts of her life and career are in C. L. Sulzberger, *A Long Row of Candles: Memoirs and Diaries, 1934–1954* (1969); L. C. Gray, "McCormick of the *Times*," *Current Hist.*, July 1939, pp. 27, 64; *Current Biog.*, 1940; Matthew Hoehn, ed., *Catholic Authors* (1948); *Time*, March 22, 1948, and May 8, 1950; *Newsweek*, March 20, 1950; and *Dict. Am. Biog.*, Supp. Five. See also John Hohenberg, *The Pulitzer Prizes* (1974), pp. 132–33, and Ishbel Ross, *Ladies of the Press* (1936), pp. 366–68. An obituary appeared in the *N.Y. Times*, May 30, 1954. A birth record was provided by the General Register Office, London; baptismal record by St. Austin's Presbytery, Wakefield, England; marriage record by the Court of Probate, Cuyahoga Cty., Ohio; death record by the N.Y. City Dept. of Health. Mack Burke gave information on the O'Hare family.]

SANDRA GIOIA TREADWAY

McCORMICK, Katharine Dexter, Aug. 27, 1875–Dec. 28, 1967. Philanthropist.

Katharine Dexter McCormick spent a large part of inheritances from her father and husband in efforts to promote woman suffrage, birth control, and higher education for women. She was born in Dexter, Mich., the second and last child of Wirt and Josephine (Moore) Dexter. Although her father, one of Chicago's most successful corporate attorneys, made his fortune in the midwest, New England was important in Katharine Dexter's heritage: her paternal great-grandfather had served in John Adams's cabinet; her grandfather led the New England migration to Michigan; and her mother had been a schoolteacher from Springfield, Mass. The sudden deaths of Wirt Dexter in 1889 and of his son in 1894 left Josephine and Katharine Dexter with a fortune and the freedom to organize their lives as they wished. They moved to Boston, where Josephine Dexter bought a mansion on Commonwealth Avenue; she purchased another on Lake Geneva in Switzerland.

Josephine Dexter instilled an intense consciousness of ancestry and social status in her daughter; she also took an active interest in the movement for woman's rights. Endowed with self-possession and indomitable will, Katharine Dexter was not satisfied with the life of a lady and sought a "thorough and practical" scientific education at the Massachusetts Institute of Technology (MIT), which she found admirable because of "its almost insurmountable difficulties" and policy of "permitting the survival of only the fittest of its students." She spent three years as a special student preparing for the entrance examinations, majored in biology, and received a B.S. in 1904 with a senior thesis on "Fatigue of the Cardiac Muscles in Reptilia."

Katharine Dexter married Stanley McCormick, a childhood friend and comptroller of the International Harvester Corporation, in her mother's Swiss chateau in September 1904. Within a year he began to exhibit symptoms of severe mental illness; he was forced to resign from International Harvester in May 1906, was hospitalized in October, and declared legally incompetent in 1909. The prominent psychiatrists who treated him attributed the compulsive and bizarre behavior that made it impossible for Stanley McCormick to function as a businessman or husband to a series of frustrations involving long-standing difficulties with his parents and older brothers, marital impotence, and an overwhelming sense of guilt induced by his relationship with his wife.

Katharine McCormick conducted a long search for a cure for her husband and consulted a series of experts, including behavioral psychologists, psychiatrists, and endocrinologists. In the late 1920s, she quarreled with the psychoanalysts working with her husband and disputed their efforts to limit her access to him. She found specialists who testified that his illness might be schizophrenia, which they thought might be traced to hormonal deficiencies, and fought a successful court battle to have the psychoanalysts dismissed from her husband's care (1930). Her interest in hormones led her to establish the Neuroendocrine Research Foundation at Harvard Medical School (1927–47), and to subsidize a journal, *Endocrinology*. But the endocrinologists failed to develop a cure for schizophrenia, and Stanley McCormick was kept as happy as possible on a baronial estate in Santa Barbara, Calif., until his death in 1947. Before then, Katharine McCormick had only limited use of her husband's income because she shared its management with members of his

family under court supervision. While she was able to spend large sums on schizophrenia research, her other philanthropic spending was limited to the income from her father's estate.

McCormick had become active in the woman suffrage movement in 1909 when she spoke at the first open-air suffrage demonstration in Massachusetts. With MARY WARE DENNETT, she led a small group of women who organized ninety-seven outdoor rallies (sometimes risking physical confrontation with police and hecklers) and conducted an intensive lobbying campaign in the Massachusetts state legislature. McCormick also served as one of CARRIE CHAPMAN CATT's lieutenants in the National American Woman Suffrage Association (NAWSA), providing subsidies for the *Woman's Journal,* and serving as treasurer and vice president of the association. During World War I she chaired NAWSA's War Service Department and worked as a member of the Women's Committee of the Council of National Defense.

McCormick next turned to the birth control movement. During the war she had met MARGARET SANGER in Boston, where Sanger was agitating for the release of a man arrested for distributing birth control leaflets. In the 1920s she was one of the European travelers who helped keep Sanger's Clinical Research Bureau open by smuggling diaphragms into the United States; Josephine Dexter's Swiss chateau served as a meeting place for both the International Suffrage Alliance and the 1927 World Population Conference. For twenty years McCormick intermittently supported contraceptive research projects brought to her attention by Sanger without achieving a major breakthrough. As a sponsor of endocrine research over the years, she developed considerable expertise as a judge of biomedical projects, and devoted a great deal of energy to the analysis of promising leads. In 1952 she confessed to Sanger that she was "feeling pretty desperate" over the lack of a "foolproof" female birth control method.

In March 1952, however, she found in the biologist Gregory Pincus, codirector of the Worcester Foundation for Experimental Biology (WFEB), a scientific entrepreneur with the commercial contacts necessary to realize the Sanger-McCormick dream of "a physiological contraceptive." Pincus, a pioneer in the study of the hormonal aspects of mammalian reproduction, was testing the therapeutic properties of large numbers of synthetic steroid compounds for the pharmaceutical house G. D. Searle. When McCormick asked him in June 1953 to develop a new contraceptive, he had already experimented with progesterone as an ovulation suppressant with modest funds provided by the Planned Parenthood Federation of America (PPFA). Neither the Federation nor Searle recognized the potential of this concept. McCormick did, perhaps because the WFEB had participated in Neuroendocrine Research Foundation projects. She thus provided Pincus with both the social justification and the necessary funds to develop "the pill," a combination of synthetic progesterone and estrogen marketed as Enovid in 1960.

Once assured that Pincus's project would succeed, McCormick turned her attention to building dormitories for women at MIT. She explained to Sanger: "This has been my ambition for many years but it had to await the oral contraceptive." The completion of Stanley McCormick Hall West (1962) and East (1968) provided first-class accommodations for 342 women, thereby effectively ending the long-standing excuse that MIT could not increase its female enrollment because no housing was available.

McCormick brought a personal style to her philanthropy that was fast disappearing as the rich learned to spend their money through tax-privileged foundations run by professional altruists. All of her giving reflected intensely personal concerns. Her donations, for the art museum in Santa Barbara, the dormitories at MIT, and the five million dollar endowment for the PPFA in her will, were given as memorials to Stanley McCormick. Katharine Dexter McCormick died in Boston of a stroke in 1967, convinced that the oral contraceptive represented a major contribution to the autonomy of women.

[The MIT Historical Collections has an excellent collection of McCormick photographs. Her undergraduate essays and class notes, as well as addresses delivered at the ceremony dedicating Stanley McCormick Hall East, are in the Institute Archives and Special Collections of the MIT Libraries. The most revealing source of all might be the dormitories themselves, which were partly furnished with objects McCormick had collected. A detailed account of Stanley McCormick's illness and of his wife's conflict with his psychoanalysts is contained in three boxes of "Medical Notes, Stanley McCormick," in Records of Saint Elizabeths Hospital, Nat. Archives. The McCormick Family Papers, State Hist. Soc. of Wis., are closed. The Margaret Sanger Papers in the Sophia Smith Coll., Smith College, document the collaboration between Sanger and McCormick in the development of the pill. McCormick contributed a chapter on "War Service of Organized Suffragists" to Ida Husted Harper, ed., *The History of Woman Suffrage*, V (1922), pp. 720–40. Her suffrage work is described in *The History of Woman Suffrage*, VI (1922). James Reed provides a brief biography and analysis of McCormick's role in the American birth control movement in *From Private Vice to Public Virtue: The Birth Control Movement and American Society since 1830* (1978), chap. 26. A death record was provided by Mass. Dept. of Public Health.]

JAMES REED

McCULLERS, Carson, Feb. 19, 1917–Sept. 29, 1967. Writer.

Carson McCullers, novelist, playwright, and short story writer, was born Lula Carson Smith in Columbus, Ga.; she was the older daughter and eldest of three children. Her father, Lamar Smith, was a watch repairman and jewelry store owner whose family had come south from Connecticut at the end of the nineteenth century; her mother, Vera Marguerite (Waters), traced her ancestors to Irish settlers who had immigrated to South Carolina before the revolution.

Lula Carson Smith was an introverted, quirky child passionately devoted to music, religion, reading, and the shaping of fantastic stories. At six she revealed an uncommon talent for picking out tunes on the piano; by ten she was practicing long hours and dreaming of fame on the concert stage. When she was fifteen, however, an attack of rheumatic fever made her doubt her stamina and she soon decided to become a writer instead. She had already read hundreds of books by the Brontës, Dostoevski, Gogol, Tolstoi, Flaubert, Hawthorne, Melville, Faulkner, and other great nineteenth- and twentieth-century novelists, and she had composed bizarre works in imitation of several modern masters. As she later recalled: "My first effort at writing was a play. At that phase my idol was Eugene O'Neill and this first masterpiece was thick with incest, lunacy, and murder . . . I tried to put it on in the family sitting room, but only my mother and my eleven-year-old sister would cooperate . . . After that I dashed off a few more plays, a novel, and some rather queer poetry that nobody could make out, including the author" (quoted in *Twentieth Century Authors,* p. 868). Among those lost adolescent works were *The Faucet*, a play set in New Zealand (where anything might happen); *The Fire of Life*, a two-character verse play in which Christ debates with Nietzsche; and *A Reed of Pan*, a novel about a jazz musician seduced by jazz.

At seventeen, having graduated from high school in Columbus (1933), Lula Carson Smith traveled to New York, ostensibly to study at the Juilliard School of Music and in the writing program at Columbia. The interest in Juilliard was sustained to please her family, for her deepest desire was to write fiction. She had planned to share an apartment with a young woman from Georgia, but in a confused sequence of events, the tuition money was lost or stolen and she soon found herself on her own. Through the winter of 1934–35, she briefly held jobs as typist, waitress, pianist, and dog walker, enrolled in writing courses at Columbia, and worked when she could on her own short fiction. Most of the apprentice stories were not to appear in print until after her death but "Wunderkind"—the tale of a prodigy's failure—was published in the December 1936 issue of *Story* magazine, just before her twentieth birthday. By then she was dating (James) Reeves McCullers, whom she had met the previous summer in Columbus. He was a handsome, high-spirited southerner, recently free from a four-year stint in the army; he hoped to study journalism and anthropology in New York and eventually to become a writer.

In November 1936 Carson Smith (she had dropped the name Lula as a teenager) suffered a recurrence of rheumatic fever, the childhood illness that was to exercise so powerfully negative an influence on her life. At the urging of Reeves McCullers she went back to Columbus to recuperate. Settled there, she began to sketch out a novel about a deaf mute and his friend.

The following year, alternating between good health and bad, Carson Smith continued to work on her novel, and on the 20th of September, she and Reeves McCullers were married. Jobs were scarce and when Reeves was hired as an investigator for the Retail Credit Corporation, the couple went to live where the work was, first in Charlotte, then in Fayetteville, N.C. News about her career was more promising: when she submitted six chapters and an outline of "The Mute," the Houghton Mifflin Company offered her a contract and the promise of a $500 advance.

Strains appeared very early in the McCullers' marriage. Although Reeves had ambitions to be an author, he had little ability and not time enough to write. Carson was *only* a writer, with a large brimming talent, small gifts for reciprocity, and no patience for domestic responsibilities. When money tightened and the sexual identities of each partner became more blurred, mutual resentments increased, quarrels multiplied, and the couple moved to New York hoping to benefit from the publication of Carson McCullers's novel. Celebrity came faster than anyone could have predicted. Within weeks of its appearance in June 1940, the newly titled *The Heart Is a Lonely Hunter* was enthusiastically praised for its remarkable insight into the lives of estranged and disadvantaged adults in a southern textile town, and the twenty-three-

year-old author was hailed as one of the most brilliant new writers in America.

That fame might solve the McCullers' marital problems proved to be an illusion; their seesaw relationship was never to remain level for long. Carson McCullers quickly found herself in situations she was too inexperienced and unstable to handle. In early summer, after meeting many well-known literary figures, she fell painfully in love with Annemarie Clarac-Schwarzenbach, a mannishly beautiful, neurotic Swiss writer, who did not return her passion. In August, at the Bread Loaf Writers' Conference in Vermont, she worked hard revising her second novel, *Reflections in a Golden Eye*. But she drank too much, awkwardly cultivated celebrities, and was regarded by many people as a sympathetic, gifted, but self-destructive eccentric. By turns and sometimes all at once, she could be shy and expansive, honest and untruthful, generous and vindictive, morose and amusing, feverish and serene. Emotionally (if not literally) promiscuous, she had an insatiable need for love, but was so often anxiety-ridden, compulsive, and self-dramatizing that she could rarely respond to other people in a mature way. As the novelist Rosamond Lehmann once said: "I found her fascinating and lovable, but . . . a terrific psychic drain. She made enormous emotional demands."

After the hectic summer of fame, she was back with her husband in September, restless, unhappy, anxious to write more and to move in literary circles, and eager for relationships with women. The McCullers talked of divorce but decided temporarily to separate; they did divorce the following year and Reeves McCullers reenlisted in the army. She soon joined an artists' cooperative at 7 Middagh Street in Brooklyn Heights, a notable ménage that included at different times W. H. Auden, GYPSY ROSE LEE, Richard Wright, Paul and Jane Bowles, and many other writers and musicians.

The years from 1941 through 1944 proved to be Carson McCullers's most creative period. Although *Reflections in a Golden Eye* received mixed notices, the handling of grotesque subject matter (perversion, voyeurism, and mutilation) revealed a powerful if unfocused talent. "A Tree. A Rock. A Cloud." was chosen for the *O. Henry Prize Stories* in 1942; the evocative, bittersweet "The Ballad of the Sad Café" was selected for *Best American Stories* two years later, and became one of the most widely admired tales of the decade. Encouraged by fellowships from the Yaddo colony (1941), the Guggenheim Foundation (1942), and the American Academy of Arts and Letters (1943), she completed the manuscript of what would prove to be her strongest and most universally praised work, *The Member of the Wedding*.

After World War II, McCullers continued to be regarded as an extraordinarily promising writer. In 1945 she and Reeves remarried; a year later she published *The Member of the Wedding*, won another Guggenheim, and began a lifelong friendship with Tennessee Williams. In 1947—just past thirty—she suffered two paralyzing strokes; in 1948 her marriage broke up again and she tried to commit suicide. In 1949 she was back with Reeves and adapting the novel for the stage. This turbulent decade ended with her greatest public triumph: on Jan. 5, 1950, *The Member of the Wedding* (starring Ethel Waters and Julie Harris and directed by Harold Clurman) opened in New York to spectacular acclaim.

In response to this success, Houghton Mifflin published McCullers's three novels and seven stories in an omnibus volume (1951). V. S. Pritchett, reviewing the British edition, called its author "a genius . . . and the most remarkable novelist to come out of America for a generation." McCullers was, in Gore Vidal's recollection, "*the* young writer" of the period, "an American legend from the beginning."

From this point on, however, the life story of Carson McCullers becomes the history of declining health and talent. The promise of the 1940s was never fulfilled. If she had moments of jubilation and creativity, she had months of misery and despair. In 1952, she was elected to coveted membership in the National Institute of Arts and Letters. The following year, she and her husband bought a house near Paris, where they lived on and off for two years, but they quarreled constantly about money, sex, professional rivalry, and many other things. Reeves McCullers, at loose ends and despondent, took drugs and fell into fits of wild abusiveness. Carson McCullers, terrified, returned alone to Nyack, N.Y., where her widowed mother had recently bought a house. Soon afterward, she learned that her husband had killed himself in November 1953.

Given the severity of the stresses under which she labored (a favorite aunt and her mother also died in the mid-1950s), the play and novel Carson McCullers published in 1958 and 1961 were victories of stoicism although failures of art. *The Square Root of Wonderful*, a maladroit comedy of manners, closed after forty-five performances in New York; *Clock Without Hands*, an ambitious, long-studied novel about race, was devoid of energy and convincing social observation. Her earlier books continued to be widely read and appreciated, however. Each of the first four volumes sold more than 500,000 copies in hardcover and paperback editions and several of her works were adapted for the stage and movies.

By the early 1960s, it had become clear to many people that Carson McCullers's reputation would rest on this small body of skillfully finished early work. Her art seemed fixed at an early stage of development; adolescents and unreflective grotesques remained her most fully realized subjects. Her most memorable achievements in fiction were two teenage girls (Mick Kelly in *The Heart Is a Lonely Hunter* and Frankie Addams in *The Member of the Wedding*) and an eccentric set of primitive misfits in "The Ballad of the Sad Café." As the years passed, her adult characters and her analyses of social and political life in the American south came to appear less plausible and substantial, and her work was often weakened by a tendency to claim for the characters greater significance than their actions or the portentous narrative commentary could convincingly give them.

The Member of the Wedding, "The Ballad of the Sad Café," several stories, and parts of other novels have qualities likely to continue to attract readers: brilliantly perceived adolescent dreamers; passages of lyric power and bleak atmospheric effect; queer, original comedy; and an affecting sympathy for the solitary lives of the inarticulate and the disfigured. *The Member of the Wedding* is often called McCullers's best because it remains complete in itself—a small, but engaging story of joy, frustration, and growing up. The plot, limited to a few days in the life of a twelve-year-old girl, is more artfully managed than the contrived murder story of *Reflections in a Golden Eye*, or the evocative, ambitious, but ultimately mechanical quest pattern in *The Heart Is a Lonely Hunter*. Tonally, the work is one of the few sentimental comedies of the period to escape the charge of being maudlin; stylistically, it is the freshest and most inventive of her novels and stories.

To the continual afflictions of her last decade, McCullers responded with gallantry and spirit. A heart attack, breast cancer, pneumonia, and a bone-crushing fall occurred in grim succession between 1958 and 1964; yet she received guests, traveled, and worked fitfully on unfinished manuscripts. In August 1967, she suffered several strokes and lapsed into a coma from which she never regained full consciousness; she died in Nyack, N.Y., at the age of fifty.

[A collection of McCullers's early stories, *The Mortgaged Heart*, edited by her sister, Margarita G. Smith, appeared in 1971. The most comprehensive and reliable account of her life is Virginia Spencer Carr, *The Lonely Hunter* (1975). It has detailed genealogies of the Carson, Waters, Smith, and McCullers families, and a bibliography of Carson McCullers's writings. See also a brief sketch in *Twentieth Century Authors* (1942). The most thorough checklists of critical essays about her work are to be found in three editions of the *Bull. of Bibliography:* April 1959; Sept.-Dec. 1964; Oct.-Dec. 1970. For criticism after 1970, see the annual issues of the *MLA Intl. Bibliography.* Oliver Evans published a book-length study, *The Ballad of Carson McCullers* (1966). A revised version of Lawrence Graver's 1969 essay in the Univ. of Minn. Pamphlets on American Writers series appears in Maureen Howard, ed., *Seven American Women Writers of the Twentieth Century* (1977). Of particular interest for the study of McCullers's work are Chester Eisinger, *Fiction of the Forties* (1963), pp. 243–58; Richard M. Cook, *Carson McCullers* (1975); and Louis D. Rubin, Jr., "Carson McCullers: The Aesthetics of Pain," *Virginia Quart. Rev.* (1977), pp. 265–83. A death record was provided by the N.Y. State Dept. of Health.]

LAWRENCE GRAVER

McDANIEL, Hattie, June 10, 1895?–Oct. 26, 1952. Actress, singer.

A large woman with an expressive face and imposing voice, Hattie McDaniel won fame in the 1930s for her film portrayals of brash, worldly-wise maids, including Mammy in *Gone With the Wind,* the role which earned her an Academy Award. Like other great black performers before her, she realized and accepted the limitations of the roles in which she was cast—but within those limits she reached for power, asserting the strength and humanity of the characters she interpreted.

She was born in Wichita, Kans., the thirteenth child of Henry and Susan (Holbert) McDaniel. A Baptist minister, Henry McDaniel was a former slave, Civil War soldier, and minstrel man who raised a gifted family; Hattie's sister Etta and brother Sam also appeared later in Hollywood films. Hattie began her performing life singing in church choirs as a child. In 1913 her family moved west, to Denver, where Hattie completed two years at East Denver High School. In 1915 she was heard over radio singing with Professor George Morrison's Orchestra and the following year won a gold medal from the Woman's Christian Temperance Union for a dramatic recitation of "Convict Joe." Not long afterward her brother Otis persuaded their parents to allow her to go on tour with his tent show. Thus McDaniel continued her show business apprenticeship, performing minstrel material on the Shrine and Elks circuits. By 1925 she was a headliner on the Pantages vaudeville circuit, later playing a part in a traveling production of *Show Boat.* Idled in Milwaukee in

the late 1920s, McDaniel took a job as a maid at Sam Pick's Suburban Inn. When her chance came for an audition, she sang "St. Louis Blues" and won a starring spot in the club's show, one she held for the next two years.

In 1931 Hattie McDaniel moved to Hollywood, seeking work in the movies. She made her debut in *The Golden West* in 1932 and appeared in over sixty films in the next seventeen years, becoming one of the most successful black movie performers. Yet she was never able to rely entirely upon her film career for support, complementing her screen roles with radio work. Her first broadcasts were in Los Angeles, as Hi-Hat Hattie on "The Optimistic Donuts Show" (1931–32). She was later heard as Mammy in the "Show Boat" variety program during the early 1930s, and on major network programs with Amos 'N' Andy and Eddie Cantor. McDaniel's background as a singer and vaudeville comedian served her well in this medium. Even when her film career faded in the late 1940s, she continued to entertain a large radio audience in the role of Beulah, a wise and comic maid.

Hattie McDaniel's screen career was built upon the image of the verbally flip, clever maid whose knowledge of human nature is wider and wiser than that of the bourgeois sorts who employ her. Hattie McDaniel filled these roles with an ironic energy, using her massive figure, enormously mobile face, and rich voice to transform the meek servant into a knowing critic of the ways of the masters. When asked why she played only these stereotypical domestics, McDaniel replied: "It's better to get $7,000 a week for playing a servant than $7.00 a week for being one." That was her practical response; her artistic response was equally direct. She created a series of memorable characters whose inescapable humanity could be enjoyed by both white and black audiences. In *Alice Adams* (1935), *Show Boat* (1936), *Saratoga* (1937), and *The Mad Miss Manton* (1938), she managed to embody the conventional virtues of the faithful servant, while preserving a sense of pride and autonomy in her characters. McDaniel's control over her own artistic vision built toward her portrayal of Mammy in *Gone With the Wind* (1939). Named best supporting actress for this performance, she became the first black American to win an Academy Award.

Hattie McDaniel was married three times. Nothing is known about her first husband, except that he died young. In 1941 she married James Lloyd Crawford, a Los Angeles real estate agent whom she later divorced. Then in 1949 McDaniel married Larry C. Williams, an interior decorator; a year later, this marriage also ended in divorce.

During World War II, McDaniel appeared in several films a year; she also chaired the black section of the Hollywood Victory Committee, organizing entertainments for segregated black troops. Her social activism later extended beyond the war effort when she promoted fundraising benefits for the education of black youth; she also engaged in a successful antidiscrimination suit involving the purchase of her California home. After the war, roles for blacks in films moved away from comic women, and McDaniel's career faltered. She introduced Beulah to television, but the role had little of the strength of her earlier characterizations. Suffering from cancer in her last two years, Hattie McDaniel died in October 1952 at the Motion Picture Home and Hospital in Los Angeles.

[Photographs and documents of Hattie McDaniel and other members of her family are in the Margaret Herrick Library, Acad. of Motion Picture Arts and Sciences, Beverly Hills, Calif. McDaniel's career is fully assessed in Donald Bogle, *Toms, Coons, Mammies, Mulattoes and Bucks: An Interpretive History of Blacks in American Films* (1973). See also Thomas Cripps, *Slow Fade to Black: The Negro in American Films, 1900–1942* (1977), and Roland Flamini, *Scarlett, Rhett, and a Cast of Thousands: The Filming of Gone With the Wind* (1975). There is a description of McDaniel in Lena Horne, *Lena* (1965). Accounts of her life and career can be found in *Current Biog.*, 1940; *Dict. Am. Biog.*, Supp. Five; and Mabel Smythe, ed., *The Black American Reference Book* (1976). Obituaries appeared in *N.Y. Times*, Oct. 27, 1952; *Variety*, Oct. 29, 1952; *N.Y. Amsterdam News*, Nov. 1, 1952. Printed sources list McDaniel's birth date as 1898. The 1895 birth year was given by her brother Samuel on McDaniel's death certificate, supplied by Calif. Dept. of Health Services.]

JOSEPH T. SKERRETT

MacDONALD, Jeanette, June 18, 1903?–Jan. 14, 1965. Film actress, singer.

Jeanette MacDonald was an enchanting and distinctive comedian who became a major movie star only when she played it straight, more or less, in the all-out operetta style for which her name (and that of her costar Nelson Eddy) became, and remained, almost a synonym. But it was the great Ernst Lubitsch, Hollywood's acknowledged master of risqué and sophisticated comedy, who discovered her and formed her early screen personality. Her "Americanness" and her straitlaced temperament both challenged and baffled him; their rapport from the start was in their common sense of humor. MacDonald was the quintessential Lubitsch heroine—as closely allied to his mockery, wit, and peculiar sophistication, as she was later on

to the bathos and genteel naiveté of *Maytime, New Moon,* and *The Firefly.* But in nearly all her films, she performed with the zest, infectious good nature, and that inexplicable radiance in front of a camera that characterizes only the greatest of movie stars.

Jeanette Anna MacDonald was the youngest of three daughters born in Philadelphia to Anna M. (Wright) and Daniel MacDonald, both of Scottish descent. Her father was a building contractor, an active Republican, and a serious Presbyterian. Nonetheless he and his wife seem to have encouraged all three of their daughters in amateur theatrical appearances. Elsie, the oldest, later ran a dancing, singing, and acting school in Philadelphia; Edith, known as Blossom, also became a dancer and actress.

Jeanette made her debut at six, singing in a charity show. During her school years she sang in local choirs and at lodges and churches, and was one of Al White's "Six Sunny Song Birds," touring eastern resort towns in summer. By January 1920 she had moved to New York and was a chorus girl on Broadway, appearing with Blossom in the *Demi-Tasse Revue.* Within one year she was playing a featured role in a Broadway show. When *Irene* went to Boston she went with it—and ended her formal education at the tenth grade. Her studies thereafter were exclusively with voice and dance coaches, and at the Berlitz language schools, where she learned to be fluent in both French and Spanish.

Throughout her early career, MacDonald was seen primarily as a dancer, although she later said she hated dancing and did it only "to keep the wolf from the door." Her first leading role on Broadway came in 1923: ads for *The Magic Ring* touted "the girl with gold-red hair and sea-green eyes," and she was soon a critics' favorite. After more than 600 performances as the ingenue lead, in New York and on tour, she returned to New York in 1925, opening in *Tip-Toes* in December of that year. She starred in *Yes, Yes, Yvette* in 1927, and in *Sunny Days* in 1928, and toured extensively in both shows. It was in the short-lived *Angela* (1928, with Eric Blore), that movie star Richard Dix saw her and asked her to make a screen test for Paramount.

Nothing came of the test until Ernst Lubitsch saw it in 1929 when he was looking for an actress to play in his momentous first sound film, *The Love Parade,* with Maurice Chevalier. Lubitsch went to Chicago to see MacDonald in the unsuccessful musical comedy *Boom! Boom!,* and signed her for the coveted film role: as Queen Louise of Sylvania, a kingdom solely and exclusively concerned, it seems, with the problem of her virginity. The movie was an enormous success, and a milestone in the development of talking-film techniques. Lubitsch's *Monte Carlo* (1930) cast MacDonald in this same sexy operetta mode: singing "Beyond the Blue Horizon" at the window of a speeding train and playing a countess who develops an embarrassing yen for her hairdresser—who turns out (happily) to be a count.

Screen musicals went out of favor with the public, however. Under contract to Paramount, MacDonald was loaned to other studios for some minor, mostly nonsinging films. After a triumphant European concert tour in 1931 (the crowds that greeted her arrival in France were claimed to be the biggest since Lindbergh), MacDonald rejoined Lubitsch at Paramount—again teamed with Chevalier—in *One Hour with You*. It became one of 1932's top moneymaking films. She and Chevalier were together again in Rouben Mamoulian's delightful *Love Me Tonight* (1932)—and then, for a final time, in Lubitsch's *The Merry Widow* (1934). Also her last film with Lubitsch, *The Merry Widow* was a triumph for both of them and the best film of MacDonald's career. Her parodic talent, her gift for ardent nonsense, her ability to convey sexual longing in a direct, pure, unembarrassing way—all were qualities exactly and deeply suited to Lubitsch's comedy of dry astonishment.

But *The Merry Widow* was a box-office disappointment. And so, ironically, began MacDonald's superstar period: as a singing and romantic partner to baritone Nelson Eddy in a series of operetta films for Metro-Goldwyn-Mayer (MGM), designed—at Louis B. Mayer's instruction—for the kind of "family audience" that spurned the Lubitsch film. MacDonald at first resisted doing *Naughty Marietta* (1935), but its unexpected and stunning success led directly to *Rose Marie* (1936) and *Maytime* (1937), both with Eddy, and both runaway hits. So was *San Francisco* (1936), with MacDonald as a smalltown choir-singer reluctantly involved with Clark Gable as a Barbary Coast gambler. The tension with Gable was interesting and her performance was one of the best of her career. In *The Firefly* (1937), the studio tried pairing her with another singer, Allan Jones, but reverted to the MacDonald–Eddy formula with *The Girl of the Golden West* (1938), *Sweethearts* (1939), and *New Moon* (1940). The famous team never recaptured the astonishing success of their first three movies—and their seventh film, *Bitter Sweet* (1940) was an outright failure. MGM made one final attempt, casting them in a "sophisticated" vehicle: *I Married an Angel* (1942). But the result pleased no one. After that, MacDonald continued the concert tours of the United States she had begun in 1939, even made a long-deferred debut in opera (in Montreal in May 1943 as Juliette in Gounod's *Roméo et Juliette*), but made only four more films. *The Sun Comes Up* (1949) was her twenty-ninth and final movie—a tearjerker about an orphan and his dog. Even here MacDonald managed some nice comic moments.

On June 16, 1937, she married film actor Gene Raymond (b. Raymond Guion). The union was close, lifelong, and childless. Jeanette MacDonald died in 1965 at Methodist Hospital in Houston, Texas. Her last words were to Raymond: "I love you." She had been awaiting open-heart surgery.

[The Billy Rose Theatre Coll., N.Y. Public Library, has a collection of scrapbooks and clippings which cover the whole of MacDonald's career. The Jeanette MacDonald Coll., Dept. of Special Collections, Univ. of Calif., Los Angeles, contains five volumes of scrapbooks and mounted clippings, reviews, photographs, and programs. An interview, taped in June 1959, is in the Popular Arts Project of the Oral Hist. Coll., Columbia Univ. For biographical information see Lee Edward Stern, *Jeanette MacDonald* (1977); James Robert Parish, *The Jeanette MacDonald Story* (1976); and De Witt Bodeen, "Jeanette MacDonald," *Films in Review*, March 1965, pp. 129–44. Eleanor Knowles, *The Films of Jeanette MacDonald and Nelson Eddy* (1975) has a discography. *Biog. Encyc. and Who's Who of the Am. Theatre* (1966) gives a full list of MacDonald's credits. See also Miles Kreuger, ed., *The Movie Musical from Vitaphone to "42nd Street"* (1975). MacDonald's birth date is variously reported as 1901, 1903, 1906, and 1907; no birth record is available. The 1903 date, used by David Thomson, *Biog. Dict. of Cinema* (1975), conforms best to the facts of her early career. A death record, giving a 1907 birth date, was provided by the Texas Dept. of Health. A biobibliography by Christine Schelshorn assisted with research. Samson Raphaelson, Rouben Mamoulian, and Walter Reisch all offered vivid personal recollections of MacDonald in Hollywood. An obituary appeared in the *N.Y. Times*, Jan. 15, 1965.]

JAMES HARVEY

MacDOWELL, Marian Griswold Nevins, Nov. 22, 1857–Aug. 23, 1956. Patron, musician.

Marian MacDowell, founder of the MacDowell Colony, was born in New York City, the third of five children and eldest of three daughters of David Henry and Cornelia (Perkins) Nevins. Both of Marian's parents were descendants of old Connecticut families: her father's had migrated from Scotland around 1727, her mother's from England in 1636. (The Perkins line included at least twelve governors, thirty-six judges, and, later, a president of Yale University.) In 1860 the Nevinses moved to Waterford, Conn., when Marian's father, a prosperous broker-banker, retired. The family lived at Shaw Farm, a home acquired from Marian's maternal grandmother.

After her mother's death in 1866, Marian Nevins briefly attended a school founded in New London by two of her aunts, Lucretia and Caroline Perkins. But most of her education came from her self-taught father. A serious girl, she became accustomed to assuming responsibility for others at an early age, helping her father raise her two younger sisters. At the age of ten, she discovered the piano and studied for four years with her aunt Caroline. In the summer of 1880, Nevins went to Germany, intending to study with Clara Schumann and attempt a career as a concert pianist; instead, she took lessons for two and a half years from Edward Alexander MacDowell, soon to become America's first internationally known composer. Marian Nevins and Edward MacDowell were married in New York on July 9, 1884; a ceremony also took place in Waterford on July 21.

After the marriage, Marian MacDowell abandoned her own career in music to further her husband's. In Germany, where they lived from 1884 to 1888, largely on an inheritance from her mother, Marian MacDowell was homemaker, secretary, copyist, and critic. She continued this supporting role in Boston, where Edward MacDowell taught and gave piano recitals for eight years, and in New York, where he became Columbia University's first professor of music in 1896. These years devoted to her husband were not easy ones for Marian MacDowell: complications following a stillbirth in 1886 kept her from having children, and she suffered several extended illnesses, which may have been in part a result of frustration over the lack of an outlet for her own energy and talents.

In 1904 Edward MacDowell left Columbia in a well-publicized dispute with the university's president and board of trustees over the direction of the music department. Shortly after resigning, MacDowell, a victim of syphilis, began to deteriorate physically and mentally. The Mendelssohn Glee Club of New York, which he had conducted from 1896 to 1898, initiated a fund-raising drive for his support. But on Jan. 23, 1908, before the drive was completed, Edward MacDowell died. At the suggestion of Marian MacDowell, the money raised—about $30,000—was given to the Edward MacDowell Memorial Association, incorporated in 1907. It was to be used to realize the composer's wish that Hillcrest, the Peterborough, N.H., summer estate where he had worked in a woodland studio, be used by other artists—composers, writers, painters, and sculptors—who could live and

work there inexpensively and undisturbed. Shortly before her husband's death, Marian MacDowell had deeded this property to the Association, retaining the lifetime right of residence and management: from Hillcrest, and from the $30,000 gift to the Association, she forged the MacDowell Colony.

For almost fifty years, the MacDowell Colony was its founder's absorbing passion. Beginning in 1910 and continuing until she was past eighty, Marian MacDowell gave nationwide lecture-recitals in which she told of the Colony's work and played Edward MacDowell's piano music. The proceeds—some $6,000 or $7,000 a year—were used along with funds solicited from organizations and individuals to support and expand the Colony. She purchased more land in Peterborough, designed and built studios and living quarters, ran a farm which raised much of the Colony's food, and established fellowships for artists who could not afford even the nominal cost of room and board. As corresponding secretary for the MacDowell Association, she also helped select colonists, and produced pageants and festivals to publicize the Colony.

By the 1930s, what had seemed an impractical dream had become a major influence on the country's artistic life. The MacDowell Colony's value was spotlighted by the success of such colonists as Aaron Copland, MABEL DANIELS, WILLA CATHER, DuBose Heyward, Thornton Wilder, ELINOR WYLIE, and Edwin Arlington Robinson, a resident for more than twenty seasons. Colonists received personal attention from their tiny, unfashionably dressed manager and patron, an excellent listener with a quick wit, hearty laugh, and sympathetic understanding of the artistic temperament. Providing her artists with basket lunches and protecting them from intruders, Marian MacDowell worked to create an atmosphere free of distractions and untainted by scandal.

From 1908 to 1945, under Marian MacDowell's unpaid management—she supported herself largely through royalties from her husband's music—the Colony grew from 135 acres, one studio, and one dormitory, to over 700 acres, twenty-four studios, three dormitories, a dining room—recreation center, and a library. Though always modestly acknowledging the help of others, MacDowell was proud of the colonists' many awards and of her own, which included several honorary degrees, the *Pictorial Review*'s $5,000 Achievement Award for 1923, the Henry Hadley Medal for outstanding service to music (1942), and a grant from the National Institute of Arts and Letters for distinguished service to the arts (1949).

Old age and ill health curtailed MacDowell's

activities at the Colony after 1945. Nearly blind, she spent most of her last ten years at the Los Angeles home of Nina Maud Richardson (1885–1969), her close companion, intended biographer, and heir; since the twenties, the perky, literary Richardson had served as MacDowell's assistant and, later, as her "eyes" at the Colony. Marian MacDowell died in Los Angeles in 1956 at the age of ninety-eight and was buried beside her husband in a two-grave woodland cemetery near the Colony.

Through her founding and nurturing of the Colony, MacDowell made an unprecedented contribution to the creative arts in America. This career, carried out when she was past fifty and without administrative training, illustrates what a woman could accomplish on her own with talent, determination, and dedication to a cause. The MacDowell Colony became not only Edward MacDowell's memorial but also its founder's.

[Marian MacDowell's unpublished memoirs and much of her extensive, mostly unpublished correspondence are found in two somewhat overlapping collections in the Library of Congress: the Music Division's, containing Edward and Marian Mac-Dowells' more personal papers, and the Manuscript Division's, containing the files of the MacDowell Colony. Other primary materials include the Griswold-Perkins family papers at the Univ. of Va. and genealogical data gathered by members of the Nevins and MacDowell family. The most important published writings by Marian MacDowell are: "Edward MacDowell: Some Reminiscences of the American Composer's Fledgling Years by His Widow," *Musical America*, Feb. 15, 1955; "MacDowell's 'Peterborough Idea,'" *Musical Quart.*, Jan. 1932; and *Random Notes on Edward MacDowell and His Music* (1950). Some of the statements in these writings are contradictory or inaccurate, especially regarding chronology. The published accounts of Marian MacDowell's life are fairly extensive but generally thin or sentimental. The longest is Nancy McKee's popularized *Valiant Woman* (1962), but the best are probably Rollo Walter Brown, "Mrs. MacDowell and Her Colony," *Atlantic Monthly*, July 1949, and Carl Carmer, "Marian MacDowell: Woman with a Possible Dream," *Yankee*, April 1952. The most thorough and scholarly study of the Mac-Dowells is Margery Morgan Lowens, "The New York Years of Edward MacDowell" (Ph.D. diss., Univ. of Mich., 1971). Useful recollections of the MacDowells include John Erskine, *My Life in Music* (1950); Henry T. Finck, *My Adventures in the Golden Age of Music* (1926); Hamlin Garland, *Roadside Meetings* (1930), and *Companions on the Trail* (1931); and Templeton Strong, "Edward MacDowell as I Knew Him," *Music Student*, Aug. 1915–July 1916. Helpful comments on Marian Mac-Dowell's management of the MacDowell Colony are contained in Hermann Hagedorn, *Edwin Arlington Robinson* (1938); Herbert Kubly, "The Care and

Feeding of Artists," *Horizon*, March 1963; Chard Powers Smith, *Where the Light Falls* (1965); and Margaret Widdemer, *Golden Friends I Had* (1964). See also the yearly reports published by the Mac-Dowell Colony since 1914. An obituary of Marian MacDowell appeared in the *N.Y. Times*, Aug. 25, 1956. Legal documents consulted include wills and marriage and death certificates. Arnold Schwab is preparing a full-length biography of Marian Mac-Dowell. George M. Kendall and Conrad S. Spohnholz provided useful assistance.]

ARNOLD T. SCHWAB

MACK, Nila, Oct. 24, 1891–Jan. 20, 1953. Radio producer and writer, actress.

Nila Mack wrote, produced, and directed one of the most popular children's radio shows ever aired. The award-winning "Let's Pretend," heard on Saturday mornings from 1934 until 1954, featured classic stories and fairy tales acted by children.

Nila Mack was born in Arkansas City, Kans., the only child of Margaret (Bowen) and Carl Mac. Her father was an engineer who had run the first train on the Santa Fe railroad into Indian territory. His family, from Scotland, were originally named MacLoughlin. The name was shortened to Mac; Nila later added the "k" because "Mac" was too often assumed to be a nickname.

In 1907 Carl Mac was killed in a train wreck. Margaret Mac opened a dancing school where her daughter played the piano accompaniment. Well known for her precocious ability in music and drama, Nila Mack also played the piano for the local open-air theater and acted and sang in regional entertainments. As a dancer, she won 208 cakes in local cakewalk contests.

After graduating from high school in Arkansas City, Nila Mack went to Ferry Hall School, a Presbyterian girls' finishing school, in Forest Park, Ill. From there she moved to Boston to study voice, dancing, and French.

Nila Mack's first professional work was as an actress with traveling repertory companies. Her mother closed the family home and they traveled together. Left in Metropolis, Ill., with no further bookings when one troupe ran out of money, Nila and Margaret Mac with Roy Briant, an actor with the company, established their own theater; Briant was manager, Nila Mack played the piano, and her mother sold tickets. This venture also failed, and Mack and Briant joined another traveling troupe. They were married on March 20, 1913, in St. Anthony, Idaho.

Shortly before World War I, Nila Mack and Roy Briant settled in Chicago, where they collaborated in writing scripts for motion pictures. Briant left for California to become a screenwriter, and Mack continued to tour, working for some time with the actress ALLA NAZIMOVA, who became a close friend. She was called back to California in 1927 to care for her husband, who had become ill; he died in December of that year.

Moving to New York, Mack went into vaudeville, writing and performing many of her own pieces. In 1928, she appeared on Broadway in *Eva the Fifth* and the following year in *Buckaroo*. Her radio career also began in 1929, when she joined the Columbia Broadcasting System (CBS). She played in Radio Guild productions, and had comedy roles in "Nit-Wits" and "Night Club Romances."

She had to abandon her engagements with CBS, however, to return to Arkansas City to care for her mother. There she became program director of the Arkansas City radio station, learning to do everything from selling and writing continuity for a show to announcing it. In 1930 Mack returned to CBS in New York City to direct "The Adventures of Helen and Mary," a children's program which had premiered June 8, 1929. Helen and Mary were played by child actresses, with the remainder of the roles going to adults. The name of the program became "Let's Pretend" in 1934. More important, during these first four years Mack changed the format of the show so that all tales were classic and all roles in the stories were played by children, a major innovation in broadcasting.

The program was a hit. In addition to winning numerous accolades, it served as a stepping stone for such young stars as Nancy Kelly, Skippy Homeier, and Roddy McDowell. When asked to take the job, Mack had declared that she didn't like children. But her sensitivity, creativity, imagination, broad background, and spirited nature drew out the best abilities of the young performers and made the show a success.

In its heyday, from 1934 until 1952, the show played to live audiences. For several years, CBS did not allow commercials on its prestigious children's program but in 1943 economic pressure led the network to sell the show to Cream of Wheat, its sponsor until 1952. Each program opened with a rousing audience rendition of "Cream of Wheat is so good to eat and I have it every day," followed by announcer "Uncle Bill" Adams's query: "How do we travel to Let's Pretend?"

Working from the theory that fairy tales are children's guides to simple, eternal truths, Mack preached the triumph of goodness over evil. Her princes were charming, her dragons fiery and tough; courtesy and kindness counted; the

good guys prevailed, and each story taught a lesson. Most of the shows were based on the tales of the Brothers Grimm, Hans Christian Andersen, Andrew Lang, and the Arabian Nights. With the help of an imaginative soundman, Mack, who wrote all the adaptations for the show, transported her listeners to long ago and far away lands of talking horses and enchanted forests. She did not believe in leaving children hanging in suspense from week to week; each drama had the battles in the middle of the half hour, with the villain receiving just punishment at the end.

Some shows became traditional seasonal presentations. During the Christmas season, "House of the World," an original script by Mack, presented the triumph of Good Will over Intolerance, Greed, Selfishness, and Poverty. "Heavenly Music" was performed at Easter, "The Leprechaun" for St. Patrick's Day, "Fairer than a Fairy" at Halloween, and "The Little Lame Prince" during the annual March of Dimes campaign to combat infantile paralysis.

"Let's Pretend" began in the middle of the depression, when fantasy provided an escape from the harsh realities of surrounding poverty. During more than twenty years of continuous broadcasting, it won nearly sixty awards from radio magazines, women's clubs, and school and college associations, including the coveted George Foster Peabody Award (1943) as the "outstanding children's program."

Nila Mack was described by *Newsweek* in 1943 as "large, plump, hard-boiled and shrewd." Her acquaintances described her as high-spirited, friendly, and humble. She always enjoyed signing autographs and meeting fans, and loved the attention showered on her when she returned to Arkansas City.

Arthur Anderson, a child actor for "Let's Pretend," later remembered her relationship with the actors as "something unusual in show business—a personal and continuing friendship and mutual dependence . . . our annual collective Christmas presents were sincere expressions of affection and Nila, being sentimental, would go all to pieces at receiving them." Nila Mack died of a heart attack in her New York apartment in January 1953. "Let's Pretend" continued for a year after her death.

[The Museum of Broadcasting in New York City has seven recordings of "Let's Pretend" and copies of some of the show's scripts. Press releases and a list of her adaptations are available from CBS Audience Services. A selection of stories, *Let's Pretend*, was published in 1948. For information on Mack and the program see *Current Biog.*, 1952; Ruth Adams Knight, *Stand By for the Ladies!* (1939), pp. 95–100; Frank Buxton and Bill Owen, *Radio's Golden*

Age (1966); John Dunning, *Tune in Yesterday* (1976), pp. 353–55; "Two Women Who Give Air's Prodigious Progeny Their Start," Nov. 16, 1935, and "Mack and the Beanstalk," June 28, 1943, both in *Newsweek;* an article in *Variety,* Aug. 21, 1946; and "Witches and Giants," *Time,* Sept. 8, 1952. Obituaries appeared in the *N.Y. Times* and *Kansas City Times,* Jan. 21, 1953, and in the Arkansas City papers. See also a letter from Arthur Anderson, *Variety,* Jan. 28, 1953. An affidavit of birth, provided by the Kans. Board of Health, is the source for Mack's mother's name; it lists her father as Don Carlos Buell Mac. A biobibliography by Betsy Wilson assisted with research; information was also provided by Cleo Budd of the Arkansas City public library.]

JANET BEYER

MACKLIN, Madge Thurlow, Feb. 6, 1893– March 14, 1962. Physician, geneticist.

Advocate of medical genetics, a term she coined, and a pioneer researcher in the inheritance of disease, Madge Macklin promoted both the inclusion of genetics courses in the medical curriculum and the founding of genetics departments in North American medical schools. Born in Philadelphia, she was the fourth of five children and the third of four daughters of Margaret (De Grofft) and William Harrison Thurlow, an engineer. The family moved to Baltimore where Madge Thurlow attended public schools. She excelled in mathematics, beginning calculus at the age of twelve. When her parents returned to Philadelphia she remained in Baltimore with a teacher, Nelly Logan, to complete her senior year at Western High School and to attend Goucher College.

After earning her A.B. in 1914, Madge Thurlow received a fellowship to study physiology at Johns Hopkins Medical School (1914–15), and then entered the medical program. In 1918, while still a student, she married Dr. Charles C. Macklin, associate professor of anatomy at Hopkins. Despite a difficult pregnancy during her fourth year, she received her M.D. with honors in 1919.

In 1921 the Macklin family, now including two children (Carol, b. 1919, and Sylva, b. 1921) moved to Canada, where Charles Macklin was appointed professor of histology and embryology at the University of Western Ontario in London. Madge Macklin received a part-time appointment as an instructor in the same department at a time when it was unusual for a husband and wife to work together. (Her early papers were on histology, some jointly written with her husband.) In 1930 she was promoted to assistant professor, still part-time

and poorly paid. Her three daughters (Margaret was born in 1927) were cared for by a housekeeper, but Charles and Madge Macklin were always home for lunch and when the children returned from school.

Madge Macklin made fundamental contributions to the statistical methodology of human genetics at a time when this subject was still in its infancy. Impatient with research that did not use proper controls, she analyzed data she had carefully gathered from family histories and studies of twins. Her major research interest was the hereditary aspects of cancer, and her studies provided convincing evidence that hereditary factors, along with environmental ones, were involved in many specific types of cancer (such as gastric cancer and breast cancer). Madge Macklin's human genetics studies, like the animal experiments of MAUD SLYE, helped call the attention of the medical profession to the genetic aspects of cancer. She stressed the therapeutic utility of such information, which would alert the physician to be on the watch for early signs of tumors in patients with a family history of cancer. Macklin also investigated other topics in medical genetics, as evidenced, for example, by her monograph on hereditary abnormalities of the eye.

With missionary zeal, throughout the 1920s and 1930s Madge Macklin urged that genetics be added to the medical curriculum. In 1938, at a time when only one medical school in North America had a compulsory separate course in genetics, she prophesied that in twenty-five years all first class medical schools would have departments of medical genetics and that all medical students would be trained in the fundamentals of the subject. By 1946, 38 percent of American medical schools assigned some time to genetics and by 1953, 55 percent included courses in the subject. To a great extent this change was due to Macklin's research, which helped demonstrate to a skeptical profession the clinical value of genetics in diagnosis, therapy, prognosis, and prevention of disease.

Macklin became an avid supporter of the controversial eugenics movement, which sought to improve the human race by controlling breeding. Although by the 1930s many geneticists had discarded eugenics as scientifically ill-founded, Macklin persisted. In 1930 she helped establish the Canadian Eugenics Society, served on its executive committee between 1932 and 1934, and acted as director in 1935. She also published some two dozen articles on the subject. Viewing eugenics as a branch of preventive medicine, she believed that physicians ought to "determine who are physically and mentally qualified to be parents of the next generation" and specifically

advocated compulsory sterilization of schizo-
phrenics as "unfit."

Despite her international reputation, groundbreaking research, and superb teaching skills,
Macklin was never promoted beyond assistant
professor. She was limited to teaching embryology to first-year students and assisting in her
husband's histology course, and was never allowed to teach a course on medical genetics
at Western Ontario. Always outspoken in expressing her views, Macklin was involved in
some clashes with her colleagues and the administration. In 1945 she was notified that her
appointment at Western Ontario, always ses-
sional, would not be renewed. The following
year she was appointed research associate in
cancer research by the National Research Council and moved to Ohio State University in Columbus, where she was also lecturer in medical genetics. Her husband remained at Western
Ontario and she returned to her home in London
for vacations and holidays.

Macklin received many honors during her
career, including an honorary LL.D. from
Goucher (1938) and the Elizabeth Blackwell
Medal of the American Medical Women's Association (1957). In 1959 she was elected president of the American Society for Human
Genetics.

Macklin retired from Ohio State in 1959 and
returned to London to care for her ailing husband, who died a few months later. She spent
the last three years of her life with her daughters and grandchildren in Toronto and died
there of a heart attack in 1962.

[Macklin's articles include "Should the Teaching of
Genetics as Applied to Medicine Have a Place in the
Medical Curriculum," *Jour. Assoc. Am. Med. Col-
leges*, Nov. 1932; "The Teaching of Inheritance of
Disease to Medical Students: A Proposed Course in
Medical Genetics," *Annals Internal Med.*, April
1933; "The Need of a Course in Medical Genetics in
the Medical Curriculum: A Pivotal Point in the
Eugenic Program," in International Eugenics Congress III, *A Decade of Progress in Eugenics*, 1934;
"Genetical Aspects of Sterilization of the Mentally
Unfit," *Canadian Med. Assoc. Jour.*, Feb. 1934; "Origin of the Socially Inadequate," *Jour. Heredity*, Aug.
1934; "The Value of Accurate Statistics in the Study
of Cancer," *Canadian Public Health Jour.*, 25
(1934), 369–73; "Genes and the Unconscious,"
Jour. Heredity, Feb. 1935; "The Inheritance of Disease and Its Relationship to the Practice of Medicine," *Med. Woman's Jour.*, April 1938; "The Case
for Inheritance of Schizophrenia," *Jour. Heredity*,
May 1939; "Inheritance and Human Cancer," *Ohio
State Med. Jour.*, Aug. 1947. A bibliography of her
work (1915–48) is available from the Goucher College Alumnae Assoc. For discussions of Macklin and
her work see Hubert C. Soltan, "Madge Macklin—
Pioneer in Medical Genetics," *Western Ontario Med.*

Jour., Jan. 1967; Murray L. Barr, *A Century of
Medicine at Western: A Centennial History of the
Faculty of Medicine, University of Western Ontario*
(1977); "Ohio State Researcher's Work Is Basis of
Article on Cancer," *Columbus Dispatch*, March 27,
1953; Ruth and Edward Brecher, "Can You Inherit
Cancer?" *Redbook*, April 1953; Mary Jane Hogue,
"The Contribution of Goucher Women to the Biological Sciences," *Goucher Alumnae Quart.*, Summer
1951. The *London Free Press* of Canada has articles
following her career (1938–57) and an obituary in
1962. Some information was provided by Carol
Macklin Kimber. Death certificate provided by Office of the Registrar General, Toronto, Ontario.]

BARRY MEHLER

McLAREN, Louise Leonard, Aug. 10, 1885–
Dec. 16, 1968. Labor educator.

Louise Leonard McLaren, founder of the
Southern Summer School for Women Workers,
was born in Wellsboro, Pa., the eldest of four
children, three daughters and a son, of Estella
(Cook) and Fred Churchill Leonard. Her parents, both of English descent, were born in
the farming region near Cowdersport, Pa.
Estella Cook, reared in an orphanage after the
early death of her father and mother, had been
a schoolteacher. Fred Leonard was a graduate of
Yale University and a successful lawyer. Elected
to Congress on the Republican ticket in 1895,
he was later United States Marshal for the
Western and Middle Districts of Pennsylvania
and president of the First National Bank of
Cowdersport.

Louise Leonard attended Miss Beret's School
for Girls in Harrisburg. Completing the course in
1904, she enrolled at Vassar College, where she
obtained an A.B. in 1907, then began teaching
history, first in high school in Watertown, N.Y.,
then at the Lock Haven (Pa.) Teachers College. In 1914 Leonard left teaching to become
YWCA industrial secretary in the coal mining
region of Wilkes Barre, Pa. Four years later,
she was transferred to Baltimore as the metropolitan industrial secretary, and in 1920 she
was named national industrial secretary for the
south, a region which would engage her imagination and hold her interest for the next twenty-
five years.

As industrial secretary, Leonard traveled extensively through the south, seeking ways to
organize young women workers in industry. She
viewed the enormous economic changes occurring in the region between 1920 and 1925 as
part of an international process of industrialization and sought to help southern workers understand their relationship to workers in other regions. While still based in New York, Leonard

also attended Columbia University for further study in economics (A.M., 1927). Her thesis, "Similar Trends in Two Industrial Revolutions," compared the process of industrialization in England and the southern United States.

Leonard had encountered difficulties organizing southern women workers into a YWCA dependent to a large degree on the support of mill owners and businessmen. As a result, she decided to organize the Southern Summer School for Women Workers in Industry, an independent, southern-based organization of women workers modeled on the Bryn Mawr Summer School for Women Workers, founded in 1921, the Brookwood Labor College, and the workers' education programs of the International Ladies' Garment Workers' Union and the Amalgamated Clothing Workers of America. In 1926 she brought together a committee of educators, industrial workers, and trade unionists to plan the school.

The American Fund for Public Service promised a grant, if an equal amount could be raised in southern communities. To that end, Leonard established a network of organizational and financial support which included members of local YWCA boards, and of the League of Women Voters and the American Association of University Women. Forming workers' education committees, these groups raised money to send young women from their communities to the school. Once established, the Southern Summer School drew increasing support from organized labor.

From among women she had known in the YWCA and at Columbia, Leonard recruited a faculty that included graduates of women's colleges in the south and northeast. They viewed workers' education as a means to social change and saw themselves as training leaders for a broadly based southern labor movement. As director Leonard emphasized the value to them of interchange among women where "there was no line drawn between the faculty and the students as is the rule in academic life."

The first Southern Summer School met in 1927, on the campus of Sweet Briar College in Virginia. (The school was never able to purchase a permanent site; it rented facilities each year in various locations near Asheville, N.C.) The students, all white, were "a carefully chosen group of twenty-five, representing all the typical industries of the South" (*Am. Federationist*, Dec. 1927, p. 1487).

Aware of the limitations of a literary and artistic emphasis in some workers' education programs, Leonard consciously sought to organize a school that would do more than improve the lot of individuals. The curriculum empha-

sized economics and industrial history, while also offering English, labor dramatics, and health education. Because most southern workers had been born on farms and were only first- or second-generation workers in industry, Leonard thought it necessary to develop "social attitudes appropriate to the Machine Age." She sought to teach workers analytical skills and to help them understand the effects of industrialization on their lives. Within the school, working with the faculty as a cooperative community, students obtained a sense of autonomy and gained the confidence for self-expression.

For Louise Leonard, the Southern Summer School became a lifework. For seventeen years she served as its director and full-time organizer. Often working at reduced salary when the School's fund-raising efforts fell short, she traveled during the year, recruiting students and supporters, educating both groups of women about the human costs of a rapidly industrializing economy, and coordinating workers' education programs among former Southern Summer School students. Totally dependent on her salary, she sacrificed to make ends meet; traveling much of the time, she did not have a permanent home. In 1930 Leonard married Myron McLaren, a professor at St. John's College in Annapolis, Md. She continued her work in the south unabated, and when McLaren lost his job in the depression, she supported them both.

In the early 1930s Louise Leonard McLaren's organizing tasks became more difficult as the School's closer ties to the labor movement threatened to topple the fragile coalition she had built between middle-class women's organizations and labor. When the CIO organizing drive gained strength in the south in 1935, McLaren struggled to interpret labor's aims to reform-minded southern women.

Under Louise McLaren's leadership, more than 300 working-class women came to summer residence sessions; the Southern Summer School succeeded in creating through its workers' education programs a grass-roots constituency of educated local leaders across the south. In 1938, with the encouragement of the trade unions, the School expanded its program to include men. But with the improved employment opportunities occasioned by World War II, workers had little time to attend a residence school, and the Southern Summer School held its final residence session in 1942. Seminars and training programs for labor groups in southern communities continued for two more years. In 1944 McLaren resigned as director, left the south, and moved permanently to New York City.

In New York, McLaren turned to more overtly political work, serving as an organizer for the CIO Political Action Committee in the 1944 elections. After the election, however, she faced the difficulties of finding a position. The social gospel of McLaren's YWCA experience, the reformist impulse of her educational work, and the socialist economic theory which inspired her to establish the Southern Summer School appeared outmoded in 1945. She held a series of jobs with New York-based organizations, including the American Cancer Society and the Girl Scouts of America. Finally, a teaching and research position with the American Labor Education Service (ALES) brought McLaren back into workers' education until her retirement at sixty-eight.

Louise McLaren died of heart disease in East Stroudsburg, Pa., in 1968 at eighty-three. Dedicated, hardworking, and imbued with an unfailing sense of optimism, she had a vision of a humane and cooperatively run industrial society that provided a model for several generations of southern women workers.

[The principal manuscript source is the Southern Summer School Papers in the ALES Coll., Catherwood Library, N.Y. State School of Industrial and Labor Relations, Cornell Univ. McLaren correspondence is available in the Mary C. Barker Papers, Emory Univ. Special Collections, and the Highlander Folk School Papers, State Hist. Soc. of Wis. Articles by McLaren include "New Summer School for Women Workers," *Am. Federationist*, Dec. 1927, pp. 1487–90; "A School in the Old South," *Labor Age*, Dec. 1928, pp. 22–23; "The South Begins Workers' Education," *Am. Federationist*, Nov. 1928, pp. 1–6; "Southern Summer School," *Jour. Adult Education*, Oct. 1932, pp. 452–54; "Southern Summer School," *Jour. Adult Education*, Oct. 1936, pp. 502–3. "South's Problems Faced at Workers' Own School," *Jour. Electrical Workers and Operators*, May 1929, pp. 233, 277; "Summer Schools for Workers in Industry," *Progressive Education*, Nov. 1932, pp. 503–7; "Workers' Education in the South," *Am. Teacher*, Nov. 1928, pp. 8–10; "Workers' Education in the South," *Vassar Quart.*, May 1935, pp. 100–5; "A Workers' School and Organized Labor," *Am. Teacher*, Dec. 1929, pp. 10–13. There are references to her work in Theodore Brameld, ed., *Workers' Education in the United States* (1941); Eleanor G. Coit and Mark Starr, "Workers' Education in the U.S.," *Monthly Labor Rev.*, July 1939; Alice Hanson Cook and Agnes M. Douty, *Labor Education Outside the Unions: A Review of Postwar Programs in Western Europe and the United States* (1958); Florence H. Schneider, *Patterns of Workers' Education: The Story of the Bryn Mawr Summer School* (1941). Further information was provided by Myron McLaren. A death certificate was supplied by Pa. Dept. of Health.]

MARY E. FREDERICKSON

MADELEVA, Sister. *See* WOLFF, Sister Mary Madeleva (Mary Evaline).

MAHONY, Marion. *See* GRIFFIN, Marion Lucy Mahony.

MALONE, Annie. *See* TURNBO-MALONE, Annie Minerva.

MANKIN, Helen Douglas, Sept. 11, 1894–July 25, 1956. Lawyer, state legislator, congresswoman.

Helen Mankin, the first woman elected to Congress from Georgia, was born in Atlanta, third of the five children and second of the four daughters of Hamilton and Corinne (Williams) Douglas. Her father, of Scottish ancestry, grew up in Virginia and taught school in Iowa. Her mother, of English descent, was a graduate of the Rockford (Ill.) Female Seminary (later Rockford College), whose family had migrated to Iowa from Rhode Island. Both earned law degrees from the University of Michigan (1887), then moved to Atlanta where Hamilton Douglas practiced law and founded Atlanta Law School. Corinne Douglas—excluded as a woman from the Georgia bar—cared for her growing family, taught school, and became an innovator in women's education.

Helen Douglas attended Atlanta public schools, graduated from Washington Seminary (1913), and earned an A.B. at Rockford College in 1917. In Europe during 1918–19 she drove an ambulance for an American hospital unit attached to the French army. Returning home, she earned an LL.B. from Atlanta Law School in 1920. That year she and her mother, then over sixty, were admitted to the Georgia bar and joined the Douglas family firm.

As a woman lawyer in Atlanta Helen Douglas felt like a "freak," and she decided to explore beyond her conservative surroundings. In May 1922 she and her sister Jean began a 13,000-mile automobile tour of North America, which the *Los Angeles Times* (Aug. 31) called "a 1922 touring record for women drivers." Helen Douglas sent daily descriptions of their travels to the *Atlanta Georgian*. After more travel in Europe she returned to Atlanta, and in 1924 opened her own law office.

Douglas had no corporate clients, and those she served as a lawyer were often poor and black. To supplement her income she gave lectures at Atlanta Law School. She also became active in city politics, serving in 1927 as woman's manager of I. N. Ragsdale's successful mayoral campaign. In September of that year she married Guy Mark Mankin, a mechanical engineer and widower with a seven-year-old son, Guy Jr. During the next five years Helen Mankin went with her husband wherever his work took him—to Cuba, Brazil, Argentina, and later to New York and Chicago.

In 1933 the couple moved back to Atlanta, and Helen Mankin resumed her law career. In 1935, after lobbying in vain among state legislators for ratification of a child labor amendment to the federal Constitution, she decided to try "from inside": in the Democratic primary of September 1936 she was elected state representative from Fulton County over five male opponents. The fifth woman to sit in the Georgia legislature, she was reelected four times, serving from 1937 to 1946—longer than any woman before her.

Tall and broad-shouldered, Helen Mankin became known in the state legislature as independent, outspoken, and abrasive. An opponent of Georgia's powerful Governor Eugene Talmadge, she worked for progressive legislation in the areas of child welfare, education, electoral reform, and women's rights. She championed Governor Ellis Arnall's liberal administration (1943–46), including his poll-tax repeal and enfranchisement of eighteen-year-olds.

When Governor Arnall called a special election for Feb. 12, 1946, to fill the unexpired term of Fifth District congressman Robert Ramspeck who had resigned, Mankin left the legislature to seek the office. Negroes, then suing under a 1944 Supreme Court decision to end Georgia's white primary, doubled their registration for this special election as they could vote freely in it. Of the eighteen candidates in the race, only Mankin actively sought black support and, by a margin smaller than her vote in the heavily black Ashby Street precinct of Atlanta, she won Ramspeck's seat. Eugene Talmadge, running again for governor, dubbed her "the Belle of Ashby Street" and heaped scorn on "the spectacle of Atlanta Negroes sending a Congresswoman to Washington." Mankin refused to disavow her black support, proclaiming: "I'm proud of every one of those votes and I hope I will get them again." She also drew support from the CIO, becoming the focus of a coalition of union members, blacks, and progressives —an alliance that the region's dominant groups had feared since the days of the Populist uprising in the 1890s.

Although not a radical, in Washington Mankin was regarded as a Georgia maverick. A consistent supporter of the administration, she was one of the few southerners who supported President Harry S Truman's veto of the Case anti-strike bill—a measure that labor bitterly opposed.

Mankin was renominated in the no longer all-white Democratic primary of July 1946 by a 10,000-vote popular majority over her opponent, James C. Davis. But Davis claimed victory according to Georgia's peculiar county-unit system, which awarded a county's assigned unit vote—varying from two to six—to the candidate receiving a plurality of its popular vote in a primary. Total unit votes, rather than an overall majority, determined victory. Long unused in the Fifth District, this system was revived to nullify the Negro vote and "to beat Mrs. Mankin—nothing else," according to W. Schley Howard, a former congressman. Mankin received six unit votes, Davis eight. Mankin challenged the outcome and the State Democratic Executive Committee, loyal to Arnall, put both candidates on the November general election ballot. But Talmadge, having won the Democratic gubernatorial primary in a one-party state, had her name removed when he took control of the committee before the general election.

Mankin organized a last-minute write-in candidacy but encountered violent opposition from a white-supremacy group working closely with Davis's staff; nonetheless, she received 19,527 write-in votes to Davis's 31,444 regular ballots. The Eightieth Congress supported Davis when Mankin challenged his right to a seat. Racial disturbances in the south sparked national demands for civil rights laws, which further excited southern tempers; in 1948, when Mankin again ran against Davis, she was widely condemned for upsetting the regional pattern and was decisively defeated.

Helen Mankin continued to practice law but never again ran for public office. In 1949 she launched a federal suit, *South v. Peters,* against the county-unit system. The Supreme Court ruled against her, stating that the federal courts must not intervene in political issues arising from a state's geographic distribution of voting strength—a ruling that was not reversed until 1962.

In the last years of her life, Helen Mankin visited Israel and lectured in the United States on Zionist causes. She was also a part-time talent scout for the Atlanta Crackers, a minor league baseball team. She died in 1956 in Atlanta as the result of injuries suffered in an automobile accident.

[For Helen Mankin's account of her travels see *Atlanta Georgian* and *Sunday-American,* May-Nov. 1922, and July-Dec. 1923. Both papers are available on microfilm at the Atlanta Public Library. Other sources include Anna Holden, "Race and Politics: Congressional Elections in the 5th Dist. of Ga., 1946–1952" (M.A. thesis, Univ. of N.C., 1955); *Hearings, Contested Election Case of Helen Douglas Mankin v. James C. Davis from 5th Cong. Dist. of Ga.* (1947); C. A. Bacote, "The Negro in Atlanta

Politics," *Phylon, The Atlanta Univ. Rev.*, vol. 16, no. 4 (1955); Supreme Court decisions *Cook v. Fortson*, 329 U.S. 675, *South v. Peters*, 339 U.S. 276, and *Gray v. Sanders*, 372 U.S. 368; *Biog. Directory of the Am. Congress, 1774–1961;* and *Current Biog.*, 1946. *Atlanta Constitution* and *Atlanta Journal*, 1936–48, and the Hapeville, Ga., *Statesman*, March-June 1946, contain articles about Mankin's political activities. Obituaries appeared in *Wash. Post*, July 28, 1956, and Wash. *Evening Star*, July 27, 1956. Information was also obtained from interviews with Ellis Arnall, former state senator G. Everett Millican, former Ga. congressmen James A. Mackay and James C. Davis, and George Stoney, Mankin's campaign manager. Mankin's birth date is given as 1896 in printed sources. The 1894 date is confirmed by the 1900 U.S. Census and by her sister Jean Douglas Smith. Death certificate was provided by the Ga. Dept. of Health.]

LORRAINE NELSON SPRITZER

MARION, Frances, Nov. 18, 1888–May 12, 1973. Screenwriter.

A novelist, film director, and artist, Frances Marion is best remembered as one of Hollywood's most respected and highest paid scriptwriters, at her peak earning $17,000 per week. She was born Marion Benson Owens in San Francisco, the daughter of Len Douglas Owens, a partner in a prosperous advertising firm, and Minnie (Hall) Owens, an accomplished pianist. She had one older brother and one younger sister. Of Irish and Welsh stock, her father, who was ruined financially by the San Francisco earthquake and fire, hailed from Iowa, while her mother, whose ancestors were of Creole origins, came from California.

Marion Owens attended the Hamilton Grammar School, Saint Margaret's Hall in Burlingame, the University of California at Berkeley, and the Mark Hopkins Art School. In 1906 she married Wesley de Lappé, a nineteen-year-old instructor at the Mark Hopkins School. Following their divorce in 1909, while studying art and posing for advertisements she first took the name Frances Marion. In 1911 she married Robert Pike; this union also soon ended in divorce. She worked as a reporter for the *San Francisco Examiner* and as an illustrator for producer and theatrical manager Oliver Morosco in 1914 before starting her career, at age twenty-six, at the Bosworth Studios with LOIS WEBER.

At the studio, according to her account, she "played extra bits, worked in the cutting-room, read scripts and dared suggest changes, and even hauled furniture around to make the sets more attractive" (Bodeen, p. 76). Her first original scenario was for *The Foundling* (1916),

with Mary Pickford (died 1979), who became a good friend. Marion soon acquired a contract to write for William A. Brady of the World Company. In 1917, already a prolific and successful screenwriter, she moved on to Paramount. Her credits in the next years, for Paramount and other studios, included *Poor Little Rich Girl* (1917), which starred Pickford; *Just Around the Corner* (1922), which she directed; *Stella Dallas* (1925); and *The Son of the Sheik* (1926). In November 1920 she married Fred Thomson, trained at Princeton to be a minister like his father. A track and field champion who loved horses, Thomson became one of the most successful cowboy stars of the silent screen, earning $10,000 a week in 1925. Together they produced sixty-eight westerns for which she wrote, without credit, many of the screenplays. Though in her autobiography *Off With Their Heads* (1972) Frances Marion discusses the difficulties some couples experience with dual careers, her marriage to Fred Thomson was, by her account as well as others', successful. Before Thomson died in 1928, from tetanus, they had one son, Fred, Jr. (b. 1926), and adopted another, Richard Gordon (b. 1927). Though Marion arranged to be free during their summer vacations, the boys spent much time with live-in servants or in private schools. Fred Thomson, Jr., recalls, however, that if her family needed her, she put her work aside. Even when she was most successful, she discouraged her sons from entering the movie business, which she termed "dirty work." Having little formal education herself, she stressed the importance of education, and, according to her son, accumulated a Gatsbylike library.

Frances Marion's fourth marriage to director George Hill in 1930 was an unhappy one. Though the films they worked on together, such as *The Big House* (1930), *Min and Bill* (1930), and *The Secret Six* (1931), enhanced both of their reputations, their private life was a failure. They were divorced in 1931. She explained the divorce by saying he drank too much. In 1934, while he was working with her on *The Good Earth*, George Hill committed suicide. In addition to her collaborations with Hill, during these years Marion wrote the scripts for *Anna Christie* (1930), *The Champ* (1931), *Dinner at Eight* (1933), and *The Prizefighter and the Lady* (1933). Both *The Big House* and *The Champ* earned her Academy Awards. Credited altogether with over a hundred scripts, she was also a script consultant on many other projects, most made with director Irving Thalberg.

Frances Marion wrote in bed very early in the morning. She smoked between three and four packs of cigarettes a day, and her bed was "pockmarked with cigarette burns"; she once set fire to herself. A keen observer who had a knack for spotting talent as well as a good story, she applied her research skills to give her films a special kind of authenticity. For example, she spent a week in San Quentin preparing for *The Big House*. Marion was aware that movies are a business, as she made clear in *How to Write and Sell Film Stories* (1937), a work she considered one of her strongest contributions. She wrote: "It may be good art, but it is not good business to send an audience home depressed and blue" (p. 87). She sought to write scripts with heightened emotional and dramatic effects which would satisfy the audience's expectations.

Though her manual stresses the importance of creating original stories for the screen, many of her own scripts were adaptations. Marion's ability to translate a play or novel into film was uncanny. She knew what to eliminate because she sensed what would and would not work visually. Though she has been criticized for being unfaithful to the text by turning *The Scarlet Letter* (1926) into a boy-girl love story, her talent for quickly establishing strong human emotions on film justifies the important place she holds in the history of American film.

Affected by the death of Irving Thalberg and increasingly disillusioned by the changes she saw in Hollywood, Frances Marion turned her attention away from the movies after 1937. Her novel, *Valley People* (1935), describes her love for northern California, a place she had fled earlier because of her ambition to become a part of the movies. She wrote five other novels, numerous short stories, and, in the years after 1937, devoted much of her time to studying and making sculpture. A generous and unpretentious woman who used her Oscars as doorstops, Frances Marion died in 1973 in Los Angeles of a ruptured aneurysm.

[The Frances Marion Coll. at Doheny Library, Univ. of Southern Calif., contains clippings, photographs, correspondence, and other materials. The Museum of Modern Art, N.Y. City, has prints of some of Marion's films, as well as selected scripts. A valuable source is *The Reminiscences of Frances Marion* (1958), Popular Arts Project, in the Oral History Coll., Columbia Univ. *Off With Their Heads* includes a detailed filmography and numerous photographs. Kenneth W. Munden, ed., *The American Film Institute Feature Films, 1921–1930* (1971), includes story synopses and credits. De Witt Bodeen, "Frances Marion," parts I and II, *Films in Review*, Feb. 1969, pp. 71–91, and March 1969, pp. 129–52, includes Marion's remark that her career was often aided by women, and also contains a bibliography and filmography. See also Ernest Corneau, *The Hall of Fame of Western Film Stars* (1969); Samuel Marx, *Mayer and Thalberg: The Make-Believe*

Saints (1972); and Mark W. Estrin, "Triumph and Ignominy on the Screen," in Gerald Peary and Roger Shatzkin, eds., *The Classic American Novel and the Movies* (1977), pp. 20–29. Gavin Lambert's review of *Off With Their Heads*, in *Academy Leader*, Nov. 1972, pp. 14–19, provides interesting information about Marion's career. Obituaries appeared in the *N.Y. Times*, May 14, 1973; *Newsweek*, May 28, 1973; and *Time*, May 28, 1973. Additional information was provided by Marion's sons, Fred Thomson, Jr., and Richard Thomson, and by Martha Lorah and Katherine Page Porter. Marriage and death certificates supplied by Calif. Dept. of Public Health.]

PHILIPPE PEREBINOSSOFF

MARSH, Mae, Nov. 9, 1895–Feb. 13, 1968. Film actress.

Mae Marsh, whose ability to play pathos to the limits of cinematic art was unequaled in silent film, was born Mary Warne Marsh. Her father, Charles Marsh, traveled across the southwest as an auditor for the Santa Fe Railroad. Mary was born in Madrid, N. Mex.; each of her five siblings—two older and two younger sisters and one younger brother—was born in a different state. Charles Marsh died when Mary was four; her mother, Mary (Warne) Marsh, moved the family from Texas to San Francisco, where she soon remarried. When the earthquake killed Marsh's stepfather and the great fire destroyed her home, the family moved again, this time to the Los Angeles area.

Marsh attended, but never liked, public school and the Convent of the Sacred Heart in Hollywood. Equally unhappy with her summer job as a telephone operator, she accompanied her sister, Marguerite Loveridge, to film studios until she was herself given a job in a Mack Sennett one-reeler in January 1912. Loveridge had joined D. W. Griffith's Biograph company the previous January, and when Sennett no longer needed her younger sister's services, she encouraged her to cross the lot to work for Griffith. Marsh probably made her first appearance in *A Siren of Impulse*, a Mary Pickford vehicle. Although films at the time appeared without acting credits, Griffith, knowing Pickford would not brook another Mary in the company, renamed his newest actress Mae Marsh.

Mae Marsh had supporting roles in three films between January and March 1912. Then Pickford, Blanche Sweet, and Mabel Normand all turned down the role of "Lily White," the heroine in *Man's Genesis*, because they felt the costume was too risqué and because they wanted to save their talent for the lead in Griffith's next picture, *The Sands of Dee*. Marsh was awarded the part and, in a characteristic gesture, Griffith announced that "as a reward for her graciousness Miss Marsh will also receive the role of the heroine in *The Sands of Dee*." Unlike the other actresses in the company, Marsh had no previous stage training; even that worked to her advantage, however. "I am inclined to favor beginners," Griffith noted. "They come untrammelled by so-called techniques, by theories, by preconceived ideas" (Evans, p. 18). When Pickford left the company in 1913, Griffith groomed Marsh as her replacement.

Along with most of the company, Mae Marsh followed Griffith when he left Biograph for the Reliance-Majestic Company, in October 1913. She appeared in seven films for Reliance, most notably as "Apple Pie Mary" in *Home Sweet Home* (1914), her most popular role up to that time. While with Reliance, Marsh was consistently partnered with Robert (Bobby) Harron, with whom she had first appeared in *Man's Genesis*; they quickly became one of the most appealing juvenile teams in film.

Marsh was elevated to international stardom by her performance in *The Birth of a Nation* (1915, originally titled *The Clansman*). As Flora Cameron, "the little sister," she throws herself into a ravine in order to prevent being raped. Critics were ecstatic over her performance, and felt she could never equal her success. She quickly proved them wrong: the following year, in the modern sequence of *Intolerance*, Marsh, as the "Little Dear One," reached the height of silent-screen acting. The image of Marsh, sitting in the courtroom, her hands displaying her agitated emotions, epitomizes "youth-in-trouble forever" (Kael, p. 106). Marsh portrayed similar emotions as an orphan in *Hoodoo Ann* (1916), as a gamin in *A Child of the Paris Streets* (1916), and as a child of nature in *The Wild Girl of the Sierras* (1916), all made for the Triangle Film Corporation under Griffith's supervision, and all costarring Bobby Harron.

In 1916, Mae Marsh was earning $85 a week working for Triangle. That fall, the newly formed Goldwyn Company offered her a two-year contract paying $2,000 a week the first year and $3,000 a week the second. Marsh was averse to leaving her mentor, but Griffith dismissed such loyalty: "Take it and when you're finished, come back to me" (Rosenkrantz and Silverstein, p. 213). Accepting the contract, Marsh moved to New York, taking her mother and younger sisters, to begin work at the Goldwyn studio in Fort Lee, N.J. Touted as the original "Goldwyn Girl," she made thirteen films, claiming to like only two: *Polly of the Circus* and *The Cinderella Man* (both 1917). Her final screen appearance with Harron was in *Sunshine Alley*, the same year. Marsh's Goldwyn films displayed none of the realism of her earlier films, and her reputation began to recede.

After making three mediocre films in Hollywood and attempting a stage career in an English comedy, *Brittie*, which closed on tour in 1921, Marsh left to make films in England. *Flames of Passion* (1922) and *Paddy the Next Best Thing* (1923) were as popular as her Griffith films, and her success with British audiences was great. But she could not tolerate the climate, and returned to New York to work again with Griffith. As Teazie, "an orphan seduced by a candidate for the ministry" (Dunham, p. 321), in *The White Rose*, Marsh regained her star stature. She observed: "It's a Mae Marsh part, which means I play a poor kid who gets herself into a terrific emotional tangle" (Evans, p. 25). This last pairing between the best of realistic screen actresses and directors was also their most successful. Marsh appeared in a German film, *Arabella* (1924), and a final silent film, *The Rat* (1925), costarring Ivor Novello, but she never again fully utilized her talent.

Mae Marsh had married Louis Lee Arms, a publicist she met while filming *Polly*, on Sept. 21, 1918. They had three children: Mary (b. 1919), Brewster (b. 1925), and Marguerite (b. 1928). After a short time in the army, Louis Arms became a land developer in southern California, investing both his and his wife's money. The loss of close to $500,000 in the 1929 stock market crash forced them into bankruptcy. Soon afterward, Mae Marsh collapsed and was hospitalized for a near fatal attack of peritonitis. She returned to the screen to play a supporting role in the 1932 remake of *Over the Hill*, her first talkie. Confessing that it was "hard for me to learn lines," Marsh completed her film career as a character actress, performing cameo roles in over a hundred films between 1932 and 1963. (Thirty-six of these were made by John Ford, who saved her from impoverishment in 1939.) Even in small roles, she made a lasting impression on the film audience, especially in *The Grapes of Wrath* (1940), *Jane Eyre* (1943), and *Titanic* (1952). In 1968 she died in Los Angeles of a heart attack.

Mae Marsh's cascading hair and exquisite facial features—including large, dolorous eyes—were suited perfectly to the demands of the movie camera. Her expressive skill made her believable as the ordinary woman, caught in the everyday traps of woman's condition. As Griffith observed: "Every other motion picture star I have known was 'made' by long training and much hard work, but Mae Marsh was born a film star. Destiny itself seemed to have been her coach in acting" (Evans, p. 28).

[*The Reminiscences of Mae Marsh* (1956), Popular Arts Project, in the Oral History Coll., Columbia Univ., offers little biographical detail but does convey some of her winsome personality. Clipping collections at both the Billy Rose Theatre Coll., N.Y. Public Library, and the Harvard Theatre Coll. provide slim material but good photographs. Marsh wrote two books: *Screen Acting* (1921), a how-to book which also contains autobiographical information; and *When They Ask Me My Name* (1932), a children's book of verse. An oral history is included in Bernard Rosenkrantz and Harry Silverstein, ed., *The Real Tinsel* (1970). For biographical accounts see Harold Dunham's article in *Films in Review*, June-July 1958, and his letter, supplying missing film credits, in the March 1959 issue; David Thomson, *A Biog. Dict. of the Cinema* (1975); Anthony Slide, *The Griffith Actresses* (1973); and H. Stern, "On Mae Marsh," *Film Culture*, Spring/Summer 1965. For earlier details see R. Bartlett, "There Were Two Little Girls Named Mary," *Photoplay*, March 1917; and Delight Evans, "Will Mae Marsh Come Back?" *Photoplay*, March 1923. Evelyn Mack Truitt, *Who Was Who on Screen* (2d ed., 1977), gives a complete list of film credits. Various historical accounts of early American cinema and D. W. Griffith include discussion of Marsh. Robert Henderson's monumental *D. W. Griffith: The Years at Biograph* (1970) and *D. W. Griffith: His Life and Work* (1972) are the most authoritative. For an intelligent discussion of Griffith's actresses, particularly their shared social status and similar physical stature, see Alexander Walker, *Stardom* (1970). Pauline Kael, "A Great Folly, and a Small One," *New Yorker*, Feb. 24, 1968, lends credence to the immortality of Marsh's screen image. Obituaries appeared in the *N.Y. Times*, Feb. 14, 1968, and *Variety*, Feb. 21, 1968. No birth or school records are available; death record was provided by the Calif. Dept. of Health Services.]

HARRIETTE L. WALKER

MARTIN, Anne Henrietta, Sept. 30, 1875–April 15, 1951. Suffragist, feminist, essayist.

Anne Henrietta Martin, the first woman to run for the United States Senate, was born in Empire City, Nev., the second of seven children and eldest of four daughters of William O'Hara and Louise (Stadtmuller) Martin. Her father, a politician and wealthy Reno banker and merchant, descended from Irish and English ancestors. Her mother, whose parents had emigrated from Bavaria, grew up in New York. Martin's father encouraged her to develop her intellect, and his populist ideas influenced her social conscience. Her mother, while dismayed at her preference for thinking over sewing, was a loyal supporter of Martin's political activities.

Martin received her elementary education in the Carson City, Nev., school run by Hannah Keziah Clapp and Elizabeth Babcock. She attended Bishop Whitaker's Academy in Reno, then transferred to the University of Nevada, where she received an A.B. in 1894. She received a second A.B. in 1896 from Stanford University and an A.M. in history, under the direction of MARY SHELDON BARNES, the following year. A tennis champion during her school years in Nevada and California, Martin was also a proficient golfer, rider, and climber. She began an academic career in 1897 by founding and heading the history department at the University of Nevada. From 1899 to 1901 she studied at Chase's Art School, at Columbia University, and at the Universities of Leipzig and London. Martin resigned as head of the department after her father's death in 1901 but remained at the University of Nevada to lecture in art until 1903. She attempted to expose the mismanagement of her father's estate by his partners, but her mother rejected her advice in favor of that of her brothers. She then arranged to receive her portion of the inheritance and left for extended travel in Europe and Asia. Her impotence in the family councils, she recalled later, "suddenly made a feminist of me! . . . I found that I stood alone in my family against a man-controlled world."

While in England from 1909 until 1911, Martin joined the militant suffragettes led by Emmeline Pankhurst and on Nov. 18, 1910, was arrested for demonstrating. During that period she also began writing on social issues, under the name Anne O'Hara, and joined the Fabian Society. Martin returned to Nevada in 1911 a committed suffragist and was elected president of the Nevada Equal Franchise Society (NEFS) in February 1912. Under her leadership the NEFS conducted an exhausting campaign for ratification of a state suffrage amendment which triumphed at the polls on Nov. 3, 1914.

After 1914 Martin became involved in national suffrage activity, serving on the executive committees of both the older, established National American Woman Suffrage Association (NAWSA) and its offshoot, the smaller, more militant Congressional Union (CU). At its founding convention in June 1916 she became the chairman of the National Woman's party (NWP), the political wing of the CU in the twelve suffrage states; when the two branches united in 1917 under the name National Woman's party, she became vice chairman and legislative chairman. Based in Washington, D.C., from 1916 to 1918, Martin organized congressional districts to put pressure on congressmen to vote for suffrage and was one of the NWP's abler speakers. When the NWP adopted the English tactic of holding the party in power responsible for legislative delays, she helped organize a campaign in 1916 among voting women in the west to withhold votes from Democrats, particularly President Woodrow Wilson. She was also among those arrested July 14, 1917, for picketing the White House. In the spring of 1918 Martin resigned her positions in the NWP and returned to Nevada to launch her campaign for the senatorial seat vacated by the death of Francis G. Newlands.

As a suffragist, Martin was one of many able leaders; as a candidate for the United States Senate in 1918, and again in 1920, she was a pioneer in modeling an active political role for women even though she polled only 20 percent of the vote. She offered her candidacy as an opportunity for women to use their votes and political skills more directly and in their own interest rather than by helping men in ladies' auxiliaries or by trying to influence them through lobbying. MABEL VERNON, Elizabeth Kent, and Margaret Long became her principal campaign supporters, but Martin also attracted brief but intense assistance from CHARLOTTE PERKINS GILMAN and SARA BARD FIELD, the talents of several NWP organizers, and steady backing from women in Nevada communities.

Martin chose to bypass the male-dominated political parties and took her case to the people as an independent. Her platforms merged her concerns for women's economic and political equality with other progressive issues. In addition to supporting the Sheppard-Towner bill to improve the welfare of mothers and infants, she advocated controls over land and natural resources to protect farmers, miners, and other laborers from monopolies and profiteers; supported prohibition; called for amnesty for political prisoners and conscientious objectors; and opposed the League of Nations as a breeder of wars.

Moving in 1921 to Carmel, Calif., where she made a home for her mother, Martin wrote extensively for American and British magazines and became active in the Women's International League for Peace and Freedom (WILPF). She addressed her essays primarily to women: urging them to overcome the "inferiority complex" caused by centuries of male domination and contribute the special insight they possessed as women to the governing of society; advising them to challenge men's control of culture through "sex solidarity"; imploring them to support women for office who agreed to put women's issues first. She assailed CARRIE CHAPMAN CATT for guiding the League of Women Voters toward education instead of direct political involvement. Although an early supporter of the Equal Rights Amendment, she criticized the NWP's leadership for continuing to beg

men for legal rights instead of seeking direct political power.

Martin was a member of the national board of the WILPF (1926–36), served as western regional director (1926–31), and attended its world conferences in Dublin (1926) and Prague (1929) as a delegate. She resigned in 1936, protesting the ineffectiveness of the WILPF leadership, and joined the Peoples Mandate to Governments to End War. Until her death in Carmel of a stroke in 1951, she resided there and in Reno, and continued to speak to women's clubs and write essays and poetry.

Underlying Martin's many national and international interests was her commitment to achieving equal participation for women at all levels of politics. As she proclaimed, "equality for women is a passion with me." She was impatient with abstract notions of legal equality and token advances. Although she shared her generation's assumption that women were responsible for home and family, she insisted that they apply their unique perspective and special strengths to every sphere of activity outside the home.

[The Anne Martin Coll., consisting of general and campaign correspondence, notes, manuscripts, pamphlets, photographs, and an excellent collection of clippings on suffrage and on Martin's senatorial campaigns, is in the Bancroft Library, Univ. of Calif., Berkeley, as is Mabel Vernon's correspondence concerning Nevada suffrage and the senatorial campaigns. Also useful are the oral history interviews with Alice Paul, Mabel Vernon, and Sara Bard Field, Regional Oral Hist. Office, Univ. of Calif., Berkeley. A small collection at the Nev. Hist. Soc., Reno, includes the sketchbooks Martin kept as a student at Bishop Whitaker's Acad. Several interviews in the Oral Hist. Project, Univ. of Nev., mention her. The Margaret Long Coll. in the Norlin Library, Univ. of Colo., contains diaries of campaigns and several photographs. The NWP Papers, Library of Congress, include considerable Martin correspondence. Martin's essays appeared in *Good Housekeeping, The Nation, The New Republic, The Independent, Current History, N.Y. Times Mag., Reconstruction, Sunset, Time and Tide, English Rev., Encyc. Britannica.* With Mary Austin she wrote *Suffrage and Government: The Modern Idea of Government by Consent and Woman's Place in It, With Special Reference to Nevada and Other Western States,* a 1914 NAWSA pamphlet; another well-known suffrage article is "The Story of the Nevada Equal Suffrage Campaign: Memoirs of Anne Martin," *Univ. of Nev. Bull.,* Aug. 1948. On her career, see Ann Warren Smith, "Anne Martin and a History of Woman Suffrage in Nevada, 1869–1914" (Ph.D. diss., Univ. of Nev., 1976) and Kathryn Anderson, "Practical Political Equality for Women: Anne Martin's Campaigns for the U.S. Senate in Nevada, 1918 and 1920" (Ph.D. diss., Univ. of Wash., 1978). Published articles include Dennis

Myers, "In Such a Cause: The Story of Anne Martin," *Sagebrush*, Univ. of Nev. at Reno, Sept. 18, 1973; Phillip I. Earl, "Nevada's Suffragets: Battle for the Vote," *Nevada Highways and Parks*, Fall 1974; Patricia Stewart, "Nevada's Contribution to Women's Rights," *The Nevadan*, Oct. 1973, and an entry in *Dict. Am. Biog.*, Supp. Five. The *Reno Eve. Gazette* published the most complete obituary April 16, 1951, and a commentary on her political career April 21, 1951. Death certificate supplied by Calif. Dept. of Health Services.]

KATHRYN ANDERSON

MARTÍNEZ, María. *See* CADILLA DE MARTÍNEZ, María.

MASON, Lucy Randolph, July 26, 1882–May 6, 1959. Labor and social reformer.

Lucy Randolph Mason was for sixteen years public relations representative for the Congress of Industrial Organizations (CIO) in the southeast (1937–53). She carried forth into the twentieth century the liberal commitment to human rights, to community service, and to the advancement of the public welfare for which her ancestors were known and revered in the history of the south. A fifth generation descendant of George Mason, Lucy Mason was born at Clarens, the home of her great-aunt, on Episcopal Seminary Hill, near Alexandria, Va., the second of three daughters and the third of six children of Lucy (Ambler) and Rev. Landon Randolph Mason.

Although the names of Mason and Randolph insured Lucy Mason from her birth the social distinction and high position of the First Families of Virginia, the family finances were meager, derived solely from "a pittance stipends" which her father earned as an Episcopal minister. Her mother, also the daughter of an Episcopal minister, diligently cared for her family and aided her husband in his work; she shared his "strong sense of social responsibility" and made zealous efforts to improve conditions in the Virginia state penitentiary. Strongly influenced by her parents' commitment to human welfare through Christian community service, in her career Mason defended the rights of prisoners, workers, blacks, and other economically and politically disadvantaged groups throughout the south.

Family finances did not afford Mason a college education. At twenty-two, she taught herself stenographic and typing skills, and spent the following ten years working as a stenographer in Richmond and volunteering her little free time to the Richmond Young Women's Christian Association (YWCA). In 1914 Mason became the industrial secretary of the Richmond YWCA,

working to generate public support for workmen's compensation and for protective labor legislation for women and children. She resigned in January 1918, after her mother's death, to care for her aged and ailing father. Supported by her brother John, she continued to volunteer her time to various social agencies, serving as a member of the Union Label League, and as president of the Richmond Equal Suffrage League and of the Richmond League of Women Voters (LWV). She chaired the Committee on Women in Industry of the National Advisory Committee on Labor and contributed to the LWV publication, *The Shorter Day and Women Workers*, which argued for the passage of a nine-hour-day bill for women.

After her father's death in 1923, Mason returned to the Richmond YWCA as general secretary, a position which she held until 1932. Through her work, she stimulated the growth of the YWCA commitment to social and industrial reform, especially as it aided the black community. She chaired the subcommittee on the economic status of women for the Negro Welfare Survey Committee of the Richmond Council of Social Agencies and in 1931, under the auspices of the National Consumers' League, she visited six southern states speaking on behalf of child labor legislation and shorter hours for women. In the same year she wrote *Standards for Workers in Southern Industry*. The first pamphlet of its kind, it reported on industrial growth in the south and demonstrated the need for regulation.

Mason's successful reform efforts in the conservative city of Richmond led to an invitation in 1932 to become executive secretary of the National Consumers' League. Moving to New York, she worked with the League until 1937. There, Mason continued to struggle for better conditions for working women, minimum wage laws, and child labor and social security legislation; in 1937 she testified at a joint congressional hearing for the Fair Labor Standards Act.

During the hearings, CIO president John L. Lewis asked her to join the Textile Workers Organizing Committee. In July 1937, at the age of fifty-five, Mason returned to the south and began to work as a "roving ambassador." She helped CIO unions "wherever or whenever and in whatever way" (*To Win These Rights*, p. 22), and, as public relations representative for the southeast, sought to promote understanding of the need for unionism. Believing strongly that organized labor must attach the community's leaders to its cause, she corresponded and visited with newspaper editors, ministers, educators, and elected officials. Her extensive responsibilities also included the distribution of information to community leaders through cir-

461

cular letters which argued the case of unionism and pinpointed repeated violations of the National Labor Relations Act in southern industry.

Mason also addressed college and university groups and organized a variety of regional conferences on labor and social welfare issues. Acting as a liaison between local unions and the national union leadership, she negotiated on behalf of workers when strikes ensued. In addition, she publicized civil rights violations and brought civil liberties cases to the attention of local and federal officials, including President Franklin D. Roosevelt.

Although southern community leaders frequently equated unionism with communism, social unrest, and racial strife, Mason was relatively successful during her early years with the CIO in generating support for unionism and in championing the rights of the worker. But the national defense crisis of 1940 to 1942 quickly eroded the few achievements of preceding years. Fearing that growing union strength, especially in defense industries, would undermine efforts for national preparedness, the south extended its attack on unionism; at least ten southern states introduced antisabotage legislation intended to restrict and/or eliminate the unions' right to strike and bargain collectively. Mason unsuccessfully protested such legislation to Governor Eugene Talmadge and to ELEANOR ROOSEVELT, with whom she corresponded and visited regularly.

Between 1942 and 1952 Mason continued as public relations representative, but for reasons of health she abandoned her role as troubleshooter and traveled less extensively. Continuing to advance the cause of the underprivileged, and working closely with religious and community organizations, she concentrated her efforts on political action, particularly in her adopted state of Georgia. Although she no longer involved herself in specific labor conflicts, Mason actively sponsored candidates and lobbied for legislative and judicial decisions favorable to labor. She championed the cause of civil liberties, particularly for blacks, organized voter registration campaigns, worked for the elimination of the poll tax, and promoted a national program of health and medical insurance.

Ill health forced Mason to reduce her responsibilities with the CIO in the spring of 1951 and she turned to writing her autobiography, *To Win These Rights*, published in 1952. During that year she received the Social Justice Award of the National Religion and Labor Foundation. Mason retired from the CIO early in 1953; she died six years later in Atlanta.

Lucy Randolph Mason combined southern femininity with progressive and liberal fem-

inism. Intelligent and diplomatic, she committed her life to political and social action and succeeded where others had failed, garnering the respect even of those southern leaders who did not or could not embrace her ideology. As a review of her autobiography noted: "Her story is an example of the South generating its own change. It is the South, in the person of a Virginia woman of good family and good heart, calmly making a revolution" (Stevenson, p. 495).

[There is an extensive collection of Mason's papers, including correspondence and copies of her publications, at Duke Univ., Durham, N.C. The Samuel Chiles Mitchell Papers, Series A, Southern Hist. Coll., Univ. of N.C., Chapel Hill, also contain Mason correspondence. Her publications include: "The CIO and the Negro in the South," *Jour. Negro Education*, Fall 1945; "I Turned to Social Action Right at Home," in Liston Pope, ed., *Labor's Relation to Church and Community* (1947); "It's NOT the Same Old South as CIO Makes a Stand in Dixie," *The CIO News*, Nov. 17, 1941; "Labor," in a Nat. Council of Churches publication, *Toward Lasting Peace* (1952); "Southerners Look at the South," *North Georgia Rev.*, 1938–39; "What Christianity Means to Me, By Three CIO Leaders," *The Witness*, March 26, 1953; "Work and Color," *The Nation*, Sept. 27, 1952; *Love Thy Neighbor* (1950); and *The Churches and Labor Unions* (1950). Mason's work is discussed in: Lawrence Lader, "The Lady and the Sheriff," *New Republic*, Jan. 5, 1948; Elizabeth Stevenson, "Promise in the South," *The Nation*, Nov. 29, 1952; George Brown Tindall, "The 'Colonial Economy' and the Growth Psychology: The South in the 1930's," *South Atlantic Quart.*, Autumn 1965; and Matthew Josephson, *Sidney Hillman, Statesman of American Labor* (1952). The Committee on Women in Industry is discussed in Emily Newell Blair, *An Interpretative Report* (1920). Margaret Lee Neustadt, "Miss Lucy of the CIO— Lucy Randolph Mason, 1882–1959" (M.A. thesis, Univ. of N.C., 1970), is informative but lacks interpretation. Obituaries appeared in the *Atlanta Constitution*, May 7, 1959, and the *N.Y. Times*, May 8, 1959.]

NANCY ANN WHITE

MASSEE, May, May 1, 1881–Dec. 24, 1966. Editor, children's literature specialist.

May Massee exerted a major influence on children's books for almost forty years. Her "genius," RUTH SAWYER recalled, was that "of discovering what each artist had to give to his work and, having discovered this, [finding] how best he could use it, bring it to fulfillment" (*Horn Book Mag.*, April 1967). Born in Chicago, she was the third of four daughters of Charlotte Maria (Bull) and Francis Spink Massee, both of English Puritan descent, and both born in upstate New York. One daughter died before May was born; she had a younger brother. The family moved to Milwaukee when she was five, and she grew up and attended the public schools there. She remembered herself as a "lonely little girl," too much younger than her classmates to have any friends. Graduating from high school at sixteen, she spent two years at the state normal school in Milwaukee and then taught elementary school for a year. After a winter spent in White Water, Wis., working with a librarian, she enrolled at the Wisconsin Library School in Madison. From there she went for two years to the Armour Institute in Chicago as an assistant librarian.

Massee left the Armour Institute with the intention of organizing libraries in western Illinois, but she met Theresa West Elmendorf, the first woman president of the American Library Association, who encouraged her to join the public library staff at Buffalo, N.Y. At first resistant to working in the children's room, she eventually chose to take it over and spent five years there. "I've never had a better time in my life anywhere," she remembered in a 1965 interview. During those years she also taught summer courses across the country.

Despite her enjoyment of library work, she was attracted by an offer to become editor of *The Booklist,* a publication of the American Library Association, and in 1913 moved to Chicago to take the job. The magazine grew, as did Massee's reputation. When Doubleday, Page publishers decided after the end of World War I to open a children's department, they came to her. Because she believed "pioneering is more fun than anything else," in 1922 she went to New York to create the second children's book publishing department in the United States. (The first had been organized in 1919 by Louise Seaman at Macmillan.) She remained at Doubleday until 1933. In that year, Massee founded the Viking Press children's book department, where she served as editor and director for twenty-seven years.

An unprecedented interest in books for children had developed in the beginning decades of the twentieth century. For the first time, articles and reviews of children's books regularly appeared in major newspapers and periodicals. In 1916 the influential Bookshop for Boys and Girls was organized by BERTHA MAHONY (MILLER). Children's rooms in public libraries were opened in increasing numbers and in 1924 Bertha Mahony established *Horn Book Magazine,* the first magazine devoted totally to reviews and criticism of children's literature.

May Massee's experience as a teacher and children's librarian, and her respect for chil-

dren's books as literature, enabled her to have a significant effect on the course of American publishing for children. Her personality was persuasive; her demeanor haunting. She was willing to take risks and was passionately devoted to the establishment of high critical standards for children's books. Long before it was considered desirable, Massee published books with minority group protagonists, regarding these books as "most truly American"; she also published stories set in Russia, Albania, Norway, and Hungary. The appearance of her own translation from the German of Eric Kästner's *Emil and the Detectives* in 1950 caused publishers to reevaluate the translated book. Recalling her own first experience, in the second grade, of reading about children from other lands who yet seemed her "sisters," Massee wanted to publish books "that would bring the joy of living of all the world's children to our children" (*Publishers Weekly,* March 11, 1950).

Massee was also a source of encouragement to authors wishing to try something new. In 1939 she published Marie Hall Ets's *The Story of a Baby,* one of the earliest books dealing with the growth of a baby from conception to birth. She welcomed Carl Sandburg's idea for the *Rootabaga Stories* and supported Morton Schindel of Weston Woods Studios when he talked to her about making iconographic films based on children's books. She worked hard to rid the field of the condescending phrase "juvenile books," preferring instead to call them junior books. As editor at both Doubleday and Viking she never lost sight of the child.

May Massee "aspired to produce important books, and succeeded" (Bader, p. 198). During her lifetime authors, illustrators, book designers, and critics praised her critical acumen in relation to illustration, text, and design and her endorsement of such new methods of production as offset lithography. In 1923 at Doubleday she published the "epoch-making" *ABC Book,* by Charles B. Falls, "the beginning in America of color printing unsurpassed in the picture books of any country," according to noted librarian Alice Jordan (*Massee Collection,* 1972, p. 13). Her appreciation of excellence in illustration later led her to seek out and to publish the work of such fine artists as Elizabeth MacKinstry, Boris Artzybasheff, Ludwig Bemelmans, and James Daugherty. Massee was the first woman member of the American Institute of Graphic Arts and in 1959 the first woman to be awarded the Institute's gold medal "for the production of beautiful books."

Many books published under Massee's direction became modern classics, including *The*

Story About Ping (1933), written by Marjorie Flack and illustrated by Kurt Wiese, and *The Story of Ferdinand* (1936), written by Munro Leaf and illustrated by Robert Lawson. Consistently, the books she edited won the most prestigious awards in children's literature. Four received the Randolph Caldecott medal for "the most distinguished American picture book for children," while more than twenty others received Caldecott honor citations. There were ten winners of the Newbery Medal for "the most distinguished contribution to American literature for children," and more than thirty other books edited by Massee earned Newbery honor citations.

Until her retirement in 1960, May Massee directed Viking's publications for children from her distinctive office, decorated by her close friend the architect Eric Gugler. Central to his design was a medallion of Taurus the Bull, Massee's sign of the zodiac, which she treasured as a symbol of the creative life. Around the top of the walls, Gugler carved in Latin her motto: "Nothing too much, not even moderation." Warm and generous with her friends, May Massee was also an awesome woman. During more than thirty-five years as editor of books for children, her work was her passion and her reason for being. She continued as advisory editor for Viking until her death at home in New York of a stroke on Christmas Eve 1966.

The recipient of the Constance Lindsay Skinner Medal (1950) for "achievement in the realm of books," Massee was also honored by the establishment of a collection in her name at the library of the Kansas State Teachers College at Emporia (later Emporia State University); her office was transported intact to the library. In an article written at the time of the opening of the collection in June 1972, author and editor Annis Duff summarized Massee's career: her "forceful influence brought children's books to a peak of excellence never before achieved in this or any other country."

[The May Massee Coll. at Emporia State Univ. includes the books published under her direction, examples of illustration and of iconographic films, reminiscences of Massee, correspondence, articles and transcripts of speeches, and interviews with her. A book title catalog, *The May Massee Collection*, was published in 1979. Nine taped interviews, *The Reminiscences of May Massee* (1964–66), are in the Oral History Coll., Columbia Univ. The Am. Inst. of Graphic Arts Medal citation and Massee's acceptance speech are in the *Horn Book Mag.*, Aug. 1969, pp. 275–77. The most complete list of articles written by Massee as well as about her is in Robin Gottlieb, *Publishing Children's Books in America, 1919–1976, An Annotated Bibliography* (1978). The *May Massee Collection: Creative Publishing for*

Children (1972), a pamphlet published in conjunction with the opening of the Massee Memorial Coll., contains two articles: "May Massee: Who Was She?" by Elizabeth Gray Vining, and "The May Massee Collection: What Is It?" by Annis Duff, and a photo of Massee. Additional articles about Massee and the collection appear in *Horn Book Mag.*, April 1972, pp. 220–22, and *Wilson Library Bull.*, Oct. 1972, pp. 186–91. The July-Aug. 1936 issue of *Horn Book Mag.* was devoted to Massee; it has biographical information and reminiscences by artists, authors, booksellers, designers, and librarians. For additional biographical data see *Who's Who in Amer.*, 1948–49 and 1962–63. Barbara Bader, *American Picturebooks from Noah's Ark to the Beast Within* (1976), contains a number of references to Massee and an overview of the development of picture books in the United States. Obituaries appeared in the *N.Y. Times*, Dec. 27, 1966, and *Publishers Weekly*, Jan. 2, 1967. There was a memorial tribute in *Publishers Weekly*, Feb. 20, 1967. Massee's nieces Elizabeth Fitton Folin and Edith Fitton Pine and her nephew Stuart Massee Fitton provided useful family information.]

BARBARA F. HARRISON

MAURY, Antonia Caetana De Paiva Pereira, March 21, 1866–Jan. 8, 1952. Astronomer.

Antonia Maury, noted for her outstanding contributions to stellar spectroscopy, was born in Cold Spring, N.Y., the oldest of the three children of Rev. Mytton and Virginia (Draper) Maury. Her father was an Episcopalian priest and editor of *Maury's Geographical Series* (1875–95). Her mother was the daughter of John William Draper, a physician, who made the first daguerreotype photograph of the moon (1840) and the first photograph of the spectrum of the sun (1843). His son, Henry Draper, also a physician, was the first to photograph a stellar spectrum successfully (1872). Though Maury's immediate ancestors were of British descent, she inherited most of her physical characteristics, particularly her sparkling dark eyes, from a Portuguese maternal great-grandmother. Antonia Maury's only sister, Carlotta Joaquina (1874–1938), became a well-known paleontologist.

Mytton Maury was his daughter's first teacher; he had her reading Vergil by the age of nine. In 1887 she graduated from Vassar College where she earned honors in astronomy, physics, and philosophy, and came under the influence of MARIA MITCHELL, America's first woman astronomer. A year after graduation she began work at Harvard University under the observatory's Henry Draper Memorial.

The Memorial had been endowed in 1886 by MARY ANNA PALMER DRAPER, in memory of her husband, for work on photographic stellar spectra. Maury was employed to classify the bright northern stars from spectra photographed with the eleven-inch telescope that had originally belonged to her uncle. The spectra were obtained by passing the starlight through one or more glass prisms placed in front of the objective lens of the telescope. This produced for each star a band of color, broken by lines or bands characteristic of the composition and physical conditions in the star's atmosphere.

Unfortunately Maury soon encountered disappointments. With an ever-inquiring mind, she was a deliberate worker, paying exquisite attention to minute detail and to every peculiarity in the spectra she examined. She was also an intellectual dreamer, seldom conscious of the passage of time. Professor E. C. Pickering, director of the observatory, had already set up a classification scheme of his own, whereby the various spectra were arranged simply in order of complexity of appearance. He expected Maury to work according to a schedule and to adopt and refine his system, then apply it to the prompt mass production of a catalog. Instead, she meticulously set up an independent system, which also incidentally demonstrated that Pickering's classes, designated *A* through *O*, did not logically follow in strict alphabetical order.

Inevitably her progress would have been slow, but the emotional stresses engendered by Pickering's impatience and disapproval decelerated it further. Her scientific spirit became her chief handicap, as Pickering apparently considered her attempts to understand why the spectra could be arranged into one or more discrete sequences a waste of time. His feelings also seem to have been influenced by the elegant Mary Anna Draper's dislike for her niece-by-marriage, who was apt to be oblivious to dress, protocol, and the demands of authority. Letters to Pickering from Mytton Maury, recommending and defending his daughter, could only have aggravated the situation. After frequent absences, Maury finally left Harvard in 1896. She stayed away for over two decades, teaching and lecturing at Cornell and elsewhere. She had previously taught science at the Gilman School in Cambridge, Mass. (1891–94).

In 1905, the Danish astronomer Ejnar Hertzsprung discovered that among stars of the same color, some were dwarfs, others giants in luminosity. Such differences, he reasoned, should be reflected in the spectra of the stars. In all of the catalogs of spectra published up to that time, only Maury's revealed what he sought. She had assigned subdivisions *a*, *b*, and *c* to her major classes to indicate the relative widths of lines among spectra that otherwise were alike. All of the stars with her "*c*-characteristic" (very narrow lines) turned out to be Hertzsprung's high-luminosity giant stars. He wrote Pickering in praise of Maury's work, but Pickering persistently maintained that the Harvard spectra were of inadequate quality to reveal the very distinctions whose validity Hertzsprung had established. Forty-six years after her catalog was published, the American Astronomical Society awarded Maury its Annie J. Cannon Prize (1943) for this early contribution, since hailed as one of the most important advances in modern observational astronomy and the cornerstone for much theoretical astrophysics.

In addition to developing her classification system, Maury was the first to compute periods of revolution for the component stars of the first two spectroscopic binaries ever discovered. The first was found by Pickering and the second by herself, both in 1889. Spectroscopic binaries—double stars too close together to be observed visually as double—can be recognized as such in their spectra. When Maury returned to Harvard in 1918, she determined the orbits of several spectroscopic binaries. She then analyzed the changes in the more than 300 spectra of the extraordinarily complex binary beta Lyrae in order to understand the behavior of the atmospheres of the component stars. Her treatise on this work was published in 1933, and though she officially left Harvard in 1935, she continued to pay annual visits there until 1948 in order to check on the accuracy of her predictions. Young astrophysicists at the time were skeptical about her theory, but their own subsequent efforts were not more successful. During these later years Maury was happy at Harvard; Harlow Shapley, director of the observatory from 1920 until 1952, understood and encouraged her.

Besides astronomy Maury enjoyed a wide range of cultural interests. She was an ornithologist, an all-round naturalist, and a conservationist both of historic sites and artifacts and of natural resources. She fought actively for the preservation of the western redwood forests, which were endangered by wartime lumber needs. For three years after leaving Harvard, she was custodian of the Draper Park Observatory Museum, the former home of the Drapers in Hastings-on-Hudson, N.Y. She continued to live in Hastings-on-Hudson until her final illness and died at the age of eighty-five in a hospital in Dobbs Ferry, N.Y. Always intrigued by the advancement of astronomy, Antonia Maury marveled at the vast expanse of the known universe, wistfully philosophizing: "But the human brain is greater yet, because it can comprehend it all."

[The two most important publications by Antonia Maury are her catalog, *Spectra of Bright Stars* (1897), Annals of Harvard College Observatory, vol. 28, part I, and *The Spectral Changes of beta Lyrae* (1933), in the same series, vol. 84, no. 8. Ejnar Hertzsprung's papers about her work, "Zur Strahlung der Sterne," are in the *Zeitschrift für Wissenschaftliche Photographie*, 1905, vol. 3, p. 429, and 1907, vol. 5, p. 86. Further evaluation of her work is found in K. Aa. Strand, "Hertzsprung's Contributions to the HR Diagram," pp. 55–59, and David H. DeVorkin, "The Origins of the Hertzsprung-Russell Diagram," pp. 72–75, both in A. C. Davis Philip and David DeVorkin, eds., *Dudley Observatory Report*, no. 13, Dec. 1977. For information on Maury's years at Harvard see Bessie Zaban Jones and Lyle Gifford Boyd, *The Harvard College Observatory* (1971); and Solon I. Bailey, *The History and Work of the Harvard Observatory, 1839–1927* (1931). Maury's ancestry on her father's side is traced in Anne Fontaine Maury, ed., *Intimate Virginiana, A Century of Maury Travels by Land and Sea* (1941). Known facts about her life apart from her career are sparse. The most extensive references are in the *Dict. Scientific Biog.*, vol. IX, and in a Harvard undergraduate thesis, Pamela E. Mack, "Women in Astronomy in the United States, 1875–1920" (1977). The exact dates of Maury's tenure at Harvard cannot be ascertained. The dates given in *Am. Men of Science* are used here because Maury would have supplied these. A death record was provided by the N.Y. State Dept. of Health.]

DORRIT HOFFLEIT

MAYER, Maria Gertrude Goeppert, June 28, 1906–Feb. 20, 1972. Physicist.

Maria Goeppert Mayer, the first woman to receive the Nobel Prize for theoretical physics, was born in Kattowitz, Upper Silesia, then a province of Germany. In 1910 the Goepperts moved to the German university town of Göttingen where she grew up, the only child of an academic family in a society profoundly conscious of rank and respectful of learning.

Her father, Friedrich Goeppert, was a pediatrician and professor of medicine at the University of Göttingen; five generations of Goepperts before him had been professors. His wife, born Maria Wolff, was a former schoolteacher and a proficient musician.

Maria's childhood was often solitary, and headaches kept her from school for weeks at a time. Her father, to whom she was particularly close, urged her to avoid self-pity; he also encouraged her to exercise her curiosity, to be daring, adventurous, a risk-taker. Above all he urged her never to sink into wifehood, motherhood, and dullness. Frau Goeppert agreed. Although by nature an extremely protective mother, she respected her husband's point of view, both as an eminent pediatrician and as head of the family.

At fifteen Maria entered a three-year private school that prepared girls for the university. The school closed three years later, in 1924, for lack of funds, but she passed the abitur examination for university entrance in Göttingen and became a student of mathematics there. The university, then a great mathematical center, had also begun to attract some physicists of note, including Max Born and James Franck.

Maria Goeppert was an acknowledged beauty. Her undergraduate years were full of parties and the suitably chaperoned entertainments of a small, elegant society where everyone knew everyone else. Her father died in 1927; that year Maria Goeppert turned her interest to physics and began work on quantum mechanics under Born, feeling an almost sacred obligation to become a professor as her father would have liked. In 1928 the German government awarded her a fellowship for a term at Girton College, Cambridge (England). There she attended lectures by the great Australian physicist Ernest Rutherford and perfected her English pronunciation.

In January 1929 an American chemist, Joseph E. Mayer, came to Göttingen on a Rockefeller fellowship to do experimental physics with James Franck. Maria Goeppert and Joseph Mayer were married in 1930. That same year she completed her Ph.D. with a dissertation on the theory of double emission and absorption of light quanta; much quoted since, it was a fundamental contribution to the field. The Mayers left Germany in 1930 for Baltimore, where Joseph Mayer joined the physics department at Johns Hopkins University.

There was no post for Maria Mayer, however, because of the university's nepotism rules. With Karl Herzfeld, a physical chemist, she did research in theoretical physical chemistry. She later published (in collaboration with A. L. Sklar) a significant paper on the excited electron states of the benzene molecule, the result of her early work at Hopkins. The first attempt to predict the electron spectrum of a relatively complicated molecule, it led to her best-known work of this period, an investigation into the theory of dyes. She collaborated with Max Born on a long article in the *Handbuch der Physik* on the lattice theory of crystals and also wrote a number of important papers on molecular physics and solid-state theory, most in collaboration with Herzfeld. Building on Enrico Fermi's formulation of nucleon-neutrino interaction, she developed the theory of double-beta decay, a logical extension of her dissertation subject.

In the spring of 1933 Maria Mayer gave birth to her first child, Maria Anne. While she was pregnant with her second child, Peter, born in 1938, she collaborated with her husband on a textbook on statistical mathematics. They completed the book after Joseph Mayer had left Johns Hopkins for Columbia University; *Statistical Mechanics* (1940) by Mayer and Mayer became a classic. Nonetheless, the Columbia physics department acknowledged Maria Mayer only as the wife of a chemist husband and had neither a post to offer her, nor an office. Harold Urey, chairman of the chemistry department, welcomed her, but the usual nepotism rules prevailed. Later, however, she taught for one year at Sarah Lawrence College.

The Mayers made valuable friendships in New York City, with Urey, and with Fermi, a recent refugee from Italian fascism. When the United States government decided to build an atomic weapon, part of the project was located at Columbia. Urey was chosen to head this program, a secret research group called the Manhattan Project, and he invited Maria Mayer to join him.

She did so with some reluctance. Her husband was away from home five days a week on war-related research, and she did not want to deprive the children of both parents. Yet the possibility of having a real job doing important research was irresistible. Maria Mayer hired an English nanny and went to work half-time with Urey in what was known as the S.A.M. Laboratory. She never stopped worrying about spending less time with her children, but she loved the work.

In 1946, both Mayers were invited to the University of Chicago, he as full professor, she as associate professor. Because of a nepotism rule she had no salary, but she accepted the position with pleasure—Fermi, James Franck, Edward Teller, and Urey would all be there. Later promoted to full professor (unpaid) she set herself the task of learning nuclear theory. At the Argonne National Laboratory nearby she was able to earn a half-time salary as senior physicist.

About a year after her arrival in Chicago Mayer began a collaboration with Teller on a theory of the origin of the elements. As she began to assemble and organize the most extensive catalog possible of nuclear properties of the abundant stable elements she found certain regularities in the numbers of nuclear particles in these elements. These "magic numbers," as they became known, were indisputable but their origin remained mysterious. She was determined to find the explanation, although Teller had long since lost interest in their collaboration and most others were skeptical. Joseph Mayer found the magic numbers fascinating, however, and

Fermi discussed them frequently with Maria Mayer.

The persistent evidence for the numbers' existence led Mayer to begin to consider a shell model for the nucleus. This model envisioned the nucleus as formed by concentric shells of protons and neutrons held in place by an averaging-out of the forces generated by the particles, a comparable structure to that posited for the atom, in which electrons move in paths or shells around the nucleus. The most stable elements are those in which the orbiting shells of electrons are so tightly bound to the nucleus that they do not easily form (by the loss or gain of electrons) new chemical combinations; in these elements the number of electrons is "magically" identical. The shell model for the nucleus had been previously considered by other physicists, drawn to it as was Maria Mayer by the similarity between these magic numbers in ordinary atomic physics and the repeated occurrence of certain stable numbers of nuclear particles. Before 1946, however, the experimental evidence was unconvincing. Mayer published a short paper in *Physical Review* in 1948 putting forth a shell theory of the nucleus, but without any further justification than the amassing of evidence for the magic numbers.

It was Fermi, in 1949, who made the chance remark, "What about spin-orbit coupling?" (Spin-orbit coupling, once likened by Mayer to a roomful of waltzers, is the simultaneous orbiting and spinning of electrons in their movement around the nucleus, some moving clockwise, some counterclockwise, still others orbiting in one direction and spinning in the other.) Mayer began a calculation that assumed that spin-orbit coupling existed within the nucleus and—unlike the spin-orbit coupling of electrons, which was weak and opposite in sign—in nuclei was very strong. She realized immediately that this was both the explanation she had been seeking of the magic numbers and proof for the shell theory of the nucleus. With spin-orbit coupling the number of possible paths along which the nuclear particles could travel increased; those paths or shells which were most tightly bound in place were those in which the magic numbers occurred.

The shell model came to be considered the central idea of nuclear structure, but in 1949 few were convinced. Fermi believed in the shell model, as did the experimental physicists at Argonne and Joseph Mayer, who repeatedly urged Maria Mayer to publish. But she held back, partly because her past history had not made for self-assertiveness in her scientific career. Finally, in December 1949, she submitted two papers to the *Physical Review*. Almost simultaneously a paper advancing the same theory, written by a German physicist, Hans D. Jensen, was received by the same journal. When the shell model began to gain general acceptance, Mayer and Jensen met in 1950, and in 1955 they published a book, *Elementary Theory of Nuclear Shell Structure*. In 1959, when the Mayers were offered full professorships at the University of California in San Diego, a full-time salary went with her post.

Within weeks of their arrival in California, Maria Mayer suffered a devastating stroke that left her with impaired use of one hand and arm. In 1963 she shared the Nobel Prize for Physics with Eugene Wigner and Hans Jensen. Mayer continued to write and do research, mostly on problems of shell theory and beta decay; she published several important articles during the 1960s. She was plagued by steadily declining health, however, especially heart trouble which required the use of a pacemaker. In February 1972 Maria Mayer died in San Diego of heart failure.

[Mayer wrote a brief account of her life to accompany publication of her Nobel Prize address in *Les Prix Nobel en 1963* (1964). A tape-recorded interview with her, made in Feb. 1962, is in the Archive for the Hist. of Quantum Physics, Univ. of Calif. at Berkeley. She contributed a memoir, centering on her research experience, to a series by Nobel laureates in science obtained in 1964 for the Oral History Coll., Columbia Univ. A biographical memoir by Robert G. Sachs, "Maria Goeppert Mayer, 1906–1972," in the Nat. Acad. of Sciences *Biographical Memoirs*, vol. 50 (1979), contains a bibliography of Mayer's work. For further biographical information see Joan Dash, *A Life of One's Own* (1973), and Mary Harrington Hall, "An American Mother and the Nobel Prize—A Cinderella Story in Science," *McCall's*, July 1964. See also Laura Fermi, *Atoms in the Family* (1954). Obituaries appeared in the *N.Y. Times* and *Wash. Post*, Feb. 22, 1972. Death certificate provided by Calif. Dept. of Public Health.]

JOAN DASH

MENDENHALL, Dorothy Reed, Sept. 22, 1874–July 31, 1964. Physician.

Dorothy Reed Mendenhall, known for her early research on Hodgkin's disease and her contributions to maternal and child health care, was born in Columbus, Ohio, second daughter and youngest of three children of Grace (Kimball) and William Pratt Reed. Both parents descended from seventeenth-century English settlers of America. Her father, a shoe manufacturer, died in 1880, leaving the family well off financially. Dorothy was educated at home by her maternal grandmother, with whom the family lived in Columbus from 1878 on, and later by a governess. Spending summers at the Kimball family home in Talcottville, N.Y., she also traveled in Europe with her mother and sister at various times between 1887 and 1890.

Dorothy Reed entered Smith College in 1891 and received a B.L. in 1895. Although she first considered a career in journalism, a course in biology convinced her to choose medicine instead. Learning that the recently opened Johns Hopkins Medical School admitted women, Reed applied; after completing required courses in chemistry and physics at the Massachusetts Institute of Technology, she entered Hopkins in September 1896. Reed and fellow medical student Margaret Long became the first women employed by a United States naval hospital when, during the summer of 1898, they assisted in the operating room and bacteriological laboratories at the Brooklyn Navy Yard Hospital. Reed obtained her M.D. degree in 1900, and took an internship at Johns Hopkins Hospital under Dr. William Osler. In 1901 she received a fellowship in pathology.

As a fellow, working with Dr. William Henry Welch, Reed taught bacteriology, assisted at autopsies, and undertook research on Hodgkin's disease, then believed to be a form of tuberculosis. This theory she conclusively disproved and, observing a particular blood cell in every case studied, demonstrated that its presence was a distinctive characteristic of the disease. The finding received international acclaim, and the cell became known as the Reed cell (also called the Sternberg-Reed or Reed-Sternberg cell).

Although she wanted to continue her work in pathology, Reed refused reappointment because of the lack of opportunities for women to advance at Hopkins. She left in June 1902 to accept an interim residency at the New York Infirmary for Women and Children, and in January 1903, she became the first resident physician at the new Babies Hospital in New York. During the summer of 1903 her sister died, leaving three children for whose education Reed took responsibility. She also managed her mother's finances from her senior year in college until her mother died in 1912, and became a shrewd investor.

On Feb. 14, 1906, Dorothy Reed married Charles Elwood Mendenhall, whom she had known since childhood. They moved to Madison, Wis., where he was professor of physics at the University of Wisconsin. For eight years Dorothy Mendenhall stayed home to bear and raise her children: Margaret (b. 1907), who died a few hours after birth as a result of bad obstetrics which also left Mendenhall with injuries and puerperal fever; Richard (b. 1908), who died in 1910 following a fall; Thomas Corwin (b. 1910), who later served as president of Smith College; and John Talcott (b. 1912), who became professor of surgery at the University of Wisconsin in Madison.

The second phase of Mendenhall's career began in 1914 when, having obtained full-time domestic help, she returned to professional life as field lecturer in the department of home economics at the University of Wisconsin. Motivated by the loss of her first-born, she began a study of infant mortality, an interest which lasted throughout her career. By gathering epidemiological data for the Wisconsin State Board of Health as she lectured across the state, preparing correspondence courses for new and prospective mothers, and writing bulletins on nutrition for the United States Department of Agriculture, she demonstrated an unusual talent for bringing together the work of various governmental agencies. In Madison in 1915 she organized the first infant welfare clinic in the state, under the aegis of the Attic Angel Association, a volunteer group concerned with public health, and the Visiting Nurse Association; she remained as its chairman until 1936. Eventually four other clinics were opened, and in 1937 her efforts were rewarded as Madison achieved recognition for having the lowest infant mortality rate of any city in the United States.

Mendenhall's interest in maternal and child welfare was also reflected in her work as a medical officer for the United States Children's Bureau. Beginning in 1917, when she joined her husband, then on war duty in Washington, D.C., she continued this work intermittently until 1936, while also maintaining her position at the University of Wisconsin. In 1919 she did a comprehensive survey of war orphanages in Belgium and France, and nutritional studies of children in England. For the Bureau's Children's Year (1918–19), Mendenhall worked on the nationwide drive to weigh and measure all children under six. This project called attention to the prevalence of malnutrition and developed norms for height and weight from birth through age six. She also represented the Children's Bureau at the International Child Welfare Conference (1919) and helped to design the minimum standards for health centers adopted at the conference.

Several of Mendenhall's publications were widely read and respected, including one she prepared in 1918 for the Children's Bureau, *Milk: The Indispensable Food for Children*. The same year, she wrote a definitive bulletin on the nutritional value of powdered milk at the request of the American Red Cross. She also prepared six chapters for the famous Children's Bureau publication, *Child Care and Child Welfare: Outlines for Study* (1921). In 1926 Mendenhall undertook a survey comparing infant and maternal mortality rates in Denmark and the United States. This influential study, published by the Bureau as *Midwifery in Denmark* (1929), concluded that American mortality rates were higher because of unnecessary interference in the natural process of childbirth and recommended the education of midwives on the Danish model.

At the University of Wisconsin Mendenhall developed a correspondence course, the "Nutrition Series for Mothers," for the department of agriculture in 1918. She introduced the first course in sex hygiene in the 1920s and lectured to seniors on "The Child from Conception through Infancy and Care of Mothers." She also maintained an active interest in the career of her husband. Following his death in 1935, she gradually withdrew from active work and, after traveling through Central America and Mexico, settled in Tryon, N.C. Mendenhall later moved to Chester, Conn., where she died at age eighty-nine of arteriosclerotic heart disease.

Dorothy Reed Mendenhall was described by her colleagues as a strikingly beautiful woman, determined and dedicated as a student and researcher, and as a teacher and physician. She drew courage and comfort from her daily reading of Marcus Aurelius, a copy of whose writings was her constant companion from the age of sixteen. Among the many tributes to her accomplishments was the Dorothy Reed Mendenhall Scholarship Fund at Johns Hopkins University, established by members of her family in 1957 "to help a deserving woman medical student." In 1965 Sabin-Reed Hall at Smith College was dedicated in honor of FLORENCE SABIN, a fellow student at both Smith College and Johns Hopkins Medical School, and Dorothy Reed Mendenhall.

[Dorothy Reed Mendenhall's papers, which include a journal, letters, essays, sketches, college and medical school memorabilia, pamphlets, articles, course outlines, lecture notes, account books, and a manuscript autobiography, are in the Sophia Smith Coll., Smith College. The autobiography is available only with the permission of Thomas C. Mendenhall. The Children's Bureau records, Nat. Archives, Washington, D.C., contain over 1,100 pages of Mendenhall correspondence, 1914–40. Among her publications are: "On the Pathological Changes in Hodgkin's Disease with Especial Reference to Its Relation to Tuberculosis," *Johns Hopkins Hospital, Reports*, vol. 10, no. 3, 1902, pp. 133–96; "A Case of Acute Lymphatic Leukaemia without Enlargement of the Lymph Glands," *Am. Jour. Medical Sci.*, Oct. 1902;

"Prenatal and Natal Conditions in Wisconsin," *Wis. Medical Jour.*, March 1917, pp. 353–69; "The Work of the Children's Bureau," *Smith College Quart.*, May 1919, pp. 211–14; "Preventive Feeding for Mothers and Infants," *Jour. Home Economics*, Oct. 1924; *What Builds Babies*, Children's Bureau, Publication Folder No. 4, 1925. Useful, though not entirely accurate accounts of Mendenhall's life and career can be found in Jean Bergman, "Dorothy Reed Mendenhall," State Hist. Soc. of Wis. Women's Auxiliary, *Famous Wisconsin Women*, 6 (1976), 48–53, and Gena Corea, "Dorothy Reed Mendenhall: 'Childbirth Is Not a Disease,'" *Ms.*, April 1974. A chapter on Dorothy Reed Mendenhall is included in *Upstate* (1971), the memoir of her mother's cousin Edmund Wilson. Obituaries appeared in the Madison, Wis., *Capital Times*, July 31, 1964, and the *Wis. State Jour.*, Aug. 1, 1964. Additional information for this article was provided by Thomas C. Mendenhall, John T. Mendenhall, Louisa Fast, Alice Clark, and Peyton Rous. Death certificate supplied by Conn. Dept. of Health.]

ELIZABETH D. ROBINTON

MESTA, Perle, Oct. 12, 1889–March 16, 1975. Political hostess, businesswoman, diplomat, feminist.

Perle Mesta, widely known Washington, D.C., "Hostess with the Mostes'," successful businesswoman and vigorous supporter of women's rights, was born in Sturgis, Mich., the first of three children and elder of two daughters of William Balser and Harriet Elizabeth (Reid) Skirvin. She was named Pearl Reid Skirvin but later officially changed the spelling of her first name to Perle. At the time of her birth, her father, of Irish, Scottish, and English descent, was a successful oil prospector in Galveston, Texas. Her mother, whose ancestors were French, was a graduate of the University of Kansas. In 1906 the family moved to Oklahoma City, where William Skirvin built and operated the Skirvin Hotel. Pearl Skirvin was educated in private schools in Galveston and studied piano and voice at the Sherwood School of Music in Chicago.

On Feb. 12, 1917, in New York City, she married George Mesta, a wealthy engineer and founder of Pittsburgh's Mesta Machine Company. During World War I he served as a consultant in Washington, and it was then that Perle Mesta began to meet Washington political and social leaders. After the war the Mestas traveled extensively in Europe, where George Mesta had business interests. They became frequent guests at the White House after the election of Calvin Coolidge, to whose campaign George Mesta had contributed substantial sums.

After her husband died in 1925, Mesta moved from Pittsburgh, a city in which she had never felt at home, to Washington, D.C. Inheriting the bulk of stock in the Mesta Machine Company, she joined the board of directors and learned the business. During the 1930s she also invested successfully, along with her father, in oil and real estate in the southwest. With the inheritance she received after her father's death in 1944, she continued to invest shrewdly, buying and profitably managing, for example, a large Arizona cattle ranch.

Meanwhile, she began to take an active interest in politics, working in 1936 with the Oklahoma State Council of Republican Women on Alfred M. Landon's campaign. In 1937 she was an Oklahoma representative to the Republican National Policy Committee. She also began lobbying for the Equal Rights Amendment (ERA), joining the National Woman's party in 1938 and becoming a member of its executive council. Mesta was named international publicity chairman for the World Woman's party, which was founded in 1938, at the urging of Alice Paul (1885–1977), to influence world opinion and monitor global progress on women's rights.

After Wendell Willkie's defeat in 1940, Mesta left the Republican party to protest the failure of party conservatives to support his candidacy. In 1942, while lobbying for the ERA, she met Senator Harry S Truman, and the following year organized a party for him during a Democratic rally in Oklahoma City. She developed a close and lasting friendship with the Trumans, and her importance as a Washington hostess rose with Truman's career. "I decided that the way I was best equipped to serve the Democratic Administration was by bringing important people together," she wrote. Her parties were large, openhanded, well planned, and very successful. A Christian Scientist who never drank, she said that a party gave her the same elation that liquor gave others. When Truman became president the role of first hostess fell to Mesta, as Bess Truman disliked giving large parties. She was also an untiring fund raiser for Truman and the Democratic party, helping to rescue the Democratic National Committee from financial ruin during the 1948 presidential campaign.

In 1949 President Truman appointed Perle Mesta Envoy Extraordinary and Minister Plenipotentiary to Luxembourg. Her long experience with the steel industry as a director of the Mesta firm strengthened her qualifications for the post in the little duchy, then one of the world's leading steel producers. As a feminist, she was pleased that Luxembourg was ruled by a woman, Grand Duchess Charlotte, and believed that if she did well as minister "it would clear the way for the appointment of other women to diplomatic and other government posts" (Lyons,

p. 51). In spite of Mesta's qualifications, the press saw the appointment as a reward for her parties.

On her first morning one of her staff asked Mesta how she wanted to be addressed. "You can call me Madam Minister," she replied. The line, shortened to "Call me Madam," was widely reported, and became the title of a successful musical comedy about an American woman ambassador. Ethel Merman exuberantly sang Irving Berlin's "The Hostess with the Mostes'," and Mesta herself was amused by the title. As ambassador Mesta traveled throughout Luxembourg and entertained extensively. She also established a scholarship fund for Luxembourg students to study in the United States, provided that they return and use their education to benefit their country.

In 1953 Mesta retired as ambassador and returned to Washington, spending the summers at her home in Newport, R.I., where she had been entertaining political figures since the 1930s. In the capital she was again a prominent hostess but, although she was a friend of the Eisenhowers, no longer part of the administration. Her name remained synonymous with "political hostess," however, and her unparalleled reputation as a party giver continued to be the touchstone by which Washington hostesses were measured.

Mesta remained close to her family throughout her life and at various times lived with her sister, Marguerite, and her sister's three children, to whom she was devoted. After she broke her hip in a fall and her health deteriorated, she moved back to Oklahoma City in February 1974 to be near her brother, O. William Skirvin. She died there of hemolytic anemia at the age of eighty-five.

[Perle Mesta's papers are held by her brother. *Perle: My Story* (1960), written with Robert Cahn, is the most complete source of biographical information. Of the many articles in newspapers and popular magazines, especially between 1947 and 1953, a few provide substantive information. These include "Widow from Oklahoma," *Time*, March 14, 1949; Flora Lewis, "Madame Minister to Luxembourg," *N.Y. Times Mag.*, Dec. 25, 1949; and Sylvia R. Lyons, "They Called Her Madam," *Good Housekeeping*, May 1955. Obituaries appeared in the *N.Y. Times*, March 17, 1975, and the *Wash. Post*, March 18, 1975; death record provided by Okla. Dept. of Health.]

JACQUELINE VAN VORIS

MEYER, Agnes Elizabeth Ernst, Jan. 2, 1887– Sept. 1, 1970. Journalist, writer, philanthropist.

Agnes Elizabeth Ernst was born in New York City, the youngest of four children and only

daughter of Frederick H. and Lucie (Schmidt) Ernst, immigrants from northern Germany. Before her third birthday, the family moved to Pelham Heights, N.Y., where Frederick Ernst established a prosperous law practice. The freedom with which Agnes roamed the rural village was tempered by the order and discipline which pervaded the Ernst home. Educated in the local school, the children were infused with Lutheran religion and western culture at home and received instruction in language and literature from a German tutor. Agnes's admiration for her father and his encouragement of her intellectual and artistic development made him the central figure in her young life.

In 1899 the family returned to New York City where Agnes graduated from Morris High School in 1903. Her delight in intellectual stimulation was clouded by her father's increasing self-indulgence, his indifference to his family and law practice, and his opposition to her further schooling. The disillusioned daughter financed her education at Barnard College with scholarships and a variety of jobs. Her initial interest in science and mathematics shifted to literature and philosophy, in which she was profoundly influenced by John Dewey. Impatient with poor teaching, an authoritarian atmosphere, and a lifeless curriculum, she rebelled against the college which she would later serve with financial support and as a member of its board of trustees.

Upon graduation in 1907 Agnes Ernst persuaded the editor of the *New York Sun* to take her on as one of its first women reporters. One year later she left the *Sun* for Paris, where her studies at the Sorbonne were soon eclipsed by involvement in literary and artistic circles which included Edward Steichen, Leo and GERTRUDE STEIN, and the sculptors Rodin and Brancusi. Returning to New York in 1909, on Feb. 12, 1910, she married Eugene Meyer, an international financier and multimillionaire twelve years her senior. This tumultuous marriage of two strong-willed individuals survived until his death in 1959, sustained by mutual fascination and respect and by its ability to accommodate Agnes Meyer's determination to pursue her own interests. Their first child, Florence, was born in 1911, followed by Elizabeth (1913), Eugene III (1915), Katharine (1917), and Ruth (1921). Chafing at the restrictions of domesticity, Meyer cultivated friendships with artists, took graduate courses at Columbia University, and embarked on foreign trips alone. Her studies of Chinese and Chinese art resulted in close friendship with Charles L. Freer and her first book, *Chinese Painting as Reflected in the Thought and Art of Li Lung-mien, 1070–1106* (1923). The limited emotional support she afforded her children was balanced in part by the rich intellectual and cultural environment she and her husband provided them and by family pack trips, cruises, and excursions to Europe.

From 1917 to 1933 Eugene Meyer served the federal government in several major economic posts. The family maintained homes in Washington, D.C., where Agnes Meyer was a popular hostess, and at Seven Springs Farm, the family estate at Mt. Kisco, in Westchester County, N.Y. Encouraged by William L. Ward, Republican boss of the county, she became active in party politics. From 1923 to 1941 she chaired the Westchester County Recreation Commission, which promoted an innovative array of cultural and recreational programs.

Her husband's purchase of the *Washington Post* in 1933 afforded a new vehicle for Agnes Meyer's literary ambitions. A part-owner, she was denied a formal role in the paper's management, although it remained in the family: the Meyers' son-in-law, Philip L. Graham, became publisher in 1946 and was succeeded by his wife, Katharine Meyer Graham, in 1963. Meyer contributed a critical series on the Works Progress Administration to the *Post*; she also wrote articles on recreation for various periodicals and published reviews and translations of works by Thomas Mann. Her twenty-year friendship with Mann was one of several intense relationships with prominent men. Although she eventually counted such women as ELEANOR ROOSEVELT and VIRGINIA GILDERSLEEVE among her close friends, she valued male friendships over those with members of her own sex.

As a young woman Agnes Meyer had remained aloof from the woman's movement and evinced little concern for social problems. Her work on the recreation commission expanded her social vision; but it was her experiences during World War II that solidified a commitment to social reform which dominated the remainder of her public life. The positive reaction to her reports for the Associated Press on Britain's home front prompted a similar study of American communities. Traveling throughout the United States, Meyer wrote a series of articles which documented inefficiencies in production and awakened the public to the failures of communities to meet the basic needs of their swelling populations. A subsequent study of postwar conditions included articles on veterans, migratory workers, overcrowded schools, and racial discrimination.

Like some other social critics of the time, Meyer saw the nation's problems as stemming in part from the selfishness, materialism, and narrow vision of the American woman who ne-

glected her primary vocation, motherhood. More constructively, she promoted establishment of the Department of Health, Education, and Welfare and federal aid to education; Lyndon B. Johnson described her as the person who most influenced his education policies. Meyer also supported expansion of social security, improved health services, and integration and economic opportunity for racial minorities. Better coordination of social services and citizen responsibility were two persistent themes in her reform efforts. Outspoken and firm in her opinions, she took on the Catholic church in the battle over federal aid to education and denounced the redbaiting of Senator Joseph McCarthy and his allies.

During the 1950s and 1960s Meyer's public activities continued unabated despite a drinking problem and various illnesses. She contributed articles to several periodicals and in 1953 published her autobiography, *Out of These Roots*. She also served on government commissions on health, education, the status of women, and employment. In 1956 Meyer promoted Adlai Stevenson's presidential candidacy, and she transferred her political allegiance to the Democratic party in 1960. Her philanthropic activities, which began with support of the New School for Social Research in 1919, included the Eugene and Agnes E. Meyer Foundation, which granted millions of dollars to a variety of projects. In the early 1960s she founded and funded organizations devoted to the improvement of public education: the Urban Service Corps and the National Committee for Support of the Public Schools.

Meyer's contributions to education and social welfare were recognized with fourteen honorary degrees and with awards from the Women's National Press Club, the NAACP, the AFL-CIO, and the National Conference of Christians and Jews. She died of cancer at the age of eighty-three at Seven Springs Farm.

[The Agnes E. Meyer Papers in the Library of Congress contain abundant correspondence, a diary, an unpublished memoir, and nearly complete collections of her speeches, articles, and other writings. Extracts from her diary for Dec. 1930 to May 1933 are included in *The Reminiscences of Eugene Meyer* in the Oral History Collection, Columbia Univ. The Beinecke Rare Book and Manuscript Library at Yale Univ. holds correspondence and other records of Meyer's friendships with Paul Claudel and Thomas Mann. Meyer's other books are *Journey Through Chaos* (1944), which contains her World War II articles, and *Education for a New Morality* (1957), a collection of lectures. Merlo J. Pusey, *Eugene Meyer* (1974), provides information about her family and social life. See also Josephine Ripley, "Agnes Meyer—Practicing Citizen," *Christian Sci-*

ence Monitor, June 10, 1967, and the entry in Current Biog., 1949. Obituaries appeared in the Sept. 2, 1970, issues of the Wash. Post and N.Y. Times, and in Newsweek, Sept. 14, 1970. A death record was provided by the N.Y. State Dept. of Health.]

SUSAN M. HARTMANN

MEYER, Annie Nathan, Feb. 19, 1867–Sept. 23, 1951. Publicist, writer, antisuffragist.

Annie Nathan Meyer, a founder of Barnard College, was born in New York City, the youngest of the two daughters and two sons of Annie Augusta (Florance) and Robert Weeks Nathan. Her anomalous career as an antisuffrage feminist contrasted sharply with that of her elder sister MAUD NATHAN, a prominent suffragist who was president of the New York Consumers' League.

Annie Nathan Meyer took pride in her descent from one of the oldest and most distinguished Sephardic Jewish families in the United States: her first cousins included EMMA LAZARUS and Supreme Court Justice Benjamin Cardozo. Her own parents shared little in this distinction. When in 1875 Robert Nathan faced bankruptcy after heavy losses in the stock market, the family moved to Green Bay, Wis., where a friend found him a job as general passenger agent for a railroad. The child Annie observed the disintegration of her parents' marriage and her mother's life, as Annie Augusta Nathan turned to drugs, threatened suicide, and finally died in a Chicago hospital in 1878. The children were sent back to their grandparents in New York.

Annie Nathan had been taught at home by her mother. Although she briefly attended public school during the single year the family lived in Chicago, she was largely self-taught. During her eighteenth year she and six friends organized a club, the Seven Wise Women, modeled on MARGARET FULLER's gatherings, to study the work of women writers. During the same year she passed the qualifying examinations for the Collegiate Course for Women at Columbia College. Annie Nathan was dismayed to find that women were expected to take examinations that included questions based on lectures from which they had been barred. She coolly refused to answer some questions on the ground of that exclusion.

Annie Nathan withdrew from the Collegiate Course when on Feb. 15, 1887, she married Alfred Meyer, a prominent physician who campaigned effectively for publicly funded tuberculosis sanatoriums. Reviewing her Columbia experience, and realizing that the trustees might be convinced to support a separate college if Columbia did not have to pay for it, Annie Nathan Meyer committed herself to finding in-

dependent funding for an affiliated women's college. With librarian Melvil Dewey and the writer MARY MAPES DODGE, she prepared a memorial to the trustees; with the assistance of ELLA WEED, who would chair the academic committee of the new college, she persuaded fifty prominent New Yorkers to sign it. In an effective article in The Nation (Jan. 26, 1888), Meyer appealed to civic pride, insisting on the need for a woman's college with high academic standards. She also suggested that the school be named after the late Columbia president Frederick A. P. Barnard, a long-time advocate of coeducation.

Meyer recruited Barnard's first board of trustees and claimed that she had identified almost all of the initial contributors. The first substantial donation was from her husband, and she signed the lease for the college's first building. Resentment of her assumption of full credit for creating the college lingered; though honored at Barnard's fiftieth anniversary, she was not given the prominent role she thought her due.

Meyer was an active trustee of Barnard from 1893 to 1942 and raised money for the college. Particularly concerned to maintain a Jewish presence at Barnard, she wanted both to protect Jewish students against slights, and to see that they represented, as she wrote in 1927 to VIRGINIA GILDERSLEEVE, the "desirable type of Jewess." She played an unusual role in recruiting black students. When ZORA NEALE HURSTON was admitted without the scholarship she needed, Meyer found independent sources of funds for her and continued to take an interest in Hurston's career. In 1925 Meyer wrote a play, Black Souls, about the vulnerable position of the liberal black intellectual. Although James Weldon Johnson and other friends in the NAACP endorsed it, the play was not produced until 1932, and then only when Meyer subsidized a production at the Provincetown Playhouse; Hurston coached the offstage singers. In the 1940s, Meyer donated a collection of books on black history and literature to Hunter College, and was disappointed when her plan for a Negro Cultural Library at Hunter was not realized.

Throughout her life Meyer was a prolific writer. She wrote three novels, an autobiography and several books of nonfiction, articles and short stories which appeared in Harper's, The Nation, and Century, and twenty-six plays. The Advertising of Kate had a brief Broadway production in 1922. Several of her plays had amateur productions throughout the country and The New Way, which dealt sympathetically with women's careers, was performed on radio in

1926. The Annie Nathan Meyer Drama Library was established at Barnard in 1937.

The Meyers' marriage was a happy one. They had one daughter, Margaret (b. 1894). Nurses helped to raise the child, who graduated from Barnard in 1915. Shortly after her marriage in 1923, Margaret Meyer died in what her mother referred to as "an accident with a pistol."

Torn between admiration for professional competence and repudiation of the single-minded selfishness that she thought accompanied ambition, Meyer was deeply ambivalent about the value of women's work in the public sector. Admiration for competence was the theme of her first book, *Women's Work in America,* a collection of essays on the status of women in a wide variety of fields, which she edited in 1891. In her short novel *Helen Brent, M.D.* (published anonymously in 1892) and her play *The Dominant Sex,* Meyer wrote bitterly of the popular expectation that women give up their professional ambitions upon marriage. On the other hand, she tended to believe that all but the most extraordinary married woman should renounce professional ambition. Despite the volume of her own literary production, she did not think of herself as a professional writer; in fact she earned little from her work and subsidized the publication of several of her books and the production of her plays. Bitter complaints that women who were active in reform politics neglected their families appeared repeatedly in Meyer's work, most notably in her essay "Woman's Assumption of Sex Superiority" (*North American Rev.*, Jan. 1904).

Meyer was particularly offended by those who suggested that women were purer and better than men and promised a refashioned social order if women were given the vote. She gave antisuffrage speeches and testified against woman suffrage even for school board elections. In 1917 she chaired a committee of the American Home Economics Association which urged women to serve the war by economizing in their kitchens; the committee received contributions from antisuffrage associations. After suffrage was accomplished, Meyer, a prolific writer of letters to the editor, periodically reminded her readers that votes for women had not ushered in a new era of social responsibility. Nevertheless, she took pride in having been one of the first women to ride a bicycle on the streets of New York and to use the tennis courts in Central Park.

Pride in her Jewish-American ancestry—she was a Daughter of the American Revolution—directed some of Meyer's fund-raising efforts. She raised money for the purchase of a portrait of Isaac Moses by the Museum of the City of New York in 1933 and for a performance of Ernest Bloch's *Sacred Music* in 1934. Although an early critic of the Nazi regime in Germany, she was also an ardent opponent of Zionism, skeptical of the dual allegiance which she feared it implied.

In 1931, Meyer drafted an autobiography, but she could find no publisher for it. Portions were printed in 1935 as *Barnard Beginnings*; a revised, chattier version was published as *It's Been Fun* at the time of her death in New York City of a heart attack in 1951.

Contemporaries found Annie Nathan Meyer eccentric, even difficult, especially after her daughter's death. Her significance lies in her role as one of the founders of a distinguished academic institution; her career remains intriguing as an unresolved amalgam of encouragement for the full development of women's talents and distrust of those who would restructure women's roles.

[The Annie Nathan Meyer Papers of the American Jewish Archives in Cincinnati contain personal correspondence, MSS. of both published and unpublished work, newspaper clippings, family photographs, photocopies of the minutes of the Barnard College board of trustees, and correspondence concerning the college. Other relevant material is in the Barnard College Archives. Among her other publications are *Robert Annys: Poor Priest* (1901), *My Park Book* (1898), and *The Dreamer: A Play in Three Acts* (1912). Her best-known short story is "Vorbei," *Harper's,* Nov. 1893, pp. 927–32. Robert Lewis Taylor, "Profiles: The Doctor, the Lady and Columbia University," *New Yorker,* Oct. 23 and 30, 1943, is a lively but acerbic sketch of the Meyers late in their lives. Stephen Birmingham, *The Grandees* (1971), pp. 310–19, stresses the tension between Annie and Maud Nathan, and must be used with caution. Biographical articles appear in the *Dict. Am. Biog.,* Supp. Five, and the *Encyc. Judaica,* 1971. Photographs of Meyer late in her life are included in *It's Been Fun.* An obituary appeared in the *N.Y. Times,* Sept. 24, 1951. A biobibliography prepared by Judith Solar assisted in the research for this article.]

LINDA K. KERBER

MILLER, Bertha Everett Mahony, March 13, 1882–May 14, 1969. Bookseller, editor, children's literature specialist.

Bertha Mahony Miller, originator of the *Horn Book Magazine,* was born in Rockport, Mass., the eldest of four children and the first of two daughters of Daniel and Mary Lane (Everett) Mahony. Her father, whose parents had immigrated to the United States in 1848 from County Kerry, Ireland, was the passenger agent for the local Boston and Maine Railroad station. Bertha's mother, an accomplished music teacher, came, by contrast, of old Yankee stock; her maternal ancestors were master mariners on Cape Ann, her father a New Hampshire lawyer and state legislator. Growing up, Bertha saw little of her mother's relatives, as they did not fully approve of the marriage to Mahony.

Much of Bertha's childhood was spent out-of-doors, roaming the woods and upland meadows near her home on Cape Ann. Both parents shared a passion for books and music, and from Bertha's infancy they sang folksongs to her and invented endless stories, Daniel Mahony recalling his boyhood among the blueberry pastures and salt marshes of Ipswich Bay. This sense of place, and the family traditions surrounding it, profoundly influenced her later beliefs about children's literature, art, and education.

Bertha Mahony's life changed dramatically at the age of eleven with the death of her mother. Despite the burden of increased household responsibilities, she graduated at nineteen from Gloucester High School with an outstanding record. She went on to attend a training class at the high school and to serve there as a student-teacher for a year (1901–02), before entering Simmons College for Women, opening that fall in Boston. Since her family could not support her through a four-year program, Mahony enrolled in a special one-year secretarial course intended for college graduates; she completed the program with distinction in 1903.

After Simmons, Mahony worked for the first time with books as shop assistant at the New Library, a bookstore and lending library in Boston. The owner frequently entrusted her with the management of the shop, but Mahony felt she regarded her as an inferior, awakening bitter childhood memories of Yankee prejudice against the Irish. In 1906, through the support of one of the New Library's patrons, she moved to the Women's Educational and Industrial Union (WEIU), a nonprofit, social service agency begun by prominent Boston women. Working there as assistant secretary to president MARY MORTON KEHEW and treasurer Helen Peirce, she learned about organizational management and assumed responsibility for the Union's publicity and informational leaflets. She also organized an amateur theater group, The Children's Players. Her search for material suitable to this group exposed Mahony for the first time to children's literature as a specialty and led her to two of the growing field's leading figures—Alice M. Jordan of the Boston Public Library and ANNE CARROLL MOORE of the New York Public Library —both of whom had created popular children's rooms in their institutions. Inspired by their innovative work, and by an article in the *Atlantic*

Monthly endorsing bookselling as an appropriate profession for educated women, Mahony began to plan her own reading room. In October 1916, with financial support from the WEIU Board of Directors, she opened the Bookshop for Boys and Girls, within the Union's Boston headquarters.

One of the many innovations of Mahony's bookshop was *Books for Boys and Girls—A Suggestive Purchase List* (1916, 1917, 1919, 1922); it included more than a thousand titles with brief descriptive notes. Another of her inventions was the Caravan, a mobile extension of the bookshop which toured New England during the summer months. But it was the homelike character of the bookshop itself, with its easy chairs, carpeting, and fireplaces, that best expressed Mahony's philosophy—that given a comfortable setting and good books, a child could begin to "think truly and . . . feel deeply."

In 1919 Mahony was joined in the bookshop by Elinor Whitney, a teacher of English at Milton Academy. Together they expanded the shop to include a room for adults stocked with books about children, started a storytelling series, and initiated art exhibits featuring work by both children and adults. Mahony's fruitful collaboration with Whitney continued for fifty years. In 1924 they founded the *Horn Book Magazine*, the first American magazine concerned exclusively with children's literature. Named after the sixteenth-century child's lesson-sheet, its purpose was to "blow the horn for fine books for boys and girls." As editor, Mahony attracted contributions over the years from distinguished writers, illustrators, librarians, and educators in the United States and abroad. Though she felt her own writing was inferior, she contributed editorials and columns that were often richly autobiographical and passionate.

In 1932, Mahony married William Davis Miller, president of W. F. Whitney Company, a furniture concern that made colonial reproductions. Subsequently, Bertha Miller divided her time between Boston and the Millers' century-old farmhouse in Ashburnham, Mass. With Elinor Whitney's marriage in 1936 to William Field, headmaster of Milton Academy, the compatible association between the two women expanded to include their husbands. The Millers and Fields decided that year to form, with the magazine's printer, Thomas Todd, a publishing company, Horn Book, Inc. The incorporation ended Bertha Miller's long and productive relationship with the WEIU.

Horn Book, Inc., became a major force in the discovery and promotion of children's writers and artists. During World War II, reflecting Bertha Miller's international interests, the company published such authors as WANDA GÁG, Beatrix Potter, and Nora Unwen. Miller's achievements later brought her the Constance Lindsay Skinner Award from the Women's National Book Association (1955), a tribute from the American Library Association (1959), and the Regina Medal from the Catholic Library Association (1967). After her death, the Jordan-Miller Memorial Course in Children's Literature was instituted at the Boston Public Library, and in 1974 the University of Southern California opened its Bertha Mahony Miller Seminar Room.

Miller's career in children's literature was capped effectively in 1959 by the appearance of *A Horn Book Sampler*, which demonstrated the range and reliability of her critical instincts. Her husband died that year; she remained as chairman of the board of Horn Book, Inc., but her activities were limited toward the end of her life by arteriosclerosis. Bertha Miller died at her Ashburnham home in May 1969 of a stroke.

[Miller's unpublished MSS., as well as her published writings and a bound set of the magazine, are in the offices of the *Horn Book Mag.*, Boston. Her joint publications with Elinor Whitney Field include *Realms of Gold in Children's Books* (1929), *Contemporary Illustrators of Children's Books* (1930), *Five Years of Children's Books* (1936), *Newbery Medal Books: 1922–1955* (1955), and *Caldecott Medal Books: 1938–1957* (1957). With others she compiled or edited *Illustrators of Children's Books, 1744–1945* (1947), *Illustrators of Children's Books, 1946–1956* (1958), and *Writing and Criticism: A Book for Margery Bianco* (1951). There is a biography by Eulalie Steinmetz Ross, *The Spirited Life: Bertha Mahony Miller and Children's Books* (1973), which includes a bibliography of Miller's writings by Virginia Haviland. For descriptions of the Bookshop see Annie Carroll Moore, "The Bookshop for Boys and Girls," *ALA Bull.*, July 1917, and Alice Jordan, "The Bookshop That Is Bertha Mahony Miller," *Atlantic Bookshelf*, June 1939. The Oct. 1969 issue of *Horn Book Mag.* was dedicated to Miller and contains tributes by her colleagues and an editorial by Elinor Whitney Field. A critical evaluation of the magazine can be found in Joan B. P. Olson, "An Interpretive History of the *Horn Book Magazine*, 1924–1973" (Ph.D. diss., Stanford Univ., 1976). Obituaries appeared in *Boston Globe*, May 15, 1969, and *Simmons Rev.*, Summer/Fall 1969; there was a tribute in the London *Times*, Nov. 15, 1969. Further material provided by Elinor Whitney Field and Frances C. Darling. Death certificate furnished by Mass. Dept. of Public Health.]

JANET NELSON FRIEDELL

MILLER, Emma Guffey, July 6, 1874–Feb. 23, 1970. Democratic party official, suffragist, feminist.

Mary Emma Guffey was born at Guffey Station, Westmoreland County, Pa., the last of three daughters and six children. Her father, John Guffey, descendant of a Scotsman who settled before 1760 in Westmoreland County, was engaged in the coal, oil, and gas industries. Emma's mother, Barbaretta (Hough) Guffey, of English ancestry, was also a descendant of pioneers in western Pennsylvania. John Guffey was active in politics, as were his brother James and Emma's brother Joseph, who became a United States senator; all were leaders of Pennsylvania's Democratic party. Emma Guffey was brought up as a loyal Democrat, and became a prominent figure in both the Democratic party and the National Woman's party, helping to lead the fight for full participation of women in politics.

After attending public elementary and high schools in Greensburg, Pa., Emma Guffey entered the fashionable Alinda Academy in Pittsburgh, where her family moved in 1891. Coming to Bryn Mawr College in 1895, she gained a reputation for wit and high spirits; she was also inspired by the feminism of its president, M. CAREY THOMAS. She graduated in 1899 with an A.B. in history and political science.

After graduation she taught briefly at the McDonald Preparatory School in Allegheny, Pa., and later in Japan. There, in 1902, Emma Guffey met Carroll Miller, an engineer and corporation executive. They were married Oct. 28, 1902, lived for five years in Japan, and then settled in Pennsylvania. They had four sons: William Gardner III (b. 1905), twins John and Carroll, Jr. (b. 1908), and Joseph (b. 1912). Carroll Miller could afford domestic help, freeing his wife to undertake a busy social and political schedule.

Emma Miller was a joiner. Between 1910 and 1920 her affiliations ranged from women's clubs and parent-teachers' organizations to the National Consumers' League and suffrage groups. She became an active speaker for the suffrage movement, and believed that women could best demonstrate their political power by working in the ranks of the major parties. In 1920 she campaigned for Democratic candidates and in 1924 won election from her ward as delegate to the Democratic National Convention. Her stirring seconding speech for Gov. Alfred E. Smith and her attack on the Ku Klux Klan prompted one excited admirer to put her name in nomination for president and she received one and a half votes. Again in 1928, Miller, an Episcopalian with sincere religious convictions, seconded the presidential nomination of Al Smith, a Catholic, and offended anti-Catholic elements by supporting him vigorously.

Throughout the 1920s Miller also directed her political efforts toward mobilizing women, helping to organize a network of Democratic women's clubs into the Pennsylvania Federation of Democratic Women. She grew impatient with the nonpartisan League of Women Voters, which she had joined in 1921, and resigned from the state executive board in 1925. In 1929 she joined the Women's Organization for National Prohibition Reform, founded by PAULINE MORTON SABIN, and until 1933 served on its advisory council, writing and speaking against prohibition. In 1930 an aroused concern with disarmament caused her to resign from the Daughters of the American Revolution as a protest against its militarism. She tried thus to respond both to humanitarian principles and political realities.

An early and active supporter of Franklin D. Roosevelt, Emma Guffey Miller increased her influence within her party in the 1930s; she also became a more militant advocate of women's rights. In 1932 she won a seat as Democratic National Committeewoman from Pennsylvania, which she retained until her death, and in 1932 and 1936 she seconded Roosevelt's nomination as president. In Pennsylvania, she was appointed to the state welfare commission and chaired the Pennsylvania National Youth Administration advisory board. Her nonpolitical positions included membership on the board of trustees of Slippery Rock (Pa.) State Teachers College, near Wolf Creek Farm, which the Millers had operated and used as a summer home since 1920.

Beginning in 1933, when Carroll Miller was appointed to the Interstate Commerce Commission, the family's main residence was in Washington, D.C. Proximity to the center of party power offered Emma Miller new opportunities. She worked with MARY DEWSON, head of the Women's Division of the Democratic National Committee, to expand women's political awareness, and ELEANOR ROOSEVELT asked her help in responding to requests from Pennsylvania citizens. Miller's advocacy of women's political activism, however, brought her into conflict with both Dewson and Roosevelt. The dispute took shape over the 1936 election for vice chairman of the Democratic National Committee, a position which Dewson had previously held and for which Miller was drafted. The real issue was disagreement over the style of leadership of the Women's Division. In an exchange of letters with Eleanor Roosevelt in July 1937, Miller urged that "more direct methods" be used to enlarge women's roles in the party. Roosevelt agreed with Dewson, whom she supported for the vice chairmanship, that political consid-

erations should precede women's concerns and defended her conduct of the Women's Division.

By the late 1930s Miller's campaign for an end to federal government discrimination against women had convinced her of the need for the Equal Rights Amendment (ERA). She became an ardent advocate of the amendment, speaking in its favor at meetings of the National Woman's party, in radio broadcasts, and in 1938 before the Senate Judiciary Committee. In 1940 Miller worked unsuccessfully for adoption of the ERA into the Democratic party platform, but in 1944 she persuaded her fellow members of the Platform Committee to support the amendment. Startling opponents by reading a letter from Eleanor Roosevelt (who had previously opposed the ERA) declaring that she would "mak[e] no statement on the Equal Rights Amendment," Miller then played a key role in getting the amendment into the platform (*Equal Rights*, Aug.-Sept., 1944). Increasingly active in the National Woman's party during the 1940s and 1950s, she became a close associate of its founder, Alice Paul (1885–1977). From 1960 to 1965 she chaired the party, and was life president from 1965 until her death.

Although handicapped in the late 1940s and 1950s by arthritis and a partial hearing loss, Miller, who was widowed in 1949, remained a colorful figure in the Democratic party. She campaigned vigorously for Harry S Truman and supported Adlai Stevenson in 1952 and 1956. With a speaking style that was pungent, witty, and forcefully partisan, Miller was a popular campaigner. During her career in politics she acquired a nickname, "the old gray mare." It seemed to describe her stubborn determination, and she enjoyed it. When she was asked to resign as Democratic National Committeewoman at the age of ninety-two, she insisted, "They can throw me out but I will not resign. I'll die with my boots on."

Although neither an intellectual nor a theoretician, Emma Miller could use ideas effectively and was often a superb tactician. Above all else she was a political partisan and her partisanship may have interfered with her feminism. She never ran for public office, perhaps out of deference to her brother, Sen. Joseph Guffey, and her achievements were limited by her acceptance of party discipline. Yet she was one of the most effective women in American politics between the two world wars, and one of the most persistent supporters of women's political equality.

Emma Guffey Miller last attended a Democratic National Convention in 1968, her twelfth appearance as a delegate. She died of a heart attack in 1970, at Grove City, Pa.

[The collection of Emma Guffey Miller's papers at the Schlesinger Library, Radcliffe College, includes correspondence, speeches, notes, clippings, copies of published articles, photographs, and memorabilia. Material on Miller can also be found in the Franklin D. Roosevelt Library, Hyde Park, N.Y.; the Harry S Truman Library, Independence, Mo.; the Washington and Jefferson College Library, Washington, Pa.; the papers of the League of Women Voters, Library of Congress; the archives of the Nat. Woman's party. Many articles and letters by Miller as well as references to her are published in the Bryn Mawr *Alumnae Bull.*, 1920–46; the *Democratic Digest*, 1932–48; and *Equal Rights*, 1937–48. Texts of some of her speeches appear in the *Official Proc.*, Democratic National Convention for 1924, 1928, 1932, and 1936. Among her other publications are "Romance of the National Pike," *Western Pa. Hist. Mag.*, Jan. 1927, and "Equal Rights: a Debate," *N.Y. Times Mag.*, May 7, 1944. For background on Miller and her family see John N. Boucher, *History of Westmoreland County Pennsylvania*, vol. 3 (1906), and Joseph F. Guffey, *Seventy Years on the Red Fire Wagon* (1952). Obituaries appeared in the *N.Y. Times*, Feb. 25, 1970, and the *Wash. Post*, Feb. 25, 1970; death certificate from Pa. Dept. of Health. Information for this article was also provided by William G. Miller, Judge Genevieve Blatt, and Louise Wright. A formal portrait of Emma Miller is in the Alva Belmont House, headquarters of the Nat. Woman's party, Washington, D.C.]

KEITH MELDER

MILLER, Frieda Segelke, April 16, 1889–July 21, 1973. State and federal official, labor reformer.

Frieda Miller, second director of the Women's Bureau of the United States Department of Labor, was born in La Crosse, Wis., the older of two daughters of Erna (Segelke) and James Gordon Miller, a lawyer. Both her father, who was born in Germany, and her mother, born in La Crosse, were members of a close-knit German community. After her mother died suddenly when Frieda was five, her father sent his daughters to live with their maternal grandparents, Augusta and Charles F. Segelke, who directed Segelke, Kohlhaus, and Company, a large manufacturing firm. Miller's interest in labor began at her grandfather's factory where skilled artisans with long service records were loyal to their employer. Her early environment shaped her gradualist approach to labor questions, an approach which looked to law and mediation to settle disputes between worker and employer.

When she was thirteen, her grandfather disappeared in a boating accident and two months later her father died. Her grandmother and an aunt raised her to maturity. She became a tall, robust, sandy-haired woman who took little time for personal appearance—pulling her hair back in a knot and dressing in sturdy clothing. The loss of her parents and her grandfather caused her to look inward for security, to work hard for success, and to keep her own counsel.

Miller attended the La Crosse public schools and graduated from Milwaukee-Downer College in 1911 with an A.B. in liberal arts. She studied labor economics and political science from 1911 to 1915 at the University of Chicago, completing all doctoral requirements but a dissertation. Tired of being a student, she sought the security of paid employment, and began her work in labor relations in 1916 as a research assistant in the department of social economy at Bryn Mawr College. She left the college in 1917 to work as executive secretary of the Philadelphia Women's Trade Union League (WTUL) and represented the League in 1920 on the administrative committee that set up the Bryn Mawr Summer School for Women Workers in Industry.

Frieda Miller's lifelong companionship with Pauline Newman, then an organizer for the WTUL, began in Philadelphia. They resigned from League work in 1923 to travel together to Europe for the Third International Congress of Working Women. Miller then went to Germany where she adopted a daughter, Elisabeth (b. 1923). Returning with the baby to New York City in 1924 to share a home and child care with Pauline Newman, who became a representative of the International Ladies' Garment Workers' Union (ILGWU), she duplicated in her adult life the female home environment which she had known in childhood.

In New York Miller found work as a factory inspector for the Joint Board of Sanitary Control of the ILGWU. Encountering dirty and unsafe conditions in many factories, she had difficulty in securing employers' agreements to improve them. In 1926 she completed a well-received study for the State Charities Aid Association, recommending changes in the housing of elderly residents on Welfare and Staten Islands, which led to work the following year as a research investigator for the New York Welfare Council.

Miller became friendly with FRANCES PERKINS, then industrial commissioner of New York, who in 1929 appointed her head of the state labor department's Division of Women in Industry. When New York passed a minimum wage law in 1933, Frieda Miller directed studies to determine fair wages for women in industries and set up boards to secure the compliance of employers; she continued throughout her years in the department to focus on securing higher wages for women workers.

Miller's activities expanded when in 1936, through Perkins's influence, she became one of the first United States delegates to the League of Nations' International Labor Organization (ILO), a permanent world body for the improvement of labor standards. Appointed by President Franklin D. Roosevelt to attend the ILO's 1936 Inter-American Regional Conference in Santiago, Chile, and other ILO Conferences, she also served on the ILO Advisory Committee on Women Workers and was the first woman elected to the organization's executive board. Her international work brought publicity and prestige to her state office work.

In 1938 Gov. Herbert H. Lehman appointed her to fulfill the unexpired term of Elmer F. Andrews as the state's industrial commissioner. New York was the second state to inaugurate a state unemployment insurance act and payments under the act had recently begun. It was Miller's task to organize a system for implementation and to secure compliance from employers. Under her administration the Labor Department collected unemployment insurance taxes from 300,000 employers and paid benefits to 3,000,000 unemployed workers. Her major emphasis, however, was on reemployment, and she revamped the New York State Employment Service, increasing job placement by 50 percent within a year. Resigning in 1942 after the election of a Republican governor, Miller became special assistant on labor to United States Ambassador to Great Britain John G. Winant.

In 1944 Frieda Miller was the choice of Secretary of Labor Frances Perkins to succeed MARY ANDERSON as director of the federal Women's Bureau. Miller's major focus as director was on the problems of the postwar reemployment of women. To this end she initiated a survey of 13,000 women workers in war industries to determine their peacetime skills and goals. Foreseeing that women would return to low wages in clerical and service industries, she also directed the Bureau to examine postwar job opportunities for women.

In 1945 Miller created the Labor Advisory Committee of the Women's Bureau, for the first time inviting trade union women to come to the Bureau. Until 1950 representatives of fifteen unions met at the Bureau every month, bringing their labor problems and raising issues of importance to women workers. After the war, many women workers were laid off and separate job categories and different pay levels for men and women once again came into effect. In response, Miller organized in 1946 a series of conferences of union leaders and representatives of national women's groups to discuss postwar employment problems and develop a reconversion blueprint to secure equal opportunity and equal pay. One such conference developed model standards for union contracts.

Throughout her tenure at the Women's Bureau, Miller continued her emphasis on equal pay and equal access to jobs for women. She testified before Congress for the proposed Equal Pay Act of 1945–46 and, although she opposed the Equal Rights Amendment as a threat to laws protecting women in industry, she shifted the emphasis of the Bureau away from protective legislation toward issues of equality in the workplace.

Frieda Miller resigned from the Women's Bureau in 1952 at the request of the incoming Republican administration but continued her work for the ILO, visiting countries in the Far East and South America in 1955 and 1956 to investigate and report on the changing economic status of women laborers. Remaining active in her seventies, she served in the 1960s as a representative at the United Nations (UN) for the International Union for Child Welfare and conducted an international child welfare survey. Miller left the UN in 1967 and moved in 1969 to the Mary Manning Walsh Home in New York City, where she died of pneumonia in 1973. She was, as Frances Perkins described her, a practical administrator who understood the economic problems of both employers and employees. Thousands of women workers in New York and throughout the country benefited from her efforts on their behalf.

[An extensive collection of Frieda Miller's papers, including her private letters, diaries, public papers, reports, published articles, and many newspaper accounts of her career, is at the Schlesinger Library, Radcliffe College. The records of the Women's Bureau, including Miller's reports and publications, are in the Nat. Archives, Washington, D.C. Biographical sketches appear in *Current Biog.*, 1945; *Independent Woman*, July 1943, p. 201; *N.Y. Times*, July 30, 1938, and Aug. 28, 1938; *Christian Science Monitor*, Nov. 22, 1940; and *Who's Who in Labor* (1946), p. 424. Information about her family is in Benjamin F. Bryant, ed., *Memoirs of La Crosse County* (1907), pp. 394–95; Marie Kroner, *The Story of the Segelke and Kohlhaus Manufacturing Company, 1857–1960* (1972); La Crosse *Daily Press*, Oct. 5 and 8, 1894; *La Crosse Daily Republican and Leader*, Oct. 13, 1894, and Dec. 15, 1902. An obituary appeared in the *N.Y. Times*, July 22, 1973. An interview with Pauline Newman was very helpful.]

DEE ANN MONTGOMERY

MINER, Dorothy Eugenia, Nov. 4, 1904–May 15, 1973. Museum curator and librarian, art historian.

Dorothy Miner, medievalist and first Keeper of Manuscripts at the Walters Art Gallery, was born in New York City, the only daughter of Roy Waldo and Anna Elizabeth (Carroll) Miner. She had a twin, Dwight, and a younger brother. Their mother, of Irish ancestry, came from Wilkes-Barre, Pa., their father from an old New England family of British descent. Both parents had given up religious vocations—he as an Episcopalian minister, she as a Catholic nun. Roy Miner became a marine biologist, working at the American Museum of Natural History, where he was named Curator of Marine Life in 1922. A charming and dynamic man, he exerted a powerful influence on his family. Through him, his daughter was introduced both to the classics and to the museum world. Anna Miner was a woman of intelligence and keen wit. Devoted to her family, she had a remarkably sweet disposition, apparently inherited by her daughter. Until World War I the Miners lived near Columbia University, moving in professional and intellectual circles closely tied to that institution. Both Dorothy Miner's family and her social milieu valued hard work and scholarly achievement.

Through the sixth grade, Miner attended the Graham School in New York City which was run by relatives. She then entered the academically oriented Horace Mann School for Girls. After her graduation in 1922, she enrolled at Barnard College, where she majored in English and classics and was elected to Phi Beta Kappa. From an early age, she had been interested in art and in the Middle Ages. Her undergraduate studies in medieval literature, history, and architecture provided a firm foundation for her later specialization in manuscript studies.

After graduating from Barnard in 1926, Miner went to Bedford College, University of London, as the first Barnard International Fellow. Her time in Europe may have prompted her change of focus from medieval literature to art history. The 1920s had seen a general development in American universities of graduate studies in art history, and in such specific fields as medieval manuscript illumination, the subject of Miner's work with Meyer Schapiro at Columbia University in 1928–29. Under the supervision of this brilliant scholar, she began her doctoral dissertation on a Carolingian Apocalypse manuscript, which she continued in Europe as a president's fellow in 1929–30. Her later employment in a museum, where the doctorate was not required, may have diverted her attention from completing this project.

A turning point in Dorothy Miner's life came in 1933–34, when she was hired by the Pierpont Morgan Library in New York City to help prepare an exhibition of illuminated manuscripts. The exhibition, held at the New York Public Library, was the first in the United States devoted entirely to this field. Presiding as director of the Morgan Library was the formidable and colorful BELLE DA COSTA GREENE, who became Miner's friend and mentor and recommended her for the post of Keeper of Manuscripts at the Walters Art Gallery in Baltimore, scheduled to open as a public museum in fall 1934.

Dorothy Miner was one of five young people hired to bring order to the vast collections of William and Henry Walters, which encompassed over 20,000 objects of diverse media and historical and geographical origins. The staff represented the first generation of professionally trained art historians employed in American museums. In addition to her responsibilities for the manuscript collection, Miner served as curator of Islamic and Near Eastern Art, developing her knowledge in this area on the job. For many years she also headed the reference library. In 1934 she became unofficial editor of Walters publications, and from 1938 to 1969 she edited the *Journal of the Walters Art Gallery*, making it a model for other museum publications. Miner also edited the many catalogs of Walters collections written by others, spending great time and energy in achieving high standards of excellence.

The years before World War II were marked by exciting discoveries, as previously unknown objects constantly surfaced from the Walters treasure troves. Miner was instrumental in consulting outside scholars on these finds and in encouraging them to publish their research. Her headquarters, the Walters Rare Book Room, became a setting for both official and informal teaching and learning. The casual visitor, the neophyte student, and the distinguished scholar were all made to feel welcome.

Miner is best known for the organization of great exhibitions which constituted pioneer surveys in their fields. Comprehensive and imaginatively designed, these shows illuminated American as well as Walters holdings for the scholarly world and for the general public. Accompanying catalogs, written or coauthored by Miner, have become standard reference works: they include *Early Christian and Byzantine Art* (1947); *Illuminated Books of the Middle Ages and Renaissance* (1949); *The World Encompassed* (1952), on maps and cartography; *The History of Bookbinding, 525–1950* (1957); *The International Style* (1962); and *2000 Years of Calligraphy* (1965).

Despite the extraordinary range of her activities, Dorothy Miner found time to write. Almost all of her articles are concerned with manuscripts and early printed books and focus on works from the Walters collections. The hallmark of her scholarship is her sensitivity to the handwritten book as an integrated physical object. Her gifts as a writer, whether in her evocation of the texture of a leaf or of a total design aesthetic, give her work an eloquence rarely found in the scholarship of this field. Miner was also a leading authority on the techniques for copying illustrations in manuscripts. Above all, she enjoyed the results of "manuscript sleuthing," extracting the secrets of their history from clues contained within the books themselves.

Shortly before her death from cancer in Baltimore in May 1973, Miner received a copy of a festschrift, *Gatherings in Honor of Dorothy Miner*, which reflected both the professional esteem of her colleagues and her many warm social relationships with scholars around the world. Miner also kept close ties with her family and with her school and college friends, and participated actively in many cultural and learned societies.

Dorothy Miner never married. The major focus of her life was her work and she belongs to the tradition in which the single woman was the accepted model for professional achievement. Her rich and enduring legacy includes her warm, witty, and generous character as well as her wide-ranging contributions to scholarship.

[Miner's professional correspondence is preserved at the Walters Gallery. A complete bibliography of her writings is included in Ursula E. McCracken, Lilian M. C. Randall, and Richard H. Randall, Jr., eds., *Gatherings in Honor of Dorothy Miner* (1974), which also contains a photograph. An outstanding example of Miner's work as an editor is *Studies in Art and Literature for Belle da Costa Greene* (1954), which includes her moving tribute to Greene. Dorothy Miner and Grace Frank, *Proverbes et Rimes* (1937), foreshadows later approaches to manuscript studies. For her attitude on the medieval book see "Manuscript Sleuthing," *Bull. of the Walters Art Gallery*, Nov. 1950, and "The Development of Medieval Illumination as Related to the Evolution of Book Design," *Catholic Life Annual*, 1958, pp. 1–20. "Since DeRicci—Western Illuminated Manuscripts Acquired Since 1934," *Jour. of the Walters Art Gallery*, 1966–67, pp. 69–103, and 1968–69, pp. 41–117, describes her manuscript acquisitions for the Walters. Two studies on medieval workshop practices are "More About Medieval Pouncing," *Homage to a Bookman: Studies in Honor of H. P. Kraus* (1967), pp. 87–107, and "Preparatory Sketches by the Master of Bodleian Douce MS 185," *Kunsthistorische Forschungen Otto Pächt zu Ehren* (1972), pp. 118–28. Miner's *Dragons and Other Animals* (1960) was the first children's coloring book based on medieval woodcuts. A posthumously published lecture, *Anastaise and Her Sisters, Women*

Artists of the Middle Ages (1974), is a pioneer study. There is no biography; a longer study by the author will appear in a forthcoming volume on women scholars and the visual arts. For biographical information see *Who's Who in American Art* (1973), p. 515; Richard H. Randall, Jr., "In Memoriam: Dorothy Miner," *Jour. of the Walters Art Gallery*, 1977, pp. v–vii; "Dorothy E. Miner," *Bull. of the Walters Art Gallery*, Oct. 1973; Madeleine Hooke Rice, "Dorothy Miner," *Barnard College Alumnae Monthly*, March 1938, pp. 9–10. See also *Medieval Art 1060–1550: Dorothy Miner Memorial* (1974), a catalog of an exhibition at the Univ. of Notre Dame. Obituaries appeared in the *N.Y. Times* May 17, 1973; the *Library of Congress Information Bull.*, May 25, 1973; *AB Bookman's Weekly*, June 11, 1973; and *Gesta*, 1974. Death record provided by the Md. Dept. of Health.]

CLAIRE RICHTER SHERMAN

MINOKA-HILL, Lillie Rosa, Aug. 30, 1876– March 18, 1952. Physician.

Lillie Rosa Minoka, a Mohawk Indian later adopted by the Oneidas, was born on the St. Regis reservation in New York state. According to family tradition, her Mohawk mother died shortly after childbirth. Her father, Joshua G. Allen, a Quaker physician from Philadelphia, had his daughter remain with her maternal relatives until she was old enough to attend school. Years later Minoka-Hill recalled coming to Philadelphia as a child of five, "looking and feeling strange . . . [a] little wooden Indian who hardly dared look right or left." Renaming her Rosa because she was "too dark to be a lily," Allen taught her about her tribal heritage and sent her to the Grahame Institute, a boarding school. There she received the training of a proper Quaker girl, and graduated from the high school in 1895.

Eager to live the Quaker precept to "do good," Minoka planned to enter nursing, but her family deemed medical school more appropriate for an educated woman. Before beginning her medical education, Allen sent her to study French for a year in Quebec, where she lived in a convent. Reminded of her earlier association with Catholicism at St. Regis and impressed by the sisters and their work, she became a Catholic; Allen accepted her decision. Returning to Philadelphia, she entered the Woman's Medical College of Pennsylvania, graduating in 1899. After interning at the Woman's Hospital in Philadelphia, she attended indigent immigrant women at the Woman's Clinic, a dispensary connected with the Woman's Medical College, and established a private practice with fellow graduate Frances Tyson. Working at Lincoln Institute, a government boarding school for Native Americans, she met Anna Hill, an Oneida student, who introduced Minoka to her brother Charles Abram Hill, a graduate of Carlisle Institute. When Minoka married Hill in 1905, and settled on his farm in Oneida, Wis., she understood that he wanted a farmer's wife and agreed to give up her practice.

Farm life in Oneida was primitive compared to the city life Minoka-Hill had known. Living in a small house with no running water, she learned to prime a pump and cook on a woodstove. Before long she was drawn back into practice. On the reservation she talked with Oneida medicine men and women, adding their herbal remedies to her medical school knowledge of botanics. Neighbors who distrusted the sole physician in Oneida began to seek her services. Local Brown County physicians, including her family doctor, Norbert Kerstin, encouraged her to treat them, although she did not hold a Wisconsin medical license. Soon Charles Hill proudly accepted his wife's unofficial medical practice.

Minoka-Hill had six children in nine years: Rosa Melissa (b. 1906), Charles Allan (b. 1906), Norbert Seabrook (b. 1912), Alfred Grahame (b. 1913), and twins Jane Frances and Josephine Marie (b. 1915). Charles Hill died in 1916 leaving his wife only a mortgaged farm and a few farm animals. Philadelphia friends counseled her to return east, but she refused, later explaining: "While in college, I resolved to spend some time and effort to help needy Indians. In Wisconsin I found my work." When the lone physician left Oneida in 1917, Minoka-Hill became the town's only trained doctor. Although her children fell ill during the influenza epidemic of 1918–19, she continued to minister to her neighbors and friends.

From then on Minoka-Hill's "kitchen-clinic," stocked with herbals and medicines supplied by physicians from nearby Green Bay and by her old friend Frances Tyson, became the focal point of medical practice in the community. Patients appeared at her door anytime from seven in the morning to ten at night; in exchange for her services, they gave her food or worked on her farm. A dedicated healer, Minoka-Hill traveled long distances to deliver babies or treat patients, many of them suffering from two ever-present realities of reservation life: malnutrition and tuberculosis. Sometimes she took her younger children with her, at other times, she sent a neighbor to look after them; of necessity they learned to be independent, and to care for each other.

The depression temporarily wiped out the small trust fund left to Minoka-Hill by her father, weakening her already precarious financial situation. Without a Wisconsin medical license, she had never been able to admit patients to the hospital, and had referred those needing such care to Brown County physicians. Now, in addition, the Federal Relief Office in Oneida could neither refer patients to her nor reimburse her for her services. Encouraged by Green Bay physicians who loaned her the $100 application fee, Minoka-Hill took the two-day examination and received her Wisconsin license in 1934, thirty-five years after she had graduated from medical school.

Dr. L. Rosa Minoka-Hill practiced in Oneida for the remainder of her life. As before, she adjusted her fees for services and medicines to a patient's ability to pay: in 1931 she received fifteen dollars to deliver one baby, two chickens for another, and nine dollars for a third. "If I charged too much," she said, "I wouldn't have a very good chance of going to heaven." In addition to attending to medical problems, she taught nutrition, sanitation, and general preventive medicine. A heart attack in 1946 forced her into semiretirement; though she no longer made housecalls, her kitchen-clinic remained open to neighbors.

Named outstanding American Indian of the year in 1947 by the Indian Council Fire in Chicago, Minoka-Hill received many other honors as well. The Oneida tribe adopted her with the name You-da-gent ("she who serves"). Giving her an honorary lifetime membership, the State Medical Society of Wisconsin also financed her 1949 trip to the American Medical Association national convention and her fiftieth college reunion. Minoka-Hill died in 1952 of a heart attack in Fond du Lac, Wis. A memorial to her outside Oneida reads: "Physician, good samaritan, and friend to all religions in this community, erected to her memory by the Indians and white people. 'I was sick and you visited me.'"

[The Archives Division, State Hist. Soc. of Wis., has a clippings file on Minoka-Hill, her application for a medical license, and photographs. In the Manuscript Division is Sally Rogow, "Indian Doctor: Rosa Minoka Hill, M.D.," an unpublished biography; because of internal inconsistencies and lack of documentation, it must be used cautiously. The Alumnae Office, Medical College of Penna., has newspaper clippings and other biographical information. For published biographical sources see: Victoria Brown, "Dr. Rosa Minoka Hill," *Uncommon Lives of Common Women: The Missing Half of Wisconsin History* (1975), pp. 65–66; "An Indian Physician Remembers," *The Crusader: The Wis. Anti-Tuberculosis Assoc.*, May 1951; Marion E. Gridley, *American Indian Women* (1974), pp. 79–80; Robert E. Ritzenthaler, "The Oneida Indians of Wisconsin," *Bull. Public Museum of the City of Milwaukee*, vol. 19 (1950); and short articles in the *Wis. Medical Jour.*, Nov. 1947 and July 1949. Obituaries appeared in *Wis. Medical Jour.*, April 1952, and *N.Y. Times*, March 19, 1952. Conflicting versions of Minoka-Hill's parentage and place of birth have appeared in published sources. Information was provided by Norbert S. Hill and Jane Hill O'Loughlin, children of Minoka-Hill, and Carol O'Loughlin Smart, a granddaughter. Marriage certificate from Clerk of Orphans' Court Division, Philadelphia. Death certificate from Wis. Dept. of Health and Social Services. Will of Joshua G. Allen, Feb. 13, 1903, provided by Register of Wills, Philadelphia.]

RIMA D. APPLE

MITCHELL, Abbie, Sept. 25, 1884–March 16, 1960. Singer, actress.

Abbie Mitchell was born in New York City where she would later earn acclaim as a singer and actress. Her career, which began when she was thirteen years old, reflects significant stylistic and ethnic milestones in the musical and theatrical life of America. She was the only child of a Jewish father from a merchant family named Mitchell and a Negro mother, Luella (Holliday) Mitchell. A maternal aunt, Alice Payne, reared the child in Baltimore where she attended school.

In the summer of 1898 Abbie Mitchell met and sang for Will Marion Cook (1869–1944), who had written the music for *Clorindy: The Origin of the Cakewalk*. He selected her for the chorus of this musical comedy which opened in New York and launched her professional career along with a new era for Negroes in the American theater. In 1899 she married Cook and joined a circle of prominent Negro theatrical personalities which included, in addition to Cook, vaudevillians Bob Cole, J. Rosamond Johnson, Bert Williams, and George Walker, composer-singer Harry T. Burleigh, and poet Paul Laurence Dunbar.

During the next several years, Mitchell appeared with Black Patti's Troubadours, a revue featuring SISSIERETTA JONES, and in two of her husband's productions, *Jes Lak White Folks* (1899) and *The Southerners* (1904). In 1900 a daughter, Marion Abigail, was born to Abbie Mitchell and Will Cook, and in 1903 a son, Will Mercer. While Marion was left in the care of relatives, Mercer, from his infancy, traveled abroad with his mother on several occasions. She remained closer to her son, who became a university professor and a United States ambassador to Niger and then Senegal.

Abbie Mitchell first won recognition abroad for her singing role in the Bert Williams and George Walker production *In Dahomey*, for which Cook composed the music. The show was produced by its star players, the famed vaudeville team of Walker and Williams, who took it to London in 1903. During that engagement, the cast appeared in a command performance for King Edward VII at Buckingham Palace. In 1905–06 Mitchell sang in New York and later toured Europe with the Memphis Students (known at first as the Nashville Students), a group of jazz musicians organized by her husband. During the next two years, she appeared in *Bandana Land* by Cook and *The Red Moon* by Cole and Johnson. By 1908 her marriage had ended in divorce but her musical association with Cook did not end.

Mitchell continued primarily as a singer until 1915 when she became a leading dramatic actress with the all-black stock company of the Lafayette Theatre in Harlem, appearing there for the next five years. She then returned to Europe as a singer with Cook's Southern (American) Syncopated Orchestra. During the remainder of the 1920s and through the 1930s, her stature as a singer and as an actress grew.

The vocal training Mitchell received from her study with Harry T. Burleigh and Emilia Serrano in New York, as well as with Jean de Reszke in Paris, enabled her to develop an extensive concert repertoire. She sang recitals at concert halls in Chicago, New York, Atlanta, and San Francisco, winning special praise in those cities, as in Europe, for her lieder interpretations. Her programs also highlighted operatic arias in addition to songs by Burleigh, Will Marion Cook, FLORENCE PRICE, and Margaret Bonds (1913–1972), her close and longtime friend. Her tours included performances at numerous colleges and churches throughout the eastern and southern United States. During this period Mitchell also taught voice at Tuskegee Institute in Alabama (1931–34) and sang on National Broadcasting Company radio shows. In the summer of 1934 she sang Santuzza with Todd Duncan as Alfio in *Cavalleria Rusticana* in New York. In 1935 she was the original Clara in George Gershwin's *Porgy and Bess*.

As a dramatic actress, Abbie Mitchell had co-starred with Rose McClendon and Jules Bledsoe in the Pultizer Prize-winning play, *In Abraham's Bosom*, produced in 1926. She next appeared with Helen Hayes in *Coquette* (1927). On succeeding Rose McClendon in Langston Hughes's *Mulatto* (1937), she encountered a ban on the play in Philadelphia, imposed by that city's mayor who feared ill feeling between whites and blacks over the theme of the drama. With the production of Lillian Hellman's *The Little Foxes* in 1939, she returned to the New York stage in the role of Addie.

Though she played no more starring roles, Mitchell remained active in the theater, becoming executive secretary of the Negro Actors

Guild of America. Instead of concertizing, she lectured and taught voice until a lengthy final illness ended her long dual career. In her waning years, her fame diminished and her former husband's music was no longer in vogue. Nevertheless, until her death in New York City in 1960, she continued to be known as Abbie Mitchell, widow of Will Marion Cook.

[The Schomburg Center for Research in Black Culture, N.Y. Public Library, has a file of newspaper clippings about Abbie Mitchell. Biographical sketches appear in Edith Isaacs, *The Negro in the American Theatre* (1947, 1969), p. 36, and Wilhelmena S. Robinson, *Historical Negro Biographies*, in the *International Library of Negro Life and History* (1967), pp. 229–30. See also Maude Cuney-Hare, *Negro Musicians and Their Music* (1936), pp. 369–71; James Weldon Johnson, *Black Manhattan* (1930, 1968), p. 103; Lindsay Patterson, ed., *The Negro in Music and Art*, in the *International Library of Negro Life and History* (1967), pp. 191–93; Harry A. Ploski and Warren Marr, eds., *The Negro Almanac: A Reference Work on the Afro-American*, 3d ed. (1976), p. 834; Mabel M. Smythe, ed., *The Black American Reference Book* (1976), p. 688; and the entry on Will Marion Cook in *Dict. Am. Biog.*, Supp. Three. Newspaper reviews of her performances include those in the *Chicago Daily News*, Oct. 22, 1930; *N.Y. Sun*, April 22, 1927; *N.Y. Daily News*, Feb. 17, 1939; *Amsterdam News*, March 4, 1939. An obituary appeared in the *N.Y. Times*, March 20, 1960. Additional information was provided by her son, W. Mercer Cook.]

GEORGIA A. RYDER

MITCHELL, Lucy Sprague, July 2, 1878–Oct. 15, 1967. Educator, writer, college administrator.

Lucy Sprague Mitchell was born in Chicago, the fourth of six children and third of three daughters of Lucia (Atwood) and Otho Sprague. Both the Sprague and Atwood families came from England in the seventeenth century, eventually settling in Vermont. In 1870, Otho and Lucia Sprague left Vermont for Chicago. There Otho Sprague joined a small grocery concern established by his brother Albert and Ezra Warner, another former Vermont farm boy. Sprague Warner and Company shortly became one of the largest wholesale grocery businesses in the world.

Lucy Sprague's father embodied the conventional New England virtues of thrift, ambition, and moral probity. Her mother, a "gay, gypsy creature whom Father tried conscientiously to reform," was exceptionally musical and artistic, but so shy and self-deprecating that her daughter pitied as well as loved her. At the Otho Sprague household, play, self-expression, any outward display of affection were considered lightmindedness, Mitchell later recalled; fear, humility, and a sense of guilt were symbols of grace.

Introspective and extremely nervous and shy, Lucy Sprague tried to escape her lonely and unsatisfactory life by keeping secret notebooks of poetry, allegories, and stories about herself and a large imaginary family. She came to feel that she was two people—the person who participated in the daily round of activities and a critical, onlooker self whom she called "the thing in the corner." Until Lucy was twelve, the Sprague children were tutored at home by a governess. Following her family's move to Chicago's elegant Prairie Avenue in 1890, she was sent to a private school for girls, but had to leave as she went "to pieces" whenever she entered the classroom. Books became her chief source of education as she systematically read her way through her father's huge library.

Young Lucy Sprague came to know several faculty members at the University of Chicago. Most influential were John Dewey, whose Laboratory School aroused her first interest in education, and ALICE FREEMAN PALMER, the former Wellesley College president. Sprague became a beloved "only daughter" for the childless Palmer, who opened a "new world" for her, introducing her to such women as MARION TALBOT and SOPHONISBA BRECKINRIDGE. Also influential was JANE ADDAMS, whose Hull House had attracted Otho Sprague's support. When her father broke decisively with Addams in 1894 over her support of the Pullman workers' right to strike, Lucy Sprague sided with Addams, creating a family rift that never healed. She developed a sense of shame and guilt at being rich, feeling she was a "'pampered darling' . . . bound by my father's wealth to a world of people whose standards I couldn't accept."

In 1893, family health problems forced the Spragues to leave Chicago for the Sierra Madre region of southern California. Lucy Sprague's two youngest brothers had both died from contagious diseases in the preceding years, and her sister Nancy now underwent a devastating mental collapse. Her mother fell into a profound depression. Otho Sprague, meanwhile, continued to suffer recurrent hemorrhages from the tuberculosis he had contracted during the Civil War. Lucy Sprague served as the family nurse for over a year. She was then sent to the Marlborough School in Los Angeles. This time, she thoroughly enjoyed her school adventure, and rebelled mightily when she was forced to return to her nursing duties after graduation.

She was rescued by an invitation to live in Cambridge, Mass., with Alice Freeman and

George Herbert Palmer, and to attend Radcliffe College. Over her father's initial objections, Sprague entered Radcliffe in the fall of 1896. Active in student affairs, she majored in philosophy, taking courses with William James, Josiah Royce, George Santayana, Hugo Munsterberg, and George Palmer, and graduated with honors in philosophy in 1900. Returning to California, she resumed her role as family nurse, and began to study landscape gardening at the Throop Institute, but she considered her course there unsuccessful. Unhappy at home and in her work, Sprague rapidly deteriorated.

Again she was rescued by the Palmers, who took her with them to Europe. Alice Palmer died unexpectedly in Paris, however, and Sprague returned to Cambridge with the grief-stricken widower. She remained for several years, helping with housekeeping, taking some graduate courses at Harvard, and becoming secretary to Radcliffe's dean. In 1906, when President Benjamin Wheeler of the University of California at Berkeley offered her a job working with women students, she accepted, insecure about her lack of training but happy to leave behind the "vicarious" and restricted life she had led at Professor Palmer's.

Sprague was appointed dean of women and assistant professor of English, one of the first two women to hold a regular faculty position at the University of California. She was an innovative and dynamic dean, abandoning the traditional "motherly" conception of the role to focus on expanding educational and social opportunities for women students. Sprague attempted to improve housing conditions for students, started courses in sex education, worked to strengthen women's organizations, and held weekly receptions at her home; she also urged students to examine social conditions in the San Francisco community. In 1911, wanting to explore the possibility of training women students for careers other than teaching, she took a four-month leave in New York City to work with such pioneers in the development of women's professions as LILLIAN WALD, FLORENCE KELLEY, MARY RICHMOND, Pauline Goldmark, and JULIA RICHMAN. The time spent with Richman, principal of a Manhattan high school, proved especially significant and Sprague came to see public education as the most constructive way to deal with social problems. It was also, she said, "the synthesis of all my interests, all my hopes for humanity."

Returning to California, Sprague resigned as dean in 1912. In May of that year she married Wesley Clair Mitchell, an economist at the University of California whose strong commitment to her life goals had eventually persuaded her that marriage would not prevent her from continuing her independent work. Marriage proved a turning point professionally as well as personally. Following the couple's move to New York City, where Wesley Mitchell wished to pursue at first hand his pioneering work on business cycles, Lucy Sprague Mitchell began in earnest her work in the education of children. She took courses at Teachers College, Columbia University, with John Dewey and others, worked as a volunteer visiting teacher in the public schools for Harriet Johnson and the Public Education Association, conducted psychological tests on normal and retarded children in city schools, and taught nursery school and kindergarten classes at Caroline Pratt's new Play School. In 1916, her first cousin, ELIZABETH SPRAGUE COOLIDGE, offered to support an educational venture of the Mitchells' choosing for a period of ten years. With her husband and Harriet Johnson as cofounders, Lucy Mitchell established the Bureau of Educational Experiments (chartered in 1950 as the Bank Street College of Education). She became chairman of the Bureau, a private educational corporation formed to teach and do research concerning "progressive education and educational experiments."

At the same time the Mitchell family was expanding. Within five years of their move to New York, there were four children; the oldest son and the only daughter, the Mitchells' third child, were adopted. "It was a highly focused life," Mitchell later recalled, "with everything concentrated on children, each aspect of my work illuminating the others." Her husband's support was crucial. She believed that his support of her career and his acceptance of her as an independent person enabled her to overcome the guilt and self-doubt that were legacies of her childhood and to establish herself as a confident and productive woman.

For four decades, Lucy Sprague Mitchell guided the Bureau of Educational Experiments in its pioneering work in early childhood education. Throughout, she gave generous financial support to the institution, always bridling, however, at being thought of as a patron rather than a worker. As head of its governing board she directed the Bureau's institutional growth, combining great skills in management with her insistence that the governance of the institution remain a cooperative endeavor. Inspired by her leadership, it became a place where professional women could extend the boundaries of traditional female interest in children in an innovative and independent manner that was both scientifically rigorous and nurturant.

Mitchell was also instrumental in setting the

direction of the Bureau's educational philosophy. Influenced by Dewey and other associates in the progressive education movement, she believed that learning should be an active and dynamic process of discovery, and that it required both "intake" (or direct observation) and "outgo" (the creative expression of experience). Theory was never isolated from practice: Mitchell's primary objective was always to study children's development—mental, emotional, and physical—in order to adapt schools to each stage of growth. Perhaps her greatest achievement was to foster a continuing correspondence between educational theory, practical classroom techniques, and research in child development.

Mitchell was most active in the institution's teacher-training and writing programs. Motivated by her experience as a teacher at Caroline Pratt's City and Country School, ELISABETH IRWIN's Little Red School House, and the Bureau's Nursery School, she became convinced of the need to train the "whole teacher," who could help stimulate vivid and creative experiences that would foster the growth of the "whole child." In 1931, she and her colleagues established the Cooperative School for Teachers. Mitchell gave courses in children's language and the environment at the school and helped to design a curriculum that allowed teachers to develop an "experimental, critical and ardent" approach to education, one that combined a "scientific attitude" with "the attitude of the artist." In 1943, she fulfilled a long-standing goal with the inauguration of a series of public school workshops, extending the educational innovations pioneered by the Bureau.

The Writers Workshop, originated by Mitchell in 1938, aimed to help writers of children's books to understand the developmental needs and interests of children and to assist them in acquiring techniques that utilized direct language and the sounds, rhythms, and imagery of children's speech; many well-known children's authors have participated in the workshops. Mitchell herself wrote, coauthored, or edited six books for adults and twenty for children. Most influential was the *Here and Now Story Book* (1921, 1971), which argued that stories for young children should derive from the world of their experiences, and that their form should correspond to children's play with words and sounds. In *Two Lives: The Story of Wesley Clair Mitchell and Myself* (1953), Mitchell created an unusual form, combining autobiography with a biography of her husband and the story of their marriage.

After Wesley Mitchell's death in 1948, Lucy Sprague Mitchell again felt besieged by loneliness and feelings of inadequacy. She retired from Bank Street in 1956, having reluctantly assumed the title of president in 1950. Moving to Palo Alto, Calif., to be near one of her children, she lived alone until a few years before her death of arteriosclerotic heart disease. In her last years, she wrote poems about her marriage and the state of her emotions, eventually emerging from the grief-stricken "second adolescence" of her widowhood to rediscover a new sense of self-worth and creativity.

Mitchell's focus on children's education, her husband's encouragement, and her inherited wealth enabled her to bring unity, as she termed it, into the life of a professional woman. Many contemporaries commented on her ceaseless energy, her iron will, and what seemed to some a cold, impersonal brusqueness. Most of her colleagues, however, found her witty and sympathetic, even charismatic. Tall and beautiful, she dressed in long skirts and embroidered blouses, wearing silver chains or intricate beads and a velvet band around her neck, her thick hair piled on top of her head. Gypsylike yet aristocratic, Mitchell blended in her person as in her character those qualities of emotion and rationalism, artist and scientist, that formed a large part as well of her educational design.

[The Lucy Sprague Mitchell Papers at Columbia Univ. contain drafts of published and unpublished MSS., papers relating to her work with the Bureau, and some family correspondence and memorabilia. The library of the Bank Street College of Education has material on the history of the institution and most of Mitchell's publications. The Bancroft Library, Univ. of Calif., Berkeley, has some documents relating to her work as dean. An oral history, *The Reminiscences of Lucy Sprague Mitchell* (1964), was made by the Regional Oral Hist. Office, Univ. of Calif., Berkeley. Other important books by Mitchell include *Young Geographers* (1934, 1963, 1971), which illustrates Mitchell's concept of "relationship thinking," and *Our Children and Our Schools* (1950), a description of the public school workshops. Mitchell also wrote numerous articles on children's education which appeared in educational journals and popular magazines. Remembrances of Mitchell are included in Bank Street College's *Lucy Sprague Mitchell Memorial Dedication Ceremony* (1971) and its *Lucy Sprague Mitchell: An Hour of Remembrance* (1967). A brief article on her by Mary Phelps and Margaret Wise Brown appeared in *Horn Book Mag.*, May–June 1937; see also *Nat. Cyc. Am. Biog.*, LIII, 375–76. A biography by Joyce Antler is in preparation. Obituaries appeared in the *N.Y. Times*, Oct. 17, 1967, and in *Publishers Weekly*, Oct. 30, 1967. Valuable information and reminiscences were provided by her sons, Arnold, Sprague, and John Mitchell, by Margaret Coolidge and other family members, and by many associates and former students, including Barbara Biber, Charlotte Winsor, Claudia Lewis, Elizabeth Gilkerson,

Jack Niemeyer, Sally Kerlin, and Arthur Burns. Death certificate from Calif. Dept. of Public Health.]

JOYCE ANTLER

MONROE, Marilyn, June 1, 1926–Aug. 5, 1962. Film actress.

Marilyn Monroe was born Norma Jean Mortenson in Los Angeles, but she was raised as Norma Jean Baker. Her mother, Gladys (Monroe) Baker Mortenson, a film splicer, had had two children from her marriage to Jack Baker. The son died in infancy; the daughter was raised by Baker's family. A second marriage, to Mortenson, had ended before Norma Jean's birth. The adult Monroe came to believe that her father had been C. Stanley Gifford, who had been her mother's coworker and steady companion in the period preceding and just after Norma Jean's birth.

Gladys Baker had to work to support her daughter, and Norma Jean spent her childhood and youth in a series of temporary residences. Her mother visited her regularly, but when Norma Jean was seven Gladys Baker was committed to a state mental hospital with an illness diagnosed as paranoid schizophrenia; Baker's mother, father, and brother had also been hospitalized with a similar condition. Grace McKee, a coworker and friend of Gladys Baker, became Norma Jean's guardian. When she married a man named Goddard some years later, Norma Jean joined the household. In the meantime she had lived in various foster homes and spent nearly two years, from ages nine to eleven, at the Los Angeles Orphan's Home Society.

Norma Jean Baker attended high school in Los Angeles, but dropped out in the eleventh grade before her marriage on June 19, 1942, to James Dougherty, an aircraft factory worker. They lived briefly in Van Nuys, Calif., and then moved to Santa Catalina Island, off the southern California coast, where Dougherty worked as an instructor for the Maritime Service. In 1944 he went to sea on a merchant freighter; Norma Jean Dougherty moved in with her in-laws and got a job assembling target airplanes at the Radio Plane Company in Van Nuys. It was there she was chosen as a model by an army photographer to illustrate an article on women workers for *Yank* magazine.

Those photographs caught the attention of other photographers and of a modeling agency and Norma Jean Dougherty enrolled in a three-month evening course in modeling. She soon quit her factory job and was working regularly as a model, posing for advertising and promotional photographs, magazine covers, and cal-

endars. Her goal was a motion picture contract, and in the spring of 1946 she took up a six-week residence in Las Vegas, Nev., in order to obtain a divorce from Dougherty: contracts were rarely given to aspiring actresses who were married.

Shortly after returning from Las Vegas, she met with Ben Lyon, head of the casting department of Twentieth Century-Fox. He arranged a silent color screen test for her, which would emphasize her appearance and play down her acting inexperience. When Darryl F. Zanuck, then Fox production head, was shown the test he immediately authorized a contract. On Aug. 26, 1946, she signed with Fox for seventy-five dollars a week, but was told that she needed a more appropriate name as an actress. Ben Lyon suggested "Marilyn" as a first name, and Baker chose her mother's maiden name, Monroe, as a surname. Norma Jean Baker Dougherty thus became Marilyn Monroe.

Marilyn Monroe's first motion picture contract, for an initial six months and renewable at the option of the studio, lasted a year. She appeared in only two films, serving the studio more as a model and hostess than as an actress. Out of work, she began taking lessons in acting at the Actors Lab, and performed for the first time in a stage play. In the spring of 1948 Columbia Pictures signed her to a six-month contract, cast her in one film, the musical *Ladies of the Chorus*, and released her. As a free-lance actress she picked up two more small roles, one in a Marx Brothers film, *Love Happy* (1950). It was in this period of unemployment and uncertainty that Monroe posed nude for the calendar photograph that would become notorious after her rise to fame.

Monroe's career took a turn for the better after she met Johnny Hyde, an important talent agent with the William Morris Agency. Hyde became her agent and her intimate companion, escorting her around Hollywood and instructing her in the movie community's styles and mores. He secured her first two important screen roles, in *The Asphalt Jungle*, directed by John Huston, and in *All About Eve*, directed by Joseph L. Mankiewicz (both 1950). In both films she plays inexperienced young women who are protégées of worldly older men, parts that resembled her life situation. For *All About Eve* she was signed again to a contract by Twentieth Century-Fox.

At a time when the old studio system, with large numbers of players under contract, was breaking down, Monroe became a studio employee, subject to the traditional Hollywood method of developing a star by creating a stereotypical image and capitalizing on it as long as box office response was favorable. Fox promoted Monroe as their "blonde bombshell" of the 1950s, sexy, shapely, and none too bright. Along with Elizabeth Taylor, a brunette, she was one of the most successful of Hollywood's manufactured sex queens, and the moviegoing public responded to her physical beauty and the comic naïveté of her screen character. By 1953 a heavy publicity campaign and ten more pictures under her Fox contract had made her famous.

Monroe's romance with baseball star Joe DiMaggio, also in 1953, vastly increased public interest in her private life. They were married on Jan. 14, 1954. Shortly thereafter she made a tour of United States army posts in South Korea, a highly publicized event that evoked riotous enthusiasm from the soldiers and demonstrated her remarkable appeal as a sex symbol. The exploitation of her sex appeal, and the public clamor it called forth, contributed, however, to the rapid deterioration of Monroe's marriage to DiMaggio. They were divorced within the year, on Oct. 27, 1954.

Whether Monroe was an actress as well as a sex object was a subject of greater concern to her than to her public. After completing *The Seven Year Itch* in 1954, she had appeared in some two dozen films. In most of these she portrayed a dumb blonde seeking a rich husband, and the few parts that differed from this stereotype cast her in an even less favorable light— as the unfaithful wife, for example, in the melodramatic *Niagara* (1953). In retrospect, one can see more clearly her talent as a comedian, and the distancing self-parody she brought to her conventionalized roles. But her subtle undercutting of her movie persona was unrecognized by many of her admirers and unsatisfying to her.

In late 1954 Monroe sought to break her Twentieth Century-Fox contract, and moved from Hollywood to New York. There she began studying at the Actors Studio under the direction of Lee and Paula Strasberg and took part in forming an independent company, Marilyn Monroe Productions. After protracted negotiations a new agreement was reached with Fox. She would be required to make only four films for Fox over a seven-year period, and would be granted power to approve the studio's choice of directors. Meanwhile, through her own company she could make any other picture she wished.

Her first film under the new arrangement was *Bus Stop* (1956). Though Monroe played yet another sort of dumb blonde, she brought to the role a poignancy and emotional depth not previously seen in her performances. This was immediately followed, however, by a reversion to type in *The Prince and the Showgirl* (1957), the only film produced by her own corporation. In *Some Like It Hot* (1959), directed by Billy Wilder, she created the most memorable of her performances in the self-parodying comedy style.

On June 29, 1956, Monroe married the playwright Arthur Miller. Over the next several years, very much wanting children, she twice became pregnant; in both cases, physical complications prevented her carrying the child to term. During this time Monroe was suffering increasingly from mental and emotional disturbances. Erratic behavior and outbursts of temperament marked her work on the productions of *The Prince and the Showgirl* and *Some Like It Hot*. Her relation with Miller deteriorated, though he wrote the screenplay for her final completed film, *The Misfits* (1961). It provided her deepest and most complex screen role, as yet another dumb blonde, but with feelings of vulnerability and compassion, and the capacity to love. Monroe and Miller were divorced on Jan. 24, 1961.

During 1961 Monroe was briefly hospitalized in a New York clinic for mental patients. She returned thereafter to California and began working on a film at Fox, but was discharged in June 1962 for her repeated failures to appear. Six weeks later she died at her home in Los Angeles, apparently from an accidental overdose of sleeping pills.

In death as in life Marilyn Monroe became a symbol. Perhaps no other American woman of the twentieth century has embodied as fully as Monroe the exploitation of sexuality in the mass media and the marketing of a woman as a sexual icon. She sought the role and she sought later, with limited success, to transcend it. Before her early death, and more frequently thereafter, Monroe's image and her career were transformed into novels, paintings, plays, and motion pictures, both as myths and as cautionary tales.

In her last few years Monroe tried through psychoanalysis to overcome her emotional disturbances, to understand her motivations and drives. She spoke about herself in almost therapeutic terms: she was the homeless waif who needed both to give and receive love, who expressed her longing by exuding an aura of desire and sensuality that came, through her screen image, to circle the globe and dominate an era.

[More books have been written about Marilyn Monroe than about any other American motion picture actress. Biographies include Fred Lawrence Guiles, *Norma Jean* (1969), Edwin P. Hoyt, *Marilyn: The Tragic Venus* (1965, 1973), and Maurice Zolotow, *Marilyn Monroe* (1960). Robert F. Slatzer, *The Life* and Curious Death of Marilyn Monroe (1974), reproduces important documents, such as her birth certificate. Among the memoirs are James E. Dougherty, *The Secret Happiness of Marilyn Monroe* (1976); Eunice Murray with Rose Shade, *Marilyn: The Last Months* (1975); Norman Rosten, *Marilyn: An Untold Story* (1973); and Lena Pepitone and William Stadiem, *Marilyn Monroe: Confidential* (1979). Critical studies are Norman Mailer, *Marilyn* (1973), with extensive photographs; Joan Mellen, *Marilyn Monroe* (1973); and Edward Wagenknecht, ed., *Marilyn Monroe: A Composite View* (1969). Michael Conway and Mark Ricci, eds., *The Films of Marilyn Monroe* (1964), gives a complete filmography, with stills from and representative reviews of each film. Monroe's *My Story* (1974) was written around 1954 as part of the effort to launch Marilyn Monroe Productions and is of little value. Birth and death records were provided by Calif. Dept. of Public Health.]

ROBERT SKLAR

MOORE, Anne Carroll, July 12 1871–Jan. 20, 1961. Children's librarian.

Anne Carroll Moore was a woman of vision; a pioneer in a new field, she helped establish the Children's Division of the New York Public Library at the turn of the century. Her imaginative and sound approach to children's reading created imitators across the country.

Her father, Luther Sanborn Moore, of Irish descent, was a lawyer and a strong influence on her life. Her mother was Sarah Hidden (Barker) Moore, whose ancestors had come to New England in the 1630s. Her daughter remembered her as bringing "to everyday life a beauty and serenity of personality, a social ease and a sound judgment on which my father relied at every turn." Anne, born Annie, was the youngest of ten, the only one of the three daughters to survive. Her family was warm and supportive, and childhood a happy period she frequently remembered in later life. Born in Limerick, Maine, she attended Limerick Academy, and Bradford (Mass.) Academy for Women, from which she graduated in 1891. In January 1892 tragedy struck; her parents died within two days of each other from influenza. That same year her sister-in-law died in childbirth, forcing her to assume for two years the role of mother to two young nieces, and ending her dream of becoming a lawyer.

She remained with her brother in Maine until 1895, when she entered the library school of Pratt Institute in Brooklyn, N.Y. The following year she accepted MARY WRIGHT PLUMMER's invitation to head the new children's department at the Institute. The first library area designed especially for children, it illustrated the new belief that a children's library should be a haven for desultory reading as well as study, a place where children would be free to handle, examine, and browse through books at will. In ten years at Pratt, she set about learning all she could about children's books, and there she initiated the storytelling hours that were to be a major feature of her later work. There, too, she developed her concept of a children's library as a "mental resource," an educational rather than a social service institution. In 1900, at a meeting of the American Library Association (ALA), she helped initiate and became first chairman of the Club of Children's Librarians; it later became the Children's Services Division of the ALA.

In 1905 Arthur Bostwick, head of the newly organized circulation department of the New York Public Library (NYPL), invited Moore to come there to work in the children's division. She became supervisor of work with children in 1906 and remained at the NYPL until 1940, becoming herself an institution and helping to create the profession of librarian for children. To improve her ability to work with children she combed schools, settlement houses, and the streets of New York in an attempt to "investigate childhood itself" and acquired a knowledge of child psychology and behavior. In her approach to young readers, she revolutionized library concepts and practices. She abolished the age limit that prevented children from using some branch libraries. To bring city children closer to nature, she made displays of flowers and vegetables appropriate to the season. She also created a variety of special events, art exhibitions, and holiday celebrations, inaugurated reading lists of recommended books, introduced storytelling sessions, and brought guest speakers to the library, all in the interest of stimulating the inner growth of children. She also emphasized the necessity of a relationship between the Children's Library and the public schools.

By 1908 Moore had gained professional status for children's librarians at the more than thirty branches of the NYPL and established salary guidelines for them. She enjoyed the branch libraries and visited them frequently, insisting that all the librarians become familiar with the individual personalities of the branches as shaped by their neighborhoods.

In 1913 Moore became involved in the Leo Frank case. She worked arduously on behalf of the young New York Jew who was accused of murder in Atlanta, and even traveled there to plead for his release. He had been one of her library children at Pratt Institute. Her books, *Nicholas: A Manhattan Christmas Story* (1924) and *Nicholas: The Golden Goose* (1932), were inspired by another of her library children, a lonely boy who visited the Children's Library every day.

Anne Carroll Moore's influence extended far beyond the NYPL through her writings and lectures, as well as through the work of many of her subordinates who established children's libraries elsewhere or, like her friend RUTH SAWYER, carried on the storytelling tradition Moore sponsored. In 1918 the publisher Ben W. Huebsch asked her to deliver a series of eight lectures, the success of which led Frederick G. Melcher, editor of *Publishers Weekly* and Franklin K. Mathiews, leader of the Boy Scouts of America, to propose that she help them establish an annual Children's Book Week; the first one took place at the NYPL the following year. Also in 1918 she began to review books on a continuous basis for *The Bookman*, a literary monthly, and to produce her "Children's Books Suggested as Holiday Gifts," which became an annual list issued by the NYPL from 1918 to 1941. She loved to compile reading lists for publication, feeling it was a creative act. She also edited a page of literary criticism of children's books entitled "The Three Owls" for the *New York Herald Tribune* from 1924 to 1930. (After 1936 the column appeared in *Horn Book Magazine.*) Very influential, it was once called "the yea or nay of all children's literature." Moore liked folk tales and fantasy and disliked children's books that were designed for moral or therapeutic ends, rather than as works of literature.

Anne Carroll Moore approached life with great intensity. She traveled extensively, loved England and its traditions, and brought her discoveries back to the children who frequented the library. She had a passionate devotion to cooking, was a circus buff, an art lover, and felt a mystic communion with nature. Very little attached to material things, she lived in a series of apartments, some of them squalid, and showed no interest in clothes, except for a passion for expensive shoes, gloves, and handbags. For many years she carried an eight-inch wooden doll named Nicholas, the hero of her books, in her purse; invitations were issued in its name, stationery devised for it, and friends and strangers judged by their reactions to it. When it was lost a group of children had an exact duplicate made for her, much to the dismay of some friends who had hoped to see the last of it. A perfectionist, she was severely demanding and "scarcely anyone escape[d], at one point or another, an encounter of great bitterness in relation to her" (Sayers, p. 120). Toward her family and friends she was fierce, but also loving and generous, helping to finance the education of her nieces and nephews.

Moore received many awards, including two honorary doctorates, the first Constance Lindsay Skinner Gold Medal awarded by the Women's National Book Association (1940), and the Regina Medal from the Catholic Library Association (1960). She was bitter and angry at her enforced retirement in October 1940 at the age of seventy. Although she continued to write, teach, and lecture, she felt lonely and displaced and spent the next decade paying frequent anguished visits to "her" library. When she reached eighty she finally began to accept her retirement and discovered the benefits of leisure time. Anne Carroll Moore died in New York in January 1961, at eighty-nine; she had made a permanent imprint not only on the New York Public Library but also on the world of children's books.

[Moore compiled three collections of her columns, *Roads to Childhood: Views and Reviews of Children's Books* (1920), *New Roads to Childhood* (1923), and *Cross Roads to Childhood* (1926). Her articles include "Seven Stories High," in *Compton's Pictured Encyc.* (1932); "The Choice of a Hobby," in the 1934 edition of *Compton's;* and "Books for Young People," *Bookman*, March 1920. Frances L. Spain, ed., *Reading Without Boundaries* (1956), contains a bibliography of Moore's writings and of articles about her through 1955. An important source is Frances Clarke Sayers, *Anne Carroll Moore: A Biography* (1972), which covers every aspect of Moore's career, and develops a fascinating study of a complicated and visionary woman. There is also a useful article in Frances Clarke Sayers, *Summoned by Books* (1965). A moving tribute to Moore by Ruth Sawyer appears in *Horn Book Mag.*, July-Aug. 1950. See also Barbara Holbrook, "Anne Carroll Moore, of the Golden Age," *Wilson Bull.*, Dec. 1938; I. Parin D'Aulaire, "Miss Moore in Brooklyn: A Reminiscence," *Horn Book Mag.*, Oct. 1964; Ernestine Evans, "Anne Carroll Moore Fills Eighty Years," *Publishers Weekly*, July 28, 1951; Nina C. Brotherton, "Anne Carroll Moore," *Library Jour.*, Sept. 1, 1941; and Frances Clarke Sayers, "Postscript: The Later Years," *Horn Book Mag.*, April 1961. Moore's objections to E. B. White's *Stuart Little* are recorded in "Anne Carroll Moore Urged Withdrawal of *Stuart Little*, E. B. White Reports," *Library Jour.*, April 15, 1966. See also the entries in the *Dict. Am. Library Biog.* (1978) and in Thomas Kunitz and Howard Haycraft, eds., *Junior Book of Authors* (1934). Obituaries appeared in *Publishers Weekly*, Jan. 30, 1961; *Library Jour.*, Feb. 15, 1961; and the *N.Y. Times*, Jan. 21, 1961. A memorial article by Frederick Melcher was in *Publishers Weekly*, Feb. 13, 1961.]

ALMA L. KENNEY

MOORE, Marianne Craig, Nov. 15, 1887–Feb. 5, 1972. Poet, critic, editor.

Marianne Moore, the younger child of Mary

(Warner) and John Milton Moore, was born in Kirkwood, Mo. She grew up with her brother, John Warner, her "bulwark" by a year and a half, soaking up the love and piety of their mother and their grandfather, Rev. John Riddle Warner, pastor of the Kirkwood First Presbyterian Church. Even in her seventies her memories of Kirkwood remained shiny, a keepsake of childhood joy in her grandfather's manse. She remembered "rides through Forest Park in a brougham" and "roses and clematis in our yard . . . bluejays, persimmons about the size of a small plum on our upper porch to benefit by frost."

But Moore's father is conspicuously absent from her scenes of memory. He did not emerge until an interview in 1957 in which she called him "something of a visionary . . . obsessed with the idea of building a smokeless furnace." The son of a Portsmouth, Ohio, foundry owner, John Moore married Mary Warner in June 1885, and took her to Newton, Mass., where his scheme failed. With a wife and infant son to care for, he was beset by financial problems, which badgered him into a breakdown. Mary Warner Moore returned to Kirkwood with her son to care for her father's house. Later Marianne Moore was to add, axiomatically, "Our mother lost him early, and we never saw him."

John Riddle Warner died in February 1894 and Mary Warner Moore traveled east to spend an interim with cousins near Pittsburgh. She then moved to Carlisle, Pa., where she accepted a position as English teacher at Metzger Institute, a girls' school, and set about to rear her brood shrewdly and devoutly.

Marianne Moore grew up among books—Lang's fairy tales, the Jacob Abbott *Rollo* volumes, above all the Bible. She developed a flair for outdoor sketching—milkweed pods, a stalk of jointed grasses. There were summer tennis matches, outings to nearby parks, and excursions to the lodge on the mountain crag owned by their close friends, Rev. George Norcross and his family. The months were punctuated by midweek prayer meetings and musicales. The Moores' family life was a private world, with fairy tale touches like the heirloom from her Kirkwood home, the pair of girandoles with glass prisms that Mary Warner Moore liked to call "The Enchanted Forest."

The inner family circle remained intact until Warner Moore left in the fall of 1904 to enter Yale College, followed by Marianne to Bryn Mawr in 1905. Their three-way correspondence of the next years allows the outsider to trespass into the Moores' enchanted woodland where all (who mattered) wore animal names. Mary Warner Moore was Fawn, Warner became Tur-

tle, and Marianne was Tibby or 'Gator, from the baby alligator she had treasured in Kirkwood once upon a time. In 1908 Kenneth Grahame's *The Wind in the Willows* became the family's book of delight, for it confirmed their fantasy. Moreover, the book lent them lifelong identities: Mole for mother, Badger for Warner, and Rat for Marianne.

The years at Bryn Mawr expanded Marianne Moore's world. Academically her efforts in English composition promised well but lacked substance. Most of her gusto fed into her biology courses, with long hours spent in the laboratory sketching the magnified details of the jellyfish or of the grasshopper's jointed leg. By her sophomore year she had begun to publish stories and poems in *Tipyn o'Bob*, the college literary monthly.

Graduation in 1909 left Marianne Moore adrift. That June she enrolled at the Carlisle Commercial College where she drilled for a year, learning Pitman shorthand and typewriting; then she accepted a position at the Lake Placid Club, the New York Adirondack resort run by the librarian Melvil Dewey. Here she spent three months helping to revise the Dewey Decimal Index and chafing at chores. On free days she wandered the mountain trails, with sketch pad for company.

By the spring of 1911 Mary Warner Moore had decided upon a trip abroad, even though it meant separation from Warner. Sailing in late May, she and her daughter landed in Liverpool and began a literary tour through England and Scotland, ending with ten days in France, then home in mid-August. Marianne Moore had kept busy sketching scenes and vistas, silently making observations to be defined in her poems.

Carlisle meant the workaday world again. Marianne Moore joined the business department faculty at the United States Indian School in Carlisle, where through 1914 she taught commercial arithmetic, typewriting, stenography, even a commercial law course designed to teach the Indians their contractual rights. The few poems she wrote she submitted to *The Lantern*, the Bryn Mawr literary annual.

Warner Moore graduated from the Princeton Theological Seminary in 1914 and two years later was installed as pastor in Chatham, N.J. His mother and sister moved to Chatham to keep house for him. But with United States entrance into World War I, Warner was sworn into the navy as acting chaplain. Soon married, he remained in the navy as a career officer until his retirement in 1948. Marianne and Mary Warner Moore relocated themselves to St. Luke's Place in New York's Greenwich Village.

By June 1914, Marianne Moore was ready to

inch her way into "the new poetry." HARRIET MONROE's *Poetry: A Magazine of Verse*, already in its second year in Chicago, had presented Ezra Pound's new corps of London poets, "Les Imagistes," especially H.D. (HILDA DOOLITTLE), a transplanted American whose poems were to become the centerpiece of Imagism. Moore submitted a sheaf of poems under the collective title of "Tumblers, Pouters and Fantails," but these did not reach print in *Poetry* until May 1915. Her formal debut in the literary world came on April 1, 1915. The London magazine *The Egoist*, often receptive to Imagists—indeed, H.D. was then assistant editor—published her two poems "To a Man Working His Way Through the Crowd" and "To the Soul of 'Progress.' " Moore's poems in *Poetry* are chiefly exercises in versecraft, akin to her Bryn Mawr pieces. *The Egoist* poems, however, strike a new direction, the first celebrating the artist's "lynx-eyed" certainty, the other assailing the "millstone" mindlessness of war. Moore's early appearance in magazines cordial to Imagists explains largely why literary history has assigned her to their company. In later years she disavowed any formal literary ties whatsoever.

The poetic movement in Chicago soon diverted its surplus vitality to Greenwich Village, where experimental magazines flourished. Alfred Kreymborg, rebuffed by *Poetry*, edited *The Globe*, to be followed by *Others*, which encouraged poets, especially those unknown others working in the new forms. In his autobiography, *Troubadour*, Kreymborg described the artists' circle around him which Marianne Moore frequently joined. He lingered to remember her, "an astonishing person with Titian hair, a brilliant complexion and a mellifluous flow of polysyllables which held every man in awe." William Carlos Williams, in his *Autobiography*, recalled that "Marianne was our saint—if we had one—in whom we all instinctively felt our purpose come together to form a stream. Everyone loved her."

The December 1915 issue of *Others* published five of Moore's poems, a widely experimental group, and she began to publish in the yearly *Others Anthology* as well. When Kreymborg's interest in poetry waned, she turned back to *The Egoist*, engaging the notice of T. S. Eliot, an assistant editor in 1917. Meanwhile her appearance in that year's *Others Anthology* led Ezra Pound to praise her for "logopoeia or poetry . . . which is a dance of the intelligence among words and ideas." In 1918, coaxing her into the literary circle, Pound offered to steer a book of her verse into print but cautioned: "You will never sell more than five hundred copies, as your work demands mental attention." Marianne Moore was all diffidence in her answer: "My

work jerks and rears and I cannot get up enthusiasm for embalming what I myself accept conditionally." With this self-appraisal she withdrew from Pound's proposal despite the fact that her poems had been appearing on both sides of the Atlantic since 1915.

Others was defunct by 1919, but in November of that year Scofield Thayer and Dr. James Sibley Watson, both men of private wealth and of artistic commitment, bought control of *The Dial*, announcing their intention to convert the political journal into a magazine devoted to the fine arts. Several months later Marianne Moore was welcomed into the circle of *The Dial*, which became the foremost American literary group in the twenties: in the April 1920 issue her poem "England" appeared, recalling "England/ with its baby rivers and little towns."

In 1921, without her knowledge and without her consent, the Egoist Press in London published her first booklet of twenty-four *Poems*, the collection "made and arranged by H.D. and Mr. and Mrs. Robert McAlmon." This note of accreditation with which Moore prefaced *Observations* (1924), the American edition of this book with additions, suggests her nicety of mind. She later amended her literary debt solely to H.D. and Bryher (the pen name of novelist Winifred Ellerman McAlmon). Curiously, H.D. and Marianne Moore had been classmates at Bryn Mawr but known to one another only by sidelong glances. In 1915 H.D. had written to ask whether Marianne Moore was indeed the same medieval lady in green dress she recalled from the Bryn Mawr May Fête freshman year.

Starting with *Observations*, Moore's books included notes which itemized her indebtedness to sources, many in family conversation. Her mother's sayings—aphoristic, biblical, caustic—became the substance of her diary jottings. Beginning in 1914, her notebooks comment tellingly on the Moores' day-by-day life at home and outside. Another series of diaries meticulously registers Marianne Moore's reading from 1907 to 1969, with sentences, even paragraphs, copied out in her "Kufic script." These private diaries became the wellsprings of her poetry. Some were as pinpointedly indexed as *Observations*: "spectrum, a fish, 20; as food, 11." Clearly, Marianne Moore's stint with Melvil Dewey's index staff had imprinted itself upon her intellectual regimen.

Moore's publication of *Observations* brought her *The Dial* Award of 1924, given in 1922 to T. S. Eliot. With this announcement came considerable prestige as well as two thousand dollars. Marianne Moore had noticeably stepped forward into the American literary scene.

The Dial was to absorb almost all of Moore's

creative energy until it ceased publication in 1929. Her writings—poems, book reviews, essays on art and literature—flowed into its issues. She came to function as an editorial mind, picking and choosing along with Thayer and Watson until her editorship became fact in 1925 when she began to write the monthly editorial "Comment." She left a loving memory, "*The Dial*: A Retrospect," chronicling both its fastidiousness and the generosity it fostered. But nowhere did she mention the vexations she encountered as Watson and Thayer became inaccessible, pursuing other interests. In July 1929 *The Dial* quietly announced its end. That year Warner Moore, now a commander in the navy, was reassigned to the Brooklyn Navy Yard. Marianne and Mary Warner Moore followed close behind, reestablishing themselves at 260 Cumberland Street, where literary callers continued to seek out the pair.

It remained for T. S. Eliot to escort Moore to fuller literary prominence. In 1935 her *Selected Poems* was published with Eliot's introduction, a gentle and deeply felt testament to her "original sensibility and alert intelligence and deep feeling." Eliot pointed out her masterful use of light rhyme (she herself came to call it "soft rhyme"), which lent her poems the elegant movement of a minuet. Yet in her "complicated, formal patterns" he failed to note the presence of syllabic verse, each poem uniquely shaped, like a snowflake. Her two-part poem "The Jerboa" measures out into stanzas repeating 5–5–6–11–10–7 syllables each line. Lapses occur, some due to the needs of revision. But her precision of mind sought to trace an exact shape for each poem. Significantly, *Selected Poems* carried "A Postscript," in which M.C.M. obliquely credited that one member of her family "who thinks in a particular way . . . in these pages, the thinking and often the actual phrases are hers."

With the publication of her slim volume *The Pangolin and Other Verse* (1936), Marianne Moore now stood at half century, her place in literary history assured despite the modesty that was her lifelong calling card. Although lionized in later life, Moore passed her major years in quiet devotion to her mother, her brother, and her art of poetry. Other slim volumes followed: *What Are Years* in 1941 and *Nevertheless* in 1944. Their contents detail animal lore and objects of virtu alongside such poems as "What Are Years?" and "In Distrust of Merits," poems of moral gravity, no doubt prompted by World War II. In 1946 she received a grant of one thousand dollars from the American Academy of Arts and Letters and began a translation of La Fontaine's Fables. Her election to the National Institute of Arts and Letters followed in 1947, the year which broke the enchanted family circle: in July, after long illness, Mary Warner Moore died at the age of eighty-five. Moore's *Collected Poems* in 1951 was dedicated to her mother.

The year 1952 started a shower of poetry prizes: the Bollingen Prize, the National Book Award, the Pulitzer Prize; and in 1953 the Gold Medal for Poetry from the National Institute of Arts and Letters. *The Fables of La Fontaine*, which had possessed her for almost ten years, reached publication in 1954; *Predilections*, a sampler of essays, in 1955. That year she was elected one of the chosen-fifty of the American Academy of Arts and Letters. More slim volumes followed: *Like a Bulwark* (1956), *O To Be a Dragon* (1959), *A Marianne Moore Reader* (1961). In 1962 a dramatic version of Maria Edgeworth's *The Absentee* appeared along with Moore's retelling of *Puss in Boots, The Sleeping Beauty & Cinderella*. *The Arctic Ox* came in 1964, then *Tell Me, Tell Me* in 1966.

Changing neighborhood conditions in Brooklyn led Warner Moore to urge Marianne to leave the Cumberland Street apartment in 1966, after thirty-seven years, and to return to Greenwich Village. Now in her seventies Moore was truly the majesty of American poets, courted and quoted on all sides. The *Life* magazine public recognized her in tricorn hat and flowing cape, photographed at the Central Park Zoo or at Yankee Stadium, rooting for the Brooklyn Dodgers. But poetry readers knew her for her elegant disquisitions, weaving fact into patterns of moral certitude. Her taste for obliquity and her deep sense of privacy often combined to riddle her meaning. In 1967 her *Complete Poems* was published with the forestatement "Omissions are not accidents. M.M.," referring to her firm withdrawal of poems from the canon and to her no-nonsense revision of other poems.

In February 1972, Marianne Moore died in New York City at the age of eighty-four. Her funeral service, held at her former neighborhood church, the Lafayette Avenue Presbyterian Church of Brooklyn, was "An Act of Thanksgiving to Almighty God for the Life and Work of Marianne Craig Moore." The occasion was witnessed by a royal blue-bound booklet, its cover gold-stamped with her lines: "Beauty is everlasting/ and dust is for a time."

[The Moore family holdings—letters, poetry MSS., the conversation notebooks and reading diaries, even "The Enchanted Forest" itself—were acquired in 1969 by the Philip H. and A. S. W. Rosenbach Foundation in Philadelphia. *The Marianne Moore Newsletter*, published semiannually since 1977 by the Rosenbach Foundation, offers choice pieces from its Moore Archives. [Ruth Stephan], "Selections from a Poet's Reading Diary and Sketchbooks," in *The Tiger's Eye*, Oct. 1947, provides an indication of the riches now banked in those archives. Until scholars can piece together the mosaic of Moore's mind and poetic art, the most trustworthy authority on Moore is Moore herself. Several first-person pieces are available: Donald Hall's interview with her in the *Paris Rev.*, Winter 1961, and his second interview in *McCall's*, Dec. 1965; Moore's "Ten Answers" (to questions by George Plimpton) in *Harper's*, Nov. 1964, and her *Poetry and Criticism* (1965); Grace Shulman's "Conversation with Marianne Moore" in *Quarterly Rev. of Lit.*, XVI (1969), nos. 1–2. More literary in form is Winthrop Sargeant's profile, "Humility, Concentration, and Gusto," in the *New Yorker*, Feb. 16, 1957; it should be read alongside the poet's own intricately rewritten copy of that issue in the Moore Archives. Moore's letters of the 1960s indicate that she was then working on a memoir, which the Rosenbach Foundation plans to edit for publication. The first checklist for scholars was *The Achievement of Marianne Moore: A Bibliography 1907–1957*, comp. E. P. Sheehy and K. A. Lohf for the New York Public Library (1958). It has been swallowed, errors and all, by Craig S. Abbott in *Marianne Moore: A Descriptive Bibliography* (1977). Abbott has also assembled *Marianne Moore: A Reference Guide* (1978). Of special help to textual scholars is *A Concordance to the Poems of Marianne Moore*, ed. Gary Lane (1972), although this concordance has been derived from Moore's *Complete Poems* in which her textual omissions and revisions were drastic. The work of poets and critics who delight in Moore's art of poetry include several omnium-gatherum volumes: the Marianne Moore issue of the *Quart. Rev. of Lit.*, IV (1948), no. 2; Tambimuttu, ed., *Festschrift for Marianne Moore's Seventy Seventh Birthday* (1964); Charles Tomlinson, ed., *Marianne Moore* (1969). Also useful are a pamphlet by Jean Garrigue, *Marianne Moore* (1965); Nicholas Joost, *Years of Transition: The Dial, 1912–1920* (1967); A. Kingsley Weatherhead, *The Edge of the Image* (1967); Donald Hall, *Marianne Moore: The Cage and the Animal* (1970). The first study based on a search of the Moore Archives is Laurence Stapleton, *Marianne Moore: The Poet's Advance* (1978). An obituary and a tribute appeared in the *N.Y. Times*, Feb. 6, 1972.]

S. V. BAUM

MOOREHEAD, Agnes, Dec. 6, 1900–April 30, 1974. Actress.

Agnes Moorehead was one of the few actresses of this century who had the courage to sublimate her image to her craft. Throughout her forty-four-year career, Moorehead acted primarily in character parts: the neurotic mother, the spinster aunt, the dowager queen. To each role—whether on stage, in radio, in film, or on television—Moorehead brought the same high degree of professionalism. Her forceful nature,

near-perfect diction, and gothic beauty impressed critics and audience alike, and secured for her a place in film history.

Agnes Moorehead was born in Clinton, Mass., the older of two daughters of Presbyterian minister John Robertson and Marie (McCauley) Moorehead, a one-time professional singer. Of Scottish and Irish ancestry, she was strongly influenced by her father's religious and educational views and by her mother's keen appreciation of the lively arts. The family moved to Hamilton, Ohio, in 1904. Eight years later they moved again, to St. Louis where Agnes attended public school and first performed on stage, in summer theater.

Though even as a child she knew she wanted to be an actress, Moorehead took her father's advice and first obtained a formal education before embarking on an acting career. From 1920 to 1923 she attended Muskingum College, a religious college founded by her uncle, near her family's farm in New Concord, Ohio; she was granted an A.B. degree in 1928. Moorehead taught school in Soldier's Grove, Wis., and performed on radio in St. Louis—where she was heard as "the female tenor"—before enrolling at the American Academy of Dramatic Arts in New York City in 1927. Two years later she graduated with honors.

Moorehead began her acting career in 1929 with minor roles for Theatre Guild productions, but the depression forced her into broadcasting. This economic necessity proved fortunate as her work during radio's golden age brought her widespread acclaim. A consistently hard worker, Moorehead was in thousands of radio shows, often as many as six a day. She appeared regularly in such shows as "Cavalcade of America," "The Shadow," and "March of Time." In the latter series she occasionally portrayed then first lady ELEANOR ROOSEVELT—the only actress allowed to do so. Moorehead was one of the women screaming in the background in the Mercury Theatre of the Air's 1938 production of "War of the Worlds." Her performance did not go unnoticed; Orson Welles and John Houseman invited Moorehead to join the Mercury Players, and she was quick to accept. Following stage productions of *Dear Abigail* and *Julius Caesar*, the group moved to Hollywood in 1940.

Moorehead credited Welles with her success in film: "He thought I could play anything . . . if it was a strange part, he said, 'Give it to Agnes. She can play it' " (Steen, p. 108). Roles in two Welles films established her reputation: the first was her vivid and imaginative portrayal of Kane's mother in *Citizen Kane* (1941). For her role as the neurasthenic Aunt Fanny in *The*

Magnificent Ambersons (1942), she won both the New York Film Critics' Award and an Academy Award nomination. The public's response to Moorehead's characterization led directly to her radio appearance the next year in Suspense Theatre's "Sorry, Wrong Number," a performance "rarely, if ever equalled on the air." She repeated this role many times and, although she was not offered the film role, her recording of it later won a gold record.

Most of Moorehead's income throughout her career came from films; during the 1940s her average earnings were over $6,000 a week. Although she often appeared in lesser films, she did receive three more Oscar nominations—all for supporting roles—in *Mrs. Parkington* (1944), *Johnny Belinda* (1948), and *Hush . . . Hush, Sweet Charlotte* (1964).

For three seasons (1951–53) Moorehead appeared as part of the First Drama Quartet, which also included Charles Boyer, Cedric Hardwicke, and Charles Laughton. She considered their international tour of *Don Juan in Hell* the highlight of her acting career. First staged in 1951, *Don Juan in Hell* was often revived, the last time in 1972. The association with Laughton, like that with Welles, sustained Moorehead in her professional life. At Laughton's suggestion, she put together a one-woman show, "The Redhead." Comprised of bits and pieces from sources as varied as the Bible and James Thurber, the show had a United States tour in 1954. She traveled with it intermittently for the next ten years, and later took a revised version, "Come Closer, I'll Give You an Earful," on an international tour.

Moorehead continued to move with ease from one entertainment medium to another. Making the transition to television, she gained wide recognition for her role as Endora in the series "Bewitched" from 1963 to 1971. Although she was nominated four times for an Emmy for that role, her only television award, for best actress in a single performance, was given for her appearance in an episode of "Wild, Wild West." She concluded her career teaching in her own acting school and lecturing on acting techniques at various colleges. Her final stage appearance was in the 1973 revival of *Gigi*.

In 1930 Agnes Moorehead married John G. Lee, an actor she had met while studying dramatics. A continuous disparity between their professional successes made the union difficult. Shortly after adopting a son, Sean (b. 1949), they were divorced in 1952. The next year Moorehead married Robert Gist, also an actor and many years her junior. They were soon separated but not divorced until 1958. Unlike most actresses, Moorehead was reticent about her private life, believing it was better to remain a mystery to the public. She was not without personal vanity or eccentricity—she insisted that her favorite color, mauve, be used whenever possible.

In her later years Moorehead's deeply ingrained religious beliefs surfaced as a kind of fundamentalism, leading to conflict with her son during the 1960s. Agnes Moorehead died of cancer in 1974 at the Rochester (Minn.) Methodist Hospital. At her request, she was buried in Ohio next to her father.

[The extensive Agnes Moorehead Coll., bequeathed to the Univ. of Wis., Madison, is on reserve at the State Hist. Soc. of Wis. It contains used and rejected scripts, personal correspondence, performance paraphernalia, and more than 100 scrapbooks, a few going back as far as 1928. The only full-length biography, written from a fundamentalist viewpoint, is Warren Sherk, *Agnes Moorehead, A Very Private Person* (1976). Calvin Beck, *Scream Queens* (1978), devotes a chapter to Moorehead, and a brief oral history, "The Character Player: Agnes Moorehead," is in Mike Steen, *Hollywood Speaks!* (1975). The most comprehensive (and responsible) single treatment is by Ronald Bowers in *Films in Review*, May 1966; he details Agnes Moorehead's personal life and career. An article by Bowers after Moorehead's death also appears in the Aug.-Sept. 1974 issue of *Films in Review*. Among the numerous magazine articles about Moorehead are those in *Life*, June 9, 1947, and Nov. 5, 1951; *Newsweek*, Feb. 3, 1947; *Time*, Sept. 10, 1945; *TV Guide*, July 17, 1965; and *Cue*, Oct. 21, 1944. Of the fan magazines, *Photoplay* had the least sensational pieces (July 1970, Dec. 1971, and Aug. 1974). A discussion of "Sorry, Wrong Number" appeared in *Life*, Sept. 24, 1945. See also *New Yorker*, April 19, 1952; *Sight and Sound*, Aug. 1955; *Current Biog.*, 1952; and *Biog. Encyc. and Who's Who of the Am. Theatre* (1966). An obituary appeared in the *N.Y. Times*, May 2, 1974. Moorehead manipulated biographical accounts of her personal life, often contriving or fabricating details; therefore, sources, especially those concerning her education, are generally unreliable. Her date of birth is most often given as 1909; the 1900 date is verified by a birth certificate provided by the town clerk, Clinton, Mass.; death record from Minn. Dept. of Health. Family information was given by Alice Flinn.]

MARSHA MC CREADIE

MORGAN, Agnes Fay, May 4, 1884–July 20, 1968. Biochemist, nutritionist.

Agnes Fay Morgan was born Jane Agnes Fay in Peoria, Ill., the third of four children of Patrick John Fay and his second wife, Mary (Dooley) Fay. Both parents came from poor but landowning families in Galway, Ireland. On coming to the United States, Patrick Fay worked first as a laborer, but later became a builder. Although neither of her two brothers attended college, Agnes Fay was such an outstanding student at Peoria High School that she received a full college scholarship from a local benefactor. She started at Vassar College, but soon transferred to the University of Chicago, where she received a B.S. in chemistry in 1904 and an M.S. in 1905. Her mentor was Julius O. Stieglitz, noted analytical chemist and chairman of the department, who encouraged her to analyze foodstuffs. It was several years, however, before Fay realized that there was a future for a woman chemist in the fledgling field of nutrition. First she taught chemistry at Hardin College in Mexico, Mo. (1905–06), the University of Montana (1907–08), and the University of Washington (1910–12), where she organized an honor society for women in chemistry.

While at Montana, in 1908, Agnes Fay married Arthur Ivason Morgan, a student of Latin and Greek, who was also a high school teacher and football coach. Theirs was a very stable marriage, and neither dominated the other. She followed him to a teaching job in Seattle, but three years later he actively encouraged her to return to Chicago to get her Ph.D. in physical and organic chemistry, which she received in 1914. The following year, Agnes Morgan accepted an offer from University of California president Benjamin Ide Wheeler, and the couple moved to Berkeley.

Morgan's initial position was as assistant professor in the division of nutrition in the College of Agriculture. In 1919 she and Mary Patterson became cochairmen of a newly established department in the College of Letters and Science; Morgan was in charge of household science and Patterson of household arts. By 1923, the year her only child, Arthur Ivason, Jr., was born, Morgan was a full professor. But she was restless. She did not believe that "arts" belonged in home economics, as her field was then called, and eventually household arts became a separate department named decorative arts. In 1938 the by-then vastly expanded department of household science became the department of home economics, and in 1951 it was again divided, with food science moving to the Davis campus and nutritional science staying in Berkeley. Morgan chaired both departments until her retirement in 1954. From 1938 until 1954 she also held the title of biochemist in the Agricultural Experiment Station.

Morgan later recalled that when she first came to Berkeley, the field of nutrition was so new that she immediately started several research projects in order to have "something to teach." Still, she organized what meager material was available and in 1915 introduced the first scientific human nutrition course at the uni-

versity. A stern but evenhanded teacher, Morgan expected much from her students. Hers was the first home economics department to make chemistry an integral part of the curriculum. She required students to take a special biochemistry course as a prerequisite for her course in nutrition, and saw to it that they were well grounded in research methods.

Morgan maintained a very active research laboratory and ensured that her colleagues did the same. The bulk of her research was addressed to problems of practical concern in nutrition and food chemistry, such as the nutrient content of foods and the stability of proteins and of vitamins during food processing, storage, and preparation. She was also concerned with establishing standards for adequate human nutrition. Her basic research focused on the effects of vitamin D, parathyroid hormone, and composition of the diet on calcium and phosphorus metabolism, and on the metabolic action of the B vitamins, and of ascorbic acid and carotene. Her most outstanding contribution, independently observed by others as well, was the finding that pantothenic acid (a B vitamin) was essential for adrenal function and for normal pigmentation of hair and skin. Ever alert to practical implications, she immediately suggested that silver fox, then a fashionable fur, could be produced artificially by incipient pantothenic acid deficiency. Morgan's contributions to basic research earned her the prestigious Garvan Medal of the American Chemical Society in 1949 and the Borden Award from the American Institute of Nutrition (AIN) in 1954. In 1951 Berkeley colleagues chose her to be the faculty research lecturer, the first woman to be so honored, and in 1959 she was elected the eleventh fellow of the AIN.

Agnes Fay Morgan's real love, however, was administration. Of all her accomplishments she was proudest of having built up one of the foremost home economics departments in the country, which was housed in a magnificent new building dedicated in 1961 as Agnes Fay Morgan Hall. She also organized and chaired numerous national and international meetings and symposia on nutrition. As nutritional adviser for several governors, Morgan was responsible for a 1939 study of the food at San Quentin Prison and in 1960 served on a committee which investigated the toxic effects of agricultural pesticides. During World War II she initiated and chaired the California Nutrition War Committee (1940–42) and worked for the United States Office of Scientific Research and Development (1942–45), studying the nutritive value of dehydrated food. Tireless as an advocate for scientific nutrition, she fought food faddists and quacks. At

Berkeley she founded Alpha Nu, a local honor society for women in home economics, as well as a national society for women in chemistry, Iota Sigma Pi.

Agnes Fay Morgan was an outstanding politician, and she brought to all her activities a measure of detachment, never being so emotionally involved as to make compromise impossible. She is remembered as "easy to get along with and surprisingly pleasant to be with" by her son, an international authority on foods in his own right. Morgan remained fully active in academic and public affairs until her death of a heart attack in Berkeley in 1968.

[Morgan's professional papers, in the Bancroft Library, Univ. of Calif., Berkeley, contain correspondence, reports, MSS. of papers and speeches, reprints of articles, her unpublished "History of Nutrition and Home Economics in the University of California, Berkeley, 1914–1962," research and lecture notes, photographs, and other material. The department of nutrition, Univ. of Calif., Berkeley, has a bibliography and curriculum vitae. She was the author of over 250 articles and, with Irene Sanborn Hall, *Experimental Food Study* (1938), a textbook on food preparation. She also wrote the histories of several of the societies in which she had been active, including a *Directory and History of the Alpha Nu Honor Society* (1927, 1940), and *A History of Iota Sigma Pi, National Honor Society for Women in Chemistry* (1963). Biographical sketches include Ruth Okey, Barbara Kennedy Johnson, and Gordon MacKinney, "Agnes Fay Morgan, 1884–1968," *In Memoriam,* Univ. of Calif., May 1969; "Biographical Notes from History of Nutrition, Agnes Fay Morgan, May 4, 1884–July 20, 1968," *Jour. Am. Dietetic Assoc.,* Dec. 1968; Wyndham D. Miles, *American Chemists and Chemical Engineers* (1976), pp. 348–49. A summary of her career as well as assessments of her work are included in "Landmarks of a Half Century of Nutrition Research: A Symposium Honoring Doctor Agnes Fay Morgan's Fiftieth Anniversary at the Univ. of Calif., May 8, 1965," *Jour. Nutrition,* Feb. 1967, Supp. 1, part II. An obituary appeared in the *N.Y. Times,* July 23, 1968. There is a portrait of Morgan in the entrance hall of Agnes Fay Morgan Hall, Univ. of Calif., Berkeley. Additional information for this article was provided by Arthur I. Morgan, Jr. Death certificate supplied by Calif. Dept. of Health Services.]

I. D. RAACKE

MORGAN, Ann Haven, May 6, 1882–June 5, 1966. Zoologist, ecologist.

Ann Morgan was born in Waterford, Conn., the elder daughter and first of three children of Stanley Griswold and Julia (Douglass) Morgan. As a child she loved to explore the woods and streams near her home. After completing her secondary education at Williams Memorial Institute in New London, she entered Wellesley

College in 1902. She transferred two years later to Cornell University, where she received her A.B. in 1906.

After college, Ann Morgan served three years as an assistant and instructor in zoology at Mount Holyoke College before returning to Cornell for graduate study. She received her Ph.D. in 1912 with a dissertation on the biology of mayflies, directed by James G. Needham at Cornell's Limnological Laboratory. Needham, she wrote later, helped her to see things in the water, a gift Morgan passed on in a series of publications, beginning in 1911, on the aquatic biology of insects. Her enthusiasm for her dissertation topic was such that freshmen in her general biology lab section at Cornell nicknamed her "Mayfly Morgan."

She returned to Mount Holyoke as an instructor in zoology, becoming an associate professor in 1914, and a full professor four years later. In 1916 Morgan was chosen chairman of the department of zoology, a position she retained until her retirement in 1947. While making her home at South Hadley, she devoted her summers to research and instruction at a variety of institutions, including the Marine Biological Laboratory at Woods Hole, Mass. (1918, 1919, 1921, 1923), and the Tropical Laboratory in Kartabo, British Guiana (1926).

Morgan thought of herself as a general zoologist rather than as a specialist in one of the field's narrower subdivisions. Although she first achieved distinction with her careful studies of aquatic insects, she progressively expanded her range to include the habits and conditions of hibernating animals and the broader issues of conservation and ecology. In all these pursuits she demonstrated the ability to communicate her observations and insights graphically to her audience—through lectures, scholarly articles, and books of general interest. The latter, enhanced by Morgan's clear, declarative prose and her equally instructive drawings and photographs, have enjoyed continuing popularity.

Morgan's *Field Book of Ponds and Streams: An Introduction to the Life of Fresh Water* (1930) has served readers in a number of ways. It introduced those new to the subject to the lively multitudes sheltered in rapidly flowing streams, and amateur naturalists have employed it to develop techniques for collecting, preserving, and mounting specimens. The book is more than a nature guide or taxonomic handbook, though. Morgan includes a full discussion of the habits and habitat of each animal group, emphasizing the concept of the ecological niche, or the specific place and function of the group in the wider ecosystem.

Similarly, Morgan's *Field Book of Animals in*

Winter (1939) combines an attention to detail with conceptual insights. While field work for the book was conducted primarily in the northeastern United States, its relevance goes beyond that geographical area to the basic ecological issue of how animals survive the rigors and crises of winter. Morgan later collaborated with Encyclopaedia Britannica Films to make "Animals in Winter" (1949), a film based on her book and designed for classroom use.

In the 1940s and 1950s Ann Haven Morgan devoted her energy to reforming the science curriculum. Eager to see ecology and conservation taught in schools and colleges in conjunction with such subjects as geography, zoology, and sociology, she gave a series of summer workshops for teachers in those fields and served on the National Committee on Policies in Conservation Education. Morgan brought her integrated, ecological perspective to bear in her last book, *Kinships of Animals and Man: A Textbook of Animal Biology* (1955). Written to serve introductory zoology courses, the work explores the concept of kinship as it relates both to behavior patterns within specific animal groups and to the competitive and cooperative relationships between those groups. Her text stresses the need, finally, for human beings to cooperate with and preserve their natural environment: "Now that the wilderness is almost gone, we are beginning to be lonesome for it. We shall keep a refuge in our minds if we conserve the remnants."

Ann Haven Morgan died of stomach cancer at her home in South Hadley, Mass., at the age of eighty-four. Until the end of her life she continued to work as a science educator, expressing concern about the global threats to the natural habitat while supporting local conservation efforts in the Connecticut River Valley she knew so well.

[Morgan's first articles, on mayflies, appear in the June 1911 and June 1912 issues of *Annals of the Entomological Soc. of America;* her dissertation, "A Contribution to the Biology of May-flies," can be found in the Sept. 1913 issue of the same journal, pp. 371–413. Reports of her research and abstracts related to aquatic biology, physiology, and winter biology appear in *Anatomical Record,* 1926, 1927, 1929, 1930, 1932, 1933, 1935; some of these papers were jointly authored. See also two articles by Morgan on science teaching, published in *Mount Holyoke Alumnae Quart.:* "Science and the New Curriculum," April 1930; and her tribute to Cornelia Maria Clapp, "An Adventure in Teaching," May 1935. Morgan is included in *Am. Men of Science,* 5th ed. (1933). Her selection as one of three women among 250 leading scientists in that edition is discussed in *Time,* March 20, 1933, p. 38. See also *Am. Men and Women of Science,* 10th ed. (1961). Obit-

uaries appeared in *N.Y. Times,* June 6, 1966, and *Holyoke* (Mass.) *Transcript-Telegram,* June 6, 1966. A tribute to Morgan by Charles P. Alexander appeared in *Eatonia,* a newsletter for ephemeropterists published jointly by the Univ. of Utah and Florida A & M Univ., Feb. 15, 1967. Clippings and manuscript materials were supplied by Williston Memorial Library, Mount Holyoke College; records by Cornell Univ. Archives; biobibliography by Annette G. Brownlee; and personal information by Isabelle B. Sprague. Death certificate furnished by Mass. Dept. of Public Health. Morgan used the name Anna until after she received the Ph.D.]

MURIEL BLAISDELL

MORGAN, Anne Tracy, July 25, 1873–Jan. 29, 1952. Philanthropist.

Known chiefly for her extensive organization of relief work in France during and after two world wars, Anne Morgan was the third daughter and youngest of four children of international financier John Pierpont Morgan and Frances Louisa (Tracy) Morgan. Born on her family's estate at Highland Falls, N.Y., Morgan was educated at home and in New York private schools. She led a secluded life till late in her twenties; when questioned as a child, however, as to what she planned to be, she announced that she planned never to marry and would be "something better than a rich fool, anyway" (Lehr, pp. 17–18).

In 1903, with a group of socially prominent women under the leadership of FLORENCE JAFFRAY HARRIMAN, Morgan helped to found the Colony Club in New York. This was the city's first social club for women and its clubhouse provided members with the facilities commonly afforded men by their clubs. Anne Morgan did not restrict herself to such socially exclusive projects, however. In 1909 she worked with the women's division of the National Civic Federation to establish a clubroom and restaurant in the Brooklyn Navy Yard where nutritious food was served at cost to workers. In the same year Morgan, an advocate of trade unions, actively supported women shirtwaist strikers and worked as a volunteer factory inspector in New York and New Jersey, examining working conditions for women. This led her, in 1910, to take an active role in founding the Working Girls' Vacation Association (later the American Woman's Association), designed to help working women save for much-needed vacations.

While organizing the Colony Club, Morgan became close friends with ELISABETH MARBURY, a theatrical and literary agent. Through Marbury, Morgan began to emerge from the seclusion of her youth and to meet professional and creative people both in the United States and at the Villa Trianon, a house near Versailles owned jointly by Marbury and the decorator ELSIE DE WOLFE.

By 1913, when Morgan inherited three million dollars from her father's estate, she had bought Marbury's interest in the Villa Trianon and had added a wing. When war broke out in 1914, Morgan and De Wolfe offered the French government the use of the house, thus beginning the relief and reconstruction work in France that was to make Morgan internationally famous. A founder of the American Fund for French Wounded, in 1917 she was active in forming the American Committee for Devastated France, and served as its executive chairman. The first goal of this organization was the restoration of the devastated region of Aisne, northeast of Paris. By 1918, 7,500 acres had been restored and planted and more than 800 farms reconstructed. After the armistice the committee continued its work of agricultural rehabilitation and also established health centers, kindergartens, orphanages, libraries, community centers, and camps. Between 1918 and 1924 the organization raised and disbursed over five million dollars for medical aid, food, and reconstruction. The American Committee's original headquarters, the chateau of Blérancourt near Soissons, was later made a Franco-American museum through Morgan's efforts. She was awarded the Croix de Guerre with palms by the French government in 1917 and was made Commander of the Legion of Honor in 1932, the first American woman thus honored.

Morgan resumed her work with the American Woman's Association in 1924, heading a fund-raising committee for a projected New York clubhouse. This campaign to provide a home and recreational facilities for 1,200 professional women of moderate means succeeded beyond predictions. In 1928, the year the twenty-seven-story clubhouse opened, Morgan became president of the association, an office she held until 1943.

Convinced that another European war was inevitable, Morgan founded the American Friends of France (AFF), a committee that was to be concerned chiefly with feeding and sheltering noncombatants. By the time hostilities broke out in 1939, three relief centers had been set up to receive evacuees from areas near the Maginot line. The AFF, with Morgan's leadership, later helped to evacuate large numbers of refugees into unoccupied territory. Morgan was forced to leave France in early 1940 but returned in 1941, 1945, and 1946 to survey relief needs. She continued her war relief work until 1948, when, in ill health, she retired to her Mount

Kisco, N.Y., estate. She died there of a heart attack in 1952.

Tall, handsome, an incessant smoker with a deep voice and a commanding presence, Morgan possessed unusual executive ability. Indefatigably active, she considered leisure dangerous. She inherited not only her father's energy but also his antipathy for publicity; yet she was willing to come under public scrutiny for the sake of her work. In 1921 she sponsored the Benny Leonard–Ritchie Mitchell prize fight to benefit the American Committee for Devastated France, raising several thousand dollars and enduring much public criticism in the process. A lifetime member of St. George's Episcopal Church in New York, she also belonged to the Society of Colonial Dames and, in spite of taking little interest in politics, to the Women's National Republican Club. Though she disclaimed being a feminist, many of the projects to which she contributed both her organizational ability and money were designed to benefit working and professional women. In 1927, she envisaged a time when women "will take their places beside men as partners, unafraid, useful, successful and free."

[Articles by Morgan include "The American Girl: Her Education, Her Responsibilities, Her Recreation, Her Future," *Woman's Home Companion*, Nov., Dec. 1914, and Feb., April 1915; "Women Must Choose: Safety or Adventure in Business," *Good Housekeeping*, May 1932; "Rekindling Home Fires in France," *Delineator*, Feb. 1918; "What Must Be Done in France," *Forum*, May 1918. With Mary Margaret McBride, Morgan wrote "Sidelights on the Woman Question," March 26, 1927 (from which the final quote is taken), and "Copy Cats," Oct. 6, 1928, both in the *Sat. Eve. Post*. For articles about Morgan see Margaret K. Leech, "Profiles: Lady Into Dynamo," *New Yorker*, Oct. 22, 1927; Mary F. Watkins, "Anne Morgan: An Intimate Portrait," *The Woman Citizen*, Aug. 1927; and "A Life of Rebuilding the Wreckage of War," *Life*, Feb. 11, 1952. For additional information see Elizabeth Drexel Lehr, *King Lehr and the Gilded Age* (1935); Elisabeth Marbury, *My Crystal Ball* (1923); Elsie De Wolfe, *After All* (1935); Herbert L. Satterlee, *J. Pierpont Morgan: An Intimate Portrait* (1939); *Nat. Cyc. Am. Biog.*, E, 333; *Current Biog.*, 1946; *Dict. Am. Biog.*, Supp. Five. Morgan's obituary appeared in the *N.Y. Times*, Jan. 30, 1952; death record provided by N.Y. State Dept. of Health. Also helpful were the personal recollections of Aileen Osborn Webb.]

MARY TOLFORD WILSON

MORGAN, Julia, Jan. 26, 1872–Feb. 2, 1957. Architect.

Julia Morgan, whose prolific and trailblazing career helped open the field of architecture for women, was born in San Francisco and raised in Oakland, Calif., the second in a family of two girls and three boys. Her father, Charles Bill Morgan, was a native of Litchfield, Conn., who dabbled in various ventures in San Francisco with negligible success. The family's comfortable life style was underwritten by the inheritance of Julia's mother, Eliza (Parmalee) Morgan, daughter of a millionaire cotton broker from New York. Of the two parents, Eliza Morgan exerted the stronger influence on the children, and she especially prodded her daughters to achieve. Both Julia and her younger sister, Emma, excelled early in scholarship. Though she was undersized and sickly, Julia defied her family's protectiveness, stealing forbidden workouts on her brothers' athletic equipment and performing daring athletic feats in the barn.

After graduating from Oakland High School, Morgan entered the University of California at Berkeley. Probably influenced by architect Pierre LeBrun, her mother's cousin and the designer of the Metropolitan Life Insurance Tower in New York, Morgan decided to study architecture. She became the first woman student in the University's College of Engineering, whose curriculum included subjects taught in architecture schools.

In her senior year she met Bernard Maybeck, who was to be one of the major influences in her life. Maybeck, then teaching descriptive geometry at the university, also taught an informal class in architecture in his home. It was probably there that Morgan formed a resolve to attend Maybeck's alma mater, the École des Beaux-Arts of Paris. Following her graduation from Berkeley in 1894, Morgan performed drafting assignments for Maybeck until her departure for Paris in 1896. She made at least two attempts to pass the École's entrance examination before she became, in 1898, the first woman to be admitted to its Architectural Section. Four years later, she was its first woman graduate.

Returning then to California, Morgan became the first woman in the state to be granted an architect's license. She worked for John Galen Howard on two University of California structures—a mining building and a Greek theater—both of them financed by PHOEBE APPERSON HEARST. Impressed by Morgan's talent, Phoebe Hearst commissioned her to remodel her own residence at Pleasanton and to collaborate with Maybeck in designing a castle and dependent "village" at Wyntoon. Mrs. Hearst is also believed to have influenced Morgan to open her own architecture office in San Francisco, in 1904.

Morgan, a shy but decisive young woman, found plenty of work, some of it steered to her

by Phoebe Hearst. Among her early commissions were a Mission-style bell tower for Mills College and several informal redwood shingle houses, notable for tasteful, unostentatious detailing without and for meeting a client's needs within. But the commission that established Morgan's reputation was the rebuilding of the luxurious Fairmont Hotel, which the 1906 earthquake-fire had left a charred and buckled ruin. After completing the Fairmont she was in demand for residences, stores, churches, offices, and educational buildings. Among the latter were the Berkeley Baptist Seminary and a library, gymnasium, and social hall for Mills College. Her rambling, shingled St. John's Presbyterian Church, a Berkeley architectural landmark, was built between 1908 and 1910.

Morgan worked in a variety of motifs, but increasingly her favorite style was Spanish Revival, which the newly available inexpensive cement made economic. Numerous commissions came from women and from women's institutions that took a feminist pride in her success. Among these was the YWCA, which commissioned her to design a series of residence halls in cities and towns throughout California and, in 1913, their Asilomar Conference Center at Pacific Grove, near Monterey. Although not a campaigning feminist, Morgan employed a number of women architects and draftsmen, many just out of school; she also gave anonymous financial aid to women students.

During the early years of her practice, Morgan took a partner, Ira W. Hoover, but their association was soon dissolved. After that Morgan never shared direction of her practice, preferring to maintain personal control over all aspects of her commissions. She ran her office in the atelier style she had known in Paris, making it a learning place for those who worked there.

After World War I she began her work for publisher William Randolph Hearst, who over the next two decades would provide nearly one-third of the work of her entire career. In 1919 he commissioned Morgan to build a castle and guest houses on the Hearst family ranch at San Simeon, midway between San Francisco and Los Angeles. It was a challenging and unprecedented task that required incorporating architectural sections of castles and monasteries that Hearst had purchased in Europe. Hearst also commissioned Morgan to design newspaper facilities for him in San Francisco and Los Angeles, and additional pleasure palaces in California and Mexico. In order to handle her Hearst commissions while continuing her regular practice, Morgan increased her staff to thirty-five and engaged a plane and pilot.

Morgan's dedication to her work was such that she had virtually no other interests; her social life was restricted to her family. She lived in San Francisco, but frequently ferried across the Bay to Oakland to be with her reclusive mother and her married sister, who had taken a law degree but never practiced.

The volume of her work reached its peak in the late 1920s, despite the debilitating effects of a maladroit mastoid operation that left her face permanently distorted and her speech and balance impaired. In 1929 came the erection of the handsome women's club-hotel, the Berkeley City Club, whose detailing echoed Hearst's castle at San Simeon. Hearst also endowed the construction of a women's gymnasium at the University of California, specifying that Morgan and Maybeck collaborate on it.

During the depression Morgan's was one of the few San Francisco architecture offices that did not have to retrench, even though the work for Hearst had almost ceased by the mid-1930s when his publishing empire fell into financial difficulty. She and Maybeck collaborated on designs for the new campus of Principia College at Elsah, Ill. Her YWCA work continued in California, and she also designed YWCAs in Salt Lake City and Honolulu. Many of the elegant touches of her palaces found their way into these admirably functional buildings by way of economical building materials. Morgan's skill with steel-reinforced concrete brought her all of the institutional work she could handle until the advent of World War II, with its labor and material shortages. She reduced her practice during the war years, retiring in 1946. After that, she traveled extensively until her death of a stroke in San Francisco in 1957.

Julia Morgan was modest in the extreme and studiously avoided publicity in her lifetime. But architectural scholars have come to recognize her as one of the prime form-givers of her region in the first half of the twentieth century. Her work was outstanding not only for its thoroughness, diversity, and volume (more than 800 structures) but also for its stylistic innovation and influence. Her early redwood shingle houses contributed to the emergence of the Bay area shingle style. She was also a decade ahead of most of her contemporaries in using structure as a means of architectural expression. Unlike the work of most San Francisco architects of her time, Morgan's was reflective of that being done outside the Bay area. She did shun the International Style, which she felt was alien to her. Otherwise, she was creatively eclectic; though she drew suggestions from classical and other styles, her interpretations were always original.

[Collections of Julia Morgan's drawings are held by the Univ. of Calif. at Berkeley, in the Bancroft Library and in the Environmental Design Documents Coll. Early articles about Morgan include Jane Armstrong, "Woman Architect Who Helped Build the Fairmont Hotel," *Architect and Engineer of Calif.*, Oct. 1907; Walter T. Steilberg, "Some Examples of the Work of Julia Morgan," *Architect and Engineer*, Nov. 1918; Julian C. Mesic, "Berkeley City Women's Club," *Architect and Engineer*, April 1931. Later articles are Sara Boutelle, "The Long-Distance Dreamer Who Altered the Look of California," *Calif. Monthly*, April 1976; Bernice Scharlach, "The Legacy of Julia Morgan," in *Calif. Living Magazine*, the *San Francisco Sunday Examiner and Chronicle*, Aug. 24, 1975. Books with material on Julia Morgan are Oscar Lewis, *Fabulous San Simeon* (1958); Elinor Richey, *Eminent Women of the West* (1975); Richard W. Longstreth, *Julia Morgan Architect* (1977). Morgan's obituary appeared in the *Calif. Monthly*, May 1957; death record provided by Calif. Dept. of Public Health. Interviews with Julia Morgan's nephew Morgan North and his wife, and with Walter T. Steilberg, were a prime source for this article.]

ELINOR RICHEY

MOSES, Anna Mary Robertson (Grandma), Sept. 7, 1860–Dec. 13, 1961. Painter.

The primitive painter known as Grandma Moses was born near Greenwich, N.Y., one of ten children of a farm family. Her story established her as something of a myth: the startling and gratifying metamorphosis of an old, obscure country woman into an overnight artistic sensation and commercial success; but it is more interesting that her achievement is remarkably of a piece with the whole of her life.

In 1945, at the request of her agent, Otto Kallir, who handled the sales of her much-in-demand paintings, Grandma Moses was persuaded to "write" an autobiography. It is a painstaking, ungrammatical, misspelled, and inadequate effort, yet touching in the insights it affords, like her pride in her family heritage. Her ancestors, of Scots-Irish descent, were early emigrants to the area where she was born, New York where it borders on Vermont. Hezekiah King, her paternal great-grandfather, fought at Ticonderoga in the Revolutionary War. "From the Kings I got art, from the Robertsons inventive faculty, from the Shanahans thrift, the Devereaux generousity" ("I, Anna Mary Robertson," *American Primitive*). Her mother, Margaret (Shanahan) Robertson, was the daughter of more recent immigrants, who had come from Ireland in the 1830s. She describes her father, Russell King Robertson, as "a farmer and an inventor and beleaver in beauty and refindment." He liked to paint (one of his landscapes hung in Grandma Moses's house), and he encouraged his children to draw on sheets of white paper he bought for a penny. She squeezed grapes and berries to color her scenes, or utilized the red paint with which her father marked his sheep. About her efforts, her father "would say, 'oh, not so bad' but my mother was more practical, thought that I could spend my time other ways."

She left her home at age twelve to earn her living as a hired girl, describing the experience as "a grand education for me, in cooking, House Keeping, in moralizeing and mingleing with the out side world." Her only formal schooling was some scattered months in a country schoolhouse near her home. On Nov. 9, 1887, when she was twenty-seven, she married Thomas Salmon Moses, a farm worker. They moved south hoping to locate a more prosperous living, settling on a dairy farm in the Shenandoah Valley near Staunton, Va. She bore ten children there, five of whom died. Anna Mary Moses lived the typical days of a hard-working farmer's wife, her time consumed with birthing, mothering, cooking, baking, berrying, preserving, and attending to daily farm chores. During the lighter work periods of the winter months, she did carpet-weaving, quilting, and embroidering to earn extra dollars. She made butter into "pound prints," selling the product as far from home as Sulphur Springs, and she ventured into potato chips, "which was a novelty in those days."

In 1905 the couple and their five remaining children moved back to a farm in Eagle Bridge, N.Y., among their relations. Grandma Moses's husband died in 1927, when she was sixty-seven. She turned over the running of the farm to her youngest son, Hugh, but kept busy herself producing cookies, canned fruits, jams, rugs, yarn pictures, quilts, dolls. When arthritis set in and fine handwork became too painful to pursue, she turned back to "dabbling in oil." For her first painting intended for framing, her daughter-in-law reported that she found some exterior house paint and "an old piece of canvas which had been used for mending a threshing machine cover." She worked in her bedroom at an old kitchen table, under a single 150-watt light bulb. Later, she preferred "tempered presd wood, the harder the better . . . I go over this with linseed oil, then with three coats of flat white paint."

Along with her other products, her pictures were put on sale at the Woman's Exchange in Thomas's Drug Store in Hoosick Falls, N.Y. Louis Caldor, an art collector, saw Grandma Moses's work there while summering in the area in 1938. He bought those, inquired where the artist lived, went out to the farmhouse, and purchased fifteen additional paintings, three of which were included in an exhibit of "Contemporary Unknown American Painters" held in 1939 at the Museum of Modern Art. In October 1940, the Galerie St. Etienne in New York City, directed by Otto Kallir, set up a one-woman show. Grandma Moses became an immediate and overwhelming success. She was then eighty years old.

She had begun to paint by copying what was at hand—the sources she had used for her yarn pictures—Christmas and greeting cards, nineteenth-century color reproductions in the few books she had access to, illustrations and advertisements in magazines, and the Currier and Ives prints which most influenced her. But in a very short time she moved on to original subjects: scenes from her childhood held in idyllic and mythmaking tableau—apple picking, maple sugaring, arriving at Grandmother's for Thanksgiving, bringing in the Christmas tree from the snowy woods—and pristinely serene townscapes.

By 1943 there was a large commercial demand for the work of an artist so winning and congenial and so uniquely accessible to a wide public (even in price) in the simplicity of her style, her subjects, and the charm of her personal story. Her public responded to a strength that shone through her work, as luminous as the white undercoat with which she carefully prepared each painting, in the form of a victory snatched from the hardscrabble rural American existence—a victory with which other Americans identified in their quite different struggles. Each modest scene, seemingly aiming for nothing beyond a pleasing depiction, created for others a peaceable kingdom with which to connect, what Louis Bromfield called "a sense of space, and 'of the whole' . . . a satisfactory relationship with the universe" (Introduction, *American Primitive*). Her "primitivism" appealed as well to the ultrasophisticated; the composer Cole Porter was one of the earliest admirers and collectors of her work.

Though her work was shown at major museums, and is included in the permanent collection of the Metropolitan Museum of Art in New York, Grandma Moses's achievement has not been seriously discussed or appraised by disinterested art critics. She was entirely self-taught, never having "even seen a real painter at work. I mean one that has taken lessons." She seemed at a loss to describe the techniques by which she achieved her effects. Though she has been praised for her "decorative" qualities and "a kind of design and composition found in Persian and Moslem Indian paintings" (Bromfield), she is generally criticized for "faulty and awkward technique." It was widely reported that she painted belt-line fashion to fulfill "orders" for duplicates of particular paintings. Though she denied working on numbers of paintings at the same time, she did indeed make copies on demand and payment—a response which came directly and naturally out of her life as a working farmer and producer. She referred to them as "those dreadful orders" and preferred to create original works of the valleys in which she had lived—the Shenandoah and the brilliantly varied landscape of the New York–Vermont border country. She painted into her nineties, incredibly gaining in assurance and artistic discretion, producing in all about a thousand pictures of fair size and perhaps half as many postcard-sized. She was 101 when she died in Hoosick Falls, N.Y., of arteriosclerotic heart disease in December 1961. Two of her ten children survived her, along with nine grandchildren and thirty great-grandchildren.

[The autobiographical material drawn on for this article comes from the sketch, "I, Anna Mary Robertson," included in Otto Kallir, ed., *Grandma Moses: American Primitive*, with an introduction by Louis Bromfield (1973). This volume also includes biographical material supplied by Dorothy Harrison Moses, the daughter-in-law with whom Grandma Moses was living. An expanded autobiographical reminiscence, also edited by Otto Kallir, is *Grandma Moses: My Life's History* (1951). Harold Schoenberg's patronizing article, "Grandma Moses: A Portrait of the Artist at 99," appeared in the *N.Y. Times Mag.*, Sept. 6, 1959. See also William Howard Armstrong, *Grandma Moses* (1970); Katharine Kuh, "Grandma Moses," *Sat. Rev.*, Sept. 10, 1967; and Helen Yglesias, "Grandma Moses—Farmwife into Legend," *Starting: Early, Anew, Over, and Late* (1978). Her obituary appeared in the *N.Y. Times*, Dec. 14, 1961; death record provided by Office of the Registrar, Rensselaer Cty., N.Y.]

HELEN YGLESIAS

MUDGE, Isadore Gilbert, March 14, 1875–May 16, 1957. Librarian, bibliographer.

Isadore Mudge, authority on reference works and outstanding reference librarian of her day, was born in Brooklyn, N.Y., the first of three daughters and two sons of Alfred Eugene and Mary Gilbert (Ten Brook) Mudge, both natives of Ann Arbor, Mich. Her maternal grandfather, a Baptist minister, was a professor and later university librarian at the University of Michigan, and her father, who became a successful lawyer, graduated from its college and also studied law there. The Mudges were both deeply interested in the education of their children. Each of the two daughters and two sons who survived childhood attended college and entered a profession.

Isadore Mudge graduated from Adelphi Academy in Brooklyn in 1893 and then entered Cornell University, of which her paternal step-grandfather, Charles Kendall Adams, had been president. An excellent student, she was strongly influenced by medieval historian and librarian George Lincoln Burr, a rigorous teacher of research methods.

Mudge graduated from Cornell in 1897 with a Ph.B. degree. In October 1898 she enrolled in the New York State Library School at Albany, then the leading institution for formal library education in the United States; she graduated at the head of her class with a B.L.S. degree in 1900. It was a propitious time to enter the library field: libraries were proliferating, librarianship was becoming more complex, and capable, well-educated librarians were at a premium. Though most of the top posts were filled by men, women did hold important positions in both public and academic libraries.

Mudge's first job was with KATHARINE L. SHARP, head of both the library and the library school at the University of Illinois at Urbana, who engaged her in 1900 as a reference librarian and as an assistant professor to teach reference work and book selection. In 1903 Mudge left Illinois to become head librarian at Bryn Mawr College. With her as cataloguer went Minnie Earle Sears, whose career was also to be a distinguished one and who became Isadore Mudge's close friend, companion, and collaborator. On a year's leave of absence in 1907 to travel in Europe, Mudge, with Sears, worked on their *Thackeray Dictionary*, which was published in 1910. Mudge did not return to Bryn Mawr, and from 1909 to 1911 she held various part-time jobs. In 1910 she assumed a responsibility that would become a lifelong labor—the editorship of what became known as the *Guide to Reference Books*, issued by the American Library Association. Succeeding ALICE B. KROEGER, Mudge compiled the third through sixth editions of this work (1917, 1923, 1929, 1936), plus supplements. Comprehensive and scholarly, it became the best-known, most authoritative, and most highly regarded work of its kind.

In the spring of 1911 Mudge was named reference librarian at Columbia University—the library appointment she wanted. Columbia was a congenial and stimulating place that offered, moreover, a virtually free field for a gifted librarian to build both a career and a library service. Under the presidency of Nicholas Murray Butler the university was rising to preeminence, but, as at most American universities, its library had not yet developed correspondingly. In her thirty-year career at Columbia, Mudge was a key force in raising the library to first rank. She created, almost from nothing and not without a struggle, a reference department geared in both its great collection and its services to assisting and instructing advanced students and faculty members. A pioneer in defining and working out new library functions for the new age in American higher education—the age of big universities, of the professionalization and institutionalization of scholarship, and, eventually, of great library collections—Mudge transformed academic library service and set a standard of competence and usefulness in the library profession.

Mudge's influence was felt also through her formal teaching. She taught briefly at the library school of Simmons College (1910–11) and then intermittently at the New York Public Library School. When the Columbia University School of Library Service opened in 1926, she began teaching there and the following year became associate professor. Her bibliography course, embodying her principles of reference work and emphasizing systematic approaches to seeking information, left a deep impression upon the students, as did her personality and quality of mind. It also served as a model for similar courses at other library schools.

Besides the four editions of the *Guide to Reference Books*, Mudge prepared an annual review of new reference books for the *Library Journal* from 1911 to 1929. She also produced seminal writings on reference work, including a pamphlet, *Bibliography* (1915), which remains a standard work; wrote book reviews and articles; and prepared scholarly bibliographies. In many of these enterprises she was helped substantially by Minnie Earle Sears, with whom she also collaborated on a *George Eliot Dictionary* (1924). In addition, she was active in professional organizations, where she advocated better bibliographical control of library resources on a regional and national scale and supported cooperative efforts to improve libraries' ability to furnish information.

Isadore Mudge was a brilliant, determined woman, generous with her knowledge and her energy. Her manner at times might have been brusque, her tolerance for incompetence limited, and, as she grew older, her devotion to principle sometimes rigid, but she was essentially a modest, kind, approachable person devoted to the cause of fine scholarship. She was admired and respected for her integrity, her vast knowledge and high scholarly standards, and above all for her keen mind and total professionalism. Her private life was an active one, socially and culturally. She took a deep interest in her one surviving brother and his family, traveled extensively, went to concerts

and the theater, and liked to garden. She enjoyed entertaining her many friends in her apartment near the Columbia campus and in the Westchester County country house that she and Sears purchased around 1930 and shared until Sears's death in 1933.

In 1941 Mudge retired from the Columbia Library, and in 1942 from teaching; thereafter she lived mostly in her Westchester home until illness and infirmity finally necessitated nursing home care. She died of cancer in 1957 at Johns Hopkins Hospital in Baltimore. The following year the American Library Association established the Isadore Gilbert Mudge Citation, awarded annually for a "distinguished contribution to reference librarianship."

[The chief manuscript sources are at Columbia Univ., in the Univ. Archives, the Rare Book and Manuscript Library, the Columbiana Coll., and the School of Library Service Archives. Also available are *The Reminiscences of Isadore Mudge* (1955), Nicholas Murray Butler Project, and *The Reminiscences of Constance M. Winchell* (1963), both in the Oral History Coll., Columbia Univ. Mudge's "The Development of the Reference Department of the Columbia University Libraries" (1941) is in the Rare Book and Manuscript Library; a copy titled "Thirty-Year Report, 1911–1941" is in the Butler Library Reference Dept. A short article by Mudge about her information searches, "Spot of Brightness," appears in *Columbia Library Columns*, May 1960 (along with a photograph of her as a college student). The best and most comprehensive source of information about Mudge is John Neal Waddell, "The Career of Isadore G. Mudge: A Chapter in the History of Reference Librarianship" (Ph.D. diss., Columbia Univ., 1973), which contains a bibliography of works by and about her, including unpublished sources. Austin P. Evans recalls Mudge in "God Almighty Hates a Quitter," *Columbia Library Columns*, Nov. 1952, and Laurel L. Grotzinger sketches her career in comparison with other leading women librarians in "Women Who 'Spoke for Themselves,' " *College and Research Libraries*, May 1978. Biographical articles, with bibliographies, appear in *Dict. Am. Library Biog.* (1978) and *Encyc. of Library and Information Sci.*, vol. XVIII (1976). Obituaries appeared in the *N.Y. Times*, May 18, 1957; *Library Jour.*, June 15, 1957; and *College and Research Libraries*, July 1957. Death certificate issued by Md. State Dept. of Health.]

PHYLLIS DAIN

MULLER, Gertrude Agnes, June 9, 1887–Oct. 31, 1954. Businesswoman, inventor.

Gertrude Muller, manufacturer of child care products and child safety expert, was born in Leo, Ind., the second of three daughters and the third of the five children of Victor Herbertus and Catherine (Baker) Muller. Gertrude's father, son of one of the town's founders, ran the general store and the post office, owned a gravel pit, two farms, and an apple orchard, and was a town trustee. His parents had emigrated from Germany. The Mullers were socially prominent and well-to-do until Victor Muller's sudden death in 1893. Catherine Muller chose to return with her children to her birthplace, Fort Wayne, Ind.

During Gertrude's later childhood the Muller family was often poor. Catherine Muller took in boarders and made and sold doughnuts. With time, she acquired some property, earning a reputation for a keen business sense. After attending local public schools, Gertrude Muller received a year of secretarial training at the International Business College, Fort Wayne. She supplemented her meager academic training with extensive reading, particularly in the areas of health, nutrition, and human development.

Muller's first jobs were with local Fort Wayne businesses. She became a stenographer for the General Electric Company (1904–10), then joined the Van Arnam Manufacturing Company, which made toilet seats and was owned by a family friend. After four years as assistant to the president, Muller became assistant manager.

At about this time, Muller's younger sister undertook a trip with her small daughter. While they were in the lobby of a fancy hotel, the covering slipped off the clumsy toilet seat she was carrying for the child. Embarrassed, the young mother complained to her sister, who decided to develop a more convenient product. Together they designed the "toidey seat," a collapsible seat that could be placed on a regular toilet or on its own small base. The first seats were made by Van Arnam, and Muller tried to sell them through plumbers. When this strategy failed, Muller in 1924 established her own enterprise, Juvenile Wood Products Company, and began marketing through department stores and baby shops.

Juvenile Wood Products grew steadily, though it remained during Muller's presidency a family concern. Her older sister, Mary Katherine, who had a master's degree in child psychology from Columbia University, abandoned a teaching career and joined the company as vice president and assistant for educational promotion and research. Many other relatives found employment with the company, especially during the depression. New products regularly appeared in the company's line: a "toidey two-steps" to help toddlers climb onto the toilet or up to the sink; the "comfy-safe auto-seat" to allow children to ride safely and see out the car

windows; a folding booster seat; and other home-care and traveling aids.

All products were intended to foster increasing independence with age, a philosophy of childrearing gently expounded in the literature packed with each item. Muller wrote most of the material, including the best-known pamphlet, "Training the Baby" (1930; 26th printing, 1950), which came with every toidey seat and was also distributed by pediatricians and used in home economics courses. It encouraged parents to make their baby comfortable and to be relaxed about toilet training, helping their children acquire good habits while developing pride in caring for themselves.

Safety was also of utmost importance in product design. Auto crash studies were conducted to improve the car seat. As a result of this work the National Safety Council made Muller a member of the National Veterans of Safety, one of the first three women so honored, and she was a guest at the White House Conference on Highway Safety (1954). Muller traveled extensively, selling her products and addressing medical and home economics conventions. She was a member of the American Home Economics Association, the Business and Professional Women's Club, and other organizations. In 1944, with increasing use of plastics, Muller's company was renamed the Toidey Company.

Outside of her business Muller devoted much of her time to her family, living with and supporting her mother and helping to put several nieces and nephews through college. She was active in the Fort Wayne community as a member of the Congregational church, which she joined as an adult, and through the Women's Club, the Art School, and other clubs. During World War II Muller dressed up as Uncle Sam to encourage local war bond sales. For pleasure she rode and kept horses, collected antiques, and played piano.

Gertrude Muller was a tall, dynamic woman. Sophisticated and broad-minded, she was happy and comfortable traveling and meeting people. She continued as president of the Toidey Company until her death in Fort Wayne in 1954 from cancer of the spine. The company was both a highly successful business and a tangible expression of Muller's efforts to develop a set of products and an associated philosophy to encourage safety and progressive childrearing.

[The best published source is Catherine Miller, "Gertrude Muller: The Babies' Industrialist," in *Hidden Heroines*, Fort Wayne Public Library (1976). Articles about Muller and her company appeared in the Fort Wayne *News-Sentinel*, May 3, 1940, May 21, 1944, and March 20, 1948; and in the Indianapolis *Star*, May 4, 1947. All are accompanied by photographs. Details of education and early employment are from *Who's Who in the Midwest* (1952). Obituaries appeared in both the Fort Wayne *News-Sentinel* and the Fort Wayne *Journal Gazette* on Nov. 1, 1954. Additional information

was provided by Muller's niece Helen Cox Stange of Princeton, N.J., who has a collection of Muller family photographs and memorabilia.]

TERRY KAY ROCKEFELLER

N

NICE, Margaret Morse, Dec. 6, 1883–June 26, 1974. Ornithologist.

Margaret Morse Nice, internationally renowned ornithologist and scholar, was born in Amherst, Mass., the second of three daughters and fourth of seven children of Anson Daniel and Margaret Duncan (Ely) Morse. Her father, a native of Vermont whose English ancestors had settled in Connecticut in the seventeenth century, was professor of history at Amherst College. Her maternal ancestors were Scots-Irish, and her mother's father had a coffee and sugar business in New York City.

Margaret's parents and Amherst College provided an intellectual environment. In the rural setting of her home she first became intrigued by the habits of birds, writing about them at age twelve in her own weekly paper, "Fruit Acre News." She attended a private grade school, The Kindergarten, and Amherst High School, and in 1901 followed her mother and a great-aunt to Mount Holyoke College. Initially interested in languages, she later turned to the natural sciences. A winter spent in Italy with her maternal step-grandmother delayed her graduation until 1906, when she received an A.B. She then entered Clark University in Worcester, Mass., where she was a fellow in biology from 1907 to 1909.

On Aug. 12, 1909, Margaret Morse married Leonard Blaine Nice, a fellow graduate student at Clark. In 1911 the couple moved to the vicinity of Harvard Medical School, where Blaine Nice studied medicine, and in 1913 went to Norman, Okla., where he headed the physiology department at the University of Oklahoma. The Nices had five daughters: Constance, born in 1910; Marjorie, born in 1912; Barbara, born in 1915; Eleanor, born in 1918 (d. 1928); and Janet, born in 1923. Meanwhile, Margaret Nice had published her first brief ornithological paper, "The Food of the Bob-white," in the *Journal of Economic Entomology* in 1910. The product of more than two years' research, this article demonstrated its author's patience in observing and recording data. It also foreshadowed

her consuming interest in behavior. During this period, Nice also studied child psychology, and in 1915 received an A.M. in psychology from Clark University. Between 1915 and 1933 she published eighteen articles on child psychology based upon observations of her own children.

During the early 1920s, however, Margaret Nice found herself increasingly absorbed by the study of birds. She was encouraged to study bird behavior, to concentrate her efforts, and to publish by Althea Sherman, an amateur ornithologist from Iowa almost twice her age, who warned Nice against the distractions of household duties.

Her first account of Oklahoma bird life, published in 1920, was followed by thirty-five articles about the state's birds, culminating in 1924 in *The Birds of Oklahoma*, the first complete study of the subject, coauthored with her husband. A prolific author, she wrote or coauthored 250 research reports and related publications between 1920 and 1965. Although most of Nice's early work was limited to listing the various bird species and recording their abundance and distribution, her interest in behavioral studies was stimulated in part by observations of captive birds that had been injured or taken from their nests, and which she kept as pets. (Guests long recalled the presence of sparrows at the dinner table.)

In 1927, the Nices moved to Columbus, Ohio, where Blaine Nice taught at Ohio State University. There Margaret Nice began her most significant work, on the life history of the song sparrow. Their house was located near the east bank of the Olentangy River, in a lowland wilderness area between two bridges. The area was visited by many nesting and migrating bird species including the common and interesting song sparrows. Margaret Nice began to apply the principles advanced by the English ornithologist H. Eliot Howard in *Territory in Bird Life* (1920), which had demonstrated that small birds defended their territories. By placing colored bands on the birds which she named and numbered, she could follow their individual behavior and thus outline the life history of a particular species, as no one had before. Her series of publications on the song sparrow, beginning in 1930, included the important two-part *Studies in the Life History of the Song Sparrow* (1937, 1943) brought out by the Linnaean Society of New York. Renowned for her extraordinary scholarship, she also wrote the semipopular *The Watcher at the Nest* (1939). Her song sparrow work established her reputation as one of the world's foremost ornithologists and behaviorists. Ernst Mayr has said that Nice "almost single-handedly, initiated a new era in American ornithology . . . She early recognized the importance of a study of bird *individuals* because this is the only method to get reliable life history data."

The Nices moved to Hyde Park near the University of Chicago in 1936 when Blaine Nice was appointed to the faculty of the Chicago Medical School. There Margaret Nice had fewer opportunities to observe and collect data about living birds. As she wrote to her daughter Marjorie, "a great city is no proper home for me." Although she kept "censuses" of the birds in Jackson Park, and often observed birds on the lake, she worked mostly at her desk. Much of her writing after 1937 was therefore based on observations made previously. Although often slowed by illness after 1942, she continued to publish until 1965, in several languages, on such diverse subjects as behavior, territorialism, courtship, sexual dominance, incubation periods, life histories, ecology, and conservation.

Always interested in educating the public to the importance of preserving as well as studying wildlife, in her later years Nice became increasingly outspoken about conservation issues. In correspondence and in print, she condemned the unrestricted use of pesticides, the killing of albatrosses on Midway Island, and the misuse of wildlife refuges. She also maintained her involvement in a number of ornithological and conservation organizations, in the United States and abroad, and, as associate editor of the journal *Bird-Banding* (1935–42, 1946–74), kept up a prodigious output of reviews. Through her knowledge of German, Dutch, and other languages, she introduced American ornithologists to the most important European publications. Over the years she also exchanged information with prominent ornithologists in the United States and abroad.

Although Nice resented being referred to as a housewife, and stressed her training as a zoologist, she served as an inspiration to other essentially nonprofessional ornithologists. As Kenneth C. Parkes observed, her "career demonstrated to countless others that a housewife without a doctorate, raising four children, could, by studying the birds in her own backyard, make 'the outstanding contribution of the present quarter century to ornithological thinking in America.'" Never a faculty member of a university, she received few grants and little secretarial assistance. Her husband provided funds for her travels and researches, as well as moral support, encouragement, and his own time and assistance in some of her efforts.

Margaret Morse Nice received many honors, including an honorary D.Sc. in 1955 at her fiftieth reunion at Mount Holyoke College. In 1969 the Wilson Ornithological Society, which Nice had served as president in 1938 and 1939 (thereby becoming the first woman president of any major American ornithological society), initiated the Margaret Morse Nice Grant-in-aid. This grant, limited to self-trained amateur researchers, recognized the special nature of Nice's contributions to the field. She died in Chicago of arteriosclerosis at the age of ninety, just a few months after her husband.

[There are seventeen boxes of Margaret Morse Nice's personal and professional papers at the Cornell Univ. Libraries, including correspondence, manuscripts of books and articles, and notes. The Wilson Ornithological Soc. has three folders of correspondence concerning editorial problems of *The Wilson Bulletin* and *Bird-Banding*. The *Mount Holyoke Alumnae Quarterly* contains entries contributed by her between 1906 and 1963. Milton B. Trautman's "A Partial Bibliography of Margaret Morse Nice" (1976) is available through the Museum of Zoology, Ohio State Univ. Other important works by Nice are the two-part "Zür Naturgeschichte des Singhammers," *Journal für Ornithologie*, Oct. 1933, and Jan. 1934, and "The Theory of Territorialism and Its Development," in [American Ornithologists' Union] *Fifty Years' Progress of American Ornithology, 1883–1933* (1933), pp. 89–100. See also Nice's "Some Letters of Althea Sherman," *Iowa Bird Life*, Dec. 1952. The major biographical sources are Nice's autobiography, *Research Is a Passion with Me* (1979), and Milton B. Trautman, "In Memoriam: Margaret Morse Nice," *The Auk*, July 1977. See also W. J. Beecher, "The Song Sparrow Lady," *Newsletter*, Chicago Acad. of Sciences, Dec. 1, 1977; and the obituaries by Kenneth C. Parkes in *The Wilson Bull.*, Sept. 1974, and by the editor of *Bird-Banding*, 1974. For information about ornithology, and Nice's place in the field, see Erwin Stresemann's *Ornithology: From Aristotle to the Present* (1975), particularly the foreword and the epilogue on American ornithology by Ernst Mayr. Helpful information for this article was provided by Edward S. Morse, Marjorie Nice Boyer, Joseph Hickey, Ernst Mayr, the Mount Holyoke College Alumnae Office, and Clark University. A death record was provided by the Ill. Dept. of Public Health.]

MILTON B. TRAUTMAN

NICHOLS, Ruth Roland, Feb. 23, 1901–Sept. 25, 1960. Aviator.

Ruth Nichols, who held more than thirty-five "firsts" for women in various aviation categories, was born in New York City, the first of four children (two girls and two boys) of Erickson Norman and Edith Corlis (Haines) Nichols. Her father, a descendant of Leif Ericson, was a stockbroker and ardent sportsman who had gained some notoriety as one of Theodore Roosevelt's Rough Riders. Edith Nichols came from a long line of Quakers, and her strict rules of conduct added to the "multiple and complicated fears" which Ruth Nichols recalled as marking her childhood.

Until the age of twelve Nichols lived in a high-stooped brownstone in Manhattan, making frequent visits to her "Aunt Polly" Haines, her lifelong confidante, in nearby Yonkers. In 1913 the family moved to suburban Rye, N.Y. Nichols attended Miss Masters School in Dobbs Ferry, graduating in 1919. Her unique graduation gift from her father—a plane ride with World War I ace Eddie Stinson—changed the direction of her life. From then on, Nichols later recalled, her heart "remained in the sky."

Despite strong family opposition, in the fall of 1919 Nichols entered Wellesley College, planning eventually to become a doctor. After two years, her mother persuaded her to leave school, hoping she would "forget about a career and take her proper place in society." Going to Florida with her family, in Miami Nichols met Harry Rogers, a well-known flying boat pilot. She began secretly to take flying lessons from him, continuing them when her family returned to New York.

Although she returned to Wellesley in 1922 and graduated in 1924, Nichols's consuming desire was to fly. Soon after her graduation she became the first woman in the world to receive an international hydroplane license. Later, in 1927, she was one of the first two women to receive a transport license issued by the Department of Commerce.

Returning in 1926 from a world cruise, Nichols worked briefly in a New York City bank. On New Year's Eve 1927, Harry Rogers invited her to be copilot on a recordmaking nonstop flight from New York to Miami. The flight, on Jan. 3, 1928, gained Nichols considerable notoriety and Sherman Fairchild, president of Fairchild Airplane and Engine Company, offered her a job in sales promotion. Later that year she became involved in the attempt to establish a nationwide chain of Aviation Country Clubs, the first of which opened at Hicksville, Long Island, in the summer of 1928. Soon after,

Nichols planned the first sportsman-pilot tour of the United States, flying to forty-six states in 1929 to publicize the club plan and survey aerial conditions throughout the country. The stock market crash in October of that year and the ensuing depression cast a pall over the future of social and sports aviation, however.

Nichols had entered some flying competitions during her Country Club tours. But she did not begin serious competition until the spring of 1930, when Col. Clarence Chamberlin persuaded her to give up her work with the clubs and join the sales department of his Crescent Aircraft Company. Nichols entered a period in her life of almost constant competitive flying and record attempts.

In 1931, her "big year," Nichols established or broke three women's records. Establishing a new altitude record (28,743 feet) in March, the following month she broke the world's speed record for women (previously held by AMELIA EARHART), with a speed of 210.754 miles per hour. Nichols attempted the first transatlantic flight by a woman in June, only to crash land in New Brunswick on the first leg of the trip. Badly injured but tenacious, she flew again as soon as she could move about. In October she donned a steel brace to support her back, and established a world's distance record for women by flying from Oakland, Calif., to Louisville, Ky. The day after this flight, Nichols's beloved Akita (her Lockheed Vega monoplane) burst into flames on the runway in Louisville, delaying further her planned second attempt to fly the Atlantic.

Nichols raised money in 1932 to rebuild her plane, and participated in a "good will tour" in support of the International Congress of Women to be held in Chicago in 1933. The transatlantic flight she planned for the spring of 1932 never materialized and in May of that year Amelia Earhart became the first woman to fly solo across the Atlantic. Nichols then planned a New York to Paris flight, only to be boxed in by winter weather. Embarking instead on what was to be a record New York to Los Angeles run, during which she dropped campaign literature for President Herbert Hoover, Nichols had another costly mishap with her newly refitted plane.

Returning to her family's home in Rye, Nichols spent most of the next few years on the ground, giving lectures and raising funds for a round-the-world flight. In 1935 Clarence Chamberlin offered her a job as copilot on his large Condor transport planes, and together they embarked on a widespread barnstorming tour of the northeast. In October, as they were attempting an emergency landing at the Troy, N.Y., airport the plane missed the runway and burst into flames. Nichols was thrown from the plane and critically injured.

Her recovery was slow and agonizing, and she did not regain her commercial pilot's license until the spring of 1937. Nichols took a job that spring with the Emergency Peace Campaign, a Quaker organization based in Philadelphia that was attempting to educate the public about the imminent danger of international conflict and to suggest peaceful resolutions. Deeply affected by this work, Nichols sought other ways to combine her aviation skills with her humanitarian sensibilities.

When war broke out in Europe in September 1939, Nichols began to plan Relief Wings, a civilian air ambulance service. The service was inaugurated in May 1940 and by the fall of 1941 centers had been established in thirty-six states. When the United States entered the war in December 1941, Nichols made Relief Wings's assets available to the government-financed Civil Air Patrol.

During the war years, Nichols worked as a volunteer Red Cross nurse's aide and gave flying lessons. She also secured a flight instructor's rerating, qualifying her to fly multiengine aircraft. Then late in 1948 she was asked to serve as a pilot the following summer on a world tour on behalf of the United Nations International Children's Emergency Fund (UNICEF), an endeavor Nichols later regarded as "the crystallization of [her] life's desire and training." On the final leg of the trip, in August 1949, an Italian plane on which Nichols had volunteered as a stewardess overshot Shannon airport in Ireland and plunged into the sea. After a perilous night on a crowded life raft, Nichols and her companions were rescued, uninjured, and she returned to the United States a few days later.

In the early 1950s Nichols revived her dream of an air ambulance service; she was asked in 1954 to become adviser to the national commander on matters pertaining to aeromedical administration for the Civil Air Patrol. Always open to new challenges, Nichols became in 1955 the first woman to pilot a twin engine executive jet and she set new women's records for speed and altitude in 1958, piloting a jet faster than 1,000 miles an hour at an altitude of 51,000 feet. Nichols lived the last few years of her life in a New York apartment, where she was found dead in September 1960, an apparent suicide. She was fifty-nine.

Ruth Nichols was best remembered by friends and colleagues for her courage. Cofounder with Amelia Earhart of the Ninety-Nines, an international organization of women pilots, she was also instrumental in involving women at all levels of the aviation industry. Forever a pioneer, Nichols's final dream was to pilot a space ship.

[The Wellesley College Archives has an extensive clippings file on Nichols. The best biographical source is her autobiography, *Wings for Life* (1957). There is a chapter on Nichols in Jean Adams and Margaret Kimball, *Heroines of the Sky* (1942), and in Charles Plenck, *Women with Wings* (1942). Anne Stoddard, ed., *Topflight Famous American Women* (1946), provides an emotional and inaccurate account of Nichols's career. Brief entries appear in *Who's Who in America* (1961–68), and *Who's Who of American Women*, IV (1958). An obituary appeared in the *N.Y. Times*, Sept. 26, 1960.]

CHRISTOPHER CORNOG

NORRIS, Kathleen Thompson, July 16, 1880– Jan. 18, 1966. Writer.

Kathleen Norris was born in San Francisco, the first of three daughters and second eldest of six surviving children of Josephine (Moroney) and James Alden Thompson, a bank manager. Although Hawaii-born, James Thompson was of a Boston family; Josephine Moroney's parents had crossed overland from Missouri to California. Both parents dabbled in the arts: her father, an avid reader, was twice president of the Bohemian Club, while her mother played piano and frequently attended concerts. In *Family Gathering*, her 1959 autobiography, Kathleen Norris depicted her parents as popular although not socially ambitious members of San Francisco's "Irishtocracy." She remembered the lively and optimistic James Thompson as "the real influence" in her youth. The family was close-knit and affectionate, and her pious Roman Catholic mother permitted no angry words to be spoken in the home. Throughout her career, her family and her Irish-American background provided most of the material for Norris's best-selling novels.

Around 1890 James Thompson moved his family from San Francisco northeast across the Bay to the redwood-shaded village of Mill Valley on the slopes of Mt. Tamalpais. There his children received little formal education, intermittently attending a country school and being taught at home by their parents or tutors. Kathleen Thompson also briefly attended a Dominican convent school in San Rafael, but her main source of knowledge was her father's library of books and eastern magazines. Even when the family took an apartment in San Francisco so the children might attend school regularly, she did not enroll. Instead, she remained at home to help her mother look after the younger children.

When she was nineteen, tragedy disrupted Kathleen Thompson's domestic tranquility. Her mother succumbed to pneumonia at Thanksgiving time, 1899, and by Christmas her father was dead, leaving savings of less than $500. She and her older brother, Joe, turned breadwinners. She took care of children and invalids and worked as saleslady, bookkeeper, and librarian. She also began to write. After studying composition for a short time at the University of California at Berkeley and making a few freelance sales, she ventured into journalism. She worked briefly as society editor for the *Bulletin,* and then in 1906 for the *San Francisco Call,* before the San Francisco *Examiner* took her on as a reporter. She loved "press business" and throughout her career as a novelist accepted occasional journalistic assignments. In San Francisco press circles she met Charles Gilman Norris, younger brother of the novelist Frank Norris, whom she married in New York in 1909.

Her long, successful career as a novelist began during her first year of marriage. Free of responsibility for her siblings, she applied her pen to supplement her husband's twenty-five-dollar-a-week salary as art editor of *American Magazine.* After placing a few short stories, she expanded one into the novel *Mother,* published in 1911, the year after the birth of her son Frank. *Mother,* a wholesome story of San Francisco family life, was based on the Thompson family and their friends; it was instantly successful.

Her family and her years as a San Francisco reporter provided an endless source of material for the novels and serials which thereafter flowed at the rate of two a year. Their casts were ordinary people with ordinary yearnings; their plots demonstrated the rewards of virtue, and of thrift, diligence, and courage. Norris's writings invariably affirmed the traditional roles of women as wives and mothers, although she favored woman suffrage and associated with suffragists. Her unsubtle, predictable, romantic tales, written in an easy fluent style, all had happy endings. When she varied her formula in the more ambitious and realistic *Certain People of Importance* (1922), the book was unpopular. Over five decades she produced eighty-one novels, two autobiographies (the first, *Noon,* appeared in 1925), a play, short stories, poems, magazine articles, newspaper pieces, and, in the late 1940s, a "soap opera" radio serial.

The Norrises divided their time between a house in Palo Alto, Calif., a New York apartment, and a country home south of San Francisco. Kathleen Norris was an attractive, humorous hostess, entertaining many literary celebrities. They adopted a second son, William Rice Norris, in 1918; twin daughters, Josephine

and Gertrude (b. 1912), had died in infancy. In addition, Norris remained close to her extended family, especially to her sister Teresa, who married the poet William Rose Benét. A few years after Teresa's premature death in 1919, Norris gained custody of the three Benét children.

As the preservation of marriage was her recurrent fictional theme, so she nurtured her own marriage, which was enduring and affectionate, a triumph over marked philosophical differences. Charles Norris, a year her junior, was an Episcopalian, while Kathleen Norris remained a devout Catholic. Moreover, he completely disagreed with her espousal of prohibition and pacifism. As a charter member of the isolationist America First group, she spoke out in the 1930s in favor of disarmament; she also opposed United States participation in World War II. After the war, she campaigned against the testing of nuclear weapons. She also lectured frequently against capital punishment, although she kept this and other controversial issues out of her writings. Charles Norris, also a dedicated writer, acted as his wife's agent and shielded her from domestic concerns, even selecting her wardrobe. In her autobiographies she generously credited him with assisting her career. He died of a heart ailment in 1954.

Kathleen Norris was one of the most popular and commercially successful authors of her time, her books selling ten million copies. She won no literary awards nor honorary degrees, however. From the outset critics called her fiction sentimental, slight, and contrived, though they praised its warmth and honesty and lauded her powers of observation. Despite their sentimentality, her novels present a painstaking, accurate depiction of Irish-American life and are thus of continuing documentary value.

In the late 1950s Kathleen Norris was crippled by arthritis and spent four years in a San Francisco hospital. In 1963 she moved to the home of her son Frank, a San Francisco gynecologist, and lived there until her death of congestive heart failure in 1966. As industrious as any of her earnest heroines, she had practiced her craft into her eightieth year.

[The Kathleen Norris Papers at the Stanford Univ. Library, Stanford, Calif., include letters and MSS.; typescripts and galleys of her published works; and a collection of Charles Norris's papers. The Bancroft Library at the Univ. of Calif., Berkeley, has transcripts of interviews with Kathleen Norris and with her brother, a bibliography of her works, and additional manuscripts and letters. The Calif. State Library in Sacramento also has a variety of material on her. No book-length biography has yet appeared, but Alexander Woollcott, *While Rome Burns* (1935) contains a revealing sketch. Factual sources on her life include *WPA Biographies of California Authors* (1942); *Twentieth Century Authors* (1942) and its *First Supplement* (1955); *Nat. Cyc. Am. Biog.*, C, 366–67; and *Time*, Jan. 28, 1935, pp. 65–66. *Family Gathering* contains many photographs of the author and her family. Her writings are discussed in Joyce Kilmer, *Literature in the Making* (1917); Isabella Taves, *Successful Women* (1943); Joseph Collins, *The Doctor Looks at Biography* (1925); and Kenneth Rexroth, "Mrs. Norris' Story," *N.Y. Times Book Rev.*, Feb. 6, 1955. See also obituaries in *N.Y. Times*, Jan. 19, 1966, and *Publishers Weekly*, Jan. 31, 1966. Additional material was provided by a biobibliography prepared by Marilyn L. Boardman and an interview with the author's son Dr. Frank Norris. A death record was provided by the Calif. Dept. of Public Health.]

ELINOR RICHEY

NORTON, Mary Teresa Hopkins, March 7, 1875–Aug. 2, 1959. Congresswoman.

Mary Norton, United States Congresswoman from 1925 to 1951, was born in Jersey City, N.J., the eldest of three daughters and the second surviving child of Thomas and Maria (Shea) Hopkins. Of the four children born before her, only her brother James lived beyond infancy. Both her mother and her father, who worked in construction, were staunch Roman Catholics who had migrated from Ireland in the mid-nineteenth century. Before her marriage, Maria Hopkins had worked as a governess for a doctor's family in New York City.

Although family sacrifices were made to educate James (who was intended for the priesthood), Mary Hopkins did not complete her elementary school education. Her father opposed college for women but Norton later said that, if her mother had lived, her younger sisters would have received a college education. Mary was seventeen when her mother died and she, with the help of a housekeeper, assumed responsibility for the household. When her father remarried four years later, Mary and her sisters took an apartment in New York City. There, the three young women attended Packard Business College and subsequently held secretarial positions. Norton later reported that this experience of independence and self-reliance served as excellent preparation for her public career.

On April 21, 1909, she married a widower, Robert Francis Norton, who worked in the management of a Jersey City cooperage firm. Grieved by the death in infancy of her only child, Robert Francis, Jr., in September 1910, and by the knowledge that she could bear no more children, Mary Norton turned to public service. With the encouragement of the pastor of Saint Joseph's Church in Jersey City, and the assistance of a group of parish women, in 1912 she helped launch the Queen's Daughters' Day Nursery, a nonsectarian day care center for children of working women. She worked for the nursery for fifteen years—three as secretary and twelve as president.

While seeking municipal funds for the nursery, Norton met a powerful local political leader—Mayor Frank Hague. He helped her to obtain money for the nursery, and also launched her on the political career which occupied the next thirty years of her life. In June 1920 Hague urged the initially reluctant Norton to represent Hudson County on the Democratic State Committee of New Jersey. Women had won the right to vote, so Hague intended to see to it that they voted as Democrats and that they participated actively in the party organization, rather than in such nonpartisan organizations as the League of Women Voters. Agreeing to his plans, Norton became the first woman member of the State Committee, and served as either vice chairman or chairman from 1921 to 1944.

In 1923 through Hague's influence, Norton became the first Democratic woman elected to the Hudson County Board of Freeholders. She convinced the board of the need for a maternity hospital, to be constructed in Jersey City at county expense. Hague made it one of his pet projects, and the Margaret Hague Maternity Hospital became one of the best hospitals of its kind in the nation.

Norton resigned from the board in 1924 to become a candidate for the House of Representatives from the Twelfth Congressional District of New Jersey. Despite large Democratic losses elsewhere, she was elected, the first woman Democrat elected to Congress without being preceded by her husband and the first woman sent to Congress by an eastern state. Asked by a reporter to pose in her kitchen holding a frying pan, the new congresswoman assured him that she "did not intend to do any cooking in Congress and thought that such a picture would be ridiculous." Norton embarked on her congressional career with the tacit support of her husband, who maintained such a low profile that she was referred to as a widow long before she became one in 1934.

In the House, she achieved prominence as an early proponent of the repeal of prohibition. She was appointed to three committees. As a member of the Veterans Affairs Committee, she obtained funds for the first veterans' hospital in New Jersey. She chaired the District of Columbia Committee from 1932 to 1937, becoming the first woman to head a congressional committee. Championing home rule for the District and overseeing its affairs with unprecedented diligence, Norton was sometimes referred to as the District's "first woman mayor."

When the chairman of the Labor Committee died unexpectedly in 1937, Norton succeeded him. She was plunged immediately into a long battle, ultimately successful, for passage of the Fair Labor Standards Act. The law, which set a minimum wage and maximum hours for unorganized workers, aided women workers by eliminating sex-based pay differentials. Throughout the ten years that she chaired the committee, Norton defended New Deal labor legislation against conservative attempts to undermine it. In addition, in every session from 1944 until she retired in 1951, she introduced legislation to establish a permanent Fair Employment Practices Commission to combat racial discrimination. Despite her efforts, not one of these bills made it out of committee. Also in 1944, foreseeing the problems women workers would encounter at the end of the war, Norton submitted a bill providing that wage determination under the War Disputes Act, the Fair Labor Standards Act, and other laws would apply to workers regardless of sex. In 1947, when Republicans obtained control of the House, Norton resigned from the Labor Committee and was appointed instead to the Administration Committee. When the Democrats regained control in 1949, she became head of that committee, overseeing House finances.

Norton was a dedicated champion of the working woman, and staunchly defended the principle of equal pay for equal work. During World War II, she sought federal funds for day care centers and, after the war, argued for their continued support by the government under the Lanham Act. She also advocated active political participation by women as voters, party members, and candidates. However, Norton refused to support the Equal Rights Amendment, as did a majority of the women in the 1930s and 1940s who favored protective legislation. And, as a devoted Catholic, she opposed MARGARET SANGER and the birth control movement, and testified against the Gillett Bill for dissemination of birth control information.

Norton was the recipient of three honorary degrees, as well as many other honors. In 1945 President Harry S Truman appointed her adviser and alternate delegate to the International Labor Organization Conference in Paris. She received the Woman of Achievement Award from the Women's National Press Club in 1946 and the Siena Medal from Theta Phi Alpha as the outstanding Catholic woman of the year in 1947.

Norton's retirement from Congress in 1951 at seventy-five coincided with the end of the Hague regime in Hudson County and with renewed Republican dominance in Congress. In later years, she served as head of the Woman's Advisory Committee of the Defense Manpower Administration under the secretary of labor. She also wrote her autobiography, which, perhaps because of its favorable bias toward Hague, remains unpublished. She died of a heart attack in Greenwich, Conn., at the age of eighty-four.

[The papers of Mary Norton are deposited in the N.J. Coll., Alexander Library, Rutgers Univ. They include certificates of election, correspondence, speeches, writings, photographs, press clippings about her political career, and the typescript of her autobiography. Also in the Norton papers is a "Summary of the Legislative Career of Representative Mary T. Norton," prepared by Angeline Bogucki, Legislative Reference Service, Library of Congress (1950). Among her writings are "Woman in Industry," in Marion T. Sheehan, ed., *The Spiritual Woman* (1955); "No! Says Rep. Norton," *Wash. Daily News*, Nov. 30, 1940; "America's Door-Key Children," Sept. 1942, and "Full Employment," July 1945, both in the *Democratic Digest*. The *Biog. Directory of the Am. Congress, 1794–1961; Current Biog.*, 1944; and *Nat. Cyc. Am. Biog.*, XLVI, 258, contain entries on Norton. An obituary appeared in the *N.Y. Times*, Aug. 3, 1959. Dates appearing in this article were verified through the Bureau of Vital Statistics, Jersey City, and St. Joseph's Church, Jersey City. Additional information was supplied by Norton's niece and former clerk on the House Labor Committee Marion McDonagh Burke; a biobibliography prepared by Carol Goldfarb assisted in the research for this article.]

CARMELA A. KARNOUTSOS

NOTESTEIN, Ada. *See* COMSTOCK, Ada.

O

O'CONNOR, Flannery, March 25, 1925–Aug. 3, 1964. Writer.

Flannery O'Connor was born in Savannah, Ga., the only child of Regina (Cline) and Edward Francis O'Connor. Her parents christened her Mary Flannery, which she later shortened to Flannery for professional purposes.

Her childhood was serene. Precocious and independent, she seems to have enjoyed the company of her parents more than that of other children, and later described herself as having always been quite pleased to be an only child. Even in childhood she liked to write; she kept journals and composed poems, stories, and essays.

Early on, O'Connor discovered an affinity for "chickens," her generic term for the varied flocks she bred and watched over. She liked peculiar birds: frizzled chickens, or those with one green eye and one orange. The star of her first collection was a chicken who walked backward, and when O'Connor was six Pathé News came to photograph them both for a newsreel. She liked to say that it was the high point of her life, after which all was anticlimax.

Flannery O'Connor became acquainted with sorrow early. When she was twelve, her father fell ill, without hope of recovery. He gave up his real estate business and the O'Connors left Savannah, returning to Regina O'Connor's family home in Milledgeville, a beautiful old town in north central Georgia. Her mother's family on both sides, the Clines and the Treanors, were landowners in the region, and Flannery went to live in the great rambling antebellum house where her mother, with fifteen brothers and sisters, had grown up. Here, when she was fifteen, Edward O'Connor died of lupus erythematosus, the same illness that was later to strike his daughter.

The loss of her much-loved father, preceded by the three-year hush of a long, slow dying, brought her, sooner than most, to a serious engagement with the religious faith that was to become so essential to her life and work. The Clines and the Treanors, as well as the O'Connors of Savannah, were traditionally Roman Catholic, rarities in an almost completely Protestant region, and Flannery O'Connor's faith, even during childhood, was deep and strong. The social position of her family spared her some of the pains local prejudice might have cost her. Nevertheless, living as she did in profound commitment to a system of beliefs and values, and to an institution that was isolated and suspect in the community, may later have helped her to disregard critical incomprehension and hostility and to proceed calmly with her knotty and enigmatic work.

She was not withdrawn or aloof, however. Graduating from Peabody High School in 1942, she became a lively and sociable participant in activities at the Georgia State College for Women (later Georgia College), in Milledgeville. Pursuing a three-year accelerated wartime program in sociology, O'Connor soon found

that her interests lay elsewhere. She became a regular contributor of poems and prose, as well as stylish satirical cartoons, to the college literary magazine; she was also editor of the senior yearbook. Receiving her A.B. in 1945, she went that September to the Graduate School of Fine Arts at the University of Iowa, where she joined the Writer's Workshop under the direction of Paul Engle. Her struggle there and thereafter was for excellence, not for recognition, which came almost at once. In 1946 she sold her first story, "The Geranium," to *Accent* magazine. In her second year at Iowa, she won the Rinehart-Iowa prize for what became *Wise Blood*, the money to be considered as an advance on royalties should the firm of Holt, Rinehart decide to publish the novel. She took her MFA in June 1947, and, in 1948, accepted an invitation to Yaddo, the retreat for writers and artists in Saratoga Springs, N.Y., where she continued work on the novel. Soon, however, she found herself in hopeless disagreement with her editor at Holt, Rinehart, who found the work in progress bizarre. He proposed to redirect her into more conventional channels; she demurred, and obtained a release that permitted her to change publishers. At Harcourt, Brace she found as her editor Robert Giroux, who became a lifelong friend. When she left Yaddo for New York City in March 1949, she met, through Robert Lowell (whom she had known at Yaddo, and who greatly admired her), Robert and Sally Fitzgerald. Two happy years followed, while she was living with the couple and their troupe of small children atop the Redding Ridge in Connecticut. Here she substantially finished *Wise Blood*, occasionally publishing chapters in literary quarterlies, and here she planned to stay indefinitely. In December 1950, however, just as she was about to go to Georgia for Christmas with her mother, she felt alarmingly unwell, and by the time she reached Milledgeville she was on the point of death.

Her illness was diagnosed as lupus which, although still extremely dangerous, had become more or less controllable by medications developed since her father's death. Flannery O'Connor's life was saved by cortisone and a brilliant doctor, but it was more than a year before she was mobile again. When she learned her true situation, she accepted it stoically, and began to reconstruct her life within the limitations now placed upon her. During the first year of her illness, she and her mother had moved to Andalusia, a handsome dairy farm near Milledgeville recently bequeathed to her mother. Regina O'Connor proposed to operate the farm, and Flannery O'Connor settled in to make a permanent home there. One of her first acts was to add to her flocks a pair of peacocks, a bird now associated with her in the minds of her readers. She had forty peafowl, raised by herself, when she died.

Under the intelligently austere care of her mother, her health was more or less stabilized and maintained. She was able to establish working habits that enabled her to produce a steady, if slow, flow of stories that were like no one else's in their force and strangeness, and were always distinguished by their craftsmanship. The style and content of her fiction gave rise to the myth of a solitary and scornful personality, but this is contradicted by those who knew or met her, by her letters to friends, and by accounts of the warm hospitality she and her mother dispensed to countless visitors. Moreover, she did all she could for a number of struggling writers who submitted their work to her for criticism. She loved the south and the pace of life there, and came to feel that she had been brought back exactly where she belonged.

Wise Blood appeared in 1953. It is the story of Hazel Motes, a backwoodsman so profoundly religious by nature that if he is not to embrace the severe fundamentalist faith in which he has been reared, he must perforce make a religion of attacking it. He is, inevitably, defeated. Cut off from any gentle or authoritative interpretation of Christianity, hence subject to his own nature, he atones with characteristic violence by blinding himself. He awaits his death, and salvation, in darkness and solitude—a kind of primitive Protestant saint. The book was widely misunderstood as an attack on religion: it seemed hard for critics and readers to realize that O'Connor's sympathies lay with any religious man, however misguided his subjective interpretation of Christ, rather than with his secularized counterpart. In a note introducing the second edition in 1962, she explained it as "a comic novel about a Christian malgré lui written by an author congenitally innocent of theory, but one with certain preoccupations. That belief in Christ is to some a matter of life and death has been a stumbling block for readers who would prefer to think it a matter of no great consequence. For them, Hazel Motes's integrity lies in his trying with such vigor to get rid of the ragged figure who moves from tree to tree in the back of his mind. For the author, his integrity lies in his not being able to."

In 1955, a collection of short stories, *A Good Man Is Hard to Find and Other Stories,* was published, and critical acclaim, if not universal understanding, increased. O'Connor's short stories were less difficult to penetrate, but even they were charged with harshness and grotesquerie and denounced as lacking in "a sense of beauty" and in "compassion." Unruffled, O'Connor continued on her way, professing herself amused, and in any case making no concession to obtuse objections and misinterpretations.

At about this time, the steroid drugs that kept the lupus under control began to erode her bones, and her hip joints could no longer sustain her slight weight; she was forced to resort to crutches. Even so, she continued to work for the few hours a day her strength permitted, and even to travel to colleges and writers' gatherings to give talks and readings. Her stories, and chapters from her new novel in progress, sold readily, and a Ford Foundation grant, wisely invested, added to her financial independence.

Administrative changes at Harcourt, Brace led O'Connor to move to Farrar, Straus & Cudahy where Robert Giroux again became her editor; she remained with that firm (later Farrar, Straus and Giroux) to the end. In 1959 her second novel, *The Violent Bear It Away,* appeared. This book centered on the efforts of another fugitive from Christ—Francis Marion Tarwater, an intractable country boy—to escape his destiny, which is primarily to baptize his little cousin, an idiot. He finally does so, against his own will, as he deliberately drowns the child. The homosexual rape of Tarwater by a stranger completes the submission the rebel had sought to avoid and, passionately converted, he sets off on his lonely way as a "prophet." In the mind of his creator, Tarwater is no freak, but a true prophet; his defeated adversary is his uncle and self-appointed savior, Rayber, a secular sociologist who tries, and fails, to deflect him. O'Connor had no illusions as to the reception of a novel predicated upon the essential importance of a baptism. In a note on her own work, she wrote: "I have found . . . that my subject in fiction is the action of grace in territory held largely by the devil. I have also found that what I write is read by an audience which puts little stock either in grace or the devil."

By this time, however, she was everywhere recognized as a highly original writer of fine and supple prose, with an incomparable ear for comic speech, and remarkable architectonic ability. Her books were translated and published not only in Europe but also as far away as Japan. Prizes and honors came yearly, and her work was widely anthologized.

In 1963, O'Connor's health took a turn for the worse. An operation, always dangerous for lupus patients, became absolutely necessary. It was successful as such, but the doctors' fears were realized; the lupus, reactivated after years in remission, raged out of control. After a few months of steady decline—which did not deter her from writing two of her most admired stories, "Judgement Day" and "Parker's Back"—she died in August 1964 of kidney failure.

Flannery O'Connor was not an activist or militant, either as a woman or on behalf of minority groups. She did not think in large social terms, and it was all she could do, in her circumstances, to write as much as she did. Her concern, humanly and as an artist, was with individuals: when individuals understood themselves and their universe, she held, social solutions would inevitably follow. "Everything that rises must converge," a sentence she took from Teilhard de Chardin, became the title of her last collection of stories (posthumously published in 1965); it suggests O'Connor's long evolutionary view of social conflicts and her hopes for their resolution. A statement of Joseph Conrad's, she said, corresponded with her own intentions: "My task . . . is, by the power of the written word, to make you hear, to make you feel—it is, before all, to make you *see*. If I succeed, you shall find there, according to your deserts, encouragement, consolation, fear, charm, all you demand—and, perhaps, also that glimpse of truth for which you have forgotten to ask."

Her energies were all turned to this effort. Faced early and late with misunderstanding of her stories and novels, she was able to say with wry patience that she could "wait a hundred years for readers." She didn't have to; whether or not the intent of her tales was always clearly seen, admiration for their solidity and complexity has continued to grow. On all three levels of meaning that she strove to embody or find—natural, symbolic, and anagogical—each story stands firmly on its own as a rendering and criticism of human experience. Altogether without sentimentality, Flannery O'Connor gave to her lonely, freakish, often maimed, and usually violent characters a dignity and significance that can never again be denied them.

[Some of Flannery O'Connor's papers are in the O'Connor Coll. in the library of Georgia College, Milledgeville, Ga. The remainder are in the possession of her mother, Regina Cline O'Connor. In addition to the books mentioned above, O'Connor wrote the introduction to a book by the Dominican Nuns of Our Lady of Perpetual Help Cancer Home in Atlanta, Ga., *A Memoir of Mary Ann* (1962). *The Complete Stories of Flannery O'Connor* appeared in 1971. Her occasional prose was collected by Sally and Robert Fitzgerald, eds., *Mystery and Manners* (1969). Sally Fitzgerald has also edited *The Habit of Being: Letters of Flannery O'Connor* (1979) and is preparing a biography. There is an abundance of critical material. For a bibliography of work by and about O'Connor see Robert E. Golden, *Flannery O'Connor and Caroline Gordon: A Refer-ence Guide* (1977). Especially useful discussions of her work are Stanley Edgar Hyman, *Flannery O'Connor* (1966); Carter W. Martin, *The True Country: Themes in the Fiction of Flannery O'Connor* (1969); David Eggenschwiler, *The Christian Humanism of Flannery O'Connor* (1972); Miles Orvell, *Invisible Parade: The Fiction of Flannery O'Connor* (1972); Martha Stephens, *The Question of Flannery O'Connor* (1973). An obituary appeared in the *N.Y. Times,* Aug. 4, 1964.]

SALLY FITZGERALD

O'CONNOR, Julia. *See* PARKER, Julia O'Connor.

O'HARA, Anne. *See* MARTIN, Anne Henrietta.

OMLIE, Phoebe Jane Fairgrave, Nov. 21, 1902–July 17, 1975. Aviator.

Phoebe Fairgrave Omlie, whose career extended from the barnstorming days of the early pilots to the period of growing aviation bureaucracy, was born in Des Moines, Iowa, only daughter and second child of Andrew and Madge (Traister) Fairgrave. Her father, born in Ohio of Scottish and English parents, was a saloonkeeper and had a stable, though modest, income. Her mother's parents came from Illinois and Indiana.

When Phoebe was twelve, the family moved to St. Paul, Minn. She attended Madison School and Mechanic Arts High School, graduating in 1920. For a few months she studied at the Guy Durrel Dramatic School in St. Paul and worked briefly as a secretary, but quickly discovered that office work was not for her. Unable to forget an air show she had seen, Phoebe Fairgrave bought four rides in an airplane at Curtiss Field, then used an inheritance from a grandfather to buy her own airplane at a cost of $3,500.

Hoping to explain this expenditure to her parents, Fairgrave, still only seventeen and untrained as a pilot, went to the offices of Fox Moving Picture Company and sold $3,500 worth of assorted aerial stunts for the movie series *The Perils of Pauline*. Years later she recalled: "Dad thought I was crazy. Mother had more faith. She thought that if I was going to do it I was going to do it and that's all there was to it." Madge Fairgrave's faith in the set purpose of her daughter's mind was fully justified.

Phoebe Fairgrave's resolution belied her diminutive stature, which sometimes proved a handicap, as when most instructors at Curtiss refused to teach her to fly because she was "too young and too little." One instructor agreed. He was Vernon Omlie, former army captain and World War I bombing instructor and at the time a stunt pilot and teacher for Curtiss. In the two years before their marriage on Jan. 22, 1922, he taught her to fly and piloted her while she fulfilled the contract with Fox and barnstormed the country in "death-defying" acts, which included wing-walking and parachuting. "It was not the approach to aviation that either of us wanted but, since aviation was not taken seriously then, it was the only way to make a living at it," she said later.

The Omlies did have opportunities to demonstrate the practicality of aviation. In 1921, during a forest fire in the northwest, they acted as aerial spotters, and during the Mississippi flood of 1927 they patrolled levees, flew in medicine and supplies, took out stranded survivors, and carried mail.

In competitive flying Phoebe Omlie set a number of records and recorded several firsts for women aviators. In April 1921, at eighteen, she became the first woman in the world to do a double parachute drop (using two parachutes cut loose at separate intervals). The following July 10 she set a new world's record parachute jump for women, jumping from 15,200 feet. During the next ten years she received the first federal pilot's license and the first aircraft and mechanic's license ever issued to a woman; she was also the first woman to enter the Ford National Reliability Air Tour (1928). In 1929 Omlie set an altitude record for women of 25,400 feet and won the Women's Air Derby. She set four records at the National Air Races in Cleveland, Ohio, in 1929 and 1930, and the next year won the Transcontinental Handicap Air Derby and set another record at Cleveland.

Together Phoebe and Vernon Omlie opened the first airport in Tennessee at Memphis and established one of the first flying schools in the country. Phoebe Omlie's business career in aviation began when she instructed in and operated the Memphis school in 1923. Much of her racing was done in Monocoupe airplanes, and though aircraft manufacturers commonly sponsored pilots by furnishing aircraft, it was an unusual distinction for the Mono Aircraft Corporation to appoint Omlie as assistant to the president of the company, a position she held from 1928 to 1931. She toured the United States and South America, promoting the company's aircraft and the cause of aviation.

Omlie joined politics and aviation when in 1932 she suggested the use of a plane in the presidential campaign of Franklin D. Roosevelt. She flew over 5,000 miles in the campaign, ferrying speakers for the Democratic National Committee. After the election she visited President Roosevelt and reportedly reminded him that Napoleon I had a woman as his chief-of-air-staff (in charge of balloons). Roosevelt ap-

pointed her to the post of technical adviser, to serve as liaison between the National Advisory Committee for Aeronautics and the Bureau of Air Commerce. The first woman government official in aviation, she held the post from 1933 until 1936.

After Vernon Omlie's death in a commercial airplane crash in 1936, Phoebe Omlie resigned her government position and returned to Tennessee to work toward the realization of some of their mutual goals: tax reforms to return aviation taxes to aviation usage and the establishment of state government-sponsored schools for training civilian pilots. She succeeded in both efforts, and the Tennessee schools later became the model for the national Civilian Pilot Training program. Omlie also helped to implement and teach a preparatory curriculum in aviation introduced into Tennessee's high schools, and later copied by other states.

In 1941 Omlie returned to Washington, D.C., to serve as senior private flying specialist with the Civil Aeronautics Administration (CAA). In that capacity she further promoted the national air marking work which she and AMELIA EARHART had begun years before. Their aim was to aid pilots by painting markers on roofs throughout the country. Omlie also headed and coordinated a joint Works Progress Administration and Office of Education project to train 5,000 airport ground personnel. During this period, incensed by the removal of women from the Civilian Pilot Training schools, she asked to be loaned to Tennessee in order to open a school for the training of women instructors. The school won national publicity, and the program spread to other states. Her instructors ended up teaching in the very schools from which they had been removed. In 1942 the National Education Association gave her a citation for her contribution to American education.

Returning to Washington in 1943, Omlie held a series of posts with the CAA. In 1952, deeply troubled by what she called the socialization of the aviation industry, she resigned. Distressed and disillusioned, Phoebe Omlie then invested most of her life savings in a cattle ranch in Mississippi, but the ranch failed and she lost her investment. Little is known about the ensuing years, except that she became increasingly concerned about federal intervention in all phases of life, and tried to organize support for the return of control of school systems to the states. In 1967 she revisited Washington to lobby for this cause, and told a reporter: "I'm a crusader." Omlie's dwindling funds helped to bring the crusade to a halt, although until her death of lung cancer in Indianapolis, Ind., in 1975, she continued her attempts to coordinate various conservative groups around the country into a coherent organization.

[Information about Omlie's early life and beginning in aviation may be found in the files of the *St. Paul* (Minn.) *Pioneer Press* and in the alumni records of the St. Paul Mechanic Arts High School. The Tenn. Dept. of Transportation, Bureau of Aeronautics, has a file on Omlie that includes newspaper clippings on her training program for women flight instructors. The best published source is Charles Planck, *Women With Wings* (1942), which devotes several chapters to her career and includes tables of her competitive flying records. Jean Adams, Margaret Kimball, and Jeanette Kimball devote a colorful chapter to her in *Heroines of the Sky* (1942). See also Gene Slack, "Tennessee's Airwomen," *Flying*, May 1943, and *Who's Who in Aviation*, 1942–43. Additional information for this article was provided by Patricia Harpole, Earl M. Rogers, Lida Lisle Greene, Madge Rutherford Minton, Nick A. Komons, and Patricia O'Malley Strickland. Death certificate supplied by Ind. Board of Health.]

GENE SLACK SCHARLAU

OVINGTON, Mary White, April 11, 1865– July 15, 1951. Civil rights reformer.

Mary White Ovington, a founder and board chairman of the National Association for the Advancement of Colored People, was born in Brooklyn, N.Y., the third of four children, and second of three daughters. Her parents, Ann Louise (Ketcham) and Theodore Tweedy Ovington, endowed her with a legacy of abolitionism and Unitarian free thought that paved the way for her career as a social reformer. Theodore Ovington's china and glass importing firm, Ovington Brothers, provided the income for a comfortable and cultured upper-middle-class life throughout most of Mary White Ovington's childhood and adolescence.

The most powerful intellectual influence on the young Ovington was the Rev. John White Chadwick, minister of the Second Unitarian Church in Brooklyn Heights. Under his guidance, she was tutored in a gospel of optimistic evolutionism, social reform, and woman's rights. Her early education at private schools in Brooklyn Heights was capped by three years at Packer Collegiate Institute (1888–91), followed by two years at Radcliffe College (1891–93), then known as the Harvard Annex. There, Ovington's moderate reform inclinations took a more radical turn under economic historian William J. Ashley. Henceforth she always looked at social problems through the analytical framework of class.

When the depression of 1893 played havoc with her father's business, Ovington was forced to leave college. She became registrar of Pratt Institute in Brooklyn and then head worker (1895–1903) at Greenpoint Settlement, a Pratt-sponsored project housed in a model tenement, which she helped to found. Located in a working-class, immigrant district, the settlement was an invaluable training ground for Ovington's later work with blacks, whose problems she always believed were due as much to class as to race. She became vice president of the Brooklyn Consumers' League and assistant secretary of the Social Reform Club in New York. The Reform Club linked her to progressive reform throughout the city and cemented her belief in socialism; she joined the Socialist party of America about 1905.

Abolitionists William Lloyd Garrison and Frederick Douglass were family heroes, but Ovington's parents taught her that emancipation and the Reconstruction amendments had put an end to "the Negro problem." It was not until 1903, when she was thirty-eight, that a speech by Booker T. Washington at the Social Reform Club made Ovington aware of racial discrimination in the north. From that time until her death Mary White Ovington's life was dedicated to the achievement of racial equality. Becoming a fellow of Greenwich House, a settlement headed by MARY KINGSBURY SIMKHOVITCH, and doing social work there among blacks, Ovington began in 1904 a study of black Manhattan. Focusing particularly on housing and employment problems, her work resulted in 1911 in publication of *Half a Man: The Status of the Negro in New York*. In the course of her research, Ovington met New York's black leaders, learned from them about community problems, began a correspondence with black scholar W. E. B. Du Bois, tried unsuccessfully to establish a settlement house for blacks, and lived for a time as the only white in a black tenement. She reported on what she learned for several publications, including the *New York Evening Post* and *Charities*. Her close associations with blacks brought her occasional notoriety: lurid newspaper accounts followed a biracial dinner in a New York restaurant at which she had sat next to a black man.

For a time her reformist energies focused almost exclusively on two organizations that were precursors of the National Urban League: the National League for the Protection of Colored Women and the Committee for Improving the Industrial Condition of Negroes in New York. But for her deepening friendship with Du Bois, she might have become a founder of the gradualist Urban League. Instead, her sympathies lay with the militant neoabolitionists of Du Bois's Niagara Movement and she became one of a select number of white associate members.

Ovington joined a handful of white reformers in founding the NAACP. Following a virulent race riot in Springfield, Ill., in August 1908, a meeting was called the following May that led to the formation of the biracial protest group, initially known as the National Negro Committee. The goals of the new organization—to end racial discrimination and segregation and to push for the attainment of legal and civil rights, including the franchise—were radical for their day, and challenged Booker T. Washington's leadership of the black community. From the start, Ovington was a member of the inner circle that made key decisions and set the organization's tone. She was also involved at its New York headquarters on a day-to-day basis.

For almost forty years she served the NAACP in numerous decisionmaking positions: board member, interim executive secretary, chairman of board committees, vice president, acting chairman of the board, chairman, and treasurer. But her influence went far beyond her official duties: no matter what the title, she was a minister without portfolio who helped articulate policy, raise money, create new branches, lobby against discrimination, and organize the national office. Above all, she was a conciliator and a buoyant spirit in the face of persistent racism.

Ovington had a genius for personal relations that was indispensable. If conflicts between key leaders had not been contained, there would have been no NAACP. For there was not enough institutional momentum—no stable of dependable big donors, few well-established branches, no string of courtroom or legislative victories—to ensure its survival. Ovington's central role was to keep publicity director Du Bois and chairman Oswald Garrison Villard at arm's length, at least for a time. Although Ovington tried to act as mediator, she was partial to Du Bois. She considered him the great genius of his race and the man who made the NAACP a credible force in black communities; he was not only a powerful personality but also the sole black among the NAACP national leadership. For his part, Du Bois regarded her as a friend and loyal ally. He also considered her one of two white associates who was entirely free of race prejudice. Her mediation lasted until late 1914, when Villard resigned as chairman.

By January 1919, when Mary White Ovington took over as chairman of the board, the NAACP could boast of 44,000 members in 165 branches and a number of symbolic if practically insignificant victories before the United States Supreme Court. Blacks had been appointed to most executive positions at the national office, in keeping with her view that qualified blacks should assume most of the leadership even as

the NAACP remained open to all races. This organizational maturity, combined with Ovington's cordial relations with executive secretary James Weldon Johnson, the first black to hold the job, determined the shape of her leadership. Her work in this period focused on organizational nuts and bolts—fund raising and the maintenance of branches—and continued in-house diplomacy. Ovington's diplomatic skills were reserved for patching up relations with disaffected branches and for dealing with Du Bois, whose prickly personality made it difficult for her to be both boss and friend.

Ovington's reform interests were varied. A feminist, pacifist, and anti-imperialist, she invariably subordinated these concerns to her NAACP work. She used the platform of The New Review, for instance, to call for the "destruction of masculine despotism" and to chide her socialist colleagues for their indifference to the plight of blacks and women. As NAACP chairman, she tried, unsuccessfully, to pressure suffrage organizations into lobbying for voting rights for black women. Although not a strict pacifist (she believed violence had been necessary to destroy slavery), she opposed United States participation in World War I. And she encouraged NAACP efforts in the 1920s to end United States occupation of Haiti and European colonialism in Africa (via Du Bois's Pan African Congress movement).

Perhaps her single most important contribution as chairman came in 1923 after several years of fruitless lobbying in Congress on behalf of the Dyer Anti-Lynching bill; she persuaded the NAACP to redirect its energies, for over a decade, toward securing equal federal aid for black and white school systems. The decision was a key first step toward the direct assault on separate-but-equal school systems that was not begun in earnest until the late 1940s.

In January 1932, Ovington resigned as chairman and became NAACP treasurer. The resignation was a sign that under executive secretary Walter White, whom she labeled a "dictator," she could no longer be the conciliator she once was, even though she agreed with him on key substantive issues. As an elder NAACP stateswoman, Ovington took a major role in the debates triggered by the depression. When Du Bois, no longer on speaking terms with her because of ideological differences, championed "voluntary segregation" in 1934, she stood by the NAACP's goal of integration. When the Committee on Future Plan and Program sketched out an NAACP future based on economic radicalism, she again sided with traditionalists like White and assistant secretary Roy Wilkins. Although she was still a socialist, she believed that advocacy of radicalism would destroy the NAACP's base in the black middle class without assuring a new constituency to replace it. In both cases, her views coincided with the majority view in the NAACP inner circle.

Always reticent about herself, Ovington's writings nonetheless provide insight into her character and beliefs. In her "Book Chats," reviews distributed to some 250 newspapers by the NAACP News Service during the 1920s, Ovington applauded the cultural pluralism and vitality of the Harlem Renaissance, even while chastising its writers for what she regarded as a preoccupation with sex. Her enthusiasm was tempered too by her reluctance to embrace the exaltation of race found in some Renaissance literature. Ovington also wrote *Portraits in Color* (1927), profiles of black leaders; *The Walls Came Tumbling Down* (1947), an autobiography that is better described as a popular history of the NAACP; *The Shadow* (1920), a poorly written novel of mistaken racial identity; and several children's books.

Throughout her life, Ovington remained close to her family. She lived and often traveled with her mother until the latter's death in 1927. She then lived alone for a time in a Greenwich Village apartment (which she sublet to black friends, insisting that they remain despite threats from other tenants). When the depression reduced her income, she moved in with her brother and sister-in-law; after retiring from the NAACP in 1947, she lived with a sister in Auburndale, Mass. In her final years, Ovington suffered from hypertension and bouts of depression. She died in July 1951 at a nursing home in Newton Highlands, Mass.

[The most important manuscript sources are: the Mary White Ovington Papers, Archives of Labor History and Urban Affairs, Wayne State Univ.; Papers of the NAACP, Library of Congress; W. E. B. Du Bois Papers, Univ. of Mass., at Amherst; Oswald Garrison Villard Papers, Harvard Univ.; Joel E. Spingarn Papers, Howard Univ. and the N.Y. Public Library. Other autobiographical accounts are an unpublished fragment in the Ovington Papers at Wayne State and the "Reminiscences" Ovington wrote for the black weekly, *Baltimore Afro-American*, Sept. 1932–Feb. 1933. Ovington also wrote *Hazel* (1913) and *Zeke: A School Boy at Tolliver* (1931), both novels for juveniles; *The Upward Path, a Reader for Colored Children* (1920), compiled with Myron Thomas Pritchard; and *The Awakening* (1923) and *Phillis Wheatley* (1932), both plays designed to recruit members to the NAACP. Among Ovington's more significant magazine articles are "The Status of the Negro in the United States," *New Review*, Sept. 1913, pp. 744–49; "Socialism and the Feminist Movement," *New Review*, March 1914, pp. 143–47; "The United States in Porto Rico," *New Republic*, July 8, 1916, pp. 244–46, and July 15, 1916, pp. 271–73. Ovington's role in the NAACP is explored to some extent in Charles Flint Kellogg, *NAACP: A History of the National Association for the Advancement of Colored People, 1909–1920* (1967), and B. Joyce Ross, *J. E. Spingarn and the Rise of the NAACP, 1911–1939* (1972). The only biography is Daniel W. Cryer, "Mary White Ovington and the Rise of the NAACP" (Ph.D. diss., Univ. of Minn., 1977). Death certificate provided by Mass. Dept. of Public Health.]

DANIEL W. CRYER

OWEN, Ruth Bryan. See ROHDE, Ruth Bryan Owen.

P

PARK, Maud May Wood, Jan. 25, 1871–May 8, 1955. Suffragist, civic leader.

Maud Wood Park, first president of the League of Women Voters, was born in Boston, the eldest of three children (two girls and one boy) of James Rodney and Mary Russell (Collins) Wood. James Wood, who had been a scout for Ulysses S. Grant during the Civil War, was a member of the Boston police force, and later founded his own detective agency. Maud Wood attended the St. Agnes School in Albany, N.Y., graduating in 1887 as class valedictorian.

She taught school first in Bedford, Mass., and then at Chelsea High School, saving enough money to enter Radcliffe College in 1895.

A brilliant student, she graduated summa cum laude after three years. At Radcliffe, as at the St. Agnes School, Wood found herself surrounded by antisuffragists. One of two students in a class of seventy-two to favor votes for women, Wood and her friend INEZ HAYNES GILLMORE (IRWIN) brought ALICE STONE BLACKWELL to Radcliffe to present the case for suffrage; both young women joined the Massachusetts Woman Suffrage Association (MWSA) soon after. In 1897, while still a student, Wood secretly married Charles Edward Park, a Boston architect. After making their marriage public in 1898, the couple lived near Denison House, a settlement in Boston's South End, where Maud Wood Park was introduced to the work of social reformers. Charles Park died in 1904.

Park was active in suffrage and civic work in Boston for more than fifteen years. She was elected chairman of the MWSA in 1900. The following year, at the request of the wealthy Boston philanthropist and suffragist PAULINE AGASSIZ SHAW, she became executive secretary of the Boston Equal Suffrage Association for Good Government (BESAGG), an organization which sought to "combine efforts to secure suffrage for women with direct activities for civic betterment." As leader and cofounder of BESAGG, which became a forum for the social feminist concerns of the younger and more progressive faction of the Massachusetts woman's movement, Park helped to organize the first Boston Parent-Teacher Association, encouraged immigrant women to form civic clubs, and strove to convert Bostonians to woman suffrage.

Park also did much to enlist the interest of college-educated women in suffrage. Having been surprised to find herself the youngest delegate present at a 1900 meeting of the National American Woman Suffrage Association (NAWSA), the following spring she and Inez Haynes Gillmore organized the first chapter of the College Equal Suffrage League (CESL). An able organizer and charismatic speaker since her college debating days, in 1904 Park began to organize CESL chapters in New York state. For the next three years she traveled around the country organizing college women. In 1908, NAWSA finally agreed to sanction a national CESL. Park, who had resigned from her Massachusetts suffrage positions in 1907, became vice president, a position she held until the organization disbanded in 1916.

Park continued to travel for another three years. After visiting the western suffrage states and spending some time in a San Francisco settlement, in March 1909, with fellow suffragist Mabel Willard, she departed for a round-the-world trip to study women in other countries, especially in Asia. The eighteen-month tour, financed by Pauline Shaw, provided the material for a series of well-paid lectures which Park gave around the country on her return. On August 20, 1908, she had secretly married Robert Hunter, a member of the Hartford Players and a New York theatrical agent. Separated by their work, Park and Hunter did not live together, but met in hotels during Park's lecture tours and later spent vacations together in her Maine home. This second marriage, never made public, was known only to a few close friends.

Returning to Boston in 1910 to resume her paid position with BESAGG, Park discovered that the tactics of Massachusetts suffragists now included open-air meetings, parades, and publicity stunts. She initially found the street meetings distasteful, but soon adjusted her speaking style to them. Although the novel techniques helped to revitalize the suffrage movement in the state, the Massachusetts referendum campaign of 1915, which Park helped to organize, was unsuccessful. Following NAWSA's adoption in 1916 of the "winning plan" of CARRIE CHAPMAN CATT to combine agitation for a federal suffrage amendment with continued campaigns at the state level, Park was persuaded by Catt to join NAWSA's Congressional Committee. In January 1917 she went to Washington, D.C., to head the "front door lobby," a designation that symbolized the idealism of the woman suffrage movement.

Park and her colleagues, while eschewing bribery and offers of political favors, ran an efficient and pragmatic campaign that depended on reasoned arguments, persuasion, and careful grassroots organization. Through an intricate political network they kept informed of the suffrage views of each member of Congress. They also used any social and political influence they could muster. Park's colleague Helen Hamilton Gardener worked on her next-door neighbor, speaker of the House of Representatives Champ Clark, to win him over to the creation of a woman suffrage committee in order to circumvent the "gentlemen's agreement" to defer general legislation while war measures were being considered. The new committee reported favorably on the suffrage amendment, which the House passed in January 1918 by a two-thirds majority. The Senate followed in June 1919, and the nineteenth amendment was officially proclaimed as adopted in August 1920 following ratification by the states.

In 1919 Park "reluctantly agreed" to become the first president of the League of Women Voters (LWV), the nonpartisan organization to educate the new voters which Catt had proposed as the successor to NAWSA. Elected to office the following year, she assumed a social feminist stance. Park asserted that the League's purpose should be to promote "reforms in which women will naturally take an interest in a greater degree than men—protection for working women, for children, public health questions, and the care of dependent and delinquent classes, extension of the Children's Bureau, extension of education's power in government."

From the moment she accepted, she later recalled, "I felt as if an avalanche of work had fallen upon me."

Euphoric over their recent victory, feminists in the LWV adopted a program of thirty-eight legislative measures. The League, which attracted only a fraction of the former membership of NAWSA and was constantly short of funds, participated with nine other women's organizations in the Women's Joint Congressional Committee (WJCC), organized in 1920 to work together for social feminist goals and to continue the front door lobby. Park became its permanent head. As a new conservatism settled over Washington, social legislation faced rough sledding, but the WJCC was largely responsible for two important pieces of legislation: the Sheppard-Towner Maternity and Infancy Protection Act of 1921 and the Cable Act of 1922 which granted independent citizenship to married women. The League also served as a pressure group for the Children's Bureau and worked in the states to end child labor and promote other social measures.

As League president, Park alternated her work in Washington with lecture tours around the country, trying to persuade young women to join the organization. Despite her successes, these years were often difficult. In early 1924 she fell ill with a serious strep infection and did not fully recover for several months. The same year a vicious red-baiting campaign was launched against the women's movement, and conservatives attempted to link the League with the "international socialist-pacifist movement." (Park was a staunch Republican.) The child labor amendment also went down to defeat in the states.

At the same time, Park faced a disturbing break with her old colleague and friend Carrie Chapman Catt, who had devoted most of her time to the peace movement after 1920. Unfamiliar with the efforts of the WJCC, Catt publicly claimed in 1922 that the LWV had been responsible for the passage of Sheppard-Towner. When Park tried to soothe ruffled feathers by emphasizing the joint collaboration of several women's organizations, Catt accused Park of favoring Republican women and of undermining the League. Catt was so angry that she did not even reply to Park's letter offering to resign the presidency. Park continued in that office until 1924 when, sick and emotionally exhausted, she handed the gavel of the LWV to BELLE SHERWIN.

After retiring from the League, Park began work on a vacation home in Cape Cottage, Maine, and lectured in eastern cities and on college campuses, assessing the state of the women's movement. She reappeared in Washington to support the World Court Committee in 1925 and served in 1926 as a legislative counselor for the LWV. The following year she extended her lecture tour to the southern states and made a last public visit to Washington to support the extension of the Sheppard-Towner Act, an effort that failed.

Following the death of Robert Hunter in 1928, Park, who had studied drama at Radcliffe, took up playwriting. *Lucy Stone*, written in 1936, was performed by the Federal Theatre Group in Boston three years later. In 1943 Park and Edna Stantial, a former secretary of BESAGG, prepared a large body of materials related to the women's movement in Massachusetts which they gave to Radcliffe College. These became the nucleus of the Woman's Rights Collection of the Schlesinger Library. Park sold her Maine house in 1946, and moved to Boston, where she at first lived in hotels and then with Guy and Edna Stantial in Melrose, Mass. She died in Reading, Mass., in 1955 of a stroke.

Park was in many ways typical of the generation of suffrage leaders who succeeded ANNA HOWARD SHAW and JULIA WARD HOWE. She and her colleagues brought a tough-minded efficiency and militancy to the suffrage movement that contributed to the success of the final push for the nineteenth amendment. She later said that while Catt had been the architect of the nineteenth amendment, she had been the builder, and her *Front Door Lobby*, published posthumously in 1960, remains a fascinating account of her years in Washington. The reticence that so marked her personal life worked to her advantage as a lobbyist, for politicians and movement leaders alike knew that she could be trusted with a confidence. A woman of great executive ability, Park seemed to thrive on appeals for membership and funds, and on grassroots organizing. Admitting that she often found it easier to speak to groups than to individuals, she was nevertheless a woman of great charm who drew both men and women to her cause. She rarely used notes, but she impressed most of her hearers by her concise, well-organized, and personal delivery. Her old friend Inez Haynes Irwin said of Park in 1955: "I was always admiring the length, breadth and height of her mind. It had great floor space."

[Some of Park's papers, mostly clippings, typewritten notes, photographs, and plays, can be found in the Woman's Rights Coll. at the Schlesinger Library, Radcliffe College, along with records of the MWSA, CESL, and BESAGG. Information about Park's work can also be found in the manuscript collections of the LWV, WJCC, NAWSA, and the papers of

Carrie Chapman Catt, all in the Library of Congress. Some of Park's papers are still in the possession of Edna Lamprey Stantial of Chilmark, Mass. Park edited and contributed several chapters to *Victory, How Women Won It; A Centennial Symposium 1840–1940* (1940). For biographical accounts see Lois Bannister Merk, "The Early Career of Maud Wood Park," *Radcliffe Quart.*, May 1948; Catherine I. Hackett, "The Lady Who Made Lobbying Respectable," *Woman Citizen*, April 19, 1924; the entry in *Dict. Am. Biog.*, Supp. Five; *Nat. Cyc. Am. Biog.*, A, 526–27. For the context of Park's work in the woman's movement and some biographical information see Lois Bannister Merk, "Massachusetts and the Woman Suffrage Movement" (Ph.D. diss., Radcliffe College, 1956; rev. microfilm ed., Library of Congress, 1961). See also Sharon Hartman Strom, "Leadership and Tactics in the American Woman Suffrage Movement: A New Perspective from Massachusetts," *Jour. Am. Hist.*, Sept. 1975, 296–315; Eleanor Flexner, *Century of Struggle: The Woman's Rights Movement in the United States* (1959); J. Stanley Lemons, *The Woman Citizen: Social Feminism in the 1920s* (1973). Edna Stantial provided information useful in the preparation of this article. A copy of the marriage license provided by Conn. Dept. of Health confirms Park's marriage to Robert Hunter; death record provided by Mass. Dept. of Public Health.]

SHARON HARTMAN STROM

PARKER, Dorothy Rothschild, Aug. 22, 1893– June 7, 1967. Writer.

Dorothy Parker was born during her parents' vacation in West End, N.J. Shortly after, the family moved back to the West Seventies in New York City; there, fittingly, destined to be an urban muse, she spent her girlhood. The youngest and perhaps unwanted child of Eliza (Marston) and J. Henry Rothschild, she had an older brother and a sister nine years her senior. She was never close to either and in later years spoke of them and her family seldom; she disliked, vehemently and unforgivingly, her father and stepmother.

Henry Rothschild was Jewish by descent; his first wife, Dorothy's mother, was Scottish. A solid member of the middle class, Rothschild worked in the garment industry. After Eliza Rothschild's early death, he remarried a strict and, if her stepdaughter is to be believed, cruel Roman Catholic. The young Dorothy Rothschild was sent for her primary education, over her protest, to New York's Blessed Sacrament Convent. Later, she attended the progressive, academically rigorous Miss Dana's School in Morristown, N.J.; she received her diploma in 1911. Some time between her father's death in 1912 and 1916, she began her real life, the only life she ever found worth discussing in later years: she found a room by herself at a boarding-house on 103d Street and Broadway in New York City, and she took on the city in a permanent gesture.

An ardent supporter of suffrage, though not an activist one, a chain smoker, ultra-feminine in her petite, dark beauty, addicted to large floppy hats and an eccentric version of haute couture, flattering and acid by turns, "masculine" in her ambition and tough brilliant wit, Dorothy Rothschild was ready to enter, and star in, the exciting creative life just starting its legendary swirl in prewar New York. She supported herself by playing the piano for a dancing school. Then in 1916, Frank Crowninshield, the dapper editor of the modish pioneering magazine *Vanity Fair*, accepted one of her poems for publication, and soon found her a job writing advertising captions for *Vogue*, which he also edited: "Brevity is the soul of Lingerie" is perhaps the most famous.

In 1917, Dorothy Rothschild married Edwin Pond Parker II, a conventional Wall Street man from an old Hartford, Conn., family. That year she joined the *Vanity Fair* staff, becoming its drama critic in 1919. She became intimate friends with Robert Sherwood, soon to be a famous playwright, and Robert Benchley, on his way to popularity as one of America's greatest twentieth-century humorists. From this triumvirate and the newspaper group consisting of Franklin P. Adams, Alexander Woollcott (both writers for the *New York World*), and Harold Ross, who would found *The New Yorker* in 1925, developed the famous cluster of metropolitan wits who lunched at the Algonquin Hotel's Round Table and exchanged highly formal criticisms off and on the printed page. In the most bitter moments of her later years, Parker would still fondly say of these early days: "We had more fun!" When she was fired in January 1920 from her *Vanity Fair* job for a drama review too cutting to please the powerful theatrical interests whose advertising sustained the periodical, Benchley and Sherwood resigned too, in protest.

All three eventually found jobs elsewhere. For a time Benchley and Parker shared an office and attempted to go into business as free-lance writers. They failed. By 1922, she was writing for the *Saturday Evening Post*'s comic page, "Short Turns and Encores." In public, her softly murmured one-liners made comic history. To a young man complaining superciliously that he couldn't bear fools, she replied: "That's odd. Your mother could." Another young man she pronounced "a rhinestone in the rough." Parker incarnated "style" in an urban age that valued nothing more highly. No party of the Smart Set could succeed without her, and few had to try. But by the midtwenties a pattern emerged of success cut short by what seems almost willful failure. That, as well as less psychological concerns, began to alter Parker's life.

Edwin Parker had gone off to war in 1918. When he returned in 1919, the marriage foundered. He drank, liked Hartford, and had little to say. Parker drank, but life in Hartford was unthinkable, and although she tried to make up witty stories about "Eddie," he came to bore her. They separated soon after the war, not without pain, and divorced in 1928. Succeeding love affairs brought Parker misery. To court unhappiness, as some say Parker did, is hardly the same thing as enjoying it. In 1923, after an abortion, Parker tried unsuccessfully to commit suicide. She tried again in 1925. The woman whose bons mots were among New York's most prized self-advertisements, was having, as she told a bartender, "not much fun."

Writing helped, but not enough. A play, Close Harmony, a satire of suburban life on which she collaborated in 1924 with Elmer Rice, failed. In 1926, a collection of her light, ironic, bitter, skillful verse, grimly entitled Enough Rope, was put out by Boni and Liveright and became a hit. Its success meant surprisingly little to her. Poet Parker mocked her own masochism: "I loved them until they loved me." She repeated her poetic success with Sunset Gun in 1928, Death and Taxes in 1931, and Not So Deep As a Well in 1936. Critics were enthusiastic about her elegant toughness and the public was impressed by Parker's sophisticated style, her tone of ennui amid pain, her role, in Irwin Edman's words, as "a Sappho who could combine a heartbreak with a wisecrack." Her readers had little inkling how great was the pain, how deeply Parker despised the ennui and distrusted the wisecracks.

One way out was politics and, though her politics were sometimes confused, Parker was never less than serious about them. In 1927, the anarchists Nicola Sacco and Bartolomeo Vanzetti were executed in Boston on the day after her thirty-fourth birthday. Parker, always on the side of the underdog, had campaigned actively against the death sentence; she was never the same after what she and countless others considered their murder. She continued nonetheless to move, like many of the Algonquinites, among the rich set of the Jock Whitneys and Averell Harrimans, accepting their hospitality and the drinks that she increasingly needed, although never writing kindly of them. She could support striking waiters at the Waldorf-Astoria and cross a picket line at the club '21' within days; yet she meant something genuine, if unclear,

when she said in 1934: "I am a communist." She worked against Franco in the Spanish civil war, and in old age told an interviewer that going to Spain was "the proudest thing" she ever did. She came to reject the wit of the old Algonquin circle, her own included, as "a shield, but . . . not a weapon." In Hollywood, where she went in the early thirties with her second husband, Alan Campbell, she made her antifascist, proleft views conspicuous enough to get herself, and the politically conservative Campbell, blacklisted in the 1940s. When she died in 1967, she left most of her estate to Martin Luther King, Jr.

Like other writers who went to Hollywood for the money it offered, Parker found the experience hateful: "I never did a picture I was proud of, and there never was a picture that was proud of me." About money in itself, Parker never cared: she earned much, spent more, and in later days, nearly starving, would leave large checks in her possession uncashed. But she wrote to earn money, and Hollywood offered a great deal. With Campbell and on her own she worked on the scripts of more than twenty films, including the original version (1939) of A Star Is Born. The other films were negligible except for The Little Foxes (1941), for which she and Campbell wrote additional dialogue and scenes for her friend Lillian Hellman's screenplay. She was proud, however, of her involvement with the Screenwriters' Guild in their struggle to unionize the profession.

Parker's conflict-laden relationship with the mediocre writer Campbell, bisexual and eleven years her junior, evolved over the years into a routine of contempt and complaisance with surprising staying power; it survived marriage (1933), divorce (1947), remarriage (1950), separation (1953), and reunion (1956), lasting until Campbell's death in 1963. They had both welcomed her pregnancy in 1935; a miscarriage in her third month was tragic.

Despite their ups and downs, despite Dorothy Parker's drinking, and her penchant for young, beautiful shallow men who exploited and humiliated her, in the late 1920s and the 1930s she found her literary voice, and a brilliant one it was. In 1929, she received the O. Henry short story prize for "Big Blonde," the painful saga of Hazel Morse, an aging, alcoholic whore totally dependent on men, who tries in vain to kill herself. Parker had begun to publish her sketches in the midtwenties in The Bookman, Scribners, and The New Yorker, and she continued to produce stories through the midforties. They are, as she well knew, her special claim to fame. In 1930, Parker brought out a collection called Laments for the Living; in 1933, After Such Pleasures. In addition, she did a skillful and witty job reviewing books for *The New Yorker* as "Constant Reader" beginning in the late twenties. She sprinkled her page with devastating judgments: over A. A. Milne's *The House at Pooh Corner,* she reported, "Tonstant Weader Fwowed Up." Writing for *Esquire* in the fifties, she early hailed such controversial talents as Vladimir Nabokov and SHIRLEY JACKSON. Parker's last play, *Ladies of the Corridor* (1953), despite its commercial failure, was a painfully honest, if loosely structured, study of women; it yielded two interesting short stories, "I Live on Your Visits" and "Lolita."

Dorothy Parker was probably, as Edmund Wilson and others believed, the only real artist in the Algonquin group. Gifted with a perfect ear, she was, with Ring Lardner whom she admired deeply, the greatest dialogue writer of her age. With the exception of Ernest Hemingway, she was the clearest, sharpest stylist among her contemporaries, possessed, in her phrase, of a "disciplined eye and a wild mind." Mistress of what she called the "he said, she said" story, Parker recounted the utter barrenness of New York society men and women: their alcoholism, their malicious games, their careless exploitation of their social inferiors, maids, blacks, poor relatives. Parker's special subject was oppression, particularly female oppression, and the most common misreading of her work is to take her apparent contempt for her society women at face value. Her compassion, founded on shrewd power of analysis, is as omnipresent as her satire; she usually lets the readers see, if they will, why her upper-class women cannot act, or change, just as she implicitly exposes the system of exploitation that crushes her more attractive victims. Her stories reveal that Parker was more profoundly political as an artist than she was as an activist.

Parker's female characters are all prisoners of the present. Her finest stories, with the exception of "Big Blonde," occur in a matter of hours, or even minutes, and the reader is given no information that reaches beyond the confines of that fixed span. It is always punitively *now,* in Parker's witty hell, and now is always a social occasion. Parker demonstrates woman's lot as the compulsion to overarticulate; she perceives feminine socialization as a process by which a girl learns that silence is intolerable and her women talk themselves, as they are meant to, into inferiority. Economics eluded Parker; men offhandedly dictating society's menus, not men aggressively running capitalist enterprises, were the incarnations of the ruling class who fascinated and angered her. She never depicted female solidarity, but no one etched more sharply

the obstacles in its way. Women in Parker's tales are in deadly competition for a limited number of the exceedingly paltry prizes only men can award them; and they scorn each other and themselves for being dumb enough to compete. They suffer pain without dignity, the shallow hysterical pang that springs from social climbing, rejection, and insecurity. Comic for the disarray of values it signifies, the pain she chronicles is nonetheless sharp, awful, unmistakable, and makes genuine politics, not to speak of social change, impossible.

Parker as a writer never regained the heights she attained in the thirties. She accomplished little after 1953; in New York City, in June 1967, alcohol and a heart attack finally finished off the small woman who had written so often of death. In the fifties, she judged herself with characteristic harshness: "I didn't make it" as a writer, she told a *Paris Review* interviewer. Years before, she'd confessed to a friend that she was "wasting" her talent by drinking, by living the New York life. Waste there was indeed; and suffering fully proportionate to the wit she summoned to shape it into the sharp bitter structures of her prose. But Parker was, as she had hoped, "a tough quotable female humorist," and more. Destined to scrutinize society in its most meaningless and cruel phases, Parker analyzed and charted waste itself. We will never cease to need her brilliantly etched maps of our empty places.

[Parker's work, with the exception of the plays which were published separately in the year of their production, can be found almost complete in *The Collected Dorothy Parker* (1973). Parker's most important statements about her work are in Malcolm Cowley, ed., *Writers at Work: The Paris Review Interviews* (1958), and in Donald Ogden Stewart, *Fighting Words* (1940). There is an interview with Parker (June 1959) in the Popular Arts Project, Oral History Coll., Columbia Univ. *Contemporary Authors: Permanent Series* has a bibliography and a complete list of film credits. The standard and readable biography is John Keats, *You Might As Well Live: The Life and Times of Dorothy Parker* (1970); he lamentably fails to date or locate Parker's individual pieces. Also useful are Lillian Hellman's chapter on Parker in *An Unfinished Woman: A Memoir* (1969); Wyatt Cooper, "Remembering Dorothy Parker," *Esquire,* July 1968; Richard Lauterback, "The Legend of Dorothy Parker," *Esquire,* Oct. 1944; Robert E. Drennan, *The Algonquin Wits* (1968); James R. Gaines, *Wits End: Days and Nights of the Algonquin Round Table* (1977); Margaret Case Harriman, *The Vicious Circle: The Story of the Algonquin Round Table* (1951); Vincent Sheean, *Personal History* (1937); William Shenahan, "Robert Benchley and Dorothy Parker," *Rendezvous,* vol. 3 (1968); and Alexander

Woollcott, "Our Mrs. Parker," in *While Rome Burns* (1934). Interesting contemporary dramatizations of Parker are found in George Oppenheimer, *Here Today* (1931); George C. Kaufman and Moss Hart, *Merrily We Roll Along* (1934); and Charles Brackett, *Entirely Surrounded* (1934). Lillian Hellman is Parker's literary executor. The *N.Y. Times* obituaries of June 8 and 10, 1967, are laudatory and anecdotal.]

ANN DOUGLAS

PARKER, Julia Sarsfield O'Connor, Sept. 9, 1890–Aug. 27, 1972. Labor leader and organizer.

Julia O'Connor Parker, union organizer best known for her leadership of New England telephone workers, was born in Woburn, Mass., the second daughter and youngest of four children of John and Sarah (Conneally) O'Connor. Her parents had emigrated from Ireland to Massachusetts, where John O'Connor earned his living as a leather currier. Julia attended parochial schools in Woburn and public high school in Medford, Mass.; upon her graduation in 1908 she began work as a telephone operator in Boston. Her involvement in the labor movement, which lasted forty-five years, began in March 1912 when she joined the newly formed Boston Telephone Operators' Union, organized by the International Brotherhood of Electrical Workers (IBEW) with the assistance of the Women's Trade Union League (WTUL). Quickly rising to prominence in the new union, O'Connor was part of the nine-woman committee that achieved the union's recognition in negotiations with top national company officials after a threatened strike in 1913.

The WTUL, established in 1903 to organize women workers and promote protective legislation, introduced O'Connor to larger social and political causes. She became involved with the league in 1912, serving as president of the Boston chapter from 1915 to 1918 (the first working woman to attain that office), and as a member of the national executive board from 1917 to 1926; in 1919 she went as a delegate to the First International Congress of Working Women. From 1914 until 1916 she was a workers' representative on the board appointed by the Massachusetts Minimum Wage Commission to determine a minimum wage for women retail workers. For four months in 1916, O'Connor attended the WTUL's training school in Chicago; she emerged critical of what she considered the school's condescension toward its worker-students and its insufficient attention to field organizing. Her feelings reflected a larger conflict of values within the WTUL between working women who stressed union organizing

and their middle-class allies, more concerned with legislative reform.

Following a near-strike in Boston in 1913, telephone operators across the country began to organize, but they were denied full representation in the IBEW, largely because of the male members' fear of "petticoat rule." An autonomous department for the telephone operators was finally established within the IBEW in 1918, and O'Connor was elected its president, a post she held until 1938. During World War I, when the telephone service came under government ownership, O'Connor served as the only labor representative on the Ryan Commission, whose function was to advise Postmaster General Albert Burleson on wages and working conditions in the telephone service. In January 1919, protesting Burleson's hostility toward organized labor, O'Connor resigned from the commission, and in April she led the New England Telephone Operators' Union in a six-day strike to compel action on its long-ignored wage demands. Completely paralyzing telephone service in five New England states, the strike was one of the few in the wave of postwar strikes to end on favorable terms for the workers.

On leave of absence from her IBEW post for four months, O'Connor visited Europe in 1921 to observe labor conditions in Great Britain, Ireland, France, Germany, and Italy. A highly talented and prolific writer, O'Connor described British and Irish working conditions in a series of articles for *The Union Telephone Operator*, the magazine of the IBEW Telephone Operators' Department. Active in the postwar peace movement, O'Connor delivered a 1921 Armistice Day address calling for an end to war and militarism at the Women's Mass Meeting on Disarmament in Washington, D.C.

In the postwar climate of hostility to organized labor, the Telephone Operators' Department quickly declined from its peak in 1919, when it had boasted 18,000 members in 200 locals. Confronted with Bell Telephone's efforts to form a company union, and shrewdly anticipating the loss of jobs that would result from the telephone dial system, in 1923 O'Connor called for a strike for shorter hours and higher wages in New England, the only region in which the union continued to be strong. But some leaders of operators' locals, accusing O'Connor of authoritarianism, failed to respond to the strike call, and the two-month strike ended in the union's total defeat. The telephone operators would not return to the IBEW for nearly fifty years.

O'Connor continued her activity in the labor movement after her marriage in 1925 to Charles Austin Parker, a reporter for the *Boston Herald*.

The couple secured the services of a housekeeper to care for their two daughters, Sarah, born in 1926, and Carol, born in 1928. An ardent supporter of Franklin D. Roosevelt, Julia O'Connor Parker was associated with the labor division of the Democratic National Committee in the presidential campaigns of 1932, 1936, and 1940. Under the National Recovery Administration, as IBEW representative, she testified in 1934 at hearings to determine labor standards in the telephone industry. Parker assailed the dial system because it displaced telephone operators, caused extra effort for the customer, and demeaned telephone work.

From 1939 until her retirement in 1957, Parker was employed as an organizer for the American Federation of Labor (AFL). Required to spend much time away from her Boston home, she placed her daughters in boarding schools. After managing successful campaigns among chemical workers in New York state, she was assigned to the AFL's southern campaign, working throughout the south and southwest from 1944 until 1947. In early 1945, Parker toured industrial establishments in Britain as part of a four-woman delegation sent by the United States Office of War Information to study war production and labor conditions. The AFL transferred her in 1947 from the south to its Boston regional office, where for the remainder of her career she participated in campaigns to organize Bridgeport Brass, General Electric, and the Fore River shipyards. Surviving her husband by twelve years, Julia O'Connor Parker died in Wayland, Mass., in 1972 of arteriosclerotic heart disease.

[The most useful sources on Julia O'Connor Parker's career are *Life and Labor*, publication of the National WTUL; the papers of the National WTUL at the Library of Congress, Washington, D.C.; the IBEW's *Jour. of Electrical Workers and Operators;* and *The Union Telephone Operator*, publication of the Telephone Operators' Dept., IBEW. Julia O'Connor's "History of the Organized Telephone Operators' Movement" appeared in a six-part series in *The Union Telephone Operator*, Jan.-June 1921. See also Gladys Boone, *The Women's Trade Union Leagues in Great Britain and the United States* (1942); Alice Henry, *The Trade Union Woman* (1915); Mass. Minimum Wage Commission, *Preliminary Report on the Effect of the Minimum Wage in Mass. Retail Stores*, Bull. No. 12, Nov. 1916; Stephen H. Norwood, "Laboring Women: The New England Telephone Operators' Union 1912-23" (M.A. thesis, Columbia Univ., 1975). An interview with Sarah Parker Swerbilov yielded valuable information about her mother's career and family background. An obituary appeared in the *Boston Globe*, Aug. 29, 1972; death record provided by Mass. Dept. of Public Health.]

STEPHEN H. NORWOOD

PARKHURST, Helen, March 7, 1887–June 1, 1973. Educator.

Helen Parkhurst, founder of the Dalton Plan of Education, was born in Durand, Wis., the eldest of three children (two boys and one girl) of Ida (Underwood) and James Henry Parkhurst. Her father, of English and Welsh ancestry, was a hotel keeper and civic leader. Her mother, of Scottish ancestry, was a teacher. Ida Parkhurst's influence was strong and supportive. Even as a young girl Helen knew she wanted to teach. She spoke later of a "fortunate childhood" made possible by parents who allowed her to "roam and learn at her own will."

After attending primary and secondary schools in Durand, Helen Parkhurst received her B.S. from the River Falls Normal School of Wisconsin State College in 1907. Her career had begun even before college graduation, when she was hired in 1904 by the rural school district in Pepin County, Wis., to teach in a one-room school serving forty farm boys of all ages. She met this challenge by using each corner of the room for a different subject and by having the older boys help the younger ones when she was not instructing them. In 1909–10, while teaching at the Edison School in Tacoma, Wash., Parkhurst realized that some of the ideas she had developed originally out of necessity were innovative and productive. Influenced also by *Mind in the Making*, a book by an American psychologist and educator, Edgar James Swift, she continued to test and develop her ideas. In 1910 she formulated her Laboratory Plan, a system intended to reorganize the physical and social structure and alter the purpose of a school. It was later renamed the Dalton Plan after the Massachusetts town that in 1918 first used it in a public school.

Parkhurst's plan was based on her belief that children learn most effectively in a situation that permits freedom of choice and allows them to progress at their own pace. To this end curriculum became secondary to living and working together in a shared, common community. She explained that "there is no such thing as a *subject* on the Dalton Plan. With us it is *living* on the Dalton Plan." Freedom, interaction with teachers and students of all ages, and budgeting of time were the three main features of the plan. Within that framework there were three objectives: to tailor each student's program to his or her interests and abilities, to enhance the student's sense of responsibility toward others, and to promote both independence and dependability. Instead of classrooms there were subject laboratories and each student was free to move from one to the other as individual programs dictated. School work was broken up into contracts, one for each month of the year. Each student agreed to accomplish monthly assignments in different subjects at an individually determined pace.

Although Parkhurst was determined to have her own school in which to put her theory into practice, this goal was not easily attained. For several years she trained others to teach—from 1911 to 1913 at the Central State Teachers College in Ellensburg, Wash., and from 1913 to 1915 as head of the primary training department at Central State Teachers College in Stevens Point, Wis. In 1914, on leave from Stevens Point, Parkhurst was appointed by the Wisconsin State Department of Education to report on the Montessori method of education. She enrolled in the International Montessori Teachers Training, in Rome, then being taught by Maria Montessori herself. Parkhurst became a disciple. Montessori later asked her to direct her exhibition classroom at the San Francisco World Exhibition. In 1917–18 Parkhurst headed the teacher training department of the Montessori training college in New York, the first person authorized by Montessori to train teachers.

By then Parkhurst was living in New York City, where she had moved in 1916. With enormous energy, strong will, and great ambition, she set out to establish her school. In New York she gained the financial backing of some prominent businessmen, and started her first classes in a private school she named the Children's University School. Renamed the Dalton School in 1920, it was extraordinarily successful and educators soon came from all over the world to observe Parkhurst's plan in action. In 1922 her book, *Education on the Dalton Plan*, was published in England; it was subsequently translated into fifty-eight languages. During the 1920s and 1930s Parkhurst was honored for her work by many countries and was decorated by both the Chinese Republic and the Emperor of Japan, whose citation declared her "officially married to her work." In 1957 Queen Juliana of the Netherlands honored her for her influence on Dutch education.

Though Parkhurst became internationally known, it was only in England and Japan, where several Dalton schools still existed in the 1970s, that the Dalton Plan really took hold. In the United States there was initial enthusiasm but, except for the school in Massachusetts and the prestigious one in New York, the plan as such was never accepted in its totality. Like other progressive education plans it emphasized flexibility, responsibility, and creative interaction, and like them it was modified and adapted to particular needs.

In 1942 Parkhurst resigned from the Dalton School after more than twenty years as its head, and went to Yale University (M.A., 1943), where she was the first Yale Fellow in Education. As a fellow, she taught sociology as well as continuing her own research. After 1947, Parkhurst entered yet another stage in her career, becoming an award-winning broadcasting celebrity. From 1947 to 1950 she did a weekly program, first on radio and later on television, called "Child's World," in which children discussed their problems. Other programs included "Growing Pains," a radio series for teenagers, and "The World of Sound," a program with blind children. She also made some 300 recordings with children on psychological subjects which were used in psychology courses throughout the country.

Parkhurst's energy never slackened; from 1952 to 1954 she taught at the College of the City of New York and during the period from 1950 to 1963 she also found time to publish three books. Working fourteen to sixteen hours a day at the age of eighty-six, Parkhurst was writing a book about Montessori and another on her childhood memories when she died of a pulmonary embolism in New Milford, Conn., in 1973. A lecture hall at the University of Wisconsin at Stevens Point is dedicated to her memory.

[The archives of the Dalton School in New York City contain much material, including unpublished lectures, reports, and an extensive bibliography on the Laboratory Plan and its implementation. Yale Univ. has tapes of some lectures given by Parkhurst while she was a Fellow in Education. Parkhurst's other books are *And They Found Jimmy* (1947), a novel; *Exploring the Child's World* (1951); *Growing Pains* (1962); and *Undertow* (1963). Biographical sources are few. Most helpful were papers, press releases, and biographical notes from the archives at the Univ. of Wisconsin at Stevens Point, where some of her papers and recordings are kept. See also Evelyn Dewey, *The Dalton Laboratory Plan* (1922) and the entry on Parkhurst in the *Biog. Dict. of Educators* (1978). Her brother, A. Alden Parkhurst, gave insights into early family relationships and into Helen Parkhurst's character and temperament. An obituary appeared in the *N.Y. Times*, June 4, 1973; death record provided by Conn. Dept. of Health.]

MARILYN MOSS FELDMAN

PARSONS, Louella Oettinger, Aug. 6, 1881– Dec. 9, 1972. Journalist.

Louella O. Parsons, the influential Hollywood columnist, achieved a power few women of her time could approach. A *New York Times* obituary noted that she "ruled as a queen," and imperial titles aptly described both the range of Parsons's influence and the personal manner in which she exercised it in an industry that crowned and deposed the stars who ruled the American popular imagination.

Born in Freeport, Ill., to Joshua and Helen (Wilcox) Oettinger, of German and Jewish descent, Louella Oettinger's early life was thoroughly small town and middle class. Her father, who died when Louella was eight, had married into a clothing manufacturing family and was a prosperous clothier by the time of his death in 1890. Of five children born to the Oettingers, only Louella, the eldest child, and a younger brother survived. Growing up in Dixon, Ill., and nearby towns, Louella remained in the narrow confines of the world to which she was born. She graduated from Dixon High School in 1901, attended Dixon College and Normal School, and, on Oct. 31, 1905, married a local realtor, John D. Parsons, with whom she had her only child, Harriet, in 1906. The marriage, never a happy one, ended, according to Parsons's account, with John Parsons's death in World War I. Some evidence, however, suggests a divorce. She was married for a second time, probably to Jack McCaffrey, a riverboat captain (Eells, pp. 38–40). But Parsons's romanticized versions of her life included neither the divorce nor a second unsuccessful marriage.

Blurring the lines between fact and fantasy played an important part in the career Parsons began in 1910 as a reporter for the *Chicago Tribune*. She supplemented her meager salary by writing scenarios for the pioneer motion picture production company, Essanay Studios, where she first met the movie people who would remain her friends and material for the rest of her career. The job at Essanay resulted in Parsons's first book, *How to Write for the Movies* (1915), a manual for aspiring screenwriters. But Parsons always considered herself a newspaperwoman first. In 1914 she began writing one of the earliest movie columns in the United States, for the *Chicago Record-Herald*. Thereafter, news for Parsons meant news about the movies and the people who made them.

As she was developing this form of news into an art, both Parsons's power and that of her Hollywood subjects increased. She moved to New York in 1919 to write first for the *New York Morning Telegraph* and then for the *New York American*. In 1923 Parsons became movie editor of the Hearst-owned *American,* and in 1925 publisher William Randolph Hearst made her movie editor for Universal News Service. After a year spent in Palm Springs, Calif., recovering from tuberculosis, she moved her operations to Hollywood in 1926. From then on, her

special talent, Hearst's powerful support, and the enormous scope of the Hearst syndicate placed Louella O. Parsons at the center of a Hollywood world which each year grew in significance as a playground and battlefield of twentieth-century culture.

Parsons developed a technique perfectly fitted to the requirements of this world in which actors and actresses became "personalities" whose lives and work merged to become mythological creations. Her columns freely mixed details about the private lives and public careers of her favorites, making them more accessible to an audience whose loyalty depended on its ability to identify with the stars. At the same time, she allowed her readers to experience vicariously the glamour of her subjects' lives. Parsons could make or destroy careers because few, even of the most prominent stars, could survive without the audience identification and participation which her column provided.

Throughout the thirties and forties, Parsons consolidated her power and position (frequently challenged by competitors, above all by HEDDA HOPPER) as the liaison between Hollywood and the world. Her news reached readers across the country and abroad through a network of syndicated columns reported to have numbered over six hundred. Parsons's ambition was matched only by her energy. While writing a daily column, she frequently contributed features to movie magazines; hosted a number of successful radio programs, most notably "Hollywood Hotel" (1934–38); appeared in a film of the same name; went on a theater tour; and wrote two semiautobiographical books, *The Gay Illiterate* (1944) and *Tell It to Louella* (1961).

Parsons was often criticized—for her weight, her grammar, and her frequent factual errors— but she was feared, and her power awed even the great movie moguls. She was also loved, for her exuberance, her generosity, and her genuine commitment and service to the industry she publicized. "Tell It to Louella" became Parsons's informal by-line and few failed to obey. She loved to play with and entertain the greats of the world she managed—Clark Gable, Mary Pickford, Rita Hayworth, among others— at the same time that she used them, sometimes viciously, for her own ends. With a network of informants, she worked tirelessly to describe to an eager public a world, part fact, part fiction, in which acting for a camera, frequent marriages and divorces, and extravagant galas and premieres all merged into a haze of illusion.

On Jan. 5, 1930, Parsons married Henry Watson Martin, a physician. Their happy marriage lasted until his death in 1951. Her real and often public affection for Docky, as she called him, and her lifelong pride in and solicitude for her daughter, Harriet, strong as they were, never interfered with her service to Hollywood. Through her marriage, Parsons became a deeply committed convert to Catholicism, a faith which provided her with strength and consolation through the height of her career and during her later lonely years in a changed Hollywood. Although she wrote her last by-line in 1964, the power and the glamour had faded by the late 1950s, and Parsons's efforts to keep up with the latest stars and the teenage rock music world were to no avail as Hollywood and Parsons had passed their zenith. "Hollywood," Parsons concluded in *Tell It to Louella,* "is and has been my life." She died after a long series of illnesses, of a stroke, in Santa Monica, Calif., in 1972.

[Parsons's columns appeared in the *L.A. Examiner,* 1926–65. She also wrote *Jean Harlow's Life Story* (1937). Tapes of her radio broadcasts are available at the Doheny Library, Univ. of Southern Calif. *The Reminiscences of Louella O. Parsons* is in the Oral Hist. Coll., Columbia Univ. Parsons's published accounts of her life were abbreviated and embroidered. George Eells provides further essential details and some corrections in *Hedda and Louella* (1972). Biographical information is also contained in Thomas Wood, "The First Lady of Hollywood," *Sat. Eve. Post,* July 5, 1939; "Hollywood's Back Fence," *Time,* Jan. 24, 1944; and *Current Biog.,* 1940. Robert Sklar, *Movie-Made America* (1975), and Ezra Goodman, *The Fifty Year Decline and Fall of Hollywood* (1961), provide background on the world within which Parsons prospered. W. A. Swanberg, *Citizen Hearst* (1961) profiles the publisher whose support and newspaper power underwrote Parsons's influence. Obituaries appeared in the *L.A. Times* and the *N.Y. Times,* Dec. 10, 1972. A birth record was supplied by Stephenson Cty. Clerk, Freeport, Ill. A marriage certificate for Parsons and Martin, from the Calif. Dept. of Health Services, gives evidence for a second marriage and gives her mother's maiden name as Wilcox, not Stine, as it appears in other sources. A death record was provided by the Calif. Dept. of Health Services.]

PAULA S. FASS

PATTERSON, Alicia, Oct. 15, 1906–July 2, 1963. Newspaper editor and publisher.

Alicia Patterson was born in Chicago to a Scots-Irish newspaper family whose beginning in the business she traced back to her great-great-grandfather, James Patrick, who founded an Ohio weekly in 1819. Her great-grandfather, Joseph Medill, directed the *Chicago Tribune* from 1855 to 1899; her grandfather, Robert W. Patterson, was an editor of the *Tribune* under Medill; and her father, Joseph Medill Patterson, was first an editor of the *Tribune* and later founder of the New York *Daily News.* More-

over, her father's sister, ELEANOR MEDILL PATTERSON, owned and operated the *Washington Times-Herald.*

Alicia Patterson was the second of three daughters of Joseph Patterson and his first wife, Alice (Higinbotham) Patterson, daughter of a partner in Chicago's Marshall Field & Company department store. She recalled her mother as a brave woman who had ridden in an airplane as early as 1911 and hunted on horseback.

Alicia's earliest years were spent rather humbly on a farm in Libertyville, Ill., where her father, avowing socialism, had exiled himself from the *Tribune.* He returned to the *Tribune* and a substantial income about 1910, and sent his four-year-old daughter for a time to Berlin to live with a family and learn German. During her childhood, Alicia's father tried to train her in personal courage with demanding tests, including jumping horses and high diving; she felt he raised her to be the son he did not have.

Her early education was in Chicago, at the Francis Parker School and the University School for Girls, but she was later sent to a series of finishing schools. Dropped by schools in Lausanne, Switzerland, and in Maryland for infractions of rules, she surprised her parents by graduating second in her class from the Foxcroft School in Virginia. But she had not reformed; she was dropped from another school in Rome and, accompanied by her mother and a sister, led a prankish life in Europe until she was nineteen, when she returned to Chicago for her coming-out party.

Even in her early adulthood her father persistently managed her life, although he did little to encourage her interest in the newspaper business. When she announced her desire for a career, however, he gave her a job on the New York *Daily News,* which he had founded in 1919. Beginning in 1927, she spent some months in the *News* promotion department before getting her chance as a reporter. A raw cub, she was assigned a major story on a divorce case and committed an error in the names of the principals that, so the story goes, involved the paper in a libel suit. In addition, she had displeased her father by joining her fellow reporters in the local speakeasies. She was peremptorily sacked and sent back to Chicago.

Still directing her life, her father encouraged her marriage, in 1927, to James Simpson, Jr., son of the chairman of the board of Marshall Field & Company. They separated after a year and were divorced in 1930. Meanwhile, Patterson traveled to Indochina to hunt game, and, with her father, learned to fly. She became a transport pilot and, in 1930, set two women's speed records for intercity flights. On Dec. 23, 1931, she married a friend of her father, Joseph W. Brooks, an insurance broker and aviator. She dabbled in journalism through the 1930s, writing articles on flying for the family's monthly magazine, *Liberty*, and returning to the *Daily News* in 1932 as a part-time book reviewer.

The marriage to Brooks gradually dissolved and ended in divorce in 1938. Then in 1939 Patterson's life took a new, definite turn. On July 1, she married Harry F. Guggenheim, sixteen years her senior, heir to a copper fortune and a former ambassador to Cuba. She later called him "the man who emancipated me from purposelessness." He urged her to find a serious life's work and, because her talent and inclination lay in newspaper work, they scouted the east for a newspaper to buy. Ultimately they purchased the remnants of the short-lived *Nassau Daily Journal*, with a small plant in Hempstead, Long Island.

Guggenheim held 51 percent of the stock in the new enterprise, and Alicia Patterson 49 percent, but from the start she was in full charge of creating the newspaper. *Newsday* had no corporate connection with the McCormick-Patterson enterprises and Joseph Patterson offered only informal counsel. Against his advice, Alicia Patterson produced a three-column tabloid in a neat, modern typographical format, which soon won awards. Through her policy of keeping separate columns for news and advertisements she improved the paper's appearance. She selected the name, *Newsday*, from entries in a contest.

Newsday's first issue appeared on Sept. 3, 1940, in a printing of 30,000; there were 11,000 paid subscriptions. At the time, the new publisher hoped only to overtake the other daily in Nassau County, which had a circulation of nearly 32,000. This goal was reached by the time *Newsday* was two years old. Profitability was a more distant objective, and before the paper broke even, around 1947, it had required an investment of $750,000.

But the costly early years had prepared the way for *Newsday* to take full advantage of the postwar population expansion in its two home counties, Nassau and Suffolk. Intense, irreverent coverage of local news, striking investigative journalism, the establishment of editions directed to particular areas, and aggressive circulation-seeking policies all contributed to its success. The paper expanded to a larger plant in Garden City, N.Y., in 1949; by 1954, its circulation exceeded 200,000. In her success, Patterson had the help of an able staff, but it was her decisions and, sometimes, her fiery temper, that shaped the paper. She intended, she said

in 1959, to make *Newsday* "readable, entertaining, comprehensive, informative, interpretive, lively, but still sufficiently serious-minded so that no Long Islander will feel compelled to read any New York City paper."

Patterson was also responsible for the independent political character of *Newsday*. The paper supported both Republican and Democratic presidential candidates, while on the local level it successfully opposed an established Republican machine. When in 1940 and 1960 she and her husband differed during a campaign, Guggenheim published a separate statement, while his wife offered *Newsday*'s endorsement in an editorial.

Her political independence was one of the causes of her growing estrangement from her father. Joseph Patterson, an early New Deal supporter, broke with Franklin D. Roosevelt on foreign policy, but *Newsday* continued to support the administration. His second marriage, to a long-time associate, the journalist Mary King (1885–1975), ended Alicia Patterson's hopes that she might eventually have a voice in operating the *Daily News*. About a year before his death in 1946, Joseph Patterson changed his will to leave control of the *News* to a trusteeship, with his wife sitting in a trustee's chair originally reserved for his daughter.

Alicia Patterson spent her remaining years concentrating on *Newsday*, which, under her guidance, became the largest suburban newspaper in the country and the twelfth largest evening newspaper in the United States. For exposing a labor racketeer, the paper won a Pulitzer Prize for public service in 1954. Patterson hoped one day to retire and be succeeded by her niece and nephew, Alice and Joseph Medill Patterson Albright. But on June 20, 1963, she entered Doctors Hospital in New York City for surgery on ulcers; she died twelve days later when doctors could not stop the bleeding. For the first time in 143 years no member of the Medill-McCormick-Patterson dynasty was running a newspaper. Harry Guggenheim took charge of *Newsday* as acting editor and publisher and remained its chief executive officer until May 1970, when he sold his interest to the Times Mirror Company, publishers of the *Los Angeles Times*.

Although her chief legacy was the creation of a successful and intelligent newspaper, Alicia Patterson also provided in her will for the encouragement of young journalists. With a million-dollar endowment, the Alicia Patterson Fund has given a year of travel and study to dozens of its fellows.

[The most detailed accounts of Alicia Patterson's life

are her own "This Is the Life I Love," as told to Hal Burton, *Sat. Eve. Post*, Feb. 21, 1959 (source of the quotations); Charles Wertenbaker, "The Case of the Hot-Tempered Publisher," *Sat. Eve. Post*, May 12, 1951; "Alicia in Wonderland," *Time*, Sept. 13, 1954; and the entry in *Current Biog.*, 1955. Obituaries appeared in *Newsday*, July 3, 1963; the *N.Y. Times*, July 3, 1963; *Editor & Publisher*, July 13, 1963. Information on *Newsday* can be found in *The Newsday Story* (1977), a pamphlet published by the newspaper; Jerry Walker, "Alicia's Newsday Has 'The Patterson Touch,' " *Editor & Publisher*, Aug. 14, 1948; and in the Pulitzer Prize exhibit files on microfilm in the journalism library, Columbia Univ. For background on the McCormick-Patterson family see John Tebbel, *An American Dynasty* (1947), and Leo E. McGivena and others, *The News: The First Fifty Years of New York's Picture Newspaper* (1969). A biobibliography prepared by Sarah Collins provided valuable assistance in the research for this article.]

JAMES BOYLAN

PEARCE, Louise, March 5, 1885–Aug. 10, 1959. Pathologist, physician.

Louise Pearce, one of the principal figures in developing the drug tryparsamide to control African sleeping sickness, was born in Winchester, Mass., the eldest of two children and only daughter of Susan Elizabeth (Hoyt) and Charles Ellis Pearce, a cigar and tobacco dealer. Both parents came from nearby Chelsea, Mass. The family moved to California some time after 1889, and Louise attended the Girls' Collegiate School in Los Angeles (1900–03). She received her A.B. in physiology and histology from Stanford University in 1907, and after spending two years as a student at the Boston University School of Medicine, entered the Johns Hopkins University School of Medicine with advanced standing in 1909. She received her M.D. in 1912 and then took a year's internship at the Johns Hopkins Hospital. In 1913 she joined the Rockefeller Institute for Medical Research (later Rockefeller University) in New York City as a fellow in the laboratory of Simon Flexner, director of the Institute.

Following Paul Ehrlich's introduction in 1910 of Salvarsan, an organic compound containing arsenic, for the treatment of syphilis, Flexner hoped to find new arsenical drugs that would be effective against sleeping sickness (trypanosomiasis). The disease, which was caused by a microscopic parasite, *Trypanosoma gambiense*, and transmitted by the tsetse fly, was then disastrously prevalent in equatorial Africa. Flexner assigned Pearce and Wade Hampton Brown, a pathologist in his laboratory, to test compounds synthesized by two of the Institute's chemists, W. A. Jacobs and Michael Heidel-berger. Finding a compound, later known as tryparsamide, to be highly effective in destroying the infectious agent in animals, Pearce and Brown announced the happy result in the *Journal of Experimental Medicine* in 1919.

To test the drug on humans, Pearce went alone in May 1920 to what was then Léopold-ville in the Belgian Congo. With laboratory and hospital facilities placed at her disposal, during the next few months she treated seventy-seven patients in all stages of the disease. Working on a scientifically planned program, beginning with graded single doses of tryparsamide, and following the results through microscopic tests, she achieved spectacular results: the parasites were driven from the circulating blood within days and totally eradicated within weeks. Mental symptoms cleared up and general health was restored in a large proportion of even the severest cases. This triumph of combined chemical, pathological, and clinical skills deeply impressed the Belgian government, which awarded Pearce the Order of the Crown of Belgium. In 1953 the still grateful Belgians summoned her to Brussels to receive the King Leopold II Prize—a check for $10,000—and a second decoration, the Royal Order of the Lion. Her three colleagues in the investigation were also honored.

Pearce was promoted to the rank of associate member of the Rockefeller Institute in 1923. Thereafter her story is one of patiently detailed experimental study of major problems in the biology of infectious and inherited disease. Working closely with Wade Hampton Brown, she made important contributions to syphilology and to cancer research. From 1920 to 1928 the two investigators worked out a thorough description of experimental syphilis in rabbits, which they found resembled human syphilis in many respects. Their observations were therefore valuable to students of immunity in the human disease and to physicians engaged in treating syphilitic patients. They also discovered in one of their rabbits a small cancer of the scrotum which they were able to propagate by implanting bits of the diseased tissue in other rabbits. The Brown-Pearce tumor, for many years the only known transplantable tumor of the rabbit, was studied in cancer research laboratories all over the world.

Around 1929 Pearce and Brown began the selective breeding of rabbits in order to study the congenital malformations and spontaneous diseases they had often observed in their animals. Three devastating epidemics of rabbit pox, a virus disease resembling human smallpox, delayed their progress, but Pearce and her junior colleagues isolated the virus—thus gaining for science from the disaster. The colony outgrew the Institute's animal house, and in 1935, Pearce, Brown, and hundreds of rabbits were transferred to the animal pathology branch in Princeton, N.J. By 1940 more than two dozen hereditary diseases and deformities were represented in the rabbit colony. By then Brown had suffered an incapacitating illness, and Pearce carried on the research alone. Following Brown's death in 1942, Pearce discontinued almost all breeding and began to write up their findings on achondroplasia and osteopetrosis. She took the remaining records with her when she retired in 1951, and published a few more papers, but the files contained far more data than she could work up; after her death they were destroyed.

One of the foremost American women scientists of her day, Pearce received numerous honors. She was visiting professor of syphilology at Peiping Union Medical College (1931–32). A member of many medical and public organizations, including the scientific advisory council of the American Social Hygiene Association, she did much to advance the cause of women in medicine and science. Especially important was her contribution to the Woman's Medical College, Philadelphia, which she served first as an elected member of the Board of Corporators (1941–46) and then as president (1946–51).

Preeminently the professional physician-scientist, Dr. Pearce left few traces of her personality in the official record. Surviving friends recall her as a cordial and hospitable woman, who appreciated the social amenities, and had a fondness for fine clothes, jewelry, books, and art. A vigorous individual, possessed of an incisive mind, Louise Pearce not only held her own in conversation with male colleagues, but also enlivened the rather sedate atmosphere of the Rockefeller Institute.

Pearce spent her last years at Trevenna Farm, the home she shared in Skillman, N.J., with the novelist Ida A. R. Wylie. A frequent vacationer in England and France, she fell ill on shipboard returning from Europe in 1959, and died a short time later in New York Hospital.

[There is no collection of Pearce's papers, but her correspondence with Simon Flexner during her 1920 stay in Africa is in the Flexner Papers, Library of the Am. Philosophical Soc., Phila. There is a file on Louise Pearce, consisting of scattered correspondence, newspaper clippings, and photographs, in the Archives of the Medical College of Pa.; minutes of the Board of Corporators for the period 1941–51 are also available there. The Johns Hopkins Medical School has Pearce's personal collection of books on syphilis, which she bequeathed. Pearce's experiences in the Belgian Congo are recorded in "Studies on the Treatment of Human Trypanosomiasis with Tryparsamide," *Jour. of Experimental Med.*, Dec. 1, 1921,

Supp. I. An extensive bibliography, and a photograph, are included in the memorial of Pearce by Marion S. Fay in *Jour. of Pathology and Bacteriology*, Oct. 1961, pp. 542–51. See also the memorials in *Trans. and Studies of the College of Physicians of Phila.*, April 1961, pp. 167–68, and *Jour. Am. Med. Women's Assoc.*, Aug. 1960, p. 793; for an account of the campaign against sleeping sickness see George W. Corner, *A History of the Rockefeller Institute* (1964), pp. 144–49. Useful information was provided by Thomas B. Turner of Johns Hopkins. Pearce's given name on both her birth certificate, which was supplied by the Mass. Dept. of Public Health, and in the 1900 U.S. Census appears as Louisa. See also *Boston City Directory*, 1880–1890. An obituary appeared in the *N.Y. Times*, Aug. 11, 1959; confirmation of death date, which is sometimes given as Aug. 9, 1959, came from N.Y.C. Dept. of Health.]

GEORGE W. CORNER

PELL, Anna Johnson. *See* WHEELER, Anna Johnson Pell.

PENNINGTON, Mary Engle, Oct. 8, 1872– Dec. 27, 1952. Chemist, refrigeration specialist.

Mary Pennington, authority on refrigeration of perishable food, was born in Nashville, Tenn., the elder of two daughters of Henry and Sarah B. (Molony) Pennington. Soon after her birth, the family moved to West Philadelphia to be nearer to Sarah Pennington's Quaker family, the Engles. There Henry Pennington established a large label manufacturing business and shared his hobby of gardening with his older daughter.

It was a library book on medical chemistry, not botany, however, that sparked an interest in science in the twelve-year-old Mary, who startled her teachers by requesting instruction in chemistry. After graduation from high school, she gained admission in 1890 to the Towne Scientific School of the University of Pennsylvania, where she studied chemistry and biology. Her parents, although surprised by her pursuit of a scientific career, supported her studies. By 1892 Pennington had completed the requirements for a B.S., but was denied the degree because of her sex, receiving instead a certificate of proficiency. She continued her graduate work, majoring in chemistry, and received a Ph.D. from the University of Pennsylvania in 1895. After two more years at the university, as a fellow in botany, she then spent a year at Yale as a fellow in physiological chemistry.

Returning to Philadelphia in 1898, the enterprising Pennington was not discouraged by the lack of opportunities for women scientists. After consulting a number of local physicians and obtaining their promises of business, she opened her own Philadelphia Clinical Laboratory. There she conducted bacteriological analyses and quickly won a reputation which led to her appointment as a lecturer at the Woman's Medical College of Pennsylvania, a position she held until 1906. She was also the head of the city health department's bacteriological laboratory, where her first assignment directed her to the problem of impure milk. Her research into methods of preserving dairy products led her to develop standards of milk inspection that were subsequently adopted by health boards throughout the country. In persuading producers and processors that cleanliness and improved methods of preservation could be profitable, Pennington developed the approach she would follow in ensuing years.

Dr. Harvey W. Wiley, chief of the Bureau of Chemistry of the United States Department of Agriculture, and an old friend of the Pennington family, followed Mary Pennington's Philadelphia career with interest. By 1905 he had asked her help in checking on reports of successes in preserving food by refrigeration. She passed civil service examinations as M. E. Pennington, and in 1907, before Department of Agriculture officials were aware of her sex, she was appointed as a bacteriological chemist. Wiley named her chief of his bureau's new Food Research Laboratory in 1908. In the same year she attended the First International Congress of Refrigeration, surprising the other delegates —all male—by delivering an address in Wiley's place.

At Pennington's insistence, the new laboratory was established in Philadelphia. Its mission was to aid implementation of the 1906 Pure Food and Drug Act. Under Pennington's direction, it became a center for research in the handling and storage of food. Her early studies, aimed at devising methods to prevent the spoilage of eggs, poultry, and fish, resulted in the development of techniques subsequently adopted by the food warehousing, packaging, transportation, and distribution industries. Pennington supervised a staff that eventually grew from four to fifty-five, but always remained involved in the practical work of the laboratory as well as in negotiations between government agencies and food dealers. After firsthand investigations of the poultry industry, for example, she invented a sharp-pointed knife whose use in killing chickens made it easier to pluck and handle them.

Pennington came to public attention during World War I when she conducted experiments with railroad refrigerator cars. The story spread that she rode in the cars to check their tempera-tures; in fact, she rode in the caboose. Twenty-five years later refrigerator cars were still built according to the standards she recommended in 1917. Her work during the war with the perishable products division of Herbert Hoover's Food Administration earned her a Notable Service Medal.

In 1919 Pennington left the Department of Agriculture to direct the research and development department of the American Balsa Company, manufacturers of insulating materials, in New York City. The job paid double her government salary. Three years later she again set out on her own, establishing a consulting office in New York. Her clients were packing houses, shipping firms, and warehousers, who sought her expertise in the handling, transportation, and storage of perishables. The work sent her on trips across the United States; she spent about half her time on the road, logging up to 50,000 miles a year.

During her years as a consultant, Pennington continued her pioneering work on food preservation, and developed a new interest—frozen foods. Her accomplishments ranged from the design and construction of refrigerated warehouses, coolers, and household and industrial refrigerators to original research on frozen poultry and frozen food processing. Over the years, she wrote and published extensively in technical journals, government bulletins, and magazines; she was also coauthor of a book, *Eggs* (1933).

Known widely for her pioneering work, she received several honors, including, in 1940, the American Chemical Society's Garvan medal, which annually honors a woman chemist. She was the first female member of the American Society of Refrigerating Engineers and the first woman elected to the Poultry Historical Society's Hall of Fame. She never retired; at the time of her death she was vice president of the American Institute of Refrigeration, and still maintained her New York office.

Pennington lived a quiet personal life, returning from her frequent travels to a penthouse apartment on Riverside Drive. There she raised flowers on her terrace, and enjoyed serving her friends foods bought frozen, according to principles she had developed. She remained all her life a member of the Society of Friends. Mary Pennington died in New York at the age of eighty.

[Correspondence documenting Pennington's work in the U.S. Dept. of Agriculture is in the files of the Bureau of Chemistry in the Nat. Archives. A number of her bulletins, articles, and speeches are listed in the *Dict. Catalog of the Nat. Agricultural Library, 1862–1965*, vol. 47 (1969). For biographical material see Edna Yost, *American Women of Science* (1943); Alice Goff, *Women Can Be Engineers* (1946); Ethel Echternach Bishop, "Mary Engle Pennington," in Wyndham Miles, *Am. Chemists and Chemical Engineers* (1976); Barbara Heggie, "Profiles: Ice Woman," *New Yorker*, Sept. 6, 1941. Obituaries appeared in the *N.Y. Times*, Dec. 28, 1952; *Chem. and Engineering News*, Jan. 1953; *Refrigerating Engineering*, Feb. 1953; *Am. Egg and Poultry Rev.*, Jan. 1953; and *Ice and Refrigeration*, Feb. 1953. Information was also furnished by Mary Betts Elderfield and Ethel Echternach Bishop.]

VIVIAN WISER

PEREIRA, Irene Rice, Aug. 5, 1907–Jan. 11, 1971. Painter.

Irene Rice Pereira, a leading geometric abstract painter in the 1930s and 1940s, was born in Chelsea, Mass. She was the second of four children and three daughters of Hilda (Vanderbilt) Rice, a native Bostonian of Dutch-German descent, and Emanuel Rice, a Pole who had immigrated to the United States as a child. When Irene was about five her father moved the family and his grain business to Pittsfield, Mass. Soon after, they settled in nearby Great Barrington, where Emanuel Rice owned a bakery. Approximately three years later the family moved again, spending a year in Boston before settling in Brooklyn, N.Y.

Hilda Rice sketched routinely at home, a habit that encouraged her two older daughters, Juanita and Irene, to pursue painting as a career. Irene Rice attended Brooklyn's Eastern District High School, switching from the academic to the commercial course in 1922 when her father died. Forced to work as a secretary to help support the family, she attended night classes in dress design at the Traphagen School, in art and design at Washington Irving High School, and in literature at New York University. From childhood on she maintained an interest in literature and a determination to become a poet.

Although still employed as a secretary, by the age of nineteen Rice was determined to be an artist. In 1927 she enrolled in night classes at the Art Students League, where she studied first with Richard Lahey and then with Jan Matulka, in whose class she met the painter Burgoyne Diller and the sculptor David Smith. (Smith remained a close friend throughout his life.) Although she received conventional instruction in life drawing, painting, and composition, Rice was also exposed to more up-to-date ideas, particularly Cubism.

In 1929 Irene Rice married Humberto Pereira, a commercial painter born in Barbados. They settled in Greenwich Village, where she was to reside nearly all her life. Completing her studies at the League by 1931, she left New York and embarked on a trip to Europe and North Africa. In Paris Pereira studied briefly at the Académie Moderne where Amédée Ozenfant was then serving as critic. Ozenfant was a founder of Purism, the art movement that, in the aftermath of Cubism, sought a reconciliation between pure form and the imagery of real life. Her experience at the Académie encouraged Pereira, when she returned to New York in 1932, to begin a series of paintings of machinemade objects: generators, funnels, ventilators. The major painting of this period is *Man and Machine* (1936). Another significant experience during the year abroad occurred on an expedition to the North African desert. Her deep response there to the infinity of space equaled in intensity the perception she had formed, as a child, of light as the embodiment of life-giving spirit.

Following her return to New York, Pereira began to emerge as an important artist. Three individual exhibitions were held in 1933, 1934, and 1935 at the American Contemporary Art Gallery in New York City. In 1936 and 1937 she taught design synthesis and a materials lab at the Design Laboratory, a school founded under the Federal Art Project and planned to resemble the Bauhaus, uniting fine arts with commercial design. She also began to explore the physical properties of a broad range of materials, including plastic, glass, metal, and paper. Turning completely to abstraction in 1937, she attempted to represent in her painting her response to light and space, which had evolved into a personal vision of the structure and meaning of the universe. Believing that light, shadow, and space might be expressed directly by materials and construction rather than represented illusionistically, by 1938 Pereira began to use geometric forms placed nonillusionistically flush with the surface, the whole given textural interest by a variety of paint techniques and materials. At the same time, she sought aesthetic equivalents for modern mathematical and scientific discoveries. By 1940 she was experimenting with multiplane constructions using transparent materials, principally parchment and glass.

In the late 1930s and early 1940s Pereira was involved with the politics of contemporary art in the United States and was an active member of the American Artists' Congress. Her work was appreciated by both camps of advanced thinking among artists of the pre-World War II generation, the surrealists and the post-cubist abstractionists, although she was stylistically closer to the latter group. In 1939 she showed both at the Julien Levy Gallery—Levy was the earliest champion of surrealism in New York—and with the American Abstract Artists, a group committed to geometric abstraction. Three years later Pereira's paintings were included in exhibitions at Art of This Century, Peggy Guggenheim's gallery where Marcel Duchamp, Max Ernst, and André Breton served as jurors for group shows and where the younger American artists of what was to become the New York School exhibited their work. In 1944 she received her own show at this gallery and first exhibited her paintings on glass in two planes.

Pereira's journey to artistic individuality in these years was accompanied by personal isolation. Her first marriage ended in divorce in 1938, and her younger sister, Dorothy, with whom she had close bonds, died in 1941. However, in 1942 Pereira married George Wellington Brown, an engineer, with whom she shared her growing interest in experimentation with materials. Professionally, she continued to be known as I. Rice Pereira.

Appreciated by friends for her fastidious taste, Pereira excelled as a cook and dressed fashionably, often in clothes made from her own designs. Simultaneously working on several pieces, she regularly painted nine hours a day and wrote at night. A mastectomy in 1943 forced her to become ambidextrous.

Major recognition came as Pereira's paintings were bought by museums and included in important group shows, for instance, "Fourteen Americans" at the Museum of Modern Art (1946). In 1953 she was given a major retrospective by the Whitney Museum of American Art. However, during the 1950s Pereira was rejected by modernism's major New York forum, the Museum of Modern Art, because of what were perceived as her philosophical and aesthetic differences from the then prominent New York School. Divorced from her second husband in 1950, Pereira married the Irish poet and translator George Reavey, who introduced her to literary circles where she felt more at home than in the New York art world of the time. She found museum, gallery, and magazine people increasingly involved with "chaos, and the disappearance of man into a void," and with existentialism rather than with the idealistic philosophy (particularly that of Giordano Bruno) by which she was influenced. Her philosophy was elaborated in several books, including *Light and the New Reality* (1951) and *The Transformation of Nothing and the Paradox of Space* (1952).

Divorced from Reavey in 1959 and still alienated from the art world, Pereira found comradeship with such prominent women in literature and the arts as Caresse Crosby, Frances Steloff, the owner of the Gotham Book Mart, Charmion von Wiegand, and Sybil Moholy-Nagy. In 1963 she converted to Catholicism. Suffering from emphysema, Pereira was forced by deteriorating health to abandon her beloved Greenwich Village. She died in 1971 in Marbella, Spain, where she had been under the care of her brother.

[The Irene Rice Pereira Papers at the Schlesinger Library, Radcliffe College, contain autobiographical MSS., correspondence, and diaries. These are available on microfilm at the Archives of Amer. Art. in Washington, D.C. The Emily Genauer Papers at the Archives contain important letters describing Pereira's philosophy. Pereira's published writings include *The Nature of Space* (1956); *The Lapis* (1957); *Crystal of the Rose* (1959), a volume of poems; *The Transcendental Formal Logic of the Infinite: The Evolution of Cultural Forms* (1966). The best collected bibliography is in the catalog published by the Andrew Crispo Gallery in 1976. Important secondary sources are John I. H. Baur, *Loren MacIver, I. Rice Pereira* (1953), the catalog of the Whitney show; *Current Biog.*, 1953; James Harithas, "I. Rice Pereira, American Painter-Writer," *Vogue*, June 1970, p. 129; Gilbert Rohde, "The Design Laboratory," *Am. Mag. of Art*, Oct. 1936, pp. 638–43; and Eleanor Tufts, *Our Hidden Heritage: Five Centuries of Women Artists* (1974), pp. 233–38. Obituaries appeared in the *N.Y. Times*, Jan. 13, 1971, and *Newsweek*, Jan. 25, 1971. Additional information has been supplied by James Rice, the artist's brother, and Djelloul Marbrook, her nephew.]

ELISABETH SUSSMAN

PERKINS, Frances, April 10, 1880–May 14, 1965. Social reformer, federal official.

The first female cabinet member in the nation's history, Frances Perkins brought to her position as secretary of labor three decades of commitment to social reform. Of Franklin D. Roosevelt's original cabinet appointments, only she and Harold L. Ickes endured from 1933 to 1945.

Born in Boston, Mass., she was the older of two daughters. She was christened Fannie Coralie Perkins, but later changed her name first to Frances C. Perkins and then, simply, to Frances Perkins. When she married in 1913, she insisted upon retaining her maiden name, a decision that she subsequently defended in court.

The daughter of Frederick W. and Susan (Bean) Perkins, Frances Perkins grew up in a comfortable, middle-class, Republican household of devoted Congregationalists whose origins reached back to the farms in northern Maine. Two years after her birth, the family moved from Boston to Worcester where her father started a wholesale-retail stationer's business. In Worcester, Perkins received her primary and secondary education; her father enrolled her in the Worcester Classical High School, an overwhelmingly male institution.

From 1898 to 1902, Perkins earned her A.B. at Mount Holyoke College in South Hadley, Mass. Although she majored in chemistry and physics, she was particularly influenced by an economic history course with Anna May Soule: Soule's students surveyed working conditions in industrial Holyoke, and they also read Jacob Riis's *How the Other Half Lives*, a book to which Perkins would repeatedly return. In her senior year, she heard an address by FLORENCE KEL-LEY, general secretary of the National Consumers' League, and it was Kelley, recalled Perkins, who "first opened my mind to the necessity for and the possibility of work which became my vocation" (Columbia Oral History Coll., Book 2, p. 260).

Upon leaving Mount Holyoke, Perkins moved through a series of part-time teaching positions, engaged in volunteer work with various social organizations in Worcester, taught for a full year at Monson (Mass.) Academy, and then in the autumn of 1904 accepted an offer to teach physics and biology at the Ferry Hall School in Lake Forest, Ill. She began to spend her free hours at Chicago settlement houses, especially Hull House. Making her rounds to collect wages for workers who had been cheated, she also visited the homes of the poor and received her first exposure to labor unions.

Perkins headed east in 1907, and for the next two years she served as general secretary of the Philadelphia Research and Protective Association. While in Philadelphia, she joined the Socialist party, and she also found time for graduate courses in economics and sociology at the University of Pennsylvania. Influenced by Simon N. Patten, she came to the conclusion that practical remedies—not the more visionary doctrines of the socialists—held out the best chance for improving the lot of the nation's labor force. In the election of 1912 she supported not Eugene V. Debs but Woodrow Wilson.

In the meantime, Perkins had left Philadelphia for New York City, the place she would call home until her death. Recipient of a fellowship from the Russell Sage Foundation, she participated in a survey of the Hell's Kitchen district during the summer of 1909, earned an A.M. in economics and sociology at Columbia University (1910), and published her first article, "Some Facts Concerning Certain Undernourished Children," in *The Survey* (Oct. 1910). Of far greater significance, Perkins succeeded Pauline Goldmark as secretary of the New York Consumers' League (1910–12).

Perkins's tenure with the Consumers' League,

though brief, was extraordinarily eventful. Working closely with Florence Kelley, Perkins drew attention to sweatshop conditions in bakeries and lobbied in Albany for industrial reform. She also taught at Adelphi College, took additional courses at Columbia, marched in suffrage parades, and spoke at street corners on behalf of votes for women. Moreover, she witnessed the Triangle Shirtwaist Company fire of March 25, 1911, in which 146 workers, mainly women and children, died. Perkins emerged from the experience with unshakable memories—memories of young women poised on window ledges in attitudes of prayer before they jumped to their deaths.

Aroused to a new burst of energy, Perkins in 1912 worked for passage of a fifty-four-hour bill in the New York legislature. Thanks in part to the cooperation she received from State Senator Alfred E. Smith, the measure came to a vote. At that point, however, an amendment was tacked on that exempted canneries from the fifty-four-hour limitation. Faced with the choice of swallowing this watered-down version, or, as Kelley recommended, scuttling the entire proposition, she accepted compromise. Perkins, as a friend approvingly described her, was "a half-loaf girl: take what you can get now and try for more later" (Martin, p. 98). Perkins had her bill, and the next year cannery workers were also covered.

In the aftermath of the Triangle fire, Perkins resigned as secretary of the New York Consumers' League (she continued to sit on the board of directors) and took a similar position with the Committee on Safety of the City of New York, an organization designed to aid the State Factory Investigating Commission. Traveling throughout the state, Perkins unmasked employers who were jeopardizing the health and safety of their workers. By the time the Commission had disbanded in 1915, the New York legislature had passed a number of progressive measures. These successes, her biographer has noted, led Perkins "to develop a lifelong conviction that the best way to improve conditions for workers was through legislation, not unions" (Martin, p. 120).

In a private ceremony on Sept. 26, 1913, Frances Perkins married Paul Caldwell Wilson, an economist for the Bureau of Municipal Research in New York. Some time in the spring of 1915, she lost an infant shortly after its birth but then, in 1916, a daughter—Susanna Winslow Wilson—was born. Even with her new responsibilities as wife and mother, Perkins kept busy with unpaid jobs. In 1918, however, her husband lost most of his money through imprudent investments, and volunteer work was no longer a possibility. During the 1920s, her husband became ever more susceptible to prolonged depression and sporadic employment. From 1930 to his death in 1952, Paul Wilson spent considerably more than half his time in institutions. Perkins paid him almost weekly visits, even when secretary of labor. Never self-pitying about her predicament, Perkins was fortified by a deep religious faith (she had become a devout Episcopalian); she was also sustained by the causes to which she was so strongly devoted.

When Alfred E. Smith ran for governor in 1918, Perkins had worked in his campaign. Smith triumphed, and he appointed her to an $8,000-a-year position as a member of the New York State Industrial Commission. The first woman to occupy this post, and the highest-paid state employee in the United States, Perkins took charge of the Bureau of Mediation and Arbitration, reorganized the Factory Inspection Division, and went into the field to settle strikes. At Smith's urging, she formally joined the Democratic party and traveled to San Francisco in 1920 for her first Democratic National Convention. Over the next three decades, she exerted influence upon Democrats to include social legislation in the party platform, particularly legislation affecting women.

When Smith lost his 1920 reelection bid, Perkins marked time as executive secretary of the Council on Immigrant Education, and then came back to her old position when Smith, in 1922, won the first of three successive gubernatorial contests. On the New York State Industrial Board (previously called the Industrial Commission), Perkins administered the Workmen's Compensation Act: in this capacity, she almost invariably sided with those who had been injured. Moreover, she concerned herself with child labor. On Jan. 1, 1926, Smith named her to the chairmanship of the Industrial Board, and two years later he appointed her industrial commissioner of the state of New York, an office to which Franklin D. Roosevelt also appointed her during his two terms (1929–33) as governor.

Using the leverage her powerful offices allowed, Perkins from 1927 to 1933 helped give New York state a reputation as a model of progressive approaches to employer-employee relations. Restoring the New York Bureau of Women in Industry, she advocated protective legislation for women rather than the Equal Rights Amendment advocated by Alice Paul (1885–1977) and the National Woman's party. She also watched with satisfaction as the fifty-four-hour law became forty-eight, cheered the extension to all workers of one day's rest in seven, and strengthened factory inspections. Although frustrated by the legislature's failure to enact a minimum wage law, she kept this issue at the top of her reform agenda.

With the stock market crash of 1929, Perkins faced new tests. Spending more time in Albany, she enrolled Susanna in private school, and also continued to retain governesses. Appalled by Herbert Hoover's optimistic unemployment estimates, she denounced the president's cautious response to the depression. Meanwhile, she urged Governor Roosevelt to act. As one of the governor's inner circle, she sat with the New York Committee on the Stabilization of Industry, testified in Washington on behalf of the Wagner-Garner Emergency Relief and Construction Act, battled for state unemployment insurance, advocated regional solutions to joblessness, and assisted New York's Temporary Emergency Relief Administration. Sent to Great Britain by Roosevelt, she studied that nation's public employment offices and system of unemployment compensation.

A frequent guest in the Roosevelt home, Perkins by 1932 had fully recovered from an initial skepticism about the governor, a skepticism dating back to the days when, as a young assemblyman, he had initially dragged his heels about the state's fifty-four-hour law. Perkins never hesitated in backing Roosevelt's presidential ambitions, and she openly supported him well in advance of the Chicago nominating convention. But because her husband's health was reaching a particularly critical juncture, her role in the campaign was limited. In the wake of Roosevelt's triumph, rumors began to circulate that Perkins might well become the first woman appointed to the cabinet.

When she learned that women such as JANE ADDAMS, GRACE ABBOTT, and MARY DEWSON were pushing for her nomination as secretary of labor, Perkins wavered. Believing that a person from the ranks of organized labor should receive the appointment, she suggested that a female trade unionist be named. As her resistance crumbled, she wanted Roosevelt to know that she expected the administration to dedicate itself to liberal social policies and that she would have to spend her weekends with her family in New York. Unfazed, Roosevelt insisted she accept, for he considered her "his most loyal friend," a person who had "no axe . . . to grind" (Bernstein, p. 10). Perkins at last relented. "I had been taught long ago by my grandmother," she recalled, "that if anybody opens a door, one should always go through" (Bernstein, p. 10). Perkins entered the portal, and on March 4, 1933, she was sworn in at the age of fifty-two.

When organized labor learned of the appointment, the reaction, as Robert Moses put it, was "a good deal like that of habitués of a waterfront saloon toward a visiting lady slummer—grim, polite, and unimpressed" (*Fortune*, p. 78). Perkins fielded the criticism from labor leaders graciously, humbly indicated that she considered her position anomalous, and lauded William Green, the president of the American Federation of Labor. Her performance was effective, and labor soon learned that the broad-faced, earnest woman in the tricorn hat was a friend.

From 1933 to 1945, Perkins's devotion to Roosevelt was unflagging. When Roosevelt addressed labor, Perkins almost invariably assisted with the speech. As the New Deal took shape, Perkins helped draft legislation, including the Federal Emergency Relief Act, the public works section (Title II) of the National Industrial Recovery Act, the Civilian Conservation Corps Act, the National Labor Relations Act, the Walsh-Healey Government Contracts Act, the Social Security Act, and the Fair Labor Standards Act. Roosevelt valued her advice in making several of his appointments, and he depended on her to maintain harmonious relations with union leaders. At Perkins's urging, Roosevelt brought the United States into the International Labor Organization in 1934.

Perkins also displayed an adroitness in implementing New Deal legislation, and her efforts on behalf of the National Recovery Administration (NRA) were especially herculean. When, for instance, she attempted to address steel workers in Homestead, Pa., neither the employers nor town officials would provide her with a suitable hall. Chased away from the mill, she spotted the United States flag flying atop the local post office. Marching resolutely onto federal property with a throng of steel workers trailing in her wake, she fielded questions about NRA, listened attentively as workers complained of United States Steel's coercive tactics, and assured the men they now had the right to organize and bargain collectively.

Employers, distressed by Perkins's prolabor stance, frequently accused her of encouraging union violence. Perkins, in response, held that "collective bargaining . . . and labor's efforts to organize are not disorder" (*Fortune*, p. 7). During the bloody labor wars of 1934—the San Francisco Dock Strike, the Minneapolis Truck Strike, the Great Textile Strike—she leaned on employers to bargain in good faith. Knowing full well that owners had far more power than their employees, she publicly upbraided some of the nation's most recalcitrant executives.

Candid talk and determined action earned Perkins the enmity of the political right, and in 1939 Representative J. Parnell Thomas offered a resolution instructing the House Judiciary Committee to inquire whether she should be impeached for refusing to deport Harry Bridges, the Pacific coast longshoremen's leader accused of being a communist. In a dramatic appearance before the Judiciary Committee, Perkins called for fair play for the embattled Bridges, and Thomas's impeachment effort fizzled.

Right-wingers had no legitimate reason to worry about Perkins's alleged radicalism. Just as she deplored hardheaded employers, she exhibited little patience with militant unionists or with labor's fratricidal combat. Her efforts to unite the AFL and the CIO inspired John L. Lewis to call her "woozy in the head." Toward the Communist party, she expressed disdain. Its principles and methods, she once stated, were "destructive and disintegrating . . . unsound and untrue" (*Fortune*, p. 94).

Perkins made some of her greatest contributions during the New Deal years, not to abstruse philosophical debate, but to the unglamorous, day-to-day work of rebuilding the Department of Labor. Under Perkins's guidance, the Immigration and Naturalization Service was purged of racketeers, the Bureau of Labor Statistics was greatly expanded, the Division of Labor Standards was established, the Women's and Children's Bureaus turned in highly competent performances, and an upgraded Federal Mediation and Conciliation Service gained the confidence of most labor leaders. While union spokesmen could not always afford to extol her in public, most came to feel that the Department of Labor had developed into an effective instrument of government—one that promoted the welfare of wage earners. To feminists, however, Perkins had erred when she publicly stated that during the depression married working women should leave their jobs so that unemployed men could be hired.

That the labor department was led by a woman through the nation's most severe depression never disappeared as an issue, but it certainly receded. Those who attended the Broadway musical "I'd Rather Be Right" must have considered ludicrous its portrayal of the cabinet's only female member as a person interested solely in chitchat. The contrary was true: she had followed her father's advice not to squander her time "with vaporings" (*Fortune*, p. 78). Typical Perkins speeches contained not idle speculation but facts and figures, leading one reporter to describe her as a "colorless woman who talked as if she swallowed a press release" (*N.Y. Times*, May 15, 1965). While she could be pedantic to the point of being schoolmarmish, she could also be feisty and humorous. Once she was asked whether her sex had handicapped her in public life. "Yes," she replied, "in climbing trees" (*N.Y. Times,* May 15, 1965).

At the outbreak of World War II, Perkins balanced her disdain for the "outrageous inhumanity of the Axis nations" (*Survey,* Feb. 1946, p. 38) with a desire to uphold gains made by the working class during the New Deal years. She tried unsuccessfully to dissuade Roosevelt and FBI Director J. Edgar Hoover from fingerprinting aliens, opposed the forced conscription of labor, and fought to uphold labor standards despite the exigencies of total mobilization. On women's issues, she continued to steer a moderate course: she opposed the registration of female workers for national labor service; she spoke against the creation of child care centers under the wartime Lanham Act; and, to the dismay of more advanced feminists, she once again opposed the Equal Rights Amendment.

With the death of President Roosevelt, Perkins served briefly under Harry S Truman. Resigning from Labor effective July 1, 1945, she returned to duty when Truman asked her to join the Civil Service Commission; she served in this capacity until the inauguration of Dwight D. Eisenhower in 1953. In the meantime, Perkins augmented her income by delivering public lectures, most of them on university campuses. She also found time to write *The Roosevelt I Knew* (1946, 1964), a book, as she conceded, unabashedly "biased in his favor."

On Dec. 31, 1952, her husband died, and Perkins was now free to leave New York City for longer periods of time. In the fall of 1957 at the age of seventy-seven, she began an affiliation with Cornell University's School of Industrial and Labor Relations, and her professorship there lasted until her death, in New York City following a series of strokes, in May 1965.

Throughout her career, Perkins displayed considerable modesty toward her own accomplishments. She should have been less self-effacing, for hers had been a remarkable life. Her selfless dedication to social justice had been unwavering. Her imprint upon wages and hours legislation, social security, and the Department of Labor had been enormous. She had made her way through a world of men without losing a strong sense of her own identity in particular, or her commitment to the interests of women in general. Resolute without being doctrinaire, she had been, as her college motto had enjoined her to be, "stedfast"—steadfast in creating a more just industrial society. That was to be her most enduring monument.

[Frances Perkins's papers were dispersed to several repositories, notably the Schlesinger Library, Radcliffe College, and the Franklin D. Roosevelt Library at Hyde Park. The most significant collection outside the Nat. Archives, however, is at Columbia Univ., especially her 5,000-page deposition for the Columbia Oral History Coll. The Dept. of Labor Records at the Nat. Archives are essential, in particular those of the Office of the Secretary: General Subject File. There are interesting glimpses of Perkins in the Federal Mediation and Conciliation Service Records, at the Federal Records Center, Suitland, Md., as well as in the Franklin D. Roosevelt MSS. Perkins began work on a biography of Alfred E. Smith, which Matthew and Hannah Josephson completed as *Al Smith, Hero of the Cities: A Political Portrait Drawing upon the Papers of Frances Perkins* (1970). Perkins's articles are voluminous in number, almost always succinct, and tend to recite findings of surveys in which she participated. Her livelier, more self-revealing efforts include "Do Women in Industry Need Special Protection?" *Survey,* Feb. 15, 1925, pp. 529–31; "Eight Years as Madame Secretary," *Fortune,* Sept. 1941, pp. 76–79ff.; and "The People Mattered," *Survey,* Feb. 1946, pp. 38–39, a warm tribute to Harry Hopkins. Of secondary works on Perkins, the most exhaustive is George W. Martin's highly favorable biography, *Madam Secretary: Frances Perkins* (1976). Irving Bernstein, *Turbulent Years: A History of the American Worker, 1933–1941* (1970), is a rich evocation of labor struggles during the 1930s and of Perkins's role therein. Helpful articles on Perkins's earlier years include Augusta W. Hinshaw, "The Story of Frances Perkins," *Century,* Sept. 1927, pp. 596–605, and Inis W. Jones, "Frances Perkins, Industrial Crusader," *World's Work,* April 1930, pp. 64–67, 114. For her years as secretary of labor see Russell Lord, "Madame Secretary: A Profile," *New Yorker,* Sept. 2, 9, 1933, a generally favorable treatment, and Marguerite Young's hostile attack, "Frances Perkins, Liberal Politician," *Am. Mercury,* Aug. 1934, pp. 398–407. Of the many obituaries see in particular *N.Y. Times,* May 15, 1965. Perkins gave her birth year as 1882, but the birth record provided by the Mass. Dept. of Public Health gives 1880.]

CHARLES H. TROUT

PERRIN, Ethel, Feb. 7, 1871–May 15, 1962. Physical education specialist.

Ethel Perrin was born to Ellen (Hooper) and David Perrin, a merchant, in Needham, Mass. She had a brother eight years her senior. Educated in private schools, Perrin enrolled at the Howard Collegiate Institute, a boarding school in West Bridgewater, Mass., in 1888. There she was first exposed to formal physical training in twice-weekly lessons given in a makeshift gymnasium by a graduate of Dudley Allen Sargent's Boston gymnastics school. Sargent's method reflected the period's interest in formal gymnastics and in the curative effect of exercise for women.

Graduating in 1890, Perrin enrolled at Amy Morris Homans's fledgling Boston Normal School of Gymnastics (BNSG). There she and Senda Berenson, who also had an illustrious career in physical education, were strongly influenced by Homans's conviction that physical training prepared women physically and mentally for motherhood. Perrin became a partisan of Swedish gymnastics, which was taught at the school "as a sort of religion." After completing her training in 1892, Perrin was invited to teach at the BNSG. She later described the Swedish system as the "I yell, you jump method."

During her years at BNSG Perrin coauthored *One Hundred and Fifty Gymnastic Games* (1902) with five other BNSG alumni, and, with Mary Seely Starks, another graduate, wrote *A Handbook of Rhythmical Balance Exercises* (1906). In 1899 she represented the school at the Conference on Physical Training organized at the behest of the National Education Association (NEA). The conference developed the principle of modification—the belief that men's sports should be modified to suit women's perceived physical and social limitations. This theory, which dominated women's sports through the first two-thirds of the twentieth century, guided Perrin's thinking throughout the rest of her career.

After leaving the BNSG in 1906 Perrin substituted as director of physical education at Smith College (1906–07) and at the University of Michigan (1907–08). During this period she began to modify her approach to teaching gymnastics, which became more informal and individualized. In 1908 she became the girls' physical education director at Detroit's Central High School, in charge of the first girls' gymnasium in the city's schools. A year later she was appointed supervisor of physical education for the Detroit public schools. There she instituted a program of nonspecialized, modified, minimally competitive, and largely intramural sports for girls, while building a department of 7 professionals into one of 365.

Remaining in Detroit until 1923 (the last three years as assistant director of health education), Perrin gained influence nationwide through her writings and other activities. The State of Michigan Course of Study in Physical Education, which she designed in 1914 with Wilbur P. Bowen and others, was used across the United States, becoming a model for public school physical education courses. Active in such young or expanding organizations as the NEA, the American Physical Education Association (APEA), and the Middle West Physical Education Society, Perrin participated in shaping their policies and helped to modernize and professionalize her field. In 1920 she became the first female vice president of the APEA. When a coalition of government, community, and education groups organized in 1923 as the National

Amateur Athletic Federation (NAAF)—becoming the country's largest athletic association—Perrin was named an executive officer of its Women's Division. In this position she helped to set standards for women's physical education programs throughout the country.

In 1923 Perrin left the Detroit public school system to become associate director of the Health Education Division of the American Child Health Association (ACHA). For the next thirteen years she traveled, spoke, and wrote extensively on the role of physical education in health education. In the 1925–26 school year alone, she gave eighty-one talks at various colleges and school districts. Her publications in this period included *Play Day: The Spirit of Sport* (1929), coauthored with Grace Turner under the imprint of the NAAF Women's Division.

The minimally competitive, "play for its own sake" athletic philosophy that Perrin and her colleagues advocated for women was held out as an alternative to the exclusive, commercialized, specialized approach characteristic of men's athletics. But it was based on the belief that women's physical potential was limited, and Perrin opposed the early rudiments of the equal rights sports movement for women. For example, through the ACHA and the Women's Division of the NAAF, she campaigned against women's expanding participation in the Olympics and for modified rules as in women's basketball. She argued that menstruation handicapped women and that strenuous, competitive effort undermined rather than promoted female health.

In 1936, when the ACHA was subsumed under the American Association for Health and Physical Education, Ethel Perrin retired and turned to dairy farming at her Rocky Dell Farm in Brewster, N.Y. She became in 1946 the eleventh person and second woman to receive the Luther Halsey Gulick Award for distinguished service in physical education. Perrin died at her farm in 1962 at the age of ninety-one.

[A curriculum vitae and other biographical material on Ethel Perrin are in the Wellesley College Archives, which also holds the BNSG records; the BNSG became the department of hygiene at Wellesley. Perrin's articles appeared in the *Am. Physical Education Rev.*, *Sportswoman*, *Jour. Health and Physical Education*, and *Mary Hemenway Alumnae Assoc. Bull.* Characteristic of her writings are "Athletics for Women and Girls," *Playground*, March 1924, pp. 658–61; "More Competitive Athletics for Girls—But of the Right Kind," *Am. Physical Education Rev.*, Oct. 1929, pp. 473, 476; "When Sport Takes On a New Significance," *Sportswoman*, Feb. 1931, pp. 7–8, 29; and "The Confessions of a Strict Formalist," *Jour. Health and Physical Education*,

Nov. 1938. An autobiographical sketch appeared in *Research Quart.*, Supp., Oct. 1941, pp. 682–85. Other major sources of biographical information are Janice W. Carkin, "Recipients of the Gulick Award" (Ed.D. diss., Stanford Univ., 1952), which evaluates Perrin's philosophy and contributions to physical education; Marjorie Bouve, "Ethel Perrin—Humanist," *Sportswoman*, March 1931, pp. 7–8; Jay B. Nash, "The Gulick Award, 1946," *Jour. Health and Physical Education*, Sept. 1946, pp. 405, 448; and Dorothy La Salle, "In Memoriam—Ethel Perrin," *Jour. Health, Physical Education and Recreation*, Sept. 1962, pp. 76, 79. The only information about her early life comes from the 1880 U.S. Census, which indicates that Ethel Perrin lived in Newton, Mass., with her mother, her brother, and an aunt. Birth record supplied by Mass. Dept. of Public Health.]

STEPHANIE L. TWIN

PESOTTA, Rose, Nov. 20, 1896–Dec. 7, 1965. Labor organizer and leader.

Rose Pesotta was born Rose Peisoty in the city of Derazhnya in the Russian Ukraine. Her parents, Itsaak and Masya Peisoty (the name became Pesotta in the United States), were grain merchants who tended together a small business inherited from Masya Peisoty's aunt. Rose was the second of their six daughters and eight children. While not wealthy, the family seems to have lived comfortably, employing a hired girl to help with the housework. Itsaak Peisoty was a leader in the town's Jewish community and an important part of its intellectual and cultural life. Rose, like her sisters, learned Hebrew and Russian at home, then attended Rosalia Davidovna's private girls' school for two years. After that she was tutored at home, reading widely through the eclectic assortment of literary and political works scattered about the house and attic. When her older sister, Esther, was radicalized at the age of fifteen, Rose followed after, joining a Derazhnya underground democratic circle, whose anarchist teachings she adhered to all her life. She brought the idealism and spirit of these early days to her later career as a trade union organizer.

In 1913, resisting pressure from her parents to marry, Rose Peisoty migrated to New York, where her sister was already working in a shirtwaist factory. Rose took a similar job within the year, joining Local 25 of the International Ladies' Garment Workers' Union (ILGWU), the organization which remained her base for the next fifty years. In 1915 she helped Local 25 set up the ILGWU's first education department, and five years later was elected to the local's executive board. Taking advantage of the growing workers' education movement, she attended the

Bryn Mawr Summer School for Women Workers in 1922 and then studied at Brookwood Labor College (1924–26). True to her anarchist commitments, she actively defended Sacco and Vanzetti after their conviction, while opposing attempts by communists to take over the ILGWU, a position which earned her the trust of the union's leaders.

In the late 1920s, the ILGWU turned to Pesotta for help in organizing women garment workers. She became a paid staff member in 1933, when the union sent her to Los Angeles to organize dressmakers in a notoriously antiunion environment. Her success there drew national attention and contributed to her election as a vice president of the ILGWU in 1934. For the next ten years, Pesotta traveled to such cities as San Francisco, Seattle, Boston, and San Juan, organizing for the union. A charismatic person, she had the ability to break through ethnic and religious barriers in her work, as she demonstrated in Montreal in 1937, winning a drive among predominantly Catholic, French-Canadian garment workers despite the opposition of local labor leaders and the church. Her reputation was such that the ILGWU lent her to striking auto workers in Flint, Mich., and to rubber workers in Akron, Ohio, during the massive industrial organizing drives of the late 1930s. In her many campaigns, as she emphasized in a 1942 speech, Pesotta tried to avoid "ruling from the top," seeking instead to "train the workers to take care of themselves."

Pesotta's popularity among workers earned her a degree of autonomy at the ILGWU. Still, her independent, outspoken approach created some tension among the union's top leaders who, she often felt, did not fully support her. She attributed part of her isolation within the leadership to her position as the only woman vice president on the union's General Executive Board. In 1942, she chose to return to her old shop as a sewing machine operator, and two years later she refused to run for a fourth term as vice president. At the convention she denounced what she asserted was the union's policy of having only one woman on its governing board despite the fact that 85 percent of its 305,000 members were women: "Some day I hope the membership will take this so-called rule and throw it out the window."

Pesotta's outburst was characteristic. A vital and volatile woman, she could rise from depression and despair to periods of inspired activity. All her life she shared warm friendships with a large group of men and women. Twice in the 1920s and again in the 1950s, she lived with men in relationships that were never formalized, preferring the freedom of long and deeply rooted friendships to the ties of marriage. After 1928, when her mother arrived from Russia, the two lived together sporadically and maintained an affectionate relationship. Pesotta was also close to her niece Dorothy Rubin.

After she returned to the ranks, Rose Pesotta resided in the ILGWU's cooperative apartments in New York City; she still engaged in various union activities. She also wrote two autobiographical books: *Bread upon the Waters* (1944), devoted to her years as an organizer, and *Days of Our Lives* (1958), which recalled her childhood in Russia. When she learned she had terminal cancer, she went to Miami, Fla., where she died in December 1965. She left behind a union stronger for the thousands of members she brought to it.

[The major collection of Pesotta papers, consisting of diaries, letters, and clippings, is at the N.Y. Public Library. Additional letters can be found in the David Dubinsky Papers, and scattered through other collections, at the ILGWU Archives, N.Y. City. The Jewish Labor Bund Archives in N.Y. City house a single file of Pesotta letters relating mainly to the 1920s. Pesotta wrote occasional articles on her organizing experiences published in various issues of *Justice*, the ILGWU newspaper, during the 1930s. Her short convention speeches can be found in the ILGWU *Proceedings* for 1922, 1924, 1934, 1937, 1940, 1944. Her work is discussed in several articles, including John C. Cort, "Trouble in Montreal," *Commonweal*, June 15, 1945, pp. 214–17; Maxine Seller, "Beyond the Stereotype: A New Look at the Immigrant Woman, 1880–1924," *Jour. Ethnic Studies*, Spring 1975, pp. 59–70; and Alice Kessler-Harris, "Organizing the Unorganizable: Three Jewish Women and Their Union," *Labor Hist.*, Winter 1976, pp. 5–23. Pesotta is cited in *Who's Who in Labor* (1946), p. 277; an obituary appeared in the N.Y. *Times*, Dec. 8, 1965. Information was provided by Sonya Farber, Leon Stein, and Henoch Mendelsund; death certificate from Fla. State Registrar.]

ALICE KESSLER-HARRIS

PHILLIPS, Irna, July 1, 1901–Dec. 22, 1973. Radio and television writer.

Irna Phillips, one-time Queen of the Soap Operas, was the youngest of ten children (several of whom did not survive to maturity) born to Betty (Buxbaum) and William S. Phillips, German Jews who migrated to Chicago in the latter half of the nineteenth century. William Phillips, who died when Irna was eight, owned a small dry goods and grocery store above which the family lived. Years later, Irna remembered herself as "a plain, sickly, silent child, with hand-me-down clothes and no friends," who sought emotional refuge in books and make-believe.

As a student in the Chicago public schools,

Irna Phillips dreamed of becoming an actress, but at the University of Illinois (she had transferred from Northwestern), a drama coach warned that, despite her talent, she had "neither the looks nor the stature to achieve professional success." After graduating in 1923 with a B.S. in education, a disheartened Phillips taught speech and drama for a year at a junior college in Fulton, Mo., and then for five years at a normal school in Dayton, Ohio.

In 1930, Chicago radio station WGN, for which she had worked without pay during her vacations, asked Phillips to write and perform in "a family drama." The result was "Painted Dreams" (sometimes considered radio's first soap opera), a ten-minute daily serial set in Chicago and centering on the widowed Mother Monahan (acted by Phillips and presumably based on her mother), her grown daughter, and neighbors. For the first time in her life, Phillips later recalled, she was happy.

Two years later, when WGN prevented the transfer of "Painted Dreams" to the National Broadcasting Company, Phillips quit the station to sell the network a "new" soap, "Today's Children," a barely disguised version of her earlier serial. By 1938, when Phillips discontinued "Today's Children" (apparently in response to her mother's death and despite sponsor protests), it had become radio's most popular daytime serial.

A year earlier, Phillips had launched two other soaps destined for more enduring fame: "The Road of Life," featuring medical intern Dr. Jim Brent, and "The Guiding Light" (created with Emmons Carlson), featuring the Rev. John Rutledge and by the 1970s the longest running soap in broadcast history. With this substitution of professional people for the simple, humbly educated characters who had until then been heroes and heroines of daytime radio, Phillips established a personal trademark and triggered a proliferation of soap-opera doctors, lawyers, nurses, social workers, and educators.

Other successes followed, among them "Woman in White" (1938), "The Right to Happiness" (1939), "Lonely Women" (1942)— in 1943 it became "Today's Children" as Phillips recycled an old title—and "The Brighter Day" (1948). Her formula, Phillips confided, was to appeal to the "instincts" of self-preservation, sex, and family (*Fortune*, June 1938). By 1943, with five serials running concurrently and six assistant writers cranking out daily dialogue, she was earning $250,000 a year, making her, reported *Time*, "America's highest-paid aerial litterateuse."

Meanwhile, as Phillips later recalled, she was "weather[ing] several unhappy love affairs," including one with a man who refused to marry her when he learned she could not bear children. She never married, but at forty-two (her mother's age when she was born), she adopted an infant boy (Thomas Dirk Phillips) and a year and a half later, a girl (Katherine Louise Phillips).

Television meant the beginning of the end for radio soap opera but not for Phillips, who has been called "the single most important influence on television soaps" (Edmondson and Rounds, p. 40). Over more than twenty years, her television credits included "The Guiding Light" (1952), "The Brighter Day" (1954), "The Road of Life" (1954), "Another World" (1964), "Days of Our Lives" (1965), and "Love Is a Many-Splendour'd Thing" (1967), as well as television's most successful daytime serial, "As the World Turns" (1956). In 1964, she became a consultant to "Peyton Place," television's first successful evening serial.

In 1973, Phillips died in Chicago of a heart attack. For a woman who had subjected her heroines to nearly unremitting travail and at least occasional ecstasy, Phillips had, to all appearances, led a remarkably uneventful personal life, sharing her mother's bedroom until she was thirty-seven, and, according to her son, preferring always the companionship of a handful of old friends and colleagues.

Together with Elaine Carrington and Frank and Anne Hummert, Irna Phillips created soap opera. Among her specific contributions are said to be the tease ending, the use of organ music to set mood and bridge scenes, and the "cross over" or appearance of a major character from one serial in a subordinate role on another. She was also among the first to employ such stock devices as the amnesia victim and the murder trial.

Despite such ploys, critics have usually considered Phillips's serials less melodramatic and better written than most. They were also less frenetic, each episode typically built around two characters engaged in serious discussion. Sententiousness, too, marked her style, whether in Reverend Rutledge's sermons (collected in book form, they sold almost 300,000 copies one year) or in the sentimental epigraphs which frequently opened her shows.

Phillips's soaps, true to the genre, featured virtuous, long-suffering heroines whose lives centered on marriage and motherhood. Though keenly aware of the ironic distance between this female domesticity she celebrated and her own eager pursuit of a career, Phillips was always an outspoken foe of feminism, warning it would weaken women's commitment to home and encourage sexual license.

In her last years, Phillips increasingly deplored the trend of TV soaps toward sensationalism—"rape, abortion, illegitimacy, men falling in love with other men's wives . . . murder, followed by a long, drawn-out murder trial." Yet her own television serials had exploited, even pioneered such subjects ("As the World Turns" sired soapland's first illegitimate baby), and her radio serials, though more diffident about sex, had helped pave the way. The heroine of "Right to Happiness" fell in love four times (once with her widowed mother's fiancé), married twice, divorced one husband, accidentally shot the other, was tried for his murder, and bore a child in jail—all in the space of four years.

Politically, too, Phillips had been willing to violate taboos, but her sponsors proved more timid. In the mid-1960s, they prevented her efforts to have her stories reflect such contemporary social issues as the struggle for civil rights.

From time to time, Phillips attributed her success as a writer to everything from her limited vocabulary ("my greatest asset") to the inspiration of her mother. A more likely explanation lies, as one history of soap opera suggests, in "her superb inventiveness, her vast energy, and her unwaveringly clear sense of the emotional center of the audience mind" (Edmondson and Rounds, p. 40).

[Irna Phillips's papers, including correspondence and scripts, are at the Univ. of Wis., Madison. Her soaps also include, on radio, "Masquerade" (1946), which ran for a year and a half and, on television, "Our Private World" (spin-off of "As the World Turns"), which lasted only one summer (1965). For a time, too, she was writer of radio's "Young Dr. Malone." "Every Woman's Life Is a Soap Opera," by Irna Phillips as told to Helen Markel, McCall's, March 1965, gives Phillips's own sentimental but highly revealing account of her life and career. Helpful discussion of Phillips's place in the history of soap opera is provided by: John Dunning, Tune in Yesterday (1976); Madeleine Edmondson and David Rounds, From Mary Noble to Mary Hartman (1976); and Raymond William Stedman, The Serials (1971). Also valuable is the entry in Current Biog., 1943. Other fairly comprehensive articles based on interviews with Phillips include "Life as Soap Opera: The Story of Irna," Chicago Daily News, Jan. 12–13, 1974; "Script Queen," Time, June 10, 1940; and "Writing On: Irna Phillips Mends with Tradition," Broadcasting, Nov. 6, 1972. See also "Irna Phillips's Ghost Writers," Variety, Aug. 5, 1942; "Queen of the Soap Operas," Newsweek, July 13, 1942; "The World Has Turned," N.Y. Times Mag., Sept. 8, 1968; and Maurice Zolotow, "Washboard Weepers," Sat. Eve. Post, May 29, 1943. A death certificate was supplied by the Ill. Dept. of Public Health. Further information was provided by Phillips's son, Thomas Dirk Phillips.]

EVELYN CATHERINE SHAKIR

PHILLIPS, Lena Madesin, Sept. 15, 1881–May 21, 1955. Feminist, lawyer, organization executive.

Lena Madesin Phillips, a founder of both the National and International Federations of Business and Professional Women's Clubs, was born Anna Lena Phillips in Nicholasville, Ky., to William Henry and Alice (Shook) Phillips. She was their only child, but she had three half brothers and a half sister from her father's previous marriage. From the age of eleven, when she changed her name to Lena Madesin (a corruption of *médecin*) in honor of her half brother George who was then studying medicine in France, she preferred to be called Madesin.

The Phillipses were among the original settlers to come from Virginia to Nicholasville in 1780. William Phillips achieved prominence in Jessamine County politics, continuously winning election as county judge from 1874 to 1917. Alice Phillips raised her daughter in the strict Southern Methodist church. A talented musician herself, she imbued Madesin with the desire to become a concert pianist. Her daughter later recalled: "My father gave me his personality, but my mother impressed it with her character and ideals . . . Under the spur of her will and ambition I obtained an excellent educational foundation" (Sergio, p. 11).

After graduating in 1899 from Jessamine Female Institute in Nicholasville, Phillips entered the Woman's College of Baltimore (later Goucher College). She switched to Baltimore's Peabody Conservatory of Music in 1902 to study the concert piano; however, a fall which damaged the nerves in her right arm ended her concert career. She returned to Nicholasville, and tried for twelve rather unhappy years to make a career out of music despite the frustration of her ambitions. For two years she headed the music department at Jessamine Institute, then tried unsuccessfully to sell the popular songs she had composed. After her mother died in 1908, Phillips ran the household for her father, and, two years later, opened a music academy with a friend. She taught music, organized musical groups, and also campaigned with Judge Phillips until June 1915, when she suffered a nervous breakdown.

When she recovered, Phillips set out in an entirely new direction, entering the University of Kentucky Law School that autumn. In 1917 she became the first woman to graduate from the law school, receiving an LL.B. with honors. She had barely begun practicing law in Nicholasville when World War I changed her life. Her work as secretary-treasurer of the Kentucky War Fund Committee of the National War Work Council of the YWCA attracted the attention of the organization's national officers, who asked Phillips to become one of its eleven field secretaries. She declined the offer, saying, "I would not leave my father, my home, my profession, for anything of which there are eleven" (Sergio, p. 33). She did agree to undertake a national survey of business and professional women and in 1918 became the executive secretary of the YWCA's National Business Women's Committee. Her work with the committee, which had been initiated to coordinate the business women's war efforts, showed Phillips the need for an ongoing organization to advance the interests of business and professional women, to aid the entry of more women into the professions, and to promote cooperation among women. To these ends, she planned a meeting, with YWCA support, which was held in St. Louis in 1919. There the National Federation of Business and Professional Women's Clubs (NFBPWC) was founded, and Phillips was elected its first executive secretary. In that capacity she established the organization's executive offices and engineered the publication of the first issues of *Independent Woman*, its official journal.

Intending to pursue her legal career, Phillips resigned as executive secretary in 1922 and enrolled at New York University Law School, receiving an LL.M. in 1923. In New York she began living with Marjory Lacey-Baker, an actress; they remained together until Phillips's death. Admitted to the New York bar in 1924, she set up her own law practice, and became one of the city's leading women lawyers. In the late 1920s, however, she became increasingly absorbed in the work of the NFBPWC. After resigning as executive secretary, Phillips had served as membership chairman from 1922 to 1926 and was elected president from 1926 to 1929. Then and later she sought to keep the NFBPWC alive to social and feminist issues. At the 1924 convention she fought to have the federation support the child labor amendment despite its being denounced as communist. In the 1920s Phillips strongly advocated equal pay for women, and in 1933 she endorsed the Equal Rights Amendment. With Phillips's backing, the 1934 convention of the NFBPWC passed a declaration which read in part: "Because there can be no economic security for any class or group unless there is economic security for all, we demand for women employment, appointment, salaries and promotions on equal terms with men." She also tried to involve the organization in peace efforts, such as endorsement of arms limitation and the World Court.

In the late 1920s Phillips sought another

means to promote international understanding. Beginning in 1928, she undertook a series of tours through Europe, aiming at the establishment of an international federation of business and professional women. In 1930, a year after she stepped down as president of the national federation, becoming honorary president, the international federation became a reality. Phillips was elected president and led the IFBPWC until 1947, when she became honorary founder-president. She continued to travel to Europe nearly every year to promote the international federation. During World War II, she toured Great Britain and Sweden as a representative of the Office of War Information (OWI) and met with members of the federation in those countries. In 1945 the OWI assigned her to a special mission on behalf of business and professional women in Europe.

In addition to her ongoing activities on behalf of the federations, and her leadership of a number of other women's, consumers', and educational organizations, Phillips was a prolific writer. A frequent contributor to *Independent Woman* and other magazines, in 1935 she had given up her law practice altogether to become the associate editor of *Pictorial Review*. Besides providing an income, the position allowed her to speak to greater numbers of women than ever before. She wrote a column which appeared monthly until *Pictorial Review* ceased publication in 1939.

In the 1940s Phillips twice ran unsuccessfully for political office. Always interested in politics, in the 1920s she had been a delegate to the Democratic National Convention and served as campaign manager in the successful bids of Joseph V. McKee for local offices in New York. Her federation activities precluded active involvement in politics until 1942 when, having moved to Westport, Conn., she was an unsuccessful Democratic candidate for the Connecticut legislature. Her most controversial political venture was her 1948 candidacy for lieutenant governor of Connecticut on the Progressive party ticket. Her abiding concern for peace led her into Henry Wallace's party, and in a 1948 letter to a friend she anticipated the attacks her decision would provoke: "I have taken my stand with Henry Wallace . . . Of course it is worth one's reputation to do so. A Communist is now being discovered under every bush and I am prepared to be smeared once more."

In her continued efforts to expand the international federation, Phillips set out in May 1955 for a conference in Beirut, Lebanon, to study the organization of professional women in the Middle East. En route she died in Marseilles, France, following surgery for a perforated ulcer.

[The Lena Madesin Phillips Papers, which include personal and professional correspondence, news clippings, articles, speeches, and photographs, are at the Schlesinger Library, Radcliffe College. The only biography, Lisa Sergio, *A Measure Filled: The Life of Lena Madesin Phillips Drawn from Her Autobiography* (1972), is based on the papers; all quotations come from this source. Biographical sketches can be found in "Women in Business," *Ladies' Home Journal*, Nov. 1928; *Dict. Am. Biog.*, Supp. Five; and *Current Biog.*, 1946. Brief histories of the federations founded by Phillips are Geline MacDonald Bowman, *A History of the National Federation of Business and Professional Women's Clubs, Inc., 1919–1944* (1944), and Phyllis A. Deakin, *In Pride and with Promise* (1970). Information was provided by the Univ. of Ky. Libraries. Obituaries appeared in the *N.Y. Times*, May 22, 1955, and *Independent Woman*, June–July 1955. While most sources give a May 20, 1955, date, the date of death Marseilles time was May 21, 1955. Death record from U.S. Dept. of State.]

J. STANLEY LEMONS

PINCHOT, Cornelia Elizabeth Bryce, Aug. 26, 1881–Sept. 9, 1960. Politician, suffragist.

Cornelia Pinchot was born in Newport, R.I., to Lloyd Stevens and Edith (Cooper) Bryce. Her great-grandfather was iron magnate Peter Cooper, the philanthropist-patron of Cooper Institute; her grandfather, Edward Cooper, was a conservative Democrat and anti-Tammany mayor of New York City. Lloyd Bryce served variously as a congressman, novelist, editor-publisher of the *North American Review*, political adviser to Theodore Roosevelt, and United States minister to the Netherlands.

The younger daughter and second of the Bryces' three children, Cornelia inherited her family's privileges along with its social conscience. Raised in Newport society and educated in Long Island private schools, the beautiful, red-haired Leila, as she was known, traveled extensively, won blue ribbons at hunts and horse shows, and joined other society women for balloon flights. She moved with poise from the receiving line to the picket line, campaigning for woman suffrage in the early 1900s and championing the working girl. As vice chairman of the New York City Conference on Unemployed Women, she helped stage a Venetian Pageant at the Waldorf-Astoria in 1914 to raise funds for a sewing room and a free employment exchange.

Her parents' friendship with Theodore Roosevelt brought Cornelia Bryce invitations to group discussions in the library at Roosevelt's Oyster Bay estate. Roosevelt recognized her keen political mind and through participation in his circle, she caught the eye of his conservationist protégé Gifford Pinchot, sixteen years her senior. Pinchot and Cornelia Bryce were married on Aug. 15, 1914; they devoted their honeymoon to Pinchot's campaign as the Progressive party candidate for the United States Senate from Pennsylvania. He lost to the incumbent in this first attempt, but the Pinchots successfully made Pennsylvania their political base for the next three decades, settling down in Grey Towers in Milford, where their only child, Gifford Bryce, was born in 1915.

While remaining close to her husband, a proponent of woman suffrage, Cornelia Pinchot renounced the traditional role of the well-bred political wife to work through her own channels. As secretary of the Pennsylvania Woman Suffrage Association (1918–19), she donated funds and lobbied to ensure the state legislature's ratification of the nineteenth amendment. She followed that successful effort by committing herself formally to the Republican party, serving on its state committee as the first woman representative from her county, and becoming treasurer of the Pennsylvania Republican Women's Committee. Concluding that the Women's Committee was not sufficiently powerful within the party structure, she then organized an independent body, the State Council of Republican Women.

Cornelia Pinchot's political influence was enhanced by her husband's election as governor of Pennsylvania in 1922, a victory to which she contributed significantly by organizing support among women in the state. Throughout Gifford Pinchot's first term in office (1923–27), she championed women's rights, asking the state legislature to investigate the legal and economic status of women in the home and at work, and opposing repeal of Pennsylvania's direct primary, which she felt guaranteed women a voice in selecting party candidates. Like her husband, she was an ardent prohibitionist. As first lady, Cornelia Pinchot became a confident public speaker, with a reputation for being quite blunt before some audiences. She told an assembly of the Daughters of the American Revolution, for example, that she hated genealogists. Maintaining a similar frank approach throughout her life, she informed delegates to a United Nations Scientific Conference on the Conservation and Utilization of Resources in 1949 that their meeting was "upside-down Humpty-Dumpty nonsense," since it had no policymaking authority.

Cornelia Pinchot made her own bid for office in 1928, an unsuccessful attempt to unseat the Republican incumbent from Pennsylvania's Fifteenth Congressional District. Her platform stressed support for prohibition and opposition to the electric power monopoly, positions central to her husband's political efforts as well. She

tried twice more to win the congressional nomination and attempted briefly in 1934 to follow Gifford Pinchot as governor, but never gained elective office.

During her husband's second term in the governor's mansion (1931–35), Cornelia Pinchot devoted particular attention to the problems of organized labor and of hard-pressed women and child workers. Appointed by her husband to a state committee to investigate sweatshops, she came into conflict with the president of the Pennsylvania Manufacturers Association and with the state GOP boss. She also made personal appearances and radio addresses advocating minimum wage laws for women and children, encouraged women to unionize, and gave financial aid to summer schools training women as union organizers. In the spring of 1933, she paraded with textile strikers in the Lehigh Valley, creating the kind of "skillful propaganda" which *The New Republic* believed improved mill conditions. The following January, Pinchot supported striking Brooklyn laundry workers, arriving at the employees' entrance in the governor's chauffeured limousine and flamboyantly advertising their cause to the press. She gained further notice late in 1935, when she effectively ran the state of Pennsylvania for several months while her husband was hospitalized.

Cornelia Pinchot remained an active and outspoken figure in the 1940s, even after her husband's death in 1946. She represented the United States at the International Women's Conference in Paris in 1945 and made headlines by calling for nationalization of all uranium deposits and for United Nations' control of atomic research. As president of the Washington chapter of the Americans United for World Organization, she appealed for international disarmament. In 1947 Pinchot was elected to the board of the Americans for Democratic Action, and in the same year undertook a four-month tour of Greece and the Balkans to study the effects of guerrilla warfare.

Cornelia Bryce Pinchot spent her last years in Washington, D.C., frequently entertaining political figures at her home there. She died in Washington of a stroke in September 1960, at the age of seventy-nine, and was buried at the Pinchot estate in Milford, Pa., beside her husband.

[Cornelia Pinchot's voluminous papers, numbering about 250,000 items, are held in the Manuscript Div., Library of Congress. For her views on women's economic rights see Cornelia Bryce Pinchot, "Women Who Work," *Survey*, April 15, 1929, pp. 138–39. Contemporary accounts of her activities include Elizabeth Frazer, "Mrs. Gifford Pinchot, Housewife and Politician," *Sat. Eve. Post*, Aug. 26,

1922; "Mrs. Pinchot Backs the 'Baby Strikers,'" *Literary Digest*, May 20, 1933, p. 9; and two items in *New Republic*, May 24, 1933, p. 30, and June 7, 1933, p. 84. A thorough review of her career during the 1920s and 1930s is provided by John W. Furlow, Jr., "Cornelia Bryce Pinchot: Feminism in the Post-Suffrage Era," *Pennsylvania Hist.*, Oct. 1976, pp. 329–46. Her father, Lloyd Bryce, is included in *Dict. Am. Biog.*, II; for her husband see Nelson McGeary, *Gifford Pinchot, Forester-Politician* (1960), which also contains information on Cornelia Pinchot. Obituaries appeared in the *N.Y. Times* and *Wash. Post*, Sept. 10, 1960. Death certificate furnished by D.C. Dept. of Public Health.]

BONNIE FOX SCHWARTZ

PITTS, ZaSu, Jan. 3, 1898?–June 7, 1963. Actress.

ZaSu Pitts, one of the leading comediennes of both silent and talking films, played in more than 150 movies in a career that spanned over forty-five years and encompassed much of the history of Hollywood. Yet she is perhaps best remembered and honored for two dramatic roles given her by director Erich von Stroheim, in *Greed* (1924) and *The Wedding March* (1928).

Born in Parsons, Kans., ZaSu Pitts was the second daughter and one of four children of Rulandus Pitts, a native of New York, and Nellie (Shea) Pitts, of Irish ancestry. She was taken by her parents at an early age to Santa Cruz, Calif., where, after her father's death in 1908, her mother ran a boardinghouse. Pitts attended public schools, graduating from Santa Cruz High School in 1914. A year later, encouraged by her family because of a gift for mimicry which had attracted local attention, Pitts went to Hollywood to seek a career in the movies. Her mother and two brothers followed her shortly thereafter.

Her first opportunity, and her first success, came in 1917 with her discovery by FRANCES MARION, at that time scenarist for Mary Pickford (died 1979). Her first film, *The Little Princess* (1917), with the popular Pickford, was directed by Marshall (Mickey) Neilan. In 1918 she appeared in *How Could You, Jean?* under the direction of the ill-starred William Desmond Taylor. In these early roles Pitts developed her distinctive woebegone manner. It was, she said later, patterned after a schoolteacher whom she imitated to the delight of the other pupils.

A fan magazine article in 1919 dubbed Pitts "The Girl with the Ginger Snap Name," and her distinctive first name always remained part of her trademark. She insisted on its being written ZaSu, with each syllable capitalized, as she claimed it was devised in honor of two paternal aunts named El*iza* and *Su*san. The correct pronunciation was "zay-zoo," she once said,

but everyone in Hollywood pronounced it "zazz-zoo" (to rhyme with "has zoo"), and she was never known to have objected.

Beginning her career as a youthful character actress, Pitts always stressed personality rather than looks in her film work. Under a full-page portrait of her, a 1923 fan magazine caption stated that ZaSu Pitts was "getting so pretty that she's been forced to abandon the wistful ugly duckling parts that brought her before the public eye." Yet she resisted studio publicity which tried to change her image. One of the few published pieces bearing her signature (though probably ghostwritten) was titled "Youth in Character Work." It appeared in a 1924 Hollywood volume, *The Truth About the Movies, By the Stars*, published just as she had completed *Greed*, for which von Stroheim had cast her despite studio objections that she was "not sexy enough for the role."

From an artistic viewpoint, Pitts's association with Erich von Stroheim was the high point of her career. Paul Rotha, in his authoritative *The Film Till Now* (1931), stated that the "brilliant performance of ZaSu Pitts as the hoarding wife . . . has never been equalled by any other American actress at any time." Many other critics have also rated that performance a classic, as they did her characterization of the lame princess in von Stroheim's *The Wedding March*. Pitts's last silent role was a dramatic one opposite Emil Jannings in *The Sins of the Fathers* (1928).

With the arrival of talking pictures, it was expected that Pitts's high-pitched cracking voice would rule her out for serious dramatic roles, and indeed thereafter she was almost invariably typecast as a fluttery comedienne. One exception occurred when, on von Stroheim's recommendation, Lewis Milestone employed her as the mother in the World War I tragedy, *All Quiet on the Western Front* (1930). Preview audiences are reported to have laughed so at her tragic scenes that they had to be reshot with Beryl Mercer in the role.

Von Stroheim himself used Pitts once more, in 1932, in his last, ill-fated, Hollywood directorial assignment, *Walking Down Broadway*, which was shelved and released much later in a truncated version as *Hello, Sister!* In this film, Pitts had a striking role in which she evidenced for her roommate, Boots Mallory, feelings "not quite motherly, not quite sisterly, but a great deal more than either." Peter Noble concluded that the sexual ambiguity of her "obsessional jealousy" toward the other girl "was so unusual that it went over the heads of the regular Fox critics and censors" (Noble, pp. 101–102). It is, at any rate, probably the first serious reference to lesbianism in a major Hollywood film.

As a comedienne, Pitts starred in thirteen shorts with Thelma Todd at Hal Roach Studios and several feature-length comedies with Slim Summerville at Universal Pictures, in the early 1930s. She also played major comedy roles in a number of outstanding movies: *The Guardsman* (1931), the only film ever to star Alfred Lunt and Lynn Fontanne; *Ruggles of Red Gap* (1935), probably her favorite, in which she played the western maid who marries the perfect English butler, portrayed by Charles Laughton; *Mrs. Wiggs of the Cabbage Patch* (1934); and *Nurse Edith Cavell* (1939). Her last film, released after her death, was Stanley Kramer's *It's a Mad, Mad, Mad, Mad World* (1963). She described her memorable type of character-ization as "pathetic comedy."

ZaSu Pitts was married to Hollywood boxing promoter Thomas S. Gallery on July 24, 1920; she gave birth to a daughter, Ann, in 1923. In 1926, on the death of actress Barbara LaMarr who was one of Pitts's closest friends, she and Gallery adopted LaMarr's son, Donald Michael. When the couple were separated in late 1926 (they were divorced in 1932), the two children remained with Pitts. On Oct. 8, 1933, she was secretly married in Minden, Nev., to former tennis champion and Pasadena real estate broker John Edward Woodall.

In the late 1930s Pitts made personal appearances at major motion picture theaters, and during World War II she toured in several stage plays, including *Her First Murder* and *Ramshackle Inn*, in which she made a short-lived Broadway debut. In 1953 she toured in a revival of *The Bat*. She also did considerable work in radio and later in the new medium of television, in which she was featured on "The Gale Storm Show" and "Oh, Susanna." By the late 1950s Pitts was largely retired. She died of cancer in 1963 in Los Angeles.

[Information about Pitts is in the Robinson Locke Coll., the Chamberlain and Lyman Brown Agency Coll., and the clipping file, all in the Billy Rose Theatre Coll., N.Y. Public Library; in the Harvard Theatre Coll.; and in the Margaret Herrick Library of the Acad. of Motion Picture Arts & Sciences, and in the library of the Am. Film Institute, both in Beverly Hills, Calif. A book of her candy recipes, *Candy Hits by ZaSu Pitts*, was published in 1963. Early accounts of her life and career include Jim Tully, "ZaSu Pitts," *Vanity Fair*, Aug. 1928, and Frank Condon, "From Eliza and Susan," *Sat. Eve. Post*, April 30, 1932. Other sources of information are King Vidor, *A Tree Is a Tree* (1952); Peter Noble, *Hollywood Scapegoat: The Biography of Erich von Stroheim* (1972); Frances Marion, *Off with Their Heads* (1972); David Thomson, *A Biog. Dict. of the Cinema* (1976), which includes an annotated list of her films; Leslie Halliwell, *The*

Filmgoer's Companion (1977). Since birth records were not kept in Kansas before 1911, there is no documentary evidence that ZaSu was actually Pitts's given name at birth. Most published sources give Pitts's birth date as Jan. 3, 1898; however, the 1900 U.S. Census lists the second daughter of Rulandus and Nellie Pitts as Yazan, born in March 1894; there is no census record of a child born in 1898. Obituaries appeared in the *N.Y. Times* and *N.Y. Herald Tribune*, June 8, 1963; marriage and death certificates from the Calif. Dept. of Health Services.]

HAROLD J. SALEMSON

PLATH, Sylvia, Oct. 27, 1932–Feb. 11, 1963. Writer.

Sylvia Plath, poet and novelist, was born in Boston, the first of two children of Aurelia (Schober) and Otto Emil Plath. Her German-born father, who came to America in his teens, was a noted entomologist, an authority on bees, and a professor of biology at Boston University. Her mother, born in Boston to Austrian parents, had taken an A.M. in English and German, and had been a student of her husband (twenty-one years her senior) in Middle German. Devoted to literature, she taught English in secondary school until her marriage.

In 1940, when Sylvia was eight, her father died following amputation of his leg—a complication of a diabetic condition for which he had refused treatment, mistakenly believing himself to have cancer. Aurelia Plath, left to support Sylvia and her younger brother Warren, began to teach medical-secretarial courses at Boston University. In 1942 she moved the family from the seaside home in Winthrop, Mass., that Sylvia had loved to a house in Wellesley which they shared with her Schober grandparents.

The trauma of her father's death, a motivating force in Plath's life and work, appears in her writing as ending not only an idyllic childhood but her wholeness. In her earlier poetry the self that survives her father has been amputated from reality; it is incomplete, false, because an essential part of her has been buried with him: "The day you died I went into the dirt" ("Electra on Azalea Path"). But in her later work, nostalgia and guilt turn to rage at having been abandoned by the "autocrat" father she "adored and despised."

From an early age, Plath was a disciplined, prizewinning student and a prolific writer with strong literary ambitions (her first poem was published shortly after her father's death). Though by nature a compulsive achiever, she was concerned to appear the well-rounded American girl. She was tall, good-looking, fashion-conscious, athletic, and defensive about being brainy.

In 1950, after graduating from Bradford High School, she entered Smith College on a scholarship endowed by the popular novelist Olive Higgins Prouty (d. 1974), who became a friend and mentor. There Plath's academic perfectionism increasingly placed a strain on her psychic resources. A month spent in New York, in the summer of 1953, as guest managing editor for *Mademoiselle* magazine stimulated her but also inflamed her self-doubts. Deeply depressed, she returned to Wellesley, underwent several traumatic electroshock treatments, and nearly succeeded in killing herself with sleeping pills. Hospitalized at Prouty's expense in McLean Hospital, a private institution in Belmont, Mass., she began to confront her "Electra complex," her guilt over her father's death, and her resentment at her closeness to her mother whom she had made a vicarious participant in her life, partly to recompense her for the sacrifices she had made.

Plath returned to Smith in 1954. Bolder, more adventurous, she dyed her hair blonde and embarked on a series of affairs. She graduated the following year summa cum laude, with several poetry awards and a prize for her English honors thesis on the "double" in Dostoyevsky. The topic reflected her fascination with true and false selves.

After graduation in 1955 she went on a Fulbright fellowship to England to study for an English tripos at Newnham College, Cambridge. There she met the young English poet Ted (Edward James) Hughes, a recent Cambridge graduate. Of working-class origins, unlike Plath he lived without regard for social conventions. His impact on her was immediate and profound: he was a "violent Adam," "the only man in the world who is my match"; "he . . . will work with me to make me a woman poet like the world will gape at." Hughes even filled somehow that "huge, sad hole I felt in having no father." But she also described him as having been ruthless, "used to walking over women"; his best self had been hidden, but she would reform him.

Plath and Hughes were married on June 16, 1956. From the outset they conceived of their union in elevated and mythic terms, as a partnership dedicated to poetry. They shared advice, criticism, and literary sources. Plath's poetry to this time had been highly literary, often self-consciously clever, always technically skilled. She was fascinated by elaborate rhyme-schemes and metrical forms, and wrote slowly, with constant reference to her thesaurus. Hughes suggested writing exercises to help her relax her inhibitions; later he invented exercises to facilitate access to the unconscious.

He also fired her with enthusiasm for Robert Graves's *The White Goddess*. Plath's loss of her father and later her break with Hughes were both readily translated into Graves's myth of the cyclical union and separation of the goddess of poetic inspiration (symbolized by the moon) and a god. Love/hate relationships with several beautiful, childless women, such as her sister-in-law Olwyn Hughes ("Amnesiac"), could also be understood in Graves's terms. Other influences among her very extensive reading include Theodore Roethke, D. H. Lawrence, Yeats, Dylan Thomas, T. S. Eliot, Auden, Blake, and Virginia Woolf. She also read widely in the literature of mysticism and the occult.

After completing her degree at Cambridge in 1957, she returned with Hughes to the United States, she to teach at Smith, he at the University of Massachusetts. Though a brilliant instructor, she came to feel that "the security and prestige of academic life [was] Death to writing." They spent the next year in Boston where Plath and the young poet ANNE SEXTON attended a poetry seminar taught by Robert Lowell. Plath was impressed by their less restrained, less public style of poetry, one which drew freely on extreme personal experience. In late 1959, just before leaving for England— where she and Hughes had decided to settle— she wrote "The Stones," which presented her 1953 breakdown as an experience of symbolic death and the rebirth of a new self. It was the first intimation of the voice she would later fully possess.

By early 1960, Plath and Hughes were living in a London flat where their daughter, Frieda Rebecca, was born on April 1. Plath's first book of poems, *The Colossus*, was published that year in England, where it was well-reviewed. But Hughes's literary success was by this time much greater, and he had already published two books of poems. From the beginning, Plath put his career above her own, typing for him, acting as his literary agent, and in other ways promoting his work.

Plath had a miscarriage in early 1961, but she was soon pregnant again; she was determined to have many children. For this, and to be able to write in peace, they needed more room. Later that year, they moved to an old manor house in the Devon countryside. Soon after, Plath received a grant to work on her novel, *The Bell Jar* (published in England in 1963 under the pseudonym Victoria Lucas). Centering around her 1953 breakdown, this tale of coming of age in the 1950s represented, in social and personal terms, her quest for wholeness, for an authentic self. Plath sometimes referred to the book as a "potboiler," perhaps reflecting her uneasiness with its satire of people (like Olive Prouty) whom she cared about. She hoped, nonetheless, to achieve a steady income by "breaking into the women's slicks" with stories like "I Lied for Love." Unsuccessful in this, she published short stories in literary magazines.

On Jan. 17, 1962, her son, Nicholas Farrar, was born at home in Devon. For several months afterward Plath wrote little poetry, but she did complete *Three Women,* a verse-play set in a maternity ward. In July she discovered that Hughes was having an affair with a woman who with her husband had sublet their London flat. Plath negotiated for a separation, while hoping for a reconciliation. But in October Hughes moved to London. She asked for a divorce and he agreed; she began legal proceedings but they were not completed before her death the following year.

Plath linked the breakup of her marriage to Hughes's disenchantment with domesticity and his desire to enjoy his growing fame (he soon came to be considered the foremost poet of his generation). But class differences also played a part and she felt he was paying her back for having "reformed" him. Her intensity was also a strain on Hughes, who remarked that it made the atmosphere they lived in an "intense claustrophobic heightening of colors."

Her abandonment by Hughes released in Plath a rage and determination to end her long self-effacement—"I shall be a rich, active woman, not a servant-shadow as I have been"—and launched her into the explosive last poems on which her reputation rests, nearly all of them written in the last eight months of her life. They form a mythicized autobiography, a mythic system analogous to that of *The White Goddess* (she borrows, for example, Graves's emblematic colors) that expresses the desire to free her hidden true self by destroying both her false self and the victimizing male in relation to whom it had evolved. In "Stings," she speaks of having "a self to recover, a queen"; in "Daddy," she symbolically identifies husband and father, and ritually kills both.

In a remarkably short time, while she was "almost fully occupied with children and house-keeping," Sylvia Plath "underwent a poetic development that has hardly any equal on record for suddenness and completeness" (Hughes, *Poetry Book Soc. Bull.*). The late poems were composed, Hughes has recalled, "at great speed, as she might take dictation, where she ignores metre and rhyme for rhythm and momentum." The experience of motherhood had stimulated her creativity, put her in touch with her deepest resources, and by 1961 her painstakingly developed poetic skills had come to be effortlessly

available. Hughes's desertion focused it all. Plath spoke of her drive to write as a kind of possession; she became a channel for words, images, themes that magically and instinctually surged up whole from the unconscious. The last poems abound with luminous, precise, almost hallucinatory imagery: "The blood jet is poetry,/ There is no stopping it"; red poppies are "little bloody skirts"; her dead father is "marble-heavy, a bag full of God." In this molten state, everything she observed or experienced manifested the underlying themes in her life and poetry: the war between true and false selves, between an ecstatic apprehension of the multiplicity of the world, and her cold pure drive toward an ultimate, unchanging self.

Plath's crisis was spiritual as well as psychological. While most of the poems express the desire for rebirth from a spoiled history, rebirth —at the very end—came to mean transcending the ego itself, overcoming what she called the "stigma of selfhood." A few days before her death she was, Hughes reports, in a "strange, terribly exalted mood." She told him: "I have seen God, and he keeps picking me up." But at the same time she wrote in "Mystic": "Once one has seen God, what is the remedy?" How can such a vision be integrated into a life still in bondage to the ego?

She drew strength from the knowledge that she was writing her best poems—"they will make my name"—and she was deep into a new autobiographical novel, which would conclude with the promise of a new self. In December she moved with her children to a London flat, delighted that it was in a house where Yeats once lived, and had plans to consult a psychiatrist. But England's worst winter in over a century further undermined her already declining health and morale. On Feb. 5, 1963, she wrote "Edge," in which the moon, like a cold muse, calmly regards the final scene of a tragedy: a "perfected" woman whose "dead/Body wears the smile of accomplishment." Six days later she ended her life by putting her head in her oven and turning on the gas.

In October 1963 ten of her most powerful poems, unprecedented in their frankness and sustained incandescence, were published in *Encounter* magazine; they caused an immediate sensation which was amplified when *Ariel*, a collection of her late poems, appeared in England two years after her death. With the American editions of *Ariel* (1966, with an introduction by Robert Lowell) and *The Bell Jar* (1971), a virtual cult of Sylvia Plath developed in her own country. Plath was hailed as a "naive prophet" of women's liberation. But her significance as a poet transcends the particular moment. She is, as

A. E. Dyson has said, "among the handful of writers by which future generations will seek to know us and give us a name."

[Aurelia Schober Plath has edited *Letters Home* (1975), a selection of Plath's correspondence, with photographs. The uncut versions of these letters, together with published and unpublished poems and prose writings and memorabilia, are in the Plath MSS., Lilly Library, Indiana Univ. MSS. of her late poems, diaries and journals, and other material are in the possession of Ted Hughes. Plath's thesis, "The Magic Mirror: A Study of the Double in Two of Dostoevsky's Novels," is in the Sophia Smith Coll., Smith College. Other books by Plath include *Crossing the Water* (1971), mostly "transitional" poems, and a second collection of late poems, *Winter Trees* (1971), which also contains her play *Three Women*. Uncollected or previously unpublished poems appear in *Pursuit* (1973); *Crystal Gazer and Other Poems* (1971); *Lyonnesse* (1971); and *Fiesta Melons* (1971), all privately printed. *Johnny Panic and the Bible of Dreams* (1977), with an introduction by Ted Hughes, is a selection of stories, articles, and excerpts from Plath's notebooks. An Oct. 1962 interview with Plath is included in Peter Orr, ed., *The Poet Speaks* (1966). Selections from the interview and Plath's reading of some of her poems are on an Argo record, *The Poet Speaks* (1965). See also Plath's statement on poetry in *London Mag.*, Feb. 1962. A "Biographical Note" by Lois Ames is appended to the U.S. edition of *The Bell Jar*. The only full-length biography, Edward Butscher, *Sylvia Plath: Method and Madness* (1976), is detailed but misogynistic and not completely reliable. *Sylvia Plath: The Woman and the Work* (1977), edited by Butscher, contains several valuable reminiscences. Ted Hughes has commented on Plath's development in "Sylvia Plath," *Poetry Book Soc. Bull.*, Feb. 1965, and "Notes on the Chronological Order of Sylvia Plath's Poems," in Charles Newman, ed., *The Art of Sylvia Plath* (1970), a useful compilation of reminiscences and critical essays which also contains a bibliography. Nancy Hunter Steiner, *A Closer Look at Ariel: A Memory of Sylvia Plath* (1973), is an informative but catty memoir by a college roommate. A. Alvarez, "Sylvia Plath: A Memoir," in *New American Rev.*, no. 12 (1971), contains an account of Plath's death that was disputed by Hughes; see their exchange of letters in the London *Times Lit. Supp.*, Nov. 19 and 26, 1971. Alvarez also wrote an obituary of Plath in the London *Observer*, Feb. 17, 1963. A critical essay by Harriet Rosenstein, "Reconsidering Sylvia Plath," appeared in *Ms.*, Sept. 1972; she also wrote a dissertation, "Sylvia Plath: 1932–1952" (Brandeis Univ., 1973). See also Eileen Aird, *Sylvia Plath* (1973), and Margaret Dickie Uroff, *Sylvia Plath and Ted Hughes* (1979). Judith Kroll, *Chapters in a Mythology: The Poetry of Sylvia Plath* (1976), is a critical study with substantial biographical information. Further information was acquired from Ted Hughes and Aurelia Plath.]

JUDITH KROLL

POLLITZER, Anita Lily, Oct. 31, 1894–July 3, 1975. Suffragist, feminist.

Anita Pollitzer, suffragist and lifelong equal rights advocate, was born in Charleston, S.C., the third daughter and last of four children of Clara (Guinzburg) and Gustave Morris Pollitzer, a cotton exporter and civic activist. Her paternal grandparents emigrated in the mid-nineteenth century from Vienna to New York where her father was born. The family later moved to Beaufort, S.C. Clara Pollitzer, born in Baltimore, Md., the daughter of a rabbi who had emigrated with his wife from Prague in 1848, graduated from Hunter College and taught German before her marriage.

Anita Pollitzer spent her childhood years in Charleston with summers in Beaufort. A precocious child, she could read, write, and play the piano before she entered school. Following her graduation in 1913 from Memminger High and Normal School, a summer of study at Winthrop College, in Rock Hill, S.C., sparked her desire to major in art; in the fall she entered Teachers College, Columbia University. Shortly after receiving her B.S. degree in art and education in 1916, she became interested in the woman suffrage movement, met Alice Paul (1885–1977), and enrolled in the National Woman's party (NWP). From that time forward her life centered around the work of the NWP.

Alice Paul quickly perceived that the diminutive, attractive Pollitzer, with her dark hair, deep blue eyes, and winning southern manner, could effectively serve the party as organizer and charm the craggiest of politicians. She dispatched Pollitzer to a succession of states in the final years before ratification of the nineteenth amendment to the Constitution. So began a career of travel, lobbying, speaking, and organizing. As a Silent Sentinel picketing in Washington in January 1917 to urge President Woodrow Wilson to endorse the amendment, Pollitzer was arrested and detained for a time. In August 1920, on the day before Tennessee, the thirty-sixth and last state, ratified the amendment, she dined with state legislator Harry T. Burn, persuading him to cast the deciding vote.

Pollitzer gave the seconding speech at a Seneca Falls anniversary ceremony in 1923, when the NWP proposed to place before Congress a new Equal Rights Amendment (ERA). For the next four decades she never let flag her labors for this cause. She wrote letters, meticulously kept current lists of congressional supporters, contributed to the NWP publication *Equal Rights*, spoke on radio and television, and appeared before Senate and House committees. Then in 1953, because of an added proviso that would have exempted protective legislation for women, she as ardently battled to defeat the amendment.

Other women's issues commanded the attention of the NWP and so of Anita Pollitzer: the right of American women married to foreign nationals to keep their citizenship, equitable labor codes under the National Industrial Recovery Act with equal pay scales for both sexes, and a married woman's right to paid employment by the government. Following Alice Paul's lead, she also entered fully into the work of the International Woman Suffrage Alliance, and supported suffrage for European women. Shortly after obtaining an A.M. degree in international law at Columbia University in 1933, she assumed the post of vice chairman in the World Woman's party, another of Paul's ventures. She went as delegate in 1945 to the San Francisco conference of the United Nations and worked for women's equality in the United Nations charter and in other international conventions.

In 1928 Pollitzer married Elie Charlier Edson, a free-lance press agent. With her husband's unqualified encouragement, she continued her NWP work. She kept her maiden name. Neither Pollitzer nor Edson earned much money, and they lived mainly on income derived from securities given her by relatives and a legacy from his mother.

Pollitzer had early moved into Alice Paul's inner leadership circle, and held several major offices in the NWP. When Paul stepped down as NWP chairman in 1945, Pollitzer, her choice as successor, received 155 of 197 votes cast. A faction led by Paul's rival, Doris Stevens (1892–1963), refused to acknowledge Pollitzer as party head and initiated a lawsuit "to bring about [by] legal means democratic executive control." But in 1947 a federal district judge ruled Pollitzer and her duly elected administration to be legal party heads. Pollitzer remained chairman until 1949. Consensus held that she rendered able, even brilliant, leadership, although some members deplored her subjection "to Miss Paul's views . . . passions and moods," and others believed Paul deliberately held Pollitzer back, preventing her from becoming the national leader of women she might have been. In fact, the two women complemented each other, Pollitzer acknowledging Paul's superiority as party strategist and eagerly and effectively carrying out the policies Paul designed.

In 1953 Pollitzer helped prevent the NWP from yielding its autonomy in an ill-conceived fund-raising scheme. Letters on this and other party matters show her persistence as well as her incisive mind. Her faith that the ERA would become part of the Constitution never wavered; her perennial optimism and sunny disposition no doubt fortified her energies, for only old age at last slowed her activities. In addition to party labors, she taught art and English, and worked as a volunteer for an antivivisection society. She also wrote a biography (never published) of Georgia O'Keeffe, a classmate in art at Teachers College. It was Pollitzer who had first shown O'Keeffe's work to photographer and art patron Alfred Stieglitz, thus beginning their very significant creative partnership.

Pollitzer lived a quieter life in the 1960s, often visiting her family in Charleston, including her sisters, Mabel and Carrie Pollitzer, who had been prominent locally in the suffrage campaign. She attended few meetings at NWP headquarters in Washington, but continued to serve the party by writing letters and telephoning. In 1971, the year her husband died, she suffered a stroke from which she did not fully recover. For four years she was cared for by nurses in her apartment near Columbia University; she died in the home of one of them in Queens, N.Y.

[The main sources of information about Anita Pollitzer are in her papers, in the possession of Constance Myers, which contain correspondence, lectures, articles, NWP bulletins and memoranda, and many photographs. The O'Keeffe-Pollitzer correspondence is in the Beinecke Library, Yale Univ., and the Miriam Holden-Pollitzer letters are at Princeton Univ. The NWP Papers in the Library of Congress contain considerable Pollitzer material. Some official correspondence and materials concerning the NWP lawsuit are in the Schlesinger Library, Radcliffe College. Taped interviews with Mabel and Carrie Pollitzer, her nephew William Pollitzer, and her friend Laura Bragg are in the South Caroliniana Library, Columbia, S.C. Pollitzer's article on O'Keeffe, "That's Georgia," appeared in the *Sat. Rev. Lit.,* Nov. 4, 1950, pp. 41–43. Scattered references to Pollitzer's part in the suffrage campaign, many in her own words, are found in Inez Haynes Irwin, *The Story of the Woman's Party* (1921). Loretta Ellen Zimmerman, "Alice Paul and the National Woman's Party, 1912–1920" (Ph.D. diss., Tulane Univ., 1964), contains references to Pollitzer's suffrage work. Her labors on behalf of the ERA are mentioned in Susan Deubel Becker, "An Intellectual History of the National Woman's Party, 1920–1941" (Ph.D. diss., Case Western Reserve Univ., 1975), and Marjory Nelson, "Ladies in the Streets: A Sociological Analysis of the National Woman's Party, 1910–1930" (Ph.D. diss., SUNY, Buffalo, 1976). See also a biographical sketch in *Equal Rights,* Nov.–Dec. 1945, and Elise Pinckney, "Anita Pollitzer: She Found a Career in Her Belief of Equal Rights for Women," *South Carolina Mag.,* March 1954. Obituaries appeared in the *N.Y. Times,* July 5, 1975, *Charleston News and Courier,* July 8, 1975, and *Charleston Evening Post,* July 7, 1975.]

CONSTANCE ASHTON MYERS

POOL, Judith Graham, June 1, 1919–July 13, 1975. Physiologist.

Judith Pool was born in Queens, N.Y., the eldest of the two daughters and one son of Leon Wilfred and Nellie (Baron) Graham. Her mother, a native of New York, was a schoolteacher; her father, a stockbroker, was English by birth. Both parents were Jewish. After graduating from Jamaica High School, Judith Graham attended the University of Chicago, where she was a member of Phi Beta Kappa and Sigma Xi. In 1938, during her junior year, she married Ithiel de Sola Pool, a student in political science. She received a B.S. in 1939 and stayed on at Chicago, pursuing graduate studies and working as an assistant in physiology. In 1942 the Pools moved to Geneva, N.Y., where they both held posts at Hobart and William Smith Colleges, she as an instructor in physics, he as assistant professor of political science. During this time they had two sons, Jonathan Robert (b. 1942) and Jeremy David (b. 1945). Judith Pool received her Ph.D. from the University of Chicago in 1946.

During the next four years Pool worked at a variety of teaching, research, and secretarial jobs. The family moved to California in 1949 when her husband received an appointment at Stanford University's Hoover Institution on War, Revolution, and Peace. Judith Pool returned to laboratory work in 1950 as a research associate at the Stanford Research Institute. In 1953 she joined the staff at Stanford University's School of Medicine as a research fellow (and trainee) supported by a Bank of America-Giannini Foundation grant for hemophilia research. It was here that she began her work in blood coagulation, and she published her first paper on the topic a year later. Pool continued her work at Stanford for the remainder of her life except for one year spent in Oslo, Norway (1958–59), under a Fulbright research fellowship. Her daughter, Lorna, was born in 1964. Her second marriage, in 1972, was to Maurice Sokolow, professor of medicine and hematology at the University of California, San Francisco. Both marriages ended in divorce, the first in 1953, the second in 1975.

Judith Pool's research was mainly concerned with muscle physiology and blood coagulation. Her studies of muscle were the basis for her dissertation, directed by the well-known neurophysiologist, Ralph Waldo Gerard. She determined the electrical potential of the membrane of a single isolated muscle fiber—a landmark discovery at the time.

Her research in the area of blood coagulation helped to revolutionize the treatment of hemo-philia. Working with two associates she developed cryoprecipitate, a cold-insoluble protein fraction of whole blood plasma which contains the antihemophilic factor (AHF) or factor VIII and which is used for transfusion to correct the bleeding defect in hemophilia. This procedure of cold precipitation of AHF, first published in 1964, has become standard in blood banks for making "cryo"—the name given to the "wet" antihemophilia factor concentrate used in the treatment of hemophilia—and in industry as the first step in processing blood plasma in the preparation of dry therapeutic AHF concentrates.

Pool also worked on many topics related to coagulation, sometimes alone but often with various colleagues. Her extensive research on the measurement of blood coagulation factors provided material for a number of published articles. She gave special attention to the measurement of an inhibitor of AHF that develops in the blood of about 10 percent of hemophiliacs who have had repeated transfusions —a complication that makes the bleeding disorder even worse.

The great value of cryoprecipitate was promptly recognized and Pool's accomplishments were widely acclaimed. She gave lectures at several institutions and congresses, including the Paul M. Aggeler Memorial Lecture in 1974, and she became a member of the national scientific advisory committees of the National Institutes of Health and the American Red Cross Blood Program. She received the Murray Thelin Award from the National Hemophilia Foundation in 1968 and the Elizabeth Blackwell Award from Hobart and William Smith Colleges in 1973. Her last honor, the Professional Achievement Award, came from the University of Chicago in the spring of 1975. After her death the National Hemophilia Foundation renamed its Research Fellowship Awards the Judith Graham Pool Research Fellowships.

Pool was an independent investigator in coagulation from 1954 until her death—an unusual situation for a person with only one year of training in such a complex field. She remained a research fellow at Stanford until 1956, advancing to senior research associate (1956–70), and senior scientist (1970–72). By this time a famous scientist, Pool was promoted to full professor in 1972, without having been in the lower professorial ranks. In her last years, she devoted much effort to making more and better opportunities in science available to women, both in her own institution and nationally. Soon after its founding, she was elected copresident of the Association of Women in Science (1971); she was also the first chairwoman of the Professional

Women of Stanford University Medical Center (organized in 1970).

Judith Pool died of a brain tumor in 1975 at Stanford University Hospital. Shortly before, she recorded a farewell message to family and friends: "The last few years of my life have been, I think, very unusual in that they have amounted to an experience for me of feeling overrewarded, overrecognized, overgratified beyond what anyone could expect, so there is no possibility of feeling cheated or regretful about what I will not have had as a result of dying earlier than expected. Quite the converse; it has almost been embarrassing in the other extreme." She was fifty-six.

[Biographical material, news releases, and lists of Pool's publications are located in the archives of Stanford Univ. Medical Center. The collection includes a "Memorial Resolution for Judith Pool, 1919–1975," by Marion E. Smith, and a review of her life and work by F. C. Grumet. Her most important publications include her paper on muscle physiology (written with R. W. Gerard), "Membrane Potentials and Excitation of Impaled Single Muscle Fibers," *Jour. Cellular and Comparative Physiology*, vol. 28, no. 99, 1946; her first paper on blood coagulation (written with T. H. Spaet), "Ethionine-Induced Depression of Plasma Antihemophilic Globulin in the Rat," *Proc. of the Soc. for Experimental Biology and Medicine*, Oct. 1954; her major work (written with E. J. Hershgold and A. R. Pappenhagen), "High Potency Antihaemophilic Factor Concentrate Prepared from Cryoglobulin Precipitate," *Nature*, July 18, 1964; and her last published paper, "Cryoprecipitate: Its Preparation and Clinical Use," in K. M. Brinkhous and H. C. Hemker, eds., *Handbook of Hemophilia* (1975). She also published (with J. P. Bunker), "The Case for More Women in Medicine: The Stanford Program," *New England Jour. Medicine*, July 1, 1971. Information on Pool's life and work can be found in Robert and Suzanne Massie, *Journey* (1975); K. M. Brinkhous, "Judith Graham Pool, Ph.D. (1919–1975): An Appreciation," *Thrombosis and Haemostasis*, April 30, 1976; and an entry in *Who's Who in America*, 1974–75. The Brinkhous article contains a photograph. An obituary appeared in the *N.Y. Times*, July 15, 1975. Information was provided by Jeremy David Pool and by Theodore H. Spaet. Death certificate was obtained from the Calif. Dept of Health.]

K. M. BRINKHOUS

PORTER, Helen Tracy Lowe. *See* LOWE-PORTER, Helen Tracy.

POST, Emily Price, Oct. 27, 1872–Sept. 25, 1960. Adviser on etiquette, writer, interior decorator.

Emily Price Post was born in Baltimore, the only child of Josephine (Lee) and Bruce Price, an architect. Both her parents descended from British immigrants who arrived before the Revolution. Her maternal grandfather, Washington Lee, was a wealthy Wilkes-Barre, Pa., mine owner; her paternal grandfather, William Price, was a lawyer and judge. Bruce Price, a decisive influence on his daughter, was becoming nationally famous by the time of Emily's birth. In 1877 he moved his business to New York; his wife and daughter followed. Emily was guided by governesses and enrolled in a neighboring finishing school, Miss Graham's. Reared in a genteel, upper-class New York setting, she was taught deportment and knowledge of the polite arts. Her personal beauty and carriage were exceptional, and attracted the favorable comments of the era's most vocal social umpire, Ward McAllister.

Shortly after her debut Emily Price married, in 1892, Edwin M. Post, a businessman and investor and a sportsman. As a girl she had spent many summers in Tuxedo Park, N.Y. (a wealthy community planned by Bruce Price), where her parents owned a house; after her marriage she continued to live there for periods of the year, and on Staten Island. In time Edwin Post purchased a house in Manhattan. The Posts spent a lengthy honeymoon in Europe, and she returned there frequently, sending home long, witty letters. Family friends persuaded her to show these letters to publishers, and, receiving encouragement from the editor of *Ainslee's* magazine, she turned them into a novel which was serialized and then published as *The Flight of a Moth* (1904).

During these early years of marriage two sons were born, Edwin M., Jr. (1893) and Bruce Price (1895). But the marriage ended in divorce in 1905. A growing estrangement was sharpened by Edwin Post's extramarital affairs, one of which was exposed by the blackmailing editor of *Town Topics*, Col. William D. Mann. Faced with the need to supplement her small income and raise her sons, Mrs. Price Post, as she chose to be known after her divorce, turned to freelance writing. During the next twenty years she turned out essays, short stories, and half a dozen novels. Most ran in journals like *Ainslee's* and *Everybody's*. She concentrated upon the life of the rich, the heady atmosphere of social climbing and new wealth. Her stories featured an international set, paying special attention to their standards of love, marriage, and taste. Post knew this class well, and her readers devoured the details of great country weekends, formal balls, sailing voyages, and romantic dalliances with the nobility.

A spirit of adventure also characterized her own activities. With her older son, Edwin, she traveled by automobile from New York to California in 1915, to visit the Panama-Pacific Exposition and to publicize the pleasures of transcontinental motoring in its heroic age. Publishing her tour journal first in serial and then in book form (*By Motor to the Golden Gate*, 1916), she complemented this venturesomeness with a continuing interest in domestic life, particularly interior decoration. Influenced by her father's architectural career, she enjoyed making architectural models and redoing the homes of friends.

As a successful writer and a former debutante, Post was approached in 1921 by Richard Duffy, an editor at Funk and Wagnalls, who suggested she create a guide to American etiquette. At first reluctant, she surveyed the existing literature and found it wanting. In a furious burst of energy she worked for ten months and produced a book published in 1922 as *Etiquette in Society, in Business, in Politics, and at Home*. Almost immediately Emily Post became a celebrity, identified in the public mind with authoritative rulings on standards of social behavior. The popularity of the book rested on its wit, judgment, sense of humor, and knowledgeability. It met the needs of postwar Americans who wanted to rationalize their newly complex social relationships. By codifying an immense mass of traditions and informal regulations, by burying some myths and allaying some suspicions, Post did what the first American dictionary makers had done a century earlier: defined appropriate usage with special bows to colloquial needs. Ironically, during a decade associated with the overthrow of taboos associated with marriage, courtship, dress, drinking, and party-giving, a traditionalist's guide to the perplexed became a best seller.

During the next twenty years over 650,000 copies of the book were sold; it moved through a number of important revisions and eventually took on the title of *Etiquette: The Blue Book of Social Usage*. Post also wrote a column which first appeared in *McCall's* and was later syndicated in more than 150 newspapers, and she appeared weekly on the radio. For a decade she received thousands of letters each month. Organizing a cooperative apartment house in New York City, she left Tuxedo Park and also built a summer home in Edgartown, Martha's Vineyard. There she gardened, entertained her grandchildren, and found time to work on several editions of her favorite book, *The Personality of a House* (1930), a guide to home decoration, and to write smaller works on child behavior, letter writing, and traveling. Her younger son, an architect, died suddenly in 1927, but her son Edwin became an adviser,

managing the Emily Post Institute, founded in 1946 to handle her small empire. In 1960, the year she died, a tenth edition of *Etiquette* was issued; like previous editions, it reflected large social changes by modifying once sacrosanct rules. Although cataract surgery interrupted her activities in later years, Post remained active until her death at her New York apartment.

Emily Post was a peculiarly American phenomenon, mediator between a mobile, democratic society and an abstract ideal of social maturity. Aristocratic ambitions led many to accept her as a certified instructor while fear of outraging the mysterious standards of "society" gave her words weight with the middle classes. Readers were fascinated by her thoroughness, reassured by her practicality, and flattered by the fantasies Post permitted to surface; there was almost no question of behavior she refused to tackle. "You may have had a successful hunting trip and wish to send the President a brace of pheasants," she wrote in her Washington section. But she advised against presenting a gift in person because the secret service disliked small packages. Responding to restaurant-going habits, Post not only advised on seating but treated alcoves and built-in benches along the wall; her chapters on dining behavior noted the problems of left-handed children. Willing to sacrifice tradition when necessary, she often did so sadly. In the 1945 edition, Post acknowledged doubts about retaining advice on opera- and theater-going as they illustrated "an extreme formality of deportment that may never return." But she included the chapter unchanged, arguing that "the opera will lose much of its prestige if its manners grow lax."

Nevertheless, she moved with the times. There is no reason, Post wrote in the 1945 edition, why a man invited to dine with a woman friend should be embarrassed to have her "take the check and pay it." "Mrs. Grundy," she concluded, "has lost nearly all of her influence during the war."

Emily Post accepted her celebrity with good humor. Sympathetic with rather than condescending toward her millions of followers, she took seriously questions about table settings, bridal invitations, mourning customs, and dress codes, spicing her descriptions with fictional families like the Oldworlds, the Onceweres, the Highbrows, and the Wellborns. In the absence of a court, a peerage, and a royal family, Emily Post became the nation's lawgiver on matters of social usage, and entered the language as the final arbiter of proper behavior.

[In addition to her novels and the books mentioned, Emily Post published many articles on various aspects of etiquette, such as "How to Be Happy

Though a Parent," *Collier's*, July 20, 1929, pp. 17, 41; "One Servant in the House," *American Home*, May 1931, pp. 113–14; and "Etiquette of Smoking," *Good Housekeeping*, Sept. 1940, p. 37. Her other books include *How to Behave Though a Debutante* (1928), a collection of sketches that had been published anonymously in *Vanity Fair; How to Give Buffet Suppers* (1933); *Time Etiquette* (1935); *The Secret of Keeping Friends* (1938); *Motor Manners: The Blue Book of Traffic Etiquette* (1949); and *The Emily Post Cookbook* (1951). The only book about her, *Truly Emily Post* (1961), written by her son Edwin, is anecdotal and not always reliable, but evocative. The best biographical source is James L. Cate, "Keeping Posted," *Univ. of Chicago Mag.*, May/June 1972, pp. 24–34. Among the many contemporary portraits see the profile, *New Yorker*, Aug. 16, 1930, pp. 22–25, by Helena Huntington Smith; Margaret Case Harriman, "Dear Mrs. Post," *Sat. Eve. Post*, May 15, 1937, pp. 18–19, 52–58; Hildegard Dolson, "Ask Mrs. Post," *Reader's Digest*, April 1941, pp. 7–12, an abridgement of an article in *Independent Woman*, April 1941; an entry in *Current Biog.*, 1941; and Geoffrey Hellman, "The Waning Oomph of Mrs. Toplofty," *New Yorker*, June 18, 1955, pp. 80, 88. An obituary appeared in the *N.Y. Times*, Sept. 27, 1960. Various published sources list her year of birth as 1873 and the day as Oct. 3 or 30; the Oct. 27, 1872, date was supplied by Post's grandson William G. Post from a handwritten entry in a family copy of a 1905 book entitled *The Post Family*.]

NEIL HARRIS

POST, Marjorie Merriweather, March 15, 1887–Sept. 12, 1973. Philanthropist, businesswoman.

Marjorie Merriweather Post was the only child of Charles William Post, founder of the Postum Cereal Company, and Ella Letitia (Merriweather) Post, both descendants of early seventeenth-century English settlers. Like her parents, Marjorie Post was born in middle-class surroundings in Springfield, Ill., but she grew up in Battle Creek, Mich., where her father moved in 1891 seeking treatment for a debilitating digestive disorder at the sanitarium of Dr. John Harvey Kellogg. Although he regained his health only after becoming a Christian Scientist, C. W. Post, then an inventor and farm implement salesman, nevertheless profited from the sanitarium's health food ideas. After experimenting with various cereal combinations, he concocted and successfully marketed Postum, Grape Nuts, and Post Toasties.

To prepare his daughter to inherit his multimillion dollar business, Post supplemented her education at the Battle Creek public schools and at Mount Vernon Seminary in Washington, D.C. (1901–04), with a thorough training in business operations and techniques. She sat in on business meetings, toured factories, and was quizzed about what she had learned. He even taught her to box. Father and daughter remained close even after he divorced her mother and remarried in 1904.

A year later Marjorie Post married Edward Bennett Close, a lawyer from an old New York family. They had two daughters, Adelaide Brevoort (b. 1908) and Eleanor Post (b. 1909). After her father committed suicide in 1914, Marjorie Post Close inherited the Postum Cereal Company. Represented on the board of directors by her husband (women were not welcome, and she only became a board member in 1936), she was consulted about major decisions. She divorced Close in 1919 and the following year married Edward Francis Hutton, a wealthy Manhattan stockbroker. The Huttons had one daughter, Nedenia Marjorie (b. 1923), who became the actress Dina Merrill.

In 1923 E. F. Hutton became chairman of the board of the Postum Cereal Company and took an active role in Postum's rapid expansion during the 1920s. At the same time, Marjorie Post Hutton, impressed by a frozen goose served on one of her yachts, became an enthusiastic early proponent of frozen foods. For several years she tried, against her husband's advice, to persuade Postum's board to purchase the patents and food freezing equipment of Clarence Birdseye, and in 1929 she succeeded. After acquiring Birdseye's General Foods Company, Postum, already a public corporation, was renamed the General Foods Corporation and grew into the largest food industry in the United States, multiplying Marjorie Post's inherited fortune several times.

Marjorie Post and E. F. Hutton (who reportedly opposed her support for Franklin D. Roosevelt and her first efforts to use her money for public charity) were divorced in 1935. The same year she married Joseph Edward Davies, a wealthy Washington, D.C., lawyer and later the ambassador to the Soviet Union (1936–38) and to Belgium (1938–39). Renowned for her beauty, vitality, and charm, Marjorie Post Davies enjoyed entertaining and, during her sojourns with her third husband in Moscow and Brussels, maintained her reputation as a lavish hostess. Divorced from Davies in 1955, she was married one more time, in 1958, to Herbert Arthur May, head of the Westinghouse Corporation. They were divorced in 1964, and she resumed the name Marjorie Merriweather Post.

For her entertaining, Post built various sumptuous estates filled with precious decorative art objects. Mar-A-Lago, her Hispano-Moresque winter estate in Palm Beach, Fla., was decorated with Dutch Delft, Venetian, Portuguese, and Louis XVI furnishings. Camp Topridge, a summer retreat in the Adirondacks, housed a fine collection of American Indian arts and crafts. In Washington, D.C., Post's Georgian residence, Hillwood, where she catered to the political and diplomatic society of the capital, displayed her priceless collection of antiques, tapestries, jades, porcelains, china services, silver, and glassware, including many treasures which had once belonged to European monarchs. Her collection of tsarist art objects—Russian imperial portraits, Fabergé Easter eggs, chalices, icons, porcelains, and jewelry—is considered the finest outside the Soviet Union. Post's decorative art treasures went on public view at Hillwood after her death there of acute pericarditis at the age of eighty-six.

Marjorie Post prided herself on using her fortune constructively, and she contributed generously to charity and the arts. During World War I, she provided funds for the Red Cross to build, equip, and run a 2,000-bed hospital at Savenay, France. From 1929 to 1935, she supported a New York City Salvation Army food kitchen, where she was known as the Lady Bountiful of Hell's Kitchen. The principal benefactor of Mount Vernon College (previously Mount Vernon Seminary), serving for many years on the school's board of directors, and of C. W. Post College in New York (later part of Long Island University), Post also helped the Boy Scouts build a service center in Washington, D.C. In addition to a large contribution toward the construction of the John F. Kennedy Center for the Performing Arts in Washington, she gave over a million dollars to the National Symphony Orchestra and sponsored the orchestra's Music for Young America concerts, which offered free spring concerts for schoolchildren visiting the capital. Post's largess was acknowledged by many awards from a variety of institutions and five foreign countries. She also had numerous private charities, including gifts to former employees.

Described even in advanced age as a remarkably handsome woman, Marjorie Merriweather Post worried about her diet, exercised religiously, and avoided cigarettes and alcohol. Fearful of infection from other people's germs, she at one time owned her own Pullman car. Post said she learned from her father that money should be used to help other people, and she also attributed her organizational talents to him. C. W. Post had, she claimed, once said of her: "If [she] were cast ashore on a desert island [she'd] organize the grains of sand."

[Post's personal papers, photographs, and family portraits are located at the Hillwood Museum, Washington, D.C. Hillwood was willed to the Smithsonian Institution (but was later returned to the Post family and became a private museum); Camp Topridge to N.Y. state; Mar-A-Lago to the U.S. government. Recollections of her childhood are included in *The Reminiscences of Marjorie Merriweather Post* (1964), in the Oral Hist. Coll., Columbia Univ. Nettie Leitch Major, "Marjorie Merriweather Post," in *C. W. Post: The Hour and the Man* (1963), and William Wright, *Heiress: The Rich Life of Marjorie Merriweather Post* (1978), are the major biographies. Post was the subject of a number of popular magazine articles, the most comprehensive being Arthur Bartlett, "Lady Bountiful," *New Yorker*, Feb. 4, 11, and 18, 1939; "Post Hostess with the Mostest," *Time*, Sept. 24, 1973; "Mumsy the Magnificent," *Time*, Feb. 3, 1967; and "A World Unique and Magnificent," *Life*, Nov. 5, 1965. Post's collection of tsarist art objects is discussed in two books by Marvin C. Ross, *The Art of Karl Fabergé and His Contemporaries* (1965) and *Russian Porcelains* (1968). On Sept. 13, 1973, the *N.Y. Times*, *Wash. Post*, and *Wash. Star News* carried long obituaries. Death certificate was supplied by D.C. Dept. of Public Health.]

NANCY BOURGERIE MEO

POUND, Louise, June 30, 1872–June 28, 1958. Scholar, teacher, athlete.

Louise Pound, who made pioneering contributions to American philology and folklore, was born in Lincoln, Neb. She was the middle of three children and older of two daughters of Stephen Bosworth and Laura (Biddlecombe) Pound, who had moved from New York state in 1869. Her father, a lawyer, was a district court judge and a state senator; her mother had been a teacher. Both parents were descended from seventeenth-century English colonists.

Lincoln offered significant cultural opportunities, particularly for select families like the Pounds: "It may have been mud-flats on the outside, but it was Boston within." Through courses at the University of Nebraska, Laura Pound had become proficient in German language and literature. She had also developed an interest in botany, finding prairie specimens hitherto unidentified. Because the program offered in the public schools was "too stereotyped," she decided to teach her three children at home. In 1886 Louise Pound entered the university's preparatory Latin School by examination, and in 1888 she enrolled as a freshman at the university.

Pound received a B.L. with a diploma in music (piano) from the University of Nebraska in 1892, having been class orator and poet, associate editor of a college paper, women's state tennis champion, and university champion in men's singles and doubles, for which she earned a man's varsity letter. She began her teaching career as a fellow in English at the university

557

in 1894 and received her A.M. there in 1895. Meanwhile she earned a string of bars for "century runs" (cycling one hundred miles in twelve hours) and was at various times coach, captain, and member of a winning women's basketball team. After attending summer sessions at the University of Chicago in 1897 and 1898, Pound determined to take the Ph.D. in Germany for reasons of economy and relative brevity. She succeeded in obtaining the degree from Heidelberg in far fewer than the usual seven semesters. "Winning that degree in two semesters was the hardest thing I ever did," she stated in a newspaper interview in 1945.

In 1900 Pound returned to the University of Nebraska, where she was to teach for forty-five more years. Athletically, she was a ranking woman golfer (for over twenty-five years) and figure skater. "Gave up tennis in the second decade of the century," she wrote in her eighties. "Bi-focal glasses wrecked my ground strokes." She became a full professor in 1912 and had visiting professorships during summers at the University of California, Berkeley (1923), Yale University (1928), the University of Chicago (1929), Columbia University (1930), and Stanford University (1931). Her teaching load during the regular academic year was heavy, and there were no sabbaticals. She taught a wide range of subjects and pioneered in teaching American literature and language at a time when most university departments offered only English literature. Her students remembered her as a great teacher—knowledgeable, inspiring, and interested in their lives and work long after graduation.

Despite the heavy teaching load, Pound accomplished an enormous amount of scholarly work, much of it innovative. A notable contribution was her demolition of the once widely held notion of the cooperative origin of ballads. Pound argued for the reasonableness of individual composition and the relative modernity of the genre. In *Poetic Origins and the Ballad* (1921), she pointed to evidence in the ballads of knowledge of rhyme and stanza form and demonstrated their dissimilarity to genuine products of folk improvisation.

Perhaps her major contribution was her role in establishing the scholarly study of American speech and folklore. A number of her studies concerned etymology and modern changes in the English language as spoken in the United States, work which, when she began it, was not considered respectable by either English or American philologists. H. L. Mencken wrote that Pound's "early work put the study of current American English on its legs." This area of her work has been partly recorded in the journal *American Speech*, of which she was a founder and senior editor (1925–33). She was also editor of the University of Nebraska *Studies in Language and Criticism* (1917–40).

The middle west figures prominently in Pound's studies of folklore, from *Folk-Song of Nebraska and the Central West: A Syllabus* (1915), the first state collection of its kind, to her last volume, *Nebraska Folklore*, published posthumously in 1959. She chose to remain in Nebraska in part because of her attachment to her sister Olivia and to the family home, a three-story modified Victorian house where she had a tower-room library and study. There were usually several women students who lived at the house and provided domestic service. Her work, however, received national recognition, and in 1955 her professional career was crowned by her election, at eighty-two, as the first woman president of the Modern Language Association. The same year she was elected to the Nebraska Sports Hall of Fame, the only woman on the roster. As she wrote to a friend and former student: "First woman again.—Life has its humors."

Louise Pound was a strikingly beautiful woman. Her red hair, which retained its color, was worn wrapped about her head in a braid. As a student she had founded the Order of the Golden Fleece, to which only women who were natural redheads could belong. Throughout her life Pound was an advocate of women's education and supported efforts to improve the position of women within the University of Nebraska. She was willing, too, to speak to women's groups throughout the state, and no doubt influenced mothers to send their daughters—who otherwise might not have gone—to the university.

She was not only outspoken in her defense of the rights of women but also capable of dramatic demonstration: in the 1920s Pound set up a desk in a hallway outside her classroom to protest her assignment to an office irrationally distant from the site of her teaching. Among the many professional organizations to which Pound belonged, "closest to her heart" was the American Association of University Women, which she served as national vice president (1937–44).

Louise Pound died in Lincoln at eighty-five of a heart attack. She had been, as her student B. A. Botkin recalled, "a great teacher because she was a great person."

[The extensive papers of the Pound family—Louise, her mother, her brother, Roscoe (dean of the Harvard Law School), and her sister, Olivia—include letters, articles, clippings, autobiographical and genealogical material, scrapbooks, class notebooks from the 1890s, and many reprints of scholarly articles. These are held in the archives of the Neb. State Hist. Soc. in Lincoln. Additional items including photographs are in the archives of the Univ. of Neb., Lincoln. *Selected Writings of Louise Pound* (1949), a good introduction to her work, has a lengthy bibliography compiled by Mamie Meredith and Ruth Odell, as well as a list of her many professional societies, activities, and honors. Some autobiographical material was published in Louise Pound, "The Class of 1892—Fifty Years After," *Neb. Alumnus*, May 1942, and in Sara Mullin Baldwin and Robert Morton Baldwin, eds., *Nebraskana* (1932), pp. 963–64. Biographical material includes Hartley Alexander, "Louise Pound," *Neb. Alumnus*, Oct. 1933; "For Members Only," *PMLA*, April 1955; B. A. Botkin, "Pound Sterling: Letters from a 'Lady Professor,'" *Prairie Schooner*, March 1959; J. R. Johnson, *Representative Nebraskans* (1954), pp. 154–58; an affectionate tribute by Roscoe Pound, "My Sister Louise," *Boston Globe*, June 30, 1957; and *Nat. Cyc. Am. Biog.*, XLVI, 538. For H. L. Mencken's acknowledged debt to Pound see *The American Language: An Inquiry into the Development of English in the United States*, Supp. I (1962), p. vi. For a description of Lincoln during Pound's formative years see Bernice Slote's introduction to *The Kingdom of Art: Willa Cather's First Principles and Critical Statements, 1893–1896* (1966), especially pp. 6–7. Obituaries appeared in the *N.Y. Times*, June 29, 1958; *Western Folklore*, July 1959, pp. 201–2; *Names*, March 1959, pp. 60–62; and *Southern Folklore Quart.*, June 1959, pp. 132–33. Additional information was provided by Belle Farman, Wilbur G. Gaffney, Elizabeth Grone, Robert and Virginia Knoll, Grace Loveland, and Bernice Slote. Death certificate supplied by Neb. Dept. of Health.]

EVELYN H. HALLER

POWDERMAKER, Hortense, Dec. 24, 1896– June 15, 1970. Anthropologist.

Hortense Powdermaker, an adventurous investigator whose work made an enduring contribution to anthropology in her generation, was born in Philadelphia, the second child of Minnie (Jacoby) and Louis Powdermaker, a middle-class businessman. Except for her paternal grandmother who came from England, her grandparents were German Jewish immigrants to Philadelphia. Both grandfathers were successful businessmen in that city, but Louis Powdermaker's fortunes fluctuated. Hortense Powdermaker grew up keenly aware of small social distinctions, a sensitivity which she later made good use of in her anthropological studies.

The family moved to Reading, Pa., when Hortense was about five, and seven or eight years later settled in Baltimore, where she was confirmed in a Reform synagogue. There were three other children in the family: an older sister, Florence Powdermaker (1894–1966), who became a distinguished psychiatrist, and a younger

sister and brother. Hortense felt dominated by her older sister, and throughout her life struggled with her own resulting feelings of inadequacy. She also at an early age rebelled against "the business values and the social snobbery" of her family.

Powdermaker attended Western High School in Baltimore and graduated from Goucher College in 1919 with a major in history. She was somewhat detached from college social life, both because she was a day student and because, as a Jew, she was not invited to join a sorority. She developed an interest in socialism and in the labor movement and spent one spring vacation working in a men's shirt factory. After graduation Powdermaker worked in New York City for the Amalgamated Clothing Workers and was sent to Cleveland and Rochester as a union organizer. She enjoyed the work but came to feel that in the union she would always be an outsider.

In 1925 she went to London where she registered at the London School of Economics for a class in anthropology taught by Bronislaw Malinowski and found that "Anthropology was what I had been looking for without knowing it." She became one of Malinowski's first graduate students while he was developing his theory of functionalism and exploring the relation of psychoanalysis to anthropology. These approaches thereafter shaped her work. During her London years, Powdermaker lived most of the time in Bloomsbury and spent summers in the South Tyrol near the Malinowski villa. She received a Ph.D. from the University of London in 1928 and left the following year to do her first field work. Her first book, *Life in Lesu* (1933), was the product of her ten months in a small village in New Ireland, an island in the southwest Pacific.

Associated with the Institute of Human Relations at Yale University between 1930 and 1937, she came to know Edward Sapir, whose interest in culture and personality greatly stimulated her own thinking. With Sapir's help, Powdermaker obtained support from the Social Science Research Council for what became one of the first community studies to be done in the United States by an anthropologist, and between 1932 and 1934 she spent twelve months in Indianola, Miss. She also helped psychologist John Dollard get started in Indianola and was chagrined when his research converged with hers and was published first. A more comprehensive study than Dollard's *Caste and Class in a Southern Town* (1937), Powdermaker's *After Freedom* (1939) is notable for its descriptions of social distinctions within the black and white communities and for its comments on the black church. Powdermaker later published a related paper reflecting her psychoanalytic interests, "The Channeling of Negro Aggression by the Cultural Process" (*Am. Jour. Sociology,* May 1943).

In 1938 Powdermaker was named instructor in anthropology at Queens College in New York City where she taught until her retirement, becoming professor in 1954. She set high standards for the joint department of anthropology and sociology which she founded, and she was proud of the accomplishments of her students. A popular lecturer, Powdermaker was especially successful in communicating the excitement of her profession. She taught briefly at several other universities and was lecturer in cultural anthropology at the William Alanson White Institute of Psychiatry, Psychoanalysis, and Psychology (1944–52), and in the department of psychiatry at the New York College of Medicine (1958). During World War II Powdermaker lectured at Yale in the Army Specialized Training Program for the southwest Pacific and wrote a short book for high school students, *Probing Our Prejudices* (1944). She was vice president and chairman of the Anthropology Section of the New York Academy of Sciences (1944–46) and vice president (1945–46) and president (1946–47) of the American Ethnological Society.

Interested in the movies ever since her field work in Mississippi, Powdermaker spent the year 1946–47 in Hollywood gathering material for the book that made her famous, *Hollywood, The Dream Factory* (1950). In it she analyzed the social structure of the moviemaking community and showed how it affected the content of the movies. Powdermaker was frustrated by Hollywood, critical of its values, and uncomfortable with her research, for she was not able to be a participant-observer—the anthropologist's ideal role in field work—as she had been elsewhere. But her interest in mass communications continued, and she spent a sabbatical year (1953–54) studying social change and the effects of mass media in Northern Rhodesia (later Zambia). *Copper Town* (1962) contains good field data, but reflects her struggle to comprehend a rapidly changing situation.

Powdermaker's last and best book was *Stranger and Friend: The Way of an Anthropologist* (1966), an account of her field work experiences. She had long been able to give a vivid picture of life in other cultures, as in such articles as "From the Diary of a Girl Organizer," in *The Amalgamated Illustrated Almanac* (1924), and "At Home on the Equator: Letters from the South Seas," in the February 1934 *Atlantic Monthly.* But *Stranger and Friend,* a long look back at her entire career, is distinguished by its perspective, by the insight into

her own person Powdermaker gained from extensive psychoanalysis, and by its intention of conveying to young anthropologists the actual experience of field work. It is a classic statement by an anthropologist of why and how one seeks to enter and understand other societies. She also wrote the article on field work for the *International Encyclopedia of the Social Sciences* (1968).

Powdermaker received an honorary degree from Goucher College in 1957 and in 1965 won the Distinguished Teacher Award given by the Alumni Association of Queens College. Retiring in 1968, she moved to Berkeley, Calif., where she began a study of the youth culture and worked on lectures on women and culture. She died in Berkeley of a heart attack in 1970.

Hortense Powdermaker was a short, plump woman, keenly interested in clothes and in her personal appearance. She liked to talk, she liked parties, and she was a frequent and gracious hostess and a good cook. A sensitive and intuitive person, she could wound sharply when she was despondent but could soothe and encourage in an uncannily comforting way when her own inner turmoil subsided. She was not close to her family but had many friends among students and colleagues who appreciated her ready wit, warmth, and honesty. For a number of years she shared her apartment with a foster son, Won Mo Kim.

Powdermaker's strengths as a scholar were her inquiring mind, keen intuition, and an inner drive that made her work very hard. A lifelong commitment to social justice helped to shape her choice of problems for study. Although she was not a significant theorist, in her ability to sense new areas where anthropological methods might be fruitfully applied, as in her studies of the American south, of Hollywood, and of contemporary Africa, she was a pioneer.

[Powdermaker directed in her will that her personal papers be destroyed. There are some letters in the Alfred L. Kroeber Papers, and in the university archives, both in the Bancroft Library, Univ. of Calif., Berkeley. A collection of photographs taken in the field are at the Lowie Museum, also at Berkeley. Her published papers also include "Vital Statistics of New Ireland as Revealed in Genealogies," *Human Biology,* Sept. 1931, pp. 351–75; with Joseph Semper, "Education and Occupation Among New Haven Negroes," *Jour. Negro Hist.,* April 1938, pp. 200–15; "The Anthropological Approach to the Problem of Modifying Race Attitudes," *Jour. Negro Education,* Summer 1944, pp. 295–303; "An Anthropological Approach to the Problem of Obesity," *Bull. N.Y. Acad. of Medicine,* 1960, pp. 5–14; and two tributes to her teacher, "Commemoration of Professor Bronislaw Malinowski," *Bull. Polish Inst. of Arts and Sciences in*

America, Jan. 1943, pp. 203–7, and "Further Reflections on Lesu and Malinowski's Diary," *Oceania,* June 1970, pp. 344–47. The major source of information about Powdermaker's life is *Stranger and Friend,* although it includes little on her teaching, other professional activities, and private life. See also Margie H. Luckett, ed., *Maryland Women* (1931), pp. 351–52; *New Yorker,* March 5, 1949, pp. 21–22; *Current Biog.,* 1961; and Winifred G. Helmes, ed., *Notable Maryland Women* (1977), pp. 285–89. Another useful source is an obituary by Eric R. Wolf, accompanied by a bibliography, a photograph, and a tribute by George L. Trager, in *Am. Anthropologist,* June 1971, pp. 783–87. An obituary also appeared in the *N.Y. Times,* June 17, 1970. Gerald D. Berreman, Ernestine Friedl, Theodora Kroeber-Quinn, and Nancy Scheper-Hughes supplied additional information for this article. The dates of her birth and graduation from college given in most printed sources are incorrect. The 1919 graduation date was confirmed by Goucher College. Birth certificate provided by Philadelphia Dept. of Records; death certificate by Calif. Dept. of Health Services.]

JOAN T. MARK

PRICE, Florence Beatrice Smith, April 9, 1888–June 3, 1953. Composer, instrumentalist.

Florence Price, whose music was played by American orchestras during the 1930s and 1940s, was important as the first black woman symphonic composer in the United States. Born in Little Rock, Ark., she was the second daughter and third child of James H. and Florence (Gulliver) Smith. Her father, a dentist, had been born of free black parents in Delaware in 1843. He learned dentistry in Philadelphia, went to Chicago to practice, and, after the Great Fire of 1871, moved to Arkansas. Her mother, a musically trained elementary school teacher, came from Indianapolis.

Florence Smith was educated in the black schools of Little Rock. She received her early musical training from her mother and began composing as a young girl, reportedly publishing her first work at age eleven. Valedictorian of her class, at fourteen she went to the New England Conservatory in Boston to study piano and organ, graduating in 1906. Smith taught at Shorter College in North Little Rock, Ark., from 1906 to 1910 and at Clark University in Atlanta until 1912, when she returned to Little Rock to marry Thomas J. Price, an attorney.

After her marriage on Sept. 12, 1912, Florence Price taught music privately, remaining active professionally after the birth of her children: a son, Thomas, who died in infancy, Florence Louise (b. 1917), and Edith (b. 1921). In 1927 the family moved to Chicago where Price continued her studies at the Chicago Musical College, the American Conservatory, and other area colleges and universities. She also taught piano, organ, and composition, and performed as an organist and pianist.

During the 1920s Price entered several composition contests, and in 1925 and 1927 her "Memories of Dixieland" and "In the Land of Cotton" won second place in the Holstein competition sponsored by *Opportunity* magazine. In 1931 she took an honorable mention in the Wanamaker Prize competition, and in 1932 won four prizes in this contest, among them first place in the symphonic division for her Symphony in E Minor. (Her composition student Margaret Bonds [1913–1972], who subsequently had a very successful career as a composer, was a prizewinner in the same contest.) The Wanamaker Prize brought Price to the attention of Frederick Stock, conductor of the Chicago Symphony, who presented the Symphony in E Minor at the Century of Progress Exposition in 1933. It was the first performance by a major American orchestra of a symphony by a black woman.

The Symphony in E Minor is in a romantic style, and uses such ethnic materials as the juba rhythm in classic forms, somewhat in the manner of Dvořák. In other symphonies, concertos, and program works for orchestra Price also drew occasionally on the spirit and rhythms of black music, including spirituals. She did not use jazz rhythms, however, nor did she quote preexistent tunes. Her work is close in spirit and style to that of the other black symphonists whose compositions were played in the early 1930s—William Grant Still, the first black male composer to have his work performed by an American orchestra, and William Dawson. The oldest of the three, Price received her professional musical education at an earlier period, and her musical tastes therefore reflect the styles of the turn of the century.

By 1928 Schirmer and McKinley were publishing Price's works, particularly her teaching pieces. Her later publications, brought out by a number of publishers, included songs, piano pieces, short choral works, and piano teaching pieces. Her songs, however, remain the works by which she is best known. She joined the American Society of Composers, Authors and Publishers (ASCAP) in 1940, and her larger works became available through this organization in manuscript form.

During her life Price's symphonic works were played by the orchestras of several cities, including those of Detroit, Pittsburgh, and Chicago, and by the Chicago Women's Symphony, with which she played her Piano Concerto in F Minor in 1934. Her *Three Negro Dances* were in the repertory of the New York City

Symphonic Band and the United States Marine Band. Songs and spiritual arrangements, the best known of which are "My Soul's Been Anchored in the Lord" and "Songs to a Dark Virgin," were sung by Marian Anderson and other concert singers. Price was very active in the Chicago Club of Women Organists, and her organ music, published by Lorenz, Summy and Galaxy, was played by organists in the Chicago area.

Thomas Price died in 1942. During the next decade Florence Price continued to perform and compose. She wrote a second violin concerto in 1952, and on Feb. 18, 1953, the Television Pops Concert by members of the Chicago Symphony included her *Suite of Negro Dances*. She died of a stroke at Saint Luke's Hospital in Chicago in 1953. In 1964 the Chicago public schools honored her memory by naming a new elementary school for her.

[A collection of original manuscripts and other documents is held by Elmer Robinson and Lawrence Robinson, Price's son-in-law and grandson. There is also a small collection of correspondence, published and unpublished scores, programs, photographs, and other materials, as well as correspondence from Price's daughter Florence Price Robinson to Mary Hudgins and Barbara Jackson, in Special Collections, Univ. of Ark. Library, Fayetteville. Price's works are partially listed in *ASCAP Symphonic Catalogue* (1959) and Ora Williams, *American Black Women in the Arts and Social Sciences: A Bibliographic Survey* (1973), which also lists recordings. Information about her and some assessment of her work can be found in Verna Arvey, "Outstanding Achievements of Negro Composers," *Etude*, March 1942; *ASCAP Biog. Dict. of Composers, Authors and Publishers*, 1948, 1952, 1966; Margaret Bonds, "A Reminiscence," *International Library of Negro Life and History: The Negro in Music and Art* (1967); Maude Cuney-Hare, *Negro Musicians and Their Music* (1936); Shirley Graham, "Spirituals to Symphonies," *Etude*, Nov. 1936; Barbara Garvey Jackson, "Florence Price, Composer," *The Black Perspective in Music*, Spring 1977; Eileen Southern, *The Music of Black Americans: A History* (1971). Mildred Denby Green, "A Study of the Lives and Works of Five Black Women Composers" (Ph.D. diss., Univ. of Okla., 1975), includes also an extensive, but not complete, list of Price's works. Obituaries appeared in *Etude*, Aug. 1953; *Musical America*, July 1953; and *Musical Courier*, July 1953; death record supplied by Ill. Dept. of Public Health. Photographs can be found in the articles by Graham and Jackson.]

BARBARA GARVEY JACKSON

PRIEST, Ivy Maude Baker, Sept. 7, 1905–June 23, 1975. Republican party worker, federal and state official.

Ivy Baker Priest, who became treasurer of the United States, was born in Kimberly, Piute County, Utah, the eldest of seven children (four boys and three girls) of Orange Decatur and Clara (Fearnley) Baker. Her father, grandson of an early Utah settler, was a miner with five years of schooling. He met his future wife, then a domestic worker, while on a Mormon mission to England. During Ivy's school years, the family lived in Bingham, Utah, a mining town twenty-eight miles southwest of Salt Lake City. After Orange Baker was injured in a mining accident, his wife opened a boardinghouse where she fed thirty miners with the help of her eldest daughter and two hired girls. Clara Baker was known as "Mrs. Republican" because of her activity in grassroots politics in Bingham. Young Ivy helped by baby-sitting for voters on election day.

Ivy Baker graduated from Bingham Canyon High School, but her family's poverty prevented her from attending college or studying law, as she had planned. She worked as a ticket seller in a movie theater before an early, unsuccessful marriage (1924–29) to Harry Howard Hicks. The couple lived in North Carolina where Harry Hicks worked as a traveling salesman.

Ivy Baker Hicks rejoined her family, then in Salt Lake City, at the onslaught of the depression. She helped out her parents, who received church welfare, by working as a long distance telephone operator, and later entered department store merchandising while teaching American history in night school.

On Dec. 7, 1935, she married Roy Fletcher Priest, a traveling wholesale-furniture dealer twenty-one years her senior. This marriage to a mature man, considerably shorter than she, proved eminently successful. She was happy to be a housewife in Bountiful, Utah, even as her husband encouraged her political activities.

A tall, trim, and vivacious brunette, who favored decorative hats, Ivy Baker Priest was a dynamic public speaker. Her organizing ability led her up the ranks of the Republican party. She was successively president of the Utah Young Republicans (1934–36); cochairman of the Young Republicans for eleven western states (1936–40); Republican committeewoman from Davis County, Utah; president of the Utah Legislative Council (1937–39); and Republican national committeewoman from Utah (1944–52). She ran unsuccessfully for the Utah State Legislature in 1934 and for Congress in 1950 against the Democratic incumbent, Reva Beck Bosone, a lawyer. During the 1930s, Priest had also been a leader in efforts to enact the first minimum wage law for working women in Utah.

Her four children, Patricia Ann (b. 1936), Peggy Louise (b. 1938), Nancy Ellen (b.

1941), and Roy Baker Priest (b. 1942), were born during this period of heavy political activity. Indeed, she had been encouraged by her husband and mother to resume her political work following the death of her daughter Peggy in 1939. Priest confronted the potential conflict between work and motherhood in her autobiography, *Green Grows Ivy*, maintaining that "her career grew out of her desire to be a better mother and to assume the responsibilities of community life." Elsewhere she gave a religious justification for her dual role: "We have a belief in the Mormon Church that each of us is given a separate set of talents. Our objective in life is to use these talents to the utmost, wherever they lead us." Priest's mother encouraged her emotionally and practically, even moving in to care for the children at busy times, as did a maternal aunt. Following a stroke, Roy Priest retired from his business at the age of sixty-eight, and assumed the title "home manager."

Ivy Baker Priest was an early supporter of Dwight D. Eisenhower's undeclared presidential candidacy in 1952. After his nomination she was appointed assistant chairman of the Republican National Committee, in charge of women's affairs. Long a proponent of increasing women's participation in politics, her successful efforts during the campaign led to her appointment as the thirtieth treasurer of the United States, the second woman to hold the position. As treasurer, she headed the banking facility of the federal government, and was responsible for all money received, for outgoing checks, and for issuing much of the nation's paper currency. Although she had no training for this work, it was an essentially political post, and she impressed the official staff with her good sense and administrative skill. She averaged ten speeches a month; she and Oveta Culp Hobby were the most visible women in the administration.

Active in the American Red Cross, the Utah and National Safety Councils, the International Soroptimist Club, and the National Society for Crippled Children and Adults, Priest lent her name and skills to many good works. The recipient of several honorary degrees, she was chosen as one of the twenty outstanding women of the twentieth century by the Women's Newspaper Editors and Publishers Association. In 1959 she was named Mother-in-Law of the Year.

After serving as treasurer during the eight years of Eisenhower's administration, she retired in 1961 to California. Roy Priest had died in 1959, and on June 20, 1961, she married Sidney William Stevens, a Beverly Hills real estate developer, who died in 1972.

In 1966 she ran successfully for the post of treasurer of California, her first elective office, and served under Governor Ronald Reagan for two four-year terms. The first woman to seek the post, she acquitted her charge to invest California's revenues for high return. In 1968 she placed Ronald Reagan in nomination for the United States presidency, becoming the first woman to nominate a candidate for that office.

Declining to run for a third term because of poor health, Ivy Baker Priest died of cancer in June 1975 in Santa Monica, Calif.

[Ivy Baker Priest's papers, still in the possession of her family, will be deposited at the University of Utah. Her lively autobiography, *Green Grows Ivy* (1958), is the best source on her life through her appointment as U.S. treasurer. The State of Utah Dept. of Development Services maintains a file of newspaper clippings about her. Short entries can be found in *Current Biog.*, 1952; *Nat. Cyc. Am. Biog.*, I, 252; and *Who's Who in Am.*, 1974–1975. See also Eleanor Roosevelt and Lorena Hickok, *Ladies of Courage* (1954), pp. 247–52. Obituaries appeared in the Salt Lake City (Utah) *Tribune* and the *N.Y. Times*, on June 25, 1975. Nancy Priest Valenzuela provided helpful information.]

CLAUDIA L. BUSHMAN

PUTNAM, Bertha Haven, March 1, 1872–Feb. 26, 1960. Historian.

Bertha Putnam, authority on medieval English legal and economic history and professor at Mount Holyoke College for twenty-nine years, was born in New York City, the eldest of the four daughters of George Haven and Rebecca Kettel (Shepard) Putnam. Both families migrated to Massachusetts from England in the seventeenth century. George Haven Putnam served in the Union army during the Civil War and later took over his father's publishing firm, which became G. P. Putnam's Sons. A Republican turned Democrat, he was active in reform movements in New York City. Rebecca Putnam had attended Antioch College, but left during her second year to nurse in a military hospital. She taught Greek and Latin at Worcester (Mass.) High School, and after her marriage she worked to introduce kindergartens into New York City schools and to improve the working conditions of salesgirls. The Putnams lived in comfortable circumstances, enjoying contacts with authors and men of affairs in the United States and England.

Bertha Putnam attended Miss Audobon's School and Miss Gibbons's School in New York City; when she was ten she persuaded her mother to teach her Greek. She received an A.B. from Bryn Mawr College in 1893 and then taught Latin at the Bryn Mawr School in Baltimore. After her mother's death in 1895, she returned to New York to act as hostess for her father until his second marriage in 1899 to EMILY JAMES SMITH PUTNAM. Bertha Putnam taught special classes at the Brearley School for four years. She also attended graduate school at Columbia University (1895–97, 1900–03), and earned her Ph.D. in 1908. That year she was appointed instructor in history at Mount Holyoke College, advancing to assistant professor in 1912 and full professor in 1924.

Bertha Putnam was above all a scholar. Her primary interest, stimulated by historian Charles M. Andrews at Bryn Mawr and by sociologist F. W. Giddings at Columbia, lay in the field of medieval English legal and economic history. Her dissertation grew out of her concern with legislation affecting the working man; it was published in 1908 as *The Enforcement of the Statutes of Labourers during the First Decade after the Black Death, 1349–1359*. In studying this early labor legislation she investigated its enforcement by special justices of laborers, and was thus led to study the justices of the peace to whom this responsibility was later given. During her research in the Public Record Office in London she identified records that had previously been misclassified and, consequently, overlooked. The justices of the peace—their powers and their practices—became the subject of her writings and the basis of her lasting reputation; subsequent work has not fundamentally altered her findings. Her frequent trips to England in connection with her research led to lasting friendships with English scholars.

In her teaching Bertha Putnam was as thorough and well organized as she was in her research. Her lectures were stimulating and informative, and her high standards, enthusiasm, and delight in her subject infected her students at Mount Holyoke. With NELLIE NEILSON, chairman of Mount Holyoke's history department, she did much to develop a distinguished department and to assist honor and graduate students as well as younger faculty members. Putnam also aided many younger scholars by providing them with opportunities for publication.

Bertha Putnam was a generous and forthright person with a lively sense of humor. She was strict in her adherence to her own high standards. After the development of a heart condition about 1916 forced her to abandon the outdoor activities she had enjoyed as a girl, she adopted the strict work schedule which made possible her many accomplishments.

Putnam received many honors during her career, including fellowships from the American Association of University Women and research grants from the American Council of Learned Societies. In 1938 she was the first woman and nonlawyer to receive a research grant from Harvard Law School. Two years later the Mediaeval Academy of America awarded her its first Haskins Medal for a volume she edited, *Proceedings Before the Justices of the Peace in the Fourteenth and Fifteenth Centuries, Edward III to Richard III* (1938), the result of thirty years of original work. In 1945 she received an honorary LL.D. from Smith College and in 1949 was elected a fellow of the Mediaeval Academy.

After her retirement from Mount Holyoke in 1937, Putnam lectured for a year at Bryn Mawr College and continued her scholarly work until an attack of shingles in the late 1940s left her partly blind. She died of arteriosclerosis in South Hadley, Mass., in 1960.

To Bertha Putnam the recognition of women as scholars was of supreme importance. She always insisted that this recognition be earned by hard and dedicated work. Her own success serves as a prime example of what she believed and practiced.

[Putnam's published works include *Early Treatises on the Practice of the Justices of the Peace in the Fifteenth and Sixteenth Centuries* (1924) and *The Place in Legal History of Sir William Shareshull, Chief Justice of the King's Bench, 1350–1361* (1950); she was editor of *Kent Keepers of the Peace, 1316–1317* (1933) and *Yorkshire Sessions of the Peace, 1361–1364* (1939). Her most important articles are "The Justices of Labourers in the Fourteenth Century," *English Hist. Rev.*, vol. 21 (1906), and "The Transformation of the Keepers of the Peace into the Justices of the Peace 1327–1380," *Royal Hist. Soc., Transactions*, 4th ser., vol. 12 (1929). Margaret Hastings and Elisabeth G. Kimball, "Two Distinguished Medievalists—Nellie Neilson and Bertha Putnam," *Jour. British Studies*, Spring 1979, discuss Putnam as scholar and teacher. George Haven Putnam, *Memories of My Youth, 1844–1865* (1914), and *Memories of a Publisher, 1865–1915* (1916), contain background information on Putnam's father; Corinna Lindon Smith, *Interesting People* (1962), provides information about her mother. A biobibliography prepared by Marjorie Markoff and an entry in *Nat. Cyc. Am. Biog.*, XLIII, 22–23, give useful details. Obituaries appeared in the *N.Y. Times*, Feb. 27, 1960; *The Times* (London), March 4, 1960; *Archives* (Journal of the British Records Association), vol. 4 (1960). Death certificate provided by the Mass. Dept. of Health.]

ELISABETH G. KIMBALL

R

RAND, Marie Gertrude, Oct. 29, 1886–June 30, 1970. Experimental psychologist.

Gertrude Rand, a leading researcher in the field of physiological optics, was born in Brooklyn, N.Y., the third child of a large family. Her parents were Mary Catherine (Moench) and Lyman Fiske Rand, later president of a manufacturing company. After graduating from Girls High School in Brooklyn in 1904, she followed a Rand tradition by entering Cornell University, where she earned her A.B. in 1908 with a major in experimental psychology. She went on to study psychology at Bryn Mawr College under Clarence Errol Ferree, who directed her dissertation on the sensitivity of the retina to color. After receiving her A.M. and Ph.D. at Bryn Mawr in 1911, she continued to work there with Ferree as postdoctoral fellow (1911–12), Sarah Berliner Research Fellow (1912–13), and associate in experimental psychology (1913–27). Rand married Clarence Ferree in 1918. Retaining her maiden name professionally, she collaborated productively with her husband until his death in 1942.

During their years at Bryn Mawr, Rand and Ferree did experimental work on the effects of general illumination on color perception and also developed techniques for measuring the light sensitivity and color discrimination of various parts of the retina. Their efforts led eventually to the Ferree-Rand perimeter, which mapped the retina for its perceptual abilities and became an important tool for diagnosing vision problems. From 1924 to 1927 Rand served on the National Research Council's committee on industrial lighting; with her husband, she designed industrial and hospital lighting systems.

In 1928 Rand moved with her husband to the Wilmer Ophthalmological Institute of the Johns Hopkins University School of Medicine. Rand taught there as an associate professor first of research ophthalmology, then of physiological optics, before becoming associate director of the Research Laboratory of Physiological Optics in Baltimore in 1935. Besides their academic work during this period, Rand and Ferree served as consultants for industries and agencies concerned with lighting technology. They developed new instruments and lamps for ophthalmologists and glare-control lighting systems for public places, notably the Johns Hopkins University Hospital and New York's Holland Tunnel, probably their most important illumination project.

In 1943, following Ferree's death, Rand moved to New York City to become a research associate at the Knapp Foundation of the Columbia University College of Physicians and Surgeons. Returning to her earlier work in color perception, she collaborated at Columbia with Legrand Hardy and M. Catherine Rittler in experiments on the detection and measurement of color blindness. In the early 1950s they developed the Hardy-Rand-Rittler plates for testing color vision. Unlike existing systems which simply identified individuals with abnormal color vision, the plates made it possible to identify the type and degree of defect for each subject. Thus Rand's careful, experimental work enabled ophthalmologists and psychologists to draw clearer conclusions from the tests they administered. Retiring in 1957, Gertrude Rand spent her last years in Stony Brook, Long Island, where she died at the age of eighty-three.

The range of Rand's work was wide, having implications for several research specialties and for industries associated with lighting technology. She was a modest, unassuming woman who tended to underestimate the value of her work, but colleagues were quick to recognize her gifts. At ease in collaboration with men, she shared credit with them on an equal basis and earned the respect of the many doctoral and, later, medical students she guided. She advised government and military offices about optics and lighting during World War II, and later became the first woman elected a fellow of the Illuminating Engineering Society (1952); the society subsequently awarded her its Gold Medal for 1963. Rand was also the first woman to win the Edgar D. Tillyer Medal of the Optical Society of America for outstanding research in vision (1959). In 1971, a year after Rand's death, her former student Louise Sloan became the second woman to receive the Tillyer Medal.

[Some materials on Rand, including alumni information forms, are on file at the Cornell Univ. Archives. Rand contributed more than 100 articles to the literature of her field, most coauthored with her husband and other collaborators. She also coauthored a text with Ferree, *Radiometric Apparatus for Use in Psychological and Physiological Optics* (1917). For a biographical sketch and selected bibliography see Kenneth N. Ogle, "Gertrude Rand: Edgar D. Tillyer Medalist for 1959," *Jour. Optical Society of Am.*, Oct. 1959, pp. 937–41; the article includes a photograph of Rand. See also *Am. Men of Science*, 9th ed. (1955); and *Lighting News*, Aug. 1963 and Nov. 1963. An obituary appeared in *N.Y. Times*, July 3, 1970. Information from 1917 N.Y. City Directory; birth certificate provided by N.Y. City Municipal Archives.]

ELIZABETH GARBER

RANKIN, Jeannette Pickering, June 11, 1880–
May 18, 1973. Suffragist, congresswoman,
pacifist.

Jeannette Rankin was the first woman elected
to the House of Representatives and the only
member of Congress to oppose the entry of the
United States into both world wars. Born on
Grant Creek Ranch, six miles from Missoula in
Montana Territory, she was the oldest of seven
children, six girls and one boy. Her mother,
Olive Pickering, of English ancestry, left her
New Hampshire home in 1878 to become an
elementary schoolteacher in Missoula; the next
year she met and married John Rankin, a successful rancher and lumber merchant whose
family had migrated from Scotland to Canada
around 1800.

The Rankin household represented an amalgam of western informality and upper-middle-
class expectations. Thus, as a child Jeannette
exhibited seemingly contradictory personality
traits; she could be creative, open-minded, and
cooperative while also being stubborn and high-
handed with her siblings. Despite a generally
permissive upbringing, the Rankin children appeared driven to succeed. Most pursued professional careers: Harriet became dean of women
at the University of Montana; Mary an English
instructor at the same university; Edna a lawyer
and pioneer in the field of planned parenthood;
and Wellington one of Montana's most famous
trial lawyers. The ambitions of all the Rankin
women were aided in part by the open, loosely
structured nature of frontier society which provided numerous career opportunities for women.
Jeannette Rankin's candidacy for national office
prior to the passage of the nineteenth amendment was possible because Montana had already
enfranchised its women.

Rankin attended public schools in Missoula,
graduating from the University of Montana in
1902 with a B.S. in biology. She did not like
school and considered herself a very poor student who "only went on because it was the
thing to do." Partly because of this sense of
intellectual inferiority, Rankin remained a shy,
retiring person throughout college. After teaching briefly in country schools following graduation, she served a short apprenticeship as a
seamstress and occasionally supported herself by
taking in sewing.

Her father's death in 1904 and her mother's
increasing withdrawal from normal household
activities led Rankin to assume full responsibility
for her younger siblings; she remained closer to
members of her immediate family, especially her
brother, than to the friends she made later in her
career. Wellington Rankin became her adviser

and financial backer; she was never completely
self-supporting and received regular installments
from the family estate all her life.

Following her father's death Rankin spent
several busy but restless years at home. In 1908
she left to study at the New York School of
Philanthropy, and subsequently practiced for a
brief time as a social worker in Montana and
Washington. Unhappy with her newly chosen
profession, Rankin entered the University of
Washington in 1909. While a student there she
joined the successful Washington state campaign for woman suffrage in 1910. This experience marked a turning point in her life: a
meeting with New Jersey journalist and former
suffrage campaigner Minnie J. Reynolds convinced her that the quest for peace should be
incorporated into the suffrage movement.

Rankin officially launched her own political
career in Montana on Feb. 2, 1911, when she
urged the state legislature to grant women the
right to vote. During the next twelve months
she gained valuable organizational and oratorical skills by working for suffrage groups in
New York, California, and Ohio. In 1913 she
became a field secretary for the National American Woman Suffrage Association, spending the
next two years lobbying for female suffrage in
fifteen states; her half dozen campaign trips to
Montana helped to win the vote for women
there in 1914.

By 1916 Rankin faced a serious career choice:
she could continue to work for national suffrage, become a lobbyist for social legislation,
or run for Congress from Montana. Choosing the
last, she campaigned successfully on a progressive Republican platform calling for woman
suffrage, protective legislation for children,
tariff revision, prohibition, and "preparedness
that will make for peace."

On April 6, 1917, four days after she had
been introduced in Congress as its first female
member, Rankin voted against United States
entry into World War I. Both CARRIE CHAPMAN
CATT and Alice Paul (1885–1977), leaders of
the prowar and antiwar suffragists respectively,
attempted to influence her decision. "I want to
stand by my country, but I cannot vote for
war," she declared on the floor of the House.
Fifty-six members of Congress voted with her
on this memorable occasion; contrary to popular
accounts, she did not cry, although some of the
men did.

Wellington Rankin had urged her to cast "a
man's vote" for war, but she maintained that
public sentiment in Montana was overwhelmingly against the war. In the 1930s, she developed a more sophisticated "revisionist" defense
of her vote, asserting: "I knew we were asked to

vote for a commercial war, that none of the idealistic hopes would be carried out, and I was aware of the falseness of much of the prowar propaganda" (Schaffer, p. 83). Whatever her reasons, her first antiwar vote had an enormous impact on her long public career. "It was not only the most significant thing I ever did," she later said, "it was a significant thing in itself." This single act publicly identified Rankin as a pacifist for the first time, and from then until her death fifty-six years later she campaigned against United States involvement in all wars.

During the remainder of her first term in Congress Rankin sponsored legislation to aid women and children, especially during wartime, and continued to work for a federal suffrage amendment. Montanans, however, became increasingly disenchanted with her pacifism as the war continued. Unable to run again for the House of Representatives in a statewide election—the legislature had divided Montana into two congressional districts—Rankin decided to become the state's first woman senator.

When she lost the Republican nomination for the Senate she continued in the race as a candidate of the newly organized National party, an amorphous group of Non-Partisan League farmers, prowar socialists, antiwar progressives, and prohibitionists. From the start it was a hopeless campaign, made even more so by the fact that Catt came out in favor of Rankin's Democratic opponent, Thomas J. Walsh.

Defeated in her bid for the Senate, Rankin finished her term in Congress and then accompanied JANE ADDAMS and FLORENCE KELLEY to Zurich in 1919 as a delegate to the Second International Congress of Women, which became the Women's International League for Peace and Freedom (WILPF). When they returned to the United States, Kelley appointed Rankin field secretary of the National Consumers' League; between 1920 and 1924 Rankin lobbied on Capitol Hill for the Sheppard-Towner bill to combat infant and maternal disease and conducted educational campaigns in the Mississippi Valley favoring laws to regulate working conditions for women. During these years she also became a field secretary and board member of the WILPF and a supporter of S. O. Levison's plan to outlaw war.

In 1924 Rankin established a second home near Athens, Ga., while retaining her legal residence in Montana. She spent most of her winters in Georgia, living in several spartan cottages which she continually remodeled. She founded the Georgia Peace Society in 1928, which became the home base of her pacifist operations until its demise from lack of funds on the eve of World War II.

In 1925, after about ten months, Rankin resigned as WILPF field secretary when it proved impossible to finance her elaborate plan for organizing western members. Moreover, like many other western suffragists, she found it difficult to work with the national leaders of the WILPF, especially its strong-minded executive secretary, Dorothy Detzer. A similar dissatisfaction involving conflicting personalities and strategies prompted her resignation in 1929 as a lobbyist for the Women's Peace Union, an organization she had supported since 1921 and whose sole purpose was to outlaw war by passing a constitutional amendment.

In 1929 Rankin began a ten-year association with the National Council for the Prevention of War (NCPW), as a Washington lobbyist and field organizer. This affiliation ended as a result of disagreements over salary cuts and her own feeling that her organizational work was not sufficiently appreciated by other NCPW leaders, especially executive director Frederick J. Libby. She also opposed her coworkers' support of the foreign policies of President Franklin D. Roosevelt.

After leaving the NCPW, Rankin again ran for Congress from Montana as a Republican pacifist. Capitalizing on her influential family connections, on the widespread public antiwar sentiment in Montana, and on the backing of labor and women, she defeated liberal Democrat Jerry J. O'Connell. She argued in Congress against Lend-Lease, the draft, military expenditures, and repeal of the neutrality legislation of the 1930s. On Dec. 8, 1941, the day after Pearl Harbor, she cast the single vote against American entry into the Second World War. Again there were no tears; again her brother urged her to vote yes. But this time she stood alone in the House and ultimately in Montana, losing any chance for reelection in 1942.

During the remainder of the 1940s Rankin ranched in Montana, redesigned yet another cottage in Georgia, cared for her ailing mother, and, most important, began to travel extensively abroad to study the pacifist methods and ideas of foreign countries. She displayed intense interest in Gandhi's work in India and visited that country seven times between 1946 and 1971. "I traveled around the world," she declared in 1972, "and stayed long enough to know how the Americans were dominating underdeveloped countries" (Berkeley Oral History Project, p. 12). Throughout the 1950s she quietly opposed all manifestations of the cold war, including United States involvement in Korea.

The war in Vietnam revitalized both her spirits and her career. She had been out of the national limelight for over two decades when the Jeannette Rankin Brigade was organized in 1967. An incongruous coalition of feminists, pacifists, hippies, rock musicians, antiwar students, and assorted radicals, the brigade demonstrated against the war in Washington, D.C., on Jan. 15, 1968. Shortly afterward, Rankin decided (at the age of eighty-eight) to run again for Congress to "have somebody to vote for" and to oppose a third world war if necessary. But it was not to be.

Rankin had long suffered from what is known as tic douloureux, a disease that causes painful inflammation of a facial nerve. For years she had tried to control the condition with alcohol injections and aspirin, but with age the pain had become incapacitating. In 1968, instead of running for a third term, she underwent surgery which was only partly successful. Nonetheless, Jeannette Rankin's long career ended as it had begun, amid a flurry of travel, public appearances, and antiwar statements. She died of a heart attack in Carmel, Calif., in 1973.

Rankin's life epitomizes the experience of a western woman among a generation of female pacifists who, like Jane Addams, believed in a global society of peace—one they conceived of in terms of "community and world housekeeping." There has probably never been such an influential generation of pacifists, and Jeannette Rankin remains one of its most memorable representatives.

[The papers of Jeannette Rankin at the Schlesinger Library, Radcliffe College, provide information for limited portions of her life; few of her private letters before World War II were preserved and the records for her first term in Congress are incomplete. A major source is the oral history of Rankin, "Activist for World Peace, Women's Rights, and Democratic Government" (1974), at the Bancroft Library, Univ. of Calif., Berkeley. Rankin's letters to the NCPW from 1929 to 1939 are in the Swarthmore College Peace Coll. Hannah Josephson, *First Lady in Congress: Jeannette Rankin* (1974), remains the only published biography, although a more thorough one by Norma Smith is forthcoming. Ronald Schaffer, "Jeannette Rankin: Progressive Isolationist" (Ph.D. diss., Princeton Univ., 1959), represents an older interpretation, but is based on documents that were either lost or passed into private hands in the 1960s. Other works include: John C. Board, "The Lady from Montana: Jeannette Rankin" (M.A. thesis, Univ. of Wyo., 1964); Katherine Cheek, "The Wit and Rhetoric of Jeannette Rankin" (M.A. thesis, Univ. of Ga., 1970); Ted Carlton Harris, "Jeannette Rankin: Suffragist, First Woman Elected to Congress, and Pacifist" (Ph.D. diss., Univ. of Ga., 1972); and Doris Buck Ward, "The Winning of Woman Suffrage in Montana" (M.A. thesis, Univ. of Mont., 1974). For published articles see: Mackey Brown, "Montana's First Woman Politician—A Recollection of Jeannette Rankin Campaigning," *Mont. Business*

Quart., Autumn 1971, pp. 23–26; Belle Fligelman Winestine, "Mother Was Shocked," *Montana: The Mag. of Western Hist.*, July 1974, pp. 70–79; Ted Harris, "Jeannette Rankin in Georgia," *Ga. Hist. Quart.*, Spring 1974, pp. 55–78; and Joan Hoff Wilson, "'Peace Is a Woman's Job . . .': Jeannette Rankin's Foreign Policy," *Montana: The Mag. of Western Hist.*, Jan., April 1980. Death certificate was provided by the Calif. Dept. of Public Health.]

JOAN HOFF WILSON

RAPOPORT, Lydia, March 8, 1923–Sept. 6, 1971. Social work educator.

Lydia Rapoport was born in Vienna, Austria, the younger of two children of Eugenia (Margulies) and Samuel Rappoport (his spelling of the name). Her Polish-born mother, although a trained teacher, did not engage in her profession but devoted herself to family duties. Her father, who had studied law in Vienna, worked in the grain trading business before migrating in 1928 to the United States, where he was employed in New York City as a translator. The rest of the family remained in Vienna until 1932 so that Lydia's brother could complete his gymnasium education.

In New York Lydia Rapoport attended public schools and majored in sociology at Hunter College. Elected to Phi Beta Kappa, she received her A.B. in 1943 and immediately enrolled in the accelerated course at Smith College School for Social Work. She received her master's degree the following year, when she was only twenty-one. From Smith, Rapoport went to Chicago, where she worked first as a child guidance counselor at the Institute for Juvenile Research, then as an intake supervisor at the Child Guidance Clinic at the Bobs Roberts Hospital of the University of Chicago, and later as a supervisor at the Jewish Children's Bureau and the Michael Reese Hospital. She earned a certificate in child therapy from the Chicago Institute for Psychoanalysis and became a specialist in the diagnosis and treatment of emotionally disturbed children.

In 1952 Rapoport won a Fulbright fellowship and left Chicago to study at the London School of Economics. While there she met Richard Titmuss, one of the architects of the national health service, and Dame Eileen Younghusband, a leading English social work scholar and educator, both of whom became her lifelong friends.

Returning from England in 1954, Rapoport decided to live in California to be near her brother and his family. She became a supervisor at the California State Mental Hygiene Clinic for students of the School of Social Welfare at the University of California, Berkeley. A year later she joined the faculty of the school as an assistant professor, teaching social casework. Receiving tenure in 1963 and promotion to full professor in 1969, Rapoport founded the Community Mental Health Program at Berkeley, an advanced program for graduate social workers interested in developing special skills in community mental health work. An effective and inspiring teacher, she frequently gave special institutes and seminars in the fields of social work she developed as specialties: crisis theory, consultation, and supervision. In addition, she taught at the summer programs at Smith College School for Social Work and the University of Chicago School of Social Service Administration.

Lydia Rapoport's major research and writings were completed during her years on the Berkeley faculty and during a year of study with Erich Lindemann at the Harvard School of Public Health (1959–60). Out of her exchanges with specialists in public health came her most important contribution: a theoretical framework for what she termed crisis-oriented brief treatment, an approach she subsequently developed as a specialty within social casework. Her work drew on the central concepts of personality, stress, and learning theories, and utilized the preventive orientation of public health rather than the medical model of treatment.

Lydia Rapoport also helped to formulate a theoretical basis for defining consultation and supervision as distinct social work functions. She explored the role of the social worker as a consultant, analyzed the function of the supervisor in social work practice and education, and set guidelines for the relationship between supervisor and student or supervisee.

In 1963 Rapoport traveled to Israel to be visiting professor at the Baerwald School of Social Work of Hebrew University in Jerusalem for a year. There she assisted in setting up a standard undergraduate curriculum in the country's schools of social work. Although she had never closely identified with her Jewish heritage, she soon acquired a profound affection for the new country and its people.

On a leave from her Berkeley post, Rapoport moved to New York in January 1971 to become the first United Nations Inter-Regional Adviser on Family Welfare and Family Planning. In July of that year she became ill and underwent emergency intestinal surgery; seven weeks later she died in New York of acute bacterial endocarditis. At the time of her death, she was about to begin a study of the roles of social workers in introducing family planning in social service programs in Israel.

In a 1960 paper, "In Defense of Social Work: An Examination of Stress in the Profession,"

Rapoport wrote: "No other profession is as self-examining and critically self-conscious as social work" (Katz, p. 49). The major legacy of her own scholarship was a commitment to examining the theoretical basis for social casework and to defining the necessary skills for the social work practitioner and educator.

[Lydia Rapoport's major writings can be found in Sanford N. Katz, ed., *Creativity in Social Work: Selected Writings of Lydia Rapoport* (1975), which also includes a biographical sketch and an analysis of her contribution to social work. A brief account of her career is in Ernest Greenwood, Gertrude Wilson, and Robert Apte, "Lydia Rapoport," *In Memoriam* (Univ. of Calif., July 1975). Obituaries appeared in the San Francisco *Chronicle*, Sept. 8, 1971; and Oakland *Tribune*, Sept. 8, 1971. The Lydia Rapoport Endowment Fund at Smith College School for Social Work, established by Rapoport's friends, supports the Lydia Rapoport Distinguished Visiting Professorship.]

SANFORD N. KATZ

RAWLINGS, Marjorie Kinnan, Aug. 8, 1896–Dec. 14, 1953. Writer.

Marjorie Kinnan Rawlings was born in Washington, D.C., the older child and only daughter of Arthur Frank and Ida May (Traphagen) Kinnan. Of largely Scots and Scots-Irish descent on both sides, the family traced its American heritage back to the seventeenth century. Arthur Kinnan was an attorney in the United States Patent Office who also owned a farm in Maryland. Growing up in Washington, Marjorie attended public school and developed an early interest in writing. As a young girl she played "Story Lady," entertaining the boys (but not the girls) in the neighborhood with her imaginative tales. Early in 1913 her father died. The next year, after completing high school, she moved with her mother and younger brother to Madison, Wis., where she enrolled at the university. Active in the campus dramatic society, she was elected to Phi Beta Kappa in her junior year and received the A.B. in 1918.

For a year after graduation Marjorie Kinnan worked as an editor and publicist for the YWCA at its national headquarters in New York City. In May 1919 she married the writer and boating enthusiast Charles A. Rawlings, and moved with him to Rochester, N.Y. During the next decade she wrote advertising copy and newspaper features, working for the *Louisville Courier-Journal* (1920–21) and the *Rochester Journal* (1922–23). She also produced a syndicated verse column, "Songs of a Housewife" (1925–27), but attempts to publish her fiction proved unsuccessful.

In 1928 Charles and Marjorie Rawlings bought a large orange grove at Cross Creek, near Hawthorne, in north central Florida, where her plan to become a professional writer was realized. In 1930 *Scribner's Magazine* bought her short collection of character sketches, "Cracker Chidlings: Real Tales from the Florida Interior," as well as her more ambitious story of a farm couple facing starvation, "Jacob's Ladder." The stories attracted the attention of Maxwell Perkins, renowned editor for the Scribner publishing firm, who began to work with her. Rawlings went to live for several weeks in the Big Scrub country not far from Cross Creek, with an old woman and her moonshiner son, and projected new fictions about the rural Floridians.

The year 1933 was momentous for Rawlings, as her story "Gal Young Un," published in *Harper's* the year before, won first prize in the O. Henry Memorial Award contest, and her first novel, *South Moon Under*, about the lives and lore of Florida moonshiners, appeared. (Like several of her later books, the novel became a Book-of-the-Month Club selection.) Shortly after the novel's publication, the author and her husband, who did not share her commitment to life in the Florida back country, recognized at last their basic incompatibility and were divorced.

Marjorie Rawlings continued to live in and about Cross Creek for the next few years, traveling briefly to Hampshire, England, to gather material for her second novel, *Golden Apples* (1935). Far below *South Moon Under* in quality, the novel was hampered by Rawlings's clumsy handling of her English protagonist and the high society he encounters. Turning back to more familiar themes, she began work on *The Yearling* (1938), inspired by Maxwell Perkins's earlier suggestion that she write "a book about a boy," an adventure tale evocative of *Huckleberry Finn* or *Kim* and set in the Florida woods. Rawlings was well suited to the task. Since adolescence, she had written yearningly in her fiction of little boys. Occasionally she might treat of a small girl, but never with the intensity she brought to an adult's fondness for a son-figure. While working on *The Yearling* at a North Carolina resort, Rawlings encountered such a child, an orphan boy who strongly appealed to her and whom she featured in her stories "A Mother in Mannville" (1936) and "Mountain Prelude" (1947).

The Yearling proved the high point of Rawlings's career. It enjoyed measured critical and enormous popular success. Movie rights were sold to MGM—though it was not until 1946 that an MGM motion picture version of *The Yearling* was finally released—and the book won the Pulitzer Prize for fiction in 1939. Other tributes followed, including membership in the National Institute of Arts and Letters, and several honorary degrees.

In 1941 Rawlings married Norton Sanford Baskin, an old friend of hers who operated a hotel and restaurant in St. Augustine, Fla., where the two then resided. She paid tribute to her adoptive home in *Cross Creek* (1942), a memoir of her "life in the woods" which warrants comparison to Thoreau's *Walden*. Although well received, *Cross Creek* embroiled its author in a long-drawn-out lawsuit by one of her Cross Creek neighbors, Zelma Cason, who felt libeled by its portrait of her. (Eventually, the Florida Supreme Court found in favor of the plaintiff, but the author had to pay only nominal damages.)

Rawlings won a second O. Henry Memorial Award in 1945 for her story "Black Secret," which had appeared earlier that year in *The New Yorker*. Two years later she purchased an old farmhouse in Van Hornesville, N.Y., to serve as her summer home. Her husband remained tied to his work in Florida, and subsequently they were together for only part of each year. As she had earlier used Cross Creek, Rawlings now employed the farmlands of upstate New York as a fictional locale, combining that setting with family lore concerning her maternal grandfather Traphagen to produce *The Sojourner* (1953). While less popular than *The Yearling* and disparaged by some critics, the novel remains one of her serious achievements, a subtle repudiation of society and its vanities.

Rawlings's next subject was to have been a biography of Ellen Glasgow, but ill health interrupted her research; she died of a stroke in St. Augustine, Fla., in December 1953. Her body was laid to rest in Antioch Cemetery not far from Cross Creek. At the funeral service a friend read from her memoir of that place: "Who owns Cross Creek? The red birds, I think, more than I . . ."

Fierce undercurrents of emotion, attraction and repulsion, energized Rawlings's work, the inspired writings as well as the "interesting trash instead of literature" (as she once called some of her fiction). She had a longing for solitude and an aversion to city life, powerfully expressed in the character of Penny Baxter in *The Yearling*. More important is her pervasive sympathy for young boys in her fiction, contrasted to her generally unsentimental handling of mothers and wives. Described by Cross Creek acquaintances as a moody, cantankerous person herself, Rawlings wrote vividly of angry women who "get back" at their husbands or children, as with Ma Baxter in *The Yearling* or Amelia Linden in *The Sojourner*. From such powerful elements the author fashioned both slapdash commercial pieces and works of art, yielding a few books and several stories which have earned her a secure place in twentieth-century American literature.

[There is a collection of Rawlings's papers, including manuscripts and letters, in the Library of the Univ. of Fla. at Gainesville. Other books by Rawlings include a collection of stories, *When the Whippoorwill—* (1940); a "conversational cookbook," *Cross Creek Cookery* (1942); a children's story, *The Secret River* (1955); and an anthology, *The Marjorie Rawlings Reader* (1956), ed. Julia Scribner Bigham. (Bigham's introduction discusses Maxwell Perkins's work with Rawlings.) There are two published biographies, generally complementary: Gordon E. Bigelow, *Frontier Eden: The Literary Career of Marjorie Kinnan Rawlings* (1966), and Samuel I. Bellman, *Marjorie Kinnan Rawlings* (1974), which includes a frontispiece photograph. Among useful essays on Rawlings are Harry Evans, "Marjorie Kinnan Rawlings," *Family Circle*, May 7 and 14, 1943; Gordon Bigelow, "Marjorie Kinnan Rawlings' Wilderness," *Sewanee Rev.*, Spring 1965, pp. 299–310; Samuel Bellman, "Marjorie Kinnan Rawlings: A Solitary Sojourner in the Florida Backwoods," *Kansas Quart.*, Spring 1970, pp. 78–87; and Samuel I. Bellman, "Writing Literature for Young People: Marjorie Kinnan Rawlings' 'Secret River' of the Imagination," *Costerus*, vol. 9 (1973). Sketches of her can be found in *Current Biog.*, 1942; *Nat. Cyc. Am. Biog.*, G, 432–33; and *Dict. Am. Biog.*, Supp. Five. An obituary appeared in the *N.Y. Times*, Dec. 16, 1953; death certificate furnished by Fla. Dept. of Health.]

SAMUEL IRVING BELLMAN

REBAY, Hilla, May 31, 1890–Sept. 27, 1967. Museum director, painter.

In the formation of the Solomon R. Guggenheim Museum Hilla Rebay realized her dream of creating a museum for the art to which she devoted her life. Born the Baroness Hildegard Anna Augusta Elisabeth Rebay von Ehrenwiesen in Strassburg, Alsace, she and her elder brother were raised in Germany. An artistically gifted child, she was encouraged by her parents to develop her talents. Her mother, the former Antonie von Eicken, had come from a cultivated and artistic family, which at one time had held mining interests in the Ruhr; her Bavarian father, Baron Franz Joseph Rebay von Ehrenwiesen, was a career army officer who attained the rank of general during World War I. His letters to Hilla, as she was called, reveal a serious, but gentle and supportive, father, who encouraged her in her artistic studies while worrying about her frail health and nerves. He

too was artistic, and filled several homes with handcarved furniture of professional skill.

Hilla attended girls' schools in Strassburg, Freiburg, and Cologne. She took regular art classes at her schools and with tutors, showing considerable skill at portraiture. At the age of nineteen, in 1909, she was sent to Paris and enrolled at the Académie Julian, where she remained until 1910. While taking all the conventional art courses, she also became aware of the more experimental art being done outside the schools. During this Paris period, she developed an interest in theosophy, and like many another twentieth-century artist, she became a lifelong devotee of Oriental mysticism.

Rebay spent most of 1911 as an advanced student in Munich. She exhibited at the Cologne Kunstverein in 1912; in 1913 she was accepted in the Munich Spring Secession exhibition and the Salon des Artistes Indépendants in Paris. From then on she signed her work Hilla v. Rebay or Hilla Rebay.

A meeting with Hans Arp in Zurich in 1916 was catalytic for Rebay's future. Arp, the proponent of the theory of spontaneous generation of form, encouraged her to work in the most advanced abstract style and to believe in herself and in the validity of this art form. He introduced her to Herwarth Walden, director of the radical Berlin art gallery, Der Sturm, where Rebay exhibited in 1917 and 1919. There she saw works by many of the artists she would later collect, most notably the nonfigurative paintings of the pioneer abstractionist Wassily Kandinsky. In his work, spontaneously created color-forms based loosely or not at all on natural objects were, as he explained, the expression of the inner emotion of the artist's soul.

At Der Sturm she also met Rudolf Bauer, a painter who was to play a disastrous role in her life. Her blind admiration for Bauer's painting, which was studiously derived from Kandinsky's, allowed Rebay to cast Bauer in the role of genius. So that he might work without distraction, she undertook to support him for the rest of his life. Accepting her assistance as his due, Bauer never evidenced any gratitude.

At thirty-five, Hilla Rebay was not prospering in her work or in her life. She was entangled in the unhappy liaison with Bauer, and still supported by her parents. To escape she moved to Italy in 1925, finally establishing her independence. Convinced that nonobjective art was thriving in the United States she decided to emigrate, and in 1927 the vivacious and talented baroness arrived in New York. When she realized her error concerning the influence of nonobjective painting there, it became her mission to promote and encourage this art form.

Through family connections she met Irene and Solomon R. Guggenheim, and she conveyed her enthusiasm for nonobjective painting to the nearly seventy-year-old multimillionaire and his wife. Having convinced them to begin to collect in this area, in 1929 she started to introduce the Guggenheims to artists' studios and galleries in Europe and the United States. They acquired works by Calder, Chagall, Delaunay, Gabo, Kandinsky, Klee, Marc, Moholy-Nagy, Mondrian, Pevsner, Picasso, Gleizes, Léger, and Seurat, which led to plans for a permanent public home for the collection and formed the nucleus of the future museum's holdings. When the Solomon R. Guggenheim Foundation was incorporated in 1937, Rebay was named curator.

Only twelve years after her arrival in the United States Rebay supervised, in 1939, the opening of the museum in temporary quarters at 24 East 54th Street, in New York City, where it was known as both the Museum of Nonobjective Painting and Art of Tomorrow. She became the museum's first director. Aware of the work accomplished by such American women as ISABELLA STEWART GARDNER and GERTRUDE VANDERBILT WHITNEY who had preceded her in the formation of public art collections, Rebay felt closest to KATHERINE DREIER, whose collection of twentieth-century art and support of artists she deeply respected. The two women, brought together in 1930 by Kandinsky and Mondrian, remained cordial friends until Dreier's death; Rebay felt that she was carrying on in the tradition Dreier had begun.

Guggenheim's faith in Rebay's leadership of the museum was firmly underscored when, in 1942, he agreed to begin the permanent building which he and Rebay had contemplated more than a decade before. Also in 1942, Hilla Rebay was denounced as a German spy; she was deeply hurt to discover that it was Rudolf Bauer, now in the United States—with her support—and jealous of her role at the museum, who had spread the rumors leading to the accusation. Rebay was cleared of the charge, and in 1943 she invited Frank Lloyd Wright to discuss plans for the design of the proposed museum (completed in 1959). Wright and Rebay became close, if argumentative, friends; he called her "a magnificently human projectile." (She became an American citizen in 1947.)

The supportive Solomon Guggenheim's death in 1949 was a great blow to Rebay. Her zealous advocacy both of nonobjective painting and of Bauer had earned her as many detractors as adherents; few were neutral. In 1952 the other trustees forced Rebay to resign from the museum, which perhaps had grown beyond her.

The museum was renamed for Solomon R. Guggenheim, and its emphasis changed from nonobjective painting to a more inclusive survey of twentieth-century art. For a decade Rebay remained active in the arts; she also established a foundation for the encouragement of nonobjective painting. But with old age and illness, she withdrew entirely. Hilla Rebay died a lonely and disappointed woman at her home in Greens Farms, Conn. But the museum created initially by her taste, vision, and energy became a public monument.

[The Hilla von Rebay Foundation Archive, containing a large collection of correspondence and personal papers, is maintained by the Solomon R. Guggenheim Museum. Rebay's writings include "Nonobjective Art," *Southern Literary Messenger*, Dec. 1942, pp. 472–75, and numerous exhibition catalogs including *Wassily Kandinsky Memorial* (1945) and *Laszlo Moholy-Nagy Memorial* (1947). Partly because of Rebay's own vagueness about dates, the biographical material previously published about her is inaccurate. Furthermore, her life and work have generally been treated in a superficial manner. An obituary in the *N.Y. Times*, Sept. 29, 1967, borders on slander. Knowledgeable articles include Dore Ashton, "Naissance d'un grand musée," *XXᵉ Siècle*, Dec. 1968, pp. 137–39; Katharine Kuh, "The Vision of Hilla Rebay," *N.Y. Times*, May 7, 1972, sect. 2, p. 21; Lawrence Campbell, "The Museum of Non-objective Painting Revisited," *ART News*, Dec. 1972, pp. 40–41; and Hans Richter, *Begegnungen von Dada bis heute* (1973), pp. 162–85. Joan M. Lukach is preparing a documentary biography of Hilla Rebay and her role in the creation of the Solomon R. Guggenheim Museum.]

JOAN M. LUKACH

REED, Dorothy. *See* MENDENHALL, Dorothy Reed.

REICHARD, Gladys Amanda, July 17, 1893–July 25, 1955. Anthropologist.

Head of what was for many years the only undergraduate department of anthropology in a woman's college in the United States, Gladys Reichard was also a dedicated field worker who made a lifelong study of the culture and language of the Navaho Indians. She was born in Bangor, Pa., the younger of two daughters of Noah W. Reichard, a respected family physician, and Minerva Ann (Jordan) Reichard. Minerva Ann Reichard died when her daughters were young, and Dr. Reichard later remarried. The Reichard family was of Pennsylvania Dutch heritage and the Quaker household was intellectually oriented. After her graduation from Bangor High School in 1909, Gladys Reichard began teaching, first in a country school in Northampton County, Pa., and then, from 1911 to 1915, at the elementary school in Bangor.

In 1915 Reichard enrolled at Swarthmore College, from which she was graduated four years later with honors, a major in classics, and the Lucretia Mott Fellowship for graduate study. Stimulated by a course in anthropology she had taken at Swarthmore, she decided she wanted to study with Franz Boas, professor of anthropology at Columbia University. In the fall of 1919 she moved to New York where Boas soon became the central intellectual influence in her life.

Of all the women students and associates who gathered around Franz Boas and, in public or in private, called him "Papa Franz," Gladys Reichard was most like a daughter. Her personal and intellectual loyalty to him was nearly absolute, and in return Franz Boas took care of her, providing jobs, fellowships, grants, and publishers as they were needed. While she was in graduate school she lived for a year in the Boas home.

Gladys Reichard had thought that she might study the evolution of culture and perhaps archaeology, but under Boas's tutelage she turned to linguistics. She received an A.M. in 1920, and in 1920–21 assisted Boas in his classes at Barnard College; she also taught at the Robert Louis Stevenson School in New York City. In 1925, she received her Ph.D. with a dissertation on the grammar of the Wiyot Indians in California, among whom she had done field work during 1922–23. After her year in California, Reichard had returned to Barnard in 1923 as instructor in anthropology; she taught there for the rest of her life, becoming assistant professor in 1928 and professor of anthropology in 1951.

Around 1923 Gladys Reichard had begun a close relationship with Pliny Earle Goddard (1869–1928), curator of ethnology at the American Museum of Natural History, who became the other great influence in her life. He interested Reichard in the Navaho Indians, whom she visited in 1923; the following year she traveled with him for six weeks on the Navaho reservation gathering genealogies which became the basis for her *Social Life of the Navaho Indians* (1928). Goddard wanted to know a culture not as an abstraction but as it was experienced by individuals, and this concern, along with the meticulous recording of data and the interest in language and in art styles which she learned from Boas, came to characterize Reichard's work. She was not interested in theory nor, generally, in comparative studies. Throughout her career she was bluntly

critical of those who, in her view, moved too quickly from observation to theory.

Reichard spent 1926–27 in Hamburg, Germany, on a Guggenheim fellowship, studying Melanesian design. From Europe she went to Idaho to do an analysis of Coeur d'Alene grammar for the *Handbook of American Indian Languages* (1938), but after Goddard's sudden death in 1928, she turned again to her Navaho studies. Her book *Melanesian Design* (1933) was awarded the A. Cressy Morrison Prize in Natural Science by the New York Academy of Sciences in 1932.

She edited Goddard's unpublished texts and then, from 1930 on, spent four summers living with a Navaho family near Ganado, Ariz., learning to speak the Navaho language and to weave rugs. Although several studies had been made of Navaho weaving, none had been done from the point of view of the weaver, which was Reichard's primary interest. *Spider Woman* (1934) is both a record of what a woman weaver thinks and does and one of the first good accounts of the field work experience. Reichard later wrote a more technical volume on weaving, *Navaho Shepherd and Weaver* (1936), and a fictionalized account of the daily life of a Navaho family, *Dezba, Woman of the Desert* (1939); she and her sister, Lilian, also took the photographs for *Dezba*.

In the summer of 1934 Reichard ran the Hogan School at her Navaho family's compound. Sponsored by the Bureau of Indian Affairs, the school made the first attempt to teach native speakers to write the Navaho language. It was a success, but the need to complete the Coeur d'Alene grammar kept her from undertaking it a second summer.

Gladys Reichard had observed Navaho ceremonials as she was learning to weave, and gradually she concentrated on the study of Navaho religion. Her early lack of interest in religion was transformed as she gathered information on sand paintings and legends. In 1950 she summed up twenty years of research in her major work, *Navaho Religion: A Study of Symbolism.*

Reichard returned to the study of language with *Navaho Grammar* (1951). This work was controversial, however, since she had never accepted a new system of transcription for Navaho worked out by Edward Sapir and Harry Hoijer. Her methods, which lacked both statistical and structural orientation, were outdated, but she continued her linguistic work with "A Comparison of Five Salish Languages," published after her death in the *International Journal of American Linguistics* (1958–60).

A reserved person with a few deep friendships, Reichard felt most at home in the southwest. From 1940 on, she spent nearly every summer and two sabbaticals in Flagstaff, Ariz., near the Museum of Northern Arizona; she planned to retire to Flagstaff. She died there in 1955, of a stroke, one week after an earlier stroke had hospitalized and partly paralyzed her.

Although in her own time Reichard was eclipsed by the greater fame of such other of Boas's students as RUTH BENEDICT and Margaret Mead (1901–1978), the depth and quality of her ethnographic recording has gradually gained recognition. A 1977 study by Gary Witherspoon, *Language and Art in the Navajo Universe*, is dedicated to Reichard, and the author views himself as carrying on the task she began, that of interpreting the Navaho world view to those outside it.

[Gladys Reichard's papers are at the Museum of Northern Arizona in Flagstaff and include book reviews, correspondence, photographs of Navaho and other Indians and of the southwest, Navaho word lists, texts, and sandpainting copies. Her letters to Franz Boas are in the Boas Papers, Am. Phil. Soc. Library, Philadelphia. Reichard's important works not cited above include *Sandpaintings of the Navajo Shooting Chant* (1937), with Franc J. Newcomb; *Navajo Medicine Man: Sandpaintings and Legends of Miguelito* (1939); *Prayer: The Compulsive Word* (1944); and *The Story of the Navaho Hail Chant* (1944). A memorial booklet published by Barnard College contains tributes by Ruth L. Bunzel, Frederica de Laguna, and Margaret Mead, a bibliography compiled by Nathalie F. S. Woodbury, and a photograph of Reichard. See also *Barnard College Alumnae Monthly*, Nov. 1950; Esther S. Goldfrank, "Gladys Amanda Reichard, 1893–1955," *Jour. of Am. Folklore* (1956), pp. 53–54, and *Plateau* (1955), p. 48; an obituary by Marian W. Smith, *Am. Anthropologist* (1956), pp. 913–16; and the *N.Y. Times* obituary, July 26, 1955. Death record from Ariz. Dept. of Health. Katharine Bartlett, Ruth L. Bunzel, Nathalie F. S. Woodbury, Leland C. Wyman, and Duane E. Miller, mayor of Bangor, Pa., supplied additional information. Leland C. Wyman of Jamaica Plain, Mass., has letters from Reichard concerning problems in Navaho ritual. A biobibliography by Steven G. Laughlin provided assistance with research.]

JOAN T. MARK

REID, Helen Miles Rogers, Nov. 23, 1882–July 27, 1970. Newspaper publisher.

Helen Rogers Reid was born in Appleton, Wis., the eleventh and last child and sixth daughter of Benjamin Talbot and Sarah Louise (Johnson) Rogers. Of largely English ancestry, Helen's parents traced their American genealogy to the early eighteenth century. Her father was

a hotel operator with interests also in mining and lumbering, her mother a housewife much occupied with childrearing. The family was moderately well off by community standards, but Benjamin Rogers's death in 1885 left them in somewhat reduced though still genteel circumstances. Helen Rogers attended the First Ward public school in Appleton until she was ten, then received a scholarship to Grafton Hall, an Episcopal seminary for girls in Fond du Lac, Wis. In 1899 she enrolled in Barnard College as one of its first midwestern students; to pay her way, she tutored, did clerical work, and served as assistant housekeeper in a dormitory. Concentrating in Greek and zoology, she wrote a senior thesis on "The Physiology of Minute Crustacea" and received her A.B. in 1903.

Casting about for a job, Helen Rogers sought and obtained the position of social secretary to ELISABETH MILLS REID, daughter of the financier Darius Ogden Mills, and wife of Whitelaw Reid, proprietor of the *New York Tribune*. The Reids lived sumptuously in a Florentine fortress on Madison Avenue, with a dinner table for eighty and the wealth and social prestige to fill it with interesting people. Helen Rogers worked eight years for Elisabeth Reid, moving between the United States and London, where from 1905 until his death in 1912, Whitelaw Reid was ambassador to the Court of St. James. During these years, Rogers met the Reids' only son, Ogden Mills, just out of Yale but not intellectually inclined. In a match much favored by his mother, he and Helen Rogers were married in Wisconsin on March 14, 1911.

At the outset, Helen Rogers Reid took only a passing interest in the *Tribune*, which her husband inherited on his father's death. In 1913 she gave birth to a son, Whitelaw, followed two years later by a daughter, Elizabeth (who died as a child, in 1924). Helen Reid's main public activity after her daughter's birth was as state treasurer for the New York suffrage campaign, raising more than a half-million dollars for the decisive 1917 effort. Her commitment to women's rights stemmed from her college years, she later told a reporter: "When I was in Barnard, working my way through, the necessity for complete independence of women was borne in upon me." In speeches through her life, she advocated that women should work and be economically independent of their husbands, and that men should take greater responsibility in the home and in raising children; she also believed women should be conscripted for some form of military service.

In 1918 Helen Reid became an advertising solicitor for the anemic *Tribune*. The Reid family was said to have poured fifteen million dollars into the paper between 1898 and 1918, but it had remained unprofitable, and Ogden Reid had done little but supervise in a very general way. Helen Reid helped to reduce the paper's deficit substantially, bringing to the business the shrewd managerial instincts her husband lacked. Within two months of joining the advertising department, she became its director, a post she held under various titles for the next twenty-nine years. Acting with what one associate called the "persistence of gravity," she prodded salesmen and tirelessly pursued potential advertisers, doubling the *Tribune's* advertising linage between 1918 and 1924. With a keen business sense she also promoted the 1924 acquisition of the *New York Herald,* merging it with the *Tribune* into the *New York Herald Tribune* at a cost of five million dollars to the Reids. With its expanded circulation and staff, the *Herald Tribune* became one of the nation's major newspapers.

Over the next two decades, as vice president of the *Herald Tribune,* Helen Reid came to play an important role in determining policy. She was responsible for its concentration on the middle-class suburbs and for its emphasis on gardening news and allied features of special interest to suburban women. She expanded the paper's Home Institute, a widely known experimental and test kitchen, and hired Clementine Paddleford as food writer. And she saw to the appointment of women in other areas as well, including that of IRITA VAN DOREN as editor of *Books,* the Sunday literary supplement, and MARIE MATTINGLY MELONEY as director of the annual Forum on Current Problems (1930) and later as editor of *This Week,* the paper's Sunday fiction and articles supplement. Reid also brought syndicated foreign affairs columnist DOROTHY THOMPSON to the paper. By the 1940s the *Herald Tribune* had more women staff members than any other daily paper in the United States.

Outside the newsroom, Helen Reid became a force in civic and national life. Filling the power vacuum created by her husband, she represented the paper in Republican politics. It was she, for example, who traveled to Marion, Ohio, in 1920 after the election of Warren G. Harding to discuss cabinet appointments and to let Harding know, subtly, that the *Tribune's* support depended on the quality of his choices. In later years, she supported and advised the presidential campaigns of Wendell L. Willkie and Dwight D. Eisenhower. According to Clare Boothe Luce: "In those years, New York Republicanism was Helen Reid." Reid's political influence was evidenced at the dinners she gave for public opinion molders and leaders. It was her custom at these dinners to throw out a question

of the moment and go around the table for comments; some guests gave their opinions seated; others, sensing they were in the presence of "Queen Helen," rose and addressed her as if she were a public meeting.

On her husband's death in 1947, Helen Reid succeeded him as president of the Herald Tribune corporation. Control of the newspaper remained within the family for the next ten years; in 1953, Reid became chairman of the board, yielding the presidency to her elder son, Whitelaw. Then two years later, at the age of seventy-two, she resigned the chairmanship but continued on the board, Whitelaw taking her place as chairman while her youngest child, Ogden (b. 1925), became president, publisher, and editor. Neither son proved adept as a newspaper owner, however, and in 1957 the family sold all but a small interest to John Hay Whitney, who operated the failing property until 1966. As the *New York World Tribune,* it expired finally in May 1967.

A trustee of Barnard College (1914–56), Helen Reid served as chairman of the Board of Trustees there from 1947 to 1956. She spent her last years quietly on the Reid family estate in Purchase, N.Y., and at her apartment in New York City, where she died in July 1970.

[Helen Reid's papers are in the Reid Family Coll., Library of Congress. There is also material on Reid, including letters on trustee matters, in the Barnard College Archives; some letters are still held by family members. Useful articles on Reid include Mona Gardner, "Queen Helen," *Sat. Eve. Post,* May 6 and 13, 1944; Don Wharton, "The Girl Who Made Good," *Today,* July 11, 1936; and *Current Biog.,* 1952. See also Harry Baehr, Jr., *The New York Tribune Since the Civil War* (1936). Obituaries appeared in the *N.Y. Times,* July 28, 1970, and *Barnard Alumnae,* Fall 1970. Information was supplied by Louise Fitzsimons and by Reid's son Whitelaw Reid.]

ALDEN WHITMAN

RICE PEREIRA, Irene. *See* PEREIRA, Irene Rice.

RICHTER, Gisela Marie Augusta, Aug. 15, 1882–Dec. 24, 1972. Classical archaeologist, museum curator.

Gisela Richter was born in London, England, the third of four surviving children and second daughter of Jean Paul and Luise Marie (Schwaab) Richter. (A third daughter died in infancy.) Her father, a British subject, partly German and partly French in origin, was a noted art historian and connoisseur of Italian painting. Luise Richter, born in Broussa, Turkey, where her father had started a silk industry, was also an art critic and writer. Both daughters continued their parents' interest: Irma (a year older than Gisela) became a painter, while the brothers branched out, the elder becoming a lawyer and the younger an orientalist.

Gisela Richter began school in Florence, Italy, where her family lived until she was ten, and continued at Maida Vale High School after the Richters moved to London in 1892. Her father trained the girls in connoisseurship of painting. When Gisela was fourteen, she and Irma attended lectures by Emanuel Loewy at the University of Rome. These lectures and frequent visits to the museums of Rome "proved a turning-point in my life," Richter later wrote. "I became enamoured of Greek and Roman art and decided to become an archaeologist." Entering Girton College, Cambridge, in 1901, she found the work "all-absorbing," especially that with her don, Katharine Jex-Blake, who taught classical languages and history. Archaeology lectures seemed "rather elementary" after Rome. In the fall of 1904, for her fourth undergraduate year, Richter went to the British School of Archaeology in Athens. The only woman at the school, she was not allowed to live there, staying instead at a pension where she became friends with several women from the American School of Classical Studies. Richter's study in Athens led to a bachelor's thesis on Attic vases, published in the British School's *Annual* for 1904–05.

In the autumn of 1905 HARRIET BOYD (HAWES), the American excavator of Gournia, then in her early thirties, invited Gisela Richter to come with her to the United States. She introduced Richter to Edward Robinson, vice director of the Metropolitan Museum of Art in New York City, who offered Richter a temporary job planning an exhibit of Greek vases. In June 1906, when she left for England to visit her family, Robinson promised her a permanent post beginning that autumn. Her family consented, but insisted, lest she become an exile, that she return each summer. The three months away from the museum became a permanent pattern; Richter spent much of the time visiting museums and conferring with the principal scholars in her own and related fields. She became an American citizen in 1917, but remained in close touch with an international circle of scholarly friends throughout her career.

Gisela Richter was named assistant curator of classical art at the Metropolitan Museum in 1910, rising to curator in 1925. During these years a steady stream of important acquisitions made by the museum's purchasing agent, John Marshall, raised the Metropolitan's classical holdings to the level of a great collection. As Richter exhibited and published these works, she became expert in all classes of Greek, Etruscan, and Roman art except for architecture. After Marshall died in 1928, Richter became responsible for acquisitions. Vigorously and with brilliant success, she pursued Marshall's tradition of making major additions to the collection. Most important and most influential on her own scholarship was her purchase in 1932 of a nearly intact early archaic marble statue of a young man (kouros), a work initially suspected as a forgery by some authorities. The successful effort to authenticate the kouros and fix its place in the history of Greek art led to the publication of *Kouroi* (1942), in which Richter established a chronology based on the steady development of realism in the rendering of anatomical features. Richter's grasp of the technical problems facing Greek sculptors was enhanced by her own experiments with sculpture in marble and by the advice of her sister, Irma, who collaborated with her on *Kouroi*. Archaic art became Richter's special interest, and a series of exhaustive studies of various types of archaic Greek sculpture made her a leading authority in this field.

Formally retired in 1948, Gisela Richter remained at the Metropolitan to finish work on museum publications before moving with her sister to Rome in 1952. Irma Richter died in 1956. Gisela Richter remained until her death in their apartment near the American Academy, whose excellent library supplied her research needs. In these Roman years she produced for the Phaidon Press a series of books, thorough, comprehensive, and beautifully illustrated. Many were reworkings of earlier books, brought up to date and often greatly enlarged. The great success of her *Handbook of Greek Art* (1959) compensated the press for the lavish production of the more specialized works. This *Handbook*, like the earlier *Sculpture and Sculptors of the Greeks* (1929), became a standard source for English-speaking students. Richter was less interested in cultural differences than in time as the principal dimension of change: the chronological frameworks she set up in her books have proved to be enduring foundations for scholarship, requiring modification but not demolition as new knowledge enters the field.

In her personal life, Richter's lifelong friendship with her sister was the dominant relationship. Gisela and Irma Richter avoided rivalry and enhanced each other's achievement; the same spirit was reflected in Richter's many personal and professional associations with other women. Among those from whom Richter learned, and whose support she acknowledged, were the potter Maude Robinson, who gave

Richter lessons in her craft, and Marjorie Milne, who lent Richter philological and epigraphical expertise as her assistant curator at the Metropolitan. Richter does not seem to have sought marriage or children of her own and seems always to have preferred to think of herself as young. Later in life, however, she enjoyed visits from children of old friends as well as from her grandnephew. She was unfailingly helpful to younger scholars throughout her mature life.

Richter received a great many honorary degrees, but never paraded them. As a young scholar employed in degree-conscious America, she was practical enough to apply for degrees on the basis of her publications, receiving a Litt.D. from Trinity College, Dublin (1913), and an A.M. (1933) and later a Litt.D. from Cambridge. Her great passion, however, was always the beautiful object and the discovery of the realities surrounding it. So she could honestly express surprise, on receiving a gold medal for archaeological achievement from the Archaeological Institute of America in 1968, at being honored for doing what she most enjoyed. Gisela Richter died in her sleep in her Rome apartment in December 1972, and was buried beside her sister in Rome's Protestant Cemetery.

[The most informative single source is Gisela Richter, *My Memoirs, Recollections of an Archaeologist's Life* (1972), illustrated with photographs. Richter describes her career at the Metropolitan Museum in "The Department of Greek and Roman Art: Triumphs and Tribulations," *Metropolitan Museum Jour.*, 1970, pp. 73–95. Her other major works include *The Craft of Athenian Pottery* (1923), *The Portraits of the Greeks*, 3 vols. (1965), and *Korai: Archaic Greek Maidens* (1968). Among her most important museum publications are *Red-Figured Athenian Vases* (1936), *Handbook of the Greek Collection* (1953), and *Catalogue of Engraved Gems, Greek, Etruscan, and Roman* (1956). Scholarly obituaries by Cornelius Vermeule, *Burlington Mag.*, May 1973, p. 329, and Homer Thompson, *Am. Phil. Soc. Year Book*, 1973, pp. 144–50, derive most of their biographical material from the *Memoirs*. Vermeule assesses her achievement as a museum curator, Thompson as an archaeologist. An obituary appeared in the *N.Y. Times*, Dec. 26, 1972; *Who's Who in America*, 1972–73, gives her final list of her degrees, awards, academies, and books. A biobibliography by Monica Blanchard was useful in locating information on Richter's parents and sister.]

EVELYN B. HARRISON

RINEHART, Mary Roberts, Aug. 12, 1876– Sept. 22, 1958. Writer.

Mary Roberts Rinehart, best-selling author and founder of the had-I-but-known school of crime novels, was born in Allegheny, Pa., the older of two daughters of Cornelia (Grilleland) and Thomas Beveridge Roberts, a sewing machine salesman. In her autobiography, *My Story* (1948), she recalls a nominally happy childhood which contained, nonetheless, a profound fear of economic and personal loss. Her mother's fierce energy went into maintaining appearances and keeping an immaculate house, taking in boarders as a last resort when times were bad. The Robertses were Covenanters, and the God they worshipped was one of wrath. Mary Roberts's "abiding sense of sin" and her feeling that danger lurked in the midst of happiness became components of her work, especially her crime novels.

When a woman doctor moved into their neighborhood, Roberts envied the bag and buggy, symbols of a status few women possessed. After she graduated from Allegheny High School at sixteen, however, her desire to go to medical school had to be postponed because of her youth and poverty. She enrolled at the Pittsburgh Training School for Nurses, where she faced a new world of industrial poverty and violence. The experience left her with "a terrible and often devastating pity and compassion" for the victims of society.

Roberts graduated in 1896, the year after her father's suicide, which deepened her sense of tragedy. She hoped for a measure of stability in her marriage in April 1896 to Stanley M. Rinehart, a young surgeon. Three sons, Stanley, Jr., Alan, and Frederick, were born during the next five years, before she was twenty-five, and she became, in her own words, "an almost excessively devoted" mother. She put aside early ambitions to write, but in 1903 when the family's security was threatened by stock market losses, she sat down at a rickety card table and within a year had sold forty-five stories. Her first published book, *The Circular Staircase* (1908), established her preeminence in the genre she unwittingly had founded—the fusion of the detective story with the humorous novel. Rinehart produced sixty more books, but, even when she employed a full-time secretary and worked in an office, she refused to define herself as "a career woman," and consistently reiterated the primacy of her family over her writing.

Her work during World War I was untiring: she served as a European correspondent in 1915, toured camps in the United States as a representative of the secretary of war, and returned to Paris to report the armistice. Her imagination took fire from stories of the war and she saw it as a chance to regain her sense of adventure. Several popular novels of the time expressed her commitment to the war, although, as a wife and mother of men in the army, she also feared its toll. *The Amazing Interlude* (1917) and *Dangerous Days* (1919) had heroines who fulfilled woman's true task—as Rinehart saw it—service. In *Bab: A Sub-Deb* (1917) a teenager, "tired of being told that the defense of our Dear Country is a masculine matter," breaks up an espionage ring to show the value of women in wartime.

During the postwar years the Rineharts moved to Washington, D.C., where Stanley Rinehart worked for the Veterans' Bureau. Spending summers on a Wyoming ranch, Mary Rinehart became concerned about the plight of the Blackfeet Indians and used her influence to raise money for them, even threatening an exposé in the *Saturday Evening Post*. In 1921 her husband resigned his post in order to manage her business affairs. Rinehart had become a late convert to the cause of woman suffrage, convinced by arguments of economic equality. She wrote many pieces for magazines about the so-called New Woman, but concluded, reluctantly but realistically, that the world had changed more than women, and that the old roles were hard to fit into a new setting.

Rinehart wrote several plays, among them the very successful *The Bat* (1920), coauthored with Avery Hopwood, who delighted her by complimenting her criminal mind. A revival of *The Bat*, with ZASU PITTS, was filmed for television in 1953 after the play closed, and three movie versions were made; the last, in 1959, starred AGNES MOOREHEAD.

After her husband's death in 1932 Rinehart moved to New York City. In 1937 she covered the coronation of George VI, and during World War II she served as an air raid warden. She was in the headlines in 1947 when her cook tried to kill her, and in 1948 her Bar Harbor, Maine, home was destroyed by fire. Ill health, serious accidents, several operations, and the tragic scalding death of her mother intensified her feeling that life offered no security. She finally became an Episcopalian, not so much because she believed in God but because she "was afraid He might exist and must be placated." After surgery for breast cancer, Rinehart courageously published her story, in the hope that it would help frightened women ("I Had Cancer," *Ladies' Home Jour.*, July 1947). When she died in her sleep at her home in New York in 1958, on her desk was the manuscript on which she was working, a very personal memoir of her girlhood entitled "To My Sons."

Mary Roberts Rinehart was said to have been on the best-seller lists longer and more often than any other American author. With the possible exception of the Tish stories—tales of three intrepid spinsters whose exploits, according to

her son, represented what Rinehart saw herself as doing had she not married—her work has not survived contemporary criticism. Nonetheless, the heroines of her stories are interesting women for whom murder and war are synonyms for liberation. Violence jolted the hidebound spinster and repressed maiden into action and responsibility. Her ambiance of domestic violence is itself a statement. "There's somebody dead in the linen closet," a typical beginning, followed by a heroic if somewhat muddled solution, illustrated Rinehart's belief that women got rather more done than men although they never took themselves so seriously.

The happy endings in her stories were required by her conviction that optimism is central to American life, by her refusal to depress her children, and by her editors' demands. She was aware of the "fatal facility" that made her write too much, too fast—she had real trouble finding a pen that wrote quickly enough for her. "I am frankly a story teller," she said in 1917. "Someday I may be a novelist." When her sons founded their own publishing firm, Rinehart felt she "owed them a best seller" every year, and so the serious work she hoped to accomplish was left undone. But the power of her writing was such that after *The Man in Lower Ten* (1909) was published, railroad passengers avoided that bunk for years, and she had fan letters from readers as diverse as Theodore Roosevelt and GERTRUDE STEIN.

[Manuscript collections containing Rinehart correspondence and other materials are at the Univ. of Pittsburgh, the N.Y. Public Library, and Houghton Library, Harvard Univ. In addition to her many novels, collections of short stories, and plays, and her autobiography, first issued in 1931 and expanded in 1945, Rinehart published several travel books and numerous articles in magazines. Two articles which focus on her views of herself as a writer are "Writing Is Work," *Sat. Eve. Post*, March 11, 1939, pp. 10–11, and "The Detective Story," in George H. Doran, ed., *Mary Roberts Rinehart: A Sketch of the Woman and Her Work* (1925). The best account of her life and her work is Jan Cohn, "A Pittsburgh Centennial: Mary Roberts Rinehart," *Carnegie Mag.*, Sept. 1976, pp. 300–7. See also *Nat. Cyc. Am. Biog.*, C, 486–87; Geoffrey T. Hellman, "Mary Roberts Rinehart," *Life*, Feb. 25, 1946, pp. 55–61; *Twentieth Century Authors* (1942) and its *First Supplement* (1955); W. J. Burke and Will D. Howe, *American Authors and Books* (1962), which lists her works; and Chris Steinbrunner and Otto Penzler, *Encyc. Mystery and Detection* (1976), which details the stage and film versions of her plays and novels. A biography by Jan Cohn, *Improbable Fiction: The Life of Mary Roberts Rinehart* (1980), appeared while this article was in press. Obituaries appeared in the *N.Y. Times*, Sept. 23, 1958; *Newsweek* and *Time*, Oct. 6, 1958; and the *Sat. Eve. Post*, Oct. 25, 1958. Additional information for this article was provided by Frederick Rinehart and William Sladen.]

BARBARA WELTER

RIPPIN, Jane Parker Deeter, May 30, 1882–June 2, 1953. Social worker, Girl Scout executive, journalist.

Jane Deeter Rippin was born in Harrisburg, Pa., the third of five children and youngest of three daughters of Sarah Emely (Mather) and Jasper Newton Deeter. Both parents descended from central Pennsylvania colonial families. The Deeter children lived in Mechanicsburg with their mother, while their father worked in the Mather family business in Harrisburg, returning home on weekends.

During Jane's girlhood her mother, at the age of fifty, told her family that she would no longer be responsible for anyone but herself. A gifted singer, she hired extra household help and paid their wages from money she earned by giving private voice lessons. Although she never did routine housework again and spent a great deal more time by herself, she remained the psychic center of the household.

Jasper Deeter did not believe in spending money on educating girls, and, although he sent both sons to private schools, all three daughters went to public school. Ruth, the eldest, worked in the family business but earned enough raising geese to send her sisters to college. Jane Deeter received her B.S. from Irving College in Mechanicsburg in 1902. Upon graduation she began working as assistant to the principal of Mechanicsburg High School.

In 1908, with her sister's encouragement, Deeter embarked on her career in social work, becoming assistant superintendent of the Children's Village, an orphanage and foster home in Meadowbrook, Pa. Two years later she moved to Philadelphia to become a caseworker for the Society for the Prevention of Cruelty to Children, and became immediately involved in the problems of youths in the city. Making friends in the social work community, in 1911 Deeter organized a cooperative boardinghouse, called the Coop, with five other women. Before the first winter they allowed two men to join as auxiliary members; their task was to shovel coal for the furnace. Though membership changed over the years, the house served as a model of cooperative living.

On Oct. 13, 1913, Jane Deeter married James Yardley Rippin, one of the first male members of the Coop. He was an architect, woodworker, and contractor, who always encouraged his wife in her career. The couple fashioned an egalitarian and mutually supportive marriage which survived various fluctuations in their fortunes. Most often her salary was their main source of income.

The year after her marriage, Jane Deeter Rippin received her A.M. from Irving College and was appointed chief probation officer of Philadelphia. When her father learned she was to receive $5,000 a year, he forbade her to accept the position because he did not believe any woman deserved such a high salary. Rippin took the job and her father disowned her. He never again saw her voluntarily, although she took him into her home two years later in his final illness.

Rippin proved to be an innovative manager and an able politician. She had charge of the probation work of five courts: domestic relations, petty criminal for unmarried mothers, juvenile, miscreants, and women's court for sex offenders. Her staff increased from 3 to 365 persons, largely because she instituted extensive social and psychological examinations and assigned an advocate social worker for each person brought to the court.

After a hard struggle with local politicians, in 1917 Rippin opened the first multipurpose municipal detention home for women offenders. Reflecting her strong belief in alternatives to traditional incarceration, the women's building served as a diagnostic and treatment center, with a court and an employment agency, as well as a dormitory-style prison. Keenly aware of women's and children's needs, Rippin installed day nurseries in courts dealing with families and fought a losing battle for a special center for women alcoholics.

In the fall of 1917 Rippin was asked by the War Department's Commission on Training Camp Activities to supervise work with women and girls who gathered around military camps in the southwest. It was her responsibility to enforce the prohibition of liquor and prostitution near military bases. Organizing the surrounding communities, she succeeded in establishing voluntary centers for girls and women which provided alternatives to delinquency. In 1918 Rippin became director of the commission's section on women and girls. During her term, her staff raised more than $500,000 and worked with more than 38,000 delinquent women. She also sponsored a study of the causes of delinquency; its recommendations helped to inspire the establishment of the United Service Organization (USO) in 1941.

As a part of that study, Rippin examined girls' organizations in the United States and became interested in the potential of the Girl Scouts to keep adolescent girls occupied in wholesome pursuits. Appointed national director of the Girl

Scouts, Inc., in 1919, she served until 1930, presiding over the transformation of the Girl Scouts from the highly personalized form developed by its founder, JULIETTE LOW, into an efficient, modern organization. Under her direction, membership grew from 50,000 to 250,000; regions and regional councils were formed; and camps and training schools (two of them designed by James Rippin) were established. Rippin actively promoted the growth of international scouting and helped in the development of the World Association of Girl Guides and Girl Scouts in 1928. A very effective fund raiser, she also initiated the annual cookie sale. Perhaps most important to the ultimate success of the organization, however, Rippin established a framework in which professional staff and volunteers could cooperate. She herself led a troop as a volunteer during her entire tenure as national director.

An enormously hard worker and an equally demanding boss, Rippin inspired her staff to spread the scouting movement across the country. She loved her Girl Scout work and left only because of failing health, continuing to be an active member of the National Advisory Council for the rest of her life.

In 1931 Rippin became director of research for women's news for the Westchester County Publishers, a chain of more than fifty local newspapers. In her role as a journalist, she was again successful. Often addressing relevant issues affecting women, she also enthusiastically covered traditional women's affairs, especially women's clubs and garden news.

Jane Deeter Rippin suffered her first serious stroke, which left her partially paralyzed and aphasic, in 1936. With singular determination, she spent months learning to recognize, pronounce, and write single words and then sentences. Over several years she regained her ability to write and speak and overcame her paralysis. Rippin continued to work for the newspapers and participate in community activities until her final stroke, March 13, 1953. She remained unconscious until her death at home in Tarrytown, N.Y., almost three months later.

[The largest single body of information on Jane Deeter Rippin is housed at the Girl Scouts of the U.S.A. Archives in New York City. The collection includes extensive typed notes from Rippin's personal letters and interviews conducted by Vera Watson Schmidt for a biography of Rippin which was never written. A June 20, 1976, interview with Dorris Hough by Mary Aickin Rothschild, also in the archives, contains valuable information about what it was like to work for Rippin. A list of organizations to which she belonged appears in the entry in *Who Was Who in America*, III (1960). For a concise summary of her career see the obituary in the *N.Y.*

Herald Tribune, June 3, 1953, which was partially written in advance by Rippin. Obituaries also appeared in the June 3, 1953, *N.Y. Times* and *Tarrytown* (N.Y.) *Daily News*. Additional information for this article was provided by Evelyn Koch and by Rippin's nieces, E. Jean Deeter and Martha D. Crawford. Death certificate was supplied by N.Y. State Dept. of Health.]

MARY AICKIN ROTHSCHILD

ROBERTS, Lydia Jane, June 30, 1879–May 28, 1965. Nutritionist, home economics educator.

Lydia Roberts, a leader in nutrition studies and a specialist in the nutrition of children, was born in Hope Township, Barry County, Mich. She was the third of four children and youngest of three daughters of Warren and Mary (McKibbin) Roberts. Her father, a carpenter, moved the family to Martin, Mich., a farming area, shortly after Lydia's birth, and there she attended grammar and high school.

In 1899 Lydia Roberts completed the one-year course at Mt. Pleasant Normal School (later Central Michigan University). After teaching for several years in Michigan, the urge to travel took her first to Montana, where she taught in schools in Miles City and Great Falls, and then briefly to Virginia. In 1909 Mt. Pleasant Normal School awarded her a Life Certificate, which qualified her to teach in any Michigan elementary school, rural or urban. Returning to Montana, Roberts taught third grade in Dillon and served as teacher-critic in Western Montana College until 1915 when, at the age of thirty-six, she entered the University of Chicago with advanced standing.

Motivated by an interest in the relation between diet and health developed during a summer of work at a Montana children's institute, Roberts resumed her education in order to gain greater understanding of the feeding of children. That subject remained a lifelong concern and one focus of a career which recorded major accomplishments in nutrition education and research and in community nutrition. The period when she entered Chicago saw the pioneering efforts of Elmer McCollum, Thomas Osborne, Lafayette Mendel, and others in the recognition of vitamins and minerals as essential trace nutrients in foods. Roberts majored in home economics, a department of which KATHARINE BLUNT, a biochemist, had recently become chairman. Encouraged by Blunt to continue her studies in foods and nutrition after receiving her B.S. in 1917, Roberts completed her M.S. in 1919. Her master's thesis, "A Malnutrition Clinic as a University Problem in Applied Nutrition," was based on work being done at a child nutrition clinic set up by Blunt in collaboration with the Rush Medical College. Her practical efforts at the clinic also led Roberts to develop a course in child feeding.

In 1919 Lydia Roberts became assistant professor of home economics at the University of Chicago. For the next decade, a period of dramatic growth in the profession of home economics as well as in the department, she continued her studies and her practical work on nutrition of children. She made skillful use of her students as coworkers in gathering information which became the basis for the book *Nutrition Work With Children* (1927). A classic in its field, the book served as her dissertation for the Ph.D. in home economics which Roberts received in 1928, along with a promotion to associate professor.

When Blunt left Chicago in 1929, Roberts headed a three-member committee to administer the department while a nationwide search was conducted for a replacement. Finally, in June 1930, the position was offered to Roberts; she served as chairman and full professor until her mandatory retirement in 1944. During this fourteen-year period she maintained a heavy schedule of administration, teaching, and research on the nutritional needs of children. That research contributed to knowledge of caloric, protein, vitamin, and mineral requirements; characteristically, it was geared to practical application. Roberts lived during this period with her elder sister Lillian, a secretary in one of the university offices. A friendly, outgoing person, she was an effective administrator and teacher who set high standards for herself and expected them as well in her associates and students.

While meeting her responsibilities in Chicago, Roberts was also active on a number of national committees. In 1929 she served on three committees of the White House Conference on Child Health and Protection, the most important being the Committee on Nutrition. Later she became a longtime member of the Council on Foods and Nutrition of the American Medical Association, and of the Food and Nutrition Board of the National Research Council. On the Food and Nutrition Board she played a leading role in setting up recommendations for the addition of selected vitamins and minerals to flour and bread as a wartime measure to insure improved nutrition. Her support helped gain acceptance of the enrichment program by the industries involved.

After retirement from the University of Chicago, Roberts accepted a faculty appointment at the University of Puerto Rico. The invitation came from the university's chancellor, who

knew of her 1943 nutrition survey of the island for the United States Department of Agriculture. Roberts made Puerto Rico her new home, engaging vigorously in nutrition studies there until her death. She chaired the home economics department at the university from 1946 to 1952, and even after her second retirement continued an active program aimed at improvement of the nutrition of Puerto Rican families.

With her colleague, Rosa L. Stefani, Roberts undertook a study of the food habits of the people; the results were published in 1949 as *Patterns of Living in Puerto Rican Families*. The culmination of her work was a nutrition improvement project undertaken in a rural community and reported in *The Doña Elena Project* (1963). An experimental effort to tie economic assistance to nutrition education, the project brought a new road, electric power lines, and improved sanitary facilities along with agricultural services and practical instruction in nutrition to an isolated mountain area. It became the model for a program established throughout the island.

Lydia Roberts's active life came to an end in Rio Piedras when, still working at age eighty-five, she collapsed at her desk. She died of massive bleeding resulting from a ruptured abdominal aneurysm. Although she received many honors, Roberts derived her greatest satisfaction from the improvement in the nutrition of children arising out of her studies and practical projects.

[Roberts's master's thesis was published in the March 1919 *Jour. Home Economics*. A revised edition of *Nutrition Work With Children* appeared in 1935; third and fourth editions, prepared by Ethel Austin Martin, were published as *Roberts' Nutrition Work With Children* in 1954 and 1978. Ethel Martin has also published "The Life Works of Lydia J. Roberts," *Jour. Am. Dietetic Assoc.*, Oct. 1966, pp. 299–302. The best biographical study is Franklin C. Bing, "Lydia Jane Roberts—A Biographical Sketch," *Jour. Nutrition*, Sept. 1967, pp. 1–13. Another good profile is Ethel Austin Martin, "Lydia Jane Roberts, June 30, 1879–May 28, 1965," *Jour. Am. Dietetic Assoc.*, Aug. 1965, pp. 127–28. Death certificate supplied by Puerto Rico Dept. of Health.]

AARON J. IHDE

ROBERTS, Mary May, Jan. 30, 1877–Jan. 11, 1959. Nurse, editor.

Mary May Roberts was the eldest of four children, two girls and two boys, of Henry W. and Elizabeth Scott (Elliot) Roberts, both of Scots-English ancestry. She was born in Duncan City, Mich. (later part of Cheboygan), a company town owned and operated by the sawmill firm for which her father worked. As a child, she attended the company school and enjoyed the company-built toboggan slides and skating pond. A serious and energetic girl, she excelled at her school work and graduated in 1895 from high school in nearby Cheboygan as valedictorian of her four-member class. Despite opposition from her father, Roberts applied to the Jewish Hospital Training School for Nurses in Cincinnati. Henry Roberts's conviction that his daughter could not "stick it out"—he handed her a return ticket as she boarded the train for school —"somehow made her instantly determined to see the thing through, no matter what," Roberts recalled (*Nursing Outlook*, Feb. 1959, p. 72).

Mary Roberts excelled at nursing school, despite supervision that "partook largely of the mental quality of a policeman on his beat," as she characterized it later. After graduating in 1899, she held a variety of hospital posts: clinic nurse at the Baroness Erlanger Hospital in Chattanooga, Tenn. (1899); superintendent of nurses at the Savannah Hospital in Georgia (1900–03); and assistant superintendent of nurses at Jewish Hospital in Cincinnati (1904–06). She then did private duty nursing in Evanston, Ill., before returning to Cincinnati in 1908 to become superintendent of nurses at the Christian R. Holmes Hospital. Remaining there until the outbreak of World War I, she played an active role in the Ohio nurses' organizations. In 1917 Roberts left her hospital post to work for the American Red Cross, recruiting nurses for military service and later serving as chief nurse and director of the Army School of Nursing unit at Camp Sherman, Ohio.

Mary Roberts left the American Red Cross in 1919, at the age of forty-two, with a solid yet unexceptional career in hospital nursing behind her. She entered Teachers College, Columbia University, to work for a college degree. These years of study brought her "a vastly increased vision and spacious-mindedness and more new found enthusiasm for nursing," Roberts later wrote. More important, Roberts's years at Teachers College brought her a new career. She attracted the favorable attention of the *American Journal of Nursing*'s editorial board, and, after receiving a B.S. and diploma in nursing school administration in 1921, Roberts, along with Katherine De Witt, succeeded SOPHIA PALMER as the *Journal*'s coeditors. In 1923 Roberts became sole editor. In justifying the appointment of an unknown Ohio nurse to this prestigious position, the board explained to its readers that "her point of view will not be that of a person who has long been in the limelight, but that of a majority of our able women."

However like the average nurse Mary Roberts

may have been in some respects, she soon displayed a journalistic skill and executive ability that placed her in the limelight. During three decades of chaotic growth for the profession, as increased demand for nurses created pressure to lower educational requirements and economic uncertainty jeopardized hard-won working conditions and wages, Roberts used her position to campaign for higher professional standards. Her aggressive editorial policy exemplified what she called the "most desirable of editorial qualities —an awareness of what is about to become important." Creating an extensive network among nurses all over the country, Roberts constantly surveyed the profession, identifying its problems and advocating solutions. Under her editorship, circulation went from 20,000 to 100,000, and the *Journal* won widespread respect.

Roberts's influence on nursing extended beyond the pages of the *Journal*. One of her most significant achievements was the plan she sponsored in 1932 making the National League of Nursing Education the education department of the American Nurses' Association (ANA). Another was the Nursing Information Bureau of the ANA, which she ran from 1934 to 1948 for the benefit of both nurses and the public. Roberts also represented the nursing profession on a number of projects involving the medical profession as a whole, including the influential Committee on Costs of Medical Care organized in 1927 to survey the cost and distribution of health services.

In 1949 Mary Roberts retired as editor of the *American Journal of Nursing*, retaining the title of editor emeritus. While continuing to play an active role in the profession, she put most of her energy into the writing of nursing history, publishing the classic *American Nursing: History and Interpretation* (1954) and *The Army Nurse Corps—Yesterday and Today* (1957). She died in New York City at age eighty-one after suffering a stroke while at work on an editorial in the *Journal* offices.

Throughout her career Roberts received a number of awards, including the International Red Cross Florence Nightingale Medal (1949) and the Mary Adelaide Nutting Award for Leadership in Nursing (1949). She was particularly proud of the Mary M. Roberts Fellowship in Journalism established in her honor by the *American Journal of Nursing* in 1950. Described by her coworkers as a hard taskmaster, Roberts nonetheless won both love and respect for her warmth, openness, and sense of humor, and gained a reputation for discretion and wise counsel. For a generation of nurses, "Miss Roberts *was* the *Journal*," and in this role she became "one of the greatest teachers, the most indefatigable investigators, and the most potent educational influences on modern nursing" (*Am. Jour. Nursing*, Oct. 1950, p. 583, and May 1949, p. 266).

[The major manuscript source is the Am. Jour. of Nursing Co.–Mary M. Roberts Coll. in the Nursing Archive, Mugar Library, Boston Univ., which contains correspondence, manuscripts, scrapbooks, biographical materials, and photographs. Material on Roberts's early life can be found in the collection of Cheboygan history privately owned by Ellis Olson. The main source for Roberts's writings is the *Am. Jour. Nursing*. For her regular contributions to this and other nursing journals see *Nursing Studies Index*. Biographical articles include Katherine De Witt, "Mary M. Roberts," *Biographic Sketches, 1937–40*, published by the Nat. League of Nursing Education and available from the Mugar Library; Edith Patton Lewis, "Mary M. Roberts: Spokesman for Nursing," *Am. Jour. Nursing*, March 1959, pp. 336–43; "Mary M. Roberts Retires as Editor," *Am. Jour. Nursing*, May 1949, pp. 261–71. See also "The Journal's Golden Anniversary," *Am. Jour. Nursing*, Oct. 1950, pp. 583–84. Obituaries appeared in the *N.Y. Times*, Jan. 12, 1959, and *Nursing Outlook*, Feb. 1959, pp. 72–73.]

NANCY TOMES

ROBESON, Eslanda Cardoza Goode, Dec. 15, 1896–Dec. 13, 1965. Writer, civil rights reformer.

Eslanda Robeson was born in Washington, D.C., the only daughter of Eslanda (Cardoza) and John Goode. Her father, who came from Chicago, was probably of West Indian descent; he worked as a clerk in the War Department. Her mother came from the prominent Charleston, S.C., Sephardic Jewish family of Cardozo (spelling of the name varies). Eslanda's grandfather, Francis Lewis Cardozo, was a black statesman and educator who had been secretary of state and secretary of the treasury in South Carolina during Reconstruction and principal after the Civil War of Avery Institute, one of the first schools for blacks in South Carolina.

After her father's death in 1902, Eslanda moved to New York City with her mother and two brothers. She attended New York City public schools and at the age of sixteen enrolled in the household science course at the University of Illinois, remaining there for two years (1912–14). In the summer of 1916 she transferred to Teachers College of Columbia University where she majored in chemistry and earned a B.S. in 1920. She then worked as a surgical technician and chemist at Presbyterian Hospital of Columbia University, probably the first black woman to hold this position.

Eslanda Goode met Paul Robeson while he was a student at Columbia University Law School; they were married in 1921 after a brief courtship. Eslanda Robeson exerted a strong influence on her husband, actively encouraging him to pursue a career in the theater. Convinced that opportunities for blacks in the legal profession were limited, he agreed. In the fall of 1925, she left her job at Columbia-Presbyterian Hospital and accompanied her husband to London for his much-heralded appearance there in the Provincetown Players' production of Eugene O'Neill's *Emperor Jones*. Their only child, Paul Jr., was born in 1927. During most of his childhood he was cared for by his maternal grandmother, leaving Eslanda Robeson free to manage her husband's career. For several years she was responsible for their finances and for booking concert tours in the United States and Europe.

Eslanda Robeson's first book, a biography entitled *Paul Robeson, Negro*, appeared in 1930. It offered a rather simplistic portrait of its subject, but it demonstrated her admiration for her husband and made clear her role in motivating him toward the realization of his tremendous potential as an artist. The book also reflects some of the marital strains which led the Robesons to separate from 1930 until 1933.

The couple had settled in London in 1928. For the next twelve years Eslanda Robeson maintained a residence in England, finding racial discrimination less pronounced there than in the United States. In England, too, she was able to develop her growing interest in Africa. She had access there to a wealth of information about Africa through the British press and films, as well as from African students. In 1935 she enrolled at London University to take classes in anthropology, continuing to study there until 1937, and at the London School of Economics in 1938. She toured Africa for six months in 1936 with her son, gathering material for a book.

During the 1930s, Eslanda Robeson also traveled through Europe and made several trips to the Soviet Union, the first in 1934. A close observer of the worsening political situation in Europe, she became an ardent antifascist. With Paul Robeson, she went to Spain during the civil war there to show her support for the Spanish Republic.

After the outbreak of World War II in Europe, the Robesons returned to the United States. They settled in Connecticut and Eslanda Robeson continued her study of anthropology as a doctoral student at the Hartford Seminary. In 1945, *African Journey*, the book based on her earlier travels, was published. Robeson's approach to Africa was more descriptive than analytical: she detailed the living habits and the economic and cultural customs of various tribes, illustrating them with photographs she had taken. Reviewers praised the book as both a provocative and enlightening account of the African peoples and an important treatise on the color line. Drawing on her training as an anthropologist, Robeson was one of the first Americans to demonstrate the urgent need for reform among the colonial powers. She also emphasized the important source of pride for Afro-Americans provided by Africa's rich heritage, which had been largely ignored or misrepresented in the United States. During the 1940s, Eslanda Robeson became a popular lecturer, bringing the subjects of Africa, race relations, and colonialism to colleges, churches, and public gatherings.

After the war, Eslanda Robeson's writings focused especially on the issue of colonialism. She viewed the war as a turning point for emerging nations in Asia and Africa and saw the United Nations as a potential mediator between the European powers and their colonies in the postwar struggle over liberation. In 1945 she attended the founding convention of the UN as a representative for the Council on African Affairs, a private organization chaired by Paul Robeson and concerned with colonial problems. Throughout the 1950s she covered UN activities for the New World Review (formerly called Soviet Russia Today). Robeson's hopes for a new international order soured as relations worsened between the United States and the Soviet Union, but she was confident that the remnants of colonialism could not long resist the rising tide of nationalism in Asia and Africa.

During these postwar years, Eslanda Robeson also drew attention for her outspoken criticism of American foreign policy and her favorable view of the Soviet Union. She contended that the issue of communism was often raised to avoid confronting the serious economic, social, and political problems caused by generations of racism and colonialism. In 1948 she joined in establishing the Progressive party and actively campaigned for Henry A. Wallace for president; she ran as the Progressive party's candidate for secretary of state in Connecticut in 1948, and in 1950 for congresswoman-at-large from that state.

These political stands led to an extended period of personal and financial hardship for both Eslanda and Paul Robeson who, unable to obtain passports, could not leave the United States from 1950 to 1958. In addition, both were subjected to congressional investigations. In July 1953 she was called before the Senate Permanent Subcommittee on Investigations, chaired by Senator Joseph R. McCarthy. Robeson refused to discuss her political beliefs, citing not only the fifth amendment to the Constitution but also the fifteenth, which guarantees equal rights regardless of race and color. Angered, McCarthy told her she had no special rights because of her race and overruled her. In response Robeson reminded the committee that she had spent her life fighting racial discrimination. "You're white and I'm colored and this is a very white committee," she observed. She continued to challenge the committee's questioning, leading McCarthy to observe that it was only out of "special consideration" that she did not receive a citation for contempt.

Eslanda Robeson's views on postwar America were elaborated in An American Argument (1949), a dialogue with PEARL BUCK. Robeson focused her criticism on the failure of the United States to be a complete democracy, especially for blacks. She was an early advocate of legislation as an important strategy for securing racial justice and equality, but believed that a strong, united black protest was necessary to initiate the process of reform.

The 1954 Supreme Court decision (Brown v. Board of Education) outlawing segregation in public schools, combined with the Montgomery, Ala., bus boycott and the emerging leadership of Martin Luther King, Jr., provided the momentum for the kind of protest movement Robeson had in mind. In 1957 she joined King's Prayer Pilgrimage to Washington, D.C., to urge implementation of the Supreme Court decision. Although she lived abroad for the next five years, she followed the civil rights movement closely and wrote enthusiastically about the sit-ins and freedom rides and about the 1963 March on Washington.

Eslanda Robeson died in New York City of cancer in 1965. The impact of her views was dulled by the political climate of the 1950s, but she provided a challenging perspective during a time of conformity, and a conscience that should have been heeded.

[There is a clipping file on Eslanda Robeson at the Schomburg Coll., N.Y. Public Library. Her books provide autobiographical information; see also her articles in the New World Rev., 1952–65. Other biographical sources include obituary notices in the New World Rev., Jan. 1966, pp. 8–13; The Worker, Dec. 19, 1965; the N.Y. Times, Dec. 16, 1965; and the entry in Current Biog., 1945. Information also appears in studies of Paul Robeson. See Edwin Embree, 13 Against the Odds (1944); Dorothy Gilliam, Paul Robeson, All-American (1976); Edwin Hoyt, Paul Robeson, the American Othello (1967); and Marie Seton, Paul Robeson (1958).]

PATRICIA A. SULLIVAN

ROBINSON, Rubye Doris Smith, April 25, 1942–Oct. 7, 1967. Civil rights reformer.

Rubye Doris Smith Robinson, a leading figure in the Student Non-Violent Coordinating Committee (SNCC), was, according to James Forman, "one of the few genuine revolutionaries in the black liberation movement." By the time of her death at twenty-five she had become the key figure in managing the unwieldy and unpredictable existence of SNCC, the most radical of the civil rights organizations in the 1960s.

Rubye Doris Smith was born in Atlanta, the second of seven children (three girls and four boys) of Alice (Banks) and John Thomas Smith, both of whom had been born in Georgia. Alice Smith was a beautician and ran the family store; John Thomas Smith was a self-employed mover who later became a minister.

The Smiths placed a high priority on education. When Rubye's older sister, Mary Ann, was sent to a church-run kindergarten, Rubye Doris, then three, insisted on going. By age four, she was in first grade, and throughout her years in public elementary school she was ahead of her age group. At thirteen she watched on television the bus boycott by blacks in Montgomery, Ala., to protest segregation; later she remembered that seeing the old people "walking, walking" led to her determination to be politically active.

Rubye Doris Smith was sixteen when she finished high school and entered Spelman College in Atlanta. She was a sophomore on Feb. 1, 1960, when the Greensboro, N.C., lunch-counter sit-in occurred. The powerful impact of this demonstration led to others. Rubye Smith, with her sister, joined students from Atlanta University Center (the Atlanta Committee on Appeal for Human Rights) in a sit-in campaign against restaurants connected with government buildings. In April 1960 she traveled with other Atlanta students to Raleigh, N.C., for the founding meeting of SNCC.

As the sit-in demonstrations continued across the south, arrests multiplied. In February 1961, after the arrest of students participating in a demonstration in Rock Hill, S.C., Smith traveled there with a SNCC support contingent. They were also arrested, and Rubye Smith and the others spent thirty days in jail, the first time civil rights workers arrested for sitting-in had chosen to adopt the tactic of jail-without-bail and serve their full sentence.

Rubye Doris Smith's strength and determination did not develop in isolation. She came from a strong family: her grandfather, Pleas Banks, had waited alone with a gun on the front porch of his house in Barnesville, Ga., when a white man threatened to lynch his son. Alice Smith was dedicated to the development and harmony of her family and her energy and skill were often needed to abate conflict between Rubye Doris

and her father, who felt that his daughter's political decisions placed her life and future in needless jeopardy. Even as a child Rubye Doris was independent, her mother recalled: "Once she was clear, she was going to do it whether it was what you wanted or not."

Her involvement in the civil rights struggle deepened in the spring of 1961 when she responded to a call for reinforcements from Freedom Riders jailed in Birmingham, Ala. The Freedom Rides, initiated by the Congress of Racial Equality (CORE) and continued by SNCC, challenged the legality of state-mandated segregation in interstate travel throughout the south. Smith's efforts to raise money for the trip drew little support; many Atlanta blacks thought the Freedom Rides too dangerous. She went to Birmingham, and on May 20, with nine students from Nashville, left for Montgomery, where the group was attacked by a mob of angry whites. On May 24, Smith and eleven other Freedom Riders boarded a bus for Jackson, Miss. There they were arrested for trying to use the white restrooms, charged with breach of peace and refusal to obey officers, and given a two-month suspended sentence and a $200 fine. Smith decided to go to jail rather than pay. She shared a cell in the Hinds County jail with as many as twenty-three others, and finished out her sentence—accompanied by an increasing number of Freedom Riders—in the maximum security unit of the Parchman State Penitentiary. Her role in the Rides was characteristic: an active participant, she also identified the kind of support the group needed and set about organizing people to serve that need.

Upon her release, Smith joined the summer voter registration project newly organized by SNCC in McComb, Miss. She also attended a training seminar for student activists at Fisk University, where arguments arose over the response SNCC would make to black youths who had thrown rocks during local demonstrations. Smith agreed with those who found it understandable that blacks would strike back. With these incidents, SNCC began to view nonviolence as a tactic rather than a way of life, a philosophical difference between their policies and those of Martin Luther King, Jr.

In fall 1961 Rubye Doris Smith returned to Spelman, while also greatly increasing the time she spent with SNCC. She took an active part in large demonstrations in Albany, Ga., in December, urging unsuccessfully that there be further demonstrations and more pressure on the city's power structure. For most of the summer of 1962 she worked with SNCC projects in Cairo, Ill. The following spring she became a full-time staff member of SNCC, working as administrative assistant to executive secretary James Forman. At twenty-one she was aware of a clear purpose in her life. She felt a sense of urgency: the conditions under which blacks lived had to be changed, and she and fully-committed black students like her had the opportunity to make a difference.

Between 1963 and 1967, Rubye Doris Smith functioned as the administrative and logistical center of SNCC. She presided over the Sojourner Motor Fleet, cars needed to carry the voter registration drive into rural areas, organized student recruits, met the day-to-day needs of the field staff, and responded to emergencies. Compassionate and responsive to individual needs, Smith also knew that a delicate balance had to be maintained between civil rights workers and local community activists; her rage knew no bounds when she discovered staff members behaving irresponsibly or against instructions. The need to bring order to a loosely knit, highly individualized staff created the most pressure in Smith's work.

During the summer of 1964, SNCC joined with CORE, NAACP, and the Southern Christian Leadership Conference in the Mississippi Summer Project, a major voter registration drive. Because of the large number of volunteers needed, most had to provide their own subsistence, making it very difficult for blacks to participate. Believing that civil rights work in the south should be led by blacks, Rubye Smith initiated a concerted drive for southern black volunteers. She was also in the forefront of those who questioned SNCC's ability to survive under the combined pressure of the influx of white volunteers and the involvement with other civil rights groups in an umbrella organization.

During the fall of 1964 a series of events underlined and enlarged Rubye Doris Smith's impact on SNCC's political direction. During a staff retreat called in the aftermath of Mississippi Summer to discuss SNCC's future direction, Smith carried out the daily tasks of the organization, making policy decisions as the need arose and without clear guidelines from the policymaking body. In September she went with nine other SNCC staff members to Africa, an experience which affected her profoundly and furthered her growing commitment to black nationalism. On her return, she urged SNCC to develop connections with Africa, one of the first staff members to suggest this step.

Smith also played a decisive role in the conflict that arose that fall over the role of women in the movement. The leadership, in general, was male-dominated, although the majority of participants were women. At SNCC most of the central office staff were women but—with the exception of Rubye Smith—they were assigned primarily to clerical tasks. She joined a sit-in at James Forman's office, organized by other women on the staff to protest their limited role and to demand that women have access to field assignments and other positions of responsibility. But she resisted further action directed to SNCC's internal needs, fearful that it would deflect energies from the organization's central purpose, the improvement of conditions for blacks throughout the country.

In November 1964, Rubye Smith married Clifford Robinson, a veteran who became chief mechanic for the Sojourner Motor Fleet. Their son, Kenneth Touré—named for Sékou Touré, the president of Guinea whom Smith had met in Africa—was born the following July. Neither marriage nor motherhood lessened her intense involvement in the movement and in the summer of 1966 Rubye Doris Smith Robinson succeeded James Forman as executive secretary of SNCC. Under chairman Stokely Carmichael, SNCC began to make the transition to black nationalism. When field secretary Willie Ricks raised the cry of black power on the June 1966 James Meredith March in Mississippi, Robinson strongly supported the new direction.

Although she may have had indications of her illness by 1966, Robinson remained active until a few months before her death from lymphoma in Atlanta. Associates remembered her as a leader, an organizer, and a fighter. Her coworker Stanley Wise recalled: "Rubye Doris was probably the nearest thing I ever met to a free person. I mean really free, free in the sense that be you Black or white, you could not commit a great indignity or injustice about Rubye and have it go undealt with . . . Rubye just stood up to *anybody* . . . That's just not the way Blacks acted in the south. As a result, she made you stand taller."

[There is no manuscript collection; all of Robinson's papers remain in the possession of her family. For biographical and background information see: Howard Zinn, *SNCC: The New Abolitionists* (1964); James Forman, *The Making of Black Revolutionaries* (1972); and August Meier and Elliott Rudwick, *CORE: A Study of the Civil Rights Movement, 1942–1968* (1973). Cleveland Sellers recalls Smith's impact on him in *The River of No Return: The Autobiography of a Black Militant and the Life and Death of SNCC* (1973), with Robert Terrell; an interview with her (as "Sarah") appears in Josephine Carson, *Silent Voices: The Southern Negro Woman Today* (1969). An obituary appeared in the *N.Y. Times*, Oct. 10, 1967; death record provided by the Ga. Dept. of Human Resources. A biobibliography by James P. Posey assisted with research. Especially valuable were interviews with Courtland Cox, Ivanhoe Donaldson, Judy Richardson, Reginald Robinson, Alice Banks Smith, Annette Jones White, and Stanley Wise.]

BERNICE JOHNSON REAGON

ROCHESTER, Anna. *See* HUTCHINS, Grace.

ROGERS, Edith Nourse, March 19, 1881–Sept. 10, 1960. Congresswoman.

Edith Nourse Rogers, Republican congresswoman from the Fifth District in Massachusetts and the sixth woman to be elected a representative, rode the crest of the veterans' movement to serve in the House of Representatives for thirty-five years, the longest stay of any woman elected to the Congress. She succeeded her husband, John Jacob Rogers, who had served the same district for twelve years. A member of the minority party for most of her career—the Republicans had a majority only in the Eightieth and Eighty-Third Congresses—Rogers was the first Republican woman to chair a major committee, Veterans' Affairs, and a nationally recognized proponent of veterans' legislation.

Born Edith Frances Nourse in the mill and shipping town of Saco, Maine, she was the only daughter and younger of two children. Both parents—Edith Frances (Riversmith) and Franklin T. Nourse—were natives of Maine and descendants of seventeenth-century Puritan settlers in Massachusetts. Edith Nourse spent her first fourteen years in Saco. The Nourse family was fairly well-to-do and her girlhood was marked by stability; Edith was educated by a tutor and her brother attended a private academy. Her father, a Harvard graduate, was the mill agent or manager of one of the largest textile mills and a power wielder in local politics. Her mother, who left the Congregational church to join her husband at the Episcopal, engaged in volunteer work to aid the poor. The Episcopal church remained important to their daughter.

In January 1895, Franklin Nourse accepted the position of mill agent for the second largest cotton textile company in Lowell, Mass., and the family moved into a larger orbit. In Lowell, Edith Nourse attended a small private girls' boarding school, Rogers Hall, graduating in 1899. Her parents then selected a finishing school, Madame Julien's in Neuilly, near Paris, and gave her travel on the Continent. Returning to Massachusetts, she participated in social, welfare, and church activities in Lowell and attended luncheon and theater parties in Boston.

In the fall of 1907 the popular socialite married John Jacob Rogers, a graduate of Harvard University and its Law School. The marriage united two prosperous Yankee Republican families. John Rogers began a successful law practice

in Lowell with his brother-in-law, then turned to politics in 1911. Running as a regular Republican, he triumphed over a Progressive, a Democrat, and a Socialist to win election to Congress in 1912. In six subsequent elections he carried Lowell and, customarily, all the other cities and towns in the district.

The couple's move to Washington provided the setting that changed Edith Nourse Rogers's life. She and her husband lavishly entertained the political and diplomatic community, although initially she sought not to intrude on his official role. In 1917, however, when he joined other members of the House Foreign Affairs Committee on a "secret" but unofficial mission to Britain and France, she insisted on accompanying him. In England she volunteered at the YMCA hut in London; on the Continent, she accompanied her husband to battle zones as a member of a Red Cross party and visited base and field hospitals. Returning to Washington in early 1918 she joined the Red Cross as a Grey Lady and worked seven days a week at Walter Reed Hospital. This was the real turning point for her: henceforth she exchanged the role of socialite for that of patriot dedicated to aiding veterans. Her husband enlisted briefly in the field artillery while retaining his seat in Congress; she continued at Walter Reed as the soldiers' "angel of mercy," working there until 1922.

After the war John Rogers held to his major interest in foreign affairs but also began to respond to pressures on Congress for aid to World War I veterans. He joined the American Legion as a charter member, and Edith Rogers joined the auxiliary. In 1922 President Warren G. Harding appointed her a dollar-a-year inspector of veterans' hospitals; Presidents Calvin Coolidge and Herbert Hoover later renewed the appointment. With her travels throughout the country she began to be recognized as an authority on the adequacy of medical service to veterans.

Edith Rogers made her first foray into the politics of the Fifth Congressional District in 1924 when she served as a Coolidge presidential elector. She became secretary of the electors, the first woman to make the official delivery of the vote. In 1924 John Jacob Rogers, at the peak of his career, fell ill with Hodgkin's disease; he died in March 1925. Ex-servicemen, along with family, businessmen, and leading Republicans in Lowell and elsewhere joined in urging Edith Nourse Rogers (she unfailingly used this name after 1925) to run for her husband's seat. At first expressing reticence, she then agreed, saying she thought her husband would wish her to carry out his policies. But she would not campaign, she said, as that would not be dignified. Rogers saw her candidacy as an extension of her profession, transferring her work for veterans to the congressional arena. Concern over electing a woman was neutralized in press coverage by arguing that "the office seeks the woman" and by stating that Edith Nourse Rogers was not a suffragist. It was never revealed that both she and her husband had earlier been ardent advocates of suffrage.

Rogers won the June primary by 84 percent against two opponents in an exceedingly low turnout, and went on to win the special June 30 election by 72 percent, the first of her eighteen election successes. Like her husband, she eventually captured the entire district, and withstood threats from State House Democrats in Boston who sought to "carve up" this Republican area as the Commonwealth gained Democratic strength while losing three congressional seats in reapportionment. At first she eliminated opposition in her own party and from the early 1940s on had no primary contests. In Democratic landslides during the New Deal, split-ticket voting gave her victories with more than 60 percent of the votes. Also from 1942 on, she carried every city and town, gaining 72 to 100 percent of the total vote. In three campaigns she had no Democratic opponent.

Rogers became a tenacious legislator. Her first committee assignments included World War Veterans' Legislation. Subsequently she also had sixteen years on the Civil Service Committee and fourteen on Foreign Affairs. When reorganization in the Eightieth Congress restricted each member to one major committee (1947), she stayed on Veterans' Affairs as the ranking member. Backing for her from veterans' organizations compelled the Republicans to recognize her seniority and give her the committee chairmanship.

The "welfare of veterans" was, according to Rogers, her "greatest interest in life." Veterans' legislation was not an issue—everyone was for it. Yet the two major organizations, the American Legion and the Veterans of Foreign Wars, with their auxiliaries, furnished formidable pressures for greater and greater benefits and climbed in membership from 885,000 in the mid-1920s to more than 5,000,000 in the mid-1950s. Rogers carried many of their bills and fought their skirmishes on the floor. When she was chairman, 77 to 80 percent of her bills dealt with veterans, though few of these were ever enacted. During her career she introduced 1,242 bills and slightly over half, 629, dealt with veterans' and armed services' matters. Notably, she was the author of the bill to establish the Women's Army Corps and was one of the major drafters of the G.I.

Bill of Rights. She also sponsored the Korean Veterans Benefits bill and a permanent Nurse Corps in the Veterans Administration, and easily won legislation to support the development of prosthetic appliances and appropriations for automobiles for amputees.

In foreign policy, another major interest, Rogers was sometimes ahead of public opinion but often merely reflected it. In 1933 she was one of the first to speak in the House against Hitler's treatment of the Jews. Before World War II she favored the fortification of Guam. Later, she supported both the House Committee on Un-American Activities and Senator Joseph McCarthy. In 1954, however, she opposed a proposal by then Vice President Richard Nixon to send troops to Indochina, contending that this was not the arena in which to strike at communism.

Rogers's relationship with her constituency was intensely personal. She openly courted Democrats; one of her last appointments was of a Democrat to a postmastership. Campaigning the year round, she maintained a well-staffed district office, providing services paid for out of her income from inheritances. Rogers diligently aided the textile and leather industries in her district, opposing foreign competition, attacking wage differentials between north and south, and authorizing expansion of State Department trade groups. She also continually sought and obtained funds for improvement and flood control for the Merrimack River Basin. Unflagging in her efforts to get defense contracts for her district, after World War II she tried for an atomic energy plant and for contracts to do nuclear research. Rogers is credited with having brought to Massachusetts more than a billion dollars of civil and military manufacturing contracts.

A "tearing beauty" in her youth, in old age a "mother figure," Rogers has been described as vivacious, charming, and hard-working, a woman who decorated herself daily with an orchid or gardenia. At times, however, she could be a "hair shirt," capable of conducting her own filibuster to force the Republican leadership to action. In the House, she generally voted with the Republican majority. Her party unity score varied (in the early 1950s from 60 to 92 percent), but it was generally above 80 percent. After 1954, however, her attendance in the House became less frequent and by 1960 her unity vote had dropped to a low of 33 percent.

Rogers had occupied more floor time and filled more space in the *Congressional Record* as the years wore on. In the twenties she was concerned primarily with private and New England measures and with some national interest measures, in the thirties, forties, and early fifties with veterans' legislation, defense, and foreign affairs. In the late 1950s she focused again on private, New England, and national interest bills, giving less attention to substantive questions and more to procedural and courtesy matters.

At times Rogers was enlightened in her ideas about women, yet she also supported stereotypical views. Immediately upon her election she said that she hoped everybody would "forget as soon as possible" that she was a woman. Asked in 1928 about women and politics she responded that the home and children should come first, noting that if she had children she would not be able to handle her political obligations. In Congress she fought child labor, and worked for a forty-eight-hour week for women and for equal pay for equal work. While praising "gracious charm and simplicity" as feminine virtues, in speeches she extolled the professional and political accomplishments of achieving women of the past and spoke optimistically about the position of women in her day.

Rogers's many honors came primarily as a result of her accomplishments for veterans. She received medals, awards, citations, certificates of merit, and honorary life memberships. In 1950 the American Legion gave her the Distinguished Service Medal, and almost every veterans' organization as well as a number of foreign governments followed with some kind of recognition. A half dozen colleges and universities awarded her honorary degrees and a public school in Lowell, the parade grounds at Fort Devens in Ayer, Mass., the WAC museum in Alabama, and the Bedford (Mass.) Veterans Hospital were given her name.

She did not remarry. Scandal threatened her in 1949 at the age of sixty-seven when she was named in a contested divorce and maintenance suit brought by the wife of one of her longtime staff members, naval Captain Harold A. Latta Lawrence. Several months later, however, the district court judge ordered all reference to Rogers removed from the record. Lawrence continued to manage her campaigns, became coexecutor of her estate, and inherited her house in Saco.

The *Congressional Record* furnishes some evidence of a slowing of Rogers's mental and physical powers for several years before her death. She seems to have become embittered with the House Republican leadership and apparently developed a sense of persecution, but neither the press nor her office staff acknowledged the effects of her advancing age. In her nineteenth election campaign and in her eightieth year, she appeared politically invincible. But seriously failing health led to hospitalization in Boston (under the assumed name of Edith White to avoid jeopardizing her campaign). Suffering a heart attack, she died in Boston three days before the primary election. The almost fifty-year political hegemony of the Rogerses was concluded. Her legacy remains.

[The Rogers Papers in the Schlesinger Library, Radcliffe College, contain records from the files of her years in office: letters, voting records, speeches, news releases, campaign materials, scrapbooks, news clippings, citations and awards, photographs, and memorial addresses delivered in Congress in 1961. A handwritten, undated genealogy of the Nourse (or Nurse) family and Mabel Hill's typewritten romantic but unreliable biography of Rogers and her husband through the 1920s were in the collection of the late Captain Harold A. Latta Lawrence, Saco. The evaluation of Edith Nourse Rogers's congressional career is derived from an analysis of the *Congressional Record*, 63d Cong., 1913, through the 87th Cong., 1961, and reports of the Veterans' Affairs Committee, 79th through 86th Cong. Her voting record in Congress covering party unity is included in the *Congressional Quart. Almanac*, vol. I (1945), and subsequent volumes. The files of the *Boston Globe* and *Boston Herald-American* and microfilm of the *Lowell Sun* and the *Lowell Courier-Citizen*, the *N.Y. Times*, and the *Wash. Post* also provided material on her career. General accounts of Edith Nourse and John Jacob Rogers appear in *Congressional Directory* for the 63d Cong., 1913, through the 86th Cong., 2d sess., 1960; *Biog. Directory of the Am. Congress, 1774–1961* (1961), pp. 1536, 1537; *Current Biog.*, 1942; and Hope Chamberlain, *A Minority of Members: Women in the U.S. Congress* (1973). For background on Saco and the Nourses see Roy P. Fairfield, *Sands, Spindles and Steeples: A History of Saco, Maine* (1956). The best recent history of Lowell is Arthur L. Eno, Jr., ed., *Cotton Was King: A History of Lowell, Massachusetts* (1976). Verification of vital statistics for Rogers, her husband, and other members of her family come from the baptismal records of the Trinity Episcopal Church, Saco; city offices in Lowell, Boston, and Washington, D.C.; secretaries' reports of the classes of 1870 and 1904, Harvard College; and the 1880 U.S. Census. Obituaries of Edith Nourse Rogers appeared in both the *N.Y. Times* and the *Wash. Post*, Sept. 11, 1960. Information was provided by James Thomas Dorris and John Cronin of the *Boston Herald-American;* Thomas Winship and Robert Healy of the *Boston Globe;* Edward Harley, Special Collections, Lowell City Library; Janet Fenderson; John McCormack; Henry Cabot Lodge; Bradford Morse; Helen Nesmith, whose scrapbook adds color to her friend's career; Rogers's niece by marriage, Betty Flather; Roy Slack; and Judith Sessions and Patricia Donegan of the Mount Vernon College Library. Mary Clayton Crozier conducted the research in Boston, Cambridge, Saco-Biddeford, and Lowell, and Daniel Danik researched the *Congressional Record*, newspapers, and Massachusetts election statistics.]

VICTORIA SCHUCK

ROGERS, Mother Mary Joseph (Mary Josephine), Oct. 27, 1882–Oct. 9, 1955. Founder, religious order.

Mary Josephine Rogers, who founded the Maryknoll Sisters of St. Dominic, was born in Roxbury, Mass., the fourth of eight children and first of three daughters of Abraham and Mary Josephine (Plummer) Rogers. Her father's parents had emigrated from Ireland in the 1820s; her mother was of English and Irish descent. Both parents were born in Massachusetts.

Mary Josephine Rogers attended public school in Jamaica Plain, Mass., and graduated from West Roxbury High School. She went on to Smith College, where she completed her A.B. in June 1905. She later remarked that if she had not attended Smith, she would not have founded a missionary congregation. During her college years she became aware of the enthusiastic Protestant mission study groups on campus, and when she returned in 1906 as an assistant in zoology, she was asked to promote some kind of religious organization for Catholic undergraduates. Because she felt unprepared to lead a Bible study group, as was first suggested, Rogers formed a mission study class, destined eventually to become the Smith Newman Club. Seeking guidance for her work as faculty adviser, she consulted Rev. James Anthony Walsh, director of the Society for the Propagation of the Faith, in Boston; in him she found a lifelong coworker and friend. She began immediately to assist Walsh in his promotion of mission activity and by 1908 was willing to resign her position at Smith and return to Boston so that she could give more time to their work. She enrolled that year in Boston Normal School, received a teacher's diploma in 1909, and taught in Boston for the next three years, while helping Walsh with the editing of his mission magazine, *Field Afar.* In 1912 Walsh opened Maryknoll, a seminary near Ossining, N.Y., to prepare American priests for service in mission areas.

Moving to Maryknoll in September 1912, Rogers soon became the recognized leader of a group of women who had come there to assist Walsh in his new endeavor. Gradually other women joined them and the desire to become a religious community developed. After a difficult search for a community that could spare sisters to provide the required ascetical training for the new group, members of the Sisters Servants of the Immaculate Heart of Mary came to Maryknoll from Scranton, Pa., in June 1914 to begin this work. By 1916, however, Walsh, Rogers, and the other sisters concluded that the simpler, more flexible Rule of St. Dominic would be more compatible with missionary life.

Maryknoll's petitions to Rome for canonical status as an official religious congregation began in July 1916. In April 1917 a Dominican sister from Sinsinawa, Wis., came to teach the Maryknoll sisters Dominican spirituality. Their first and second requests to Rome for official recognition were refused because the sisters lacked the necessary financial independence and autonomy of government. Finally, on Feb. 14, 1920, the decree erecting a new religious institute, the Foreign Mission Sisters of St. Dominic, arrived and the sisters' official period of novitiate began. In 1921 the first group of twenty-one made their vows, and during that year six sisters went to China. Since 1920 Maryknoll women had been at work among the Japanese in California and in Seattle. The first general chapter of the new order met in 1925, and elected Mary Josephine Rogers, now Mother Mary Joseph, as superior general.

The close cooperation between the priests and the sisters of Maryknoll continued. Walsh's advice still influenced the sisters, but Mother Mary Joseph's views also influenced the priests, so a fraternal rather than a paternal relationship developed. On a visit to the Far East, Mother Mary Joseph discovered that the priests' health suffered from bad nutrition, the result in part of their ignorance about buying and preparing food; she subsequently designed a course on the subject for the seminarians. She also prepared a manual of courtesy for the priests and seminarians, concerned that, without domestic pressure from women, the men might develop careless manners that could offend the Chinese.

As a religious superior, Mother Mary Joseph insisted that the best service of God and man required the best possible use of human talents and energies within a framework of religious devotion. The sacrificial element, always essential to religious consecration, would, she felt, come naturally from the difficult work that the sisters had chosen rather than from a proliferation of penitential exercises. She never "tried" sisters who were in training to evaluate their spiritual progress, believing that their responses to the challenges of their lives would provide proof enough.

Emphasizing the value of prayer and meditation, Mother Mary Joseph insisted that every Maryknoll sister should be a contemplative in action. In 1933, without any precedent for such an arrangement among active communities of religious women, she established a contemplative branch, a cloistered Maryknoll to support the work of the congregation through constant prayer.

As the leader of a mission order, Mother Mary Joseph emphasized the duty of service and the necessity of professional preparation. While deeply concerned with the worship of God, and with the preservation of the faith, she saw service of God especially in the service of human beings, an unusual point of view in the pre-Vatican II era. Under Mother Rogers's leadership, Maryknoll sisters worked to enable indigenous women in developing areas to serve their own people. To this end, ten independent religious sisterhoods were founded with Maryknoll help. Although five of these had to be disbanded when the Communist regime took over in China, the remainder were still active in the 1970s. Women from mission areas who wished to join Maryknoll were also welcomed into the order, as were members of the Chinese congregations who succeeded in escaping from mainland China.

Mother Mary Joseph also insisted that all Maryknoll sisters, from the United States and abroad, be fully qualified for their work. In an era when many sisters taught or provided other services without professional preparation, Maryknoll sisters did not. Although the congregation did not devote itself to any one specific form of service, most sisters taught, nursed, or engaged in some form of social service. A sister's profession was determined by the needs of the people in her area and by her own aptitudes, previous training, and tastes.

At first most Maryknoll sisters went to the Orient, but over the years the order increasingly diversified its mission areas, going to Africa, Micronesia, the Middle East, and eight Latin American countries. The life and work of Mother Mary Joseph Rogers resulted in the service of more than 1,100 American women in developing areas, and more than 300 working with cultural minorities in the United States. In addition, more than 170 women had come to the congregation from mission areas.

Mother Mary Joseph was reelected as superior general at every chapter, until, in 1947, she declined reelection because she knew that the dispensation from Rome necessary for the continuance of the same leadership after so long a time would not be granted. Those who knew her best remark that Mother Mary Joseph was not "perfect" in the rigid tradition, so much as she was "great" in the possession of a rare breadth of vision, warmth of heart, and a faith strong in its response to God and to the challenge of events. A large woman, with striking eyes, she had an intense interest in contemporary affairs, a magnetic personality, and a keen sense of humor. As a spiritual leader, her central emphasis was on loving human relationships as both a means and a consequence of the establishment of a deep relationship with God. Until her death from peritonitis at St. Vincent's Hospital in New York City, Mother Mary Joseph remained a vital and constructive influence in the congregation she founded.

[Nearly all the important original sources, including extensive diaries, are available in the Archives of the Maryknoll Sisters' Motherhouse, Maryknoll, N.Y. Sister Jeanne Marie Lyons, *Maryknoll's First Lady* (1964), is a popularly written but thoroughly researched biography. Sister Camilla Kennedy is preparing a doctoral dissertation on the spirituality of Mother Mary Joseph for the St. Louis Univ. Dept. of Theology. See also *Dict. Am. Biog.*, Supp. Five. Interviews with Mother Mary Coleman, former superior general of the Maryknoll Sisters, with Sister Jeanne Marie Lyons, and with Mother Mary Joseph's niece, Elizabeth Novak Schmick, supplemented documentary sources, as did material from Sister Barbara Hendricks, president of the order. An obituary appeared in the *N.Y. Times*, Oct. 10, 1955. Photographs are available at the Maryknoll Motherhouse.]

JOAN BLAND, S.N.D.

ROHDE, Ruth Bryan Owen, Oct. 2, 1885–July 26, 1954. Congresswoman, diplomat, lecturer.

Ruth Bryan was born in Jacksonville, Ill., eldest of three children (two daughters and a son) of Mary Elizabeth (Baird) and William Jennings Bryan. Her father's forebears, Irish and English, had been long settled in Virginia before migrating to the Illinois frontier, where her grandfather, Silas L. Bryan, was a circuit judge and legislator. On the maternal side, Scottish and English forebears left colonial New England for upper New York state and later for Illinois. Mary Baird Bryan was a remarkable woman who left a strong imprint on her daughter's character. College-educated, she studied law after her marriage and was admitted to the Nebraska bar in 1888. Far abler than her husband in intellect and judgment, she enabled him to make the most of his political talents. Their eldest daughter's attributes reflect a union of her parents' qualities. From her father came an extraordinary power of expression, facility in personal relations, courage, and a handsome presence; from her mother, a constructive intelligence, ambition, and ceaseless drive.

When Ruth was two, her parents left Jacksonville for Lincoln, Neb. She was five when Bryan was elected to the first of two terms in Congress. She often accompanied her mother to the House gallery, and occasionally sat beside her father on the House floor, listening with "awed delight" to his brilliant performance in the tariff debates. After the historic "cross of gold" speech stampeded the Democratic National Convention into nominating Bryan for the presidency in 1896, the candidate's tightly knit family participated in his precedent-setting campaign of nationwide travel. Appealing directly to the voters, Bryan was accompanied by his wife, who also handled the correspondence, and frequently by his children as well; eleven-year-old Ruth acknowledged the letters from admirers who had named children for her father. Much later, she served as her father's secretary and campaign manager on his third and last try for the presidency in 1908. From childhood, therefore, Ruth Bryan had an insider's view of politics, acquiring both political knowledge and the capacity to absorb defeat as well as victory with composure and grace.

After intermittent education in the Lincoln public schools, she entered Monticello Female Academy (later Monticello College) in Godfrey, Ill., in 1899. Two years later she enrolled at the University of Nebraska, but cut her academic career short by marrying an artist, William Homer Leavitt, on Oct. 3, 1903. Two children were born, Ruth in 1904 and John Baird in 1905, before the marriage ended in divorce in 1909. While studying voice in Germany in 1909, she met Reginald Altham Owen, officer in the Royal (British) Engineers, whom she married on May 3, 1910. The couple was stationed in Jamaica until Major Owen was recalled to England in 1913. Her second son, Reginald, was born there the same year.

While Major Owen saw continuous service in the Egypt-Palestine campaigns, sustaining injuries that made him a chronic invalid, his wife served for fifteen months as secretary-treasurer of the American Woman's War Relief Fund in London, along with LOU HENRY HOOVER. In 1915 she and her two-year-old son went to Cairo, where she served for three years as an operating room nurse in a voluntary unit attached to a military hospital. At the war's end, she returned to the United States with her husband and son, and joined her parents in Coconut Grove, Fla. There Ruth Owen's fourth child, Helen Rudd, was born in 1920.

At the age of thirty-five, with a husband and children to support, Ruth Owen turned to the lyceum and Chautauqua platforms as her father had done. Having inherited his oratorical gifts as well as his prestige, she enjoyed considerable success. She also participated actively in civic, cultural, and patriotic organizations in fast-growing Miami. The newly established University of Miami named her vice chairman of the board of regents in 1925 and she later taught public speaking there (1927–28). Her textbook, *The Elements of Public Speaking* (1931), based

in part on personal experiences, is of more than passing interest.

In 1926 she was drawn into politics, entering the Democratic primary in Florida's Fourth Congressional District, which comprised the coastal counties from Jacksonville to Key West. She faced formidable obstacles. In Florida, which had voted against the nineteenth amendment, prejudice against women was clamorous, and the Democratic organization opposed her candidacy. She lost, but by less than 800 votes. After Major Owen's death in December 1927, she ran again for Congress the following year, aided and encouraged by her mother. Adopting her father's campaign tactics, she traveled over her large district in an attention-getting green Ford, talking to voters and soliciting the aid of editors in every community. She won the election to the Seventy-first Congress by a wide margin to become the first congresswoman from the south.

Her defeated opponent challenged her election on the grounds that her citizenship status was obscure. Under a 1907 law, she had forfeited citizenship in 1910 by marrying an alien, and had not regained it under the Cable Act until 1925. The question at issue was: whether on election day she had been a citizen for seven years as required by the Constitution. The Elections Committee of the House of Representatives, charged with the power to determine the eligibility of its members, met in December 1928 to decide the question. Acting as her own counsel, and arguing on feminist grounds, Owen brilliantly defended her eligibility and condemned both the original law and the procedural flaws in the Cable Act that had made her repatriation difficult. The dramatic impact of the well-publicized "trial" focused attention on the Cable Act, which had been enacted in 1922 in response to strong feminist demands for "independent citizenship." The ensuing corrective amendments stand as Owen's greatest legislative achievement.

Although less ardent a feminist than her mother, Owen became the first congresswoman after JEANNETTE RANKIN to concentrate on feminist issues. She introduced and vigorously supported legislation to create a cabinet-level Department of Home and Child, and fought for appropriations to send delegates to international conferences on health and child welfare. Mindful of her constituents, she secured a law to protect citrus growers, and initiated legislation to set aside the Everglades Swamp as a national park. Despite her father's lifelong antitariff position, Owen, prudently responding to her district's protectionist views, voted for the Smoot-Hawley Tariff (1929).

Owen's political and religious views departed from those of her parents, but the supportive family ties were never broken. The prestige of the family name lingered on to color her congressional career. A place was created for her on the Foreign Affairs Committee, making her the first woman to serve on a major congressional committee. Reelected in 1930, when she ran for a third term two years later she fell victim to antiprohibition sentiment. Although she had proposed a referendum on the issue, she was unable to counter her opponent's attacks on her as the daughter of the great "dry crusader." Abiding by the wishes of her district, she voted for repeal of the eighteenth amendment in the lame duck session of the Seventy-second Congress.

In April 1933, President Franklin D. Roosevelt named Owen envoy extraordinary and minister plenipotentiary to Denmark, making her the first American woman to hold a major diplomatic post. Her ministerial tasks were to improve trade relations, damaged by the impact of the Smoot-Hawley Tariff, and to create a fresh image of the United States. Both tasks were well suited to her talents. Taking with her three of her children and three grandchildren, she attracted favorable press attention as representing the fulfillment of family life. She learned Danish, entertained graciously, and traveled extensively, recording an official trip to Greenland in *Leaves From a Greenland Diary* (1935). Returning to the United States on home leave, on July 11, 1936, she married Börge Rohde, Captain of the King's Guard and Gentleman in Waiting at the Court of King Christian X, at the Hyde Park home of Franklin and ELEANOR ROOSEVELT. It was her stated intention to retain her American citizenship and return to Denmark as minister, but marriage to a Dane automatically made her a Danish citizen. Unwittingly possessed of dual citizenship, she could no longer serve in her ministerial capacity, and she resigned her post.

The Rohdes lived thereafter in the United States. Ruth Rohde returned to the lecture platform, served on numerous boards and commissions, and wrote several books, including *Look Forward, Warrior* (1942), a forcefully written proposal for international cooperation. President Roosevelt named her special assistant to the State Department to aid in drafting the United Nations Charter, and in 1949 President Harry S Truman appointed her an alternate delegate to the United Nations General Assembly. From 1948 onward she chaired the executive committee of the Speakers' Research Committee of the United Nations.

The recipient of many awards and several honorary degrees, Ruth Rohde traveled to Denmark in 1954 to acknowledge the Order of Merit conferred on her by King Frederick IX for her contribution to Danish-American friendship. She died in Copenhagen of a heart attack, and her ashes were buried there.

To the end of her life Ruth Rohde remained a majestically handsome woman, famous as a hostess who combined political acumen with personal grace, and for her ceaseless activity in civic and international causes. Her career conveyed a message on the political status of women in a transitional period. She served admirably as a vivid and courageous trailbreaker to whom overcoming obstacles—often of her own making —appeared effortless. For the same reason she could not well serve as a model.

[Ruth Bryan Owen Rohde also wrote travel books and retellings of Scandinavian folk tales, including *Denmark Caravan* (1936), *The Castle in the Silver Wood and Other Scandinavian Fairy Tales* (1939), *Picture Tales from Scandinavia* (1939), and *Caribbean Caravel* (1949). The principal source for the social and political background of her early life is the candid memoir of her parents, *Memoirs of William Jennings Bryan: By Himself and His Wife Mary Baird Bryan* (1925). See also Paolo Coletta, *William Jennings Bryan*, I, *Political Evangelist, 1860–1908* (1964); *Current Biog.*, 1944; and *Dict. Am. Biog.*, Supp. Five. For Rohde's congressional career see *Biog. Directory of the Am. Congress* (1961), *Congressional Record*, 71st and 72nd Congresses, and Hope Chamberlin, *A Minority of Members: Women in the U.S. Congress* (1973). On the contested election case see *Committee Print*, U.S. House of Representatives, Committee on Elections, no. 1, Jan. 17, 1930: "Arguments and Hearings in the Contested Election Case of William C. Lawson v. Ruth Bryan Owen" (1930). For background on the Cable Act and a discussion of her case see J. Stanley Lemons, *The Woman Citizen: Social Feminism in the 1920s* (1973), pp. 63–69, 235–37. *The Woman's Journal* has good coverage of the Cable Act and its consequences in 1922–23; see *The Woman Citizen* for commentary on the 1928–29 hearing. Among the many press articles about Rohde, the most useful are C. Lowe, "Our First Woman Diplomat," *Pictorial Rev.*, Feb. 1934; "Ruth Bryan Owen: First Woman Diplomat," *Christian Century*, April 26, 1933; "Mr. Roosevelt's New Deal for Women," *Literary Digest*, April 15, 1933; "Lady Lame Duck's Farewell," *Literary Digest*, Feb. 25, 1933. A biobibliography prepared by Libby Atwood proved useful in research for this article. Obituaries appeared in the *N.Y. Times*, July 27, 1954, and *Newsweek*, Aug. 9, 1954.]

LOUISE M. YOUNG

ROMBAUER, Irma Louise von Starkloff, Oct. 30, 1877–Oct. 14, 1962. Food writer.

The author of the most popular American

cookbook in the mid-twentieth century was born Irma von Starkloff in St. Louis, Mo. She was the younger of two daughters of Hugo Maximilian and Clara (Kuhlman) von Starkloff; her father also had two sons by an earlier marriage. Hugo von Starkloff, a physician and surgeon, was descended from a very old Stuttgart family; he had come to the United States in the 1850s. Her mother also emigrated from Germany to St. Louis and in 1873 helped SUSAN BLOW to start the first public school kindergarten in the United States.

When Irma was twelve her father was appointed United States consul in Bremen, Germany. She was educated at boarding schools in Switzerland, and learned to speak German and French fluently, an asset that in later life enabled her to do food research in three languages. After years of schooling and traveling through Europe, she returned to St. Louis in 1894 and for a time attended the school of fine arts at Washington University. She had become, in every sense, the young lady of the period. She danced well, knew music, did stitchery, and was versed in various other arts—not, however, the art of cookery.

On Oct. 14, 1899, Irma von Starkloff married a young lawyer named Edgar Roderick Rombauer. She knew absolutely nothing about domestic duties, so her husband, an avid camper and enthusiastic camp cook, coached her in the kitchen. Like other celebrities in the food world, she learned to cook through necessity rather than through choice. But her interest grew, and as the family became more successful and she found herself entertaining more often, she acquired greater confidence in cooking and learned to shop for the best the markets could offer. In a few years she had established a reputation as a delightful hostess who had a way with food.

Her husband, who was active in politics as a reformer and served briefly as speaker of the St. Louis House of Delegates and for many years as president of the city's Urban League, died in February 1930. By this time Rombauer's daughter, Marion (1903–1976), and son, Edgar (b. 1907), were married and had set up their own households. They asked her to write a little cookbook of the recipes they had grown up with. This she did, drawing on an earlier compilation gathered for a Unitarian church-sponsored cooking course she had given in the 1920s, and adding bits of her sage advice and a good measure of her wit. The book of 500 recipes, privately printed and published in 1931, was called Joy of Cooking. It sold some 3,000 copies. Rombauer then rewrote and enlarged it, changing the format of her recipes to the step-by-step

method that became her permanent style, and began to look for a publisher.

By chance Irma Rombauer met the president of the Bobbs-Merrill publishing firm, who agreed to look over her book. This proved a momentous step for both publisher and author. The first Bobbs-Merrill edition of The Joy of Cooking was published in 1936. It did not become a best seller at once, although it sold well initially and continued to sell. In 1943 Rombauer revised the book, incorporating in it Streamlined Cooking, which she had published in 1939. Suddenly it caught on, and the rest is history. The Joy of Cooking set sales records that only FANNIE FARMER's Boston Cooking-School Cook Book had broken in previous years. It also was one of the first cookbooks to offer a money-back guarantee. During the next thirty years The Joy of Cooking received many encomiums and became a part of almost every American home. It has also had a few dissenters, as does any classic volume: there are those who claim they cannot follow Fannie Farmer or Julia Child.

The book went through a third revision, published in 1952, with Marion Rombauer Becker named for the first time as coauthor. In later years Rombauer turned over much of the responsibility for the book to her daughter, who had assisted with the work from the beginning. She herself was always ready to answer queries, however, and she replied to fan letters in longhand. She also continued to travel and remained active in a variety of civic and cultural organizations. She was a woman of versatile interests and always stimulating company, possessed of both a charming sense of humor and a modest but knowing approach to living.

Rombauer's other two books, Streamlined Cooking and Cook Book for Boys and Girls (1946), were eclipsed by the overwhelming popularity of The Joy of Cooking, which set a standard for cookbooks in an age when there was great dissension among food writers. Even the most devoted followers of European or Oriental cooking are apt to have a copy on their shelves to use for its information if not for its recipes. (Rombauer herself was a fan of Chinese cooking and discussed the possibility of applying Chinese techniques to everyday practices in American kitchens, an idea that later came into fashion.) The book covers a tremendous amount of ground, and can usually be depended on to yield a recipe for practically anything in the contemporary kitchen. Its influence has been vast, and if it has not created a distinctive style of cooking or set a trend, it never touched any cook it did not enrich.

Irma Rombauer died in St. Louis in 1962 of

an acute heart attack, having suffered a stroke eight years earlier. Revisions of *The Joy of Cooking* continued under the supervision of her daughter. Marion Becker carried on the work with dedication, although she did prepare one edition that broke away from many of the principles her mother had established; it included far too many French and Italian recipes, and robbed the book of some of the delicious Rombauer humor and personality. Irma Rombauer is one of the great women of American cookery and deserves to be known in her original state of joy.

[Further editions of *The Joy of Cooking* appeared under Marion Rombauer Becker's direction in 1963 and 1975. Her son, Ethan Becker, is preparing a new edition. The fullest account of Rombauer's life is contained in *Little Acorn: The Story Behind the Joy of Cooking, 1931–1966* (1966), which is available from the Bobbs-Merrill Co. Other sources of information about Rombauer and her book include Harry B. Wilson, "St. Louis Queen of Cookbooks," *Coronet*, Oct. 1950; Jane Nickerson, "They Wanted to Cook Like Mother," *N.Y. Times Book Rev.*, Aug. 12, 1951; an entry in *Current Biog.*, 1953; and obituaries in the *N.Y. Times*, Oct. 17, 1962, and *Time*, Oct. 26, 1962; death record from Mo. Dept. of Health. Assistance in the research for this article was provided by a biobibliography prepared by Kathleen McDonough.]

JAMES BEARD

ROOSEVELT, Anna Eleanor, Oct. 11, 1884–Nov. 7, 1962. Social reformer.

Anna Eleanor Roosevelt was born in New York City, the first child of Elliott and Anna (Hall) Roosevelt. Descended on both sides from distinguished colonial families active in commerce, banking, and politics, Eleanor seemed destined to enjoy all the benefits of class and privilege. By the time she was ten, both her parents had died, as had a younger brother, leaving Eleanor and her second brother, Hall, as the only survivors.

From that point forward, Eleanor Roosevelt's life was characterized by paradox. A woman of remarkable self-control, she yet reached out to touch the world in profoundly emotional ways. Although committed to the traditional idea of women as primarily responsible to husband and family, she personified the strength of the independent woman. Both by fate and by will, she became the most important public woman of the twentieth century.

Eleanor Roosevelt remembered herself as "a solemn child, without beauty. I seemed like a little old woman entirely lacking in the spontaneous joy and mirth of youth." She experienced emotional rejection early: her mother called her "granny" and, at least in Eleanor's memory, warmly embraced her son while being only "kindly and indifferent" to her little girl. From most of her family young Eleanor received the message that she was "very plain," almost ugly, and certainly "old-fashioned." When her parents died, she went to live with her maternal grandmother, who was equally without warmth. As a cousin later remarked: "It was the grimmest childhood I had ever known. Who did she have? Nobody."

In fact, she had one person—her father. "He was the one great love of my life as a child," she later wrote, "and . . . like many children, I have lived a dream life with him." Described by his friends as "charming, impetuous . . . generous, [and] friendly," Elliott Roosevelt developed with Eleanor an intimacy that seemed almost magical. "As soon as I could talk," she recalled, "I went into his dressing room every morning and chattered to him . . . I even danced with him." She dreamed of the time when she and her father "would have a life of our own together."

But Elliott Roosevelt's capacity for ebullient play and love also contained the seeds of self-destruction. He was never able to provide stability for himself and his family, and his emotional imbalance caused his banishment from the household. He nourished the relationship with Eleanor through letters to "father's own little Nell," writing of "the wonderful long rides" that he wanted them to enjoy together. But when his long-awaited visits occurred, they often ended in disaster, as when he left Eleanor with the doorman at his club, promising to return but going off on a drunken spree. The pain of betrayal was exceeded only by a depth of love for the man who she believed to be "the only person who really cared."

The emotional void caused by her father's death persisted until, at the age of fifteen, she enrolled at Allenswood, a girls' school outside of London presided over by Marie Souvestre. The daughter of the French philosopher and radical Emil Souvestre, she passionately embraced unpopular causes, staunchly defending Dreyfus in France and the cause of the Boers in South Africa. Souvestre provided for Eleanor a deeply needed emotional bond, confiding in her as they toured the continent together, and expressing the affection that made it possible for the younger woman to flower. Roosevelt remembered the years at Allenswood as "the happiest years" of her life: "Whatever I have become since had its seeds in those three years of contact with a liberal mind and strong personality."

Souvestre's imprint was not lost when Eleanor Roosevelt returned to New York City at seventeen to come out in society. In the rush of parties and dances, she kept her eye on the more serious world of ideas and social service. She plunged into settlement house work and at eighteen joined the National Consumers' League, headed by FLORENCE KELLEY. The League was committed to securing health and safety for workers, especially women, and as Roosevelt visited factories and sweatshops, she developed a lifelong commitment to helping the poor. She also joined the Junior League and taught calisthenics and dancing at the Rivington Street Settlement House. Much of Eleanor Roosevelt's subsequent political activism can be traced to this early involvement in social reform.

At the same time, Eleanor Roosevelt was secretly planning to marry her cousin Franklin Roosevelt. Like Elliott Roosevelt, his godfather, Franklin was spontaneous, warm, and gregarious. But Franklin Roosevelt also possessed good sense and singleness of purpose. Eleanor Roosevelt saw in him the spark of life that she remembered from her father; he, in turn, saw in her the discipline that would curb his own instincts toward excess.

After their marriage on March 17, 1905, the young Roosevelts settled in New York City while Franklin finished his law studies at Columbia University. For the next fifteen years Eleanor Roosevelt's public activities gave way to other concerns. Sara Roosevelt, Franklin's mother, objected to her work at the settlement house because she might bring home diseases. The Roosevelts' first child, Anna, was born within a year (1906), James the next year, and two years later Franklin. Eleanor Roosevelt cherished her children, but it was not a happy time. Her mother-in-law dominated the household, and she came to feel that "Franklin's children were more my mother-in-law's children than they were mine." But she did not rebel. She feared hurting her husband and losing his affection, and she experienced a profound sense of inadequacy about her abilities as a wife and mother that continued throughout her life. The death of her third child, seven months after his birth, only reinforced her pain and unhappiness. Three additional children were born in the next six years—Elliott in 1910, Franklin Jr. in 1914, and John in 1916. But motherhood could not be fulfilling in a household ruled by a mother-in-law who told the children they were hers: "Your mother only bore you."

Between 1910 and the beginning of World War I, Eleanor Roosevelt's activities revolved increasingly around her husband's growing political career. Elected as the Democratic assemblyman from Dutchess County, N.Y., in 1910, Franklin Roosevelt rapidly became a leader of insurgent anti-Tammany forces in Albany and Eleanor Roosevelt found herself organizing frequent social-political gatherings. In 1913 he was appointed assistant secretary of the navy and she became expert at hosting multiple social events while managing a large household and moving everyone to Campobello in New Brunswick during the summer, then to Hyde Park, and back to Washington.

The entry of the United States into World War I in 1917 provided Eleanor Roosevelt, as her biographer Joseph Lash has noted, with "a reason acceptable to her conscience to free herself of the social duties that she hated, to concentrate less on her household, and plunge into work that fitted her aptitude." She rose at 5:00 A.M. to coordinate activities at Washington's Union Station canteen for soldiers on their way to training camps, took charge of Red Cross activities, supervised the knitting rooms at the navy department, and spoke at patriotic rallies. Her interest in social welfare led to her drive to improve conditions at St. Elizabeths Hospital for the mentally ill, while her sensitivity to suffering came forth in the visits she paid to wounded soldiers. "[My son] always loved to see you come in," one mother wrote. "You always brought a ray of sunshine."

After Franklin Roosevelt's unsuccessful campaign for the vice presidency in 1920, the Roosevelts returned to New York where Eleanor became active in the League of Women Voters. At the time of her marriage, she had opposed suffrage, thinking it inconsistent with women's proper role; now she coordinated the League's legislative program, drafted laws providing equal representation for men and women, and worked with Esther Lape and Elizabeth Read on the League's lobbying activities. In 1922 she joined the Women's Trade Union League (WTUL)—then viewed as "left-leaning"—and found there friends as well as political allies. In addition to working for maximum hour and minimum wage laws for women, she helped raise funds for WTUL headquarters in New York City and developed warm ties to its leaders, including ROSE SCHNEIDERMAN and MAUD SWARTZ, both immigrants.

When her husband was paralyzed by polio in 1921, Eleanor Roosevelt's public life expanded still further as she became his personal representative in the political arena. With the aid of Louis Howe, Franklin Roosevelt's political mentor who had become her own close friend, she first mobilized Dutchess County women, then moved on to the state Democratic party, organizing all but five counties by 1924. "Organization," she noted, "is something to which [the men] are always ready to take off their hats." No one did the job better. Leading a delegation to the Democratic National Convention in 1924, she fought for equal pay legislation, the child labor amendment, and other planks endorsed by women reformers.

By 1928, Eleanor Roosevelt had become a political leader in her own right. Once just a political wife, she gradually extended that role into a vehicle for asserting her own personality and goals. She headed up the national women's campaign for the Democratic party in 1928, making sure that the party appealed to independent voters, to minorities, and to women. After Franklin Roosevelt's election as governor of New York, she was instrumental in securing FRANCES PERKINS's appointment as the state's industrial commissioner. She dictated as many as a hundred letters a day, spoke to countless groups, and acted as an advocate of social reform and women's issues.

Eleanor Roosevelt's talent for combining partisan political activity with devotion to social welfare causes made her the center of an ever-growing female reform network. Her associates included Marion Dickerman and Nancy Cook, former suffragists and Democratic party loyalists; MARY DEWSON, who was president of the New York Consumers' League from 1925 to 1931; and MARY DREIER of the WTUL. She walked on picket lines with Rose Schneiderman, edited the *Women's Democratic News,* and advised the League of Women Voters on political tactics. Not only did her political sophistication grow, but she also learned to uphold her beliefs even if she caused "disagreement or unpleasant feelings." By standing up for women in politics, she provided a model for others to follow.

During the 1932 campaign which led to her husband's election to the presidency, Eleanor Roosevelt coordinated the activities of the Women's Division of the Democratic National Committee, working with Mary Dewson to mobilize thousands of women precinct workers. After the election, Dewson took over direction of the Women's Division. She corresponded daily with Eleanor Roosevelt both about appointing women to office and about securing action on issues that would appeal to minorities, women, and such professional groups as educators and social workers. Together they brought to Washington an unprecedented number of dynamic women activists, including ELLEN WOODWARD, Hilda Worthington Smith, and Florence Kerr. MARY ANDERSON, director of the Women's Bureau, recalled that women government officials had formerly dined together in a small university club. "Now," she said, "there are so many of them that we need a hall."

Eleanor Roosevelt also provided a national forum for transmitting the views and concerns of these women. At regular press conferences for women reporters, she introduced MARY MCLEOD BETHUNE and other women leaders to talk about their work with the administration. These sessions provided new status and prestige for the female press corps; they also underlined the importance to Eleanor Roosevelt of women's issues and created a community of women reporters and government workers.

Eleanor Roosevelt's own political role was best seen in the 1936 reelection drive when she used the educational approach developed by the Women's Division in 1932 as a primary campaign weapon. More than 60,000 women precinct workers canvassed the electorate and for the first time women received equal representation on the Democratic platform committee, an event described by the *New York Times* as "the biggest coup for women in years."

Eleanor Roosevelt's fear that there would be no active role available to her as first lady had been unfounded. She toured the country repeatedly, surveying conditions in the coal mines, visiting relief projects, and speaking out for the human rights of the disadvantaged. Through her syndicated newspaper column "My Day," which first appeared in January 1936, and through radio programs and lectures, she reached millions and communicated to the country her deep compassion for those who suffered. At the White House, in turn, she acted as advocate of the poor and disenfranchised. "No one who ever saw Eleanor Roosevelt sit down facing her husband, and holding his eyes firmly, say to him 'Franklin, I think you should . . . or, Franklin surely you will not' . . . will ever forget the experience," Rexford Tugwell wrote. She had become, as columnist Raymond Clapper noted, a "Cabinet Minister without portfolio— the most influential woman of our times."

But if Eleanor Roosevelt had achieved an unparalleled measure of political influence, it was in place of, rather than because of, an intimate personal relationship with her husband. Probably at no time after their first few years together did Franklin and Eleanor Roosevelt achieve the degree of intimacy that she once described as caring so much that a look and the sound of a voice would tell all. Not only did Sara Roosevelt remain a dominant presence, but Franklin had embarked on his own interests and enthusiasms, often different from those of his wife. The dissimilarities in their temperaments became a permanent barrier. While he loved to party, she held back, telling her daughter Anna in a letter from Warm Springs, Ga., in 1934, that she "always felt like a spoil-sport and policeman here."

During his years as assistant secretary of the navy, Franklin Roosevelt had often indulged his fun-loving instinct, causing a lasting breach in the marriage. When his wife was away, his frequent companion had been Lucy Mercer, Eleanor's social secretary. Over time, their relationship became intimate. Eleanor Roosevelt learned of the affair in 1918 and offered to divorce him. Although Franklin refused her offer, and Sara Roosevelt engineered an agreement for them to stay together if her son stopped seeing Lucy Mercer, Eleanor Roosevelt's marriage would never again achieve the magical possibility of being "for life, for death."

Some observers have connected Eleanor Roosevelt's reemergence as a public figure with her profound anger at her husband's betrayal. Yet her activism predated her discovery of the Mercer affair, going back to World War I and ultimately to the settlement house years. The Lucy Mercer affair, like Franklin's polio, reinforced her move toward public self-assertion, but did not in itself cause a transformation. What it did cause was a gradual reallocation of emotional energy away from her husband. Throughout the 1920s a warmth of tone and feeling continued in her letters to and about him. Yet gradually their lives became more separate. She might be jealous of his secretary, Missy LeHand, or even of her daughter Anna, for the ease with which they supplied Franklin Roosevelt with fun and enjoyment. But part of her also accepted the idea that others must provide what she could not give. In a poignant piece entitled "On Being Forty-five," written for *Vogue* in 1930, Eleanor Roosevelt wrote that by middle-age a woman must recognize that the romantic dreams of youth are over. The forty-five-year-old woman "must keep an open and speculative mind . . . [to] be ready to go out and try new adventures, create new work for others as well as herself, and strike deep roots in some community where her presence will make a difference to the lives of others."

Taking her own advice, Eleanor Roosevelt transferred her emotional attachments to others. In 1926 she had moved with Nancy Cook and Marion Dickerman into Val-Kill, a newly constructed cottage at Hyde Park. The event accurately symbolized her growing detachment from Franklin and his mother. Although she returned to "the big house" at Hyde Park when her husband was present, it was always with a sense of resentment and regret. She and Dickerman purchased Todhunter, a private school in New York City where Eleanor Roosevelt taught three days a week even after Franklin was elected governor of New York. The three women also jointly managed a furniture crafts factory at Val-Kill. After 1920, she and Louis Howe developed profound bonds of affection and support, each carrying the other loyally through crises with Franklin and the vicissitudes of party politics. Harry Hopkins, director of the WPA, also became an intimate. But her most carefree relationship was probably that with Earl Miller, a former state trooper and subsequently a bodyguard for the Roosevelt family who became a close companion. Miller encouraged her to drive her own car, take up horseback riding again, and develop confidence in her personality.

With these and others, Eleanor Roosevelt developed a rich emotional life. Although she frequently appeared cold and distant, she passionately cared for her children and friends. Writing to her daughter Anna on Christmas Eve in 1935, she noted: "It was hard to decorate the tree or get things distributed without you . . . and if anyone says much I shall weep." She expressed similar affection in daily letters to LORENA HICKOK, the former journalist and assistant to Harry Hopkins, who moved to Hyde Park after a falling-out occurred between Eleanor Roosevelt and Marion Dickerman and Nancy Cook in the late 1930s. Most surprising of all, perhaps, she poured out her feelings to distant correspondents, answering the many pleas for help which came to her with either a sensitive letter, an admonition to a federal agency to take action, or even a personal check. The poor wrote to her because they knew she cared, and in caring, she found an outlet for her powerful emotional needs.

The same compassion was manifested in Eleanor Roosevelt's advocacy of the oppressed. Hearing about the struggle of Appalachian farmers to reclaim their land, she became a champion of the Arthurdale (W.Va.) Resettlement Administration project and devoted her lecture fees as well as her influence to help the community. She invited to the White House representatives of poor southern textile workers and northern garment workers, seating them next to the president at dinner so that he might hear of their plight. She and Franklin Roosevelt had worked out a tacit understanding which permitted her to bring the cause of the oppressed to his attention, and allowed him, in turn, to use her activism as a means of building alliances with groups to his left. Although the president frequently refused to act as she wished, the dispossessed at least had an advocate.

Largely because of Eleanor Roosevelt, the issue of civil rights for black Americans received a hearing at the White House. Although like most white Americans she had grown up in an environment suffused with racism and nativism, she was one of the few voices in the administration insisting that racial discrimination had no place in American life. As always, she led by example. At a 1939 Birmingham meeting inaugurating the Southern Conference on Human Welfare, she placed her chair so that it straddled the black and white sides of the aisle, thereby confounding local authorities who insisted on segregation. She resigned in the same year from the Daughters of the American Revolution after they denied the black artist Marian Anderson permission to perform at Constitution Hall. Instead, and in part through Eleanor Roosevelt's intervention, Anderson sang to 75,000 people from the Lincoln Memorial.

Eleanor Roosevelt also acted as behind-the-scenes lobbyist for civil rights legislation. With alacrity she accepted the suggestion of Walter White, executive secretary of the NAACP, that she act as an intermediary with the president in the association's attempt to secure legislation defining lynching as a federal crime. She also agreed to be a patron of an NAACP-sponsored exhibit in New York City of paintings and drawings dealing with lynching, and attended the showing. Although she lost out in her campaign for the president's strong endorsement of an antilynching bill, she had communicated to him her anger that "one could get nothing done." Continuing to speak forthrightly for the cause of civil rights, she addressed the NAACP's annual meeting in June 1939 and joined the biracial protest organization a few weeks later. As the threat of war increased, Eleanor Roosevelt joined her Negro friends in arguing vigorously for administration action to eliminate discrimination in the armed services and in defense employment. Although civil rights forces were not satisfied with the administration's response, the positive changes that did occur were due in large part to their alliance with Eleanor Roosevelt.

She brought the same fervor to her identification with young people. Fearing that a whole generation might be lost to democracy because of the depression, she reached out to make contact with them. Despite warnings from White House aides, between 1936 and 1940 Eleanor Roosevelt became deeply involved in the activities of the American Student Union and the American Youth Congress, groups committed to a democratic socialist program of massively expanded social welfare programs. She advanced their point of view in White House circles, and invited them to meet the president. Although she was later betrayed by some of her young allies who followed the Communist party line and denounced the European war as imperialistic after the Nazi-Soviet Non-Aggression Pact

of 1939, she continued to believe in the importance of remaining open to dissent. "I have never said anywhere that I would rather see young people sympathetic with communism," Eleanor Roosevelt wrote. "But I have said I would rather see the young people actively at work, even if I considered they were doing things that were a mistake."

With the onset of World War II, Roosevelt persisted in her efforts for the disadvantaged. She insisted that administration officials consult women activists and incorporate roles for women as a major part of their planning for wartime operations, and she intervened repeatedly with war production agencies as well as the military to advocate fairer treatment for black Americans. When it seemed that many New Deal social welfare programs would be threatened by war, Eleanor Roosevelt became their defender. Increasingly she devoted herself to the dream of international cooperation, aware more than most of the revolution rising in Africa and Asia, and of the dangers posed by the threat of postwar conflict.

But her energies in the war were directed primarily to human needs. When Jewish refugees seeking a haven from Nazi persecution received less than an enthusiastic response from the State Department, Eleanor Roosevelt served as their advocate. Families separated by war always found an ally when they sought her help, and wounded veterans in army hospitals far from home received from her visits the cherished message that someone cared.

As the war proceeded, the worlds of Franklin and Eleanor Roosevelt became still more separate. They were frequently adversaries and the president was less able to tolerate her advocacy of unpopular causes. In search of release from the unbearable pressures of the war, he had come to rely on the gaiety and laughter of his daughter Anna, and other women companions, including Lucy Mercer Rutherford, who, unknown to Eleanor, was with Franklin Roosevelt in Warm Springs when he died of a cerebral hemorrhage in April 1945.

With great discipline and dignity, Eleanor Roosevelt bore both the pain of Franklin's death and the circumstances surrounding it. Her first concern was with carrying forward the policies in which they had both believed despite their disagreements. Writing later about their relationship, she commented: "He might have been happier with a wife who had been completely uncritical. That I was never able to be and he had to find it in some other people. Nevertheless, I think that I sometimes acted as a spur . . . I was one of those who served his purposes." What she did not say was that Franklin Roosevelt had served her purposes as well. Though they never retrieved their early intimacy, they had created an unparalleled partnership to respond to the needs of a nation in crisis.

Not long after her husband's death, Eleanor Roosevelt told a reporter: "The story is over." But no one who cared so much for so many causes, and was so effective a leader, could long remain on the sidelines. Over the next decade and a half, she continued to be the most effective woman in American politics. In long letters to President Harry S Truman, she implored the administration to push forward with civil rights, maintain the Fair Employment Practices Commission, develop a foreign policy able to cope with the needs of other nations, and work toward a world system where atom bombs would cease to be a negotiating chip in international relations.

Appropriately, President Truman nominated Eleanor Roosevelt as a United States delegate to the United Nations. There she argued, debated, and lobbied for the creation of a document on human rights that would embody standards which civilized humankind would accept as sacred and inalienable. Finally on Dec. 10, 1948, the Universal Declaration of Human Rights, fundamentally shaped by her, passed the General Assembly. Delegates rose in a standing ovation to the woman who more than anyone else had come to symbolize the cause of human rights. Even those in the United States who had most opposed her applauded: "I want to say that I take back everything I ever said about her," Michigan Senator Arthur Vandenberg commented, "and believe me, it's been plenty." At times during the New Deal a figure of scorn among some conservatives, Eleanor Roosevelt was fast becoming a national heroine.

The cause of world peace and the desire to help the victims of war quickly became central to Roosevelt's efforts. In moving speeches that vividly portrayed the suffering wrought by war, she sought to educate the United States to its postwar responsibilities. She had traveled through England noting the names of all the young men who had died during the war, she told an audience. "There is a feeling that spreads over the land," she said, "the feel of civilization that of itself might have a hard time coming back." If the United States wished to avoid such a world, it must help those who had suffered, and avoid isolationism.

Although Eleanor Roosevelt disagreed profoundly with some of the military aspects of United States foreign policy, she supported the broad outlines of its response to the Soviet Union

in the developing cold war. In debates at the UN she learned quickly that Soviet delegates could be hypocritical, and on more than one occasion she responded to their charges of injustice in America by proposing that each country submit to investigation of its social conditions—a suggestion the Soviets refused. She refused in 1947 to support the newly formed Progressive party with its platform of accommodation toward the Soviet Union, and instead spearheaded the drive to build Americans for Democratic Action, a group which espoused social reforms at home and support of Truman's foreign policy.

Throughout the 1950s Eleanor Roosevelt remained a singular public figure, able to galvanize the attention of millions by her statements. She became one of the staunchest advocates of Israel, argued vigorously for civil rights, and spoke forcefully against the witch hunts of McCarthyism. When Dwight D. Eisenhower became president in 1953 she resigned her UN post, but she continued to work tirelessly through the American Association for the United Nations to mobilize public support for international cooperation. She also gave unstintingly of her time to the election campaigns in 1952 and 1956 of her dear friend Adlai Stevenson, who brought to politics a wit and sophistication that she admired.

The private sphere, however, remained most precious. "The people I love," Eleanor Roosevelt wrote her friend and physician David Gurewitsch, "mean more to me than all the public things. I only do the public things because there are a few close people whom I love dearly and who matter to me above everything else." The Roosevelt children remained as much a trial as a comfort. After Franklin Roosevelt's death, she lived at Val-Kill with her secretary, Malvina Thompson (1893–1953), and her son Elliott and his family. More often than not, family gatherings degenerated into bitter arguments. But her grandchildren brought joy as did friends, old and new.

As she entered her seventies, Eleanor Roosevelt had become the first lady of the world. Traveling to India, Japan, and the Soviet Union, she spoke for the best that was in America. Although she did not initially approve of John F. Kennedy and would have much preferred to see Adlai Stevenson nominated again in 1960, she lived to see the spirit of impatience and reform return to Washington. In 1962 she sponsored hearings in Washington, D.C., where young civil rights workers testified about the judicial and police harassment of black protesters in the south.

It was fitting that Eleanor Roosevelt's last

major official position was to chair President Kennedy's Commission on the Status of Women, to which she was appointed in December 1961. More than anyone else of her generation she had exemplified the political independence and personal autonomy that were abiding themes of the women's movement. Eleanor Roosevelt had not been a militant feminist and, like most social reformers, she had opposed the Equal Rights Amendment (ERA) until the mid-1940s, believing that it would jeopardize protective labor legislation for women. During the depression she accepted the popular view that, at least temporarily, some married women should leave the labor force to improve the chances of the unemployed. On occasion, she also adopted male-oriented definitions of fulfillment. "You are successful," she wrote in a 1931 article, "when your husband feels that he has been a success and that life has been worthwhile."

But on the issue of women's equality as in so many other areas, Roosevelt most often affirmed the inalienable right of the human spirit to grow and seek fulfillment. Brought up amidst anti-Semitic and anti-Negro attitudes, she had transcended her past to become one of the strongest champions of minority rights. Once opposed to suffrage, she had grown to exemplify women's aspirations for a full life in politics.

Eleanor Roosevelt participated in the activities of the Women's Commission until August 1962, testifying on behalf of equal pay laws at a congressional hearing in April of that year. She died at her home in New York City in November from a rare form of tuberculosis. Twenty years earlier she had written: "You can never really live anyone else's life, not even your child's. The influence you exert is through your own life and what you've become yourself."

Despite disappointment and tragedy, Eleanor Roosevelt had followed her own advice. "What other single human being," Adlai Stevenson asked at her memorial service, "has touched and transformed the existence of so many? . . . She walked in the slums . . . of the world, not on a tour of inspection . . . but as one who could not feel contentment when others were hungry." Because of her life, millions of others may have experienced a new sense of possibility. She would have wished for nothing more.

[The Eleanor Roosevelt Papers at the Franklin Delano Roosevelt Library, Hyde Park, N.Y., represent the most comprehensive collection of material available. Of particular interest are her correspondence with Walter White of the NAACP, material about her family, especially her father, and drafts of articles and lectures. Other relevant collections at Hyde Park are the papers of Mary Dewson, Hilda Worthington Smith, and Lorena Hickok; the papers

of the Women's Div. of the Democratic Nat. Committee; and those of Anna Roosevelt Halsted. Several manuscript collections at the Schlesinger Library, Radcliffe College, bear directly on Eleanor Roosevelt's life: see especially the papers of Mary Anderson, Mary Dewson, Mary Dreier, and Ellen Woodward. Of Eleanor Roosevelt's own writings the most valuable are *This I Remember* (1949); *This Is My Story* (1937); *Autobiography* (1961); and *It's Up To The Women* (1933). She also wrote a monthly column, "If You Ask Me," for the *Ladies' Home Jour.* from June 1941 to spring 1949 and in *McCall's* after 1949. The best place to begin reading about her is Joseph Lash's excellent two-volume biography, *Eleanor and Franklin* (1971) and *Eleanor: The Years Alone* (1972). Other books that cast light upon the Roosevelt family include James Roosevelt, *My Parents: A Differing View* (1976), and Elliott Roosevelt, *An Untold Story* (1973), both of which offer personal views by the Roosevelt children. Another useful biography is Tamara Hareven, *Eleanor Roosevelt: An American Conscience* (1968).]

WILLIAM H. CHAFE

ROSENBERG, Ethel Greenglass, Sept. 28, 1915–June 19, 1953.

Ethel Rosenberg was born on the Lower East Side of New York City, the only daughter of Barnet and Tessie (Felt) Greenglass. Her mother was born in Austria; her father, born in Russia, had a home repair shop for sewing machines in the basement of their Sheriff Street tenement. Ethel had an older half brother, Samuel, and two younger brothers, Bernard and David. She died in the electric chair at Sing Sing prison at the age of thirty-seven, the day after her fourteenth wedding anniversary, accused of conspiracy to commit espionage and condemned by the testimony of David Greenglass and his wife, Ruth.

Growing up, Ethel Greenglass was ambitious to break away from her neighborhood; she dreamed of success as an actress and singer. She attended the local public schools before entering nearby Seward Park High School where, hoping to go to college, she took the general rather than clerical course. An excellent student, she was allowed to skip a year and graduated in 1931. From junior high school on, she sang and acted in school plays, despite her mother's bluntly voiced disapproval. Ethel Greenglass graduated into the depression, however; she enrolled in a six-month stenographic course and took a job, in the summer of 1931, with the National New York Shipping and Packing Company.

But she did not entirely abandon her ambitions. She joined the Clark House Players, an amateur theatrical group, and played several leading roles in her three years with them, including one as the sister of a man awaiting execution. Seeking ways to eke out her seven-dollar weekly salary, Ethel Greenglass also entered the amateur night competitions that were a feature of depression-era entertainment, singing on the Major Bowes circuit in theaters in New York and New Jersey. She continued to live at home, giving most of her salary to her mother, but managing to save enough to take singing lessons. Her greatest success was her acceptance as the youngest member of a professional choir, the Schola Cantorum.

As the depression deepened, Ethel Greenglass became increasingly involved in political action. She helped organize the union at the National Company and in August 1935 was on the strike committee and an active participant in what became a major city-wide strike for better wages and for recognition of the Ladies Apparel Shipping Clerks Union. Ethel Greenglass and other strike leaders were fired; in September she brought a complaint to the newly formed National Labor Relations Board which ruled five months later that she should be reinstated. By then, however, she was working as a stenographer for the Bell Textile Company.

In 1936, singing at a fund-raising rally for the International Seamen's Union, she met Julius Rosenberg, almost three years her junior and then an engineering student at the City College of New York. Like Ethel Greenglass, he had graduated young from Seward Park High School; he lived with his family, Jewish immigrants from Poland, less than a block from the Greenglasses. Rosenberg had been an outstanding student of Hebrew, and intensely religious. His idealism redirected by the case of Tom Mooney, the unjustly imprisoned California labor leader, he joined the Communist party sometime in the 1930s. By 1936 he was thinking of leaving college to devote his time to political action, but Ethel Greenglass urged him not to give up his chance for an education.

They married on June 18, 1939; Ethel Rosenberg later recalled "the turbulence and struggle, the joy and beauty of the early years . . . Together we hunted down the answers to all the seemingly insoluble riddles which a complex and callous society presented" (*Death House Letters*, p. 39). She continued to work at Bell Textile, and became a member of the women's auxiliary of her husband's union, the Federation of Architects, Engineers, Chemists and Technicians (FAECT); with the other women she helped to raise funds for children orphaned by the civil war in Spain. For some months in 1940 Ethel Rosenberg worked as a clerk-typist for the United States Bureau of the Census. In the fall of 1941 Julius Rosenberg received an appointment as a junior engineer with the United States Signal Corps, a job he held—with promotions—until 1945.

With this new position, Ethel Rosenberg's life also changed. She turned to volunteer activity, continuing to work with the FAECT auxiliary. Welcoming United States entry into World War II as a continuation of the left's fight against fascism, she joined the Lower East Side Defense Council, a volunteer civil defense organization. The Rosenbergs moved into Knickerbocker Village, a new low-cost housing project which remained their home for the rest of their lives together. Neighbors later told FBI agents that they stayed very much to themselves, and were very close: they "adore[d] each other," one observed. Ethel Rosenberg, another said, was "always poorly dressed"; she seemed to have "even less money" than other project residents.

With the birth of their first child, Michael, in 1943, Ethel Rosenberg's outside activities gradually ceased. She was ill for some months in 1944 and 1945, suffering from symptoms she attributed to a spinal curvature that had troubled her since childhood. By the time Robert was born, in 1947, the energies she had once given to acting and singing and to political work were turned almost entirely to home and family; there was little encouragement from the organized political movements on the left for women to take a public role. She took a course in child psychology at the New School for Social Research, learned to play the guitar, and attended a course on music for children at the Bank Street School.

Michael was high strung and difficult. Ethel Rosenberg feared that her anxieties and her permissiveness were at fault, and sought help for him in 1947 from a social worker at the Jewish Board of Guardians. This concern, as well as mounting pressure on the family because of their political activities and the continuing disapproval and rejection that had marked her relationship with her family, led her to seek psychiatric help for herself in 1949. Julius Rosenberg had been fired from the Signal Corps in 1945 on political grounds; he had been laid off later that year from a job with Emerson Radio. With David Greenglass, he attempted to start his own business, a machine shop. It was never successful, and they both lost money.

In 1950 Harry Gold, a Philadelphia chemist who claimed to be the United States contact for confessed British spy Klaus Fuchs, identified David Greenglass as his source of information in passing atomic secrets. Greenglass claimed that his brother-in-law had recruited him for espionage work. Julius Rosenberg was arrested in July 1950 and imprisoned.

After his arrest, Ethel Rosenberg had to conclude the business of the failed machine shop, care for her home, and try to quiet her children's anxieties. A woman with few friends, she was isolated, avoided by acquaintances and neighbors fearful of guilt by association; her only support came from her husband's family. On Aug. 2, 1950, she was called to appear before a Grand Jury. After her second appearance, nine days later, she too was arrested. Her bail was set at $100,000, and she was sent to the Women's House of Detention in New York City.

She remained there for eight months, with no specific charges brought to support her arrest as part of a "conspiracy to commit espionage." In July, James McInerney, head of the Justice Department's Criminal Division, had said there was not enough evidence to proceed against Ethel Rosenberg, although noting her potential usefulness as a lever against her husband (JR Headqtrs. file, vol. 3, no. 188). Not until February 1951 were any charges made; they came only from Ruth Greenglass, who, according to a summary report in the FBI files (the original interview has not appeared), claimed that Ethel Rosenberg had typed the information allegedly brought to her husband by David Greenglass (JR Headqtrs. file, vol. 18, no. 922). No such typed notes were ever produced as evidence in the trial, nor had there been any mention in David Greenglass's prior testimony of his sister's involvement. Ruth Greenglass admitted to complicity in the crime for which her husband was later convicted, but she was never indicted.

Knowing the weakness of their case against Ethel Rosenberg, the government yet persisted, hoping to force Julius Rosenberg to a confession. They hoped, too, to make an example of her. At a meeting of the Joint Congressional Committee on Atomic Energy on Feb. 8, 1951, United States Attorney Myles Lane acknowledged: "The case is not too strong against Mrs. Rosenberg. But for the purpose of acting as a deterrent, I think it is very important that she is convicted, too, and given a stiff sentence." She and Julius Rosenberg were brought to trial in March; they were convicted of conspiracy.

In April FBI Director J. Edgar Hoover recommended a thirty-year sentence for Ethel Rosenberg, because she was "the mother of two small children" and "would, in a sense, be presumed to be acting under the influence of her husband" (JR Headqtrs. file, vol. 19, no. 944). Assistant United States Attorney Roy Cohn favored the death penalty, but noted: "If Mrs. Rosenberg were sentenced to a prison term there was a possibility she would talk" (J. Edgar

Hoover to D. M. Ladd, April 3, 1951, *Kaufman Papers*). But trial judge Irving Kaufman had already determined on the death sentence for both the Rosenbergs (memo, A. H. Belmont to D. M. Ladd, March 16, 1951, JR Headqtrs. file, vol. 17, no. 894), and his decision remained.

The Rosenbergs continued to protest their innocence, as they did until the end of their lives. Ethel Rosenberg was held for two years in virtual solitary confinement at Sing Sing prison, the sole woman prisoner, her only companions the matrons assigned to guard her. She was allowed a weekly visit with her husband, with a wire mesh screen between them. After a year's absence, she began to see her children at infrequent intervals.

Ethel and Julius Rosenberg had to communicate mainly by letters; many of these were released for publication in an attempt to raise money for the support of their sons. Despite the sometimes self-conscious prose that marks what were at once private and public communications, Ethel Rosenberg's letters provide a passionate and articulate record of her torment over the loss of husband and children and her anxiety over her children's future. Her pride and anger are clear too (as they are in other documents of the Sing Sing years). She was subjected to great pressure from the government, from her mother and her brothers, and from press and public images of her as an unnatural mother and a domineering wife. (President Dwight D. Eisenhower justified his refusal to grant her clemency by claiming: "It is the woman who is the strong and recalcitrant character, the man is the weak one.") But she refused to accede to those pressures in order to save her life or provide her children with a mother.

The letters also reveal Ethel Rosenberg's passion to write. They provided an outlet long denied her to express herself to a listening public; at the beginning, she saw her imprisonment as an opportunity to serve as a symbol of those who were being victimized by anticommunist hysteria. Her hold on her emotional equilibrium was sometimes precarious, and she suffered periods of breakdown. Her psychiatrist was allowed to visit her and, at the end, she expressed her deep gratitude to him, wanting him to share her "triumph—For I have no fear and no regrets—only that the release from the trap was not completely effectuated and the qualities I possessed could not expand to their fullest capacities" (*We Are Your Sons*, pp. 265–66).

A series of legal appeals kept Julius and Ethel Rosenberg alive for two years after a sentence of death was passed. The courts refused to consider new evidence which was presented by defense lawyers, however, and the government refused to accede to the pleas for clemency which poured in from countries around the world. Ethel Rosenberg wrote on June 16, 1953, asking President Eisenhower as an "affectionate grandfather . . . sensitive artist . . . [and] devoutly religious man" (*We Are Your Sons,* pp. 252–55) to grant them their lives. He refused; she died three days later, telling her sons in her last letter to them: "Always remember that we were innocent and could not wrong our conscience."

[The files released by the FBI in connection with the Freedom of Information Act suit brought by the Rosenbergs' sons, Michael and Robert Meeropol, are at the office of the Fund for Open Information and Accountability, Inc. (FOIA) in N.Y. City; they can be seen by appointment. Quotations from FBI files (JR Headqtrs. file) are from material in the FOIA archive. FBI documents relating to Judge Kaufman's handling of the case were published in 1976 by the Nat. Committee to Reopen the Rosenberg Case as *The Kaufman Papers.* Unpublished letters are in the possession of the family. The trial transcript is on file at Fed. District Court for Southern N.Y. at Foley Square, *U.S.* v. *Rosenbergs, Sobell, Yakovley, and Greenglass* (Cr. No. 134–245). In 1952 the trial transcript was sold in book form by the Nat. Committee to Secure Justice in the Rosenberg Case; a microfilm of the transcript was published by the Fund for the Republic (1954). Selected letters were published as *Death House Letters* (1953); others appear in a book on the case by Robert and Michael Meeropol, *We Are Your Sons: The Legacy of Ethel and Julius Rosenberg* (1975). An important early book, Virginia Gardner, *The Rosenberg Story* (1954), gives biographical information on Ethel Rosenberg, as does an excellent article by Ellie Meeropol and Beth Schneider, "The Ethel Rosenberg Story," *Off Our Backs,* Sept.-Oct. 1975. The most thoroughly researched discussion of the case, which includes evidence of the Rosenbergs' innocence not introduced at the trial, is Walter and Miriam Schneir, *Invitation to an Inquest* (1973). Other books in support of the Rosenbergs are William A. Reuben, *The Atom Spy Hoax* (1954), an expanded version of his series of articles in the *National Guardian,* 1951–53; John Wexley, *The Judgment of Julius and Ethel Rosenberg* (1955); Malcolm D. Sharp, *Was Justice Done?* with an introduction by Harold C. Urey (1956); Alvan Goldstein, *The Unquiet Death of Julius and Ethel Rosenberg* (1975); and a book by the Rosenbergs' codefendant, Morton Sobell, *On Doing Time* (1974). Upholding their conviction are Louis Nizer, *The Implosion Conspiracy* (1973), and Jonathan Root, *The Betrayers* (1966). See also the article on Julius and Ethel Rosenberg in *Dict. Am. Biog.,* Supp. Five; Sol Stern and Ronald Radosh, "The Hidden Rosenberg Case," *New Republic,* June 23, 1979, which argues for Ethel Rosenberg's innocence of the charges against her; and Jon Steinberg, "The

Rosenbergs Framed Again," *Seven Days,* July 20, 1979.]

CAROL HURD GREEN

ROSENTHAL, Ida Cohen, Jan. 9, 1886–March 28, 1973. Manufacturing executive.

Ida Rosenthal was born in Rakov, near Minsk, Russia, the eldest of the four girls and three boys of Abraham and Sarah (Shapiro) Kaganovich. (The surname was changed to Cohen when the family came to the United States.) Her father was a Hebrew scholar and her mother kept a small general store to help support the family. At the age of sixteen Ida went to Warsaw, where she worked as a dressmaker, taking lessons in Russian and mathematics in her spare time. She left for the United States around 1904, following her sister Ethel and William Rosenthal, a young man who had left Russia to escape the tsarist draft. Her parents emigrated in 1909, and her father and three of her brothers organized A. Cohen & Sons of New York City, wholesalers of silverware, clocks, and cut glass.

An accomplished seamstress, Ida Cohen settled in Hoboken, N.J., and supported herself as a dressmaker. On June 10, 1906, she married William Rosenthal and together they continued in the dressmaking business. They had a son, Lewis (1907–1930), and a daughter, Beatrice, born in 1916. When they moved their dressmaking shop from Hoboken to New York's Washington Heights in 1918, they had some fifteen to twenty employees. In the early 1920s Enid Bissett, a friend of Ida Rosenthal, persuaded her to become a partner in a dress shop on fashionable Fifty-Seventh Street. The women, dissatisfied with the fit of their garments on the boyish figures that were then stylish, pioneered in designing the modern brassiere. To replace the plain strip of cloth with hooks at the back that was the brassiere of the day, Rosenthal and Bissett designed a garment, to be given away with their dresses, which had a few tucks that formed "cups" for the breasts. Since their customers returned to buy the giveaways, they went into the business of manufacturing them. Together with William Rosenthal they incorporated the Maiden Form Brassiere Company in 1923, with an initial investment of $4,500. (The name was changed to Maidenform, Inc. in 1960, to conform with the trade name of the company's product.) The Rosenthals held two-thirds of the common stock, Enid Bissett one-third. When poor health forced Bissett's retirement in the 1940s, the Rosenthals remained the principal managers. William Rosenthal, president of the company, was in charge of design, and, in the early years, of production as well. He created standard brassiere sizes which were the precursors of the A, B, C, and D cup sizes. Ida Rosenthal, treasurer of the company, managed sales and finances.

Under five feet in height, brown-eyed and vivacious, Ida Rosenthal was a dominant force in the business. A reporter later remarked that while others in the organization might "know design, or production, or standards . . . Mrs. R. knows everything" (*Fortune*, p. 130). The business was a success from the beginning. Sales increased each year in the 1920s. In 1924 the factory, having outgrown the New York premises, was moved to Bayonne, N.J. Maiden Form's growth in the 1930s owed much to the change in women's fashions: the boyish look was replaced by the softly curved female figure. But the success of the firm also rested upon careful management, innovative design, mass production, the introduction of a modified piecework system as an incentive to labor, and an aggressive sales organization.

By 1938 Maiden Form had annual gross earnings of more than $4,500,000, a figure that would reach $40,000,000 by 1964. During World War II Maiden Form was given priority in obtaining materials, Ida Rosenthal later claimed, because women workers who wore an "uplift" brassiere were less fatigued than those who did not. In the late 1940s, at the suggestion of Mary Filius, a copywriter for a New York advertising agency, the Rosenthals launched a highly successful twenty-year advertising campaign that featured young women dreaming of themselves in a variety of situations, dressed, above the waist, only in their Maidenform bras: "I dreamed I went shopping in my Maidenform bra," exclaimed the first of many models. At midcentury Maiden Form had 9,000 retail outlets, and its volume of sales was increasing by almost $1,000,000 yearly.

Upon the death of her husband in 1958 Ida Rosenthal became president of the company, and in 1959 chairman of the board. She also moved from their eighteen-room house on Long Island to a small Manhattan apartment, where she lived for the rest of her life.

In the 1960s Rosenthal spent much of her time traveling to keep in touch with Maidenform's worldwide interests in more than one hundred countries. She explained: "Quality we give them. Delivery we give them. I add personality" (*Time*, p. 92). With some 4,000 employees, the company had offices, plants, and warehouses in five states, Puerto Rico, Trinidad, England, and Canada. Maidenform expanded into sportswear in 1961. Two years later Ida Rosenthal went to the Soviet Union as a member of an industrial study exchange team, returning

home enthusiastic about future markets there. At the age of eighty, she was still making at least two business trips a year to Europe and elsewhere.

Ida Rosenthal also had many philanthropic interests. She and her husband founded Camp Lewis, a Boy Scout camp in Sussex County, N.J., established the Judaica and Hebraica Library at New York University, and contributed significantly to setting up the Albert Einstein College of Medicine of Yeshiva University. A director of the Bronx Lebanon Medical Center and of the Bayonne Industrial YMCA, she was in addition active for many years in the Anti-Defamation League of B'nai B'rith.

Over the years several family members worked for Maidenform, including Ida Rosenthal's daughter, Beatrice Coleman, who eventually took over the business. Ida Rosenthal died of pneumonia in New York City in 1973 at the age of eighty-seven, after several years' illness.

[The few published sources on Ida Rosenthal are often contradictory as to basic facts. For biographical information see *Nat. Cyc. Am. Biog.*, LVII, 339–40. Discussions of the development of Maidenform include "Maidenform's Mrs. R.," *Fortune*, July 1950, pp. 75–76ff.; "Ida Rosenthal," *Time*, Oct. 24, 1960, p. 92; and Caroline Bird, *Enterprising Women* (1976). Additional information came from the *N.Y. Times*, Dec. 9, 1965, and from scattered items in *Fortune*, *Newsweek*, and the *N.Y. Times*. The biographical sketch of William Rosenthal in *Nat. Cyc. Am. Biog.*, XLVIII, 41–42, and his obituary in *N.Y. Times*, April 14, 1958, were helpful. Ida Rosenthal's obituary appeared in the *N.Y. Times*, March 30, 1973. Assistance was provided by Beatrice Coleman and by Hyman J. Cohen, Ida Rosenthal's brother.]

IRENE D. NEU

ROSENTHAL, Jean, March 16, 1912–May 1, 1969. Lighting designer.

The start of Jean Rosenthal's career coincided with the beginnings of her profession. A pioneer in lighting design, she believed that "the most successful and brilliant work a lighting designer does is usually the least noticeable." Rosenthal considered hers a subservient art, a high craft serving the creative purposes of other artists. Nevertheless, she insisted that lighting affects "how you see what you see, how you feel about it, and how you hear what you are hearing."

She was born Eugenie Rosenthal in New York City, the only daughter and second of three children of Pauline (Scharfman) and Morris Rosenthal. Her parents, both the children of Jewish tailors, had emigrated from Rumania in the 1880s. Both were doctors of medicine, and

Pauline Rosenthal had an additional degree in psychiatry. Jean and her brothers attended in succession the Ethical Culture School in the Bronx, William Fincke's experimental Manumit School in Pawling, N.Y., and the Friends Seminary in Manhattan, from which she graduated in 1928. Rosenthal recalled that her parents encouraged her to take advantage of all that the city offered: she regularly attended the theater, opera, and symphony; she read the critics and columnists of the day; and she was infected by the excitement of innovations in music, dance, and painting.

To complete her schooling, Rosenthal did not go on to college, but enrolled in the Neighborhood Playhouse School of the Theatre (1929–30), although she had no idea what she wanted to do. Finding that she wanted neither to act nor to dance, Rosenthal became technical assistant to faculty member Martha Graham and discovered that she had what she called "a useful way of seeing things." She applied to George Pierce Baker, then teaching drama at Yale University, and after a five-minute interview he enrolled her in the drama program. There, from the lighting instructor Stanley McCandless, whom she called "the granddaddy of us all," she learned a "specific and orderly attitude" which demanded that "there *must be* a technique and a method for organizing" ideas in theater lighting.

Leaving Yale in 1933, Rosenthal was employed by the Federal Theatre Project as a technician in charge of wagon theaters in the New York City parks. The experience provided her with a thorough education in production and led to a job in another Federal Theatre group with producer John Houseman. Rosenthal followed Houseman when he took a leave of absence in 1936 to produce *Hamlet*, with Leslie Howard, and took over when the man who was to install the lighting fell ill. When, along with Houseman, Orson Welles, and the rest of the group, she was fired from the Federal Theatre Project, she became Welles's technician in charge of lighting for the Mercury Theatre. Within a year she was directing the production staff. Word soon spread in the profession that the stunning and original lighting for Welles's modern *Julius Caesar* (1937) had been created by the small, dark-haired woman with the huge blue eyes named Jean Rosenthal. In 1940, in order to ensure a steady income for herself, Rosenthal founded the Theatre Production Service, which supplied equipment and design for college and community theaters.

Her "professional home was always 'on Broadway,'" although her earliest and continuing association was with what she termed lyric rather than commercial theater. In addition to her work for the Mercury, Rosenthal designed the lighting for Martha Graham's dance company—to which she always gave first priority; the New York City Ballet and its predecessor, the Ballet Society; Gian Carlo Menotti's operas; and the opera season at New York's City Center. Her influence on lighting for the dance was worldwide. Instead of fixed light for visibility and a minimum change of color, which resulted in a two-dimensionally lit stage, she used side light to edge the bodies of dancers, giving them the quality of sculpture moving in space. She also introduced pale palettes of light which enhanced the beauty of the form, light cues which anticipated the movement of the dancers, and subtle transitions which helped the dancers appear effortless. Just as Martha Graham expanded dance tradition to create new forms, so Jean Rosenthal's lighting helped to transform the appearance of dance performances, including that of traditional European ballets.

As her reputation grew, Rosenthal was offered her choice of productions in the commercial theater. She made memorable contributions to such hits as *Becket* (1960) and the 1964 production of *Hamlet* with Richard Burton. Rosenthal worked with Mike Nichols on *The Odd Couple* (1965), *Plaza Suite* (1968), and *Luv* (1969), and with other directors. The formidable list of productions in which "lighting by Jean Rosenthal" was a mark of excellence also included the musicals *West Side Story* (1957), *Hello, Dolly!* (1964), *Fiddler on the Roof* (1964), and *Cabaret* (1966).

Outside New York, Rosenthal lit Shakespeare in Connecticut and opera in Dallas and Chicago. She also designed the lighting for buildings across the country, including the Pan American terminal at the John F. Kennedy Airport in New York and theaters in Canada and Australia as well as the United States. Of these she considered the Los Angeles Music Center to be the most successful and practical.

Rosenthal was a master of lighting techniques, but her most important contribution, widely adopted by her successors, was an attitude. She thought about each production as a whole, eschewing obtrusive effects, lighting the air in which actors moved rather than the scenery, underlining the dramatic mood of the moment. John Houseman credited her in large part with "bringing organization and order into the lighting of shows," and her system of writing cues so that the results could be repeated uniformly was copied throughout the profession.

During what time she had for it, her private life was happy, shared with a few cherished friends and enriched by a close relationship with her family. Marion Kinsella, an artist and her lighting assistant, shared Rosenthal's New York apartment and her house on Martha's Vineyard for many years. For recreation Rosenthal loved walking on country roads or the beach, and trips to Europe. Gourmet cooking was her hobby.

Jean Rosenthal died of cancer in New York in 1969. During the terminal days of her illness, she was taken in a wheelchair to the theater to carry out the last assignment she was able to fulfill, the lighting for a new dance created by Martha Graham. Many of her major contributions exist only in faulty memories and dusty work sheets, but before she died she began a collaboration on a book tracing her career and her ideas about lighting design. In *The Magic of Light* (1972) she wrote: "Lighting design, the imposing of quality on the scarcely visible air through which objects and people are seen, begins with *thinking* about it."

[The Jean Rosenthal Papers at the Wis. Center for Theater Research consist of lighting notes for a number of productions, 1949–61. There are some lighting plots and memorabilia in the Billy Rose Theatre Coll., N.Y. Public Library. All quotations in the article are from Jean Rosenthal and Lael Wertenbaker, *The Magic of Light* (1972). The research material and transcripts of the tapes Rosenthal made for the book are in the Lael Wertenbaker Coll., Mugar Library, Boston Univ. The fullest biographical account is Winthrop Sargeant, "Please, Darling, Bring Three to Seven," *New Yorker*, Feb. 4, 1956, pp. 33–59. Her career is chronicled in "Personality of the Month: Jean Rosenthal," *Dance Mag.*, Oct. 1959. John Houseman, *Run-Through* (1972) tells of his association with Rosenthal, including an account of her work on *The Cradle Will Rock. The Biog. Encyc. and Who's Who of the Am. Theatre* (1966) gives a nearly complete list of her credits. Her obituary appeared in the *N.Y. Times*, May 2, 1969. Additional information was supplied by her brother Leon Rosenthal.]

LAEL WERTENBAKER

RUBINSTEIN, Helena, Dec. 25, 1870–April 1, 1965. Entrepreneur, philanthropist.

From a legendary twelve pots of face cream, Helena Rubinstein created a multimillion dollar cosmetics industry; at one time she employed 30,000 people all over the world. Born in Cracow, Poland, she was the eldest of eight daughters (a brother died in infancy) of Augusta (Silberfeld) and Horace Rubinstein, an egg merchant. She attended the University of Cracow, studied medicine briefly in Switzerland, and around 1902 immigrated alone to Australia, where an uncle lived.

Rubinstein brought with her twelve pots of her mother's face cream, developed by chemist Jacob Lykusky. Australian acquaintances, impressed by her fair complexion, begged her so frequently for the cream that she obtained a loan and opened a modest shop in Melbourne. Besides selling her "Creme Valaze," she instructed women individually on the art of proper skin care, an innovation at that time. Her shop prospered because of the praise of well-known clients, and Rubinstein never forgot the value of publicity and personal endorsement. Phenomenally energetic, she worked eighteen hours a day, setting a pattern for life. She loved her work with a passion not often directed to other areas of her life, and came to believe that she was "confident and relaxed only in business" (*My Life for Beauty*, p. 39).

By 1908 her sister Ceska had joined her in Australia to take over management of the business. Helena Rubinstein sailed for London with $100,000 in capital to begin what would become an international organization. To broaden her knowledge of cosmetics, she studied briefly in Paris with a dermatologist, and then in Vienna under Emmie Litz, who returned with her to the fashionable salon she had established in a London mansion. Impressed by the vivid decors of Léon Bakst and Alexandre Benois for the Ballet Russe, Rubinstein adopted their electric color combinations when decorating her salons.

In 1908 Rubinstein married American journalist Edward Titus; they had two sons, Roy (b. 1909) and Horace (b. 1912). The family moved to Paris where Rubinstein opened another salon, but with the coming of World War I, they fled to the United States (1915). They bought a home in Greenwich, Conn., and lodged the two children in boarding schools; Rubinstein then opened a new salon in New York City. By 1917 she had salons in San Francisco, Boston, and Philadelphia, and department stores clamored for her preparations. With the postwar eagerness to try new things, her business expanded. Movie and theater stars helped launch new beauty trends, and Madame, as she was known, created the vamp look for THEDA BARA.

In 1918 Rubinstein and her husband returned to her business in Paris. Edward Titus founded Black Mannequin Press, which published D. H. Lawrence and other modern writers; Rubinstein entered the world of art, beginning to amass what became tremendous collections of paintings, sculpture, and jewelry. Their apartment became a center for artists seeking commissions, among them Braque, Modigliani, Chagall, and Dufy. The sculptor Jacob Epstein introduced her to African sculpture, a lifelong interest. Rubinstein bought art and jewelry indiscriminately and in vast quantities, explaining, "I'm a business woman, I'm used to buying in bulk" (James, p. 41). In 1942 Salvador Dali painted her chained by ropes of emeralds to a high rock, enslaved by her possessions, an interpretation that Madame vigorously disputed. She was, in fact, surprisingly casual with her treasures, and once kept a million dollars' worth of jewelry (some once owned by Catherine of Russia) in a cardboard dress box beneath her bed.

Not a classic beauty, Rubinstein was small (four feet ten) and elegant. She wore her black hair in a severe chignon; dressed in high fashion, she loved masses of jewelry and crimson lipstick and nail polish. Her manners were often earthy, and her behavior paradoxical; although capable of great acts of generosity, she carried her lunch in a brown paper bag and practiced strange and irrational economies in her household.

Rubinstein's marriage faltered in the late twenties and she was divorced in 1937 or 1938. She blamed the breakdown on her devotion to business: "I realize what a failure I must have been at that time as a wife, even as a mother" (*My Life for Beauty*, p. 72). In an attempt to slow down she sold her American business to a Wall Street firm, Lehman Bros., only to buy it back a year later after the Wall Street crash, for a fraction of its cost.

Although Rubinstein never followed prescribed beauty routines herself, because "it takes time and time is one thing I haven't got" (James, p. 38), she was brilliant and innovative in developing a business based on these routines. She instituted a program to train salesgirls to teach women skin care, devised a diet plan for beauty modeled on her personal experience at a Swiss health spa, and inaugurated a "Day of Beauty" at her salons, in which clients underwent a full eight hours of reconditioning. Rubinstein also developed medicated skin creams and waterproof mascara, but her emphasis on the medicinal value of her preparations led her into conflict with the Food and Drug Administration. She loved innovative promotional techniques, excelling in the use of colorful stunts, decorative motifs, and imaginative packaging. Rubinstein's feud with ELIZABETH ARDEN, who also maintained a salon on Fifth Avenue, was legendary; it took a baroque turn in 1938 when Arden hired away Rubinstein's general manager and eleven members of his staff, and Madame retaliated by hiring Arden's ex-husband, Thomas J. Lewis.

Once described as a "matriarch . . . both mother and ruler of the tribe" (James, p. 43), Rubinstein took many members of her family into the business, including several sisters, a nephew, a niece, and her son Roy. In 1938 she married Prince Artchil Gourielli-Tchkonia, a Russian prince twenty years her junior, and established a male cosmetics line bearing his name. Gourielli died in 1956; her son Horace died two years later.

Rubinstein was active in philanthropic causes and was particularly generous to Israel. She founded the Helena Rubinstein Pavilion of Contemporary Art in Tel Aviv where her exquisite collection of miniature rooms is housed. The Helena Rubinstein Foundation, created in 1953, gave funds to organizations concerned with health, medical research, and rehabilitation, supported the America-Israel Cultural Foundation, and provided scholarships for Israelis.

In 1959 Helena Rubinstein officially represented the United States cosmetics industry at the American National Exhibition in Moscow. She never retired: in her last years, when her health began to fail, she often conducted business meetings from her lucite bed, its headboard and footboard illuminated with fluorescent lighting. She died in New York City in April 1965, at ninety-four.

[Rubinstein's autobiography, *My Life for Beauty* (1964) is informative. Patrick O'Higgins, *Madame* (1971) emphasizes the last ten years of her life when he was her personal assistant; it is entertaining, but gossip-strewn and often unreliable. Maxine Fabe, *Beauty Millionaire* (1972), is a children's book. For further biographical information see T. F. James, "Princess of the Beauty Business," *Cosmopolitan*, June 1959; Jo Swerling, "Beauty in Jars and Vials," *New Yorker*, June 30, 1928; and *Current Biog.*, 1943. Other sources include "We Can't All Be Beautiful," *American Mag.*, June 1936; "Helena Rubinstein in Her Paris Home," *House and Garden*, Jan. 1938; H. Bauer, "Beauty Tycoon," *Collier's*, Dec. 4, 1948; "Beauty's Handmaiden," Jan. 26, 1953, and "Beauty Merchant," April 9, 1965, both in *Time*; "Madame," *Newsweek*, April 12, 1965; and two articles in *Life*, "Madame Rubinstein, the Little Lady from Krakow," July 21, 1941, and "A Tiny, Tireless Tycoon of Beauty," May 15, 1964. Articles on Rubinstein's art collection include G. O'Donnell, Feb., April, and July 1957, and S. A. Parvin, "Miniature Rooms of Helena Rubinstein," May and July 1965, all in *Hobbies*; and "Imaginary U.S.A.," *Look*, Oct. 20, 1953. Although Rubinstein's birth date is sometimes given as 1882, she confirms the 1870 date in her autobiography. An obituary appeared in the *N.Y. Times*, April 2, 1965.]

ALMA L. KENNEY

RUDKIN, Margaret Fogarty, Sept. 14, 1897–June 1, 1967. Businesswoman.

Margaret Rudkin, who at forty started the Pepperidge Farm bakeries with a few loaves of home-baked whole wheat bread, was born in

New York City, the oldest of the five children of Joseph I. and Margaret (Healy) Fogarty. While she later claimed that her mother "never even boiled an egg," Margaret learned something about good food and its preparation as a girl from her Irish grandmother, with whom the family lived in a narrow, four-story brownstone house in the Tudor City area of Manhattan. Her grandmother died when Margaret was twelve and the family moved to Flushing, Long Island, where she attended public schools, graduating as valedictorian of her high school class. She then went to work as a bookkeeper for a small local bank, the first woman hired there, and prepared herself for a business career.

In 1919 Margaret Fogarty moved to the firm of McClure, Jones & Co., member of the New York Stock Exchange. There she dealt directly with customers and met Henry Albert Rudkin, a polo-playing partner in the firm; twelve years her senior, he shared her New York origins and Irish descent. The two were married on April 8, 1923, and had three sons: Henry Jr. (b. 1924), William (b. 1926), and Mark (b. 1929). Prospering on Wall Street, the Rudkins purchased 125 acres near Fairfield, Conn., built a Tudor mansion there, and christened their estate after an old pepperidge tree which stood on the grounds.

In its early days, Pepperidge Farm boasted a garage for five automobiles and stables for twelve horses. The Rudkins' devotion to hunts and horse shows was curtailed by the depression, however, and by a serious polo accident that forced Henry Rudkin to be away from work for six months. Margaret Rudkin sold the horses and all but one automobile, dismissed her full-time servants, and sought new ways to raise money on the farm, starting with homegrown apples and turkeys.

Margaret Rudkin began baking bread at Pepperidge Farm in 1937. According to one popular account, she made her first loaf as part of a special diet for her youngest son's asthma, following a doctor's suggestion that chemical additives in commercially baked bread might be aggravating his condition. (In her official account of Pepperidge Farm, written in 1962, Rudkin notes simply that the bakery grew out of her "interest in proper food for children.") Relying only on cookbooks, she set out to make stone-ground whole wheat bread: her initial effort was "as hard as rock and about one-inch high." Eventually Rudkin arrived at a formula that pleased both family and friends, and in the summer of 1937 she went into business. In August she sold her first batch of loaves wholesale to her own grocer in Fairfield.

Because her recipe relied on fresh, relatively expensive ingredients, like butter and whole milk, Rudkin's bread initially sold at more than twice the price of its mass-produced competitors. Yet demand grew quickly, enabling her to hire several more workers that fall and move the baking from the kitchen to a corner of the garage. There she began to make white bread of unbleached flour, testing the product on the manager of Charles & Co., a famous specialty food store in New York City; she came away with an order for twenty-four loaves a day, delivered personally for the first few weeks to Grand Central Station by Henry Rudkin on his way to Wall Street.

The early success of Rudkin's bakery was closely tied to publicity. Her bread received its first important notice on Nov. 20, 1937, with an article in the *New York Journal and American,* "Society Woman Turns Baker to Supply Elite With Healthful Bread." Enthusiastic articles followed in the New York press from the *Herald Tribune's* Emma Bugbee and the *World Telegram's* Helen Worden, who described the bread's creator as "slim and sophisticated, with gorgeous red hair, green eyes and a milk-white skin." The single most important boost for Pepperidge Farm, though, was J. D. Ratcliff's article, "Bread, de Luxe," which appeared in the December 1939 issue of *Reader's Digest* and yielded Rudkin orders from all over the United States, Canada, and several foreign countries. On the strength of an expanding reputation, she borrowed $15,000 in 1940 to move the bakery from Pepperidge Farm proper to a former auto salesroom and hospital in Norwalk, Conn. Weekly volume exceeded 50,000 loaves there the first year, with white bread the major item, although the company continued to produce whole wheat bread and add to its roster of baked goods.

Over the next two decades, Pepperidge Farm grew to become a major national firm. Henry Rudkin gradually gave up his Wall Street activities to handle finances and marketing as chairman of the company, while Margaret Rudkin served as president, overseeing the bakery's daily operations. In 1947 production shifted to a new $625,000 plant in Norwalk, and plants were later opened in Pennsylvania (1949) and Illinois (1953). Pepperidge Farm began advertising nationally in the 1950s, with Margaret Rudkin appearing in television commercials. She also played a part in two important acquisitions during the decade, purchasing a frozen pastry line from a firm in New Hampshire and cookie recipes from the Delacre company of Belgium.

In 1960 the Rudkins sold their business to the Campbell Soup Company. Pepperidge Farm had then reached profits of $1,300,000 on annual sales of $32,000,000, assets the Rudkins exchanged for Campbell stock worth about $28,000,000. Under the agreement, Margaret Rudkin became a director of Campbell Soup while continuing to run Pepperidge Farm. In 1962 she yielded the presidency to her son William and succeeded her husband as chairman, a post she held until September 1966, five months after her husband's death. Ill with breast cancer, for which she had first undergone surgery in 1956, Margaret Rudkin died in June 1967 at the Yale-New Haven Hospital.

Margaret Rudkin brought to Pepperidge Farm both her commercial flair and a consuming interest in the product. While servants helped her at times with the housework, she frequently did her own cooking and her fondness for food led her to collect ancient cookbooks. In 1957 the company's 1,000 employees (who were paid somewhat more than similar workers elsewhere) contributed a dollar each and celebrated the bakery's twentieth anniversary by buying her a copy of the fifteenth-century classic *De Honesta Voluptate et Valetudine*. She drew on this later in writing *The Margaret Rudkin Pepperidge Farm Cookbook* (1963), which became a best seller. In the months before her death, Rudkin donated her cookbook collection to the Pequot Library in Southport and made generous gifts as well to the Yale-New Haven Hospital and other institutions. The Rudkin tradition of quiet generosity extended to individuals as well, notably Benjamin Sonnenberg, the publicity man who suggested the 1939 *Reader's Digest* article. In addition to employing him on the usual fee basis, Margaret and Henry Rudkin gave him a 5 percent interest in the business. By 1960, this was worth more than $1,000,000.

[*The Margaret Rudkin Pepperidge Farm Cookbook* (1963, 1970) includes an autobiographical account. Rudkin also describes the origins and growth of her bakery in the 25th anniversary issue of *The Conveyor*, published by Pepperidge Farm in 1962. See also the March 1973 issue of *The Conveyor*, which traces the history of the company over thirty-five years. Other accounts of Rudkin's life and career include: "Rudkin of Pepperidge," *Time*, July 14, 1947; John Bainbridge, "Striking a Blow for Grandma," *New Yorker*, May 22, 1948; W. B. Hartley, "The Story of Pepperidge Bread," *Coronet*, Aug. 1953; *Current Biog.*, 1959; "Champion of the Old Fashioned," *Time*, March 21, 1960; "Pepperidge Farm Sold to Campbell Soup," *N.Y. Times*, Nov. 18, 1960; and "Mrs. Rudkin Revisited," *New Yorker*, Nov. 16, 1963. An obituary appeared in *N.Y. Times*, June 2, 1967; death certificate furnished by Conn. Dept. of Health.]

TOM MAHONEY

RUSSELL, Jane Anne, Feb. 9, 1911–March 12, 1967. Biochemist, endocrinologist.

Jane Anne Russell was born in Los Angeles County in what is now Watts, Calif., the youngest of five children (three girls and two boys) of Josiah Howard and Mary Ann (Phillips) Russell. Her parents, both of English descent, were poor; they had moved to California at the turn of the century, probably from Maryland. Josiah Russell worked at ranching, served as deputy sheriff, and built a homestead near Los Angeles.

An outstanding student, especially proficient in mathematics, Jane Russell went for two years to Polytechnic High School in Long Beach; she graduated in 1928, second in her class. She entered the University of California at Berkeley at seventeen and graduated first in her class four years later. For her outstanding achievement she received the Kraft Prize, a Phi Beta Kappa key, a Stewart Scholarship, and the University Gold Medal.

Entering the graduate school at Berkeley, Russell at first supported herself by working as a technician for the chairman of the biochemistry department, Edward S. Sundstroem. In 1934, however, she received the California Fellowship in Biochemistry, and the Rosenberg Fellowship the following year. She was also accepted as a Ph.D. candidate in the Institute of Experimental Biology under Herbert M. Evans, who was directing massive research programs on vitamins and hormones. Under the supervision of Leslie L. Bennett, Russell was assigned to investigate the role of pituitary hormones in carbohydrate metabolism. By the time she received her doctorate in 1937 she had already published six papers on the subject, with several more in press. Particularly influential was an article in *Physiological Reviews* on the relation of the anterior pituitary to carbohydrate metabolism (1938). Her interest in carbohydrates led her to collaborate with Carl and GERTY CORI at Washington University, St. Louis, Mo.

After receiving her degree, Russell stayed at the Institute for another year supported by a Porter Fellowship from the American Physiological Society. In 1938 she moved to Yale University as a National Research Council Fellow. Already a recognized world authority in her field, she had demonstrated that during periods of carbohydrate deprivation some unknown pituitary factor (later shown to be growth hormone) was necessary to maintain adequate levels of tissue carbohydrate, including blood glucose. Russell's pioneering contributions demonstrated the existence of checks and balances which govern carbohydrate metabolism, and laid a foundation for future studies on the mechanisms of body growth, maintenance, and breakdown.

Jane Russell had an extraordinarily lucid and disciplined mind, in part a result of her early mathematical training. Her particular genius lay in devising relatively simple experiments capable of yielding decisive answers to important questions. At Yale, in the department of physiological chemistry under C. N. H. Long, she continued her studies on the hormonal regulation of carbohydrate metabolism for the next twelve years. Her most important contribution was to show that the carbohydrate regulating activity of pituitary extracts was contained in the growth hormone discovered by H. M. Evans and prepared in crystalline form by Alfred Ellis Wilhelmi, a close collaborator whom she married on Aug. 26, 1940.

Russell worked first with the aid of two fellowships, and then from 1941 to 1950 as an instructor. Her lack of formal recognition by Yale became a much-cited example of academic discrimination against women, especially after Russell had received the prestigious Ciba Award in 1946 for hormonal studies as well as other distinctions usually reserved for full professors. Starting in 1949 she participated in the peer-review system of research grant applications to the National Institutes of Health (NIH) and in 1950 she served as vice president of the Endocrine Society.

Russell and Wilhelmi moved to Emory University in Atlanta, Ga., in 1950, he as professor and chairman of the department of biochemistry and she as assistant professor. Thus started a decade of great activity for Russell. In the laboratory, she extended her studies on the metabolic effects of growth hormone to nitrogen metabolism; her results led her to theorize that this hormone was needed not only for growth in the young, but also for preventing the breakdown of essential structural proteins—a concept shown to be correct by later studies. An outstanding teacher as well as researcher, she developed a remarkable clarity of style as a lecturer and took great pride in her students.

Russell wielded substantial influence in science-policy organizations and received much public recognition. She served on the NIH study section on metabolism and endocrinology (1950–54) and on the National Research Council Committee for the Evaluation of Post-Doctoral Fellowships (1955–58), and was a member of the National Science Board—a major honor. In 1961 she shared the Upjohn Award of the Endocrine Society with Alfred Wilhelmi, and that year was also designated Woman of the Year in Professions in Atlanta. In 1958 she was elected to the editorial board of the American Physiological Society, and became section editor for metabolism and endocrinology in 1962.

Despite her more than seventy publications and numerous other accomplishments, formal academic recognition was slow in coming. Though promoted to associate professor in 1953 —already a belated move—promotion to full professor eluded her for another twelve years; when it finally came in 1965, she was fatally ill. She died of mammary cancer in Atlanta in 1967, after five years of painful illness.

Jane Russell greatly valued her marriage and her home; she was close to her family and cared for her aged mother. Skilled in gardening and sewing, she was a virtuoso knitter, whose sweaters were almost as famous as her laboratory work. She possessed extensive knowledge about California, and retained a lifelong love for her native state.

[The Archives at Emory Univ. contain a file of clippings, a curriculum vitae, and a list of publications. Some letters from Russell to Herbert M. Evans are in the Manuscript Div., Bancroft Library, Univ. of Calif., Berkeley. Information about Russell's life can be found in C. N. H. Long, "In Memoriam: Jane A. Russell," *Endocrinology*, Oct. 1967; J. R. K. Preedy, "Jane Russell Wilhelmi (1911–1967)," Memorial Oration, Durham Chapel, Emory Univ., March 15, 1967; Jay Tepperman, "Remembering Jane," read on the occasion of the first Jane Russell Wilhelmi Memorial Lecture, Emory Univ., March 19, 1976; and an entry in *Who Was Who in America*, IV (1968). Alfred E. Wilhelmi provided useful information.]

I. D. RAACKE

RYAN, Anne, July 20, 1889–April 18, 1954. Artist.

Anne Ryan was born in Hoboken, N.J., the oldest of four children and only daughter of John and Elizabeth (Soran) Ryan. Her father, a prosperous Irish Catholic banker who wrote poetry in his spare time, died in 1902. Her mother had committed suicide a year earlier; the children were brought up by their grandmother. Also in 1904, when she was fourteen, Anne Ryan enrolled at the Academy of St. Elizabeth's Convent, in Convent Station, N.J. She completed preparatory school there and continued into St. Elizabeth's College. In 1911, she left college to marry a young law student, William J. McFadden.

Twin children, William and Elizabeth, were born the next year; a third child, Thomas, was born in 1919. After some years of strain, caused in part by her desire to live in a world beyond the domestic circle, the McFaddens were legally separated in 1923. Ryan (who resumed her maiden name) wrote poems, worked on a novel, and spent time with artists in New York City's Greenwich Village; she published a volume of poetry, *Lost Hills*, in 1925.

Leaving her children in school in the United States, Ryan went in 1931 to Majorca, her first and only visit to Europe. She chose Majorca not only because it was beautiful and unspoiled but also because it was an inexpensive place to live. In her two years abroad, she wrote poems, stories, and articles, some of which appeared in *The Literary Digest* and *Commonweal*, and worked on a full-length study—never published —of Fra Junipero Serra. Her twins joined her for the summer of 1932 and with them she traveled to Paris, where for the first time she saw a wide variety of contemporary painting.

Forced by the economic pressure of the depression to leave Spain in 1933, Ryan returned to the United States and lived with her younger son in Greenwich Village. She continued to write, and for a time supported herself by running a restaurant. Increasingly she became interested in painting, as she came to know the work of the many gifted young artists who lived in the Village during the days of the Federal Arts Project and the American Abstract Artists group. Almost fifty, she began to paint in response to the excitement around her. Her efforts were encouraged by her friends Hans Hofmann and Tony Smith. In 1941 Ryan joined Atelier XVII, the printmaking workshop which the British surrealist Stanley William Hayter had moved to New York from Paris at the outbreak of World War II. There she encountered the work of sophisticated European artists, and was much influenced by the biomorphic linear abstraction which characterized Hayter's own work at the time. She produced a number of woodblock prints and engravings during this period.

The chief turning point in Ryan's artistic development was her exposure in 1948 to the collages of the German master Kurt Schwitters shown at the Rose Fried Gallery shortly after his death early in 1948. Ryan was enormously excited by Schwitters's use of materials, by the way material fragments could be transposed into abstract form, and by the power that could be communicated on such a small scale. Immediately she began to collect materials and to experiment with the medium.

Ryan's first works reflected the Schwitters influence most directly, in that she used bits of such everyday things as postage stamps and tickets—fragments of printed and pictorial mat-

ter—to make her compositions. Gradually, however, she developed a repertory of materials which became distinctly individual: very fine papers—including the handmade papers of Douglas Howell—and a range of textiles, printed or plain but always with a distinctive weave and texture. With these she worked for the next six years until her death, producing a large body of abstract compositions.

Many of her works were very small, in contrast to the big, overall painting most characteristic of the milieu in which she worked, but they possessed an individual voice and authority. Ryan's discovery of her own materials, and of the aptness of collage to her sense of a mystical perfection lying beyond consciousness, lent a new, personal dimension to the medium. Her work, Hilton Kramer noted, had "the air of a private communication, of something confided with affection and delicacy" (*N.Y. Times*, Feb. 3, 1968, p. 25).

During the 1940s and early 1950s, Ryan participated in exhibitions in New York and elsewhere, including the Whitney Annual (1951, 1953), the Brooklyn Museum Print Annual (1947–53), and the 1951 exhibition of "Abstract Painting and Sculpture in America" at the Museum of Modern Art. In 1950 she joined the gallery of Betty Parsons, noted as one of the early supporters of avant-garde art. During this period Anne Ryan also continued to write, and in the fifties several stories were published: "Fear" in *Botteghe Oscure*, 10 (1952); "She Was Divorced" in *Folder* (1954); "Liedrica" in *Paris Review*, 5 (1954); and "The Darkest Leaf," published posthumously in *Botteghe Oscure*, 22 (1958). Her stories comment on the conflict between the sacred and the mundane; they possess, in Donald Windham's words, "the fault, or virtue, of viewing contemporary events as though they are timeless." In a 1942 journal Ryan, looking back on the stories she once wrote, had noted: "I have had the best agent in New York and yet she has never been able to place a single line anywhere. I still believe" (quoted in Windham, p. 271).

It is as a visual artist, however, most particularly in the medium of collage, that Anne Ryan made her chief contribution and it is her collages that earn her a place in the history of American art. Looking back on her work the poet John Ashbery saw it as part of "the way of American art"; comparing her compositions to the work of Charles Ives, John Cage, and MARIANNE MOORE, he noted that Ryan's art also goes "beyond 'mysteries of construction' . . . into mysteries of being which, it turns out, have their own laws of construction" (Ashbery, p. 74).

In her last years Anne Ryan shared a house

in Greenwich Village with her daughter. She
suffered a stroke in the spring of 1954 and died
in April at her son's home in Morristown, N.J.

[Ryan's papers at the Archives of Am. Art, Washington, D.C., include correspondence, notebooks, MSS.,
documents, and an unpublished memoir by her
daughter, Elizabeth McFadden. The catalog of the
exhibition *Anne Ryan Collages,* Brooklyn Museum,
March 13–April 21, 1974, contains an introduction

by Sarah Faunce, a chronology, a list of exhibitions,
and a bibliography. Donald Windham, "A Note on
Anne Ryan," *Botteghe Oscure,* 22 (1958), has biographical information as well as commentary on her
writing. See also John Ashbery, "A Place for Everything," *ART News,* March 1970, and a review of the
1974 exhibition by Peter Frank in *Art in America,*
Sept. 1974. Elizabeth McFadden provided helpful
information.]

SARAH C. FAUNCE

S

SAARINEN, Aline Milton Bernstein, March 25,
1914–July 13, 1972. Art critic, television commentator.

Aline Saarinen was born in New York City,
the only daughter and the middle of three children of Allen Milton and Irma (Lewyn) Bernstein, both amateur painters. Her father, a native of New York City, headed an investment
and industrial counseling firm. Bernstein's parents encouraged her to pursue artistic and cultural interests. In the twenty-fifth anniversary
report of his Harvard class, her father described
his family as "high-brow"; he also noted that
Aline's ambition at fourteen was to be the Jane
Austen of her day. She later remembered her
girlhood goal as wanting to be "intelluptuous."
On her first trip to Europe, when she was nine,
her older brother, Charles, introduced her to the
splendors of French châteaus and Gothic ca-
thedrals; it was the beginning of a lifelong
commitment to art and architecture.

Bernstein attended the Fieldston School in
New York City, graduated in 1931, and went
on to Vassar College where the art courses she
took with John McAndrew and Agnes Rindge
were influential in her choice of a career. She
was also active in campus journalism. An excellent student, she was elected to Phi Beta
Kappa in her junior year, awarded a Vassar
College Fellowship, and graduated with an
A.B. in 1935.

Almost immediately after graduation, on June
17, 1935, Aline Bernstein married Joseph H.
Louchheim, a public welfare administrator; they
had two sons, Donald (b. 1937) and Harry (b.
1939). She enrolled in the fall of 1935 at the
Institute of Fine Arts, New York University,
and graduated in 1941 with an A.M. in the history of architecture. During World War II she
put aside a career in art to serve as executive
secretary of the Allegheny County Rationing

Board in Pittsburgh and to work as a Red Cross
nurse's aide in Washington, D.C., while her husband served in the navy.

In February 1944, having returned with her
family to New York City, Aline Louchheim
joined the staff of *Art News* magazine; from
1946 to 1948 she was its managing editor. She
later claimed she had been given the job because
she could spell the name of the fifteenth-century
artist "Pollaiuolo." Her solid preparation in art
and journalism and her tremendous drive and
energy were the more likely causes, however.
In 1946 the magazine sponsored a book, *5000
Years of Art: A Pictorial History,* with commentary by Aline Louchheim. It was warmly praised
in the *New York Times* (March 23, 1947) as a
reflection of her personal experience rather than
a catalog of art. In December 1947, she became
associate art editor and art critic for the *Times.*
During the next several years, she wrote on such
topics as abstract art, the role of museums, and
advertising in relation to art collecting for the
Times, Atlantic Monthly, House Beautiful, and
other publications. For her discussions of works
of art as interpretations of the period in which
they were made, she received significant accolades, including the International Award for
Best Foreign Criticism at the Venice Biennale
(1951) and the American Federation of Arts
Award for best newspaper criticism (1953).

Aline and Joseph Louchheim were divorced
in 1951. Two years later she interviewed the
noted Finnish-born architect Eero Saarinen,
then at the beginning of an extraordinary period during which he designed such buildings
as the General Motors Technical Center in Warren, Mich. (1948–1956), and the Dulles International Terminal outside Washington, D.C.
(1958–1962). In an admiring article, Louchheim
praised him for "giving form or visual order to
the industrial civilization to which he belongs
. . . His buildings [have] become an expression

613

of our way of life." They were attracted to one another personally and, after Saarinen divorced his wife, they married in 1954. She moved to Bloomfield Hills, Mich., where his architectural firm had its headquarters, changed her by-line at the *Times* to Aline B. Saarinen, and became associate art critic, a status she retained until 1959. In December 1954, they had a son, Eames, named for the designer Charles Eames.

The years with Eero Saarinen were productive for both. His office underwent tremendous expansion and he was busy designing the best buildings of his career. From 1954 to 1963 Aline Saarinen did public relations for his firm. With the aid of a Guggenheim fellowship awarded in 1957, she wrote *The Proud Possessors* (1958), a biographical study of major American art collectors whom she interpreted as paradigms of taste for their respective periods. It became a best seller and launched Aline Saarinen as a public personality.

Eero Saarinen died unexpectedly in September 1961, leaving ten major buildings under construction. Aline Saarinen moved with the firm to New Haven, Conn., a change planned before his death, and became in a sense the public guardian of her husband's reputation. In 1962 she published *Eero Saarinen on His Work*.

Aline Saarinen's third career began when she was almost fifty. She came into television, she later noted, by the "backdoor of art," having been asked in 1962 to appear on television to discuss Rembrandt's "Aristotle Contemplating the Bust of Homer" which the Metropolitan Museum of Art had recently purchased at an exorbitant price. Her informal and engaging manner, and her ability to be "highbrow without being highblown," led to more interviews and eventually to a career as a television art critic. Her association with Eero Saarinen no doubt contributed to her aura, but, as she stated, her success was due "25% to Eero and 75% to me." In the fall of 1963 she became the art and architecture editor for the new "Sunday" show on the National Broadcasting Company (NBC) network and art critic for the daily "Today" show. With her usual verve she discussed topics from city planning to postage stamp design, and made such flamboyant gestures as listing the six worst manmade objects. She also won wide acclaim for her numerous specials and documentaries such as "The Art of Collecting" (NBC, Jan. 19, 1964).

In October 1964 Saarinen became the third woman correspondent for NBC News, following Pauline Fredericks and Nancy Dickerson. Outspoken and authoritative, she turned her skill for trenchant observation to diverse topics, ranging from presidential inaugurations to economic discrimination against women. As the moderator of "For Women Only," a panel show with questions from the audience, Saarinen dealt with such timely issues as abortion and birth control. In 1971, she was named chief of NBC's Paris News Bureau. The first woman ever to head an overseas television news bureau, she held the position until her death. She thrived on the intensity and total involvement her career demanded, once commenting that the "pace is dreadful. You almost have to be a widow to do it."

Saarinen received many honors, including two honorary degrees. She was the only woman member of the Fine Arts Commission in Washington, D.C. In 1964, President Lyndon Johnson offered her the post of ambassador to Finland, but she declined.

Aline Saarinen died of a brain tumor in New York City in July 1972. In a 1966 lecture at Vassar she had commented that while "everyone is exposed to the raw material of experience, not everyone contends with it, not everyone imposes his style upon it." Saarinen not only created her own style but in so doing also played an important role as a translator of art and culture for the American public.

[Aline Saarinen's papers are at the Archives of Am. Art, Washington, D.C. They have not been microfilmed and are restricted for an unspecified period. For biographical information see *Current Biog.*, 1956, pp. 534–35; Joan Walker, "Women and the News," *Cue*, Aug. 14, 1965; "Art Expert or TV Personality?" an interview with Saarinen in the *N.Y. Post*, April 25, 1970; and articles in *Time*, July 2, 1956, and Nov. 3, 1967, and *Newsweek*, June 21, 1965. Eero Saarinen's obituary was in the *N.Y. Times*, Sept. 6, 1961; see also Allen Temku, *Eero Saarinen* (1962) and Rupert Spade, *Eero Saarinen* (1971). Obituaries of Aline Saarinen appeared in the *Wash. Post* and the *N.Y. Times*, both July 15, 1972. Memorial articles appeared in the *N.Y. Times*, July 23 (by John Canaday), Sept. 13, and Sept. 15, 1972.]

MARGARET SUPPLEE SMITH

SABIN, Florence Rena, Nov. 9, 1871–Oct. 3, 1953. Physician, medical researcher.

Florence Sabin was born in Central City, Colo., the second of two daughters of Serena (Miner) and George K. Sabin, who had both migrated from New England to the Colorado mining country. Two younger brothers died in infancy. Florence spent her early childhood in mining communities where her father worked as an engineer. Following her mother's death shortly after childbirth on Florence's seventh birthday, she and her sister, Mary, lived with relatives in Chicago and then Vermont. In 1889 she followed her sister to Smith College. There she became aware of the issues of women's rights for which she would quietly battle for the remainder of her life; there too she became interested in the burgeoning biological sciences.

By the time she graduated with a B.S. in 1893 Florence Sabin had decided to study medicine, an early but unfulfilled interest of her father's. Needing first to earn enough to pay for her medical education, she taught mathematics in a Denver school for two years, then taught in Smith College's zoology department for a year. In 1896 she was part of the fourth class admitted to the Johns Hopkins Medical School, where she experienced the best medical education then available in the United States.

When Sabin began her study of medicine, anatomy had just recently begun to emerge from its long descriptive phase to become an experimental science through studies in embryology and histology, subjects which would occupy her early career. Sabin was a fine all-around medical student, winning one of the four highly prized internships in internal medicine with William Osler at Johns Hopkins Hospital upon graduation. But it was Franklin P. Mall, professor of anatomy, who proved to be the strongest and most lasting influence upon her subsequent work. Mall's hallmark in teaching, as it would be Sabin's later as well, was to stimulate students to learn on their own, never to be so precise as to rob them of the joys of discovery. While she was still a student, Sabin undertook a project under Mall's guidance leading to the construction of a three-dimensional model of the mid- and lower brain. Adapted for publication in 1901, *An Atlas of the Medulla and Midbrain* was quickly adopted as a popular text.

After completing her internship in 1901, Sabin chose to continue her work in anatomical and histological research. For a year she was supported by a fellowship from a group of Baltimore women who aided women's education. Then in 1902 she became an assistant in the department of anatomy, the first woman on the Hopkins medical faculty. (Her male colleagues at this time still referred to her as Miss rather than Dr. Sabin.) When she rose to the rank of full professor in 1917, she was again the first woman at the university to achieve that rank.

During her early Hopkins years, Sabin concentrated her research mainly upon the origins of blood cells and the lymphatics, small vessels that transport lymph fluid. Probably her most significant scientific contribution was the demonstration that the lymphatics arise in the embryo by a series of small buds directly from the veins. By skillful injection of lymph channels with colored solutions, and by the use of small pig embryos rather than the larger ones commonly used for such studies, she provided the histological evidence that controverted the older theory that the lymphatics arose from tissue spaces and then grew toward the veins. This work led to a number of widely cited papers and a chapter in the influential *Manual of Human Embryology* (1910–12) edited by Mall and Franz Keibel.

On numerous summer trips to German laboratories Sabin brought back fresh ideas and new techniques. One for which she is usually given much credit is supra vital staining, the use of a nontoxic stain to study cells while still alive so that their vital processes may be observed. Though she used and helped popularize this important technique in her studies of the developing blood cells, one of her students, Herbert M. Evans, deserves the credit for its refinement and introduction in the United States.

Sabin's twenty-five-year teaching career in the Hopkins anatomy department was a busy and satisfying period of her life. Soon after her appointment as an instructor in 1902, she began to help Ross Harrison teach the histology course; when he left for Yale in 1907 she took over the course. After Mall's death in 1917, Lewis Weed, who had been one of Sabin's students, succeeded to the chairmanship of the department. With disappointment but not apparent rancor, she continued to teach at Hopkins until 1925. A student in 1909 described her lectures as "very rapidly spoken" because "she was so enthusiastic in trying to correlate the scientific and medical aspect of anatomy," and also reported that Sabin would "tear up her notes after each lecture so that she would have to work it over the next year." She had many devoted students, a number of whom she influenced to follow scientific careers. Several became leaders in anatomy, immunology, and hematology. She won the respect and affection of medical students unaccustomed to women professors by her personal dignity, her generosity, and her contagious enthusiasm for medical science, all traits which made her a superb teacher.

Indeed, important as her scientific research at Hopkins was, her teaching, and later her public service in Colorado, probably led to more lasting contributions. She shared with Mall a belief in the intimate connection between research and teaching: "Research lifts teaching to a high plane. No one can be a great educator unless he himself is an investigator." As she explained in her presidential address to the American Association of Anatomists, which elected her its first woman president in 1924: "All the class can be taught in the spirit of research, which means that it is more important for the student to be able to find out something for himself than to memorize what someone else has said."

In 1925 Florence Sabin became the first woman elected to membership in the National Academy of Sciences, as well as the first of her sex to receive a full membership at the Rockefeller Institute in New York. At the Institute, where she worked for thirteen years in the second phase of her career, she headed a section that studied the cellular aspects of immunity. Her work was an extension of her earlier study of the development of blood cells in the embryo and in adult bone marrow, in which she recognized the prominence of the mononuclear blood cells. With coworkers at the Institute she elucidated the role of the monocytes in antigen-antibody reactions and the role of the various fatty acids of the tubercle bacillus in the production of the typical cellular reactions to that bacterium.

Her ties to Baltimore remained close, and she worked on the biography of her mentor, which was well received when it was published in 1934 as *Franklin Paine Mall: The Story of a Mind.* Sabin's study of Mall was partly autobiographical in that many of the attitudes toward research, medical education, and techniques of teaching she ascribed to Mall were also ones to which she adhered.

Sabin retired to her native state in 1938 to live with her sister, Mary, with whom she had been close despite so many years of geographical separation. She remained active on a number of national advisory boards and carried on an extensive correspondence with her many former students and colleagues. In 1944 she began the third, and perhaps most remarkable, phase of her career when she was asked by Colorado Governor John Vivian to serve on his Post-War Planning Committee and assist in assessing the state's health needs. Colorado had long considered itself a haven for those who sought to improve their health; it thus came as a shock when Sabin and the subcommittee on public health that she chaired publicized the facts about an inefficient, politically controlled board of health hampered by insufficient funds, poorly trained staff, and inadequate laws.

This persistent and dynamic woman in her middle seventies became known throughout her state as the "little doctor," and was seen as a potent political force. In her crusade for basic public health reforms in Colorado she used her long years of experience and her scientific skills very effectively. She gathered pertinent facts, traveled, spoke, and wrote extensively. With simple but overwhelming evidence, she persuaded colleagues on committees, legislators,

and state officials to support a reorganized and better financed public health program. She worked tirelessly for successful passage of a series of health laws drafted by her committee and known as the Sabin program. In 1947 Mayor James Quigg Newton of Denver persuaded her to accept appointment as chairman of the Interim Board of Health and Hospitals of Denver, a post she held until 1951. In her Sippy Memorial Address to the western branch of the American Public Health Association, of which she had been president in 1948, she demonstrated that at the age of eighty-one she was still actively concerned and informed about environmental health issues.

Florence Sabin died in Denver in 1953 of a heart attack just short of her eighty-second birthday. Among the many honors she had received as a scientist, as a woman, and as a civic reformer were numerous honorary degrees and buildings named for her at the University of Colorado School of Medicine and at Smith College. One of the two Coloradans represented by statues in the United States Capitol, she was one of the foremost women medical scientists of her era.

[The Florence Rena Sabin Papers at the Am. Phil. Soc. Library in Philadelphia contain a bibliography, biographical material, and extensive correspondence. The Florence Rena Sabin Coll. in the Sophia Smith Coll., Smith College, includes biographical and genealogical information, scientific studies, lecture notes, notebooks, memorabilia, and photographs, as well as correspondence; many letters to her sister, Mary, and to Ella Strong Dennison shed light on her personal concerns as well as her scientific career. Her numerous scientific papers appeared for the most part in *Contributions to Embryology* (a publication of the Carnegie Institution, Washington, D.C.), *Science,* and publications of the institutions where she worked. The most complete book about Sabin, which includes a bibliography, is Elinor Bluemel, *Florence Sabin: Colorado Woman of the Century* (1959). Mary K. Phelan, *Probing the Unknown* (1969), is for younger readers. The best treatment of Sabin's scientific contributions is Philip D. McMaster and Michael Heidelberger, "Florence Rena Sabin," *Biog. Memoirs Nat. Acad. of Sciences,* 34 (1960), 271–319, which also contains a bibliography. See also Vincent T. Andriole, "Florence Rena Sabin—Teacher, Scientist, Citizen," *Jour. Hist. Medicine and Allied Sciences,* July 1959, pp. 320–50; George W. Corner, *A History of the Rockefeller Institute, 1901–1953* (1964), pp. 238–39; Lawrence S. Kubie, "Florence Rena Sabin, 1871–1953," *Perspectives in Biology and Medicine,* Spring 1961, pp. 306–15; John H. Talbott, *A Biographical History of Medicine* (1970), pp. 1181–83; Edna Yost, *American Women of Science* (1943), pp. 62–79; and the entries in *Dict. Am. Biog.,* Supp. Five, and *Dict. Scientific Biog.,* vol. 12 (1975). An obituary appeared in the *N.Y. Times,* Oct. 4, 1953. Death certificate supplied by Colo. Dept. of Public Health.]

GERT H. BRIEGER

SABIN, Pauline Morton, April 23, 1887–Dec. 27, 1955. Prohibition repeal leader, Republican party official, interior decorator.

Pauline Morton Sabin, a leader of the movement to repeal the eighteenth amendment, was the younger of two daughters of Paul and Charlotte (Goodridge) Morton. She was raised in a political family: her grandfather, J. Sterling Morton, was United States secretary of agriculture (1893–97), as well as senator and governor of Nebraska; her father, a railroad executive and later president of the Equitable Life Assurance Society, served as secretary of the navy from 1904 to 1905. In addition, her uncle founded Morton Salt, and she inherited several million dollars from the company fortune. Born in Chicago, Pauline Morton attended private schools there and in Washington, D.C.; she also traveled abroad and developed a lasting interest in the fine and decorative arts.

On Feb. 2, 1907, she married James Hopkins Smith, Jr., a wealthy New York yachting and sports enthusiast. They had two sons, Paul Morton (1908–1956) and James Hopkins (b. 1909), who became assistant secretary of the navy for air (1952–56). At the beginning of World War I, after her husband left to serve in the French ambulance corps, Pauline Smith obtained a divorce and began an interior decorating business. She gave up the business when, on Dec. 28, 1916, she married recently divorced Charles H. Sabin, president of Guaranty Trust Company of New York. Pauline and Charles Sabin maintained an estate at Southampton, Long Island, as well as a house in New York City, and were active in New York's social elite.

Soon after remarrying, she renewed her interest in politics, sharing her father's allegiance to the Republican party despite her husband's active support for the Democrats. In 1919 Pauline Sabin was elected to the Suffolk County Republican Committee and the following year joined the party's state executive committee. She helped establish the New York-based Women's National Republican Club, serving as its president from 1921 to 1926. When women were added to the Republican National Committee, as advisers in 1923 and full members a year later, Sabin became New York's first woman representative. She was a delegate to the Republican National Conventions of 1924 and 1928, cochaired Sen. James Wadsworth's unsuccessful 1926 reelection campaign, and directed

women's activities for the Coolidge and Hoover presidential campaigns in the east. A skillful organizer and fund raiser, she favored a business-minded and isolationist government. She also consistently encouraged women to participate more actively in politics.

Pauline Sabin first began to criticize national prohibition in 1926 in defending Wadsworth's opposition to the eighteenth amendment. Earlier she had favored the law. In June 1928 she wrote in *The Outlook* that prohibition was diverting and corrupting public officials; rather than protecting children from temptation, the widely violated law was causing them to grow up "with a total lack of respect for the Constitution and for the law." Elsewhere, she expressed concern over growing federal government power as represented by the liquor ban and the steps taken to enforce it. In March 1929 she resigned from the Republican National Committee and a month later denounced the Hoover administration for supporting prohibition. She enlisted a group of other socially prominent, upper-class women and on May 28 in Chicago announced formation of the Women's Organization for National Prohibition Reform (WONPR). The WONPR cooperated closely with the all-male Association Against the Prohibition Amendment, in which Charles Sabin had been active since the early 1920s, but remained independent of that older society and eventually grew much larger than its counterpart. By its first national convention in April 1930, the WONPR had 100,000 members, and by 1933 it claimed 1,500,000, making it over three times the size of the Woman's Christian Temperance Union.

Small, slender, and attractive, Pauline Sabin was the WONPR's national chairman, driving force, and most visible representative—writing, speaking, appearing on the cover of *Time,* testifying before congressional committees, lobbying both parties, and building support for repeal. The membership, publicity, and grassroots campaigning of the WONPR destroyed the myth that all women favored prohibition and encouraged the political revolt against the liquor ban. Sabin's group became the first antiprohibition organization to endorse the 1932 Democratic repeal platform and ticket. When the repeal amendment was ratified in December 1933, the WONPR disbanded.

Pauline Sabin cochaired Fiorello La Guardia's 1933 New York mayoral campaign. After repeal, however, her political involvement waned, although she served on the American Liberty League's executive committee and campaigned for Alfred M. Landon in 1936. She was widowed Oct. 10, 1933, and on May 8, 1936, married a widower, Dwight F. Davis, former secretary of war (1925–29), governor general of the Philippines (1929–32), and donor of the international tennis trophy, the Davis Cup. In May 1940, Pauline Davis was named director of volunteer special services of the American Red Cross. Under her wartime leadership, the number of Red Cross volunteers working in blood banks and canteens, making bandages and garments, serving as nurse's aides, and assisting families of servicemen grew from 53,000 to over 4,000,-000. She resigned in December 1943, after a dispute over policy issues.

After 1943 Pauline Davis remained active in Washington society, serving as a consultant on White House redecoration during the Truman administration. She also cared for her elder son's three children. For three years before her death she suffered from amyotrophic lateral sclerosis; she died of bronchopneumonia in Washington in 1955.

[Although no collection of Pauline Morton Sabin papers survives, much information regarding her activities can be found in the WONPR files of the Pierre S. du Pont Papers at Eleutherian Mills Hist. Library and in the archives of the American Red Cross. The principal published sources of information on her antiprohibition activities are Grace C. Root, *Women and Repeal: The Story of the Women's Organization for National Prohibition Reform* (1934), and David E. Kyvig, "Women Against Prohibition," *Am. Quart.*, Fall 1976. The *Time* cover story of July 18, 1932, is the most useful of numerous contemporary magazine or newspaper accounts. For her resignation from the Red Cross, see Foster Rhea Dulles, *The American Red Cross: A History* (1950). See also *Dict. Am. Biog.*, Supp. Five. Obituaries appeared in the *N.Y. Times* and *Wash. Post*, Dec. 28, 1955. Her son, James Hopkins Smith III, also provided useful information. Death record from D.C. Health Dept.]

DAVID E. KYVIG

SAGE, Kay Linn, June 25, 1898–Jan. 8, 1963. Painter.

Kay Sage, painter and poet, was born in Albany, N.Y., where her great-grandfather had been a lumberman and a benefactor of Cornell University. Her father, Henry Manning Sage, who attended Yale, became president of the family business, the Sage Land Improvement Company; he was also a Cornell trustee and a New York state senator. Her mother, Anne Wheeler (Ward) Sage, was unconventional and restless and never quite adjusted to the conservative and socially prominent Sage family. To escape, Anne Sage traveled regularly to France, always taking Kay, the younger and her favorite of her two daughters.

In "China Eggs," an unpublished autobiography written in 1955, Kay Sage recalled her childhood love of Paris, where she rode donkeys, pushed hoops, and went on the merry-go-rounds in the Tuileries. Her parents divorced before she was ten and from then on her life was split between Italy, where her mother rented the same villa in Rapallo every year, and the United States, where her father (and, usually, her sister) lived and where Kay sometimes went to school.

Kay Sage's education was haphazard, as her mother did not hesitate to take her out of school to travel. Between January 1911 and March 1914 she was a student at the fashionable Brearley School in New York City, although for some months in 1913 she was in Europe. She became fluent in French and Italian, as well as English, although a later poem comically notes that while she can "write in all of these . . . at best, they are translations, / I think in Chinese" (from *The More I Wonder*). Sage felt particularly at home on ships, suspended between continents, or floating down the Nile, but Italy soon became her country, as Paris had earlier been her city. In 1914, with the beginning of World War I, Sage came back to the United States. She went to the Foxcroft School in Virginia for a year, then to the Corcoran Art School in Washington, D.C., where she seldom attended classes. She had drawn and painted all her life, but had little use for instruction.

When the war ended, Kay Sage returned to Italy. Moving to Rome in order to study art seriously, she took life study courses at the Scuolo Libera delle Belli Arti and other academies, always staying away when the professor came to criticize. In Rome she met Onorato Carlandi, an artist who had a deep influence on her, teaching her "to think as I hadn't thought to think before." The only woman admitted to his group of artists who went once a week to paint in the Roman Campagna, she later remembered these as "the happiest days of my life."

It was during these years that the surrealists were transforming the art world in Paris. Sage, in Rome, married an Italian prince, Ranieri di San Faustino, in 1925. The marriage ended in divorce in 1935 and there seems little to be said about Sage's painting during those ten years. She had her first solo show in 1936, in Milan; the following year she moved to Paris. Most of her work in the late 1930s, in contrast to her early landscapes and portraits, was abstract.

André Breton, leader of the surrealist group in

Paris, saw Kay Sage's paintings at the Salon des Surindépendants; he identified them as the work of a man because of their strength. Through acquaintance with Breton and other surrealists, Kay Sage met the painter Yves Tanguy; they were immediately attracted to each other. In 1939, however, with the outbreak of World War II, Sage returned to the United States. There she immediately set out to help those who were left in Paris. With the help of Yvon Delbos, French minister of education, she organized a series of one-man shows for artists working in Paris; Yves Tanguy inaugurated the series. Sage and Tanguy were married on Aug. 17, 1940, and shortly after moved to Woodbury, Conn. That year she had her first solo exhibition in the United States, at the Pierre Matisse Gallery in New York City. Sage and Tanguy lived in an old farmhouse, where each had a studio, and where they frequently entertained such friends as the artists Hans Richter, Alexander Calder, and Marcel Duchamp; gallery owner Julien Levy, in whose gallery Sage had a 1944 show; and curator James Thrall Soby.

Yves Tanguy died suddenly in 1955 and Kay Sage became more and more reclusive. She continued to paint and to write poetry in both French and English until 1958, when her eyesight began to fail. After a double cataract operation, she never regained complete vision; she stopped painting. In 1959, she took an overdose of barbiturates but recovered. Catherine Viviano, her dealer for fourteen years, organized, at her own expense, a retrospective exhibition of Sage's work in order to give her the will to live and continue painting. Sage began a series of collages and objects made of tinfoil, doorknobs, eyeglass lenses, and other such materials and completed a book of poems, *Mordicus* (1962), printed and illustrated by Jean Dubuffet. She also worked on cataloguing the work of Yves Tanguy, but her reconciliation with life was superficial. On Jan. 8, 1963, at her home in Connecticut, she shot herself through the heart and died.

In a characteristically meticulous will, Sage asked that her work be distributed by three close friends: James Thrall Soby, John Monagan, and Catherine Viviano. Through their efforts, major museums and colleges throughout the United States own her paintings, as well as the works of art she had collected and cherished. She bequeathed to the Museum of Modern Art in New York City nearly one hundred works of art from her extensive collection. In addition, she left to the Museum the largest legacy of unrestricted purchase funds it had yet received.

Kay Sage never talked about her paintings,

believing they could "speak for themselves." The paintings speak of infinity, space, and obstacles. In Sage's paintings, as in Tanguy's, the landscapes appear to come from another planet, but in her work there are constructions, scaffoldings, rigging, and towers, familiar objects from our modern world presented in a dreamlike fashion. These objects are carefully structured and harmonious, but some of them have collapsed, as if pushed by an adverse force that has disappeared after destroying their delicate balance. The colors in her paintings are at once subtle and glowing, reminiscent of the sulphurous light before a thunderstorm. Occasionally, bright mysterious objects dot the landscapes, providing a respite along an endless journey. The figures in the landscapes are human, but veiled, walking blindly to their destiny. The paths they follow look mysterious, tantalizing, and sometimes treacherous, leading to vast surfaces on the sea or on the desert. In 1955 she wrote: "I walk very quickly over a thin layer of ice. Below, the lake is deep. I am alone. There is nothing, even on the horizon. If I stop, even for a second, the ice breaks, and down I go . . . There is no other side."

[Sage's papers in the Archives of Am. Art, Washington, D.C., include correspondence, photographs of her work, and "China Eggs," the most complete record available of her life. Sage's other published works are *Piove in Giardino* (1937), as Kay di San Faustino; *Demain, Monsieur Silber* (1957); *The More I Wonder* (1957); *Faut dire c'qui est* (1959); and *Yves Tanguy, A Summary of His Work* (1963). For biographical information see Régine Tessier Krieger's introduction to *Kay Sage, 1898–1963,* catalog of an exhibition at the Hubert F. Johnson Museum of Art, Cornell Univ., which contains a chronology and partial bibliography; *A Tribute to Kay Sage* (1965), catalog of an exhibition at the Mattatuck Museum, Waterbury, Conn., with an introduction by Talcott Clapp; and the catalog of the Catherine Viviano Gallery, *Kay Sage Retrospective, 1937–1958* (1960), with an essay by James Thrall Soby. See also Paul Cummings, *Dict. Contemporary Am. Artists* (1977); Linda Nochlin and Ann S. Harris, *Women Artists* (1977). Discussions of her work include Ralph M. Pearson, *The Modern Renaissance in American Art* (1954, 1968), pp. 284–86; James Thrall Soby, "Double Solitaire: Retrospective Exhibition at Wadsworth Atheneum," *Sat. Rev.,* Sept. 4, 1954, pp. 29–30, on a Sage-Tanguy exhibition; Julien Levy, "Tanguy, Connecticut, Sage," *ART News,* Sept. 1954, pp. 24–27; a brief review by Margaret Breuning, "A Kay Sage Retrospective," *Arts,* May 1960; and two articles in *Time,* "Serene Surrealist," March 13, 1950, p. 49, and "Séance in Connecticut," Aug. 30, 1954, p. 58. A biobibliography by Christie D. Stephenson lists further reviews of Sage exhibitions.]

RÉGINE TESSIER

ST. DENIS, Ruth, Jan. 20, 1879–July 21, 1968. Dancer.

Ruth St. Denis was born Ruth Dennis, in New Jersey, the eldest child of Thomas Laban and Ruth Emma (Hull) Dennis, both born in England. Her father's family had migrated to Boonton, N.J., where Thomas Dennis later enlisted in the New Jersey Cavalry in the Civil War. The Hulls came in the 1840s to Canandaigua, N.Y., in the heart of the "burned-over district" of religious revivalism, where Emma Hull became a staunch Methodist. In 1872 Hull graduated from the University of Michigan Medical School, but a nervous breakdown prevented her practice of medicine, and she drifted to the Eagleswood colony of artists and intellectuals near Perth Amboy, N.J. There she met Thomas Dennis. He divorced his first wife in 1878 and entered a common-law marriage with Emma Hull, who was pregnant. Their hasty exchange of vows in an artist's studio haunted their daughter, who as Ruth St. Denis became extraordinarily sensitive to social proprieties, as well as fearful of pregnancy. In 1884 the Denises moved to a farm near Somerville, N.J., joined by Thomas Dennis's adolescent son by his first marriage; their own son, Brother, was born in 1885. The family took in paying boarders, for Thomas Dennis, a machinist and amateur inventor, drank heavily and was unemployed.

Ruthie Dennis escaped family quarrels by playacting and practicing Delsarte poses before the family boarders. Extroverted and athletic, she once answered the taunts of a schoolmate at the local one-room Adamsville school by bashing his head with a rusty coal shovel. She studied dancing in Somerville until anxious relatives financed a term at Dwight Moody's Northfield Seminary in Massachusetts during the fall of 1893. There she argued with the famed evangelist over the merits of the theater and fled home in time to star in her mother's amateur production of "The Old Homestead." Emma Dennis took her protégée on to New York for an audition with Karl Marwig, "master of dance" for the producer Augustin Daly, and during the week of Jan. 29, 1894, "Ruth," as she was billed, made her debut as a skirt dancer at Worth's Museum. For a decade thereafter she appeared in roof garden concerts and variety revues, helping to support both parents, who were then separated. During 1896–97 she attended the Packer Collegiate Institute in Brooklyn, N.Y., excelling in French, but forsook further schooling for acting-dancing roles on the legitimate stage.

While touring with David Belasco's *Madame*

DuBarry in 1904, she spotted the advertisement for Egyptian Deities cigarettes which provided the catalyst for the Oriental style of her solo dance career. Her interest in Orientalia and mysticism had grown after her discovery of Christian Science; under the influence of the actor Edmund Russell she explored ancient religions, appearing with Russell in the Sanskrit drama *Sakuntala* in 1905. These influences led to the creation of "Radha," an Oriental dance-drama which launched her fame. She unveiled "Radha" in a "smokers' concert" (attended primarily by men) at the New York Theatre on Jan. 28, 1906, and first used her stage name, Ruth St. Denis, at a performance in March of that year. "Radha" proved a blueprint for later St. Denis dances, with its virginal female deity, its Manichean theme, and its iconographic movements.

St. Denis toured Europe during 1906–09 and returned home with the cachet of international success to tour America as a solo dancer. Her mother remained her most rigorous critic and barred the door to St. Denis suitors. In 1914, however, Emma Dennis's mental condition deteriorated and she soon entered a sanitarium, beginning a period for St. Denis of several years of responsibility for the care of both parents.

St. Denis found new inspiration and guidance from the divinity student-turned-dancer Ted Shawn, who had come to her New York studio in 1914 hoping to become her student. They were married on Aug. 13, 1914. Moving to Los Angeles in 1915 they founded Denishawn, the company and school which became the seedbed of American modern dance, counting among its students Martha Graham, DORIS HUMPHREY, and Charles Weidman. Ted Shawn was the organizational genius behind the school, while "Miss Ruth" contributed lofty philosophical monologues and solo dance demonstrations, ever the grand lady on and off stage.

Essentially a soloist, St. Denis felt trapped in the lavish Denishawn productions and in 1919 broke away briefly with her own company of Ruth St. Denis Concert Dancers to perform "music visualizations," the translation of musical compositions into movement. Economic necessity forced her back into Denishawn, an instance of the recurring tension in her career between experimentation and popular art. She once wrote bitterly that "the 'caviar to the many' is tragedy for the artist . . . and paradoxically my whole art life has been a slow tragedy."

Unlike her contemporary, ISADORA DUNCAN, who revolutionized movement, St. Denis was destined to be a dance popularizer, and throughout the 1920s she brought dance to small-town

America as the central icon in Denishawn productions. In 1925–26 the company toured the Orient and brought its repertoire home for touring, including the exquisite St. Denis solo, "White Jade." A new Denishawn house was built in New York, but with the depression, both Denishawn and its founders' marriage dissolved. Separated in 1931 but never divorced, Shawn and St. Denis argued over extramarital affairs, professional jealousy, her fear of pregnancy, and his preference for males. Shawn left to form his own company of male dancers while St. Denis embarked on a bitter decade of meager earnings and professional eclipse. Outmoded in the context of the emerging modern dance, St. Denis formed the Society of Spiritual Arts, intended to further dance as a form of worship, gave private concerts, wrote poetry, and performed in churches until the end of the decade when she began that transformation into myth which resurrected her career.

With her designation as dance director of Adelphi College in New York in 1938, the publication of her autobiography in 1939, and her triumphant revival of "Radha" at Shawn's Jacob's Pillow in 1941, St. Denis earned the title of "First Lady of American Dance." In 1940 she founded the School of Natya in New York with the dancer La Meri, and in late 1942 moved to Hollywood, where her brother provided a studio-home. From this base she performed in concerts and plays for two more decades. Her keen intellect and earthy wit were undiminished, and she never lost the ability to project her personal magnetism on stage. The culmination of the mythmaking process came in 1964 with her Golden Wedding celebration concert with Shawn, with whom St. Denis had maintained a long-distance friendship. On July 21, 1968, St. Denis died in Hollywood of a stroke. Her ashes were buried at Forest Lawn Cemetery, where her grave marker bears the lines of a St. Denis poem: "The Gods have meant/That I should dance,/And by the Gods/I will!"

[A vast collection of Ruth St. Denis's diaries, letters, musical scores, photographs, and personal documents is housed in the Special Collections of the Univ. Research Library, the Univ. of Calif. at Los Angeles, with an additional collection particularly rich in correspondence, iconography, and film housed in the Dance Coll. of the N.Y. Public Library. St. Denis's own published writings include her impressionistic autobiography, *An Unfinished Life* (1939), and a volume of poetry, *Lotus Light* (1932). She also wrote extensively in popular journals and in *The Denishawn Mag.* (1924–25). Ted Shawn paid tribute to her early career in the lavish *Ruth St. Denis: Pioneer and Prophet* (1920) and added valuable information in his own memoir,

One Thousand and One-Night Stands (1960). St. Denis's friend Walter Terry has written the only biography, the affectionate *Miss Ruth: The 'More Living Life' of Ruth St. Denis* (1969); see also Elizabeth Kendall, *Where She Danced* (1979). Christena L. Schlundt's contributions include a chronology and index of dances (1906–32), *The Professional Appearances of Ruth St. Denis and Ted Shawn* (1962); a dissertation, "The Role of Ruth St. Denis in the History of American Dance" (Univ. of Calif. at Claremont, 1958); "Into the Mystic With Miss Ruth," *Dance Perspectives* (1971); and "An Account of Ruth St. Denis in Europe, 1906–1909," *Am. Assoc. for Health, Physical Education, Recreation Research Quart.*, 1960. Dance history surveys with sections on St. Denis include Charles and Caroline Caffin, *Dancing and Dancers of Today* (1912); Troy and Margaret Kinney, *The Dance* (1914); Margaret Lloyd, *The Borzoi Book of Modern Dance* (1949); Paul Magriel, ed., *Chronicles of the American Dance* (1948); Lillian Moore, *Artists of the Dance* (1938); Don McDonagh, *The Complete Guide to Modern Dance* (1976). Walter Terry, "The Legacy of Isadora Duncan and Ruth St. Denis," *Dance Perspectives* (1960) is a useful analysis. The year of St. Denis's birth has been variously given as 1877, 1878, 1879, and 1880; no birth certificate exists. The Jan. 20, 1879, date is based on several sources: the date on her tombstone and on her death certificate; the U.S. Census (1880) for Perth Amboy, N.J.; an affidavit in the Thomas L. Dennis file, Bureau of Pensions, in the U.S. Navy Archives, Washington, D.C. A death certificate was provided by Calif. Dept. of Public Health.]

SUZANNE SHELTON

SANDOZ, Mari, May 11, 1896–March 10, 1966. Writer.

Mari Sandoz, biographer, historian, teacher, and writer of fiction, was the oldest of the three daughters and three sons of Jules Ami Sandoz and his fourth wife, Marie Elizabeth (Fehr), both German-Swiss immigrants. Her father, a medical student at the University of Zurich, emigrated from Neuchâtel in 1881 and homesteaded in northwestern Nebraska in 1884. Her mother came from Schaffhausen.

Born Marie Susette at Jules Sandoz's first homestead beside the Niobrara River in Sheridan County, her earliest education sprang from the demands of an isolated frontier household. She learned to trap, hunt, skin, bake, and care for the younger children. What another child might have gleaned from books, she learned from the region's storytellers—trappers, cattlemen, Indians—who gathered round the family's wood stove. Her father's wide-ranging intellectual interests—he was a well-known horticulturist, as well as a locator for settlers and an avid participant in local politics—stimulated her natural curiosity and conveyed a sympathy for the world's disinherited. Her mother's harsh and difficult life, and her courage, created in her daughter both admiration and pity.

At nine, speaking Swiss-German and a few words of English, Marie Sandoz began school, walking six miles a day. She quickly learned to read and was soon devouring novels and magazines despite her father's objections to fiction. Hawthorne, Conrad, and Hardy were favorite authors. After only four and a half years of schooling, and despite absences when snow-blinded at twelve and during a bad case of jaundice, Sandoz passed the rural teachers' examination at age sixteen. For the next seven years she taught in schools in Sheridan and Cheyenne (Neb.) counties. In May 1914 she married Wray Macumber, a homesteader from Iowa; they were divorced in August 1919. Sandoz did not speak publicly about her marriage, although she signed her early stories Marie Macumber.

In the summer session of 1922 Sandoz enrolled as an "adult special" at the University of Nebraska in Lincoln, beginning a ten-year period of intermittent study concentrated on English and writing. She supported herself through a variety of jobs, working in a drug laboratory, as an assistant in the university's English department, and as a proofreader. She had decided to become a writer almost as soon as she learned to write, and at ten had published a story in the *Omaha Daily News*. The first issue of *Prairie Schooner* (1927) opened with her story, "The Vine." Her father had once told her that he considered "artists and writers the maggots of society." But his dying wish, in 1928, that she write "of his struggles as a locator, a builder of communities, a bringer of fruit to the Panhandle," gave her a subject rich and complex enough for her developing art. Living frugally but joyfully, despite her disappointment at the rejection of many stories, Sandoz devoted herself to the biography of Old Jules. In it, she recreated not only the struggles of her family but also the story of Nebraska as it moved from pioneer days into the twentieth century.

At the height of the depression in 1933, when the judges of the *Atlantic* nonfiction contest (conducted by the *Atlantic Monthly* magazine) rejected the manuscript of *Old Jules,* Mari Sandoz decided to give up; she burned more than seventy-five stories and returned, despondent, to her family's sandhills homestead. Her spirit soon revived. When she went back to Lincoln in 1934, to a research job at the Nebraska State Historical Society, she resubmitted *Old Jules* to the *Atlantic* judges. In 1935 it won their $5,000 prize for the most interesting

and distinctive work of nonfiction and was selected by the Book-of-the-Month Club. These events marked a turning point in Sandoz's career.

Old Jules (1935) became the first of the Trans-Missouri series which examines the long history of human occupation in the region between the Missouri River and the Rocky Mountains. The series includes *Crazy Horse* (1942), a biography of a chief of the Oglala Sioux; *Cheyenne Autumn* (1952); and three books about the men who used the land's resources, *The Buffalo Hunters* (1954), *The Cattlemen* (1958), and *The Beaver Men* (1964). These volumes are distinguished by the breadth of Sandoz's vision of this immense territory, the accuracy of her research, and the beauty of her prose. To convey her sense of "the hardship, the violence and gaiety" of life on the high plains, as well as her feeling for the "deep, complex, and patterned interrelationships" of American Indian cultures she developed a style characterized by figures of speech drawn from nature, regional idioms, and rhythmical use of language. In *Crazy Horse* she fulfilled her purpose of expressing the Indian's "relationship to the earth and the sky and all that is in between." *Cheyenne Autumn* narrates the epic flight of a band of northern Cheyenne to their homeland on the Yellowstone River. Together they reveal Mari Sandoz's understanding of her Plains Indian neighbors.

Sandoz's novels and short fiction reflect the concern for social justice evidenced in the Trans-Missouri series as well as her interest in fundamental human conflict and the relation of people to the land. *Slogum House* (1937), a novel about Nebraska in pioneering times, explores the psychology of a domineering "will-to-power individual" who turned "every honest, good, and beautiful thing about her to her end." Sandoz viewed her next book, *Capital City* (1939), as "a microscopic study of a unit of modern democratic society selling itself into fascism" (Meredith, p. 385). Though neither novel was as well received as her historical works, they are serious experiments in allegorical fiction. Like her later novels—*The Tom-Walker* (1947), *Miss Morissa: Doctor of the Gold Trail* (1955), and *Son of the Gamblin' Man* (1960)—they are eminently readable.

Vitality, good humor, generosity, a "rapport with persons of all ages and backgrounds," and a capacity for intense activity typified Sandoz throughout her career (Switzer, p. 113). For many summers she taught creative writing: at the University of Colorado (1941) and at Indiana University (1946), and for several years at the summer Writers' Institute at the

University of Wisconsin (1947–53; 1955–56). She won appropriate honors: among them an honorary degree from the University of Nebraska (1950) and an award from The Westerners, Chicago Corral, for her preservation of the cultural history of the west (1955).

After 1943 she lived simply and alone in New York City's Greenwich Village, continuing her habit of working long hours on research and writing. The move enabled her to be near her publishers and to use eastern research libraries. She had a mastectomy in 1954 and another ten years later. During this period, in addition to the three late novels, she published two short novels for young readers, *The Horsecatcher* (1956) and *The Story Catcher* (1963), as well as *These Were the Sioux* (1961), a perceptive account of custom and belief which also contains many fine chapters on Sioux women, and *Love Song to the Plains* (1961). During the last year and a half of her life she finished *The Battle of the Little Big Horn* (1978) and *The Christmas of Phonograph Records: A Recollection* (1966). Mari Sandoz died of cancer in March 1966, in St. Luke's Hospital, New York City. She was buried, according to her wishes, in the sandhills of Nebraska.

[The principal manuscript sources are in the Mari Sandoz Coll. at the Univ. of Nebraska in Lincoln. Materials there include her research files, a vast accumulation of notes and interviews, MSS., correspondence, maps, and her extensive cross index for the research material. Other MSS. and many photographs are held by the Mari Sandoz Corporation, Gordon, Neb. Many of her short writings were collected in *Hostiles and Friendlies* (1959), which has a biographical introduction to each selection, and *Sandhills Sundays and Other Recollections* (1970), which also contains a Sandoz chronology and a checklist of her writings. *Making of an Author: From the Mementoes of Mari Sandoz* (1972), a booklet by her sister, Caroline Sandoz Pifer, includes letters, stories, articles, and many early photographs. Helen Arlene Winter Stauffer, "Mari Sandoz: A Study of the Artist as Biographer" (Ph.D. diss., Univ. of Neb., 1974), analyzes the three biographies of the Trans-Missouri series. Two essays based on personal acquaintance are Dorothy Nott Switzer, "Mari Sandoz's Lincoln Years: A Personal Recollection," *Prairie Schooner*, Summer 1971, and Mamie J. Meredith, "Mari Sandoz," in Virginia Faulkner, ed., *Roundup: A Nebraska Reader* (1957), pp. 382–86. See also LaVerne Harrell Clark, "The Indian Writings of Mari Sandoz: 'A Lone One Left from the Old Times,' " *American Indian Quart.*, Autumn 1974 and Winter 1974–75; and Scott L. Greenwell, "The Literary Apprenticeship of Mari Sandoz," *Nebraska Hist.*, Summer 1976, and "Fascists in Fiction: Two Early Novels of Mari Sandoz," *Western American Lit.*, Summer 1977. Dates of her marriage and divorce were obtained from the Sheridan Cty. Court

and the District Court, Sheridan Cty., Neb. *Contemporary Authors* and *Twentieth Century Authors* give Sandoz's birth year incorrectly as 1901, as does her obituary in the *N.Y. Times*, March 11, 1966; 1896 is confirmed by all other sources. Caroline Sandoz Pifer provided information about her sister and the family in an interview with Sheryll Patterson-Black.]

                                                                           GAIL BAKER

SANGER, Margaret, Sept. 14, 1879–Sept. 6, 1966. Birth control reformer.

Margaret Sanger, leader of the American birth control movement, was born Margaret Louise Higgins in Corning, N.Y., the sixth of eleven children and third of four daughters of Anne (Purcell) and Michael Hennessey Higgins, owner and operator of a stone monument shop. Anne Higgins maintained the Roman Catholic faith of her Irish ancestors, but Michael Higgins, who ran away from a Canadian farm as a teenager to fight with the Union army, was an outspoken champion of the ideas of the atheist Robert Ingersoll and of the single-tax advocate Henry George. The two eldest Higgins daughters sacrificed their ambitions to family need and worked to supplement a family income that always seemed inadequate to Margaret Higgins. She associated both her mother's tubercular cough and the family's financial insecurity with her parents' high fertility. Anne Higgins died when she was forty-nine, prematurely aged, in her third daughter's view, by the endless drudgery of raising eleven children on the income provided by a man who was usually too busy arguing great social issues to attend to business. Michael Higgins lived past eighty. The contrast between her parents' fates was one source of Margaret Sanger's ambition to win reproductive autonomy for women.

Despite her determination to escape the family martyrdom of her mother and her sisters, Margaret Higgins loved her father as "a philosopher, a rebel, and an artist." He encouraged independence in his children and treated her as an intellectual ally with whom he discussed the free silver issue as well as woman suffrage and dress reform. Yet Michael Higgins, a physically imposing man, also expected from his children the deference due a Victorian patriarch. While Margaret Higgins shared her father's ideal of self-reliance, she longed for the security and status precluded by his controversial opinions and indifference to business, and her childhood was shaped by rebellion against authority. After an eighth grade teacher mocked a new pair of elegant gloves, a gift from her eldest sister, she refused to continue school in Corning. Her two older sisters then paid her tuition at Claverack College, a private coeducational preparatory school in the Catskills. Although she had to work in the kitchen for room and board, Higgins loved the genteel Claverack and "never wanted to return home."

After three happy years at Claverack, Higgins took a job teaching first grade to immigrant children in Little Falls, N.J., but discovered that she was "not suited by temperament" for the task. Obeying her father's summons, she returned to Corning, where her mother was dying of tuberculosis. Michael Higgins expected her to manage his household with the stoic resourcefulness of a traditional wife, but she resented the burden, particularly after he locked her out of the house one night for returning past his ten o'clock curfew. She escaped Corning a second time by entering the new nursing school of White Plains (N.Y.) Hospital.

The arduous duties of a nurse probationer were interrupted by a series of operations for tubercular glands, a condition that Higgins believed she had contracted while nursing her mother. In 1902 she was completing two years of practical nursing and had just been accepted into a three-year degree program when she married William Sanger, an architect who hoped to establish himself as an artist. Reluctant to marry because she felt that she was wasting both her sisters' sacrifices for her education and her own ambition, she explained to one sister: "He made me marry him, now or never he said." Pregnant within six months, Margaret Sanger spent most of her confinement at an Adirondack sanatorium. She delivered a son, Stuart, with great difficulty in 1903, and was sent back to the sanatorium by her doctor, who feared that she would be an invalid for life. Developing a revulsion against the treatment, however, she decided to attempt a normal life no matter what the consequences and the following year returned to her family in New York City on her own initiative.

Her health improved, and the Sangers built a home in suburban Westchester County; a second son, Grant, was born in 1908 and a daughter, Margaret (Peggy), in 1910. About this time Margaret Sanger became conscious of an increasing dissatisfaction with her life as a housewife. She had been drawn to William Sanger by the qualities of idealism and enthusiasm that he shared with her father. But, after eight years of marriage, the chance that he would become a serious artist seemed increasingly remote. The Sangers sought to thwart a growing estrangement through joint participation in radical politics, and they left their Hastings-on-Hudson home for a Manhattan apartment. Margaret Sanger began working as a home nurse on the Lower East Side "in order to earn my share" and enlisted in the radical labor movement as an activist in the International Workers of the World (IWW) effort to organize textile workers in the northeast.

Sanger made important contributions to the IWW strike efforts of 1912–13 in Pennsylvania, Massachusetts, and New Jersey. Together with ELIZABETH GURLEY FLYNN she organized the evacuation of strikers' children from Lawrence, Mass., a tactic that aroused national sympathy for the workers and was a key factor in the success of the strike. IWW leader William (Big Bill) Haywood found Sanger especially useful because she did not fit stereotypes usually associated with radicals. She was a petite mother of three, native born, and a trained nurse. But Sanger gradually lost the reticence expected of a lady as she learned from EMMA GOLDMAN and other radical women that issues of economic justice might be joined with feminist demands for recognition of the right of women to control their bodies. Responding to an urgent demand among women of all classes for information about venereal disease, birth control, and sex education, Sanger, as a nurse and mother, easily established herself among radicals as a speaker and writer on sexual reform. She gradually became convinced that women needed a distinctive voice representing them as an interest group in the struggle for social justice, and she adopted the position that sexual reform was the paramount issue for women, a cause that had to precede the struggle for higher wages and control of the work place.

Sanger's alienation from radical colleagues resulted in part from conflicts with William Sanger. He bitterly opposed the intimate friendships that had developed between his wife and a number of their friends. The discovery of her own capacity for sexual expression provided Margaret Sanger with a deep sense of personal power. Convinced that the sexual liberation of women would unleash great reservoirs of energy that had formerly been repressed or misdirected, she rejected her husband's demand that she be faithful to him, but her decision was painful. During this period she became acutely conscious of the condescension toward women of many male radicals, who expected women to subordinate their particular concerns to the class struggle.

Sanger's emerging feminist consciousness was also spurred by repression of her publications. Beginning in November 1912, she published a series of articles about female sexuality in the socialist weekly *The Call*. An article about syphilis for the Feb. 9, 1913, issue was declared unmailable by the United States Post Office under the Comstock Act of 1873, whose sweeping provisions also banned information on contraception and abortion. Venereal disease exacted a terrible toll from women denied knowledge of their bodies, but the numerous deaths from abortions among Sanger's patients in the tenements of the Lower East Side provided an even more horrifying symbol of female degradation.

Sanger claimed that, of all her experiences as a midwife and visiting nurse, the death of one of her clients from a self-induced abortion was the traumatic event that led her to focus all her energy on the single cause of reproductive autonomy for women. In the story of Sadie Sachs, a truck driver's wife who was scornfully refused contraceptive advice by a doctor and instructed instead to have her husband sleep on the roof, Sanger found a compelling myth. She used it to convey her outrage at the suppression of knowledge that women needed, whether their primary concern was the support of their families or the desire for greater personal freedom. Sanger's feeling of having been trapped by marriage, as well as her resentment of her mother's premature death, made the suffering of tenement mothers her own. There seemed to be no justice for these women, whose "weary misshapen bodies . . . were destined to be thrown on the scrap heap before they were thirty-five." Thus in 1914 Sanger, then living apart from her husband, set out to remove the stigma of obscenity from contraception and to establish a nationwide system of advice centers where women could obtain reliable birth control information.

Her first task was an investigation of birth control methods with the goal of discovering a safe, effective, female-controlled contraceptive. Native-born Americans had dramatically lowered their birth rates in the nineteenth century through sexual restraint within marriage, induced abortion, and contraception, but they paid a high cost in the form of sexual frustration, infection, and guilt. American moral leaders almost unanimously condemned these practices on religious and nativist grounds, claiming that the native-born women's revolt against their "natural" role would lead to "race suicide." These fears provided one motive for the late nineteenth-century suppression of contraceptive information, particularly through the Comstock Act. Although numerous contraceptive devices, including spermicidal douches, "womb veils" (diaphragms), a "safe period," and condoms, were described in nineteenth-century marriage manuals, physicians did not conduct contraceptive research. After surveying the medical literature and finding that no female methods had

been clinically tested, Sanger traveled to Europe in search of better birth control technology. She returned in early 1914 determined to spread the good news that sex could be separated from procreation, although women would have to discover through individual experimentation which method was best.

Sanger hoped to mobilize a mass demand for legalization of birth control through publication, beginning in March 1914, of her militantly feminist journal, *The Woman Rebel*, which the post office declared unmailable even though it gave no specific contraceptive advice. She continued to publish the journal and, after being indicted for violation of the postal code, departed for Europe in October 1914. Left behind were her instructions for mass distribution of her how-to-do-it pamphlet *Family Limitation*, which provided the most detailed and informed discussion of contraceptive technique then available in English. Critics pointed to questionable recommendations such as the use of laxatives to induce menstruation, but she had shown that women did not have to accept the void left by medical reluctance to provide contraceptive information.

During a year of exile in Europe, Sanger became an intimate friend of Havelock Ellis, author of *Studies in the Psychology of Sex*. Under his influence she began to develop a more cautious propaganda that exploited the rhetoric of social science and sought to win social elites to the cause. Ellis's permissive view of sexuality provided Sanger with a model of human nature more congenial to feminism than that of his great rival Freud. In the Netherlands Sanger found contraceptive advice centers staffed by midwives and was allowed to attend classes in the fitting of the spring-loaded vaginal diaphragm, a device that had been popularized by that country's first female physician, Aletta Jacobs. While she was away, William Sanger had been entrapped by an agent of the New York Society for the Suppression of Vice for handing out a copy of *Family Limitation*. This event and the pneumonia death of the Sangers' daughter in 1915 aroused great public sympathy for her. Probably as a result, within six months of her return to the United States in October 1915, the government dropped its earlier charges against her. Deeply distressed by her daughter's death, Sanger more than ever sought personal redemption through her cause and began a nationwide tour that convinced her the time had come to open a birth control advice center in the United States.

Staffed by Sanger and her younger sister, Ethel Byrne, the Brownsville clinic opened in October 1916 and provided 488 Brooklyn mothers with contraceptive advice during the ten days before it was closed by the police. The trial and imprisonment of the "birth control sisters" helped make Sanger a national figure, and, in appealing her case, she won a clarification of the New York law that forbade distribution of birth control information. Judge Frederick Crane ruled that the 1873 statute under which Sanger had been arrested was reasonable because it allowed doctors to prescribe condoms for venereal disease. In rejecting Sanger's claim that the law was unconstitutional because it forced women to risk death in pregnancy against their will, Crane established the right of doctors to provide women with contraceptive advice for "the cure and prevention of disease," thus widening the venereal disease clause to include women.

Sanger interpreted the Crane decision as a mandate for doctor-staffed birth control clinics. Although she continued to send revised editions of *Family Limitation* to those who asked for help, she adopted the strategy of lobbying for "doctors only" bills that removed legal prohibitions on medical advice. This pragmatic concession to the self-conscious professionalism of doctors was bitterly opposed by MARY WARE DENNETT, Sanger's chief rival for leadership of the movement in the early 1920s.

Sanger's attempt to cultivate support among doctors was part of her shift of strategy as a reformer. Gradually she broke her ties with old comrades, played down her radical past, stressed eugenic arguments for birth control, and found financial angels among socialites and philanthropists. Such support allowed her in 1921 to organize the American Birth Control League, the national lobbying organization which later became the Planned Parenthood Federation of America (1942). Having divorced William Sanger in 1920, she completed her social transition in 1922 by marrying millionaire J. Noah Slee, the manufacturer of Three-in-One Oil. Slee kept his promises to respect her autonomy and to fund her cause, and, although Sanger continued to enjoy intimate friendships with other men, their marriage lasted until Slee's death in 1943.

By 1923 Sanger had developed the network of support that allowed her to open, and to keep open, the Birth Control Clinical Research Bureau in New York City. The first doctor-staffed birth control clinic in the United States, it was one of Sanger's most important achievements. Under the medical direction of Hannah Stone (1893–1941), a careful clinical record was established demonstrating the safety and effectiveness of contraceptive practice. Irresponsible claims by medical men that diaphragms caused

cancer and madness, and did not work anyway, were refuted. The Bureau also served as a teaching facility where hundreds of physicians received instruction in contraceptive technique at a time when it was not a part of the medical school curriculum. Perhaps the Bureau's most important role was as a model for the nationwide network of over 300 birth control clinics established by Sanger and her supporters by 1938. Staffed mainly by women doctors and supported by the efforts of women volunteers, these clinics provided access to reliable contraceptive advice and were responsible for important improvements in the effectiveness of contraceptive practice.

In order to keep her clinics open, Sanger tirelessly raised money to make up budget deficits. Until she could convince an old friend, Herbert Simonds, to found the Holland Rantos Company in 1925 (with funds provided by Slee), she smuggled European-manufactured diaphragms into the United States. She also fought a series of court battles to establish the legality of the birth control clinic, and in 1936 realized her goal of reversing the Comstock Act's classification of birth control as obscenity. In *United States* v. *One Package*, a case initiated by Sanger's national Committee on Federal Legislation for Birth Control, a federal court ruled that new clinical data forced reinterpretation of the 1873 law to permit the mailing of contraceptive materials intended for physicians. The decision made possible the 1937 resolution of the American Medical Association recognizing contraception as a legitimate medical service that should be taught in medical schools.

After the *One Package* case, Sanger played a less important role in the American birth control movement and moved from New York to Tucson, Ariz., where she and Slee had built a home for their retirement. Her occasional suggestion that women stop having children until their demands for reproductive autonomy were met and her desire to ease restrictions on medical abortions seemed out of step during a period when the birth rate hovered around the replacement level; instead, prominent social scientists argued that depopulation was a cause of the depression and fretted over the disparity between birth rates in the western democracies and those in Nazi Germany. By the late 1930s Sanger's brand of feminism was deemed counterproductive by new leaders who hoped to gain acceptance of their cause from supporters of voluntary health organizations. They replaced "birth control" with "family planning" in an effort to broaden the appeal of the movement and sought to restrict contraceptive advice to those whose health would be threatened by pregnancy. This trend distressed Sanger, who believed in helping as many women as possible.

After World War II and the discovery of the so-called population explosion, Sanger's vision began to command new respect, and in 1952 she played a creative role in the founding of the International Planned Parenthood Federation, which she served as first president. Despite her role in promoting the diaphragm, she had never been satisfied with it and raised large sums throughout her career for research on promising leads ranging from spermatoxins to foam powders. In 1952 she helped to realize her dream of a female-controlled physiological contraceptive when she brought the work of the biologist Gregory Pincus to the attention of KATHARINE DEXTER MCCORMICK, who subsidized the development of the birth control pill first marketed in 1960.

When Margaret Sanger died of congestive heart failure in 1966 after a four-year stay in a Tucson nursing home, her goal of reproductive autonomy for all women remained unattained, but she had done more than any other individual to give women control over their bodies.

[Over 500 boxes of personal and organizational papers are divided among the Library of Congress, the Sophia Smith Coll. at Smith College, and the Am. Birth Control League Papers at Houghton Library, Harvard Univ. The Sophia Smith Coll. also has a microfilm of the Sanger papers in the Library of Congress, as well as the papers of the Planned Parenthood Federation of America. Sanger left two autobiographies, *My Fight for Birth Control* (1931) and *Margaret Sanger: An Autobiography* (1938). Her other major books are *Woman and the New Race* (1920), *The Pivot of Civilization* (1922), *Happiness in Marriage* (1926), and *Motherhood in Bondage* (1928). She published three important journals: *Woman Rebel* (1914), *Birth Control Review* (1917–40), and *Human Fertility* (1940–48). Major studies of her career are Harold Hersey, *Margaret Sanger: The Biography of the Birth Control Pioneer* (1938); Lawrence Lader, *The Margaret Sanger Story and the Fight for Birth Control* (1955); David Kennedy, *Birth Control in America: The Career of Margaret Sanger* (1970); Emily Taft Douglas, *Margaret Sanger: Pioneer of the Future* (1970); and Madeline Gray, *Margaret Sanger: A Biography of the Champion of Birth Control* (1979). In addition, several historians have given extended attention to Sanger's career in broader studies: Linda Gordon, *Woman's Body, Woman's Right: A Social History of Birth Control in America* (1976); Sheila Rothman, *Woman's Proper Place: A History of Changing Ideals and Practices, 1870 to the Present* (1978); and James Reed, *From Private Vice to Public Virtue: The Birth Control Movement and American Society Since 1830* (1978), which contains an annotated bibliography. The source of Sanger's birth date is the family Bible in the Sophia

Smith Coll.; Gray, p. 13, explains how discrepancies in the date were resolved. Death certificate supplied by Ariz. Dept. of Health.]

JAMES REED

SAVAGE, Augusta Christine, Feb. 29, 1892–March 26, 1962. Sculptor.

Augusta Savage was born in Green Cove Springs, Fla., the seventh of fourteen children of Rev. Edward and Cornelia (Murphy) Fells. She was the third child and second daughter of the nine children (five girls and four boys) who lived to maturity. Edward Fells, who earned his living as a house painter, was a deeply religious man who assisted local Methodist ministers in conducting church services.

Augusta Fells attended public schools in Green Cove Springs and studied briefly at the state normal school in Tallahassee (later Florida A & M University). From an early age, she had shown an interest in modeling the local red clay into figures. Edward Fells, thinking Augusta's models were the "graven images" prohibited in the Bible, punished her whenever he found her creations, but she persisted and he came eventually to accept her modeling.

Augusta Fells married John T. Moore in 1907; her only child, Irene Connie Moore, was born the following year. John Moore died when Irene was a small child and in 1915 Augusta Moore moved to West Palm Beach, Fla. Some time in the mid-1910s, she married James Savage, a laborer and carpenter; they were divorced in the early 1920s. She remained close to her daughter; they shared a home for much of Augusta Savage's life and Irene Moore provided emotional and financial support for her mother's art.

At a Palm Beach county fair Savage's clay models won a special prize of $25; additional donations from the public brought her fair earnings to $175. Advised to go to New York City to develop her talent, she eventually arrived there in 1920 with $4.60, found a job as an apartment caretaker, and set out to learn to be a sculptor. Solon Borglum, a prominent New York sculptor, directed her to Cooper Union, which had a four-year tuition-free art program. Beginning there in October 1921, she continued to take courses at the school until 1924, doing much of her study with the sculptor George Brewster. She lost her job soon after starting at Cooper Union, but the school's directors granted her a scholarship for her living expenses.

In early 1923, Augusta Savage applied for admission to a summer school to be held under the patronage of the French government at the

Palace of Fontainebleau. "Without thinking it necessary to mention my race," she made a preliminary deposit and was preparing to have two recommendations sent to the selection committee for American students when she was informed that they had decided not to approve her application. Subsequently, Ernest Peixotto, chairman of painting and sculpture for the committee, admitted that Savage had been rejected because she was not white. Hurt and disappointed, she decided to make the story public to prevent "other and better colored students" from being kept out of the school. Savage's black and white supporters appealed to the committee to reverse its decision and to President Warren G. Harding and the French government to intervene. Although these efforts were unsuccessful, committee member sculptor Hermon MacNeil invited Savage to study with him that summer.

It would be six years before Savage secured the European training that would help her transcend the academicism she had learned at Cooper Union. Yet, the Fontainebleau incident was a significant influence on her career, making her a well-known black artist and a heroine to many. To some influential white artists and gallery owners, however, she appeared a troublemaker who should be avoided. At the same time, Savage was becoming known independently as a portrait sculptor. In late 1922 she had completed a bust of W. E. B. Du Bois and was working on one of Marcus Garvey. In later years, she also did busts of Frederick Douglass, Eugene Kinckle Jones, W. C. Handy, James Weldon Johnson, Edwin Bowes, Walter Gray Crump, and Theodore Upshure.

Several other disappointments followed for Savage. In October 1923 she married Robert L. Poston, a journalist and an associate of Marcus Garvey; Poston died the following March. Awarded a scholarship in 1925 to cover tuition and working materials at the Academy of Fine Arts in Rome, Savage was unable to go because she lacked the funds to pay for her travel and living expenses. She worked in laundries to collect the needed money but spent most of her earnings helping her parents and other family members.

In 1929, Savage won the first of two successive Julius Rosenwald fellowships, awarded for "Gamin," an appealing portrait of a young Harlem boy and one of the best executed of her character studies. Seeking to learn the most advanced techniques in portrait sculpture, she went to Paris where she studied with Felix Beauneteaux at the Grand Chaumière and later with Charles Despiau. Savage's work was exhibited at several galleries in Europe, winning citations at the Salon d'Automne and the Salon Printemps at the Grande-Palais in Paris and a medallion at the French government's Colonial Exposition.

By early 1932, Savage had returned to New York City. She turned again to sculptured portraits, and also established a school, the Savage Studio of Arts and Crafts, where she later provided studio space for artists involved in the Works Progress Administration's Federal Art Project (FAP). Exhibitions by Savage's students attracted favorable publicity during the 1930s. Savage herself was asked to exhibit her sculpture before wider and larger audiences in the 1930s and early 1940s.

By 1936, Savage had become an assistant supervisor of the FAP for New York City and in December 1937 she was named the first director of the Harlem Community Art Center. Responsible for increasing the number of blacks employed by the FAP, Savage was also influential as a teacher. Several of her students, including William Artis, Norman Lewis, and Jacob Lawrence, went on to become nationally recognized artists.

During these years Savage received several honors. In 1934 she became the first black elected a member of the National Association of Women Painters and Sculptors, and she was one of four women and the only black woman commissioned to produce a piece of sculpture for the New York World's Fair of 1939–40. Her statue, "Lift Every Voice and Sing," featured a sixteen-foot-tall harp with strings leading from a frieze of singing black youth; a kneeling figure in front offered the gift of black music to the world. Praised by Alain Locke as "a magnificently dramatic idea," it received wide publicity.

Savage had taken a leave of absence from the Harlem Community Art Center to do the World's Fair sculpture. When she sought to return, she was disappointed to find that she had been replaced. She next became president of a corporation that in June 1939 opened the Salon of Contemporary Negro Art, the first gallery in the United States devoted to the exhibition and sale of works of black artists. Although it served a great need, the gallery went out of existence a few years after its founding because of lack of funds. Subsequently, Savage withdrew from active promotion of art and art education in New York City and her own work declined in volume and significance.

About 1945, Savage moved to rural Saugerties, N.Y., hoping to find new ideas for her work. There she raised and sold chickens and eggs, did some portrait sculptures of tourists, and on occasion taught children in nearby summer camps. She remained in Saugerties until a few months before her death in Bronx, N.Y., of cancer in 1962.

Despite the barriers created throughout her life by racism and poverty, Augusta Savage produced a substantial number of works of high artistic quality. Critics have argued that her best work was her bronze and plaster portrait sculpture, although she also showed ability in several other mediums. Her portraits of Du Bois and Marcus Garvey capture the dignity and strength of those militant black leaders, while her narrative skills are displayed in the wood-carving "Envy," where a symbolic distortion and twisting of the human figure dramatize the negative impact of that emotion. "Green Apples" uses contortion for different purposes, showing a beautifully modeled nude youngster whose body is doubled over with pain from eating green apples.

Savage herself was modest about her achievements: "I have created nothing really beautiful, really lasting, but if I can inspire one of these youngsters to develop the talent I know they possess, then my monument will be in their work" (Poston, p. 67). Her own suffering and struggles as an artist led her to sacrifice time she might have spent in producing her own work to teach others how to develop their talent, even when they could not pay. Augusta Savage left as her legacy not only significant works of art but also significant artists to achieve the recognition often denied to her.

[There is no manuscript collection. The Schomburg Coll., N.Y. Public Library, and Savage's daughter, Irene Moore Allen, have clippings, artwork, and other memorabilia. A list of works and exhibitions and a bibliography appear in Theresa Dickason Cederholm, *Afro-American Artists: A Bio-bibliography and Directory* (1973), pp. 247–48. Savage published "Augusta Savage: An Autobiography," *Crisis*, Aug. 1929, p. 269. Various newspaper and magazine interviews rely on quotations and information supplied by Savage. The most valuable of these are: Eric Walrond, "Florida Girl Shows Amazing Gift for Sculpture," an undated clipping in the Schomburg Coll., which includes a poem by Savage and one written about her; "Young Sculptress Defies Adversity That Dogged Her Steps, Now Studies in Paris," *Norfolk Journal and Guide*, Oct. 19, 1929, also in the Schomburg Coll.; T. R. Poston (her brother-in-law), "Augusta Savage," *Metropolitan Mag.*, Jan. 1935; and Harmon Foundation, *Negro Artists: An Illustrated Review of Their Achievements* (1935). See also *Current Biog.*, 1941. The most useful critical evaluations are Elton Clay Fax, "Augusta Savage: An Appraisal," *AMSAC* (Am. Soc. for African Culture) *Newsletter*, 1962, and the chapter on Savage in Romare Bearden and Harry Henderson, *Six Black Masters of American Art* (1972). See also Alain Locke, ed., *The Negro in Art: A Pictorial Record of the Negro Artist and of*

the *Negro Theme in Art* (1940), and James A. Porter, *Modern Negro Art* (1943, 1969). Obituaries appeared in the *N.Y. Times*, March 27, 1962, and the *N.Y. Amsterdam News*, March 31, 1962. Savage's birth date generally appears as 1900; the 1892 date is confirmed by the 1900 U.S. Census and by a death certificate, provided by the N.Y. City Dept. of Health. Irene Allen provided useful information; a biobibliography by Frances Pollard Fugate further assisted with research.]

DE WITT S. DYKES, JR.

SAWYER, Ruth, Aug. 5, 1880–June 3, 1970. Children's author, storyteller.

Ruth Sawyer, who made major contributions to the art of storytelling, was born in Boston's Back Bay, the only girl in a family with four older sons, all born four or five years apart. Her father, Francis Milton Sawyer, was a successful importer, a descendant of an old New England family who had been Tory sympathizers. Her mother was Ethalinda J. (Smith) Sawyer, of Lexington, Mass., also descended from an old New England family, but on the revolutionary side.

A well-to-do family, the Sawyers moved to New York in 1881 and established themselves on the Upper East Side. Ruth Sawyer received loving but strict care from her parents and found it difficult growing up as the youngest and a girl in a household of adults and older brothers. But she had her beloved Irish nurse, Johanna, who captivated Ruth with tales from Donegal.

Until she was seven Ruth Sawyer had a French governess; she later spent three years at Miss Brackett's, the New York school run by ANNA BRACKETT, which she described in *Roller Skates*. Francis Sawyer died in 1894, when Ruth was fourteen; because of uncertain finances the family spent a year in its summer home near Camden, Maine, later the basis for her book, *The Year of Jubilo*. When they returned to New York, she studied for a year at the Packer Collegiate Institute in Brooklyn (1895–96).

In 1900, after graduation from Garland, a kindergarten training school in Boston, Ruth Sawyer helped to organize kindergartens for the many children in Cuba orphaned by the Spanish-American War. In recognition of this service, she received a scholarship to Teachers College, Columbia University, where she studied folklore and received a B.S. in education (1904). While at Columbia she became a volunteer storyteller and also had the significant experience of hearing British storyteller Marie Shedlock tell stories of Hans Christian Andersen. Also important for her own storytelling was the invitation of the New York Public Lecture Bureau to offer folk tales in story hours for foreign-born groups; for two years she told stories in such varied settings as the Bowery, the Seamen's Mission, and a boys' reformatory at Fordham. Her first storytelling at the New York Public Library occurred in 1910 and initiated a long friendship with ANNE CARROLL MOORE, the library's supervisor of work with children.

In 1905 and again in 1907, Sawyer went to Ireland to do feature articles on commission for the *New York Sun*. There she associated with the great traditional storytellers, including Padraic Colum and James Stephens. Riding a little Irish pony through Donegal, she met rural folk and heard the old *seanachies*. In Dublin, at the studio of the poet and painter AE (George Russell), she contributed "Rip Van Winkle" and "The Tar Baby" to storytelling sessions and was lovingly called "the sister of Tom Sawyer."

In 1911 Ruth Sawyer married Albert C. Durand, whom she had met in New York while they were finishing their studies—she at Columbia, he at the Manhattan Eye and Ear Infirmary. The couple moved to Ithaca, N.Y., where Dr. Durand had set up a practice in ophthalmology. There they had two children: David (b. 1912) and Margaret (b. 1916). While the children were growing up, Ruth Sawyer (the name she used professionally) continued to tell stories and began to write in earnest —both novels and children's stories. The first two novels were *The Primrose Ring* (1915) and *Seven Miles to Arden* (1917), the latter appearing serially in the *Ladies' Home Journal*. More important and enduring, however, were her contributions to children's literature. Her early books for children included *This Way to Christmas* (1916), *Child's Yearbook* (1917), and *The Tale of the Enchanted Bunnies* (1923).

In 1931 Ruth Sawyer's interest in children's literature took a new turn when she went to Spain for a year of collecting stories—an adventure motivated by an earlier fascination with Washington Irving's *Tales of the Alhambra* and *Conquest of Granada*. The result of this travel was *Toño Antonio* (1934), published by Viking Press; it was then that Ruth Sawyer became a close friend of Viking's children's book editor MAY MASSEE. Subsequent results of the Spanish adventure were *Picture Tales from Spain* (1936) and a book on travel, *My Spain* (1962).

By 1935 her reputation as a storyteller brought Ruth Sawyer an invitation from the United States Department of Justice to tell stories at the Federal Reformatory for Women in Alderson, W. Va. Between 1935 and 1945 she spent a month each year at Alderson.

It was in 1936 that Sawyer first achieved wide recognition, for her autobiographical story *Roller Skates*, the story of a spirited little girl discovering New York City on her own at the turn of the century when her parents were abroad. The book, which introduced new urban subject matter into literature for children, won the John Newbery Medal (given annually by the American Library Association for the most distinguished book for children) in 1937; its sequel, *The Year of Jubilo*, also autobiographical, appeared in 1940. Many other stories followed, among them *Old Con and Patrick* (1940); *The Long Christmas*, (1941); *The Little Red Horse* (1950); *Journey Cake, Ho!* (1953), illustrated by her son-in-law, Robert McCloskey; *The Enchanted Schoolhouse* (1956); *Dietrich of Berne and the Dwarf King Laurin* (1963), with Emmy Mollès; and *Daddles, the Story of a Plain Hound-Dog* (1964). In *The Way of the Storyteller* (1942; rev. ed. 1962) Ruth Sawyer explained her conception of storytelling as a creative art. The book, which also includes eleven tales retold for storytellers, became a standard guide for practitioners and teachers.

During six decades of giving the children's book world an original and creative outpouring, Sawyer received several honors. In 1958 the College of St. Catherine in St. Paul, Minn., established the Ruth Sawyer Collection of rare books in the field of children's literature. In 1965 she received both the Regina Medal of the Catholic Library Association and the Laura Ingalls Wilder Medal (American Library Association) for a "substantial and lasting contribution to children's literature." In the same year a storytelling festival was held in her honor in Provincetown, Mass.

After Albert Durand's retirement in 1946, the Durands moved to Hancock, Maine. Later they moved to Florida—and then to Boston, where Ruth Sawyer spent one winter telling stories at the Boston Public Library. Finally, they moved to the Hancock House Nursing Home in Lexington, Mass., where Dr. Durand died in 1967; Ruth Sawyer died there three years later of a gastrointestinal hemorrhage, two months before her ninetieth birthday.

[In addition to the collection at St. Catherine's College, there is material pertaining to Sawyer in the May Massee Coll., Emporia (Kans.) State Univ. The major source of information is Virginia Haviland, *Ruth Sawyer* (1965), which incorporates material from the author's interviews with Sawyer. See also Ruth Sawyer's "Acceptance Paper" and a biographical note by Jacqueline Overton in *Newbery Medal Papers* (1955); and *Junior Book of Authors* (1951). An obituary appeared in *Horn*

Book Mag., Aug. 1970; death record provided by Mass. Dept. of Public Health.]

VIRGINIA HAVILAND

SCHNEIDERMAN, Rose, April 6, 1882–Aug. 11, 1972. Labor organizer, social reformer.

Rose Schneiderman was born Rachel Schneiderman in Saven, a small village in Russian Poland, the first of Adolph Samuel and Deborah (Rothman) Schneiderman's four children (two girls and two boys). Growing up in an impoverished but close-knit Orthodox Jewish family, Rose spent her early childhood in Saven and in Khelm, an industrial city, where her father worked as a tailor and her mother, a skilled seamstress, made custom uniforms for Russian army officers. She remembered her father as gentle, easygoing, and intellectual, her mother as assertive and outspoken. Deborah Schneiderman also believed in female education and insisted that her daughter attend school. At four, Rose began attending a traditional Hebrew school, or *cheder*–highly unusual for a girl–and at six, she began Russian public school. Later, in the United States, despite frequent interruptions in her education, she completed the ninth grade.

The Schneidermans migrated to the United States in 1890 and settled on New York's Lower East Side. In the winter of 1892, Samuel Schneiderman became ill with meningitis and died within a few days, leaving his wife pregnant with her fourth child. For several years the family depended upon charity to supplement what Deborah Schneiderman could earn by taking in boarders and home sewing. Despite their mother's resourcefulness, Rose and her brothers spent over a year in Jewish orphanages. When she returned home, Rose took on the tasks of housework and child care while her mother was at work.

At thirteen Rose began work, spending three years as a department store cash girl and sales clerk–jobs that paid just over $2.00 for a work week that often stretched to seventy hours. Despite her mother's objection that industrial work was not genteel, in 1898 she took a better paying job in a cap factory. Initially she knew nothing of trade unionism, but her outlook changed after a stay with a socialist family in Montreal. In 1903 Rose Schneiderman launched her union career. With two other women, she organized her shop into the first female local of the Jewish Socialist United Cloth Hat and Cap Makers' Union. Schneiderman emerged as an effective leader, and her local soon grew to a membership of several hundred. She served as

its secretary and as one of the union's delegates to the New York Central Labor Union. During the capmakers' successful thirteen-week strike in 1905 against employers' attempts to institute an open shop policy, she walked picket lines and led strike meetings.

Although she remained a member of the union throughout her life, after 1907 Schneiderman increasingly devoted herself to the Women's Trade Union League (WTUL), which she considered "the most important influence in my life." A coalition of workers and middle- and upper-class reformers, the WTUL was dedicated to unionizing working women and to lobbying for protective legislation. MARGARET DREIER ROBINS, then president of the New York branch, persuaded Schneiderman to join in 1905, despite her initial doubts that an organization with so many wealthy women could understand the needs of working women or accomplish much for them. Schneiderman became a vice president of the New York WTUL the following year. A stipend provided by IRENE LEWISOHN enabled her to quit factory work, devote herself to the league as its East Side organizer, and continue her education briefly at the Rand School of Social Science, a socialist night school dedicated to workers' education. In 1910 she accepted a position as the New York league's full-time organizer. Remaining active in the New York organization, the strongest branch of the WTUL, for thirty-five years, she and MARY DREIER became its most important leaders.

Under league auspices, Schneiderman played a key role in the successful organizing drives of the International Ladies' Garment Workers' Union (ILGWU) from 1909 through 1914. By conducting strikes in virtually every branch of the women's clothing industry, the ILGWU brought several hundred thousand workers, a majority of them women, into the union, and transformed itself into a powerful organization. Schneiderman was instrumental in organizing and raising funds for ILGWU Local 25 (shirtwaistmakers), sat on that union's executive board, and was one of the leaders of the shirtwaistmakers' strike, the "Uprising of the Twenty Thousand." She also organized ILGWU Local 62 (white goods workers), served briefly as that union's president, and helped lead its 1913 strike.

For Schneiderman, the early years of trade union work were exhilarating and fulfilling. The shy, lonely young woman developed into a militant organizer and dynamic speaker, well known for her strong views and a fiery temperament that matched her flaming red hair. Although less than five feet tall, she could rivet audiences' attention on street corners, in union halls, and at mass rallies. In the aftermath of the 1911 Triangle factory fire, in which 146 shirtwaistmakers died, it was Schneiderman's impassioned speech at the Metropolitan Opera House that best expressed the workers' outrage at the horrors of the sweatshop system. "I would be a traitor to these poor burned bodies," she told the audience, "if I came here to talk good fellowship. . . . Every year thousands of us are maimed. The life of men and women is so cheap and property is so sacred" (*All for One,* pp. 100–1).

Schneiderman found it difficult to reconcile her commitment to the labor movement with her desire to improve conditions for women workers. Although often at odds with other WTUL leaders about what she considered their lack of commitment to immigrant women, in the end she found it easier to collaborate with members of the league than with male colleagues in the labor movement. As a national organizer for the ILGWU in 1915 and 1916—one of the few women organizers in a union with a largely female membership—she felt isolated and frustrated by the union officers' lack of confidence. She especially resented an effort by male organizers to lead a strike that she had planned, and returned to the WTUL in 1917.

By this time Schneiderman had also developed an interest in broader political and educational movements. Viewing the ballot as a means of attaining protective legislation for working women, she became a committed suffragist, working as a National American Woman Suffrage Association speaker and organizer in the Ohio referendum campaign in 1913, and active as well in the 1915 and 1917 New York state campaigns. She helped to form the short-lived New York State Labor party in 1919 and ran as the party's candidate for United States senator the following year. She traveled to Europe in 1919 with MARY ANDERSON as part of the WTUL delegation to the Paris Peace Conference, and helped organize the International Congress of Working Women at that time. An ardent believer in education as a means of advancement, she was among the organizers of the Bryn Mawr Summer School for Women Workers which opened in 1921.

The WTUL remained her major interest. In 1918 Schneiderman was elected president of the New York league, a position she held until 1949. She became president of the National WTUL as well in 1926, but that body had already lost much of its dynamism. An effective administrator and fund raiser, as head of the New York league Schneiderman concentrated less on organizing than on promoting workers' education and on lobbying for protective legislation. She succeeded in raising funds to purchase a club-house, which became an educational as well as social center for working women. Increasingly, Schneiderman devoted her energies to lobbying in Albany for minimum wage and eight-hour-day laws for women workers. Like other advocates of protective legislation, she vigorously opposed the Equal Rights Amendment, and, as national league president, concentrated in the late 1920s on opposing the efforts of the National Woman's party to secure its ratification.

Her league activities brought Schneiderman in touch with prominent politicians and reformers, most notably Franklin and ELEANOR ROOSEVELT. Their long friendship began when Eleanor Roosevelt joined the New York WTUL in 1922. Schneiderman became a frequent guest at the Roosevelts' homes in New York City and Hyde Park and, after 1929, at the governor's mansion in Albany. During these visits, she and WTUL leader MAUD SWARTZ often talked about the labor movement and helped to shape the Roosevelts' views on labor relations. Close associates, including FRANCES PERKINS, believed that as a result of these conversations, Franklin Roosevelt saw the trade union movement "in a new light." For her part, Schneiderman was proud of her friendship with the Roosevelts and the opportunity it gave her to experience a way of life so far removed from her own origins.

As president, Franklin Roosevelt in 1933 appointed Schneiderman to the labor advisory board of the National Recovery Administration (NRA). The task assigned to the board was to insure that the wages and hours provisions of the codes drawn up by various industries were fair to workers. As the only woman member, Schneiderman concentrated on codes for industries that employed large numbers of women. She later called her two years with NRA "the most exhilarating and inspiring of my life."

In 1935, after the act that had established the NRA was declared unconstitutional, Rose Schneiderman returned to the Bronx, where she shared an apartment with her mother. She also returned to the WTUL which resumed its organizing efforts. Under her leadership, the league successfully organized New York women laundry workers (who through Schneiderman's negotiations were also able to affiliate with the Amalgamated Clothing Workers of America) and the city's hotel workers. The two protective measures for which she worked hardest, the eight-hour day and a minimum wage, were enacted into New York law during the 1930s, due in part to her coordination of WTUL lobbying efforts. In addition to her league work, from 1937 to 1943 Schneiderman also held the post of secretary of the New York State Department of Labor. Always an activist, she found this largely administrative position frustrating, and resigned because "there was not enough for me to do."

Schneiderman was still president of the National WTUL when it disbanded in 1950. The year before she had retired as president of the New York league, but remained an active member until it too closed its doors in 1955. Thereafter she retired from public life and lived quietly in Manhattan, where she had moved following her mother's death in 1939. In her autobiography, written in her eighties, she expressed satisfaction at the progress American workers had made since her days as a capmaker. She spent the last five years in the Jewish Home and Hospital for the Aged in New York, where she died at the age of ninety.

The dominant theme in Rose Schneiderman's career was her commitment to the labor movement. As a feminist unionist, her special contribution to that movement had been to work for the advancement of women in the workplace and in the unions, efforts that often brought her into conflict with male union leaders. As her own circumstances changed, she came to have more in common with the reformers than with the working women she sought to help, but her commitment to their cause never faltered.

[Rose Schneiderman's papers, consisting primarily of correspondence, NYWTUL materials, and memorabilia, are located at the Tamiment Library, N.Y. Univ. Other useful material on her career is contained in the papers of the NYWTUL, located in the N.Y. State Labor Library, Dept. of Labor, N.Y. City, and the Nat. WTUL Papers, Library of Congress. The most helpful published work is Schneiderman's autobiography, *All for One* (1967). She was an occasional contributor to the Nat. WTUL's journal, *Life and Labor;* see especially "The White Goods Workers of New York," May 1913. See also her early article, "A Cap-Maker's Story," *Independent,* April 27, 1905. For information on the NYWTUL see Nancy Schrom Dye, "The Women's Trade Union League of New York, 1903–1920" (Ph.D. diss., Univ. of Wis., 1974); "Creating a Feminist Alliance: Sisterhood and Class Conflict in the New York Women's Trade Union League," *Feminist Studies,* 2 (1975); and "Feminism or Unionism? The New York Women's Trade Union League and the Labor Movement," *Feminist Studies,* 3 (1975). See also Robin Miller Jacoby, "The Women's Trade Union League and American Feminism," *Feminist Studies,* 3 (1975), and "The British and American Women's Trade Union Leagues: A Case Study of Feminism and Class" (Ph.D. diss., Harvard Univ., 1976). For information on Schneiderman's relationship with the Roosevelts see Frances Perkins, *The Roosevelt I Knew* (1946), and Joseph Lash, *Eleanor and Franklin* (1971). Schneiderman's reform interests are emphasized by Gary Edward Endelman, "Solidarity Forever: Rose Schneiderman and the Women's Trade Union League" (Ph.D. diss., Univ. of Del., 1978). See also *Current Biog.,* 1946, *Biog. Dict. Am. Labor Leaders* (1974), *Who's Who in Labor* (1946), and the obituary in the *N.Y. Times,* Aug. 12, 1972. Some sources list Schneiderman's birth date as April 6, 1884, but *All for One* and the death certificate provided by the N.Y. City Dept. of Health give it as April 6, 1882.]

NANCY SCHROM DYE

SCOTT, Ann London, July 29, 1929–Feb. 17, 1975. Feminist, poet.

Ann London Scott was born Claire Ann in Seattle, Wash., to Daniel Edwin and Claire (Chester) London, both of British ancestry. In 1935 the family moved to San Francisco, when Daniel London received an offer to become manager of the St. Francis, a luxury hotel, where Ann and her younger sister, Mimi, had memorable escapades.

Ann London was a voracious reader and an excellent student, especially during her high school years at the intellectually competitive Dominican Convent School in San Rafael, Calif. In 1947 she entered Stanford University, but found it difficult to combine the serious study required of a scholarship student with the social life of a San Francisco debutante. When her fellowship was not renewed, she transferred in 1949 to the University of Washington. There a longtime interest in poetry drew her away from sorority life. Gravitating toward new friends in the arts, she married on Nov. 23, 1951, Paul de Witt Tufts, a young musician from a Washington farm family; the marriage was considered inappropriate by her family and did not survive their student years.

After graduation in 1954, she returned to San Francisco, briefly renewing old associations and experimenting with various jobs. She was most attracted to the San Francisco of beat writer Jack Kerouac and Lawrence Ferlinghetti's City Lights bookstore. A second marriage followed in October 1956, to an impecunious Jewish poet, Gerd Stern. A son, Jared London, was born in 1957. The marriage caused further estrangement from her parents, who objected to her bohemian lifestyle; it ended in 1961.

Determined to create a new life for herself and her son, Ann London, now thirty-two, returned that fall to the University of Washington to work toward a doctorate in literature. Her parents encouraged her, providing supplemental financial support and a summer home for their grandson. By the time she left Seattle four years later, she had begun a dissertation on Shakespeare's use of language, published her poetry in such journals as *Sage, Choice,* and

Poetry Northwest, and found a promising teaching position at the State University of New York (SUNY) at Buffalo. Students responded to her wit and warmth, and colleagues respected her intelligence. Although she received her Ph.D. in 1968, delay in completing her dissertation cost her a tenured position in the English department. She remained on the staff until 1972, when she moved to Baltimore.

In 1969 personal and professional developments coincided to change the direction of her life. She married Thomas Jefferson Scott, a gentle and sensitive artist; the marriage brought her happiness and greater self-confidence. She responded angrily to the fact that male colleagues whom she regarded as her intellectual inferiors had received tenure. Supported by her husband and the local chapter (which she had founded) of the National Organization for Women (NOW), Ann Scott embarked on a study of sex discrimination at SUNY, Buffalo— an action that rapidly propelled her into a new career as a feminist and activist dedicated to social change.

Elected in 1970 to the Board of Directors of the national NOW, Scott became convinced that changes in legislation affecting education, employment, and reproductive choice were essential if the cultural changes advocated by feminists were to have meaning. As NOW's Federal Contract Compliance Officer, she sought to ensure equal employment opportunities for women not only in universities but also in industry and broadcasting. With fellow NOW leader Lucy Komisar she lobbied members of Congress and national organizations to pressure the Department of Labor to change affirmative action guidelines to include women in regulations governing hiring and promotions for firms holding federal contracts. They applied similar pressure to the Federal Communications Commission, enlisting other organizations in support of a petition filed by a public interest law firm to include women in affirmative action guidelines applying to all local stations holding an FCC license. As NOW's vice president for legislation, Scott worked to secure passage of both the 1972 Equal Employment Opportunity Act Amendment and the Equal Rights Amendment. She possessed remarkable powers of persuasion, an ability to broaden alliances, and a political sophistication that won her the admiration of legislators and fellow lobbyists. Creator of a national NOW lobbying network, Scott was also a member of the national board of Common Cause and of the Leadership Conference on Civil Rights. She regarded the efforts of all these organizations as part of a larger struggle for economic and social justice. In 1974 she became associate director of the American Association for Higher Education.

Scott died of cancer in Baltimore in 1975, after valiantly struggling with the disease for over a year. Helping to write her own obituary, she expressed a wish to be remembered as a poet and a feminist. Her enduring contribution was to the women's movement, to which she brought not only her much needed political skills but also the example of her hard-won control over her own life.

[Material on Scott's feminist activities is in the possession of Lucy Komisar and in the NOW Legal Defense Fund Files. A collection of unpublished poems by Scott is in the possession of Jerome Mazzaro, SUNY, Buffalo. Scott's sex discrimination study was published as "The Half-Eaten Apple: A Look at Sex Discrimination in the University," *The Reporter,* SUNY, Buffalo (May 14, 1970). Scott's feminist activities are described in the NOW newsletter, Jan.-Feb. 1975, and in the obituary by Lucy Komisar, *Ms.,* June 1975. An obituary also appeared in the *N.Y. Times,* Feb. 19, 1975. Komisar, Mazzaro, Thomas Scott, Claire London, and Anita Gardner provided valuable information. Birth certificate obtained from Washington State Board of Health; death certificate from Md. Dept. of Health.]

JANE DE HART MATHEWS

SCUDDER, Ida Sophia, Dec. 9, 1870–May 24, 1960. Physician, missionary.

Ida Scudder, founder of the Christian Medical College and Hospital, Vellore, South India, was born in Ranipet, Madras Presidency, India, the sixth and youngest child and only daughter of Sophia (Weld) Scudder and John Scudder II. Her father, born in Ceylon, was the youngest of seven sons and two daughters who followed the first American medical missionary, John Scudder, into the Indian mission field. Her Vermont-born mother, although initially adjudged by the Reformed Church mission board as too frail to accompany her husband, survived sixty-four years in India, the last twenty-five as her daughter's unofficial hostess, assistant, and adviser.

Ida's early days in the mission bungalow in Vellore included traumatic experiences during a devastating famine and cholera epidemic. In 1878 the family returned to live for four years on a farm near Creston, Neb. When her father resumed his duties in India in 1882, followed a year later by her mother, the thirteen-year-old Ida was left in Chicago under the strict tutelage of an uncle, Rev. Henry Martyn Scudder, and his wife. The feelings of loneliness and parental abandonment common to missionary children sent home for a safe education were exacerbated in 1887 when her uncle joined the Japan mission, after placing Ida in Dwight Moody's

Northfield Seminary in Massachusetts. There the popular and mischievous blonde became a student leader, but confessed feelings of rejection and loneliness to her diary.

Despite her parents' expectations and the powerful model of Scudder missionary service—four generations of the family eventually contributed 1,100 years of missionary service in India—Ida determined to share her classmates' conventional middle-class life. Still hostile to a missionary career, she left Northfield without graduating in 1890 because her mother was ill and her parents needed her help in their isolated new post in Tindivanam. There her determination to return to the United States broke down when in a single dramatic night she was summoned to help deliver three women in childbirth, all of whom died. She had protested her lack of training and urged her father's more experienced services, but the husbands refused to allow a man to attend their wives.

In 1895 Ida Scudder matriculated in the Woman's Medical College of Pennsylvania, transferring in her final year to Cornell Medical College for the superior clinical training available there. She received her M.D. in 1899. Involved in preparations for her return to India and in fund raising for a hospital there, Scudder was distracted by insistent marriage proposals from a Philadelphia medical student. Rejecting these, as she had earlier proposals, she later commented that " 'I never could have carried on my work in the hospital and school if I had had the responsibility of bringing up a family of my own' " (Jeffery, pp. 185–86). Her students and the thousands of children she delivered and sometimes informally adopted substituted for a family.

Scudder also nurtured several close and long friendships, beginning with her Northfield classmate, Annie Hancock, who accompanied her to India in 1900 and was active as an evangelistic worker in Vellore until her death in 1924. An even closer companion was Gertrude Dodd, twelve years her senior, who joined her in India as an unofficial self-supporting Reformed Church missionary in 1916. Dodd gave generously from her inheritance to support students at the medical college founded by Scudder and to meet emergency needs; she also served as college bursar and registrar. The two women signed their cables "Scuddodd," and lived and traveled together until Dodd's death in Florida in 1944.

When her father died of cancer within five months of her arrival in Vellore in 1900, Scudder was deprived of the experienced guidance she had planned to substitute for an internship. She found herself mistrusted by his former pa-

tients because of her age and sex, and restricted to a tiny missionary bungalow room with only the assistance of her mother and the cook's wife acting as nurse. Nonetheless, she treated thousands of cases while also supervising construction of the small Mary Taber Schell Hospital, which opened in 1902. To her heavy case load she added weekly tours of the countryside, which developed eventually into a system of itinerant roadside clinics. Through these clinics, medical teams provided treatment and rudimentary public health education to a vast rural population.

As the hospital's only surgeon for twenty-two of the years before the appointment of a second surgeon in 1932, Scudder became convinced that the medical needs of India's women could not be met by government or mission facilities. In 1909 the training program for Schell Hospital nurses was expanded into a full-fledged nursing school. Overcoming great obstacles, promoting interdenominational support, and negotiating subsidies from the Madras government, she next opened the Union Mission Medical School for Women in 1918. Combining the roles of surgeon, instructor, and administrator, and with the help of supporting groups outside India, she not only weathered the depression but significantly expanded facilities. In 1938, however, new government regulations requiring university affiliation for the granting of medical degrees seemed to doom the medical school. The septuagenarian Scudder returned to the United States in 1941 and attempted to raise funds under difficult wartime conditions. She traveled for four years, although dispirited by the death of Gertrude Dodd and by the alienation of supporters such as LUCY PEABODY, who accused her of disloyalty to the cause of women's education when she concluded that the only way to save the college (renamed the Christian Medical College in the 1940s) was to make it coeducational. She persisted, and permanent affiliation with the University of Madras was announced in 1950, the fiftieth anniversary of her service in India. Finally, the founder could retire to her bungalow near Kodaikanal, in the Palani Hills, where she remained active, even playing tennis into her eighties. She died at her home in her ninetieth year.

Ida Scudder received important assistance from a loyal staff and thousands of American and British supporters. Yet, from the premature opening of the medical school during wartime and a cholera epidemic, to the controversial decision not to close the school in 1938, it was her tenacious dedication to her dream, her remarkable vitality and gift for personal relations combined with simple faith, that made the difference between a routine missionary career and her extraordinary contribution. In the 1970s the Christian Medical College and Hospital in Vellore, by then an Indianized institution, had over 2,000 staff members.

[The Scudder papers at the Schlesinger Library, Radcliffe College, contain family and personal correspondence, Dorothy Wilson's MSS. for her biography, diaries and notebooks, printed material on the hospital and medical college, and many photographs. There are also a few letters at the Ida Scudder Auditorium Museum at the Christian Medical College in Vellore. Other MS. material has apparently been destroyed. Her missionary reports and correspondence with her denominational board have not been located in the Reformed Church Archives, New Brunswick, N.J., nor in the N.Y. offices of either the Foreign Mission Board or the Vellore Christian Med. Board. Except for promotional brochures and brief articles in denominational periodicals such as "Glimpses of My Life," *Church Herald* (Sept. 3, 1954), Scudder published only such professional accounts as "Methods of Training Indian Medicals," *Baptist Missionary Rev.* (Dec. 1919), and reports on her innovative surgical techniques in *Proc. of the First All-India Obst. & Gynaec. Congress* (Madras, 1936). The most recent biography is Dorothy C. Wilson, *Dr. Ida: The Story of Dr. Ida Scudder of Vellore* (1959; rev. ed. 1964); it is not annotated, but is based on interviews and research in papers surviving in Vellore in 1957. Also popular and undocumented, but somewhat more detailed for the early years and for her medical work, is M. Pauline Jeffery, *Dr. Ida: India, The Life Story of Ida S. Scudder* (1938; rev. ed. 1950). Short hagiographic summaries are Sheila Smith, *Doctor Ida* (1950), and Carolyn Scott, *The Doctor Who Never Gave Up* (1970). Dorothy Jealous Scudder, "A Thousand Years in Thy Sight, the Story of the Scudders of India" (1970), a MS. in the Reformed Church Archives, includes three chapters on Ida Scudder. See also D. C. Wilson, *Twelve Who Cared* (1977); Stephen Neill and others, eds., *Concise Dict. of the Christian World Mission* (1971); Sherwood Eddy, *Pathfinders of the World Missionary Crusade* (1945), pp. 128–39; and Sally Knapp, *Women Doctors Today* (1947), pp. 65–78. An obituary in the *N.Y. Times,* May 25, 1960, has several discrepancies in chronology.]

VALENTIN RABE

SCUDDER, Vida, Dec. 15, 1861–Oct. 9, 1954. Social reformer, scholar.

Vida Scudder was born Julia Davida in Madura, India, the only child of David Coit Scudder, a Congregationalist missionary, and Harriet Louisa (Dutton) Scudder. In 1862 David Scudder drowned and Harriet Scudder returned with her infant daughter to the Dutton home in Auburndale, Mass. Both Scudders and Duttons were old New England families; Vida,

a delicate, sensitive child, grew up surrounded by doting grandparents, distinguished aunts and uncles, and a devoted mother.

Vida Scudder spent much of her childhood in Europe where she absorbed, as much from her mother as from their travels, the devotion to beauty and tradition which marked her life. She also attended private schools in Boston, and in the religious excitement of the 1870s she and her mother were confirmed by Phillips Brooks in the Episcopal church.

In 1878 Vida joined the first class of Girls' Latin School in Boston and in 1880 entered Smith College, her first ordinary association with her peers and her first and only separation from her mother until Harriet Scudder's death in 1920. Scudder learned the value of true feminine friendship during her college years; throughout her life her deeper friendships were with women.

During a postgraduate term at Oxford University in 1884 Scudder attended the last lectures of John Ruskin and became aware of the "plethora of privilege" in her life. She came away filled with a social radicalism for which there was no outlet in the Boston to which she returned in 1885. Brooding, groping, bored, she accepted a position in the English department at Wellesley College in 1887, choosing Wellesley over Smith so she could remain with her mother. From the outset her teaching was animated by both a great love of letters and a growing social concern, a combination also seen in two of her earliest books, *The Life of the Spirit in Modern English Poets* (1895) and *Social Ideals in English Letters* (1898).

Teaching gave her self-confidence, but her worry about "privilege unshared" persisted. This concern led her in 1887 to initiate plans for a college settlement, the beginning of what became the College Settlements Association. In 1889 the first settlement opened on Rivington Street in New York City. Scudder, as secretary of the electoral board of the association, promoted its work on college campuses, and in 1893 took a year's leave of absence from Wellesley to join HELENA DUDLEY in the official opening of Denison House in Boston's South End. For the next twenty years she was the prime mover at Denison House, supplying "the ideas" while Helena Dudley, the headworker, provided "the human warmth and contacts."

In 1889 Scudder became a member of William D. P. Bliss's Society of Christian Socialists, a charter member of the Brotherhood of the Carpenter, and an active worker in the Christian Social Union. But settlement work and friendships with the women in settlement neighborhoods turned her attention to the practical side of the labor question. Denison House became a meeting place for several labor groups. Vida Scudder and Helena Dudley were elected delegates to the Boston Central Labor Union.

The mental and spiritual strain of conflicting interests brought on a breakdown in 1901. Her mother was puzzled if not disappointed by her radicalism and Scudder was often in conflict with the Wellesley College administration over her socialist activities. Her outspoken opposition to a Rockefeller gift had led to direct disagreement with the Wellesley trustees in 1900. Moreover, she constantly reproached herself for the many personal compromises she felt obliged to make in following such diverse careers.

After two years of enforced idleness, traveling in Europe (1901–02), Vida Scudder returned to Boston filled with enthusiasm and new ideas. She formed an Italian Circle at Denison House for new immigrants and took an active part in organizing the Women's Trade Union League. Realizing that the moral and intellectual disunion in society demanded more radical solutions, she also began to participate more actively in church and socialist groups.

In 1911 Scudder was a founding member of the Episcopal Church Socialist League, designed to encourage the application of Christian principles to industrial and social relations. Believing that Christians committed to socialism should also make their views heard outside the church, she joined the Socialist party in 1911. In *Socialism and Character* (1912) she tried to reconcile the apparent differences between Christianity and socialism.

Through her socialist connections Scudder was asked to speak in Lawrence, Mass., during the 1912 textile strike. Her speech and that of Wellesley colleague Ellen Hayes led to demands for their resignation, and Vida Scudder was asked to suspend for that year the course for which she had become famous, "Social Ideals in English Literature." Realizing that her radicalism also hindered the work at Denison House, she resigned from most of her activity there and in 1912 moved with her mother to Wellesley.

In 1919 Florence Converse (1871–1967) and her mother joined the Scudder household. Poet, novelist, and assistant editor of the *Atlantic Monthly* (1908–30), Converse had been Scudder's student at Wellesley. She had become Scudder's most intimate friend, her comrade in radical causes and companion in the deepest spiritual experiences. Until Scudder's death they shared "both jokes and prayers."

When the United States entered the war in 1917, Vida Scudder supported Wilson's decision, causing a painful break with many pacifist friends, whose right to dissent she nonetheless supported strongly. In 1919, anxious to keep alive the spark of radicalism in the Episcopal church, Scudder organized the Church League for Industrial Democracy, bringing together both liberal and radical church members committed to the cause of social justice. She was also active in reorganizing the Intercollegiate Socialist League into the League for Industrial Democracy and here formed a lasting friendship with Norman Thomas.

In the postwar years Scudder moved toward pacifism. In 1923 she joined the Fellowship of Reconciliation and that summer gave a series of lectures at a meeting of the Women's International League for Peace and Freedom in Podebrady near Prague. She looked hopefully at the Russian revolution but soon realized that any revolution which did not proceed "from a Christian conception of man" could not provide a solution to social ills. Often called a communist, she actually anticipated the later Christian-Marxist dialogue. By the mid-1930s Scudder had become and remained an absolute pacifist.

In 1928 Scudder retired from Wellesley and a new phase in her career began. Years of research on the early history of the Franciscans resulted in her major work, *The Franciscan Adventure* (1931), and established her as a leading Franciscan scholar. In 1930 she became the first dean of the Summer School of Christian Ethics held at Wellesley and in 1931 she lectured weekly at the New School for Social Research in New York. Her greatest contribution to the growth of Christian social thought in America came, however, through her writing. The author of sixteen books, on literary, religious, and political subjects, she continued to explore every new path that might lead to social redemption. Her autobiography, *On Journey,* published in 1937, provides a perceptive review of seventy-five years of social history and of her own religious ideals.

More than most of her companions in social movements, Vida Scudder was able to harmonize the demands of an active career with an intense spiritual life. The Society of the Companions of the Holy Cross, a group of Episcopal women to which she had belonged since 1889, provided consistent strength and support. Through the society she organized institutes on such topics as Franciscan studies, the church's responsibility toward racial groups, and penal reform. In 1945, almost eighty-five, she addressed the annual Conference on Christian Social Thinking at the Episcopal Theological School in Cambridge, Mass., on "Anglican Thought on Property."

Although age curtailed her activity in the next decade, her interest never waned. In 1952 she published *My Quest for Reality,* a sequel to her autobiography. She died suddenly in 1954 of asphyxiation, caused by choking on a piece of food, in her home in Wellesley.

[Most of the Vida Scudder MSS. have been lost. Of those remaining, the most valuable collections are in the Wellesley College Archives, the archives of the Society of the Companions of the Holy Cross, Adelynrood, So. Byfield, Mass., and the Smith College Library. Smith also has six handwritten journals, a draft of *On Journey.* See also the records of the College Settlements Assoc. in the Smith College Library and the Denison House records in the Schlesinger Library, Radcliffe College. Among her other books are *The Witness of Denial* (1895); *Introduction to the Study of English Literature* (1901); *A Listener in Babel: Being a Series of Imaginary Conversations* (1903); *Saint Catherine of Siena as Seen in Her Letters* (1905); *The Disciple of a Saint* (1907); *Le Morte d'Arthur of Sir Thomas Malory and Its Sources* (1917); *The Church and the Hour: Reflections of a Socialist Churchwoman* (1917); *The Social Teachings of the Christian Year* (1921); *Brother John: A Tale of the First Franciscans* (1927); *Father Huntington* (1940). She also prepared editions of a variety of English literary and historical works, and several volumes of religious interest as well. The most complete bibliography of her work is in Sister Catherine Theresa Corcoran, S.C., "Vida Dutton Scudder: The Progressive Years" (Ph.D. diss., Georgetown Univ., 1973). Secondary material is scarce but see Arthur Mann, *Yankee Reformers in an Urban Age* (1954); Theresa Corcoran, S.C., "Vida Dutton Scudder: Impact of World War I on the Radical Woman Professor," *Anglican Theological Rev.,* Spring 1975; and Peter J. Frederick, "The Professor as Social Activist," *New England Quart.,* Sept. 1970. There are references to Scudder in Florence Converse, *Wellesley College: A Chronicle of the Years, 1875–1938* (1939); Alice Payne Hackett, *Wellesley, Part of the American Story* (1949); Dorothy Burgess, *Dream and Deed: The Story of Katharine Lee Bates* (1952); Mercedes Randall, *Improper Bostonian: Emily Greene Balch* (1964). See also *Dict. Am. Biog.,* Supp. Five. A copy of *On Journey* to which many snapshots of Vida Scudder have been added is in the Wellesley College Archives. An obituary appeared in the *N.Y. Times,* Oct. 11, 1954; death record from the Mass. Dept. of Public Health.]

THERESA CORCORAN, S.C.

SEARS, Eleonora Randolph, Sept. 28, 1881–March 26, 1968. Sportswoman.

A popular Boston socialite in her day, Eleonora Sears devoted her enthusiastic energies to sports, pursuing her activities with determination and dedication. She was beautiful, outspoken, and independent, and delighted in doing the unusual. The first national women's squash champion, Sears was dubbed "pioneer in women's sports" by the *New York Times.* Horses were her most enduring passion; she owned and bred them, was an expert rider and jumper, and was the first woman to play polo. She also participated in tennis, sailing, golf, swimming, trapshooting, and walking, and even tried football, baseball, and ice hockey.

Eleonora Randolph Sears was born on Boston's fashionable Beacon Hill, the younger of two children and only daughter of Frederick Richard and Eleonora Randolph (Coolidge) Sears. Both parents descended from early English settlers of Massachusetts, and her mother was the great-granddaughter of Thomas Jefferson. Her father's family had a successful business in real estate and shipping. Raised in an atmosphere of luxury, she was educated by private tutors both at home and in Paris where she and her family accompanied her grandfather, Thomas Jefferson Coolidge, who served as minister to France (1892–93).

One of the earliest interests in Eleonora Sears's varied sporting career was tennis. Niece of the first national tennis champion, Richard Dudley Sears, she was by 1903 acclaimed as the tennis queen of Newport, R.I., for her victories in club tournaments. Her aggressive style of play and overwhelming desire to win were always exciting to spectators. She was four times National Women's Doubles champion—twice with HAZEL HOTCHKISS (WIGHTMAN), in 1911 and 1915, and twice with Molla Bjurstedt (Mallory), in 1916 and 1917—and won the National Mixed Doubles championship with Willis Davis in 1916. She also contributed to the revolution in women's tennis dress by rolling up her shirt sleeves to play.

One of Eleonora Sears's most daring escapades, publicized nationwide, occurred in 1912 at a practice session for a men's polo team in Burlingame, Calif. Riding onto the field astride her horse, rather than sidesaddle as convention dictated to women, and wearing jodhpurs, she requested permission to be on the team. The request was denied, and she so startled the spectators by her audacity and appearance that the Burlingame Mothers' Club issued a resolution asking Eleonora Sears to "restrict herself to the normal feminine attire in the future." She completely ignored the resolution and took to wearing trousers even when she was not riding.

Although her breakthroughs into previously all-male sports opened doors for other women, Eleonora Sears never saw herself as a leader of a feminist crusade. Her motive was only to be able to participate in the sports she loved, and her position as an affluent Boston society woman gave her the license to do the unconventional.

She played on the squash courts of the Harvard Club when women were officially forbidden to enter the building. There were hardly any women squash players in 1918 when she took up the game, but ten years later enough interest had developed so that the first women's national championships were held. Not surprisingly, Eleonora Sears was the winner, and she continued in tournament play until the age of seventy. Often referred to as the "Mother of Squash," she was at one time president of the United States Women's Squash Racquets Association and captain of its international team.

Some of Sears's most publicized achievements were her long-distance walks. She acquired the habit of taking long walks from her father, and she frequently walked from the Sears's Beacon Street home to their summer house in Prides Crossing, Mass., a distance of twenty miles. In her early thirties she covered the 108 miles between Burlingame and Del Monte, Calif., in nineteen hours and fifty minutes. Sometimes accompanied by Harvard athletes, she often walked the forty-seven miles from Boston to Providence, R.I. In 1926 she recorded her best time between the two cities: nine hours and fifty-three minutes. Dressed in her usual hiking costume of a short coat and skirt, socks rolled down to her heavy hiking boots, and a felt hat, she was always followed by her chauffeur-driven car.

Eleonora Sears's sporting achievements were extensively reported in the newspapers, but few knew about her investments in the sporting world. For years she provided the financial support for the United States Equestrian Team, and team members frequently competed in the Olympics on horses she lent them. Her money also helped to keep the National Horse Show an annual event. As a longtime member of the Boston Skating Club, Sears contributed generously to the rebuilding program after a fatal plane crash in France in 1961 practically eliminated the American skating team. Her efforts to save the Boston Mounted Police were legendary in the Boston area. When an economy move threatened in 1957 to eliminate the horses from the ranks of police work, Sears not only came forth with the necessary money but donated some of her horses to the department.

Eleonora Sears spent the last five years of her life in Palm Beach, Fla. She remained relatively healthy and vigorous until 1968, when she died of leukemia in a West Palm Beach hospital. An avid sportswoman, a leader in society, a controversial figure because of her independent ways, she had "blazed a pathway for women which never had been taken before" (Menke, p. 1065).

[The major sources of material on Eleonora Sears are newspaper clippings and magazine articles. Short sketches of her accomplishments are included in John Durant and Otto Bettman, *Pictorial History of American Sports* (1954); Phyllis Hollander, *One Hundred Greatest Women in Sports* (1976); and Frank Menke, *The Encyclopedia of Sport* (1969). Colorful accounts of her character are in Cleveland Amory, *The Proper Bostonians* (1947), and "Bostonian Unique—Miss Sears," *Vogue*, Feb. 15, 1963, pp. 80–83. Agnes Rogers, *Women Are Here to Stay* (1949), contains several photographs. The fullest biographical account is the obituary in the *N.Y. Times*, March 27, 1968; a biography by the author is in preparation. Obituaries also appeared in the *Boston Globe*, March 27, 1968; *Time*, April 5, 1968; and *Newsweek*, April 8, 1968. Death certificate was supplied by the Fla. Dept. of Health and Rehabilitative Services.]

JOANNA DAVENPORT

SEEGER, Ruth Crawford. *See* CRAWFORD-SEEGER, Ruth.

SETON, Grace Gallatin, Jan. 28, 1872–March 19, 1959. Suffragist, feminist, explorer, writer.

Grace Gallatin Seton described herself as "one of those people who were born believing in suffrage." Fighting for women's rights throughout her life, she set up the Biblioteca Femina, a collection of books by women. She also traveled to areas previously seen by few western women, and wrote about the common struggle for equality of women from widely varying cultures.

Her father, Albert Gallatin, who arrived penniless in Sacramento, Calif., from New York state in the early 1860s, eventually became president of the largest hardware, iron, and steel house on the west coast. He married Clemenzie Rhodes of Hudson, Mich., the daughter of a Methodist preacher and circuit rider whose family had emigrated from England in the seventeenth century. Grace was the youngest of their two daughters and one son.

In 1881 Grace Gallatin's parents were divorced. Her mother, taking only Grace with her, first returned to her family and then remarried and moved to New York City. Grace had little contact with her siblings and her father, who soon remarried, although she became close to her sister much later in life. She attended the Packer Collegiate Institute in Brooklyn, graduating in 1892. Later she studied commercial and hand bookmaking and printing.

During a trip to Europe in 1894 Grace Gallatin met Ernest Thompson Seton, a naturalist and writer. They were married in New York City in 1896. Because Grace Seton preferred society and city life and Ernest Seton preferred the country, they compromised by spending winters in an apartment in New York City and summers at a series of country estates. From about 1912 until 1914 they lived in England. In the early years of their marriage, Grace Seton assisted her husband with the design, organization, and editing of his books.

Eager to share her husband's interests, Grace Seton also joined him on his camping trips. He wrote that "she was a dead shot with the rifle . . . and met all kinds of danger with unflinching nerve." In her first book, *A Woman Tenderfoot* (1900), she described her trip on horseback through the Rockies, suggesting designs for camping clothes that gave women freedom and looked "equally well on and off the horse." Her enthusiasm for outdoor life later led her to help organize the Camp Fire Girls (1912).

After an earlier miscarriage, in 1904 Grace Seton gave birth to her only child, a daughter christened Ann and nicknamed Anya, who became a well-known writer. Anya was brought up mainly by governesses. Uninterested in being a homemaker and unable to cook or sew, Seton always had servants. Frequently away from home, during World War I she organized and directed a woman's motor unit in France which brought food and aid to the soldiers directly behind the trenches. She was decorated by the French government for her service.

Active in the suffrage campaign from the age of seventeen, Seton served as vice president and later president of the Connecticut Woman's Suffrage Association (1910–20). After World War I, she focused her concern on women writers. As president of the National League of American Pen Women (1926–28 and 1930–32), she doubled the number of branches of the organization. Her most important accomplishment was the establishment of the Biblioteca Femina, a collection of 2,000 volumes and 100 pamphlets, many of them not found in libraries, by women from thirty-seven countries on five continents. The Biblioteca, which helped gain recognition for women writers, originated during Seton's tenure as chairman of letters of the National Council of Women (1933–38), when she organized and presided over a conclave of women writers during the 1933 International Congress of Women in Chicago. It was later donated to the Northwestern University Library.

A committed activist, Grace Seton belonged to and held office in a large number of organizations. She claimed that her entry in *Who's Who in America* was longer than that of any other woman writer. As a member of the Republican party, she campaigned for Herbert Hoover and Thomas E. Dewey and fought for equal status for women in the Republican National Committee. In addition, she belonged to various social clubs, and articles about her often appeared on society pages.

During the 1920s and 1930s, in addition to trips to Europe, Seton visited Japan, China, Egypt, India, South America, and Indochina. Unwilling to confine herself to the typical tourist sites, she sought places where "all normalcy and security is gone." Thus she rode a donkey on a caravan through the Libyan desert and an elephant on a safari through the jungles of Vietnam, organized a tiger hunt in India, and went to see a military uprising in China "first-hand." Besides lecturing and publishing numerous articles, Seton wrote a series of five books about her travels. These first-person narratives include extensive discussions of each country's history, customs, social structure, and political system, as well as analysis of the status of women. She sought out the Moi tribes in Vietnam, the subject of her last book, *Poison Arrows* (1938), as an example of a matriarchal culture. Generally apolitical in her writing, Seton for instance praised both the British rulers and the anti-British nationalist leaders in *A Woman Tenderfoot in Egypt* (1923).

After World War I, Grace Seton and her husband, both strong-willed and competitive, followed independent careers that rarely overlapped. By the late 1920s they had separated, and they were divorced in 1935. A beautiful woman, even in her later years, she had many male friends and suitors as well as a wide circle of women friends.

An early interest in mysticism and eastern religions strengthened as Seton became older. In the 1940s she was a follower of Yogananda, traveling to his ashrams in Washington, D.C., and Los Angeles. Many of her poems, collected in *The Singing Traveler* (1947), express eastern beliefs. From middle age Seton suffered from arthritis, wearing an Indian bracelet to guard her from its effects and spending her winters in warm climates. Her daughter lived with her from 1930 until her death of a heart attack in Palm Beach, Fla., in 1959.

[The Sophia Smith Coll. at Smith College has some of Seton's correspondence, a clipping file, notes on her travels, MSS., and pamphlets. In the Schlesinger Library at Radcliffe College are letters on her work with various women's organizations. Her other books include *Nimrod's Wife* (1907), *Chinese Lanterns* (1924), *Yes, Lady Saheb* (1925), and *Magic Waters* (1933). Biographical information can be found in *Nat. Cyc. Am. Biog.*, XLVII, 80–81; *Women of Achievement* (1940), p. 38; John J. A'Becket, "Mr. and Mrs. Seton-Thompson at Home," *Harper's Bazaar*, Feb. 3, 1900; Helen Buckler, Mary F. Fiedler, and Martha F. Allen, *Wo-He-Lo: The Story of Camp Fire Girls, 1910–1960* (1961); and Ernest Thompson Seton, *Trail of an Artist-Naturalist*

(1940), pp. 343–50. For material on her father see *Nat. Cyc. Am. Biog.*, XXXVII, 407–8, and Betty Foot Henderson, "Families in the Mansion," *Golden Notes*, May 1973, pp. 2–4. James J. Hogaboam, *The Bean Creek Valley* (1876), has some information about the Rhodes family. Seton's obituary appeared in the *N.Y. Times*, March 20, 1959. Additional invaluable information was provided by Seton's daughter, Anya Seton Chase, and her granddaughter, Clemency Chase Coggins. Death certificate from Fla. Dept. of Health and Rehabilitative Services.]

JOAN FEINBERG

SEWELL, Edna Belle Scott, Aug. 1, 1881– Oct. 22, 1967. Farm women's leader.

Edna Sewell, first director of the Associated Women of the American Farm Bureau Federation (AFBF), was born on a farm near the small town of Ambia, Benton County, Ind., the oldest of the three daughters and two sons of Clinton and Emma (Albaugh) Scott, both of Irish ancestry. Her father was a farmer and, for a time, a pharmacist; her mother, a homemaker. Edna Scott attended a one-room district school in the rural area where her father farmed, and graduated from the high school in Oxford, the Benton County seat. Although she did not go to college, she continued to read and study throughout her adult life.

Girls married early in the community where Edna Scott lived. On Dec. 29, 1897, she married Charles W. Sewell, who was already well established as one of the county's better farmers. He took his bride to live in the oldest farmhouse in the county, and in that primitive dwelling she mastered the skills of a farm wife—baking, sewing, cleaning, canning, maintaining a sizable vegetable garden—and gave birth to her two children: Greta Geneive in 1900, and Gerald Scott in 1903 (d. 1945).

In 1906 the Sewell family moved to the small town of Otterbein, Ind., to a more up-to-date farm dwelling that was close to both church and school. Edna Sewell became organist and Sunday school superintendent at the Methodist church, and joined other social organizations such as the local chapter of the Order of the Eastern Star.

Her career as a leader of American farm women began in 1908, when she was asked to address a meeting of the Benton County Farmers' Institute. Her paper, entitled "The Woman in the Home and Community," attracted the attention of Professor William C. Latta of Purdue University, who invited her to give similar speeches in other counties; by 1913 she was listed as a regular speaker on the Farmers' Institute roster. These county institutes, the earliest form of systematic agricultural extension in the United States, were organized by and for farmers but were intended to promote the well-being of the entire community. In her own town Sewell organized in 1913 a farmers' social club, which later helped construct the area's first cooperative grain elevator and became the nucleus for a local chapter of the American Farm Bureau Federation.

Edna Sewell gradually became known throughout the state for her efforts to help farm women improve their lives. Purdue University offered her a unique opportunity in 1916 when, in connection with its home economics department, she organized and helped direct the first three home improvement tours ever conducted in the United States. These tours demonstrated to farm wives new and efficient ways of caring for their families and homes. Sewell also served for one year at Purdue as assistant leader of Home Demonstration agents, and in 1920 helped establish a short course in home economics to be taught in connection with the Indiana State Fair.

Sewell gained nationwide recognition through her association with the AFBF, an independent organization of farmers founded in 1920 to develop agriculture and to protect the interests of farmers across the nation. At the organization's second annual meeting she stepped in at the last moment as a replacement speaker and gave an extremely effective and widely publicized talk. "There isn't a man here this evening," she maintained, "no matter how good a farmer or how capable a manager he may be, who is capable enough to manage and direct all the affairs of his farm and homestead unless he has in close partnership with him an up-to-date woman to help him." Her speech prompted the federation to pass a resolution recognizing that the strength of the farm home was essential to the stability of American agriculture, and that the admission of women as members could significantly extend the organization's influence. "We welcome to our councils the farm women of our nation," the resolution declared.

In 1921 Secretary of Agriculture Henry C. Wallace invited Edna Sewell to come to Washington as one of Indiana's seven delegates to President Harding's National Agricultural Conference. She became a second vice president, head of the women's department, and a member of the board of the Indiana Farm Bureau—a position she held for nine years. In 1927 the AFBF established under Edna Sewell's directorship a Home and Community Department, which in 1934 became the Associated Women of the AFBF. She remained its head until her retirement, directing public relations work, supervising the federation's congressional lobbying activities, promoting the development of education and health-care systems, working for war relief abroad, and speaking at meetings and conferences throughout the country. She helped organize chapters in North Carolina and Tennessee, and in 1947 and 1950 traveled to Europe as the federation's delegate to the triennial conferences of Associated Country Women of the World. In addition to her work for the federation, Sewell was a consultant on rural health to the American Medical Association, which awarded her a citation for distinguished service in that field.

Sewell officially retired in 1950, but continued to make public appearances and to serve on a number of committees. She was honored many times for her accomplishments, receiving distinguished service awards from such institutions as the University of Wisconsin (1933), and the AFBF (1950). Charles Sewell had continued to farm until his death in 1933. Hiring a family to run the farm, Edna Sewell remained there, continuing to be active in federation affairs until her death in 1967 of kidney failure at a nursing home in Lafayette, Ind.

[The best source for information about the life and career of Edna Belle Scott Sewell is an autobiography written when she was seventy-three years old; the manuscript is in the possession of family members. An essay of hers, entitled "My Country 'Tis of Thee," appeared in the *Progressive Farmer* in 1951. Considerable information about her life can be found in press releases and other materials from the files of the AFBF, Cornell Univ. Libraries, Dept. of Manuscripts. For an account of the Associated Women and of Sewell's role in the organization see Orville M. Kile, *The Farm Bureau Through Three Decades* (1948). "Where Are They Now?" *The Hoosier Farmer*, Oct. 1964, contains information about the later part of her life. The Indianapolis *News*, April 21, 1956, and the Lafayette (Ind.) *Journal and Courier*, March 22, 1958, printed articles citing her honors and accomplishments. Obituaries appeared in the Indianapolis *Star*, Oct. 24, 1967, and the Lafayette *Journal and Courier*, Oct. 23, 1967. A death record was provided by the Ind. Board of Health.]

REBECCA A. SHEPHERD

SEXTON, Anne Gray Harvey, Nov. 9, 1928–Oct. 4, 1974. Poet.

Anne Sexton began writing seriously at the age of twenty-eight. From that time until she died, she made her poetry a critical battleground for sanity, identity, and fame; the poet's business of ordering experience through language became her means of holding on to life.

Daily life was often very difficult for Anne Sexton; from 1954 on, she had frequent break-downs, spent considerable time in mental institutions, and attempted suicide several times. But she did not want to be known as "the mad-suicide poet," and her poetry is often obsessed instead with the will to live. Her books, especially the early ones, are filled with poems about love, life, family, her children; even the poems which clearly court death are full of the strain of the struggle.

She once wrote, "Poetry saved my life"—she had begun writing poetry as mental therapy—but her motivation was not only therapeutic. Few poets were so openly demanding of praise and admiration, so immensely concerned to be taken seriously, to be thought more important than popular. She worried that her public image misrepresented her private self; as she wrote to Erica Jong, after meeting her at a reading: "That isn't the real me, the woman of the poems, the woman of the kitchen, the woman of the private (but published) hungers. Perhaps you knew that? Perhaps I didn't seem like a god-damn show-off after all" (*Self-Portrait*, pp. 413–14). On stage—as she always was in public—Anne Sexton was glamorous, self-confident, full of style and posture. Behind the scenes, however (as is especially evident in her published letters) she was obsessively lacking in self-confidence, starving for praise and approval, frightened both of life and of death.

In March 1956, Anne Sexton was for the second time admitted to a mental hospital. In November she tried to kill herself. Until that time, her life seems to have been at once suburbanly regular and eccentrically disturbing. Unlike other successful women poets of her generation, she was neither academic, intellectual, nor urban. Born in Newton, Mass., she was the third of three daughters of Mary Gray (Staples) and Ralph Churchill Harvey. Her father was a successful wool merchant, owner of his own company; Mary Harvey had attended Wellesley College and had literary interests. Sexton always maintained that her mother was her sternest critic. Although many of her adult letters to her family were filled with love and intimacy, there were times when she felt she was essentially unwanted, "the mistake/ that Mother used to keep Father/ from his divorce" ("Those Times," *Live or Die*).

The Harveys lived in suburban Wellesley, Mass., where Anne attended public schools. Graduating in 1947 from Rogers Hall, a preparatory school for girls in Lowell, Mass., she very briefly attended Garland Junior College in Boston, before eloping on Aug. 16, 1948, with Alfred "Kayo" Muller Sexton II. He was the son of an affluent, conservative family who were not at all pleased with the impetuous marriage nor with their son's withdrawal from college to support his wife. After Kayo's naval service, the Sextons settled in the suburbs of Boston and Kayo went into the Harvey family business. "All I wanted," Sexton remarked in 1968, "was a little piece of life, to be married, to have children . . . I was trying my damnedest to lead a conventional life, for that was how I was brought up, and it was what my husband wanted of me." But this life worried her. "You can't build little picket fences to keep the nightmares out" (Kevles, p. 160). The pressures of isolation and of society's expectations were troubling: "A woman who writes feels too much/ . . . As if cycles and children and islands/ weren't enough, as if mourners and gossips/ and vegetables were never enough" ("The Black Art," *All My Pretty Ones*).

In addition, Sexton did not look the part of the contented suburban matron. She was strikingly handsome; a tough-looking, undeniably sexy woman who in her late twenties had worked as a model for the Hart Agency in Boston. Yet her poems suggest that she was constantly uneasy about her sexual identity. Addressing her daughter, she wrote: "I, who was never sure/ about being a girl, needed another/ life, another image to remind me" ("The Double Image," *To Bedlam and Part Way Back*).

On July 21, 1953, Anne Sexton gave birth to her first child, Linda Gray. Joyce Ladd was born on Aug. 5, 1955. Although she was intensely devoted to her children, it is clear that Sexton found motherhood extremely difficult and demanding. Seven months after Joyce's birth she suffered a severe breakdown and was admitted to a mental hospital; some months later, after her suicide attempt, her children were sent to live with their grandparents. Joyce spent her first three years with her father's parents. Anne Sexton convalesced at her parents' home and saw her children only occasionally. As she recovered, her mother became ill. In "The Double Image," she explored her guilt about abandoning her child (the poem is addressed to Joyce) and feeling, irrationally, responsible for her mother's cancer. "She turned from me, as if death were catching . . . as if my dying had eaten inside of her./ That August you were two, but I timed my days with doubt." Later, she began to see Joyce more regularly and finally reestablished her maternal claims; she cared for her mother, who had come to live with the Sextons, for most of 1957 and 1958.

The year 1959 was one of intense depression as well as brave self-examination. On March 10 Mary Harvey died of cancer; three months later Ralph Harvey died of a stroke. And in October,

Anne Sexton underwent major surgery. The poems in her first book, *To Bedlam and Part Way Back* (1960), reflect the depression, but mostly the bravery.

Earlier, she had quite systematically and consciously learned about writing poetry. In 1957, she enrolled in John Holmes's poetry workshop at the Boston Center for Adult Education; in 1958 she worked at Antioch with W. D. Snodgrass—who was to become a lifelong friend—and in the same year, she was accepted into Robert Lowell's writing seminar at Boston University. There she met and became friends with SYLVIA PLATH, George Starbuck, and Maxine Kumin—her closest and most treasured friend from that time on. Lowell was a testing and a tasking teacher and his influence was significant and permanent. He encouraged Sexton and wrote, for the cover of her first book: "Her poems stick in my mind. I don't see how they can fail to make the great stir they deserve."

The poems received the attention Lowell anticipated, and Sexton's career as a poet began. In 1961, she taught poetry at Harvard and was a scholar in poetry at the Radcliffe Institute for Independent Study. *All My Pretty Ones* (1963) was nominated for a National Book Award; *Live or Die* (1966) was awarded the Pulitzer Prize in 1967. She received an honorary Phi Beta Kappa from Harvard (1968) and a Guggenheim fellowship (1969). In the spring of 1972 she held the Crashaw Chair in Literature at Colgate University. Later that year Anne Sexton became a full professor at Boston University, where she had been a very successful teacher since 1969.

After 1968, however, her poetry was turned out at an increasingly rapid and distressingly uncontrollable rate: *Love Poems* (1969), *Transformations* (1971), *The Book of Folly* (1972), *The Death Notebooks* (1974). *The Awful Rowing Towards God* (1975) and *45 Mercy Street* (1976) were published posthumously. With the possible exception of *Transformations*, grotesquely but marvelously retold fairy tales, the late poetry is strangely, dangerously possessed by an undisciplined longing for dark belief. Although she talks about hope for mercy, the poems mainly settle on despair.

Books appeared and honors were conferred at an astonishing rate, but that was apparently not enough to support an increasingly desperate, unhappy, and unstable personal life. In 1973 she was twice hospitalized and the same year requested and was granted a divorce. In October 1974, Anne Sexton committed suicide at her home in Weston, Mass.

Her last poems had become increasingly undisciplined and she was herself extremely dissatisfied with much that she wrote. But Anne Sexton's poetry at its best reflects the woman who insisted on life, not death, who wrote, "I say *Live, Live* because of the sun,/ the dream, the excitable gift" ("Live," *Live or Die*). And that is the poetry that will survive.

[In addition to the books cited, a collection, *Selected Poems*, was published in England in 1964. A selection of her letters, *Anne Sexton: A Self-Portrait in Letters*, ed. Linda Gray Sexton and Lois Ames, appeared in 1977. There is no full-length biography. J. D. McClatchy, ed., *Anne Sexton: The Poet and Her Critics* (1978), a collection of critical essays, contains a chronology and a full though not complete bibliography of primary and secondary sources. See also Barbara Kevles, "The Art of Poetry xv: Anne Sexton," *Paris Rev.*, no. 52 (1971), an interview. Her obituary appeared in the *N.Y. Times*, Oct. 6, 1974; death record provided by Mass. Dept. of Public Health.]

JANE MCCABE

SHAMBAUGH, Jessie Field, June 26, 1881– Jan. 15, 1971. Rural educator.

Jessie Field Shambaugh, "Mother of 4-H," was born Celestia Josephine, the fifth of eight children and third of five daughters of Solomon Elijah and Celestia Josephine (Eastman) Field. Her parents, both former educators, moved west from Illinois in 1869, and were sodbusters in Shenandoah, Page County, Iowa, where Jessie was born. As a small child, Jessie Field accompanied her father to Farm Institute meetings where the dynamic "Uncle" Henry C. Wallace, editor of *Wallace's Farmer,* inspired her with the ideals of farm life. She attended Fairview, a country school, in Grant Township. Although rheumatic fever when she was thirteen interrupted her education for a year, she graduated from Shenandoah High School in 1899.

While attending Western Normal College in Shenandoah, Field began her career as an educator: she was asked to teach the spring term of 1901 at the Goldenrod School in Page County. To foster a feeling of pride and self-worth in her students, and to teach them improved farming techniques and home management, she formed at the school her first Boys Corn Club and Girls Home Club, the forerunners of 4-H clubs. After receiving her A.B. from Tabor College, in Fremont County, Iowa, in 1903, Field taught in Antigo, Wis. (1903–04), and Shenandoah (1904–05), and then became principal of the Jefferson School in Helena, Mont. (1905–06). At a time when few young women attained such positions, she was elected superintendent of schools in Page County in the fall of 1906.

As superintendent, Field was innovative in her emphasis on the practical value of education. Her goal was to make the schools more vital and useful to farm youth. In 1909 she published *Farm Arithmetic,* a book of problems applicable to rural living which was widely used in Iowa schools. To educate youth about scientific and improved farming techniques, she called on the colleges and Farm Institutes to offer their assistance.

Believing that friendly competition was a useful teaching device, Field began in 1906 to establish a Boys Corn Club and a Girls Home Club in each of the 130 schools in Page County. With the assistance of Perry G. Holden, a professor in the extension department of the Iowa State College of Agriculture, she taught improved farming techniques. Club activities, conducted after school, included seed corn, milk, and livestock judging, and competition in home crafts and road dragging (grading of dirt roads with teams of horses pulling logs). In 1908, under Field's leadership, the Page County Boys Agricultural Club was organized. Field's students won many honors, including first prize at the International Corn Show in Omaha (1909). In 1912, Field won first place as the Adult Corn Judge at the Iowa State Agricultural College.

While Field was superintendent, her schools served as models for exemplary rural education and attracted national attention. In 1909, under the sponsorship of the Southern Board of Education of Nashville, Tenn., fifteen superintendents from southern states visited the Page County schools; they reported that Field was "a genius" and "a prophet in her own country." Educational journals commended the schools' innovative teaching methods and their farm youth clubs.

To encourage student participation in rural organizations, Field designed a three-leaf clover pin, to represent technological, agricultural, and domestic science. First distributed as an award in 1910, the letter "H" was placed on each leaf, symbolizing "Head," "Hands," and "Heart" with a kernel of corn and the word "Page" in the center. A fourth "H" was later added, representing "Home" and then "Health." The idea of the farm clubs, symbolized by the pin, was the beginning of 4-H, which evolved over the years into a national organization sponsored by the Department of Agriculture.

In 1910 Jessie Field organized the first Page County Boys Farm Camp, where seminars on new farming techniques were held. A girls' camp was added in 1911. Growing in popularity, these camps were later sponsored by 4-H. In *The Corn Lady: The Story of a Country Teacher's Life,* published in 1911, Field described her work in the rural schools and as an organizer of farm youth groups.

Resigning from her superintendency, Field moved to New York City in May 1912 to become the National YWCA secretary for small town and country work. Upset that "the city continues each year to claim an immense number of the best country people" ("The Country Girl"), Field felt that the YWCA could counter this movement by improving the domestic, social, and religious lives of women living on farms and in small towns. During her years in New York, Field also published with Scott Nearing *Community Civics* (1916), a textbook for rural adolescents.

In 1917, at thirty-five, Jessie Field returned to Iowa to marry Ira William Shambaugh, twenty years her senior, who owned a grain mill. After the stillbirth of a son in 1919, they adopted a son, William H., the following year. After she recovered from pernicious anemia, Jessie Shambaugh gave birth to their daughter, Phyllis Ruth, in 1922; she later had two miscarriages.

Shambaugh published *A Real Country Teacher: The Story of Her Work* in 1922; it includes the letters previously published in *The Corn Lady*, adding an update, "Fifteen Years Later," and a supplement devoted to farm arithmetic problems. As a wife and mother, she continued to advise 4-H groups and to perform welfare work, becoming a charter member of the Page County Social Welfare Board. In 1971 after a hip fracture, Jessie Shambaugh died in Clarinda, Iowa, of pneumonia at the age of eighty-nine.

[The Nat. Board, YWCA, N.Y. City, has Shambaugh's booklet *College Women and Country Leadership* (1915) and a 1913 speech, "The Country Girl." Other articles by Shambaugh, all in the *Jour. Education*, are "Educating the Country Boy and Girl," May 5, 1910; "The Best Teachers for the Country," Nov. 17, 1910; and "Polly Stanton's Eight Week Club," Dec. 24, 1914. For information on her work see "The Best Rural Schools in America," *Page County History, Iowa* (1942), pp. 42–48; A. E. Winship, "Ideal Rural School Work," *Jour. Education*, June 24, 1909, pp. 688–90; Franklin M. Beck, *The 4-H Story: A History of 4-H Club Work* (1951); and Faye Whitmore and Manila Cheshire, *The Very Beginnings* (1963), an account by friends of Shambaugh who were 3-H and 4-H members. Obituaries appeared in *Des Moines Register and Tribune*, Jan. 16, 1971; *Council Bluffs Nonpareil*, Jan. 17, 1971; and *N.Y. Times*, Jan. 18, 1971. Additional information was provided by Shambaugh's daughter, Ruth Shambaugh Watkins, and by Faye Whitmore and Manila Cheshire. Death record was provided by the registrar of Page Cty., Iowa.]

JANICE NAHRA FRIEDEL

SHAVER, Dorothy, July 29, 1897–June 28, 1959. Business executive.

Dorothy Shaver, whose enthusiastic promotion of American designers helped bring American fashion to international attention, was born in the small Arkansas town of Center Point. She was the eldest of three daughters (the youngest died in childhood) and the third of five children born to James D. and Sallie (Borden) Shaver.

She was descended from seventeenth-century English, Welsh, and German migrants. Dorothy's father was a lawyer and chancery court judge; his father was Robert Glenn ("Fighting Bob") Shaver, a Confederate general. Sallie Shaver was the daughter of Benjamin Borden, an editor of the *Arkansas Gazette*.

Soon after Dorothy's birth, her family moved twenty miles north to Mena, a larger community. She grew up there, sang in the Episcopal church choir, graduated from high school with honors, and at eighteen was ready to marry a law student of whom her father disapproved. Judge Shaver cooled the romance by sending her to the University of Arkansas. After two years there, she moved on to the University of Chicago for a year, majoring in English. Her younger sister, Elsie, was also in Chicago, studying art.

Encouraged by having earned $600 for illustrating a Marshall Field catalog, Elsie Shaver decided in 1920 to seek her fortune in New York. When she booked her train passage, Dorothy decided to go along "for the ride." In New York, Elsie sold some advertising art, continued her studies, and for her amusement made some impish dolls of rags and raffia. Dorothy Shaver, who had read that the Kewpie dolls of ROSE O'NEILL were earning her a fortune, had Elsie make up a family of her dolls and undertook to sell them. Her opportunity, and the beginning of her career, came through Samuel Wallace Reyburn, a distant cousin through the Bordens, who had come from Arkansas to New York in 1914 to be treasurer of Lord & Taylor, the famous Fifth Avenue specialty store. By 1920 he had become president of both Lord & Taylor and of the Associated Dry Goods Corporation, which owned it. Shown Elsie's dolls during a Sunday call, Reyburn gave the sisters advice on production and distribution. The dolls, called "The Little Shavers," were sold through Lord & Taylor and other outlets, earning the sisters a sizable income for four years.

By 1924 Elsie had lost interest in the dolls and Dorothy Shaver began her career with Lord & Taylor. She worked first in the comparison shopping bureau, checking prices in rival stores, and two months later was made its director. In 1925 she became director of interior decoration and fashion. At her suggestion, the store established a bureau of fashion advisers, formed to improve the quality of the store's merchandise by working directly with designers and producers. This innovation soon became a standard component of retail stores. Elected to the store's board of directors in 1927, the following year she imported from France a $100,000 collection of modern art and decorative objects, including some Picassos, Braques, and Utrillos, which earned the store fame and profits. In 1931, she was made vice president in charge of advertising, publicity, and the bureau of fashion.

From this time on Shaver focused on American designers and American fashion. Paris still dominated fashion, but through her emphasis on American designers as best qualified to meet the fashion needs of American women, and through her constant promotion of this idea at Lord & Taylor, Shaver contributed substantially to making New York the center of the fashion world. Among the many American designers whom she brought to public attention were CLAIRE MCCARDELL, Lilly Daché, Anne Fogarty, William Pahlmann, Rose Marie Reid, and Pauline Trigère. Shaver was also largely responsible for the creation of the annual Lord & Taylor American Design Awards, begun in 1938.

Between 1931 and 1945, when she became president of the store, Shaver's innovations were many, distinctive, and profitable. Unusual window displays (including the Christmas bell windows, in which no merchandise was displayed but music was piped to the outside from gold bells), the store's characteristic seasonal awnings, and the bright reds and greens used throughout the interior drew crowds, as did the creation of the first fashion department exclusively devoted to teenagers. It all helped. Though Associated Dry Goods paid no dividends between 1931 and 1943, Lord & Taylor paid dividends in every depression year except 1933.

Shaver was also largely responsible for launching Lord & Taylor's branch store program, which began with the Manhasset, Long Island, branch in 1941. During World War II, she served as consultant to the quartermaster general on merchandise and women's uniforms and was also active in the Red Cross and American Women's Volunteer Services.

In 1945, Shaver was elected president of Lord & Taylor at a salary of $110,000, the largest on record for any woman in the country, a fact that was widely publicized (though *Life* magazine noted that this was only a quarter of the salary paid to a man in a similar position). Shaver's promotion brought her some matrimonial offers and a flood of pleas for help from individuals

and organizations. She continued, however, to live with her sister in a New York apartment and a summer home at Tannersville, N.Y. She weighed the pleas and expanded her civic and charitable activities; she also broadened the Lord & Taylor Awards to honor distinguished service in medicine, the arts, housing, education, and international relations.

Shaver's efforts continued to be reflected in expanding profits. Lord & Taylor's sales, which were $30 million a year when Shaver became president, reached $50 million six years later and soared to $100 million in 1959, when Associated Dry Goods paid record dividends. Shaver had been made a director of the holding company in 1946.

In 1946 and 1947, Associated Press editors voted Dorothy Shaver the outstanding woman in business. The American Woman's Association gave her its 1950 award for feminist achievement and in 1953, she received the first award of the Society of New York Dress Designers for "outstanding support of American design." Shaver was also a trustee of the Parsons School of Design and a fellow of the Metropolitan Museum of Art, where she was instrumental in the formation of the museum's Costume Institute.

In 1959, Shaver suffered a mild stroke in New York and apparently recovered only to be felled by a second at her summer home. She died of a stroke at the Columbia Memorial Hospital at Hudson, N.Y. Shaver's American Design Awards were discontinued, but in 1976, as part of the store's 150th anniversary celebration, one was revived: an annual Dorothy Shaver Rose Award for "an outstanding individual whose creative mind has brought new beauty and deeper understanding to our lives."

[Dorothy Shaver's papers, principally texts of her speeches, were given by her sister to the Smithsonian Institution. Biographical sketches of Shaver appear in *Current Biog.*, 1946, and the *Nat. Cyc. Am. Biog.*, H, 134–35, with portrait. Biographical articles include S. J. Woolf, "Miss Shaver Pictures the Store of Tomorrow," *N.Y. Times*, Jan. 5, 1947; Jeanne Perkins, "No. 1 Career Woman," *Life*, May 12, 1947; and a chapter in Isabella Taves, *Successful Women and How They Attained Success* (1943). Lord & Taylor's public relations operation under Dorothy Shaver was described by Tom Mahoney and Rita Hession in *Public Relations for Retailers* (1949). Shaver's obituary appeared in the *N.Y. Times*, June 29, 1959; death record from N.Y. State Dept. of Health.]

TOM MAHONEY

SHERWIN, Belle, March 25, 1868–July 9, 1955. Suffragist, civic leader.

Belle Sherwin was born in Cleveland, Ohio, the oldest of the four daughters and one son of Henry Alden and Mary Frances (Smith) Sherwin; two of her siblings died in childhood. Both parents were of colonial English ancestry. Her maternal grandfather left New York for Ohio's Western Reserve in 1836. Her father, born in Vermont, migrated to Cleveland about 1860. From modest beginnings in wholesale trade he prospered and, as founder of the paint manufacturing Sherwin-Williams Company, became one of Cleveland's leading industrialists and influential citizens. His oldest daughter inherited his intellectual acuity and executive gifts as well as his devotion to the work ethic. Growing up in an atmosphere of increasing affluence tempered by moral zeal, she early showed signs of charting her own course.

Following primary education in Cleveland's public schools, Belle Sherwin attended St. Margaret's School in Waterbury, Conn. In 1886 she entered Wellesley College, attracted by its stated purpose "to educate learned and useful teachers," and by its dynamic president, ALICE FREEMAN (PALMER), and the faculty of women scholars she had recruited. Among the faculty members who encouraged interest in social reform and served as role models, KATHARINE COMAN, professor of history and economics, was a particularly strong influence on Sherwin. Receiving a B.S. in 1890, Sherwin maintained a lifelong association with Wellesley. Elected a trustee in 1918, she served until 1943 and remained as trustee emerita until 1952. For thirty years she chaired the Building and Grounds Committee, contributing with good judgment and generous gifts to the development of the Wellesley campus.

After graduating from college, Sherwin taught history briefly at St. Margaret's School before pursuing graduate study in history at Oxford University (1894–95). She made a further trial of teaching history at Miss Hersey's School for Girls in Boston, but the constraints imposed on teachers in private schools, combined with her reluctance, since she was financially independent, to limit her choices too narrowly, prompted her return to Cleveland in 1899. She ventured first into social work at Alta House, organizing English classes for Italian immigrants. In 1900 she organized the Cleveland Consumers' League and for several years directed its investigative activities. She became a board member of the newly established Visiting Nurses' Association (VNA) in 1902 and served as chairman of the committee on recruitment and training. Within the next decade, she integrated the VNA into the Cleveland Welfare Federation, upgraded visiting nurse training,

and established a secure place for the visiting nurse in Cleveland's public health system.

Sherwin's reputation as an administrator made her a natural choice to head the war work of Cleveland women in 1917 and to move on rapidly to chairmanship of the Woman's Committee of the Ohio branch of the United States Council of National Defense. She coordinated the activities of sixty women's organizations in carrying out programs of food conservation and production, industrial recruitment, and social welfare. This experience strengthened and disciplined her native talent for what she later defined as "the art of getting things done."

Belle Sherwin's involvement in the suffrage movement began in 1910 when she joined the College Equal Suffrage League during MAUD WOOD PARK's organizing visit to Cleveland. Her welfare activities remained primary, however, until 1916, when a group of wealthy Cleveland women organized a militant branch of the National Association Opposed to Woman Suffrage which rapidly polarized Cleveland women. In order to provide those antagonized by the extremists on both sides with a forum for rational debate, Sherwin organized the Women's City Club. When her war service ended in 1919, she became president of the Cleveland Suffrage Association and a supporter of CARRIE CHAPMAN CATT's plan to perpetuate the suffrage coalition until women had mastered the use of the ballot.

In 1920 the National American Woman Suffrage Association reconstituted itself as the National League of Women Voters; the following year, at the first League convention after ratification of the suffrage amendment, Belle Sherwin was elected vice president and chairman of the department charged with training women for their civic duties. From an office in her Cleveland home soon emanated a stream of programs for citizenship classes, instructions on state electoral requirements and on voting, and analyses of political processes. But the poor showing of women in the 1920 and 1922 elections demonstrated that crash programs in civics would not motivate political participation. Sherwin concluded that the lessons had to be learned "from the alphabet upward, and the experience of centuries encapsulated." The necessary psychological reorientation called for the development of innovative methods of political education, a task Sherwin undertook upon her election in 1924 as the League's second president, succeeding Maud Wood Park.

When Sherwin took over, the organization was united in its desire to win a share in governing the country but divided as to methods. Each of its semiautonomous standing committees, which represented the different segments of the suffrage coalition, had its own program and specialists. Sherwin saw the possibility of fusing aims and methods. Establishing a residence in Washington, D.C., she made the national headquarters there the functioning center of authority and communications by drawing in previously dispersed activities and systematizing procedures. Since the "art of getting things done" interested her more than specific programs, she directed her conciliatory skills toward achieving consensus on program and policy among the conflicting factions.

The ten years of Sherwin's presidency established the character of the League of Women Voters as a nonpartisan, goal-oriented organization, politically accountable for its policies, and respected for the accuracy and objectivity of the educational materials prepared by its research staff. The institutional structure, educational techniques, and administrative procedures established during this period were largely attributable to her leadership. Under Sherwin, "study before action" became the operative principle of the League. The research and discussion which preceded the formulation of legislative goals and political action to achieve those goals became the means of the members' political education. This decisionmaking process characterized the League's work long after her departure and has largely accounted for its legislative achievements. Sherwin likened the League to "a university without walls . . . whose members enter to learn and remain to shape the curriculum," in the meantime acquiring habits of independent political judgment and disciplined action.

Sherwin's greatest gift as an organizer and administrator was the ability to detect and develop talent. Those who worked most closely with her admired her as a great teacher whose intellectual credentials were evidenced in all of her work. She was a skillful politician, holding together the disparate elements in the organization by a mixture of conciliation and persuasion. Although generous and just, she was a severe taskmaster and impatient with trivialities. She possessed both dignity and style, and wore easily the mantle of authority; none doubted that her quiet self-assurance masked a resolute and forceful character.

In 1934 Sherwin was succeeded as president of the League by MARGUERITE WELLS. That year President Franklin D. Roosevelt appointed her to the Consumers' Advisory Board of the National Recovery Administration; she was also appointed to the Federal Advisory Committee of the United States Employment Service.

Despite long absence, Sherwin never ceased identifying herself as a citizen of Cleveland. In 1942 she sold her Georgetown home and returned to her native city. Still intellectually vigorous and active, she divided her time during the next decade between Winden, the family estate at Kirtland, and a townhouse she designed. Her final years were shadowed by ill health. She died of bronchopneumonia at her Cleveland home at the age of eighty-seven.

[The League of Women Voters of the U.S. Records in the Manuscript Div., Library of Congress, contain official minutes, letters to state presidents, and speeches during her presidency, as well as correspondence with League officers and others. A small collection of materials is in the Belle Sherwin Papers at the Schlesinger Library, Radcliffe College. Articles about Sherwin's work appeared in the League's *Woman Citizen*, 1919–23 and 1926–27, and *Woman's Journal*, 1928–31. The *Cleveland Plain Dealer* and *Cleveland Press* gave generous coverage of her career from 1917 to her retirement. Other printed sources include Virginia Abbott, *The History of Woman Suffrage and the League of Women Voters in Cuyahoga County, 1911–1945* (1949); Irene M. Bowker, *Public Health Nursing in Cleveland, 1895–1928* (1930); Avis D. Carlson, "Trail-Blazers in Citizenship," *Survey Graphic*, Sept. 1945, a brief history of the League; Florence Converse, *Wellesley College: A Chronicle of the Years 1875–1938* (1939); Jean Glasscock, ed., *Wellesley College, 1875–1975: A Century of Women* (1975); J. Stanley Lemons, *The Woman Citizen: Social Feminism in the 1920s* (1973), which contains a useful bibliography; and *How Ohio Mobilized Her Resources for the War: A History of the Activities of the Ohio Branch, Council of National Defense, 1917–1919* (1919). For family background see the autobiography of her nephew, Orville Prescott, *The Five-Dollar Goldpiece* (1956). Obituaries appeared in the *N.Y. Times* and the *Cleveland Plain Dealer*, July 10, 1955. Sherwin's niece, Sarah Prescott Michel, furnished a genealogy of the Smith-Sherwin families and valuable personal reminiscences. Additional information about the League years was provided by Julia H. Carson, Beatrice Pitney Lamb, and Marguerite Owen. Death certificate supplied by Ohio Dept. of Health.]

LOUISE M. YOUNG

SHERWOOD-HALL, Rosetta. *See* HALL, Rosetta Sherwood.

SIMKHOVITCH, Mary Kingsbury, Sept. 8, 1867–Nov. 15, 1951. Settlement worker, housing reformer.

Mary Simkhovitch, founder of Greenwich House, was born in Chestnut Hill, Mass., the older of two children and only daughter of Laura (Holmes) and Isaac Franklin Kingsbury. Both parents came from old New England families; the Kingsburys' considerable wealth rested on large real estate holdings in the Boston area. Her paternal grandmother had been a student of MARY LYON at the Ipswich Female Seminary; her maternal grandfather, Cornelius Holmes, an ardent abolitionist. Laura Holmes Kingsbury enjoyed advanced educational opportunities for a young woman of her time, attending normal school; she taught before her marriage. Mary Kingsbury Simkhovitch described her mother as "primarily an intellectual person. Domestic duties worried rather than interested her." Her father, having served in the Union army, returned to assume a political career, first in the Custom House, then in the Massachusetts state legislature, and finally as town clerk of Newton.

Mary Kingsbury graduated from Newton High School in 1886. She decided against attending a women's college and instead chose to commute to Boston University, a school she later described as "more like a midwestern college" than the "restrained and narrow" eastern women's schools. In 1890 she received her A.B. and was elected to Phi Beta Kappa. While at Boston University Kingsbury met the Rev. W. D. P. Bliss and HELENA STUART DUDLEY, both of whom exerted a strong influence upon her. Bliss, a Fabian socialist, editor of *The Encyclopedia of Social Reform*, and pastor of the Episcopal Church of the Carpenter, attracted a broad spectrum of workers, labor leaders, bourgeois reformers, and academics to his church. Dudley, head of Denison House, a settlement house in Boston's South End, was part of a reform circle of women academics and scholars that included VIDA SCUDDER. Like the Church of the Carpenter, Denison House provided an open forum for the discussion of social theory and the exploration of social problems.

During her college years Kingsbury first encountered slum life as leader of a teenage girls' club at St. Augustine's Episcopal Church; this experience marked the beginning of her interest in housing reform. It was here as well that she learned one of the basic principles that would characterize her settlement house philosophy: "Before any help can be given the situation must be felt, realized and understood at first hand . . . Only that which is lived can be understood and translated to others."

For two years following her college graduation, Kingsbury taught high school Latin in Somerville, Mass. In 1892 she began graduate study in economic history and sociology at Harvard Annex (later Radcliffe College). She continued her contacts with Boston's black neighborhoods as well, serving on St. Augustine's casework committee. In 1893 Kingsbury received a scholarship from the Women's Educational and Industrial Union to continue her studies in Berlin. Accompanied by her mother she spent a year studying history and sociology at the University of Berlin. There she renewed her friendship with EMILY GREENE BALCH, with whom she took classes and toured Italy and southern Germany. At the year's end, Balch and Kingsbury attended the last major International Socialist Trade Union Congress in London.

Returning to the United States, Mary Kingsbury continued her graduate studies at Columbia University with James Harvey Robinson, E. R. A. Seligman, and Franklin Giddings. There her long-developing concern with the problems of the city and industrialization took a more decisive direction. Concluding that "sociology and economics and history could surely turn out to have a reality and a validity for one if one could gain a wider personal experience," she left Columbia in 1897 to become the head resident of the College Settlement House. Located on Rivington Street in New York's Lower East Side, the College Settlement House had been founded in 1889 by graduates of the women's colleges. Ensconced on the Lower East Side, Kingsbury commenced Yiddish lessons and became exposed to the full excitement of American social criticism as it developed among members of New York's Jewish working class. There too she met the city's leading social reformers and settlement house leaders. Working with tenants' groups, she became involved in housing reform and assisted the Outdoor Recreation League, founded at the College Settlement House.

In 1899 Mary Kingsbury married Russian-born Vladimir Simkhovitch, whom she had met in Berlin. A professor of economic history at Columbia University, he shared her interest in social reform. Their two children, Stephen (b. 1902) and Helena (b. 1904), were brought up with the help of a governess largely on the Simkhovitch farm in Whitehouse, N.J., where their parents visited them on weekends. The family spent summers in Maine.

Between 1898 and 1901 Mary Simkhovitch served as chief resident of the Friendly Aid House on East Thirty-third Street. She found that the values and goals of this Unitarian church-supported settlement, which emphasized religious and moral uplift (the outmoded approach of the city mission movement) contrasted sharply with those of the all-female, nonsectarian College Settlement. The women alumnae at the College Settlement had emphasized cooperation with neighborhood residents and a willingness to experiment with a variety of novel, often radical, economic and social theories. The trustees of Friendly Aid House also attempted to restrict her political activities. In

1901 Simkhovitch organized the Association of Neighborhood Workers upon the principles she felt should guide the settlement house movement.

The following year she led an exodus from the Friendly Aid House and organized Greenwich House on Jones Street; it later moved to Barrow Street. Under her leadership Greenwich House assumed a prominent position in the settlement and social reform movements. Under its auspices or with its financial encouragement, a number of seminal economic and community studies were undertaken on the problems of dilapidated housing, unemployment, racism, and the assimilation of immigrant groups.

Underlying Mary Simkhovitch's directorship of Greenwich House was her belief that settlements should function as catalysts in the creation of community cohesion and indigenous leadership. "If social improvements are to be undertaken by one class on behalf of another," she said, "no permanent changes are likely to be effected." Another guiding principle was that settlements should connect the neighborhood to broader social reform movements.

By the 1920s Simkhovitch had developed two rather distinct areas of interest, reflecting her philosophical commitments. She became deeply involved in the cultural life within the neighborhood, and, in the larger world beyond Greenwich Village, she maintained close ties with the liberal and urban wing of the Progressive movement. She worked within Greenwich House to support neighborhood theater, to establish a settlement music school, to turn local schools into neighborhood centers, and to encourage local residents to assume leadership roles. Maintaining her interest in neighborhood parks and recreational facilities, begun while she was a resident at the College Settlement, in 1911 she was appointed a member of the Mayor's Public Recreation Commission, and in 1925 she chaired the New York City Recreation Committee. Between 1898 and 1917 Simkhovitch served on the executive board of the National Consumers' League, working closely with FLORENCE KELLEY. She also taught at Barnard College (1907–10) and at Teachers College, Columbia University (1910–13). Her political activity included speaking widely for Theodore Roosevelt during the 1912 presidential campaign as well as canvassing for woman suffrage. However, Simkhovitch broke with many of the women in the settlement movement when she supported the First World War.

Her major reform interest centered on improving public housing. In 1907 she helped found the Committee on the Congestion of Population and served as its chairman. "Our idea was to show that overcrowding was responsible for many of the city's ills," she later explained. With her lifelong commitment to housing reform, Simkhovitch illustrates the continuum between Progressive and New Deal reform. From 1931 to 1943 she served as president of the Public Housing Conference, whose purpose was to mobilize support for a major, permanent federal housing program. Following Franklin D. Roosevelt's election as president, Simkhovitch was instrumental in gaining inclusion in the National Industrial Recovery Act of a provision for the first federally financed low-income public housing. In 1934 Mayor Fiorello La Guardia appointed her vice chairman of the New York City Housing Authority; three years later she helped to draft the public housing bill that finally passed as the Wagner-Steagall Housing Act. While enthusiastically advocating pioneering efforts in large-scale public housing, Simkhovitch never lost sight of the importance of restoration of old buildings and the reconstruction of small-scale traditional neighborhoods. "Many of my city planner friends," she wrote in 1938, "think it foolish to engage in housing unless it is on an impressive scale. I suppose a woman looks at it differently . . . My life at Greenwich House has taught me not to despise small things." Her ideal remained the organic community combining business, housing, recreation, and educational and cultural institutions.

In 1946 Mary Simkhovitch retired as director of Greenwich House, though she continued to serve as vice chairman of the New York City Housing Authority. She died at Greenwich House in 1951.

[The Mary Kingsbury Simkhovitch Papers at the Schlesinger Library, Radcliffe College, contain biographical and genealogical material, speeches, articles, correspondence, and files of Greenwich House, the Greenwich Village Assoc., and the N.Y. City Housing Authority. Simkhovitch's *Neighborhood: My Story of Greenwich House* (1938) is an account of her life and of the settlement. Her other major writings are *Standards and Tests of Efficiency in Settlement Work* (1911), *Votes in the Tenements* (1914), *The City Worker's World in America* (1917), *The Settlement Primer* (1926), *The Church and Public Housing* (1934), *The Red Festival* (1934), *Group Life* (1940), *Quicksand: The Way of Life in the Slums* (1942), and *Here Is God's Plenty: Reflections on American Social Advance* (1949). Biographical sketches appear in *Current Biog.*, 1943; *Dict. Am. Biog.*, Supp. Five; and *Encyc. Social Work* (1971). Allen F. Davis, *Spearheads of Reform: The Social Settlements and the Progressive Movement, 1890–1914* (1967), places Simkhovitch's work in a larger perspective. Her role in the development and passage of federal housing legislation is discussed in Timothy L. McDonnell, *The Wagner*

Housing Act: A Case Study of the Legislative Process (1957). An obituary appeared in the *N.Y. Times*, Nov. 16, 1951. A biobibliography by Russell Merritt greatly assisted in the research for this article. Birth order information from 1880 U.S. Census.]

CARROLL SMITH-ROSENBERG

SLYE, Maud Caroline, Feb. 8, 1869–Sept. 17, 1954. Pathologist.

Maud Slye was born in Minneapolis, the second of three children and younger daughter of Florence Alden (Wheeler) and James Alvin Slye. She came from an educated but relatively poor family whose ancestors can be traced back to colonial times. James Slye was a lawyer and author. Florence Slye, who had an interest in poetry, hoped that her daughter would become an artist or a writer, but Maud Slye's love of nature led her toward a career in biology. The family moved to Iowa where Maud attended public schools, first in Des Moines and then in Marshalltown. After graduating from Marshalltown High School in 1886, she worked as a stenographer in St. Paul, Minn., where the family moved following her father's death. She matriculated at the University of Chicago in September 1895, reputedly entering the university with forty dollars in her possession. For three years she carried a full academic load and worked her way through school as a secretary to president William Rainey Harper; the strain led to a nervous breakdown.

She recuperated while visiting relatives in Woods Hole, Mass., and then completed her undergraduate studies at Brown University, where she received an A.B. in 1899. Maud Slye next served as professor of psychology and pedagogy at Rhode Island State Normal School until 1905. Professor Charles Otis Whitman, whom she had met earlier at the Woods Hole Marine Biological Laboratory, invited her in 1908 to join him as a graduate assistant in the biology department of the University of Chicago at a small stipend.

Her first research after returning to Chicago involved a study of so-called "waltzing mice," which apparently suffered from a nervous disorder. Her attention soon turned, however, from the inheritance of nervous disorders to the inheritance of cancer. Several investigators had suggested that heredity might play an important role in cancer, but there was little evidence at the time for this view. Slye began carrying out breeding experiments with mice to investigate this subject, drawing upon her own meager funds to support her work. There were days when she ate very little so that she might have money to feed her mice.

In 1911 Maud Slye joined the staff of the newly established Sprague Memorial Institute at the University of Chicago, which provided her with more adequate facilities and funds for her research. The Institute's director, pathologist H. Gideon Wells, encouraged her in her work and agreed to confirm her microscopic analyses of tissue samples. In 1913 she was ready to present her first paper on her cancer research. On the basis of breeding experiments involving 5,000 mice, 298 of whom had spontaneously developed cancers, she concluded that the susceptibility to cancer was inherited and that contagion was not a factor in its transmission.

Slye devoted the rest of her career to further pursuit of this line of research. In 1919 she became director of the Cancer Laboratory at the University of Chicago, and in 1922 she was promoted from instructor to assistant professor of pathology. Four years later she became associate professor of pathology, a position that she held until her retirement in 1944. A tireless worker, she raised and kept pedigrees on over 150,000 mice during her career. In the early years, Slye took care of the mice by herself, performing the autopsies, and preparing and examining the tissue slides. Later, Harriet Holmes, a trained pathologist, offered to serve as a laboratory assistant at no salary. She prepared tissue samples for microscopic analysis and coauthored several papers on cancer.

Maud Slye's laboratory was described as a "mouse Utopia." She kept it scrupulously clean and took excellent care of the animals to ensure that the susceptibility to cancer in certain mice would not be masked by their dying young from other diseases. In addition, she apparently developed a real affection and concern for her laboratory animals. For many years she refused to take a vacation for fear of leaving her laboratory in the care of anyone else.

At first Slye postulated that susceptibility to cancer was due to the presence of a single Mendelian recessive character. She recognized, however, that a mouse susceptible to cancer would not necessarily develop the disease unless exposed to an irritant that stimulated the growth of a cancerous tumor. The question of the nature and cause of cancer was controversial, and her views were subjected to various criticisms. By 1936, sufficient evidence had come to light that more than one gene was involved in cancer to force her to modify her position. Her revised theory held that two genetic factors were involved, one determining the type of cancer (carcinoma, sarcoma, leukemia), the other the location of the tumor. Even this view was later shown to be an oversimplification of the genetics of cancer. Although her theory has not withstood the test of further research, her extensive and meticulous studies helped to establish clearly the role that heredity plays in determining susceptibility to cancer. Her contributions were recognized by various honors, including gold medals from the American Medical Association (1914) and the American Radiological Society (1922), the Ricketts Prize of the University of Chicago (1915), and an honorary D.Sc. from Brown University (1937).

Slye believed that cancer (and other diseases) could be bred out of the human species as she had bred the disease out of certain strains of mice. She repeatedly called for the establishment of a central record bureau for human cancer statistics in the hope of determining the heredity and external factors involved in cancer so that these could be avoided as far as possible.

As a woman in science, she was sometimes called upon to combat stereotypical views of women. When asked whether she was ever afraid of mice, she responded that she did not believe that women in general feared mice any more than men did. In another incident, she had to deny a malicious rumor that she had refused to show her research results to certain scientists visiting her laboratory and had broken down and cried when pressed to do so.

Outside of her research, her chief interests were poetry, music, gardening, sailing, and her two dogs. Slye, who lived with her sister, published two volumes of poetry, *Songs and Solaces* (1934) and *I in the Wind* (1936). One of her poems describes her choice of a career in science over marriage and motherhood:

'Twas not for me to go the happy road
Of flower-decked bride, and mother whose rich arms
Clasped all her babies . . .
My feet were set upon the service path,
Whose glory of the day is toil,
Whose peace at night is the peace of dreams
That reach beyond the stars! (Jaffe, *Outposts*, pp. 159–60).

On August 16, 1954, Maud Slye was hospitalized with a heart attack. She suffered a second, fatal attack in Billings Hospital, Chicago, a month later.

[The Joseph Regenstein Library, Univ. of Chicago, has a collection of Maud Slye Papers that consists almost exclusively of reports and records of her cancer research, but also includes three folders of correspondence. Materials on Slye, including a curriculum vitae, are available from the Office of Public Information, Univ. of Chicago. Most of Slye's important papers can be found in the *Jour. Cancer Research.* See also her lectures on "Heredity in Relation to Cancer," in *Our Present Knowledge of Heredity* (1925), pp. 101–56, and on "Genetics of Cancer and Its Localization," in Henry B. Ward, ed., *Some*

Fundamental Aspects of the Cancer Problem (1937), pp. 3–16. The only book-length biography of Maud Slye is a popular, undocumented work by J. J. McCoy entitled *The Cancer Lady: Maud Slye and Her Heredity Studies* (1977). Useful biographical sketches are included in *Current Biog.*, 1940, pp. 743–45, and in Bernard Jaffe, *Outposts of Science* (1935), pp. 129–60; an abbreviated version of the latter article was published in Ray Compton and Charles Nettles, eds., *Conquests of Science* (1939), pp. 255–68. On her work see also John A. Menaugh, "Rearing Mice to Save Men," *Minneapolis Sunday Jour.*, Feb. 5, 1933. There are obituaries in the *N.Y. Times* and *Chicago Tribune*, Sept. 18, 1954. A biobibliography prepared by Nancy Korpal assisted in the research for this article. Published sources give Maud Slye's birth date as Feb. 8, 1879. The 1869 date comes from the 1880 U.S. Census. The superintendent of Marshalltown schools has confirmed the 1886 graduation date, and has also found an 1880 record which lists Slye as eleven years old. Information from St. Paul City Directory, 1889–98.]

JOHN PARASCANDOLA

SMITH, Lillian, Dec. 12, 1897–Sept. 28, 1966. Writer, civil rights reformer.

Lillian Smith expressed the central theme of her life and work when she wrote: "Future generations will think of our times as the age of wholeness, when the walls began to fall; when the fragments began to be related to each other." In the writings for which she is best known and in her less recognized roles as director of a girls' camp and editor of a little magazine, Smith probed and challenged the racist, sexist, and economically exploitative walls that fragmented her place and time.

Born in Jasper, Fla., Lillian Eugenia Smith was the seventh of ten children, the third of four daughters of Calvin Warren and Annie Hester (Simpson) Smith. Her adult writings record experiences of belonging to a loving and financially comfortable family. But they also depict traumatic episodes of growing up in the racially segregated and economically stratified south. Smith's parents subjected their children to periodic religious revivals and severe sexual taboos which shattered Lillian's sense of well-being. They also encouraged her to love her black nurse and black playmates and then taught her to denigrate them, raising questions about the relations between white and black that were too painful to ask but too enduring to be forgotten.

To these uncertainties were added the death of her older brother Dewitt from typhoid in 1911, and a reversal in family fortunes. Her father lost the family business in 1915 and the Smiths moved permanently to their summer cottage in Clayton, Ga. Lillian Smith, an aspiring musician, attended Piedmont College in Demorest, Ga., for a year (1915–16), then left school to help her parents.

She twice began studies at the Peabody Conservatory in Baltimore, Md., in 1917 and again in 1919. In the intervening year she served as principal of a rural Georgia school, assisted by her youngest sister, Esther, the family member closest to her in sympathies and values.

Some time after her return to Baltimore, Smith fell in love with a fellow musician. But neither then nor later did marriage seem to be a serious possibility. Usually silent on this subject, Smith once confided: "All my life I have felt burdened by having to make promises that extend too far into the future . . . it is why I never married. My family did not believe in divorce . . . and I could not commit myself wholly and irrevocably."

In the fall of 1922 Lillian Smith accepted the position of music director at Virginia School, an American Methodist institution in Huchow, China. There western imperialism and indigenous politics quickened her awareness of the destructiveness of divisions based upon race and class. In 1925 her parents fell ill and she had to return to Clayton to manage their major source of income, Laurel Falls Girls Camp. Thus diverted from a career in music, Smith returned to the south where she would spend most of her life, establish a vocation as a writer, and enjoy with fellow southerner Paula Snelling a rich lifelong partnership.

Smith and Snelling first worked together at Laurel Falls, where Snelling, a counselor, supported Smith in transforming the traditional camp into a unique and nationally renowned undertaking. To encourage the campers to confront the emotional, biological, and social forces in their lives, Smith introduced programs in the arts, staffed by experts, including (in drama) her sister Esther.

Family reliance on Lillian Smith's abilities and loyalty continued to influence the direction of her life. For two winters, 1925–26 and 1926–27, she was executive secretary to her recently widowed brother, Austin, and companion to his preschool daughter. The death of her father in 1930 left Smith responsible for her invalid mother (who died in 1938). Her frequent involvement in the personal crises of her relatives led Smith to reflect that "one wants to [help], one wouldn't do anything else, but one's own dreams, one's own life just sort of dwindles away."

Some of this sense of life dwindling away led Smith, in concert with Paula Snelling, to found a little magazine. First published in 1936, it was called *Pseudopodia,* later renamed *The North*

Georgia Review, and finally, *South Today.* The first white southern journal to publish the work of black scholars and artists, *South Today* also gave space and encouragement to aspiring women writers and examined such sensitive topics as lynching. The magazine grew from a small literary undertaking to a substantial journal of interdisciplinary thought, achieving near the end of its existence in 1945 a circulation of 10,000.

While working on *South Today,* Smith was writing books and pursuing wide-ranging studies of Freudian psychology, philosophy, anthropology, and literature, entirely self-directed. She also traveled, living in Brazil for several months in 1938 and going twice to India, first in 1946 and with Snelling in 1955.

In 1944 Lillian Smith's first novel was published. *Strange Fruit* is a story of interracial love and of the later pathological effects of sexual and racial conditioning in childhood. The book was banned in Massachusetts for "obscenity." The literary historian Bernard DeVoto and a local bookseller challenged the ban; a trial ensued, ending in victory for the censors. A wider ban, by the United States Post Office, was quickly lifted at the intervention of ELEANOR ROOSEVELT. The novel was later adapted for the stage by Lillian and Esther Smith and played in Canada and on Broadway.

Smith's second book, *Killers of the Dream* (1949), unequivocally denounced segregation and questioned the moral and psychological health of Smith's racist countrymen, some of whom reacted with hostility. She began to feel that, as a result, her work was being "smothered." Although she received a succession of honors and was from the time of *Strange Fruit* always in demand as a lecturer and magazine contributor, the sales, reviews, and promotion of her later work never matched those of her first two books.

The 1950s brought further hardship. *The Journey,* a book on "the meaning of ordeal, its creative and destructive effects," was completed in 1953, shortly after Smith underwent surgery for breast cancer. In *Now Is the Time* (1955) Smith appealed for southern support of the 1954 Supreme Court decision on desegregation; it was the most poorly promoted of any of her books. Also in 1955 came the shock of a major fire. Set by young whites, it destroyed several manuscripts and notes for books, including two autobiographical novellas and an estimated 13,000 letters and private papers. An earlier accidental fire in 1944 had consumed important files, and yet another episode of arson by unknown intruders occurred in 1958.

While still reeling from the losses of the 1955

blaze, Smith began the novel *One Hour*. A complex story about intelligent people succumbing to mindless hysteria, the work—published in 1959—held clear implications for the McCarthy era in which it was written. A family reminiscence, *Memory of a Large Christmas*, was published in 1962.

Lillian Smith's final book, *Our Faces, Our Words* (1964), focused on the nonviolent civil rights movement, reflecting Smith's close identification with the black struggle for equality and justice. Black leaders valued her work; she was a friend of Martin Luther King, Jr., and John Lewis of the Student Nonviolent Coordinating Committee cited her as one of the three major influences in his life. In addition, she was honored by leading black universities (Howard, Atlanta, and Fisk) and was for many years a member of the executive board of the Congress of Racial Equality (CORE). When CORE disavowed nonviolence Smith resigned, interpreting the emerging language of black power as yet another source of fragmentation.

At the time of her resignation Lillian Smith was gravely ill with cancer. She continued to write, working on a collection of essays and a book for and about contemporary youth. Also left unfinished was a manuscript for a novel, tentatively titled "Julia." This, along with the autobiography which Smith had hoped to write, would, in the judgment of Paula Snelling, "have been her major, deeply felt and pondered works on the seductive subject of gender."

Smith died at Emory University Hospital in September 1966. Her body is buried on Old Screamer, the Georgia mountain where Laurel Falls Camp was located and where much of her writing had been done.

[Most of Lillian Smith's papers are at the Univ. of Ga. at Athens; the collection includes personal and business correspondence, fan mail, Camp Laurel papers, and some MSS. Papers relating to *South Today*, deposited before the 1955 fire and representing the bulk of manuscript sources on the magazine, may be found at the Univ. of Fla. in Gainesville. The Julius Rosenwald Fund Papers at Dillard Univ., New Orleans, also include Smith papers. An original, complete collection of *South Today* is at the Univ. of Ga. A major collection of Smith's writings appeared posthumously in 1978. *The Winner Names the Age*, ed. Michelle Cliff, is introduced by Paula Snelling's reminiscence, "In Re Lillian Smith." A brief biography, *Lillian Smith,* by Louise Blackwell and Frances Clay, was published in 1971. The most substantive article-length studies on Smith are Morton Sosna, "Lillian Smith: The Southern Liberal as Evangelist," *In Search of the Silent South* (1977); Margaret Sullivan, "Lillian Smith: The Public Image and the Personal Vision," *Mad River Rev.*, Summer/Fall 1967; Redding Sugg, Jr., "Lillian Smith and the Condition of Women," *South Atlantic Quart.*, Spring 1972; Jo Ann Robinson, "Lillian Smith: Reflections on Race and Sex," *Southern Exposure*, Winter 1977. See also Margaret Sullivan, *A Bibliography of Lillian Smith and Paula Snelling with an Index to South Today* (1971). An anthology of pieces selected from *South Today* was published by Helen White and Redding Sugg, Jr., as *From the Mountain* (1972). Obituaries which best capture the fullness of Smith's life are George P. Brockway in *Sat. Rev.*, Oct. 22, 1966, and Margaret Long in *The New South*, Fall 1966. Esther Smith shared information from the family Bible and other family materials. Paula Snelling allowed the writer to examine materials on Laurel Falls Camp that survived the fire of 1944 and a five-page "Lillian Smith Chronology," which the subject wrote shortly before her death, outlining the major phases of her life.]

JO ANN ROBINSON

SMITH, Rubye Doris. *See* ROBINSON, Rubye Doris Smith.

SOMERVILLE, Nellie Nugent, Sept. 25, 1863–July 28, 1952. Suffragist, state legislator.

Nellie Nugent Somerville, only surviving child of William Lewis and Eleanor Fulkerson (Smith) Nugent, was of English, Welsh, and Irish descent. Nellie (baptized, but never called, Eleanor) was born on her grandmother's plantation near Greenville, Miss. Her father was in the Confederate army at the time; federal soldiers had shot her grandfather and burned the family home in Greenville shortly before her birth. Her young mother survived barely two years, and though Nugent remarried, he was widowed again in a few months. Until his marriage to Aimee Webb in 1870, the care of his daughter fell largely to her devout and strong-willed grandmother, S. Myra Smith. In 1872 Nugent moved his family to Jackson, the state capital, where he quickly rose to leadership in the bar and in time became one of the wealthiest men in Mississippi.

By the time Nellie was twelve, five other children had been born, and she was sent to Whitworth College, a boarding school in Brookhaven, Miss., characterized by very plain living. After two years its president confessed that this bright child had exhausted his school's resources, and she went on to Martha Washington College in Abingdon, Va. She received her A.B. in 1880, finishing with a nearly perfect record. Despite these formal educational experiences, she acquired most of her considerable learning in political theory, theology, history, and public affairs on her own.

After graduation her father suggested that she read law in his office, but she preferred the in-

important cultural resource for the neighborhood and also came to serve as a model for later schools of its kind. Essentially a conservatory, the school offered individual instruction by highly qualified teachers at little or no cost. There were as many as 500 students, not all of them young. Emphasis was placed on learning music, rather than on competition, and performers' names did not always appear on the programs for student concerts. In addition, the school provided instructors and advice for any group in the settlement that wished to add music to its programs, and offered frequent concerts and performances open to all. In 1936 Aaron Copland wrote a play-opera, *The Second Hurricane*, specifically for performance by Henry Street students; the production was directed by Orson Welles. Copland also taught at Henry Street, and such other noted figures as the conductor John Barbirolli and Wagnerian soprano Kirsten Flagstad visited and assisted the school. Spofford encouraged the founding of other such music schools. Her "highest hope for American music [was] a shifting of emphasis from over-professionalism to personal participation in music shared as a common experience of life" (*Etude*, July 1939).

After her retirement, Grace Spofford became involved in international music relations and represented the United States at more than twenty international music and music education conferences in Europe and the Middle East. Between 1954 and 1963 she was three times elected chairman of music of the International Council of Women, and for ten years served in the same capacity for the National Council of Women of the United States. During her tenure, the National Council sponsored the recording of orchestral works by five women composers: MABEL DANIELS, Miriam Gideon, Mary Howe, Julia Perry, and Louise Talma. In 1964 and again in 1966 she was a delegate to the International Music Council, the music wing of UNESCO.

Spofford's long career in the cause of music earned her many honors, including a 1968 award from the National Federation of Music Clubs for distinguished service to music in the field of human rights. In an autobiographical sketch written in 1969, when she was eighty-two, Grace Spofford listed herself as still active in the National Council on Arts and Government, the People-to-People Music Committee, the National Music Council Committee on Music in UNESCO, and many other organizations. She also cited her activities with the Unitarian Church of All Souls in New York City and with the International Association for Liberal Christianity and Religious Freedom.

This tireless woman who lived her life for others, for the young, for music, and who traveled gladly, kept a diary throughout her long life. In the final volume, on Friday, May 31, 1974, she noted, "No therapy. Wrote letters. I am coming to my better self."

Grace Spofford's better self in fact had guided her through all her eighty-six years. The initiative and self-reliance which had led her to seek and obtain the Curtis Institute post kept her in touch with the professional world of music throughout her retirement and final bout with a broken hip, hospital, nursing home, and advanced age. She died of a heart attack on June 5, 1974, in New York City; the evening before she had commented on the music at a program at the nursing home—her final contribution to the art.

[The Sophia Smith Coll. at Smith College houses a large collection of Spofford's papers. In addition to correspondence that includes the 1969 autobiographical sketch, there are diaries, a box of photographs including the subject at all stages of her life, birth certificate, clippings, and scrapbooks. The Genealogy Dept. of the Haverhill Public Library also has clippings on Spofford and her family. There is some biographical information and a photograph in the article on recipients of the Elizabeth Mathias Award in *The Triangle* of Mu Phi Epsilon, Fall 1970. See also *Who's Who Am. Women*, 1974–75. The best description of the Henry Street Music School is Myles H. Fellowes, "The 'Musical Lighthouse' of New York's East Side," *Etude*, July 1939. Articles also appeared in *Musical America*, May 1952; *Newsweek*, June 2, 1952; and the *Christian Science Monitor*, April 26, 1952. An obituary appeared in the *N.Y. Times*, June 7, 1974. Dorothy Barko recounted the circumstances of Grace Spofford's last days.]

VERNON GOTWALS

STANLEY, Louise, June 8, 1883–July 15, 1954. Home economist, federal official.

Louise Stanley, the first woman to direct a bureau in the United States Department of Agriculture (USDA), was born in Nashville, Tenn., to Gustavus and Eliza (Winston) Stanley. Her parents died before she was four years old so she and her younger brother were raised by an aunt. Stanley attended the Peabody Demonstration School and Ward's Seminary in Nashville. Her intellectual ability and money inherited from her parents enabled her to secure several academic degrees: an A.B. from Peabody College at the University of Nashville in 1903; a B.Ed. from the University of Chicago in 1906; and an A.M. from Columbia University in 1907. She then studied biochemistry at Yale University with Lafayette B. Mendel, receiving a Ph.D. in 1911.

The years Stanley devoted to her education coincided with the emergence of home economics as a promising profession, offering many able women employment opportunities and the chance to combine scientific interests with educational programs. Joining the home economics faculty at the University of Missouri in 1907, she was department chairman by 1917, a post she held until 1923.

Stanley's influence rapidly extended beyond the university as she joined with other progressive reformers, educators, and scientists to improve the quality of life in American homes and, specifically, to secure federal support for home economics education. Following passage of the Smith-Hughes Act (1917), which provided funds for agricultural, industrial, and home economics education in the public schools, Stanley played a significant role, as head of the American Home Economics Association's legislative committee, in the campaign for additional federal encouragement of home economics.

When the Bureau of Home Economics was formed in the USDA in 1923, Louise Stanley was selected by Secretary of Agriculture Henry C. Wallace as the department's first female bureau chief. During her tenure, the foundations were carefully laid for effective and growing programs of research and public education. Under her direction, research in nutrition, undertaken in the 1920s, led to the four basic diet plans for families at different economic levels, developed by Hazel K. Stiebeling. These were widely utilized in government programs during the depression and World War II, and for later war relief programs abroad. Stanley also directed the first national survey of rural housing and the Consumer Purchase Study (1938–41), which compiled information on family income, expenditures, and savings. Breaking down consumption patterns by regional and residential categories, this large-scale study established base year prices for the cost-of-living index, a significant economic indicator. The Bureau also conducted time and motion studies of housekeeping methods and did studies of body measurements which encouraged the standardization of clothing sizes.

Stanley believed family well-being was the primary goal of the Bureau's work, an attitude that sometimes brought her into conflict with agricultural interests. On one occasion in the 1930s farmers and members of Congress objected to the dietary plans, claiming that the Bureau was using public funds to discourage consumption of wheat and sugar. Stanley continued to defend consumer interests and good

nutrition and was supported in her efforts by a coalition of women's organizations.

During World War II Stanley's appointment as special assistant to the administrator of agricultural research gave her an opportunity to develop home economics internationally. Her particular interest was Latin America, and she directed nutrition surveys and educational programs in Brazil, Venezuela, and Mexico. In 1943 she participated in the United Nations Conference on Food and Agriculture, and she was actively involved in the work of the United States National Commission for UNESCO. Following her retirement in 1950, Stanley served as consultant for home economics in the Office of Foreign Agricultural Relations of the USDA until 1953.

Throughout her career, Stanley consistently aimed to serve those she considered most needy and to defend blacks and others whom she considered victims of injustice. Objecting to discriminatory membership policies, Stanley refused to join the Daughters of the American Revolution although she was eligible. Her concern for the rural poor in the United States later expanded to include those living in poverty in other countries.

Stanley's personal life was closely intertwined with her public career. She was part of an extensive network of professional colleagues, and became a mentor for younger women interested in home economics. It was perhaps her professional interest in family life and children that motivated her in 1929 to adopt a daughter, Nancy.

Louise Stanley died of cancer in Washington, D.C., in 1954. Among her many honors, the Latin American scholarship established in 1953 by the American Home Economics Association and the School of Home Economics building at the University of Missouri, dedicated in 1961, bear her name. An effective national leader, Stanley succeeded in institutionalizing home economics at the federal level and hastened the evolution of home economics as an accepted academic discipline, a valid subject for scientific research, and a respected profession for women. Her greatest contribution to her profession was the example and the encouragement she provided to later generations of home economists.

[The *Jour. Home Economics* includes many articles written by and about Stanley. The main source of information about her career is Helen T. Finneran, "Louise Stanley: A Study of the Career of a Home Economist, Scientist and Administrator, 1923–1953" (M.A. thesis, American Univ., 1966). The USDA *Yearbook for 1962* also describes Stanley's career and includes a photograph of her, while other departmental publications describe the work of the

Bureau and contain data from studies. Also see Paul Betters, *The Bureau of Home Economics* (1930), and Marie Dye, *Home Economics at the University of Chicago, 1892–1956* (1972). Obituaries appeared in the *N.Y. Times* and *Wash. Post,* July 16, 1954, and in *Jour. Am. Dietetic Assoc.* and *Jour. Home Economics,* Sept. 1954. Additional information for this article was provided by Hazel K. Stiebeling and Sadye F. Adelson, and by Stanley's daughter. Death certificate supplied by D.C. Health Dept.]

CHARLOTTE W. CONABLE

STERN, Catherine Brieger, Jan. 6, 1894–Jan. 8, 1973. Educator.

An innovator in the teaching of elementary mathematics and reading, Catherine Stern was born Käthe Brieger, second of four children and only daughter of Oscar and Hedwig (Lyon) Brieger, residents of Breslau, Germany. Her father and two grandfathers were prominent physicians and she grew up in a tightly knit circle of medical and academic families. Hedwig Brieger, who combined family care with work in an early volunteer kindergarten, shared an extraordinary intimacy with Käthe, passing on to her daughter an abiding interest in the education of children.

The Briegers were prosperous and had at least one private tutor; Käthe Brieger studied formally as well at the Mädchen Gymnasium in Breslau (1904–12) and then at the University of Breslau, concentrating in physics at the urging of her father. After his death in 1914, she taught briefly in the Mädchen school; her graduate research was further delayed by World War I, during which she served in a hospital. Brieger persisted, however, and in January 1918 she obtained her Ph.D. in mathematics and physics from Breslau.

Vivacious, talented, and serious, Käthe Brieger combined her scientific training with a fondness for language and literature. Fluent in French, she also produced plays and wrote poetry to her Breslau companions. Among them was Rudolf Stern, like her a member of a medical family, who went on to become a physician and researcher. She and Stern were married on April 19, 1919; in forty-three years, she wrote after his death in 1962, "we were, almost every day, together." A daughter, Toni, was born in 1920 and a son, Fritz, in 1926.

As a young mother, Stern's interest in the education of children grew both practically and theoretically. From 1921 to 1923 she studied the official Montessori teaching method and conducted a preschool at home. In 1924 she opened Breslau's first Montessori kindergarten—later expanded to an after-school club for older children and a teacher-training institute. Although she had domestic help, she continued to work by choice within her home, obtaining state certification to teach at grade school levels there; her daughter was among her pupils. While directing her school during the 1920s Stern designed the first of the materials for teaching reading and arithmetic for which she later became known, and wrote articles for various journals. In 1932, at the insistence of her friend and adviser chemist Fritz Haber, she published *Methodik der täglichen Kinderhauspraxis,* which discussed her teaching experiences within a theoretical framework; she followed this with *Wille, Phantasie und Werkgestaltung* (1933), a vivid discussion of the practical aspects of running a kindergarten.

Stern's educational doctrine, which renounced drills and routines in an effort to adapt learning "to the natural development of the child," found little encouragement in Hitler's Germany. Her situation was further aggravated by the fact that, while raised as Lutherans, both she and her husband came from Jewish families and so were subject to the persecutions of the Nazis. Although the Sterns first attempted to emigrate via Paris in 1933, it was not until 1938 that they, along with Hedwig Brieger (who went to live in Canada), left Germany for good. They arrived that October in New York City. There Käthe became Catherine Stern, and took United States citizenship in 1944.

Working as a teacher, researcher, lecturer, and author, Stern continually refined and improved the mathematics and reading approaches she had developed in Germany. Her teaching materials were designed to reduce dependence on rote memorization by encouraging young children to explore relationships fundamental to the understanding of reading and arithmetic. She made numbers concrete by fashioning colored blocks of lengths varying from one to ten units which fit into corresponding slots on boards or within frames. With these devices, children could count, add, subtract, divide, or multiply, while gaining insight into the basic structure of mathematics. The eight-slot, for example, could house either four two-unit blocks or two four-unit blocks, illustrating the commutative principle.

Similarly, Stern's approach to reading broke language down into concrete units. In contrast to traditional approaches in reading, which focused either on recognition of whole words by their overall shapes, or on the association of individual letters with single sounds which must then be blended, Stern began with what novice readers already knew, the spoken language. She challenged children first "to take spoken words apart and to put them together again," and then to analyze and reassemble written words in the same fashion. By stressing the correspondence of spoken sounds with letter clusters, Stern helped children approach reading, spelling, and writing as integral parts of the same constructive process.

Catherine Stern's teaching methods received vital support from Max Wertheimer, founder of the school of Gestalt psychology in Berlin, whom she met in New York in 1940. Wertheimer, whose educational theory stressed that learning by insight is more productive for both student and teacher than learning by memorization, found this ideal embodied in Stern's materials. From 1940 until Wertheimer's death in 1943, Stern served as his research assistant at the New School for Social Research. There, funded by grants from the New York Foundation and Oberländer Trust, she studied Gestalt theory, gave lecture-demonstrations in Wertheimer's classes, and began a book primarily for teachers, published later as *Children Discover Arithmetic* (1949), relating her techniques to Gestalt principles. In turn, Wertheimer cited her materials in his book, *Productive Thinking* (1945, 1959), and devised for them the title, *Structural Arithmetic*, under which they were published for classroom use by Houghton Mifflin in the United States (1951, 1965, 1966; in England they became known as the Stern Apparatus).

Catherine Stern conducted the experimental Castle School in Manhattan from 1944 to 1951 with her daughter Toni Stern Gould and Margaret J. Bassett, later her daughter-in-law. The school was one of the first to teach children of two to four years number concepts and reading. Stern summarized her Castle School approach in *The Early Years of Childhood: Education Through Insight* (1955), with Toni S. Gould, and later coauthored another book with Gould, *Children Discover Reading* (1965). In the meantime, she continued to teach, lecture, and do research, obtaining grants from the Carnegie Corporation (1958–62). She was also consulted by the School Mathematics Study Group, proponents of the new math program.

Catherine Stern was a very private person, indifferent to public acclaim or conventional honors and devoted to her close friends and family. Many of her early teaching experiences involved family members; later, each of her grandchildren enjoyed her tutelage, and her daughter and daughter-in-law carried on her work. She read avidly; her passions ranged from detective stories to foreign languages. A few months before her death she returned to the study of Italian. Stern remained professionally active until her death in New York City in January 1973, following a stroke.

After her death, Stern's materials continued to be employed in classrooms throughout northern Europe, Israel, and North America. In the United States, her mathematics tools have proved particularly useful in the field of special education. Catherine Stern anticipated by a quarter of a century some of the key ideas of the "modern mathematics" movement and, in the field of early education, her lifework served as an argument against teaching based on rote drill, and for an approach stressing insight and understanding.

[Stern's memoirs (unpublished MS.) and other autobiographical statements are held by her son, Fritz Stern. She collaborated on the *Structural Reading* series, published by Singer/Random House (1963, 1966, 1972, 1978). A revised edition of *Children Discover Arithmetic* (1971), with Margaret Bassett Stern, contrasts Catherine Stern's approach to that of the "new math." M. B. Stern's "Structural Arithmetic and Children with Learning Disabilities," *Bull. of the Orton Soc.*, 1977, pp. 171–82, places Stern's arithmetic methods in a Piagetian context. See also Kenneth Lovell, *The Growth of Basic Mathematical and Scientific Concepts in Children* (1961); Martin Mayer, *The Schools* (1961); and Rudolph Arnheim, *Visual Thinking* (1969). There is a biographical sketch and photograph in *Nat. Cyc. Am. Biog.*, LVII, 661. An obituary appeared in *N.Y. Times*, Jan. 9, 1973. Personal information supplied by Margaret B. Stern and Fritz Stern. Grant records furnished by Carnegie Fdn.; death record by N.Y. Dept. of Health.]

RICHARD D. TROXEL

STEWART, Isabel Maitland, Jan. 14, 1878– Oct. 5, 1963. Nursing educator.

Isabel Maitland Stewart was born in Raleigh, Ont., Canada, the third daughter and fourth of nine children of Francis Beattie and Elizabeth (Farquharson) Stewart. The Farquharsons moved to Canada from Aberdeenshire, Scotland, in 1866, the Stewarts in 1871. Francis Stewart was a substantial farmer and sawmill owner in Fletcher, Ont., but when Isabel was in her early teens the business failed. Her father then moved his family to Manitoba, where, as an unordained Presbyterian missionary, he conducted services in rural communities. Isabel Stewart early exhibited a sense of responsibility for her family, "taking charge" and ruling in what her older brother termed a "benevolent autocracy." She later recalled the "adventurous and free" spirit of the pioneer west where she spent her young adulthood. She and her friends considered themselves "new women" and planned careers; living in a region where men far outnumbered women, they disdained marriage as commonplace.

Stewart's parents encouraged the education of their daughters as well as their sons. She attended schools in Pilot Mound, Man., Chatham, Ont., and Winnipeg, where she qualified for teaching certificates. Once she was old enough, Stewart, like her brothers and sisters, supported her education by teaching in local schools. Though she considered a career as a teacher of high school English and history, Stewart turned to nursing. Her family and most of her friends opposed her decision, believing that as a nurse she would be wasting a good education. But she was encouraged by the enthusiasm of two nurse friends and by her desire for adventure, to see and experience more of life. In 1900 Stewart entered the Winnipeg General Hospital School of Nursing. As a student nurse, she spent long hours on the wards and received limited formal training. A smallpox epidemic at Winnipeg General, which developed an impressive spirit of comradeship among the staff, confirmed her choice of a career.

Graduating in 1903, Stewart practiced private nursing for two years, relieved a district nurse in Winnipeg for several months, and returned for two years to Winnipeg General as nurse supervisor. She also joined with a group of other graduates to form an alumnae association and the Manitoba Association of Graduate Nurses, was cofounder of an alumnae journal, and contributed articles to the *Canadian Nurse*. Her experiences both as a student and as a teacher of nurses colored her later ideas about nursing education. She believed that nurses should learn in the classroom as well as on the wards, and throughout her career initiated and supported efforts to strengthen the theoretical component of nurse training. Far from satisfied with the education offered by Canadian nurse training schools, she responded enthusiastically to news of innovations in nursing education in the United States under the leadership of ADELAIDE NUTTING.

Returning from a summer trip to Great Britain in 1908, she entered the hospital economics program at Teachers College, Columbia University, which Nutting headed. Though her original aim had been to return to Canada to establish a preparatory course for Canadian nurses, Isabel Stewart remained at Teachers College for the rest of her professional life. She received a B.S. in 1911 and an A.M. in 1913; held the positions of assistant, instructor, and assistant professor; and in 1925 succeeded Adelaide Nutting as Helen Hartley Jenkins Foundation Professor of Nursing Education and director of the department.

When Stewart entered Teachers College, the program was chiefly concerned with the training of nurse administrators. In 1910, when an endowment by Helen Hartley Jenkins permitted the creation of an expanded nursing education department, Stewart persuaded Nutting to set up a program to train teachers, the first of its kind. Stewart was given full responsibility for this program from its inception, designing and teaching the first courses and planning and supervising the practice teaching. Under Nutting and Stewart, the department became the preeminent center for advanced work in the field, attracting students from all over the world. As director, Stewart further expanded its offerings. During her tenure, some students from the department for the first time qualified for doctoral degrees.

A leader in various professional organizations, Stewart was active in efforts to raise the status of nursing and to introduce higher standards for training. In particular, as secretary and then chairman of the education committee of the National League of Nursing Education, she was instrumental in the design of the influential national curricula, published by the League in 1917, 1927, and 1937 as guidelines for evaluating nursing school instruction. She organized the subcommittees which accomplished most of the work on the first curriculum, and she personally wrote most of it. In addition she directed the two revisions, which stressed the need for nurses to consider the mental and social impacts of illness; recommended more courses in the basic sciences, psychology, sociology, and public health; and introduced the case study method and other innovations in teaching techniques. Stewart is credited with initiating the idea of standardized tests in nursing, and with reviving interest in the comprehensive study and grading of nursing schools. Completed in 1934, the study paved the way for the first system of voluntary accreditation in 1939. She also worked to improve standards of nursing education through the Association of Collegiate Schools of Nursing, an organization she helped to found in 1932, which promoted the establishment of nursing schools in colleges and universities, and as chairman of the education committee of the International Council of Nurses.

During two world wars Stewart served in leadership roles. In the first, she chaired the curriculum committee of the Vassar Training Camp, which recruited college graduates to serve as nurses and gave them preliminary training. She also wrote most of the materials used in the campaign to recruit nurses for the war effort. In World War II, she chaired the committee on educational policies and resources of the National Nursing Council for War Service (1940–42), in which capacity she advocated federal appropriations for nursing education; she also served as a consultant to several government agencies.

Isabel Stewart reached her largest audience through her research and writing. Her *Opportunities in the Field of Nursing* (1912) was one of the earliest publications offering vocational guidance in nursing. Two books, *The Education of Nurses: Historical Foundations and Modern Trends* (1943) and *A Short History of Nursing* (in five editions), became the standard sources on their subjects. Because she treasured the traditions of nursing and valued research, Stewart promoted the preservation of nursing documents, supporting the growth of the Adelaide Nutting Historical Nursing Collection at Teachers College and of local history collections.

Stewart's interests extended beyond nursing. A liberal, with a keen interest in politics, she was for many years a member of the Foreign Policy Association. She was also an early and vigorous supporter of better education and economic justice for women. At the age of sixteen, she had written an essay on woman suffrage, and during her early years at Teachers College had joined Adelaide Nutting, LILLIAN WALD, and many of her colleagues in suffrage parades up Fifth Avenue.

Before and after her retirement in 1947, Stewart's contributions to education were recognized by many honors, including the Mary Adelaide Nutting Award from the National League of Nursing Education (1947), a medal from the government of Finland (1946), and several honorary degrees. In 1961 Teachers College established the Isabel Maitland Stewart Research Professorship in Nursing Education. In retirement Stewart, indefatigable and generous as ever, continued to be consulted by former colleagues and students. She died suddenly in 1963 at the home of a nephew in Chatham, N.J., of a heart attack.

[Major sources of biographical data include the Isabel Maitland Stewart Papers in the archives of the nursing education department, Teachers College, Columbia Univ., and *The Reminiscences of Isabel Maitland Stewart* (1960), Oral History Coll., Columbia Univ. *Opportunities in the Field of Nursing* was reprinted in 1920, 1925, and 1930. The first four editions of *A Short History of Nursing from Ancient to Modern Times* (1920, 1925, 1931, 1938) were written in collaboration with Lavinia L. Dock; the fifth, entitled *A History of Nursing from Ancient to Modern Times* (1962), was a joint effort with Anne L. Austin. "A List of the Published Writings of Isabel Maitland Stewart" (1967), comp. Anne Austin and available from Nursing Education

Alumnae Assoc., Teachers College, contains the titles of Stewart's pamphlets, forewords, introductions, and periodical articles. Information about her career and assessments of her impact on nursing education can be found in Stella Goostray, "Isabel Maitland Stewart," *Am. Jour. of Nursing*, March 1954; Mary M. Roberts, *American Nursing: History and Interpretation* (1955); "Isabel M. Stewart Recalls the Early Years," *Am. Jour. of Nursing*, Oct. 1960; Teresa E. Christy, *Cornerstone for Nursing Education: A History of the Division of Nursing Education of Teachers College, Columbia University, 1899–1947* (1969); Stella Goostray, *Memoirs: Half a Century of Nursing* (1969); Helen E. Marshall, *Mary Adelaide Nutting: Pioneer of Modern Nursing* (1972). See also Gladys Bonner Clappison, *Vassar's Rainbow Division* (1918). Useful biographical information was provided by Henry E. Sharpe and Margaret E. Hart. Obituaries appeared in *Nursing Outlook*, Nov. 1963; *Am. Jour. of Nursing*, Nov. 1963; *N.Y. Times*, Oct. 7, 1963. A birth record was supplied by Ontario Office of the Registrar General; death record provided by N.J. Dept of Health.]

ANNE L. AUSTIN

STRANG, Ruth May, April 3, 1895–Jan. 3, 1971. Educator.

Ruth Strang, a leader in the field of educational guidance, was born in Chatham, N.J., the only daughter and youngest of three children of Charles Garrett and Anna (Bergen) Strang. Her father's ancestors, Huguenots, had emigrated from France, her mother's ancestors from the Netherlands, both arriving in America during the colonial era. Charles Strang, a farmer who faced hard work and financial stringencies, moved with his family several times during Ruth's childhood, first from New Jersey to South Jamaica, Long Island, where he worked a farm inherited from his father, and then to Phoenix, Ariz. After recuperating there from bronchitis, he sold the Long Island farm and the Strangs settled finally in Brooklyn, where Ruth attended her fourth elementary school. Despite her mother's sympathetic presence, she later recalled growing up in an "atmosphere of anxiety."

Ruth Strang's secondary school years, at Adelphi Academy, were happier, introducing her both to the classics and to women's athletics. She had to give up hopes of attending Wellesley College on graduation, however, when her father discouraged the idea (although he had helped her older brother Benjamin through Columbia). She entered Pratt Institute in Brooklyn, N.Y., instead, completing a two-year normal program in household science in 1916. Strang worked briefly as an interior decorator and cared for her ailing mother before becoming a home economics teacher in a poor district of New York City (1917–20). Then, in the face of strong opposition from home and school advisers, she decided to continue her education at Teachers College, Columbia University. With close guidance and support from several faculty members, she earned her B.S. in 1922 and her Ph.D. four years later. In her graduate education as in her later career, Strang pursued a wide range of educational interests, supervising health education at the Horace Mann School, contributing to an experimental reading project for deaf and mute children, and serving as a research assistant and instructor in psychology.

On receiving her doctorate, Ruth Strang accepted a research fellowship from Teachers College to investigate national trends in student personnel administration. The project focused on the role of deans of girls and women in American schools, and Strang coauthored two books on the subject. Subsequently she chaired the Research Committee of the National Association of Deans of Women (1930–39)—which later became the National Association for Women Deans, Administrators, and Counselors—and edited its *Journal,* one of the leading publications in the guidance field, from 1938 to 1960. In the late 1920s Strang taught three summers at the Women's College at the University of North Carolina (Greensboro). She also completed one of her most widely consulted works, *An Introduction to Child Study* (1930), which she revised several times during her career.

In 1929 Strang became assistant professor of education at Teachers College, where she remained for three decades, becoming full professor in 1940 and helping to make its department of guidance and student personnel administration a major center for graduate study. Strang not only taught guidance, she practiced it, serving as a model to many who profited from her advice. Living alone in a room near the college, Strang, a careless housekeeper, devoted most of her social energies to the success and friendship of her students. Her style was informal, and she favored casual dress and sneakers.

Besides her work in guidance, to which Strang devoted over one-third of her roughly four hundred articles and books, she pursued a second major interest in the teaching of reading. She directed the High School and College Reading Center, begun at Teachers College in 1932, and wrote *Problems in the Improvement of Reading in Secondary Schools and High Schools* (1938), along with many other books and articles on the subject. Her work in this area supported the development of reading and communication centers at many American schools and colleges.

The remainder of her scholarly efforts were distributed among the fields of health education, testing, psychology and mental health, the teaching of gifted children, group work, and rural education. Active in professional organizations, she served as president of the National Association of Remedial Teachers (1955), and as a three-term member on the board of directors of the National Society for the Study of Education.

Reaching the mandatory retirement age of sixty-five, Ruth Strang left Teachers College in 1960 to serve as professor of education and direct the reading development center at the University of Arizona (1960–68). She then held a visiting professorship at the Ontario Institute for Studies in Education (1968–69), before retiring to Amityville, N.Y. Suffering from arteriosclerosis in her final years, she died in Amityville in January 1971.

An instinctive moralist, Strang described herself as a Puritan, consciously dedicated to work, duty, self-improvement, and service. This ethic was tempered by a romantic humanism, however; she cited Emerson in her writings and brought to her vision of good education both a dislike for social engineering and a nostalgic fondness for the small, rural community of neighborliness and cooperation. She wanted a school to be such a community in miniature and accordingly emphasized face-to-face teaching, while arguing that the most important lessons are "caught, not taught." Strang did not originate or revolutionize this approach, nor did she conduct groundbreaking research, but she was a gifted synthesizer, communicating important professional ideas and innovations to workers in the field. Her career epitomized the progressive education movement with its vigorous competence, its faith in gradual change, and its utter dedication to the life of service.

[The best source is Robert J. Havighurst, ed., *Leaders in American Education: The Seventieth Yearbook of the National Society for the Study of Education* (1971), pt. II, pp. 365–411. The volume devotes a chapter to Ruth Strang, including a revealing autobiographical statement by Strang shortly before her death, a selective bibliography, and a thoughtful analysis by Charles Burgess. A more thorough bibliography appears in Amelia Melnik, "The Writings of Ruth Strang," *Teachers College Record,* May 1960, pp. 464–76. See also *Current Biog.,* 1960; an editorial statement, Jan. 1961, pp. 69–70, and an obituary, Spring 1971, pp. 97–98, in *Jour. Nat. Assoc. of Women Deans and Counselors.* An obituary also appeared in *N.Y. Times,* Jan. 5, 1971. Personal information was supplied by Strang's faculty colleagues at Teachers College. Death certificate obtained from N.Y. State Dept. of Health.]

FREDERICK D. KERSHNER, JR.

STRONG, Anna Louise, Nov. 24, 1885–March 29, 1970. Radical journalist, writer.

When Anna Louise Strong died in Peking at the age of eighty-four, journalists noted both the distance between the People's Republic of China and her birthplace in Friend, Neb., and the persistence of the pioneer spirit which had brought her such a distance. An internationally known propagandist for the Soviet Union and for the People's Republic, she was the eldest of three children (two daughters and a son) of Congregational minister Sydney Dix Strong and Ruth (Tracy) Strong. Her ancestors on both sides migrated from England in the 1630s. The family moved as Sydney Strong became pastor of various churches, going to Mount Vernon, Ohio, in 1887 and then to Cincinnati in 1892. There Anna attended a public and then a private school, finishing eight grades in four years. Her father became pastor of an Oak Park, Ill., church in 1897 and she went to high school there, graduating at fifteen. She studied in Europe before beginning college at Oberlin (from which both of her parents had graduated) in 1902. At her mother's insistence, she transferred to Bryn Mawr in 1903.

That year Ruth Strong died at sea as she and her husband were returning from a tour of South African missions. A religious and ambitious woman, she was the strongest influence on her daughter's life. As president of the Women's Home Missionary Union of Ohio and Illinois, she was also influential in gaining positions for her husband.

Anna Louise Strong returned to Oberlin in 1904. After receiving her A.B. in 1905, she went in March 1906 to the University of Chicago. There she successfully defended her dissertation, published as *The Psychology of Prayer,* to gain her Ph.D. in philosophy in 1908. By then, however, her interests had shifted to reform work and the following year she joined her father in organizing a "Know Your City" civic betterment program in Seattle, the site of his new ministry. A committed pacifist, Sydney Strong shared his sense of mission with his favorite child. She went on to organize similar programs in other northwestern cities. Their success led the Russell Sage Foundation to invite her to serve as assistant director of the New York Child Welfare Exhibit in 1911. Although she left Russell Sage later that year, she continued to direct child welfare exhibits, which became popular with urban social reformers, from Kansas City to Dublin, Ireland. During one such exhibit, in St. Louis, Strong became engaged to Roger Baldwin, the future director of the American Civil Liberties Union. They failed to marry because of Sydney Strong's opposition and her own conclusion that Baldwin was not a committed Christian.

Strong was in the employ of Russell Sage again in late 1913, but in September 1914 went to Washington to become director of exhibits under JULIA LATHROP at the Children's Bureau. Resigning in the fall of 1915, she returned to the west coast. The following year Strong joined CRYSTAL EASTMAN's Anti-Preparedness League and arranged antiwar rallies in the middle west. She turned decisively to politics later that year, returning to Seattle to run unsuccessfully for the state legislature. She was, however, elected to the Seattle School Board. Following United States entry into World War I, Strong, who had since 1912 considered herself a socialist, anonymously wrote antiwar and anticapitalist articles for the socialist *Seattle Daily Call.* Her attendance at anticonscription meetings and her defense of those who worked against the draft led to her recall from the school board in March 1918. Writing under the pseudonym of Anise, Strong found a refuge in becoming feature editor of the *Seattle Union Record,* a labor paper. On Feb. 4, 1919, she published an editorial, "No One Knows Where," which justified and in great part launched the Seattle General Strike of 1919. It made her even more notorious.

With the collapse of Seattle labor's solidarity, in 1921 Strong left for Poland under the auspices of the American Friends Service Committee to assist famine victims there. From Lincoln Steffens and others, she had heard exciting tales of the revolution in Russia, and she next went there hoping to make her life in the revolution. In Moscow, she found favor by teaching Trotsky English and defending Lenin's New Economic Policy in her book *The First Time in History* (1924). She identified strongly with the Bolsheviks and became a great admirer of Trotsky. Her attempts to join the Communist party were rebuffed, however. Wanting to do more for the revolution, Strong raised money to establish the John Reed Children's Colony, set up for the many children and teenage refugees left homeless by the Volga famine, and for the American Working School, a trade school in Moscow. Both ventures failed, and Strong's revolutionary idealism had to be channeled into her career as writer, journalist, and lecturer. From the mid-1920s until the late 1940s she alternated periods of work in the Soviet Union with regular trips to the United States to lecture and raise funds.

Anna Louise Strong went to China for the first time in 1925. Anticipating there the revolution she continued to seek, Strong returned to Hankow in 1927. She arrived in time to join Russian adviser Michael Borodin and a group of

Russians and Chinese fleeing from the wrath of Chiang Kai-shek, who had turned against his communist allies. Strong became the diarist for this caravan as they raced for safety in Siberia.

Strong also continued to seek ways to publicize the revolution in the Soviet Union. In 1930 she founded the English-language *Moscow News* to provide information to Americans working there. Two years later, when arguments among the editors led Strong to decide to abandon the paper, Stalin intervened at her request and brought about a decision to reorganize the paper into a daily. In her 1935 autobiography, *I Change Worlds*, Strong offered this episode, with its revelation of both Soviet administrative methods and Stalin's abilities as a leader, as the crucial event of her life. But her dissatisfaction with the newspaper returned and Strong resigned to cover the Spanish civil war in 1936–37 and to report from China in 1938–39.

Strong had entered into a common law marriage in 1932 with Joel Shubin, a Communist party member and an editor of the Moscow *Peasant's Gazette*. Often separated because of her travels, they were together for a few months in 1939 when he became a director of the Soviet Pavilion at the 1939 New York World's Fair. Strong was then in the United States writing a book on the New Deal, *My Native Land* (1940), undertaken at the suggestion of ELEANOR ROOSEVELT.

The German invasion of the Soviet Union in 1941 prevented Strong from being with Shubin when he died there in 1942. Stranded in the United States, she defended Stalin's policies in her 1941 book, *The Soviets Expected It*, became technical adviser for an MGM film, *Song of Russia*, and wrote her first novel, *Wild River* (1943), about Russian heroism in the face of the German invasion. Given a United States passport and accredited to the *Atlantic Monthly*, Strong returned to Moscow in 1944 and accompanied the Red army that year as it drove the Germans back across Poland.

Still seeking the Chinese revolution, Strong traveled there again in 1946. She lived at Communist Chinese headquarters at Yenan in 1946–47 and obtained there her famous interview with Mao Tse-tung in which he proclaimed that all reactionaries were paper tigers (published in English in *Amerasia*, April 1947). She was eager to remain with Mao, but he urged her to go and publicize the revolution abroad. Her publication of the thought of Mao Tse-tung led to accusations that she was a spy and she was deported from the Soviet Union in 1949, an early manifestation of Sino-Soviet tensions.

Strong returned to the United States, where she was publicly shunned by party members until the Soviet Union exonerated her in 1955. Three years later she returned again briefly to Moscow and then left to take up permanent residence in Peking. In 1962 she began to publish a newsletter, *Letter from China*, which became a regular source of information about Chinese positions in the Sino-Soviet debate and gave readers in the West a glimpse of life in China. Remaining an active partisan, she traveled to Tibet, Laos, and to North Vietnam three times to demonstrate her solidarity with the revolutionary cause. She explained to a friend: "I have to do what I want to do . . . I have to go on." In 1965 Mao Tse-tung honored her on her eightieth birthday and the following year the Red Guard made her an honorary member. But the Chinese Cultural Revolution struck too close to her in 1968 as her closest friends and associates were arrested as left deviationists. She decided in 1969 to return to the United States to work against the war in Vietnam, but died in Peking the following year of heart disease, unable to accomplish this last goal. She was buried in Peking's National Memorial Cemetery of Revolutionary Martyrs, near the grave of AGNES SMEDLEY.

Anna Louise Strong remained faithful to her belief that her most important role was to popularize the thought of Lenin, Stalin, and Mao Tse-tung for the masses. Her remarkable loyalty to the communist cause despite denunciation and spy charges reveals a woman of tremendous will and blinding devotion to her ideals.

[The Anna Louise Strong, Sydney Dix Strong, and Tracy Strong, Sr., Papers are located at the Univ. of Wash., Seattle. Correspondence with Eleanor Roosevelt, mostly between 1937 and 1939, is in the Franklin D. Roosevelt Library, Hyde Park, N.Y. There is abundant autobiographical material in other books by Strong: *Red Star in Samarkand* (1929), *Road to the Grey Pamir* (1931), *I Saw the New Poland* (1946), *China's Millions* (1928), and *The Chinese Conquer China* (1949). For her account of her expulsion from Moscow see "Jailed in Moscow," *N.Y. Herald Tribune*, March 27–April 1, 1949. Her article, "The Thought of Mao Tse-tung," appeared in *Amerasia*, June 1947. She also put out a newsletter, *Today*, from 1950 to 1956. For recollections of Strong by her colleagues see: Philip Jaffe, "The Strange Case of Anna Louise Strong," *Survey*, Oct. 1964; Rewi Alley, "Some Memories of Anna Louise Strong," *Eastern Horizon*, vol. 9, nos. 2 and 3 (1970). See also David Milton and Nancy Dall Milton's account of Anna Louise Strong during the Cultural Revolution in *The Wind Will Not Survive* (1976); an entry in *Current Biog.*, 1949; entries in *Twentieth Century Authors* (1942) and *First Supplement* (1955), both of which include a bibliography; Robert L. Friedheim, *The Seattle General Strike* (1967), especially pp. 110–12; Robert W. Pringle, Jr., "Anna Louise Strong: Propagandist of

Communism" (Ph.D. diss., Univ. of Va., 1972); and Stephanie F. Ogle, "Anna Louise Strong: Seattle Years" (M.A. thesis, Seattle Univ., 1973). An obituary appeared in the *N.Y. Times*, March 30, 1970.]
                                                    STEPHANIE F. OGLE

SUCKOW, Ruth, Aug. 6, 1892–Jan. 23, 1960. Writer.

A writer whose fiction explored the life and landscape of Iowa, Ruth Suckow was born in that state, in the small town of Hawarden. Her parents, William John and Anna Mary (Kluckhohn) Suckow, were both children of German immigrants; Ruth visited her grandparents often as a child, acquiring a sense of family history that enriched her later work. She was deeply influenced by her father, a Congregational minister who held pastorates in several Iowa towns, including Hawarden and Algona, where Ruth began elementary school. In her autobiographical essay, "A Memoir" (1952), she recalls listening to her father's sermons with their "purity and economy of style," composing her earliest tales in the privacy of his study, and following his vocation by baptizing kittens and conducting "funeral services for birds, mice and broken dolls." Ruth's relationship with her mother was more difficult. Troubled by a thyroid condition which "destroyed her beauty as well as her health," Anna Suckow found little fulfillment in the social duties of a minister's wife, focusing her ambitions on Ruth and her older sister and only sibling, Emma. Growing up, Ruth found it difficult to accept her mother's demanding love: "I suffered from it."

In 1907 the Suckows moved to Grinnell, Iowa, where Ruth completed high school while her father worked as a field secretary for Grinnell College. She entered Grinnell in 1910. Although she studied English there and contributed a few stories to campus magazines, her first passion was for the stage. Seeking more training as a dramatic reader and actress, she left Grinnell at the end of her junior year to complete a two-year program at the Curry School of Expression in Boston (1913–15). She then operated her own "school of expression" briefly in Manchester, Iowa, where her father held a pastorate, before joining her ailing sister in Denver, Colo. There at the University of Denver, Suckow earned her A.B. (1917) and A.M. (1918) in English.

Living in Colorado, Suckow's ambitions shifted decisively from acting and teaching to writing. She focused initially on verse, publishing her first poems in 1918, and to support her craft, studied beekeeping with a woman outside Denver. After her mother's death in 1919, she returned to live with her father in Iowa. Aside

from a few winter visits to New York City, she spent the next six years in her home state, raising honey at her apiary in Earlville, writing poems, and producing a series of short stories set in rural and small-town Iowa which became the cornerstone of her literary reputation. In 1921 her story, "Uprooted," about an aging farm couple whose children convene to decide their parents' fate, appeared in *The Midland*, for which she subsequently served as assistant editor. *The Midland*'s editor, John T. Frederick, urged her to send samples of her work to H. L. Mencken, who promoted her heartily: "I lately unearthed a girl in Iowa," he wrote to Sinclair Lewis, "who seems to me to be superb." Between late 1921 and 1923, a procession of stories by Suckow appeared in Mencken's *The Smart Set*, and in 1924 *The Century Magazine* followed suit, serializing her novella *Country People*, published later that year by Alfred A. Knopf. Knopf subsequently collected her first stories under the title *Iowa Interiors* (1926), which won enthusiastic reviews. This early work is remarkable for its dramatic economy and its acute, unsentimental vision of rural life. Swiftly and graphically, Suckow captures the plight of her characters, like the farm wife in "Renters" who is being evicted from her land: "She could smell the rich ripening corn in the hot night. It swelled her bitterness."

Now an established author, Ruth Suckow sold her Earlville apiary late in 1926 and moved to New York City. Within four years she completed three novels: *The Bonney Family* (1928), *Cora* (1929), and *The Kramer Girls* (1930). These, like Suckow's earlier work *The Odyssey of a Nice Girl* (1925), portray the struggles of young women to forge identities apart from the customs and expectations of their midwestern friends and families. While uneven in quality, without at times the keen, objective edge of her best work, these novels are nonetheless honest, avoiding easy solutions—Suckow's young protagonists find refuge neither in nostalgic homemaking nor in heroic self-reliance.

In March 1929 Ruth Suckow married Ferner Nuhn, a writer and critic. Born in Iowa in 1903, Nuhn appreciated and supported Suckow's effort to explore their native region in fiction; he later published *The Wind Blew from the East: A Study in the Orientation of American Culture* (1942). For several years after their marriage, Suckow and Nuhn lived variously in California, New Mexico (1929), and Iowa (1930–32); they spent summers as well at the Yaddo and MacDowell Colonies (1933–34). Through most of this period Suckow worked steadily on her longest and most substantial novel, *The Folks* (1934). Following six members of an Iowa family, the Fergusons, from the first decade of the twentieth century to the dawn of the depression, *The Folks* relates personal to social and historical change more effectively than any of her previous work. In one of the novel's briefest and most intriguing episodes, the Fergusons' youngest child shocks his parents by bringing home his new bride, the strong, sullen, and radical daughter of poor Russian immigrants: "He wanted to take all this that was alien on himself and somehow absorb it."

In a sense, *The Folks* was Ruth Suckow's summary work. As E. H. Walton suggested in the *New York Times*, she seemed to commit to it "all her knowledge and careful observation." While Suckow continued to produce novels and stories after 1935, her output in her last twenty-five years was relatively slender. Yet she was by no means idle. From about 1934 she lived in the Washington, D.C., area, where her husband worked for the Department of Agriculture; President Franklin D. Roosevelt appointed Suckow in 1936 to the Farm Tenancy Committee. By 1937 she and her husband had settled in Cedar Falls, Iowa, where they spent most of the next decade writing, running a rental agency inherited from Ferner Nuhn's father, and encouraging local interest in literature and the arts. She remained in touch during these years with her literary friends and mentors, including Robert Frost, DOROTHY CANFIELD FISHER, and Norwegian novelist Sigrid Undset (Suckow's work appeared in translation throughout Scandinavia). *New Hope*, Suckow's seventh novel and her most lyrical and nostalgic vision of an Iowa community, appeared in 1942.

A pacifist, Suckow supported conscientious objectors during World War II by visiting civilian public service camps; after the war she joined her husband as an active member of the Society of Friends. She began to suffer from arthritis during this period, and partly for reasons of health, moved with Ferner Nuhn to Tucson, Ariz., in 1948. In the spring of 1952 they settled finally in Claremont, Calif., where Suckow completed her last novel, *The John Wood Case* (1959). She died at home in January 1960.

Technically, perhaps, Ruth Suckow was not a virtuoso novelist. In longer works her urge to analyze in depth the motives and misgivings of her characters sometimes led her away from the taut description and sharp dialogue which grace her best short narratives, tales which drew the admiration of critics and artists alike. Sinclair Lewis found her early stories "lucid, remarkably real, firm," and Robert Frost praised her second collection, *Children and Older People* (1931), as "without guile or thesis . . . just stories of life

vividly restored." Suckow was not exclusively a realist, though, or a "regional painter" aiming for highly polished vignettes. Her overruling object, and the goal which led her to longer, more elaborate narratives like *The Folks*, was to do justice in fiction to the emotional quandaries of the family—or as her Iowans refer to their assorted relatives, "the relationship." To the study of such relationships Suckow brought great versatility, imagining the very old and very young with equal skill and realizing the guilt and affection tying one generation to the next. The result is a body of work examining common characters—and the forces that pull them apart and bind them together—with exceptional faithfulness.

[Ruth Suckow's papers, including correspondence, photographs, MSS., and clippings, are in the Special Collections Dept., Univ. of Iowa Libraries, Iowa City. For a description of some of the correspondence held there see Frank Paluka, "Ruth Suckow: A Calendar of Letters," *Books at Iowa*, Oct. 1964, and April 1965. Clippings and family photographs are also located at the Ruth Suckow Memorial Library in Earlville, Iowa. Several of her early works are anthologized in *Carry-Over* (1936). Suckow's autobiographical essay, focusing on her childhood and her religious development, appears in *Some Others and Myself* (1952). See also Ferner Nuhn, ed., "Cycle of the Seasons in Iowa: Unpublished Diary of Ruth Suckow," *The Iowan*, Oct.-Nov. 1960; Dec.-Jan. 1960–61; Feb.-March 1961; April-May 1961. An extended bibliography of publications by and about Suckow appears in Leedice McAnelly Kissane, *Ruth Suckow* (1969), which also includes a chronology, biographical information, and an analysis of the fiction. Other full-length studies include Margaret O'Brien Stewart, "A Critical Study of Ruth Suckow's Fiction" (Ph.D. diss., Univ. of Illinois, 1960); and Margaret Steward Omrcanin, *Ruth Suckow: A Critical Study of Her Fiction* (1970). Margaret Matlack Kiesel has contributed two helpful articles: "Ruth Suckow's Grinnell," *Grinnell Mag.*, Nov.-Dec. 1975; and "Iowans in the Arts: Ruth Suckow in the Twenties," *Annals of Iowa*, Spring 1980. Biographical sketches can be found in *Twentieth Century Authors* (1942), p. 1368; Harry Warfel, *American Novelists of Today* (1951), pp. 416–17; and *Nat. Cyc. Am. Biog.*, XLVII, 352–53. Obituaries appeared in *N.Y. Times*, Jan. 24, 1960; and *Annals of Iowa*, Spring 1960. A biobibliography by Alice Medin assisted with research; death certificate provided by Calif. Dept. of Public Health.]

STEPHEN G. HYSLOP

SWINDLER, Mary Hamilton, Jan. 3, 1884–Jan. 16, 1967. Archaeologist, classicist.

Mary Hamilton Swindler was one of the most quietly influential classical archaeologists in

America. For six decades she was a central part of the work in classics and archaeology at Bryn Mawr College, helping to make Bryn Mawr a distinguished archaeological center. She was born in Bloomington, Ind., the second of the three surviving children and second daughter of Ida M. (Hamilton) and Harrison T. Swindler, a merchant. After attending Bloomington High School, she obtained both the A.B. (1905) and the A.M. (1906) in Greek from Indiana University. Her career at the university can be followed in many reviews of her theatrical performances and accounts of her successes as an intramural basketball player.

Mary Swindler entered Bryn Mawr on a Greek fellowship in 1906 and remained there nearly all her life. Soon after her arrival she first displayed her powers of observation and analysis in the field of ancient painting. Her article on a Greek vase exhibited at the Academy of Natural Sciences in Philadelphia assigned the red-figured body to a painter called the Master of the Penthesilea School and the signed foot to a lost black-figured cup by Nikosthenes. The article, published in 1909 in the *American Journal of Archaeology*, marked her as a scholar of promise and early authority.

Aided by the Mary E. Garrett European Fellowship, Mary Swindler studied in Berlin in 1909 and then went on to the American School of Classical Studies in Athens. This experience, which provided intense exposure to sites, monuments, and museums, was so valuable that she always encouraged all her students to visit Athens and the European museums. Later she raised an annual fellowship for Bryn Mawr students to study abroad, and founded a museum at Bryn Mawr to permit teaching from original works of art. When she returned to the American School as visiting professor in 1938, her lectures were so popular that the director had to limit the attendance.

At Bryn Mawr Mary Swindler earned her Ph.D. in 1912 and rose to the rank of professor of classical archaeology by 1931. Her dissertation, *Cretan Elements in the Cults and Ritual of Apollo* (1913), was characteristic of Bryn Mawr interests at the time. The Cretan or Aegean world being uncovered in her student days remained a favorite subject and was treated authoritatively in her major published work, *Ancient Painting* (1929). A remarkable book, its contents ranged from Paleolithic cave paintings and ancient Egyptian and Near Eastern painting to late antique mosaics and the early Christian catacombs. It was the first of its kind, supported at every point by precise scholarly references and large bibliographies, as well as a wealth of small, clear illustrations. Mary

Swindler looked hard at every piece, and brought a formidable technical and aesthetic judgment to focus on it. *Ancient Painting* is impressive not only for its ambition, size, and learning, but also for the simplicity and power of the descriptive prose. The international reputation earned her by *Ancient Painting* was further enhanced by Swindler's editorship of the *American Journal of Archaeology* from 1932 until 1946. The first woman editor-in-chief, she not only changed the format and increased the journal's coverage and circulation, but also made it a truly international publication. This was perhaps her greatest scholarly achievement, and at the same time her students and colleagues benefited from the new discoveries that came to her desk as editor.

With tremendous energy and vitality in those years, she began yet another monumental undertaking. To be titled "The Beginnings of Greek Art," this work was designed to follow the processes of creativity in Greece from Neolithic times through the Bronze and Dark Ages until the emergence of a preclassical style in the seventh century B.C. However, Mary Swindler's sense of perfection prevented her from ever being satisfied with the manuscript, while the burden of her duties and, later, failing eyesight and ill health kept her from completing it.

At Bryn Mawr, Mary Swindler's modest yet vigorous, direct, and humorous style of teaching inspired generations of undergraduates. She instilled in students a sense of form and color, set fragments of antiquity in historical and literary perspective, and encouraged excellence. A beautiful woman, she had a lifelong vision of the comic, and a profound distaste for the shoddy and the sentimental. At seminars in her apartment, she challenged graduate students with recent problems or chapters from her book, and then served them tea, English muffins, and cherry jam. It is reported that she used a rowing machine to keep fit during the tedious hours of editing the *Journal*. Until the end of her life she kept an enormous file of archaeological clippings and photographs, which she pasted on shirt cardboards collected from her male colleagues.

Warm-hearted and generous, Mary Swindler not only aided many of her own students but was also instrumental in finding the means to help refugee scholars from Nazi Germany obtain positions in the United States. When she retired from Bryn Mawr in 1949 on a very modest pension, she had barely provided for herself, so she continued to teach, at the University of Pennsylvania (1949–50), the University of Michigan (1950–53), and again at Bryn Mawr (1953–56). Even when she retired fully she read everything, and continued to help students informally.

Mary Hamilton Swindler was honored by Indiana University with an LL.D. (1941), with the Achievement Award of the American Association of University Women (1951), and, as one of the three outstanding scholars in the humanities in 1959, with a grant from the American Council of Learned Societies. She was a fellow of the Royal Society of Arts in London and of the German Archaeological Institute. Mary Swindler died of bronchopneumonia in 1967 in Haverford, Pa. She left generations of classicists and archaeologists whose professional achievements testify to her influence both in the United States and abroad.

[Mary Swindler's college and later career can be traced in excerpts from student and alumni publications provided by the Ind. Univ. Archives. A biographical sketch by Dorothy Burr Thompson, "Mary Hamilton Swindler," *Am. Jour. Archaeology*, Oct. 1950, pp. 292–93, also contains a bibliography. See also Sara Anderson Immerwahr, "Mary Hamilton Swindler," *Bryn Mawr Alumnae Bull.*, 1966–67, no. 3, pp. 26–27. An obituary appeared in the *N.Y. Times,* Jan. 18, 1967. Birth record supplied by Monroe Cty. Health Dept., Bloomington, Ind.; family information by Indiana State Library; death certificate by Pa. Dept. of Health.]

EMILY VERMEULE
SARA ANDERSON IMMERWAHR

SWITZER, Mary Elizabeth, Feb. 16, 1900–Oct. 16, 1971. Federal official.

Mary Switzer, leader in the rehabilitation of the disabled, was born in Newton Upper Falls, Mass., the oldest child of two daughters and a son of Margaret (Moore) and Julius F. Switzer, a manual worker. Her father left the family, and when Mary was eleven her mother died. Mary and her sister subsequently lived with two maternal aunts and an uncle, a machinist. "Uncle Mike" Moore greatly influenced Mary Switzer: Irish patriot, woman suffragist, and socialist, he taught her about the world and encouraged her to do something useful with her life.

Brought up as a Roman Catholic, Switzer attended public schools and graduated from Newton Classical High School in 1917. Through a scholarship and a variety of jobs, she was able to attend Radcliffe College, where she majored in international law and helped to found the reformist Inter-Collegiate Liberal League. Above all, she experienced "the excitement that comes from the stirring of the mind."

After receiving an A.B. in 1921, Switzer moved to Washington and obtained a position with the District of Columbia Minimum Wage Board. There she met other capable women in government, among them Isabella Stevenson Diamond, who became librarian of the Treasury Department and with whom Switzer made her lifelong home. For a dozen years, her work remained somewhat routine. After the first job, she served briefly as executive secretary of the Women's International League for Peace and Freedom, but soon entered the federal civil service. Beginning in 1922 as a junior economist in the Treasury Department, she established a niche for herself preparing reports on current news and opinion for Secretary Andrew W. Mellon and for President Herbert Hoover as well.

Switzer's career got off the ground with her appointment in 1934 as assistant to the assistant secretary of the treasury, Josephine Roche (1886–1976), who assigned her to oversee the United States Public Health Service. Through her work on an interdepartmental committee, she had a hand in consolidating health and welfare programs into a new Federal Security Agency (FSA), and later in its elevation to the Department of Health, Education, and Welfare. In 1939 Switzer joined the FSA as assistant to the administrator, Paul McNutt, with responsibility for health and medical matters. During World War II she participated in the highly confidential War Research Service and in the Procurement and Assignment Service for medical personnel. For her war work Switzer received the President's Certificate of Merit, the first of a long series of honors. Later she advanced to the international scene and helped to set up the World Health Organization. In these activities she demonstrated a gift for organization and action which brought her not only promotion but also prestige and influence in circles of government, medicine, and social work, as well as on Capitol Hill.

In 1950 Switzer was appointed director of the Office of Vocational Rehabilitation (OVR), then part of the FSA. Already interested in this field of service, she now enjoyed autonomy in a position that called forth all her talents. Established in 1920, the OVR allocated grants-in-aid to the states in order to develop the ability of handicapped persons to work, but the program had reached only a few selected cases. Switzer set out with dynamic energy to make it "meet the total vocational needs of the mentally as well as the physically handicapped," to see that it became "responsible for meeting the . . . needs of all the people." An exceptionally skilled administrator, she developed and shaped vocational rehabilitation in the United States to such an extent that well after her death former colleagues could still say that the program "is the shadow of Mary Switzer."

"I am amazed at myself," she remarked in 1951, "at how readily and easily I have fallen into the habit and pattern of an operator." Exercising her authority to the full, Switzer coordinated the efforts of state and federal agencies and private organizations toward a single goal: to assist all the disabled to find satisfying work. Even as federal grants increased, she insisted that the states should play an important role, and she herself visited all the state agencies. Largely through her efforts, the landmark Vocational Rehabilitation Act of 1954 provided funds for research, for training of specialists, and for construction of comprehensive rehabilitation centers. As director of her agency and as chair of countless committees, Mary Switzer sparked conferences, wielded the power of the purse, and obtained appropriations to make services broadly available to groups formerly shunted aside as hopeless, including the mentally retarded.

To energy and dedication, Switzer added diplomatic skill. A liberal Democrat, she survived political shifts. "No bureaucrat," she believed, "really comes of age until he or she has found the answer to accommodating to successive changes in administration, both inter- and intra-party, and growing in the process." Vital to success were her relations with Congress; she not only testified convincingly before committees but kept on excellent personal terms with powerful legislators who found themselves unable to refuse her the sizable appropriations she requested. In her pleasure at receiving a prestigious Albert Lasker Award in 1960, Switzer also observed that the splendid publicity came at a timely moment—"just as I was negotiating with the appropriations committee."

She cared most for people. Hard work did not dampen her ebullient personality, and she remained accessible even when papers piled high. "She made light shine around her," said John Gardner, a former secretary of health, education, and welfare. "As you move up," she ad-

jured her nephew, then a young rehabilitation worker, "never forget the people you're working for—get out and touch them." Ties of affection linked her to her sister and to her brother and his family. She credited Isabella Diamond with teaching her "the advantage of a balanced life," with "interests as broad as life is—baseball—to Grand Opera—the circus—a bird with a broken wing, and the way to organize life to enjoy all" (Switzer, "Hope," p. 19).

In 1970, as administrator of the Social and Rehabilitation Service in the Department of Health, Education, and Welfare, Mary Switzer retired—or, as she insisted, merely left in order to head the Washington office of the World Rehabilitation Association. She died in Washington of cancer the following year.

[The Mary E. Switzer Papers at the Schlesinger Library, Radcliffe College, are voluminous. They contain correspondence, speeches, reports, articles, and other material, but little that is personal. Her short article "Hope, the Anchor of Life," *Radcliffe Quart.*, Feb. 1959, is quite revealing. The Dept. of Health, Education, and Welfare has compiled a typescript list of "Articles by Miss Mary E. Switzer," and there is a pamphlet by Isabella Diamond, "Mary Elizabeth Switzer, 'The Dedicated Bureaucrat.'" A brief biography can be found in *Current Biog.*, 1962. An excellent photograph appears on the cover of *Medical World News*, March 3, 1967, accompanying an article, "Getting the Disabled on Their Feet." See also three works by Howard A. Rusk, "Career in Rehabilitation," *N.Y. Times*, March 1, 1970, "Mary Elizabeth Switzer: A Tribute," *Rehabilitation Record*, Jan.-Feb. 1972, pp. 1–2, and *A World to Care For* (1972), pp. 214–15, 293; and C. Warren Bledsoe, "Dedication to Mary Elizabeth Switzer (1900–1971)," *Blindness: Am. Assoc. of Workers for the Blind Annual*, 1972, pp. ix–xii. Obituaries appeared in the *N.Y. Times*, Oct. 17, 1971, and *Am. Speech and Hearing Assoc.*, Dec. 1971, p. 729. Death certificate supplied by D.C. Dept. of Public Health. Additional information for this article was provided by Ann Switzer, Richard Moore Switzer, Arthur J. Switzer, Isabella Diamond, Anne Verano, Frances Curtis, Charles Schottland, Joseph V. Hunt, and Milton Cohen.]

JEAN CHRISTIE

T

TABA, Hilda, Dec. 7, 1902–July 6, 1967. Educator.

Professor, author, and leader in curriculum development, Hilda Taba was born in south-

eastern Estonia, the eldest child of the four daughters and five sons of Robert and Liisa (Leht) Taba. Her parents, both Lutherans and native Estonians, had had elementary schooling and her father a secondary education as well. He taught school for forty years while her mother assisted on the family farm; the land was part of the compensation for teaching.

Although far from wealthy the Tabas encouraged education, and all their children went to college through a combination of hard work and scholarships. Hilda Taba received an A.B. from the University of Tartu, Estonia, in 1926. With the aid of a scholarship for graduate work in the United States, she came to Bryn Mawr College, where she received an A.M. in education and psychology in 1927. She then pursued doctoral study at Teachers College, Columbia University (Ph.D., 1933). Returning to Estonia during this time, she taught there for two years.

In her dissertation, *Dynamics of Education: A Methodology of Progressive Educational Thought* (1932), written under William Heard Kilpatrick, Taba acknowledged her debt to Boyd H. Bode's writings and to the "inspiration and help" of John Dewey in "classroom and conferences." Her mentors were the leading philosophers of the progressive education movement, and although she was critical of certain aspects of the movement, many of the techniques and theories she later developed were rooted in progressive principles.

Taba became involved in the Progressive Education Association's major project of the 1930s: its Eight-Year Study designed to extend the principles of progressive education to secondary schools and to provide freedom for those schools to innovate without jeopardizing their students' chances of acceptance to college. Taba was director of curriculum research at the participating Dalton School in New York City; later, she became a staff associate, evaluating student development in the thirty secondary schools involved in the study. Ralph W. Tyler, the evaluation research director, was an important intellectual and professional associate. Taba's appointments as assistant professor at Ohio State University (1936–38) and at the University of Chicago in 1938 were a result of her work with the Eight-Year Study.

While on leave from Chicago (1945–48), Taba became director of an intergroup education project, sponsored by the American Council on Education and financed by the National Conference of Christians and Jews. This project was designed to study intergroup relations in the areas of race, creed, and national origins, and their advancement within the educational system through revised teaching materials and methods. As director of the Center for Intergroup Education at the University of Chicago (1948–51), Taba continued to direct experimental programs in human relations, helped develop curriculum, and conducted workshops for

educators. She wrote, edited, or coauthored numerous books and articles based on these projects.

When Taba became professor of education at San Francisco State College in 1951, she embarked on the most productive years of her professional career. Her most important book, *Curriculum Development: Theory and Practice* (1962), conceptualized a systematic approach to curriculum planning and design, incorporating concepts from the social sciences; it became a classic in the field. Taba sought to bridge the traditional gap between theory and practice by inverting the conventional sequence: rather than trying to impose a design, she advocated beginning at the classroom level with units planned by teachers. She was firmly convinced that teachers must be involved in curriculum development and could make important contributions to curriculum theory.

Taba continued to work closely with teachers and school districts in the federally funded projects she directed. Her research on teaching strategies and children's thinking culminated in her *Teachers' Handbook for Elementary Social Studies* (1967), designed to teach students how to use specific facts to develop basic concepts and generalizations in a spiral curriculum. A companion project involved the development of an elementary social studies curriculum using this inductive approach to teach children thinking skills. In the 1970s Addison-Wesley published the Taba Program in Social Science, a textbook series for grades one through eight based on her concepts.

A prolific writer, creative thinker, and effective teacher, Hilda Taba possessed a probing intellect and a vibrant personality. Friends remember her as a warm and caring person with tremendous energy and a zest for living. Her interests included music, traveling, theater, gardening, swimming, and reading.

Taba died in Burlingame, Calif., in 1967 of peritonitis at the age of sixty-four. Although much of her pioneering work has since been surpassed, in her lifetime Taba influenced the areas of curriculum, student evaluation, human relations, social studies, and teaching for critical thinking. Some of her ideas remained influential in the 1970s; when the Association for Supervision and Curriculum Development singled out a dozen "great persons" in the history of curriculum for their bicentennial yearbook (O. L. Davis, ed., 1976), Hilda Taba was one of two women to be included.

[Among the nearly two dozen works written or coauthored by Hilda Taba are *Adolescent Character and Personality* (1949), with Robert Havighurst; *Diagnosing Human Relations Needs* (1951); *Lead-*

ership Training in Intergroup Education (1953); *School Culture* (1955); and *Teaching Strategies for the Culturally Disadvantaged* (1966), with Deborah Elkins. She also contributed over fifty articles to education journals and yearbooks. For analyses of Taba's ideas and methods see Selma Greenberg, *Selected Studies of Classroom Teaching* (1970); James E. Davis, "Taba Program in Social Science," *Social Education*, Nov. 1972, pp. 761–63; Roger L. Brown, "Taba Rediscovered," *Science Teacher*, Nov. 1973, pp. 30–33; and Wayne C. Hall, Jr., and Charles B. Myers, "The Effect of a Training Program in the Taba Teaching Strategies on Teaching Methods and Teacher Perceptions of Their Teaching," *Peabody Jour. Education*, April 1977, pp. 162–67. The main sources on her life are the brief accounts in *Nat. Cyc. Am. Biog.*, LIV, 113–14, which includes a photograph, and the *N.Y. Times* obituary, July 8, 1967. See also Patricia A. Moseley, "Hilda Taba, Curriculum Worker," in O. L. Davis, ed., *Perspectives on Curriculum Development, 1776–1976* (1976), pp. 214–15. The entries in *Leaders in Education* (1948), *Who's Who of Am. Women* (1968–69), and *Biog. Dict. of Am. Educators* (1978) contain a number of factual errors. Information was provided by Ralph W. Tyler and by a brother, Paul Taba. Death record was obtained from the Calif. Registrar of Vital Statistics.]

NATALIE A. NAYLOR

TAEUBER, Irene Barnes, Dec. 25, 1906–Feb. 24, 1974. Demographer.

Irene Barnes Taeuber was born in Meadville, Mo., the second of four children (two girls and two boys) of Lily (Keller) and Ninevah C. Barnes; her younger brother died in infancy. Her father, who alternated between farming and barbering, served for many years as justice of the peace. A restless man, he once left the family for over a year. Irene was very close to her mother and to her maternal grandparents who had come to Missouri from Ohio. She treasured over the years the memory of her Keller grandparents reading to her when she was severely ill with scarlet fever.

After graduating from public high school, Irene Barnes went to college against her father's wishes. She attended Northeast Missouri State Teachers College in Kirksville for a year, and then transferred to the University of Missouri. With her mother's encouragement, she supported her education through scholarships and a variety of jobs. She majored in sociology, but was particularly influenced by a biology professor, W. C. Curtis. After earning her A.B. in 1927, she continued her study of sociology, and received an A.M. from Northwestern University (1928) and a Ph.D. from the University of Minnesota (1931), where Pitirim Sorokin was an important influence.

Two years earlier she had married Conrad Taeuber, a fellow graduate student in sociology. While completing their dissertations, they both worked as research assistants for J. H. Kolb at the University of Wisconsin, gaining experience in rural demography and statistics. Then, in an arrangement unusual during the depression, both Taeubers received appointments in the department of economics and sociology at Mount Holyoke College in 1931, Irene as instructor, Conrad as assistant professor. In 1934, Conrad Taeuber accepted a research appointment with the Federal Emergency Relief Administration, and subsequently had a distinguished career as administrator, statistician, and demographer in the United States Department of Agriculture, the Food and Agriculture Organization of the United Nations, and the United States Bureau of the Census. The Taeubers had two sons, Richard Conrad (b. 1933) and Karl Ernst (b. 1936). Both children later worked in fields related to their parents' interests—Richard in statistics and econometrics, Karl in demography and sociology. Irene Taeuber took time out from teaching after the birth of her first child; while the children were young, she limited herself to part-time work so that she could be at home when they returned from school.

Irene Taeuber became involved in what was to be her life work early in 1935, when she helped Frank Lorimer, secretary of the newly organized Population Association of America (PAA), prepare a periodic bibliography of recent and current articles on population. The following year, when the Office of Population Research (OPR) was established at Princeton University under the direction of Frank W. Notestein, she became a staff member there and coeditor of *Population Index*, the successor of the publication on which she had been working. She was affiliated with the OPR for the rest of her life, commuting from her home in Hyattsville, Md., to Princeton every week or two.

Working mainly from her Library of Congress study, she shouldered the major responsibility for *Population Index* from 1937 to 1954, and also wrote a quarterly column, "Current Items." After the death of Louise K. Kiser, who had been a coeditor since 1942, she asked to be relieved of responsibility for the journal in order to devote more time to her own research. Despite an international reputation and a prodigious scholarly output which amounted to sixteen books and monographs (most of them coauthored) and some 250 articles, it was not until 1961 that she was promoted to senior research demographer, a position she held until her retirement in 1973. Never one to emphasize the difficulties of working in a man's field, she nevertheless felt that she did not have as much clerical and research assistance as did her male colleagues at the OPR.

Irene Taeuber became a demographer at a time of rapid expansion of the field. The governmental agencies established during the New Deal recognized the policy implications of population studies, as did the League of Nations, which in 1939 commissioned the OPR to study the future populations of European countries as a basis for postwar planning. Taeuber became deeply involved in this work, especially after America's entry into World War II, when the OPR, at the request of the Department of State, began to investigate Asian populations. She agreed to study Japan and after the war made several trips there, developing a lifelong love of the Far East. With the help of scholars and official agencies, she compiled historic demographic data on Japan; she did not know the language, but was quick to understand Japanese statistical tables. When *The Population of Japan* appeared in 1958, Japanese demographers proclaimed it the best work on the subject, a veritable Encyclopedia Demographica Japonica. In his foreword to this definitive work, Notestein predicted that it would "prove a landmark of demographic analysis." When it was translated into Japanese in 1965, the book provided a major stimulus for indigenous demographic analysis.

Possessing the instincts of the true scholar, Taeuber in her population studies covered more than a dozen countries, including those in Africa, Latin America, and Oceania. With her husband she coauthored *The Changing Population of the United States* (1958) and *People of the United States in the Twentieth Century* (1971), works of interest to historians as well as planners. In the view of her Princeton colleague, Clyde V. Kiser, Taeuber's work was distinguished by her interest in the social, economic, and cultural determinants of population trends. Indicative of this concern were her efforts to visit rural villages and to establish ties with local residents. The only woman among a group of four who made a study tour of the Far East for the Rockefeller Foundation in 1948, she emphasized the roles of women and children in her section of the report, published as *Public Health and Demography in the Far East* (1950). At the time of her death she was accumulating materials for a book on China. A paper of November 1973 presented to the American Public Health Association demonstrated that, despite the absence of hard data that plagued all students of Chinese population, she was making headway in inferring population and other trends. Data that be-

came available after her death confirmed her findings that the Chinese were rapidly bringing their fertility under control.

Believing that the researcher could make contributions to policy, but also insisting on the distinction between scholarship and propaganda, Irene Taeuber served as a consultant for many governmental and international organizations. Widely recognized for her achievements, she was president of the PAA (1953–54) and vice president of the International Union for the Scientific Study of Population (1961–65), the first woman to be elected to either position. During the 1960s, she received two honorary degrees as well as distinguished service medals from the Universities of Missouri and Minnesota. She was also visiting professor at Johns Hopkins University (1961–65). Colleagues at Princeton and elsewhere considered her a great if unofficial teacher.

Irene Taeuber was admired for her warm human qualities as well as for her professional attainments. Sensitive to the feelings of persons of other cultures, she befriended many of the young Japanese and other foreign students who came to the OPR, and was the recipient of many confidences. Despite their busy work schedules, she and her husband devoted time on weekends to gardening—she was as meticulous about her roses as about her research—and to entertaining. Although beset by arthritis in her later years, she continued to work. Death came quickly at her home in February 1974 from pneumonia complicating severe emphysema.

[Irene B. Taeuber's papers, consisting of research materials, including notes and MSS., and correspondence, are in the Western Hist. Manuscript Coll., Univ. of Missouri. The major published sources are Frank W. Notestein, "Irene Barnes Taeuber, 1906–1974," *Population Index*, Jan. 1974, pp. 3–17, which includes an extensive bibliography, and Ansley J. Coale, "Irene Barnes Taeuber, 1906–1974," *The Am. Statistician*, Aug. 1974, pp. 109–10. See also the *N.Y. Times* obituary, Feb. 26, 1974. *Am. Men of Science*, 11th ed. (1968) contains entries on all four Taeubers. For background information on demography see Philip M. Hauser and Otis Dudley Duncan, eds., *The Study of Population: An Inventory and Appraisal* (1959), especially "The Development and Status of American Demography," by Rupert B. Vance, pp. 286–313. Further information was provided by Conrad Taeuber, Clyde V. Kiser, and Minoru Muramatsu. A death record was provided by the Md. Dept. of Health.]

NATHAN KEYFITZ

TAFT, Jessie, June 24, 1882–June 7, 1960. Psychologist, social work educator.

Jessie Taft was born Julia Jessie in Dubuque,

Iowa, the oldest of the three daughters of Amanda May (Farwell) and Charles Chester Taft, both of whom came from Vermont. Except for a year in an isolated part of Florida where Charles Taft had purchased land, the family lived in Iowa throughout Jessie's childhood and adolescence, moving from Dubuque to Des Moines. There her father had a prosperous wholesale fruit business and the family led a comfortable middle-class life. Amanda Taft's progressive deafness increasingly isolated her from her children, and during her childhood Jessie was particularly close to an aunt who, with her invalid husband, lived with the family.

After graduating from West Des Moines High School, Jessie Taft went on to receive an A.B. from Drake University in 1904. Eager for knowledge, she spent the following year at the University of Chicago, where she received a Ph.B. degree in 1905. She then went home to teach mathematics, Latin, and German at West Des Moines High School for four years before a fellowship in philosophy enabled her to return to the University of Chicago to work on a doctorate.

The years at Chicago were of major importance both personally and professionally. There Taft studied philosophy and psychology with George Herbert Mead, James H. Tufts, and Addison W. Moore. She read the works of William James, John Dewey, Josiah Royce, and Havelock Ellis, and became particularly interested in the writings of women such as Olive Schreiner, CHARLOTTE PERKINS GILMAN, IDA TARBELL, GRACE ABBOTT, and EDITH ABBOTT. Her Ph.D. dissertation, published in 1915 as *The Woman Movement from the Point of View of Social Consciousness,* defined the problem of women—and society as a whole—as the need to resolve the dualism between the world of social relationships in the home and the material world of the wage earner. At Chicago Taft met Virginia Robinson, who became a lifelong personal friend, professional partner, and living companion.

On leave from the university in the spring of 1912, Taft spent six months in New York with Robinson, interviewing women committed to prisons and reformatories for a study initiated by KATHARINE BEMENT DAVIS. After receiving her Ph.D. in 1913, she returned to New York, working first for Davis as assistant superintendent of the New York State Reformatory for Women in Bedford Hills. Then, in 1915, she became director of the Social Services Department of the New York State Charities Aid Association's Mental Hygiene Committee. Her major responsibility was to promote mental hygiene programs in the state, but she also worked with individual cases at the New York Hospital Mental Hy-

giene Clinic and established the Farm School in New Jersey for children referred to the clinic because of problems in school.

Taft's reputation as a therapist as well as mental hygiene consultant and expert on social casework with children grew rapidly after her move to Philadelphia in 1918. There she became director of the new Department of Child Study of the Seybert Institution, a temporary shelter for children awaiting placement. In 1920 the Bureau of Children of the Pennsylvania Department of Welfare and the Children's Aid Society of Pennsylvania took over her department, and she greatly expanded the mental hygiene services offered to the children served by these agencies. Under her leadership, the department also participated in training staff, finding placements, and counseling foster parents. As a speaker, Taft was in great demand by social workers, teachers, nurses, and parents. In her numerous talks and papers during this period she developed her views on foster care, adoption, and the role of the caseworker and the agency in the helping process. Her personal experience informed these writings: in 1921 Taft and Robinson adopted a nine-year-old boy, Everett Taft, and later they adopted a six-year-old girl, Martha Taft. They lived in a home the two women purchased in Flourtown, Pa.

In 1924 Jessie Taft first met Otto Rank, who became a major influence on her life and work. In Rank's concept of the will she found "a key to my own as well as to my patients' psychology," and in 1926 she underwent analysis with him. A major opportunity to apply to social work the ideas she adopted from Rank's theories came in 1934, when Taft joined the faculty of the Pennsylvania School of Social Work (later the University of Pennsylvania School of Social Work). Until her retirement in 1950, she served as professor of social casework and, with Robinson, who had been at the school since 1918, she built the school's curriculum and shaped its distinctive ideology, which came to be known as functionalism.

During the decade which followed her arrival at the Pennsylvania School, Taft played a major role in the controversy which developed in social work education between the Freudian, or diagnostic, approach to casework practice and the Pennsylvania School's functional approach. Taft defined her concept of function in casework as the particular social service offered by an agency, which determined the interaction between client and worker. In a 1937 article she distinguished between the Freudian "psychology of cure" and a "psychology of helping." Whereas the Freudian approach emphasized diagnosis and treatment plans determined by the therapist, functional casework put the client at the center of an "internal, self-determined growth process to be released with the aid of the therapist." While Taft stressed that Rank was not responsible for the concept of function, she identified his contribution to her theories and practice as the recognition of the effects on the therapeutic process of time limitations and of the will of both therapist and client.

Taft wrote many articles on functionalism and its implications for social work education. She also published *The Dynamics of Therapy in a Controlled Relationship* (1933) and a two-volume translation of the work of Otto Rank, *Will Therapy: An Analysis of the Therapeutic Process in Terms of Relationship* (1936) and *Truth and Reality: A Life History of the Human Will* (1936). She devoted much of her time in retirement to a biography of Rank which was published in 1958. Taft died in a Philadelphia hospital of a stroke in 1960.

Jessie Taft identified herself above all as a professional, believing that "the professional self is the real self, the self that carries value, the immortal self." Described as forceful and straightforward, she attracted friends and associates alike by her vitality. She was, according to a colleague, "the living exponent of her own credo of the power of the positive will, a lover and liver of life" (quoted in Robinson, p. 9).

[Taft's foreword to *Otto Rank, A Biographical Study Based on Notebooks, Letters, Collected Writings, Therapeutic Achievements and Personal Associations* (1958) contains autobiographical notes detailing her relationship to him. The major source of biographical information is Virginia Robinson, ed., *Jessie Taft, Therapist and Social Work Educator: A Professional Biography* (1962), which contains biographical chapters by Robinson, selections from Taft's major works tracing the development of her interests, and a bibliography of her writings. A brief biographical article may be found in the *Encyc. Social Work* (1965). An article about the origins and development of the functional school of social work in the *Encyc. Social Work* (1977) is also useful. An obituary appeared in *Social Service Rev.*, Sept. 1960. Death certificate supplied by Pa. Dept. of Health.]

JUNE AXINN

TAMIRIS, Helen, April 24, 1902?–Aug. 5, 1966. Dancer, choreographer.

Helen Tamiris was born Helen Becker on the Lower East Side of New York City, the only daughter and youngest of five children of Isor and Rose (Simoneff) Becker, who were Russian Jewish immigrants. Her father worked as a tailor. Of her brothers, one became a painter, another a sculptor and musician. Helen knew early that she wanted to be a dancer. She began dance lessons at the Henry Street Settlement House with IRENE LEWISOHN and Blanche Talmud. Against her father's wishes she auditioned for the Metropolitan Opera Ballet School and was accepted on scholarship to study under prima ballerina Rosina Galli. After graduating from high school, Becker joined the Metropolitan's company in 1920. She also studied ballet at the studio of Michel Fokine and natural (modern) dancing at an ISADORA DUNCAN studio.

Leaving the Metropolitan Ballet after the 1922–23 season, Becker toured South America in the summer of 1923 as second soloist with the Bracale Opera Company which went broke in Bogotá. Returning to the United States she danced in nightclubs and revues, appearing in Chicago in 1924 at the Villa Venice nightclub as the Senorita Tamiris. The name came from a poem about a Persian queen: "Thou art Tamiris, the ruthless queen who banishes all obstacles." Later that year she was a featured dancer in the Music Box Revue in New York with FANNY BRICE and Bobby Clark, performing in a Chinese dance and as the Red Queen in an "Alice in Wonderland" sketch.

In 1927 Tamiris decided to leave her career in musical revues for the less remunerative but more challenging concert stage. She produced her first solo program on Oct. 9, 1927, at the Little Theatre in New York; in addition to choreographing and performing the dances, she also designed and made her costumes. The beautiful, energetic, red-haired Tamiris premiered twelve works: they included "1927," to music by George Gershwin; "The Queen Walks in the Garden," a dance to no music; and "Subconscious," in which, according to a contemporary review, Tamiris appeared nude for "one long and devastating moment." In her second solo concert, on Jan. 29, 1928, she danced to two Negro spirituals; in later years her dances for spirituals became her most famous works. Tamiris saw herself as engaged in a crusade to reform dance. On the program for her second concert, she printed a manifesto which declared that the principal duty of an artist is "to express the spirit of his race." Dance was not to be circumscribed by rules or tradition: "Dancing is simply movement with a personal conception of rhythm . . . The dance of today must have a dynamic tempo and be vital, precise, spontaneous, free, normal, natural and human."

In 1928 Tamiris traveled to Europe, dancing first in Paris and then at the Salzburg Festival in Austria, the first American woman invited to perform there. She also gave a concert in Berlin in February 1929. Later that year she opened her School of American Dance in New York City. In her initial concert after her return she included "Revolutionary March," the first example of her developing belief that dance should make a social statement.

From 1930 to 1939 Tamiris was active in the growth of the new art form termed modern dance. With her contemporaries Martha Graham, DORIS HUMPHREY, and Charles Weidman she formed the Dance Repertory Theatre, the first of her several attempts at "creative collaboration." The organization lasted two seasons (1930 and 1931) before conflict among the various personality styles forced the experiment to a close. She then trained and choreographed for her Group, which appeared with her in concerts from 1931 and became a mature entity in 1934 with the performance of Tamiris's cycle "Walt Whitman Suite," a lyrical blending of Whitman and jazz.

In developing her social dances during the early 1930s, Tamiris encountered criticism both from those who believed modern dance should be a pure art form and from revolutionary dancers who saw her message as not explicit enough. With the founding of the Federal Theatre Project in 1935, Tamiris organized the Dance Association and convinced HALLIE FLANAGAN, the Project's director, that dancers should be recognized as a separate group. From the beginning of the Dance Project in January 1936 until 1939 when the entire Federal Theatre Project was closed down by Congress, Tamiris put aside her personal career to devote her energies to bringing modern dance with social themes to a wide audience. Most important of her dances during these years were *How Long, Brethren?* (1937), based on seven Negro songs of protest, and *Adelante* (1939), her brilliant dance on the theme of the civil war in Spain. (In *Adelante* she billed herself for the first time as Helen Tamiris, rather than the more exotic Tamiris.) During these years Tamiris and her Group also gave benefit concerts for the *Daily Worker* and appeared in a pageant at the Lenin Memorial Meeting in Madison Square Garden (1936), leading critics to describe her as a "Red sympathizer."

In 1937 Tamiris's Dance Association merged with two other dancers' groups to form the American Dance Association (ADA), intended to look after the economic needs of dancers and to further the cause of dance generally; Tamiris became first president of the ADA. In the same year she received the first *Dance Magazine* award for group choreography for *How Long, Brethren?*

In the years just after the demise of the Federal Theatre, Tamiris divided her time between concert and nightclub performances and public and political benefits. In 1940 she opened a New York studio where she taught and gave performances with her Group; "Liberty Song," one of her most successful works, was presented there in 1941. The following year she played two six-week engagements at the popular nightclub, the Rainbow Room. In 1943 she choreographed for the United States Department of Agriculture a production designed to promote wartime meat rationing; she appeared as Porterhouse Lucy, the Black Market Steak. Tamiris and Daniel Nagrin, her former student and longtime dance partner, performed in a twenty-five city tour of "The People's Bandwagon" in 1944, part of Franklin D. Roosevelt's reelection campaign. Tamiris and Nagrin were married on Sept. 3, 1946; they separated in January 1964 but did not divorce. Tamiris had been married in the early 1930s to James Fuller, who was not connected with the theater.

In 1944 Tamiris's career took a new direction as she began to choreograph for Broadway musicals. The first two, *Marianne* and *Stovepipe Hat*, were flops. But *Up in Central Park* (1945), with its famous skating ballet, ran for over 500 performances in New York, toured nationally (1946–47), and was made into a film (1948), and Tamiris was well-established and in demand. Working from her belief that "the choreographer must respect . . . the script," she had the rare ability, dance critic John Martin noted, "to see a show whole." A revival of *Showboat* (1946) and *Annie Get Your Gun* (1948) were enormous hits. In 1949 she won the Antoinette Perry Award for the best choreography of the season for *Touch and Go*. By 1955 she had worked on ten more shows, including *Fanny* (1954) and *Plain and Fancy* (1955). Nagrin assisted his wife in staging most of the musicals; he also performed, most notably as The Wild Horse in *Annie Get Your Gun*. Success affected Tamiris's politics. As dance critic Walter Terry commented, the "comfort of a mink coat and a bank balance seemed to make her more conservative."

With her husband she founded the Tamiris-Nagrin Dance Company in 1960 but the company disbanded when Tamiris and Nagrin separated. Her last work as a choreographer was *The Lady from Colorado*, done in 1964 for the Central City, Colo., Opera Association. In 1965 Tamiris was artist in residence at Indiana University. Later that year she entered the Jewish Memorial Hospital in New York, suffering from cancer; she died there in August 1966. In her will she left one-third of her estate "for the benefit of American Modern Dance"; a fund, the Tamiris Foundation, was established to continue her contributions to this unique American art form.

[The Tamiris scrapbooks and all her papers were given to the Dance Coll., N.Y. Public Library; also there are many photographs of Tamiris and her Group and films of Tamiris performing "Negro Spirituals" and "Dances for Walt Whitman." Christena L. Schlundt, *Tamiris, A Chronicle of Her Dance Career, 1927–1955* (1972), is the most useful and complete study. Tamiris is discussed in John Martin, *America Dancing* (1968); Joseph Mazo, *Prime Movers: The Makers of Modern Dance in America* (1977); Don McDonagh, *The Complete Guide to Modern Dance* (1976); and Walter Terry, *The Dance in America* (1971). See also John Martin, "The Dance: Tamiris," *N.Y. Times*, Dec. 1, 1946, and *Biog. Encyc. and Who's Who of the Am. Theatre* (1966). Most printed sources give Tamiris's birth date as 1905; both Daniel Nagrin and Tamiris's close friend, Florence Becker Lennon, say she was born in 1902. They provided further helpful information as did Bruce Becker, Tamiris's nephew, and her friend Ann Mackenzie Payne. A biobibliography by Margaret Cline assisted with research.]

IRIS M. FANGER

TAYLOR, Lily Ross, Aug. 12, 1886–Nov. 18, 1969. Classicist.

Lily Ross Taylor was born in Auburn, Ala., the eldest of three children of William Dana Taylor, a well-known railway engineer, and his first wife, Mary (Ross) Taylor. Both parents were born in Alabama. Mary Taylor died in 1895, and in 1897 William Taylor married Annie L. McIntyre; three more children were born of this marriage.

In Lily Ross Taylor's childhood the family often accompanied her father where his work took him, as when she attended the preparatory department of Pritchett College, Glasgow, Mo. When in 1901 her father was appointed professor of railway engineering at the University of Wisconsin, she went to Madison High School and obtained her A.B. at the university in 1906. She majored in mathematics at first, but in her junior year a course on Lucretius with Moses Slaughter convinced her that her real interest was in Roman studies. She entered the graduate school of Bryn Mawr College in 1906, studied for a year at the American Academy in Rome (1909–10), and received her Ph.D. from Bryn Mawr in 1912. Her thesis became her first book, *The Cults of Ostia* (1912). In this and her second book, *Local Cults in Etruria* (1923), she amplified evidence from literary sources with archaeological and inscriptional material.

Appointed instructor in Latin at Vassar College in 1912, Taylor remained until 1927, rising to the rank of professor. In 1917 she became the first woman fellow of the American Academy in Rome, but soon joined the American Red Cross to serve in Italy and the Balkans during and after World War I. Her fellowship at the American Academy was renewed for 1919–20. In 1927 she was appointed professor of Latin and chairman of the department at Bryn Mawr College.

As a scholar, building on the work of the nineteenth century, Lily Ross Taylor made major contributions to the more dynamic twentieth-century interpretation of Roman political history and religion. Her third book, *The Divinity of the Roman Emperor* (1931), took her into a wider and more speculative area than her earlier studies of local religious cults. She discussed the origin of the cult of the emperor and its possible sources in the thought of earlier Rome, of the Hellenistic kingdoms, and of Persia. This book involved a study of the close relationship between the religious and political life of Rome, on which her later work shed further light. It also led to her subsequent research on the political structure of the Roman Republic.

Her insatiable curiosity about institutions and how people function within them inspired and enlivened her research, as did her intense interest in contemporary events and politics. These qualities, as well as a deep love of Latin literature, made her an outstanding teacher. "My aim as a teacher," she said, "is to make my students feel that they are walking the streets of Rome, and seeing and thinking what Romans saw and thought" (Broughton, *Am. Philosophical Soc. Year Book*, p. 178). When in 1942 she became dean of the graduate school at Bryn Mawr, she gave up her chairmanship, but continued to teach. Her achievements in the classroom were recognized by the Life Magazine Teachers Award (1952).

In addition to her duties at Bryn Mawr, during the 1940s Lily Ross Taylor also served as an associate editor of *Classical Philology* and principal social science analyst in the Office of Strategic Services in Washington, D.C. (1943–44). Active in various professional organizations, she became president of the American Philological Association in 1942; earlier, she had served as vice president of the American Institute of Archaeology (1935–37). In 1947 she was the first woman to be appointed Sather Professor of Classics at the University of California, and she delivered the Sather Lectures, published as *Party Politics in the Age of Caesar* (1949). This lively study demonstrates the importance of the individual leader and the absence of any real parties at the end of the Republic, and shows how factions were formed, how they broke down, and how the electoral and legislative processes could be manipulated.

After her retirement from Bryn Mawr College in 1952, Lily Ross Taylor was professor in charge of the Classical School of the American Academy in Rome until 1955, when she returned to live in Bryn Mawr. In 1956–57, as Phi Beta Kappa Visiting Scholar, she lectured around the country. During the late 1950s and early 1960s she was visiting professor at several universities and spent a year as a member of the Institute for Advanced Study at Princeton. In 1960 Taylor published her second study of Roman political institutions, *The Voting Districts of the Roman Republic: The Thirty-five Urban and Rural Tribes*. A detailed analysis of the geographical distribution of the tribes in which Roman citizens were registered and in which they voted, it also included data on individual tribe members. Appointed Jerome Lecturer at the American Academy in Rome and the University of Michigan (1964–65), Taylor published her lectures as *Roman Voting Assemblies* (1966). Her last book, it deals with the complex organization and workings of the assemblies in which Romans voted, and contains an illuminating description of the construction of voting places and ways of casting votes.

Lily Ross Taylor's capacity for work, to the end of her life, was remarkable. She was sustained by excellent health and retained the vitality of thought and expression which, along with her sense of humor, engaged her host of friends. She also enjoyed travel, especially in Italy where her fluent Italian made easy those explorations on which, in her seventies, she could walk the legs off younger friends.

Taylor always maintained close relations with her brothers and sisters and their many children. From 1932 until her death she lived with Alice Martin Hawkins, who gave Lily Ross Taylor intellectual companionship and took over the domestic duties which bored her. The recipient of honors and awards throughout her career, Taylor was elected to the American Philosophical Society and made a fellow of the American Academy of Arts and Sciences. In 1952 she received the Achievement Award of the American Association of University Women; in 1960 Bryn Mawr gave her its Citation for Distinguished Service at the seventy-fifth anniversary of the college. She was also given the Award of Merit of the American Philological Association (1962), and the Cultori di Roma gold medal given by the city of Rome (1962). She was working on a book about the Roman Senate when in 1969 at the age of eighty-three she was killed by a hit-and-run driver in Bryn Mawr.

[The Bryn Mawr College Archives contains MSS. of unpublished lectures, notes on work in progress, a small amount of professional correspondence, and many letters received by Agnes Michels on the occasion of Lily Ross Taylor's death, as well as a few photographs of her. In addition to her books, Taylor published seventy articles and over sixty reviews. A bibliography of her publications to 1966 was published by Bryn Mawr College. A 1977 French edition of *Party Politics in the Age of Caesar*, translated as *La Politique et les Partis à Rome au Temps de César*, by Elisabeth and Jean-Claude Morin, with an introduction by Elizabeth Deniaux, contains a complete bibliography. Accounts of her life and career include Agnes Kirsopp Michels, "Lily Ross Taylor," Am. Philological Assoc. *Proceedings*, 1969, pp. xviii–xix; T. R. S. Broughton, "Lily Ross Taylor (1886–1969)," *Am. Phil. Soc. Year Book 1970* (1971), pp. 172–79; T. R. S. Broughton, "Lily Ross Taylor," *Gnomon*, Nov. 1970, pp. 734–35; Agnes Michels, "Lily Ross Taylor," *Bryn Mawr Alumnae Bull.*, Winter 1970. A lecture by T. R. S. Broughton, "Roman Studies in the Twentieth Century," given at a convocation in her honor at Bryn Mawr, Feb. 28, 1970, is kept in the College Archives. Obituaries appeared in the Philadelphia *Inquirer* and *Evening Bulletin*, Nov. 19, 1969; *N.Y. Times*, Nov. 20, 1969; and *London Times*, Nov. 27, 1969. Family background was supplied by Taylor's niece Mary Reed Naish, as well as by Thomas Owen, *Hist. of Ala. and Dict. of Ala. Biog.*, vol. 4 (1921). Additional information was provided by T. R. S. Broughton; death record provided by Pa. Dept. of Health.]

AGNES KIRSOPP MICHELS

TERRELL, Mary Eliza Church, Sept. 23, 1863–July 24, 1954. Community leader, social reformer, lecturer, suffragist.

Mary Church Terrell was born in Memphis, Tenn., the first of two children and the only daughter of Louisa (Ayres) and Robert Reed Church. Her mother, a house slave before emancipation, afterward became the proprietor of a successful hair store in Memphis. When Louisa Church divorced her husband in the late 1860s, she left the south and, for more than thirty years, operated a beauty parlor in New York. Robert Church was born in Holly Springs, Miss., in 1838, the son of Captain Charles B. Church, a white man, and Emmeline, a slave. He worked on his father's Mississippi River boats until a Union fleet drove them from the river; he then opened a saloon in Memphis. Investing his savings in local real estate after a yellow fever epidemic drove prices down, he became by the 1880s the south's first black millionaire.

Mary Eliza, called Mollie, spent her early years in a comfortable home on the outskirts of Memphis, protected from the problems that most blacks faced. She knew her white grandfather as a kindly gentleman who filled her arms with fruit and flowers when she visited him. Only her maternal grandmother, dark-skinned Eliza Ayres, told her tales of slavery and gave her some perception of her African heritage. After her parents' divorce, Mollie was sent north to school. Boarding with a black family in Yellow Springs, Ohio, she attended the model school on the Antioch College campus for two years, followed by two years in public schools. She moved to Oberlin, Ohio, in 1875, for high school (graduating in 1879) and college. Energetic and high-spirited, she skated, swam, danced, rode horseback, and read widely. At Oberlin College, where she enrolled in the four-year classical course instead of the two-year "ladies' course," she was an editor of the *Oberlin Review.* The fact that she was often the only black student in her class, and sometimes the only woman, spurred her to excel, to prove that she was the equal of her companions in every way. Encountering little overt discrimination, she schooled herself to ignore occasional snubs or to defuse them by exercising diplomacy.

Graduating from Oberlin in 1884, she returned to Memphis. Although she had trained herself for a life of usefulness, her father wanted his daughter to be a "real lady" and forbade her to work. At the end of an unhappy winter as his hostess, she disregarded his wishes and joined the faculty of Wilberforce University in Xenia, Ohio. From Wilberforce she moved to Washington, D.C., in 1887 to teach Latin at the M Street High School, the capital's secondary school for blacks. In 1888, her father, by then reconciled to her activities, offered to send her abroad to study. For over two years, she toured western Europe, perfecting her knowledge of French, German, and Italian, and taking advantage of cultural opportunities. Cordially received wherever she went, she rejoiced in the absence of racial barriers and considered remaining abroad. But, recognizing that she had had a better education than any other black woman in the United States, and than most whites, she felt it her duty to return in 1890 to her teaching position in Washington "to promote the welfare of my race."

Church's marriage on Oct. 28, 1891, to Robert Heberton Terrell, who had been her supervisor at the M Street High School, ended her teaching career, since married women were not permitted to work in the District schools. Robert Terrell, one of the first blacks to graduate from Harvard (1884), was a school principal and lawyer. In 1901 he was appointed justice of the peace for the District of Columbia by Theodore Roosevelt and was soon made a judge of the municipal court, a position he held until his death in 1925; he was the only black federal judge.

The first years of the Terrells' marriage were marred by the death of three children, each of whom lived only a few days. Believing that they might have survived with better medical care than Washington's segregated hospital afforded, Mary Terrell went to New York for the birth, in 1898, of her daughter Phyllis. In 1905, she adopted her brother's daughter, Mary, four years older than Phyllis.

A devoted mother who supervised every detail of her daughters' upbringing, Terrell was also deeply involved in community work. For eleven years, from 1895 to 1901, and again from 1906 to 1911, she was a member of the District of Columbia Board of Education, the first black woman to receive such an appointment. In 1896, she became president of the newly organized National Association of Colored Women; after serving three terms, she was in 1901 voted honorary president for life. During the 1890s she also began her career as a public speaker. Long concerned with women's rights issues, she addressed the 1898 convention of the National American Woman Suffrage Association on "The Progress of Colored Women." In 1904, Terrell traveled to the convention in Germany of the International Council of Women, where she spoke in flawless German and French on the problems and progress of black women.

By the turn of the century, Mary Church Terrell had become a professional lecturer, bringing the story of black America to leading forums and college campuses across the country. Sugarcoating her message with such titles as "Uncle Sam and the Sons of Ham" and "The Bright Side of a Dark Subject," she campaigned against lynching, disfranchisement, and discrimination, and highlighted black achievements. Handsome, well-dressed, with a skin color that she described as "swarthy," she sometimes passed for white when traveling in order to avoid the indignities of Jim Crow, but never without resentment at the deception or fear of exposure. While her daughters were young, she limited her lecture tours to three weeks at a time, leaving her mother in charge of her household.

Between lectures, Terrell wrote on black history and life for newspapers and liberal magazines. A charter member of the National Association for the Advancement of Colored People, she became a familiar figure on Capitol Hill and at the White House as she led delegations to protest injustice and to urge corrective legislation.

During World War I, as a patriotic duty, she took a clerkship in the War Department, only to be humiliated by a transfer to an all-black section. Although she was forbidden to work with white women in federal offices, she was then, and later, associated with some of the nation's most progressive women. She picketed the White House with the National Woman's party on behalf of suffrage and, in 1919, traveled to Zurich to address the second congress of the Women's International League for Peace and Freedom. For several years after the war she was a member of the executive committee of the league. With the passage of the nineteenth amendment, she served as director of work among colored women in the east for the Republican National Committee, later performing a similar function for the 1930 senatorial campaign of RUTH HANNA MCCORMICK (SIMMS).

After Robert Terrell's death in 1925, Mary Church Terrell continued her speaking and writing career. She had long planned to write an uncompromising account of the hurdles that black women faced: "Be sure to be courageous and tell everything," she admonished herself in a 1919 diary. But when her book was published in 1940 as *A Colored Woman in a White World* it had become conventional autobiography. A lifetime of meeting rebuffs with "a more or less genuine smile" had kept her from expressing the emotions that she sometimes revealed in her diaries.

In the last decade of her life, however, age seemed to free her from the shackles of convention. While universities gave her honorary degrees and women's organizations feted her, she stepped up her efforts to fight for first-class citizenship. She was eighty-five when she broke down the color bar in the American Association of University Women. In 1950, she was one of a group attempting to desegregate the John R. Thompson restaurant in Washington, D.C. When the effort failed, she brought suit and, at eighty-nine, was leading picket lines in the campaign to desegregate the capital's lunchrooms. Victory came when, in 1953, the Supreme Court upheld the 1872–73 acts banning discrimination in places of public accommodation in the District of Columbia.

During the McCarthy period, when protest was muffled, she urged clemency for ETHEL ROSENBERG, and pleaded for the life of Rosa Lee Ingram, a Georgia sharecropper who had killed a white man. She was planning a second trip to Georgia on Ingram's behalf when, two months before her ninety-first birthday, she died of cancer in Annapolis, Md.

[Mary Church Terrell's *A Colored Woman in a White World* (1940, reprinted with supplementary chapters, 1968) is the main source for her biography. All quotes are taken from this volume. It must be checked carefully, however, with letters, diaries, and scrapbooks in the Mary Church Terrell and Robert H. Terrell Papers, Library of Congress, and with diaries in the possession of Phyllis Terrell Langston. The Library of Congress papers also include articles and speeches by Mary Church Terrell and some photographs. Papers concerning her work with the Nat. Assoc. of Colored Women are in the Nat. Archives for Black Women's History, Nat. Council of Negro Women, Washington, D.C. Gladys B. Shepperd's *Mary Church Terrell—Respectable Person* (1959) adds little new information. Annette E. and Roberta Church, *The Robert R. Churches of Memphis: A Father and Son Who Achieved in Spite of Race* (1974), includes biographical material on Robert Reed Church. A brief biography of Robert H. Terrell can be found in A. B. Caldwell, ed., *History of the American Negro and His Institutions*, vol. VI (1922). See also Elizabeth Lindsay Davis, ed., *Lifting as They Climb: An Historical Record of the National Association of Colored Women* (1933); Charles Kellogg, *NAACP*, vol. I (1967); August Meier, *Negro Thought in America, 1880–1915* (1963); *Dict. Am. Biog.*, Supp. Five. Obituaries appeared in the *N.Y. Times*, July 29, 1954, and the *Wash. Post*, July 29, 1954; death record provided by Md. Dept. of Health. Interviews with Phyllis Terrell Langston, Dorothy Porter, and Annie Stein provided personal details and a valuable account of Terrell's last years.]

DOROTHY STERLING

THOMPSON, Clara [Mabel], Oct. 3, 1893–Dec. 20, 1958. Psychiatrist, psychoanalyst.

Clara Thompson was born in Providence, R.I., of American parents who had grown up within the religious and seafaring tradition of the area around Narragansett Bay. She was the older of two children, her brother, Frank, being six years younger. Her father, T. Franklin Thompson, a self-made man, worked briefly as a tailor—having learned this skill from his father —and then as a traveling salesman for a wholesale drug company, ultimately becoming its president. As a child, Thompson was always called "Mabel" by her family in order to avoid confusion with her mother, Clara (Medbery) Thompson, a quiet but forceful housewife. As an adult, Thompson hated the name Mabel, and she became simply Clara Thompson.

Shortly after the birth of her brother, the family moved from a small house near the center of Providence to their own large two-family house on the outskirts of the city, which was inhabited over the years by various relatives, including her Medbery grandparents, who lived in the first-floor flat, and her widowed paternal grandmother. Clara Thompson's lifelong love of the sea and of adventure seems to have emerged from her association as a child with her grandparents. Her grandmother Thompson drew her pictures of ships and told her about her Swedish-born grandfather, then long dead, who had run away to sea when he was nineteen and had earned his living thereafter as a rigger for whaling ships. In adult life, Thompson sometimes referred to herself as "the Swede," although three of her grandparents were American-born. Her grandfather Medbery had his own romantic tales of making his way as a young boy to California, trying belatedly to follow the trail of the forty-niners in search of gold. By the time Thompson knew him, he earned his living as a peddler of vegetables and a lamplighter for the city.

The move into an extended family setting also exposed the child to the wide-ranging and strongly held religious beliefs of different adults. Members of her family belonged to the Free Baptist sect, which, like Rhode Island, was founded on the principle of the separation of church and state. Family arguments over interpretations of the Bible coincided in time with a wider theological argument among all Baptists generally over Calvinist theology versus the Arminian doctrine of the Free Baptists. By 1913, the argument had been largely resolved both regionally and locally, but the imprint of that struggle stayed with Thompson. Within her profession, she insisted on an eclectic dialogue, while avoiding unproductive arguments over doctrinal details.

Thompson reported that she was a tomboy until she reached puberty, participating in a carefree way and as an equal in the various outdoor activities of boys her age. She credited her father with helping her to achieve a somewhat lighthearted childhood. When, at twelve, she was baptized by total immersion, she did not take the experience very seriously, by her own account, splashing about delightedly in the waters. But the somewhat Calvinist values for proper behavior for a girl her age, as dictated by the Medbery women—her mother and grandmother—gradually changed the nature of her life. Shortly after she entered the Classical High School in 1908, she announced that she had decided to become a medical missionary in India, thus resolving the conflict between her love of adventure and the religious dedication prescribed by the Medbery women; at the same time, she overcame any anticipated opposition to being the first person in the family to go to college—and a woman at that. Studies now became her first priority, although she continued to be active in sports and excelled in debating. In 1912 she graduated from high school with top honors.

That fall she began her premedical training, as a commuter, at Pembroke College, the women's college affiliated with Brown University. Here she found a new intellectual stimulation sharply at variance with the religious debates at home, and she began to arrive at the painful decision to become a physician but not a missionary, much to the consternation of her mother. She began to refer to herself as "Clara," sometimes varying it by calling herself "Maggie," the heroine of George Eliot's *Mill on the Floss;* this book mirrors Thompson's life as well as Eliot's. She went through a rather acute period of turmoil and confusion, marked by great loneliness interspersed with intense relationships with classmates. Near the end of her undergraduate work, her romantic interest in a major in the Army Medical Corps was terminated by her refusal to abandon her medical career—his condition for marriage. At about the same time, she stopped going to church regularly and began to express the rights of a free person rather than a Free Baptist. Later her estrangement from her mother was intensified when she began to experiment openly with what was then defined as free love.

Thompson graduated from Brown in 1916, with membership in both Sigma Xi and Phi Beta Kappa, and entered Johns Hopkins Medical School that fall. In her second year, her friendship with a fellow student, Lucile Dooley (1884–1968), a psychotherapist who was preparing for a career as a medically trained psychoanalyst, became crucial for her own professional development. Through Dooley, Thompson spent one summer at St. Elizabeths Hospital in Washington, D.C., where she came under the influence of William Alanson White. By the time Thompson finished her medical training, she had decided on a career in psychiatry and psychoanalysis. After completing her clinical requirements, she began a three-year residency in psychiatry under Adolf Meyer in the Henry Phipps Psychiatric Clinic at Hopkins. Meyer accorded her increasing responsibility until she decided in 1925 to undergo psychoanalysis, a decision he considered politically unwise at that time in a university setting.

As an outcome, Thompson left Phipps and began the private practice of psychoanalysis in Baltimore, receiving support for this move from Harry Stack Sullivan, then at Sheppard and Enoch Pratt Hospital near Baltimore. Thompson had met Sullivan in 1923, and their friendship and active collaboration continued until his death in 1949; she described the relationship as the longest and most important in her life. In the late 1920s, Sullivan persuaded Thompson to study psychoanalysis under Sandor Ferenczi in Budapest and then teach him, in the apprenticeship fashion of the period—a plan that was implemented intermittently over several years. After Thompson's return from Budapest in 1933, she began to live and practice in New York City, where Sullivan was already living.

In the 1930s Sullivan and Thompson were particularly influenced by the influx of psychoanalysts from Europe, and welcomed both Erich Fromm and KAREN HORNEY to their ongoing weekly intellectual interchange, playfully designated the Zodiac group; each member was identified with an animal—Thompson was a puma and Horney a water buffalo. Thompson and Sullivan had already been engaged, since the Baltimore days, in a dialogue on the delineation of cultural forces in the development of female adolescence; and she wrote the chapter entitled "Notes on Female Sexuality" for Sullivan's book *Personal Psychopathology*, completed in 1933. While the various intermittent members of the Zodiac group must all be credited for major collaboration on a more clinically sound formulation of female sexuality, the collaboration between Thompson and Horney, which lasted for almost a decade, was particularly significant since it combined the clinical observations of two perceptive women who had grown up in different cultures. In 1943, Thompson wrote her most important paper on women, " 'Penis Envy' in Women," in which she denied any biological basis for penis envy, tracing it to cultural pressures. The major part of her writings on women, which combined significantly the biological, psychological, and cultural determinants of women's behavior, was discovered after her death in an uncompleted book. During her lifetime, her ideas found their greatest influence through the wide professional range of her many students, including physicians, social workers, teachers, and nurses.

The collaboration among members of the Zodiac group was marred in 1943 by a schism in the American Institute of Psychoanalysis. Fromm was forced to resign from this Institute when Horney refused to make an exception for him as a lay psychoanalyst, in spite of his membership in the International Psychoanalytic Institute. Thompson and Sullivan resigned in protest. At that time, Thompson set up her own training institute as a New York branch of the Washington School of Psychiatry, which later became the William Alanson White Institute of Psychiatry, Psychoanalysis, and Psychology in New York. Thereafter Fromm and Thompson shared the direction of that Institute for over a decade. In the early 1950s, Thompson again manifested her independence when she threatened to bring suit, under the Sherman Anti-Trust Act, against the American Psychoanalytic Association, which was attempting to bar from membership anyone who trained or taught at the William Alanson White Institute.

Over the years, Thompson gained a reputation as an expert clinician, teacher, and administrator. She held many important posts in mental hospitals and professional organizations, beginning with her election as the first president of the Washington–Baltimore Psychoanalytic Society in 1930. Her first teaching experience was an innovative course in mental hygiene at the Institute of Euthenics at Vassar College in 1929. From 1936 to 1941, she was an analyzing instructor for the New York Psychoanalytic Institute, and she headed the William Alanson White Institute from 1946 until her death.

Clara Thompson's chief joy in life was centered around her summer holidays in Provincetown, Mass.; after she met the Hungarian artist Henry Major in the late 1930s, they spent the summers together there until his death. He continued to maintain his marriage to a woman who had been Thompson's speech therapist at one time. Major represented, like others of Thompson's Hungarian friends, a particular release from the restrictions of her girlhood. But the relationship had its own measure of frustration, since Thompson felt an affection for Major's wife and had to accept the reality of his continued relationship with his wife during the winter months. In 1947, Major became fatally ill; in the summer of 1948, he returned to Provincetown as usual, where Thompson nursed him through his last illness.

Although Thompson became over the years a source of generosity and warmth for a large group of dedicated students and trainees, she retained a certain shyness, even a surface blandness in her relationships with most people, mixing friendliness with a capacity for periodic withdrawal. After Major's death in 1948, Sullivan's death in 1949, and Fromm's increasing involvement in Mexico in the 1950s, she maintained an even more stoical life, although she continued to be productive.

In 1957, she had an unsuccessful operation for cancer; and although she told her brother and his family the medical reality, she acted toward colleagues and students as if there were no remaining problem. She died at her apartment in New York City in December 1958. Her grave is in the same Provincetown plot as that of Henry Major, at her request. The bronze marker gives her name as Clara M. Thompson, as decided by her family. Her friend Barbara Malicoat had small seashells placed on each corner of the marker to echo the sea motif that Thompson had arranged for Major's grave. In the end the conflicts of her life as an independent and intelligent woman seemed to fall into some kind of simple order, so that her family experience, her early religious training, her love of the sea and of the Hungarian artist had come together.

[A selection of Thompson's papers was published posthumously by Maurice R. Green as *Interpersonal Psychoanalysis* (1964); a shorter selection, focusing on women, appeared as *On Women* (1971). Thompson also wrote, in collaboration with Patrick Mullahy, *Psychoanalysis: Its Evolution and Development* (1950), based on a series of lectures at the Washington School of Psychiatry and the William Alanson White Institute. For her early formulations on women see "Notes on Female Adolescence," in Harry Stack Sullivan, *Personal Psychopathology* (1972), pp. xxi–xxii, 245–64. A bibliography of Thompson's writings may be compiled by incorporating articles in *Interpersonal Psychoanalysis* with her bibliography from 1930–47 published in *Psychiatry*, May 1947, pp. 237–38. The main source of published information on Thompson's family and professional life is Maurice R. Green's "Her Life," the final section of *Interpersonal Psychoanalysis;* the book also contains a photograph. For a history of her major professional affiliations see Thompson, "The History of the William Alanson White Institute," available from the Institute's office; and the "History of the Washington Psychoanalytic Society" (1969), by Douglas Noble and Donald L. Burnham, available at the office of that society. Brief summaries of her professional significance can be found in the *N.Y. Times* obituary, Dec. 21, 1958, and in *Psychiatry*, Feb. 1959, p. 87. Dates and factual information about family history came from birth certificates, her parents' marriage certificate, death certificates, and grave markers. Additional information came from Maurice R. Green, Frank and Peg Thompson, Barbara Malicoat, and from personal acquaintance.]

HELEN SWICK PERRY

THOMPSON, Dorothy, July 9, 1893–Jan. 30, 1961. Journalist.

Dorothy Thompson, newspaper columnist and political commentator, was born in Lancaster, N.Y., eldest of the three children and two daughters of Peter and Margaret (Grierson) Thompson. Her English-born father was a Methodist clergyman noted for his pulpit eloquence; her mother was of English and Scottish parentage. In 1900 the family moved to Hamburg, N.Y., near Buffalo. Dorothy's mother died the following year, and in 1903 her father married Elizabeth Abbott. Two years later the family moved to nearby Gowanda, N.Y., where Dorothy entered the local high school. She did not get along well with her moralistic stepmother, and in 1908 her father sent her to Chicago to live with relatives. There she attended the Lewis Institute, a private school offering both high school work and a two-year college program.

Entering Syracuse University as a junior in 1912 on a scholarship available to children of Methodist ministers, she won a reputation as a gifted and articulate student with a propensity for monopolizing conversations and for forming intense attachments with other young women. Caught up in the surge of woman suffrage activity, she joined the Syracuse Equal Suffrage League. Upon graduating in 1914 she took a publicity job in Buffalo with the state woman suffrage association; in the successful New York suffrage campaign of 1917 she lectured widely in the upstate region. After briefly sharing an apartment in Greenwich Village with Barbara De Porte, a Cornell graduate, in 1918–19 Thompson spent some months in Cincinnati as publicity director for the Social Unit, a New York based reform organization dedicated to awakening political consciousness in the slums.

A European trip with Barbara De Porte in July 1920 saw the modest beginnings of Thompson's career in journalism. Her interview with the Irish independence leader Terence MacSwiney and a story done with De Porte on striking Fiat workers in Rome were both carried by the International News Service (INS). When De Porte returned to London to marry, Thompson spent a few months in Paris and then early in 1921 went to Vienna as a publicist for the American Red Cross and unsalaried correspondent for Cyrus Curtis's *Philadelphia Public Ledger*. Shortly after her arrival, with the aid of Marcel Fodor, Hungarian-born correspondent for the *Manchester Guardian* who became a lifelong mentor and friend, she wrote a first-hand account of the attempt of Charles, grandnephew of Emperor Franz Josef, to reestablish the Hapsburg monarchy. Thanks in part to this coup she was placed on salary and in 1924 made Central European bureau chief for the *Ledger* and the *New York Evening Post* (another Curtis newspaper), with headquarters in Berlin. A full-fledged journalist at last, she savored the role to the full, covering developments in Berlin, Vienna, Warsaw, and elsewhere with growing professional ability, while assiduously cultivating what her biographer has called "the Thompson legend in which the intrepid girl reporter, braving unimaginable perils to get the news, becomes as much a part of the story as the events she is covering" (Sanders, p. 81).

Thompson found the febrile cultural atmosphere of Vienna and Berlin in the 1920s intensely stimulating. An affair with Josef Bard, a Hungarian Jew with saturnine good looks, vague literary ambitions, and a reputation as a playboy led to their marriage early in 1922. Bard's amorous adventuring did not diminish, however, and in 1927 they were divorced. She speculated that his "talent for treachery" might be "a Jewish talent . . . I am afraid I am becoming anti-Semite" (Sheean, p. 19).

In 1927 she toured the Soviet Union for the *Evening Post*, producing a perceptive series of articles, later published as *The New Russia* (1928). Resigning from the Curtis newspapers in March 1928, on May 14 of that year, in London, she married the recently divorced novelist Sinclair Lewis, whom she had met the preceding year in Berlin. Returning to America they purchased the 300-acre "Twin Farms," in South Pomfret, Vt., which would be for Thompson a center of stability through many marital and professional vicissitudes. Their only child, Michael, was born June 30, 1930. She also acquired an eleven-year-old stepson, Wells Lewis, to whom in time she became deeply attached; he was killed in World War II.

Marriage and motherhood did not long interrupt her career. Recrossing the Atlantic late in 1930, she spent much of the next five years in Europe, with summer visits to Twin Farms and periodic lecture tours throughout the United States. In articles for the *Saturday Evening Post* and other magazines she documented the ominous turn of events in Central Europe and especially in Germany. A 1931 interview with Adolf Hitler for *Cosmopolitan* magazine, later expanded into a book (*I Saw Hitler!* [1932]), enhanced her reputation and increased her lecture audiences. In a judgment she soon had cause to regret, she portrayed Hitler as "inconsequent and voluble, ill-poised, insecure"— a man of "startling insignificance" who would never be able to seize supreme power.

During the 1932 holiday season, spent with Lewis in Semmering, Austria, Thompson conceived a second child, but it was eventually lost in a miscarriage. On the same holiday she became involved in an intense erotic relationship with the Baroness Hatvany of Budapest, a longtime friend who under the pen name Christa Winsloe had written the lesbian novel *Mädchen in Uniform*. In a diary entry Thompson reviewed the "Sapphic" undercurrent of her sexual life and the "incredible feeling of sisterhood" it evoked, but concluded that she sought only "warm friendship" in such relationships, and that physical homosexuality was for her unsatisfactory and even distasteful. For the next several years, Baroness Hatvany was Thompson's frequent traveling companion and guest at Twin Farms. While Sinclair Lewis professed tolerance toward his wife's female friends, his 1932 novel *Ann Vickers,* a satirical portrayal of the woman suffrage movement, dismayed many of them. "Sometimes I think you don't see me at all, but somebody you have made up, a piece of fiction like Ann Vickers," Thompson wrote him shortly after its publication (Sanders, pp. 178–80).

There were other strains on the marriage as well. While Thompson's reputation was growing, Lewis's was on the wane. He won the Nobel Prize for literature in 1930, but much of his subsequent work was undistinguished. Though his 1935 novel *It Can't Happen Here*, dealing with a fascist takeover in America, reflected his wife's influence, he did not in general share her preoccupation with politics and world events. Lewis's drinking produced further conflicts; after 1933 their lives increasingly diverged and by 1937 they had separated. They were divorced in 1942.

Between Hitler's rise to power in 1933 and the United States's entry into war in 1941, Dorothy Thompson emerged as one of the nation's most powerful voices denouncing Hitlerism and demanding American intervention against the fascist threat. Her expulsion from Nazi Germany in July 1934 attracted worldwide notice, and two articles on fascism in *Foreign Affairs* (July 1935 and April 1936) enhanced her standing as a serious political commentator. After February 1936 her column "On the Record" appeared regularly in the *New York Herald Tribune*, the voice of the eastern, internationalist wing of the Republican party; it was soon carried by some 170 newspapers. A shrewdly intuitive thinker rather than a profound political analyst, in her columns Thompson gave her own inimitable stamp to observations on events abroad by such journalist friends and advisers as William L. Shirer and John Gunther, Max Ascoli, émigré authority on Italian fascism, and others. In 1937, while maintaining a heavy lecture schedule, she added a monthly column in the *Ladies' Home Journal* and became a regularly featured NBC radio commentator. The two most influential women in America, it was said in these years, were ELEANOR ROOSEVELT and Dorothy Thompson.

The plight of refugees aroused Thompson's particular attention in the late 1930s. She helped many European acquaintances to secure visas to the United States, often offering them temporary shelter. On a public level, she insistently called on the United States to develop a coordinated political strategy for dealing with the growing tide of refugees. Her article "Refugees, A World Problem" (*Foreign Affairs*, April 1938) was influential in bringing about the July 1938 international refugee conference at Evian-les-Bains, France, called by President

Franklin D. Roosevelt, which led to the creation of an Intergovernmental Committee on Refugees. Thompson's efforts were honored at a dinner in New York on May 6, 1941, where messages from President Roosevelt and Winston Churchill were read and representatives of refugee and antifascist groups paid her tribute.

Some, however, even among her ideological supporters, found Thompson strident and emotionally self-indulgent. When a collection of her columns appeared in 1939 as *Let the Record Speak*, one reviewer suggested that it be retitled *Let the Record Shout*. In these years, nonetheless, she was read, listened to, quoted, and talked about. Her confident, authoritative style, expressed in simple declarative sentences and short staccato paragraphs liberally sprinkled with exclamation points, appealed deeply to people frightened and confused by events abroad.

In the 1940 presidential campaign Thompson first proposed a bipartisan ticket of Franklin D. Roosevelt for president and the Republican Wendell Willkie for vice president. When this idea was ridiculed, she dramatically switched her support from Willkie to Roosevelt, declaring that his world leadership role outweighed all domestic considerations. This led to the termination of her *Herald Tribune* contract in 1941, and she switched to the Bell syndicate, whose flagship newspaper was the liberal *New York Post*. Initially, the outbreak of war served only to intensify her activities: she lectured, wrote, broadcast regularly (including, in 1942, a series of anti-Hitler talks in German broadcast to Germany via shortwave), and worked for refugees as a member of the Emergency Rescue Committee. At a more fundamental level, however, the coming of the war brought Dorothy Thompson to a turning point in her career. Once the great debate of the 1930s was resolved in favor of intervention and war, she was robbed of her great subject. "Politically," observed a friend, "she was like a great ship left stranded on the beach after the tide has gone out" (Sanders, p. 341).

In the immediate postwar years, seeking a new issue upon which to focus her journalistic energies, she turned from Europe to the Middle East, and specifically to the touchy issue of Zionism. Her reputation as a strong supporter of the movement to establish a Jewish nation in Palestine went back as far as 1920, when she had met Chaim Weizmann and other Zionist leaders in London, but in 1946 she emerged as a sharp critic of the movement. The sources of this about-face, which dismayed many American Jews, were complex. One cause was the emergence of a new militancy among Zionists in Palestine, of which she became aware on a trip to the Middle East in the spring of 1945. In her column for July 29, 1946 (soon after a bomb planted by Zionist militants in Jerusalem's King David Hotel resulted in ninety-one deaths) she urged British and American Zionists to repudiate Zionist extremism.

In addition, Thompson had consistently advocated a broad approach to the problem of resettling refugees, utilizing all possible nations, while certain Zionist organizations placed a high and sometimes exclusive priority on channeling European Jewish refugees to Palestine. In her 1938 book, *Refugees, Anarchy or Organization?* she had even suggested that Palestine, with its deepening Arab-Jewish conflicts, was unsuitable as a haven for the masses of European Jewry. Her long-standing interest in refugees also made her particularly sensitive to the plight of Palestinian Arabs uprooted by the creation of the state of Israel in 1948.

Gradually Thompson moved toward a fixed anti-Zionist, pro-Arab position, and this issue came to dominate her columns and lectures as fascism had earlier. In 1950 she toured the Middle East on a trip covertly financed by the State Department. The following year she helped found and became president of the American Friends of the Middle East (AFME), financed in part by the Arabian American Oil Company and apparently, although unknown to Thompson, by the Central Intelligence Agency. Though the organization's aim, in her view, was not to oppose Israel but to publicize "the problems and achievements of other Middle Eastern states" (Sanders, p. 337), in practice it functioned mainly as a conduit for anti-Israel pronouncements, particularly on the Palestinian refugee issue.

Thompson's partisanship aroused sharp criticism not only from American supporters of Israel but also from editors and readers who felt that her reputation for journalistic independence was being compromised. As early as 1947 the *New York Post*, which had a large Jewish readership, dropped her column, and the number of newspapers carrying it declined steadily thereafter. She resigned the presidency of AFME in 1957, in response to criticism, but did not modify her views. Her newspaper columns now lacked their earlier zest, and readers often found them vacillating and contradictory, though reflecting a generally rightward drift on domestic issues, as in her 1952 endorsement of Dwight D. Eisenhower for the presidency. The final column appeared in 1958.

Her magazine writing, primarily the monthly *Ladies' Home Journal* column which continued until her death, covered a broad range of subjects. While occasionally displaying the old polemical fire—particularly when the subject was progressive education or the decline of morality and the family—increasingly they dealt with noncontroversial matters, including her endless battle against obesity. Initially ambivalent about her role as a mother, Thompson found relations with her son often difficult; her *Journal* columns, however, frequently upheld the values of motherhood. In the early 1950s she often adopted a strongly anticommunist position, but later in the decade she wrote more frequently of the need for world disarmament and portrayed the cold war as more of a cultural and ideological than a military struggle.

In her private life, Dorothy Thompson achieved a measure of tranquillity. On June 16, 1943, she married Maxim Kopf, an Austrian émigré artist of modest talent and easygoing ways. The marriage was amicable and lasted until Kopf's death in 1958. In November 1960, after a visit to Sinclair Lewis's birthplace, she published an affectionate, although shrewdly objective, profile of him in the *Atlantic Monthly*, demonstrating that her journalistic skill and her fundamental decency of spirit had survived the ravaging years. She died of a heart attack in Lisbon, Portugal, early in 1961. Her estate, in excess of $600,000, went mainly into a trust fund for her two grandchildren.

Like HARRIET BEECHER STOWE in the 1850s, Dorothy Thompson emerged in the 1930s as a person whose outlook, preoccupations, and intellectual style were uncannily relevant to the larger issues of the period. Her ability to penetrate to the emotional heart of complex situations and her propensity for viewing world events and leaders in black-and-white moral terms were well suited to the convulsive decade which witnessed the rise of Adolf Hitler. When the Nazis rose to dominance she was unsparing in expressing her contempt for their racist ideology. She was equally vehement in denouncing their attacks on the "decadence" of the Weimar period, for it was that cultural milieu which had allowed her to overcome the taboos of her early life and explore unacknowledged dimensions of her nature. For a brief but crucial span of years, she played an opinion-molding role that assured her a place not only in journalistic history but also in the larger sweep of world events in the twentieth century.

[The voluminous collection of Thompson papers at the Syracuse Univ. Library includes correspondence, family papers, MSS. of speeches, broadcasts, and other writings, notes and research materials for her columns, typescripts of both newspaper and magazine columns, diaries, photographs, and copies of articles about her. Books not mentioned above are *Once on Christmas* (1939), a memoir of her girlhood; *Dorothy Thompson's Political Guide* (1938); *Listen, Hans* (1942), a compilation of her wartime propaganda broadcasts; and *The Courage to Be Happy* (1957). On her post-1946 anti-Zionism see her "America Demands a Single Loyalty," *Commentary*, March 1950. For the "Dorothy Thompson legend" in full-blown form see "Girl from Syracuse" and "Rover Girl in Europe," *Sat. Eve. Post*, May 18 and 25, 1940. The *Reader's Guide to Periodical Literature*, 1927–1961, is the best source for listings of articles by and about her. There is no fully satisfactory biography. Marion K. Sanders, *Dorothy Thompson: A Legend in Her Time* (1973), and Vincent Sheean, *Dorothy and Red* (1963), an account of her marriage to Sinclair Lewis, both draw selectively on her papers. See also *Current Biog.*, 1940; *New Yorker*, April 20 and 27, 1940; Mark Schorer, *Sinclair Lewis* (1961); American Council for Judaism, *Information Bull.*, Aug. 15, 1946 (reprint of her column of July 29, 1946); and David S. Wyman, *Paper Walls: America and the Refugee Crisis, 1938–1941* (1968). Although her birth date is often given as 1894, the U.S. Census (1900) confirms the 1893 date. An obituary and editorial appeared in the *N.Y. Times*, Feb. 1, 1961.]

PAUL BOYER

THOMPSON, Helen Mulford, June 1, 1908– June 25, 1974. Orchestra manager, organization executive.

Helen Thompson was the driving force behind the development of symphony orchestras throughout the United States from 1950 to 1970. Born in Greenville, a small town in Illinois, she retained an affinity for small towns and cities and believed that in them lay the future of American symphonic music.

Helen was the second of three surviving children and younger daughter of Jobe Herbert and Lena (Henry) Mulford, both of English heritage. Her father, a druggist by trade, played the clarinet and was actively involved in the town band and Sunday school orchestra. Recruiting his own children to fill the gaps in those ensembles, he assigned Helen to the violin at the age of six. In high school, she was concertmistress of the school orchestra and then, from 1926 to 1927, studied music at DePauw University in Indiana. Deciding against further music studies, she worked for two years in a library and on her savings enrolled in 1929 at the University of Illinois, where she majored in sociology and psychology and graduated Phi Beta Kappa in 1932. At Illinois, she took a chemistry course taught by a graduate assistant, Carl Denison Thompson, who went on to become a research chemist for Union Carbide. He and Helen Mulford were married in Waukegan, Ill., on April 8, 1933.

Helen Thompson was employed as a social worker, directing and supervising casework for public and private agencies in Illinois, Wisconsin, and New York state from the year before her marriage until 1940. Carl Thompson was then relocated to the Union Carbide plant in Charleston, W.Va., where on May 4, 1940, their son, Charles Denison, was born, prompting Helen Thompson to retire from social work. She did not confine herself to the role of housewife, however, but joined the newly formed Charleston Symphony in 1940 as a second violinist. She became its volunteer manager soon thereafter. To increase concert attendance and improve the orchestra's quality, Thompson employed a number of innovative techniques, placing an ad at one point in the *Chemical and Engineering News* for "chemists who are also symphony musicians." The notice attracted talent to Charleston and attention to its young orchestra. Later Thompson helped the orchestra obtain as director the American-born Antonio Modarelli, formerly conductor of the Pittsburgh Symphony. Modarelli greatly influenced Thompson's ideas on orchestral repertoire, management, and community relations.

In 1943 Thompson, striving to gain more publicity and engagements for her orchestra, became affiliated with the nascent American Symphony Orchestra League (ASOL), founded in Chicago the year before to serve civic orchestras. As the League expanded during the 1940s, Thompson's role grew with it. In 1948 she became the editor of its *Newsletter* (later *Symphony News*), where her talents as an organizer and publicist for civic orchestras drew notice. One of those who recognized her abilities was Max Risch, a building contractor and amateur bassoonist, who in 1950 made an anonymous donation of $2,000 to the League, stipulating that Helen Thompson be appointed its first full-time paid executive. Thompson moved the League's headquarters into her home, and from that point on, as several who later worked with her asserted, "Helen Thompson was the League." Her official title at the ASOL shifted in 1963 from executive secretary and treasurer to executive vice president and treasurer, and she remained the organization's key figure until her departure in 1970.

In her work for the ASOL, Thompson sometimes lobbied publicly for its interests, as in 1951 when she appeared before a congressional committee to argue successfully for the repeal of the 20 percent excise tax on symphony tickets. More often, though, she worked through private channels. Meeting with conductors, managers, and board members of most of the country's orchestras, Thompson identified firsthand their mutual problems and concerns, and developed programs in response. To improve orchestra management, for example, the ASOL cosponsored the nation's first course in that subject in 1952. In the same year, realizing that opportunities for conductor training in the United States were inadequate, Thompson combined with Eugene Ormandy and the Philadelphia Orchestra to found the Conductors Workshop. Thompson also instigated music critic workshops and promoted a dialogue between conductors and composers. As Gerald Deakin of the American Society of Composers and Publishers pointed out, it was "through her help and her good work . . . that the contemporary composer [was] able to get . . . performances in the United States."

Author of *The Community Symphony Orchestra: How to Organize and Develop It* (1952), and several other studies, Thompson later coedited with Leslie White a *Survey of Arts Councils* (1959). Reflecting her skills as a researcher, the ASOL became the best source for accurate statistical data on symphony orchestras in the United States, a fact the Ford Foundation recognized in 1966 by appointing Thompson its primary consultant for grants to American orchestras.

Helen Thompson combined intelligence with a well-honed business and organizational sense, reflected in the growth of the ASOL. By 1970, when she resigned her position there, the League had grown from 72 member orchestras to 1,400, becoming one of the nation's most representative professional groups in the performing arts.

In April 1970, Thompson became manager of the New York Philharmonic. The first woman since the early 1930s to manage one of the Big Five orchestras, she played an important part in the Philharmonic's campaign to expand its public educational services. Reaching the Philharmonic's compulsory retirement age of sixty-five in 1973, Thompson then left New York for California, where she formed her own arts consulting and research firm. She died of a heart attack in Carmel, Calif., in June 1974.

During her career, Helen Thompson used her considerable influence in the American musical establishment wisely and impartially to raise performance standards. As her friend David Hatmaker commented, she brought to America's developing orchestras the "sophistication and knowledge and expertise" they needed.

[Interviews conducted by Diane Jordan with David Hatmaker, Gerald Deakin, Carl Thompson, and others who knew Helen Thompson are stored in the archives of the Music Educators Nat. Conference Hist. Center, McKeldin Library, Univ. of Md., College Park. There are ASOL files at the ASOL office, Vienna, Va., and in an ASOL archive, Special Collections, George Mason Univ. Library, Fairfax, Va. Studies published by Thompson for the ASOL include *Report of Study on Governing Boards of Symphony Orchestras* (1958) and *A Report on Conductor Study and Training Opportunities* (1960). For Thompson's activities at the ASOL see the twentieth anniversary issue of *Newsletter of the American Symphony Orchestra League*, April–May 1962; "Helen Thompson Remembered, 1908–1974," *Symphony News*, Oct.–Nov. 1974. Diane Jordan is preparing a master's thesis, "Helen M. Thompson and the Conductors Workshop of the American Symphony Orchestra League: 1952 to 1970," at the Univ. of Md. See also Gail Stockholm, "New Philharmonic Manager: 'Penchant for Being Ahead of the Game," *Music and Artists*, April–May 1970. Thompson's contributions are cited in two books: Philip Hart, *Orpheus in the New World: The Symphony Orchestra as an American Cultural Institution* (1973); and Howard Shanet, *Philharmonic: A History of New York's Orchestra* (1975). Obituaries appeared in the *N.Y. Times*, June 26, 1974, and *Symphony News*, Aug.–Sept. 1974. Information supplied by Carl Thompson; birth certificate by Ill. Dept. of Public Health; marriage license by clerk of Lake Cty., Ill.; and death certificate by Calif. Dept. of Health Services.]

DIANE MARIE JORDAN

THORNE, Florence Calvert, July 28, 1877–March 16, 1973. Labor researcher and editor.

Florence Thorne was born in Hannibal, Mo., the second of three daughters of Stephen and Amanthis Belle (Mathews) Thorne. Her father, a native of Georgia whose family had moved there from New York, had fought for the Confederacy during the Civil War. In 1870 Stephen Thorne went to Hannibal, where he taught school and later became a partner in a grocery establishment. Amanthis Thorne was descended from Sir George Calvert, the first Lord Baltimore; the Mathews family, which had migrated from Kentucky to Missouri, were among the earliest settlers in Marion County, Mo.

Florence Thorne attended public schools and graduated valedictorian of Hannibal High School in 1896. Entering Oberlin College the following year, she studied Latin, Greek, and Middle English. With its heavily northern student body, Oberlin was an eyeopener for a young woman raised in a southern tradition. She left in 1899 to teach for a year in Eastman, Ga., and then returned to Hannibal, where she taught history, English, and civics in the public schools (1902–12). Beginning in 1903, she completed her undergraduate education, studying history and political science during the summer sessions of the University of Chicago, which awarded her a Ph.B. in 1909.

In her last undergraduate quarter at Chicago, Thorne received her first introduction to the trade union movement through a course taught by economist Robert F. Hoxie. The class met many of Chicago's labor leaders and Thorne found her academic study leading out into "a real life struggle." Continuing at Chicago in graduate school, in the summer of 1910 she began a thesis on the American Federation of Labor (AFL). During the course of the research, she met AFL president Samuel Gompers. In a long, unhurried interview in Chicago, Gompers strongly impressed Thorne; he offered her the opportunity to do research in the files at AFL headquarters in Washington, D.C. She accepted, spending the summer of 1911 in the AFL offices, where Gompers dropped by frequently to discuss her work. In the fall, she returned to Hannibal to teach. The following year Gompers, impressed by her abilities and her "understanding of human problems," wired Thorne offering her the assistant editorship of the *American Federationist*. She took the post and began a forty-year career with the AFL, during which she served first as one of Gompers's key aides, and later as the organization's research director.

From 1912 to 1917, Thorne's role at the AFL was shaped by her close working relationship with its chief. She became Gompers's confidential assistant, occasional speechwriter, and gatekeeper, controlling access to the president. She later referred to these years with Gompers as her "apprenticeship." Studying his life and policies first-hand, she came to understand the larger problems of organized labor and gradually assumed major responsibilities at the AFL headquarters. Although Gompers was listed as editor of the *American Federationist*, Thorne assumed responsibility for all editorial work and wrote many articles. She also interested Gompers in the idea of labor-oriented research, and carried out studies of legislation, politics, and economics.

America's entry into World War I interrupted Thorne's work for the AFL. Like Gompers, she enthusiastically supported the war effort and in 1917 was appointed to the Subcommittee on Women in Industry of the Advisory Committee of the Council of National Defense. The following year she left the AFL to serve in the Department of Labor, where as assistant director of the Working Conditions Service in the War Labor Administration, she helped promote health, safety, and better worker-employer relationships in wartime industries.

After the war, Thorne assisted Gompers in preparing his autobiography. She spent five years researching and writing the manuscript, submitting a draft of each chapter to him for approval; Gompers acknowledged her help in the book's foreword. In 1924, before the work was completed, Gompers died. Thorne, who was with him at the time, wrote and signed the last chapter of *Seventy Years of Life and Labor: An Autobiography*, which was published in 1925.

Although closely tied to Gompers, Florence Thorne's commitment to the AFL continued after his death. She reassumed her editorial responsibilities under the new president, William Green, serving also as his administrative assistant. Green supported her efforts to institutionalize research. In 1926 Thorne put together a volunteer research staff and initiated the first unemployment reporting by local unions. (No national unemployment statistics were available at the time.) Recognizing the importance of such work, the AFL formally organized the research department with a paid staff and appointed Thorne director in 1933.

Through the depression years, Thorne's research staff played an influential role at the AFL. Under her direction, the department provided unions with information for collective bargaining and for National Recovery Administration code negotiations. Her work also contributed to the development of social security and unemployment benefits and to child labor regulation. At the same time, she sought to encourage the confidence of union executives in their researchers. Earlier, Thorne had experienced the suspicion trade union officials often harbored for intellectuals: "It is very difficult to give these labor men advice," she wrote a friend in 1921. Thorne countered such resistance by insisting that the experts' function was to give information, not to make decisions or policy. "Ours is a service function," she pointed out in 1941, and "leadership and responsibility must rest with those we serve." Despite this policy, she did not always limit herself to behind-the-scenes activities. Thorne often represented the AFL on delegations, acting during World War II as a member of the Federal Advisory Commission for Employment Security and as a labor adviser to the International Labor Organization.

Thorne resigned from the AFL in 1953, shortly after George Meany became president. Aside from work on a biography, *Samuel Gompers, American Statesman* (1957), and occasional trips abroad, she spent her retirement quietly in the Virginia home she shared with her friend Margaret Scattergood, Thorne's

colleague in research at the AFL since 1928. Originally a Baptist, Thorne converted to Catholicism shortly before her death of pulmonary emboli in Falls Church, Va., in March 1973.

A small slender woman, she usually wore lace cuffs and ruffles, and skirts that brushed the floor, which gave her a "deceptively mild turn-of-the-century look." Strongly identifying with her Calvert ancestors, she was dedicated to individual freedom, and shared with Gompers the belief that workers should rely on their own initiatives rather than on government action. Accordingly, Thorne opposed protective legislation, arguing that economic action through trade unions should be "the main effort for promoting the welfare of women." Even as she shunned publicity and personal credit, Thorne made a major contribution to the development of labor research, by bridging the gap between research experts and labor leaders.

[A large collection of Florence Thorne's official papers are in the AFL Papers, State Hist. Soc. of Wis. Relevant files include those of the Research Director, the *American Federationist*, and the Office of the President for the Gompers era. Other letters can be found in the precommerce section of the Herbert Hoover Papers at the Hoover Library, West Branch, Iowa, and in the Selma Borchardt Papers at Wayne State Univ. The State Hist. Soc. of Mo. and the Marion County Hist. Soc. contain information about Thorne's family background. See also interviews conducted in 1957 with Florence Thorne and her successor as research director at the AFL, Boris Shishkin, in the Oral Hist. Coll., Columbia Univ. Useful secondary sources include Bernard Mandel, *Samuel Gompers: A Biography* (1963), and Philip Taft, *The A.F. of L. in the Time of Gompers* (1957). Obituaries appeared in *N.Y. Times* and *Wash. Post*, March 17, 1973, and in *AFL-CIO News*, March 24, 1973. Personal information was furnished by Margaret Scattergood, academic records by Hannibal Public Schools and Oberlin College, and a death certificate by the Va. Dept of Health.]

ELIZABETH FONES-WOLF

THURSTON, Matilda Smyrell Calder, May 16, 1875–April 18, 1958. Missionary, educator.

Matilda Calder Thurston, founder and first president of Ginling College for Women in Nanking, China, was born in Hartford, Conn. Both her father, George Calder, a carpenter who migrated to the United States from Scotland, and her mother, Margery (Patterson) Calder, who came from northern Ireland, were staunch Presbyterians. The eldest of three children, Matilda Calder had a sister and a brother. She recalled her childhood as uneventful; she had few friends and minimal social life outside her tightly knit family. Her closest companion was her sister and her deepest interest was school. She joined the church in 1888, "taking the step entirely of my own accord."

After graduating from the Hartford public schools, Matilda Calder left home for the first time to enter Mount Holyoke College, where she delighted in the intellectual stimulation of the college atmosphere. Decisive in her choice of career were the visit of a missionary delegation during her senior year and her enrollment in a mission study class on India. One of twenty-four Mount Holyoke students who joined the Student Volunteer Movement for Foreign Missions (SVM), an organization founded in 1886 to encourage college youth to enter the mission field, she resolved to become a missionary.

After receiving her B.S. degree from Mount Holyoke in 1896, Calder taught for four years in Connecticut secondary schools. She continued volunteer church work and attended SVM summer conferences at Northfield, Mass. Enthusiasm generated at these meetings strengthened her determination to volunteer for foreign mission service, a step she took in 1900. She was by this time acquainted with her future husband, John Lawrence Thurston, son of a minister and member of the SVM. A graduate of Yale University, he was a student at Hartford Seminary.

Calder taught at Central Turkey College for Girls, Marash, for two years, then returned to marry Lawrence Thurston in 1902. Her husband had helped organize the Yale University Mission, which decided to concentrate on educational work in China. Shortly after their marriage, the Thurstons sailed for China. After only a few months studying Chinese and seeking a location for Yale-in-China, they were forced by Lawrence Thurston's ill health to return to the United States in August 1903. He died in California of tuberculosis on May 10, 1904.

Matilda Thurston spent the next two years as SVM secretary, visiting branch associations in eastern colleges, and then returned to China to the Yale mission in Changsha, Hunan. For five years she taught in the boys' preparatory school and worked in the hospital attached to the mission. The revolution of 1911 broke out as she was departing for home furlough, and numerous westerners fled the civil conflict in interior China. Anticipating that the revolution would open new opportunities for educated women, refugee missionaries in Shanghai formulated plans for a women's Christian college in central China. Though one or two mission schools provided education for women at the junior college level, no four-year women's college then existed

in China, and coeducation was considered unacceptable.

Thurston returned to China in 1913 under the auspices of the Presbyterian Board of Foreign Missions, one of five societies pledging support to the proposed interdenominational school. In November of that year she was elected first president of the institution, later named Ginling College for Women, and assumed primary responsibility for finding a campus, gathering a faculty, and publicizing the venture among potential applicants, particularly in Christian middle schools.

Ginling opened with six faculty members and eight students in September 1915. The curriculum was modeled on that of American liberal arts colleges but included four years of Chinese. As in most mission institutions, religious courses and activities were required and instruction was largely in English. Thurston added to her administrative duties the teaching of astronomy, advanced mathematics, synoptic Gospels, and the life of Jesus; she also conducted a choir and gave regular chapel talks in Chinese. On her furloughs to the United States she made use of her SVM contacts to plead the cause of Ginling. Close ties were established with Smith College, which made annual contributions. Teachers from both Smith and Mount Holyoke frequently came to Ginling on short-term assignments.

Although Ginling remained a women's college while other schools introduced coeducation, its enrollment expanded to 152 in 1926 and to over 200 during the 1930s. The school increasingly attracted the daughters of the well-to-do as well as Christians of modest means. Majors in the social sciences were popular, though Ginling also became known for its courses in the sciences, English, music, and physical education. Most graduates became teachers, mainly in middle schools.

During the 1920s Chinese nationalists criticized the Christian schools for their foreign atmosphere, western administration, and religious requirements. Thurston resigned the presidency in 1928 in favor of one of Ginling's first graduates, Wu Yi-fang. Until 1936 she remained as adviser and took a special interest in supervising building construction on the campus, whose architecture combined Chinese form and western techniques.

Three years in the United States (1936–39) preceded three years in China as treasurer and aide to war and relief organizations. When the Japanese occupied Nanking, Thurston was interned. Repatriated in 1943, she lived with her sister, Helen Calder, in Auburndale, Mass. Despite declining health, she cooperated with Ruth

M. Chester in writing a history of Ginling College (1955). She died in Auburndale of the effects of arteriosclerosis in 1958.

In 1952 the People's Republic of China reorganized all institutions of higher education into a national system, and Ginling was amalgamated with other institutions in Nanking. Though Ginling graduated only about 1,000 students before its demise, it claimed to have awarded the first bachelor's degrees to women in China. Thurston saw the school and its students as pioneers, and she hoped through education to open new opportunities for professional careers for women as well as to extend Christian influence. She expected Ginling alumnae to assume leadership positions and tried to instill a sense of obligation to China, to the Christian cause, and to the goal of achieving greater independence and respect for women.

A member of the first graduating class characterized Matilda Calder Thurston as a genteel and dignified lady general, respected, demanding, and beloved. Thurston herself took pride in the fact that almost half of the alumnae of the first decade studied abroad and that many attained national prominence in education, medicine, and other professions.

[The Mount Holyoke College Hist. Coll. has some Thurston correspondence, materials on Ginling College, and a memorial tribute by Mrs. Way-sung New, delivered at the Wellesley, Mass., Congregational Church, April 28, 1958. Additional Thurston correspondence and other manuscript materials on Ginling are located at the United Board for Christian Higher Education in Asia, N.Y. City. The Presbyterian Hist. Soc., Philadelphia, has a biographical folder on Thurston which contains a brief autobiography submitted in her 1900 application for mission service. The papers of Lawrence Thurston at the Yale Univ. Library contain some correspondence and a copy of *Ginling College Mag.*, June 1928, which was dedicated to Matilda Thurston. Information on her public career is available in Matilda Thurston, "Ginling College," *Educational Rev.*, July 1918, pp. 242–43, and in her book, *Ginling College.* Reuben Holden, *Yale in China, The Mainland, 1901–1951* (1964), and Henry B. Wright, *A Life With a Purpose: A Memorial of John Lawrence Thurston, First Missionary of the Yale Mission* (1908), describe the founding of the Yale Univ. Mission and the trip to China to locate a site. Obituaries were published in the *N.Y. Times*, April 20, 1958, and *Boston Globe*, April 22, 1958. Additional information for this article was provided by a biobibliography by Susan E. Shehee and by Anne Calder Piskor, Thurston's niece. Death certificate supplied by Mass. Dept. of Public Health.]

JESSIE G. LUTZ

TILLY, Dorothy Eugenia Rogers, June 30, 1883–March 16, 1970. Civil rights reformer.

Dorothy Rogers Tilly, a leader of Methodist church work in the southeast and founder of the Fellowship of the Concerned, was born in Hampton, Ga., the third daughter and fourth of eleven children of Richard Wade and Frances (Eubank) Rogers. Both of her parents were descendants of early English settlers of Virginia. From 1896 to 1901 Richard Rogers, a Methodist minister, was president of Reinhardt Junior College in Waleska, Ga. Frances Rogers, the daughter of a planter, was a graduate of Wesleyan College in Macon, Ga.

Both parents sought to instill in their offspring a love of learning and compassion for the less fortunate. Dorothy Tilly remembered hearing as a child "the troubles of people . . . as they flowed over our doorsteps. They hurt me deeply." The eight Rogers children who survived infancy all received a college education. Dorothy Rogers graduated with honors from both Reinhardt College (1899) and Wesleyan (Ga.) College, where she received her A.B. in 1901. Two years later, on Nov. 24, 1903, she married Milton Eben Tilly, an Atlanta chemical distributor. They had one son, Eben Fletcher, born in 1904.

Tilly credited her husband with calling to her attention the plight of southern blacks. In the 1920s he insisted upon her accompanying him on morning drives through black slums, and she watched children raiding garbage cans behind Atlanta's fashionable Piedmont Hotel. When she protested, he responded, "If [seeing this] . . . hurts you enough, you will tell other people and they will do something" (Smith, p. 66). Milton Tilly promised financial assistance for her projects and consistently encouraged her efforts to promote social change. Theirs was an especially happy marriage.

In the 1910s and 1920s Tilly became prominent in the Women's Missionary Society of the North Georgia Conference of the Methodist Episcopal Church, South. She served as secretary of children's work and taught courses at Lake Junaluska, N.C., and elsewhere. Around 1929, she became director of the summer leadership school at Paine College in Augusta, Ga., which trained black Methodist women as community leaders.

In 1931 Dorothy Tilly joined the Commission on Interracial Cooperation (CIC) and the Association of Southern Women for the Prevention of Lynching (ASWPL). She was soon named to the national executive committee of the ASWPL and made secretary of its Georgia chapter. With JESSIE DANIEL AMES, founder of the ASWPL, she investigated lynchings in Georgia and crusaded for better treatment of blacks in the south. Meanwhile she continued her work for the

Methodist church, serving as secretary of Christian social relations for the Women's Society of Christian Service of the southeast.

Tilly's work on behalf of racial justice in the south led to her appointment in 1945 to President Harry S Truman's Committee on Civil Rights. She was the only white woman and one of only two southerners on the committee. Tilly encouraged committee members not to single out the south as the only racist section of the nation, but she fully endorsed the committee's condemnation of segregation as morally wrong. When the committee report, *To Secure These Rights,* was issued in 1947, Tilly spoke on its behalf in more than twenty states. She denounced segregation in the nation's capital and publicly began to support integration in the south.

Meanwhile she became a field worker and later the director of women's work for the Southern Regional Council (SRC), which succeeded the CIC in 1944. For the SRC Tilly investigated a race riot in Columbia, Tenn., and the lynching of four blacks in Monroe, Ga., in 1946. She also launched a crusade against the Ku Klux Klan and helped lead successful campaigns to persuade the legislatures of Georgia and South Carolina to pass antimask laws.

In September 1949, under SRC sponsorship, Tilly started a new group to carry on the aims of the ASWPL, which had dissolved in 1942. The new interracial and interfaith organization, which came to be called the Fellowship of the Concerned, drew its members from churches and synagogues in twelve southern states. An informal network of women who shared a religiously motivated commitment to "equal justice under the law," its original aim was to promote fair treatment of blacks in the courts. Tilly believed that if prominent women attended trials of blacks accused of crimes, judges, juries, and prosecuting attorneys would be less likely to violate the defendants' civil rights. Fellowship members were urged to report to Tilly on their activities, which also included accompanying registered black women voters to the polls and educating law enforcement authorities on methods of averting race riots and lynchings.

By 1950 the Fellowship of the Concerned had more than 4,000 members, many of whom found it prudent to conceal from their husbands that they were attending the organization's workshops. Tilly became an effective fund raiser, frequently obtaining the money to pay the expenses of workshop delegates. Starting in 1953, in anticipation of the 1954 *Brown* v. *Board of Education* Supreme Court decision, the Fellowship shifted its focus and began to hold workshops to promote support for integrated schools; it

also directed attention to the United Nations and to human rights.

From the 1930s on Tilly engaged in a wide variety of activities in addition to her work for the Fellowship and for the Methodist church. An advocate of United States participation in the League of Nations and an opponent of war, she joined CARRIE CHAPMAN CATT's Committee on the Cause and Cure of War. She served as president of its Georgia chapter in 1936 and was later named head of the southeastern branch. In 1943 Tilly joined the private Emergency Committee for Food Production, and in 1944 led its lobbying effort in Washington to extend the life of the Farm Security Administration. She was also a trustee of Wesleyan (Ga.) College, and was active in the Americans for Democratic Action and the American Civil Liberties Union. In December 1949, she was one of six people sent to Israel by the American Christian Palestine Committee to study the status of Jerusalem.

Barely five feet tall, aristocratic, addicted to hats with roses, sincerely religious, and a staunch prohibitionist, Tilly never shunned controversy, and was frequently honored for her courage. Segregationists detested her, calling her a communist and a parasite. Tilly kept a phonograph near her telephone and played a recording of the Lord's Prayer whenever she received a threatening phone call. After a Ku Klux Klan plot to bomb her house was uncovered in the 1950s, the mayor of Atlanta arranged for police protection and installed a street light in front of her home.

In the late 1950s and throughout the 1960s, despite bone fractures which frequently confined her to a wheelchair, Tilly refused to curtail her activities and traveled to numerous meetings and speaking engagements. The death of her husband in 1961 and the assassinations of John F. Kennedy and Martin Luther King, Jr., profoundly distressed her. At the last meeting of the Fellowship of the Concerned in the fall of 1968 she was so weak that her speech could barely be heard. Late in 1969 her son had her admitted to a nursing home in suburban Atlanta, where she died of respiratory arrest a few months later.

[The Dorothy Rogers Tilly Papers at Emory Univ. contain correspondence, clippings, biographical information, records of her work for the Methodist church and the Committee on Civil Rights, and a scrapbook. Other manuscript material is in the CIC and ASWPL papers at Atlanta Univ.; the SRC papers, which will be placed at Atlanta Univ.; and the Winthrop (S.C.) College Archives, where articles, letters, and other materials on Tilly have been deposited. Other sources of information include

Margaret Long, "Mrs. Dorothy Tilly, a Memoir," *New South*, Spring 1970; Beulah Mackay, "Dorothy Tilly: Pioneer," *The Church Woman*, March 1964; Sarah Cunningham, "A Woman Beyond Her Times," *The Church Woman*, Dec. 1966; Helena Huntington Smith, "Mrs. Tilly's Crusade," *Collier's*, Dec. 30, 1950; Ruth Collins, "We Are the Inheritors," *Response*, July-Aug. 1971; Morton Sosna, *In Search of the Silent South* (1978); Arnold Shankman, "Dorothy Tilly, Civil Rights, and the Methodist Church," *Methodist Hist,*. Jan. 1980, pp. 95–108; and Jessie Arndt, "Women's Crusade Spurs Fair Treatment of Negroes in Southern U.S.," *Christian Sci. Monitor*, Jan. 9, 1953. Obituaries appeared in the *Atlanta Journal*, March 17, 1970, and the *Atlanta Constitution*, March 18, 1970. Additional information was provided by Eben Tilly and Thelma Stevens.]

ARNOLD SHANKMAN

TOKLAS, Alice Babette, April 30, 1877–March 7, 1967. Writer.

Alice B. Toklas was born in San Francisco. Her mother, Emma Levinsky, born in Brooklyn, N.Y., was the daughter of German Jews: Louis Levinsky, who went to California during the 1849 Gold Rush and made money in mining and merchandising, and Louis's cousin, Hanchen Lewig, who was interested in music and culture. Toklas's father, Ferdinand, a Polish Jew, had immigrated to the United States in 1865, to become another successful western merchant.

Toklas was raised comfortably. Educated in private schools in San Francisco and Seattle, where her family moved around 1890, she entered the music conservatory of the University of Washington in 1893. Her mother's illness helped to end her formal education and also brought the family back to San Francisco. Emma Toklas died in 1897 and Alice Toklas assumed responsibility for the family home and for her only sibling, a brother ten years younger than she. For the next decade, she scrupulously fulfilled her domestic obligations without sacrificing all her other interests. She read Henry James. She studied the piano, with some hope of becoming a concert performer. She was aware of local Bohemian circles. She was both a dutiful daughter and a woman with exotic impulses at discreet variance with family standards.

In 1907, impulse overcame duty. Toklas traveled to Europe with Harriet Levy, one of several close women friends. In September, in Paris, Toklas met GERTRUDE STEIN, whose family she had known in California. Symbolically and literally, her life began again. In her memoirs, *What Is Remembered* (1963) Toklas recalled, "Gertrude Stein . . . held my complete attention,

as she did for all the many years I knew her until her death, and all these empty ones since then." By 1910, Toklas had fully settled into the famous home and salon at 27 rue de Fleurus that Stein then shared with her brother Leo. For more than thirty years, the two women were physically, emotionally, and socially inseparable. Except for an American lecture tour in the 1930s, they remained in Europe. Though aging Jews, they survived the German occupation of France during World War II. Like Stein, Toklas resisted open talk about their private world and their sexuality. Her public labels were often "secretary" or "companion." Nevertheless, Stein and Toklas created a lesbian relationship that has become legendary.

After Stein's death in July 1946, Toklas fiercely nurtured her literary reputation. She also established a separate public identity. She talked and lectured. She wrote: some journalism; her highly selective memoirs; the shrewd, incisive, opinionated, gossipy letters later published and praised; and two cookbooks, contributions to a genre she cherished and used. Her texts are, as her talk was, pungent, efficient, observant, often ironic and acerb. *The Alice B. Toklas Cook Book* (1954), which her friend Sir Francis Rose illustrated, is a famous confection of anecdote, advice, comment, and gourmet extravaganzas. Because the editing of the second, *Aromas and Flavors of Past and Present* (1958, with Poppy Cannon) displeased her, she tended to distance herself from it.

In 1957, Toklas returned to the Catholic church into which she claimed to have been baptized as a child. (Biographers have been unable to verify the claim.) She hoped that by joining the church she would be ensured of a posthumous reunion with Stein. Though her last years were both willful and interesting, loneliness and illness disfigured them, as did financial insecurity and quarrels that Stein's heirs initiated over Stein's estate. Increasingly fragile, lame from the effects of arthritis, and blind, Toklas died in Paris on March 7, 1967, and was buried there, next to Stein.

Both Victorian and twentieth-century elements characterize Toklas's history. She explicitly, self-consciously, and apparently happily accepted the role of loyal "wife" to Stein's "husband," of mother to Stein's prodigal child. She organized her "marriage" meticulously. She guarded Stein passionately, often jealously, and believed in and applauded her "genius." With her printing of the Plain Editions of Stein's writings, she even served as her publisher. The stability of her devotion, inseparable from the couple's mutual dependence, clearly helped Stein to work. Yet, Toklas was also unconventional. Although she acted on occasion like a powerful wife, she repudiated the securities of heterosexual marriage. She simultaneously integrated several marginal subcultures, those of the Jew, the American westerner, the American expatriate in Europe, the artist's mate, and the homosexual. She was committed to tradition and change, to service and independence. Because of this paradox, two lives reflect her achievement: Stein's and her own.

[Toklas's letters after Stein's death were well edited by Edward Burns, *Staying on Alone: Letters of Alice B. Toklas,* with an introduction by Gilbert A. Harrison (1973); see also *Dear Sammy: Letters from Gertrude Stein and Alice B. Toklas,* with a memoir by Samuel M. Steward (1977). Linda Simon, *The Biography of Alice B. Toklas* (1977), is a solid, mature, accomplished biography. For a helpful review see Donald Sutherland, "The Biography of Alice B. Toklas," *New Republic,* Aug. 20 and 27, 1977. Other sources of information and interpretation are books about Stein and Stein's own work, both her quasi-disguised autobiographical writing and the celebratory, playful *Autobiography of Alice B. Toklas,* written in 1932 and published in 1933, with photographs.]

CATHARINE R. STIMPSON

TOUREL, Jennie, June 22, 1900?–Nov. 23, 1973. Opera and concert singer.

Jennie Tourel was born in Vitebsk, Russia, one of four children, three girls and a boy, of a Jewish couple, Solomon and Pauline (Schulkin) Davidson. Her father was a banker, and although the family lost much of their wealth when they fled Russia in 1918, they remained well off. Living first in Danzig and then in Berlin, they settled eventually in Paris. Jennie Davidson's studies of voice and piano began before her arrival in France, but the only teacher identifiable by name is Anna El-Tour, an émigré Russian artist, with whom she studied voice in Paris for two years in the late 1920s. Otherwise, Tourel (as she called herself, reversing the syllables of her teacher's name) was largely self-taught. Later she identified the Spanish mezzo Conchita Supervia and the lieder singer Marya Freund as major influences; she also admired Madeleine Grey and her friend Eva Gauthier.

After numerous concert appearances, by 1931 she had made her opera debut as Jennie Tourel at the Opéra-Russe in Paris. In 1933 she joined the Opéra-Comique, appearing immediately in the stellar role of *Carmen.* Emil Cooper, conductor of the Opéra-Russe, arranged for her first appearance in the United States; during the 1930–31 season of the Chicago Opera she sang in Ernest Moret's *Lorenzaccio,* took the role of Lola in Mascagni's *Cavalleria Rusticana,* and

shared the stage with MARY GARDEN in the world premiere of Hamilton Forrest's *Camille.* Visiting the United States again in 1937, she made her debut at the Metropolitan Opera as Mignon in Thomas's opera by that name. Until World War II, Tourel sang throughout France; her roles included Charlotte in Massenet's *Werther,* Cherubino in Mozart's *The Marriage of Figaro,* and the title roles in *Mignon* and in Bizet's *Djamileh.* She left Paris in June 1940, just days before the Nazis entered the city. Delayed by illness in Lisbon and then forced to wait in Cuba for a visa, she did not arrive in the United States until January 1941, too late to be included in the Metropolitan Opera's roster of singers for that season.

Soon after her arrival, Tourel was invited by Wilfred Pelletier to sing Carmen and Mignon under his baton in Montreal. She later sang these and other roles in Havana, Toledo, Chicago, Philadelphia, Boston, Toronto, and Baltimore. In New York, she sang Lisa in Tchaikovsky's *Pique Dame* with the New Opera Company, and, in 1944, presented her uniquely sensitive Carmen during the debut season of the New York City Opera. Tourel returned to the Metropolitan Opera in March 1944 to sing Mignon. Within a few seasons, she presented Adalgisa in Bellini's *Norma* and offered audiences the original mezzo version of Rosina in Rossini's *The Barber of Seville,* the first time that version was heard at the house.

Tourel's American concert career began spectacularly in October 1942, when she performed with Toscanini and the New York Philharmonic in Berlioz's dramatic symphony *Roméo et Juliette.* Virgil Thomson, then critic of the *New York Herald Tribune,* reported: "She is a singer in the great tradition. Her voice is beautiful, her diction clear, her vocalism impeccable and her musicianship tops." Following her many performances of Berlioz and her later offerings of Mahler, the music of these two composers acquired new popularity. Tourel also successfully rendered the songs of then little-known South American composers such as Villa-Lobos. She sang with Koussevitzky and the Boston Symphony and, with Stokowski and the National Broadcasting Company Orchestra, gave the American premiere of Prokofiev's cantata *Alexander Nevsky.* Also with Stokowski, she was soloist in Bach's *Saint Matthew Passion* at the Metropolitan Opera House in April 1943. She became an American citizen in 1946.

Tourel was particularly responsive to unfashionable music and to the contemporary composers. She created the role of Baba the Turk in the 1951 Venice premiere of Stravinsky's *The Rake's Progress,* and promoted Hindemith's song cycle *Das Marienleben*. She also sang the songs of Ned Rorem and Francis Poulenc, Debussy's *Chansons de Bilitis*, Ravel's *Chansons Madécasses*, and Joaquín Nin's *Pano Murciano*. Tourel collaborated often with Leonard Bernstein. In 1944 in Pittsburgh she gave the first performance of his *Jeremiah* symphony. She also sang in this work in the summer of 1973, in her last public appearance in Israel, with whose musicians and people she felt a kinship.

Tourel, who had a decided gift for making and holding close friends, particularly among men, kept her personal life private. She was married three times: first in Paris to Bernhard Michlin, a businessman; later to the artist Leo Michaelson; and from 1955 to 1957 to Dr. Harry Gross, a heart specialist. All three marriages ended in divorce. She began teaching in 1957 and joined the faculty of the Juilliard School in 1964. Her public master classes at Carnegie Recital Hall beginning in 1963 drew many nonsingers along with professionals.

In the 1950s, Tourel achieved success in concert versions of less familiar operas, most often with the American Opera Society—notably in Rossini's *Otello* and Offenbach's *La Grande Duchesse de Gérolstein*. She appeared on National Educational Television as the countess in *Pique Dame* in 1971 and the following year she returned to staged opera in Pasatieri's *Black Widow* for the Seattle Opera. Shortly before her death from lung cancer in New York in 1973, Tourel, with her indefatigable energy, appeared in the speaking role of the Duchess of Krakenthorp in Donizetti's *La Fille du Régiment* with the Chicago Lyric Opera.

Jennie Tourel combined a first-rate musical intelligence with great emotional and intuitive gifts. Everything she sang, from the complex music of Hindemith to the sensuous compositions of Debussy, was deeply felt. Her legendary aptitude for languages originated in her childhood, when she heard Russian and French within the family. Later she learned German, Italian, Spanish, Portuguese, and Hebrew; she had acquired English before she arrived in the United States. Her voice was remarkable, a rich, deep mezzo with a range through high C, but even more remarkable was the way she cultivated it. A perfectionist, she never stopped working, refining and polishing what were already superb performances. She never had trouble winning audiences, captivating them with her distinctive style of performance, but the more sophisticated the audience, the more they appreciated her artistry.

[Biographical material on Tourel, particularly her early life, is scanty, and much of it is inaccurate. Articles about her include Robert Jacobson, "The Gist of Jennie," *Musical America*, June 1963; Richard Dyer, "The Spell of Jennie Tourel," *N.Y. Times*, Sept. 22, 1974; *Time*, Jan. 27, 1947, pp. 44–45; and entries in *Current Biog.*, 1947, and *Baker's Biog. Dict. of Musicians* (1978). An attempt to sort out fact from fiction is made by Robert Offergeld, "Some Notes on the Future of Jennie Tourel," *Stereo Rev.*, Nov. 1975. She is also discussed in David Ewen, *Encyc. of the Opera* (1955) and *Musicians Since 1900: Performers in Concert and Opera* (1978), and Irving Kolodin, *The Metropolitan Opera* (1966). Obituaries appeared in the *N.Y. Times*, Nov. 25, 1973, and *Opera News*, Jan. 12, 1974. A memorial by Leonard Bernstein, "Jennie Tourel—1910–1973," appeared in the *N.Y. Times*, Dec. 9, 1973. Additional information for this article was provided by Friede Rothe, Tourel's longtime manager, and by Robert Offergeld. No birth record is available. Tourel claimed that she was born in 1910 in Montreal; however, recent sources, including Offergeld, Ewen, *Baker's*, and the obituary in *Opera News*, give the year as 1900. Offergeld indicates that early passports supply this date as well as the correct place of birth. Both Friede Rothe and the U.S. Office of Passport Services say Tourel was born in 1903; the passport office, however, incorrectly lists the birthplace as Montreal.]

ELAINE BRODY

TOWLE, Charlotte Helen, Nov. 17, 1896–Oct. 1, 1966. Social work educator.

Charlotte Towle was born in Butte, Mont., the second of four children (three girls and a boy) of Emily (Kelsey) and Herman Augustus Towle. Her father's Scottish ancestors had settled in New Hampshire around 1640. As a young man Herman Towle had moved from Indiana to Montana, where he became a prosperous jeweler. Emily Towle, who was of French and Scottish ancestry, had been a schoolteacher before her marriage.

In their home in Butte, a copper city, the Towle children heard discussions of absentee ownership, labor-management conflict, unemployment, and, especially, party politics, in which both parents took a keen interest. The young Towles attended public schools with children of immigrants from many lands. After Charlotte graduated from Butte High School in 1915, she and her older sister were sent to a junior college in Virginia. The next year she transferred to Goucher College with the hope of becoming a writer, but she decided to major in education so that she could earn her living. In her senior year Towle enrolled in an elective course in social work and did field work with the Baltimore Prisoners' Aid Society and the American Red Cross. Upon graduating with an A.B. in 1919, she was convinced that she wanted a career in social work.

In Baltimore, Denver, and then in Thermopolis, Wyo., Charlotte Towle was a Red Cross caseworker from 1919 until 1921. She then worked for the United States Veterans Bureau, first in San Francisco (1922–24) and then at the neuropsychiatric hospital in Tacoma, Wash. (1924–26). Towle received a Commonwealth Fund fellowship in 1926 to study at the New York School of Social Work (later the Columbia University School of Social Work). Dissatisfied with the traditional casework of the day, in which the agency and the worker were central, she sought an alternative in psychiatric social work. Although the school did not offer an academic degree, Towle was attracted by its highly individualized programs which were designed for students who already had social work experience. After studying for a year with leaders in the social casework field and with well-known psychiatrists, Towle emerged with a firm base in psychoanalytic theory and with a wide-ranging interest in all that had to do with human behavior. Spending a year in Philadelphia as director of the home-finding department of the Children's Aid Society (1927–28), she also taught part-time at the Pennsylvania School of Social Work, where she came to know JESSIE TAFT and Virginia P. Robinson (1884–1977), who became leaders of the so-called functional school of social work. She then went to the Institute for Child Guidance in New York, where she supervised students from the New York and Smith College schools of social work. In 1931–32 Towle was a full-time field instructor in the New York School, working with students placed at the Institute.

Charlotte Towle's long association with the University of Chicago began in 1932 when she accepted the invitation of EDITH ABBOTT, dean of the School of Social Service Administration (SSA), to develop a program in psychiatric casework. She went to Chicago with a sense of mission: she was to do pioneering work in an institution known primarily for its interest in social welfare policy, a setting which many of her friends in the east considered hostile to psychiatric casework. But, although Towle came to be considered a leader in the so-called diagnostic or psychosocial school of social work, she refused to be labeled, and worked effectively with all groups in the profession.

Appointed as assistant professor at the SSA in 1932, Towle was promoted to associate professor in 1935 and to professor in 1944. She spent her first Chicago years in developing new courses and field placements in psychiatric casework. She also produced several important journal articles and published her first book, *Social Case Records from Psychiatric Clinics* (1941).

The experience of the depression increased Towle's sensitivity to the impact of social and economic adversity upon human personality. It also strengthened her belief that all caseworkers, not just those who specialized in psychiatric social work, needed a depth of understanding of human behavior. Once she had the psychiatric sequence in order, Towle therefore took the lead in developing generalized casework courses; a single generic course replaced separate courses in family, child welfare, medical, and psychiatric casework. This change, which was considered an important innovation in the 1940s, soon became common in other schools. In 1954 Towle was invited to the London School of Economics for a year to help develop a unified training program for social workers founded on the generic casework approach.

At the SSA Towle also became known for her teaching of social work instructors. From her early courses in supervision, she developed a course on dynamics of learning, in which she sought to integrate learning theory and dynamic psychology. Out of this course came her last book, *The Learner in Education for the Professions* (1954). Still later, she devoted much of her time to developing a new course in human behavior to be taught by social workers rather than by psychiatrists.

Towle frequently served as a consultant to social agencies in Chicago and elsewhere. In 1944 the Bureau of Public Assistance of the United States Social Security Board, headed by JANE HOEY, asked her to develop a manual for its workers who dealt with needy families in local agencies administering old-age assistance, aid to the blind, and aid to dependent children. In *Common Human Needs*, published by the United States Government Printing Office in 1945, Towle wrote of the inalienable right to food, shelter, and health care, and of the duty of the public assistance worker to help clients prove their eligibility for help. Those were dangerous words. Protests from journalists, and later from the president of the American Medical Association, who accused Towle of advocating socialism, caused the government, under order of the director of the Federal Security Administration, to discontinue the manual and to destroy its stock. In response to counterprotests from social workers and others, the American Association of Social Workers began publishing the work, which was translated into several languages and was still in print in the late 1970s. (Towle again ran afoul of the government before her 1954 trip to England, when her passport was delayed until she could explain her membership in two allegedly subversive organizations and her signature on a petition for clemency for Julius and ETHEL ROSENBERG.)

Over the years Towle served on many committees of professional organizations and held important advisory posts with the Veterans Administration (1946–48), the American Red Cross (1945–48), and the Mental Health Division of the United States Public Health Service (1947–49; 1953). For many years she was also a member of the editorial board of the *Social Service Review*. Her contributions to the profession were recognized by several honorary degrees and by the Florina Lasker Award for distinguished service to the field of social welfare (1956) and the Distinguished Service Award of the National Conference on Social Welfare (1962).

Charlotte Towle lived near the University of Chicago campus with her older sister Mildred and with Mary E. Rall, a social worker and later district supervisor in the United Charities of Chicago. Towle and Rall shared a love of the out-of-doors and vacationed together in New England. Although her salary was limited, Towle for many years provided some support for her parents and siblings, including Mildred, who had been partly crippled in an accident.

After her official retirement in 1962, Towle continued teaching on a part-time basis for two years and then worked two more years for the Scholarship and Guidance Association before retiring completely. She died of a stroke while on vacation in North Conway, N.H., in 1966. After her death she was honored by a memorial fund, established by friends and former students, which has been used for lectures to alumni of SSA in various parts of the United States and for special symposia in Chicago.

[Teaching materials, unpublished autobiographical notes, clippings, photographs, bibliographies, and other material may be found in the Charlotte Towle Coll. in the Dept. of Special Collections, Univ. of Chicago Library. The Charlotte Towle Memorial Library of the Spence-Chapin Adoption Service, N.Y. City, contains a complete set of Towle's books and professional articles, as well as memorabilia and some letters to members of the board. Some of Towle's most important articles have been collected in Helen Harris Perlman, ed., *Helping: Charlotte Towle on Social Work and Social Casework* (1969). A biographical sketch, tributes by friends and colleagues, and a bibliography are included in SSA *Newsletter*, Autumn/Winter 1966–67. A brief biography appears in *Encyc. of Social Work* (1977), vol. 17, pp. 1956–57. Material on her early teaching may be found in Shirley C. Hellenbrand, "Main Currents in Social Casework, 1898–1936: The Development of Social Casework in the United States" (Ph.D. diss., Columbia Univ. School of Social Work, 1965). In 1969 the Charlotte Towle Memorial Symposium on Comparative Theoretical Approaches to Social Casework resulted in the volume *Theories of Social Casework*, ed. Robert W. Roberts and Robert H. Nee (1971). An obituary appeared in the *N.Y. Times*, Oct. 2, 1966. A birth certificate was supplied by Mont. Bureau of Vital Statistics; death certificate supplied by town clerk of Conway, N.H. Additional information was provided by John H. Towle and Elise Towle Nickerson, her brother and sister, and by Mary E. Rall.]

RACHEL B. MARKS

TRAUBEL, Helen Francesca, June 16, 1899–July 28, 1972. Opera and concert singer.

Helen Traubel, Wagnerian soprano and, throughout the fifties, a beloved presence in American popular entertainment, was born into a prominent middle-class family of German descent in St. Louis. Her maternal grandfather founded the Apollo Theater there, the first to present important German drama in the middle west. Her father, Otto Ferdinand Traubel, a druggist and a man of many talents and interests, exerted a great influence upon his daughter's life, although he died when she was twelve. Her mother, Clara (Stuhr) Traubel, chose marriage over a singing career; according to her daughter, she possessed "the most exciting and thrillingly beautiful soprano voice I have ever heard." Traubel inherited not only voice, but also physique from her mother: her five-foot-nine 175-pound frame was very much that of the Stuhr women. Helen and her older brother Walter had a rich and varied childhood, filled with music (she had seen about thirty operas by age twelve) and the enjoyment of local vaudeville and St. Louis Browns baseball; Traubel bought a small interest in that woebegone team in 1950, "for sentimental reasons."

By her early teens Traubel was substituting for her mother in a church choir, and in that period she sang her first concert for money. In 1916 she became the pupil of Louise Vetta-Karst, a brilliant St. Louis voice teacher who for nearly eighteen years was at once Traubel's closest friend and "my most overbearing tyrant and female Svengali." The prize pupil left high school after her sophomore year to devote herself fully to her vocal training, and for many years she sang little in public beyond church work. In 1922 she married Louis Franklin Carpenter, a St. Louis car salesman; they separated after a short time.

Traubel made her debut in 1924 with the St. Louis Symphony Orchestra under Rudolph Ganz, a close friend and supporter who featured her in two midwest tours. In 1926 she sang the "Liebestod" in a Ganz concert at Lewisohn Stadium in New York, and gained her first offer from the Metropolitan Opera. She refused because she felt unready, but she did consent to a concert tour for the noted impresario Arthur Judson. Ever conscious of her vocal development, she left Judson after four months to return to her studies in St. Louis.

After another decade of Lulu Vetta-Karst, church singing, and local concertizing, Traubel sang under the American "Pope of Music," Walter Damrosch, at the 1935 St. Louis Sängerfest. Damrosch was so won over by this local "unknown" that he rewrote his opera *The Man Without a Country* to include a part for her. A private performance brought another (refused) Met offer, as well as a radio contract from the National Broadcasting Company (NBC). In the spring of 1937, Traubel finally made her Met debut in the world premiere of the Damrosch opera. She received critical acclaim, but her success was overshadowed by the opera's failure. Her radio successes, however, were bringing the phenomenon of an American-born, American-trained Wagnerian soprano to the appreciative attention of a large public. In fall 1937 she appeared for the first time with Kirsten Flagstad and her future partner, Lauritz Melchior.

The following year she divorced Louis Carpenter to marry William L. Bass, who became her manager and principal adviser. The first year of their marriage was one of financial hardship because Traubel had stopped her radio career and returned to her studies, this time with Giuseppe Boghetti, teacher of Marian Anderson. The characteristically cautious Traubel rejected $25,000 worth of radio contracts to live on stew, spaghetti, and voice lessons.

Her Town Hall debut, Oct. 8, 1939, elicited reviews of the kind she had learned to expect ("remarkable beauty and eloquence," "consummate artistry"); they hailed a career that was, at last, truly launched. She made her Carnegie Hall debut two weeks later. Traubel's somewhat scandalous nonrelationship with the Met came to an end when the management agreed to her choice of role for her second debut, Dec. 28, 1939, when she appeared to rave reviews as Sieglinde in *Die Walküre*. A few months later, she gave a brilliantly successful concert in Philadelphia singing a program identical to one which Flagstad had sung there just ten days before. This gesture of rivalry symbolizes a basic fact of the Traubel career: it took place during the Age of Flagstad (only four years her senior). Despite Traubel's enormous success, she was fated always to be compared with the great Norwegian in her central repertoire, the three *Ring* Brünnhildes, and Isolde. Still, they were friendly colleagues, and any direct rivalry ended when Flagstad returned to Norway in 1941. When she returned for the 1950–51 season, she insisted to

Metropolitan manager Rudolf Bing that she share the Wagner roles with Traubel: "She is a great singer, and I will not be the one to push her aside."

Throughout the forties Traubel reigned as "Queen of the German Wing" of the Met, the greatest American Wagnerian since LILLIAN NORDICA, and the new partner of Lauritz Melchior. The Associated Press twice voted her "Woman of the Year in Music"; she won a raft of major musical awards and two honorary doctorates; and in the 1942–43 season she became the first American-born, entirely American-trained singer to do Isolde and all three Brünnhildes in a season.

Her career became international with tours of Canada, Cuba, Mexico, and South America. In the early 1950s she made two world tours, including a historically triumphant stint in Japan. She was, however, essentially American, a symbol of what the homegrown variety could accomplish in a world dominated by hallowed European traditions, traditions she often defied—most controversially when she traded Brünnhilde's armor for flowing gowns designed by Adrian of Hollywood.

By the mid-1940s Traubel was feeling the restraints of her devotion to opera, and she turned to a variety of new interests. During World War II she experimented with popular music in USO concerts, with rousing success. In 1948, captivated by the enthusiasm and determination of her fellow Missouri singer Margaret Truman, Traubel became "background adviser" to the president's daughter; the role ballooned into a major problem as she futilely attempted to convince her to resist the blandishments of show business opportunists. Traubel's commanding figure and booming laughter became famous to a vast new audience as she appeared on NBC television in 1950 with Jimmy Durante, Red Skelton, Ed Sullivan, and others. In yet another realm of activity, she wrote a short mystery novel, *The Ptomaine Canary* (1949), which was syndicated in 200 papers. Its lightness of spirit brought it a better reception than its more ambitious successor, *The Metropolitan Opera Murders* (1951), in which a large, statuesque Wagnerian soprano with a golden voice and a booming laugh escapes murder and finds romance. Her last book, her autobiography *St. Louis Woman*, was written in collaboration with Richard Hubler and published in 1959.

For all her success, Traubel was unable to pursue her dual career as Met diva and popular entertainer for long. Her 1953 decision to add the role of nightclub entertainer to her activities was too much for Rudolf Bing, who in effect made her choose between nightclubs and the

Met; the result of their very public argument was that she chose nightclubs, leaving the Met for good after her last 1953 Isolde, and accusing her erstwhile boss of "rank snobbery." She further demonstrated her versatility by starring in the successful MGM musical *Deep in My Heart* (1954) and in the Rodgers and Hammerstein show *Pipe Dream* (1955). In 1964 she appeared again with Jimmy Durante, and in 1967 made another movie appearance, in *Gunn*. She died of a heart attack in Santa Monica, Calif., in 1972.

Helen Traubel made hundreds of recordings for RCA and Columbia, the most famous that of the Immolation scene from *Götterdämmerung*, in which she is accompanied by Arturo Toscanini and the NBC Symphony Orchestra—the first recording that Toscanini ever consented to make with a singer. Traubel had a huge song repertoire, but she sang only ten roles in opera, all but two of them Wagnerian. Her talent, her versatility, and her generous embrace of life won her a much larger place in the American consciousness than could ever have been expected for a Wagnerian "specialist." She was a joyous, confident presence who for a time brought some liberation to an all-too-stratified American culture.

[The best single source of biographical information —and reviews, both good and bad—is *St. Louis Woman*; it is not entirely reliable, however. She claims there a 1903 birth date and alters other dates to suit; her birth certificate, giving 1899, is available from the St. Louis Div. of Health. It also lists her middle name as Frances. Charles O'Connell's often very revealing book, *The Other Side of the Record* (1947), has an excellent chapter on Traubel and the politics of recording. She is given passing notice in all Metropolitan Opera and other opera histories; there is an interesting negative view in Quaintance Eaton, *Miracle of the Met* (1968). She received much coverage in the press throughout her career (*Time, Newsweek*, the major papers); the nightclub vs. opera issue inspired much comment (see *Life*, Oct. 12, 1953, and *Musical America*, Oct. 1953, which inclines toward Bing). A *N.Y. Times* obituary, July 30, 1972, and accompanying article are good, but not entirely accurate. Irving Kolodin's notice in *Sat. Rev.*, Aug. 19, 1972, and Edwin McArthur's in *Opera News*, Sept. 1972, are informative and affectionate. A death record was provided by the Calif. Dept. of Public Health.]

JOHN SWAN

TUCKER, Sophie, Jan. 13, 1884–Feb. 9, 1966. Entertainer.

Sophie Tucker was born Sophia Kalish in Russia to Jennie (Yacha) Kalish, a Russian Jew on her way to Boston to join her husband, who at some point took the name Charles Abuza. In the early 1890s the Abuzas moved to Hartford, Conn., where they opened a restaurant. Sophie, the second of four children and the first of two girls, attended the Brown School in Hartford and worked in the restaurant. She hated the work and wanted to become an entertainer. Instead, shy because she weighed 145 pounds at age thirteen, she played piano for her sister at amateur shows. In her autobiography, *Some of These Days* (1945), Tucker recalled: "Gradually, at the concerts I began to hear calls for 'the fat girl' . . . Then I would jump up from the piano stool, forgetting all about my size, and work to get all the laughs I could get." She concluded that "maybe in show business size didn't matter if you could sing and could make people laugh."

In 1903, Sophie Abuza married Louis Tuck, a local beer wagon driver. She soon had a son, Bert, and when her husband could not support his family, they separated. In 1906 she left Bert to be raised by her family, with her support, and went to New York to get into show business. Changing her name to Tucker, she literally sang for her supper and began to work her way up. According to her autobiography, when she entered an amateur show the manager hollered: "This one's so big and ugly the crowd out front will razz her. Better get some cork and black her up." Many white entertainers then used blackface makeup, but men like Al Jolson chose to do it. Tucker had to—because of her looks; in American show business, a woman's size and shape did matter. She hated the blackface, but felt she needed it. She made her professional debut in New York Dec. 9, 1906, at the 116th Street Music Hall, and was soon hailed as the "World-Renowned Coon Shouter." Certain that her 165 pounds would keep her out of "pink tights and a spangled G string," in 1908 she joined a burlesque show. Only when her luggage did not arrive for a show did Tucker attempt a performance without the makeup. Although she worried about appearing without a "disguise," the audience loved the way she belted out her zesty ragtime tunes. She was through with blacking up. In 1909 she won a spot in Ziegfeld's *Follies*, but lost it when the female stars refused to compete with the show-stopping new performer.

In vaudeville Tucker achieved stardom by developing a distinctive stage personality and making her size an asset. In 1910 she began singing double-entendre songs like "Nobody Loves a Fat Girl, But Oh How a Fat Girl Can Love." Being "big and gawky," she explained, "I made a song such as that funny but not salacious." In 1911 she played in two musical comedies in Chicago and introduced "Some of

These Days," which was to become her trademark. With new confidence and an act blending catchy rags, suggestiveness, and humor, Tucker rose quickly in vaudeville, her career reaching its first peak in 1914 when she played the prestigious Palace Theatre in New York. When jazz began to replace ragtime, Tucker organized a jazz band and billed herself as "The Queen of Jazz." After her father's death in 1915, she began to sing sad, sentimental ballads. Her success with them led her to dramatize songs, introducing them with skits and monologues that gave them an aura of realism and enhanced their emotional impact. By 1920 her act was essentially complete. She used her booming voice, emotional delivery, and suggestive humor on material that ranged from bouncy jazz tunes to tear-jerking ballads.

After five years in a New York nightspot, Tucker in 1922 made the first of many tours of England, where her emotional, honky-tonk style made her a star. Her English popularity was to sustain her throughout her career. Following a big-time American vaudeville tour which began at the Palace, she returned to England in 1925, winning great acclaim in London's fashionable Kit Kat Klub and in English music halls. With the demise of American vaudeville in the early 1930s, the country's top nightclubs became the scene of her greatest American successes. In 1934 Tucker returned to England, where music halls continued the live variety tradition, on a tour that climaxed with her command performance for King George V. Between 1929 and 1945 she made eight movies, two of them British, and continued to play in musicals like *Leave It to Me* (1938) and *High Kickers* (1941). Although she appeared regularly on radio and later on television, Tucker was always best with live audiences. The restrictions of the mass media inhibited her wide-open, earthy style. "I couldn't even say 'hell' or 'damn,'" she complained about radio, "and nothing, honey, is more expressive than the way I say 'hell' or 'damn.'"

In her personal life Tucker was caught between traditional values and new realities. She wanted to be with her family and son, but her profession required continual travel, which kept them apart. In marriage, part of her wanted to be led by a strong man, but another part wanted independence and power. She never found a solution to this dilemma. After divorcing Louis Tuck in 1913, Tucker married Frank Westphal, her pianist, in 1914. They were divorced in 1919, and a third marriage, in 1928, to Al Lackey, a fan who had become her personal manager, also ended in divorce, in 1933. In each marriage, she was the provider and leader.

In addition to supporting her family, Tucker was an active fund raiser and philanthropist. She established the Sophie Tucker Foundation in 1945 and ten years later endowed a chair in the theater arts at Brandeis University. She helped to organize vaudevillians in the controversial American Federation of Actors (AFA), which elected her president in 1938. Conflicts with Actors' Equity ended with the AFA being absorbed in Equity's American Guild of Variety Artists. But the performers ended up with a strong union.

By the late 1930s, Sophie Tucker had become an entertainment institution. Her fame in itself made her an attraction, but it was her explosive live performances which sustained her popularity for over fifty years in the United States and England. Like FANNY BRICE, Eddie Cantor, and other unique performers of her generation who served long apprenticeships before live audiences, Tucker was a consummate performing artist with a distinctive stage personality. "I'm the 3-D Mama with the Big Wide Screen," she boomed to a new generation of fans. Audiences never tired of her, and she never retired. In 1962 she gave another command performance in London, and, only four months before her death in New York in 1966, she was enthralling audiences there at the Latin Quarter. In many ways, the song Sophie Tucker first sang in 1928 was prophetic: she *was* "The Last of the Red Hot Mamas."

[The Sophie Tucker Coll. in the Billy Rose Theatre Coll., N.Y. Public Library, contains nearly 300 scrapbooks, as well as reviews, clippings, photographs, memorabilia, and some correspondence. There is a file of clippings in the Harvard Theatre Coll. The best published source of information on her life and career is her autobiography. The entry in *Current Biog.*, 1945, essentially summarizes the autobiography. *Biog. Encyc. and Who's Who of the Am. Theatre* (1966) lists the major facts about her career. Tributes to her long career in show business appeared in *Newsweek*, Oct. 5, 1953; *Theatre Arts*, Oct. 1953; and the *N.Y. Times Mag.*, Sept. 27, 1953. The *Cumulative Dramatic Index, 1909–1949* (1965) contains a bibliography of articles about her. An obituary in the *N.Y. Times*, Feb. 10, 1966, describes her career. The year and place of her birth appear in the U.S. Census, 1900.]

ROBERT C. TOLL

TURNBO-MALONE, Annie Minerva, Aug. 9, 1869–May 10, 1957. Entrepreneur, philanthropist.

Born in Metropolis, Ill., Annie Turnbo-Malone was the tenth of eleven children of Robert and Isabella (Cook) Turnbo. Family tradition claims that Robert Turnbo, a farmer, fought with Union troops in the Civil War, his wife and children fleeing Kentucky to find refuge in Metropolis. Orphaned before school age, Annie Turnbo was reared by her elder siblings. After attending public school in Metropolis, she lived with a married sister in Peoria, Ill. There she attended high school before withdrawing because of frequent illness. Fascinated as a child with dressing her sisters' hair, she later claimed to have studied chemistry, thus learning to make her unique mixture for enhancing the sheen and texture of hair.

In 1900, while living in the all-black town of Lovejoy (now Brooklyn), Ill., Annie Turnbo manufactured and sold her "Wonderful Hair Grower." In 1902 she moved her thriving business to St. Louis, where she and three assistants sold her products door-to-door, giving free hair and scalp treatments to attract clients. A brief marriage in 1903 to a Mr. Pope ended after he attempted to interfere in her business.

Impressed with the demand for her products during the 1904 St. Louis World's Fair, Turnbo launched an extensive advertising campaign in the black press. She held press conferences, toured the southern states, and recruited women whom she trained to administer and sell her products. According to Claude Barnett, founder of the Associated Negro Press, one of her agents in St. Louis in 1905 was SARAH BREEDLOVE (Madame C. J.) WALKER. In 1906, competition from what Turnbo called "fraudulent imitations" led her to copyright the trade name "Poro" for her products and merchandising system. By 1910 she had built a national enterprise. Though many companies sold hair straighteners and pomades at the time, Poro's sales appear to have outstripped the field because of Turnbo's system of franchised agent-operators.

On April 28, 1914, Turnbo married Aaron Eugene Malone, an ex-teacher and traveling Bible salesman. In 1918, with profits soaring, Annie Turnbo-Malone built an impressive five-story factory and beauty-training school in the heart of St. Louis's upper-middle-class black neighborhood. Envisioning a campuslike environment, she named it Poro College. The building's modern facilities were used not only for manufacturing and training but also for religious, fraternal, civic, and social functions. The National Negro Business League made its headquarters at Poro College and black St. Louisans, denied admittance to the city's restaurants and hotels, cherished Poro's hospitality.

Annie Turnbo-Malone displayed an abiding interest in the improvement of material and cultural life for blacks. She advertised Poro College as a "constructive force in the development of the race," and her pamphlets dwelled upon the virtues of cleanliness, good grooming, thrift, and industry. Annual brochures called for "ambitious women to enter a profitable profession" and promised economic independence as Poro agents. Turnbo-Malone personally supervised the training of Poro's "beauty-culturists" with a benevolent, if autocratic, concern for their welfare; one of her several annual awards was given to those who invested in real estate or helped their parents to do so. In St. Louis Poro employed 175 people; in addition, its franchise schools and supply stations in North and South America, Africa, and the Philippines created jobs for almost 75,000 women.

In addition to her business acumen, Annie Turnbo-Malone had an instinctive grasp of popular tastes. A Poro girls' orchestra captured headlines in the 1920s. Exotic African coiffures graced Poro advertisements; even the name "Poro" was said to derive from a West African organization devoted to physical perfection.

Poro profits reportedly made Annie Turnbo-Malone a millionaire. Her income tax in 1924—close to $40,000—was publicized as the highest in Missouri. Yet she lived modestly; her money, she explained, belonged to God and should "draw interest in human character." She gave thousands to the local black YMCA and to Howard University Medical School and donated $25,000 to the 1925 St. Louis YMCA campaign, "to show that the Negro . . . is willing to bear his share of responsibility." In 1919, she gave the site for the St. Louis Colored Orphans' Home and raised most of the costs of construction; she served on the Home's executive board from 1919 to 1943. In 1946, over her protest, the trustees renamed it the Annie Malone Children's Home. Turnbo-Malone received many honorary degrees specifically acknowledging her philanthropy.

Retaining control of her business, however, was not easy. In 1927 Aaron Malone filed suit for divorce, demanded half of her business, and forced Poro College into a court-ordered receivership. Black St. Louis split in partisan uproar. For political reasons, many sided with Aaron Malone, who had become prominent in local and state Republican politics (partly because of contributions from his wife's business). But black churchmen, the black press, Poro workers, and such leaders as MARY MCLEOD BETHUNE rallied in behalf of Turnbo-Malone, one editorial noting that Poro College had prospered "without the guiding hand of man." An out-of-court settlement on May 9, 1927, affirmed her sole ownership of Poro, and a divorce was granted. Bitter memories lingered, though, and in 1930 Turnbo-Malone moved her business to Chicago's South Parkway, where she bought an entire city block.

In 1937, settlement of a long-standing suit, in which a disgruntled former employee claimed credit for her success, forced the sale of the St. Louis property.

A symbol of respectability and success into her old age, Annie Turnbo-Malone died in 1957 of a stroke at Chicago's Provident Hospital. Childless, she willed her establishment and diminished fortune to her nieces and nephews.

[The Claude A. Barnett Papers at the Chicago Hist. Soc. contain correspondence, clippings, photographs, press releases, publications, and typescript biographies of Annie Turnbo-Malone. Research materials on Poro College and the Children's Home are also available in the Western Hist. Coll., Univ. of Missouri–St. Louis. Turnbo-Malone's national stature is recognized in J. L. Nichols and W. H. Crogman, *Progress of a Race* (1920); Carter Woodson, *The Negro in Our History* (1927); Edwin R. Embree, *Brown Americans: The Story of a Tenth of the Nation* (1943); E. Franklin Frazier, *The Negro in the United States* (1969). Her career is also cited in Eva DelVakea Bowles, "Opportunities for the Educated Colored Woman," *Opportunity*, March 1923, and in Gladys Porter, *Three Negro Pioneers in Beauty Culture* (1966), in the Moorland-Spingarn Coll., Howard Univ. Brief sketches appear in the *Official Manual—State of Missouri* (1971–72); the *Missouri Hist. Rev.*, July 1973; the *Jour. of Negro History*, vol. 9 (1924); and *The Ville: The Ethnic Heritage of an Urban Neighborhood* (1975). Obituaries appeared in the *St. Louis Argus*, May 17, 1957; the *St. Louis Post-Dispatch* and *St. Louis Globe-Democrat*, May 12, 1957; and the *Chicago Daily Defender*, May 13, 15, and 16, 1957. Julia Davis, former associate of Annie Turnbo-Malone, provided additional information.]

JEANNE CONWAY MONGOLD

TUVE, Rosemond, Nov. 27, 1903–Dec. 20, 1964. Literary scholar, teacher.

Rosemond Tuve was born in Canton, a small South Dakota town between the Big Sioux and the prairies, the only daughter of Anthony Gulbrandssen and Ida Marie (Larsen) Tuve. Her father was a mathematician and the president of Augustana, a small Lutheran college in Canton, where her mother had also taught music. Her four grandparents all had come from Norway. Her three brothers became successful scientists: George Lewis (mechanical engineering), Merle Anthony (physics), Richard Larsen (physical chemistry).

Of her early life she writes: "As the third child among four I chiefly did what my three brothers thought was important, such as learning the Morse code to take down their wireless messages, and playing in neighborhood gangs, but I learned without noticing it before I was ten to care about most of the things I have since thought or written about—and no doubt was equally inescapably made ready to miss the rest." Her father died when she was fourteen, and the family moved to Minneapolis "to put safely into the University of Minnesota my next oldest brother . . . to prevent him from saving the family fortunes by going on the boards with a Chicago opera company."

At sixteen Rosemond Tuve entered the university high school, graduating in 1920. Staying on at Minnesota as a college student, from 1923–24 she was the student assistant of the renowned Old English scholar Friedrich Klaeber. She claimed that she learned to type overnight in order to get the position. Between sophomore and junior years she taught fourth and fifth grades in the "tiny prairie town" of Toronto, S.D. After receiving the A.B. cum laude in 1924, she borrowed one thousand dollars to go to Bryn Mawr, where she received the A.M. the following year and was awarded the Bryn Mawr European Fellowship. Debts forced her to postpone the fellowship to accept a position at Goucher College, where she taught for two years (1926–28) while also attending seminars at Johns Hopkins.

In 1928, with the additional bounty of an American Association of University Women fellowship, Rosemond Tuve was finally able to go to England. She took up residence in Somerville College, Oxford, where she completed the B.Litt. courses and passed the *viva*. Unable to fulfill the residence requirements, she returned to teach English at Vassar (1929–31) with summers teaching at the Bryn Mawr Summer School for Women Workers in Industry, "an experience which left me forever (I hope) left of center, at least of where this country has taken to placing the center." In 1931 she received her Ph.D. from Bryn Mawr and returned to France to see her dissertation through the press: *Seasons and Months: Studies in a Tradition of Middle English Poetry* (1933, 1974). She stayed on in Oxford, London, and Ireland, and after a second year with friends in Somerset, went to Connecticut College in 1934.

It was at Connecticut that she established herself; for twenty-eight years it was home, providing nurture and appreciation. Minnesota and Bryn Mawr had started her out as a medievalist; Connecticut confirmed her as the foremost American literary scholar of the Renaissance. *Elizabethan and Metaphysical Imagery* (1947) was the first successful attempt to deal with Renaissance logic and rhetoric as those subjects impinge on poetic images. It was also the most comprehensive effort of traditional historical criticism to answer the ahistorical premises of the New Criticism.

This concern with the proper understanding of poetic images continued throughout her career. *A Reading of George Herbert* (1952)—which began as a refutation of William Empson's reading of "A Sacrifice"—developed out of Tuve's deep understanding of the ways in which Renaissance readers understood Herbert's images. The same concern for the proprieties and subtleties of Renaissance images informs *Images and Themes in Five Poems by Milton* (1957) and the posthumous *Allegorical Imagery* (1966). These books and numerous articles and reviews established her reputation as learned, judicious, and vivacious.

Connecticut College lacked one thing that Rosemond Tuve grew to know she required: a group of graduate students with whom she could share her learning, and whom she could train as she herself had been trained by her teachers to serve the poets. During her last ten years at Connecticut she held visiting lectureships at Minnesota (1952), Harvard (1956), Aarhus, Denmark (1960), and Princeton (1961). In all of these institutions her formidable learning and unorthodox teaching induced many others to serve the poets in ways that they had not thought possible. She also received a number of awards during these years: an honorary degree with her brother Merle from Augustana College (1952), a Fulbright fellowship to study at

Oxford (1957–58), and a $10,000 prize for extraordinary scholarly achievement from the American Council of Learned Societies (1960).

In 1963 Rosemond Tuve joined the faculty of the University of Pennsylvania. She died the following year in her home at Bryn Mawr of a stroke. Deeply religious, compassionate, humane and jovial, intelligent and learned, she served the Lord and the poets and showed two generations of Renaissance scholars the way, if they had but the patience and perseverance to heed.

[The most complete bibliography of Tuve's writings is in Thomas P. Roche, Jr., ed., *Essays by Rosemond Tuve: Spenser, Herbert, Milton* (1970), which also includes a photograph. Tuve's letters to Thomas Roche, 1960–64, will eventually be placed in the Princeton Univ. Library. Autobiographical information appears in *Twentieth Century Authors, First Supplement* (1955), pp. 1011–12, from which all quotations are taken, and the Vita on pp. 231–32 of her *Seasons and Months*. For further biographical details see *Contemporary Authors: Permanent Series*, I, 637–38, and the brief appreciation by Dorothy Bethurum in "For Members Only," *Publications of the Modern Language Assoc.*, June 1960, p. i. Assistance with research was provided by a biobibliography by Patricia Buck Dominguez. A death record was supplied by Pa. Dept. of Health.]

THOMAS P. ROCHE, JR.

V

VAN BLARCOM, Carolyn Conant, June 12, 1879–March 20, 1960. Nurse, midwife.

Carolyn Van Blarcom was born in Alton, Ill., the second of two daughters and fourth of six children of William Dixon and Fanny (Conant) Van Blarcom. Her father's ancestors were Dutch, her mother's English. Carolyn spent most of her childhood in Alton, where her father, a native of Passaic, N.J., was a financier. He apparently abandoned his family sometime prior to 1893, leaving his wife to care for six growing children. Fanny Van Blarcom, a native of Troy, N.Y., and a fluent linguist and pianist, managed to raise her family in a middle-class fashion despite the absence of her husband.

Most of Carolyn Van Blarcom's early education was informal and conducted at home, where her mother served as her principal teacher. A bout with rheumatic fever at the age of six left her extremely weak and made formal schooling

impracticable; her health was further impaired by the onset of rheumatoid arthritis. These illnesses kept her bedridden for long periods throughout her life.

At the age of fourteen, when her mother died, Van Blarcom went east to live with her grandfather, Alban Jasper Conant, a portrait painter, and other relatives. In 1898, despite the resistance of her family, she enrolled in the prestigious three-year course of study at the Johns Hopkins Hospital Training School for Nurses. Sickness kept her from her assignments for over a year, but she performed so ably that upon her graduation in 1901 she was invited to become a member of the nursing school faculty. For the next four years Van Blarcom served as an instructor in obstetrics and as the assistant superintendent of nurses at the Johns Hopkins Hospital Training School.

Upon leaving Johns Hopkins in 1905, Van Blarcom went to St. Louis, where she helped to reorganize a training school for nurses. Her work was interrupted for three years by her worsening arthritic condition. When her health improved, she accepted the directorship of the Maryland Tuberculosis Sanatorium at Sibillisville. Her success there led to a similar post at a sanatorium near New Bedford, Mass., which she upgraded from a bleak, underequipped clinic to a well-funded and much-emulated hospital. Her organizational ability and executive skills attracted widespread attention, and in 1909 she was appointed secretary of the New York State Committee for the Prevention of Blindness. There she seized the opportunity to play a leading role in investigating the causes of blindness and in educating the public to ways in which it could be prevented.

Van Blarcom found that an eye infection called ophthalmia neonatorum was the leading cause of preventable blindness among newborns. It could almost always be avoided by applying a solution of silver nitrate, but many birth attendants—approximately 50 percent of whom were midwives—were unfamiliar with this relatively simple procedure. This finding prompted Van Blarcom, working with the Committee for the Prevention of Blindness and a grant from the Russell Sage Foundation, to conduct a study of midwifery practices in the United States, England, and fourteen other countries. The results of this investigation, published in Van Blarcom's most important work, *The Midwife in England* (1913), demonstrated that the United States was "the only civilized country in the world" that did not protect its mothers and infants by providing for the training and licensing of midwives.

The book established Van Blarcom as one of the foremost midwife reformers in the United States. She herself was the first American nurse to become a licensed midwife. She wrote articles for medical journals and popular periodicals, addressed health conferences throughout the United States and abroad, and helped establish a midwives' school in affiliation with Bellevue Hospital in New York City. In 1916 she became secretary of the Illinois Society for the Prevention of Blindness, and in World War I was director of the Bureau of Nursing Service of the Atlantic Division of the American Red Cross.

Van Blarcom expanded her efforts in behalf of mothers and infants during the 1920s. She served as health editor for the *Delineator* and published three books. Her textbook *Obstetrical Nursing* (1922) was so popular that it eventually appeared in six editions. A comparable book for the lay person, *Getting Ready to Be a Mother* (1922), went through four editions.

Another work, *Building the Baby*, was published in 1929.

Carolyn Van Blarcom's chronic ill health forced her into retirement during the 1930s. She briefly resumed her career during World War II to direct the nurses' aid training program of the American Red Cross chapter in Pasadena, Calif. Although Van Blarcom was not one to engage in self-pity, she did bemoan the fact that her recurrent illness often hindered her nursing activities. During the post-World War II years, her health further deteriorated. She died in Arcadia, Calif., of bronchopneumonia in 1960.

[Manuscript materials, including letters by Van Blarcom, are located at the Alan Mason Chesney Medical Archives, Johns Hopkins Medical Institutions; at the Inst. of the Hist. of Medicine, Johns Hopkins Univ.; and at the headquarters of the Johns Hopkins Nurses Alumni Assoc., Baltimore. Biographical sketches appear in *Biog. Cyc. Am. Women*, 3 (1928), 228–37; and in Meta Rutter Pennock, *Makers of Nursing History* (1940), which also includes a likeness. Obituaries were published in *Alumnae Mag.*, Johns Hopkins Hospital School of Nursing, Oct. 1960; and in *Am. Jour. Nursing*, June 1960. Assistance was also given by Van Blarcom's niece Eleanor Van Blarcom Hughes. Death certificate was obtained from the Calif. Dept. of Health.]

JUDY BARRETT LITOFF

VAN DOREN, Irita Bradford, March 16, 1891– Dec. 18, 1966. Literary editor.

Irita Van Doren, who directed the *New York Herald Tribune's Book Review* for thirty-seven years, was born in Birmingham, Ala., the oldest of two daughters and two sons of Ida Henley (Brooks) and John Taylor Bradford. Her unusual given name was coined by her mother from Ida and Marguerite. Both parents were of English descent, her father born in Florida, her mother in Alabama. The family moved to Tallahassee, Fla., when Irita was four. Her father, a merchant and owner of a sawmill, was killed by a discharged workman when she was nine; her mother, an accomplished musician and a good cook, then supported the family by giving music lessons and selling preserves. The children helped pare fruit, while one read aloud from Dickens or Trollope. On one occasion Ida Bradford used a small legacy to take her daughters to New York and introduce them to the theater, museums, concerts, and opera, a cultural investment which became a determining influence on Irita's future career.

Irita Bradford graduated from the Florida State College for Women at Tallahassee (later Florida State University) in 1908 at the age of seventeen, and the next year received a master's degree. She then left for New York to pursue doctoral studies in English at Columbia University. There she met Carl Van Doren, who later became a major literary critic and Pulitzer Prize-winning biographer; they were married on Aug. 23, 1912. The Van Dorens had three daughters: Anne (b. 1915), Margaret (b. 1917), and Barbara (b. 1920). They divided their time between New York and an old farm, Wickwire, which they purchased at Cornwall, Conn. The marriage ended in divorce in 1935.

Irita Van Doren joined the editorial staff of *The Nation* in 1919 and became literary editor in 1923. When in 1924 the *New York Herald Tribune* launched a Sunday supplement entitled *Books,* later known as the *Book Review,* the editor, Stuart Sherman, chose her as his assistant. Upon Sherman's death in 1926, Van Doren succeeded him. During the next thirty-seven years, she came to exert a broad cultural influence, not only in New York but across the country, as booksellers followed the *Review*'s reports and bought accordingly. Van Doren drew around her a brilliant group that included her brother-in-law, Mark Van Doren, and such other Columbia lights as Joseph Wood Krutch and John Erskine, as well as writers from the broader literary world, among them Stephen Vincent Benét, Carl Sandburg, and John Gunther. French and English authors—André Maurois, Rebecca West, Virginia Woolf, and Harold J. Laski—were also friends and contributors.

Irita Van Doren helped to shape her times not only because of the post she held but also because of the person she was. She made the *Book Review* "one of the liveliest, best balanced, best written, and most authoritative" of American literary publications. Through her wide acquaintance in the literary world, she convinced famous writers to become contributors, despite the modest fees she could afford to offer. During a career that stretched from the era of GENE STRATTON-PORTER's enormously successful sentimental novels to that of Norman Mailer, Van Doren's editorial policy remained catholic. Books should be appraised, she believed, "from the point of view from which they are written so that they will ultimately find the audience for which they are intended."

Irita Van Doren's literary activities extended beyond her editorship of the *Book Review.* Beginning in 1938, she presided over the Book and Author luncheon series cosponsored by the *Herald Tribune* and the American Booksellers Association and designed to bring together contemporary writers and the reading public. Though many publishers wished to gather Van Doren's informative, incisive introductions of her author-guests into a book, she gently refused, describing herself as the nonwriting Van Doren. She served on the editorial board of *The American Scholar* (1935–66) and on the board of directors of the *Herald Tribune* during the years when the Reid family owned the newspaper. She retired from the *Book Review* in 1963 to become consultant to William Morrow & Co., the publishers.

Outside the publishing world, Irita Van Doren had friends as diverse as Virgil Thomson and Houdini. She assisted her longtime friend, the industrialist and 1940 Republican presidential candidate Wendell Willkie, in the preparation of his speeches and of his influential book, *One World* (1943). She is also said to have counseled him in the phrasing of his letter to President Franklin D. Roosevelt after Pearl Harbor, supporting the administration but stating Willkie's unwillingness to accept a post in it (Barnard, p. 136).

Van Doren received several honors, including the Constance Lindsay Skinner Award in 1942. She was known throughout the writing and publishing field for her personal warmth, her professionalism, and her serene management of her private life. She maintained close relationships with her daughters while supervising two homes and a domestic staff.

Irita Van Doren had sparkling dark eyes, dark hair, later turning gray, and a trim figure which remained youthful. She suffered a stroke in July 1966, rallied, but died five months later in New York of a heart attack. Her ashes, like those of her ex-husband, were scattered at the family home in Cornwall, Conn.

[Irita Van Doren's papers, containing correspondence, manuscripts of speeches, articles, poems, and book reviews, are at the Library of Congress. Mark Van Doren, "Irita Van Doren," an unpublished typescript (n.d.) in the author's possession, is an intimate and affectionate memoir. For biographical facts see *Current Biog.,* 1941, which also includes a portrait. A detailed account of her work as editor appeared in " 'Books' Covers the World of Books," *Publishers Weekly,* Sept. 30, 1939, pp. 1338–47. Printed estimates of her influence include John K. Hutchens, "Irita Van Doren (1891–1966)," *Authors Guild Bull.,* Jan.-Feb. 1967; Maurice Dolbier, "Salutation to an Emeritus," *N.Y. Herald Tribune,* June 9, 1963; and "Irita Van Doren," *Publishers Weekly,* Jan. 2, 1967, p. 39. Van Doren as confidante and adviser to Wendell Willkie is discussed in Ellsworth Barnard, *Wendell Willkie: Fighter for Freedom* (1966), and in Joseph Barnes, *Willkie: The Events He Was Part Of—The Ideas He Fought For* (1952). Obituaries appeared in the *N.Y. Times,* Dec. 19, 1966, and *Publishers Weekly,* Dec. 26, 1966. Additional information came from Louis M. Starr, Jean Stipicevic, and Van Doren's daughters, Margaret Bevans and Barbara Klaw, as well as from personal acquaintance.]

GERALD CARSON

VAN HOOSEN, Bertha, March 26, 1863–June 7, 1952. Surgeon, feminist.

Bertha Van Hoosen, a founder and first president of the American Medical Women's Association, was born on a farm in Stony Creek, Mich., the younger of two daughters of Joshua and Sarah Ann (Taylor) Van Hoosen. Her father, whose parents had migrated from Holland, was a self-made man who lacked formal education. Born in Canada, he had purchased a comfortable homestead in Stony Creek with money earned digging gold in California; soon after he married the daughter of the farm's former owners. Sarah Van Hoosen was a teacher whose grandfather had migrated with his family from New York state in 1823 to pioneer in the Michigan Territory.

Bertha Van Hoosen attended district public schools, graduated from high school in Pontiac, Mich., in 1880, and then entered the literary department of the University of Michigan, as her sister Alice had done. After receiving her A.B. in 1884, she enrolled in Michigan's medical department, despite her mother's objections and her father's consequent refusal to finance her training. She later attributed her choice of career to the independence and the opportunity to "mitigate suffering and save life" that medicine afforded (*Petticoat Surgeon,* p. 55). To pay her way, she did obstetrical nursing, demonstrated classroom anatomy, and taught school. Graduating in 1888, Van Hoosen felt her medical training at Michigan to have been clinically inadequate. She devoted the next four years to clinical residence at the Woman's Hospital in Detroit, the Kalamazoo (Mich.) State Hospital for the Insane, and the New England Hospital for Women and Children in Boston.

Van Hoosen opened a private practice in Chicago in 1892. It developed slowly at first, but she kept active during the lean years by teaching anatomy and embryology at the Woman's Medical School of Northwestern University and by giving public health lectures to such organizations as the Kindergarten Association. Her competence as a physician eventually overcame the handicap of being female, and within five years she had more paying patients than she could handle. She also began to make her mark on Chicago's medical community. After the Woman's Medical School closed in 1902, she became professor of clinical gynecology at the Illinois University Medical School (1902–12), despite strong opposition to the appointment of a woman. She was later named professor and head of obstetrics at Loyola University Medical School (1918–37), thus becoming the first woman to head a medical division at a coeducational university. She attended at several Chicago hospitals, and in 1913 became chief of the gynecological staff at Cook County Hospital, the first time a woman physician received a civil service appointment; in 1920 she also became chief of the obstetrical staff there.

Throughout her career, Bertha Van Hoosen devoted herself to women's health concerns. Although a brilliant general surgeon, like many women physicians of her generation she was particularly interested in obstetrics and treated mostly women and children. She helped develop better methods of prenatal care and in 1930 established the first human breast milk bank in Chicago. An enthusiastic feminist, she lectured for many years on sex education to the Committee on Social Purity of the Chicago Woman's Club.

Van Hoosen also pioneered in the use of scopolamine-morphine anesthesia in childbirth. Known as twilight sleep, the popular German method became a cause célèbre for some American feminists who demanded in 1914 that physicians recognize the right of every woman to choose painless delivery. Van Hoosen, who had been experimenting with the method since 1904, considered it "the greatest boon the Twentieth Century could give to women." She was in a minority among her medical colleagues, many of whom considered twilight sleep unsafe, but by 1908 she had delivered 2,000 healthy babies with the help of scopolamine, and later published her research in a book, *Scopolamine-Morphine Anaesthesia* (1915), and two articles.

Van Hoosen, who confessed to the ambition of being "as good a doctor as the best man," did much to advance the position of women in medicine. She trained over twenty women surgeons, many of whom served as missionaries in China, and were proud to be considered her "surgical daughters." A peppery perfectionist, this small outspoken woman with flaming red hair and a temper and sense of humor to match had a profound impact on medical students, especially women, who found her a demanding but inspiring teacher. Van Hoosen also assisted other women physicians, traveling as far as Detroit to consult with and perform operations for nonsurgical colleagues.

As her medical career advanced, Van Hoosen became increasingly irritated by her anomalous position as a woman physician in relation to her male colleagues. She smarted at the fact that the Chicago Gynecological and Obstetrical Society still barred women members, and felt isolated at

American Medical Association conventions. Consequently, in 1915 she called a meeting of Chicago medical women which led to the formation of the American Medical Women's Association (AMWA). As the first president of AMWA, she fought unsuccessfully for the right of women physicians to serve in the armed forces during World War I. Although many of her colleagues were suspicious of separatism, Van Hoosen remained convinced that a woman's organization was a necessity as long as women physicians experienced discrimination. Over the years she served the AMWA in numerous capacities.

Though she never married, Bertha Van Hoosen found a family in her widowed sister Alice and her beloved niece, Sarah Van Hoosen Jones, whom she treated like a daughter. Despite their early objections to her choice of medicine, her parents later gave her support. Always vibrant and full of energy, she performed her last operation in 1951 at the age of eighty-eight. She died a year later of a stroke at a convalescent home in Romeo, Mich.

[The Bentley Historical Library, Univ. of Michigan, has correspondence, diaries, and clippings on Van Hoosen's years at the Univ. of Michigan and on her professional activities, and correspondence with her sister and niece. The AMWA Coll., Cornell Univ. Archives, has numerous references to her, and the Chicago Hist. Soc. has some newspaper and magazine clippings on her public career. A reference to her dissatisfying term as resident physician at the New England Hospital is in the New England Hospital MSS. in the Sophia Smith Coll. at Smith College. Van Hoosen's autobiography, *Petticoat Surgeon* (1947) is the best source of information on her career and private life. Her articles on twilight sleep are "The New Movement in Obstetrics," *Woman's Med. Jour.*, June 1915, pp. 121–23, and "Scopolamin Anesthesia in Obstetrics," *Current Research in Anesthesia and Analgesia*, May-June 1928, pp. 151–54. She also wrote a short history of AMWA, "Looking Backward," *Jour. Am. Med. Women's Assoc.* (JAMWA), Oct. 1950, pp. 406–08. Tributes include Mabel E. Gardner, "Bertha Van Hoosen, M.D.," *JAMWA*, Oct. 1950, pp. 413–14 (with photograph); Rose V. Menendian, "Bertha Van Hoosen: A Surgical Daughter's Impressions," *JAMWA*, April 1965, pp. 349–50; and "Bertha Van Hoosen, M.D. (1863–1952)," *JAMWA*, July 1963, pp. 533–43. A death record was provided by Mich. Dept. of Health.]

REGINA MARKELL MORANTZ

VAN KLEECK, Mary Abby, June 26, 1883– June 8, 1972. Social researcher and reformer.

Mary Abby van Kleeck was born in Glenham, N.Y., the second daughter and youngest of three children of the Reverend Robert Boyd and Eliza (Mayer) Van Kleeck. Her mother was the daughter of a founder of the Baltimore and Ohio Railroad; her father, an Episcopal minister of Dutch ancestry, came from a family of clergymen. A member of the National Society of Colonial Dames, Mary Van Kleeck—she later changed the capitalization of her last name—was proud of her Dutch heritage. After her father's death in 1892, the family moved to Flushing, N.Y., where Mary was educated in public schools. Graduating from Flushing High School in 1900, she went on to Smith College and received her A.B. in 1904.

The following year the socially conscious minister's daughter began her long and influential career as a social investigator. As a fellow of the College Settlements Association, she conducted research on girls in New York City factories and child labor in tenements (1905–06) and then, as industrial secretary of the Alliance Employment Bureau, began her investigations of women's employment. The Russell Sage Foundation, which had supported her studies since 1908, made them an integral part of its committee on women's work established in November 1910. From these beginnings came the foundation's department of industrial studies, which, except for the brief period 1918–19, van Kleeck served as director until she retired in 1948.

The department functioned from the start as a research rather than a propaganda agency. But, like other Progressives, van Kleeck believed that the facts, once publicized, would provide the essential impetus for action. Her own research led to a series of pioneering studies, including *Artificial Flower Makers* (1913), *Women in the Bookbinding Trade* (1913), and *Wages in the Millinery Trade* (1914). Her work, and that of her collaborators—some of them her students at the New York School of Philanthropy, where she taught from 1914 to 1917— influenced judicial opinion and helped shape protective legislation. A tireless perfectionist, van Kleeck testified at committee hearings, worked closely with public and private agencies, and served on Mayor John Purroy Mitchel's Committee on Unemployment in 1915. Concerned about the economic opportunities of middle- as well as working-class women, she served as president of the Intercollegiate Bureau of Occupations, an organization designed to help women find work in fields other than teaching.

As one of the nation's leading experts on women's employment, Mary van Kleeck became an influential figure in Washington, D.C., during World War I. After earlier advisory work, she joined the army's Ordnance Department at the beginning of 1918 as director of the women's branch of its industrial service section. There she drew up standards for the employment of women in war industries that were ultimately adopted by the War Labor Policies Board. (She was herself a member of the Board, 1918–19.) With strong endorsement from the Women's Trade Union League, van Kleeck was appointed director of the women in industry service, set up in the Department of Labor in July 1918. Gathering information by field visits, negotiating with employers and with other government agencies, the service sought to avoid or correct substandard conditions of employment. It was perhaps most important as the forerunner of the permanent, peacetime Women's Bureau. When van Kleeck resigned her post after a year, her assistant director, MARY ANDERSON, succeeded her.

Returning to the Russell Sage Foundation in 1919, van Kleeck led the department of industrial studies in new directions. The department had already begun to focus on broad issues of labor and unemployment that affected men as well as women. After the war it turned to the experiments in employer-employee relations—the operation of company unions, wage earners' participation in management, and other plans—then taking place throughout the country. The department also developed an interest in unemployment statistics, and during the twenties and thirties investigated the economic roots of insecurity and the causes of workers' dissatisfaction, notably in the coal industry. Throughout this period, van Kleeck kept up her interest in matters concerning women's employment, remaining in close touch with the Women's Bureau. Like other reformers of her generation, she opposed the Equal Rights Amendment which she feared would undo protective legislation for women.

A woman of great intelligence, van Kleeck commanded attention whenever and wherever she spoke. As a sought-after member of government committees, she served on the President's Conference on Unemployment (1921) and Committee on Unemployment and Business Cycles (1922–23). Her humanitarian interests were broad: she chaired the executive committee that established the National Interracial Conference held in Washington (1928), helped to draft a report to the International Labor Organization on the economic position of women (1936), and was a member of the executive committee of Hospites, a relief organization that offered employment and financial aid to refugees from Nazi Germany in the mid-1930s. Van Kleeck remained active in the field of social work in the United States and abroad, lecturing at the Smith College School of Social

Work in the 1920s, and serving as president of the Second International Conference of Social Work, Frankfurt-am-Main, in 1932. She was also a trustee of Smith College from 1922 to 1930.

The urgencies of World War I and the depression, together with a strong Episcopal faith that led her to Christian socialism, changed van Kleeck from a Progressive-style moral reformer, interested in alleviating working conditions for women, into a bold social critic. The change was dramatically illustrated during the early days of the New Deal. When FRANCES PERKINS appointed her to the Federal Advisory Council of the United States Employment Service in August 1933, van Kleeck resigned after one day, citing her objections to New Deal policies that she believed weakened labor unions, gave increased power to monopolies, and failed to recognize the right of workers to bargain collectively.

By this time she had come to believe that a fundamental reconstruction of American society was necessary. In *Miners and Management* (1934), a study of union-management cooperation in the Rocky Mountain Fuel Company owned by Josephine Roche (1886–1976), van Kleeck advocated socialization of all industry. Collective ownership would, she believed, set free not only the workers but also the rest of society, and would be wholly in keeping with a democratic political system. In *Creative America* (1936), a synthesis of her political and social views, she argued strongly against private ownership of the means of production. Her proposals for accomplishing change were not extreme, however. Rather, she continued to argue for a strong labor movement and an economic base of modified collectivism.

Believing that economic crises were worldwide and interlocking, van Kleeck became increasingly involved in international affairs. As associate director of the International Industrial Relations Institute from 1928 to 1948, she organized and participated in conferences designed to further international economic cooperation and to use social and economic planning to improve the world's productive capacity. With Mary L. Fleddérus, director of the Institute and a close friend who joined the department of industrial studies in 1937, van Kleeck wrote *Technology and Livelihood* (1944), an analysis of changes in labor requirements and employment opportunities growing out of technological developments.

Stirred by the commitment of Soviet socialism to common ownership and the elimination of private profit, van Kleeck joined Soviet-American friendship societies and traveled to the

Soviet Union. Beginning in the early thirties, she defended Soviet foreign policy, advocated five-year plans for the United States, and contributed articles praising Soviet society to the *Daily Worker, Soviet Russia Today,* and *New Masses.* In the decades that followed, she maintained her loyalty to the ideals of Soviet socialism.

Van Kleeck continued to write and lecture in the 1940s and developed new interests in community organization, disarmament, and the peacetime use of atomic energy. In 1948, after forty years, she retired from the Russell Sage Foundation. That year she supported the presidential campaign of Henry A. Wallace and herself ran unsuccessfully for the New York state senate as the candidate of the American Labor party. Her radical sympathies led to a subpoena in March 1953 from the Senate Permanent Subcommittee on Investigations, chaired by Joseph McCarthy.

A woman of great integrity with a keen and penetrating mind, Mary van Kleeck possessed considerable human sympathy and great determination to improve conditions for working people. Her sense of a Christian duty to promote progressive social change found expression in lifelong affiliation with the Episcopal League for Social Action, social service arm of the Episcopal church, and with the Church League for Industrial Democracy. She was also a member of the Society of the Companions of the Holy Cross, the Episcopal organization of women devoted to contemplation and to the study of social issues.

Van Kleeck retired to Woodstock, N.Y. In 1972, shortly before her eighty-ninth birthday, she died in Kingston, N.Y., of a heart attack.

[The papers of Mary van Kleeck, including clippings, addresses, articles, industrial studies, and scrapbooks, are in the Sophia Smith Coll., Smith College. Additional material is in the Archives of Labor History and Urban Affairs of Wayne State Univ. and in the Nat. Archives, Social and Industrial Branch. Van Kleeck's publications include: "Working Hours of Women in Factories," *Charities and the Commons,* Oct. 6, 1906; "Child Labor in New York City Tenements," *Charities and the Commons,* Jan. 18, 1908; *Working Girls in Evening Schools* (1914); and *A Seasonal Industry* (1917), as well as her investigations and those she directed, which are published by the Russell Sage Foundation. She collaborated in the preparation of Charles S. Johnson, *The Negro in American Civilization* (1930). Details about her personal life are scarce; see her entry in *Who's Who in America,* 1972–73. Information concerning her career may be found in John M. Glenn, Lilian Brandt, F. Emerson Andrews, *Russell Sage Foundation 1907–1946,* 2 vols. (1947), and in Mary Anderson, *Woman at Work* (1951), writ-

ten with Mary Winslow. An obituary appeared in the *N.Y. Times,* June 10, 1972; death certificate was supplied by N.Y. State Dept. of Health.]

ELEANOR MIDMAN LEWIS

VAN WATERS, Miriam, Oct. 4, 1887–Jan. 17, 1974. Penologist, social worker.

Miriam Van Waters, the leading figure in female corrections from the 1920s through the 1940s, was born in Greensburg, Pa., the second of four daughters and five children of George Browne and Maude (Vosburg) Van Waters. (The eldest daughter died in infancy.) In 1888 George Van Waters, an Episcopal minister who preached a vigorous social gospel, moved his family to Portland, Oreg., and began church colonization work throughout the northwest. An adventurous child, Miriam once got up in the middle of the night to join a cougar hunt. She received a classical education at home and then at St. Helen's Hall, a local school begun by her father, from which she graduated in 1904. As a teenager, she assumed significant responsibilities at home because of her father's pastoral absences and the prolonged trips to Pennsylvania of her homesick mother. Aided by two uncles, she cared for her sometimes rebellious sisters, managed the rectory, and attended to visiting clergymen. But she was often lonely, once writing her mother: "We have so little home life."

Van Waters continued her active pace at the University of Oregon, where she founded and edited a literary magazine, wrote for the college newspaper, and participated in dramatic productions. She graduated with honors in philosophy in 1908 and two years later earned an A.M. degree in psychology. Encouraged by her Oregon professors, Van Waters applied for a fellowship at Clark University in Worcester, Mass., then headed by the psychologist G. Stanley Hall. She received the award but soon encountered difficulty working with Hall, refusing to use data on female delinquency to confirm Hall's recapitulation theory. (He maintained that repeated delinquent behavior meant that an individual's development was mired in a "primitive" period of history.) After this clash Van Waters continued her work with anthropologist Alexander Chamberlain and received her Ph.D. in 1913. Her dissertation, "The Adolescent Girl Among Primitive Peoples," anticipated the work of RUTH BENEDICT and Margaret Mead (1901–1978) in its appreciation of diverse cultures and awareness of the force and legitimacy of female sexuality.

Even before she began her dissertation, Miriam Van Waters had shown more interest in reform movements than in an academic career.

In 1911 she visited Judge Harvey H. Baker's Boston Juvenile Court, observing the results of parent neglect and inadequate educational and recreational facilities, and two years later she was appointed an agent of the Boston Children's Aid Society, in charge of young girls appearing before the court. Here she became aware of the special burdens of female delinquents, most of whom were charged with sexual offenses and, under the prevailing Victorian code, were assumed to be "morally insane" and incapable of rehabilitation. Van Waters challenged this view by improving court health care services and by vigorously seeking foster homes for her charges. Her reputation flourished but the effort exhausted her, and in 1914 she returned to Portland to head Frazer Hall, the county juvenile detention center. Her work had just begun when she learned she had tuberculosis; her career was interrupted for three years.

During her recovery, Van Waters visited college friends in Los Angeles. There, in 1917, she passed a civil service examination and was appointed superintendent of the county juvenile home. Her success in improving conditions at the home led in 1919 to a supplementary appointment to head El Retiro, an experimental county home for delinquent girls, which she called a "preventorium." The routine was distinguished by a degree of inmate self-government, by the payment of wages to inmates, and by the availability of choice of vocational training. A halfway house donated by the Los Angeles Businesswomen's Club aided the transition from the home to jobs. As in her subsequent work, Van Waters tried to give the girls a sense of belonging and infused institutional life with emotional intensity through dramatic productions, poetry readings, and celebrations of birthdays, holidays, and graduations. She also criticized the judicial double standard which penalized women more severely than men for sex offenses. Her distinctive influence, however, derived from her close identification with the rebellious young women whose sexuality she sought to justify and guide rather than suppress.

Van Waters's work at El Retiro attracted the attention of Chicago philanthropist ETHEL STURGES DUMMER, who provided her with funds to complete a national study of schools for delinquent girls. In "Where Girls Go Right," published in *Survey Graphic* in 1922, she praised institutions that met United States Children's Bureau standards for humane care and condemned schools practicing corporal punishment. With Dummer's continued aid, she wrote two books, *Youth in Conflict* (1925) and *Parents on Probation* (1927), in which she related delin-

quency to adult enthusiasm for mechanized civilization.

In 1920 Miriam Van Waters passed the California bar exam and was appointed referee of the Los Angeles Juvenile Court. This job provided professional visibility and her dynamic speeches at penal and social work conventions further enhanced her reputation. In 1927 Felix Frankfurter invited her to evaluate juvenile facilities in Boston for the Harvard Law School Crime Survey. Two years later she was appointed a consultant to the National Commission on Law Observance and Enforcement (the Wickersham Commission), for which she prepared a study of juvenile offenders against federal law. In *The Child Offender in the Federal System of Justice* (1932) she condemned the failure of district courts to utilize juvenile court procedures or to supervise juvenile reformatories.

Stimulated by the social and intellectual life in Cambridge, Van Waters seized the opportunity to succeed the late JESSIE HODDER in 1932 as superintendent of the Massachusetts Women's Reformatory at Framingham. There Van Waters carried on Hodder's liberal policies of conditional release and day service indenturing and, like Hodder, permitted some inmates to keep their children in the institution's nursery. She also increased medical and psychological services and added a distinctive touch by organizing numerous clubs for inmates, whom she preferred to call students. The clubs reflected Van Waters's emphasis upon self-government as well as her acceptance of prevalent social divisions; black prisoners, for example, had their own club. In the 1930s and 1940s, however, the Framingham institution was considered avant-garde. Miriam Van Waters, enjoying the support of Gov. Leverett Saltonstall and Commissioner of Corrections Francis Sayre, was at the peak of her career.

She also continued to play the leading role within her family. When her father's investments failed, she contributed to the education and support of her siblings. Her brother Ralph and his wife Bertha held various jobs at Framingham, and her mother lived there after she was widowed. Attractive and vivacious, Miriam Van Waters had a number of suitors, but never married. In 1932 she adopted a child, Sarah Ann (b. 1922), whom she had first met as a seven-year-old ward of the Los Angeles Juvenile Court. Sarah Ann Van Waters, who married young, had three children, and was divorced in 1949, had a troubled life. She was killed in an automobile accident in 1953.

On Nov. 10, 1947, Miriam Van Waters's life changed abruptly when an Italian prisoner from

Boston's North End committed suicide at Framingham. Commissioner of Corrections Elliott McDowell, under pressure from the Hearst press (always critical of Van Waters for her opposition to capital punishment), conducted a lengthy series of investigations. He charged her with condoning lesbianism, illegally permitting ex-inmates to become institution employees, and failing to supervise indenture for day work or adult education. In January 1949 McDowell fired Van Waters, but a special governor's commission reversed his decision. Her defense was publicized and paid for by the Friends of Framingham, which rallied supporters of liberal penology, and by her friends throughout the nation. At the crowded and dramatic final hearings, the group's lawyer disproved most of McDowell's charges.

Van Waters returned to Framingham to be emotionally welcomed by the inmate choir singing the "Te Deum." She remained superintendent until 1957, reaping plaudits for her defense of liberal penological principles and receiving several honorary degrees. The reformatory program itself was much reduced. Under pressure from the department of corrections, the nursery was phased out, day work severely curtailed, and visits by former inmates forbidden.

In her later years Miriam Van Waters reaffirmed her beliefs in speeches and articles and in 1963 she began to write a book entitled "Redemption in Prison." Until her death of pulmonary disease in 1974, she continued to live in Framingham, not far from the reformatory.

[The Miriam Van Waters Papers in the Schlesinger Library, Radcliffe College, contain personal and professional correspondence and drafts of articles and speeches, and of "Redemption in Prison." Related collections are the Ethel Sturges Dummer Papers and the Friends of the Framingham Reformatory Papers, also in the Schlesinger Library. Information about Van Waters's work for the Boston Crime Survey and for the Wickersham Commission is in the archives of the Harvard Law School. She wrote many articles and book reviews, the most distinguished of which are "Adolescence," *Encyc. Social Sciences*, vol. I (1930); "Juvenile Delinquency and Juvenile Courts," *Encyc. Social Sciences*, vol. VIII (1932); "Philosophical Trends in Modern Social Work," Nat. Conference of Social Work, *Proceedings*, 1930. The only published biography, Burton J. Rowles, *The Lady at Box 99* (1959), is entertaining but hagiographic. Janet T. St. Goar, "Extending the Boundaries: Miriam Van Waters, Superintendent of the Massachusetts Reformatory for Women, 1932–1958" (B.A. honors thesis, Harvard Univ., 1978), is a more serious study. See also *Current Biog.*, 1963. Obituaries appeared in the *N.Y. Times*, Jan. 18, 1974, and *Boston Globe*, Jan. 19, 1974.

Additional information for this article was provided by Mason Wilson and Kathleen Marquis. Death certificate supplied by Mass. Dept. of Public Health.]

ROBERT M. MENNEL

VERNON, Mabel, Sept. 10, 1883–Sept. 2, 1975. Suffragist, feminist, pacifist.

Mabel Vernon, tireless fund raiser, organizer, and speaker for the causes of women's rights and world peace, was born in Wilmington, Del., the youngest of seven children of George Washington and Mary (Hooten) Vernon. She had five brothers and one sister; four half brothers and one half sister from her father's first marriage also lived in Wilmington. Her father, whose family had migrated to America from Wales in the eighteenth century, was the editor and publisher of the *Wilmington Daily Republican* until his death in 1901. He was of Quaker background, but the family worshipped at a Presbyterian church. Mabel Vernon attended the small, private Miss Bigger's School and graduated from the Wilmington Friends School in 1901, returning there to study German after a month at Smith College. She entered Swarthmore College in 1903 and earned her A.B. in 1906.

At Swarthmore Vernon met Alice Paul (1885–1977), a fellow student, and it was this friendship that later focused her interest in women's rights. To support herself after college, Vernon taught German and Latin at Radnor High School in Wayne, Pa. Meanwhile her interest in the suffrage movement was already growing, and she served as an usher at the Philadelphia National American Woman Suffrage Association (NAWSA) convention in 1912. When Paul asked her to work as a suffrage organizer in 1913, Vernon left teaching and, working for a small salary, devoted full time to the cause. She brought to it the skills developed as an award-winning college debater, and she became the first national suffrage organizer for NAWSA's militant offshoot, the Congressional Union for Woman Suffrage, which in 1917 merged with the National Woman's party (NWP). In 1914 Vernon was sent to Nevada to work with ANNE MARTIN in the campaign for ratification of that state's suffrage amendment. The next year she arranged SARA BARD FIELD's transcontinental auto campaign for woman suffrage.

Vernon is credited with one of the first acts of militancy of the suffragists' campaign, interrupting President Woodrow Wilson in a Washington, D.C., speech of July 4, 1916. She was a vocal member of a small commission that met with Wilson in May 1917 to demand support for a federal suffrage amendment. That same year she picketed the White House and was among the first suffragists to be sent to prison. She spent three days in the District of Columbia jail, and after her release traveled through the midwestern and northwestern states to explain the NWP actions to the public.

Vernon's activities in this period were as varied as her interests. She served as campaign manager for the 1918 and 1920 senatorial campaigns of Anne Martin, and, after passage of the suffrage amendment by Congress in 1919, spoke out for its ratification. For a time she left political activity, acting as superintendent for the Swarthmore Chautauqua, organizing meetings and lecturing on feminism. In 1923 she returned to school and earned her A.M. in political science from Columbia University (1924). But women's rights continued to engage her, and in 1924–25 she traveled across the country supporting women candidates for Congress. She then returned to the NWP as executive secretary to work for the Equal Rights Amendment. In what was considered her most impressive speech, she championed the NWP's unsuccessful membership bid at the Tenth Congress of the International Woman Suffrage Alliance in Paris (1926).

In 1930 Vernon joined the Women's International League for Peace and Freedom (WILPF), moving on from the NWP to devote herself to the causes that would become her life's work: peace and disarmament. As campaign manager, she organized a transcontinental Peace Caravan in 1931, gathering signatures for petitions to be presented at the 1932 World Disarmament Conference in Geneva. She represented the United States at the WILPF conferences in Zurich in 1934 and in Geneva in 1935. Vernon also acted as campaign director in 1935 for the Peoples Mandate to End War, a committee of the WILPF which stressed a worldwide campaign for peace. By 1944 Vernon had come to focus her efforts specifically on Latin America. She served as director of the renamed Peoples Mandate Committee for Inter-American Peace and Cooperation, and chaired the committee from 1950 until her retirement in 1955.

Vernon applied the methods used in the suffrage fight to the cause of peace, often working behind the scenes to raise money and organize petition drives. She led the United States delegation of the Peoples Mandate to the Inter-American Conference for the Maintenance of Peace in 1936 in Buenos Aires, spoke at the Pan American Conference at Lima in 1938, and was a member of the Inter-American delegation at the founding of the United Nations in San Francisco in 1945. In 1942 she was awarded the Diploma de Honor by the Ecuadorean Red Cross and in 1944 received the Al Merito from Ecuador in recognition of her longtime commitment to peace.

Vernon shared her Washington, D.C., apartment with Consuelo Reyes-Calderon, a close friend and Peoples Mandate colleague, from 1951 until her death there in 1975 of arteriosclerotic heart disease. She was remembered—and often praised during her lifetime—as an articulate speaker with a strong and resonant voice, and as a successful fund raiser. Above all, it was her political acumen—reflected in endless canvassing, petitioning, lobbying, even picketing when necessary—which made Mabel Vernon an effective as well as loyal and energetic advocate of equality and peace.

[The Anne Martin Coll., at the Bancroft Library, Univ. of Calif., Berkeley, contains the Mabel Vernon correspondence, 1914–20, as well as an excellent file of clippings on suffrage and on Martin's senatorial campaigns. Information about Vernon's activities with the WILPF and the Peoples Mandate can be found in the Swarthmore College Peace Coll. The most valuable source on Vernon's life and career is her own oral history, *Speaker for Suffrage and Petitioner for Peace* (1976), taken in 1972 and 1973 by the Regional Oral Hist. Office, Univ. of Calif., Berkeley. The appendix of the oral history contains newspaper articles, photographs, information on the WILPF and the Peoples Mandate, and a transcription of the memorial service for Vernon. It also contains her article, "A Suffragist Recounts the Hard-Won Victory," which appeared in the *Am. Assoc. of Univ. Women Jour.*, April 1972. Oral histories of Alice Paul and Rebecca Hourwich Reyher at the Berkeley Regional Oral. Hist. Office contain additional information on Vernon. See Blanche Wiesen Cook, ed., *Crystal Eastman: On Women and Revolution* (1978) for Vernon's speech at the 1926 Congress of the Internat. Woman Suffrage Alliance. Inez Haynes Irwin, *Story of the Woman's Party* (1921), and Doris Stevens, *Jailed for Freedom* (1920, 1976) provide useful information about Vernon's suffrage work. An obituary appeared in the *Wash. Post*, Sept. 4, 1975. Birth order information from 1880 and 1900 U.S. Census. Death certificate supplied by D.C. Dept. of Human Resources.]

LUCY EVE KERMAN

VON MISES, Hilda. *See* GEIRINGER, Hilda.

VORSE, Mary Heaton, Oct. 9, 1874–June 14, 1966. Journalist, writer.

Mary Heaton Vorse was born in New York City into comfort and the expectation of social position; she became an ardent champion of labor and a vivid example of the arduous life of the working writer. Her father, Hiram Heaton, from an old New England family, had owned the Red Lion Inn in Stockbridge, Mass. Her mother, Ellen (Blackman), also had five considerably older children by an earlier marriage; her ancestors had come from England to New England in 1635. Mary was the Heatons' only child. Retired while his daughter was growing up, Hiram Heaton provided his family with a comfortable income based partly on his wife's real estate holdings in California. They spent the summers in Amherst, Mass., and many winters in Europe, where Mary Heaton attended school and was tutored by her mother. At sixteen, she went for a time to Paris to study art; her sketchbooks reveal a competent if derivative style.

In 1898, Mary Heaton married Albert White Vorse, a boat-loving explorer and writer. They lived in Europe and in New York, where their children were born: Heaton in 1901 and Ellen in 1907. Mary Heaton Vorse's first book, *The Breaking In of a Yachtsman's Wife*, appeared in 1908.

The year before, Mary and Albert Vorse had bought the seventeenth-century Captain Kibbee house in Provincetown, Mass. It became a centrally important place for her. In *Time and the Town* (1942), she described her symbiotic relationship with the house; later, in her eighties, writing many lists of the activities of sixty years, she noted with sorrow the many months of every year that she had to spend away from home. Vorse also discovered Provincetown for other New York writers. Because of her enthusiasm, Hutchins Hapgood and his wife, Neith Boyce, came there, as well as SUSAN GLASPELL, George Cram Cook, and Max Eastman, the group that was to become the nucleus of the original Provincetown Players. It was on the Vorse wharf that the first company production was given, and Mary Vorse remained a godmother to the several theater groups which carried on the Players' name.

Vorse's secure world of family and friends fell apart in 1910: in one day her husband and her mother died. She had much admired her brisk and remarkable mother, and vividly captured Ellen Heaton's refusal to let her children make her old in what is perhaps her best book, *Autobiography of an Elderly Woman* (1911, 1974). Unable to depend on her father, who had lost most of his income as a result of the 1906 California earthquake, Vorse turned to her writing as a source of support. She had for some time been writing stories in the vein of *Stories of the Very Little Person* (1911), warm, comic tales of her daughter, and she knew that stories about marriage and children always found a ready market. Vorse later said that her involvement in the cause of labor had its source in her anger and

concern over the miserable lives led by workers' children.

It was that interest which brought Vorse to Lawrence, Mass., during the 1912 textile mill strike. Investigating the disappearance of a trainload of food designated for striking workers' children, she discovered the appalling living conditions of mill families. Her anger was transformed into a lifelong commitment to labor, a commitment deepened by her association with the radical journalist Joseph O'Brien, with whom she covered the Lawrence strike. There they joined ELIZABETH GURLEY FLYNN (who remained a lifelong friend), Big Bill Haywood, and Carlo Tresca in demanding a political solution to the continuing oppression of labor. Vorse chose not to join a radical political party, however, maintaining a fiercely partisan support of labor without the confines of a political ideology.

Vorse and O'Brien were married in 1912; their son, Joel, was born in January 1914. Their passionate and intense marriage ended with his death in 1915, shortly after Vorse returned from Europe, where she attended the peace-seeking international congress of women at The Hague and wrote of the misery of war. Mary Heaton Vorse (she retained that name for professional purposes) married again in 1920, but divorced two years later. Her third husband, Robert Minor, a cartoonist, was secretary of the Communist party of the United States. She returned to Europe in 1918–19, partly on a Red Cross assignment, to record the aftermath of war, and went to the Soviet Union in 1921 and 1922, reporting on the Russian famine for the Hearst papers.

Living in Provincetown, she resided in New York when on assignment, leaving her children at home in the charge of a governess. When Vorse was at home, she devoted every morning to writing—in bed—and tolerated no interruption. Her schedule often annoyed her children, but writing was a matter of family survival. During the late 1920s and 1930s, Heaton Vorse became her frequent companion in covering labor uprisings.

Mary Heaton Vorse was a continuous presence during the great labor struggles from Lawrence in 1912 through the Chrysler strike of 1950. Her books and articles in such periodicals as *Harper's Magazine, The Nation,* and *The New Republic* provide a history of the evolution of labor militancy. In the early days, when unions pitted themselves against management in a fierce battle to exist, she reported on the mass unemployment in New York in the winter of 1914, the strike by metal miners of Minnesota's Mesabi Range in 1916, and the attempts to murder the leaders of the Industrial Workers of the World (IWW). Her book *Men and Steel* (1920) gives a vividly detailed picture of the great steel strike of 1919–20. There is anger and compassion in her work on striking textile workers in Passaic, N.J., and in the 1930 novel *Strike!*, a thinly fictionalized account of the textile strike in Gastonia, N.C., where she was accredited as an organizer of the Amalgamated Clothing Workers of America.

During the 1930s, Vorse's writings mirror a change in working-class protest, with workers' demands focusing, after passage of the Wagner Act, on a decent wage. Vorse was on the scene in Flint, Mich., in 1937 where she supported the striking auto workers and with JOSEPHINE HERBST wrote a living newspaper to dramatize the protest of the sitdown strikers. Violence directed at strikers had not abated, however. That same year, in Muncie, Ind., Heaton Vorse was wounded while covering the steel strike. Almost immediately afterward, while Mary Vorse was standing on a women's picket line in Youngstown, she received a grazing wound from a policeman's bullet.

That type of armed struggle ended with World War II, and Vorse reported that the business community was coming to recognize that the economic benefits of high wages and contented workers were good for the economy. She was particularly impressed by the skill of Walter Reuther and the United Auto Workers (UAW) in meeting the needs of union members by cooperating with the community. Returning to Youngstown in 1949 to report on the steelworkers' strike for old age pensions, Vorse described it as "a restrained, almost a puritanical strike," supported, in the name of the town's prosperity, by merchants, real estate agents, and even policemen. A 1953 *Nation* article on the "State of the Unions" described joint management-labor support of better working conditions, higher wages, and old age insurance. "American labor," she commented, "has swung away from its old ideas of a class struggle almost without realizing it."

Still active as a journalist in her late seventies, in 1952 Mary Heaton Vorse reasserted her view that to be prolabor was not necessarily to be prounion when she exposed the corruption rampant along New York's waterfront. Attacking the longshoremen's union for cooperating with stevedore companies in an illegal hiring system, she applauded the wildcat strikes along the waterfront, as workers attempted to cast off their corrupt union.

Never free, according to her friend Dorothy Day, of the need to help "support her children and even her children's children" (Day, p. 158), Vorse continued to turn out occasional pieces and to write fiction, the domestic romances which she called "lollipops." Known among her friends as a wit, she wrote several humorous pieces and she published a number of travel articles. In 1939 she had traveled to Europe, reporting on the Sudeten Germans of Czechoslovakia, the German invasion of Poland, and Paris immediately before the occupation. From 1945 to 1947, she returned to Europe on a hard-won assignment from the United Nations Relief and Rehabilitation Administration. She had worked as a publicist for the National Consumers' League in the 1920s, and for the Bureau of Indian Affairs in the mid-1930s (as an editor on *Indians at Work*); she began a history of the Massachusetts Consumers' League in the 1950s.

Although ill health curtailed some of her activities in the 1960s, she was able to accept the United Auto Workers' Social Justice Award in 1962. She died four years later at her home in Provincetown. Mary Heaton Vorse's significance in her lifetime is at interesting odds with her later obscurity. Working as she did on the edges of many histories—literary, theatrical, radical, labor—she fell from view once she no longer had a by-line.

[The extensive collection of Vorse's papers at the Archives of Labor History and Urban Affairs, Wayne State Univ., Detroit, contains personal and business correspondence, clippings, drafts and MSS., and various documents and autobiographical jottings. Papers relating to her work with the Mass. Consumers' League are at the Schlesinger Library, Radcliffe College. *The Reminiscences of Mary Heaton Vorse* (1957) are in the Oral History Coll., Columbia Univ. Vorse's books on labor also include *Labor's New Millions* (1938, 1969). She published more than 190 short stories between 1905 and 1942 in such magazines as *Woman's Home Companion, Good Housekeeping, Everybody's Mag., McClure's, Atlantic Monthly, Harper's Monthly Mag.* (later *Harper's Mag.*), and the *New Yorker*. An extensive list of her publications appears in an excellent bio-bibliography prepared by Rusty Byrne. Biographical material is scarce. There is an enthusiastic chapter, "The Rebel Girl," in Murray Kempton, *Part of Our Time: Some Ruins and Monuments* (1955), and reminiscences of her in Dorothy Day, *The Long Loneliness* (1952), pp. 158–60. Entries on Vorse appear in *Twentieth Century Authors* (1942) and *First Supplement* (1955). An obituary appeared in the *N.Y. Times*, June 15, 1966. Further information provided by Beatrix Faust, Miriam De Witt, and Catherine Huntington. Vorse's birth date frequently appears as 1881. The 1874 date is confirmed by the Archives of Labor History and Urban Affairs and by the 1880 U.S. Census. A death certificate was obtained from the Mass. Dept. of Public Health.]

LESLIE GOULD
CAROL HURD GREEN

W

WALDO, Ruth Fanshaw, Dec. 8, 1885–Aug. 30, 1975. Advertising executive.

Ruth Waldo, a leader in the advertising business in an era of tremendous growth, was born and reared on a farm in the village of Scotland, in eastern Connecticut. She was the only daughter and first of three children of Gerald and Mary (Thomas) Waldo, descendants of eighteenth-century settlers. After attending Windham High School in Willimantic, Conn., she entered Adelphi College, where she concentrated in languages (A.B. 1909). She received an A.M. from Columbia University in 1910 and became a social worker in New York City. After four years she began to look for a field with more opportunity for advancement. Waldo had made the acquaintance of Helen Resor, whose husband, Stanley, was negotiating to buy the J. Walter Thompson Company advertising agency from its founder; when the Resors invited her to join the company as an apprentice copywriter at fifteen dollars a week in 1915, she accepted.

Between 1915 and 1930, Ruth Waldo established a solid reputation as a talented and creative copywriter for the Thompson Company, dividing her time among its Chicago, London, and New York offices. These years saw the national advertising of branded consumer products in magazines and newspapers, backed by million-dollar budgets, become standard practice for large businesses. In Waldo's first fifteen years in advertising, it was almost exclusively an art of the written word and of the commercial artist's talent for illustration. As space costs rose, and the challenge posed by color photography and printing became more evident, the need to get and hold the reader's attention placed new demands on writers. And as the share of family income that was disbursed by housewives grew rapidly, "creativity" came to mean the ability to appeal to women, not only in their functions as wives and mothers, but as individuals.

Waldo became an authority in such matters at the Thompson Company; after playing an important part at the London office in the early 1920s, she returned to New York, where she supervised women's copy for the entire agency beginning in 1930. While her poise would probably have marked her as someone with more clout than a secretary, Waldo helped establish the idea at the New York headquarters that female copywriters should wear their hats at work, thus leaving no room for misunderstanding. Soon clients, male account executives, writers, and art directors found nothing remarkable in the growing number of hatted women on the eleventh and twelfth floors of the Graybar Building.

During the 1930s and 1940s, Waldo and her colleagues carried out a series of advertising campaigns whose slogans became household phrases. Notable was that devised in 1942 for Pond's, one of the agency's oldest and largest accounts. "She's lovely! She's engaged! She uses Pond's!"—with its society lady elegantly endorsing a low-price cold cream intended for the millions—was emblematic of Waldo's approach to cosmetics, household items, foods, and other products purchased principally by women. Waldo left the business side of agency-client relations to the account executives of the company, who were exclusively male, but she knew that it was first-class copy that the client was really paying for, and in creative matters she usually managed to get her own way.

Ruth Waldo was proud of what she called her hobby—"getting on successfully with people, especially difficult people"—and she coped equally well with economic realities, adapting her approach shrewdly to accommodate depression, then war, and the television-based advertising boom that followed. In 1944 she was appointed vice president of the J. Walter Thompson Company, becoming one of the most prominent women in her field. At her retirement in 1960 she was no prouder of being the J. Walter Thompson Company's first woman vice president than she was of being the first of several, most of whom she trained.

Like her friends Helen and Stanley Resor, Waldo was devoted to her work and it remained her consuming interest. One of her close associates later described her in the *J. Walter Thompson News* as an "intelligent, 'high-intensity' woman, small and birdlike, with a high-pitched, 'chirpy' voice." She was a hard taskmaster, and suffered fools poorly, but she gained a reputation for fairness and honesty in a profession that has been famous for neither.

Waldo never married, and lived well within her means, saving a good deal of money over the years. Concerned with peace issues, she joined the Society of Friends in 1953 and on retirement established a trust fund, with the principal later divided between Adelphi University and the American Friends Service Committee. She spent her last years in Connecticut, first in Willimantic, then after 1967 in an apartment in Bridgeport, where she died in 1975 at the age of eighty-nine. She bequeathed her eighteenth-century Waldo homestead to the public.

[Ruth Waldo published an article, "Invention—the Essence of Advertising," *J. Walter Thompson News Bull.*, Dec. 1929, pp. 9–12. For background information on the agency during her years there see the second section of *Advertising Age*, Dec. 7, 1964, commemorating the centennial of the J. Walter Thompson Co. An obituary appeared in the *N.Y. Times*, Sept. 5, 1975, and a tribute in *J. Walter Thompson News*, Oct. 1975. There are tributes in publications of Adelphi Univ., Garden City, N.Y.: *Adelphi Now*, Jan. 1976, p. 11; and *Planned Giving Today*, Sept.-Oct. 1977, pp. 1–3. Waldo's college transcript supplied by Adelphi; other information furnished by Bridgeport Public Library, Religious Society of Friends, N.Y. City, and her brother Russell H. Waldo. A copy of her will was provided by Bridgeport Probate Court.]

ALBRO MARTIN

WALLER, Judith Cary, Feb. 19, 1889–Oct. 28, 1973. Broadcasting executive.

Judith Cary Waller, pioneer broadcaster and first manager of radio station WMAQ, Chicago, was born in Oak Park, Ill., the oldest of four daughters of John Duke Waller, a physician and surgeon, and Katherine (Short) Waller, daughter of the first president of what became MacMurray College, in Jacksonville, Ill. Waller's father was of moderate means, but one of his sisters was wealthy and treated Judith Waller to a year's tour of Europe after her graduation from Oak Park High School in 1908. On her return she enrolled in business college and then worked for several firms, including the J. Walter Thompson advertising agency in both Chicago and New York.

In 1922 Walter Strong, business manager of the *Chicago Daily News*, whom Waller had met on her European trip, asked her to run the radio station recently purchased by the newspaper. Although she had never even heard of a radio station and doubted her ability to run one, she accepted the offer and became manager of WGU, one of the first stations to go on the air in Chicago. Located in the nation's third largest market, the station, which soon changed its call letters to WMAQ, was from its inception an important broadcasting property.

From the beginning Waller showed a talent for programming. Noting that a competing Chicago station was playing jazz and popular music, she developed a classical music format for her station. Her first program featured a visiting opera star, with a piano and violin accompaniment. Radio carried no advertising then, so to attract talent to WMAQ Waller used the lure of publicity in the *Daily News*. She called regularly on music schools, lyceums, and Chautauqua agencies to invite their performers to appear on WMAQ. When they accepted, she wrote the publicity for the paper, then went to the studio where she produced and announced the program. She and one engineer comprised the entire staff.

Waller was an innovator in many diverse programming areas. She produced the first play-by-play broadcast of a college football game in 1924 when the University of Chicago played Brown. She was also directly responsible for convincing Chicago Cubs owner William Wrigley, Jr., to permit WMAQ to carry all the team's home games in 1925. At Waller's direction, WMAQ broadcast both political conventions in 1924 and Coolidge's inauguration in 1925. She was also responsible for the first broadcast of the Chicago Symphony Orchestra, and played an important role in the immense success of "Amos 'N' Andy." For two years Waller negotiated with Charles Correll and Freeman Gosden, originators of the show, then known as "Sam 'N' Henry," and with *Daily News* executives, to bring the program from rival WGN to WMAQ. Finally, on March 19, 1928, the first broadcast of "Amos 'N' Andy" was heard on WMAQ. The program's meteoric climb to popularity in both network radio and television confirmed again Waller's remarkable talent as well as her tenacity in programming.

The program with which she was most closely associated in the public mind was the prestigious "University of Chicago Round Table," which was originated by WMAQ in 1931 and later carried by the National Broadcasting Company (NBC) network. For over twenty years it set the standard for intellectual excellence in broadcasting. The program exemplified Waller's enthusiasm for the great potential of radio and later television as educational media. Earlier she had broadcast lectures from Northwestern University and had introduced a series of educational programs into the Chicago schools. Later she was responsible for the creation of "Ding Dong School," the first successful television program for preschoolers.

Waller's career closely paralleled the development of the broadcasting industry. She participated directly in all four of the national radio conferences called in the 1920s by Secretary of Commerce Herbert Hoover. In response to a dispute with the American Society of Composers, Authors and Publishers (ASCAP) over payment of music copyright holders, she joined with other broadcasting representatives in forming the National Association of Broadcasters (NAB). Waller was also active in the debate over the introduction of advertising into broadcasting, and she used her station's newspaper ties to promote the growth of radio news.

Preeminent among the broadcasting pioneers, Waller truly worked for the spirit of public trusteeship embodied in both the Radio Act of 1927 and its successor, the Communications Act of 1934, rather than adopting the more common private profit approach. Her conviction that radio should serve the public interest enabled Waller to step down without objection from the positions of vice president and general manager of WMAQ, which she had become in 1929, to become educational director of NBC's Central Division when the network bought the station in 1931; she later became public service director.

During her years with NBC, Waller pursued her interest in education in various ways. She served on the Federal Radio Education Committee, and on the Educational Standards Committee of the NAB, and as a board member of the University Association for Professional Radio Education. In the summer of 1942 she worked with Northwestern University to establish a program for persons aiming for jobs in broadcasting. Waller became codirector of the resulting NBC-Northwestern University Summer Radio Institute. In 1946 she wrote a textbook, *Radio, the Fifth Estate,* which was widely used in college and university broadcasting courses.

In an industry not noted for its acceptance of women in positions of leadership, Judith Cary Waller won universal respect and admiration from her male colleagues. Upon her retirement from NBC in 1957, she was praised for her "tough, original, critical mind, and an aversion to stuffiness." After retirement she remained active, heading television workshops at Purdue University and lecturing at Northwestern. She died of a heart attack in 1973 at eighty-four in Evanston, Ill., where she had shared a home with a sister.

[The primary sources of biographical material are two taped interviews with Waller, conducted in 1951 and 1965, in the Broadcast Pioneers Library, Washington, D.C. That library also has transcripts of speeches delivered by Waller as well as reports and correspondence concerning the Federal Radio Education Committee. Tapes of other speeches are in the Northwestern Univ. oral history archives. The only substantial account of her career is Mary E. Williamson, "Judith Cary Waller: Chicago Broadcasting Pioneer," *Journalism History,* Winter 1976–77. An obituary appeared in the *Chicago Tribune,* Oct. 29, 1973, and in the *Evanston* (Ill.) *Rev.,* Nov. 1, 1973; death record from Ill. Dept. of Public Health. Information was also supplied by Waller's former assistant at WMAQ-TV, Betty Ross West, and by former associates Sydney Eiges and Williams S. Hedges.]

MARY E. WILLIAMSON

WARD, Winifred Louise, Oct. 29, 1884–Aug. 16, 1975. Children's theater specialist.

Winifred Ward, the most influential figure in children's theater from the 1930s through the 1950s, was born in Eldora, Iowa, the youngest of three daughters and third of four children of George William and Frances Allena (Dimmick) Ward. Her parents, both of English ancestry, met and married when George Ward attended law school in Washington, D.C., and later migrated to Eldora, where they became prominent middle-class citizens. George Ward served as mayor, school board member, and county attorney; Frances Ward devoted her time to raising children and participating in civic activities. Winifred Ward remembered her mother as "the dominating force in my early life. She was large and capable, able to do well anything she undertook, but preferring always the big things." To her daughter, Frances Ward represented the world outside their small Iowa town, and on visits to her maternal grandparents in Washington, D.C., an excitingly different environment opened to Winifred Ward.

As a child, Ward was particularly impressed by her father's dramatic readings and her mother's cultured musical tastes, as well as by the presentations she witnessed at the local Chautauqua assemblies. After finishing her public school training in Eldora in 1902, she entered the Cumnock School of Oratory in Evanston, Ill. Completing the diploma course in oratory in 1905, she directed plays and declamation contests in Eldora for two years before returning to the Cumnock School for the postgraduate course in oratory (1907–08). Ward taught for the next eight years in the public schools of Adrian, Mich., then, in 1916, entered the University of Chicago, where she earned her Ph.B. in English.

Completing her college work in 1918, Ward was invited to join the faculty of the Cumnock School (which in 1920 became the Northwestern University School of Speech). It remained the focal point for her entire career. During her first ten years there, Ward, with the support of the school's dean, Ralph Dennis, expanded the speech education curriculum from two to twelve courses and negotiated the use of the Evanston Public Schools for field testing her ideas concerning the educational possibilities of story dramatization with children. She became supervisor of dramatics in the Evanston schools, a position she held until her retirement in 1950. In addition, in 1925, with Alexander Dean, head of the University Theatre, and Dennis, and under the sponsorship of Northwestern, Ward cofounded the Children's Theatre of

Evanston. This theater, which she directed until 1950, provided children with high quality productions of worthwhile drama and served as a laboratory where university students could develop their abilities as actors, producers, directors, and technicians. Unlike the handful of other children's theaters established in the United States during the 1920s, Ward's theater used college students in all adult roles and children from the public schools in juvenile parts. It was therefore a joint university/community venture both serving education and promoting the arts.

As Northwestern grew and attracted students and teachers from all parts of the United States, Ward acquired a national audience for her work. A prolific and effective writer as well as a teacher and director, she addressed that audience in numerous articles and several books. Her first book, *Creative Dramatics* (1930), showed her debt to the progressive education movement, which advocated a child-centered approach to instruction. In it she made a careful, even rigid, distinction between drama *with* children and drama *for* children. In creative dramatics, the name she gave to her concept of drama with children, the emphasis was always clearly on the process of creating, thus making the creative act a vehicle for the education of the child. Conversely, in children's theater—drama for children—the emphasis was on the product, or the aesthetic credibility of the thing created. She further expounded this idea in her next book, *Theater for Children* (1939).

In contrast to her first two books, which were written for trained specialists, Ward's *Playmaking With Children* (1947) was intended for "young people who wish to learn how to guide boys and girls in playmaking, or creative dramatics" and for "experienced *classroom* teachers who have the desire and the philosophy but not the technique of teaching improvised drama" to children ages five through fourteen. The most comprehensive manual for inexperienced creative dramatics leaders, *Playmaking* became the standard text in the field. Her last book—the first of its kind—was *Stories to Dramatize* (1952), an ambitious compilation of stories drawn from world literature suitable for dramatization with children; it, too, became a standard text. In addition to this book, Ward published many articles after her retirement.

Besides her accomplishments in teaching, directing, and writing, Ward became involved in national professional organizations such as the American Educational Theatre Association (AETA). When AETA was founded in 1936, Ward was invited to chair a committee on children's theater. Through the committee, she developed a connection between leaders in cre-

ative dramatics and children's theater by founding at Northwestern in 1944 the Children's Theatre Conference, later known as the Children's Theatre Association (CTA), a division of AETA. The CTA has been described as "the most significant organization contributing to the growth of children's theatre in the United States."

Ward never married but throughout her adult life was surrounded by intelligent and creative people. One close friend was Harold Ehrensperger, editor and also a teacher at Northwestern. Another was Charlotte Chorpenning, a playwright whom Ward had encouraged to write for children. Over the many years of their friendship they collaborated on numerous productions at the Children's Theatre of Evanston. Hughes Mearns, artist and teacher, with whom she long corresponded, was one of the strongest influences on her work. She was closest to Hazel Easton, her colleague at Northwestern and housemate of over fifty years. Winifred Ward died in Evanston of a stroke in 1975.

[The most important source of information on Ward's life and career is the Winifred Ward Papers, Northwestern Univ. Archives, which include biographical material about Ward and her family, personal and professional correspondence, Ward's history of the Children's Theatre of Evanston, creative dramatics materials, speeches, reviews, articles, scrapbooks, programs, and other memorabilia. Also in the collection is the most comprehensive study of Ward's life, Jan A. Guffin, "Winifred Ward: A Critical Biography" (Ph.D. diss., Duke Univ., 1975), which contains a bibliography of her work. An issue of *Children's Theatre Rev.*, vol. XXV, no. 2, 1976, devoted to Ward was expanded into a pamphlet, Ruth Beall Heinig, ed., *Go Adventuring! A Celebration of Winifred Ward: America's First Lady of Drama for Children* (1977). It includes an autobiographical sketch written in 1918 and a summary of Guffin's dissertation, as well as personal appreciations, photographs, and excerpts from correspondence. Books which help place Ward's work in a national context include Nellie McCaslin, *Theatre for Children in the United States: A History* (1971), and Geraldine Brain Siks and Hazel Brain Dunnington, eds., *Children's Theatre and Creative Dramatics* (1961). Additional information was provided by Hazel Easton, by Ward's niece Louise Nuckolls, and by Geraldine Brain Siks, Ward's former student and professional associate for many years. Death record supplied by Ill. Dept. of Public Health.]

JAN A. GUFFIN

WEBSTER, Margaret, March 15, 1905–Nov. 13, 1972. Director, actress, writer.

Margaret Webster, whose achievements as a director of Shakespeare in America are unrivaled, was born prematurely in New York City where her father, Benjamin Webster III, was then appearing on stage. He and his wife, Mary Louisa (May Whitty), were both superior British stage performers who fostered high theatrical sense and sensibility in their only child. (A son, born Christmas 1903, had died at birth.) During her first three years, Margaret remained in the care of close family friends while her parents toured and appeared on Broadway, often separately. The family then returned to London, where Margaret went to private schools; from the onset of World War I, she attended country boarding academies, graduating from Queen Anne's School, Caversham, in 1923. That same year she underwent two successful operations to correct an eye disorder which had marred her sight from birth.

Although as a child Margaret Webster resented the separations necessitated by her parents' professional commitments, she thrived in the artistic atmosphere at home and determined at an early age to become a great actress. Making her first stage appearance at eight, reciting the prologue to the York Nativity Play in a special matinee performance directed by Ellen Terry, she continued to appear in amateur productions, both in and out of school.

Webster decided against formal education and enrolled instead in the Etlinger Dramatic School in London in 1924. She made her first professional appearance the same year, as a chorus member in *The Trojan Women*, and, soon after, was engaged by a longtime family friend, John Barrymore, to portray a gentlewoman in his London production of *Hamlet* (1925). The bustling theater between the wars offered Webster a unique opportunity to improve her craft. She understudied Sybil Thorndike in *Saint Joan* (1925), joined the Macadona Players, graduating from minor to major roles in their Shaw repertory and touring Great Britain in 1926, and then appeared with J. B. Fagan's Oxford Company, a collegiate enterprise well known for its presentation of Chekhov's plays. Webster attained her most valuable stage experience beginning in 1928 while a member of Sir Philip Ben Greet's Players, a troupe famous for its consistently commendable production of Shakespeare. She played major roles: she might act Viola in the afternoon, Portia in the evening, and Lady Macbeth, sleepwalking up and down a fire escape, the next day. As a member of the Old Vic Company, led by John Gielgud, during the 1929 season Webster took on second leads; she returned to the company three years later to portray Lady Macbeth.

In 1934, Margaret Webster began to direct drama. Her first endeavor consisted in part of directing eight hundred Kentish countrywomen in the final scene of *Henry VIII*. Departing from traditional methods, Webster gave individual direction, thus ensuring a balanced staging while demonstrating to each actress her importance in the drama. Such innovation, founded on her empathy with performers, became Webster's signature.

Upon her return to London from the Moscow Theatre Festival in 1935, Margaret Webster's career took a decisive turn. She began to enlist more directorial than acting assignments. Her work, particularly for *Lady from the Sea* (1936) and *Old Music* (1937), gained increasingly good notices and led to an invitation from her former colleague British actor Maurice Evans to direct *Richard II* in New York. Convinced by his belief that there was an audience for Shakespeare in the United States, but frightened by the task of directing unknown work (*Richard II* had not been seen since 1878) for an audience new to her, Webster crossed the Atlantic for the first time in twenty-nine years. The production drew rave reviews and had a record run. For the next thirteen years Margaret Webster's name would be linked to that of William Shakespeare. She became devoted to the production of his plays and to the parallels his works, "the abstract and brief chronicles of time" (*Hamlet*, II, i, 511–12), offered to modern conditions.

After garnering respectable notices as Masha in the Alfred Lunt–Lynn Fontanne production of *The Sea Gull* (1938), Webster again directed Evans, this time in *Hamlet*. Conceived as two separate productions, one cut and one uncut version, Webster labored over various play editions, adamant in her dedication to textual fidelity. "Inevitably I applied an actor's ear and a knowledge of stage practices to arguable points," she recalled. She and Evans felt there would be small demand for the uncut version so she asked him to bill it as "Shakespeare's *Hamlet* in its entirety. Eight minutes shorter than *Gone With the Wind*" (*Don't Put Your Daughter on the Stage*, pp. 26, 37). The response was overwhelming and the reviews were glorious; the shorter version was quickly eliminated, and the production subsequently went on two national tours. The Webster-Evans team followed with *Henry IV, Part I* (1939), an equally triumphant production; they had proved the existence of an American audience for Shakespeare. That same year, Webster, working alone, staged and directed four abbreviated Shakespearean comedies for the Merrie Old England exhibition at the New York World's Fair.

Meanwhile, Webster's parents had moved to Hollywood. They appeared occasionally, but always notably, in film, and worked actively in such war-related efforts as the successful plan to rescue English orphans, all children of theatrical families, and bring them to the United States. Margaret Webster shared in these efforts. In 1940 she spent six months at the Paramount studio before she decided film was not her medium. She had had the unusual opportunity of directing her parents: Ben Webster in *The Young Mr. Disraeli* (1937) and Dame May Whitty (she had been made a Dame of the British Empire for her humanitarian efforts during World War I) in *The Trojan Women* (1941) and *Therese* (1945). Her mother recalled: "The last time I was in Boston I was teaching Peggy to speak. This time she's teaching me to act" (*Don't*, p. 141). Her father died in 1947, her mother the year after.

The 1940s produced the maturation of Margaret Webster's directorial effort and the evolution of her style, both anchored in her commitment to the spoken word. While working with a Shakespearean play, she sought inspiration in the text itself and rarely relied on scholarly interpretation. In 1942 she wrote her superb first book, *Shakespeare Without Tears*, which included her credo for directors: "We must know our author and our audience and see to it that the actors interpret justly between them." Abhorring gimmicks and stage trickery, she took infinite pains to see that her actors relied on neither.

Webster returned to New York in the fall of 1940 to direct Maurice Evans and Helen Hayes in the Theatre Guild's production of *Twelfth Night*. The following year she again directed Evans, this time with Judith Anderson in *Macbeth*. Although these productions were well-mounted and well-received, they lacked the inspiration of her previous efforts. For her next project, she cast Paul Robeson in the title role of *Othello*, and faced "every possible hostility and prediction of doom" (*Don't*, p. 112). Although an active proponent of civil rights, Webster based her selection rather on the "paramount importance to the play, to its credibility and to the validity of every character in it" (*Shakespeare*, p. 178) of having a black portray the Moor. *Othello* premiered at the Brattle Theatre, Cambridge, Mass., in August 1942, and opened in New York in October 1943, four years after the project's inception. Webster portrayed Emilia, as well as directing and partially producing the play; she was especially proud of this production and of the many obstacles it helped to overcome.

After a short respite from Shakespeare, during which she first directed *The Cherry Orchard* and then replaced Eva Le Gallienne in the lead-

ing role (1944–45), she mounted her last great Shakespearean revival. For a production of *The Tempest* (1945), she daringly cast Canada Lee, a black boxer, as Caliban, and Vera Zorina, a ballet dancer, as Ariel, and employed a revolving stage, flying apparatus, and a small orchestra. Again, critical acclaim attended the run.

Margaret Webster, with Le Gallienne and producer Cheryl Crawford, founded the American Repertory Theatre (ART) in 1946. Although it was originally conceived as a resident company, funded by local subsidy, for a major metropolitan area other than New York, ART found its home on Columbus Circle. The founders were motivated by the difficulties each had had while working within the established commercial theater and they strongly believed that ART would fulfill the demands of the non-Broadway theatergoer. After one season, in which Webster both acted and directed, ART failed financially. Webster attributed its demise to the critics' inability to foster noncommercial drama and to the lack of public subsidy for the arts.

Webster went on to form her own bus-and-truck troupe, the Margaret Webster Shakespeare Company (Marweb). Modeled after Ben Greet's players, the group of twenty-two actors and eight staff members barnstormed America. Beginning in 1948, and for two years after, Marweb performed in gymnasiums, auditoriums, and civic centers, in thirty-six states and four Canadian provinces. Presenting *Hamlet*, *Macbeth*, *Julius Caesar*, and *The Taming of the Shrew*, they afforded many their first exposure to Shakespeare or to drama of any kind. The troupe was a financial as well as a popular success; moreover, many young performers gained there valuable training unavailable elsewhere in the United States. Exhausted, but elated by a sense of accomplishment, the company disbanded in 1950. Webster rightly claimed that this was her greatest contribution to the theater.

In November 1950 Margaret Webster became the first woman to direct a production of the New York Metropolitan Opera Company when she directed *Don Carlos*, the season's opener. For six months she had concentrated on the technical aspects of operatic staging, ingeniously using toy soldiers to block the opera. When the production went into staging, she requested that all cast members—including the chorus, a heretofore unheard-of request—participate in full rehearsals. Her efforts were so successful that she continued to direct opera throughout the 1950s: *Aïda* (1951) and *Simon Boccanegra* (1960), both at the Met; *Troilus and Cressida* (1955), *Macbetto* (1957), *The*

Taming of the Shrew and *The Silent Woman* (both 1958), at the New York City Opera.

Webster also continued to act and to direct drama, most notably with the New York City Theatre Company. Her career suffered severely, however, after José Ferrer (who had portrayed Iago in her production of *Othello*) named her before the House Committee on Un-American Activities (HUAC) in May 1951. She underwent a series of ugly experiences: first, the United States government denied her a passport but, because she still held dual citizenship, England granted her one; then she was dismissed from consideration for pending broadcasting assignments; and, finally, she received no offers to work in the theater. Webster had worked for and been associated with many political organizations, most of them theater-connected, but none was communist-oriented. Even after she appeared before HUAC in May 1953 and was cleared of all charges, Webster, like so many of her colleagues, was stung and humiliated by condemnation and fear. She found work in England, however, where she directed *The Merchant of Venice* at Stratford-upon-Avon in 1956, *Measure for Measure* the following year at the Old Vic, and Noel Coward's *Waiting in the Wings* in London in 1960. Webster, with characteristic wit, referred to this period as one of "transatlantic schizophrenia."

She regained something of her former position in the United States when the Department of State invited her in 1961 to travel to South Africa under its auspices. As a member of the American Specialists Program, Webster lectured, gave concert readings of Shakespeare and George Bernard Shaw, and directed a production of Eugene O'Neill's *A Touch of the Poet* throughout the country, for both black and white audiences.

During the remainder of the 1960s, Webster divided her time between residencies at various American universities, where she taught and staged drama, and performances of one-woman shows, an endeavor she had begun in the early 1940s. She retired to her Martha's Vineyard retreat to write her family's history, *The Same Only Different* (1969), and her autobiography, *Don't Put Your Daughter on the Stage* (1972), thus fulfilling her lifelong mission "to keep language a live and beautiful thing." When Margaret Webster died in 1972 in London, one of Britain's finest theater families came to an end.

[The Margaret Webster Theatre Coll., Library of Congress, contains the bulk of her personal and professional papers; additional family material is in the British Museum and the Harvard Theatre Coll. Material relating to Marweb is in the Billy Rose Theatre Coll., N.Y. Public Library, which also has clipping files on Webster and on individual productions; material concerning her Theatre Guild association is in the Guild's archive, Beinecke Library, Yale Univ. Webster adapted a play from German, *Royal Highness* (pub., 1949); revised *Shakespeare Without Tears*, issued in Great Britain as *Shakespeare Today* (1957); and wrote *Shakespeare and the Modern Theatre*, Fifth Lecture on the Helen Kenyon Lectureship at Vassar College (1944). A bibliography of her magazine and periodical articles appears in *Cumulated Dramatic Index, 1909–1949*, and in Ely Silverman, "Margaret Webster's Theory and Practice of Shakespearean Production in the United States, 1937–1953" (Ph.D. diss., N.Y. Univ., 1969), which also includes an interview with her and citations of reviews and works about her. Other dissertations include Janet Carroll, "A Promptbook Study of Margaret Webster's Production of *Othello*" (La. State Univ., 1977) and Ronald Wolsey, "Margaret Webster: A Study of her Contributions to American Theatre" (Wayne State Univ., 1973). Biographical essays appeared in *Current Biog.*, 1940, 1950, and in the *New Yorker*, May 20, 1944; a list of credits is in *Biog. Encyc. and Who's Who of the Amer. Theatre* (1966). Obituaries appeared in *N.Y. Times*, Nov. 14, 1972, and London *Times*, Nov. 14, 1972; see also Laurence Olivier's tribute, London *Times*, Nov. 16, 1972.]

HARRIETTE L. WALKER

WEED, Ethel Berenice, May 11, 1906–June 6, 1975. Military officer.

Ethel Weed, Women's Army Corps officer in occupied Japan and advocate of the rights of Japanese women, was born in Syracuse, N.Y. She was the oldest of the three daughters and one son of Grover Cleveland and Berenice (Benjamin) Weed, both of British ancestry. Ethel attended school in Syracuse until her father, an engineer who had learned his trade through correspondence courses, moved the family to Cleveland, Ohio, in 1919. Grover Weed was a well-read man who enjoyed games, music, and travel and who encouraged his children to be adventurous. Berenice Weed, a homemaker, was very close to her oldest child and supported her efforts as a social reformer.

Ethel Weed attended Lakewood High School in Cleveland and Western Reserve University, earning an A.B. in English in 1929. She was the first of her family to seek a college degree. After graduation, she worked for eight years as a feature writer at the *Cleveland Plain Dealer*, and then, for a brief period, worked and traveled in Europe. In 1937 she returned to Cleveland to pursue a public relations career and until 1941 was assistant executive secretary of public relations for the Women's City Club. She then opened her own office, handling publicity for various women's and other civic organizations.

In May 1943 Ethel Weed closed her business and joined the Women's Army Corps (WAC), a decision she made after talking with a WAC recruiter whose public relations tour to Cleveland she had arranged. Following basic training, she was sent to Officers' Candidate School at Fort Oglethorpe, Ga., and was commissioned as a second lieutenant in August 1944. As an army public relations officer she did recruiting until 1945. At Officers' Candidate School Weed had heard about a course in Japanese studies to be held at Northwestern University to prepare a select group of twenty women officers for assignment in Japan once the war ended. Intrigued by the prospect of working in the Far East, she applied and was accepted.

Japan surrendered in August 1945, and Ethel Weed and her fellow WACs were soon dispatched to Yokohama on the first American convoy sent to Japan. Their mission was to help set up an Allied Occupation under Gen. Douglas MacArthur to demilitarize and democratize Japan. When Weed reported to General Headquarters in Tokyo in October 1945, she was given the title of Women's Information Officer in the Civil Information and Education Section, and assigned the task of formulating policy and developing "programs for the dissemination of information pertinent to the reorientation and democratization of Japanese women in [the] political, economic, and social fields." Operating initially from a borrowed table set up in a corner of General Headquarters, she began her work by developing a circle of Japanese women leaders who became her consultants and close associates. Most of these women had been leaders in the prewar suffrage movement and advocates of other women's rights causes in the 1920s and 1930s.

Weed's first big assignment was to promote women's suffrage, which had been granted in December 1945. American officials, confident that women would be a force for peace, wanted to assure a high turnout in the first postwar election on April 10, 1946. Weed undertook an extensive campaign to encourage women to vote, using radio shows, motion pictures, displays, press conferences, and other promotional methods. Despite press predictions that as few as 10 percent of the eligible women would vote, the women's turnout was an astonishingly high 67 percent, not far behind the rate for men. The election brought an unprecedented thirty-nine women into parliament, and Weed was widely credited for the successful outcome.

Another major area of her activity was promoting the development of women's clubs and organizations on a democratic basis. Drawing on her experience with women's clubs in Cleveland,

Weed helped women leaders organize, and in some cases reorganize, such groups as the Women's Democratic Club, the Japanese Association of University Women, the Housewives' Federation, and the Japanese League of Women Voters. A pamphlet she prepared on how to run organizations according to democratic principles was widely used by women's groups throughout Japan. In recognition of her efforts in this and related areas, Ethel Weed received an Army Commendation Ribbon on Sept. 23, 1946.

During 1946 the Occupation initiated a number of legal reforms to improve the status of Japanese women. Weed worked closely with legal experts in revising the Civil Code, providing women freedom of choice in marriage, and equality under property, divorce, and inheritance laws. She also conducted a series of speaking tours throughout Japan to win women's support for such reforms. In 1947 she was instrumental in the formation of a Women's and Minors' Bureau within the newly established Japanese Ministry of Labor and from 1947 to 1952 she acted as the Bureau's defender, ensuring that the ministry would not restrict its funds. She also organized two major trips to the United States, in 1950 and 1951, for groups of Japanese women leaders. Her most important achievement, however, was to help women's groups understand and make use of their new legal rights.

Weed had resigned from the WACs in 1947 with the rank of first lieutenant, continuing her duties with civilian status until the last days of the Occupation. In April 1952 she returned to the United States. For a time she pursued a doctorate in East Asian studies at Columbia University, but she did not complete the degree. In 1954 Weed and her cousin, Thelma Ziemer, established the East and West Shop in New York City, a bookshop specializing in works on Asia. They moved the shop to Newton, Conn., in 1969.

Over the years, Ethel Weed maintained contact with a large circle of Japanese women from Occupation days. In 1971 she returned to Japan as their guest, and was honored by prominent government and civic leaders for her efforts on behalf of Japanese women. She died of cancer in Newton, Conn., in 1975.

[The Women's Affairs Activity File, Nat. Records Center, Suitland, Md., includes memos, correspondence, reports, clippings, and other materials in English and Japanese relating to Weed's work as Women's Information Officer of the Civil Information and Education Section of the Occupation (1945–52). A smaller collection of her personal papers, clippings, and correspondence remains with the family. Correspondence between Weed and

Mary Beard is in the Beard Coll. at Smith College. An account of Ethel Weed's activities in the Allied Occupation appears in Japanese in Shukan Shincho, ed., *Makkasa no nihon* (1970), and in Susan J. Pharr, "Soldiers as Feminists: Debate Within U.S. Occupation Ranks over Women's Rights Policy in Japan," in Merry I. White and Barbara Molony, eds., *Proceedings of the Tokyo Symposium on Women* (1979). A forthcoming book by Susan Pharr on political women in Japan provides background on Occupation initiatives in the area of women's rights and Japanese women's responses to those initiatives. Articles on Weed's career appeared in the *Cleveland Plain Dealer*, Aug. 25, 1944, Dec. 3, 1945, and March 17, 1946; the *Cleveland News*, Oct. 2, 1946; and the *Christian Science Monitor*, Sept. 4, 1946. Assistance was provided by Dr. Elizabeth (Weed) Van Hamersveld.]

SUSAN J. PHARR

WELLS, Marguerite Milton, Feb. 10, 1872– Aug. 12, 1959. Suffragist, civic leader.

Marguerite Milton Wells, third president of the National League of Women Voters, was born in Milwaukee, the eldest of four children (three daughters and one son) of Nellie (Johnson) and Edward Payson Wells. She was descended on both sides from seventeenth-century English settlers in New England, one of whom, Thomas Welles, was an early governor of Connecticut. Her father came as a young man to Minneapolis in 1868, met and married her mother, originally of Farmington, Maine, and together they moved to the very edge of the settlement in the then Dakota Territory. There at Jamestown he began a career in banking, railroading, and politics that made him one of the great figures in the development of the upper Mississippi Valley west.

Marguerite Wells spent her childhood and youth with unbroken prairie at her door. The town and subsequently the state were organized as she grew up, and the experience of watching a heterogeneous group of people forming a community and living under a government they themselves had created made an indelible impression on her, nurturing her conviction that democracy could indeed work. She took a precocious interest in government and once persuaded her father, a member of the territorial legislature, to let her accompany him to the all-male party caucus. Dressed as a boy in a slicker, with a cap pulled down over her short bobbed hair, she was exhilarated by the talk she heard and returned home to write an account of it in rhyme.

At fifteen she took teacher's examinations and taught a summer session in a one-room Dakota school. Later she attended Miss Hardy's school in Eau Claire, Wis., and in 1891 entered Smith College, where she rapidly won distinction as a scholar, receiving a B.L. in 1895. Her association with Smith was to be a long one, for in 1915 she was asked to become a permanent trustee, a post she held until her resignation in 1930; five years later Smith conferred on her an honorary LL.D.

Apart from two years of teaching in New Jersey, Wells spent the first decade after her graduation from college alternating long periods of travel and residence in Europe with stays at home in Minneapolis, where her family had now permanently settled. In both settings she characteristically took responsibility for other members of her close-knit family, her mother in recurrent illness and her younger sisters during stages of their education in Europe. When in Minneapolis she pursued volunteer work, serving on innumerable civic and charitable boards.

Then suddenly, in 1917, came a critical turning point in her life. It is possible that she sensed that her powers had not yet found an object that challenged them. Whatever the cause, she came home one day, resigned from every public office that she held, and went directly to the headquarters of the Minnesota Woman Suffrage Association to offer her services. Never attracted to causes, she had nevertheless come to the conclusion that the issue of woman suffrage must be decided once and for all so women could turn their energies to more important public questions. Working closely with CLARA UELAND, president of the Association, she threw herself into the final stages of the suffrage struggle, organizing and leading Minnesota's successful campaign to ratify the nineteenth amendment.

At the convention of the National American Woman Suffrage Association in St. Louis in 1919, the president, CARRIE CHAPMAN CATT, suggested that a league be formed to educate the newly enfranchised voter. Marguerite Wells, who remembered the day and hour that she read Catt's words, was caught up by the idea. While Catt thought that the task might be completed in five years, Wells saw the possibility that this fresh infusion of women into the electorate could contribute something of permanent importance to the functioning of government in the United States. The National League of Women Voters, born in 1920 out of the old suffrage movement, took up this challenge. For the next twenty-five years Wells poured her talents into the organization, serving first as president of the Minnesota League for ten years, simultaneously as a member of the National Board, and, succeeding BELLE SHERWIN, as the League's national president from 1934 to 1944.

In the burst of creative educational activities Wells inspired in the early Minnesota years, she soon came to realize that it was through political action on specific legislation or in working for specific governmental reforms that League members learned best the realities of political life. Here failure often taught as much as success. She saw the League's inability to secure ratification of the child labor amendment in crucial states and the failure to prolong the life of Sheppard-Towner, the Maternity and Infancy Act of 1921, as vivid proof not only of the power of entrenched special interests but also of the absence of a voice speaking for the public interest. Here, Wells perceived, was the nub of the problem.

If the League were to supply that voice effectively, Wells wrote in 1930, "there must be a nucleus of people in each community who would carry a continuing responsibility for government and would give an intelligent and disinterested political leadership on issues as they arose." To train such people, and to sustain them in an organized way with current political knowledge and know-how was the real reason for being of the League of Women Voters, she felt. More than any other single individual, Wells became the architect of the League's philosophy of government over these years.

With the collapse of democratic governments one after another, as Hitler overran western Europe in the spring of 1940, the fate of democracy everywhere seemed in jeopardy. Wells saw this as the League's great opportunity and her letters to state League presidents during the war years, published in 1944 under the title *Leadership in a Democracy, Marguerite Milton Wells,* convey brilliantly her vision and her sense of urgency.

Within this context she began the effort to get the League to educate beyond its own membership. In *A Portrait of the League of Women Voters at the Age of Eighteen,* written in 1938, she had noted the danger in the League's increasing preoccupation with study, when the need was for action in the outside world where political decisions are made. Asking the League to change its habits, she was pulling it in unaccustomed directions.

She sought as well to bring about a restructuring of the League that would make it possible for the national office to work more directly with members. The League's structural problem, apparent for some time, was thrown into high relief in January 1941 at the beginning of the great debate on Lend-Lease. Members received information and calls for action only from state League offices, many of whom failed to forward the material sent by the national, and the force of the League's work on this critical issue was thus severely weakened. With this in mind, at the National Convention in 1944, when she was retiring from the presidency, Wells proposed for debate a plan to restructure the League. What she sought was open consideration of the issues by the Convention and a conscious choice of direction for the future. Wells's hope was never realized, however, because the Convention became absorbed in the election of a new president, rejecting the official nominee and nominating another from the floor. The plan was thus sidetracked. Pieces of the proposed changes found their way slowly into League practice in subsequent years.

Marguerite Wells was not a feminist in any orthodox sense nor was the League of Women Voters an organization that focused on women's issues as such. Wells strongly supported efforts to remove the legal disabilities of women but felt such action in itself would not alter public attitudes. In her view the latter would come only as more women succeeded in responsible jobs. That she underestimated the difficulties women were to encounter in getting those jobs may have been due, in part, to the freedom she enjoyed as a single woman, with education, private income, and rare intellectual endowments. More important, however, was the fact that her focus was on the broader problem, the League's overall objective, of making the democratic process in government work.

Small of stature, agile, with snapping black eyes and characteristic flashes of humor, she was a magnetic personality and a natural leader. Her mind fastened on one of the most elusive problems of political science, the role of the electorate in a democracy. What did the system demand of the individual, the citizen, the governed, but likewise of the person who was ultimately responsible through the vote for what happened? There were no easy answers. She was unpersuaded by theories that class structure or the power of money were the sole sources of political evil. Like the Founding Fathers, whose writings she read avidly, she pinned her faith on the belief that, if informed and given time, a majority of men and women would act wisely. An advancing arteriosclerosis clouded her last years and she died of pneumonia at her sister's home in Minneapolis in 1959.

[The Wells Family Papers, 1861–1932, Minn. League of Women Voters Papers, 1919–60, and Minn. Woman Suffrage Papers, 1894–1921, in the Minnesota Hist. Soc. Archives, St. Paul, are the richest sources of information about Marguerite Wells. The official records of the Nat. League of Women Voters are in the Library of Congress. A small collection of Wells papers in the Schlesinger

Library, Radcliffe College, contains material on the 1944 League convention and on Wells in retirement. The clipping collection of the *Minneapolis Tribune*, 1920–59, includes articles from several Minneapolis newspapers tracing her activities. A privately printed volume, *Welles-Wells Family, 1636–1936* (1936), which is in the Minn. Hist. Soc. Archives, contains a fascinating account of the career of Edward Payson Wells. See also *Mother's Letters* (1930), selected by Marguerite M. Wells, and *Autobiography of Stuart Wilder Wells* (1956). Among Wells's own writings see especially "Some Effects of Woman Suffrage," in the Am. Acad. of Political and Social Sci. *Annals*, May 1929. Biographical information can also be found in Mary C. Brown, "Among Those We Know," *Golfer and Sportsman*, Jan. 1940. Avis D. Carlson, "Trail-Blazers in Citizenship," *Survey Graphic*, Sept. 1945, is a brief history of the League of Women Voters. Mary Wells provided helpful assistance. Death certificate supplied by Minn. Dept. of Health.]

JEANNETTE BAILEY CHEEK

WHEELER, Anna Johnson Pell, May 5, 1883– March 26, 1966. Mathematician.

Anna Johnson was born in Hawarden, Iowa, to Andrew Gustav and Amelia (Frieberg) Johnson. She was the second of three daughters, and third of four children. Her parents were Swedish immigrants, her father a furniture dealer and undertaker in Akron, Iowa.

After attending Akron High School, Anna Johnson obtained an A.B. degree from the University of South Dakota in 1903. There her exceptional mathematical ability was noticed and nurtured by a professor, Alexander Pell, who later became her husband. Pell encouraged her to go on to graduate study in mathematics, and she received A.M. degrees from the University of Iowa in 1904 and from Radcliffe College in 1905. She then won an Alice Freeman Palmer Fellowship from Wellesley College to attend Göttingen University during 1906–07. She studied there with the noted German mathematician David Hilbert, but she left without taking a degree.

In Göttingen, in July 1907, she married Pell, whose wife had died in 1904. Pell, a former Russian revolutionary whose real name was Sergei Degaev, had escaped from Russia in the 1880s after being implicated in the celebrated murder of a secret police inspector. Coming to the United States with a price on his head, he had changed his name and begun a new career as a mathematician. The couple returned to the University of South Dakota, but Alexander Pell soon resigned to teach at the Armour Institute of Technology in Chicago. Anna Pell completed her Ph.D. at the University of Chicago in 1910

under Eliakim Hastings Moore, then chairman of the mathematics department. She had hoped, she wrote, "for a position in one of the good universities like Wisconsin, Illinois, etc.," but she found "there is such an objection to women that they prefer a man even if he is inferior both in training and in research." When Alexander Pell suffered a stroke in 1911, she temporarily took over his teaching responsibilities. Her first regular faculty position was at Mount Holyoke College, where from 1911 to 1918 she taught classes, continued her research, and took care of her ailing husband.

In 1918 Anna Pell went to Bryn Mawr College, where she remained until her retirement in 1948. She continued to be extremely active not only as a teacher of mathematics, and later as head of the department, but also as a researcher. Alexander Pell died in 1921, and in 1925 she married Arthur Leslie Wheeler, a classics scholar and colleague, who that year became professor of Latin at Princeton University. The Wheelers moved to Princeton, but she continued to lecture part-time at Bryn Mawr College. She moved back to Bryn Mawr in 1932 after her husband's sudden death.

Anna Pell Wheeler's mathematical ability was widely respected. At Göttingen Hilbert had interested her in integral equations, and much of her subsequent work was focused in this area. She extended and generalized some of Hilbert's results. Particularly noteworthy was her work on biorthogonal systems of functions and their applications to integral equations. In 1927 Wheeler was invited by the American Mathematical Society to deliver the Colloquium Lectures, an annual series of three or four lectures by a distinguished research mathematician. Wheeler was the first woman, and as late as the 1970s remained the only woman, so honored. Her lectures, on quadratic forms in infinitely many variables, and their applications, surveyed the broader scene in which her own research had played a part for twenty years.

Wheeler had a reputation for being a fine teacher who imbued her students, both graduate and undergraduate, with her own all-consuming love of mathematics. Seven women working under her direction received doctorates at Bryn Mawr. Keenly aware of the difficulties encountered by women as mathematicians, Wheeler often took her students to mathematical meetings and urged them to participate on an equal professional basis with men. She herself was active in the American Mathematical Society, serving on both its council and board of trustees, and in the Mathematical Association of America. An able administrator, Wheeler also strove to enhance the reputation of the Bryn

Mawr mathematics department. Recognizing that research was a necessary part of an instructor's development, she advocated reduced teaching loads and encouraged her faculty in their research efforts. She organized exchange programs with other colleges in the Philadelphia area, and in 1933 Wheeler succeeded in attracting the eminent German-Jewish algebraist Amalie Emmy Noether (1882–1935) to Bryn Mawr College.

During her second marriage Wheeler and her husband built a summer home in the Adirondacks which they named "Q.E.D." There she spent many happy hours and became an avid bird watcher and wildflower enthusiast. She was also generous in inviting her students to Q.E.D. Despite recurrent attacks of arthritis, after her retirement Wheeler continued to attend mathematical meetings and to support and encourage women in mathematics. Early in 1966 she suffered a stroke and died a few months later in Bryn Mawr at the age of eighty-two.

[A listing of Anna Pell Wheeler's publications to 1931 appears in Johann Christian Poggendorff, *Biographischliterarisches Handwörterbuch zur Geschichte der exakten Wissenschaften* (1940), vol. VI, part 4, p. 2861. Not included are two papers: "Linear Ordinary Self-Adjoint Differential Equations of the Second Order," *Am. Jour. of Mathematics*, 1927, pp. 309–20, and "Spectral Theory for a Certain Class of Non-Symmetric Completely Continuous Matrices," *Am. Jour. of Mathematics*, 1935, pp. 847–53. The Colloquium Lectures were never published. Church records of the Immanuel and Union Creek Lutheran Churches, Akron, Iowa, contain information about the Johnson family. A scrapbook of letters from colleagues and students compiled at Wheeler's retirement is in the Bryn Mawr Archives. Louise S. Grinstein and Paul J. Campbell, "Anna Johnson Pell Wheeler, 1883–1966," Assoc. for Women in Mathematics *Newsletter*, Sept. and Nov. 1978, includes a brief biography, discussion of her research, and bibliography. An account of the memorial service held at Bryn Mawr College as well as a photograph appear in the *Bryn Mawr Alumnae Bull.*, Summer 1966, pp. 22–23. Other sources include an entry in *Am. Men of Sci.*, vol. I (1955), and an obituary in the *N.Y. Times*, April 1, 1966. A death certificate was supplied by the Pa. Dept. of Health. Invaluable information was provided by Wheeler's niece Jean Hoagland Owens, and by Ruth Stauffer McKee, Fern Roy, and Paul J. Campbell.]

LOUISE S. GRINSTEIN

WHITE, Eartha Mary Magdalene, Nov. 8, 1876–Jan. 18, 1974. Social welfare and community leader, businesswoman.

Eartha White, known as the Angel of Mercy

to thousands of poor, ill, elderly, and homeless people, was born in Jacksonville, Fla. She was the daughter of Mollie Chapman, a black woman, and a young white man of good family whose name was never revealed. Soon after birth she was adopted by Lafayette and Clara (English) White. Clara White, the daughter of freed slaves, had worked as a domestic and cook, and as a stewardess on several steamship lines. Lafayette White, himself an ex-slave, had served with the Union army during the Civil War as a member of the 34th Regiment, Company D, United States Colored Troops. The Whites instilled in Eartha a deep pride in her Afro-American heritage; many years later she established an Afro-American museum to preserve and transmit that heritage.

Eartha White attended Stanton School in Jacksonville (grades one to eight), where one of her teachers was Mary Still, whose family had been abolitionists and supporters of the Underground Railroad in Pennsylvania. In 1888, fleeing an epidemic, Clara and Eartha White moved to New York City (Lafayette White had died in 1881). During the next six years they returned to Jacksonville intermittently, but Eartha attended schools in New York: Dr. Reason's school, Madam Hall's school, where she studied hairdressing and manicuring, and Madame Thurber's National Conservatory of Music, where one of her voice teachers was the famed Harry T. Burleigh. In 1895 she was invited to join the Oriental-American Opera Company, one of the first black opera companies in the United States. She remained with the company for a year, touring within the country and in Europe and the Orient.

During this period Eartha White met James Lloyd Jordan, a young black man from South Carolina. They became engaged, but a month before the wedding Jordan died. Eartha White returned to Jacksonville. From 1896 to 1898 she attended the Florida Baptist Academy, teaching subsequently in nearby Bayard and at the Stanton School. An energetic woman, she also worked for a time as a secretary at the Afro-American Life Insurance Company, and risked her life to save the firm's records during the great fire of 1901 that destroyed Jacksonville. From 1905 to 1930 White owned a series of small businesses: a dry-goods store, a general store, an employment agency, a janitorial contracting service, a real-estate business, and a steam laundry (where she claimed she could "clean anything but a dirty conscience"). She invariably started each venture on a small scale, worked hard to build it up, sold it for a profit, and started a new one. She continued to buy and sell real estate for most of her life, using the profits to support her public-service activities. White also became the city's first black social worker and census taker.

In all these endeavors Eartha White was very much the follower of Booker T. Washington; in 1900 she had joined hands with him in Boston as a charter member of the National Negro Business League. Like Washington, she believed that education, business success, and racial uplift could be effective instruments against prejudice. She protested segregation, but in a somewhat muted and supremely dignified way, believing cooperation to be the best means toward achieving racial equality. White devoted her life to encouraging others, through her own example, to become informed, active, and responsible citizens.

Many organizations and groups benefited from White's skills. She became a speaker for organizations like the Colored Citizens' Protective League, which she helped organize in 1900, revived the Union Benevolent Association to aid elderly Civil War veterans (1901), and raised funds for the Colored Old Folks' Home (built in 1902). For many years she operated the only orphanage for black children in Duval County— possibly the only one in the entire state. In 1904 she organized the Boys' Improvement Club and launched a campaign called "Save 1,000 Boys from Juvenile Court," to raise money for a recreation center. When this project failed, White induced a friend to donate land for a park, and used her personal funds to hire a recreation worker; not until 1916 was the city council persuaded to take over the operation. For over fifty years White conducted Sunday Bible classes at the county prison and worked to improve conditions for the inmates; the men routinely sought her assistance after their release.

During World War I Eartha White was the director of War Camp Community Services and Coordinator of Recreation in Savannah, Ga. She was the only woman chosen to participate in the Southeast War Camp Community Service Conference, held in Jacksonville. Later, she was the only Negro to attend a White House meeting of the Council of National Defense.

Active in politics as well, White became a precinct worker for the Republican party and campaigned for moderate candidates. In 1920 she headed the Negro Republican Women Voters, and won praise for her leadership. She also became the only woman member of the Duval County Republican Executive Committee.

Eartha White's zeal for community service was inspired by her adoptive mother, who always made generous contributions of food and clothing to the ill and needy. In 1928, eight years after Clara White's death, Eartha White established in her memory the Clara White Mission—considered by many to be her most important work and Jacksonville's counterpart to Chicago's Hull House. White herself lived at the mission with the transients and the downtrodden. During the depression, the mission became the center of black relief activities: more than 2,500 persons received either food packages or soup at the kitchen in February 1933 alone. The mission also served as headquarters for numerous Works Progress Administration activities.

With the coming of World War II, White became an honorary colonel in the Women's National Defense Program. She set up canteen service and managed various Red Cross activities in a building she donated for a servicemen's center. In 1941 she worked with A. Philip Randolph to organize a march on Washington as a protest against job discrimination. Although the march was never made, the movement led to the issuance by President Franklin D. Roosevelt of Executive Order 8802 banning discrimination in employment in defense industries and in the federal government, and to the establishment of the Fair Employment Practices Committee that same year.

The Clara White Mission became a base for the establishment of Eartha White's many other service agencies: a maternity home, a child placement center and orphan home, the Harriet Beecher Stowe Community Center, and a tuberculosis rest home, among others. In 1967 White's proudest achievement, the Eartha M. M. White Nursing Home, was completed. Begun with her personal funds and supported by a federal grant, this 120-bed institution had facilities for physical therapy, occupational therapy, and recreational activities for county and state welfare patients.

Over the years Eartha White became one of Jacksonville's most decorated citizens. Already the holder of honorary degrees, in 1969 she was given the Good Citizenship Award by the local Jaycees. In 1970 she received the Lane Bryant Volunteer Award, and in 1971 the American Nursing Home Association gave her its Better Life Award. Two years later the National Negro Business League honored White, its longtime official historian, with the Booker T. Washington Symbol of Service Award.

Eartha White remained active well into her nineties. Confined to a wheelchair, she still attended civic and government meetings, but it was the mission and the nursing home that always received the largest share of her attention. She died of heart failure in Jacksonville in 1974, at the age of ninety-seven.

[The Eartha White Coll. at the library of the Univ. of North Fla. contains over 1,000 documents, letters, photographs, and other items. Biographical material is also located at the Clara White Mission, Jacksonville, Fla. The Booker T. Washington Papers at the Library of Congress, and the Rollins College Archives, Winter Park, Fla., contain primary source material relevant to White's career. Information on White's adoption can be found in the Deed Books, Nassau Cty. Courthouse, Fernandiana Beach, Fla.; at the Duval Cty. Courthouse in Jacksonville; and in Nat. Archives, Record Group 94. Information about White's life and work can be found in Fred Wright, "Eartha White," *Floridian*, Aug. 1, 1971; C. Frederick Duncan, "Negro Health in Jacksonville," *The Crisis*, Jan. 1942; L. W. Neyland, *Twelve Black Floridians* (1970); and Harold Gibson, "The Most Unforgettable Person I Have Met," *Reader's Digest*, Dec. 19, 1974. The last two contain many inaccuracies. Interviews with White in her later years were printed in *St. Petersburg Times*, Aug. 1, 1971, and *N.Y. Times*, Dec. 4, 1970. Obituaries appeared in *N.Y. Times, Jacksonville Journal*, and *Florida Times-Union*, Jan. 19, 1974; and in the Nat. Business League's *National Memo*, Jan. 1974. Death certificate was obtained from the Fla. Dept. of Health.]

DANIEL SHAFER

WHITE, Edna Noble, June 3, 1879–May 4, 1954. Educator, home economist.

Edna Noble White, a pioneer in child development, nursery school education, and parent education, was born in Fairmount, Ill., the younger daughter and second of three children of Angeline (Noble) and Alexander L. White. Her father, a native of Logan, Ohio, was one of Fairmount's most respected citizens; he was manager of a firm dealing in lumber, hardware, and agricultural implements and held several posts in the town government. Her mother, born in Indiana, was well educated and active in community affairs.

After graduating from the Fairmount High School and receiving her A.B. from the University of Illinois in 1906, Edna White taught in the Danville, Ill., high school and at the Lewis Institute in Chicago before joining the home economics faculty of Ohio State University in 1908. Within seven years she became a full professor, head of the department, and supervisor of the home economics extension service. Her work during flood disasters and during World War I as director of Ohio food conservation for the Council of National Defense earned her a reputation beyond the state. When LIZZIE MERRILL PALMER, widow of Senator Thomas W. Palmer of Michigan, left three million dollars for the founding and maintenance of a school to train young women for motherhood and home-

making, White was chosen in 1919 to be its founding director.

There was no precedent for the kind of school and research center Edna White developed at the Merrill-Palmer Institute in Detroit during her twenty-seven years as director. When the Institute opened in 1920 it was the second center for child development research in the country (the first was the Iowa Child Welfare Station, founded in 1917), and it was for many years the only such center not affiliated with a university. Edna White was determined to go beyond the traditional interpretation of motherhood training as merely practical instruction in homemaking skills, and to prove that the physical, mental, and emotional development of children was worthy of study at the college level. From a first class of twelve children and six students recruited from Michigan State University, the Institute grew to attract the attention of educators throughout the world. Initially, courses lasted six months; later a one-year residency requirement was set for master's degree candidates.

The Merrill-Palmer laboratory nursery school, unlike nursery schools in England that were established primarily for the physical care of poor children, was designed to help college students and parents learn more about children and to provide opportunities for research on child development and parent education. The growth of the school, founded in 1922, coincided with the development in the United States of the parent education movement, which reached its height between 1925 and 1935.

Gathering together specialists in pediatrics, nutrition, psychology, education, home economics, and social work, Edna White organized the staff so as to integrate their knowledge and methods into the development of an all-round view of the child; she thus initiated one of the first interdisciplinary efforts in the new field of child development. Weekly meetings of the entire staff were held, and independent research by specialists was discouraged. Focusing at first on the preschool child, the Institute soon broadened its view to include all phases of child development from conception to adulthood and began some of the first longitudinal studies of children. Another innovation was the shift from the individual child to the family as the unit of study. The fame of the Institute reached distant parts of the world: the King of Siam, greeting visitors from Detroit, is said to have welcomed them as from the home of Merrill-Palmer.

Believing that the Institute should serve the community, Edna White initiated at the city and state levels programs such as the Visiting Housekeepers and the Detroit Youth Council;

many of these programs were later taken over by other institutions. Above all, she believed: "Merrill-Palmer must never crystallize its program or become static in what it does. If this ever happens, it can never justify its existence."

White disseminated her ideas on child development and parent education as a leader in numerous organizations. She was president of the American Home Economics Association from 1918 to 1920 and chairman of its advisory committee on child development and parent education. In 1923 she became an adviser to Lawrence K. Frank, chief architect and administrator of the fund which established the nationwide network of Rockefeller institutes for child development research. She also served as chairman of the National Council on Parent Education from 1925 to 1937, and during the depression as chairman of the National Advisory Committees on Nursery Schools and Parent Education of the Works Progress Administration.

After her retirement from Merrill-Palmer in 1947, Edna White served with the American Mission to Greece to help organize the study of child development and family life in Greek universities. Later, she developed and administered a gerontology program in Detroit. She received honorary degrees from four colleges and universities. During most of her adult life she lived with her sister and acted as foster mother to her brother's two sons. She died suddenly of a heart attack at her home in Highland Park, Mich., in 1954.

[Biographical material, photographs, copies of articles by and about Edna White, and historical sources on the Merrill-Palmer Institute are in the Merrill-Palmer Archives in Detroit. Her publications include: *A Study of Foods* (1914), with Ruth A. Wardall; "Nursery Schools (United States)," in *Encyc. Britannica*, 14th ed. (1929); "Parent Education in the Emergency," *School and Society*, Nov. 24, 1934; "The Nursery School—A Teacher of Parents," *Child Study*, Oct. 1926; "The Objectives of the American Nursery School," *The Family*, April 1928; "The Role of Home Economics in Parent Education," *Bull. Am. Home Economics Assoc.*, Jan. 1929; "The Scope of Parent Education in America," in *Towards a New Education* (1929, Report, 5th Internat. Conference, New Educational Fellowship, Elsinore, Denmark). Illuminating anecdotes about Edna White and the Institute are included in the oral histories of Pauline P. W. Knapp (1971), Lawrence K. Frank (1963), and Lois Meek Stolz (1968), in the Milton J. E. Senn Coll., Nat. Library of Medicine, Bethesda, Md. For information on White's career see Lawrence K. Frank, "The Beginnings of Child Development and Family Life Education in the Twentieth Century," *Merrill-Palmer Quart.*, Oct. 1962; Dorothy Tyler, "A Study of Leadership in the Making of an Institution," *Social Forces*, May 1932; *Merrill-Palmer Institute Report, 1920–1940*; and Harry Overstreet and Bonaro W. Overstreet, *Leaders for Adult Education* (1941), pp. 105–8. Obituaries appeared in the *Merrill-Palmer Quart.*, Fall 1954, and the *Detroit News*, May 5, 1954. White's birth date appears in some printed sources as 1880. The 1879 date is confirmed by the 1880 and 1900 U.S. Censuses and by the death certificate, provided by the Mich. Dept. of Health. Information was also obtained from Lois Meek Stolz and Dorothy Tyler and from a biobibliography by Iris B. Durden.]

ALICE SMUTS

WHITE, Helen Constance, Nov. 26, 1896–June 7, 1967. Scholar, teacher, novelist.

Helen White was born in New Haven, Conn., the first of four children of John and Mary (King) White. In 1901, Helen's family moved to Roslindale, Mass., where her father, of Irish Catholic descent and formerly a clerk with the New York, New Haven and Hartford Railroad, entered the civil service. Growing up, Helen White enjoyed a close relationship with her two younger sisters: all three went on to become teachers of English. At Girls' High School in Boston from 1909 to 1913, her teachers encouraged her interest in literature, and in such social issues as woman suffrage and the condition of Boston's immigrants.

In 1913, Helen White entered Radcliffe College, where in four years she earned both an A.B., summa cum laude, and an A.M. in English. She then served as assistant in English at Smith College from 1917 to 1919, before joining the English department at the University of Wisconsin to teach and study for her doctorate. She completed the Ph.D. in 1924 and remained at Madison, which became her second home after Boston: she consistently presented herself as "from" these two places and two educational traditions, eastern women's and midwestern coeducational. Promoted from instructor to assistant professor at Wisconsin in 1925, White became a full professor in 1936, the only woman then at that level in the college of Letters and Science. White later served as chairman of the English department, from 1955 to 1958 and again from 1961 to 1965.

A committed teacher, Helen White also successfully combined three other pursuits: scholarly research in medieval and Renaissance literature, the writing of novels on turning points in the history of ideas in the Catholic church, and public service in education. White's scholarly work is characterized by attention to the social and intellectual traditions within which writers work. Her dissertation, *The Mysticism of William Blake*, published in 1927, explores the history of mystical thought and illustrates

White's concern for the connections between religion and literature, an interest reflected in such later works as *The Metaphysical Poets: A Study in Religious Experience* (1936), *Social Criticism in Popular Religious Literature of the Sixteenth Century* (1944), and *Prayer and Poetry* (1960).

Similarly, White's fiction presents the social environment in which new ideas are developed and religious values lived out. Her first novel, *A Watch in the Night* (1933), concerning a thirteenth-century Franciscan, was first choice of the Pulitzer Novel Committee, although Caroline Miller's *Lamb in His Bosom!* received the prize that year because of its American setting. White's second novel, *Not Built with Hands* (1935), is the story of Matilda, Countess of Tuscany. Matilda, White said, fascinated her as the suffragists had; she is a political leader who consciously acts out of women's values. Dedicated to White's mother, the novel features a strong mother-daughter relationship. White wrote four more novels, continuing the pattern of carefully observed everyday life in times of ideological change.

In the field of education, Helen White served as president of the American Association of University Women (AAUW) from 1941 to 1947. She believed that women should support the war effort and be subject to the draft; she also emphasized the responsibility of educated women to use their trained intelligence for peaceful social change. "We must not forget," she wrote in 1944, "that the great problem of the world is the replacement of force as the arbiter of men's destiny."

After World War II, Helen White demonstrated her commitment to educational service as a member of the United States Educational Mission to Germany (1946), and the National Commission for UNESCO (1946–49). She was also a board member of Catholic educational foundations and committees as well as the National Conference of Christians and Jews (1940–49). The recipient of numerous honorary degrees and several major grants during her career, including both Guggenheim (1928–30) and Huntington Library (1939–40) fellowships, White helped in turn to promote the careers of students and fellow scholars, acting on an advisory board of the Whitney Foundation, a selection committee for Marshall Scholars, and as president of the Modern Humanities Research Association (1963). She was also president of the American Association of University Professors from 1956 to 1958.

For all White's professional responsibilities, generations of Wisconsin students knew her chiefly as a devoted and slightly eccentric teacher. She admitted to making more than her "due contribution to the saga of the absent-minded professor" (*Current Biography*, p. 670); a dull set of seminar papers once put White to sleep in class, and she found that students' presentations became more lively as a result. "I have often thought since then," she wrote later, "that it would be better for teachers to fall asleep than to leave all the sleeping to the students." Known as "the lady in purple," White stayed with the color because it was easy to coordinate for travel. The same pragmatic approach was apparent in her advice to students. Dissertations and novels, personal organization and professional advancement, all were subject to her standard advice: "Get on with it."

After her retirement as chairman of the English department in 1965, White received an appointment to the University of Wisconsin Institute for Research in the Humanities. She suffered from heart disease in her last years and died of a stroke in Norwood, Mass., in June 1967. Through her full career as a teacher, novelist, and policymaker, Helen White maintained an integrated view of the importance of the life of the mind and demonstrated the potential of educated women to serve society.

[White's files, including newspaper clippings, MSS., and some correspondence, are in the Univ. Archives, Memorial Library, Univ. of Wis., Madison. In addition to the books cited, White's scholarly works include *English Devotional Literature (Prose) 1600–1640* (1931), *The Tudor Books of Private Devotion* (1951), and *Tudor Books of Saints and Martyrs* (1963). Her other novels are *To the End of the World* (1939), *Dust on the King's Highway* (1947), *The Four Rivers of Paradise* (1955), and *Bird of Fire: A Tale of St. Francis of Assisi* (1958). White cites the influence of her high school teachers in "An English Professor Examines Her Role in Teacher Education," *Jour. General Education*, April 1966, pp. 31–39. She discusses her education and development as a literary critic in "Criticism in Context," *College English*, Oct. 1965, pp. 17–23, and in *Changing Styles in Literary Studies*, Presidential Address of the Modern Humanities Research Assoc. (1963). As the organization's president from 1941 to 1947, White published a number of articles in the *AAUW Jour.*, including "University Women in War and Peace," Fall 1944, pp. 3–7. Biographical sources include *Current Biog.*, 1945; *Catholic Authors* (1948), pp. 782–84; *Twentieth Century Authors* (1955), p. 1072; *Contemporary Authors*, vol. 5–8, pp. 1234–35; and *Nat. Cyc. Am. Biog.*, LIII, 460–61. See also Jane Agard's article in State Hist. Soc. of Wis. Women's Auxiliary, *Famous Wisconsin Women*, 6 (1976), 73–79, and an obituary, *AAUW Jour.*, Oct. 1967, p. 29. A biobibliographical report on Helen White was prepared by Susan Simenz; death record from Mass. Dept. of Public Health.]

BARBARA HILLYER DAVIS

WIGHTMAN, Hazel Virginia Hotchkiss, Dec. 20, 1886–Dec. 5, 1974. Athlete.

Hazel Hotchkiss Wightman, whose name became synonymous with the game of tennis, was born in Healdsburg, Calif., the only daughter and fourth of five children of William Joseph and Emma Lucretia (Grove) Hotchkiss. Descended from seventeenth-century immigrants, her paternal grandparents had moved west from Kentucky in 1850; her maternal grandparents had come from Virginia after the Civil War. William Hotchkiss was a well-to-do rancher and cannery owner. Her parents encouraged Hazel, a frail child, to play baseball and football with her brothers. In 1900 the family moved to Berkeley. Two years later she saw her first tennis—a sport thought more proper for ladies—and won her first tournament. In 1909 she claimed the first of her record forty-four national titles, going on in 1909, 1910, and 1911 to win all three national events, Singles, Doubles, and Mixed. As late as 1978, this feat had never been duplicated. In 1924 she won Olympic Gold Medals in Doubles and Mixed and Wimbledon Doubles. She was a National Squash Champion in 1927 and runner-up in National Badminton Mixed. Hazel Hotchkiss Wightman's last national title came in 1954, and her final appearance in a national tournament was in 1960, at the age of seventy-three.

Hotchkiss graduated from the University of California at Berkeley in 1911. The next year she married George William Wightman, member of a prominent Boston family, a former Harvard tennis player and later a wealthy lawyer. The couple had five children. She was nursing her first child, George, in 1913 when she defeated the national champion at the Longwood Cricket Club in Chestnut Hill, Mass., a club that was to be identified with her name. Her father wrote that he was glad she was continuing to play, and that it was important for married women to keep up their interests. In 1919, after the birth of two more children, Virginia and Hazel, she won the National Singles again. Dorothy was born in 1922 and William in 1925. She was divorced from George Wightman in 1940, and thereafter lived in a large house near Longwood, which became the tournament home for the dozens of young women tennis players she taught and encouraged.

Born shortly after tennis was introduced into the United States, Wightman was a molder of the game. Her famous rivalry with May Sutton of southern California marked the real beginning of women's tennis. While Sutton introduced hard-hitting into women's tennis, Wightman launched the volleying game, hitherto thought possible only for men. This style capitalized on her quickness and alertness, offsetting her size of barely five feet. To free her arm for overhead smashes, she wore sleeveless dresses, contributing to the revolution in dress. Her game was "skillful, versatile and heady," according to the *San Francisco Call*. "She went up into the air to volley a ball like a fox terrier after a butterfly" (undated clipping, International Tennis Hall of Fame).

The extended rivalry with Sutton attained a strained grimness, yet Wightman kept herself under control, proving that "an athlete can be fiercely competitive and at the same time . . . perform with authentic sportsmanship" (Wind, "From Wimbledon," pp. 116, 118). Another remarkable asset was her ability to concentrate on her game. "Nothing bothered Hazel," Dick Williams, her Olympics Doubles partner, later commented. "She had marvelous anticipation and coordination—but her concentration was incredible."

In 1919 Wightman conceived the idea of an "International Cup" so that women players might have an objective comparable to that offered men by the Davis Cup. When she presented the Cup, with the hope of setting up matches among British, French, and American women, the International Lawn Tennis Federation vetoed the idea as expensive and without interest. Only the arrival in this country of some of the best British players and the need of the West Side Tennis Club of New York for an event to inaugurate its stadium led to the first Wightman Cup Match in 1923. Wightman played five times (1923, 1924, 1927, 1929, and 1931) and was team captain in thirteen competitions. The success of the Wightman Cup matches proved that women's tennis could flourish independent of men's.

In the 1920s Wightman embarked on her long career as a teacher of tennis. In *Better Tennis* (1933), she offered readers the advice she gave students: "Shoulders high, arms out"; "Skip before and after hitting"; "Cultivate a buoyant spirit." A later edition added an alphabetical series of maxims from "Always Alert" to "Xceed Xpectations" and "Zip Zip." Her success with such champions as Sarah Palfrey, Helen Wills, and her rival Helen Jacobs proved the keenness of her judgment and the soundness of her methods. But it was ordinary players with whom she most enjoyed working. "I have a special feeling about the awkward and shy ones. By doing something well that other people admire they will gain confidence and poise." In 1922 she started free clinics, open to all, at Longwood. She ran tournaments at all levels and opened her home to tournament players from champions to twelve-year-olds.

Although originally shocked by the idea of professional tennis for women, Wightman came to support demands for equal purses. She presented the first equal pay check at the United States National Championships in 1973.

"A bouncy, warm, unpretentious accumulation of unnervous energy," Hazel Wightman also possessed an "inalterable determination to help her neighbor" (Wind, "Run, Helen," p. 31). In addition to her work with young tennis players, she served the Red Cross in Boston for fifty years and supported the Boston Children's Hospital for over forty.

Her long career brought honors: the United States Lawn Tennis Association Service Bowl was donated in her honor and she was elected to the International Tennis Hall of Fame. On the fiftieth anniversary of the Wightman Cup, in 1973, she was made an honorary Commander of the British Empire by Queen Elizabeth II.

The Californian who had become, according to the *Boston Globe*, the "epitome of the Bostonian grande-dame" died of a heart attack in her Newton home just before her eighty-eighth birthday.

[Scrapbooks and other papers and mementos of Hazel Hotchkiss Wightman are at the Internat. Tennis Hall of Fame, Newport, R.I. A taped interview, made June 7, 1972, is part of the Boston Tradition in Sports Coll., Boston Public Library. Major articles about her include two by Herbert W. Wind: "Run, Helen," *New Yorker,* Aug. 30, 1952, and "From Wimbledon to Forest Hills," *New Yorker,* Oct. 13, 1975. See also Melvin Maddocks, "The Original Little Old Lady in Tennis Shoes," *Sports Illustrated,* April 10, 1972; Barbara Klaw, "Queen Mother of Tennis," *Am. Heritage,* Aug. 1975; Edwin S. Baker, "Hazel Hotchkiss Wightman," *Tennis USA,* Aug. 1973. The program for the fiftieth anniversary of the Wightman Cup matches at the Longwood Cricket Club contains a biographical article by Nancy Norton and several pictures of Hazel Wightman. Obituaries appeared in the *N.Y. Times* and the *Boston Globe,* Dec. 6, 1974, and in *Tennis USA,* Jan. 1975. Commemorative pieces containing biographical information include "Hazel Hotchkiss Wightman, 1886–1974," *Boston Globe,* Dec. 8, 1974; Larry Eldridge, "Hazel H. Wightman," *Christian Sci. Monitor,* Dec. 12, 1974; and an article in Kappa Kappa Gamma, *The Key,* Spring 1975. Death record provided by Mass. Dept. of Public Health.]

NANCY NORTON

WILDER, Laura Ingalls, Feb. 7, 1867–Feb. 10, 1957. Writer.

When Laura Ingalls Wilder was sixty-five years old, in 1932, she published *Little House in the Big Woods,* the first of the fictionalized memoirs of her western girlhood that would make her reputation. It was followed by *Farmer Boy* (1933), *Little House on the Prairie* (1935), *On the Banks of Plum Creek* (1937), *By the Shores of Silver Lake* (1939), *The Long Winter* (1940), *Little Town on the Prairie* (1941), and *Those Happy Golden Years* (1943), all narrative rich in quotidian detail. They immediately found a large audience; all except *Farmer Boy* were Newbery honor books, and the entire series was reprinted, with new illustrations by Garth Williams, in 1953. In 1974 a weekly television series was begun, loosely based on the books, and they have been translated into at least fourteen languages and Braille. In 1954 the American Library Association established the Laura Ingalls Wilder Award, given every five years to the author who, over a period of years, has made a substantial and lasting contribution to literature for children. She was its first recipient.

Laura Elizabeth Ingalls was born in Pepin, Wis., the second child and second of four daughters of Caroline (Quiner) and Charles Philip Ingalls; a son died in infancy. Seeking better land and easier farming, they moved repeatedly throughout Laura's childhood: by covered wagon to Missouri in 1869, and then on to Kansas in 1870, where they squatted illegally on Indian land. They returned to Wisconsin in 1871 and then went to Walnut Grove, Minn. (which would figure in her books as Plum Creek). The family lived briefly in Burr Oak, Iowa, where Charles Ingalls managed a small hotel in 1876. It was a period of her life so dismal that it did not figure in any of Laura's books. In 1877 they returned briefly to Walnut Grove, then in 1879 moved permanently to De Smet, S. Dak., where Charles Ingalls worked briefly for the railroad and took out a homestead claim. Laura and her three sisters grew up in De Smet.

Like many of their contemporaries, the family not only broke the soil for each of their successive farms, but built their own houses, dug their own wells, raised and preserved their own food, made most of their own clothes. They were usually deeply in debt; they sold the farm at Walnut Grove after a summer drought and grasshoppers. Laura and her sisters were aware of the financial pressures on their parents, and they were always deeply involved in the household economy, to which women's work was integral. When she wrote her books, Wilder recounted this labor in explicit detail. There are accounts of how to build a log cabin, how to stitch a sheet, and what to feed the chickens. Domestic work is respected, but never romanticized. On the eve of her own marriage, Laura hesitated: "I don't want to marry a farmer . . . a farm is such a hard place for a woman" (*The First Four Years*, pp. 3–4).

Laura Ingalls's education was sporadic. It took place in a series of one-room schools, beginning with the Barry Corner School in Pepin when she was four. Not until the winter of 1880, when she was thirteen, did her schooling take on any regularity. She attended the school in De Smet whenever it was in session, until she was nearly sixteen, and briefly again after her first teaching position, though she never formally graduated.

It was always assumed that Laura Ingalls would contribute to family expenses (especially for the schooling of the eldest daughter Mary, who was blind). Occasionally she worked in town, once sewing shirts for twenty-five cents a day. Although teachers were required to be sixteen, a complaisant member of a local school board administered the test for a certificate for her in December 1882, two months before her sixteenth birthday. She went immediately to her first job, a brief winter session at a small settlement twelve miles from home. The woman in whose home she boarded suffered a severe depression in the fierce Dakota winter, and Laura Ingalls remembered the experience as a warning of the effect the frontier could have on a woman not strong enough to resist it.

On Aug. 25, 1885, Laura Ingalls married Almanzo James Wilder, ten years her senior. His parents had moved from New York state to Spring Valley, Minn., and from there Wilder and his brother had left home to stake out their own claims near De Smet. In her account of the wedding in *These Happy Golden Years* Laura Ingalls announces that she will not say obey. " 'Are you for woman's rights . . .?' Almanzo asked in surprise. 'No,' Laura replied, 'I do not want to vote. But I can not make a promise that I will not keep.' "

Almanzo Wilder filed both a homestead and a tree claim. But the early years of their marriage were a succession of tragedies: crop failures, increasing debts, the death of an infant son. The house burned to the ground; both contracted diphtheria, from which Almanzo Wilder never seems to have recovered fully. After two years in western Florida and a brief return to De Smet, they set out again, searching for a healthier climate. Using money Laura Wilder had earned as a seamstress, they bought a small farm in Mansfield, Mo., in the Ozarks, where they remained for the rest of their lives. Wilder raised chickens and fruit on a substantial scale. From August 1919 until September 1927 she was secretary-treasurer of the Mansfield Farm Loan Association, through which farmers could borrow money from the Federal Land Bank in St. Louis. Laura Wilder was its sole paid officer, and she handled loan applications and transfers of funds with skill and efficiency.

The Wilders' only surviving child, Rose, was born on the Dakota homestead on Dec. 5, 1886; a boy, born in 1889, died twelve days after his birth. Rose Wilder was educated in one-room rural schoolhouses in Mansfield and became a telegrapher, a field newly open to women. After her marriage in 1909 to Gillette Lane (they divorced in 1917), she had a brief but successful career as one of the first female real estate agents in California, and then began to write for the *San Francisco Bulletin* and for *Sunset* magazine. An extraordinarily prolific writer, Rose Wilder Lane became a nationally known journalist. In the 1930s she was a vigorous critic of President Franklin D. Roosevelt and the New Deal, and she later worked for conservative causes. When she published the *Woman's Day Book of Needlework* in 1963 she saw it as a "pro-American, anti-Socialist" statement celebrating traditional women's folk art. In 1965, age seventy-nine, she traveled to Vietnam on assignment for *Woman's Day*, reporting that the communist threat there should be halted before it reached the Philippines, Australia, and even Hawaii. She died on Oct. 30, 1968.

Rose Wilder Lane had encouraged her mother to write; indeed she served her as agent, editor, and even collaborator. Although the first editor of the *Little House* books publicized them as the artless accounts of an unsophisticated pioneer woman, Laura Ingalls Wilder served a very long apprenticeship. She wrote columns about farm households for the *Missouri Ruralist* between 1911 and 1924, and about poultry for the *St. Louis Star;* she also sold a few articles to *McCall's* and *Country Gentleman*. In 1915 she went to San Francisco for the Panama-Pacific International Exposition, the longest trip of her life, explicitly "to see a lot of new things to write" (*West From Home*, p. 5). She made herself Lane's pupil: "Rose and I are blocking out a story of the Ozarks for me to finish when I get home. If I can only make it sell, it ought to help a lot" (*West From Home*, p. 67).

Not until 1931 did Wilder begin her first book, *Little House in the Big Woods*. Rose Wilder Lane directed the negotiations with the Knopf publishing house and then with Harpers which ultimately published the series; her literary agent was involved in handling the subsequent volumes. Letters between Wilder and Lane in the 1930s show their continuing dialogue on the shaping of plot, characterization, and style.

Little House in the Big Woods was successful

as soon as it was published. The account of a self-sufficient family, making it through hard times on their own, always providing security for their children, had an obvious message in the depression years. Praise continued to build. Reviewers admired the spare prose, "aways dignified and restrained, often elegant," and the lack of sentimentality. In the last years of her life, Wilder carried on extensive correspondence with children who read her books. Almanzo Wilder died in 1949, aged ninety-two. Three days after her own ninetieth birthday, in February 1957, Laura Ingalls Wilder died in Mansfield of a stroke.

The *Little House* books were written from the perspective of a child; indeed the manuscript revisions show Wilder's care in making sure that this point of view was consistently maintained. After Wilder's death, an unfinished manuscript was published as *The First Four Years* (1971). In tone and characterization it differs markedly from the previous books. The young couple face an unremitting series of calamities: drought, debt, illness, and death. In earlier books similar experiences had been described as challenges that could be overcome. But the happy security of childhood vanishes in *The First Four Years,* where parents no longer stand as a buffer between their daughter and the cruel reality of the frontier.

Wilder's books did not lose their popularity; twenty years after her death it was estimated that the total sale of all her books since their original publication was more than twenty million copies. They remain a rich chronicle of a woman's life—as child and adult—on the plains frontier, with "a dramatic force that derives from honesty and accuracy" (E. B. White, *Horn Book Mag.,* Aug. 1970, p. 349). They retain their immediacy. "Now is now," thinks the child Laura at the end of *Little House in the Big Woods.* "It can never be a long time ago."

[Small collections of Laura Ingalls Wilder's correspondence are held by the Detroit Public Library; the Pomona (Calif.) Public Library; the Laura Ingalls Wilder/Rose Wilder Lane Home and Museum, Mansfield, Mo. (which also has artifacts and documents); and the Laura Ingalls Wilder Memorial Society in De Smet. The Society also maintains the Ingallses' 1879–80 home and the school Wilder attended. Wilder donated manuscript drafts of *The Long Winter* and *These Happy Golden Years* to the Detroit Public Library. Examiner's reports of Wilder's conduct of the Mansfield Farm Loan Assoc. are in the records of the Farm Credit Admin., Record Group 103, Nat. Archives. Some Rose Wilder Lane correspondence is in the Dorothy Thompson Papers, Arents Research Library, Syracuse Univ.; her letters to Fremont Older, editor of the *San Francisco Bulletin,* are in the Bancroft Library,

Univ. of Calif., Berkeley. Other papers of both Wilder and Lane are held by Lane's executor, Roger Lea MacBride, of Charlottesville, Va. The first editions of the *Little House* books were illustrated by Helen Sewell. A special edition of the *Horn Book Mag.,* Dec. 1953, includes comments by Garth Williams on his illustrations for the new edition of the series published that year, and by Virginia Kirkus on the decision to publish *Little House in the Big Woods.* Wilder's diary of the trip from De Smet to Mansfield in 1894 was published as *On the Way Home* (1962), with an introduction by Rose Wilder Lane. The letters Wilder wrote during her visit to San Francisco were published in *West From Home: Letters of Laura Ingalls Wilder to Almanzo Wilder—San Francisco 1915* (1974). Two of Rose Wilder Lane's books, *Let the Hurricane Roar* (1933) and *Free Land* (1938), are concerned with themes similar to those in Wilder's books, treated from an adult viewpoint. *Rose Wilder Lane: Her Story* (1977) is a fictionalized biography, loosely based on letters and diaries, written by Roger Lea MacBride. The most subtle scholarly analyses of Wilder's prose appear in two articles by Rosa Ann Moore, "Laura Ingalls Wilder's Orange Notebooks and the Art of the *Little House* Books," *Children's Literature* (1976; annual of the Modern Language Assoc. Seminar on children's literature), pp. 105–19, and "The *Little House* Books: Rose-Colored Classics," *Children's Literature* (1978), pp. 7–16. The only biography is Donald Zochert, *Laura: The Life of Laura Ingalls Wilder* (1976), which emphasizes the period of Wilder's life described in the *Little House* books, with a brief final chapter on the years after 1894. William Anderson, curator of the Wilder Memorial Soc., emphasizes the later years of her life in *Laura Wilder of Mansfield* (1974). The most significant of Rose Wilder Lane's books are *The Peaks of Shala* (1923), *Hill-Billy* (1926), *Let the Hurricane Roar* (which was reprinted in 1976 as *Young Pioneers*), and *Free Land.* An obituary of Laura Ingalls Wilder appeared in the *N.Y. Times,* Feb. 12, 1957; of Rose Wilder Lane, Nov. 1, 1968. A death record was provided by the Div. of Health of Mo. Preparation of this article has been facilitated by a biobibliography prepared by Ivy Lerner.]

LINDA K. KERBER

WILHELMI, Jane Russell. *See* RUSSELL, Jane.

WILLEBRANDT, Mabel Walker, May 23, 1889–April 6, 1963. Lawyer, federal official.

Mabel Walker Willebrandt, hailed by her contemporaries as the "First Lady in Law," was assistant attorney general of the United States from 1921 to 1929. Born in a homestead cabin in Woodsdale, Kans., she was the only child of Myrtle (Eaton) and David William Walker. Her mother was born in Illinois, her father, who was of German ancestry, in Pennsylvania. Mabel shared their nomadic frontier life as they variously taught and edited newspapers in Missouri and Oklahoma. Reading at home and learning through setting type in her father's office, she was thirteen before she entered the sixth grade in Kansas City, Mo., for her first formal schooling. She then attended Park College, Parkville, Mo., until expelled for expressing her religious differences with the administration.

By seventeen Mabel Walker had passed her teaching examinations. Moving with her parents to the lumber town of Buckley, Mich., she taught in the local public school. In February 1910 she married the principal, Arthur F. Willebrandt. To treat his tuberculosis the couple went to Tempe, Ariz., where in addition to nursing her husband Mabel Willebrandt completed a degree program at the State Normal School in 1911 and taught briefly in Phoenix. With her husband and mother-in-law she moved to Los Angeles, where she became the youthful principal of Buena Park School, and then of Lincoln Park grammar school in South Pasadena. She wanted to study medicine but, as no night classes were available, she began instead to take law classes at the University of Southern California, where her husband was also a law student. Her job as principal supported them both. Admitted to the bar in 1915, Mabel Willebrandt received an LL.B in 1916 and an LL.M. in 1917.

Her concern with the problem of legal assistance for the poor led Willebrandt to press for the establishment of a public defender's office in Los Angeles. Soon after its inception in 1915, she was appointed to the nonsalaried post of assistant public defender with special responsibilities for cases involving women. While simultaneously developing a private practice, she worked on the defense of over 2,000 women; her vigorous and sympathetic handling of prostitution cases resulted in a changed practice in court procedures as judges began to mandate the appearance of both man and woman before the bench. She spoke persuasively before a joint session of the legislature for a married women's property bill (1918) and worked for legislation that would forbid corporations and banks from practicing law in California. In addition, Willebrandt was active in civic and political affairs, and in professional women's clubs. She served on the legislative committee of the California Bar Association, and became a member of the Republican State Committee.

During World War I, Mabel Willebrandt was appointed head of the Legal Advisory Board for draft cases for district eleven, the largest draft board in Los Angeles. Subsequently, she was recommended by Senator Hiram Johnson and by every member of the bench in southern California for the post of assistant attorney general in the Harding administration. During his interview with her, President Warren G. Harding noted that the only thing against her was her age, a condition, she noted, that would be solved by time. She later reminisced, however: "I was a young lawyer, much too young (only 32) when appointed for the responsibilities heaped on me."

Only the second woman to receive an appointment as assistant attorney general and the first to have an extended term (ANNETTE ABBOTT ADAMS, appointed in 1920, served less than a year), Willebrandt began her service under the controversial Attorney General Harry M. Daugherty. She was responsible for the division in the Justice Department which dealt with tax, prison, and prohibition matters. Much of her effort was expended in corporate, estate, and income tax cases; her arguments in such cases have been credited with establishing the foundation for interpretations of the income tax amendment (Griswold and Knoeller interviews).

Her most publicized activities, however, were in the area of prohibition. Before her appointment, Willebrandt had not been a prohibitionist; in office, she was determined to uphold the law. The major obstacles, she noted in *The Inside of Prohibition* (1929), were political interference, official incompetence, and public indifference. She especially chafed at the indifference of Treasury Secretary Andrew W. Mellon, and described many United States marshals' offices as "filled with broken down politicians, fond of drink and low company" (Winter, p. 63). Congressional drinking was particularly repugnant, especially the sight of a "Senator in drunken condition holding onto his desk to block legislation." The performance of some United States attorneys in bringing cases to trial ranged from inefficient to obstructionist. Under Daugherty's successor, Harlan Fiske Stone, she was able to secure the dismissal of several attorneys hostile to the prosecution of prohibition violations. Angered at the dismissal of a protégé, California Senator Morgan Shortridge later blocked Willebrandt's hoped-for appointment to the federal bench in California.

Despite the obstacles, major cases were broken under Willebrandt's direction. In 1923, the Big Four of Savannah, allegedly the largest bootleg ring in the country, was cracked, as were the Cincinnati operations of bootlegger George Remus (O'Donnell, p. 16). The attorney general's annual report for 1925 noted that of 48,734 cases brought by Willebrandt's division between June 1924 and June 1925, 39,072 ended in convictions. Willebrandt submitted

278 cases *on certiorari* to the Supreme Court dealing with the defense, clarification, and enforcement of the prohibition amendment and the Volstead Act. She also argued over forty Supreme Court cases, a total that has rarely been exceeded; particularly noteworthy were her victories in cases controlling liquor sales on American and foreign vessels.

Earning the title of "Prohibition Portia," Willebrandt wrote and spoke extensively urging public support of the law. She consistently argued that the government should aim at the major offenders, complaining that "going after the hip pocket and speakeasy cases" was "like trying to dry up the Atlantic Ocean with a blotter" (O'Donnell, p. 16). At the time, she challenged allegations that the eighteenth amendment was unenforceable, but later concluded that it "covered too much territory" and that local enforcement should have been left to local authorities (Willebrandt memoir, Stone MSS.).

In her efforts to enforce the law, Willebrandt proposed the reallocation of federal judges to respond more flexibly to prohibition case loads, the transfer of enforcement from the Treasury to the Justice Department, better articulation of law enforcement agencies, and stiffer, more consistent sentences for convicted offenders. She also recommended J. Edgar Hoover to head the Bureau of Investigation (Mason, p. 150).

If Mabel Willebrandt's prohibition efforts proved frustrating and controversial, her prison work was universally applauded. Her "energy and resourcefulness" led to the establishment in West Virginia of Alderson, the first federal prison for women. The first warden, MARY B. HARRIS, was her choice. She also effected the establishment of the Chillicothe, Ohio, reformatory for young male offenders, worked to reform the administration of the Atlanta prison, and brought in professional Sanford Bates as chief of the Bureau of Prisons.

In 1928 Willebrandt became a central figure in the heated presidential campaign. The first woman to chair a committee at a Republican National Convention, she skillfully handled the credentials disputes and effectively seated thirty-five contested delegates for candidate Herbert Hoover. Soon after, she was accused of planning a series of raids on New York speakeasies to coincide with the Democratic National Convention, meeting to nominate Alfred E. Smith. Most controversial were her speaking tours. A strong, vital speaker, who had briefly toured on the Redpath Chautauqua circuit, Willebrandt was dispatched to the midwest, border south, and far west. In Ohio in September she urged 2,500 pastors of the Methodist Episcopal church to support Hoover because the enforcement of prohibition "must be in the hands of those who believe in it." Smith immediately attacked her for bringing religion into the campaign, the hostile *New York Times* urged Hoover to silence her, and an *Independent* editorial announced "Mrs. Willebrandt Runs Amuk." Dry forces cheered her as Deborah, "a woman of God carrying a great message." Dismayed at the furor, Willebrandt secured a statement from the Republican party speakers bureau that she spoke under its auspices; she later declared that she had twice asked the bureau to excuse her from giving the speech (*Inside of Prohibition*, pp. 11–12). *Collier's* concluded in an October issue: "No other woman has ever had so much influence upon a presidential campaign as this one."

Following Hoover's election, Willebrandt decided to return to private practice and in May 1929 he accepted her resignation with regret. She had met all the responsibilities of public office while facing major challenges in her personal life. Physically strong, she faced an increasing hearing disability. In a letter to her mother in October 1923, the night before arguing a case before the Supreme Court, she worried: "Each time it's such a struggle not to be terrified over my ears. They talk so low—the Justices." After an eight-year separation, her marriage ended in divorce in 1924. Believing that life was not complete without children, and having failed to have any of her own after an early miscarriage, she adopted two-year-old Dorothy Rae in 1925. She shared the care of Dorothy with her housemates, LOUISE STANLEY, chief of the Bureau of Home Economics, and Annabel Matthews (1883–1960) of the legal department of the Treasury, as well as with nurse-cook Rose Gainor, and the Walkers, who made frequent visits.

After 1929 Willebrandt renewed her private practice, establishing offices in Washington and California. In a flurry of press attacks, Methodists and other dry forces decried her work with her client the California Grape Growers and their affiliate, Fruit Industries Ltd., which produced a grape concentrate that could be fermented in the home. Later Willebrandt helped the beleaguered grape growers to obtain $20,000,000 in Federal Farm Board funds.

Other major clients reflected such new industries as aviation and communication. Willebrandt served as Washington counsel for the Aviation Corporation and compiled the first comprehensive review of common law and state and national statutes on the control of air space; subsequently she was the first woman to head a committee of the American Bar Association, the Committee on Aeronautical Law. She was a friend of aviators AMELIA EARHART and Jacqueline Cochran, and obtained her own pilot's license in the 1940s.

In the communications industry, Willebrandt represented the Screen Directors Guild and was instrumental in gaining the guild's first victory in a 1938–39 labor struggle with producers. She was also the attorney for many Hollywood figures, including Clark Gable, JEAN HARLOW, and W. S. Van Dyke. In 1932 she represented Indiana station WJKS in a case that established the authority of the Federal Radio Commission to allocate radio licenses from over- to under-utilized regions.

Concerned with the position of women and the law, Willebrandt served as national president of the women's legal fraternity Phi Delta Delta from 1922 to 1926 and worked to bring talented women lawyers into the Justice Department. She urged that women should lead in ending sex discrimination in law and business "by accepting a fair field for all, with no particular favors to the fair" (*New York Times,* Sept. 20, 1929).

Maintaining homes in Washington and California and a farm in Gettysburg, Pa., Willebrandt managed a warm social life despite her arduous work schedule. Her deep concern for others, vividly demonstrated in her early teens by her insistence that her parents adopt a homeless young girl, was later evident in her continued help to many of the women she met through her public defender cases. Attractive, outgoing, and vital, she built deep and lasting friendships, and was an accomplished hostess, known for large Sunday gatherings at her farm. On one of her Gettysburg holidays, she began a lively discussion of religion with a Roman Catholic priest visiting from nearby Emmitsburg, Md. Raised in the Christian Church, she had become a Christian Scientist in the mid-1920s. In 1952 her reading and reflection led to her conversion to Roman Catholicism.

She died of lung cancer at her home in Riverside, Calif., in April 1963. Reviewing her long career of firsts, her friend Judge John J. Sirica observed: "If Mabel had worn trousers she could have been President."

[A small collection of Willebrandt Papers at the Library of Congress contains clippings, family papers and correspondence, and material relating to her work in the 1920s. Her long memoir written to Alpheus Mason in 1951 is in the Harlan Fiske Stone Papers at the Library of Congress. Information on her work with Alderson prison, and with prohibition and tax law are in the Archives of the Justice Dept. Her monograph, *The Inside of Prohibition,* was published in 1929. Willebrandt's articles appealing for public observance of prohibition appeared in the *Ladies' Home Journal,* July 1929; *The Woman Citizen,* Feb. 23, 1924; and *Good Housekeeping,* April 1924. "First Impressions," on child rearing, was in *Good Housekeeping,* May 1928. Biographical articles include "Who's Who–and Why," *Sat. Eve. Post,* Sept. 27, 1924; Alice Winter, "First Lady in Law," *Ladies' Home Journal,* June 1925; "First Legal Lady of the Land," *Literary Digest,* March 31, 1923; Jack O'Donnell, "Can This Woman Make America Dry?" *Collier's,* Aug. 9, 1924; Avery Strakosch, "A Woman in Law," *Sat. Eve. Post,* Sept. 24, 1927; Frances Parkinson Keyes, "Homes of Outstanding American Women," *Better Homes and Gardens,* March 1928; and John S. Martin, "Mrs. Firebrand," *New Yorker,* Feb. 16, 1929. For background information on her prohibition and Justice Department years see Thomas M. Coffey, *The Long Thirst* (1975), and Alpheus T. Mason, *Harlan Fiske Stone: Pillar of the Law* (1956); for Alderson and prison reform, Mary B. Harris, *I Knew Them in Prison* (1936), and Sanford Bates, *Prisons and Beyond* (1936); for aviation, Jacqueline Cochran, *The Stars at Noon* (1954); for the Screen Directors Guild, Frank Capra, *The Name Above the Title* (1971), and Robert C. Cannon, *Van Dyke and the Mythical City, Hollywood* (1948, 1977). Obituaries appeared in the *L.A. Times,* April 8, 1963, and the *N.Y. Times,* April 9, 1963. A death record was provided by Calif. Dept. of Public Health. Interviews with her daughter, Dorothy Rae Van Dyke, and with her friends and associates Grace Knoeller, Paula Knoeller Gore, John J. Sirica, May Lahey, Erwin N. Griswold, and Myra Dell Collins were valuable.]

DOROTHY M. BROWN

WILLIAMS, Anna Wessels, March 17, 1863–Nov. 20, 1954. Physician, bacteriologist.

Anna Wessels Williams, who gained national recognition for her contributions to the understanding of infectious diseases and to effective diphtheria immunization, was born in Hackensack, N.J. She was the second child and second daughter of six children (three girls and three boys) of William and Jane (Van Saun) Williams; there were also half sisters and brothers from her father's first marriage. Anna Williams's family was religious. Her mother especially was an avid supporter of missions for the First Reformed (Dutch) Church of Hackensack. Her father, English by birth, had been a private school teacher; in 1875 he became a trustee of the State Street Public School where Anna began her formal education at age twelve. Before then, her parents had taught their children at home, not approving of the public schools and unable to afford private education. At the State Street School Williams became interested in science when she looked under a teacher's "wonderful microscope."

A diploma from the New Jersey State Normal

School in Trenton in 1883 and a brief teaching stint (1883–85) preceded her choice of a medical career. The decision came in 1887 when her sister Millie lost her baby and almost died. Greatly disturbed by the doctors' inability to intervene, that fall Anna Williams entered the Woman's Medical College of the New York Infirmary. Her father gave his full support, and her mother withdrew her initial objections when Williams suggested she might become a medical missionary. After obtaining an M.D. degree in 1891, Williams remained at the New York Infirmary until 1893 as an instructor in pathology and hygiene. She also served as assistant to the chairman of the department of pathology and hygiene (1891–95), and as a consulting pathologist (1902–05).

In 1894 Williams volunteered to assist in the diagnostic laboratory of the New York City Department of Health, the first municipally operated diagnostic laboratory in the nation, which had opened the year before. There Williams assisted the director, William Hallock Park, an early exponent of applied bacteriology, in his effort to find a more effective antitoxin for diphtheria, a leading cause of childhood deaths. By the end of her first year, she had published two papers, and in 1895 she became a full-time staff member with the title of assistant bacteriologist.

Early in 1894 Williams isolated a strain of the diphtheria bacillus (later classified as *Corynebacterium diphtheriae*) from a case of mild tonsillar diphtheria. This strain, known throughout the world as Park-Williams #8 or occasionally as the Park strain, possesses an unusual capability for generating toxin, and remains in use for commercial toxin production. (Park was on vacation at the time of isolation, but he oversaw subsequent experimental and clinical trials; due to his position as laboratory director and the nature of the collaborative research much of the credit has been attributed to him.) Williams's discovery greatly facilitated antitoxin production and enabled New York City to undertake its successful campaign against diphtheria. By the autumn of 1894 antitoxin was made available to physicians without charge for patients who could not afford to pay. The program was soon adopted by public health authorities throughout North America and Great Britain. Two decades later the New York City public health laboratories championed the active immunization of children with modified toxins, and in this work Anna Williams also played a role, albeit a less central one. Due to these pioneering efforts diphtheria became a rare disease in many countries, including the United States.

Williams had the ability to work on a multiplicity of problems; in addition to her work on diphtheria, between 1894 and 1896 she investigated the bacteriology of streptococcal and pneumococcal infections. In 1896 she went to the Pasteur Institute in Paris to obtain a toxin for scarlet fever which she hoped would yield an antitoxin comparable to that used in the treatment of diphtheria. Although her endeavors were unsuccessful, her visit there led her to another advance in disease control in the United States. When Williams returned to the New York City Laboratories in September she brought with her a culture of rabies virus. Through her efforts, sufficient vaccine was prepared from this culture so that by 1898 large-scale rabies vaccine production could be undertaken.

In her effort to find a rapid method of diagnosing suspected rabid animals, Williams noted the consistent appearance of a distinctive body or cell in infected brain tissue from proven cases. Concurrently, Adelchi Negri, an Italian physician, published in 1904 his observations of the presence and significance of these cellular inclusions, which became known as "Negri bodies"; they have remained the criterion for the pathological diagnosis of rabies. Undaunted, Williams, in 1905, published a new rapid method for preparing and staining brain tissue in order to detect Negri bodies. This was a major step forward in rabies diagnosis and subsequent control; her staining method was not improved upon until 1939. The significance of this work was recognized when the American Public Health Association, at its annual meeting in 1907, established a Committee on the Standard Methods for the Diagnosis of Rabies and named Williams its chairman.

Williams also studied chronic inflammatory eye infections then being diagnosed as trachoma which were rampant among underprivileged school children in New York City. Trachoma leads to scarring and sometimes blindness and "trachoma centers" had been established throughout the city. Williams's studies were undertaken in cooperation with the Division of Child Hygiene, under the directorship of S. JOSEPHINE BAKER. After seeing over 3,000 cases, Williams found that more benign infections than trachoma were responsible and the centers were closed.

Meanwhile, the New York City Research Laboratories had grown rapidly and in 1905 Williams was named assistant director, a post she held until her retirement in 1934. Team work became well organized under her leadership and the staff, which included many women, greatly expanded. During World War I Williams was appointed to an influenza commission jointly sponsored by the research laboratory, medical schools, and an insurance company. At the request of the War Department she directed a training program at New York University for workers for war service in medical laboratories in the United States and in Europe. She also participated in the program for the detection of meningococcal carriers in the military.

Williams was a prolific writer. In 1905 she joined Park as coauthor of the second edition of *Pathogenic Microörganisms Including Bacteria and Protozoa: A Practical Manual for Students, Physicians and Health Officers.* Park and Williams, as the text was widely known, enjoyed immense popularity; its final, eleventh, edition (1939) was published after Park's death. In 1929, also with Park, she wrote *Who's Who Among the Microbes,* a book for lay readers—a first of its kind. Williams's intensive studies of streptococci, which extended the work of others including George and GLADYS DICK, helped demonstrate that several toxins are involved in streptococcal infections. In 1932 she published a definitive monograph, *Streptococci in Relation to Man in Health and Disease.*

On March 31, 1934, Williams was forced to retire when Mayor Fiorello La Guardia, despite petitions from her colleagues, refused to make an exception to the mandatory retirement principle. Retiring to Woodcliff Lake, N.J., ten years later she moved to Westwood, N.J. There she lived with her sister, Amelia Wilson, until her death in 1954 from heart failure.

Among her honors, Williams was the first woman to be elected to an office in the laboratory section of the American Public Health Association, serving as vice chairman (1931); the following year she became chairman of the section. She was also honored at a testimonial dinner given by the New York Women's Medical Society in 1936 for her significant services to the city, and for advancing the cause of women doctors. In her acceptance speech, Williams, whose achievements had been overshadowed by her close association with Park, characteristically mentioned the names of the coworkers—many of them women—who had contributed to her own success.

[The Anna Wessels Williams Papers, which include an autobiographical manuscript, correspondence, clippings, and photographs, are located in the Schlesinger Library, Radcliffe College. Williams published in several scientific journals between 1893 and 1935, especially *Collected Studies* of the Research Laboratories of the N.Y. City Health Dept., 1905–26, and the *Monthly Health Bull.,* N.Y. City Health Dept., 1911–18. Her major works include: "Persistence of Varieties of the Bacillus Diphtheriae and of Diphtheria-Like Bacilli," *Jour. Medical Research,* June 1902; "The Etiology and Diagnosis of Hydrophobia," *Jour. Infectious Diseases,* May 1906; "A Study of Trachoma and Allied Conditions in the Public School Children of New York City," *Jour. Infectious Diseases,* March 1914; "Relationship of the Streptococci Causing Erysipelas," *Am. Jour. Public Health,* Dec. 1929; "The Etiology of Influenza," *Proceedings* of the N.Y. Pathological Soc., Jan.-May 1918. Miscellaneous studies may be found in *Women's Medical Jour.,* April 1909 and April 1910; *Am. Jour. Obstetrics and Gynecology,* April 1933; *Annals of Otology, Rhinology and Laryngology,* Sept. 1934; and *East African Medical Jour.,* Oct. 1934. Secondary works include: Wade W. Oliver, *The Man Who Lived for Tomorrow: A Biography of William Hallock Park* (1941), an excellent source, containing several letters from Williams to Park; Esther P. Lovejoy, *Women Doctors of the World* (1957); *New York Health Department Centennial, 1866–1966* (1966); *Who Was Who in America,* V (1969–70); and Elizabeth D. Robinton, "A Tribute to Women Leaders in the Laboratory Section of the American Public Health Association," *Am. Jour. Public Health,* Oct. 1974. Obituaries appeared in the *N.Y. Times,* Nov. 21, 1954, and the Bergen *Evening Record,* Nov. 22, 1954. Some family information from U.S. Census, 1880. Annis Thomson provided useful information. Death certificate provided by N.J. Dept. of Health.]

ELIZABETH D. ROBINTON

WILSON, Edith Bolling Galt, Oct. 15, 1872– Dec. 28, 1961.

Edith Bolling Wilson, second wife of Woodrow Wilson, twenty-eighth president of the United States, was born in Wytheville, Va., the seventh of eleven children and fourth of five daughters of William Holcombe and Sallie (White) Bolling. The Bollings were among the oldest families in Virginia (Edith's grandmother seven times removed was POCAHONTAS) and had been plantation owners before the Civil War. His plantation devastated and his slaves gone, William H. Bolling moved to the backwater town of Wytheville in southwestern Virginia, opened a law practice, and soon became a judge of the circuit court.

Edith Bolling grew up in genteel poverty in an extended family which included both grandmothers and two aunts. She enjoyed a happy childhood and remained extremely close to her family. Her father, a devout Episcopalian, influenced her greatly. Her formal education consisted of a year's attendance at Martha Washington College, a finishing school in Abingdon, Va., and a second year at Powell's School in Richmond. What skills Bolling acquired, she learned for the most part at home from her paternal grandmother. Although she wrote that she loved hearing the classics read to her as a child, she apparently did little reading before her marriage to Woodrow Wilson. Her penmanship was primitive; as late as 1915 her letters were almost illegible. However, she possessed keen native intelligence and was a shrewd judge of character. She also had a lively wit, was a great raconteur, and possessed charm, warmth, and impeccable manners according to Victorian standards.

In the early 1890s Edith Bolling went to Washington, D.C., to visit her sister Gertrude Bolling Galt, whose husband, Alexander, was a partner in his father's jewelry and silver goods store, Galt's. Norman Galt, a cousin of Alexander and also a partner in the store, became her constant suitor. They were married in 1896. Norman Galt soon became sole owner of the store, and the couple prospered and moved in upper-class circles in Washington. For Edith Galt, the marriage was not a happy one. The Galts had one child, a boy, born in 1903, who lived only three days; she was incapable of having children afterward.

After Norman Galt's death in 1908, Edith Galt delegated the responsibility for running the business to trusted and able employees. She traveled frequently to Europe, entertained, and attended the theater. An avid motorist, she owned the first electric car in Washington. Among a number of young women she befriended was Alice Gordon, who was being courted by Cary T. Grayson, Woodrow Wilson's physician and aide. Through Grayson, in late 1914 Edith Galt became acquainted with Wilson's cousin Helen Woodrow Bones, mistress of the White House after ELLEN AXSON WILSON's death in August 1914. The two women soon became intimate friends. About mid-March 1915, an accidental meeting with the president in the White House led to an invitation to dinner.

Wilson, who had suffered severe depression and loneliness since Ellen Wilson's death, was at once smitten by Edith Galt. He wrote his first letter to her on April 28, 1915, and professed his love on May 4. From that day until near the time of their marriage, he wrote her at least one and often two long letters a day, except when they spent several weeks together at his summer home in Cornish, N.H. Edith Galt said that she was "dead to love"; Wilson rekindled her capacity for love. Insecure and uncertain whether she had the qualities that a first lady should possess, she hesitated in accepting his offer of marriage. Wilson persuaded her that she not only was fully capable but was absolutely indispensable as a lover and helpmate. On June 29 she agreed to marry him. They announced their engagement on October 6 and were married in her home on Dec. 18, 1915. The dark and

gloomy White House became bright and gay again after the marriage, for Edith Wilson loved parties and was a gracious hostess.

From the time of their marriage until Woodrow Wilson's death in 1924, Edith Wilson rarely left her husband's side. She had a keen interest in all aspects of domestic and foreign problems, and he kept her completely informed. They read diplomatic dispatches together; he read all his important state papers to her before he prepared the final text; and she decoded messages in the president's secret code. In 1919 she went with him to the Paris Peace Conference.

Edith Wilson had strong opinions and expressed them vigorously to her husband. He valued her advice; indeed, he seems to have regarded her as his wisest and certainly most trusted counselor. However, he made important decisions upon the basis of his own independent conclusions. Her most important role was to provide him with the companionship and love that was indispensable to his happiness and well-being.

She is known to have engaged in only one political intrigue. In late 1916 she made a compact with Col. Edward M. House that she would persuade her husband to dismiss his secretary, Joseph P. Tumulty, and House would persuade the president to dismiss Secretary of the Navy Josephus Daniels. Thus importuned, President Wilson asked Tumulty to resign but relented when his secretary begged to stay on; House did not keep his part of the bargain.

Much controversy has arisen about Edith Wilson's role in governing during Woodrow Wilson's illness following a massive stroke on October 2, 1919. Her sole concern was the health and recovery of her husband, and she accepted the judgment of his physicians who, when she suggested that it might be best for him to resign, replied that resignation would impair his chances for recovery. She insisted that she never made an important political decision during the period of her husband's illness, and there is abundant documentary evidence confirming the truth of her assertion. Her method was, first, to go over important letters and reports with Tumulty; together they decided which should be shown to the president. She then took the documents to him and either read them aloud or, when he had strength enough, let him read them. He then instructed her what to say in reply, and she wrote on the documents, "The President instructs . . ." or "The President believes . . ." The single known instance when Edith Wilson tried to influence her husband at this time occurred during the height of the controversy over the Treaty of Versailles. According to her own account, she begged the president to accept Sen. Henry Cabot Lodge's reservations to the treaty, which would have specified the limits of United States obligations to the League of Nations. Wilson's refusal to do so is considered a crucial factor in the defeat of the treaty.

The Wilsons moved to a home on S Street in Washington upon Woodrow Wilson's retirement in 1921. Edith Wilson was a faithful nurse and companion to her husband until his death on Feb. 3, 1924. During the balance of her life she encouraged and took great interest in organizations and projects perpetuating her husband's memory and ideals, such as the Woodrow Wilson Foundation, the Woodrow Wilson Birthplace Foundation, the Woodrow Wilson School of Public and International Affairs of Princeton University, and the publication of his papers. She retained ownership of Galt's until 1934, when she sold it to her employees. Her active interest in political affairs never diminished, and one of her last public appearances was at the inauguration of President John F. Kennedy. Edith Wilson died quietly in her home of heart failure in December 1961.

[The basic sources are the Edith Bolling Wilson Papers and the Woodrow Wilson Papers, both in the Library of Congress. All the letters between Woodrow Wilson and Edith Bolling Wilson, as well as many of her other letters, will be published in forthcoming volumes of Arthur S. Link and others, eds., *The Papers of Woodrow Wilson*. No adequate historical literature on her life exists. Her autobiography, *My Memoir* (1938), is anecdotal and often unreliable. Alden Hatch, *Edith Bolling Wilson* (1961), and Ishbel Ross, *Power with Grace: The Life Story of Mrs. Woodrow Wilson* (1975), both rely heavily upon *My Memoir*. Accounts of the Galt-Wilson courtship and marriage appear in Ray Stannard Baker, *Woodrow Wilson; Life and Letters: Facing War, 1915–1917* (1937), and Arthur S. Link, *Wilson: Confusions and Crises, 1915–1916* (1964). An obituary appeared in the *N.Y. Times*, Dec. 29, 1961.]

ARTHUR S. LINK

WOLFF, Sister Madeleva (Mary Evaline), May 24, 1887–July 25, 1964. College administrator, religious educator, poet.

Mary Evaline Wolff, who became a leader of Catholic education for women, was born in Cumberland, Wis., the second of three children and only daughter of August Frederick and Lucy (Arntz) Wolff. A third brother died in infancy. Affectionately nicknamed Eva, she had a happy childhood in the small island lumber town. Eva Wolff imbibed an esteem for education from her parents. Her mother, the daughter of German immigrants, had been a schoolteacher before her marriage. August Wolff, who

had emigrated from Germany as a child, was a skilled harnessmaker who also served as mayor of Cumberland. It was taken for granted that Eva would go to college, and, after deferring entrance for a year because of family finances and her youth, she enrolled at the University of Wisconsin at Madison in 1905 intending to specialize in mathematics.

A chance reading of a magazine advertisement for St. Mary's College, Notre Dame, Ind., led her to transfer to that college in 1906. There she encountered Sister Rita Heffernan, whose genius for literature, teaching, and friendship brought Eva Wolff not only to write poetry but also to redirect her life. In December 1908 Wolff entered the novitiate of the Holy Cross sisters who conducted St. Mary's. Taking the religious name of Sister Madeleva, she set herself to learn the ways of prayer and the meaning of poverty, chastity, and obedience as practiced by her order. In 1909 she received her B.A. from St. Mary's and was assigned to teach at the college.

Membership in the community, in which she made a permanent profession of vows in 1914, reinforced a contemplative habit of mind, and directed her into the professions of teaching and administration; it also provided the context for her poetry. She earned an M.A. in English from neighboring Notre Dame University in 1918. From 1919 to 1922 she taught at Sacred Heart Academy in Ogden, Utah; between 1922 and 1924 she commuted between her teaching in Woodland, Calif., and the University of California at Berkeley, where she completed a Ph.D. in 1925.

Chaucer's Nuns and Other Essays, and her thesis, *Pearl: A Study in Spiritual Dryness,* both published in 1925, illustrated her critical talents. It was as a poet that Sister Madeleva became noteworthy, however. Never a prolific writer, between 1915 and 1964 she composed slightly over two hundred poems. Her first collection, *Knights Errant* (1923), displayed her control of classic forms and a lyric brilliancy. By 1927, when the *Penelope* collection appeared, she had fully adopted the colloquial idiom, or "syntax of prose," which became her trademark. Then and later her poetry offered a unique blend of artistry, wry humor, and a bold imagery used to express both a love relationship with God and a wide range of human emotions.

Her struggles to create poetry came during hours of chronic insomnia and recurrent hospitalization for exhaustion in the midst of an extremely active life. For over thirty years she served as a college president: first of St. Mary-of-the-Wasatch in Salt Lake City, Utah (1926–33), and then, after a year's interlude in Europe, of her alma mater St. Mary's (1934–61). During her presidency, many outstanding thinkers, literary critics, and dramatists came to St. Mary's and both a library and fine arts center were built. She also made curricular innovations, organizing interdisciplinary sequences around the medieval trivium and drawing on the concepts of Christian humanism as advanced by British historian Christopher Dawson.

Sister Madeleva's concern with both religious education for women and the formal training of women religious led in the 1940s to two major developments. In 1943, St. Mary's created the first Catholic graduate program in theology open to women. The program trained women to teach religion at the college level at a time when no Catholic university admitted women as graduate students in theology. By the time St. Mary's program closed in 1969–after Marquette and Notre Dame Universities opened their theology programs to women–it had awarded seventy-six doctorates and over three hundred master's degrees.

Her concern with the education of women religious on a broader scale led Sister Madeleva in 1948 to organize a new section of the National Catholic Education Association (NCEA) to focus on that subject. Papers from a panel she led at the 1949 NCEA convention, published that year as *The Education of Sister Lucy*, supplied the basis for the reform of training programs organized in the 1950s under the leadership of the Sister Formation Conference. As a result of Sister Madeleva's concern, women entering religious communities began to work toward college degrees prior to being assigned to apostolic work and women's education for ministry became more commensurate with that afforded men through the Catholic seminary system. *Conversations with Cassandra* (1961) distilled the essence of Sister Madeleva's confidence in women's potential and her belief in the role of higher education in the development of women's powers.

Recognition of Sister Madeleva's abilities and achievements came in the form of numerous honors and offices. She was vice president of the Indiana Conference of Higher Education and the recipient of six honorary degrees as well as several awards for her poetry. Keenly interested in ecumenical affairs as the daughter of a Lutheran father and a Catholic mother, at one time she chaired the Indiana section of the National Conference of Christians and Jews.

Sister Madeleva retired in 1961, leaving a college which had sharpened its sense of mission and gained in national prestige. Her retirement years were brief. She continued an extensive speaking schedule and personal correspondence; served in a consultative capacity to her successor; indulged in her hobby of gardening; continued to write; and turned, in hours of silence, to the contemplative reading of Dante's *Paradiso*. Much to her frustration, the episodes of extreme exhaustion which had continually plagued her worsened and necessitated her spending whole months in bed. On July 23, 1964, in Boston, she underwent an operation for a nonmalignant condition; she died there two days later of septicemia. The body she had described in one of her poems as "woven" by her mother, and "textured through with life and time and place," was laid to rest.

[Principal collections of Sister Madeleva's papers are in the St. Mary's College Archives and in the St. Mary's Convent (General Motherhouse) Archives. In addition to her initial works mentioned above, she published nine books of poetry between 1935 and 1955. All of her earlier poems are reprinted in *The Four Last Things: Collected Poems* (1959). *A Child Asks for a Star* appeared posthumously in 1964. The Columbia Broadcasting System televised her script, "Praise Be My Lord," Dec. 24, 1963. Other writings include her autobiography, *My First Seventy Years* (1959), and *A Lost Language and Other Essays on Chaucer* (1951). Her literary essays appeared in *The Bookman, Commonweal, Thought,* and the *Am. Benedictine Rev.* Essays on biographical themes and educational philosophy include "Saint Hilda of Whitby," in Clare Boothe Luce, ed., *Saints for Now* (1952); *Addressed to Youth* (1944); "Education for Immortality," in *A College Goes to School,* a volume she edited (1945); *Theology and the Teacher* (1953). Biographical detail appears in Sister Mary Immaculate Creek, *A Panorama: 1844–1977* (1977); Barbara C. Jencks, *The Sister Madeleva Story* (1961); *Twentieth Century Authors* (1942); *Catholic Authors, 1930–1947;* and *Current Biog.,* 1942. See also Carol Frances Jegen, "Women in Theology," *Listening: Jour. of Religion and Culture,* Spring 1978, and Sister Maria Concepta McDermott, *The Making of a Sister-Teacher* (1965). St. Mary's alumnae quarterly, *Courier,* has also published several articles by and about Sister Madeleva. Obituaries appeared in the *N.Y. Times,* July 26, 1964, and *The CPSA [Catholic Poetry Society of America] Bull.,* July-Aug. 1964.]

KAREN KENNELLY, C.S.J.

WOLFSON, Theresa, July 19, 1897–May 14, 1972. Labor economist and educator.

Theresa Wolfson was born in Brooklyn, N.Y., the first of three children and only daughter of Adolph and Rebecca (Hochstein) Wolfson. Theresa's parents were Russian-Jewish radicals who had immigrated to the United States a few years before her birth. During her childhood, Adolph Wolfson worked as a news dealer until the family bought a large house, where both parents shared the tasks of keeping boarders. Wolfson attended Eastern District High School in Brooklyn and then entered Adelphi College. While an undergraduate she helped organize a chapter of the Intercollegiate Socialist Society (later the League for Industrial Democracy), and in the summer of 1916, took a job investigating wage standards in the ladies' garment industry.

After receiving her A.B. from Adelphi in 1917, Wolfson continued her involvement in social and economic issues, serving as a health worker for the Meinhardt Settlement House in New York City and speaking occasionally at socialist rallies. This partisan commitment did not survive the factional struggles that followed the October Revolution of 1917. Thereafter, her socialism was of the heart and her belief in industrial democracy transcended party politics.

From January 1918 to June 1920, Wolfson worked as a field agent and investigator for the National Child Labor Committee, a job that took her to a number of states in the south and midwest, and provided the impetus for her first published articles. These studies confirmed what was to become one of her guiding principles: that a worker's ability to deal effectively with society depended on a sound education.

While working for the National Child Labor Committee, Wolfson was courted by Iago Galdston, a medical student beginning a career in public health. The two were married on July 19, 1920, and Galdston, who later switched to psychiatry, took a job at the Union Health Center of the International Ladies' Garment Workers' Union (ILGWU). For the next several years Wolfson, who retained her maiden name, pursued graduate studies in economics at Columbia University and held two jobs that brought her into close touch with the problems of working women. From 1920 to 1922, she campaigned for minimum wage legislation and the eight-hour day under the auspices of the New York Consumers' League. She then investigated the seating, posture, and fatigue of sewing machine operators for the ladies' garment industry's Joint Board of Factory Control. In the process she collected data for her master's thesis, completed at Columbia in 1923. In 1925, convinced that workers could achieve economic and social justice only through trade unions, she moved to the ILGWU, where she served as education director of the Union Health Center for two years. The virtual exclusion of women from trade union leadership disturbed her, however, and she decided to devote her doctoral thesis to exploring the reasons for their absence. This study, which earned Wolfson a Ph.D. from the

Brookings Institution in 1926, became her first book, *The Woman Worker and the Trade Unions*, published the same year.

During the 1920s, Wolfson found a practical focus for her social convictions in the workers' education movement, a loosely organized network of trade unionists, socialists, and academics who believed that effective trade unionism required educated workers trained for leadership. Wolfson had been contributing to this effort since 1921, teaching labor history and economics to workers in a variety of union-sponsored schools; in 1928 she began teaching at the Bryn Mawr Summer School for Women Workers. Wolfson pursued a traditional academic career as well, starting in September 1928 as an instructor at the Brooklyn branch of Hunter College, which became Brooklyn College two years later. She remained there as a professor of economics and labor relations until her retirement.

Along with her busy teaching schedule, she raised two children: Richard (b. 1926) and Margaret Beatrice (b. 1930). Wolfson's marriage to Galdston grew strained, ending in divorce in 1935; three years later she married Austin Bigelow Wood, professor of psychology at Brooklyn College.

Wolfson's work for the balance of her career was animated by her belief in the potential of industrial democracy to create a just society. She kept her faith in trade unionism, at a time when unions were threatened with schismatic attacks from the left and accusations from the right. She believed that unions could be democratized through broader participation by women and the unskilled, and by education. Workers, she maintained, "cannot hope to solve the problems of their industry or of their economic world without specific information concerning both." Wolfson did not limit her educational efforts to blue-collar workers; during the thirties and forties, she played a prominent role in summer schools for office workers, and in the white-collar workshops sponsored by the American Labor Education Service.

As a member of the public panel of the War Labor Board (1942–45), Wolfson urged a continuing role for wage-earning women in the American economy after the conflict. Women who have worked in wartime industries, she wrote in 1943, should not "be cast aside like an old glove." After the war, Wolfson took a new direction, joining the national panel of arbitrators of the American Arbitration Association, which provided a base for resolving union-management disagreements. For her efforts at mediating industrial disputes, she was corecipient of the John Dewey award of the League for Industrial Democracy in 1957.

A vital person and an inspiration to her students and colleagues, Wolfson retired from Brooklyn College in 1967. She went on to teach women in the continuing education program at Sarah Lawrence College. Wolfson died in Brooklyn in May 1972. In her memory, her former students at Brooklyn College donated a collection of books to the college she had served so long.

[Theresa Wolfson's personal letters and papers are still in the possession of her family; most are held by her daughter, Margaret Frank. There are some Wolfson letters in the papers of her brother, the dramatist Victor Wolfson in the Twentieth Century Archives, Boston Univ. Professional correspondence, a curriculum vitae, and a complete bibliography prepared by Wolfson are in the Labor-Management Documentation Center, Catherwood Library, Cornell Univ. The Special Collections Div., Brooklyn College Library, contains a brochure reprinting eulogies delivered in services for Wolfson held at Community Church, June 3, 1972. Significant published works include two books Wolfson coauthored: *Labor and the N.R.A.* (1934) and *Frances Wright, Free Enquirer: The Study of a Temperament* (1939). The progress of Wolfson's thought can be traced in a number of articles: "People Who Go to Beets," *Am. Child,* Nov. 1919, pp. 217–39; "Posture and Fatigue," *Survey,* April 8, 1922, pp. 52–53; "Where Are the Organized Women Workers?" *Am. Federationist,* June 1925, pp. 455–57; "Schools the Miners Keep," *Survey,* June 1, 1926; "Trade Union Activities of Women," *Am. Acad. of Political and Social Sci., Annals,* May 1929, pp. 120–31; "Industrial Unions in the American Labor Movement," *New Frontiers,* Feb. 1937, pp. 3–52, with Abraham Weiss; "Should White Collar Workers Organize?" *Independent Woman,* Nov. 1936; "Union Finances and Elections," Am. Acad. of Political and Social Sci., *Annals,* Nov. 1946, pp. 31–36. No biography of Wolfson exists, but Victor Wolfson published a fictionalized account of the family, *My Prince! My King!* (1962). Information was provided by Margaret Frank and Victor Wolfson. An obituary appeared in the *N.Y. Times,* May 15, 1972.]

ALICE KESSLER-HARRIS

WONG, Anna May, Jan. 3, 1905–Feb. 3, 1961. Actress.

In a career spanning four decades, Anna May Wong achieved a measure of stardom despite her humble origins, but never realized her lifelong ambition to be an actress of the first rank. She was the second of eight children and second daughter of Wong Sam Sing and Lee Gon Toy, who gave her the Chinese name Liu Tsong at birth. Little is known about her parents, who were of Chinese descent, except that they operated a laundry business, one of the few occupations open to Asians in the United States at the turn of the century. Born and raised in Los Angeles, she attended public schools while helping in the family laundry.

Wong exhibited a keen interest in film early in life. As a youngster she often played truant and frequented the local nickelodeon. This precocious interest brought her into conflict with her father, who considered the world of film disreputable, unfit for a proper Chinese-American daughter. Strong-willed and fiercely independent, she decided upon an acting career in her early teens and, defying her father, began to make the rounds of the casting offices.

At the age of fourteen, Wong appeared as an extra in her first film, *The Red Lantern* (1919). She later attributed her appearance in it to James Wang, an actor who recruited Chinese extras. Subsequently, she appeared in minor roles in other silent films, all with sinister Asian characters. She played her first leading role in a minor film, *The Toll of the Sea* (1922), as a Chinese Madame Butterfly who renounces her true love by dutifully committing suicide after he finds a woman of his own race. Critics praised her performance in this film whose antimiscegenation theme recurs in her later films.

In 1924 Wong savored her first taste of fame by appearing in a lavish, landmark production, *The Thief of Bagdad,* starring Douglas Fairbanks. Though she performed only a supporting role as a "Mongol slave," her beauty and grace captured the public eye. Highly photogenic, with high cheekbones, expressive eyes, and jet black hair with horizontal bangs set against an ivory complexion, she became a favorite of photographers as a glamorous, exotic figure. Accordingly, she was groomed as Hollywood's "oriental siren." Her success coincided with the production of a number of new films which used China, Chinatown, or London's Limehouse district as background for crime and mystery, and in which Chinese were generally associated with evil, intrigue, treachery, and even savagery. By 1928 she had appeared in more than twenty silent films, most of them of this genre, including *Mr. Wu* (1927), *The Devil Dancer* (1927), and *Chinatown Charlie* (1928).

In 1928, tired of being typecast as an oriental villain in minor roles, Wong set off for Europe to seek international fame. She went abroad under contract to Richard Eichberg, an independent German producer. For her performance in her first German film, *Song* (1928), she was acclaimed by Berlin critics. After a decade of struggle in Hollywood she gained recognition in Europe by landing several leading screen and stage roles, reaching the pinnacle of her success during the late 1920s and the early 1930s. From

1928 to 1930 she was cast in leading roles in German, English, and French melodramas, including *Piccadilly* (1929) and *The Flame of Love* (1930). As talkies succeeded silents, Wong learned German and French; she also revealed new talents for singing and dancing. In March 1929 she made her stage debut in *The Circle of Chalk* with Laurence Olivier in London. Neither the play, based on a Chinese legend, nor her lead performance was favorably reviewed. Responding to criticism, she took voice lessons to cultivate a British accent.

Fresh from her European achievements, Wong returned to America in the fall of 1930. The depression years proved to be her most lucrative. In October 1930 she appeared on Broadway for the first time, playing a cunning, vengeful "half-caste Chinese moll" in the successful play *On the Spot*, by Edgar Wallace. During her absence from the United States, Sax Rohmer's Dr. Fu Manchu, a character personifying the so-called yellow peril, whose avowed purpose was the wholesale subjugation of the white race, came into vogue in Hollywood. In 1931 Wong returned there to perform the title role of *Daughter of the Dragon* (1931), based on Rohmer's *Daughter of Fu Manchu.*

Her other American and British films of this period were in the main suspenseful melodramas. Notable among these were *Shanghai Express* (1932), *A Study in Scarlet* (1933), *Limehouse Blues* (1934), *Chu Chin Chow* (1934), and *Java Head* (1935). In 1935 Metro-Goldwyn-Mayer offered her the supporting role of the vindictive concubine in *The Good Earth*, a screen adaptation of PEARL S. BUCK's best-selling novel. Wanting the lead role of O-lan instead, Wong spurned the offer of this only unsympathetic role in a film featuring an all-white cast portraying Chinese characters. On her first visit to China in January 1936, Chinese officials, to her surprise and dismay, chastised her harshly for her negative portrayals of Chinese characters. She explained that such roles were the only ones open to her.

With the Sino-Japanese conflict intensifying, Wong returned home to perform for the first time in a film sympathetic to the Chinese. Reflecting changes in Sino-American relations, *Daughter of Shanghai* (1937) represented a favorable shift in Hollywood's portrayal of Chinese. Her remaining major roles in the 1930s were all in undistinguished class B mystery films, including *Dangerous to Know* (1938) and *King of Chinatown* (1939). During World War II she appeared only in a couple of Pacific war films. Off screen, she raised money for various China relief funds and entertained American troops. In the last two decades of her life, Wong faded into middle-aged obscurity, managing to work only intermittently in film and television. After a long absence, she returned to the screen in a suspenseful melodrama, *Portrait in Black* (1960), as Lana Turner's mysterious maid. Her last film, *The Savage Innocents*, was released in 1961, the year she died of a heart attack at the Santa Monica, Calif., home she shared with her brother Richard.

Anna May Wong was a person of contrasts and contradictions whose career was shaped by sex and race discrimination. To pursue her career, she had to defy her parents. Yet she retained a strong sense of family responsibility and loyalty; she helped to support her large family and even sent her widowed father and several siblings to China in 1934 for a lengthy visit. Scorned by many of her own people who were affronted by her screen caricatures of Chinese, she herself was disenchanted with the negative racial stereotypes which, ironically, made her acting career possible. Throughout her long career, the film industry adhered to a general policy of racial exclusion, reserving major Asian roles in class A films for white performers. Circumscribed by forces beyond her control, Wong did not have a real chance to realize her true worth as an actress. Even in death, this pioneer Asian-American actress was unable to escape her Hollywood image as the "foremost Oriental villainess" (*Time*, Feb. 10, 1961, p. 78).

[Published materials about Anna May Wong are fragmentary and scattered; most should be used with care. An article by Judy Chu, "Anna May Wong," *Gidra*, Jan. 1974, is reprinted in Emma Gee, ed., *Counterpoint: Perspectives on Asian America* (1976), pp. 284–89. See also Betty Willis, "Famous Oriental Stars Return to the Screen," *Motion Picture*, Oct. 1931; J. Parker, ed., *Who's Who in the Theatre* (1936), p. 1551; and Conrad Doerr, "Anna May Wong," *Films in Review*, Dec. 1968, pp. 660–62. A list of her film credits is in Evelyn Mack Truitt, *Who Was Who on Screen* (1977). For a study of American screen treatment of Asian characters and settings see Eugene Franklin Wong, "On Visual Media Racism: Asians in the American Motion Pictures" (Ph.D. diss., Univ. of Denver, 1978). Obituaries appeared in the *N.Y. Times, N.Y. Herald Tribune*, and *L. A. Times*, Feb. 4, 1961. A biobibliography prepared by Rexanne D. Newnam assisted in the research for this article. Additional information was provided by Richard Wong and Terence Tam Soon, who also made available his private collection of material on Anna May Wong. Birth certificate supplied by Registrar-Recorder, Los Angeles Cty.]

EMMA GEE

WOOD, Sara Bard Field. *See* FIELD, Sara Bard.

WOODSMALL, Ruth Frances, Sept. 20, 1883–May 25, 1963. YWCA leader.

General secretary of the World's YWCA from 1935 to 1947 and a crusader for women's rights, Ruth Woodsmall was born in Atlanta, the younger daughter and last of four children of Hubert Harrison and Mary Elizabeth (Howes) Woodsmall. Woodsmall's English ancestors had migrated to the United States as early as 1621, her Bavarian forebears in the mid-eighteenth century; both groups settled largely in New England, New Jersey, and Pennsylvania. Her father, a Union soldier during the Civil War, was a lawyer who also obtained a degree in religion and became an active teacher and worker for the Baptist Home Mission Society. (Ruth Woodsmall later joined the Baptists as well.) Her mother, an educated southern gentlewoman, supported the family by teaching painting and decorative arts after her husband's death in 1889. The family moved to Indianapolis, where Ruth grew up.

Eager to continue her ancestors' traditional involvement in higher education, Ruth Woodsmall attended Franklin College in Indiana (1901–03), Indiana University (1903–05), and the University of Nebraska, where she received her A.B., Phi Beta Kappa, in 1905. In addition to summer graduate work at Columbia University and the University of Heidelberg, she studied at Wellesley College, earning an A.M. in German there in 1906. Woodsmall began work that year as a high school principal in Ouray, Colo., serving subsequently as a German and English teacher in Reno, Nev., Pueblo, Colo., and Colorado Springs. In 1916 she left teaching to travel for a year through India and the Far East, observing social conditions and developing insights later applied in her international efforts for the YWCA.

Beginning in 1917 with the United States' entry into World War I, Woodsmall spent more than three decades with the YWCA. Her first assignment, with the National Board of the United States, included War Work Council service, directing Hostess Houses near bases in the United States and France. After the armistice, she entered Germany with the army of occupation and later visited Poland to evaluate postwar conditions. Woodsmall's comprehensive field surveys in Baltic and Balkan countries (1918–20) helped to initiate YWCA activities there.

In 1920 Woodsmall became executive secretary of the YWCA in the Near East (Turkey and Syria) and also secretary of the YWCA Eastern Mediterranean Federations (Turkey, Syria, Palestine, and Egypt). Her special field research in these countries, carried out with the help of American business and welfare organizations, yielded contributions to a social survey of Constantinople (1920–21) as well as a comprehensive study of American philanthropy in the Near East (1924). A traveling fellowship from the Laura Spelman Rockefeller Memorial Foundation in 1928 enabled Woodsmall to begin a two-year critical study of the changing status of Moslem women in Syria, Lebanon, Turkey, Egypt, Palestine, Transjordan, Iraq, Iran, and India. Her report, issued in 1930, was later published as *Moslem Women Enter a New World* (1936). It was regarded as a seminal work as it revealed the dramatic transition being made from the strict observance of Islamic tradition to a more liberal interpretation of the status and role of Moslem women. Woodsmall expanded the scope of her research in the early 1930s, studying the roles of women in Burma, India, China, and Japan as a member of the Laymen's Foreign Mission Inquiry. This, and her related work for the International Missionary Council in Japan, led to another book, *Eastern Women Today and Tomorrow* (1933).

Woodsmall returned to the United States in 1932 to serve as an international affairs staff specialist on the National Board of the YWCA. Then in 1935 she resettled in Geneva, Switzerland, to launch her twelve-year tenure as general secretary of the World's YWCA. Woodsmall brought to this task her unerring diplomatic skills, combining an earnest appreciation for diverse customs and cultures with an ability to emphasize the problems faced in common by women around the world. Energetic, resourceful, and courageous, she also had a special gift for attracting and sustaining a large, varied circle of friends with whom she shared her private and public life.

Drawing on all of these qualities, Woodsmall continued to explore the changing status of women in a variety of settings, from Nazi Germany in the 1930s to Latin America during World War II. The World's YWCA Council regarded her field reports both as resources for evaluating the social and other conditions that effectively restricted women's advancement, and as guides for directing an organization with a distinctly Christian orientation in its efforts to redress those problems. These reports, along with her many other writings during her tenure as general secretary, provide a remarkably complete record of the YWCA's structure, goals, and achievements; they also document a critical era of world history. Her work for the YWCA was recognized by honorary degrees from the University of Nebraska and Indiana University.

Stepping down as general secretary in November 1947, Woodsmall continued to work for the YWCA's Special Service in China, Japan, Korea, and several other Asian countries until April 1948. The following year she returned to government service, remaining in Occupied Germany until 1954 as Chief of Women's Affairs, first under the Military Government and then under the United States High Commission for Germany. In this capacity, she helped German women rebuild channels of communication with women of other nations, a contribution acknowledged in 1962 with a Commander's Cross of the Order of Merit of West Germany. Complementing her work in Germany, she was an adviser for the United Nations Commission on the Status of Women at meetings in Beirut (1949) and Geneva (1952), and contributed in Paris to the UNESCO Working Party on the Equality of Access of Women to Education (1951).

Ruth Woodsmall devoted the last decade of her life principally to research and writing. Aided by two Ford Foundation grants, she effectively updated her earlier pioneering studies of near and far eastern women in two books: *Study of the Role of Women, Their Activities and Organizations in Lebanon, Egypt, Iraq, Jordan and Syria* (1955) and *Women and the New East* (1960). She was living in New York City in May 1963, when she died at the age of seventy-nine. Friends later scattered her ashes in the woods near Geneva, where she had spent many happy and productive years.

[Ruth Woodsmall's personal and professional papers are preserved in the Sophia Smith Coll., Smith College. Extensive files (1904–60) include family, personal, and professional correspondence, diaries, brief autobiographical and biographical sketches, records, reports, photographs, and clippings. No definitive biography exists, but the following articles contain information on Woodsmall: Anna Rice, "To Ruth Woodsmall, for Twelve Years General Secretary of the World's Y.W.C.A.," *Woman's Press*, Nov. 1947, pp. 19, 46; "Personalities and Projects: Social Welfare in Terms of Significant People," *Survey*, March 1949; Ethel Johnson, "Lady Ulysses," *Independent Woman*, April 1949, pp. 105–6; Jean Storke Menzies, "Changing Roles of Women Studied by World Traveler," *Santa Barbara News-Press*, Nov. 3, 1957; Norma Green, "Books in Review," *Nebraska Alumnus*, March 1961, p. 23; "Tributes" [to R.F.W.], *World YWCA* (1964), pp. 1–11. See also *Current Biog.*, 1949. An obituary appeared in the *N.Y. Times*, May 27, 1963. Personal and career information was furnished by Woodsmall's niece Marlen E. Neumann and by her friend and associate Elizabeth Palmer.]

MARY-ELIZABETH MURDOCK

WOODWARD, Ellen Sullivan, July 11, 1887–Sept. 23, 1971. Federal official, state legislator.

Born in Oxford, Miss., Ellen Sullivan Woodward went from Mississippi state politics to become a leading New Deal official, administering both relief programs for women and the federal arts and writers projects. Ellen was the fourth of five children of William Van Amberg and Belle (Murray) Sullivan, and the second of three daughters. Her parents, descendants of seventeenth- and eighteenth-century Scottish and Irish immigrants, enjoyed a respected position in the community. William Sullivan, the first law graduate of Vanderbilt University, served as a Mississippi congressman (1897–98) and United States senator (1898–1901). He was particularly close to his children after his wife's death in 1894 and often permitted Ellen to accompany him as he argued his cases in court. He once told a friend his young daughter "had no such thing as fear of anyone in her composition." Ellen Sullivan's informal education in civic affairs continued during her life in Washington as an adolescent. She graduated from Oxford High School and received a diploma from Sans Souci College in Greenville, S.C., in 1905, and a music certificate from Washington (D.C.) College.

Noted for her intelligence and beauty, Ellen Sullivan was a socially prominent young woman. On June 27, 1906, she married Albert Young Woodward, an attorney who served successively as a state district judge, city attorney, and member of the Mississippi legislature. Their son, Albert Y. Woodward, Jr., was born in 1909. As a young matron in Louisville, Miss., Ellen Woodward became a leader in community affairs. She also conducted her husband's successful campaign for the legislature. After Albert Woodward's sudden death on Feb. 6, 1925, she succeeded him in the 1926 legislative session, defeating her male opponent decisively. The second woman to serve in the Mississippi House of Representatives, Ellen Woodward was supported by her colleague NELLIE NUGENT SOMERVILLE. Her service on legislative committees on libraries, higher education, the liquor traffic, and eleemosynary institutions presaged her later work for women and children.

As a widow and the mother of a teenage son, Woodward declined to seek reelection and in late 1926 accepted a more remunerative position with the Mississippi State Board of Development as director of civic development. Promoted to executive director of the board in 1929, she served until 1933. She also held executive or trustee posts with a variety of charitable institutions and with the first Mississippi State Board of Public Welfare. Wide public recognition and her own political astuteness led to her election as a delegate to the 1928 Democratic

National Convention. In 1932 she was named the Mississippi Democratic Committeewoman, but resigned the post in 1934 because of her federal employment.

Through her vigorous work in Franklin D. Roosevelt's 1932 presidential campaign, Woodward came to the attention of MARY DEWSON, head of the Women's Division of the Democratic National Committee. When Harry L. Hopkins, director of the federal Works Progress Administration (WPA), sought an assistant to direct women's work programs, Dewson urged Woodward's appointment. In September 1933, Ellen Woodward came to Washington to become assistant administrator in charge of emergency relief programs for women; she remained in Washington for the rest of her life. During the New Deal she instituted or supervised direct relief and work relief programs that assisted nearly 500,000 women who were heads of families or had no other means of support. Believing in the traditional values of home and children, Woodward sponsored programs which developed women's work within that context. The largest of the projects promoted household training, sewing rooms, school lunchroom management, rural library development, and public health services. Most of Woodward's forty-eight state directors were women.

In July 1936, Woodward's duties expanded when she became director of the WPA cultural projects for writers, musicians, actors, and artists, administering programs for an additional 250,000 persons. As director of the Women's and Professional Division of the WPA, she was the second highest-ranking woman in the federal government, outranked only by FRANCES PERKINS. Under Woodward's administration, federal involvement in state cultural projects increased. Central to her work was her belief that men and women should receive equal pay for equal work and that emergency programs should train women for future gainful employment. She once said, "Unemployment and unhappiness are synonymous. Our programs aim to end both." Woodward's competence and tact, as well as her keen political sense and humanistic approach to the problems of the needy, won her the support of ELEANOR ROOSEVELT, with whom she maintained close professional and personal ties.

Directing a politically sensitive agency while also dealing with artists and writers was far from easy. She was sympathetic to the experimental aims of the cultural projects, and defended them tenaciously but unsuccessfully in her 1938 appearance before the congressional investigating committee headed by Martin Dies. After Hopkins's resignation from the WPA, Wood-ward accepted a presidential appointment to the three-member Social Security Board, taking the seat vacated by Dewson. She was reappointed in 1943.

In accepting the Social Security post, Woodward said she welcomed the "opportunity for service where my deepest interests lie—security for the home and family." She directed her efforts to the expansion of social security for women and dependent children, focusing her attention during World War II on the opening of new job opportunities for women, the extension of unemployment insurance coverage for women, and the promotion of women in postwar policymaking. From 1943 to 1946 she was a member of the United States delegation to the United Nations Relief and Rehabilitation Administration, serving as a member of the Standing Technical Committee for Welfare and as an observer of German camps for displaced persons. In July 1946, when the Social Security Board was abolished, President Harry S Truman appointed Woodward director of the Office of Inter-Agency and International Relations of the Federal Security Administration (FSA). As the FSA liaison officer with the United Nations and the State Department, she attended the 1947 Lake Success organizational meeting of the UN Economic and Social Council.

Ellen Woodward retired from government service on Jan. 1, 1954. She remained active in many women's organizations, including the National Federation of Business and Professional Women's Clubs, for which she had been national chairman for public affairs from 1944 to 1946. In 1971, she died of arteriosclerosis at her Washington home.

[The Woodward Papers and Scrapbooks in the Miss. Dept. of Archives cover her entire career; they include extensive correspondence, memoranda, public documents, speeches, and photographs. A smaller collection of her papers is in the Schlesinger Library, Radcliffe College. Other pertinent manuscripts are in the Eleanor Roosevelt, Harry Hopkins, and Mary Dewson Papers at the Franklin D. Roosevelt Library, Hyde Park, N.Y. The Truman Library in Independence, Mo., has a number of letters endorsing her 1946 appointment. Numerous Woodward articles and speeches appeared in the leading women's popular magazines and professional journals during the 1930s and 1940s. *Holland's* contains two biographical articles (March 1936 and June 1944); several issues of the *Democratic Digest* contain news items of her work and party activities. Two dissertations discuss Woodward's work: Elsie L. George, "The Women Appointees of the Roosevelt and Truman Administrations: A Study of Their Impact and Effectiveness" (American Univ., 1972) and Susan Ware, "Political Sisterhood in the New Deal: Women in Politics and Government, 1933–

1940" (Harvard Univ., 1978). Woodward's WPA administration is evaluated in William F. McDonald, *Federal Relief Administration and the Arts* (1969); Jane DeHart Mathews, *The Federal Theatre, 1935–1939: Plays, Relief, and Politics* (1967); Richard McKinzie, *The New Deal for Artists* (1973); Jerre Mangione, *The Dream and the Deal: The Federal Writers' Project, 1935–1943* (1972). Obituaries appeared in Wash. *Evening Star*, Sept. 24, 1971, Jackson (Miss.) *Clarion-Ledger*, Sept. 26, 1971, and Winston County (Miss.) *Journal*, Sept. 30, 1971. Numerous photographs of Woodward and of WPA women's projects are in the Miss. Dept. of Archives.]

MARTHA H. SWAIN

WRIGHT, Mary Clabaugh, Sept. 25, 1917–June 18, 1970. Historian.

Mary Wright was a leading figure in the study of modern Chinese history during the 1950s and 1960s when it came of age as a major discipline in the United States. During the 1950s, as a collector and curator of the modern China collection at the Hoover Institution on War, Revolution and Peace at Palo Alto, and then during the 1960s as professor of history at Yale, she inspired new work, fostered the structural development of the field, and set a brilliant example in her own teaching, research, and publication.

Mary Oliver Clabaugh was born in Tuscaloosa, Ala., the second of five children and eldest of four daughters of Samuel Francis and Mary Bacon (Duncan) Clabaugh. Her father, a native of Birmingham and graduate of the University of Alabama, was a successful business executive, publisher of the *Tuscaloosa News* (1910–14), and later head of life insurance companies in Birmingham. Her mother was born in Eutaw, Ala., attended Agnes Scott College, and graduated from the University of Alabama.

Mary Clabaugh was thus born into a well-established family rooted in Alabama. From an early age she enjoyed outdoor life and sports, especially swimming, tennis, and horseback riding. A pacesetter for her three younger sisters, she was also a leader in high school and college. At Ramsay High School in Birmingham, she became president of the student body and of the National Honor Society; while at Vassar College, which she entered on scholarship in 1934, she was president of the student Political Union.

Graduating from Vassar as a member of Phi Beta Kappa, she began her postgraduate studies at Radcliffe College in the fall of 1938 in European history. She soon became interested in the history of China, a country she had visited briefly in 1934. A new field, modern China was then taught in less than a dozen American universities. Chinese diplomatic documents had just been published and at Harvard it was also possible to study the Chinese language and begin to use Chinese sources for research. Mary Clabaugh's imagination responded to this challenging opportunity and her passion for thoroughness soon had her deeply involved.

At twenty-one her beauty and southern accent were accompanied by an extraordinary intellectual vitality. She met another, more advanced, graduate student, Arthur Frederick Wright (1913–1976), whose interests complemented and supported hers to a remarkable degree. Arthur Wright, after receiving his A.B. from Stanford University in 1935, had turned away from automotive America, represented by his father's burgeoning automobile sales and service business, and elected to begin studies of Chinese Buddhism at Oxford. After receiving the B.Litt. (Oxon.) in 1937, he came to Harvard to pursue both Chinese and Japanese, a young man of great charm and gaiety with broad aesthetic interests and a strong intellectual commitment to the humanities, especially the history of thought.

Arthur and Mary Wright were married in an Episcopal service in Washington, D.C., on July 6, 1940, and at once departed for Kyoto to spend a year on fellowships pursuing their doctoral researches. Their plan was to spend a second year in Peking (then Peiping) and in fact they did so, but it would be seven years before they returned to the United States. During 1940–41 Arthur and Mary Wright lived in a Japanese house in Kyoto, studying both Japanese and Chinese with half a dozen teachers. Determined not to forgo the arduous on-the-spot training so necessary for their careers as area specialists, they moved to the bustling city of Peking in June 1941 to a fine house, formerly part of a prince's palace. Under the pro-Japanese local government, American funds were hard to convert, but they visited Peking's sites and enjoyed the well-served social life that continued in the Sino-foreign community. They tried to allay the natural concern of their families by arguing that few other Americans were leaving Peking and that the city would not be a military target.

After December 1941, when war began for America with the Japanese attack on Hawaii, life in Peking continued pleasantly, though precariously, until March 24, 1943, when Peking's enemy aliens were finally interned in a camp which they administered themselves at Weihsien, Shantung. The indignities, hard work, and comradeship of the next two-and-a-half years in camp were a contrast to Peking. Arthur

Wright was a butcher, water-carrier, and fire-man, among other things, Mary Wright a washer of dishes and clothes, but she also baked cakes and studied Russian.

When evacuated from Wei-hsien on Oct. 17, 1945, the Wrights returned to Peking to get back to their studies. Suddenly a new world of practical action opened up. The Hoover Library began a program to collect contemporary materials on the Chinese revolution. Arthur and Mary Wright became its China representatives and arranged to visit major cities on American army planes. In October 1946 they visited the Chinese Communist party capital at Yenan, met Mao Tse-tung, dined with Chu Te, and saw the many model institutions. Later during three weeks in Nanking Mary Wright secured some 3,000 volumes from Nationalist government offices. She also saw postwar conditions and found materials in Shanghai, Hankow, Hong Kong, Macao, and Taiwan. The collection program became essentially hers, benefiting from her initiative, persistence, and persuasiveness with people. From being a postwar displaced scholar out of funds she became an operator in the American establishment in China. She also became an expert on Chinese contemporary materials. In April 1947 the Wrights returned to the United States. That year Arthur Wright completed his Ph.D. at Harvard and accepted appointment in the history department at Stanford. Mary Wright became China curator at the Hoover Library under Harold Fisher. Her experience of China in turmoil before, during, and after World War II had prepared her unusually well to be a historian.

Mary Wright's Radcliffe Ph.D. was completed in 1951, but conversion of the thesis into a book was delayed by circumstances that seldom equally affect the work of male historians: Charles Duncan Wright was born on May 9, 1950, Jonathan Arthur Wright on Jan. 9, 1952. *The Last Stand of Chinese Conservatism: The T'ung-chih Restoration, 1862–1874* was published in 1957.

In approaching the postrebellion China of the 1860s, Mary Wright had begun with foreign relations, for which the Chinese documents were first published in 1932. But the demands of the subject—how the dynasty was restored both by appeasing the British, French, and Russian invaders and by using foreign arms to suppress the Taiping, Nien, and other rebels— soon led her into a much larger undertaking, a study of the Ch'ing administration of the 1860s in all its aspects, using the 4,000-volume dynastic *Veritable Records* published in 1936, of which she obtained her own copy. The result was a "first"—a detailed study of the ideology,

problems, successes, and failures of an entire generation of Chinese and Manchu leaders who struggled to preserve an ancient and outdated order "amid lengthening shadows," as she put it. *The Last Stand* was the most daring, ambitious, and significant single work in its field and marked her at once as a major historian. Her new understanding of the Ch'ing officials whose writings she pursued so voraciously naturally led her to give credit to their aims and hopes; but she found the old China incapable of genuine remaking short of revolution. Later work has in some respects modified her picture, but her book of 1957 is still a milestone. It set a model of studying modern China from the inside.

While Mary Wright had done some lecturing under the Stanford history department, she was not made a faculty member. In the Hoover Library, where she became assistant professor in 1951 and associate professor in 1954, she had built up a unique collection of materials through her contacts around the world. She had also sponsored a series of half a dozen bibliographic studies of major topics such as the Overseas Chinese, the Chinese Red Army, the student movement. But she did not want to be classed primarily as a library curator. In 1959 Arthur and Mary Wright were invited to the history department at Yale, he as professor, she as associate professor, making her the first tenured woman in the faculty of arts and sciences. This coup, combined with Yale's strength in Chinese language and literature, made that university overnight a major center of Chinese studies. The Wrights avoided setting up special arrangements for Chinese history and kept it in the mainstream of history teaching, with the Yale stress on undergraduate instruction. In 1953–54 they had spent a first sabbatical in Japan; in 1962–63 the family of four, plus a congenial tutor for the boys, traveled through Europe and South Asia and again spent several months on sabbatical in Japan. Both parents, though by now heavily engaged in the organizational activity of American academic life, remained strongly family-centered.

Mary Wright's interest in modern China had moved on to the overwhelming fact of revolution and she set herself to study the processes at work. In August 1965 she presided over a research conference on the Chinese Revolution of 1911 from which emerged in 1968 *China in Revolution: The First Phase, 1900–1913*. Mary Wright's long introduction, "The Rising Tide of Change," is notable for its comprehensive interest in the whole Chinese scene and the spectrum of issues of interpretation. Her eloquent thesis, that "the foreign omnipresence" in China and the danger of intervention to protect foreign interests were major factors that "stopped the revolution short and brought Yuan Shih-k'ai to power," has been the starting point for much further work.

In the organizing of the China field, Mary Wright founded the Society for Ch'ing Studies and its journal *Ch'ing-shih wen-t'i*, and served on a central developmental agency, the Joint Committee on Contemporary China. She received several honorary degrees and became the first woman trustee of Wesleyan University at Middletown, Conn.

A kinetic imagination and a passion for thoroughness, when combined, are hard taskmasters. Mary Wright's achievements in family life, teaching, research, and increasingly in the public scene taxed her strength, and at age forty-eight she suffered a nervous exhaustion. She got back into action, but only to find herself in late 1969 a victim of inoperable lung cancer. Typically, she took charge of this emergency, set her affairs in order, saw her family and friends, spent a spring fortnight with her husband in Florence, and died at her home in Guilford, Conn., on June 18, 1970.

History is of course rewritten by each generation and historians live by this fact. Their influence is in their writings, their students, and their example. Mary Wright was a pioneer in several respects. She entered the China field out of intellectual curiosity pure and simple, responding to its challenge as unknown territory. Her original training at Harvard was very brief and she had to find her way later in both language work and source materials. Her husband was of enormous help to her at every turn, but she remained at all times an equal coworker pursuing her own career, not subordinate to his. Her intellectual vigor is evidenced in her books. Her beauty, which did not fade, enhanced her symbolic role as a woman professor. But her outstanding trait was total commitment to the task at hand, whether it was defending Owen Lattimore, campaigning for Adlai Stevenson, opposing the Vietnam War, criticizing a sloppy manuscript, or advocating the publication of a good one. She was eloquent both in denunciation and in advocacy, and a force to be reckoned with in any meeting. Perhaps the primary example she set, as at the time of her death, was one of intellectual realism and courage.

[There is no collection of Mary Clabaugh Wright's papers, but the Archives of Stanford Univ. contain the papers of the Asian Survey Project, in which she participated. The Radcliffe College Archives contain some of Mary Wright's letters from Japan and China, 1940–45. *The Last Stand* was reprinted in 1966 with a new preface and added notes. Important articles by Mary Wright include "From Revolution to Restoration: The Transformation of Kuomintang Ideology," *Far Eastern Quart.*, Aug. 1955, pp. 515–32, and "The Adaptability of Ch'ing Diplomacy: The Case of Korea," *Jour. of Asian Studies*, May 1958, pp. 363–81. Other publications through 1965 are listed in the *Cumulative Bibliography of Asian Studies, 1941–1965*, vol. IV (1969), p. 699. The *N.Y. Times* carried news stories about Mary Wright on Nov. 4, 1956, and May 7, 1964; see also *Who Was Who in America*, V (1973). There are obituaries by John K. Fairbank in *Am. Hist. Rev.*, Oct. 1970, pp. 1885–86, and Jonathan Spence in *Jour. of Asian Studies*, Nov. 1970, p. 131; an obituary also appeared in the *N.Y. Times*, June 19, 1970. A death record was provided by Conn. Dept. of Health. Mary Wright's sister, Jean Clabaugh Hiles, provided family letters and useful information. A biobibliography prepared by Mary Jane Conger was also helpful.]

JOHN K. FAIRBANK

WRIGHT, Muriel Hazel, March 31, 1889–Feb. 27, 1975. Historian, community leader.

Muriel Hazel Wright, the first of two children of Eliphalet Nott and Ida Belle (Richard) Wright, was born near Lehigh, Choctaw Nation (later Coal County, Okla.). Eliphalet Wright was half Choctaw Indian; his father, a graduate of Union Theological Seminary and chief of the Choctaw Nation (1866–70), had married a Presbyterian missionary teacher of colonial American ancestry. Ida Wright, of English and Scottish ancestry, was a graduate of Lindenwood College in St. Charles, Mo., who also came to the Choctaw Nation as a Presbyterian missionary. At the time of Muriel's birth, her father, a graduate of Union College and Albany (N.Y.) Medical College, was practicing medicine and serving as company physician for the Missouri-Pacific Coal Mines.

Education was a priority in the Wright family, and in 1895, when Muriel was old enough to enroll in school, they moved to Atoka, a major town in the region. There she attended Presbyterian and Baptist elementary schools until 1902. The family then returned to their farm near Lehigh, and Ida Wright tutored her two daughters at home. In 1906 Muriel Wright set out for schooling in the east, entering Wheaton Seminary (later Wheaton College) in Norton, Mass. During her two years at Wheaton she excelled in her studies.

When in 1908 her family moved to Washington, D.C., where her father served as resident delegate of the Choctaw Nation to the United States government, Wright joined them. In Washington she studied privately, taking French, piano, and voice lessons. After the family's return to Lehigh, Muriel Wright enrolled at the newly founded East Central State Normal School in nearby Ada, Okla., in 1911. Upon graduation the following year, she embarked upon a teaching career. Her first position was in Wapanucka, Okla., and, after a year in nearby Tishomingo, Wright returned to Wapanucka in 1914 as high school principal. As principal she also taught Latin, English, and history, coached the girls' basketball team, and directed the senior play.

A desire for further education attracted Wright to New York in 1916, where she began work on a master's degree, studying history and English. The outbreak of World War I forced her to return to Oklahoma in 1917. She served as principal of the Hardwood District School in Coal County, near the Wright farm, from 1918 to 1920 and from 1922 to 1924. Again she acted as both teacher and administrator, and she introduced a student-administered assistance program for children who could not afford school supplies.

Although Wright briefly returned to teaching (1942–43), she devoted most of her career to researching and writing about the Oklahoma Indians and their role in shaping the history of Oklahoma, the west, and American culture in general. Her work found an audience beyond her home state, and she achieved national recognition for her editing of *The Chronicles of Oklahoma*, the quarterly journal of the Oklahoma Historical Society. A contributor beginning in 1922, she served as associate editor (1943–55) and then editor (1955–73), raising the publication's standards of scholarship while encouraging diversity in submissions. During Wright's tenure, *The Chronicles* published several series of documents, including the "Oklahoma War Memorial–World War II" (1943–49), her unique collection of historical and biographical records from the war era.

Her own writing, published in *The Chronicles* and many other periodicals, has been praised for its "depth of research in primary sources, personal interviews, the use of topography and geography, enthusiasm, insight, creativity and thoroughness" (Fischer, p. 19). Among Wright's other literary achievements are the four-volume work *Oklahoma: A History of the State and Its People* (1929), written with Joseph B. Thoburn, and three widely used standard texts of Oklahoma history. A grant from the Rockefeller Foundation assisted her in preparing *A Guide to the Indian Tribes of Oklahoma* (1951), a reference work cited for distinction by the American Association for State and Local History.

Muriel Wright remained dedicated to her Choctaw heritage throughout her life. After Oklahoma became a state in 1907, the Choctaw tribe had begun the long and complicated process of transferring tribal lands to private hands. As secretary of the Choctaw Committee from 1922 to 1928, Wright was involved in settling the multifarious economic and business affairs of the tribe. She subsequently helped to organize the Choctaw Advisory Council and served as its secretary (1934–44) during a period of continuing efforts to make a final settlement of Choctaw properties. Wright was also among those Native Americans who fought for just government recompense for the plunder of Indian territory following Oklahoma statehood. Another lasting contribution reflecting a life-long interest was her initiation with George Shirk of a statewide historical marker program. Wright's dedication and efforts on behalf of the program helped make Oklahoma a leader in identifying and preserving historic sites. In one instance she succeeded in blocking an attempt to remove the Choctaw Council House from Tuskahoma.

Frequently honored for her accomplishments, Wright was elected to the Oklahoma Hall of Fame (1940) and received a Distinguished Service Citation from the University of Oklahoma (1949) for her historical writing, civic work, and service to her tribe. In 1971 the North American Indian Women's Association recognized her as the outstanding Indian woman of the twentieth century. After retiring in 1973, she maintained an office at the Oklahoma Historical Society, continuing to write and plan future projects, including a biography of her father. Muriel Wright died of a stroke in 1975 in Oklahoma City.

[Biographical material on Muriel Wright is limited. The Okla. Hist. Soc. Div. of Library Resources has a collection of Wright's papers that is not yet open to research. An article she wrote about her father, "A Brief Review of the Life of Doctor Eliphalet Nott Wright," appeared in *Chronicles of Okla.*, June 1932. Probably the best and most accessible source of information about her life is the tribute by Le Roy H. Fischer, "Muriel H. Wright, Historian of Oklahoma," *Chronicles of Okla.*, Spring 1974, pp. 3–21, which is accompanied by a bibliography of her writings. Another tribute is Lucyl A. Shirk, "Muriel H. Wright: A Legend," *Chronicles of Okla.*, Fall 1975, pp. 397–99. *Who's Who in Oklahoma* (1964) has a short piece, as does Lu Celia Wise, *Indian Values Past and Present* (1978). An obituary appeared in the *Daily Oklahoman*, Feb. 28, 1975. Interviews with Harriet O'Leary James, Patricia Lester, and Martha Blaine provided additional information. Death certificate supplied by Okla. Dept. of Health.]

RUTH ARRINGTON

WURSTER, Catherine Bauer. *See* BAUER, Catherine Krouse.

Y

YEZIERSKA, Anzia, 1880?–Nov. 21, 1970. Writer.

Anzia Yezierska, whose work was celebrated in the 1920s and then fell into eclipse, wrote fiction and essays about poor Jewish immigrants from New York's Lower East Side whose experiences she shared. In the 1970s renewed interest in ethnic and feminist themes led to a rediscovery of her significance.

Yezierska never knew the date of her birth. She invented one, Oct. 19, 1883, but was probably born in 1880 or 1881, in the village of Plinsk near Warsaw in Russian Poland. She was the third youngest of eight or nine brothers and sisters, the children of Bernard and Pearl Yezierska—an impecunious Talmudic scholar and a housewife. When they emigrated to America, some time between 1890 and 1895, the family name was changed to "Mayer" by immigration inspectors, and Anzia was renamed "Hattie Mayer." Yezierska took back her own name before she began publishing her stories.

In 1915 her first published story, "The Free Vacation House," depicted the humiliation of the poor by unfeeling charities; in 1919 "The Fat of the Land" won the O'Brien prize for the best short story of the year. Both stories were included in Yezierska's first volume, *Hungry Hearts* (1920). That book was purchased by Samuel Goldwyn for $10,000, and she went to Hollywood to work on the screenplay. The film appeared in 1922, after Yezierska had refused a screenwriter's contract and returned to the New York life she thought essential to her creativity.

Her early efforts to free herself from poverty—working in sweatshops and laundries—and from an oppressive family situation, were fictionalized in *Bread Givers* (1925). The book was significantly subtitled "A struggle between a father of the Old World and a daughter of the New." One route to escape was through education. Yezierska, who had attended public school briefly and gone to night classes in East Side settlement houses, had invented a high school education that got her accepted as an unclassified student at Teachers College, Columbia University, in 1900. Four years later she had received a diploma in domestic science which she then taught, unhappily, for a few years—she loathed the subject but it was the only free education she could get. In *Arrogant Beggar* (1927) she described with some bitterness charitable patrons who provided financial aid for such a student.

Yezierska always identified with the poor and oppressed. A strong individualist, there is no evidence that she belonged to any radical parties. Around 1910, however, she lived for a time in a house set up by the Rand School to encourage a community of socialist thinkers. In 1910 she married Jacob Gordon, an attorney, but the marriage was annulled in a few months. The following year she married Arnold Levitas, who taught in vocational high schools and wrote textbooks. Yezierska desired only a religious ceremony, rather than the legally binding civil ceremony, so when their daughter Louise was born in 1912 she was formally adopted by her father to legitimize her.

Yezierska hated cooking and housekeeping, disappointing her sociable husband's expectations. She left him temporarily in 1914, taking her daughter with her for a year to visit a sister in Los Angeles. Hiring a nursemaid, she took a job and began to write. In 1916, the year after her first story was published, she returned to New York, quit the marriage, and left her daughter with the father. Unable to obtain more than substitute teaching, she decided impetuously to enlist the aid of John Dewey at Columbia to secure accreditation. Her dynamic, striking presence (auburn hair, velvety white skin, blue eyes, short robust figure) and the stories she showed him impressed Dewey. Unprecedentedly, he allowed her to audit his seminar on social and political philosophy. Through the academic year 1917–18 their relationship became a romantic attachment. Their short-lived—probably not consummated—affair deeply affected them both. Dewey encouraged her to write, inspiring her with self-confidence at a critical juncture of her career, as can be seen in one of the poems he wrote to her:

Generations of stifled worlds reaching out
Through you
Aching for utt'rance, dying on lips
That have died of hunger,
Hunger not to have, but to be (Boydston, p. xxvi).

She fictionalized her experience as translator on Dewey's project among Philadelphia Poles in *All I Could Never Be* (1932)—one of several stories about an aspiring girl of the people who encounters an upper-class man.

Between that book and the autobiographical novel *Red Ribbon on a White Horse* (the title comes from a ghetto proverb, "Poverty becomes a wise man like a red ribbon on a white horse") in 1950, her reputation and fortune declined sharply. In the 1950s she wrote several reviews of books with ethnic and immigrant themes for the *New York Times;* in the 1960s she published a few essays and stories on aging in *The Re-*

porter, Commentary, and smaller journals. Aside from anthology pieces culled from *Hungry Hearts* and *Children of Loneliness* (1923) on the meaning of America to immigrants—"A deathless hope—a world still in the making"—her work was little known.

Yet even in her extreme age Yezierska kept writing. The title of her last published story, "Take Up Your Bed and Walk" (*Chicago Jewish Forum*, 1969), testifies to her spirit. In her last year of life, almost blind after cataract operations, she dictated her work. She had left New York by then to live near her daughter, and died of a stroke in a nursing home in Ontario, Calif., on Nov. 21, 1970.

Yezierska's novels often read like soap opera and her style can be overwrought ("She longed to throw herself at his feet and weep. Ach! America—God from the world! Ach!" *Salome of the Tenements*, 1922), yet 1920s critics responded to her portrayal of direct, strong emotions. No critic hinted at her years of preparation (including a writing course at Columbia in 1918), or noted that the translation of Yiddish vernacular spoken by her characters resulted from careful artifice and craft, not untutored genius. *Bread Givers* is a strong book; *Red Ribbon on a White Horse* is well-made and subtle. The narrator's accounts in *Red Ribbon* of Hollywood, of her relationship with a Dewey-inspired character, of palmy Algonquin days, hard times, and the Works Progress Administration Writers' Project—one of her coworkers was Richard Wright—and finally an interlude in Vermont in search of a simple and emotionally fulfilling life, convince that who touches this book touches a person.

[The collection of Yezierska's papers at Boston Univ. —including some MSS., personal correspondence, and published and unpublished materials—is largely disappointing. The YIVO Inst. for Jewish Research in N.Y. City contains a few scattered letters of little significance. There is no biography or extended critical study; there is a dissertation by Ralda Sullivan, "Anzia Yezierska, an American Writer" (Univ. of Calif., Berkeley, 1975). The best evaluation of her life, work, and importance is Alice Kessler-Harris, introduction to *Bread Givers* (1975). Jo Ann Boydston, introduction to *The Poems of John Dewey* (1977), illuminates admirably the Dewey relationship. *Twentieth Century Authors* (1942) contains a good photograph but is factually unreliable; the *First Supplement* (1955) is appreciative. Irving Howe, *World of Our Fathers* (1976), pp. 268–70, emphasizes her struggle with her father. A collection of Yezierska's stories, *The Open Cage* (1980), includes a sensitive essay by Alice Kessler-Harris and a moving and informative afterword by Yezierska's daughter, Louise Levitas Henriksen. Yezierska's accounts of her life in interviews and writings are often fictionalized, and the date of her birth remains a question. Kessler-Harris gave 1885 in her introduction to *Bread Givers* but now agrees (correspondence with author) with the 1880 date given by Louise Henriksen, based on the dates of her attendance at Teachers College, internal evidence in stories, and her probable age at the time of her daughter's birth. An obituary appeared in the *N.Y. Times*, Nov. 23, 1970; death record from Calif. Dept. of Public Health.]

JULES CHAMETZKY

YURKA, Blanche, June 19, 1887–June 6, 1974. Actress.

Blanche Yurka was born in Saint Paul, Minn., the third of four children of Anton and Karolina (Novak) Jurka. Both parents had emigrated from Bohemia, then part of the Austro-Hungarian Empire, to the large Czech colony in Chicago. From her father, Blanche inherited scholarly and artistic interests, a nature not easy to intimidate, and the joy of staging and acting in plays. Her mother, who spoke no English, had an unfortunate first marriage which ended in divorce. But Mila, Blanche Jurka's half sister, was as close to her as her older sister Rose and her two brothers. In Saint Paul, Blanche finished grade school before her father lost his job teaching Czech at Jefferson School and accepted a position as executive secretary for the Czech Benevolent Society in New York. He moved his family there in 1900.

In New York Blanche Jurka began singing lessons before entering Wadleigh High School (1901–03), where she proved an erratic student. Music fascinated her, however, and she appeared in an amateur production of Balfe's *The Bohemian Girl*, which later supplied her with the title of her memoirs. She studied first at the Metropolitan Opera School (1903–05) and made her stage debut as the Grail-bearer in a 1903 Metropolitan production of *Parsifal*. Dismissed from the school for injuring her voice by singing the role of Leonora in an amateur production of *Il Trovatore*, she went to the Institute of Musical Art (1905–07), the predecessor of the Juilliard School, which released her for the same reason. Having lost her chance at a career in opera, she finally accepted the suggestion of the Institute's director: "Why not go on the stage?" With customary persistence, she obtained an audition from David Belasco, who, she claimed, told her: "Your diction is clear and pure. Your voice has good timbre. I can sense that you have temperament. We must find out if you can act" (*Bohemian Girl*, p. 37).

She soon had a small part in Belasco's *The Rose of the Rancho* (1906), and the following year received a contract from the impresario. (It was apparently at this time that she changed the spelling of her last name.) But her rise to stardom was slow, even disheartening. Beginning with *The Warrens of Virginia* (1907), and for a decade thereafter, Yurka alternated between stock company and touring productions, most notably appearing in three plays with E. H. Sothern. Her first real success was in *Daybreak* (1917), with JANE COWL, a play which ran twelve weeks on Broadway before touring. She also toured in *The Naughty Wife*, then returned to New York to play in *Allegiance* (1918), which failed after forty-four performances. It was during an engagement in *The Law Breaker* (1922) that she met Ian Keith (born Ian Keith Ross), whom she married in September 1922. An actor whose career never reached great success, Keith's charm was offset by his jealousy; they were separated in 1925 and divorced in 1928.

From the early 1920s through the mid-1930s Blanche Yurka achieved her greatest success as an actress. For 125 performances she played Gertrude to John Barrymore's Hamlet (1922). Because Barrymore at forty-two seemed a little old to be her son, she vented her irritation by making herself as youthful as possible. Her greatest popular success was in a slight melodrama called *The Squall* (1926), which played one year on Broadway and toured for another. Artistically, however, Yurka had already established herself in the part of Gina in *The Wild Duck* (1925), a role she modeled upon her mother. She also acted in *Hedda Gabler* (1929) and *Lady from the Sea* (1929), prompting critics to rave that she was making Ibsen one of the most popular playwrights of the day. Tall and imposing, with a voice and style of acting well suited to classical drama, Yurka was enthusiastically received in Norman Bel Geddes's production of *Electra* (1932). The following year she read the narrator in André Obey's *Lucrece*, enjoying a passionate interest in "well-spoken words." She won critical acclaim in 1935 when she replaced Edith Evans as the nurse in *Romeo and Juliet*, with KATHARINE CORNELL.

Although her reputation rests firmly on classical drama, Blanche Yurka had other interests. In 1935 she started a career in the movies, performing in more than twenty films from *A Tale of Two Cities* (1935), in which she created a memorable Madame DeFarge, to *Thunder in the Sun* (1959). Beginning in 1936 she produced a series of successful one-woman shows in which she recreated scenes from classical drama. During World War II Yurka gave generously to the war effort with her time and talent, always emphasizing the cause of good theater. Both

before and after the war she toured with theater groups through Europe.

Always a perceptive and forthright critic of the theater to which she had devoted her life, Yurka was also an independent and dynamic woman. She supported the actors' strike in 1919, later vigorously defended American actors and acting against the British invasion of American theaters, and endorsed TALLULAH BANKHEAD's defense of the Federal Theatre Project at the 1939 Senate Appropriations Committee hearings. While noting that the Federal Theatre needed improvement, Yurka observed: "After all, you do not chloroform a child who happens to have the measles." When the occasion demanded, she could and did castigate Broadway for poor productions. After World War II she was more active in Hollywood than in New York, and her enthusiasm for theater waned.

Her growing distaste for "the passion for ugliness that seems so much a part of our theatre today," expressed in a Nov. 6, 1955, letter to the *New York Times*, led her to announce her retirement that year. However, she could not long remain away from the theater. During the ensuing years, Yurka combined intermittent stage appearances with a career as a writer. Her enthusiasm for the theater illuminates *Dear Audience* (1959), a fascinating introduction to the art she loved; she went on to edit two collections of plays before writing *Bohemian Girl* (1970). Visiting Athens under the United States International Exchange of Artists to open the Greek Drama Festival in 1957, Yurka appeared in a reading of EDITH HAMILTON's translation of *Prometheus Bound*. Few good roles came during her last years—the brevity of her part as the cook in *Dinner at Eight* (1966) shocked her—and she made her final stage appearance in *The Madwoman of Chaillot* in 1970.

Historians tend to chronicle Yurka as an actress of strong-willed women and, indeed, in such roles she left her mark upon American acting. She died in New York City shortly before her eighty-seventh birthday.

[The Blanche Yurka Coll. in the Billy Rose Theatre Coll., N.Y. Public Library, contains correspondence, reviews, photographs, and programs. Clippings can also be found in the Robinson Locke Scrapbooks at that library, and in the Harvard Theatre Coll. The most complete published source, despite some errors in dates and chronology, is *Bohemian Girl: Blanche Yurka's Theatrical Life* (1970), a well-written autobiographical account. It also has excellent photographs. Yurka edited *Three Scandinavian Plays* (1962) and *Three Classic Greek Plays* (1964). "Speed Mania the Curse of Modern Drama," *Theatre Mag.*, May 1929, pp. 20, 58, indicates the kind of criticism she could write. *The Biog. Encyc. and*

Who's Who of Am. Theatre (1966), pp. 937–38, lists her credits. See Louis Sheaffer's interview in the *N.Y. Times,* Nov. 6, 1955, and the interview in *Opera News,* April 3, 1971, pp. 12–13. For other observations on her work see William C. Young, *Famous Actors and Actresses of the American Stage* (1975), II, 1209–14 (which contains some inaccuracies); Arthur William Row, "A Star Who Is a

Luminary," *Poet Lore,* Spring 1928, pp. 132–33; John Mason Brown, *Two on the Aisle* (1938), pp. 68–71. An obituary appeared in the *N.Y. Times,* June 7, 1974. Information on the original spelling of Yurka's name came from the 1900 U.S. Census. A biobibliography prepared by Hampton Marshall Auld assisted in the preparation of this article.]

WALTER J. MESERVE

Z

ZAHARIAS, Mildred Ella (Babe) Didrikson, June 26, 1911?–Sept. 27, 1956. Athlete.

Babe Didrikson, the extraordinarily versatile athlete who broke records in several sports, acquired her nickname as a girl because she reminded her playmates of Babe Ruth. Born in Port Arthur, Texas, she was the sixth of seven children and the fourth girl of Norwegian immigrants, Ole Nickolene and Hannah Marie (Olson) Didriksen. Babe Didrikson later changed the spelling of the name to what she believed to be the Norwegian form (Johnson and Williamson, *Whatta-Gal,* p. 36). Her father was a carpenter who refinished furniture and built his family's house; her mother, who had won skating championships in Norway, sometimes worked as a practical nurse and on occasion took in washing. In 1915 the Didriksens moved to a working-class neighborhood in Beaumont, Texas, where Babe grew up playing sandlot baseball with the boys.

A high school basketball star, she was hired as a typist in February 1930 by Melvin Mc-Combs, who ran the women's athletic program of the Employers Casualty Company of Dallas. Industrial athletic programs for women were common, since opportunities for women in college athletics were few. A three-time All-American, Didrikson led the company's semiprofessional basketball team, the Golden Cyclones, to two finals and a national championship. This rapid transition from small-town girl to national star may have accounted for the ambitious Didrikson's arrogance and boastfulness, which alienated her teammates.

She soon had more to boast about. Introduced to track, by 1932 Didrikson had set American, Olympic, or world records in the eighty-meter hurdles, javelin, high jump, broad jump, and baseball throw. In the 1932 Amateur Athletic Union (AAU) championships she entered eight events and won five, tied one, and finished fourth in another, thus single-handedly winning

the team title. Limited to three events in the 1932 Olympics, she won gold medals in the javelin and hurdles. Tying the winner in the high jump, she was given the second place silver medal because of her unorthodox style. The Olympics brought fame and adulation from both press and public, to which Didrikson responded with naive pride and brash wit.

Fame was one thing, but there was no competitive context in which a woman athlete could earn a living. After being suspended by the AAU for allegedly accepting a car and appearing in a Chrysler Corporation advertisement, Didrikson turned professional in December 1932. She spent a week with a vaudeville act in which she ran on a treadmill and displayed her real ability as a harmonica player. Later she toured for a season with a mixed basketball team, Babe Didrikson's All Americans. She drew so well that, after pitching in some major league spring training games in 1934, she played 200 games with a traveling, bearded baseball team called the House of David. For pitching an inning or two, she received $1,500 a month—and much scorn.

Despite her singular success, Didrikson was often classed with other women athletes as a joke. No woman athlete can be taken seriously, Paul Gallico claimed; they are "at best second-rate imitations of the gentlemen" (Gallico, *Farewell to Sport,* p. 244). Didrikson resented this kind of stereotyping and also objected to being called a "muscle moll," complaining that "they seem to think I'm a strange, unnatural being . . . The idea seems to be that Muscle Molls are not people" (Didrikson, "I Blow My Own Horn," p. 104). In later years, she liked to tell about the dressmaking prize she had won at a state fair, and talked of her interest in cooking and gardening.

In 1932 Didrikson made the fateful decision to try golf, at the urging of her friend the sportswriter Grantland Rice. During the spring and summer of 1933, in Los Angeles, she received free golf lessons from Stan Kertes. In November 1934, in her first tournament, the Fort Worth Women's Invitational, she shot seventy-seven to qualify, but lost in the first round. Then in April 1935, in the hostile upper-class atmosphere of the River Oaks Country Club in Houston, she won the Texas Women's Amateur Championship, her first tournament victory. Immediately, the United States Golf Association branded her a professional. With only two professional tournaments for women then in existence, it was back to barnstorming, this time with a top male golfer, Gene Sarazen. She earned $150 per day plus a retainer from Wilson, the sporting goods manufacturers.

In 1938 Didrikson qualified for a men's tournament in Los Angeles, where she was by then living, and was paired with George Zaharias, a prosperous professional wrestler and promoter. They were married in St. Louis on Dec. 23, 1938. George Zaharias successfully took on the management of his wife's career and made it possible for her to sit out the three years necessary to regain amateur status. From 1940 to 1943, she played in professional tournaments but refused the cash prizes. In 1940 she won the Western Opens, her first tournament victories since 1935. With the postwar resumption of a full schedule of tournaments, she put together a string of fourteen consecutive titles, climaxed by the British Women's Amateur Championship in 1947. She was the first American to win that prestigious title. In winning tournaments, Zaharias played a short, sharp game, a fact obscured by the fame of her 245-yard drives.

After turning professional in August 1947, Babe Didrikson Zaharias and five others founded the Ladies Professional Golf Association in January 1948, with the Wilson Company providing $15,000 prize money for nine tournaments. Zaharias was the leading money winner in 1949, 1950, and 1951. In 1952 she had a hernia operation; the following year she developed cancer of the rectum and had a colostomy. Fifteen months later she won her third United States Women's Open title by twelve strokes. But the cancer recurred in the spring of 1955, and she died in a Galveston hospital the following year.

Babe Didrikson Zaharias converted women's golf to an exciting power game, breaking seventy, the women's four-minute mile; she also made it entertaining. She played to the galleries with wisecracking repartee which some found damaging to the image of the woman athlete; but her sense of theater gave women's golf the color it needed. A hustler, a practical joker, and at times a prima donna, she was above all competitive and aggressive. A "remarkably fierce spirit" matched her extraordinary physical attributes, and the combination of physical coordination, hard work, and temperament produced her records. In launching big-time women's golf, she led the way for other women's sports.

Golf made Babe Didrikson famous and earned her most of the $1,000,000 she accumulated in her lifetime. But it was her versatility which made her unique. In addition to her successes at basketball and baseball, she won tennis tournaments and a diving championship, and had a bowling average around 170. The Associated Press chose her six times as Woman Athlete of the Year; in 1950 they named her the Woman Athlete of the Half-Century. Not an overt campaigner for women's equality, "everything that was natural about Babe led her to sports, traditionally a man's world" (Johnson and Williamson, *Whatta-Gal*, p. 21). Her skills and accomplishments made her a symbol of what women could achieve in that arena.

[A collection of letters to Zaharias's friends William (Tiny) and Ruth Scurlock are in the John Gray Library at Lamar Univ., Beaumont, Texas. Shortly before her death she collaborated on an autobiography with Harry Paxton, *This Life I've Led* (1955). She also wrote "I Blow My Own Horn," *American Mag.*, June 1936, and *Championship Golf* (1948). Most thorough and objective of the accounts of her life are three articles in *Sports Illustrated*, Oct. 6, 13, and 20, 1975, by William Oscar Johnson and Nancy P. Williamson, and their book based on the articles, *"Whatta-Gal": The Babe Didrikson Story* (1977). Betty Hicks's account "Babe Didrikson Zaharias," *Womensports*, Nov. and Dec. 1975, contains some errors, but is a revealing assessment by an opponent. Representative of hostile male opinion is Paul Gallico, *Farewell to Sport* (1938). Grantland Rice, *The Tumult and the Shouting: My Life in Sport* (1954), offers an enthusiastic appreciation. Articles about her appeared frequently in national magazines through the thirties and forties and after her operation for cancer. See also *Current Biog.*, 1947. Babe Didrikson Zaharias claimed various birth dates, and no birth certificate is available. The 1911 date was chosen on the basis of information supplied to her biographers by one of her sisters. Obituaries appeared in the *N.Y. Times*, Sept. 28, 1956, and in the Oct. 8, 1956, issues of *Life, Time,* and *Newsweek;* death record provided by Texas Dept. of Health. Photographs are in her autobiography and in the works by Johnson and Williamson. A biobibliography by Jacqueline Pratt provided assistance in research.]

NANCY NORTON

ZIMBALIST, Mary Louise Curtis Bok, Aug. 6, 1876–Jan. 4, 1970. Music patron, philanthropist.

Mary Curtis Zimbalist was best known for her support of musicians and musical organizations, notably the Curtis Institute of Music, founded in Philadelphia in 1924. She was born in Boston, the only child of the publisher Cyrus Hermann Kotzschmar Curtis, of Portland, Maine, and Louisa (Knapp) Curtis. Three months after her birth, the family moved to Philadelphia, where printing prices for Curtis's *People's Ledger* were lower. Mary Louise Curtis grew up in a musical atmosphere: her father played the organ, her mother sang, and they all attended concerts. She studied the piano and specialized in music at the Ogontz School for Young Ladies.

By 1883 Cyrus Curtis had become the sole owner and Louisa Curtis editor of the *Ladies' Home Journal*. Having boosted *Journal* circulation to over a million, Curtis also purchased the *Saturday Evening Post* in 1897. These ventures ensured the growth of the Curtis Publishing Company, which came to stand for high quality editorial work and glorified middle-class values. In 1889 Edward William Bok, a Dutch immigrant and self-made publishing success, succeeded Louisa Curtis as editor of the *Ladies' Home Journal*. An active philanthropist in later life, Edward Bok spearheaded a successful endowment campaign for the Philadelphia Orchestra and willed over two million dollars to charities. On Oct. 22, 1896, he and Mary Louise Curtis were married. They had two sons, William Curtis (b. 1897) and Cary William (b. 1905).

Mary Bok devoted her life to music through a variety of philanthropic activities in which she always maintained a practical involvement. After her mother's death in 1910 she gave funds for a building in her honor to house the Settlement Music School, which served the children of a disadvantaged neighborhood of Philadelphia. Grateful for all that music had given her, Bok aspired to communicate self-respect and good citizenship through exposing others to music. Her most ambitious contribution was the founding of the Curtis Institute of Music, named for her father, in October 1924.

Considered a pioneering undertaking in music education at the time, the Institute offered courses in musicianship and academic subjects in addition to applied instruction. Bok aimed at producing "all-around" musicians, and the school also provided students with opportunities such as recitals, lectures, and contact with leading artists. Close ties were cultivated with the Philadelphia Orchestra; its conductor, Leopold Stokowski, led the student orchestra, and many of the orchestra's principals joined the faculty. In addition, Bok and her family were active both on the orchestra's board of directors and in the school's administration.

Among those who attended the Curtis Institute over the years were Samuel Barber, Gian Carlo Menotti, and Leonard Bernstein. A more direct beneficiary of Bok's patronage was the futurist composer George Antheil, whom she began to assist in 1921. Despite fundamental aesthetic conflicts, this unlikely artist-patron collaboration and friendship survived for nineteen years the tempestuous course of Antheil's career. Though she frequently disapproved of his behavior as well as his music, Bok always responded generously to Antheil's requests for supplements to the allowance she granted him.

In 1927 Mary Bok substantially increased her initial grant of $500,000 to the Curtis Institute. With the total endowment raised to $12,500,-000, the school was able to abolish tuition. Bok also provided living expenses for needy students and their families, lent grand pianos, and sponsored tours of Europe. The Rockport summer music colony established near the family summer home in Maine likewise grew out of her generosity.

In 1930 Bok's husband died, and she nursed her father through his final illness until his death in 1933. In memory of her father, she later donated the Curtis organ in Irvine Auditorium to the University of Pennsylvania, had his home organ rebuilt for Christ Church, and presented the world's largest movable pipe organ to the Academy of Music in Philadelphia. On July 6, 1943, Mary Bok married Efrem Zimbalist. A Russian-born concert violinist, Zimbalist had joined the Curtis Institute's faculty in 1928 and became its director in 1941.

Mary Bok Zimbalist's philanthropy at times extended outside the music world. Civic and harbor improvement programs, jobs for the unemployed during the depression, and construction of libraries and the Bok Amphitheater were among her charitable undertakings in Rockport and Camden, Maine. She also donated the Annie Russell Theater to Rollins College in Winter Park, Fla.

Mary Zimbalist died of heart failure in Philadelphia at ninety-three. A tribute to her on the fiftieth anniversary of the Curtis Institute, which she had served as president for forty-five years, described her as "calm, wise, gracious, understanding, tolerant, a lady of exquisite taste and poise: a woman of enormous strength and determination." Although conservative tastes placed her in opposition to much of modern and popular music, she endeavored to remain publicly neutral, in unswerving belief that the music would speak for itself.

[Manuscript sources include a collection at the Curtis Institute, which contains drafts of correspondence, commencement speeches, newspaper clippings, and photographs. It is available to scholars by appointment only. The Grace Spofford Papers in the Sophia Smith Coll., Smith College, contain personal as well as official correspondence between Spofford, the first dean of Curtis, and Zimbalist. The Music Div., Library of Congress, holds her correspondence with George Antheil; see Wayne D. Shirley, "Another American in Paris: George Antheil's Correspondence with Mary Curtis Bok," *Quart. Jour. of the Library of Congress,* Jan. 1977. The Hist. Soc. of Pa. has a cross-section of material, including the Cyrus Curtis Papers, and the George H. Lorimer Papers (*Post* series), mostly concerning business, and Charles J. Cohen's 1924 Rittenhouse Square scrapbook, which contains a letter from Zimbalist with a brief autobiographical sketch. The most useful published source on Zimbalist's life and career is *Overtones,* the Curtis Institute newsletter, published with her support from 1929 until 1940. The fiftieth anniversary issue (1974), edited by Nellie Lee Bok, contains a tribute and biographical sketch with photographs. Early Curtis Institute catalogs are also of interest. An entry appears in *Baker's Biog. Dict.,* 6th ed. Sources of information about her family include entries on Cyrus Curtis and Edward Bok in *Dict. Am. Biog.,* Supp. One; Edward Bok, *A Man From Maine* (1923), a biography of Cyrus Curtis, and his autobiography, *The Americanization of Edward Bok* (1920). Also see Robert A. Gerson, *Music in Philadelphia* (1940), and Herbert Kupferberg, *Those Fabulous Philadelphians: The Life and Times of a Great Orchestra* (1969). An obituary appeared in the *N.Y. Times,* Jan. 6, 1970; death certificate supplied by Pa. Dept. of Health.]

DEBORAH B. THOMAS

CLASSIFIED
LIST OF BIOGRAPHIES

Agriculture and Rural Life

Chase, Mary Agnes
Cunningham, Minnie Fisher
Hagood, Margaret Loyd Jarman
Lowry, Edith Elizabeth
Sewell, Edna Belle
Shambaugh, Jessie Field
Stanley, Louise

Anthropology and Folklore

Cadilla de Martínez, María
Deloria, Ella Cara
Densmore, Frances Theresa
Hurston, Zora Neale
Pound, Louise
Powdermaker, Hortense
Reichard, Gladys Amanda
Sawyer, Ruth

Archaeology

See Classics and Archaeology

Architecture

Barney, Nora Stanton
Bauer, Catherine Krouse
Griffin, Marion Mahony
Hayden, Sophia Gregoria
Morgan, Julia
See also Landscape Architecture

Art

Ames, Blanche Ames

Brooks, Romaine
Dreier, Katherine Sophie
Fuller, Meta Vaux Warrick
Griffin, Marion Mahony
Halpert, Edith Gregor
Hesse, Eva
Hoffman, Malvina Cornell
Huntington, Anna Vaughn Hyatt
Johnson, Adelaide
Liebes, Dorothy Wright
Miner, Dorothy Eugenia
Moses, Anna Mary Robertson (Grandma)
Pereira, Irene Rice
Rebay, Hilla
Richter, Gisela Marie Augusta
Ryan, Anne
Saarinen, Aline Milton Bernstein
Sage, Kay Linn
Savage, Augusta Christine
Swindler, Mary Hamilton
See also Photography

Astronomy

Maury, Antonia Caetana De Paiva Pereira

Aviation

Nichols, Ruth Roland
Omlie, Phoebe Jane Fairgrave
Willebrandt, Mabel Walker

Biochemistry

See Medicine: Researchers; Nutrition

Classified List

Biology

Carson, Rachel Louise
Harvey, Ethel Browne
Hyman, Libbie Henrietta
Morgan, Ann Haven
Nice, Margaret Morse

Birth Control

Ames, Blanche Ames
Kleegman, Sophia Josephine
Levine, Lena
McCormick, Katharine Dexter
Sanger, Margaret

Botany

Braun, Emma Lucy
Chase, Mary Agnes
Eastwood, Alice
Ferguson, Margaret Clay

Broadcasting

Allen, Gracie
Berg, Gertrude Edelstein
Brice, Fanny
Gordon, Dorothy Lerner
Hennock, Frieda Barkin
McDaniel, Hattie
Mack, Nila
Moorehead, Agnes
Phillips, Irna
Saarinen, Aline Milton Bernstein
Thompson, Dorothy
Waller, Judith Cary

Business

Adler, Polly
Arden, Elizabeth
Auerbach, Beatrice Fox
Barney, Nora Stanton
Carnegie, Hattie
Frederick, Christine McGaffey
Gilbreth, Lillian Moller
Grossinger, Jennie
Halpert, Edith Gregor
Hawes, Elizabeth
Knopf, Blanche Wolf
Liebes, Dorothy Wright
Mesta, Perle
Morgan, Julia

Muller, Gertrude Agnes
Pennington, Mary Engle
Post, Marjorie Merriweather
Rosenthal, Ida Cohen
Rubinstein, Helena
Rudkin, Margaret Fogarty
Shaver, Dorothy
Turnbo-Malone, Annie Minerva
Waldo, Ruth Fanshaw
Weed, Ethel Berenice
White, Eartha Mary Magdalene

Chemistry

Carr, Emma Perry
Pennington, Mary Engle
See also Medicine: Researchers; Nutrition

Children's Literature

Arbuthnot, May Hill
Brown, Margaret Wise
Forbes, Esther
Irwin, Inez Haynes Gillmore
Massee, May
Miller, Bertha Mahony
Mitchell, Lucy Sprague
Moore, Anne Carroll
Sawyer, Ruth
Wilder, Laura Ingalls

Civil Liberties

Flynn, Elizabeth Gurley
Hughan, Jessie Wallace
Kenyon, Dorothy
King, Carol Weiss

Civil Rights

Ames, Jessie Daniel
Baker, Josephine
Barker, Mary Cornelia
Bass, Charlotta Spears
Bethune, Mary McLeod
Fauset, Crystal Dreda Bird
Gaines, Irene McCoy
Hansberry, Lorraine
Haynes, Elizabeth Ross
Jemison, Alice Mae Lee
Lampkin, Daisy Elizabeth Adams
Ovington, Mary White
Robeson, Eslanda Cardoza Goode
Robinson, Rubye Doris Smith

Classified List

Roosevelt, Anna Eleanor
Smith, Lillian
Terrell, Mary Church
Tilly, Dorothy Eugenia Rogers

Classics and Archaeology

Goldman, Hetty
Hamilton, Edith
Richter, Gisela Marie Augusta
Swindler, Mary Hamilton
Taylor, Lily Ross

College Administration

See Education

Community Affairs

Auerbach, Beatrice Fox
Barron, Jennie Loitman
Bowen, Louise deKoven
Butler, Selena Sloan
Carter, Eunice Hunton
Cunningham, Minnie Fisher
Davis, Frances Elliott
Dummer, Ethel Sturges
Gaines, Irene McCoy
Gellhorn, Edna Fischel
Haynes, Elizabeth Ross
Hogg, Ima
Jemison, Alice Mae Lee
Kohut, Rebekah Bettelheim
Lampkin, Daisy Elizabeth Adams
Sherwin, Belle
Terrell, Mary Church
Wells, Marguerite Milton
White, Eartha Mary Magdalene
Wright, Muriel Hazel

Conservation

Akeley, Mary Lee Jobe
Braun, Emma Lucy
Carson, Rachel Louise
Eastwood, Alice
Morgan, Ann Haven
Nice, Margaret Morse

Consumer Affairs

Brady, Mildred Edie
Campbell, Persia Crawford

Dewson, Mary Williams
Herrick, Elinore Morehouse
Kenyon, Dorothy
Kyrk, Hazel
Mason, Lucy Randolph
Perkins, Frances
Stanley, Louise

Cookery

Davis, Adelle
Rombauer, Irma Louise von Starkloff
Rudkin, Margaret Fogarty
Toklas, Alice Babette

Dance

Burchenal, Elizabeth
Castle, Irene
Chace, Marian
Humphrey, Doris
St. Denis, Ruth
Tamiris, Helen

Demography

Hagood, Margaret Loyd Jarman
Taeuber, Irene Barnes

Economics

Balch, Emily Greene
Campbell, Persia Crawford
Kyrk, Hazel
Rochester, Anna (*see under* Hutchins, Grace)
Wolfson, Theresa

Education

College Founders and Administrators

Bethune, Mary McLeod
Blunt, Katharine
Clapp, Margaret Antoinette
Comstock, Ada Louise
Drexel, Mother Mary Katharine
Flanagan, Hallie Mae Ferguson
Gildersleeve, Virginia Crocheron
Lloyd, Alice Spencer Geddes
Meyer, Annie Nathan
Mitchell, Lucy Sprague
Thurston, Matilda Smyrell Calder
White, Edna Noble
Wolff, Sister Madeleva (Mary Evaline)

Classified List

School Founders and Administrators

Andrus, Ethel Percy
Arbuthnot, May Hill
Barker, Mary Cornelia
Bethune, Mary McLeod
Brown, Charlotte Eugenia Hawkins
Burroughs, Nannie Helen
Cooke, Flora Juliette
Cooper, Anna Julia Haywood
Frazier, Maude
Hamilton, Edith
Jarrell, Helen Ira
Kohut, Rebekah Bettelheim
Lloyd, Alice Spencer Geddes
Lusk, Georgia Lee Witt
McLaren, Louise Leonard
Parkhurst, Helen
Shambaugh, Jessie Field
Stern, Catherine Brieger

Writers and Researchers

Arbuthnot, May Hill
Fisher, Dorothy Canfield
Goodenough, Florence Laura
Gruenberg, Sidonie Matsner
Littledale, Clara Savage
Mitchell, Lucy Sprague
Stern, Catherine Brieger
Strang, Ruth May
Taba, Hilda

Other

Barker, Mary Cornelia
Barron, Jennie Loitman
Blaine, Anita McCormick
Borchardt, Selma Munter
Butler, Selena Sloan
Dummer, Ethel Sturges
Fisher, Dorothy Canfield
Hughan, Jessie Wallace
Jarrell, Helen Ira
Meyer, Agnes Ernst
Terrell, Mary Church
Ward, Winifred Louise
See also Physical Education

Engineering and Industrial Design

Barney, Nora Stanton
Clarke, Edith
Flügge-Lotz, Irmgard
Gilbreth, Lillian Moller
Muller, Gertrude Agnes
Pennington, Mary Engle
Rand, Marie Gertrude

Entertainment

Allen, Gracie
Baker, Josephine
Brice, Fanny
Castle, Irene
Garland, Judy
Henie, Sonja
Holiday, Billie
Joplin, Janis Lyn
Lee, Gypsy Rose
Tucker, Sophie
See also Broadcasting; Dance; Film; Music;
    Theater

Exploration

Akeley, Mary Lee Jobe
Seton, Grace Gallatin

Fashion

Bernstein, Aline Frankau
Carnegie, Hattie
Chase, Edna Woolman
Hawes, Elizabeth
Liebes, Dorothy Wright
McCardell, Claire
Rosenthal, Ida Cohen
Shaver, Dorothy

Feminism

Ames, Blanche Ames
Barney, Nora Stanton
Bass, Mary Elizabeth
Beard, Mary Ritter
Blair, Emily Newell
Cadilla de Martínez, María
Dock, Lavinia Lloyd
Hawes, Elizabeth
Irwin, Inez Haynes Gillmore
Johnson, Adelaide
Kenyon, Dorothy
Laughlin, Gail
Lee, Muna
Lovejoy, Esther Pohl
McCormick, Katharine Dexter
Martin, Anne Henrietta
Mesta, Perle
Miller, Emma Guffey
Phillips, Lena Madesin
Pollitzer, Anita Lily
Rohde, Ruth Bryan Owen
Sanger, Margaret
Scott, Ann London

Seton, Grace Gallatin
Van Hoosen, Bertha
Vernon, Mabel

Film

Bara, Theda
Barry, Iris
Bauchens, Anne
Bow, Clara Gordon
Deren, Maya
Garland, Judy
Gish, Dorothy
Grable, Betty
Hayward, Susan
Henie, Sonja
Holliday, Judy
Hopper, Hedda
McDaniel, Hattie
MacDonald, Jeanette
Marion, Frances
Monroe, Marilyn
Moorehead, Agnes
Parker, Dorothy Rothschild
Parsons, Louella Oettinger
Pitts, ZaSu
Wong, Anna May
Yurka, Blanche

Geology

Edinger, Tilly
Gardner, Julia Anna
Goldring, Winifred
Knopf, Eleanora Frances Bliss

Government and Politics

Appointees

Adams, Annette Abbott
Anderson, Mary
Bethune, Mary McLeod
Brunauer, Esther Caukin
Campbell, Persia Crawford
Clapp, Margaret Antoinette
Flanagan, Hallie Mae Ferguson
Frazier, Maude
Harriman, Florence Jaffray Hurst
Hennock, Frieda Barkin
Hoey, Jane Margueretta
Lee, Muna
Mesta, Perle
Miller, Frieda Segelke
Priest, Ivy Maude Baker

Rohde, Ruth Bryan Owen
Roosevelt, Anna Eleanor
Stanley, Louise
Switzer, Mary Elizabeth
Van Kleeck, Mary Abby
Woodward, Ellen Sullivan

Congresswomen

Lusk, Georgia Lee Witt
Mankin, Helen Douglas
Norton, Mary Teresa Hopkins
Rankin, Jeannette Pickering
Rogers, Edith Nourse
Rohde, Ruth Bryan Owen

Other Elected Officials

Fauset, Crystal Dreda Bird
Ferguson, Miriam Amanda Wallace
Frazier, Maude
Laughlin, Gail
Lusk, Georgia Lee Witt
Mankin, Helen Douglas
Priest, Ivy Maude Baker
Somerville, Nellie Nugent
Woodward, Ellen Sullivan

Party Workers and Officials

Adams, Annette Abbott
Bass, Charlotta Spears
Blair, Emily Newell
Cline, Genevieve Rose
Cunningham, Minnie Fisher
Dewson, Mary Williams
Fauset, Crystal Dreda Bird
Gaines, Irene McCoy
Harriman, Florence Jaffray Hurst
Miller, Emma Guffey
Pinchot, Cornelia Elizabeth Bryce
Priest, Ivy Maude Baker
Sabin, Pauline Morton

Wives of Presidents

Coolidge, Grace Anna Goodhue
Roosevelt, Anna Eleanor
Wilson, Edith Bolling Galt

History

Beard, Mary Ritter
Bowen, Catherine Shober Drinker
Clapp, Margaret Antoinette
Cooper, Anna Julia Haywood
Forbes, Esther

Classified List

Green, Constance McLaughlin
Hyslop, Beatrice Fry
Putnam, Bertha Haven
Wright, Mary Clabaugh
Wright, Muriel Hazel

Home Economics

Blunt, Katharine
Frederick, Christine McGaffey
Gilbreth, Lillian Moller
Kyrk, Hazel
Morgan, Agnes Fay
Roberts, Lydia Jane
Stanley, Louise
White, Edna Noble

Housing Reform

Bauer, Catherine Krouse
Simkhovitch, Mary Kingsbury

International Affairs

Brunauer, Esther Caukin
Dean, Vera Micheles
Lee, Muna
McCormick, Anne Elizabeth O'Hare
Roosevelt, Anna Eleanor
Thompson, Dorothy
Woodsmall, Ruth Frances
See also Peace

Journalism

Bass, Charlotta Spears
Brady, Mildred Edie
Burgos, Julia de
Craig, Elisabeth May Adams
Cunningham, Minnie Fisher
Fleeson, Doris
Furman, Bess
Gilmer, Elizabeth Meriwether (Dorothy Dix)
Gordon, Dorothy Lerner
Herbst, Josephine
Herrick, Elinore Morehouse
Hickok, Lorena
Higgins, Marguerite
Hopper, Hedda
Jemison, Alice Mae Lee
Littledale, Clara Savage
Lloyd, Alice Spencer Geddes
McCormick, Anne Elizabeth O'Hare
Meyer, Agnes Ernst

Parsons, Louella Oettinger
Patterson, Alicia
Post, Emily Price
Reid, Helen Miles Rogers
Rippin, Jane Parker Deeter
Roosevelt, Anna Eleanor
Saarinen, Aline Milton Bernstein
Strong, Anna Louise
Thompson, Dorothy
Van Doren, Irita Bradford
Vorse, Mary Heaton

Labor

Anderson, Mary
Barker, Mary Cornelia
Bloor, Ella Reeve
Borchardt, Selma Munter
Christman, Elisabeth
Cohn, Fannia Mary
Dickason, Gladys Marie
Dreier, Mary Elisabeth
Flynn, Elizabeth Gurley
Hawes, Elizabeth
Herrick, Elinore Morehouse
Hutchins, Grace
Jarrell, Helen Ira
Kellor, Frances
McLaren, Louise Leonard
Mason, Lucy Randolph
Miller, Frieda Segelke
Norton, Mary Teresa Hopkins
Parker, Julia Sarsfield O'Connor
Perkins, Frances
Pesotta, Rose
Schneiderman, Rose
Thorne, Florence Calvert
Van Kleeck, Mary Abby
Vorse, Mary Heaton
Wolfson, Theresa
See also Social Research

Landscape Architecture

Farrand, Beatrix Jones

Law

Adams, Annette Abbott
Allen, Florence Ellinwood
Barron, Jennie Loitman
Bartelme, Mary Margaret
Borchardt, Selma Munter
Carter, Eunice Hunton
Cline, Genevieve Rose

Classified List

Hennock, Frieda Barkin
Kenyon, Dorothy
King, Carol Weiss
Laughlin, Gail
Mankin, Helen Douglas
Phillips, Lena Madesin
Willebrandt, Mabel Walker
See also Penology and Criminology

Librarianship

Eastman, Linda Anne
Haines, Helen Elizabeth
Moore, Anne Carroll
Mudge, Isadore Gilbert

Literature

Editors and Publishers

Anderson, Margaret Carolyn
Beach, Sylvia Woodbridge
Fauset, Jessie Redmon
Heap, Jane (*see under* Anderson, Margaret
  Carolyn)
Knopf, Blanche Wolf
Loveman, Amy
Moore, Marianne Craig
Van Doren, Irita Bradford

Scholars

Pound, Louise
Scudder, Vida Dutton
Tuve, Rosemond
White, Helen Constance

Translators

Bogan, Louise
Doolittle, Hilda (H.D.)
Hamilton, Edith
Lee, Muna
Lowe-Porter, Helen Tracy
Moore, Marianne Craig

Writers

Barney, Natalie
Barry, Iris
Blair, Emily Newell
Bogan, Louise
Bowen, Catherine Shober Drinker
Buck, Pearl

Burgos, Julia de
Cadilla de Martínez, María
Doolittle, Hilda (H.D.)
Fauset, Jessie Redmon
Ferber, Edna
Field, Sara Bard
Fisher, Dorothy Canfield
Forbes, Esther
Hamilton, Edith
Herbst, Josephine
Hurst, Fannie
Hurston, Zora Neale
Irwin, Inez Haynes Gillmore
Jackson, Shirley Hardie
Keller, Helen
Lee, Gypsy Rose
Lee, Muna
Lowe-Porter, Helen Tracy
Luhan, Mabel Dodge
McCullers, Carson
Mitchell, Lucy Sprague
Meyer, Annie Nathan
Moore, Marianne Craig
Norris, Kathleen Thompson
O'Connor, Flannery
Parker, Dorothy Rothschild
Plath, Sylvia
Post, Emily Price
Rawlings, Marjorie Kinnan
Rinehart, Mary Roberts
Sandoz, Mari
Seton, Grace Gallatin
Sexton, Anne Gray Harvey
Smith, Lillian
Suckow, Ruth
Toklas, Alice Babette
Vorse, Mary Heaton
White, Helen Constance
Wilder, Laura Ingalls
Wolff, Sister Madeleva (Mary Evaline)
Yezierska, Anzia

Magazine and Journal Editing

Abbott, Edith
Brady, Mildred Edie
Chase, Edna Woolman
Dean, Vera Micheles
Isaacs, Edith Juliet Rich
Littledale, Clara Savage
Miller, Bertha Mahony
Miner, Dorothy Eugenia
Roberts, Mary May
Strang, Ruth May
Swindler, Mary Hamilton
Wright, Muriel Hazel
See also Literature: Editors and Publishers

Classified List

Mathematics

Flügge-Lotz, Irmgard
Geiringer, Hilda
Hagood, Margaret Loyd Jarman
Stern, Catherine Brieger
Wheeler, Anna Johnson Pell

Medicine

Physicians

Alexander, Hattie Elizabeth
Andersen, Dorothy Hansine
Apgar, Virginia
Bass, Mary Elizabeth
Cori, Gerty Theresa Radnitz
Dick, Gladys Rowena Henry
Dunbar, Helen Flanders
Dunham, Ethel Collins
Frantz, Virginia Kneeland
Fromm-Reichmann, Frieda
Goldsmith, Grace Arabell
Hall, Rosetta Sherwood
Hamilton, Alice
Horney, Karen Danielsen
Jordan, Sara Claudia Murray
Kleegman, Sophia Josephine
L'Esperance, Elise Strang
Levine, Lena
Lovejoy, Esther Pohl
Macklin, Madge Thurlow
Mendenhall, Dorothy Reed
Minoka-Hill, Lillie Rosa
Pearce, Louise
Sabin, Florence Rena
Scudder, Ida Sophia
Thompson, Clara
Van Hoosen, Bertha
Williams, Anna Wessels

Researchers

Alexander, Hattie Elizabeth
Andersen, Dorothy Hansine
Cori, Gerty Theresa Radnitz
Dick, Gladys Rowena Henry
Evans, Alice Catherine
Frantz, Virginia Kneeland
Goldsmith, Grace Arabell
Hazen, Elizabeth Lee
L'Esperance, Elise Strang
Macklin, Madge Thurlow
Mendenhall, Dorothy Reed
Pearce, Louise
Pool, Judith Graham
Russell, Jane Anne

Sabin, Florence Rena
Slye, Maud
Williams, Anna Wessels

Microbiology

See Medicine: Researchers

Military

Blanchfield, Florence Aby
Gildersleeve, Virginia Crocheron
Rogers, Edith Nourse
Weed, Ethel Berenice
Woodsmall, Ruth Frances

Music

Bauer, Marion Eugénie
Coolidge, Elizabeth Sprague
Crawford-Seeger, Ruth Porter
Daniels, Mabel Wheeler
Densmore, Frances Theresa
Diller, Angela
Eames, Emma Hayden
Farrar, Geraldine
Fields, Dorothy
Garden, Mary
Garland, Judy
Harrison, Hazel Lucile
Holiday, Billie
Jackson, Mahalia
Joplin, Janis Lyn
Leginska, Ethel
McDaniel, Hattie
MacDonald, Jeanette
MacDowell, Marian Griswold Nevins
Mitchell, Abbie
Price, Florence Beatrice Smith
Spofford, Grace Harriet
Thompson, Helen Mulford
Tourel, Jennie
Traubel, Helen Francesca
Zimbalist, Mary Louise Curtis Bok

Nursing

Arnstein, Margaret Gene
Blanchfield, Florence Aby
Breckinridge, Mary
Davis, Frances Elliott
Dock, Lavinia Lloyd
Gardner, Mary Sewall
Goodrich, Annie Warburton

Classified List

Roberts, Mary May
Sanger, Margaret
Sherwin, Belle
Stewart, Isabel Maitland
Van Blarcom, Carolyn Conant

Nutrition

Blunt, Katharine
Davis, Adelle
Goldsmith, Grace Arabell
Morgan, Agnes Fay
Roberts, Lydia Jane
Stanley, Louise

Paleontology

See Geology

Peace

Barney, Nora Stanton
Balch, Emily Greene
Hamilton, Alice
Harkness, Georgia Elma
Hughan, Jessie Wallace
Hull, Hannah Hallowell Clothier
Hutchins, Grace
Martin, Anne Henrietta
Rankin, Jeannette Pickering
Scudder, Vida Dutton
Suckow, Ruth
Terrell, Mary Church
Vernon, Mabel

Penology and Criminology

Bartelme, Mary Margaret
Bowen, Louise deKoven
Bronner, Augusta Fox
Dewson, Mary Williams
Dummer, Ethel Sturges
Harris, Mary Belle
Glueck, Eleanor Touroff
Rippin, Jane Parker Deeter
Van Waters, Miriam
Willebrandt, Mabel Walker

Philanthropy

Blaine, Anita McCormick
Bowen, Louise deKoven

Coolidge, Elizabeth Sprague
Dummer, Ethel Sturges
Grossinger, Jennie
Hoey, Jane Margueretta
Hogg, Ima
Hurst, Fannie
McCormick, Katharine Dexter
Meyer, Agnes Ernst
Morgan, Anne Tracy
Post, Marjorie Merriweather
Rubinstein, Helena
Tucker, Sophie
Turnbo-Malone, Annie Minerva
Zimbalist, Mary Louise Curtis Bok

Philosophy

Arendt, Hannah

Photography

Akeley, Mary Lee Jobe
Arbus, Diane Nemerov
Bourke-White, Margaret
Johnston, Frances Benjamin
Lange, Dorothea

Physical Education

Bancroft, Jessie Hubbell
Burchenal, Elizabeth
Kellor, Frances
Perrin, Ethel
See also Sports

Physics

Anderson, Elda Emma
Mayer, Maria Gertrude Goeppert
Rand, Marie Gertrude

Political Science

Arendt, Hannah
Dean, Vera Micheles

Politics

See Government and Politics

Classified List

Psychiatry and Psychoanalysis

Dunbar, Helen Flanders
Fromm-Reichmann, Frieda
Horney, Karen Danielsen
Levine, Lena
Thompson, Clara

Psychology

Bronner, Augusta Fox
Bühler, Charlotte Bertha
Frenkel-Brunswik, Else
Gilbreth, Lillian Moller
Goodenough, Florence Laura
Rand, Marie Gertrude
Strang, Ruth May
Taft, Jessie
Taba, Hilda

Public Health

Anderson, Elda Emma
Apgar, Virginia
Arnstein, Margaret Gene
Breckinridge, Mary
Davis, Frances Elliott
Dick, Gladys Rowena Henry
Dock, Lavinia Lloyd
Dunham, Ethel Collins
Evans, Alice Catherine
Gardner, Mary Sewall
Goldsmith, Grace Arabell
Hamilton, Alice
Hazen, Elizabeth Lee
Jarrett, Mary Cromwell
L'Esperance, Elise Strang
Lovejoy, Esther Pohl
Mendenhall, Dorothy Reed
Pearce, Louise
Pennington, Mary Engle
Sabin, Florence Rena
Van Blarcom, Carolyn Conant
Williams, Anna Wessels

Radio and Television

See Broadcasting

Religion

Boole, Ella Alexander
Burroughs, Nannie Helen
Cameron, Donaldina Mackenzie
Drexel, Mother Mary Katharine
Dunbar, Helen Flanders
Hall, Rosetta Sherwood
Harkness, Georgia Elma
Hull, Hannah Hallowell Clothier
Jackson, Mahalia
Kohut, Rebekah Bettelheim
Lowry, Edith Elizabeth
Lyman, Mary Ely
Rogers, Mother Mary Joseph (Mary Josephine)
Scudder, Ida Sophia
Scudder, Vida Dutton
Thurston, Matilda Smyrell Calder
Tilly, Dorothy Eugenia Rogers
Wolff, Sister Madeleva (Mary Evaline)

Science

See Astronomy; Biology; Botany; Chemistry; Geology; Medicine; Nutrition; Physics

Settlements

Balch, Emily Greene
Bowen, Louise deKoven
Cameron, Donaldina Mackenzie
Diller, Angela
Dock, Lavinia Lloyd
Hamilton, Alice
Ovington, Mary White
Scudder, Vida Dutton
Simkhovitch, Mary Kingsbury
Spofford, Grace Harriet
White, Eartha Mary Magdalene

Socialism and Radicalism

Bambace, Angela
Bloor, Ella Reeve
Flynn, Elizabeth Gurley
Herbst, Josephine
Hughan, Jessie Wallace
Keller, Helen
King, Carol Weiss
Robeson, Eslanda Cardoza Goode
Rosenberg, Ethel Greenglass
Scudder, Vida Dutton
Strong, Anna Louise
Van Kleeck, Mary Abby

Social Reform

Abbott, Edith
Balch, Emily Greene

Cameron, Donaldina Mackenzie
Dewson, Mary Williams
Dock, Lavinia Lloyd
Dreier, Mary Elisabeth
Hamilton, Alice
Keller, Helen
Kellor, Frances
Kenyon, Dorothy
Mason, Lucy Randolph
Perkins, Frances
Roosevelt, Anna Eleanor
Schneiderman, Rose
Scudder, Vida Dutton
Simkhovitch, Mary Kingsbury
Terrell, Mary Church
Van Kleeck, Mary Abby
See also Birth Control; Civil Liberties; Civil
   Rights; Consumer Affairs; Feminism; Housing
   Reform; Labor; Peace; Socialism and Radicalism;
   Suffrage; Temperance and Prohibition

Social Research

Abbott, Edith
Colcord, Joanna Carver
Dewson, Mary Williams
Hagood, Margaret Loyd Jarman
Haynes, Elizabeth Ross
Kellor, Frances
Lundberg, Emma Octavia
Miller, Frieda Segelke
Ovington, Mary White
Van Kleeck, Mary Abby
Wolfson, Theresa
See also Labor

Social Welfare

Andrus, Ethel Percy
Bremer, Edith Terry
Buck, Pearl
Dummer, Ethel Sturges
Keller, Helen
Kohut, Rebekah Bettelheim
Lee, Rose Hum
Lowry, Edith Elizabeth
Morgan, Anne Tracy
Switzer, Mary Elizabeth
White, Eartha Mary Magdalene
See also Community Affairs; Women's Organizations

Social Work

Abbott, Edith
Bremer, Edith Terry

Cannon, Ida Maud
Colcord, Joanna Carver
Coyle, Grace Longwell
Dewson, Mary Williams
Glueck, Eleanor Touroff
Hamilton, Gordon
Hoey, Jane Margueretta
Jarrett, Mary Cromwell
Lundberg, Emma Octavia
Rapoport, Lydia
Rippin, Jane Parker Deeter
Taft, Jessie
Towle, Charlotte Helen
Van Waters, Miriam

Sociology

Glueck, Eleanor Touroff
Hagood, Margaret Loyd Jarman
Lee, Rose Hum
Taeuber, Irene Barnes

Sports

Henie, Sonja
Pound, Louise
Sears, Eleonora Randolph
Wightman, Hazel Hotchkiss
Zaharias, Mildred Ella (Babe) Didrikson
See also Physical Education

Suffrage

Allen, Florence Ellinwood
Ames, Blanche Ames
Ames, Jessie Daniel
Barney, Nora Stanton
Beard, Mary Ritter
Blair, Emily Newell
Bloor, Ella Reeve
Bowen, Louise deKoven
Burns, Lucy
Cadilla de Martínez, María
Chase, Mary Agnes
Cunningham, Minnie Fisher
Dewson, Mary Williams
Dock, Lavinia Lloyd
Dreier, Katherine Sophie
Dreier, Mary Elisabeth
Field, Sara Bard
Gellhorn, Edna Fischel
Hull, Hannah Hallowell Clothier
Irwin, Inez Haynes Gillmore
Johnson, Adelaide
Lampkin, Daisy Elizabeth Adams

Classified List

Laughlin, Gail
McCormick, Katharine Dexter
Martin, Anne Henrietta
Miller, Emma Guffy
Park, Maud Wood
Pinchot, Cornelia Elizabeth Bryce
Pollitzer, Anita Lily
Rankin, Jeannette Pickering
Reid, Helen Miles Rogers
Schneiderman, Rose
Seton, Grace Gallatin
Sherwin, Belle
Somerville, Nellie Nugent
Terrell, Mary Church
Vernon, Mabel
Wells, Marguerite Milton

Antisuffrage

Meyer, Annie Nathan

Temperance and Prohibition

Boole, Ella Alexander
Norris, Kathleen Thompson
Somerville, Nellie Nugent
Willebrandt, Mabel Walker

Prohibition Repeal

Miller, Emma Guffey
Sabin, Pauline Morton

Theater

Adams, Maude
Bankhead, Tallulah Brockman
Barrymore, Ethel
Berg, Gertrude Edelstein
Bernstein, Aline Frankau
Cornell, Katharine
Crothers, Rachel
Draper, Ruth
Ferber, Edna
Fields, Dorothy
Flanagan, Hallie Mae Ferguson
Gersten, Berta
Hansberry, Lorraine
Helburn, Theresa
Holliday, Judy
Isaacs, Edith Juliet Rich
Jones, Margo
McCullers, Carson
Mitchell, Abbie
Moorehead, Agnes
Rosenthal, Jean

Ward, Winifred Louise
Webster, Margaret
Yurka, Blanche

Women's Organizations

American Association of University Women

Brunauer, Esther Caukin
Comstock, Ada Louise
Gildersleeve, Virginia Crocheron
White, Helen Constance

League of Women Voters

Ames, Jessie Daniel
Blair, Emily Newell
Cunningham, Minnie Fisher
Gellhorn, Edna Fischel
Mason, Lucy Randolph
Miller, Emma Guffey
Park, Maud Wood
Sherwin, Belle
Wells, Marguerite Milton

National Association of Colored Women

Bethune, Mary McLeod
Butler, Selena Sloan
Gaines, Irene McCoy
Haynes, Elizabeth Ross
Lampkin, Daisy Elizabeth Adams
Terrell, Mary Church

National Council of Negro Women

Bethune, Mary McLeod
Brown, Charlotte Eugenia Hawkins
Carter, Eunice Hunton
Lampkin, Daisy Elizabeth Adams
Terrell, Mary Church

National Federation of Business and Professional Women

Laughlin, Gail
Phillips, Lena Madesin

National Woman's Party

Barney, Nora Stanton
Beard, Mary Ritter
Burns, Lucy
Dock, Lavinia Lloyd
Field, Sara Bard
Irwin, Inez Haynes Gillmore
Laughlin, Gail
Lee, Muna

Classified List

Martin, Anne Henrietta
Mesta, Perle
Miller, Emma Guffey
Pollitzer, Anita Lily
Vernon, Mabel

Women's International League for Peace and Freedom

Balch, Emily Greene
Hull, Hannah Hallowell Clothier
Martin, Anne Henrietta
Rankin, Jeannette Pickering
Terrell, Mary Church
Vernon, Mabel

Women's Trade Union League

Anderson, Mary
Balch, Emily Greene
Christman, Elisabeth
Dreier, Mary Elisabeth
Miller, Frieda Segelke
Parker, Julia Sarsfield O'Connor
Schneiderman, Rose

YWCA

Bremer, Edith Terry
Brown, Charlotte Eugenia Hawkins
Carter, Eunice Hunton
Coyle, Grace Longwell
Fauset, Crystal Dreda Bird
Haynes, Elizabeth Ross
McLaren, Louise Leonard
Mason, Lucy Randolph
Phillips, Lena Madesin
Shambaugh, Jessie Field
Woodsmall, Ruth Frances

Other

Ames, Jessie Daniel
Cline, Genevieve Rose
Fuller, Meta Vaux Warrick
Kohut, Rebekah Bettelheim
Morgan, Anne Tracy
Rippin, Jane Parker Deeter
Sewell, Edna Belle
Tilly, Dorothy Eugenia Rogers
Weed, Ethel Berenice